CollegeBoard

2011
Book of Majors

2011

Book of Majors

CollegeBoard

Fifth Edition

The College Board, New York

The College Board

The College Board is a not-for-profit membership association whose mission is to connect students to college success and opportunity. Founded in 1900, the College Board is composed of more than 5,700 schools, colleges, universities, and other educational organizations. Each year, the College Board serves seven million students and their parents, 23,000 high schools, and 3,800 colleges through major programs and services in college readiness, college admission, guidance, assessment, financial aid and enrollment. Among its best-known programs are the SAT®, the PSAT/NMSQT®, the Advanced Placement Program® (AP®), SpringBoard® and ACCUPLACER®. The College Board is committed to the principles of excellence and equity, and that commitment is embodied in all of its programs, services, activities and concerns.

For further information, visit www.collegeboard.com.

Copies of this book may be ordered from College Board Publications, P.O. Box 8670, Reston, VA 20195, or online at www.collegeboard.com. The price is $26.99.

Editorial inquiries concerning this book should be directed to College Planning Services, The College Board, 45 Columbus Avenue, New York, NY 10023-6992.

Library of Congress Control Number: 2006903733

ISBN-13: 978-0-87447-904-1

Printed in the United States of America

Contents

Special academic programs 1278

Preface

The *College Board Book of Majors* is the only book of its kind that provides a complete, all-in-one source for what students exploring majors need to know: what the majors are about, *and* where they can be studied.

The 200 majors profiled in Part I of this book are primarily undergraduate programs, taught at the associate or bachelor's degree level. These majors represent not only those that are most widely offered, but also those that students most often express interest in.

Each profile of a major is compiled from detailed questionnaires submitted by college professors teaching in the field. Where appropriate, information from secondary sources—including professional and academic associations, national newspapers, and the federal Department of Labor's *Occupational Outlook Handbook* was also used. Additional insights are included from college students enrolled in these majors.

In Part II of this book are brief descriptions of more than 900 majors contained in the current version of the *Classification of Instructional Programs* (*CIP* for short), developed by the National Center for Educational Statistics for the U.S. Department of Education.

In Part III, those 900 majors are listed alphabetically, with the colleges and graduate schools that offer them presented state by state. Each college listing also indicates at which degree level or levels the major can be studied (certificate, associate, bachelor's, master's, doctorate, or first-professional). Following these are 31 special academic programs, similarly arranged alphabetically, with state-by-state listings of the colleges offering them.

What's New

Based on student interest, we've added descriptions of two new majors in Part I: Digital art and Sports communications. In addition, each profile in Part I has been reviewed by the editors, with special emphasis on the latest career trends. The contact information that appears in the "For more info" section of each profile has also been verified and updated.

About the College Data

The data in the college listings were provided by the schools themselves in the College Board's Annual Survey of Colleges, conducted in the spring of 2010. Colleges reported their programs of majors according to the *CIP* (even though the names they give majors may differ slightly from the *CIP* titles).

The information provided by the colleges was verified by a staff of editors to ensure that the data are as complete and accurate as possible. However, program changes occur, and readers are urged to contact colleges directly to confirm facts related to their major of choice.

To be eligible for inclusion, a college must be accredited by a national or regional accrediting association recognized by the U.S. Department of Education, and offer at least an associate degree. Graduate programs are listed only for those schools that also have undergraduate programs. An alphabetical index of every major profiled in Part I and/or listed in Part III appears at the end of this book.

Acknowledgments

Many people helped with the creation and publication of this book, and it is a pleasure to acknowledge them here:

First of all, thanks are due to Renee Gernand, whose efforts, assistance, and guidance were essential to the successful completion of this book. "What to know about majors" and the introductions to the major categories in Part I were written by Barbara Kram. Michael Polizzi and Regina Sampogna provided editorial assistance for this edition. The enormous task of collecting and verifying the college information in Part III of this book was conducted by Stan Bernstein and the editorial staff of the Annual Survey of Colleges. Thanks also to the staff at Content Data Solutions, Inc., who provide the technological savvy that helps us turn our data into books.

The professors, who made gifts of their knowledge, insights, and enthusiasm for their subjects, are individually acknowledged in the list of contributors beginning on the following page. It is a privilege to forward those gifts along to the students who, we all hope, will find guidance in this book.

Tom Vanderberg
Senior Editor, College Planning Services
The College Board

List of contributors

Agriculture

Arthur Cameron
Professor of Horticulture
Michigan State University

Stephanie Doores
Associate Professor of Food Science
Penn State University Park

Lee A. Edgerton
Director of Undergraduate Studies, Department of
    Animal Sciences
University of Kentucky

Karen S. Kubena
Professor, Department of Nutrition&Food Science
Texas A&M University

Donald W. Larson
Professor, Department of Agricultural, Environmental,
    and Development Economics
Ohio State University

Kenneth L. Larson
Professor Emeritus, Department of Agronomy
Iowa State University

Murray H. Milford
Professor Emeritus, Department of Soil and Crop
    Sciences
Texas A&M University

M. Edward Rister
Professor of Agricultural Economics
Texas A&M University

Marianne Sarrantonio
Associate Professor of Sustainable Agriculture
University of Maine

H. Jerry Schurink
Director of Equine Studies and IHSA Team Coach
University of Massachusetts Amherst

Douglas L. Young
Professor, College of Agricultural, Human and Natural
    Resource Sciences
Washington State University

Architecture

Michael Bednar
Professor of Architecture
University of Virginia

Philip N. Pregill
Professor and Chair, Landscape Architecture
California State University: Pomona

Alfred D. Price
Associate Professor, Department of Urban and Regional
    Planning
State University of New York at Buffalo

John B. Wright
Professor of Geography and Planning
New Mexico State University

Area, ethnic, and gender studies

Lynne S. Abel
Associate Dean for Undergraduate Education, College of
    Arts and Sciences
Cornell University

Sandra Lipsitz Bem
Professor of Psychology
Cornell University

Bernard Haykel
Associate Professor of Middle Eastern and Islamic
    Studies
New York University

Daniel Horowitz
Professor of American Studies
Smith College

Theresa Chang-whei Jen
Professor and Director, East Asian Studies
Lauder Institute, Wharton School, University of
    Pennsylvania

Reynaldo F. Macías
Professor of Chicana/o Studies, Education & Applied
    Linguistics
University of California: Los Angeles

R. Baxter Miller
Professor of English and Director, Institute for African
    American Studies
University of Georgia

Eleuteria Hernández
Student Affairs Officer, Department of Chicana/o
    Studies
University of California: Los Angeles

Peter W. Rees
Associate Professor of Geography and Former Director,
    Latin American Studies Program
University of Delaware

Kathryn W. Shanley
Associate Professor, Native American Studies
University of Montana

Biological sciences

Austin E. Brooks
Treves Professor of Biology
Wabash College

William H. Coleman
Professor of Biology
University of Hartford

Carter Denniston
Professor, Genetics and Medical Genetics
University of Wisconsin–Madison

Robert S. Greene
Professor of Biology
Niagara University

Eileen Gregory
Professor of Biology
Rollins College

Kenneth F. Haynes
Professor, Department of Entomology
University of Kentucky

Donald L. Lovett
Associate Professor, Department of Biology
The College of New Jersey

Douglas Meikle
Professor and Chair, Department of Zoology
Miami University

Amanda Norvell
Assistant Professor, Department of Biology
The College of New Jersey

C.O. Patterson
Associate Professor, Department of Biology and
    Molecular and Environmental Plant Sciences
Texas A&M University

Gregory M. Raner
Associate Professor, Chemistry and Biochemistry
University of North Carolina at Greensboro

Dean E. Wendt
Assistant Professor, Biological Sciences Department and
    Center for Coastal Marine Science
California Polytechnic State University

Business

Gedas Adomavicius
Assistant Professor, Carlson School of Management
University of Minnesota

Stephen J. Brown
David S. Loeb Professor of Finance
Stern School of Business, New York University

Peter Bycio
Professor, Department of Management and
    Entrepreneurship
Williams College of Business, Xavier University

Wayne F. Cascio
U.S. Bank Term Professor of Management
University of Colorado at Denver

Diane Kaufman Fredette
Chair and Professor, Construction Management
    Program, School of Architecture
Pratt Institute

Lorin M. Hitt
Alberto Vitale Term Associate Professor of Operations
    and Information Management
The Wharton School, University of Pennsylvania

Susan Ivancevich
Associate Professor of Accounting
University of North Carolina at Wilmington

Carol A.B. Jordan
Eminent Scholar of Risk Management and Insurance
Troy State University

Ann-Mary Kapusta
Associate Dean, McDonough School of Business
Georgetown University

Mark Lee Levine
Professor, Burns School of Real Estate and Construction
    Management
University of Denver

Charles J. Metelka
Professor, Department of Hospitality and Tourism
University of Wisconsin–Stout

Patricia Rigia
Professor and Director, Fashion Merchandising Division,
    School of Business
University of Bridgeport

Stephen Spinelli, Jr.
Vice Provost for Entrepreneurship and Global
    Management
Babson College

Debbie M. Thorne
Associate Vice President for Academic Affairs and
Professor of Marketing
Texas State University: San Marcos

Communications

Thomas A. Bowers
James L. Knight Professor and Interim Dean, School of
Journalism and Mass Communication
University of North Carolina at Chapel Hill

John Doolittle
Associate Director, Center for Teaching Excellence, and
Associate Professor
American University

Bruce E. Gronbeck
A. Craig Baird Distinguished Professor of Public Address
University of Iowa

Joel A. Kline
Assistant Professor of Business and Economics and
Director, Digital Communications Program
Lebanon Valley College

Keith Strudler
Department Chair and Assistant Professor of
Communication
Marist College

Patsy G. Watkins
Associate Professor and Chair, Lemke Department of
Journalism
University of Arkansas

Computer and information sciences

Champlain College
Program Director and Assistant Professor of Computer
and Digital Forensics

Tom Dowd
Assistant Professor, Department of Interactive Arts and
Media
Columbia College Chicago

Sampath Kannan
Associate Dean of Engineering
University of Pennsylvania

Anne Marchant
Associate Professor, Applied Information Department
George Mason University

Kathryn M. Stewart
Chair, Computer Technology
Tallahassee Community College

Murray Turoff
Professor Emeritus, Information Systems Department
New Jersey Institute of Technology

Education

Mary C. Clement
Associate Professor of Teacher Education
Berry College

Jeanneine P. Jones
Professor of Middle Grades Education
University of North Carolina at Charlotte

Dawn Eddy Molloy
Faculty Research Associate
University of Maryland

Lynda M. Nilges
Associate Professor, Department of Physical Education
University of South Carolina

Susan J. Olson
Professor and Chair, Department of Educational
Foundations and Leadership
The University of Akron

Engineering

Stanley M. Barnett
Professor of Chemical Engineering and Pharmaceutics
University of Rhode Island

Roger H. Compton
Dean and Professor of Naval Architecture
Webb Institute

Roger D. Doherty
A.W. Grosvenor Professor of Materials Engineering
Emeritus
Drexel University

Lyle. D. Feisel
Dean Emeritus, Watson School of Engineering and
Applied Science
State University of New York at Binghamton

Audeen W. Fentiman
Chair, Nuclear Engineering Program
Ohio State University

Stephan Grilli
Chair and Professor of Ocean Engineering
University of Rhode Island

Edward A. Hiler
Dean of Agriculture and Life Sciences Emeritus
Texas A&M University

Keith D. Hjelmstad
Professor of Civil Engineering
University of Illinois at Urbana–Champaign

Charles A. Kliche
Professor, Mining Engineering and Management
Department
South Dakota School of Mines and Technology

C. Patrick Koelling
Associate Professor, Grado Department of Industrial and
    Systems Engineering
Virginia Polytechnic Institute and State University

Brian A. Rock
Associate Professor of Architectural Engineering
University of Kansas

Malcolm L. Spaulding
Professor of Ocean Engineering
University of Rhode Island

Alfred G. Striz
Professor and L.A. Comp Chair in Engineering
University of Oklahoma

Calvin L. White
Professor of Materials Science and Engineering
Michigan Technological University

Frank H. Young
Professor Emeritus of Computer Science and Software
    Engineering
Rose-Hulman Institute of Technology

Engineering technology

Harold L. Broberg
Associate Dean of Engineering, Technology, and
    Computer Science
Indiana University–Purdue University Fort Wayne

Pierre Catala
Senior Lecturer Emeritus
Texas A&M University

Paul Clarke
Lead Instructor, Drafting and Engineering Technology
MiraCosta College

Thomas M. Hall, Jr.
Professor and Head, Department of Engineering
    Technology
Northwestern State University

James Kamm
Professor of Mechanical Engineering Technology
University of Toledo

Mark R. Steinle
Professor, Department of Trades and Technology
Casper College

Indrajith Wijayratne
Associate Professor of Surveying
Michigan Technological University

English language and literature

Jonathan Fink
Creative Writing Fellow in Poetry
Emory University

David A. McMurrey
Program Chair, Technical Communications
Austin Community College

Brett C. Millier
Reginald L. Cook Professor of American Literature
Middlebury College

James G. Taaffe
Emeritus Professor of English
University of Alabama

Family and consumer sciences

Eva L. Essa
Foundation Professor and Chair, Human Development
    and Family Studies
University of Nevada: Reno

Sally L. Fortenberry
Associate Professor and Internship Coordinator,
    Department of Design, Merchandising and Textiles
Texas Christian University

Bonita A. Glatz
Professor of Food Science and Human Nutrition
Iowa State University

Penny A. Ralston
Professor and Dean Emeritus, College of Human
    Sciences
Florida State University, Tallahassee

Paul Sorgule
Dean of Culinary Arts and Hospitality
Paul Smith's College

Anne L. Sweaney
Professor and Head, Housing and Consumer
    Economics, College of Family and Consumer
    Sciences
University of Georgia

Health

Debra L. Agard
Assistant Dean, Office of Student Affairs
University of Illinois at Chicago College of Pharmacy

Marcia A. Armstrong
Director, Medical/Laboratory Technology and
    Phlebotomy Programs
University of Hawaii: Kapiolani Community College

Paula Owens Ashby
Assistant Director of Academic Services and Chief
    Health Professions Advisor
University of Maryland: Baltimore County

Jean E. Bartels
Chair and Professor of Nursing
Georgia Southern University

Georgine W. Bills
Program Director, Respiratory Therapy
Weber State University

Stan S. Cooke
Professor and Head of Department of Communication
    Disorders
Western Kentucky University

Susan S. Deusinger
Director, Program in Physical Therapy
Washington University School of Medicine

Anne E. Dickerson
Professor and Chair, Department of Occupational
    Therapy
East Carolina University

Leonard H. Friedman
Associate Professor of Public Health
Oregon State University

Paul N. Gonzales
Director, Radiologic Technology Program
Fresno City College

Rosann M. Ippolito
Associate Director, Physician Assistant Program
Northeastern University

Mary Anne Marsh
Chair, Department of Nursing
Dickinson University

Connie L. Peterson
Assistant Professor
James Madison University

Professor Nicholas G. Popovich
Head, Department of Pharmacy Administration
University of Illinois at Chicago College of Pharmacy

Susan H. Stadler
Director, Veterinary Technician Program
Lehigh Carbon and Northampton Community College

Annmary E. Thomas
Assistant Professor, Emergency Medical Services
    Program
Drexel University

Olivia Bennett Wood
Associate Professor and Director, Didactic Program in
    Dietetics
Purdue University

Nancy C. Zinser
Professor and Chair, Dental Health Services
Palm Beach Community College

Humanities

D. Terence Langendoen
Professor Emeritus, Department of Linguistics
University of Arizona

Richard T. Lee
Brownell Professor of Philosophy
Trinity College

Michael D. Richards
Samford Professor of History
Sweet Briar College

Kenneth S. Rothwell, Jr.
Associate Professor and Chair, Department of Classics
University of Massachusetts Boston

Tobin Siebers
Professor and Chair, Department of Comparative
    Literature
University of Michigan

Joseph Ugoretz
Professor of English and Director of Teaching and
    Learning with Technology
Borough of Manhattan Community College

Languages

Theresa A. Antes
Associate Professor of French and Linguistics
University of Florida

Scott Cook
Associate Professor of Chinese
Grinnell College

Michael Fishbein
Lecturer in Arabic
University of California: Los Angeles

Melissa Frazier
Professor of Russian Language and Literature
Sarah Lawrence College

H. Mack Horton
Professor of Japanese Literature
University of California, Berkeley

Mike Kemp
Professor, Department of ASL and Deaf Studies
Gallaudet University

María Negroni
Assistant Professor
Sarah Lawrence College

Robert E. Proctor
Joanne Toor Cummings '50 Professor of Italian
Connecticut College

Heidi Thomann Tewarson
Professor and Chair, Department of German Language
and Literature
Oberlin College

Legal studies

Diane Curtis
Prelaw Advisor
University of Massachusetts Amherst

Jeffrey J. Davis
Assistant Professor of Political Science
University of Maryland, Baltimore County

Lenore M. Molee
Associate Professor and Coordinator of Paralegal Studies
Program, Department of Legal Studies
Montclair State University

Mathematics

James Alexander
Chair, Department of Mathematics
Case Western Reserve University

David M. Bressoud
DeWitt Wallace Professor of Mathematics
Macalester College

Michele Marini
Undergraduate Administrator, Department of Statistics
Virginia Polytechnic Institute and State University

Multi/interdisciplinary studies

Stephen M. Buhler
Professor of English
University of Nebraska–Lincoln

Joseph F. Cimini
Associate Professor, Department of Sociology &
Criminal Justice
University of Scranton

Caroline Higgins
Professor of History and Convener, Peace and Global
Studies
Earlham College

Richard S. Lewis
Associate Professor of Psychology and Neuroscience
Pomona College

Ann Milkovich McKee
Assistant Professor and Director, Undergraduate
Historic Preservation
Goucher College

Eve Walsh Stoddard
Professor of English and Chair, Global Studies
Department
St. Lawrence University

Natural resources and conservation

Eric M. Hallerman
Professor and Head, Department of Fisheries and
Wildlife Sciences
Virginia Polytechnic Institute and State University

David H. Hirth
Associate Professor and Chair, Wildlife and Fisheries
Biology Program
University of Vermont

Steven E. Jungst
Professor, Department of Forestry
Iowa State University

David K. Loomis
Associate Professor, Human Dimensions Research Unit,
Department of Natural Resources Conservation
University of Massachusetts Amherst

Michael Maniates
Professor of Environmental Science and Political
Science
Allegheny College

David E. Smith
Professor, Department of Environmental Sciences
University of Virginia

Parks and recreation

Lowell Caneday
Professor of Leisure Studies
Oklahoma State University

Stephen W. Jefferson
Chief Undergraduate Adviser and Undergraduate
Program Director, Sport Management Program
University of Massachusetts Amherst

Physical sciences

Neta A. Bahcall
Eugene Higgins Professor of Astrophysics
Princeton University

Dave Esser
Professor and Program Coordinator, Department of
Aeronautical Science
Embry-Riddle Aeronautical University

Richard G. French
Professor and Chair, Astronomy Department, and
Director, Whitin Observatory
Wellesley College

Ronald E. Johnson
University Professor and Associate Professor of
    Oceanography
Old Dominion University

Stanley T. Jones
Professor and Chair, Department of Physics &
    Astronomy
University of Alabama

James P. Koermer
Professor of Meteorology
Plymouth State University

Jonathan W. Peterson
Associate Professor of Geology and Environmental
    Science
Hope College

Bahram Roughani
Professor and Department Head of Physics
Kettering University

James N. Spencer
Emeritus William G. and Elizabeth R. Simeral Professor
    of Chemistry
Franklin & Marshall College

Protective services

Daniel Klenow
Professor and Chair, Department of Sociology,
    Anthropology, and Emergency Management
North Dakota State University

Dennis R. Longmire
Professor, College of Criminal Justice
Sam Houston State University

Frank Vozzo
Associate Professor of Forensic Science
Russell Sage College for Women

Thomas J. Woodford
Associate Professor and Department Head, Fire
    Protection and Safety Technology
Oklahoma State University

Public administration

Danny L. Balfour
Professor and Director, School of Public and Nonprofit
    Administration
Grand Valley State University

Tuesday L. Cooper
Dean, Long Island Center
Empire State College

Irene Queiro-Tajalli
Professor and Executive Director of Undergraduate
    Education, School of Social Work
Indiana University–Purdue University Indianapolis

Religion and theology

Kamran S. Aghaie
Assistant Professor of Islamic Studies
University of Texas at Austin

Sandra Billy
Director, Center for Sacred Music
Virginia Wesleyan College

Shmuel Bolozky
Professor of Hebrew
University of Massachusetts Amherst

John A. Grim
Professor of Religion
Bucknell University

Andrew E. Hill
Professor of Old Testament
Wheaton College (IL)

Richard B. Pilgrim
Professor Emeritus, Department of Religion
Syracuse University

Shelley Shepherd
Preministerial studies advisor
Southern Methodist University

David G. Truemper
Professor and Chair of Theology
Valparaiso University

Social sciences

David L. Browman
Chairman, Interdisciplinary Program in Archaeology
Washington University in St. Louis

Gregory A. Elmes
Professor of Geography, Department of Geology and
    Geography
West Virginia University

Jacqueline Johnson
Assistant Professor, Sociology
Fordham University

Andrew A. Latham
Associate Professor of Political Science and Associate
    Director, Center for Scholarship and Teaching
Macalester College

Robert Mandel
Professor and Chair, International Affairs Department
Lewis and Clark College

Lee McCann
Professor of Psychology
University of Wisconsin–Oshkosh

Baron Perlman
Professor of Psychology
University of Wisconsin–Oshkosh

John J. Siegfried
Professor of Economics
Vanderbilt University

Visual and performaing arts

Sven Anderson
Assistant Professor, Computer Art and Printmaking
State University of New York College at Oneonta

Chrystelle Trump Bond
Professor of Dance and Founding Chair, Dance
    Department
Goucher College

Lilly Ann Boruszkowski
Associate Professor
Southern Illinois University Carbondale

David B. Brownlee
Professor of the History of Art
University of Pennsylvania

Jo Anne Caputo
Professor
Cleveland Institute of Music

Meredith Davis
Professor of Graphic Design
North Carolina State University College of Design

Bevin Engman
Associate Professor of Art
Colby College

David B. Greene
Professor of Arts Studies Emeritus
North Carolina State University

Janine King
Associate Professor and Chair, Department of Interior
    Design
University of Florida

Anthony J. LaMagra
Professor and Director of Music Emeritus
Manhattanville College

Judy Lochhead
Professor of Music and Graduate Program Director
State University of New York at Stony Brook

Ronald Naversen
Professor of Scenic Design
Southern Illinois University Carbondale

Fred Niles
Professor and Chair, Department of Visual Arts
University of Dayton

Donald Poynter
Animation Instructor
School of Visual Arts

Mary Stephens
Director of Fashion Design, Advanced Study Programs
Fashion Institute of Design and Merchandising

Diane Timmerman
Professor of Theatre
Butler University

Allen Winold
Professor Emeritus of Music
Indiana University Bloomington

How to use this book

Find a major, find a college

If you are thinking about college majors, this book offers a lot of help.

If you have no idea what you want to study in college, it can help you discover majors that might appeal to you.

If there are several majors that interest you, it can help you make an informed choice.

If you already know what you want to major in, it can help you prepare for the program by letting you know what to expect. (Or it might present a completely different but more attractive option you never knew existed—which just might be the best help of all.)

But choosing a major is only half the job—you also have to find a college that offers it, at the degree level that is right for you, and in a place where you want, or need, to be. This book helps you do that, too. (The description of Part II below will tell you how.)

Part I: Full Descriptions of Majors

According to the U.S. Department of Education's *Classification of Instructional Programs (CIP)*, there are over 900 fields of study—majors, that is. Part I describes 200 of these in full detail; all are briefly described in Part II.

Major categories

The 200 profiled majors are grouped into 26 broad categories, arranged alphabetically. Each category begins with a short write-up about the field of study as a whole, to guide your exploration of the majors and the colleges that offer them. You'll get a feel for the different ways colleges approach the majors, insights from professors, and guidance on questions to ask as you explore the majors in the group.

The category introductions are just a starting point. You'll want to read all the details in the individual profiles of the majors that interest you.

The profiles

Each profile is based on information gathered from college professors teaching in the field. The major is described as it is generally taught at colleges across the United States, not just at a particular school. Throughout, the term *college* refers to any institution of higher education—two-year college, four-year college, university, technical school, professional school, and so on.

How did we pick the majors to profile? First, we looked at the majors that high school students (almost 2 million of them) said they were most interested in when they completed a brief questionnaire on their SAT registration forms. Then we examined which majors are most widely offered at colleges across the country, to be sure a broad spectrum was represented. And we added a few that we believe are noteworthy or up-and-coming (like Game design and Emergency management/homeland security), even if they are not among the most popular or the most available.

Almost all the profiled majors are for undergraduate study, either at the two-year associate degree level or in a four-year bachelor's degree program. For the few majors that are available only as graduate programs (physical therapy, for instance), we've described the undergraduate course of study that will prepare you for grad school. We also describe preprofessional programs (such as prelaw and premedicine) that are technically not majors.

The following headings correspond to what you will find in the profiles.

Name of major: This is the generic name of the major that is most often used and most widely recognized. You are likely to see variations in individual college catalogs, but they should be similar to the name shown here.

Also known as: Colleges don't always agree on what to call a major; alternative names that you might come across are listed here.

What it's about: This paragraph gives you a quick idea of the subject area the major covers and the careers it prepares you for.

Is this for you? This section should help you select a major according to what you like to do or to study, what you are good at, and what your personal qualities are. We've listed some characteristics common to students who have succeeded in the major. They are not requirements, and you certainly don't have to match them all, or even any of them; your interest in a particular field may be based on something totally different and be just as valid.

Recommended high school prep: The course units recommended here refer to years of study in a four-year high school. "Math 3" refers to Algebra I, geometry, and Algebra II; "lab science 3" includes earth science, biology, and either chemistry or physics, each with a lab component. "Social studies 3" includes U.S. history, world history, and either geography or government/economics.

The recommended courses tend to be similar for all majors, because a well-rounded high school curriculum, with courses in English, math, science, social studies, and a foreign language, is generally required for admission to most colleges, regardless of major. The recommendations will differ with respect to additional units or elective courses that can help you prepare for a particular major. But these are suggestions only; your high school may not teach some of the courses mentioned here.

What if you don't know what you want to major in? Preserve your options by taking the most rigorous courses you can. The College Board recommends four years of English, four years of math (including Algebra I, Algebra II, Geometry, and pre-Calculus or Calculus), a minimum of two years of lab science (some colleges require more), three years of social science and history, and at least two years of the same foreign language. Your school counselor will have the best advice as to whether your choice of high school courses will support your college goals.

Did you know...? Included here are important aspects or interesting facts about the major, or the careers it may lead to, that many students entering the major are not aware of.

Typical courses in the major: This list is a sampling of courses commonly offered in the major, in roughly the order of sequence they are taken. Some colleges offer fewer courses than these and some more, and course titles may vary.

Concentrations: You can sometimes concentrate your studies, or specialize, in a certain area within your major. The concentrations listed here are not available at all colleges. Concentrations that are generally not available until grad school are listed separately.

What the study of this major is like: This section tells you what you'll actually study in a major, and how the major is generally taught and learned. We've described differences in emphasis, requirements, and philosophies among colleges that offer the major, to help you evaluate the program at the colleges you are considering. You will also get a sense of what your academic lifestyle will be like, and what challenges to expect.

Other majors you might like: This section lists majors that are related by subject matter, approach, or the interests and characteristics of the students who study them. Some of the related fields are obvious, but some may surprise you; they are included to help you cover all the bases, or perhaps to suggest an option you may not have known about. Majors in **bold type** are fully profiled in this book. Those in regular type are described in Part II.

Questions to ask colleges: These questions are designed to help you find colleges that have strong programs for your major, or that approach the subject area in a way that is compatible with your goals and interests. Good for college visits, interviews, or an email to the Web sites of the colleges you are considering.

Career options and trends: This section lists job titles in careers the major may lead to—an asterisk indicates a type of job that graduates most often pursue. Also described are any additional education, certification, or licensure requirements for the careers listed, plus trends occurring or likely to occur in careers related to the major.

Insider's viewpoint: We asked professors to tell something about what appeals to them about the major. We also asked college students actually enrolled in the major to give some pointers or insights, or to describe their experiences as a major in class, internships, or field studies.

For more info: Contact information is provided here for associations (educational and business) that you should investigate to explore further the major and/or related careers. Most of these associations have robust sections for students, although sometimes you have to drill down to find them.

Part II: Brief Descriptions of Majors

Adapted from the latest version of the U.S. Department of Education's *Classification of Instructional Programs* (*CIP*), these descriptions cover the whole spectrum of majors offered by colleges throughout the United States, and are included to supplement the college listings in Part III. Each description indicates the scope of the major and, where appropriate, the jobs for which you are prepared. Some of these majors are only available at the graduate degree level.

Part III: College Listings

Colleges Listed by Major and State

Here you will find the colleges that offer the major (or majors) you are interested in. The majors are presented alphabetically, and under each major is a state-by-state list of the colleges that teach it. Some colleges listed here do not offer majors in the traditional sense but provide in-depth specialization that is very similar to the course work usually required for a degree.

A lot more majors are listed here than are profiled in Part I. There are over 900, in fact—all the undergraduate majors and graduate programs offered by the schools responding to the College Board's Annual Survey of Colleges. The names of the majors conform to the *CIP*, but individual colleges may use different names in their course catalogs.

Levels of study

Are you looking for a two-year program or a four-year program? Going on to graduate school? Thinking about beefing up your credentials with a certificate in your career area? Then you need to know that the colleges offering the major you want also offer it at the right level of study for you.

In the list of colleges by major, the different degree levels offered for each major are designated by the following letters found after the college name:

C Certificate or diploma
A Associate degree
B Bachelor's degree
T Teacher certification
M Master's degree
D Doctorate
P Professional degree (e.g., J.D., M.D.)

Certificate or diploma. Certificates are awarded to students who complete nondegree programs, which usually take one year or less and are most frequently offered in technical and vocational fields of study. Entry requirements for the programs may vary; for some you might need only a high school diploma or equivalent, while for others (accounting, for example) you might have to have some college under your belt.

Associate degree. The degrees most frequently earned at this level are the associate of arts (A.A.) (in the context of academic degrees, arts refers to the humanities, not to painting and drawing) and the associate of science (A.S.). The associate in applied science (A.A.S.) is also used for technological or vocational fields. Usually two years in length, associate degree programs are most often found at community colleges and technical schools, but they are also offered at many four-year colleges. Associate degrees in transfer programs are designed to provide the first two years of a four-year bachelor's degree at most colleges.

Bachelor's degree. Programs in which you earn a bachelor's (sometimes called a baccalaureate) degree usually take four years, but some programs can be completed in three years and some take five. The bachelor of arts (B.A.) and the bachelor of science (B.S.) are the most common; both include general education courses, a major, and electives. Some programs offer specialized degrees, such as the bachelor of fine arts (B.F.A.) or bachelor of architecture (B.Arch.). There are no absolute, or universally accepted, differences between the degrees, and colleges may vary in whether they give an arts or a science degree to graduates in a particular program.

Teacher certification. Each state sets its own certification standards, and all colleges that prepare teachers are accredited by the state in which they are located. Students must meet both bachelor's degree requirements and state certification requirements. Most states require candidates to pass an examination in the field they plan to teach.

Master's degree. Master of arts (M.A.) and master of science (M.S.) programs are graduate degrees in the liberal arts and sciences, intended for students with B.A. or B.S. degrees,

and usually take one or two years to complete. Among other master's degree programs are the master of business administration (MBA), the master of library science (M.L.S.), and the master of social work (M.S.W.) In some fields, such as law and medicine, the master's degree follows the professional degree (J.D., M.D.).

Doctorate. The most common type of doctorate is the doctor of philosophy (Ph.D.), awarded in most of the humanities, the arts, and the sciences. Examples of other programs are the doctor of education (Ed.D.) and the doctor of public health (D.P.H.). Doctoral programs usually consist of course work and independent research culminating in a dissertation or other formal presentation of the results of independent study. Length of study varies widely, and is usually self-determined.

Professional degree. These programs provide the academic prerequisites to become licensed in a recognized profession, such as medicine, law, or veterinary medicine. At least two years of prior college-level study are required for entrance into the program, and the total registered time of study must equal six academic years. Professional degrees are awarded in the following fields:

Chiropractic	D.C., D.C.M.
Dentistry	D.D.S., D.M.D.
Divinity/Ministry	D.D., M.Div.
Law	L.L.B., J.D.
Medicine	M.D.
Optometry	O.D.
Osteopathic medicine	D.O.
Pharmacy	Pharm.D.
Podiatry	D.P.M.
Rabbinical/Talmudic studies	M.H.L., Rav.
Veterinary medicine	D.V.M.

Special academic programs

In addition to majors, minors, and concentrations, many colleges offer other ways to enhance, focus, or further shape your undergraduate education. For each of the following programs, there is a state-by-state listing of colleges that offer them.

Combined bachelor's graduate program. In this program, you study at both the undergraduate and the graduate levels. Usually, you can earn a bachelor's degree and a master's or a professional degree in less time than if you pursued the two degrees separately.

Double major. Colleges listed here allow you to complete the requirements of two majors at the same time.

External degree. If you want or need to earn a college degree with minimal or no classroom attendance, an external degree program allows you to do so through independent study, distance learning, proficiency exams, and demonstrated personal experience.

Semester at sea. You spend a semester on a research vessel, doing field work in the marine sciences and taking academic course work.

Student-designed major. This program allows you to create for yourself a major that is not formally offered by the college. You develop your major, which is likely to be nontraditional and interdisciplinary, with the approval of a college officer or a committee.

Teacher certification. Colleges that have certification programs can prepare you to meet state requirements for teaching in elementary and secondary schools. [See a more detailed explanation of teacher certification in "Levels of Study" above.]

United Nations semester. The colleges listed here let you take courses at a college in the New York City area while you participate in an internship program at the United Nations.

Urban semester. You spend a semester in a major city, such as New York, Chicago, Los Angeles, or Houston, experiencing life in an urban center while pursuing course work, seminars, and/or internships related to your major.

Washington semester. You take an internship program with a government agency or department in the Washington, D.C., metro area. You can earn field service credit for your work and may also take courses at area colleges.

Alphabetical index of majors

A page reference in bold indicates a full profile of the major begins on that page. Otherwise, the page references are to the "Colleges listed by major" in Part III.

What to know about majors

What is a major?

Your college major is the subject that you will take the most courses in and learn most about. It's the area of study that your degree will be in, after you complete the required courses.

As an undergraduate, you will most likely work toward a two-year Associate of Arts (A.A.) or Associate of Science (A.S.) degree, or a four-year Bachelor of Arts (B.A.), Bachelor of Science (B.S.), or Bachelor of Fine Arts (B.F.A.) degree.

Whatever your major, you'll probably take up to half your courses in the liberal arts, to fulfill what's known as "general education" or "core" requirements. This group of subjects includes the humanities, such as literature, the fine arts (such as music and art), philosophy, and history; foreign languages; the social sciences (like anthropology, psychology, economics, political science, and sociology); math; and the biological sciences (such as zoology) and the physical sciences (for example, astronomy, chemistry, geology, and physics). Most students take these general education requirements in the first two years of a four-year program. Many two-year colleges also have liberal arts requirements.

Why so much work outside your major? Colleges want to make sure that you have a well-rounded education—that you become familiar with a wide variety of subjects. If you're an English major, for example, you're likely to benefit more from your literature courses if you also explore, say, psychology and history. If you're a math major, you'll need to be able to communicate your ideas. Think of general education as a foundation of knowledge to support your major studies. The liberal arts expose you to new ideas, and open your mind to many ways of thinking and understanding the world.

How to choose a major

You may have no idea, at the moment, what you want to study in college. A good way to zero in on a major is to think of what interests you and what you are good at. Examine your academic strengths and the subjects that inspire you to learn. Which are your favorite classes in high school? Where did you get the best grades?

What activities do you enjoy, either in or outside school? Are you a whiz at creating cartoons on the computer? Does teaching a younger sibling to cook give you pleasure? Do you love working with your hands or being outdoors? Maybe you're a political junkie who can't get enough current events. Or do you make sense of the world by learning about the past? Any of these skills and interests might suggest a major (for instance, animation, chef training, forestry, journalism, archaeology).

For many students, hobbies and extracurricular activities are as important as class work. If that's you, then maybe your major will relate to your experience in community or volunteer work, religious activities, camping or Scouting, sports or the arts.

What are your values and your vision of the future? What do you see yourself doing for a living? Do you plan to go on to graduate or professional school? Do you want to make sure that you are financially comfortable above all else? Maybe you see yourself as a leader and a motivator of others. Can you picture yourself doing scientific research or working in health care? Do you like to work outdoors? Are you an artist? Have you always wanted to be a teacher? Think about what matters to you and how your priorities may affect your choice of a major.

Then, look around and ask yourself how the world affects you. Are there careers, like nursing, that have a shortage of professionals, so that a degree in the subject should be a passport to a good job? Are you worried that, in a global economy, many jobs may be shipped overseas? If so, you may want to choose a major based on the likely needs of the job market. (You can go to www.bls.gov/oco for more information.)

Look inside yourself and look outside at other forces in your life. Before you know it, you'll start to make some choices about what to study.

When to decide on your major

Many first-year college students are undecided about their majors, and there's nothing wrong with needing more time to make a decision. Most four-year colleges expect you to declare (choose) your major at the end of your second year or at the beginning of your third year. That gives you time to take courses, including the liberal arts requirements, in a number of fields before you settle on a major.

During your first two years as an undergraduate, you can usually take some electives—nonrequired courses that interest you. If you have not yet decided on a major, you can use your electives to sample several areas of study—for instance, you might take introductory courses in two or three fields that you are considering as a major. Whether you choose electives as a way to test-drive a major or simply to learn more about a subject that appeals to you, electives will give you the opportunity to explore new ideas.

For some degrees, however, you will want to declare a major as soon as possible. That's because some majors have requirements that you'll have to meet in your first year or two of college. An example is nursing: you may have to qualify for the major by achieving a certain grade-point average in prerequisite courses before being admitted to the college's nursing program. Another example is an education major: you may need certain grades in liberal arts courses in order to qualify for a teaching program. Being accepted by a college doesn't guarantee that you'll get into the program you want at the college. Before you begin your first year, find out what's required, so you can work out your education plan.

Applied and academic majors

You can divide majors into two big groups. One group consists of the *applied majors*. These programs prepare you for a specific career by giving you the knowledge and skills you'll need in a particular line of work. When you go to work in that field, you'll put into action the information and skills you learned in college. Some examples are food science, landscape architecture, finance, real estate, journalism, special education, electrical engineering technology, nursing, veterinary technology, and forensic science. Applied majors also prepare you for the special licensing or certifications you'll need in jobs like accounting, teaching, occupational therapy, and social work.

The other big group covers the *academic majors*. Many of these majors are in the arts and sciences and include the humanities, science, and math. The academic majors don't necessarily lead to specific careers, though. They prepare you for graduate studies or for professions in which a wide range of skills and creative talents are valued—the ability to communicate, to understanding people, to read, to think about the world, or to work with numbers. Some examples of academic majors are African-American studies and Latin American studies, English, history, mathematics, chemistry, economics, and communications. (Colleges don't always agree on which majors fall into the liberal arts category. You'll find both applied and academic majors in this book.)

Applied and academic majors each have advantages and disadvantages. For the academic majors, the downside is that you will enter the job market without specific job training; you might have to settle for a lower starting salary. On the plus side, your academic training enables you to understand texts, express yourself verbally, and analyze and solve problems. Employers value these skills because they help you adapt to change. Academic majors also prepare you for graduate school in many fields. In graduate school, you can continue your education as you work toward a master's degree (M.A. or M.S.) or, maybe a doctorate degree (Ph.D.) or professional degree (law degree, medical degree).

The applied majors are popular choices because students can target their college work to launch a career. But by committing to a particular field, you will probably have fewer options, and you'll have to worry about job cycles and economic slumps in your field, or the possibility that your education and training will become out of date.

The right major at the right college

Which comes first, your choice of a major or your choice of a college? You should have some idea of what you want to study as you search for colleges because you'll want a school with a strong program in that area. Look for colleges that offer the majors you like and the related majors, too (they are listed with the majors profiled in this book). If you choose a college that teaches several majors that appeal to you, you'll be less likely to have to transfer to another college if, for any reason, you change your major.

Is a two-year or a four-year college right for you? Many two-year colleges, usually called community colleges, offer excellent training for a variety of careers, such as engineering technology, business administration, and support services in health care.

Another option is to earn a two-year associate degree in a transfer program. You'll study the equivalent of the first two years of a bachelor's degree program, and then transfer the credits when you apply to and are accepted by a four-year college. But be sure to find out which courses will be accepted for credit at the four-year college you would apply to.

As you start thinking about majors, it's good to know how colleges work. For instance, many small, private colleges are known for their liberal arts offerings. Larger universities often emphasize graduate programs. Most big-name schools, including state universities, are made up of several colleges. Sometimes it's clear what an undergraduate college or school in a university system, such as the college of agriculture or the school of nursing, has to offer. But sometimes the name of a college doesn't provide many clues. For instance, the college of arts and sciences and the school of business administration, in the same university system, might both offer a major in economics. But the course requirements might differ, and so might the admission requirements. As you look for a major, do some research on colleges. You can find more information on official college Web sites (their Internet addresses usually end in .edu).

When you scout about for the right college, you'll probably read books, magazines, and Web sites that rank the most competitive schools—that is, label one college as the best, another as the next best, and so on. Keep in mind, though, that rankings can't convey many of the features of a college, and that a listing may be based on factors that are not very important to you. So before examining a ranking, try to find out what the ratings were based on.

Your choice of college depends on what's right for you, and only you can come up with the college list that really matters. To help find colleges with good programs in the majors of interest to you, check out "Questions to ask colleges" in the major profiles in this book.

Concentrations, minors, double majors, and special programs

When you get to college, you may have even more options besides the choice of major. For example, you might select a concentration that allows you to specialize in a topic within your major, by taking a cluster of courses in the subject area. If you major in history, for instance, you might concentrate on Europe during the Middle Ages; or as a studio arts major, you might concentrate on painting. The availability of a concentration will vary from major to major and from college to college. Occasionally, a concentration may be required. In music performance, for example, you may have to choose a particular instrument that you'll concentrate on. Concentrations are less common in smaller colleges, and some programs offer concentrations only in graduate school.

Another option is to add a minor to your major. A minor is course work in which you explore another field, but not as widely or as deeply as for your major. You might minor in a subject that complements, or adds strength to, your major, such as a minor in business administration with a major in public relations, or an Arabic-language minor with a major in international relations. Then again, you could minor in a subject that's not related to your major, to give your brain a break from the type of work you do in your major courses. For example, computer science majors might enjoy studying creative writing, too.

Some colleges let you take a double major in related or even unrelated fields. In a double major, you complete two majors at the same time. For example, you could major in art history and in fine/studio arts, or in anthropology and Native American studies. You can even combine an academic and an applied major—for example, majoring in linguistics and in computer science. Double majors aren't for everyone, because college is tough enough without taking required courses for two majors. But it's something to think about if you can handle the workload and want to boost your academic résumé.

Another option to consider is a combined bachelor's and graduate degree. For many of these joint degrees, you are accepted into both programs when you apply to college. That way, you won't have to apply to grad school after you finish your undergraduate degree. These special programs (listed in Part III of this book) often include three years of study for a bachelor's degree, and then you begin the graduate program in your fourth year. The advantage is that you can complete both degrees in less time than it would take to earn the two degrees in the traditional way (often saving a

year). As an example, you could earn a bachelor's degree in biology plus a master's in physical therapy in six years. Some schools of education offer five-year programs combining a bachelor's in education and a Master of Teaching degree.

Even if you know what major you want, adding concentrations, minors, or double majors, or entering combined programs, expands your choices of what to study in college. And here's another option: at some colleges you can create your own major or work with a professor on an independent project.

Preprofessional programs

Sometimes college is a stepping stone to... more college. That's not a bad thing. The more education people have, the lower their unemployment and the higher their earnings. Also, lawyers, doctors, and other health care professionals, including pharmacists, dentists, and physical therapists, must have professional degrees. Many members of the clergy and business executives also earn advanced degrees.

To prepare you for advanced studies, some colleges offer preprofessional programs. These are advisory programs, or "tracks," that lead you through a group of requirements that you can fulfill in almost any major.

Take law school, for example. More students earn law degrees than any other professional degree. In law school, the emphasis is on the writing, reading, and understanding of documents and texts. These skills are needed in nearly every undergraduate college course. So if you intend to apply to law school, you have a wide choice of undergrad majors, including history, political science, English, philosophy, criminal justice, the sciences, math, engineering, and a foreign language.

Medical schools do not insist that applicants have specific undergraduate majors, either. However, it's no surprise that most med school applicants major in the biological sciences. Others study the physical or social sciences, or one of the liberal arts. Med school applicants are typically required to have taken five year-long courses in math and science, as well as some general education courses. The requirements, and the number of credits and labs they include, are spelled out by the college in its pre-med program.

The best thing you can do, if you plan to go to law school or medical school or to graduate programs, is to get excellent grades in your undergraduate work. You'll also need to prepare for the appropriate professional school or grad school entrance exam.

Switching majors

Many students switch majors in college. This can be risky depending upon how far along you are in your college career, because you may have to spend more time than you'd planned, and more money, to finish your degree. But your original major might not be right for you, or an elective course might spark within you a passion for another field of study. Many options are open to you, even after you enroll in college.

If you find yourself in a major that you want to change, be sure to check with your college academic adviser. Like a high school counselor who can give you guidance, a college academic adviser can help you sort through electives, choose a major, change your major, and steer you toward completion of your degree.

Planning for now and for later

You don't have to feel overwhelmed by the choice of a major and of a college. Having a lot of choices can only benefit you. Think about your interests and talents while you read about the majors. Once you narrow the selection to a few majors you like, do some research on college programs in those majors (you might also ask about the credentials, or qualifications, of faculty members, and about the availability of libraries, computers, and labs).

You can also visit the Web sites of professional associations for specific careers and of leading employers of graduates in a particular major (employers may include corporations, small businesses, nonprofit organizations, and various levels of government). A look at the job descriptions and career opportunities will give you an idea of the educational requirements that employers expect. Web sites for professional associations are included in the descriptions of majors in this book.

Thinking about a career as you are deciding on a major and a college is understandable, but try to remain flexible. The world is changing so rapidly that the jobs in demand when you declare a major may be different after you graduate. That's just one good reason to choose a major that fits the person you are. Do that, and success will follow.

Glossary

Academic adviser. A professor assigned to help students choose appropriate courses each semester. Many students consult their adviser for help in selecting a major. At some schools, when a student declares a major, he or she is assigned an adviser who teaches in the student's chosen field of study.

Academic year. A measure of the academic work that a student is expected to accomplish. Each college defines its own academic year, but federal regulations set minimum standards. Every program must have a defined academic year that contains a minimum of 30 weeks of instructional time. For undergraduate programs, a full-time enrolled student is expected to complete at least 24 semester or trimester hours, 36 quarter hours, or 900 clock hours over the 30-week period.

Accelerated program. A college program of study completed in less time than is usually required, most often by attending classes in summer or by taking extra courses during the regular academic term. Completion of a bachelor's degree program in three years is an example of acceleration.

Accreditation. Recognition by an accrediting organization or agency that a college meets acceptable standards in its programs, facilities, and services. National or regional accreditation applies to a college as a whole. Some programs or majors within colleges, such as engineering or nursing, may be accredited by professional organizations. The descriptions of majors in Part 1 of this book discuss program accreditation if it is significant in the field.

Adjunct professor. A member of the faculty who is not on the track for tenure and may teach part-time or full-time. Some colleges may refer to adjuncts as "lecturers" or "visiting professors." See also *professor* and *teaching assistant*.

Advanced placement. Admission or assignment of a first-year student to an advanced course in a subject, on the basis of evidence that the student has completed the equivalent of the college's first-year course in that subject.

Advanced Placement Program® (AP®). An academic program of the College Board that provides high school students with the opportunity to study and learn at the college level. AP offers more than 30 courses and exams in a wide variety of subject areas. High schools offer the courses and administer the exams to interested students. Most colleges in the United States accept qualifying AP Exam scores for credit, advanced placement, or both.

Adviser. See *academic adviser*.

Applied study. The practice of putting theoretical knowledge to practical use, as in the use of engineering principles to design machinery.

Area studies. A program of study that focuses on the history, geography, economics, politics, and culture of a region of the world—for example, Latin America, Eastern Europe.

Articulation agreement. An agreement between two colleges to facilitate the transfer of students from one college to the other without duplication of course work.

Associate degree. A degree granted by a college or university after the satisfactory completion of a two-year, full-time program of study. In general, the Associate of Arts (A.A.) or Associate of Science (A.S.) degree is granted after students complete a program similar to the first two years of a four-year college curriculum. The Associate in Applied Science (A.A.S.) is awarded by many colleges on completion of technological or vocational programs of study.

Bachelor's, or baccalaureate, degree. A degree received after the satisfactory completion of a four- or five-year, full-time program of study (or its part-time equivalent) at a college or university. The bachelor of arts (B.A.), bachelor of science (B.S.), and bachelor of fine arts (B.F.A.) are the most common bachelor's degrees. Policies concerning their award vary from college to college.

Calendar. The system by which a college divides its year into shorter periods for providing instruction and for awarding credit. The most common systems are those based on the semester, the trimester, the quarter, and the 4-1-4 calendar.

Capstone course. A senior-year course in which students use information and skills learned in previous course work to address a topic, issue, or set of problems.

Carnegie unit. A unit of credit given for successful completion of one year's study of a college preparatory or academic subject in high school. Some colleges refer to Carnegie units as academic units. The name comes from the Carnegie Foundation for the Advancement of Teaching.

Case study. A means of learning by studying a specific example. For instance, students of hotel management might observe the work of an actual hotel to learn how to conduct a marketing survey, hire and train staff, and advertise.

Certificate. An award for completing a particular program or course of study, usually given by two-year colleges or vocational or technical schools for non-degree programs of a year or less.

College. The generic term for an institution of higher learning; also a term used to designate divisions within a university. A university may consist of various colleges: of arts and sciences, of engineering, of music, of agriculture, of architecture, and more. When a university is divided into colleges, students usually have to apply for admission to a specific college. Colleges in a university usually have their own requirements. For example, the college of arts and science may require two units of a foreign language, and the college of music may require an audition.

College calendar. See *calendar*.

College-Level Examination Program® **(CLEP®).** Thirty-three examinations in composition and literature, foreign languages, history and social sciences, science and mathematics, and business that provide students the opportunity to earn college credit by achieving a qualifying score. These exams are sponsored by the College Board and administered by colleges year-round.

College preparatory subjects. Areas of study required for admission to, or recommended as preparation for, college. College prep subjects usually include English, history and social studies, foreign languages, mathematics, science, and the arts.

Combined bachelor's/graduate degree. A program in which students complete a bachelor's degree and a master's degree or first-professional degree in less than the usual amount of time. In most programs, students apply to undergraduate study and begin the graduate program in their fourth year of college. Graduates of the program are awarded both bachelor's and graduate degrees. At some colleges, this option is called a joint degree program.

Combined liberal arts/career program. A program in which a student typically completes three years of study in a liberal arts field and then two years of professional or technical study (for example, engineering). Graduates of the program are awarded a Bachelor of Arts degree and a Bachelor of Science degree. The combination is also referred to as a 3+2 program.

Community/junior college. A college offering two-year programs leading to an associate degree. Community colleges are public institutions, while junior colleges are privately operated on a not-for-profit basis. Most two-year colleges offer both vocational programs (also called "career" or "terminal" programs), as well as the first two years of a four-year program ("academic" or "transfer" programs). Students in the vocational program usually go directly into a vocation after graduation, while students in the academic program usually intend to transfer to a four-year institution or an upper-division college.

Concentration. A specialized branch of study within a major. For example, students majoring in psychology might choose a concentration in personality and social psychology; in fulfilling the requirements of the major, they would select courses focusing on personality and social psychology. In some programs, a concentration consists of a few courses in the area of specialty; in others, students may take 30 to 40 credits in their chosen area. A concentration may help students prepare for graduate study.

Cooperative education (co-op). A career-oriented program in which students divide their time between traditional academic study and employment in business, industry, or government. Students are typically paid for their work. Under a cooperative plan, students normally need five years to earn a bachelor's degree, but graduates have the advantage of about a year's work experience in addition to their studies.

Core curriculum. A group of courses, in varied areas of the arts and sciences, designated by a college as one of the requirements for a degree. See also *general education requirements.*

Course load. The number of class hours the student is permitted to schedule, in a given semester or quarter. It is usually 16–18 hours on a semester calendar, and 15–16 hours on a quarter calendar.

Credit hour. A standard unit of measurement for a college course. Each credit hour represents one classroom hour per week. Credit hours are used to determine the total number of hours needed to complete the requirements of a degree, diploma, certificate, or other formal award.

Curriculum. A set or program of courses. Students complete a certain curriculum, often consisting of liberal arts courses, electives, and courses in their major, to earn their degree.

Degree. An award given by a college or university certifying that a student has completed a course of study. See *bachelor's degree, associate degree, graduate degree.* See also *certificate.*

Department. A group of related programs of study within a college. The Romance languages department, for example, may include programs in French, Italian, and Spanish. Some colleges have only a few departments, and some have a wide variety. Most departments offer several majors. A biology department might offer majors in marine biology, in microbiology, and in botany, for example.

Discipline. An academic area of study. Literature, history, social science, natural science, mathematics, the arts, and foreign language are disciplines; each takes a certain approach to knowledge

Discussion section. A supplement to a large lecture course in which students meet with either the professor or a teaching assistant, usually once a week, to discuss the lectures and assigned reading.

Distance learning. An option for earning course credit off campus, via cable television, Internet, satellite classes, DVD or videotape, correspondence courses, or other means.

Doctoral degree. See *graduate degree.*

Double major. Any program in which a student completes the requirements of two majors at the same time.

Dual enrollment. The practice of allowing students to enroll in college courses while still in high school.

Elective. A course that is not required for one's chosen major or the college's core curriculum, and can be used to fulfill the credit hour requirement for graduation.

Ethnic studies. A group of courses that focus on the culture, society, literature, and history of an ethnic group such as African Americans or Hispanic Americans.

Exchange student program. Any arrangement that permits a student to study for a semester or more at another college in the

United States without extending the amount of time required for a degree.

External degree program. A system of study in which a student earns credit toward a degree through independent study, college courses, proficiency examinations, and personal experience. External degree colleges generally have no campus or classroom facilities.

Field of study. See *major*.

Fieldwork. Study that takes place outside the classroom and provides students with hands-on experience in their major. Geology majors may spend time in a ravine studying rock formations; major in food science may spend time in a hospital kitchen.

Professional degree. A degree granted on completion of academic requirements to become licensed in a recognized profession. The programs of study require at least two years of college work for entrance, and at least six years of college work for completion.

4-1-4 calendar. A variation of the semester calendar system that consists of two terms of about 16 weeks each, separated by a one-month intersession used for intensive short courses, independent study, off-campus work, or other types of instruction.

Full-time student. An enrolled student who is carrying a full-time academic workload (other than correspondence courses). What makes up a full-time workload is determined by the institution and is applicable to all students enrolled in a program.

General education requirements. Courses that give undergraduates background in the primary academic disciplines: natural sciences, social sciences, mathematics, literature and language, and fine arts. Most colleges require students to take general education courses in their first and second years, as a way to sample a wide range of courses before choosing a major. At some colleges, general education courses are referred to as the core curriculum; at others, a few courses within the general education requirements are core courses that all students must take.

Grade point average (GPA). A system used by many schools for evaluating the overall scholastic performance of students. Grade points are usually determined by first multiplying the number of hours given for a course by the numerical value of the grade, and then dividing the sum of all grade points by the total number of hours carried. The most common system of numerical values for grades is: $A = 4$, $B = 3$, $C = 2$, $D = 1$, and E or $F = 0$.

Graduate degree. A degree (sometimes called a postgraduate degree) pursued after a student has earned a bachelor's degree. The master's degree, which requires one to three years of study, is usually the degree earned after the bachelor's. The doctoral degree requires further study. First-professional degrees are also graduate degrees.

Honors program. Any special program for very able students that offers the opportunity for educational enrichment, independent study, acceleration, or some combination of these.

Humanities. The branches of learning that usually include art, the classics, dramatic art, English, general and comparative literature, journalism, music, philosophy, and religion. Many colleges divide their offerings into three divisions: humanities, social sciences, and natural sciences.

Independent study. Academic work chosen or designed by the student, with the approval of the department concerned, and pursued under an instructor's supervision. The work is usually undertaken outside the regular classroom structure.

Interdisciplinary major. See *multidisciplinary major*.

International Baccalaureate (IB). A high school curriculum offered by some schools in the United States and other countries. Some colleges award credit for completion of this curriculum. Please visit the organization's website for further information.

Internship. A short-term, supervised work experience, usually related to a student's major field, for which the student earns academic credit. The work can be full- or part-time, on or off campus, paid or unpaid. Student teaching and apprenticeships are examples.

Junior college. See *community college*.

Laboratory course. A course, usually supplemented by lectures, in which students perform scientific experiments under the supervision of a professor or a teaching assistant.

Land-grant university. One of the universities established by the federal government in 1862. The institutions were intended to educate the agricultural workforce the country needed. Many are now large universities teaching a wide range of subjects, but they still offer numerous agriculture-related majors.

Lecture course. A midsize or large course, in which the instructor speaks from prepared notes on a topic relating to the assigned reading or laboratory work. Lectures are usually supplemented by discussion sections or laboratories.

Liberal arts. The study of the humanities (literature, the arts, and philosophy), history, foreign languages, social sciences, mathematics, and natural sciences. The liberal arts and humanities stress the development of general knowledge and reasoning ability rather than specific skills.

Liberal arts/career combination. See *combined liberal arts/career program*.

Licensure. The procedure in which graduates pass one or several examinations and are awarded a license to practice a profession. For example, an accounting major must take a licensing exam after graduation to become a certified public accountant (CPA). Some of the majors described in this book prepare students to take licensing examinations after earning their bachelor's degree.

Lower-division courses. Courses that students are expected to take in their first two years of college. These courses lay the foundation for further study in the subject area.

Major. The field of study in which students concentrate, or specialize, during their undergraduate study. At most colleges, students take a third to a half of their course work in the major; the rest is devoted to liberal arts requirements and electives. In academic majors, students generally take a third of their courses in their academic field, which they usually must choose by the beginning of their junior year. In career-related, or applied, programs, such as nursing and engineering, students may take up to half their courses in their major. See *concentration* and *minor*.

Master's degree. See *graduate degree*.

Matriculation. The process in which a student is accepted, pays fees, and enrolls in classes, officially becoming a student at the college. This term is applied only to first-year students or to transfer students' first enrollment.

Minor. Course work that is not as extensive as that in a major but gives students some specialized knowledge of a second field. Students may choose a minor in the department of their major (for example, a major in comparative literature with a minor in German literature), or in a different department (for example, a biology major with a minor in philosophy). College catalogs describe the requirements for minors.

Multidisciplinary major. A major that uses the perspectives of many disciplines, or academic subjects, simultaneously, to explore problems, events, or situations. For example, women's studies uses anthropology, history, sociology, literature, and psychology to examine women in various times and cultures.

Pass/fail course. A course in which a student's achievement is noted only as either passing or failing. In some cases, the course may be offered only as a pass/fail course. In others, a student, with the instructor's permission, may take a regular course on a pass/fail basis.

Placement test. A battery of tests designed to assess a student's aptitude and level of achievement in various academic areas so that he or she can select the most appropriate courses.

Portfolio. A physical collection of examples of a student's work assembled to provide a representation of the student's achievements and skill level.

Postgraduate degree. See *graduate degree*.

Practicum. A course, usually taken in the third or fourth year of college, in which classroom learning is put into practice in a clinic (for students in medical fields) or in a classroom (for education majors). Students are supervised by a working professional during this phase of their education.

Preprofessional program. An advising program and recommended course of study for undergraduate students intending to pursue a professional degree after college. Although there is no prescribed major for entrance to professional school, students planning for a career in law, ministry, or a medical profession need to take an undergraduate program that lays the groundwork for their training. Premed students, for example, must complete certain science courses. Preprofessional advisors help students plan their undergraduate studies and to prepare for admission to professional school.

Prerequisite. A course that must be taken as preparation for more advanced course work in a particular field. For example, introductory calculus would be a prerequisite for differential mathematics. College catalogs usually indicate whether a course has a prerequisite.

Professor. A member of the faculty at a college or university who either has tenure or is on the "track" for tenure. See also *adjunct professor* and *teaching assistant*.

Program. See *major*; see also *honors program*.

PSAT/NMSQT® (Preliminary SAT/National Merit Scholarship Qualifying Test). A preparatory tool for the SAT that is administered by high schools to sophomores and juniors each year in October. The PSAT/NMSQT serves as the qualifying test for scholarships awarded by the National Merit Scholarship Corporation.

Quarter. An academic calendar period of about 12 weeks. Four quarters make up an academic year, but at colleges using the quarter system, students make normal progress by attending three quarters each year. In some colleges, students can accelerate their progress by attending all four quarters in one or more years.

Reserve Officers' Training Corps (ROTC). Programs conducted by some colleges in cooperation with the U.S. Air Force, Army, and Navy. Naval ROTC includes the Marine Corps (the Coast Guard and the Merchant Marine do not sponsor ROTC programs). Local recruiting offices of the military services themselves can supply detailed information about these programs, as can participating colleges.

SAT®. A college entrance exam that tests critical reading, writing and mathematics skills, given on specified dates through the year at test centers in the United States and other countries. The SAT is used by most colleges and sponsors of financial aid programs.

SAT Subject Tests™. Admissions tests in specific subjects given at test centers in the United States and other countries on specified dates throughout the year. The tests are used by colleges for help in both evaluating applicants for admission and determining course placement, and exemption of enrolled first-yearstudents.

School. One name for a subdivision of a university. For example, the administrative unit that offers nursing courses may be called the "college of nursing" at one institution, and the "school of nursing" at another.

Semester. On a college's calendar, a period of about 16 weeks. Colleges on a semester system offer two periods of instruction, fall and spring, a year; there may also be a summer session (usually a shorter, more concentrated period of time).

Semester at sea. A program for credit, usually for students majoring in oceanography, marine biology, or related fields, in which students live for part of a semester on a ship, usually a research vessel. Academic courses are generally taken in conjunction with the sea experience or at other times during the semester.

Seminar. A course, with a small enrollment, that focuses on a specific topic. Class discussions, student presentations, and student writing are usually emphasized over lectures and exams.

Short course. A course, generally a seminar, offered during the middle term at colleges on a 4-1-4 calendar, or sometimes offered as a one-credit class during a regular term. Students often take short courses, which usually focus on limited topics of general interest, on a pass/fail basis.

Specialization. See *concentration*.

Student-designed major. An academic program that allows a student to construct a major that the college does not formally offer. Often nontraditional and multidisciplinary, the major is developed with the approval of a college officer or committee.

Student teaching. A program in which education majors, in their fourth year, teach in a local school, under the supervision of a licensed teacher.

Studio course. A course in which students create works of art and/or design, under the guidance of an instructor, rather than receive information through lectures.

Study abroad. An arrangement by which a student completes part of the college program—typically the third year but sometimes only a semester or a summer—studying in another country. A college may operate a campus abroad, or it may have a cooperative agreement with another U.S. college or with an institution in the host country.

Teacher certification. A college program designed to prepare students to meet the requirements for certification as teachers in elementary and secondary schools.

Teaching assistant. A graduate student who aids a professor by grading papers, leading discussion sections, and/or supervising labs.

Tenure. Permanent appointment to the faculty of a college. Professors who have tenure cannot be dismissed from the faculty except for gross misconduct.

Term. The shorter period into which colleges divide the school year. Some colleges are on the semester system, in which students complete two semesters, or terms, each year. Others are on the quarter system, in which they attend three quarters each year. Many colleges offer a summer term, so that students can attend college year-round and thus receive their degree more quickly, or can finish incomplete credits. See also *calendar*.

Terminal degree. The highest degree that can be earned in a particular field. For most faculty members, it is the doctoral degree. In certain fields, however, a master's degree is the highest level.

Terminal program. An education program designed to prepare students for immediate employment. These programs usually can be completed in less than four years beyond high school and are available in most community colleges, career colleges, and vocational-technical institutes.

Thesis. A long research paper written as a requirement for a degree. At some colleges, departments may require an undergraduate thesis for a bachelor's degree. At others, an undergraduate thesis may be required of students only in certain programs. Theses are usually written under the supervision of a faculty adviser over a semester or an entire academic year.

3+2 program. See *combined liberal arts/career program*.

Transcript. A copy of a student's official academic record, listing all courses taken and grades achieved.

Transfer program. An education program in a two-year college (or four-year college that offers associate degrees), designed primarily for students who plan to continue their studies in a four-year college. See also *community/junior college*.

Transfer student. A student who attends a college—typically for a period ranging from a single term up to three years—and then is accepted by and enrolls in another college. A transfer student may receive credit for all or some of the courses successfully completed before the transfer.

Trimester. An academic calendar period of about 15 weeks. Three trimesters make up one year. Students normally progress by attending two of the trimesters each year and in some colleges can accelerate their progress by attending all three trimesters in one or more years.

Two-year upper-division college. A college offering bachelor's degree programs that begin with the third year. An entering student must have completed the first and second years at another college.

Undergraduate. A student in the first, second, third, or fourth year of an academic program leading to an associate or bachelor's degree, as opposed to a graduate student, who has earned a bachelor's degree and is pursuing a master's, doctoral, or professional degree.

United Nations semester. A program for credit in which students generally take courses at a college in the New York City metropolitan area while participating in an internship program at the United Nations.

University. An institution of higher learning that incorporates together several colleges and graduate schools. When a university is divided into colleges, students usually have to apply for admission to a specific college. Colleges within a university will have different requirements.

For example, a college of arts and science may require two units of a foreign language, and the college of music may require an audition.

Upper division. The third and fourth years of study. See also *two-year upper-division college*

Upper-division courses. Courses taken during the third and fourth years of study. Often numbered 300, 400, or 500, these courses build on the foundation of knowledge gained during the first two years and provide an in-depth exploration of the topic.

Urban semester. A program for credit in which students of diverse majors spend a semester in a major city, such as New York, Philadelphia, Chicago, Denver, or San Francisco, experiencing the complexities of an urban center through course work, seminars, and/or internship related to their major.

Virtual university. A degree-granting, accredited institution in which all courses are delivered by distance learning, with no physical campus.

Washington semester. A program in which students participate in an internship program with a government agency or department in the Washington, D.C., metropolitan area. Students earn field service credit for their work and frequently take courses at area colleges.

Weekend college. A program that allows students to take a complete academic course by attending classes only on weekends. The program, generally restricted to a few areas of study at a college, requires more than the traditional number of years to complete.

Part I: Full Descriptions of Majors

About Part I

Here you will find in-depth descriptions of 195 undergraduate majors, plus 5 preprofessional programs. These profiles are grouped into 26 broad categories. See the Table of Contents for a complete listing.

The headings below correspond to what you will find in the profiles. For more on how to interpret the profiles, read "How to Use This Book" on pages 11 to 15.

Name of major: This is the generic name of the major that is most often used by colleges.

Also known as: Alternative names that you might come across are listed here.

What it's about: This gives you a quick idea of the subject area the major covers and the careers it prepares you for.

Is this for you? This section should help you select a major according to what you like to do or to study, what you are good at, and what your personal qualities are.

Recommended high school prep: The course units recommended here refer to years of study in a four-year high school.

Did you know ...? Included here are important aspects or interesting facts about the major that many students entering the major are not aware of.

Typical courses in the major: This list is a sampling of courses commonly offered in the major, in roughly the order of sequence they are taken.

Concentrations: You can sometimes concentrate your studies in a certain area within your major. The concentrations listed here are not available at all colleges.

What the study of this major is like: This section tells you what you'll actually study in a major, and how the major is generally taught and learned.

Other majors you might like: Some of these will be obvious, but some may surprise you. We encourage you to consider them with an open mind. Majors in **bold type** are fully profiled in this book. Those in regular type are briefly described in Part II.

Questions to ask colleges: Good for college visits, interviews, or an email to the Web sites of the colleges you are considering.

Career options and trends: This section lists job titles in careers the major may lead to—an asterisk indicates a type of job that graduates most often pursue. Also described are any additional education, certification, or licensure requirements for the careers listed, plus trends occurring or likely to occur in careers related to the major.

Insider's viewpoint: We asked professors and students to give some insight or describe what appeals to them about the major.

For more info: Contact information is provided here for associations (educational and business) that you should investigate to explore further the major and/or related careers.

Agriculture

Agriculture is an ancient practice that has become a cutting-edge science and industry. It's all about the production of crops, livestock, feed, and fiber. People need agriculture for the basics like food and clothing.

"The things that we do have a major impact on everyone—everyone must eat," says Bonita A. Glatz, a food science professor at Iowa State University.

Farmers and ranchers have gotten pretty good at growing and raising crops and food. The big push in agriculture now is to increase the quality and quantity of plant and animal products, while preserving the ecology of our systems. Things are really getting technical. In many majors, agricultural study is a type of applied biology or applied chemistry. It's a science. So if you study agriculture in a four-year program, you're likely to get a solid science background followed by an in-depth exploration of chemistry, biochemistry, genetics, pathology (study of diseases), meteorology (weather), economics, or education.

Is agriculture for you? People who study and work in farming represent a wide variety of skills and interests. If you care about people, animals, or planet Earth, you might consider an agricultural major. Do you have a passion for vegetable gardening or horseback riding? Maybe you love nature, plants, or the outdoors. Perhaps you want to protect the environment or help developing countries that are struggling with poverty and malnutrition. Many students bring experience in farming and ranching with them to college. During college, they gain an interest in economics and business or a particular branch of agriscience. You don't have to come from a farming background or plan to work on a farm to be an ag major. But you will need quantitative skills—math and statistics—to study this field.

What about job prospects? We all need agricultural products, but the industry is so efficient that we don't need as many farms and traditional farm jobs as we did in the past. Farms are merging so that we have fewer and larger farms now. Agriculture is big business. That means a smaller number of jobs for farmers and ranchers. On the other hand, the business of farming and the global scale of food distribution expand the role of other things like agribusiness and agricultural economics. In fact, students in these two majors will take many of the same classes. The difference is that agribusiness students will probably have a career path toward management in a food company. Agricultural economics is more analytical and good preparation for either research or business. Your choice of major and level of degree affect your job prospects.

What's hot in the field

If you're thinking that agriculture is just plants and soil, no way. Computers, telecommunications, and other high-tech tools play a huge role. "Precision agriculture guided by geographic information systems, satellite guidance, and computer-equipped tractors increases production and conserves natural resources," explains Professor Douglas L. Young of Washington State University.

What else is happening? You've probably seen news stories about environmental regulations or about real estate development in what were once rural areas. These trends may require agriculture students to learn more about the environment and resource economics. "The sustainability of the way we produce food is becoming more important as fuel, transportation and food safety issues are intensifying," says Professor Marianne Sarrantonio, who coordinates the sustainable agriculture program at the University of Maine. She sees increasing demand for graduates in that field.

Another new area of study is the economics of biotechnology. The job picture is also bright for students in food science, partly because people's tastes change and consumers are learning more about nutrition, health, and wellness. And don't forget food safety and biosecurity. They couldn't be more important. Other hot jobs are in plant breeding and genetics, financial management, information systems, and teaching.

From field to table, from the plant to the planet, agriculture requires more knowledge and education than ever before. Today's agricultural professionals have business, economic, scientific, and technical skills and expertise.

It's no surprise that during graduate-level studies, students focus on a very specific area. For example, in agronomy, grad students zoom in on things like crop production and physiology; or soil sciences including soil chemistry, microbiology, and biochemistry. If you're interested in a business track, keep in mind that nearly all agribusiness professions require advanced degrees; grad studies veer toward agricultural marketing or agricultural trade.

But not all colleges and universities define majors in the same way. Colleges vary in the areas of study they emphasize. The differences could stem from the regional climate and its specific crop or soil suitability, or even a college's size and priorities. In college catalogs and on the Internet, look under agricultural sciences, biological sciences, environmental sciences, and natural resources. And be sure to go to the Web sites of the land-grant universities and the big state schools, which dominate agricultural education. Another section in this book related to agriculture is Natural resources and conservation. There you'll find majors in forestry, fisheries, and environmental studies.

Here are some Web sites to get you started thinking about your future in agriculture: the U.S. Department of Agriculture (www.usda. gov), the U.S. Food and Drug Administration (www.fda.gov), the National FFA Organization (www.ffa.org), and the American Farm Bureau (www.fb.com).

Agricultural business

Also known as:

Agribusiness

What it's about:

Agricultural business deals with the management, marketing, and financing of food and fiber, "from the field to the table." You study principles from agricultural sciences, economics, business, and statistics in preparation for a career in agribusiness, farming, natural resources, government, and related areas.

Is this for you?

You might like this major if you also like: 4-H projects and competitions; debating; organizing or leading a club or other group activity; solving problems; sports. A concern for the problems of developing countries that are struggling with poverty and malnutrition might also lead you to this major.

Consider this major if you are good at: attention to detail; critical reading/thinking; leadership; organizing; persuading/influencing; quantitative analysis; teamwork *...or have...* initiative; verbal skills; writing skills.

Recommended high school prep:

English 4, math 3 (including precalculus), lab science 3 (including biology and chemistry), social studies 3, and a foreign language 2–3. If available, take a computer course covering basic office applications and spreadsheets.

Did you know...

...that to be successful in agricultural business, you must know math and statistics? Many students are surprised by the idea, as well as by the need for excellent writing and speaking skills.

Typical courses in this major:

Introduction to agribusiness
Managerial accounting
Economics (micro and macro)
Statistics
Farming technologies
Production management
Farm and ranch management
Human resources management
Agricultural marketing
International trade
Agricultural finance
Farm management laboratory
Agricultural history and law
Agricultural policy
Business/environmental law
Management information systems

Concentrations:

In college: agricultural economics; agricultural marketing; farm and ranch management; agricultural finance; environmental economics; crop or animal production; international agriculture and trade.

If you go on to grad school: econometrics; agricultural policy; rural and community economic development.

What the study of this major is like:

The agricultural business major prepares you to apply business and economic principles to the production and marketing of food and other agricultural products and to the management of natural resources. In order to make economically and environmentally sound decisions in this field, you need to understand accounting, economics, finance, labor, marketing, management, and public policy, as you analyze and deal with business and environmental risk; identify and respond to changes in the demand for food products and services; and improve profitability.

You learn principles associated with best practices for product development, profit maximization, and investment planning. You become familiar with accounting tools like balance sheets, income statements, and cash flow statements. You are taught to use quantitative tools such as statistics, accounting methods, computer programs, and investment analysis to solve management and planning problems.

You also learn the importance of risk management in an industry in which prices can zigzag (because of the uncertainties of worldwide markets) and production is at the mercy of weather, pests, and natural disasters. To thrive despite the risks, you must make smart use of futures markets, insurance, contracting, machinery maintenance, emerging technologies, and labor management. You also take supporting courses in data analysis, international studies, biological sciences, social sciences, and written and oral communication. A number of agribusinesses offer internships that give you a chance to get some real business experience.

Many majors are challenged by such requirements as calculus and courses in the humanities and social sciences. Third- and fourth-year team and individual projects—which can sometimes conflict with off-campus employment or other activities—require long hours of work. But problem-centered assignments help you build a solid foundation for future employment.

Leading agricultural colleges may emphasize agribusiness, marketing, farm/ranch management, technology, natural resource economics, or statistics/econometrics, but most colleges offer courses in all these areas. If you are interested in other areas, such as international agricultural development or rural development, explore the catalogs or Web sites of various programs to see what they offer. If you want to combine an agribusiness degree with another field (for instance, wine grape production), examine course offerings and prerequisites in departments such as crop and soil sciences. The agricultural business major is also offered at the two-year associate degree level; the program is generally geared for transfer into a four-year agribusiness program.

Other majors you might like:

Economics
Business administration and management
Accounting
Agronomy and crop science

Animal sciences
Forest resources production
Range science
Agricultural and biological engineering
Geography
Farm and ranch management
International business
Aquaculture

Questions to ask colleges:

Does the program feature the latest technologies being applied to agricultural production?

What ties do the faculty members have to the industry? Are undergrads given assistance in finding internships?

Where have recent graduates gone to work?

Career options and trends:

Agribusiness manager or marketer*; farmer or rancher*; loan officer*; government agency employee; production supervisor; financial analyst; commodity merchandiser.

The long-term trend toward consolidation into fewer and larger farms is projected to continue, further reducing the number of jobs for farmers and ranchers but increasing employment opportunities for agricultural managers since owners of these farms rarely live on their land. Most graduates obtain jobs in business and industry. There is demand for managers and specialists trained in accounting, credit analysis, marketing, and international trade. Job prospects are generally good, especially if you are willing to relocate.

For more info:

United Agribusiness League
54 Corporate Park
Irvine, CA 92606-5105
(800) 223-4590
www.ual.org

Agricultural economics

What it's about:

The agricultural economics major teaches you to understand agriculture from both the national and the international perspective. You apply economic principles to the study of agricultural trends, productivity, investment, and the use and conservation of natural resources.

Is this for you?

You might like this major if you also like: social studies; math; business; government; working with numbers; looking at the big picture; environmental issues.

Consider this major if you are good at: critical reading/thinking; leadership; math; persuading/influencing; quantitative analysis; teamwork *...or have...* initiative; verbal skills; writing skills.

Recommended high school prep:

English 4, math 4 (including precalculus), lab science 3, social studies 3; and a foreign language 3. If possible, take courses in computer science, economics, and statistics. A foreign language is especially helpful because agricultural markets are increasingly global.

Did you know...

...that most graduates in this major, contrary to popular belief, do not farm? While nearly 20 percent of all jobs in the United States are in the food and fiber industries, fewer than 3 percent of the employees in those industries actually work on a farm.

Typical courses in this major:

Accounting
Economics (micro and macro)
Statistics
Quantative methods in agricultural economics
Agricultural marketing and sales
Agricultural price analysis
Agribusiness management
Agricultural cooperatives
Agricultural finance
Agricultural policy
Commodity futures markets
International trade and finance
Agricultural and business law
Environmental resources development
Rural economic development
Professional career development

Concentrations:

Farm and ranch management; marketing; finance; environmental economics; rural development; international economic development.

What the study of this major is like:

Economics is the study of the way societies use available resources to meet people's needs. Since farming is the largest user of the earth's resources, agricultural economics is a wide-ranging field. You are most likely to benefit from the major if you have a broad educational background. Your general education courses may include English, speech, data analysis, chemistry, physics, economics, the natural and social sciences, history, literature, and the arts.

Many of the courses offered in this major are the same as in the agricultural business major, and sometimes it's hard to distinguish the two. Both majors cover economic principles, technical agricultural sciences, and business management tools. Whereas the agricultural business major provides management, operational, and production skills for business careers in the industry, agricultural economics focuses analytically on a broader range of issues to prepare you for graduate study or for careers in research and public policy as well as in business. You explore the relationship between agriculture and other sectors of the economy; you evaluate responses to economic problems created by the changing agricultural environment. You learn quantitative problem solving and qualitative reasoning, as well as how to make ethical judgments.

You also take upper-level electives in your chosen concentration, which may focus on public policy and regional development issues; natural resource allocation and environmental issues; management and production; or international trade. In many programs, a capstone project teaches you to debate concepts and integrate them into a wider perspective. Some colleges require you to do an internship or declare a minor. You may be able to earn college credit by participating in a study-abroad program.

Typically, you need good preparation in math and science to succeed in this major. Joining a student chapter of a national agricultural association will help you to learn more about the field, make valuable career contacts, and find internships and job opportunities.

Programs are typically found in colleges of agriculture at land-grant universities. Some smaller, four-year private and public colleges offer a similar major, particularly in regions where agriculture is a significant industry. Admission and course requirements differ slightly among colleges. Some colleges combine agricultural business and agricultural economics into one program. There may also be differences in the areas of concentration offered.

Other majors you might like:
Agricultural business
Farm and ranch management
Agricultural education services
Environmental studies
Finance
Development economics
Mathematics
Statistics
Management information systems
Global studies
Public policy analysis
International business

Questions to ask colleges:
How much emphasis is placed on math and quantitative analysis?

How does the agricultural economics program differ from the agribusiness major? Are courses in the agricultural technical sciences included?

Is a senior capstone project required? What sort of projects have recent graduates submitted?

Career options and trends:
Agricultural statistician; agricultural consultant; government agency employee (e.g., USDA); financial analyst; bank manager or loan officer; sales representative; natural resources manager; public policy analyst; commodities broker, trader, or merchandiser.

The food and fiber industries are changing rapidly, because of corporate mergers and consolidations, the increasing reliance on telecommunications, and the growth of global trade and competition. As a result, companies want educated, productive, and flexible employees who can adapt in a rapidly shifting world market.

Demand for economists in general remains fairly constant, in good times and bad. Opportunities for agricultural economists in particular are increasing, as is the diversity, globalization, and high-tech nature of the profession.

Insider's viewpoint:
"I have enjoyed almost all the classes that are offered through this major, especially those dealing with commodities, farm planning, and managerial and decision-making economics. All of these classes deal with real-world situations; they are not all just about theories and concepts."

—Christopher, senior, University of Wisconsin

For more info:
Agricultural & Applied Economics Association
555 East Wells St., Suite 1100
Milwaukee, WI 53202
(414) 918-3190
www.aaea.org

Agronomy and crop science

What it's about:

This major provides the theoretical and practical knowledge needed for the efficient and sustainable production of food, fuel, feed, and fiber. You will gain a broad understanding of the diversity of, and relationships among, plants, soils, and climates. You will also explore the ethical, cultural, and environmental issues facing professionals in agriculture and natural resources.

Is this for you?

You might like this major if you also like: 4-H or FFA (Future Farmers of America) projects and competitions; Boy/Girl Scouts; science and math; the Weather Channel; gardening; outdoor activities; collecting or observing insects; seed collecting; issues relating to world hunger and the environment.

Consider this major if you are good at: attention to detail; critical reading/thinking; leadership; organizing; quantitative analysis; research; teamwork *...or have...* initiative; manual dexterity; verbal skills.

Recommended high school prep:

English 4, math 3 (including precalculus), lab science 4 (including biology, physics, and chemistry), social studies 3, and a foreign language 2–3. Take as much math and science as you can, and a computer science course if available. Courses that help you develop good writing and oral communication skills are also important.

Did you know...

...that a farm background is not essential for a major in agronomy?

Typical courses in this major:

Plant pathology
Entomology
Pest management
Soil fertility
Weed science
Ecology
World food issues
Sustainable agriculture
Genetics
Weather and climate
Seed science and technology
Global climate change
Plant breeding
Crop management and production
Soil science
Statistics

Concentrations:

In college: agroecology; crop and soil management; plant breeding; pest management; seed production and technology; soil conservation; turfgrass management; climatology; biotechnology.

If you go on to grad school: agricultural meteorology; crop production and physiology, with specializations in seed science and weed science; plant breeding; and soil science, with specializations in soil chemistry, physics, morphology, genesis, biology, fertility, and management.

What the study of this major is like:

Agronomists work to provide consumers with a sufficient supply of food; to help producers increase profitability and efficiency; and to protect the environment. As an agronomy and crop science major, you learn how the plant and soil sciences are used in the production of abundant, high-quality food, fuel, feed, and fiber. Crop and plant sciences relate primarily to the genetics, breeding, physiology, and management of crops. Soil science covers the physics, chemistry, origin, microbiology, fertility, and management of soil. Majors also study weather and climate.

You generally begin with courses in soil science, crop production, botany or biology, geology, chemistry, English, and statistics. In addition, you study the physical and social sciences, communications, economics, and math. You'll be encouraged to take at least one course in plant pathology, entomology, weed science, and soil fertility/plant nutrition. As you learn more about the discipline, you may develop specific interests in crop science, soil science, or climatology. You can generally double-major (or minor) in agronomy/crop science and agribusiness, agricultural journalism, animal science, environmental sciences, or extension education.

Core courses (natural sciences, math, English, and social sciences) are usually taught in a lecture/lab format. Upper-level agronomy and crop science courses focus on problem solving, real-life situations, and professional competency. Integrated into the instruction is an emphasis on teamwork, leadership, communication, critical analysis, and management skills, as well as sustainability principles and ethical values.

Your course work is often supplemented by field trips, industrial tours, or seminars on agronomy issues. Majors can participate in regional and national contests with crop and soil judging teams. You are also encouraged to seek internships and summer/part-time employment in government agencies, agricultural businesses (seed, fertilizer, agricultural chemicals), conservation centers, pest control companies, or other areas relating to food, fuel, feed, and fiber production. You can generally earn academic credit for such work.

Colleges may vary in their emphasis on the role of science in response to world hunger and pollution. If you plan to go on to grad school, you generally need to complete an undergraduate program that stresses agronomic, biological, mathematical, and physical sciences.

Other majors you might like:
Forestry
Sustainable agriculture
Plant sciences
Atmospheric science
Plant protection/pest management
Range science
Soil science
Biochemistry
Agricultural and biological engineering

Genetics
Turf management
Agricultural education services

Questions to ask colleges:
Are internships and summer work opportunities available? When you evaluate a curriculum, you should take into account the availability of internships and exchange programs that provide work in the profession and study-abroad experiences.

Does the program provide learning experiences at a working farm or in a campus greenhouse?

Does the program include courses covering leadership qualities and skills, especially in communications, ethics, and decision-making?

Career options and trends:
Agricultural business manager*; plant breeder; seed production specialist*; environmental and natural resources manager; farm manager; government agency employee*; range management specialist; crop and soil management specialist; soil conservationist and surveyor*.

Demand for Agronomists is expected to be good. The need to provide sustainable sources of food, energy, and raw materials will grow as our global population grows, and this need will become even more pressing if the trend towards loss of arable land continues.

Agronomy is increasingly international—you should expect to travel during your career. The "green revolution" occurring in developing countries calls for expertise in seed physiology, soil science, and plant breeding, to counter the effects of pests, disease, and drought. The role of genetic engineering will increase in importance as well, and you should expect a greater emphasis on biorenewables and food management and safety practices.

For more info:
American Society of Agronomy
677 South Segoe Rd.
Madison, WI 53711-1086
(608) 273-8080
www.agronomy.org

Animal sciences

What it's about:

The animal sciences major deals with the breeding, raising, and management of livestock and poultry, and the foods and products obtained from them. The care and welfare of companion or captive animals may also be covered.

Is this for you?

You might like this major if you also like: working with large animals; biology; Animal Planet; working outdoors; physical challenges; 4H groups; farmwork.

Consider this major if you are good at: attention to detail; caring/nurturing; critical reading/thinking; math; organizing; quantitative analysis *...or have...* initiative; patience; physical stamina; writing skills.

Recommended high school prep:

English 4, math 4 (including precalculus or calculus), lab science 4, social studies 3, and a foreign language 2–3. If available, take an advanced biology course.

Did you know...

...that this major is not for the squeamish? You have to be willing to get up close and personal with the animals, and not mind the aroma—or maybe even like it.

Typical courses in this major:

Animal behavior
Animal biology
Animal evaluation
Nutrition
Livestock management
Poultry science
Dairy science
Endocrinology
Genetics
Growth and development
Lactation
Livestock marketing
Reproductive physiology
Artificial insemination practices
Companion animal management
Meat science and processing

Concentrations:

In college: reproductive physiology; genetics and breeding; endocrinology; animal nutrition; animal behavior.

If you go on to grad school: reproductive physiology; genetics and breeding; endocrinology; animal behavior.

What the study of this major is like:

Like most science majors, you will spend at least 40 percent of your time in courses in the humanities, social sciences, natural sciences, and math—typically during your first two years. A solid foundation in the biological and physical sciences will help you get the most from the animal science courses you will take in your third and fourth years.

Biological concepts and animal science terminology are usually presented in lectures; you then get hands-on experience in class demonstrations and labs. You will also be encouraged (in some programs, required) to gain practice outside the classroom, by participating in an internship, research project, livestock judging competition, or extension work.

Because animal agriculture is a process that depends on cooperation among professionals and technicians, your courses will probably include teamwork activities. In fact, communication skills are essential in this discipline. You will also benefit from sharpening your understanding of math and chemistry. Most students who transfer out of animal sciences do so because they are having difficulty with one or both of these subjects.

Most colleges offer several options in the major: a production track, business/management track, science track, or preveterinary track. Colleges in regions with a livestock industry may focus on production systems and offer plenty of hands-on training. Colleges with strong research programs may emphasize the biology of animal growth and reproduction, biotechnology, and genetics. Some programs stress compatibility with the preprofessional requirements of veterinary medicine and human medicine, as well as with grad school requirements. A business option will emphasize agricultural economics.

If a species is prominent in the area around a college, its presence will likely be reflected in the expertise of the faculty and the courses offered. You can strengthen your ability to observe similarities and differences if you study not only the commonly found species but others as well.

Other majors you might like:
Zoology
Livestock management
Wildlife and wilderness management
Veterinary technology
Biochemistry
Aquaculture
Dairy science
Entomology
Food science
Microbiology
Poultry science
Agricultural and biological engineering

Questions to ask colleges:
Does the program have adequate resources, including labs and animal facilities, to provide practice in the animal handling skills you will need professionally? Access to facilities in which you can study meat, dairy, and other food processing and testing is also desirable.

Are there opportunities to participate with faculty members in their research programs? Such experiences are essential if you wish to go on to a graduate or professional program.

Career options and trends:
Livestock production manager*; artificial breeding technician; research technician; vocational agriculture teacher; sales representative for agricultural supplier*; extension agent; farm or ranch manager; veterinarian*.

According to the Bureau of Labor Statistics, employment in this field is projected to be strong, growing faster than average through 2018.

For certain positions, such as consulting work, it may be desirable or necessary to be certified by ARPAS (American Registry of Professional Animal Scientists). To become a veterinarian, you must obtain a doctorate of veterinarian medicine (D.V.M.) and pass a licensing exam.

An understanding of environmental issues associated with animal production; concerns about animal welfare; and a sense of the ethical issues associated with animal product development are increasingly important to animal scientists. Global issues, such as growing populations, decreasing arable land, and climate change, will create opportunities for innovative professionals.

Insider's viewpoint:
"I liked being able to apply to real life the knowledge I gained through my classes. It's enjoyable to consult with a farmer on the best way to manage his dairy cattle, or to help a horse owner formulate a diet for her dressage horse."

—Kristen, senior, University of Maryland

For more info:
American Society of Animal Science (ASAS)
2441 Village Green Place
Champaign, IL 61822
(217) 356-9050
www.asas.org

Equestrian studies

Also known as:
Equine studies

What it's about:
This major deals with horses and horsemanship (in Latin, *equus* means "horse"). You learn the scientific principles needed for the care, breeding, and conditioning of horses; the business principles needed for managing horse-related enterprises and facilities; and the equitation and training skills needed for teaching horseback riding and for training horses.

Is this for you?
You might like this major if you also like: horses and horseback riding; working outdoors; sports and competition; tutoring; business activities; taking care of animals.

Consider this major if you are good at: attention to detail; caring/nurturing; coaching; counseling; memorizing; organizing *...or have...* a sense of responsibility to your work; initiative; patience; physical stamina.

Recommended high school prep:
English 4, math 3, lab science 3, social studies 3, and a foreign language 2–3. If available, take anatomy and physiology.

Typical courses in this major:
Equine anatomy and physiology
Equine nutrition
Equine breed types and selection
Stable management
Equine lameness and disease
Stud farm management
Equine breeding lab
Equine business management
Equine health management
Management of equine events
Equine breaking and training
Equitation (riding) classes
Care and prevention of athletic injuries
Teaching horsemanship
Entrepreneurship

Concentrations:
Equine business management.

What the study of this major is like:
As an equestrian studies major, you learn to understand the horse and its role in society today. If you have little familiarity with horses, you take handling and riding courses and gain practice in caring for horses and horse tackle. If you are more experienced, you are taught how to break and train horses, instruct riders, and ride at an advanced level (such as dressage and jumping). To learn how to live and work responsibly with horses, all majors study the animal's history and its health and safety needs. Most likely, you will also explore various horse-related enterprises, such as feed sales, racing, breeding, and equine publications.

In general, programs allow students at all levels to be stimulated by their course work. You typically begin with general science courses (for example, biology and chemistry) and then specialize, taking courses in anatomy and physiology, equine breeds, and types and selection. In higher-level courses, such as a breeding lab, you apply what you learn. Equitation courses (involving actual horseback riding) are also taught at beginning, intermediate, and advanced levels.

Many programs offer a two-year associate of science or applied science degree. You can usually choose one of three tracks—equestrian, equine science, or equine business management. In the equestrian track, you concentrate on horsemanship, teaching, and training skills, as you prepare to enter the field of horse training and riding instruction. The science and business tracks generally prepare you to transfer to a four-year program.

In a four-year program, a concentration in science and preveterinary courses focuses on biology, chemistry, math, and equine health and breeding and usually leads to a Bachelor of Science degree. An equine management track includes business subjects and stresses industry-oriented courses, such as stable or stud farm management, equine economics, and equine marketing. At some colleges, equestrian studies (or equine science) is offered only as a concentration in an animal sciences program.

Other majors you might like:
Animal sciences
Physical education
Horse husbandry/equine science
Veterinary technology
Wildlife and wilderness management
Sports and fitness administration
Athletic training
Biology
Zoology
Entrepreneurial studies

Questions to ask colleges:
What are the graduates of the equine degree program doing in the industry now? The answer should indicate whether the program is a strong one.

Career options and trends:
Horse care technician; assistant manager/trainer; farrier (individual who shoes horses); riding instructor; equine massage therapist; veterinarian; biomedical technician; nutritional consultant; pharmaceutical representative.

Jobs as a professional horse trainer are very hard to come by; graduates might find positions as assistant trainers at best, or, more probably, as managers, assistant managers, and grooms. Graduates with a solid science background can investigate alternative career opportunities in the biomedical field and in the pharmaceutical and nutritional industries.

Today, horses represent a larger financial commitment than in years past. As a result, employers in the industry look for better-educated, more qualified personnel than previously.

Insider's viewpoint:
"I look at every student and every horse similarly. Each is an individual that needs support and the freedom of self-expression in order to grow and realize his or her full potential."

—H. Jerry Schurink, Director of Equine Studies, University of Massachusetts Amherst

For more info:
United States Pony Clubs, Inc.
4041 Iron Works Parkway
Lexington, KY 40511
(859) 254-7669
www.ponyclub.org

Farm and ranch management

What it's about:

By combining courses in economics, business, and agriculture, this major prepares students to manage a farm, a ranch, and other rural businesses and to do commercial and professional work related to agriculture.

Is this for you?

You might like this major if you also like: working outdoors; using equipment; rural communities; team sports; animals.

Consider this major if you are good at: attention to detail; critical reading/thinking; organizing; quantitative analysis; research; teamwork *...or have...* initiative; manual dexterity; physical stamina.

Recommended high school prep:

English 4, math 3, lab science 3, social studies 3, and a foreign language 2–3. Three years of vocational agriculture is recommended, if available; as well as two years of computers and speech, and an accounting course.

Typical courses in this major:

Introduction to agricultural economics
Microeconomic theory
Marketing agricultural products
Principles of farm and ranch management
Equipment operation and maintenance
Financial management in agriculture
Accounting principles
Animal health and nutrition
Feedlot management
Livestock production
Advanced farm and ranch management
Agricultural price analysis
Agricultural commodity futures
Agricultural policy
Macroeconomics of agriculture
Rural entrepreneurship

Concentrations:

Crop production; animal husbandry; agricultural mechanization; agricultural marketing.

What the study of this major is like:

Your course work in this major provides a foundation in accounting, finance, marketing, management, economics, and technical production and/or processing. You use computer applications to integrate what you learn into a comprehensive set of entrepreneurial skills. Although you will be expected to study subjects in a number of academic and technical disciplines, you will have flexibility when it comes to identifying your specialty field.

At some colleges, the program emphasizes accounting and a traditional farm and ranch management-oriented curriculum. At others, more attention is placed on technical applications; some colleges may relax their focus and teach general rural entrepreneurship. And while some cover a variety of business, economic, and technical subjects, others stress the application of those subjects to a comprehensive business plan. Programs may also vary in the extent to which they explore risk management.

This major provides opportunities for you to learn and apply business and economic principles, concepts, and tools to a broad spectrum of rural management areas. Career opportunities include the operation of your own farm, ranch, or other rural business; professional farm and ranch management; and agricultural real estate appraisal. During college, you can benefit from interning with a rural lending institution or business.

Other majors you might like:

Range science
Agronomy and crop science
Veterinary technology
Animal breeding
Dairy science

Sustainable agriculture
Mining and mineral engineering
Entomology
Heavy equipment maintenance
Operations management
Turf management
Entrepreneurial studies

Questions to ask colleges:

What are the experiences and interests of faculty members who teach the core courses?

What computer resources are available, and how are they used in the curriculum?

How are "real-world" professionals involved in the program? People employed in rural management can help prepare you for challenges you may face in your career.

Career options and trends:

Farmer*; rancher*; business owner or manager*; farm/ranch appraiser; rural loan officer*; consultant; farm machinery company representative.

The number of self-employed farmers and ranchers continues to decline; farm/ranch consolidation, increased agricultural productivity, and the high cost of running a farm or ranch are all contributing factors. However, with fewer people wanting to become farmers, job prospects are projected to be favorable over the next decade for those who want to go into farming.

If you are good at integrating business, economics, and technical expertise, you may be able to take advantage of other types of rural entrepreneurial opportunities that are increasing. A growing number of small-scale farmers have found success in "niche" (closely targeted) markets, organic farming, farmers' markets, and agricultural and marketing cooperatives. In fact, organic farming, while still a small part of the overall U.S. food supply, is one of the fastest-growing sectors in agriculture.

For more info:
National FFA Organization (formerly Future
   Farmers of America)
P.O. Box 68960
6060 FFA Drive
Indianapolis, IN 46268-0960
(317) 802-6060
www.ffa.org

Food science

What it's about:
In the food science major, you integrate and apply your knowledge of chemistry, biology, nutrition, and engineering as you learn to preserve, process, package, and distribute foods that are wholesome, affordable, and safe to eat.

Is this for you?
You might like this major if you also like: science and math; cooking; hands-on learning; working individually or in teams; applying scientific principles to real-world problems.

Consider this major if you are good at: attention to detail; critical reading/thinking; quantitative analysis; research; teamwork *...or have...* initiative; lab skills; manual dexterity; verbal skills.

Recommended high school prep:
English 4, math 4 (including precalculus), lab science 4 (including chemistry, biology, and physics), social studies 3, and a foreign language 2–3. Chemistry is essential; courses in health and nutrition are helpful if available.

Typical courses in this major:
Introduction to food science
Agricultural economics
Food chemistry
Food microbiology
Food engineering
Packaging and distribution
Nutrition
Dairy foods processing
Plant foods processing
Meat processing
Food laws and regulations
Sensory analysis
Food quality control and management
Unit operations

Concentrations:
Food chemistry; food-processing technology; packaging; safety and quality assurance; sensory evaluation; food microbiology; food engineering; nutrition.

What the study of this major is like:
Food science is an interdisciplinary program. It brings together principles from the natural sciences, the social sciences, engineering, and business to shed light on the nature and characteristics of food and the nutritional needs of people of various ages, cultures, and lifestyles.

The first two years of a typical food science program consist of required core courses in general chemistry, organic chemistry, and biochemistry; biology; general microbiology; physics; calculus; statistics; human nutrition; communications; and humanities. Most courses have a practical, hands-on laboratory work or project assignment in which you put into practice the facts and concepts you've learned in the classroom.

The course of study is rigorous, but it lays a solid foundation for the food science courses you take in the third and fourth years. Because scientists, technicians, producers, and business people work together in the food industry, you need to develop good communication skills and to understand the differing perspectives these individuals represent.

In upper-level courses, you learn and apply technology to the sanitary processing, preservation, storage, and marketing of foods. You become skilled at using food science instruments and processing equipment. You also receive extensive training in laboratory techniques. Internships with industry or government agencies provide valuable experience.

Special emphasis may vary among colleges, depending on the particular strengths of the faculty members or the needs of local industry. Programs that stress basic science, as it applies to food and food ingredients, focus on food microbiology, food chemistry, or food engineering. Other programs are more commodity-oriented; they focus on dairy processing, meat processing, or plant processing. You may be encouraged to take a minor concentration in food marketing, consumer education, nutrition, business, or economics.

Other majors you might like:
Food and nutrition studies
Dietetics
Agricultural and biological engineering
Animal sciences
Dairy science
Plant sciences
Agricultural business
Microbiology
Chemical engineering
Biotechnology
Restaurant/food services management
Culinary arts and chef training

Career options and trends:
Food technologist; research and development scientist; quality assurance manager; food inspector; process engineer; packaging technologist.

A graduate degree (master's or doctorate) is required for a position as a research scientist or extension food technologist.

Employment can be found with manufacturers of retail food products, as well as with companies that supply food ingredients, processing equipment, and packaging materials, or are involved in institutional food service. Positions are also available in various government agencies and in independent testing laboratories.

Prospects are generally good in this field, even during economic downturns. Job growth will be driven in part by the demand for new food safety measures, and heightened public awareness of diet, health, food safety, and biosecurity issues.

For more info:
Institute of Food Technologists (IFT)
525 West Van Buren, Suite 1000
Chicago, IL 60607
(312) 782-8424
www.ift.org

Horticulture

What it's about:

Horticulture is a diverse field that includes plant biology, physical sciences, systems management, and the arts. Horticulturists study fruits, vegetables, herbs, trees, shrubs, flowers, and ornamental perennials and annuals, as well as the operation and management of field and greenhouse production, and the design and construction of gardens and landscapes.

Is this for you?

You might like this major if you also like: being outdoors; working with your hands; the arts; science; gardening clubs; arboretums; the environment.

Consider this major if you are good at: attention to detail; caring/nurturing; creativity; critical reading/thinking; math; memorizing; organizing; spacial thinking/analysis; teamwork *...or have...* manual dexterity.

Recommended high school prep:

English 4, math 3, lab science 3 (including biology, chemistry, and physics), social studies 3, visual arts 1, and a foreign language 2–3.

Typical courses in this major:

Plant biology
Plant propagation
Plant taxonomy and identification
Soil science and plant nutrition
Plant genetics
Greenhouse management
Floriculture production
Vegetable production
Nursery management
Organic and sustainable plant production
Fruit production
Viticulture (grapes and wine making)
Plant physiology
Landscape design
Plant pathology
Entomology

Concentrations:

In college: floriculture; environmental horticulture; ornamental horticulture; field crops; nursery management; greenhouse operations; landscape design; fruit crops.

If you go on to grad school: plant breeding and genetics; plant pathology; environmental plant physiology; horticulture management.

What the study of this major is like:

As a horticulture major, you study the biological and physical sciences as they relate to plants and plant growth (the effects of temperature, light, moisture, and nutrition) and to the environment. You will probably be required to take general and organic chemistry, and math at least through trigonometry. You should also expect to take a computer systems course.

Because many graduates eventually take on managerial positions, curricula often include horticultural business management and economics. You are encouraged to develop problem-solving and quantitative reasoning skills. To help you learn the techniques of sustaining production systems, your course work combines principles of biological sciences, ecology, and horticultural technology. You usually concentrate in one of the following:

General horticulture is the study of crops, including fruits, vegetables, and herbs.

Landscape design and construction trains you in plant materials, irrigation control, and other aspects of landscape maintenance.

Floriculture examines the production, marketing, and use of cut flowers and potted plants. You learn about plant breeding, nutrition, disease, and insect pests; effects of the environment on plant growth; floral design; and interior plantscaping.

Olericulture/vegetable science covers the production and marketing of vegetables and herbs. You explore greenhouse, field, organic, and inorganic production techniques; plant breeding, nutrition, disease, and insect pests; and related human health issues.

Environmental horticulture teaches you about urban and natural landscapes. You learn how native plants are selected, produced, and installed to restore disturbed habitats. Environmental ethics and issues relating to sustainability are also covered.

Ornamental horticulture studies landscape and greenhouse crops, including trees, shrubs, potted plants, and foliage plants.

Greenhouse operations is the study of the construction and operations of greenhouses, with an emphasis on producing ornamental and vegetable crops.

Nursery operations focuses on the outdoor or protected production of ornamentals, perennials, fruit trees, and other crops.

Turfgrass management explores the production, marketing, installation, and maintenance of grasses used in golf courses, athletic fields, parks, and commercial and residential landscapes.

Although you learn horticultural basics in the classroom, your training involves plenty of hands-on work, such as greenhouse production or landscape design. In most programs, you get to know your professors and interact with students of diverse interests and ages. Horticulture clubs are often an important part of your academic (and perhaps social) life.

Generally, research horticulture is conducted at land-grant universities, which usually have good facilities and strong programs. The most significant differences among programs relate to the fact that horticulture generally focuses on crops specific to a state or a region. For example, you would not go to Minnesota to study banana production!

Other majors you might like:
Botany
Plant sciences
Forestry
Entomology

Natural resource conservation
Sustainable agriculture
Landscaping/groundskeeping
Turf management
Agricultural and biological engineering
Landscape architecture
Fine/studio arts

Questions to ask colleges:
Does the program utilize teaching greenhouses and field plots?

Which areas of specialization are available? If, like most entering students, you don't know which area of horticulture to pursue, you should look for a strong program that offers a range of possibilities.

Career options and trends:
Plant production manager; manager of garden center or retail florist; golf course or resort landscape manager; fruit or vegetable grower; greenhouse grower; nursery manager; landscape designer; organic producer; viticulturalist (wine grower); research technician.

According to the Bureau of Labor Statistics, horiculture is one of the fastest growing segments of agriculture and a great place to get started in the field. Opportunities exist in landscaping, ornamentals, organic production, health aspects of plants, and greenhouse operations. More efficient production often means more sophisticated techniques, so there is a market for well-trained, motivated, creative professionals. In an exciting trend, horticulture and education join forces to set up "children's gardens" as an imaginative method of teaching and learning.

For more info:
American Society for Horticultural Science (ASHS)
113 South West St.
Suite 200
Alexandria, VA 22314-2851
(703) 836-4606
www.ashs.org

Soil science

What it's about:
Soil science applies principles of biology, chemistry, mathematics, geology, and physics to one of the most important and dynamic natural resources—often abused, sometimes reclaimable, and only slowly renewable. Soil science majors examine the nature and properties of soils and gain the skills needed for wise use, conservation, and management of this resource.

Is this for you?
You might like this major if you also like: nature and the outdoors; working with your hands; science and math; solving complex and multi-faceted problems; farming; gardening; environmental issues.

Consider this major if you are good at: attention to detail; critical reading/thinking; organizing; quantitative analysis; spacial thinking/analysis *...or have...* initiative; manual dexterity; verbal skills.

Recommended high school prep:
English 4, math 4 (including precalculus), lab science 4 (including earth science, biology, physics, and chemistry), social studies 3, and a foreign language 2–3. If they are available, take a computer science course and an environmental science course.

Did you know...
...that soil is not just dirt, but a complex, varied ecosystem that makes up as much as one third of our environment? Critical for life, this natural resource is often taken for granted; but after years of being studied and put to a variety of uses, soils still hold many secrets for scientists to unlock.

Typical courses in this major:
General and organic chemistry
Quantitative soil analysis
Meteorology
Geology
Soil chemistry
Soil morphology, genesis, and taxonomy
Soils and land use
Soil fertility
Environmental soil management
Soil microbiology
Agronomic crop science
Soil contaminants
Plant and soil water relations
Soil physics
Introductory plant pathology
Hydrogeology

Concentrations:
Generally, none in college; but if you go on to grad school: soil microbiology; soil chemistry; soil mineralogy; soil physics; soil conservation; soil management; soil fertility; forest soils; land reclamation.

What the study of this major is like:
Soil scientists have prime responsibility for determining the distribution of soils on the landscape, assessing their characteristics, and predicting their suitability for different purposes. Professionals also help promote practices that will conserve or reclaim soils. Majors learn to describe soils in the field, recognize their uses and limitations, and make recommendations for erosion control, reclamation practices, water movement, and soil improvement.

Soil science is sometimes a concentration within agronomy and crop science; geology and earth science; environmental science; or natural resources and conservation majors. Whether you major or concentrate in soil science, you need a solid foundation in chemistry, biology, physics, and mathematics, along with courses in the humanities and the social sciences. Courses in geology, geography, economics, plant sciences, statistics, nutrition, and genetics are often recommended or required.

In your first and second years, you may be discouraged by the emphasis on university core and basic science courses—soils are hardly mentioned. But if you master the basics, you will likely be rewarded later: in upper-level, soil-oriented courses, you will be expected to apply what you've learned earlier. Because many courses are in lecture-laboratory format, you will spend more hours a week in class/lab than students who take only lecture classes. On the other hand, you generally learn more through hands-on experimentation and probably have to spend less out-of-class time reading and writing.

You are usually encouraged (if not required) to do summer internships and/or part-time work with field soil scientists. Many organizations that employ graduates—such as contractors, mining companies, government agencies, power companies, and landscaping firms—also offer summer internship opportunities.

Relatively few colleges, other than the land-grant state universities, offer the number of credit hours in soil science needed for certification or licensure as a soil scientist. Among those that do, some may emphasize agronomic applications, and others may focus on environmental aspects; but generally there are few differences. Look for a program that is strong not only in soil science but also in the basic sciences.

Other majors you might like:
Horticulture
Environmental science
Natural resources and conservation
Agronomy and crop science
Landscape architecture
Microbiology
Range science
Agricultural and biological engineering
Botany
Farm and ranch management
Geology/earth science
Biochemistry

Questions to ask colleges:
Does the program have a soil judging team? This competitive activity helps you solidify your understanding of soil morphology, classification, interpretations, and landscape distribution, and provides a way to meet other people in the field.

Are the teaching labs well equipped for soil analysis? Are agricultural research stations, as well as farm, forest, and/or range lands, close by and accessible?

Career options and trends:
Soil surveyor*; researcher; field soil scientist with federal or state agricultural or environmental agency, or with private industry*; environmental consultant; soil chemistry consultant; hazardous waste specialist.

Several states require certification or licensing in order to practice as a professional soil scientist. Requirements vary but usually involve taking a certification exam and three to five years of experience.

Soil scientists find more jobs in nonagricultural areas than agricultural. Traditionally, most jobs were in government agencies, but opportunities have been growing in the private sector, especially in environmentally related fields. Overall, the number of job opportunities is much greater than the number of graduates in this field.

Insider's viewpoint:
"I interned with a field soil scientist to run soil transects and update the soil surveys in Delaware. I worked outside almost every day in the summer, investigating the different soils in the lower part of Delaware, and scientifically classifying these soils so that they can be mapped and correlated."

—Kristin, sophomore, University of Delaware

For more info:
The Soil Science Society of America (SSSA)
677 South Segoe Rd.
Madison, WI 53711
(608) 273-8080
www.soils.org

Soil science education home page:
http://soil.gsfc.nasa.gov

Sustainable agriculture

Also known as:
Agroecology
Environmental agriculture

What it's about:
Sustainable agriculture is an ecological approach to farming that conserves and protects natural resources while profitably providing healthy food to local communities.

Is this for you?
You might like this major if you also like: science; working outdoors; community service; involvement with social justice or environmental issues. Most students in this major actually don't have much farming experience, but they usually enjoy working with others on socially meaningful projects, such as hunger awareness activities or farmland preservation workshops.

Consider this major if you are good at... synthesizing ideas; organizing; critical reading/thinking; advocating and persuading; doing research; writing *...or have...* initiative, creativity, a love of nature and a desire to help bring positive change in society.

Recommended high school prep:
English 4, math 3, lab science 3 (including biology and chemistry), social studies 3, and a foreign language 2-3. If available, take a course in environmental studies or ecology.

Did you know...
...that sustainable agriculture does not mean farming "the old-fashioned way" or rejecting modern technology? Rather, it combines the best practices of the past with current science and cutting-edge "green" technologies.

Typical courses in this major:
Principles and practices of sustainable agriculture
Agroecology
Cropping systems
Weed ecology and management
Integrated pest management
Soil science
Organic soil management
Organic vegetable and fruit production
Crop ecology
Watershed ecosystem analysis
Human nutrition
Land use history and planning
Resource and environmental economics
Environmental policy and law
Rural sociology
Agriculture and environmental ethics

Concentrations:
Entomology; plant pathology; agricultural economics; rural sociology

What the study of this major is like:
Since sustainable agriculture is as much a way of life as a system of farming, it is taught as an interdisciplinary major, blending agricultural, physical, environmental, and social sciences.

The program typically starts with a combination of basic science courses (biology, chemistry and plant science) and courses that will introduce you to the methods and concepts of sustainable agriculture, such as how to boost crops without chemical fertilizers, or how to protect against pests using natural, rather than synthetic, controls. You are also introduced to the social dimensions of agriculture, such as how to maintain family farms and how to establish and support local food supply chains.

Upper division courses go into more detail in these areas, and you will begin to work on projects that pull together what you have learned. Most colleges have a student farm, or provide hands-on internships, where you will have ample opportunities to put theory to practice.

Students participate in all levels of planning and operations on the student farm. They determine how much land will be planted with a variety of vegetable and herbs, based on the markets they are likely to have. They order seed, prepare the soil, and start transplants in the greenhouse. As classes wind down in the spring, they begin planting their vegetable seeds and transplants, then manage them throughout the summer (weeding, fertilizing, controlling pests). Harvesting begins when the earliest crops are ready, usually in mid-summer.

Some student farms operate a farm stand at their site, or participate in local farmers' markets. Others supply the college cafeteria with produce or sell to local restaurants. Many operate a Community Supported Agriculture (CSA) program, in which community members purchase a "share" of the farm's produce.

How this all works can vary at different colleges. Students may work under the supervision of an experienced farm manager on many student farms, or they may manage the farm themselves, with faculty and farm staff available for help and advice as needed.

Back in the classroom, you will be taught in a variety of styles, including traditional lectures and class discussion. There may also be a service-learning project, where you work in a group to help the local farming community.

The main difference between colleges offering this major is whether their primary focus is on classroom science and theory, or on hands-on practical training. Many try to blend both approaches. Some offer training opportunities in such areas as tractor safety and repair, farm equipment maintenance and operation, or pesticide application certification.

Other majors you might like:
Agronomy and crop science
Farm and ranch management
Agricultural education services
Global studies
Plant protection/pest management
Urban, community, and regional planning
Agricultural and biological engineering
Botany
Food and nutrition studies
Solar energy technology

Environmental studies
Natural resources and conservation

Questions to ask colleges:
Is this major housed in a school of agriculture with special admission requirements?

How much contact will students have with working farms and farmers?

What opportunities exist for summer on-farm jobs?

What are recent grads doing now?

Career options and trends:
Farmer or farm manager*; organic farm certifier; agricultural educator*; Natural Resources & Conservation Service (NRCS) agent; crop consultant; community farm manager*; community food bank manager; agribusiness employee.

The U.S Department of Agriculture foresees strong growth in the sustainable agriculture industry, fueled by rising consumer demand for organic food and the growing trend to "buy local" produce. And because everyone must eat, employment of agricultural and food scientists is projected to be fairly stable even during difficult economic times.

For more info:
Sustainable Agriculture Research and Education
1400 Independence Ave. SW
Washington, D.C. 20250-2223
(202) 720-5384
www.sare.org

National Sustainable Agriculture Information
    Service (ATTRA)
P.O. Box 3657
Fayetteville, AR 72702
(800) 346-9140
http://attra.ncat.org

Architecture

In the fall of 1980, a professor gave his architecture class an assignment: to enter a national design competition for a memorial honoring those who had served in the Vietnam War. You may already know the rest. One student's vision was chosen unanimously by the experts and was built on the National Mall in Washington, D.C. The Vietnam Veterans Memorial was designed by a Yale University undergraduate, Maya Lin.

Of course, very few people start their careers so successfully. Lin created an inspiring physical environment in an urban park by integrating architectural and landscape design. What was once an ordinary space became a national treasure.

"Students who want to understand the connections between people and the environment and want to do something to improve the world" should consider majoring in architecture, suggests Professor John B. Wright of New Mexico State University.

"It is thrilling to recognize that the physical shape of our destiny is in our own hands," says Alfred D. Price, School of Architecture and Planning, State University of New York at Buffalo. "Good environmental design, sound planning, engaging architecture, responsible landscape design can, do, and will make a difference."

To learn architecture, you study many things: humanities, math, natural sciences, architectural history, graphics, design, photography, economic development, environmental planning, geography, and more.

You don't have to be a great artist to be an architect, but design is a big part of the program. Some schools are based more in studio art and creative expression, while other colleges take the engineering angle to solve problems through analysis. In between are colleges that do both.

"The median approach is one that integrates creative artistic responses with methodical analysis, the art and science of design, the poetic and the practical," notes Professor Michael Bednar of the University of Virginia. "The best way to assess the design philosophy is by speaking with faculty and students. Viewing student work is another useful means of assessing a school's design direction."

Still another helpful guide is the college's list of required courses for majors in architecture, planning, landscape, or environmental design. That list will tell you what's covered in the degree program. Keep in mind that some bachelor's degree programs take five years. On the graduate level, concentrations include ecological planning, urban design, land use, building conservation, transportation, universal design, and community development. Among the emerging fields of study are environmental and sustainable architecture.

Your model campus

Okay, let's get real. You probably won't be designing a national memorial anytime soon. But you can plan your studies and prepare for work in the highly professional field of architecture. Some architects work for government or nonprofit organizations; some are employees of contractors, real estate developers, or engineering firms; many are independent professionals who are hired as consultants. Specific jobs include architect, landscape architect, neighborhood and community planner, industrial designer, conservator, graphic designer, and other careers. Employment prospects will be favorable for those with backgrounds in environmentally friendly and energy efficient design, as more and more buildings today are being built to "green" standards.

Look for architecture and related majors in schools of architecture, colleges of environmental design, colleges of arts and sciences or natural resource management; and departments of geography, landscape architecture, and public administration. You might even look at schools of engineering for some city planning studies.

And while you're comparing colleges, ask about the design studios. After all, you'll be spending plenty of time there working on projects.

"Students spend long hours individually designing their projects and making drawings and models to express their design intentions," explains Bednar. "Drawings are in all media from informal sketches to formal presentations."

Ask how often the design studios meet and if you can get into the studio after class. Are the studios equipped with state-of-the-art computer hardware and specialized software? What are the other facilities and libraries like?

The faculty's credentials may be an attraction at a particular college. Are professors accomplished, practicing architects? If so, what do their designs look like? Has the work of students in the department been recognized nationally in recent years as outstanding?

Do you have particular interests such as the environment, urban planning, historical preservation, or high-tech design? If so, look for colleges with those priorities. And see if the program is accredited. One accreditation to look for is by the National Architectural Accrediting Board.

And don't forget to think about your degree options. What is the first degree you'll earn? Is it an accredited professional degree or a preprofessional degree that will qualify you to apply to grad school? Will your undergrad program take four or five years? For each type of degree, you'll want to find out about the requirements and the career options.

Important sources of information include the American Institute of Architects at www.aia.org; the Association of Collegiate Schools of Architecture at www.acsa-arch.org; the American Planning Association at www.planning.org; and the American Society of Landscape Architects at www.asla.org.

One last thing: be ready for a pretty competitive field if you choose to study an architectural major. Maya Lin only got a B in that class!

Architecture

What it's about:

Architecture majors prepare for the professional practice of architecture by learning how to design buildings and other aspects of the built environment.

Is this for you?

You might like this major if you also like: drawing; photography; making models; crafts of all kinds; science; art; history; cities; landscapes.

Consider this major if you are good at: creativity; critical reading/thinking; organizing; persuading/influencing; quantitative analysis; sketching ideas; spacial thinking/analysis ...*or have...* initiative; manual dexterity; visual sensitivity.

Recommended high school prep:

English 4, math 4 (including precalculus), lab science 4 (including physics), social studies 4, visual arts 1, and a foreign language 3–4. If they are available, courses in environmental science, drafting/technical drawing, and computer science are also recommended.

Did you know...

...that artistic talent is not essential to be successful in this major?

Typical courses in this major:

Architectural history
Architectural graphics
Design fundamentals
Architectural design
Architectural theory
Construction materials and methods
Structural design
Environmental controls
Site design
Engineering mechanics
Computer-aided design (CAD)
Construction economics

Concentrations:

Generally, none in college; but if you go on to grad school: historic preservation; urban design; environmental design; architectural engineering.

What the study of this major is like:

The architecture major combines courses in the liberal arts and sciences with architecture. Along with technical and design skills, architects must understand the culture they work in (humanities), the physical world (physical sciences), and human relations (social sciences). They must also be familiar with the history of art and architecture.

After two years of liberal arts, you begin studying architecture by taking courses in visual and graphic skills. Courses in history and theory of architecture teach you how the built environment was formed, and the role of related disciplines.

The most important courses in every architecture program are the design studio courses. In beginning studios, you learn to design objects, furniture, and rooms. Intermediate studios stress the design of small buildings, such as museums, libraries, and schools. In your final year, you design larger buildings for urban areas.

In the studio, you work on a series of projects. Your instructor assigns a project, outlines expectations, and provides resources. As you develop your design, you benefit from group feedback from fellow students. The project itself, which includes drawings and models you've created in various media, will be evaluated by faculty members for its strengths and weaknesses. Studio work can also include field trips, documentation, photography, interviews, research, model making, and graphic analysis. Your work is supported by classes in construction technology, computer graphics, and design theory.

Be ready to spend long hours on your projects. The studio is both a supportive and a competitive environment—design work is stimulating, spontaneous, and often difficult. To be successful, you need to be resourceful and to have good critical-thinking and time management skills. You will also need to become technically savvy with 3D modeling tools and other design software.

Programs can take different approaches to architectural design. In one approach, based in studio art, you are encouraged to express yourself creatively. In an opposite, engineering-oriented approach, you analyze the needs of a project and evaluate various solutions. Balanced programs, which emphasize both the art and the science of design, combine artistic responses and methodical analysis. But even balanced programs can vary: some may use historical models; others may draw on cultural philosophies; still others may favor social or environmental ethics. You may have difficulty telling how a college approaches architectural design if the focus is not clearly stated in the catalog. The best way to find out is to speak with faculty members and students and to view student work.

In order to work as a professional architect, you need to be licensed by the state where you will practice. Requirements vary from state to state, but generally you must satisfy both an educational and internship requirement, and pass an examination. A professional degree from a school with a program accredited by the National Architectural Accrediting Board (NAAB) will satisfy any state's educational requirements.

Other majors you might like:

Civil engineering
Architectural history /criticism
Historic preservation
Real estate
Environmental design
Industrial design
Drafting and design technology
Housing and human environments
Physics
Interior design
Construction management
Marine engineering /naval architecture

Questions to ask colleges:

How are the design studios set up?

How often do they meet and how many students are in each section?

Is the studio space you are assigned available to you exclusively, 24/7?

What role do computers play in the studio process?

Do the faculty members practice architecture?

What kind of buildings have they designed?

Career options and trends:

Architect; urban planner; landscape architect; architectural historian; graphic designer; industrial designer; construction manager.

Recently, more architects are working for contractors or real estate developers as employees than as independent professionals that are hired as consultants. Many also work for public agencies or for corporations as in-house architects.

Employment opportunities for architects are expected to increase through 2018 to meet the needs of a growing population. Architects with knowledge of sustainable design will be in particular demand because of environmental concerns and rising energy costs.

Insider's viewpoint:

"The combination of the poetic and the practical, the art and the science, is what has always attracted me to this field. An architect needs to use both sides of the brain simultaneously to produce good architectural design."

—Professor Michael Bednar, University of Virginia

For more info:

Association of Collegiate Schools of Architecture
1735 New York Ave., N.W.
Washington, DC 20006-5292
(202) 785-2324
www.acsa-arch.org

Environmental design

What it's about:

This major will prepare you to design public and private spaces, indoor and outdoor, in a way that shapes, restores, preserves, and sustains both the built and the natural environments. It can also ready you for professional practice as an environmental designer or architect.

Is this for you?

You might like this major if you also like: drawing; nature study; natural and physical sciences; joining volunteer activities; model-building; computers; crafts; photography; cities; landscapes. Most students in this major share a passionate concern both for the environment and for people.

Consider this major if you are good at: attention to detail; creativity; critical reading/thinking; math; organizing; spacial thinking/analysis; teamwork *...or have...* manual dexterity; patience; writing skills.

Recommended high school prep:

English 4, math 4 (including precalculus), lab science 4 (including biology, chemistry, and physics), social studies 4, visual arts 1, and a foreign language 3-4. Drawing (freehand) is important. A course in computer-aided drafting is helpful, since much of your college course work will use that technique, but it's not required.

Typical courses in this major:

Architectural and landscape drawing
Behavior and environment
Materials and methods
Construction technology
Environmental control systems
Urban history
Computer-aided design
Landscape design
Community planning
Architectural history
Landscape ecology
Law and urban land use
Site systems and engineering
Geographical information systems (GIS)
Restoration and reclamation ecology
Facilities planning and design

Concentrations:

Landscape and horticultural design; urban planning and design; facilities planning; designing for universal access; designing for special populations (elderly, physically-challenged, etc.).

What the study of this major is like:

In this major, you study the various aspects of the environment from a design point of view. You learn to consider the built, natural, and human components of space and place holistically. Your goal will be to create designs for structures and spaces that harmonize these components, while meeting the requirements of function, environmental safety, and ecological sustainability.

For this reason environmental design is an interdisciplinary major that combines creative concepts in architecture, landscape, interiors, and environmental graphics (signs and information boards) with courses covering social science, health science, environmental science, and physical science.

These topics are taught through a combination of lecture courses, research seminars, field assignments, and studio workshops. In your first two years of study, you'll fulfill your college's general education requirements in the liberal arts and sciences, along with required introductory and foundation courses in environmental design. In your third and fourth years you will spend almost all your time on upper-level elective courses within a concentration of your choice, such as urban and regional planning or landscape design.

What's most distinctive about this major are the studio or workshop courses. They require a far greater time commitment than usual—for both class work and projects outside class. Especially in your third and fourth years, you'll understand why design students are known for burning the midnight oil.

Workshops and internships introduce you to real-world exercises in planning and design. You might work with a local public, private, or nonprofit organization to analyze the economic, social, political, and design issues involved in a community planning or development project. Or you might work hands-on in a machine and assembly shop, learning about construction methods and materials.

In the studio, you'll learn that for any given problem, there is no single solution, as there is in math or chemistry. Designers continually revise their concepts, each time seeking to refine and improve their ideas. Critical-thinking skills, good judgment, and the capacity for reflection and healthy self-criticism are key to success.

An environmental design program can usually be distinguished from ones taught at other colleges by its primary focus. Some programs emphasize traditional physical design; others feature research-based design for special-needs populations; still others stress community-based approaches to planning.

Programs that highlight physical design are usually found in schools of architecture, interior design, landscape design, or possibly engineering (for industrial or product design). Programs at colleges that are more research-oriented will have formal research centers that are doing important new work, and that work should be described on their websites. Programs that are geared toward planning and policy (which are most common) are closely allied with departments of city/urban/regional planning.

Other majors you might like:

Landscape architecture
Interior design
Urban studies
Parks, recreation, and leisure studies
Environmental studies
Historic preservation
Industrial design
Geology/earth science
Construction management

Land use planning
Housing and human environments
Drafting and design technology

Questions to ask colleges:

Are there specialized, dedicated computing facilities for environmental design majors, or is access shared with all other students at the campus computing center?

Are the program's design studios equipped with state-of-the-art hardware and software?

Does the program use faculty members or administrative staff as academic advisers for undergraduates?

Has any student work received national recognition in recent years?

Career options and trends:

City or community planner*; neighborhood housing specialist; architect; interior designer; landscape architect; construction manager*; facilities planner/manager*; real estate developer.

All architects must be licensed, as must most landscape architects and interior designers, depending on the state in which they intend to practice.

Because there are relatively few graduates in this field, employment prospects are good. However, demand for designers and planners is greatest where populations are growing, so it might be necessary to relocate in order to find a job. In recent years, the employment opportunities have been most notable in the South, the West, and the Southwest.

For more info:

Environmental Design Research Association
  (EDRA)
Post Office Box 7146
Edmond, OK 73083-7146
(405) 330-4863
www.edra.org

Landscape architecture

What it's about:

Landscape architecture explores contemporary issues related to the design, planning, and management of the constructed landscape. You learn fundamental techniques of site design and planning and receive studio training in advanced areas such as urban and regional landscape design and planning.

Is this for you?

You might like this major if you also like: tackling environmental concerns; environmental art; gardening; arboretums; outdoor activities; drawing and graphic expression.

Consider this major if you are good at: active listening; attention to detail; creativity; critical reading/thinking; organizing; quantitative analysis; spacial thinking/analysis; teamwork *...or have...* initiative; verbal skills.

Recommended high school prep:

English 4, math 3, lab science 4 (including physics), social studies 3, and a foreign language 2. If possible, take a year of computer drafting, one to two years of art, and a business course.

Did you know...

...that landscape architecture can range from designing a skateboard park to an entire wilderness area? It's not just about the trees and shrubs around buildings.

Typical courses in this major:

Fundamentals of design
Computer-aided drafting (CAD)
Landscape planning
Landscape design
Landscape technology
Graphic communications
Applied ecology
Landscape construction
Plant materials
Plant identification
Plane surveying
Landscape architectural history
Landscape architectural theory

Concentrations:

Landscape restoration; landscape technology; ecological planning.

What the study of this major is like:

Landscape architects plan, design, and manage outdoor settings, such as parks and areas around buildings, to make these displays useful, beautiful, and in harmony with nature. As a landscape architecture major, you work with the land: drawing, painting, and mapping it; describing it; examining and analyzing it; and imagining what it might become in the future. You learn about the complex ecology of natural landscapes and the even more complex human ecology of urban landscapes.

Landscape architecture is a studio-based program that requires you to become thoroughly familiar with the ways in which natural vistas can be created or changed. First you learn traditional techniques of site planning and design, including drawing and computer graphics, and the principles and vocabulary of design. In addition to the studio curriculum, you take courses in graphic communications, history and theory, materials, and professional practice. You study ecological systems, learn to identify and work with a broad range of locally grown plants, and analyze the relationships between social and political institutions, on the one hand, and the land, on the other.

Later you study advanced techniques that include urban design, landscape technology, and regional planning and analysis. Building on your foundations, you shape increasingly complex landscapes and develop detailed drawings, specifications, and other means of bringing your plans to life. In a typical studio course in your third or fourth year, you might design a park, a public garden, or a plaza; plan a site for an apartment house or a sports arena; or develop a management program for a natural reserve. In construction courses, you learn how to produce the detailed drawings for projects like these.

As a major, you might join college organizations devoted to environmental issues, urban design, and regional landscape awareness. You can often find volunteer opportunities that include mentoring high school students about landscape architecture. Some students participate in community planning groups. At the conclusion of a four- or five-year program, you should be qualified to enter the profession, with a private firm or a public agency.

Landscape architecture departments differ a great deal in the approach they take to the major. Some programs focus on physical design, while others concentrate on sustainability and regeneration (to protect natural settings and to ensure their survival). Still other programs stress both physical design and ecological issues. Geographic and social distinctions may also influence the focus of a particular program. Programs at colleges in cities are more likely to devote themselves to urban landscape design than programs in suburban or rural areas. Another reason for differences in programs is that some colleges encourage faculty members to conduct research, whereas in other programs, instructors spend more time in professional practice. Finally, some programs are based on a four-year curriculum and award a Bachelor of Science in Landscape Architecture (B.S.L.A.), while others offer a five-year degree, the Bachelor of Landscape Architecture (B.L.A.), which requires you to complete additional studio and lecture courses.

Other majors you might like:

Environmental design
Environmental studies
Landscaping/groundskeeping
Horticulture
Land use planning
Mining and mineral engineering
Urban forestry
Graphic design
Parks/recreational/leisure facilities management
Environmental engineering

Botany
Turf management

Questions to ask colleges:

Does the program offer a degree in four years or in five years? What is the academic focus of the program? What are the professional and academic activities of the faculty members?

Career options and trends:

Landscape architect; landscape construction manager; political advocate; urban planner; environmental agency manager; natural resource manager.

Most states require landscape architects to be licensed or registered, based on the Landscape Architect Registration Examination (LARE) and one to four years work experience. Some states also require an additional state-specific exam focusing on local laws and environments.

Most graduates of landscape architecture programs work in private consulting firms as designers, planners, or managers. Landscape architects can also work in city planning, recreation, and parks departments at the local level and in land management agencies such as the National Park Service, National Forest Service, and Bureau of Land Management at the federal level. In addition, the training you receive in landscape architecture provides a foundation for other careers related to shaping the environment, such as landscape restoration.

Employment prospects are projected to be strong, but new graduates my face strong competition for entry-level jobs. Demand for landscape architects will be driven by growth in development, the need to comply with environmental regulations and security requirements, and continued efforts to restore and preserve lands, wetlands, and ecosystems.

For more info:

American Society of Landscape Architects (ASLA)
636 Eye Street, N.W.
Washington, DC 20001-3736
(202) 898-2444
www.asla.org

Urban, community, and regional planning

What it's about:

The urban, community, and regional planning major focuses on creating livable, responsibly financed, and environmentally healthy communities. You learn about transportation, economic development, housing, land-use regulations, infrastructure management, and preservation of parks and other open spaces. Planners shape surroundings that are appropriate to the needs of urban, suburban, or rural residents.

Is this for you?

You might like this major if you also like: the outdoors; maps; architecture; history; working with people; exploring cities and small towns; environmental and social causes; community service activities.

Consider this major if you are good at: attention to detail; creativity; organizing; persuading/influencing; spacial thinking/analysis; teamwork *...or have...* initiative; patience; verbal skills; writing skills.

Recommended high school prep:

English 4, math 3, lab science 3, social studies 3, and a foreign language 3–4. If possible, also take classes in geography, environmental issues, statistics, and computer applications.

Typical courses in this major:

Planning theories
Planning practice
Regional studies
Technology of urban life
History of cities
Urban and landscape design
Social issues
Land use regulation and law
Transportation planning
Economic development
Community development
Housing
Environmental planning
Geographic information systems (GIS)
Cartography
Field/design project

Concentrations:

Generally, none in college; but if you go on to grad school: land use regulation; transportation planning; urban design; community development (including housing, economic development, and social issues).

What the study of this major is like:

To create a livable community, planners must reduce conflicts between competing interests (real estate developers and residents, for example) and ensure that the development is fiscally, structurally, and environmentally sound. As an urban, community, and regional planning major, you explore such topics as physical and environmental geography, urban studies, transportation, land use and real estate law, community development and economic development, mapping, statistics, economics, history, political science, and human geography.

In this major, courses are mostly in lecture format, although there are some design classes. Your course work will cover a range of tools and techniques—from computer modeling to group decision-making; from statistical programming to brainstorming and values clarification. You will often work in groups, addressing difficult questions as a team: Can a community learn to recycle, conserve resources, and protect wildlife? Are a community's transportation systems appropriate for conditions anticipated in the next hundred years? How can a city upgrade the standard of living of its low-income residents? How can conflicts be resolved between developers and architectural preservation groups? How can volunteer groups, corporations, and governments work together to solve problems? Together with your team, you may visit project sites and tour development areas.

Generally, majors do internships with public planning agencies, nonprofit groups, or private businesses. Independent projects (usually research papers) are also common. Students often have the most trouble with "spatial thinking"—understanding how the landscape is structured and how communities function. After a few required courses, though, most students catch on. Group projects and small classes tend to create a friendly, supportive environment.

Planning programs may be housed in departments of geography, landscape architecture, or public administration, or in their own department. Planning programs tend to break down into three areas of concentration: urban, rural/regional, and environmental. Although all programs focus on land use regulations, the first two approaches emphasize distinct types of communities, and environmental planning deals with issues like pollution, environmental impact statements, cleanup of toxic waste sites, and natural hazards such as flooding and earthquakes. Because planning overlaps with many other fields, you may double-major in planning and another subject, or minor in a related field.

Planning is a hands-on major—you learn to analyze a situation, to imagine a better one, and to determine how to bridge the gap. Planning offers you a career in which you can conserve nature and help build a better world.

Other majors you might like:

Civil engineering
Urban forestry
Emergency management/homeland security
Landscape architecture
Land use planning
Historic preservation
Housing and human environments
Environmental design
Public administration
Urban studies
Political science
Sociology

Career options and trends:

Land use planner; geographic information systems director; transportation planner; grant writer; housing coordinator; parks/open space planner; architect; cartographer.

Planners also find work in local government agencies dealing with zoning and community/economic development; fish and game agencies; and parks, transportation, and environment departments; in federal agencies such as the Forest Service, Environmental Protection Agency, Defense Mapping Agency, Housing and Urban Development, and Natural Resources Conservation Service; in environmental consulting companies, engineering firms, real estate companies, land development companies, and surveyors' offices; and in nonprofit groups such as the Nature Conservancy, Trust for Public Lands, and American Farmland Trust.

With cities and rural areas growing in all regions of the country, there is a high demand for planners in the United States. Employment prospects will be best for those with a masters degree as well as those with strong technical skills, and also for planners who can help communities prepare for both natural and man-made disasters.

Insider's viewpoint:

"All-time famous misperception about the major: planning equals architecture. Planning is a very political field, and the program recognizes this in its courses. If you don't like politics, you might not like planning."

—Kacey, senior, Cornell University

For more info:

American Planning Association (APA)
1776 Massachusetts Ave., N.W., Suite 400
Washington, DC 20036-1904
(202) 872-0611
www.planning.org

Area, ethnic, and gender studies

At first glance, these majors seem to be devoted to the interests of a minority of people. Not so. These studies embrace the vast majority of the world's population.

"The primary objective of the curriculum, regardless of race or color, is education for positive and productive citizenship," says R. Baxter Miller of the University of Georgia's Institute for African American Studies. "One would see oneself as a thoughtful and creative agent of cultural transformation and change—a guardian of the true implementation of American democracy."

From the studies of indigenous peoples to those from faraway lands, these majors help students understand other cultures and their own.

"Most students don't realize the inextricable connections between the Middle East with our own Western history and traditions—we are in fact part of the same civilizational unit," says Professor Bernard Haykel of New York University. "By engaging in Middle Eastern studies, one acquires an entirely novel way of looking at one's own identity and develops a much broader understanding of the world we live in."

In some majors, such as Latin American studies, language is central. "To me the most important aspect of this field is the opportunity to learn about and communicate with a variety of peoples and cultures," says Professor César G. López of Scripps College.

The women's studies major cuts across many cultures. Women hold up half the sky, as the Chinese proverb goes. The major explores gender, sexuality, power, inequality, racism, class issues, oppression, and the connection between these topics.

The area, ethnic, and gender studies majors cover everything imaginable—history, culture, language, literature, anthropology, political science, religion, the arts—you name it. If these subjects appeal to you, you might check other sections in this book: Humanities, Languages, Multi/interdisciplinary studies, Religion and theology, Social sciences, and Visual and performing arts.

"The American studies major enables students to understand the world around them from a variety of perspectives," says Daniel Horowitz of Smith College. "It enables students to understand how the nation's history, literature, arts, politics, and society illuminate their nation's experiences."

The culture of work

Okay, let's look at these studies from the shameless, self-serving, capitalistic perspective of what they can do for you. Fortunately, many of the subjects taught in area and ethnic majors translate to valuable job skills. For example, "area studies" means just what it sounds like, the study of a particular region of the world. Such majors are great preparation for jobs with companies that do business in the region being studied. It's a big plus in today's multicultural workplaces and in the expanding global markets, especially Asia.

If you speak an Asian language, Arabic, or Spanish, you automatically have a marketable skill. "Spanish is today the second language in the United States after English," says López. "There is a big demand for teachers at all levels. In some states, the knowledge of Spanish is necessary for medical personnel (especially pediatricians), lawyers, and social workers."

Clearly, Middle Eastern experts are also in demand. "In the post-9/11 world, and because of the political and economic turbulence in the Middle East, the United States, at the level of the public and private sectors, will be intensely engaged in the region for years if not decades to come," says Haykel. "Persons with language and other skills pertaining to the Middle East will easily find gainful and rewarding employment."

In addition to language, critical thinking and human understanding are aspects of these majors that are essential in professions including communications, law, teaching, public service, social services, labor relations, business, counseling, Foreign Service/diplomacy, and humanitarian work.

When choosing a school, look for colleges of arts and sciences or liberal arts, and divisions of humanities or social sciences. While you're at it, see how the college balances the humanities and the social sciences. Is the curriculum mostly language-based or does it focus more on history and political science? If the emphasis is on history, the courses may concentrate on a time period, such as the Middle Ages or the present. If the focus is on language, look into the quality of the school's language labs. Also, what are the library holdings to support your studies and research? Will you be studying abroad as a requirement or as an elective?

Ethnic and gender majors are so broad that no one college can cover them all. Check the core requirements to get a feel for the program. Do the courses build on one another? Is the major supported with its own department? How many full-time faculty members are in the department? Are they prominent, published scholars? Do the professors teach undergraduates?

Oddly, no matter which of these diverse majors you may choose, your studies will be influenced by a dead white guy, Socrates. The Greek philosopher's method of teaching was to ask the class questions. Students learned through participation and conversation, and that's how these majors are often taught. The technique makes the quality of the faculty even more important.

African-American studies

Also known as:

Black studies

What it's about:

The major in African-American studies includes the history, politics, traditions, literature, art, and lives of North American peoples of African descent. Traditional assumptions about race are tested and examined to help students make enlightened choices for themselves and their society. The primary objective of this major is to prepare all students, regardless of race or color, for positive, productive citizenship.

Is this for you?

You might like this major if you also like: community involvement; reading; debating; travel; foreign languages; sports; music; dance; theater; politics.

Consider this major if you are good at: caring/nurturing; creativity; critical reading/thinking; leadership; persuading/influencing ...*or have...* initiative; verbal skills; writing skills.

Recommended high school prep:

English 4, math 3, lab science 3, social studies 4, and a foreign language 2–3. Courses in government, economics, music, and art are also recommended.

Did you know...

...that in business and government, there is an increasing demand for graduates trained in multiculturalism? In a society in which power is distributed unequally, multiculturalists can mediate disputes between individuals or communities of different ethnic or racial backgrounds.

Typical courses in this major:

American history to 1865
African-American politics
History and cultures of Africa
Multiculturalism in modern America
Modern African-American experience
Caribbean history and society
Christianity and colonialism in Africa
African-American religions
African-American society
African-American folklore
African-American poetry
Modern African literature
African-American music
Women in African-American cinema
Seminar in race and ethnicity

Concentrations:

In college: African-American history; African-American language, literature, and art; social and political inquiry.

If you go on to grad school: African-American literature; African-Hispanic literature; African-American drama; African-American psychology, African-American sociology, African-American religions.

What the study of this major is like:

African-American studies is an interdisciplinary major in the liberal arts and social sciences. You learn through a Socratic method that takes place within a human laboratory of constant challenges. Learning reveals a discrepancy between tradition and dissent in American life; a vitality of diversity in redefining the ideal of freedom. Majors develop the ability to communicate highly charged cultural and emotional issues into well-reasoned proposals subject to logical debate and resolution.

Your introductory courses examine the history of African-Americans, prepare you for interdisciplinary work, and place black history in the context of world history. You examine the works of anthropologists, economists, political scientists, psychologists, theologians, and sociologists. In most introductory courses, you also study music, dance, and the arts of African-Americans.

Throughout the program, the emphasis is on how people of color see themselves and how others see them. You examine the heritage of slavery from the perspectives of both the slaveholder and the slave: you are asked to reconcile opposing viewpoints, sort out the emotions and motivations of whites and blacks alike, explore your own feelings about race, and reach a balanced conclusion about the effects of slavery on whites and blacks today.

Advanced courses, which build on this introduction, provide in-depth analysis and allow you to develop a concentration reflecting your interests.

Courses in art and literature cover such topics as slave and folk songs of the mid-nineteenth century; the Harlem Renaissance of the 1920s; contemporary rap; the poetry of Langston Hughes, Margaret Walker, Gwendolyn Brooks, Sonia Sanchez, and Amiri Baraka; and the stories, novels, and other works of Frances Harper, Richard Wright, Jean Toomer, Ralph Ellison, James Baldwin, Alice Walker, and Toni Morrison.

Courses taught from a historical, sociological, and political viewpoint explore the impact of social class, status, and power relations on African-Americans, as members of the current social structure and as descendants of the African diaspora (forced migration). After studying such issues as the civil rights movement, affirmative action, the role of African-American women, and urban families, you examine ways of turning theory into public policy. Most programs require you to take one or two courses in the history and cultures of the African continent.

Programs can usually be distinguished by the emphasis they give to politics, humanities, and the social sciences. One program may stress the formulation of public policy, whereas another focuses on theory. One may take a somewhat radical approach; another, a more traditional one. Some may emphasize arts, literature, and drama; others may focus on social and multicultural issues; still others may be stronger in history. You can probably learn about a program's orientation by speaking with graduates and faculty members.

Other majors you might like:
African studies
Latin American studies
Chicano studies
Jazz studies
American literature
Intercultural /diversity studies
Islamic studies
Caribbean studies
Women's studies
Urban studies
Anthropology
Sociology

Questions to ask colleges:
How do faculty members and majors interact in and out of class? Which events and activities help majors bond as a unified group?

Which outstanding graduates in the discipline have come out of the program in the last decade or so?

Career options and trends:
African-American studies prepares students for careers in education, social service, public administration, business, and a range of other areas. It is also excellent preparation for graduate or professional study in law, business, religion, medicine, or social work.

As the population becomes more diverse, multiculturalists, who can explain reasons behind conflicts, help create bonds among employees, and strengthen the body politic by promoting education and equality, will be of increasing value to society

Insider's viewpoint:
"It's only in my ethnic studies classes that I've learned about the Civil Rights movement, the brown power movement, the women's rights movement, and gay liberation. This is all stuff that the departments called history don't teach."

—Ronald, senior, University of California: Berkeley

For more info:
National Council for Black Studies
Georgia State University
P.O. Box 4109
Atlanta, GA 30302-4109
(404) 413-5131
www.ncbsonline.org

Association for the Study of African American Life
    and History
Howard University, C. B. Powell Building, Suite
    C142
525 Bryant St., N.W.
Washington, DC 20059
(202) 865-0053
www.asalh.org

American studies

What it's about:

The American studies major uses a wide variety of materials and approaches to give you a comprehensive understanding of American society and values. As an interdisciplinary program, it integrates courses in American history, literature, popular culture, and contemporary social concerns.

Is this for you?

You might like this major if you also like: the History Channel; movies; talk radio; studying media and popular culture; biographies; debating; antiquing; traveling and sight-seeing; learning about people who are different from you.

Consider this major if you are good at: creativity; critical reading/thinking; research ...*or have...* curiosity; initiative; self-motivation; sense of adventure; verbal skills; writing skills.

Recommended high school prep:

English 4, math 3, lab science 3, social studies 4, and a foreign language 3.

Did you know...

...that, in this major, you often analyze forms of cultural expression, such as songs, novels, magazines, and movies?

Typical courses in this major:

American civilization
Women in American society
American literature
American film
The American wilderness
American art and architecture
American folklore
Ethnicity in America
American regional cultures
Religion in America
American music
American popular culture
American eras
Contemporary America
American political culture
Native American cultures

Concentrations:

In college: ethnic studies (including a focus on specific groups); media studies; popular culture studies; gender and/or gay and lesbian studies.

If you go on to grad school: American literature; American history; cultural theory.

What the study of this major is like:

American studies is an interdisciplinary major that relies on a number of approaches to study the United States. Although history and literature were once the focus of the field, the major now also draws on such disciplines as sociology, anthropology, political science, African-American studies, film studies, women's studies, theater criticism, and music. By analyzing the United States in terms of, for example, region, ethnicity, gender, and class, you learn to understand the world around you from a variety of perspectives, including that of trans-nationalism, the ways in which people and ideas cross national borders. While programs vary according to faculty strengths and college requirements, all have a common aim: to explore American society and values, past and present.

Among the typical core courses are those focusing on a chronological period (the 1890s; the 1960s), a topic (the West; individualism and community), or a scholarly approach (literary criticism; cultural analysis). In your first and second years, you usually take survey courses that trace American society from colonization to the present. Topics in the first semester may include immigration (history), the rise of American architecture (art), and the evolution of colonial politics (political science), all as part of the study of pre-Revolutionary society. In the next semester, you may focus on family life and urbanization (sociology), the rise of advertising (history), and the origins of American realism in the 1880s and 1890s (art and literature).

During your third and fourth years, you are likely to concentrate on a few subjects. You consult with a faculty adviser and develop an area of interest. In history and literature (a popular concentration), for instance, your course work might include political history, modern literature, and film. To explore American pluralism (the nation's diverse population), you can enroll in courses on ethnic studies, sociology, religion, and history. Majors are usually stimulated by this interdisciplinary approach—you may gain a greater appreciation of literature, art, and film by studying the country's political and economic development.

American studies programs usually include fourth-year seminars (or capstone courses), which build on your previous work. Although these seminars vary from one program to the next, most use in-depth readings to examine the development of American society and culture. In some programs, you can also pursue a special research project.

The interdisciplinary focus of American studies encourages you to spend a good deal of time with other undergrads and with faculty members. Instructors are usually easy to talk to, and classes tend to be relatively small. Thus, the strong bond with other students you are likely to develop should make the program as enjoyable as it is useful.

Other majors you might like:
American literature
Political science
Sociology
Art history
Anthropology
African-American studies
Women's studies
Latin American studies
Geography
Native American studies
Chicano studies

Questions to ask colleges:
What are the core requirements in the program? Most strong programs have core courses that bring together the diverse fields the major draws from. Also, it is good to have some flexibility when choosing your courses.

Are the primary loyalties of the faculty members (as teachers, advisers, and program developers) to American studies rather than to other fields?

How extensive are offerings in American history, American literature, fine arts, film studies, African-American studies, Hispanic-American studies, sociology, women's studies, and American government?

Career options and trends:
High school teacher; writer; journalist; literary or media critic; political consultant.

Many graduates with American studies degrees are employed in helping professions (such as social service), museums, historical societies, and communications. Communications fields such as the media, Internet, advertising, television, and film attract graduates who can interpret American culture from a variety of perspectives. With graduate or professional training, majors can pursue careers in higher education (college teaching), museum administration, law, medicine, public policy, and business.

Insider's viewpoint:
"I don't know how many times I've heard people say, 'Oh, what's American studies? The study of America?' A lot of people think it's a basket-weaving discipline, but I've gotten a lot of calls from potential employers who didn't care what I studied, they just cared that I studied it well."

—Michael, senior, University of Colorado

For more info:
American Studies Association (ASA)
1120 19th St., N.W.
Suite 301
Washington, DC 20036
(202) 467-4783
www.theasa.net

Asian studies

What it's about:

The major in Asian studies is designed to provide a background in Asian languages and cultures. Programs may concentrate on one area of Asia (Japan, China, Korea, Southeast Asia, or South Asia) or focus on a comparative study of the entire region. Students usually study an Asian language and take a range of social science and humanities courses to gain insight into Asian societies, history, politics, and economics.

Is this for you?

You might like this major if you also like: exploring other cultures and societies; travel; new experiences; learning a foreign language; art; literature; mythology; learning about philosophies and religions.

Consider this major if you are good at: attention to detail; memorizing; research *...or have...* curiosity; verbal skills; writing skills.

Recommended high school prep:

English 4, math 3, lab science 3, social studies 4, and a foreign language 4.

Typical courses in this major:

Asian language (I, II)
Religions of India
Buddhist thought and values
Introduction to Asian art
Classical Asian civilizations: China and Japan
Asian politics and economic development
Masterpieces of Asian literature
Political philosophy in Southeast Asia
Japanese art and culture
Chinese calligraphy
Modern Japan
The Chinese-American experience
Political power in contemporary China
Premodern Japanese literature
Music of Asia
Tibetan civilization

Concentrations:

An Asian language; East Asian literature; South Asian literature; politics and history; anthropology; geography; art history.

What the study of this major is like:

In the major in Asian studies, you study the languages, cultures, religions, societies, politics, and economic characteristics of all of Asia or one of its primary subdivisions: Japan, China, Southeast Asia, or South Asia. The program usually includes interdisciplinary courses that survey a wide range of topics in the social sciences and humanities, providing you with an historical and contemporary overview of the region. With this background, you choose additional courses in fields such as history, anthropology, political science, art history, literature, and religion.

Programs may cover traditional aspects of Asian culture, the impact of the prominent religions (Hinduism, Buddhism, Islam, Taoism, and Shinto), the history of art (architecture, music, literature, and film), the role of women, and interaction with the West.

Central to any program is the study of an Asian language (for example, Chinese, Japanese, Korean, Thai, Hindi). All programs require at least two semesters (most require four) of language study. Learning the language will enrich your appreciation of the cultures of Asia. Intensive summer programs in the United States and Asia, together with one-year programs in Asia, enable you to obtain additional language training and practice. Many Asian studies programs encourage students to spend a summer or a year in Asia. The experience can be very rewarding.

In general, work in Asian studies builds a feeling of solidarity among fellow majors. In addition, faculty members, who share a commitment to increasing your knowledge about and contacts with Asia, tend to be accessible and supportive. With more than half the world's population and the fastest-growing economies, Asia is, and will be, a dominant force in the twenty-first century. Asian studies majors are likely to find opportunities to help foster understanding and to enhance communications between Asian and Western societies.

Other majors you might like:
Asian-American studies
Chinese
Linguistics
Anthropology
Archaeology
Geography
Global studies
Religious studies
Islamic studies
International business
International relations
Art history

Career options and trends:
International trade consultant; importer/exporter; journalist; Foreign Service officer; ESL teacher.

Graduates in Asian studies often pursue careers in education, government, journalism, communications, international business, the travel industry, and international law. Teachers with special knowledge of Asia are needed at graduate, undergraduate, and secondary levels. There are positions in government agencies (State Department, development agencies, CIA) and in private foundations and international agencies. Businesses, particularly banks, seek Asia specialists to work overseas; international law firms also provide opportunities for Asia generalists and specialists. As is usually the case, the more language training you have, the more job opportunities will be available to you.

Insider's viewpoint:
"I like interesting stories, so Asian history, culture, and politics really fascinate me. There is so much that has happened in Asia in the past fifty years, not to mention the wealth of history that dates back as far or farther than some of the more widely recognized cultures."

—Min, senior, University of California: Berkeley

For more info:
Association for Asian Studies
1021 East Huron St.
Ann Arbor, MI 48104
(734) 665-2490
www.aasianst.org

Chicano studies

Also known as:
Mexican American studies

What it's about:
This major is an interdisciplinary, comparative exploration of the history, sociology, politics, culture, and economics of Mexican-origin communities in the United States, studied within a regional, national, and global context. The field also examines other Latino and indigenous populations of the Americas, and the ways they influence Chicano communities.

Is this for you?
You might like this major if you also like: community involvement; reading; talking about social justice issues; music, dance, theater, and art; Chicano/Latino culture; languages. Students who see themselves heading for the "helping professions" or wish to give back to their communities are often attracted to this major.

Consider this major if you are good at: attention to detail; creativity; critical reading/thinking; leadership; organizing; research ...*or have...* initiative; patience; verbal skills; writing skills.

Recommended high school prep:
English 4, math 3, lab science 3, social studies 4 (including history and geography), and a foreign language 3–4. If available, economics and sociology are also recommended.

Did you know...
...that Chicano studies is not an "identity, feel-good" major for Chicanos only? While it may be particularly advantageous for Mexican-American and other *raza* students to learn about their history and cultures, non-Latinos can also benefit from exploring one of the fastest-growing populations in the United States.

Typical courses in this major:
History of Chicano Los Angeles
Recent Chicano literature
Farmworker movements, social justice, and
  AFL-CIO
Chicano folklore and oral tradition
Contemporary Chicano theater
Music of Latin America
Chicana feminism
Barrio popular culture
Immigration and Latino identity
Border consciousness
The Mexican mural
Health in Chicano/Latino populations
Mexican Americans and U.S. education
U.S.–Mexico relations
Bilingual writing workshop
Interracial dynamics in American society

Concentrations:
Generally, none in college; but if you go on to grad school: Barrio, community and urban studies; Chicano languages and literature; political, economic, and social issues; Chicano/Latino history and culture; Chicano/Latino music, art, theater

What the study of this major is like:
Topics in this major cover a wide range of issues. You'll study both the history of Mexican-origin peoples and the conditions in which they are living today—primarily in the United States but also across North America and around the world.

You'll explore this group from within, by looking at its literature, art, music, theater, oral history, and folklore. And you'll also explore the group from an external focus, by looking at the way the U.S. society and government has treated Chicanos over time. During this exploration you'll compare how the experience of Chicanos is similar to or different from the experiences of other groups in the United States and elsewhere in the world.

In Chicano studies, majors analyze the world with an eye toward social justice, and the scholarship emphasizes social change, social ethics, and equity. The program focuses on the real world; a service learning component, included in many of your courses, involves interaction with the Chicano community. Even as an undergraduate, you'll have an opportunity to engage in research training.

Some students are challenged by the breadth of the field and its interdisciplinary nature—they may have difficulty synthesizing the various perspectives. And this major does not shirk the hard issues—the focus on inequality, stereotypes, and discrimination can be unsettling at first.

Most programs encourage students to be scholar-activists (in the sense of being civically engaged); as a result, extracurricular activities, volunteerism, and commitment to the community are emphasized. Many programs also expect students to participate in academic advising and governance, as part of their responsibility for their own education and development, by taking part in departmental committees and student senates, or by designing student-initiated courses.

Where this major is housed within a college (under social sciences, humanities, or the arts) can affect the content and curriculum of the program. The geographic location of the college itself is also important to consider—having access to large concentrations of Chicanos in Los Angeles, for example, as opposed to smaller communities elsewhere, can make a difference in the service learning and civic engagement aspects of the program. At some colleges, courses might be taught in English, Spanish, or bilingually, and some programs require a Spanish (or Mexican-indigenous) language competency.

Other majors you might like:
Anthropology
Sociology
Urban, community, and regional planning
Intercultural/diversity studies
ESL teacher education
Latino studies
Journalism
Caribbean studies

Latin American studies
Native American studies
Labor studies
Geography

Questions to ask colleges:
How many students take this major?

How often are required courses offered?

Will I meet with a faculty adviser or a counselor? How often is this person available?

Are classes normally large or small?

Career options and trends:
Chicano studies (like most liberal arts majors) is not "vocational" preparation for an occupation. It is as useful in the job market as most other liberal arts majors (history, English, etc.). Since most Chicano studies majors are bilingual and biliterate, however, they are attractive job candidates in many fields, especially business, education, and government. Majors often go on to graduate or professional school to prepare for careers in law, health and medicine, teaching, and social work.

Insider's viewpoint:
"I love this major because for the first time in my life I feel empowered. I love learning about my own history, but at the same time learning about others who have also been marginalized and the struggles they face."

—Robert, senior, University of California: Los Angeles

For more info:
National Association for Chicana and Chicano Studies (NACCS)
P.O. Box 720052
San Jose, CA 95172-0052
www.naccs.org

Mujeres Activas en Letras y Cambio Social
http://malcs.net

European studies

What it's about:

European studies is an interdisciplinary major for students who want to increase their understanding of the languages, cultures, societies, history, and economics of the peoples of Europe and European civilization, from antiquity to the present.

Is this for you?

You might like this major if you also like: learning a foreign language; reading; travel; exploring different cultures; history; politics; current events; art; music; philosophical discussions.

Consider this major if you are good at: critical reading/thinking; languages; research ...*or have...* initiative; verbal skills; writing skills.

Recommended high school prep:

English 4, math 3, lab science 3, social studies 4, and a foreign language 4. Courses in music, art, government, and economics are also recommended.

Typical courses in this major:

Greece and Rome
Cities of Europe
Medieval Europe
United States and the European Economic Union
Post-Communist Russia
Baroque art
Indo-European comparative mythology
European cinema
Folk music of Eastern Europe
Irish nationalism
Modern Britain
Women in Italian culture
The Mediterranean world, past and present
Don Quixote
Dante's *Divine Comedy*
The Third Reich and the Holocaust

Concentrations:

Comparative literature; international relations; government and politics; history and culture of a particular country (for instance, Italian studies, Russian studies), region (Mediterranean, Scandinavian), or historical period (the Renaissance, Europe since 1945).

What the study of this major is like:

The study of European civilization—past and present—is a vast interdisciplinary undertaking. It covers several millennia of political, social, and economic history; the development of art, music, religions, philosophy, and literatures in more than a dozen languages; monumental contributions to science, mathematics, and technology; and the study, often comparative, of politics, religion, philosophy, and the arts in present-day Europe. If you find a wide variety of topics and disciplines to choose from liberating rather than overwhelming, then this major might be a good choice.

Usually you are introduced to this wealth of material in one of two ways: in a survey course in European civilization, or in a course that deals with a particular era of European history (the Renaissance, the Age of Reason, the Romantic period) or with the culture of a single country in modern Europe (France, Germany, Spain). Occasionally, both approaches are used. You also begin to fulfill the language requirement—most programs expect you to take a language (other than English) through the intermediate level.

Within a framework that ensures that you acquire both a historical and a contemporary perspective, you are given wide latitude to work out the rest of your studies. In other words, you will mostly design the major yourself, to fit your own interests, talents, and background.

For example, if you have studied Latin and have an interest in the medieval period, you might take further work in Latin and courses in the history, philosophy, theology, and literature of the Middle Ages. Or if you know some German and enjoy reading about Germany today, you can, after basic work in economics and comparative politics, focus on the challenges of reunification. Perhaps you have learned Polish at home; after preparation in history and comparative politics, you might concentrate on Poland's transition from a socialist country under the former Soviet Union to a democracy. As another example, if examining the relationships between music, painting, and literature in early-twentieth-century Europe appeals to you, why not obtain the needed background in music and art history and complete the major with appropriate courses in the humanities?

European studies programs may recommend, or even require, that you spend a semester or a year (usually the third year) in Europe. Living and studying in Europe and using a language other than English (except in the United Kingdom and Ireland) can be an extraordinary experience. Colleges that do not have a study-abroad program usually honor work taken under the auspices of another institution. Or you can enroll at a European university whose credits will transfer to your college at home.

You may be required, in your final year, to complete a capstone project related to your area of concentration. Most likely, you will do a research paper or thesis, based on independent study or on participation in a seminar.

Other majors you might like:

International business
Linguistics
Anthropology
History
Geography
Global studies
Tourism/travel management
Journalism
Architectural history/criticism
Classics
Medieval and Renaissance studies
Art history

Questions to ask colleges:

Does the program include a study-abroad semester or year with an affiliated European university? Are the costs comparable to those for your college at home? Do students remain registered while abroad, and do all credits earned overseas count toward the major and general degree requirements?

Is there an adviser to help students design their areas of concentration?

Can students "test out" of the language requirement? Can the language requirement be fulfilled by study abroad in a university in which the instruction is not in English?

Career options and trends:

The European studies major is not designed to lead to any particular profession, but rather to prepare you for a wide variety of careers. Government service, international business and finance, travel and tourism, journalism, law, management, public relations, teaching—are all possible career paths. Many of these careers require graduate or professional study, for which the major is a strong foundation.

For more info:

Council for European Studies
Columbia University /1203A International Affairs
  Building, MC 3310
420 West 118th St.
New York, NY 10027
(212) 854-4172
www.councilforeuropeanstudies.org

Latin American studies

What it's about:

Latin American studies is an interdisciplinary major that provides you with comprehensive training in the Spanish and Portuguese languages, as well as Latin American literature, history, politics, geography, anthropology, art and music, and economics.

Is this for you?

You might like this major if you also like: traveling; Hispanic culture; history; learning about international politics and trade; discovering connections across subject areas; languages.

Consider this major if you are good at: attention to detail; creativity; critical reading/thinking; leadership; learning languages; organizing; spacial thinking/analysis; teamwork *...or have...* initiative; verbal skills; writing skills.

Recommended high school prep:

English 4, math 3, lab science 3, social studies 4 (including history and geography), and a foreign language 3-4. If they are available, economics and sociology are also recommended.

Did you know...

...that the most widely spoken indigenous language in the Americas is Kechwa (also spelled Quechua), the language of the Incas? About a quarter of the population of Peru still speaks Kechwa, and for many it is the only language they speak.

Typical courses in this major:

Introduction to Latin American studies
Latin American history
Latin American economics
Latin American geography
Latin American art
Latin American anthropology
Latin American literature
Current Latin American politics
High civilizations of the Americas
Peoples and cultures of modern Latin America
Latin American environmental issues
Colonial rule in Latin America
Revolutionary change in Latin America
The United States and Latin America

Concentrations:

Economics; history; political science; Spanish literature; Portuguese literature; geography; sociology; anthropology; international business; particular geographic areas.

What the study of this major is like:

As a Latin American studies major, you examine the diverse area in the Western Hemisphere that stretches from Mexico to the southern tip of Chile and Argentina. Some programs also include the islands of the Caribbean. You focus on the region's evolution and its relationship to other parts of the world, particularly the United States. Because the major is interdisciplinary, it makes use of courses and faculty members from a number of departments. For example, by taking courses offered by the departments of art history, political science, and ecology, you look at Latin America from artistic, political, and environmental perspectives.

All Latin American studies majors begin with a core of social sciences, natural sciences, and humanities requirements (such as math and English composition), along with courses specific to Latin America. After getting an overview of the region, you choose a concentration—usually from such disciplines as anthropology, political science, sociology, history, geography, business, agriculture, journalism, art history, government, ecology, Portuguese, or Spanish.

Some programs require you to take your concentration in one department (for example, Mexican history within the history department). At other colleges, concentrations may cut across departments (such as a Latin American business and economics concentration that draws from business and economics departments).

Most likely, you will be required to take at least two years of either Spanish or Portuguese—the chief languages of Latin America (Portuguese is the language of the continent's largest nation, Brazil). Languages such as Kechwa, Kaqchikel Maya (still spoken in Guatemala), and Haitian Creole (a mixture of European and Native languages) may also be available. You are encouraged to study for a summer, semester, or year in Latin America, in a program sponsored by your own or another college. Some students double-major—in Latin American studies and, for example, geography, economics, history, or political science.

Your courses vary in size, and language courses are generally small. The major typically attracts U.S. and foreign students, from both Hispanic and Anglo cultures, and you can expect to interact with a diverse group of people. In many programs, Portuguese is not stressed as much as Spanish. Also, some programs have a strong emphasis on literature and culture, while others focus on politics and international economics.

Other majors you might like:
Chicano studies
Spanish
Portuguese
International economics
Women's studies
History
Geography
International business
Anthropology
Caribbean studies
International relations
Sociology

Questions to ask colleges:
Is the program balanced across all subject areas, from the arts to social studies? Is the program geographically balanced, or is more emphasis given to certain countries or regions?

Does the program offer opportunities for students to study in Latin America?

Career options and trends:
International business manager/consultant; export-import manager; translator/interpreter; journalist; Foreign Service officer.

Careers in the Foreign Service are usually open only to U.S. citizens.

Graduates also pursue careers in government (CIA, State Department, or developmental agencies), non-governmental organizations (NGOs), teaching (such as teaching English in Latin America), international business (especially marketing and banking), social work (especially with agencies that work in Latin America), the travel industry, or law. Diplomatic service may require additional specialized training; translators and teachers usually need certification. Some graduates participate in the Peace Corps before beginning a career.

The presence of substantial numbers of recent immigrants from Latin America in many parts of the United States is likely to generate additional jobs—particularly in education, health care, social services, translation, journalism, and government—for those with a Latin American studies background.

Insider's viewpoint:
"I find myself easily bored by routine things. I can't imagine sitting through class after class of one discipline, like you have to do in English or business. In Latin American studies, your classes come from all different majors: language, government, history, economics, anthropology."

—Jennie, senior, University of Texas at Austin

For more info:
Latin American Studies Association (LASA)
416 Bellefield Hall
University of Pittsburgh
Pittsburgh, PA 15260
(412) 648-7929
http://lasa.international.pitt.edu

Native American studies

What it's about:

The Native American studies major provides an overview of tribes that are indigenous to the United States (including Alaska) and a history of cross-cultural relations from first contact with Europeans up to the present. You study tribal literatures, art, dance, song, religious traditions, philosophies, educational institutions, political and economic structures, and ecological perspectives.

Is this for you?

You might like this major if you also like: tackling social justice and/or environmental issues; Native American culture; non-traditional religions; mythology; other cultures.

Consider this major if you are good at: creativity; critical reading/thinking; persuading/influencing; research; teamwork ...*or have...* initiative; verbal skills; writing skills.

Recommended high school prep:

English 4, math 3, lab science 3, social studies 4, and a foreign language 3–4.

Typical courses in this major:

Cultures of Native North America and Alaska
Tribal governments
Contemporary issues in Native American studies
Oral and written traditions of Native Americans
Native American health and healing
Native American religion and philosophy
Native American arts
Contemporary indigenous issues and literatures
Native American history until 1865
Ecological perspectives of Native Americans
Sociology of Native Americans
Native Americans and film
Research and methods in Native American studies
Gender issues in Native American studies
Indigenous worldview perspectives
Native language study/linguistics

Concentrations:

Concentrations can be based on discipline, e.g., anthropology, political science, sociology, literature, or history; or on a particular region, e.g., North America, Mexico, Central America, or South America.

What the study of this major is like:

As a major in Native American studies, you must first catch up on any significant history you may not have covered in high school—in particular, the treatment of Native American tribal cultures by Europeans settling the Americas. Because your studies will include information not often presented in mainstream education and media, your first courses in the major may leave you feeling both dismayed and inspired. You will learn Native perspectives on a range of subjects, including the treaty-making process through which European Americans obtained access to and/or ownership of land and resources. In upper-level courses, you delve more deeply into art, literature, government, and religion; regions such as Alaska and the Southwest; and historical development, such as U.S.–Native contact before 1865.

Most faculty members who teach Native American studies have degrees in a subject such as history, anthropology, or English, but they draw from a variety of disciplines to develop their courses. For example, a course on present-day issues might incorporate writing by Native Americans (literary studies), as-told-to autobiographies (anthropology or literature), tribal arts and crafts (contemporary or historical art), sociological information (sociology), tribal newspapers (journalism), historical documents (history), court cases (law), or archaeological study (archaeology). Thus, because of the variety of academic approaches and cultural perspectives, the Native American studies classroom experience can be varied and exciting.

You may have a few large historical-overview courses, but most classes will be small groups that foster discussion and encourage you to sharpen your researching and writing abilities. Your two biggest challenges will be to deepen your cross-cultural understanding and to enhance your communication skills. Although much of your course work will consist of research and writing, you might also do projects, field studies, or interviews that take you off campus. And Native American elders, community activists, artists, scholars, and other visiting speakers may give on-campus talks that enrich your studies.

Native American studies programs tend to focus on the regions in which the college resides; for example, colleges in the Southwest are likely to have specialized courses on the Native American cultures and languages of Arizona and New Mexico, and on the connections between these tribal groups and those of Mexico and Latin America. Programs often have a disciplinary emphasis or strong link to another academic department, such as anthropology, social work, or history. These bonds exist because many Native American studies programs have grown out of traditional academic departments. Some programs are known for a particular strength; one college, for example, might support a project on Native voices and the media, while another offers a joint master's degree in Native American studies and law.

Native American studies can offer fresh perspectives that may give you a sense of purpose. Majors often strive to make a difference; they learn all they can about indigenous thought, traditions, values, and contributions to the global community. Their goal is to help Native Americans retain land and resources and revitalize cultural practices and beliefs.

Other majors you might like:
American history (U.S.)
Anthropology
Environmental studies
Linguistics
Latin American studies
Chicano studies
Musicology/ethnomusicology
Archaeology

Historic preservation
Sociology
Social work
Community health services

Questions to ask colleges:
Does the program cover Latin America, Alaska, or Canada, or does it focus on the United States, particularly on the lower 48 states? Although each type of program has merits, you should consider whether your interests fit a program's emphases.

Career options and trends:
Teacher*; park ranger; government officer (e.g., Indian Health Service, Bureau of Indian Affairs)*; lawyer (American Indian law); social worker*.

A state certificate or license is required for teaching in public schools. A law degree and license are required for practicing American Indian law off-reservation. Civil service exams are needed for most government employment.

Native American studies majors also pursue careers in environmental monitoring, business, Native American cultural preservation, tourism, tribal and nontribal criminal justice, health professions, and Native language preservation.

States are increasing their requirements for certification in Native American studies. Businesses are demanding an understanding of cultural diversity from employees, and social service and law enforcement agencies are looking for culturally appropriate ways to approach the populations they serve. These developments should increase employment opportunities for graduates with in-depth knowledge of Native American issues and traditions.

For more info:
American Indian Higher Education Consortium
121 Oronoco St.
Alexandria, VA 22314
(703) 838-0400
www.aihec.org

Near and Middle Eastern studies

What it's about:

Near and Middle Eastern studies focuses on a vast, culturally diverse geographic area that extends from North Africa to Central Asia. Using interdisciplinary and comparative approaches, you study the cultures and languages of the region. In addition, you examine the area's history, from antiquity to the present day, with particular focus on the period after the emergence of Islam.

Is this for you?

You might like this major if you also like: the History Channel; travel; adventure; languages; politics; reading about international events and military affairs; learning about other religions and cultures; languages written in unfamiliar alphabets.

Consider this major if you are good at: attention to detail; critical reading/thinking; memorizing; research *...or have...* curiosity; patience; verbal skills; writing skills.

Recommended high school prep:

English 4, math 3, lab science 3, social studies 3, and a foreign language 2-3. You are not expected to have studied the region in high school, but it is helpful if you can study a Near and Middle Eastern language. Other useful languages (especially if you intend to go to grad school in the field) are German and French.

Did you know...

...that some of the languages of the Middle East—Persian for instance—are among the easiest to learn? Arabic, on the other hand, is among the more difficult.

Typical courses in this major:

Arabic
Arabic literature in translation
Modern Near and Middle Eastern history
Near and Middle Eastern politics
Turkish
Islamic history and civilization
Islamic religion
People of the Near and Middle East
Hebrew
Persian
Islam and politics
Christianity, Judaism, and Islam
The United States and the Near and Middle East
Colonialism, imperialism, and nationalism
Palestine, Zionism, and Israel
Art in the Islamic world

Concentrations:

Geographic areas; area languages (Arabic, Turkish, Persian, Hebrew, etc.); area literature; disciplines with Near and Middle Eastern focus (such as Turkish history).

What the study of this major is like:

In a typical program, you take an introductory survey course covering the geography, history, and religious traditions of Asia Minor, Southwestern Asia, the Arabian Peninsula, and North Africa. In your second year, you take one or two specialized courses in history, political science, anthropology, religion, or literature translation. You should begin language study early enough to complete at least three years of Arabic and two years of Turkish, Persian (also known as Farsi, the language of Iran), or Hebrew. (At some colleges, you can take other languages, such as Armenian, Kurdish, or Berber.) If Middle Eastern language courses are not offered, try to take them at a neighboring college or as independent study, particularly if you plan to apply to grad school in the field.

You'll study languages in small classes, with professors who are generally native speakers. Learning a language will probably take at least four semesters of intensive daily study. Once you learn to decipher an unfamiliar alphabet and master the grammar, you may feel exhilarated to be able to read the works of contemporary as well as medieval authors from the Near and Middle East.

While studying a language, you attend lecture courses and seminars (in English) that address history, literature, politics, and other aspects of the region. Seminars usually have only about 10 to 20 students, and all of them are expected to take part in class discussion. In general, majors passionately debate current events; they readily observe links between the past and the present. Many majors spend a semester or a year abroad at a university (for example, the American University of Beirut, American University of Cairo, and Hebrew University of Jerusalem).

Near and Middle Eastern studies programs are differentiated mainly in two ways. First, programs concentrate either on the classical and medieval periods or on the modern period. Second, programs have either a language-and-literature approach or a discipline-based approach (historical, anthropological, political, philosophical, for example). Programs that stress the classical and medieval tend also to emphasize languages and literatures; the modern-oriented programs tend to take the discipline-based (or even multidisciplinary) approach. Some programs have a good mix of the medieval and the modern, and they include, as well, languages, literature and discipline-based studies.

Other majors you might like:
Arabic
History
Journalism
Linguistics
Archaeology
Art history
Islamic studies
Peace and conflict studies
Religious studies
Judaic studies
Ancient Near Eastern/Biblical languages
International relations

Questions to ask colleges:
What is the program's definition of Near and Middle Eastern studies? For example, a major may not fit the needs of students interested in contemporary issues and politics. Such students may be better served by majoring in history or political science and taking a Near and Middle Eastern language on the side.

Career options and trends:
Foreign Service Officer; international business or trade consultant; teacher; college professor; translator/interpreter; intelligence analyst; journalist; social worker.

Careers in the Foreign Service are usually open only to U.S. citizens.

Because of the political and economic turbulence in the Near and Middle East, the United States (including both the public and the private sector) will be intensely engaged in the region for years to come. People with language and other skills pertaining to the region should have a relatively easy time finding rewarding jobs.

Insider's viewpoint:
"Not only are there many areas of Middle Eastern history yet to be discovered (e.g., unknown and unedited medieval manuscripts), but what I teach and write about the Middle East has real contemporary relevance."

—Professor Bernard Haykel, New York University

For more info:
Middle East Studies Association (MESA)
University of Arizona
1219 North Santa Rita Ave.
Tucson, AZ 85721
(520) 621-5850
http://www.mesana.org

Women's studies

Also known as:
Feminist, gender, and sexuality studies

What it's about:
Women's studies is an interdisciplinary major that examines the connections between gender, sexuality, power, and inequality. You study such issues as oppression of women and sexual minorities; class exploitation; racism; and women's cultural and historical roles, both in the U.S. and around the world.

Is this for you?
You might like this major if you also like: thinking about the differences between men and women; seeing connections between ideas, people, and systems; thinking about issues in a comprehensive way.

Consider this major if you are good at: critical reading/thinking; organizing; persuading/influencing; research; teamwork *...or have...* tolerance for ambiguity; writing skills.

Recommended high school prep:
English 4, math 4, lab science 3, social studies 4, and a foreign language 3. If it is available, take statistics.

Typical courses in this major:
Women's history
Women in the economy
Women and literature
Gender, race, and class
Biological basis of sex differences
Feminism, state, and public policy
Feminist theories
Gender and colonization
Gender and language
Gender and sexuality in cross-cultural perspective
Gender inequality
Global perspectives on gender
Gender, sexuality, and law
History of sexuality
Women in cinema
Sociology of marriage

Concentrations:
Race, class, and ethnicity in the United States; lesbian, bisexual, gay, and transgender studies; global perspectives; feminist theory; women's history; movements, institutions, and social policy; gender, science, and health; women's art and literature.

What the study of this major is like:
If you are curious about gender and sexuality issues, women's studies is a good major to choose. It seeks to understand what it means now, and has meant in the past, to be a woman. You examine differences among women themselves, as well as the concept and uses of gender—that is, the changing definitions that societies attach to being women and men. Because gender can reflect and determine differences in power and opportunity, majors learn to analyze economic and social systems, ask searching questions about equality, and discuss ways in which society can be transformed. In addition, you explore the political and cultural effects of race, class, age, nationality, sexual identity, and ethnicity.

Women's studies began in the late 1960s as an attempt to make up for the lack of information, in most college courses, about women. What started as an effort to fill in the gaps has become a comprehensive analysis of the role of women in all areas of life. Besides supplying research about women, the major questions accepted beliefs and unexamined norms. Almost every discipline in the arts, humanities, and social sciences contributes to women's studies. For many majors in the field, women's studies becomes a window on the rest of the world.

A typical program includes courses offered within women's studies as well as courses offered by other departments. You will probably take an introductory women's studies course; a series of electives in the humanities, social sciences, and, where possible, natural sciences. A capstone experience is usually required in the form of a fourth-year seminar, fieldwork or internship project, or independent study. Many programs also require courses in feminist theory as well as in race, ethnicity, or non-Western culture.

Over the years, the major has concerned itself not only with *what* is taught but also *how* the material is taught. Classes seek to foster dialogue and to create a safe arena in which to debate. Course work often includes various methods of presentation, group activities, self-defined papers and projects, and invitations to tie theory to your own experience. Most programs offer the flexibility to tailor your program to meet your needs and interests. Many students double-major in a traditional liberal arts discipline and in women's studies.

Colleges may vary in their name for the major—the most common are gender and sexuality studies, feminist studies, and women's studies—and the differences in the name may signal variations in emphases. Because the field is wide-ranging, most programs cannot cover everything. Therefore, you should read course catalogs to find out which aspects individual programs emphasize.

Other majors you might like:
African-American studies
European studies
Native American studies
Latin American studies
American literature
Anthropology
Comparative literature
Psychology
Sociology
Human development and family studies
History
Gay/lesbian studies

Questions to ask colleges:
Are the faculty members permanent, full-time professors? What are some faculty research projects?

Do the courses build on and connect to one another? Are they offered regularly?

What research opportunities are available to undergraduates?

You should make sure that the college supports women's studies as a serious field of inquiry.

Career options and trends:
Some women's studies graduates go on to activist careers in social and political issues or social services. Others find jobs in education (all levels), business, public policy and administration, health services, communications, and film, and (with appropriate graduate degrees) in college teaching, research, law, and medicine.

Insider's viewpoint:
"The way I understand women's studies, it's a critique of traditional disciplines and so it was a way of looking at things I'd seen my entire life from a different viewpoint."

—Paulette, senior, Oberlin College

For more info:
National Women's Studies Association (NWSA)
7100 Baltimore Ave., Suite 203
College Park, MD 20740
(301) 403-0407
www.nwsa.org

Biological sciences

The biological sciences are no less than the study of life itself. Biologists often see the big picture by looking through a microscope.

Studies focus on animals, plants, and microbes, all on the levels of molecules and cells; organs, such as the heart; organisms (individuals of a species); populations (such as migrating birds); and environments, such as rain forests. Some biologists research particular life forms. Botanists study plants, marine biologists investigate sea life, and entomologists look into the world of insects.

Professors talk about the many fields of biology as explorations into the frontiers of biochemistry, biotechnology, and the rapidly growing areas of genetics and molecular and cellular biology.

"The complexity of living organisms represents an ideal outlet for satisfying the need to discover," says biochemist Gregory M. Raner of the University of North Carolina at Greensboro.

"Molecular biology is for people who are constantly asking why," notes Eileen Gregory of Rollins College. And according to the botanist C. O. Patterson of Texas A&M University, "New discoveries and invention of new techniques have generated an explosion of understanding and interest in this field."

Many scientific journeys in biological and medical research are aimed at improving health through vaccines, medicines, and cures for cancer, heart disease, AIDS, Alzheimer's, and other diseases. Some researchers venture into realms of genetic engineering, immune system therapies, and stem cell research. These emerging fields are reflected in new majors, which include bioengineering, genomics, biostatistics, and molecular modeling.

The life sciences prepare you to work in any number of professions—as a clinician, research assistant or technician, or scientist. Biotech labs, pharmaceutical companies, hospitals, and medical testing firms all hire biologists, as does the government, which has increased funding for research.

Employment growth in the biological sciences is slowing somewhat. However, scientists are needed to put new discoveries to use, such as fighting disease with gene therapies. Naturally, the more education, training, and experience you have, the better the job you're likely to get. For instance, a four-year Bachelor of Science degree is a must for most nonresearch jobs in the life sciences. Researchers usually need even more education. A master's degree is okay for some researchers but a doctorate (Ph.D.) is required in the competition for other research jobs. No matter what level you study, professors say, you'll need to know chemistry as well as biology from the get-go.

Colleges great and small

When you compare biology programs, keep in mind the size of the colleges. While smaller colleges provide a solid foundation in the biological sciences, many of the newer majors are offered only at large universities. Also, larger universities have more funding for research. On the other hand, small colleges often pride themselves on the quality of their teaching. Find out if the college's faculty members are active in research and have published their work. Ask, too, whether undergrads can do research, in the college or on an internship. It's valuable experience, especially if you plan to go for a graduate degree and need an edge by getting hands-on experience.

"One of the most important things a graduate admission committee looks for is a good letter of recommendation from a respected researcher in whose laboratory you have participated," suggests Carter Denniston, professor of genetics at the University of Wisconsin, Madison.

You can study practically any area in biology in graduate school, including hot topics like microbial, plant, and animal genetics. Genetics is now central to biology, providing "general concepts and techniques for the study of inheritance, development, disease, and evolution in all living organisms and viruses," Denniston says.

You may find that molecular biology, virology, or another course you want is offered only at the graduate level—it all depends on the college. Some examples of graduate programs are bacterial physiology, pharmacogenetics, community and evolutionary ecology, environmental or conservation biology, toxicology, immunology, and neurobiology.

When you study biology, expect to do class work, fieldwork, and especially laboratory work. You'll spend a lot of quality time in the lab. So, if possible, compare the labs and equipment, as well as courses and faculty members, in the colleges you may apply to. Find out if your studies will cover a range of biology topics or zero in on one aspect of the life sciences, such as molecular or cellular biology or biochemistry. The course list will give you an idea of what the college stresses. And rcmcmber, some colleges are geared for premed students—those who plan to become doctors.

When searching for colleges with bio programs, look for colleges or divisions of arts and sciences, biological sciences, colleges of medicine, natural science and mathematics, health sciences, or applied science and technology.

Your career as a researcher begins now. Start your college search by reading about the majors in this section and visiting the American Instititute of Biological Sciences's Web site (www.aibs.org). For information about other majors related to the life sciences, go to the sections on Agriculture, Health, and Natural resources and conservation.

Biochemistry

What it's about:

Biochemistry majors study the principles that enable living things to function as they do. Combining knowledge of chemical structure and of the behavior of molecules with a "big picture" view of biological processes helps you understand how "life" occurs at its most basic level.

Is this for you?

You might like this major if you also like: all areas of science; all varieties of living things; new technologies; mysteries (novels, movies, computer games) and puzzles; finding out how things work; seeking answers to fundamental questions about nature and living things.

Consider this major if you are good at: attention to detail; creativity; critical reading/thinking; math; memorizing; quantitative analysis; research; spacial thinking/analysis; teamwork *...or have...* initiative; manual dexterity.

Recommended high school prep:

English 4, math 4 (including precalculus or trigonometry), lab science 4 (biology, chemistry, physics, earth science), social studies 3, and a foreign language 2–3. Take as many advanced or honors-level science courses as you can. Any computer courses would also be useful.

Did you know...

...that many students in this major find biochemistry easier to learn than the more traditional branches of science? This is because you study the basic principles in a familiar context: the world of living organisms. In fact, many students do better with chemistry and physics when the material is linked to principles of biology.

Typical courses in this major:

Analytic chemistry
Organic chemistry
Calculus
Physics
Microbiology
Physical chemistry
Biochemistry
Quantitative analysis
Cell biology
Genetics
Inorganic chemistry
Physiology
Immunology
Physical biochemistry

Concentrations:

Biotechnology; toxicology; pharmacology; cell biology; immunology; neurochemistry; genetics; hematology; bacteriology.

What the study of this major is like:

Biochemists, who study the chemistry of organisms, relate the principles of chemistry to the functions of living systems. Biochemistry majors learn how to recognize the chemical nature of biological molecules by taking many of the core courses needed for a chemistry degree. You will also take courses that introduce you to human metabolism; DNA replication (how cells reproduce themselves) and the conversion of genetic information into functional cell components; human and mammalian physiology; and real-world applications of biotechnology.

Many people define biochemistry too narrowly; they think that it is simply a fifth division of chemistry, along with physical, inorganic, organic, and analytical. In reality, biochemistry includes all of the traditional divisions of chemistry and extends beyond the physical sciences into the life sciences and medicine as well.

Most courses in biochemistry are in lecture format and may include laboratory work. In many courses, you'll have plenty of homework, especially problem sets to complete and daily reading assignments. Most programs strongly encourage you to do some type of research. You may also be required to give oral presentations. Usually the biggest challenges students face is scheduling their courses and managing their time. Students sometimes take light course loads early on, not realizing that they are simply shifting the weight of their work to their third or fourth year, when courses become more challenging and time-consuming. You can help balance your workload by developing and sticking to a study plan.

There are many different approaches to the study of biochemistry. At some colleges the program emphasizes the chemical nature of biological systems. These programs are usually in departments of chemistry or physical science. Biochemistry programs in life science or medical departments may focus on physiology or molecular and cellular biology. Probably the best way to determine the emphasis of a program is to examine the required courses for the major. A program that does not require physical or inorganic chemistry would be likely to emphasize the biological aspects of biochemistry, with less attention to the chemistry of biomolecules. In contrast, a stress on chemistry might indicate a commitment to the fundamental aspects of biological interactions.

Other majors you might like:
Cell biology and histology
Microbiology
Molecular biology
Clinical nutrition
Neuroscience
Pharmacy
Chemistry
Biotechnology
Clinical/medical laboratory technology
Biomedical engineering
Chemical engineering
Forensic science

Career options and trends:
College professor*; physician*; research technician; research scientist*; science teacher.

Graduate or professional school after college is required for careers in medicine and scientific research. To teach in college you will need at least a master's degree and preferably a Ph.D. Additional credits in education and certification are usually needed for teaching in high school as well.

A major in biochemistry is a logical choice to prepare for medical, dental, or veterinary school, or for health and agricultural careers in such areas as toxicology, biomedical engineering, clinical chemistry, plant pathology, and animal sciences. Industries that may employ biochemistry majors include biotechnology, pharmaceutical, and medical testing and diagnostic firms. Biochemistry majors who also obtain a certificate in specialized lab training (DNA sequencing, in vitro cell biology, genetic engineering, for example) will improve their prospects.

For more info:
American Society of Biochemistry and Molecular Biology
9650 Rockville Pike
Bethesda, MD 20814
(301) 634-7145
www.asbmb.org

Biology

Also known as:
Life science

What it's about:
Biology is the study of the structure, function, heredity, and evolution of all living things—microorganisms, fungi, plants, and animals. These life forms are studied at the levels of molecule, cell, organism, and population. Through lab work and fieldwork, you acquire a basic understanding of organisms, their habitats, and the processes that govern their life activities.

Is this for you?
You might like this major if you also like: pets; wildlife; gardening; wellness/fitness activities; environmental issues; outdoor activities (hiking, canoeing, rock climbing, etc.); zoos; insects.

Consider this major if you are good at: attention to detail; creativity; critical reading/thinking; memorizing; organizing; quantitative analysis; research; teamwork ...*or have...* critical observation; manual dexterity; patience.

Recommended high school prep:
English 4; math 4 (including trigonometry and precalculus); lab science 4 (including earth science, biology, chemistry, and physics); social studies 2; a foreign language 2–3; and a computer applications course. Because biology is increasingly quantitative, a strong foundation in the physical sciences and math is essential.

Did you know...
...that mathematics is becoming increasingly important in biological research and innovation? If you are strong in both areas you will be in a good position for 21st century jobs.

Typical courses in this major:
Genetics
Cell biology
Microbiology
Molecular biology
Developmental biology
Immunology
Animal or plant physiology
Comparative anatomy and embryology
Animal behavior
Plant biology
Invertebrate biology
Parasitology
Aquatic biology
Environmental biology
Ecology
Evolution

Concentrations:
In college: biochemistry; botany; environmental science; microbiology; molecular biology; neuroscience; zoology.

If you go on to grad school: anatomy; behavioral biology; bioinformatics, cell biology; developmental biology; evolutionary biology; genetics; immunology; limnology; mycology; ornithology; paleontology; parasitology; pharmacology; physiology (animal and plant); systematics (animal and plant).

What the study of this major is like:
As a biology major, you'll focus on the way organisms solve the problems they face in their environments. In addition, you'll seek answers to the question most biology programs ask: How have ecological and hereditary factors contributed to the evolution of plants, animals, and microbes?

Generally, biology courses are taught through a combination of lectures and coordinated labs. Some professors provide opportunities for collaborative activities and online assignments as well. In the lab, hands-on experiences include observational exercises and open-ended experiments; for both types of work, you analyze data and then write reports.

After the intro courses, which stress the primary concepts, processes, and vocabulary of biology, you'll examine many of the subjects in greater depth. In cell biology and physiology, for instance, you analyze the link between the structure and function of cells—how they divide and then differentiate (take on new forms and new tasks). You'll observe cells through the microscope and do data-gathering experiments on different kinds of cells.

In genetics, you identify the molecular and cellular aspects of heredity in animals and in plants. You may also cover topics such as human hereditary disorders and DNA technology. Labs usually require you to work independently on fruit flies, molds, bacteria, and viruses. In ecology, you study the relation of plants and animals to their environment. Most likely, you'll follow up field-work with data analysis based on varied computational and statistical methods.

Courses beyond the intro level may include botany and more-specialized courses in seed plants, algae, fungi; invertebrate zoology and more-specialized classes in entomology (insects), protozoology (amoebas and other one-celled forms); and vertebrate zoology and more-specialized courses in ornithology (birds), ichthyology (fish), and so on.

Again, as you observe the relationship between function and structure, you'll consider how evolution has led to the diversity of the animal and plant kingdoms. In labs, you dissect fresh and preserved material, and sometimes apply culture techniques. Microbiology concentrates on the structure, function, genetics, and ecology of bacteria and viruses. Molecular biology and biochemistry are concerned with the substances that help regulate living systems. In these and other advanced courses, you read, analyze, and discuss current biology literature and often conduct independent research. Some advanced courses offer extended fieldwork.

The greatest challenge for biology majors is to deal with the large amount of information you must learn. Also, in most semesters you have to take two or even three lab courses. The most successful majors keep up-to-date with their assignments and learn to manage their time effectively. An upside of the workload, though, is that you often do lab projects with a partner or a small team of students, so you have the benefit of a support group and a chance to develop friendships with other majors.

Although most biology programs cover all aspects of the field, programs may emphasize different areas of biology. For example, one department might focus on cellular and molecular biology, while another emphasizes the organism or environmental studies. Some programs feature extended field trips to unique habitats, such as rain forests, mountains, or deserts. Another difference among programs is the amount of emphasis placed on undergrad research. Requirements for the major may also vary from college to college, particularly in the number of chemistry, physics, and math courses you must complete before you graduate.

Other majors you might like:
Agronomy and crop science
Environmental science
Wildlife and wilderness management
Forestry
Horticulture
Veterinary technology
Marine biology
Anthropology
Biomedical engineering
Entomology
Zoology
Biotechnology

Questions to ask colleges:
Are there opportunities for independent study and research?

Are the lab facilities up-to-date and sufficient for the number of students in the program?

Is this primarily a premed program, or do many of the graduates go on to pursue the science of biology in grad school and industry?

Career options and trends:
Teacher*; naturalist; industrial or university researcher*; lab technician; state or federal government biologist; health care professional (physician, dentist, vet, nurse)*; health care administrator; sales/marketing representative (pharmaceutical/biotech).

You will need to go on to graduate or professional school for a career in research or medicine, or to teach at the college level. Additional education credits and certification is usually needed to teach in high school as well.

According to the Bureau of Labor Statistics, about 40 percent of all biologists work for federal, state, and local government agencies (environmental, agricultural, health), and most of the others work in the pharmaceutical and biotech industries. Job growth in the biotech field continues to be strong but is expected to slow down after rapid expansion in the biotechnolgy industry. Biologists with diverse knowledge and training, particularly in math and computer science, will enjoy the best prospects and demand.

Insider's viewpoint:

"I'm not premed, but a lot of people in my classes are. They're really, really competitive. For me, I'm taking the class because it's interesting to me, but for them, they have to get 100 percent on everything, so the curve is really high."

—Romi, sophomore, University of California: Los Angeles

For more info:
American Institute of Biological Sciences (AIBS)
1444 I (Eye) St., N.W.
Suite 200
Washington, DC 20005
(202) 628-1500
www.aibs.org

Biotechnology

What it's about:

The biotechnology major combines the molecular life sciences and engineering. You learn how to use living cells, cellular and molecular processes, and genetic information to solve problems and to create new products.

Is this for you?

You might like this major if you also like: science and technology (a lot); science fairs; putting theory to practical use; building things; running your own business; working with people.

Consider this major if you are good at: attention to detail; creativity; critical reading/thinking; organizing; quantitative analysis; research; teamwork *...or have...* initiative; patience; verbal skills.

Recommended high school prep:

English 4, math 4 (including precalculus), lab science 4, social studies 3, and a foreign language 2–3. Take computer science if offered. If possible, participate in a summer research program for high school students, available at many research institutes (such as Roswell Park Cancer Institute Summer High School Research Program).

Did you know...

...that biotechnology involves nanotechnology—working with materials (genes and DNA) that are invisible without powerful microscopes?

...that biotechnology is one of the oldest technologies? Humankind has been using the biological processes of microorganisms—such as yeast—for over 6,000 years. On the other hand, 70 percent of all biotechnologically produced medicines now on the market were approved since the early 1990s.

Typical courses in this major:

General biology I & II
Cell biology
Cell physiology
Microbiology
Developmental biology
Organic chemistry
Biochemistry
Immunology
Virology
Tissue culture methods
Bioanalytical techniques
Plant biotechnology
Genetic engineering
Genomics (gene function)
Bioinformatics
Proteinomics

Concentrations:

Bioinformatics; genomics; protenomics; toxicogenomics; pharmacogenomics; bioprocess; molecular modeling; computational chemistry.

What the study of this major is like:

In biotechnology, which combines molecular life sciences and engineering, you use living matter to develop products and services in agriculture (plant growth hormones, food additives), health care (vaccines, improved medicines and vitamins), the environment (detoxification of chemicals), and other areas. The study of biotechnology has greatly expanded with the sequencing of the human genome, as well as many other genomes. In fact, all of life's processes are now open to study—from the human to the bacterial.

As a biotechnology major, you learn to use several technologies to explore organisms: genetic engineering (changing gene characteristics for a specific purpose); bioprocessing (using separating and purifying techniques); immunobiochemistry; protein engineering; and biocatalysis (using enzymes to produce a biochemical reaction). In fact, biotechnologists need all the tools of the biochemist, the molecular biologist, the immunologist, and even the engineer, to prepare a product or an application on a large scale for the marketplace.

Because biotechnology course work covers all the life sciences (including areas such as exobiology and nuclear transfer cell therapy), you are likely to find subjects that interest you. The major is taught in both lecture and lecture/lab formats. In some classes, you may work on research projects with faculty members—an experience worth seeking out. You might also be required to complete independent research. An individual research project in biotechnology at the undergraduate level is a big undertaking. But producing an original contribution will give you a taste of what science has to offer—a chance to do something unique.

You can find biotechnology offered at the four-year bachelor's degree level, the two-year associate degree level, and even as a ten-week certificate program. Community colleges across the country have been increasing their offerings in this field in order to match growth in the industry, particularly in the areas of medical, pharmaceutical, and agricultural manufacturing.

Differences among biotechnology programs occur because of differences in the size of the institutions and the funding available for the undergraduate program. At well-funded institutions, the program may be good, but teaching may be less valued than research. At small institutions, teaching is often the primary concern, but funding may be nonexistent. If there's a balance between size and funding, faculty members can be active in research but still have the time and interest to help undergraduates.

Other majors you might like:

Agricultural and biological engineering
Microbiology
Biochemistry
Applied physics
Biological/physical sciences
Forest technology
Chemical engineering
Biomedical technology
Biomedical engineering
Clinical/medical laboratory technology
Environmental engineering
Bioinformatics

Career options and trends:

Biomedical researcher*; biochemical development engineer; environmental health and safety specialist; pharmaceutical product development researcher or engineer*; forensic scientist; medical diagnostician; biotechnology industry researcher, engineer or manager*; quality control analyst or engineer; regulatory affairs specialist.

The biotechnology field is large and growing, so job opportunities will be strong in the foreseeable future. The fastest employment growth is projected to occur in the pharmaceutical and medical manufacturing industry and in firms providing research and testing services.

Insider's viewpoint:

"I'm doing independent research with a professor in the med school, and I'm working directly under the president of a biotech company, helping him with scientific literature research. These experiences help me tremendously; I learned how to network and overcame the fear of talking to professors. In addition, there's the research experience itself. It's very hard-core and takes a lot of endurance, patience, and stamina. Being single-minded is key."

—Clare, senior, University of California: Davis

For more info:

Biotechnology Industry Organization (BIO)
1201 Maryland Avenue, S.W.
Suite 900
Washington, DC 20024
(202) 962-9200
www.bio.org

National Center for Biotechnology Information
National Library of Medicine
Building 38A
Bethesda, MD 20894
(301) 496-2475
www.ncbi.nlm.nih.gov

Botany

Also known as:

Plant biology

What it's about:

Majors in botany study all aspects of plant life, which ranges from the smallest to the largest organisms on earth. Courses teach both microscopic and field investigation techniques.

Is this for you?

You might like this major if you also like: discovering new things, observing nature, gardening, hiking, working and playing outdoors, natural history.

Consider this major if you are good at: attention to detail; creativity; logical reasoning; quantitative analysis; research; teamwork ...*or have...* manual dexterity; observation skills; patience.

Recommended high school prep:

English 4, math 4 (including precalculus and statistics), lab science 4 (including biology, chemistry and physics), social studies 3, and a foreign language 2–3.

Typical courses in this major:

General biology
Biochemistry
Microbiology
Genetics
Plant anatomy and physiology
Field ecology
Plant evolution
Photosynthesis
Plant taxonomy and systematics
Mycology (fungi)
Pteridophytes (ferns)
Phycology (algae)
Lichens and bryophytes
Vascular plant morphology
Paleobotony

Concentrations:

In college: plant physiology; plant ecology; plant genetics.

If you go on to grad school: paleobotany; plant genomics; plant development and hormonal regulation; plant cell biology; plant systematics; community and evolutionary ecology.

What the study of this major is like:

Although people have been studying plants for thousands of years, discoveries made and techniques developed in the last few decades have generated an explosion of interest in botany. This is indeed an exciting time in the plant sciences.

Introductory courses in botany (first- and second-year courses) usually have both lecture and lab components. In courses that include fieldwork, you study organisms in their natural habitats, where you may observe interesting examples of anatomical and physiological adaptations to features of the environment. While even a handheld lens can provide vital information about many species, most botanical studies rely on sophisticated tools. That's why it's useful to take as many courses as possible that offer hands-on experience with a range of equipment and techniques.

In cell biology courses, you will study the biochemical pathways that maintain and promote life through each of the cell's parts. In plant anatomy and plant physiology, you will explore the unique nature of plants: how cells are organized; how organs are formed and function; and how growth, development, and reproduction processes are coordinated. Plant ecology focuses on the way individual plants integrate into communities of organisms and the way plants respond to their environment—for example, how plants coexist with animals that eat them or how plants use animals to help them pollinate and reproduce.

The diversity of plants is so great that you may, at first, feel overwhelmed by the amount of information available. But as you examine plants more closely, you will see that most of the basic features of plants are the same for nearly all species. Rather than try to learn every detail about every kind of plant, you can begin to focus on one plant group.

Some colleges stress ecology and the evolution of plants, while others emphasize molecular and ultrastructural studies. At many colleges, you must complete a set of core courses in biology before beginning specialized botany courses; on other campuses, you may take botany courses in your first year.

Because botanists spend a lot of time in the lab or in the field, they tend to dress comfortably and informally. Likewise, they often have laid-back attitudes. Nevertheless, they work hard, both physically and intellectually. Some botanists visit unexplored regions looking for new species, even putting themselves in danger in the search. Others rarely stray outside their lab, although they may put in 16-hour days carrying out complex experiments. Because plants function on their own schedules, without regard for human convenience, botanists usually plan their days (and nights) to meet the needs of their research organisms. So a botanist may be in the lab at 3:00 a.m. to observe the unfurling of a flower bud, the division of a growing cell, the opening and closing of stomata—but the thrill of discovery makes any loss of sleep worth while.

Other majors you might like:

Horticulture
Genetics
Ecology
Plant pathology
Agricultural and biological engineering
Wood science/paper/pulp technology
Agronomy and crop science
Range science
Landscape architecture
Herbalism
Floriculture
Forestry

Questions to ask colleges:

Is there access to a nearby nature reserve or other protected, undisturbed area? For plant ecology studies, this would be very valuable.

Is there a well-equipped herbarium on campus? It would be useful for taxonomic and systematics work. For most areas of research in botany, modern, fully equipped labs are essential.

Career options and trends:

Laboratory technician; manager of a nature conservancy or environmentally protected area; technical artist, illustrator, or photographer; curator of a museum, herbarium, or arboretum; pharmaceutical researcher or investigator; plant breeder.

Employment opportunities are generally good, with higher salaries closely linked to advanced education and training and/or experience. The two areas showing most rapid expansion are the molecular biology of plants, and field studies of protected or endangered plant species.

Insider's viewpoint:

"Think about botany in relation to horticulture and decide if the science of plants sounds interesting or if the growing of plants is more interesting to you. I, myself, love both but I really wanted to learn the science."

—Deborah, senior, University of Wisconsin

For more info:

American Society of Plant Biologists (ASPB)
15501 Monona Drive
Rockville, MD 20855-2768
(301) 251-0560
www.aspb.org

Botanical Society of America (BSA)
P.O. Box 299
St. Louis, MO 63166-0299
(314) 577-9566
www.botany.org

Cell biology and histology

What it's about:

Cell biology emphasizes the cell as the basic unit for examining characteristics common to all living organisms. Histology is the study of how cells are organized into functional units called tissues, and how tissues are organized into organs.

Is this for you?

You might like this major if you also like: microscopes and lab work; math and science, especially biology and chemistry.

Consider this major if you are good at: attention to detail; creativity; critical reading/thinking; math; organizing; quantitative analysis; research ...*or have...* initiative; manual dexterity; patience.

Recommended high school prep:

English 4, math 3, lab science 4 (including biology, chemistry and physics), social studies 3, and a foreign language 2–3. Take as many advanced or honors science courses as possible.

Typical courses in this major:

Physics
Calculus
Organic chemistry
Cell biology
Molecular biology
Genetics
Biochemistry
Cell physiology
Immunology
Developmental biology
Neurobiology
Structural biology
Virology
Histology/microanatomy
Microscopy/microtechnique
Electron microscopy

Concentrations:

Generally, none available.

What the study of this major is like:

Cell biology is often offered as a concentration within the broad-based major in biology; in some cases it is offered as a major in cellular and molecular biology. Histology, also called microscopic anatomy, may be included under histotechnology, cytotechnology, microtechnique, or even microscopy. Histology is usually taught as a course within a major or as a separate associate's degree or certification program.

In cell biology, the focus is on the cell as the basic unit of life. You will explore the fundamental processes that are common to all living cells, and investigate the unique characteristics and processes of more specialized cell types such as lymphocytes and neurons. Additionally, you should acquire a broad, general foundation in biology, chemistry, and physics.

Most of your classes will involve lectures. However, as is usual for science classes, most of your learning will take place in the lab. In cell biology laboratory sections, you will take part in various aspects of research. You may also have the opportunity to participate in research on your own, either on an independent-study project mentored by faculty members or on an internship.

Since cellular biology and molecular biology are two rapidly growing areas in biology, the amount of information you will have to deal with can be overwhelming. You'll find that the work requires both attention to detail and the ability to appreciate and comprehend broad concepts. As a biologist, you should be ready to take initiative and to work cooperatively with others. Although you will often study alone, you will sometimes work in pairs or in small groups in the lab. Because of the emphasis on real-life learning, many laboratory experiments cannot be completed within a typical laboratory period (3 hours). Therefore, you can expect to work outside of class, either alone or in small groups. Keep in mind, too, that much of the laboratory learning may at first seem repetitious; but this valuable experience will help you master the hands-on research skills you'll need.

In some colleges, the biology degree offers a broad exposure to the hierarchy of living things, spanning molecules, cells, organisms, ecologies, and ecosystems. In other colleges, the biology major focuses on molecular, cellular, or biochemical processes. If you select a broad-based program, it is possible that you may discover a field that interests you more than the one you initially selected. In a narrower program, you might have fewer options if you decide to make a change. With a strong background in basic biology, however, you can take supplemental courses in graduate school to keep yourself competitive with students coming from more specialized undergraduate programs.

Other majors you might like:
Molecular biology
Microbiology
Biochemistry
Chemistry
Zoology
Botany
Genetics
Biomedical engineering
Chemical engineering
Biomedical technology
Biotechnology
Clinical/medical laboratory technology

Questions to ask colleges:
What is the laboratory enrollment size? Do full-time faculty members, teaching assistants, or adjunct instructors teach laboratory courses? What type of access do undergraduates have to laboratory equipment?

Career options and trends:
Research scientist; physician or health care professional; research assistant or technician; regulatory compliance officer; college professor.

For work as a research technician, certain laboratories require certification in areas such as histotechnology.

Cell biology is a fast-moving field, so it is hard to predict trends. Today's discoveries may become tomorrow's ordinary tools and techniques.

For more info:
American Society for Cell Biology (ASCB)
8120 Woodmont Ave.
Suite 750
Bethesda, MD 20814-2762
(301) 347-9300
www.ascb.org

Entomology

Also known as:

Insect biology

What it's about:

Entomology deals with the biology and economic importance of insects and their relatives. If you are interested in understanding the diversity of insects in all their habitats, or their impact on human health and resources, you may find this major a better match than the broader life sciences majors.

Is this for you?

You might like this major if you also like: bugs, of course; nature and the environment; farming and agriculture; lab sciences.

Consider this major if you are good at: attention to detail; critical reading/thinking; organizing; quantitative analysis; research; teamwork ...*or have*... curiosity; initiative; verbal skills.

Recommended high school prep:

English 4, math 4, lab science 4, social studies 3, and a foreign language 2–3. Take a course in computer science or computer applications if one is available.

Did you know...

...that not many students major in this subject? Those who do, therefore, have more opportunity for one-on-one interactions with their advisers and professors.

...that over a million different species of insects have been identified so far? Some experts believe that there may be another 30 million species yet to be discovered.

Typical courses in this major:

General biology
Microbiology
Chemistry
General entomology
Insect physiology
Insect taxonomy and systematics
Field crop insects
Horticultural entomology
Livestock entomology
Insect behavior
Aquatic entomology
Beekeeping
Agricultural entomology (pest management)
Medical entomology
Forest entomology
Urban entomology

Concentrations:

Generally, none in college; but if you go on to grad school: evolution and behavior; molecular entomology; pest management

What the study of this major is like:

Entomology evolved into a field of its own because of the enormous impact insects have on humans. Some entomologists teach farmers how to use efficient, environmentally safe methods of pest control. Others work in forest management or in ornamental plant industries to protect trees from destructive bugs. Still others, employed by public health agencies, help ranchers deal with insects that plague livestock. Entomologists also conduct basic research in ecology, physiology, toxicology, genetics, and biotechnology, since insects can serve as test organisms for the examination of principles common to all animal life.

Before you begin study in entomology, you take introductory courses in plant and animal biology and in chemistry (including organic chemistry). Because entomology is a biological science, you will be taking biology courses throughout your undergraduate studies. From a general entomology course you progress to advanced classes in the morphology, taxonomy, physiology, ecology, and behavior of insects. Other advanced courses may deal with the importance of insects to human health and welfare (for example, pest management or medical entomology). Elective courses include plant physiology, plant pathology, nematology (nematodes or roundworms), microbiology, parasitology, agricultural engineering, agronomy, sociology, and economics.

Laboratories are an important part of many entomology courses. In some courses, you may even be required to collect insects. You will probably be encouraged to conduct an independent research project under the supervision of a professor. The electives you choose should reflect your educational and career objectives. If, after college, you plan to go directly into pest management, you should take courses in other agricultural sciences, such as weed science or plant pathology. If, on the other hand, you would like to go to graduate school, take advanced courses in biology and entomology that relate to your interests.

Entomology is not generally offered as an undergraduate major except in large public research universities and land grant colleges. Some programs may focus more on pest management (usually those in agricultural departments); others emphasize basic science.

Other majors you might like:
Plant protection/pest management
Environmental science
Ecology
Sustainable agriculture
Zoology
Agricultural and biological engineering
Agronomy and crop science
Wildlife biology
Animal sciences
Aquatic biology/limnology

Questions to ask colleges:
What are the opportunities for independent research?

How flexible is the major in meeting my career objectives (for example, pest management or basic science)?

Do graduates get jobs that relate to their major in entomology?

Career options and trends:
Urban or agricultural pest management specialist*; government research technician or scientist; university research technician*; industry researcher; industry technical or sales representative; university extension agent.

Entry-level positions in industry and government may be obtained with a bachelor's degree, but a graduate degree is required for most research and upper-level jobs.

For more info:
Entomological Society of America
10001 Derekwood Lane
Suite 100
Lanham, MD 20706-4876
(301) 731-4535
www.entsoc.org

Genetics

What it's about:

Genetics began when an Austrian monk examined the heredity of simple traits in peas. It now serves as the framework for the biological sciences, by providing concepts and techniques for studying inheritance, development, disease, and evolution in all living organisms and viruses. As a major in genetics, you gain a solid background from which you can specialize in most areas of biology.

Is this for you?

You might like this major if you also like: science and technology; finding out how things work; solving puzzles; natural and human history; research; learning about medicine and evolution.

Consider this major if you are good at: attention to detail; creativity; critical reading/thinking; math; quantitative analysis; research *...or have...* manual dexterity; patience; writing skills.

Recommended high school prep:

English 4, math 4 (including calculus), lab science 4 (including biology, physics, and chemistry), social studies 3, and a foreign language 2–3. Be sure to take all available computer science courses.

Typical courses in this major:

Calculus
Organic chemistry
Inorganic chemistry
Biochemistry
Statistics
Physics
General biology
Principles of genetics
Advanced genetics
Human genetics
Molecular genetics
Quantitative genetics and breeding
Evolutionary genetics
Population genetics
Developmental genetics
Genetic data analysis

Concentrations:

Generally, none in college; but if you go on to grad school: human genetics; plant genetics; animal genetics; microbial genetics; viral genetics; developmental genetics; population genetics; cytology; quantitative genetics; behavioral genetics.

What the study of this major is like:

Genetics majors usually begin with a solid grounding in chemistry, biochemistry, and general biology. Math and statistics requirements vary from college to college. Within the major, your work can be diverse, including courses in classical genetics, molecular biology, plant and animal genetics, population genetics, cytology, human genetics, microbial genetics (bacteria and viruses), behavioral genetics, and specialized courses related to model organisms (such as maize, roundworms, or mice) or to laboratory skills such as molecular genetics techniques.

Some colleges do not have the undergraduate major "genetics," but they offer similar courses under "molecular biology." Most programs contain a mix of lecture, laboratory, and independent research opportunities; in addition, some programs have a capstone course in which you read original research papers and discuss them. To be a successful major, you should be committed to genetics and have good study habits. Some students find genetics challenging because it is a research-oriented major. If you don't like research (many people don't), then genetics is probably not for you. But if you love working in the lab at all hours, you should do well.

If you plan on going for a Ph.D. in genetics or another biological science, pick a college that offers quality undergraduate research opportunities. A graduate admissions committee will probably expect you to supply a letter of recommendation from a respected researcher in whose laboratory you worked.

Genetics is a good undergraduate major for students heading for medical school, veterinary school, and most other graduate programs in biology. On the other hand, you don't have to major in genetics to get into a graduate program in the field. Graduate programs accept majors in biochemistry, bacteriology, biology, zoology, botany, and other biological sciences.

Other majors you might like:
Biomedical engineering
Agricultural and biological engineering
Botany
Zoology
Genetic counseling
Biotechnology
Forensic science
Animal breeding
Biomedical technology
Biochemistry
Molecular biology

Career options and trends:
Genetics counselor*; medical or veterinary doctor*; genetics researcher or investigator*; lab bench scientist or technician, or lab manager; science writer; executive, manager, or sales rep in the biotechnology industry; clinical and medical geneticist.

A degree from a professional school and licensing are required for those wishing to become physicians or veterinarians, and most jobs in genetic research require a Ph.D.

The biotechnology industry has a number of career opportunities for students with just a baccalaureate. The aggressive growth that occurred in that industry in the past has slowed somewhat but is still going strong, and is expected to remain strong for the foreseeable future. There is also an increasing need for people with a solid background in both genetics and communications.

For more info:
Genetics Society of America (GSA)
9650 Rockville Pike
Bethesda, MD 20814-3998
(301) 634-7300
www.genetics-gsa.org

Marine biology

What it's about:
Students in marine biology explore the diversity of sea life, the functioning of marine ecosystems, and the chemical and physical nature of the oceans. As a marine biology major, you will gain a broad understanding of the processes that control life in underwater environments.

Is this for you?
You might like this major if you also like: the sea and shore; boats and boating; water sports; aquariums; the outdoors; nature; travel; science and technology.

Consider this major if you are good at: attention to detail; creativity; critical reading/thinking; leadership; math; quantitative analysis; research; spacial thinking/analysis; teamwork ...*or have...* communication skills; initiative.

Recommended high school prep:
English 4, math 4 (including precalculus), lab science 4 (including earth science, chemistry and physics, and field biology if available), social studies 3, and a foreign language 2-3. You will need calculus and computer skills in college. The ability to communicate well, in writing and in speaking, is important in this field, so don't neglect your English courses. If possible, participate in a summer internship program at an aquarium or a research center.

Did you know...
...that marine biology covers more than fish and sea mammals? You study everything from the microscopic, single-cell plants that float in the oceans, to ecosystems like coral reefs, kelp forests, and the intertidal zone (at the edge of the sea where tides ebb and flow) and widely differing environments, such as hydrothermal vents miles below the ocean's surface and the frigid waters of the Antarctic Ocean.

...that this major requires a sound training in chemistry? Chemistry is important in understanding the building blocks of life, such as DNA and proteins, and the way the biological world affects and is affected by the physical world undersea.

Typical courses in this major:
Chemical oceanography
Physical oceanography
Ichthyology
Invertebrate biology
Marine botany
Deep-sea biology
Fisheries biology
Limnology (freshwater environments)
Marine ecology
Marine mammals
Aquaculture
Coastal ornithology
Marine policy
Plankton biology
Phycology (algae)
Computer modeling

Concentrations:
Generally, none in college; but if you go on to grad school: vertebrates; invertebrates; coastal ecology; coral reef ecology; fisheries biology; marine mammals

What the study of this major is like:
Marine biologists study the ocean as a system—how underwater species relate to one another as food and prey and how various species depend on the ocean's physics and chemistry. As a major, you will have in-depth exposure to this complex ecosystem and will gain insight into environmental problems, such as the consequences of global climate changes and ocean pollution. And you will examine the consequences of humankind's reliance on the seas.

Courses cover the form, structure, development, evolution, physiology, biochemistry, and genetics of marine systems, including fisheries. Emphasis is placed on the spatial and regional distributions of species—for example, whether they inhabit coastal or open ocean, cold or warm water, deep or shallow water. You may study why certain species are endangered and how they can be protected, or you can pursue special interests, such as the economics of harvesting marine organisms for food and energy.

During the first two years, majors take basic courses including math, chemistry, physics, and biology. You may also take a first-year survey, with field trips, of marine environments. In your second year, you might conduct laboratory examinations of the ecology, physiology, and behavior of marine organisms. Upper-level work focuses on the chemical and physical characteristics of the ocean. In addition, you will probably take courses in conservation, marine resources, and policy (coastal law, pollution, economic resources of the ocean).

The coursework is generally a mix of lectures, laboratory activities, and, especially in the third and fourth years, fieldwork. Many students do summer internships or research outside college, and a senior thesis—an independent research project, conducted under faculty supervision and summarized in a written report—is often required.

A frequent challenge for majors is to develop a co-ordinated path through the field. Marine biology is not a distinct area of study; rather, it draws heavily on other disciplines such as biology, chemistry, and physics. Avoid taking just a collection of survey courses from various areas of science. Instead, try to explore one field of marine biology in depth. Also, majors often spend a lot of time on fieldwork. But although they work hard, they generally enjoy what they do.

Because marine biology is such a broad area, different programs have different emphases. For example, professors at some colleges may concentrate on open-ocean rather than near-shore species; at other colleges, faculty members may have expertise in marine mammals and know little about fisheries. Some colleges offer a biological concentration within a broader oceanography major. Take a look at course catalogs, which should reflect colleges' emphases.

Other majors you might like:

Oceanography
Aquaculture
Ecology
Environmental biology
Ocean engineering
Environmental science
Aquatic biology/limnology
Zoology
Marine engineering/naval architecture
Water, wetlands, and marine management
Fishing and fisheries

Questions to ask colleges:

In which area of marine biology do faculty members have the most expertise?

Which types of marine field research or internships are available to undergraduates?

Career options and trends:

Government resource manager*; science teacher; fisheries biologist; laboratory research technician*; environmental consultant*; staff member at a museum or aquarium.

The job market is tight in this field. A strong math background and computer skills will give you a competitive edge, especially in the fisheries industry. Most research and academic positions will require a graduate degree.

Insider's viewpoint:

"A misconception is that fieldwork, such as scuba diving and cruises, is all fun and games. Taking a midnight dive—and my fifth dive of the day—in the pouring rain or being seasick is not fun."

—Amy, senior, University of San Diego

For more info:

American Fisheries Society (AFS)
5410 Grosvenor Lane
Bethesda, MD 20814
(301) 897-8616
www.fisheries.org
www.marinecareers.net

Microbiology

What it's about:

The microbiology major focuses on the biology of microscopic organisms, such as bacteria, algae, and fungi. Your goal is to understand the function of microbes in agriculture, medicine, ecology, and biotechnology. You will also receive training in sterile procedures; the identification, enumeration, and growth of microorganisms; the evaluation of antimicrobials and antibiotics; and the practice of microbial genetics.

Is this for you?

You might like this major if you also like: science projects; gardening; environmental causes; microscopes; caring for people; keeping things organized.

Consider this major if you are good at: attention to detail; creativity; critical reading/thinking; organizing; quantitative analysis; research; spacial thinking/analysis; teamwork *...or have...* manual dexterity.

Recommended high school prep:

English 4 (a writing course would be helpful), math 4 (including precalculus or calculus), lab science 4 (including chemistry and physics), social studies 3, and a foreign language 2-3. If possible, take a course in statistics and in computer science.

Did you know...

...that the study of microorganisms is not just about germs and disease? Oil prospecting, soil use and management, agriculture, development of nanosystems, genetic engineering, uses and misuses of microbes in military activities, and monitoring for microbes are just some of the many applications.

Typical courses in this major:

General biology I, II
Organic chemistry
Inorganic chemistry
Cell biology
Genetics
Bacteriology
Biochemistry
Microbial ecology
Bioinformatics/computational biology
Advanced microbiology
Bacterial physiology
Medical bacteriology
Immunology
Virology
Recombinant DNA techniques
Mycology and parasitology

Concentrations:

Generally, none in college; but if you go on to grad school: bacteriology; virology; mycology (fungi); phycology (algae); microbial physiology; genetics; biotechnology.

What the study of this major is like:

As a microbiology major, you will probably begin by familiarizing yourself with microscopes. You'll get an overview of the diversity, structure, function, growth, reproduction, genetics, physiology, preservation, and control of microorganisms. You'll then learn to grow and catalog a wide variety of microorganisms, including bacteria, algae, fungi, protozoa, and viruses. When you progress to biochemistry and molecular genetics, the work becomes more abstract. In labs and lectures, you use critical-thinking skills to prepare and conduct experiments. As you advance, your work focuses on bacterial mutants, the documentation of agents (including viruses, which are not usually seen directly), and measurements with biochemical tools.

Microbiology majors develop laboratory procedures that enable them to study a type or a group of microorganisms. Students sometimes have trouble attending to the many important details and thoroughly applying sterile procedures and techniques. You must work well in a group, even if you are doing an individual research project. Majors have to cooperate in order to maintain and use shared equipment and materials safely, often under sterile conditions. Sometimes you need to develop new skills for a particular project, such as the ability to search gene databases. For most investigations, you'll need to understand the molecular biology and biochemistry of both hosts and parasites. To be successful in this field, you should be willing to learn unfamiliar methodologies and adapt to unexpected situations.

Some colleges emphasize a premedical curriculum in biology, and give less attention to other biological sciences. In such programs you may be limited to broader applications in microbiology. Other colleges emphasize environmental science or molecular biology rather than a more integrated approach to the diverse areas within microbiology. Most small colleges offer solid foundations in the biological sciences, teaching concepts (such as the theories behind evolution, genetics, respiration, photosynthesis, and biochemistry) as well as technical skills. Conceptual skills are useful because the field of microbiology is changing rapidly, and certain technologies and methods might one day be out-of-date.

Other majors you might like:
Clinical/medical laboratory technology
Biotechnology
Biomedical engineering
Cell biology and histology
Zoology
Genetics
Biochemistry
Entomology
Chemistry
Soil science
Ecology
Agricultural and biological engineering

Questions to ask colleges:
Do undergraduates learn lab techniques and practical skills that would qualify them for entry into the job market? Where do most majors go after graduation—medical school, graduate school, or employment?

Career options and trends:
Physician*; veterinarian; high school and college teacher; research technician*; environmental scientist; hospital administrator; biotechnologist*; health care professional (respiratory therapist, phlebotomist, etc.); government agency microbiologist.

Graduates with a degree in microbiology find positions in health care and in the biotechnology, agricultural, food, and pharmaceutical industries. Job opportunities are projected to grow faster in this field than in the biological field as a whole. Job growth remains strong in the biotechnology industry, especially in the areas of pharmaceutical and medical manufacturing. Health care is a particularly strong field even in tight job markets.

Insider's viewpoint:
"I had a misconception of what people do in labs. I thought you just go there and do your experiments. In fact it's far more involved. You think about the experiments, you talk to your instructor, you talk to other students who work with you, and you go to conferences. It's a very different culture. You're not completely isolated."

—Julio, senior, San Francisco State University

For more info:
American Society for Microbiology (ASM)
1752 N St., N.W.
Washington, DC 20036-2904
(202) 737-3600
www.asm.org

Molecular biology

Also known as:
Cell and molecular biology

What it's about:
As a major in molecular biology, you investigate the basic mechanisms of life by studying the macromolecules—proteins, for example—essential to living organisms. Using chemical analysis, you explore metabolism, gene function and regulation, cell differentiation, and development. Special emphasis is placed on the role of proteins and nucleic acids in cellular processes.

Is this for you?
You might like this major if you also like: science clubs and projects; new technology; thinking creatively and abstractly; exploring the inner workings of things. Molecular biology is for people who are constantly asking "Why?" and are not satisfied until something is completely explained.

Consider this major if you are good at: attention to detail; critical reading/thinking; math; quantitative analysis; research; spacial thinking/analysis; teamwork *...or have...* initiative; manual dexterity; perseverance.

Recommended high school prep:
English 4, math 4 (including calculus and statistics), lab science 4 (including biology, chemistry, and physics), social studies 3, and a foreign language 2–3. Take as many advanced science courses as possible, and a course in computer science if available.

Did you know...
...that you must have an understanding of chemistry when you study living organisms? The ability to apply chemical principles to the function and structure of cells is the basis of molecular biology.

Typical courses in this major:
General biology (I, II)
General chemistry (I, II)
Organic chemistry (I, II)
General physics (I, II)
Cellular biology
General molecular biology
General microbiology
Biochemistry
Plant molecular biology
Molecular genetics
Biostatistics
Endocrinology
Nucleic acid chemistry
Developmental biology
Protein isolation and characterization (lab)
Writing in molecular biology

Concentrations:
Generally, none in college; but if you go on to grad school: bioinformatics; structural biology; computational biology; molecular medicine; functional genomics; molecular genetics; pharmacogenetics.

What the study of this major is like:
As a molecular biology major, you focus on subcellular components. You'll investigate cellular mechanisms (including cell metabolism and genetics) and learn to apply principles of chemistry to biological systems.

Most likely, you'll begin with an introduction to the essential macromolecules, especially the structure and function of proteins and nucleic acids. Then you'll conduct an in-depth study of DNA replication and function. You also focus on protein biosynthesis and enzyme regulation. In the required biochemistry courses, you cover metabolic pathways for energy and precursor production.

Cellular biology courses combine molecular and biochemical information to describe the production of cellular material. Because successful molecular biologists need well-developed analytical skills, most majors enroll in biostatistics and quantitative analysis courses. You are also expected to have strong computer skills. If you don't have experience with database searches, spreadsheets, and presentation software, you should take technology courses in your early college years.

Advanced courses focus on the interaction of specific proteins and the role of DNA in the regulation of cellular processes. In biotechnology courses, you begin to apply these principles to real-world problems. In bioinformatics and computational biology, you'll learn to use information obtained from genome sequencing. Besides lectures and seminars, most courses have labs in which you practice basic research techniques, including DNA and protein isolation, purification, and manipulation. Advanced courses generally require you to do an independent research project.

Majors spend a considerable amount of time working independently in the lab. The field of molecular biology depends on experimentation, so you must develop excellent laboratory skills and good hand-eye coordination. You spend additional out-of-class time reading journals and writing scientific reports. Although you need to be creative, you also have to develop an organized approach to problem solving, be able to memorize technical terms, and do complex data analysis and application. Most students in molecular biology study and work in groups; teamwork is essential to success. In addition to lightening individual workloads, study groups provide a strong support system.

Other majors you might like:
Biochemistry
Cell biology and histology
Agricultural and biological engineering
Biomedical engineering
Neuroscience
Microbiology
Genetics
Clinical/medical laboratory technology
Biomedical technology
Physics

Chemistry
Forensic science

Questions to ask colleges:
What is the primary focus of the program? At some colleges, the program may emphasize one aspect of biology (such as genetics) or a particular group of organisms; while other colleges may focus on the chemistry/biochemistry aspects. You may also have to choose between a biotech track and a preprofessional (premed) track.

Which lab equipment is available for undergraduates? Because the field of molecular biology is highly dependent on experimentation, undergrads must develop excellent lab skills.

Career options and trends:
University researcher/professor; medical or pharmaceutical researcher*; forensic scientist; health professional (such as physician, nurse)*; genetic counselor; high school teacher; agricultural researcher; laboratory technician*; public health officer.

Research positions may require a graduate degree.

Technological developments such as genome sequencing and DNA arrays have significantly increased the role of molecular biology research in the field.

For more info:
American Society for Biochemistry and Molecular Biology (ASBMB)
9650 Rockville Pike
Bethesda, MD 20814-3996
(301) 634-7175
www.asbmb.org

Zoology

Also known as:
Animal biology

What it's about:
Zoology majors study animals—their origin, cell structure, genetics, physiology, behavior, ecology, and life processes. They also receive training in molecular biology techniques, quantitative field sampling, and statistical analysis.

Is this for you?
You might like this major if you also like: all creatures great and small; natural history museums; the outdoors; lab work and fieldwork; identifying animals; bird watching; anatomy; environmental issues.

Consider this major if you are good at: attention to detail; critical reading/thinking; memorizing; organizing; quantitative analysis *...or have...* communication skills; initiative; manual dexterity; patience.

Recommended high school prep:
English 4, math 4 (including precalculus or calculus), lab science 4, social studies 3, and a foreign language 2–3. If they are available, take additional science courses in anatomy, physiology, or genetics.

Did you know...
...that the proper pronunciation of this major is "zo" (like "no") -ology, not "zoo" –ology? The word "zoo" is actually a mispronounced abbreviation for "zoological park."

Typical courses in this major:
Animal behavior
Animal physiology
Comparative anatomy
Ecology
Endocrinology
Genetics
Entomology (insects)
Evolutionary biology

Herpetology (reptiles and amphibians)
Invertebrate biology
Limnology (ponds and lakes)
Mammalogy
Ornithology
Parasitology
Primatology
Vertebrate zoology

Concentrations:
In college: Conservation or environmental biology; ecology and evolution; entomology; marine biology; neurobiology; physiology.

If you go on to grad school: anatomy and histology; ornithology (the study of birds); herpetology; developmental zoology; endocrinology; invertebrate zoology; parasitology; population biology.

What the study of this major is like:
As a zoology major, you explore how animals function. You study the way an organism acquires energy and material for growth and reproduction, and examine animals' interaction with their own kind as well as with other living and nonliving things. You also consider how animals have evolved.

In your first year, you will probably enroll in introductory courses in both biology and chemistry. Biology courses cover the significant concepts, from molecular biology to ecosystem ecology. In your second and third years, you take focused core courses, such as anatomy, cell biology, ecology, evolution, genetics, and physiology. Zoology majors usually study at least two years of chemistry, a year of physics, and some advanced math such as calculus. In your third and fourth years, you select upper-level electives specific to zoology.

In most zoology courses, you study the basic concepts in lectures; then, in a lab or field setting, you are introduced to data collection and techniques of analysis. Zoology majors usually spend about the

115

same amount of time in lectures and in labs. After the first year, many majors do independent research projects with faculty members or sometimes with graduate students. Most first-year majors face serious challenges, especially in the first semester. Introductory biology and chemistry are generally taught in greater depth and more rigorously than in high school. If you do not complete the assignments on time, you may find it difficult to keep up with the work as the semester progresses. You need to call on your self-discipline in lectures, the laboratory or fieldwork, and no-nonsense studying.

Course offerings tend to mirror the research activities of the faculty. Different zoology departments may emphasize one area of biology or zoology over others. For example, some departments focus on molecular and cell biology and feature courses that explore how the parts of organisms (such as molecules and tissues) function. Other departments may stress whole organisms and populations and offer courses in ecology, environmental biology, and taxonomic groups (entomology, invertebrate zoology, ornithology, for example). Because most high school biology classes take only a brief look at the diversity of the animal kingdom, your interests may change in college as you encounter new areas of study. A department with a well-balanced curriculum that offers a wide variety of courses may give you the most options.

Other majors you might like:
Anthropology
Biology teacher education
Ecology
Evolutionary biology
Microbiology
Wildlife and wilderness management
Animal sciences
Livestock management
Marine biology
Veterinary technology
Entomology
Aquatic biology/limnology

Questions to ask colleges:
Is the major broad-based or does it concentrate on one particular area of zoological study?

What percentage of zoology majors are admitted into medical and other professional schools?

Which facilities are unique to the zoology program (such as a breeding facility), and which facilities are shared with other biological programs (electron microscope, computers)?

Career options and trends:
Health care professional; park ranger or guide; research assistant; teacher or college professor; environmental consultant; staff member at an aquarium, zoo, or animal park; veterinarian or veterinarian technician.

There will continue to be demand for those looking to enter the field of zoology, although opportunities will be limited because of the small size of this field. The best prospects are in the health care, biomedical, and environmental industries. A graduate or professional degree is necessary for most research, academic, and medical positions. A doctorate is generally required for work as a zoologist. Summer employment in a medical, environmental, or other career area is increasingly expected of job applicants.

For more info:
American Institute of Biological Sciences (AIBS)
1444 I (Eye) St., N.W.
Suite 200
Washington, DC 20005
(202) 628-1500
www.aibs.org

Business

Business has been tough lately, as we all know. But according to the National Association of Colleges and Employers (www.naceweb.org), prospects for students graduating later in this decade remain strong, mostly because of a rapidly aging workforce. Even if the economy rebuilds slowly, there will be a need for managers in all sectors of business to get things done.

Do you have what it takes to succeed in business? Business abilities cover a wide range of talent—"people skills" and communication, technical expertise, math and analytical skills, leadership, teamwork, and creativity— as well as commitment to integrity.

The main subject areas in business are topics that everyone should know something about.

"Knowledge of finance is an essential life skill," says Stephen J. Brown of the Stern School of Business, New York University.

"The same management concepts that ensure that the resources of a business organization are used effectively and efficiently can and should be applied to the choices one makes in life generally," observes Peter Bycio, Williams College of Business, Xavier University.

No matter what you're interested in, a knowledge of business can enhance your career.

"Entrepreneurship is applicable to any number of other careers," says Stephen Spinelli, Jr. of Babson College. "If someone has a passion for theater, studying business can help that person create, grow, and manage a theater company. Engineers, doctors, and lawyers need entrepreneurial skills to grow and succeed. The list goes on and on."

One way to think about business studies is to group them into functions, like finance, accounting, and marketing. Some majors cut across these functions. For instance, if you study business management or management information systems, you'll need to know about all aspects of operations and administration. Still other business majors, such as real estate, insurance, fashion merchandising, hospitality, and construction management, take you into specific industries or professions.

If you study business, you'll learn more than how to use a spreadsheet. Understanding human behavior is so important that many business programs contain courses in sociology, psychology, and the humanities.

Trends in business may also affect what you'll study. Current economic forces include globalization of companies and markets, a shift from manufacturing to service industries, corporate mergers, rapid developments in technology, changes in government regulations, price pressures, and shifting demographics. These trends have resulted in the creation of such business majors and courses as risk management, information management, e-commerce, supply chain management, and entrepreneurship. "We live in a world in which *change* may be the only constant," says Professor Diane Kaufman Fredette of Pratt Institute. "Given this trend, *managing change* has become an increasingly critical skill for construction managers."

On the undergraduate level, colleges have different philosophies of teaching business. Some colleges focus on quantitative, analytical, and technological aspects of business, while others emphasize strategy and management. Some programs get you ready to apply to grad school by teaching all about business theory. Other schools, taking a more practical, hands-on approach, prepare you for a business career with your bachelor's degree. Sometimes bachelor's and master's degrees are combined in a five-year program. A two-year degree is what you need for some jobs in hospitality and fashion merchandising.

Is grad school for you?

Each year, more than 150,000 students get master's degrees in business administration. That's a lot of competition for top jobs. Is the MBA a one-way ticket to a corner office? Not necessarily, but a survey of MBA students by the Graduate Management Admission Council shows that 91 percent of the students polled felt that their degree was of outstanding value, even as the economy remained stagnant. Wall Street, however, is not the immediate goal it once was. The recent financial meltdown means MBA's need to think of alternative routes to success, according to Diane Riemer, assistant director for graduate career services at Boston University's School of Management. She advises students to think of a "bridge strategy" where jobs can be stepping stones toward an ultimate career.

What do grad students in business actually study? It all depends on the major. Graduate tracks might include quality management; franchise, distributorship, and license ownership; corporate or international finance; investment banking; compensation and labor relations; information technology and systems; marketing research; and accounting information systems.

In the meantime, think about where you might go as an undergrad. Often, the location of the college dictates its business offerings. If the school is in an urban area and you're studying finance, for example, the program may prep you to work in financial services, which have offices in the city, rather than in financial management in suburban businesses.

Here are a few things to ask at all business-degree levels when comparing colleges: How long has the major been offered? Who are the faculty members? Are they full-time professors, or adjunct (part-time) professors (who are business professionals), or a combination? It's good to learn from the experts, but if they're on campus only a few hours a week, can you contact them easily? Are courses lecture-oriented, project-oriented, or action-oriented, and do you have a preference? How is technology used in class?

What kinds of resources do students have? Seed funding? Business-plan competitions? Internships? Access to industry experts? Do student organizations have chapters on campus? What kind of job placement assistance and career counseling will you get after you graduate? What career paths do most graduates follow? Which employers interview business majors on campus?

Make it your business to find out about colleges that offer these majors. They include schools of business, management, commerce, business administration, and arts and sciences.

Accounting

What it's about:

Accounting is known as the language of business. The major prepares you to gather, record, analyze, interpret, and communicate financial information about an individual's or an organization's performance and risks. You study such topics as financial statement preparation and analysis, risk assessment and control, management decision-making, tax preparation and planning, management of accounting information systems, auditing, and fraud.

Is this for you?

You might like this major if you also like: computers; leadership roles; working with numbers; interacting and working with people; seeing both the details and the "big picture" when analyzing situations.

Consider this major if you are good at: attention to detail; critical reading/thinking; leadership; organizing; quantitative analysis; teamwork ...*or have...* people skills; verbal skills; writing skills.

Recommended high school prep:

English 4 (including writing), math 3 (including trigonometry), lab science 3, social studies 3, and a foreign language 2–3. If possible, also take communications, speech, and computer courses.

Did you know...

...that accounting is not just about crunching numbers? Communication and critical-thinking skills are essential for success in the profession, because accountants spend most of their time advising, analyzing, communicating, and managing. The profession is often viewed as the fast track to upper-level management positions like controller, chief financial officer (CFO), or chief executive officer (CEO).

Typical courses in this major:

Introductory accounting
Intermediate accounting
Advanced accounting
Auditing
Cost accounting
Taxation
International accounting
Accounting information systems
Government and not-for-profit accounting
Financial statement analysis

Concentrations:

Generally, none in college; but if you go on to grad school: financial accounting; accounting information systems; cost accounting; managerial accounting; forensic accounting.

What the study of this major is like:

Accounting is a popular major available at most colleges, often housed in a school of business or management. Otherwise, accounting may be offered as part of a program in the liberal arts or sciences, usually in the economics or social sciences department. The accounting major includes both technical and application-based course work. The technical nature of some courses makes them well suited to the lecture format, which is often supplemented with interactive learning tools such as case analyses, computer simulations, and research projects. Many courses are taught as seminars, with plenty of student participation; some courses include hands-on, real-world experience.

Undergraduate concentrations are rare. You take courses in economics and finance, business law, business organization and management, marketing, and computer information sciences. You learn to measure costs, compile data, and determine how the data affect efficiency and profitability. After your introductory accounting courses, you study financial statements and how they are used to make business decisions. You also study such topics as risk assurance, e-commerce accounting and control, fraud investigation, internal auditing, and ethics.

One of the more challenging areas you may face as a major is financial accounting. Many students find it difficult at first—comprehending it can be like solving a complex puzzle. But once you master the subject, its framework and logic become second nature.

In addition to your accounting curriculum, you are usually required to take a range of liberal arts and science courses. Especially important are those in history and foreign languages (finance has become global). Because good communication is vital to the profession, you will also benefit from classes that sharpen your writing, speaking, and problem-solving skills.

In some accounting programs, you focus on theory. Other programs take an applied approach that stresses the skills you will need as an accountant. Some programs also have a niche emphasis, such as internal auditing or accounting information systems. Although some programs still have separate undergraduate and master's degrees, others offer a five-year program—a bachelor's and a master's are awarded jointly at graduation. These programs have become more popular with the phasing in of the rule requiring students who want to become a certified public accountant (CPA) to complete 150 credit hours of course work.

The accounting major prepares you for careers in public or managerial accounting. Public accountants work with auditing firms to produce credible financial reports; managerial accountants work with management to monitor an organization's financial health. Managerial accountants often need special knowledge about taxes, budgeting, and investing. While often helpful, a CPA designation is not essential for internal auditing, corporate accounting, and government accounting.

Other majors you might like:
Finance
Management information systems
Accounting technology/bookkeeping
Information systems
Statistics
Economics
Insurance
Public administration
Real estate
International business
Marketing
Theater arts management

Questions to ask colleges:
Does the program encourage internships?

Is course work primarily applied (analysis-based) or conceptual (theory-based)?

Are bachelor's and master's degrees offered in separate programs or in a unified, five-year program?

Career options and trends:
Auditor*; tax accountant/adviser*; risk assurance/information technology consultant*; corporate accountant*; financial planner; fraud examiner; government investigator (IRS, FBI).

The job outlook for accountants is very good. The best prospects will be for those with CPA certification or an MBA in accounting. To become a CPA, you must pass the national CPA exam, and also meet the certification requirements of the state where you want to practice; most states require a period of professional work experience and the equivalent of five years of college (150 credit hours).

Large-scale business scandals have put accounting, auditing, and fraud investigations in the spotlight. CFOs and auditors have greater responsibilities and tighter rules governing their behavior. Thus the demand for well-qualified accounting professionals should remain high. The growth of global business will also lead to more demand for those with knowledge of international accounting rules.

For more info:
American Accounting Association (AAA)
5717 Bessie Drive
Sarasota, FL 34233-2399
(941) 921-7747
www.aaahq.org

American Institute of Certified Public Accountants
1211 Sixth Ave.
New York, NY 10036-8775
(212) 596-6200
www.aicpa.org

Business administration and management

What it's about:
This major teaches you how to plan, organize, lead, and control the human, financial, and physical resources of an organization to achieve business goals. As a manager, you will be expected to meet the many demands of your employer, your organization's internal and external customers, and society in general.

Is this for you?
You might like this major if you also like: working with people; starting and running a business; the *Wall Street Journal*; debating; organizing or leading a club or group activity; solving problems; taking risks; competing; sports; helping others to succeed.

Consider this major if you are good at: attention to detail; critical reading/thinking; leadership; organizing; persuading/influencing; quantitative analysis; teamwork *...or have...* initiative; verbal skills.

Recommended high school prep:
English 4, math 4 (including precalculus), lab science 3, social studies 3, and a foreign language 2-3. If available, take calculus and a computer course covering basic office applications and spreadsheets.

Did you know...
...that this is by far the most popular major? That means you'll have lots of company—and a wide choice of colleges that offer this major.

...that math skills are important for a business degree? Quantitative analysis is required for several areas of business, such as accounting, finance, and business statistics.

Typical courses in this major:
Accounting I, II
Business law
Economics
International trade and business
Business finance
Human resources
Managing information technology
Managerial communication
Principles of marketing
Business statistics
Production management
Operations management
Organizational design and development
Leadership
Quality planning and improvement
Strategic formulation and implementation

Concentrations:
Accounting; entrepreneurship; finance; international business; leadership; marketing; organizational behavior; production operations management

What the study of this major is like:
Few people can avoid management. One day, you will probably either be a manager or work for one. The business management and administration major prepares you to serve as an effective, responsible manager in business, government, or nonprofit sectors. Managers have both the opportunity and the duty to make a difference: receiving good service can reflect good management; an employee's unethical behavior can reflect poor management; and good managers make sure that organizations generate value for their stakeholders on a sustained basis.

In the major, you typically learn how to achieve goals by planning (defining goals and deciding how to achieve them), organizing (deciding what resources need to go where to best support the plan), leading (influencing people to work toward accomplishing goals), and controlling (monitoring progress toward achieving goals and adjusting initial plans as needed). You study how managers respond to the complex, ever-changing expectations of employees, bosses, customers, governments, the legal community, and society as a whole. Majors begin with basic courses in accounting, marketing, and finance. You then take specialized courses, such as organizational behavior, human resources management, supervisory skills, and international management. In your fourth year, you usually take a capstone course in business strategy or business policy; applying what you have learned, you explore the way an organization interacts with the outside world and operates internally.

Most management programs offer internships, usually for a semester, to help you gain experience, learn about possible careers, and relate classroom learning to the workplace. Most internships award academic credit and require you to submit material to be graded. Some internships can lead to future job opportunities. Many colleges offer a semester-abroad program that lets you practice your management skills in another country. Because the policies and practices of employees, customers, organizations, and their competitors can reflect—positively or negatively—on the society in which they are located, managers must understand the cultural expectations of their host country.

Nevertheless, the objective of the major is to prepare you to lead others in an organization. Most management courses stimulate your persuasive and creative abilities—memorizing facts is generally not top priority. Courses are typically taught through lectures, videos, case studies, and, perhaps, role-playing. Professors use case studies to develop your problem-solving and analytical skills, to teach you to defend ideas logically, and to push you to challenge the ideas of others. You analyze actual business problems, develop realistic responses, and present your recommendations to professors and classmates. Working managers are often brought in to share their experiences. You use computers for spreadsheet programs, databases, and other programs that help you conduct statistical analysis, prepare financial projections, and do marketing research. If you choose this major, you should be ready to work hard.

Although most agree on a definition of general management, different colleges may have different emphases. Some programs take a quantitative approach and focus on decision-making techniques. Other programs may emphasize a management function such as leadership or an area of general management—for example, human resource management or organizational behavior. Differences among programs are also reflected in their readiness to adapt to changes in the field. For example, supply chain management, project management, and entrepreneurship are emerging topics. Some programs will be relatively conservative in their approach to such topics, offering only a course or two at first, while others may develop new concentrations or even new majors.

Other majors you might like:

Agribusiness operations
Entrepreneurial studies
Marketing
International business
Construction management
Emergency management/homeland security
Music management
Parks/recreational/leisure facilities management
E-commerce
Public administration
Economics
Nonprofit/public organization management

Questions to ask colleges:

Is the program accredited by the Association to Advance Collegiate Schools of Business? If so, the program has been examined for quality from a number of perspectives.

Are there internships or co-op programs available in this major?

Do companies recruit on campus?

Career options and trends:

Management trainee or assistant manager*; sales or account representative*; corporate executive; management consultant; franchise or small business owner; human resources specialist; systems analyst; financial analyst; venture capitalist.

The job outlook mirrors the economic times, but organizations are always looking for good managers. As the world of business grows more complex, risky, and global in scope, the need for professional managers increases. Job growth is particularly expected within management consulting firms specializing in information technology, health care, and marketing.

An MBA is usually essential if you want to climb the corporate ladder; but many well-known companies will help you obtain this advanced degree while you're working.

Insider's viewpoint:

"Some classes, like accounting or information systems, are a much bigger time commitment. But I would estimate that on average, I spend about four hours per class per week on homework. However, that doesn't include the group projects, which take much more time. Business-school classes have many more group projects than any other classes I've taken."

—Dan, junior, University of Washington

For more info:

Association to Advance Collegiate Schools of
  Business (AACSB)
777 South Harbor Island Blvd.
Suite 750
Tampa, FL 33602-5730
(813) 769-6500
www.aacsb.edu

American Management Association (AMA)
1601 Broadway
New York, NY 10019
(877) 566-9441
www.amanet.org

Construction management

What it's about:

Construction management is the art of orchestrating all the components necessary to complete a building project within budget and on time. This major combines courses in business management, technology, and the liberal arts to provide the practical knowledge and critical thinking skills that a leadership role in construction requires.

Is this for you?

You might like this major if you also like: the outdoors; running a group project; working in teams; taking responsibility; working with your hands; achieving goals and results; watching construction sites.

Consider this major if you are good at: attention to detail; leadership; multi-tasking; organizing; persuading/influencing; quantitative analysis; spacial thinking/analysis; teamwork *...or have...* verbal skills.

Recommended high school prep:

English 4, math 3 (including trigonometry), lab science 3, social studies 3, industrial arts 2, and a foreign language 2. Spanish is recommended because it is spoken by many workers in the construction industry. If available, courses in business, accounting, and computer-aided drafting (CAD) are also helpful.

Did you know...

...that the ability to think in three dimensions is essential in this field? Before giving instructions or solving problems, construction managers often have to visualize how a structure should take shape.

Typical courses in this major:

Principles of management
Principles of accounting
Labor relations
Business law and ethics
Project scheduling
Construction estimating
Blueprint reading
Specifications
Construction materials
Structural methods
Mechanical and electrical systems
Environmental compliance
Project budgeting and cost management
Construction law, codes, and regulations
Site logistics
Safety management

Concentrations:

Construction technology; safety management; planning and logistics

What the study of this major is like:

Construction management is both an on-site job (making sure that the project is going smoothly and according to plan) and a desk job (dealing with bids, contracts, insurance, and other paperwork). A successful manager has expertise in three areas: construction, management, and people skills.

This major helps you develop this expertise by blending business management training with technical know-how. Course work covers creative problem solving, emerging technologies, best practices, and ethical principles. The goal is to prepare you to become a professional manager who can combine business acumen with an awareness of the diverse interests of the developer, contractor, owner, architect, and engineer.

Beginning with basic studies of blueprints and drawings, construction materials and techniques, you progress to an understanding of more complex components such as site logistics, specifications, cost estimating, and design, mechanical, structural, electrical, and legal issues. You learn to consider construction drawings as a picture not only of the planned structure but also of the complex process involving five dimensions—which include time and money, referred to as "schedule" and "budget."

Crunching numbers may not sound much like construction work, but nothing gets built before a budget is in place. That's why courses in estimating and accounting are usually required. You'll learn, step by step, how to figure the costs for everything from building materials to labor. You'll practice looking for clues in floor plans, and you'll get a handle on competitive bidding.

Many students enjoy the technical and graphic aspects of the major but find that writing skills do not come as easily. To help bring these skills together, most programs require a capstone project in the final year. For that you research a topic of your own interest and present a professional quality report to be reviewed by faculty or invited professionals.

Most programs include practical exposure to the profession. Lectures and lab courses are supplemented by opportunities for internships in which you do hands-on work under the guidance of a mentor. Actual construction experience is as essential as a degree when it comes to finding a job after graduation.

While construction management can be considered a business major, it is usually housed in a school or department of technology, engineering, or architecture. The emphasis on business management skills may vary depending on the overall strength of the college's business program. Architecturally based programs usually focus on design and on a team approach to problem solving.

This major is offered at both the associate degree and the bachelor's degree level. Four-year programs include more business management skills and liberal arts requirements. Two-year programs usually concentrate on construction technology.

Other majors you might like:
Civil engineering
Construction technology
Architectural engineering
Land use planning
Operations management

Real estate
Surveying technology
Geology/earth science
Mining and mineral engineering
Historic preservation
Heavy/earthmoving equipment operation
Architecture

Questions to ask colleges:

Is the program accredited by the American Council for Construction Education (ACCE)?

Do the professors incorporate their field experience into their classroom instruction?

What kinds of hands-on experiences are provided? Is there an internship program?

Career options and trends:

Construction manager; general contractor; site inspector; cost estimator; specifications writer; contract administrator.

Even though the construction industry has been hard hit lately, the Bureau of Labor Statistics still projects good job prospects for construction managers because there are not enough graduates in this field to meet expected demand. As the economy recovers and stimulus projects break ground, that demand will become more acute. Employment in this field will always be subject, however, to cyclical fluctuations in the industry.

Prospects will be best for those with a bachelor's degree and construction work experience gained through internships and summer jobs.

For more info:

American Council for Construction Education
1717 N. Loop 1604 E.
San Antonio, TX 78232
(210) 495-6161
www.acce-hq.org

Construction Management Association of America
7926 Jones Branch Drive, Suite 800
McLean, VA 22102
(703) 356-2622
www.cmaanet.org

E-commerce

Also known as:
Digital business strategy

What it's about:
This major focuses on how to use marketing concepts, business strategies, economics, and computer science to develop new businesses, or to transform an existing business, through the use of the Internet and related information technology.

Is this for you?
You might like this major if you also like: computers; social networking; starting or running a business venture; new technology; taking risks; science fiction; advertisements; buying and selling.

Consider this major if you are good at: attention to detail; creativity; leadership; math; organizing; persuading/influencing; quantitative analysis; research *...or have...* computer skills; initiative.

Recommended high school prep:
English 4, math 3, lab science 3, social studies 3, and a foreign language 2–3. If available, take a computer science course and an economics course that covers microeconomics.

Did you know...
...that e-commerce is not solely about technology, but rather the linking of technology and new business approaches? So you don't have to be a computer geek to do well in this major.

...that most of the interesting applications of e-commerce are likely to be in established businesses rather than in start-up ventures? This makes the long-term prospects of an e-commerce-related career more stable and broadens the types of job opportunities available.

Typical courses in this major:
Management information systems
Introduction to e-business
E-commerce marketing
E-commerce strategy
Law of electronic commerce
Strategic management
Entrepreneurial management
Venture capital
New venture initiation
Business application development (programming)
Internet technology
Computer networking and communications
Systems analysis and design
World Wide Web design
Business transformation/reengineering

Concentrations:
Business to consumer (B2C) e-commerce; business to business (B2B) e-commerce; electronic marketing; business strategies; computer technology.

What the study of this major is like:
While you might think e-commerce has been around your whole life, e-commerce as a discipline, or academic subject, is still in its infancy. New technologies and creative individuals are continually remaking e-commerce and keeping it interesting. How many other disciplines transform themselves so extensively every few years? Another factor that makes e-commerce exciting is that you can apply your ideas quickly; you may have the satisfaction of producing immediate results.

The e-commerce major usually begins with a combination of general courses in technology and management fundamentals. Next, you take courses focusing on how e-commerce can be used in creating businesses or improving the performance of existing businesses. In many of your courses, you'll examine recent developments in electronics, such as smart phones, and then identify opportunities to apply the new tools. You may also focus on finding technological solutions to classic business problems—for instance, figuring out how computers can help deliver customized products more efficiently. Because much of your work involves exploring ways to apply technology, you will probably spend considerable time brainstorming with others on team projects.

The biggest difference among programs is whether they emphasize technology or business. Almost all programs have a mix of the two areas, but the number of technology or business offerings can vary dramatically. Some programs focus almost entirely on technology. In these programs, courses usually deal with computer programming, network technology, and the development of Web content. Other programs focus on management issues, such as marketing, business case analyses, business plan development, or business strategies made possible by the Internet. In still other programs, you cannot take e-commerce as a stand-alone major; you must combine it with a major in computer science, management, marketing, or information technology. Ask yourself if you are more business or technology oriented to figure out which programs are a better fit for you.

Other majors you might like:
Marketing
Business administration and management
Information technology
Electrical and communications engineering
Economics
Digital media
Entrepreneurial studies
Management information systems
Web/multimedia management
Advertising
Computer engineering
Consumer merchandising

Questions to ask colleges:
Does the program focus primarily on the technological aspects or the business aspects of e-commerce?

Are the courses staffed with regular faculty members or with outside professionals and visiting professors? Are the faculty members engaged in the field? How do they keep current with fast-changing developments?

Career options and trends:
Web developer*; Internet business developer (analyst or manager); network engineer; product manager/marketing manager; business alliance manager; technology analyst*; venture capitalist/fund manager; investment banking analyst; market analyst*; Internet applications designer.

The long-term employment prospects for e-commerce and related professions are very strong. The Bureau of Labor Statistics describes the growth of e-commerce as "explosive" and notes that the expansion of the wireless Internet will spur the need for managers with both business savvy and technical proficiency. Technology constantly improves, and each advance presents new business opportunities.

Insider's viewpoint:
"It's exciting to be in a field where things thought to be impossible only a decade before become commonplace."

—Professor Lorin Hitt, Wharton School of Business

For more info:
Association for Computing Machinery (ACM)
2 Penn Plaza
Suite 701
New York, NY 10121-0701
(800) 342-6626
www.acm.org

Entrepreneurial studies

Also known as:

Enterprise management

What it's about:

The entrepreneurial studies major teaches you how to recognize, evaluate, and respond to new business opportunities. You learn to use management skills to set up and run your own business or franchise, or to apply your creativity and energy to increase the productivity of an existing business.

Is this for you?

You might like this major if you also like: thinking of better ways to do things; learning new ideas, exploring new places, and meeting new people; starting or running a business; puzzles; sports; competition; taking charge of a group activity; taking risks.

Consider this major if you are good at: creativity; critical reading/thinking; leadership; organizing; persuading/influencing; teamwork *...or have...* initiative; perseverance; self-confidence; verbal skills.

Recommended high school prep:

English 4, math 3, lab science 3, social studies 3, and a foreign language 2–3. If available, take a business course, an economics course, and statistics.

Did you know...

...that entrepreneurship is about more than creating a new business? There are opportunities to apply entrepreneurial thinking to the corporate world, socially focused projects, venture capital financing, and a host of other possibilities.

...that in this major, risk and failure are rewarded? Because many businesses disappear within the first five years of operation, most entrepreneurship professors expect students to explore risky ideas that have a greater than 50 percent chance of failing. If an opportunity is worth taking, most likely it will be risky (otherwise, someone would have already taken it).

Typical courses in this major:

Foundations of entrepreneurship
Living the entrepreneurial experience
New ventures and the business plan
Entrepreneurial finance
Managing a growing business
Family business
Social enterprise management
Investor relations and funding
Business and tax planning
Entrepreneurial marketing
New product design and development

Concentrations:

New-venture creation; entrepreneurial finance; corporate entrepreneurship; family-controlled enterprise management; franchise, distributorship, and license ownership; entrepreneurial economics.

What the study of this major is like:

Entrepreneurial studies is the liberal arts major of business school. To be successful as an entrepreneurial major, you need to be able to see the "big picture" and still remain focused enough to take action. You can apply entrepreneurial thinking to almost any field of study—from liberal arts and social sciences to mathematics and physics—and to a variety of careers. If you have a passion for, say, theater, you can use what you learn in entrepreneurial studies to help you create, grow, and manage a drama company. An engineer with an entrepreneurial studies degree can develop innovations that are not just new, but that people will want and buy. Doctors and lawyers who work on their own can use entrepreneurial skills to make their private practices develop and thrive. Business executives can use their entrepreneurial skills to capitalize on opportunities from within their companies. This major prepares you not only for a career but also for life.

Almost all entrepreneurship programs require you to complete a core of business courses. Most programs also offer courses in developing a business plan and in entrepreneurial finance. Good programs blend academic exercises such as case studies and class discussion with hands-on experience creating an enterprise or working with an existing organization. They also provide a variety of specialty paths that may include social entrepreneurship, management of a growing business, and family-controlled enterprises.

The challenges you will face depend on the rigor of the program you attend. Students in strong programs often have to deal with real-world experiences that are outside the bounds of traditional academic activities—for instance, handling professional vendors or actual customers. In general, entrepreneurship can be emotionally demanding because you must make a personal commitment, to your stakeholders (investors, employees, your family, society), that you will create value or improve social conditions. And you don't commit to try—you commit to *do*.

The most obvious difference among programs is how much the sponsoring school or college focuses on entrepreneurship. The programs generally evolve as follows: first, a handful of entrepreneurs and management professors teach a course or two on new-venture creation; then a division of professors teach a number of concentrations in the discipline (such as new ventures or financing) with little interaction with other departments; finally, the college (or school of business) reshapes it curriculum, teaching business in the context of entrepreneurship.

Other majors you might like:
E-commerce
Business administration and management
Franchise operations
Marketing
Consumer economics
Farm and ranch management
Real estate
Small business administration/management
Arts management
Economics

Development economics
Finance

Questions to ask colleges:
How many full-time faculty members teach and research entrepreneurship as their principal endeavor? Do any of the professors have real-world experience or background as entrepreneurs?

How long has the major been offered at this college?

Which career path do graduates from the college generally follow: start-up? industry? finance?

Which kinds of resources are available for students (such as incubator space, seed funding, business plan competitions, access to industry experts and sources of funding)?

Career options and trends:
Business owner/new-venture creator*; investment banker; consultant*; sales and marketing professional*; venture capitalist; operations manager.

Entrepreneurship remains strong in both good and bad economic periods. When the economy is strong, entrepreneurs find an abundance of opportunity, and companies and consumers have more money to spend on the emerging products and services that entrepreneurs provide. When the economy is weak and jobs are scarce, entrepreneurs will spend their time creating a job rather than looking for one.

For more info:
Junior Achievement Inc.
One Education Way
Colorado Springs, CO 80906
(719) 540-8000
www.ja.org

National Foundation for Teaching
  Entrepreneurship (NFTE)
120 Wall St.
29th Fl.
New York, NY 10005
(800) 367-6383
www.nfte.com

Fashion merchandising

What it's about:

The major in fashion merchandising introduces you to all areas of the industry, including design, product development, textiles, buying, marketing, advertising, importing and exporting, sales, and retail management. You learn how to identify and acquire the fashions that customers want, and to sell those fashions.

Is this for you?

You might like this major if you also like: shopping at secondhand stores, consignment shops, and tag sales; fashion magazines; art and photography; travel; interesting people; learning about different cultures; clothes, fabrics, and fashion accessories; cosmetics; keeping up with trends; thinking creatively.

Consider this major if you are good at: attention to detail; creativity; critical reading/thinking; leadership; organizing; stress management; teamwork ...*or have...* an eye for color and design; initiative; verbal skills; writing skills.

Recommended high school prep:

English 4, math 3, lab science 3, social studies 3, and a foreign language 3–4. Courses in art, art history, and business are also recommended. Because the fashion industry operates in the global marketplace, a foreign language is highly desirable.

Typical courses in this major:

History of fashion
Textiles
Sales
Advertising
Marketing
Fashion buying
Merchandising accounting
Fashion show
Consumer behavior
Retail management
International fashion marketing
Mass marketing
Product pevelopment
Computer-aided design (CAD)

Concentrations:

In college: fashion buying; textiles; marketing and advertising; visual merchandising; retail management; apparel production.

If you go on to grad school: production; supply chain management.

What the study of this major is like:

The fashion merchandising major prepares you for a wide variety of career opportunities in the business of marketing and distributing fashion products. Fashion merchandising is an exciting field, reflecting a fast-paced global industry that shapes worldwide trends. The glitz of fashion shows and fashion magazines is the result of creative and analytical thinking, market research, and hard work.

You can learn to manage a retail firm, buy goods for a firm, or work with designers in planning an apparel manufacturer's fashion message. To acquire the communication, analytic, and computer skills necessary to succeed in this competitive industry, you will probably begin with courses in writing, speech, mathematics, history, social science, and natural science. During your first and second years, you take courses such as fashion analysis and textiles, which provide an introduction to the field. In advanced courses, you learn to organize and operate a retail clothing business; to plan, promote, and manage merchandise inventories; and to calculate retail figures for a profitable business. You may also study historical and multicultural costumes—you can later draw on this interesting subject to develop special promotions or store events.

Fashion merchandising programs can lead to either two-year (associate) or four-year (bachelor's) degrees. Associate degree programs generally include courses on the fashion industry, textiles, buying, advertising, sales, and retail management. Sometimes students who have earned a bachelor's degree in another field obtain an associate degree in fashion merchandising. Bachelor's programs in fashion merchandising include traditional liberal arts courses and professional courses in product development, importing and exporting, marketing textiles, product design, retail management, and business law. At some colleges, you can minor in marketing, textiles, and design. Many programs offer field experiences for college credit. Associate degree programs generally offer one opportunity for an industry internship. In bachelor's programs, you may be able to take more than one internship, as well as to study abroad for a semester.

The program is a combination of traditional academic courses and less traditional fashion merchandising courses. The academic courses, which are generally lectures and discussions or laboratory sessions, usually require tests and papers. The fashion merchandising classes generally include lots of hands-on work. Most faculty members and academic advisers have extensive industry experience and do not teach only from textbooks. Fashion merchandising courses are often enriched by field trips and guest speakers. Some programs offer study tours of major U.S. fashion markets (such as New York, Dallas, and Los Angeles) or of European fashion centers. In advanced courses, you are assigned group projects to help you become an effective team player. Many fashion merchandising majors hold jobs while carrying a full-time class load.

Some colleges offer only associate degree programs; some offer only bachelor's degree programs; and some offer both. Certain colleges allow you to move from an associate degree directly into the bachelor's program with no loss of credit. Other associate degree programs provide credit transfer arrangements with four-year colleges.

Other majors you might like:

Marketing
Retailing
Hospitality administration and management
Fiber/textile arts

Fashion and apparel design
Commercial/advertising art
Photography
Anthropology
Psychology
Clothing, apparel and textile studies
Family and consumer sciences
Cosmetic services

Questions to ask colleges:

Do faculty members keep current in their field by continuing to work in the industry? Do they maintain contacts in the field?

Is help available for students looking for internships? Is there a cooperative education program? Students who make contacts in the industry and do networking are likely to receive job offers before graduation.

Career options and trends:

Fashion designer; buyer*; fashion marketing executive*; showroom account executive*; fashion editor; textile designer*; import/export specialist; fashion advertising director; visual merchandiser*; merchandise manager.

Many majors think that the only careers open to them are fashion design and retail buying. However, a survey has identified 31 additional fashion careers, including computer-assisted apparel design; color forecasting; storyboard design; catalog production; mall management; private label development; Web-based retailing; online direct marketing; and fashion consulting. Experience on the job and good networking skills should lead to promotions and future job offers.

For more info:

International Textile and Apparel Association (ITAA)
6060 Sunrise Vista Drive
Suite 1300
Citrus Heights, CA   95610
(916) 723-1628
www.itaaonline.org

Finance

What it's about:

The finance major provides you with a general understanding of financial decision-making and an insight into the way financial markets perform. Emphasis is on the financial management function in firms and not-for-profit organizations, the valuation of financial securities, and the appropriate management of financial risk.

Is this for you?

You might like this major if you also like: family business discussions; the *Wall Street Journal*; doing research; following the stock market; investment clubs.

Consider this major if you are good at: attention to detail; creativity; critical reading/thinking; math; quantitative analysis; research; teamwork *...or have...* mental stamina; writing skills.

Recommended high school prep:

English 4, math 4 (including precalculus), lab science 3, social studies 3, and a foreign language 2-3. If possible, take computer science, economics, and statistics courses. Calculus is also helpful, although not required.

Did you know...

...that even though this major deals with money, you should not count on getting rich quick? Most entry-level positions open to undergraduate finance majors involve hard work and long hours. Students who have become successful have usually exerted considerable effort early on in their career.

...that even bright, well-motivated students often think that finance is a difficult major and that the language of finance is incomprehensible? Most majors quickly learn, however, that the subject matter is made up of simple, straightforward concepts.

Typical courses in this major:

Financial management
Financial institutions and markets
Corporate finance
Futures and options
Portfolio analysis
International finance
Investment banking
Real estate finance
Risk and insurance
Working capital management
Bank management
Investments
Accounting
Economics

Concentrations:

Corporate finance; real estate finance; investment banking.

What the study of this major is like:

In many business schools, finance classes are offered only to students in their second year or higher; because of the technical nature of the material, you'll need to have mastered a number of foundation courses. During your first two years, your general education requirements usually include mathematics, humanities, natural sciences, and social sciences courses. Most programs also require three to six credits each of economics, statistics, and accounting.

After completing the prerequisites, majors take introductory courses in finance and other functional areas of business, such as accounting, management, marketing, and management of information systems (MIS). Usually you must also take one or more courses in financial management/corporate finance and in financial institutions and markets, most of them taught in a large lecture format.

Your first finance course will probably focus on corporate financial analysis, as well as on valuation principles for financial assets such as stocks and bonds. Emphasis is on the tools of analysis, including the evaluation of financial statements and the time value of money calculations. Subsequent classes cover investments and portfolio managements, corporate finance, banking and financial institutions, and international finance. Then you're likely to take smaller classes or seminars on a variety of finance subspecialties that interest you. Because of the critical relation of economics and accounting to finance, most finance programs require at least 12 to 15 semester hours of course work in both economics and accounting.

Many finance courses require the use of computers for problem solving, to improve your facility with spreadsheet programs, statistical and financial analysis, financial forecasting, and the preparation of financial reports. Electives may be in statistics, economics, accounting, computer applications, and communications.

Most of your classes will demand a level of familiarity and comfort with quantitative analysis. This subject area may well be your biggest challenge. The style of teaching varies according to subspecialty. Most advanced corporate finance and financial management courses are taught by means of case analysis; you are presented with a situation and, either individually or as a group, you prepare a presentation. Some areas (particularly derivative securities and futures and options classes) are math-oriented; if you have not covered precalculus or other advanced math in high school, you may have to play catch-up.

Programs typically differ on whether they emphasize financial markets, investment and financial management, or corporate finance. The split will often reflect the college's evaluation of job opportunities in the locality. For example, colleges close to financial centers may stress financial markets and investments, on the assumption that many graduates will head for the financial services sector. Colleges in other regions may emphasize financial management, on the assumption that most graduates will seek employment in the finance departments of nearby corporations.

Other majors you might like:

Accounting
Actuarial science
Banking/financial services
Business administration and management
Economics
Financial planning
International finance
Investments/securities
Insurance
Management science
Real estate
Credit management

Questions to ask colleges:

What is the emphasis of the program? If you want to work in a corporate setting, a program that focuses on financial management would seem appropriate. If you'd rather work in the financial services sector, then you might prefer a program featuring the financial markets and investments.

Career options and trends:

Stockbroker; security sales representative; financial analyst; investment banker; commercial banker; portfolio or mutual fund manager; financial planner; government regulator.

To be a stockbroker or to engage in securities sales and trading, you must pass the general securities registered representative examination (Series 7), administered by the National Association of Security Dealers (NASD). Portfolio managers and other investment management professionals typically acquire the postgraduate chartered financial analysts (CFA) certification, administered by the Association for Investment Management and Research (AIMR). Certification requirements for other positions vary on a state-by-state basis.

Employment in the financial services sector will always be affected by the state of the economy on Wall Street. Demand for financial analysts and personal financial advisors, however, is projected to grow modestly over the next decade, according to the Bureau of Labor Statistics. Increased government oversight of the securities industry should create job opportunities in regulatory agencies.

A sound training in finance is considered useful for any general management position. Banks often employ finance majors in a variety of areas, from corporate lending to trust operations. Corporations hire graduates as financial managers, as financial controllers, or in international financial operations. Brokerage and investment banking firms offer opportunities as account executives or financial consultants for clients. Insurance companies and real estate developers also offer entry-level opportunities. Competition can be tough in this field, and those with an MBA or other certifications will have the best employment prospects.

Insider's viewpoint:

"I like to think of this field as 'advanced common sense.'"

—Professor Stephen J. Brown, Stern School of Business, New York University

For more info:

Financial Management Association International
University of South Florida College of Business
   Administration
4202 East Fowler Ave., BSN 3331
Tampa, FL 33620-5500
(813) 974-2084
www.fma.org

Hospitality administration and management

Also known as:
Hotel, restaurant, and tourism management

What it's about:
Hospitality management is a career-oriented program focusing on anticipating and satisfying the needs of the traveling visitor/guest. It prepares you for professions in the travel, lodging, food service, and recreation industries.

Is this for you?
You might like this major if you also like: travel; meeting new people; cooking; giving parties; working with people; sports; learning about different cultures; socializing in large groups; leadership roles.

Consider this major if you are good at: attention to detail; creativity; critical reading/thinking; leadership; math; teamwork ...*or have...* initiative; verbal skills; writing skills.

Recommended high school prep:
English 4, math 3, lab science 3, social studies 3, and a foreign language 3–4. Courses covering accounting and geography would also be helpful. The Hospitality Business Alliance (www.nraef.org) has spearheaded the School to Career Partnership of hotels, restaurants, high schools, and colleges. High school students can earn credits that are transferable to two- and four-year colleges.

Did you know...
...that the hospitality and tourism industry is one of the top three employers in the U.S., and is estimated to be the largest industry in the world? Whether for a business conference, a rock concert, or a family wedding, the industry can provide the transportation, accommodations, meals, sound systems, security—whatever is needed to make the event happen.

Typical courses in this major:
Introduction to tourism
Management principles
Marketing
Employee labor relations
Facilities design
Lodging administration
Resort operations
Hospitality law
Hospitality finance/accounting
Geography of tourism
Festival and event management
Food service operations

Concentrations:
Casino management; community economic development; time-share management; hotel/motel management; club management; restaurant management; tourism and service management.

What the study of this major is like:
Hospitality is serious business, a fact that is often overshadowed by media images of a carefree vacation destination. The major requires a wide variety of business courses. In addition, you can expect hands-on experiences, including restaurant operation, front-office management, and housekeeping supervision. The program usually requires co-op service or an internship (which may be paid); study abroad opportunities are especially valuable in this major.

Often the faculty members have industry experience in addition to academic credentials. Moreover, there are generally several active student associations that arrange industry speakers, on-site facility visits, and fund-raisers to finance these activities.

When comparing programs, remember that there is no one best format. Colleges may take advantage of their closeness to large hotels, casinos, small resorts, or other establishments that attract business travelers and international visitors. Majors housed in a college of business tend to offer modified versions of traditional business courses. An emphasis on food and beverage operations is also a feature at some colleges. Customer/guest contact is the cornerstone of any variation of the major.

The hospitality industry thrives on outgoing, creative people. There is no routine day. The industry strives to produce satisfied guests by customizing their experience, and in a well-managed facility, employees know how to to meet the challenge. The ability to pay attention to detail is also required. A hospitality property rarely has a second chance to make a good impression. It is also a well-recognized reality that students in this major will have to adjust to the fact that they will be working while almost everyone else around them is playing! Finally, expect to travel.

Other majors you might like:
Geography
Tourism/travel management
Hotel/motel administration/management
Resort management
Interior design
Restaurant/catering management
Landscape architecture
Culinary arts and chef training
Security services management
Sports and fitness administration
Parks, recreation, and leisure studies
International business

Questions to ask colleges:
Do the faculty members have industry experience?

To what extent has the college invested in the excellence of the major by providing course-linked restaurant laboratories, design labs, computer simulations, and, in some cases, hotel facilities operated by students?

Career options and trends:
Restaurant manager; hotel/resort manager; club manager; convention and visitor's bureau director; supplier salesperson; convention and meeting planner; festival and event organizer; caterer; state tourism department employee.

This industry is sensitive to the business cycle, but opportunities always exist if you are willing to travel or relocate. Technological advancements in the form of "virtual meetings" and "virtual vacations" are having an impact on the industry (a simulation of a vacation destination may serve as an ideal preparation for an actual visit), and people who can manage that technology will be in demand. Security is a major concern and represents a rapidly growing career opportunity. However, travel agents have been hit hard by the popularity of self-service, Web-based travel planning.

Insider's viewpoint:
"We're doing a design-your-own-resort project, and you have to go into what type of people you want to come, what type of buildings you want to have, and where you're going to put everything. Our teacher wants us to get a realistic view of how difficult and expensive it is to develop a resort."

—Jennifer, senior, San Francisco State University

For more info:
American Hotel & Lodging Association (AHLA)
1201 New York Ave., N.W.
Suite 600
Washington, DC 20005-3931
(202) 289-3100
www.ahla.com

National Restaurant Association
1200 17th St., N.W.
Washington, DC 20036-3097
(202) 331-5900
www.restaurant.org

Human resources management

Also known as:

Personnel management

What it's about:

Majors in human resources (HR) management study employment-related issues that affect men and women at work. You study topics such as recruitment, staffing, training, performance management, compensation, labor relations, and health and safety, in order to support the goals and strategies of business organizations.

Is this for you?

You might like this major if you also like: working with people; working with numbers; serving people; helping people reach their goals; team sports; clubs; tutoring; camp counseling.

Consider this major if you are good at: counseling; listening; negotiating; organizing; quantitative analysis; teamwork *...or have...* patience; verbal skills.

Recommended high school prep:

English 4, math 3, lab science 3, social studies 3, and a foreign language 2–3. If available, the following courses would also be helpful: statistics, psychology, geography, speech, computer applications, accounting, and business.

Typical courses in this major:

Organizational behavior
Managing individuals and teams
Recruitment and staffing
Occupational safety and health
Employment law
Statistics
Compensation and benefits
Training and development
Performance management
Employee and labor relations
International human resources management

Concentrations:

Generally, none in college; but if you go on to grad school: compensation; labor relations.

What the study of this major is like:

This major prepares you to work with employees in business and nonprofit organizations. The field of human resources management is exciting because it is continually evolving. Frequent developments in the law, in judicial rulings, in technology (for example, the Internet), and in research in many specialty areas of the field require that HR professionals constantly "reinvent" themselves.

As a major, you begin with a sound foundation in the humanities, fine arts, mathematics, and social sciences, including philosophy, psychology, and sociology. In your third and fourth years, you mix business administration and HR management course work. Business administration courses include marketing, finance, accounting, statistics, information systems, and organizational behavior. Human resources management courses include the following:

Employment law. Your study of laws dealing with civil rights, pay, benefits, and health and safety, as well as important court rulings on employment relationships, will help you advise employees of their rights and obligations at work.

Recruitment and staffing. You learn how to attract potential employees and how to decide which ones to hire. Tools in decision-making include interviews, psychological and performance tests, reference checking, and screening devices to identify the most-qualified candidates.

Training and development. You learn how to create and evaluate programs designed to enhance the skills and productivity of individuals and teams.

Compensation and benefits. You focus on designing and putting in place improved systems of pay, benefits, and incentives. Key topics include social security, unemployment and workers' compensation programs, pensions, and life and health insurance.

Employee and labor relations. You examine the history and legal framework of labor-management relations, including collective bargaining, strikes, and dispute-resolution mechanisms (such as arbitration) in union and nonunion companies.

International human resources management. You examine the role of HR management in international business.

The chief difference among programs is in their emphasis on quantitative (numbers-oriented) study. For example, engineering colleges that offer the HR management major tend to require a background in mathematics. A familiarity with statistics can be a big help in courses like compensation and benefits. Staffing can also be highly quantitative, especially if professors assign readings in the research literature. Liberal arts colleges generally require fewer math courses.

Other majors you might like:
Human services
Occupational therapy
Occupational health/industrial hygiene
Industrial engineering
Psychology
Sociology
Labor/industrial relations
Counselor education
Family/community services
Hospitality administration and management
Medical records administration
Human resources development

Questions to ask colleges:
Is there an active student association chapter for HR majors on campus? Is there a professional association chapter nearby? If so, students can work as administrative aides and attend the meetings, make connections with people who have similar interests, and hear invited speakers discuss cutting-edge issues in the field.

Career options and trends:
Human resources manager; management consultant; compensation consultant; labor lawyer; office manager; pension manager; recruiter.

Employment in this field is projected to grow at an above-average rate through 2018, although subject to fluctuations in the economy. Many HR responsibilities are outsourced (the work is contracted to be done outside the organization), especially such tasks as benefits administration and claims processing. Some other responsibilities may be handled by computerized human resources information systems. There will also be some job growth due to increased demand for specialists with experience in international human resources management and information systems.

To remain relevant and in demand, professionals in the field need to build HR systems that "fit" the business strategy of their organization. Doing so will demonstrate the value of their services in quantifiable terms.

For more info:
Society for Human Resource Management (SHRM)
1800 Duke St.
Alexandria, VA 22314
(800) 283-7476
www.shrm.org

American Society for Training and Development (ASTD)
1640 King St., Box 1443
Alexandria, VA 22313-2043
(703) 683-8100
www.astd.org

Insurance

Also known as:
Risk management

What it's about:
As an insurance major, you learn how to help people and businesses manage risk, recover from losses, and plan for the future. You study the legal principles underlying insurance; the types of insurance (including liability, life, property); employee benefits and pension plans; the role of insurance in financial planning; risk assessment and loss evaluation; the preparation of insurance contracts (underwriting); and the way insurance companies operate.

Is this for you?
You might like this major if you also like:

Consider this major if you are good at: attention to detail; building relationships; communicating; leadership; math; quantitative analysis; teamwork *...or have...* initiative; writing skills.

Recommended high school prep:
English 4, math 3–4, lab science 3, social studies 3, and a foreign language 3. If possible, take courses in statistics and computer applications. Courses in accounting and economics, if available, are also recommended.

Did you know...
...that insurance is an important part of business planning and creation? Many people think a career in insurance involves only selling policies and adjusting claims. But in a global economy, risk management is vital to the economies of all nations.

Typical courses in this major:
Principles of insurance
Property and liability insurance
Personal insurance
Insurance operations
Corporate risk management
Insurance accounting
Surplus lines and reinsurance
Life and health insurance
Employee benefits
Estate planning
Financial planning
Ethics of insurance

Concentrations:
Risk management; property and casualty insurance; employee benefit planning; estate planning; financial planning.

What the study of this major is like:
Individuals, families, and businesses invest in insurance to protect and provide for themselves if, one day, their situation changes or disaster strikes. Because people and businesses are increasingly looking to shield themselves from liability lawsuits (in which they may be held responsible, or liable, for harm to another) and losses resulting from serious illness, theft, or death in the family, job prospects in the insurance field continue to grow.

As an insurance professional, you will need to be a "people person" and, in particular, be successful at relationship building. You should enjoy challenges, problem solving, and multitasking. And because every insurance contract represents an act of "utmost good faith," you must also have a sense of integrity and responsibility.

In your first two years of study, you typically concentrate on the liberal arts (English, history, and sociology, for example). A core of business courses (such as accounting, economics, and management information systems) either overlaps with or follows your liberal arts courses. You usually take specialized insurance courses in your third and fourth years. These courses may focus on property loss and legal liability, as well as on employee-related plans dealing with health, disability, and retirement.

In many courses, you'll explore methods of minimizing the impact of such problems (risk management); then you'll analyze how well these methods work.

Because insurance providers are regulated by the government, you need to become thoroughly familiar with the laws and rules that apply. You learn how to assess the risks taken by profit-seeking and nonprofit organizations—and how to respond to disaster. In classes on contracts, there is a lot of required reading. You also need to develop critical-thinking skills—the skills insurance underwriters and risk managers use in assessing potential losses to which organizations may be exposed.

Courses in the major build on and relate to each other, so as you progress through your studies, you'll be applying what you learned in previous courses. Many programs encourage or require you to do internships that make use of the material you've studied in class. Internships are a good way to interact with industry professionals before you graduate.

Some programs, especially those preparing you for graduate school, are highly theoretical in their approach to insurance. Other programs take a more practical approach, teaching you the knowledge and skills you need if you plan to enter the workplace with a bachelor's degree. Some colleges incorporate the insurance major into their finance programs.

Other majors you might like:
Actuarial science
Fire protection and safety technology
Finance
Real estate
Accounting
Financial planning
Statistics
Economics
Human resources management
Security services management
Entrepreneurial studies
Medical insurance specialist

Career options and trends:
Commercial lines underwriter*; property risk analyst*; liability risk analyst*; claims adjuster*; risk

manager; broker/agent; financial planner; actuarial trainee; reinsurance intermediary or reinsurance underwriter.

Insurance executives report that one of their most critical problems is to find enough entry-level candidates educated in the professional areas discussed here.

For more info:
American Institute for CPCU/Insurance Institute
  of America
720 Providence Rd.
Suite 100
Malvern, PA 19355-0716
(800) 644-2101
www.aicpcu.org

American Risk and Insurance Association
716 Providence Rd.
Malvern, PA 19355-3402
(610) 640-1997
www.aria.org

International business

What it's about:

This major prepares you to think globally and manage complexity in an international environment and in cultures other than your own. While learning basic business management techniques and practices, you study how business is conducted in and between nations and how it is affected by the financial systems, government policies, cultural differences, management styles, and other factors that apply.

Is this for you?

You might like this major if you also like: travel; new ideas, people, and places; adventure; unusual challenges; leadership roles.

Consider this major if you are good at: creativity; critical reading/thinking; leadership; teamwork ...*or have...* cross-cultural sensitivity; initiative; patience; self-confidence; verbal skills; writing skills.

Recommended high school prep:

English 4, math 4 (including precalculus), lab science 3, social studies 3, and a foreign language 4. If possible, take calculus.

Did you know...

...that your first position will likely be a domestic, not an overseas, assignment? Within two years after graduation, you probably will not be overlooking the Eiffel Tower but will be employed stateside, working for either a domestic or a foreign multinational corporation, a bank with international operations, or perhaps an international organization such as the United Nations or the World Bank.

Typical courses in this major:

International finance
Derivatives and financial markets
International marketing
Intercultural communication
Global logistics
International operations
Advanced seminar in international business
Economics
Accounting
Management
Business in specific regions

Concentrations:

In college: international economics and trade; marketing; finance.

If you go on to grad school: developing nations; public policy; banking and finance in different regions of the world; business–government relations; international security.

What the study of this major is like:

The international business major provides you with a solid foundation in accounting, marketing, finance, and management. It includes courses that train you to analyze information about overseas businesses and that encourage you to think globally when making work-related decisions. Business environments vary from country to country, and it is increasingly important for managers to understand the causes and consequences of the differences.

As a major, you begin with basic business courses and then advance to ones with an international focus. These courses may examine how money and capital (equipment and other goods) move within and between countries; how technology is transferred between nations; and what management skills are practiced abroad. You analyze the international economic scene, study competition and interdependence, and assess cultural distinctions among nations. You may learn how to market goods and services from the United States and to evaluate the strength of overseas investments. Because an understanding of politics and government is essential to the practice of international business, you should take electives in these areas.

Most programs require you to master a foreign language. Many international business majors gain experience by studying abroad for a semester, a summer, or even a year. Sometimes there are opportunities to visit foreign companies and meet with managers working in U.S. companies.

Although some students think that the international business major is less difficult than other business majors, they soon discover it's not the case. In this major, you are expected to take a variety of demanding courses, such as international marketing, international finance, international management, and international operations. The combination of international business and another major, such as finance or marketing, can be especially challenging.

When comparing programs at different colleges, you'll find that some take an interdisciplinary approach, stressing a wide range of knowledge, with extensive offerings in the liberal arts as well as business; while others may emphasize specific areas of business, such as the ethical dilemmas you may encounter as you do international work.

Other majors you might like:
Accounting
Finance
International relations
Marketing
Tourism/travel management
Global studies
Comparative literature
International marketing
Foreign languages/literatures
Latin American studies
Asian studies
Development economics

Questions to ask colleges:
Do most of the students select international business as a solo major or as a double major?

What is the career track of the most recent graduates?

Is there a study-abroad requirement? How is it financed?

Is there a language requirement?

Are there internship opportunities with an international focus?

Career options and trends:
Derivatives trader; investment banker*; management consultant*; real estate developer; government employee; financial analyst*; brand manager; import/export manager.

Because almost all business has become global, qualified managers with an international perspective are increasingly in demand. In many quarters, in fact, graduates are assumed to have a global view of the world. Now more than ever, with the world a less certain place and with the growing volatility of the economy, business leaders who can operate effectively in a variety of cultural environments are needed.

Insider's viewpoint:
"It is exciting to see a student from Kansas form a worldview, or a student from New Jersey who had never traveled beyond the East Coast corridor discover that, contrary to her prior beliefs, the United States is not the center of the universe."

—Professor Ann-Mary Kapusta, Georgetown University

For more info:
AIESEC International
Teilingerstraat 126
3032-AW
Rotterdam, the Netherlands
+31 10 443 4383
www.aiesec.org

Washington International Trade Association (WITA)
1300 Pennsylvania Ave., N.W.
Suite 350
Washington, DC 20004
(202) 312-1600
www.wita.org

Management information systems

Also known as:
Information technology

What it's about:
In this major, you learn how to apply information technology to solve business problems. MIS prepares you to understand the function of information technologies and systems in business organizations, and it provides the knowledge and skills you will need when you analyze, design, develop, and manage information systems.

Is this for you?
You might like this major if you also like: team sports; computers and electronics; solving problems; working with people; reading; tutoring.

Consider this major if you are good at: attention to detail; creativity; critical reading/thinking; leadership; math; organizing; research; teamwork *...or have...* communication skills; initiative.

Recommended high school prep:
English 4, math 4 (including precalculus), lab science 3, social studies 3, and a foreign language 2–3. If available, take calculus, a writing course, a business or economics course, and an introductory computer science course.

Did you know...
...that computers and technology are not the sole focus of this major? The functional areas of business (operations, finance, accounting, marketing, etc.) and the information itself, as well as the people who will use the information, are primary concerns you must deal with.

Typical courses in this major:
Programming for systems development
Systems analysis and design
Database design
Database management and administration
Networks and telecommunication
Financial information systems
E-commerce
Information services management
Emerging technologies
Advanced software development
Data warehousing
Decision support technologies
Project management and practice

Concentrations:
Information systems design and development; information technology infrastructure; information services management; e-commerce; software development; information technology (IT) strategy.

What the study of this major is like:
As a management information systems major, you must be comfortable with all types of computers, software, and communications (such as wireless phone systems). You study the design, development, and maintenance of information support systems; the ways in which they support business processes and managerial decision making; managerial approaches to effective systems development; and emerging technologies used by information systems. You learn critical-thinking and problem-solving skills so you can handle changing situations and apply the right technology to problems as they arise.

Because you'll be working in organizations and businesses, you must also learn how they operate, by studying finance, human resources, marketing, and accounting. In addition, you are often encouraged to take courses in sociology and psychology and to sharpen your communication skills (writing, speaking, and listening). By understanding human behavior and perfecting your "people skills," you learn how to be a successful link between technology and the people who use it.

Management information systems courses are taught in a variety of ways, including lectures. In labs you can use various software packages to help you with your course work: readings, quizzes, homework assignments, midterm and final examinations, individual and group projects, and term papers. Students interested in research may have opportunities to work on an independent project under the supervision of a faculty member.

When searching for an MIS job, you should have some experience in a business setting. Many programs offer local internships to give you hands-on experience, which is particularly useful for systems analysis (which emphasizes analyzing business processes) and consulting (in which you may work with several industries).

Management information systems programs may emphasize different aspects of the curriculum. For example, some programs may focus on technology-related topics, while other programs may cover more managerial topics. You can usually determine a program's focus by looking at its course offerings.

Other majors you might like:

Business communications
E-commerce
Organizational behavior studies
Software engineering
Management science
Computer engineering technology
Emergency management/homeland security
Organizational communication
Information technology
Computer forensics
Medical informatics
Computer networking and telecommunications

Questions to ask colleges:

How many classes make use of computer labs (or other advanced facilities) as part of the course work? Practical experience is essential in this field.

Are the faculty members actively involved in research or the local business community? It's important for the faculty and the curriculum to keep up with the rapid change in this field.

Is the equipment in the computer labs kept current with changing technology and maintained with good tech support? Students should learn in a technical environment similar to the one they will work in professionally, so a fairly rapid upgrade/replacement cycle is necessary.

What sort of network access is available? Are the classrooms connected to the Internet and campus networks, either by "port per seat" or wireless networking?

Career options and trends:

Systems analyst/designer*; software developer (programmer)*; database administrator*; consultant; project manager; chief information officer (CIO); researcher.

Job opportunities are generally excellent for students with MIS knowledge and good business sense. Heightened concern over "cyber security" is also spurring demand for managers proficient in computer security issues; in fact, such knowledge is almost a prerequisite.

Students who have very specific interests and career goals ("information security analyst for medical information systems," for example) usually have excellent opportunities for specialization after they graduate. In addition, the job market rewards students who double-major and match MIS with finance, marketing, operations, or accounting.

For more info:

Association for Information Systems (AIS)
P.O. Box 2712
Atlanta, GA 30301-2712
(404) 413-7441
www.aisnet.org

Association for Computing Machinery (ACM)
1515 Broadway
New York, NY 10036-5701
(800) 342-6626
www.acm.org

Marketing

What it's about:

Marketing is concerned with the process of developing customer relationships, uncovering business opportunities, and delivering products and services to buyers. Marketing majors learn to analyze customers and their needs, and to make decisions about product design and quality, pricing, advertising, selling, and distribution.

Is this for you?

You might like this major if you also like: buying and selling; looking at quality TV commercials, magazine ads, and store window displays; online social networking; working in teams; involvement with student groups; volunteerism; part-time work; thinking about what motivates people; shopping.

Consider this major if you are good at: creativity; critical reading/thinking; leadership; persuading/influencing; quantitative analysis; research; teamwork *...or have...* initiative; verbal skills; writing skills.

Recommended high school prep:

English 4, math 3, lab science 3, social studies 3, and a foreign language 2–3. If available, take computer classes that teach word processing and spreadsheet applications.

Did you know...

...that marketing isn't just about advertising and sales? Actually, it is much broader and more strategic in focus, requiring a strong understanding of accounting, economics, finance, management, information technology, and other areas.

Typical courses in this major:

Principles of marketing
Retailing
Professional selling
Sales management
Consumer behavior
Marketing communications/promotion
E-commerce/Internet marketing
Services marketing
Product development and management
International marketing
Marketing research
Marketing management
Marketing strategy
Advertising principles

Concentrations:

Generally, none in college; but if you go on to grad school: market research; e-commerce; advertising management; product management.

What the study of this major is like:

Marketing focuses on important business measures that have a central role in company performance and success, such as customer satisfaction, sales revenue, and market share. As a major in marketing, you will explore the role of marketing in business performance and examine the functions of marketing professionals.

Questions you will ask include these: How does marketing affect society, and how does society affect marketing? In which ways is research important to marketing? On what basis do consumers and industrial buyers make purchasing decisions? How are products developed, priced, and distributed? How do organizations communicate with prospective customers through advertising, personal selling, social networking websites, and publicity? What are the steps involved in developing, conducting, and evaluating marketing strategies? What impact do international environments have on marketing?

Marketing is an intellectually stimulating and demanding subject. Analytical, creative, and communication skills are important to success in the profession. Consequently, marketing majors spend about half their time taking courses in the liberal arts. You must also take a number of business courses, including economics, statistics, accounting, finance, computer information systems, and management.

These courses may challenge you, but they are fundamental for exploring the field. For instance, you'll familiarize yourself with the two primary types of marketing. In business-to-business (B2B) marketing, products such as computers, copying machines, steel, and chemicals are sold to other businesses. In business-to-consumer (B2C) marketing, in contrast, individuals buy products (called, appropriately, "consumer products") such as appliances, cars, packaged goods (food, soap), and services such as insurance and banking. Courses in marketing principles and marketing management teach you to develop and implement plans to market products and services.

Other courses specialize in a single aspect of marketing management. Market research—usually required of all majors—teaches you to use surveys, experiments, test markets, and other techniques to obtain the information you need in making effective marketing decisions. In advertising management, you study the development, testing, execution, and monitoring of advertising campaigns. (Marketing majors are usually not involved in the creative aspects of advertising—design and production.) Courses in sales management focus on the psychology of effective selling and the recruiting, selecting, organizing, training, and motivating of salespeople. In marketing channels courses, you learn about the institutions (retailers, wholesalers, industrial distributors) that work as intermediaries between manufacturers and buyers.

Most marketing courses combine lecture with discussion. Majors usually complete a number of team and individual projects that involve research, analysis, critical thinking, creativity, information technology, writing skills, and oral presentations.

Strong marketing programs focus on ideas and theories while providing you with experiences and teaching you skills that can be easily applied in the workplace. Differences in programs may involve the relative emphasis on project-oriented, hands-on courses; the availability and use of technology; the availability of internships and student competitions; and the degree to which quantitative (math-related) skills are woven into the curriculum. Location, potential employers, and faculty members may add unique aspects to a program.

Other majors you might like:

Advertising
Fashion merchandising
Selling/sales operations
Family and consumer sciences
Economics
Public relations
Sociology
Political communications
Sports communications
Tourism promotion
Business statistics
Psychology

Career options and trends:

Sales representative*; sales manager; advertising and integrated marketing communications manager*; retail manager*; entrepreneur/business owner; product manager; marketing researcher; marketing consultant; customer service manager.

The broad nature of marketing leads to a positive job outlook. Since marketing is used in business, nonprofits, and government agencies, job opportunities can be found even during economic downturns. Marketers are generally paid well, and the field is especially lucrative for those who earn commissions or bonuses based on performance.

For more info:

American Marketing Association (AMA)
311 South Wacker Drive, Suite 5800
Chicago, IL 60606
(800) AMA-1150
www.marketingpower.com

Real estate

What it's about:

The real estate major provides you with an understanding of the economic and social principles that affect how real property—buildings and land—is developed, financed, operated, and traded.

Is this for you?

You might like this major if you also like: working independently; making decisions; interacting with people; building things; travel; buying and selling; playing Monopoly.

Consider this major if you are good at: caring/nurturing; critical reading/thinking; negotiating; organizing; persuading/influencing; teamwork *...or have...* initiative; patience; verbal skills; writing skills.

Recommended high school prep:

English 4, math 3, lab science 3, social studies 3, a foreign language 2–3. If they are available, take a course in statistics and a course that teaches business fundamentals and/or general legal principles.

Did you know...

...that real estate is not simply about building, buying, or selling a home? Professionals who handle appraisals, valuation, investments, and similar activities for multimillion dollar projects around the world need sophisticated training. Think about it—all businesses must operate at some physical location that they either lease or own. In either case, someone must develop the property, and someone must handle the financial transactions.

Typical courses in this major:

Real estate principles and practices
Real estate law
Financing
Appraising
Real estate investments
Residential real estate
Commercial real estate
Taxation
International real estate
Computer applications for real estate analysis
Global perspectives in real estate
Management of income properties
Real estate securities and syndications
Real estate practicums (practical applications)

Concentrations:

Real property development; construction management; real estate finance and mortgage lending; international real estate; real estate law; real estate asset management; appraising; market analysis; and a combination of real estate and almost any other professional subject offered by a typical college of business.

What the study of this major is like:

In real estate, which is an interdisciplinary field, you study various areas of business and you learn to communicate well, both in speaking and in writing. As a major, you probably won't take real estate courses until after you complete course work in the liberal arts and introductory business courses such as accounting, economics, and statistics. Then you take an introductory course covering the language of real estate, ethics, brokerage (the buying and selling of real estate), appraisal (the valuation of real estate), contracts, and property management.

In higher-level courses, you learn about the law of property ownership, transfer, and land-use control; methods of financing property purchases and sales; the effect of tax laws on real estate investments; management of office buildings and apartment buildings; and marketing techniques. In addition, you gain development and redevelopment skills, including ways of salvaging abandoned properties. You might also have the opportunity to do a residential or commercial practicum, managing the construction or development of an actual piece of property.

Real estate classes typically follow a lecture-discussion format and use case studies and computer software as problem-solving tools. Some programs in real estate focus on physical elements (sites and structures) and have studio courses to teach physical planning and construction. Other programs concentrate on theory. Try to determine which type of program interests you the most. You might be attracted to theory-oriented programs if you are considering a job in planning or government. If you want to go into the real estate business, look for programs that emphasize real-world interaction between the real estate and business communities.

The real estate field, which is constantly changing, is a challenging area. To creatively meet the needs of owners, landlords, tenants, purchasers, financiers, and others involved in property transfers, real estate professionals must understand the many aspects of the business and work well with a variety of individuals and representatives. For example, you might have to locate a site for an office building; determine how to finance the transaction; figure out a tax-saving strategy; and work with teams of attorneys, accountants, and other professionals. Successful real estate professionals need initiative, patience, and stamina to see projects through; various technical skills; and an ability to see the "big picture" of a real estate deal.

Although many graduates work in established sectors of the industry, others establish their own businesses or manage their own investments. In addition to financial rewards, the real estate field can give you the chance to set your own flexible schedule.

Other majors you might like:
Construction management
Finance
Building/property maintenance
Urban, community, and regional planning
International business
Environmental studies
Landscape architecture
Architecture
Construction technology
Surveying technology
Housing and human environments
Historic preservation

Questions to ask colleges:
How well are the computer applications used in this major kept up-to-date with advances in technology in the current real estate market?

Can students combine a real estate major with another, such as accounting, finance, international business, or entrepreneurial studies?

What are the research opportunities, internships, or other ways for students to interact with faculty members and the real estate community as a way to gain practical experience?

Career options and trends:
Real estate broker or sales agent; appraiser; consultant; mortgage banker; financial analyst; developer; tax assessor; real estate asset manager.

In order to work as a real estate sales agent or broker, you must pass a state real estate licensing exam.

Opportunities in the real estate field can be found in global and international real estate, REITs (real estate investment trusts), corporate positions, investment houses, financial and tax planning organizations, low-income housing, and government agencies dealing with housing, building regulation, and property management.

The real estate field tends to be cyclical. Swings in the economy, especially interest rates, affect agents and brokers the most. The real estate market is slowly recovering from the recent downturn, but to varying extent across the country. The time it will take to recover will also vary by region.

However, there are a wide variety of employment opportunities in the industry. After all, everyone needs a place to live, and a place to work. With or without cycles, this fact won't change.

For more info:
National Association of Realtors (NAR)
430 North Michigan Ave.
Chicago, IL 60611-4087
www.realtor.org

Communications

Wherever you get the news—online, TV, radio, newspaper or magazine—you're probably aware that reporters, photographers, editors, designers and producers work on it. But a news organization is also a business. Many professionals focus on the advertising and business operations.

"Advertising pays the bills and some see it growing in influence on the news product," observes Patsy G. Watkins of the University of Arkansas's journalism department.

A major in communications—which might be in advertising, digital media, journalism, pubic relations, radio and television, or in communications itself—is a gateway to jobs on the content and business sides of broadcasting, telecommunications, and other media and sectors. You might become a writer, designer, producer, or announcer; or you might work in sales, management, human resources, the legal department, or research.

"Most students began their post-baccalaureate work, not in the communications field but in general business and industry, usually sales," says Professor Bruce E. Gronbeck of the University of Iowa.

"Students considering broadcast media don't realize how satisfying it is to work in less visible positions which are crucial to the success of any media production," says Professor John Doolittle of American University. "News producers, radio sales staff, video shooters, and Web designers are in very demanding and rewarding jobs."

"Understanding business and the needs of the commercial world is integral to succeeding in the field," adds Professor Joel A. Kline of Lebanon Valley College. "Opportunities are also found in public relations and the government."

New jobs in communications are linked to the latest technologies. Emerging majors on campus get students up-to-date on computer-assisted, electronic, and interactive communications; visual journalism and video graphics; strategic communications; health communications; human interface design; new media; multimedia arts; and Internet advertising and marketing. Many media are coming together so students will have to be familiar with a variety of methods of communication.

"To communicate requires writing skills, visual skills, and technological skills. When students master these perspectives, they can enter many different fields," Kline says.

Get the story on colleges

To choose a college, do some investigative reporting. Get out your notebook or video camera, burn some shoe leather, check the library, read guidebooks; if possible, visit colleges and talk to people who may be helpful. Or send e-mails instead (look on a college's Web site for details). Either way, get the scoop about colleges, including schools of journalism, communications, mass communications, media studies, business, humanities, social sciences, liberal arts, and arts and sciences.

Colleges have many different ways of covering communications.

"The single most important dividing line is between programs that are practically oriented and those that are built around a liberal arts philosophy," explains Gronbeck. "Some colleges offer professionally oriented courses, believing that students are completing a business-type degree aimed at the communication industries. Others are constructed around the philosophy that 'communication' is such a general notion that training should be focused on the analytical and speaking/writing skills that students can bring to any entry-level position."

If you did a TV series on choosing a college, it would have five episodes: Faculty, Courses, Facilities, Internships, and Jobs. Here are some ideas for your script.

Episode One: Faculty. Are they experienced professionals? What are the backgrounds of instructors teaching the courses? Are professors easy to meet with outside class?

Episode Two: Courses. When must you declare your major and what are the required courses? Is the focus on technical skills or creative and thinking skills?

Episode Three: Facilities. What's in the computer lab? How new is the broadcast equipment like cameras and editing platforms? How often is the hardware and software updated? How much access will you have to the studios and labs? Can you work for the campus newspaper, radio or TV station, or other publications and outlets? Are they run by the faculty or independently?

Episode Four: Internships. What kinds of internship programs are offered and what are the typical assignments? Will the college help you land an internship at a broadcast or other outlet (on or off campus)? Is the campus near a city with lots of communications opportunities? Will you put together a portfolio or reel of your projects to show your talents to future employers? (At this point in your script, cut to an interview with an expert like advertising maven Thomas A. Bowers, University of North Carolina at Chapel Hill.) "Potential employers will ask for samples of work the student did on campus publications or at internships. Having such experience is absolutely essential."

Episode Five: Jobs. Will you get help finding a job after graduation? Where are graduates working now and what kinds of work are they doing? How many go on to law school or graduate work in communication studies? (Show a graphic here of the top five careers for graduates, then cut to Watkins.) "A variety of career opportunities are available for people with skills in researching, writing, and presenting information clearly."

Fade to black and roll credits.

Advertising

What it's about:

Advertising majors learn to create and distribute paid messages in communication media in order to persuade people to accept an idea, change attitudes, or to take action. Your studies include analysis of customers, markets, and media, as well as advertising's history, regulation, and social and economic effects.

Is this for you?

You might like this major if you also like: writing; art and design; being curious about a wide variety of subjects; keeping up on current trends and current events.

Consider this major if you are good at: active listening; attention to detail; creativity; critical reading/thinking; quantitative analysis; spacial thinking/analysis; teamwork *...or have...* initiative; verbal skills; writing skills.

Recommended high school prep:

English 4, math 3, lab science 3, social studies 3, and a foreign language 2–3. Courses in art, business, and computer applications are also recommended.

Did you know...

...that most advertising agencies hire copywriters and art directors who have attended portfolio-preparation schools that offer specialized, advanced training to college graduates? Such preparation has become essential for creative positions.

...that creativity in advertising is not limited to copywriting and design? Creativity—the approach to a familiar problem from a fresh perspective—is important, as well, in media planning, research, and account development.

Typical courses in this major:

Principles of advertising
Copywriting
Advertising design
Media planning
Advertising campaigns
Advertising management
New media and Internet design
Creative strategy
Market research
Account planning
Advertising sales
Retail advertising
Consumer behavior
Social and economic aspects of advertising
Mass media law
Marketing

Concentrations:

Copywriting; design; account management.

What the study of this major is like:

Advertising programs are usually found in schools of journalism and mass communications and are influenced by the strong liberal arts emphasis in such institutions. Don't be surprised to find out that you will probably be required to choose two-thirds of your courses from outside the major. A typical major consists of four or five advertising courses; a few courses in news writing, mass media law, and ethics; and many liberal arts courses. You are advised or required to take at least one course in marketing, usually taught in a school of business.

Advertising courses are a mix of theory and practical experience. You are introduced to concepts and principles that you will use when you develop advertising campaigns. In most courses, you will be expected to make oral presentations, an essential part of advertising. Because much of the work in advertising is done by teams of people, advertising courses typically require group projects. All advertising courses stress clear, concise writing.

Courses in the major cover such areas as copywriting, in which you learn to create the text of your ads; media planning, in which you decide where your ads will appear (TV, online, and so on); and research, in which you explore ways to conduct surveys and other analyses of your "targets": those whom the ads are intended to persuade. Advertising art and design is usually not a big part of this major at most colleges. If you have artistic talent and intend to pursue a career in advertising art, you should consider majoring in commercial art or graphic design instead.

You should be prepared to balance several responsibilities and assignments at one time. In addition, you may be frustrated occasionally by the difficulty of arranging project meetings with group members who are equally time-pressed (this is actually good preparation for the real world). Courses in research or in media planning require some quantitative analysis, so you might have to brush up your math skills.

It may be difficult to land a full-time job after graduation without some experience. Opportunities to get experience include internships at an advertising agency, newspaper, or broadcasting station, and part-time jobs with a campus newspaper or radio station. Colleges in or near cities can usually offer more internship and employment opportunities than rural colleges can. Although studying advertising in an accredited program is not essential for employment in the profession, the major can help open doors for you. Because of its stress on broad knowledge, critical analysis, and communication skills, it can be valuable preparation for other careers as well.

Other majors you might like:
Journalism
Broadcast journalism
Marketing
Commercial/advertising art
Public relations
Business administration and management
Communications
English
Graphic design
Photojournalism
Fashion merchandising
Web page/multimedia design

Questions to ask colleges:
What is the professional experience of the professors? In a strong program, at least some of the professors have worked as professionals in advertising.

What are the opportunities for internships and other hands-on experience? Potential employers often ask for samples of work you did for campus media organizations or on internships.

Career options and trends:
Copywriter*; media planner*; account executive*; advertising salesperson; account planner.

After graduate study, you may pursue work as an advertising research specialist.

When businesses suffer, advertising budgets often take the first hit. However, with more advances in technology and other non-traditional means of advertising and promotion, employers will be looking for new and different ways to better reach their customers. If you understand how the various forms of media are evolving and can apply that understanding, you will be at an advantage.

Insider's viewpoint:
"I love the fact that our knowledge of human behavior will never be complete and that even the best advertising campaigns will not always be successful. Long live the independent-minded consumer!"

—Professor Thomas A. Bowers, University of North Carolina at Chapel Hill

For more info:
Accrediting Council on Education in Journalism and Mass Communications (ACEJMC)
Stauffer-Flint Hall, University of Kansas
1435 Jayhawk Blvd.
Lawrence, KS 66045-7575
(785) 864-3973
www.ku.edu/~acejmc

Communications

What it's about:

In the communications major, you examine the many ways in which information and ideas are exchanged in modern society. You may study the history of political and religious speeches; write reviews of TV programs and films; explore the sociology of interpersonal and group dynamics; evaluate the impact of the media on individuals and society; and inquire into the ethics of communication.

Is this for you?

You might like this major if you also like: group discussions; blogging; writing; tutoring or camp counseling; volunteering for political/service organizations; movies, radio, and television; student government; making presentations; working on the school newspaper, Web site, or yearbook.

Consider this major if you are good at: active listening; caring/nurturing; creativity; critical reading/thinking; leadership; spacial thinking/analysis; teamwork ...*or have...* verbal skills; writing skills.

Recommended high school prep:

English 4, math 3, lab science 3, social studies 3, and a foreign language 2–3. If possible, take courses in speech, journalism, debate, and theater. It is also valuable to work on the yearbook or newspapers; at a radio station; as a DJ at dances; or with political, service, or outreach organizations.

Did you know...

...that after college, most majors begin working in business and industry—usually in sales? Communications is one of the most popular gateways into a wide variety of jobs in business and industry.

Typical courses in this major:

History of public address
Interpersonal communications
Organizational communications
Communications theory
Introduction to rhetoric
Media criticism
Interviewing
Radio/TV/film production
Introduction to digital media
Public relations
Public speaking
Argumentation
Mass media and society
Group communications
Persuasion
Ethical and legal foundations of media practices

Concentrations:

In college: speech communications; journalism; advertising; public relations; political communications; broadcasting; film studies; media studies; theater arts.

If you go on to grad school: rhetorical studies; communications technologies; new media/technologies; computer-assisted communications.

What the study of this major is like:

The study of communication is as old as the writings of the ancient Greeks on rhetoric and politics. Today, social and electronic communications are explored from historical, critical, theoretical, ethical, and sociological perspectives.

The communications major blends practical training with a liberal arts education. To fulfill humanities requirements, you will probably select courses in history, communications theory, media criticism, social science, and public policy. Most courses in communications include both theory and practice. For example, you will be expected to analyze situations and then communicate your conclusions through speaking, writing, negotiating, listening, or producing.

Typically, you begin the major with either an introductory course or communication skills courses (public speaking, reporting, radio production).

Large lecture classes are supplemented by small discussion sections. In performance and production courses, which are usually small, you present oral or media work for evaluation. Media production courses train you in preproduction (planning and writing), production (shooting), and postproduction (editing). Some colleges have up-to-date studios, whereas others send you to work in the field. In courses in public speaking, interviewing, group communications, and argumentation, you learn to prepare and deliver messages and to listen carefully to what others have to say.

Third- and fourth-year courses generally emphasize theory and research, history and criticism, and advanced practical work. You may read and discuss videotapes of presidential speeches, First Amendment court cases, or other documents that call on your critical-thinking skills. You are graded on your mastery of the readings, your contributions to class discussions, and your ability to analyze what you have read and observed.

Internships are a popular feature of many programs: you may spend a few hours a week or an entire semester getting on-the-job experience in a workplace that interests you, such as a radio station, an advertising firm, an insurance agency, a cable TV company, or a customer relations department. You may also spend a semester abroad studying the politics, theater, mass media, or cinema of another culture.

The biggest difficulty in choosing a college or a program is to sort through the many communications programs that are available. Some may focus on speech; media studies; dramatic or theater arts; broadcasting, film, or multimedia arts; humanities or social sciences; or print or electronic journalism. Some programs may also stress speech disorders, pathology, or audiology.

The most important distinction to consider is whether a program focuses on practical applications or is based on a liberal arts philosophy. Programs that emphasize skills and a professionally oriented curriculum offer a business-type degree aimed at the communications industries, such as journalism, sales, and health services. Other programs stress the analytical, speaking, and writing skills useful for a wide variety of entry-level positions. Some programs also encourage you to take elective courses outside the major, to give your studies a particular focus. For example, you might take electives in social work to prepare for a career in the service industries, or political science electives if you plan to work for the government.

Other majors you might like:
Journalism
Business communications
Media studies
Design/visual communications
Multimedia
Graphic design
Photography
English
Drama and theater arts
Technical and business writing
Speech/rhetorical studies
Web page/multimedia design

Questions to ask colleges:
What are the five most frequent careers graduates pursue? How many majors each year go on to law school, an MBA program, or graduate work in communications?

Is there an internship program? If so, what are some typical assignments?

Does the college have the up-to-date electronic equipment that prepares students for the communications technologies they'll be using on the job?

Career options and trends:
Sales associate*; staff worker in political, governmental, or social service organizations*; business/industry management trainer*; communications research specialist; communications consultant.

Communications majors also go on to careers in law, management, human resources, the broadcasting industry (radio, TV, cable), the telecommunications industry, research, public advocacy, and agencies of the municipal, state, and national governments.

Because this major often leads to careers in business and sales, graduates usually find work quickly. Entry-level positions in radio, television, and cable operations are still obtainable, mostly because of turnover. Entering the film industry remains difficult. Social service positions are relatively stable.

Insider's viewpoint:

"We had to research the court system and the communication theory that was tied to it. We looked at footage from the Rodney King case, and 'Court TV' and 'Judge Judy.' Bringing all of these elements together, deciding what was most important, and then arguing our conclusion took a lot of critical thought."

—Molly, senior, University of Colorado

For more info:

National Communication Association (NCA)
1765 N St., N.W.
Washington, DC 20036
(202) 464-4622
www.natcom.org

Digital media

Also known as:
New media design and studies
Interactive media

What it's about:
Digital media is an interdisciplinary major that combines new communication technology with art, business, English, and computer science. A degree in digital media prepares you to develop and manage digital communications media for a wide range of applications.

Is this for you?
You might like this major if you also like: writing; Web site design; art; business; computers; explaining ideas with writing and graphics.

Consider this major if you are good at: attention to detail; creativity; critical reading/thinking; organizing; quantitative analysis; spacial thinking/analysis; teamwork *...or have...* initiative; writing skills.

Recommended high school prep:
English 4, math 3, lab science 3, social studies 3, and a foreign language 2–3. If possible, take a journalism or writing course, as well as an intro to computer science or programming course, a Web site design course, and a computer graphics course.

Did you know...
...that you don't need a strong art background in order to succeed in this major? Since digital media is interdisciplinary, almost anyone with an interest in technology can find an enjoyable area of concentration.

Typical courses in this major:
Introduction to computer programming
Fundamentals of networks and databases
Two-dimensional design
Multimedia design
Writing for digital media
E-commerce
Information law and ethics
Introduction to digital design
Project management seminar
Web site management
Senior project

Concentrations:
In college: design; art history; e-commerce and e-business; programming and network infrastructure; writing for digital media; teaching technology.

If you go on to grad school: multimedia design; educational instructional design.

What the study of this major is like:
Digital media blends theoretical and applied concepts. The major requires you to develop skills in many different areas, some of which will be new to you when you begin college. Few high school students are familiar with the complete digital media field, including the computer programming, graphics, business, and writing topics that most colleges teach in this major.

Early on in your first semester, you should be ready to do a lot of reading in your studies. Although a digital media program has many hands-on applications, the theory behind the field comes from your readings. Most programs teach only basic math; they focus, instead, on creative projects. Because you take fewer math courses than computer science and engineering majors, the digital media course load is generally more manageable.

You do much of the creative work—writing, art, and media programming—in a computer lab. Here you transform an idea into a completed project. Other ways of approaching digital media, such as from business, law, and ethics perspectives, are usually presented in a lecture or discussion format. Students are sometimes stressed by the amount of creative projects they are expected to complete in a semester. Developing texts, graphics, and media programs for several courses can be a strain, especially for students who are not used to using computers as instruments for stimulating the imagination.

Because digital media is an emerging field, the content of majors varies among colleges. Many colleges teach only visual and written components; they focus on the design of a communication instead of its technology or commercial elements. Some colleges combine technology and commercial elements into a program that stresses business technology. Other schools do not treat the program as interdisciplinary and offer it from the art department, with an emphasis on graphic design.

Other majors you might like:
Web page/multimedia design
Graphic design
Web/multimedia management
Information technology
Business communications
Media studies
E-commerce
Digital art
Technical and business writing
Management information systems
Animation

Questions to ask colleges:
Do the program's faculty members have both academic and applied experience in the field? A mixture of academic researchers, consultants, and practitioners ensures that you learn about a wide variety of digital media.

Does the program seek to develop students' creative and critical-thinking skills or only to develop software competency?

Career options and trends:
Multimedia designer; information architect; Web site content manager; e-business analyst; graphic artist; public relations manager; technology support specialist; sales and marketing specialist; Webmaster; e-business manager.

Some technology positions need network or application certifications that are relevant to the type of products the company uses or installs.

There is demand for digital media specialists in all areas where communication is a primary function—marketing, public relations, advertising, government, education, the arts—but to be successful requires an understanding of the needs of business and the commercial world.

For more info:
Information Technology Association of America
   (ITAA)
1401 Wilson Blvd.
Suite 1100
Arlington, VA 22209
(703) 522-5055
www.itaa.org

Internet Society (ISOC)
1775 Wiehle Ave.
Suite 102
Reston, VA 20190-5108
(703) 326-9880
www.isoc.org

Journalism

What it's about:
Beginning with a broad introduction to the liberal arts and sciences, journalism majors learn how to find information and how to communicate their findings through writing, speech, and other forms of expression, including multimedia tools such as digital video. You also practice the skills you'll need for working with a newspaper, radio and TV station, advertising or public relations agency, and Web media.

Is this for you?
You might like this major if you also like: reading and writing; being in the know; current events; history; politics; photography; Web surfing; sports; movies; digging for facts; research; adventure; working independently or in groups.

Consider this major if you are good at: attention to detail; creativity; critical reading/thinking; meeting deadlines; organizing; research *...or have...* curiosity; initiative; perseverance; verbal skills; writing skills.

Recommended high school prep:
English 4, math 3, lab science 3, social studies 4, and a foreign language 3–4. Being active on your high school media—newspaper, yearbook, literary magazine, and/or, if available, television and radio—is also recommended. But many students enter college with little or no high school journalism experience and do very well.

Did you know...
...that there is a strong emphasis on writing skills in this major? You will be required to write, write, write—whether for print or online news, broadcast news, or advertising and public relations.

...that to succeed in this major, you must do more than merely go to class? You have to connect personally with faculty members, seek out mentors (instructors or others who give you guidance and support), make professional contacts, and get real-world experience through school media and internships.

Typical courses in this major:
News reporting methods and techniques
Copyediting
Magazine writing
Photojournalism
Writing for the Web
Feature writing
Public affairs reporting
Broadcast news
Media law
Ethics
Newspaper management
Digital media
The documentary
Sports writing and reporting
Political reporting
Media campaigns

Concentrations:
In college: broadcast journalism; print journalism; public relations; newmedia technology; photojournalism.

If you go on to grad school: specialized reporting (such as political, financial, international, agricultural); investigative reporting; documentary studies.

What the study of this major is like:
Students who plan to enroll in a journalism program often say they have so many interests they can't decide on a major—they want to major in everything. As a journalism major, in fact, you'll have the chance to explore many subjects. You may even be able to make a difference in people's lives—for example, by reporting about someone unfairly convicted of a crime, or by developing a promotional campaign for a nonprofit agency.

Majors typically take many courses in the liberal arts and sciences, to gain a broad understanding of history, geography, political science, economics, literature, and the natural sciences. This comprehensive background will help you understand the context of the information you will, as a journalist, gather and report.

In the past 10 years there has been a shift from the traditional form of print journalism (newspapers, books) to more online media. In order to deal with this change in dynamic, schools are seeking to better blend the fundamental courses in journalism (emphasizing the *Associated Press Stylebook*) with classes in new media and the business of journalism.

Overall, your course work emphasizes writing, reporting, and technology skills, as well as professional practices and values. Assignments develop your ability to express yourself using language, computers, software, and recording equipment. You also take courses in media law and ethics. Most journalism programs arrange for you to intern with a professional media organization.

Typically, about 60 percent of your courses will cover skills and 40 percent will be "topical" courses, devoted to a particular subject. Skills course work is heavily hands-on, with a great deal of personal instruction. The main challenges you are likely to face are heavy writing assignments and the emphasis on meeting deadlines. Journalism course work is very much project-based—you will probably have assignments in most of your courses, every semester. Frequently, course projects involve helping local community groups to develop ad campaigns or publications. You are also encouraged to participate in one or more of the college media outlets: you might report for a student newspaper, magazine, or radio station.

Electives you can choose might include sports journalism; government and the media; electronic publishing; Web design; computer-assisted reporting; television documentary studies; gender and the media; television and society; visual literacy; business reporting; and the presidency and the press.

At some colleges, you can't become a journalism major until you have completed a certain number of credits, and you can't join a student media organization until a specified point in your academic progress. Other schools admit you as a major in your first year and encourage you to join student media organizations from day one. Generally, the policy depends on the size of the school; larger schools tend to be more restrictive.

And in some journalism programs, you will be trained to work in the most important types of media—print, broadcast, and the Internet—rather than specialize in one of these areas. This curriculum follows what is called the "convergence" approach. Other programs have specialty divisions, but you can also choose to develop skills in a second area of journalism. For example, a still photojournalist may also learn video shooting and editing.

Other majors you might like:
History
Radio and television
Communications technology
Community organization/advocacy
Public relations
Political science
Sports communications
Peace studies
Marketing
International relations
Media studies
Global studies

Questions to ask colleges:
What student media are available? How and when can a student join the college newspaper, radio station, or other type of media? Is there faculty supervision, or are the media outlets independent?

Is there an internship program? Is an internship required? Are students assisted in finding internships?

Are students and student organizations encouraged to enter regional and national competitions?

Career options and trends:
Print or online news reporter, editor, or photographer*; broadcast reporter, producer, or anchor*; advertising copywriter*; public relations manager*; magazine or Web editor; freelance writer (magazine, Web, newsletter); photojournalist; news outlet manager; Web designer.

There is stiff competition for reporting jobs at large newspapers, broadcast stations, and national magazines, so most entry-level positions are in small-town or suburban media. Large newspapers and broadcasters require 3 to 5 years of postgraduate experience and usually prefer job applicants who have a degree and/or experience in a specific subject area, such as economics, business, science, or politics.

While job prospects for newspaper journalists is in decline, some growth is projected in broadcast journalism, and strong growth is predicted for employment in online media. Recent surveys of journalism graduates indicate that the best-paid entry-level jobs are with Internet organizations.

Insider's viewpoint:

"We came into class one morning, and the professor gave us the topic for a newspaper story and said we had an hour and a half to complete it. We had to run around campus gathering information and opinions, which is difficult at 8:30 a.m. because no one is awake yet. It was good experience, though."

—Courtney, senior, SUNY Binghamton

For more info:
American Society of Newspaper Editors (ASNE)
11690B Sunrise Valley Drive
Reston, VA 20191-1409
(703) 453-1122
www.asne.org

American Society of Magazine Editors (ASME)
Magazine Publishers of America
810 Seventh Avenue, 24th Floor
New York, NY 10019
(212) 872-3700
www.magazine.org/asme

Public relations

Also known as:
Image management
Organizational communication

What it's about:
Public relations majors examine how to manage the public image and communications of an organization or individual (such as an entertainer or a political candidate). You learn how to shape the appropriate message, and you'll explore the best ways to get your message across. You also master technical and managerial skills, such as writing and producing printed and visual materials; and study strategic planning and problem solving.

Is this for you?
You might like this major if you also like: writing; public speaking; planning parties, club activities, or fund-raising events; team sports; working on the school newspaper.

Consider this major if you are good at: creativity; critical reading/thinking; organizing; persuading/influencing; research; teamwork *...or have...* initiative; verbal skills; writing skills; "people skills".

Recommended high school prep:
English 4, math 3, lab science 3, social studies 4, and a foreign language 3–4. If available, take a journalism course, a business course, and a computer applications course.

Did you know...
...that this field involves technical and analytical skills, not just communication skills? Some students think that public relations is a "soft" business major; but the job of a PR professional is not only about managing image and message, but also about showing how the results of these efforts affect the bottom line. To do this effectively requires familiarity with statistics, research methods, finance, and communications technologies.

Typical courses in this major:
Fundamentals of public relations
Writing for mass media
Writing for the Web
Media planning
Principles of advertising
Public relations research
Public relations writing
Speech writing
Media law and ethics
Media campaigns
Visual communications and graphic design
Video production
Image management
Crisis management
Case studies in public relations management

Concentrations:
Corporate public relations; consumer relations; employee relations; public affairs; nonprofit public relations; financial or investor relations; publicity and media relations; international public relations.

What the study of this major is like:
Public relations courses address three aspects of professional work. One group of courses—writing, graphic design, and video production—focuses on the techniques you'll need in publicizing a client's message: the how of communication.

The second group of courses—social sciences, humanities, natural sciences, mathematics, foreign language, business, and fine arts—provides an understanding of the social and cultural environment: the what of communications.

The third group of courses, which explore why clients communicate with the public, includes public opinion, research methods, strategic planning, problem solving, and ethics. You learn how to obtain and evaluate feedback from the public and how to incorporate the information into business strategies.

Most public relations programs are offered by schools or departments of journalism or mass communications. Sometimes the major is in a department of speech or communications, where it may be called organizational communications. Wherever the major is housed, you take about 25 percent of your courses in public relations, primarily in writing and other skills and in methods of planning, developing, and implementing public relations campaigns (or projects). The rest of the courses are usually in the liberal arts and sciences.

Majors are encouraged to complete a minor or to take most of their electives in business (including accounting, finance, and marketing), especially if they plan to do public relations work for a corporation or for a firm that represents corporate clients.

A highlight of the major is an internship, which may be required, during the academic year or in the summer. On-the-job experiences allow you to apply, in the real world, the principles and techniques you learned in the classroom. When looking for that first job after graduation, you'll need a portfolio of articles, scripts, presentations, or other work that illustrates your ability. Writing for your college TV or radio station or student newspaper is another excellent way to gain experience and material for your portfolio.

Many public relations courses are taught in a laboratory format; you complete in-class writing, editing, and production assignments. Other courses use the case study approach, in which you evaluate an actual or hypothetical public relations presentation. This type of exercise helps you develop skills in problem solving and critical analysis. In-class discussion and debate give you the opportunity to express and defend your opinions. You will most likely be required to participate in a capstone project, in which you plan, develop, implement, and evaluate a public relations campaign, working alone or in a group organized along the lines typically encountered in the working world.

Other majors you might like:
Advertising
Journalism
Marketing

Music management
Public administration
Community organization/advocacy
Human resources management
Media studies
Graphic design
Organizational behavior studies
Hospitality administration and management
Science, technology, and society

Questions to ask colleges:
Is the program accredited by the Association for Education in Journalism and Mass Communication?

How does the program include technical and research skills in the curriculum?

Career options and trends:
Public relations manager; corporate communications manager; publicist; media relations specialist; event planner; speech writer; public opinion researcher; public relations agency representative; promoter; nonprofit or educational fund-raiser.

Over the next decade or so, employment opportunities in the public relations field are expected to grow much faster than in many other professions. Nevertheless, there will be stiff competition for entry-level jobs because the major is so popular. In fact, there is currently a shortage of public relations instructors around the country. Prospects will be best for graduates who combine their public relations degree with business courses and who have internship or related work experience.

For more info:
Public Relations Society of America (PRSA)
33 Maiden Lane
New York, NY 10038
(212) 460-1400
www.prsa.org

Radio and television

What it's about:

The radio and television major prepares you for a career in all areas of these two types of media, including writing, editing, production, performance, and sales. In addition, you develop an understanding of the history, structure, regulation, and functions of the electronic media and explore the ethical issues you may encounter when you deal with radio and TV audiences.

Is this for you?

You might like this major if you also like: telling or writing stories; knowing about everyday events and issues; expressing your ideas and opinions; technology; taking pictures or making videos.

Consider this major if you are good at: active listening; attention to detail; creativity; critical reading/thinking; organizing; teamwork ...*or have...* initiative; verbal skills; writing skills.

Recommended high school prep:

English 4, math 3, lab science 3, social studies 3, and a foreign language 2–3. If possible, participate in student media activities such as radio and TV stations, newspapers, and yearbooks.

Did you know...

...that you don't have to be "on the air" to have a satisfying job in radio or television? Most news producers, radio sales staff, video shooters, and Web designers have demanding but rewarding careers. You are also more likely to find a job behind the scenes.

Typical courses in this major:

Introduction to mass communication
History of broadcasting
Writing for the electronic media
Fundamentals of video production
Radio/television news producing
Mass media and society
New communications technology
Media law and regulation
On-air performance
Interactive media
Sound design/production
Studio television production
Marketing and sales

Concentrations:

In college: television production; radio production; broadcast news; media management; media studies; integrated media/multimedia/new media; audio recording; media sales; media promotion.

If you go on to grad school: telecommunications policy; audience studies; law and policy; media and society; international communication; screenwriting.

What the study of this major is like:

In this major, you quickly discover that radio and television production requires teamwork. You must learn to cooperate with others on the job and to be both a follower and a leader. Any glamour that the mass media might have had for you can swiftly fade when you are faced with deadlines, difficult-to-meet standards for scripts, and technical problems. Opportunities to practice and polish your writing, performance, and other creative skills make your training both demanding and satisfying.

In a four-year program, about 50 percent of your courses are in the liberal arts—history, literature, social sciences, and natural sciences—and most of these are taken in your first two years. An introductory course in mass media provides an overview of the social, political, economic, and historical factors that affect all media in our society. Elective courses in the major allow you to focus on one media or the other, or to concentrate on certain aspects of the industry.

In addition to lecture classes, you receive hands-on experience in lab courses and field assignments. This training can include working in a production studio, interviewing people outside of class, or using specialized communication gear such as audio and video recorders, editing equipment, and lighting. Two-year programs are usually more technically oriented, or designed for specific occupations in the industry.

Colleges near large cities usually offer numerous opportunities for internships and part-time employment during the academic year. On the other hand, newspapers and radio stations in rural or suburban communities may allow you to do the kind of work that students in metropolitan areas would not be permitted to do. Student-run radio and television organizations can provide you with excellent outside-of-class opportunities. Colleges with a tradition of media-related programs, such as journalism, advertising, and the arts, are likely to emphasize those areas in their radio and television offerings.

Other majors you might like:
Journalism
Film/cinema studies
Electrical and communications engineering
Drama and theater arts
Business communications
Recording arts
Photographic/film/video technology
Cinematography and film/video production
Media studies
Broadcast journalism
Photojournalism
Telecommunications technology

Questions to ask colleges:
What kinds of equipment are available? Is the equipment updated as necessary, and adequate to meet the needs of everyone in the program?

What kind of jobs do graduates of the program typically obtain?

Career options and trends:
Producer*; news reporter*; station manager; production assistant*; camera operator; disk jockey; Web master; sales executive; entertainment lawyer.

Mergers, new technology, and the growth of alternative media sources are reshaping the radio and TV industries. Corporate media "families" may now include cable and/or broadcast TV stations, film studios, radio stations, newspapers, magazines, and Internet companies.

If you have skills and experience that can be applied in two or more areas, such as the ability to write for both TV news and the Web, you may have a better chance of getting a job with a media company. All job seekers face keen competition in this field, but camera operators and editors are projected to have the best job prospects.

For more info:
International Radio and Television Society (IRTS)
420 Lexington Ave., Suite 1601
New York, NY 10170
(212) 867-6650
www.irts.org

National Broadcasting Society, Alpha Epsilon Rho (NBS, AERho)
P.O. Box 4206
Chesterfield, MO 63006
(636) 536-1943
www.nbs-aerho.org

Sports communications

What it's about:

Students of sports communications prepare for careers as sports journalists or public relations professionals specializing in sports. In this major you will examine the relationships between sport, communication, and society, and study the impact of sports media. You will also learn practical skills in areas such as sports reporting, broadcasting, promotion, and various media production methods.

Is this for you?

You might like this major if you also like: all types of sports (not just those that are popular); writing; keeping a journal or blog; reading; coaching; describing or explaining things to others; fact-checking and research.

Consider this major if you are good at: attention to detail; creativity; critical reading/thinking; organizing; teamwork *...or have...* initiative; patience; verbal skills; writing skills.

Recommended high school prep:

English 4, math 3, lab science 3, social studies 4, and a foreign language 3. Courses in journalism and speech are helpful. If possible, participate in student media activities such as a school website, newspaper, or yearbook.

Did you know...

...that you don't have to be an athlete to excel in this major? In fact, the ability to look critically at sport is more likely to bring success. That requires a different perspective than that of a player or a fan.

...that this major focuses on writing? Students are often surprised by how much time they spend practicing their writing skills.

Typical courses in this major:

Introduction to journalism
Media writing
Sports reporting
Sports broadcasting
Sports and society
The business of sports media
Sports and film
Sports event management
History of sports media
Sports marketing
Sports and gender
Sports psychology
Sports law and ethics
Public and media relations in sports
Audio production and performance
Principles of television production

Concentrations:

Sports broadcasting; sports public relations.

What the study of this major is like:

Students sometimes come into this major thinking it is a "fun" major. In actuality, the major is demanding and takes lots of hard work. And you have to work when everyone else is having fun — attending sporting events.

You'll be held to strict newsroom standards, and deadlines are real, as they are in the real world. Most professors won't accept late assignments at all. They also tend to be sticklers for accuracy and good spelling, just like editors.

Sports communications involve a lot more than team scores and statistics. You will look at sports in new ways, examining the role of sports in society and considering issues such as gender, race, performance enhancing drugs, and other tough topics. You'll study the history, economics, psychology, and cultural significance of sports of all kinds. This major combines critical thinking with a deep understanding of the field.

Your studies begin with a broad foundation of courses that range from the theoretical to the applied. Most four-year programs require a solid grounding in the liberal arts and humanities in order to provide a broad cultural context. General introductory courses in communications, media, and journalism are often required.

Introductory courses provide an in-depth study of the field. You will study the practice and effects of sports communications and will likely write research papers on these topics. You will likely study the economics of sports media and examine sports marketing and management as well. Most of these courses will be taught in lecture and discussion classes.

In later courses you will move into more applied areas, such as sports reporting, sports public relations, and sports broadcasting. These courses usually start with lecture/discussion formats, and then focus more on field work and real world practice. For example, in a sports reporting course, students often attend, cover, and write about sporting events and write "game stories." You'll also try your hand at columns, features, and possibly in-depth investigative reporting. In a sports broadcasting course you learn production and postproduction methods along with play-by-play announcing. In all of these courses, writing will be emphasized.

In many schools, internships are an integral part of this major. You might intern with media organizations, sports organizations, sports advertising and promotion companies, and other groups that perform the many affiliated functions of sports communications. Some schools may also have a capstone class that allows students to work in-depth on a particular sports communication project.

As you explore colleges, you'll see a difference between schools that offer a B.A. (bachelor of arts) and a B.S. (bachelor of science) degree in this major. Those in the former will be geared toward journalism and focus more on the liberal arts. Those in the latter are usually geared more toward broadcasting and offer more technical classes. Some programs require a minor, concentration, or dual degree in kinesiology—the study of human movement.

Other majors you might like:

Radio and television
Broadcast journalism
Photojournalism
Media studies
Business communications
Athletic training
Physical education
Sports and fitness administration
Physical therapy
Hospitality/recreation marketing
Golf management
Parks, recreation, and leisure studies

Questions to ask colleges:

Does the school have broadcasting facilities or a studio? Is there a journalism lab?

Are there internship opportunities with off-campus sports organizations and events?

Does the school offer sports that interest you?

What kind of jobs do graduates of the program typically obtain?

Career options and trends:

Sports journalist*; sports broadcaster*; sports writer; sports marketing specialist; sports public relations specialist*; team publicist; statistician; event planner; promoter; sports information director*; production assistant; public address announcer.

There are few areas of public interest as popular as sports. The huge demand for sports information is fueling increased coverage on cable networks and the Internet, which in turn creates new jobs for sports communications professionals. At the same time, the information industry as a whole is in great flux as different media forms migrate online.

Competition for jobs is keen in all areas of sports communications. Sports journalists, broadcasters and writers who can work in an online environment and in multiple mediums will have the the best prospects.

For more info:

National Collegiate Baseball Writers Association (NCBWA); Football Writers Association of America (FWAA); United States Basketball Writers Association (USBWA)
www.sports writers.net

Associated Press Sports Editors (APSE)
National Sports Journalism Center
Indiana University-Purdue University Indianapolis
535 West Michigan Street
Indianapolis, IN 46202
http://apsportseditors.org

Computer and information sciences

Computer science is making a comeback as college major. After years of declining enrollment, the Computing Research Association reports an 8 percent uptick in the number of students in computer science programs. This is good news for those in the industry who were worried about the nation's ability to compete in a global economy.

Apparently, fear of jobs going overseas were overblown, as more IT jobs are available in the United States today than at the height of the dot com boom, reports the Association for Computing Machinery.

The demand for workers in this field still far exceeds supply—in fact, computer occupations are consistently projected by the Department of Labor to be among the fastest-growing fields in the United States. Employment in network systems analysis and related services is expected to grow by 34 percent through 2018.

"One thing I can say for sure is people with a good computer science education in the next 15 years will have tons and tons of opportunities to choose from," Microsoft Chairman Bill Gates told students at the University of Michigan. "If there's a great field to go into, this is it."

If you're leaning toward a computer major, you probably already have a good deal of experience using computers for communicating with friends, doing homework, and gaming. Maybe you've used graphics, animation, or multimedia systems. People probably come to you for help with their computers. You may also enjoy doing math and puzzles and building mechanical or electronic gadgets.

But how do you turn your familiarity with computers into a challenging and rewarding college education and career? First, get to know how the various computer sciences are taught and which areas of the field attract your interest.

Computer science provides a foundation in the theory and design of computer systems. The information sciences majors add an understanding of the way people use the technologies. After all, an information system includes not just the computers, programs, and networks but also the way individuals, organizations, and society use these powerful tools. Computer forensics blends computer science and law enforcement, while game design draws on both technical and artistic skills.

"One can view the world of computing as a continuum," explains Anne Marchant, Department of Applied Information Technology, George Mason University. "At one end, you have fields like computer science and electrical engineering that focus on the development of hardware and software. At the other end, you have fields like information science ... and management information systems. Information technology is in the middle. Practitioners in the field of IT integrate technologies to build and administer information infrastructure."

Since computers influence just about every profession, you may also be interested in other chapters in this book that discuss majors including management information systems, digital media, electrical and communications engineering, computer engineering technology, drafting and design technology, graphic design, and animation. Computer sciences are also applied to emerging areas of study such as bioinformatics, mobile/wireless computing, digital media design, and cognitive science.

The program for you

When you enter the workplace as a college grad, you'll need the latest skills and knowledge of sophisticated software, the Internet, networking and wireless technologies and a variety of programming tools and languages in order to make computers work for people.

Problem solving is a mission for computer programmers, according to Kate Stewart, Department of Technology and Professional Programs, Tallahassee Community College. "Students who truly enjoy the challenge of creating software that serves a user's needs are passionate and addicted to the process of design and development."

When you are comparing colleges, look for adequate lab facilities and a wide selection of courses. See if you'll have access, from your home or dormitory, to the Internet and the computer networks you'll need. Will you have to invest in hardware and software? Find out if research or internship opportunities are open to you. Also, be aware that colleges stress different aspects of computer science. Some colleges may be more theoretical, others more hands-on or business oriented. If possible, conduct some research on faculty members to see what they've published. Are their priorities similar to yours?

"Each orientation has its strength, and you should consider your overall goal—graduate school or employment. You should also consider the industry needs of the geographic area you hope to reside in," Stewart suggests.

Some concentrations in undergraduate majors include computer systems, database management, programming, robotics, interface design, systems analysis, information systems management, multimedia, data communications and networking, e-commerce, and Web development.

Learning never ends in these cutting-edge fields. Advanced and graduate studies include computer architecture, compilers, operating systems, programming languages, networks and security; advanced database applications, knowledge systems, artificial intelligence, medical or biological informatics; data mining, software engineering; algorithm analysis, programming languages, and artificial intelligence.

Look for these majors in colleges of computing, engineering, information technology, applied sciences, liberal arts and sciences, and in business schools. Also check colleges of engineering, because some programs combine electrical and computer engineering.

For more information, visit the Association for Computing Machinery (www.acm.org), the Institute of Electrical and Electronics Engineers (www.ieee.org), the Society for Industrial and Applied Mathematics (www.siam.org), and the Association for Information Systems (www.aisnet.org and www.isworld.org).

Computer forensics

Also known as:

Digital forensics
Cyber forensics

What it's about:

Computer forensics majors learn how to analyze computer systems, networks, and data storage devices for evidence related to criminal acts; how to preserve and present digital evidence for legal actions; and how to troubleshoot computer security problems and protect against system intrusions.

Is this for you?

You might like this major if you also like: pursuing elusive clues, solving complex problems, open source software, trying new operating systems, law enforcement shows, math and science.

Consider this major if you are good at: attention to detail; quantitative analysis; research; teamwork; communicating with others ...*or have...* self reliance; initiative; patience; math skills; writing skills.

Recommended high school prep:

English 4, math 4 (including precalculus), lab science 3 (including physics), social studies 3, and a foreign language 2-3. If possible, take a course in criminal justice, and as many computer courses as you can.

Did you know...

...that computer forensics is not like the forensics made popular on TV? This major is not about using computers to examine physical evidence in criminal cases, but rather it focuses on digital evidence found on computers, computer networks and digital devices.

Typical courses in this major:

Criminal law and procedure
Introduction to criminal justice
Criminal evidence and investigation
Operating systems
Forensic science
Forensic accounting
Digital forensics I, II
Analysis of digital media
Investigative interviewing
Computer and network security
Network forensics
Cybercrime
Digital investigation
Statistics
Technical writing
E-discovery

Concentrations:

Network forensics, digital media analysis, network security, law enforcement, e-discovery.

What the study of this major is like:

This major combines the study of information systems, computer security, law, and criminal procedure with technical courses in the analysis and deconstruction of digital devices and data found on computer storage systems.

Students starting out in this major are often surprised by the number of criminal justice courses required. By the time you take your first technical digital forensic course, you will be well grounded in legal theory and practice as well as computer theory and operating systems.

After your foundation courses you will tackle the process of analyzing digital devices in order to find evidence pertaining to crimes. Most of these courses are a combination of lecture and laboratory, where you learn to apply theories and best practices to hand-on analysis of computer forensic images and traces. You will conduct computer lab projects both in class and for homework, and also participate in group projects.

You will also learn how to write detailed reports of your analysis of digital devices and to present your findings both orally and in writing. This may be another surprise if you think this major is only about technical skills. But the ability to express yourself clearly is vital, because digital forensic examiners must work collaboratively with detectives and prosecutors to present their case, and to explain how data on digital devices supports or contradicts findings. This often requires giving testimony in court.

Typically during your third and fourth years of study you will participate in an internship, obtaining real life experience working in a local digital forensics firm, laboratory or law enforcement agency. The length of your internship may vary depending on the program, but the experience is invaluable both for your training and your job prospects.

In upper level courses you will also be introduced to the subjects of forensic accounting and white collar crime. You'll probably study alongside business and accounting majors, learning the painstaking and detailed work involved in examining business accounts, personal financial transactions, and the methods used by criminals to launder money.

Seniors often conduct their own research in new and highly technical aspects of digital forensics. It's a good idea to also participate in computer forensics associations or clubs in order to broaden your knowledge outside the classroom and make connections in the field.

Many programs are very law enforcement centric; but there is another side to computer forensics relating to commerce, e-discovery (the disclosure in civil lawsuits of electronically held information) and computer security outside the prosecution of crimes. If you want to widen your career options, look for colleges with programs that cover both aspects of computer forensics or offer a minor or concentration in network security.

Other majors you might like:
Forensic science
Information systems
Computer/systems security
Emergency management/homeland security
Criminology
Behavioral sciences

Criminal justice and law enforcement
Police science
Information technology
Computer engineering technology
Management information systems
Psychology

Questions to ask colleges:

What other areas of the industry besides law enforcement can your program prepare me for?

Is the computer forensics major part of a larger division or school within the college? A program housed in the Computer Science department will be different than a program housed under Criminal Justice.

Does the program require or encourage an internship? What support does the college offer in finding internships?

What are the general education course requirements for this major?

Career options and trends:

Digital forensics examiner/analyst*; computer forensics technologist; information systems security officer*; systems analyst; system engineer; database analyst; computer forensics associate

Job prospects are good, especially in law enforcement, where the increase in computer and internet crime is forcing agencies to create technology task forces and to hire digital examiners. The FBI predicts that before long up to fifty percent of its cases will require a computer forensic expert.

The need for computer security is also pushing demand for digital media and systems analysts throughout industry. The Bureau of Labor Statistics projects employment of such analysts to grow much faster than average through 2018.

Applicants for law enforcement or government positions must pass security clearances and often undergo a lie detector test. Be aware that if you pursue a career in law enforcement, child pornography cases can be as much as seventy percent of the work load for state level digital forensic laboratories.

Computer programming

What it's about:

Computer programming majors learn how to write various programming languages used for software development and operating systems. Topics covered include software installation and maintenance, program customization and linking, debugging, and prototype testing.

Is this for you?

You might like this major if you also like: puzzles and brain teasers; computer games; learning new technology; figuring out creative solutions to challenging problems.

Consider this major if you are good at: attention to detail; creativity; critical reading/thinking; math; organizing; teamwork *...or have...* listening skills; patience; verbal skills; writing skills.

Recommended high school prep:

English 4, math 3, lab science 3 (including physics), social studies 3, and a foreign language 2–3. Take as many computer courses as you can. Courses that cover business and communication are also helpful

Did you know...

...that the core of computer programming is to figure out how to meet users' needs, not just to know how the computer works? That's why communication skills are important.

Typical courses in this major:

Computer literacy
Introduction to computer technology
Business communications
Operating systems
Networking essentials
C++ programming
Java programming
Object oriented programming
Visual basic programming
Database design
Database systems
Multimedia applications
Web page development
Scripting languages
Network security

Concentrations:

Generally, none available.

What the study of this major is like:

In this major you learn how to talk to computers—using programming languages to tell a computer how to do what you want it to. If you are interested in a higher-level study of the theory and design of computer systems, consider a major in computer science. But if you want to dive right into coding, this could be the major for you.

Course work in computer programming gives you an understanding of software design and development strategies; basic hardware principles; elementary network concepts; database design and implementation techniques; and a combination of Web, multimedia, and security concepts. Most of these topics are taught through a combination of lectures and lab work. Lectures cover techniques, strategies, vocabulary, and concepts. The lab time allows you to put into practice what you've learned.

It's not rote learning. Because a successful computer programmer must have the ability to analyze a user's needs and then develop an efficient piece of software that meets those needs, the program's emphasis is on building strong problem-solving and communication skills. Stress is also placed on cultivating habits of patience and attention to detail.

You will probably spend a lot of time outside of class acquiring these skills and habits. Each programming language and/or topic may present specific challenges. As might be expected, many students find that they are stronger in some areas than in others—for example, they have an easier time understanding hardware than programming concepts, or they have particular difficulty anticipating how changes in code will affect outcomes. In the beginning, some assignments will drive you nuts.

But if you are prepared at the outset to dedicate the extra time and effort required to patiently think about, design, implement, and debug your work, you should find that the rewards outweigh the frustrations. The satisfaction you get when a project is completed and functioning properly is addictive—as you encounter each assignment, problem solving becomes a mission. But there's no getting around the fact that this is a rigorous major. It takes practice, patience, and dedication.

This major is offered mostly at two-year (community) colleges and technical schools. If you come across a four-year program, it's most likely a higher-level computer science major. Colleges use many different names for their computer majors, so go by the description in the course catalogue, not the name.

As you explore colleges, you will notice that the major can vary widely in focus. At some schools, the concentration is on software (mostly programming); at others, the emphasis is on Web page design and management. Some majors are geared toward industry-recognized certifications (Cisco or Microsoft, for example); others are applications oriented (computer graphics, data entry, etc.); still others deal mostly with systems and networking. Examine the descriptions closely to see which programs best match your goals.

And as you think about your goals, remember that programmers can never stop learning; to stay employable, you'll have to keep up with the state of the art.

Other majors you might like:
Information technology
Mathematics
Computer engineering technology
Information systems
Computer science
Medical office computer specialist
Animation

Computer graphics
Database design/management
Management information systems

Career options and trends:

Computer programmer*; web developer/administrator*; database administrator; network administrator; help desk operator; PC support/technician; network support/technician*.

Industry-recognized vendor certifications, such as those offered by Cisco, Microsoft, CompTia, or C-Tech, are good credentials to take into the job market. Learning a variety of programming languages and tools for networking, database management, and Internet applications will also increase your chances of landing a job.

Job prospects are good for those with a bachelor's degree and experience with a variety of programming languages. Basic or routine programming jobs, however, continue to be shifted to countries with educated workers and low wages, like India and China. For future job security, combine your technical savvy with knowledge of some other business or scientific field, so you'll know both how to use programming tools and how to apply them to a specific goal.

For more info:

Association for Computing Machinery (ACM)
1515 Broadway
New York, NY 10036
(800) 342-6626
www.acm.org

Institute of Electrical and Electronics Engineers
   (IEEE)
445 Hoes Lane
Piscataway, NJ 08854
(732) 981-0060
www.ieee.org

Computer science

What it's about:

The computer science major trains you in the theory and design of computing systems and software, as well as in important application areas. Your course work balances the need to keep up-to-date with the latest technology with the need to acquire a conceptual foundation that will last throughout your career.

Is this for you?

You might like this major if you also like: mathematical and logical puzzles; using programming to solve real-world problems or explore mathematics; giving precise and elegant explanations for how things work; building mechanical or electronic gadgets.

Consider this major if you are good at: active listening; attention to detail; creativity; critical reading/thinking; math; quantitative analysis; research; teamwork *...or have...* mental stamina; writing skills.

Recommended high school prep:

English 4, math 4 (including precalculus), lab science 3, social studies 3, and a foreign language 2–3. If possible, take discrete mathematics, calculus, a computer science course, and physics (covering electricity and magnetism).

Did you know...

...that companies like Microsoft have more jobs for computer-science graduates with bachelor's degrees than they can fill? But while high-end computer jobs in the United States may be abundant, the Commerce Department confirms that the outsourcing of low-end, routine jobs is on the rise.

...that mathematical ability and logical thinking are the core skills you need for this major? You don't need to learn programming in high school. In fact, many students come to college thinking they know how to program, only to find that they have to relearn the subject from a more analytical perspective.

...that there are many interdisciplinary areas of study within the computer science major? Cognitive science connects computer science and psychology, linguistics, philosophy, and neuroscience. Bioinformatics and computational biology combine computer science and biology. Digital media design links computer science to the fine arts and communications.

Typical courses in this major:

Introduction to program design
Data structures
Computer system organization
Mathematics for computer science
Automata and formal language theory
Algorithms
Digital system design
Operating systems
Software engineering
Compilers
Principles of database design
Computer graphics
Artificial intelligence
Robotics

Concentrations:

In college: theoretical computer science; computer systems; artificial intelligence; databases; graphics; robotics; computational biology; computational linguistics; multimedia.

If you go on to grad school: computer architecture; compilers; operating systems; programming languages; networks and security; robotics and computer vision; natural language processing; algorithms and complexity; bioinformatics.

What the study of this major is like:

In this major you study many abstract concepts, and examine fundamental notions such as mathematical proof, knowledge, computability, and randomness in a new light. But computer science, of course, also focuses on the computer.

Because using a computer to communicate requires precision, you must learn to use precise programming languages. During your core training, you'll be asked to think about many questions: Why are programming languages designed the way they are? How do you translate a real-world problem into a carefully worded set of instructions—a program—that a computer can execute (or follow) to produce the solution? What goes on inside a computer when a program is being executed? How is the computer constructed to enable it to function? What impact do computers and programs have on a variety of fields?

Computer science programs vary in the amount of core training they provide. A solid foundation will help you solve problems in application areas. Some programs focus on skills that are immediately applicable, while others emphasize abstract, conceptual ideas to ensure that what you learn will be able to help you to adapt to rapid changes in technology. In addition, some programs assume that students have pretty sophisticated backgrounds in math and logic. In other programs, students aren't necessarily expected to have such in-depth, high-level preparation.

Designing and analyzing computer programs requires a mathematical creativity that you may find challenging. Furthermore, you will encounter a multitude of programming environments and languages and may struggle to master them. Projects and assignments typically require long hours of work. On the whole, the computer science major is intellectually demanding, but the field is young and full of possibilities. Once you acquire a mathematical and logical foundation, you can quickly reach the point where you are conceiving and evaluating ideas on your own. If you are attracted to abstract thinking as well as to practicality, computer science can offer you the best of both worlds.

Other majors you might like:
Computer engineering
Electrical and communications engineering
Computer hardware engineering
Computational mathematics
Cognitive science
Software engineering

Systems engineering
Robotics technology
Information technology
Computer engineering technology
Computer graphics
Digital media

Questions to ask colleges:
Does the computer science program include aspects of electrical engineering? If you are interested in the circuitry of computers, examine a school's course list carefully. Because schools may differ in the way they divide the content of electrical engineering and computer science, the circuitry of computers is not taught in all computer science departments.

Career options and trends:
Senior programmer*; systems analyst*; network administrator; database manager; software developer*; financial analyst*.

Job prospects are excellent, especially for computer system designers, database administrators, and computer security specialists, which are projected to be among the nation's fastest growing occupations for the forseeable future. There are minor fluctuations in the market and small ups and downs in the salaries for entry-level jobs. But the shortage of students choosing this field will increase demand for those that do.

Insider's viewpoint:
"Networking and Graphics are my favorite classes. Networking is the backbone for communications nowadays, and there is much to be done to increase security, speed, and availability. Graphics is simply fun. In my Graphics class, we created a video game, a flight simulator, and a ray tracer that produces highly realistic pictures."

—Amy, senior, University of Maryland

For more info:
Association of Computing Machinery (ACM)
1515 Broadway
17th Floor
New York, NY 10036-5701
(800) 342-6626
www.acm.org

Game design

Also known as:
Game development
Video game design

What it's about:

Game design and development blends art, science, and technical proficiency to produce computer games. In this major you learn how to design, program, test, and produce interactive games for a variety of platforms.

Is this for you?

You might like this major if you also like: telling stories (especially visually); intricate puzzles; comics; reading fiction, biography, history; experimentation; the give and take of working in group projects.

Consider this major if you are good at: teamwork; creativity; attention to detail; quantitative analysis; critical reading/thinking; time management ...*or have*...curiosity; initiative; leadership skills; writing skills; a strong visual imagination.

Recommended high school prep:

English 4, math 4 (including precalculus), lab science 3 (including physics), social studies 4, and a foreign language 2–3. If available, take courses in creative and technical writing, introductory programming, and art/media history.

Typical courses in this major:

Introduction to game development
Game design I, II
Sound and music for games
Computer animation
Fundamentals of 3D graphics
Simulation design
Digital game studies
Programming for games
Physics for games
Narrative writing for games
Story development for interactive media
Game culture
Engine-based design
Game production
Game criticism
Multiplayer network programming

Concentrations:

In college: game development, game sound design, game programming, game art/animation.

If you go on to grad school: game studies/theory, game production and management.

What the study of this major is like:

Courses in game design revolve around the five main components of a production team: design (fun and gameplay), art (2D and 3D animation, and interface), programming (game code and structure), sound (sound effects and music), and management (project scheduling and planning). The background of game culture (theory and criticism, sociology, marketing) is also covered.

Introductory classes focus on the fundamentals in each area, providing a foundation and framework for later classes. Some classes in the major are entirely focused on one topic, but more often the various components of game design and development are integrated.

This integrated approach will carry through in group projects as well. Game design is rarely a solo endeavor, so it is extremely important that you learn to work in a team that collectively provides the creative and technical expertise necessary to create a game that is not only fun and challenging, but also technically and artistically sound.

Classes combine theoretical presentation and discussion with hands-on practical instruction. You will be exposed to multiple game engines and production tools, and will be encouraged to experiment with new gameplay ideas and techniques. Classes are very often goal-oriented and focused on

181

the completion of a final group project. Many classes also delve into problem-solving techniques specific to each stage of game development.

Class structure can be loose and informal, but demanding. The ability to think critically and to take and receive useful criticism is required. Participation and interaction are key to the learning process. That's because games are an active medium that requires thought and response. They must challenge the user to not just watch something happen, but to make decisions that change outcomes in surprising ways.

Most game design programs are focused on preparing the student for a career in game development, but more and more schools are offering another focus that emphasizes social-conscious games, sometimes referred to as "serious games." Some colleges, especially those with graduate programs, also teach the use of game engines and game technology for alternative applications, such as virtual environments. Games are also used in other areas such as in education, training, simulation, and advertising.

Two-year or certificate programs are usually focused on creating technically adept workers, especially in the areas of 3D animation and programming, but contain little creative or artistic emphasis. An associate degree will qualify you for an entry-level job, but a bachelor's will help you into higher-level design positions.

Other majors you might like:

Animation
Computer graphics
Digital media
Graphic communications
Graphic design
Cinematography and film/video production
Creative writing
Web page/multimedia design
Instructional media
Software engineering
Drafting and design technology
Computational mathematics

Questions to ask colleges:

How long has the college offered this major? Are your graduates finding jobs in the industry?

What kind of facilities and software library does the school have to support game studies?

Do faculty have game industry experience?

Are there internship opportunities?

How many team-oriented game projects do students typically work on? Is there a focus on portfolio development?

How much extra-curricular support is there for independent game production?

Career options and trends:

Game designer; game artist; game producer; game tester; game sound designer.

Even in a slowing economy, the demand for computer and video games is expected to remain strong, and the need for skilled game designers is likely to increase. Nevertheless, the game industry is very competitive; so be prepared to present a wide variety of completed works (games, models, etc.) that show a range of abilities.

Insider's viewpoint:

"I love this field because of the creative possibilities. You can tell stories, visit odd places, be someone you can never be in real life and help save the day; and at the same time explore serious issues of social justice and cultural heritage."

—Professor Tom Dowd, Columbia College Chicago

For more info:

International Game Developers Association
19 Mantua Road
Mt. Royal, NJ 08061
www.igda.org

Information systems

Also known as:

Information science

What it's about:

Information systems is about bringing computers and people together. Majors learn how to conceive, design, and implement computer applications, systems, and information technology (IT) that meet the specific needs of individuals, businesses, and many other types of organizations.

Is this for you?

You might like this major if you also like: using computers to solve problems or accomplish tasks; showing others how to use computers; having your own Web site; playing computer games; working on team projects; tutoring. If you enjoy working both with computers and with people, this major could be a good choice.

Consider this major if you are good at: attention to detail; communicating; critical reading/thinking; math; organizing; teamwork *...or have...* initiative; listening skills; writing skills.

Recommended high school prep:

English 4, math 4 (including precalculus), lab science 4 (including physics), social studies 3, and a foreign language 2–3. If available, take courses that cover computer science and applications, psychology or sociology, speech, and writing.

Did you know...

...that in this major, you learn the same technology skills as a computer science major, but you must also develop good communication skills? An ability to communicate well with nontechnical users and to write specifications accurately is essential for students in this field.

Typical courses in this major:

Introduction to programming
Introduction to data structures
Operating systems
Systems analysis
Information retrieval and data mining
Object-oriented programming
Web development and e-commerce
Human and computer interaction
Principles of database design
Database applications
Multimedia systems
Computer graphics
Simulation and modeling
Game design
Decision support systems
Advanced information systems

Concentrations:

In college: computer interface design; systems analysis and design; decision support systems; information systems management; multimedia, visualization, and graphics; data communications and networking; management information systems; e-commerce and Web development.

If you go on to grad school: networking and security; advanced database applications; information systems assurance (IS auditing and security); computer-mediated communications; knowledge systems; artificial intelligence and expert systems; medical or biological informatics.

What the study of this major is like:

This major prepares you to bring computers and people together to solve problems. Computers are fast and logical; people are slower and intuitive, but also creative and insightful. To develop useful information systems and computer applications for business, government, science, and society, you need to understand both the benefits and the dangers that can occur when humans interact with computers. You must learn how humans solve problems, as well as how organizational processes work.

Generally, about half your course work is devoted to general education—math, science, speech, writing, social sciences, humanities, and electives, most of which you complete during your first two years. The work is geared to help you explore the way people solve problems and the way group and organizational processes function. What you learn can be translated into the design and implementation of computer systems and applications.

The technical skills you'll learn are similar to those taught in the computer science major. Although computer studies begin in your first year, you take most computer courses in your third and fourth years. Core requirements are generally spread evenly over the following areas:

Computer and programming concepts. Basic information and skills you'll use for developing computer hardware, computer operating systems, and computer programs.

Data and file structures. Basic ideas and techniques you'll use in creating the logical and physical structures of data and files.

Database management. Instruction that enables you to design, construct, and use database systems.

Data communications. Basic ideas, terms, design, and applications you'll need for developing data communications and networks.

Systems analysis and design. Tools and techniques you'll use in analyzing and developing computer-based systems.

In the lab, you'll be taught a variety of computer languages and systems. You are usually required to learn at least one high-level computer language well enough so that you can create programs in it. Electives and advanced courses may be offered in interface design, multimedia systems, expert systems, e-commerce and Internet applications, and computer-aided modeling and systems engineering.

The field of information systems is rapidly evolving; new material is constantly being developed. Among the essential things you learn as a major is how to master the professional literature and how to keep up with new developments.

Leading information systems programs are accredited by the Computing Sciences Accreditation Board (CSAB). Ideally, a program should encourage you to pursue an area of concentration but not to overemphasize that area (that is, not to take more than about five courses in one application). In fact, most courses should concentrate on concepts that cut across application areas—that can be useful in any number of situations.

Other majors you might like:

Computer science
Behavioral sciences
Communications
Web page/multimedia design
Information technology
E-commerce
Management information systems
Digital media
Electrical and communications engineering
Software engineering
Computer education
Emergency management/homeland security

Questions to ask colleges:

Are faculty members actively engaged in research? This is an important indicator of a good program. If instructors are doing research in areas that interest you, that's another good sign.

Are faculty members using the Web and group communications to extend discussions outside the classroom? If they are not, perhaps they are somewhat behind the times.

What types of computer networks are available on campus? Can the computer facilities be accessed from off-campus over the Internet? Are majors required to have their own laptops or other equipment?

Is this program accredited by the Computer Science Accreditation Board (CSAB)?

Career options and trends:

Systems analyst*; trainer/consultant; database administrator; information systems manager*; applications programmer.

Fear about computer jobs being outsourced overseas has discouraged many students from entering this field, but that fear is unjustified—more jobs are being created state-side than there are applicants to fill them.

Employment is expected to increase by over 30 percent through 2018, mostly due to a large number of new jobs being created.

Because of advances in Internet and mobile technology, however, you should be prepared to continually upgrade your skills throughout your career in order to remain employable.

Insider's viewpoint:

"We study a lot about design issues, figuring out what users find attractive, what they think is the easiest to read on Web pages, things of that sort. We're learning how to make things simpler, more accessible, because people in the computer industry have a tendency to make things hard."

—Erin, junior, Florida State University

For more info:

Association for Information Systems (AIS)
P.O. Box 2712
Atlanta, GA 30301-2712
(404) 651-0348
www.aisnet.org

Association for Computing Machinery (ACM)
1515 Broadway
New York, NY 10036
(800) 342-6626
www.acm.org

Information technology

What it's about:

As an information technology (IT) major, you'll study the ways in which information and computing systems support business, research, and communications needs.

Is this for you?

You might like this major if you also like: using computers to solve real-world problems; experimenting with computer hardware and software; playing computer games; being online.

Consider this major if you are good at: attention to detail; creativity; critical reading/thinking; math; organizing; research; teamwork *...or have...* patience; verbal skills; writing skills.

Recommended high school prep:

English 4, math 4 (including precalculus), lab science 4 (including physics), social studies 3, and a foreign language 2–3. If available, take courses that cover computer science and applications, Java programming, psychology or sociology, and business.

Did you know...

...that there are more IT jobs now than at the height of the dot-com boom? A recent report by the Association for Computing Machinery found that the 2 to 3 percent of IT jobs that are outsourced overseas each year are more than made up for by new jobs created in the U.S.

Typical courses in this major:

Fundamentals of programming
Computer systems and architecture
Database management
Web development
Information security
Introduction to computer science
Problem solving and algorithm design
Networking
Computer forensics
IT ethics and social issues
Probability and statistics
Discrete mathematics
Technical writing
Speech communication
Human and computer interaction
Systems analysis and design

Concentrations:

In college: Web development; networking; database management; digital communications; applications development.

If you go on to grad school: information security; data mining; computer forensics; medical information systems

What the study of this major is like:

Sometimes it's difficult to figure out how the IT major differs from other computer majors. It might help to imagine all the computer fields arranged along a line.

At one end are fields like computer science and computer engineering, which focus on the development of hardware and software. At the other end are topics like information systems, which explores the ways computers and people work together, and management information systems, which examines the application of computers to specific business processes, such as accounting or inventory control.

IT is in the middle, where technologies and concepts from both ends are integrated to build and administer an information infrastructure—systems, networks, applications, hardware, and software.

As a result, IT majors develop a breadth of knowledge through introductory courses in a range of subjects, including Web development, database management, networking, information security, programming, and human-computer interaction. They then acquire in-depth understanding by concentrating elective courses on a particular area.

For example, you may decide to specialize in Web development and take classes such as Web page design and database development for the Web. Or you may be drawn to digital communications and take classes in telecommunications networks.

Courses in discrete mathematics and probability and statistics are usually required. You won't need to take as much math as in other computer or engineering majors, but the work can still be challenging. Most programs also require supporting courses in natural science, business, speech, and writing. You will be encouraged to minor in a related field such as business, visual arts, or communication.

Classes usually combine lectures, hands-on lab experience, projects, presentations, and online applications. Teamwork is emphasized, along with writing, research, and presentation skills. In most four-year programs, you'll be expected to do a senior project in which you will collaborate with other students to solve an IT problem. This learning approach mirrors the real world of IT.

The academic lifestyle of an IT major is fast paced and energized. Most likely you'll be taught by instructors from the industry, who bring real-world experience to the classroom and are up-to-date on the latest developments.

A good IT program should offer a balance between theory and applied skills. You'll want to see plenty of hands-on lab experience, but not so much that you'll be acquiring only technical skills or short-term (vendor-specific) knowledge. Programs administered by schools of business may include more courses in finance, accounting, marketing, and management, while majors that have evolved from computer science departments may require more math and programming.

IT is available in many two-year programs at community colleges, where you can get a good grounding in the field. If you go that route, though, you should think about continuing on to a four-year program at some point—you'll have better career prospects with a bachelor's degree.

Other majors you might like:
Management information systems
Computer engineering technology

Systems engineering
Bioinformatics
Information systems
Software engineering
Library science
Communications
Applied mathematics
Medical office computer specialist
Behavioral sciences
E-commerce

Questions to ask colleges:
Are professors working in the field, applying the latest trends in information technology?

Will the college help me find an internship?

Is the program recognized by the Accreditation Board for Engineering and Technology (ABET)?

Career options and trends:
IT project manager; tech support; network administrator; Web developer; Web site administrator; information security analyst; database administrator; applications developer; software tester.

Job growth for IT professionals is predicted to remain strong through 2018. Businesses continue to depend heavily on networks and are particularly concerned about cyber-security. Some IT jobs (such as routine programming and customer support) are being outsourced overseas; but in diminishing numbers, relative to the number of new jobs being created. Jobs that require on-site support or are security related will remain domestic. Job prospects are also better for those who can combine IT with other areas of business, such as e-commerce or supply chain management.

Women students are often attracted to IT because of the opportunities for collaborative work, particularly in health-related fields and in government.

For more info:
Association for Computing Machinery (ACM)
1515 Broadway
New York, NY 10036
(800) 342-6626
www.acm.org

Education

To be an educator, you have to be educated. It makes sense that education is the field with the most graduate degrees awarded, both masters' and doctorates. It's second only to business in the number of all degrees earned. And it is one of the few fields showing good job prospects during these recessionary times.

Teaching is something you should know about already. You've seen teachers in action for many years now. You can probably think of a teacher who has influenced your vision of the future.

"This is truly a career where you can influence the hearts and minds of young teenagers, ensuring them a healthier and more productive adulthood," says Jeanneine Jones, a professor of middle school education at the University of North Carolina at Charlotte. "Students touch my life and I touch theirs; they teach me and I teach them. It's a wonderful relationship built on mutual respect and pervasive caring."

You may be wondering why a middle school teacher like Jones is working at a college. She became a university instructor so she can pass on her skills and knowledge to the next generation of teachers. To become a teacher isn't easy. To begin with, you have to prove that you're a good student in your first year or two of college. Then you may qualify to enter an education program. There you learn two big things—the subject you'll be teaching and how to teach it. You'll also have to work as a student teacher for a semester, under the watchful eye of an experienced educator. That's similar to the way doctors learn—by working for real. Finally, teachers take a test to get certified. Many states require another test to show that you know the subject(s) you'll be teaching.

Education is a hot topic lately. Things are changing: as part of it's economic recovery plan, the government is spending more money on education than ever before in order to ensure that all students can participate and compete in the global economy. Public schools are under pressure to prove that kids are learning.

Teaching may not be a breeze, but it can make you walk on air. "The sense of accomplishment that I feel after teaching a class is as good as climbing to the top of a mountain," says Professor Mary C.

Clement of Berry College. "I feel that I have won the lottery when students 'get' the lesson presented and when something that they learned in my class helps them to attain success."

Making the Grade

In a way, you have already begun your teaching career by working hard in school to master a number of academic subjects.

"Studying to be a teacher involves learning the subject you plan to teach extremely well, so students must be prepared to complete a major or the equivalent if they are going to teach a subject like math, English, French, history, or physics," Clement advises.

Why not talk to some of your teachers about their college years and how they chose their schools? They may tell you that some universities have separate divisions of education, while others offer the education major as part of studies like arts or sciences.

When comparing education programs, you'll find that some emphasize teaching reading and literacy and that colleges use technology in different ways. However, the standards for a major are mostly set by the state in which the college is located. When you finish your bachelor's degree, you'll need to be certified in the state where you'll teach. Specific certifications go with particular types of teaching, like early childhood, elementary, middle school, secondary (high) school, special education, and physical education. In general, look for a program that's been approved by the National Council for Accreditation of Teacher Education (www.ncate.org). And be sure to ask the college about the percentage of its grads who become certified.

Of course, teaching isn't the only career that educators pursue. Other jobs include administrator (like your principal), school counselor, school psychologist, curriculum director, and education researcher; or you might be interested in becoming a corporate trainer to use your teaching skills in the business world.

Employment prospects are good, partly because many teachers are expected to retire soon. Also, as states and schools try to improve education and boost course requirements for students, more and better-qualified teachers are needed. Teaching jobs are likely to increase at all grade levels through 2018. Job opportunities vary, of course, depending on the region and the subject. Teachers of foreign languages, math and science, and bilingual education are especially in demand.

Teachers often go to grad school to obtain certifications and credentials such as an "endorsement," which allows you to teach a particular subject, like reading. Other grad students in education focus on advanced work in their subjects so that they become experts in their field who can inspire and enlighten students.

"It is my philosophy that teachers are not just subject matter experts, but dispensers of hope for students of all ages," offers Clement.

With any luck, you've had a teacher like that. With hard work and dedication, you may become one.

Early childhood education

What it's about:

This major prepares you to teach infants and children through age eight, in all subjects through grade 3. You receive practicum/internship experience with small children in a variety of settings, such as day care, before- and after-school programs, pre-K (kindergarten) programs, early start, and K through grade 3 classrooms.

Is this for you?

You might like this major if you also like: working with very young children; watching them grow and change; volunteer or part-time work at day care or community centers; crafts; games; puppet shows; team sports; being creative; tutoring.

Consider this major if you are good at: active listening; caring/nurturing; coaching; communicating; critical reading/thinking; empathizing with children's thoughts and feelings; teamwork *...or have...* an open mind; manual dexterity; patience; physical stamina.

Recommended high school prep:

English 4, math 3, lab science 3, social studies 3, and a foreign language 2–3. In addition, take a course in family and consumer science (home economics), especially if there is a child development component; and courses in psychology and sociology, if available.

Did you know...

...that early childhood is perhaps the most flexible field in education, with numerous areas in which to gain expertise? In fact, with just a few additional courses, you can pick up credentials in special education, child development, or literacy for early childhood along with your major, thus increasing your career possibilities.

Typical courses in this major:

Child development and learning
Parent–child relations
Curriculum methods in early education
Early childhood children's literature
Music methods
Arts and the child
Early childhood language arts
Early childhood mathematics
Social development and play
Educational psychology
Classroom management and behavior
Instructional resources and technology
Professional issues or foundations of education
Inclusion methods for special-needs students
Diversity of learners methods
Early childhood health and physical education

Concentrations:

Generally, none available.

What the study of this major is like:

Most early childhood education programs require a broad, general background in education; a core of professional courses that include education basics, knowledge of curriculum, and teaching methods; and opportunities to observe and student-teach in a variety of settings and at a variety of age and grade levels.

Because the early childhood curriculum focuses on a variety of subjects, you should take general education courses similar to those required in colleges of liberal arts and sciences. Your goal is to learn communication, critical-thinking, and problem-solving skills while you study the humanities, math, biological and physical sciences, social sciences, history, health, and physical education. You may be expected to complete a minor, or concentration, in one of the general education areas. If so, general education courses would make up between two-thirds and three-fourths of your undergraduate course work.

In professional education courses, you study the history and philosophy of early childhood education as well as early childhood growth and development. You also explore curriculum and classroom organization, by planning, putting into practice, and evaluating a program appropriate for young children. Since preschoolers learn through play, you learn how to introduce language arts, social skills, and basic math and science concepts through play and other hands-on activities. In addition, you learn how to introduce academics at the kindergarten and early primary grade levels. You may also take courses on teaching special-needs children in the regular classroom.

Your professional education includes fieldwork, called practicums, in which you observe and participate in programs for young children in settings such as elementary schools, child care centers, and Head Start programs. You conclude with student teaching or an internship, as you take on increasing responsibility for a class. Most programs require you to do a semester of student teaching in pre-K through grade 3 settings, or perhaps several student-teaching assignments at different age or grade levels.

As an early childhood education major, you will probably be taught in lectures, small-group interactive projects, discussions, demonstrations, and presentations. You may take part in distance-learning through video segments and hear expert speakers. In your third and fourth years, you will spend a great deal of (unpaid) time working with children in schools; keep that point in mind if you plan to hold a job during college. While you are student-teaching (also unpaid), you will have no time for a job, so plan to save money for that final semester.

Early childhood programs may emphasize different teaching philosophies. Many programs include all models and theories, and let you pick the approach that best suits you. Others may focus on one model, such as the Bank Street or the Montessori approach. In general, most quality programs follow standards set by the National Association for the Education of Young Children (NAEYC).

In all states, to be licensed to teach pre-K–3, you must have a four-year degree. Some states do not offer the early childhood teaching certificate but provide instead a "kindergarten endorsement" on an elementary teaching certificate. In these states, early childhood education may be a minor offered to elementary education majors. Some institutions offer teacher certification for early childhood education only at the graduate level. Many states are moving to requiring a master's degree or the equivalent for continued teacher certification. If you think you may relocate, check to see if the state you are moving to will honor the degree you plan to pursue.

Other majors you might like:
Elementary education
Middle school education
Special education
Teacher assistance
Communication disorders
Sociology
Human development and family studies
Behavioral sciences
Psychology
Social work
Child development
Child care management

Questions to ask colleges:
Where do students complete their fieldwork, practicum, internship, and student teaching? When do these projects occur in the program? How many hours are required? What kind of support do students receive in the assignments? What choices, if any, do students have in these placements? Are the settings rural, urban, suburban, metropolitan, or a mix?

What are the prerequisites for full admission into the early childhood major (e.g., required courses, GPA, cutoff scores on the SAT, ACT, or PRAXIS I exams)? Do I need a background check?

Career options and trends:
Teacher assistant or aide; pre-school teacher*; kindergarten teacher*; child care administrator; family service coordinator.

An associate degree is usually required for teacher aides or teacher paraprofessionals to work in public school classrooms. These persons may work with small children as well as older children with disabilities.

Center directors often have a master's degree, but it is not a requirement.

In general, the shortage of early childhood/ elementary education teachers is less severe than for teachers of older students. However, the South (Florida, Georgia, and the Carolinas) and the West (Arizona, Texas, Nevada, and California) have a higher demand for early education teachers because of their increasing numbers of young children. Job prospects continue to be better in urban and isolated rural areas. In many regions, teachers who are willing to relocate and who hold more than one license/certification, such as in early childhood and special education or ESL (English as a second language), will have an advantage.

For more info:
National Association for the Education of Young
  Children (NAEYC)
1313 L St., N.W.
Washington, DC 20005
(800) 424-2460
www.naeyc.org

Elementary education

What it's about:
Elementary education majors prepare to teach children in the elementary grades, which can range from K (kindergarten) through 8, depending on the school system. In addition to learning how to teach specific subjects, such as reading and math, you study the way children develop socially and intellectually, and you get hands-on professional experience in teaching and learning.

Is this for you?
You might like this major if you also like: working with children; tutoring; team sports; volunteer or community service; public speaking; problem solving.

Consider this major if you are good at: active listening; communicating; creativity; critical reading/thinking; organizing; persuading/influencing ...*or have...* enthusiasm; flexibility; patience; physical stamina.

Recommended high school prep:
English 4, math 3, lab science 3, social studies 3, and a foreign language 2–3. Take any computer science or applications courses available. Four years of Spanish is highly recommended, because fluency in that language would be a great asset for a teacher.

Typical courses in this major:
Child development and learning
History and philosophy of education
Curriculum methods in elementary education
Teaching language arts
Teaching mathematics
Teaching science
Teaching social studies
Reading fundamentals
Educational psychology
Classroom management and behavior
Educational assessment and measurement
Instructional resources and technology
Special education needs and issues
Schooling in a culturally diverse society

Concentrations:
Generally, none available.

What the study of this major is like:
Almost all elementary education programs offer a liberal arts foundation, a professional education core that includes course work in teaching methods, and a variety of student-teaching experiences in elementary school settings. The goal is to prepare you for state certification to teach in the elementary grades. States have different rules, and there may be special requirements for teaching kindergarten through third grade (K–3) or grades 6–8. In addition to completing the elementary education major, many states require students to pass tests in subject matter, communications, and knowledge of methods, in order to be certified. Some states also require a second major in a particular subject area (e.g., language arts) or specialty (e.g., reading).

Most elementary school teachers instruct one class in several subjects, using a wide range of tools, such as games, music, artwork, films, books, and computers. Therefore, you should probably take between 50 and 60 percent of your course work in the humanities, social sciences, natural sciences, technology, and mathematics—mostly during your first two years. Generally, you do not become fully admitted into the major until your second year, after you meet certain requirements. They vary among colleges, so be sure to find out what they are before you enroll in a program.

In methods courses, you focus on ways to instruct children, and you develop your capacity to solve problems that may arise as you introduce reading, language arts, mathematics, science, and social studies to young children. You also gain practice in planning lessons, evaluating learning, and managing the classroom. Some elementary education majors can minor in early childhood or special education.

Throughout the major, practical experiences in schools are typically interwoven with classroom studies. As you observe, assist, and teach elementary children, what you've learned in your classes becomes more meaningful and more useful. Student teaching, which normally occurs in your last semester, is often the high point of the elementary education major. This experience, under the supervision of both college and school instructors, gives you a big boost in your goal of becoming a teacher.

Other majors you might like:
Early childhood education
Middle school education
Special education
Teacher assistance
Reading teacher education
Communications
Family/consumer sciences education
Behavioral sciences
Psychology
Social work
Child development
Sociology

Questions to ask colleges:
Is the program accredited by the National Council for Accreditation of Teacher Education?

Career options and trends:
Besides teaching in the elementary schools, majors who pursue appropriate graduate training can become school administrators, educational researchers, curriculum specialists, reading specialists, or school counselors.

Currently there is no shortage of elementary school teachers, and enrollment of elementary school children is projected to rise slowly overall; but these factors will vary by region. Fast-growing states in the South and West—particularly California, Texas, Georgia, Idaho, Hawaii, Alaska, and New Mexico—will experience the largest enrollment increases. Minority teachers and teachers who are

bilingual in Spanish are in short supply, and demand for these will grow with the rising enrollment of minority and Spanish-speaking children.

While certification requirements vary by state, all states require a bachelor's degree and completion of an approved teacher education program with a prescribed number of subject and education credits as well as supervised student teaching. About one-third of the states also require technology training, and some require specific minimum grade point averages as well.

Insider's viewpoint:
"Most of the assignments focus on analyzing classroom practices—tell why you like it, how you'd change it. Then you plan your own lessons and implement those plans."

—Kau'i, senior, University of Hawaii

For more info:
National Association for the Education of Young
 Children (NAEYC)
1313 L St., N.W.
Washington, DC 20005
(800) 424-2460
www.naeyc.org

Middle school education

Also known as:
Junior high education

What it's about:
This major prepares you for an entry-level license or certification to teach specific content areas (such as language arts, mathematics, social studies, or science) in middle school, intermediate school, or junior high school, which may include grades 4–9, depending on the school system.

Is this for you?
You might like this major if you also like: community service; working with youth; reading; writing; public speaking; tutoring; coaching; helping friends and others with their problems; leadership roles in high school.

Consider this major if you are good at: caring/nurturing; counseling; critical reading/thinking; leadership; organizing; persuading/influencing; teamwork ...*or have...* patience; physical stamina; verbal skills.

Recommended high school prep:
English 4, math 3, lab science 3, social studies 3, and a foreign language 2–3. Course work that helps you develop your reading and communication skills is essential.

Did you know...
...that elementary school teachers teach children, and high school teachers teach content, but middle school teachers teach content to children?

...that the middle school years are commonly labeled the turning point in the life span? Middle school teachers can have a real impact on young people, encouraging them to become healthy, productive adults.

Typical courses in this major:
Introduction to middle school education
Early adolescent learners
Classroom management
Specific subject curriculum
Content methods
Philosophy of middle grades education
Curriculum of middle grades education
Reading and writing across subject areas
Research and analysis of middle grades education
Health and safety issues in middle schools
Instructional design and technology
Teaching students with special needs
Schooling in a culturally diverse society

Concentrations:
Specific content areas, such as science, math, language arts, social studies, and music.

What the study of this major is like:
As a middle school education major, you have the opportunity to make a real difference in the life of young adults. Although early adolescents are often portrayed as defiant and confused, people who work with middle school students generally agree that they are sensitive, stimulating, motivated, and eager to contribute to the world around them.

Majors study the developmental and learning styles of the 10- to 15-year-old and examine the ways in which students can be given structure and guidance, as well as a sense of independence and personal responsibility. You will also take about six to eight courses in one or two subject areas, such as language arts, mathematics, social studies, and science. As a whole, the program prepares you to enter a school knowing what to teach, how to teach, and the needs of your audience.

Although courses contain some lectures, they feature hands-on work experiences, called practicums or clinical hours, in local public and private schools. These are included in the course assignments and are a critical part of your workload.

They are designed to help you transfer campus discussions and studies into successful classroom applications.

These experiences culminate in a full semester of student teaching in your last year. It will enable you to master the material you've been studying and to practice your presentation of it under the supervision of both college and middle school instructors. Perhaps even more important, your student-teaching semester will help you deal with the frustrations often associated with teaching, including enforcing classroom discipline, managing your time, and motivating unresponsive students.

While colleges vary, all strong programs should require the study of at least one content area. They should also communicate an in-depth understanding of adolescent development and middle school philosophy. Courses should cover lesson plan design, effective teacher behavior, and classroom management. Finally, you should be given opportunities to apply your course work in local schools and related community programs, especially in a challenging, well-supported student-teaching semester.

Other majors you might like:
Child development
Secondary education
Special education
ESL teacher education
Bilingual/bicultural education
Human development and family studies
Native American education
Liberal arts and sciences
Juvenile corrections
Youth ministry
Social work
Psychology

Questions to ask colleges:
Does this college have a clearly identified middle school program, which includes a professor to coordinate it? Do core faculty members have experience teaching in grades 6–8?

Does the surrounding region have strong middle schools for student-teaching work?

Career options and trends:
Middle school teacher*; secondary school teacher*; elementary school teacher; school counselor; school administrator*.

An additional, but related, license or certification is required for teaching at the elementary or secondary school level. An advanced degree is necessary for positions as a school counselor, administrator, or supervisor.

This area of education is one of the most marketable in the country, but demand will vary by region and subject specialty. Currently, those most in demand are qualified to teach mathematics, science (especially chemistry and physics), bilingual education, foreign languages, and computer science.

Insider's viewpoint:
"Once I really, really know these children, they emerge as stimulating, and stimulated, young adults who are sensitive, capable, and productive citizens. They touch my life and I touch theirs, they teach me and I teach them. It's a wonderful relationship built on mutual respect and caring."

—Professor Jeanneine P. Jones, University of North Carolina at Charlotte

For more info:
National Middle School Association (NMSA)
4151 Executive Parkway
Suite 300
Westerville, OH 43081
(800) 528-6672
www.nmsa.org

Physical education

What it's about:

Physical education majors prepare to teach physical education (PE) or to coach sports in public or private schools, kindergarten through twelfth grade (K–12).

Is this for you?

You might like this major if you also like: helping people; sports and competition; physical exercise; good health habits; coaching; tutoring; a sense of humor.

Consider this major if you are good at: caring/nurturing; coaching; critical reading/thinking; leadership; persuading/influencing; sports, gymnastics, or dance; teamwork *...or have...* patience; physical stamina; verbal skills; writing skills.

Recommended high school prep:

English 4, math 3, lab science 3, social studies 3, and a foreign language 2–3. If possible, take extra physical education credits to enhance your skills, or serve as a physical education assistant in addition to participating in team sports. Knowledge of or fluency in a foreign language (especially Spanish) will make you more marketable.

Did you know...

...that this is not the easy major many people think it is! Learning to teach physical education means more than playing games. You must love sports and also enjoy teaching a variety of subjects to children and adolescents. In addition, you will be expected to continue your educational and professional development throughout your career.

Typical courses in this major:

Biology
Physics
Anatomy and physiology
Human growth and development
Motor learning and development
Observation and analysis of motor skills
Physical education teaching methods
Methods for teaching lifetime fitness
Physical education curriculum
Multicultural education
Educational psychology
History and philosophy of physical education
Tests and measures in physical education
Administration of physical education programs
Adapted physical education
Coaching effectiveness

Concentrations:

Elementary school physical education; secondary school physical education; adapted physical education; athletic coaching.

What the study of this major is like:

If you want to become a physical education teacher, you should generally enjoy many types of sports and exercise. Since few children and adolescents are elite athletes, knowing how to work with students at all skill levels is essential. Another plus is to feel comfortable speaking to groups and to be a skillful communicator. In addition, you should be warm and caring in your approach to young people. Good physical education teachers are role models of active, healthy lifestyles.

As a PE major, you take general education courses during your first two years. Then you enroll in science courses that focus on how the human body is affected by exercise and sports and how performance can be improved. Other courses include child development, psychology, and curriculum and instruction, and you'll have opportunities to work with children in supervised field settings. Although you will probably be required to take part in numerous recreational activities and sports, don't expect to get much academic credit. At the end of most programs, you'll do student teaching.

Many majors are challenged by the lab sciences that are often required (for example, anatomy and

199

physiology and biology). In your third and fourth years, you typically take practicum courses, which give you extensive teaching practice in local schools. You'll learn to teach such subjects as sport skills, gymnastics, dance, lifetime activities, and fitness to diverse students in a range of settings. Practicum courses can be nerve-racking, though, because you teach real kids in real schools. After practicums, you usually do your student teaching. During this semester-long assignment, you gradually assume the full responsibilities of a teacher. Student teaching is often challenging, as you experience both the difficulties and the rewards of the profession.

Requirements for teaching certification vary from state to state. But programs that are approved by the National Council for Accreditation of Teacher Education (NCATE) meet the standards that ensure effective teaching preparation. In many states, to obtain a teaching certificate, you also need to earn acceptable scores on competency exams (for example, the PRAXIS I and II), and some physical education programs require you to pass competency exams in order to graduate. Most physical education programs will qualify you to be certified to teach K–12. However, in some programs you can major in elementary school physical education or secondary school physical education. If you enjoy working with young children, for example, you might seek out a program that specializes in elementary physical education.

Other majors you might like:
Athletic training
Exercise sciences
Sports and fitness administration
Parks, recreation, and leisure studies
Health teacher education
Physical therapy
Occupational therapy
Biology
Food and nutrition studies
Dance therapy
Recreational therapy
Community health services

Questions to ask colleges:
How much hands-on teaching experience is given in an actual school setting? Good programs should provide ample practical experience leading up to student teaching.

Is the program NCATE accredited?

Career options and trends:
Physical education teacher (K–12)*; recreation supervisor (community or private setting); aerobic dance instructor; physical trainer.

The demand for physical education teachers across the United States is not as high as it is for teachers in areas such as math and science, bilingual education, and special education. However, some districts (especially urban and rural) need teachers in all subject areas, including physical education.

Obtaining a minor in another teaching area or athletic coaching can really improve your career prospects. A physical education teacher who is dual certified (can teach physical education and an academic subject, or can teach physical education and coach a sport) is much more marketable. Increasing awareness of the growing problem of childhood obesity should also increase demand for PE teachers who can help combat this problem.

For more info:
American Alliance for Health, Physical Education,
  Recreation and Dance (AAHPERD)
1990 Association Drive
Reston, VA 20191-1598
www.aahperd.org

Secondary education

Also known as:

High school teacher education

What it's about:

This major prepares you to be a high school teacher. You learn the curriculum and methods of teaching a specific subject (math, science, English, history, foreign language, and so forth), organization and management of a classroom, needs of diverse learners, and the role of high schools in today's society.

Is this for you?

You might like this major if you also like: Scouting; 4-H; extracurricular activities; sports; coaching; tutoring; working at summer camps; leading, not following. Idealism is a good attribute for teachers.

Consider this major if you are good at: caring/nurturing; creativity; organizing; persuading/influencing ...*or have...* initiative; patience; verbal skills; writing skills.

Recommended high school prep:

English 4, math 3, lab science 3, social studies 3, and a foreign language 2–3. Take a course in psychology, if one is offered. You should take a four-year sequence in the subject you plan to teach; if advanced or honors courses in that subject are available, taking those is highly recommended.

Did you know...

...that majoring in education as an undergraduate is generally the quickest way to become a teacher? If you decide after college to become a teacher, you will probably need to return to college for two more years.

...that in many states, you may have to undergo a criminal background check and be fingerprinted before observing or student-teaching in a public school district?

Typical courses in this major:

Introduction to secondary education
Issues and trends in secondary education
Adolescent behavior and development
Educational psychology
History and foundations of education
Educational technology
Specific subject curriculum
Specific subject instructional methods
Classroom management
Diversity/multicultural education
Teaching students with special needs
Testing in the classroom

Concentrations:

Generally, none available.

What the study of this major is like:

The secondary education major provides a foundation in the arts and sciences, in-depth study in a particular subject, and courses in teaching procedures. To achieve their goals, most students take a double major or the equivalent.

In introductory courses, which may include visits to schools to observe and interview teachers, you will explore the conditions of today's schools, the diversity of students, and the role of schools in today's society. Educational psychology courses focus on the way children and teenagers learn and provide strategies for motivating learners and for meeting the needs of all students, including those with disabilities, language deficiencies, and emotional problems. You will also take at least one special education course.

In content-based course work, you learn *what* to teach; how to prepare lesson plans, unit plans, and tests; and how to meet state and national teaching standards. In methods courses, you learn *how* to teach. For these upper-level courses, you may spend three to five hours a week in local schools before you begin student teaching.

A course in classroom management provides strategies for organizing time, space, and materials, as well as guidelines for creating a management style that suits your needs. In other courses you gain practice in giving lectures, doing demonstrations, running audio/visual equipment, and maintaining classroom discipline. Future science teachers learn how to supervise laboratory work; students interested in vocational education learn how to give students hands-on experience with tools and equipment.

Your final activity as a major is a semester of student teaching—working with a teacher, every school day for the entire day. You still pay full tuition and fees during student teaching, and you are not paid by the school district. You may also have to travel a considerable distance from campus, and it is difficult to hold a part-time job while you student-teach. Graduates say that this semester is the most challenging, but often the most useful, time of their college years.

At some colleges, you are required to double-major in the subject area you plan to teach; at others you major in your subject area and minor in secondary education or a teacher certification program. Many colleges gear their programs to the certification requirements of the state in which they are located; keep this point in mind when you are considering where to apply to college.

Other majors you might like:

Middle school education
Special education
ESL teacher education
Liberal arts and sciences
Agricultural education services
Human resources management
Juvenile corrections
Psychology
Social work
Sociology

Questions to ask colleges:

Is the program accredited by both the state body for teacher certification and by the National Council for Accreditation in Teacher Education (NCATE)?

How are student-teaching placements made? Are they assigned or do students have a choice? For how long is the full-time student-teaching placement, and how far away from campus may it be located?

Does this teacher education program require minimum exam scores for admission? Since some states require candidates to have a certain ACT, SAT, or PRAXIS I score in order to be granted a teaching license, many colleges now require such scores for admission to the major.

Career options and trends:

High school teacher*; school principal or assistant*; school superintendent or assistant; curriculum director; school counselor; educational writer; program director in Scouting, 4-H, youth programs, churches, or other organizations.

Although states have different certification requirements, most require you to have a bachelor's degree (and in some states, an additional year or a master's degree) in a program accredited by the state and by either the Teacher Education Accreditation Council (TEAC) or NCATE; to complete a major (or the equivalent) in your chosen subject area(s); and to pass a state exam, the Praxis II exam, or another test.

Additional licensing or certification and an advanced degree are necessary for a position as a principal, superintendent, or other upper-level administrator.

The acute shortage of math and science high school teachers in many parts of the United States is being called the "silent crisis." Shortages also exist for foreign languages, bilingual education, and special education. Teachers who earn certification in more than one subject are highly employable, and so are teachers who choose to work in non-English-speaking or disadvantaged communities. Graduates with ESL training are also in demand.

For more info:

American Federation of Teachers (AFT)
555 New Jersey Ave. N.W.,
Washington, DC 20001
(202) 879-4400
www.aft.org

Special education

What it's about:

The special education major prepares you to meet the educational, social, emotional, and vocational needs of infants, children, and youth with disabilities. Your professional preparation includes specialized course work, field experiences with children with disabilities, and student teaching.

Is this for you?

You might like this major if you also like: helping people, especially people who appear to be different; working with people one-on-one; multitasking.

Consider this major if you are good at: caring/nurturing; coaching; counseling; critical reading/thinking; leadership; organizing; teamwork *...or have...* initiative; patience; verbal skills.

Recommended high school prep:

English 4, math 3, lab science 3, social studies 3, and a foreign language 2–3.

Did you know...

...that, because special education serves a wide range of students, special educators work in many settings, both in and out of schools? Besides schools, settings include hospitals, private practice environments, health care centers, and correctional facilities.

...that many states and the federal government offer scholarships and loan forgiveness to students entering the special education field?

Typical courses in this major:

Introduction to psychology
Introduction to sociology
Statistics
Human development
Introduction to special education
Educational assessment
Behavior management
Curriculum and instruction
Speech/language development
Content area courses (e.g., reading, math)
Computers/technology for teachers
Educational policy and law
Integrated fieldwork
Student teaching

Concentrations:

In college: early childhood, elementary, or secondary special education; learning disabilities; mental retardation; autism; deaf/hard of hearing; visual impairments; severe/profound disabilities; emotional/behavioral disorders.

If you go on to grad school: policy studies; vocational training; transition to adult services; educational administration.

What the study of this major is like:

Special education refers to instruction that is specifically designed to meet the needs of infants, children, and youth with disabilities; special education services cover infants through 21-year-olds. To become a special education professional, you must develop skills in educational assessment and instruction for students with disabilities and in working with their families. Your course work usually includes lectures and field placement, or hands-on activities, such as assisting in a special education classroom.

In your first and second years as a major, you will probably take introductory and core courses in education, psychology, and child development, along with general studies. In your third year, you explore the types of disabilities you are likely to encounter in your work. In addition, you observe classrooms and obtain supervised field placement experience.

In field placements, you receive hands-on experience working with children with disabilities in a special education setting, such as a regular classroom, resource room, self-contained classroom, vocational-technical school, or institution. During your first field placement experiences, you spend most of your time observing the teacher with whom you are placed; but as you progress, you gradually assume greater responsibility. In your fourth year, you take advanced courses in special education, along with electives, and do student teaching. By then, you will do most, if not all, of the teaching.

Being a special education teacher often means being an "educational manager"—the person who coordinates all the education and training a child receives. Many students with disabilities require the services of several professionals (such as school psychologists, speech therapists, occupational therapists). As a special educator, you need to know what role these professionals will play in a student's education and how their work relates to yours. In fact, you and the other service providers will function as a multidisciplinary team—each contributing professional and personal skills for the benefit of the child.

Several features distinguish special education programs. First, colleges vary in their approach to special education. For example, some colleges offer dual programs in elementary and special education, with less emphasis on special education than in a program focusing on that field alone. Further, some programs offer a generalized treatment of special education, while in others you can specialize by age level or type of disability. While some programs take four years to complete, others take five; some offer graduate credits and/or degrees in conjunction with the bachelor's program. Colleges also differ in the amount of required field experiences. Finally, special education programs may be distinguished by their philosophies. Programs may differ according to their emphasis on inclusion of individuals with disabilities in community settings and on using research to inform your teaching.

Majors are expected to demonstrate professional behavior from the first semester they are placed in classrooms. Professional behavior includes punctuality, time management, and the ability to interact as an adult with students, school staff, and students' parents. Opportunities to establish a network of potential job contacts begin the day you start your field placement. A career in special education is rewarding, exciting, and intellectually challenging.

Other majors you might like:
Communication disorders
Child development
Audiology/speech pathology
Education of learning disabled
Education of physically handicapped
Early childhood education
American sign language (ASL)
Art therapy
Occupational therapy
Physical therapy
Recreational therapy
Human development and family studies

Questions to ask colleges:
How much and which types of fieldwork are required? Where are students placed and who supervises field placements? What ages or disability types are students being prepared to teach?

Does the special education program have a more selective admissions process than other divisions of the college?

Which certification do students earn? Is certification transferable to other states?

Is the program focused on special education, or is training split between general and special education? Does the program provide graduate credits?

Career options and trends:
Special education teacher*; special education instructional assistant; special education advocate; educational administrator*; parent educator; psychologist; lobbyist; policy analyst; educational researcher.

The special education major prepares you to work in a school or institutional setting. With graduate study, students often pursue careers as administrators of special education. Advanced training may also lead to a career as a speech/language pathologist, audiologist, physical therapist, occupational therapist, school psychologist, school counselor, evaluation specialist, teacher trainer, parent/community coordinator, rehabilitation counselor, vocational/special needs teacher, or adaptive physical education instructor. A state certificate or license is required for teaching in public elementary and secondary schools.

Job opportunities in special education are excellent. All areas of special education are in the process of evolving, especially at the early childhood and secondary/transition levels. All regions of the country are experiencing shortages of special education teachers, and long-term projections indicate that the shortages will continue.

Insider's viewpoint:

"It is exciting to be in a profession that continually offers intellectual challenges, while serving individuals who have historically been relegated to the fringe of society."

—Dawn Eddy Molloy, University of Maryland

For more info:

American Association of Colleges for Teacher
    Education (AACTE)
1307 New York Ave., N.W.
Suite 300
Washington, DC 20005
(202) 293-2450
www.aacte.org

Engineering

Have you ever wondered how a DVD works? Or what makes a metal magnetic? Do you enjoy brain teasers? Can you twist a wire hanger into something useful? Do you secretly love the math story problems that other students dread? You, my friend, might be an engineer.

But it's not enough to be mechanically inclined or have the ability to visualize in 3-D. To become an engineer takes an awful lot of work.

"Realize that engineering is not a 'party' major. You will have to work harder than your friends, but the rewards and satisfaction are worth it," says Lyle D. Feisel, a dean emeritus at the State University of New York at Binghamton.

Engineers design systems, components, and processes to make life better. Whenever a plane takes off, a computer boots up, the lights go on, a car is driven, a building constructed, a medical device used, a phone call made, a photo taken, or a product sold, it all comes down to engineering. When engineers show up for work, they may do research, development, production, construction, operations, quality improvement, management, technical sales, consulting, or teaching. Jobs in the field and studies of engineering cover materials, mining and metals, manufacturing, marine engineering, and mechanics—and those are just the ones that start with "m."

Anyone who goes into engineering can look forward to lifelong learning about leading-edge science—nuclear and alternative energy, information technologies, integrated circuits, aerospace and defense, global positioning systems, genetic research.

Colleges offer more than 30 engineering majors. The most common majors offered are electrical, mechanical, civil, chemical, and computer engineering. More than half of engineers find work in these areas. Some new majors include architectural engineering, biochemical engineering, robotics, environmental engineering, manufacturing engineering, nanotechnology, biomaterials, and energy management technology.

Did you know that engineers earn some of the highest salaries for people with a bachelor's degree? And that's not all; since fewer students are choosing engineering, overall job opportunities are expected to be good. Of course, jobs depend on how the economy is doing. But even during economic downturns, many engineering efforts—like building a bridge—are based on long-term plans that will continue through lean times.

Where will you go?

As you look at colleges of engineering, you'll see that many undergraduate programs look alike because standards are in place. If a program is good enough, it is "ABET-accredited" by the organization formerly known as the Accreditation Board for Engineering and Technology (but whose official name now is just the acronym).

How do colleges differ? Mostly in their approach. Some schools are more hands-on and mechanical, giving you a sort of job training through work in laboratories. Other colleges focus on theoretical concepts and abstract mathematical modeling to prepare you for graduate school. Graduate tracks include math, basic science, engineering sciences, design, and research. Some specific graduate areas are wireless engineering, hydrosystems, biochemical or pharmaceutical engineering, and software user interface design.

It's important to find out if the school is a research college that attracts talented professors. Also judge the quality of facilities like the design, computing, and testing laboratories and the libraries. Other factors to look at are admissions criteria, location, tuition and fees, and financial aid. How about work-study programs, part-time employment on campus, internships, or cooperative work to help finance your engineering education? It's okay to ask what recent graduates are doing. Have they gone on to grad school? Or have they taken jobs? If so, where? What percent of recent graduates got hired right away?

The one thing that will always come up is the need for strong math and science preparation on your part. Once you're at college, expect heavy math, statistics, basic science, and lab work for the first two years, followed by applied science and engineering courses later.

"Engineers are problem solvers, but many engineering students become disillusioned early in their studies because they fail to see the applicability of the abstract mathematical principles they encounter in their freshmen and sophomore years," warns Edward A. Hiler, a dean emeritus at Texas A&M University. "Perseverance is necessary, and is well rewarded later in college and in their careers."

Only about one-third of engineering graduates finish their degree in four years. Most students take nine or more semesters to graduate. Studies often finish with a capstone course. That's a real-world project putting together everything you've learned. Ask the college about the types of projects students have done in the past.

Keep in mind that when you look up engineering majors in college catalogs and on the Internet, you might see some combinations and hybrids. Aerospace engineering and aviation might be called aeronautics. Industrial engineering is also known as industrial and systems engineering. Think it through.

Read more about the particular engineering majors in this section and about the field in general by going to the Junior Engineering Technical Society (www.jets.org), American Society for Engineering Education (www.asee.org), and ABET (www.abet.org).

Aeronautical/aerospace engineering

What it's about:

As an aeronautical/aerospace engineering major, you study the design and development of high-speed transportation vehicles such as aircraft, spacecraft, missiles, launch vehicles, deep space probes, dirigibles, hang gliders, unmanned aerial vehicles (UAVs), and space habitats. In addition, you examine the physics of the flow of air, water, and plasma around these vehicles.

Is this for you?

You might like this major if you also like: anything to do with aircraft, spacecraft, or space exploration; model aircraft building; flying; hang gliding; physics; astronomy; science fiction; computer programming; designing things; problem solving. If you instinctively look up when you hear an airplane, you know you have the aerospace bug.

Consider this major if you are good at: attention to detail; creativity; critical reading/thinking; leadership; math; organizing; quantitative analysis; spacial thinking/analysis; teamwork *...or have...* imagination; initiative.

Recommended high school prep:

English 4, math 4 (including precalculus), lab science 4, social studies 3, and a foreign language 2–3. If you must choose, take physics and chemistry over biology or earth science. Also, if possible, take a year of computer literacy, a computer programming course, and calculus.

Typical courses in this major:

Introduction to aerospace engineering
Thermodynamics
Strength of materials (with lab)
Aerodynamics (with lab)
Aerospace structures
Flight mechanics
Control systems
Aerospace propulsion
Flight controls
Space science and systems
Aerospace vehicle design
Robotics lab
Intelligent systems
Space mission design
Systems engineering
Computer-aided design (CAD)

Concentrations:

In college: aerodynamics; aerospace structures; propulsion; controls; aerospace vehicle design; intelligent systems; space science and systems.

If you go on to grad school: theoretical mechanics; heat transfer; numerical modeling.

What the study of this major is like:

For all engineers, the academic program usually consists of two years of science and engineering basics, followed by two years of specialty courses. In the aeronautical/aerospace engineering major, most of your general education electives and required courses (such as English, history, and social science) are taught in the lecture format, but some of the science courses also have labs. You will probably be required to take four semesters of calculus and analytic geometry, one semester of chemistry, two semesters of physics, one semester of differential equations, and courses in computer programming and in numerical methods.

Most likely, your engineering studies will begin with an overview course, often containing team projects and reports. You then take statics/dynamics, thermodynamics, electrical science, and materials science, courses that are normally taught as lectures, with homework and exams, and sometimes project reports. Advanced general engineering courses, such as computer programming, graphics, strength of materials, and controls, are also taught as lectures, but they often have lab sessions in which you work with a team on experimental or computer projects and on written reports. Most programs also require a fourth-year capstone course featuring a team experimental or vehicle design project.

You can probably specialize in either aeronautics (aircraft) or astronautics (spacecraft) at the undergraduate level. Although most programs cover both areas, usually with less emphasis on space, some colleges offer only one or the other. Aerospace courses, such as propulsion, flight mechanics, avionics, and vehicle/system design, have varied formats, but they often contain open-ended design projects (including reports) that you can do on your own or with a team. Technical and experimental electives—such as CAD, FEM (finite element method), courses from other engineering departments, and aerospace-specific courses such as space mission design and robotics lab—have varied formats featuring lectures, lab experiments, or design work.

As an aeronautical/aerospace engineering major, you need to sharpen your ability to visualize in three dimensions, in order to understand complex physical systems. The required work, as you would expect, is harder than in high school. New college students are not always good at budgeting their time, or at studying on their own; developing these skills in high school will give you a leg up. You must also learn how to work with a team. The demands of this major (including project reports and computer projects) leave little time for extracurricular activities. But if you have the time, you can usually join a technical society or a design/build/fly team. Tech societies often organize trips to aerospace companies or professional conferences.

There are four types of aeronautical/aerospace engineering programs approved by the Accreditation Board for Engineering and Technology (ABET): aeronautical engineering programs with a brief introduction to space; space programs with a short introduction to aeronautical engineering; aeronautics and astronautics programs that cover the two areas more or less equally; and aerospace options in fields such as mechanical engineering and engineering mechanics. Accredited programs regularly undergo standardized outside review. On the other hand, some of the best programs in the United States do not seek accreditation. Programs may also differ in their emphasis. Some colleges stress open-ended problems (design) rather than questions with specific answers (analysis). Some programs may include more hands-on experiences, and others, more computer simulations. Even standard aeronautical/aerospace engineering programs may sometimes set a particular emphasis, such as on intelligent systems, information technology, or space telecommunications.

Other majors you might like:

Aeronautics and aviation science
Aeronautical/aerospace engineering technology
Mechanical engineering technology
Astronomy
Astrophysics
Atmospheric sciences
Applied physics
Instrumentation technology
Marine engineering/naval architecture
Aviation management
Materials science
Nuclear engineering

Questions to ask colleges:

Which of the four ABET accredited aeronautical/aerospace engineering programs does this college offer?

Which facilities (such as wind tunnels, computer labs, and design labs) are available? What designing, building, and flying opportunities exist on a regular basis?

Career options and trends:

Design engineer*; project engineer*; fighter pilot; flight test engineer; research engineer.

Majors usually enter the aerospace industry, which loosely includes the prime aerospace contractors and their chief suppliers, the propulsion industry, academia, NASA, the Federal Aviation Administration, Department of Defense research and development (R&D), other government agencies, and the airlines (to be a pilot, you need rigorous training and licensing). Careers fall into the following areas: R&D, manufacturing, maintenance, marketing/planning, and computer applications technology.

Engineers generally work in groups devoted to specific disciplines, such as systems engineering, structures, aerodynamics, controls, and human factors.

The aeronautical/aerospace engineering industry tends to be cyclical but is projected to grow over the next decade or so: increased defense spending and the need to replace much of the commercial fleet with "next-generation" aircraft are creating job opportunities for graduates. The aerospace industry is distributed across the country, from the West Coast (Seattle, Los Angeles) to the Midwest (St. Louis and Forth Worth) and the South (Atlanta). Workplaces are normally in or near large cities and cultural centers.

Insider's viewpoint:

"I like building things that fly. I also like the fact that aero/astro is a combination of mechanical engineering, electrical engineering, and physics. I'm excited by the cutting edge stuff we do, the hands-on work."

—Stuart, senior, Massachusetts Institute of Technology

For more info:

American Institute of Aeronautics and
   Astronautics (AIAA)
1801 Alexander Bell Dr.
Suite 500
Reston, VA 20191-4344
(800) 639-2422
www.aiaa.org

NASA/Educational Programs
300 E St., S.W.
Washington, DC 20546
(202) 358-1110
www.nasa.gov

Agricultural and biological engineering

Also known as:
Bioengineering
Biosystems engineering

What it's about:
Majors in agricultural and biological engineering learn to apply principles from the physical, biological, and engineering sciences to come up with improved methods of producing food, fiber, timber, and renewable energy sources; to preserve environmental quality; to tackle problems affecting plant and animal systems; and to develop products from biological resources.

Is this for you?
You might like this major if you also like: farming and agriculture; working on machinery and equipment; the outdoors; biology, chemistry, and math; scientific research; computers. If you are drawn to engineering, but would also like to do something about world hunger and environmental pollution, this major might be a good choice for you.

Consider this major if you are good at: creativity; critical reading/thinking; leadership; math; quantitative analysis; spacial thinking/analysis; teamwork *...or have...* a social conscience; initiative; verbal skills.

Recommended high school prep:
English 4, math 4 (including trigonometry and precalculus), lab science 4 (including biology, chemistry and physics), social studies 3, and a foreign language 2-3. Try to take as many math and science courses as possible, including life sciences, and if they are available, courses in calculus and computer science. You should also take courses in writing and speech, because all engineers must be able to communicate effectively.

Typical courses in this major:
Agricultural engineering design
Biochemistry
Water resources engineering
Power and machinery
Engineering properties of biological materials
Biological and agricultural energy systems
Soil science
Instrumentation and measurement
Transport processes
Bioenvironmental systems design
Hydrology
Food process engineering
Biosystems engineering
Electrical energy applications
Engineering mechanics
Fluid mechanics

Concentrations:
Agricultural process engineering; environmental and natural resources engineering; machine systems design; bioenvironmental controls; biomaterials systems; soil and water resources; food engineering; biochemical engineering.

What the study of this major is like:
The agricultural and biological engineering major, which focuses on theory, analysis, and design, includes supplementary lab work and project development. In core courses, you explore the nature of biological materials and study hydraulic systems, irrigation, agricultural machinery design, and erosion control. You take math, including calculus and differential equations; science, including biology, chemistry, physics, biochemistry, materials science, and plant and animal physiology; and basic engineering courses. In addition, you study the humanities and social sciences, and perhaps computer programming and numerical analysis. To enhance your ability to work with others, you sharpen your oral and written communication skills.

Some students become disillusioned because they don't see how the abstract mathematical principles they encounter in their first and second years apply to the major. But self-discipline, commitment, and perseverance pay off in the third and fourth years, when you explore practical applications in the upper-level courses.

Majors can generally concentrate in several areas, such as food engineering (which focuses on production, nutrition, packaging, factory design, and preservation); soil and water engineering (irrigation, soil science, drainage and hydraulic structure design, and erosion control); or machine design (various topics, such as the automation of animal feeding for large-scale farming). Many colleges offer cooperative education programs that provide opportunities for full-time employment during alternating academic terms. You will probably be eligible for these programs after completing the basic engineering course work. Most colleges include a capstone design course integrating concepts from previous courses.

Agricultural and biological engineering programs may vary in the emphasis they place on different areas of the field. For example, programs may stress natural resource and environmental engineering, food systems engineering, machinery systems engineering, or biological systems engineering. In addition, some programs prefer a hands-on, practical approach, while others focus on the theories behind agricultural and biological engineering.

Other majors you might like:
Aquaculture
Applied physics
Biomedical engineering
Forest engineering
Environmental engineering
Food science
Agronomy and crop science
Agricultural equipment technology
Environmental science
Biotechnology
Biochemistry
Genetics

Career options and trends:
Environmental engineer; design engineer; project engineer; product development engineer; soil and water conservationist; irrigation engineer; bioengineer; food engineer.

As the world's population grows and our global ecosystem becomes more fragile, the contributions of agricultural and biological engineers will be increasingly important to society. Employment growth for agricultural engineers will be generated by demand for more efficient crop production as well as the use of agriculture as renewable energy resources.

Opportunities for biological engineers is expected to grow much faster than average, as demand increases for more advanced medical equipment that can be used in a cost-effective manner. Career opportunities are also available in such related fields as medicine, pharmacy, and bioinstrumentation.

For more info:
American Society of Agricultural and Biological
  Engineers (ASABE)
2950 Niles Rd.
St. Joseph, MI 49085
(269)429-0300
www.asabe.org

Architectural engineering

What it's about:

Architectural engineering combines architecture and engineering to focus on the links between design and construction. Professionals in this discipline work with both architects and other engineers to ensure the timely, effective design and construction of buildings and other structures and systems.

Is this for you?

You might like this major if you also like: building things; discovering how things work; drawing; model making; working with your hands; working in teams; art; history; studying different architectural styles. If you are interested in architecture and have excellent math and science abilities, architectural engineering may be a good major for you.

Consider this major if you are good at: attention to detail; creativity; designing and drafting; math; quantitative analysis; spacial thinking/analysis; teamwork ...*or have...* patience; verbal skills; writing skills.

Recommended high school prep:

English 4, math 4 (including calculus or precalculus), lab science 4 (including physics and chemistry), social studies 3, and a foreign language 2–3. Take as many math, science, and English courses as possible. High school physics and chemistry are essential, but geology, biology, and environmental science are also relevant. Courses in computer skills, freehand drawing, CAD, and speech, if available, are good preparation, too.

Typical courses in this major:

Architectural design fundamentals
Thermal/fluid sciences
Energy conservation in buildings
Architectural history
Soil mechanics
Seismic analysis and design
Construction materials and methods
Architectural graphics
Steel and reinforced concrete design
Computer-aided design (CAD)
Lighting and power systems
Fire protection and plumbing design
Environmental systems design
Structural analysis
Construction finance and economics
Specifications and contracts

Concentrations:

Heating, ventilating, and air-conditioning (HVAC) systems; plumbing, piping, and fire protection; energy conservation and solar energy; electrical, lighting, communications, and control systems; structures; construction; acoustics; facility management.

What the study of this major is like:

Historically, architecture at most universities was housed in engineering schools, and architectural engineers were generally viewed as architects with a technical background. But in the late 1970s, many architecture programs, seeing themselves as more artistic than scientific, separated from engineering to form their own schools. Architectural engineering then redefined itself as a hybrid engineering discipline, focused on the analysis, design, and construction of building systems—functions that had once been part of architecture and civil, mechanical, and electrical engineering. But because architectural engineers still receive some architectural training, they are valuable links between architects and traditional engineers working on construction projects.

Both architecture and engineering are challenging fields that require dedication, passion, and stamina. If you are trying to decide between the two majors, architectural engineering might be a good solution. Typically, architectural engineering programs have competitive admissions standards. Therefore, you should take as many rigorous courses in high school as you can.

Even if you had introductory calculus in high school, you will probably be required to take engineering calculus courses in college. Majors typically complete four courses in advanced math, two in physics, one in chemistry, two in English, and several humanities electives. You can also expect to take a series of courses in structures—including statics, dynamics, strength of materials, and steel/concrete design—and some courses in mechanical and electrical systems and basic engineering sciences, such as circuits, thermodynamics, and fluid mechanics. While requirements may vary, most programs include at least one year's worth of architectural design and architectural history courses.

Course work includes lecture classes, lab sessions, and both independent and team projects. Because your work will be challenging, you must become excellent at time management and develop superior study skills. Summer internships are beneficial for obtaining that first full-time, post-graduation position.

All the programs approved by the Accreditation Board for Engineering and Technology (ABET) have similar basic requirements, usually covered in the first two years. However, colleges may differ in their emphasis on architecture, science, or engineering. If you are interested in design, you might choose a program that stresses architectural content, but if you are scientifically inclined, you may want to focus on engineering. Also, some programs include many electives that allow concentrations, whereas other programs are not as flexible. Architectural engineering courses are generally offered through a number of departments, so you may encounter a variety of philosophies and teaching styles.

Training to be a good architectural engineer is hard work. But careers in the field are often intellectually (and financially) rewarding—and you'll appreciate seeing your designs actually built!

Other majors you might like:
Drafting and design technology
Civil engineering
Structural engineering
Construction engineering
Marine engineering/naval architecture

Physics
Construction technology
Fire protection/safety technology
Heating/air conditioning/refrigeration technology
Urban, community, and regional planning
Environmental design
Architectural history/criticism

Questions to ask colleges:
How long will it take to earn a degree? Most bachelor's degree programs take four years, but a few take five years.

Is the program accredited by ABET? Most architectural engineers seek professional registration after graduation, and a degree from an accredited program is required.

Do undergraduates have open access to up-to-date design, computing, and testing laboratories? Are the facilities dedicated to the architectural engineering program, or are they shared with other engineering majors? Are design studios set aside for senior projects?

Career options and trends:
Consulting engineer*; analytical or design engineer*; architect*; engineering manager; construction manager.

Architectural education has become less technical and other engineering fields have become more general. As a result, architectural engineers are in demand because of the unique combination of design and analytical skills they possess. Graduates with concentrations in mechanical and electrical systems are in higher demand than grads with concentrations in construction and structural areas, who face competition from civil and construction engineers. Many architectural engineers move swiftly from design positions to project management and administration. Some soon start their own firms.

For more info:
Architectural Engineering Institute (AEI)
1801 Alexander Bell Dr.
Reston, VA 20191-4400
(800) 548-2723
www.aeinstitute.org

Chemical engineering

What it's about:

Through the study of math and the natural sciences, chemical engineering majors learn to develop products for businesses, government, and consumers; they also look for solutions to regional or global problems, such as pollution. Like most engineers, chemical engineers turn technological advances in the lab into useful materials and services beyond the university walls.

Is this for you?

You might like this major if you also like: science and math (of course); exploring the basic nature of things; lab work and technology.

Consider this major if you are good at: attention to detail; creativity; critical reading/thinking; math; memorizing; organizing; quantitative analysis; teamwork ...*or have...* initiative; writing skills.

Recommended high school prep:

English 4, math 4 (including calculus or precalculus), lab science 4 (including biology, chemistry and physics), social studies 3, and a foreign language 2–3. If possible, take other advanced mathematics or science courses.

Did you know...

...that Frank Capra, the director of *It's a Wonderful Life*, earned a chemical engineering degree at Stanford?

Typical courses in this major:

General chemistry
Organic chemistry
Physical chemistry
Physics
Calculus
Differential equations
Computer programming
Statistics
Microbiology
Materials engineering

Energy and material balances
Thermodynamics
Heat mass and momentum transfer
Chemical and biological reaction engineering
Engineering economics
Chemical and pharmaceutical plant design

Concentrations:

Biochemical engineering; biomolecular engineering; biomedical engineering; environmental engineering; materials engineering; thin films and surface science; pharmaceutical engineering.

What the study of this major is like:

Chemical engineers convert the discoveries that physical or biological scientists make in the laboratory into products used by industry, the military, and ordinary consumers. In addition, they play an important role in the new areas of biotechnology (the development of medical treatments), nanotechnology (the science of miniaturization), and information technology. As a chemical engineering major, you are trained to design and develop many of the processes and products necessary for modern industrial society, including antibiotics and other medicines, natural and synthetic fibers, semiconductors, fuel cells, synthetic fuels, petroleum-based fuels and hydrogen, body parts and organ substitutes, and environmental pollution prevention and cleanup. In your work, the primary goal is to create products and processes that are safe and economical.

Chemical engineering programs in the United States are approved by the Accreditation Board for Engineering and Technology (ABET), in cooperation with the American Institute of Chemical Engineers (AIChE). These programs begin with courses in the natural sciences, math, and computer programming. In most programs, you will also be required to study speech and writing as well as the humanities and social sciences. Programs may vary in their focus; they may emphasize materials engineering, bioengineering, environmental concerns, modeling and computer applications, or some or all these areas. Physics and biochemistry or biophysics courses may be included as electives.

One of the most important courses you take as a major is energy and material balances—the basis for the design and evaluation of biological, chemical, energy, and environmental processes. Thermodynamics teaches you to determine the energy efficiency of chemical and biological processes, including those in the human body. In other courses, you learn about the economics of alternative designs, life-cycle analysis, and mathematical analysis by computer simulation. You'll need to get a good background in mathematics to do, for example, rigorous analyses of chemical plant processes. In a capstone course, you may design an entire process for the production of chemicals, fuels, electronic devices, or drinking water from the oceans; or you may design devices for kidney dialysis or blood oxygenators.

Other majors you might like:
Biotechnology
Biochemistry
Agricultural and biological engineering
Biomedical engineering
Materials engineering
Polymer/plastics engineering
Metallurgical engineering
Soil science
Environmental engineering
Chemical technology
Forensic science
Clinical/medical laboratory technology

Questions to ask colleges:
Does the college help students find internships while in school, and jobs after graduating?

Ask to see the facilities, particularly the computer rooms and student work areas. You should also ask for a list of graduate schools, companies, and government agencies that the previous 100–200 graduates enrolled in or were offered jobs by.

Career options and trends:
Consulting engineer; product designer/engineer; research and development engineer; production engineer or plant manager; sales representative; environmental engineer.

Careers are available in the environmental, pharmaceutical, materials, fuel, and specialty chemical industries. Growth opportunities for chemical engineers will be located in service-providing industries, such as professional, scientific, and technical services. Positions in the alternative energy, biotechnology and nanotechnology fields are also rapidly expanding. Engineering positions will require state certification in addition to the required degrees.

Insider's viewpoint:
"Go to class and get involved; just get through those first two years and you're golden."

—Travis, senior, Penn State

For more info:
American Institute of Chemical Engineers (AIChE)
3 Park Ave.
New York, NY 10016-5991
(800) 242-4363
www.aiche.org

Civil engineering

What it's about:

Civil engineering majors learn to apply the principles of science and math to the planning, construction, and maintenance of facilities, both public and private, that are essential to industrialized society. Civil engineers work on buildings; on such large-scale projects as bridges, dams, highways, environmental control systems, and water purification systems; and on other structures in both the urban and rural environments.

Is this for you?

You might like this major if you also like: learning how things work (building things, taking things apart); thinking big; brain teaser puzzles; math and science; achieving practical results; outdoor activities; watching construction sites. If you like to solve problems by dividing them up into logical parts (divide and conquer), then civil engineering might be a good choice. Projects tend to be large in scope, and you should have the patience for complexity and long-term commitments.

Consider this major if you are good at: attention to detail; math; organizing; quantitative analysis; research; spacial thinking/analysis; teamwork *...or have...* initiative; interpersonal skills; mechanical facility; verbal skills.

Recommended high school prep:

English 4, math 4 (including trigonometry, geometry, and calculus or precalculus), lab science 3–4 (including chemistry and physics), social studies 3, and a foreign language 2–3. Courses in computer applications, business, and economics are also helpful.

Typical courses in this major:

Engineering graphics
Structural analysis and design
Soil mechanics
Statics
Dynamics
Strength of materials
Surveying
Environmental engineering
Construction materials
Fluid mechanics
Water resources
Engineering economics
Transportation engineering
Geotechnical engineering
Construction management
Hydraulics and hydrology

Concentrations:

Structural engineering; geotechnical engineering; environmental engineering; construction; transportation engineering; hydrosystems (hydraulics, hydrology, water resources).

What the study of this major is like:

Civil engineers plan, analyze, design, and erect structures (such as buildings, bridges) and systems (transportation, water supply). Civil engineering is often called "the people-serving profession" because many of its projects serve the public good. To tackle complex problems, civil engineers use principles of math and science, as well as their creativity. Civil engineering works are generally large-scale, one-of-a-kind projects, usually requiring cooperation among professionals from a variety of disciplines.

Differences among civil engineering programs are minimal because of the requirements established by the Accreditation Board for Engineering and Technology (ABET). Programs include a broad range of courses in mathematics (especially calculus and differential equations); basic sciences (chemistry, physics, and possibly geology or biology); engineering sciences; engineering design; and the humanities and social sciences. In addition, programs may include courses in computers, English composition, speech, report writing, engineering economics, and statistics.

You can expect to take most professional courses during your last two years of study. In civil engineering, probably more than in any other engineering field, you can concentrate in a number of areas. Some typical concentrations include the following:

Structural engineering. The planning and design of large structures, including bridges, buildings, towers, dams, offshore drilling, and exploration facilities.

Environmental engineering. The planning and design of facilities for water purification; control of air and water pollution; solid water management; and disposal of hazardous materials.

Geotechnical engineering. The analysis and design of foundations and retaining walls; the development of excavation and construction techniques for tunnels, dams, and storage systems for hazardous materials.

Hydrosystems. The analysis and design of dams, floodwalls, pumping stations, aqueducts, canals, harbor and coastal facilities, irrigation and drainage systems, and navigable waterways.

Transportation engineering. The analysis and design of facilities for highways, airports, railways, aerospace systems, and pipelines.

Most courses are taught in lecture format, but some have lab components. In most technical courses, you learn primarily by solving "story problems": scenarios are described to the class, and you must determine which theories are applicable, which information is superfluous, which information is missing, and so on. Later courses often have open-ended problems, possibly involving teamwork or research. Like all engineering majors, this one is very demanding. Because many of your courses build on one another, you need to keep up with your studies.

Other majors you might like:
Mechanical engineering
Civil engineering technology
Industrial engineering
Materials science
Architecture
Architectural engineering
Construction management

Ocean engineering
Physics
Urban, community, and regional planning
Geology/earth science
Surveying technology

Questions to ask colleges:
Is there a student chapter of the American Society of Civil Engineers (ASCE) on campus?

Does the college offer a five-year combined bachelor's/master's degree program? (More than one-third of civil engineering graduates go on to earn a master's degree.)

Does the college offer a five-year cooperative study program in which you alternate periods of study with related employment?

Career options and trends:
Consulting engineer*; city engineer or official at a state or federal agency (e.g., EPA, Department of Transportation)*; construction engineer; researcher in a government laboratory, forensic engineering firm, or university.

Civil Engineers often need a professional engineer's (PE) license to practice. In some states, structural engineering (SE) has a separate licensure. Increasingly, a master's degree is required for entry-level positions or advancement.

Since many civil engineering projects are large in scope, they create numerous jobs that last a long time. As a result, employment may remain strong for some time after an economic downturn. Thus, hiring trends in civil engineering may lag behind national trends.

Insider's viewpoint:
"I love civil engineering because it is a field with a fascinating balance between the certainty of science and uncertainty of the natural environment."

—Professor Keith Hjelmstad, University of Illinois

For more info:
American Society of Civil Engineers (ASCE)
1801 Alexander Bell Drive
Reston, VA 20191-4400
(800) 548-2723
www.asce.org

Electrical and communications engineering

Also known as:
Electrical and computer engineering

What it's about:
Electrical and communications engineering deals with the design, manufacture, and operation of the range of devices and systems that depend on electricity—from wireless telephones to giant power generators. You examine superconductors, wave propagation, energy storage, fiber optics, reception, and amplification, from both a theoretical and an applied perspective.

Is this for you?
You might like this major if you also like: tinkering (putting things together, taking them apart, making them work); music; ham radio; computers.

Consider this major if you are good at: attention to detail; creativity; math; organizing; quantitative analysis; spacial thinking/analysis; teamwork; vsualization ...*or have...* initiative; writing skills.

Recommended high school prep:
English 4, math 4 (including precalculus or calculus), lab science 3-4 (including physics), social studies 3, and a foreign language 2-3. Advanced or honors courses in math and physics are recommended, as well as courses in computer applications and writing.

Did you know...
...that more engineers are employed in electrical engineering than in any other branch of engineering? According to the U.S. Bureau of Labor Statistics, nearly one-third work in California, Texas, New York, and New Jersey, where many large electronics firms are located.

Typical courses in this major:
Electric circuits and systems
Electromagnetics
Control systems
Electromechanical energy conversion
Digital circuits
Materials science
Microwaves and high-speed circuits
Signal processing
Semiconductor electronics
Instrumentation
Microprocessor systems
Fields, matter, and waves
Communications systems
Physics of electronic devices
Fiber optics and photonics
Electrical engineering practicum

Concentrations:
In college: communications systems; electric power; electronic design; electromagnetics; computer systems; digital systems; control systems; telecommunications.

If you go on to grad school: physical electronics; bioengineering; wireless engineering; electronics packaging; photonics; microwave engineering.

What the study of this major is like:
Most electrical and communications engineering programs begin with an introduction to the design process that stresses engineering fundamentals and suggests some of the careers you might pursue after graduation. You also start with mathematics, physics, and some chemistry courses that are the basis for many engineering courses you will take later on.

Your other courses cover engineering science and design, humanities, social sciences, and electives that correspond to your concentration. In humanities and social sciences courses, you see how the work that engineers do impacts society. You will probably participate in a significant design project in your fourth year, or perhaps earlier. Most students find the experience rewarding because it brings together what you've learned in various courses and helps you understand what engineering can accomplish. These projects, which are usually team efforts and may involve professional engineers and instructors, often require a written report and perhaps several oral presentations.

You learn by attending lectures and by working on computers, but especially by doing homework. Working through your homework problems and making sure you understand the concepts they illustrate is essential. Most engineering students do homework in small groups, but you should find out what your professors' policies are—sometimes instructors prefer that you work independently. You'll also take a number of lab courses, in which you explore abstract principles you learn in the classroom. Labs also provide opportunities to develop teamwork skills and your ability to write clear technical reports.

Your education does not necessarily take place entirely on campus. You will probably take a number of field trips to engineering labs and factories. You may also work as an engineering summer intern—an invaluable experience that can help when you seek your first job. In addition, many international programs allow engineering students to work or study abroad while earning academic credit.

Although there is much similarity among programs, there are also variations in coverage or emphasis. Some programs stress computer engineering; others may have more courses in digital communication technology and information science. All programs prepare graduates for entry into the profession, but some devote more attention to preparing students for graduate school. Graduates from these programs, which tend to emphasize theory over application, may need more on-the-job training before they can work independently in industry.

The ABET (Accreditation Board for Engineering and Technology) standards for approving engineering programs in the United States require that programs clearly state their objectives. These goals (published in college catalogs) might help you clarify a program's focus to see if it fits your interests. As in all areas of engineering, your education never really ends, because of the need to keep up with the rapid advances in electrical and communications technology.

Other majors you might like:
Mechanical engineering
Engineering physics
Systems engineering
Metallurgical engineering
Software engineering
Electrical engineering technologies
Rehabilitation engineering/assistive technology
Computer science
Physics
Neuroscience
Electrical drafting/CAD/CADD
Computer engineering technology

Questions to ask colleges:
Is computer engineering considered part of the electrical engineering major, or a separate major?

Are co-op educational experiences available?

How do you prepare graduates to work in an industry where outsourcing of engineering services is a growing trend?

Career options and trends:
Production engineer*; design engineer; engineering manager; systems analyst; consulting engineer*; field engineer; research engineer.

Licensure (or registration) as a professional engineer (PE) is often required of engineers working in the public sector (for instance, for power companies and government agencies) but not of engineers working for private firms. Although some electrical engineers (EEs) are licensed, most are not.

As the economy rebounds, job prospects are likely to be favorable, especially for graduates who have had engineering intern experience. Consulting engineering firms are expected to generate the fastest job growth. Because most products today involve electricity and electronics, EEs are found in almost every industry at every level, doing all kinds of work—from designing integrated circuits to performing instrumentation on a ship in the Antarctic Ocean.

Industrial engineering

What it's about:

Industrial engineering is the most "people-oriented" of the engineering fields. As a major, you learn to plan, design, and implement complex systems for industry that take into account the needs and capabilities of individuals and groups, as well as the availability of information, equipment, and materials. Industrial engineers (IEs) find ways to increase both productivity and customer satisfaction in all kinds of organizations, from hospitals to steel foundries, and they are the only engineers educated as quality and productivity improvement professionals.

Is this for you?

You might like this major if you also like: helping people; working in teams; math and science; figuring out how to do things more easily; working with numbers; debating; solving puzzles and brain teasers.

Consider this major if you are good at: attention to detail; communicating ideas; creativity; critical reading/thinking; leadership; math; organizing; persuading/influencing; quantitative analysis ...*or have...* initiative; listening skills.

Recommended high school prep:

English 4, math 4 (up to precalculus), lab science 4 (including biology, chemistry and physics), social studies 3, and a foreign language 2–3. English is important because industrial engineers must effectively communicate the ideas and procedures they develop. If available, courses in speech, psychology, and economics are also helpful.

Did you know...

...that industrial engineers are more widely distributed among manufacturing businesses than any other type of engineer? And IEs also work in unexpected places, like Disney World and other theme parks.

Typical courses in this major:

Production planning and control
Operations research
Quality control
Supply chain logistics
Human factors
Ergonomics
Facilities planning and design
Discrete event computer simulation
Engineering management
Engineering economics
Probability and statistics
Materials handling and control
Computer modeling
Information systems
Robotics
Safety management

Concentrations:

Generally, none in college; but if you go on to grad school: manufacturing; operations research; ergonomics; management systems.

What the study of this major is like:

While other engineers produce things, industrial engineers create or improve the systems and procedures used in making or doing things. The work that IEs do has been around a long time, and the profession has been recognized since the 1920s. In the early 1900s, two of industrial engineering's founders, Frank and Lillian Gilbreth, helped determine the "one best way" for hospitals to perform surgery and train doctors, nurses, and technicians. As a result, operating times dropped drastically and survival rates increased. Today, IEs serve as integration engineers, focusing on the way the numerous components of industrial or service systems work as a unit. In figuring out how to improve a procedure, IEs seek to reduce or eliminate the many areas of waste, especially of time, money, materials, and energy.

IEs concern themselves with the design of workplaces, ergonomic and safety studies, and productivity. They design factories (workstations, automated procedures, and robotics; material handling systems; and control systems) and determine the "best way" to manufacture goods. But the word "industrial" refers to more than just manufacturing; today, IEs work in (or with) providers of health care, lodging, and food service; in defense and government; and in such businesses as transportation and communications. A typical task might involve getting a package from San Francisco to Dûsseldorf overnight.

Your first two years as a major are similar to those of most engineering students. You take courses in math, the physical sciences, and engineering sciences such as statics, thermodynamics, and electrical circuits. These two years can be intellectually challenging, and you may wonder whether you'll ever get to your chosen field of study, industrial engineering; perseverance and patience will pay off. In your third and fourth years, you explore topical areas of the major and take supporting math and statistics courses. Here, most students begin to identify their fields of interest.

You can expect to receive a diverse education in computer systems, design, and management, as well as in the physical and social sciences, including economics. Because IEs focus on organizations and the people in them, you will need to take arts and humanities courses. Your schedule will be full, with little room for electives.

Among different industrial engineering programs, requirements are similar and philosophies are fundamentally the same. Most programs stress manufacturing, operations research (applying mathematical modeling and analysis to problems), or "general" industrial engineering, which covers all or most topical areas. A few undergraduate programs have an in-depth focus on safety management, logistics, quality control, or human factors.

Other majors you might like:
Systems engineering
Business administration and management
Management science
Materials engineering

Industrial technology
Information systems
Psychology
Occupational safety/health technology
Management information systems
Human resources management
Economics
Organizational behavior studies

Questions to ask colleges:
How extensive and state-of-the-art are the computer lab facilities, and how accessible are they to undergrads? For industrial engineering majors, the computing equipment is essential because of the specialized (and often expensive) software they use.

Which types of research projects are under way? The answer will provide insight into the interests and strengths of the faculty.

Career options and trends:
Consulting industrial engineer*; manufacturing/production supervisor*; plant manager or chief operating officer; quality engineer; safety engineer; systems engineer; materials manager; operations analyst*; process engineer.

The Bureau of Labor Statistics projects strong job growth through 2018, as firms look for new ways to reduce costs and raise productivity, and to make their operations more "green." Demand for IEs is increasing in service industries, such as banking and insurance; health care; transportation and distribution; environmental protection; and information processing.

For more info:
Institute of Industrial Engineers (IIE)
3577 Parkway Lane, Suite 200
Norcross, GA 30092
(800) 494-0460
www.iienet.org

Marine engineering/naval architecture

What it's about:

Marine engineers and naval architects design, build, operate, and maintain a wide variety of oceangoing vehicles, from recreational boats to ships at sea. Marine engineering concentrates on ship machinery, including propulsion, electrical, mechanical, and control systems. Naval architecture focuses on ship design, including hull shape, structure, power requirements, and performance.

Is this for you?

You might like this major if you also like: anything to do with ships and the sea; boating; competitive sailing; working with machinery; drawing, drafting, and design; model ship building; radio-controlled boat building; math and science.

Consider this major if you are good at: attention to detail; creativity; critical reading/thinking; making decisions; math; quantitative analysis; spacial thinking/analysis *...or have...* communication skills; initiative; patience.

Recommended high school prep:

English 4, math 4 (including trigonometry and calculus), lab science 3–4 (including chemistry and physics), social studies 3, and a foreign language 2–3. Take as much math and science as you can. Courses that prepare you to communicate well are also important. Knowledge of a foreign language would be useful, as the maritime industry is, by its nature, global. If possible, take courses in spreadsheet applications, manual graphics, and computer-assisted design (CAD).

Typical courses in this major:

Foundations of ship design
Hullform and hydrostatics
Intact and damaged stability
Ship structures
Resistance and powering
Seakeeping and maneuvering
Ship production
Marine power systems
Solid mechanics
Thermodynamics
Marine hydrodynamics
Marine electronics
Marine dynamics
Sailing craft design
Small craft design

Concentrations:

Generally, none in college; but if you go on to grad school: structural analysis; hydrodynamics; autonomous vehicles; maritime business; marine power systems; sailing yachts; energy conversion; nuclear propulsion; control systems; robotics.

What the study of this major is like:

Marine engineering and naval architecture has wide-ranging applications to ships and boats, from tankers to trawlers, submarines to sailboats, military ships to personal watercraft. It encompasses a variety of engineering challenges, including stability, seakeeping, engine selection, space utilization, structural design, model testing, propeller design, high-speed submarine dynamics, and historical ship performance.

The major usually stresses general technical content and design. Programs tend to be more applied than theoretical, although both facets are covered. Hands-on lab experiences are essential. As part of a long tradition, you take capstone courses in ship design. Field trips and practical work experience are also highly useful and instructive.

As a major, you will face challenges typical of any engineering program. Some students have a hard time with the spatial visualization of complex three-dimensional shapes. In addition, you may have to develop the ingenuity and patience needed in tackling the open-ended engineering problems that are often solved through repetitive trials. You should be prepared to spend plenty of time on your course work, especially on design courses. At the end of the program, you will be rewarded with comprehensive knowledge and a confidence in your ability to do the work. You will understand "the big picture" of the engineering and design of ships.

Although entry requirements are uniform, the various marine engineering and naval architecture programs reflect the expertise and interests of the teaching faculty. Some programs emphasize the analysis of marine vehicles; some, the design of marine vehicles; others, a particular category of ships or boats; and still others, a combination of these fields. In some programs, industry experience is incorporated into the curriculum. Also, some institutions consider their marine engineering and naval architecture programs to be subsets of larger engineering programs.

Other majors you might like:
Ocean engineering
Marine science/Merchant Marine
Electrical and communications engineering
Nuclear engineering
Oceanography
Mechanical engineering
Fishing and fisheries
Military technologies
Aircraft powerplant technology
Marine maintenance/fitter/ship repair
Drafting and design technology

Questions to ask colleges:
Do majors have access to a marine towing tank as an integral part of their academic program? Other facilities to inquire about: model basin, gravity wave tank, propeller tunnel, CAD computer laboratories.

How is the curriculum split between marine engineering and naval architecture studies? Does the school's marine engineering curriculum emphasize design or ship operations?

Is there a summer internship program in the marine industry?

Career options and trends:
Naval architect*; marine engineer*; yacht designer; naval officer; ship's officer (Merchant Marine); shipyard engineer.

Majors in marine engineering and naval architecture also pursue careers in ship operations and marine commerce. After additional professional or graduate study, you may find work in admiralty law or research. It is not necessary to be registered as a professional engineer (PE) to obtain employment, but it is a respected credential. Registration requirements vary, but they generally involve two examinations and a period of work experience.

For the near future, the job market in the marine transportation industry is projected to be tight. Ship design, building, and operations have become an increasingly international business. However, as a result of global events and technological advances, significant changes are occurring in military ship design; therefor strong demand for naval vessels should offset declining domestic construction of commercial vessels. Good job prospects for marine engineers are also expected because of the need to replace workers and the limited number of students pursuing this field.

For more info:
Society of Naval Architects and Marine Engineers
    (SNAME)
601 Pavonia Ave.
Jersey City, NJ 07306
(800)798-2188
www.sname.org

American Society of Naval Engineers (ASNE)
1452 Duke St.
Alexandria, VA 22314-3458
(703) 836-6727
www.navalengineers.org

Materials engineering

Also known as:

Materials science and engineering

What it's about:

This major focuses on the materials used by all engineers: ceramics, metals, polymers, and combinations of these (composites). The major provides a rigorous exposure to the principles governing the fabrication, properties, and applications of these materials. Because a primary task of engineers is to create various types of products from a wide variety of ingredients, the study of materials is a gateway to almost any engineering field or project.

Is this for you?

You might like this major if you also like: chemistry, physics, and math; exploring the nature of things. Are you fascinated by the architecture of materials at the atomic and molecular levels? Do you wonder what things are made of—for example, computers, milk cartons, DVD players? Have you asked yourself, "Why are some plastics hard, while others are soft?" Would you rather work on a range of engineering projects than be limited to a particular field? If your answer is yes, read on.

Consider this major if you are good at: attention to detail; creativity; critical reading/thinking; math; organizing; quantitative analysis; spacial thinking/analysis; teamwork *...or have...* initiative; manual dexterity; writing skills.

Recommended high school prep:

English 4, math 4 (including precalculus), lab science 4 (including chemistry and physics), social studies 3, and a foreign language 2–3. If it is available, take a course that covers both integral and differential calculus. Courses that help you develop writing and speaking skills are essential in engineering.

Did you know...

...there are such things as "magnetic liquids" (magneto-rheological fluids), that you can morph from a fluid to a solid simply by moving your hand through them, and "memory metal" (Nitinol), which, after being bent and twisted, returns to its original shape with a blast of hot air? The discovery of materials like these, and the development of applications for them, is the fun part of materials engineering.

Typical courses in this major:

Introduction to materials
Thermodynamics of materials
Kinetics of materials
Physical metallurgy
Processing and properties of ceramics
Composites
Fundamentals of polymers
Polymer processing
Mechanical behavior of solids
Materials engineering design
Materials characterization laboratory
Engineering computational laboratory
Degradation of materials
Failure analysis
Phase equilibria
Senior design project

Concentrations:

In college: biomaterials; ceramic materials; composites; electronic materials; metals and alloys; nanomaterials; polymeric materials

If you go on to grad school: materials processing; process and microsection modeling; smart materials.

What the study of this major is like:

Materials are a common denominator among all branches of engineering because, without them, engineers cannot work. When designing systems, other engineers (civil, chemical, electrical, mechanical) frequently collaborate with materials engineers to select the most appropriate materials. Materials engineering can be done at the atomic level (as in fiber reinforcement to make a graphite fishing rod) or at the macroscopic level (as in the manufacture of appliances, cars, and bridges). In fact, everything we see and use—from skyscrapers to computers—is made of materials derived from the earth. As a major, you learn to develop materials to meet specific needs.

Programs normally include math, communications, computer science, natural sciences (especially chemistry and physics), humanities, social sciences, engineering science, and engineering design courses. As a major, you study the physical and chemical properties of materials, transport phenomena, strength of materials, and tools for structural and chemical characterization. You use differential and integral calculus to solve equations governing the behavior of solids. In design courses, you gain practice in devising materials, components, systems, or processes to meet particular objectives. In various courses you will employ a variety of tools (such as electron microscopes, and software for modeling the behavior of materials and components) and ways of processing material (such as microgravity processing).

Typically, materials engineering classes are small (about 20 students), allowing for close interaction between students and faculty members. You learn primarily through lectures, presentations, and hands-on laboratories. You are encouraged to develop your oral and writing skills. Because much of the subject matter is conceptual, you must learn how to visualize solid materials in three dimensions.

Course requirements are similar at most colleges. All programs focus on the relation, in solids, of processing, microstructure, and property. Some colleges may stress mechanics of materials, thermodynamics, or kinetics. Other programs emphasize a particular material, such as ceramics or polymers. Differences in approach generally reflect faculty members' interest and expertise.

This major is often referred to as a science as well as an engineering discipline, because much of the science (chemistry and physics) of engineering materials is still being developed. You will find that most programs have a high ratio of graduate research students to undergraduate majors. This usually results in many opportunities for undergraduates to take part in important research on new materials, such as carbon nano tubes, for example.

Other majors you might like:
Materials science
Ceramic sciences/engineering
Polymer/plastics engineering
Metallurgical engineering
Mining and mineral engineering
Physics
Chemical engineering
Agricultural and biological engineering
Biotechnology
Manufacturing engineering
Industrial engineering
Hazardous materials technology

Questions to ask colleges:
Is the program accredited by the Accreditation Board for Engineering and Technology (ABET)?

Are faculty members engaged in research?

Is there a graduate program in materials science or engineering on campus? Are there opportunities for undergraduates to join in research, or to pursue independent study projects?

What types of lab facilities and equipment (such as electron microscopes) do undergrads have access to?

Career options and trends:
Applications engineer*; production engineer; metallurgist; polymer engineer*; industrial research and development staff member*; technical writer.

Every year, fewer than 1,000 students receive bachelor's degrees in this discipline. For this reason and because of the interdisciplinary nature of the field, there are a wide variety of job opportunities. While manufacturing in general is declining, job growth should be strong for materials engineers working on nanomaterials and biomaterials. Salaries are competitive with those in other fields of engineering.

For more info:

Materials Research Society (MRS)
506 Keystone Drive
Warrendale, PA 15086-7573
(724) 779-3003
www.mrs.org

The Minerals, Metals, and Materials Society (TMS)
184 Thorn Hill Rd.
Warrendale, PA 15086-7514
(724) 776-9000
www.tms.org

The Materials Information Society (ASM
   International)
Materials Park, OH 44073-0002
(800) 336-5152
www.asminternational.org

Mechanical engineering

What it's about:

Mechanical engineering deals with the forces and energy at work in thermal and mechanical (solid and fluid) systems. You learn the engineering principles underlying the generation, transmission, and utilization of these energies, and the design, production, and application of mechanical devices and systems.

Is this for you?

You might like this major if you also like: mechanical devices; learning how things work; computers; cars; solving problems; math and science.

Consider this major if you are good at: attention to detail; creativity; organizing; quantitative analysis; research; spacial thinking/analysis *...or have...* manual dexterity; verbal skills; writing skills.

Recommended high school prep:

English 4, math 4 (including precalculus), laboratory science 4 (including chemistry and physics), social studies 2, a foreign language 2–3. If it is available, take a computer science course.

Typical courses in this major:

Statics
Dynamics
Circuit analysis
Engineering graphics
Mechanical design fundamentals
Computer modeling
Mechanical vibrations
Solid mechanics
Energy systems
Mechanical systems
Fluid mechanics
Automatic controls
Thermodynamics
Materials science
Manufacturing systems
Heat transfer

Concentrations:

Automatic controls; energy systems; materials engineering, design; manufacturing systems; thermal systems; automotive engineering.

What the study of this major is like:

In mechanical engineering, you focus on mechanics (fluids and solids) and heat as forms of energy. You learn about the forces and motions that affect mechanical performance. Before you build a device, you use math to determine what the machine will do. You learn to model—to visualize a piece of equipment and to convey to others what it would do. And you learn what's involved in manufacturing the machinery you design—for example, a vehicle, an acoustic system, an engine.

All engineering disciplines start out the same way: with courses in math (calculus through differential equations) and numerical analysis; natural science (chemistry, physics, and perhaps biology or materials science); humanities and social science; and basic engineering science. In your second year, you will be introduced to mechanical engineering, in courses that include the design of thermal and mechanical systems. Training in engineering design, which is now largely computer-based, involves modeling, simulation, analysis, and synthesis.

Programs generally emphasize theory and analysis as well as design, with appropriate supporting labs and project work in such areas as these:

Engineering mechanics. Static and dynamic forces within and on structures; equivalent force systems; dynamics; stresses and strains; and strength of materials.

Materials. Properties of materials; physical metallurgy; and metallic and other materials including polymers, ceramics, and composites.

Electrical systems. Electrical circuits; direct and alternating current; electrical machinery; digital and

231

analog electronic devices; circuits; and control systems.

Thermal systems. Fluid mechanics; thermodynamics; combustion; refrigeration; heat transfer; energy systems; and internal combustion engines.

Mechanical systems. Kinematics and mechanisms; modeling of multicomponent systems; control of mechanical systems; vibrations; component design and analysis; machine design; and dynamics of machinery.

Manufacturing systems. Modern manufacturing systems; robotics; computer-aided manufacturing systems; artificial intelligence; and computers integrated in manufacturing.

Specialty course work or technical electives typically include in-depth study of acoustics and noise control; advanced control system design; applied solar energy; automotive engineering; biomechanics and biomedical engineering; biotechnology; computer-aided design; composite materials; direct energy conversion; energy conservation; energy system analysis; environmental control systems; gas dynamics; heating, ventilating, and air conditioning; nondestructive testing; numerical modeling and simulation; packaging engineering; propulsion systems; polymer processing; robotics; and turbomachinery.

Because computers are used in the solution of many engineering problems, the major includes a great deal of programming and numerical analysis.

Many colleges offer cooperative education programs, which provide opportunities for full-time employment during alternating academic terms. Such programs are generally available after you have completed the basic engineering course work.

Other majors you might like:
Mechanical engineering technology
Aeronautical/aerospace engineering
Nuclear engineering
Robotics technology
Marine engineering/naval architecture
Electrical and communications engineering
Physics
Industrial engineering

Materials engineering
Drafting and design technology

Career options and trends:
Consulting engineer; industrial engineer; plastics fabrication engineer; safety engineer; test engineer; automotive engineer; manufacturing engineer; design engineer; research and development engineer.

Mechanical engineers are engaged in a wide range of careers in industry, business, government, and universities. They interact with people and machines in research, design, development, testing, manufacturing, operations, marketing, sales, and management. Continued demand for graduates trained in mechanical engineering is projected for the near future, especially in industries fostering emerging technologies.

Insider's viewpoint:
"There is a lot of freedom in a mechanical engineering major. I feel like I'm learning a thought process as opposed to a trade, and this thought process is more powerful than anything you could memorize from a book."

—Alison, junior, Colorado State University

For more info:
American Society of Mechanical Engineers (ASME)
3 Park Avenue
New York, NY 10016-5990
(800) 843-2763
www.asme.org

Metallurgical engineering

What it's about:

In this major, you study the structure, properties, and performance of metals and alloys. Metallurgical engineering is a distinct discipline, although it is closely related to the more inclusive fields of materials science and materials engineering, which address similar relationships in all classes of materials (such as metals, ceramics, polymers, and fabrics).

Is this for you?

You might like this major if you also like: chemistry, physics, and math; exploring the nature of things. Have you ever asked yourself, "Why is glass transparent and steel shiny? Why do some steels rust and others don't? What makes some metals magnetic and other not?" If so, this major might interest you.

Consider this major if you are good at: attention to detail; creativity; critical reading/thinking; math; organizing data; quantitative analysis; spacial thinking/analysis; teamwork *...or have...* initiative; patience; writing skills.

Recommended high school prep:

English 4, math 4 (including trigonometry and calculus or precalculus), lab science 3–4 (including chemistry and physics), social studies 3, and a foreign language 2–3.

Did you know...

...that most high school students considering metallurgical engineering envision a career in a steel mill or foundry? Such careers are actually in the minority. Many metallurgical engineers work in the aerospace industry, processing exotic alloys; in the microelectronics industry, contributing to advances in electro-optical materials; or in the biomedical industry, developing implants and biomedical sensors.

Typical courses in this major:

Structure and properties of materials
Mechanics of materials
Mechanical behavior of solids
Metallurgical thermodynamics
Physical metallurgy
Chemical metallurgy
Extractive metallurgy
Processing and properties of metals
Transport phenomena in metallurgy
Casting and solidification processing
Metallurgical engineering design
Degradation of materials
Engineering economics
Senior design project

Concentrations:

In college: physical metallurgy; extractive metallurgy.

If you go on to grad school: programs may focus on a specific alloy, processing technique, or application.

What the study of this major is like:

Although metallurgical engineering builds on a tradition of metalworking that is thousands of years old, it is sufficiently complex that materials and processes are continuously being discovered. Until fairly recently, high-temperature superconductivity, amorphous metals, buckyballs, and carbon nanotubes were unknown. Yet, if you consider the many elements on the periodic table, the ways in which they can be combined, and the possibilities for processing them to achieve novel structures, you will realize that the universe of achievable materials has barely been explored.

As an undergraduate in a program approved by ABET (Accreditation Board for Engineering and Technology), you must complete two years of math (including calculus and differential equations) and at least a year of both chemistry and physics. Majors typically take at least 48 semester credits of engineering-related courses, divided between general engineering courses (such as statics, design, and programming) and metallurgical core courses.

The core courses stress the relationships among the structure, properties, processing, and performance of metals and alloys. You study the structure of a metal on scales ranging from the bonding between individual atoms to the interaction of macroscopically visible components in engineered composites (such as fibers and particles). You use advanced techniques including optical and electron microscopy; X-ray diffraction; mechanical testing; thermal analysis; and electrical, magnetic, and optical characterization of materials.

Other courses cover the mechanical, chemical, and physical properties of alloys. Typically, you are required to take at least one course on mechanical properties and one course on physical properties (electrical, magnetic, optical). Often courses on electrochemical behavior of material (such as corrosion) are also required.

You study processing in courses that range from the thermodynamics of materials and the kinetic processes that govern movement of atoms and molecules, to the applied aspects of materials processing, such as sintering, casting, or vapor deposition of metals and alloys.

The desired performance of metals and alloys is governed by their properties, as well as factors such as cost, availability, and recyclability. Performance is usually incorporated into a number of courses and then emphasized in a major design project—which you probably undertake during your last year—that integrates knowledge and skills from earlier courses.

Most departments are relatively small and informal. Depending on the college, classes have from 10 to 50 students. Because metallurgical engineering depends on the application of advanced experimental techniques, you may take more lab classes than students in other engineering majors. Most majors get to know faculty members and fellow students, and many programs have student societies that help you become integrated into the profession before you graduate.

There are significant differences in emphasis among various departments across the United States. Some programs focus exclusively on metals; some include other classes of materials (ceramics, composites, and so on.). While some programs emphasize extractive processing of commodity metals, others concentrate on physical metallurgy and the application of engineering alloys. A careful examination of third- and fourth-year core and elective courses gives you a good indication of a program's emphasis.

Other majors you might like:

Materials engineering
Ceramic sciences/engineering
Chemical engineering
Electrical and communications engineering
Materials science
Chemistry
Physics
Metallurgical technology
Electrical engineering technology

Career options and trends:

Industrial metallurgist*; industrial researcher; research scientist at a university; quality control specialist; production engineer; production supervisor.

Because metallurgical and materials engineers work in all segments of the manufacturing economy, employment prospects for graduates tend to be less affected by downturns in a single industry than are some other engineering disciplines. Demand for metallurgical and materials engineers will likely be sustained by the need for fuel-efficient transportation; by advances in biomaterials, computers, and information technology; and by increased spending on national defense.

For more info:

The Minerals, Metals, and Materials Society (TMS)
184 Thorn Hill Rd.
Warrendale, PA 15086
(724) 776-9000
www.tms.org

Mining and mineral engineering

Also known as:

Natural resources engineering

What it's about:

Mining engineering is the application of scientific principles to the discovery, appraisal, and extraction of minerals from the earth and the sea. The engineer may work in underground mines or mines on the Earth's surface, overseeing the recovery of mineral resources from the natural environment; processing the extracted materials; ensuring safety; and restoring the land.

Is this for you?

You might like this major if you also like: rocks and rock collecting; fossil collecting; working outdoors rather than in an office; camping, fishing, hiking; the prospect of working with large, complex equipment.

Consider this major if you are good at: leadership; math; quantitative analysis; spacial thinking/ analysis; teamwork ...*or have...* initiative; patience; verbal skills; writing skills.

Recommended high school prep:

English 4, math 4 (including trigonometry, calculus or precalculus), lab science 3–4 (including chemistry and physics), social studies 3, and a foreign language 2–3. Courses in written and oral communication are also important.

Did you know...

...that according to the U.S. Bureau of Mines, for every American, every year, the equivalent of 40,000 pounds of new minerals, and energy equal to that produced by 30,000 pounds of coal, are harvested? With so much demand for extraction, mining engineers can choose to work in diverse environments, in many areas of the world. So if you're looking for a well-paid career with opportunities for advancement, then mining engineering could be a good major for you.

Typical courses in this major:

Physical geology
Structural geology
Engineering mechanics
Fluid mechanics
Thermodynamics
Ore and mineral deposits
Petrology
Mineral economics
Mining methods
Mine surveying
Mine planning and design
Ground control and rock mechanics
Rock blasting and fragmentation
Mineral or coal processing
Environmental reclamation
Mine health and safety

Concentrations:

In college: surface mining; underground mining; hard-rock mining; soft-rock (coal, phosphate, clays) mining; placer mining; quarry and industrial-minerals mining.

If you go on to grad school: rock mechanics; rock slope engineering; mine planning and design; geostatistical techniques; explosives engineering; mine health and safety; mine environment and reclamation; mine management.

What the study of this major is like:

Mining and mineral engineering is more hands-on than many other engineering fields. Like other areas of engineering, though, it is a highly technical field. These days, mining operations routinely use technologies such as global positioning, radio telemetry of data, satellite communications, computer-aided design, automation, and robotics. The equipment gets bigger and better; the industry's health and safety record continues to improve; and the productivity of miners in the United States (and, generally, worldwide) keeps increasing.

Mining engineers spend a considerable portion of their time out in the field. Accordingly, most majors consider themselves outdoorsy types. Often, students in the major started out in another science or engineering discipline. They took a summer internship at a mine operation, enjoyed the experience, and changed majors after returning to college in the fall.

Your course work generally includes math and science, basic engineering, mining engineering, geology, and the humanities and social sciences. Many courses, especially in mining and geology, are taught as a combination of lectures and laboratory experience. On the whole, though, most courses are still conducted as lectures. The greatest challenge most students encounter is to complete some of the other required engineering courses—for example, an electrical engineering course. Most programs in the United States are small, compared with better-known programs such as mechanical engineering. Therefore, students normally work in small groups with their instructors. Teamwork is emphasized; you'll get to know your colleagues and professors well.

Many of the eastern colleges offering degrees in mineral engineering specialize in coal mining, whereas western colleges tend to specialize in hard-rock mining. Graduates of eastern colleges most often find work in the coalfields of the eastern and central states, whereas their counterparts in western colleges usually find jobs in the central and western part of the country. Although some colleges have a practical orientation, a few emphasize undergrad research and the utilization of research conducted by faculty members and graduate students. Some programs have started offering specializations in areas such as quarry mining, underground construction, and management.

Other majors you might like:
Structural engineering
Geotechnical engineering
Environmental engineering
Natural resources and conservation
Mining technology
Surveying technology
Geology/earth science
Range science

Heavy/earthmoving equipment operation
Ocean engineering
Petroleum engineering
Geography

Questions to ask colleges:
Does the program specialize in a particular area of mining engineering?

Are summer internships or co-op education programs available?

Are field trips part of the curriculum, so that students can visit mines and gain real-world experience?

Career options and trends:
Mine engineer*; construction engineer*; mine manager*; environmental engineer; sales/technical representative.

In the United States, only about 125 students graduate each year with a degree in mining engineering. Recent studies have concluded that over 300 new graduates per year will be needed just to keep up with retirements. Starting salaries are expected to rise dramatically with this increase in demand.

Globalization is another trend affecting this field. Mining engineers frequently find opportunities overseas to introduce advances in technology or to assist in the development of the mining economy.

Insider's viewpoint:
"Mining engineering is as much of a lifestyle choice as a career choice."

—Professor Charles Kliche, South Dakota School of Mines and Technology

For more info:
Society for Mining, Metallurgy, and Exploration
    (SME)
8307 Shaffer Parkway
Littleton, CO 80127-4102
(800) 763-3132
www.smenet.org

Nuclear engineering

Also known as:
Radiological engineering

What it's about:
Nuclear engineering focuses on the application of radioactive materials and radiation to meet many of society's needs. The generation of electricity by nuclear power plants typically receives the most attention, but other applications include nuclear medicine, space power, environmental research, and the use of radiation in industrial processes and research.

Is this for you?
You might like this major if you also like: math and science, especially physics; science fairs; science fiction; working in teams; building things.

Consider this major if you are good at: attention to detail; creativity; math; quantitative analysis; spacial thinking/analysis; teamwork ...*or have...* initiative; persistence; verbal skills; writing skills.

Recommended high school prep:
English 4, math 4 (including precalculus or calculus), lab science 3–4 (including chemistry and physics), social studies 3, and a foreign language 2–3. If available, courses in computer programming and technical writing would be valuable.

Did you know...
...that every year, two million nuclear medical procedures are performed in the United States? These procedures include cancer radiation treatments, nuclear magnetic resonance imaging (MRI), gamma knife surgery, boron neutron capture therapy, brain scans, and other applications to diagnose disease.

...that before its nuclear properties were discovered, uranium was used for coloring glass?

Typical courses in this major:
Introduction to nuclear science and engineering
Nuclear reactor theory
Nuclear fuel cycle
Radiation safety
Thermal hydraulics for nuclear plants
Radiation interactions with matter
Materials for nuclear applications
Radiation detection
Radiation shielding
Nuclear power systems
Nuclear engineering design
Engineering ethics

Concentrations:
In college: health physics; radiation protection.

If you go on to grad school: nuclear power; nuclear fusion; nuclear medicine; radioactive waste management; instrumentation and control; probabilistic safety assessment; nuclear reactor theory.

What the study of this major is like:
Nuclear engineers can work with radioactive materials and radiation in a variety of ways. Some are employed at large commercial power plants that produce electricity, while others work on smaller nuclear reactors that generate power for naval vessels, spacecraft, or equipment operating at remote locations. Some nuclear engineers focus on medical applications; others devote their efforts to radioactive waste disposal and environmental restoration of sites that have been contaminated.

As a nuclear engineering major, you will be introduced to these and other applications of radiation and radioactive materials. Primarily, though, you will learn the fundamentals that are essential for nuclear engineers preparing themselves for a number of possible careers. In your courses, more than likely, you will explore the nature of radiation and radioactive decay; naturally occurring radioactive materials; the detection of radiation; its interaction with matter (its effects on humans and other living things, as well as on materials in the power plant); the principles of radiation protection; the fuel cycle; and the environmental impact of nuclear facilities. At most colleges, courses contain some material that engineering students often consider to be soft science. But these topics (including ethics, economics, and regulation of nuclear facilities) are critical to professionals in the discipline.

Most of your courses are taught as lectures; you'll have a variety of out-of-class assignments, such as finding solutions to problems, developing or applying computer models to analyze reactors or other nuclear systems, and working on team research or design projects. Several courses have a laboratory component, in which you work with detection equipment and perhaps with a research reactor or a simulator (if your college has such equipment). Lab experiments are generally done in teams. You frequently spend one or more terms as a co-op or intern, working at a nuclear facility and learning firsthand what nuclear engineers do. Positions as co-ops, interns, or assistants on faculty research projects provide excellent opportunities to apply the theoretical material you learned.

A unique challenge students face is the public's ignorance about—and sometimes fear of—radiation, nuclear power, nuclear waste, and related topics. Professionals in this field need to educate themselves about the industry and learn to talk about it with laymen, in language they can understand. Most nuclear engineers belong to a professional organization, such as the American Nuclear Society. Nuclear engineering students are generally encouraged to begin participating in the ANS while they are still in college.

There are several areas in which nuclear engineering programs may vary among colleges. Some focus on nuclear power engineering; some focus on radiological engineering/health physics; and some include both subjects. At some colleges, the curriculum emphasizes theory, whereas others offer a good deal of practical application, including visits to nuclear facilities or hands-on lab courses. The curriculum may be geared toward students going on to graduate school, toward those who plan to work in the industry after completing a Bachelor of Science degree, or it may combine the two orientations.

Other majors you might like:

Radiation protection/health physics technology
Nuclear engineering technology
Hazardous materials technology
Applied math
Environmental engineering
Marine engineering/naval architecture
Nuclear medical technology
Nuclear power technology
Physics
Applied physics
Medical radiologic technology/radiation therapy
Radiologic technology/medical imaging

Questions to ask colleges:

What are the primary research areas of the nuclear engineering faculty members? Are undergraduate students encouraged to become involved in research?

What opportunities are available for co-op or intern positions in the nuclear industry, and what co-op and/or intern positions have recent students in the program held?

What lab facilities do undergrads have an opportunity to use?

Career options and trends:

Health physicist; radiation safety officer; nuclear reactor operator*; nuclear equipment design engineer; consulting engineer*; researcher at a national laboratory; government employee (U.S. Navy or Department of Energy)*; instrumentation design specialist; radioactive waste manager or environmental restoration specialist.

Approximately a third of the nuclear workforce is expected to retire in the next decade, and a shortage of new engineers is projected. While no commercial nuclear power plants are currently under construction in the United States, nuclear engineers will be needed to operate existing plants; they will also be needed in the areas of nuclear medicine technology, national defense, fusion research, waste management, and regulatory compliance. Salaries of nuclear engineers are among the highest for all engineers.

An exciting development in the nuclear industry is the worldwide effort to design a generation of nuclear power plants that are safer, more efficient, and more economical than existing plants. In addition to generating electricity, some of these plants are being designed to produce hydrogen to support the "hydrogen economy," desalinate water, provide industrial process heat, and burn nuclear waste.

Insider's viewpoint:

"I purchased a book from the bookstore with the misleading title 'Introductory Nuclear Engineering.' I managed to read up to chapter 3 until it made no sense whatsoever. In high school, I took physics, chemistry, anatomy, and math up to precalculus. These courses were necessary to even understand the first three chapters of that book."

—Robert, junior, University of Tennessee: Knoxville

For more info:

American Nuclear Society (ANS)
555 North Kensington Ave.
La Grange Park, IL 60526
(708) 352-6611
www.ans.org

Nuclear Energy Institute (NEI)
1776 I St., N.W.
Suite 400
Washington, DC 20006-3708
(202) 739-8000
www.nei.org

Ocean engineering

Also known as:
Coastal engineering

What it's about:
Ocean engineers apply a variety of engineering disciplines to develop systems that operate in ocean and coastal waters. The profession includes such project areas as the construction and maintenance of facilities such as ports, harbors, and dikes; ocean drilling, dredging and salvage operations; underwater construction; and management of the ocean environment. This field should not be confused with marine engineering, which focuses primarily on the mechanics and operation of seagoing vessels.

Is this for you?
You might like this major if you also like: water sports (boating, diving, sailing, swimming, rowing, and surfing); math, science, and technology; designing and building things; the coastal and offshore environments.

Consider this major if you are good at: attention to detail; creativity; critical reading/thinking; math; quantitative analysis; research; spacial thinking/analysis; teamwork *...or have...* initiative; verbal skills.

Recommended high school prep:
English 4, math 4 (including precalculus), lab science 4 (earth science, biology, chemistry and physics), social studies 3, and a foreign language 2–3. If available, advanced or honors courses in math and physics are recommended. Since ocean engineering is, by its nature, a global discipline, facility with a foreign language can be valuable.

Typical courses in this major:
Marine structures
Coastal structures
Oceanography
Marine hydrodynamics
Mechanics of materials
Diving technology
Passive and active circuits
Fluid mechanics
Ocean measurements and instrumentation
Fundamentals of ocean mechanics
Wave mechanics and littoral (seashore) processes
Underwater acoustics
Engineering materials
Marine geomechanics
Ocean resources engineering
Nearshore environmental engineering

Concentrations:
Generally, none in college; but if you go on to grad school: ocean instrumentation and seafloor mapping; underwater acoustics; marine hydrodynamics and water wave mechanics; environmental engineering; marine geomechanics; coastal and offshore structures.

What the study of this major is like:
During your first two years as an ocean engineering major, you focus primarily on mathematics, chemistry, physics, and engineering fundamentals. You will probably take courses in calculus and analytic geometry; differential equations; statics/mechanics; electrical engineering; and engineering economics. Other general education requirements may be distributed throughout the curriculum. Electives, which will fill most of your third and fourth years, may include these:

Ocean acoustics. Sound is often the only way to sense the underwater environment or to transmit information underwater. You study the influence of water properties on sound speed and refraction; sonar systems; and sounds generated by ships and marine life.

Hydrodynamics. This field covers the behavior of water; floating and submerged objects; lift and drag forces; wave forces on beaches, vessels, and offshore platforms; and basic seakeeping.

Ocean measurements. You explore the principles of sensors, measurement, and electronics as applied to the ocean environment. You may also study seafloor mapping and underwater acoustics.

Ocean resources engineering. Here you examine systems to develop the energy, mineral, and living resources of the sea; the use of the ocean for waste disposal; and related environmental and economic issues.

Marine geomechanics. This focuses on the behavior of the seabed and sediments, dredging, cables and pipelines, and foundations for offshore and coastal structures.

Coastal engineering. Topics include ports and harbors, inlets, and barrier islands; nearshore environmental engineering; beach dynamics; flood hazards; and coastal structures such as piers.

Your fourth year will be dominated by a capstone project, in which you apply the knowledge and skills you've learned to a real-world design problem. It is usually a group project involving analysis, data collection, design, and a final presentation and report, and may also include scale-modeling, construction, and testing.

Programs are generally rigorous and comprehensive, requiring hardworking and dedicated students. Courses are typically taught as lectures, some with associated lab work and experimental projects. There is usually a great deal of fieldwork required, which most students enjoy. You may also take hands-on courses that focus on designing and building a system or structure, such as an autonomous underwater vehicle (AUV). Ocean engineering courses are sometimes supplemented by classes offered by other departments of engineering (chemical, civil, environmental, electrical, and/or mechanical), math, computer science, and grad schools of oceanography. Programs may be approved by the Accreditation Board for Engineering and Technology (ABET).

Other majors you might like:
Oceanography
Marine engineering/naval architecture
Environmental engineering

Marine biology
Marine science/Merchant Marine
Civil engineering
Water, wetlands, and marine management
Environmental science
Construction technology
Geology/earth science
Physics
Geography

Questions to ask colleges:
Are offshore or shoreline field experiences offered? What laboratory and experimental facilities are available? The extent of hands-on learning opportunities is a good indication of the strength of the program.

Career options and trends:
Coastal engineer*; civil engineer; underwater acoustician*; geotechnical engineer*; offshore engineer; marine engineer.

Job opportunities remain strong in the fields of coastal engineering; environmental engineering and pollution control; ocean instrumentation; dredging engineering; acoustics; ocean systems; and consulting. As nations increasingly rely on the oceans to meet the growing demand for resources, ocean engineers will be needed to meet these demands effectively and wisely.

For more info:
Marine Technology Society (MTS)
5565 Sterrett Place
Suite 108
Columbia, MD 21044
(410) 884-5330
www.mtsociety.org

Association of Coastal Engineers
c/o Angie Gross, Executive Secretary
5550 Northwest 111th Boulevard
Applied Technology and Management Inc.
Gainesville, FL 32653
www.coastalengineers.org

Software engineering

What it's about:

As a software engineering major, you study the techniques used in constructing large, complex software systems. The discipline covers the analysis, specification, design, construction, testing, and maintenance of software systems. Software engineers build systems that empower users, increasing their capabilities and improving the way they work.

Is this for you?

You might like this major if you also like: solving puzzles and complex problems; abstract thinking; planning and organizing activities and events; explaining things; working in groups.

Consider this major if you are good at: attention to detail; creativity; critical reading/thinking; giving directions; logical reasoning; organizing; teamwork ...*or have...* math skills; writing skills.

Recommended high school prep:

English 4, math 4 (including calculus or precalculus), lab science 3-4, social studies 3, and a foreign language 2-3. If possible, take advanced or additional classes in discrete mathematics, computer science, and writing.

Did you know...

...that software engineers don't have to be passionate, compulsive programmers? Many students who major in one of the computing fields never did computer programming in high school.

Typical courses in this major:

Fundamentals of software development
Introduction to computer science
Systems analysis
Programming language concepts
Discrete mathematics
Statistics
Software architecture and design
Software construction and evolution
Software requirements and specification
Database systems
Operating systems
Software testing and quality assurance
Software project management
Senior project/capstone experience

Concentrations:

In college: commercial applications; computer engineering; scientific computing; embedded systems.

If you go on to grad school: systems analysis; software development methodologies; software testing and quality assurance; software project management; software reengineering and evolution; user interface design; software metrics.

What the study of this major is like:

Software engineers do much more than program computers; they use their talents to help nonexperts benefit from the computer in their daily activities. They also create tools that enable computer users to work efficiently, economically, and effectively.

Most students don't realize that software engineering uses concepts from engineering, computer science, and mathematics, as well as from management, psychology, economics, politics, art, sociology, and language arts. To be successful in the discipline, you need good writing and oral presentation skills and the ability to use mathematical thinking (abstraction, logical reasoning), to work effectively in teams, and to understand computer programming. In addition, you must be able to learn new practices and procedures quickly, so that you can apply them soon after they are introduced.

In your first two years as a major, you take basic courses in computer science and math (including calculus and discrete mathematics) and other general education courses. Your last two years will focus on software engineering and related areas. Most programs have a capstone course in which you complete a software development project. The project requires you to put into practice what you have learned in previous courses, as a means of preparing you for a professional career. Courses in computer science and software engineering often involve group projects. Some courses have scheduled laboratories, but you can often do lab work at other times as well. If you delay your group project and lab assignments until just before the deadline, the result may be poor-quality work—and you will probably learn less as you play last-minute catch-up.

The earliest undergrad programs in software engineering date from the 1990s, and many colleges have not yet developed separate software engineering programs. Colleges may still offer numerous software engineering courses, however, provided by computer science, computer engineering, and/or electrical engineering programs. Software engineering, computer engineering, and computer science are not completely separate fields; they have significant amounts of overlap. Software engineering programs that are housed in electrical and computer engineering departments tend to focus on hardware issues. On the other hand, software engineering programs in departments of computer science (or math and computer science) tend to emphasize software, and their orientation is likely to be theoretical and mathematical.

As you study college catalogs, be aware that similarly named programs may actually contain different content—and programs with different names may, in fact, be very similar. Variation is to be expected in a field as new as software engineering.

Other majors you might like:

Computer science
Computer engineering
Digital media
Electrical and communications engineering
Management information systems
Game design
Animation
Artificial intelligence/robotics
E-commerce
Computer engineering technology
Bioinformatics
Applied mathematics

Questions to ask colleges:

What is the nature of the capstone course? What kinds of projects have been done in the past?

How good is the campus computer network? Are appropriate software tools available for software engineering students?

Do faculty members have experience building large software systems?

Are there any opportunities for summer internships or co-op work experiences? Are there opportunities for students to use their technical skills in campus jobs?

Career options and trends:

Software engineer*; software developer*; software or systems analyst*; senior programmer; systems programmer; database administrator.

Jobs in all computing fields are increasing at a good clip even during tough economic times. Software engineering opportunities are projected to be excellent, especially for those with interpersonal skills and business sense.

There is an important warning about entry-level jobs in computing fields: change in the computer industry is constant and rapid. A job you may want to prepare for as you begin college will probably be completely different by the time you graduate. Therefore, computer majors must be prepared for a life of constant learning.

For more info:

Association of Computing Machinery (ACM)
1515 Broadway,
New York, NY 10036-5701
(800) 342-6626
www.acm.org

Institute of Electrical and Electronics Engineers
   Computer Society (IEEE-CS)
1828 L Street, N.W.
Suite 1202
Washington, DC 20036
(202) 371-0101
www.computer.org

Engineering technology

What's the difference between engineering (covered in the previous section) and engineering technology? To begin with, engineering programs always lead to bachelor's degrees and, often, graduate degrees. Engineering technology programs can lead to either an associate degree or a bachelor's degree (currently, most students earn associate degrees). Second, engineering is more theoretical and employs higher-level math and physics, to prepare you for a career in product design or systems research. Engineering technology gives you more practical experience with the installation, maintenance, and operation of components and instruments.

Let's look at a specific example from this section: telecommunications technology. "While engineering programs typically prepare you for equipment design, graduate school and research, telecommunications technology programs are usually oriented toward using existing equipment for system and network design," explains Professor Pierre Catala of Texas A&M University. "Telecom engineering technicians maintain all the networks and sophisticated gear that make the World Wide Web, satellite and space probe transmissions, and e-commerce possible."

In this case, the associate degree (technician) programs in engineering technology usually deal with the testing, operation, initial software configuration, and maintenance of telecommunications equipment. Bachelor's degree (technologist) programs in engineering technology expand into design, implementation, configuration, and management of telecommunications networks.

"Engineering technologists bridge the gap between technicians and engineers with an understanding of both operations and design," says Thomas M. Hall, Jr. a professor at Northwestern State University. "Engineering technology graduates solve the problems of today, while research engineers solve the problems of tomorrow."

Mechanical engineering technologists are another example. "Now that mechanical engineering technology and other branches of engineering technology are offered as four-year Bachelor of Science programs, the industry has begun to accept engineering technology graduates as full engineers," suggests Professor James Kamm, University of Toledo.

The same level of application-related education and training goes into other engineering technologies—computer, electrical, construction, drafting, and surveying.

"Electrical engineering technology programs apply math and science to the real world," Hall says of his specialty.

With these majors, you can make an immediate impact working in manufacturing, field service, systems engineering, and applied design. Jobs include technicians, salespeople, network administrators, support specialists, drafters, designers, computer-aided design (CAD) operators, project managers, field supervisors, and inspectors.

The employment outlook depends on the specific industry. For instance, jobs continue to be generated in the computer and software industries, while signals are mixed as to how jobs will fare in the manufacturing and construction sectors. Long-term infrastructure projects resulting from economic stimulus spending should create job opportunities for all types of engineering technologists over the next decade.

A bachelor's degree in one of the engineering technologies improves your chances. So do professional licenses and certifications.

Design for learning

If you choose one of these college majors, you won't have your nose in a book all day. "The hallmark of any engineering technology program is the extensive laboratory experience," says Hall. In addition to labs and class, some colleges offer field experience, and cooperative educational (co-op) programs, in which you combine your academic studies with on-the-job training.

When comparing colleges, get a feel for how much they stress fundamentals compared to the latest gizmos. You want to learn the state-of-the-art technology, but you'll also need to know the principles, because technologies are changing. The newest tracks include wireless communications, 3-D modeling and animation, geographic information systems, and environmental and energy management technologies.

Think about whether you're going for a two-year associate degree or a four-year bachelor's degree. The associate degree is for technical training, current technologies and hands-on, nuts-and-bolts preparation for an entry-level job. A bachelor's degree in engineering technology, like an engineering degree, means more math and science, to help you analyze complex problems. Some programs also delve into the business or management side. The B.S. degree can be a launching pad to graduate work in geomatics (three-dimensional computerized mapping), engineering economics, network engineering, and management information systems.

Here are some things to think about or to ask people: What is the college's philosophy and approach? Does the college see its role as preparing talent for local industry? If so, which companies are they and what kind of jobs are likely? What is the background of some of the professors? If they're from industry, the courses will probably be more practical; if the faculty members have academic backgrounds, the courses will be more theoretical and scientific.

Ask if the program is approved by the leading commission in the field, like the Accreditation Board for Engineering and Technology (www.abet.org) for some specialties. How large are the lab classes and what type of equipment is used? Is it the kind used in industry? Is the program equipped to teach how computers interface with engineering technology? What is the seating capacity of the lab facilities?

In most other majors, you want to know the ratio of students to faculty members, but in these majors you may also want to ask about the ratio of students to computers.

Computer engineering technology

What it's about:

The computer engineering technology major will prepare you for a career in a number of fields: computer networking, telecommunications, computer electronics, programming, wireless and data communications and networks, embedded system design, and robotics. Offered at both the associate and bachelor's degree levels, this major is designed to meet the needs of technically inclined students who prefer hands-on teaching and learning to the more theoretical, mathematics-oriented computer science and engineering disciplines.

Is this for you?

You might like this major if you also like: working and playing with computer hardware and software; electronics; math and science; figuring out why things work the way they do; mathematical and logical puzzles; solving complex problems.

Consider this major if you are good at: attention to detail; critical reading/thinking; math; memorizing; organizing; quantitative analysis; teamwork ...*or have...* initiative; patience.

Recommended high school prep:

English 4, math 3–4, lab science 3 (including physics), social studies 3, and a foreign language 2–3. Precalculus, computer-aided design (CAD), and other computer programming and applications courses are also recommended, although not required.

Typical courses in this major:

Basic electricity and electronics
Digital systems and microprocessors
Object-oriented software development
Programming fundamentals I, II
Operating systems
Digital/communications
Computer architecture
Assembly language applications
Electronics computer-aided design
Data structures and file processing
Digital testing techniques
Wide-area networking
Local-area networking
Systems administration
Technical writing and communications

Concentrations:

Local-area and wide-area networking (LAN/WAN); systems administration; communications systems; microprocessors; programming languages; software engineering; hardware engineering; industrial automation systems; robotics.

What the study of this major is like:

This major provides you with practical training and skills in courses covering hardware and software, electronics, programming, and supporting topics. Most programs in computer engineering technology focus on both the hardware and the software aspects of the applications, including the interfacing of computers and systems; in contrast, most electrical engineering technology programs concentrate primarily on hardware and secondarily on related software.

Hands-on training in applications and equipment is the primary teaching method, but you'll also learn theoretical aspects to help you adapt to new technology in the future. You begin with the basics of electricity and electronics, including analog and digital circuit analysis. Then you'll be introduced to the fundamentals of microprocessors and operating systems; programming; and applications that use word processors, spreadsheets, and high-level and low-level computer languages.

Other required courses zero in on mathematical and communication skills, and you'll learn enough about the industrial and business environment to perform effectively on the job. In labs, you work on a variety of microprocessor systems and devices, as you gain experience in installing, diagnosing, operating, and servicing computer systems and related equipment.

Upper-level courses, in which you get an in-depth look at the hardware and software used in industry and business, are usually wide ranging enough to allow for specialization. Topics include networking technology and security; advanced programming; digital testing technology; data communications; hardware description languages; embedded system design; industrial instrumentation; and industrial automation systems.

Because many areas of computer application are important in industry and business, colleges vary in the aspects of the major that they emphasize. For instance, some programs may focus on computer-use topics such as programming, Internet technology, and database systems, while others may stress technical applications such as industrial networking, Web-based control, electronic devices, Web services, and other aspects of enterprise networking.

Two-year associate degree programs are more likely to focus on specific occupations or systems than are programs designed for a four-year bachelor's degree. In bachelor's programs, you'll study more math (in particular, differential equations, sets and logic, and calculus), alongside courses in the humanities and sciences. Coupled with business electives, a four-year degree will generally increase your employment options. Many students begin in the less-costly two-year program and then transfer into the last two years of a bachelor's program, usually with enough job skills to work as they continue their education.

In computer engineering technology, lifelong learning really counts—you have no choice but to continue your education if you want to remain employable. Technological advances come so rapidly that even people with good jobs have to keep their skills up-to-date. After all, employers are often looking to put the latest technologies to profitable use. Continuing education opportunities are plentiful, however, and many employers will help you take advantage of them.

Other majors you might like:
Game design
Software engineering
Digital media
Electrical and communications engineering
Management information systems
Computer programming
Computational mathematics
Robotics technology
E-commerce
Information technology
Recording arts
Applied mathematics

Questions to ask colleges:
How often are the lab facilities upgraded with the latest hardware and software? Be sure that the new equipment includes various operating systems in the Microsoft, Apple, and Unix/Linux categories.

Is the program approved by the Technology Accreditation Commission of the Accreditation Board for Engineering and Technology (TAC/ABET)?

Are co-op education and internships available? If so, take advantage of them. Real-world experience will greatly enhance your employment opportunities.

How successful have graduates been in getting jobs in the specialty areas emphasized by the college?

Career options and trends:
Systems analyst; consulting engineer*; network administrator*; database administrator; systems administrator; software engineer (applications or systems); support specialist*.

Certification in a particular application, program language (such as JAVA), or system (Linux) may be of value to employers using them. Some vendors and software firms may require certification if you will be working with their products.

The job titles listed above are among the fastest-growing careers, according to the U.S. Bureau of Labor Statistics, which also projects computer and data processing services to be the most rapidly growing industry in the economy. The employment outlook is favorable for graduates who can set up and maintain computer networks, information and Internet technology, and computer-based electronic systems.

However, computer support, like many technical fields, is becoming increasingly competitive internationally. As a result of the expanding knowledge economy, countries in Eastern Europe and Asia are producing labor pools of relatively low-cost, highly trained computer specialists; and some computer support positions are being outsourced overseas.

But don't let that spook you—job creation is outpacing job destruction in this field, and you can prepare yourself for the competition by obtaining a broad-based education, developing interpersonal and business skills, and remaining alert to the areas of greatest demand, such as e-commerce and communications security.

For more info:

Institute of Electrical and Electronics Engineers (IEEE)
445 Hoes Lane
Piscataway, NJ 08855
(732) 981-1686
www.ieee.org

Association for Computer Machinery (ACM)
1515 Broadway
New York, NY 10036-5701
(800) 342-6626
www.acm.org

Construction technology

What it's about:

The construction technology major provides practical training and broad-based education in general, structural, and construction engineering principles; in planning and design; and in construction management.

Is this for you?

You might like this major if you also like: working in groups or teams; working with your hands; carpentry; the outdoors; achieving goals and results; watching construction sites.

Consider this major if you are good at: attention to detail; coaching; critical reading/thinking; leadership; math; organizing; persuading/influencing; spacial thinking/analysis; teamwork *...or have...* initiative.

Recommended high school prep:

English 4, math 3 (including trigonometry), lab science 3 (including physics and chemistry), social studies 3, industrial arts 2, and a foreign language 2. If they are available, take courses in computer-aided drafting (CAD) or mechanical drawing.

Did you know...

...that the construction industry is the second-largest employer in the United States, after the federal government?

Typical courses in this major:

Planning and scheduling
Safety, security, and environmental impact
Blueprint reading
Site surveying, planning, and design
Cost estimating
Architecture and urban form
Construction practices and methods
Computer-integrated construction (CIC)
Electrical systems
Groundwater hydrology
Soils and foundations
Construction materials and systems
Reinforced concrete design
Materials handling
Structural steel design
Technical report writing

Concentrations:

Structural design; construction management; construction engineering.

What the study of this major is like:

This major will provide you with a breadth of training, from management to carpentry, business law to asphalt paving. While the particular emphasis may vary, all programs feature hands-on, practical learning experiences in labs or in the field, in conjunction with classroom lectures.

You are encouraged to apply your skills through cooperative (co-op) experiences and independent studies. Most lecture classes use demonstrations and video aids, and in the labs you are introduced to construction methods and problems, which you work on either through simulations or with actual materials and equipment. Concepts and training come together in field experiences on construction sites.

Construction technology is usually taught in one of two ways. In one, the program follows the traditional engineering track: you apply mathematical theories and equations to explain abstract engineering principles. Courses cover such topics as statics, applied thermodynamics, and fluid mechanics. The other method is to pattern the curriculum after business management courses, with emphasis on lectures, reading, and case studies. Programs feature course content in contract management, plans and specifications, estimation of costs, building codes, labor relations, team dynamics, project management, and environmental and land-use concerns. In programs that are geared toward construction management, most students earn a four-year Bachelor of Science degree.

Either approach will give you sufficient technical training to be familiar with the methods used in residential, commercial, industrial, and public-works construction. Architectural drafting and computer-aided design (CAD), blueprint reading, and the basics of surveying are also likely to be core requirements.

In a two-year associate degree program, which focuses on the technical aspects of construction, you will study the basics of structural design, construction methods and practices, and project management. Bachelor's degree programs include courses in mathematics, natural sciences, business, humanities, social sciences, and written and oral communications. In upper-level course work, you concentrate on advanced engineering, design, and management principles.

A valuable part of a strong construction technology program is co-op educational experience: you combine your academic studies with paid, on-the-job training, either during regular semesters or over the summer. Independent study opportunities—which are often available through student chapters of professional organizations such as the Associated Builders and Contractors, the Associated General Contractors of America, and the National Society of Professional Engineers—are another way to supplement your classroom and lab training.

Other majors you might like:

Civil engineering
Construction management
Structural engineering
Architectural engineering technology
Drafting and design technology
Historic preservation
Housing and human environments
Surveying technology
Heating/air conditioning/refrigeration technology
Heavy/earthmoving equipment operation
Parks, recreation, and leisure studies
Theater design and technology

Questions to ask colleges:

Do the lab facilities have enough computers and construction equipment to offer adequate training in the wide range of problems this program explores, such as soil analysis, materials testing, CAD, surveying?

Is the program approved by the Technology Accreditation Commission of the Accreditation Board for Engineering and Technology (TAC/ABET)?

Career options and trends:

Field engineer; job expeditor; project manager; field supervisor; site inspector; scheduler; contract administrator; estimator; designer.

Employment opportunities are expected to recover in the construction industry, because of a shortage of professionals who can handle the increasing complexity of projects, technology, and regulatory standards, and because of the need to replace much of the country's aging infrastructure. Job prospects will be best for graduates with a bachelor's degree and previous construction work experience.

For more info:

Associated Builders and Contractors (ABC)
4250 N. Fairfax Drive, 9th Fl.
Arlington, VA 22203
(703) 812-2000
www.abc.org

National Association of Women in Construction (NAWIC)
327 South Adams St.
Fort Worth, TX 76104
(800) 552-3506
www.nawic.org

Drafting and design technology

Also known as:

Computer Aided Drafting and Design (CADD)

Technical drawing and design

What it's about:

The major in drafting and design technology, which can lead to either an associate degree or a bachelor's degree, prepares you for a career in industry or in another design-related field. You learn how to make drawings, plans, and computer-aided drafting (CAD) models and simulations that will be used in constructing a building, manufacturing a product, or developing a creative project such as marketing materials.

Is this for you?

You might like this major if you also like: learning new tricks on the computer; being precise; working independently as well as in groups; contributing to large projects; drawing; making models; planning how things fit together.

Consider this major if you are good at: attention to detail; concentrating; creativity; critical reading/thinking; math; organizing; spacial thinking/analysis ...*or have...* manual dexterity; patience.

Recommended high school prep:

English 4, math 3, lab science 3 (including physics), social studies 3, industrial arts 2, and a foreign language 2–3. If they are available, take courses in computer-aided drafting or mechanical drawing, computer applications, and a fine arts drawing class.

Did you know...

...that in this major, you learn another language—a graphic language? Known as the "the language of industry," drafting is a universal method of communication that is understood by technicians, engineers, designers, and architects all over the world.

Typical courses in this major:

Blueprint reading

Technical drawing

Computer-aided drafting (CAD) I, II

Engineering design graphics

Construction materials

Manufacturing processes

Solid modeling

Machine drafting

Architectural drafting

Business and technical writing

Geometric dimensioning and tolerancing

Descriptive geometry

Building codes

Architectural delineation

Electromechanical design

Product design

Concentrations:

Product design; architectural drafting.

What the study of this major is like:

Drafters and designers are important links between great ideas and actual products, buildings, processes, or services. As a drafting and design technology major, you study idea generation and sketching, product specification, working and assembly drawings, product realization and construction, and manufacturing processes and materials.

Few disciplines have been changed more by computers than drafting and design. You may be taught basic drafting on the drawing board, but you will certainly be trained to use computer-aided-drafting software and solid modeling software. "CAD" no longer refers just to drawing—it is now the first step in the programming of automated production equipment. Also, CAD is the principal ingredient in the trend away from making prototypes of products the old-fashioned way, by hand. More and more engineers are creating prototypes on modeling software and then testing them through computer simulation.

In most drafting and design courses the instructor will introduce a concept through a lecture and demonstration; then students complete an assignment to reinforce the concept. In a final project, you will show what you've learned: you'll develop an idea of your own choosing into a usable design. Your project and other work may be included in a portfolio that will be helpful during your job search.

What are the challenges? The ability to see an object in three dimensions is a skill that most majors must learn—it rarely comes naturally. Majors who are not familiar with computers may also have difficulty mastering CAD software while also learning the basics of computer operating systems.

The major is usually offered at two-year technical and community colleges. Programs may have different philosophies, requirements, and emphases. Philosophically, they may differ in the importance they place on teaching the fundamentals versus introducing students to the latest technology. Some colleges emphasize a theoretical, scientific orientation, while others focus on the "nuts and bolts" essentials that are needed for real-world jobs. Finally, programs may differ in the emphasis they place on certain industries. Community colleges in particular often reflect the local industries they serve. This emphasis can be seen in the types of courses and CAD software the program offers.

Other majors you might like:
Graphic design
Architectural technology
Surveying technology
Architectural engineering technology
Mechanical engineering technology
Industrial design
Medical illustrating
Digital media
Animation
Cartography
Computer science
Geology/earth science

Questions to ask colleges:
What types of computer software and hardware are used in the courses? Are they up-to-date? Is the software widely used in key industries? Is it used in the industry or geographic location you are considering?

What is the seating capacity of the lab facilities? Are the computers connected to a campus network? Are open labs available for homework and projects? What is the student-to-computer ratio?

Career options and trends:
CAD operator*; drafter or designer*; engineering technician; design engineer; CAD systems manager; technical illustrator.

Engineering positions such as design engineer usually require a four-year degree, although some designers earn these positions through progressive work experience.

The job outlook for drafting technicians is generally good. While the manufacturing base is declining, the number of industries and fields using CAD is expanding; as is the use of technical drawings and models in the production process. CAD modeling is also being used for product packaging and marketing activities.

Students who gain a strong understanding of the fundamentals and then keep up-to-date with the latest technology will be most likely to advance in their careers. But CAD systems are becoming more powerful and easier to use, making it easier for basic tasks to be handled by other workers or outsourced. This will reduce demand for lesser skilled drafters.

Insider's viewpoint:
"Drafting is a great field because of the opportunities it offers my students. What other field allows you to complete a degree or certificate program in two years or less, get a good-paying job, and continue your education while being paid for the valuable experience you are gaining?"

—Professor Paul Clarke, MiraCosta College

For more info:
American Design and Drafting Association (ADDA)
105 East Main St.
Newbern, TN 38059
(731) 627-0802
www.adda.org

Electrical engineering technology

Also known as:
Electrical and computer engineering technology

What it's about:
This major gives you practical training in a wide-ranging field of electrical engineering, including electronics, computers, communications, automatic controls, robotics, instrumentation, power systems, and computer-aided design (CAD). At the associate degree level, the focus is on operation, repair, and maintenance. At the bachelor's degree level, you also study the analysis, design, and development of electrical and electronic devices, systems, and processes.

Is this for you?
You might like this major if you also like: anything that involves math, science, electronics, and computers; tinkering and kit building; figuring out why things work the way they do.

Consider this major if you are good at: attention to detail; critical reading/thinking; math; organizing; quantitative analysis; spacial thinking/analysis; teamwork ...*or have...* initiative; patience.

Recommended high school prep:
English 4, math 3-4, lab science 3 (including physics), social studies 3, and a foreign language 2-3. Precalculus, calculus, computer-aided drafting, and other computer programming and applications courses are also recommended, although they are not required.

Did you know...
...that employers often prefer to hire engineering technologists rather than traditional engineers for positions in manufacturing, field service, systems engineering, and applied design? That's because engineering technologists combine an understanding of theory and design with hands-on operational experience.

Typical courses in this major:
Fundamentals of electricity
Control systems
Statics
Analog and digital electronics
Electronic system drafting (CAD)
Telecommunications systems
Electrical power and machines
Project management
Optical technology
Laser technology
Robotics
Data communications and computer networks
Technical writing
Transmission networks
Industrial electronics
Capstone project

Concentrations:
Electronics; electrical power and machinery; digital systems; computers and microprocessor systems; instrumentation; automation and control systems; telecommunications; information technology; electrical computer-aided drafting (CAD).

What the study of this major is like:
Students in electrical engineering technology (EET) programs like to build things, fix things, and make things work—or make them work better. They like to get their hands on the systems and the lab equipment. EET programs provide exactly that experience for you. The hallmark of any engineering technology program is the extensive laboratory experience—and EET is no exception.

EET programs apply math and science to the real world. Technical courses usually begin in your first year, along with general education courses in math, science, and the humanities. Sometimes students are surprised, and challenged, by the nontechnical course requirements; but employers expect EET graduates to acquire more than technical savvy. To prepare for a good job, you'll need to sharpen your skills in oral and written communication, teamwork, and project management; develop professional, ethical, and social responsibility; and be aware of contemporary issues.

In a bachelor's program, you are introduced to design concepts; and some courses stress calculus applications. Your first two years will lay a foundation in mathematics, chemistry, physics, and computer applications. In the third and fourth years, courses take an in-depth, technical approach and allow for specialization. You use software programs to simulate and design electrical systems and circuits, and to analyze complex problems.

Two-year associate degree programs provide technical training in circuit analysis, electronics, digital logic, microprocessors, communications, and control systems, with an emphasis on specific applications. The goal is to prepare you for entry-level employment as a technician.

The best students in EET programs learn, work, and play together. Often, student chapters of professional organizations, such as the Institute of Electrical and Electronics Engineers (IEEE) and the Instrumentation, Systems and Automation Society (ISA), offer a variety of programs and opportunities for students.

The field of EET is very broad. Typically, colleges with EET programs design a curriculum that is appropriate for both graduates and employers in the region. While all programs may touch on a range of topics, many emphasize one or more areas, such as robotics or industrial automated systems. In these areas of concentration, you get in-depth training and develop expertise; but be sure, when you are selecting a college, that its program matches your own interests.

Programs at various colleges can differ in other ways as well. Some rely heavily on the traditional classroom and laboratory settings; others make extensive use of field experience, co-op programs, or internships. In most programs, you will study with faculty members who have broad industrial experience. But in colleges that concentrate on theory and design, faculty members tend to have academic backgrounds.

Other majors you might like:
Computer engineering technology
Robotics technology
Applied mathematics
Telecommunications technology
Instrumentation technology
Electrocardiograph technology
Information technology
Laser/optical technology
Electrical drafting/CAD/CADD
Electrician
Avionics maintenance/technology
Radio and television

Questions to ask colleges:
Is the program approved by the Accreditation Board for Engineering and Technology (ABET)?

Does the program emphasize any particular areas within the broad field of EET?

Career options and trends:
Electrical/electronic technician; electrical engineering technologist; field service technician; systems technologist; communications engineer; design engineer; manufacturing process technologist; technical assistant; technical salesperson; technical writer.

According to the U.S. Bureau of Labor Statistics, employment for electrical engineering technologists is expected to grow at a moderate rate for the near future; job increases will be fueled by a demand for more sophisticated electrical and electronic products, controls, and processes. Most jobs are in electronic machinery and equipment manufacturing, instrumentation, and service industries.

For more info:
Institute of Electrical and Electronics Engineers
   (IEEE)
445 Hoes Lane
Piscataway, NJ 08855
(732) 981-0060
www.ieee.org

Mechanical engineering technology

What it's about:

As a major in mechanical engineering technology, you will learn to apply engineering principles and technical skills to the design and development of a wide variety of projects involving mechanical systems and the products that they create.

Is this for you?

You might like this major if you also like: achieving practical results; working on something different every day; math and science.

Consider this major if you are good at: attention to detail; creativity; critical reading/thinking; math; quantitative analysis; spacial thinking/analysis ...*or have...* initiative; patience; writing skills.

Recommended high school prep:

English 4, math 3, lab science 3 (including physics), social studies 3, and a foreign language 2–3. Your math classes should cover algebra and precalculus, and a class in computer-aided drafting or mechanical drawing would also be helpful.

Did you know...

...that math skills, rather than mechanical ability, are the most important indicator of success in this major? While high school calculus is not required, algebra and geometry are essential.

Typical courses in this major:

Fundamentals of mechanics
Computer-aided design (CAD)
Statics
Strength of materials
Thermodynamics
Fluid mechanics
Electrical circuits
Electromechanical control systems
Heating, ventilation, and air conditioning systems
Manufacturing processes
Stress and vibration analysis
Dynamics of systems
Machine design
Technical communications
Mechanical measurement and devices
Quality control systems

Concentrations:

In college: computer-aided design (CAD); thermodynamics; fluid mechanics; control systems; computer-controlled automation; materials science; machine design.

If you go on to grad school: engineering management; engineering economics.

What the study of this major is like:

Many people believe, incorrectly, that students who major in mechanical engineering technology must be amateur mechanics who love to work on, or under, cars. Although some majors do become automotive engineers or technicians, many others find good jobs as energy conservation engineers, plant managers, technical sales representatives, technical writers, robotics experts, and designers of alternative energy systems.

What's more, mechanical engineering technicians (METs) are no longer thought of simply as workers who simply assist mechanical engineers. Now that mechanical engineering technology and other branches of engineering technology are offered as four-year Bachelor's of Science programs, the industry has begun to accept graduates as full engineers. In fact, METs and mechanical engineers (MEs) often compete for the same jobs. Although MEs are more likely to get the jobs requiring a strong science background (for example, working with NASA or other research facilities), METs and MEs are usually considered equally qualified for a wide variety of jobs. There is even a procedure for METs to become registered as Professional Engineers (PEs).

The biggest difference between MEs and METs is in their education. MEs take more courses that require abstract thinking and heavy calculus loads; METs, on the other hand, take mostly applied, or practical, courses, with less calculus. At the undergraduate level, MEs prepare themselves for graduate school and employment as researchers, while METs are trained to get an engineering job—their only graduate school possibilities are in management or business. But the skills in design, application, and troubleshooting that METs and other engineering technology majors learn provide a significant career boost.

The mechanical engineering technology curriculum is diverse. You begin with physics; in your examination of machines, you'll observe the forces that are applied to mechanical devices and the forces that they generate. You'll learn, too, how engineers predict the way these forces are transmitted, multiplied, and/or reduced. You'll also study fluid mechanics: some machine systems rely on fluids to transmit either power or control. On the other hand, some fluid systems depend on machines, such as pumps, to distribute liquids (think of soup on an assembly line being poured into cans). In your class on thermodynamics, the science of heat, you'll concentrate on energy—how to make it work, how to use it more efficiently, how to find it in unexpected places (the sources of alternative energies). You study heat in automobile engines as well as in electric power plants. You also learn graphic arts by taking courses in computer-aided design (CAD) in both two- and three-dimensional formats.

Two-thirds of your courses deal primarily with problem solving—in the type of problem solving that engineers call "design," you'll use equations to determine important properties of a situation. For this work, you'll need a solid understanding of mathematics (including some calculus applications), as well as good critical-thinking skills, so that you can apply the math logically. You also take courses that develop your mechanical skills, usually by doing laboratory activities. Because, in some cases, laboratories simulate work environments, you'll have the chance to become familiar with instruments and equipment used in industry. Some equipment is based on cutting-edge technology, but most of the equipment in engineering labs is traditional, even timeless, such as pressure gauges, thermometers, material testers, and machine tools (metal cutting machines). Most programs end with a senior capstone design project.

Other majors you might like:
Biomedical technology
Robotics technology
Industrial technology
Aeronautical/aerospace engineering technology
Automotive engineering technology
Agricultural equipment technology
Drafting and design technology
Heavy equipment maintenance
Machine tool technology
Manufacturing technologies
Technical and business writing

Questions to ask colleges:
Is the program approved by the Accreditation Board for Engineering Technology (ABET)? If so, it will probably require an advanced level of calculus and have advanced courses that focus on abstract engineering, rather than on specific types of jobs in industry.

Career options and trends:
Plant manager; consulting engineer; manufacturing engineer; design engineer; sales engineer.

Consulting engineers typically are certified as Professional Engineers (PEs) by the state they work in. When you know where you'll be working, you should find out how a graduate of an engineering technology program becomes a PE in that state, since rules may differ from state to state.

Mechanical engineers and technicians are typically the most sought after of all the engineering disciplines, and entry-level salaries are good. Many graduates begin their careers performing CAD functions. Once they learn the product or service, they take on more responsibility for its actual design. Employment opportunities follow the national economy; sometimes jobs are more difficult to find or starting salaries are lower than normal, but graduates can almost always find a job.

Surveying technology

Also known as:

Geomatics engineering

What it's about:

Using specialized equipment and techniques, surveying technology majors learn how to measure the physical features of the earth. You gather data to determine land boundaries, locate existing and proposed engineering structures, make topographic maps of the earth's surface, and perform computations and computer-assisted drafting.

Is this for you?

You might like this major if you also like: drafting; drawing; working outdoors; geography and maps; solving practical problems; working with precision and detail.

Consider this major if you are good at: attention to detail; math; organizing; research; spacial thinking/analysis; teamwork *...or have...* communication skills; initiative; manual dexterity; physical stamina.

Recommended high school prep:

English 4, math 3, lab science 3 (including physics), social studies 3, and a foreign language 2–3. Math courses should cover algebra, geometry, trigonometry, and perhaps precalculus. If possible, also take courses in drafting and computer science or computer applications.

Did you know...

...that surveyors can map in three dimensions? They use the computerized technology known as geomatics, which processes information received from satellites and from sensors and imaging systems in the air, sea, and ground. Geomatic surveying is important for the building and monitoring of large engineering projects.

Typical courses in this major:

Calculus and analytic geometry
Basic statistics
Physics
Surveying fundamentals
Advanced surveying
Engineering and construction surveying
Measurement error analysis and adjustment
Geodetic datums and coordinate systems
Photogrammetry
Land information systems
Real estate law
Boundary surveying principles
Technical writing
Soil mechanics
Statics and strength of materials
Hydrology and drainage

Concentrations:

In college: geodetic (large-area) surveying; mine surveying; hydrographic surveying; cartography; photogrammetry (aerial surveying); geographic information science.

If you go on to grad school: geomatics (three-dimensional computerized mapping); geodesy; remote sensing.

What the study of this major is like:

In this major, you study the technologies used in making accurate measurements on earth. These measurements include distances, directions, and elevations that can be calculated directly or indirectly with optical or electromechanical instruments. The most recognizable device is the tripod-mounted *theodolite*, which measures horizontal and vertical angles. You will also learn to gather measurements by using tools such as aerial photographs, global positioning system (GPS) satellites, geographic information systems (GIS), and satellite remote sensing imagery. In addition to taking measurements, you'll acquire skills in analyzing the information you collect and in making conclusions and recommendations.

Courses are laboratory-oriented. In outdoor lab work, you explore different surveying techniques and gain practice in using the equipment. In indoor labs, you use specialized software to do survey computations and related drafting. Because most survey technology programs have small enrollments, students often become a closely knit group whose members help each other. In most schools, organizations representing students in the major are affiliated with state or national professional surveying organizations.

This major is offered at either the associate (two-year) or the bachelor's (four-year) degree level, depending on the college. Many programs prepare students to obtain state licensure for professional practice. These programs usually consist of courses on boundary determination, land development, and related state and federal statutes. Programs at some colleges may emphasize engineering and construction surveying, while other programs may stress mapping and the management of geographic information. Although a bachelor's degree from any accredited surveying technology program will make you eligible to apply to graduate school, an undergraduate program that gives you a strong grounding in math may better prepare you for graduate studies.

After graduation, your work location and responsibilities may change as you progress in your career. Early on, you will probably work mostly outdoors, performing different types of surveys. Senior surveyors usually become partners in surveying/engineering companies and hold management positions.

There are several career tracks open to you, in addition to assisting professional surveyors as a technician. *Photogrammetrists* prepare detailed maps of remote or inaccessible areas, using aerial photographs and other imaging systems. *Geodetic surveyors* measure large areas of the earth's surface, using technology such as satellite remote sensing. *Geophysical surveyors* map prospecting sites for subsurface exploration. *Hydrographic surveyors* survey harbors, rivers, and other bodies of water to determine depths, shorelines, bottom topography, and other nautical features.

In most states, to become a professional land surveyor, you must have a license or registration. Requirements vary but generally include the completion of a two-part examination, conducted by the National Committee of Examiners for Engineering and Surveying, and a period of apprenticeship. An increasing number of states also require a bachelor's degree. Licensure is not required unless your practice includes work related to property boundaries. Certification as a survey technician is available through national professional societies.

Other majors you might like:

Cartography
Civil engineering
Drafting and design technology
Real estate
Forest engineering
Landscape architecture
Geology/earth science
Geography
Construction management
Land use planning
Mining and mineral engineering
Instrumentation technology

Questions to ask colleges:

Does the program offer an associate degree, a bachelor's degree, or both?

Is the program accredited? Most programs in this major are approved under one of three commissions of the Accreditation Board for Engineering and Technology (ABET): the Engineering Accreditation Commission, the Applied Science Accreditation Commission, or the Technology Accreditation Commission.

What surveying equipment is available for laboratory work? Are students trained in the latest surveying technologies?

Are the students required to purchase any supplies other than textbooks?

Career options and trends:

Surveying technician*; drafting technician; photogrammetric technician; professional land surveyor*; GIS manager; consultant.

Job prospects for surveying technicians are likely to increase faster than average over the next decade or so. Opportunities will be greatest for those who have a bachelor's degree and proficiency in advanced technologies such as GPS and GIS. Resurgent growth in construction, which is also projected for the long term, should create demand for surveyors to lay out projects and to define areas in need of environmental protection.

Insider's viewpoint:

"Being a person who loves the outdoors, I prefer surveying to any other engineering related field."

—Professor Indrajith Wijayratne, Michigan Technological University

For more info:

American Congress on Surveying and Mapping (ACSM)
6 Montgomery Village Ave.
Suite 403
Gaithersburg, MD 20879
(240) 632-9716
www.acsm.net

American Society of Photogrammetry and Remote Sensing (ASPRS)
5410 Grosvenor Lane
Suite 210
Bethesda, MD 20814-2160
(301) 493-0290
www.asprs.org

Telecommunications technology

What it's about:

In the telecommunications technology major, students are trained in the installation, management, operation, and maintenance of telecommunications equipment and systems, such as those used in telephone, data, Internet, and wireless networks. Graduates of associate degree (technician) programs typically handle the testing, operation, initial software configuration, and maintenance of telecommunications equipment. Bachelor's degree (technologist) programs, in contrast, prepare you to design, implement, configure, and manage telecommunications networks.

Is this for you?

You might like this major if you also like: amateur or ham radio; working and playing with computers; connecting systems (computers, home entertainment systems); electronics.

Consider this major if you are good at: attention to detail; creativity; critical reading/thinking; math; memorizing; organizing; teamwork *...or have...* initiative; patience; verbal skills; writing skills.

Recommended high school prep:

English 4, math 3–4 (trigonometry and precalculus), lab science 3, social studies 3, and a foreign language 2–3. If they are available, take courses in computer office applications (word processing, spreadsheets, and databases) and introductory computer programming.

Did you know...

...that telecommunications covers a lot more than just communicating by phone, cell, or instant messaging? Telecom engineering technicians maintain all the networks and sophisticated gear that make the World Wide Web, satellite and space probe transmissions, and e-commerce possible. These networks form the fabric of the global economy.

Typical courses in this major:

Communication systems
Electrical circuits and systems
Data communications
Telephony
Digital transmission
Central offices
Local-area networks and wide-area networks
Internet protocols (IP) for data and voice
Fiber optics
Telecom testing techniques
Wireless systems
Radio frequency design
Network planning and design
Satellite networks
Microwave link design
Network management

Concentrations:

In college: data communications; local-area networks (LAN); wide-area networks (WAN); telephony (transmission and switching); wireless systems (wireless LAN, microwave links, satellites); fiber optics.

If you go on to grad school: network engineering; traffic engineering; telecom regulations; international telecommunications; management of information systems (MIS).

What the study of this major is like:

Telecommunications technology professionals design, install, manage, operate, and maintain the equipment and systems (such as telephone, data, Internet, and wireless networks) that make possible today's fast-paced exchange of information. Telecom technicians and technologists work to create the right balance between sophistication and cost effectiveness while setting up networks and ensuring that they function properly.

To become an engineering technologist, you must complete a four-year bachelor's degree program

263

that prepares you to design, implement/configure, and manage telecommunications networks. Two-year associate degree programs, which train you to become a technician, typically cover the testing, operation, initial software configuration, and maintenance of telecommunications equipment.

As a major, you learn to design both local and long distance telecommunications networks (LANs and WANs). You also learn the principles of cellular telephone networks and receive a strong foundation in LAN administration.

Although the major is mostly system- or network-oriented, you generally take additional electronics and computers courses that cover basic electricity, solid-state fundamentals, digital concepts, and microprocessors. You learn about central office switching, analog and digital carrier circuits, broadband design and analysis, fiber optics, coaxial and twisted pair splicing, outside plant construction, and specific computer applications. And because communication skills are important, development of your writing and speaking abilities is an essential part of your training.

You are taught through lectures, videotapes, and presentations from industry visitors. Almost all your courses have accompanying labs, in which you get hands-on experience, working with a variety of tools and electronic testing equipment. Starting in your second year, you work on many team projects. To prepare you for the industry, you write reports and term papers and give oral presentations to other students. In addition, you can join a telecom student society—the field trips and other interesting activities that such groups usually sponsor are good opportunities for you to meet industry professionals.

While most electrical engineering programs prepare you for graduate school, research, or a job designing new equipment, telecommunications technology programs train students to use existing equipment for system and network design. Telecom technology programs also have fewer math requirements but a much greater emphasis on hands-on experience. Some four-year programs focus on the business or management side of telecommunications.

Other majors you might like:
Electrical engineering technology
Radio and television
Recording arts
Information technology
Computer engineering technology
Communications
Electrical drafting/CAD/CADD
Communications systems installation/repair
Digital media
Medical records technology
Technical and business writing
Management information systems

Questions to ask colleges:
How large are the lab classes? What types of equipment are used? The ability to learn on up-to-date, accessible, "real-industry" equipment is an important factor in selecting a program.

How "wired"—and wireless—is the campus? How many types of network technologies are available?

Career options and trends:
Design engineer; network developer*; network administrator*; network applications support specialist; test engineer; radio frequency (RF) engineer*; sales engineer; facilities engineer; telecom manager.

The telecom industry is transitioning from wired to wireless, and introducing new technologies and services at a fast pace. Although this transition will create jobs, gains will be offset by declines in maintenance work—the new equipment doesn't require as much. The rapid pace of change and technological development in this industry will create the most opportunities for college-educated technologists with the training, knowledge, and skills to oversee these changes.

For more info:
IEEE Communications Society
3 Park Ave., 17th Fl.
New York, NY 10016
(212) 705-8900
www.comsoc.org

English language and literature

English is a major major, to borrow from Joseph Heller. More bachelor's degrees are earned in English than in any of the other liberal arts.

The English language dates back to Anglo-Saxon, yet it's perfectly suited to the digital age. English lends itself well to computer and multimedia communications because it's dense in meaning and conveys more ideas in less time and space than many other tongues do. The spread of American culture and business internationally has also popularized the language.

To study English is to grasp its Germanic roots and shake loose its literary leaves, from *Beowulf* to Weblogs. Students who choose to study English must be ready to read as many as 500 pages each week.

"One of the most important interests or activities for a creative writer is engaged reading—to try and understand how a text influences a reader's emotions or intellect," explains Jonathan Fink, a poet who teaches at Emory University.

Fortunately, if you like high school English, you're probably already an avid reader and a skilled writer. These talents aren't just for budding novelists, either. Corporations, nonprofit organizations, and government agencies all need good writers to take advantage of online communications, desktop publishing, and video editing tools.

"The discipline's emphasis on analytical skills and on careful writing prepares students for a variety of professions and occupations far beyond the world of teaching," says Professor Emeritus James G. Taaffe of the University of Alabama.

English majors go on to journalism, publishing, advertising, technical writing, management, law, and other careers. Graduate students specialize in genres, or types of literature, such as fiction, poetry, children's books, sci fi, and even hypertext—interactive fiction online. Other graduate areas include linguistics, film, and drama. Some grad students latch on to a specific historical period—say, nineteenth-century American literature. Multicultural literature, which might focus on works by African Americans or by women, is an emerging area these days. (See the section on Area, ethnic, and gender studies for related majors.)

"For a student, the number of possibilities for graduate study is encouraging; for a graduate, the competition for employment in creative writing can be daunting," cautions Fink. College English teaching positions are also hard to come by, so be flexible in planning a career using your English smarts. Technical or business writing may be an outlet if you're a good communicator with an interest in technology and multimedia.

"Increasingly, even liberal arts majors such as those in American literature are asked to have high-level technical skills," notes Professor Brett C. Millier of Middlebury College. "Many careers, ranging from magazine editing to investment banking, require strong research skills."

Read Up on Colleges

Look for these majors in colleges of arts and sciences or arts and letters, and in departments and schools of English, liberal arts, and humanities.

When comparing colleges, you should do some reading, research, and critical analysis of your own. You'll notice that two-year colleges usually prepare students for the workplace and technical communications jobs. If that's your goal, find out if you'll be ready for an entry-level job when you get your associate degree. Also for technical writers, scope out the software at the college and find out how widely it's used in the real world. See if the college has partnerships and internships with industry to get your foot in the door.

Most English majors go to four-year colleges, which have an academic slant.

"Inquire about whether the department is committed to a cultural studies approach or whether its focus is on critical theory," Taaffe advises. Cultural studies requires intense reading of literature to put it into a social or historical context. In critical theory, instead of reading and interpreting a work, you explore what other people, especially writers over the years, have said about it.

Other points to consider: Check out the college library, its books and journals. Is the library catalog online? Will you have access to the *Oxford English Dictionary* (*OED* to you), which traces how words have been used over the centuries? Can you access digitized materials offsite?

The faculty is most important. You want class time with the top profs. How many lower-division and upper-division courses are taught by graduate students instead? Are any of the leading professors called "emeritus"? That means they don't teach anymore.

Will you have the chance to work on a literary journal or publications? Does the university often host visiting writers on campus? Are other literary or cultural opportunities nearby?

If American lit is your passion, ask if it's a department of its own. How many courses are offered and in what depth? Are they huge lectures or smaller seminars? Keep in mind that you'll read modern writers, but even as an American literature major, you'll curl up with the masters of English literature—including Chaucer, Shakespeare, and Milton—during your college years.

American literature

What it's about:

As an American literature major, you study the principal literary movements and the fiction, non-fiction, poetry, and drama of the United States. You examine how American literature has developed historically and learn about the intellectual, economic, geographic, and social forces that have shaped U.S. culture.

Is this for you?

You might like this major if you also like: reading; expository and critical writing; contemporary literature; literature in its cultural and historical context; creative writing.

Consider this major if you are good at: active listening; attention to detail; creativity; critical reading/thinking; research ...*or have...* initiative; verbal skills; writing skills.

Recommended high school prep:

English 4, math 3, lab science 3, social studies 3, and a foreign language 2–3.

Did you know...

...that even American literature majors should take Chaucer, Shakespeare, and Milton?

Typical courses in this major:

Survey of American literature
The American novel
American drama
Native American literature
Melville
Faulkner
The American Renaissance
American poetry
African-American literature
Literature by American women
American autobiography
American poetry
Senior seminar

Concentrations:

In college: comparative studies; creative writing.

If you go on to grad school: a particular historical era (e.g., 18th, 19th, 20th centuries); a particular genre (e.g., fiction, poetry).

What the study of this major is like:

Although American literature is comparatively young, its writings are rich and varied. The tradition began in the oral songs and tales of Native Americans and continued in the literature of European exploration and settlement, through the seventeenth century. In New England, the Puritans developed a prolific literary culture that included histories, biographies, poetry, and sermons. The Puritan influence was transformed, in the mid-nineteenth century, by Nathaniel Hawthorne, Ralph Waldo Emerson, Henry Thoreau, Emily Dickinson, and Harriet Beecher Stowe. Although New England dominated American writing until the Civil War, authors elsewhere in the North (Benjamin Franklin, James Fenimore Cooper, Herman Melville, and Walt Whitman) and in the South (William Byrd, Thomas Jefferson, and Edgar Allan Poe) created a distinctive, significant literature. Other lively, often subversive traditions flourished: fugitive slave narratives, Native American protest speeches, folk songs, and frontier humor.

Since the Civil War, American literature has undergone a cultural explosion. As an American literature major, you will follow the development of this legacy, by exploring the rise of realism in fiction (William Dean Howells, Henry James, Stephen Crane, Edith Wharton, Theodore Dreiser); the growth of midwestern, western, and southern regionalism (Willa Cather, Sherwood Anderson, Frank Norris, John Steinbeck, Flannery O'Connor, Eudora Welty); America's leadership in international modernism in poetry (Ezra Pound, T. S. Eliot, Marianne Moore, Wallace Stevens, William Carlos Williams); the modernist novels of Ernest Hemingway,

F. Scott Fitzgerald, William Faulkner; the emergence of major dramatists (Eugene O'Neill, Arthur Miller, Tennessee Williams); the prominence of African-American literature (Langston Hughes, Zora Neale Hurston, Richard Wright, Ralph Ellison, James Baldwin); the self-conscious affirmations of post-World War II fiction (Saul Bellow, Vladimir Nabokov, Norman Mailer, John Updike); the grimness of post-World War II poetry (Robert Lowell, John Berryman, Elizabeth Bishop, Sylvia Plath); the revolt of the Beat Generation (Jack Kerouac). The course work also highlights the achievements in Native American writings in English (N. Scott Momaday, Leslie Silko, James Welch, Louise Erdrich); literature by and for women (Adrienne Rich, Ann Beattie, Joan Didion, Toni Morrison); and a powerful array of ethnic literatures.

If you major in American literature, you will probably take an introduction-to-literature course and then three or four courses covering (in historical order) the literary traditions of the United States. You may then take a seminar or two on a single author, and you elect your concentration—usually either comparative studies or creative writing. You also take several electives—in American poetry, or African-American literature, for example—in preparation for advanced study in your fourth year. Fourth-year work usually consists of a seminar or two, a comprehensive exam, and, if you are eligible, an honors thesis.

American literature is studied today basically as it has always been studied. While computers help you write papers more easily and have easier access to resource materials, you still do the important work by reading a book and your professor still lectures in front of a chalkboard. Your academic routine will be generally low-tech, quiet, and relatively solitary. You must read a great deal—sometimes 400 or 500 pages in a week—and typically write several papers for each course.

Not many colleges offer an American literature major, so most students study American literature within the context of an English major. English departments may vary as to how many courses in American literature are offered, and there may be gaps in historical sequence. Departments may also vary in their course offerings in emerging fields such as ethnic American literatures, or reject the idea of "cultural studies" of literature altogether.

Other majors you might like:
English
American studies
African-American studies
Publishing
Native American studies
American history (U.S.)
Media studies
English literature (British)
Comparative literature
Political science
Women's studies
Creative Writing

Questions to ask colleges:
Is American literature taught within an English department or on its own? If it is taught within an English department, how many courses in the field are offered in a typical year, and how much depth can students achieve?

How big are the courses—are they all large lecture courses, or are there also medium-size courses and seminars? Are there courses in emerging fields like African-American literature or ethnic American literatures?

Career options and trends:
High school teacher; journalist; editor; college professor.

American literature majors do well in a variety of fields because careers ranging from magazine editing to investment banking often require strong research skills.

For more info:
American Studies Association (ASA)
1120 19th St., N.W.
Suite 301
Washington, DC 20036
(202) 467-4783
www.theasa.net

Creative Writing

What it's about:

As a creative writing major, you study the creation and construction of poetry, fiction, drama, nonfiction, and screenwriting. You examine the works of established writers and develop your own original work (poems, stories, dramas, etc.), and submit your work to professors and peers for discussion and analysis.

Is this for you?

You might like this major if you also like: reading; drama; poetry; fiction; film; language; self-expression; the subtle meanings of words and sentences. Creative writing majors find pleasure in weighing, balancing, and selecting words for their ability to convey meaning through image, tone, rhythm, and scene.

Consider this major if you are good at: attention to detail; creativity; critical reading/thinking; organizing; persuading/influencing *...or have...* emotional stamina/endurance; initiative; patience; perception; verbal skills; writing skills.

Recommended high school prep:

English 4, math 3, lab science 3, social studies 4, and a foreign language 4. If available, take courses that encourage you to write and to think about how art is constructed. Also, activities such as working on a student literary journal or newspaper are recommended.

Typical courses in this major:

Introduction to creative writing
Poetry writing
Fiction writing
Journalism
Composition
Playwriting
Screenwriting
Argumentation
Advanced creative writing
Expository writing
Memoir/creative non-fiction writing
Topics in English composition

Concentrations:

Poetry; fiction; playwriting; screenwriting; creative nonfiction.

What the study of this major is like:

The creative writing major closely resembles the English major. Much of the course work is similar, and you study works of drama, prose, and poetry, as well as composition. But in creative writing, you develop your own literary voice in workshops that are taught by practicing writers who know first-hand the challenges and struggles of the writing process.

In general, your course work is divided among writing workshops, literature courses, and liberal arts requirements in the sciences, mathematics, and other humanities. In most programs, your writing samples and performance in writing courses is examined before you are admitted into the workshops.

Most introductory creative writing courses combine several forms of writing. Similar to survey courses in the arts, an introductory course in creative writing usually encourages you to write fiction, poetry, and, often, drama. You will also examine the history of several forms of writing and analyze the works of contemporary authors.

"Forms" courses are similar to a traditional literature course, but with a focus on an aspect of writing not usually covered in core courses. The topics may range from contemporary short story or memoir to an examination of the struggles involved in revision. Most upper-level courses are divided by genre, which allows you to focus more in-depth on your own poetry, fiction, or drama. You will also probably be required to submit a thesis project—usually a collection of poems, stories, or essays.

Upper-level workshops also focus on a particular form. In essay writing, you study techniques of analysis and persuasion, explore the relation between voice and purpose, and learn how to design an argument. In poetry writing, you experiment with meter, image, tone, and organization. In fiction courses, you may focus on characterization, narrative, scene, dialogue, or plot. In most courses, members of the class analyze each other's work with guidance from the instructor. Because writing is such a solitary endeavor, most students consider this feedback to be the most valued aspect of the major.

Being a creative writing major requires maturity, patience, and determination. The challenges you are likely to face are generally those that all writers encounter: Where do I get ideas? How can I overcome writer's block? How can I choose the most appropriate way to express my ideas? You will also need to set writing and revision schedules for yourself; this task can be hard, because the amount of time creative work takes is often unpredictable. Unlike majors that have clearly mapped out paths to success, creative writing challenges you not only to follow the guidance of professionals, but also to rely heavily on your own initiative and conviction.

Creative writing may be offered as an independent major, as a concentration in the English major, or as an independent minor. Because content and approach vary widely in creative writing programs, you should examine the writing of professors at the colleges you are considering. Look for writers whose work addresses some of your own interests and concerns.

Other majors you might like:
English
Drama and theater arts
Journalism
Publishing
Comparative literature
Advertising
Philosophy
Psychology
Business communications
Radio and television
Fine/studio arts
Technical and business writing

Questions to ask colleges:
Does the college have a visiting-writers program that invites authors to campus?

What opportunities are there for students to become involved in literary journals or readings?

How many creative writing majors does the college currently enroll?

Career options and trends:
Freelance writer; copywriter for advertising or marketing; editor; content manager for Web site or other electronic publishing venue.

Not many authors make a living from their writing. Creative writing majors do find employment, however, in related fields like teaching, advertising, journalism, television, radio, film, and publishing; or, they ply their language skills in graduate programs in law, medicine or business. Most university-level teaching positions require an advanced degree.

Recently, there has been an increase in the number of graduate creative writing programs. For a student, the increased possibilities for graduate study are encouraging; for a graduate, the competition for employment in the field of creative writing can be daunting.

Insider's viewpoint:
"The longer I struggle with the creation and motivation of my invented characters, the more I am able to translate that empathy to individuals I encounter in 'real' life."

—Professor Jonathan Fink, Emory University

For more info:
Associated Writing Programs
George Mason University
Mail Stop 1E3
Fairfax, VA 22030
(703) 993-4301
www.awpwriter.org

Poets & Writers, Inc.
90 Broad St.
Suite 2100
New York, NY 10004
(212) 226-3586
www.pw.org

English

What it's about:

English majors read, discuss, and write about literature. Literary works include poetry, prose, and drama but may also be drawn from film, journalism, and television. Study focuses on the critical, historical, linguistic, and cultural contexts of these works. In addition, you practice your own writing, developing your language-use and composition skills.

Is this for you?

You might like this major if you also like: reading; writing; discussion; languages; film; music; theater; dance; working independently.

Consider this major if you are good at: attention to detail; creativity; critical reading/thinking; persuading/influencing; research ...*or have...* initiative; patience; verbal skills; writing skills.

Recommended high school prep:

English 4, math 3, lab science 3, social studies 3, and foreign language 3.

Did you know...

...that the major requires a lot of library research, as well as reading and writing assignments? Even if you are an avid reader, you must plan your time carefully in order to complete your work.

...that the study of English literature covers not just the text of a work but also its context—how, when, and why it was produced, as well as how it has influenced generations of readers?

Typical courses in this major:

Survey of English literature
Chaucer
Shakespeare
Milton
History of the English language
Medieval literature
Victorian literature
The Romantics
Modern English grammar
English drama
American literature
Continental literature
Critical theory
New voices in literature
Poetry
The modern short story

Concentrations:

Creative writing; critical theory; drama; film; linguistics; ethnic literatures; literature of a particular period.

What the study of this major is like:

An almost universal first-year requirement of this major is a semester- or year-long chronological (or thematic) survey of English and American literature, which lays the groundwork for further courses in particular genres or literary time periods. Classes are usually small, and you are expected to contribute to class discussion and to write term papers—usually two per course.

Upper-level courses present a more formal study of literature. You learn how to read critically, how to determine the contexts of literature, and how literature creates and reflects the culture from which it springs. In addition, you study point of view, explication, tone, irony, metaphor, image, structure, and allusion. You also explore the ways in which texts affect audiences' beliefs and emotions, and the ways in which literature sheds light on our lives.

Besides the core courses, most programs offer a broad selection of electives focusing on genre study, critical theory, individual authors, and other topics. Courses in writing encourage you to practice the techniques you learn by reading the works of others. You'll become increasingly sensitive to the subtleties of language and to the influences of what you read and hear. In both literature and writing courses, you will examine the logic of an argument, the ways experiences are organized, and reactions to psychological and emotional persuasion. Your studies may conclude with a seminar on a particular theme or subject approached from a variety of directions. And there will likely be a lengthy term project for that seminar.

In addition to classes, most programs provide opportunities to attend readings presented by guest speakers, topical seminars, and more formal lectures given by faculty members. It is also common for English majors with similar interests to meet informally outside of class (usually at the local watering hole) to discuss their work and to exchange ideas and opinions.

Other majors you might like:
Communications
Drama and theater arts
Chicano studies
African-American studies
Comparative literature
Public relations
Medieval and Renaissance studies
Film/cinema studies
English teacher education
History
Philosophy
Classics

Questions to ask colleges:
What are typical class sizes? Which classes have prerequisites? English classes are popular and often, especially at larger colleges, getting into classes is competitive. If you see a course in the catalog that you must take, be sure to ask about it, so you know you have at least a chance of being enrolled.

Does the college offer both U.S. and foreign library catalogs online? Does it offer access to the *Oxford English Dictionary* and *Early English Books Online*? You might research the college's holdings of books and journals to see what is available in the library and online.

Career options and trends:
Elementary, middle, or high school teacher; college professor; editor; journalist; technical writer.

The English major also prepares you for broad career options, including opportunities in publishing; radio, television, and online communications; social work; and management. With graduate or professional study, you can pursue a career in law, medicine, or other field.

A state certificate or license is required for teaching in public schools. College-level teaching positions in English are few and difficult to obtain.

Insider's viewpoint:
"Have an idea of where you want to go with the major. Many people choose English because they don't know what else to do or they think it's easy. Having a career goal, like journalism in my case, helps a lot."

—Courtney, senior, SUNY Binghamton

For more info:
Modern Language Association (MLA)
26 Broadway
3rd Floor
New York, NY 10004-1789
(646) 576-5000
www.mla.org

Technical and business writing

Also known as:
Professional writing

What it's about:
As a technical and business writing major, you learn how to adapt technical information to specific audiences and types of media (text, images, animation, audio, video). You also learn to manage the technical communication process—the steps you go through before, during, and after you write.

Is this for you?
You might like this major if you also like: working with computers; science and technology; reading; tutoring; working with different types of people; being precise; expressing yourself in writing and in person.

Consider this major if you are good at: attention to detail; concentrating; creativity; critical reading/thinking; organizing; research; teamwork ...*or have...* initiative; verbal skills; writing skills.

Recommended high school prep:
English 4, math 3, lab science 3, social studies 3, and a foreign language 2–3. Courses in business and computer science or applications are also recommended.

Did you know...
...that you don't need technical expertise to go into technical and business writing? The "technical" part of the major isn't nearly as scary as some students think. And the major doesn't deal just with computers. What is most important is the ability to work with many different people and to communicate clearly and carefully.

Typical courses in this major:
Foundations in technical communications
Technical editing
Software documentation
Product documentation
Correspondence and report writing
Graphics for technical communications
Documentation process and management
Writing grant proposals
Web authoring
Science writing
Business writing
Multimedia for training and tutorials
Usability testing for technical communications
Internationalizing/localizing documentation

Concentrations:
Internet publishing; scientific writing; business writing; writing for the arts.

What the study of this major is like:
In this major you learn how to translate technical texts into "ordinary" language so that people with no special training can understand them. You also learn how to manage the overall process of technical communications—in particular, determining what type of work you are expected to create (such as a draft copy) and when you need to deliver the completed project. In addition, you gain practice in tracking and reviewing your work, and in writing up your decisions as documentation plans and proposals.

Courses on the internationalization and the localization of information focus on ways to make information understandable to a broad audience or to a specific audience. In other courses you study editing and usability testing, as well as financial, legal, and ethical issues. Most programs include a research component where you learn how to gather information from print and electronic sources, conduct interviews, and design surveys and questionnaires.

The curriculum also introduces you to "visual writing"—the use of layout and design, tables and graphs, illustrations, and other ways to highlight and structure text. By the time you graduate, you will have experience with desktop publishing, image editing, graphics, multimedia, and other types of software.

Your studies generally prepare you for entry-level technical communications jobs. Four-year programs may concentrate on theory and research, along with general education courses in the sciences and humanities. Two-year programs at community colleges and technical schools focus more on training you for entry into the workforce.

Other majors you might like:
Desktop publishing
Information systems
Web page/multimedia design
Creative Writing
Management information systems
Public relations
Design/visual communications
Drafting and design technology
Digital media
Business communications
Computer graphics
Medical records administration

Questions to ask colleges:
Is there an open lab where majors can use publishing software? Which software programs does the program make available, and how often are they upgraded? Are software applications used in various industries featured in the courses?

Does the program have partnerships and internships with local businesses?

Career options and trends:
Workplace technical communicator*; software documentation writer; Web site editor/writer; information architect; product planner; marketing technical communicator.

Employment of technical writers is expected to increase. As a result of rapid growth in technology and electronics, both at home and in the workplace, there will be more need to interpret technical information into users guides, training materials and instruction manuals.

The role of the technical communicator is evolving as businesses look for ways to manage content most effectively—that is, to enable one text to be published in different media forms. Also, the profession may join forces with related areas such as quality assurance and technical support.

For more info:
Society for Technical Communication (STC)
901 North Stuart St.
Suite 904
Arlington, VA 22203-1822
(703) 522-4114
www.stc.org

Association for Computing Machinery (ACM)
1515 Broadway
New York, NY 10036
(800) 342-6626
www.acm.org

Family and consumer sciences

People who study and work in the family and consumer sciences home in on living.

"A general major addresses the study of individuals, families, and communities to understand people's basic needs of food, clothing, shelter, and relationships—and to seek solutions to problems," says Professor Penny A. Ralston of Florida State University.

On the undergraduate and graduate levels, students specialize in the social and behavioral sciences, like child development and family relations, and in such fields as consumer economics, apparel design and merchandising, housing and living environments, and applied sciences in food, nutrition, and textiles. Those who choose family and consumer sciences tend to be creative, analytical, and caring. "The desire to help others and the opportunity to make a difference in people's lives" lead students to these majors, according to Professor Anne L. Sweaney of the University of Georgia.

Colleges have dozens of names for this category. The old name, "home economics," just doesn't cut it anymore. Instead, new and dynamic fields of family and consumer sciences are taught in schools, colleges, and departments of human sciences, human ecology, human resources, humanities and social science, business management, professional studies, arts and sciences, applied sciences, applied technology, or even education.

The majors differ at each college, so be sure to do your homework if you're planning to go into housing, human and family studies, apparel and textiles, or culinary arts. Find out if the program focuses on the industrial or the creative aspects of the field. In housing majors, for instance, the industrial approach emphasizes business functions like residential property management, while creative programs stress space design and planning. Culinary arts or apparel studies might also focus on one approach or the other.

Finding your college home

When choosing a college, see how many credits you'll take in general education courses in comparison with specific courses in your major. The issue here is, does the college mostly look at the "big

277

picture" or does the program plunge into the occupation in a practical way?

"At some, especially larger, institutions, there may be more opportunity to specialize in one area of the major, while other colleges may treat the major in a more integrated and holistic manner, with broad, contextual courses," explains Professor Eva L. Essa of the University of Nevada, Reno.

Talk to an adviser on campus about what's important at that college. How much of your work will be in the classroom, and how much hands-on experience will you get? If you major in housing and human environments, will you work in the housing industry or do service work in the community to learn problem solving? Can you do an internship at a preschool if you're majoring in family studies, or at a restaurant if you're majoring in culinary arts? Will the college help you find the position? Will you be paid?

"Culinary arts programs will require students to complete internships in the field," says Paul Sorgule, a dean at Paul Smith's College. "These 'real-life' experiences can be a gateway to a permanent job after graduation."

Also ask how much real-world experience the faculty members have. As Sorgule puts it, "Not all chefs make the best teachers, but no teacher can be effective teaching the culinary arts without the experience to back up theory." That's good advice in many areas of study.

You might also find out what other courses you will take in college. Perhaps physical sciences to learn about foods or textiles? How about a foreign language as an academic and professional enhancement? For that matter, you might want to take courses at other parts of the university to learn topics from other colleges or departments. Ask if that's okay.

Other questions for colleges: What types of careers do their graduates pursue? What is the employment rate for graduates with the major you want?

Job prospects will differ depending on your major. For example, the apparel industry can go up or down with the economy and is extremely competitive. Production has moved overseas, where wages are low. Culinary and housing professionals enjoy fields with high employment even in shaky economic times. In addition to private industry, many of these fields of study can lead to work in the public sector and steady government jobs for teachers and social workers.

Family and consumer sciences are also great preparation for further studies in and outside of the field. Graduate students might specialize in adult development and the aging population. In apparel, graduate programs include textile engineering and retail marketing; housing grads might choose real estate or city and regional planning.

Two good general Web sites are those of the American Association of Family and Consumer Sciences (www.aafcs.org), and the National Council on Family Relations (www.ncfr.org). Also read about related majors in this book, including fashion merchandising and hospitality administration and management in the Business section, food science in the Agriculture section, and the majors in the section on Public administration.

Clothing, apparel, and textile studies

What it's about:

The apparel and textiles major includes the design, production, marketing, and use of garments, fabrics, and fibers. You learn about technology applications, manufacturing systems, product development, buying, promotional techniques, clothing and material design and customization, and quality control in the apparel and textiles industries.

Is this for you?

You might like this major if you also like: combining colors, fabrics, and shapes; using your imagination; sewing; drawing; sketching; shopping; history; fashion magazines; predicting trends.

Consider this major if you are good at: creativity; critical reading/thinking; leadership; math; persuading/influencing; quantitative analysis; research; teamwork ...*or have...* initiative.

Recommended high school prep:

English 4, math 2, lab science 2, social studies 3, and a foreign language 3. If possible, take courses in computer/graphic arts, photography, business, accounting, and family and consumer studies (for example, fashion design)

Did you know...

...that this major requires you to have a working knowledge of computer applications such as Excel, Access, and PowerPoint? Knowledge of creative software, such as PhotoShop and Publisher, is also helpful.

Typical courses in this major:

Textile fundamentals
Apparel design
Sociology of clothing
Clothing construction
Mass production of apparel
Figure and fashion illustration
Promotion and marketing principles
Historic textiles and costumes
Textiles in non-apparel uses
Tailoring
Product development
Advanced textile testing and analysis
Computer-aided design
Merchandise buying and management
Contemporary fashion designers
Textile and apparel economics

Concentrations:

In college: buying; product development; textile production; apparel design and production; fashion promotion and marketing; interior merchandising.

If you go on to grad school: retail marketing; costume design; textile design; textile science; historic costume and textiles; curating and preservation; textile economics.

What the study of this major is like:

This major is typically taught in laboratory, studio, and lecture settings. In most classes you apply what you learn by completing projects or papers. You will probably be expected to make presentations to the class, so good oral communications are an asset. Your work may occasionally be evaluated by industry professionals. Especially in senior-level courses, you will apply critical-thinking skills in analytical and persuasive writing. Many classes invite guest speakers to discuss up-to-date trends and requirements of the industry.

Understanding consumer behavior, likes, and wants will contribute to your potential success in this field. Therefore, many colleges require internships in which you earn credit while getting firsthand experience in the industry. You can also participate in field trips or off-campus study programs in manufacturing and fashion centers, including retail stores, design houses, textiles factories, museums, and historic sites in areas such as New York, Dallas, and Europe.

This major may be offered in a college of arts and sciences or in a college of family and consumer sciences (formerly home economics), and may lead either to a Bachelor of Science degree (with an emphasis on physical science) or a Bachelor of Arts (humanities). In some Bachelor of Science programs, you take chemistry to fulfill the science requirement. Bachelor of Arts programs usually require fewer core courses and more general education courses. Colleges that focus on retailing do not offer creative courses as part of the major. Programs in other colleges may focus on design, product development, or textiles. Many colleges require you to take two semesters of foreign language and at least one semester of economics, and to be proficient in computer systems.

Apparel and textiles majors tend to be outgoing and self-motivated. Most colleges host an industry-related organization like Fashion Group International. Depending on the campus, you might participate in the Student Marketing Association, Student Retail Federation, or the Advertising and Public Relations Club. Majors who are active in the community or have a part-time job may conduct fashion shows for fund-raisers, organize clothing drives, or set up programs to recycle textiles, apparel, and shoes.

Other majors you might like:

Fashion and apparel design
Textile science
Fashion merchandising
Textile sciences/engineering
Retailing
Marketing
Family and consumer sciences
Advertising
Fiber/textile arts
Theater design and technology
Interior design

Questions to ask colleges:

In what ways do faculty members and students become involved in related local industries? How many faculty members have had industry experience? How frequently do industry professionals serve as guest speakers in classes?

What types of off-campus study programs are available? Does the program require an internship prior to graduation?

What types of careers do graduates in this major pursue after graduation? Where do most graduates relocate to for their first industry job?

Career options and trends:

Buyer; product developer; product manager; market researcher; fashion coordinator; fashion reporter; fashion or textile designer; pattern maker; visual merchandising manager.

The apparel and textiles major can prepare you to work as a merchandise coordinator with a national-brand wholesale firm; an in-store sales associate or manager with a major retailer; a production assistant with a manufacturing firm; an educational representative for a fabric, pattern, sewing machine, or notions firm; a textile and apparel advertiser and promoter; or a quality control analyst. With specialized training, you may work as a textile chemist, textile engineer, or museum costume curator.

The apparel and textiles industries are strongly affected by the national economy and consumer spending. In good times, the industry expands so rapidly that firms have a difficult time hiring enough people; but when the economy suffers, the industry may not hire entry-level employees and may even close stores. Be aware that most of the labor-intensive activities (especially apparel manufacturing) have moved to developing countries, where wages are significantly lower.

For more info:

International Textile and Apparel Association
   (ITAA)
6060 Sunrise Vista Dr.
Suite 1300
Citrus Heights, CA 95610
(916) 723-1628
www.itaaonline.org

Fashion Group International, Inc. (FGI)
8 W. 40th St.
New York, NY 10018
(212) 302-5511
www.fgi.org

Culinary arts and chef training

What it's about:

Culinary arts and chef training programs prepare you for a career in the food service industry as a chef, executive chef, pastry chef, restaurant manager, food and beverage director, food service director, or restaurateur. Chefs today are managers of people, products, and facilities. They have a responsibility to provide quality food and experiences in a safe, sanitary environment.

Is this for you?

You might like this major if you also like: cooking and presenting different kinds of food; serving others; people of diverse backgrounds; expressing yourself in artistic ways; travel; creating something and receiving immediate feedback.

Consider this major if you are good at: coaching; counseling; leadership; multi-tasking; organizing; spacial thinking/analysis; teamwork *...or have...* initiative; manual dexterity; physical stamina.

Recommended high school prep:

English 4, math 3, lab science 3, social studies 3, and a foreign language 2–3. If possible, also take a basic computer applications course.

Did you know...

...there is much more to this major than cooking? Being a professional cook is a hands-on career, but chefs need a strong foundation in math applications, problem resolution, decision making, human resources management, team building, and critical-thinking skills.

Typical courses in this major:

Professional cooking
Foundations of baking
International cooking
Advanced cooking
Banquets and catering
Garde-manger (cold food preparation)
Fabrication and charcuterie
Nutrition
Food science
Restaurant management
Food service sanitation
Menu planning and purchasing
Food and beverage control
Human resources management

Concentrations:

Pastry arts; baking.

What the study of this major is like:

Training to be a chef requires discipline. The field demands a strong work ethic; empathy; a dedication to excellence; and self-assessment, organizational, multitasking, and timing abilities. A successful chef is good at following through on projects, always aware that the job must get done.

Like many academic programs, programs in culinary arts require dedication to research, reading, writing, and computation. However, as a chef-in-training, you must work long hours, under the critical eye of instructors and the dining public. Most colleges insist you follow the conservative uniform and grooming standards of the industry. In chef training programs, you work with others, performing as part of a team, and you are evaluated and receive critiques as a group member. At most colleges you will spend 15–40 hours a week in the kitchen (depending on the semester), beginning as early as 5 a.m. and often working into the evening. At the same time, you must complete assignments for courses in cooking, liberal arts, and management.

Training programs include internships that can be anywhere in the country. Traditionally, internships are paid positions, although some are not. Most students use these real-world experiences as a way to obtain permanent jobs after graduation.

Many colleges offer degrees in culinary arts and related services. As you investigate the schools you arc considering, keep in mind their philosophies and methodologies. Most programs require hands-on experience, although some emphasize it more strongly than others. In some programs, general education courses are optional. Other programs include both cooking and liberal arts courses.

Recently, some colleges have started offering bachelor's degrees in culinary arts. Besides stressing the technical skills that can make you a successful chef, they encourage you to be a decision maker, team builder, manager, and leader.

If you think you'd like to be a chef, you should pursue a balanced education. A chef must understand the finances of an operation, be well read and able to design restaurant menus that match a profiled guest, know how environments affect human behavior, and be a good communicator.

Other majors you might like:

Restaurant/food services management
Food and nutrition studies
Food science
Dietetics
Hospitality administration and management
Baking/pastry arts
Nutrition sciences
Human resources management
Italian studies
Entrepreneurial studies

Questions to ask colleges:

Which types of industry experience does the faculty have? Not all chefs make good teachers, but it is hard to be an effective teacher in the culinary arts without some experience to back up the theory.

Is the program accredited by the American Culinary Federation? How current are the facilities?

Career options and trends:

Cook; sous chef; executive chef; food and beverage director; restaurant manager; restaurateur.

Increasingly, serious chefs are seeking certification through the American Culinary Federation as chef de cuisine, executive chef, pastry chef, or master chef. A certificate in sanitation from the National Restaurant Association is also useful.

Since dining out has become essential to the American lifestyle, the culinary business continues to grow, even during tough economic times. Job opportunities are expected to be about average through 2018. Finding a position should not be difficult, although many positions are part-time, resulting in high turnover rates as people leave the profession for full-time positions. Competition should be keen for jobs in the top kitchens of higher end restaurants which pay better but have low turnover.

A bachelor's degree is becoming the standard for positions at the chef level, and within the next decade or so, a master's degree may be necessary. The major companies are winning the battle for customers, so even though 80 percent of the restaurants in the United States are privately owned, restaurant chains have the ability and cash flow to reward their employees. The chains are therefore likely to offer the most career opportunities.

Insider's viewpoint:

"Chefs are designers of experiences that are the basis for building relationships, mending disagreements, creating partnerships, confirming friendships, celebrating accomplishments, and recognizing personal and professional achievements."

—Paul Sorgule, Paul Smith's College

For more info:

American Culinary Federation (ACF)
180 Center Place Way
St. Augustine, FL 32095
(800) 624-9458
www.acfchefs.org

National Restaurant Association
1200 17th St., N.W.
Washington, DC 20036
(202) 331-5900
www.restaurant.org

Family and consumer sciences

Also known as:

Human sciences

Home economics

What it's about:

The major in family and consumer sciences focuses on individuals, families, and communities from ecological and interdisciplinary perspectives. The purpose of the major is to help you understand the problems they face—especially those related to the basic needs of food, clothing, shelter, and relationships—and to seek solutions.

Is this for you?

You might like this major if you also like: children and families; community service; leadership roles; helping people make decisions and solve problems.

Consider this major if you are good at: active listening; caring/nurturing; critical reading/thinking; leadership; research; teamwork ...*or have...* initiative; verbal skills; writing skills.

Recommended high school prep:

English 4, math 3, lab science 4 (including biology and chemistry), social studies 3, and a foreign language 2–3. If possible, take at least one year of family and consumer sciences.

Did you know...

...that you need a background in chemistry to do well in courses like food science, nutrition, and textiles, which are usually included in the major?

Typical courses in this major:

Personal and family financial management

Child development

Family relations

Consumer economics

Housing and interior design

Food science

Fundamentals of nutrition

Nutrition in the life cycle

Community nutrition

Apparel production and analysis

Consumer textiles

Human development

Concentrations:

Child development; family relations; consumer economics (including personal finance); apparel design; fashion merchandising; textiles; housing and interiors; food and nutrition; family and consumer science education.

What the study of this major is like:

The family and consumer sciences major is the interdisciplinary study of factors that can affect the well-being of people of all ages. As you explore a range of subjects—from social and behavioral sciences, such as child development and family relations, to applied sciences, such as food science, nutrition, and textiles—you must be open to different approaches to understanding individuals, families, and communities.

The major begins with course work in the liberal arts. You then choose courses in areas such as family studies, housing, clothing and textiles, food science and nutrition, and personal/family finances and resource management.

The information you learn will be applied to individual and family concerns. For example, you might translate a family's nutritional problems into strategies for selecting better diets, or you may determine how children's developmental needs can be met in different settings, such as child care and community centers. For your last year, you will select a practicum, or internship, that will provide both the work experience and the contacts needed in any job search. Some programs offer opportunities for international or cross-cultural internships.

At large institutions the program may be located in divisions of human ecology, human sciences, or family and consumer sciences. Generally, the number of required courses depends on the size of the program. Larger programs usually provide more flexibility, so that you can focus on an area of your choice.

Family and consumer sciences majors gain not only an in-depth appreciation of the subject matter but also a broad understanding of the environments in which consumers and families live, work, and, sometimes, struggle. As a graduate, you'll have a variety of career options, particularly if you choose to specialize. Course work and internships or other supervised practical experiences prepare you for professional roles in business, government, education, and human services.

Other majors you might like:

Human services
Psychology
Environmental design
Culinary arts and chef training
Dietetics
Gerontology
Fashion and apparel design
Interior design
Business administration and management
Community health services
Sociology
Youth services

Questions to ask colleges:

How much access do majors have to advisers? Students pursuing the general major in family and consumer sciences often look for a flexible program. You'll need appropriate guidance on how to handle practicums, internships, honors, and undergraduate research.

Career options and trends:

High school teacher; child care professional; family services professional; community agency administrator; sales representative; product designer; financial planner.

With appropriate course work, you can become certified as a family life educator and, with an examination, as a family and consumer sciences professional.

In the light of increasing globalization, family and consumer sciences majors should consider international opportunities, including study abroad. The experience can lead to jobs with national or international health organizations and strengthen your credentials for human service and education positions. Also, there is a critical shortage of secondary school teachers in this field. With additional coursework, you can become certified to teach.

For more info:

American Association of Family and Consumer
  Sciences (AAFCS)
400 N. Columbus St.
Suite 202
Alexandria, VA 22314
(703) 706-4600
www.aafcs.org

National Council on Family Relations (NCFR)
3989 Central Ave., N.E.
#550
Minneapolis, MN 55421
(888) 781-9331
www.ncfr.org

Food and nutrition studies

What it's about:

The food and nutrition studies major covers the processing and preparation of food before it is eaten (food science) and the role of nutrients in human metabolism (nutrition). You study food safety, quality, and nutritional content; food product and recipe development; the planning of diets to maintain wellness and nutrition counseling.

Is this for you?

You might like this major if you also like: cooking, tasting, and experimenting with recipes; sports and exercise; helping others; science (especially biology and chemistry) and math; knowing what you eat and how it is made; working with others to tackle problems.

Consider this major if you are good at: attention to detail; caring/nurturing; critical reading/ thinking; leadership; math; organizing; teamwork *...or have...* initiative; verbal skills; writing skills.

Recommended high school prep:

English 4, math 3 (including trigonometry and pre-calculus), lab science 4 (including biology, chemistry, and physics), social studies 3, and a foreign language 2–3. If possible, also take speech.

Did you know...

...the differences between the food and nutrition studies major, the food science major, and the dietetics major? Food science primarily focuses on food production and safety—what happens before it gets into your kitchen. Dietetics programs prepare you to become a licensed health professional as either a registered dietician (RD) or a dietician technician (DTR). Food and nutrition studies spans much of what is covered in both, with a broader, interdisciplinary approach to healthy eating and living.

...that this major requires strong science and math skills? The basic courses are the same as those taken by biology or chemistry majors. Food and nutrition studies can be thought of as an applied biology or an applied chemistry major, with the focus on food, nutrition, and human health.

Typical courses in this major:

Biology
Biochemistry
Microbiology
Physiology
Chemistry
Physics
Mathematics
Statistics
Nutrition
Community nutrition
Food chemistry
Food microbiology
Food preparation
Food product development
Food processing
Sensory evaluation

Concentrations:

In college: consumer-related issues; food processing; food product development; food safety; wellness studies; clinical nutrition; community nutrition; pre–health professional track for entry into graduate or medical school.

If you go on to grad school: food chemistry; food microbiology; sensory and quality evaluation; nutritional biochemistry; nutritional toxicology.

What the study of this major is like:

The food and nutrition studies major is usually found at large universities in schools of home economics, agriculture, human ecology, family and consumer sciences, health and human services, or applied sciences. At some institutions, food science and nutrition are separate majors; at others, they are one major and you may specialize in either food science or nutrition. The breadth of the major can vary from narrow, emphasizing only food science, nutrition, or dietetics, to broad, covering many aspects of food and nutrition studies.

In your first two years, you take courses such as chemistry, biochemistry, physiology, and microbiology, often in large lecture classes that break into smaller discussion and laboratory sections. The science and math requirements are similar to most other science- or health-related majors. If you plan to focus on dietetics or nutrition education (working with individuals and families to promote health), you also take courses in education and communication. To prepare for work in the business world, you should take business administration, marketing, computers, and public relations courses. Courses in sociology and psychology are also helpful.

You'll likely enroll in an introductory nutrition or food science course during your first two years, but you probably won't take many courses in the major until you have completed the basic science courses. In the beginning, you may feel lost in large lecture classes. Because these courses are prerequisites for the major rather than part of it, you may wonder about their relevance; but you'll soon see how they relates to your career goals.

You may usually concentrate on either food science or nutrition or both. In food science, you learn about food preparation, processing, packaging, storage, and distribution. You also learn what makes food pleasing to our sense of sight, smell, and taste. In nutrition courses, you study food selection, preparation, consumption, and digestion. You take courses in food chemistry and in basic and advanced nutrition. Although emphasis is placed on the chemistry of these processes, you also study the psychological and behavioral aspects of eating.

In addition to lectures, most courses have laboratory work, to provide you with hands-on experience in, for example, identifying microorganisms in foods. In laboratory sessions, you often work in teams to conduct short-term experiments and independent projects. Upper-level class sizes are usually small. Courses may be taught as lectures or as discussion sections on subjects such as community nutrition, assessment methods, and nutrition and disease. Individual and team projects are often included.

Summer jobs or internships provide real-world experiences that relate to academic course work. You can also work with faculty members on research projects during the academic year; these experiences are valuable when you apply for jobs or acceptance into graduate school or internship programs. The Institute of Food Technologists and the American Dietetic Association approve or accredit undergraduate programs, but some colleges offer nonaccredited programs instead. The level of science courses required for the major varies and is usually lower in nonaccredited programs. The laboratory facilities also vary from one college to another.

Technology has drastically changed the way food is grown, harvested, packaged, transported, and sold. Our understanding of the relation of nutrition to health, especially in the causes and treatment of chronic diseases, has greatly increased and an enormous variety of products are available from all over the world. At the same time, fad diets, eating disorders, substance abuse, and nutrient-drug interactions threaten health and well-being. Careers in food and nutrition studies provide many opportunities for making important contributions to our world.

Other majors you might like:

Food science
Chemistry
Dietetics
Culinary arts and chef training
Nutrition sciences
Sports and fitness administration
Food service
Institutional food production
Pharmacy
Restaurant/food services management
Hospitality administration and management

Career options and trends:

Food purchasing manager; test kitchen/recipe developer*; product researcher/developer; dietitian*; nutrition counselor*; community nutritionist; food editor (for newspaper or magazine); inspector for the Food and Drug Administration or the Department of Agriculture.

To become a registered dietitian (RD), you must complete a prescribed set of undergraduate courses and a supervised internship program and take the registered dietitian's examination (see the description for the dietetics major in the section on Health).

The food industry itself, and the demand for all types of industry professionals, remain quite stable; population growth and the marketability of new food products provide more job opportunities. Because of current concerns, food safety specialists should have no trouble finding work. Also with the increasing interest in nutrition, the development of enhanced foods, and the emergence of wellness programs, the demand for nutritionists and dietitians is likely to continue.

Insider's viewpoint:

"Ever since I became a nutrition major, I am eating better, exercising more, and basically living a healthier lifestyle. I honestly believe that this lifestyle has aided me in my studying and my overall college performance."

—Kate, senior, Rutgers University

For more info:

Institute of Food Technologists (IFT)
525 West Van Buren, Suite 1000
Chicago, IL 60607
(312) 782-8424
www.ift.org

American Society for Nutrition (ASN)
9650 Rockville Pike
Suite 4500
Bethesda, MD 20814
(301) 634-7050
www.nutrition.org

Housing and human environments

What it's about:

As a housing and human environments major, you study various aspects of housing, including needs assessment, financing, legislation, equipment, energy conservation, and housing alternatives. Your goal is to gain an in-depth understanding of housing as a product, an environment, a service, and a process for sheltering a diverse, changing population adequately, accessibly, and affordably.

Is this for you?

You might like this major if you also like: helping others; community or volunteer service; interior design; working on team projects.

Consider this major if you are good at: caring/nurturing; critical reading/thinking; leadership; persuading/influencing; research *...or have...* initiative; patience; verbal skills; writing skills.

Recommended high school prep:

English 4, math 3, lab science 3, social studies 3, and a foreign language 2–3.

Typical courses in this major:

Housing in contemporary society
Advanced housing theories
Housing alternatives
Housing policy
Housing counseling
Household technology and systems
Family demographics and policy
Interiors and furnishings
Kitchen and bath design
Real estate
State and local developments
Special needs housing
Family resource management
Property management
Principles of family finance

Concentrations:

Property management; public policy; interiors.

What the study of this major is like:

All housing and human environment majors receive a background in liberal arts, mathematics, natural sciences, and social studies before choosing a concentration. You study housing issues (safety, types of dwellings, ownership) and learn how housing policies, particularly financial programs, government regulation, and taxation, affect families. You also study factors influencing family well being, such as poverty and access to health care, education, and other public services. You might examine consumer legislation and lobbying efforts by housing advocates. Economics and other business courses are often required.

Most programs emphasize learning through experience. You can often do an internship in your area of interest and earn a limited amount of course credit (and sometimes pay) for your work. A positive internship may even lead to a job offer. Another advantage is the mentoring you receive from your field supervisor—a relationship that may last beyond your internship. Guest speakers, field trips, and community service projects can also enhance your studies. For example, students in one program worked with AARP to publicize predatory lending practices. They delivered literature to senior citizens who were at risk of being targeted by dishonest lenders.

Every housing and human environments program is unique. Some focus on space planning and design, with courses in environmental or interior design, and in preparation for kitchen and bath certification. In others, where there is emphasis on the residential property management industry, you use your academic experience to tackle real-life problems that may occur among residents of multifamily dwellings. Still other programs focus on the socioeconomic and policy aspects of housing, where you take additional courses in political science or economics. Before you decide on a program, study the catalogs from different colleges to make sure your interests match a program's strengths.

This major provides you with opportunities to work in both public and private housing arenas. You will be able to apply what you learn in your personal as well as your professional life. Students seeking degrees in housing can be creative in designing programs and career paths to match their interests and abilities, but they all share the desire to help shape the present and future accommodations of our society.

Other majors you might like:

Real estate
Home furnishings
Construction technology
Social work
Historic preservation
Public administration
Urban, community, and regional planning
Construction management
Interior design
Sociology
Civil engineering

Questions to ask colleges:

Are there opportunities to take courses in other majors such as real estate, social work, journalism, and computer science?

What opportunities are there for students to work on service projects in the community, such as Habitat for Humanity, homeless shelters, or homebuilder shows? What kinds of internships are available?

Career options and trends:

Commercial real estate broker*; residential property manager*; construction project manager; residential home loan officer; area housing administrator*; housing counselor; mortgage originator; homebuilder; banking officer; research analyst.

Housing majors find jobs with real estate companies, state and federal agencies, public utilities, historic preservation firms, financial/mortgage institutions, and trade organizations.

Opportunities in this field may be closely related to strength of the housing market, though positions can be found even in tough economic times. As the population ages, there are many employment possibilities involving housing for older adults. Also, as the housing stock itself ages, many consumers are remodeling. These factors are providing good career opportunities for graduates of housing programs.

For more info:

Housing Education and Research Association (HERA)
Montana State University Extension Service
P.O. Box 173580
Bozeman, MT 59717-3580
(406) 994-3451
www.housingeducators.org

National Apartment Association (NAA)
4300 Wilson Blvd.
Suite 400
Arlington, VA 22203
(703) 518-6141
www.naahq.org

Human development and family studies

Also known as:
Human ecology

What it's about:
The human development and family studies major prepares you to investigate how individuals interact as members of a family and how individuals and families interact with the larger social and economic community. You also study the impact of life cycle changes on individuals, families, and societies.

Is this for you?
You might like this major if you also like: taking care of children or the elderly; learning family histories; helping people work out their problems.

Consider this major if you are good at: caring/nurturing; counseling; critical reading/thinking; leadership; organizing; teamwork *...or have...* initiative; verbal skills; writing skills.

Recommended high school prep:
English 4, math 3, lab science 3, social studies 3, and a foreign language 2–3. If possible, take courses in economics, sociology, and psychology.

Typical courses in this major:
Lifespan human development
Child guidance and parenting
Family finance
Communications in human development
Early childhood education
Human sexuality
Administration of child and family services
Family education and intervention programs
Child socialization
Family interaction
Death and dying: a family and lifespan perspective
Children and families in a multiethnic society
Work and family systems
Families and public policy
Contemporary family issues
Issues in family health

Concentrations:
In college: early childhood education; child development; adolescent development; adult development and aging; family studies; consumer education; family resource management

If you go on to grad school: consumer economics; work and family studies; financial planning and counseling; marriage and family therapy.

What the study of this major is like:
If you major in human development and family studies, you explore the biological, psychological, and sociological development of individuals and families. Courses are designed to help you learn about people in various contexts (including communities and society) and to study them within appropriate theoretical frameworks. Theory and research are coordinated with supervised field experiences.

Generally, you take two introductory courses: one in lifespan development, which covers both continuity and change in individuals from conception to death; the other in the study of families. More advanced courses dealing with such subjects as death and dying and family interaction deepen your understanding. Other courses, such as family education and intervention programs, and the administration of child and family services, have a more practical purpose. Still others, on research and communication, are focused on auxiliary skills.

Professors in human development and family studies use a wide variety of teaching methods, including lecture, discussion, Web-based instruction, field study, and community internship. You are expected to build on and integrate the information and skills you learn as you progress in the program, and to develop your analytical skills and demonstrate good written and oral communication abilities. Most courses include written assignments, essay exams, and opportunities for discussion. An important element in most programs is the fourth-year internship, which is customized to help you consolidate your learning in a semester-long community-based experience.

At some institutions, especially the larger ones, you will probably have greater opportunity to focus your studies on a particular area. These colleges may concentrate on a specialized area such as infant development or family communication and, as a result, offer fewer courses that explore topics from a wider social perspective. Other colleges have a more integrated, holistic approach to human development and family studies, offering a broader, more comprehensive program.

Other majors you might like:

Psychology
Sociology
Early childhood education
Gerontology
Funeral services/mortuary science
Child care management
Occupational therapy
Adult development/aging
Child development
Food and nutrition studies
Work/family studies
Social work

Questions to ask colleges:

How available are supervised practicum sites, such as an infant program, a preschool, or a family-counseling center, where hands-on involvement and observation are carried out?

How many credits are required in general education, in the major, and in elective courses? How accessible and supportive is student advisement? To what extent do students have opportunities to design courses of study to meet their individual interests?

Career options and trends:

Counselor*; early childhood educator*; child care or youth program administrator*; human services agency administrator*; family life educator; family

or consumer advocate; child care curriculum coordinator; senior center coordinator; family financial planner.

Human development and family studies majors also find work in child care licensing, Child Life programs, parent education, and human resources.

With a graduate degree, you can pursue counseling certification as a Marriage and Family Therapist (MFT). If you plan to work in parent education or as a family life educator, you will need to fulfill additional requirements and become a Certified Family Life Educator (CFLE).

The job outlook is very good. There will be strong demand for well-trained human service workers and teachers in this field for some time.

For more info:

National Council on Family Relations (NCFR)
3989 Central Ave., N.E.
Suite 550
Minneapolis, MN 55421
(888) 781-9331
www.ncfr.org

Health

If you're looking for a major that leads to job security and satisfaction, you've come to the right place. Health care is a growth industry. Because the population is aging and people are living longer, over 3.2 million new health care jobs will be needed by 2018, according to the U.S. Bureau of Labor Statistics—more than any other field. And that's on top of the need to replace about 2 million health care workers who will retire or leave the profession. At the same time, fewer students are moving into the health professions and related sciences lately. Shortages of workers are expected across the board.

"Today's growing health care system has created unlimited employment opportunities for nurses in practice, education, and research," says Professor Jean E. Bartels of Georgia Southern University School of Nursing.

"This is an industry that truly combines high tech with high touch," notes Leonard H. Friedman of the Department of Public Health, Oregon State University. "I can think of no professional activity that is more important, worthwhile, or ultimately satisfying."

How will you prepare for a demanding and in-demand career as a clinician, therapist, technician, or other health professional? Look for colleges that specialize in health education. They include schools or divisions of medicine or allied health; nursing schools; colleges of pharmacy, health sciences or services, health occupations, or health professions; and schools of arts and sciences, professional studies, human environmental sciences, health and human sciences, or medical sciences.

The names of the colleges may vary, but the health studies in each field—respiratory therapy, for example—should be very much alike. That's because of groups like CoARC, ARC-PA, AUPHA, and CAPTE. What's with the alphabet soup? Those letters stand for the names of accrediting groups. For instance, more than 130 physician assistant programs nationwide have gotten a professional OK from the Accreditation Review Commission on Education for the Physician Assistant (but you can call it ARC-PA for short). Having standardized courses means that college programs cover similar material to prepare students for professional certification or licensing. Accreditation is the stamp of approval that you'll want your college to have.

Do you want to be a doctor, dentist, or veterinarian? Each field requires specific preprofessional undergraduate courses even though the fields aren't actually majors. That's right—you may know what you want to be but not know what to major in as an undergraduate! For example, premedical studies is a program of prerequisite courses for entrance into medical school. But premed students still have to pick an academic major, and most choose a science such as biology. A preprofessional adviser at college will help you choose a major, prepare for the graduate school entrance examination, arrange the interview, get letters of recommendation, and find volunteer or paid clinical, research, and community service opportunities.

Look for colleges with a strong record of placing students into medical, dental, or veterinary school. For other health studies, ask how long the program has had its gold star from the group that oversees education and training in the profession. (See the individual majors in this section for accrediting bodies.) Also, is it a full accreditation or just something pending? Is the college itself accredited or only the particular program?

Get a complete history

Even with standards in place to nail down core skills and knowledge, programs can differ. Some may take a clinical, practical, hands-on approach to teaching, while others are geared toward theory or research. Some go past the basics into cutting-edge science.

Ask about the three main types of studies you'll do: class/lecture, lab, and clinical internships. Find out about the credentials and experience of the faculty members. What is the ratio of students to teachers? Will the top professors actually do the teaching, or are most courses taught by grad students? Will you be able to do research? Are the labs and equipment up-to-date? What kind of fieldwork or clinical experience is the college set up to give you? Will you work in a hospital? Is it near campus? Will you need to take a licensing exam to work in your professional area? What percent of grads pass that exam?

Also, find out if you're looking at a two-year or a four-year degree program. Different levels of degrees prepare you for different types of work. A dental hygiene or laboratory technician program typically takes two years. Radiologic technicians need an associate degree but can add a bachelor's degree to learn a particular type of medical imaging technology. Veterinary technicians typically have two-year associate degrees.

Nurses at the baccalaureate level are qualified to work in nearly all health care settings, while two-year degrees prepare entry-level LPNs—licensed practical nurses—with lesser responsibilities that vary from state to state.

Is graduate school for you? Physicians, dentists, and veterinarians aren't the only health care professionals with advanced degrees. Pharmacy is a six-year doctoral (Pharm.D.) program starting with two years of preprofessional requirements. You'll need to go beyond a four-year degree for physical therapy programs; the doctorate has become the degree of choice to work in that field. Occupational therapists must also have at least a master's degree. Some nurses study at the graduate level to learn clinical specialties like neonatal (newborn) acute care.

If you're interested in health care but don't want to be a clinician or provide direct patient care, you might go into health care administration or work as a clinical or medical lab technician. Ten of the top 20 fastest growing occupations are healthcare related.

In many health specialties, you'll need continuing professional education to keep up with new technologies and therapies. State licenses may require it. If you want the career benefits of working in health care, your education is only just beginning.

Athletic training

Also known as:
Sports medicine

What it's about:
This major prepares you to become a certified athletic trainer (ATC), a health care professional who knows how to prevent, evaluate, and treat the injuries and related illnesses sustained by physically active people.

Is this for you?
You might like this major if you also like: helping people; sports and competition; problem solving; science and medicine; physical exercise; working with people; tutoring.

Consider this major if you are good at: caring/nurturing; organizing; persuading/influencing; teamwork ...*or have...* a sense of humor; initiative; manual dexterity; physical stamina; verbal skills; writing skills.

Recommended high school prep:
English 4, math 3, lab science 4 (take all possible lab sciences), social studies 3, and a foreign language 2–3 (Greek or Latin would help with medical terminology). If available, take a course in anatomy or physiology, and try to obtain First Aid and CPR certification. If possible, work as a team manager, attend summer athletic training camps, or volunteer in sports medicine clinics.

Did you know...
...that more than 60 percent of certified athletic trainers have a master's degree or higher? While the minimum degree needed for many jobs is a bachelor's, you'll significantly improve your career prospects if you have one to two years of graduate school.

Typical courses in this major:
Prevention and care of athletic injuries
Assessment of extemity injuries
Assessment of illnesses
General medical conditions and disabilities
First Aid and emergency care
Therapeutic modalities
Therapeutic exercise and rehabilitation techniques
Human anatomy
Human physiology
Exercise physiology
Kinesiology or biomechanics
Nutrition
Strength and reconditioning
Pharmacology
Pathology
Psychosocial intervention

Concentrations:
Generally, none in college; but if you go on to grad school: health promotion; exercise physiology; biomechanics; exercise psychology; physical education teaching certification; anatomy.

What the study of this major is like:
As an athletic training major, you study academic and clinical sciences. You'll be trained to watch for injuries that may occur in the gym or on the field and to determine, through examination, whether an injury requires First Aid and whether a doctor or an ambulance should be called. You'll also prepare yourself to become a member of a health care team, so that (under a physician's direction), you can administer treatment: whirlpool baths, ultrasound, electrical stimulation, taping, splints, and exercise.

As you work with coaches, physicians, administrators, and athletes, you develop leadership and communication skills. When you complete the program and pass the required exam, you qualify for national certification—the entry-level standard for this profession.

Your first year or two of courses include general studies in the humanities, basic sciences (anatomy, physiology, and chemistry), and an introduction to athletic training. You also learn more about the profession and the major. In some colleges, you must then be accepted into the program. As a major, you are required to complete a minimum of four semesters of clinical experience, in addition to your course work. You'll probably receive at least 800 hours of directed clinical experience, usually in a range of sports: contact and noncontact; male and female; team and individual. Clinical settings are both on- and off-campus, or perhaps in sports medicine clinics in hospitals or private settings.

Most courses include both lecture and laboratory sessions. In lab and clinical courses, you develop practical application (psychomotor) skills and apply them in real-world situations. The biggest challenge most majors face involves time management. Your day might consist of classes during the morning, clinical work for several hours every afternoon, perhaps a class in the evening, and even sports competitions on weekends. You'll have to devote a lot of time to clinical work, but you won't want to neglect your other course assignments. Probably most important, you are responsible for keeping sensitive medical information confidential, and you must always act professionally.

The biggest difference among programs often depends on the orientation of the department that runs the major. Programs in a sports or exercise science department tend to require more science-based courses; those housed in departments of kinesiology or physical education may require more courses in sports training; and programs in a health science or health education department may stress such areas as prevention of injuries. Philosophical differences among programs show up in the way students are selected and assigned to clinical experiences. In some programs, you begin clinical education during your first semester, while other programs require one or two years of courses and observation before you are admitted to the major and begin your clinical education. In addition, some programs offer many off-campus opportunities in sports medicine clinics and at local high schools, while others provide clinical opportunities only on campus.

Other majors you might like:
Physical therapy
Recreational therapy
Sports and fitness administration
Sports communications
Occupational therapy
Exercise sciences
Physical education
Health/physical fitness
Emergency medical technology (EMT paramedic)
Physician assistant
Parks, recreation, and leisure studies
Hospitality administration and management

Questions to ask colleges:
Is this program accredited by the Commission on Accreditation of Athletic Training Education (CAATE)? Only graduates of an accredited program are eligible to take the national certification exam.

What is the application process to be formally accepted into the major?

What is the school's passing rate on the Board of Certification exam?

Where are some of the graduates employed—in which settings, in which schools, and with which teams?

Where are clinical rotations completed?

Career options and trends:
High school athletic trainer*; college athletic trainer*; clinical athletic trainer (sports medicine clinic or hospital); industrial athletic trainer; professional sports athletic trainer; medical sales representative.

Strong job growth is projected through 2018, mostly in the health care industry. Fitness and recreation sports centers also will provide many new jobs, and opportunities are emerging in the armed services and performing arts.

Positions with sports teams are harder to come by. Many high schools require a teaching license in addition to the athletic training certification. Sports medicine clinics were once a primary source for entry-level employment, but this market has become saturated; and high-profile colleges and universities, as well as professional sports, have limited turnover.

"This is a great major for people who love the human sciences because you get just enough of basic science but you are not inundated with chemical formulas and learning why starfish are in phylum Echinodermata."

—Caleb, sophomore, University of Southern California

For more info:
National Athletic Trainers' Association (NATA)
2952 Stemmons Freeway
Suite 200
Dallas, TX 75247-6916
(214) 637-6282
www.nata.org

Commission on Accreditation of Athletic Training
    Education (CAATE)
2201 Double Creek Drive
Suite 5006
Round Rock, TX 78664
(512) 733-9700
www.caate.net

Clinical/medical laboratory technology

What it's about:

Clinical/medical lab technicians examine blood and other body fluids to search for clues in the diagnosis of various diseases. In this major, you are trained to perform general tests in all medical laboratory areas, such as blood banking and hematology; clinical chemistry; urinalysis; immunology; and medical microbiology.

Is this for you?

You might like this major if you also like: solving problems; challenges; puzzles; computers; science and technology; knowing why and how things work; working with precision and accuracy.

Consider this major if you are good at: attention to detail; critical reading/thinking; organizing; quantitative analysis; spacial thinking/analysis; teamwork ...*or have...* manual dexterity; patience; verbal skills.

Recommended high school prep:

English 4, math 3, lab science 3 (biology, chemistry, physics), social studies 3, and a foreign language 2–3. Take computer technology and advanced chemistry if available.

Did you know...

...that 70 to 80 percent of all medical decisions are based on laboratory data? The practice of medicine would be impossible without the tests performed by clinical/medical laboratory technicians.

...that the ability to communicate well, both in writing and in speaking, is important in this field? Technical skills alone do not get the job done—results must be communicated accurately and completely.

Typical courses in this major:

Introduction to the clinical laboratory
Clinical chemistry
Hematology
Immunology
Immunohematology
Microbiology
Quality assessment
Anatomy and physiology
College algebra
General chemistry and lab
English composition
Urinalysis/body fluids
Clinical internship

Concentrations:

In college: clinical chemistry; hematology; immunology; clinical microbiology; urinalysis.

If you go on to grad school: clinical/laboratory facilities management; molecular diagnostics.

What the study of this major is like:

A career in clinical/medical laboratory technology is an excellent choice if you want to work in health care, but not directly with patients. As a clinical/medical laboratory technician, you apply your knowledge of, and skills in, the basic sciences to testing in such settings as health care, research, industry, or government agencies.

Laboratory technicians work with medical teams of pathologists, other specialists, and scientists to determine the absence, presence, extent, or cause of disease, and to provide data for evaluating the effectiveness of treatment. The field offers opportunities to learn and grow. As procedures are developed to detect both old and new diseases, the laboratory remains in the forefront of medicine. In addition to an array of precision instruments and electronic equipment, successful laboratories need well-trained, responsible staff.

The clinical/medical laboratory technology major is offered as both a two-year associate degree and a four-year bachelor's degree. This major may be found in departments of biology, chemistry, natural sciences, or life sciences, and in schools of health professions, allied health and/or nursing, or medicine.

Because classes are usually small and labs generally have fewer than 18 students, teamwork and group learning are encouraged. To gain a sound foundation for your clinical studies, you are likely to begin with a number of science courses. You'll take courses in anatomy and/or physiology, genetics, and microbiology, and perhaps advanced cell physiology. In chemistry courses, you'll focus on inorganic and organic compounds and biochemistry. Algebra and statistics may also be also required; courses in chemical analysis and computer science are useful. Many students find the large amount of information presented in a two-year program a bit overwhelming, especially if they have not been full-time college students before entering the program.

In this major, the emphasis is on laboratory practice. Unlike traditional science majors, in which the lab work illustrates theories you learn in the classroom, clinical/medical laboratory technology uses theory to support the lab work. You learn by doing, in order to understand the theoretical and clinical significance of lab procedures. In most programs you spend the equivalent of one semester learning the theory, procedures, equipment, and practices of clinical laboratory science in a working laboratory. During this time, you learn to test body fluids and tissues and practice what you learn in class. Most majors find laboratory work the most exciting and interesting part of the program.

To be eligible for national certification exams, you should attend an accredited program—one that meets the standards set by the National Accrediting Agency for Clinical Laboratory Science (NAACLS). Programs at different colleges may meet the standards in different ways—for example, by teaching courses in a different order, making use of online programs or courses, or varying the required clinical internship from none to several hundred hours.

Other majors you might like:
Chemistry
Biochemistry
Biomedical technology

Molecular biology
Cytotechnology
Microbiology
Forensic science
Phlebotomy
Biotechnology
Dental laboratory technology
Clinical laboratory science
Radiologic technology/medical imaging

Questions to ask colleges:
Is the program accredited?

Are the lab facilities dedicated to this major?

In a two-year program, is there an articulation agreement with a four-year college to accept transfer credit for these courses?

Is space guaranteed in the clinical facility for the internship?

Career options and trends:
Clinical/medical laboratory technologist*; microbiologist*; laboratory director; forensic analyst; biotechnician; research technician; technical/marketing sales representative.

Clinical/medical laboratory technicians work in a variety of practice settings, such as hospitals, for-profit laboratories, clinics, nursing homes, public health facilities, business, and industry. Supervisory or management positions usually require Clinical Laboratory Scientist (CLS) certification.

The long-term employment for medical laboratory technicians looks bright. According to the Bureau of Labor Statistics, there will be a shortage in this field over the next decade or so, with nearly twice the number of positions as graduates to fill them.

For more info:
American Society for Clinical Laboratory Science (ASCLS)
6701 Democracy Blvd., Suite 300
Bethesda, MD 20817-1574
(301) 657-2768
www.ascls.org

Communication disorders

What it's about:

At the undergraduate level, this major is primarily a preprofessional program designed to give training in the identification and treatment of human communication disorders, in preparation for professional training in a master's degree program in either speech-language pathology or audiology. You learn about the normal processes of human communication and the problems that may occur, including disorders of articulation, language, hearing, cognition, swallowing, and voice.

Is this for you?

You might like this major if you also like: helping people; problem solving; using technology; working with children; working with older adults.

Consider this major if you are good at: attention to detail; caring/nurturing; counseling; creativity; math; persuading/influencing ...*or have...* initiative; patience; verbal skills; writing skills.

Recommended high school prep:

English 4; math 3, lab science 3, social studies 3, and a foreign language 2–3. Take anatomy and psychology if they are available.

Typical courses in this major:

Survey of communication disorders
Phonetics
Normal speech and language development
Audiology
Anatomy and physiology
Articulation disorders
Language disorders
Aural rehabilitation
Diagnostics
Augmentative communication

Concentrations:

In college: childhood speech; language disorders.

If you go on to grad school: speech-language pathology; audiology; adult and neurological communication disorders; childhood and developmental communication disorders.

What the study of this major is like:

The major in communication disorders emphasizes both normal and abnormal growth and development. Professionals (such as speech-language pathologists and speech, language, and hearing scientists) deal with infants, children, adolescents, adults, and the elderly, in schools, hospitals, businesses, private practice, universities, research laboratories, and government agencies.

The undergraduate major prepares you for professional study at the master's degree level. As a major, you explore normal and defective hearing and speech, and then learn to identify and evaluate communication disorders and available treatment. The typical program is sequential—courses are based on the knowledge and skills you developed in previous course work.

In introductory courses, you study normal voice, speech, and language processes and the symptoms of disorders. Taking anatomy and physiology teaches you how people produce and perceive speech. You will read research reports on speech disorders, in order to apply findings to treatment programs and to determine what further research should be done. You may study stuttering, aphasia, and other common disorders.

While you pursue your major, you complete requirements in academic areas that support the core courses, including biology and physical sciences, behavioral and social sciences, and other liberal arts and sciences course work. Majors usually get clinical experience by working (under close supervision) in the college speech and hearing clinic with children and adults.

Although most courses follow the lecture format, you may also work with interactive computer instruction. Academic standards for the major are high, because the majority of students will continue on to a master's program. In fact, most states require an advanced degree for certification in this field. To be successful in this major, you need a strong background in math, science, and writing. Anatomy and neurology require a lot of memorization, and you may have difficulty managing your time as a result of heavy clinical requirements. But students in this major tend to bond into closely knit groups and assist each other through the program.

Other majors you might like:
Child development
Psychology
Gerontology
Special education
Education of speech impaired
Linguistics
Audiology/speech pathology
American sign language (ASL)
Anthropology
Speech teacher education
Education of deaf/hearing impaired
Speech/rhetorical studies

Questions to ask colleges:
What are the academic requirements for admission into the major, both at the undergraduate and at the graduate level? Are students admitted into the program as freshmen, or must they qualify for admission after their first or second year in college?

Is a combined bachelor's/graduate degree program available?

Is the undergraduate program broad-based, or is it geared toward either childhood disorders or adult disorders?

Career options and trends:
School speech/language therapist*; speech pathologist*; audiologist; speech scientist.

The American Speech–Language–Hearing Association (ASHA) sets standards for national certification in speech-language pathology or audiology (check their Web site for updates). Currently, this certificate requires a master's degree, passing a national exam, and at least 36 weeks of supervised professional employment in the field. State teacher certification is required for teaching students with speech and language disabilities in the public school system. Most states also have professional license requirements for speech pathologists employed in a health care setting.

Employment prospects in this field are expected to grow faster than average through 2018. As awareness and identification of speech and language disorders in children becomes more prevalent, the number of positions available in educational settings will increase. Opportunities for speech-language pathologists in private practice should also increase as hospitals, schools, and nursing care facilities have begun contracting out for these services in an effort to control costs. Demand for audiologists will keep pace with the increasing population of older Americans facing hearing loss.

Insider's viewpoint:
"We're required to have a lot of clinical hours, and we have to get them in a lot of different areas, including adults and children, diagnostics, and treatment. So it's the fun part and it's also the hard part, to make sure you get all those hours in."

—Cara, graduate student, University of Pittsburgh

For more info:
American Speech–Language–Hearing Association (ASHA)
2200 Research Blvd.
Rockville, MD 20850-3289
(800) 498-2071
www.asha.org

Dental hygiene

What it's about:

As a major in dental hygiene, you obtain the knowledge and clinical skills needed to prevent and treat oral diseases in order to protect teeth and gums—and to preserve patients' general health. Courses in basic and dental sciences, as well as clinical training in patient care, prepare you to become a licensed dental hygienist.

Is this for you?

You might like this major if you also like: working with your hands; routines and schedules; working with people; detail-oriented activities; crafts.

Consider this major if you are good at: caring/nurturing; counseling; following directions; multitasking; organizing; teamwork *...or have...* manual dexterity; patience; verbal skills.

Recommended high school prep:

English 4, math 3, lab science 3 (including chemistry), social studies 3, and a foreign language 2–3. Take a basic computer/keyboarding course and a health course, if available.

Did you know...

...that while an associate degree in dental hygiene is offered at many two-year colleges, it may actually take longer than two years to complete? That's because most schools require you to take prerequisite courses before admission into the program.

Typical courses in this major:

Pharmacology
Histology
Pathology
Radiology
Microbiology
Chemistry
Dental anatomy
Preventive dentistry
Dental materials
Dental hygiene techniques
Nutrition
Office emergencies
Office management
Introduction to clinic procedures

Concentrations:

Generally, none available.

What the study of this major is like:

Registered dental hygienists are licensed health care professionals. To become licensed, you must graduate from an accredited dental hygiene program and pass state and national exams.

The primary responsibility of dental hygienists is to assist patients in maintaining oral and dental health. Majors in dental hygiene are therefore required to master a wide range of skills related to health and patient education. Although training differs among states, you are usually taught to perform patient assessments (including medical histories; blood pressure testing; head, neck, and mouth examinations; and oral cancer screenings); remove deposits from the teeth (oral prophylaxis); use agents such as fluoride to help prevent decay; work with dental X rays; and advise patients on maintaining healthy lifestyles.

You first take anatomy, physiology, and pathology to explore the functions of the human body, the process of disease, and the biological and physiological basis of health. Courses in dental hygiene sciences provide the foundation for dental hygiene care and clinical practice. Learning takes place in the classroom, in laboratories, and in clinical experiences. In your first year, you develop skills by practicing on models and then, under professional supervision, by treating patients. Your course work emphasizes providing dental hygiene services to diverse groups of patients in clinical settings. Because much of a dental hygienist's time is spent interacting one-on-one with patients, you take courses in psychology, speech, sociology, and patient management to develop strong communications and interpersonal skills.

Dental hygiene programs are full-time courses of study. Course material must be covered in a certain sequence, because new courses build on past work. Throughout your clinical experience, you will continue to apply what you've learned in your courses. Outside experiences may include visits to patients in public health clinics, hospitals, child care centers, nursing homes, and correctional facilities. You may also participate in health fairs, health education presentations, and elementary school activities. Some programs send you to work in dental offices in the community to gain real-world experience.

Dental hygiene programs may be located in community colleges or four-year institutions. Some programs are affiliated with dental schools. In the two-year associate degree program, the curriculum should be accredited by the American Dental Association (ADA). The associate degree is the minimum required for entry-level certification. Bachelor's or master's degree programs prepare you to work in industry, education, or research. If you have dental assisting experience or are a graduate of an ADA-accredited dental-assisting program, some colleges give you transfer credit for your experience, so that you do not have to repeat material you have already covered.

Other majors you might like:
Clinical/medical laboratory technology
Dental laboratory technology
Physical therapy
Makeup artist
Public health education
Ophthalmic technology
Physician assistant
Radiologic technology/medical imaging
Medical records technology
Dietetics
Social work
American sign language (ASL)

Questions to ask colleges:
Is the program accredited by the ADA? If not, your degree will not be recognized by state licensing bodies and you will not be eligible to take the national board exam.

Which courses must be taken before entry into the program?

Where is the clinical component performed? Most programs have on-site clinical facilities, but some may require travel to nearby locations.

Career options and trends:
Dental hygiene practitioner*; clinical instructor; clinical researcher.

In order to become a registered dental hygienist and obtain a state license, you must pass a national written examination, and a state or regional clinical examination.

This field is ranked among the fastest growing occupations. Most dental hygienists work in private dental offices, but many work in clinics, schools, nursing homes, hospitals, universities, managed health care organizations, and correctional institutions. As health care expands to include dental professionals as part of an interdisciplinary team of health care providers, practice settings available to dental hygienists will also expand.

For more info:
American Dental Hygienists' Association (ADHA)
444 North Michigan Ave., Suite 3400
Chicago, IL 60611
(312) 440-8900
www.adha.org

Dietetics

What it's about:

Dietetics prepares you to provide for the nutritional needs of people in conditions of both wellness and ill health. Your studies include the basic sciences, nutrition and food science, principles of management, and behavioral and social sciences. Bachelor degree programs prepare you to become a registered dietitian (RD), and associate degree programs prepare you to be a dietitian technician (DTR).

Is this for you?

You might like this major if you also like: cooking and eating; watching cooking shows on TV; reading about nutrition and health in magazines; science fairs and projects; sports; health and fitness activities; helping people.

Consider this major if you are good at: attention to detail; caring/nurturing; counseling; critical reading/thinking; science; teamwork *...or have...* initiative; verbal skills.

Recommended high school prep:

English 4, math 3, lab science 4 (including chemistry and physics), social studies 3, and a foreign language 2–3. If possible, take advanced biology and chemistry; courses on health, foods, and nutrition are also recommended.

Did you know...

...that this is a great major for entrepreneurs? The food industry is the fourth largest in the world. Almost any food- or health-related setting needs dietitians, and nutrition is essential to health, from birth to old age.

Typical courses in this major:

Organic chemistry
Biochemistry
Anatomy and physiology
Microbiology
Food science
Food chemistry
Basic nutrition
Advanced nutrition and metabolism
Medical nutrition therapy
Maternal and child nutrition
Geriatric nutrition
Public health *or* Community nutrition
Quantity food production and procurement
Diet selection and management

Concentrations:

Clinical nutrition; health and fitness; institutional food management.

What the study of this major is like:

All dietetics programs must be approved by the Commission on Accreditation for Dietetics Education (CADE). To become a registered dietitian, you must complete an accredited program and earn at least a four-year Bachelor of Science degree. Your course work includes biochemistry, microbiology, and anatomy, as well as industry-related subjects such as culinary arts, food service systems management, and food and nutrition sciences. In courses like communications, computer science, and sociology, you learn the necessary business skills and "people skills."

You must also complete a supervised practice program in dietetics (typically 6 to 12 months)—either while you're in college or afterward—and pass an exam administered nationally by the Commission on Dietetic Registration (CDR). Programs that combine your degree work and the practice program are called coordinated programs in dietetics (CPD). Programs that postpone the supervised practice work until after you graduate are called didactic programs in dietetics (DPD). You should choose which program is best for you before you enroll.

If you plan to become a dietitian technician, you must complete a CADE-accredited dietetics program while you earn at least a two-year associate degree. You take courses in food and nutrition, food service systems management, and general science, together with at least 450 hours of supervised practice in a health care facility or food service organization. After you graduate, you must pass the CDR's nationally administered registration examination. If you think you might later want to become an RD, check with the dietitian program you are considering to see if it has formal arrangements (known as an articulation agreement) with CPD and DPD programs to accept some or all of your credits. Otherwise, check directly with the CPD or DPD programs you are considering to see if your courses will receive transfer credit.

Course work in the dietetics major includes lecture, labs, individual and group projects, and required practical experience and/or summer internships. In courses with labs, you'll be kept very busy, so you must organize your time efficiently. Programs may differ in aspects of the curriculum that work best for faculty members. For example, a program in a research-based university may emphasize science, whereas in a small college, it may stress food service systems management. As a result, some programs may be more academically challenging than others, and some may offer opportunities beyond the basic requirements. To find out about a program's emphasis, look at the catalog. Faculty members' areas of expertise will be reflected in the courses they teach.

Sometimes people confuse registered dietitians, dietitian technicians, and nutritionists. Although in some states you need to be licensed to call yourself a nutritionist, the definition often varies. In every state, however, only professionals who are certified by the Commission on Dietetic Registration (CDR) can legally use the titles "registered dietitian" and "dietitian technician."

Other majors you might like:
Culinary arts and chef training
Food and nutrition studies
Pharmacy
Sports and fitness administration
Physician assistant
Occupational therapy
Restaurant/food services management
Hospitality administration and management
Nutrition sciences
Public health education
Gerontology
Food science

Questions to ask colleges:
Does the program help identify opportunities for summer jobs and entry-level job?

What percent of the program's graduates pass the certification examination to become an RD?

What is the acceptance rate of graduates into dietetic practice programs?

Career options and trends:
Registered dietitian (RD) in clinical, administrative, or private practice*; registered dietitian technician (DTR) working in a school or health care facility*; restaurant manager; extension educator; research dietitian; chef; food industry representative.

According to the National Bureau of Labor Statistics, job prospects for dietitians will likely increase, especially in home health care and social services. Employment in hospitals is expected to show little change over the next decade or so because of anticipated slow growth and reduced length of patients' hospital stays. Faster growth, however, is anticipated in nursing homes, residential care facilities, and physician clinics. Rising public interest in nutrition and obesity disorders will also spur demand.

While job prospects are good for all dietetics majors, the best and most plentiful jobs go to graduates who are RDs.

For more info:
American Dietetic Association
120 South Riverside Plaza, Suite 2000
Chicago, IL 60606
(800) 877-1600
www.eatright.org

Emergency medical technology (EMT paramedic)

Also known as:
Emergency medical services (EMS)

What it's about:
In this major, you develop the problem-solving, critical-thinking, and management skills necessary to function independently in prehospital settings. You learn how to recognize, assess, and manage medical emergencies; to supervise ambulance personnel; and to carry out medical interventions, from basic responses such as bandaging to high-level techniques such as administering medication, providing cardiac care, and performing advanced airway measures.

Is this for you?
You might like this major if you also like: working with all types of people; helping people in times of crisis; fast action; sports; technology, science, and medicine; taking command.

Consider this major if you are good at: attention to detail; caring/nurturing; critical reading/thinking; organizing; persuading/influencing; teamwork; thinking on your feet ...*or have...* initiative; patience; self-confidence; verbal skills.

Recommended high school prep:
English 4, math 3, lab science 3–4 (biology and chemistry most important), social studies 3, and a foreign language 2–3. If available, take a course on anatomy or physiology; and try to obtain First Aid and CPR certification.

Did you know...
...that being a paramedic requires more responsibility than putting people into the back of an ambulance and driving them to the hospital? The job involves interacting with other community organizations, family members, and hospital personnel. In many communities, you are crossed-trained with other public safety responders, such as police officers and firefighters.

Typical courses in this major:
Anatomy and physiology
College math
Pathophysiology
Pharmacology
Bioterrorism
Medical and trauma assessment
Emergency care analysis and intervention
Communications and computer operations
Crisis scene management
Accounting and budgeting
Advanced cardiac life support
Prehospital field techniques
Vehicle rescue
Equipment operation and maintenance
Prehospital trauma life support
Professional standards

Concentrations:
In college: pharmacology; trauma assessment; anatomy and physiology; emergency care and analysis.

If you go on to grad school: emergency management; ambulatory care.

What the study of this major is like:
Emergency medical services (EMS) providers help people in life- or health-threatening situations. The most highly trained prehospital EMS providers are EMT (emergency medical technician) paramedics, who care for patients on site and then help get them to hospitals. As workers or volunteers for ambulance services, fire departments, hospitals, and government-based services, EMTs may be called in to help someone suffering from a broken toe one hour, and someone else having a massive heart attack the next.

If you major in emergency medical technology, you usually take courses such as anatomy and physiology, disease process, pharmacology, cardiology, medical and trauma assessment, hazardous material, bioterrorism, and vehicle rescue. Liberal arts courses teach you how to communicate and work with patients and with other health professionals. Courses are taught in a number of ways, ranging from lecture format to Web-based scenario practice. In classrooms and labs, you learn and practice skills such as intravenous (IV) insertion, intubations, and defibrillation.

In addition to course work, you do clinical rotations in hospitals and with paramedic units. During clinical rotations, you gain experience in making decisions, assessing patients' condition, and providing appropriate treatment—always under close supervision. Because paramedics must be familiar with all types of injury and illness, your clinical rotations cover a range of patients, including adult, pediatric, and geriatric patients, as well as a wide variety of conditions, including chest pain, respiratory distress, broken bones, and spinal cord injuries. You may work in a cardiac intensive care unit, an operating room, an emergency department, a trauma unit, a burn unit, or a behavioral unit.

In your paramedic unit rotation, you work in the field, answering calls with a qualified instructor. You learn how to care for patients under often-difficult conditions. Some programs require one paramedic field rotation, whereas others call for two—one in a suburban ambulance and one in an urban ambulance. Most EMT majors are enrolled full-time, and some find it hard to balance study time with clinical rotations and course work. Still, most majors find, in the end, that being well trained to help others is worth the effort they have put into studying.

Emergency medical technology programs are found in colleges, EMT academies, and hospitals. Most are similar, emphasizing critical-thinking, problem-solving, and clinical skills. Some programs provide training in entry-level management. Others focus on paramedic studies and do not include management or education courses. The majority of programs offer a two-year associate degree or certificate program; but if you plan to move up quickly into management or supervisory roles, you should consider pursuing a four-year Bachelor of Science degree.

Other majors you might like:
Physician assistant
Nursing (RN)
Athletic training
Community health/preventative medicine
Respiratory therapy
Occupational safety/health technology
Forensic science
Emergency management/homeland security
Hazardous materials technology
Fire protection and safety technology
Paralegal studies
Social work

Questions to ask colleges:
Where are the clinical rotations done (for instance, in trauma centers or in a local hospital)? Where are the prehospital rotations done?

What system is used to track and record the required number of student-patient contacts necessary for certification?

Are graduates of the program eligible to sit for the National Registry Examination for paramedics?

Career options and trends:
Paramedic*; emergency room technician; fire fighter; police officer; occupation health officer; state office of EMS employee; Federal Emergency Management Agency (FEMA) employee; infection control officer; EMS coordinator; EMS supervisor.

Most states require certification through the National Registry Examination for Paramedics, which makes it easier to relocate from state to state. Municipal or federal employment usually requires you to take a civil service exam as well.

EMS employment is projected to have higher than average growth through the year 2018.

For more info:
National Association of Emergency Medical
   Technicians (NAEMT)
P.O. Box 1400
Clinton, MS 39060-1400
(800) 34-NAEMT
www.naemt.com

Health care administration

What it's about:
The health care administration major prepares you to manage the business activities of a wide variety of organizations that make up the health care delivery system, such as hospitals, clinics, nursing homes, insurance companies, and public health agencies.

Is this for you?
You might like this major if you also like: organizing or leading a club or group activity; solving problems; team sports; working with different types of people; starting and running a business; debating; health and science issues; community service projects.

Consider this major if you are good at: active listening; attention to detail; leadership; organizing; persuading/influencing; quantitative analysis; teamwork *...or have...* initiative; verbal skills; writing skills.

Recommended high school prep:
English 4, math 3, lab science 4, social studies 3, and a foreign language 2-3. While not a specific requirement, evidence of leadership either in high school or in the community is desirable. Additionally, a course in public speaking would be helpful.

Did you know...
...that the majority of undergraduates pursuing health administration are women?

Typical courses in this major:
Introduction to health care
Organizational behavior
Statistics
Epidemiology
Health policy
Ethics
Strategic planning
Marketing health care
Economics of health care
Accounting
Management information systems
Public health
Health law
Health care management
Financial management
Human resources management

Concentrations:
Long-term health care; health information systems; physician practice management.

What the study of this major is like:
If you want to work in health care delivery but do not want to become a clinician, health care administration is the perfect major. You will learn how to make health care available to individuals and how to manage organizations such as nursing homes, clinics, welfare departments, rehabilitation centers, and hospitals. The program teaches you to manage finances, deal with personnel, understand and comply with the laws that affect health care delivery, and oversee other aspects of administration.

Health care administration is a "people business." As a health care administrator, you'll spend most of your time dealing with physicians, nurses, patients and their families, payers, regulators, government agencies, and media representatives. Although majors must be organized and willing to work hard, the most important quality health care administrators need is good interpersonal skills. To be successful, you should feel comfortable working with diverse groups of people; communicate well (writing, speaking, and listening); be able to assume a leadership role when necessary; accept criticism without taking it personally; juggle multiple demands; take into account information from a variety of sources when making decisions; and be ready to improve your organization.

Majors take courses in three broad areas—liberal arts, general management, and health services management. In liberal arts courses, you study communications (especially public speaking), mathematics (especially statistics), critical thinking, and social context (including philosophy, sociology, psychology, political science, and economics). For general management, you examine theories of management, the functional areas of management (such as accounting, computer applications, human resource management, marketing, and strategic management courses), and leadership skills. Health services management courses cover health and disease, health services organization and delivery, financial management, law and government regulation, and health policy.

Health services management courses begin in your third year. Your classes will primarily be lecture/discussion. Many courses use the case method: groups of students examine a question or a problem and come up with a number of solutions. Most programs require a supervised, field-based internship (in the summer or for a semester). Additional practicum experience is highly recommended. Experience in either paid or volunteer positions can make all the difference when you begin your job search.

There are two challenges that most majors face. The first is time management—courses (particularly at the upper level) are intense and require numerous papers and extensive reading. The second challenge is public speaking—an essential skill for health care professionals. In upper-level courses, you often work to overcome both challenges by participating in study groups.

Programs may have different emphases, depending on where they are housed. For example, programs in business schools stress finance and similar subjects, whereas programs in schools of public health or health sciences stress subjects like community response to infectious diseases. As a major, you should seek out courses that balance your studies. If your program has a business focus, be sure to enroll in courses in public health; similarly, if the program is in a health sciences/public health school, you should think about minoring in business.

Other majors you might like:

Business administration and management
Occupational health/industrial hygiene
Insurance
Funeral services/mortuary science
Health services administration
Biotechnology
Psychology
Public administration
Human services
Social work
Community health services
Management information systems

Questions to ask colleges:

Is the program a certified member or candidate member of the Association of University Programs in Health Administration? Certification by AUPHA indicates that the program has met national standards in facilities, program support, curriculum, and outcomes measures.

Are student chapters of health care professional organizations available on campus? These clubs give students valuable leadership and networking opportunities.

Career options and trends:

Health plan administrator; health policy analyst; hospital or health system management*; nurse management; nursing home administrator*; physician group practice administrator*; public health administrator; pharmaceutical sales representative.

State licensure is usually required to run a skilled-care nursing home. Administrators of public health departments or agencies typically have a clinical background either in nursing, social work, or equivalent field of practice.

As the healthcare industry expands and changes, more managers will be needed to ensure that business operations continue to run smoothly. The most significant trend for likely employment is in the areas of long-term care and physician group-practice management. The increasing number of acute care hospitals is also opening up employment opportunities. But keep in mind that to move up from an entry-level management position, you'll probably need a master's degree and at least five years' experience.

For more info:

Association of University Programs in Health
    Administration (AUPHA)
2000 14th St. North
Suite 780
Arlington, VA 22201
(703) 894-0940
www.aupha.org

American College of Healthcare Executives
    (ACHE)
One North Franklin, Suite 1700
Chicago, IL 60606
(312) 424-2800
www.ache.org

Medical Group Management Association (MGMA)
104 Iverness Terrace East
Englewood, CO 80112
(303) 799-1111
www.mgma.org

Licensed practical nursing

Also known as:
Vocational nursing

What it's about:
The practical nursing major is a one- or two-year program that prepares you to assist registered nurses and physicians in providing general nursing care. After you graduate, you will be eligible to take the National Council Licensing Examination for Practical Nurses (NCLEX-PN). Passing the exam allows you to be certified by a state board of nursing as a licensed practical/vocational nurse (LP/VN).

Is this for you?
You might like this major if you also like: working with others; caring for peoples' physical, psychological, and emotional needs; physical and social sciences; learning about the human body.

Consider this major if you are good at: caring/nurturing; communicating; critical reading/thinking; making decisions; math; organizing; teamwork *...or have...* manual dexterity; patience; physical stamina; positive attitude.

Recommended high school prep:
English 4, math 3, lab science 3 (including biology and chemistry), social studies 3, and a foreign language 2–3.

Typical courses in this major:
Nursing (lecture and clinical courses)
Nutrition
Pharmacology
English composition
Chemistry
Anatomy and physiology
Microbiology
Psychology
Developmental psychology
Sociology

Concentrations:
Generally, none available.

What the study of this major is like:
Licensed practical nurses (LPNs)—also called licensed vocational nurses (LVNs) in some states—play an essential part in hospital care: monitoring patients' condition and reporting changes to nurses and physicians; taking temperature and blood pressure; helping patients do rehabilitative exercises; giving medications; bathing patients; changing bandages; and collecting laboratory samples. With the growing shortage of registered nurses (RNs) throughout the world, the role of the LPN continues to evolve. For example, intravenous (IV) therapy for patients used to be provided only by RNs. In some states, certified LPNs can now perform IV therapy.

The major includes general education, science, and nursing courses. Behavioral and social science courses stress the elements of human behavior, growth and development, interpersonal relationships, and cultural diversity. Nursing courses generally cover the nursing process, basic and advanced nursing skills, communication, disease, medications, dosage calculations, lab tests, treatments, ethics, legal/professional issues, and patient care from birth to death.

Behavioral and social science courses are typically in lecture format. Nursing and natural science courses include both lecture and laboratory/clinical experiences. Your initial lab courses allow you to safely practice your nursing skills. Before working with patients, you need to become knowledgeable, competent, and confident. You then move out into the real world for your clinical practice work, where you are supervised as you care for patients in acute care or long-term care facilities.

The most likely challenge you may face is to recognize how difficult the work can be and to devote the necessary time and effort to it. To participate actively in class, you must prepare the required class presentations and written work. Many programs expect you to maintain a minimum grade point average. After you graduate, you must complete a national exam.

To become an LPN, you can pursue either a one-year vocational program at a technical school or a two-year associate degree at a college. As you compare programs, consider your career plans. If you see yourself as a bedside nurse working under the supervision of a registered nurse, doctor, or dentist, then a one-year vocational program is enough. On the other hand, if you think you might want to advance further in nursing, you should start with an accredited two-year program where you can transfer credits to other programs. Because nursing courses vary among colleges, it may be hard to transfer—so if you need to transfer, meet with the director of the new program and provide a description of the courses you have completed. Try to get credit for what you have learned.

Other majors you might like:
Nursing (RN)
Dietetics
Physician assistant
Psychology
Dental hygiene
Physical therapy
Art therapy
Gerontology
Medical office administration
Human development and family studies
American sign language (ASL)
Emergency medical technology (EMT paramedic)

Questions to ask colleges:
Is the nursing program approved by the state board of nursing?

What are the admission, curriculum, progression, and graduation requirements? You should find out before you enroll, so you won't have any surprises later.

What percent of the school's graduating nurses pass the NCLEX-PN?

Career options and trends:
Specialty certification is available to LPNs in areas such as long-term care, pharmacology, I.V. therapy, and gerontology. To advance to higher levels of nursing—to become, say, a registered nurse or a certified nurse specialist in pediatrics, you will most likely need a bachelor's or master's degree, work experience in the particular area of nursing, and a passing grade on a certification exam.

Employment prospects for LPNs are excellent because of a severe shortage of nurses worldwide. The majority of LPNs work in hospitals, clinics, long-term-care and nursing home facilities; but other employment opportunities are available in rehabilitation centers, public health agencies, industrial/occupational health offices, private doctor's offices, and schools. Employment growth is expected in the areas of community and home health nursing, because insurance companies are mandating shorter hospital stays, and more patients will require nurses to aid recovery at home.

Insider's viewpoint:
"Nursing is not just medication administration; you are there for the patients when they are throwing up or have diarrhea. One must think about those things as well: can you handle that?"

—Josette, A.S. candidate, Riverside Community College

For more info:
National Federation of Licensed Practical Nurses (NFLPN)
605 Poole Drive
Garner, NC 27529
(919) 779-0046
www.nflpn.org

National Association for Practical Nurse Education & Service (NAPNES)
1940 Duke St.
Suite 200
Alexandria, VA 22314
(703) 933-1003
www.napnes.org

Nursing (RN)

What it's about:

This major prepares students to be frontline providers of health care. Registered nurses design, manage, and coordinate care for individuals, families, groups, communities, and larger populations. Nursing students learn how to attend to the sick and the injured; how to rehabilitate, counsel, and educate patients; and how to work as part of a health care team in many settings.

Is this for you?

You might like this major if you also like: caregiving; volunteer work; making a difference in people's lives; science; autonomy and independence; a fast pace; working in groups; challenges.

Consider this major if you are good at: active listening; caring/nurturing; critical reading/thinking; leadership; math; organizing; problem solving; teamwork *...or have...* initiative; patience; verbal skills.

Recommended high school prep:

English 4, math 4 (including precalculus, calculus, or statistics), lab science 3 (including biology and chemistry), social studies 3, and a foreign language 2-3. If available, courses in psychology, growth and development, nutrition and health are recommended, as are speech and writing courses. A computer applications course would also be helpful.

Did you know...

...that nurses aren't just doctors' helpers? Nurses are independent primary health care providers, whose responsibilities range from directly treating patients to developing and supervising complex nursing care systems. In the United States, RNs—who outnumber physicians by more than four to one—are involved in just about every type of health care service.

Typical courses in this major:

Psychology
Anatomy and physiology
Microbiology
Chemistry
Nutrition
Fundamentals of practice in nursing
Pharmacology
Physical assessment
Nursing leadership
Sociology
Mental health
Environmental and occupational health
Adult, pediatric, and geriatric care
Maternal/child and neonatal care
Medical and surgical care
Home health care

Concentrations:

Generally, none in college; but if you go on to grad school: family primary care; women's health; pediatrics; adult primary care; geriatrics; neonatal acute care; adult acute care.

What the study of this major is like:

Generally, you take courses in English, social sciences, the humanities, and the natural sciences during your first two years as a major. In your nursing program, you apply your education in liberal arts and sciences to learn the principles of nursing theory. You evaluate research to determine its benefit to nursing practice; examine nurse–client relationships and the organization of health care delivery; study ethical and practical issues related to terminal illness and death; and examine ways of providing health promotion services and illness care to culturally diverse communities.

Some programs require a fourth-year internship in which you receive academic credit while gaining clinical experience. You may work (under supervision) in hospitals, long-term care facilities, schools, community health organizations, mental health/psychiatric institutions, and other settings. There may also be opportunities for paid summer work experience.

You do not specialize at the undergraduate level. Graduates of nursing programs are generalists, able to assume roles in acute care, long-term care, and community-based facilities. After completing your undergraduate degree, you must pass the National Council Licensing Examination for Registered Nurses (NCLEX-RN) in order to work in the field.

Perhaps the biggest surprise for beginning students in nursing is the intensity and rigor of the subject matter and clinical practice requirements. Because nurses, who often work independently, must be responsible and accountable, they are expected to master a great deal of specialized (often technical) knowledge and theory.

Being a nursing major requires time management and a commitment to long hours of both course work and clinical practice. Usually you will need to study for several hours for every hour of class time. Clinical practice generally involves 16 hours a week of work in a variety of health care settings. Before and after clinical practice, you develop case studies, care plans, and education projects related to your client population. Also, early in your studies, you must begin preparation for the NCLEX-RN exam.

Programs can grant an associate degree in nursing (A.D.N.) or a Bachelor of Science degree in nursing (B.S.N.). For an A.D.N. (usually from a community college), you complete the program in two to three years and are prepared for entry-level registered nurse practice at the bedside.

The four-year B.S.N. prepares you to work in the full range of health care settings, including hospitals; critical care, long-term care, rehabilitation, outpatient care, public health, community health, and mental health facilities; private homes; and neighborhood clinics. It also prepares you for graduate work. In addition to the liberal arts and sciences courses, B.S.N. programs feature more in-depth nursing courses, including theory, research, pharmacology, pathophysiology, physical assessment, and nutrition. You also receive training in specific areas such as community and public health nursing, medical-surgical nursing, maternal-child nursing, pediatric nursing, mental health nursing, and nursing leadership and management.

Other majors you might like:

Education of physically handicapped
Human services
Communication disorders
Psychology
Licensed practical nursing
Physical therapy
Music therapy
Gerontology
Food and nutrition studies
Human development and family studies
American sign language (ASL)
Emergency medical technology (EMT paramedic)

Questions to ask colleges:

Is the program accredited by the Commission on Collegiate Nursing Education (CCNE) or the National League for Nursing Accrediting Commission (NLNAC)?

What is the NCLEX-RN passing rate for graduates?

What types of laboratories are available for the program, and how well equipped are they?

What are the types and locations of clinical sites used for student practice opportunities?

Career options and trends:

Advanced nurse practitioner*; nurse educator*; clinical nurse specialist; nurse anesthetist; nurse midwife; nurse researcher; nurse administrator*.

For advanced or specialty practice, a bachelor's or master's degree and certification based on examination and clinical practice requirements are essential.

The United States is in the midst of a national nursing shortage that is projected to intensify as the population ages and the demand for new health care services and technologies increases. It is anticipated that by the year 2020, there will be a severe shortage (more than 800,000 RNs) in the number of nurses needed in the nation's health care system.

"Put on your seat belt; you are in for a wild ride. You will feel emotions you have never felt before."

—Jenn, class of 2000, Golden West College

For more info:

American Association of Colleges of Nursing (AACN)
One Dupont Circle, N.W.
Suite 530
Washington, DC 20036
(202) 463-6930
www.aacn.nche.edu

National Student Nurse Association (NSNA)
45 Main St., Suite 606
Brooklyn, NY 11201
(718) 210-0705
www.nsna.org

American Nurses Association (ANA)
8515 Georgia Avenue, Suite 400
Silver Spring, MD 20910
(800) 274-4262
www.ana.org

Occupational therapy

What it's about:

Occupational therapy is the use of "occupation" (work, self-care, and play/leisure) to help people who are affected by developmental, psychosocial, or physical problems to achieve or regain independent function, enhance development, and prevent injury. You must have a master's degree or higher in order to be certified as an occupational therapist. In college you take the prerequisite courses needed to be admitted into the graduate program.

Is this for you?

You might like this major if you also like: working with individuals from diverse backgrounds; hobbies, activities, or interests involving fine hand (motor) skills; solving problems or puzzles in creative ways, even when there are no right or wrong answers; technology; physical activity; working in groups.

Consider this major if you are good at: active listening; caring/nurturing; counseling; creativity; critical reading/thinking; organizing; teamwork ...*or have...* initiative; manual dexterity; verbal skills; writing skills.

Recommended high school prep:

English 4, math 3–4, lab science 3 (including biology, chemistry, and physics), social studies 3, and a foreign language 2–3. Courses in the arts, music, and, if available, psychology or human behavior would be helpful

Did you know...

...that creativity and problem solving are important in this profession? After you learn the knowledge and skills to be an OT, you must be able to apply them to the unique situations and individuals you encounter in the various areas of practice that make up the profession.

Typical courses in this major:

Biology
English composition
Anatomy and physiology
General psychology
Developmental (life-span) psychology
Human development
Ergonomics
Statistics
Sociology
Anthropology
Mechanical physics
Kinesiology
Neuroscience
Gerontology
Leadership and management
Research methods

Concentrations:

Generally, none in college; but if you go on to grad school: occupational science; psychiatric disabilities; physical disabilities; pediatrics; rehabilitation technology

What the study of this major is like:

Occupational therapists help people who may have conditions that make it hard for them to function. These conditions may include developmental problems (such as learning disabilities), psychosocial issues (eating disorders), physical problems (arthritis or repetitive stress injury), the aging process (difficulty seeing or hearing), poverty, or cultural differences. OTs start by considering people's surroundings, evaluating their performance of everyday tasks, and assessing their personal goals. Then they use various activities to help the clients function with greater independence and to make the most of their abilities. Finally, OTs determine how well the therapy has worked.

To become an OT, you must pass the National Board for Certification in Occupational Therapy examination (NBCOT). Those who pass the exam are awarded the title "Occupational Therapist Registered" (OTR), and are eligible for state licensure.

As of January 1, 2007, in order to qualify for the exam, you must graduate from an accredited graduate program in OT, at either the master's or doctorate degree level. In college, this major is now primarily a preprofessional program made up of prerequisite courses that will prepare you for admission into a graduate program in OT.

These prerequisite courses generally include one year (two semesters) of anatomy and physiology, English, statistics, and sociology, and usually three semesters of general and developmental psychology. In addition, most graduate programs require you to be certified in CPR (cardiopulmonary resuscitation) and to have at least 50 hours of volunteer experience working with a licensed OTR. A course in mechanical physics (related to movement and/or principles of movement) is often recommended, although not required.

You can major in anything you want in college so long as you take the prerequisite courses, but the most popular majors are biology, psychology, sociology, anthropology, liberal arts, and anatomy. Quite a few colleges offer a combined bachelor's/master's program that allows you to enter as a college freshman, and continue straight through to the OT graduate degree in five years.

Once you get into the graduate program, the curriculum includes the study of normal maturation, development, and function; the effect of diseases, trauma, and aging; and the varied ways in which therapists can help people whose ability to do normal activities is threatened or impaired. Programs generally consist of lecture courses; lab courses, in which you practice and analyze skills; and fieldwork training in clinical settings.

In courses on occupational therapy theory and practice, you do closely supervised fieldwork, where you observe and then treat clients in hospitals, schools, or other facilities. As you advance in the program this fieldwork becomes full-time, for a minimum of 24 weeks; also under the supervision of a qualified occupational therapist.

Fieldwork is the most demanding part of your studies because you must apply, in a real-world setting, what you've learned in class and the lab. However, students typically enjoy fieldwork immensely, and their enthusiasm helps them complete the program.

Other majors you might like:

Physical therapy
Gerontology
Child development
Art, dance, or music therapy
Psychology
Special education
Athletic training
Recreational therapy
Human services
Exercise sciences
Human resources management
Biomedical engineering

Questions to ask colleges:

Is the program approved by the Accreditation Council for Occupational Therapy Education?

Is there a combined bachelor's/graduate degree option? If so, what are the requirements to move on into the graduate part of the program?

What kinds of internships or volunteer experiences working with OTs are available?

Career options and trends:

Occupational therapist*; researcher; industrial ergonomist; instructor; master clinician; health care administrator.

In addition to requiring successful completion of the NBCOT exam, most states have licensing standards. Practitioners must also renew their certification every three years.

Job prospects are excellent—as society ages, occupational therapists will be more in demand. Because the profession has been underutilized, many areas of practice have yet to be developed. In addition to hospitals, schools, rehabilitation centers, and long-term-care facilities, emerging areas of practice include evaluation, rehabilitation, and training for driving skills; consultation on accessibility design and home modification; ergonomics and workplace modification; assistive device development; services for those with impaired vision; and private practice in community health services.

For more info:

American Occupational Therapy Association (AOTA)
4720 Montgomery Lane
P.O. Box 31220
Bethesda, MD 20824-1220
(800) 377-8555
www.aota.org

National Board for Certification in Occupational Therapy (NBCOT)
12 South Summit Ave.
Suite 100
Gaithersburg, MD 20877-4150
(301) 990-7979
www.nbcot.org

Pharmacy

What it's about:

Pharmacists apply a knowledge of medicines to patient needs. As a pharmacy student, you learn how to counsel patients, dispense drugs, monitor drug therapy, minimize side effects, and work with physicians, nurses, and other health care professionals. Pharmacy is no longer an undergraduate major. The entry-level degree is now the Doctor of Pharmacy (Pharm.D.) first-professional degree, a four-year program that usually follows two years of college-level prepharmacy courses.

Is this for you?

You might like this major if you also like: chemistry; community service activities; meeting different kinds of people; helping people; learning; reading; being independent.

Consider this major if you are good at: attention to detail; counseling; critical reading/thinking; multitasking; organizing; quantitative analysis; teamwork *...or have...* initiative; verbal skills; writing skills.

Recommended high school prep:

English 4, math 4 (including precalculus), lab science 4 (including biology, chemistry and physics), social studies 3, and a foreign language 2–3. Courses that develop communications skills (writing and speech) are also important. Latin can be helpful, but is not necessary. Computer skills are essential.

Did you know...

...that pharmacists do much more than fill prescriptions? While about half of all pharmacists work in community pharmacies, many others are employed as clinical education specialists, researchers, government agency employees (e.g., in the Food and Drug Administration), or work in the pharmaceutical industry as scientists, consultants, product development managers, or marketing reps.

Typical courses in this major:

Physiology
Pathophysiology
Biochemistry
Microbiology
Molecular biology
Pharmaceutics
Pharmacology/medicinal chemistry
Immunology
Nonprescription medications and self-care
Dietary supplements and herbal medicines
Biostatistics
Professional communication
Pharmaceutical care
Pharmacy law and ethics
Health systems management
Physical assessment

Concentrations:

Generally, none available.

What the study of this major is like:

Typically, the pharmacy (Pharm.D.) major is a six-year doctorate program that requires two undergraduate years of prepharmacy courses, followed by four academic years (or three calendar years in an accelerated program, with summer semesters) of professional education. The prepharmacy curriculum usually includes courses in writing and speech, biology, general chemistry, organic chemistry, microbiology, calculus, human anatomy and physiology, social and behavioral sciences, economics, English, and humanities. Some prepharmacy programs also require physics courses and computer competency.

But you do not have to do prepharmacy training in order to be accepted into the professional pharmacy program; you must simply complete the prerequisite courses in college. For example, many pharmacy applicants are chemistry, biochemistry, or biology majors, and their pharmacy prerequisites are usually covered by courses they took to complete their major. Be aware that admissions requirements may vary greatly among professional pharmacy programs. To be considered for admission in about half the programs, you must submit Pharmacy College Admission Test (PCAT) scores.

At the graduate level, you focus on the physiology and biochemistry of the body, and on appropriate medication therapy, to diagnose, treat, or prevent disease. In medicinal chemistry (biochemistry of medicinals, immunology, biotechnology) and pharmacology courses, you study the effects of various classes of medications on the body. In courses on pharmaceutics/drug delivery systems, you learn how drugs are administered to, absorbed into, and eliminated from the body. Pharmacotherapy focuses on choosing and implementing medication therapies, including patient evaluation and counseling; risk assessment; prescribing, preparing, and dispensing; symptom management; and evaluation of results. In pathophysiology courses, you examine the way disease affects the body; pharmacokinetics explores the body's reactions to medications over time, as well as the measurement of blood levels to determine dosage; and in pharmacognosy, you study drugs derived from plants.

You'll be trained to dispense medication safely and to educate patients about their prescription and nonprescription (over-the-counter) therapies. Further, you learn to work with, and advise, physicians on medication selection. You also take courses in pharmacy management, pharmacy law, pharmacoeconomics, managed care, and pharmaceutical marketing.

All professional programs have the equivalent of three years of classroom instruction involving lectures, discussion sessions, laboratories, and practice-related activities. Integrated into this time is an "Introductory Pharmacy Practice Experience" which continues in a progressive manner until the "Advanced Pharmacy Practice Experiences" (clerkship rotations) which occur during the fourth year. During your clerkship rotations you apply what you have learned, completing 1,500 hours or more of hands-on practice in hospitals, clinics, community pharmacies, or other patient care settings.

Some colleges offer a bachelor's degree in pharmaceutical sciences or pharmacology, which can prepare you for a career in the pharmaceutical industry or for graduate study or medical school; but such a degree will not make you eligible for licensure as a pharmacist. Another option is the two-year associate degree (or diploma or certificate, depending on the program) that trains you to become a pharmacy technician. Pharmacy technicians work under the close supervision of pharmacists, performing technical tasks such as stocking, packaging, and pricing medications, and maintaining records and inventories of prescriptions, medications, and supplies.

Other majors you might like:
Biochemistry
Clinical/medical laboratory technology
Chemistry
Substance abuse counseling
Health care administration
Pharmacy assistant
Public heath
Community health/preventative medicine
Microbiology
Medical records administration
Small business administration/management
Dietetics

Questions to ask colleges:
Does the college offer a six-year prepharmacy/ Pharm.D. program for entering students? If so, what are the requirements (such as GPA) for continuing on into the professional program? What percentage of the prepharm students continue? If a state school, do in-state students get preference?

Are students required to take the PCAT before admission into the Pharm.D. program? If so, what is the score range for admission?

Do students get help in obtaining summer internship opportunities?

What is the range of clerkship opportunities available during the last professional year? How does the college assign students to these clerkships, and do students often have to relocate to attend them?

Career options and trends:

Community pharmacist*; hospital staff pharmacist*; long-term care facility pharmacist; managed care pharmacist; public health service pharmacist; clinical specialist; clinical drug researcher; quality control supervisor.

Every state requires a license to practice pharmacy. To qualify, you must serve an internship period and pass a national board exam and a state exam. Continuing professional education is required for license renewal.

Some positions in research, clinical pharmacy, teaching, or other specialty area may require an advanced graduate degree (master's or Ph.D.), and/or further training in a residency program or fellowship.

The job outlook is excellent, with good employment opportunities projected through 2018. Also, fewer Pharm.D. degrees are expected to be granted than the number of jobs created. The retail sector will be influenced by such trends as automated dispensing and wider use of pharmacy technicians to meet the growing demand at lower cost; expansion of chain drugstores and of mail order firms; and increased involvement by managed care and Medicare.

For more info:

American Association of Colleges of Pharmacy
   (AACP)
1426 Prince St.
Alexandria, VA 22314
(703) 739-2330
www.aacp.org

Physical therapy

What it's about:

Physical therapists (PTs) are licensed health care professionals who work to prevent, diagnose, and treat conditions that affect a person's movement and functional independence. Although you have to go to graduate school to earn a degree in physical therapy, a variety of undergraduate majors can prepare you for a professional PT program.

Is this for you?

You might like this major if you also like: helping people; sports and exercise; dance; gymnastics; science and technology; learning and discovery; problem solving; understanding other people's perspectives; seeking and using feedback.

Consider this major if you are good at: active listening; caring/nurturing; creativity; critical reading/thinking; organizing; persuading/influencing *...or have...* initiative; patience; physical stamina; verbal skills.

Recommended high school prep:

English 4, math 3, lab science 3 (including biology and chemistry), social studies 3, and a foreign language 2–3. In addition, it may be helpful to participate in a job-shadowing program at a local hospital.

Did you know...

...that physical therapists have considerable flexibility in their career paths? You can serve as a clinician, teacher, researcher, consultant, administrator, or in some combination of these roles. Also, both full-time and part-time opportunities exist in physical therapy, so that you can pursue other personal and professional goals if you wish.

Typical courses in this major:

Biology
Human development
Anatomy
Physiology
Physics
General (inorganic) chemistry
Mathematics
Statistics
Psychology
Sociology
Ethics
Neuroanatomy
Orthopedics
Health policy
Physical therapy exercise
Kinesiology

Concentrations:

Generally, none available.

What the study of this major is like:

To become a physical therapist, you must complete the prerequisites in college and then take a full-time, three-year, graduate-level program. Some colleges offer "3 + 3" programs, which enable you to complete both college and graduate work in six years.

Currently, the professional degree in physical therapy is either a master's degree (M.S.P.T. or M.P.T.) or the Doctorate in Physical Therapy (D.P.T.). The D.P.T. emerged in response to a significant shift in the roles and responsibilities of the physical therapist; PT education now requires a depth and breadth like that in other professional health care fields, such as medicine, dentistry, and optometry. A large number of professional programs have either converted to the D.P.T. degree, or have indicated an intention to do so.

Although various undergraduate majors, including biology, psychology, chemistry, or engineering, may help you get into a professional physical therapy program, you must be interested in movement as a primary component of health, and be committed to the study and application of the science of movement in the context of health care. As an undergraduate, you should take courses in the natural sciences, social sciences, and humanities, as well as in quantitative and analytical fields. A broad liberal arts education will help you hone your interpersonal skills, think critically, provide evidence-based care, and learn how to serve diverse populations.

Prerequisite course work for admission to professional programs can include anatomy, kinesiology, athletic training, exercise science, neuropsychology, social psychology, human development, physiology, physical education, and special education. Many graduate PT programs also require computer literacy, certification in CPR, and competence in medical terminology (a knowledge of Latin and Greek roots). Many also require a certain number of hours of volunteer clinical experience. You should plan each semester in college to be sure that you fulfill all the requirements for admission to grad school.

What can you look forward to in grad school? Most programs begin with basic science courses such as anatomy (generally dissection-based), neuroscience and motor control, exercise physiology and pathophysiology, and the psychosocial aspects of health and disability. You then apply what you learn to clinical practice, through guided clinical experiences. The core of your curriculum involves studying clinical sciences in neurology, cardiology, pediatrics, and orthopedics and acquiring patient management skills that you can use in diagnosing problems, planning interventions, and assessing results. Your clinical competence will be judged by a variety of clinical internships that you must complete.

Other majors you might like:

Psychology
Biomedical engineering
Anthropology
Exercise sciences
Occupational therapy
Nursing (RN)
Athletic training
Sports and fitness administration
Dance therapy
Social work
Dietetics
Respiratory therapy

Questions to ask colleges:

Does the college offer a combined pre-PT/graduate program? If so, what are the requirements for admission and for continuing on into the professional program?

How are students advised about, and assisted in, meeting prerequisites for grad school?

What are the opportunities for volunteer experience in physical therapy settings?

Career options and trends:

Clinician; private practitioner; clinical administrator; clinical educator.

Physical therapists work in hospitals, extended-care facilities, home health agencies, public and private schools, industry, programs for people with developmental disabilities, and private clinics.

All states require physical therapists to pass a licensure exam before they can practice, after graduating from an accredited PT educational program. A number of states require continuing education to maintain licensure.

Physical therapy is now about prevention as well as rehabilitation. Clients include individuals in good health, as well as those at acute stages of illness; in schools and fitness facilities as well as in hospitals and nursing homes; and of both young and old ages. Therefore, the job outlook is excellent; health care, health promotion, and prevention opportunities abound.

For more info:

American Physical Therapy Association (APTA)
1111 N. Fairfax St.
Alexandria, VA 22314
(800) 999-2782
www.apta.org

Physician assistant

What it's about:

Physician assistants (PAs) are licensed to practice medicine under the supervision of a doctor. Working as part of a health care team, PAs take medical histories, examine and treat patients, order and interpret laboratory tests and X-rays, make diagnoses, and prescribe medications.

Is this for you?

You might like this major if you also like: working both independently and as part of a team; taking responsibility; solving problems for others; volunteer work in hospitals or clinics.

Consider this major if you are good at: active listening; attention to detail; caring/nurturing; critical reading/thinking; handling emergencies; leadership; organizing; teamwork; time management *...or have...* initiative; self-confidence; verbal skills.

Recommended high school prep:

English 4, math 3–4 (statistics would be helpful), lab science 3–4 (biology and chemistry most important), social studies 3, and a foreign language 2–3.

Did you know...

...that in some programs, PA majors attend many of the same classes as medical students? PA education and physician education differ not so much in the curriculum but in the amount of training.

...that PAs often work autonomously? In rural or inner-city clinics, where a physician may be available only one or two days a week, PAs may be the principal care providers; they consult with the supervising physician as needed. PAs also make house calls and go to hospitals and nursing homes to check on patients and report back to the physician.

Typical courses in this major:

Anatomy
History taking and physical diagnosis
Pharmacology
Microbiology
Behavioral sciences
Clinical medicine
Obstetrics and gynecology
Pediatrics
Geriatrics
Psychiatry
Surgery
Critical care
Medical laboratory sciences
Radiology
Health care delivery
Ethics

Concentrations:

Generally, none available.

What the study of this major is like:

All states require that new PAs complete a program approved by the Accreditation Review Commission on Education for the Physician Assistant, Inc. (ARC-PA). PA programs are located within sponsoring institutions such as universities, four-year colleges, community colleges, and hospitals. The credential offered by a program (certificate, associate degree, bachelor's degree, or master's degree) depends on the institution; more than half award a master's degree, and most PA graduates earn at least a bachelor's. No matter what degree is granted, every accredited PA program must meet the standards established by the ARC-PA, by offering courses in the basic medical sciences, behavioral and social sciences, clinical sciences, health policy, and professional practice, as well as supervised clinical practice. The average length of PA training is 26 months.

For admission, many PA programs require you to have completed at least two years of college and participated in some health care work. Many applicants enter PA programs from other health care professions, such as nursing and emergency medical technology. Prerequisites (including health care experience, courses, degree, and test scores) and application deadlines vary, so be sure to research PA programs well in advance.

In general, PA education includes one year of classroom studies followed by a year of supervised clinical experience (rotations) in health care institutions. You take courses in anatomy, microbiology, clinical medicine, clinical pharmacology, physical diagnosis, medical ethics, geriatric and home health care, biochemistry, pathology, and disease prevention. In addition to lectures, there are many opportunities for you to learn in small groups and refine your clinical skills under faculty supervision. During your second year, you spend at least 40 hours a week at your clinical rotation sites, including internal medicine, family medicine, emergency medicine, obstetrics and gynecology, pediatrics, general surgery, and psychiatry.

After completing the PA program, you must pass the national exam administered by the National Commission on Certification of Physician Assistants (NCCPA). In addition to national certification, you must then be licensed or registered by the state in which you practice. The profession is committed to lifelong learning, and PAs must recertify by examination every six years and complete 100 hours of continuing medical education every two years.

Other majors you might like:

Optometric assistant
Licensed practical nursing
Radiologic technology/medical imaging
Athletic training
Funeral services/mortuary science
Respiratory therapy
Medical records administration
Medical illustration
Forensic science
Biology
Biomedical engineering

Questions to ask colleges:

How much heath care experience is required for admission to the PA program? Which types of experiences qualify?

Does the program participate in the Central Application Service for Physician Assistants (CASPA)? This service collects and authenticates applicant materials for distribution to participating programs.

What is the first-time pass rate for recent graduates taking the Physician Assistants National Certifying Examination?

Career options and trends:

Many PAs work in primary care areas, such as internal medicine, pediatrics, and family medicine. Others work in specialty areas, such as general and thoracic surgery, emergency medicine, orthopedics, and geriatrics. PAs specializing in surgery provide pre- and postoperative care, and may work as assistants during major surgery.

Employment opportunities are excellent and projected to grow at an above-average pace, because of the nation's expanding health care needs and efforts to contain costs. Demand for PAs will be high in areas and settings where there is a shortage of physicians, such as rural and inner-city clinics. Technology that allows interactive consultations with off-site doctors ("telemedicine") will also increase the role of PAs.

For more info:

Physician Assistant Education Association (PAEA)
300 North Washington St.
Suite 505
Alexandria, VA 22314-2544
(703) 548-5538
www.paeaonline.org

Predental

What it's about:

Predental studies consists of the courses you need to take in college in order to get into dental school. It's not a major by itself, so you have to choose a major in addition to completing the predental requirements. Predental programs also provide guidance to help you prepare for dental school.

Is this for you?

You might like this major if you also like: helping people of all kinds; science and technology; working with your hands; arts and crafts; model making; playing a musical instrument; problem solving.

Consider this major if you are good at: attention to detail; caring/nurturing; creativity; critical reading/thinking; math; memorizing ...*or have...* integrity; manual dexterity; motivation; verbal skills.

Recommended high school prep:

English 4, math 4 (including precalculus and calculus), lab science 4 (including biology, chemistry, and physics), social studies 4 (including economics), and a foreign language 3–4 (Spanish recommended). If available, courses in psychology, speech communication, business, and computer science are also recommended.

Did you know...

...that cleaning and filling teeth are just a few of the jobs a dentist performs? Since many medical conditions that affect the whole body are revealed in the mouth, dentists are on the forefront of the early detection of disease.

Typical courses in this major:

Inorganic (general) chemistry
Organic chemistry
Biology
Zoology
Biochemistry
Physics
Calculus
College mathematics
English
Psychology
Cell biology
Genetics
Anatomy and physiology
Speech communication
Computer science
Sculpture

Concentrations:

Generally, none available.

What the study of this major is like:

Sometimes students are surprised to learn that taking part in studio arts or playing a musical instrument is good preparation for a career in dentistry. But it makes sense—dentists must be able to visualize three-dimensional objects from diagrams, have good eye–hand coordination, and perform detailed tasks in very small spaces. Perhaps you didn't realize that it takes some artistic ability to give people beautiful smiles.

In a predental program, however, science rather than the sculptural arts will occupy most of your time. You must take two semesters each of biology, general chemistry, organic chemistry, and physics. Many dental schools also expect you to take calculus and biochemistry. Courses in English and perhaps psychology are in the mix too. On top of all that, you will have to fulfill the requirements for the major you select.

Most students choose a science major, since the courses dovetail with the predental requirements. However, you don't have to follow that path if you don't want to. Many predental students select a nonscience major, and dental school admissions offices are satisfied with that option; in fact, they like to accept students from a variety of academic backgrounds, as long as the applicants excelled in their science courses. Choosing a nonscience major, though, may create some course-scheduling conflicts that might make it difficult to graduate in four years. The trick is to keep your goal in mind, but also to follow your bliss—you'll do best in a major you like.

Your predental adviser will play a critical role in helping you navigate your undergraduate career. He or she will assist you in planning your course work, choosing a major, coping with difficulties that may arise, and finding internships or community service opportunities. You will appreciate your adviser's help most during the process of applying to dental school: evaluating your prospects, lining up interviews and letters of recommendations, and preparing for the Dental Admission Test (DAT).

What you do outside class is another important aspect of a predental program. It's a definite plus to get related experience, such as "job-shadowing" a dentist or volunteering in a dental office. Many communities have Healthcare for the Homeless organizations, which provide oral care to people who are unable to visit a dentist; these groups often use student volunteers. Successful dental school candidates usually devote 15–20 hours a week to such activities during the school year and 40–50 hours a week over the summer.

Just how hard is it to get into dental school? Nationally, the mean GPA of successful dental school applicants is in the 3.1–3.2 range. The percentage of students who are accepted depends on the number of applicants per year, but is usually between 40 and 60 percent. Most dental schools are state institutions that give preference to residents of their state.

Here's something to consider: more than half the dental schools in the United States cooperate with colleges to offer joint programs that enable you to achieve both a bachelor's degree and a dental degree in less time than if you pursued the two programs separately. If you are interested, look at the latest edition of the *Official Guide to Dental Schools,* published by the American Dental Education Association.

Other majors you might like:
Biology
Biochemistry
Chemistry
Dental laboratory technology
Biomedical technology
Entrepreneurial studies
Anthropology
Occupational therapy
Communication disorders
Medical office administration
Forensic science

Questions to ask colleges:
How many predental and premedical students does the institution have? (The premedical and predental populations are often considered as one.)

How many predental students get into dental school after one application? After two or more applications?

Is the predental adviser easily accessible, particularly when students apply to dental school?

Is there help to obtain dentistry-related internship or volunteer experiences, during both the school year and school breaks?

Does the college have a combined bachelor's/D. D.S. program or other special relationship with dental schools?

Is there a DAT prep course available on campus?

Career options and trends:
Dentist*; oral surgeon*; orthodontist; dental or medical laboratory technician.

During dental school you must pass Parts I and II of the National Board Dental Examination. After dental school you will have to become fully licensed in the state(s) in which you want to practice. Like most licensed professionals, dentists are required to complete a certain amount of continuing education credits each year.

The demand for dentists is strong and growing, because the population is increasing and improved public oral hygiene has enabled people to keep their teeth longer! Also, many dentists who were educated in the 1960's and '70's will be retiring soon.

For more info:

American Dental Education Association (ADEA)
1400 K St., N.W., Suite 1100
Washington, DC 20005
(202) 289-7201
www.adea.org

American Student Dental Association (ASDA)
211 E. Chicago Ave., Suite 700
Chicago, IL 60611
(800) 621-8099 ext. 2795
www.asdanet.org

Premedicine

What it's about:

If you want to be a medical doctor, osteopathic doctor, or podiatrist, you must go to medical school, and that means you have to take certain courses in college. Premedicine is not itself a major—just those prerequisite courses. It's also an advising program to help you get into medical school.

Is this for you?

You might like this major if you also like: helping people; science and technology; anatomy; learning and discovery; problem solving; *ER*. You will spend many years studying and training to become a doctor, so a desire to heal and prevent disease must be a strong motivator.

Consider this major if you are good at: attention to detail; counseling; critical reading/thinking; math; memorizing *...or have...* compassion; initiative; integrity; motivation; verbal skills.

Recommended high school prep:

English 4, math 4 (including precalculus and calculus), lab science 4 (including biology, chemistry, and physics), social studies 4, and a foreign language 3–4 (Spanish recommended). If available, courses in psychology, statistics, and computer science are also recommended. It is also advisable to do volunteer work at a local hospital or other health facility.

Did you know...

...that you don't need a 4.0 to get into medical school? You should be an excellent student, but medical schools look at applicants as more than the sum of their grade point averages and MCAT test scores.

...that some colleges offer a seven-year program that combines undergraduate and medical studies and culminates in an M.D.?

Typical courses in this major:

Inorganic chemistry
Biology
Calculus
Organic chemistry
Physics
Psychology
Cell Biology
Genetics
Sociology
English
Statistics
Biochemistry
Computer science
Bioethics
Neuroscience
Medicinal chemistry

Concentrations:

Generally, none available.

What the study of this major is like:

"Declaring" premed may be as simple as checking off a box on your college application or filling out a form during orientation. In any event, you should contact the premed adviser at your college as soon as you enroll.

The adviser's role is critical to your success in college. He or she will help you plan your premedical course work, choose a major, overcome any academic difficulties, and find internships or community service opportunities. You will also receive help applying to med school, preparing for the Medical College Application Test (MCAT), securing and sending letters of recommendation, preparing for interviews, and making a successful transition to medical school.

The premed science requirements include a full year (two semesters) each of general chemistry, biology, organic chemistry, and physics. Some medical schools also require either one or two semesters of calculus. Other courses that, although not required, will help you prepare for the MCAT and medical school are cell biology, biochemistry, genetics, molecular biology, and physiology. Because there is a two- to three-year sequence in the required science courses, you should take general chemistry and biology in your first year, no matter what you decide to major in.

It is important to know that premed is not just about science. Medical schools look for well-rounded students who possess a broad background in the humanities and social sciences. For example, English courses will provide an opportunity to sharpen your writing skills, a philosophy course will help you develop critical thinking skills and a moral compass, and psychology courses can help you understand the connection between mind and body. At most colleges you can usually fulfill the nonscience premed requirements by taking courses in the core liberal arts program.

Because the premed requirements emphasize science, the field in which their interests lie, most premed students choose a science major—but about 15 to 20 percent do not. Not only can students pursue a nonscience major, but most medical schools, seeking diversity, look with favor on applicants who take this route. If you are considering a nonscience major, however, you should realize that you must excel in the science courses you do take and that because of scheduling conflicts between premed and major-course requirements, you may not be able to graduate in four years.

During college you will need to pace yourself. Avoid taking more than two science and/or math courses per semester, and if you want to enter med school right after college, plan to complete your science/math requirements by the end of your third year, so that you can take the MCAT and then apply to med school during your fourth year. In addition, to be competitive you should consider taking honors and independent-study courses. Your premed advisor will help you juggle this challenging course load.

A premed program is not just about schoolwork, either. A successful premed student usually spends an average of 15–20 hours per week in extracurricular activities (clinical, research, or community service work) during the academic year, and 40–50 hours per week during school breaks. When selecting colleges, look to see if opportunities for such experiences are easily available nearby, and if you will receive help in obtaining them.

Other majors you might like:
Biology
Biochemistry
Chemistry
Music therapy
Physician assistant
Biomedical engineering
Psychology
Sociology
Anthropology
Health care administration
Emergency medical technology (EMT paramedic)
Neuroscience

Questions to ask colleges:
How many premed students are there at this college? How many are accepted into medical school?

Is the premed adviser easily accessible, particularly when students apply for medical school?

Is assistance available to obtain clinical, research, and community service experience during the school year and school breaks?

Is there an MCAT prep course available on campus?

Career options and trends:
Medical doctor*; osteopathic doctor*; podiatrist; physician assistant; physician/scientist*; optometrist; physical therapist; pharmacist; radiologist.

Medical school graduates must complete the United States Medical Licensing Examination (USMLE), Parts I–III. Physicians must be licensed in each state in which they want to practice; there are some interstate and regional agreements between and among states. In addition, in order to maintain their licenses, physicians must complete a certain amount of continuing medical education (CME) credits each year.

There is a particular need for general practitioners, geriatricians, psychiatrists, and podiatrists. In addition, because of a growing interest among patients in alternative cures and treatments, there is expected to be an increased demand for naturopathic physicians.

For more info:
Association of American Medical Colleges (AAMC)
2450 N Street, N.W.
Washington, DC 20037
www.aamc.org

The Student Doctor Network
P.O. Box 1160
Sunset Beach, CA 90742
www.studentdoctor.net

Preveterinary

What it's about:
If you love animals and are good at science, you might be thinking you want to go to veterinary medical school after college. Because there are only twenty-eight vet schools in the United States, however, being accepted is a challenge. A program in preveterinary studies will help you become a competitive candidate by guiding you through the college courses and extracurricular experience that vet schools require. But keep in mind that prevet studies is not itself a major—you'll still have to pick one.

Is this for you?
You might like this major if you also like: all creatures great and small; people too; science and nature; volunteering at the local shelter or animal rescue center. Prevet students have a passion for animals, both sick and well, and the people who own them.

Consider this major if you are good at: attention to detail; caring/nurturing; critical reading/thinking; math; memorizing *...or have...* integrity; motivation; patience; verbal skills.

Recommended high school prep:
English 4, math 4 (including precalculus and calculus), lab science 4 (including biology, chemistry, and physics), social studies 4, and a foreign language 3-4 (Spanish recommended). If available, courses in psychology, statistics, speech, and computer science are also recommended. It is strongly suggested that you have experience working with animals.

Did you know...
...that veterinary school is actually more competitive than medical school? That's because there are very few veterinary schools and many applicants. The prevet science requirements are the same as for premed, plus additional courses such as zoology, microbiology, or animal science. But don't be discouraged—you should be able to reach your goal if you have faith in yourself and stay focused.

Typical courses in this major:
Inorganic (general) chemistry
Organic chemistry
Biology
Biochemistry
Zoology
Physics
Calculus
Speech communication
Statistics
English
Animal science
Genetics
Comparative anatomy
Microbiology
Animal nutrition
Business management

Concentrations:
Generally, none available.

What the study of this major is like:
The preveterinary curriculum usually includes courses in biochemistry, biology, general chemistry, organic chemistry, physics, and English. Some veterinary schools require additional course work in microbiology, biochemistry, nutrition, or animal science. You may also be expected to take courses in the humanities and social sciences.

Nonscience courses are important because veterinary schools prefer well-rounded students. What is more, these courses help you develop the skills you'll need as a vet. For example, courses in psychology can help you understand the behavior of animals as well as that of their owners; business courses will be valuable if you, like most vets, run your own practice.

In addition to academics, you will need to acquire hands-on experience working with both small and large animals under the eye of a veterinarian. Practical experience might involve breeding, rearing, feeding, and showing various kinds of animals, including pets, livestock, laboratory animals, zoo animals, or wildlife. Some vet schools set a minimum number of hours for such work, usually 200, but successful applicants usually have much more than that.

At most colleges, preveterinary studies is not a major; it's an advising program—and the prevet adviser at your college will be a very important to you. You'll get assistance in selecting and scheduling courses, choosing a major, dealing with difficulties that may crop up, and finding internships and other extracurricular opportunities. Your adviser will also be a big help when you apply to veterinarian school.

You might wonder whether you can pursue a prevet program while taking a nonscience major. Yes, it is possible; but because veterinary schools require their students to become familiar with so many different species, a solid science background is strongly recommended. Students with a nonscience interest are usually encouraged to have a science major but a nonscience minor. If you are still committed to a nonscience major, go for it—but you might need more than four years to finish college.

About a third of the twenty-eight accredited vet schools in the United States offer joint programs with undergraduate colleges, ranging in length from six to eight years. Admission to these highly competitive programs is open to excellent students who, as high school seniors, are committed to pursuing a career as a veterinarian. If you are interested, review the latest edition of *Veterinary Medical School Admissions Requirements*, available from Purdue University Press.

Because managing the work load while maintaining academic excellence in all your courses is a challenge, you must be highly motivated and committed to your goal of becoming a veterinarian. Success also requires a four-year plan at the outset that allows you to fulfill all the requirements at a pace you can handle. But remember—college offers a wonderful opportunity to grow as a person and should not be a total grind. Your prevet adviser can help you achieve the right balance.

Other majors you might like:
Animal sciences
Biology
Zoology
Anthropology
Biochemistry
Chemistry
Wildlife and wilderness management
Agricultural and biological engineering
Genetics
Veterinary technology
Wildlife biology
Equestrian studies

Questions to ask colleges:
How many prevet students does the college have, as opposed to other pre–health profession students?

How many students are accepted into vet school after one application? After two or more applications?

Is there a knowledgeable prevet adviser who is easily accessible, particularly when students apply to vet school?

What kind of opportunities are available to gain practical experience working with animals, and where are these opportunities located?

Does the college have a combined D.V.M. program or other special relationship with vet schools?

Career options and trends:
About 75 percent of veterinarians today work in private practice. The rest are employed in a variety of areas, such as teaching at colleges and universities; conducting biomedical research in the public or private sector; or working for local, state, or federal agencies, departments of agriculture, and public health services that regulate or protect animals as well as people. Practice settings may also include race tracks, zoos, animal shelters, aquariums, and wildlife management facilities.

After graduating from veterinary school, you will have to meet the licensure requirements of the state(s) where you want to practice. In addition, like most licensed professionals, you must complete a certain amount of continuing education credits each year.

Job prospects are excellent, because there simply are not enough graduates each year to meet demand.

For more info:

Association of American Veterinary Medical
  Colleges
1101 Vermont Ave., N.W., Suite 301
Washington, DC 20005
(202) 371-9195
www.aavmc.org

American Veterinary Medical Association
1931 N. Meacham Rd., Suite 100
Schaumburg, IL 60173-4360
(847) 925-8070
www.avma.org

Radiologic technology/medical imaging

Also known as:
X ray technology

What it's about:
Radiologic technologists, also called radiographers, use X ray equipment to perform diagnostic imaging examinations of internal parts of the body. Experienced radiographers may perform more complex imaging procedures, such as computed tomography (CT) scans and magnetic resonance imaging (MRI).

Is this for you?
You might like this major if you also like: science and technology; art and photography (radiologic technology is said to be a combination of science and art); medical illustrations; working in teams; thinking about what's inside the human body.

Consider this major if you are good at: attention to detail; caring/nurturing; creativity; critical reading/thinking; organizing; quantitative analysis; spacial thinking/analysis; teamwork *...or have...* initiative; manual dexterity; writing skills.

Recommended high school prep:
English 4, math 3, lab science 3 (including biology and physics), social studies 3, and a foreign language 2–3. Participating in a job-shadowing program in radiologic technology at a local hospital would be most helpful, and you will need CPR certification before you begin your clinical courses in college.

Did you know...
...that radiologic technology is not always neat and clean? Occasionally a technologist must perform unpleasant examinations, and sometimes physical stamina is required for lifting patients and positioning them properly.

...that radiation is natural? Each year, you are exposed to an amount of naturally occurring "background radiation" from the atmosphere, the Earth's crust, and cosmic rays, that is 50 times stronger than a typical dental X ray.

Typical courses in this major:
Radiologic physics
Radiographic positioning
Imaging equipment
Medical terminology
Human anatomy and physiology
Radiographic exposure
Radiobiology and protection
Radiographic pathology
Clinical practice
Cross-sectional anatomy
Health law and ethics
Principles of radiation exposure

Concentrations:
Radiation biology; fluoroscopy; and anatomical positioning.

What the study of this major is like:
Radiographers take X rays of parts of the body to create films that are used in diagnosing medical conditions. Closely following physicians' instructions and radiation-use regulations, radiographers prepare, position, and protect patients (for example, by using lead shields); position and operate radiographic equipment; and develop the film. In addition, they may help to decide which types of equipment to buy; maintain equipment; keep patient records; and manage an office or department.

If you choose to study radiologic technology/medical imaging, you can pursue a certificate, an associate degree, or a bachelor's degree. There are more two-year associate degree programs than four-year bachelor's programs, and some hospitals offer certificate programs. Most formal training programs are accredited by the Joint Review Committee on Education in Radiologic Technology (JRCERT) and have similar requirements in anatomy, physiology, algebra, and physical science. Bachelor's degree programs offer more concentrations in specialty areas, such as radiation therapy, nuclear medicine, ultrasound, CT scan, or MRI, than are available in associate degree programs.

As a major in radiologic technology/medical imaging, you split your time among classroom lectures, laboratory activities, and clinical internship work. You must fulfill both general requirements (such as English, algebra, psychology, political science, sociology, and speech courses) and radiologic-specific course work. For the major, you study anatomy, physiology, biology, pathology, physics, radiation safety, patient care procedures, principles of imaging, medical ethics, and medical terminology. You learn to use computers and operate highly advanced medical equipment.

You must also develop your communication skills in order to work with patients and with other health care professionals as part of an effective team. In laboratories, you apply what you learn in the classroom, experimenting with patient positioning and X ray equipment. During hands-on clinical training, you work in actual radiology departments with physicians, nurses, and radiographers, again practicing what you learned in the classroom and laboratory.

Other majors you might like:
Laser/optical technology
Clinical/medical laboratory technology
Respiratory therapy
Electrical engineering technology
Computer science
Nuclear medical technology
Photographic/film/video technology
Physician assistant
Ophthalmic technology
Neuroscience
Animation
Radiation protection/health physics technology

Career options and trends:
There is an acute shortage of radiologic technologists that is expected to continue. As the population ages, the demand for diagnostic imaging will likely increase. This situation should not only guarantee employment but also generate improved compensation and working conditions.

In addition to becoming a staff X ray technician, you can—with on-the-job training, home study, and continuing education—go into a specialty area of radiography, such as heart catheterization; CT or MRI; ultrasound; mammography; nuclear medicine; radiation therapy; commercial sales; equipment repair; radiation health physics; education; or administration.

Although most jobs are found in hospitals, greater employment growth is projected in doctors' offices, clinics, and diagnostic imaging centers, because of the strong shift toward outpatient care. Radiologic technologists who are qualified for more than one type of diagnostic imaging technology, such as radiography and sonography or nuclear medicine, will be the most sought after.

Depending on where you work, you may have to be certified, registered, or licensed; and the differences between these credentials can be confusing. Certification is awarded by the American Registry of Radiologic Technologists (ARRT) to those who complete the required education and training and pass the national exam. Certification qualifies you to practice anywhere in the U.S. and is generally required for employment. Registration, which is voluntary but preferred by many employers, is an annual renewal of the certificate; it indicates that you have complied with ARRT's continuing education requirements. Licensing is required by most states in order to practice. Each state administers its own licensing process, but most require only ARRT certification and a fee.

For more info:
American Society of Radiologic Technologist (ASRT)
15000 Central Ave., S.E.
Albuquerque, NM 87123-3917
(800) 444-2778
www.asrt.org

Respiratory therapy

What it's about:

This major trains you to work with physicians, nurses, and other health care professionals in the diagnosis, treatment, and rehabilitation of patients whose heart, circulation, or lungs are functioning abnormally. Working mostly in hospitals, respiratory therapists manage the ventilation of critically ill patients, or provide immediate and long-term care to patients with breathing disorders.

Is this for you?

You might like this major if you also like: helping people; working with technology; science.

Consider this major if you are good at: attention to detail; critical reading/thinking; math; organizing; persuading/influencing; teamwork *...or have...* initiative; manual dexterity; verbal skills.

Recommended high school prep:

English 4, math 3, lab science 3 (including biology, physics, and chemistry), social studies 3, and a foreign language 2–3. If they are available, take courses in health, sociology, psychology, interpersonal communications, and computer skills.

Typical courses in this major:

Human anatomy and physiology
Medical terminology
Cardiopulmonary pathophysiology
Pharmacology
Respiratory therapy procedures
Physical assessment
Mechanical ventilation
Neonatal and pediatric care
Critical care
Home care
Pulmonary function testing
Sleep disorders and their treatment
Microbiology
Pulmonary rehabilitation
Pulmonary diagnostics

Concentrations:

In college: neonatal/pediatric respiratory care; adult critical care; home care/extended care; polysomnography (sleep disorders, sleep medicine); cardiovascular technology; and pulmonary function testing.

If you go on to grad school: perfusion technology; extracorporeal circulation; health education; management/administration.

What the study of this major is like:

Respiratory therapists typically treat patients of all ages on all floors, in the emergency room, in clinics—in short, all over the hospital. They may attend to premature newborns; heart attack, stroke, drowning, or shock victims; and older patients with chronic diseases such as emphysema or asthma.

Respiratory therapists often deal with high-stress situations, working in intensive care units and participating in all cardiac resuscitations ("Code Blue"). They work with a variety of medical professionals and assist with other cardiac procedures such as pacemaker insertions, cardiac catheterization, and cardioversion. Besides hospitals, respiratory therapists can be employed in patients' homes, long-term-care facilities, diagnostic labs, and rehabilitation and educational facilities. And although sleep disorders have only recently become widely known, over half the professional staff in sleep labs now are respiratory therapists.

As a respiratory therapy major, you must fulfill general education requirements, including college algebra, chemistry, physics, English, computer and information literacy, communications, and social science (psychology or sociology). In the major, you take courses in anatomy, physiology, microbiology, pharmacology, diseases of the heart and lungs, and medical terminology, as well as technical courses that deal with procedures and clinical tests.

After examining the way the heart and lungs function, learning how to evaluate their condition, and determining which injuries, diseases, and disorders can seriously threaten cardiopulmonary (heart and lung) function, you are taught how to treat patients who have problems with their breathing and circulation. You gain practice in administering medications and using techniques and equipment (gases, humidity, equipment function and sterilization, arterial puncture and blood gas analysis, expansion therapies) to improve oxygen delivery to vital organs. You also spend time in hospitals applying what you have learned and providing patient care under supervision.

The program features lectures, laboratory work, and clinical practice. You learn theory in class, have hands-on experience with equipment in a laboratory setting, and then practice direct patient care under the supervision of faculty. Observing and caring for critically ill patients can be stressful and requires maturity. You will also have to adapt to the rigorous course work and the hours you must spend in the laboratory and clinical settings. You will be doing patient care during actual shifts, which are usually 12 hours long and may include afternoons and nights. You should therefore plan to attend classes, labs, and clinical courses full-time. As a result, you may not be able to have a job in addition; try to save money for your education before you enroll.

Respiratory therapy programs vary in length as well as in the degree or credential that graduates earn. Some programs offer two-year associate or four-year bachelor's degrees, preparing you for a career as a registered respiratory therapist (RRT). Shorter programs offer certificates and prepare you for work as an entry-level certified respiratory therapist (CRT).

Other majors you might like:
Cardiovascular technology
Physician assistant
Occupational therapy
Renal/dialysis technology
Clinical/medical laboratory technology
Licensed practical nursing
Gerontology
Biomedical technology

Social work
Recreational therapy
Radiologic technology/medical imaging

Questions to ask colleges:
Is the program approved by the Committee on Accreditation for Respiratory Care (CoARC)?

How many hospitals are used for clinical training, and where are they located?

After completing the program, are students eligible to take the National Registration Exam offered by the National Board for Respiratory Care (NBRC)? What is the first-time pass rate for recent graduates?

Career options and trends:
Respiratory therapist*; advanced-practice respiratory therapist; polysomnography technologist (sleep tech); cardiac ultrasound technician; perfusionist (operates bypass during heart surgery).

You must pass the NBRC examination to become a certified respiratory therapist, which allows you to practice as a CRT in every state that requires a license.

Respiratory therapists are employed in acute care hospitals, long-term care facilities, home health care, equipment and pharmaceutical sales, education, sleep laboratories, and health promotion. Employment forecasts for RTs indicate a continuing need for more therapists for the next decade or so. Therapists with cardiopulmonary care skills, or experience working with newborns and infants, will be especially in demand.

For more info:
American Association for Respiratory Care (AARC)
9425 N. MacArthur Blvd.
Suite 100
Irving, TX 75063
(972) 243-2272
www.aarc.org

Veterinary technology

Also known as:
Animal health technology

What it's about:
This major prepares you to work under the supervision of veterinarians, zoologists, and lab specialists to provide animal care and clinical assistance. Veterinary technicians (VTs) serve as receptionists, practice managers, radiologic/imaging technicians, medical and surgical nurses, anesthetists, pharmacy and laboratory technicians, animal behavior educators, and client liaisons.

Is this for you?
You might like this major if you also like: animal or pet training; the sciences; volunteering at the local shelter; 4H groups; farmwork; getting involved in animal welfare issues; meeting people; talking about animals.

Consider this major if you are good at: attention to detail; caring/nurturing; critical reading/thinking; organizing; problem solving; teamwork ...*or have...* initiative; patience; verbal skills.

Recommended high school prep:
English 4, math 3, lab science 4, social studies 3, and a foreign language 2–3. If your high school offers an advanced science track, try to take one or more of the following: anatomy and physiology, microbiology, nutrition, and genetics.

Did you know...
...that veterinary technicians spend a great deal of their time working not only with animals but with people? Students who find satisfaction in this field possess good "people skills" and can function well as team players.

Typical courses in this major:
Animal anatomy and physiology
Parasitology
Clinical laboratory techniques
Animal nutrition
Large animal clinical procedures
Small animal clinical procedures
Veterinary pharmacology and anesthesia
Animal disease
Veterinary radiology and surgical nursing
Lab animal science and exotics
Externship/internship

Concentrations:
Generally, none available.

What the study of this major is like:
VTs perform a wide range of activities, doing everything veterinarians do expect making diagnoses, performing surgery, and prescribing medicine. VTs assist veterinarians with client appointments, client education, and management of the practice. They work as medical and surgical animal nurses, animal physical therapists, animal dental hygienists (cleaning teeth), and diagnostic laboratory technicians (working with laboratory specimens). In laboratory animal medicine, VTs do experimental procedures, keep records, analyze data, write reports, and take care of animals. In the pet food industry, VTs work in sales, marketing, and research.

As a veterinary technology major, you would probably earn a two-year associate degree in applied science. Introduction to veterinary technology courses usually cover office procedures, vocational opportunities, regulatory issues, and client communication. In addition to other core courses, most programs require general education courses, in English, applied mathematics (algebra, statistics), social science, humanities, and biological science (microbiology). To be successful in this career, you need to do well in science. You should also develop computer and communication skills, as well as critical-thinking skills, such as patient assessment, and decision-making abilities.

In all programs, you must work as a student intern/extern for a minimum of 240 hours at specific types of veterinary sites. This experience allows you to explore various vocational opportunities (such as jobs in companion animal and large-animal care, and in biomedical research) and to develop the skills you learned during your early training. In your intern/externship, you are also exposed to specialized clinical areas such as cardiology, emergency medicine, and exotic animals.

Veterinary technology programs are career-oriented; if you complete the curriculum, you should be ready to work in a veterinary facility. Most programs incorporate traditional lecture format, computer self-study, guest speakers, "wet labs" (for hands-on work such as dentistry), and scheduled and open laboratory time. You also have opportunities to work with a variety of species and are usually responsible for caring for the animals housed on campus.

Programs accredited by the American Veterinary Medical Association Committee on Veterinary Technician Education and Activities (AVMA CVTEA) have a required content, to ensure that you are properly prepared for a career. But programs may vary. Some provide additional instruction in laboratory animal science and medicine, clinical diagnostic techniques, or large-animal or exotic species care. Programs may incorporate distance learning or online training into their curriculum or vary their scheduling (offering day and/or night courses). Some programs prepare you to become a veterinary assistant (VA); but take note that VAs do *not* receive an equivalent form of training as VTs.

Other majors you might like:
Biology
Animal sciences
Wildlife and wilderness management
Animal breeding
Equestrian studies
Dairy science
Zoology
Genetic
Biotechnology
Wildlife biology

Questions to ask colleges:
Is the program accredited by the American Veterinary Medical Association (AVMA)?

How many courses provide hands-on experience with animals, and which species of animals will students work with?

What kind of veterinary sites are offered to students for their externship experience, and where are they located?

Career options and trends:
Many states provide licensure for veterinary technicians. The terminology will vary (certified, registered, licensed), as will the requirements. Most states require that you graduate from an accredited program and pass the National Veterinary Technician Board Examination.

Job prospects in this field are excellent, as there is currently a shortage of formally trained veterinary technicians, and demand is projected to increase in all veterinary practice areas and industrial fields.

Some of the areas in which graduates find job opportunities are small-animal and large-animal veterinary clinics; companion animal practice; pet food and pharmaceutical companies (technical research assistance or sales); laboratory animal research; animal diagnostic laboratories; zoos and wildlife centers; wildlife rehabilitation; and government regulatory agencies. Research and academic institutions usually require a bachelor's degree.

For more info:
National Association of Veterinary Technicians in America (NAVTA)
50 South Pickett St.
Suite 110
Alexandria, VA   22304
(703) 740-8737
www.navta.net

Humanities

In the humanities, it's not so much *what* you know as *how* you know it. In these liberal arts majors, you'll learn how to learn by honing skills in research, reading, writing, and thinking.

"Liberal arts is a major for students who enjoy learning, who want to spend their college time getting an education and exploring new ideas, rather than strictly preparing for a specific career," says Professor Joseph Ugoretz, Manhattan Community College.

What are the humanities? You could write a whole term paper on that question. They cover history, philosophy, comparative literature, the classics, linguistics, and many other subjects, including the liberal arts. Perhaps in keeping with the spirit of these studies, their exact definition is open to interpretation.

When you search for colleges offering humanities majors, look for schools and divisions of arts and sciences, arts and letters, liberal arts, general studies, literature, science, and social sciences. Other sections in this book include related majors in Languages, English language and literature, Social sciences, and Religion and theology.

By now you may be worried that studying the humanities is like trying to nail Jell-O to the wall. But it's not. The fact is that more associate degrees are awarded in the humanities than any other major by far. And a college degree is something you really *can* hang on the wall!

It turns out that the humanities provide a wealth of understanding that can transfer to many other studies and careers. Liberal arts majors are able to "take advantage of openings in the job market that may be closed to others who are less broadly prepared," Ugoretz points out.

Many humanities students go on to advanced degrees and pursue careers in law, medicine, business, and teaching. History and the classics are two majors that often lead to a Master of Arts in Teaching degree.

Cross training for the mind

Some humanities, such as liberal arts, allow students to find themselves academically. (Examples of new liberal arts programs include multimedia design and writing for the Internet.) Other humanities majors are specialized. Linguistics, which teaches us how language works, is also a good place to sharpen your computer programming skills. "Linguistic training is excellent preparation for employment in high-tech industry, particularly when combined with computer science or information science training," says Professor Emeritus D. Terence Langendoen of the University of Arizona, Tucson. The humanities sometimes merge with each other and with other fields to create new areas of thought. For example, philosophy and computer science together give rise to the study of artificial intelligence. Linguistics and philosophy combine to become cognitive sciences. Whew! You won't find gut courses here.

Even though the humanities cover a lot of ground, colleges pretty much take the same approach to these majors. That means if you transfer from one college to another, your humanities credits will likely be accepted. But check to make sure the credits from your first college will go toward your degree at the second one, especially if you transfer from a two-year to a four-year college.

When choosing a college, always consider the faculty factor. Who teaches the undergrad classes? Is it the regular faculty (that's who you want) or graduate students (who may be less able to inspire you)?

"The best way to find out about a particular department's undergraduate curriculum is to talk to a current student, a recent graduate, or one of the faculty members," says Professor Richard T. Lee of Trinity College. "Even an e-mail correspondence with a faculty member will give the student some feel for the program."

Another issue: Does the major you want have its own department? That's a sure sign it's an important curriculum at the college. Also ask about class size. Will you have the opportunity to take small classes and seminars with fewer than 20 students?

Essential to these majors are the college's library, archives, and databases, to give you access to the storehouse of knowledge that the humanities encompass.

You may want the freedom to explore other subjects and courses, so find out how many electives you can take. If it's a big university, can you take courses at other colleges in the university system? If it's a small college, are any of the top profs planning a leave of absence or sabbatical during the time you plan to attend?

Speaking of leave of absence, you may want one yourself. To strengthen skills and enhance experience, humanities majors often take time to study abroad. See if the college has a strong program.

In a world that's changing rapidly, nobody knows exactly what skills and knowledge will be needed down the road. The humanities provide a kind of cross training for the mind that can prepare you for more specialized studies and career development later. Knowing how to know may be one of the most sought-after abilities in the workplace of the future.

Classics

Also known as:
Greek and Latin

What it's about:
Classics is the study of the languages, literatures, and civilization of the ancient Greco-Roman world, including both ancient Greek and Latin. Course work usually involves reading classical texts in these two languages (with discussion in English); but in some programs, the readings may be in English translation.

Is this for you?
You might like this major if you also like: the History Channel; archaeology; languages; debate; computer programming; music; theater.

Consider this major if you are good at: attention to detail; creativity; critical reading/thinking; memorizing; organizing; research ...*or have...* initiative; linguistic ability; patience; verbal skills.

Recommended high school prep:
English 4, math 3, lab science 3, social studies 4, and a foreign language 4. If possible, take Latin. French, Italian, and German are also useful.

Did you know...
...that classics can appeal to both "techie" students and "fuzzy" students (those who like art, literature, and philosophy)? To master Latin and Greek, you develop the same kind of mental discipline that is typical of physicists or computer programmers. Some computer companies, in fact, hire classicists because they, like programmers, insist on obeying the language rules. Classicists even distinguished themselves as code breakers in World War II.

...that classics is a leader in the use of computer technology in the humanities? Because the discipline is based on intensive study of a set of texts, databases were developed to help classicists analyze these works. These databases are now part of the regular research tools for students and professionals.

Typical courses in this major:
Elementary Greek
Intermediate Greek (Plato, Homer)
Elementary Latin
Intermediate Latin (Caesar, Ovid)
Ancient philosophy
Classical art and archaeology
Greek and Roman civilization
Athenian democracy
Classical mythology
Tragedy and comedy
Elegiac poetry
Lyric poetry
Epic and lyric: Virgil and Horace
Livy and Tacitus
Homer
Herodotus

Concentrations:
In college: classics and philosophy; classics and archaeology; classics and religion; classics and ancient history; classics and art.

If you go on to grad school: Greek literature (in ancient Greek); Latin literature (in Latin); Latin teacher education.

What the study of this major is like:
"Classics" refers to the literature of the ancient Greeks and Romans. Its themes, forms, and images have inspired generations of readers and writers. In the classics major, you learn Latin, Greek, or both and, in the process, learn about language itself. You explore different methods of interpreting literature—methods that consider audience, context, transmission of the text, and modern theory. You also gain practice in distinguishing between reliable and unreliable sources and in using evidence to understand others' arguments and to create your own. These skills are useful in any career.

You will almost certainly study the oldest surviving classical text (and one of the oldest texts of Western literature): Homer's *Iliad*. Homer probably composed this epic in the ninth century B.C., but he incorporated songs and themes from far earlier times. Homer reveals a society just beginning to develop the intellectual, cultural, and political life of the Greek city-state.

You are introduced to the more lyrical works of later Greek poets, such as Sappho and Pindar. Aeschylus, Sophocles, and Euripides created tragedies, and Aristophanes wrote comedies for democratic Athens. Their plays are still powerful, beautiful, and funny. The works of other Greek writers—Herodotus, Thucydides, Plato, Aristotle, and Demosthenes—were devoted to history, philosophy, rhetoric, and literary theory. As a classics major, you'll consider the questions about human existence, knowledge, politics, ethics, and beauty that these writers asked and that still interest us today.

Latin literature begins with the lively comedies of Plautus in the third century B.C., when Rome was already a great power. Your reading of Latin works includes the comedies of Terence, the philosophical poetry of Lucretius, the love poetry of Catullus, Caesar's accounts of his conquest of Gaul (roughly, modern France), and the orations of Cicero; these works all are part of the turbulent culture of the late Roman Republic.

In the early years of the empire founded by Augustus in 29 B.C., the great Latin writers flourished: the poets Virgil, Horace, and Ovid; the satirist and poet Juvenal; the historians Livy and Tacitus; and the statesman and playwright Seneca. In addition to their works (and despite Horace's conviction that poetry is the most enduring of all monuments), you'll examine the practical Roman creations: architectural and civil engineering works, legal codes, and principles of governing. Like the literature, these achievements have shaped Western society.

In classics departments, classes are often small, so you should have regular contact with faculty members. Individual professors may offer different approaches. Some might emphasize the learning of the languages, whereas others may stress literary interpretation or the analysis of the social and intellectual contexts of the written works. It's helpful to have both sides represented in a department.

Although students often expect classics majors to be stuffy and conservative, most of them aren't. Qualities typical of classics majors are intellectual curiosity about the ancient world, a willingness to accept the challenge of learning no-longer-spoken languages, and an urge to do something unconventional. Most classics majors take their academic work (but not necessarily themselves) seriously; learning Greek and Latin can be difficult. You will probably spend most of your time working alone, although students occasionally work together outside class—for example, upper-level students sometimes tutor lower-level students. Indeed, majors tend to have a shared feeling of enthusiasm and commitment. Beyond acting as curators of a great literary tradition, they discover new meaning in the works of the ancient Greeks and Romans, so that the classic texts remain alive and relevant.

Other majors you might like:

Comparative literature
Medieval and Renaissance studies
History
Philosophy
Archaeology
Linguistics
Liberal arts and sciences
Judaic studies
Ancient studies
Ancient Near Eastern/Biblical languages
Architectural history and criticism
Speech/rhetorical studies

Questions to ask colleges:

Do students have access to databases such as the *Thesaurus Linguae Graecae* and the L'Année philologique Web site?

Career options and trends:

A recent survey of business recruitment officers shows that employers appreciate the intellectual stamina, communication and analytical skills, ability to handle complex information, and broad perspective that Classics majors bring to the workplace. Classics majors pursue careers in law, medicine, journalism, education, finance and banking, marketing, management, government, computer programming, publishing, speechwriting, TV production, and the ministry.

Since the 1990s, Latin-class enrollments have increased by well over 50 percent, and so has the demand for high school Latin teachers.

Insider's viewpoint:

"What most appeals to me is the intellectual challenge of tackling a text written in a complicated, long-dead language, and the thrill of discovery in decoding it. Every time I meet with my Greek and Latin students it is to unravel something that was written over two thousand years ago."

—Professor Kenneth S. Rothwell Jr., University of Massachusetts Boston

For more info:

American Philological Association (APA)
292 Logan Hall, University of Pennsylvania
249 S. 36th St.
Philadelphia, PA 19104-6304
(215) 898-4975
www.apaclassics.org/

National Committee for Latin and Greek (NCLG)
www.promotelatin.org

American Classical League (ACL)
Miami University
Oxford, OH 45056
(513) 529-7741
www.aclclassics.org/

Comparative literature

What it's about:

As a comparative literature major, you study the literature of different countries, cultures, and languages. You explore poetry, prose, and drama and consider the relation of literature to other arts and other fields of study. The major requires you to study at least two bodies of literature (one of which may be English) in their original languages.

Is this for you?

You might like this major if you also like: travel; literature; art; foreign languages; different cultures; debating; philosophy.

Consider this major if you are good at: active listening; attention to detail; creativity; critical reading/thinking; research ...*or have...* initiative; linguistic ability; verbal skills; writing skills.

Recommended high school prep:

English 4, math 3, lab science 3, social studies 4, and a foreign language 4 (one language). If possible, take a year of world literature and all available world history courses.

Typical courses in this major:

Great books of Western culture
Medieval epic
Tragedy
Romanticism
Baroque and Neoclassicism
Proust, Mann, and Joyce
History and the novel
The novel of the self
Myths and legends
Literature of China and Japan
Literature of the Americas
Gender and interpretation
Narrative technique

Concentrations:

Literature of a particular nation or culture.

What the study of this major is like:

Comparative literature majors study subjects that cross national, historical, and language boundaries. Topics include literary movements (for example, Romanticism), literary periods (the Renaissance), literary forms (the novel), literary issues (the treatment of science and technology), and literary theory and criticism. You'll study at least two bodies of literature (American students usually choose English or American literature as one of the fields) and at least one foreign language.

Then you'll focus on comparisons and contrasts between the two cultures and their literature. You may also explore the connections between literature and other artistic fields, such as painting, photography, film, or sculpture, or between literature and other academic areas, such as anthropology, psychology, or history. The field is strongly interdisciplinary, and the possibilities for comparative study are nearly endless. And if you'd enjoy reading works of literature from as many societies as you can, this is the major for you.

Most programs require one or more courses that introduce you to comparative analysis and to new approaches to reading. You may focus on the text alone; or on the society and the times in which it was written; or on the link between the text, its author, and its readers. Which traditions did an author draw upon? What influences can be seen underlying a poem, play, or novel?

In advanced courses you may read works in the language in which they were written. Most colleges offer the study of English, French, Spanish, German, Latin, and Greek language and literature; others offer Russian, Japanese, Chinese, Arabic, Polish, or others. Because you study these bodies of literature in their own language departments, you come across a variety of critical approaches. Many programs also require a capstone project—such as researching and writing a fourth-year thesis.

Comparative literature departments and classes are usually small, and tend to identify with a particular literary theory, interpretative tradition, and attitude toward language study. The major requires a lot of reading and writing, sometimes in a foreign language. Also, you should be ready, willing, and able to see the world from a perspective that differs from the one you are familiar with. Therefore, study abroad can be an exciting and important part of your college work. By graduation, most students have developed a powerful connection to at least one other culture—its literature, art, and unique view of life.

Other majors you might like:

Anthropology
Medieval and Renaissance studies
Area, ethnic, and gender studies
Linguistics
English
Philosophy
Film/cinema studies
Global studies
Art history
International business
Creative Writing
Religious studies

Questions to ask colleges:

Are the professors full-time comparative literature faculty members or are they borrowed from other departments?

Is a senior thesis required? If so, do students receive help from comparative literature faculty members?

Does the department have a club for majors? Do majors help plan events (such as speakers and readings)?

Career options and trends:

Comparative literature majors pursue jobs in journalism, business, cultural institutions, education, publishing, law, government, radio, television, and film. Graduate or professional school is also a popular option. Prospects are best for majors who have mastered another language.

Insider's viewpoint:

"In comparative literature the implicit nationalism of most programs of literary study is rare. Comparatists like to ride the fence, so to speak, which means that you have an investment in more than one place."

—Professor Tobin Siebers, University of Michigan

For more info:

American Comparative Literature Association (ACLA)
University of Texas
1 University Station B5003
Austin, TX 78712-0196
(512) 471-8020
www.acla.org

History

What it's about:

History is the study of the record of past human experience. Working with written, oral, visual, and artifacts, history majors examine the causes, contexts, and chronologies of historical events to understand how human experiences have both remained the same and changed over time.

Is this for you?

You might like this major if you also like: reenactments; the History Channel; model building; museums; historical novels; collecting stamps, coins, etc.; other cultures and other times; genealogy and family history.

Consider this major if you are good at: attention to detail; critical reading/thinking; organizing; persuading/influencing; research *...or have...* curiosity; initiative; patience; verbal skills; writing skills.

Recommended high school prep:

English 4, math 3, lab science 3, social studies 4, and a foreign language 4. If possible, take a year of both European and American history. One year of civics or government would also be beneficial.

Did you know...

...that the study of history is not confined to just books and documents? For example, to research the history of the blues, you might include such sources as posters, music recordings, photographs, oral histories, newspaper clippings, and business contracts.

Typical courses in this major:

Survey of European history
Western civilization
Ancient Greece
Tudor and Stuart England
Precolonial Africa
U.S. constitutional history
Modern Latin America
Renaissance and Reformation
French Revolution
East Asian civilization
Ancient Rome
Modern England
American history
U.S. economic history
Medieval history
Historical research

Concentrations:

Geographical regions (for example, European civilization, Russian history); time periods (medieval and early modern studies); themes (law and society, environmental history).

What the study of this major is like:

As a history major, you examine the causes, contexts, and narratives of past events. Historians now study a wide range of subjects, but most historians work with either political or social history. Although historians employ their own methods, they also make use of those of many other disciplines. Some "studies" majors include history; for instance, American studies generally has a literary or historical emphasis, whereas Russian/Slavic studies tends to focus on political science or international relations.

Courses usually focus on time periods, nations, geographic areas, historical perspectives, and themes, often in combination (for example, civil rights in the United States, or women in nineteenth-century Europe). Your course work helps you to understand the purposes, principles, and methods of the study of history, and to grasp both the particulars and the universals of societies past and present. You also explore questions of judgment and interpretation.

There are prerequisites for advanced work, but you do not necessarily have to take courses in a fixed, chronological order. You devise a program that meets your interests and also fulfills requirements found in most colleges: one or two introductory courses, one or more courses that acquaint you with cultures and histories other than your own, a course in historical methods, and a research seminar.

Some programs offer an introductory course that teaches the basics of history while featuring a particular topic, such as immigration in American history. Other lower-level courses may cover the history of Europe, the United States, and, perhaps, the non-Western world. Upper-level courses are usually seminars in areas you find most interesting. There is generally a capstone course that may explore great historical writing, the different genres of the subject, or the construction of chronologies from the raw materials of human experience.

As a major, you read extensively and develop writing skills through essay exams, book reviews, and research papers (you must become familiar with computer-aided research, especially if your research project has a social science focus). Because history majors often do archival research and interviewing, and your classes rely on lectures and discussion, you'll need to sharpen your listening and speaking skills.

The main challenge you will face as a major is to find source material for your research studies. At first, you'll interpret documents presented to you. Eventually, though, you must choose a question you want to answer (such as, what was the route of the Underground Railroad?) and then decide how to locate the books and other sources that will help you come up with an answer. With the encouragement of instructors and others in the field, you should quickly become an independent historian.

Other majors you might like:

Classics
Medieval and Renaissance studies
European studies
Asian studies
Art history
Anthropology
International relations
Political science
Archaeology

African-American studies
Public history/archives
Journalism

Questions to ask colleges:

Is the curriculum heavily focused on European and American history, or are there courses on the non-Atlantic world?

What are the library's strengths and weaknesses? Which journals does the library subscribe to and which archives (if any) does it control? Does the library make online databases available and offer online access to journals?

What kinds of connections does the department have with local historical societies, museums, historical sites, or the history departments of other colleges in the area?

Career options and trends:

College professor; high school teacher*; lawyer; museum curator or archivist*; journalist.

History majors learn how to locate, synthesize, and present information—valuable training for almost any career. Graduate and professional schools also value the education history majors receive. Few majors actually become historians—and college level teaching positions are extremely competitive—but employment options are many and varied, including government service, business, teaching in elementary and secondary schools, law, medicine, and other professions.

Insider's viewpoint:

"I used to read every book I could get my hands on about the Holocaust, about sixteenth-century France. If you think about it, every novel you read, if it's not set in the present, is a historical novel. Studying history is an extension of that love of literature; it's like watching a very long movie."

—Emily, sophomore, Northwestern University

For more info:

American Historical Association (AHA)
400 A St., S.E.
Washington, DC 20003-3889
(202) 544-2422
www.historians.org

Liberal arts and sciences

What it's about:

The liberal arts and sciences major provides you with a well-rounded education in the sciences, humanities, mathematics, and languages. You gain the ability to reason critically, communicate effectively, and understand relationships across broad fields of knowledge. This generalist background prepares you for a wide range of endeavors rather than for a specific career.

Is this for you?

You might like this major if you also like: reading; writing; discussing new ideas; arguing; reasoning.

Consider this major if you are good at: creativity; critical reading/thinking; persuading/influencing; quantitative analysis; teamwork *...or have...* initiative; patience; verbal skills; writing skills.

Recommended high school prep:

English 4, math 3, lab science 3, social studies 3, art 1, and a foreign language 3.

Did you know...

...that liberal arts and sciences is not just another term for "undecided"? Choosing this major is a decision to prepare for a world in which new and unexpected careers are invented every day.

Typical courses in this major:

English literature
Biological concepts
Environmental science
American history since 1865
World religions
Philosophy
Psychology
Sociology
Fundamentals of economics
Cultural anthropology
Philosophy
Probability and statistics
Foreign language I, II
Communications
Music history
Art history

Concentrations:

A wide range is available; among them are gender studies, multicultural studies, social sciences, literature and linguistics, natural sciences.

What the study of this major is like:

If you enjoy learning and want to spend your college years exploring new ideas rather than preparing for a specific career, you might consider majoring in liberal arts. The liberal arts program is typically offered only as an undergraduate major. Most liberal arts courses include a great deal of reading, writing, and discussion, and classes tend to be small.

As a liberal arts major, you will be required to study a wide range of subjects, some of which may be new to you or may be in areas in which you have not excelled in the past. Even though you might prefer studying literature, you will have to take classes in history and mathematics. Science lovers will have to take classes in poetry and music.

Most liberal arts programs have a required "core"— meaning you must take at least an introductory course in each of certain designated areas (although you usually have a choice of courses in each area). The areas include the fine arts (such as art history, music, drama); social sciences (economics, sociology, history); natural sciences (chemistry, biology); mathematics; humanities (literature, philosophy); and a foreign language. Some programs also require a semester of study abroad, or some other cross-cultural experience.

In addition to a core of required courses, you will likely be offered a wide range of electives from a wide range of subjects. You might find this freedom to choose very liberating; or you might find it confusing or intimidating. In either case, you would be wise to ask your academic adviser for help in designing a course of study that is relevant to your talents and interests.

Because the liberal arts program includes basic college subjects, you will meet students from many disciplines and be exposed to the perspectives of many academic areas. For the liberal arts major, college is an opportunity to discover and refine goals rather than to work single-mindedly on a predetermined regimen. This major allows you to be flexible with your schedule and to follow specific interests over several semesters in various related courses. Although your reading and writing assignments tend to be heavy, the variety of the subject matter keeps your work fresh and interesting. You will have opportunities to see connections between different subjects and to broaden and deepen your learning.

As a survey of college subjects, the major tends not to vary much, in emphases, requirements, and philosophies, from one college to another. The similarity will come in handy if you should want to transfer to another institution. At the two-year or community college level, students intending to continue on to a four-year college usually prefer this major. Generally, most of your liberal arts credits will be accepted at other colleges, and you will be well prepared for upper-level courses.

Other majors you might like:
Humanities
Journalism
English
American studies
Mathematics
Natural sciences
Communications
Global studies
Environmental studies
Women's studies
Classics
Philosophy

Questions to ask colleges:
Is this major housed in its own department, or is it pulled together from different departments?

How easy is it to transfer to other majors?

Are students eligible to take classes at other colleges while they are enrolled in the program? Is there a study-abroad program?

Career options and trends:
Teacher*; lawyer*; doctor; journalist*; filmmaker.

Career paths for liberal arts and science majors are wide open: they include journalism, teaching, business and industry, sales, social work, government, film, entrepreneurship—almost any area of human endeavor. The major is also an excellent foundation for an advanced or professional degree leading to careers in law, medicine, engineering, or teaching.

For liberal arts majors, the job outlook is positive, even in difficult times. Because the curriculum is flexible in terms of career preparation, graduates can take advantage of openings in the job market (including jobs that don't even exist yet) that may be closed to others who are less broadly prepared.

For more info:
American Academy for Liberal Education
1050 17th St., N.W.
Suite 400
Washington, DC 20036
(202) 452-8611
www.aale.org

Linguistics

What it's about:

As a linguistics major, you learn what makes human languages special: how they are spoken, written, and understood. You'll also examine many of the world's languages—how they are related and how they have changed over time—as well as methods of analyzing languages for their characteristic and distinctive properties.

Is this for you?

You might like this major if you also like: learning new languages; traveling; exploring other cultures; your own heritage culture; crossword puzzles and word games like Scrabble; figuring out where people come from by their accent; word origins.

Consider this major if you are good at: active listening; attention to detail; creativity; critical reading/thinking; organizing; research ...*or have...* initiative; patience; verbal skills.

Recommended high school prep:

English 4, math 3, lab science 3, social studies 3, and a foreign language 4. It may be helpful to divide your foreign language studies between two languages. If possible, take a year of computer programming.

Did you know...

...that there are more than 5,000 languages spoken in the world today and that many of them are threatened with extinction before the end of this century? Linguists are leading the efforts to document these languages and to help their speakers preserve them, in written and oral form, for future generations.

...that linguistic training is excellent preparation for employment in high-tech industry, particularly when combined with training in computer science or information science? Linguistics also prepares you for further study in any area in which knowledge of how language works is useful.

Typical courses in this major:

Introduction to linguistics
Phonetics
Phonology
Syntax
Semantics
Morphology
Dialectology
Languages of the world
Language and mind
Language and society
Historical linguistics
Writing systems
Structure of a particular language
Psycholinguistics

Concentrations:

In college: a language or group of languages, e.g., Germanic languages (such as English, German, Dutch); Romance languages (Spanish, Portuguese, French, Italian); Semitic languages; or East Asian languages. However, few undergraduate linguistics programs are large enough to support concentrations.

If you go on to grad school: phonetics/phonology; morphology/syntax; semantics; typology; psycholinguistics; sociolinguistics; computational linguistics; historical linguistics; structure of a language or group of languages.

What the study of this major is like:

Linguistics focuses on the similarities among the world's languages, as well as on the unique characteristics of individual languages, in order to understand those traits and the people who speak the languages. The major usually begins with an introductory course, followed by courses in phonetics and phonology (the study of speech sounds), morphology (the structure and function of words), syntax (the way words combine to form phrases or sentences), and semantics (meaning and use of words).

In addition, the major may include the study of specific languages, or families of languages, and the communities or societies that speak them. You might undertake comparative and historical studies of both well-known and little known languages and dialects. You might explore how children acquire language; how people produce and comprehend written, spoken, and signed language; how language disorders are diagnosed and treated; how languages can be taught most effectively; how the use of particular languages and dialects has been fostered (or discouraged) by government policy; and how computers can be programmed to recognize and produce language.

Most students find linguistics intellectually challenging—in a word, hard. In introductory courses, you will most likely be given samples from languages you don't know and be asked to describe the languages. Once you get the hang of it, you will probably enjoy such exercises and be ready for the next stage of training, in which you'll explore linguistic theories and their explanation of observed data. At first, this approach may be frustrating, because you won't understand how the theories work. But once you feel comfortable doing a linguistic experiment, you might begin a project for an advanced course or an undergraduate thesis. You may, in fact, find yourself working on cutting-edge studies while still an undergraduate.

There are two major approaches to the study of human language: formal and functional. Formal study emphasizes the structure of languages and requires good data-handling and reasoning skills. Functional study emphasizes the use of language and may involve laboratory or field research and statistics. Most linguistics programs stress one or the other of these approaches. A few (mostly larger) departments combine them successfully.

Other majors you might like:

Native American studies
Anthropology
Classics
Speech/rhetorical studies
Communications
Computer science
Foreign language teacher education
Language interpretation/translation

Philosophy
Psychology
Communication disorders
American sign language (ASL)

Questions to ask colleges:

Is the major offered by a linguistics department, by another department that includes linguistics, or as an interdisciplinary program? Are courses in the core areas of linguistics (phonology, syntax, semantics) regularly offered?

Is there a strong study-abroad program that enables students to learn a language or strengthen skills in one they already know?

Can students do independent research with a faculty member in linguistics, work in a linguistics lab, or do an industry internship (for example, in computational linguistics) as part of the undergraduate degree?

Career options and trends:

High school language teacher*; college professor*; translator; consultant.

The linguistics major can also prepare you for jobs in international business, government service, public relations, software design, marketing, publishing, advertising, English as a second language (ESL) teaching and research, health-related professions (speech pathology and language disorders), industrial research and development (speech recognition, text analysis and interpretation, electronic dictionary preparation, artificial intelligence, and speech synthesis), and law. Some of these fields require graduate study.

Linguists are playing a prominent role in high-tech industry, primarily in information retrieval and analysis and in speech technology. While technology has made this work easier in some ways, it will never replace the need for individuals with strong language skills. As business and commerce becomes more international in the global economy, opportunites are expected to increase for translators and interpreters. Good language teachers are always needed in the United States and overseas (especially English teachers), as are speech and language therapists.

"I volunteered as a conversation partner for foreign students, which was fun and provided some insight into how people learn foreign languages. Anything that puts you in contact with native speakers of as many languages as possible is great, because for linguistics classes you very often need native consultants to provide data."

—Andrea, senior, University of Washington

For more info:

Linguistic Society of America (LSA)
1325 18th St., N.W.
Suite 211
Washington, DC 20036-6501
(202) 835-1714
www.lsadc.org

Center for Applied Linguistics (CAL)
4646 40th St., N.W.
Washington, DC 20016-1859
(202) 362-0700
www.cal.org

Philosophy

What it's about:

Philosophy is the study of the fundamental questions about the nature of being, knowledge, right and wrong, and our place in the physical world. You explore the key philosophical texts and traditions, and examine the nature of argument and reasoning. You'll also consider the ways philosophy affects other fields of inquiry, such as physics, religion, and computer science.

Is this for you?

You might like this major if you also like: puzzles and games; thinking about what life is about; debate and argument; science fiction or other imaginative literature; thinking differently from the way other people do.

Consider this major if you are good at: attention to detail; creativity; critical reading/thinking; organizing ...*or have...* patience; verbal skills; writing skills.

Recommended high school prep:

English 4, math 3, lab science 3, social studies 4, and a foreign language 3-4. If possible, take a course in philosophy or a humanities course that includes philosophical works. Any course that requires a lot of reading will also be beneficial.

Did you know...

...that it is a rare and valuable ability to know what an argument is? Employers are often grateful to find someone who can write clear prose and think logically.

Typical courses in this major:

Problems of philosophy
History of philosophy
Ethics
Political theory
Logic
Epistemology
Philosophy of religion

Aristotle
Kant
Aesthetics
Metaphysics
Theory of knowledge
Philosophy of science
Plato
Locke
Hegel

Concentrations:

In college: history of philosophy; ethics; logic.

If you go on to grad school: epistemology; metaphysics.

What the study of this major is like:

Philosophy majors participate in a tradition of thought as old as civilization and as new as artificial intelligence. Philosophy is the most general field of study. Every religious or moral belief, every detail from science—even ordinary information—can be viewed as subject matter. Philosophy majors are encouraged to contemplate the universe, both human and nonhuman. At the same time, they are trained to become disciplined, imaginative thinkers who can persuasively support their positions.

Many questions that philosophers ask are often asked by children: How did the world begin? Do animals have their own language? Could I be someone else? Part of the fascination of philosophy is that it can reveal the complexity and subtlety of simple matters. On the other hand, philosophy tries to expose the muddled thinking we read and hear every day.

Beginning courses in philosophy are designed for students with little background, because few high schools teach philosophy. Most college programs have introductory courses in philosophical problems, which may include such topics as ethics (moral conduct), metaphysics (the nature of reality), logic, epistemology (the study of knowledge), and aesthetics (the nature of art). Another introductory course surveys the history of philosophy beginning with the Greeks, and usually takes one or two years to complete.

As you progress through the major, you will read works by Plato, Aristotle, Aquinas, Descartes, Hume, Kant, Hegel, Wittgenstein, John Dewey, and other important writers on such issues as the nature of consciousness, "truth," and social justice. Increasingly, though, you will be expected to think from a philosophical perspective on your own. A substantial paper or thesis is usually required in your senior year.

Philosophy can present you with ideas that may at first seem overly abstract, incomprehensible, or pure fantasy. You may also have trouble seeing the connection between the philosophical concepts you study and the issues that matter in your daily life. In addition, philosophy courses seldom begin with easy material and then progress to the more difficult. Philosophers circle back on questions again and again. When studying philosophy, you can expect to progress from confusion to some clarity, but not from one small but clear concept to another well-defined concept. This situation frustrates some students and excites others.

Most philosophy departments at large universities are strong in certain areas of philosophy, such as ethics and moral philosophy, philosophy of language, history of philosophy, or political philosophy. Some departments focus on the sciences, some on the humanities, and a few take a religious approach. Departments at colleges that do not have graduate programs tend not to be specialized. Most departments, however, offer undergraduates a full range of courses. You can generally assume that the more professors in the department, the greater the variety of subjects taught.

Other majors you might like:
English
Religious studies
Political science
History
Mathematics
Music, general
Physics
Classics
European studies
Asian studies
Legal studies
Theology

Questions to ask colleges:
Is there an opportunity to take small classes (under 20 students) and seminars? Is there a philosophy club? Do students have any role in the department's activities, such as helping to select outside speakers?

Career options and trends:
Philosophy majors find their training useful in a variety of fields. The analytic skills developed in college are easily transferable to a number of professional areas. Students of philosophy tend to have the flexibility and capacity for growth that employers find valuable. Many graduates accept jobs in business, journalism, computer science, public administration, teaching, publishing, and public relations.

Teaching positions at the college level are very competitive and require a Ph.D.

Insider's viewpoint:
"Philosophy unites living and thinking in a way that few other disciplines do. It is a matter of giving yourself over to a life of questioning and searching, with no holds barred. It rewards honesty, courage, and curiosity. Philosophy at its best is not a way to make a living, but a way to be alive."

—Professor Richard T. Lee, Trinity College

For more info:
The American Philosophical Association (APA)
University of Delaware
31 Amstel Ave.
Newark, DE 19716-4797
(302) 831-1112
www.apaonline.org

Languages

People don't realize that the United States has no official language. There's a movement afoot to give English the nod (and English has its own section in this book). But what about the 34 million Americans who speak Spanish at home? Or the 7 million who speak Asian tongues? Knowing more than one language is a valuable skill in business, government, and the nonprofit sectors here and around the world.

"More students would consider language majors if they knew how important proficiency in a foreign language is in the workplace today," says Professor Theresa A. Antes, University of Florida, Gainesville. "Many employers will hire an applicant who is proficient in a foreign language over one who is not."

Language skills are growing in importance because of Internet communications, global business, the integration of the European Union, unrest in the Middle East, and the emergence of China as a participant in international affairs and commerce.

Regarding China, Professor Scott Cook of Grinnell College says, "Students may not realize just how important China is in the world and how many job opportunities a Chinese degree may open up for them."

The significance of Arabic is not in doubt, with the Middle East so prominent in the news. "Knowledge of Arabic is indispensable for a firsthand acquaintance with events in the region," says Professor Michael Fishbein, University of California: Los Angeles.

The world is your oyster (and your ostra, Auster, huître, ostrica) if you master languages. Consider these pearls of opportunity: employment in international relations, diplomacy, intelligence gathering, journalism, law, medicine, tourism, and the arts; jobs as translators/ interpreters, Foreign Service specialists, and environmental specialists; and positions in a nongovernmental organization, the computer industry, and international banking and business.

"It used to be assumed that all students pursued a degree in French in order to teach at the high school level, but demands of the global economy have changed that scenario," Antes says.

La Dolce Vita

Studying a language requires much more than memorizing vocabulary and learning grammar rules. And the rewards go beyond career enhancement.

"Learning to speak Italian enables one to combine good employment with fine living," notes Professor Robert E. Proctor, Connecticut College. "There's always something new to discover," he says of Italy.

"Once you take Russia as your focus," observes Professor Melissa Frazier of Sarah Lawrence College, "concepts like 'East' and 'West,' 'Europe' and 'Asia' become more tentative, and your understanding of the world around you much more complicated and also much more interesting."

Japanese is a subject of inexhaustible riches, according to H. Mack Horton, University of California, Berkeley. Sure, Japan is the world's second-largest economy, but he's talking about intellectual enrichment. "The Japanese major is a gold mine for anyone with an abiding curiosity about the human condition," he says.

Just as languages differ, so do college programs. At some colleges, you'll choose between studying the language/linguistics, or the literature/culture, of the countries where the language is spoken. By the way, there are also separate majors called area studies, which emphasize the history, culture, politics, and economics of a region rather than its language and literature. As an example, German (language/literature) is a different major from German studies. It's good if colleges offer both types. (See the chapter on Area, ethnic, and gender studies.)

Many graduate programs combine language studies with studies of other things, such as the arts, political science, religious studies, sociology, and economics. Graduate tracks in literature may concentrate on a particular period—classical or modern—or on a genre, such as poetry or drama. (Some colleges teach literature in translation, so find out if you'll be reading works in the original language.)

Here are some questions to ask: What are the possibilities for study abroad? Are the study-abroad programs offered through the university, so you can be sure credits will be transferred? Are tuition and fees the same as those for courses on campus?

How many faculty members are native speakers? What are their specializations? If you want to learn a particular dialect, make sure a faculty member teaches it. How big are the classes? To master a language, you'll want the chance to speak in class.

In choosing a college, look for facilities that include a library with computers and databases. Are computers set up to access the Web and handle word processing in the language? How good is the library's collection? What about language labs? Does the college receive news and other TV programming in the language?

Will your college experience include social opportunities to meet and converse with others who speak the language in dorms or the cafeteria? Is a community of native speakers nearby? Are activities and lectures offered to promote studies on and off campus?

Resources for more information include the Association for Asian Studies, at www.aasianst.org; Modern Language Association, at www.mla.org; American Council on the Teaching of Foreign Languages, at www.actfl.org; Association of Professional Schools of International Affairs, at www.apsia.org; and National Foreign Affairs Training Center (Foreign Service Institute), at www.state.gov.

This section also covers American Sign Language. For more information about the classics and linguistics majors, turn to the Humanities chapter.

American Sign Language (ASL)

What it's about:

American Sign Language (ASL) is a visual language used by the Deaf community in the United States and Canada. In this major you learn how to sign, and study the literature, grammar, and history of this language and its use among members of the Deaf community in North America.

Is this for you?

You might like this major if you also like: taking risks; interacting with people from different cultures and with different points of view; helping others; breaking down barriers.

Consider this major if you are good at: critical reading/thinking; memorizing; spacial thinking/analysis *...or have...* cultural sensitivity; initiative; manual dexterity; patience; physical stamina; verbal skills.

Recommended high school prep:

English 4, math 3, lab science 3, social studies 3, and a foreign language 3–4.

Did you know...

...that ASL is not based on English? Its syntax has more in common with Japanese, and is also completely different from British Sign Language.

...that there are cross-cultural issues you might not be aware of? Deaf Culture is a distinct group that has its own language and customs. Students who hear can sometimes cross invisible cultural lines without realizing it.

Typical courses in this major:

Comparative analysis of ASL and English
ASL literature
ASL classifiers
ASL incorporated numbers and fingerspelling
Introduction to methods of teaching ASL
Introduction to Deaf studies
Deaf Culture
History of the Deaf community
Communication in gestures
Senior thesis/seminar

Concentrations:

In college: ASL teacher education; ASL interpretation.

If you go on to grad school: ASL linguistics; Deaf studies with an emphasis on ASL.

What the study of this major is like:

When you begin learning American Sign Language, you can expect to be fascinated by it. Language acquisition research shows that picking up the basics of ASL shouldn't take you a long time. But although you may at first think that ASL is easy, you will probably realize, soon enough, that mastering the language can be a challenging, sometimes tedious experience.

ASL does not "mime" spoken English and is not structured like English at all. ASL has its own rules for the creation of words, phonetics, and grammar quite unlike those for spoken languages. ASL also involves more than hand gestures—facial movements are also part of the grammatical structure, and meaning is also derived from the signer's use of the surrounding space.

You may also have difficulty communicating with Deaf people because they sign quickly; for many, ASL is their native language. And after you become proficient in ASL, you may still feel stalled in your ability to interact with members of the Deaf community. But if you persevere and don't let yourself be discouraged by the frustrations of being unable to understand them at times and of occasionally being rejected, you will eventually qualify as a skilled interpreter.

Some colleges offer courses in Signed English, in the belief that this form of communication can enhance Deaf children's English literacy skills. This practice is not widely accepted in the Deaf community, however.

If you think you may want to become an ASL teacher, keep in mind that while this is not impossible, such training is intended, primarily, for Deaf students. ASL-trained people who hear can more easily find jobs as general teachers of the Deaf, ASL interpreters, or counselors.

Other majors you might like:
Communication disorders
Education of Deaf/hearing impaired
Special education
Audiology/hearing sciences
Linguistics
Sign language interpretation
Anthropology
Human services
Foreign languages/literatures
Audiology/speech pathology
Child development

Questions to ask colleges:
Are there Deaf teachers? Are there adequate ASL labs?

Does the program provide interaction with the local Deaf community? Is there group support for students who are new to Deaf Culture and may experience culture shock?

Career options and trends:
ASL interpreter; high school teacher; ASL specialist.

The American Sign Language Teachers Association offers three levels of certification: Provisional, Qualified, and Professional. ASL interpreters earn certifications from the Registry of Interpreters for the Deaf or from the National Association of the Deaf.

Legislative mandates that incorporate ASL into foreign language curriculums is increasing the demand for ASL high school teachers all over the United States. In metropolitan areas, the job market for ASL interpreting is both very hot and very competitive. The hourly rates are excellent (but freelance interpreters receive no fringe benefits). The increasing use of video relay services, which allow individuals to conduct video calls using a sign language interpreter over an Internet connection, will also increase demand for interpreters.

Insider's viewpoint:
"I enjoy watching my students acquiring the language. They appear to be intimidated on the first day of classes but by the end, they are animated with the use of their faces, hands, and bodies when they communicate."

—Professor Mike Kemp, Gallaudet University

For more info:
American Sign Language Teachers Association (ASLTA)
P.O. Box 92445
Rochester, NY 14692-9998
www.aslta.org

National Association of the Deaf (NAD)
8630 Fenton St.
Suite 820
Silver Spring, MD 20910
(301) 587-1788
www.nad.org

Arabic

What it's about:

Arabic majors learn to understand, read, and speak Modern Standard Arabic; read and analyze the key works of classical and modern Arabic literature; and study Islam and Middle Eastern history.

Is this for you?

You might like this major if you also like: learning languages; Arabic and Islamic culture; history; travel; religious issues and thought.

Consider this major if you are good at: attention to detail; critical reading/thinking; memorizing; organizing; research *...or have...* linguistic ability; patience; verbal skills; writing skills.

Recommended high school prep:

English 4, math 3, lab science 3, social studies 4, and a foreign language 3–4. If possible, take Arabic. Otherwise, take another language with a case system (where nouns and adjectives are inflected depending upon the grammar of the sentence), such as German, Russian, or Latin. World history, comparative religion, and literature courses are also helpful.

Did you know...

...that Arabic is the classical language of Islamic civilization and is the language preferred for religious expression by Muslims everywhere, whether or not their native language is Arabic? Much of classical Arabic literature also covers history, biography, travel literature, poetry, and philosophy from a nonreligious perspective.

Typical courses in this major:

Literary Arabic
Islamic texts
Classical Arabic texts
Philosophical and Kalam texts
Modern Arabic literature
Arabic media
Shi'ia in Islamic history
Contemporary Islamic thought
History of the Arabs
Spoken Egyptian Arabic
Spoken Moroccan Arabic
Western Islamic art
Survey of the Middle East from 500 to the present
Islamic civilization: premodern Islam
Islamic civilization: Islam and the modern world

Concentrations:

Generally, none in college; but if you go on to grad school: classical Arabic literature; Islamic texts; modern Arabic literature.

What the study of this major is like:

If you major in Arabic, you can expect to devote plenty of time to learning the language. According to the U.S. Foreign Service, Arabic, along with Chinese and Japanese, is among the languages that adults have most trouble learning. Arabic has a complicated phonetic system and grammar, as well as a system of usage that is not even remotely related to English. In addition, the formal Modern Standard Arabic is very different from informal, colloquial Arabic. Students often feel that they are learning two languages at the same time, so be prepared to work hard and to persevere.

To become proficient in listening to, speaking, reading, and writing Arabic, you'll have to study long hours outside class, completing homework assignments, reading and preparing texts for discussion, researching topics for reports and papers, and reviewing. Arabic courses may use videotapes and CDs, in addition to textbooks. You should gain as much exposure to the language as possible; for example, you can use the Web to access Arabic newspapers and radio broadcasts. An exciting development in recent years is the availability of up-to-the-minute journalism in Arabic online.

Undergraduate Arabic courses usually include language, literature, culture, history, and Islamics (the study of the religion). You should plan to spend at least one summer in an Arabic-speaking country, or possibly in a semester- or year-abroad program. Most American institutions have adopted the proficiency method of language teaching. In other words, Arabic is no longer taught purely as a classical language, with stress on grammar and translation. So even if you are interested primarily in modern or classical literature, you'll be expected to learn to pronounce the language correctly and to acquire a reasonable fluency in speaking.

Because only a few students major in Arabic, you'll have more opportunities to receive individual attention from faculty members than you would in most other majors. You will also have ample opportunity to meet other Arabic majors. Friendships often form across cultural borders: for example, between Muslim and Christian students or between students with a Middle Eastern background and those of European or African origin.

Other majors you might like:
Near and Middle Eastern studies
Linguistics
Ancient Near Eastern/Biblical languages
History
Religious studies
Art history
Musicology/ethnomusicology
Political science
Classics
Islamic studies
Judaic studies
International relations

Questions to ask colleges:
Does the program have a special focus? One program may emphasize modern literature, another linguistics, or Islamic thought. Look for a program that will satisfy your own interests.

Is the library committed to keeping the Arabic and Middle Eastern collections up-to-date? Library resources are extremely important for the study of Arabic.

Do computers have access to the Web in Arabic, and can they handle Arabic word processing?

Career options and trends:
College professor*; translator/interpreter*; Foreign Service Officer*; journalist.

Jobs in the U.S. Foreign Service are usually open only to U.S. citizens. To become a FSO, you must pass the Foreign Service Examination.

The importance of the Middle east in world affairs is pushing demand for speakers of Arabic. More jobs are available in intelligence, translation, and journalism for people with expertise in Arabic and the Middle East. More universities are establishing Arabic programs and are hiring faculty members in the field.

For more info:
American Association of Teachers of Arabic
    (AATA)
3416 Primm Lane
Birmingham, AL 35216
(205) 822-6800
www.aataweb.org

Middle East Studies Association of North America
University of Arizona
1219 North Santa Rita Ave.
Tuscon, AZ 85721
(520) 621-5850
www.mesana.org

Chinese language and literature

What it's about:
The Chinese major prepares you to interact with and understand the modern Chinese world, while introducing you to China's long and rich cultural tradition. It typically combines three to four years of language study (modern Mandarin) with courses in literature, philosophy, history, and other fields.

Is this for you?
You might like this major if you also like: Chinese culture; studying languages; history; travel; different ways of thinking about the world.

Consider this major if you are good at: attention to detail; creativity; critical reading/thinking; memorizing ...*or have...* initiative; linguistic ability; patience; persistence; verbal skills; writing skills.

Recommended high school prep:
English 4, math 3, lab science 3, social studies 4, and a foreign language 4. Be sure to take as much foreign language as possible; Chinese is preferable but in no way required. World history courses are also recommended.

Did you know...
...that you don't need to know any Chinese before you begin college? If you have solid study habits, the language, as difficult as it may be, is highly learnable.

Typical courses in this major:
Elementary Chinese
Intermediate Chinese
Advanced Chinese
Advanced classical Chinese
Traditional Chinese literature
Modern Chinese fiction
Modern Chinese film
Modern Chinese theater
Chinese philosophy
Chinese religion
Chinese history
East Asian civilization
Chinese linguistics
Chinese gender and women's studies
Chinese music
Chinese art

Concentrations:
Chinese language; Chinese literature; Chinese calligraphy.

What the study of this major is like:
For English speakers, Chinese is easy to learn, but difficult to master. Once you learn the four tones and basic vocabulary, speaking the language should not be hard, because the grammar is user-friendly.

If you major in Chinese, be ready to immerse yourself in the language. Language courses typically meet five days a week and are often conducted in Chinese only. The classes may consist of alternating grammar and drill sessions. You learn to speak, listen, read, and write Chinese. In your first year or two, greater emphasis is placed on speaking and listening. Most language programs introduce Chinese written characters almost immediately, although some instructors wait until you establish a solid foundation in the spoken language.

By your third year, the emphasis will likely shift, to take in more written materials, such as newspaper articles and fairly simple literature. Your fourth-year courses usually include advanced literature and perhaps a course in classical Chinese. Although classical Chinese is grammatically different from modern Chinese, learning it will increase your understanding of Chinese as a whole. Language courses are supplemented by English-taught courses in literature, philosophy, and history. Such courses typically focus on lecture and discussion and require written papers in English.

As a Chinese major, you should expect a demanding workload, especially in the language courses, although your studies should be enjoyable if you are well prepared. Your greatest challenge will be to get off to a good start—to develop solid study habits and establish a strong foundation for future language study. You should advance quickly in your first year; but in your second year, your progress, though no less real, may be less noticeable. In your second year you focus on memorization and the acquisition of characters and vocabulary, which can be frustrating if you have not mentally prepared yourself for it. After the second year, students generally feel more confident as they begin to gain mastery of the language. For real fluency, you should study in a Chinese-speaking community or country for at least a semester, preferably a year.

The Chinese major may be housed in departments that teach only modern languages, teach East Asian languages and culture, teach East Asian languages and literature, teach comparative literature, teach linguistics, or offer second-language education, including bilingual education. The biggest difference among Chinese programs is the balance between courses in language study and in area studies (for example, the literature, religion, and history of a region). Often, if a program requires only two years of language study but offers a number of courses in area studies, the reason is not a matter of philosophy but rather of necessity. The program may not have enough professors to offer more than two or three years of Chinese. You would then take area studies courses from faculty members in other departments.

Other majors you might like:
Asian studies
Linguistics
Asian-American studies
Comparative literature
Foreign language teacher education
Philosophy
History
Chinese studies
East Asian studies
International relations
East Asian languages
Art history

Questions to ask colleges:
How many years of Chinese are offered on campus? A small liberal arts college that offers three or four years of the language should be considered to have, for its size, a substantial program.

How many other departments offer China-related courses? How many hours a week do language courses meet? A college that offers less than five hours per week at the first- and second-year levels is cutting corners.

How large is the Chinese community on campus? What kinds of activities promote Chinese studies on campus, including guest lecturers, Chinese tables, Chinese houses, or Lunar New Year celebrations?

Career options and trends:
Chinese language teacher*; ESL teacher; Foreign Service Officer; administrator or analyst for an international NGO (nongovernmental organization); translator/interpreter; journalist.

An increasing number of Chinese language majors are hired by firms dealing with overseas markets. Various branches of government and international organizations need experts in Chinese languages and culture. The Foreign Service is usually open only to U.S. citizens who pass an exam.

As China prospers economically and grows in political importance, job opportunities related to China continue to increase. However, fluency in Chinese alone may not get you a foot in the door; you also need training in another field—for instance, if you want to do business in China, you should take economics courses, and preferably pursue an MBA degree later on. College faculty positions in Chinese are not easy to come by, so you should not consider seeking a doctorate in Chinese unless you have a deep commitment to the field.

For more info:
Association for Asian Studies (AAS)
1021 East Huron St.
Ann Arbor, MI 48104
(734) 665-2490
www.aasianst.org

French

What it's about:
Majors in French study the language, literature, and culture of France and other areas of the French-speaking world.

Is this for you?
You might like this major if you also like: French culture; studying languages; literature; art; traveling.

Consider this major if you are good at: active listening; attention to detail; critical reading/ thinking; memorizing ...*or have...* linguistic ability; perseverance; verbal skills; writing skills.

Recommended high school prep:
English 4, math 3, lab science 3, social studies 4 (including European and world history), and French 4. If possible, also take a second foreign language; Spanish, Italian, and Latin are especially recommended.

Did you know...
...that there are many career opportunities available to French majors besides teaching? In addition to language and literature classes, you can often choose among topics such as French for business, French for medicine, cultural studies, or film studies to expand your options in the global economy.

...that, in many programs, the courses in elementary French are considered prerequisites and do not count toward your major? So if you can, take at least two years of high school French; then you can begin studying at the intermediate level in college.

Typical courses in this major:
French composition
French conversation
French grammar
Stylistics
French literature
French phonetics
Structure of French
French theater
Realism and naturalism
Twentieth-century poetry

Concentrations:
French literature and culture; French language and linguistics; foreign language education.

What the study of this major is like:
As a French major, you study the language, literature, and culture of the people of France and other French-speaking regions. Traditionally, Parisian French (the language spoken in France's capital) and the culture of France have dominated the major. But since World War II, the French major has broadened to include the language and cultures of nations formerly under French control, such as Algeria, the Ivory Coast, Lebanon, and Indochina (now Southeast Asia). The widened perspective reflects the importance of French, which has been an international language (one used in diplomacy and global trade) since the eighteenth century.

Most programs provide a combination of language and literature courses. While you work on fluency and accuracy in language courses, you learn about the culture by studying various French texts. In a series of grammar, composition, and conversation courses, you read, listen to, speak, and write French. In literature courses you may examine the classics: the theater of Molière, Corneille, and Racine; the poetry of the Renaissance; the novels of Flaubert. You may also view films or read newspapers, magazines, and technical reports.

To succeed as a French major, you must be willing to spend a good deal of time outside class memorizing word forms, listening to cassettes, working with multimedia materials, and doing other language-learning activities. In fact, you'll probably spend twice as much time preparing for class as you spend in class. Although many French majors have been exposed to the language before college, you can begin studying French in your first year and start your course work for your major in your third year. Generally, you must complete at least 12 semester-length courses in upper-level French.

Many students learning a foreign language in the United States face the challenge of working in a sort of intellectual vacuum. You're most likely to succeed in the French major if you seek out opportunities to practice the language with native speakers, attend French club meetings, eat dinner at a French table, or even live in a language house.

At many colleges, study abroad is strongly encouraged, in either a summer program or your third year. Many French departments also sponsor film series, lectures, theatrical performances, and informal social gatherings where you can speak and hear French. Keep in mind that you'll usually have to look for such opportunities yourself. Although they are essential for gaining proficiency in French, they are not necessarily required.

If you want to teach French in elementary or high school, the Bachelor of Science in Education is the logical choice; for all other careers or if you wish to go on to grad school, the Bachelor of Arts probably makes sense.

Other majors you might like:
Comparative literature
Linguistics
International relations
Latin
Business
Art history
History
French teacher education
Romance languages
European studies
European history
French studies

Questions to ask colleges:
How many faculty members are native or near-native speakers? When do students have contact with native speakers?

What is the variety of specializations among the faculty members? Is there one literature specialist who teaches all courses, or are there several, who specialize in different centuries or genres? Is there a linguist on the faculty?

Career options and trends:
High school teacher*; Foreign Service Officer*; interpreter/translator.

French majors also go on to jobs in tourism, international relations, the computer industry, international business, journalism, and publishing. With appropriate graduate degrees, you can work in research, law, diplomacy, banking, and marketing. A state certificate or license is required for teaching in public elementary and secondary schools. Translation work usually requires that you get specially certified.

Many states are predicting a shortage of high school French teachers in the near future, due to the expected retirement of older teachers. To a lesser extent, a shortage of college faculty members is also expected. The computer industry has provided numerous jobs for linguists and translators, and this trend will probably continue.

For more info:
Modern Language Association (MLA)
26 Broadway, 3rd Fl.
New York, NY 10004-1789
(646) 576-5000
www.mla.org

American Association of Teachers of French
Southern Illinois University
Mailcode 4510
Carbondale, IL 62901-4510
(618) 453-5731
www.frenchteachers.org

German

What it's about:

This major primarily teaches the language and literature of Germany, Austria, and much of Switzerland. By examining genres, literary movements, and individual authors and themes, you expand your capacity for literary analysis and appreciation.

Is this for you?

You might like this major if you also like: German culture and heritage; languages; travel; history; philosophy; literature; music; art; architecture; science.

Consider this major if you are good at: attention to detail; creativity; critical reading/thinking; memorizing; organizing *...or have...* initiative; patience; perseverance; verbal skills; writing skills.

Recommended high school prep:

English 4, math 3, lab science 3, social studies 4, and foreign language 4. If possible, social studies should include both European history and art history. Language should be German, and a year of Latin is useful. One year of classical music (orchestra, lessons) is also recommended.

Did you know...

...that beginning and intermediate language courses often do not count toward your major?

...that in almost every German department, there are opportunities, including stipends, for study abroad?

...that German is often required for graduate study in fields such as art, music history, and philosophy?

Typical courses in this major:

Introduction to German literature I, II
Conversation and composition
German history and thought
The age of Goethe

Romanticism
Realism
Fin-de-siècle Vienna
Thomas Mann
Franz Kafka
German drama
German women writers
Jewish contributions to German culture
Postwar literature
Migration literature
German film
Modern German literature

Concentrations:

German literature of a particular period; German cinema; German area studies; Germanic linguistics; German intellectual history.

What the study of this major is like:

If you major in German language and literature, you must first concentrate on the language. You need a good knowledge of grammar in order to write properly, so, even if you know how to speak German and have a wide vocabulary, be prepared to polish your skills. You then use the language to explore increasingly complex texts in courses that are taught in German and tend to have small enrollments.

Like other literature majors, German language and literature includes the study of literary theory. You are introduced not only to classical German literature but also to recent works. You read eighteenth- and nineteenth-century authors such as Goethe, Schiller, and Heine, and major figures from the early twentieth century such as Kafka, Rilke, Dürrenmatt, and Brecht. You also read contemporary writers such as Frisch, Sebald, Böll, and Grass. Many German departments teach the literature and film of postwar divided Germany (1945–89) or of recent immigrants (for example, Italian, Turkish). You thus explore questions of multiculturalism and diversity as they are emerging in Europe today.

Some colleges offer a German studies major—a more interdisciplinary approach that emphasizes cultural expressions other than literature, such as music, art, film, philosophy, science, and history. German studies may cover anything from the works of great philosophers such as Kant, Hegel, Nietzsche, and Marx, the writings of Freud, the German contribution to music and art, to the role of women in contemporary German culture.

The major typically includes time abroad, in either academic or work programs. Generally, colleges that have their own programs abroad offer courses taught by special staff; students live in dormitories, apartments, or local homes. Most of the stronger junior-year-abroad programs accept students from various institutions. Colleges without their own programs generally permit, or even encourage, qualified students to attend them. Many American colleges and other organizations can help you find vacation employment in German-speaking countries, to strengthen your command of the language and appreciation of the culture.

Other majors you might like:
Comparative literature
Linguistics
European studies
Music, general
Philosophy
History
Political science
German studies
Germanic languages
German teacher education

Questions to ask colleges:
Does the program teach literary works primarily in the original German or in translation? How will previous language training be credited?

Is there a German house or dormitory on campus that students can live in? Which types of study-abroad programs does the program offer? Does the program provide stipends?

Career options and trends:
College professor*; high school teacher*; interpreter/translator*; international lawyer.

German majors tend to pursue a rich variety of careers. Many enter jobs in government, business, library and information science, tourism, or journalism. With appropriate professional study, you can pursue a career in law or medicine. A mastery of German is valuable in almost any academic field, as well as in international business and diplomacy. A graduate degree is usually necessary for obtaining a job in a German field. An additional state certificate or license is required for teaching in public elementary and secondary schools.

Insider's viewpoint:
"I took a class with a professor who made me realize that German was a new way in which I could communicate my life experiences and emotions. A lot of German literature tends to be highly emotionally charged, and it takes a strong person to deal with it."

—Sabrina, junior, Oberlin College

For more info:
Modern Language Association (MLA)
26 Broadway, 3rd Fl.
New York, NY 10004-1789
(646) 576-5000
www.mla.org

American Association of Teachers of German (AATG)
112 Haddontowne Court, #104
Cherry Hill, NJ 08034-3668
(856) 795-5553
www.aatg.org

Italian

What it's about:

As an Italian major, you study the language and literature of Italy, usually in the broader context of Italy's culture, history, and society.

Is this for you?

You might like this major if you also like: Italian culture and heritage; Romance languages; traveling; art; history; nature; food; architecture; music; film.

Consider this major if you are good at: active listening; caring/nurturing; critical reading/thinking; leadership; memorizing *...or have...* initiative; patience; verbal skills; writing skills.

Recommended high school prep:

English 4, math 3, lab science 3, social studies 4 (including European history and art history), and a foreign language 4. If possible, take Latin. If Latin is not available, take French or Italian.

Typical courses in this major:

Elementary Italian
Intermediate Italian
Advanced Italian
Italian composition and conversation
Masterworks of Italian literature
Dante's *Divine Comedy*
Twentieth-century literature
Italian theater
Italian civilization
Renaissance literature
Nineteenth-century literature
Italian cinema

Concentrations:

Italian language and literature; Italian culture and society; Italian and linguistics.

What the study of this major is like:

If you don't know the language, you begin with elementary Italian, a two-semester course in which you study basic grammar and learn to listen to, speak, read, and write Italian. After this course (or if you know basic Italian before entering college), you take intermediate Italian, a two-semester course usually taught in Italian, in which you review grammar and practice listening, speaking, reading, and writing.

Most intermediate courses include poetry and prose, and introduce you to Italian history, culture, and contemporary Italian society. Intermediate Italian also prepares you for a possible third year abroad, which all language majors are encouraged to pursue. Most study-abroad programs require two years of college Italian because the courses are taught entirely in Italian. In advanced Italian, which emphasizes conversation and composition, you discuss and write about historical and contemporary aspects of Italian culture and civilization.

Italy's greatest poet is Dante Alighieri, author of *The Divine Comedy*, a work in three parts that profoundly influenced the development of modern Italian. You are usually required to read either part or all of this poem in the original language. Most programs in Italian also include study of Italian Renaissance literature, especially the writings of Boccaccio and Petrarch, sometimes the epic poems of Ariosto and Tasso, and often the writings of Machiavelli and Galileo. Most colleges expect majors to explore the works of nineteenth-century Romantic writers, such as the novelist Alessandro Manzoni, author of *I promessi sposi* (*The Betrothed*).

Twentieth-century literature, a popular course among majors, includes the best Italian fiction writers of our time—Pirandello, D'Annunzio, Moravia, Pasolini, Ginsburg, and Calvino—and the poets Montale, Ungaretti, Saba, and Quasimodo. At some colleges you can take a course in masterworks of Italian literature, an in-depth examination of one or more great writers, or a survey course on writers from Dante to the present. In many programs, films are shown in the contemporary literature course; or a course in Italian cinema may be offered, devoted to the works of such famous directors as De Sica, Visconti, Fellini, Antonioni, Pasolini, and Bertolucci. You may also have one or more required courses in Italian opera.

Learning a language is like playing a musical instrument; you have to practice every day. Most students find that reading serious literature in Italian is a challenge, because building a vocabulary takes time and effort. But the more time you spend reading Italian, the sooner you will be able to read effortlessly. Colleges may offer different literature and cultural courses, depending on the interests of the faculty members, and may vary in the way they teach these subjects. Approaches can range from a textual and linguistic analysis, to a cultural and historical orientation, to interpretations of the text based on recent theories of art and literature, such as feminist literary theory.

Other majors you might like:
Linguistics
Romance languages
Classics
Art history
Comparative literature
Latin
Medieval and Renaissance studies
Culinary arts and chef training
Spanish
Italian studies
Music, general
European studies

Questions to ask colleges:
Who teaches the Italian language courses? Some colleges believe that teaching language and teaching literature and culture are separate specializations that require different instructors. Other colleges adopt a liberal arts approach that encourages each faculty member to teach all areas of Italian, from elementary language to Dante, and to introduce students to culture and literature when they teach language courses.

Career options and trends:
College professor*; high school teacher; art historian; interpreter/translator.

Italian majors also go on to careers in music, film, the arts, research, government, NGOs (nongovernmental organizations), diplomacy, law, fashion design, tourism, international politics, or international business. Graduate study is required for some of these careers.

Italy is "in." New York and Los Angeles are filled with upscale Italian restaurants. College students want to study in Italy; their parents want to vacation there. College enrollments in Italian courses continue to rise. More high schools are offering Italian. The need for people fluent in both English and Italian is growing.

For more info:
National Italian American Foundation (NIAF)
1860 19th St., N.W.
Washington, DC 20009
(202) 387-0600
www.niaf.org

American Association of Teachers of Italian (AATI)
www.aati-online.org

Japanese

What it's about:

This major focuses on Japanese spoken and written language, often in both premodern and modern forms. Students are generally exposed to Japanese literature through reading primary texts in either the original or in English translation, as well as through secondary sources.

Is this for you?

You might like this major if you also like: Japanese culture; learning difficult languages; travel; anime and *manga*; word games; poetry; calligraphy; interacting with different cultures

Consider this major if you are good at: attention to detail; critical reading/thinking; memorizing; research *...or have...* Linguistic ability; Motivation; Self Discipline; patience; verbal skills; writing skills.

Recommended high school prep:

English 4, math 3, lab science 3, social studies 4, and a foreign language 4. Be sure to take as much foreign language as possible; Japanese is preferable but not required. World history courses and classes involving writing and research are also recommended.

Did you know...

...that the Japanese use several different writing systems? In earlier times, there was even one form of writing for men and another for women.

Typical courses in this major:

Elementary Japanese
Intermediate Japanese
Advanced Japanese
Reading Japanese—newspapers and periodicals
East Asian cultures
Survey of Japanese literature in translation
Introduction to Classical Japanese
Introduction to Japanese linguistics
Readings in modern Japanese literature
Japanese history
The world of premodern Japan
The Tale of Genji
Japanese theater: ghosts, masks and actors
Religion and philosophy in premodern Japan
Japanese cinema
Writers and thinkers: modern Japan in the world

Concentrations:

Generally, none in college; but if you go on to grad school: Premodern literature, modern literature, linguistics.

What the study of this major is like:

This major is for those who really like to challenge themselves. Modern Japanese is one of the most difficult languages to learn. Its grammar is the reverse of that of English, and its writing system is very complex, involving two different syllabary sets (*hiragana* and *katakana*) and between two thousand and three thousand characters (*kanji*), most with at least two different readings. Despite its difficulty, though, Japanese has become a highly popular language major.

Unless you have had experience speaking Japanese, you will spend the first year acquiring the basics of the grammar and writing system. In many colleges, lecture courses are taught in English and may meet once or twice a week; they are coupled with smaller practice or recitation classes, conducted in Japanese and meeting daily.

Often beginning Japanese courses focus on the everyday side of the language. You might learn how to talk about weather, food, shopping, or school, and how to read menus, street maps, signs, and letters to and from friends. You may even have an opportunity to send e-mail in Japanese. Since Japanese majors often go on to work in business, practical details like these are important.

During the first and perhaps second year, you will probably also take one or two literature survey courses in English translation, which will involve considerable reading, class discussion, quizzes and exams, and papers of varying length.

In the third and fourth years, you will spend more time with electives in your areas of interest, such as modern literature, drama, film, or courses built around specific themes or questions, such as love in classical and modern Japan, the life of the pre-modern warrior, and representations of gender in literature.

If Japanese is offered within a broader major in Asian or East Asian studies, as it is at many smaller colleges, the language requirement is often only two years. Courses relating to other Asian countries may be required as well.

You are unlikely to learn enough, even after two or three years of courses in the language, to read Japanese high school texts or newspapers easily, much less to work in business or as a translator. A year of study in Japan is extremely helpful for attaining conversational fluency. Keep in mind, however, that the university experience in Japan is very different from that in the United States; the academic year starts in April, and your credits may not all transfer.

Other majors you might like:
Asian studies
Linguistics
International relations
Comparative literature
International business
Asian-American studies
Anthropology
East Asian studies
Animation
Global studies
Geography

Questions to ask colleges:
How many full-time professors does the program have?

How many years of Japanese-language courses does the program offer?

Does the program offer a study-abroad or exchange program, or access to Japanese television and other media?

Career options and trends:
Japanese-language teacher*; ESL teacher; interpreter or translator; journalist; Foreign Service officer*.

Knowledge of Japanese is an asset for almost any career path. There is significant demand for people with good Japanese-language ability and knowledge of Japanese culture in the areas of international business and the travel industry, and those who possess a Ph.D. have a much better chance of obtaining a faculty position in a college or university than is true for other fields.

Japanese companies, either in Japan or elsewhere, often hire non-Japanese with good language ability for translation, writing, or research duties, although the growth potential in such positions may be limited.

Insider's viewpoint:
"There is so much to read, and so few people outside Japan who can read it; you can go into the library and peruse ancient Japanese works that may not have been read by anyone else at the university."

—Professor H. Mack Horton, University of California: Berkeley

For more info:
Association for Asian Studies (AAS)
1021 E. Huron St.
Ann Arbor, MI 48104
(734) 665-2490
www.aasianst.org

Russian

What it's about:

In this major, you learn the Russian language and investigate the Russian-speaking world. You learn oral and written communication, and you explore the historical, geographic, and cultural factors that have contributed to the development of the Russian language.

Is this for you?

You might like this major if you also like: Russian literature; international politics; Russian culture; Russian/world film, dance, theater, and music.

Consider this major if you are good at: attention to detail; creativity; critical reading/thinking; learning languages; memorizing ...*or have...* initiative; patience; persistence; verbal skills; writing skills.

Recommended high school prep:

English 4, math 3, lab science 3, social studies 3 (including a year of world history), and a foreign language 4. Although any language experience is helpful, another inflected language (for example, Latin or German, whose nouns change form for gender) can be especially useful.

Did you know...

...that many opportunities exist for study abroad in Russia? There are now excellent programs in a variety of Russian locations.

Typical courses in this major:

Elementary Russian
Intermediate Russian
Advanced Russian
Russian theater and drama
The Russian short story
The Russian novel
Phonetics and intonation
Conversation and composition
Survey of Russian literature
Alexander Pushkin
Nikolai Gogol
Dostoyevsky and Tolstoy
Anton Chekhov

Concentrations:

In college: Russian literature; Russian language.

If you go on to grad school: Slavic literatures/languages/linguistics (such as Russian); non-Slavic Eurasian literature/language/linguistics (focusing on the Caucasus, Central Asia, and other areas); folklore; drama; literary theory; specific literary genres or periods.

What the study of this major is like:

Russian, the language of one of the world's greatest bodies of literature, is valuable in international relations, business, and science. Russian majors study the language and read the literature; you may also study Russian culture and civilization, Russian and European history, and related disciplines.

The Russian major usually requires three to four years of language study, or an equivalent combination of language study and advanced literature/culture courses in the original Russian, survey courses in Russian literature/culture in translation, or Russian-related courses in other departments. Lecture and seminar courses in Russian departments offer you the opportunity to read the classics of Russian literature, but they have also become increasingly interdisciplinary, incorporating, for example, the study of film, contemporary society, or intellectual history. Russian literature today is not studied in geographic isolation, and many departments offer you the option of studying the language, literature, and cultures of other eastern European, central European, and Eurasian countries. You can sometimes count courses in other literature programs toward your major.

During your first two years, you are usually required to take at least 5-6 hours a week of language classes and labs. Some colleges offer intensive language courses, which require 8-12 hours a week. In upper-level language courses, you learn to communicate effectively with Russian speakers on a variety of topics. The choice of courses at the advanced level depends on the department and the strength of its program. Several offerings allow you to pursue your own interests. During your fourth year, you may participate in a seminar on a literary topic.

As a major, you spend a significant amount of time studying a language that most English speakers don't find easy. Fortunately, your classes are likely to be small and your teachers and classmates a quirky, interesting, and highly motivated bunch. All Russian majors should seriously consider the option of studying for a summer, a semester, or, best of all, a year abroad. Although the culture shock can at first be extreme, students often find that their time in Russia is the most personally and intellectually rewarding experience of their college career.

Other majors you might like:

Linguistics
Comparative literature
History
Political science
Geography
Anthropology
International relations
International business
Russian/Slavic studies
Slavic languages
Central/Middle/Eastern European studies

Questions to ask colleges:

Are there student- or department-sponsored activities, such as Russian tables and Russian clubs, lectures, film screenings, musical gatherings, or dinners? Most good Russian departments have enthusiastic students looking for opportunities to satisfy, outside the classroom, their love of things Russian.

Career options and trends:

High school teacher; college professor; Foreign Service Officer; interpreter/translator.

Russian majors also enter the fields of international law, international business, not-for-profit work, health care, social work, environmental affairs, and journalism. Although strong language skills are most important for Russian majors looking for work in these areas, some employers may want you to have at least a master's degree. Translating work usually requires that you get specially certified. Careers in the Foreign Service are usually open only to U.S. citizens.

Politics always plays a role for Americans looking for work related to Russia, no matter how apolitical that work may seem. In the post-Soviet world, visa regulations, laws of international business, and the degree of U.S. involvement in the region are in a state of uncertainty and will remain so for some time. If you are looking for work in or with Russia, you should keep up-to-date on current events. A focus on Eurasia is of increasing importance for all jobs.

Insider's viewpoint:

"For me the defining marker of Russian-ness is the question 'what is Russia?'—a question that Russians are still trying to answer in a post-Soviet, post-modern world. The endlessly creative ways Russian writers have tried to resolve the issue of their own identity is fascinating for me as a literary scholar."

—Professor Melissa Frazier, Sarah Lawrence College

For more info:

American Association of Teachers of Slavic and Eastern European Languages (AATSEEL)
P.O. Box 569
Beloit, WI 53512-0569
(608) 361-9697
www.aatseel.org

American Association for the Advancement of Slavic Studies (AAASS)
Harvard University
8 Story St., 3rd Fl., Box 14
Cambridge, MA 02138
(617) 495-0677
www.fas.harvard.edu~aaass/

Spanish

What it's about:

As a Spanish major, you learn the Spanish language and explore the literature and culture of Spain, Latin America, and the Latino communities living in the United States.

Is this for you?

You might like this major if you also like: Spanish culture and heritage; community service; travel; politics; history; languages; reading.

Consider this major if you are good at: attention to detail; creativity; critical reading/thinking; memorizing; persuading/influencing; teamwork ...*or have...* patience; verbal skills; writing skills.

Recommended high school prep:

English 4, math 3, lab science 3, social studies 4, and a foreign language 4. Studying Spanish is, of course, useful, but any other Romance language (such as Italian, French, or Latin) is also highly recommended. If possible, take a year of Latin American history.

Did you know...

...that Spanish is the official language of more countries than any other language except English? Depending on the methodology used, Spanish is also ranked as either the second or third most spoken language on earth. It is unlikely to ever catch number one, however—Mandarin Chinese.

Typical courses in this major:

Elementary Spanish
Intermediate Spanish
Advanced Spanish
Spanish literature in translation
Culture and civilization
Business Spanish
Latin American novels
Applied linguistics
Spanish Renaissance
Miguel de Cervantes
Phonetics
Latin American literature in translation
Iberian peninsular literature

Concentrations:

Spanish literature; Latin American literature; Spanish and Portuguese literature; language teaching; international trade; translation.

What the study of this major is like:

During your first and second years in college, your primary focus is on learning and using the Spanish language. Almost all of your classes are conducted in Spanish, so you can hone your basic skills (speaking, listening, reading, writing) rapidly.

During your third and fourth years, you work on advanced speaking and writing skills, learning phonetics and doing creative writing in Spanish. You also study literature, usually that of both Spain and Latin America. The broad range of Spanish-language literature may include the medieval epic *El Cid* and the literature written when Christians, Jews, and Moors shared the Iberian Peninsula; the early Renaissance Spanish classic *La Celestina*; the picaresque novel *Lazarillo de Tormes*; the writings of the mystics; the great Spanish dramatists of the Golden Age (Lope de Vega, Tirso de Molina, Calderón de la Barca); the baroque masterpiece *Don Quixote*; and neoclassical, Romantic, realist, and modernist works. The literature of Latin America includes such authors as Borges, García Márques, Fuentes, and Vargas Llosa. You may also watch films produced in Spanish-speaking regions.

In general, you will be asked to do research and write papers on different topics. Oral practice is important when learning a language. This is accomplished outside of class by working in language labs, meeting with language assistants, doing field or community work, attending lectures and poetry readings in Spanish, or even participating in the construction or maintenance of a Spanish Web site.

Many Spanish departments have different styles and philosophies. Individual faculty members also vary in their approaches to teaching. Some stress grammar over oral communication or, when teaching literature, the social and intellectual context of a work over the literary aspects. The program may offer courses in teaching methods and applied linguistics, often in collaboration with the school of education. Many programs—responding to the number of students looking to use Spanish in their careers—offer business Spanish and medical Spanish, as well as courses in the history and culture of Spain and Latin America (independent of courses offered by the history department).

The biggest challenge you will encounter is to immerse yourself in the Spanish language without falling back on English when you don't know how to express your ideas. Almost all programs encourage you to spend a semester, a summer, or a year of study—often during your third year—in a Spanish-speaking country. The lifestyle of the Spanish major is one of its most appealing features. Latin culture offers good food, music, literature, and social life—and it usually influences class dynamics. Students tend to work in groups and find it rewarding as a way to relax and make friends.

Other majors you might like:
Comparative literature
Linguistics
Language interpretation/translation
ESL teacher education
European studies
Spanish/Iberian studies
Latin American studies
History
Linguistics
Chicano studies
Spanish teacher education
International business

Questions to ask colleges:
Does the program recognize the varieties of the language as spoken throughout the Spanish-speaking world, or does it focus only upon how Spanish is spoken in Spain?

Does the library provide access to computers and databases? How extensive is the library's catalog in the field?

Career options and trends:
College professor; interpreter/translator; high school teacher; ESL teacher.

Spanish majors can also find jobs in business, banking, social services, government, and international organizations. A state certificate or license is required for teaching in public elementary and secondary schools. Translating work usually requires that you get specially certified. With appropriate advanced degrees, you may also work in medicine, law, and other professions, where you will be especially valued in bilingual Spanish/English-speaking communities.

For more info:
Modern Language Association (MLA)
26 Broadway, 3rd Fl.
New York, NY 10004-1789
(646) 576-5000
www.mla.org

Latin American Studies Association (LASA)
University of Pittsburgh
416 Bellefield Hall
Pittsburgh, PA 15260
(412) 648-7929
http://lasa.international.pitt.edu

Legal studies

Sometimes you have to know what something isn't before you can know what it is.

The programs in this chapter will not qualify you to take the bar exam and become a lawyer. To do that, you must go to law school to get a graduate degree called a juris doctor (J.D.), or doctor of jurisprudence (in simpler terms, doctor of law).

If you want to be an attorney, you can take nearly any undergraduate major, not just the ones in this chapter. That's true even if you take prelaw. "Students interested in legal careers major in every possible field. There is no required course of study for admission to law school," says Diane Curtis, prelaw adviser at the University of Massachusetts, Amherst.

"Prelaw is not a major or a specific course of study," Curtis explains. "At the overwhelming majority of colleges and universities, it is an advising program designed to assist students to explore future legal careers, and to help with the law school application process."

Okay. Now that you know what this chapter isn't, let's move on to what is. (See? You are thinking like a lawyer already.)

Whether you choose a prelaw program or not, if you are planning on going to law school, you must be prepared to take the most challenging undergraduate courses from the toughest professors and get good grades. "In your undergraduate classes, you need to acquire the core knowledge and skills upon which your legal education will be built," Curtis says. "Since law deals with a wide variety of human conflicts, the more you know about the diversity of human experience, the better prepared you will be to study law."

Legal studies is a major by itself, and can lead to any number of careers—lawyer, professor, teacher; legal assistant, paralegal, librarian, mediator, arbitrator; a job in the courts, or in other areas of government or politics; police or corrections work; business.

Is legal studies the right field for you? Students who gravitate toward the program tend to have leadership potential; analytical, problem-solving, and quantitative skills; a talent for persuasion or counseling; a powerful memory; research abilities; and a gift for communicating. Interests often include history, current events, politics, debating, student government, community service, and social justice.

"Legal studies is a fascinating field because...virtually every aspect of our lives is touched in some way by the law, and a knowledge and awareness of the legal system is beneficial regardless of the career path a student might take," says Jeffrey J. Davis, assistant professor of political science at the University of Maryland.

The Paper Chase

To find legal studies majors, look at a college's school of government or political science, or sociology department. For paralegal studies, check out colleges of arts and science or business and management.

Programs differ. Those geared toward training students to become paralegal and legal assistants offer more practice- and skills-oriented courses than programs that prepare you for law school, other graduate school, or for careers in government or business. Ask yourself if you're more likely to succeed in rigorous academic and theoretical courses or in hands-on training for law-related work. If you're considering a paralegal or legal assistant program, see if it's approved by the American Bar Association. Whether it's a two-year or four-year paralegal or legal assistant program, expect to study areas and foundations of the law in a very demanding environment requiring loads of reading and writing.

You may be bound for law school or for a legal career straight out of college. In either case, be sure to research the institution. Do your due diligence. Find out if the college's faculty members or advisers have law degrees themselves. Have they actually practiced law? Does the college arrange for graduates to have internships with attorneys and/or judges? Are participatory activities available, such as mock trial, moot court, or debate team?

For prelaw programs, it's a good idea to register with a prelaw adviser as early as possible in your college career, to get on track academically. Your adviser can also help you explore the different legal specialities and work environments. (A few examples: litigating criminal cases in court, doing corporate law at a big firm, devoting yourself to government service.) Ask what percentage of students who see an adviser gain admission to one or more law schools. See whether advisers will help you after you graduate. Is an LSAT prep course offered? Does the school have a network of attorney-alumni that undergraduates can contact? (Note that some institutions compress B.A. and J.D. curriculums into a joint six-year program.)

While there will always be a need for lawyers, competition for openings is keen because of the large number of students graduating from law school each year (over 43,000 in 2009). For paralegals and legal assistants, job opportunities are projected to grow rapidly as employers try to reduce costs by hiring paralegals to perform tasks formerly done by lawyers.

For more information, go to the American Bar Association (www. abanet.org). Who knows? You may become a member of that organization one day.

Legal studies

What it's about:

This major examines the law and legal issues from the perspectives of the social sciences and the humanities. Taking a theoretical rather than a practical approach, students explore the origins, evolution, function, and effects of the law as a social phenomenon. Legal studies is not a prelaw program, and this major will not qualify you to take the bar examination or to work as a lawyer. If your goal is to become an attorney, you must attend law school after college.

Is this for you?

You might like this major if you also like: history; philosophy; current events; politics; debating; student government; community service activities; issues relating to social justice; reading and writing.

Consider this major if you are good at: attention to detail; counseling; creativity; critical reading/thinking; leadership; persuading/influencing; research ...*or have...* initiative; verbal skills; writing skills.

Recommended high school prep:

English 4, math 3, lab science 2, social studies 4, and a foreign language 3–4. Other recommended courses include business law, philosophy, sociology, psychology, statistics, and comparative government and politics.

Did you know...

...that while legal studies is a good prelaw major, it won't increase your chances of getting into law school? Law schools don't favor any specific college major.

...that combining a science or technology major with a major or minor in legal studies is a good marriage for the career-minded? The areas are increasingly intertwined, in both law and business.

Typical courses in this major:

American politics and government
Philosophy of law
Civil rights and liberties
Legal and judicial process
Legal reasoning
Constitutional law
Law, crime, and social justice
International law
Comparative law
Business law
Legal history
Environmental law
Law and literature
Legal ethics
Legal research and writing
Women and the law

Concentrations:

Criminal justice; government and politics; international and comparative law; business and commercial law

What the study of this major is like:

Shortly after the September 11, 2001, terrorist attacks, President George W. Bush signed the Patriot Act. This law made it easier for the government to guard against terrorist activity by allowing such tactics as searches without notice. But many people believe that the measure endangers the civil rights and civil liberties of both citizens and immigrants.

Does it make sense to trade in some civil rights for greater protection against terrorism? Will the government's greater access to our private lives make us safer? As a legal studies major, you'll take an in-depth look at these and other important issues.

While legal studies is not a prelaw program, it is a good major for prelaw students because it will help you to develop your ability to think clearly and to analyze arguments critically. It is also an excellent major if you are leaning toward a career in public service or planning to study business or the social sciences in grad school.

The major is academically rigorous. It requires excellent reading comprehension skills and sharp analytical ability. Reading and writing assignments can be substantial. You should be ready to engage in intense discussion of thorny legal problems, study actual court cases, do computer research using legal databases, and write a senior thesis.

Course work, which is usually interdisciplinary, focuses on the legal process, legal institutions, and how they operate in society. For example, you might examine crime and punishment from the viewpoint of psychology, philosophy, and anthropology, or use legal doctrines to study international business models in a globalized economy. A course in comparative law will expose you to systems that differ from those in the United States, such as European civil law or Islamic Sharia. Legal studies is based on the idea that an understanding of the foundations of law and justice requires the application of a broad range of academic disciplines, as well as a critical analysis of human behavior and institutions.

In most programs you will have a chance to participate in moot courts (arguing an artificial appeal), mock trials (playing a role in an artificial trial) and to serve internships with judges, private lawyers, prosecutors, defense attorneys, or in government offices. This aspect of the major can give you a close perspective on a legal career prior to deciding on law school.

At some colleges this major emphasizes training for the paralegal and legal assistant professions. These programs, which may be available at the two-year, or associate degree, level, often provide practice-oriented courses in specific areas of law, such as real estate or contracts. Generally, four-year colleges that house the major prepare students for law school, for graduate school, or for careers in government and business. These programs offer courses in a variety of disciplines, and are usually more rigorous academically and more theoretical.

Other majors you might like:
Political science
Criminology

Sociology
History
Public policy analysis
Environmental studies
International relations
Labor studies
Behavioral sciences
Peace studies
Criminal justice and law enforcement
Public administration

Questions to ask colleges:
Do any of the faculty members have law degrees, and have they actually practiced law?

Does the school assist with internships with lawyers and/or judges in the area?

Is there a mock trial, moot court, or debate team?

Is there an active legal studies club?

Career options and trends:
Lawyer*; government official*; paralegal; public interest advocate; business executive; law enforcement officer; journalist.

To practice law, you must go to law school, pass a bar exam, and be certified by the bar of the state in which you will practice.

As a liberal arts program, legal studies can prepare you for a variety of careers in business and public service, as well as in the law. The major will also qualify you to apply to graduate school in the humanities and social sciences, or to professional school in teaching, public policy, business and health administration, and social work.

For more info:
American Bar Association
321 N. Clark St.
Chicago, IL 60610
(800) 285-2221
www.abanet.org

Paralegal studies

What it's about:

This major prepares you to conduct legal research; draft legal documents; and perform investigatory, record-keeping, and other administrative duties under the supervision of an attorney or a court officer. Paralegal education is not the equivalent of law school training and does not qualify you for, or make you eligible to take, a bar examination.

Is this for you?

You might like this major if you also like: public speaking; Mock Trial competitions; debate; student government; politics; public service; reading; research; social justice issues.

Consider this major if you are good at: attention to detail; critical reading/thinking; leadership; organizing; research; teamwork *...or have...* initiative; patience; verbal skills; writing skills.

Recommended high school prep:

English 4, math 3, lab science 3, social studies 3, and a foreign language 2–3. If possible, take an introductory law or political science course.

Did you know...

...that the paralegal profession is one of the five fastest growing career fields in the United States? Today, paralegals perform much of the work that was once done by lawyers. As a result, paralegals have a great deal of responsibility and play an essential role in providing legal services to the public. Some paralegals even represent clients before local, state, and national administrative agencies.

Typical courses in this major:

Litigation/civil procedure
Criminal law and procedure
Computerized research
Legal writing
Real estate law
Business law
Wills, trusts, and probate law
Family law
Immigration law
Intellectual property law
Evidence
Ethics
Personal injury/tort law
Environmental law
Alternative dispute resolution
Elder law

Concentrations:

Generally, none available.

What the study of this major is like:

As a paralegal studies major, you learn practical, job-related skills along with the underlying legal theory. You study substantive law (the particular disciplines, or areas, you can practice) and procedural law (how you practice—such as rules of evidence and pre-trial paper work). Legal research and writing are essential parts of the curriculum and often are the most challenging elements for students. Your course work also stresses communication skills (oral, nonverbal, and interpersonal), computational and organizational skills, an ability to think critically, and an appreciation of legal ethics. You use computer-based resources to help you with your work.

You are encouraged to learn through hands-on work; therefore, internships, practicums, or clinical experience are highly recommended and sometimes required. Internships and similar experiences give you the chance to obtain firsthand knowledge about the practice of law and may even lead to a full-time position after graduation. Most paralegal programs have active student organizations, which build camaraderie among participants by organizing law-related events on or near the campus.

This major is offered at two-year, community and junior colleges; four-year colleges; and business and proprietary schools devoted solely to providing this training. Because there is no uniformly accepted educational standard for entry into the paralegal field, content, length, and admissions requirements vary among colleges.

The American Bar Association approves paralegal education programs that meet its guidelines. Although seeking ABA approval is voluntary on the part of the college, the bar association's standards are rigorous and, therefore, helpful in evaluating a program. However, there are some quality programs that have chosen not to seek ABA approval. A complete listing of paralegal education programs approved by the ABA is found on its Web site (www.abanet.org). Additionally, the American Association for Paralegal Education (AAPE) has a set of minimum program requirements that must be adhered to by member institutions and can be found on the AAPE website.

When deciding among programs, you may also want to consider local or regional standards, particularly with regard to future job opportunities. Check with your local or regional paralegal associations for additional information about educational standards for paralegals in your area.

Other majors you might like:
Criminal justice and law enforcement
Political science
Sociology
Office management
Physician assistant
Technical and business writing
Real estate
Social work
Insurance
Criminology
Legal studies
Labor studies

Questions to ask colleges:
Is the paralegal studies program approved by the American Bar Association? Is the institution a member of the American Association for Paralegal Education and therefore guided by its requirements?

Are faculty members practicing attorneys and/or paralegals?

Do students have access to the resources they need to do legal research (such as a law library)?

Are students taught how to use computerized legal research systems (WESTLAW or Lexis-Nexis)?

Career options and trends:
The Bureau of Labor Statistics projects strong growth in this field. Graduates also pursue careers as private investigators, law librarians, human resources personnel, court personnel, mediators, arbitrators, special advocates, estate and trust officers, real estate professionals, insurance agents, risk managers, contract managers, legal administrators, corporate compliance officers, and government workers.

Although there is no mandatory certification of paralegals, voluntary certification is sponsored by the two paralegal professional associations. The National Association of Legal Assistants sponsors a national certification exam, several state-specific exams, and certification for specialty areas of law. The National Federation of Paralegal Associations offers the Paralegal Advanced Competency Examination (PACE).

Many states, through the legislature, court system, or bar association, have issued ethics opinions dealing with a paralegal's use of title, the scope of duties, the unauthorized practice of law, and how clients may be billed for paralegal services. You should examine and review these opinions prior to obtaining employment as a paralegal.

For more info:
National Association of Legal Assistants (NALA)
1516 South Boston Ave., Suite 200
Tulsa, OK 74119
(918) 587-6828
www.nala.org

American Association for Paralegal Education (AAfPE)
19 Mantua Road
Mt. Royal, NJ 08061
(856) 423-2829
www.aafpe.org

Prelaw

What it's about:

Prelaw is not a major or a prescribed course of study, and it is not a requirement for law school. Rather, it is an advising program designed to help you prepare for law school while in college, explore future legal careers, and manage the law school application process. You must obtain a bachelor's degree to apply to law school, but you can major in anything you want.

Is this for you?

You might like this major if you also like: history; philosophy; current events; politics; debating; student government; community service activities; social justice issues; problem solving; reading and writing. The law plays a role in almost every field—from sports to music to banking—and many potential law students have a wide variety of hobbies and interests.

Consider this major if you are good at: attention to detail; critical reading/thinking; leadership; organizing; persuading/influencing; research *...or have...* initiative; intellectual curiousity; verbal skills; writing skills.

Recommended high school prep:

English 4, math 3, lab science 2, social studies 4 (including economics and government, if available), and a foreign language 3-4. Other recommended courses include philosophy, sociology, psychology, statistics, and speech.

Did you know...

...that only one-third of law school applicants come directly from college? Many law schools like to see applicants that have gained some work experience after college.

Typical courses in this major:

Principles of economics
English composition
U.S. history to 1865
U.S. history from 1865 to present
Western philosophy
Introduction to psychology
Ethics
Logic
Social anthropology
Law and literature
American government and politics
Scientific methods
Computer science
English literature
Principles of accounting
Expository writing

Concentrations:

Generally, none available.

What the study of this major is like:

Because "prelaw" is not a major but an advising program, there are no admission requirements—just register with the prelaw adviser as early as you can. You will still have to pick a college major before the end of your second year.

While many prelaw students choose majors that are considered traditional preparation for law school, such as English, history, political science, legal studies, economics, or business, none of these disciplines are preferred by law schools. You can major in art, music, math, computer science, a foreign language—anything that will lead to a bachelor's degree. What matters is that you take courses that will help you develop the skills law schools are looking for and that will help you do well on the Law School Admission Test (LSAT).

Just what are those skills? According to the American Bar Association (ABA), a likely candidate for law school is good at critical thinking and reading; writing, speaking, and listening; research; and task management and organization. Law schools also look for applicants who value service and justice and who have an understanding of the historical, cultural, and political influences on society; of human behavior and sociology; and of basic math and science.

Your prelaw adviser will assist you in selecting courses and extracurricular activities that can give you the grounding you need. A useful approach is to choose challenging courses from demanding professors. Get as much practice as you can in critical thinking and writing. Seek out courses in which you will be expected to write several papers and will receive detailed feedback. Literature courses offer practice in close reading, and a course in logic is often recommended for reasoning and analysis.

If you like math or science, you might want to consider a major in one of those areas. Scientific or technical knowledge can make you marketable in specialized fields such as patent law or environmental law.

In evaluating an applicant's extracurricular activities or internships, law school admissions committees are flexible. Still, they favor activities that indicate a candidate's sense of service and justice and that helps reveal his or her interests and experiences. While a law-related internship will not give you an edge, it is an excellent way to see what lawyers do and to determine if their work is what you would enjoy doing.

If you choose prelaw, be prepared to take your college work seriously. Admission to law school is competitive, so aim for an above-average GPA—3.5 and higher is preferable, although 3.0 to 3.5 is still acceptable, if coupled with a good LSAT score. Other factors such as letters of recommendation and extracurricular activities are relatively minor compared with the GPA and the LSAT score. The higher these numbers are, the more options you will have when choosing law schools.

But don't worry about law school right now. Enjoy college, and be open to the ideas and options you will discover there. There will be plenty of time to focus on a legal career later. Major in what interests you—you will do better in classes that excite and challenge you.

Other majors you might like:

Accounting
English
Journalism
Environmental studies
Women's studies
Liberal arts and sciences
Peace and conflict studies
Philosophy
Criminal justice and law enforcement
Political science
Real estate
History

Questions to ask colleges:

How much individual attention is the prelaw adviser able to give each student? What kinds of services are offered?

What kind of resources does the school offer to students seeking law-related internships?

Does the school have a network of attorneys who graduated from the college that undergraduates can contact?

Do you offer LSAT preparation courses?

Career options and trends:

Private practice lawyer*; government attorney*; corporate attorney*; paralegal; legislative aid; journalist; business executive; public interest lawyer; public official; legal editor.

Prelaw advising helps prepare the student for law school, not for a career. To become a practicing attorney, you must obtain a J.D. degree from a law school, pass a state bar exam, and be admitted to the bar in a specific jurisdiction (state or federal). But there are many law-related careers that do not require admission to the bar.

There will always be a need for lawyers, regardless of how business is doing. The general economy often has an impact on first-year attorneys' salaries but not on job availability overall. Certain areas of practice, such as real estate, are more likely than others to be affected by economic cycles.

Mathematics

Is the probability high that you will study mathematics? If so, you may be interested to know that the number of students getting bachelor's degrees in math continues to decline. But the silver lining may be that by studying math, you can rise above other students and job seekers.

"There is a steady, strong demand for math majors," says Professor David M. Bressoud of Macalester College. "Many employers (as well as graduate schools in professions such as law and medicine) will give preferential treatment to graduates with a degree in math."

Then why don't more students major in math? The work is intense. But students don't realize it's also very creative.

"Mathematics is not just learning a bunch of formulas," says Professor James Alexander of Case Western Reserve University. "Mathematics ranges from the purely theoretical studies to highly integrated with engineering and the physical and social sciences; and many majors, including applied mathematics, are available."

Professor Bressoud points out, "Mathematics is about understanding basic, abstract structures to discover progressively deeper and more refined patterns that give profound insights into the workings of the world around us."

And don't forget statistics. Virginia Tech's Michele Marini calls statistics "an undiscovered gem of a major."

As a likely math student, you'll choose from many colleges offering mathematics, applied mathematics, statistics, and related programs. Look for these majors in colleges, divisions, or schools of sciences, mathematical sciences, physical sciences, engineering, arts and sciences, and humanities.

You'll want a college that shares your interests. For instance, some colleges put more emphasis on applied mathematics to prepare you for the workplace, while other programs stress advanced topics in analysis, algebra, geometry, and related areas—rigorous preparation for grad school. Graduate tracks include statistics, applied mathematics, computational mathematics, algebra, number theory, analysis, logic, geometry, and topology (the bending and stretching of geometric forms). Other advanced studies cover computing/ information science, operations research, and control theory; or industrial statistics, environmental statistics, and bioinformatics (computerized health and medical stats).

When comparing colleges, ask if computers are used in the classroom or if it's mostly "chalk and talk," as instructors like to call their lectures. Is statistics required for nonstatistics majors? How often are key courses like modern algebra taught? Do students enter math competitions? Or help the faculty members with research? Have any students been published as co-writers? What kind of capstone or senior project is required?

Also ask how many students go on to graduate school. How successful are students at getting jobs after graduation? What kinds of jobs are they getting?

Career permutations and combinations

You'll find that the job outlook is good for students with a math education.

"The study of mathematics is excellent preparation for a host of employment opportunities in business, finance, insurance, communications, electronics, scientific research of any type, and any field that has challenging problems to solve," Bressoud says. "Mathematics lies behind the models of the physical world that are used in predicting weather or in understanding subatomic particles. It lies at the root of economics as well as ecology. It provides the tools for analyzing medical, sociological, or psychological research. It explains electricity and magnetism, radio waves, and quantum tunneling, as well as the hidden patterns of business cycles."

If you major in applied math, you'll be preparing for a career in which you use your math skills in a particular industry or for a particular purpose.

"The Bachelor of Science degree in applied mathematics includes a solid foundation in mathematics as well as a professional core that is specific to computing and information science, operations research, systems engineering, control theory, and statistics," explains Alexander.

If you're going for applied math, see if you can shave college time through a five-year integrated program leading to a Bachelor of Science degree in math and a master's degree in your specialty.

Your math and statistics skills can be used in almost any type of business or research effort.

"I can work on a psychological problem one week, work on U.S. census data the next, and then work on health issues," says Marini.

"The importance of a math background is the ability to think abstractly and conceptually. This is especially important because technology changes rapidly and more specialized skills are likely to be outmoded soon," Alexander notes.

Careers in math include all sorts—engineering, business, and management consulting; high school or college teaching; working for a government agency; as a financial analyst; or as an actuary in the insurance industry. An advanced degree is an enhancement in nearly all math work.

For more information, visit the Mathematical Association of America (www.maa.org), the American Mathematical Society (www.ams.org), the American Statistical Association (www.amstat.org), and the Society for Industrial and Applied Mathematics (www.siam.org).

In this book, see also the sections on Computer and information sciences, Engineering, and Multi/interdisciplinary studies.

Applied mathematics

What it's about:

In the applied mathematics major, you receive a solid grounding in mathematics as well as professional training in your chosen area of application. Possible application areas are computing and information science, operations research, systems engineering, control theory, and statistics.

Is this for you?

You might like this major if you also like: seeing how math explains natural phenomena; understanding the theory behind the way computers and other mechanical things work.

Consider this major if you are good at: attention to detail; creativity; critical reading/thinking; math; organizing; quantitative analysis; teamwork ...*or have...* initiative; patience; writing skills.

Recommended high school prep:

English 4, math 4, lab science 3, social studies 3, and a foreign language 2-3. Try to take as many mathematics classes as possible. Also, if available, take courses in computer programming and statistics.

Did you know...

...that you can become an applied mathematics major if you have an interest in math and in an application such as engineering—you don't necessarily have to decide between your two interests?

Typical courses in this major:

Calculus
Differential equations
Linear algebra
Discrete mathematics
Numerical analysis
Physics
Computer science
Probability theory
Logic design and computer architecture
Systems design
Signals, systems, and control engineering
Optimization theory and technique
Data analysis and linear models
Multivariate analysis and data mining
Theoretical statistics
Time series

Concentrations:

In college: computing/information science; systems engineering; statistics.

If you go on to grad school: operations research; control theory.

What the study of this major is like:

As an applied mathematics major, you have two homes. You spend plenty of time studying math—in your third and fourth year, you will most likely take at least two math courses per semester. In addition, you'll enroll in classes in the application area you choose. By searching for connections between math and its applications, you combine knowledge from your two bases. In a kind of conceptual loop, you apply abstract principles of math to your area of interest, and then translate functions of that application back into more general mathematics. For example, in a control theory course, you learn how to construct a feedback mechanism, such as a robot. In a math course, you explore the math behind the mechanism. Your task is to discover the link between what you've learned in the two courses.

The material in math courses and in many applications courses is presented in lecture formats. You are expected to spend considerable time outside class getting comfortable with the material. Some applications courses may involve laboratories or computer programming.

Although a Bachelor of Science degree prepares you to start a career, many professionals return for more specialized training by pursuing a master's degree. Some colleges offer a five-year integrated program leading to a Bachelor of Science degree in applied mathematics and a Master of Science degree in your chosen application area or in applied mathematics. Colleges may also have different mathematics requirements. No matter which technical field you go into, a strong mathematical background—one that teaches you to think abstractly and conceptually—is essential. Because technology changes so rapidly, specific engineering skills can soon become out-of-date. If you have a good grounding in math, though, you should be able to adapt to advances in technology.

Other majors you might like:

Computer science
Management information systems
Aeronautical/aerospace engineering
Statistics
Systems engineering
Management science
Astrophysics
Applied physics
Mathematics/computer science
Computational mathematics
Information systems
Economics

Questions to ask colleges:

How are the different majors offered in the math department distinguished? Do they contain distinctly different content?

How well do relevant departments (such as physics and engineering) cooperate? Are there adequate facilities, particularly in the applications areas, for course work and research?

How easy is it to switch majors? You'll be introduced to many exciting disciplines during your course work, which may spark new interests.

Career options and trends:

Engineer*; statistician*; actuary; management consultant; financial mathematical analyst.

Demand is always strong for people who are strong in math. Traditionally, jobs requiring a math background have been found primarily in the technical and engineering fields; but going forward the best career prospects are for those who can apply math to the life and medical sciences.

Insider's viewpoint:

"As a mathematician, I'm excited about being able to bring my knowledge to bear on other areas of knowledge. I love having problems brought to me by researchers from a wide variety of disciplines, from science and engineering to social science and medicine."

—Professor James Alexander, Case Western Reserve University

For more info:

Society for Industrial and Applied Mathematics (SIAM)
3600 Market St., 6th Floor
Philadelphia, PA 19104-2688
(215) 382-9800
www.siam.org

Mathematical Association of America (MAA)
1529 18th St., N.W.
Washington, DC 20036
(800) 741-9415
www.maa.org

Mathematics

What it's about:

Math majors develop the ability to explore, conjecture, and reason logically, as well as to use mathematical methods to solve problems. Mathematics is both a discipline and a tool used extensively in the sciences, medicine, engineering, and industry.

Is this for you?

You might like this major if you also like: music, especially composition; art, especially as it relates to shape, balance, and design; playing with abstractions; intellectual challenges; solving puzzles; philosophy; writing that is succinct and precise.

Consider this major if you are good at: attention to detail; creativity; critical reading/thinking; math; organizing; quantitative analysis; spacial thinking/analysis ...*or have...* initiative; patience.

Recommended high school prep:

English 4, math 4 (including precalculus and trigonometry), lab science 4 (including physics), social studies 3, and a foreign language 2–3. Calculus and statistics would be helpful, but are not required.

Did you know...

...that high-level math is not about memorizing procedures? It is about understanding basic, abstract structures to discover deeper, more refined patterns that give insights into the workings of the world around us. Like music, math is the creative exploration of possibilities within prescribed rules and parameters.

Typical courses in this major:

Single-variable calculus
Multivariable calculus
Elementary statistics
Discrete mathematics
Linear algebra
Differential equations
Modern algebra
Modeling
Combinatorics
Number theory
Modern geometry
Topology
Complex analysis
Real analysis

Concentrations:

In college: statistics; applied mathematics; discrete mathematics; computational mathematics.

If you go on to grad school: number theory; functional analysis; geometric analysis; topology; logic.

What the study of this major is like:

Mathematics deals with how basic patterns and processes can be turned into abstract representations. As a math major, you work with increasingly abstract concepts in analytic, algebraic, and geometric math.

Analysis (the mathematics of dynamic change) begins with calculus. Calculus was developed in the seventeenth century to analyze changes in physical quantities—for example, the minimum distance between two planets or the maximum profit of a business enterprise. Through calculus, you can determine the lengths of curves and the volumes of solids, or investigate the acceleration of moving objects. Analysis continues with differential equations, in which you use the knowledge of the way things interact to predict their future state. Real analysis, complex analysis, and functional analysis provide tools that deal with unexpected phenomena.

Modern algebra involves integers, counting problems, and symmetries. It begins with linear algebra (probably the most useful undergrad course) and continues with combinatorics and number theory. You also study structures known as groups, rings, and fields, in order to explore such questions as "is pi rational?"

Discrete mathematics and combinatorics consider the finite nature of certain problems—for instance, in how many ways can a fixed number of vehicles visit multiple locations, and which schedule would be the least costly? Modern geometry and topology study the world of transformations and explore the deeper meaning of concepts such as shape, area, and distance.

Traditionally, math has been taught entirely through lectures, but this approach is changing. Many math courses now make use of computers; you do projects that help you explore a topic in depth; and in written assignments, you clarify difficult concepts. In addition, lectures themselves have changed. Today, many professors understand the importance of describing how particular mathematical concepts came about and of showing how mathematical insights can be applied outside the classroom.

Majoring in mathematics can be an intense experience. There are always new ideas to be mastered. Learning how to rely on precise definition, how to tackle an unfamiliar problem, and how to construct a proof is sometimes difficult. Many math majors find it helpful to form supportive study groups, in which participants share their struggles and insights. Activities such as annual CO-MAP modeling competitions are built on teamwork; good mathematics programs build strong camaraderie among majors.

Some colleges emphasize applied math or allow you to take an applied mathematics track. These programs typically replace advanced courses in analysis, algebra, and geometry with advanced work in statistics, operations research, and modeling. It is usually a less intense major that can be excellent preparation for the workplace.

Other majors you might like:
Engineering
Economics
Physics
Computer science
Accounting
Finance
Business statistics
Actuarial science

Mathematics teacher education
Information systems
Music theory and composition
Philosophy

Questions to ask colleges:
How does the program incorporate computers into math classes? Is there an emphasis on writing?

In which competitions do math students participate?

Do any of the faculty members use students to help with their research? Have any instructors published a joint paper with a student?

Is a capstone project or fourth-year thesis required?

Career options and trends:
Operations researcher*; business consultant; high school teacher*; statistician*; financial or securities analyst; college professor; actuary.

There is a steady, strong demand for math majors. Many employers (as well as graduate schools in professions such as law and medicine) will give preferential treatment to graduates with a degree in math. The study of mathematics is excellent preparation for a host of employment opportunities in business, finance, insurance, communications, electronics, scientific research of any type, and any field that has challenging problems to solve.

Insider's viewpoint:
"Be careful; it's a difficult field. All the classes I'd ever taken before were 'standard' math, very real-world-based math, application-based math, which is a far cry from the abstract reality of a math major's world."

—John, sophomore, Case Western Reserve University

For more info:
The Mathematical Association of America (MAA)
1529 18th St., N.W.
Washington, DC 20036
(800) 741-9415
www.maa.org

Statistics

What it's about:
Statistics is the practical science of dealing with data—information in the form of numbers, often from many sources. In this major, you study the most efficient ways to collect data and to analyze and interpret it. Statistics, which forms the backbone of all research methods, includes the study of experimental design, regression analysis (the relationships between measurements), probability, and sampling theory.

Is this for you?
You might like this major if you also like: math; quantitative problems; figuring out how things work and how to make them work better; dealing with numbers; puzzles.

Consider this major if you are good at: active listening; attention to detail; critical reading/thinking; math; quantitative analysis; research; teamwork ...*or have...* patience; writing skills.

Recommended high school prep:
English 4, math 4 (including calculus), lab science 3, social studies 3, and a foreign language 2–3. If possible, take statistics.

Did you know...
...that statistics includes much more than just tallying batting averages or shooting percentages? Using statistics, you can perform a wide range of tasks, such as deciding which people should fill out a certain survey or ensuring that a medication up for approval works better than medicines currently on the market.

...that statisticians are in high demand and are often well paid? Think of an area of study that interests you. You can usually find statisticians giving work-related advice to professionals in that field.

Typical courses in this major:
Statistical methods I, II
Statistical theory I, II
Experimental design and analysis of variance
Regression analysis
Statistical computing
Sample survey theory
Applied time series analysis
Technical writing
Probability
Statistical quality control
Calculus

Concentrations:
In college: actuarial science.

If you go on to grad school: industrial statistics; environmental statistics; bioinformatics.

What the study of this major is like:
Statistics is the science of handling data in the most effective way. It's not just a branch of mathematics, but a separate discipline that uses a great deal of math and relies heavily on computers. Most statistics departments are in colleges of liberal arts and sciences, but several are in business colleges and a few are in colleges of engineering or agriculture. Combined departments of mathematics and statistics also exist, primarily in small- to medium-size institutions.

If you want to complete an undergraduate degree (B.S.) in statistics, be prepared to take a fairly vigorous math curriculum. In your first year, you concentrate on general courses and mathematics, including a year of calculus. Introductory courses in statistics and computers most often begin in the second year, after you have developed sufficient math skills. In your third year, statistics becomes the dominant part of your studies.

Courses in the applied techniques of describing and analyzing data to extract information require strong skills in algebra and computing. For courses focusing on probability and the mathematical theory of statistics, you'll need to sharpen your abilities in calculus and in logic. In courses that deal with the preparation of sample surveys, small groups of students design a study, collect and analyze the data, and present a report of the results. If you plan on going to graduate school, you should study advanced calculus.

To be a successful statistician, you must understand both the theory and the application of statistics. In an important application, statisticians routinely advise scientists and researchers in business, government, nonprofit organizations, and industry on how to handle data in a wide variety of projects. The work that statisticians do demands not only mathematical tools but also communication, teamwork, and technical writing skills, as well as familiarity with the concepts and terminology of the business or organization they're assisting. In fact, statisticians must rely on the business executives or professionals in these organizations to supply the data they'll be examining. Therefore, courses in the natural sciences, humanities, and social sciences are essential. You are strongly encouraged to strengthen your oral and written communication skills by taking writing and speech courses or participating in related extracurricular activities.

Statistics programs that emphasize actuarial science tend to focus on preparing you for actuarial exams. Other programs concentrate on a particular discipline. For example, biostatistics is more likely to be taught in a college that has a medical education program. In still other programs, geared to preparing students to pursue advanced degrees, the math curriculum is usually much more rigorous.

Other majors you might like:

Accounting
Information systems
Genetics
Economics
Systems science/theory
Econometrics/quantitative economics
Computational mathematics
Actuarial science
Applied mathematics
Systems engineering
Operations research
Business statistics

Career options and trends:

Actuary; data analyst*; statistician*; statistical analyst*; statistical programmer; professor*; project statistician.

The Bureau of Labor Statistics projects employment opporunities for those skilled in statistics to grow through 2018. Statisticians work in a wide variety of areas, including manufacturing, pharmaceuticals, insurance, government agencies, consulting firms, and agricultural research. Statistics majors also find jobs in actuarial science, statistical programming, operations research, and mathematical analysis. A graduate degree can increase your career opportunities.

Most high school students haven't heard of statistics and thus don't consider it as a major; this situation seems unlikely to change. Therefore, there are always more jobs available than there are college graduates to fill the positions.

Insider's viewpoint:

"I can work on a psychological problem one week, work on U.S. census data the next, and then work on health issues in an animal species. I have the constant opportunity to learn new things about subjects that I have no formal education in."

—Michele Marini, Instructor, Virginia Tech

For more info:

American Statistical Association (ASA)
732 North Washington St.
Alexandria, VA 22314-1943
(888) 231-3473
www.amstat.org

Multi/interdisciplinary studies

If you've ever written a college application essay, you've probably tried to tap your knowledge and experience in many areas in order to answer an interesting or important question. That's what multi/interdisciplinary studies are like. These majors take more than one path of learning to arrive at understanding.

The world is not just black and white. To get the flavor of multi/interdisciplinary studies, don't think chocolate or vanilla. Think swirl or twist. By mixing areas of study, we can effectively answer questions like these: Why do we think and behave the way we do? How does the mind relate to the body? Can we ever live in peace? If you want that broad perspective, you need to study the finer points of more than one subject. Each of these majors covers many topics and the majors are very different from one another. In this chapter you'll flash back to the fall of Rome and glimpse the future frontiers of science.

Multi/interdisciplinary fields include Medieval and Renaissance studies, neuroscience, gerontology, global studies, and peace studies. Gerontology, for example, looks at aging from many angles—biological, behavioral, and social.

"Almost every aspect of the human aging process impacts on most academic disciplines—arts and sciences, business administration, education, government, law, medicine, mental health, nursing, public health, public relations, and communication," says Professor Joseph F. Cimini, University of Scranton.

Global studies also casts a wide net. "The global studies major is based on new approaches to knowledge and combining political economy and cultural studies with comparative regional studies," explains Professor Eve Walsh Stoddard of St. Lawrence University. "It emphasizes the interconnections and interactions, as opposed to studying discrete, separate topics."

The same goes for neuroscience, which combines studies of the nervous system and behavior. Neuroscience is found within other sciences such as biology, chemistry, physics, and psychology, but also in mathematics, computer science, philosophy, economics, and cognitive science. "Neuroscience has a huge impact in many areas of science and beyond," says Professor Richard Lewis, Pomona College.

A glimpse at graduate studies in just three majors suggests how relevant multi/interdisciplinary studies can be. In gerontology, graduate tracks include elder law, geriatric nursing, personal care/assisted living, and retirement planning. In global studies, graduates might specialize in peace and conflict studies, international relations, or environmental issues. In neuroscience, graduate studies include behavioral or cognitive functions of the nervous system.

No easy questions

You can probably picture the reaction at the Thanksgiving table when you come home from college and tell everyone you're considering a multi/interdisciplinary major. "Huh?" they may ask. If that happens, calmly explain the importance of knowing about more than one thing—and that these majors combine various in-depth studies to meet a new need, like caring for a growing population of old people, or understanding a complex problem like war.

At that point, the focus should shift to the turkey. But if anyone's still listening, tell them how you carefully chose your college and your major.

Why would you choose an interdisciplinary major? Maybe you enjoy making connections between cultures or exploring the unknown. Perhaps you have good interpersonal skills, like to solve problems, are socially or politically active, or love to volunteer. Those are the types of students who are interested in these majors.

To pinpoint your multidisciplinary or interdisciplinary major requires a lot of legwork. You'll need to find out as much as you can about the major and how it fits into the college's courses. What is the history of the major at the college? What is the expertise of the faculty members? Is your major supported by related activities, speakers, or conferences? What exactly will your degree be in? Can you declare a double major, a minor, or a concentration in another subject? How about an independent study or self-guided learning in something that you're passionate about? What are graduates doing—going to professional or grad school, teaching, or pursuing business careers? What opportunities exist for off-campus and experiential study?

Just as there are no easy answers when you study these diverse fields, there are no easy questions when looking at colleges that offer them. You'll need to know if study abroad is required. If so, what are the costs and are they greater than studying on campus? Can your financial aid be applied toward study abroad? In a major that fuses two or more fields, is one stressed more than the other? Which department is the major under? Does the college offer career help, field experience, research opportunities, or a mentoring program to get real-world skills or find a job?

Students interested in these combined majors should look for colleges of arts and sciences, liberal arts, social sciences, or professional studies; schools of humanities; and divisions of interdisciplinary majors or life sciences. In this book, also read the sections on Area, ethnic, and gender studies; the Humanities; and the Social sciences.

Gerontology

Also known as:
Elder studies

What it's about:
Gerontology majors study the processes of aging and the resulting biological, behavioral, and social changes that affect older people's lives. The practical application of gerontology involves providing services to older adults and their families.

Is this for you?
You might like this major if you also like: helping people; community service activities; family relationships; interacting with older adults.

Consider this major if you are good at: caring/nurturing; counseling; creativity; critical reading/thinking; organizing *...or have...* a sense of justice; initiative; interpersonal skills; patience; verbal skills; writing skills.

Recommended high school prep:
English 4, math 3, lab science 3, social studies 3, and a foreign language 2–3. If possible, take a service-learning class—one that combines community service experience with learning.

Did you know...
...that according to estimates, by the year 2030 there will be about 72 million older persons in the United States, more than twice as many as there were in 1997?

Typical courses in this major:
Social problems of aging
Aging around the world
Aging and the life cycle
Aging and human behavior
Aging and the community
Health and aging
Crime and aging
Social policy and aging
Aging and death
Special topics in gerontology
Psychology of aging
Housing needs of older adults
Physical activity programs
Services for older adults
Food for the elderly

Concentrations:
In college: health care; human services; long-term-care administration; social work.

If you go on to grad school: elder law; community advocacy; estate and financial planning; geriatric nursing; human development; nursing home administration; personal care/assisted living; recreation/leisure; retirement planning.

What the study of this major is like:
The gerontology major prepares you to understand the process of aging and to work for organizations that serve older adults (such as Area Agencies on Aging; family services; long-term-care facilities; federal, state, and local government agencies; retirement communities; and business and industry institutions). If you plan to pursue a career administering or developing programs for a government agency, you should take courses in finance and accounting, and, probably, program planning and evaluation. In addition, oral and written communications skills and computer literacy are essential.

In this major, your course work will include both the liberal arts and preparation for an entry-level practice in human services or advanced work in gerontology/aging studies, social work, public administration, social welfare, or related fields. Your courses in the major are interdisciplinary and cover topics that explore what it is like to grow old, how an individual typically progresses through the life cycle, and what an aging population means to society.

In courses on the aging process, you examine, first, the physical and intellectual changes that occur from middle age to the end of life, including intellectual stability and Alzheimer's disease. Later courses deal with the influence of family and community on older people's quality of life; topics include the changing role that families play, ways in which members of minority and ethnic groups experience aging, and influences of social class on aging. Your third area of study will focus on the laws, programs, and institutions that help or hinder the process of aging in the United States and other countries. You examine programs such as Social Security, Medicare, and Medicaid, and the ways in which government influences private programs through tax incentives and regulation.

Some gerontology programs emphasize research and statistics. Others stress theory. Still others may focus on casework. The traditions of the college, as well as any religious affiliation, will likely determine the orientation of its gerontology program.

The gerontology major is not more, and not less, challenging than most social science programs. The subject matter is generally taught in lecture courses, with opportunities for service learning, internships, special-topic courses, guided independent study, and faculty-student research projects. As a major, you will probably spend substantial time volunteering or interning in both profit-making and not-for-profit agencies that provide services for the elderly in areas like housing, health, mental health, transportation, education, recreation, and social work. For example, you may visit senior citizen centers, volunteer in nursing homes, work part-time in retirement communities, or have field experiences in a government program.

Other majors you might like:

Urban, community, and regional planning
Human development and family studies
Exercise sciences
Health care administration
Human services
Nursing (RN)
Occupational therapy
Physical therapy
Psychology
Social work

Anthropology
Women's studies

Questions to ask colleges:

Are guided independent-study courses, community-service learning experiences, and internships available?

Can students declare double majors, a minor, or a concentration?

What library and electronic media resources support gerontology study?

How successful are graduates of the program in graduate and professional schools, as well as in careers?

Career options and trends:

Research gerontologist; geriatric physician; elder law attorney*; gerontology research assistant; long-term care administrator*; advocate for older adults; long-term care caseworker*; area agency on aging staff member*.

Additional employment possibilities for gerontology graduates include program development positions in recreation, education, and social services; administration of nursing homes, housing projects, and government programs; and service roles in multipurpose senior citizen centers, mental health agencies, and human resources departments of corporations and not-for-profit organizations.

Employment prospects are excellent in this field. An aging population with increasing life spans ensures continued demand for professionals knowledgeable in gerontology and elder care issues.

For more info:

Gerontological Society of America (GSA)
1220 L St., N.W.
Suite 901
Washington, DC 20005
(202) 842-1275
www.geron.org

Association for Gerontology in Higher Education
1220 L St., N.W.
Suite 901
Washington, DC 20005
(202) 289-9806
www.aghe.org

Global studies

What it's about:

Global studies is an interdisciplinary major that combines politics, economics, and cultural studies with comparative regional studies. You learn to view individuals, communities, states, economies, cultures, and ecologies in larger, internationally oriented contexts.

Is this for you?

You might like this major if you also like: current events; politics; international popular culture; world music; other cultures; travel; geography; history; peace and/or social justice movements.

Consider this major if you are good at: creativity; critical reading/thinking; leadership; research; spacial thinking/analysis *...or have...* initiative; verbal skills; writing skills.

Recommended high school prep:

English 4, math 3, lab science 3, social studies 4, and a foreign language 4. If possible, take courses in world history, economics, statistics, and world geography.

Typical courses in this major:

Introduction to global studies
Introduction to international relations
Introduction to anthropology
Modern world history
The international economy
The global environment
Ethnic conflict and nationalism
Comparative education
Topics in world literature
Global women's issues
Global social movements
Global climate change
Cultural geography
Intercultural studies
Regional perspectives

Concentrations:

Peace and conflict studies; international relations; international economics; gender issues; environmental issues; media and communications; specific regions.

What the study of this major is like:

The global studies major can be challenging, because the field is immense and it requires you to think in ways you might not be accustomed to. Your global studies course work combines aspects of history, economics, geography, and culture. As a major, you will move back and forth between two perspectives: the big-picture approach, in which you examine world systems and world history, and the case studies approach, in which you take an in-depth look at specific regions or nations.

Topics you'll consider include mass migrations, the effects of colonialism, and questions of cultural influence—for instance, can globalization be labeled a synonym for Americanization? Your courses will be taught in lecture or discussion format; students usually do research projects on areas they want to pursue. Language study and experiential learning (such as study-abroad) are important. You will also benefit from reading, and watching, the news and checking the Internet for alternative perspectives.

The global studies major may differ from college to college. Some colleges require you to study abroad and to learn the language of your host area; some have a capstone fourth-year independent project; and some allow you to design the focus of your major. Although certain programs have their own core courses and may have dedicated full-time faculty members, programs in other colleges may be a collection of courses from various departments, sometimes coordinated by only one faculty member.

Some colleges offer a broad range of international courses; others have a smaller number, perhaps restricted to fewer regions of the world. In some colleges, the cost of study abroad is the same as on-campus study; in others, you cannot take all your financial aid with you when you study abroad. Also, the types of concentrations offered can vary among colleges.

Other majors you might like:
International business
Peace and conflict studies
Geography
Sociology
Anthropology
Religious studies
Intercultural/diversity studies
International relations
Women's studies
Journalism
Economics
Linguistics

Questions to ask colleges:
What kinds of study-abroad opportunities are offered? For example, a strong global studies program should offer both on-campus studies of, and off-campus opportunities in, the developing countries outside Europe. Also, look for colleges that make it affordable to study abroad.

Does the program cover a range of topics? Most global studies programs include the social science disciplines (sociology, anthropology, politics, history, economics) within an international framework. But does the program also touch on the arts, communications, and ecology and climate?

Career options and trends:
High school teacher*; international NGO (nongovernmental organization) worker*; Peace Corps volunteer; government/State Department worker*.

Global studies majors also go on to work in international business and international banking. A state certificate or license is required for teaching in secondary public schools. Working for the State Department usually requires language proficiency.

As political, social, economic, and environmental concerns continue to bring the world closer to us, job opportunities in the global studies field continue to grow. These days, it is crucial that you strengthen your qualifications by living abroad or learning to speak a second language.

For more info:
Global Studies Association (GSA)
Oxford Brookes University
Headington
Oxford, UK OX3 0BP
+44 (0) 18 65 483 752
www.globalstudiesassociation.org

International Studies Association (ISA)
324 Social Sciences
University of Arizona
Tuscon, AZ 85721
(520) 621-7715
www.isanet.org

Social Science Research Council (SSRC)
One Pierrepont Plaza, 15th Floor
Brooklyn, NY 11201
(212) 377-2700
www.ssrc.org

Historic preservation

What it's about:

Majoring in historic preservation will teach you the theories and practices of preserving historically significant buildings, structures, and landscapes for future generations. You'll study the history of architecture, the principles of conservation and restoration, and the tools and techniques used in documenting, maintaining, and protecting cultural resources.

Is this for you?

You might like this major if you also like: exploring old buildings; antiquing; storytelling; detective work; reading about history and other cultures; travel; photography; visiting museums and historic sites

Consider this major if you are good at: attention to detail; creativity; critical reading/thinking; leadership; research; spacial thinking/analysis; teamwork *...or have...* initiative; verbal skills; writing skills.

Recommended high school prep:

English 4, math 3, lab science 4 (including physics), social studies 4, visual arts 2, and a foreign language 3–4. History courses offer the best preparation for this major. If they are available, courses in art history, photography, drafting/technical drawing, and speech communication are also recommended.

Typical courses in this major:

Foundations of architecture
Architectural history
American architecture
Documentation and recording
History and theory of preservation
Preservation planning and policy
Material resources of preindustrial America
Preservation law and finance
Landscape preservation
Researching historic structures and sites
Technology and materials for building conservation
Designing for an existing context
Exterior and interior rehabilitation
Social and cultural landscapes
Codes and requirements
Site development, interpretation, and management

Concentrations:

Building conservation; landscape preservation; documentation and research; preservation planning; site management

What the study of this major is like:

This major trains students to be the stewards of America's historic buildings, structures, and landscapes. The program, which involves a mix of lectures and hands-on experience, presents the theory and history of preservation and the tools and techniques used in documenting, maintaining, and protecting cultural resources.

You'll learn the nuts and bolts of the profession—investigation of the history of a building using local records and archives, analysis of its construction and style, and examination of physical evidence. By pulling all the information together, you'll be able to determine the significance of the structure. And you'll come to understand how preserving historic buildings and sites provides the community with a renewed appreciation of its heritage.

Your classes will cover a wide range of subjects, such as landscape architecture and urban planning, architectural history, conservation techniques, public relations, as well as land-use, real-estate, and tax policies. Then in individual and group projects, these interrelated topics will be applied to specific buildings, sites, structures, and objects as well as to the community as a whole.

The fieldwork is what distinguishes the historic preservation major. You deal directly with old stones, timbers, and documents. Some colleges have specialized laboratories for this work; most programs team with local or regional historic sites and agencies to supplement their on-campus facilities and to provide extended learning opportunities for their students.

All programs have similar core requirements that include courses on preservation theory and philosophy, architectural history, documentation techniques, and public policy principles. Programs differ in the amount of emphasis given to fieldwork and in the types and variety of elective courses and internship opportunities offered. The specific nature of each program usually depends on which academic department the historic preservation major is housed in and where the college itself is located.

Programs housed in schools of architecture tend to be more technically oriented—they emphasize the built environment through documentation and technology courses and through projects in adaptive use and design. Programs housed in planning departments focus more on public policy. If the major is in the history department, the emphasis will be on general research using documentation from the past. And the location of the college itself largely determines the types of internships and on-site fieldwork available. As might be expected, smaller communities have a feel and an influence that differ from those of urban areas.

One of the biggest challenges of this rewarding major is the research component. You'll use a variety of research techniques, including nontraditional primary sources such as the building itself. Time management is very important, because many projects require you to be self-motivated and self-directed. A keen sense of curiosity and a good dose of patience will serve you well as you work beyond the classroom and in your future career.

Other majors you might like:

American studies
Archaeology
Housing and human environments
Art history
Architectural history/criticism
Geography
Cultural resource management
History

Architectural engineering
Museum studies
Urban, community, and regional planning
Public policy analysis

Questions to ask colleges:

Are internships or fieldwork required for this major? What types are available, and how does the college help students obtain them?

Is the college connected to local preservation organizations, agencies, and historic sites?

What types of jobs have graduates of the program obtained?

Career options and trends:

Historic preservation consultant; cultural resource manager; historic site manager or curator; urban planner.

Planners and developers have come to realize that it is often more economical to restore than to build anew. Because of the growing trend to adapt and reuse historic buildings by modifying and repurposing the interiors, a greater number of skilled professionals with formal preservation training will be needed.

For more info:

National Trust for Historic Preservation
1785 Massachusetts Ave., N.W.
Washington, DC 20036-2117
(800) 944-6847
www.preservationnation.org

National Council for Preservation Education
www.uvm.edu/histpres/ncpe

Medieval and Renaissance studies

What it's about:

Medieval and Renaissance studies explores the ideas, achievements, and practices of the period A.D. 500–1660. These eras comprise the heart of most modern cultures of the West and Near East, affecting current literature, philosophy, art, history, religion, and politics.

Is this for you?

You might like this major if you also like: the History Channel; drama; music; Renaissance fairs; foreign languages and cultures; Shakespeare; painting; sculpture; architecture; discovering the origins of social attitudes and practices.

Consider this major if you are good at: attention to detail; creativity; critical reading/thinking; organizing; research; spacial thinking/analysis ...*or have...* initiative; writing skills.

Recommended high school prep:

English 4, math 3, lab science 3, social studies 4, and a foreign language 3–4. If possible, take at least one European history class as well as an art history, music history, or theater history class.

Did you know...

...that this major offers you opportunities to do focused, original research based on your own interests? You might be drawn to examples of devout worship or bawdy storytelling. You may concentrate on a specific author or artist, and then study the society in which he or she worked. Or you might consider the social forces that shaped the hospital, the parliament, and the organization of work according to clock time; study the evolution of jury trials or the idea of human rights; or trace the spread of ideas after the printing press was invented.

Typical courses in this major:

The great cathedrals
Medieval art
Leonardo da Vinci
Classical drama
Dante and medieval theology
Religion of late antiquity
Arthurian legend
Science and Islam
Chaucer/Shakespeare/Milton
Age of the Baroque
Judaism in the Middle Ages
The Italian Renaissance
England: Reformation to revolution
Spanish medieval literature
Music and the Church
Medieval philosophy

Concentrations:

In college: a particular author, artist, nation, monarch (e.g., Elizabeth I), or cultural practice.

If you go on to grad school: the medieval period; the Renaissance; a particular religious tradition, philosophic tradition, or art form.

What the study of this major is like:

If you major in medieval and Renaissance studies, you will analyze the historical and cultural features of the sixth through seventeenth centuries in Europe and the Middle East; be able to read at least one relevant language; become familiar with the primary artistic, intellectual, and social developments of the period; and recognize medieval and Renaissance contributions to modern thought and culture.

In this major, you should take a variety of courses in a number of academic areas: architecture, art history, classics, religious studies, English, history, modern languages, music, philosophy, and theater arts, among others. Although some courses may be in lecture format, most are seminars highlighting student discussion, independent research, and presentations (as individuals and in groups). Several courses may be devoted to interdisciplinary topics, such as the medieval or Renaissance city, the iconographic tradition, Shakespeare's world, encounters with Islam, and voice and verse. Because many central documents of the period were written in languages other than English, a reading knowledge of Latin, French, German, Spanish, or Italian—whichever suits your interests—is generally required.

Many programs have a strong focus on either English or history; others emphasize England or Europe; still others stress the Renaissance to the near-exclusion of the Middle Ages. Sometimes the focus of a program is evident in the basic course offerings or in specially presented topics or seminars. At other times, the focus is apparent only when you look into the faculty's research interests. If certain aspects of the major appeal to you, check into the emphases of the colleges you are considering to make sure you don't end up feeling frustrated or restricted.

Student and faculty gatherings are often an excellent source of information and community for medieval and Renaissance studies majors. At such meetings, you can hear about the latest research and get to know both professors and other students with similar interests. Many programs encourage you and your classmates to attend local stage and musical performances, museum exhibits, lectures, and conferences. As a medieval and Renaissance studies major, you can look forward to having stimulating exchanges with students and faculty members and to making genuine academic discoveries.

Other majors you might like:
English
History
Art history
Archaeology
Classics
Philosophy
Architectural history/criticism
Comparative literature
European studies
Religious studies
Italian studies
Drama and theater arts

Questions to ask colleges:
How many departments contribute to the medieval and Renaissance studies faculty? Is there an undergraduate research program? Is an undergraduate thesis required or encouraged? Which relevant study resources or activities are available on campus? Is there a larger academic community (such as a related graduate program) that undergraduate majors can easily access?

Career options and trends:
A degree in Medieval and Renaissance studies, like all liberal arts degrees, gives you a well-rounded education rather than training for a particular career. The degree is excellent preparation for graduate or professional school, and for careers in law, medicine, businesses, the arts, journalism, museology, and teaching.

For more info:
Medieval Academy of America (MAA)
104 Mount Auburn St., 5th Fl.
Cambridge, MA 02138
(617) 491-1622
www.medievalacademy.org

Renaissance Society of America (RSA)
City University of New York
365 Fifth Ave., Room 5400
New York, NY 10016-4309
(212) 817-2130
www.rsa.org

Neuroscience

Also known as:

Psychobiology

What it's about:

Neuroscience is the interdisciplinary study of the nervous system and behavior. It covers issues such as the molecular and cellular basis of neuronal function, nervous system structure, systems of neurons as processors of information, the representation of functions in the brain, the evolutionary development of the nervous system, neural correlates of behavior, and mechanisms of nervous system disorders. The neuroscience major prepares you for graduate study in neuroscience or a related field and for careers requiring a solid foundation in science.

Is this for you?

You might like this major if you also like: thinking about how we think; anatomy; computers; science; exploring the unknown; probability-based reasoning; complex problems.

Consider this major if you are good at: attention to detail; creativity; critical reading/thinking; math; quantitative analysis; research; teamwork *...or have...* manual dexterity; verbal skills.

Recommended high school prep:

English 4, math 4 (including precalculus), lab science 4 (including biology, chemistry, and physics), social studies 4, and a foreign language 3–4. Your courses in English and social studies are just as important as your math and science courses.

Did you know...

...that areas of neuroscience are found not only in traditional science fields, such as biology, chemistry, physics, and psychology, but also in mathematics, computer science, philosophy, economics, and cognitive science?

...that the curriculum for neuroscience at most colleges parallels a pre-med program?

Typical courses in this major:

General chemistry
Organic chemistry
General biology
Calculus
Statistics
Physics
Introductory psychology
Introductory neuroscience
Neurobiology
Behavioral neuroscience
Cognitive neuroscience
Systems neuroscience
Neuropharmacology
Sensory neuroscience
Developmental neuroscience

Concentrations:

Neurobiology; comparative and evolutionary neuroscience; systems neuroscience; behavioral neuroscience; social neuroscience; cognitive neuroscience; computational neuroscience.

What the study of this major is like:

Neuroscience addresses interesting questions. How do we think? Why do we behave the way we do? What is the relationship between the mind and the brain? How does the brain give rise to consciousness? How do nature and nurture influence our behavior? But neuroscientists seek answers to these questions in the lab sciences.

You shouldn't think of becoming a neuroscience major unless you enjoy laboratory research approaches to exploring these issues. Like other life sciences majors, neuroscience students spend many hours in labs. All neuroscience programs will expect you to obtain a firm grounding in the basics, including biology, chemistry, physics, math, psychology, and statistics. Some students may be frustrated by taking so many courses that do not deal specifically with the major. But your understanding of the nervous system will depend on your familiarity with scientific fundamentals.

Neuroscience may be the broadest major that exists. It is based in the life sciences but has connections to the social sciences and humanities. To date, there is no agreed-on sense of what is essential for the neuroscience curriculum. Each program differs in some ways from all the others. At each school that offers the major, the nature of the program is determined by the faculty members who teach the courses. Few colleges have hired instructors specifically to develop undergraduate programs in neuroscience. Instead, professors develop departmental majors such as biology and psychology. Therefore, the major depends on which areas of neuroscience are valued in the departments that contribute faculty members to the program. Look carefully at course offerings to see if the courses in the major match your interests.

Neuroscience is in an exciting phase because techniques have been developed that provide new ways to explore the brain. The human brain is the most complex phenomenon in nature. Answers to many neuroscientists' questions are beginning to surface, but much remains unknown. If you expect final answers, you will be frustrated by the brain's complexity. If you are excited by a sense of discovery, then you should do well in neuroscience.

Other majors you might like:
Molecular biology
Psychology
Behavioral sciences
Chemistry
Philosophy
Biopsychology
Information systems
Neurobiology/physiology
Biomedical engineering
Robotics technology
Biological/physical sciences
Electroencephalograph technology

Questions to ask colleges:
What are the areas of faculty expertise?

Will students get a background in molecular and cellular aspects of neuroscience? Will students get training in neuroanatomy, neuropharmacology, neurophysiology, and neurochemistry?

How much emphasis is placed on behavior? How much emphasis is placed on cognitive neuroscience, social neuroscience, computational neuroscience, and comparative and evolutional neuroscience?

Career options and trends:
Physician*; college professor/researcher*; high school teacher; science writer; research technician (e.g., with a drug company or research lab); electroneurodiagnostic technician.

Neuroscience is becoming an important area within the sciences. Medical and academic prospects are relatively good in this field. Increasingly, universities are hiring in this area, especially in fields that have not had neuroscience representation, such as computer science, mathematics, and cognitive science.

Insider's viewpoint:
"I enjoy learning about the human brain and all of the bodily and spiritual connections to it, to help understand people around me as well as myself. Being able to spout off about the brain is also great at parties."

—Candace, senior, University of Rochester

For more info:
Society for Neuroscience (SfN)
1121 14th St., N.W.
Suite 1010
Washington, DC 20005
(202) 962-4000
www.sfn.org

Peace and conflict studies

What it's about:

As a peace and conflict studies major, you explore strategies for constructing a just and peaceful world. You study issues of war, sexism, racism, and poverty; nonviolent social change; and conflict resolution. The approach is both theoretical and experience-based.

Is this for you?

You might like this major if you also like: social and political activism; service-related activities; volunteer activities; creative writing; theater; art; community building; human rights issues.

Consider this major if you are good at: caring/nurturing; creativity; critical reading/thinking; leadership; organizing; persuading/influencing; teamwork *...or have...* initiative; people skills; verbal skills; writing skills.

Recommended high school prep:

English 4, math 3, lab science 3, social studies 4, and a foreign language 4.

Did you know...

...that peace and conflict studies is less about mastering material and more about learning a process of action and reflection? There is a substantial hands-on component to this major. Most students complete internships in the United States and abroad.

Typical courses in this major:

Theory and practice of nonviolence
History of nonviolence
The global political economy
Introduction to international relations
Philosophical inquiry: peace and justice
Contemporary social theory
Postcolonial theory
Conflict resolution
Methods of peacemaking
Philosophy of social science
International law
Theories of international relations
Issues before the United Nations
Marxism
Urban political economy
Feminism, ecology, and peace

Concentrations:

Interpersonal and intergroup conflict resolution; international war and peace; social, economic, and/or environmental justice.

What the study of this major is like:

As a peace and conflict studies major, you spend part of your time in class, learning theory and history, and part of your time in lab situations—in settings (such as internships) where you can develop peacemaking skills and put them to good use. Many courses require you to write papers and present oral reports based on group projects. You become accustomed to analyzing problems locally and globally.

Peace and conflict studies may be a program on its own or an interdepartmental major including courses from different departments. Many programs have been influenced by the traditional peace churches (Quakers, Mennonites, Church of the Brethren) or by Catholic social thought, although some are not affiliated with any religion.

Some programs are global in scope; others tend to focus on the United States. In either case you will be encouraged to explore a non-western culture and issues of human diversity. Some programs also require proficiency in a foreign language equivalent to two years of college-level study. Internships and hands-on learning are encouraged more on some campuses than on others; some programs even offer their own international, off-campus study programs.

Most peace and conflict studies majors take their education very seriously. You will have significant interaction with faculty members who serve as teachers and mentors both in and out of the classroom. Majors frequently make friends they keep long after graduation.

Other majors you might like:
International relations
Women's studies
Gay/lesbian studies
Environmental studies
Religious studies
Philosophy
Labor/industrial relations
Emergency management/homeland security
Legal studies
Intercultural/diversity studies
Political science
Near and Middle Eastern studies

Questions to ask colleges:
Does the program sponsor peace-related activities, speakers, conferences, and so on?

How many faculty members participate in the program?

Do the students have a say in the design of their education? What opportunities are there for off-campus and experience-based study?

Have graduates found work in peace and justice efforts?

Career options and trends:
College professor*; nongovernmental organization (NGO) worker*; lawyer*; minister or other member of the clergy*; government worker; public relations manager; international business consultant; human resources manager.

Peace and conflict studies majors also enter graduate and professional schools to become doctors, lawyers, teachers, and caregivers. Many people who eventually teach peace and conflict studies do not pursue graduate training in the field. Instead, they specialize in a discipline that lends itself to a peace perspective, such as sociology, economics, political science, history, or philosophy.

In the United States, mediation and conflict resolution are becoming increasingly promising fields. Also, a peace and conflict studies degree can be useful for positions in a wide range of nongovernmental organizations.

For more info:
Peace and Justice Studies Association (PJSA)
University of San Francisco
2130 Fulton Street, 5th Floor
San Francisco, CA 94117-1080
(415) 422-5238
www.peacejusticestudies.org

Natural resources and conservation

If you are considering the majors in this section, you probably already know about disappearing forests, threats to wildlife habitats, and other ways that humans hurt the environment. The good news is that, by learning about natural resources and conservation, you should be able to do something about these problems. "Students for whom environmental studies is the right major are those who take pleasure in making a difference," says Professor Michael Maniates of Allegheny College. "They have compelling interest in environmental issues and deep-felt concern about current patterns of assault on the environment and what this means for future generations."

If you the love the outdoors, enjoy camping trips or Scouting, or have a passion for bird watching, these majors may be right for you.

Many areas of study, including programs that mix several subjects, fall under this category. "Environmental science zips together a working knowledge of physics, chemistry, and biology," says Professor David E. Smith, University of Virginia. "Environmental *science* programs focus on the natural sciences, whereas environmental *studies* also emphasizes the social sciences as they relate to environmental issues."

Why should you study the social sciences if your interest is in the environment? "Many students enter natural resource and conservation programs in the belief or expectation that they will not be dealing with political, economic, or social areas of study," says Professor David K. Loomis, University of Massachusetts Amherst. "Managing natural resources is in many ways accomplished by managing people. There is no distinct separation between society and our natural resources."

As a professional in these fields (and forests, wetlands, and waterways!), you will spend a great deal of time working with the public. In fact, public awareness of the urgency to protect the environment increases funding and jobs in conservation. It's weird, but a healthy job outlook stems in part from an unhealthy environmental outlook.

"Americans are concerned about the environment, and this awareness has created a stable need for environmental professionals in both the government and private sector," Smith says.

Fields, forests, and fisheries

Careers in natural resources management and conservation include research, teaching, consulting, law, journalism, policymaking, government regulation, and advocacy. Some new areas of study and work include conservation biology and watershed management. Okay, now, get out the bug spray and consider these specific jobs: environmental consulting, engineering, and policy analysis; community recycling and energy-conservation projects; research in health risks from pollutants; or working as an outdoor educator, field naturalist, forester, or park ranger; endangered species officer; fisheries biologist, manager, or ecologist. To get a job in wildlife work, such as wildlife biologist or operations officer, you'll face more competition.

When you compare colleges, you'll see that they differ in the way they achieve balance between the scientific and the human pieces of the environmental puzzle.

"This difference is fine and welcome, so long as the program incorporates significant insight from other disciplines and features courses and projects that allow students to effectively combine the skills and ideas they're learning from different fields," advises Maniates.

The issues of accreditation and certification are also huge. That's because some jobs in conservation require specific credentials, like state certifications. See whether your area of interest has certifications and find out if the college degree comes with a certification or a way to earn it. Accreditation is different from certification: certification is for you, while accreditation is for the college. Look for college programs accredited by the professional association for your specialty.

Here are some other questions for colleges: What's the most important course in the program? The answer should reveal that college's priorities. Is your major a full-fledged degree area or just a concentration under another major—like wildlife under zoology?

Are internships available for what you're studying? Are the laboratories up-to-date? Will you get field experience? Are good field sites near the university? The location of the college may suggest a strong program—for instance, in fisheries or regional forestry. Also ask about the variety of classes open to you and how many electives you can take. Explore where students go after graduation. But most of all, read the catalog descriptions of the faculty members.

"College and university programs are only as good as their faculties," Smith emphasizes. "The faculty should be fully engaged in all aspects of scholarship, both teaching and research." Look for opportunities to do supervised research and independent study in a topic that's important to you, especially if you're planning to go to grad school. Graduate studies include environmental policy and law; land use, sprawl, and urban planning; water, wetlands, and marine resources management; forest management/resources and wood science; and fisheries science and management.

For information, go to the Ecological Society of America (www.esa.org). Read about related majors in the sections on Agriculture; Parks and recreation; and the Physical sciences.

Environmental science

What it's about:

The interdisciplinary field of environmental science spotlights two concerns: the interaction of the physical and biological processes that shape our natural environment, and the application of scientific methods and research to environmental problems.

Is this for you?

You might like this major if you also like: complex puzzles; exploring the outdoors; using computers; taking a journey to an unknown destination; working on real-world problems; learning how the environment works.

Consider this major if you are good at: attention to detail; creativity; critical reading/thinking; math; organizing; quantitative analysis; research; teamwork *...or have...* initiative; patience; writing skills.

Recommended high school prep:

English 4, math 4 (including precalculus), lab science 4 (earth science, biology, chemistry, physics), social studies 3, and a foreign language 2–3. If they are available, take courses in environmental studies or sciences, ecology, computer applications, and calculus or statistics.

Did you know...

...how important a background in the physical sciences and the life sciences is in this field? If you were investigating the oxygen concentration in a lake or the impact of acid rain on a forest, you would have to evaluate both the physical and the biological processes, and their interaction, to show how the environment works.

Typical courses in this major:

Environmental modeling and methodology
Physical geology
Fundamentals of ecology
Hydrology and water resources
Atmosphere and weather
Population and the environment
Geographic information systems (GIS)
Remote sensing
Global biogeochemistry cycles
Climatological analysis
Biochemistry
Coastal processes
Management of forest ecosystems
Environmental impact assessment
Waste management systems
Marine biology/ecology

Concentrations:

Environmental biology; environmental chemistry; environmental geology; environmental physics; aquatic ecology; terrestrial ecology; environmental health; environmental protection; natural resource management.

What the study of this major is like:

Because problems that affect the environment are complex, environmental science requires an imaginative approach that includes a working knowledge of physics, chemistry, and biology. As a major, you will probably be expected to gain a clear understanding of a wide range of physical and biological processes. For example, you may be required to take classes that deal with the water cycle and its effect on sediments and rocks. You will also study atmospheric science, geoscience, ecology, environmental chemistry, hydrology, and land and resource analysis. When you complete the required subjects, you should be ready to construct a course of study that emphasizes your own strengths and interests.

Fieldwork, which is often an important part of your education, can offer intellectual challenges and the sort of real-world risks that laboratory research can't provide. You may have additional opportunities to do supervised research in which you work closely with faculty members in the field or the laboratory. Paid summer research internships or fellowships at research sites throughout the country are also available; these opportunities supplement your academic course work. For a variety of reasons, environmental science is collaborative; many individuals contribute their special talents as they work in research or investigative groups to solve problems. Therefore, you should develop your communication skills (writing, reading, speaking, listening) and learn the terminology, or distinct vocabulary, of the profession.

Computer skills are also essential; a strong program will provide experience with data analysis, digital mapping, remote sensing, and geographic information systems (GIS). The opportunity to conduct professional-level research in a senior capstone project is another indicator of a good program.

People sometimes confuse environmental science and environmental studies, but these programs differ in key ways. In general, environmental science focuses on the natural sciences (chemistry, biology, physics) as they relate to the environment, whereas environmental studies emphasizes the social sciences (such as economics, policy, or law) as they relate to environmental issues. Environmental science majors study the natural sciences on a deeper level, while environmental studies majors gain additional opportunities through their exposure to the social sciences. Be sure to investigate the programs that interest you to see that you understand the goals and requirements of each.

Other majors you might like:
Environmental engineering
Petroleum engineering
Ecology
Natural sciences
Soil science
Hazardous materials technology
Hydrology/water resources science
Geology/earth science
Geography
Atmospheric science
Oceanography
Environmental health

Questions to ask colleges:
Are the faculty members in this program engaged in both teaching and research? Professors who are active in research can, and do, incorporate aspects of their research into their teaching.

Are undergraduates given opportunities to participate in supervised research and/or independent study? These activities are valuable regardless of which career path you take after graduation.

Career options and trends:
Researcher; college professor or high school teacher; environmental consultant; environmental lawyer; resource manager in industry; regulatory compliance specialist; state or federal government regulator; staff member of an advocacy group.

A master's degree is required for most entry-level research and teaching positions, and a Ph.D. is usually necessary for high-level research.

Job prospects are generally very good in the government, academic, and private sectors for students with undergraduate and graduate degrees, although a master's degree is usually preferred. Because of increasing pressures on the environment from expanding populations and economic development, demand for environmental scientists in both government and industry is projected to grow, both in the United States and abroad. Opportunities should be especially strong in companies that provide regulatory compliance services.

Coupling a major in environmental science with a minor in business, public administration, or health will also improve your job prospects.

For more info:
Ecological Society of America (ESA)
1990 M St., N.W.
Suite 700
Washington, DC 20036
202-833-8773
www.esa.org

Environmental studies

What it's about:

Environmental studies integrates insights and tools from natural and engineering sciences, social sciences, and humanities to explore the effects of human activities on the natural world. In this major, you identify environmental problems, analyze their causes, and learn how to develop a range of solutions.

Is this for you?

You might like this major if you also like: community service; environmental causes; the outdoors; camping trips; Scouting; fishing; hunting; bird watching; working on problems without easy answers; making the world a better place.

Consider this major if you are good at: advocating; attention to detail; creativity; critical reading/thinking; organizing; quantitative analysis; teamwork ...*or have...* curiosity; initiative; writing skills.

Recommended high school prep:

English 4, math 3, lab science 3 (earth science, biology, chemistry), social studies 3, and a foreign language 2-3. If it is available, take a course in environmental science/studies or ecology.

Did you know...

...that most undergraduates majoring in environmental studies are women?

Typical courses in this major:

Introduction to environmental studies
Ecology
Conservation biology
Environmental chemistry
Geology
Environmental politics
Environmental philosophy and ethics
Environmental and ecological economics
Tools of environmental analysis
Wildlife management
Land use planning

Environmental education
Environmental history
Environmental health
Energy technologies, supply, and policy

Concentrations:

Environmental policy and law; terrestrial ecosystems; aquatic ecosystems; conservation biology and biodiversity; environmental education; environmental ethics and philosophy; environmental preservation; land use and urban planning; energy production and conservation.

What the study of this major is like:

The rapidly growing interest in environmental studies as an undergraduate major results from an increasing awareness of the human impact on the environment. Environmental studies differs from environmental science and environmental engineering in its greater emphasis on the social sciences and humanities. As an environmental studies major, you enroll in a number of academic subjects to examine the causes of, and possible solutions to, environmental problems.

Programs can differ greatly from college to college. Typically, you begin by taking introductory courses in the natural sciences and the social sciences, with at least half your courses in biology, chemistry, and geology. If you have a strong interest in natural science, you might combine a concentration in science with courses in environmental studies.

Many programs offer courses and projects that allow you to integrate, or combine, what you learn from different fields. Some may focus on the natural sciences, while others offer advanced courses in the social sciences, environmental economics, and environmental history. Economic analysis is often the basis of solutions to problems such as pollution and resource depletion (overuse). Classes in environmental politics will help you understand the context in which policies and programs are created and carried out. Some programs also cover environmental issues in foreign countries—for example, the erosion of beaches in the Caribbean islands—and global concerns like the greenhouse effect. In programs that include humanities, you are encouraged to take courses in environmental philosophy and ethics as well as in art, religion, and literature, as a way of examining the links between human activity and the environment.

Programs in environmental studies tend to argue that human society is undermining the ecological foundations of life and that we must fundamentally change behavior if we are to prosper as a species—we must go beyond recycling or planting trees in order to tackle looming environmental threats. For some students, this claim can be unsettling. Most programs value your ability to think critically about problems and to develop innovative solutions, but a problem-solving emphasis is likely to make certain demands on you. Instead of learning facts about specific environmental problems, you are encouraged to analyze them, because the environmental challenges we will face in twenty years will probably differ significantly from the ones that confront us today.

In environmental studies, your course work is often rewarding and eye-opening. You can get hands-on experience in responding to environmental threats through fieldwork, service-learning programs, and internships. However, careers in the field increasingly require technical training at advanced levels, usually graduate work. The liberal arts education in environmental studies does not replace specialized training, but it provides excellent preparation for such training.

Other majors you might like:

Geography
Political science
Economics
Environmental engineering
Global studies
Geology/earth science
Forestry
Urban, community, and regional planning
Sustainable agriculture
Ecology

Environmental health
Wildlife and wilderness management

Questions to ask colleges:

In which courses do you apply ideas from various fields to resolve environmental problems? Some programs ask you to take a variety of courses from different disciplines but offer few opportunities to integrate, or tie together, what you've learned.

What internships are available? How well do these internships complement, or enrich, the course offerings?

Has the number of students majoring in the program grown over the past few years and, if so, are faculty members being brought in to accommodate the increased interest?

Are there faculty members whose primary responsibility is teaching and advising environmental studies students? Sometimes the program's professors are "on loan" from other programs, which may hold first claim to the instructors' time.

What is the most important course in the curriculum? The answer will tell you about the focus of the program. Compare that focus with your own interests.

Where are recent graduates of the program working? If they have landed jobs that sound interesting, that's a good sign.

Career options and trends:

Environmental consultant*; environmental lobbyist; environmental engineer; park naturalist; specialist in environmental communications; specialist in regulations compliance; environmental educator.

As environmental problems are becoming more of a concern throughout the world, the job market is expanding. Career opportunities exist in toxic waste disposal, management of environmental organizations, journalism, community recycling and energy conservation, and environmental and economic development in nonindustrial countries. With appropriate graduate work, you can pursue a career in air or water quality planning, solid waste planning, land use planning, fisheries and wildlife management, policy analysis, environmental law, laboratory research, or resource economics.

"I love the excitement of working directly on problems that scare us all at least a little bit. It's hard, as a professor or as a student, to be bored by the subject: the issues are too large, the stakes too high, the rewards too great."

—Professor Michael Maniates, Allegheny College

For more info:

National Wildlife Federation
11100 Wildlife Center Drive
Reston, VA 20190-5362
(800) 822-9919
www.nwf.org

Association for the Study of Literature and
   Environment (ASLE)
www.asle.umn.edu

Fishing and fisheries

What it's about:

The major in fisheries explores the biology and ecology of fishes and other aquatic species; the bodies of water that are their habitats; and the human use, management, and production of aquatic species. Courses cover both basic science and applied aspects of commercial and recreational fishing activities.

Is this for you?

You might like this major if you also like: fishing, boating, or hiking; working with your hands as well as your mind; keeping an aquarium or raising live animals; learning about living creatures and natural ecosystems.

Consider this major if you are good at: attention to detail; creativity; critical reading/thinking; problem solving; quantitative analysis; spacial thinking/ analysis; teamwork *...or have...* initiative; verbal skills.

Recommended high school prep:

English 4, math 3, lab science 3, social studies 3, and a foreign language 2-3. Courses in advanced biology, environmental science, precalculus, and computer literacy are also recommended.

Typical courses in this major:

Evolutionary biology
Genetics
Fisheries techniques
Ichthyology
Fish ecology
Limnology
Aquatic animal nutrition
Economics
Aquatic entomology
Freshwater ecology
Statistics
Policies, laws, and regulations
Principles of aquaculture
Fisheries management

Concentrations:

Fisheries management; fisheries science; aquaculture.

What the study of this major is like:

Fisheries management is a science-based field that requires you to understand and apply principles of biology, ecology, statistics, and social sciences. Professionals who work in fisheries management do not simply sample, assess, and stock fish populations; they also improve habitats for certain species to protect biodiversity (for example, helping endangered species recover) and interact with the public. Fisheries managers must also be able to communicate technical information in person and in writing.

You begin your studies by establishing a strong foundation in fields such as biology, chemistry, mathematics, and English. You will also probably take an introductory course in natural resources management in your first year. Your second-year studies generally include plant and evolutionary biology, physical sciences, and social sciences, along with an introduction to principles of fisheries and wildlife management. Through your first two years, the prime method of instruction is lectures, supplemented by laboratories in biology and chemistry and some fieldwork in natural resources management. Many majors tend to feel most challenged by course work in chemistry and calculus.

In your third and fourth years, course content becomes more fisheries-oriented; fieldwork and hands-on learning is more important. Your third year generally includes foundation courses, such as field techniques, ichthyology (the study of fishes), and fish ecology. The fourth year usually features such key courses as freshwater ecology, human dimensions of fisheries and wildlife management, aquaculture, and a capstone course in fisheries management. The capstone course generally combines everything you have learned; groups of students devise action plans for solving real-world problems in fisheries management. In your third and fourth years, classes are smaller and you have more opportunities to interact personally with your professors and with other majors. In fact, majors typically study in groups and socialize after hours. Many of them enroll in the local chapter of a professional society and begin to feel part of the profession.

You will be encouraged to learn from practical experience by volunteering to help graduate students with fieldwork or laboratory work, by participating in internships in fisheries management agencies or nongovernmental organizations, or by conducting independent research projects. In these activities, you can identify and explore areas of technical specialization. You can also establish professional contacts that may prove helpful if you look for an entry-level position after graduation. Of students graduating with bachelor's degrees, roughly one-quarter move on to graduate studies and three-quarters obtain entry-level jobs in the field.

Some of the programs emphasize fisheries science, which encourage you to solve management problems by understanding fish ecology. Science-based programs are essential if you are considering going to graduate school and pursuing a challenging career in fisheries science. Other programs stress instruction in practical fisheries management and aim to produce entry-level managers for state or federal fisheries management agencies. Programs may also differ in the amount of hands-on learning available and in the opportunities for participation in research and internships. Often, universities with graduate programs in fisheries offer more opportunities for learning outside formal classes.

Other majors you might like:
Aquaculture
Marine biology
Ocean engineering
Parks, recreation, and leisure studies
Zoology
Aquatic biology/limnology

Marine engineering/naval architecture
Marine science/Merchant Marine
Underwater diving
Oceanography
Natural resources management/policy
Water, wetlands, and marine management

Questions to ask colleges:
What sorts of facilities are offered? Do they include laboratories, experimental ponds, raceways (canals), and aquaria, as well as access to nearby streams, rivers, or reservoirs?

Are there opportunities for doing hands-on learning and for gaining practical research experience? Is there a graduate program, so that undergraduates can learn by helping graduate students with their research? Are undergraduates encouraged to undertake independent research projects?

Career options and trends:
Fisheries manager*; conservation officer; fish ecologist; fish culturist*; endangered species management officer; environmental consultant; fisheries research scientist; fisheries and wildlife journalist.

Many state and federal fisheries management agencies require their employees to become certified fisheries scientists under the program administered by the American Fisheries Society. Certification requires formal education and professional experience. Although entry-level jobs can be obtained with a bachelor's degree, an advanced degree will lead to a more rewarding career.

Not all jobs focus on management of sport and commercial fisheries, and many address recovery of endangered species, public education, development of public policy, and other areas. Most jobs in fisheries combine physical work outdoors with intellectual engagement—the talents, skills, and energies of fisheries managers seldom go unused.

Private-sector employment has grown in response to our increased awareness of environmental issues. Fisheries professionals are employed by environmental consulting firms, forest products companies, public utilities, and conservation groups. Aquaculturists can work in both public agencies and private firms.

Employment of captains and crews in the fishing industry is declining, because of foreign competition, stock depletion, and habitat destruction. The good news is that these same factors should spur demand for professionals trained in fisheries science and management.

Insider's viewpoint:

"Fisheries management is maturing as a field of applied science, and it is exciting to witness and participate in its application. For example, during my own career, I have witnessed the restoration of Great Lakes fisheries, the rise of aquaculture, and the emergence of conservation science and management. Many are the days that I smile inwardly and think, 'I get paid to do what I love.'"

—Professor Eric Hallerman, Virginia Polytechnic Institute and State University

For more info:

American Fisheries Society (AFS)
5410 Grosvenor Lane
Bethesda, MD 20814
(301) 897-8616
www.fisheries.org

World Aquaculture Society
143 J. M. Parker Coliseum
Louisiana State University
Baton Rouge, LA 70803
(225) 578-3137
www.was.org

Forestry

What it's about:

This major deals with the management, conservation, and preservation of forest ecosystems. Integrating what you learn in the physical, biological, and social sciences helps you appreciate the numerous benefits and resources of forests, including wood and fiber products, biodiversity, recreation, water, wilderness, and wildlife.

Is this for you?

You might like this major if you also like: the great outdoors; math and science; maps; geography; arboretums; building things; working with people; helping others accomplish their goals.

Consider this major if you are good at: critical reading/thinking; leadership; managing people; organizing; quantitative analysis; teamwork ...*or have...* initiative; patience; verbal skills.

Recommended high school prep:

English 4, math 4 (including pre-calculus), lab science 4 (earth science, biology, chemistry, and physics), social studies 3, and a foreign language 2–3. If they are available, courses in statistics, environmental science or ecology, and computer applications are also recommended. Many agencies, such as county conservation boards, state and national parks, and the U.S. Forest Service, provide summer employment opportunities in forestry.

Did you know...

that the amount of forest land in the United States is down only about one-third from what it was when the Pilgrims landed, and is about the same as it was a century ago? Because of forest management policies, forest growth exceeds harvesting by 33 percent each year—a reassuring statistic, because, for every individual in the United States, the equivalent of a full-grown tree is turned into wood and paper each year.

Typical courses in this major:

Botany
Forest soils
Forest management and policy
Forest measurements
Forest economics
Silviculture
Forest ecology
Forest growth and yield
Wildlife management
Resource allocation
Aerial photo interpretation
Geographic information systems (GIS)
Harvesting and production technology
Hydrology
Wood science
Composite products

Concentrations:

In college: forest resource management; urban forestry; wood products; wood science; fire management.

If you go on to grad school: forest biology; forest economics; forest biometry; forest ecology.

What the study of this major is like:

Forestry programs begin with general course work in English, mathematics, chemistry, physics, speech, and statistics. In your first year, you generally take introductory forestry courses and do field studies conducted by forestry faculty members. Because forestry is a broad field, you typically have to choose an area of concentration. You may pick your concentration as early as your first year or as late as the end of your second year. You then begin course work in your chosen area. Nonforestry courses, such as business management, industrial engineering, and technical report writing, help you prepare for work in the field.

Many aspects of a forestry education are hands-on. Some courses are taught in the field so that you can experience for yourself the complexities of the forest and apply theories learned in the classroom to real situations. Most problems encountered in forestry represent new challenges, arising from new circumstances, and your task may be to come up with appropriate solutions. Therefore, critical thinking, analysis, and problem-solving skills are essential.

In laboratory sessions, you do statistical analysis of data collected in the field and study biological relationships among different species of trees, as well as between trees and other living organisms in the forest. You are encouraged to use your summers to work in forestry-related jobs. Many programs offer credit for these experiences, most of which are paid jobs in private industry; with county, state, or federal government agencies; or with other resource management agencies. Working in the field improves your understanding of forestry and your chances of finding a permanent job after graduation. You should also become active in professional organizations so you can practice the teamwork and leadership skills that are central to a successful forestry career.

There are four main types of forestry programs. Some programs train students to be forestry technicians and usually grant two-year degrees that allow graduates to work in field jobs related to forestry. Other programs prepare you for both field and supervisory work, such as being a district ranger, forest supervisor, regional forester, or chief forester with the U.S. Forest Service; a consulting forester; or a forester with a state department of natural resources. These are usually four-year Bachelor of Science programs. Other programs prepare you to work in wood science, with either a B.S. degree or an advanced degree. Still other programs are intended primarily for graduate students. And some forestry programs offer a combination of the four options. In addition, some programs focus on forestry in a particular region of the United States, while others offer a generic, broad-ranging approach.

Other majors you might like:
Botany
Wildlife and wilderness management
Forest resources production
Surveying technology
Landscape architecture
Horticulture
Environmental studies
Ecology
Land use planning
Wood science/pulp/paper technology
Entomology
Forest engineering

Questions to ask colleges:
Is the program accredited by the Society of American Foresters or the Society of Wood Science and Technology? If it is, then you know that the curriculum is reviewed periodically by an outside team of professionals, and that it meets accepted standards.

What types of field laboratory experiences are offered, and in what types of environments? What forestry-related facilities (research labs, habitats, remote sensing equipment, greenhouses, preserves) are on or near campus?

Career options and trends:
Forester with the U. S. Forest Service or state agency*; park ranger*; urban forester; industrial forester or timber manager*; arborist; wood product sales; consulting forester.

Generally, not much job growth is projected in the forestry field, and overall employment is expected to decline in the timber industry. Nevertheless, there is increasing demand for graduates in the areas of wood science, urban and community forestry, and natural resource conservation or interpretation. The growing public demand for protection and responsible management of forest resources should create opportunities in research, testing, and compliance services.

For more info:
Society of American Foresters (SAF)
5400 Grosvenor Lane
Bethesda, MD 20814-2198
(301) 897-8720
www.safnet.org

Society of Wood Science and Technology (SWST)
www.swst.org

Natural resources and conservation

What it's about:

Natural resources and conservation is a broad, interdisciplinary field of study that addresses the management, protection, use, restoration, and enjoyment of the Earth's resources. Training is provided in a number of academic areas, including biology and other natural sciences, social sciences, economics, and environmental studies.

Is this for you?

You might like this major if you also like: outdoor activities such as camping, fishing, hunting, hiking, and canoeing; traveling; photography; debating; getting involved in environmental causes; politics; business and economics; leading or organizing school activities.

Consider this major if you are good at: creativity; critical reading/thinking; integrative thinking; leadership; quantitative analysis; research; teamwork ...*or have...* initiative; verbal skills; writing skills.

Recommended high school prep:

English 4, math 3, lab science 3, social studies 4, and a foreign language 2–3. If they are available, courses in environmental studies, economics, and computer applications are also recommended.

Did you know...

...that the management of natural resources is in many ways accomplished by the management of people? There is no distinct separation between society and the natural world. Many students begin this major expecting an in-depth examination of the environment. They soon learn, however, that they must also take courses in the social sciences, and that as professionals they will spend a great deal of time working with the public.

...that much of the work in this field is done indoors? This is especially true as you advance in your career.

Typical courses in this major:

Biology
Ecology
Chemistry
Plant and animal identification
Economics
Human dimensions
Natural resources management
Environmental policy
Conservation law
Wildlife and fisheries conservation
Geographic information systems (GIS)
Measurements and sampling techniques
Environmental communication
Soils and land use
Politics and ecology
Ecotourism

Concentrations:

Natural resources policy; outdoor recreation; resources management; environmental law and policy; environmental education; wildlife rehabilitation; wetlands restoration; coastal zone management.

What the study of this major is like:

Historically, professionals working in the natural resources and conservation field focused on specific academic areas, or disciplines, such as forestry or wildlife biology. Today, leading programs combine a range of courses; as a result, all majors become familiar with several fields, including forestry, wildlife, fisheries, physical sciences (such as chemistry), and social sciences (economics and political science). In addition, you take writing and, often, public speaking courses. Majors learn to integrate, or link, many disciplines and apply them to natural resource issues.

Many natural resources and conservation courses are taught in the traditional lecture and discussion format. Other courses focus on fieldwork, such as plant or animal identification and sampling techniques. Some courses combine the two, with a lecture/discussion session followed by fieldwork. An increasing number of courses require group projects, designed to prepare you for the type of work you may do after you graduate.

Natural resources and conservation programs vary a great deal in their emphases, degree requirements, and philosophies. Some programs have well-defined requirements that offer little flexibility, while others can accommodate almost any reasonable curriculum you want to pursue. At the same time, accreditation (offered by the Society of American Foresters) and individual certification (offered by SAF, the American Fisheries Society, and The Wildlife Society) ensure that all programs follow professional guidelines. All programs that are accredited must meet the same standards of quality and course requirements.

Some programs place more emphasis on either the biophysical or the socioeconomic aspects of natural resources and conservation. The combination of disciplines available at a college can also create differences among programs. For example, some programs cover only forestry or wildlife conservation. Even though such programs might be of high quality, your study and career options are somewhat limited. Other colleges have larger, integrated programs that offer you more possibilities. For instance, a college might combine wildlife and fisheries conservation, forestry, and natural resource studies into a single program.

Other majors you might like:
Biology
Geography
Geology/earth science
Political science
Oceanography
Range science
Agronomy and crop science
Emergency management/homeland security
Natural resources management/policy
Ecology
Sustainable agriculture
Mining and mineral engineering

Questions to ask colleges:
Which field experiences or other opportunities for hands-on learning are offered to undergraduates? Where do the activities take place? Is there access to nearby nature preserves, field stations, or research centers?

How flexible is the program regarding electives—can students design a course of study that reflects their interests?

Is the program accredited? What certification requirements can be fulfilled through this program?

Career options and trends:
Wildlife biologist; fisheries manager; forester; park ranger; conservation law enforcement officer; natural resources manager; government agency employee (EPA, state conservation department, etc.); natural resources policy analyst; environmental lawyer; environmental educator.

The various professional disciplines in this field have different certification requirements. You should investigate the certification options and their importance in the area of natural resources you are most interested in. Also, many careers in the discipline require graduate study.

While the rate of job growth has slowed recently, job trends remain promising. The broad nature of this field provides a variety of career options in both government and industry. Most students with a bachelor's degree will find employment, but prospects are better if you have a master's degree or higher. Also, many employees in public natural resources management agencies are reaching retirement age. As with any occupation, there are times of greater or lesser demand, but highly motivated, well-trained graduates should be able to find employment.

Insider's viewpoint:
"Economics and policy are an integral part of natural resources management; these 'practical' concerns are necessary to be able to effectively deal with natural resources in today's society. If you're not cut out for the economics, look somewhere else for a major."

—Zeb, senior, University of Delaware

For more info:
Society of American Foresters (SAF)
5400 Grosvenor Lane
Bethesda, MD 20814-2198
(301) 897-8720
www.safnet.org

The Wildlife Society (TWS)
5410 Grosvenor Lane
Suite 200
Bethesda, MD 20814-2144
(301) 897-9770
www.wildlife.org

Wildlife and wilderness management

Also known as:

Conservation biology

What it's about:

Wildlife and wilderness management is an area of applied ecology that deals with the conservation of animal populations, ranging from those that are regularly hunted to those that are considered endangered, and the habitats in which these animals are found.

Is this for you?

You might like this major if you also like: outdoor activities such as hiking, camping, fishing, and hunting; science; Scouting; caring for animals; bird watching; natural history museums; zoos; travel; learning about the natural world.

Consider this major if you are good at: attention to detail; creativity; critical reading/thinking; leadership; organizing; quantitative analysis; teamwork *...or have...* initiative; physical stamina; verbal skills; writing skills.

Recommended high school prep:

English 4, math 3, lab science 4, social studies 3, and a foreign language 2–3. Any course in environmental studies is recommended, if available. Advanced biology would also be a plus, but is not required.

Did you know...

...that this is the best major at most universities for students who have a strong interest in field-oriented ecology? Biology programs typically cater to premed students and emphasize "skin-in" biology. Wildlife programs attract students interested in animal populations and emphasize "skin-out" biology.

Typical courses in this major:

Biology
Anatomy
Chemistry, general and organic
Statistics
Principles of wildlife management
Terrestrial wildlife ecology
Wetlands wildlife ecology
Field methods for wildlife management
Ornithology (study of birds)
Mammalogy
Entomology (study of insects)
Conservation biology
Genetics
Behavioral ecology
Systematic botany
Conservation law and policy

Concentrations:

Wildlife biology; wildlife conservation; habitat management; wetlands conservation.

What the study of this major is like:

Wildlife and wilderness management programs began as game management programs in the 1950s. Back then, people thought game species (mostly birds and mammals) were the only wildlife that needed to be managed. But human population growth inevitably affects animal populations by loss or change of habitat, reduction of food supply, presence of pollutants, and other human-related factors. In recent years, more and more rare and endangered species have been added to the list of wildlife in need of active management.

Wildlife professionals have come to realize that many species that are neither hunted nor endangered are also in need of our attention. Examples include declining populations of amphibians, birds of prey, and neotropical migrant birds; they could all become endangered if they do not receive immediate assistance. As a result of changes in attitudes toward the natural world, many wildlife and wilderness programs study a much broader array of species, and teach the skills needed to protect them, than those traditionally covered in game management programs.

As a wildlife major, you study both resource management and biology. Most of your courses are in biology, but you must also take chemistry, mathematics (through elementary calculus), and statistics. Anatomy and vertebrate zoology courses, such as ornithology and mammalogy, are important, too. Because wildlife biologists must be able to identify plants, at least one plant taxonomy course is generally required. Most other courses in a wildlife and wilderness management program are field-oriented and deal with ecology.

You will probably have to take several lab courses each semester in order to graduate in four years. Most lab courses (beyond introductory biology and chemistry) are strongly field oriented. Wildlife and wilderness management deals with animals living in natural environments; you must therefore be prepared to work with animal populations and their habitats. In the field, you gain experience in identifying birds and mammals, estimating their populations, and analyzing their habitats—you acquire firsthand knowledge of how and where the animals that you study in the classroom live. At many colleges, summer courses give you an opportunity to work full-time on field projects.

If you are comparing wildlife and wilderness management programs, look carefully at the courses offered to see whether programs you are considering favor traditional game management, or whether their courses reflect a broader, more modern conservation-biology focus.

Other majors you might like:
Forestry
Zoology
Botany
Entomology
Range science
Veterinary technology
Animal sciences
Biology
Natural sciences
Land use planning
Wildlife biology
Ecology

Questions to ask colleges:
Is the wildlife program a full major, or just a concentration within another major, such as zoology or forestry?

Does the school offer (or require) a broad array of natural resources management courses beyond those in the wildlife major?

What opportunities are there to do course-related field experience or to become involved in graduate student or faculty research? Are there good field sites near the campus? Is there a study-abroad program in this major?

Do the courses required for the major satisfy The Wildlife Society's standards for certification?

Career options and trends:
Wildlife biologist; research biologist; environmental educator; environmental consultant; university professor; park or field naturalist; conservation biologist; wildlife manager.

The job outlook continues to be very competitive. Students hoping to enter this field should complete at least a four-year Bachelor's of Science degree. Field experience gained through internships and temporary jobs remains an important way to obtain a permanent job. A graduate program leading to a Master's of Science degree can enhance your marketability for full-time employment and for advancement in the field.

Insider's viewpoint:
"A challenge of the major is low pay. It's also a really competitive field. There are a lot of people wanting to go into it."

—Chad, junior, Oregon State University

For more info:
The Wildlife Society (TWS)
5410 Grosvenor Lane
Suite 200
Bethesda, MD 20814-2144
(301) 897-9770
www.wildlife.org

Parks and recreation

If you choose to study parks and recreation, you will become something of an expert in leisure, and that may mean you'll get teased a bit.

"Students in this major should expect some 'razzing' regarding their chosen major," admits Professor Lowell Caneday of Oklahoma State University.

But you may end up laughing all the way to the bank, because several mega-trends suggest that working at playing will be a hot job market in the future. Employment in recreation, parks, and leisure services is expected to increase over the long term. One reason is that when economies rebound there is pent up demand for recreational activities. Also, folks are living longer, more active lives. Students seem to get it, because recreation and sports majors have been among the fastest growing over the last ten years.

Hmmm, let's see... A popular group of majors. A growing market segment. A college career devoted to studying what people do for fun. Sounds like a slam dunk. But these majors aren't just a walk in the park or a day at the beach. College is college, and you will have to buckle down.

The foundations for academic preparation in recreation, park, and leisure studies include behavioral sciences: human growth and development, normal and abnormal psychology, cultural and environmental sociology, learning and leadership theory, motivation and consumer behavior.

People in this field run programs and supervise and administer activities in many settings: state and national parks, campus recreational programs, hospitals, long-term-care facilities, youth service agencies, military recreational facilities, forest recreation, commercial settings, church outings, corporate and employee recreational destinations, resorts and cruise ships, and camps.

Graduate students dive into topics like leisure services management and therapeutic recreation, or follow business tracks in commercial recreation and tourism management.

Fans know that sports management is also big. Even if you can't swish a trey, you can become a pro at sports marketing, sports and the law, sports finance and business, college sports, events management, and labor relations.

Sports management "is concerned with the operation of many types of sports organizations, ranging from professional teams and leagues to national and international amateur sports organizations, federations, conferences, and associations," says Professor Stephen W. Jefferson, University of Massachusetts Amherst. Sports management is linked to professions including broadcasting, community relations, finance and accounting, law, licensing, and merchandising.

A park-like campus

Start your college search by looking at divisions and schools of education, physical education, and recreation; health and human services; arts and sciences; forestry and natural resources; and yes, business. Where the college stands in its approach to these majors may depend on where it sits.

"Since these programs may be found in a wide variety of academic units or divisions on college campuses, differences between programs can be expected depending upon the 'academic home,'" says Caneday. "Programs housed in education or human services divisions focus on human behavior, whereas programs offered by forestry or natural resources divisions emphasize the natural environment. Programs in business divisions will likely stress management, economics, finance, and business practices."

Compare schools by considering whether the program plays an important role in the college's family of offerings or is just an add-on to a department devoted to other majors. Does the college have diverse courses such as program design in leisure services; natural resource recreation; sport marketing, management, and law?

Is the program accredited? If so, it has passed an external review by the likes of the National Recreation and Park Association (www.nrpa.org), the American Association for Leisure and Recreation (www.aahperd.org/aalr), or other recognized body. Parks and recreation programs that are accredited must teach conceptual foundations, professional practices and service delivery, programming strategies, assessment, planning, evaluation, management, and legislative and legal issues. Accredited programs also offer field experience. There's more than one type of accreditation, so ask which kind the college has.

In addition to accreditation, you will need to be certified for some jobs in therapeutic recreation, so ask what the pass rate is for recent grads on their national certification examinations. (See, these majors aren't so easy after all.)

Other questions: What is the placement rate of graduates, and where are they finding jobs? What research are faculty members doing, and are undergraduates helping? Will regular faculty members teach your classes or will graduate assistants? You want the veterans, not the rookies.

In sports management programs particularly, find out if the college has a good network of graduates that gives you a chance to rub elbows with professionals, do networking, and find internships. An internship might be a tryout for a great job.

"A major in recreation, park, and leisure studies provides the foundation to work in a career focusing on improving the quality of life for all," Caneday observes.

That would certainly make the teasing worthwhile.

Parks, recreation, and leisure studies

Also known as:
Leisure sciences

What it's about:
This major focuses on the environments, behaviors, and experiences of people during recreation. You examine people's motivations for choosing a pastime, investigate the effects of their behaviors, and develop skills to manage a variety of recreation and leisure services, enterprises, and organizations.

Is this for you?
You might like this major if you also like: working with different types and ages of people; voluntary service programs such as Scouting, 4-H, YM/YWCA; sports; games that require physical and social interaction; leading or organizing group activities.

Consider this major if you are good at: active listening; caring/nurturing; counseling; creativity; leadership; organizing; persuading/influencing ...*or have...* initiative; verbal skills; writing skills.

Recommended high school prep:
English 4, math 3, lab science 3, social studies 3, and a foreign language 2–3. If possible, also take courses in writing, computer applications, communications (speech, drama, or debate), psychology, and sociology.

Did you know...
...that jobs related to parks, recreation, and leisure are among the fastest-growing areas of employment according to the United States Department of Labor? In addition, a career in this field is identified as one of the top ten most satisfying jobs among working people surveyed.

Typical courses in this major:
Introduction to parks, recreation, and leisure
History of leisure
Philosophy of leisure
Recreation for special populations
Recreation leadership
Program and event planning
Area and facility design
Computer applications in leisure services
Evaluation of leisure services
Administration of leisure services
Legal issues in leisure services
Marketing recreation enterprises
Outdoor recreation
Commercial recreation

Concentrations:
Leisure services management; therapeutic recreation; natural resources recreation; tourism; program management; commercial recreation.

What the study of this major is like:
"Leisure" is actually a complex, multifaceted concept that differs from person to person. As a major in parks, recreation, and leisure studies, you encounter many different aspects and applications, from the operation of community leisure services to the provision of therapeutic recreation. Your studies are generally built upon behavioral science courses, such as human growth and development, normal and abnormal psychology, cultural and environmental sociology, learning and leadership theory, and motivation and consumer behavior.

Professors may employ a variety of teaching techniques and learning styles. Most classes feature lectures supported by appropriate technology, questioning, and group interaction; in many classes, you'll do laboratory work, or applied experiences, in which you organize, deliver, and evaluate leisure services for specific populations. In fact, all accredited programs in the major require one or more fieldwork activities, either as part of your regular courses, as internships for credit, or as employment or voluntary service.

Parks, recreation, and leisure studies has been identified as a "discovery" major, meaning most students learn about it only after arriving at college; so you may find second- or third-year students beginning the major with you. The two biggest challenges of the major are, first, the combination of theory, applied learning, and service delivery experience that is necessary to develop a complete perspective; and second, time management. Don't be surprised by how demanding this major can be.

Programs in parks, recreation, and leisure studies may be found in a variety of academic divisions. Therefore, differences between programs may depend upon a program's academic home. Programs housed in education or human services divisions focus more on human behavior, whereas programs offered by forestry or natural resources divisions emphasize the natural environment. Programs in business divisions will likely stress management, economics, finance, and business practices.

Besides fieldwork, the accreditation standards require all students to learn conceptual foundations; professional and service delivery practices; programming and assessment strategies; planning; and evaluation, management, legislative, and legal issues. Concentrations can prepare you for service in therapeutic recreation, park and recreation management, not-for-profit management, military recreation, correctional leisure services, natural resources recreation, sports management, tourism management, and other specialties.

Other majors you might like:
Landscape architecture
Physical education
Tourism/travel management
Recreational therapy
Sports communications
Hospitality administration and management
Gerontology
Forestry
Athletic training
Sports and fitness administration
Exercise sciences
Family/community services

Questions to ask colleges:
Is the program accredited by The National Recreation and Park Association (NRPA)? If you are interested in a specific concentration, be sure to ask if that aspect of the program is also accredited.

Where do students complete their internships? What additional field experience is expected or required of students? What is the "pass rate" for recent graduates on the national certification exams?

Career options and trends:
Activities director (sports, aquatics, outdoor pursuits, etc.); program supervisor; department administrator; facilities manager; park ranger; certified therapeutic recreation specialist.

Majors find jobs in campus recreation, hospitals, long-term-care facilities, YM/YWCAs and other youth service agencies, commercial outfitters, corporate recreation services, resorts and cruise ships, camps, and similar areas.

Most public park and recreation agencies will expect you to have the certified park and recreation professional (CPRP) credential offered by the NRPA. Numerous skill-based certifications, in such areas as first aid, aquatic facility management, challenge-course programming, and outdoor/environmental education, may also be required.

Long-term trends that are fueling employment growth include increasing affluence within a growing population; longer and more energetic retirement lives; expanding leisure opportunities through technology; and increased expectations of populations that have been underserved in the past. These trends are likely to continue well into this century.

For more info:
National Recreation and Park Association (NRPA)
22377 Belmont Ridge Rd.
Ashburn, VA 20148
(800) 626 6772
www.nrpa.org

Sport and fitness administration

What it's about:

The sports and fitness administration major prepares you to apply the principles of business, coaching, and physical education to the management of athletic programs, sports teams, fitness facilities and health clubs, and sport recreation.

Is this for you?

You might like this major if you also like: mathematical and logical puzzles; playing sports; managing fantasy league sports teams; attending sports events; interacting with athletes; tracking sports statistics.

Consider this major if you are good at: attention to detail; coaching; critical reading/thinking; leadership; math; teamwork *...or have...* initiative; patience; verbal skills; writing skills.

Recommended high school prep:

English 4 (including a writing course), math 4 (including precalculus), lab science 3, social studies 3, and a foreign language 2–3. If possible, take an economics course and any business courses that are offered.

Did you know...

...that successfully managing athletes, sports teams, or sports facilities involves a lot of math, logic, and other business skills?

Typical courses in this major:

History of sports
Sociology of sports
Kinesiology (exercise science)
Human anatomy and physiology
Sports and fitness marketing
Sports communications
Sports finance
Sports law
Athletic program management
Fitness program management
Labor relations and professional sports
Facilities management
Media relations
Economics of sports
Community relations
Principles of coaching

Concentrations:

In college: professional sports; sports communication; sports broadcasting; fitness management; recreation and tourism; sports marketing; sports finance; sport agency; facilities and event management.

If you go on to grad school: social-historical foundations of modern sports; sports economics; sports organizational behavior and development; sports management policy; labor relations.

What the study of this major is like:

Sports are fun and exciting, but sports are also a business. Whatever aspect of sports and fitness administration you pursue, you will most likely need a solid business foundation. In most sports and fitness administration programs, you take courses in accounting, finance, management, economics, and marketing (and perhaps computer science and precalculus) before you begin sports-specific business courses.

Within the major, you generally take three types of courses. The first type is devoted to theory—the sociology, psychology, physiology, and history of sports. The second explores the fundamentals of business and management. The third type involves the application of management theory to specific aspects of the sports and fitness industry, such as marketing and public relations; sports law; business operations for sports, health, and fitness organizations; the organization of and management of events; media relations; broadcasting; and college athletics.

Because sports management is relatively difficult to break into, most programs include a fieldwork component or encourage you to get hands-on experience and to make valuable connections through internships. The types of internships offered by programs vary. Some colleges have connections to sport industries or are located near sports or broadcasting facilities that are willing to hire interns. You may also be able to work in facilities on campus or at college-sponsored events.

In addition, programs at different colleges may have different emphases. Some programs focus on college athletics—how to create and nurture competitive teams, meet budgets, and maybe even coach. In programs that focus on spectator sports, you learn how to attract and satisfy fans. Programs that stress participant sports and fitness teach you how to find and manage individual athletes, or how to manage and operate health clubs and spas. Fitness-oriented programs will stress health related courses such as anatomy and physiology, nutrition, injury prevention, and physical training.

Other majors you might like:

Athletic training
Physical education
Public relations
Business administration and management
Marketing
Sports communications
Physical therapy
Entrepreneurial studies
Equestrian studies
Fishing and fisheries
Hospitality administration and management
Tourism/travel management

Questions to ask colleges:

Are there adequate facilities for students to do hands-on activities as part of their course work? For example, are there places where students participate in selling tickets, running events, or marketing? The answers should help you determine the quality of the program.

Is the sports and fitness program offered as its own major or is it simply a minor (sometimes offered through a business school) or a concentration in some other field? The answer to this question can give you an idea of the size of the program as well as the college's commitment to it.

Does the curriculum include an internship track that might lead to job opportunities in the field? If so, are a wide variety of internships available, including positions in such areas as facility management, events management, sports agency, or sports marketing? Check to see that the internship placement opportunities match your own interests.

Does the program have a strong alumni network? Often a good alumni network results in better internship opportunities and job openings.

Career options and trends:

Athletic director; health club manager; sports broadcaster; promoter; sports agent or scout; fitness program coordinator; general manager.

Sports managers are concerned with the operation of many types of organizations: professional teams and leagues, college athletic departments and conference offices, and national and international amateur sports organizations. Sports and fitness administration graduates also serve the sport industry through club and facilities management, marketing and event promotion, and sports clothing and equipment sales and distribution.

Job prospects are generally excellent—the sports and fitness industry is strong and growing. There are minor fluctuations from year to year and small ups and downs in salaries for entry-level jobs, but even in tighter markets, sports fitness and administration majors who have initiative are in demand.

For more info:

North American Society for Sport Management (NASSM)
NASSM Business Office, West Gym 014
Slippery Rock University
Slippery Rock, PA 16057
(724) 738-4812
www.nassm.com

American Alliance for Health, Physical Education, Recreation and Dance (AAHPERD)
1900 Association Drive
Reston, VA 20191-1598
(800) 213- 7193
www.aahperd.org

Physical sciences

If someone asked you why the sky is blue, would you tell them about wavelengths? If so, you know something about the laws of nature, and that's what the physical sciences are all about. Areas of study in this group include aeronautics and aviation science, astronomy, astrophysics, atmospheric science, chemistry, geology (earth science), oceanography, and physics. The most popular major is chemistry, where students earn more than half of all bachelor's degrees in the physical sciences.

"Chemistry is the entry point for many careers in science. Almost every interesting question has chemistry at its base," says Professor James N. Spencer, Franklin and Marshall College. "As we learn about life processes, drug action, synthetic fuels, and behavior, the more evident it is that chemical processes are vitally important to understanding."

Physics is another top major and a foundation for many of these studies. It covers the principles of mechanics (forces, energy, and the basic laws of motion), electricity and magnetism, quantum mechanics, and thermodynamics (the theory of heat).

"There are no limits on what physics can do for us, but there are serious challenges in what we can do with physics," says Professor Bahram Roughani, who teaches applied physics at Kettering University. "That is why preparing the next generation of physicists is crucial for society."

The physical sciences are exciting and exacting. How deep is the ocean? What will tomorrow's weather be? When did the world begin? Better get out your calculator to answer physical science questions.

"You are usually required to complete an introduction to probability and statistics course, and mathematics through first-year calculus," says Ronald E. Johnson, professor of oceanography at Old Dominion University. "You then apply this knowledge at increasingly complex levels."

The climate is the same in atmospheric science. "Most students don't realize that meteorology is an applied physical science that is mathematically intensive and challenging. It involves developing sophisticated quantitative and conceptual skills. Mathematics is heavily used," says Professor James P. Koermer, Plymouth State College.

"Astronomy is a quantitative physical science, and upper-level astronomy courses usually require substantial preparation in physics and mathematics," adds Professor Richard G. French of Wellesley College. "I love being able to reach into the toolkit of mathematics and physics to help untangle the mysterious objects that we see."

Make a quantum leap

You've worked hard in high school and studied all the math offered. Soon you'll be ready for the next level: choosing a college with a great physical sciences program. Look for these majors in colleges of arts and sciences or engineering, and schools or divisions of science. For aeronautics, look for schools of aviation or transportation.

Here are a few things to consider: Find out if you need to come in with stellar math skills or if the college will help you catch up. Ask if your major is in the physical sciences department or has its own department. The setup may affect the course sequence and which courses you can take. "A wide range of courses offered on a reasonable time schedule is a good indication of a quality program," Johnson says.

Every college is different, just as every student is different. Some departments put more emphasis on lab work than others. Ask if introductory courses have a lab component. Some colleges require undergrads to do a research project. Ask if you'll have the chance to do research with faculty members or if you'll work independently. See what recent projects students have done.

Try to get an idea of the college's approach. Is the program more about applying the science or learning it in an academic sense? "Some colleges may emphasize work in observational astronomy more than theoretical astrophysics, some may do the reverse. A good, balanced program is best," suggests Professor Neta A. Bahcall, Princeton University. "Evaluate the quality of the program—the faculty, facilities, teaching and research programs, as well as the mentorship available."

As for the faculty, how many professors have advanced degrees and will those professors be your teachers (or will your instructors be grad students)? Have a look at the faculty members' publications to see what they're researching. Find out if you'll be studying hot new majors like nanotechnology or environmental aspects of the physical sciences.

Also ask about the quality of the laboratories, computers, and other equipment. How much access will you have to the best stuff, like the most powerful telescope on or near campus? Will you go on expeditions like coastal field exercises in oceanography?

What are former students doing? Are graduates successful at landing jobs in government and industry? Jobs in the physical sciences include scientist, researcher, teacher or professor, policymaker, writer, data analyst, software developer, pilot, astronaut, broadcaster, and medical doctor. Be sure to explore your graduate school options for advanced sciences. (See the majors in this section for examples of graduate studies.)

Aeronautics and aviation science

Also known as:
Air transportation
Airline/commercial pilot

What it's about:
The aviation science major prepares you for a career as a flight crew member on commercial aircraft, a corporate pilot, or other type of pilot. In your training to become an aviation professional, you will be encouraged to develop your mathematical and problem-solving skills. Emphasis is placed on crew resource management, safety, and the principles involved in aircraft operations.

Is this for you?
You might like this major if you also like: flying; travel; mathematical and logical puzzles; working with machinery; interacting with people; looking up at every airplane that flies over.

Consider this major if you are good at: attention to detail; leadership; math; memorizing; spacial thinking/analysis; teamwork *...or have...* manual dexterity; mental stamina; verbal skills.

Recommended high school prep:
English 4, math 4 (including precalculus), lab science 3 (including a physics course that covers electricity and magnetism), social studies 3, and a foreign language 2–3. It is not necessary to have flight experience.

Did you know...
...that this major covers a variety of subjects? Math and physics are obviously important, but your course work will also help you acquire problem-solving and communication skills, as well as good judgment.

...that an increasing number of men and women enter professional flying careers directly out of college, without military training?

Typical courses in this major:
Aeronautics
Flight instruction
Meteorology
Aerodynamics
Aircraft performance
Aircraft engines
High speed, long range navigation
Aircraft systems and components
Flight physiology
Crew resource management
Jet transport systems
Flight safety
Flight technique analysis
Turbojet techniques and crew procedure
Electronic navigation and flight control systems
International flight operations

Concentrations:
In college: airline pilot; corporate pilot; law enforcement aviation; agricultural aviation; military pilot (ROTC).

If you go on to grad school: aviation education technology; aviation management; aviation/aerospace operations; safety systems; human factors in aviation systems; space studies.

What the study of this major is like:
As an aviation science major, you combine flight training and academic studies, preparing for a career as a professional flight crew member on a jet transport aircraft, a corporate pilot, or a military pilot. Generally, you spend your first two years learning basic physics, mathematics, and communications skills, as well as fundamental aeronautics. You study how aircraft are designed and how they work, including the function of flight systems and controls and of navigation systems. You also study the procedures and government regulations for flight crew operations, radio communications, air safety, air traffic, and navigation.

In your third and fourth years, you take advanced training courses and study high-level aeronautical science. With the aid of both aircraft trainers and simulator trainers, you practice flying, navigating, and operating aircraft. These exercises help you sharpen your abilities to react quickly and effectively, by analyzing situations and solving problems. As in all flight-related courses, the paramount emphasis is on safety.

In addition to flight training, some programs offer courses in the human factors of aviation, which may include cockpit resource management, aviation psychology, and aviation accident investigation and analysis. In conjunction with courses in business, economics, communications, and management, you are prepared for a variety of careers in the aviation industry besides flying.

Depending on the strength of the program, by the time you graduate you may be qualified to take commercial and airline crew examinations given by the Federal Aviation Administration, or you may have already earned FAA certification as an instrument-rated commercial pilot.

Other majors you might like:
Aviation management
Aeronautical/aerospace engineering
Atmospheric science
Physics
Transportation management
Geography
Air traffic control
Aircraft powerplant technology
Avionics maintenance/technology
Military technologies

Questions to ask colleges:
Are faculty members experienced in the aviation industry? Professionally experienced instructors can do more than teach you about aircraft and how to fly them; they can also give you valuable insights into the aviation industry.

Which FAA certifications (private pilot, multi-engine, commercial, and others) and ratings do students qualify for at the completion of their training? How much of the costs of obtaining the certifications are covered by tuition?

How many and which types of aircraft and simulators are available for student flight training? You will need sufficient access to appropriate, well-maintained aircraft and adequate simulator time.

Is the program accredited by the Aviation Accreditation Board International (AABI)?

Career options and trends:
Passenger airline pilot*; corporate pilot*; military pilot*; aircraft dispatcher; flight instructor; natural resources pilot; firefighting pilot; law enforcement pilot; aerial applicator.

All pilots who are paid to transport passengers or cargo must have a commercial pilot's license with an instrument rating issued by the FAA, which requires a minimum of 250 hours of flight experience. Requirements for the airlines are much higher. You must have an airline transport pilot's license (minimum of 1,500 hours); obtain night, instrument, and multiengine ratings; and pass FAA written and flight examinations. Depending on the airline, you may have to be certified for specific types of aircraft and pass psychological and aptitude tests.

Jobs in the airline industry are closely tied to the economy. During times of recession, as well as decreased air travel for other reasons, airlines will be forced to lay off flight crews, normally for a few months only. Competition for jobs is expected to be strong, even with a projected growth in passenger travel and the approaching retirement age of a considerable number of pilots. The fastest growth should occur among regional commuter airlines, although at lower pay scales.

More pilots with civilian rather than military training are entering the airline profession; but military pilots continue to have a competitive advantage because they usually have more flight experience in sophisticated equipment.

Insider's viewpoint:
"Aviation allows one to meet individuals from many cultures, and get paid to have a god's-eye view of humanity below."

—Professor David Esser, Embry-Riddle Aeronautical University

For more info:

Aviation Accreditation Board International (AABI)
3410 Skyway Drive
Auburn, AL 36830-6444
(334) 844-2431
www.aabi.aero

Federal Aviation Administration (FAA)
800 Independence Ave., S.W.
Washington, DC 20591
(866) 835-5322
www.faa.gov

Women in Aviation, International (WAI)
Morningstar Airport
3647 State Route 503 South
West Alexandria, OH 45381
(937) 839-4647
www.wai.org

Applied physics

Also known as:
Engineering physics

What it's about:
Applied physics combines pure physics with math, science, and engineering principles, and applies them to practical ends. It is especially geared toward advanced and emerging technologies such as nanotechnology, medical and advanced imaging, and renewable energies.

Is this for you?
You might like this major if you also like: learning how things work; working in teams; learning about new technologies; relating theoretical concepts to practical uses; participating in science fairs and competitions or summer science camps.

Consider this major if you are good at: thinking creatively; math; quantitative analysis; spatial thinking/analysis; attention to detail; research ...*or have...* initiative; curiosity; verbal skills; writing skills.

Recommended high school prep:
English 4, math 4 (including precalculus or calculus), lab science 4 (including physics and chemistry), social studies 3, and a foreign language 3. Take as many additional math and science courses as you can.

Did you know...
...that applied physicists usually don't design anything in particular? That's for the engineers. Rather, applied physicists use physics concepts or conduct research to develop new technologies or solve an engineering problem.

Typical courses in this major:
Calculus and analytic geometry
Classical mechanics
Quantum mechanics
Electricity and magnetism
Thermodynamics
Physics of waves
Optics
Acoustics
Materials science
Nanotechnology
Applied nuclear physics
Fiber optics
Optoelectronics
Solid state physics
Computer modeling
Statistical mechanics

Concentrations:
In college: acoustics; optics; nanotechnology; biophysics; computational physics; space science; environmental science; microelectronics.

If you go on to grad school: accelerator physics; biomedical and health physics; laser physics; microfluids; plasma physics; quantum information science.

What the study of this major is like:
Besides its "practical" emphasis, the principal way that this major differs from the traditional physics major is the greater breadth and flexibility that it offers. Introductory and upper-level courses integrate other related disciplines such as engineering, computer science, chemistry and biology, and you have a much greater choice of electives and concentrations.

For example, courses in applied optics may combine knowledge of fiber optics, lasers, and LEDs with electrical devices, controls, and communication systems in order to explore ways to increase data transfer rates or Internet bandwidth. Or, courses in applied materials could combine the physics of electronic, magnetic, and optical materials with the engineering behind materials processing to examine possible applications of nanotechnology.

Courses are often taught in a combination of approaches. The basic courses may be either a traditional lecture and lab or a combined lecture/lab setting. More advanced courses include group projects, independent research work, and a senior thesis project. (More rigorous programs may require a high-level senior research thesis that makes an "original contribution" to the field.)

Ideally, course work is combined with extended work co-op or internships that provide hands-on experience, enabling you to see the connection between physics concepts and their application in real-world cases.

Among colleges there are varying requirements for an applied physics degree, ranging from two terms of elective lab courses added to a traditional physics program, to a more rigorous four-year plan. In the later case there may be a required sequence (concentration) of courses in a specific field of applied physics such as acoustics, optics, medical physics, and the like; plus a sequence of technical courses (minor) in a field outside physics such as engineering; plus a co-op experience or summer internship; plus a thesis.

As you consider this degree, be aware that a high level of preparation in high school mathematics is necessary to grasp the advanced physics concepts you will be facing. You should expect to engage in teamwork with other students in group projects, as well as individual problem solving and independent research. This is a challenging degree that requires a passion for learning, discipline, and good time management skills.

Other majors you might like:
Applied mathematics
Biophysics
Biomedical engineering
Architectural engineering
Environmental engineering
Nuclear engineering
Industrial design
Aeronautics and aviation science
Aeronautical/aerospace engineering
Radiologic technology/medical imaging
Robotics
Entrepreneurial studies

Questions to ask colleges:
How does your applied physics major differ from traditional physics or engineering majors?

Is there a co-op or internship requirement? If so, is there placement assistance?

Are there a thesis requirement for this degree?

What facilities and laboratories are available for each area of emphasis in applied physics?

Career options and trends:
Optical engineer*; medical physicist; researcher*; acoustics engineer*; materials scientist*; laser technologist.

The applied physics major will open the door to almost any technical industry, but most opportunities will require a master's degree. A bachelor's degree may qualify you for entry-level positions related to engineering, computer science, environmental science, and some nonscience fields, such as sales. There is also a strong demand for high school physics teachers, but most states require new teachers to obtain a master's degree within a certain time.

The Bureau of Labor Statistics projects favorable prospects through 2018 in applied research, development, and related technologies, particularly for physicists with good oral and written communication skills and some knowledge in areas outside of physics, such as economics, information technology, or business management.

The fastest job growth will be in the biomedical, environmental, alternative energy, and similar advanced and emerging technologies.

For more info:
American Institute of Physics (AIP)
One Physics Ellipse
College Park, MD 20740-3845
301-209-3100
www.aip.org

American Physical Society (APS)
One Physics Ellipse
College Park, MD 20740-3844
(301) 209-3200
www.aps.org

Astronomy

What it's about:

Astronomy majors study the universe beyond our atmosphere, beginning with the underlying physical principles. You observe and investigate the planets, stars, and galaxies, as you learn methods of inquiry such as optical astronomy, radio astronomy, and theoretical astronomy.

Is this for you?

You might like this major if you also like: observing the changing patterns in the sky—the constellations, phases of the moon, and eclipses; news about space exploration and technology; science museums; computers; taking things apart and putting them back together to see how they work.

Consider this major if you are good at: attention to detail; creativity; critical reading/thinking; math; quantitative analysis; research; spacial thinking/analysis; teamwork *...or have...* initiative; paticnce.

Recommended high school prep:

English 4, math 4 (including precalculus or calculus), lab science 4 (including physics), social studies 3, and a foreign language 2–3. If possible, take an introduction to computer science course and a writing course. Also, take as many advanced science courses as you can.

Did you know...

...that astronomers spend only a small part of their time looking through telescopes? In fact, astronomers spend most of their time analyzing data with computers. Most people think that astronomy is about stargazing, but it is actually a quantitative science with plenty of math and physics.

Typical courses in this major:

Stars, galaxies, and cosmology
Planetary astronomy
Observational astronomical techniques
Planetary geology
Archaeoastronomy and the history of astronomy
Computer science
Multiwavelength astronomy
Calculus
Quantum physics
Planetary physics
Galactic astronomy
Extragalactic astronomy and cosmology
Stellar structure and evolution
Astrophysical techniques
Observational radio astronomy
Observational optical astronomy

Concentrations:

In college: observational astronomy; planetary science; extragalactic astronomy and cosmology; multiwavelength astronomy.

If you go on to grad school: radio astronomy; interstellar processes; planetary physics; stars and stellar structure; dynamical astronomy; galactic structure; astronomical instrumentation.

What the study of this major is like:

Students of astronomy examine the key components of the universe, such as the stars and planets, and the physical and mathematical laws that govern them. In cosmology, you analyze current theories about the origins and future of the universe; planetary astronomy describes the surfaces and makeup of the planets and moons in the solar system. Usually, the solar system and stars, galaxies, and cosmology are covered in two separate courses. Most likely, you'll attend weekly laboratory sessions in which you study such topics as the constellations and the motions of the sky, the properties of gravity and of light, and the operation of telescopes.

Once you complete the survey courses, the pace quickens. If you are serious about majoring in astronomy, you should plan your program of study to ensure that you take the required upper-level courses in physics and mathematics. Typically, these courses are the equivalent of a major in physics and a minor in math.

Most astronomy departments offer at least one course in astrophysics; as the theoretical side of astronomy, it explores the formation and evolution of stars, galaxies, and the universe itself. Many students find this investigation to be challenging, because it requires fluency in the language of math and physics. To learn why a star shines, for example, you need a basic understanding of mechanics, electricity and magnetism, thermodynamics and statistical mechanics, quantum mechanics, special relativity, and nuclear physics.

Most astronomy departments offer upper-level courses in observation through telescopes. You may have opportunities to carry out independent projects, typically using a digital (CCD) camera and requiring computer analysis of the observations. Even on research projects, you can often get by with relatively small telescopes. For a taste of professional astronomy, you may be able to do research, during the summer, at national observatories, or at some universities and colleges.

Departments with a strong physics orientation might emphasize astrophysics rather than observational techniques; those with strong connections to a research observatory might stress the development of instrumentation and hands-on astronomy. At some colleges, planetary astronomy is offered in coordination with the departments of geology and/or atmospheric science. Some departments offer two tracks in the astronomy program: one leads to broad, general knowledge of the field; the other, which includes intensive work in physics and mathematics, prepares you for graduate study.

Other majors you might like:

Astrophysics
Planetary sciences
Atmospheric sciences
Computer science
Geology/earth science
Physics
Aeronautical/aerospace engineering
Mathematics
Aeronautics and aviation science

Questions to ask colleges:

What observing facilities are available on or near campus? Can undergraduates use the largest telescope? Is there a digital camera on the telescope? Are there computers that can be used to analyze the observations?

What opportunities are available for undergraduates to participate in research during the academic year or over the summer? Are there opportunities for independent study? What are some recent projects by astronomy majors? Is there an astronomy club?

Career options and trends:

Most astronomers working in the field do research at universities, observatories, or laboratories, or teach at the high school or college level. A small number work in planetariums and science museums. An advanced degree is required.

The major in astronomy provides excellent preparation for careers in fields other than the physical sciences. Astronomy majors have become engineers, neurosurgeons, trial lawyers, insurance executives, and business leaders.

Insider's viewpoint:

"There's a lot of acronyms, special terminology for things. There's a lot of data: when people give talks they list names of stars, not "Rigel" or the sun, but they'll give the names and numbers. It takes a few years of experience to comprehend those."

—David, junior, University of Texas at Austin

For more info:

American Astronomical Society (AAS)
2000 Florida Ave., N.W.
Suite 400
Washington, DC 20009-1231
(202) 328-2010
www.aas.org

American Association of Variable Star Observers
49 Bay State Rd.
Cambridge, MA 02138
(617) 354-0484
www.aavso.org

Astrophysics

What it's about:

Astrophysics, which focuses on the theoretical side of astronomy, presents the basic physical laws of the formation, evolution, and behavior of stars, galaxies, and the universe itself.

Is this for you?

You might like this major if you also like: using a telescope; math; computers; science fiction; abstract thinking; logical solutions; working through complex problems.

Consider this major if you are good at: attention to detail; creativity; critical reading/thinking; math; quantitative analysis; research; spacial thinking/analysis ...*or have...* imagination; initiative.

Recommended high school prep:

English 4, math 4 (including precalculus or calculus), lab science 4 (earth science, biology, chemistry, and physics), social studies 3, and a foreign language 2–3. Take as much advanced math and science as you can. Courses in language arts and computer skills are also important.

Did you know...

...the difference between astrophysics and astronomy? Some people in the field say there isn't any, because all astronomers use physics to understand their findings. Basically, astronomy places greater emphasis on observing, measuring, and gathering data about celestial bodies and phenomena, while astrophysics concentrates on the physical processes of outer space and the origin and future of the universe.

Typical courses in this major:

Principles of astrophysics
Waves and particles
Quantum mechanics
Differential equations
Stars and star formation
Topics in modern astronomy
Galactic astronomy
Extragalactic astronomy
Cosmology
The early universe
Plasma astrophysics
The interstellar medium
High-energy astrophysics
General relativity

Concentrations:

Theoretical astrophysics; observational astronomy; cosmology; high-energy astrophysics.

What the study of this major is like:

Astrophysics is a rigorous major, with plenty of physics and mathematics (much like the physics major itself), especially in your first two years. You typically take courses in upper-level astronomy, astrophysics, physics, and math; you also do independent research projects in observational or theoretical astrophysics. Your course work generally includes topics such as stars and stellar evolution, galaxies and extragalactic astronomy, cosmology, relativity, and the physics of space plasma.

You should be prepared to spend time in an observational astronomy lab and perhaps to research and write a senior thesis. Most programs place a great deal of emphasis on both independent and collaborative research. Independent projects can cover any research topic in the field, from planets to the Big Bang. You use computers for all projects, including data analyses, investigation through telescopes, and theoretical modeling of the universe. If you are interested in the solar system, you should probably take additional geology courses.

Some colleges do not distinguish between astrophysics and astronomy; others design the astrophysics major primarily as a stepping-stone to graduate study in the field and offer astronomy as a less rigorous science major for liberal arts students. If you see yourself working with equations more than with telescopes to unlock the secrets of the universe, then a strong astrophysics program might be for you.

Other majors you might like:
Physics
Aeronautical/aerospace engineering
Astronomy
Planetary sciences
Geology/earth science
Geophysics//seismology
Nuclear engineering
Mathematics
Computer science
Aeronautical/aerospace engineering technology
Philosophy

Questions to ask colleges:
What opportunities are there for undergrads to work individually with faculty members on research projects?

Such opportunities are desirable for any science major, but they are particularly important for astrophysics majors because research is fundamental to the field.

Is the department of astronomy and astrophysics separate from the physics department?

Are the physics courses that are needed to fulfill requirements offered on a regular basis?

How much time do undergraduates get at either on-campus or off-campus observatories?

Career options and trends:
Professor*; researcher*; science teacher; software developer.

Most jobs are in basic research and development, and in college-level teaching; a doctoral degree is the usual educational requirement for these positions. A bachelor's or master's degree is sufficient for some jobs in applied research and development and in teaching at the high school level. A degree in astrophysics also prepares you for a wide variety of technical careers in industry, especially the computer science, space, and aeronautical fields.

Insider's viewpoint:
"It's very demanding, very time-consuming. The physics and math are really hard. It's a lot of late nights, problem sets, and labs. But I think it's worth it; it's so interesting. I don't want to go to college and not be challenged."

—Allison, sophomore, Harvard University

For more info:
American Astronomical Society (AAS)
2000 Florida Ave., N.W., Suite 400
Washington, DC 20009
(202) 328-2010
www.aas.org

Atmospheric science

Also known as:
Meteorology

What it's about:
In the atmospheric science major, you gain a broad understanding of the Earth's atmosphere, including its composition, structure, processes, and weather systems. Most programs are highly interdisciplinary and rely heavily on math, physics, and chemistry to develop the underlying theories and principles governing atmospheric behavior.

Is this for you?
You might like this major if you also like: the outdoors; computers; aviation; sailing; scientific inquiry and analysis; the Weather Channel; dealing with changing situations.

Consider this major if you are good at: attention to detail; critical reading/thinking; math; organizing; quantitative analysis; spacial thinking/analysis; teamwork *...or have...* a strong work ethic; initiative; patience.

Recommended high school prep:
English 4, math 4, lab science 4 (earth science, biology, chemistry, and physics), social studies 3, and a foreign language 2–3. If it is available, calculus is recommended, as are courses in communications, environmental science, and computer applications.

Did you know...
...that this major is not only about weather maps and TV forecasting? It is an applied physical science that requires you to develop sophisticated skills in math and in abstract thinking. Atmospheric science is essential in such fields as air pollution control, agriculture, air and sea transportation, defense, and the study of trends in the earth's climate, including global warming, droughts, or ozone depletion.

Typical courses in this major:
Climatology
Atmospheric thermodynamics
Observations and instrumentation
Weather communications
Weather analysis and forecasting
Atmospheric dynamics
Air pollution
Mesoscale meteorology
Micrometeorology
Tropical meteorology
Radar meteorology
Remote sensing systems
Stormwater hydrology
Atmospheric boundary layer
Biosphere and carbon cycle

Concentrations:
In college: broadcast meteorology; climatology; mesoscale meteorology; synoptic meteorology; air quality and pollution.

If you go on to grad school: atmospheric physics and dynamics; atmospheric modeling; air chemistry; climate change; cloud physics; tropical meteorology; paleoclimatology; remote sensing; satellite meteorology.

What the study of this major is like:
The major in atmospheric science builds on a core of mathematics, physics, and chemistry. (In fact, you might be required to take enough math courses to earn a math minor.) Your first two years generally include math every semester, a two-semester sequence in chemistry, and a two-semester sequence in physics. In some colleges, you take descriptive, introductory-level meteorology courses during your first few semesters. Other programs may hold off on meteorology until you complete the required math and science courses. In your third and fourth years, you apply math, physics, and chemistry to gain a scientific understanding of how the atmosphere works. Most

weather analysis and forecasting courses are offered at this level. Many programs also offer internships, practicums, and research opportunities.

Although some meteorology courses are primarily in a lecture format, most of them usually have associated laboratories. As with other science and engineering majors, you can expect to spend more time in classes than students in nonscience disciplines, because of longer laboratory courses. Nonscience majors may spend 15 hours per week in class; science and/or engineering majors probably spend closer to 20 hours.

At first, many students are challenged by the math and chemistry requirements, especially if their backgrounds are weak in these areas. Perhaps the biggest hurdle to clear, though, is calculus-based physics, which is the most time-consuming course many students have taken. A solid understanding of physics takes patience and commitment—you should expect to do a great deal of work in this area. But once these potential stumbling blocks have been passed, most students can complete a meteorology program if they remain focused and continue to work hard.

A few colleges emphasize a particular area of atmospheric science, such as weather analysis and forecasting, theoretical meteorology, physical meteorology, or climatology. If you are interested in becoming a weather forecaster, choose a college that emphasizes weather analysis and instrumentation. If you might like to become a broadcast meteorologist for radio or TV, look for programs that will help you develop strong communication skills, with courses in speech, journalism, and related areas.

Other majors you might like:
Chemistry
Geology/earth science
Aeronautics and aviation science
Oceanography
Geography
Agronomy and crop science
Instrumentation technology
Environmental science
Aeronautical/aerospace engineering
Radio and television

Questions to ask colleges:
Does the program meet the minimum guidelines established by the American Meteorological Society? Do graduates possess the minimum requirements needed for entry-level forecasters with the National Weather Service?

Does the program have reliable access to real-time weather data? Does the program support weather visualization tools to access these data? If you are interested in broadcasting, you should also ask if the program has access to studio facilities.

Does the program have any student organizations, such as a student chapter of the American Meteorological Society or the National Weather Association?

Career options and trends:
Operational meteorologist*; certified consulting meteorologist (CCM); broadcast meteorologist*; researcher*; forensic meteorologist.

To be a CCM, you must be certified by the American Meteorological Society (AMS), which requires at least a B.S. degree, experience, a passing grade on AMS exams, and professional references.

Most atmospheric scientists work as weather forecasters, known professionally as operational meteorologists. As long as you are willing to relocate and be flexible, entry-level jobs in forecasting are generally available. A master's degree will improve your job prospects and chances for advancement; it is usually required for positions involving research and development.

Opportunities in broadcasting are rare and highly competitive. The federal government is the largest employer of atmospheric scientists, but hiring in the public sector is expected to decline. This situation should be offset by increased opportunities in private industry, spurred by continuing improvements in weather forecasting. Demand is projected to grow for consulting firms that can give weather-sensitive industries more detailed and closely targeted information than the National Weather Service.

Chemistry

What it's about:

Majors in chemistry study the composition, structure, and properties of matter, as well as the reactions that transform one form of matter into another. Because it is an experimental science, students learn to design and perform the investigations that will lead to a better understanding of the physical world.

Is this for you?

You might like this major if you also like: solving problems; lab experiments; taking things apart; working independently; using math; questioning why things are the way they are.

Consider this major if you are good at: attention to detail; critical reading/thinking; math; quantitative analysis; research; teamwork *...or have...* curiosity; initiative; perserverance; writing skills.

Recommended high school prep:

English 4, math 4 (including precalculus or calculus), lab science 4 (earth science, biology, chemistry and physics), social studies 3, and a foreign language 2-3. If it is available, also take a computer science course.

Did you know...

...that the chemistry major provides preparation for many careers, even outside science? The thorough grounding in math, critical thinking, and computers that the major offers can qualify you for work in areas you might not have expected, such as banking, business, and law.

Typical courses in this major:

General chemistry
Inorganic chemistry
Organic chemistry
Physical chemistry
Analytical chemistry
Biochemistry
Thermodynamics
Quantitative analysis
Instrumental analysis
Environmental chemistry
Spectroscopy and crystallography
Biochemistry
Polymer and materials chemistry

Concentrations:

In college: analytical chemistry; inorganic chemistry; organic chemistry; physical chemistry.

If you go on to grad school: physical and theoretical chemistry; polymer chemistry; materials chemistry; forensic chemistry; medicinal chemistry; environmental chemistry.

What the study of this major is like:

Chemists provide the expertise to create products you encounter every day, such as medicines, fabrics, and synthetic materials. As a major, for example, you learn ways to control the chemical reactions that produce ceramics, semiconductors, insulators, polymers with unusual properties, and molecules essential for life. In your examination of atoms bonding to form molecules, you observe how the properties of substances depend on which atoms are combined, and how.

Chemistry has traditionally been divided into four areas: organic, inorganic, physical, and analytical. Organic chemistry is the study of carbon compounds, whereas inorganic chemistry is the study of all other elements. Physical chemists investigate the structure and properties of matter, and analytical chemists devise the procedures used in identifying and measuring the individual components of complex mixtures.

Chemistry majors usually take a core curriculum that includes courses in all four areas before they concentrate in one area. Your concentration may require you to take advanced courses that explore the methods for synthesizing natural products; that introduce you to the instruments and techniques used in analyzing unknown compounds; or that show you how to use lasers to study a molecular collision. You will also be expected to take courses in math, physics, and, probably, biology.

All chemistry majors spend a great deal of time performing experiments in the laboratory. The lab experience teaches you to observe the world around you, to draw conclusions from these observations, and to challenge currently accepted beliefs. A typical week's classes consist of about three 50-minute classroom sessions and a two- to four-hour lab. Advanced students take independent study courses, in which they work with a professor on a research project. There is generally little time for electives. On top of lecture classes and lab work, you should expect to work on daily problem sets and put in considerable time studying and writing reports.

Some colleges award Bachelor of Arts degrees in chemistry; others award Bachelor of Science degrees; still others offer both. But regardless of which degree is offered, most chemistry programs emphasize critical-thinking and laboratory skills. The American Chemical Society specifies the course requirements that enable a bachelor's degree program to qualify graduates for ACS certification, which most employers look for.

Other majors you might like:
Atmospheric science
Environmental science
Clinical/medical laboratory technology
Soil science
Chemical engineering
Materials engineering
Biochemistry
Molecular biology
Chemical technology
Forensic science
Pharmacy
Chemistry teacher education

Questions to ask colleges:
Are research opportunities and equipment available for all students? Doing worthwhile research is especially important if you intend to go on to grad school.

What do most chemistry majors do after obtaining their degree—go to medical school or graduate school, or go into industry? If one area predominates, it may reflect a particular emphasis in the program.

Does the program qualify graduates for ACS certification?

Career options and trends:
Industrial or pharmaceutical research chemist*; physician, pharmacist, or other medical professional*; pharmaceutical sales representative; high school chemistry teacher*; chemical lab technician; food scientist; government inspector (for FDA or EPA); crime lab analyst or forensic chemist; occupational safety specialist; environmental consultant.

Graduates entering this field may find competition for jobs, particularly in the declining chemical manufacturing industry; job opportunities will be more plentiful in pharmaceutical and biotechnology firms. Research and testing firms will experience healthy growth as manufacturers outsource research and testing formerly done by in-house chemists. Another area of opportunity is environmental research and regulatory compliance. Chemists with a master's or doctorate degree will be in most demand, although those with a bachelor's degree should be able to find work as assistant research scientists in smaller firms.

Insider's viewpoint:
"I really enjoyed organic chemistry, despite the many horror stories I heard beforehand. There is a certain thought process that goes along with orgo and once that process is understood, it becomes logical. Understanding why reactions go the way they do simplifies many problems."

—Christina, junior, University of California: Davis

For more info:
American Chemical Society (ACS)
1155 16th St., N.W.
Washington, DC 20036
(202) 872-4600
www.chemistry.org

Geology/earth science

What it's about:

Geology/earth science is the study of the earth and the forces that act on it. Topics include the history and formation of planet Earth; the behavior of the solids, liquids, and gases that it is composed of; and the interaction between the biosphere—the living things that call the earth their home—and the planet's inorganic, or nonliving, substances.

Is this for you?

You might like this major if you also like: the outdoors; history; archaeology; gems; dinosaurs; rock climbing; hiking and camping; collecting; environmental issues; a broad range of scientific inquiry, from the unimaginably big to the very small.

Consider this major if you are good at: attention to detail; creativity; critical reading/thinking; math; quantitative analysis; spacial thinking/analysis; teamwork *...or have...* initiative; patience; physical stamina; verbal skills; writing skills.

Recommended high school prep:

English 4, math 4 (including precalculus), lab science 4 (earth science, biology, chemistry, and physics), social studies 3, and a foreign language 2–3. Courses in computer science or applications are recommended, if available; and you will benefit if you can obtain a basic understanding of geographic information systems, either in school or on your own.

Did you know...

...that geology isn't just about rocks—it is a scientific discipline closely linked to chemistry, biology, and physics? It is not a place to avoid these other sciences, but rather a place to apply them. The field is becoming increasingly quantitative, so math skills are a definite advantage.

Typical courses in this major:

Physical geology
Historical geology
Paleontology
Structural geology
Mineralogy
Petrology
Surficial geology
Geophysics
Geochemistry
Hydrogeology
Field geology
Stratigraphy and sedimentation
Geologic hazards
Tectonics
Geographical information systems
Earth resources

Concentrations:

In college: geochemistry; geophysics; environmental geology.

If you go on to grad school: paleontology; petrology; petroleum geology; mineralogy; hydrology; tectonics; paleomagnetics; structural geology and tectonics; geological engineering; geochronology.

What the study of this major is like:

Geology/earth science students first take introductory courses in physical and/or historical geology that teach you basics: rock, mineral, and fossil identification; landform evolution; plate tectonics; and the geological time scale. Topical courses, such as environmental geology, planetary geology, or oceanography, may also serve as introductions to the major. Most introductory courses and upper-level courses have weekly three- to four-hour laboratories or field trips of various lengths. To learn other essential geology/earth science tools, you take year-long courses in chemistry, physics, mathematics, and biology.

Upper-level courses are often arranged in sequence: you take courses in a specific order so that you learn the skills and knowledge needed to continue. For instance, a semester or year of mineralogy provides the analytic skills (such as the use of the petrographic microscope) essential for later courses in petrology. Paleontology, sedimentation, and stratigraphy often form a sequence covering the origin of sedimentary rocks and the fossil organisms they may contain. Geomorphology and glacial geology courses focus on processes that shape the earth's surface. Courses in resources—energy, minerals, and water—examine their origin, as well as the exploration, recovery, and use of these essential commodities.

A unique aspect of geology/earth science is its emphasis on the history of the earth—a recurring theme of many courses in the major. Another trademark is its reliance on fieldwork. Because the field is to a geologist what the library is to a historian, most geology/earth science courses include fieldwork as well as lab work. Some undergraduate departments require a semester-long or summer course in field geology, and most graduate departments require such a course for admission. Many summer courses, which average four to five weeks and are based at permanent facilities in the western states, offer intensive training in geological mapping and in preparing reports. After completing the third year and a field course, the best-qualified majors may be able to find summer jobs as geological field assistants or interns in industry or government.

Visualizing in three dimensions, and comprehending the large scale of many geological phenomena, can be challenging at first. And although geologists are typically not regimented in their activities, you cannot afford to be undisciplined. Because deadlines in geology/earth science courses are usually farther apart than in many other majors, you must figure out a long-term time management plan.

The main philosophical differences among programs are in applied rather than purely academic geological science. If you are interested in using your geological training to tackle concrete problems, you will probably be more comfortable in a department that focuses on hydrogeology, petroleum geology, environmental geology, and exploration seismology. Such departments have more of an engineering perspective, and may even have a geological engineer or civil engineer on staff. In more academically focused departments, faculty members include petrologists, mineralogists, paleontologists, and tectonists.

Other majors you might like:
Atmospheric science
Geography
Oceanography
Soil science
Surveying technology
Environmental science
Mining and mineral engineering
Planetary sciences
Geological engineering
Petroleum engineering
Landscape architecture
Science teacher education

Questions to ask colleges:
Are field trips and field instruction built into most, if not all, of the courses?

How many geology majors take chemistry, biology, physics, or math beyond the minimum requirements?

How accessible are facilities and instrumentation housed in other departments, like chemistry, for use by geology majors?

Do any of the faculty members have experience working as professional geologists outside the academic setting (e.g., industry)?

Career options and trends:
Earth science teacher*; engineering geologist; environmental hydrologist*; petroleum geologist; government agency staff geologist; researcher*.

A Ph.D. degree is required for most research positions in colleges and universities and in government.

The petroleum industry is a cyclical business, but over the long term, there will be opportunities in the energy sector, especially for those willing to work overseas. In other industries, the need to comply with environmental regulations will create opportunities for environmental geoscientists, especially hydrologists and engineering geologists.

For more info:
Geological Society of America (GSA)
P.O. Box 9140
Boulder, CO 80301-9140
(303) 357-1000
www.geosociety.org

Oceanography

What it's about:

Oceanography majors study the oceans—their origins; movement; and biological, chemical, geological, and physical components. As an interdisciplinary science, oceanography draws on the natural sciences to increase our understanding of the ocean environments of planet Earth.

Is this for you?

You might like this major if you also like: the coast and the sea; science and math; exploring the unknown; water sports such as boating, diving, surfing, sailing; travel; environmental issues; asking questions such as "how did that bottle get to our beach?"

Consider this major if you are good at: attention to detail; creativity; critical reading/thinking; math; quantitative analysis; research; teamwork ...*or have...* initiative; writing skills.

Recommended high school prep:

English 4, math 4 (including precalculus or calculus), lab science 4 (earth science, biology, chemistry, and physics), social studies 3, and a foreign language 2–3. Courses in writing, computer science, and environmental science are also recommended, if available.

Typical courses in this major:

Physical oceanography
Chemical oceanography
Geological oceanography
Biological oceanography
Waves and tides
Fluid mechanics
Meteorology
Marine ecology
Environmental physiology of marine animals
Sedimentology
Marine pollution
Barrier islands and coastal lagoons
Oceanic and atmospheric processes
Polar oceanography
Estuarine oceanography
Sampling techniques and field studies

Concentrations:

Biological oceanography; chemical oceanography; geological oceanography; physical oceanography; marine resource management.

What the study of this major is like:

Scientists know more about the surface of the moon than they do about the depths of the oceans. Oceanography is an interdisciplinary science that makes use of principles of biology, chemistry, geology, physics, geophysics, mathematics, botany, zoology, meteorology, and geography.

You begin the major by taking math, physics, biology, geology, and chemistry. Usually you must complete an introduction to probability and statistics course, and mathematics through first-year calculus. (In some programs, an earth science education track requires only precalculus.) As you study oceanography at increasingly complex levels, you explore the methods and instruments of research and do fieldwork, collecting data to analyze and interpret.

In your third year, you will probably choose to concentrate in biological, chemical, geological, or physical oceanography. In biological oceanography, you study the distribution, abundance, and production of plants, animals, and nutrients in the oceanic ecosystem; the emphasis is on the investigation of bacteria, phytoplankton, zooplankton, and other organisms living at the bottom of the sea.

Chemical oceanography examines the complex chemistry, distribution, and cycling of dissolved substances, nutrients, and gases in seawater, especially the mechanisms that control these elements and compounds. Geological oceanography focuses on marine sediments, examines the theory of ocean basin formation, and surveys shoreline formation. In physical oceanography, you observe and predict the seas' motion, from small tidal changes to the giant circular currents. Important areas of research include the distribution of physical properties (temperature, salinity, sea ice), and air-sea interaction, with its effect on climate.

In accompanying laboratories, you apply lecture and reading material in a practical setting. By your fourth year, you are ready to do solid fieldwork and to assist faculty members in their research. Most programs finish with a yearlong capstone field study course in ocean and earth science.

Some oceanography majors have trouble completing the math requirements. It helps if you focus on math in high school and in your first two years of college—especially if you are thinking of concentrating in physical oceanography. It is also important to complete your introductory science courses during your first two years. Because oceanography is an integrated field, most of your concentration courses will include material from biology, chemistry, geology, and physics. And since oceanography requires a lot of fieldwork, you should learn, early on, how to translate the theoretical material in textbooks to the practical activities in the lab. Another recommendation is to do volunteer work on faculty research projects, both in the lab and in the field. Many majors experience field exercises, aboard a research ship bound for distant seas—a highlight of their college career.

Other majors you might like:
Marine biology
Ocean engineering
Fishing and fisheries
Marine engineering/naval architecture
Water, wetlands, and marine management
Geology/earth science
Atmospheric science
Environmental science
Geography
Aquaculture
Marine science/Merchant Marine
Underwater diving

Questions to ask colleges:
What types of offshore or coastal field exercises are offered to undergraduates? Are research opportunities with faculty members also available?

Does the program emphasize a particular concentration within oceanography? Some colleges stress physical oceanography, others take a biological or environmental slant, and some integrate oceanography and atmospheric science. A wide range of courses offered on a reasonable schedule indicates a quality program.

Career options and trends:
Middle school or high school earth science teacher; government, faculty, or industry researcher; government agency staff oceanographer (U.S. Geological Survey, National Oceanographic and Atmospheric Administration, state environmental protection agencies); marine technician.

The largest employers of oceanographers, besides colleges and universities, are the federal and state governments. Careers in private industry are also available, primarily in engineering, geology, geophysics, environmental quality, marine policy, and marine fisheries. More students are entering this field than in the past, so competition is increasing, especially for biological oceanographers. Most jobs require an advanced degree. There is strong demand, however, for qualified earth science teachers in middle and high schools.

Insider's viewpoint:
"I went on a research cruise with Scripps (Institution of Oceanography) with kids from across the country. We sailed to Samoa for the quarter, dredging the bottom of the ocean to pick up volcanic rocks in hope of dating these submarine volcanoes. I worked the night shift, and even though there were hardships, I found that it pushed me."

—Teresa, junior, University of California: Los Angeles

For more info:
The Oceanography Society
P. O. Box 1931
Rockville, MD 20849-1931
(301) 251-7708
www.tos.org

Physics

What it's about:

Physics is the study of the basic laws of nature, including mechanics, sound, electricity and magnetism, optics, heat, and quantum theory. You explore matter and systems, and the particles within them to see how they exchange energy and momentum with their surroundings, exert forces on one another, and move under the influences of these forces.

Is this for you?

You might like this major if you also like: math; computers; electronics; tinkering with things to see how they work; learning about the natural world; abstract thinking; logical solutions; solving puzzles.

Consider this major if you are good at: attention to detail; creativity; critical reading/thinking; math; organizing; quantitative analysis; spacial thinking/ analysis ...*or have...* imagination; manual dexterity; patience.

Recommended high school prep:

English 4, math 4 (including precalculus or calculus), lab science 4, social studies 3, and a foreign language 2–3. Take as many advanced science courses as possible, but don't neglect language arts and social studies.

Did you know...

...that a lot of math is required in this major? Your math courses will probably include calculus, linear algebra, differential equations, complex variables, and statistics.

Typical courses in this major:

Modern physics
Classical mechanics
Electricity and magnetism
Thermodynamics
Statistical mechanics
Quantum mechanics
Computational physics
Advanced laboratory
Solid-state physics
Electronics
Nuclear physics
Wave motion
Particle physics
Optics
Acoustics

Concentrations:

In college: applied physics; biophysics; computational physics.

If you go on to grad school: atomic/molecular physics; elementary particle physics; nuclear physics; condensed matter; optics; plasma physics; solid-state physics; astrophysics.

What the study of this major is like:

Physics courses examine phenomena as different as the structure and evolution of the universe, on the one hand, and the fundamental particles from which all matter is made, on the other. As a major, you begin with courses that introduce you to the principles of physics: mechanics (forces, energy, and the laws of motion); electricity and magnetism (the emission of electromagnetic radiation by charged particles); quantum mechanics (the particle nature of electromagnetic waves, the wave nature of particles, energy levels, and the effect of the uncertainties of nature on particle behavior); and probably thermodynamics (the theory of heat). These courses emphasize the logical, mathematical structure of the principles of nature, as well as important applications of these principles. For example, you learn about the nature of light, atomic structure, and the properties of solids, including the semiconductors that have revolutionized our world. As you advance in the major, the math becomes more complex, so strong computation skills are imperative.

467

Physics courses stress problem-solving skills. You will be assigned homework sets consisting of increasingly difficult problems. Most courses are taught in lecture format, but there are several laboratory courses as well. Physics is an experimental science, and your course work will show the relation between experiments and the theories derived from them. Because some of the advanced material is conceptually and mathematically challenging, physics majors often work together. Collaborating with others is one of the highlights of physics study. In the end, of course, you must be able to work on your own, on exams and certain assignments. As a physics major, your goal is to become an independent thinker, a problem solver, and a researcher.

The main challenge most physics majors face is the conceptual complexity of the subject. You will have to visualize abstract concepts, some of which may not immediately make sense. Although the task can be hard, understanding a difficult concept can give you great satisfaction. Another challenge you may encounter is to find solutions to complicated problems. Simply selecting a formula won't help; you must comprehend the principles at work and determine a strategy for unraveling the puzzle. Solutions often require lengthy mathematical computations.

Most physics departments have an undergraduate organization that encourages you to take part in the life of the department. In the departments, interaction between faculty members and students is generally high. You can often participate in independent research with faculty members. Although most physics programs have similar curricula, the sequence of courses might differ—for example, some programs introduce the modern fields of physics (relativity, quantum theory) earlier on than in other programs. In many programs, the introductory courses are taught with combined lectures and labs. But some programs place more emphasis on laboratory work than others do. There may also be variations among departments in the use of technology in instruction. And in some programs, you must complete a research project as part of your degree requirements.

Other majors you might like:

Architecture
Mathematics
Astrophysics
Philosophy
Computer science
Engineering physics
Civil engineering
Aeronautical/aerospace engineering
Nuclear engineering
Radiologic technology/medical imaging
Technical and business writing
Nuclear medical technology

Questions to ask colleges:

Are the physics courses listed in the course catalog offered on a regular basis? Often they are not, so you should find out which courses will actually be available to you in your third and fourth years.

What are the opportunities for undergraduate research? This is an important consideration if you intend to go on to grad school.

How accessible are the computers in the physics labs and outside of class?

Is there an active SPS (Society of Physics Students) chapter on campus?

Career options and trends:

Researcher*; engineer*; high school teacher; professor; laboratory technician; computer programmer*; financial analyst.

Certification in education is required for teaching in public high schools; a Ph.D. is essential for teaching in college.

Most physicists work in research and development, in industry, government, or academia. A Ph.D. is generally required for basic research, but with a master's degree, you can get an entry-level position in manufacturing and applied research and development.

Nanotechnology is becoming an important field. In this discipline, physicists, chemists, and engineers explore the properties and applications of materials of increasingly small size ("nano" means "one-billionth"). In fact, physics in general is growing more interdisciplinary, as it overlaps with chemistry, engineering, biology, and other fields.

Students who double-major in physics and engineering or business, or pursue these areas in grad school, have greater job options. But a bachelor's degree in physics can open doors in many fields that value analytical skills. There is a strong demand for high school physics teachers.

Insider's viewpoint:

"Being a woman in physics now is not as weird because you learn to adapt to the culture. I just went to the CERN laboratories in Switzerland, and out of the eight people who were invited, I was the only woman. You just get used to that."

—Sarah, senior, Columbia University

For more info:
American Institute of Physics (AIP)
One Physics Ellipse
College Park, MD 20740-3843
(301) 209-3100
www.aip.org

PhysLink.com
5318 East Second St., #530
Long Beach, CA 90803
www.physlink.com

Protective services

Working in the protective services is not exactly like what you see in the movies or on some TV crime dramas. The detective doesn't crack the case alone, and the true hero in a disaster may not be a first responder, but someone working behind the scenes. It may not be glamorous but the contributions of professionals in protective services are just as essential as the TV shows depict.

"Both crime prevention and justice delivery are important matters for society at large," says Professor Dennis R. Longmire, Sam Houston State University. "Being able to engage in studies related to these important issues is both fulfilling and exciting." And while the challenges presented to emergency management planners "are as varied as the types of disasters any community may face," notes Daniel J. Klenow, a professor at North Dakota State University, "they are also opportunities to create a safer and more resilient community."

Criminal justice professionals work in a wide variety of settings, in both industry and government. Most work for federal, state, or local government, but some private firms, such as security companies or correctional service providers, receive government contracts for certain types of work.

What types of jobs are we talking about here? Criminal justice majors go on to become police officers, security officers, probation officers, parole officers, and other law enforcement agents. Those who major in emergency management/homeland security can become disaster response coordinators, business continuity analysts, or FEMA program managers. Forensic science majors, who learn to analyze evidence, work as evidence technicians, fingerprint analysts, firearms experts, and as scientists like chemists, DNA or dental experts, anthropologists, pathologists, and psychiatrists. Of course, the fire service is another important branch of public safety. Professionals in those ranks include fire protection consultants; fire marshals or inspectors; environmental, health, and safety experts; and loss control personnel, who often work in the insurance business.

For better or worse, many jobs are available in occupations that protect people and property. "Crime is a 'growth industry,'" Longmire says. "Any of the careers associated with it continue to experience increased demands for new and highly qualified workers."

Law enforcement and corrections agencies are regularly looking for police recruits and officers. If you want to be among the Finest, as the police are rightly known, or the Bravest—the firefighters—it helps to go to college. In many communities, you need a college degree to become a police officer.

"The field of criminal justice continues to become increasingly professionalized. What this means is that positions that were once filled by workers who only held high school degrees now require college-level workers who can exercise increasingly complex and demanding discretion," Longmire explains.

Several national trends contribute to the growing importance of these fields. Mandatory minimum prison sentences have swelled the prison population and created the need for workers in corrections agencies and industries. Other laws have increased the use of DNA and fingerprints, so hiring is also taking place in forensic sciences. The needs of the various agencies merged into the Department of Homeland Security keep the job market strong.

"There will always be demand for scientists in crime labs, police, and security agencies," predicts Professor Frank Vozzo of Russell Sage College.

First and second degrees

These majors reside in many types of colleges, and in divisions and departments within colleges. Look for criminal justice, public administration, social sciences, natural sciences, applied arts and sciences, applied arts and technology, behavioral science, anthropology, human services, engineering, and engineering technologies.

You'll notice that protective services majors are multidisciplinary—they require you to study many subjects to understand complex topics like criminal behavior or the way the justice system works. For instance, the criminal justice major mixes sociology, psychology, and public administration, and colleges strike different balances among those fields. Majors in emergency management/

homeland security may focus more on natural disasters than on terrorism. Forensics combines science and the law with varying emphasis on each. The fire and safety programs may differ in whether they stress practical skills or theoretical studies.

Read up on the colleges of interest and their programs and ask some questions about finding work with an associate, bachelor's, or graduate (master's, doctorate, or law) degree. Look for schools that offer internship programs in agencies for your field. Ask about the professional and academic credentials of the faculty members. You can learn a lot from a former cop as an instructor, but you really need professors who are also highly educated and keep current with the latest trends and techniques in law enforcement and forensic sciences. Like the faculty, the college labs need to be up-to-date. Also find out if the program is accredited and if you will need professional certification.

Graduate tracks in criminal justice include criminological theory, private and public security, and criminal justice administration or management. Graduates in forensics specialize in administration, analytical chemistry, forensic toxicology (poisons), molecular biology, genetics or serology (blood) as they relate to forensics. In the fire service, grads may become professionals in industrial hygiene or in computer fire modeling.

Some of the newest majors in these fields include victim studies, international security studies, terrorism and security analysis, bioinformatics (clinical databases), and fire and emergency management.

"The field of criminal justice is filled with exciting and important issues that are constantly changing," says Longmire.

That's not just on TV, but in real life.

Criminal justice and law enforcement

What it's about:

The major in criminal justice and law enforcement administration focuses on how society responds to criminal behavior. Areas of study include policing, the courts, and the sentencing of both adult and juvenile violators. Don't confuse this major with criminology, which is primarily concerned with the sociopathic and psychological bases of criminal behavior.

Is this for you?

You might like this major if you also like: working with people; helping others; membership in religious or community groups; "service" activities; public speaking; debating; mystery games; crime stories.

Consider this major if you are good at: attention to detail; counseling; leadership; organizing; persuading/influencing; problem solving; teamwork *...or have...* composure during crises; initiative; patience; verbal skills; writing skills.

Recommended high school prep:

English 4, math 3, lab science 3, social studies 3, and a foreign language 2–3. If they are available, take courses in psychology and philosophy.

Did you know...

...that criminal justice professionals are primarily involved in the delivery of human services to their communities? Many courses you will take draw from psychology, social work, and public-service-related disciplines.

...that criminal justice professionals work in both the public and the private sectors? While most of them work for government agencies (federal, state, and local), some are employed by private security agencies, as well as by private correctional agencies that contract with the government. Criminal justice positions are also available in all branches of the military.

Typical courses in this major:

Introduction to the criminal justice system
Legal aspects of law enforcement
Criminology
Courts and criminal procedure
Fundamentals of criminal law
Human behavior
Comparative criminal justice systems
Law and society
White-collar crime
Research methods
Criminal profiles
Forensic sciences
Correctional systems and practices
Police systems and practices
Criminal investigation
Professionalism and ethics

Concentrations:

In college: law enforcement; forensic studies; corrections.

If you go on to grad school: criminological theory; private and public security; criminal justice administration; criminal justice management; research methods and statistics.

What the study of this major is like:

Course work in criminal justice includes the behavioral sciences, especially sociology, psychology, and social work. You examine theories about the causes of crime, as well as ways to organize public agencies for both crime prevention and crime control. Courses in research methods and criminal statistics are often required. In most programs, you can concentrate in either law enforcement (policing) or corrections (including probation, prisons, and parole), but you must still take courses on a wide variety of subjects related to the administration of justice. All programs emphasize effective communication skills: the ability to speak well is essential, because there is extensive public contact in the criminal justice profession; you must know how to write well because written reports are an integral part of the work.

Since the discipline of criminal justice is actually a blend of sociology, psychology, and public administration, colleges may vary in the emphasis they place on these areas. Programs that developed out of sociology tend to stress theories of crime causation that focus on the problems that plague society. In contrast, programs that emerged from psychology tend to see crime primarily in terms of individual background, motivation, and behavior. And degree programs that evolved out of public administration are usually more interested in issues of law enforcement than in crime causation itself.

All programs require students to explore the constitutional and legal aspects of the administration of justice. However, some colleges place less emphasis on these courses than others. Those that do so tend to focus on the scientific study of crime causation and require students to take more courses in research methods and in statistics.

In general, courses involve classroom lectures, supplemented by out-of-class reading and other homework assignments. Many programs deliver some of their course work online, and some even offer complete degree programs through nontraditional, Web-based methods. Many programs will also allow you to accumulate academic credit through internships with criminal justice agencies, in which you work under the supervision of a professor as well as a criminal justice professional. Some programs provide the opportunity to travel to foreign countries to examine the cross-cultural and international issues facing criminal justice professionals around the world.

Other majors you might like:
Criminology
Corrections
Police science
Legal studies
Psychology
Security/loss prevention
Public administration
Forensic science
Human services
Juvenile corrections
Sociology
Security services management

Questions to ask colleges:
Does the program place students in internships with appropriate public or private agencies? Wide-ranging experience in such agencies can help graduates seeking jobs in those agencies or similar organizations.

What are the academic and professional backgrounds of the faculty members? Some programs employ former law enforcement personnel who have had little or no academic training. Their teaching style often relies on the telling of "war stories." These instructors may be interesting, but they may not provide the most current and useful information in the field.

Career options and trends:
Police officer*; security officer; probation officer*; parole officer*; correctional counselor; federal law enforcement agent (FBI, Secret Service, etc.).

Special certification is usually required for positions involving "special-needs offenders," such as youthful, drug- and alcohol-addicted, and mentally challenged violators of the law. Often, your college course work can be counted as partial credit toward such certification.

The field of criminal justice has become increasingly professionalized—college degrees are required where high school diplomas would once have been enough. It is also becoming more globalized, as professionals from all over the world cooperate on significant issues and cases. Job applicants who are bilingual or multilingual, or who have military experience, have a competitive edge.

Insider's viewpoint:
"My particular interest in the discipline is driven by the realization that issues associated with law enforcement and criminal justice are also associated with human rights and basic freedoms."

—Professor Dennis R. Longmire, Sam Houston State University

For more info:

Academy of Criminal Justice Sciences (ACJS)
P.O. Box 960
Greenbelt, MD 20768
(800) 757-2257
www.acjs.org

American Correctional Association (ACA)
206 North Washington St., Suite 200
Alexandria, VA 22314
(703) 224-0000
www.aca.org

American Probation and Parole Association
  (APPA)
2760 Research Park Drive
Lexington, KY 40511-8410
(859) 244-8203
www.appa-net.org

Emergency management/homeland security

Also known as:

Disaster management

What it's about:

This major studies natural as well as man-made catastrophes within a social, political, and environmental context. The interdisciplinary curriculum provides a broad overview of disaster preparedness, mitigation, response and recovery, and issues of homeland security.

Is this for you?

You might like this major if you also like: community service; working collaboratively; current affairs; learning about international issues. Students who are innovators, problem solvers, and who have leadership qualities would enjoy this major.

Consider this major if you are good at: organizing; critical reading/thinking; teamwork; attention to detail; persuading/influencing; caring/nurturing *...or have...*initiative; patience; verbal skills; writing skills.

Recommended high school prep:

English 4, math 3, lab science 3 (including chemistry), social studies 4 (including American government), and a foreign language 3–4. If available, courses in psychology, sociology, and computer applications are helpful.

Did you know...

...that this major is not about becoming a first responder? Rather, the focus is on managing disaster planning and recovery work at the organizational level, whether municipal, state, national, or international.

Typical courses in this major:

Principles of emergency management
American government
Organizational behavior
Introduction to homeland security
Disaster response and recovery
Emergency response preparedness and planning
Special populations in disasters
Sociology of disaster
Psychology of disaster
Meteorology
Chemical, biological, and radiological hazards
Geographic Information Systems (GIS)
Border and coastal security
Terrorism and anti-terrorism
Business continuity
Public policy issues in emergency management

Concentrations:

Generally, none in college; but if you go on to grad school: pandemic planning; disaster recovery; environmental hazard mitigation; homeland security management.

What the study of this major is like:

The term "emergency" has become the most common label for this major, but it can be misleading if you think it's mostly about the immediate response to a localized and unforeseen event, such as the attacks on 9/11. Some programs prefer the term "disaster management" as a better indicator that your studies will encompass events that significantly disrupt an entire social or ecological system, whether by surprise terror attack, devastating oil spill, viral outbreak, or natural disaster such as an earthquake or hurricane.

You won't be trained to be a hero—but rather as a planner and manager who can help enhance community preparedness, mitigate effects, and provide effective response and recovery efforts.

The typical teaching model involves a traditional emphasis on lectures, but your studies will be a blend of the theoretical and the practical. Many programs offer seminars that incorporate class interaction and student research. Courses that emphasize research methods and specific applications such as geographic information systems may have lab activities as well.

Since emergency management is an applied field, most programs will require some form of field experience or internship outside of class, which may be integrated into the academic year or experienced during the summer. Internship opportunities can include working with organizations (such as the local chapter of the Red Cross) and agencies involved with providing security or building community preparedness for floods, tornadoes, or public health crises.

How this major is taught at various colleges can vary significantly in terms of emphasis. Some programs focus on disaster management, government policy, and social topics related to natural and man-made disasters with little emphasis on terrorism. Others focus more directly on homeland security with specific attention to global and domestic terrorism and related events while still providing content on natural disasters. Programs that are more science oriented will focus on understanding and mitigating the effects of disasters and include courses such as meteorology, chemistry, geology, environmental science, computer modeling, and information systems.

In addition, this interdisciplinary major may be housed in a variety of academic departments which can influence its perspective, such as sociology, public policy and administration, public health, political science, or environmental studies.

Other majors you might like:
Urban, community, and regional planning
Emergency medical technology (EMT paramedic)
Hazardous materials technology
Environmental studies
Natural resources management/policy
Criminal justice and law enforcement
Criminology
Computer forensics
Computer/systems security
Management information systems
International relations
Peace and conflict studies

Questions to ask colleges:
How long have you had an emergency management program?

What is the primary focus of the program – is it sociological, political, environmental? Natural disaster planning and recovery, or anti-terrorism?

What types of internship opportunities are available?

What types of organizations are employing your graduates? How successful are your graduates in the job market?

Has this program applied for accreditation from the Foundation of Higher Education for Disaster/Emergency Management and Homeland Security?

Career options and trends:
Emergency management planner, homeland security planner, disaster response coordinator, business continuity analyst/planner, geographic information systems specialist, city emergency manager, FEMA program manager.

This is a new and rapidly expanding field. Jobs are available at all levels of government, both locally and nationally; many non-governmental organizations and relief agencies need people trained in emergency management; and there is a widespread and growing need for trained disaster planners in the private business sector (particularly the insurance industry).

Jobs are increasingly going to candidates with specific education in emergency management. The addition of a minor (business, transportation logistics, sociology, communication, natural resource management, planning, political science, etc) to your plan of study can greatly enhance employment options.

For more info:
International Association of Emergency Managers (IAEM)
201 Park Washington Court
Falls Church, VA 22046
(703) 538-1795
www.iaem.com

Fire protection and safety technology

What it's about:

In this major, you learn to evaluate and reduce potential loss of property and life in the workplace and other settings. You explore three of the most likely threats to safety: fire, accidents, and exposure to hazardous materials.

Is this for you?

You might like this major if you also like: volunteer work; firefighting; change; working with people; helping others.

Consider this major if you are good at: attention to detail; creativity; critical reading/thinking; leadership; organizing; persuading/influencing; quantitative analysis ...*or have...* initiative; verbal skills.

Recommended high school prep:

English 4, math 4 (including precalculus or calculus), lab science 4 (including chemistry and physics), social studies 3, and a foreign language 2–3. Courses in computer applications and drafting are also recommended.

Did you know...

...that professionals in fire protection and safety technology are dedicated to protecting people in all types of employment from many kinds of hazards? The major is not limited to firefighting and fire service organizations.

...that there is a big demand for the services of loss control professionals? The opportunities for women and minorities are at an all-time high, and graduates are enjoying record placement rates of nearly 100 percent.

Typical courses in this major:

Fire safety and hazards recognition
Fire suppression and detection systems
Introduction to occupational safety techniques
Studies in loss control
Fire protection management
Design and analysis of sprinkler systems
Elements of industrial hygiene
Fire protection hydraulics and water supply
Industrial safety organization
Structural designs for fire and life safety
Human factors in accident prevention
Fire dynamics
Building electrical systems
Issues in local government and fire services
Disaster and fire defense planning
Hazardous materials management

Concentrations:

In college: fire protection systems; code compliance; fire dynamics and behavior; fire investigation; industrial safety; industrial hygiene.

If you go on to grad school: computer fire modeling.

What the study of this major is like:

Programs in fire protection and safety technology prepare you for a career in loss control. The profession is divided into three areas: loss from fire; loss from physical accidents; and loss from environmental exposure. As a major, you learn to predict threats to safety in the workplace and to take steps to prevent them—for example, by designing efficient evacuation routes; by identifying objects that could injure workers; and by controlling the use of toxic materials in factories.

The curriculum introduces you immediately to issues in fire protection and safety. Therefore, you can measure your interest in a fire protection and safety technology career early on in your studies. The program includes many courses in math and in the physical sciences. Two semesters of calculus are required, as well as two semesters of chemistry and one semester of physics. Computers are an essential tool in most courses. If you know that you want to pursue this major, you should try to take classes in high school that will prepare you for college-level math and science.

Some programs include plenty of hands-on work; you do numerous lab exercises to reinforce the facts and ideas that are taught in lectures. You might be expected to take at least two or three afternoon lab sessions each semester. Industry internships are frequently encouraged, because they provide valuable experience and let you apply, in a real-world setting, what you've learned.

A number of programs gear their curriculum toward careers in the fire service. The emphasis of these programs is on practical application—you put into use the techniques you've studied, but you may or may not learn the theories behind the techniques. Courses designed specifically for fire protection may not be easily transferred to more general programs. Therefore, you should be committed to a career in fire safety if you enroll in such a program.

Other majors you might like:

Architectural engineering
Industrial engineering
Fire services administration
Occupational safety/health technology
Firefighting/fire science
Security/loss prevention
Insurance
Civil engineering
Hazardous materials technology
Construction technology
Building inspection

Questions to ask colleges:

Is the program approved by an outside professional organization, such as the International Fire Service Accreditation Congress (IFSAC) or the Technology Accreditation Commission of the Accreditation Board for Engineering and Technology (ABET/TAC)? These organizations have set standards that can help you judge the quality of a program.

Does the college support internships and co-ops? Internships are especially valuable in the broad field of fire protection and safety.

Are there enough lab facilities available? Are the faculty members and students dedicated to safety?

You may be able to get an indication of the program's commitment to safety by observing the college's own facilities.

Career options and trends:

Fire protection consultant*; environment, health, and safety engineer*; building code official/plans examiner; loss control consultant (for insurance companies)*; industrial safety engineer; deputy fire marshal/inspector.

You can become certified as a certified fire protection specialist (CFPS), an associate safety professional (ASP), a certified safety professional (CSP), or an engineer-in-training/professional engineer (EIT/PE). You can also become state-licensed as a fire prevention officer.

Fire protection engineering activities are indirectly tied to the construction industry. Upturns in construction have a significant, positive impact on job opportunities. The effects of downturns are less dramatic; because of code requirements, structures must be maintained and retrofitted as necessary. Recent emphasis on homeland security is predicted to create substantial growth in the fire protection field.

The field of safety is more closely linked to manufacturing and industrial activities, which are subject to shifts in the global economy. Homeland security concerns are expected to increase activities in safety, security, and environmental monitoring.

Insider's viewpoint:

"Testing the response of materials and structures to the assault of fire is dramatic and interesting, and protecting firefighters and occupants from the effects of fire is challenging and rewarding."

—Professor Thomas J. Woodford, Oklahoma State University

For more info:

International Fire Service Accreditation Congress (IFSAC)
1700 West Tyler
Oklahoma State University
Stillwater, OK 74078-8075
(405) 744-8303
www.ifsac.org

Forensic science

What it's about:

Forensic science is an interdisciplinary major that applies knowledge of the natural sciences, the criminal justice system, and the law to the analysis and evaluation of evidence gathered from a crime or accident scene.

Is this for you?

You might like this major if you also like: science clubs; chemistry; computers; lab experiments; amateur sleuthing; detective stories and police shows; working with precision instruments.

Consider this major if you are good at: attention to detail; math; organizing; quantitative analysis; spacial thinking/analysis; teamwork *...or have...* manual dexterity; observational skills; patience; writing skills.

Recommended high school prep:

English 4, math 4 (including precalculus), lab science 4 (including biology, chemistry, and physics), social studies 3, and a foreign language 2–3.

Did you know...

...that forensic scientists, evidence technicians, crime scene investigators, and detectives are separate people who have taken separate career paths? TV shows can give the impression that one person does it all, from discovering trace evidence to cracking the case—but most forensic science takes place in the field or in the lab, as one part of an investigatory team process.

Typical courses in this major:

Introduction to criminal justice
Analytical chemistry
Human anatomy
Instrumental analysis
Genetics
Microbiology
Molecular biology
Criminal evidence and procedure
Criminalisitics
Crime scene investigation
Statistics
Care and preservation of evidence
Fire investigation
Toxicology
Forensic anthropology
Forensic entomology

Concentrations:

In college: toxicology; forensic anthropology; crime scene investigation; forensic chemistry; trace evidence; accident and fire investigation.

If you go on to grad school: criminalistics; forensic science administration; analytical chemistry; forensic molecular biology; forensic engineering; forensic entomology; forensic DNA/serology.

What the study of this major is like:

Although trace evidence may be tiny, it is often enough to establish the particulars of a crime and lead to its solution. The forensic science major teaches you how to use scientific analysis to tie pieces of evidence to particular sources. Because analytical techniques are constantly improving, forensic scientists can more easily protect the innocent and bring the guilty to justice. In fact, investigators can often crack cases that have gone unsolved for decades.

Your first two years in the Bachelor of Science program are typically like those of a chemistry major or a premed student. You take challenging courses in biology, general and inorganic chemistry, and physics, as well as college-level statistics and calculus. Since the chemistry, biology, and math courses have sequencing requirements, you must begin them in your first semester. You will also take introductory courses in criminal justice, the social sciences, and psychology.

In your third and fourth years, you enroll in specialized lab courses, taught by or in association with forensic scientists, where you apply the scientific principles and techniques from your earlier courses to forensics. These later courses, which sometimes include independent work (such as research projects or internships), provide you with professional skills and career information. In your final year, you usually participate in a field practicum and a capstone seminar project. Although the forensic science major prepares you for direct employment as a laboratory technician, you are generally encouraged to go on to graduate school for further specialization.

Most forensic science programs have developed from existing programs in criminal justice or the natural sciences. There is considerable variation as to which areas they cover in depth. The oldest and largest programs may offer a variety of concentrations, while newer and smaller programs generally focus on one or two of the following subdisciplines:

Forensic biology, which deals with the analysis of blood and other body fluids, physical wounds, and body positions; DNA analysis; forensic chemistry, which examines trace evidence such as hairs, fibers, paint, soil; forensic anthropology, which is concerned with skeletal remains; forensic entomology, which uses insect activity in decomposing bodies to determine place and time of death; forensic toxicology, which analyzes specimens of blood, urine, or tissue for drugs, alcohol, or poison. There are other specializations in such areas as computer crime, fingerprints, firearms and explosives, and footprint, tool, and tire impressions.

Two-year or certificate programs in forensic science prepare you for careers as crime scene or evidence technicians. Training may include the collection and preservation of evidence; crime scene photography; latent fingerprint processing; and/or composite drawing. Many of these positions require you to pass a certification exam given by the International Association for Identification (IAI). Not all jurisdictions use civilian technicians for these functions, so be sure to check the rules where you intend to work.

Other majors you might like:
Criminology
Psychology
Microbiology
Biochemistry
Anthropology
Criminal justice and law enforcement
Police science
Chemistry
Materials science
Computer forensics
Emergency medical technology (EMT paramedic)
Clinical/medical laboratory technology

Questions to ask colleges:
Are internships available in crime labs or related facilities?

What opportunities do undergraduates have for field research or other hands-on training?

Career options and trends:
Forensic lab technician*; crime scene investigator*; latent fingerprint analyst; forensic engineer; forensic chemist*; forensic DNA analyst*; law enforcement officer.

In some states, only uniformed law enforcement officers investigate crime scenes. Forensic pathologists, psychiatrists, and medical examiners are licensed physicians.

Demand for forensic science professionals is projected to increase because of new technologies in the field, the needs of homeland security, and legislation requiring DNA and fingerprint sampling from members of certain groups. Prospects are best for those who have a strong background in the basic sciences (especially chemistry) and who are willing to relocate.

Insider's viewpoint:
"Don't major in forensic science as an undergrad. Get a strong science background first. Make sure this is what you want to do. Nothing is worse than getting into a field after two or more years of

higher learning and discovering it isn't your cup of tea."

—Elizabeth, M.S. candidate, John Jay College of Criminal Justice

For more info:
American Academy of Forensic Sciences (AAFS)
410 North 21st St.
Suite 203
Colorado Springs, CO 80904
(719) 636-1100
www.aafs.org

Public administration

What is public administration? Let's break it down. "Public" refers to the public sector, and that means government. "Administration" means the management of a program or an agency. So public administrators manage government programs, right? Well, that's true, but it's not the whole story. Public administration isn't just for your class treasurer. These majors also prepare students for work in nonprofit organizations and for the private (business) sector. That's because more and more, the government is outsourcing—hiring outside companies to do government work.

Why does public administration have a whole chapter in this book? Because it is the largest category of civilian jobs in the federal government. And then there are the state, county, and local government employees, like those in public welfare agencies. But it's not the quantity, it's the quality of work that counts. Public administrators run the most critical services for the most vulnerable citizens.

"Public administration is a great field for those who want to make a difference in society," says Professor Danny Lee Balfour of Grand Valley State University.

What do public administrators do? In addition to providing direct service to individuals, they have management and supervisory responsibilities, in areas like human resources management, budgeting, and policy and planning. They might also do economic development, labor relations, and court administration—almost anything requiring organizational and time management skills and a concern for people.

In human services agencies, professionals and paraprofessionals help individuals and families become self-sufficient. Jobs include substance abuse counselors, probation officers, and mental health workers. Social work is another big part of public service, even bigger than you may think.

"Unfortunately, many students equate social work only with public assistance, and their vision of a social worker is that of a case worker," says Professor Irene Queiro-Tajalli, Indiana University-Purdue University Indianapolis. "Students need to realize the wide range of employment opportunities after graduation."

As you may know, many states and the federal government have had budget problems lately. In some cases, this has led to a reduction in the public workforce or to a hiring slowdown. On the plus side, the work that public administrators do is often essential and can't be cut because it helps people get the necessities of life. The job outlook for new graduates is buoyed by an expected wave of retirement of older government workers.

Know your goals

When you look for colleges, you'll find the public administration program in schools or divisions of social science, professional studies, health studies, anthropology, sociology, social work, and public affairs.

Some public administration programs are geared toward getting you ready to work at a specific level of government—local, state, or federal. If it's local government, for instance, you'll learn skills for community development and city management. It's good to know ahead of time what level of government you're interested in. It would also be great if you had a preference for direct service (one-to-one contact like social work) or management and supervisory work.

You may not be able to make all these decisions yet. But give some thought to what type of degree you're after, because you can pursue a public administration major (and later a career) at any degree level. If it's a certificate program, find out if your course work would be eligible for transfer credits toward a college degree later.

Think about style as well as substance: What is your learning style? You may want to get both theory (book learning) and practice (getting out there and doing it!). Also, find the class size and faculty-to-student ratio that works for you. Ask if you'll do an internship or community service project before graduation. If you're juggling many responsibilities, see if classes are offered in the day and in the evening. How about online?

For studies leading to social work, you want a program accredited by the Council on Social Work Education. Most accredited programs cover topics like human behavior and social policy, and there isn't a huge difference among colleges. However, the location of the college and the needs of its surrounding community may guide the way the college prepares students to help people.

Graduate studies in social work may be organized in several different ways: by who is served (individuals, families, communities); by fields of work, such as child welfare, aging, and mental health; or by particular social problems, such as poverty and homelessness. In other areas of public administration, specialties in graduate school include management and leadership, nonprofit administration, criminal justice, urban or regional affairs, and community health.

Find out more from the National Association of Schools of Public Affairs and Administration (www.naspaa.org), the American Society for Public Administration (www.aspanet.org), and the International City/County Management Association (www.icma.org).

Human services

What it's about:

The human service major prepares you to become an aide to a professional or to practice as a professional who helps individuals, families, or communities become self-sufficient. You learn about social service delivery systems and explore the reasons why many people are unable to obtain or hold on to the basic necessities of life.

Is this for you?

You might like this major if you also like: helping people from different backgrounds; improving people's lives; volunteering in your community; working both independently and in groups.

Consider this major if you are good at: caring/nurturing; counseling; creativity; critical reading/thinking; organizing; teamwork *...or have...* initiative; patience; social skills; verbal skills; writing skills.

Recommended high school prep:

English 4, math 3, lab science 3, social studies 3, and a foreign language 3-4. If possible, take courses in speech and computer literacy. Community volunteering experience is also helpful.

Did you know...

...that being able to speak a foreign language is particularly useful in the human services field? As immigration to the United States increases, social service professionals who can communicate with non-English-speaking populations are in great demand.

Typical courses in this major:

Group dynamics/process
Intake and referral
Introduction to counseling
Introduction to criminal justice
Local, state, and federal government
Multiculturalism
Social problems
Introduction to psychology
Ethics and the law
Introduction to sociology
Human services agencies and organizations
Organizational behavior
Human development
Legal issues in human services
Medical aspects of human services
Adult development

Concentrations:

In college: criminal justice; addiction studies (drug and alcohol); counseling; youth development; advocacy; human services management.

If you go on to grad school: organizing human services; human services management and leadership; community organization.

What the study of this major is like:

As a human services major, you study a range of topics. You will most likely examine the history of the human services delivery systems in the United States; counseling and service theories; and the various philosophical approaches to the human condition, team work, and social problems. Most courses are lecture based and often feature case studies, group work, games, and class discussion. Well-rounded programs provide you with the opportunity to participate in (and often require) internships, community service learning, or practicums. Strong bachelor's degree programs will also require course requirements outside the human services major.

Generally, the challenges you encounter involve managing your time, being organized, and working effectively in groups. As in any major, expect to spend a lot of time studying. But you may be asked to apply your newly learned skills and theories earlier in your academic career than your colleagues in other majors.

Because of the range of content and skills taught in human services, the major can be housed in various departments. You can also study human services at a variety of institutions that offer certification or degree options. Before you pick a program, you should think about the level of education you plan to attain. Courses in certificate programs might not be transferable if you later wish to earn a bachelor's degree. In addition, some programs focus on direct service (one-to-one contact) and others focus on human services management (supervisory skills). You should probably look for a program that offers a variety of courses, so that you can explore many tracks within the profession. You don't need to choose your area of specialization before you enter college.

Other majors you might like:
Criminal justice and law enforcement
Urban, community, and regional planning
Public policy analysis
Family/community services
Human development and family studies
Gerontology
Community organization/advocacy
Community health services
Health care administration
Substance abuse counseling
Anthropology
Behavioral sciences

Questions to ask colleges:
What are the different types of internship or community service learning experiences available? Is the program affiliated or in partnership with local organizations?

Career options and trends:
Residential counselor; drug/alcohol counselor; case manager; probation/parole officer; client advocate; child abuse worker; mental health worker; youth worker; rehabilitation case worker; social service worker.

Certification requirements for different careers vary from state to state. For example, some states require drug and alcohol counselors to have state certification in addition to a college degree. Most human services professions have a continuing education requirement.

The aging baby boomer population is creating a demand for human services workers and professionals skilled in working with older people. The restorative justice field (in which members of the community are brought into the criminal justice process, such as sentencing and rehabilitation) is also expected to continue growing. In another trend, most states are funding drug treatment and counseling through departments of corrections, rather than the traditional human services areas. This development will further integrate the fields of human services and criminal justice.

For more info:
National Organization for Human Services (NOHS)
www.nationalhumanservices.org

Council for Standards in Human Service
    Education (CSHSE)
1935 S. Plum Grove Road
PMB 297
Palatine, IL 60067
www.cshse.org

Public administration

Also known as:
Public affairs

What it's about:
Public administration majors study the management of public and nonprofit organizations and the many aspects of public service and governance. Topics include political issues, group dynamics, public policy, health care delivery, economic development, human resources management, philanthropy, voluntarism, budgeting, public finance, information technologies, and neighborhood analysis.

Is this for you?
You might like this major if you also like: community service; student government; Boy or Girl Scouts; joining clubs or teams; environmental issues; organizing group activities.

Consider this major if you are good at: critical reading/thinking; leadership; organizing events; persuading/influencing; solving problems; teamwork *...or have...* initiative; patience; verbal skills; writing skills.

Recommended high school prep:
English 4, math 3, lab science 3, social studies 4 (including government and economics), and a foreign language 2–3. A business course is also recommended.

Typical courses in this major:
Introduction to public administration
Public budgeting and financial administration
Public human resources administration
Public policy and policy processes
Local politics and administration
Introduction to nonprofit management
Developing nonprofit resources
Volunteerism and the nonprofit sector
Public sector information technology
Grant writing
Organization theory
Community analysis
Economic development
Structure of state government
Public service ethics

Concentrations:
Public finance; economic development; community development; health administration; human resources; environmental policy; nonprofit administration; urban/regional affairs.

What the study of this major is like:
In this major you explore the ways that public administration professionals achieve managerial efficiency, program effectiveness, legal accountability, client-driven responsiveness, political representation, and organizational reform. You acquire practical skills, including analyzing agency budgets, supervising staff, designing Web pages and evaluation surveys, and writing grant proposals. You learn to recognize the moral, social, political, economic, and technical issues to consider as you design and lead programs in the public interest.

Upper-level courses deal with budgets, accounting, and financial management, as well as with specific executive and personal skills such as strategic planning, leadership, and ethical sensitivity. Majors are strongly encouraged to take a broad range of liberal arts courses, including English, history, communications, economics, political science, psychology, and sociology.

Courses frequently use case studies, simulations, and other activities to provide a sense of what real-world public administration is all about. Most programs require you do an internship, perhaps in Washington, D.C., or in a state capital, to gain experience in public or nonprofit agencies. At some institutions, cooperative programs allow you to alternate semesters (first studying in the classroom, then working in a government agency).

Programs at different colleges may vary in their organization, approach to public policy, or the level of government they emphasize. For example, some programs focus on local politics, economic and community development, and city management. Other programs prepare you for a career in state government or in the federal government. A few programs specialize in environmental policy, international development, regulatory policies, social policy, or other areas. A growing number of programs provide courses in nonprofit administration, including grant writing, volunteer management, fund-raising, and philanthropy.

A bachelor's degree opens doors to a variety of public service careers with government agencies, nonprofit organizations, and private sector firms. It also offers a good background for many graduate programs. You can enhance your marketability by taking part in paid or volunteer internships; gaining valuable skills in information technology, public relations, or planning; joining professional organizations; and developing your oral, written, and visual communication skills. The most successful students combine classroom study with real-world experience, and they network, or make contact, with professionals in the field. Increasingly, international study is playing an important role in public affairs, and you are encouraged to participate in study-abroad programs.

Other majors you might like:
Political science
Public policy analysis
Urban, community, and regional planning
Parks, recreation, and leisure studies
Public relations
Economics
Civil engineering
Urban studies
Emergency management/homeland security
Sociology
Health care administration
Environmental studies

Questions to ask colleges:
Does the program require or provide internship opportunities?

How active is the program in the field's professional associations?

Does the program specialize in particular areas? If so, which ones? Does the program focus on a level of government (local, state, or federal), or include nonprofit administration?

Career options and trends:
City manager; assistant city manager*; budget/financial officer; human resource manager; policy analyst; grant coordinator; program evaluator; volunteer coordinator; neighborhood planner; economic development coordinator.

The retirement of the baby boom generation should open up job opportunities, even at the coveted federal level. For example, the Office of Personnel Management projects that 282,000 of the executive branch's full-time civilian employees will leave within a few years.

Nonprofit organizations (neighborhood associations, religious organizations, schools, chambers of commerce, etc.) provide a good employment entry point because they offer many volunteer and internship positions through which you can acquire experience.

Insider's viewpoint:
"Public policy studies how to do things, how to use what we have to make a world. In many cases, we even try to be fair. It has amazed me to learn that there is a science, a precision, a balancing to be addressed with the precision and discipline of an artist."

—Kobi, senior, Columbia University

For more info:
American Society for Public Administration (ASPA)
1301 Pennsylvania Ave., N.W.
Suite 840
Washington, DC 20004
(202) 393-7878
www.aspanet.org

Social work

What it's about:

The social work major is a professional degree program that provides the knowledge, values, and skills needed for generalist social work practice. You learn to help individuals, families, groups, and communities prevent and respond to social problems. As a practicing social worker, you modify harmful social conditions, promote social and economic well being, and increase opportunities for people to live fulfilling, dignified lives.

Is this for you?

You might like this major if you also like: helping people in need; diversity; being a "people person"; working for social and economic justice.

Consider this major if you are good at: caring/ nurturing; counseling; creativity; critical reading/ thinking; leadership; organizing; teamwork *...or have...* initiative; respect for others; verbal skills; writing skills.

Recommended high school prep:

English 4, math 3, lab science 3, social studies 4, and a foreign language 2–3. If you can, take classes in computer science and anthropology. Spanish is a useful language to learn because of the changing makeup of the U.S. population. Volunteer work or community service activities are strongly recommended.

Did you know...

...that social work covers more than just administering public assistance? Many students' idea of a social worker is that of a caseworker. Ironically, few caseworkers are trained social workers.

Typical courses in this major:

Human behavior and social environment
Introduction to psychology
Introduction to sociology
Social work research
Social work practice
Social policy and services
Values and ethics
Diversity
Modern social problems
Populations-at-risk
Social and economic justice
Community resources
Field internship

Concentrations:

Generally, none in college; but if you go on to grad school: child welfare; family welfare; aging; health; addictions; working with individuals, groups, families, or communities; poverty, homelessness, and other social problems; social administration; social work research.

What the study of this major is like:

As a social work major, you gain a foundation in the liberal arts, with an emphasis on the social sciences. In your first two years of college, you generally take sociology, political science, economics, psychology, and human biology. In your third and fourth years, you take most of your social work courses, learning how to conduct a generalist social work practice.

In courses in social welfare policy and services, which describe the laws, programs, and benefits available to meet human needs, you consider the way social programs are developed and changed. Research courses teach basic methods and stress the evaluation of social welfare programs. At most colleges, the major emphasizes the understanding and acceptance of diversity in ethnicity, race, culture, gender, and sexual orientation.

Typically, social work professors use a variety of approaches in their courses: lectures, teamwork, role-playing, research projects, field trips, and skill-building exercises. An attractive feature of the major is the combination of theory and hands-on experience. Your most important educational experience is a supervised practicum (field internship), most likely in a social service agency. All undergraduates earning a Bachelor's of Social Work (B.S.W.) must complete at least 400 hours of field experience under the supervision of a qualified social worker.

Early in your studies, you may have difficulty applying theoretical concepts to practical situations. Programs handle this challenge by closely supervising students as they complete their internships. You may also be troubled by differences between your personal values and those of the profession. In response, most programs encourage you to examine your values as well as those of social workers and society.

In many states, you must graduate from a program accredited by the Council on Social Work Education (CSWE) in order to be licensed and certified. Because of these standards, undergraduate social work programs tend to be very similar. Differences may exist in the number of courses offered, but the choices you have are usually based more on program resources or regional mission than on program philosophies.

The sense of calling and commitment that can lead you to choose social work as a profession may generate a spirit of camaraderie and dedication among students. Although healthy competition is part of academic life, social work students often develop projects cooperatively, make group presentations, and form long-lasting professional relationships. In recent years many nontraditional and older students have found social work an attractive choice for a major and a career.

Other majors you might like:
Sociology
Psychology
Native American studies
American sign language (ASL)
Funeral services/mortuary science
Human development and family studies
Community health services
Gerontology
Youth ministry
Emergency medical technology (EMT paramedic)

Nursing (RN)
Occupational therapy

Questions to ask colleges:
Is the program accredited by the CSWE?

Which types of agencies are available for students looking to fulfill their practicum requirements?

Career options and trends:
Generalist social work practitioner; clinician; administrator; case manager; social planner; researcher.

A bachelor's degree prepares you for generalist social work in a wide range of settings, such as child welfare and public welfare agencies, hospitals and other health care facilities, schools, developmental disabilities services, services for the aged, the juvenile and criminal justice systems, industry, and business. A master's degree is required for jobs involving supervision, administration, or complex research.

All states license or regulate social workers, but regulations and procedures vary from state to state.

Job prospects are favorable for those going into social work. Generally, there will be more opportunities in the areas of mental health and substance abuse than in child, family and school social work.

Insider's viewpoint:
"When my adviser suggested I take the introductory social work class I didn't want to because I never heard anything positive about it; I associated it with child protection services and doing the dirty work. But that was before my favorite professor introduced me to macro social work and the public policy side of it: legislation, community development and economic revitalization, that sort of thing."

—Melissa, junior, Michigan State University

For more info:
National Association of Social Workers (NASW)
750 First St., N.E.
Suite 700
Washington, DC 20002-4241
www.naswdc.org

Religion and theology

The study of religion is not what you may think. It's not necessarily faith-based, or a form of worship. And it isn't always preparation for the clergy. Instead, the majors in this group often approach religion as an academic subject.

"The study of religion in the academic context is not the same as in some religious context (church, synagogue, mosque)," says Professor Emeritus Richard B. Pilgrim of Syracuse University.

"Once students realize that the study of religion does not favor or teach about a religion in order to convert or train a person in that tradition, then religion as an academic discipline begins," explains Professor John A. Grim, Bucknell University.

The academic approach to religion includes studies of civilization and society, history, language and texts, culture, music, and many other subjects.

Theology is just one of the majors in the universe of religion studies. "Theology" literally means "the study of God." This major often concentrates on a particular faith, and may have liturgical (worship) and counseling components to prepare students for graduate work in the ministry, among other careers.

"A major in theology typically includes courses in biblical studies, history of the church, history of Christian thought, ethics, and the moral life. It is also likely to include study of world religions," says Professor David G. Truemper of Valparaiso University.

Religion and theology majors are all about the big picture.

"The study of religion is only one aspect of Judaic studies," says Professor Shmuel Bolozky, University of Massachusetts Amherst. "It is also the study of the Jewish people, its role in civilization, and its interaction with the other members of society."

For its part, Islamic studies "involves a great deal of reading, researching, and writing," says Professor Kamran S. Aghaie, University of Texas at Austin. "It entails expanding one's perspective on the world and understanding different cultures."

Your Higher Education

Studying religion as part of a liberal arts education is a way to obtain skills in research, reading, writing, and thinking that are needed in graduate school and in almost any career. When you look for an institution offering religion majors, consider colleges of liberal arts or humanities or arts and sciences, divinity schools, and schools of religion or theology.

How religion is taught depends on the college. Some colleges have been set up by a particular religion, so they are faith-based. If you are preparing for the ministry, consider a religion-affiliated university with a preministry program to guide you toward a major and graduate studies. "Through advising, internship experiences, and well-chosen curricula across the disciplines in courses from biblical literature to psychology to ethics, interested men and women can determine what types of ministry suits them," says Shelley Shepherd, preministerial studies adviser at Southern Methodist University.

At other colleges, including state universities, the approach is not religious but secular. Be sure you are entering the type of program you want and double-check that any state aid you will receive applies if you study religion. It may not.

Professor Pilgrim explains the primary distinction between religious and nonreligious colleges: "The difference is between private, parochial schools where religious indoctrination or advocacy may be the main thrust in a religion or theology major, and private or public colleges or universities where religious studies is clearly an academic, scholarly enterprise," he says. "It's not always easy to tell one from the other, but prospective students need to check closely about this."

Some programs are devoted to a particular tradition, like Buddhism, Christianity, Islam, or Judaism, or to an aspect of a tradition, like the Bible or Islamic law. Other programs specialize in theoretical approaches (such as ethics, psychology, philosophy, anthropology).

"A prospective student should look for balance across approaches and cultural traditions in a religion department. Look for courses in ethics, philosophy of religion, religion and ecology, or popular religion," Grim suggests. "A basic perspective is to look for courses in Judaism, Christianity, Islam, Buddhism, Hinduism, Confucianism, or Taoism to get a sense of the commitment of the department to teaching the full spectrum of cultural religious expressions."

Whatever your likely major, check out the courses and faculty members to see if their focus matches your interests. You can reach out to educators at the college. Ask how the school can help you connect personal religious faith with intellectual and academic work. How does the program help you relate to people of other faiths? Will your studies have a global dimension? Is there a religious community nearby to provide support and stimulation? Does the college have resources such as online library subscriptions, translations, and a language lab? Are grants and scholarships available? How about an internship, mission, or social service, if such an opportunity is right for you?

In choosing a college, think about your future. Most religion students are probably planning to work in education, law, business, medicine, social activism, or social service. If you envision a career in the clergy, or plan on graduate studies, see the individual majors in this section for graduate tracks. A good general resource is the American Academy of Religion, at www.aarweb.org.

Bible studies

What it's about:

As a Bible studies major, you explore the literature of the Bible, including the historical and cultural setting of the biblical world. Emphasis is placed on the content, concepts, and theological teachings of the Bible, as well as on ways to interpret biblical literature. Some programs may require you to study Greek and Hebrew.

Is this for you?

You might like this major if you also like: archaeology; history; volunteering and service activities; exploring your spirituality; reading the Bible and biblical literature.

Consider this major if you are good at: attention to detail; caring/nurturing; creativity; critical reading/thinking; organizing; research *...or have...* patience; verbal skills; writing skills.

Recommended high school prep:

English 4, math 3, lab science 3, social studies 4, and a foreign language 3. If possible, take classes in ancient history, anthropology, classical Greek, Latin, philosophy, or world religions.

Did you know...

...that this major is much broader than you might think? It covers the rich heritage of Hebrew and Judeo-Christian religious traditions, often emphasizing interdisciplinary study. Majoring in Bible studies can lead to job opportunities for both women and men.

Typical courses in this major:

New Testament overview
Old Testament overview
Christian doctrine and systematic theology
Church history and historical theology
Biblical interpretation and hermeneutics
History of Greece
History of Rome
History of the ancient Near East
Biblical archaeology
Biblical criticism
Christian ethics
Literature of the Bible
Geography of the Bible
Contemporary social concerns
Global Christianity
Key figures in biblical or Church history

Concentrations:

In college: Church history; New Testament; Old Testament.

If you go on to grad school: apologetics; biblical criticism; biblical interpretation; biblical theology; Christian/spiritual formation; classical dogmatics; early Christianity; evangelism/missions; religion in America; systematic theology.

What the study of this major is like:

Bible studies majors encounter broad and diverse subject matter. Course work may cover biblical history, biblical literature and methods for interpreting it, key characters in the Bible, important eras and figures in Church history, historical or systematic theology and ethics, the original languages of the Bible, the culture of the biblical world, the contribution of archaeology to biblical studies, and world religions.

Bible studies is taught and learned in many ways, and classes may vary in size. Your classes may feature lectures, discussion, seminars, research, writing, oral and written examinations, special projects, and student presentations. Other learning opportunities may include independent or guided study with a small group of students (directed by a faculty member); special lectures, symposiums, and conferences conducted by guest speakers; study-abroad programs; archaeological field work; off-campus internships and social service projects; and language lab instruction in Greek or Hebrew.

The reading, research, and writing demanded by your course work will require time management, good study habits, and personal discipline. Challenges specific to the Bible studies major include mastering the subject matter; the interdisciplinary nature of the major; and the diversity of Christian thought and teaching that has emerged from Roman Catholic, Orthodox, and Protestant traditions over many centuries. You must also balance your intellectual pursuits, on the one hand, with your spiritual and religious needs and your desire to serve, on the other.

Bible studies programs may differ in their requirements. Some may emphasize the biblical languages of Greek and Hebrew. Others may require an internship or a missions or social service component. There is considerable variation in how much emphasis is given to liberal arts or interdisciplinary studies. Programs also differ in their selection of reading strategies and their choice of interpretive approaches to biblical and religious literature.

Differences in emphases and philosophies stem from several factors. The weight given to matters of history, literature, and theology often reflects the specialized training of the faculty members. Another consideration is whether the educational institution is a state-supported, public college or a private institution linked to a particular Christian denomination or other religious group. Keep in mind that each of the three branches of the Christian tradition (Roman Catholic, Orthodox, and Protestant) sustains college programs in Bible studies committed to its own historical and theological traditions—traditions that, in turn, are based on doctrines and beliefs, biblical teachings, worship practices, and the religious body's purpose in providing theological education.

Other majors you might like:
Anthropology
Archaeology
Youth ministry
Ancient studies
Preministerial studies
Sociology
Sacred music
Christian studies

Ancient Near Eastern/biblical languages
History
Missionary studies
Philosophy

Questions to ask colleges:
Does the major require biblical languages (Greek or Hebrew)?

Are faculty members involved in the ministry of the church, in social services, or in missions?

At what kinds of academic institutions (research universities, seminaries, or professional schools) did faculty members study or work?

Career options and trends:
Christian education director; youth minister; clergy member; chaplain (military, hospitals, prisons, retirement/nursing homes); college professor.

Many church denominations require those entering the clergy to be ordained. Most states require licensing for clergy conducting religious rites with civil implications, such as marriages, funerals, and burials, and some types of counseling.

Bible studies majors also pursue careers in church ministry, campus ministries, social service organizations, counseling ministries, home or overseas missions, religious education, religious publishing, religious administration, journalism, business, or law.

Insider's viewpoint:
"Jewish tradition has an expression for the love of the Hebrew Scriptures known as *simchah Torah* or 'the joy of Torah.' My passion for the study of the Bible was sparked by a professor who taught courses in Hebrew language and Old Testament studies with this sense of joy."

—Professor Andrew E. Hill, Wheaton College (IL)

For more info:
Council for Christian Colleges and Universities
  (C.C.C.U.)
321 Eighth Street, N.E.
Washington, DC 20002
(202) 546-8713
www.cccu.org

Islamic studies

What it's about:

As an Islamic studies major, you explore the history, culture, and interpretation of the Islamic faith. You may also be required to study Arabic, Persian, Turkish, or Urdu for the equivalent of two years.

Is this for you?

You might like this major if you also like: learning about Islamic culture and heritage; religious customs and writings; foreign languages and cultures; history; philosophy; understanding world events; community service activities.

Consider this major if you are good at: attention to detail; critical reading/thinking; leadership; organizing; persuading/influencing; research ...*or have...* an open mind; initiative; verbal skills; writing skills.

Recommended high school prep:

English 4, math 3, lab science 3, social studies 3, and a foreign language 2–3. If possible, take courses in the Arabic, Turkish, Persian, or Urdu language.

Did you know...

...that Islam is the fastest-growing religion in the United States?

...that most Muslims do not live in the Middle East and are not Arabs? Arabs make up less than 15 percent of the Muslim population. The nation with the largest Muslim population is Indonesia.

Typical courses in this major:

Prophet of Islam
The Qur'an
Islamic sciences
Sufism
Shi'ite Islam
Popular Islam
Modern political Islam
Islamic revolution of Iran
Women in Islam
Islamic art
Islamic architecture
Islamic law
Islamic theology
Islamic philosophy
Hadith
Muslim intellectual history

Concentrations:

Women and gender issues; Islam in America; Islamic art and architecture; Islam in South Asia (India and Pakistan); Islam in Iran; Sufism; Islamic law; modern political Islam and fundamentalism; Shi'ite Islam; popular Islam; Islamic theology and philosophy; Islamic history.

What the study of this major is like:

The Islamic studies major focuses on the diversity of Islamic society and culture found in many geographic areas, time periods, and branches of the faith (including Sunni, Shi'ia, and Ahmadiyya). Your studies begin in sixth-century Arabia with the teachings of the Prophet Muhammad and include interpretations and additions made by Islamic teachers and scholars over the centuries.

You learn about Islamic scripture, principally the Qur'an, and other texts (Hadith, Sirah, Sunnah, Tafsir) that interpret, describe, or illustrate the Qur'an and the life and teachings of the Prophet. In addition, you examine the mystical beliefs of Sufism, modern Islamic politics, gender issues in Islam, Islamic sciences, Islamic law, Islamic art, and Islamic architecture.

As an Islamic studies major, you are required to do a great deal of reading, researching, and writing. Some colleges teach Islam as a component of U.S. foreign policy studies. Others include Islamic studies in the context of comparative religions. In most colleges, though, Islam is taught from an "area studies" perspective; the focus is on culture and history rather than on religion. In all programs, you develop an understanding of different societies and expand your perspective on the world.

Other majors you might like:
Near and Middle Eastern studies
Religious studies
Arabic
Iranian/Persian languages
Asian studies
Anthropology
History
South Asian studies
Sociology
Peace and conflict studies
Medieval and Renaissance studies
Judaic studies

Questions to ask colleges:
Which approaches to Islam does the program offer? Which specialties are the strongest?

Career options and trends:
College professor; teacher; journalist; Foreign Service Officer.

Majors in Islamic studies often go on to study at professional or graduate schools to prepare for careers in the clergy, law, medicine, or social work. They also find employment in the government; in nongovernmental organizations dealing with the Muslim world; and in business, education, and publishing.

Opportunities in all areas of Islamic studies have dramatically increased, especially positions in higher education (as college professors), research, government, and think tanks. For most jobs in the field, competence in an Islamic language is highly desirable.

For more info:
Middle Eastern Studies Associations of North
   America
University of Arizona
1219 North Santa Rita Ave.
Tuscon, AZ 85721
(520) 621-5850
www.mesana.org

Judaic studies

Also known as:
Jewish studies

What it's about:
This major explores the culture and religion of the Jewish people over the course of its 3,500-year history, in both their ancestral land and the lands of dispersion (migration to Europe, North America, and Israel). Your studies are wide-ranging, including the Jewish religion, heritage, philosophy, and intellectual history; Hebrew and Yiddish languages and literature; anti-Semitism; Jewish-Gentile (non-Jewish) relations; the Holocaust; Zionism; and the State of Israel.

Is this for you?
You might like this major if you also like: foreign cultures and languages; the Bible and religion; learning about Jewish heritage; community service activities.

Consider this major if you are good at: attention to detail; creativity; critical reading/thinking; leadership; research; teamwork ...*or have...* initiative; verbal skills; writing skills.

Recommended high school prep:
English 4, math 3, lab science 3, social studies 4, and a foreign language 4. Hebrew is recommended if available, although it is not a prerequisite; knowledge of any other foreign language will help you learn Hebrew in college.

Did you know...
...that the study of religion is only one aspect of Judaic studies? The major also includes the history of the Jewish people, their role in civilization, and their interaction with other cultures. Because Jewish studies is interdisciplinary, you can explore areas suited to your interests and goals.

Typical courses in this major:
Elementary, intermediate, and advanced Hebrew
Biblical Hebrew
Ancient Israel and the ancient Near East
Judaism in the Middle Ages
Jewish law and society
Family and sexuality in Judaism
Women in Jewish history
Modern Jewish history
Anti-Semitism in historical perspective
Yiddish language and culture
The Holocaust
Jewish culture in America
Zionism and Israel
Hebrew/Israeli literature in translation
Jewish and Israeli film
Jewish mysticism

Concentrations:
In college: Jewish civilization in the ancient Near East; Rabbinical Hebrew and medieval Judaism; Jewish literature; modern Jewish religion and philosophy; Holocaust studies.

If you go on to grad school: ancient Jewish texts in related languages (Hebrew, Aramaic, Akkadian); Mishna/Talmud; medieval texts; modern Rabbinical writing; Jewish history of a particular period; Zionism and Israel studies; modern Hebrew language and literature.

What the study of this major is like:
This major allows Jewish students to explore their culture in an objective, academic setting, and it gives non-Jewish students the opportunity to broaden their understanding of Judaism, a central foundation of Western civilization, Christianity, and Islam. It is a demanding course of study; you must be willing to work hard in reading and analyzing classical texts, and in most programs you are required to obtain proficiency in the Hebrew language.

Areas covered include archaeology, Biblical times, Christian Europe, and the Islamic world. In-depth study is available in Rabbinical Hebrew and medieval Judaism, including the Mishna/Talmud and medieval Jewish philosophy. Of special interest is the modern period—the beginnings of secularization, the origins of Reform and Conservative Judaism, and the development of modern anti-Semitism, leading to the Holocaust. Examination of the State of Israel focuses on the gathering of exiles; the revival of Hebrew; the status of the Palestinians; and the historical, social, and political forces that have shaped the struggle to maintain a democracy in the Middle East.

Most classes are conducted as seminars, with plenty of outside reading and directed group discussion. A frequent attribute of programs is a close relationship between students and their professors and classmates. Majors tend to study in groups, and work together on projects. Advanced Hebrew language students often tutor beginning students (for practicum credit), an activity that fosters group interaction and friendships.

Study abroad is an important aspect of the major. Most overseas study takes place in Israel; however, travel advisories in times of conflict may require colleges to offer alternative locations, such as Prague or other European cities with strong Jewish communities. Internships in Jewish community centers, museums, synagogues, and Hillel (a prominent Jewish student organization) are also encouraged, or even required.

One significant difference among programs concerns the importance placed on achieving proficiency in Hebrew. Some departments insist that students who cannot read Hebrew documents in the original language cannot gain a genuine understanding of Jewish culture. Other programs believe that what really matters is the content, and reliable translations are sufficient. If you might want to continue your Judaic studies in graduate school, however, you will need at least intermediate-level skills in Hebrew or other Semitic language (such as Arabic or Aramaic).

Other majors you might like:

Religious studies
History

Philosophy
Archaeology
Anthropology
Hebrew
Near and Middle Eastern studies
Ancient Near Eastern/Biblical languages
Talmudic studies
Islamic studies
Linguistics
Sociology

Questions to ask colleges:

What resources does the library have in Judaic studies? Do they include online resources, educational DVDs, Israeli publications, and so on? Does the Judaica collection include both Yiddish and Hebrew texts? Is there access to Jewish and Israeli music and film?

Is there a language lab, and are there computer-assisted instructional materials for Hebrew?

Are there Judaica-related extracurricular activities on or near campus?

Career options and trends:

College professor*; teacher*; Rabbi*; director of religious education; journalist; community center administrator.

A teaching certificate is required for teaching in public school, but not necessarily for Hebrew day schools or religious schools.

Judaic studies can lead to careers in business, education, government service, social work, and other careers that require a liberal arts education. It is also sound preparation for a range of graduate or professional programs, such as law, medicine, Jewish scholarship, the rabbinate, or the cantorate.

Insider's viewpoint:

"Hebrew is a fascinating language, as all Semitic languages are, because of its special mechanisms for word formation, but also because of its revival as a spoken language in the last century. I love reading Hebrew texts, and enjoy imparting their internal beauty to my students."

—Professor Shmuel Bolozky, University of Massachusetts Amherst

For more info:

Association for Jewish Studies (AJS)
Center for Jewish History
15 West 16th St.
New York, NY 10011-6301
(917) 606-8249
www.ajsnet.org

American Academy for Jewish Research (AAJR)
420 Walnut St.
Philadelphia, PA 19106
(215) 238-1290
www.aajr.org

National Association of Professors of Hebrew
University of Wisconsin–Madison
1346 Van Hise Hall, 1220 Linden Drive
Madison, WI 53706
(608) 262-3204
http://polyglot.lss.wisc.edu/naph/

Preministerial studies

What it's about:

A preministerial studies program will help you prepare to become an ordained Christian minister, priest, or other religious leader. At most colleges it is not a major but an advising program; students planning to enter a seminary, divinity school, or full-time ministerial work after college may pursue any major they choose.

Is this for you?

You might like this major if you also like: Bible study; public speaking; reflecting on spiritual issues and discussing them with others; being a friend to turn to; taking an active role in the church community. A true calling to the ministry is sometimes clear and sometimes not; but a deep religious faith and empathy for others are often found among those who are called.

Consider this major if you are good at: caring/nurturing; counseling; creativity; leadership; organizing ...*or have...* Compassion; patience; verbal skills; writing skills.

Recommended high school prep:

English 4, math 3, lab science 3, social studies 4, and a foreign language 2–3. If available, a year of Latin or Greek would be helpful, and courses in psychology, philosophy, speech, and world religions are also recommended.

Typical courses in this major:

New Testament
Western philosophy
Old Testament/Hebrew Bible
Church history
World religions
Christian ethics
Sociology
Introductory psychology
Advanced Bible study
Expository writing
Homiletics (preaching)
Church organization and management
Evangelism
Dynamics of intercultural communication
Western civilization
Liturgical theology and practice

Concentrations:

Generally, none available.

What the study of this major is like:

Many preministerial programs are nondenominational, with no sectarian or religious requirements for admission. Most, however, are typically offered at colleges affiliated with a particular religion and focus on the history, rituals, traditions, and beliefs of that denomination. Each faith usually sets its own requirements for becoming a minister. Some religions require a graduate degree from a seminary or divinity school, while others do not; so where and how a candidate is educated varies from one faith to the next.

But common to all preministerial programs is the role of the adviser, who will help you to choose a major in line with your interests and to select courses that will prepare you for the ministry or for admission to divinity school or other graduate program—and who will, in addition, discuss with you how best to use your skills in the community. Although your adviser will assist primarily in the academic aspects of your education, he or she will be sensitive to your unique concerns as you contemplate a career in ministry.

In a typical preministerial program, the courses provide you with a strong background in biblical literature, as well as a look at the cultures that produced the sacred texts. A balanced curriculum that emphasizes the liberal arts will give you the well-rounded education you'll need as you prepare for the variety of challenges you will face as a minister. If you decide to go on to the graduate level, you will have the skills necessary there as well: how to make use of the library, do research, and write effectively.

Some preministerial programs are very flexible about what courses you can select, while other programs have specific requirements, which may include vocational experience courses and courses in cross-cultural understanding. Usually, programs with specific requirements are geared to a particular faith or tradition; so check out a school's affiliation and direction before you apply.

In addition to academic pursuits, you'll do one or more internships, practicing what you've been learning about the ministry. This experience can take a number of forms: you might visit congregation members' homes, work with young people at a Christian summer camp, teach Bible lessons, give sermons, or play sacred music.

You should also attend lectures and seminars and talk with clergy to familiarize yourself with current issues. A useful pursuit is to engage in volunteer work in the community, that will expose you to real-world problems such as poverty, homelessness, and substance abuse.

Preministerial programs are not abundant and are more likely to be found at religiously affiliated universities and colleges. It is not essential to come from a preministerial program in order to get into graduate school or enter the ministry. But a good preministerial program will give you the time to broaden your understanding, to participate in a multitude of experiences, and to determine who you are and what really matters to you.

Other majors you might like:
Religious studies
Bible studies
Judaic studies
Pastoral counseling
Philosophy
History
Sacred music
Social work
Psychology
Peace and conflict studies
Religious education
Youth ministry

Questions to ask colleges:
May I choose any major if I wish to pursue a preministerial studies path, or are there specific disciplines I must choose from?

Is there a faculty member or adviser to help students navigate the program and assist them in obtaining related internship or vocational experiences?

If the program is nondenominational, is there a club or other student organization on campus for my specific faith?

Career options and trends:
Minister; priest; religious education coordinator; theology professor; military chaplain; missionary.

Usually ministers, priests, and chaplains must go through a candidacy and ordination process through a church conference or diocese before they may become a minister. In some Christian denominations, students who wish to start the process toward ordination must secure the blessing of a bishop or other church authority well in advance of beginning a graduate program.

Fewer young people are entering the ministry as a first career these days. Job prospects are good, especially for those who have a graduate degree, or are willing to accept part-time positions or to work in rural areas. In some Christian denominations, you may have to relocate at the discretion of a bishop.

For more info:
Association for Biblical Higher Education
5575 S. Semoran Blvd., Suite 26
Orlando, FL 32822-1781
(407) 207-0808
www.abhe.org

Association of Theological Schools (ATS)
10 Summit Park Drive
Pittsburgh, PA 15275-1110
(412) 788-6505
www.ats.edu

Religious studies

Also known as:

Comparative religion

What it's about:

In the religious studies major, you become familiar with many of the world's spiritual traditions, and learn to use a range of approaches—historical, textual, psychological, philosophical, sociological, and anthropological—to examine the variety of religious experience.

Is this for you?

You might like this major if you also like: philosophy; literature; the arts; other cultures, past and present; mythology; languages; thinking about religious themes and motivations.

Consider this major if you are good at: caring/nurturing; creativity; critical reading/thinking; memorizing; research; teamwork *...or have...* an open mind; patience; writing skills.

Recommended high school prep:

English 4, math 3, lab science 3, social studies 4, and a foreign language 3-4. Take as many history courses as possible, including art history.

Did you know...

...that most religious studies majors do not intend to pursue careers as priests, imams, or rabbis? This major is mostly taught as an interdisciplinary liberal arts field that prepares you for many different career paths.

Typical courses in this major:

Introduction to religion
Judaism
Hinduism
Christianity
Buddhism
Islam
Religions of China
American religions
Existentialist theology
Religions of Japan
Religion and moral issues
Critiques of religion
Pilgrimage
Mysticism
New religious movements
Philosophy of religion

Concentrations:

In college: particular religions; groups of religions (for example, Asian); historical periods; cultural studies (Christianity in the Americas); comparative religions.

If you go on to grad school: psychology of religion; religious anthropology; ritual studies; language and scriptural studies (such as the Torah and Hebrew, the Sanskrit scriptures of Hinduism, or Taoist classics in Chinese); religion and science.

What the study of this major is like:

The study of religion includes many cultures and traditions. You learn the difference between *participating in* a religious tradition—its stories, rituals, symbols, beliefs, social and institutional structures, and customs—and *understanding* that tradition, regardless of whether or not you participate in it. By studying religion independently of participants' beliefs, you learn to think critically and imaginatively.

Your course work teaches you a variety of methods and approaches, including historical investigation, psychological inquiry, social analysis, anthropological and ethnological investigation, feminist criticism, and linguistic analysis. As you examine a range of religions, you begin to recognize and appreciate their similarities and differences.

Generally, you are not expected to enter college with a background in religion. The major typically begins with introductory courses that familiarize you with the basic elements of religion, such as

507

myth, ritual, scripture, and symbols. You can usually choose from among courses in several areas: the Western traditions of Judaism, Christianity, and Islam; the Asian traditions of Hinduism, Jainism, Sikhism, Buddhism, Confucianism, and Taoism; theoretical and philosophical approaches to the study of religion; and, occasionally, on indigenous traditions (for instance, the religious practices of Native American cultures).

Most programs require an entry-level course in at least two traditions and recommend that you take courses in both Western and non-Western traditions. At least one of your courses will examine theoretical approaches. In some programs, languages associated with religious traditions may be offered. Although you are not usually required to take a foreign language, such training is helpful, especially if you intend to continue religious studies in grad school.

Your course work examines key questions on such topics as ecology, science, gender relations, cultural and historical conflicts, the emergence of the universe, and conscious awareness. You explore the development of religious traditions over time, as well as the creativity that keeps religions relevant today. Areas that may prove difficult to deal with include unfamiliar worldviews and practices, and abstract theological and philosophical ideas. But learning to recognize other religious points of view will challenge, contradict, and then deepen your understanding.

Programs at different colleges may vary in their emphases. For example, some specialize in theoretical approaches, such as ethics, philosophy, or anthropology, while others may focus on a particular religion or an aspect of a religion (such as biblical studies or Islamic law/Shari'ah). Look for balance across approaches and traditions—for a good indication, look for courses in both Eastern and Western faiths. Also, some private colleges teach religious studies from a faith-based, rather than an academic, point of view. It is not always easy to tell, so if you have a preference, be sure to check.

Other majors you might like:
Anthropology
Peace and conflict studies

Theology
Near and Middle Eastern studies
Medieval and Renaissance studies
History
Archaeology
Philosophy
Psychology
Sociology
Global studies

Questions to ask colleges:
Which religious traditions are taught? Do course descriptions mention women, ritual, or indigenous peoples? Are topics such as the psychology of religion or science and religion covered in the curriculum?

Career options and trends:
High school teacher; college professor; social worker; journalist.

Majors in religious studies also go on to work in business, law, medicine, counseling, management, psychology, academic research, and religious vocations. Careers in many of these disciplines require graduate or professional study.

Insider's viewpoint:
"I wrote a paper on the anthropology of religious war. It really helped me see that, wow, maybe I can do this sort of thing and maybe it can be useful. I see a great need to make religious studies practical."

—Andy, junior, Cornell University

For more info:
American Academy of Religion (AAR)
825 Houston Mill Rd., N.E.
Suite 300
Atlanta, GA 30329
(404) 727-3049
www.aarweb.org

Council of Societies for the Study of Religion
c/o Rice University
P.O. Box 1892, MS-156
Houston, TX 77251-1892
(713) 348-5721
www.cssr.org

Sacred music

Also known as:

Religious music

Pastoral music

What it's about:

The sacred music major provides a broad base of information about music history, music theory, and performance skills as preparation for careers as minister of music, organist, or choir director in a place of worship. You develop a repertory of sacred music, grounded in both historical and contemporary forms of expression.

Is this for you?

You might like this major if you also like: singing; chorus; expressing your faith through music; playing an instrument; participating in worship-related activities; leading group activities; tutoring.

Consider this major if you are good at: caring/nurturing; coaching; creativity; leadership; musicianship; organizing; persuading/influencing; teamwork ...*or have...* patience; verbal skills.

Recommended high school prep:

English 4, math 3, lab science 3, social studies 3, music 1–2, and a foreign language 2–3. Participation in high school chorus (2 or 3 years) is highly recommended. Basic keyboarding skills (piano or organ) are also expected.

Did you know...

...that success in this field requires more than just musical ability? Certainly a passion for sacred music is essential; but enthusiasm and a desire to work with people can be as important as musical skills.

Typical courses in this major:

Music theory

Music history

Composition

Choral conducting

Choir training methods

Sight singing

Sacred music history

Choral literature

Hymnology

Children's choir leadership

Church music administration

Applied voice, piano, or organ

College choir, vocal, or instrumental ensemble

Concentrations:

Organ studies; conducting; worship leadership

What the study of this major is like:

Throughout history, musicians have worked alongside the clergy to lead others in worship and praise. Many consider expressing faith through music to be one of the highest forms of worship. The sacred music major helps you develop the skills you need to be successful in the profession.

Besides training in music, professionals in sacred music need skills in areas such as arts management, program planning and organization, community building, and talent development. As a professional, you are responsible for bringing the music of the religious institution to life, developing musical resources, and guiding the congregation in praise and worship. The exploration of contemporary worship music, such as music from world cultures, keeps the profession fresh.

As a major, you study basic musicianship. Theory courses review the mechanics of music (such as rhythmic and pitch notation, key signatures, triads, and scales) and explore composition (harmonic activity and structure). In sacred music history courses, you examine the development of music in worship (in the West and in traditional Asian and African cultures), liturgy, the historical significance of the sections of a worship service, and the primary works of sacred music.

Because most majors plan to be musical leaders in congregations, programs include performance and ensemble participation, conducting, choir training, and choral literature. You also study hymnology (the history and techniques of congregational singing); administrative skills; and applied instruction in voice, piano, or organ. Organ instruction is highly recommended, and some proficiency at the piano is generally expected. In addition, you may have opportunities to conduct children's and/or handbell choirs.

Because musicians serving congregations often function as performers, most programs encourage majors to participate in third-year and fourth-year solo recitals. In addition, you can attend concerts and recitals by ensembles, faculty members, and visiting artists, and perhaps intern in local houses of worship. Some programs offer workshops and conferences (on weekends or during the summer) that teach current trends and special aspects of the profession.

The sacred music program presents challenges beyond those of performance. Unlike other music programs, you are faced with questions about music's role in worship, its historical significance to modern liturgy, its place in contemporary society, and its function as "performance" or "offering." Also, at large conservatory programs, sacred music majors often find they are less respected than students majoring in performance or education. This can dishearten students who work just as hard as their peers in other concentrations do.

As a sacred music major, you earn either a Bachelor of Arts degree, which denotes a music specialty within a broad liberal arts program, or a Bachelor of Music degree, which focuses on performance and professional training. At a faith-based college, religious training may be just as important as musical training. At a music conservatory, the focus is on scholarly work and performance, and music study is offered at a more demanding level. You are expected to enter the program with considerable musical ability and to show achievement in performances throughout your college career. If the university is state-supported, certain sacred music courses may not be offered.

Other majors you might like:
Conducting
Piano/organ
Youth ministry
Music pedagogy
Music teacher education
Music history/literature
Recording arts
Music theory and composition
Voice/opera
Music management
Religious studies

Questions to ask colleges:
Are internships or other practical experiences available at local places of worship?

Does the program offer special campus activities, such as workshops/seminars/conferences related to sacred music, led by respected practitioners?

Is there ample access to organ or piano instruments for practice and rehearsals?

Career options and trends:
Choir director; organist in house of worship*; director of music ministries*; children's choir director; handbell choir director; parochial school music teacher.

Two issues present challenging opportunities for newcomers to the field: global music and contemporary worship music. Due to our growing appreciation of other cultures, the sacred music professional needs to be aware of the contributions and performance styles of other societies. Additionally, many mainstream denominations are including contemporary styles of worship, requiring the ability to blend praise choruses with traditional hymns or to incorporate instruments such as keyboards, guitar, and percussion into the worship service.

For more info:
American Guild of Organists
475 Riverside Drive
Suite 1260
New York, NY 10115
212-870-2310
www.agohq.org

Theology

What it's about:
Theology is the academic study of the beliefs and practices of a particular religion or religious community. You gain an understanding of its faith and practices by studying its history, literature, ethics, doctrines, and present-day situation. This major may also include a comparative study of world religions and practical courses in counseling, homiletics (preaching), and worship services.

Is this for you?
You might like this major if you also like: thinking about philosophical and spiritual matters; ritual and liturgy; music or drama; helping others; community activities.

Consider this major if you are good at: caring/nurturing; counseling; creativity; critical reading/thinking; leadership; research ...*or have...* initiative; patience; verbal skills; writing skills.

Recommended high school prep:
English 4, math 3, lab science 3, social studies 4, and a foreign language 2–3. If available, courses in psychology, sociology, and world literature are also recommended.

Did you know...
...that the study of theology can be both intellectually and spiritually demanding? It requires reflection on the relationship (even tension) between personal faith and critical thinking on fundamental religious questions.

Typical courses in this major:
Introduction to theology
The Old Testament
The New Testament
History of Christian thought
The early church
Medieval thought
The Reformation era
Biblical interpretation and hermeneutics
Studies in the Gospels
Studies in the Epistles
Christian doctrine
Liturgical theology and practice
Ethics
Systematic theology
Church history
World religions

Concentrations:
In college: biblical studies; history of religions; youth and family ministry; religious education; church history.

If you go on to grad school: theology and ministry; Hebrew Bible; New Testament/Christian origins; pastoral theology; liturgical studies.

What the study of this major is like:
Theological studies can be a rich and diverse major. It may be found in departments of theology, religion, philosophy and religion, or Bible studies. In most colleges, theology is taught not just as the beliefs of a particular religious community, but in a more all-encompassing spirit—that is, you learn about the theologies of your community, other communities, and the broader non-Christian world.

As a major, you explore the issues of justice, mercy, and the power attributed to God, and meditate on the problem of evil, suffering, and death in a world ruled by God. In Christian theology, you read the Bible, if possible in the original languages. By studying various religions, you learn how their followers perceive the moral life, and you evaluate the effect of faith on practical matters of worship and ethics.

Other Bible-oriented courses may examine how the books of the Bible came to be considered by Jews and Christians as sacred. Taking note of parables and metaphors in secular, or nonreligious, literature highlights the similarities and differences between the Bible and other literary works.

In church history courses, topics include the development of spirituality and worship; the relationship between religious institutions and civil governments and secular society; the impact of believers on culture and politics; and the way social and political environments affect the church. In ethics, you study the personal and social teachings of the living faith, including the challenges of medical and economic technology, and consider the ways in which believers can participate in social action and political life.

Your college experience will include a lot of reading and reflection, intense and wide-ranging conversations with other students, and exploratory visits to worshiping communities from other traditions. You typically learn through a combination of reading, lecture, discussion, and, sometimes, formal debate. Fieldwork, internships, and practicums are regular features of theological studies programs, and service learning is becoming increasingly popular.

Between your third and fourth years, you are likely to do an internship. Practical/ministerial studies also include clinical experience and frank self-reflection. The biggest challenge you may face is to take an objective look at beliefs and ideas you may have accepted unquestioningly; students are often afraid of asking hard-driving questions about their faith.

Some colleges encourage this no-holds-barred inquiry into the faith, on the basis that critical questioning (when supported by a community of believing scholars) can deepen and strengthen your faith by helping you become mature and reflective. Other colleges focus on instilling faith and strengthening your conviction, contending that careful teaching of the faith can make you a mature believer, without causing you stress by questioning your basic convictions.

Other majors you might like:
Bible studies
Religious studies
Human services
Youth ministry
Preministerial studies
Philosophy
Religious education
Social work
Anthropology
Legal studies
Peace and conflict studies

Questions to ask colleges:
How does the program help students relate to persons of other faiths in a pluralistic society?

Is there a community of faith that can provide support and stimulation?

Career options and trends:
Priest or minister; teacher; youth minister; director of religious education; journalist; social worker; parish administrator; vocational counselor.

Like other liberal arts majors, theology prepares you for a variety of careers in education, business, government, public affairs, and social work. A theology degree is excellent preparation for graduate study in divinity, which enables you to work in pastoral positions. Most mainline Christian church bodies are suffering from severe shortages in pastoral and other ministry positions.

For more info:
American Academy of Religion (AAR)
825 Houston Mill Rd., N.E.
Suite 300
Atlanta, GA 30329-4205
(404) 727-3049
www.aarweb.org

Association of Theological Schools (ATS)
10 Summit Park Drive
Pittsburgh, PA 15275-1110
(412) 788-6505
www.ats.edu

Social sciences

Social sciences are the most popular academic majors in American four-year colleges and second only to business among all categories of majors chosen. More than 195,000 bachelor's degrees are given in the social sciences each year, including nearly 90,000 in psychology alone. It seems we can never know enough about our fellow human beings.

These majors cover the world inside and out, from archaeological digs that investigate the beginnings of humankind, to satellite global positioning systems that pinpoint where we are today. (You'll study GPS in the geography major.) Anthropology explores our origins, cultures, and evolution from prehistory to the present. Sociology, the study of groups of people, covers places, spaces, and races. Psychologists probe the way we behave and think. Economists track resources. Political scientists gauge power. And experts in international relations tackle global conflicts, poverty, oppression, and the flip side—peace, wealth, and freedom.

"I love this field because it addresses the 'big' issues, problems and challenges that confront humanity today to provide tools and insights that can help us create a more just, humane, and peaceful world," says Professor Andrew A. Latham of Macalester College.

These majors touch on many fields, and the knowledge and skills you'll learn can be applied later along many career paths.

"Economics graduates find jobs in education, government, industry, public policy, and planning. Many become business managers," says Professor John J. Siegfried, Vanderbilt University. "The field is also excellent preparation for law school, business school, and, more recently, medical school. Many students with a B.A. or a B.S. degree enter general management training in large corporations. Others start out in sales or analyst positions."

As is often the case, jobs are harder to get for students with just a bachelor's degree, if the economy is slow. But because the social sciences make students think, use numbers intelligently, write well, and understand people, these majors are good overall training for the workplace.

"More students would consider international relations if they knew how valuable this major is as a flexible basis for future careers," notes Professor Robert Mandel, Lewis and Clark College, of his department, whose grads are likely to be in demand in today's global workplace.

"For political science majors," Latham says, "developing the intellectual tools necessary to understand politics equips students with some of the skills required for leadership in their chosen field."

Mixing art and science

These majors cover a lot of bases, so, in addition to schools of social sciences, look into colleges of humanities, liberal arts, arts and sciences, arts and letters, behavioral sciences, life sciences, and education, as well as preprofessional divisions. For economics, be sure to check out business programs.

But wait, are social sciences really humanities or are they really sciences?

"The study of political science can be both 'scientific' and 'humanistic,'" Latham explains. "Some schools favor methods that are more scientific or quantitative, some more humanistic or qualitative."

Another example of this blend is in geography. "Two main specializations within geography are physical geography and human geography," says Professor Gregory A. Elmes of West Virginia University. "Purely physical geography is akin to the natural sciences with emphasis on theory, laws, and experimental evidence. Within human geography are the more conventional systematic elements, such as cultural, economic, and urban studies."

When choosing a college program, ask if it's more about humankind or research, the people or the numbers. Are you mostly theorizing about the subject or analyzing it? Or both? Some majors, including psychology, can lead to either a Bachelor of Arts or a Bachelor of Science degree.

Ask colleges which electives you should take with your major, like history with international relations. How much math will you need to know? What are the degree requirements and what special courses can you take? Do most students in the major finish their degree in four years?

Learn the strengths of the faculty members. Do they know about other fields so they can help you draw connections to other disciplines? Are full professors teaching undergraduates? Do the profs also teach the labs and offer advising? What kind of research are the faculty members doing? Will you get a chance to do research with them? How big are the classes? Are libraries, book collections, journals, and computers and software adequate and up-to-date?

Are scholarships and internships available for undergrads? What kinds of jobs do grad students often get? Find out if your major has a graduate program, where you could go for a master's or a Ph.D. (See the individual majors in this section for graduate concentrations, careers, and sources of information.)

Also in this book, read about related majors in the sections on Area, ethnic, and gender studies; Business; Education; Engineering technology; Family and consumer sciences; Humanities; Multi/interdisciplinary studies; Natural resources and conservation; and Public administration. You see, the social sciences are everywhere.

Anthropology

What it's about:

Anthropology is the study of people—their origins, physical nature, and social behavior. Anthropology majors explore human cultural and biological evolution and the way all peoples, from prehistoric times to today, adapt to their environment; form families, clans, tribes, and nations; regulate behavior through laws and government; worship and celebrate; communicate; educate their young; and adapt to change.

Is this for you?

You might like this major if you also like: traveling; learning about different peoples and cultures; *National Geographic*; reading; history; geography.

Consider this major if you are good at: attention to detail; foreign languages; observing; research ...*or have...* initiative; verbal skills; writing skills.

Recommended high school prep:

English 4, math 3, lab science 3 (including biology), social studies 4, and a foreign language 3-4. If available, courses in sociology and government are also recommended.

Typical courses in this major:

Biological anthropology
Introduction to archaeology
Cultural anthropology
Primate behavior
Archaeological field methods
Religion and culture
Music and culture
Language and culture
Mythology
Human origins and evolution
Culture and personality
Native American cultures
Forensic anthropology
Human population genetics
Old World prehistory
Peoples and cultures of Africa, Asia, etc.

Concentrations:

Archaeology; physical/biological anthropology; linguistic anthropology; cultural anthropology; urban anthropology; applied anthropology; cultural resource management.

What the study of this major is like:

Majors in anthropology focus on the similarities and differences between human beings and other primates, as well as on the similarities and differences among human populations. Anthropologists are interested in all aspects of what it means to be human.

You learn how people in different parts of the world live their lives and adapt to their environments. Most programs require courses in each of the four main subdivisions of anthropology: physical anthropology, cultural anthropology, linguistic anthropology, and archaeology. Elective courses allow you to follow your interests—a specific country or cultural unit, such as Japan or Mexico, or a topic, such as political systems, child-rearing practices, music, or art.

Physical anthropology (also known as biological anthropology) investigates when and where human beings first appeared; you may even handle stone tools, skeletal materials, and plaster casts of the remains of people who lived many centuries ago. You may spend time in a local zoo observing chimpanzees and other primates to compare their actions with human behavior. In addition, you'll examine genetic evidence, as you trace human biological origins and evolutionary development.

Cultural anthropology explores specific cultures or concentrates on aspects shared by all cultures—religion, politics, law, or ecology. Cultural anthropologists study the diversity found in contemporary societies, from the few remaining peoples who hunt and gather roots and berries to those who shop in supermarkets and live in metropolitan areas such as Tokyo, New York, and London.

In linguistic anthropology, you examine the relationship of language to other aspects of culture. For instance, you study methods of communication—including body language, dialects, jargon, and slang; you observe how the language people use reflects their perception of and interaction with the world around them.

Archaeology, which deals with excavating, analyzing, and interpreting physical and cultural remains, is increasingly studied as an independent major or graduate program. Most anthropology programs offer introductory courses and opportunities to study field methods during a summer session.

Some programs encourage students to apply what they learn to contemporary problems facing the United States or other industrial societies; this approach is usually called applied anthropology.

As a rule, instructors will have spent a year or more living and studying among the peoples they are teaching about; the firsthand experience of living for extended periods in other cultures is an important part of anthropological training. In fact, fieldwork in other cultures sets anthropology apart from other social sciences and usually results in engaging lectures.

Most colleges offer courses in the four main subdivisions of anthropology, but few have courses in all the specialized subjects or include all regions of the world with equal thoroughness. If you are interested in a specific society, such as Japan, or a specific topic, such as legal anthropology, you should read course catalogs carefully to see if a particular program covers the topics you want.

Other majors you might like:
Archaeology
Sociology
Linguistics
Classics
Genetics
Geography
History
Psychology
Native American studies
Human development and family studies

Religious studies
Urban studies

Questions to ask colleges:
Are majors encouraged to spend a semester or term abroad? The opportunity to relate what you have learned in your anthropology courses to your own experiences with another culture is the best way to grasp the theories and methods of anthropology. Some programs consider fieldwork so important that they make a term abroad a requirement.

Career options and trends:
Social worker; genetic counselor; field archaeologist; teacher of English as a second language (ESL); cultural artifact specialist; educator; national/state park interpreter; environmental impact assessment researcher; travel agent/guide/consultant; museum administrator or technician.

Some occupations, such as field archaeologist, genetic counselor, and museum technician, may require additional specialized training and experience; graduate study is usually required for research, social work, and teaching.

Anthropology provides good preparation for a wide variety of jobs—in government, business, social services, the news media, museums, and education—that require an understanding of cultural and national differences and the ability to work with people from a variety of backgrounds.

Insider's viewpoint:
"Come prepared to think. This isn't a major for people who like to sit back and listen to others talk. Also, you need an open mind to study anthropology, because part of what you have to learn is that the way other people think is no less developed, no less 'right,' than the way you think."

—Chris, senior, Williams College

For more info:
American Anthropological Association (AAA)
2200 Wilson Blvd.
Suite 600
Arlington, VA 22201
(703) 528-1902
www.aaanet.org

Archaeology

What it's about:

Archaeology majors investigate extinct societies and the history of living societies. By excavating, analyzing, and interpreting cultural remains, you reconstruct lifeways and study why and how human cultures have changed over the last 2.5 million years.

Is this for you?

You might like this major if you also like: Scouting; collecting; detecting; discovery; history; mummies; ancient civilizations.

Consider this major if you are good at: attention to detail; creativity; critical reading/thinking; organizing; research; spacial thinking/analysis *...or have...* curiosity/thirst for knowledge; initiative; patience; writing skills.

Recommended high school prep:

English 4, math 3, lab science 3, social studies 3, and a foreign language 3–4. Computer skills and an additional language are useful but not mandatory.

Did you know...

...that archaeological "digs," or investigations, require systematic and detailed data collection, often in remote locations? While there is excitement in discovery, the process can be slow and somewhat tedious, often based upon minute and fragmentary evidence.

Typical courses in this major:

Introduction to archaeological theory and methods
Survey of world prehistory
Greco-Roman studies
Egyptology
Chinese and Japenese dynastic history
Paleolithic cultures
Origins of New World civilizations
Sub-Saharan African cultures
Central Asian archaeology
Origins of Australian and Polynesian cultures
Megalithic and Celtic archaeology
Field excavation
Zooarchaeology
Paleoethnobotany
GIS (Geographic Information Systems)
Forensic archaeology

Concentrations:

In college: classical archaeology; anthropological archaeology.

If you go on to grad school: maritime archaeology; zooarchaeology; paleoethnobotany; environmental archaeology; aDNA (ancient DNA) analyses; forensic archaeology; cultural resources management; GIS (Geographic Information Systems) and spatial analysis; rock art analyses; and regional studies, such as Egyptology, Hittite archaeology, Mayan archaeology.

What the study of this major is like:

First- and second-year archaeology courses are survey lectures that provide the tools to get you involved in the more interesting aspects of the discipline. For example, you need to learn where and when a culture existed before you go out into the field and study it. Your third- and fourth-year courses, usually seminars of about 5 to 15 students, focus on specific issues, areas, and problems of anthropological or classical archaeology.

For anthropological archaeology, you take lab courses ranging from the preliminary analyses of excavation materials to advanced labs in specialty fields, such as zooarchaeology (the analysis of animal remains); geoarchaeology (the use of geologic methods to interpret an excavation site); paleoethnobotany (the analysis of plant remains); forensic archaeology (the recovery of buried criminal evidence); spatial analysis (use of GIS technology); or historical archaeology (the archaeologic record of historic events).

If you concentrate in classical archaeology, your work shifts to literature-and-language studies and intensive investigation of Greek, Roman, Egyptian, or Chinese cultures. In both trajectories, students often prepare an honors thesis, the product of an independent study.

Most students participate in one or more semester-abroad excavation projects, which sometimes take place during the summer. There are many possibilities; selecting the one best for you is often a challenge. For some, the issue is cost; to attend a field school, you must pay for room and board, transportation, and perhaps tuition. Also, if you need to work during the summer to help pay for school, field projects can interfere. Another consideration is the type of data you need to collect. Although the field school is a good place to do research for an honors thesis, you may have trouble knowing which kind of data your project requires. Your college advisers should provide you with suggestions.

Archaeology professors are often working on their own field research projects, so you may be able to help with the analysis of earlier excavations or participate in the excavations on a current project. If you develop an interest in a geographic area or an ancient culture other than those your instructors are pursuing, you might work on a project with some of their colleagues. Also, colleges with a grad program may allow you to work with master's or doctorate degree students on their research projects. Advanced students often make good mentors.

Working together in the field and on thesis projects can be fun and exciting. Students often develop a strong camaraderie and pick up on each other's enthusiasm. Most programs offer colloquiums, in which students meet to hear an undergrad, grad student, faculty member, or distinguished visitor give an informal presentation on work in progress.

Other majors you might like:
Art history
Anthropology
Geology/earth science
Classics

Environmental studies
Architectural history/criticism
History
Historic preservation
Bible studies
Medieval and Renaissance studies
Ancient studies
Classical/ancient Mediterranean/Near Eastern studies

Questions to ask colleges:
Does the program offer undergrad concentrations in classical and/or anthropological archaeology? Learning about both approaches provides you with a broader grasp of archaeology and may offer you more graduate and post-graduate opportunities.

Does the college have a grad program in archaeology? What kinds of archaeological labs are available? Are there opportunities for students to go on excavation projects? The presence of a grad program usually indicates a stronger program for undergraduates, with more facilities and field opportunities.

Where do the faculty members conduct their field research? If you are already interested in a particular region, you should go to a college that will allow you to work in that area.

Career options and trends:
College professor; museum curator; cultural resource management specialist; state or federal government archaeologist; park ranger.

If you go into cultural resource management or, to a lesser extent, other archaeological fields, you are strongly encouraged to meet the training and certification requirements of the Register of Professional Archaeologists (www.rpanet.org), which includes obtaining an advanced degree.

Employment prospects for archaeologists are strong. Less than half of all archaeologists work in traditional areas such as teaching and museums. The majority now work for state or federal government agencies or in the private sector. Probably as many as two-thirds of all archaeologists hold positions that did not exist a generation ago.

Insider's viewpoint:

"I thrill to the excitement of discovery, finding the first known example of geophagy (the practice of eating earth when food is scarce) in the Andes, discovering evidence for a new trade route, pulling the disparate pieces of the puzzle together and figuring out the lifeways of past human cultures."

—Professor David L. Browman, Washington University in St. Louis

For more info:

Society for American Archaeology (SAA)
900 Second St., N.E.
Suite #12
Washington, DC 20002-3560
(202) 789-8200
www.saa.org

Society for Historical Archaeology (SHA)
9797 Key West Avenue
Suite 100
Rockville, MD 20850
(301)-990-2454
www.sha.org

Economics

What it's about:

The economics major provides a framework for analyzing issues such as inflation, unemployment, monopoly, and economic growth. You learn how economic systems function to provide goods and services. As you study theory, policy, and trends, you explore ways to deal with the economic problems that confront individuals, businesses, and nations.

Is this for you?

You might like this major if you also like: Thinking about issues such as wealth, poverty, discrimination, the environment, and trends in the global economy; working with numbers; reading about current events in newspapers and news magazines; investment clubs.

Consider this major if you are good at: attention to detail; logical reasoning; math; organizing; quantitative analysis ...*or have...* initiative; writing skills.

Recommended high school prep:

English 4, math 4, lab science 3 (including physics), social studies 4 (including American/U.S. history, world history, government/civics, and economics), and a foreign language 2–3. If possible, take a computer science course.

Did you know...

...that economics is concerned with choices people make in all areas of their lives, not just choices related to financial matters?

Typical courses in this major:

Principles of microeconomics
Principles of macroeconomics
Economic statistics
Money and banking
Business and government
International trade
International finance
Urban economics
Environmental economics
Labor economics
Public economics
Industrial organization
Economic history
Poverty and discrimination
Health economics
Law and economics

Concentrations:

Generally, none in college; but if you go on to grad school: microeconomic theory; macroeconomic theory; econometrics; labor economics; monetary economics; industrial organization; public economics; international economics; economic history; economic development.

What the study of this major is like:

Economics is about choices and change. By investigating how people make decisions, economists can predict how people will react to change. Economics can help people to understand the causes of economic problems and to devise ways to avoid them. It is a practical discipline that plays an important role in the formulation of policies on such issues as taxation, energy policy, retirement security, international trade, health care, the environment, and the rate of inflation.

If you like rigorous analysis and problem solving, economics can be intellectually appealing. It uses simplified models to explain and predict economic behavior in a complicated, disorderly world. For example, when the interest rate goes down, what happens to mortgage rates and to the cost of new cars? Economics emphasizes insights derived from observation. It teaches you to isolate the most important facts and to focus on their implications.

As a major, you will probably begin with introductory and intermediate microeconomics (the study of individual firms, consumers, and workers) and macroeconomics (the study of economy-wide income, employment, and prices), and an economic statistics course. Later, in electives—such as international trade and finance, environmental economics, labor, public finance, or comparative economic systems—you see how basic principles come to bear in specific applied fields. Your standard tools of analysis are graphs and algebra. Most of your classes will be taught as lectures, and you can expect to do plenty of problem sets.

Some programs focus on theoretical analysis; others favor data analysis. Programs may also vary in their definition of economic practice. According to some professionals, an economist's main job is to model the economy as it might be—to develop theories that predict the consequences of policies. Other economists see their job as collecting data that describe the economy as it is. Still others examine the social, cultural, and political factors that influence the economy.

Although few economics departments have enough staff to offer courses in all the applied fields, most programs emphasize universal, fundamental principles. However, if you are interested in applying economics to a particular problem, be sure to choose a college that has the courses you'll need.

Other majors you might like:

Agricultural economics
Business administration and management
Accounting
Applied mathematics
Business/managerial economics
Finance
Psychology
Entrepreneurial studies
Statistics
Econometrics/quantitative economics
International business
International relations

Questions to ask colleges:

How much math do you need to succeed in the major? Is it enough to do well in algebra, or is calculus or even more advanced math necessary? The answers can help you plan what courses to take in both high school and college.

Is there a capstone experience such as a senior seminar, thesis, or independent-study project?

Career options and trends:

Business economist; economic consultant; government economist; investment banker; market researcher.

Graduates also find jobs in education, industry, public policy, and planning. In addition, the field is excellent preparation for law school, business school, and, recently, medical school. Many students with a B.A. or B.S. degree in economics enter training programs in large corporations and may become business managers. Others start out in sales or analyst positions. Economics majors can also consider teaching positions; high schools in particular are expected to have a growing need for economics instructors.

Insider's viewpoint:

"It's hard to understand and accept the fact that there are economic theories that support either conservative or liberal policies and that, although these theories contradict each other, they are both viable."

—David, senior, Cornell University

For more info:

Council for Economic Education
122 East 42 Street, Suite 2600
New York, NY 10168
(800) 338-1192
www.councilforeconed.org

Geography

What it's about:

Geography is the science of space and place on the earth's surface. You examine how people, regions, and environments interact to create and sustain the world in which we live. Using a multidisciplinary approach, you study local, regional, and global geography.

Is this for you?

You might like this major if you also like: maps; current affairs; *National Geographic*; travel; backpacking; biking; environmental issues; Model UN; computer graphics; other people and cultures.

Consider this major if you are good at: Integrating information from different sources; attention to detail; creativity; critical reading/thinking; research; spacial thinking/analysis ...*or have...* graphical skills; initiative; verbal skills; writing skills.

Recommended high school prep:

English 4, math 3, lab science 3, social studies 4, and a foreign language 2–3. If they are available, also take ecology and AP human geography.

Typical courses in this major:

Human geography
Physical geography
Urban geography
World regional geography
Cultural geography
Economic geography
Remote sensing
Political geography
Cartography
Natural resources
Energy and the environment
Urban and regional planning
Weather and climate
Social geography
Geographic Information Systems (GIS)
Human-environmental relations

Concentrations:

In college: physical geography; environmental geography; human geography; spatial skills (tools and techniques); regional or area studies.

If you go on to grad school: human-environment relations; geographic information science; environmental geoscience; atmospheric and climatic studies; geomorphology; urban and regional systems; development studies.

What the study of this major is like:

Geography includes much more than the memorization of place names, capitals, and longest rivers. It investigates the way people from a variety of localities relate to their environment and the way their surroundings shape their lives. As a major, you gain a broad understanding of the way humans have adapted to, changed, and organized their physical environments. Geography draws from related fields, such as anthropology, economics, political science, and biology.

Two main specializations in the major are physical geography and human geography—and discussions often focus on their overlap. Physical geographers study climates, landforms, vegetation, soils, and water. In human geography, the emphasis is on people's perception, use, and modification of space, as individuals and communities create and sustain the places they call home. Topics the two groups examine include the effects, on both human activity and the natural world, of global warming, desertification, deforestation, loss of biodiversity, groundwater pollution, fire, and flooding.

The major begins with first-year courses that introduce you to facts, ideas, and tools. Besides human geography and physical geography, you take statistics, regional geography (such as courses on Africa or North America), and skills (such as cartography or remote sensing). Then you can concentrate in an area such as environmental geography, geographic education, or geographic information processing. You may be required to complete an independent research project—a capstone experience that pulls together numerous topics and skills. Sometimes you can meet the requirement by participating in a field course. You should also take courses in other departments that relate to your concentration.

Because geography is not usually emphasized in high school, few students begin college as geography majors. Many pick this major in their second or third year of college, so your classmates are often a mixture of upper- and lower-division students. Your course work includes a rich mixture of lectures, lab, and library and field research. As you progress, you spend more time in specialized computer labs for cartography, GIS, and remote sensing; and in labs for physical geography (soils, geomorphology, and fluvial and glacial processes).

Frequently, the best place to learn is in the field. For example, you can spend a semester collecting, analyzing, and presenting local data, or you can study overseas. Often, the hardest part of being a geography major is integrating varied subject matter and approaches. In particular, you need to appreciate the perspectives of both the natural and the social sciences.

Because of geography's roots in both the natural sciences and the humanities, programs are offered in a wide variety of divisions and schools. Undergrad programs are often influenced by the emphasis and philosophy of connected graduate programs. Some programs rely heavily on graduate teaching assistants and part-time faculty members. Many specialized courses—such as medical geography; social and physical planning; population and demographics; and race, ethnicity, and class—are based on the research interests of faculty members. But the most noticeable differences are among programs that stress either physical or human geography. Some colleges have successfully bridged the two by focusing on human-environment relations.

Other majors you might like:
Cartography
Environmental engineering

Urban, community, and regional planning
Global studies
Mining and mineral engineering
Landscape architecture
International relations
Area/ethnic/cultural studies
Wildlife and wilderness management
Surveying technology
Natural resources and conservation
Geology/earth science

Questions to ask colleges:
Are there labs for GIS, remote sensing, and cartography? Which software packages are available? How many computer seats are dedicated to geography majors?

Are there certificate programs in GIS, remote sensing, or applied geography? Where and how large is the library/map collection? Which digital data sources are available (for example, population census and aerial photographs)?

What field trips are required or recommended for graduation?

Career options and trends:
Cartographer; GIS manager; economic development analyst; energy analyst; environmental engineer; engineer in photogrammetry (aerial surveying); land use planner; land surveyor; remote sensing specialist; water resources planner.

Engineering jobs such as surveying require certification. Increasingly, certification is a requirement for GIS-related jobs. Planning jobs are available to geographers without specific qualifications, but a master's degree or equivalent in planning is strongly recommended.

The hottest job market in the field is for graduates with experience in geographic information systems and remote sensing.

Insider's viewpoint:
"I do everything from calculus to paper writing to map analysis. There is incredible variety in the work involved in my major and that's one of the things I love about it. Things stay interesting."

—Carolyn, senior, Arizona State University

For more info:

Association of American Geographers (AAG)
1710 16th St., N.W.
Washington, DC 20009-3198
(202) 234-1450
www.aag.org

National Geographic Society (NGS)
1145 17th St. N.W.
Washington, DC 20036-4688
(800) 647-5463
www.nationalgeographic.com

University Consortium for Geographic
  Information Science (UCGIS)
P.O. Box 15079
Alexandria, VA 22309
(703) 799-6698
www.ucgis.org

International relations

What it's about:

International relations is the study of the causes, consequences, and efforts to resolve global patterns of conflict and peace, poverty and wealth, and freedom and oppression. As a major, you examine nations and international organizations to understand political, economic, military, and cultural interactions on the international level.

Is this for you?

You might like this major if you also like: world history; travel; maps; flags; "big picture" issues; stamp collecting; languages; politics.

Consider this major if you are good at: attention to detail; creativity; critical reading/thinking; leadership; persuading/influencing *...or have...* initiative; patience; verbal skills; writing skills.

Recommended high school prep:

English 4, math 3, lab science 3, social studies 4 (especially world history), and a foreign language 4.

Typical courses in this major:

U.S. foreign policy
International organizations
International law
African politics
Latin American politics
European politics
Russian and East European politics
Northeast Asian politics
South Asian politics
Middle East politics
Global environmental issues
International relations theory
National security
International conflict
International political economy
Global human rights issues

Concentrations:

International law and organization; international business; human rights; international political economy; national security; international environmental issues; transnational studies; comparative and regional perspectives; U.S. foreign policy.

What the study of this major is like:

This major draws from many disciplines, such as political science, economics, history, sociology, and foreign languages.

You typically begin with an introduction to international relations (usually offered by the political science department), intro courses in micro- and macroeconomics, one or two courses in world history, and a course in sociology or anthropology. Generally, in your third and fourth years you take courses in U. S. foreign policy, international organizations (especially the United Nations), regional issues, diplomacy, national security, and in economics, law, the environment, and human rights, all from a global perspective.

Courses typically incorporate insights from several disciplines and focus on significant current issues. Other requirements may include a seminar in your area of concentration, as well as proficiency in a related foreign language. International travel is recommended to deepen your understanding of other societies.

Although much of the material is presented in lectures, you listen to, and may participate in, serious debate on how the theories of international relations can be most effectively applied. Global discussions, such as those at regional conferences, frequently involve controversial topics. In most colleges, therefore, you will encounter a wide variety of viewpoints on international issues. Exams generally stress interpretive essays rather than single-answer questions. In addition, you will be expected to write papers that combine solid research with independent thinking.

Many majors are overwhelmed, at first, by the broad scope of international relations and the rapidly changing state of world affairs. Because the discipline does not have a fixed body of absolute truths, you must make full use of your critical-thinking and analytical skills. You should expect ongoing challenge and a constant questioning of your views.

There are several differences in the way the major is taught. Often, the program is a multidisciplinary subject of study administered by a committee of professors from various departments. There are few actual departments of international relations, because most professors who teach the subject hold positions in political science, history, or economics departments. Programs may also vary in emphases. While most programs focus on political science, history, and economics, some emphasize language and literature. In addition, a few colleges stress the worldview of the United States, while most attempt to represent a more global perspective.

Some programs may require you to specialize in a global region, although most permit you to be a generalist with a functional, rather than a geographic, specialty (such as business/economics, security/conflict, or human rights). In other programs, the focus is almost entirely on sovereign states. Still others examine transnational and subnational forces (such as humanitarian organizations, terrorist groups, multinational corporations, and separatist groups like the Basques, the Tibetans, and the Tamils). A program may emphasize concepts and theories or practical cases in world affairs. Some programs cover most of the twentieth century, while others focus on recent issues.

Other majors you might like:

International business
Political science
History
Geography
Global studies
Comparative literature
Asian studies
Islamic studies
Peace and conflict studies
Linguistics

Journalism
Emergency management/homeland security

Questions to ask colleges:

Do students in the program pursue internships for undergraduate credit? How are overseas programs integrated into the major?

Career options and trends:

Graduates in international relations are usually eligible for entry-level positions in the federal Civil Service (especially the departments of State, Defense, Agriculture, and Treasury). Many graduates take positions with members of Congress, congressional committees, or the CIA. Other options are United Nations work, international journalism, paralegal positions with law firms and public service legal agencies; jobs in banks and other firms doing international business; and positions with humanitarian organizations such as Amnesty International. A graduate degree in international relations enhances your career options, especially in the Foreign Service and international business.

Graduates with international relations training are in high demand. Globalization is accelerating, and many jobs now have an international component. People who have cultural sensibilities and understand international political, economic, and military issues are much needed.

Insider's viewpoint:

"I just like the fact that the news is part of my major. What I learn in class I can apply to what I read in the news or on the Internet or see on TV. I like having a sense of what's outside the bubble of my university and the United States."

—Sean, senior, Baylor University

For more info:

International Studies Association (I.S.A.)
324 Social Sciences Building
University of Arizona
Tuscon, AZ 85721
(520) 621-7715
www.isanet.org

Political science

Also known as:
Government

What it's about:
As a political science major, you explore the origins, historical development, and functions of government and political power. You study the ways in which electoral, legislative, judicial, and administrative structures vary among countries; the reasons why governments change, fall, and engage in wars; and the behavior of public officials and other citizens who take part in politics.

Is this for you?
You might like this major if you also like: history; current events; politics; debating; student government; community service activities; issues relating to social justice.

Consider this major if you are good at: critical reading/thinking; leadership; quantitative analysis; research; teamwork ...*or have...* initiative; verbal skills; writing skills.

Recommended high school prep:
English 4, math 4, lab science 2, social studies 4, and a foreign language 3–4.

Typical courses in this major:
U.S. government
Judicial processes
U.S. foreign policy
Public policy analysis
International law
Global issues
Political action groups
Comparative politics
Political theory
American political campaigns and elections
Politics of developing areas
Politics of ecological crisis
U.S. intelligence and policymaking
Contemporary political ideologies
Ethnic and racial politics
U.S. political thought

Concentrations:
U.S. politics; international relations; comparative politics; political theory.

What the study of this major is like:
The political science and government major deals with a range of domestic and international issues, including civil rights, health care, war and peace, economic development, democracy, the environment, and the role of race, ethnicity, and gender in political life.

You might begin the major with an intro course in political science or, more likely, with an intro to one or more subfields (for example, international relations). In addition, you'll probably take intro theory courses and a class on analytical methods and databased research. Intermediate and advanced courses may cover such topics as international security and global political economy, and U.S. institutions and constitutional law.

Most programs require you to minor in a related field, such as history, sociology, economics, or anthropology. You examine such issues as the principles of human behavior that underlie political activity, the actions of citizens, politicians, and public officials; overall social and economic structures and processes; the origins and development of individual political systems; and the physical and social geography in which governments exist and politics takes place. In some colleges, you study these and other subjects through the core curriculum. If there is no core curriculum, you should choose electives that cover these areas.

Many programs now require majors to complete a capstone project—usually a substantial piece of research in which you integrate the knowledge and skills you have learned, as you investigate questions that interest you. Designing a research project and writing a paper based on your research can be very rewarding.

Your classes may be in either a traditional (lectures) or an active (seminars, problem-based learning) format. You learn both individually and, especially in upper-division courses, in teams. College courses generally take an analytical approach, rather than the historical and current-events approach that students may be accustomed to in high school courses. Even at large colleges, courses above the intro level usually have relatively few students and provide opportunities for discussion among students and instructors.

Most programs offer academic and practical experience outside the classroom—for example, internships in public offices (such as those of state legislative committees, public defenders, and county attorneys) or in administrative agencies. You may spend a "Washington semester" working and studying in the nation's capital. Political science departments often participate in the college's study-abroad programs. Political science clubs and campus political organizations can also enhance the intellectual and social life of majors.

Political science programs differ widely; you should examine the description of the major at colleges you may apply to. Some colleges are more liberal, others more conservative. Some favor scientific or quantitative (math-based) approaches; others choose a humanistic or qualitative perspective.

Other majors you might like:

International relations
History
Criminal justice and law enforcement
Public administration
Public relations
American studies
Urban, community, and regional planning
Legal studies
Journalism
Peace and conflict studies
Urban studies
Military technologies

Career options and trends:

The study of political science and government can lead to careers in a wide range of fields including business, journalism, government service, public administration, nongovernmental organizations (NGOs), law, teaching, the Foreign Service, and the diplomatic corps.

Insider's viewpoint:

"A special commitment to understanding history and current events is helpful. More importantly, perhaps, political science majors should feel comfortable engaging with others on these issues, occasionally in heated debates. I love doing that."

—Brian, junior, Columbia University

For more info:

American Political Science Association (APSA)
1527 New Hampshire Ave., N.W.
Washington, DC 20036
(202) 483-2512
www.apsanet.org

Psychology

What it's about:

Psychology majors study the behavior and mental (emotional, learning, and thought) processes of animals and humans. You learn psychological principles, facts, and theories about individuals and groups, using experimental, observational, and case study methods.

Is this for you?

You might like this major if you also like: observing how animals and people act and respond; science; helping others; working with children or the elderly; working with numbers.

Consider this major if you are good at: critical reading/thinking; math; memorizing; research ...*or have...* empathy; initiative; motivation; people skills; writing skills.

Recommended high school prep:

English 4, math 4 (including trigonometry or precalculus), lab science 4 (including advanced biology or chemistry), social studies 3, and a foreign language 2-3. If possible, take computer science and statistics courses and a year of psychology. Participating in community service is also beneficial.

Did you know...

...that in psychology, animals are studied both to examine their behavior and to provide insights into human behavior?

...that this major requires you to learn scientific and statistical methods? Many students are surprised by this but then find it to be not that difficult.

...that for almost all work done as a professional psychologist, you need a graduate or professional degree?

Typical courses in this major:

Abnormal psychology
Social psychology
Personality development
Learning and memory
History of psychology
Tests and measurement
Cognitive psychology
Statistics
Child psychology
Perception
Physiological psychology
Experimental psychology
Industrial/organizational psychology
Developmental psychology
Research methods in psychology
Cross-cultural psychology

Concentrations:

In college: methodology/research; applied psychology; clinical psychology; child psychology; social psychology.

If you go on to grad school: ecological psychology; personality; sensation and perception; animal behavior; industrial and organizational psychology; sports psychology; forensic psychology.

What the study of this major is like:

The psychology major most often begins with a required one-semester intro course; continues with several other required core courses, such as in research methods, statistics, and experimental psychology; and concludes with a fourth-year capstone experience—perhaps a research seminar.

Most departments divide the major into concentrations—such as developmental psychology (which may include infant and child psychology, adolescence, gerontology, and the life span) and experimental psychology (learning, sensation and perception, and biological psychology)—and require you to take courses from each area. In addition, you can usually choose from a range of electives. You earn either a Bachelor of Science degree (which requires more math and science) or a Bachelor of

Arts degree (requiring more humanities and a foreign language); otherwise, there may be little difference in course work between the two degrees.

The subject matter of psychology is diverse. An intro course may cover the basics of motivation, perception, learning, memory, social psychology, developmental psychology, abnormal psychology, counseling psychology, and language—topics that may also be covered, in depth, in intermediate and advanced courses. In undergraduate counseling psychology, you learn about psychotherapy. Clinical psychology adds psychological assessment (testing) and program evaluation and research skills.

Some courses feature lecture and discussion, and some have research components. Labs may involve working with sophisticated equipment, or with a rat, pigeon, or other animal colony. Doing research allows you to learn scientific methods and to differentiate between commonsense notions and research-based findings. In individual and group research, you may investigate attitudes and beliefs through questionnaires; observe people in social situations; or explore differences in responses between experimental groups and control groups.

The challenges you may face include mastering statistics and becoming familiar with the methods of scientific inquiry. Learning the terminology and basic concepts of psychology will probably require some no-nonsense studying. Presenting research at a forum or conference can be a rewarding, if intimidating, experience.

Departments may vary in whether they emphasize psychology as a liberal arts or as a preprofessional program. At some colleges, the emphasis is on pure research. At others, which stress the practical application of research, there may be more opportunities to do internships in the mental health/human service and industrial/organizational areas.

Other majors you might like:
Mental health services technology
Behavioral sciences
Gerontology
Industrial engineering
Neuroscience
Human development and family studies
Criminology

Sociology
Child development
Anthropology
Human resources management
Religious studies

Questions to ask colleges:
Can students take courses that give them experience with professional or applied psychology, such as counseling or industrial/organizational work? Which courses allow students to participate in labs and/or field research?

Do faculty members help students determine if they should go on to grad school? Ideally, full-time instructors are available as advisers throughout your undergraduate education.

Career options and trends:
Social worker; school psychologist; clinical psychologist; lawyer; counseling psychologist; physician (internist, psychiatrist, or other specialist); health care administrator; psychotherapist.

Psychology majors also pursue careers in a wide variety of public, private, profit, nonprofit, business, and service organizations, working in administration/management, community relations, program development, research, human resources, public relations, military service, advertising, market research, retail, and sales.

Jobs in health care administration, social work, industrial/organizational psychology, and medicine (including psychiatry) require graduate or professional degrees. Job growth will be strong for positions in school psychology, clinical psychology, and human services/mental health, which usually require either a master's or doctorate degree, state certification or licensure, and sometimes a one-year internship. Physicians must pass the state board exams to be licensed to practice in a particular state.

Many graduate programs that teach clinical skills (such as psychotherapy, assessment, and program evaluation) are discontinuing such training at the master's level; the doctorate is becoming the entry-level degree of choice.

Insider's viewpoint:

"Don't base your decision to major in psychology on Psych 101 because it is pretty broad and boring. I found classes in social, abnormal, and adolescent psychology to be the most interesting."

—Alison, senior, University of Virginia

For more info:

American Psychological Association (APA)
750 First St., N.E.
Washington, DC 20002-4242
(800) 374-2721
www.apa.org

Association for Psychological Science (APS)
1133 15th St., N.W.
Suite 1000
Washington, DC 20005
(202) 293-9300
www.psychologicalscience.org

Sociology

What it's about:

Sociology is the study of society and social behavior. By studying how individuals act in small and large groups, as well as how such groups are formed and function, you explore social problems and public policy. You investigate a range of topics, including the intimacies of family relationships; the demographics of urban and rural spaces; and the consequences of race, gender, and class divisions across societies.

Is this for you?

You might like this major if you also like: observing human behavior; reading; research; writing; community service activities; debating; computers; politics; exploring different perspectives on social issues such as gender and race.

Consider this major if you are good at: attention to detail; creativity; critical reading/thinking; organizing; quantitative analysis; research; teamwork *...or have...* initiative; patience; writing skills.

Recommended high school prep:

English 4, math 3, lab science 3, social studies 3, and a foreign language 2–3.

Did you know...

...how much scientific research is involved in sociology? Sociologists follow strict guidelines for the collection and analysis of information, including quantitative methods used for conducting surveys, qualitative methods used for interviews and observations, analytical procedures used for coding and interpreting field notes, and statistical procedures used to analyze data.

Typical courses in this major:

Introduction to sociology
Sociological theory
Research methods
Social stratification
Deviance

Socially complex organizations
Minority groups
Juvenile delinquency
Social problems
Gender roles
Social psychology
Sociology of education
Sociology of the family

Concentrations:

In college: racial and ethnic minorities; sex and gender; criminology and delinquency; family sociology; work and occupations; urban or rural affairs; stratification.

If you go on to grad school: demography; methodology; education; social movements; gerontology; medical sociology.

What the study of this major is like:

Course work ranges from case studies of the relationships among individuals in particular social settings, to scrutiny of governments and economic systems across time. Intro courses ask questions such as "How are rules of normality established? How do these rules change? How do social institutions (such as the family) influence our choices, our perceptions of reality, and our plans for the future?" To answer these questions, you may explore the issues from several perspectives (often drawn from disciplines such as history, economics, and political science) as you make progress in your studies.

Sociology is taught mostly through lectures, supplemented by presentations, films, guest speakers, and independent research. Required courses usually include introductory sociology, research methods, theory, and statistics. Probably you'll take courses in such related areas as geography, political science, religion, and economics. Many courses deal with social policy. For example, a course on social stratification (that is, how societies are divided up) may include discussion of policies designed to reduce inequality.

Most programs require you to learn the theories and research methods that prepare you for independent projects. You'll gain practice in using academic journals, computerized databases, and other materials available at most college libraries; or you might gather and analyze data yourself, through surveys, interviews, and observations. In many programs, you will have the opportunity to do an internship at a social service agency, where you can apply what you have learned in the classroom.

There are some challenges. First, the field is so wide that you may have difficulty narrowing your interests to a specific research topic. Second, the scientific method of conducting research, especially the emphasis on statistical analysis, can cause trouble for some students. But students who master data analysis are usually rewarded. Statistics makes their research work much more efficient, and many jobs that majors take after graduation require data analysis. Finally, there is a fair amount of reading, writing, studying terminology, and evaluating different perspectives and theories that are sometimes difficult. The independent research project that some colleges require takes time, initiative, patience, and, often, creativity. Despite the academic demands of this major, though, students rarely complain that the readings are uninteresting.

Programs may vary in the number of courses required for the major. Across colleges, concentrations may also vary according to faculty members' expertise, and areas of concentration may change as new topics emerge. You can get a feel for the differences among programs by comparing courses required and concentrations offered and by looking at the types of research the professors are doing.

Other majors you might like:
African-American studies
Political science
Anthropology
Community organization/advocacy
Criminal justice and law enforcement
Chicano studies
Media studies

Parks, recreation, and leisure studies
Human development and family studies
Social work
Urban, community, and regional planning
Gay/lesbian studies

Career options and trends:
The sociology major can lead to careers in marketing, consumer research, advertising, insurance, human resources, teaching, nonprofit organizations, community development agencies, environmental groups, criminal justice (probation or parole officers), government research (in local, state, and federal agencies), law, urban planning, Foreign Service, and industrial sociology. Advanced degrees are required for work as college professors, lawyers, demographers, policy analysts, and research institute managers.

Insider's viewpoint:
"I've heard many people say statistics don't mean anything, they're just numbers, but to me they represent what goes on. When I took statistics in my first semester, I didn't understand why I had to, but in a lot of the classes it's 'ninety percent of these people...' or 'ninety-seven percent of kids...'"

—Liz, senior, San Jose State University

For more info:
American Sociological Association (ASA)
1307 New York Ave., N.W.
Suite 700
Washington, DC 20005
(202) 383-9005
www.asanet.org

Visual and performing arts

If you turned to this chapter first, you probably think of the arts as more than just entertainment or pretty pictures. You are not alone. The arts are popular majors for students who might like to pursue a career in painting, acting, dance, or other creative or expressive fields. The performing arts differ from the visual arts, so let's start with the performing arts.

If you're a singer, actor, dancer, or musician, you may already know that the intense competition for performance work limits jobs to the most accomplished artists in a given field.

"Very few performance majors are ever able to make a living through music performance alone," says Professor Sandra Billy of the Center for Sacred Music at Virginia Wesleyan College. (See the Religion and theology section for sacred music.)

Fortunately, you can break the stereotype of the starving artist. Many doors are open to trained artists. For instance, dancers and choreographers (who create dances) may not be able to break through the competition barrier, but dance teachers are needed. Arts management is another professional outlet.

"Despite limited job opportunities, there is always room for those who are highly talented and well prepared," says Jo Anne Caputo, a member of the faculty at the Cleveland Institute of Music.

You can parlay your talent and training in the arts into a rewarding career. Take another example. Theater majors are known for their ability to get ideas across. That skill is important in many professions—law, advertising, business, teaching, and even politics. President Ronald Reagan and California governor Arnold Schwarzenegger worked as movie actors before running for public office.

"Fine arts are excellent preparation for any field requiring careful thinking, synthesis, accurate observation and expression, not just art-related positions," assures Professor of Arts Studies Emeritus David B. Greene of North Carolina State University.

In the visual arts, a similar dynamic is at play, because few people earn their living from gallery exhibits and sales of their artwork. But visual and design skills can be transferred to jobs like interior and

535

fashion design; photography; and graphic design for print, video, and the Internet. Many college programs, including interactive and digital art, multimedia, Web design, and animation, apply computer technologies to the visual arts. Composers of music use computers and digital musical instruments in their craft, leading to valuable workplace skills.

If you can use digital technologies or think visually, you have prized talents in a media-driven world. "In a knowledge economy, those who make information comprehensible are valued," explains Professor Meredith Davis of North Carolina State University.

The education landscape

If someone did a painting depicting all of the country's college art programs, it would look like a Pollock, not a Mondrian. "This is a complicated educational landscape...with wildly different degree offerings," cautions Professor Davis.

Choose wisely if you plan to study the arts in college. Especially if you're interested in the fine arts, ask yourself how competitive a school you really want. "Some performance students prefer and thrive in a hyper-competitive environment. Others may prefer a less intense, more nurturing setting. It is important to find the right fit," Caputo advises.

Here are some other things to think about in choosing visual or performing arts programs: Should you study near a city with lots of concerts and galleries? Does the college have its own collection, facilities, image archive, rehearsal instruments, and studios? Do you have to audition or submit a portfolio of your artwork to be accepted?

Are you going for a B.A. degree or a B.F.A (Bachelor of Fine Arts)? The B.A. is a broader approach to art. The B.F.A. gets you ready for a career in a specific art form and might require an audition or portfolio to get into college.

If you're headed for a teaching career, you'll want a higher degree. Graduate studies in the various arts focus on recording and studio production techniques, animation, creative art therapy, and performance art, to name a few. Fine arts grad students may study a particular period, region, or medium.

Also try to get an idea of the daily life of an arts major. How many hours per week will you be taking lessons or working in a studio or at a computer? Are computer lab fees included in your tuition? Will you set your own schedule or are rehearsals preset? How crowded are studios or computer stations? Are they open late? Look at the studios, concert halls, galleries, and design technologies on campus. Nice facilities mean the school is committed to the arts.

The faculty is most important, especially in the performing arts, where students are guided by mentors. Your choice of a college may hinge on the availability of a master teacher.

In your search, you'll run across art programs in colleges of arts and sciences, liberal arts, mass communications, fine and performing arts, schools of design, schools or conservatories of music, and so on. A good Web site to get you going is www.arts-accredit.org. If you don't have a computer, ask your school counselor or local librarian to help you compare colleges and programs. Also see the Communications section for some related majors.

Animation

What it's about:

Animation majors learn a broad range of animation techniques, both traditional and contemporary. Your training covers a broad range of drawing, sound, acting, film, and storytelling skills, along with current software applications.

Is this for you?

You might like this major if you also like: filmmaking; photography; reading and writing stories; drama clubs; art clubs.

Consider this major if you are good at: attention to detail; creativity; critical reading/thinking; organizing; spacial thinking/analysis; teamwork *...or have...* imagination.

Recommended high school prep:

English 4, math 3, lab science 3, social studies 3, and a foreign language 2–3. Take as many courses in art (including studio art and art history) and computer applications as you can. A strong background in language arts (literature and writing) is also recommended.

Did you know...

...that traditional art skills are still the most important quality that successful animators have? If you have these skills, you will have an edge over those who don't. Specific knowledge of software is not essential; you will learn computer techniques in the major.

...that an interest in literature and storytelling is also important? Knowing what makes a good story is just as significant as having technical skills.

Typical courses in this major:

Figure and animal drawing
Color theory
Storyboard and narrative
Screenwriting for animators
Acting for animators
History of animation

Character animation techniques
Stop-motion techniques
Experimental animation techniques
Layout and background design
Digital ink and paint
Special effects
Sound design
Digital compositing
Digital character modeling
3-D computer animation

Concentrations:

Computer animation; character animation; stop-motion animation; special effects.

What the study of this major is like:

Do you enjoy telling stories? Do you love to draw? Do you visualize the characters and settings in some of the works you read? If so, animation might be a good major for you. The field of animation offers many ways to use your imagination, including writing stories, designing characters, and re-creating the worlds that the characters inhabit.

As an animation major, you'll first receive a firm grounding in the principles of art, and you'll explore a variety of ways to develop and tell stories. You then learn the techniques (practical as well as creative) of cinema and how to apply these techniques to both traditional and computer-assisted filmmaking.

As you advance in the program, you are introduced to various animation software packages (for example, 3D Studio Max and Maya for three-dimensional modeling and animation; Flash, Photoshop, and After Effects for compositing; Toonz for digital ink and paint). These and other software systems become part of your toolkit as you gain experience in making your own films. You'll finish with a fourth-year thesis film.

Your courses consist of lectures and demonstrations, accompanied by many hours of practice in and out of the classroom. Early in the program, you concentrate on drawing, a skill that will help you master the more advanced techniques taught later on. Ideally, animation programs challenge you to enlarge your visual vocabulary and storytelling abilities. To do so, you should have a passion for your studies and a willingness to work long hours outside of class—qualities that will serve you well in the professional world.

All strong animation programs emphasize a solid foundation in art while also teaching skills and techniques that are in demand in the real world. Because there are a number of specializations within the animation business (for example, storyboard artist, character designer, and 3-D modeler), programs may differ in the concentrations they offer.

As you progress through the major, your assignments will become more complex and instructors will review your work periodically to see how well you are integrating the skills you have learned with your creative ideas. At some colleges, passing these reviews is a requirement for continuing in the major. Your final project, the thesis film, along with a portfolio, will serve as your "résumé" in the industry.

Other majors you might like:

Computer graphics
Game design
Illustration
Graphic design
Digital art
Digital media
Photographic/film/video technology
Make-up artist
Computer engineering technology
Drafting and design technology
Web page/multimedia design
Radio and television

Questions to ask colleges:

What is the student-to-instructor ratio? Are the instructors currently working in the animation industry? In a good program, you will receive close instruction from faculty members who are familiar with the latest technology and have helpful contacts in the industry.

Are there adequate studio facilities, and are they available around the clock, so that students have a chance to complete assignments? Do the hardware and software capabilities keep current with the industry?

Are internships or apprenticeships in the animation business part of curriculum?

Career options and trends:

Art director/production designer*; storyboard/concept artist*; background/layout designer; character designer; 3-D animator (computer)*; 2-D animator; stop-motion animator; game designer; production coordinator.

Jobs are increasingly freelance in nature, with staff hired from project to project. Some portions of productions are being outsourced overseas. Developing multiple skills will give you a competitive advantage, particularly during economic downturns. In addition to film, television, advertising, and advertising productions, there are opportunities in the creation of computer games and in Web design.

For more info:

Animation World Network (AWN)
6525 Sunset Blvd.
Garden Suite 10
Hollywood, CA 90028
(323) 606-4200
www.awn.com

International Animated Film Association (ASIFA)
http://www.asifa.net/

StopMotionAnimation.com
www.stopmotionanimation.com

Art history

What it's about:

Art history majors study how works of art were created, how they were interpreted by their first audiences, and what they mean to us now. Through visual analysis and extensive reading and writing, majors achieve an understanding of the context of art—time, place, culture, influences, and traditions—and develop the ability to describe art and its meaning to others.

Is this for you?

You might like this major if you also like: visual arts and architecture; antiquing; museums and galleries; travel; model making; reading about history and other cultures; finding connections and relationships between things.

Consider this major if you are good at: active listening; attention to detail; creativity; critical reading/thinking; research; spacial thinking/analysis ...*or have...* initiative; verbal skills; writing skills.

Recommended high school prep:

English 4, math 3, lab science 3, social studies 4, art 2, music 1, and a foreign language 3–4. English and social studies courses that teach writing, speech, critical analysis, and research skills are essential, and studio art classes give valuable insight.

Did you know...

...that while the study of art history is similar in many ways to the study of literature or other cultural fields, it is unique in that you rely primarily on visual perception and on your ability to translate a nonverbal language into a verbal one?

Typical courses in this major:

Art and civilization before 1400
Asian art and temple architecture
Greek and Roman art
Egyptian art and architecture
Medieval art and architecture
The Renaissance
Michelangelo
European Baroque
Early modern architecture
Impressionism and Postimpressionism
Picasso
Postmodernism
Abstract expressionism
American art
History of photography
Introduction to museology

Concentrations:

In college: a historical period, such as ancient, medieval, or modern; a medium, such as painting, architecture, or sculpture; or the arts of a specific culture, such as America, Byzantium, or Polynesia.

If you go on to grad school: a particular artist or movement; museology and curatorship.

What the study of this major is like:

This major teaches you to differentiate among artworks by their style, materials, workmanship, and other characteristics. You can then identify (and seek to understand) the artists, cultures, and/or periods that produced the works. In addition, you consider how individual works of art and groups of works may express or symbolize ideas or emotions. Like archaeologists and anthropologists examining artifacts, you explore what a work of art reveals about a society's culture, rituals, and other aspects of civilization. Often you discover that the art's original value and meaning resulted from its connection to specific religious, political, or social practices.

In your first and second years, you generally take introductory art history courses, along with liberal arts courses in science, English, math, and history. Because art varies widely among societies (both past and present), art is often studied in association with a particular time and place (for example, Renaissance art, East African art). Thus the

540

study of art generally includes some account of the religious, political, economic, literary, and intellectual history of the culture in which a work was created. You will read about art patrons, critics, and viewers, as well as artists. Frequent field trips to local museums augment classroom slide presentations.

After the introductory courses, you take smaller lecture courses that explore art in more detail. Seminars help you develop and refine advanced skills in research and presentation. In your fourth year, you usually have the option of writing a thesis under the direction of a faculty member. Many art history majors also take courses in areas related to their particular interests, such as history, anthropology, or literature. In addition, many study two or more years of a foreign language as a way of understanding other cultures.

Art history majors usually enjoy the benefits of working in a relatively small department where your needs can be dealt with individually. Study-abroad programs are common, and you should have opportunities to participate in internships at museums, galleries, and historic sites. Keep in mind, however, that while internships in museums are attractive, many involve work in education departments that may be isolated from the museum's curatorial activity. Smaller museums often offer more interesting opportunities. Commercial galleries may hire some summer staff, although summer is generally their slow period.

Other majors you might like:
Museum studies
Architecture
Architectural history/criticism
Anthropology
Classics
Comparative literature
Area studies (European, Asian, etc.)
Historic preservation
Medieval and Renaissance studies
Archaeology
Arts management
Music history/literature

Questions to ask colleges:
What is the extent of the visual media collection (slides, digitized images, etc.)?

What opportunities are there to study original works of art in a university collection or nearby museum?

Career options and trends:
Teacher (college or high school); museum curator*; museum management/staff (education, installation, registrar, etc.)*; commercial gallery operator/assistant*; art editor; art appraiser.

Art history majors graduate with a liberal arts degree that has trained them in observation, analysis, and communication. This preparation may qualify you for many jobs in business and government. A master's degree is generally required for employment in museums, archives, auction houses, and galleries, and for teaching in high school; a Ph.D. is essential for positions as museum curators and directors, and as instructors at the college level. Art conservation usually requires specialized training and knowledge of chemistry.

Insider's viewpoint:
"It's fairly important to study a foreign language, especially if you want to go to grad school. I've been taking Italian, so I chose to concentrate on late-medieval and early-Renaissance art; I wanted to read primary documents in the original."

—Dilip, senior, Northwestern University

For more info:
College Art Association (CAA)
275 Seventh Ave.
New York, NY 10001
(212) 691-1051
www.collegeart.org

Cinematography and film/video production

What it's about:

This major prepares you to work in all aspects of film and/or video production, including producing, media writing, production management, directing, lighting, cinematography and/or videography, editing, and sound recording and mixing. The major also provides a strong foundation in media literacy, history, and theory.

Is this for you?

You might like this major if you also like: movies and television; taking photographs and making videos; reading; storytelling and creative writing; painting and drawing; the theater and stagecraft; working with computers; using technology creatively. If you like to make things and can think in visual terms, this field may be for you.

Consider this major if you are good at: attention to detail; creativity; critical reading/thinking; organizing; spacial thinking/analysis; teamwork *...or have...* discipline; initiative; verbal skills; writing skills.

Recommended high school prep:

English 4, math 3, lab science 3, social studies 3, and a foreign language 2-3. Take as many art courses as possible, especially those covering photography and media; theater and drama; and computer courses. If these subjects are not available in high school, extracurricular or community activities in these areas are highly recommended.

Did you know...

...that the digital revolution in this field has made skills in math, science, and computers increasingly important? Writing skills and social, cultural, and media literacy are also necessary—if you want to make meaningful films, you need something meaningful to say.

Typical courses in this major:

Introduction to film and video production
Advanced film and video production
Studio television production
Directing
Cinematography and/or videography
Digital editing
Screenwriting
Sound design/production
Animation and special effects
Production management
Lighting
Television programming
Media and society
Visual literacy and communication
Film history
Film, video, and television genres

Concentrations:

Directing; producing; editing; screenwriting; sound; cinematography/videography; animation; narrative production; documentary production; alternative/experimental production.

What the study of this major is like:

Terms used in film and/or video production can be confusing. Although "film" programs traditionally use motion picture cameras and celluloid (film) to capture images, they are increasingly incorporating digital video. "Video" generally refers to single-camera production using either analog or digital videotape, and is similar to filmmaking in the way its production is organized.

Most programs in cinematography/film/video provide a mix of media studies and production courses. In media studies, you explore film and video history, theory, and analysis. You learn the language, theories, and politics of using images and sound to communicate. Because media making is a social and cultural practice that overlaps with many other disciplines, most programs require a foundation in liberal arts. In production courses, you are taught basic techniques: the creative use of lenses, lighting, cameras, and film stock; the theory and practice of editing; and the art and technology of sound design and recording. Once you master the basics, you move on to intermediate and advanced production work. In many programs, your studies culminate in a thesis project, which often becomes part of a demo reel—a viewable collection of your work—that can help you in your job search.

Programs may offer concentrations in one or more areas, such as editing or cinematography. In all programs, you can expect to work as a crew member on other students' projects. By crewing for other students, you can focus in one area of production or expand your skills in several areas. For example, if you are interested in sound design, you can volunteer to record and mix students' projects. You should seek as much practical production experience as possible because anything you work on can be included in your demo reel.

In media studies, most courses consist of both lectures and screenings, and assignments include writing research papers. Typical production courses require two two-hour lectures and one two-hour lab per week. Labs, which have fewer students than lectures do, involve hands-on learning and the screening of student projects. You generally shoot required projects outside of class.

The cinematography and film/video production major is time-intensive. You often work on projects during the evenings and on weekends. Because you're most likely to get a job through skill and experience, you should take advantage of all on- and off-campus opportunities, such as volunteering at a public TV station, and also seek internships or media jobs in the summer. Students sometimes earn course credit for participation in extracurricular activities.

This major can be costly, because you will probably have to buy some of the gear. While all programs provide major equipment, most expect you to purchase your own light meter, computer hard drive, and film/tape stock, and to pay for film lab services. But there is always a market for used equipment, and you can often purchase items at reduced cost from graduating majors.

Some cinematography/film/video programs emphasize production for "the industry," while others focus on film/video as an art form. Commercially oriented programs use Hollywood production techniques and tend to stress narrative fiction or broadcast news; little attention is given to avantgarde work. An arts-oriented program, in contrast, challenges you to explore your own vision and may also emphasize experimental or documentary production. Most programs strive for a balance. Some programs emphasize individual production and require you to write, direct, and edit your own projects. Other programs operate on a crew-oriented basis: only a few student projects are picked for production, and the other students crew on these films.

Other majors you might like:
Radio and television
Photography
Digital art
Digital media
Web/multimedia management
Playwriting/screenwriting
Media studies
Theater design and technology
Animation
Photographic/film/video technology
Instructional media
Laser/optical technology

Questions to ask colleges:
What equipment does the department provide, and how available is the equipment? Are editing and sound labs open on evenings and weekends? Does the department have a television studio/sound stage?

When do students start doing actual production? (Some programs introduce students to production in the first or second year; others wait until the third year.) Do the students own the rights to the productions they produce? Who funds the productions? Does the college provide film stock, or tape, or lab services?

Does the department sponsor a film or video festival?

Career options and trends:

Independent film/videomaking*; camera operator, director of photography*; sound editor, designer, mixer; apprentice or assistant editor; production assistant*; producer; director or assistant director; production manager; screenwriter.

Employment in the industry depends on ability, as evidenced in a demo reel, or in previous jobs or internships, rather than on a college degree. However, college training is often the best way to acquire job-qualifying skills, contacts, hands-on experience, and a demo reel. Technical positions other than entry-level ones may require membership in a union or guild.

The job market in film/video is competitive. There are far more job seekers than positions, but that should not discourage you from pursing this major. Students who commit to the profession, who excel in their production skills, who develop a good work ethic, and who are attentive and enthusiastic do get jobs. Moreover, the field as a whole is projected to grow as the entertainment market expands and computers and the Internet provide opportunities for interactive productions.

Small or independent filmmakers may provide the best job prospects for beginners, because they are likely to grow more quickly as digital technology cuts production costs.

Many graduates do not hold full-time or staff jobs but work freelance; but even those who work on a television series can have months of downtime each year.

Insider's viewpoint:

"The hardest classes are critical studies in film. You've got to know the film terminology and be able to pull apart scenes and read into them. That's a little bit hard, reading what's going on behind what you see on the screen."

—Anthony, junior, San Francisco State University

For more info:

American Film Institute (AFI)
2021 North Western Ave.
Los Angeles, CA 90027
(323) 856-7600
www.afi.com

University Film and Video Association (UFVA)
Box 1777
Edwardsville, IL 62026
(866) 647-8382
www.ufva.org

Dance

What it's about:

Dance majors learn to use their bodies in motion as instruments of artistic expression. As a major, you receive intensive training in the art of dance, in a liberal arts context, to prepare you for a career as a dancer or a choreographer. You'll study dance from several perspectives: technical, choreographic, aesthetic, historical, anatomical, cultural, anthropological, psychological, and therapeutic.

Is this for you?

You might like this major if you also like: dance; music; theater; learning about different cultures. Dance students have a passion for this art form; dance is a part of their daily lives.

Consider this major if you are good at: active listening; attention to detail; creativity; critical reading/thinking; memorizing; organizing; spacial thinking/analysis; teamwork ...*or have...* perseverance; physical stamina; self-discipline.

Recommended high school prep:

English 4, math 3, lab science 3, social studies 3, and a foreign language 2–3. Your dance training should consist of ballet and modern dance, with integrated dance history and anatomy components, and courses in dance composition and motif description.

Did you know...

...that there are significant differences between a Bachelor of Arts degree in dance, in which you study dance in a liberal arts context, and a Bachelor of Fine Arts degree, in which you train for a professional career as a dancer? Since many dancers stop performing by their late thirties, these differences are important: with a B.A. rather than an B.F.A., you may have an easier time getting a job after you retire from dancing.

Typical courses in this major:

Dance technique (ballet, modern, and jazz)
Principles of choreography
Improvisation
Dance appreciation
Dance composition
Technical production for dance
Music for dance
Dance history
Motif description and labanotation
Anatomy and kinesiology for dance
Dance theory, philosophy, and criticism
Historic dances (Renaissance, Baroque, Ragtime)
The teaching of dance

Concentrations:

In college: technique and performance; choreography; dance education; dance history and criticism; dance therapy.

If you go on to grad school: dance kinesiology; dance and technology; labanotation (for scoring music and dance) and labanalysis (movement analysis)—terms named for Rudolf Laban, a dance theorist.

What the study of this major is like:

To pursue a B.F.A. degree in dance, you will take a number of studio courses in technique, choreography, partnering, company repertoire, mainstage performances, and notation—a curriculum that trains students to become performing and creative artists. In contrast, a B.A. degree in dance, which emphasizes courses in liberal arts subjects such as English, history, literature, and music, can prepare you for a career as a performing and creative artist *and* as a dance educator, administrator, historian, or critic. The B.A. is usually stronger preparation if you plan to go on to grad school or simply want to have more career options.

For a B.A. in dance, you take a minimum of 12 required credit hours in ballet, modern, and jazz dance technique courses. In-depth training in technique is essential, but a breadth of experience is also important. Technique courses may include other kinds of dance, such as ethnic, folk, social, tap, historic, or character dance.

Course work in anatomy and kinesiology (the anatomical study of movement) will enhance your technical skills by teaching you how the body moves and how to avoid injury. Courses in rhythmic analysis, percussion accompaniment, and music resources sharpen your sensitivity to rhythm and help you find or create appropriate accompaniment for your choreography. In dance notation courses, you analyze movement and record it, and read movement scores. In a course on dance philosophy, you may learn principles of aesthetics that you can apply to choreography. And when you study dance history, you'll be encouraged to develop an appreciation for dance as an innate (inborn) and universal form of human expression.

Dance majors should expect to choreograph throughout college—at first, simple dance studies and improvisations; then, later, at least one fully staged work. You learn to design costumes, to light dances, and to help produce concerts. You also learn to work cooperatively with others, to direct, to evaluate choreography (including your own), and to accept and benefit from criticism. And you perform! Some performances are informal presentations for teachers and classmates; others are theater productions before the public. If possible, take advantage of courses on teaching methods. Although many professional dancers may not plan to teach, almost all eventually do.

Daily classes in dance technique, rehearsals, and performances will cut deeply into your study time for academic subjects. To be a successful dance major, you need to have time management and stress management skills, the ability to focus clearly on the task at hand, and a commitment to produce quality work under deadline pressure.

At some colleges, the dance major is housed in the department of physical education rather than a department of fine arts, dance, or theater. Such programs usually emphasize kinesiology, physiology of exercise, health science, nutrition, and physical therapy.

Other majors you might like:
Anthropology
Sociology
Physical therapy
Dance therapy
Physical education
Theater arts management
American sign language (ASL)
Athletic training
Fine/studio arts
Drama and theater arts
Communications
Creative Writing

Questions to ask colleges:
May both dance majors and nonmajors participate in the technical dance courses?

How many and what kinds of performance opportunities are offered each semester?

What is the audition policy? Do students have to audition for entrance into the dance major, for placement in technique classes, for opportunities to perform their own choreography or to select dancers for their own choreography, to perform in someone else's choreography, or to be in the dance company?

How many hours per week are devoted to technical instruction?

Are students able to control their own rehearsal schedule or is it predetermined?

Career options and trends:
Professional dancer and/or choreographer; dance teacher; dance critic; dance scientist/kinesiologist/physical therapist; dance historian/reconstructor; dance arts administrator; dance therapist.

Certification is required for teaching, and physical therapists and dance therapists are licensed health professionals with graduate degrees in their fields.

The field is overcrowded with professional dancers and choreographers—only the most talented find regular employment. Many performance opportunities depend on funding from public and private organizations; such support is not expected to keep up with rising production costs. On the other hand, there is a great need for dance educators in public and private elementary and secondary schools. There are few positions in dance criticism or dance therapy; but opportunities are expanding in the fields of dance/arts administration, dance science, dance history and reconstruction, and dance kinesiology (which usually require a master's degree).

Insider's viewpoint:
"If you're constantly comparing yourself to others, you won't get anywhere. And don't always stand in the back corner of your class; have enough confidence in yourself to stand in the front."

—Nicole, sophomore, University of Wisconsin

For more info:
National Dance Association (NDA)
American Alliance for Health, Physical Education, Recreation and Dance
1900 Association Drive
Reston, VA 20191-1598
(800) 213-7193
www.aahperd.org

Digital art

Also known as:

Computer art

What it's about:

Digital art majors use the computer as the primary means of making art, including interactive installations, digital photography, animation, sound and video. Students are trained in various software applications and technical skills along with the fundamentals of studio art, such as drawing, design, and color theory.

Is this for you?

You might like this major if you also like: computer games; movie special effects; art history and contemporary culture; drawing; stretching your imagination; experimenting; coming up with practical solutions; learning new computer programs.

Consider this major if you are good at: Attention to detail; creativity; drawing; memorization; organizing; spacial thinking/analysis; team work ...*or have...* imagination; initiative; patience; verbal skills.

Recommended high school prep:

English 4, math 3, lab science 3, social studies 3, foreign language 2–3, art 1-2, computer science 1. Take as many courses in art and computer applications as you can.

Did you know...

...that most colleges offering this major require applicants to present a portfolio (examples of your work) that demonstrates traditional art skills as well as computer skills?

Typical courses in this major:

Drawing
Color theory
History of art and design
Multimedia design
2-D and 3-D animation
Sound design

Web design (static and dynamic)
Interactive media
Digital photography
Video art
Installation/performance media
Digital paint
3D computer modeling
Digital imaging
Scripting
Game design

Concentrations:

Computer modeling; animation; special effects; digital sound; digital design; graphic design; website design; digital photography; digital video; multimedia.

What the study of this major is like:

Digital artists make art in inventive ways, using any form of digital technology available. In this major you will gain both the artistic skills and the technological expertise you'll need to create hybrid art forms, and to stretch the boundaries of what art can be.

In a typical four-year program, the sequence of courses usually begins with foundation classes such as drawing, design, and color theory. You'll also take an intro course in which you study the history of the computer's use in art and learn basic programming skills.

In subsequent classes these foundational skills are incorporated with technologies that include interactive art and design, time-based media (sound, video and animation) and web design. Some programs offer internships as electives. Seniors usually take one or two capstone classes or complete a senior project, thesis or portfolio.

This is a time-intensive major—you should expect to work very long hours. Successful students usually spend most of the day and night working in the labs. Most courses are project based with a series of assignments that teach practical skills while you complete a finished product such as a video or animation.

Some classes involve team projects to simulate real world commercial jobs. Team projects also accelerate learning—when you work in the lab or studio with other students rather than on your own, you learn much more as you help each other solve problems. When everything works right you learn a little; when things go wrong and you have to figure out why, you learn a lot.

Like most other art programs, you will also learn from critiques of your work by peers and professors.

As you explore colleges, you'll see that some house this major in the computer science department. Such programs emphasize the programming side of the field, and usually require applicants to have strong math skills. Other colleges will house the major in the art department, and while computer proficiency is expected, they will be more interested in seeing a portfolio of your basic art skills.

Some programs combine courses from different academic departments. These programs incorporate aspects of visual and performing arts, computer science, and cultural theory. The goal of an interdisciplinary approach is to give you a broad-based artistic, technical and theoretical background that will prepare you to work in various media and adapt to rapidly changing technologies. Other programs focus more on providing training in current software applications or a particular media, such as computer animation, game art or computer music.

Most programs will allow you to specialize in a particular area or opt for a more comprehensive study of the discipline. Keep in mind that in the digital world, what is state-of-the-art today will be old hat tomorrow. It's best to look for a program that balances practical training with the fundamental concepts that will prepare you for a life-long career.

Two-year associate degree programs in digital art provide training in computer graphics, sound and animation, and prepare you for technical support positions in the field or for transfer to four-year programs.

Other majors you might like:
Animation
Computer graphics
Game design
Digital media
Photographic/film/video technology
Drafting and design technology
Software engineering
Multimedia
Graphic design
Web page/multimedia design
Instructional media

Questions to ask colleges:
What studio and lab facilities are provided and when do students have access to them? Are there any lab fees?

How up-to-date is the equipment?

Is the program part of the Art Department? Is there a relationship with the Computer Science Department?

How does the curriculum balance the study of fine arts and technology—does it emphasize one over the other?

What are recent grads doing now?

Career options and trends:
Animator*; video artist; graphic artist/designer*; game designer*; illustrator; special effects artist; web designer.

This field is expanding and always changing—many students end up doing things that they never heard of as freshmen. Until recently degree requirements were minimal to nonexistent in the game industry; but with more colleges offering this major, more companies will look for graduates with a degree in the field.

Insider's viewpoint:
"This field changes every day. I get to do whatever my imagination leads me to. It was fun when I started and still is 25 years later."

—Professor Sven Anderson, State University of New York at Oneonta

For more info:

Association for Computing Machinery's Special
   Interest Group on Graphics and Interactive
   Techniques (ACM SIGGRAPH)
www.siggraph.org

The National Association of Schools of Art and
   Design (NASAD)
11250 Roger Bacon Drive
Reston, VA 20190-5248
www.arts-accredit.org

Drama and theater arts

What it's about:

The major in drama and theater arts covers many aspects of staged plays, including theater history, literature, and criticism; acting and directing; lighting, scenery, and costume design; stage management; playwriting; and arts administration. You may specialize in one area while you obtain a broad foundation in many of the other areas.

Is this for you?

You might like this major if you also like: school and community drama clubs; speech and debate; music and art; expressing ideas and feelings; collaborating with others. Because theater encompasses many areas, a variety of personality types enjoy this major.

Consider this major if you are good at: creativity; critical reading/thinking; leadership; organizing; persuading/influencing; teamwork *...or have...* initiative; physical stamina; verbal skills; writing skills.

Recommended high school prep:

English 4, math 3, lab science 3, social studies 4, and a foreign language 2–3. In addition to any drama/theater courses available, take courses covering Shakespeare and dramatic literature, art history, music appreciation, art studio, and industrial arts (woodworking, drafting, etc.). Participation in theater, dance, or musical activities is a must.

Did you know...

...that theatrical skills are practical as well as creative? Dramatic projects must be produced within the boundaries of time, money, and labor constraints. Theater majors learn to think creatively, speak well, motivate a group, sell an idea, and get a job done on time—achievements that look good on a résumé for almost any job.

Typical courses in this major:

Introduction to theater
Theater design
Theater history
Dramatic literature
Play analysis
Acting
Directing
Production laboratory
Stagecraft
Production fundamentals
Voice for the actor
Shakespeare
Lighting design
Costume design
Scenic design
Musical theater

Concentrations:

In college: acting; directing; theater studies (history, literature, criticism); lighting design; costume design; scenic design; stage management; theater technology; production management.

If you go on to grad school: playwriting; dramaturgy.

What the study of this major is like:

The first thing to decide is whether to pursue a Bachelor of Arts or a Bachelor of Fine Arts degree. In a B.A. program, you gain a broader education, but may have difficulty competing with B.F.A. graduates in the professional world. But although the B.F.A. prepares you more rigorously for a theatrical profession, you may be less able to explore other areas of interest while you're in college.

You can generally choose from a wide variety of theater-related courses. In dramatic art courses, you study dramatic style and structure, theories of criticism, and the functions of theater artists, technicians, and managers. Theater history and dramatic literature courses cover Western theater from ancient Greece to the twentieth century. In directing courses, you learn how to analyze a script's style, form, and action, with the goal of translating the text into a staged production.

Introductory acting courses teach the fundamentals of relaxation, trust, sensory awareness, group interaction, and reaction and response. Improvisations, group exercises, and monologues are usually included. In advanced acting courses, you generally do scene work of increasing complexity in various classical and contemporary styles.

In courses in speech and voice, you practice phrasing, dialect, and breath control. Stage movement (sometimes taught as dance) develops relaxation and expressiveness. Theater history and criticism courses, often taught as lectures, involve considerable reading, discussion, and paper writing. Design and production courses are typically more hands-on; usually the lecture portion is coordinated with a laboratory session in which you work with tools and materials. For a concentration in arts administration, you study business and public relations/communications, in addition to taking theater courses.

Theater students and faculty members are typically opinionated and creative; class discussions and projects can be high-spirited. To add to the excitement, you may study, in a single day, contemporary theater in an acting course, fencing in a stage movement course, Shakespeare in a voice course, and end by rehearsing a performance art piece.

But the wide range of work is not only a blessing; if you do not have good organizational skills and time management skills, it can also be a curse. The greatest challenge that majors face is being committed to too many production projects. You must be able to withstand the rigors of nightly rehearsals, while still participating fully in your classes. Developing time management skills and the ability to take care of yourself (proper eating and sleeping) may be the most important thing you can do to ensure success as a drama and theater arts major.

The presence of a graduate theater program at an institution may have both advantages and disadvantages. Faculty members connected with a graduate program tend to be more high-powered, and production standards tend to be more professional. On the other hand, the graduate program may overshadow the undergraduate program.

The size of a program may also make a big difference: larger programs may offer a greater variety of courses and more chances to act, direct, and design, whereas at smaller colleges, there may be more production opportunities.

Other majors you might like:
Theater design and technology
Fashion and apparel design
Film/cinema studies
Cinematography and film/video production
Art history
Music management
Theater arts management
Communications
Radio and television
Digital media
Make-up artist
English

Questions to ask colleges:
What is the policy on crew hours and rehearsals? Sometimes working on a crew or attending rehearsal is tied to course work, sometimes to a noncredit requirement. There should be guidelines for time spent rehearsing and building a production.

Does the department provide assistance in obtaining internships and summer work?

Is there ample space for students to practice acting and directing? At least two performance sites are desirable.

Career options and trends:
Actor, director, technician, or designer*; drama teacher; business manager, marketer, or publicist for theater*; arts educator at regional theaters*.

Competition for jobs is fierce in the performance segment of the industry. Versatility is one way to expand your career possibilities. Although technicians and arts administrators usually find more work than actors, directors, and designers, all theater students should be able to multitask. For example, touring companies might hire actors who have the technical skills to set up and strike, or take down, a set. Regional theaters may hire graduates to teach in their educational programs or to participate in workshops or other short-term projects. Taking jobs in related areas can often open doors for future work in your specialty.

Insider's viewpoint:

"Some of the best theater I have witnessed has been in scene work for acting classes. Also, rarely produced classics, new plays, large cast shows, and alternative performance art pieces are often found on university stages, rather than in the commercial or regional theater that can't take the risk."

—Professor Diane Timmerman, Butler University

For more info:

University/Resident Theater Association
1560 Broadway, Suite 1103
New York, NY 10036
(212) 221-1130
www.urta.com

Fashion and apparel design

What it's about:

This major prepares you for a career as a designer of commercial fashions, clothing, and accessories. You are trained in all aspects of fashion design, including sketching, creative design, computer applications, draping, and flat pattern drafting. You also learn how to communicate design ideas through storyboards and fashion shows, and how to work effectively in a diversified, global industry.

Is this for you?

You might like this major if you also like: drawing; sewing; decorating; museums; pop culture; travel; fabrics; shopping; fashion magazines; art and photography; keeping up with trends.

Consider this major if you are good at: attention to detail; creativity; math; organizing; persuading/influencing; quantitative analysis; spacial thinking/analysis; teamwork *...or have...* manual dexterity; patience.

Recommended high school prep:

English 4, math 3, lab science 3, social studies 3, visual arts 2-3, and a foreign language 2-3. Also recommended, if they are available: vocational and family/home economics courses covering sewing, textiles, and apparel; drafting and design; and computer applications.

Did you know...

...that in this major, you need to feel comfortable with math? That's because you must have technical and analytical skills to design a garment from sketch to pattern to construction and finishing of the garment.

Typical courses in this major:

Fashion sketching
History of costume
Creative design theory and elements
Color and design theory
Computer-aided design
Computer pattern drafting
Computer grading, marking, and cutting
Draping
Industrial sewing techniques
Garment construction
Accessory design
Fashion industry survey
Collection development
Fashion show production
Professional practices
Portfolio development

Concentrations:

Film and TV costume design; theater costume design; footwear design.

What the study of this major is like:

The fashion and apparel design major is generally hands-on, immersing you in a working environment from day one. From sketching to pattern making, you explore the many areas of design, under the instruction of industry professionals.

In your lower-level courses, you are introduced to figure-sketching techniques and to pattern drafting. In later courses, you explore such topics as color and design theory; textiles; and industry practices, including fashion groups, storyboards, and the development of collections. In computer-aided design (CAD) work, you learn how to design garments and construct patterns using techniques that are widespread throughout the industry. Most programs require a capstone course in which you develop a complete collection. This is the final course you take, and it prepares you to begin interviewing for jobs. You should leave the program with a comprehensive portfolio and real-world experience.

Expect to work hard; majors sometimes have to pull all-nighters to complete their projects. Fashion and apparel design is a highly technical industry that requires attention to detail and patience.

Measurements must be exact, sketches must be proportional, and patterns must be cut precisely. Majors often find that the technical requirements are the most challenging. But programs are developed with these challenges in mind, and you generally have step-by-step guidance.

You will find many two-year fashion design programs leading to an associate degree, and some four-year programs leading to a bachelor's degree. The fashion design curriculum is similar in the two programs, but the first two years of B.A. programs provide a broad liberal arts background.

Programs can also be categorized by type of approach: training-based and theory-based. Elements of both types are essential for success in the industry. In the training approach, you have more opportunity to practice the skills you study in the classroom. As you construct garments from start to finish, you absorb the nuances of design, discover and solve problems, and perfect your technique. A theory-based education, in contrast, gives you a broader understanding of the industry as a whole—its history and its future.

Other majors you might like:
Commercial/advertising art
Fashion merchandising
Marketing
Fiber/textile arts
Advertising
Interior design
Metal/jewelry arts
Theater design and technology
Anthropology
Family and consumer sciences
Apparel/textile marketing
Entrepreneurial studies

Questions to ask colleges:
What ties does the college have to the fashion industry? Are the instructors industry professionals?

Does the college use the latest industry technology? How accessible are computers, and design and production facilities, after class?

If this is a four-year bachelor's degree program, are students admitted into the major at the outset, or do they have to meet requirements (such as a portfolio or high academic standing) at the end of the second year in order to continue?

Career options and trends:
Designer or assistant designer; pattern maker; grader; visual merchandiser; textile designer; technical designer; illustrator; stylist; costume designer.

As the fashion industry incorporates computer technology into every aspect of design, traditional ways of creating garments are being revolutionized. Majors in fashion should become proficient in as many of the software programs used in the fashion industry as possible. Since two-thirds of salaried fashion designers work in either New York or California, a willingness to relocate may be necessary.

As in all design fields, fashion majors face a lot of competition. Demand for designers should remain strong, however, because style-conscious consumers will always want something new to wear. The best opportunities will be in design firms that specialize in stylish, affordable, mass market clothing; opportunities will be limited in firms that cater to more specialized, higher-end customers.

For more info:
Fashion Group International
8 W. 40th St., 7th Floor
New York, NY 10018
(212) 302-5511
www.fgi.org

Fine/studio arts

Also known as:
Visual arts

What it's about:
Students majoring in the fine and studio arts learn to create images, objects, and environments using a variety of techniques and media. As you work on a number of structured assignments and independent studio projects, you sharpen your visual understanding and enhance your critical-thinking skills. Most likely, you will begin with an introduction to design and then choose a medium, such as photography or ceramics, for focused study.

Is this for you?
You might like this major if you also like: handicrafts, especially sewing, woodworking, model building, or pottery; riddles and metaphors; cooking; museums and galleries; drawing and painting; manipulating digital images; working independently; taking risks.

Consider this major if you are good at: attention to detail; creativity; critical reading/thinking; relational thinking; research; spacial thinking/analysis ...*or have...* manual dexterity; patience; persistence; verbal skills.

Recommended high school prep:
English 4, math 2, lab science 2, social studies 4, and a foreign language 3. If possible, take a variety of visual and performing arts classes, including as many object- and figure-drawing classes as you can. Some colleges will require a portfolio of your artwork for admission.

Did you know...
...that you don't need to think of yourself as "artistic" or "really creative" to major in art? Art can be taught; it need not be regarded as a mysterious gift that only a few possess. To be successful in this major, you should have a strong interest in studio art and a commitment to learning.

...that this major is work-intensive, with plenty of outside projects? Studio projects take more time to complete than regular academic assignments. To do well, you need to be disciplined, patient, attentive to detail, and good at managing your time.

Typical courses in this major:
Two- or three-dimensional basic design
Drawing
Art history
Painting
Jewelry
Illustration
Sculpture
Book arts
Digital imaging
Printmaking
Graphic design
Ceramics
Industrial design
Textile and fiber arts
Photography
Art theory

Concentrations:
In college: drawing; sculpture; printmaking; graphic design; illustration; painting; photography; book arts; textile and fiber arts; ceramics; animation; glass blowing; architecture; jewelry and metalsmithing; industrial design; film and video.

If you go on to grad school: historic preservation; performance art; art conservation; environmental works; art history; museum studies; landscape architecture; time-based media; city planning; urban design.

What the study of this major is like:
Art classes in this major take place in studios outfitted with the equipment you'll need for a particular medium, such as charcoal drawing or woodworking. Your instructors are practicing, exhibiting artists and designers. In most programs, a

basic design course is a prerequisite for upper-level courses. You will probably be required to take a series of art history courses as well, although some colleges emphasize art history more than others. By designing and producing artworks of your own and by studying the work of others, you learn to understand the ideas, values, motives, and vocabulary of artists, and you develop an appreciation of the way art was, and is, created and the important social and cultural role it plays.

Art schools offer a Bachelor of Fine Arts degree, while liberal arts colleges usually offer a Bachelor of Arts. Both degrees have their strengths. A B.F.A. program allows you to become immersed in art. Classes tend to be three or four hours long. After completing foundation courses in your first two years, you focus on your concentration (for example, painting, sculpture) for two or three years before graduating. In contrast, a B.A. program allows you to maintain a focus on art but also explore other serious interests—which are likely to serve as inspiration for the images and objects you will create. B.A. classes are generally shorter, around two hours. When you graduate, you might have done only one or two years of independent work (less than in the B.F.A. program), but you have benefited from an exposure to a multitude of issues and ideas.

Not all studio programs offer the same choices of media. Even in a single medium like painting, the philosophy of programs can differ greatly. Some colleges stress conceptual or contemporary references to shape the curriculum. Others might emphasize the traditional materials and techniques. It may be useful to review images of student and faculty work, which are often available on a college's Web site.

As a major, you balance structured, in-class assignments with independent, outside work. Instead of term papers and exams, you receive feedback through individual and group critiques and portfolio reviews, in which you learn to take and give criticism. You are encouraged to read art magazines and be aware of current exhibitions in galleries and museums. A good student learns to work steadily throughout the semester. In the studio,

don't expect to cram to make up for lost time; creativity cannot be rushed. You spend long hours and many late nights working. In effect, the studio becomes your second home and part of your social life.

While in the program, you can seek employment in galleries, studio apprenticeships to artists, and internships in architecture firms or museums. Both the B.A. and B.F.A. prepare you for continuing work toward a Master of Arts or Master of Fine Arts. The major also provides preparation for a fulfilling career as a practicing artist or commercial designer.

Other majors you might like:
Arts management
Museum studies
Medical illustrating
Film/cinema studies
Theater design and technology
Architecture
Art therapy
Digital art
Commercial/advertising art
Graphic design
Classics
Medieval and Renaissance studies

Questions to ask colleges:
How crowded are the studios? How late are they open? What security is offered for late-night work? Is there an accessible collection of art (on slides or elsewhere)? How extensive is the library's collection of art and art history books? The availability and condition of resources and facilities often reflect the institution's commitment to teaching the arts.

How many students go on to graduate school or related professional opportunities? Art is highly competitive, and the number of students who continue on in the field may point to the seriousness and success of the program.

Career options and trends:
Art teacher*; commercial artist; museum curator; architect; gallery preparator*; art therapist; studio artist; art editor or critic; art restorer/conservator; art director or administrator*.

A master's degree is generally required for employment in museums and galleries, and a Ph.D. (usually in art history) is required for positions as museum curators and directors. A master's in art education is the usual requirement for teaching in high school, and a master of fine arts (M.F.A.) for teaching at the college level. Art restoration and conservation usually requires specialized training and knowledge of chemistry.

Making a living solely from producing art is extremely difficult; most working artists have a sideline. One source of employment is the growing number of city and county arts councils that need staff for a variety of positions, including management and teaching; art therapy is also a growing field, but it requires further specialized education.

The interface between computers and art is the most important trend, for both creating art and teaching art. Illustrators are increasingly using technology, which has created new opportunities to work with animators, game designers, and in broadcast media.

Insider's viewpoint:

"Majoring in visual arts was never an easy way out. I spent more time and effort on my painting projects than some people in premed spent studying. And in the end, I believe I learned more than any academic major could have taught me: how to see the world I live in and express it to others."

—James, class of 2002, Fordham University

For more info:

College Art Association (CAA)
275 Seventh Ave.
New York, NY 10001
(212) 691-1051
www.collegeart.org

Graphic design

What it's about:

The graphic design major is about visual communication—how it is created and how it is perceived. Graphic designers plan and create print, film, and electronic communications composed of images and typography; their work ranges from books to multimedia programs, CD covers to film titles, logos to Web sites.

Is this for you?

You might like this major if you also like: books, magazines, and comics; graphic novels; coming up with practical solutions; working on the school newspaper, yearbook, or literary and arts magazines; drawing; color; working with different types of people; computers; craftsmanship.

Consider this major if you are good at: Communicating; attention to detail; creativity; critical reading/thinking; organizing; persuading/influencing; spacial thinking/analysis ...*or have...* curiosity; imagination; patience; writing skills.

Recommended high school prep:

English 4, math 3, lab science 3, social studies 3, and a foreign language 2–3. Many colleges require a portfolio (examples of your work), and your high school art classes can help you prepare one. Many colleges also offer summer or Saturday design camps, where you can develop your portfolio and get a taste of college-level instruction in design.

Did you know...

...that historically, the graphic design profession arose from the typesetting and printing trades? Practitioners came into the field through apprenticeships, without a formal education in design. Today, the complexity of contemporary communications requires graphic designers to have a deeper knowledge of how visual information works.

...that this major is about design more than computers? While graphic designers use computers extensively, knowledge of computers and software applications is not the same as knowledge of design.

Typical courses in this major:

Design analysis and theory
Typography
2-D and 3-D graphics
Factors of human perception
Packaging and display
Technical and professional writing
Drawing and illustration
Photography
Web page design
History of visual communications
Text and images
Identity and symbols
Digital imagery
Multimedia design
Motion graphics
Advertising design

Concentrations:

Advertising; multimedia; computer graphics; motion graphics (film titles and animation); Web design; identity or symbol design; information design (charts and graphs); publications; packaging; environmental graphics (signs and signage systems).

What the study of this major is like:

Graphic design programs vary widely from college to college, and a course title in a catalog does not necessarily describe the course content. But regardless of content distribution or course names, the graphic design major should prepare you to solve design problems; understand audiences; handle tools and technology (including offset printing, photography, and interactive media); apply concepts such as visual organization, information hierarchy, symbolic representation, and aesthetics; understand design history, theory, and criticism from a variety of perspectives (including art history, linguistics, and communication and information theory); and know basic business practices (such as organizing design projects and working productively with teams).

If you expect to go into advertising, you should enroll in a program that includes additional course work in marketing, audience and/or user evaluation, art direction, copywriting, and communications theory. If you want to work in time-based or interactive media, select programs with additional courses in storyboarding, computer scripting, sound editing, and interface design. For a career in planning and strategy development, seek programs that teach team problem solving; systems analysis; writing for business; and the application of management, communications, and information theories.

As a graphic design major, you learn primarily by completing hands-on projects in classes of 15–25 students. Design majors work long hours and must be self-motivated. Assignments are usually open-ended, with many right answers; they require you to think through different approaches and a variety of solutions. Your work is then evaluated by your classmates and instructors, based on how well you fulfilled the requirement of the assignment and on whether you showed an understanding of the audience and the context for which the item was intended. This approach is frequently used in all design and studio courses, and you have to learn not to take the criticism personally.

Exhibitions, auctions of visual work, costume balls, and design competitions are extracurricular activities in most colleges. Most design programs have some affiliation with the graphic design profession through clubs, portfolio reviews, field trips, internships, sponsored projects, or conferences. Generally, design programs have strong networks of graduates who can help you make the transition from college to work.

According to the accreditation requirements of the National Association of Schools of Art and Design, a Bachelor of Fine Arts degree in graphic design requires at least 65 percent of your courses to be studio art and design instruction, with at least 25 percent of those courses to be specifically related to graphic design. The B.F.A. is considered to be the professional degree for graphic design practice. In Bachelor of Arts or Bachelor of Science programs (B.A., B.S.), you will find a higher percentage of general education/liberal arts courses, and a smaller percentage of graphic design courses as part of the total art and design requirements. Two-year associate degree programs prepare you for technical support positions in the field and for transfer to four-year programs in design.

Other majors you might like:
Animation
Computer graphics
Digital art
Digital media
Drafting and design technology
Illustration
Industrial design
Communications
Advertising
Desktop publishing
Web page/multimedia design
Instructional media

Questions to ask colleges:
What studio, computer resources, and lab facilities are provided and how many hours do students have access to them? Are there any lab fees?

Is there a graphic design slide collection? What other library resources support graphic design majors?

Do students have to buy their own computer equipment? Does the college provide technical assistance for student-owned computers and/or software? Are printers, scanners, digital cameras, video and sound equipment, or other peripherals available for student use?

Career options and trends:
Art director*; graphic designer in design group or studio*; interactive/multimedia designer*; Web designer*; illustrator; exhibition designer; advertising agent; package designer; design strategist/planner; print production pre-press designer.

In a knowledge-based economy, those who make information comprehensible are valued. Success in the field of graphic design depends on talent, education, and work ethic, and students who graduate at the top of their class find jobs. Rapid technological change has created specializations in the field; as a result, specialists are in demand and more graphic designers are likely to obtain a graduate degree.

Increasingly, basic layout and design work is being outsourced to design firms overseas. Higher-level graphic design jobs that focus on "strategic design"—developing communication strategies for clients and firms—require proximity and will remain in the United States. Graphic designers with skills in Web site design and animation will have the best opportunities, as will those with knowledge or experience in marketing and business.

For more info:
American Institute of Graphic Arts (AIGA)
164 Fifth Ave.
New York, NY 10010
(212) 807-1990
www.aiga.org

The National Association of Schools of Art and
  Design (NASAD)
11250 Roger Bacon Drive
Suite 21
Reston, VA 20190-5248
(703) 437-0700
www.arts-accredit.org

Interior design

What it's about:

This major provides academic preparation for professional practice as an interior designer. You learn how to create indoor environments that are both beautiful and functional: they are intended to improve the quality of life, increase productivity, and protect the health and safety of the public.

Is this for you?

You might like this major if you also like: tours of museums and historical buildings; art; theater; math; debate; community service; working with people; making things; learning about different cultures; travel.

Consider this major if you are good at: attention to detail; creativity; critical reading/thinking; math; organizing; research; spacial thinking/analysis; teamwork *...or have...* initiative; verbal skills.

Recommended high school prep:

English 4, math 3, lab science 3, social studies 3, and a foreign language 2–3. Art and art history courses, if offered, are highly recommended. A course in computer-aided design (CAD) would be good but it is not a prerequisite. Taking part in theater or music activities can teach you disciplines and skills used by successful interior design students.

Did you know...

...that there is a difference between interior design and interior decorating? While both fields are concerned with aesthetics, decorators work only with surface adornment; they work with paint, fabric, furnishings, lighting, and other materials. Interior designers are professional space planners, who ensure that interiors meet code requirements and the practical, technical, and functional needs of a wide range of clients—commercial, industrial, and residential—in such facilities as hospitals, schools, hotels, and apartment complexes.

...that interior design is subject to government regulation? Almost half the states and the District of Columbia require interior designers to be licensed or registered after passing the National Council for Interior Design's qualification examination.

Typical courses in this major:

Principles of interior design
History of interiors and decorative arts
Drawing and design in two and three dimensions
Computer-aided design
Interior materials and finishes
Construction documents and specifications
Codes, public health, and safety
Residential interiors
Furniture design
Textiles
Acoustics and interior design
Lighting design and building systems
Environmental control systems
Interiors for special populations
Professional practice
Portfolio preparation

Concentrations:

In college: lighting design; furniture design; exhibition design; acoustics; fabric design.

If you go on to grad school: historic preservation; workplace design; institutional facilities; interior environmental health; construction management.

What the study of this major is like:

Interior design majors study all aspects of the built environment: scale, proportion, arrangement, light sources, acoustics, temperature, textures, colors, and materials. Because interior design projects are complex, you learn to employ a systematic process; you balance the client's needs and resources, on the one hand, with the goal of creating safe, attractive, and practical interiors, on the other.

To design successful interior environments, you must be trained in building construction, materials specification, lighting techniques, technical drawing, and business practices. You learn to analyze problem areas; develop detailed design solutions; and organize and oversee the project to completion. You must be familiar with building codes and fire regulations. And because interior designers usually function as members of a team rather than as individual designers, you need to be able to work well with other professionals.

Programs usually consist of a series of design courses that culminate in a senior thesis. Generally, studio courses use a hands-on approach: the professor presents a problem and you work on a solution, discussing and evaluating your progress with the instructor. As you advance through the program, you will be expected to demonstrate increasing skill in tackling such problems.

Undergraduate majors receive a generalized education in interior design. Nevertheless, some programs may emphasize architecture or environmental design, whereas others stress fine arts or family and consumer science. Programs with an architectural focus generally concentrate on three-dimensional design, construction practices, and large-scale commercial projects. These programs tend to prepare you for work in large architectural and interior design firms. Programs that concentrate on fine arts or family and consumer sciences usually focus on the decorative aspects of the field—fixtures and furniture, selection and layout, and coordination of finishes. Also some programs feature residential design, while others highlight commercial and/or institutional design. However, standards ensure that all accredited programs prepare you for entry-level professional work in either residential or commercial/institutional design.

Other majors you might like:
Housing and human environments
Environmental design
Industrial design
Architectural history/criticism
Furniture design/manufacturing
Fashion and apparel design
Psychology
Anthropology
Theater design and technology
Drafting and design technology

Hotel/motel administration/management
Art history

Questions to ask colleges:
Is the program accredited by the Foundation of Interior Design Education and Research (FIDER)? Most states that license interior designers require graduation from a FIDER-accredited program.

Are students given their own desks in the studio for the entire semester? "Cold studios" are those in which students are given work spaces for the term; "hot studios" are more like typical classrooms with drawing tables. Colleges with cold studios generally have stronger design programs.

Are the computer laboratories accessible most hours of the day? Do they provide access plotters and printers? Gaining proficiency in computer-aided design applications is essential.

Career options and trends:
Interior designer*; furniture designer; lighting designer; facilities manager; real estate broker; trade show exhibit designer; product representative.

Interior designers work for interior design firms, architectural firms, department and home furnishing stores, theme parks and resorts, and hotel and restaurant chains. Some designers do freelance work full-time, part-time, or in addition to a salaried job. Beginning designers usually receive on-the-job training and normally need one to three years of apprenticeship before they advance to higher-level positions.

Ergonomics and "green design" are trends to watch. Ergonomic design is important for an aging population and workplace safety, and concerns for environmental quality and the needs of people with allergies and asthma are driving demand for green design.

For more info:
American Society of Interior Designers (ASID)
608 Massachusetts Ave., N.E.
Washington, DC 20002-6006
(202) 546-3480
www.asid.org

Music, general

What it's about:

This liberal arts major is for those who want a generalist approach, rather than a career-specific orientation, to the subject. You study music from various perspectives: the historical development of musical styles; ear training and musicianship; the structures and theory of music; composition; music technologies; performance instruction; and music teaching.

Is this for you?

You might like this major if you also like: playing, listening, and learning about music, of course; math; travel; working independently as well as in groups; using computers. Mere enjoyment of music is not enough for success in this major —you must have a real commitment and well-developed musical skills.

Consider this major if you are good at: attention to detail; concentration; creativity; critical reading/thinking; memorizing; quantitative analysis; spacial thinking/analysis ...*or have...* patience; perseverance; physical stamina; self-discipline; verbal skills.

Recommended high school prep:

English 4, math 3, lab science 3, social studies 3, music 4, and a foreign language 3. Courses in music theory, music history, individual lessons on an instrument or in voice, and participation in performance ensembles (orchestra, band, jazz, chamber music) are highly recommended, whether available inside or outside high school. No matter what instrument you play or even if you don't intend to perform, all college music majors are expected to have basic knowledge of piano (keyboard). Even six months of lessons will help—a year is better.

Did you know...

...that this major isn't just about playing music? In some ways it is more demanding than many other majors, because you have to be both academic and musical.

Typical courses in this major:

Music history
Ethnomusicology
Music theory
Ear training and/or musicianship
Composition
Conducting
Orchestration
Keyboard competence
Sight singing
Lyric diction
Chamber ensemble
Wind ensemble
Chorus
Tonal counterpoint
Computer and electronic music
Jazz studies

Concentrations:

History or musicology; ethnomusicology; performance; conducting; theory; composition; music education.

What the study of this major is like:

Most music programs require at least four courses in music history, in which you study the musical styles and genres of different periods, as well as the most important composers. You may do advanced work in the music of a period or of a composer; the extent of change in music from one period to the next; and the connection between music and the society in which it was created. More and more colleges are teaching music produced outside Europe and North America—for example, traditional Chinese music and music of the West African coast.

Music theory courses assume that you are familiar with the fundamentals of music (rhythmic and pitch notation, key signatures, and scales). In a minimum of four theory courses, you learn the principles of four-part music. You then practice these principles in weekly writing exercises. Theory courses also teach methods of analyzing music in depth. You may do advanced work in counterpoint, analysis, or the history of music theory; or begin work in composition. In composition courses, you may use computer programs to synthesize music electronically.

The music major almost always includes work in basic musicianship—piano, sight singing, score reading, keyboard harmony, and melodic and harmonic dictation. All programs provide you with opportunities to perform in ensembles, and many require you to do so. Individual voice and instrumental lessons, as well as conducting courses, are available at many colleges. Some programs offer a music performance degree, which involves much more performance work (for example, in voice, violin, trumpet, or percussion). These programs often lead to the Bachelor of Music degree rather than to a liberal arts degree with a music major.

Instruction style may vary according to the aspect of music you are studying. Your courses may be research-oriented or lab-oriented, or you may work mostly one-on-one with your professors. The music major can be demanding, because it requires you to take numerous courses and spend many hours studying and rehearsing, both in and out of the classroom. But majors generally have a strong sense of community and of working toward a common goal. Because colleges sponsor recitals and concerts by faculty members and guest artists, students frequently meet and talk extensively with professional performers and also participate in the management of these concerts. Many colleges offer music majors the opportunity to present their own recitals when they are in their fourth year.

Colleges vary widely in their approach to the study of music. Some schools are conservatories that emphasize performance and composition. Other colleges focus on the historical and theoretical study of music. Still others seek a balance between practice and theory.

Other majors you might like:
Music management
Sacred music
Music history/literature

Music teacher education
Music therapy
Radio and television
Recording arts
Musical instrument fabrication/repair
Computer science
Electrical and communications engineering
Mathematics
Digital media

Questions to ask colleges:
Are auditions required for admission into or placement in the major? In many programs, candidates must be able to sing in tune and also take a written music exam.

What practice facilities are available and during what hours? Is digital recording equipment available?

What are the performance opportunities? What kinds of ensembles are available?

To what extent is non-Western music taught?

Career options and trends:
Professional or studio musician; composer; music teacher; recording engineer or mixer; art administrator; music publishing editor; film music editor; music therapist; music store manager; music software developer.

To become a music therapist or to teach in public schools, you must obtain certification and meet specific education requirements.

A general music major does not directly lead to careers in the profession, but like all liberal arts majors, it provides a broad, flexible foundation for a variety of occupations or for graduate school. Students at the top of their class who are willing to relocate may obtain music-related jobs after graduation, but the music industry is very competitive.

For more info:
College Music Society (CMS)
312 East Pine St.
Missoula, MT 59802
(406) 721-9616
www.music.org

Music management

What it's about:

This major provides a broad understanding of the fields of music and management. You take courses in music history, theory, and performance. In addition, you explore the methods, concepts, and principles of management, with specific focus on the music business.

Is this for you?

You might like this major if you also like: starting or running a business venture; managing or performing in a band; organizing or leading a club or group activity; solving problems; taking risks; competing; sports; helping others to succeed.

Consider this major if you are good at: attention to detail; critical reading/thinking; leadership; organizing; persuading/influencing; teamwork ...*or have...* initiative; verbal skills; writing skills.

Recommended high school prep:

English 4, math 3, lab science 3, social studies 3, music 3–4, and a foreign language 3. If they are available, these are also recommended: statistics, computer applications, economics, accounting, business, psychology, and participation in music performance such as band or orchestra.

Typical courses in this major:

Introduction to the music business
Music publishing and copyright law
Recording and broadcast industries
Contracts and other legal issues
Accounting
Economics
Introduction to marketing
Fundamentals of management
Computer applications
Music history
Basic music theory and ear training
International marketing
Concert and tour promotion
Business statistics
Music technology
Recording techniques

Concentrations:

In college: recording and studio production techniques; marketing and merchandising; arts management.

If you go on to grad school: international marketing.

What the study of this major is like:

The music management major prepares you to enter the music business world. You learn about issues such as patronage, copyright laws, and musicians' union regulations, as well as fund-raising, grant-proposal writing, and advertising techniques.

There are two main approaches to the music management major. Some colleges focus on business or management, expecting you to learn only a minimal amount about music. In these programs, you generally take a core of courses that teach methods, concepts, and principles of music management and business. A number of other programs have strong offerings in music, with only a smattering of business and management courses. Industry experts have come to demand a greater balance between the two aspects of the major. Ideally, you should choose a program that provides maximum opportunities to study both music and business/management.

For a comprehensive or music-oriented program, you may be asked to demonstrate (through an audition) the ability to play an instrument or sing, and to take a music theory placement examination. To prepare yourself, you'll need some previous music training. Such colleges also require you to enroll in a sequence of music history and theory courses, in addition to the business and management courses. In all programs, you must participate in activities promoting music and art on campus and in the surrounding community (such as campus concerts and local civic organizations) to test out the concepts and strategies you study in class. Additionally, most colleges expect you to take 30–40 percent of your total course work in humanities, mathematics, and the sciences, to ensure that you receive a well-rounded education.

Upper-level courses often require at least two internships at off-campus establishments. These internships, often in cooperation with recording studios, music publishing houses, arts organizations, symphony orchestras, or television studios, provide a unique way for you to explore the professional field under the guidance of college mentors. The biggest challenge most students encounter involves time management—balancing the development of academic skills with practical fieldwork. You also need to cultivate good "people skills."

Other majors you might like:

Radio and television
Recording arts
Musicology/ethnomusicology
Jazz studies
Public relations
Business administration and management
Hospitality administration and management
Web/multimedia management
Information systems
Theater arts management
Music history/literature
Entrepreneurial studies

Questions to ask colleges:

Are there opportunities on campus to gain experience in promoting concerts and other arts events?

Does the college have a recording studio, or a radio and/or television station, and opportunities to develop skills in audio and video work?

What connections do the faculty members and the department have with the music industry?

Career options and trends:

Business manager*; recording industry promoter or producer*; orchestra manager; booking agent; artist representative or manager; music publishing executive or editor*; television and radio promoter*;

A&R (artist and repertoire) administrator or coordinator; studio production manager; entertainment lawyer.

The field is becoming highly international, so knowledge of a foreign language (such as Spanish, French, or Japanese) is a big plus. Also, knowledge of digital technology and intellectual property rights is essential. As in all art-related fields, there is plenty of competition, but the business end of music is varied enough to provide greater opportunity. Internship experience, which is expected of job applicants in all music-related businesses, is an invaluable way to develop networking contacts and, sometimes, to receive job offers.

For more info:

American Society of Composers, Authors, and
　　Publishers (ASCAP)
One Lincoln Plaza
New York, NY 10023
(212) 621-6000
www.ascap.com

American Federation of Musicians
1501 Broadway
Suite 600
New York, NY 10036
(212) 869-1330
www.afm.org

Music performance

Also known as:
Applied music

What it's about:
The music performance major allows you to achieve a high level of technical proficiency and musical sensitivity. You are trained to play a musical instrument or to sing professionally, both as a solo and ensemble performer.

Is this for you?
You might like this major if you also like: communicating through music; listening to music; performing outside school; reading music biographies. If you have strong encouragement from your music teachers, confidence in your abilities, and a commitment to succeed, you might consider this major.

Consider this major if you are good at: attention to detail; creativity; math; memorizing; organizing; teamwork ...*or have...* aural skills; physical stamina; self-discipline.

Recommended high school prep:
English 4, math 3–4, lab science 3, social studies 3, music 3–4, and a foreign language 2–3. While not required, music courses covering large ensembles, small ensembles, solo performance, music theory, and music history are recommended. Regardless of your specific training (voice or instrument), you will be expected to have basic knowledge of the piano keyboard.

Did you know...
...that most auditions require you to sing? No matter what your instrument, you are expected to be able to use your voice intelligently and in tune.

Typical courses in this major:
Music theory
Aural skills
Music history
Individual instruction
Computer and/or electronic music
Vocal diction
Percussion
Strings
Brass
Woodwinds
Introduction to music literature
Accompanying
Instrumental ensemble
Vocal ensemble
Fundamentals of conducting
Pedagogy of the piano/voice/etc.

Concentrations:
Voice; piano; organ; individual orchestra or band instruments; jazz studies; early music; instrumental pedagogy; conducting.

What the study of this major is like:
Most music performance majors have already taken part in musical activities in high school, except perhaps for singers, whose "instruments" are not available until their voices mature. Most programs test new students to determine their background and skills. Tests may include an audition and both a written and an oral exam. If you lack necessary skills, you may have to enroll in catch-up courses.

In addition to performance work and related instruction, the major includes core courses in music theory, literature, and history. Traditionally, you attend weekly private lessons in your chosen instrument (or in voice) with your concentration instructor. You also participate in master classes, studio recitals, and solo recitals. Instrumentalists take part in chamber music coaching and performances; vocalists take part in opera coaching, workshops, and performances; and all students participate in rehearsals and large-ensemble performances.

In music theory and aural skills courses, you study harmony, rhythm, counterpoint, sight singing, ear training, melodic and harmonic dictation, improvisation, and analysis of musical structure. Mastering theory and aural skills helps you understand the way a piece of music is put together. In music history and literature courses, you will survey music through the ages and explore books and documents related to your concentration. Other courses may cover repertoire, music education, conducting, composition, and jazz studies.

Voice concentrates may need to take Italian, German, Russian, and/or French, the languages of many operas. Nonpiano concentrates must take an introduction to keyboard harmony. And almost all performance programs require you to do 25–50 percent of your course work in the liberal arts. Therefore, you must come to college with the same study skills, writing skills, and academic background as liberal arts majors.

For performance majors, time is precious; large blocks of it (besides the hours you spend in classes and studying) must be set aside for solitary practice. When you are not practicing and studying, you often perform both on and off campus and participate in competitions—leaving you very little free time. Your social life will probably center on a small group of friends who share your goals and serve as a support group.

Among various colleges, striking differences may exist in mission and atmosphere. For example, a single-purpose conservatory that enrolls top students will differ significantly from a four-year liberal arts college. Professionally oriented performance schools sometimes foster intense competition. Whereas some students thrive in such an environment, others prefer a less intense, more nurturing educational setting. You should examine your options carefully to find the right fit.

Other majors you might like:
Music management
Sacred music
Music theory and composition
Music teacher education
Music therapy
Radio and television

Recording arts
Jazz studies
Computer science
Electrical and communications engineering
Mathematics
Voice/opera

Questions to ask colleges:
What is the ratio of students to practice rooms?

How many hours of private instruction do students receive each week in their major? Can incoming students meet with the instructor to whom they will be assigned?

How will this program and the faculty members help undergraduates make the transition from student to professional life?

Career options and trends:
Orchestral musician; solo musician; ensemble musician (string quartet, jazz trio, etc.); church musician; orchestra or opera company manager; music technician/producer; music teacher (private); music teacher (public school or college); music therapist.

Performing arts are risky career choices, because they are competitive and compensation for artists is notoriously low. The recording industry is reporting a downturn in sales and earnings, and symphony orchestras and opera companies are facing decreased contributions, endowment income, and ticket sales.

Longer term, the pendulum will swing the other way and conditions should improve all around. All signs point to a future with plenty of audience for the work of performers. Teaching music shows promise, as there has been no falloff in the desire to study music. The American String Teachers Association (ASTA) projects a need for 5,000 string teachers over the next several years.

For more info:
College Music Society (CMS)
312 East Pine St.
Missoula, MT 59802
(406) 721-9616
www.music.org

Music theory and composition

What it's about:
This major consists of two related areas of study—music theory is the study of the materials, processes, and structures of music; music composition is the art of writing music. In some institutions, the two are combined into a single major; in other institutions, they are separate.

Is this for you?
You might like this major if you also like: computer science; psychology; mathematics; audio recording; languages; art; drama.

Consider this major if you are good at: attention to detail; creativity; critical reading/thinking; organizing; quantitative analysis ...*or have...* aural perception; initiative; patience; writing skills.

Recommended high school prep:
English 4, math 3–4, lab science 3, social studies 3, and a foreign language 2–3. Most colleges do not require or recommend any specific music courses at the high school level. But you must have a thorough knowledge of the fundamentals (intervals, scales, chords in treble and bass clef; simple rhythmic and metric notation) and skill in basic ear training (intervals, scales, triads; dictation of simple rhythmic, melodic, and harmonic examples). An ability to play a keyboard instrument is recommended. Courses that cover math, psychology, and computer science can be good background for music theory.

Typical courses in this major:
Aural skills
Music history
Schenkerian analysis
Analysis of twentieth-century music
Atonal music
Operatic literature
Symphonic literature
Composition seminar
Psychology of music
Music technology
Diction and song literature
Counterpoint
Piano pedagogy
Orchestration
Computer-assisted music notation
Senior thesis project

Concentrations:
Generally, none available.

What the study of this major is like:
As a music theory and composition major, you learn to understand and describe the forces that shape music. The discipline of music theory can be compared with subjects such as linguistics and psychology: you explore the principles that help determine the results, whether in music or in human behavior and language. Studying music composition is similar to studying creative writing: you combine knowledge of the principles and techniques with imagination to produce a work of art.

In beginning theory courses, you will read works on the topic by leading scholars (for example, Rameau, Schenker, Forte). When you first take composition, you may study under the guidance of a master teacher, who sets tasks or goals for you and then analyzes your work and suggests possible improvements. For both theory and music composition, you typically examine the literature—including scholarly writings and original scores—and enhance your musical skills. Advanced theory courses teach you how to formulate and test your own ideas through research; advanced composition courses usually offer you more opportunities for creative expression.

Musical skills courses include ear training and sight singing, and training in voice or in your instrument. Like all music majors, you will participate in a student ensemble, band, choir, or other group. You cannot become a good theorist or composer without also becoming a good musician.

Although some programs combine music theory and composition in a single major, other programs address them separately. But differences among individual professors of music theory and of composition are usually more significant than differences among programs. To figure out which program is probably best for you, you should talk to professors about their teaching style and expectations.

Other majors you might like:

Music performance
Jazz studies
Music history/literature
Musicology/ethnomusicology
Music management
Creative Writing
Mathematics
Linguistics
Computer science
Conducting

Questions to ask colleges:

Is the program accredited by the National Association of Schools of Music?

What opportunities does the program offer in music pedagogy?

Is electronic or computer music part of the curriculum?

Are there any audition requirements?

Career options and trends:

A bachelor's degree in this major does not prepare students for specific careers, except possibly as a private teacher, performer, or composer. Teaching in elementary, middle, and high school requires a music education degree and state certification, and teaching at the college level usually requires a doctorate degree.

For more info:

College Music Society (CMS)
312 East Pine St.
Missoula, MT 59802
(406) 721-9616
www.music.org

Society for Music Theory
University of Chicago
Department of Music
1010 East 59th St.
Chicago, IL 60637
(773) 834-3821
www.societymusictheory.org

Photography

What it's about:

The major in photography is for students interested in the art of communicating information, ideas, moods, and feelings through photographic images. You gain a broad background in both the technical and the aesthetic aspects of photography.

Is this for you?

You might like this major if you also like: nature studies; art and art classes; science and technology; working with equipment and chemicals; the school newspaper, yearbook, or photography club; working independently.

Consider this major if you are good at: attention to detail; creativity; organizing; spacial thinking/analysis; visualizing ideas or images *...or have...* initiative; patience; verbal skills; writing skills.

Recommended high school prep:

English 4, math 3, lab science 3 (including chemistry and physics), social studies 3, visual arts 3–4, and a foreign language 2–3. If available, a journalism course would be helpful, and computer applications courses are recommended.

Did you know...

...that often the same type of preparatory courses are required for photography as for other art disciplines—drawing, two-dimensional and three-dimensional design, and color theory?

Typical courses in this major:

Elementary photography
History of photography
Two-dimensional design
Black-and-white photography
Color photography
Digital photography
Materials and processes
Commercial and/or industrial photography
Portraiture
Photo editing
Studio photography
Photojournalism
Advanced photographic techniques
Lighting techniques
Biomedical and forensic practicum
Portfolio preparation

Concentrations:

In college: fine art photography; digital imaging; portraiture; biomedical photographic illustration; commercial photography; fashion photography; photojournalism.

If you go on to grad school: most graduate photography programs concentrate on fine art applications, and many are self-directed.

What the study of this major is like:

As a photography major, you begin by exploring the fundamentals of design, form, color, and composition. You learn about the nature of light and analyze how three-dimensional space is changed into two-dimensional images. In an introductory course, you study camera operation and controls (such as focus, shutter speed, and aperture setting) and their effects on photographic images; you also learn about types of cameras: digital, 35 mm, medium format, and large format field cameras that produce single negatives. You discuss contemporary issues in photography, as well as photographic history. Critiques (in which you evaluate the strengths and weaknesses of a photograph) are an essential part of your learning process.

In lower-level photography courses, your assignments center on depicting specific ideas or situations. As you progress through the major, you concentrate more on your own ideas of what to depict. You create portfolios (a group of photographs on a theme) and study many approaches to photography, such as studio techniques, color, digital applications, and alternative processes. Taking courses in other arts, such as drawing, sculpture, and painting, can enrich your work. If you are interested in documentary photography or photojournalism, you might take courses in journalism, English, and anthropology. Throughout your studies, you evaluate your strengths and interests in relation to a possible career. A final portfolio that showcases your work is the capstone to almost every degree program.

Most photography programs try to balance the technical and the creative aspects of the art. Programs often specialize in one or two areas of photography; fine arts and journalism are the most common. (Such courses may also be offered in conjunction with broader art or journalism programs.)

The biggest issue facing photography programs is the tension between traditional, "wet" darkroom practice and digital processes, so be aware of the technical practices of the programs you consider. Also, some colleges emphasize the practical, commercial aspects of photography; these programs train you to concentrate on meeting the demands of clients. Other programs, which are based in the fine arts, encourage you to express your personal point of view. Degree programs can range from two-year associate degrees to four-year Bachelor of Arts, Bachelor of Science, or Bachelor of Fine Arts degrees, each with its own emphasis.

Other majors you might like:
Cinematography and film/video production
Journalism
Graphic design
Advertising
Digital art
Fashion merchandising
Entrepreneurial studies
Photographic/film/video technology
Radiologic technology/medical imaging
Surveying technology
Computer graphics
Digital media

Questions to ask colleges:
Does the program offer training in digital technologies?

What equipment must students provide on their own, and what equipment is available for student checkout?

Is there sufficient darkroom space and access time? How many majors and nonmajors share darkroom facilities?

Career options and trends:
Photojournalist; fine art photographer; freelance photographer; commercial or industrial photographer; technical or medical photographer; digital image technician; wedding photographer; portrait photographer; animator; manager of a photo lab.

Most photographers are either working freelance or running their own businesses and studios; salaried jobs are increasingly hard to find. Competition is keen, especially for photojournalists and commercial photographers. Fine arts photographers face the same challenge as other artists: how to attract audiences who favor their particular type of work. In all areas, good business sense, creative talent, and technological savvy are necessary ingredients for success.

Insider's viewpoint:
"I like isolating segments of the environment through the frame of the camera's viewfinder. I tend to see my surroundings in a series of still images—like the stop-action aspect of a movie."

—Professor Fred Niles, University of Dayton

For more info:
Student Photographic Society
229 Peachtree St., N.E.
Suite 2200
Atlanta, GA 30303
(866) 886-5325
www.studentphoto.com

Society of Photographic Education (SPE)
2530 Superior Ave.
Suite 403
Cleveland, OH 44114
(216) 622-2733
www.spenational.org

Theatre design and technology

Also known as:
Technical theater

What it's about:
This major covers the design and production of costumes, lighting, scenery, and sound for theater, opera, and dance. Typically housed in a theater or a performing arts department, the program enables students to specialize in one or more of these areas while they gain a broad foundation in the related disciplines of acting, directing, and theater history and theory.

Is this for you?
You might like this major if you also like: building things; working with your hands; decorating; art and literature; music; photography; working collaboratively with people; organizing events; solving problems. If you enjoy plays, movies, museums, and theme parks and would like to know how these attractions are produced, you might consider working behind the scenes in theater.

Consider this major if you are good at: attention to detail; creativity; critical reading/thinking; organizing; spacial thinking/analysis; teamwork *...or have...* initiative; manual dexterity; patience; verbal skills.

Recommended high school prep:
English 4, math 3, lab science 3, social studies 3, foreign language 2-3, music 1-2, and visual arts 1-2. Courses that cover music appreciation, design (computer-aided if possible), and dramatic arts and literature are recommended, as is participation in extracurricular activities such as drama, art, and music clubs, and community organizations or summer theater companies. Industrial and/or vocational arts classes in woodworking, metalworking, drafting, and sewing are also helpful.

Did you know...
...that even though they work behind the scenes, majors in theater design and technology are often required to take performance classes such as acting or dance, and courses in theater history and theory? That's because the technician's job is to enhance the work of performers and directors, so an understanding of their craft is necessary.

Typical courses in this major:
Introduction to theater
Mechanical drafting
Scenographic techniques
Computer applications for theater
Sound
Stage management
Costume design and construction
Makeup for the stage
Lighting
Scene design and construction
Theater history
Theater graphics
Play analysis
Acting and performance courses
Art and art history courses
Portfolio development and presentation

Concentrations:
Lighting design; costume design (including makeup); scene design; technical direction; sound design; stage management.

What the study of this major is like:
This major is generally divided into design and production courses. The design component includes introductory and advanced courses in costume, lighting, scenery, and sound design. You'll study script analysis, historical research, fundamentals of visual art, drawing, rendering, and design presentation. In the production courses, you'll learn how to pattern, drape, and fit costumes on

an actor's body; construct, paint, and prop scenery; rig, hang, and focus lighting equipment; record sound effects; and place microphones or speakers for sound reinforcement. Introductory courses in these subjects teach basic vocabulary, tool usage, and procedures for design production. Some departments offer specialty courses in period styles in clothing and architecture; drawing and painting techniques; and advanced crafts, such as millinery, fabric dyeing and modification, makeup, wig construction, scene painting, properties design and construction, model making, and structural engineering for scenery.

Many production courses consist of a lecture class that addresses theory and laboratory sessions in which you have the opportunity to practice what you learn. Labs often provide the labor to implement your designs for department plays. Faculty members evaluate each assignment to determine if you are ready for projects that are more challenging. Ideally, you progress through the program by taking more advanced classes and assuming greater responsibilities in the design and production of plays. Because you'll often have to spend hours doing work outside your course requirements, you should be prepared to balance your academic and production commitments.

Most theater design and technology programs offer either a Bachelor of Arts or a Bachelor of Fine Arts degree. The B.A. program provides a liberal arts education that gives you an understanding of the world that the theater attempts to reflect; the program also prepares you for jobs you can take while pursuing the goal of working full-time in theater. The B.F.A. program trains you for a professional career in theater by offering more specialized, intensive course work. Most B.F.A. programs require auditions and/or interviews for admission and yearly performance evaluations to remain in the program. A few universities offer Bachelor of Science (B.S.) degrees in theater, which have stronger science and technology components than B.A. programs. A few junior and community colleges offer a two-year associate of arts (A.A.) degree in theater design and technology.

Other majors you might like:

Radio and television
Cinematography and film/video production
Architecture
Interior design
Theater history/criticism
Theater arts management
Fashion and apparel design
Structural engineering
Construction technology
Resort management
Interior design
Museum studies

Questions to ask colleges:

Is the program accredited by the National Association of Schools of Theater (NAST)?

Is there also a graduate program at this college? The presence of a graduate program has both advantages and disadvantages for undergrads—usually the quality of productions is high, but undergraduates may have to compete with grad students for the best design and production opportunities.

How many productions are offered per season and/or academic year? What types of theatrical works are produced (period plays, musicals, opera, dance)?

Do student designers and technicians have to audition and/or interview for positions on a production?

Career options and trends:

Regional/professional theater designer (costume, scenery, lighting, sound)*; theater technician (carpenter, scene painter, tailor or seamster, cutter/draper, electrician, sound engineer)*; technical director/production manager; art director/production designer for film and television; college or high school teacher in theater*.

The skills learned in this major are also useful in designing and working in theme parks, film, television, special effects, concerts, circuses, interior design, store and window display, apparel design, museum display and exhibition design, cruise ship tours, party design, parade and float design, architecture, and any business requiring the creation of an environment (such as multimedia and Internet) that people can view and interact with.

A bachelor's degree in Education and/or state certification is necessary to teach theater on a high school level. An advanced degree (MFA or Ph.D.) is mandatory for teaching at the college level. Technicians who have gained production experience can often find entry-level jobs with a bachelor's degree, but designers usually need to attend grad school for additional training.

Because theater is both an art and a business, it is subject to the ups and downs of local, state, and national economics and to trends in political ideology. While theater technicians enjoy more job security than actors, directors, and playwrights, they still must look for seasonal jobs at a variety of theaters.

Insider's viewpoint:

"If you're passionate about something you might as well go out and do it. Even if you're not famous or rich at least you'll be happy instead of being stuck in a cubicle. I'd rather be happy doing what I love, which is theater, than in a different job and making money."

—Emily, senior, San Jose State University

For more info:

Educational Theater Association (ETA)
2343 Auburn Ave.
Cincinnati, OH 45219
(513) 421-3900
www.edta.org

Part II: Brief Descriptions of Majors

About Part II

There are far more fields of study available at U.S. colleges and universities than are fully described in Part I of this book. To give you an idea of what they are about, Part II includes brief descriptions of the more than 900 majors recognized by the U.S. Department of Education and offered among the nation's undergraduate colleges, graduate schools, and first-professional schools.

Use the brief descriptions of majors in this Part in conjunction with Part III. They will help you get a better idea of what the colleges listed there are offering. These brief descriptions indicate the scope of the major and, where appropriate, the job or career for which it prepares you.

You won't find all of these majors at every institution. Some are very specialized fields, which are offered only by a few colleges. Some are vocational or technical in nature, and only offered by community colleges, technical institutes, or other two-year institutions. And some are only available as graduate degree programs.

Some of these briefly-described majors are mentioned in the "related majors" section of the full descriptions of majors that appear in Part I. All of these majors are listed in Part III of this book, showing which colleges and universities offer degrees for each major, and at what degree level.

If you think one of these majors sounds interesting, but you can't find a college listed in Part III that offers it at the degree level that's appropriate for you, keep in mind that there might still be ways you can study the subject in college. One way is to go to a college that offers a major in a related, broader field, and then concentrate or minor in your preferred subject. If you do this, you will then be well-prepared for a career or graduate study that focuses on the specialization you've chosen.

Brief descriptions of majors

Accounting. Includes instruction in various types of accounting, legal considerations, auditing, report procedures, planning and consulting, research methods, and professional standards and ethics.

Accounting technology/bookkeeping. Prepares students to provide technical administrative support to financial management personnel.

Accounting/business management. A combined program in accounting and business management.

Accounting/computer science. A program that combines accounting with computer science and/or computer studies.

Accounting/finance. An integrated program that trains individuals to function as accountants and financial managers.

Acoustics. Investigates the properties and behavior of sound waves under different conditions.

Acting. Prepares students to impart ideas and feelings through naturalistic and believable behavior in imaginary circumstances.

Actuarial science. Highlights the mathematical and statistical analysis of risk and its applications to insurance and other business management problems.

Acupuncture. Readies individuals to practice pulse diagnosis, acupuncture point selection, and needle insertion to treat health imbalances.

Administrative/secretarial services. Describes the duties of administrative assistants and/or secretaries and stenographers.

Adult development/aging. Investigates aging populations and the needs of older individuals in family and institutional settings.

Adult health nursing. Informs registered nurses how to provide general care for adult patients.

Adult literacy instruction. Prepares students to serve as instructors and mentors for adults in literacy programs in school, institutional, community, and private settings.

Adult/continuing education. Prepares students to instruct adult students in various types of educational programs.

Adult/continuing education administration. Readies individuals to serve the basic educational needs of undereducated adults or the needs of adults seeking further instruction.

Advertising. Focuses on commercial messages intended to promote and sell ideas, products, and services.

Aeronautical/aerospace engineering. Highlights the design, development, and operational evaluation of aircraft, space vehicles, and their systems.

Aeronautical/aerospace engineering technology. Covers the development, manufacturing, and testing of aircraft, spacecraft, and their systems.

Aeronautics and aviation science. The study of aviation, including in-flight and ground support operations.

Aesthetician/skin care. Prepares individuals to cleanse, depilate, massage, and beautify the human body.

African languages. Focuses on one or more of the languages originating in Africa.

African studies. Explores the history, society, politics, culture, and economics of Africa.

African-American studies. Investigates the history, sociology, politics, culture, and economics of the North American peoples descended from Africa.

Agribusiness operations. Investigates the management of agricultural businesses and agriculturally related operations within diversified corporations.

Agricultural and biological engineering. The study of systems used to produce, process, and store agricultural products; and the improvement of agricultural methods and biological systems.

Agricultural business. Focuses on the organization, operation, and management of agricultural enterprises.

Agricultural business technology. Explores the operation of agricultural office equipment, software, and information systems.

Agricultural communications. Prepares students to apply journalistic, communication, and broadcasting principles to develop, produce, and transmit agricultural information.

Agricultural economics. The analysis of resource allocation, productivity, investments, and trends in the agricultural sector.

Agricultural education services. Features the provision of referral, consulting, technical assistance, and educational services to gardeners, farmers, ranchers, and agribusinesses.

Agricultural equipment technology. Provides instruction in the maintenance and repair of specialized farm, ranch, and agribusiness power equipment and vehicles.

Agricultural mechanization. Readies students to sell, select, and service agricultural or agribusiness technical equipment and facilities, including computers, power units, machinery, and utilities.

Agricultural power machinery operation. Highlights the operation of specialized farm, ranch, and agribusiness power equipment.

Agricultural production. Focuses on the general planning, economics, and use of facilities, natural resources, labor, and capital to produce plant and animal products.

Agricultural supplies. Highlights the purchasing, marketing, and selling of agricultural products.

Agricultural teacher education. Prepares students to teach vocational agricultural programs at various educational levels.

Agricultural/food products processing. Readies individuals to receive, inspect, process, and package agricultural products for human consumption, animal or plant food, or other products.

Agriculture, general. The study of agricultural research and production.

Agronomy and crop science. The study of the chemical, physical, and biological relationships of crops and soils.

Air traffic control. Prepares students to manage and control air traffic, usually with additional training at the FAA Flight Control Center in a cooperative education program.

Aircraft maintenance/technology. Prepares individuals to repair all aircraft components other than engines, propellers, avionics, and instruments.

Aircraft powerplant technology. Prepares students to repair, service, and maintain all types of aircraft power plant and related systems.

Airline/commercial pilot. Focuses on the flying and/or navigation of commercial fixed-wing aircraft.

Algebra/number theory. Prepares students to express quantities by means of symbols, vectors, matrices, equations, and integer properties.

Alternative fuel vehicle technology. Describes the maintenance of alternative fuel vehicles and the conversion of standard vehicles to AFV status.

American government/politics. Features the political institutions of the United States.

American history (U.S.). Focuses on the development of American society, culture, and institutions from the Pre-Columbian period to the present.

American literature. Features the literature of the United States from the colonial era to the present.

American Sign Language (ASL). Focuses on American Sign Language as a medium of communication for deaf individuals and Deaf culture.

American studies. The study of the history, society, politics, culture, and economics of the United States.

Analysis/functional analysis. Defines the properties of equations, multivariate solutions, functions, and dynamic systems.

Analytical chemistry. Prepares students to analyze and describe the composition of matter.

Anatomy. Highlights organs, tissues, and whole bodies together with their cellular and structural components.

Ancient Greek. Highlights the Greek language and literature from its origins through the fall of the Byzantine Empire, as a secular and/or theological subject.

Ancient Near Eastern/Biblical languages. The study of the extinct Semitic and/or Non-Semitic languages spoken in the ancient Near East, including those used to write historical Jewish and Christian religious texts.

Ancient studies. Focuses on Western and non-Western cultures and related topics in the periods of prehistory and antiquity.

Anesthesiologist assistant. Trains students to assist anesthesiologists and nurses in developing and implementing patient anesthesia care plans.

Animal behavior/ethology. Highlights the psychological and neurological processes of animals.

Animal breeding. Applies the principles of genetics and genetic engineering to the improvement of agricultural animal health and the development of new animal breeds.

Animal genetics. Features animal genetics from the experimental, comparative, veterinary, and medical viewpoints.

Animal health. Investigates the prevention and control of diseases in agricultural animals.

Animal husbandry. Features the selection, breeding, care, processing, and marketing of livestock and small farm animals.

Animal nutrition. Focuses on nutrition as related to animal health, and on the production of improved animal products.

Animal physiology. The study of internal function, development, and dynamics within animal species, with comparative applications to humans.

Animal sciences. Studies the scientific principles underlying the breeding and husbandry of agricultural animals; and the production and distribution of agricultural animal products.

Animal training. Prepares individuals to teach and exercise animals for leisure, sport, show, and professional purposes.

Animation. Prepares individuals to communicate simulated real-world content through the manipulation of film, video, photographs, digital copy, and soundtracks.

Anthropology. Describes human beings, their antecedents, and their cultural behavior and institutions in comparative perspective.

Apparel/accessories marketing. Prepares students to perform operations connected with the distribution and sale of apparel and accessories.

Apparel/textile manufacture. A program that focuses on the design, development, and production of textile products and related processes.

Apparel/textile marketing. Trains students to apply marketing research and management to the products of the apparel and textile industries.

Appliance installation and repair. Readies students to mend, install, and fix major gas, electric, and microwave appliances.

Applied economics. Applies economics to the study of particular industries, activities, or the exploitation of particular resources.

Applied mathematics. Uses mathematics to find solutions to functional problems in fields such as engineering, computing and information science, and the applied sciences.

Applied physics. Combines fundamental physics, math, and engineering with a focus on specific technologies or fields, such as electrical engineering, chemistry, or computer science.

Aquaculture. Prepares students to culture, propagate, harvest, and market domesticated fish, shellfish, and marine plants.

Aquatic biology/limnology. Highlights the ecology and behavior of microbes, plants, and animals inhabiting inland fresh waters.

Arabic. The study of the language, literature, and culture of Arabic-speaking peoples.

Archaeology. Explores societies via the excavation, analysis, and interpretation of their artifactual and human remains.

Architectural drafting/CAD/CADD. Highlights the technical skills used to develop working drawings and electronic simulations for architectural and related construction projects.

Architectural engineering. Features the mathematical and scientific principles applied to the design and development of materials, systems, and methods used to construct buildings for human habitation or other purposes.

Architectural engineering technology. Prepares students to support architects, engineers, and planners engaged in designing and developing buildings and urban complexes.

Architectural history/criticism. Studies the aesthetic, technical, and social development of the built environment and the architectural profession from ancient times to the present.

Architectural technology. Prepares students to assist architects in developing plans and documentation, and in performing office services.

Architecture. Prepares students for the professional practice of architecture, with instruction in architectural design, history, and theory; building structures; site planning; and construction.

Aromatherapy. Readies individuals to provide therapeutic care through the preparation and application of essential oils.

Art. An introductory study and appreciation of the visual arts.

Art history. Studies the historical development of art as social and intellectual phenomenon, the analysis of art, and art conservation.

Art teacher education. Readies individuals to provide art and art appreciation programs at various educational levels.

Art therapy. Describes the use of art media to assess, treat, and rehabilitate individuals with physical, emotional, developmental, or mental disorders.

Artificial intelligence/robotics. Focuses on the simulation by computers of human learning and reasoning, and of human motor control and motions by computer-driven machinery.

Arts management. Trains individuals to organize and manage art organizations and facilities.

Asian bodywork therapy. Readies students to provide relief and improved health through the traditional bodywork therapies of Asia.

Asian history. Examines the development of the societies, cultures, and institutions of the Asian continent from their origins to the present.

Asian studies. Studies the history, society, politics, culture, and economics of the Asian continent.

Asian-American studies. Describes the history, sociology, politics, culture, and economics of Asian population groups who have immigrated to the United States and Canada.

Astronomy. Focuses on the planetary, galactic, and stellar phenomena occurring in outer space.

Astrophysics. The theoretical study of the physical laws underlying the formation, evolution, and behavior of stars, galaxies, and the universe.

Athletic training. Instructs students on the prevention, evaluation, and treatment of sports injuries.

Atmospheric physics/dynamics. Features the processes governing the behavior of atmospheric, terrestrial, and solar phenomena.

Atmospheric science. Investigates the earth's atmosphere and its effect on terrestrial weather, and on related environment and climate problems.

Atomic/molecular physics. Investigates the behavior of matter-energy phenomena at the atomic and molecular levels.

Auctioneering. Trains individuals for careers as auctioneers and auction managers and for meeting state licensing requirements.

Audiology/hearing sciences. Trains students to diagnose hearing loss, advise patients on how to use their remaining hearing, and select and fit hearing aids.

Audiology/speech pathology. An integrated program that prepares individuals as audiologists and speech-language pathologists.

Auditing. Prepares individuals to evaluate organizational financial and operational activities, ensure regulatory compliance, safeguard assets, and promote resource allocation.

Australian/Oceanic/Pacific languages. Focuses on the languages spoken by the Melanesian, Micronesian, and Polynesian peoples.

Auto body repair. Prepares individuals to repair, reconstruct, and finish automobile bodies, fenders, and external features.

Automotive engineering technology. Trains students in the development, manufacture, and testing of self-propelled ground vehicles and their systems.

Automotive technology. Describes the servicing and maintenance of all types of automobiles.

Aviation management. Emphasizes the management of aviation industry operations and services.

Avionics maintenance/technology. Trains individuals to maintain aircraft operating, control, and electronic systems.

Bacteriology. Features bacteria that are significant factors in causing human disease.

Baking/pastry arts. Describes bread and pastry making, decorating, marketing, counter display, and service.

Ballet. Trains individuals to express ideas and feelings through interpretation of classical dance choreography.

Banking/financial services. Describes a variety of customer services in banks, insurance agencies, and savings and loan companies.

Barbering. Focuses on facial shaving, hair cutting, styling art, facial and scalp massage, hairpiece fitting, equipment operation, and safety.

Bartending. Readies students to mix beverages and manage bars, lounges, and beverage services operations.

Behavioral sciences. Studies problems of human individual and social growth and behavior.

Bible studies. The study of the Christian and/or Jewish Bible, with an emphasis on interpreting the messages contained therein.

Bilingual/bicultural education. Focuses on the design and provision of teaching to bilingual/bicultural children or adults.

Biochemistry. Focuses on living systems, their chemical substances and pathways, and information transfer systems.

Biochemistry/biophysics and molecular biology. An integrated program focusing on the structure, function, and behavior of biological systems at molecular levels and their influence on biological activity.

Bioethics/medical ethics. A course of study that analyzes health care issues, clinical decision-making, and research procedures.

Bioinformatics. Applies computer-based technologies to biological, biomedical, and biotechnological research.

Biological immunology. Describes the biological origination and development of disease and host responses to disease.

Biological/physical sciences. A program that is either a general synthesis of the biological and physical sciences, or a specialization that draws from the biological and physical sciences.

Biology. Introductory study of living organisms and their relations to their natural environments.

Biology lab technology. Prepares students to apply scientific principles and skills in support of biologists in research, industrial, and government settings.

Biology teacher education. Trains individuals to teach biology at various educational levels.

Biomedical engineering. Studies the design and development of biological and health systems and products such as integrated biological systems, medical information systems, and artificial organs and prostheses.

Biomedical sciences. The scientific study of biological issues related to health and medicine.

Biomedical technology. Readies students to support engineers engaged in developing biological or medical systems and products.

Biometrics. Applies various computational methods to the study of problems in the biological sciences and related fields in agriculture and natural resources.

Biophysics. Applies the principles of physics to the workings of biological processes and assemblies.

Biopsychology. Highlights linkages between biochemical and biophysical activity to central nervous system functioning.

Biostatistics. Prepares students to apply statistics to biomedical research and clinical, health, and industrial issues related to humans.

Biotechnology. Combines biological sciences, biochemistry, and genetics with engineering principles to prepare new agricultural, environmental, clinical, and industrial products.

Boilermaking. Trains individuals to make and repair steam boiler components.

Botany. The study of plants, related organisms, and plant habitats and ecosystem relations.

Broadcast journalism. Prepares students to report, produce, and deliver news via radio, television, and video/film media.

Buddhist studies. Explores the Buddhist faith; along with its intellectual, cultural, social, and ritual developments.

Building inspection. The study of industrial, labor, and governmental standards to the oversight of construction projects and the maintenance of completed buildings.

Building/property maintenance. Prepares individuals to keep a building functioning and service a variety of structures.

Business administration and management. Prepares students to plan, organize, direct, and control the functions of a firm or organization.

Business communications. Prepares students to function in an organization as a composer, editor, and proofreader of business communications.

Business machine repair. Prepares individuals to install and maintain a variety of office machinery.

Business statistics. Features the description, analysis, and forecasting of business data.

Business teacher education. Prepares individuals to teach vocational business programs.

Business/commerce. The general study of business, business organization, and accounting as used in profit-making and nonprofit public and private institutions and agencies.

Business/managerial economics. The application of economic principles to the analysis of the organization and operation of business enterprises.

Cabinetmaking/millwright. Prepares students to set up, operate, and repair woodworking machinery, and to design and fabricate wooden items.

CAD/CADD drafting/design technology. Prepares individuals to create graphic representations and simulations in support of engineering projects.

Canadian studies. Describes the history, society, politics, culture, and economics of the Canadian people.

Cardiopulmonary technology. Readies individuals, under the supervision of physicians and nurses, to perform cardiovascular and pulmonary procedures.

Cardiovascular science. Highlights the heart, vascular system, and blood, and the disorders associated with the cardiovascular system.

Cardiovascular technology. Describes cardiovascular testing procedures used to aid in diagnoses and treatments.

Caribbean studies. Explores the history, society, politics, culture, and economics of the major islands and archipelagoes of the Caribbean Sea.

Carpentry. Prepares students to lay out, fabricate, install, and repair wooden structures and fixtures using hand and power tools.

Cartography. Describes mapmaking through the use of mathematical and computer techniques.

Cell biology and histology. Features the structure, function, and regulation of cells as individual units and as components of tissues and organs.

Cell physiology. Features the physiological processes, communications, and behavior of cells in the context of whole organisms.

Cellular/anatomical biology. Integrates the study of cell structure and function within the context of anatomical systems.

Cellular/molecular biology. Integrates the study of cells, cellular systems, and the molecular basis of cell structure and function.

Celtic languages. A program that focuses on the historical and modern languages spoken by the Celtic peoples of the British Isles, Continental Europe, and Asia Minor.

Central Asian studies. Focuses on the history, society, politics, culture, and economics of Inner/Central Asia, including the inhabitants of the Caspian, Amur, Tien Shan, Baikal, Gobi, Siberian, and Manchurian regions and the historical Silk Road.

Central/Middle/Eastern European studies. Highlights the Balkans, Belarus, Czech Republic, Hungary, Poland, Romania, Russia, Slovakia, and the Ukraine.

Ceramic sciences/engineering. Prepares students to design, develop, and evaluate inorganic nonmetallic materials.

Ceramics. Studies the production of artwork out of clay and similar materials.

Chemical engineering. The study of the design and development of systems employing chemical processes and the analysis of chemical problems such as corrosion, pollution, and energy loss.

Chemical physics. Combines the disciplines of physical chemistry and atomic/molecular physics to study structural phenomena.

Chemical technology. Prepares students to aid chemical and biochemical research and industrial operations.

Chemistry. Investigates the composition and behavior of matter, the processes of chemical change, and the laboratory simulation of these phenomena.

Chemistry teacher education. Prepares individuals to teach chemistry.

Chicano/Hispanic-American/Latino studies. The study of the Hispanic-American immigrant populations within the United States and Canada.

Child care management. Prepares individuals to plan, design, and manage child care facilities that meet children's developmental needs in a safe environment.

Child care service. Includes instruction in child development, nutrition, recreation, activities supervision, child abuse prevention, and parent-child relationships.

Child development. Features the intellectual, social, emotional, and biological development of children and the planning of related human services.

Chinese. Features the Chinese language and its associated dialects and literature.

Chinese studies. Investigates the history, society, politics, culture, and economics of present-day China.

Chiropractic (D.C.). Readies students for the professional practice of chiropratic, including the application of noninvasive treatments and spinal adjustments to alleviate problems caused by vertebral misalignments.

Chiropractic assistant. Prepares students to assist chiropractors by providing patient management, examinations, and treatment services.

Christian studies. Features the teachings of Jesus Christ and the subsequent movements and institutions based on Christianity.

Cinematography and film/video production. Prepares students to communicate dramatic information, ideas, moods, and feelings through the creation and production of films and videos.

Civil engineering. Studies the design, development, and evaluation of public facilities, including structural, load-bearing, transportation, water resource, and material control systems.

Civil engineering drafting/CAD/CADD. Features the technical skills necessary to develop working drawings and electronic simulations in support of civil engineers and geological engineers.

Civil engineering technology. Trains individuals in the practical application of the design and execution of public works projects.

Classical/ancient Mediterranean/Near Eastern studies. Explores the cultures, environment, and history of the ancient Near East, Europe, and Mediterranean basin from the perspectives of the humanities, social sciences, and archaeology.

Classics. Focuses on the Greek and Latin languages and literatures.

Climatology. Describes the characteristics of atmospheric elements and processes in predictive, current, and historical contexts.

Clinical child psychology. Emphasizes the developmental processes of children and associated disorders.

Clinical laboratory science. Readies students to conduct medical tests and research, manage laboratories, and consult with physicians and researchers.

Clinical nurse specialist. Trains registered nurses to deliver direct patient care in clinical settings.

Clinical nutrition. Readies students to manage nutrition programs as part of clinical therapies, and oversee health care facility food services.

Clinical pastoral counseling. Prepares clergy and other counseling professionals to respond to the emotional and spiritual needs of patients and families in emergency or dibilitating health care situations.

Clinical psychology. Describes the analysis, diagnosis, and clinical treatment of psychological disorders and behavioral pathologies.

Clinical/medical laboratory assistant. Prepares students to assist laboratory teams by performing tests, phlebotomy, and other duties.

Clinical/medical laboratory technology. Trains individuals to engage in various medical laboratory procedures and tests and to record and analyze data.

Clinical/medical social work. Describes the professional practice of social work in hospitals and other health care facilities and organizations.

Clothing, apparel and textile studies. Highlights the development, distribution, and use of textile products in terms of the consumer's needs.

Cognitive psychology/psycholinguistics. Studies the processes of learning, thinking, and associated information systems.

Cognitive science. An interdisciplinary study of the mind and the nature of intelligence.

College student counseling. Studies the provision of counseling and administrative services to students in postsecondary educational institutions and adult education facilities.

Commercial fishing. Prepares students to function as commercial fishermen or fishing operations supervisors.

Commercial photography. Focuses on artistic techniques for communicating ideas and information to business and consumer audiences, and recording events and people, by way of digital, film, still, and video images.

Commercial/advertising art. Prepares students to communicate ideas and information to business and consumer audiences via illustrations and other media.

Communication disorders. The study of speech, language, hearing, and cognitive communication problems caused by disease, injury, or disability.

Communications. Explores human communication in a variety of formats, media, and contexts.

Communications systems installation/repair. Prepares students to assemble, operate, and fix one- and two-way communications equipment.

Communications technology. Prepares individuals to function within communications industries.

Community health services. Readies students to link health care and related social services with affected recipient communities.

Community health/preventative medicine. Prepares individuals to plan and manage health services in local community settings.

Community organization/advocacy. Prepares individuals to provide services to communities, organize communities for social action, and serve as community liaisons to public agencies.

Community psychology. Trains students to analyze social problems and implement intervention strategies for addressing these problems.

Community/junior college administration. Focuses on administration at community and junior colleges and related postsecondary systems.

Comparative literature. The study of the literatures of different societies and linguistic groups from a comparative perspective.

Comparative psychology. Focuses on the behavior of group members and the relationship of those behaviors to the group's evolutionary origins.

Comparative/international education. Compares educational practices and institutions within different countries, states, and societies.

Computational mathematics. Prepares students to apply mathematics to the theory, architecture, and design of computers, computational techniques, and algorithms.

Computer education. A program that prepares individuals to teach computer education programs.

Computer engineering. Prepares individuals to design and develop computer systems and to analyze specific problems related to computer applications.

Computer engineering technology. Provides practical training in the design, development, and maintenance of computer systems, networks, and installations.

Computer forensics. Focuses on the investigative techniques used to find and analyze data that has been electronically stored or encrypted on digital media.

Computer graphics. Studies the software and hardware used to represent, display, and manipulate topological, two-, and three-dimensional objects on a computer screen.

Computer hardware engineering. Readies students to design, develop, and evaluate computer hardware.

Computer hardware technology. Highlights the design of computer hardware and peripheral systems.

Computer installation and repair. Describes the application of technical skills to install and maintain computers.

Computer networking/telecommunications. Analyzes the management of linked computer systems, peripherals, and software to maximize efficiency and productivity.

Computer programming, general. Studies the writing and implementation of programs to drive operating systems and other applications, including instruction in software design, installation, and maintenance.

Computer programming, specific applications. Prepares individuals to devise customized solutions for problems presented by individual software users.

Computer science. Focuses on computers, computing problems and solutions, and the design of computer systems and user interfaces.

Computer software technology. Prepares students to aid in developing, implementing, and evaluating computer software and program applications.

Computer support specialist. Readies students to provide technical assistance to computer users by identifying and solving hardware and software problems.

Computer systems analysis. Trains students to design and implement large-scale computer applications and networking systems.

Computer systems technology. Includes instruction in basic computer design and architecture, programming, maintenance and inspection, and problem diagnosis and repair.

Computer typography. Prepares students to execute page formats, layouts, and text composition; and to make typographical selections using computer programs.

Computer/information sciences, general. Focuses on computing, computer science, and information science as part of an interdisciplinary program.

Computer/systems security. Readies students to assess the security needs of computer systems, recommend solutions, and manage security devices and procedures.

Concrete finishing. Trains individuals to prepare, construct, and finish buildings using masonry mixtures.

Conducting. Prepares students to lead bands, choirs, orchestras, and other ensembles in performance.

Conservation biology. Specifies conservation issues that result from advancing human social, economic, and industrial pressures.

Construction engineering. Studies the planning, design, and building of facilities and structures, including structural principles, site analysis, geology, materials, contracting, project management, and graphic communications.

Construction management. Readies students to coordinate the construction process from concept development through project completion on a timely and economical basis.

Construction site management. Prepares students to supervise, manage, and inspect construction sites and buildings.

Construction technology. Provides practical training in the planning, design, execution, and management of construction projects.

Construction trades. Focuses on the building, inspecting, and maintenance of structures.

Consumer economics. Prepares students to apply economic theories to consumer behavior and individual and family consumption of goods and services.

Consumer merchandising. Highlights product and service promotion from the consumer's perspective.

Consumer services/advocacy. Features the techniques needed to protect consumers from unsafe, unreliable, and/or unhealthy products and services.

Correctional facilities administration. Trains students to provide management services for institutional facilities that house and rehabilitate prisoners.

Corrections. The study of correctional science in preparation for becoming a corrections officer in an incarceration facility.

Cosmetic services. Trains students for licensed practice in hair cutting and styling, cosmetic preparations, manicures and pedicures, and facial treatments.

Cosmetology. Prepares grooming technicians to teach their specializations in schools of cosmetology and barbering.

Counseling psychology. Highlights the provision of therapeutic services to individuals and groups experiencing psychological problems and symptoms.

Counselor education. Prepares individuals to support student development and to organize guidance services within educational institutions.

Court reporting. Readies students to record examinations, testimony, judicial orders, and other proceedings via print or electronic methods.

Crafts/folk art/artisanry. Features the aesthetics and techniques for designing objects in the handcraft or folk art traditions.

Creative writing. Describes the composition of literary forms such as the short story, poetry, and the novel.

Credit management. Includes instruction in how to perform credit, collateral, and loan processing operations.

Criminal justice and law enforcement. Prepares students to apply theories and practices of criminal justice to the management of criminal justice agencies, including police departments and private protection services.

Criminal justice studies. Focuses on the criminal justice system, its components and processes, and its legal and public policy contexts.

Criminalistics/criminal science. Highlights the reconstruction of crimes and the analysis of physical evidence.

Criminology. Highlights crime as a sociopathological phenomenon, the behavior of criminals, and the social institutions developed to respond to crime.

Critical care nursing. Readies students to provide specialized care to patients with life-threatening problems.

Crop production. Prepares individuals to cultivate grain, fiber, forage, oilseed, fruits and nuts, vegetables, and other domesticated plant products.

Culinary arts and chef training. Prepares students to provide professional chef and related cooking services, with instruction in various cuisines, recipe and menu planning, cooking techniques, kitchen supervision, food supply management, and food presentation.

Culinary arts/related services. The general study of cooking and related culinary arts, including food preparation, cooking techniques, equipment operation, sanitation and safety, and food service management.

Cultural resource management. Readies students to preserve and protect cultural heritage sites and artifacts.

Curriculum/instruction. Includes instruction in curriculum theory, design, planning, and evaluation, as well as instructional material design and evaluation.

Customer service management. Prepares students to monitor customer service performance and manage frontline customer support services.

Cytogenetics/clinical genetics technology. Readies students to analyze human chromosomes for the research and diagnosis of genetic diseases, organ transplants, and cancer treatments.

Cytotechnology. Explores the change in body cells that may indicate the early development of cancers and other diseases.

Czech. Explores the languages, literatures, and cultures of the Czech people.

Dairy husbandry. Prepares students to manage the selection and care of dairy animals and associated dairy farm facilities.

Dairy science. Prepares students to produce and manage dairy animals and products.

Dance. Explores the cultural effects of dance and prepares students to perform in one or more of the dance disciplines.

Dance therapy. A course of study that applies creative dance movement to promote client rehabilitation and physical, emotional, and mental health.

Danish. Features the Danish language as used in Denmark and Greenland.

Data entry/applications. Prepares individuals to perform basic data and text entry using varied software products.

Data processing technology. Describes the use of computers and software packages for text processing, number processing, graphics, and database management.

Database design/management. Prepares individuals to design and manage databases, including the linking of data sets to create complex searchable databases and the use of analytical search tools.

Demography/population studies. Emphasizes population models, population phenomena, and related problems of social structure and behavior.

Dental assistant. Focuses on the provision of patient care, the preparation for procedures, and the completion of office functions under the supervision of dental professionals.

Dental clinical services. Generally prepares dentists in one or more of the oral sciences and advanced/graduate dentistry specialties.

Dental hygiene. Prepares individuals to clean teeth, provide oral health education, identify oral pathologies, and manage dental hygiene practices.

Dental laboratory technology. Trains students, under the supervision of dentists, to design and construct dental prostheses.

Dentistry (D.D.S., D.M.D.). Prepares students for the professional practice of dentistry, including the evaluation, diagnosis, prevention, and treatment of diseases, disorders, and conditions of the teeth and mouth.

Design/visual communications. Focuses on effectively communicating ideas and information, and packaging products, to business and consumer audiences.

Desktop publishing. Trains students to design the layout and typography of printed and electronic graphic and textual products.

Development economics. Defines economic development and its application to the problems of specific countries and regions.

Developmental biology/embryology. The scientific study of the development and growth of animals and human beings from fertilization to birth.

Developmental/child psychology. The study of the psychological growth and development of individuals from infancy through adulthood.

Diagnostic medical sonography. Features the utilization of medical ultrasound techniques to gather data used to diagnose a variety of conditions and diseases.

Diesel mechanics. Trains individuals to maintain diesel engines in vehicles, as well as stationary diesel engines in electrical generators.

Dietetic technician. Prepares individuals to implement nutritional and dietetic plans and to provide direct client services as certified dietitian technicians.

Dietetics. A program that trains students to design and manage effective nutrition programs in a variety of settings as a registered dietitian.

Dietician assistant. Trains students to assist in planning, preparing, and serving meals to individuals with specific dietary needs.

Digital art. Focuses on the use of the computer as the primary means of creating works of art, including photography, animation and video.

Digital media. Studies the development, use, and regulation of electronic communication technologies using computer applications.

Directing/theatrical production. Readies individuals to manage the planning, design, preparation, and production of theatrical entertainment programs.

Divinity/ministry (B.Div., M.Div.). Prepares individuals for ordination as ministers or priests in any of the Christian religious traditions.

Drafting and design technology. Features the application of technical skills to create working drawings and computer simulations for a variety of applications.

Drama and theater arts. Focuses on the general study of dramatic works and their performance.

Drama/dance teacher education. A program that prepares students to teach components of drama and/or dance.

Drawing. Highlights the expression of emotions, ideas, or inner visions through lines made on a surface.

Driver/safety education. The study of driver and safety education curricula.

Drywall installation. Describes how to install, tape, and plaster drywall installations in interior and exterior construction jobs.

Dutch/Flemish. Highlights the Dutch language as used in the Netherlands, Flemish-speaking Belgium, and Suriname.

E-commerce. Trains individuals to manage, supervise, and market electronic operations, products, and services provided on the Internet.

Early childhood education. Readies individuals to teach all relevant subject matter to students ranging in age from infancy through eight years.

Early childhood special education. A program that specifies teaching infants and preschool age children with special learning needs.

East Asian languages. Highlights one or more of the Sino-Tibetan, Japanese, and Korean languages of East Asia.

East Asian studies. Focuses on the history, society, politics, culture, and economics of China, Korea, Mongolia, Taiwan, Tibet, and related borderlands and island groups.

Ecology. Prepares students to relate small-scale biological systems, such as organisms, to complex and whole systems, and to the physical environment.

Econometrics/quantitative economics. Prepares students for the mathematical and statistical analysis of economic phenomena.

Economics. Covers the production, conservation, and allocation of resources, together with the organizational systems related to these processes.

Education of autistic. Prepares students to plan and implement educational services for children or adults who are autistic.

Education of blind/visually handicapped. Readies individuals to provide services for children or adults with visual disabilities.

Education of brain injured. Highlights educational services for students who are recovering from brain injuries that affect their cognitive, perceptive, and motor functions.

Education of Deaf/hearing impaired. Prepares students to provide educational services to Deaf and hard of hearing students at various grade levels.

Education of developmentally delayed. Readies individuals to provide educational services for students who exhibit slow social, physical, cognitive, or emotional growth patterns.

Education of emotionally handicapped. Readies students to provide educational services for individuals affected by emotional conditions.

Education of gifted/talented. Studies the provision of educational services and opportunities to individuals exhibiting exceptional intellectual or artistic talent, maturity, or social leadership skills.

Education of learning disabled. Characterizes various learning disabilities and the programs designed to address them.

Education of mentally handicapped. Characterizes mental disabilities that adversely affect educational performance and the programs designed to address them.

Education of multiple handicapped. Prepares students to design and provide educational services for individuals with multiple disabilities.

Education of physically handicapped. Describes orthopedic and other physical health impairments that affect students and their educational performance.

Education of speech impaired. Describes the design and provision of educational services for children or adults with speech impairments.

Education, general. Covers learning and teaching, educational psychology, educational activities, and the social foundations of education.

Educational assessment/testing. Prepares students to design, implement, and evaluate tests, and to assess teaching tools, strategies, and curricula.

Educational evaluation/research. Highlights procedures for generating information about educational programs, personnel and methods, and the analysis of such information for planning purposes.

Educational leadership/adminstration. The description of techniques for administering a wide variety of schools, to prepare individuals as general administrators and supervisors.

Educational psychology. Studies learning environments, their effects on behavior, and the effects of nonschool experience on the educational process.

Educational statistics/research methods. The application of statistics to the analysis of educational research problems, and the development of technical designs for research studies.

Educational superintendency. Prepares students to lead and manage multi-school educational systems and school districts.

Educational supervision. Includes instruction in staffing and organization, personnel relations, and administrative duties at the school building, facility, or staff level.

Electrical and communications engineering. Trains students to design, develop, and evaluate electrical, electronic, and related communications systems.

Electrical drafting/CAD/CADD. Readies students to design working schematics and representations in support of electrical/electronic engineers and computer engineers.

Electrical engineering technology. Includes instruction in electrical circuitry, prototype testing, systems analysis and maintenance, instrument calibration, and report preparation.

Electrician. Prepares students to install, operate, maintain, and repair electric systems, as well as DC and AC motors, controls, and electrical distribution panels.

Electrocardiograph technology. Readies individuals to administer EKG and ECG examinations, and to report results to the treatment team.

Electroencephalograph technology. Prepares students, under the supervision of a physician, to study and record electrical activity in the brain and nervous system.

Electromechanical technology. Prepares individuals to support engineers engaged in developing and testing automated, servomechanical, and other electromechanical systems.

Electronics/electrical equipment repair. The study of the operation, maintenance, and repair of electrical and electronic equipment.

Elementary education. Readies individuals to teach subject matter to students in grades kindergarten through grade eight.

Elementary/middle school administration. Prepares individuals to serve as principals and masters of elementary and middle schools.

Emergency care attendant (EMT ambulance). Readies individuals to assist EMTs to transport patients and operate emergency vehicles and equipment.

Emergency management/homeland security. An inter-disciplinary field drawing on the social, natural and applied sciences to prepare students for careers in disaster preparedness, response, and recovery.

Emergency medical technology (EMT paramedic). Prepares students to recognize, assess, and manage medical emergencies in prehospital settings, and to supervise ambulance personnel.

Endocrinology. Covers the development and secretion of protein compounds by cells and glands, and the role of endocrine substances in bodily processes.

Energy systems technology. Readies students to support engineers engaged in the development of energy-efficient systems or monitoring energy use.

Engine machinist. Focuses on the construction of automotive and commercial vehicle engines.

Engineering mechanics. Investigates the behavior of structures, forces, and materials in engineering problems.

Engineering physics. Prepares individuals to apply the principles of physics to the analysis of engineering problems.

Engineering science. Focuses on the general application of various mathematical and scientific principles to the analysis and evaluation of engineering problems.

Engineering technology, general. A program that readies individuals to apply basic engineering principles and technical skills in support of engineers engaged in a wide variety of projects.

Engineering, general. Prepares individuals to solve a wide variety of practical problems in industry, social organizations, and commerce.

Engineering/industrial management. Covers the planning and operational management of industrial and manufacturing operations.

English composition. Investigates English vocabulary, grammar, morphology, syntax, and semantics, and the techniques used to express ideas in written forms.

English language and literature. Explores the English language, including its history and structure, and the literature and culture of English-speaking peoples.

English literature (British). Studies the literature of the English speaking peoples of Britain and the British Commonwealth from the origins of the English language to the present.

English teacher education. Studies the teaching of English grammar, composition, and literature programs.

Entomology. The scientific study of insects.

Entrepreneurial studies. Prepares students to perform development, marketing, and management functions associated with owning a business, and to recognize, evaluate, and respond to new business opportunities.

Environmental biology. Focuses on living populations in relation to changing environmental processes.

Environmental design. Prepares students to design total environments and living systems, both indoor and outdoor.

Environmental engineering. Studies the design, development, and evaluation of environmental systems, including pollution control, waste and hazardous material disposal, health and safety protection, and conservation.

Environmental engineering technology. Investigates the development and use of indoor and outdoor environmental pollution control systems.

Environmental health. The study of environmental factors affecting human health.

Environmental psychology. Investigates ways in which to improve the behavioral interactions between human beings and the environment.

Environmental science. Applies various scientific principles to the study of the physical environment and the solution of environmental problems.

Environmental studies. Studies environment-related issues using a combination of scientific, social, or humanistic approaches.

Environmental toxicology. Focuses on the effects of exposure to toxic chemicals, pollutants, and biohazards, the management of environmental toxins, and the development of protective measures.

Epidemiology. Studies the distribution and prevention of disease across populations.

Equestrian studies. Focuses on the horse, horsemanship, and related businesses, facilities, and equipment, and the training of horses and riders.

ESL teacher education. Studies the principles and practice of teaching English to students who are not proficient in the language or who do not speak, read, or write English.

Ethics. Investigates the theory of moral good and its application to various theoretical and practical problems.

Ethnic studies, general. An interdisciplinary study of the various minority groups in the United States and the many meanings of diversity.

European history. Studies the development of European society, culture, and institutions from its origins to the present.

European studies. Focuses on the history, society, politics, culture, and economics of the European continent.

Evolutionary biology. Describes the emergence and changes of organisms and species over time.

Executive assistant. Trains individuals to function as special assistants and/or personal secretaries for business executives and top management.

Exercise physiology. Explores the processes involved in physical or motor activity.

Exercise sciences. Focuses on the anatomy, physiology, biochemistry, and biophysics of human movement, and applications to exercise and therapeutic rehabilitation.

Experimental psychology. Investigates behavior under experimental conditions and analyzes controlled behavioral responses.

Facial treatment. Studies massage and treatment of the face, scalp, and neck.

Facilities/event planning. Prepares students to become facility and event managers and workplace consultants.

Family and consumer sciences. Studies family, work, and community settings and how people relate to their physical, social, emotional, and intellectual environments.

Family practice nurse/nurse practitioner. Readies registered nurses to provide independent general care for family groups and individuals.

Family psychology. Readies students to provide therapeutic, evaluative, and research services to families and individuals in the family unit context.

Family resource management studies. Includes instruction in financial goal-setting and management, preventing and resolving financial difficulties, and the use of relevant public resources.

Family systems. Highlights the family in its development and its significance as a system that impacts individuals and society.

Family/community services. Focuses on the development and implementation of support services for individuals, families, and localities.

Family/consumer business sciences. Investigates the relationship between the economy and the consuming individual and family.

Family/consumer sciences education. Readies students to teach vocational home economics programs.

Farm and ranch management. Prepares individuals to manage farms, ranches, or similar enterprises.

Fashion and apparel design. Trains students to design commercial fashions, apparel, and accessories, and to manage fashion development projects.

Fashion merchandising. Readies students to promote fashion product lines/brands and to organize promotional campaigns to attract retailer interest, wholesale purchasing, and supply contracts.

Fashion modeling. Highlights the display of fashion apparel and accessories in wholesale and retail settings.

Fashion/fabric consultant. Readies individuals to assist in fashion selection, style coordination, sales, fabric selection, clothing specifications, and purchasing.

Fiber/textile arts. Readies students to construct designs from woven or nonwoven fabrics and fibrous materials.

Filipino/Tagalog. Emphasizes the modern Filipino/Tagalog language as used in the Philippines.

Film/cinema studies. The study of film/video arts, as well as the basic principles of filmmaking and film production.

Finance. Readies students to plan, manage, and analyze the financial aspects and performance of business enterprises or banking institutions.

Financial planning. Prepares individuals to plan and manage the financial interests and growth of individuals and institutions.

Fine/studio arts. Prepares individuals to function as creative artists in the visual and plastic media.

Fire protection and safety technology. Studies the application of fire prevention and control skills to loss limitation, substance removal, and fire investigations.

Fire services administration. Prepares students to structure, manage, direct, and control fire departments, prevention services, and inspection and investigation offices.

Firefighting/fire science. Readies individuals to perform the duties of firefighters.

Fishing and fisheries. The scientific study of the husbandry and production of fish and shellfish populations for commercial and recreational purposes, and the management of fishing and related product processing.

Flight attendant. Readies students to perform a variety of personal services conducive to the safety and comfort of airline passengers during flight.

Flight instructor. Prepares individuals to train pilots and flight crews to fly and/or operate commercial, corporate, agricultural, public service, or rescue aircraft.

Floriculture. Explores the operation and management of florist enterprises, supply and delivery services, and flower catering services.

Food and nutrition studies. A general program that focuses on the role of foods and nutrition in human health and wellness.

Food preparation. Trains students to serve as kitchen support staff and food preparation workers.

Food science. Studies the conversion of raw agricultural products into processed forms suitable for human consumption.

Food service. Includes instruction in table and counter services, dining room operations, personnel supervision, safety, and sanitation.

Food technology/processing. Describes the manufacturing, packaging, storage, and distribution technologies and processes for food products.

Foreign language teacher education. Instructs individuals how to teach foreign languages other than French, German, or Spanish.

Foreign languages, general. A program that studies multiple foreign languages at the basic/elementary level.

Forensic chemistry. The application of chemical analysis to the investigation of crime scenes or other events.

Forensic psychology. Prepares individuals to apply clinical, counseling, and neuropsychological skills to criminal investigations.

Forensic science. Trains students to apply physical, biomedical, and social sciences to analyze physical evidence, human testimony, and criminal suspects.

Forest engineering. Highlights the mechanical devices and processes used for efficient forest management, timber production, and related systems.

Forest management. Prepares individuals for the management and administration of forest lands and related resources.

Forest resources production. Prepares students to perform technical and managerial functions as they relate to the production, harvesting, and processing of forest resources.

Forest sciences/biology. The study of environmental factors affecting forests and the growth and management of forest resources.

Forest technology. Readies individuals to assist foresters in the management and production of forest resources.

Forestry. Features the management and development of forest areas for economic, recreational, and ecological purposes.

Franchise operations. Trains individuals to manage and operate franchises.

French. The study of the language and literature of French-speaking peoples, including related dialects and creoles.

French studies. Describes the history, society, politics, culture, and economics of France.

French teacher education. Describes how to teach French language programs.

Funeral direction. Prepares individuals for professional licensure as managers of funeral homes and cemeteries.

Funeral services/mortuary science. Describes the basic elements of mortuary science, the funeral service business, and counseling.

Furniture design/manufacturing. Readies individuals to design furniture projects; assemble, finish, and repair furniture articles; and use hand and power tools.

Game design . Prepares students to apply the artistic and technical skills needed to design and develop computer games.

Gay/lesbian studies. The study of homosexuality and the public policies and legal issues surrounding the gay and lesbian community.

Gene therapy. Describes the treatment of diseases and inherited abnormalities through the modification of gene expression.

Genetic counseling. Readies students to counsel patients and families concerning inherited genetic disorders and diseases.

Genetics. The study of biological inheritance, development, disease, and evolution in all living organisms and viruses.

Geochemistry. Investigates the properties and behavior of the substances forming, and formed by, geomorphological processes of the earth and other planets.

Geography. Highlights the spatial distribution and interrelationships of people, natural resources, and plant and animal life.

Geography teacher education. Describes teaching geography at various grade levels.

Geological engineering. Prepares students to apply geological analysis to engineering problems, such as environmental recovery sites, or the geological forces acting upon structures.

Geology/earth science. The scientific study of the earth, the forces acting upon it, and the behavior of the solids, liquids, and gases comprising it.

Geophysics/seismology. The scientific study of the physics of solids and its application to the study of the earth.

Geotechnical engineering. Explores the systems used to manipulate and control surface and subsurface features at or incorporated into structural sites.

German. Highlights the German language as used in Austria, Germany, and Switzerland.

German studies. Focuses on the history, society, politics, culture, and economics of the Germanic peoples.

German teacher education. Prepares students to teach German language programs at various educational levels.

Germanic languages. A general program that focuses on one or more of the Germanic languages of Western, Central, and Northern Europe.

Gerontology. Investigates the aging process and aged human populations.

Geropsychology. Investigates the psychology of aging populations, with reference to growth and decline across the life span.

GIS technology. Prepares students to learn a system for capturing, storing, analyzing and managing data and associated attributes which are spatially referenced to the Earth.

Glazier. Readies individuals to install and repair fixtures, sheets, windows, and skylights made of glass or Plexiglas.

Global studies. Investigates global and international issues from the perspective of the social sciences and social services.

Golf management. Studies the principles and skills needed to manage golf facilities and related organizations of the golf industry.

Graphic communications. Provides technical training in the manufacture, distribution, or transmission of graphic communications, including prepress, press, and postpress operations.

Graphic design. Readies students to use artistic and computer techniques to convey technical and commercial concepts through images and typography.

Graphic/printing production. Prepares students to apply technical knowledge to perform a variety of commercial and industrial graphic communications jobs.

Greenhouse operations. Investigates the production and storage of plant species in controlled indoor environments for sale or research purposes.

Gunsmithing. Highlights the making and modification of firearms.

Hair styling. Readies individuals to shampoo, style, and set hair, and apply hair cosmetics and wigs.

Hazardous materials information systems. Readies individuals to implement, monitor, and enforce hazardous materials management and removal.

Hazardous materials technology. Focuses on basic engineering principles to aid in identifying and disposing of hazardous materials.

Health aide. Readies individuals to provide supervised care to patients, and/or perform maintenance and general assistance in health care facilities.

Health care administration. Readies individuals to develop, plan, and manage health care operations and services within health care facilities.

Health communications. Explores how people understand health and illness and the media's role in shaping health care messages.

Health management/clinical assistant. Prepares students to perform office services and clinical specialties under the supervision of physicians, nurses, or other health care professionals.

Health occupations teacher education. Trains students to teach specific vocational health occupations programs.

Health physics/radiologic health. A program of study that applies nuclear science and engineering physics to diagnostic, treatment, and therapeutic processes, and to public health protection.

Health services. Prepares for entry into specialized training programs or for concentrations in the allied health area.

Health services administration. Readies students to plan and manage health services delivery systems in the public and private sectors.

Health teacher education. Prepares individuals to educate students about health-related topics.

Health unit coordinator. Readies individuals to perform administrative and reception duties in a patient care unit.

Health unit manager. Prepares students to supervise and coordinate the operations of patient care units.

Health/medical psychology. Studies health, illness, and recovery, from the perspective that these phenomena arise from a combination of physical, behavioral, and social conditions.

Health/physical fitness. Readies students to promote physical fitness and athletic prowess, and to accomplish related research and service goals.

Heating/air conditioning/refrigeration maintenance. Describes the maintenance of heating, air conditioning, and refrigeration systems.

Heating/air conditioning/refrigeration technology. Focuses on the development and installation of air conditioning, refrigeration, and heating systems.

Heavy equipment maintenance. Trains individuals to repair and overhaul heavy equipment.

Heavy/earthmoving equipment operation. Trains students to operate and maintain heavy construction equipment involved in digging, sloping, grading, stripping, backfilling, clearing, and excavating.

Hebrew. Explores the Hebrew language in either premodern or modern forms.

Herbalism. A program that utilizes herbal medicines to prevent and cure illnesses and temporary physical disorders.

Higher education administration. Prepares students to become administrators in four-year colleges, universities, and higher education systems.

Hindu studies. A program that defines the philosophies, religious history, and cultural and social manifestations of Hinduism.

Histologic assistant. Readies individuals to process tissue samples and perform routine histologic procedures and tests.

Histologic technology. Trains students to identify tissue and cell components and relate these findings to physiological functions and to the detection and diagnoses of diseases.

Historic preservation. Studies the process of saving and restoring old structures for contemporary use.

History. The study and interpretation of the past.

History of science/technology. Describes the historical evolution of scientific theories and science applications and technologies.

History teacher education. Prepares students how to teach history programs at various educational levels.

Holocaust studies. Investigates acts of genocide in human history with particular reference to twentieth-century genocides.

Home furnishings. Includes instruction in selecting, purchasing, designing, and decorating home furnishings; floral design; accessory construction; textiles; and upholstery.

Home health attendant. Highlights the provision of support services for homebound disabled, recovering, or elderly people.

Homeopathic medicine. Features a system that uses natural substances in highly diluted forms to mimic symptoms of illness and trigger autoimmune responses.

Horse husbandry/equine science. Trains students in the care and maintenance of horses and of horse farms, stables, and tracks.

Horticultural science. Focuses on the scientific principles related to the cultivation of garden and ornamental plants, including fruits, vegetables, flowers, and landscape and nursery plants.

Horticulture. Describes the production of domesticated plants, shrubs, flowers, trees, and groundcover, and the management of horticultural services.

Hospital/health care facilities administration. Prepares students to administer hospitals, clinics, nursing homes, and other health care facilities.

Hospitality administration and management. Prepares students to serve as general managers of hospitality operations in the travel, lodging, food service, and recreation industries.

Hospitality/recreation marketing. Focuses on the provision of marketing services in the hospitality and leisure fields.

Hotel/motel administration/management. Prepares individuals to oversee operations and facilities that provide lodging services to travelers.

Housing and human environments. The study of the behavioral, social, economic, functional, and aesthetic aspects of housing, interiors, and other environments.

Human development and family studies. Studies human development and behavioral characteristics of the individual within the context of the family.

Human nutrition. Highlights the relationships between food consumption and human development and health.

Human resources development. Readies students to manage and evaluate programs to improve individual productivity, employability and job satisfaction, and organizational effectiveness.

Human resources management. Prepares students to manage the development of personnel in organizations, including recruitment, staffing, training, performance management, compensation, labor relations, and health and safety.

Human sciences communication. Focuses on communication of human sciences subject matter to various audiences through print and non-print media.

Human services. Explores the provision of human and social services to individuals and communities.

Human/medical genetics. Describes human genetics as they relate to diagnosis, genetic engineering and therapy, transplantation, and diseases and their defense.

Humanities. Combined studies in the humanities, emphasizing languages, literatures, art, music, philosophy, and religion.

Hydraulics technology. Includes instruction in hydraulics principles, pipeline and pumping systems, operational testing, and inspection and maintenance procedures.

Hydrology/water resources science. The study of the circulation, distribution, chemical and physical properties, and environmental interaction of surface and subsurface waters.

Illustration. Highlights artistic techniques to portray the concepts of authors and designers to specifications.

Industrial design. Readies individuals to convey information through forms, shapes, and packaging for manufactured products.

Industrial electronics technology. Trains individuals to assemble, manage, and service industrial electrical/electronic equipment.

Industrial engineering. Prepares students to design systems for managing industrial production processes.

Industrial equipment maintenance/repair. Readies students to fix and sustain the operation of industrial machinery and equipment.

Industrial radiologic technology. Focuses on the operation of industrial and research testing equipment using radioisotopes.

Industrial safety technology. Prepares students to implement and enforce industrial safety standards.

Industrial technology. Includes instruction in organizational behavior, industrial planning, computer applications, and report and presentation preparation.

Industrial/organizational psychology. Examines individual and group behavior in industrial and organizational settings.

Information resources management. Prepares students to plan, manage, and evaluate information services in organizations.

Information systems. Focuses on the theory and process of information collection, transmission, and utilization in traditional and electronic forms.

Information technology. Highlights the design of technological information systems as solutions to business, research, and communications support needs.

Inorganic chemistry. Covers elements and their compounds, other than the hydrocarbons and their derivatives.

Institutional food production. Focuses on the management of food service operations in institutional settings.

Institutional food service. Provides instruction in the production and service used in institutional food establishments.

Instructional media. Focuses on the techniques of creating instructional products and educational resources in various media formats.

Instrumentation technology. Readies students to apply basic engineering principles in support of engineers engaged in developing measurement systems and procedures.

Insurance. Trains individuals to manage risk in organizational settings and provide insurance and risk-aversion services to businesses and individuals.

Intercultural/diversity studies. Examines the social relations between and among majority and minority groups, and ways to promote cooperation, tolerance, and management of diversity issues.

Interior architecture. Prepares students to apply architectural principles in the design of structural interiors for living, working, and leisure purposes.

Interior design. Readies individuals to plan, design, equip, and furnish interior spaces.

International agriculture. Studies the problems of global food production and distribution, and the agricultural systems of other countries.

International business. Trains individuals to oversee international business operations.

International economics. Prepares individuals to analyze international commercial behavior and trade policy.

International finance. Trains students to manage international financial operations and related currency transactions.

International marketing. Readies students to perform marketing techniques for enterprises engaged in exporting or importing goods and services in world markets.

International public health. Focuses on public health problems in poor and developing countries and regions.

International relations. The study of international politics and institutions, and the conduct of diplomacy and foreign policy.

Investments/securities. A program that prepares students to oversee assets placed in capital markets.

Iranian/Persian languages. A program that focuses on the languages used in ancient, medieval, and modern Iran.

Ironworking. Readies individuals to make and install ornamental and reinforcing metal structures and supports.

Islamic studies. The study of the history, culture, and interpretation of the Islamic faith.

Italian. Explores the Italian language and its applications in varied settings.

Italian studies. Highlights the history, society, politics, culture, and economics of modern Italy.

Japanese. The study of Japanese literature, language, and dialects.

Japanese studies. Features the history, society, politics, culture, and economics of Japan.

Jazz studies. Studies the performance and composition of jazz.

Journalism. Focuses on gathering, processing, and delivering news.

Judaic studies. Focuses on the history, culture, and religion of the Jewish people.

Juvenile corrections. Studies the provision of correction services to underage populations.

Kindergarten/preschool education. Trains individuals to instruct students ranging in age from three to six years, in settings prior to beginning regular elementary school.

Kinesiotherapy. Readies individuals to treat the effects of disease, injury, and congenital disorders through exercise and education.

Knowledge management. The study of knowledge management in government agencies and corporations for the purpose of supporting stated goals and objectives.

Korean. The study of Korean literature, language, and dialects.

Korean studies. Examines the history, society, politics, culture, and economics of Korea.

Labor studies. Highlights work, labor organization, policy, and movements from the perspective of the social sciences and history.

Labor/industrial relations. The study of employee-management interactions and the management of issues regarding working conditions and worker benefit packages.

LAN/WAN management. A program that prepares students to oversee and regulate computer systems and performance requirements of an entire network of satellite users, including local and wide area networks.

Land use planning. Focuses on how land can be preserved, developed, and used for maximum social, economic, and environmental benefit.

Landscape architecture. Prepares students for the professional practice of landscape architecture, with instruction in geology and hydrology; soils, groundcovers, and horticultural elements; site planning; and landscape design.

Landscaping/groundskeeping. Describes the maintenance of ornamental and recreational plants and related conceptual designs.

Language interpretation/translation. Highlights the interpretation and/or translation of documents and data files, either from English or (Canadian) French into another language or vice versa.

Laser/optical technology. Readies individuals to support engineers in the development and use of lasers and other optical instruments for commercial or research purposes.

Latin. Features the Latin language and literature and its current ecclesiastical usage.

Latin American studies. Features the history, society, politics, culture, and economics of the North and South American continents outside Canada and the United States.

Latin teacher education. A program that prepares individuals to teach Latin at various grade levels.

Law (J.D.). Preparation for the independent practice of law, taking bar examinations, and advanced research in jurisprudence.

Legal administrative assistance. Instruction includes legal terminology, research, and documentation; software applications; and office procedures.

Legal studies. Applies the social sciences and humanities to the study of law and legal issues.

Liberal arts and sciences. A program that is a structured combination of the arts, sciences, and humanities, emphasizing breadth of study.

Library assistance. Includes instruction in library operation and services; acquisition, storage, and display systems; and material retrieval.

Library science. Prepares individuals for professional service as librarians and information consultants.

Licensed midwifery. Readies individuals to provide for prenatal, natural birth, and immediate postpartum care to pregnant women.

Licensed practical nursing. Prepares students, under the direction of a registered nurse, physician, or dentist, to assist in providing general nursing care.

Lineworker. Describes how to install, operate, maintain, and repair electric power cables; erect and construct pole and tower lines; and install underground cables.

Linguistics. The study of language, language development, and the relationships among languages and language groups.

Livestock management. Readies individuals to produce and manage livestock animals and the production and handling of meat and other products.

Locksmithing. Trains students to open locks, make keys, enter and change lock and safe combinations, and install and repair safes.

Logic. The systematic study of valid inference, argument, and sound reasoning.

Logistics/materials management. Prepares individuals to coordinate all logistical functions within an enterprise, such as acquisitions, receiving and handling, storage, allocation of resources, quality control, and shipping.

Machine shop technology. Trains students to make and modify metal parts used in manufacturing, repair, or design activities.

Machine tool technology. Prepares individuals to manufacture, assemble, test, and repair parts, mechanisms, and machines.

Make-up artist. Prepares students to apply cosmetics and perform specialized makeovers including wig work, masking, and related costuming for professional, artistic, security, or leisure purposes.

Management information systems. Readies individuals to manage data systems for processing and retrieving internal business information, to select systems, and to train personnel.

Management science. Highlights the application of mathematical modeling, programming, forecasting, and operations techniques to the analysis of business organization and performance problems.

Manicurist. Readies students to shape fingernails and toenails, remove unwanted skin, and apply polish and cosmetics to nails.

Manufacturing engineering. Includes instruction in the design, development, and implementation of manufacturing systems.

Manufacturing technologies. Covers the basic engineering principles used to identify and resolve production problems in the manufacturing process.

Marine biology. Emphasizes marine organisms and their interactions with the physical environment.

Marine engineering/naval architecture. Prepares individuals to design vessels operating on or under the water, and to analyze related engineering problems.

Marine maintenance/fitter/ship repair. Prepares students to repair vessel components and mechanical devices, maintain sails, and repair and balance propeller and drive shafts.

Marine science. An interdisciplinary study of all aspects of the ocean, making use of both the biological and the physical sciences.

Maritime technology/Merchant Marine. Prepares individuals to serve as captains, executive officers, engineers, and ranking mates on commercially licensed vessels.

Marketing. Prepares students to manage the development of consumer audiences and the delivery of products from producers to consumers.

Marketing research. A program that readies individuals to describe consumer behavior patterns and market environments to marketing managers.

Marriage/family therapy. Trains individuals to diagnose mental and emotional disorders within marriages and family systems, and to apply short- and long-term therapeutic strategies.

Masonry. Focuses on the laying or setting of brick, concrete block, hard tile, and marble, using hand tools.

Massage therapy. Prepares individuals to apply manual techniques for manipulating skin, muscles, and connective tissues.

Materials engineering. Focuses on the design, development and evaluation of materials used in manufacturing, the synthesis of new materials, and the analysis of materials requirements.

Materials science. Focuses on the analysis and evaluation of the characteristics and behavior of solids.

Maternal/child health. Emphasizes public health issues affecting women, children, and families.

Maternal/child health nursing. Informs registered nurses how to provide prenatal care to pregnant women and to mothers and their newborn infants.

Mathematical statistics/probability. Focuses on the mathematical theory underlying the use of statistical methods.

Mathematics. A general program that analyzes quantities, magnitudes, forms, and their relationships, using symbolic logic and language.

Mathematics teacher education. Prepares individuals to teach mathematical subjects.

Mathematics/computer science. A program with a general synthesis of mathematics and computer science, or a specialization that draws from mathematics and computer science.

Meat cutting. Prepares individuals to receive, cut, and package animal meat products in commercial establishments.

Mechanical drafting/CAD/CADD. Trains individuals to prepare working drawings and electronic simulations in support of mechanical and industrial engineers.

Mechanical engineering. Focuses on the design and development of mechanical devices and systems, including physical systems used in manufacturing; engines; power units; hydraulics; and the integration of computers and remote control with operating systems.

Mechanical engineering technology. Provides practical training in the design, development, and implementation of engineering projects involving mechanical systems.

Mechanics/repairers, general. Emphasizes the application of technical skills in the adjustment, maintenance, part replacement, and repair of tools, equipment, and machines.

Media studies. Analyzes the criticism of media, how people understand media, and the roles of media in transforming culture.

Medical administrative assistant. Prepares students to provide administrative assistance to physicians and other health professionals.

Medical claims examiner. Readies students to investigate, analyze, and evaluate medical/health insurance claims.

Medical illustrating. Focuses on the creation of visual materials to facilitate educational, research, and clinical purposes.

Medical informatics. Prepares individuals to apply computer science to medical research and clinical support, and to develop advanced imaging, database, and decision systems.

Medical insurance coding specialist. Trains students to conduct data entry, classification, and record-keeping procedures related to medical insurance documentation.

Medical insurance specialist. Covers the management of insurance operations in a medical office, facility, or organization.

Medical office administration. Focuses on the management of business functions in a medical or clinical office.

Medical office assistant. Trains individuals to perform routine administrative duties in a medical, clinical, or health care facility office.

Medical office computer specialist. Readies individuals to install, maintain, and upgrade medical software and associated hardware.

Medical radiologic technology/radiation therapy. Readies students to administer prescribed radiation treatments, manage patients, and maintain pertinent records.

Medical receptionist. Readies students to provide customer service, visitor reception, and patient services.

Medical records administration. Readies individuals to plan, design, and manage systems, processes, and facilities used to collect, store, analyze, and transmit medical records and related information.

Medical records technology. Trains individuals to classify, construct, and secure medical records under the supervision of health information administrators.

Medical scientist. Prepares graduated physicians as research scientists in various areas.

Medical staff services technology. Prepares individuals to provide personnel management, credentialing, and accreditation compliance services for health care facilities and organizations.

Medical transcription. Prepares students to execute verbatim medical minutes, reports, and orders.

Medical/clinical assistant. Readies students to support physicians by providing assistance during patient consultations and examinations.

Medication aide. Prepares students to administer prescribed medications, report patient reactions, and perform emergency and recording duties.

Medicinal/pharmaceutical chemistry. Explores the properties of compounds intended for medicinal applications, and the development of related research methods and clinical trial procedures.

Medicine (M.D.). Prepares individuals for the independent professional practice of medicine as licensed physicians.

Medieval and Renaissance studies. Explores the medieval and Renaissance periods in Europe from the perspective of the humanities and social sciences.

Medium/heavy vehicle technology. Highlights the specialized maintenance of commercial and industrial vehicles, such as trucks and buses.

Mental health counseling. Trains students to evaluate, refer, and counsel people to prevent or mediate personal conflicts and emotional crises.

Mental health services technology. Prepares individuals to assist psychiatrists, psychologists, and nurses in patient care and treatment.

Merchandising/buying operations. Prepares students to function as professional buyers of resale products and product lines for stores, chains, and other retail enterprises.

Metal building assembly. Highlights the construction of metal structures using prefabricated framing and siding components.

Metal/jewelry arts. Trains individuals to fashion artwork from gems and other stones and precious metals.

Metallurgical engineering. Covers the metal components of structural, power, transmission, and moving systems, and the analysis of engineering problems.

Metallurgical technology. Trains students to support metallurgists engaged in developing and using industrial metals and manufacturing processes.

Meteorology. Readies students to predict atmospheric motion and climate change.

Microbiology. The study of small organisms, including bacteria and viruses, as distinguished from the cellular material of larger organisms.

Middle school education. Trains individuals to guide students in the middle, intermediate, or junior high grades.

Military technologies. Prepares individuals, for various responsibilities in the armed services and related national security organizations.

Mining and mineral engineering. Studies the evaluation of mineral extraction and refining systems, including open shaft mines and prospecting equipment.

Mining technology. Prepares individuals to support engineers engaged in the development and operation of mines and related mineral processing facilities.

Missionary studies. The theory and practice of religious outreach, social service, and proselytization.

Modern Greek. A program that focuses on the development and use of the Greek language.

Molecular biochemistry. Describes the chemical processes of living organisms at the molecular level.

Molecular biology. Investigates the structure and function of biological macromolecules, with emphasis on proteins and nucleic acids, and processes such as metabolism, gene function and regulation, differentiation, and development.

Molecular biophysics. Applies physics principles to the study of living cells and organisms at the molecular level.

Molecular genetics. Covers the molecular structure and processes that regulate gene expression, information transfer, replication, and stability.

Molecular pharmacology. Highlights characteristics of drugs at the molecular level and their interaction with, and effects on, microbiological structures and processes.

Molecular physiology. Focuses on the scientific study of biochemical communications and processes at the subcellular level.

Molecular toxicology. Describes the interaction of toxic agents with biological systems at the molecular and cellular levels.

Montessori teacher education. Highlights the pedagogical principles and methods developed by Maria Montessori and her followers.

Mortuary science/embalming. Prepares students for licensure as embalmers and morticians, with instruction in embalming, restorative art, laws and regulations, and special services.

Motorcycle maintenance. Prepares students to fix motorcycles and other similarly powered vehicles.

Movement therapy. Prepares individuals to promote body awareness and optimal mental and physical functioning.

Multicultural education. Highlights the design and implementation of instructional and advising services for culturally diverse learning populations.

Multimedia. Prepares students to display ideas in either two or three dimensions, through the simultaneous use of a variety of materials and media.

Museum studies. Prepares individuals to develop, conserve, and retrieve artifacts, exhibits, and collections in museums and galleries.

Music history/literature. Highlights the evolution of music, the development of musical instruments, and the analysis and criticism of musical literature.

Music management. Explores the organization and management of music operations, facilities, personnel, bands, ensembles, and individual artists.

Music pedagogy. Studies the provision of musical instruction and tutoring to clients in private and institutional settings.

Music performance. Prepares individuals to master musical instruments or to sing, and to become solo and/or ensemble performers.

Music teacher education. Prepares individuals to teach music and music appreciation.

Music theory and composition. The study of the structures and processes of music, and the art of writing and arranging music.

Music therapy. Highlights the utilization of music to address patients' physical, psychological, cognitive, emotional, and social needs.

Music, general. An introductory study and appreciation of music and the performing arts.

Musical instrument fabrication/repair. Describes the fabrication, repair, maintenance, and tuning of musical instruments.

Musical theater. Studies acting, singing, dancing, lighting and set design, and costuming to prepare for musical performances.

Musicology/ethnomusicology. The study of the forms, methods, and functions of music in Western and non-Western societies and cultures.

Nanotechnology. A scientific field focused on building machines on the scale of molecules.

Native American education. Prepares individuals to provide teaching and administrative services to American Indian, Alaska Native, and Hawaiian Native students that attend Tribal/First Nation schools.

Native American languages. A program that focuses on the languages native to the Western Hemisphere, with an emphasis on American Indian languages and literatures.

Native American studies. Highlights the history, sociology, politics, culture, and economics of the American Indian, Aleut, Inuit, and Hawaiian peoples.

Natural resource economics. Applies economic concepts and methods to the analysis of issues such as pollution, land use planning, waste disposal, and conservation policies.

Natural resources and conservation. Focuses on the natural environment and its conservation, use, and improvement.

Natural resources management/policy. Readies students to plan, manage, and evaluate programs to protect and regulate natural habitats and resources.

Natural sciences. A combined or undifferentiated focus on one or more of the physical and biological sciences.

Naturopathic medicine. Describes an approach that combines medical knowledge with noninvasive therapies and emphasizes disease prevention, wellness, and self-healing.

Near and Middle Eastern studies. Covers the history, society, politics, culture, and economics of North Africa, Southwestern Asia, Asia Minor, and the Arabian Peninsula.

Neuroanatomy. Focuses on the scientific study of the structure and function of the brain and central nervous system.

Neurobiology/physiology. Describes the neural functions and control of physiological systems in animals and humans.

Neuropharmacology. Focuses on drugs that modify brain function, the human body, and behavior, and the development of treatment therapies.

Neuroscience. Investigates the molecular, structural, cognitive, and behavioral aspects of the brain and nervous system.

Nonprofit/public organization management. Readies individuals to manage the business affairs of foundations, educational institutions, associations, public agencies, or governmental operations.

Norwegian. The study of the language and related dialects of the Norwegian-speaking peoples.

Nuclear engineering. Focuses on systems for controlling and manipulating nuclear energy and the analysis of related engineering problems.

Nuclear engineering technology. Readies individuals to support engineers operating nuclear facilities and engaged in nuclear applications and safety procedures.

Nuclear medical technology. Features the employment of nuclides in evaluations and therapeutic applications, while monitoring for patient health and safety.

Nuclear physics. The scientific study of the properties and behavior of atomic nuclei.

Nuclear power technology. Readies individuals to support engineers in the running of nuclear reactors, and in nuclear materials processing and disposal.

Nurse anesthetist. Teaches registered nurses how to administer anesthetics and provide care for patients before, during, and after anesthesia.

Nurse midwifery. Readies registered nurses to independently deliver babies and treat mothers in the prenatal, delivery, and post-delivery periods.

Nursery operations. Studies the management of plant farms, nurseries, and facilities that develop domesticated plant products for propagation, harvesting, and transplantation.

Nursing (RN). Provides instruction in the knowledge, techniques, and procedures for promoting health and providing care for the sick and disabled, and preparation for licensure as a registered nurse.

Nursing administration. Prepares registered nurses to manage nursing personnel and services in hospitals and other health agencies.

Nursing assistant. Readies individuals, under the training and supervision of a registered nurse or licensed practical nurse, to provide nursing-related services to patients.

Nursing science. The study of clinical practices, research methodologies, and the administration of complex nursing services.

Nutrition sciences. Focuses on the utilization of food for human growth and metabolism in both normal and dysfunctional states.

Occupational health/industrial hygiene. Trains students to monitor and evaluate health and related safety standards in the workplace.

Occupational safety/health technology. Features the maintenance of job-related health and safety standards.

Occupational therapy. Prepares students to maximize patient independence and health through a mix of skills, motivation, environmental adaptations, and assistive technologies.

Occupational therapy assistant. Focuses on aiding occupational therapists by providing assistance during examinations and treatments and by keeping patient records.

Occupational/environmental health nursing. A program that prepares registered nurses to deliver nursing services to worker populations in clinical settings and at job sites.

Ocean engineering. Describes how to plan, design, and evaluate systems that monitor, control, and operate within coastal and ocean environments.

Oceanography. Features the chemical components, mechanisms, and movement of ocean waters and their interactions with terrestrial and atmospheric phenomena.

Office management. A program that prepares students to supervise and manage the operations and personnel of business offices and management-level divisions.

Office technology/data entry. Readies students to support businesses by using computer equipment for administrative purposes.

Office/clerical services. Prepares individuals, under the supervision of office managers, administrative assistants, and secretaries, to provide administrative support.

Oncology. Features the genetics, onset, and composition of cancer cells, as well as cancer behaviors and treatments.

Operations management. Readies students to direct the development, production, and manufacturing functions of an organization.

Operations research. Focuses on the development and application of simulation models to solve problems involving operational systems that are subject to human intervention.

Ophthalmic laboratory technology. Prepares individuals, under the supervision of an ophthalmologist or optometrist, to make corrective lenses and eyewear.

Ophthalmic technology. Prepares students to aid ophthalmologists and optometrists in examining and treating patients with vision disorders and eye diseases.

Opticianry/ophthalmic dispensing. Trains students to fit corrective eyewear, assist patients in selecting appropriate frames, and prepare work orders for ophthalmic technicians.

Optics. Covers light energy and its structure, properties, and behavior under different conditions.

Optometric assistant. Readies individuals to assist in providing patient care, administer examinations and treatments, and perform office functions.

Optometry (O.D.). Prepares individuals for the professional practice of optometry, focusing on the techniques for examining, diagnosing, and treating conditions of the human eye.

Organic chemistry. Investigates the properties and behavior of hydrocarbon compounds and their derivatives.

Organizational behavior studies. Focuses on the scientific study of the behavior and motivations of individuals functioning in organized groups and its application to business and industrial settings.

Organizational communication. Includes instruction in group relations within organizations; decision-making and conflict management; symbolic messages; and human interaction with computer technology.

Ornamental horticulture. Prepares students to breed, grow, and utilize ornamental plant varieties for commercial and aesthetic purposes.

Orthotics/prosthetics. Features the techniques used to design and fit orthoses and prostheses for patients with disabling conditions or limb deformity.

Osteopathic medicine (D.O.). A program that prepares individuals for the professional practice of osteopathic medicine, involving a combination of traditional medicine with principles of holistic medicine and the relationship of the musculoskeletal system to general health.

Pacific area/rim studies. Describes the history, society, politics, culture, and economics of Australia, New Zealand, and the Pacific Islands.

Painting. Readies individuals to impart ideas through the application of paints and chemical color substances to canvases.

Painting/wall covering. Prepares students to finish structural surfaces by applying protective or decorative coating materials, such as paint and wallpaper.

Paleontology. Features the reconstruction and analysis of ancient and extinct lifeforms, ecosystems, and geologic processes.

Paralegal studies. Prepares students to perform research, drafting, investigatory, record-keeping, and administrative functions under the supervision of an attorney or court.

Parasitology. Focuses on organisms that live on or within host organisms, and the role of parasites in causing injury, disease, and environmental damage.

Parks, recreation, and leisure studies. Investigates the practices involved in the provision of recreational facilities and services to the general public.

Parks/recreational/leisure facilities management. Prepares students to develop and manage park facilities and other recreational and leisure facilities.

Particle physics. Studies the basic elements of subatomic matter and energy, and the forces governing their fundamental processes.

Parts/warehousing operations. Prepares students to maintain inventory control, care for inventory, and make minor repairs to warehouse equipment.

Pastoral counseling. Prepares ordained clergy to provide nonclinical pastoral counseling.

Pathology assistant. Trains individuals to help pathologists by performing autopsies, obtaining and preparing surgical specimens, and writing autopsy reports.

Pathology, human/animal. The scientific study of tissue injury and disease, including death and disease infestation and transfer.

Peace and conflict studies. Emphasizes the origins, resolution, and prevention of international and inter-group conflicts.

Pediatric nursing. Prepares registered nurses to provide care for children from infancy through adolescence.

Perfusion technology. Trains individuals to operate equipment that supports or replaces a patient's own respiratory or circulatory system.

Permanent cosmetics/tattooing. Focuses on the application of markings, color, and cosmetic products to the body for aesthetic or clinical purposes.

Personal/culinary services. Focuses on professional services related to cosmetology, funeral services, and food service.

Personal/financial services marketing. Prepares students to perform marketing and operational tasks associated with the provision of personal and financial services.

Personality psychology. Focuses on characteristics that set the individual apart from other individuals and on how others respond to that individual.

Petroleum engineering. Readies students to develop systems for locating, extracting, processing, and refining crude oil and natural gas.

Petroleum technology. Readies individuals to implement the development and operation of oil and natural gas extraction and processing facilities.

Pharmaceutical sciences. Prepares students to understand the mechanisms of drug action on biological systems and the toxicological aspects of drugs and other substances.

Pharmacology. Emphasizes the interactions of drugs on organisms and their various uses.

Pharmacology/toxicology. The study of pharmacological and toxicological issues in biology and the biomedical sciences.

Pharmacy (Pharm.D.). A doctoral-professional program that prepares students to prepare and dispense medications, monitor drug therapy, manage pharmacy practices, and counsel patients as professional pharmacists.

Pharmacy assistant. Prepares students, under the supervision of pharmacists, to prepare medications, provide medications to patients, and to manage pharmacy business and clinical operations.

Philosophy. Focuses on ideas and their structure, including arguments and investigations about abstract and real phenomena.

Phlebotomy. Trains students to draw blood samples from patients using a variety of intrusive procedures.

Photographic/film/video technology. Readies students to operate and maintain camera and lighting equipment; and produce finished still, video, and film products.

Photography. Describes the creation of images on photographic film, plates, and digital images.

Photojournalism. Describes the use of still and motion photography in journalism.

Physical anthropology. Studies the adaptations, variability, and evolution of human beings and their living and fossil relatives.

Physical education. Readies students to coach sports and/or teach physical education programs.

Physical sciences. The study of the topics, concepts, processes, and interrelationships of physical phenomena.

Physical therapy. Readies individuals to alleviate physical and functional impairments and limitations caused by injury or disease through the use of therapeutic interventions.

Physical therapy assistant. Trains individuals to support physical therapists by providing assistance during patient examinations, treatment, and monitoring.

Physical/theoretical chemistry. Investigates the properties of matter and the relation of force to the chemical structure and behavior of molecules.

Physician assistant. Prepares students, under the supervision of a physician, to practice medicine.

Physics. The study of matter and energy, and the formulation and testing of the laws governing their behavior.

Physics teacher education. Focuses on the teaching of physics curricula.

Physiology. The study of the functions, processes, and interactions of cells, tissues, and organs, such as respiration, circulation, digestion, sensory perception, and reproduction.

Piano/organ. Readies students to develop the skills necessary to master the piano or organ, and to perform art as solo, ensemble, and/or accompanist performers.

Pipefitting. Focuses on the design, installation, and testing of piping systems and automatic fire and exposure protections systems.

Planetary sciences. The scientific study of planets, small objects, and related gravitational systems.

Plant breeding. Applies genetics and genetic engineering to the improvement of agricultural plant health and populations and the development of new plant varieties.

Plant genetics. Highlights the relation of botanical research, comparative genetics, ecology, and evolutionary studies to the genetics of plants and fungi.

Plant molecular biology. Explores molecular structures, functions, and processes specific to plants and plant substances.

Plant pathology. Highlights plant diseases, plant health, and the development of disease control mechanisms.

Plant physiology. Investigates the internal workings and systems of plants, plant-environment interaction, and plant life cycles and processes.

Plant protection/pest management. Prepares students to control animal and weed infestation of domesticated plant populations and crops; prevent/reduce economic loss; and control environmental pollution related to pest control measures.

Plant sciences. Highlights the breeding, cultivation, and production of plants and the processing and distribution of agricultural plant products.

Plasma/high-temperature physics. Highlights the properties and behavior of matter at high temperatures.

Plastics engineering technology. Includes instruction in the use of industrial polymers, plastics manufacturing and equipment, and design and operational testing procedures.

Platemaker/imager. Readies students to prepare film, digital data, and surfaces to reproduce printed or graphic images.

Playwriting/screenwriting. Describes the composition of written works for the theater and/or film.

Plumbing. Trains students to install and maintain piping fixtures and systems in home and business environments.

Podiatry (D.P.M.). Prepares individuals for the professional practice of podiatry, focusing on the prevention, diagnosis, and treatment of diseases and injuries to the foot and lower extremities.

Polarity therapy. Includes instruction in energy-based anatomy and physiology; polarity processing, bodywork, and yoga; and energetic nutrition, evaluation, and assessment.

Police science. Prepares individuals to perform the duties of police and public security officers.

Polish. Highlights the Polish language and its use in literature.

Polish studies. Covers the history, society, politics, culture, and economics of Poland.

Political communications. Focuses on human and media communication in the political process and readies individuals to function as members of political and public affairs organizations, political campaign staffs, and related media entities.

Political science. A general program that focuses on the study of political institutions and behavior.

Polymer chemistry. The study of synthesized macromolecules and their interactions with other substances.

Polymer/plastics engineering. Studies the design and development of synthesized macromolecular compounds and their application to specific engineering uses.

Population biology. Investigates the natural history, life cycle behavior, and ecosystem dynamics of single- and multi-species communities and the causes of diversity among such populations.

Portuguese. Focuses on the Portuguese language and related dialects.

Poultry science. Prepares students for the production and management of poultry animals and products.

Power/electrical transmission. Features the installation of indoor and outdoor residential, commercial, and industrial electrical systems and associated power transmission lines.

Precision production trades, general. A program that prepares individuals to apply technical knowledge in creating products using precision crafting and technical illustration.

Predental. Prepares individuals for admission to a doctoral-professional program in dentistry.

Prelaw. A four-year program, in virtually any major, that prepares individuals for admission to law school or a doctoral-professional (JD) law program.

Premedicine. Readies students for admission to a doctoral-professional program in medicine, osteopathic medicine, or podiatric medicine.

Preministerial studies. Readies students to enter a seminary or other religious ordination program, or a related religious vocation.

Prenursing. Prepares individuals for admission to professional study in nursing.

Preoperative/surgical nursing. Readies registered nurses to provide care to surgery patients and to provide tableside assistance to surgeons.

Prepharmacy. Prepares individuals for admission to a doctoral-professional program in pharmacy.

Prephysical therapy. Prepares individuals for admission to a doctoral-professional program in physical therapy.

Preveterinary. Readies students for admission to a doctoral-professional program in veterinary medicine.

Printing management. Analyzes the application of managerial skills to printing operations from design through finished product.

Printing press operator. The application of technical skills to set up, operate, and maintain printing presses.

Printmaking. Prepares individuals to render art concepts onto surfaces and transfer images, via ink or dyes, onto paper or fabric.

Psychiatric nursing. Describes the provision of nursing care to patients with mental, emotional, or behavioral disorders.

Psychoanalysis. Readies individuals to provide psychoanalytic counseling to individuals and groups.

Psychobiology/physiological psychology. Covers the biological bases of psychological functioning and their application to experimental and therapeutic research.

Psychology. The study of individual and collective behavior, the bases of behavior, and the analysis and treatment of behavior problems and disorders.

Psychology teacher education. A program that prepares students to teach general psychology at the secondary school level.

Psychometrics/quantitative psychology. Explores psychological test construction and validation procedures; problems associated with behavior measurement; and quantitative methods used in research design.

Psychopharmacology. Describes the behavioral effects of drugs, nutrients, and chemicals in laboratory and clinical settings.

Public administration. Trains students to serve as managers in the executive arm of local, state, and federal government.

Public finance. Readies individuals to tend to the financial assets and budgets of public sector organizations.

Public health. Prepares individuals to plan, manage, and evaluate public health care services.

Public health education. A program of study that promotes preventive health measures and the education of targeted populations on health issues.

Public health nursing. Prepares individuals, under the supervision of a public health agency, to provide nursing services for groups or communities.

Public history/archives. A program that applies history and administrative skills to the recording of public events and the management of related historical resources.

Public policy analysis. The study of public policy issues and decision processes.

Public relations. Prepares students to manage the media image of an organization and communicate with clients and the general public.

Publishing. Describes the creation, publishing, and distribution of print and electronic books and other text products.

Purchasing/procurement/contracts. Readies individuals to manage the process of contracting goods and services for an organization.

Quality control technology. Highlights the maintenance of manufacturing and construction standards.

Rabbinical studies (M.H.L., Rav.). A program that prepares individuals for ordination as rabbis.

Radiation biology. Emphasizes the effects of radiation on organisms and biological systems.

Radiation protection/health physics technology. Prepares students to monitor and control radiation exposure and implement preventive measures in health care, work, and natural environments.

Radio and television. Studies the planning, production, and distribution of audio and video programs, and prepares students to function as staff, producers, directors, and managers of radio and television shows.

Radio/television broadcasting. Prepares students to apply technical knowledge to the production of radio and television programs.

Radiologic technology/medical imaging. Focuses on the provision of x-ray and other medical imaging services to patients and health care professionals.

Range science. Studies rangelands, arid regions, and grasslands, and the principles of managing such resources for maximum benefit and environmental balance.

Reading teacher education. Describes how to diagnose reading difficulties and teach reading programs.

Real estate. Prepares individuals to develop, buy, sell, appraise, and manage real property.

Receptionist. Prepares students to perform frontline public relations duties for a business, organization, or answering service.

Recording arts. Prepares individuals to produce sound recordings as finished products or as components of other media productions.

Recreational therapy. Trains students to organize and direct recreational activities designed to promote health for patients who suffer from disabling conditions.

Regional studies. The study of the defined geographic subregions and subcultures within countries and societies.

Reiki. Highlights the manipulation of the body's energy field to increase healing energy.

Religious education. Prepares individuals to provide religious educational services to members of faith communities.

Religious studies. Explores the nature of religious beliefs and specific religious and quasi-religious systems.

Renal/dialysis technology. Trains individuals to administer hemodialysis treatments to patients with renal failure.

Reproductive biology. The study of reproductive processes in animals and human beings.

Resort management. Emphasizes the planning, management, and marketing of comprehensive vacation facilities, services, and products.

Respiratory therapy. Trains individuals to manage the ventilation of critically ill patients, provide respiratory care to patients with breathing disorders, and consult with other health care team members.

Respiratory therapy assistant. Highlights the administration of general respiratory care procedures under the supervision of respiratory therapists.

Restaurant/catering management. Readies individuals to plan, supervise, and manage food and beverage service operations, restaurant facilities, and catering services.

Restaurant/food services management. Trains students to manage restaurants, food services in hospitality establishments, chains and franchises, and restaurant suppliers.

Retailing. Readies individuals to perform operations associated with retail sales in a variety of settings.

Robotics technology. Prepares individuals to aid engineers and other professionals engaged in developing and using robots.

Romance languages. A general curriculum that focuses on the Romance languages of Western, Central, and Southern Europe.

Romanian. Highlights the Romanian language and related dialects.

Roofing. Readies individuals to prepare, install, and maintain exterior roofing materials and roofs.

Russian. The study of the languages, literatures, and cultures of Russian-speaking peoples.

Russian/Slavic studies. Focuses on the history, society, politics, culture, and economics of the Russian Federation.

Sacred music. Highlights the history, theory, composition, and performance of music for religious or sacred purposes.

Sales/distribution. Studies the process and techniques of direct wholesale and retail buying and selling operations and introduces individuals to related careers.

Sales/marketing education. Investigates the teaching of vocational sales, marketing, and distributive operations education programs.

Salon management. Trains individuals to manage beauty parlors, shops, and specialized salons.

Sanskrit/classical Indian languages. The study of Sanskrit and related ancient and classical Indo-Aryan languages.

Scandinavian languages. A program that characterizes one or more of the languages, literatures, and linguistics of the Scandinavian peoples.

Scandinavian studies. Studies the history, society, politics, culture, and economics of Denmark, Finland, Greenland, Iceland, Norway, and Sweden.

School librarian education. Prepares students to serve as librarians and media specialists in elementary and secondary schools.

School psychology. Prepares individuals to treat and diagnose student behavioral problems.

Science teacher education. Prepares students to teach general science subjects or a combination of biology and physical science.

Science, technology, and society. Covers the relationship, ramifications, and ethical dimensions of science and technology to public policy.

Sculpture. Features the use of clay, plaster, wood, stone, and metal to create three-dimensional works of art.

Secondary education. Readies individuals to teach a comprehensive curriculum or specific subject matter to students at the secondary school level.

Secondary school administration. Prepares individuals to serve as principals and masters of junior high, secondary, or senior high schools.

Security services management. Readies individuals to plan, manage, and supervise services providing private security protection for people and property.

Security/loss prevention. Focuses on the performance of routine inspection, patrol, and crime prevention services for private clients.

Selling/sales operations. Prepares individuals in the direct promotion of products and services to potential customers, and to function as sales representatives and managers.

Semitic languages. Focuses on the Semitic languages of Western Asia, North Africa, and Europe.

Sheet metal technology. Focuses on the forming, shaping, bending, and folding of metal, including the creation of new products, using hand tools and machines.

Shoe/leather repair. Readies students to replace, mend, refinish, and dye leather goods and footwear.

Sign language interpretation. Prepares students to be simultaneous interpreters of American Sign Language and other sign language systems, both one-way and two-way.

Sign language linguistics. Explores American Sign Language and other visual signed languages as modes of communication within the Deaf community and in relation to spoken and written languages.

Slavic languages. A general program that focuses on one or more of the Slavic languages of Central and Eastern Europe.

Slavic studies. Analyzes the history, society, politics, culture, and economics of the Slavic peoples.

Slovak. The study of the Slovak language, dialects, and literature.

Small business administration/management. A program that prepares individuals to develop and manage independent small businesses.

Small engine mechanics. Readies students to service small internal-combustion engines used on portable power equipment.

Social psychology. Explores individual behavior in group contexts, group behavior, and associated phenomena.

Social science teacher education. Studies the teaching of specific social science subjects and programs.

Social sciences. The study of human social behavior and institutions using any of the methodologies common to the social sciences and/or history.

Social studies teacher education. Prepares students to teach general social studies programs.

Social work. Studies the provision of basic support services for vulnerable individuals and groups.

Social/philosophical foundations of education. Studies education as a social and cultural institution, and the educational process as an object of humanistic inquiry.

Sociology. The systematic study of human social institutions and social relationships.

Software engineering. Prepares individuals to design, implement, validate, and maintain computer software systems using a variety of computer languages.

Soil chemistry/physics. The analysis of the nature, properties, conservation, and management of soils.

Soil science. The scientific classification of soils and soil properties, and the study of their relationship to agricultural crops.

Solar energy technology. Highlights the development of solar-powered energy systems.

Solid-state/low-temperature physics. Focuses on solids and related states of matter at low energy levels, including liquids and dense gases.

Somatic bodywork. A course of study that encourages physical and emotional balance through the provision of skilled touch principles and techniques.

South Asian languages. Features one or more of the languages, literatures, and linguistics of the peoples speaking the languages of the Indian subcontinent.

South Asian studies. Analyzes the history, society, politics, culture, and economics of Afghanistan, India, the Maldives, Burma, Pakistan, and Sri Lanka.

Southeast Asian languages. Focuses on one or more of the modern or historical languages spoken or originating in mainland Southeast Asia.

Southeast Asian studies. Covers the history, society, politics, culture, and economics of the peoples of Southeast Asia, defined as Brunei, Cambodia, Indonesia, Laos, Malaysia, The Philippines, Singapore, Thailand, and Viet Nam.

Spanish. Features the language, literature, and culture of Spanish-speaking peoples.

Spanish teacher education. Readies individuals to teach the language, literature, and culture of Spanish-speaking peoples.

Spanish/Iberian studies. Analyzes the history, society, politics, culture, and economics of the peoples of the Iberian Peninsula.

Special education. Describes the design and provision of educational services to children or adults with special learning needs.

Special education administration. Highlights the planning, supervision, and management of programs for exceptional students and their parents.

Special products marketing. Trains individuals to execute marketing and sales operations connected with the promotion of special products, including floristry, food, and home and office products.

Speech pathology. Readies individuals to evaluate patients' speaking capabilities and develop rehabilitative solutions in consultation with related professionals.

Speech teacher education. Prepares students to teach speech and language arts at various educational levels.

Speech-language pathology assistant. Trains students to become certified to work under the supervision of a licensed speech language pathologist, who helps children and adults with communication disorders.

Speech/rhetorical studies. Studies interpersonal communication from the scientific/behavioral and humanistic perspectives.

Sports and fitness administration. Highlights the organization, administration, and management of athletic programs and teams, fitness/rehabilitation facilities, and sport recreation services.

Sports communication. The theoretical study of sport and communication combined with practical skills in sports reporting, broadcasting, and public relations.

Statistics. A study of the theory and proofs that form the basis of probability and inference, and of the methods of collecting, analyzing, and interpreting data.

Structural biology. The scientific study of molecular components and how they are organized into cells and tissues.

Structural engineering. Studies the design, analysis, and structural problems of load-bearing structures such as roads, bridges, and dams.

Substance abuse counseling. Focuses on intervention techniques and therapeutic services for persons suffering from addiction.

Surgical technology. Prepares students to maintain, monitor, and enforce the sterile field and aseptic technique by surgical personnel.

Surveying engineering. Readies individuals to determine the location, elevations, and alignment of natural and man-made topographic features.

Surveying technology. Trains students to determine, plan, and position land tracts and water boundaries, and to prepare related maps, charts, and reports.

Sustainable/organic agriculture. The study of food production methods that incorporate ecology and the sociology of food into farming practices.

Swedish. Focuses on the Swedish language as used in Sweden and Finland.

System administration. Trains individuals to control the system configurations and manage the computer operations of a specific site or network hub.

Systematic biology. Features the patterns of origin, maintenance, diversification, distribution, and extinction of species.

Systems engineering. Trains individuals to design, develop, and evaluate total systems solutions to a wide variety of engineering problems.

Systems science/theory. Focuses on the solution of complex problems using data from the natural, social, technological, behavioral, and life sciences.

Talmudic studies. Prepares students for advanced Talmudic scholarship and entry to ordination programs and conventional graduate and professional schools.

Taxation. Prepares students to provide tax advice and management services to individuals and corporations.

Taxidermy. Trains individuals to reproduce life-like representations of living animals for permanent display and to manage taxidermy businesses.

Teacher assistance. Readies individuals to assist teachers in regular classroom settings or instruct and supervise special student populations.

Teacher education, multiple levels. Prepares individuals to teach students at more than one educational level.

Technical and business writing. The study of the methods and skills needed for writing and editing scientific, technical, and business papers.

Technology/industrial arts education. Trains students to teach technology education/industrial arts programs at various levels.

Telecommunications technology. Focuses on the design and implementation of telecommunications systems.

Textile science. Investigates the properties and processing of fibers, yarns, whole fabrics, dyes, and finishes.

Textile sciences/engineering. Focuses on systems that test and manufacture fiber products and the development of new and improved fibers, textiles, and their uses.

Theater arts management. Trains students to manage theaters and production companies.

Theater design and technology. Prepares students to communicate dramatic information, ideas, moods, and feelings through technical theater methods, including set design, lighting, sound, scene painting, costumes, and computer applications.

Theater history/criticism. Studies the literature, history, and analysis of theatrical productions and theater methods and organization.

Theological studies. The study of the beliefs and doctrines of a particular religious faith from the point of view of that faith.

Theoretical/mathematical physics. Prepares individuals to formulate and evaluate the physical laws governing matter-energy phenomena and to analyze experimental designs and results.

Tibetan studies. Describes the history, society, politics, culture, and economics of Tibet.

Tool and die technology. Prepares individuals to operate tools and make instruments used to form metal parts.

Tourism promotion. Trains students to perform marketing and sales operations connected with the promotion of tourism in a variety of settings.

Tourism/travel management. Readies individuals to manage travel-related enterprises and conventions and/or tour services.

Tourism/travel services. Features the provision of retail services to hotel and motel clients and customers in a variety of settings.

Toxicology. The study of toxic substances; their interaction with organisms; and their prevention, management, and counteraction.

Trade/industrial education. Prepares students to teach specific vocational trades and industries programs.

Traditional Chinese medicine/herbology. Highlights the use of natural products and prescribed medical formulae to treat health imbalances as defined in the Nei Ching Su Wen and other authorities.

Traffic/customs/transportation clerk. Prepares students to manage revenue-based transportation services and assist in the control of fleet-based traffic for businesses.

Transportation. A program that prepares individuals to apply technical skills to perform services that facilitate the movement of people or materials.

Transportation management. Readies students to coordinate physical transportation operations, networks, and systems.

Transportation/highway engineering. Focuses on the development of systems for the physical movement of people, materials, and information.

Truck/bus/commercial vehicle operation. Trains individuals to drive trucks and buses, delivery vehicles, and for-hire vehicles.

Turf management. Readies individuals to develop, plant, and manage grassed areas and produce and store turf used for transplantation.

Turkish. A program that focuses on the Turkish language in either or both of its premodern and modern variants.

Ukrainian. Focuses on the Ukrainian language and its applications in varied settings.

Underwater diving. Prepares students to function as professional deep-water or scuba divers, diving instructors, or support personnel.

Upholstery. Highlights the installation of springs, padding, covering, and finishing on furniture, seats, caskets, mattresses, and bedsprings.

Urban education. Describes issues specific to the educational needs of populations located in metropolitan areas and inner cities.

Urban forestry. Studies the development, care, and maintenance of trees and forested areas that are within or near areas of dense human habitation.

Urban studies. Emphasizes urban institutions and the forces influencing urban social and political life.

Urban, community, and regional planning. The application of planning, analysis, and architecture to the development and improvement of urban areas.

Vehicle emissions inspection/maintenance. Prepares individuals to test and service all vehicle emission systems in accordance with relevant laws and regulations.

Vehicle parts/accessories marketing. Prepares individuals to distribute and sell replacement parts and other supplies in the automotive, marine, and aviation industries.

Vendor/product certification. Prepares students to fulfill requirements set by vendors for professional qualification to install, customize, and maintain specific software products and/or processes.

Veterinary medicine (D.V.M.). Trains students for the professional practice of veterinary medicine, involving the diagnosis, treatment, and management of animal health care.

Veterinary technology. Prepares students, under the supervision of veterinarians, to provide animal health care, clinical assistance, and owner communication.

Violin/viola/guitar/stringed instruments. Prepares students to master a stringed instrument.

Virology. Examines viruses that inhabit living cells in parasitical relationships and their role in causing disease.

Vision science. The study of vision, visual processes, clinical research, and forms of treatment.

Visual/performing arts. Highlights the visual and performing arts, and prepares individuals in any of the visual artistic media or performing disciplines.

Vocational rehabilitation counseling. Prepares students to counsel disabled individuals in order for them to have fulfilling and productive lives.

Vocational/technical education. Readies individuals to teach vocational technical education programs to students.

Voice/opera. Trains students to master the human voice and to perform in concerts, choirs, operas, or other forms of singing.

Waldorf/Steiner teacher education. Features the pedagogical principles and methods developed by Rudolf Steiner and his followers.

Warehousing/inventory management. Readies individuals to support warehouse operations, inventory control, parts identification, and counter services for customers.

Watch/jewelrymaking. Readies individuals to mend and maintain time-measuring devices and jewelry items.

Water quality/treatment/recycling technology. Prepares individuals to implement engineering designs for origination and use of water storage, water-power, and wastewater treatment systems.

Water resource engineering. Describes systems for collecting, storing, moving, conserving, and controlling surface- and groundwater.

Water, wetlands, and marine management. Investigates the development, conservation, and management of freshwater and saltwater environments.

Web page/multimedia design. Readies students to produce and publish documents, images, graphics, sound, and multimedia projects on the World Wide Web.

Web/multimedia management. Covers the development and maintenance of Web servers and Web pages at Web sites.

Welding technology. A program that prepares individuals to apply technical knowledge and skills to join or cut metal surfaces.

Well drilling. Readies individuals to operate well-drilling equipment; locate, drill, and construct wells; and test and monitor wells.

Western European studies. Covers the history, society, politics, culture, and economics of historical Western Europe.

Wildlife and wilderness management. Describes the conservation and management of wildlife and wilderness areas, and the management of wildlife reservations and zoological facilities.

Wildlife biology. A program that applies biological principles to the study of vertebrate wildlife and habitats in remote and urban areas.

Women's studies. Focuses on the history, sociology, politics, culture, and economics of women and the development of modern feminism.

Wood science/pulp/paper technology. Describes the properties and behavior of wood and the development of processes for converting wood into paper and other products.

Woodworking. Trains students to shape, mark, saw, carve, sand, and repair wooden products, and to use a variety of hand and power tools.

Word processing. Highlights typing, table construction, and document formatting on personal computers.

Work/family studies. Focuses on family and consumer science concepts and the various career paths open to interested students.

Yoga teacher/therapy. Trains students to provide spiritual and physical Yoga therapy in private, institutional, and clinical settings.

Youth ministry. Studies the provision of spiritual counseling and leadership services to children, adolescents, and young adults.

Youth services. Readies students to plan, manage, and implement social services for children, youth, and families.

Zoology. Emphasizes the anatomy, structure, and behavior of animals.

Part III:
College Listings

About Part III

Once you have an idea of what you might want to study, you can use this Part to find colleges that offer the majors or academic programs you are interested in.

Colleges listed by major

All of the majors that are fully or briefly described in this book (over 900 in all) are presented here alphabetically, and under each is a state-by-state list of the colleges that teach it. After the college name you'll find letter symbols that designate the different degree levels at which the major is offered by that college:

C   Certificate or diploma
A   Associate degree
B   Bachelor's degree
T   Teacher certification
M   Master's degree
D   Doctorate
P   Professional degree

Certificate or diploma. Certificates are awarded to students who complete nondegree programs, which usually take one year or less and are most frequently offered in technical and vocational fields of study.

Associate degree. Usually two years in length, associate degree programs are most often found at community colleges and technical schools, but they are also offered at many four-year colleges.

Bachelor's degree. Programs in which you earn a bachelor's degree usually take four years, but some programs can be completed in three years and some take five.

Teacher certification. Each state sets its own certification standards, and all colleges that prepare teachers are accredited by the state in which they are located. Students must meet both bachelor's degree requirements and state certification requirements. Most states require candidates to pass an examination in the field they plan to teach.

Master's degree. Master of arts (M.A.) and master of science (M.S.) programs are graduate degrees in the liberal arts and sciences, intended for students with B.A. or B.S. degrees, and usually take one or two years to complete. Among other master's degree programs are the master of business administration (MBA), the master of library science (M.L.S.), and the master of social work (M.S.W.) In some fields, such as law and medicine, the master's degree follows the first-professional degree (J.D., M.D.).

Doctorate. Doctoral programs usually consist of course work and independent research culminating in a dissertation or other formal presentation of the results of independent study. Length of study varies widely, and is usually self-determined.

Professional degree. These programs provide the academic prerequisites to become licensed in a recognized profession, such as medicine, law, or veterinary medicine. At least two years of prior college-level study are required for entrance into the program, and the total registered time of study must equal six academic years.

Special academic programs

In addition to majors, minors, and concentrations, many colleges offer other ways to enhance, focus, or further shape your undergraduate education. For each of the more common and popular programs, there is a state-by-state listing of colleges that offer it, beginning on page 1278.

Colleges listed by major

Accounting

Alabama

Alabama Agricultural and Mechanical University *B*
Alabama State University *B, M*
Athens State University *B*
Auburn University *B, M*
Auburn University at Montgomery *B*
Birmingham-Southern College *B*
Bishop State Community College *A*
Calhoun Community College *A*
Chattahoochee Valley Community College *A*
Huntingdon College *B*
Jacksonville State University *B*
Lawson State Community College *A*
Miles College *B*
Oakwood University *A, B*
Samford University *B, M*
Southern Union State Community College *A*
Talladega College *B*
Troy University *B*
Tuskegee University *B*
University of Alabama *B, M, D*
University of Alabama
  Birmingham *B, M*
  Huntsville *B, M*
University of Mobile *B*
University of Montevallo *B*
University of North Alabama *B*
University of South Alabama *B, M*
University of West Alabama *B*
Wallace State Community College at Hanceville *A*

Alaska

Ilisagvik College *C, A*
University of Alaska
  Anchorage *A, B*
  Fairbanks *B*
  Southeast *C, B*

Arizona

Arizona State University *B, M*
Brookline College
  Phoenix *C, A*
Brown Mackie College: Tucson *A, B*
Central Arizona College *C, A*
Chandler-Gilbert Community College Pecos *A*
Coconino County Community College *C, A*
Everest College
  Phoenix *A*
GateWay Community College *C, A*
Glendale Community College *A*
Grand Canyon University *B*
Lamson College *A*
Mesa Community College *A*
Mohave Community College *C*
Northcentral University *B*
Northern Arizona University *C, B*
Northland Pioneer College *C, A*
Paradise Valley Community College *C, A*
Penn Foster College *A*
Phoenix College *A*
Pima Community College *C, A*
Prescott College *B*
Rio Salado College *C, A*

Scottsdale Community College *C, A*
University of Arizona *B, M*
University of Phoenix *A, B, M*
Western International University *C, B, M*

Arkansas

Arkansas Baptist College *A*
Arkansas Northeastern College *C*
Arkansas State University *B, M*
Arkansas Tech University *B*
Black River Technical College *A*
Harding University *B*
Henderson State University *B*
Hendrix College *B, M*
John Brown University *B*
Lyon College *B*
National Park Community College *A*
North Arkansas College *C*
Northwest Arkansas Community College *C, A*
Ouachita Baptist University *B*
Ouachita Technical College *C*
South Arkansas Community College *C*
Southern Arkansas University *B*
University of Arkansas *B, M*
University of Arkansas
  Community College at Batesville *A*
  Little Rock *B*
  Monticello *B*
  Pine Bluff *B*
University of Central Arkansas *B, M*
University of the Ozarks *B*

California

Allan Hancock College *C, A*
American River College *C, A*
Azusa Pacific University *B*
Bakersfield College *A*
Barstow Community College *C, A*
Biola University *B*
Butte College *C, A*
Cabrillo College *C, A*
California Baptist University *B*
California College San Diego *B*
California Lutheran University *B*
California Polytechnic State University: San Luis Obispo *M*
California State University
  Chico *B*
  Dominguez Hills *B*
  East Bay *B, M*
  Fresno *B*
  Fullerton *B, M*
  Long Beach *B*
  Los Angeles *M*
  Northridge *M*
  Sacramento *B, M*
  San Bernardino *B, M*
Canada College *C, A*
Cerritos College *A*
Chabot College *A*
Chaffey College *C, A*
Chapman University *B*
Citrus College *C*
City College of San Francisco *C, A*
Claremont McKenna College *B*
Coastline Community College *C, A*
College of Alameda *A*
College of Marin: Kentfield *C, A*
College of San Mateo *C, A*
College of the Canyons *C, A*
College of the Desert *C*

College of the Sequoias *C, A*
College of the Siskiyous *C, A*
Columbia College *C*
Copper Mountain College *C*
Cosumnes River College *C, A*
Crafton Hills College *C*
Cuyamaca College *C, A*
Cypress College *C, A*
De Anza College *C, A*
Diablo Valley College *C*
East Los Angeles College *A*
El Camino College: Compton Center *C, A*
Empire College *C, A*
Evergreen Valley College *C*
Folsom Lake College *C, A*
Foothill College *C, A*
Fresno City College *C, A*
Fresno Pacific University *B*
Fullerton College *A*
Gavilan College *C*
Glendale Community College *C, A*
Golden Gate University *C, B, M*
Golden West College *C, A*
Hartnell College *C*
Heald College
  Fresno *C, A*
  Hayward *C, A*
  Rancho Cordova *C, A*
  Roseville *C, A*
  Salinas *A*
  San Jose *C, A*
  Stockton *C, A*
Humphreys College *A, B*
Irvine Valley College *C, A*
Kaplan College: Panorama City *A*
LA College International *C*
La Sierra University *B, M*
Lake Tahoe Community College *C, A*
Laney College *A*
Lassen Community College *A*
Long Beach City College *C, A*
Los Angeles City College *A*
Los Angeles Harbor College *C, A*
Los Angeles Mission College *A*
Los Angeles Pierce College *C, A*
Los Angeles Southwest College *A*
Los Angeles Trade and Technical College *A*
Los Angeles Valley College *C*
Los Medanos College *C, A*
Loyola Marymount University *B*
MTI College *C*
The Master's College *B*
Mendocino College *C, A*
Merced College *C, A*
MiraCosta College *C, A*
Mission College *A*
Modesto Junior College *C, A*
Monterey Peninsula College *C, A*
Moorpark College *C, A*
Mount St. Mary's College *A, B*
Mount San Antonio College *C, A*
Napa Valley College *A*
National University *B, M*
Ohlone College *C, A*
Orange Coast College *C, A*
Oxnard College *C, A*
Pacific States University *B, M*
Pacific Union College *B*
Palo Verde College *C, A*
Palomar College *C, A*
Pasadena City College *C, A*

Pepperdine University *B*
Point Loma Nazarene University *B*
Reedley College *C, A*
Rio Hondo College *A*
Riverside Community College *C, A*
Sacramento City College *C, A*
Saddleback College *C, A*
St. Mary's College of California *B*
San Bernardino Valley College *C, A*
San Diego City College *C, A*
San Diego Mesa College *C, A*
San Diego State University *B, M*
San Francisco State University *B*
San Joaquin Delta College *A*
San Jose City College *C, A*
San Jose State University *B, M*
Santa Ana College *C, A*
Santa Barbara City College *C, A*
Santa Clara University *B*
Santa Monica College *A*
Santa Rosa Junior College *C*
Santiago Canyon College *A*
Scripps College *B*
Shasta College *A*
Sierra College *C, A*
Simpson University *B*
Skyline College *C, A*
Solano Community College *C, A*
Southern California Institute of Technology *C*
Southwestern College *C, A*
Taft College *C, A*
University of La Verne *B*
University of Redlands *B*
University of San Diego *B, M*
University of San Francisco *B*
University of Southern California *B, M, D*
University of the West *B*
Vanguard University of Southern California *B*
Ventura College *C, A*
West Hills College: Coalinga *C, A*
West Los Angeles College *C, A*
West Valley College *A*
Woodbury University *B*
Yuba Community College District *C, A*

Colorado

Adams State College *B*
Aims Community College *A*
CollegeAmerica
  Fort Collins *B*
Colorado Christian University *B*
Colorado Mountain College *C, A*
Colorado State University *B, M*
Colorado State University Pueblo *B*
Community College of Aurora *C, A*
Fort Lewis College *B*
Lamar Community College *A*
Mesa State College *B*
Metropolitan State College of Denver *B*
Morgan Community College *A*
Pikes Peak Community College *C, A*
Regis University *B*
Trinidad State Junior College *A*
University of Colorado
  Boulder *B, M*
  Denver *M*
University of Denver *B, M*

Western State College of Colorado *B*
Westwood College: Denver North *B*

Connecticut

Albertus Magnus College *B*
Asnuntuck Community College *A*
Capital Community College *C, A*
Central Connecticut State
   University *B*
Eastern Connecticut State
   University *B, M*
Fairfield University *B, M*
Gateway Community College *A*
Housatonic Community College *A*
Lincoln College of New England:
   Briarwood *A*
Manchester Community College *C, A*
Middlesex Community College *A*
Northwestern Connecticut
   Community College *A*
Norwalk Community College *C, A*
Post University *A, B*
Quinebaug Valley Community
   College *C, A*
Quinnipiac University *B, M*
Sacred Heart University *B*
Saint Joseph College *B*
Southern Connecticut State
   University *B*
Three Rivers Community College *C, A*
Tunxis Community College *C, A*
University of Bridgeport *B, M*
University of Connecticut *B, M*
University of Hartford *B, M*
University of New Haven *B*
Western Connecticut State
   University *B*

Delaware

Delaware State University *B*
Delaware Technical and Community
   College
    Owens *A*
    Stanton/Wilmington *A*
    Terry *A*
Goldey-Beacom College *A, B, M*
University of Delaware *B, M*
Wesley College *B*
Wilmington University *B*

District of Columbia

American University *B*
Catholic University of America *B*
Gallaudet University *B*
George Washington
   University *B, M, D*
Georgetown University *B*
Howard University *B*
Potomac College *A, B*
University of the District of
   Columbia *B*

Florida

Barry University *B, M*
Bethune-Cookman University *B*
Brevard Community College *C*
Broward College *C, A*
Brown Mackie College: Miami *A*
Central Florida College *A*
Central Florida Community
   College *C, A*
Clearwater Christian College *B*
College of Business and Technology:
   Flagler *C, A*
College of Business and Technology:
   Kendall *A*
Daytona State College *C, A*
Edison State College *C, A*
Flagler College *B*
Florida Agricultural and Mechanical
   University *B*
Florida Atlantic University *B, M*
Florida Gulf Coast University *B, M*

Florida Institute of Technology *A, B*
Florida International University *B, M*
Florida Memorial University *B*
Florida National College *A*
Florida Southern College *B, M*
Florida State College at Jacksonville *A*
Florida State University *B, M, D*
Gulf Coast Community College *C, A*
Hodges University *A, B*
Indian River State College *C, A*
Jacksonville University *B*
Miami Dade College *C, A*
Northwest Florida State College *C, A*
Northwood University
   Florida *B*
Nova Southeastern University *B, M*
Palm Beach Community College *A*
Pensacola Junior College *C, A*
Polk State College *A*
Rasmussen College: Fort Myers *A, B*
Rasmussen College: Ocala *A, B*
Rasmussen College: Pasco
   County *A, B*
Saint Johns River Community
   College *A*
Saint Leo University *B*
Saint Thomas University *B, M*
South Florida Community
   College *C, A*
Southeastern University *B*
Southwest Florida College *A*
State College of Florida,
   Manatee-Sarasota *C, A*
Stetson University *B, M*
Tallahassee Community College *A*
University of Central Florida *B, M*
University of Florida *B, M*
University of Miami *B, M*
University of North Florida *B, M*
University of South Florida *B, M*
University of Tampa *B*
University of West Florida *B, M*
Valencia Community College *A*
Webber International
   University *A, B, M*

Georgia

Abraham Baldwin Agricultural
   College *A*
Albany State University *B*
Altamaha Technical College *A*
Ashworth College *C, A*
Augusta State University *B*
Augusta Technical College *C, A*
Bainbridge College *A*
Berry College *B*
Brenau University *B*
Brewton-Parker College *B*
Brown Mackie College: Atlanta *A*
Chattahoochee Technical
   College *C, A*
Clark Atlanta University *B, M*
Clayton State University *B*
Columbus State University *B*
Columbus Technical College *C, A*
Dalton State College *B*
Darton College *C, A*
DeKalb Technical College *C, A*
DeVry University
   Decatur *A, M*
Emory University *B, D*
Fort Valley State University *B*
Gainesville State College *A*
Georgia College and State
   University *B, M*
Georgia Southern University *B, M*
Georgia Southwestern State
   University *B*
Georgia State University *B, M, D*
Griffin Technical College *A*
Gwinnett College *C*
Gwinnett Technical College *C, A*
Kennesaw State University *B, M*
LaGrange College *B*

Macon State College *B*
Mercer University *M*
Middle Georgia College *A*
North Georgia College & State
   University *B*
North Georgia Technical College *C, A*
Oglethorpe University *B*
Paine College *B*
Reinhardt College *B*
Savannah State University *B*
Shorter College *B*
South University: Savannah *A*
Southeastern Technical College *A*
Southern Polytechnic State
   University *B*
University of Georgia *B, M*
University of West Georgia *B, M*
Valdosta State University *B*
Waycross College *C, A*
West Georgia Technical College *A*

Hawaii

Chaminade University of
   Honolulu *B, M*
Hawaii Pacific University *A, B*
Heald College
   Honolulu *A*
University of Hawaii
   Hawaii Community College *A*
   Hilo *B*
   Kapiolani Community College *C, A*
   Kauai Community College *C, A*
   Leeward Community College *A*
   Manoa *B, M*
   Maui Community College *A*
   West Oahu *B*

Idaho

Boise State University *B, M*
Brigham Young University-Idaho *B*
College of Idaho *B*
Eastern Idaho Technical College *C, A*
Idaho State University *B*
Northwest Nazarene University *B*
Stevens-Henager College: Boise *A, B*
University of Idaho *B, M*

Illinois

Augustana College *B*
Aurora University *B, M*
Benedictine University *B, M*
Black Hawk College: East
   Campus *C, A*
Blackburn College *B*
Bradley University *B, M*
Carl Sandburg College *C, A*
Chicago State University *B*
City Colleges of Chicago
   Harold Washington College *C, A*
   Kennedy-King College *C, A*
   Malcolm X College *C, A*
   Olive-Harvey College *C, A*
College of DuPage *C, A*
College of Lake County *C*
Concordia University Chicago *B*
Danville Area Community College *C*
DePaul University *B, M*
DeVry University: Online *A*
Dominican University *B, M*
Eastern Illinois University *B*
Elgin Community College *A*
Elmhurst College *B, M*
Eureka College *B*
Fox College *A*
Governors State University *B, M*
Greenville College *B*
Harper College *C*
Heartland Community College *C*
Hebrew Theological College *B*
Highland Community College *C, A*
Illinois Central College *C, A*
Illinois College *B*
Illinois Eastern Community Colleges
   Olney Central College *A*

Illinois State University *B, M*
Illinois Wesleyan University *B*
John Wood Community College *A*
Joliet Junior College *C, A*
Judson University *B*
Kankakee Community College *C, A*
Kaskaskia College *C, A*
Kishwaukee College *C, A*
Lewis University *B*
Lewis and Clark Community
   College *A*
Lincoln College *A*
Lincoln Land Community College *A*
Loyola University Chicago *B, M*
MacCormac College *A*
MacMurray College *B*
McKendree University *B*
Midstate College *A, B*
Millikin University *B*
Monmouth College *B*
Morton College *A*
National-Louis University *C, B*
North Central College *B*
Northeastern Illinois University *B, M*
Northern Illinois University *B, M*
Northwestern College *A*
Northwestern University *M, D*
Oakton Community College *C, A*
Olivet Nazarene University *B*
Prairie State College *C*
Quincy University *B*
Rasmussen College: Aurora *A*
Rasmussen College: Rockford *A*
Richland Community College *A*
Rock Valley College *C, A*
Rockford Career College *A*
Rockford College *B*
Roosevelt University *B, M*
St. Augustine College *C, A*
Saint Xavier University *B*
Sauk Valley Community College *C, A*
Shawnee Community College *A*
South Suburban College of Cook
   County *C, A*
Southern Illinois University
   Carbondale *B, M*
Southern Illinois University
   Edwardsville *B, M*
Southwestern Illinois College *A*
Spoon River College *C*
Taylor Business Institute *A*
Trinity Christian College *B*
Trinity International University *B*
Triton College *C, A*
University of Illinois
   Chicago *B, M*
   Springfield *B, M*
   Urbana-Champaign *B, M, D*
University of St. Francis *B*
Waubonsee Community College *C, A*
Western Illinois University *B, M*
Wilbur Wright College *C, A*

Indiana

Anderson University *B, D*
Ball State University *B*
Bethel College *B*
Brown Mackie College: Fort Wayne *A*
Brown Mackie College: South
   Bend *C, A*
Butler University *B, M*
Calumet College of St. Joseph *C, A, B*
Franklin College *B*
Goshen College *B*
Grace College *B*
Harrison College
   Anderson *C, A*
   Columbus *C, A*
   Elkhart *A*
   Evansville *C, A, B*
   Fort Wayne *C, A*
   Indianapolis *C, A, B*
   Lafayette *C, A*

Muncie *C, A, B*
Terre Haute *C, A, B*
Huntington University *B*
Indiana Institute of
    Technology *A, B, M*
Indiana State University *B*
Indiana University
    Bloomington *B, M*
    East *A, B*
    Kokomo *B*
    Northwest *M*
    South Bend *M*
    Southeast *B*
Indiana University-Purdue University
    Fort Wayne *B*
Indiana University-Purdue University
    Indianapolis *B, M*
Indiana Wesleyan University *B*
International Business College *C, A*
Kaplan College: Hammond *C, A*
Manchester College *A, B, M*
Marian University *A, B*
Oakland City University *A, B*
Purdue University *B*
Purdue University
    Calumet *B*
    North Central *A, B*
Saint Joseph's College *B*
Saint Mary's College *B*
St. Mary-of-the-Woods College *A, B*
Taylor University *B*
Trine University *A, B*
University of Evansville *B*
University of Indianapolis *B, M*
University of Notre Dame *B, M*
University of St. Francis *A, B*
University of Southern
    Indiana *C, B, M*
Valparaiso University *B, M*

Iowa

AIB College of Business *A, B*
Briar Cliff University *B*
Buena Vista University *B*
Central College *B*
Clarke College *B*
Clinton Community College *C*
Coe College *B*
Des Moines Area Community
    College *A*
Dordt College *B*
Drake University *B, M*
Ellsworth Community College *A*
Graceland University *B*
Grand View University *C, B*
Hawkeye Community College *C, A*
Iowa Central Community College *C, A*
Iowa Lakes Community College *A*
Iowa State University *B, M*
Iowa Wesleyan College *B*
Kaplan University
    Cedar Falls *A*
    Cedar Rapids *A*
    Davenport *A*
    Des Moines *A, B*
    Mason City *A, B*
Kirkwood Community College *C, A*
Loras College *B*
Luther College *B*
Marshalltown Community
    College *C, A*
Morningside College *B*
Mount Mercy College *B*
Muscatine Community College *C, A*
North Iowa Area Community
    College *C, A*
Northeast Iowa Community
    College *A*
Northwest Iowa Community
    College *A*
Northwestern College *B*
St. Ambrose University *B, M*
Scott Community College *C, A*
Simpson College *B*

Southeastern Community College
    North Campus *C, A*
Southwestern Community College *A*
University of Dubuque *B*
University of Iowa *B, M, D*
University of Northern Iowa *B, M*
Upper Iowa University *B*
Wartburg College *B*
Western Iowa Tech Community
    College *A*
William Penn University *B*

Kansas

Allen County Community College *A*
Baker University *B*
Barton County Community College *A*
Benedictine College *B*
Bethany College *B*
Brown Mackie College
    Salina *A*
Butler Community College *A*
Central Christian College of
    Kansas *A, B*
Coffeyville Community College *A*
Dodge City Community College *C, A*
Donnelly College *A*
Emporia State University *B*
Fort Hays State University *B*
Friends University *B*
Highland Community College *A*
Johnson County Community
    College *A*
Kansas State University *B, M*
Kansas Wesleyan University *A, B*
Labette Community College *A*
McPherson College *B*
MidAmerica Nazarene University *B*
Neosho County Community
    College *C, A*
Newman University *B*
Pittsburg State University *B, M*
Pratt Community College *C, A*
Seward County Community
    College *C, A*
Southwestern College *B*
Tabor College *M*
University of Kansas *B, M*
University of St. Mary *B*
Washburn University *B, M*
Wichita State University *B, M*

Kentucky

Asbury College *B*
Ashland Community and Technical
    College *A*
Bellarmine University *B*
Berea College *B*
Big Sandy Community and Technical
    College *A*
Brescia University *B*
Campbellsville University *A, B*
Daymar College: Paducah *C*
Eastern Kentucky University *B*
Georgetown College *B*
Kentucky Wesleyan College *B*
Madisonville Community College *A*
Maysville Community and Technical
    College *C, A*
Morehead State University *B*
Murray State University *B, M*
National College
    Danville *C, A*
    Florence *C, A*
    Lexington *C, A*
    Louisville *C, A*
    Pikeville *C, A*
    Richmond *C, A*
Northern Kentucky University *B, M*
Owensboro Community and
    Technical College *A*
Spalding University *B*
Spencerian College *C, A*
Sullivan University *C, A, B*
Thomas More College *C, A, B*

Transylvania University *B*
Union College *B*
University of Kentucky *B, M*
University of Louisville *B, M*
University of the Cumberlands *B*
West Kentucky Community and
    Technical College *A*
Western Kentucky University *C, B*

Louisiana

Centenary College of Louisiana *B*
Delgado Community College *A*
Dillard University *B*
Grambling State University *B*
Herzing University *B*
Louisiana College *B*
Louisiana State University
    Shreveport *B*
Louisiana State University and
    Agricultural and Mechanical
    College *B, M, D*
Louisiana Tech University *B, M*
Loyola University New Orleans *B*
McNeese State University *B*
Nicholls State University *B*
Northwestern State University *B*
Our Lady of Holy Cross College *B*
Southeastern Louisiana University *B*
Southern University
    Shreveport *A*
Southern University and Agricultural
    and Mechanical College *B*
Tulane University *A, B, M*
University of Louisiana at Lafayette *B*
University of Louisiana at Monroe *B*
University of New Orleans *B, M*
Xavier University of Louisiana *B*

Maine

Andover College *A*
Beal College *A*
Central Maine Community College *A*
Husson University *A, B*
Northern Maine Community
    College *A*
Saint Joseph's College of Maine *B*
Thomas College *A, B*
University of Maine *C, B*
University of Maine
    Augusta *B*
    Machias *A, B*
    Presque Isle *B*
University of Southern Maine *B, M*
York County Community College *A*

Maryland

Allegany College of Maryland *A*
Baltimore City Community College *A*
Chesapeake College *C, A*
Frederick Community College *A*
Frostburg State University *B*
Kaplan College: Hagerstown *C, A, B*
Loyola University Maryland *B*
Morgan State University *B*
Mount St. Mary's University *B*
Prince George's Community
    College *C, A*
Salisbury University *B*
Stevenson University *B*
Towson University *B*
University of Baltimore *B, M*
University of Maryland
    College Park *B*
    Eastern Shore *B*
    University College *C, B, M*
Washington Adventist University *A, B*

Massachusetts

American International College *B, M*
Assumption College *B*
Atlantic Union College *A, B*
Babson College *B*
Bay State College *A*

Becker College *B*
Bentley University *B, M, D*
Boston College *B, M*
Boston University *B*
Bridgewater State College *B, M*
Bristol Community College *A*
Bunker Hill Community College *C, A*
Cape Cod Community College *A*
College of the Holy Cross *B*
Dean College *C*
Eastern Nazarene College *B*
Elms College *B*
Endicott College *B*
Fisher College *A, B*
Fitchburg State College *B, M*
Gordon College *B*
Greenfield Community College *C, A*
Lasell College *B*
Marian Court College *C, A*
Massachusetts Bay Community
    College *C, A*
Massasoit Community College *C, A*
Middlesex Community College *A*
Newbury College *B*
Nichols College *B*
Northeastern University *B, M*
Northern Essex Community
    College *C, A*
Roxbury Community College *C, A*
Salem State College *B*
Springfield Technical Community
    College *A*
Stonehill College *B*
Suffolk University *C, B, M*
University of Massachusetts
    Amherst *B, M*
    Boston *M*
    Dartmouth *B*
Western New England College *B, M*
Westfield State College *M*

Michigan

Adrian College *B*
Alma College *B*
Alpena Community College *A*
Andrews University *B*
Aquinas College *B*
Baker College
    of Auburn Hills *A, B*
    of Cadillac *C, A, B*
    of Clinton Township *C, A, B*
    of Flint *C, A, B*
    of Jackson *C, A, B*
    of Muskegon *C, A, B*
    of Owosso *A, B*
    of Port Huron *C, A, B*
Baker College of Allen Park *A*
Bay de Noc Community College *C, A*
Calvin College *B*
Central Michigan University *B*
Cleary University *A, B, M*
Cornerstone University *B*
Davenport University *A, B, M*
Delta College *C, A*
Eastern Michigan University *B, M*
Ferris State University *B*
Finlandia University *B*
Glen Oaks Community College *C*
Gogebic Community College *A*
Grace Bible College *B*
Grand Valley State University *B, M*
Henry Ford Community College *A*
Hillsdale College *B*
Hope College *B*
Jackson Community College *C, A*
Kalamazoo Valley Community
    College *C, A*
Kellogg Community College *C, A*
Kuyper College *B*
Lake Michigan College *A*
Lake Superior State University *B*
Lansing Community College *A*
Macomb Community College *C, A*
Madonna University *C, B*

Marygrove College C, A, B
Michigan State University B, M, D
Mid Michigan Community College A
Monroe County Community
  College C, A
Montcalm Community College A
Muskegon Community College A
North Central Michigan College C, A
Northern Michigan University B
Northwestern Michigan College A
Northwood University: Michigan A, B
Oakland University B, M
Rochester College B
Saginaw Valley State University B
St. Clair County Community
  College A
Siena Heights University A, B
Spring Arbor University B
University of Detroit Mercy B
University of Michigan M
University of Michigan
  Flint B, M
Walsh College of Accountancy and
  Business Administration B, M
Washtenaw Community College C, A
Wayne County Community College A
Wayne State University B, M
West Shore Community College A
Western Michigan University B, M

Minnesota

Academy College C, A, B
Alexandria Technical College A
Anoka Technical College C
Anoka-Ramsey Community College A
Augsburg College B
Bemidji State University B
Capella University B, M
Central Lakes College A
Century Community and Technical
  College C, A
College of St. Benedict B
College of St. Scholastica B
Concordia College: Moorhead B
Concordia University: St. Paul B
Dakota County Technical College C, A
Globe University C, A, B
Gustavus Adolphus College B
Hamline University B
Hennepin Technical College C, A
Inver Hills Community College A
Itasca Community College A
Lake Superior College A
Metropolitan State University B
Minneapolis Business College A
Minneapolis Community and
  Technical College A
Minnesota School of Business C, A, B
Minnesota School of Business:
  Blaine C, A, B
Minnesota School of Business:
  Brooklyn Center B
Minnesota School of Business:
  Rochester C, A, B
Minnesota School of Business: St.
  Cloud C, A, B
Minnesota State College - Southeast
  Technical C, A
Minnesota State Community and
  Technical College C, A
Minnesota State University
  Mankato B
  Moorhead B
Minnesota West Community and
  Technical College A
National American University
  Bloomington B
Normandale Community College A
North Hennepin Community
  College C, A
Northland Community & Technical
  College C, A
Northwest Technical College A
Northwestern College B

Pine Technical College C, A
Rasmussen College
  Eagan A
  Eden Prairie A
  Mankato A
  St. Cloud A
Rasmussen College: Brooklyn Park A
Rasmussen College: Lake
  Elmo/Woodbury A
Ridgewater College C, A
Riverland Community College C, A
Rochester Community and Technical
  College A
St. Catherine University B
Saint Cloud State University B
St. Cloud Technical College C, A
St. John's University B
St. Mary's University of
  Minnesota C, B
St. Paul College A
South Central College C, A
Southwest Minnesota State
  University A, B
University of Minnesota
  Crookston B
  Duluth B
  Twin Cities C, B
University of St. Thomas B, M
Vermilion Community College A
Walden University B
Winona State University B

Mississippi

Alcorn State University B
Antonelli College
  Jackson A
Belhaven University C, B
Copiah-Lincoln Community College A
Delta State University B, M
Jackson State University B, M
Millsaps College B, M
Mississippi College B
Mississippi Delta Community
  College A
Mississippi Gulf Coast Community
  College A
Mississippi State University B, M
Mississippi University for Women B
Mississippi Valley State University B
Northwest Mississippi Community
  College A
University of Mississippi B, M, D
University of Southern
  Mississippi B, M
Virginia College Gulf Coast A

Missouri

Avila University B
Bolivar Technical College C, A
Central Methodist University A, B
College of the Ozarks B
Columbia College B
Culver-Stockton College B
Drury University B
Evangel University A, B
Hannibal-LaGrange College B
Harris-Stowe State University B
Hickey College C, A
Lincoln University B
Lindenwood University B, M
Maryville University of Saint
  Louis B, M
Metropolitan Community College:
  Longview C, A
Metropolitan Community College:
  Penn Valley C, A
Mineral Area College A
Missouri Baptist University B
Missouri Southern State
  University A, B
Missouri State University B, M
Missouri Valley College B
Missouri Western State University B
North Central Missouri College C, A

Northwest Missouri State
  University B
Ozarks Technical Community
  College A
Park University B
St. Louis Community College
  St. Louis Community College at
    Florissant Valley C
  St. Louis Community College at
    Meramec C, A
Saint Louis University M
Southeast Missouri State
  University B, M
Southwest Baptist University A, B
State Fair Community College A
Stephens College B
Texas County Technical Institute C, A
Three Rivers Community College A
Truman State University B, M
University of Central Missouri B, M
University of Missouri
  Columbia B, M, D
  Kansas City B, M
  St. Louis B, M
Washington University in St.
  Louis B, M
Webster University C, B
Westminster College B
William Jewell College B
William Woods University B

Montana

Flathead Valley Community
  College C, A
Fort Peck Community College C
Helena College of Technology of the
  University of Montana A
Montana State University
  Bozeman M
  College of Technology: Great
    Falls A
Rocky Mountain College B
University of Great Falls B
University of Montana A, M, D

Nebraska

Bellevue University B
Chadron State College B
College of Saint Mary A
Concordia University B
Creighton University B, M
Dana College B
Doane College B
Kaplan University
  Lincoln A
Kaplan University: Omaha A, B
Metropolitan Community
  College C, A
Nebraska Wesleyan University B
Northeast Community College A
Union College A, B
University of Nebraska
  Lincoln B, M
  Omaha B, M
Western Nebraska Community
  College C, A
York College B

Nevada

College of Southern Nevada A
Great Basin College C, A
Morrison University A, B
Truckee Meadows Community
  College A
University of Nevada
  Las Vegas B, M
  Reno B, M
Western Nevada College A

New Hampshire

Franklin Pierce University A
Lakes Region Community
  College C, A

Lebanon College A
Manchester Community College C, A
NHTI-Concord's Community
  College C, A
Nashua Community College C, A
New England College B, M
Plymouth State University B
River Valley Community College A
Saint Anselm College B
Southern New Hampshire
  University A, B, M
University of New Hampshire M
White Mountains Community
  College A

New Jersey

Atlantic Cape Community College A
Berkeley College- Garret Mountain
  Campus A, B
Bloomfield College C, B
Brookdale Community College A
Burlington County College A
Caldwell College B, M
Camden County College A
Centenary College B, M
The College of New Jersey B
College of St. Elizabeth C
Cumberland County College C, A
Essex County College C, A
Fairleigh Dickinson University
  College at Florham B, M
  Metropolitan Campus B, M
Felician College B
Georgian Court University C, B
Gloucester County College C, A
Hudson County Community
  College A
Kean University B, M
Mercer County Community College A
Middlesex County College A
New Jersey City University M
Ocean County College C
Passaic County Community College A
Ramapo College of New Jersey B
Rider University B, M
Rowan University B, M
Rutgers, The State University of New
  Jersey
  Camden Regional Campus B, M
  New Brunswick/Piscataway
    Campus B, M
  Newark Regional Campus B, M
Saint Peter's College B, M
Seton Hall University B, M
Sussex County Community
  College A
Thomas Edison State College C, B
Warren County Community
  College C, A
William Paterson University of New
  Jersey B

New Mexico

Brookline College
  Albuquerque C, A
Central New Mexico Community
  College C, A
Clovis Community College A
Eastern New Mexico University B
Eastern New Mexico University:
  Roswell Campus C, A
Navajo Technical College C, A
New Mexico Highlands University B
New Mexico Junior College A
New Mexico State University B, M
Northern New Mexico College C, A
Santa Fe Community College A
University of New Mexico M
University of the Southwest B
Western New Mexico University B

New York

Adelphi University B, M
Adirondack Community College A

Alfred University B, M
Berkeley College A, B
Berkeley College of New York
City A, B
Bramson ORT College C, A
Briarcliffe College A, B
Bryant & Stratton Business Institute
Bryant & Stratton College: Albany A
Bryant & Stratton College:
Rochester A
Bryant & Stratton College:
Syracuse A
Bryant & Stratton College: Syracuse
North A
Canisius College B, M
Cazenovia College B
City University of New York
Baruch College B, M
Borough of Manhattan Community
College A
Bronx Community College A
Brooklyn College B, M
College of Staten Island B
Hostos Community College A
Hunter College B
Kingsborough Community
College A
LaGuardia Community College A
Lehman College B, M
Medgar Evers College B
New York City College of
Technology A
Queens College B, M
Queensborough Community
College A
York College B
Clinton Community College A
College of Saint Rose B, M
College of Westchester C, A
Columbia-Greene Community
College C, A
Concordia College B
Cornell University D
Corning Community College C, A
D'Youville College B
Daemen College C, B, M
Dominican College of Blauvelt B
Dowling College B
Dutchess Community College A
Elmira Business Institute C, A
Elmira College B
Excelsior College B
Finger Lakes Community College A
Fordham University B, M
Genesee Community College A
Globe Institute of Technology C, A, B
Hartwick College B
Herkimer County Community
College A
Hilbert College A, B
Hofstra University B, M
Houghton College B
Hudson Valley Community
College C, A
Iona College B, M
Ithaca College B, M
Jamestown Business College A
Keuka College B
Le Moyne College B
Long Island Business Institute A
Long Island University
Brooklyn Campus B, M
C. W. Post Campus B, M
Manhattan College B
Maria College A
Marist College B
Marymount Manhattan College B
Mercy College B, M
Mildred Elley C
Molloy College B, M
Monroe College A, B
Monroe Community College A
Mount Saint Mary College C, B
Nassau Community College A

Nazareth College B
New York Institute of
Technology A, B
New York University C, B, M, D
Niagara County Community
College C, A
Niagara University B
Nyack College B, M
Olean Business Institute A
Orange County Community College A
Pace University C, B, M
Professional Business College C, A
Roberts Wesleyan College B
Rochester Institute of
Technology C, A, B, M
Rockland Community College A
Sage College of Albany B
Saint Bonaventure University B, M
St. Francis College B, M
St. John Fisher College B
St. John's University B, M
St. Joseph's College B
St. Joseph's College: Suffolk
Campus B
St. Thomas Aquinas College B
Siena College C, B, M, T
State University of New York
Albany B, M
Binghamton B, M
Buffalo M
College at Brockport B, M
College at Fredonia B
College at Geneseo B, M
College at Old Westbury B, M
College at Oneonta B
College at Plattsburgh B
College of Agriculture and
Technology at Morrisville A
College of Technology at Alfred A
College of Technology at Delhi A
Farmingdale C
Institute of Technology at
Utica/Rome B, M
New Paltz B, M
Oswego B, M
Suffolk County Community College A
Sullivan County Community
College C, A
Syracuse University B, M
Technical Career Institutes A
Touro College C, A, B, M
University of Rochester M
Utica College B
Utica School of Commerce C, A
Wagner College B, M
Westchester Community College C, A
Wood Tobe-Coburn School A
Yeshiva University B

North Carolina
Alamance Community College C, A
Appalachian State University B, M
Asheville-Buncombe Technical
Community College A
Barton College B
Beaufort County Community
College C, A
Belmont Abbey College B
Bennett College for Women B
Caldwell Community College and
Technical Institute A
Campbell University B
Catawba College B
Central Carolina Community
College A
Cleveland Community College A
Davidson County Community
College C, A
Durham Technical Community
College A
East Carolina University B, M
Edgecombe Community College A
Elizabeth City State University B
Elon University B

Fayetteville State University B
Fayetteville Technical Community
College A
Forsyth Technical Community
College A
Gardner-Webb University B, M
Gaston College A
Greensboro College C, B
Guilford College C, B
Halifax Community College A
Haywood Community College C, A
High Point University B
James Sprunt Community
College C, A
Johnson & Wales University:
Charlotte B
Johnston Community College A
King's College C, A
Lenoir Community College A
Lenoir-Rhyne University B
Livingstone College B
Mars Hill College B
Mayland Community College A
McDowell Technical Community
College A
Meredith College B
Methodist University B
Miller-Motte Technical College C, A
Mitchell Community College A
Montgomery Community College A
Montreat College B
Mount Olive College A, B
Nash Community College A
North Carolina Agricultural and
Technical State University B
North Carolina Central University B
North Carolina State
University C, B, M
North Carolina Wesleyan College B
Pamlico Community College A
Pfeiffer University B
Piedmont Community College A
Pitt Community College C, A
Randolph Community College A
Richmond Community College C, A
Roanoke-Chowan Community
College C
Rockingham Community College A
Rowan-Cabarrus Community
College C, A
St. Augustine's College B
Salem College B
Sampson Community College A
Sandhills Community College C, A
South College A
South Piedmont Community
College C, A
Southwestern Community
College C, A
Stanly Community College C, A
Surry Community College C, A
Tri-County Community College A
University of North Carolina
Asheville B
Chapel Hill M
Charlotte B, M
Greensboro B, M
Pembroke B
Wilmington B, M
Vance-Granville Community
College A
Wake Forest University B, M
Wake Technical Community
College A
Western Carolina University B, M
Western Piedmont Community
College C, A
Wilkes Community College C, A
Wilson Community College A
Wingate University B
Winston-Salem State University B

North Dakota
Dickinson State University B

Jamestown College B
Lake Region State College A
Minot State University B
North Dakota State University B
Rasmussen College: Bismarck A, B
Rasmussen College: Fargo C, A, B
University of Mary B, M
University of North Dakota B, M

Ohio
Ashland University B
Baldwin-Wallace College C, B, M
Belmont Technical College A
Bluffton University B
Bowling Green State University B, M
Bowling Green State University:
Firelands College C, A
Bradford School C, A
Bryant & Stratton College
Eastlake A
Parma A
Capital University B
Case Western Reserve University B, M
Cedarville University B
Central Ohio Technical College A
Central State University B
Cincinnati State Technical and
Community College C, A
Cleveland State University B, M
College of Mount St. Joseph A, B
Columbus State Community
College C, A
Cuyahoga Community College
Metropolitan Campus A
Davis College C, A
Defiance College B
ETI Technical College of Niles A
Eastern Gateway Community
College A
Edison State Community College C, A
Franciscan University of
Steubenville A, B
Franklin University A, B
Gallipolis Career College A
Heidelberg University B
James A. Rhodes State College C, A
John Carroll University B, M
Kent State University B, M, D
Malone University B
Marietta College B
Marion Technical College A
Miami University
Oxford Campus B, M
Mount Union College B
Mount Vernon Nazarene University B
Muskingum University B
National College
Dayton C
North Central State College A
Northwest State Community
College C, A
Notre Dame College C, B
Ohio Business College: Sandusky C, A
Ohio Christian University A, B
Ohio Dominican University B
Ohio Northern University B
Ohio State University
Columbus Campus B, M, D
Ohio University B, M
Ohio Valley College of Technology A
Ohio Wesleyan University B
Otterbein College B
Owens Community College
Toledo C
Shawnee State University A
Stark State College of Technology A
Terra State Community College C, A
Tiffin University A, B
Trumbull Business College A
University of Akron B, M
University of Akron: Wayne College A
University of Cincinnati B, D
University of Dayton B
University of Findlay A, B

University of Northwestern Ohio *A, B*
University of Rio Grande *A, B*
University of Toledo *A, B, M*
Urbana University *B*
Ursuline College *B*
Walsh University *A, B*
Washington State Community
College *A*
Wilberforce University *B*
Wilmington College *B*
Wright State University *B, M*
Xavier University *B*
Youngstown State University *A, B, M*
Zane State College *C, A*

Oklahoma

Bacone College *A*
Cameron University *B*
Carl Albert State College *C, A*
Connors State College *A*
East Central University *B*
Eastern Oklahoma State College *A*
Langston University *B*
Northeastern Oklahoma Agricultural
and Mechanical College *C, A*
Northeastern State University *B*
Northern Oklahoma College *A*
Northwestern Oklahoma State
University *B*
Oklahoma Baptist University *B*
Oklahoma Christian University *B*
Oklahoma City University *B, M*
Oklahoma Panhandle State
University *B*
Oklahoma State University *B, M*
Oklahoma State University
Institute of Technology:
Okmulgee *A*
Oral Roberts University *B*
Rogers State University *A*
Southeastern Oklahoma State
University *B*
Southern Nazarene University *B*
Southwestern Oklahoma State
University *B*
Tulsa Community College *A*
University of Central Oklahoma *B*
University of Oklahoma *B, M*
University of Tulsa *B*

Oregon

Central Oregon Community
College *A*
Chemeketa Community College *C, A*
Clackamas Community College *C, A*
Clatsop Community College *A*
Corban College *B*
Eastern Oregon University *B*
Linfield College *B*
Mt. Hood Community College *C, A*
Northwest Christian University *B*
Oregon Institute of Technology *B*
Portland Community College *C*
Portland State University *C, B*
Southern Oregon University *B*
Umpqua Community College *A*
University of Oregon *B, M, D*
University of Portland *B*

Pennsylvania

Albright College *B*
Alvernia University *B*
Arcadia University *B*
Bloomsburg University of
Pennsylvania *B*
Bucknell University *B*
Bucks County Community
College *C, A*
Cabrini College *C, B*
California University of
Pennsylvania *B*
Cambria-Rowe Business College:
Indiana *A*
Carlow University *B*

Carnegie Mellon University *D*
Cedar Crest College *C, B*
Central Pennsylvania College *C, A, B*
Chatham University *B, M*
Chestnut Hill College *A, B*
Clarion University of
Pennsylvania *C, B*
Commonwealth Technical Institute *A*
Community College of Philadelphia *A*
Consolidated School of Business
Lancaster *A*
York *A*
DeSales University *B*
Delaware Valley College *B*
Drexel University *M*
Duquesne University *B, M*
Edinboro University of
Pennsylvania *B*
Elizabethtown College *C, A, B*
Erie Business Center *A*
Erie Business Center South *A*
Gannon University *B*
Geneva College *B*
Grove City College *B*
Gwynedd-Mercy College *A, B*
Holy Family University *B*
Immaculata University *C, A, B*
Indiana University of
Pennsylvania *A, B*
Juniata College *B*
Kaplan Career Institute: Pittsburgh *A*
Keystone College *A, B*
King's College *B*
Kutztown University of
Pennsylvania *B*
La Roche College *B*
La Salle University *A, B*
Lackawanna College *A*
Laurel Business Institute *A*
Lebanon Valley College *C, A, B*
Lehigh University *B, M*
Lincoln University *B*
Lock Haven University of
Pennsylvania *B*
Luzerne County Community
College *A*
Lycoming College *B*
Manor College *A*
Mansfield University of
Pennsylvania *B*
Marywood University *B*
Mercyhurst College *B*
Messiah College *B*
Misericordia University *B*
Montgomery County Community
College *C, A*
Moravian College *B*
Mount Aloysius College *A, B*
Muhlenberg College *C, A, B*
Neumann University *C, B*
Newport Business Institute: Lower
Burrell *A*
PJA School *C, A*
Penn Commercial Business and
Technical School *C*
Penn State
Abington *B*
Altoona *B*
Beaver *B*
Berks *B*
Brandywine *B*
DuBois *B*
Erie, The Behrend College *B*
Fayette, The Eberly Campus *B*
Greater Allegheny *B*
Hazleton *B*
Lehigh Valley *B*
Mont Alto *B*
New Kensington *B*
Schuylkill *B*
Shenango *B*
University Park *B*
Wilkes-Barre *B*

Worthington Scranton *B*
York *B*
Pennsylvania College of
Technology *B*
Philadelphia University *C, A, B, M*
Point Park University *C, A, B*
Reading Area Community
College *C, A*
Robert Morris University *C, B*
Rosemont College *B*
St. Francis University *B*
Saint Joseph's University *A, B, M*
St. Vincent College *C, B, M*
Seton Hill University *B*
Shippensburg University of
Pennsylvania *B*
Slippery Rock University of
Pennsylvania *B*
South Hills School of Business &
Technology *A*
South Hills School of Business &
Technology: Altoona *A*
Susquehanna University *B*
Temple University *B, M*
Thiel College *A, B*
University of Pennsylvania *B, M, D*
University of Pittsburgh *B*
University of Pittsburgh
Bradford *B*
Greensburg *B*
Johnstown *B*
Titusville *C, A*
University of Scranton *B, M*
Villanova University *B, M*
Washington & Jefferson College *B*
Waynesburg University *B*
West Chester University of
Pennsylvania *B*
Westminster College *B*
Widener University *B, M*
Wilkes University *B*
Wilson College *A, B*
YTI Career Institute: York *A*
York College of Pennsylvania *B, M*

Puerto Rico

American University of Puerto
Rico *A, B*
Bayamon Central University *B, M*
Caribbean University *A, B*
Huertas Junior College *A*
Inter American University of Puerto
Rico
Aguadilla Campus *A, B, M*
Arecibo Campus *A, B*
Bayamon Campus *A, B*
Fajardo Campus *A, B*
Guayama Campus *A, B*
Metropolitan Campus *A, B, M*
Ponce Campus *A, B, M*
San German Campus *A, B, M*
National College of Business and
Technology: Bayamon *A*
National College of Business and
Technology: Rio Grande *A*
Pontifical Catholic University of
Puerto Rico *B, M*
Turabo University *A, B, M*
Universidad Metropolitana *B, M*
Universidad del Este *A, B, M*
University College of San Juan *A, B*
University of Puerto Rico
Aguadilla *B*
Arecibo *B*
Bayamon University College *B*
Cayey University College *B*
Humacao *B*
Ponce *B*
Rio Piedras *B, M*
Utuado *B*
University of the Sacred Heart *B*

Rhode Island

Bryant University *B, M*

Community College of Rhode
Island *C, A*
Johnson & Wales University:
Providence *B, M*
Providence College *B*
Rhode Island College *B, M*
Roger Williams University *B*
Salve Regina University *B*
University of Rhode Island *B, M*

South Carolina

Aiken Technical College *C, A*
Benedict College *B*
Bob Jones University *B, M*
Central Carolina Technical College *A*
Charleston Southern University *B*
Clemson University *B, M*
Coastal Carolina University *B*
College of Charleston *B, M*
Columbia College *B*
Converse College *B*
Florence-Darlington Technical
College *A*
Forrest Junior College *A*
Francis Marion University *B*
Furman University *B*
Greenville Technical College *C, A*
Horry-Georgetown Technical
College *A*
Midlands Technical College *C, A*
North Greenville University *B*
Northeastern Technical College *A*
Orangeburg-Calhoun Technical
College *C, A*
Presbyterian College *B*
South Carolina State University *B*
Southern Wesleyan University *B*
Spartanburg Community College *C, A*
Technical College of the
Lowcountry *C, A*
Tri-County Technical College *A*
Trident Technical College *A*
University of South Carolina *B, M*
Wofford College *B*
York Technical College *C, A*

South Dakota

Augustana College *B*
Black Hills State University *B*
Dakota State University *B*
Dakota Wesleyan University *B*
Kilian Community College *A*
Lake Area Technical Institute *A*
Mitchell Technical Institute *A*
Mount Marty College *A, B*
National American University
Rapid City *A, B*
Northern State University *B*
Oglala Lakota College *B*
Sinte Gleska University *A*
Sisseton Wahpeton College *A*
Southeast Technical Institute *A*
University of Sioux Falls *B*
University of South Dakota *B, M*
Western Dakota Technical Institute *A*

Tennessee

Belmont University *B, M*
Carson-Newman College *B*
Columbia State Community College *A*
Cumberland University *B*
Draughons Junior College:
Nashville *C, A*
East Tennessee State University *B, M*
Freed-Hardeman University *B*
Jackson State Community College *A*
King College *B*
Lambuth University *B*
Lee University *B*
Lincoln Memorial University *B*
Lipscomb University *B, M*
Martin Methodist College *B*
Middle Tennessee State University *B*
Milligan College *B*

Nashville State Community College A
National College
   Knoxville C, A
   Nashville C, A
National College of Business &
   Technology
   National College: Bristol C, A
Northeast State Community College C
Rhodes College M
South College A
Southern Adventist University A, B, M
Tennessee State University A, B
Tennessee Technological University B
Tennessee Wesleyan College B
Trevecca Nazarene University B
Tusculum College B
Union University B, T
University of Memphis B, M
University of Tennessee
   Chattanooga M
   Knoxville B, M, D
   Martin B
Vanderbilt University M

Texas

Abilene Christian University B, M
Amarillo College C, A
Amberton University B
Angelina College A
Angelo State University B, M
Austin Community College C
Baylor University B, M
Blinn College A
Brazosport College A
Brookhaven College C, A
Cisco College A
Clarendon College A
Coastal Bend College C, A
College of the Mainland A
Dallas Baptist University B, M
El Centro College C, A
El Paso Community College C, A
Frank Phillips College C, A
Galveston College C, A
Grayson County College C, A
Hardin-Simmons University B
Houston Baptist University B, M
Houston Community College
   System C, A
Howard College C, A
Howard Payne University B
Huston-Tillotson University B
Kilgore College C, A
Lamar State College at Orange C
Lamar State College at Port
   Arthur C, A
Lamar University B
Laredo Community College C, A
LeTourneau University B
Lee College C, A
Lon Morris College A
Lone Star College System C, A
Lubbock Christian University B
McLennan Community College C, A
McMurry University B
Midland College C, A
Midwestern State University B
Mountain View College C, A
Navarro College C, A
North Lake College C, A
Northwood University: Texas B
Our Lady of the Lake University of San
   Antonio B, M
Palo Alto College A
Paris Junior College A
Prairie View A&M University B, M
Richland College C, A
St. Edward's University B
St. Mary's University B, M
St. Philip's College A
Sam Houston State University B
San Jacinto College C, A
Schreiner University B
South Plains College A

South Texas College C, A
Southern Methodist University B, M
Southwestern Adventist University B
Southwestern Assemblies of God
   University B
Southwestern University B
Stephen F. Austin State
   University B, M
Sul Ross State University B
Tarleton State University B
Texas A&M International
   University B, M
Texas A&M University B, M, D
Texas A&M University
   Commerce B, M
   Corpus Christi B, M
   Kingsville B, M
   Texarkana B, M
Texas Christian University B, M
Texas Lutheran University B
Texas Southern University B, M
Texas State University: San
   Marcos B, M
Texas Tech University B, M
Texas Wesleyan University B, M
Texas Woman's University B
Trinity University B, M
Trinity Valley Community
   College C, A
University of Dallas M
University of Houston B, M, D
University of Houston
   Clear Lake B, M
   Downtown B
   Victoria B
University of Mary Hardin-Baylor B
University of North Texas B, M, D
University of St. Thomas B, M
University of Texas
   Arlington B, M, D
   Austin B, M, D
   Brownsville - Texas Southmost
     College C, A, B
   Dallas B, M
   El Paso B, M
   Pan American B, M
   San Antonio B, M, D
   Tyler B
   of the Permian Basin B, M
University of the Incarnate Word B, M
Vernon College A
Weatherford College C, A
West Texas A&M University B, M
Western Texas College C, A
Wiley College B

Utah

Brigham Young University B, M
College of Eastern Utah C
Dixie State College of Utah B
Eagle Gate College: Layton A, B
Independence University A, B
LDS Business College C, A
Provo College A
Snow College A
Southern Utah University B, M
Stevens-Henager College: Logan B
University of Utah B, M
Utah Career College A
Utah State University B, M
Utah Valley University C, A, B
Weber State University B, M
Western Governors University B
Westminster College B, M

Vermont

Castleton State College B
Champlain College B
College of St. Joseph in Vermont A, B
Lyndon State College B
Norwich University B
St. Michael's College B
University of Vermont M

Virginia

Averett University B
Blue Ridge Community College A
Bryant & Stratton College
   Richmond A
Bryant & Stratton College: Virginia
   Beach A
Central Virginia Community
   College C, A
Christopher Newport University B
College of William and Mary M
Danville Community College A
ECPI College of Technology: Virginia
   Beach C, A
ECPI Technical College: Roanoke A
Eastern Mennonite University B
Emory & Henry College B
Ferrum College B
George Mason University B, M
Germanna Community College C
Hampton University B
J. Sargeant Reynolds Community
   College C, A
James Madison University B, M
Liberty University A, B, M
Longwood University B
Lord Fairfax Community College A
Lynchburg College B
Mountain Empire Community
   College A
National College
   Bluefield C, A
   Charlottesville A
   Danville C, A
   Harrisonburg C, A
   Lynchburg C, A
   Martinsville C, A
   Roanoke Valley C, A, B, M
New River Community College C, A
Norfolk State University B
Northern Virginia Community
   College A
Old Dominion University B, M
Patrick Henry Community College A
Radford University B
Randolph-Macon College B
Rappahannock Community
   College C, A
Regent University A, B
St. Paul's College B
Southwest Virginia Community
   College A
Stratford University:
   Woodbridge C, A, B
Thomas Nelson Community
   College A
Tidewater Community College C, A
University of Richmond B, M
University of Virginia M
University of Virginia's College at
   Wise B
Virginia Commonwealth
   University B, M
Virginia Highlands Community
   College C, A
Virginia Polytechnic Institute and
   State University B, M
Virginia State University B
Virginia Union University B
Virginia Western Community
   College A
Washington and Lee University B
Wytheville Community College A

Washington

Bellevue College C, A
Centralia College C, A
City University of Seattle C, B, M
DeVry University
   Federal Way A
Eastern Washington University B
Everett Community College C, A
Gonzaga University B, M
Green River Community College C, A

Highline Community College C, A
Lake Washington Technical
   College C, A
Lower Columbia College C, A
Peninsula College A
Pierce College C, A
Renton Technical College C, A
Saint Martin's University B
Seattle Pacific University B
Seattle University B
Skagit Valley College C, A
South Puget Sound Community
   College C, A
South Seattle Community
   College C, A
Spokane Community College A
Spokane Falls Community College A
University of Washington B, M
University of Washington Bothell B
University of Washington Tacoma B
Walla Walla University B
Washington State University B, M, D
Western Washington University B
Whatcom Community College C, A
Whitworth University B
Yakima Valley Community
   College C, A

West Virginia

Alderson-Broaddus College B
American Public University System A
Bethany College B
Bluefield State College B
Concord University B
Davis and Elkins College B
Fairmont State University B
Huntington Junior College A
Marshall University B, M
Mountain State College A
Mountain State University A, B
New River Community and Technical
   College A
Ohio Valley University B
Potomac State College of West
   Virginia University A
Shepherd University B
Southern West Virginia Community
   and Technical College A
University of Charleston B
Valley College C
West Liberty University B
West Virginia Business College: Nutter
   Fort A
West Virginia State Community and
   Technical College A
West Virginia State University B
West Virginia University B, M
West Virginia Wesleyan College B
Wheeling Jesuit University B, M

Wisconsin

Blackhawk Technical College A
Cardinal Stritch University B
Carroll University B
Carthage College B
Chippewa Valley Technical College A
College of Menominee Nation A
Concordia University Wisconsin B
Edgewood College B, M
Fox Valley Technical College C, A
Gateway Technical College A
Herzing University B
Lakeland College B
Lakeshore Technical College A
Marian University B
Marquette University B, M
Mid-State Technical College A
Milwaukee Area Technical College A
Moraine Park Technical College C, A
Mount Mary College B
Nicolet Area Technical College A
Northcentral Technical College A
Northeast Wisconsin Technical
   College A

Rasmussen College: Green Bay A
St. Norbert College B
Silver Lake College B
Southwest Wisconsin Technical
    College C, A
University of Wisconsin
    Eau Claire B
    Green Bay B
    La Crosse B
    Madison B, M
    Milwaukee B
    Oshkosh B
    Parkside B
    Platteville B
    River Falls B
    Stevens Point B
    Superior B
    Whitewater B, M
Viterbo University B
Waukesha County Technical
    College A
Western Technical College A
Wisconsin Indianhead Technical
    College A

Wyoming
Casper College A
Central Wyoming College A
Eastern Wyoming College A
Laramie County Community
    College A
University of Wyoming B, M
Western Wyoming Community
    College C, A

Accounting/business management

Alaska
Alaska Pacific University B

Arizona
Arizona State University M
University of Phoenix B, M

California
Claremont McKenna College B
Kaplan College: Panorama City A
Santa Clara University B

Colorado
CollegeAmerica
    Denver A, B

Connecticut
Mitchell College B

Florida
Florida Institute of Technology B
Santa Fe College C

Illinois
Elgin Community College C
Kaskaskia College C
University of Illinois
    Urbana-Champaign B

Indiana
National College: Indianapolis C, A, B
Purdue University B, M, D
Vincennes University C

Iowa
AIB College of Business A
Dordt College B

Kansas
Central Christian College of
    Kansas A, B
Colby Community College C

Kansas City Kansas Community
    College A
Kansas State University A
Ottawa University B
Tabor College B

Louisiana
Centenary College of Louisiana B

Maine
Husson University B, M

Massachusetts
Babson College B
Cape Cod Community College A
Eastern Nazarene College B
Elms College B
Lasell College B

Michigan
Baker College
    of Muskegon B
Oakland Community College A

Minnesota
Augsburg College B
Minnesota West Community and
    Technical College A
Walden University M, D

Mississippi
Mississippi College M

Missouri
Park University A, B
University of Missouri
    Kansas City B

Montana
Rocky Mountain College B, M
University of Great Falls B

Nevada
DeVry University: Henderson M

New York
ASA Institute of Business and
    Computer Technology A
City University of New York
    Brooklyn College M
College of Westchester A
Five Towns College A
Globe Institute of Technology C, A, B
Mercy College B
Mount Saint Mary College M
Olean Business Institute C, A
Rochester Institute of
    Technology B, M
State University of New York
    College of Agriculture and
        Technology at Morrisville A
Utica College M

North Carolina
Chowan University B
East Carolina University B

North Dakota
Dakota College at Bottineau A
University of Mary M

Ohio
National College: Cincinnati A
National College: Stow A
Ohio Christian University A, B
Stark State College of Technology A
Urbana University B

Oregon
Corban College B
George Fox University B

Pennsylvania
Chestnut Hill College A, B
Harrisburg Area Community
    College A
Keystone College B
Mount Aloysius College A, B
Newport Business Institute: Lower
    Burrell A

South Carolina
Miller-Motte Technical College A

South Dakota
Mitchell Technical Institute A

Tennessee
Bethel University B
Lambuth University B
National College: Bartlett C, A
National College: Madison A
National College: Memphis A

Texas
Cedar Valley College C, A

Utah
Stevens-Henager College: Logan A

Vermont
Champlain College B
Lyndon State College B

Virginia
Rappahannock Community
    College C, A

Washington
DeVry University
    Federal Way M
Olympic College C

Wisconsin
Herzing University A, B
Maranatha Baptist Bible College B
Marquette University M

Accounting/computer science

California
California State University
    Chico B
College of the Siskiyous A
San Jose State University B

Colorado
Colorado Mountain College A

Connecticut
Three Rivers Community College A

Iowa
Coe College B

Kansas
Central Christian College of
    Kansas A, B

Maine
Northern Maine Community
    College B, M

Massachusetts
American International College B, M

Missouri
State Fair Community College A

New Hampshire
Southern New Hampshire
    University B

New York
Schenectady County Community
    College A

Oregon
Warner Pacific College B

Puerto Rico
Inter American University of Puerto
    Rico
    Bayamon Campus B

South Carolina
University of South Carolina
    Upstate B

Texas
Houston Baptist University B
Texas State University: San Marcos M
University of Dallas M

Washington
Western Washington University B

Accounting/finance

Alabama
Faulkner University B

Arizona
DeVry University
    Phoenix M

California
DeVry University
    Fremont M
    Long Beach M
    Pomona M
    Sherman Oaks M
Westwood College: Anaheim B

Colorado
DeVry University
    Westminster M

Florida
DeVry University
    Miramar M
    Orlando M
Florida Institute of Technology M
Palm Beach Atlantic University B

Georgia
DeVry University
    Alpharetta M
    Decatur M

Illinois
DeVry University
    Tinley Park M
DeVry University: Online B, M

Indiana
DeVry University: Indianapolis M
Harrison College
    Anderson A
    Columbus A
    Elkhart A
    Evansville A
    Fort Wayne A
    Indianapolis A
    Lafayette A
    Muncie A
    Terre Haute A
Huntington University B
Purdue University B, M, D

Iowa

AIB College of Business *A*
Maharishi University of
    Management *M*

Kansas

Central Christian College of Kansas *A*

Louisiana

Centenary College of Louisiana *B*

Maine

University of Southern Maine *B*

Maryland

DeVry University: Bethesda *M*
University of Maryland
    University College *M*

Massachusetts

Babson College *B*
Eastern Nazarene College *B*
Lasell College *B*
Massasoit Community College *C*
Salem State College *B*

Michigan

Aquinas College *B*
Ferris State University *B*
Northern Michigan University *B*

Minnesota

Bethel University *B*
DeVry University
    Edina *M*
Minnesota West Community and
    Technical College *A*

Missouri

DeVry University
    Kansas City *M*
University of Missouri
    Kansas City *B*
Webster University *B*

New Hampshire

Franklin Pierce University *B*
Southern New Hampshire
    University *M*

New York

Clarkson University *B*
DeVry
    College of New York *M*
Globe Institute of Technology *C, A, B*
Rochester Institute of Technology *M*
State University of New York
    College of Agriculture and
        Technology at Morrisville *A*

North Carolina

DeVry University: Charlotte *M*

North Dakota

University of North Dakota *B*

Ohio

DeVry University
    Columbus *M*
Hiram College *B*
Lourdes College *B*
Stark State College of Technology *A*

Oklahoma

DeVry University: Oklahoma City
    Center *M*
Northeastern State University *M*
Oklahoma State University
    Oklahoma City *A*

Oregon

Corban College *B*
DeVry University: Portland *M*

Pennsylvania

DeVry University
    Fort Washington *M*
Eastern University *B*
Elizabethtown College *B*
Holy Family University *B*
York College of Pennsylvania *M*

South Carolina

York Technical College *C*

Tennessee

DeVry University: Memphis *M*

Texas

DeVry University
    Irving *M*
DeVry University: Houston *M*
North Lake College *C*

Utah

DeVry University: Sandy *M*
Eagle Gate College: Murray *A*

Vermont

Champlain College *B*
Lyndon State College *B*

Virginia

DeVry University
    Arlington *M*

Washington

DeVry University
    Federal Way *M*
Olympic College *C*
Seattle University *M*

Wisconsin

DeVry University: Milwaukee *M*
Herzing University *B*

Accounting technology/ bookkeeping

Alabama

Gadsden State Community College *A*
Jefferson Davis Community College *C*
Jefferson State Community
    College *C, A*
Northwest-Shoals Community
    College *C, A*

Alaska

University of Alaska
    Fairbanks *C, A*

Arizona

Central Arizona College *C, A*
Coconino County Community
    College *C*
Glendale Community College *A*

Arkansas

Arkansas State University
    Beebe *C*
Arkansas State University: Newport *C*
Black River Technical College *C*
Pulaski Technical College *C*
Southeast Arkansas College *C*
University of Arkansas
    Community College at Hope *C*
    Cossatot Community College of the
        C

California

College of the Siskiyous *C, A*
DeVry University
    Fremont *A*
Empire College *C*
Folsom Lake College *C*
Foothill College *C*
Imperial Valley College *C, A*
Kaplan College: Panorama City *A*
Santa Barbara City College *C, A*
Southwestern College *C*
West Hills College: Lemoore *C*

Colorado

Arapahoe Community College *C, A*
Colorado Northwestern Community
    College *C, A*
Community College of Denver *C, A*
DeVry University
    Westminster *A*
Front Range Community College *C, A*
Northeastern Junior College *C, A*
Pikes Peak Community College *C, A*
Pueblo Community College *A*
Red Rocks Community College *C, A*

Connecticut

Naugatuck Valley Community
    College *C, A*

Delaware

Delaware Technical and Community
    College
    Owens *C*
    Stanton/Wilmington *C*
    Terry *C*

Florida

Central Florida Community College *A*
Daytona State College *A*
DeVry University
    Miramar *A*
    Orlando *A*
Hillsborough Community College *A*
Lake City Community College *C*
Saint Johns River Community
    College *A*
St. Petersburg College *C, A*
Seminole Community College *C, A*
University of Miami *C*
Valencia Community College *C, A*

Georgia

Albany Technical College *C*
Athens Technical College *C, A*
Brown Mackie College: Atlanta *C*
Central Georgia Technical
    College *C, A*
DeVry University
    Decatur *A*
Georgia Highlands College *A*
Middle Georgia Technical
    College *C, A*
Savannah Technical College *C, A*
Southwest Georgia Technical
    College *C, A*

Idaho

Lewis-Clark State College *C, A, B*

Illinois

Black Hawk College *C, A*
College of DuPage *C, A*
College of Lake County *C, A*
Danville Area Community College *A*
DeVry University: Online *A*
Harper College *C, A*
Highland Community College *C*
Illinois Eastern Community Colleges
    Wabash Valley College *A*
John A. Logan College *C, A*
John Wood Community College *C, A*

McHenry County College *C, A*
Moraine Valley Community College *C*
Northwestern University *C*
Parkland College *C, A*
Triton College *C*
Waubonsee Community College *C*

Indiana

Indiana University
    Southeast *A, B*
Ivy Tech Community College
    Bloomington *C, A*
    Central Indiana *C, A*
    Columbus *C, A*
    East Central *C, A*
    Kokomo *C, A*
    Lafayette *C, A*
    North Central *C, A*
    Northeast *C, A*
    Northwest *C, A*
    Richmond *C, A*
    South Central *C, A*
    Southeast *C, A*
    Southwest *C, A*
    Wabash Valley *C, A*
Vincennes University *A*

Iowa

Des Moines Area Community
    College *C, A*
Indian Hills Community College *C*
Kaplan University
    Cedar Rapids *C*
North Iowa Area Community
    College *C*
Northeast Iowa Community
    College *C*
Vatterott College *C*
Western Iowa Tech Community
    College *C*

Kansas

Barton County Community
    College *C, A*
Kansas City Kansas Community
    College *C*

Kentucky

Draughons Junior College *C, A*
Somerset Community College *C*
Southern Ohio College
    Brown Mackie College: North
        Kentucky *A*

Louisiana

Baton Rouge Community College *A*

Maine

Kennebec Valley Community
    College *A*

Maryland

Allegany College of Maryland *C, A*
Anne Arundel Community
    College *C, A*
Carroll Community College *C, A*
Cecil College *C, A*
College of Southern Maryland *C, A*
Community College of Baltimore
    County *C, A*
Hagerstown Community College *A*
Harford Community College *C, A*
Montgomery College *C, A*
Wor-Wic Community College *C, A*

Massachusetts

Bunker Hill Community College *C*
Holyoke Community College *C, A*
Mount Wachusett Community
    College *C*
North Shore Community College *A*

Michigan
Baker College
  of Muskegon *C*
  of Port Huron *C*
Bay de Noc Community College *A*
Ferris State University *A, B*
Grand Rapids Community College *A*
Henry Ford Community College *C*
Kirtland Community College *C*
Mott Community College *A*
Northwestern Michigan College *A*
Oakland Community College *C, A*
Schoolcraft College *C, A*
Southwestern Michigan College *A*
Wayne County Community College *C*

Minnesota
Anoka-Ramsey Community
  College *C, A*
Central Lakes College *C*
Century Community and Technical
  College *C*
Dakota County Technical College *C*
DeVry University
  Edina *A*
Hennepin Technical College *C, A*
Lake Superior College *C*
Minneapolis Community and
  Technical College *C*
Minnesota State College - Southeast
  Technical *C, A*
Minnesota State Community and
  Technical College *C*
Minnesota West Community and
  Technical College *C*
North Hennepin Community
  College *C, A*
Northland Community & Technical
  College *C*
Northwest Technical College *C*
Pine Technical College *C*
Ridgewater College *C*
St. Cloud Technical College *C*
St. Paul College *C*
South Central College *C, A*

Missouri
East Central College *C, A*
St. Charles Community College *C, A*

Montana
Montana State University
  Billings *C, A*
  College of Technology: Great
    Falls *C*
Montana Tech of the University of
  Montana *C, A*

Nevada
Western Nevada College *C*

New Jersey
Bergen Community College *A*
Burlington County College *C, A*
Essex County College *A*
Raritan Valley Community College *A*
Union County College *A*

New Mexico
Central New Mexico Community
  College *C*
New Mexico State University
  Carlsbad *C*
San Juan College *C, A*
Santa Fe Community College *C*
Southwestern Indian Polytechnic
  Institute *C, A*

New York
Broome Community College *A*
Canisius College *B*
Cayuga County Community
  College *C, A*
City University of New York
  Brooklyn College *C*
Dutchess Community College *C*
Elmira Business Institute: Vestal *C, A*
Fulton-Montgomery Community
  College *A*
Genesee Community College *C, A*
Globe Institute of Technology *C, A, B*
Jamestown Community College *A*
Jefferson Community College *C, A*
Mercy College *A*
Mohawk Valley Community
  College *C, A*
Onondaga Community College *A*
Orange County Community College *C*
Pace University *M*
Rockland Community College *A*
State University of New York
  College of Agriculture and
    Technology at Cobleskill *A*
  College of Agriculture and
    Technology at Morrisville *A*
  College of Technology at Canton *A*
Tompkins Cortland Community
  College *C, A*
Ulster County Community College *A*

North Carolina
Cape Fear Community College *A*
Catawba Valley Community
  College *C, A*
Central Piedmont Community
  College *C, A*
Coastal Carolina Community
  College *C, A*
Guilford Technical Community
  College *C, A*
Martin Community College *C, A*
Southeastern Community College *C*
Wayne Community College *A*

North Dakota
Dakota College at Bottineau *A*
Lake Region State College *C, A*
Williston State College *A*

Ohio
Cincinnati State Technical and
  Community College *C, A*
Clark State Community College *C, A*
Columbus State Community
  College *C, A*
Davis College *A*
Hocking College *C, A*
Kent State University
  Ashtabula *A*
  East Liverpool *A*
  Trumbull *A*
  Tuscarawas *A*
Kent State University: Geauga *C*
Marion Technical College *A*
Miami University
  Hamilton Campus *C, A*
  Oxford Campus *C, A*
North Central State College *C*
Ohio University
  Southern Campus at Ironton *A*
Owens Community College
  Toledo *C, A*
Southern State Community College *A*
Stark State College of Technology *A*
University of Akron *C, A*
University of Cincinnati
  Clermont College *C, A*
  Raymond Walters College *C, A*
University of Rio Grande *B*
Wright State University *A*
Youngstown State University *A*

Oklahoma
Oklahoma State University
  Oklahoma City *A*
Rose State College *A*

Oregon
Blue Mountain Community
  College *A*
Clackamas Community College *C*
Klamath Community College *C, A*
Lane Community College *C, A*
Linn-Benton Community College *A*
Portland Community College *C, A*
Southwestern Oregon Community
  College *C, A*
Treasure Valley Community College *C*
Umpqua Community College *A*

Pennsylvania
Bucks County Community College *C*
Butler County Community
  College *C, A*
Community College of Allegheny
  County *C, A*
Community College of Beaver
  County *A*
Consolidated School of Business
  Lancaster *A*
  York *A*
Gannon University *A*
Harrisburg Area Community
  College *C, A*
Lehigh Carbon Community
  College *C, A*
Luzerne County Community
  College *C, A*
Montgomery County Community
  College *C, A*
Newport Business Institute: Lower
  Burrell *A*
Northampton Community
  College *C, A*
Peirce College *A*
Pennsylvania College of
  Technology *A*
Pennsylvania Highlands Community
  College *A*
South Hills School of Business &
  Technology *C*
South Hills School of Business &
  Technology: Altoona *C, A*
University of Pittsburgh
  Titusville *C*
Westmoreland County Community
  College *C, A*

Rhode Island
Bryant University *B*

South Carolina
Aiken Technical College *C*
York Technical College *C*

South Dakota
Mitchell Technical Institute *A*
Southeast Technical Institute *C*

Tennessee
Chattanooga State Community
  College *A*
Pellissippi State Community
  College *A*
Southwest Tennessee Community
  College *A*

Texas
Austin Community College *C, A*
Brookhaven College *C*
Del Mar College *C, A*
Lamar Institute of Technology *A*
Lamar State College at Orange *A*
St. Edward's University *B*
St. Philip's College *C, A*
San Antonio College *C, A*
San Jacinto College *C*
Tarrant County College *C, A*
Texas State Technical College
  Harlingen *C*
Tyler Junior College *C, A*

Utah
Salt Lake Community College *C, A*

Virginia
Piedmont Virginia Community
  College *A*
Southwest Virginia Community
  College *C*

Washington
Bates Technical College *C, A*
Bellevue College *C, A*
Bellingham Technical College *C, A*
Big Bend Community College *C, A*
Clark College *C, A*
Clover Park Technical College *C, A*
DeVry University
  Federal Way *A*
Grays Harbor College *C, A*
Lower Columbia College *C, A*
North Seattle Community
  College *C, A*
Olympic College *C, A*
Peninsula College *C, A*
Shoreline Community College *C, A*
Wenatchee Valley College *C, A*
Yakima Valley Community College *A*

West Virginia
Davis and Elkins College *A*
West Virginia Northern Community
  College *C, A*
West Virginia State Community and
  Technical College *A*

Wisconsin
Herzing University *C*
Marquette University *B*
Milwaukee Area Technical College *C*
Northcentral Technical College *C*
Western Technical College *C*
Wisconsin Indianhead Technical
  College *C*

Wyoming
Casper College *C, A*
Central Wyoming College *C, A*

Acoustics

District of Columbia
American University *B*

Pennsylvania
Penn State
  University Park *M, D*

Acting

California
American Academy of Dramatic Arts:
  West *C, A*
Chapman University *B*
College of the Desert *A*
College of the Siskiyous *C, A*
Grossmont College *C, A*
Monterey Peninsula College *C, A*
Pepperdine University *B*
University of Southern
  California *B, M*

Colorado
Colorado Mountain College *C*

Connecticut
University of Connecticut *B*
University of Hartford *B*

Florida
Daytona State College *A*
Florida State University *B, M*
Palm Beach Atlantic University *B*
University of Miami *B*

Illinois
Bradley University *B*
Columbia College Chicago *C, B*
DePaul University *B, M*
Illinois Wesleyan University *B*
Roosevelt University *B, M*
University of Illinois
  Urbana-Champaign *B*

Indiana
Purdue University *B, M*

Iowa
Coe College *B*
Drake University *B*
University of Northern Iowa *B*

Kansas
Central Christian College of Kansas *A*

Maine
University of Southern Maine *B*

Maryland
University of Maryland
  Baltimore County *B*

Massachusetts
Bard College at Simon's Rock *B*
Boston University *B, M*
Brandeis University *M*
Emerson College *B*
Salem State College *B*
Suffolk University *B*

Michigan
Central Michigan University *B*
Michigan State University *B, M*
Oakland University *B*
University of Michigan
  Flint *B*

Minnesota
Saint Cloud State University *B*
University of Minnesota
  Duluth *B*

Mississippi
Mississippi University for Women *M*

Missouri
Lindenwood University *B*
Northwest Missouri State
  University *B*
Webster University *B*

New Hampshire
Keene State College *B*

New Jersey
Cumberland County College *A*
Kean University *B*

New Mexico
College of Santa Fe *B*

New York
American Academy of Dramatic
  Arts *A*
Bard College *B*

Cornell University *M*
Five Towns College *B*
Hofstra University *B*
Ithaca College *B*
Marymount Manhattan College *B*
Pace University *B*
State University of New York
  Binghamton *B*

North Carolina
East Carolina University *B*

Ohio
Ohio University *B, M*
Otterbein College *B*
Youngstown State University *B*

Oklahoma
Oklahoma City University *B*
Oral Roberts University *B*

Pennsylvania
Arcadia University *B*
Lycoming College *B*
Northampton Community College *A*
Penn State
  Abington *B*
  Altoona *B*
  Beaver *B*
  Berks *B*
  Brandywine *B*
  DuBois *B*
  Erie, The Behrend College *B*
  Fayette, The Eberly Campus *B*
  Greater Allegheny *B*
  Hazleton *B*
  Lehigh Valley *B*
  Mont Alto *B*
  New Kensington *B*
  Schuylkill *B*
  Shenango *B*
  University Park *B*
  Wilkes-Barre *B*
  Worthington Scranton *B*
  York *B*
Point Park University *M*
Seton Hill University *B*
Slippery Rock University of
  Pennsylvania *B*
Temple University *B, M*
University of the Arts *B*

South Carolina
Coker College *B*

Tennessee
Chattanooga State Community
  College *C*
Freed-Hardeman University *B*

Texas
Baylor University *B*
Texas Christian University *B*
Texas Tech University *B, M*

Utah
Brigham Young University *B*

Vermont
Bennington College *B*

Virginia
Emory & Henry College *B*
Old Dominion University *B*
Regent University *M*
Shenandoah University *B*

Washington
Cornish College of the Arts *B*

Wyoming
Casper College *A*
Central Wyoming College *A*

Actuarial science

Arizona
Prescott College *M*

California
The Master's College *B*

Connecticut
University of Connecticut *B*

Florida
Florida State University *B*

Georgia
Georgia State University *B, M*

Illinois
Aurora University *B*
Bradley University *B*
North Central College *B*
Roosevelt University *B*
Saint Xavier University *B*
University of Illinois
  Urbana-Champaign *B, M, D*
University of St. Francis *B*

Indiana
Ball State University *B, M*
Butler University *B*
Indiana University
  Northwest *B*
  South Bend *B*
Purdue University *B*
Valparaiso University *B*

Iowa
Central College *B*
Drake University *B*
Northwestern College *B*
University of Iowa *B, M*
University of Northern Iowa *B*

Kansas
Pittsburg State University *B*

Kentucky
Bellarmine University *B*

Massachusetts
Boston University *M*
Worcester Polytechnic Institute *B*

Michigan
Central Michigan University *B*
Eastern Michigan University *B*
Michigan Technological University *T*
Spring Arbor University *B*
University of Michigan
  Flint *B*

Minnesota
University of Minnesota
  Duluth *B*
  Twin Cities *B*
University of St. Thomas *B*

Missouri
Maryville University of Saint
  Louis *B, M*
University of Central Missouri *B*

Nebraska
University of Nebraska
  Lincoln *B, M*

New Jersey
Rider University *B*
Saint Peter's College *B, M*

New York
City University of New York
  Baruch College *B*
  Queens College *B*
St. John's University *B*
Siena College *B*
State University of New York
  Binghamton *B*

North Carolina
Appalachian State University *B*

Ohio
Bowling Green State University *B*
Ohio State University
  Columbus Campus *B*
Ohio University *B*
Otterbein College *B*

Oklahoma
University of Central Oklahoma *B*

Pennsylvania
Lebanon Valley College *B*
Lincoln University *B*
Lycoming College *B*
Mansfield University of
  Pennsylvania *B*
Penn State
  Abington *B*
  Altoona *B*
  Beaver *B*
  Berks *B*
  Brandywine *B*
  DuBois *B*
  Erie, The Behrend College *B*
  Fayette, The Eberly Campus *B*
  Greater Allegheny *B*
  Hazleton *B*
  Lehigh Valley *B*
  Mont Alto *B*
  New Kensington *B*
  Schuylkill *B*
  Shenango *B*
  University Park *B*
  Wilkes-Barre *B*
  Worthington Scranton *B*
  York *B*
Robert Morris University *B*
Saint Joseph's University *B*
Seton Hill University *B*
Slippery Rock University of
  Pennsylvania *B*
Temple University *B, M*
Thiel College *B*
University of Pennsylvania *B*

Rhode Island
Bryant University *B*

South Carolina
Bob Jones University *B*

Texas
Texas Christian University *B*
University of Texas
  Dallas *B*
  San Antonio *B*

Utah
Brigham Young University *B*

Wisconsin
Carroll University *B*
Concordia University Wisconsin *B*
University of Wisconsin
  Madison *B, M*
  Milwaukee *B*

Acupuncture

Connecticut
University of Bridgeport *M*

Illinois
National University of Health
Sciences *M*

Minnesota
Northwestern Health Sciences
University *M*

New York
Swedish Institute *M*

Washington
Bastyr University *B, M, D*

Administrative/
secretarial services

Alabama
Alabama Southern Community
College *C, A*
Bevill State Community College *C, A*
Bishop State Community College *A*
Central Alabama Community
College *C, A*
Chattahoochee Valley Community
College *A*
Enterprise-Ozark Community
College *C, A*
Faulkner State Community
College *C, A*
Gadsden State Community
College *C, A*
George C. Wallace State Community
College
  George C. Wallace Community
    College at Dothan *C, A*
  Selma *C, A*
Jefferson Davis Community
College *C, A*
Jefferson State Community
College *C, A*
Lawson State Community College *A*
Lurleen B. Wallace Community
College *C, A*
Northeast Alabama Community
College *C, A*
Northwest-Shoals Community
College *C, A*
Shelton State Community
College *C, A*
Snead State Community College *C, A*

Alaska
University of Alaska
  Fairbanks *C, A*
  Southeast *A*

Arizona
Brown Mackie College: Tucson *A*
Central Arizona College *C, A*
Cochise College *A*
Dine College *C, A*
Eastern Arizona College *C, A*
GateWay Community College *C, A*
Glendale Community College *C, A*
Lamson College *C*
Mohave Community College *C, A*
Northland Pioneer College *C, A*
Paradise Valley Community
College *C, A*
Pima Community College *C, A*
Scottsdale Community College *A*
Tohono O'odham Community
College *C*

Arkansas
Arkansas Northeastern College *A*
Arkansas State University *A*
Arkansas State University
  Mountain Home *C, A*
Arkansas Tech University *C, A*
Black River Technical College *C*
East Arkansas Community
College *C, A*
National Park Community College *C*
North Arkansas College *C*
Northwest Arkansas Community
College *A*
Philander Smith College *B*
Rich Mountain Community
College *C, A*
South Arkansas Community
College *C, A*
Southeast Arkansas College *C*
University of Arkansas
  Community College at Batesville *A*
  Cossatot Community College of the
    C
  Monticello *C*

California
Allan Hancock College *C, A*
American River College *C, A*
Antelope Valley College *C, A*
Bakersfield College *A*
Barstow Community College *C*
Butte College *C, A*
Canada College *C, A*
Cerritos College *A*
Cerro Coso Community College *C, A*
Chabot College *C, A*
Chaffey College *C, A*
Citrus College *C*
City College of San Francisco *C, A*
Coastline Community College *C*
College of Alameda *C, A*
College of the Canyons *C, A*
College of the Redwoods *A*
College of the Sequoias *C, A*
College of the Siskiyous *C, A*
Columbia College *C, A*
Contra Costa College *C, A*
Crafton Hills College *C, A*
Cypress College *C, A*
De Anza College *C, A*
Diablo Valley College *C*
East Los Angeles College *A*
El Camino College *C, A*
El Camino College: Compton
  Center *A*
Empire College *C, A*
Evergreen Valley College *A*
Feather River College *C, A*
Folsom Lake College *A*
Fresno City College *C, A*
Fullerton College *A*
Glendale Community College *C, A*
Golden West College *C, A*
Grossmont College *C, A*
Hartnell College *C, A*
Heald College
  Salinas *A*
Humphreys College *C, A, B*
Imperial Valley College *C, A*
Kaplan College: Panorama City *C*
Lake Tahoe Community College *C, A*
Laney College *C, A*
Lassen Community College *A*
Long Beach City College *C, A*
Los Angeles City College *C, A*
Los Angeles Harbor College *C, A*
Los Angeles Mission College *C, A*
Los Angeles Southwest College *A*
Los Angeles Trade and Technical
  College *C, A*
Los Angeles Valley College *A*
MTI College *C, A*
Mendocino College *C, A*
Merced College *C, A*

MiraCosta College *C, A*
Mission College *A*
Modesto Junior College *C, A*
Moorpark College *C, A*
Mount San Antonio College *C, A*
Napa Valley College *C, A*
Ohlone College *C, A*
Orange Coast College *C, A*
Oxnard College *C, A*
Pacific Union College *A*
Palomar College *C, A*
Pasadena City College *C, A*
Porterville College *A*
Riverside Community College *C, A*
Sacramento City College *C, A*
Saddleback College *C, A*
San Bernardino Valley College *C*
San Diego City College *C, A*
San Diego Miramar College *C, A*
San Joaquin Delta College *A*
San Jose City College *A*
Santa Barbara City College *C, A*
Santa Rosa Junior College *C*
Shasta College *C, A*
Sierra College *C, A*
Skyline College *C, A*
Solano Community College *C, A*
Southern California Institute of
  Technology *C*
Taft College *A*
Ventura College *C, A*
Victor Valley College *C, A*
West Hills College: Coalinga *C, A*
West Los Angeles College *C, A*
West Valley College *C, A*
Yuba Community College
  District *C, A*

Colorado
Aims Community College *C, A*
Arapahoe Community College *C, A*
Community College of Aurora *A*
Community College of Denver *C, A*
Lamar Community College *A*
Otero Junior College *A*
Pikes Peak Community College *C*
Pueblo Community College *A*

Connecticut
Capital Community College *C, A*
Gateway Community College *C, A*
Goodwin College *C, A*
Housatonic Community College *C, A*
Lincoln College of New England:
  Briarwood *C, A*
Manchester Community College *C, A*
Middlesex Community College *A*
Naugatuck Valley Community
  College *C, A*
Quinebaug Valley Community
  College *C, A*
Tunxis Community College *C, A*

District of Columbia
University of the District of
  Columbia *A*

Florida
Brevard Community College *A*
Broward College *C*
Clearwater Christian College *A*
Florida State College at
  Jacksonville *C, A*
Hobe Sound Bible College *A*
Indian River State College *A*
Lake City Community College *C*
Miami Dade College *C, A*
Pasco-Hernando Community
  College *A*
Pensacola Junior College *A*
Polk State College *A*
Rasmussen College: Ocala *A*
Rasmussen College: Pasco County *A*

Saint Johns River Community
  College *A*
Santa Fe College *A*
Seminole Community College *A*
South Florida Community
  College *C, A*
State College of Florida,
  Manatee-Sarasota *A*
Tallahassee Community College *C, A*

Georgia
Albany Technical College *C*
Athens Technical College *C, A*
Atlanta Technical College *C*
Augusta Technical College *A*
Bainbridge College *C, A*
Central Georgia Technical
  College *C, A*
Chattahoochee Technical College *A*
Clayton State University *A*
Columbus Technical College *C, A*
Dalton State College *C, A*
Darton College *C, A*
DeKalb Technical College *C*
Gainesville State College *A*
Griffin Technical College *A*
Gwinnett College *C*
Gwinnett Technical College *A*
Savannah Technical College *C, A*
Southeastern Technical College *C*
Southwest Georgia Technical
  College *C, A*
Valdosta State University *B*
West Georgia Technical College *A*

Hawaii
University of Hawaii
  Hawaii Community College *C, A*

Idaho
Eastern Idaho Technical College *C, A*
Idaho State University *C, A*
Lewis-Clark State College *C, A, B*
North Idaho College *A*
University of Idaho *B*

Illinois
Black Hawk College *C, A*
Black Hawk College: East
  Campus *C, A*
Carl Sandburg College *C, A*
City Colleges of Chicago
  Harold Washington College *C, A*
  Kennedy-King College *C, A*
  Malcolm X College *C, A*
  Olive-Harvey College *C, A*
College of DuPage *A*
College of Lake County *C, A*
Danville Area Community College *C*
East-West University *A*
Elgin Community College *C*
Fox College *A*
Harper College *C*
Heartland Community College *C*
Highland Community College *C, A*
Illinois Central College *C, A*
Illinois Eastern Community Colleges
  Frontier Community College *C, A*
  Lincoln Trail College *C, A*
  Olney Central College *C, A*
  Wabash Valley College *C, A*
John Wood Community College *C, A*
Joliet Junior College *C, A*
Kankakee Community College *A*
Kaskaskia College *C*
Lake Land College *A*
Lincoln Land Community College *A*
MacCormac College *C, A*
McHenry County College *C, A*
Midstate College *A*
Moraine Valley Community
  College *C, A*
Morton College *C, A*

Northwestern College *A*
Oakton Community College *C*
Parkland College *C*
Prairie State College *C, A*
Rend Lake College *C, A*
Rock Valley College *A*
St. Augustine College *C, A*
Sauk Valley Community College *A*
South Suburban College of Cook
   County *C, A*
Southeastern Illinois College *C, A*
Spoon River College *C, A*
Triton College *C*
Waubonsee Community College *A*
Wilbur Wright College *C, A*

Indiana

Ball State University *A*
Brown Mackie College: South Bend *A*
Harrison College
   Anderson *C, A*
   Columbus *C, A*
   Evansville *A*
   Fort Wayne *C, A*
   Indianapolis *C, A*
   Lafayette *C, A*
   Muncie *C, A*
   Terre Haute *C, A*
International Business College *C, A*
Ivy Tech Community College
   Northwest *A*
Kaplan College: Hammond *C, A*
Kaplan College: Indianapolis *A*
National College: Indianapolis *A*
Vincennes University *C, A*

Iowa

AIB College of Business *A*
Clinton Community College *C, A*
Dordt College *A*
Ellsworth Community College *A*
Faith Baptist Bible College and
   Theological Seminary *A*
Hawkeye Community College *C*
Indian Hills Community College *C*
Iowa Central Community College *C, A*
Iowa Lakes Community College *C*
Iowa Western Community College *A*
Kirkwood Community College *C, A*
Marshalltown Community College *A*
Muscatine Community College *C, A*
North Iowa Area Community
   College *C, A*
Northeast Iowa Community
   College *C, A*
Northwest Iowa Community
   College *C*
Scott Community College *C, A*
Southeastern Community College
   North Campus *C, A*
Southwestern Community College *A*
Western Iowa Tech Community
   College *C, A*

Kansas

Allen County Community College *A*
Barton County Community
   College *C, A*
Central Christian College of Kansas *A*
Cloud County Community
   College *C, A*
Coffeyville Community College *A*
Colby Community College *C, A*
Cowley County Community
   College *C, A*
Fort Hays State University *A*
Fort Scott Community College *C, A*
Garden City Community College *C*
Hutchinson Community College *C, A*
Johnson County Community
   College *C, A*
Kansas City Kansas Community
   College *C, A*

Neosho County Community
   College *C, A*
Seward County Community
   College *C, A*
Tabor College *A, B*
Washburn University *C, A*

Kentucky

Big Sandy Community and Technical
   College *A*
Bluegrass Community and Technical
   College *C, A*
Daymar College
   Owensboro *C, A*
Daymar College: Paducah *C*
Eastern Kentucky University *A*
Henderson Community College *A*
Madisonville Community College *A*
Murray State University *A*
National College
   Danville *C, A*
   Florence *C, A*
   Lexington *C, A*
   Louisville *A*
   Pikeville *C, A*
   Richmond *C, A*
Owensboro Community and
   Technical College *A*
Somerset Community College *C*
Southeast Kentucky Community and
   Technical College *A*
Sullivan University *C, A*
West Kentucky Community and
   Technical College *A*

Louisiana

Delgado Community College *C, A*
ITI Technical College *A*
Louisiana State University
   Eunice *C, A*
Nunez Community College *C*
Southeastern Louisiana University *A*

Maine

Andover College *C, A*
Beal College *A*
Eastern Maine Community College *A*
Northern Maine Community
   College *A*

Maryland

Allegany College of Maryland *C, A*
Baltimore City Community College *A*
Carroll Community College *C, A*
Cecil College *C, A*
Chesapeake College *C, A*
College of Southern Maryland *C*
Community College of Baltimore
   County *C, A*
Kaplan College: Hagerstown *A*
Prince George's Community
   College *C, A*
Wor-Wic Community College *C, A*

Massachusetts

Cape Cod Community College *C, A*
Greenfield Community College *C, A*
Holyoke Community College *C, A*
Marian Court College *C, A*
Massasoit Community College *A*
Mount Wachusett Community
   College *C*
Northern Essex Community
   College *A*
Quinsigamond Community
   College *C, A*
Roxbury Community College *A*
Springfield Technical Community
   College *A*

Michigan

Baker College
   of Auburn Hills *C, A*

   of Cadillac *A*
   of Clinton Township *C, A, B*
   of Flint *C, A*
   of Jackson *C, A*
   of Muskegon *C, A, B*
   of Owosso *A, B*
   of Port Huron *C, A, B*
Bay de Noc Community College *C, A*
Delta College *C, A*
Glen Oaks Community College *C*
Gogebic Community College *A*
Henry Ford Community College *C*
Kalamazoo Valley Community
   College *C, A*
Kellogg Community College *C, A*
Kirtland Community College *C, A*
Lake Michigan College *C, A*
Lansing Community College *A*
Macomb Community College *C, A*
Mid Michigan Community College *A*
Monroe County Community
   College *C, A*
Montcalm Community College *A*
Mott Community College *A*
Muskegon Community College *C, A*
North Central Michigan College *A*
Northern Michigan University *A*
Northwestern Michigan College *C*
St. Clair County Community
   College *C, A*
Schoolcraft College *C, A*
Southwestern Michigan College *A*
Washtenaw Community College *C, A*
West Shore Community College *A*

Minnesota

Alexandria Technical College *C*
Anoka Technical College *C*
Anoka-Ramsey Community College *C*
Central Lakes College *A*
Century Community and Technical
   College *C, A*
Dakota County Technical College *C*
Fond du Lac Tribal and Community
   College *A*
Globe University *C, A*
Hibbing Community College *A*
Lake Superior College *C, A*
Mesabi Range Community and
   Technical College *A*
Minneapolis Business College *A*
Minneapolis Community and
   Technical College *C, A*
Minnesota School of Business *C*
Minnesota State College - Southeast
   Technical *C, A*
Minnesota State Community and
   Technical College *C, A*
Minnesota West Community and
   Technical College *A*
Northland Community & Technical
   College *C, A*
Northwest Technical College *C, A*
Rasmussen College
   Eagan *A*
   Eden Prairie *A*
   Mankato *A*
   St. Cloud *A*
Rasmussen College: Brooklyn Park *A*
Ridgewater College *C*
Riverland Community College *C, A*
Rochester Community and Technical
   College *C, A*
St. Paul College *C, A*
South Central College *C, A*
Winona State University *B*

Mississippi

Copiah-Lincoln Community College *A*
Hinds Community College *A*
Holmes Community College *C, A*
Meridian Community College *A*
Mississippi Delta Community
   College *C, A*

Mississippi Gulf Coast Community
   College *C, A*
Virginia College Gulf Coast *C*

Missouri

Baptist Bible College *A, B*
Crowder College *C, A*
East Central College *C, A*
Hickey College *C, A*
Jefferson College *A*
Lincoln University *A*
Metropolitan Community College:
   Longview *C, A*
Metropolitan Community College:
   Maple Woods *C, A*
Metropolitan Community College:
   Penn Valley *C, A*
Mineral Area College *C, A*
Northwest Missouri State
   University *B*
Patricia Stevens College *C*
St. Louis Community College
   St. Louis Community College at
     Florissant Valley *C, A*
   St. Louis Community College at
     Meramec *C, A*
Southeast Missouri State University *C*
State Fair Community College *C*
Texas County Technical Institute *C, A*
Three Rivers Community College *A*
University of Central Missouri *A*

Montana

Dawson Community College *C, A*
Flathead Valley Community
   College *C, A*
Fort Peck Community College *C, A*
Helena College of Technology of the
   University of Montana *C, A*
Little Big Horn College *C*
Miles Community College *A*
Montana State University
   Billings *C, A*
Montana Tech of the University of
   Montana *A*
Salish Kootenai College *A, B*
University of Montana *C, A*

Nebraska

Central Community College *C, A*
Kaplan University
   Lincoln *A*
Metropolitan Community
   College *C, A*
Northeast Community College *A*
Southeast Community College *C, A*
Western Nebraska Community
   College *C, A*

Nevada

College of Southern Nevada *A*
Everest College: Las Vegas *A*
Great Basin College *C, A*
Truckee Meadows Community
   College *A*

New Hampshire

Lakes Region Community College *C*
Manchester Community College *C, A*
White Mountains Community
   College *A*

New Jersey

Atlantic Cape Community College *A*
Bergen Community College *C, A*
Brookdale Community College *C, A*
Camden County College *C*
Cumberland County College *C, A*
Essex County College *A*
Gloucester County College *C, A*
Hudson County Community
   College *C, A*

Mercer County Community
College *C, A*
Ocean County College *C*
Passaic County Community
College *C, A*
Raritan Valley Community College *C*
Rider University *B*
Salem Community College *C*
Sussex County Community College *C*
Union County College *C, A*
Warren County Community College *C*

New Mexico
Central New Mexico Community
College *C, A*
Clovis Community College *C, A*
Dona Ana Community College of New
Mexico State University *C, A*
Eastern New Mexico University:
Roswell Campus *C, A*
New Mexico Junior College *C, A*
New Mexico State University
Alamogordo *C, A*
Carlsbad *C, A*
Northern New Mexico College *C, A*
San Juan College *C*
Santa Fe Community College *C*
Western New Mexico University *C, A*

New York
Bramson ORT College *A*
Briarcliffe College *A*
Broome Community College *C*
Bryant & Stratton Business Institute
Bryant & Stratton College: Albany *A*
Bryant & Stratton College:
Buffalo *A*
Bryant & Stratton College:
Rochester *C, A*
Bryant & Stratton College:
Syracuse *A*
Bryant & Stratton College: Syracuse
North *A*
City University of New York
Borough of Manhattan Community
College *A*
Bronx Community College *A*
Hostos Community College *A*
LaGuardia Community College *A*
Queensborough Community
College *A*
College of Westchester *C, A*
Columbia-Greene Community
College *A*
Concordia College *A*
Corning Community College *C, A*
Dutchess Community College *A*
Erie Community College
City Campus *A*
Finger Lakes Community College *C, A*
Fulton-Montgomery Community
College *A*
Genesee Community College *C, A*
Globe Institute of Technology *C*
Herkimer County Community
College *A*
Hudson Valley Community College *A*
Jamestown Business College *C, A*
Jamestown Community College *C*
Jefferson Community College *C, A*
Mildred Elley *C*
Mohawk Valley Community College *A*
Monroe Community College *C, A*
Nassau Community College *A*
Niagara County Community
College *C, A*
Olean Business Institute *C, A*
Orange County Community
College *C, A*
Rockland Community College *A*
State University of New York
College of Agriculture and
Technology at Morrisville *A*

College of Technology at Delhi *A*
Farmingdale *A*
Technical Career Institutes *C, A*
Tompkins Cortland Community
College *C*
Trocaire College *A*
Utica School of Commerce *C, A*
Westchester Community College *C, A*
Wood Tobe-Coburn School *C, A*

North Carolina
Alamance Community College *A*
Asheville-Buncombe Technical
Community College *A*
Beaufort County Community
College *C, A*
Blue Ridge Community College *C, A*
Brunswick Community College *C, A*
Caldwell Community College and
Technical Institute *C, A*
Cape Fear Community College *A*
Carteret Community College *A*
Central Carolina Community
College *A*
Central Piedmont Community
College *C, A*
Cleveland Community College *C, A*
Coastal Carolina Community
College *C, A*
College of the Albemarle *A*
Durham Technical Community
College *C, A*
Edgecombe Community College *A*
Fayetteville State University *A*
Gaston College *A*
Haywood Community College *C, A*
James Sprunt Community
College *C, A*
Johnston Community College *A*
King's College *C, A*
Lenoir Community College *A*
Mayland Community College *A*
Mitchell Community College *C, A*
Nash Community College *A*
Piedmont Community College *A*
Randolph Community College *A*
Richmond Community College *C, A*
Roanoke-Chowan Community
College *A*
Sampson Community College *A*
Sandhills Community College *A*
South College *A*
Southwestern Community
College *C, A*
Tri-County Community College *A*
Vance-Granville Community
College *C, A*
Wake Technical Community
College *A*
Wayne Community College *A*
Western Piedmont Community
College *C, A*

North Dakota
Bismarck State College *C, A*
Cankdeska Cikana Community
College *A*
Dakota College at Bottineau *A*
Dickinson State University *A, B*
Lake Region State College *C, A*
North Dakota State College of
Science *A*
Rasmussen College: Bismarck *A*
Rasmussen College: Fargo *C, A*
United Tribes Technical College *C, A*
Williston State College *C, A*

Ohio
Bowling Green State University:
Firelands College *A*
Bryant & Stratton College
Eastlake *A*
Parma *A*

Bryant & Stratton College:
Cleveland *A*
Central Ohio Technical College *A*
Columbus State Community
College *C, A*
Cuyahoga Community College
Metropolitan Campus *C, A*
Davis College *A*
ETI Technical College of Niles *C, A*
Eastern Gateway Community
College *A*
Edison State Community College *C*
Gallipolis Career College *A*
God's Bible School and College *A*
Hocking College *C, A*
James A. Rhodes State College *A*
Kent State University
Ashtabula *A*
Salem *A*
Trumbull *A*
Tuscarawas *A*
Marion Technical College *C, A*
Miami University
Oxford Campus *C, A*
Mount Vernon Nazarene
University *A, B*
National College: Cincinnati *C, A*
National College: Stow *A*
North Central State College *A*
Northwest State Community
College *A*
Ohio Business College: Sandusky *C, A*
Ohio Valley College of Technology *A*
Owens Community College
Toledo *C*
RETS College *C*
Southern State Community College *A*
Stark State College of Technology *A*
Terra State Community College *C, A*
University of Akron *C, A*
University of Akron: Wayne
College *C, A*
University of Cincinnati
Clermont College *C, A*
Raymond Walters College *A*
University of Northwestern Ohio *A*
University of Rio Grande *C, A*
Wright State University *A*
Zane State College *C, A*

Oklahoma
Carl Albert State College *A*
East Central University *B*
Eastern Oklahoma State College *A*
Langston University *B*
Murray State College *C, A*
Northeastern Oklahoma Agricultural
and Mechanical College *C, A*
Oklahoma State University
Institute of Technology:
Okmulgee *A*
Oklahoma Wesleyan University *A*
Tulsa Community College *C, A*
Western Oklahoma State College *A*

Oregon
Blue Mountain Community
College *C, A*
Central Oregon Community
College *C, A*
Chemeketa Community College *A*
Clackamas Community College *C, A*
Lane Community College *C*
Linn-Benton Community College *A*
Mt. Hood Community College *C, A*
Portland Community College *A*
Southwestern Oregon Community
College *A*
Umpqua Community College *C, A*

Pennsylvania
Baptist Bible College of
Pennsylvania *A, B*
Bucks County Community College *A*

Butler County Community College *A*
Cambria-Rowe Business College:
Indiana *A*
Central Pennsylvania College *A*
Clarion University of Pennsylvania *C*
Community College of Allegheny
County *C, A*
Community College of Philadelphia *A*
Consolidated School of Business
Lancaster *A*
York *A*
Erie Business Center *A*
Harrisburg Area Community
College *C, A*
Kaplan Career Institute: Pittsburgh *A*
Lackawanna College *A*
Laurel Business Institute *A*
Lehigh Carbon Community College *C*
Luzerne County Community
College *C, A*
Montgomery County Community
College *C, A*
Newport Business Institute: Lower
Burrell *A*
Northampton Community College *A*
Penn Commercial Business and
Technical School *A*
Pennsylvania Highlands Community
College *A*
Pennsylvania Institute of Health and
Technology *A*
Pennsylvania Institute of
Technology *A*
Reading Area Community
College *C, A*
South Hills School of Business &
Technology *C*
South Hills School of Business &
Technology: Altoona *C, A*
Westmoreland County Community
College *C, A*

Puerto Rico
American University of Puerto
Rico *A, B*
Bayamon Central University *A, B*
Caribbean University *A, B*
Columbia Centro Universitario:
Caguas *A*
Electronic Data Processing College:
San Sebastian *A*
Huertas Junior College *A*
Humacao Community College *A*
Inter American University of Puerto
Rico
Aguadilla Campus *A, B*
Arecibo Campus *A, B*
Fajardo Campus *A, B*
Metropolitan Campus *A, B*
Ponce Campus *A, B*
San German Campus *A, B*
National College of Business and
Technology: Arecibo *A, B*
National College of Business and
Technology: Bayamon *A, B*
Pontifical Catholic University of
Puerto Rico *A, B*
Universidad Adventista de las
Antillas *A, B*
Universidad del Este *B*
University College of San Juan *C, A*
University of Puerto Rico
Arecibo *A, B*
Carolina Regional College *A, B*
Cayey University College *B*
Humacao *A, B*
Ponce *A, B*
Rio Piedras *B*

Rhode Island
Community College of Rhode
Island *A*
New England Institute of
Technology *A*

South Carolina

Aiken Technical College *C, A*
Central Carolina Technical
  College *C, A*
Denmark Technical College *C*
Florence-Darlington Technical
  College *C, A*
Forrest Junior College *A*
Greenville Technical College *C, A*
Horry-Georgetown Technical
  College *C, A*
Midlands Technical College *C, A*
Northeastern Technical College *C, A*
Orangeburg-Calhoun Technical
  College *C, A*
Spartanburg Community College *C, A*
Technical College of the
  Lowcountry *C, A*
Tri-County Technical College *C, A*
Trident Technical College *A*
University of South Carolina
  Lancaster *A*
Williamsburg Technical College *C, A*
York Technical College *C, A*

South Dakota

Black Hills State University *A*
Northern State University *A*
Southeast Technical Institute *C*
Western Dakota Technical Institute *C*

Tennessee

Chattanooga State Community
  College *A*
Cleveland State Community
  College *C, A*
Columbia State Community College *A*
National College
  Knoxville *A*
  Nashville *C, A*
National College of Business &
  Technology
  National College: Bristol *C, A*
National College: Bartlett *A*
National College: Madison *A*
National College: Memphis *A*
Northeast State Community
  College *C, A*
Pellissippi State Community
  College *A*
Roane State Community College *C*
South College *C*
Southwest Tennessee Community
  College *A*
Tennessee State University *A, B*
Tennessee Temple University *A, B*
Volunteer State Community College *C*
West Tennessee Business College *C, A*

Texas

Amarillo College *C, A*
Angelina College *C, A*
Austin Community College *C, A*
Blinn College *C*
Brazosport College *C, A*
Cedar Valley College *C, A*
Central Texas College *C, A*
Coastal Bend College *C, A*
College of the Mainland *C, A*
Del Mar College *C, A*
Eastfield College *C, A*
El Centro College *C*
El Paso Community College *C, A*
Frank Phillips College *C, A*
Galveston College *C, A*
Grayson County College *C, A*
Hill College *C, A*
Lamar Institute of Technology *C, A*
Lamar State College at Orange *C, A*
Lamar State College at Port
  Arthur *C, A*
Laredo Community College *A*
Lee College *C, A*

Lone Star College System *C, A*
McLennan Community College *C*
Midland College *C, A*
Mountain View College *C*
Navarro College *C, A*
North Central Texas College *A*
North Lake College *A*
Northeast Texas Community
  College *C, A*
Odessa College *C, A*
Palo Alto College *C, A*
Panola College *C*
Paris Junior College *A*
Ranger College *C, A*
Richland College *C, A*
St. Philip's College *C, A*
San Antonio College *C*
San Jacinto College *C, A*
South Plains College *A*
Southwest Texas Junior College *A*
Southwestern Adventist University *B*
Sul Ross State University *B*
Tarrant County College *C, A*
Temple College *A*
Texarkana College *C, A*
Texas State Technical College
  Harlingen *C, A*
Texas Woman's University *B*
Trinity Valley Community
  College *C, A*
Tyler Junior College *C, A*
Vernon College *A*
Victoria College *C, A*
Weatherford College *C, A*
Western Texas College *C, A*
Wharton County Junior College *C, A*

Utah

College of Eastern Utah *C, A*
LDS Business College *C, A*
Provo College *A*
Utah State University *A, B*
Weber State University *A, B*

Virginia

Blue Ridge Community College *C, A*
Bryant & Stratton College
  Richmond *A*
Bryant & Stratton College: Virginia
  Beach *A*
Central Virginia Community
  College *A*
Dabney S. Lancaster Community
  College *A*
Danville Community College *A*
ECPI College of Technology: Virginia
  Beach *C, A*
ECPI Technical College: Roanoke *A*
J. Sargeant Reynolds Community
  College *C*
John Tyler Community College *C, A*
Liberty University *A*
Lord Fairfax Community College *A*
National College
  Bluefield *C, A*
  Charlottesville *C, A*
  Danville *C, A*
  Harrisonburg *C, A*
  Lynchburg *C, A*
  Martinsville *C, A*
  Roanoke Valley *C, A*
New River Community College *A*
Northern Virginia Community
  College *C*
Paul D. Camp Community College *A*
Piedmont Virginia Community
  College *C*
St. Paul's College *B*
Southside Virginia Community
  College *A*
Southwest Virginia Community
  College *C, A*
Tidewater Community College *A*
Virginia Baptist College *A*

Virginia Highlands Community
  College *A*
Virginia Western Community
  College *A*
Wytheville Community College *A*

Washington

Bates Technical College *C, A*
Bellevue College *C, A*
Clover Park Technical College *C*
Everett Community College *C, A*
Highline Community College *C, A*
Lake Washington Technical
  College *C, A*
Lower Columbia College *C, A*
North Seattle Community
  College *C, A*
Olympic College *C, A*
Peninsula College *C, A*
Pierce College *C, A*
Renton Technical College *C, A*
Skagit Valley College *C, A*
South Puget Sound Community
  College *C, A*
Spokane Community College *C, A*
Spokane Falls Community College *A*
Wenatchee Valley College *C*
Whatcom Community College *C*
Yakima Valley Community
  College *C, A*

West Virginia

Concord University *A*
Eastern West Virginia Community and
  Technical College *C, A*
Huntington Junior College *C, A*
Mountain State College *A*
Mountain State University *C, A*
Potomac State College of West
  Virginia University *A*
Southern West Virginia Community
  and Technical College *C, A*
Valley College *C*
West Virginia Business College: Nutter
  Fort *C, A*
West Virginia Business College:
  Wheeling *C, A*
West Virginia Northern Community
  College *C, A*
West Virginia State Community and
  Technical College *A*

Wisconsin

Blackhawk Technical College *A*
Chippewa Valley Technical College *A*
College of Menominee Nation *A*
Fox Valley Technical College *A*
Gateway Technical College *A*
Lakeshore Technical College *A*
Maranatha Baptist Bible College *A*
Mid-State Technical College *C, A*
Milwaukee Area Technical College *A*
Moraine Park Technical College *C, A*
Nicolet Area Technical College *A*
Northcentral Technical College *A*
Northeast Wisconsin Technical
  College *A*
Southwest Wisconsin Technical
  College *A*
Waukesha County Technical
  College *A*
Western Technical College *A*
Wisconsin Indianhead Technical
  College *A*

Wyoming

Casper College *C, A*
Central Wyoming College *A*
Eastern Wyoming College *A*
Northwest College *C, A*
Sheridan College *C, A*
Western Wyoming Community
  College *C, A*

Adult/continuing education

Alabama

Auburn University *B, M, D, T*
Troy University *M*
University of West Alabama *M*

Alaska

University of Alaska
  Anchorage *M*

Arizona

Prescott College *B, M*
University of Phoenix *M*

Arkansas

University of Arkansas *M, D*
University of Arkansas
  Little Rock *M*

California

Patten University *B*
Whittier College *T*

Colorado

Colorado Christian University *B*
Colorado State University *M*

Delaware

Delaware State University *D*

District of Columbia

George Washington University *M*

Florida

Florida Agricultural and Mechanical
  University *M*
Florida International University *M, D*
University of South Florida *M*

Georgia

University of Georgia *M, D, T*

Idaho

University of Idaho *M*

Illinois

Argosy University: Chicago *M*
National-Louis University *M, D*
University of Illinois
  Urbana-Champaign *M*

Indiana

Ball State University *M, D*
Indiana University-Purdue University
  Indianapolis *M*

Iowa

University of Iowa *M, D*

Kansas

Kansas State University *M, D*

Kentucky

Morehead State University *M*
University of Louisville *M*
Western Kentucky University *M*

Louisiana

Louisiana State University and
  Agricultural and Mechanical
  College *B, M, D*
Northwestern State University *M*

Maine

University of Southern Maine *M*

Massachusetts
Boston University *M, T*
Suffolk University *M*

Michigan
Michigan State University *M, D*

Minnesota
Capella University *M, D*
University of Minnesota
Twin Cities *M*
Walden University *D*

Missouri
University of Central Missouri *M, T*
University of Missouri
St. Louis *M*

Nebraska
University of Nebraska
Lincoln *M*

Nevada
University of Nevada
Las Vegas *B, M*

New York
Cornell University *D*
Elmira College *M*
State University of New York
College at Buffalo *M*

North Carolina
North Carolina Agricultural and
Technical State University *M*

Ohio
Cleveland State University *M*

Oklahoma
Northeastern State University *M*
University of Central Oklahoma *M*
University of Oklahoma *M, D*

Oregon
Oregon State University *M*
Portland State University *D*

Pennsylvania
Cheyney University of
Pennsylvania *M*
Indiana University of
Pennsylvania *M, T*
Penn State
Greater Allegheny *M*
Harrisburg *D*
University Park *B, M, D*
Temple University *M*

South Carolina
University of South Carolina *M*

Texas
Midwestern State University *M*
Texas A&M University *M, D*
Texas A&M University
Commerce *M*
Texarkana *M*
Texas State University: San Marcos *M*
University of Texas
Tyler *M*

Virginia
James Madison University *M*
Virginia Commonwealth University *M*

Washington
Eastern Washington University *M*
Seattle University *M*
Western Washington University *M*

Wisconsin
Alverno College *M*
University of Wisconsin
Madison *M, D*

Adult/continuing education administration

Arizona
University of Phoenix *M*

Florida
Nova Southeastern University *D*

Georgia
Valdosta State University *M, D*

Illinois
Bradley University *M*
Northern Illinois University *M, D*
University of Illinois
Urbana-Champaign *M, D*

Indiana
Ball State University *M*
Purdue University
Calumet *T*

Iowa
Drake University *M*
Iowa State University *M, D*

Maine
University of Southern Maine *M*

Maryland
Coppin State University *M*

Massachusetts
Harvard College *M, D*
Lesley University *M*

Michigan
Central Michigan University *M*
Grand Valley State University *M*
Marygrove College *M*
Michigan State University *M, D*

Minnesota
Walden University *D*

Mississippi
University of Southern Mississippi *M*

Missouri
University of Missouri
Columbia *M, D*

New York
Fordham University *M, D*
State University of New York
College at Buffalo *M*

North Carolina
East Carolina University *M*
North Carolina Agricultural and
Technical State University *M*
North Carolina State University *M, D*

Ohio
Ohio State University
Columbus Campus *M*

Oregon
Oregon State University *M*

Pennsylvania
Penn State
Hazleton *M*
University Park *M, D*
Widener University *M*

Puerto Rico
Universidad Metropolitana *M*
Universidad del Este *M*

South Carolina
University of South Carolina *M*

South Dakota
University of South Dakota *M, D*

Tennessee
Tusculum College *M*

Texas
Texas A&M University
Kingsville *M*
Texas State University: San Marcos *D*
University of the Incarnate Word *T*

Wisconsin
Carroll University *M*

Adult development/ aging

Arizona
Arizona State University *B, M*
Glendale Community College *C*
University of Phoenix *M*

Arkansas
University of Arkansas
Pine Bluff *C, B*

California
East Los Angeles College *C*
Folsom Lake College *C, A*

Colorado
University of Northern Colorado *B, M*

Connecticut
Gateway Community College *C, A*

Florida
Hillsborough Community College *C*

Georgia
Southwest Georgia Technical
College *C*

Maryland
College of Notre Dame of
Maryland *M*

Massachusetts
North Shore Community College *C, A*

Michigan
Eastern Michigan University *M*
Grand Rapids Community College *A*
Madonna University *C, A, B*

Minnesota
Lake Superior College *C*

New Jersey
Georgian Court University *C*

New York
City University of New York
York College *B*
Genesee Community College *C*

Mercy College *C*

Ohio
Bowling Green State University *B*
Cleveland State University *D*
Columbus State Community
College *C, A*
Stark State College of Technology *A*
University of Cincinnati
Clermont College *C*

Oklahoma
University of Central Oklahoma *B*

Pennsylvania
Gwynedd-Mercy College *B*
Harrisburg Area Community
College *C*
Pennsylvania Highlands Community
College *A*
Saint Joseph's University *M*

Rhode Island
Community College of Rhode
Island *A*

Texas
San Antonio College *C*

Virginia
Virginia Commonwealth University *M*

Adult health nursing

California
University of San Francisco *M*

Connecticut
Quinnipiac University *M*
Western Connecticut State
University *M*

Illinois
Loyola University Chicago *M*
Saint Anthony College of
Nursing *B, M*

Indiana
Goshen College *M*
Indiana University-Purdue University
Indianapolis *M*

Iowa
Allen College *M*
University of Iowa *M*

Louisiana
Louisiana State University Health
Sciences Center *M*

Massachusetts
Worcester State College *B*

Michigan
Madonna University *M*
Oakland University *M*
Wayne State University *M*

Minnesota
College of St. Scholastica *M*
Metropolitan State University *M*

Missouri
Maryville University of Saint Louis *M*

Nebraska
Clarkson College *M*

New Jersey
Seton Hall University *M*

New York
Adelphi University *M*
City University of New York
    College of Staten Island *M*
    Hunter College *B, M*
College of New Rochelle *M*
Daemen College *M*
Long Island University
    Brooklyn Campus *M*
Mount Saint Mary College *M*
State University of New York
    Binghamton *M*
    Buffalo *M*
    Stony Brook *M*
University of Rochester *M*

Ohio
Case Western Reserve University *M*
Wright State University *B*
Youngstown State University *M*

Oklahoma
University of Oklahoma *M*

Pennsylvania
Pennsylvania College of
    Technology *B*
University of Pennsylvania *M*
York College of Pennsylvania *M*

South Carolina
Medical University of South
    Carolina *M*

Tennessee
University of Tennessee
    Knoxville *M*
University of Tennessee Health
    Science Center *D*

Texas
Texas Christian University *M*

Virginia
James Madison University *M*

Wisconsin
Marian University *M*
Marquette University *M*

Adult literacy instruction

Nevada
University of Nevada
    Reno *M, D*

Advertising

Alabama
University of Alabama *B, M*

Arizona
Art Center Design College *B*
Art Institute of Tucson *B*
Northern Arizona University *B*

Arkansas
Harding University *B*
University of Arkansas
    Little Rock *B*
University of Central Arkansas *B*

California
Academy of Art University *C, A, B, M*
Art Center College of Design *B*
Art Institute
    of California: San Diego *B*
California Lutheran University *B*

California State University
    East Bay *B*
    Fullerton *B, M*
College of San Mateo *A*
Cosumnes River College *A*
Fullerton College *C*
Irvine Valley College *A*
Long Beach City College *C, A*
Los Angeles City College *A*
Los Angeles Southwest College *A*
Mount San Antonio College *A*
Orange Coast College *A*
Palomar College *C, A*
Pepperdine University *B*
San Diego State University *B*
San Jose State University *B*
Santa Ana College *C, A*
University of San Francisco *B*

Colorado
Adams State College *B*
Johnson & Wales University:
    Denver *B*
Trinidad State Junior College *A*
University of Denver *M*

Connecticut
Albertus Magnus College *B*
Middlesex Community College *C*
Quinnipiac University *B*
University of Bridgeport *B*

District of Columbia
University of the District of
    Columbia *A*

Florida
Art Institute of Fort Lauderdale *B*
Barry University *B*
Florida Southern College *B*
Florida State University *B*
Gulf Coast Community College *A*
Lynn University *B*
Miami International University of Art
    and Design *B*
Northwood University
    Florida *B*
State College of Florida,
    Manatee-Sarasota *A*
University of Central Florida *B*
University of Florida *B*
University of Miami *B*

Georgia
Art Institute
    of Atlanta *C, B*
University of Georgia *B*
Wesleyan College *B*

Hawaii
Hawaii Pacific University *B*

Idaho
Brigham Young University-Idaho *B*
University of Idaho *B*

Illinois
Bradley University *B*
Columbia College Chicago *B*
Concordia University Chicago *B*
Danville Area Community College *A*
Illinois Institute of Art: Schaumburg *B*
North Park University *B*
Northwestern University *B*
Oakton Community College *C*
University of Illinois
    Urbana-Champaign *B, M, D*
University of St. Francis *B*

Indiana
Indiana University-Purdue University
    Indianapolis *B*

Purdue University *B*
University of Southern Indiana *B*

Iowa
Drake University *B*
Iowa State University *B*
Morningside College *B*
St. Ambrose University *B*

Kansas
Pittsburg State University *B*

Kentucky
Murray State University *B*
University of Kentucky *B*
Western Kentucky University *B*

Maine
New England School of
    Communications *B*

Maryland
Montgomery College *C, A*

Massachusetts
American International College *B*
Babson College *B*
Boston University *B, M*
Emerson College *B, M*
Lasell College *B*
Salem State College *B*
Suffolk University *B*
Western New England College *B*

Michigan
Art Institute of Michigan *B*
Bay de Noc Community College *C*
Central Michigan University *B*
Ferris State University *B*
Grand Valley State University *B*
Lansing Community College *A*
Michigan State University *B, M*
North Central Michigan College *C*
Northwood University: Michigan *B*
Spring Arbor University *B*
Western Michigan University *B*

Minnesota
Art Institutes International
    Minnesota *B*
College of St. Scholastica *B*
Hennepin Technical College *C, A*
Metropolitan State University *B*
Minneapolis College of Art and
    Design *B*
North Hennepin Community
    College *C*
Rochester Community and Technical
    College *C*
Saint Cloud State University *B*
St. Cloud Technical College *C, A*
Winona State University *B*

Mississippi
Mississippi Delta Community
    College *A*
University of Southern Mississippi *B*

Missouri
Drury University *B*
Fontbonne University *B*
Lindenwood University *B*
Northwest Missouri State
    University *B*
St. Louis Community College
    St. Louis Community College at
        Florissant Valley *A*
Stephens College *B*
University of Missouri
    Columbia *B*
Washington University in St. Louis *B*
Webster University *B, M*

Westminster College *B*
William Woods University *B*

Nebraska
University of Nebraska
    Kearney *B*
    Lincoln *B*

New Hampshire
New England College *B*
Southern New Hampshire
    University *B*

New Jersey
Rider University *B*
Rowan University *B*

New Mexico
Art Center Design College *B*

New York
City University of New York
    Baruch College *B, M*
    City College *B*
Fashion Institute of Technology *A, B*
Iona College *B*
Long Island University
    C. W. Post Campus *B*
Marist College *B*
Mohawk Valley Community
    College *C, A*
Monroe Community College *A*
New York Institute of Technology *B*
Pace University *B*
Rochester Institute of Technology *B*
St. John's University *B*
Syracuse University *B, M*
Tompkins Cortland Community
    College *A*

North Carolina
Alamance Community College *C*
Appalachian State University *B*
Campbell University *B*
Halifax Community College *A*

North Dakota
Dakota College at Bottineau *C, A*

Ohio
Bowling Green State University *B*
Cincinnati State Technical and
    Community College *C*
Kent State University *B*
Marietta College *B*
School of Advertising Art *C, A*
Xavier University *A, B*
Youngstown State University *B*

Oklahoma
Northeastern State University *B*
Oklahoma Christian University *B*
Oklahoma City University *B*
University of Central Oklahoma *B*
University of Oklahoma *B*

Oregon
University of Oregon *B, M*

Pennsylvania
Gannon University *B*
Keystone College *A, B*
Luzerne County Community
    College *C, A*
Marywood University *M*
Oakbridge Academy of Arts *A*
Penn State
    Abington *B*
    Altoona *B*
    Beaver *B*
    Berks *B*
    Brandywine *B*

DuBois *B*
Erie, The Behrend College *B*
Fayette, The Eberly Campus *B*
Greater Allegheny *B*
Hazleton *B*
Lehigh Valley *B*
Mont Alto *B*
New Kensington *B*
Schuylkill *B*
Shenango *B*
University Park *B*
Wilkes-Barre *B*
Worthington Scranton *B*
York *B*
Point Park University *B*
Temple University *B*
Waynesburg University *B*

Puerto Rico
University of Puerto Rico
Carolina Regional College *B*
University of the Sacred Heart *B, M*

Rhode Island
Johnson & Wales University:
Providence *B*

South Carolina
University of South Carolina *B*

South Dakota
Southeast Technical Institute *A*

Tennessee
Chattanooga State Community
College *A*
Lee University *B*
Southern Adventist University *B*
Union University *B*
University of Tennessee
Knoxville *B*

Texas
Abilene Christian University *B*
Amarillo College *A*
Dallas Baptist University *C*
Del Mar College *A*
Lamar University *B*
North Lake College *C*
Palo Alto College *A*
Sam Houston State University *B*
Southern Methodist University *B*
Texas A&M University
Commerce *B*
Texas Christian University *B, M*
Texas State University: San Marcos *B*
Texas Tech University *B*
University of Texas
Arlington *B*
Austin *B, M, D*
El Paso *B*
West Texas A&M University *B*

Utah
Brigham Young University *B*

Virginia
Hampton University *B*

Washington
Everett Community College *C, A*

West Virginia
Bethany College *B*
Concord University *B*
West Virginia State Community and
Technical College *C*
West Virginia University *B*

Wisconsin
Marquette University *B, M*

Aeronautical/aerospace engineering

Alabama
Auburn University *B, M, D*
Tuskegee University *B*
University of Alabama *B, M*

Arizona
Arizona State University *B, M, D*
Embry-Riddle Aeronautical University:
Prescott Campus *B*
University of Arizona *B, M, D*

California
California Institute of
Technology *M, D*
California Polytechnic State
University: San Luis Obispo *B, M*
California State Polytechnic
University: Pomona *B*
California State University
Long Beach *B, M*
Northridge *M*
San Diego State University *B, M*
San Jose State University *B, M*
Stanford University *M, D*
University of California
Davis *B*
Irvine *B*
Los Angeles *B, M, D*
San Diego *B, M, D*
University of Southern
California *B, M, D*

Colorado
United States Air Force Academy *B*
University of Colorado
Boulder *B, M, D*

Delaware
Delaware State University *B*
University of Delaware *B*

District of Columbia
George Washington University *M, D*

Florida
Embry-Riddle Aeronautical
University *B, M*
Florida Institute of
Technology *B, M, D*
University of Central Florida *B, M*
University of Florida *B, M*
University of Miami *B*

Georgia
Georgia Institute of
Technology *B, M, D*

Idaho
Northwest Nazarene University *B*

Illinois
Illinois Institute of Technology *B*
University of Illinois
Urbana-Champaign *B, M, D*

Indiana
Purdue University *B, M, D*
University of Notre Dame *B, M*

Iowa
Iowa State University *B, M, D*

Kansas
University of Kansas *B, M, D*
Wichita State University *B, M, D*

Maryland
United States Naval Academy *B*
University of Maryland
College Park *B, M, D*

Massachusetts
Boston University *B, M, D*
Massachusetts Institute of
Technology *B, M, D*
Worcester Polytechnic Institute *B*

Michigan
University of Michigan *B, M, D*
Western Michigan University *B*

Minnesota
University of Minnesota
Twin Cities *B, M, D*

Mississippi
Mississippi State University *B, M*

Missouri
Saint Louis University *B*
University of Missouri
Missouri University of Science and
Technology *B, M, D*

New Hampshire
Daniel Webster College *B*

New Mexico
New Mexico State University *B*

New York
Clarkson University *B*
Cornell University *M, D*
Rensselaer Polytechnic
Institute *B, M, D*
Rochester Institute of Technology *B*
State University of New York
Buffalo *B, M, D*
Syracuse University *B, M, D*

North Carolina
North Carolina State
University *B, M, D*

Ohio
Case Western Reserve
University *B, M, D*
Ohio State University
Columbus Campus *B, M, D*
University of Cincinnati *B, M; D*
University of Dayton *M, D*

Oklahoma
Oklahoma State University *B*
Southeastern Oklahoma State
University *B*
University of Oklahoma *B, M, D*

Pennsylvania
Penn State
Abington *B*
Altoona *B*
Beaver *B*
Berks *B*
Brandywine *B*
DuBois *B*
Erie, The Behrend College *B*
Fayette, The Eberly Campus *B*
Greater Allegheny *B*
Hazleton *B*
Lehigh Valley *B*
Mont Alto *B*
New Kensington *B*
Schuylkill *B*
Shenango *B*
University Park *B, M, D*
Wilkes-Barre *B*

Worthington Scranton *B*
York *B*

Tennessee
University of Tennessee
Knoxville *B, M, D*

Texas
Rice University *M, D*
Texas A&M University *B, M, D*
University of Houston *M, D*
University of Texas
Arlington *B, M, D*
Austin *B, M, D*

Utah
Utah State University *B*

Virginia
Old Dominion University *M, D*
University of Virginia *B*
Virginia Polytechnic Institute and
State University *B, M, D*

Washington
University of Washington *B, M, D*

West Virginia
West Virginia University *B, M, D*

Aeronautical/aerospace engineering technology

Alabama
Calhoun Community College *A*

Arizona
GateWay Community College *A*

California
Antelope Valley College *C, A*
Bakersfield College *A*
Solano Community College *A*
University of California
San Diego *B*

Delaware
Delaware Technical and Community
College
Owens *A*

Florida
Daytona State College *A*

Georgia
Middle Georgia College *A*

Hawaii
University of Hawaii
Honolulu Community College *A*

Indiana
Purdue University *A, B*

Maryland
Capitol College *B*
Prince George's Community
College *A*

Missouri
Saint Louis University *B*

New York
New York Institute of Technology *B*
Vaughn College of Aeronautics and
Technology *A*

Ohio
Bowling Green State University *B*

Cincinnati State Technical and
Community College *A*
Columbus State Community
College *A*

Pennsylvania

Community College of Beaver
County *A*
Pittsburgh Institute of Aeronautics *A*

Texas

Laredo Community College *A*
LeTourneau University *B*

West Virginia

Fairmont State University *B*

Aeronautics and aviation science

Alabama

Calhoun Community College *A*

Alaska

University of Alaska
Anchorage *A, B*

Arizona

Arizona State University *B*
Chandler-Gilbert Community College
Pecos *C, A*
Embry-Riddle Aeronautical University:
Prescott Campus *B, M*

Arkansas

Northwest Arkansas Community
College *A*

California

Chabot College *A*
City College of San Francisco *C, A*
College of San Mateo *C, A*
Cypress College *C, A*
Glendale Community College *C*
Long Beach City College *C, A*
Mount San Antonio College *A*
Orange Coast College *C, A*
Pacific Union College *A, B*
Palomar College *C, A*
San Diego Mesa College *C*
San Jose State University *B*
Santa Rosa Junior College *C*

Colorado

Aims Community College *C, A*
Colorado Northwestern Community
College *A*
Metropolitan State College of
Denver *B*

Connecticut

Naugatuck Valley Community
College *A*
Three Rivers Community College *A*

Delaware

Delaware State University *B*
Wilmington University *B*

District of Columbia

University of the District of
Columbia *A, B*

Florida

Broward College *A*
Embry-Riddle Aeronautical
University *B*
Embry-Riddle Aeronautical University:
Worldwide Campus *A, B*
Everglades University: Boca
Raton *B, M*

Florida Institute of Technology *B*
Florida Memorial University *B*
Florida State College at Jacksonville *A*
Miami Dade College *A*
Palm Beach Community College *A*

Georgia

Middle Georgia Technical
College *C, A*

Illinois

Lewis University *A, B*
Quincy University *A*

Indiana

Indiana State University *A*
Purdue University *A, B*

Iowa

Iowa Central Community College *C, A*
Iowa Lakes Community College *A*
University of Dubuque *B*

Kansas

Central Christian College of Kansas *A*
Hesston College *A*

Kentucky

Eastern Kentucky University *B*

Louisiana

Louisiana Tech University *B*

Maryland

Cecil College *C, A*
Community College of Baltimore
County *C, A*
University of Maryland
Eastern Shore *B*

Michigan

Andrews University *A, B*
Delta College *C, A*
Lansing Community College *A*
Northwestern Michigan College *A*

Minnesota

Academy College *A*
Anoka Technical College *C, A*
University of Minnesota
Crookston *B*
Vermilion Community College *A*

Mississippi

Delta State University *B*

Missouri

St. Louis Community College
St. Louis Community College at
Meramec *C*

Nebraska

University of Nebraska
Omaha *B*

New Hampshire

Daniel Webster College *A, B*

New Jersey

County College of Morris *A*
Mercer County Community College *A*

New Mexico

Clovis Community College *A*
Eastern New Mexico University:
Roswell Campus *A*

New York

Dowling College *B*

Schenectady County Community
College *A*
Vaughn College of Aeronautics and
Technology *B*

North Carolina

Elizabeth City State University *B*

North Dakota

University of North Dakota *M*

Ohio

Kent State University *B*
Ohio State University
Columbus Campus *B*
Ohio University *A, B*
University of Cincinnati
Clermont College *A*

Oklahoma

National Education Center
Spartan College of Aeronautics and
Technology *C, A*
Oklahoma City Community College *A*
Oklahoma State University *B*
University of Oklahoma *B*
Western Oklahoma State College *A*

Oregon

Umpqua Community College *A*

Pennsylvania

Geneva College *A*

South Carolina

Trident Technical College *C, A*

South Dakota

South Dakota State University *B*

Tennessee

Middle Tennessee State University *B*

Texas

LeTourneau University *B*
Palo Alto College *A*
Texas Southern University *B*
Texas State Technical College
Waco *C, A*

Utah

Utah State University *A*
Westminster College *B*

Virginia

Averett University *B*
Aviation Institute of Maintenance:
Virginia Beach *C, A*
Liberty University *B*
Northern Virginia Community
College *A*

Washington

Green River Community College *A*
Highline Community College *C, A*
South Seattle Community
College *C, A*

West Virginia

American Public University
System *B, M*
Fairmont State University *B*

Aesthetician/skin care

Alabama

Gadsden State Community College *C*
Lurleen B. Wallace Community
College *C*

Northeast Alabama Community
College *C*
Snead State Community College *C*

California

San Jose City College *C*

Colorado

Pueblo Community College *C*
Red Rocks Community College *C*
Trinidad State Junior College *C*

Florida

Indian River State College *C*

Kentucky

West Kentucky Community and
Technical College *C*

Massachusetts

North Shore Community College *C*

Michigan

Kirtland Community College *C, A*

Minnesota

Minnesota State College - Southeast
Technical *C*
Minnesota State Community and
Technical College *C*
Northland Community & Technical
College *C*
Ridgewater College *C*
St. Paul College *C, A*

North Carolina

Brunswick Community College *C*
Cape Fear Community College *C*
Carteret Community College *C*
Central Carolina Community
College *A*
Davidson County Community
College *C*
Edgecombe Community College *C*
Fayetteville Technical Community
College *C*
Isothermal Community College *C*
Johnston Community College *C*
Miller-Motte Technical College *C*
Miller-Motte Technical College:
Cary *C*
Southeastern Community College *C*
Stanly Community College *C*

Puerto Rico

Ponce Paramedical College *C*

South Carolina

Horry-Georgetown Technical
College *C*

Texas

Lamar State College at Port Arthur *C*
Panola College *C*

Virginia

Dabney S. Lancaster Community
College *C*

Washington

Clover Park Technical College *C, A*
Olympic College *C*

Wisconsin

Southwest Wisconsin Technical
College *C*
Wisconsin Indianhead Technical
College *C*

Wyoming

Eastern Wyoming College *C*

African-American studies

Alabama

Talladega College *B*
University of Alabama *B*
University of Alabama
  Birmingham *B*

Arizona

Arizona State University *B*

Arkansas

University of Central Arkansas *B*

California

California State University
  Dominguez Hills *B*
  East Bay *B*
  Fresno *B*
  Fullerton *B*
  Long Beach *B*
  Los Angeles *B*
  Northridge *B*
  San Bernardino *B*
Claremont McKenna College *B*
College of Alameda *A*
Contra Costa College *A*
De Anza College *A*
East Los Angeles College *A*
El Camino College *A*
Fresno City College *A*
Laney College *A*
Los Angeles City College *A*
Los Angeles Southwest College *A*
Loyola Marymount University *B*
Merritt College *A*
Pitzer College *B*
Pomona College *B*
San Diego City College *A*
San Diego Mesa College *A*
San Diego State University *B*
San Francisco State University *B*
San Jose State University *B*
Santa Ana College *A*
Santa Barbara City College *A*
Scripps College *B*
Solano Community College *A*
Sonoma State University *B*
Southwestern College *A*
Stanford University *B*
University of California
  Berkeley *B, D*
  Davis *B*
  Irvine *B*
  Los Angeles *B, M*
  Riverside *B*
  Santa Barbara *B*
University of Southern California *B*

Colorado

Metropolitan State College of
  Denver *B*
University of Northern Colorado *B*

Connecticut

Trinity College *B*
Wesleyan University *B*
Yale University *B, M, D*

District of Columbia

Howard University *B*

Florida

Florida Agricultural and Mechanical
  University *B*
Florida International University *M*
State College of Florida,
  Manatee-Sarasota *A*
University of Miami *B*
University of South Florida *B*

Georgia

Atlanta Metropolitan College *A*
Clark Atlanta University *M, D*
Emory University *B*
Georgia State University *B, M*
Mercer University *B*
Morehouse College *B*
University of Georgia *B*

Illinois

Chicago State University *B*
City Colleges of Chicago
  Kennedy-King College *A*
  Olive-Harvey College *A*
DePaul University *B*
Dominican University *B*
Eastern Illinois University *B*
Knox College *B*
Loyola University Chicago *B*
Northwestern University *B, D*
Roosevelt University *B*
University of Chicago *B*
University of Illinois
  Chicago *B*
Western Illinois University *B*

Indiana

DePauw University *B*
Earlham College *B*
Indiana State University *B*
Indiana University
  Bloomington *B, M*
  Northwest *B*
Purdue University *B*
University of Notre Dame *B*

Iowa

Coe College *B*
Luther College *B*
University of Iowa *B, M*

Kentucky

Berea College *B*
University of Louisville *B, M*

Maine

Bates College *B*
Colby College *B*

Maryland

Johns Hopkins University *B*
Morgan State University *B, M*
Prince George's Community
  College *A*
University of Maryland
  Baltimore County *B*
  College Park *B*
  Eastern Shore *B*

Massachusetts

Amherst College *B*
Bard College at Simon's Rock *B*
Boston University *M*
Brandeis University *B*
Hampshire College *B*
Harvard College *B, M*
Mount Holyoke College *B*
Northeastern University *B*
Simmons College *B*
Smith College *B*
Suffolk University *B*
Tufts University *B*
University of Massachusetts
  Amherst *B, D*
  Boston *B*
Wellesley College *B*

Michigan

Eastern Michigan University *B, M*
Michigan State University *B, M, D*
University of Michigan *B*

University of Michigan
  Flint *B*
Wayne State University *B*
Western Michigan University *B*

Minnesota

Carleton College *B*
University of Minnesota
  Twin Cities *B*

Mississippi

University of Mississippi *B*

Missouri

University of Missouri
  Columbia *B*
Washington University in St. Louis *B*

Nebraska

University of Nebraska
  Omaha *B*

New Hampshire

Dartmouth College *B*

New Jersey

Rutgers, The State University of New
  Jersey
  Camden Regional Campus *B*
  New Brunswick/Piscataway
    Campus *B*
  Newark Regional Campus *B*
Seton Hall University *B*
William Paterson University of New
  Jersey *B*

New Mexico

University of New Mexico *B*

New York

City University of New York
  Brooklyn College *B*
  City College *B*
  College of Staten Island *B*
  Hunter College *B*
  Lehman College *B*
  York College *B*
Colgate University *B*
Columbia University *B*
Columbia University
  School of General Studies *B*
Cornell University *B, M*
Fordham University *B*
Hamilton College *B*
Hobart and William Smith Colleges *B*
Metropolitan College of New
  York *A, B*
New York University *B, M*
State University of New York
  Albany *B, M*
  Binghamton *B*
  Buffalo *B*
  College at Brockport *B*
  College at Cortland *B*
  College at Geneseo *B*
  College at Oneonta *B*
  New Paltz *B*
  Stony Brook *B*
Syracuse University *B*
University of Rochester *B*
Wells College *B*

North Carolina

Duke University *B*
East Carolina University *B*
Guilford College *B*
North Carolina State University *B*
St. Augustine's College *B*
University of North Carolina
  Chapel Hill *B*
  Charlotte *B*
  Greensboro *B*

Winston-Salem State University *B*

Ohio

Bowling Green State University *B*
College of Wooster *B*
Denison University *B*
Kent State University *B*
Miami University
  Oxford Campus *B*
Oberlin College *B*
Ohio State University
  Columbus Campus *B, M*
Ohio University *B*
Ohio Wesleyan University *B*
Owens Community College
  Toledo *A*
University of Cincinnati *B*
University of Toledo *B*
Wright State University *B*
Youngstown State University *B*

Oklahoma

University of Oklahoma *B*

Pennsylvania

Franklin & Marshall College *B*
Gettysburg College *B*
Lehigh University *B*
Penn State
  Abington *B*
  Altoona *B*
  Beaver *B*
  Berks *B*
  Brandywine *B*
  DuBois *B*
  Erie, The Behrend College *B*
  Fayette, The Eberly Campus *B*
  Greater Allegheny *B*
  Hazleton *B*
  Lehigh Valley *B*
  Mont Alto *B*
  New Kensington *B*
  Schuylkill *B*
  Shenango *B*
  University Park *B*
  Wilkes-Barre *B*
  Worthington Scranton *B*
  York *B*
Temple University *B, M, D*
University of Pennsylvania *B*
University of Pittsburgh *B*

Rhode Island

Brown University *B*
Rhode Island College *B*
University of Rhode Island *B*

South Carolina

Claflin University *B*
University of South Carolina *B*

Tennessee

American Baptist College *A, B*
University of Memphis *B*
University of Tennessee
  Knoxville *B*
Vanderbilt University *B*

Texas

Southern Methodist University *B*

Utah

Weber State University *B*

Vermont

Goddard College *B*

Virginia

College of William and Mary *B*
Old Dominion University *B*
University of Virginia *B*
Virginia Commonwealth University *B*

Washington

University of Washington *B*

Wisconsin

Marquette University *B*
University of Wisconsin
Madison *B, M*
Milwaukee *B*

African languages

California

University of California
Los Angeles *B*

Indiana

Indiana University
Bloomington *B*

Massachusetts

Wellesley College *B*

Wisconsin

University of Wisconsin
Madison *M, D*

African studies

California

Claremont McKenna College *B*
San Diego City College *A*
San Diego Mesa College *A*
Stanford University *B*
University of California
Davis *B*
Los Angeles *M*

Connecticut

Connecticut College *B*
Trinity College *B*
Yale University *B, M*

District of Columbia

Howard University *B, M, D*

Florida

State College of Florida,
Manatee-Sarasota *A*

Georgia

Agnes Scott College *B*
Emory University *B*
Kennesaw State University *B*
Mercer University *B*
Savannah State University *B*

Illinois

Illinois Wesleyan University *B*
University of Chicago *B*
University of Illinois
Urbana-Champaign *M*

Iowa

University of Iowa *B*

Kansas

University of Kansas *B, M*

Louisiana

Dillard University *B*
Tulane University *B*

Maine

Bowdoin College *B*

Massachusetts

Amherst College *B*
Bard College at Simon's Rock *B*
Hampshire College *B*
Tufts University *B, M*

Wellesley College *B*

Michigan

Lansing Community College *A*
Oakland University *B*

Minnesota

Carleton College *B*
University of Minnesota
Twin Cities *B*

New Hampshire

Dartmouth College *B*

New Jersey

Drew University *B*
Rutgers, The State University of New
Jersey
New Brunswick/Piscataway
Campus *B*
Newark Regional Campus *B*
William Paterson University of New
Jersey *B*

New York

Bard College *B*
Barnard College *B*
City University of New York
Queens College *B, T*
Colgate University *B*
Columbia University *B*
Columbia University
School of General Studies *B*
Fordham University *B*
Hobart and William Smith Colleges *B*
Hofstra University *B*
Nassau Community College *A*
St. Lawrence University *B*
State University of New York
College at Brockport *B*
Syracuse University *M*
United States Military Academy *B*
Vassar College *B*

Ohio

Bowling Green State University *B*
College of Wooster *B*
Oberlin College *B*
Ohio State University
Columbus Campus *B, M*
Ohio University *B, M*

Oregon

Portland State University *B*

Pennsylvania

Dickinson College *B*
Franklin & Marshall College *B*
Lafayette College *B*
University of Pennsylvania *B*

Rhode Island

Brown University *B*

Vermont

Middlebury College *B*

Virginia

University of Richmond *B*

Washington

University of Washington *B*

West Virginia

American Public University System *B*

Agribusiness operations

Alabama

Alabama Agricultural and Mechanical
University *M*

Wallace State Community College at
Hanceville *C, A*

Arizona

Eastern Arizona College *A*
Mesa Community College *A*

Arkansas

Arkansas State University *B, M*
Arkansas Tech University *B*
Southern Arkansas University *A*
University of Arkansas *B*
University of Arkansas
Monticello *B*
Pine Bluff *B*

California

Allan Hancock College *C, A*
Bakersfield College *A*
California Polytechnic State
University: San Luis Obispo *B*
College of the Redwoods *A*
College of the Sequoias *C, A*
Hartnell College *C, A*
San Joaquin Delta College *C, A*
Santa Rosa Junior College *C, A*
Shasta College *C, A*

Colorado

Colorado State University *B*
Northeastern Junior College *C, A*

Delaware

University of Delaware *B*

Florida

Florida Agricultural and Mechanical
University *B*
Miami Dade College *A*
South Florida Community College *A*

Georgia

College of Coastal Georgia *A*
University of Georgia *B*

Hawaii

University of Hawaii
Hilo *B*

Idaho

Brigham Young University-Idaho *A*

Illinois

Illinois State University *B, M*
Kishwaukee College *A*

Indiana

Purdue University *M*

Iowa

Dordt College *B*
Iowa Central Community College *A*
Iowa State University *B*
Iowa Western Community College *A*
North Iowa Area Community
College *A*
Northeast Iowa Community
College *A*

Kansas

Colby Community College *C, A*
Dodge City Community College *C, A*
Highland Community College *A*

Kentucky

Morehead State University *A*

Michigan

Michigan State University *C*

Minnesota

Ridgewater College *A*
Southwest Minnesota State
University *A, B*
University of Minnesota
Crookston *B*

Mississippi

Hinds Community College *A*
Mississippi State University *B*
Northwest Mississippi Community
College *A*

Missouri

Crowder College *A*
Missouri State University *B*
North Central Missouri College *C, A*
Northwest Missouri State
University *B*
Southeast Missouri State University *B*
William Woods University *M*

Nebraska

Nebraska College of Technical
Agriculture *A*
Northeast Community College *A*

New Mexico

Eastern New Mexico University *A, B*
New Mexico State University *B*

New York

Cornell University *B*
State University of New York
College of Agriculture and
Technology at Cobleskill *A, B*
College of Agriculture and
Technology at Morrisville *A, B*

North Carolina

Bladen Community College *A*
James Sprunt Community College *A*
North Carolina State University *B*
Wayne Community College *A*

North Dakota

Dickinson State University *A*
North Dakota State College of
Science *A*
North Dakota State University *B*
Sitting Bull College *A*
Williston State College *A*

Ohio

Wilmington College *B*

Oklahoma

Northern Oklahoma College *A*
Oklahoma Panhandle State
University *B*

Oregon

Chemeketa Community College *A*

Pennsylvania

Delaware Valley College *B, M*
Harrisburg Area Community
College *C, A*
Penn State
Abington *B*
Altoona *A, B*
Beaver *B*
Berks *A, B*
Brandywine *A, B*
DuBois *B*
Erie, The Behrend College *A, B*
Fayette, The Eberly Campus *A, B*
Greater Allegheny *A, B*
Hazleton *A, B*
Lehigh Valley *A, B*
Mont Alto *B*

New Kensington *B*
Schuylkill *B*
Shenango *B*
University Park *A, B*
Wilkes-Barre *B*
Worthington Scranton *B*
York *B*

South Carolina

South Carolina State University *B, M*

South Dakota

Lake Area Technical Institute *A*
South Dakota State University *B*
Western Dakota Technical Institute *A*

Tennessee

Middle Tennessee State University *B*
Tennessee Technological University *B*

Texas

Abilene Christian University *B*
Palo Alto College *C, A*
Sam Houston State University *B*
Southwest Texas Junior College *B*
Stephen F. Austin State University *B*
Sul Ross State University *B, M*
Tarleton State University *B*
Texas A&M University *B, M*
Texas A&M University
 Kingsville *B*
Texas State University: San Marcos *B*
West Texas A&M University *B, M*

Utah

Snow College *C, A*
Utah State University *M*

Vermont

Vermont Technical College *A*

Wisconsin

Fox Valley Technical College *A*
Northcentral Technical College *C*
Southwest Wisconsin Technical
 College *A*
University of Wisconsin
 Platteville *B*

Wyoming

Eastern Wyoming College *A*
Laramie County Community
 College *A*
University of Wyoming *B*

Agricultural and biological engineering

Alabama

Auburn University *B, M, D*

Arizona

University of Arizona *B, M, D*

Arkansas

University of Arkansas *B, M*

California

California Polytechnic State
 University: San Luis Obispo *B*
Santa Clara University *B*
University of California
 Los Angeles *B*

Colorado

Colorado State University *M, D*

Delaware

University of Delaware *B*

Florida

Florida Agricultural and Mechanical
 University *B*
University of Florida *B, M*

Georgia

Abraham Baldwin Agricultural
 College *A*
Fort Valley State University *B*
University of Georgia *B, M, D*

Hawaii

University of Hawaii
 Manoa *B, M, D*

Idaho

University of Idaho *B, M, D*

Illinois

Illinois Institute of Technology *M*
University of Illinois
 Urbana-Champaign *B, M, D*

Indiana

Purdue University *B, M, D*
Vincennes University *A*

Iowa

Dordt College *B*
Indian Hills Community College *A*
Iowa Lakes Community College *A*
Iowa State University *B, M, D*

Kansas

Kansas State University *B, M, D*

Kentucky

University of Kentucky *B, M, D*

Louisiana

Louisiana State University and
 Agricultural and Mechanical
 College *M*

Maine

University of Maine *B, M*

Maryland

University of Maryland
 College Park *B, M, D*

Michigan

Michigan State University *B, M, D*

Minnesota

University of Minnesota
 Twin Cities *B, M, D*

Missouri

University of Missouri
 Columbia *B, M, D*

Nebraska

University of Nebraska
 Lincoln *B, M*

New Jersey

New Jersey Institute of Technology *M*

New Mexico

New Mexico State University *B*

New York

Cornell University *B, M, D*

North Carolina

North Carolina Agricultural and
 Technical State University *B*

North Carolina State
 University *B, M, D*

North Dakota

North Dakota State University *B, M, D*

Ohio

Clark State Community College *A*
Ohio State University
 Columbus Campus *B, M, D*

Oklahoma

Oklahoma State University *B, M, D*

Oregon

Oregon State University *M, D*

Pennsylvania

Penn State
 University Park *M, D*

South Carolina

Clemson University *B, M, D*

South Dakota

South Dakota State University *B*

Tennessee

University of Tennessee
 Knoxville *B, M, D*

Texas

Laredo Community College *A*
Texas A&M University *B, M, D*

Utah

Utah State University *B, M, D*

Virginia

Virginia Polytechnic Institute and
 State University *B, M, D*

Washington

Washington State University *M, D*

Wisconsin

University of Wisconsin
 Madison *B, M, D*

Agricultural business

Alabama

Central Alabama Community
 College *A*
Faulkner State Community College *A*
Jefferson State Community
 College *C, A*
Northwest-Shoals Community
 College *C, A*

Arizona

Arizona State University *B, M*
Central Arizona College *C, A*
Cochise College *A*

Arkansas

Arkansas Northeastern College *C*
Arkansas State University
 Beebe *A*
Southern Arkansas University *B*

California

Bakersfield College *C*
Butte College *C, A*
California State Polytechnic
 University: Pomona *B*
California State University
 Chico *B*
 Fresno *B*
College of the Desert *A*

College of the Redwoods *C*
Cosumnes River College *A*
Imperial Valley College *C, A*
Los Angeles Pierce College *A*
Merced College *A*
MiraCosta College *C, A*
Modesto Junior College *A*
Mount San Antonio College *A*
Reedley College *C, A*
San Diego State University *B*
San Joaquin Delta College *A*
Santa Rosa Junior College *C*
Shasta College *A*
West Hills College: Coalinga *A*
Yuba Community College
 District *C, A*

Colorado

Adams State College *B*
Fort Lewis College *B*
Lamar Community College *A*
Morgan Community College *C*

Delaware

Delaware State University *B*
Delaware Technical and Community
 College
 Owens *A*
 Stanton/Wilmington *A*
 Terry *A*
University of Delaware *B*

Florida

Florida Southern College *B*

Georgia

Abraham Baldwin Agricultural
 College *A*
Gainesville State College *A*

Idaho

University of Idaho *B*

Illinois

Black Hawk College *A*
Black Hawk College: East
 Campus *C, A*
Carl Sandburg College *A*
Danville Area Community College *A*
Highland Community College *A*
Illinois Central College *A*
Illinois Eastern Community Colleges
 Wabash Valley College *C, A*
John Wood Community College *C, A*
Kishwaukee College *C, A*
Lake Land College *C*
Parkland College *C, A*
Rend Lake College *A*
Richland Community College *A*
Sauk Valley Community College *A*
Shawnee Community College *A*
Spoon River College *A*
University of Illinois
 Urbana-Champaign *B, M, D*

Indiana

Purdue University *M*
Vincennes University *C, A*

Iowa

Dordt College *B*
Ellsworth Community College *C, A*
Grand View University *B*
Iowa Western Community College *A*
Marshalltown Community College *A*
North Iowa Area Community
 College *A*
Northwestern College *B*
Southeastern Community College
 North Campus *A*
Southwestern Community College *A*

Kansas

Central Christian College of Kansas *A*
Coffeyville Community College *A*
Dodge City Community College *A*
Fort Hays State University *B*
Fort Scott Community College *A*
Garden City Community College *A*
Kansas State University *B, M*
Pratt Community College *C, A*
Seward County Community College *A*

Kentucky

Henderson Community College *C*
Owensboro Community and
    Technical College *A*

Louisiana

Louisiana State University and
    Agricultural and Mechanical
    College *B*
Louisiana Tech University *B*
University of Louisiana at Monroe *B*

Maine

Northern Maine Community
    College *A*
University of Maine *B*

Maryland

Garrett College *A*
Harford Community College *A*
University of Maryland
    Eastern Shore *B*

Michigan

Andrews University *A, B*
Delta College *A*
Michigan State University *C, B*

Minnesota

Minnesota West Community and
    Technical College *A*
Northland Community & Technical
    College *A*
Ridgewater College *C, A*
University of Minnesota
    Crookston *B*
    Twin Cities *B*

Mississippi

Alcorn State University *B*
Mississippi Delta Community
    College *A*
Mississippi State University *M*

Missouri

College of the Ozarks *B*
Lincoln University *B*
Missouri State University *B*
Missouri State University: West
    Plains *A*
State Fair Community College *A*
Three Rivers Community College *A*
University of Central Missouri *B*
University of Missouri
    Columbia *B*

Montana

Dawson Community College *C, A*
Miles Community College *A*
Montana State University
    Bozeman *B*
Rocky Mountain College *B*

Nebraska

Central Community College *C, A*
Concordia University *B*
Nebraska College of Technical
    Agriculture *A*
Northeast Community College *A*
Southeast Community College *A*

University of Nebraska
    Kearney *B*
    Lincoln *B*

Nevada

Great Basin College *B*

New Jersey

County College of Morris *A*

New Mexico

San Juan College *A*

New York

Cornell University *B*
State University of New York
    College of Agriculture and
        Technology at Cobleskill *B*
    College of Agriculture and
        Technology at Morrisville *A, B*
    College of Technology at Alfred *A*

North Carolina

Bladen Community College *A*
North Carolina Agricultural and
    Technical State University *B*
North Carolina State University *A*

North Dakota

Bismarck State College *C, A*
Dickinson State University *B*
Lake Region State College *C*
North Dakota State College of
    Science *A*

Ohio

Clark State Community College *A*
Ohio State University
    Agricultural Technical Institute *A*
    Columbus Campus *A, B*
Owens Community College
    Toledo *A*
University of Northwestern Ohio *C, A*
Wilmington College *B*

Oklahoma

Eastern Oklahoma State College *A*
Langston University *B*
Northwestern Oklahoma State
    University *B*
Oklahoma State University *B*
Oklahoma State University
    Institute of Technology:
        Okmulgee *A*

Oregon

Blue Mountain Community College *A*
Eastern Oregon University *B*
Klamath Community College *A*
Linn-Benton Community College *A*
Oregon State University *B*
Treasure Valley Community College *A*

Pennsylvania

Penn State
    DuBois *A*

South Carolina

Clemson University *B, M*

South Dakota

Oglala Lakota College *A*
Western Dakota Technical Institute *A*

Tennessee

Columbia State Community College *A*
Jackson State Community College *A*
University of Tennessee
    Martin *M*

Texas

Cisco College *A*
Clarendon College *A*
Frank Phillips College *C*
Hardin-Simmons University *B*
Hill College *A*
Howard College *A*
Lubbock Christian University *B*
Navarro College *A*
Northeast Texas Community
    College *C, A*
South Plains College *A*
Southwest Texas Junior College *A*
Tarleton State University *B*
Texas A&M University *B, M*
Texas A&M University
    Commerce *M*
    Kingsville *B, M*
Texas Tech University *B, M*
Trinity Valley Community College *A*
Weatherford College *C, A*
West Texas A&M University *B, M*

Utah

Snow College *A*
Southern Utah University *B*
Utah State University *B*

Vermont

Vermont Technical College *A*

Virginia

Ferrum College *B*

Washington

Skagit Valley College *A*
Spokane Community College *A*
Washington State University *B, M*
Wenatchee Valley College *C*
Yakima Valley Community
    College *C, A*

West Virginia

West Virginia University *B*

Wisconsin

Fox Valley Technical College *A*
Mid-State Technical College *C*
Moraine Park Technical College *C*
Northcentral Technical College *C*
Northeast Wisconsin Technical
    College *A*
Southwest Wisconsin Technical
    College *A*
University of Wisconsin
    Madison *B*
    River Falls *B*

Wyoming

Casper College *A*
Central Wyoming College *A*
Northwest College *A*
Sheridan College *A*

Agricultural business technology

Arkansas

University of Arkansas
    Monticello *C*

Colorado

Pueblo Community College *A*

Florida

Indian River State College *A*

Kentucky

Henderson Community College *A*

Minnesota

University of Minnesota
    Crookston *B*

New York

State University of New York
    College of Agriculture and
        Technology at Morrisville *A, B*

Texas

Texas State Technical College
    Harlingen *A*
Wharton County Junior College *A*

Virginia

Tidewater Community College *A*

Washington

Washington State University *B*

Wisconsin

Western Technical College *A*

Wyoming

Laramie County Community
    College *A*

Agricultural communications

Georgia

University of Georgia *B*

Idaho

University of Idaho *B*

Illinois

University of Illinois
    Urbana-Champaign *B*

Indiana

Purdue University *B*

Kansas

Kansas State University *B*

Missouri

University of Missouri
    Columbia *B*

Nebraska

University of Nebraska
    Lincoln *B*

North Dakota

North Dakota State University *B*

Ohio

Ohio State University
    Agricultural Technical Institute *A*
    Columbus Campus *B*

Oklahoma

Oklahoma State University *B, M*

Texas

Texas A&M University *B*
Texas A&M University
    Commerce *B*
Texas Tech University *B, M*
West Texas A&M University *B*

Washington

Washington State University *B*

Wisconsin

University of Wisconsin
    Madison *B, M*

Wyoming
University of Wyoming *B*

Agricultural economics

Alabama
Alabama Agricultural and Mechanical
  University *B*
Auburn University *B, M*
Tuskegee University *M*

Arizona
University of Arizona *B, M*

Arkansas
University of Arkansas *M*

California
San Joaquin Delta College *A*
University of California
  Berkeley *D*
  Davis *M, D*

Colorado
Colorado State University *B, M, D*
Fort Lewis College *B*

Connecticut
University of Connecticut *B, M, D*

Delaware
University of Delaware *B, M*

Florida
University of Florida *B, M, D*

Georgia
Fort Valley State University *B*
University of Georgia *B, M, D*

Idaho
University of Idaho *B, M*

Illinois
Southern Illinois University
  Carbondale *B, M*
University of Illinois
  Urbana-Champaign *B, M, D*

Indiana
Purdue University *B, M, D*

Iowa
Iowa State University *M, D*

Kansas
Highland Community College *A*
Kansas State University *B, M, D*

Kentucky
Bluegrass Community and Technical
  College *A*
University of Kentucky *B, M, D*

Louisiana
Louisiana State University and
  Agricultural and Mechanical
  College *M, D*
Southern University and Agricultural
  and Mechanical College *B*

Maine
University of Maine *B, M*

Maryland
University of Maryland
  College Park *B, M, D*

Massachusetts
University of Massachusetts
  Amherst *B, M, D*

Michigan
Michigan State University *B, M, D*

Minnesota
Northland Community & Technical
  College *A*
Ridgewater College *A*
University of Minnesota
  Twin Cities *B, M, D*

Mississippi
Alcorn State University *B*
Mississippi Delta Community
  College *A*
Mississippi State University *B, D*
Northwest Mississippi Community
  College *A*

Missouri
Northwest Missouri State
  University *B*
University of Central Missouri *B*
University of Missouri
  Columbia *B, M, D*

Nebraska
University of Nebraska
  Lincoln *B, M, D*

Nevada
University of Nevada
  Reno *B, M, D*

New Jersey
Rutgers, The State University of New
  Jersey
  New Brunswick/Piscataway
    Campus *M*

New Mexico
New Mexico State University *M*

New York
Cornell University *M, D*

North Carolina
North Carolina Agricultural and
  Technical State University *B, M*
North Carolina State University *M*

North Dakota
North Dakota State University *B, M*

Ohio
Ohio State University
  Columbus Campus *B, M, D*

Oklahoma
Langston University *B*
Oklahoma State University *B, M, D*

Oregon
Eastern Oregon University *B*
Oregon State University *B, M, D*
Treasure Valley Community College *A*

Pennsylvania
Penn State
  University Park *M, D*

South Carolina
Clemson University *B, M, D*

South Dakota
South Dakota State University *B*

Tennessee
University of Tennessee
  Knoxville *B, M*

Texas
Clarendon College *A*
Prairie View A&M University *M*
Tarleton State University *B*
Texas A&M University *B, M, D*
Texas A&M University
  Commerce *B, M*
Texas Tech University *B, M, D*

Utah
Utah State University *B, M*

Virginia
Virginia Polytechnic Institute and
  State University *B, M*

Washington
Washington State University *B, M, D*

West Virginia
West Virginia University *B, M, D*

Wisconsin
University of Wisconsin
  Madison *B, M, D*
  Platteville *B*

Wyoming
Eastern Wyoming College *A*
University of Wyoming *M*

Agricultural education services

Colorado
Colorado State University *B*
Northeastern Junior College *C*

Georgia
University of Georgia *M*

Illinois
University of Illinois
  Urbana-Champaign *B, M, T*

Iowa
Iowa State University *B*

North Carolina
North Carolina State
  University *B, M, D*

Pennsylvania
Penn State
  Abington *B*
  Altoona *B*
  Beaver *B*
  Berks *B*
  Brandywine *B*
  DuBois *B*
  Erie, The Behrend College *B*
  Fayette, The Eberly Campus *B*
  Greater Allegheny *B*
  Hazleton *B*
  Lehigh Valley *B*
  Mont Alto *B*
  New Kensington *B*
  Schuylkill *B*
  Shenango *B*
  University Park *B, M, D*
  Wilkes-Barre *B*
  Worthington Scranton *B*
  York *B*

Agricultural equipment technology

Arizona
Central Arizona College *C*

California
Shasta College *C*

Georgia
Southwest Georgia Technical
  College *A*

Idaho
University of Idaho *B*

Illinois
Spoon River College *A*

Kansas
North Central Kansas Technical
  College *A*

Minnesota
Minnesota West Community and
  Technical College *C, A*
South Central College *C, A*

Nebraska
Northeast Community College *A*

New York
State University of New York
  College of Agriculture and
    Technology at Morrisville *A*

Ohio
Ohio State University
  Agricultural Technical Institute *A*

Utah
Utah State University *B, M*

Wisconsin
University of Wisconsin
  River Falls *B*
Wisconsin Indianhead Technical
  College *C*

Agricultural/food products processing

California
California State University
  Fresno *C*

Indiana
Purdue University *B, M, D*

Iowa
Des Moines Area Community
  College *C*
Northeast Iowa Community
  College *C, A*

Kansas
Kansas State University *M, D*

Nebraska
University of Nebraska
  Lincoln *B*

North Dakota
North Dakota State University *M, D*

Oklahoma
Eastern Oklahoma State College *A*

Washington

Washington State University C, B
Wenatchee Valley College A
Yakima Valley Community College A

Wisconsin

University of Wisconsin
River Falls B

Agricultural mechanization

California

California Polytechnic State
University: San Luis Obispo B
Yuba Community College District A

Colorado

Northeastern Junior College A

Idaho

University of Idaho B

Illinois

Black Hawk College C, A
Parkland College C, A
Rend Lake College C, A
University of Illinois
Urbana-Champaign B, M, D

Indiana

Purdue University B

Iowa

Iowa State University B

Kansas

Kansas State University B

Minnesota

Ridgewater College C

Missouri

College of the Ozarks B

Nebraska

Northeast Community College A
University of Nebraska
Lincoln B, M

New York

State University of New York
College of Agriculture and
Technology at Cobleskill A, B
College of Agriculture and
Technology at Morrisville A

North Carolina

Beaufort County Community
College C, A
North Carolina State University B

North Dakota

North Dakota State University B

Ohio

Owens Community College
Toledo A

Pennsylvania

Penn State
Abington B
Altoona B
Beaver B
Berks B
Brandywine B
DuBois B
Erie, The Behrend College B
Fayette, The Eberly Campus B
Greater Allegheny B

Hazleton B
Lehigh Valley B
Mont Alto B
New Kensington B
Schuylkill B
Shenango B
University Park B
Wilkes-Barre B
Worthington Scranton B
York B

South Dakota

South Dakota State University B

Texas

Sam Houston State University B, M
Stephen F. Austin State University B
Tarleton State University B

Washington

Washington State University B

Agricultural power machinery operation

California

Shasta College C

Georgia

Southwest Georgia Technical
College A

Illinois

Black Hawk College: East Campus C

Iowa

Hawkeye Community College A
Iowa Lakes Community College A
Northeast Iowa Community
College A

Kansas

Hutchinson Community College C, A
North Central Kansas Technical
College C

Montana

Dawson Community College C, A

New York

State University of New York
College of Agriculture and
Technology at Morrisville A

North Carolina

Guilford Technical Community
College A

North Dakota

North Dakota State College of
Science A

Ohio

Ohio State University
Agricultural Technical Institute A

Agricultural production

Arizona

Tohono O'odham Community
College A

Arkansas

University of Arkansas M
University of Arkansas
Monticello A

Colorado

Northeastern Junior College C, A

Delaware

Delaware Technical and Community
College
Owens C, A

Illinois

Black Hawk College A
Highland Community College C
Illinois Eastern Community Colleges
Wabash Valley College A
John Wood Community College C
Lincoln Land Community College A
Rend Lake College C, A

Indiana

Purdue University B

Iowa

Indian Hills Community College A
Iowa Lakes Community College A
Muscatine Community College C, A
North Iowa Area Community
College A
Northeast Iowa Community
College A
Southwestern Community College A

Kansas

Barton County Community
College C, A
Cloud County Community
College C, A

Kentucky

Hopkinsville Community College C, A
Madisonville Community College C, A
Owensboro Community and
Technical College C
Western Kentucky University A

Michigan

Michigan State University C

Minnesota

Minnesota West Community and
Technical College A
Ridgewater College C, A
South Central College C, A

Missouri

Crowder College A
Mineral Area College A

Nebraska

Northeast Community College A

Ohio

Wilmington College B

Oregon

Blue Mountain Community College A

Puerto Rico

University of Puerto Rico
Utuado A

Texas

Stephen F. Austin State University B
Texas A&M University B

Virginia

Virginia Polytechnic Institute and
State University A

Washington

Big Bend Community College A
Wenatchee Valley College C, A

Wyoming

Laramie County Community
College A
Sheridan College A

Agricultural supplies

California

Modesto Junior College A

Colorado

Aims Community College C, A
Pueblo Community College A

Illinois

Carl Sandburg College C
John Wood Community College C
Joliet Junior College C, A
Kishwaukee College A

Iowa

Des Moines Area Community
College C, A
Hawkeye Community College C, A
Iowa Lakes Community College A
Kirkwood Community College C, A
Muscatine Community College C, A
North Iowa Area Community
College A
Northeast Iowa Community
College A
Southeastern Community College
North Campus A
Western Iowa Tech Community
College C, A

Kansas

Cloud County Community College A
Coffeyville Community College A

Michigan

St. Clair County Community
College C, A

North Dakota

North Dakota State College of
Science A

Texas

Sul Ross State University C, A
Tarleton State University B
Texas A&M University B

Washington

Yakima Valley Community College A

Wisconsin

Fox Valley Technical College A

Agricultural teacher education

Arizona

Prescott College T
University of Arizona M

Arkansas

Arkansas State University B, M, T
Southern Arkansas University B, T
University of Arkansas B, M
University of Arkansas
Pine Bluff B, T

California

California Polytechnic State
University: San Luis Obispo B, T
California State Polytechnic
University: Pomona B

California State University
Chico B, T
Fresno M
University of California
Davis M, T

Colorado

Colorado State University B, T

Connecticut

University of Connecticut B, T

Delaware

University of Delaware B, T

Florida

University of Florida B, M

Georgia

Fort Valley State University B, T
University of Georgia B

Idaho

University of Idaho B, M, T

Illinois

Elmhurst College B
University of Illinois
Urbana-Champaign B, M, T

Indiana

Purdue University B

Iowa

Ellsworth Community College A
Iowa State University B, M, D, T

Kansas

Kansas State University B

Kentucky

Western Kentucky University M, T

Louisiana

Louisiana State University and
Agricultural and Mechanical
College B
McNeese State University B, T
Southern University and Agricultural
and Mechanical College B
University of Louisiana at Lafayette B

Maryland

University of Maryland
Eastern Shore B, M

Minnesota

University of Minnesota
Crookston B
Twin Cities B, M, T

Mississippi

Mississippi State University B, M, T

Missouri

College of the Ozarks B, T
Missouri State University B
Northwest Missouri State
University B, M, T
University of Central Missouri B, T
University of Missouri
Columbia B, M, D

Montana

Montana State University
Bozeman B, M

Nebraska

University of Nebraska
Lincoln B, M

Nevada

Great Basin College B
University of Nevada
Reno B, T

New Mexico

Eastern New Mexico University B
New Mexico State University B, M

New York

Cornell University B, M, D, T
State University of New York
Oswego B

North Carolina

North Carolina Agricultural and
Technical State University B, M, T
North Carolina State
University B, M, T

North Dakota

North Dakota State University B, M, T

Ohio

Ohio State University
Agricultural Technical Institute A
Columbus Campus B, M, D
Wilmington College B

Oklahoma

East Central University B
Eastern Oklahoma State College A
Oklahoma Panhandle State
University B
Oklahoma State University B, M, D

Oregon

Oregon State University M

Puerto Rico

Universidad Metropolitana M

South Carolina

Clemson University B, M

South Dakota

South Dakota State University B

Tennessee

Tennessee Technological
University B, T
University of Tennessee
Knoxville B, M, T

Texas

Laredo Community College A
Lubbock Christian University B
Prairie View A&M University M
Sam Houston State University M, T
Stephen F. Austin State University T
Tarleton State University M, T
Texas A&M University M, D
Texas A&M University
Commerce M, T
Kingsville B, M
Texas State University: San
Marcos M, T
Texas Tech University M, D
West Texas A&M University T

Utah

Utah State University B

Washington

Washington State University B, T

West Virginia

West Virginia University B, M, T

Wisconsin

University of Wisconsin
Madison B
Platteville B, T
River Falls B, M, T

Wyoming

Eastern Wyoming College A
Northwest College A
University of Wyoming B

Agriculture, general

Alabama

Calhoun Community College A
Faulkner State Community College A
Gadsden State Community College A

Arizona

Arizona Western College A
Prescott College B
University of Arizona B

Arkansas

Arkansas State University B, M
East Arkansas Community College A
Mid-South Community College A
North Arkansas College A
Northwest Arkansas Community
College A
Rich Mountain Community College A
Southern Arkansas University M
University of Arkansas
Community College at Hope A

California

California Polytechnic State
University: San Luis Obispo M
California State Polytechnic
University: Pomona M
California State University
Fresno B
Stanislaus B
Feather River College A
Fresno City College C, A
Hartnell College C, A
Imperial Valley College C, A
Merced College A
Napa Valley College C, A
Shasta College A
Sierra College C, A
West Hills College: Coalinga A

Colorado

Aims Community College C, A
Colorado State University M
Fort Lewis College B

Connecticut

University of Connecticut B

Delaware

Delaware State University B, M
University of Delaware A

Florida

Florida Agricultural and Mechanical
University B, M
Gulf Coast Community College A
Pensacola Junior College A
South Florida Community College A

Georgia

Abraham Baldwin Agricultural
College B
Andrew College A
Dalton State College A
Darton College A
East Georgia College A
Gainesville State College A
Georgia Highlands College A

Middle Georgia College A
University of Georgia B

Hawaii

University of Hawaii
Hawaii Community College C, A
Maui Community College A

Idaho

University of Idaho B

Illinois

Black Hawk College A
Illinois Valley Community College A
John Wood Community College A
Joliet Junior College C, A
Kaskaskia College C, A
Lake Land College A
Parkland College A
Southern Illinois University
Carbondale B
Western Illinois University B

Indiana

Ivy Tech Community College
Columbus A
East Central C, A
Kokomo C, A
Lafayette A
North Central A
Richmond A
Southwest A
Wabash Valley A
Purdue University A, B
Vincennes University A

Iowa

Iowa Western Community
College C, A
North Iowa Area Community
College A
Southeastern Community College
North Campus A

Kansas

Barton County Community College A
Coffeyville Community College A
Garden City Community College A
Highland Community College A
Hutchinson Community College A
Pratt Community College C, A
Seward County Community College A

Kentucky

Berea College B
Morehead State University B
Murray State University A, B, M, T
Western Kentucky University B, M, T

Louisiana

McNeese State University B
University of Louisiana at Lafayette B

Maryland

Montgomery College C, A
University of Maryland
College Park B, M, D
Eastern Shore B

Massachusetts

Hampshire College B
North Shore Community College C

Minnesota

Minnesota West Community and
Technical College A
Northland Community & Technical
College C
Ridgewater College C, A
South Central College C, A

Mississippi

Alcorn State University B, M
Hinds Community College A
Mississippi Gulf Coast Community
    College C, A
Mississippi State University B, M, D

Missouri

Lincoln University B
Missouri State University B
Northwest Missouri State
    University B, M
Southeast Missouri State University B
Truman State University B
University of Central Missouri B, M
University of Missouri
    Columbia B

Nebraska

Nebraska College of Technical
    Agriculture A
Northeast Community College A
University of Nebraska
    Lincoln B, M

Nevada

Great Basin College A

New Jersey

Cumberland County College C, A

New Mexico

Mesalands Community College C, A
Navajo Technical College A
New Mexico State University B, M
Western New Mexico University A

New York

Cornell University B, M, D
State University of New York
    College of Agriculture and
        Technology at Cobleskill A
    College of Agriculture and
        Technology at Morrisville A, B

North Carolina

North Carolina State University A

North Dakota

Cankdeska Cikana Community
    College A
Dakota College at Bottineau A
North Dakota State University B
Turtle Mountain Community
    College C
Williston State College A

Ohio

Ohio State University
    Agricultural Technical Institute C, A
Southern State Community College A

Oklahoma

Cameron University B
Eastern Oklahoma State College A
Northeastern Oklahoma Agricultural
    and Mechanical College A
Northwestern Oklahoma State
    University B
Oklahoma Panhandle State
    University B
Oklahoma State University M
Redlands Community College A

Oregon

Central Oregon Community
    College A
Linn-Benton Community College A
Oregon State University B, M
Treasure Valley Community College C

Pennsylvania

Penn State
    Abington B
    Altoona B
    Beaver B
    Berks B
    Brandywine B
    DuBois B
    Erie, The Behrend College B
    Fayette, The Eberly Campus B
    Greater Allegheny B
    Hazleton B
    Lehigh Valley B
    Mont Alto B
    New Kensington B
    Schuylkill B
    Shenango B
    University Park B
    Wilkes-Barre B
    Worthington Scranton B
    York B

Puerto Rico

Universidad Metropolitana C
University of Puerto Rico
    Utuado A

South Dakota

Lake Area Technical Institute A
South Dakota State University A, B
Western Dakota Technical Institute A

Tennessee

Austin Peay State University B
University of Tennessee
    Knoxville D
    Martin B

Texas

Blinn College A
Brazosport College A
Clarendon College A
Howard College A
Kilgore College A
Laredo Community College A
Lubbock Christian University A, B
Prairie View A&M University B
Sam Houston State University B, M
Southwest Texas Junior College A
Stephen F. Austin State
    University B, M
Tarleton State University B, M
Texarkana College A
Texas A&M University B, M
Texas State University: San Marcos B
Texas Tech University B, M
Tyler Junior College C, A
West Texas A&M University B, M, D

Utah

Southern Utah University C, B

Vermont

Sterling College B
University of Vermont B
Vermont Technical College B

Virginia

Virginia Polytechnic Institute and
    State University B, M
Virginia State University B

Washington

Evergreen State College B
Washington State University B, M
Yakima Valley Community College A

West Virginia

Potomac State College of West
    Virginia University A
West Virginia University M, D

Wisconsin

Blackhawk Technical College C
Chippewa Valley Technical College A
University of Wisconsin
    Platteville M
    River Falls B

Wyoming

Casper College A
Eastern Wyoming College A
Laramie County Community
    College A
Northwest College A
University of Wyoming B

Agronomy and crop science

Arizona

Prescott College B, M
University of Arizona B

Arkansas

University of Arkansas B, M, D

California

Butte College C, A
California Polytechnic State
    University: San Luis Obispo B
California State University
    Chico B
    Fresno B, M
Merced College A
Modesto Junior College A
San Joaquin Delta College A
University of California
    Davis B

Colorado

Colorado State University B, M, D
Lamar Community College A

Connecticut

University of Connecticut B

Delaware

University of Delaware B

Florida

University of Florida B, M, D

Georgia

University of Georgia M, D

Hawaii

University of Hawaii
    Hilo B

Idaho

Brigham Young University-Idaho B
University of Idaho B

Illinois

University of Illinois
    Urbana-Champaign B, M, D

Indiana

Purdue University B, M, D

Iowa

Iowa State University B, M

Kansas

Colby Community College A
Garden City Community College A
Kansas State University B, M, D

Kentucky

University of Kentucky B, M, D

Louisiana

Louisiana State University and
    Agricultural and Mechanical
    College M, D

Michigan

Michigan State University C

Minnesota

Minnesota West Community and
    Technical College A
Ridgewater College C, A
University of Minnesota
    Crookston B
    Twin Cities M, D

Mississippi

Mississippi State University B

Missouri

College of the Ozarks B
Missouri State University B
Northwest Missouri State
    University B
University of Missouri
    Columbia M, D

Nebraska

Northeast Community College A
University of Nebraska
    Lincoln B, M, D

New Mexico

New Mexico State University B, M, D

New York

Cornell University B, M, D
State University of New York
    College of Agriculture and
        Technology at Cobleskill A
    College of Technology at Alfred A

North Carolina

North Carolina State
    University B, M, D

North Dakota

North Dakota State University M, D

Ohio

Ohio State University
    Agricultural Technical Institute A
    Columbus Campus B
Wilmington College B

Oklahoma

Cameron University B
Eastern Oklahoma State College A
Oklahoma Panhandle State
    University B
Oklahoma State University D
Redlands Community College A

Oregon

Eastern Oregon University B
Oregon State University B, M, D
Treasure Valley Community College A

Pennsylvania

Delaware Valley College B
Penn State
    Abington B
    Altoona B
    Beaver B
    Berks B
    Brandywine B
    DuBois B
    Erie, The Behrend College B
    Fayette, The Eberly Campus B
    Greater Allegheny B
    Hazleton B

Lehigh Valley *B*
Mont Alto *B*
New Kensington *B*
Schuylkill *B*
Shenango *B*
University Park *B, M, D*
Wilkes-Barre *B*
Worthington Scranton *B*
York *B*

South Carolina

Clemson University *B, M, D*

South Dakota

South Dakota State University *B, D*

Tennessee

Tennessee Technological University *B*

Texas

Clarendon College *A*
Hardin-Simmons University *B*
Stephen F. Austin State University *B*
Tarleton State University *B*
Texas A&M University *B, M, D*
Texas A&M University
  Commerce *M*
  Kingsville *M*
Texas Tech University *B, D*
West Texas A&M University *B, M*

Utah

Utah State University *B*

Vermont

University of Vermont *B*

Virginia

Virginia Polytechnic Institute and
  State University *B, M, D*

Washington

Washington State University *B, M, D*

West Virginia

Potomac State College of West
  Virginia University *A*
West Virginia University *B, M*

Wisconsin

Chippewa Valley Technical College *A*
University of Wisconsin
  Madison *B, M, D*
  Platteville *B*
  River Falls *B*

Wyoming

University of Wyoming *M, D*

Air traffic control

Alaska

University of Alaska
  Anchorage *A, B*

Arizona

Arizona State University *B*

California

Mount San Antonio College *A*

Colorado

Metropolitan State College of
  Denver *B*

Florida

Embry-Riddle Aeronautical
  University *B*
Florida State College at Jacksonville *A*

Georgia

Middle Georgia College *B*

Illinois

Lewis University *A, B*

Indiana

Purdue University *B*

Maryland

Cecil College *C, A*

Minnesota

Anoka Technical College *C, A*
Minneapolis Community and
  Technical College *A*
Saint Cloud State University *B*

Missouri

St. Louis Community College
  St. Louis Community College at
    Meramec *A*

New Hampshire

Daniel Webster College *B*

New Jersey

Thomas Edison State College *A, B*

New York

Vaughn College of Aeronautics and
  Technology *C*

North Dakota

University of North Dakota *B*

Pennsylvania

Community College of Beaver
  County *C, A*
Geneva College *A*

Texas

LeTourneau University *A*
Mountain View College *C, A*

Aircraft maintenance/technology

Alabama

Enterprise-Ozark Community
  College *C, A*

Alaska

University of Alaska
  Anchorage *C, A, B*
  Fairbanks *C, A*

Arizona

Cochise College *C, A*

Arkansas

Pulaski Technical College *C*
Southern Arkansas University Tech *C*
University of Arkansas
  Community College at
    Batesville *C, A*

California

Antelope Valley College *C, A*
Chaffey College *A*
City College of San Francisco *C, A*
College of Alameda *C, A*
College of San Mateo *C, A*
Cypress College *C, A*
Foothill College *C, A*
Gavilan College *C, A*
Glendale Community College *C, A*
Mount San Antonio College *A*
Orange Coast College *C, A*
Reedley College *C*

Sacramento City College *C, A*
San Bernardino Valley College *C*
San Diego Miramar College *C, A*
San Joaquin Valley College *A*
Solano Community College *C, A*
West Los Angeles College *C, A*

Colorado

Colorado Northwestern Community
  College *C, A*
Pueblo Community College *A*
Redstone College *C, A*

Connecticut

Housatonic Community College *A*

Delaware

Delaware Technical and Community
  College
  Owens *C*

Florida

Florida State College at Jacksonville *C*
St. Petersburg College *A*

Georgia

Central Georgia Technical College *C*
Middle Georgia College *A*
Savannah Technical College *C*

Hawaii

University of Hawaii
  Honolulu Community College *C, A*

Illinois

Lewis University *C, A, B*
Lincoln Land Community College *C, A*
Moody Bible Institute *B*
Rock Valley College *A*
Southwestern Illinois College *C, A*

Iowa

Iowa Western Community College *A*

Kansas

Central Christian College of Kansas *A*
Cowley County Community
  College *C, A*
Kansas State University *A, B*

Maryland

Chesapeake College *C, A*

Massachusetts

Middlesex Community College *A*

Michigan

Andrews University *B*
Lansing Community College *A*
Northern Michigan University *C, A*

Minnesota

Lake Superior College *C, A*
Minneapolis Community and
  Technical College *C, A*
Northland Community & Technical
  College *C, A*

Mississippi

Hinds Community College *C*

Missouri

Linn State Technical College *C, A*

Montana

Helena College of Technology of the
  University of Montana *A*

Nebraska

Western Nebraska Community
  College *C, A*

New Hampshire

Nashua Community College *A*

New Jersey

Mercer County Community College *A*
Thomas Edison State College *A, B*

New Mexico

Central New Mexico Community
  College *C*

New York

Mohawk Valley Community
  College *C, A*
State University of New York
  Farmingdale *C, A*
Vaughn College of Aeronautics and
  Technology *C, A, B*

Ohio

Cincinnati State Technical and
  Community College *C, A*
Columbus State Community
  College *C, A*

Oklahoma

Southeastern Oklahoma State
  University *B*

Oregon

Lane Community College *A*
Portland Community College *C, A*

Pennsylvania

Pittsburgh Institute of Aeronautics *A*

South Carolina

Trident Technical College *A*

South Dakota

Lake Area Technical Institute *A*

Texas

Amarillo College *C, A*
Del Mar College *C, A*
Hallmark College of Aeronautics *A*
Houston Community College
  System *C, A*
LeTourneau University *B*
Midland College *C*
St. Philip's College *C, A*
Tarrant County College *C, A*
Texas State Technical College
  Harlingen *C, A*
  Waco *C, A*
  West Texas *C, A*

Utah

Utah State University *A, B*

Virginia

Hampton University *A*
Northern Virginia Community
  College *A*

Washington

Big Bend Community College *C, A*
South Seattle Community
  College *C, A*
Spokane Community College *A*

Wisconsin

Blackhawk Technical College *C*
Fox Valley Technical College *A*
Milwaukee Area Technical College *C*

Aircraft powerplant technology

Alaska
University of Alaska
  Fairbanks *C, A*

Arizona
Cochise College *C*
Pima Community College *C, A*

Arkansas
Pulaski Technical College *C, A*
Southern Arkansas University
  Tech *C, A*

California
Antelope Valley College *C*
City College of San Francisco *C*
Long Beach City College *C, A*
Orange Coast College *C*

Florida
Embry-Riddle Aeronautical
  University *A, B*
Embry-Riddle Aeronautical University:
  Worldwide Campus *B*

Georgia
Clayton State University *A*
Georgia Military College *A*

Idaho
Idaho State University *C, A*

Illinois
Lincoln Land Community College *C*

Kansas
Kansas State University *C*

Kentucky
Somerset Community College *C, A*

Michigan
Wayne County Community College *A*

Minnesota
Minneapolis Community and
  Technical College *C, A*

Missouri
Linn State Technical College *C, A*

Nebraska
Western Nebraska Community
  College *C, A*

New Mexico
Central New Mexico Community
  College *C, A*

New York
Vaughn College of Aeronautics and
  Technology *C, A, B*

Oregon
Portland Community College *C*

Pennsylvania
Pennsylvania College of
  Technology *C, A*

South Carolina
Trident Technical College *C, A*

South Dakota
Lake Area Technical Institute *A*

Texas
Del Mar College *C, A*
Hallmark College of Aeronautics *A*
Houston Community College
  System *C, A*
LeTourneau University *B*
Midland College *C*
St. Philip's College *C, A*
Tarrant County College *C, A*
Texas State Technical College
  West Texas *C*

Washington
Clover Park Technical College *C, A*
Everett Community College *A*
South Seattle Community
  College *C, A*

Wisconsin
Blackhawk Technical College *C*
Fox Valley Technical College *A*
Milwaukee Area Technical College *C*

Airline/commercial pilot

Alaska
University of Alaska
  Anchorage *A, B*
  Fairbanks *A*

Arizona
Cochise College *C, A*
Embry-Riddle Aeronautical University:
  Prescott Campus *B*

Arkansas
Henderson State University *B*
Pulaski Technical College *A*

California
College of San Mateo *C, A*
Cypress College *C, A*
Orange Coast College *C, A*

Colorado
Pueblo Community College *C*

Florida
Embry-Riddle Aeronautical
  University *A, B, M*
Embry-Riddle Aeronautical University:
  Worldwide Campus *M*
Jacksonville University *B*
Santa Fe College *A*

Hawaii
University of Hawaii
  Honolulu Community College *A*

Illinois
Lewis University *B*
Quincy University *B*
Southern Illinois University
  Carbondale *A*
University of Illinois
  Urbana-Champaign *C, B*

Indiana
Indiana State University *B*
Purdue University *B*
Vincennes University *C, A*

Iowa
Indian Hills Community College *A*

Kansas
Kansas State University *A, B*

Kentucky
Bluegrass Community and Technical
  College *A*

Louisiana
University of Louisiana at Monroe *B*

Massachusetts
Bridgewater State College *B*
North Shore Community College *A*

Michigan
Baker College
  of Muskegon *A*
Eastern Michigan University *B*
Northwestern Michigan College *A*
Western Michigan University *B*

Minnesota
Academy College *A*
Lake Superior College *C, A*
Saint Cloud State University *B*
University of Minnesota
  Crookston *B*

Mississippi
Delta State University *B*

Missouri
Saint Louis University *B*

Montana
Montana State University
  College of Technology: Great
  Falls *A*
Rocky Mountain College *B*

New Mexico
Central New Mexico Community
  College *C, A*

New York
Jamestown Community College *A*
State University of New York
  Farmingdale *B*
Vaughn College of Aeronautics and
  Technology *A, B*

North Carolina
Guilford Technical Community
  College *C, A*
Lenoir Community College *C, A*

North Dakota
University of North Dakota *B*

Oklahoma
Southeastern Oklahoma State
  University *B*

Oregon
Central Oregon Community
  College *A*
Lane Community College *A*
Portland Community College *A*
Umpqua Community College *C, A*

Pennsylvania
Community College of Allegheny
  County *A*
Luzerne County Community
  College *A*

Rhode Island
New England Institute of
  Technology *A*

Texas
Baylor University *B*
LeTourneau University *B*

Midland College *A*
Mountain View College *C, A*
San Jacinto College *C, A*
Tarleton State University *B*

Utah
Salt Lake Community College *A*
Utah Valley University *A, B*

Virginia
Averett University *B*

Washington
Big Bend Community College *C, A*
Clover Park Technical College *C, A*
Northwest Aviation College *C, A*

Wisconsin
Fox Valley Technical College *A*
Gateway Technical College *A*

Wyoming
Casper College *A*

Algebra/number theory

New York
City University of New York
  Brooklyn College *B*

Wisconsin
Marquette University *D*

Alternative fuel vehicle technology

Arkansas
Pulaski Technical College *C*

California
College of the Desert *C*
Long Beach City College *C, A*

Illinois
Morton College *C*

Michigan
Wayne County Community College *C*

American government/ politics

Arizona
Northern Arizona University *B*

California
The Master's College *B*
Mills College *B*
University of California
  San Diego *B*

District of Columbia
Catholic University of America *M*

Florida
Florida State University *M*

Massachusetts
Brandeis University *B*
Bridgewater State College *B*
Suffolk University *B, M*

Missouri
Drury University *B*

New York
United States Military Academy *B*
Wells College *B*

North Carolina

Meredith College *B*

Ohio

Ohio Wesleyan University *B*
University of Akron *B*

Pennsylvania

Gettysburg College *B*
La Salle University *B*
Lycoming College *B*

South Carolina

Wofford College *B*

Texas

Wayland Baptist University *B*

Vermont

Bennington College *B*

Virginia

Emory & Henry College *B*

Wisconsin

Marquette University *M*

American history (U.S.)

California

Mills College *B*
Pitzer College *B*

Iowa

Morningside College *B*

Kansas

Central Christian College of Kansas *A*

Massachusetts

Bard College at Simon's Rock *B*
Brandeis University *M, D*
Elms College *B*
Harvard College *M, D*
Mount Ida College *B*
Salem State College *B*
Suffolk University *B*

Michigan

Calvin College *B*
Central Michigan University *M*

New Hampshire

Keene State College *B*

New York

Bard College *B*
College of Saint Rose *B*
United States Military Academy *B*

North Carolina

Montreat College *B*
Western Carolina University *M*

Pennsylvania

Gettysburg College *B*
La Salle University *B*
Lycoming College *B*

Puerto Rico

University of Puerto Rico
Rio Piedras *B*

Rhode Island

Salve Regina University *B*

South Carolina

Charleston Southern University *B*

Vermont

Bennington College *B*

Virginia

Emory & Henry College *M*

Wisconsin

Marquette University *D*

American literature

California

California State University
Bakersfield *B, M*
East Bay *B*
College of the Desert *A*
College of the Siskiyous *C*
San Joaquin Delta College *A*
University of California
Los Angeles *B*
San Diego *B, M, D*
University of Southern California *B*
Whittier College *B*

Colorado

Pikes Peak Community College *A*

District of Columbia

George Washington University *M, D*

Florida

Miami Dade College *A*

Illinois

Illinois Valley Community College *A*
Lincoln College *A*
Richland Community College *A*

Indiana

Purdue University
Calumet *B*

Kansas

Central Christian College of Kansas *A*

Maine

University of Maine
Fort Kent *B*

Maryland

Johns Hopkins University *D*

Massachusetts

Simmons College *B*
Tufts University *B, M, D*

Michigan

Cornerstone University *B*
Eastern Michigan University *M*
Lansing Community College *A*
Michigan State University *D*

Minnesota

Augsburg College *B*
Saint Cloud State University *B*

Missouri

University of Missouri
St. Louis *M*
Washington University in St.
Louis *B, M, D*

Montana

Miles Community College *A*

Nebraska

Creighton University *B*

New York

Bard College *B*
City University of New York
Baruch College *B*
Columbia University *B*
St. Lawrence University *B*
State University of New York
Purchase *B*

Ohio

College of Wooster *B*
Ohio Wesleyan University *B*

Pennsylvania

Gettysburg College *B*
La Salle University *B*
University of Pittsburgh
Johnstown *B*
Westminster College *B, T*

Rhode Island

Brown University *B, M, D*

Texas

North Lake College *C, A*
Texas A&M University
Commerce *B*

Vermont

Bennington College *B*
Castleton State College *B*
Marlboro College *B*
Middlebury College *B*

Washington

Everett Community College *A*

Wisconsin

Marquette University *M, D*

American Sign Language (ASL)

California

Antelope Valley College *A*
California State University
Sacramento *B*
Grossmont College *A*
Imperial Valley College *A*
National University *B*
Ohlone College *A*
San Diego Mesa College *A*
Santa Rosa Junior College *A*
Santiago Canyon College *A*
Sierra College *A*

District of Columbia

Gallaudet University *B*

Idaho

Idaho State University *A*

Indiana

Goshen College *B*
Indiana University-Purdue University
Indianapolis *B*
Vincennes University *A*

Maryland

Montgomery College *A*

Massachusetts

Bristol Community College *A*
Northeastern University *B*

Michigan

Madonna University *A, B*

Minnesota

North Central University *B*

St. Catherine University *B*
St. Paul College *A*

Missouri

William Woods University *B*

New Jersey

Union County College *A*

New York

Keuka College *B*
Nassau Community College *A*
Rochester Institute of
Technology *A, B*
University of Rochester *B*

North Carolina

Gardner-Webb University *B*

Oregon

Portland Community College *A*

South Dakota

Augustana College *B, T*

Tennessee

Maryville College *B*

Utah

Utah Valley University *B*

Virginia

Tidewater Community College *A*

American studies

Alabama

Gadsden State Community College *A*
University of Alabama *B, M*

Arizona

Arizona State University *B*
Northern Arizona University *B*

Arkansas

Harding University *B*
Hendrix College *B*
University of Arkansas *B*

California

California State Polytechnic
University: Pomona *B*
California State University
Chico *B*
Fullerton *B, M*
San Bernardino *B*
Claremont McKenna College *B*
Cosumnes River College *A*
El Camino College *A*
Folsom Lake College *A*
Foothill College *A*
Los Angeles Valley College *A*
Mills College *B*
Mount St. Mary's College *B*
Occidental College *B*
Pepperdine University *M*
Pitzer College *B*
Pomona College *B*
San Diego State University *B*
San Francisco State University *B*
Scripps College *B*
Southwestern College *A*
Stanford University *B*
University of California
Berkeley *B*
Davis *B*
Santa Cruz *B*
University of San Francisco *B*
University of Southern California *B, D*

Connecticut

Connecticut College *B*
Fairfield University *B, M*
Saint Joseph College *B*
Trinity College *B, M*
University of Connecticut *B*
Wesleyan University *B*
Western Connecticut State
  University *B*
Yale University *B, M, D*

Delaware

Wesley College *B*

District of Columbia

American University *B*
George Washington
  University *B, M, D*
Georgetown University *B*

Florida

Eckerd College *B*
Florida State University *B*
Lynn University *B*
Miami Dade College *A*
Nova Southeastern University *B*
State College of Florida,
  Manatee-Sarasota *A*
Stetson University *B*
University of Miami *B*
University of South Florida *B, M*

Georgia

Emory University *B*
Kennesaw State University *M*
Oglethorpe University *B*

Hawaii

University of Hawaii
  Manoa *B, M, D*

Idaho

Idaho State University *B*
University of Idaho *B*

Illinois

DePaul University *B*
Dominican University *B*
Elmhurst College *B*
Illinois College *B*
Illinois Wesleyan University *B*
Knox College *B*
Lake Forest College *B*
Lewis University *B*
Northwestern University *B*

Indiana

Franklin College *B*
Indiana University
  Bloomington *D*
University of Notre Dame *B*
University of St. Francis *B*
Valparaiso University *B*

Iowa

Coe College *B*
University of Iowa *B, M, D*
University of Northern Iowa *B*
Upper Iowa University *B*

Kansas

University of Kansas *B, M, D*

Kentucky

Georgetown College *B*
Lindsey Wilson College *B*

Louisiana

Tulane University *B*

Maine

Bates College *B*
Colby College *B*
University of Southern Maine *M*

Maryland

Anne Arundel Community College *A*
Goucher College *B*
Howard Community College *A*
Prince George's Community
  College *A*
Towson University *B*
University of Maryland
  Baltimore County *B*
  College Park *B, M, D*
Washington College *B*

Massachusetts

American International College *B*
Amherst College *B*
Bard College at Simon's Rock *B*
Boston College *M*
Boston University *B, M, D*
Brandeis University *B*
Elms College *B*
Emmanuel College *B*
Hampshire College *B*
Lesley University *B, M*
Mount Holyoke College *B*
Smith College *B*
Stonehill College *B*
Tufts University *B, M*
University of Massachusetts
  Boston *B, M*
  Lowell *B*
Wellesley College *B*
Wheaton College *B*
Wheelock College *B*
Williams College *B*

Michigan

Albion College *B*
Hillsdale College *B*
Michigan State University *B, M, D*
Siena Heights University *B*
University of Michigan *B, M, D*
University of Michigan
  Dearborn *B*
Wayne State University *B*

Minnesota

Carleton College *B*
Minnesota State University
  Moorhead *B*
St. Olaf College *B*
University of Minnesota
  Twin Cities *B, M, D*

Mississippi

Mississippi Delta Community
  College *A*
University of Southern Mississippi *B*

Missouri

Columbia College *B*
Lindenwood University *B, M*
Saint Louis University *B, M, D*
University of Missouri
  Kansas City *B*
Washington University in St.
  Louis *B, M*
Webster University *B*

Nebraska

Creighton University *B*

New Hampshire

Franklin Pierce University *B*
Keene State College *B*

New Jersey

College of St. Elizabeth *B*

Ramapo College of New Jersey *B*
Rider University *B*
Rutgers, The State University of New
  Jersey
  New Brunswick/Piscataway
    Campus *B*
  Newark Regional Campus *B*
Saint Peter's College *B*

New Mexico

University of New Mexico *B, M, D*

New York

Bard College *B*
Barnard College *B*
City University of New York
  Brooklyn College *B*
  College of Staten Island *B*
  Queens College *B*
Clarkson University *B*
College of New Rochelle *B*
College of Saint Rose *B*
Columbia University *B*
Columbia University
  School of General Studies *B*
Cornell University *B*
Elmira College *B*
Fordham University *B*
Hamilton College *B*
Hobart and William Smith Colleges *B*
Hofstra University *B*
Long Island University
  C. W. Post Campus *B*
Manhattanville College *B*
Marist College *B*
Nazareth College *B*
New York University *M, D*
Pace University *B*
St. John Fisher College *B*
Siena College *B, T*
Skidmore College *B*
State University of New York
  Buffalo *B, M, D*
  College at Fredonia *B*
  College at Geneseo *B*
  College at Old Westbury *B*
  Oswego *B*
  Stony Brook *B*
Syracuse University *B*
Union College *B*
Vassar College *B*
Wells College *B*

North Carolina

High Point University *B*
Lenoir-Rhyne University *B*
Montreat College *B*
Queens University of Charlotte *B*
Salem College *B*
University of North Carolina
  Chapel Hill *B*
  Pembroke *B*
Wingate University *B*

Ohio

Ashland University *B*
Bowling Green State
  University *B, M, D*
Case Western Reserve University *B*
Cedarville University *B*
Kent State University *B*
Kenyon College *B*
Miami University
  Oxford Campus *B*
Mount Union College *B*
Oberlin College *B*
University of Dayton *B*
University of Rio Grande *B*
University of Toledo *B*
Ursuline College *B*
Wittenberg University *B*
Youngstown State University *B, M*

Oklahoma

Northeastern State University *M*
Oklahoma City University *B*
Oklahoma State University *B*
Southern Nazarene University *B*

Oregon

Oregon State University *B*
Pacific University *B*
Reed College *B*
Warner Pacific College *B*
Willamette University *B*

Pennsylvania

Albright College *B*
Bucks County Community College *A*
Cabrini College *B*
Dickinson College *B*
Franklin & Marshall College *B*
Gettysburg College *B*
Lafayette College *B*
Lebanon Valley College *B*
Lehigh University *B, M*
Lycoming College *B*
Muhlenberg College *B*
Penn State
  Abington *B*
  Berks *B*
  Brandywine *B*
  Harrisburg *B, M, D*
  Worthington Scranton *B*
  York *B*
St. Francis University *B*
Temple University *B*
University of Pennsylvania *B, M, D*
University of Pittsburgh
  Greensburg *B*
  Johnstown *B*
Ursinus College *B*
West Chester University of
  Pennsylvania *B*

Rhode Island

Brown University *B, M, D*
Providence College *B*
Roger Williams University *B*
Salve Regina University *B*

South Carolina

Claflin University *B*
Erskine College *B*

Tennessee

Cumberland University *B*
King College *B, T*
Lincoln Memorial University *B*
Lipscomb University *B*
Tennessee Wesleyan College *B*
University of Tennessee
  Knoxville *B*
University of the South *B*
Vanderbilt University *B*

Texas

Austin College *B*
Baylor University *B, M*
Southwestern University *B*
Texas A&M University *B*
Texas State University: San Marcos *B*
University of Dallas *M*
University of Mary Hardin-Baylor *B*
University of Texas
  Austin *B, M, D*
  Dallas *B*
  Pan American *B*
  San Antonio *B*

Utah

Brigham Young University *B*
Utah State University *B, M*

Vermont

Bennington College *B*
Goddard College *B*
Marlboro College *B*
Middlebury College *B*
St. Michael's College *B*

Virginia

Christopher Newport University *B*
College of William and Mary *B, M, D*
Shenandoah University *B*
University of Mary Washington *B*
University of Richmond *B*

Washington

University of Washington Bothell *B*
University of Washington Tacoma *B*
Washington State University *B, M, D*
Western Washington University *B*
Whitworth University *B*

Wyoming

University of Wyoming *B, M*

Analysis/functional analysis

Maryland

University of Maryland
College Park *M*

New York

University of Rochester *M*

Analytical chemistry

Florida

Florida Institute of Technology *B*
Florida State University *M, D*

Illinois

Governors State University *M*
Illinois Institute of Technology *M*

Iowa

Iowa State University *M, D*

Massachusetts

Tufts University *M, D*

Montana

University of Montana *M, D*

Pennsylvania

West Chester University of
Pennsylvania *B*

Wisconsin

Marquette University *M, D*
University of Wisconsin
Madison *M*

Anatomy

Arizona

Mesa Community College *A*
University of Arizona *M, D*

California

California State University
Fresno *B*
Loma Linda University *D*
University of California
Irvine *M, D*

District of Columbia

Georgetown University *D*
Howard University *M, D*

Florida

Barry University *M*

Illinois

Rush University *M, D*

Indiana

Indiana University
Bloomington *M, D*
Indiana University-Purdue University
Indianapolis *M, D*

Iowa

University of Iowa *M, D*

Kansas

Central Christian College of Kansas *A*

Kentucky

University of Kentucky: College of
Medicine *D*
University of Louisville *M, D*

Louisiana

Louisiana State University Health
Sciences Center *M, D*
Tulane University *M, D*

Massachusetts

Boston University *M, D*
Tufts University *D*

Michigan

Wayne State University *M, D*

Minnesota

Minnesota State University
Mankato *B*
University of Minnesota
Twin Cities *M*

Missouri

Saint Louis University *M, D*

Nebraska

Creighton University *M*

Nevada

College of Southern Nevada *A*

New York

State University of New York
Buffalo *M, D*
Stony Brook *D*
Upstate Medical University *M, D*
Yeshiva University *M, D*

North Carolina

Duke University *B, M, D*

North Dakota

University of North Dakota *M, D*

Ohio

Case Western Reserve
University *M, D*
Kent State University *D*
Ohio State University
Columbus Campus *M, D*
University of Cincinnati *D*
Wright State University *B*

Pennsylvania

Lycoming College *B*
Temple University *D*

Puerto Rico

University of Puerto Rico
Medical Sciences *M, D*

South Dakota

University of South Dakota *M, D*

Tennessee

University of Tennessee
Knoxville *M, D*
University of Tennessee Health
Science Center *M, D*

Texas

University of Texas
Health Science Center at
Houston *M, D*
Medical Branch at Galveston *M, D*

Utah

University of Utah *M, D*

Virginia

Virginia Commonwealth
University *M, D*

West Virginia

West Virginia University *M*

Ancient Greek

Alabama

Samford University *B*

California

Loyola Marymount University *B*
Santa Clara University *B*
University of California
Berkeley *B, M*
Los Angeles *B, M*

Connecticut

Yale University *B*

District of Columbia

Howard University *B*

Florida

Florida State University *B, M*
University of Miami *B*

Georgia

Emory University *B*
University of Georgia *B*

Illinois

Augustana College *B*
Concordia University Chicago *B*
Loyola University Chicago *B*
Monmouth College *B*
Moody Bible Institute *B*
Trinity International University *M*
University of Chicago *B, D*

Indiana

DePauw University *B*
Indiana University
Bloomington *B, M, D*
University of Notre Dame *B*
Wabash College *B*

Iowa

Luther College *B*
University of Iowa *B, M*

Louisiana

Loyola University New Orleans *B*

Maryland

Washington Bible College *M*

Massachusetts

Amherst College *B*
Boston College *B, M*

Michigan

Boston University *B*
Harvard College *B, D*
Mount Holyoke College *B*
Smith College *B*
Tufts University *B*
Wellesley College *B*

Michigan

Calvin College *B*
Grand Valley State University *B*
University of Michigan *B, M*

Minnesota

Carleton College *B*
St. Olaf College *B*
University of Minnesota
Twin Cities *B, M, D*

Missouri

Washington University in St.
Louis *B, M*

Nebraska

Creighton University *B*
University of Nebraska
Lincoln *B*

New Hampshire

University of New Hampshire *B*

New York

Bard College *B*
Barnard College *B*
City University of New York
Hunter College *B*
Queens College *B*
Columbia University *B*
Elmira College *B*
Fordham University *B, M, D*
Vassar College *B*

North Carolina

Duke University *B*
Wake Forest University *B*

Ohio

John Carroll University *B*
Kenyon College *B*
Oberlin College *B*
Ohio State University
Columbus Campus *M, D*
Ohio University *B*

Oregon

Multnomah University *B*
University of Oregon *B*

Pennsylvania

Bryn Mawr College *B, M, D*
Duquesne University *B*
Franklin & Marshall College *B*
Haverford College *B*
Swarthmore College *B*
University of Scranton *B*

Rhode Island

Brown University *B*

South Carolina

Furman University *B*

Tennessee

University of Tennessee
Knoxville *B*
University of the South *B*

Texas

Baylor University *B*
Rice University *B*
University of Texas
Austin *B*

Utah
Brigham Young University *B*

Vermont
University of Vermont *B*

Virginia
Hampden-Sydney College *B*
Randolph College *B*
Randolph-Macon College *B*
University of Richmond *B*

Washington
University of Washington *B*

Wisconsin
Lawrence University *B*
University of Wisconsin
  Madison *B, M*

Ancient Near Eastern/ Biblical languages

California
Concordia University *B*
The Master's College *B*

Connecticut
Yale University *B, M, D*

Delaware
University of Delaware *B*

District of Columbia
Catholic University of America *M, D*

Illinois
University of Chicago *B, M, D*

Iowa
Luther College *B*

Kentucky
Asbury College *B*

Michigan
Calvin College *B*

New York
Columbia University *B*

Ohio
Ohio Wesleyan University *B*

Pennsylvania
La Salle University *B*

South Carolina
Columbia International University *B*

Texas
Baylor University *B*
Houston Baptist University *B*
Howard Payne University *B*

Utah
Brigham Young University *B*

Washington
University of Washington *M*

Wisconsin
Concordia University Wisconsin *B*

Ancient studies

Arizona
Prescott College *M*

California
Loyola Marymount University *B*
Santa Clara University *B*
University of California
  Riverside *B*

Connecticut
Wesleyan University *B*
Yale University *B*

Florida
University of Miami *B*

Georgia
Georgia State University *B*

Iowa
University of Iowa *B*

Kansas
University of Kansas *B*

Maine
Bates College *B*
Bowdoin College *B*

Maryland
University of Maryland
  Baltimore County *B*

Massachusetts
Mount Holyoke College *B*
Smith College *B*

Michigan
University of Michigan *B, M, D*

Minnesota
St. Olaf College *B*

Missouri
Missouri State University *M*
Washington University in St. Louis *B*

Nebraska
University of Nebraska
  Lincoln *B*

New Hampshire
Dartmouth College *B*

New York
Barnard College *B*
Columbia University *B*
Vassar College *B*

Ohio
Ohio State University
  Columbus Campus *B*
Ohio Wesleyan University *B*

Oregon
University of Oregon *B*

Rhode Island
Brown University *B*

Texas
University of Texas
  Austin *B*

Virginia
University of Richmond *B*

Anesthesiologist assistant

Georgia
South University: Savannah *M*

Ohio
Case Western Reserve University *M*

Wisconsin
Milwaukee Area Technical College *A*

Animal behavior/ ethology

Arizona
Northern Arizona University *B*

California
University of California
  Davis *D*

Massachusetts
Hampshire College *B*

New York
Canisius College *B*

North Dakota
University of North Dakota *B*

Pennsylvania
Bucknell University *B, M*

Texas
Southwestern University *B*

Wisconsin
Carroll University *B*

Animal breeding

California
Modesto Junior College *A*

Illinois
Kishwaukee College *C, A*

Iowa
Iowa State University *M, D*

Mississippi
Hinds Community College *A*

Nevada
University of Nevada
  Reno *B*

New York
Cornell University *M, D*
State University of New York
  College of Agriculture and
    Technology at Cobleskill *B*

Oklahoma
Oklahoma State University *D*

Texas
Texas A&M University *M, D*

Animal genetics

Arizona
University of Arizona *M, D*

Connecticut
University of Connecticut *M, D*

New York
Cornell University *B, M, D*

Washington
Washington State University *M, D*

Animal health

California
California State University
  Fresno *B*
Los Angeles Pierce College *A*
San Diego Mesa College *A*

Colorado
Colorado Mountain College *A*
Front Range Community College *C, A*

Nebraska
Nebraska College of Technical
  Agriculture *A*
University of Nebraska
  Lincoln *M*

Texas
Sul Ross State University *A, B*

Animal husbandry

California
Santa Rosa Junior College *C*
Sierra College *C, A*

Connecticut
University of Connecticut *A*

Idaho
University of Idaho *B, M*

Illinois
Black Hawk College *C, A*
Black Hawk College: East Campus *C*
John Wood Community College *C, A*
Parkland College *C, A*
University of Illinois
  Urbana-Champaign *B, M, D*

Indiana
St. Mary-of-the-Woods College *B*

Iowa
Ellsworth Community College *C*
Hawkeye Community College *C, A*
Iowa State University *M*

Kansas
Colby Community College *C*

Michigan
Michigan State University *C*

New York
Jefferson Community College *A*
State University of New York
  College of Agriculture and
    Technology at Morrisville *A, B*

North Carolina
James Sprunt Community
  College *C, A*
North Carolina State University *A*

Ohio
Ohio State University
  Agricultural Technical Institute *A*

Oregon
Blue Mountain Community College *A*

Puerto Rico
University of Puerto Rico
  Utuado *A*

Texas
Angelo State University *B*

Tarleton State University *B*
Texas A&M University *B*

Utah

Southern Utah University *A*
Utah State University *C*

Wyoming

Casper College *A*

Animal nutrition

Georgia

University of Georgia *D*

Illinois

Joliet Junior College *C*

Oklahoma

Oklahoma State University *D*

Animal physiology

Arizona

University of Arizona *B, M, D*

California

University of California
San Diego *B*

Colorado

Colorado State University *M, D*

Connecticut

University of Connecticut *B, M, D*

Idaho

University of Idaho *D*

Indiana

Ball State University *M*

Iowa

Iowa State University *M, D*

New York

Cornell University *B, M, D*

Ohio

Kent State University *M, D*
Ohio State University
Columbus Campus *M, D*
University of Akron *B*

Pennsylvania

Penn State
University Park *M, D*

South Carolina

Clemson University *M, D*
Medical University of South
Carolina *D*

Tennessee

University of Tennessee
Knoxville *M, D*

Texas

Texas State University: San Marcos *B*

Animal sciences

Alabama

Auburn University *B, M, D*
Tuskegee University *B, M*

Arizona

University of Arizona *B, M, D*

Arkansas

Arkansas State University *B*
University of Arkansas *B, M, D*

California

Bakersfield College *A*
Butte College *C, A*
California Polytechnic State
University: San Luis Obispo *B*
California State Polytechnic
University: Pomona *B*
California State University
Chico *B*
Fresno *B, M*
College of the Redwoods *C, A*
College of the Sequoias *C*
Cosumnes River College *A*
Los Angeles Pierce College *C, A*
Merced College *C, A*
Modesto Junior College *A*
Moorpark College *C, A*
Mount San Antonio College *C, A*
Reedley College *C*
San Joaquin Delta College *C, A*
Santa Rosa Junior College *C*
University of California
Davis *B, M, D*
West Hills College: Coalinga *C, A*
Yuba Community College District *C*

Colorado

Colorado State University *B, M, D*
Lamar Community College *A*
University of Denver *B*

Connecticut

University of Connecticut *B, M, D*

Delaware

University of Delaware *B, M, D*

Florida

University of Florida *B, M, D*

Georgia

Abraham Baldwin Agricultural
College *A*
Berry College *B*
Fort Valley State University *B, M*
University of Georgia *B, M, D*

Hawaii

University of Hawaii
Hilo *B*
Manoa *B, M*

Idaho

Brigham Young University-Idaho *A, B*
University of Idaho *B, M, D*

Illinois

Black Hawk College: East Campus *C*
John Wood Community College *A*
Southern Illinois University
Carbondale *B, M*
University of Illinois
Urbana-Champaign *B, M, D*

Indiana

Purdue University *B, M, D*

Iowa

Dordt College *B*
Iowa State University *B, M, D*

Kansas

Butler Community College *A*
Central Christian College of Kansas *A*
Fort Scott Community College *A*
Garden City Community College *A*
Kansas State University *C, B, M, D*

Pratt Community College *A*
Seward County Community College *A*

Kentucky

University of Kentucky *B, M, D*

Louisiana

Louisiana State University and
Agricultural and Mechanical
College *B, M, D*
Louisiana Tech University *B*
Southern University and Agricultural
and Mechanical College *B*

Maine

University of Maine *B, M*

Maryland

University of Maryland
College Park *B, M, D*

Massachusetts

University of Massachusetts
Amherst *B, M, D*

Michigan

Andrews University *B*
Michigan State University *C, B, M, D*

Minnesota

Globe University *B*
South Central College *C, A*
University of Minnesota
Crookston *B*
Twin Cities *B, M, D*

Mississippi

Mississippi State University *B*
Northwest Mississippi Community
College *A*

Missouri

College of the Ozarks *B*
Missouri State University *B*
Northwest Missouri State
University *B*
Southeast Missouri State University *B*
University of Missouri
Columbia *B, M, D*

Montana

Montana State University
Bozeman *M, D*

Nebraska

Northeast Community College *A*
University of Nebraska
Lincoln *B, M, D*

Nevada

University of Nevada
Reno *B, M*

New Hampshire

University of New
Hampshire *A, B, M, D*

New Jersey

Rutgers, The State University of New
Jersey
New Brunswick/Piscataway
Campus *B, M, D*

New Mexico

New Mexico State University *B, M, D*

New York

Cornell University *B, M, D*
Mercy College *B*

Niagara County Community
College *C*
State University of New York
College of Agriculture and
Technology at Cobleskill *A*
College of Agriculture and
Technology at Morrisville *A*
College of Environmental Science
and Forestry *B, M, D*
College of Technology at Alfred *A*
Ulster County Community College *C*

North Carolina

North Carolina Agricultural and
Technical State University *B, M*
North Carolina State
University *B, M, D*
Sampson Community College *C*

North Dakota

North Dakota State University *B, M, D*

Ohio

Ohio State University
Columbus Campus *B, M, D*
University of Findlay *B*
Wilmington College *B*

Oklahoma

Cameron University *B*
Eastern Oklahoma State College *A*
Langston University *B*
Oklahoma Panhandle State
University *B*
Oklahoma State University *B, M*

Oregon

Linn-Benton Community College *A*
Oregon State University *B, M, D*
Treasure Valley Community College *A*

Pennsylvania

Delaware Valley College *B*
Harcum College *A*
Penn State
Abington *B*
Altoona *B*
Beaver *B*
Berks *B*
Brandywine *B*
DuBois *B*
Erie, The Behrend College *B*
Fayette, The Eberly Campus *B*
Greater Allegheny *B*
Hazleton *B*
Lehigh Valley *B*
Mont Alto *B*
New Kensington *B*
Schuylkill *B*
Shenango *B*
University Park *B, M, D*
Wilkes-Barre *B*
Worthington Scranton *B*
York *B*

Rhode Island

University of Rhode Island *B, M*

South Carolina

Clemson University *B, M*

South Dakota

South Dakota State University *B, M, D*

Tennessee

Middle Tennessee State University *B*
Tennessee State University *B, M*
Tennessee Technological University *B*
University of Tennessee
Knoxville *B, M, D*

Texas
Abilene Christian University *B*
Angelo State University *B, M*
Central Texas College *C*
Cisco College *A*
Clarendon College *A*
Hardin-Simmons University *B*
Lubbock Christian University *B*
Palo Alto College *C, A*
Prairie View A&M University *M*
Sam Houston State University *B*
Stephen F. Austin State University *B*
Sul Ross State University *B, M*
Tarleton State University *B*
Texas A&M University *B, M, D*
Texas A&M University
   Commerce *B, M*
   Kingsville *B, M*
Texas State University: San Marcos *B*
Texas Tech University *B, M, D*
West Texas A&M University *B, M*
Western Texas College *A*

Utah
Snow College *A*
Utah State University *B, M, D*

Vermont
University of Vermont *B, M, D*

Virginia
Blue Ridge Community College *C, A*
Virginia Polytechnic Institute and
   State University *B, M, D*

Washington
Everett Community College *A*
Pierce College *A*
Washington State University *B, M, D*
Yakima Valley Community College *C*

West Virginia
Potomac State College of West
   Virginia University *A*
West Virginia University *B, M*

Wisconsin
Chippewa Valley Technical College *A*
University of Wisconsin
   Madison *B, M, D*
   Platteville *B*
   River Falls *B*

Wyoming
Eastern Wyoming College *A*
Northwest College *A*
Sheridan College *A*
University of Wyoming *B, M, D*

Animal training

Colorado
Colorado Northwestern Community
   College *C*

Massachusetts
Becker College *A*

South Dakota
National American University
   Rapid City *B*

Animation

Arizona
Art Center Design College *B*
Art Institute
   of Phoenix *B*
Art Institute of Tucson *B*
Cochise College *C*
Collins College *A, B*

Pima Community College *A*
University of Advancing
   Technology *A, B*

California
Academy of Art University *C, A, B, M*
Allan Hancock College *A*
Art Center College of Design *B, M*
Art Institute
   of California: Orange County *B*
Art Institute of California:
   Hollywood *B*
Art Institute of California: Inland
   Empire *B*
Art Institute of California:
   Sacramento *B*
Art Institute of California: San
   Francisco *B, M*
Art Institute of California:
   Sunnyvale *B*
City College of San Francisco *C*
College of the Canyons *C, A*
College of the Siskiyous *C*
East Los Angeles College *C, A*
Ex'pression College for Digital Arts *B*
Long Beach City College *C*
Loyola Marymount University *B*
National University *M*
Otis College of Art and Design *B*
Platt College
   Ontario *B*
Santa Ana College *C*
Santa Monica College *C*
Santa Rosa Junior College *C*
Silicon Valley College
   Western Career College:
     Emeryville *C, A, B*
Westwood College of Technology
   Westwood College: Inland
     Empire *B*
   Westwood College: Los Angeles *B*
Westwood College: South Bay *B*

Colorado
Art Institute
   of Colorado *B*
Colorado Mountain College *A*
Front Range Community College *C, A*
Mesa State College *C, A*
Pueblo Community College *A*
Rocky Mountain College of Art &
   Design *B*
Westwood College of Technology
   Westwood College: Denver South *B*

Connecticut
Northwestern Connecticut
   Community College *A*

Delaware
Delaware College of Art and Design *A*

District of Columbia
American University *B*

Florida
Art Institute of Fort Lauderdale *B*
Full Sail University *B*
International Academy of Design and
   Technology: Tampa *B*
Miami Dade College *A*
Miami International University of Art
   and Design *B, M*
Rasmussen College: Fort Myers *B*
Ringling College of Art and Design *B*
Southwest Florida College *C, A*

Georgia
Art Institute
   of Atlanta *A, B*
Central Georgia Technical College *C*
Savannah College of Art and
   Design *C, B, M*

Southwest Georgia Technical
   College *C*

Idaho
University of Idaho *B*

Illinois
Bradley University *B*
City Colleges of Chicago
   Kennedy-King College *C*
Columbia College Chicago *C, B*
DePaul University *B*
Elgin Community College *C*
International Academy of Design and
   Technology: Chicago *A, B*
International Academy of Design and
   Technology: Schaumburg *A, B*
Moraine Valley Community College *C*
North Central College *B*
Oakton Community College *C*
School of the Art Institute of
   Chicago *B, M*
Waubonsee Community College *C*
Westwood College: Chicago Loop *B*

Kansas
Kansas City Kansas Community
   College *C*

Kentucky
Sullivan College of Technology and
   Design *A, B*

Maryland
Cecil College *C*
Hagerstown Community College *C, A*
Howard Community College *C*
Montgomery College *C*

Massachusetts
Hampshire College *B*
Mount Ida College *B*
Northeastern University *B*
School of the Museum of Fine
   Arts *B, M*
Springfield Technical Community
   College *A*

Michigan
College for Creative Studies *B*
Davenport University *B*
Ferris State University *B*
Henry Ford Community College *A*

Minnesota
Academy College *C, A*
Art Institutes International
   Minnesota *B*
Minneapolis College of Art and
   Design *B*
Minneapolis Community and
   Technical College *C, A*
Northwestern College *B*
St. Paul College *A*

Missouri
Missouri State University: West
   Plains *A*

Nevada
Art Institute
   of Las Vegas *B*
College of Southern Nevada *C, A*

New Jersey
Bergen Community College *A*
Burlington County College *A*
Montclair State University *B*
Raritan Valley Community College *A*
Union County College *A*

New Mexico
Art Center Design College *B*
Eastern New Mexico University:
   Roswell Campus *C, A*
New Mexico State University
   Carlsbad *C*

New York
Fashion Institute of Technology *B*
Pratt Institute *B*
Rochester Institute of
   Technology *B, M*
School of Visual Arts *B*
State University of New York
   College at Oneonta *B*
Villa Maria College of Buffalo *B*

North Carolina
Fayetteville Technical Community
   College *A*

Ohio
North Central State College *A*
University of Cincinnati
   Raymond Walters College *C*
Washington State Community
   College *A*

Oklahoma
Oklahoma Christian University *B*

Oregon
Lane Community College *C, A*
Portland Community College *C*

Pennsylvania
Art Institute
   of Philadelphia *A, B*
   of Pittsburgh *A, B*
Bucks County Community
   College *C, A*
Carnegie Mellon University *M*
Lehigh Carbon Community
   College *C, A*
Philadelphia University *B, M*
University of the Arts *B*

Rhode Island
New England Institute of
   Technology *A*

South Dakota
Southeast Technical Institute *A*

Tennessee
East Tennessee State University *B*

Texas
Austin Community College *C, A*
Collin County Community College
   District *C, A*
Houston Community College
   System *C, A*
North Lake College *C*
Sam Houston State University *B*
University of the Incarnate Word *B*

Utah
Brigham Young University *B*
Salt Lake Community College *A*

Vermont
Bennington College *B*
Champlain College *B*

Virginia
George Mason University *B*
Regent University *C, B*

Washington
Art Institute of Seattle *A*

DigiPen Institute of Technology *B*
Olympic College *A*

Wisconsin
Herzing University *A, B*

Anthropology

Alabama
Auburn University *B*
University of Alabama *B, M, D*
University of Alabama
 Birmingham *B*
University of South Alabama *B*

Alaska
University of Alaska
 Anchorage *B, M*
 Fairbanks *B, M, D*

Arizona
Arizona State University *B, M, D*
Cochise College *A*
Coconino County Community
 College *A*
Eastern Arizona College *A*
Northern Arizona University *B, M*
Pima Community College *A*
Prescott College *B, M*
University of Arizona *B, M, D*

Arkansas
Hendrix College *B*
University of Arkansas *B, M, D*

California
Bakersfield College *A*
Biola University *B*
Cabrillo College *A*
California Institute of Integral
 Studies *M, D*
California State Polytechnic
 University: Pomona *B*
California State University
 Bakersfield *B*
 Chico *B, M*
 Dominguez Hills *B*
 East Bay *B, M*
 Fresno *B*
 Fullerton *B, M*
 Long Beach *B, M*
 Los Angeles *B, M*
 Northridge *B*
 Sacramento *B, M*
 San Bernardino *B*
 Stanislaus *B*
Canada College *A*
Cerritos College *A*
Chaffey College *A*
College of Alameda *A*
College of the Desert *A*
College of the Siskiyous *A*
Copper Mountain College *A*
Crafton Hills College *A*
Cypress College *A*
De Anza College *A*
East Los Angeles College *A*
El Camino College *A*
Foothill College *A*
Fresno City College *A*
Fullerton College *A*
Gavilan College *A*
Glendale Community College *A*
Golden West College *A*
Humboldt State University *B*
Imperial Valley College *A*
Irvine Valley College *A*
Lake Tahoe Community College *A*
Los Medanos College *A*
Merced College *A*
Mills College *B*
Monterey Peninsula College *A*
Ohlone College *C*

Orange Coast College *A*
Oxnard College *A*
Pitzer College *B*
Pomona College *B*
Saddleback College *A*
St. Mary's College of California *B*
San Diego City College *A*
San Diego Mesa College *A*
San Diego State University *B, M*
San Francisco State University *B, M*
San Joaquin Delta College *A*
San Jose State University *B*
Santa Ana College *A*
Santa Barbara City College *A*
Santa Clara University *B*
Santa Rosa Junior College *A*
Santiago Canyon College *A*
Scripps College *B*
Sonoma State University *B, M*
Southwestern College *A*
Stanford University *B, M, D*
University of California
 Berkeley *B, D*
 Davis *B, M, D*
 Irvine *B, M, D*
 Los Angeles *B, M, D*
 Riverside *B, M, D*
 San Diego *B, D*
 Santa Barbara *B, M, D*
 Santa Cruz *B, D*
University of California: Merced *B*
University of La Verne *B*
University of Redlands *B*
University of San Diego *B*
University of Southern
 California *B, M, D*
Vanguard University of Southern
 California *B*
West Los Angeles College *C, A*
Westmont College *B*
Whittier College *B*

Colorado
Colorado College *B*
Colorado State University *B, M*
Fort Lewis College *B*
Metropolitan State College of
 Denver *B, T*
Pikes Peak Community College *A*
University of Colorado
 Boulder *B, M, D*
 Colorado Springs *B*
 Denver *B, M*
University of Denver *B, M*
University of Northern Colorado *B*
Western State College of Colorado *B*

Connecticut
Central Connecticut State
 University *B*
Connecticut College *B*
Trinity College *B*
University of Connecticut *B, M, D*
Wesleyan University *B, M*
Yale University *B, M, D*

Delaware
University of Delaware *B*

District of Columbia
American University *B, M, D*
Catholic University of America *B, M*
George Washington University *B, M*
Georgetown University *B*
Howard University *B*
University of the District of
 Columbia *B*

Florida
Broward College *A*
Eckerd College *B*
Florida Atlantic University *B, M*
Florida Gulf Coast University *B*

Gulf Coast Community College *A*
Indian River State College *A*
Miami Dade College *A*
New College of Florida *B*
Palm Beach Community College *A*
Rollins College *B*
Santa Fe College *A*
University of Central Florida *B, M*
University of Florida *B, M, D*
University of Miami *B*
University of North Florida *B*
University of South Florida *B, M, D*
University of West Florida *B, M*

Georgia
Agnes Scott College *B*
Darton College *A*
East Georgia College *A*
Emory University *B, D*
Gainesville State College *A*
Georgia Perimeter College *A*
Georgia Southern University *B*
Georgia State University *B, M*
Kennesaw State University *B*
University of Georgia *B, M, D*
University of West Georgia *B*

Hawaii
Hawaii Pacific University *C, B*
University of Hawaii
 Hilo *B*
 Manoa *B, M, D*
 West Oahu *B*

Idaho
Boise State University *B*
College of Idaho *B*
Idaho State University *B, M*
North Idaho College *A*
University of Idaho *B, M*

Illinois
Augustana College *B*
Black Hawk College: East Campus *A*
Chicago State University *B*
DePaul University *B*
Illinois State University *B*
Illinois Wesleyan University *B*
Knox College *B*
Loyola University Chicago *B*
Monmouth College *B*
National-Louis University *B*
North Central College *B*
Northeastern Illinois University *B*
Northern Illinois University *B, M*
Northwestern University *B, M, D*
Principia College *B*
Richland Community College *A*
South Suburban College of Cook
 County *A*
Southern Illinois University
 Carbondale *B, M, D*
Southern Illinois University
 Edwardsville *B*
Southwestern Illinois College *A*
Triton College *A*
University of Chicago *B, D*
University of Illinois
 Chicago *B, M, D*
 Urbana-Champaign *B, M, D*
Wheaton College *B*

Indiana
Ball State University *B, M*
Butler University *B*
DePauw University *B*
Hanover College *B*
Indiana State University *B*
Indiana University
 Bloomington *B, M, D*
Indiana University-Purdue University
 Fort Wayne *B*

Indiana University-Purdue University
 Indianapolis *B*
Purdue University *B, M, D*
University of Indianapolis *B*
University of Notre Dame *B*
Vincennes University *A*

Iowa
Central College *B*
Cornell College *B*
Drake University *B*
Grinnell College *B*
Iowa State University *B, M*
Luther College *B*
University of Iowa *B, M, D, T*
University of Northern Iowa *B*

Kansas
Barton County Community College *A*
Kansas State University *B*
University of Kansas *B, M, D*
Washburn University *B*
Wichita State University *B, M*

Kentucky
Centre College *B*
Eastern Kentucky University *B*
Northern Kentucky University *B*
Transylvania University *B*
University of Kentucky *B, M, D*
University of Louisville *B*
Western Kentucky University *B*

Louisiana
Louisiana State University and
 Agricultural and Mechanical
 College *B, M*
Tulane University *B, M, D*
University of Louisiana at Lafayette *B*
University of New Orleans *B*

Maine
Bates College *B*
Bowdoin College *B*
Colby College *B*
University of Maine *B*
University of Maine
 Farmington *B*
University of Southern Maine *B*

Maryland
Harford Community College *A*
Howard Community College *A*
Johns Hopkins University *B, M, D*
St. Mary's College of Maryland *B*
University of Maryland
 Baltimore County *A*
 College Park *B, M, D*
Washington College *B*

Massachusetts
Amherst College *B*
Bard College at Simon's Rock *B*
Boston University *B, M, D*
Brandeis University *B, M, D*
Bridgewater State College *B*
College of the Holy Cross *B*
Hampshire College *B*
Harvard College *B, M, D*
Massachusetts Institute of
 Technology *B*
Mount Holyoke College *B*
Smith College *B*
Tufts University *B*
University of Massachusetts
 Amherst *B, M, D*
 Boston *B*
Wellesley College *B*
Wheaton College *B*
Williams College *B*

Michigan

Albion College *B*
Alma College *B, T*
Andrews University *B*
Central Michigan University *B*
Eastern Michigan University *B*
Grand Valley State University *B*
Kalamazoo College *B*
Lansing Community College *A*
Michigan State University *B, M, D*
Michigan Technological University *B*
Oakland University *B*
University of Michigan *B, M, D*
University of Michigan
  Dearborn *B*
  Flint *B*
Wayne State University *B, M, D*
Western Michigan University *B, M*

Minnesota

Carleton College *B*
Gustavus Adolphus College *B*
Hamline University *B*
Macalester College *B*
Minnesota State University
  Mankato *B, M*
  Moorhead *B*
Saint Cloud State University *B*
University of Minnesota
  Duluth *B*
  Morris *B*
  Twin Cities *B, M, D*

Mississippi

Millsaps College *B*
Mississippi State University *B, M*
University of Mississippi *B, M*
University of Southern
  Mississippi *B, M*

Missouri

Missouri State University *B*
Southeast Missouri State University *B*
University of Missouri
  Columbia *B, M, D*
  St. Louis *B*
Washington University in St.
  Louis *B, M, D*
Webster University *B*
Westminster College *B*

Montana

Montana State University
  Bozeman *B*
University of Montana *B, M*
University of Montana: Western *B*

Nebraska

Creighton University *B*
University of Nebraska
  Lincoln *B, M*
Western Nebraska Community
  College *A*

Nevada

Great Basin College *A*
Truckee Meadows Community
  College *C, A*
University of Nevada
  Las Vegas *B, M, D*
  Reno *B, M, D*

New Hampshire

Dartmouth College *B*
Franklin Pierce University *B*
University of New Hampshire *B*

New Jersey

Drew University *B*
Monmouth University *B*
Montclair State University *B, M*
Princeton University *B, M, D*

Rutgers, The State University of New
  Jersey
  New Brunswick/Piscataway
    Campus *B, M, D*
  Newark Regional Campus *B*
Seton Hall University *B*
Thomas Edison State College *B*
William Paterson University of New
  Jersey *B*

New Mexico

Eastern New Mexico University *B, M*
New Mexico Highlands University *B*
New Mexico State University *B, M*
University of New Mexico *B, M, D*

New York

Adelphi University *B*
Bard College *B*
Barnard College *B*
Canisius College *B*
City University of New York
  Brooklyn College *B*
  City College *B, M*
  Hunter College *B, M*
  Lehman College *B*
  Queens College *B, T*
  York College *B*
Colgate University *B*
Columbia University *B*
Cornell University *B, M, D*
Dowling College *B*
Elmira College *B*
Fordham University *B*
Hamilton College *B*
Hartwick College *B*
Hobart and William Smith Colleges *B*
Hofstra University *B*
Ithaca College *B*
Nazareth College *B*
New York University *B, M, D*
St. John Fisher College *B*
St. John's University *B*
St. Lawrence University *B*
Skidmore College *B*
State University of New York
  Albany *B, M, D*
  Binghamton *B, M, D*
  Buffalo *B, M, D*
  College at Brockport *B*
  College at Buffalo *B*
  College at Cortland *B*
  College at Geneseo *B*
  College at Oneonta *B*
  College at Plattsburgh *B*
  College at Potsdam *B*
  New Paltz *B*
  Oswego *B*
  Purchase *B*
  Stony Brook *B, M, D*
Syracuse University *B, M, D*
Union College *B*
University of Rochester *B*
Vassar College *B*
Wagner College *B*
Wells College *B*

North Carolina

Appalachian State University *B*
Davidson College *B*
Duke University *B, M, D*
East Carolina University *B, M*
Elon University *B*
North Carolina State University *B, M*
Peace College *B*
University of North Carolina
  Chapel Hill *B, M, D*
  Charlotte *B*
  Greensboro *B*
  Wilmington *B*
Wake Forest University *B, M*
Warren Wilson College *B*
Western Carolina University *B*

North Dakota

North Dakota State University *B, M*
University of North Dakota *B*

Ohio

Case Western Reserve
  University *B, M, D*
Cleveland State University *B*
College of Wooster *B*
Denison University *B*
Franciscan University of
  Steubenville *B*
Heidelberg University *B*
Kent State University *B, M*
Kenyon College *B*
Miami University
  Oxford Campus *B*
Muskingum University *B*
Oberlin College *B*
Ohio State University
  Columbus Campus *B, M, D*
Ohio University *B*
Ohio Wesleyan University *B*
University of Akron *B*
University of Cincinnati *B, M*
University of Toledo *B*
Wright State University *B*
Youngstown State University *B*

Oklahoma

Oklahoma Baptist University *B*
University of Oklahoma *B, M, D*
University of Tulsa *B, M*

Oregon

Central Oregon Community
  College *A*
Chemeketa Community College *A*
Eastern Oregon University *B, T*
Lewis & Clark College *B*
Linfield College *B, T*
Linn-Benton Community College *A*
Oregon State University *B, M*
Portland State University *B, M, D*
Reed College *B*
Southern Oregon University *B*
University of Oregon *B, M, D*
Western Oregon University *B*
Willamette University *B*

Pennsylvania

Albright College *B*
Bloomsburg University of
  Pennsylvania *B*
Bryn Mawr College *B*
Bucknell University *B*
Carnegie Mellon University *B*
Clarion University of Pennsylvania *B*
Dickinson College *B*
Drexel University *B*
Edinboro University of
  Pennsylvania *B*
Elizabethtown College *B*
Franklin & Marshall College *B*
Gettysburg College *B*
Haverford College *B, T*
Indiana University of Pennsylvania *B*
Juniata College *B*
Kutztown University of
  Pennsylvania *B*
Lafayette College *B*
Lehigh University *B*
Lincoln University *B*
Lycoming College *B*
Mansfield University of
  Pennsylvania *B*
Mercyhurst College *B*
Millersville University of
  Pennsylvania *B*
Muhlenberg College *C, B*
Penn State
  Abington *B*
  Altoona *B*

Beaver *B*
Berks *B*
Brandywine *B*
DuBois *B*
Erie, The Behrend College *B*
Fayette, The Eberly Campus *B*
Greater Allegheny *B*
Hazleton *B*
Lehigh Valley *B*
Mont Alto *B*
New Kensington *B*
Schuylkill *B*
Shenango *B*
University Park *B, M, D*
Wilkes-Barre *B*
Worthington Scranton *B*
York *B*
St. Vincent College *B*
Swarthmore College *B*
Temple University *B, M, D*
University of Pennsylvania *A, B, M, D*
University of Pittsburgh *B, M, D*
University of Pittsburgh
  Greensburg *B*
Ursinus College *B*
West Chester University of
  Pennsylvania *B*
Widener University *B*

Puerto Rico

University of Puerto Rico
  Aguadilla *A*
  Rio Piedras *B*

Rhode Island

Brown University *B, M, D*
Rhode Island College *B*
Roger Williams University *B*
University of Rhode Island *B*

South Carolina

College of Charleston *B*
University of South Carolina *B, M, D*

South Dakota

Augustana College *B*
University of South Dakota *B*

Tennessee

Lee University *B*
Middle Tennessee State University *B*
Rhodes College *B*
University of Memphis *B, M*
University of Tennessee
  Knoxville *B, M, D*
University of the South *B*
Vanderbilt University *B, M, D*

Texas

Austin Community College *A*
Baylor University *B*
Galveston College *A*
Palo Alto College *A*
Rice University *B, M, D*
Southern Methodist
  University *B, M, D*
Southwestern University *B*
Texas A&M University *B, M, D*
Texas A&M University
  Commerce *B*
Texas Christian University *B*
Texas State University: San
  Marcos *B, M*
Texas Tech University *B, M*
Trinity University *B*
University of Houston *B, M*
University of Houston
  Clear Lake *B*
University of North Texas *B, M*
University of Texas
  Arlington *B, M*
  Austin *B, M, D*
  El Paso *B*

Pan American *B*
San Antonio *B, M*

Utah
Brigham Young University *B*
Snow College *A*
University of Utah *B, M, D, T*
Utah State University *B*

Vermont
Bennington College *B*
Green Mountain College *B*
Johnson State College *B*
Marlboro College *B*
St. Michael's College *B*
University of Vermont *B*

Virginia
College of William and Mary *B, M, D*
Emory & Henry College *B*
George Mason University *B, M*
James Madison University *B*
Longwood University *B*
Radford University *B*
Sweet Briar College *B*
University of Mary Washington *B*
University of Richmond *B*
University of Virginia *B, M, D*
Virginia Commonwealth University *B*
Washington and Lee University *B*

Washington
Centralia College *A*
Eastern Washington University *B*
Everett Community College *A*
Highline Community College *A*
Olympic College *A*
Pacific Lutheran University *B*
University of Washington *B, M, D*
Washington State University *B, M, D*
Western Washington University *B, M*
Whitman College *B*

Wisconsin
Beloit College *B*
Lawrence University *B*
Marquette University *B, T*
Ripon College *B*
University of Wisconsin
  Madison *B, M, D*
  Milwaukee *B, M, D*
  Oshkosh *B*
  Parkside *T*
  River Falls *T*

Wyoming
Casper College *A*
Laramie County Community
  College *A*
University of Wyoming *B, M, D*
Western Wyoming Community
  College *A*

Apparel/accessories marketing

California
Art Institute
  of California: Orange County *B*

Colorado
Art Institute
  of Colorado *B*

Georgia
Gwinnett Technical College *C*

Iowa
Des Moines Area Community
  College *C, A*

Massachusetts
University of Massachusetts
  Amherst *B*

Michigan
Michigan State University *B, M*

New York
Fashion Institute of Technology *M*

North Carolina
Art Institute
  of Charlotte *B*

Ohio
Youngstown State University *B*

Oklahoma
University of Central Oklahoma *B*

Pennsylvania
Philadelphia University *B*

Rhode Island
University of Rhode Island *B*

Texas
Brookhaven College *C, A*

Wisconsin
Milwaukee Area Technical College *A*

Apparel/textile manufacture

Alabama
Lawson State Community College *C*

California
Fashion Institute of Design and
  Merchandising
  Los Angeles *A*
  San Diego *A*
  San Francisco *A*
Orange Coast College *C*

Iowa
Iowa State University *B*

Michigan
Michigan State University *B, M*

Minnesota
Minneapolis Community and
  Technical College *C*

New York
Fashion Institute of Technology *A, B*

Apparel/textile marketing

Alabama
Auburn University *B, M*

California
Allan Hancock College *C*
Fashion Institute of Design and
  Merchandising
  Los Angeles *A*
  San Diego *A*
  San Francisco *A*

Colorado
Colorado State University *B, M*

Georgia
Savannah College of Art and Design *B*

Hawaii
University of Hawaii
  Maui Community College *A*

Iowa
Iowa State University *B*

Michigan
Michigan State University *B, M*
Wayne State University *B, M*

Missouri
Northwest Missouri State
  University *B*

New York
Laboratory Institute of
  Merchandising *A, B*

North Carolina
North Carolina State University *B*

North Dakota
North Dakota State University *M*

Pennsylvania
Philadelphia University *B, M*

South Dakota
South Dakota State University *B*

Texas
University of the Incarnate Word *A, B*

Appliance installation and repair

California
Solano Community College *C, A*

Kansas
Kansas City Kansas Community
  College *C*

Kentucky
Elizabethtown Community and
  Technical College *C, A*
Somerset Community College *C*

Michigan
Bay de Noc Community College *C*

Minnesota
St. Paul College *C*

Washington
Bellingham Technical College *C, A*

West Virginia
West Virginia Northern Community
  College *C*

Applied economics

Alaska
University of Alaska
  Fairbanks *M*

Arizona
University of Arizona *B*

Florida
Florida State University *B*

Georgia
Agnes Scott College *B*
Georgia Southern University *M*

Illinois
DePaul University *M*

Iowa
University of Northern Iowa *B*

Kentucky
Western Kentucky University *M*

Louisiana
Centenary College of Louisiana *B*

Michigan
Eastern Michigan University *M*
Michigan Technological University *M*
University of Michigan *M*
Western Michigan University *M, D*

Minnesota
Augsburg College *B*
College of St. Scholastica *B*
Saint Cloud State University *M*
University of Minnesota
  Twin Cities *B*

New Hampshire
Plymouth State University *B*

New York
Ithaca College *B*
State University of New York
  Binghamton *B*
  Farmingdale *B*

North Carolina
East Carolina University *M*

North Dakota
University of North Dakota *M*

Oklahoma
University of Central Oklahoma *B*

Pennsylvania
Allegheny College *B*

Rhode Island
Bryant University *B*
University of Rhode Island *M, D*

Tennessee
Vanderbilt University *B, M, D*

Texas
Southern Methodist University *B, M*

Washington
Washington State University *M*

Wisconsin
Marquette University *M*

Applied mathematics

Alabama
Auburn University *B, M*
Oakwood University *B*
University of Alabama *D*
University of Alabama
  Birmingham *D*
  Huntsville *D*

Alaska
University of Alaska
  Fairbanks *B, M*

Arizona
Arizona State University *B, D*
Mesa Community College *A*

University of Arizona *M, D*

Arkansas
University of Arkansas
  Little Rock *B, M*
  Pine Bluff *B*
University of Central Arkansas *M*

California
California Institute of
  Technology *B, D*
California State University
  Chico *B*
  East Bay *B, M*
  Fullerton *B, M*
  Long Beach *B, M, D*
  Northridge *B, M*
Fresno Pacific University *B*
Harvey Mudd College *B*
Loyola Marymount University *B*
The Master's College *B*
Mount St. Mary's College *B*
San Diego City College *A*
San Diego State University *B, M*
San Francisco State University *B*
San Jose State University *B*
Santa Clara University *M*
University of California
  Berkeley *B, D*
  Davis *B, M, D*
  Los Angeles *B*
  Riverside *B, M*
  San Diego *B, M*
  Santa Barbara *M*
  Santa Cruz *M, D*
University of California:
  Merced *B, M, D*
University of Southern
  California *B, M, D*
University of the Pacific *B*

Colorado
Colorado School of Mines *B*
University of Colorado
  Boulder *B, M, D*
  Colorado Springs *M*
  Denver *M, D*

Connecticut
University of Connecticut *B*
University of New Haven *B*
Yale University *B, M, D*

Delaware
Delaware State University *M, D*

District of Columbia
American University *B*
George Washington University *B, M*

Florida
Florida Atlantic University *M*
Florida Institute of
  Technology *B, M, D*
Florida International University *M*
Florida State University *B, M, D*
New College of Florida *B*
University of Central Florida *M, D*
University of Miami *B*
University of North Florida *M*

Georgia
Armstrong Atlantic State
  University *B, T*
Emory University *B*
Georgia Institute of Technology *B*
University of Georgia *M*
University of West Georgia *M*
Valdosta State University *B*

Hawaii
Hawaii Pacific University *B*

Idaho
Boise State University *B*
College of Idaho *B*
University of Idaho *B*

Illinois
DePaul University *M*
Illinois Institute of
  Technology *B, M, D*
Knox College *B*
Millikin University *B*
National-Louis University *B*
North Central College *B*
Northern Illinois University *B*
Northwestern University *B, M, D*
University of Chicago *B*
University of Illinois
  Urbana-Champaign *M*

Indiana
Goshen College *B*
Indiana University
  South Bend *B*
Indiana University-Purdue University
  Fort Wayne *M*
Oakland City University *B*
Purdue University *B, M, D*
Purdue University
  Calumet *B, M*
Saint Mary's College *B*
Taylor University *B*
University of Evansville *B*
University of Notre Dame *M*

Iowa
Grand View University *B*
Iowa State University *M, D*
University of Iowa *B, D*
University of Northern Iowa *B*

Kentucky
Berea College *B*
Brescia University *B*
University of Kentucky *M*
University of Louisville *D*

Louisiana
Tulane University *M, D*

Maryland
Bowie State University *M*
Loyola University Maryland *B*
Stevenson University *B*
Towson University *M*
United States Naval Academy *B*
University of Maryland
  Baltimore County *M, D*
  College Park *M, D*

Massachusetts
Harvard College *B, M, D*
Northeastern University *M*
Tufts University *B, M*
University of Massachusetts
  Amherst *M*
  Lowell *B*
Worcester Polytechnic Institute *B, M*

Michigan
Ferris State University *B*
Kettering University *B*
Lansing Community College *A*
Michigan State University *M, D*
Oakland University *M, D*
Saginaw Valley State University *B*
University of Detroit Mercy *M*
University of Michigan *M, D*
Wayne State University *M*
Western Michigan University *M*

Minnesota
Metropolitan State University *B*

Winona State University *B*

Mississippi
Millsaps College *B*
Mississippi State University *D*

Missouri
Central Methodist University *A*
Maryville University of Saint Louis *B*
University of Missouri
  Columbia *M*
  Missouri University of Science and
    Technology *B, M*
  St. Louis *B, D*
Washington University in St. Louis *B*

Montana
University of Montana: Western *B*

Nebraska
Creighton University *B*

Nevada
University of Nevada
  Las Vegas *B, M, D*

New Jersey
Bloomfield College *B*
New Jersey Institute of
  Technology *B, M*
Princeton University *M, D*
Rutgers, The State University of New
  Jersey
  Newark Regional Campus *B*
Stevens Institute of Technology *B, M*

New Mexico
New Mexico Institute of Mining and
  Technology *B, M, D*

New York
Barnard College *B*
City University of New York
  Baruch College *M*
  Hunter College *M*
  New York City College of
    Technology *B*
Clarkson University *B*
Columbia University *B, M, D*
Columbia University
  School of General Studies *B*
Cornell University *M, D*
Dowling College *B*
Hofstra University *B, M*
Iona College *B*
Long Island University
  C. W. Post Campus *B, M*
Marist College *B*
Polytechnic Institute of New York
  University *B, M, D*
Rensselaer Polytechnic Institute *M*
Rochester Institute of
  Technology *A, B, M*
St. Thomas Aquinas College *B*
State University of New York
  Albany *B*
  Buffalo *B*
  Farmingdale *B*
  Institute of Technology at
    Utica/Rome *B*
  Oswego *B*
  Stony Brook *B, M, D*
University of Rochester *B, M*

North Carolina
Elon University *B*
North Carolina Agricultural and
  Technical State University *M*
North Carolina State
  University *B, M, D*

University of North Carolina
  Chapel Hill *B*
  Charlotte *D*
Western Carolina University *M*

North Dakota
Jamestown College *B*

Ohio
Case Western Reserve
  University *M, D*
Kent State University *B, M, D*
Ohio State University
  Columbus Campus *M, D*
Ohio University *B*
University of Akron *B, M*
University of Dayton *M*
Wright State University *B, M*

Oklahoma
East Central University *B*
University of Central Oklahoma *B, M*
University of Tulsa *B, M*

Oregon
Oregon Institute of Technology *B*

Pennsylvania
Carnegie Mellon University *B, D*
Clarion University of Pennsylvania *B*
Geneva College *B*
Indiana University of Pennsylvania *B*
La Salle University *B, T*
Lehigh University *M, D*
Penn State
  Harrisburg *B*
Robert Morris University *B*
University of Pittsburgh *B, M*
University of Pittsburgh
  Bradford *B*
  Greensburg *B*

Rhode Island
Brown University *B, M, D*
Bryant University *B*
University of Rhode Island *D*

South Carolina
Charleston Southern University *B*
Coastal Carolina University *B*
University of South Carolina *M*
University of South Carolina
  Aiken *B*
  Upstate *B*

South Dakota
University of Sioux Falls *B*

Tennessee
University of Tennessee
  Chattanooga *B*

Texas
Baylor University *B*
Lamar University *B, M*
Rice University *B, M, D*
Southern Methodist University *M, D*
Southwestern Adventist University *B*
Texas A&M University *D*
Texas State University: San
  Marcos *B, M*
University of Houston *B, M*
University of Houston
  Downtown *B*
University of Texas
  Arlington *D*
  Austin *M, D*
  Dallas *B, M, D*
  El Paso *B*
  San Antonio *M*

Utah

Utah State University *D*
Weber State University *B*

Virginia

Hampden-Sydney College *B*
Hampton University *M*
Mary Baldwin College *B*
Old Dominion University *M, D*

Washington

University of Washington *B, M, D*
Washington State University *B, M, D*
Western Washington University *B*
Whitworth University *B*

West Virginia

Alderson-Broaddus College *B*
West Virginia State University *B*

Wisconsin

Carroll University *B*
University of Wisconsin
  Madison *B*
  Milwaukee *B*
  Stout *B*

Wyoming

Casper College *A*

Applied physics

Alaska

University of Alaska
  Fairbanks *B*

California

California State University
  San Marcos *B*
University of California
  Davis *B*

Georgia

Emory University *B*
Morehouse College *B*

Michigan

Kettering University *B*
University of Michigan *M, D*

Minnesota

University of Minnesota
  Duluth *B*

Missouri

Drury University *B, T*

Oregon

Linfield College *B*

Pennsylvania

Indiana University of Pennsylvania *B*

Tennessee

Carson-Newman College *B*

Texas

Angelo State University *B*
University of Texas
  Arlington *M, T*
  Austin *M*

Utah

Brigham Young University *B*

Washington

Whitworth University *B*

Wisconsin

Carroll University *B*

Aquaculture

Alabama

Auburn University *B, M, D*
Gadsden State Community College *C*

Arkansas

University of Arkansas
  Pine Bluff *M*

Delaware

Delaware Technical and Community
  College
  Owens *C*

Florida

Hillsborough Community
  College *C, A*

Maine

Unity College *B*
University of New England *B*

New Jersey

Cumberland County College *C*

New York

State University of New York
  College of Agriculture and
    Technology at Morrisville *A*

North Carolina

Brunswick Community College *C, A*

South Carolina

Clemson University *B, M*

Texas

Texas A&M University *B*
Texas A&M University
  Corpus Christi *M*
  Galveston *B*

Washington

Grays Harbor College *C*

West Virginia

New River Community and Technical
  College *A*

Aquatic biology/ limnology

Arizona

Northern Arizona University *B*

California

University of California
  Santa Barbara *B*

Florida

Florida Institute of Technology *B*
Stetson University *B*

Kentucky

Murray State University *M*

Minnesota

Saint Cloud State University *B*

New York

State University of New York
  College at Brockport *B*
  College of Environmental Science
    and Forestry *B*

Rhode Island

Brown University *B*
University of Rhode Island *M*

Texas

Baylor University *M*
Texas A&M University
  Galveston *B*
Texas State University: San
  Marcos *B, M*

Wisconsin

University of Wisconsin
  Superior *B*

Arabic

California

Grossmont College *A*
Imperial Valley College *A*
National University *B*
University of California
  Los Angeles *B*

District of Columbia

Catholic University of America *M, D*
George Washington University *B*
Georgetown University *B, M, D*

Georgia

University of Georgia *B*

Illinois

DePaul University *B*
University of Chicago *B*

Indiana

University of Notre Dame *B*

Maryland

Howard Community College *A*
United States Naval Academy *B*
University of Maryland
  College Park *B*

Massachusetts

Bard College at Simon's Rock *B*
Wellesley College *B*

Michigan

Michigan State University *B*
University of Michigan *B, M*

Minnesota

University of Minnesota
  Twin Cities *M*

Missouri

Washington University in St.
  Louis *B, M*

New Hampshire

Dartmouth College *B*

New York

Bard College *B*
State University of New York
  Binghamton *B*
United States Military Academy *B*

Ohio

Ohio State University
  Columbus Campus *B*

Texas

University of Texas
  Austin *B, M, D*

Utah

Brigham Young University *B, M*

University of Utah *B, M, D*

Vermont

Middlebury College *M, D*

Washington

University of Washington *B*

Archaeology

Arizona

Pima Community College *C, A*
Prescott College *M*

California

California State University
  East Bay *B*
  San Bernardino *C*
Merced College *A*
Palomar College *C, A*
St. Mary's College of California *B*
Stanford University *B*
University of California
  Los Angeles *M, D*
  San Diego *B*

Connecticut

Norwalk Community College *C*
Wesleyan University *B*
Yale University *B, M*

District of Columbia

George Washington University *B*

Florida

Gulf Coast Community College *A*

Illinois

Illinois State University *M*
Richland Community College *A*
Southwestern Illinois College *A*
Wheaton College *B, M*

Indiana

Indiana University
  Bloomington *D*
University of Evansville *B*
University of Indianapolis *B*

Iowa

Cornell College *B*

Maine

Bowdoin College *B*

Maryland

Johns Hopkins University *B*

Massachusetts

Boston University *B, M, D*
Bridgewater State College *B*
Tufts University *B*
Wellesley College *B*

Michigan

Michigan Technological
  University *M, D*

Minnesota

University of Minnesota
  Twin Cities *M, D*

Missouri

University of Missouri
  Columbia *B, M, D*
Washington University in St.
  Louis *B, M, D*

New York

Bard College *B*

City University of New York
Hunter College *B*
Columbia University *B*
Cornell University *B, M*
Hamilton College *B*
State University of New York
College at Potsdam *B*

North Carolina
University of North Carolina
Chapel Hill *B*

Ohio
College of Wooster *B*
University of Akron *C*
University of Cincinnati *M, D*
University of Rio Grande *B*

Pennsylvania
Bryn Mawr College *B, M, D*
Dickinson College *B*
Haverford College *B*
Lycoming College *B*
Penn State
Abington *B*
Altoona *B*
Beaver *B*
Berks *B*
Brandywine *B*
DuBois *B*
Erie, The Behrend College *B*
Fayette, The Eberly Campus *B*
Greater Allegheny *B*
Hazleton *B*
Lehigh Valley *B*
Mont Alto *B*
New Kensington *B*
Schuylkill *B*
Shenango *B*
University Park *B*
Wilkes-Barre *B*
Worthington Scranton *B*
York *B*
University of Pennsylvania *M, D*

Rhode Island
Brown University *B, M, D*

Tennessee
Southern Adventist University *B*

Texas
University of Texas
Austin *B*

Utah
Brigham Young University *B*
Weber State University *C, A*

Virginia
Sweet Briar College *B*
Washington and Lee University *B*

Washington
Western Washington University *B*

Wisconsin
University of Wisconsin
La Crosse *B*

Wyoming
Western Wyoming Community
College *A*

Architectural drafting/ CAD/CADD

Arizona
Coconino County Community
College *C, A*
Pima Community College *C, A*

Scottsdale Community College *C, A*

California
College of the Canyons *C, A*
College of the Desert *C, A*
Hartnell College *C*
Long Beach City College *C, A*
Santa Rosa Junior College *C*
Shasta College *C, A*
Sierra College *C, A*
Silicon Valley College
Western Career College: San Jose *A*
Southwestern College *C*
Westwood College of Technology
Westwood College: Inland
Empire *A*
Westwood College: South Bay *A*

Colorado
Pikes Peak Community College *C*

Florida
Central Florida Community College *A*
Indian River State College *A*
Palm Beach Community College *C*
St. Petersburg College *A*

Georgia
Albany Technical College *C*
Atlanta Technical College *C*
Central Georgia Technical College *C*
Clayton State University *A*
Southwest Georgia Technical
College *C*

Hawaii
University of Hawaii
Honolulu Community College *A*

Illinois
Harper College *C, A*
Kaskaskia College *C, A*
Lincoln Land Community College *C, A*
Triton College *C, A*
Waubonsee Community College *C*

Indiana
Vincennes University *A*

Iowa
Clinton Community College *C, A*
Des Moines Area Community
College *C, A*
Hawkeye Community College *A*

Kentucky
Owensboro Community and
Technical College *C, A*
Sullivan College of Technology and
Design *C, A*
Western Kentucky University *A*

Maine
Southern Maine Community
College *A*

Maryland
Carroll Community College *C, A*
Community College of Baltimore
County *C, A*
Hagerstown Community College *C*
Wor-Wic Community College *C*

Massachusetts
Springfield Technical Community
College *C*

Michigan
Baker College
of Muskegon *A*
Baker College of Allen Park *A*

Bay de Noc Community College *C*
Grand Rapids Community College *A*
Lake Michigan College *C*
St. Clair County Community
College *C, A*

Minnesota
Dakota County Technical College *C, A*
Dunwoody College of Technology *A*
Hennepin Technical College *C, A*
Lake Superior College *C, A*
Minneapolis Community and
Technical College *C*
Minnesota State Community and
Technical College *A*
Northwest Technical Institute *A*
Rochester Community and Technical
College *C*
St. Cloud Technical College *C, A*

Missouri
Jefferson College *C, A*
Southeast Missouri State University *C*

Nebraska
Metropolitan Community
College *C, A*
Northeast Community College *A*
Southeast Community College *A*

Nevada
College of Southern Nevada *C*

New Jersey
Thomas Edison State College *A, B*

New Mexico
Central New Mexico Community
College *C, A*

New York
Mohawk Valley Community College *C*
State University of New York
College of Agriculture and
Technology at Morrisville *A*

North Carolina
Gaston College *C*

North Dakota
North Dakota State College of
Science *A*

Ohio
Central Ohio Technical College *A*
Marion Technical College *C*
Owens Community College
Toledo *A*

Oklahoma
Oklahoma State University
Oklahoma City *A*

Oregon
Chemeketa Community College *C*
Clackamas Community College *A*
Rogue Community College *C*

Pennsylvania
Butler County Community College *A*
Commonwealth Technical Institute *A*
Johnson College *A*
Luzerne County Community
College *C, A*
Triangle Tech
DuBois *A*
Erie *A*
Greensburg *A*
Westmoreland County Community
College *A*

Puerto Rico
Turabo University *C, A*
Universidad Metropolitana *C*
Universidad del Este *C*

South Carolina
Spartanburg Community College *C*

South Dakota
Western Dakota Technical Institute *A*

Texas
Westwood College: Fort Worth *A*
Wharton County Junior College *C*

Utah
Salt Lake Community College *A*

Washington
Bates Technical College *C, A*
Olympic College *C*

West Virginia
West Virginia State Community and
Technical College *A*

Wisconsin
Herzing University *A, B*
Waukesha County Technical
College *A*

Wyoming
Casper College *C*

Architectural engineering

Alabama
Auburn University *B, M*

California
California Polytechnic State
University: San Luis Obispo *B*
East Los Angeles College *A*
San Joaquin Delta College *A*
University of Southern California *M*

Colorado
University of Colorado
Boulder *B*

Connecticut
Norwalk Community College *A*

District of Columbia
University of the District of
Columbia *A*

Florida
Miami Dade College *A*
University of Miami *B, M*

Illinois
City Colleges of Chicago
Olive-Harvey College *A*
Dominican University *B*
Illinois Institute of Technology *B, M*
University of Illinois
Urbana-Champaign *M*

Kansas
Kansas State University *B, M*
University of Kansas *B, M*

Kentucky
Sullivan College of Technology and
Design *A*

Massachusetts
Northeastern University *B*
Tufts University *B*

Michigan
Delta College *A*
Lawrence Technological University *B*

Mississippi
Holmes Community College *A*

Missouri
University of Missouri
 Missouri University of Science and
  Technology *B*

Nebraska
University of Nebraska
 Lincoln *B, M*
 Omaha *B*

New York
State University of New York
 College of Agriculture and
  Technology at Morrisville *A*

North Carolina
North Carolina Agricultural and
 Technical State University *B, M*

North Dakota
University of North Dakota *M*

Ohio
Stark State College of Technology *A*

Oklahoma
Oklahoma State University *B*
University of Oklahoma *B*

Pennsylvania
Drexel University *B*
Penn State
 Abington *B*
 Altoona *B*
 Beaver *B*
 Berks *B*
 Brandywine *B*
 DuBois *B*
 Erie, The Behrend College *B*
 Fayette, The Eberly Campus *B*
 Greater Allegheny *B*
 Hazleton *B*
 Lehigh Valley *B*
 Mont Alto *B*
 New Kensington *B*
 Schuylkill *B*
 Shenango *B*
 University Park *B, M, D*
 Wilkes-Barre *B*
 Worthington Scranton *B*
 York *B*
Philadelphia University *B*

Rhode Island
New England Institute of
 Technology *B*

Tennessee
Tennessee State University *B*

Texas
Laredo Community College *A*
University of Texas
 Austin *B, M*

Virginia
John Tyler Community College *A*

Washington
Bates Technical College *A*

Wisconsin
Milwaukee School of Engineering *B*

Wyoming
University of Wyoming *B*

Architectural engineering technology

Alabama
Lawson State Community
 College *C, A*

Alaska
University of Alaska
 Anchorage *A*

Arizona
Mesa Community College *A*

California
Allan Hancock College *A*
Chabot College *A*
Chaffey College *C, A*
College of the Desert *C, A*
College of the Sequoias *A*
Contra Costa College *A*
Cuyamaca College *A*
Diablo Valley College *C*
East Los Angeles College *A*
El Camino College *C, A*
Fullerton College *C*
Golden West College *C, A*
Laney College *C, A*
Long Beach City College *C, A*
Los Angeles Harbor College *C, A*
Los Angeles Trade and Technical
 College *C, A*
Modesto Junior College *C, A*
Mount San Antonio College *C, A*
Orange Coast College *C, A*
San Joaquin Delta College *C, A*
Santa Monica College *C, A*
Ventura College *C, A*

Colorado
Arapahoe Community College *C, A*
Front Range Community College *C, A*
Mesa State College *B*
Pikes Peak Community College *C, A*
Westwood College: Denver North *A*

Connecticut
Capital Community College *A*
Norwalk Community College *A*
Three Rivers Community College *C, A*
University of Hartford *B*

Delaware
Delaware State University *B*
Delaware Technical and Community
 College
 Owens *A*
 Stanton/Wilmington *A*
 Terry *A*

Florida
Daytona State College *A*
Florida State College at Jacksonville *A*
Gulf Coast Community College *A*
Hillsborough Community
 College *C, A*
Miami Dade College *A*
Seminole Community College *A*

Georgia
Southern Polytechnic State
 University *B*

Hawaii
University of Hawaii
 Hawaii Community College *C*

Idaho
Brigham Young University-Idaho *A*

Illinois
Joliet Junior College *C, A*
Morrison Institute of Technology *A*
Oakton Community College *A*

Indiana
Indiana State University *B*
Indiana University-Purdue University
 Fort Wayne *A*
Indiana University-Purdue University
 Indianapolis *A*
Purdue University *A, B*
Purdue University
 North Central *A, B*

Iowa
Iowa Western Community College *A*
Western Iowa Tech Community
 College *A*

Kentucky
Eastern Kentucky University *B*
Northern Kentucky University *C, A, B*
Sullivan College of Technology and
 Design *A*

Louisiana
Delgado Community College *A*

Maryland
Montgomery College *A*

Massachusetts
Benjamin Franklin Institute of
 Technology *A*
Fitchburg State College *B*
Massasoit Community College *A*
Wentworth Institute of Technology *A*

Michigan
Baker College
 of Auburn Hills *A*
 of Flint *A*
 of Muskegon *A*
 of Owosso *A*
Ferris State University *A*
Monroe County Community
 College *C, A*
Mott Community College *C, A*
Oakland Community College *A*

Minnesota
Northwest Technical Institute *A*

Mississippi
Mississippi Delta Community
 College *A*
University of Southern Mississippi *B*

Missouri
St. Louis Community College
 St. Louis Community College at
  Meramec *A*
University of Central Missouri *B*

Nebraska
Southeast Community College *A*

Nevada
Truckee Meadows Community
 College *C, A*

New Hampshire
Keene State College *B*
NHTI-Concord's Community
 College *A*

New Jersey
Essex County College *A*
Mercer County Community
 College *C, A*

New Mexico
Eastern New Mexico University:
 Roswell Campus *A*

New York
Dutchess Community College *A*
Erie Community College
 South Campus *A*
Finger Lakes Community College *A*
Institute of Design and
 Construction *A*
Onondaga Community College *A*
Orange County Community College *A*
State University of New York
 College of Agriculture and
  Technology at Morrisville *A*
 College of Technology at
  Alfred *A, B*
 College of Technology at Delhi *A*
 Farmingdale *A, B*
Suffolk County Community College *A*

North Carolina
Cape Fear Community College *A*
Catawba Valley Community College *A*
Central Carolina Community
 College *A*
Central Piedmont Community
 College *C, A*
Coastal Carolina Community
 College *C, A*
Durham Technical Community
 College *C, A*
Fayetteville Technical Community
 College *C, A*
Forsyth Technical Community
 College *A*
Gaston College *C, A*
Guilford Technical Community
 College *C, A*
Nash Community College *A*
Pitt Community College *A*
Sandhills Community College *A*
Wake Technical Community
 College *C, A*
Wilkes Community College *C, A*

North Dakota
North Dakota State College of
 Science *A*

Ohio
Cincinnati State Technical and
 Community College *A*
Columbus State Community
 College *C, A*
Cuyahoga Community College
 Metropolitan Campus *A*
James A. Rhodes State College *C*
Marion Technical College *C*
Owens Community College
 Toledo *C, A*
Stark State College of Technology *A*
Terra State Community College *C, A*

Oregon
Chemeketa Community College *C*
Mt. Hood Community College *C, A*

Pennsylvania
Community College of Philadelphia *A*

Harrisburg Area Community
College *C, A*
Northampton Community College *A*
Pennsylvania College of
Technology *A, B*
Pennsylvania Highlands Community
College *A*
Pennsylvania Institute of
Technology *A*

South Carolina
Greenville Technical College *C, A*
Midlands Technical College *C, A*
Trident Technical College *C, A*

South Dakota
Southeast Technical Institute *A*

Tennessee
Middle Tennessee State University *B*
Nashville State Community College *A*
Southwest Tennessee Community
College *A*

Texas
Del Mar College *C, A*
San Antonio College *C, A*
Tarrant County College *C, A*
Texas Tech University *B*
University of Houston *B*

Vermont
Vermont Technical College *A, B*

Virginia
Central Virginia Community
College *A*
J. Sargeant Reynolds Community
College *A*
John Tyler Community College *C, A*
New River Community College *A*
Norfolk State University *A*
Northern Virginia Community
College *A*
Virginia Western Community
College *C, A*

Washington
Bates Technical College *C, A*
Clover Park Technical College *A*
Lake Washington Technical
College *C, A*
Spokane Community College *A*
Spokane Falls Community
College *C, A*

West Virginia
Bluefield State College *A, B*
Fairmont State University *A, B*

Wisconsin
Milwaukee Area Technical College *A*
Northeast Wisconsin Technical
College *A*
Wisconsin Indianhead Technical
College *A*

Architectural history/ criticism

Georgia
Savannah College of Art and
Design *B, M*

Illinois
DePaul University *B*
University of Illinois
Urbana-Champaign *D*

Kansas
University of Kansas *B*

New York
Bard College *M*
Barnard College *B*
Cornell University *M, D*

Ohio
Miami University
Oxford Campus *B*

Pennsylvania
Carnegie Mellon University *B, M*

Rhode Island
Brown University *B, M, D*
Roger Williams University *B*

Texas
University of Texas
Austin *M*

Virginia
University of Virginia *B, M, D*

Architectural technology

Alabama
Shelton State Community College *A*

Arizona
Coconino County Community
College *C, A*

California
Allan Hancock College *C, A*
College of the Desert *C, A*
Diablo Valley College *C, A*
Los Angeles Harbor College *C, A*
Los Angeles Pierce College *C, A*
Orange Coast College *C, A*
Southwestern College *C, A*

Colorado
Westwood College of Technology
Westwood College: Denver South *A*

Connecticut
Three Rivers Community College *C, A*

Florida
Miami Dade College *A*
Valencia Community College *A*

Illinois
Morrison Institute of Technology *A*
Rend Lake College *C, A*
University of Illinois
Urbana-Champaign *D*

Kentucky
Western Kentucky University *B*

Maine
University of Maine
Augusta *A, B*

Maryland
Montgomery College *A*

Massachusetts
Benjamin Franklin Institute of
Technology *A*
Fitchburg State College *B*
Roxbury Community College *A*

Michigan
Delta College *C, A*
Grand Rapids Community College *A*
Henry Ford Community College *A*

Washtenaw Community College *C, A*

Minnesota
Dunwoody College of Technology *A*
Northland Community & Technical
College *C, A*
Northwest Technical Institute *A*

Missouri
Washington University in St. Louis *B*

Nevada
College of Southern Nevada *A*

New Jersey
Mercer County Community
College *C, A*

New York
City University of New York
College of Staten Island *A*
New York Institute of
Technology *A, B*
State University of New York
College of Agriculture and
Technology at Morrisville *A*
College of Technology at Delhi *A*

North Carolina
Catawba Valley Community College *A*
College of the Albemarle *C, A*
Durham Technical Community
College *C, A*
Fayetteville Technical Community
College *A*
Gaston College *C, A*
Nash Community College *A*
Roanoke-Chowan Community
College *A*
Sandhills Community College *A*

North Dakota
North Dakota State College of
Science *A*

Pennsylvania
Carnegie Mellon University *B, M, D*
Pennsylvania College of
Technology *A*
Thaddeus Stevens College of
Technology *A*

South Dakota
Mitchell Technical Institute *A*

Texas
Abilene Christian University *A*
Lone Star College System *A*
North Lake College *C, A*
South Texas College *C, A*

Virginia
J. Sargeant Reynolds Community
College *A*

Washington
Bates Technical College *C, A*

Wisconsin
Milwaukee Area Technical College *A*
Northcentral Technical College *A*
Western Technical College *A*

Architecture

Alabama
Auburn University *B*
Tuskegee University *B*

Arizona
Arizona State University *B, M, D*
University of Arizona *B, M*

Arkansas
University of Arkansas *B*

California
Academy of Art University *M*
California College of the Arts *B, M*
California Polytechnic State
University: San Luis Obispo *B, M*
California State Polytechnic
University: Pomona *B, M*
NewSchool of Architecture &
Design *B, M*
Otis College of Art and Design *B*
Southern California Institute of
Architecture *B, M*
University of California
Berkeley *B, M, D*
Los Angeles *B, M, D*
University of San Francisco *B*
University of Southern
California *B, M, D*
Woodbury University *B, M*

Colorado
University of Colorado
Denver *M*

Connecticut
Connecticut College *B*
University of Hartford *B, M*
Yale University *B, M*

District of Columbia
Catholic University of America *B, M*
Howard University *B*
University of the District of
Columbia *B*

Florida
Florida Agricultural and Mechanical
University *B, M*
Florida Atlantic University *B*
Florida International University *M*
University of Central Florida *B*
University of Florida *B, D*
University of Miami *B, M*
University of South Florida *M*

Georgia
Georgia Institute of
Technology *B, M, D*
Savannah College of Art and
Design *B, M*
Southern Polytechnic State
University *B*

Hawaii
University of Hawaii
Manoa *D*

Idaho
University of Idaho *B, M*

Illinois
Illinois Institute of
Technology *B, M, D*
Judson University *B, M*
School of the Art Institute of
Chicago *M*
Southern Illinois University
Carbondale *B*
University of Illinois
Chicago *B, M*
Urbana-Champaign *B, M, D*

Indiana
Ball State University *B, M*

University of Notre Dame *B, M*

Iowa
Iowa State University *B, M*

Kansas
Kansas State University *M*
University of Kansas *M, D*

Kentucky
University of Kentucky *B, M*

Louisiana
Louisiana State University and
Agricultural and Mechanical
College *B, M*
Louisiana Tech University *B*
Southern University and Agricultural
and Mechanical College *B*
Tulane University *B, M*
University of Louisiana at
Lafayette *B, M*

Maryland
Morgan State University *B, M*
University of Maryland
College Park *B, M*

Massachusetts
Boston Architectural College *B, M*
College of the Holy Cross *B*
Hampshire College *B*
Harvard College *M, D*
Massachusetts Institute of
Technology *B, M, D*
Mount Holyoke College *B*
Northeastern University *B, M*
University of Massachusetts
Amherst *M*
Wellesley College *B*
Wentworth Institute of
Technology *B, M*

Michigan
Andrews University *B, M*
Eastern Michigan University *B*
Lawrence Technological
University *B, M*
University of Detroit Mercy *B, M*
University of Michigan *B, M, D*

Minnesota
University of Minnesota
Twin Cities *B, M*

Mississippi
Mississippi State University *B, M*

Missouri
Drury University *B*
University of Missouri
Kansas City *B*
Washington University in St.
Louis *B, M*

Montana
Montana State University
Bozeman *M*

Nebraska
University of Nebraska
Lincoln *B, M*

Nevada
University of Nevada
Las Vegas *B, M*

New Hampshire
Keene State College *B*

New Jersey
New Jersey Institute of
Technology *B, M*
Princeton University *B, M, D*

New Mexico
University of New Mexico *B, M*

New York
Barnard College *B*
City University of New York
City College *B, M*
Columbia University *B*
Columbia University
School of General Studies *B*
Cooper Union for the Advancement of
Science and Art *B, M*
Cornell University *B, M*
Hobart and William Smith Colleges *B*
New York Institute of
Technology *B, M*
Parsons The New School for
Design *B, M*
Pratt Institute *B, M*
Rensselaer Polytechnic
Institute *B, M, D*
State University of New York
Buffalo *B, M*
College of Technology at Delhi *B*
Syracuse University *B, M*

North Carolina
North Carolina State University *B, M*
University of North Carolina
Charlotte *B, M, D*

North Dakota
North Dakota State University *M*

Ohio
Kent State University *B, M*
Miami University
Oxford Campus *M*
Ohio State University
Columbus Campus *B, M*
University of Cincinnati *B, M*

Oklahoma
Oklahoma State University *B*
University of Oklahoma *B, M*

Oregon
Portland State University *B*
University of Oregon *B, M*

Pennsylvania
Carnegie Mellon University *B, M, D*
Drexel University *B, M*
Lehigh University *B*
Marywood University *B, M*
Penn State
University Park *B, M*
Philadelphia University *B*
Temple University *B*
University of Pennsylvania *B, M, D*

Puerto Rico
Inter American University of Puerto
Rico
San German Campus *B*
Universidad Politecnica de Puerto
Rico *B*
University of Puerto Rico
Rio Piedras *M*

Rhode Island
Rhode Island School of Design *B, M*
Roger Williams University *B, M*

South Carolina
Clemson University *B, M*

Tennessee
Tennessee State University *B*
University of Memphis *M*
University of Tennessee
Knoxville *B, M*

Texas
Baylor University *B*
Prairie View A&M University *B, M*
Rice University *B, M, D*
Texas A&M University *B, M, D*
Texas Tech University *B, M*
University of Houston *B, M*
University of Texas
Arlington *B, M*
Austin *B, M*
San Antonio *B, M*

Utah
University of Utah *B, M*

Vermont
Bennington College *B*
Norwich University *B, M*

Virginia
Hampton University *B*
University of Virginia *B, M*
Virginia Polytechnic Institute and
State University *B, M, D*

Washington
University of Washington *B, M*
Washington State University *B, M*

Wisconsin
University of Wisconsin
Milwaukee *B, M, D*

Aromatherapy

Vermont
Goddard College *B, M*

Art

Alabama
Alabama Agricultural and Mechanical
University *B*
Alabama State University *B*
Athens State University *B*
Auburn University at Montgomery *B*
Birmingham-Southern College *B*
Faulkner State Community College *A*
Gadsden State Community College *A*
Jacksonville State University *B*
Judson College *B*
Samford University *B*
Stillman College *B*
Troy University *B*
University of Alabama
Birmingham *B*
Huntsville *B*
University of Mobile *B*
University of Montevallo *B, T*
University of South Alabama *B*
Wallace State Community College at
Hanceville *A*

Alaska
University of Alaska
Anchorage *B*
Fairbanks *B, M*
Southeast *C, B*

Arizona
Arizona State University *B, M*
Central Arizona College *A*
Cochise College *A*
Coconino County Community
College *A*

Eastern Arizona College *A*
Northern Arizona University *B*
Phoenix College *A*
Pima Community College *A*
Prescott College *B*
Scottsdale Community College *C*
University of Arizona *M*

Arkansas
Arkansas State University *B, M*
Arkansas Tech University *B*
Black River Technical College *A*
Harding University *B*
Henderson State University *B*
Hendrix College *B*
Lyon College *B*
Southern Arkansas University *B*
University of Arkansas *B, M*
University of Arkansas
Little Rock *B, M*
Monticello *B*
Pine Bluff *B*
University of Central Arkansas *B*
University of the Ozarks *B*

California
Allan Hancock College *A*
Azusa Pacific University *B*
Berkeley City College *C, A*
Cabrillo College *A*
California Baptist University *B*
California College of the Arts *B*
California Lutheran University *B*
California State Polytechnic
University: Pomona *B*
California State University
Bakersfield *B*
Chico *B, M*
Dominguez Hills *B*
East Bay *B*
Fresno *B, M*
Fullerton *B, M*
Long Beach *B, M*
Los Angeles *B, M*
Monterey Bay *B*
Northridge *B, M*
Sacramento *B, M*
San Bernardino *B, M*
Stanislaus *B*
California State University: Channel
Islands *B*
Canada College *A*
Cerritos College *A*
Cerro Coso Community College *A*
Chabot College *A*
Chaffey College *A*
Chapman University *B*
Citrus College *A*
Claremont McKenna College *B*
College of the Canyons *A*
College of the Desert *A*
College of the Sequoias *A*
College of the Siskiyous *C, A*
Columbia College *A*
Concordia University *B*
Copper Mountain College *A*
Cosumnes River College *A*
Crafton Hills College *A*
Cypress College *A*
De Anza College *A*
Dominican University of California *B*
East Los Angeles College *A*
El Camino College *A*
El Camino College: Compton
Center *A*
Folsom Lake College *A*
Foothill College *C, A*
Fresno City College *A*
Fresno Pacific University *B*
Fullerton College *A*
Gavilan College *A*
Golden West College *A*
Hartnell College *A*
Humboldt State University *B*

Imperial Valley College *A*
Irvine Valley College *A*
La Sierra University *B*
Lake Tahoe Community College *C, A*
Laney College *A*
Lassen Community College *A*
Long Beach City College *A*
Los Angeles City College *A*
Los Angeles Harbor College *A*
Los Angeles Mission College *A*
Los Angeles Southwest College *A*
Los Angeles Valley College *A*
Loyola Marymount University *B*
Mendocino College *C, A*
Mills College *A*
MiraCosta College *A*
Mission College *C, A*
Modesto Junior College *A*
Monterey Peninsula College *C, A*
Mount San Jacinto College *A*
Notre Dame de Namur University *B*
Occidental College *B*
Orange Coast College *A*
Otis College of Art and Design *B, M*
Oxnard College *C, A*
Palomar College *C, A*
Pepperdine University *B*
Pitzer College *B*
Pomona College *B*
Reedley College *A*
Saddleback College *A*
St. Mary's College of California *B*
San Diego Mesa College *C, A*
San Francisco Art Institute *B, M*
San Francisco Conservatory of
    Music *C*
San Francisco State University *B, M*
San Jose City College *C*
San Jose State University *B, M*
Santa Barbara City College *A*
Santa Rosa Junior College *C, A*
Santiago Canyon College *C, A*
Shasta College *A*
Sierra College *C, A*
Skyline College *A*
Southwestern College *A*
Stanford University *B, M, D*
Taft College *C, A*
University of California
    Berkeley *B, M*
    Davis *M*
    Los Angeles *B, M*
    Riverside *B*
    Santa Barbara *B*
    Santa Cruz *B*
University of La Verne *B*
University of Redlands *B*
University of Southern California *M*
University of the Pacific *B*
Victor Valley College *A*
West Hills College: Coalinga *A*
West Los Angeles College *C, A*
West Valley College *A*
Westmont College *B*
Whittier College *B*
Yuba Community College District *A*

Colorado

Adams State College *A, B, M*
Colorado Mountain College *A*
Colorado State University *B*
Lamar Community College *A*
Mesa State College *B*
Metropolitan State College of
    Denver *B*
Morgan Community College *A*
University of Denver *B*
Western State College of Colorado *B*

Connecticut

Albertus Magnus College *B*
Central Connecticut State
    University *B*

Naugatuck Valley Community
    College *A*
Norwalk Community College *A*
Sacred Heart University *B*
Southern Connecticut State
    University *B, M, T*
Trinity College *B*
University of Hartford *M*
Western Connecticut State
    University *B*
Yale University *B*

Delaware

University of Delaware *B*

District of Columbia

American University *B*
Catholic University of America *B*
Corcoran College of Art and Design *B*
Georgetown University *B*
Howard University *B, M*

Florida

Barry University *B*
Broward College *A*
Daytona State College *A*
Florida Atlantic University *B*
Florida Gulf Coast University *B*
Gulf Coast Community College *A*
Indian River State College *A*
Jacksonville University *B*
Northwest Florida State College *A*
Pensacola Junior College *A*
Rollins College *B*
State College of Florida,
    Manatee-Sarasota *A*
Stetson University *B*
University of Central Florida *B*
University of Miami *B, M*
University of North Florida *B*
University of South Florida *B*
University of Tampa *B*
University of West Florida *B*

Georgia

Agnes Scott College *B*
Armstrong Atlantic State University *B*
Atlanta Metropolitan College *A*
Berry College *B*
Clark Atlanta University *B*
College of Coastal Georgia *A*
Columbus State University *B*
Darton College *A*
East Georgia College *A*
Georgia College and State
    University *B*
Georgia Perimeter College *A*
Georgia Southern University *B*
Georgia Southwestern State
    University *B*
Georgia State University *B*
Gordon College *A*
Kennesaw State University *B*
Macon State College *A*
Mercer University *B*
Middle Georgia College *A*
Morehouse College *B*
Oglethorpe University *B*
Piedmont College *B, T*
Reinhardt College *A*
University of Georgia *B, M, D*
University of West Georgia *B*
Valdosta State University *B*
Young Harris College *A*

Hawaii

University of Hawaii
    Hilo *B*
    Manoa *B, M*

Idaho

Boise State University *B, M*
Brigham Young University-Idaho *B*

College of Idaho *B*
Idaho State University *A, B, M, T*
University of Idaho *B, M*

Illinois

Augustana College *B*
Aurora University *B*
Black Hawk College: East Campus *A*
Blackburn College *B*
Bradley University *B, M*
Chicago State University *B*
City Colleges of Chicago
    Harold Washington College *A*
College of DuPage *A*
College of Lake County *A*
Columbia College Chicago *B*
Concordia University Chicago *B, T*
DePaul University *B*
Dominican University *B*
Eastern Illinois University *B, M, T*
Elgin Community College *A*
Elmhurst College *B, T*
Eureka College *B*
Governors State University *B, M*
Greenville College *B*
Illinois College *B, T*
Illinois Institute of Art: Schaumburg *B*
Illinois State University *B, M, T*
Illinois Valley Community College *A*
Illinois Wesleyan University *B*
John A. Logan College *A*
John Wood Community College *A*
Joliet Junior College *A*
Judson University *B*
Kankakee Community College *A*
Kishwaukee College *A*
Lake Forest College *B*
Lewis University *B, T*
Lincoln College *A*
MacMurray College *B*
McHenry County College *A*
Monmouth College *B, T*
National-Louis University *B*
North Central College *B*
North Park University *B*
Northeastern Illinois University *B*
Northern Illinois University *B, M*
Northwestern University *B, M*
Olivet Nazarene University *B, T*
Parkland College *A*
Rend Lake College *A*
Richland Community College *A*
Rockford College *B*
School of the Art Institute of
    Chicago *B, M*
South Suburban College of Cook
    County *C*
Southern Illinois University
    Carbondale *B*
Southern Illinois University
    Edwardsville *B, T*
Southwestern Illinois College *A*
Spoon River College *A*
Trinity Christian College *B*
Triton College *A*
Western Illinois University *B*
Wheaton College *B, T*

Indiana

Ball State University *B, M*
Bethel College *B*
Earlham College *B*
Goshen College *B*
Huntington University *B*
Indiana State University *B, M*
Indiana University
    Northwest *B*
    South Bend *B*
    Southeast *B*
Indiana University-Purdue University
    Indianapolis *B*
Manchester College *A, B, T*
Marian University *A, B, T*
Oakland City University *A, B*

Purdue University *B*
Saint Mary's College *B*
St. Mary-of-the-Woods College *B*
Taylor University *B*
University of Evansville *B*
University of Indianapolis *B, M*
University of St. Francis *B*
University of Southern Indiana *B, T*
Valparaiso University *B*
Vincennes University *A*
Wabash College *B*

Iowa

Briar Cliff University *B*
Buena Vista University *B, T*
Central College *B, T*
Clarke College *A, B, T*
Coe College *B*
Cornell College *B, T*
Dordt College *B*
Ellsworth Community College *A*
Grinnell College *B*
Iowa State University *B*
Luther College *B*
Mount Mercy College *B*
Northwestern College *B, T*
Simpson College *B*
University of Iowa *B, M, T*
University of Northern Iowa *B, M*
Upper Iowa University *B*
Wartburg College *B, T*

Kansas

Allen County Community College *A*
Barton County Community College *A*
Bethany College *B, T*
Butler Community College *A*
Central Christian College of Kansas *A*
Coffeyville Community College *A*
Cowley County Community
    College *A*
Dodge City Community College *A*
Emporia State University *B, T*
Fort Hays State University *B*
Friends University *B*
Garden City Community College *A*
McPherson College *B, T*
Neosho County Community
    College *A*
Newman University *B*
Ottawa University *B, T*
Pittsburg State University *B, M*
Seward County Community College *A*
Sterling College *B, T*
University of St. Mary *B*
Washburn University *B*
Wichita State University *B, M, T*

Kentucky

Bellarmine University *B, T*
Berea College *B, T*
Brescia University *B*
Campbellsville University *B*
Centre College *B*
Eastern Kentucky University *B*
Kentucky Wesleyan College *B, T*
Pikeville College *B*
University of Louisville *M*

Louisiana

Centenary College of Louisiana *B, T*
Delgado Community College *A*
Dillard University *B*
Grambling State University *B*
Louisiana State University
    Shreveport *B*
Louisiana Tech University *B, M*
Loyola University New Orleans *B*
McNeese State University *B*
Nicholls State University *B*
Northwestern State University *M*
Southeastern Louisiana University *B*
Tulane University *B, M*

University of Louisiana at Lafayette *B*
Xavier University of Louisiana *B*

Maine

Bates College *B*
Colby College *B*
Maine College of Art *B*
University of Maine
  Farmington *B*
  Presque Isle *B*
University of Southern Maine *B*

Maryland

Allegany College of Maryland *A*
Baltimore City Community College *A*
Bowie State University *B*
Carroll Community College *A*
College of Notre Dame of Maryland *B*
Coppin State University *B*
Frederick Community College *A*
Goucher College *B*
Hood College *B*
Howard Community College *A*
Loyola University Maryland *B*
McDaniel College *B*
St. Mary's College of Maryland *B*
Salisbury University *B*
Towson University *B*
Washington College *B, T*

Massachusetts

Anna Maria College *B, M*
Art Institute of Boston at Lesley
  University *B*
Bristol Community College *A*
Bunker Hill Community College *A*
Clark University *B*
Framingham State College *B*
Gordon College *B*
Harvard College *M, D*
Holyoke Community College *A*
Lesley University *B, M*
Massachusetts Bay Community
  College *C*
Massachusetts College of Liberal
  Arts *B*
Montserrat College of Art *B*
Mount Wachusett Community
  College *A*
Northeastern University *B*
Salem State College *B*
School of the Museum of Fine
  Arts *B, M, T*
Smith College *B*
Springfield College *B*
Suffolk University *C, B*
University of Massachusetts
  Boston *B*
Westfield State College *B, T*

Michigan

Adrian College *A, B, T*
Albion College *B*
Alma College *B, T*
Andrews University *B*
Aquinas College *B*
Calvin College *B, T*
Central Michigan University *B, M*
Delta College *A*
Eastern Michigan University *B*
Finlandia University *B*
Gogebic Community College *A*
Grand Rapids Community College *A*
Grand Valley State University *B*
Henry Ford Community College *A*
Hillsdale College *B*
Kalamazoo College *B*
Lake Michigan College *A*
Lansing Community College *A*
Marygrove College *B, T*
Michigan State University *B, M*
Mott Community College *A*
Northern Michigan University *A, B*

Northwestern Michigan College *A*
Saginaw Valley State University *B, T*
Siena Heights University *A, B*
Spring Arbor University *B, T*
University of Michigan *B, M*
Wayne State University *B, M*

Minnesota

Bemidji State University *B*
Bethel University *B*
College of St. Benedict *B*
College of St. Scholastica *B*
Concordia College: Moorhead *B*
Concordia University: St. Paul *B*
Gustavus Adolphus College *B*
Minneapolis College of Art and
  Design *M*
Minnesota State University
  Mankato *B, M*
  Moorhead *B*
Minnesota West Community and
  Technical College *A*
Northland Community & Technical
  College *A*
Ridgewater College *A*
Saint Cloud State University *B, M*
St. John's University *B*
St. Olaf College *B*
Southwest Minnesota State
  University *B, T*
University of Minnesota
  Duluth *B*
  Twin Cities *M, D*
Winona State University *B*

Mississippi

Belhaven University *B*
Hinds Community College *A*
Mississippi College *B, M*
Mississippi Gulf Coast Community
  College *A*
Tougaloo College *B*

Missouri

College of the Ozarks *B*
Columbia College *B*
Crowder College *A*
Culver-Stockton College *B, T*
Drury University *B, M, T*
Fontbonne University *B, M, T*
Hannibal-LaGrange College *A, B*
Lindenwood University *B, M*
Missouri State University *B*
Missouri Valley College *B*
Missouri Western State University *B*
Southeast Missouri State University *B*
Southwest Baptist University *B*
Truman State University *B*
University of Central Missouri *B, M*
University of Missouri
  Columbia *B, M*
  Kansas City *B, M*
  St. Louis *B*
Washington University in St. Louis *B*
Webster University *B, M*
William Jewell College *B, T*
William Woods University *B, T*

Montana

Miles Community College *A*
Montana State University
  Billings *B*
  Bozeman *B*
Rocky Mountain College *B, T*
University of Great Falls *B*
University of Montana *B, M*
University of Montana: Western *B, T*

Nebraska

Bellevue University *B*
Chadron State College *B*
Concordia University *B*
Creighton University *B*

Dana College *B*
Doane College *B*
Nebraska Wesleyan University *B*
Northeast Community College *A*
Peru State College *B*
Union College *A*
University of Nebraska
  Kearney *B, M, T*
  Omaha *B*
Wayne State College *B*
Western Nebraska Community
  College *A*

Nevada

College of Southern Nevada *A*
Great Basin College *A*
University of Nevada
  Las Vegas *B, M*
  Reno *B, M*

New Hampshire

Chester College of New England *B*
Colby Sawyer College *B*
New England College *B*
Plymouth State University *B*
Rivier College *A*
Saint Anselm College *B*
University of New Hampshire *B*

New Jersey

Brookdale Community College *A*
Caldwell College *B*
The College of New Jersey *B*
College of St. Elizabeth *B, T*
Cumberland County College *A*
Drew University *B*
Essex County College *A*
Felician College *B*
Georgian Court University *B*
Gloucester County College *A*
Kean University *B, T*
Monmouth University *B*
Montclair State University *B, M, T*
New Jersey City University *B, T*
Ocean County College *A*
Ramapo College of New Jersey *B*
Rider University *B*
Rowan University *B, T*
Rutgers, The State University of New
  Jersey
  Camden Regional Campus *B, T*
  New Brunswick/Piscataway
    Campus *B*
  Newark Regional Campus *B, T*
Sussex County Community College *A*
Thomas Edison State College *B*
William Paterson University of New
  Jersey *B*

New Mexico

Eastern New Mexico University *A, B*
New Mexico Highlands University *B*
New Mexico State University
  Alamogordo *A*
  Grants *A*
Northern New Mexico College *A*
Santa Fe Community College *A*
University of New Mexico *B, M*

New York

Cayuga County Community College *A*
City University of New York
  Brooklyn College *B*
  City College *B*
  Queensborough Community
    College *A*
Colgate University *B*
Daemen College *B*
Elmira College *B*
Fordham University *B*
Fulton-Montgomery Community
  College *A*
Genesee Community College *A*

Hartwick College *B, T*
Herkimer County Community
  College *A*
Houghton College *B*
Ithaca College *B*
Marist College *B*
Marymount Manhattan College *B*
Mohawk Valley Community College *A*
Molloy College *B*
Nassau Community College *A*
Nazareth College *B, T*
Pace University *B*
St. Thomas Aquinas College *B, T*
State University of New York
  Binghamton *B*
  Buffalo *B*
  College at Brockport *B, M*
  College at Cortland *B*
  College at Fredonia *B*
  College at Plattsburgh *B*
  New Paltz *B, M*
  Oswego *B*
Vassar College *B*
Wells College *B*

North Carolina

Appalachian State University *B*
Brevard College *B*
Caldwell Community College and
  Technical Institute *A*
College of the Albemarle *A*
Davidson College *B*
East Carolina University *B, M*
Elon University *B*
Gardner-Webb University *B*
Guilford College *B*
High Point University *B*
Lees-McRae College *B*
Mars Hill College *B, T*
Methodist University *B*
North Carolina Agricultural and
  Technical State University *B, T*
North Carolina Central University *B*
St. Andrews Presbyterian College *B*
St. Augustine's College *B*
Sandhills Community College *A*
University of North Carolina
  Asheville *B, T*
  Charlotte *B*
  Greensboro *B*
Warren Wilson College *B*
Western Carolina University *B*
Wingate University *B*
Winston-Salem State University *B*

North Dakota

Dickinson State University *B, T*
Minot State University *B*
North Dakota State University *B*
University of North Dakota *B, M*

Ohio

Ashland University *A*
Baldwin-Wallace College *B*
Bluffton University *B*
Bowling Green State University *B, M*
Capital University *B*
Central State University *B*
Cleveland State University *B, T*
College of Mount St. Joseph *A, B, T*
Defiance College *A, B, T*
Edison State Community College *A*
Hocking College *C, A*
Lourdes College *A, B*
Miami University
  Oxford Campus *B, M*
Mount Vernon Nazarene University *B*
Muskingum University *B*
Ohio Dominican University *B, T*
Ohio Northern University *B*
Ohio State University
  Columbus Campus *B, M*
Ohio University *B, M*
Otterbein College *B*

Shawnee State University *A*
Tiffin University *B*
University of Findlay *B*
University of Rio Grande *A*
University of Toledo *B*
Virginia Marti College of Art and
Design *A*
Wilmington College *B*
Wittenberg University *B*
Wright State University *B*
Youngstown State University *B*

Oklahoma

Bacone College *A*
Cameron University *B*
Carl Albert State College *A*
Connors State College *A*
East Central University *B, T*
Langston University *B*
Northeastern Oklahoma Agricultural
and Mechanical College *A*
Northeastern State University *B*
Northern Oklahoma College *A*
Oklahoma Baptist University *B, T*
Oklahoma Christian University *B*
Oklahoma City University *B*
Oklahoma Panhandle State
University *B*
Oklahoma State University *B*
Oral Roberts University *B*
Redlands Community College *A*
St. Gregory's University *B*
Seminole State College *A*
Southeastern Oklahoma State
University *B*
University of Central Oklahoma *B*
University of Science and Arts of
Oklahoma *B, T*
University of Tulsa *B, M*
Western Oklahoma State College *A*

Oregon

Chemeketa Community College *A*
George Fox University *B*
Lewis & Clark College *B*
Linfield College *B, T*
Linn-Benton Community College *A*
Marylhurst University *C, B*
Mt. Hood Community College *A*
Oregon State University *B*
Pacific University *B*
Portland State University *B*
Reed College *B*
Southern Oregon University *B, T*
Treasure Valley Community College *A*
University of Oregon *B, M*
Western Oregon University *B*

Pennsylvania

Allegheny College *B*
Arcadia University *B*
California University of
Pennsylvania *B*
Carnegie Mellon University *B, M*
Cedar Crest College *B*
Cheyney University of Pennsylvania *B*
Clarion University of Pennsylvania *B*
Community College of Allegheny
County *A*
Community College of Philadelphia *A*
Edinboro University of
Pennsylvania *B, M, T*
Gettysburg College *B*
Harrisburg Area Community
College *A*
Immaculata University *C*
Indiana University of Pennsylvania *B*
Keystone College *A, B*
Kutztown University of
Pennsylvania *B, M, T*
Lafayette College *B*
Lehigh Carbon Community College *A*
Lehigh University *B*

Lock Haven University of
Pennsylvania *B*
Lycoming College *B*
Mansfield University of
Pennsylvania *B, T*
Millersville University of
Pennsylvania *B, M, T*
Montgomery County Community
College *A*
Moravian College *B, T*
Muhlenberg College *C, B*
Penn State
Abington *B*
Altoona *B*
Beaver *B*
Berks *B*
Brandywine *B*
DuBois *B*
Erie, The Behrend College *B*
Fayette, The Eberly Campus *B*
Greater Allegheny *B*
Hazleton *B*
Lehigh Valley *B*
Mont Alto *B*
New Kensington *B*
Schuylkill *B*
Shenango *B*
University Park *B, M*
Wilkes-Barre *B*
Worthington Scranton *B*
York *B*
Shippensburg University of
Pennsylvania *B, T*
Slippery Rock University of
Pennsylvania *B*
Susquehanna University *B*
Temple University *B*
Thiel College *B*
Ursinus College *B*
Washington & Jefferson College *B*
Waynesburg University *B*
West Chester University of
Pennsylvania *B*
Westminster College *B*
Wilson College *B*

Puerto Rico

University of Puerto Rico
Rio Piedras *B*

Rhode Island

Community College of Rhode
Island *A*

South Carolina

Anderson University *B*
Benedict College *B*
Bob Jones University *B, M*
Claflin University *B*
Clemson University *B, M*
Coker College *B*
Columbia College *B*
Converse College *B*
Erskine College *B*
Francis Marion University *B*
Furman University *B, T*
Lander University *B*
Newberry College *B*
Presbyterian College *B*
University of South Carolina
Lancaster *A*
Winthrop University *B*

South Dakota

Augustana College *B*
Black Hills State University *B*
Dakota Wesleyan University *B*
Northern State University *B*
Oglala Lakota College *A*
University of Sioux Falls *B*
University of South Dakota *B, M*

Tennessee

Austin Peay State University *B*
Belmont University *B, T*
Carson-Newman College *B, T*
Columbia State Community College *A*
East Tennessee State
University *B, M, T*
Fisk University *B*
Freed-Hardeman University *B, T*
Jackson State Community College *A*
Lambuth University *B*
LeMoyne-Owen College *B*
Lincoln Memorial University *B, T*
Maryville College *B*
Memphis College of Art *B, M*
Middle Tennessee State University *B*
Rhodes College *B*
Southern Adventist University *B*
Tennessee Technological University *T*
University of Memphis *B, M*
University of Tennessee
Chattanooga *B, T*
Knoxville *B*
Vanderbilt University *B*
Watkins College of Art, Design and
Film *B*

Texas

Alvin Community College *A*
Amarillo College *A*
Angelina College *A*
Angelo State University *B, T*
Austin College *B*
Austin Community College *A*
Brazosport College *A*
Central Texas College *A*
Cisco College *A*
Clarendon College *A*
Dallas Baptist University *B*
Del Mar College *A*
El Paso Community College *A*
Galveston College *A*
Grayson County College *A*
Hill College *A*
Howard College *A*
Howard Payne University *B, T*
Kilgore College *A*
Lamar University *B*
Laredo Community College *A*
Lon Morris College *A*
Lubbock Christian University *B, T*
Midland College *A*
Midwestern State University *B*
Navarro College *C, A*
Northeast Texas Community
College *A*
Odessa College *A*
Our Lady of the Lake University of San
Antonio *B*
Palo Alto College *A*
Rice University *B*
St. Edward's University *B*
St. Philip's College *A*
Sam Houston State University *B*
San Jacinto College *A*
Southern Methodist University *B*
Southwestern University *B, T*
Stephen F. Austin State
University *B, M, T*
Sul Ross State University *B, M*
Temple College *A*
Texarkana College *A*
Texas A&M University
Commerce *B, M*
Corpus Christi *T*
Texas Lutheran University *B*
Texas State University: San
Marcos *B, T*
Texas Tech University *B, M, D*
Texas Wesleyan University *B*
Texas Woman's University *B, M*
Trinity University *B*
Trinity Valley Community College *A*
Tyler Junior College *A*

University of Houston *B*
University of Houston
Clear Lake *B*
University of North Texas *B, M, D*
University of Texas
Arlington *B*
Austin *B*
Brownsville - Texas Southmost
College *B*
El Paso *B, M*
San Antonio *B, M*
Tyler *B*
of the Permian Basin *B*
University of the Incarnate Word *B*
Wayland Baptist University *B, T*
West Texas A&M University *B, M*
Western Texas College *A*
Wharton County Junior College *A*

Utah

Brigham Young University *B, M*
Snow College *A*
Southern Utah University *B, T*
University of Utah *B, M, T*
Utah State University *B, M*
Weber State University *B*
Westminster College *B*

Vermont

Castleton State College *B*
Green Mountain College *B*
Johnson State College *B*
Marlboro College *B*
St. Michael's College *B*

Virginia

Averett University *B*
Bluefield College *B*
College of William and Mary *B*
Eastern Mennonite University *B*
Emory & Henry College *B, T*
Ferrum College *B*
George Mason University *B, M*
Hampton University *B*
James Madison University *B, M, T*
Longwood University *B, T*
Lynchburg College *B*
Mary Baldwin College *B*
Norfolk State University *B*
Old Dominion University *B, T*
Radford University *B*
Roanoke College *B, T*
Southern Virginia University *B*
University of Virginia *B*
University of Virginia's College at
Wise *B, T*
Virginia Intermont College *B*
Virginia Polytechnic Institute and
State University *B*
Virginia Union University *B*
Virginia Wesleyan College *B*

Washington

Centralia College *A*
Cornish College of the Arts *B*
Everett Community College *A*
Evergreen State College *B*
Highline Community College *A*
North Seattle Community
College *C, A*
Olympic College *A*
Pacific Lutheran University *B*
Seattle Pacific University *B*
University of Puget Sound *B, T*
University of Washington *B, M*
University of Washington Bothell *B*
Walla Walla University *B*
Western Washington University *B*
Whitworth University *B, T*

West Virginia

Bethany College *B*
Concord University *B*

Shepherd University *B*
University of Charleston *B*
West Virginia University *B, M, T*
West Virginia Wesleyan College *B*

Wisconsin

Alverno College *B*
Cardinal Stritch University *B, M, T*
Carroll University *B*
Concordia University Wisconsin *B*
Edgewood College *B*
Lakeland College *B*
Lawrence University *B, T*
Mount Mary College *B, T*
Northland College *B*
Ripon College *B, T*
St. Norbert College *B*
Silver Lake College *B*
University of Wisconsin
    Eau Claire *B*
    Green Bay *B, T*
    La Crosse *B, T*
    Madison *B, M*
    Milwaukee *B, M, D*
    Oshkosh *B*
    Parkside *B, T*
    Platteville *B*
    River Falls *B*
    Stevens Point *B*
    Stout *B*
    Superior *B, T*
    Whitewater *A, B, T*
Viterbo University *B, T*
Wisconsin Lutheran College *B*

Wyoming

Casper College *A*
Central Wyoming College *C, A*
Eastern Wyoming College *A*
Laramie County Community
    College *A*
Sheridan College *A*
University of Wyoming *B*
Western Wyoming Community
    College *A*

Art history

Alabama

Birmingham-Southern College *B*
Chattahoochee Valley Community
    College *A*
University of Alabama *B, M*
University of Alabama
    Birmingham *M*

Arizona

Arizona State University *D*
Northern Arizona University *B*
University of Arizona *B, M, D*

Arkansas

University of Arkansas
    Little Rock *B*

California

California College of the Arts *M*
California State University
    Chico *B*
    Dominguez Hills *B*
    East Bay *B*
    Fullerton *B, M*
    Long Beach *B, M*
    Northridge *B, M*
    San Bernardino *B*
Chapman University *B*
College of the Desert *A*
Cosumnes River College *A*
De Anza College *C, A*
Dominican University of California *B*
Folsom Lake College *A*
Foothill College *C, A*
Gavilan College *A*

Grossmont College *A*
Los Angeles Southwest College *A*
Los Angeles Valley College *A*
Loyola Marymount University *B*
Merced College *A*
Mills College *B*
MiraCosta College *A*
Monterey Peninsula College *A*
Occidental College *B*
Ohlone College *C*
Pepperdine University *B*
Pitzer College *B*
Pomona College *B*
San Diego City College *A*
San Diego State University *B, M*
San Francisco Art Institute *B, M*
San Jose State University *B, M*
Santa Barbara City College *A*
Santa Clara University *B*
Scripps College *B*
Sonoma State University *B*
University of California
    Berkeley *B, D*
    Davis *B, M*
    Irvine *B*
    Los Angeles *B, M, D*
    Riverside *B, M*
    San Diego *B*
    Santa Barbara *B, M, D*
    Santa Cruz *B*
University of La Verne *B*
University of Redlands *B*
University of San Diego *B*
University of San Francisco *B*
University of Southern
    California *B, M, D*
Whittier College *B*

Colorado

Colorado College *B*
Colorado State University *B*
University of Colorado
    Boulder *B, M*
University of Denver *B, M*

Connecticut

Albertus Magnus College *B*
Connecticut College *B*
Fairfield University *B*
Saint Joseph College *B*
Southern Connecticut State
    University *B, M*
Trinity College *B*
University of Connecticut *B*
University of Hartford *B*
Wesleyan University *B*
Yale University *B, M, D*

Delaware

University of Delaware *B, M, D*

District of Columbia

American University *B, M*
Catholic University of America *B*
Corcoran College of Art and
    Design *M*
Gallaudet University *B*
George Washington
    University *B, M, D*
Georgetown University *B*
Howard University *B, M*
Trinity Washington University *B*

Florida

Eckerd College *B*
Florida International University *B*
Florida Southern College *B*
Florida State University *B, M, D*
Jacksonville University *B*
New College of Florida *B*
Palm Beach Community College *A*
Rollins College *B*

State College of Florida,
    Manatee-Sarasota *A*
University of Florida *B, M*
University of Miami *C, B, M*
University of South Florida *B, M*

Georgia

Emory University *B, D*
Georgia State University *B, M*
Oglethorpe University *B*
Savannah College of Art and
    Design *B, M*
University of Georgia *B, M*
Wesleyan College *B*

Hawaii

University of Hawaii
    Manoa *M*

Idaho

Boise State University *B*

Illinois

Augustana College *B*
Bradley University *B*
Columbia College Chicago *B*
DePaul University *B*
Dominican University *B*
Illinois Valley Community College *A*
Knox College *B*
Lincoln College *A*
Loyola University Chicago *B*
North Central College *B*
Northern Illinois University *B*
Northwestern University *B, M, D*
Principia College *B*
Richland Community College *A*
Rockford College *B*
Roosevelt University *B*
School of the Art Institute of
    Chicago *B, M*
University of Chicago *B, D*
University of Illinois
    Chicago *B, M, D*
    Urbana-Champaign *B, M, D*

Indiana

DePauw University *B*
Hanover College *B*
Indiana University
    Bloomington *B, M, D*
Indiana University-Purdue University
    Indianapolis *B*
Marian University *B, T*
Purdue University *B*
University of Evansville *B*
University of Notre Dame *B, M*
University of St. Francis *B*

Iowa

Clarke College *A, B, T*
Cornell College *B*
Drake University *B*
University of Iowa *B, M, D*
University of Northern Iowa *B*

Kansas

Baker University *B*
University of Kansas *B, M, D*
Washburn University *B*
Wichita State University *B*

Kentucky

Berea College *B*
Bluegrass Community and Technical
    College *A*
Thomas More College *A*
University of Kentucky *B, M*
University of Louisville *B, D*

Louisiana

Louisiana State University and
    Agricultural and Mechanical
    College *M*
Tulane University *B, M*
University of New Orleans *B*

Maine

Bowdoin College *B*
Colby College *B*
University of Maine *B*
University of Southern Maine *B*

Maryland

College of Notre Dame of Maryland *B*
Howard Community College *A*
Johns Hopkins University *B, M, D*
Maryland Institute College of Art *B*
McDaniel College *B*
Montgomery College *A*
University of Maryland
    College Park *B, M, D*

Massachusetts

Art Institute of Boston at Lesley
    University *B*
Bard College at Simon's Rock *B*
Boston College *B*
Boston University *B, M, D*
Brandeis University *B*
Bridgewater State College *B*
Clark University *B*
College of the Holy Cross *B*
Hampshire College *B*
Harvard College *B*
Massachusetts College of Art and
    Design *B*
Mount Holyoke College *B*
Salem State College *B*
Simmons College *B*
Smith College *B*
Stonehill College *B*
Suffolk University *B*
Tufts University *B, M*
University of Massachusetts
    Amherst *B, M*
    Dartmouth *B*
Wellesley College *B*
Wheaton College *B*
Williams College *B, M*

Michigan

Albion College *B*
Alma College *B*
Andrews University *B*
Aquinas College *B*
Calvin College *B*
Eastern Michigan University *B*
Ferris State University *B*
Grand Valley State University *B*
Hope College *B*
Kalamazoo College *B*
Kendall College of Art and Design of
    Ferris State University *B*
Madonna University *B*
Michigan State University *B*
Northern Michigan University *B*
Oakland University *B*
University of Michigan *B, M, D*
Wayne State University *B, M*
Western Michigan University *B*

Minnesota

Augsburg College *B*
Carleton College *B*
Gustavus Adolphus College *B*
Hamline University *B*
Minnesota State University
    Mankato *B*
St. Catherine University *B*
Saint Cloud State University *B*
St. Olaf College *B*

University of Minnesota
  Duluth *B*
  Morris *B*
  Twin Cities *B, M, D*
University of St. Thomas *B, M*

Mississippi

Millsaps College *B*
University of Mississippi *B*

Missouri

Drury University *B*
Kansas City Art Institute *B*
Lindenwood University *B*
Missouri State University *B*
Saint Louis University *B*
Truman State University *B*
University of Missouri
  Kansas City *B, M, D*
  St. Louis *B*
Washington University in St.
  Louis *B, M, D*

Montana

University of Montana *B, M*

Nebraska

Bellevue University *B*
University of Nebraska
  Kearney *B*
  Lincoln *B*
  Omaha *B*

Nevada

University of Nevada
  Reno *B*

New Hampshire

Dartmouth College *B*
New England College *B*

New Jersey

Drew University *B*
Kean University *B*
Princeton University *B, M, D*
Rutgers, The State University of New
  Jersey
  New Brunswick/Piscataway
    Campus *B, M, D*
Seton Hall University *B*

New Mexico

College of Santa Fe *B*
Santa Fe Community College *A*
University of New Mexico *B, M, D*

New York

Adelphi University *B*
Bard College *B, M, D*
Barnard College *B*
Canisius College *B*
City University of New York
  Brooklyn College *B, M*
  City College *B, M*
  Hunter College *B, M*
  Lehman College *B, M*
  Queens College *B, M*
  York College *B*
Colgate University *B*
College of New Rochelle *B, T*
Columbia University *B*
Columbia University
  School of General Studies *B*
Cornell University *B, M, D*
Fordham University *B*
Hamilton College *B*
Hartwick College *B*
Hobart and William Smith Colleges *B*
Hofstra University *B*
Ithaca College *B*
Long Island University
  C. W. Post Campus *B*

Manhattanville College *B*
Marist College *B*
Marymount Manhattan College *B*
Nazareth College *B*
New York University *M, D*
Pace University *B*
Parsons The New School for
  Design *M*
Pratt Institute *B, M*
Saint Bonaventure University *B*
School of Visual Arts *B, M*
Skidmore College *B*
State University of New York
  Albany *B*
  Binghamton *B, M, D*
  Buffalo *B, M*
  College at Buffalo *B, M*
  College at Fredonia *B*
  College at Geneseo *B*
  College at Oneonta *B*
  College at Potsdam *B*
  New Paltz *B*
  Purchase *B, M*
  Stony Brook *B, M, D*
Syracuse University *B*
University of Rochester *B*
Wells College *B*

North Carolina

Duke University *B, D*
East Carolina University *B*
Elon University *B*
Salem College *B*
University of North Carolina
  Chapel Hill *B, M, D*
  Charlotte *B*
  Wilmington *B*
Wake Forest University *B*

Ohio

Art Academy of Cincinnati *B*
Baldwin-Wallace College *B*
Bowling Green State University *B*
Case Western Reserve
  University *B, M, D*
College of Wooster *B*
Denison University *B*
Hiram College *B*
John Carroll University *B*
Kent State University *B, M*
Kenyon College *B*
Lourdes College *B*
Miami University
  Oxford Campus *B*
Oberlin College *B*
Ohio State University
  Columbus Campus *B, M, D*
Ohio University *B, M*
Ohio Wesleyan University *B*
University of Akron *B*
University of Cincinnati *C, B, M*
University of Dayton *B*
University of Toledo *B*
Ursuline College *B*
Virginia Marti College of Art and
  Design *A*
Wright State University *B*
Youngstown State University *B*

Oklahoma

Oklahoma City University *B, M*
University of Central Oklahoma *B*
University of Oklahoma *B, M, D*
University of Tulsa *B*

Oregon

Art Institute of Portland *B*
Mt. Hood Community College *A*
Portland State University *B*
University of Oregon *B, M, D*
Willamette University *B*

Pennsylvania

Allegheny College *B*
Arcadia University *B*
Bloomsburg University of
  Pennsylvania *B*
Bryn Mawr College *B, M, D*
Bucknell University *B*
Chatham University *B*
Duquesne University *B*
Edinboro University of
  Pennsylvania *B*
Franklin & Marshall College *B*
Gettysburg College *B*
Haverford College *B*
Juniata College *B*
La Salle University *B*
Lehigh University *B*
Lycoming College *B*
Mansfield University of
  Pennsylvania *B*
Marywood University *M*
Messiah College *B*
Moore College of Art and Design *B*
Moravian College *B*
Penn State
  Abington *B*
  Altoona *B*
  Beaver *B*
  Berks *B*
  Brandywine *B*
  DuBois *B*
  Erie, The Behrend College *B*
  Fayette, The Eberly Campus *B*
  Greater Allegheny *B*
  Hazleton *B*
  Lehigh Valley *B*
  Mont Alto *B*
  New Kensington *B*
  Schuylkill *B*
  Shenango *B*
  University Park *B, M, D*
  Wilkes-Barre *B*
  Worthington Scranton *B*
  York *B*
Rosemont College *B*
St. Vincent College *B*
Seton Hill University *B*
Susquehanna University *B*
Swarthmore College *B*
Temple University *B, M, D*
University of Pennsylvania *B, M, D*
University of Pittsburgh *B, M, D*
Ursinus College *B*
Villanova University *B*

Puerto Rico

Caribbean University *M*
University of Puerto Rico
  Aguadilla *A*
  Rio Piedras *B*

Rhode Island

Brown University *B, M, D*
Providence College *B*
Rhode Island College *B*
Roger Williams University *B*
Salve Regina University *B*
University of Rhode Island *B*

South Carolina

College of Charleston *B*
Converse College *B*
Presbyterian College *B*
University of South Carolina *B, M*
Winthrop University *B*
Wofford College *B*

Tennessee

Lambuth University *B*
Middle Tennessee State University *B*
Tennessee State University *B*
University of Memphis *B, M*

University of Tennessee
  Knoxville *B*
University of the South *B*
Vanderbilt University *B, M*

Texas

Baylor University *B*
Lamar University *M*
Lon Morris College *A*
Rice University *B*
Southern Methodist University *B, M*
Southwestern University *B*
Stephen F. Austin State University *B*
Texas A&M University
  Commerce *M, D*
Texas Christian University *B, M*
Texas Tech University *B*
Trinity University *B*
University of Dallas *B*
University of Houston *B*
University of North Texas *B, M*
University of Texas
  Arlington *B*
  Austin *B, M, D*
  El Paso *B*
  San Antonio *B, M*
University of the Incarnate Word *B*

Utah

Brigham Young University *B, M*
University of Utah *B, M*

Vermont

Bennington College *B*
Marlboro College *B*
Middlebury College *B*
University of Vermont *B*

Virginia

George Mason University *M*
Hollins University *B*
James Madison University *B*
Longwood University *B*
Old Dominion University *B*
Randolph College *B*
Randolph-Macon College *B*
Roanoke College *B*
Sweet Briar College *B*
University of Mary Washington *B*
University of Richmond *B*
University of Virginia *M, D*
Virginia Commonwealth
  University *B, M, D*
Washington and Lee University *B*

Washington

Eastern Washington University *B*
Seattle University *B*
University of Washington *B, M, D*
Western Washington University *B*
Whitman College *B*

West Virginia

West Virginia University *B*

Wisconsin

Beloit College *B*
Carthage College *B*
Lawrence University *B, T*
Ripon College *B*
University of Wisconsin
  Madison *B, M, D*
  Milwaukee *B, M*
  Superior *B, M*
  Whitewater *B, T*

Art teacher education

Alabama

Alabama Agricultural and Mechanical
  University *M*
Birmingham-Southern College *B, T*

University of Alabama
Birmingham *M*

Alaska
University of Alaska
Fairbanks *T*

Arizona
Cochise College *A*
Eastern Arizona College *A*
Northern Arizona University *B, T*
Prescott College *B, M, T*
University of Arizona *B, M*

Arkansas
Arkansas Tech University *B*
Harding University *B, T*
Henderson State University *B, M, T*
Ouachita Baptist University *B, T*
Southern Arkansas University *B, T*
University of Arkansas
Pine Bluff *B, T*
University of the Ozarks *T*
Williams Baptist College *B*

California
Academy of Art University *B, M*
Azusa Pacific University *B, T*
California Baptist University *T*
California Lutheran University *B, T*
California State University
Chico *B, T*
Long Beach *B, T*
Northridge *B, T*
San Bernardino *T*
Cuesta College *A*
Humboldt State University *T*
Mills College *T*
Mount St. Mary's College *T*
Point Loma Nazarene University *B*
San Diego State University *T*
San Francisco State University *T*
Sonoma State University *T*
University of San Francisco *M*
University of the Pacific *T*
Westmont College *T*

Colorado
Adams State College *B, M, T*
Colorado State University *B, T*
Colorado State University
Pueblo *T*
Metropolitan State College of
Denver *B, T*
Rocky Mountain College of Art &
Design *B*
Western State College of
Colorado *B, T*

Connecticut
Albertus Magnus College *B, T*
Central Connecticut State
University *B, M, T*
Southern Connecticut State
University *B, M, T*

Delaware
Delaware State University *B*

District of Columbia
Corcoran College of Art and
Design *B, M*
Gallaudet University *B, T*
George Washington University *M, T*
Howard University *B*
University of the District of
Columbia *B*

Florida
Flagler College *B, T*
Florida Agricultural and Mechanical
University *B, T*

Florida Atlantic University *M*
Florida International University *B, M*
Florida Southern College *B, T*
Florida State University *M, D*
Palm Beach Atlantic University *B, T*
Palm Beach Community College *A*
Pensacola Junior College *A*
University of Central Florida *B, M*
University of Florida *B*
University of North Florida *B*
University of South Florida *B, M*
University of West Florida *B*

Georgia
Armstrong Atlantic State
University *B, M, T*
Brenau University *B*
Columbus State University *B, M*
Darton College *A*
Gainesville State College *A*
Georgia State University *B, M*
Kennesaw State University *B*
North Georgia College & State
University *B, M*
Piedmont College *M, T*
Savannah College of Art and
Design *M*
Shorter College *B*
University of Georgia *M, D, T*
University of West Georgia *M*
Valdosta State University *B, M*
Young Harris College *A*

Idaho
Boise State University *B, M, T*
Brigham Young University-Idaho *T*
Northwest Nazarene University *B*
University of Idaho *B, T*

Illinois
Augustana College *B, T*
Blackburn College *B, T*
Bradley University *B, M*
Chicago State University *B*
City Colleges of Chicago
Olive-Harvey College *A*
Columbia College Chicago *M*
DePaul University *B, M, T*
Dominican University *T*
Elmhurst College *B*
Illinois College *T*
John A. Logan College *A*
Judson University *B*
Knox College *T*
Lewis University *T*
Lincoln College *A*
McKendree University *B*
Millikin University *B, T*
Monmouth College *T*
North Central College *B, T*
North Park University *T*
Northern Illinois University *B, M, T*
Olivet Nazarene University *B, T*
Parkland College *A*
Rockford College *T*
Saint Xavier University *B*
School of the Art Institute of
Chicago *B, M*
Trinity Christian College *B, T*
University of Illinois
Chicago *B*
Urbana-Champaign *B, M, D, T*
University of St. Francis *B, M*

Indiana
Anderson University *B, T*
Bethel College *B*
Calumet College of St. Joseph *T*
Goshen College *B, T*
Grace College *B*
Huntington University *B*
Indiana State University *B, T*

Indiana University
Bloomington *B, M*
Indiana University-Purdue University
Fort Wayne *B, T*
Indiana University-Purdue University
Indianapolis *B, M, T*
Indiana Wesleyan University *B, T*
Oakland City University *B*
Purdue University *B, M, D*
Saint Joseph's College *B*
Saint Mary's College *T*
St. Mary-of-the-Woods College *B, T*
Taylor University *B, T*
University of Evansville *B, T*
University of Indianapolis *B, M, T*
University of St. Francis *B, T*
Valparaiso University *B*
Vincennes University *A*

Iowa
Briar Cliff University *B*
Buena Vista University *B, T*
Central College *T*
Coe College *B*
Cornell College *B, T*
Dordt College *B*
Drake University *T*
Graceland University *T*
Grand View University *M, T*
Iowa State University *T*
Iowa Wesleyan College *B*
Loras College *B*
Maharishi University of
Management *T*
Morningside College *B*
Mount Mercy College *T*
Northwestern College *T*
St. Ambrose University *B, T*
Simpson College *T*
University of Iowa *M, D, T*
Upper Iowa University *T*
Wartburg College *B, T*

Kansas
Baker University *B, T*
Bethany College *T*
Bethel College *T*
Friends University *B*
Garden City Community College *A*
Kansas State University *B, T*
Kansas Wesleyan University *B, T*
McPherson College *B, T*
Pittsburg State University *B, M, T*
Sterling College *T*
University of Kansas *B, M, T*
Washburn University *B*
Wichita State University *B, M, T*

Kentucky
Asbury College *B, T*
Berea College *B, T*
Brescia University *B, T*
Campbellsville University *B*
Eastern Kentucky University *B*
Kentucky Wesleyan College *B, T*
Lindsey Wilson College *B, T*
Murray State University *B, T*
Thomas More College *B*
University of Kentucky *B, M*
University of Louisville *M*
University of the Cumberlands *B, M, T*
Western Kentucky University *M, T*

Louisiana
Centenary College of Louisiana *B, T*
Grambling State University *B*
Louisiana College *B*
Louisiana State University
Shreveport *B*
Louisiana Tech University *B*
McNeese State University *B, T*
Nicholls State University *B*
Southeastern Louisiana University *B*

Southern University and Agricultural
and Mechanical College *B*
University of Louisiana at Lafayette *B*
University of Louisiana at Monroe *B*
Xavier University of Louisiana *B*

Maine
Maine College of Art *T*
University of Maine *B*
University of Maine
Presque Isle *B*
University of New England *B*
University of Southern Maine *B, T*

Maryland
Bowie State University *M*
College of Notre Dame of Maryland *T*
Hood College *T*
Maryland Institute College of
Art *B, M, T*
Mount St. Mary's University *T*
Salisbury University *T*
Towson University *B, M, T*
University of Maryland
College Park *B*
Eastern Shore *B*

Massachusetts
Anna Maria College *B, M*
Art Institute of Boston at Lesley
University *B, M*
Assumption College *T*
Boston University *B, M*
Bridgewater State College *B, M, T*
Fitchburg State College *M*
Framingham State College *M*
Harvard College *M, D*
Lesley University *B*
Massachusetts College of Art and
Design *B, M, T*
Montserrat College of Art *T*
School of the Museum of Fine
Arts *M, T*
Springfield College *B*
Tufts University *M, T*
University of Massachusetts
Dartmouth *B, M, T*
Westfield State College *B, T*

Michigan
Adrian College *B, T*
Albion College *T*
Alma College *T*
Andrews University *M*
Calvin College *B*
Central Michigan University *B*
Delta College *A*
Eastern Michigan University *B, M*
Ferris State University *B, M*
Grand Rapids Community College *A*
Grand Valley State University *T*
Hope College *B, T*
Kendall College of Art and Design of
Ferris State University *B, M*
Lansing Community College *A*
Michigan State University *B*
Northern Michigan University *B, T*
Spring Arbor University *B*
University of Michigan
Dearborn *B*
Flint *B, T*
Wayne State University *B, M, T*
Western Michigan University *B, M, T*

Minnesota
Augsburg College *T*
Bemidji State University *T*
Bethel University *B*
College of St. Benedict *T*
Concordia College: Moorhead *B, T*
Concordia University: St. Paul *B, T*
Gustavus Adolphus College *T*
Hamline University *B*

Minnesota State University
   Mankato *B, M, T*
   Moorhead *B*
Northwestern College *B*
Ridgewater College *A*
St. Catherine University *B, M, T*
Saint Cloud State University *B*
St. John's University *T*
Southwest Minnesota State
   University *B, T*
University of Minnesota
   Duluth *B, T*
   Morris *T*
   Twin Cities *B, M, T*
Vermilion Community College *A*
Winona State University *B, T*

Mississippi

Millsaps College *T*
Mississippi College *B, M*
Mississippi Delta Community
   College *A*
Mississippi Gulf Coast Community
   College *A*
Mississippi University for Women *B, T*
Northwest Mississippi Community
   College *A*
University of Southern Mississippi *M*

Missouri

College of the Ozarks *B, T*
Culver-Stockton College *B, T*
Evangel University *B, T*
Hannibal-LaGrange College *B*
Lincoln University *B*
Lindenwood University *B*
Maryville University of Saint
   Louis *B, M, T*
Missouri Southern State
   University *B, T*
Missouri State University *B*
Missouri Western State University *B*
Northwest Missouri State
   University *B, T*
Park University *T*
Southeast Missouri State
   University *B, T*
Southwest Baptist University *B, T*
Truman State University *M, T*
University of Central Missouri *B, T*
University of Missouri
   Columbia *B, M, D*
   Kansas City *B*
Washington University in St.
   Louis *B, M, T*
William Jewell College *B, T*
William Woods University *B, T*

Montana

Montana State University
   Billings *B, T*
Rocky Mountain College *B, T*
University of Great Falls *B*
University of Montana *B, T*
University of Montana: Western *B, T*

Nebraska

Chadron State College *B*
Concordia University *B, T*
Creighton University *T*
Dana College *B*
Nebraska Wesleyan University *T*
Peru State College *B, T*
Union College *T*
University of Nebraska
   Kearney *B, M, T*
   Lincoln *B*
Wayne State College *B, T*
Western Nebraska Community
   College *A*
York College *B, T*

Nevada

University of Nevada
   Reno *B, T*

New Hampshire

Colby-Sawyer College *B, T*
Franklin Pierce University *M, T*
New England College *B, T*
Plymouth State University *B, T*
University of New Hampshire *B, T*

New Jersey

Caldwell College *T*
The College of New Jersey *B, T*
College of St. Elizabeth *T*
Cumberland County College *A*
Georgian Court University *T*
Kean University *M*
New Jersey City University *M, T*
Rowan University *B*
Seton Hall University *B*
William Paterson University of New
   Jersey *B, T*

New Mexico

New Mexico Highlands University *B*
University of New Mexico *B, M*
Western New Mexico University *B*

New York

Adelphi University *B, M, T*
Alfred University *B, T*
City University of New York
   Brooklyn College *M, T*
   City College *B, M, T*
   Hunter College *B*
   Lehman College *M*
   Queens College *B, M, T*
College of New Rochelle *B, M, T*
College of Saint Rose *B, M, T*
Daemen College *B, T*
Dowling College *B*
Elmira College *B, T*
Fordham University *T*
Hofstra University *B, M, T*
Ithaca College *B, T*
Long Island University
   Brooklyn Campus *B, T*
   C. W. Post Campus *B, M, T*
Manhattanville College *M, T*
Marymount Manhattan College *T*
Molloy College *B*
Nazareth College *B, M, T*
New York Institute of
   Technology *B, T*
New York University *B, M, D*
Pratt Institute *B, M*
Roberts Wesleyan College *B*
Rochester Institute of Technology *M*
St. Lawrence University *T*
St. Thomas Aquinas College *B, T*
School of Visual Arts *M*
State University of New York
   College at Buffalo *B, M, T*
   New Paltz *B, M, T*
   Oswego *M*
Syracuse University *B, M, T*

North Carolina

Appalachian State University *B, T*
Barton College *B, T*
Brevard College *B*
East Carolina University *B, M*
Elizabeth City State University *B, T*
Greensboro College *B, T*
High Point University *B, T*
Lenoir Community College *A*
Lenoir-Rhyne University *B, T*
Mars Hill College *B, T*
Meredith College *B, T*
Methodist University *B, T*
North Carolina Central University *B, T*

University of North Carolina
   Charlotte *B*
   Greensboro *B*
   Pembroke *B, M*
Western Carolina University *B, T*
Wingate University *B, T*
Winston-Salem State University *B*

North Dakota

Dickinson State University *B, T*
Minot State University *B*

Ohio

Art Academy of Cincinnati *M*
Ashland University *B, T*
Bluffton University *B*
Bowling Green State
   University *B, M, T*
Capital University *T*
Case Western Reserve University *B, M*
College of Mount St. Joseph *B, T*
Defiance College *B, T*
Hiram College *T*
Kent State University *B, M*
Malone University *B*
Miami University
   Oxford Campus *B, M*
Mount Union College *T*
Mount Vernon Nazarene
   University *B, T*
Notre Dame College *T*
Ohio Dominican University *B, T*
Ohio Northern University *B, T*
Ohio State University
   Columbus Campus *B, M, D*
Ohio University *B, T*
Ohio Wesleyan University *B*
Otterbein College *B*
University of Akron *B, M*
University of Cincinnati *B, M, T*
University of Dayton *B, M, T*
University of Findlay *B, M, T*
University of Rio Grande *B, T*
University of Toledo *B, M, T*
Ursuline College *B, M, T*
Wilberforce University *T*
Wright State University *B, M, T*
Youngstown State University *B, M*

Oklahoma

Cameron University *B, T*
Eastern Oklahoma State College *A*
Northeastern State University *B*
Oklahoma Baptist University *B, T*
Oklahoma Christian University *B, T*
Oklahoma City University *B*
Oral Roberts University *B, T*
Southeastern Oklahoma State
   University *B, T*
Southwestern Oklahoma State
   University *B, M, T*
University of Central Oklahoma *B*

Oregon

Linfield College *T*
Portland State University *T*
Southern Oregon University *T*

Pennsylvania

Albright College *B, T*
Arcadia University *B, M, T*
Carlow University *B, M, T*
Chatham University *M*
Holy Family University *B*
Keystone College *T*
Lebanon Valley College *T*
Lincoln University *T*
Lycoming College *T*
Mansfield University of
   Pennsylvania *B, M, T*
Marywood University *B, M*
Mercyhurst College *B, T*
Messiah College *B, T*

Moore College of Art and Design *B, T*
Moravian College *T*
Penn State
   Abington *B*
   Altoona *B*
   Beaver *B*
   Berks *B*
   Brandywine *B*
   DuBois *B*
   Erie, The Behrend College *B*
   Fayette, The Eberly Campus *B*
   Greater Allegheny *B*
   Hazleton *B*
   Lehigh Valley *B*
   Mont Alto *B*
   New Kensington *B*
   Schuylkill *B*
   Shenango *B*
   University Park *B, M, D*
   Wilkes-Barre *B*
   Worthington Scranton *B*
   York *B*
Rosemont College *T*
Saint Joseph's University *B*
St. Vincent College *B*
Seton Hill University *B, T*
Temple University *B, M*
University of the Arts *M*
Washington & Jefferson College *B, T*
Waynesburg University *B*

Puerto Rico

Escuela de Artes Plasticas de Puerto
   Rico *B*
Inter American University of Puerto
   Rico
   San German Campus *B*
Pontifical Catholic University of
   Puerto Rico *B, T*
Turabo University *M*

Rhode Island

Rhode Island College *B, M*
Rhode Island School of Design *M*

South Carolina

Anderson University *B, T*
Bob Jones University *B*
Claflin University *B*
Coker College *B, T*
Converse College *T*
Francis Marion University *T*
Furman University *T*
Limestone College *B*
South Carolina State University *B, T*
University of South Carolina *B, M*
University of South Carolina
   Upstate *M*
Winthrop University *M, T*

South Dakota

Augustana College *B, T*
Black Hills State University *B*
Dakota Wesleyan University *B, T*
Northern State University *B, T*
University of Sioux Falls *B*
University of South Dakota *T*

Tennessee

Belmont University *B, M, T*
Bethel University *T*
Freed-Hardeman University *B, T*
Lambuth University *B, T*
Lincoln Memorial University *B, T*
Lipscomb University *B, T*
Memphis College of Art *M, T*
Middle Tennessee State University *B*
Southern Adventist University *B*
Tennessee Technological University *T*
Tusculum College *B, T*
Union University *B, T*
University of Tennessee
   Chattanooga *B*

Knoxville *B, T*

Texas

Abilene Christian University *B, T*
Austin College *M*
Hardin-Simmons University *B, T*
Houston Baptist University *B, M*
Howard Payne University *B, T*
Kilgore College *A*
Lamar University *B, M, T* ·
Laredo Community College *A*
Lubbock Christian University *B*
McMurry University *B, T*
St. Edward's University *B, T*
Sam Houston State University *M, T*
Southwestern University *T*
Tarleton State University *T*
Texas A&M University
  Commerce *T*
  Kingsville *B, M*
Texas Christian University *B*
Texas College *B, T*
Texas State University: San Marcos *T*
Texas Tech University *M*
Texas Wesleyan University *T*
University of Dallas *T*
University of Houston *M, T*
University of Houston
  Clear Lake *T*
University of Mary Hardin-Baylor *T*
University of North Texas *M, D, T*
University of Texas
  Arlington *T*
  Austin *M*
  El Paso *M*
  San Antonio *T*
University of the Incarnate Word *T*
West Texas A&M University *T*

Utah

Southern Utah University *B, T*
Weber State University *B*
Westminster College *M*

Vermont

Castleton State College *B, T*
Goddard College *B*
Green Mountain College *B, T*
Johnson State College *B*
St. Michael's College *B, M, T*
University of Vermont *B, T*

Virginia

Averett University *B, M, T*
Bluefield College *B, T*
Bridgewater College *T*
Eastern Mennonite University *T*
Emory & Henry College *B*
Hollins University *T*
Longwood University *B, T*
Northern Virginia Community
  College *A*
Old Dominion University *B, T*
Radford University *T*
Virginia Commonwealth
  University *B, M*
Virginia Intermont College *B, T*
Virginia Wesleyan College *B, T*

Washington

Eastern Washington University *B*
Seattle Pacific University *B, T*
Western Washington University *B, M*
Whitworth University *M, T*

West Virginia

Bethany College *B*
Concord University *B, T*
Fairmont State University *B*
Shepherd University *T*
West Liberty University *B*
West Virginia State University *B*
West Virginia University *T*

West Virginia Wesleyan College *B*

Wisconsin

Alverno College *B, T*
Beloit College *B, T*
Carroll University *B, T*
Carthage College *M, T*
Concordia University Wisconsin *B, M*
Edgewood College *B, T*
Lawrence University *T*
Marian University *B, T*
Mount Mary College *B, T*
Silver Lake College *B, T*
University of Wisconsin
  Green Bay *T*
  Madison *B, M*
  Milwaukee *B, M*
  Parkside *T*
  Platteville *B*
  River Falls *B, T*
  Stout *B, T*
  Superior *B, T*
  Whitewater *B*
Viterbo University *B, T*

Wyoming

Casper College *A*

Art therapy

Arizona

Prescott College *B, M*

Arkansas

Harding University *B*

California

California Institute of Integral
  Studies *M*
Loyola Marymount University *B*
Notre Dame de Namur University *M*

Connecticut

Albertus Magnus College *B, M*

District of Columbia

George Washington University *M*

Florida

Florida State University *M*

Illinois

DePaul University *B*
Millikin University *B*
School of the Art Institute of
  Chicago *M*
Southern Illinois University
  Edwardsville *M*

Indiana

St. Mary-of-the-Woods College *M*
University of Indianapolis *B*
Vincennes University *A*

Kansas

Bethany College *B*
Emporia State University *M*

Kentucky

University of Louisville *M*

Massachusetts

Anna Maria College *B*
Emmanuel College *B*
Lesley University *B, M, D*
Springfield College *B, M*

Michigan

Marygrove College *B*

New York

College of New Rochelle *B, M, T*
Hofstra University *M*
Long Island University
  C. W. Post Campus *B, M*
Nazareth College *M*
Pratt Institute *M*
St. Thomas Aquinas College *B*
School of Visual Arts *M*

Ohio

Bowling Green State University *B*
Capital University *B*
Ursuline College *M*

Oregon

Marylhurst University *M*

Pennsylvania

Arcadia University *B*
Carlow University *B*
Marywood University *B, M*
Mercyhurst College *B*
Seton Hill University *B, M*

South Carolina

Converse College *B*

Tennessee

Southern Adventist University *B*

Vermont

Goddard College *M*

West Virginia

West Virginia University *D*

Wisconsin

Alverno College *B*
Edgewood College *B*
Mount Mary College *B, M*
University of Wisconsin
  Superior *B, M*

Artificial intelligence/ robotics

Arizona

University of Advancing
  Technology *A, B, M*

Arkansas

East Arkansas Community College *C*

California

University of Southern California *M*

Florida

Gulf Coast Community College *A*

Georgia

Georgia Institute of Technology *D*
University of Georgia *M*

Massachusetts

Worcester Polytechnic Institute *B*

Michigan

Henry Ford Community College *C*
Wayne County Community College *A*

New Hampshire

Daniel Webster College *B*

New York

Globe Institute of Technology *A, B*
Rochester Institute of Technology *M*

Pennsylvania ·

Carnegie Mellon University *M, D*

Texas

Texas State Technical College:
  Marshall *A*

Arts management

Alabama

Spring Hill College *B*

Arizona

Northern Arizona University *B*

California

California State University
  East Bay *B*
Santa Rosa Junior College *C*
University of San Francisco *B*

Delaware

Delaware State University *B*

District of Columbia

American University *M*
Howard University *B*

Florida

Florida State University *M*
Lynn University *B*
Ringling College of Art and Design *B*

Georgia

Brenau University *B*
Savannah College of Art and
  Design *M*

Illinois

Benedictine University *B*
Columbia College Chicago *C, B, M*
DePaul University *B*
Eureka College *B*
School of the Art Institute of
  Chicago *M*

Indiana

Butler University *B*
Indiana University
  Bloomington *M*

Iowa

Buena Vista University *B*
University of Iowa *B*
Upper Iowa University *B*
Waldorf College *B*

Kansas

Kansas Wesleyan University *B*

Kentucky

Bellarmine University *B*
Bluegrass Community and Technical
  College *A*
University of Kentucky *B*

Louisiana

Dillard University *B*
Southeastern Louisiana University *B*
University of New Orleans *M*

Maine

University of Maine
  Farmington *B*
University of Southern Maine *B*

Maryland

Goucher College *M*
Howard Community College *C, A*

Massachusetts
Dean College *B*
Fitchburg State College *M*
Massachusetts College of Liberal
  Arts *B*
Simmons College *B*
Suffolk University *B*

Michigan
Adrian College *B*
Aquinas College *B*
Bay de Noc Community College *C*
Eastern Michigan University *B*

Minnesota
Art Institutes International
  Minnesota *B*
St. Mary's University of Minnesota *M*

Mississippi
Belhaven University *B*

Missouri
Culver-Stockton College *B*
Drury University *B*
Lindenwood University *B, M*
Webster University *M*

Nebraska
Bellevue University *B*
Concordia University *B*

New Hampshire
Franklin Pierce University *B*

New Jersey
Rider University *B*

New Mexico
Santa Fe Community College *A*

New York
City University of New York
  Baruch College *B*
Daemen College *B, M*
Fashion Institute of Technology *B, M*
Herkimer County Community
  College *A*
Ithaca College *B*
Long Island University
  C. W. Post Campus *B*
Pratt Institute *M*
State University of New York
  Buffalo *M*
  Purchase *B*
Wagner College *B*

North Carolina
Appalachian State University *B*
Bennett College for Women *B*
Catawba College *B*
Lees-McRae College *B*
Lenoir-Rhyne University *B*
North Carolina State University *B*
Pfeiffer University *B*
Salem College *B*
University of North Carolina
  Charlotte *M*

North Dakota
Minot State University *B*

Ohio
Owens Community College
  Toledo *A*
Tiffin University *B*
University of Cincinnati *M*
Wright State University *B*

Oklahoma
Oklahoma City University *B, M*

University of Tulsa *B*

Oregon
Art Institute of Portland *B*
University of Oregon *M*

Pennsylvania
Carnegie Mellon University *M*
Chatham University *B*
Drexel University *M*
Marywood University *B*
Messiah College *B*
St. Vincent College *B*
Seton Hill University *B*
Waynesburg University *B*

Puerto Rico
Turabo University *M*
University of Puerto Rico
  Rio Piedras *M*

South Carolina
College of Charleston *B*

South Dakota
University of South Dakota *B*

Texas
El Paso Community College *C*
Southern Methodist University *M*
Texas A&M University
  Commerce *B*

Utah
Southern Utah University *M*
Westminster College *B*

Virginia
George Mason University *M*
Mary Baldwin College *B*
Randolph-Macon College *B*
Shenandoah University *B, M*

West Virginia
West Virginia Wesleyan College *B*

Wisconsin
University of Wisconsin
  Madison *M*
  Stevens Point *B*
Viterbo University *B*

Asian-American studies

California
California State University
  East Bay *B*
  Fullerton *B*
Claremont McKenna College *B*
De Anza College *A*
El Camino College *A*
Los Angeles City College *A*
Pitzer College *B*
Pomona College *B*
San Francisco State University *B, M*
Scripps College *B*
Solano Community College *A*
Southwestern College *A*
Stanford University *B*
University of California
  Berkeley *B*
  Davis *B*
  Irvine *B*
  Los Angeles *B, M*
  Riverside *B*
University of Southern California *B*

Colorado
University of Denver *B*

Massachusetts
Hampshire College *B*

New York
Columbia University *B*

Pennsylvania
Gettysburg College *B*

Washington
University of Washington *B*

Asian bodywork therapy

New York
Swedish Institute *A*

Pennsylvania
Keystone Technical Institute *C, A*

Asian history

Massachusetts
Harvard College *D*

New York
Bard College *B*

Pennsylvania
Gettysburg College *B*

Asian studies

Alabama
Samford University *B*

California
Cabrillo College *A*
California Institute of Integral
  Studies *M, D*
California State University
  Chico *B*
  Long Beach *B, M*
  Sacramento *B, M*
  San Bernardino *M*
Claremont McKenna College *B*
Cypress College *A*
Laney College *A*
Loyola Marymount University *B*
Occidental College *B*
Pepperdine University *B*
Pitzer College *B*
Pomona College *B*
San Diego State University *B, M*
Scripps College *B*
University of California
  Berkeley *B, M, D*
  Los Angeles *B*
  Riverside *B*
  Santa Barbara *B, M, D*
University of Redlands *B*
University of San Francisco *M*

Colorado
Colorado College *B*
University of Colorado
  Boulder *B*

Connecticut
Trinity College *B*

Florida
Florida International University *B*
Florida State University *B, M*
Miami Dade College *A*
University of Florida *B*

Georgia
Georgia State University *B*

Hawaii
University of Hawaii
  Manoa *B, M*

Illinois
Augustana College *B*
Illinois Wesleyan University *B*
Knox College *B*
Lake Forest College *B*
Northwestern University *B*
University of Illinois
  Urbana-Champaign *M*

Indiana
Indiana University
  Bloomington *M, D*
Purdue University *B*

Iowa
Coe College *B*
University of Iowa *B, M*

Kentucky
Berea College *B*

Louisiana
Tulane University *B*

Maine
Bowdoin College *B*

Maryland
St. Mary's College of Maryland *B*
University of Maryland
  University College *B*

Massachusetts
Amherst College *B*
Bard College at Simon's Rock *B*
College of the Holy Cross *B*
Hampshire College *B*
Mount Holyoke College *B*
Northeastern University *B*
Smith College *B*
Tufts University *B, M*
Wellesley College *B*
Wheaton College *B*
Williams College *B*

Michigan
Calvin College *B*
Michigan State University *B, M, D*
University of Michigan *B*

Minnesota
Carleton College *B*
Macalester College *B*
St. Olaf College *B*

Missouri
Washington University in St. Louis *B*

Montana
University of Montana *B*

Nevada
University of Nevada
  Las Vegas *B*

New Hampshire
Dartmouth College *B*

New Jersey
Seton Hall University *B, M*

New Mexico
University of New Mexico *B*

New York
Bard College *B*

Barnard College *B*
City University of New York
   City College *B*
Colgate University *B*
Columbia University *B*
Columbia University
   School of General Studies *B*
Cornell University *B, M*
Hamilton College *B*
Hobart and William Smith Colleges *B*
Hofstra University *B*
Manhattanville College *B*
St. John's University *B*
St. Lawrence University *B*
Skidmore College *B*
State University of New York
   Albany *B*
   Binghamton *B*
   Buffalo *B*
   New Paltz *B*
   Stony Brook *B, T*
Union College *B*
Vassar College *B*

North Carolina
Duke University *B*
St. Andrews Presbyterian College *B*
University of North Carolina
   Chapel Hill *B*

Ohio
Bowling Green State University *B*
Case Western Reserve University *B*
Mount Union College *B*
Ohio University *B*
University of Cincinnati *B*
University of Toledo *B*

Oregon
Pacific University *B*
University of Oregon *B*
Willamette University *B*

Pennsylvania
Gettysburg College *B*
Lafayette College *B*
Lehigh University *B*
Swarthmore College *B*
Temple University *B*

Rhode Island
Brown University *B*

South Carolina
Furman University *B*

Tennessee
University of Tennessee
   Knoxville *B*
University of the South *B*

Texas
Baylor University *B*
Rice University *B*
Texas State University: San Marcos *B*
Trinity University *B*
University of Texas
   Austin *B, M*

Utah
Brigham Young University *B*
University of Utah *B, M*
Utah State University *B*

Vermont
Bennington College *B*
Marlboro College *B*
University of Vermont *B*

Virginia
Mary Baldwin College *B*
Old Dominion University *B*

University of Richmond *B*

Washington
Everett Community College *A*
Gonzaga University *B*
Seattle University *B*
University of Puget Sound *B*
University of Washington *B, M, D*
University of Washington Tacoma *B*
Washington State University *B*
Whitman College *B*

West Virginia
American Public University System *B*

Wisconsin
Carthage College *B*
University of Wisconsin
   Madison *B*

Astronomy

Arizona
Mesa Community College *A*
Northern Arizona University *B*
University of Arizona *B, M, D*

California
California Institute of
   Technology *B, D*
De Anza College *A*
El Camino College *A*
El Camino College: Compton
   Center *A*
Fullerton College *A*
Gavilan College *A*
Golden West College *A*
Orange Coast College *A*
Palomar College *C, A*
Pomona College *B*
Saddleback College *A*
San Bernardino Valley College *A*
San Diego State University *B, M*
San Joaquin Delta College *A*
Southwestern College *A*
University of California
   Los Angeles *M, D*
   Santa Cruz *D*
University of Southern California *B*

Colorado
Colorado Mountain College *C*
University of Colorado
   Boulder *B*

Connecticut
Wesleyan University *B, M*
Yale University *B, M, D*

Delaware
University of Delaware *B*

District of Columbia
Howard University *M, D*

Florida
Daytona State College *A*
Santa Fe College *A*
University of Florida *B, M, D*

Georgia
Emory University *B*
Georgia State University *D*
Gordon College *A*
University of Georgia *B*
Valdosta State University *B*
Young Harris College *A*

Hawaii
University of Hawaii
   Hilo *B*

Manoa *M, D*

Idaho
North Idaho College *A*

Illinois
Kishwaukee College *A*
South Suburban College of Cook
   County *A*
Southwestern Illinois College *A*
University of Chicago *D*
University of Illinois
   Urbana-Champaign *B, M, D*

Indiana
Indiana University
   Bloomington *B, M, D*
Valparaiso University *B*

Iowa
Drake University *B*
University of Iowa *B, M*

Kansas
Benedictine College *B*
Central Christian College of Kansas *A*
University of Kansas *B*

Maryland
Johns Hopkins University *B, D*
University of Maryland
   College Park *B, M, D*

Massachusetts
Amherst College *B*
Boston University *B, M, D*
Hampshire College *B*
Harvard College *M, D*
Mount Holyoke College *B*
Smith College *B*
Tufts University *B*
University of Massachusetts
   Amherst *B, M, D*
Wellesley College *B*
Wheaton College *B*
Williams College *B*

Michigan
Bay de Noc Community College *A*
Central Michigan University *B*
Michigan State University *M, D*
University of Michigan *B, M, D*

Minnesota
Minnesota State University
   Mankato *B*
University of Minnesota
   Twin Cities *B*
Vermilion Community College *A*

New Hampshire
Dartmouth College *B*

New Mexico
New Mexico State University *M, D*

New York
Barnard College *B*
Colgate University *B*
Columbia University *B*
Columbia University
   School of General Studies *B*
Cornell University *B, M, D*
Rensselaer Polytechnic Institute *M*
State University of New York
   Stony Brook *B*
Suffolk County Community College *A*
Union College *B*
Vassar College *B*

Ohio
Case Western Reserve
   University *B, M, D*
Ohio Northern University *B*
Ohio State University
   Columbus Campus *B, M, D*
Ohio Wesleyan University *B*
University of Toledo *B*
Wilmington College *B*
Youngstown State University *B*

Oklahoma
Tulsa Community College *A*
University of Oklahoma *B*

Pennsylvania
Bryn Mawr College *B*
Franklin & Marshall College *B*
Gettysburg College *B*
Haverford College *B*
Lehigh University *B*
Lycoming College *B*
Penn State
   Abington *B*
   Altoona *B*
   Beaver *B*
   Berks *B*
   Brandywine *B*
   DuBois *B*
   Erie, The Behrend College *B*
   Fayette, The Eberly Campus *B*
   Greater Allegheny *B*
   Hazleton *B*
   Lehigh Valley *B*
   Mont Alto *B*
   New Kensington *B*
   Schuylkill *B*
   Shenango *B*
   University Park *B, M, D*
   Wilkes-Barre *B*
   Worthington Scranton *B*
   York *B*
Swarthmore College *B*
Villanova University *B*

South Carolina
College of Charleston *B*

Tennessee
Vanderbilt University *M*

Texas
Baylor University *B*
Lon Morris College *A*
Rice University *B, M, D*
Texas Christian University *B*
University of Texas
   Austin *B, M, D*

Utah
Brigham Young University *B, D*

Vermont
Bennington College *B*
Marlboro College *B*

Virginia
George Mason University *B*
University of Virginia *B, M, D*

Washington
Everett Community College *A*
Highline Community College *A*
University of Washington *B, M, D*
Whitman College *B*

Wisconsin
University of Wisconsin
   Madison *B, M, D*

Wyoming
University of Wyoming *B*

Astrophysics

Alaska
University of Alaska
   Fairbanks *M, D*

Arizona
Arizona State University *M, D*
Northern Arizona University *B*

California
California Institute of
   Technology *B, M, D*
University of California
   Berkeley *B, D*
   Los Angeles *B*
   Santa Cruz *B*

Colorado
University of Colorado
   Boulder *M, D*

Connecticut
Connecticut College *B*
Yale University *B*

Georgia
Agnes Scott College *B*

Illinois
University of Chicago *D*

Indiana
Indiana University
   Bloomington *B*

Iowa
Iowa State University *M, D*

Massachusetts
Boston University *B*
Smith College *B*
Tufts University *M, D*
Wellesley College *B*
Williams College *B*

Michigan
Michigan State University *B, M, D*

Minnesota
University of Minnesota
   Twin Cities *B, M, D*

New Jersey
Princeton University *B, M, D*

New Mexico
New Mexico Institute of Mining and
   Technology *B, M, D*
University of New Mexico *B*

New York
Barnard College *B*
Colgate University *B*
Columbia University *B*
Columbia University
   School of General Studies *B*
Rochester Institute of Technology *D*

Ohio
Ohio University *B*

Oklahoma
University of Oklahoma *B*

Pennsylvania
Carnegie Mellon University *B*
Franklin & Marshall College *B*
Lehigh University *B*
Swarthmore College *B*
Villanova University *B*

South Carolina
College of Charleston *B*

Texas
Rice University *B, M, D*
Texas Christian University *D*

Washington
University of Washington *B*

Wisconsin
University of Wisconsin
   Madison *B, M, D*

Wyoming
University of Wyoming *B*

Athletic training

Alabama
Huntingdon College *B*
Samford University *B*
Troy University *B*
University of Alabama *B*
University of Mobile *B*
University of West Alabama *B*
Wallace State Community College at
   Hanceville *A*

Arizona
Grand Canyon University *B*
Northern Arizona University *B*

Arkansas
Arkansas State University *B*
Harding University *B*
Henderson State University *B*
John Brown University *B*
Ouachita Baptist University *B*
Southern Arkansas University *B*
University of Central Arkansas *B*

California
California Baptist University *M*
California Lutheran University *B*
California State University
   East Bay *B*
   Northridge *M*
Chapman University *B*
College of the Canyons *C*
Diablo Valley College *C, A*
Foothill College *C, A*
Fresno Pacific University *B*
Grossmont College *C, A*
Hope International University *B*
Orange Coast College *C, A*
Pepperdine University *B*
Point Loma Nazarene University *B*
San Bernardino Valley College *C*
San Diego Christian College *B*
San Francisco State University *C*
Santa Barbara City College *C, A*
Santa Rosa Junior College *C*
University of La Verne *B*
Vanguard University of Southern
   California *B*
Whittier College *B*

Colorado
Colorado State University *B*
Fort Lewis College *B*
Mesa State College *B*

Connecticut
Central Connecticut State
   University *B*
Quinnipiac University *B*
Sacred Heart University *B*

Delaware
University of Delaware *B*

Florida
Barry University *B*
Broward College *A*
Florida Gulf Coast University *B*
Florida International University *M*
Florida Southern College *B*
Florida State University *B*
Nova Southeastern University *B*
Palm Beach Atlantic University *B*
University of Central Florida *B*
University of Miami *B*
University of North Florida *B*
University of South Florida *B*
University of Tampa *B*

Georgia
Abraham Baldwin Agricultural
   College *A*
Andrew College *A*
Darton College *C*
Georgia Southern University *B*
Georgia State University *M*
North Georgia College & State
   University *B*
Valdosta State University *B*

Hawaii
University of Hawaii
   Manoa *M*

Idaho
Boise State University *B, M*
University of Idaho *B*

Illinois
Aurora University *B*
Eastern Illinois University *B*
Illinois State University *B*
Illinois Valley Community College *A*
Lewis University *B*
McKendree University *B*
Millikin University *B*
North Central College *B*
Olivet Nazarene University *B*
Southern Illinois University
   Carbondale *B*
Trinity International University *B*
Triton College *C*
University of Illinois
   Urbana-Champaign *B, M*
Western Illinois University *B*

Indiana
Anderson University *B*
DePauw University *B*
Franklin College *B*
Indiana State University *B, M*
Indiana Wesleyan University *B*
Manchester College *M*
Purdue University *B*
University of Evansville *B*
University of Indianapolis *B*

Iowa
Buena Vista University *B*
Central College *B*
Coe College *B*
Dordt College *B*
Ellsworth Community College *A*
Graceland University *B*
Loras College *B*
Northwestern College *B*
Simpson College *B*

University of Iowa *B, M*
University of Northern Iowa *B, M*
Upper Iowa University *B*

Kansas
Barton County Community College *A*
Benedictine College *B*
Bethany College *B*
Bethel College *B*
Central Christian College of Kansas *A*
Coffeyville Community College *A*
Dodge City Community College *A*
Emporia State University *B*
Garden City Community College *A*
Kansas State University *B*
MidAmerica Nazarene University *B*
Neosho County Community
   College *A*
Seward County Community College *A*
Southwestern College *B*
Sterling College *B*
Tabor College *B*
University of Kansas *B*
Washburn University *B*
Wichita State University *B*

Kentucky
Campbellsville University *B*
Eastern Kentucky University *M*
Georgetown College *B*
Northern Kentucky University *B*

Louisiana
Louisiana College *B*
McNeese State University *B*
Southeastern Louisiana University *B*
University of Louisiana at Lafayette *B*

Maine
University of Maine
   Presque Isle *B*
University of New England *B*
University of Southern Maine *B*

Maryland
Howard Community College *C*
Salisbury University *B*
Towson University *B*

Massachusetts
Boston University *B*
Bridgewater State College *B, M*
Dean College *A*
Endicott College *B*
Lasell College *B*
Massachusetts College of Liberal
   Arts *B*
Merrimack College *B*
Mount Wachusett Community
   College *C*
Northeastern University *B*
Salem State College *B*
Springfield College *B, M*

Michigan
Adrian College *B*
Aquinas College *B*
Calvin College *B*
Central Michigan University *B*
Eastern Michigan University *B*
Grand Valley State University *B*
Hope College *B*
Michigan State University *B*
Northern Michigan University *B*
Saginaw Valley State University *B*
University of Michigan *B*
Western Michigan University *B*

Minnesota
Bethel University *B*
Gustavus Adolphus College *B*
Lake Superior College *C*

Minnesota State University
  Mankato *B, M, T*
  Moorhead *B*
Northland Community & Technical
  College *A*
Ridgewater College *A*
St. Paul College *C, A*
University of Minnesota
  Duluth *B*
Winona State University *B*

Mississippi
Alcorn State University *B*
Delta State University *B*
University of Southern Mississippi *B*

Missouri
Central Methodist University *B*
Culver-Stockton College *B*
Lindenwood University *B*
Missouri Baptist University *B*
Missouri State University *B*
Missouri Valley College *B*
Park University *B*
Saint Louis University *B, M*
Southwest Baptist University *B*
William Woods University *B*

Montana
Montana State University
  Billings *B, M*
Rocky Mountain College *B*
University of Montana *B*

Nebraska
Creighton University *B*
Nebraska Wesleyan University *B*
University of Nebraska
  Lincoln *B*
Wayne State College *B*
Western Nebraska Community
  College *A*

Nevada
University of Nevada
  Las Vegas *B*

New Hampshire
Colby-Sawyer College *B*
Keene State College *B*
Plymouth State University *B*
University of New Hampshire *B*

New Jersey
Kean University *B*
Montclair State University *B*
Rowan University *B*
Seton Hall University *M*

New Mexico
New Mexico Junior College *A*
New Mexico State University *B*

New York
Alfred University *B*
Canisius College *B*
Daemen College *M*
Dominican College of Blauvelt *B*
Finger Lakes Community College *A*
Hofstra University *B*
Ithaca College *B*
Marist College *B*
State University of New York
  College at Brockport *B*
  College at Cortland *B*
Suffolk County Community College *A*

North Carolina
Appalachian State University *B*
Barton College *B*
Campbell University *B*
Catawba College *B*

Chowan University *B*
East Carolina University *B, M*
Gardner-Webb University *B*
Greensboro College *C, B*
Guilford College *B*
High Point University *B*
Lenoir-Rhyne University *B*
Mars Hill College *B*
Methodist University *B*
North Carolina Central University *B*
Pfeiffer University *B*
Shaw University *B*
University of North Carolina
  Charlotte *B*
  Pembroke *B*
  Wilmington *B*
Western Carolina University *B*
Wingate University *B*

North Dakota
Mayville State University *B*
North Dakota State University *M*
University of Mary *B*
University of North Dakota *B*

Ohio
Ashland University *B*
Baldwin-Wallace College *B*
Bowling Green State University *B*
Capital University *B*
Cedarville University *B*
Cincinnati State Technical and
  Community College *C*
College of Mount St. Joseph *B*
Defiance College *C, B*
Heidelberg University *B*
Kent State University *B*
Marietta College *B*
Miami University
  Oxford Campus *B*
Mount Union College *B*
Ohio Northern University *B*
Ohio University *B, M*
Otterbein College *B*
Shawnee State University *B*
University of Akron *C, B, M*
University of Findlay *B, M*
Urbana University *B*
Xavier University *B*
Youngstown State University *B*

Oklahoma
East Central University *B*
Northeastern Oklahoma Agricultural
  and Mechanical College *A*
Oklahoma Baptist University *B*
Oklahoma City University *B*
Oklahoma State University *B*
Southern Nazarene University *B*
Southwestern Oklahoma State
  University *B*
University of Tulsa *B*

Oregon
Concordia University *B*
George Fox University *B*
Linfield College *B*
Southern Oregon University *B*
Treasure Valley Community College *A*

Pennsylvania
Alvernia University *B*
Bloomsburg University of
  Pennsylvania *M*
California University of
  Pennsylvania *B, M*
Chestnut Hill College *C*
Duquesne University *B*
East Stroudsburg University of
  Pennsylvania *B*
Eastern University *B*
King's College *B*
Marywood University *B*

Messiah College *B*
Northampton Community College *A*
Slippery Rock University of
  Pennsylvania *B*
Temple University *B, M*
University of Pittsburgh
  Bradford *B*
Waynesburg University *B*
West Chester University of
  Pennsylvania *B*

Puerto Rico
Ponce Paramedical College *C*
Turabo University *M*
University of Puerto Rico
  Ponce *B*

South Carolina
Charleston Southern University *B*
College of Charleston *B*
Erskine College *B*
Lander University *B*
Limestone College *B*

South Dakota
Augustana College *B*
Dakota Wesleyan University *B*
National American University
  Rapid City *B*
South Dakota State University *B*

Tennessee
Carson-Newman College *B*
King College *B*
Lee University *B*
Lincoln Memorial University *B*
Lipscomb University *B*
Middle Tennessee State University *B*
Tusculum College *B*
Union University *B*
University of Tennessee
  Chattanooga *M*

Texas
Angelo State University *B, T*
Baylor University *B*
East Texas Baptist University *B*
Hardin-Simmons University *B*
Howard College *A*
Howard Payne University *B*
Lubbock Christian University *B*
McMurry University *B*
Midwestern State University *B*
South Plains College *A*
Southwestern University *B*
Stephen F. Austin State University *M*
Texas A&M University
  Commerce *B*
  Corpus Christi *B*
Texas Christian University *B*
Texas Lutheran University *B*
Texas State University: San
  Marcos *B, M, T*
Texas Tech University Health Sciences
  Center *M*
Texas Wesleyan University *B*
Texas Woman's University *M*
University of Mary Hardin-Baylor *B*
University of Texas
  Arlington *B*
  Austin *B*
  of the Permian Basin *B*
University of the Incarnate Word *B*
West Texas A&M University *B*

Utah
Brigham Young University *B, M*
Eagle Gate College: Salt Lake City *C*
Southern Utah University *B*
University of Utah *B*
Weber State University *B, M*

Vermont
Castleton State College *B*
Johnson State College *B*
Lyndon State College *B*
Norwich University *B*
University of Vermont *B*

Virginia
Averett University *B*
Bridgewater College *B*
Emory & Henry College *B*
George Mason University *B*
James Madison University *B*
Jefferson College of Health
  Sciences *B*
Liberty University *B*
Longwood University *B*
Lynchburg College *B*
Roanoke College *B*
Shenandoah University *M*
Virginia Commonwealth University *M*

Washington
Eastern Washington University *B*
Spokane Falls Community College *A*
Washington State University *B*
Whitworth University *B*

West Virginia
Alderson-Broaddus College *B*
Concord University *B*
Marshall University *B*
University of Charleston *B*
West Virginia University *B, T*
West Virginia Wesleyan College *B, M*

Wisconsin
Carroll University *B*
Carthage College *B*
Concordia University Wisconsin *B*
Marquette University *B*
University of Wisconsin
  Eau Claire *B*
  La Crosse *B*
  Stevens Point *B*

Wyoming
Casper College *A*
Central Wyoming College *A*

Atmospheric physics/dynamics

New Mexico
New Mexico Institute of Mining and
  Technology *B, M, D*

Wisconsin
University of Wisconsin
  Milwaukee *B*

Atmospheric science

Alabama
University of Alabama
  Huntsville *M, D*
University of South Alabama *B*

Alaska
University of Alaska
  Fairbanks *M, D*

Arizona
University of Arizona *M, D*

California
California State University
  Chico *B*
San Francisco State University *B*
San Jose State University *M*
Shasta College *A*

University of California
  Berkeley *B*
  Davis *B, M, D*
  Los Angeles *M, D*

Colorado

Colorado State University *M, D*
Metropolitan State College of
  Denver *B*
United States Air Force Academy *B*
University of Colorado
  Boulder *M, D*

Connecticut

Western Connecticut State
  University *B*

Delaware

University of Delaware *D*

District of Columbia

Howard University *M, D*

Florida

Embry-Riddle Aeronautical
  University *B*
Florida State University *C, B, M, D*
Gulf Coast Community College *A*
Miami Dade College *A*
State College of Florida,
  Manatee-Sarasota *A*
University of Miami *B*

Illinois

Northern Illinois University *B*
University of Illinois
  Urbana-Champaign *B, M, D*

Indiana

Purdue University *B*
Valparaiso University *B*

Kansas

University of Kansas *B, M*

Louisiana

University of Louisiana at Monroe *B*

Maryland

University of Maryland
  College Park *M, D*

Massachusetts

Massachusetts Institute of
  Technology *M, D*

Michigan

Michigan Technological University *D*
University of Michigan *B, M, D*

Minnesota

Saint Cloud State University *B*

Mississippi

Jackson State University *B*

Missouri

Saint Louis University *B, M, D*
University of Missouri
  Columbia *B, M, D*

Nebraska

Creighton University *B, M*
University of Nebraska
  Lincoln *B*

Nevada

University of Nevada
  Reno *B, M, D*

New Hampshire

Plymouth State University *B, M*

New Jersey

Princeton University *M, D*
Rutgers, The State University of New
  Jersey
  New Brunswick/Piscataway
    Campus *B*

New York

Cornell University *B, M, D*
State University of New York
  Albany *B, M, D*
  College at Brockport *B*
  College at Oneonta *B*
  Maritime College *B*

North Carolina

North Carolina State
  University *B, M, D*
University of North Carolina
  Asheville *B*

North Dakota

University of North Dakota *B, M*

Ohio

Ohio State University
  Columbus Campus *M, D*
Ohio University *B*
Shawnee State University *B*

Oregon

Oregon State University *M, D*

Pennsylvania

Millersville University of
  Pennsylvania *B*
Penn State
  Abington *B*
  Altoona *B*
  Beaver *B*
  Berks *B*
  Brandywine *B*
  DuBois *B*
  Erie, The Behrend College *B*
  Fayette, The Eberly Campus *B*
  Greater Allegheny *B*
  Hazleton *B*
  Lehigh Valley *B*
  Mont Alto *B*
  New Kensington *B*
  Schuylkill *B*
  Shenango *B*
  University Park *B, M, D*
  Wilkes-Barre *B*
  Worthington Scranton *B*
  York *B*

South Dakota

South Dakota School of Mines and
  Technology *B, M, D*

Texas

Texas A&M University *B, M, D*
Texas Tech University *M*

Utah

University of Utah *M, D*

Vermont

Lyndon State College *B*

Virginia

George Mason University *D*

Washington

Everett Community College *A*
South Seattle Community College *A*
University of Washington *B, M, D*

Wisconsin

University of Wisconsin
  Madison *B, M, D*

Wyoming

University of Wyoming *M, D*

Atomic/molecular physics

California

San Diego State University *B*
University of California
  San Diego *B*

Florida

Florida State University *D*

Massachusetts

Harvard College *B, M, D*

Minnesota

University of Minnesota
  Twin Cities *M, D*

Ohio

College of Wooster *B*
Ohio State University
  Columbus Campus *M, D*

Texas

Rice University *M, D*

Virginia

Norfolk State University *M*

Wisconsin

University of Wisconsin
  Madison *M, D*

Auctioneering

Pennsylvania

Harrisburg Area Community
  College *C*

Audiology/hearing sciences

Alabama

University of Montevallo *B*

California

San Diego State University *M*

Colorado

University of Colorado
  Boulder *D*
University of Northern
  Colorado *B, M, D*

Connecticut

University of Connecticut *D*

District of Columbia

Gallaudet University *D*

Florida

Nova Southeastern University *D*
University of Florida *D*
University of South Florida *D*

Idaho

Idaho State University *D*

Illinois

Northwestern University *M, D*
Rush University *D*

University of Illinois
  Urbana-Champaign *B, M, D*

Indiana

Ball State University *M*
Indiana University
  Bloomington *B*
Indiana University-Purdue University
  Fort Wayne *B*
Purdue University *B, M, D*

Iowa

University of Iowa *B*

Kansas

University of Kansas *D*
University of Kansas Medical
  Center *M, D*

Kentucky

University of Louisville *D*

Louisiana

Louisiana State University Health
  Sciences Center *D*

Maryland

University of Maryland
  College Park *D*

Massachusetts

Boston University *M, D*
Elms College *B*
Emerson College *B, M*
Northeastern University *M*
University of Massachusetts
  Amherst *D*

Michigan

Central Michigan University *D*
Michigan State University *D*
Wayne State University *M, D*
Western Michigan University *D*

Missouri

Missouri State University *D*
Washington University in St.
  Louis *M, D*

Nebraska

University of Nebraska
  Lincoln *D*

New Jersey

Montclair State University *D*

New York

City University of New York
  Brooklyn College *M*
  Hunter College *M*
Hofstra University *D*
State University of New York
  Buffalo *D*

North Carolina

University of North Carolina
  Chapel Hill *D*

Ohio

Cleveland State University *B, M*
Ohio State University
  Columbus Campus *B, M, D*
University of Akron *D*

Oklahoma

University of Oklahoma *D*

Oregon

Portland State University *B, M*

Pennsylvania

Bloomsburg University of
Pennsylvania *D*
La Salle University *B, M*

Puerto Rico

University of Puerto Rico
Medical Sciences *D*

Rhode Island

University of Rhode Island *D*

Tennessee

East Tennessee State University *D*
University of Memphis *D*
University of Tennessee
Knoxville *B, M, D*
Vanderbilt University *M, D*

Texas

Lamar University *M, D*
Stephen F. Austin State University *B*
Texas Tech University Health Sciences
Center *D*
University of Houston *M*
University of North Texas *D*
University of Texas
Dallas *D*

Utah

University of Utah *M, D*

Virginia

James Madison University *D*

Washington

University of Washington *M, D*

West Virginia

West Virginia University *D*

Wisconsin

University of Wisconsin
Stevens Point *D*

Audiology/speech pathology

Alabama

Auburn University *B, M*
University of Alabama *B*
University of South Alabama *B, M, D*

Arizona

Arizona State University *D*

Arkansas

Arkansas State University *B*
Ouachita Baptist University *B*
University of Arkansas *B, M*
University of Arkansas
Little Rock *B, M, D*
University of Central
Arkansas *B, M, D*

California

California State University
East Bay *B, M*
Northridge *M*
Sacramento *B, M*
Loma Linda University *B*
University of Redlands *B, M*

Colorado

University of Northern Colorado *B*

Connecticut

Southern Connecticut State
University *M*
University of Connecticut *M, D*

District of Columbia

Gallaudet University *M*
George Washington University *B, M*
University of the District of
Columbia *M*

Florida

Florida Atlantic University *M*
Florida International University *M*
Florida State University *B, M, D, T*
University of Central Florida *B, M*
University of Florida *B, D*
University of South Florida *B, M, D*

Hawaii

University of Hawaii
Manoa *B, M*

Idaho

Idaho State University *B*

Illinois

Augustana College *B*
Illinois State University *B, M, D, T*
Northwestern University *D*
Southern Illinois University
Edwardsville *B, M*
University of Illinois
Urbana-Champaign *B, M, D*

Indiana

Ball State University *B, D*
Indiana State University *B, M, T*
Indiana University
Bloomington *B, M, D*
Purdue University *B, M, D*

Iowa

University of Iowa *M, D*

Kansas

Fort Hays State University *M*
Wichita State University *D*

Kentucky

Brescia University *B*
Murray State University *B, M, T*
University of Kentucky *B, M*
Western Kentucky University *M, T*

Louisiana

Louisiana State University Health
Sciences Center *M*
Louisiana State University and
Agricultural and Mechanical
College *B, M, D*
Louisiana Tech University *B, M*
Nicholls State University *B*
Southeastern Louisiana University *B*
Southern University and Agricultural
and Mechanical College *B*
University of Louisiana at
Lafayette *B, M*
University of Louisiana at
Monroe *B, M*

Maine

University of Maine *B, M*

Maryland

Loyola University Maryland *M*
Towson University *B, M, D*

Massachusetts

Boston University *M, D*
Elms College *B*
Emerson College *B*
Northeastern University *B, M*

Michigan

Andrews University *B*

Calvin College *B*
Michigan State University *B, M, D*
Western Michigan University *B*

Minnesota

Minnesota State University
Moorhead *B*
Saint Cloud State University *B*
University of Minnesota
Twin Cities *B*

Mississippi

Delta State University *B*
University of Mississippi *B, M*
University of Southern
Mississippi *B, M*

Missouri

Missouri State University *B, M*
Saint Louis University *B, M*
University of Central Missouri *M*
University of Missouri
Columbia *B, M*
Washington University in St.
Louis *M, D*

Nebraska

University of Nebraska
Lincoln *M*

Nevada

University of Nevada
Reno *M*

New Hampshire

University of New Hampshire *M*

New Jersey

Richard Stockton College of New
Jersey *B*
William Paterson University of New
Jersey *M*

New Mexico

Eastern New Mexico University *B, M*
University of New Mexico *B, M*

New York

Adelphi University *B, M, D*
City University of New York
Brooklyn College *B*
Lehman College *B, M*
College of Saint Rose *B, M, T*
Elmira College *B*
Hofstra University *B*
Iona College *B*
Long Island University
Brooklyn Campus *B, M*
C. W. Post Campus *B, M*
Marymount Manhattan College *B*
Mercy College *B*
Molloy College *B*
New York University *B, M, D*
St. John's University *B, M, D*
State University of New York
Buffalo *B, M, D*
College at Cortland *B*
College at Fredonia *B, M, T*
College at Plattsburgh *B*
Syracuse University *B, M, D*
Yeshiva University *B*

North Carolina

East Carolina University *B, M, D*
Shaw University *B*
University of North Carolina
Chapel Hill *M, D*
Greensboro *B, M*

North Dakota

University of North Dakota *D*

Ohio

Bowling Green State University *B*
College of Wooster *B*
Kent State University *B, M, D*
Miami University
Oxford Campus *M*
Ohio State University
Columbus Campus *B, M, D*
Ohio University *B, M, D*
University of Akron *B, M*
University of Cincinnati *B, M, D*

Oklahoma

Northeastern State University *B*
University of Central Oklahoma *B*
University of Oklahoma *M, D*
University of Tulsa *B, M*

Pennsylvania

Bloomsburg University of
Pennsylvania *B*
Clarion University of Pennsylvania *B*
East Stroudsburg University of
Pennsylvania *B, M, T*
Indiana University of
Pennsylvania *M, D*
La Salle University *B, M*
Marywood University *B, M*
Temple University *B, M, D*
Thiel College *B*
University of Pittsburgh *B, M, D*
West Chester University of
Pennsylvania *B, M*

South Carolina

South Carolina State University *B, M*
University of South Carolina *D*

South Dakota

University of South Dakota *D*

Tennessee

East Tennessee State University *M*
Tennessee State University *B*
University of Memphis *M, D*
University of Tennessee
Knoxville *D*
Vanderbilt University *M, D*

Texas

Hardin-Simmons University *B*
Lamar University *B*
Stephen F. Austin State University *B*
Texas State University: San
Marcos *B, M*
Texas Tech University Health Sciences
Center *M*
Texas Woman's University *M*
University of Houston *B, M*
University of North Texas *B*
University of Texas
Dallas *B*
El Paso *M*
Pan American *B, M*

Utah

Brigham Young University *B, M*
University of Utah *B, M, D, T*
Utah State University *B, M, D*

Virginia

Hampton University *B, M*
Old Dominion University *B, M*
Radford University *M*
University of Virginia *B, M*

Washington

University of Washington *B, M, D*
Washington State University *B, M*
Western Washington University *B, M*

West Virginia

Marshall University *M*
West Virginia University *B*

Wisconsin

Marquette University *B*
University of Wisconsin
  Madison *B, M, D*
  Stevens Point *B, M, T*
  Whitewater *M*

Wyoming

University of Wyoming *B, M*

Auditing

California

San Francisco State University *C*

Illinois

University of Illinois
  Urbana-Champaign *B*

Massachusetts

Babson College *B*

Michigan

Eastern Michigan University *M*

North Dakota

Cankdeska Cikana Community
  College *A*

Pennsylvania

Carlow University *B*

Puerto Rico

Inter American University of Puerto
  Rico
  Bayamon Campus *B*

Australian/Oceanic/ Pacific languages

Hawaii

University of Hawaii
  Hilo *M*
  West Oahu *M*

Auto body repair

Alabama

Bevill State Community College *C*
Bishop State Community College *C*
Gadsden State Community College *C*
George C. Wallace State Community
  College
  George C. Wallace Community
    College at Dothan *C*
Jefferson Davis Community College *C*
Lawson State Community
  College *C, A*
Northwest-Shoals Community
  College *C*
Shelton State Community College *C*
Wallace State Community College at
  Hanceville *C, A*

Arizona

Central Arizona College *C*
Mesa Community College *C*

Arkansas

Arkansas State University
  Beebe *C*
Arkansas Tech University *C*
North Arkansas College *C*
Pulaski Technical College *C*

University of Arkansas
  Cossatot Community College of the
    C
University of Arkansas Community
  College at Morrilton *C, A*

California

Allan Hancock College *C, A*
Antelope Valley College *C, A*
Cerritos College *A*
Cerro Coso Community College *C, A*
Chabot College *A*
Chaffey College *C, A*
College of Marin: Kentfield *C, A*
Columbia College *C*
Contra Costa College *C, A*
Cuesta College *C, A*
Cypress College *C, A*
East Los Angeles College *C*
El Camino College *C, A*
El Camino College: Compton
  Center *C, A*
Fresno City College *C, A*
Fullerton College *C, A*
Gavilan College *C*
Golden West College *C, A*
Hartnell College *C, A*
Imperial Valley College *C, A*
Lassen Community College *C, A*
Long Beach City College *C, A*
Los Angeles Pierce College *C, A*
Los Angeles Trade and Technical
  College *C, A*
Mendocino College *C, A*
Merced College *C, A*
MiraCosta College *C, A*
Modesto Junior College *C, A*
Mount San Jacinto College *C*
Oxnard College *C, A*
Palomar College *C, A*
Pasadena City College *C, A*
Porterville College *C, A*
Rio Hondo College *C, A*
Riverside Community College *C, A*
Santa Monica College *C, A*
Santa Rosa Junior College *C*
Solano Community College *C, A*
Yuba Community College District *C*

Colorado

Aims Community College *C, A*
Morgan Community College *A*
Pikes Peak Community College *C, A*
Pueblo Community College *C, A*
Red Rocks Community College *C, A*
Trinidad State Junior College *C, A*

Florida

Central Florida Community College *C*
Daytona State College *C*
Florida State College at Jacksonville *C*
Hillsborough Community College *C*
Palm Beach Community College *C*
South Florida Community College *C*

Georgia

Albany Technical College *C*
Athens Technical College *C*
Central Georgia Technical College *C*
Columbus Technical College *C*
Middle Georgia College *A*
North Georgia Technical College *C*
Savannah Technical College *C, A*

Hawaii

University of Hawaii
  Hawaii Community College *C, A*
  Honolulu Community College *A*
  Kauai Community College *C, A*
  Maui Community College *A*

Idaho

Idaho State University *C, A*

Lewis-Clark State College *C, A, B*
North Idaho College *C, A*

Illinois

Black Hawk College *C, A*
Carl Sandburg College *C, A*
City Colleges of Chicago
  Kennedy-King College *C*
College of Lake County *C*
Danville Area Community College *C*
Highland Community College *C, A*
Illinois Eastern Community Colleges
  Olney Central College *A*
John A. Logan College *C, A*
Joliet Junior College *C, A*
Kaskaskia College *C, A*
Kishwaukee College *C, A*
Lake Land College *C*
Lincoln Land Community College *C, A*
Parkland College *C, A*
Prairie State College *C*
Waubonsee Community College *C, A*

Indiana

Vincennes University *C, A*

Iowa

Des Moines Area Community
  College *C, A*
Hawkeye Community College *C, A*
Indian Hills Community College *A*
Iowa Central Community College *C, A*
Iowa Lakes Community College *C*
Kirkwood Community College *C*
Northwest Iowa Community
  College *C, A*
Scott Community College *C, A*
Southeastern Community College
  North Campus *C*
Southwestern Community
  College *C, A*
Western Iowa Tech Community
  College *C, A*

Kansas

Butler Community College *C, A*
Coffeyville Community College *C*
Highland Community College *C, A*
Hutchinson Community College *C, A*
Kansas City Kansas Community
  College *C*
Manhattan Area Technical
  College *C, A*
Pittsburg State University *B*

Kentucky

Big Sandy Community and Technical
  College *C*
Bluegrass Community and Technical
  College *C*
Maysville Community and Technical
  College *C*
Somerset Community College *C, A*
West Kentucky Community and
  Technical College *C*

Louisiana

Gretna Career College *C*

Maine

Northern Maine Community
  College *C, A*

Maryland

Community College of Baltimore
  County *A*

Michigan

Alpena Community College *C*
Bay de Noc Community College *C*
Ferris State University *A*
Mott Community College *A*

Oakland Community College *C*
Washtenaw Community College *C, A*

Minnesota

Century Community and Technical
  College *C, A*
Dakota County Technical College *C, A*
Dunwoody College of
  Technology *C, A*
Hennepin Technical College *C, A*
Lake Superior College *C*
Minnesota State College - Southeast
  Technical *C, A*
Minnesota State Community and
  Technical College *C, A*
Minnesota West Community and
  Technical College *C, A*
Northland Community & Technical
  College *C, A*
Ridgewater College *C, A*
Riverland Community College *C*
St. Cloud Technical College *C, A*
St. Paul College *C, A*
South Central College *C, A*

Mississippi

East Central Community College *C*
Hinds Community College *C*
Mississippi Gulf Coast Community
  College *C*
Northeast Mississippi Community
  College *C*
Northwest Mississippi Community
  College *C*
Pearl River Community College *C, A*

Missouri

Crowder College *C*
Linn State Technical College *C, A*
Metropolitan Community College:
  Longview *C, A*
Mineral Area College *C, A*
North Central Missouri College *A*
Ozarks Technical Community
  College *C, A*
Ranken Technical College *A*

Montana

Montana State University
  Billings *C, A*
  College of Technology: Great
    Falls *A*

Nebraska

Central Community College *C, A*
Metropolitan Community
  College *C, A*
Mid-Plains Community College
  Area *C, A*
Northeast Community College *A*
Southeast Community College *A*
Western Nebraska Community
  College *C, A*

New Hampshire

Nashua Community College *A*

New Mexico

Eastern New Mexico University:
  Roswell Campus *C*
San Juan College *C, A*

New York

Erie Community College
  South Campus *A*
State University of New York
  College of Agriculture and
    Technology at Morrisville *A*
  College of Technology at Alfred *A*

North Carolina

Blue Ridge Community College *C*

Caldwell Community College and
Technical Institute *C*
Cape Fear Community College *C*
Central Piedmont Community
College *C*
Cleveland Community College *C*
Coastal Carolina Community
College *C*
Edgecombe Community College *C*
Fayetteville Technical Community
College *C*
Forsyth Technical Community
College *C*
Guilford Technical Community
College *C*
Haywood Community College *C*
Isothermal Community College *C, A*
Mayland Community College *C*
McDowell Technical Community
College *C*
Montgomery Community College *C*
Randolph Community College *C*
Sandhills Community College *C*
Surry Community College *C*
Tri-County Community College *C*
Wayne Community College *C*
Wilkes Community College *C*

North Dakota

Bismarck State College *C, A*
North Dakota State College of
Science *C, A*

Ohio

Owens Community College
Toledo *C*

Oklahoma

Oklahoma State University
Institute of Technology:
Okmulgee *A*
Western Oklahoma State College *A*

Oregon

Clackamas Community College *C, A*
Lane Community College *C, A*
Linn-Benton Community College *C*
Portland Community College *C, A*

Pennsylvania

Pennsylvania College of
Technology *C, A*
Thaddeus Stevens College of
Technology *A*

Rhode Island

New England Institute of
Technology *A*

South Carolina

Greenville Technical College *C*

South Dakota

Southeast Technical Institute *A*
Western Dakota Technical Institute *C*

Tennessee

Chattanooga State Community
College *C*

Texas

Amarillo College *C*
Central Texas College *C, A*
Eastfield College *C, A*
Grayson County College *C, A*
Hill College *C, A*
Howard College *C*
Kilgore College *C, A*
Northeast Texas Community
College *C, A*
St. Philip's College *C, A*
San Jacinto College *C, A*

South Plains College *C, A*
Tarrant County College *C, A*
Texarkana College *C*
Texas State Technical College
Harlingen *C, A*
Waco *A*
West Texas *C*
Trinity Valley Community College *C*
University of Texas
Brownsville - Texas Southmost
College *C*

Utah

Salt Lake Community College *C, A*
Utah Valley University *C, A*
Weber State University *C, A*

Virginia

Danville Community College *C*
J. Sargeant Reynolds Community
College *A*
Northern Virginia Community
College *C*

Washington

Bates Technical College *C, A*
Bellingham Technical College *A*
Clover Park Technical College *C*
Green River Community College *C, A*
Lake Washington Technical
College *C, A*
Lower Columbia College *A*
Renton Technical College *C, A*
South Seattle Community
College *C, A*
Spokane Community College *A*

Wisconsin

Chippewa Valley Technical College *A*
Fox Valley Technical College *A*
Lakeshore Technical College *C*
Milwaukee Area Technical College *C*
Moraine Park Technical College *C*
Northcentral Technical College *A*
Northeast Wisconsin Technical
College *C*
Southwest Wisconsin Technical
College *C*
Waukesha County Technical
College *C*
Wisconsin Indianhead Technical
College *C*

Wyoming

Casper College *C, A*
Laramie County Community
College *C, A*
WyoTech: Laramie *C, A*

Automotive
engineering technology

Alabama

Lawson State Community
College *C, A*

California

Barstow Community College *C, A*
Santa Barbara City College *C, A*
Taft College *C, A*

Colorado

Colorado State University
Pueblo *B*

Florida

Daytona State College *A*
Santa Fe College *C, A*
State College of Florida,
Manatee-Sarasota *A*

Georgia

Middle Georgia Technical College *C*

Illinois

Southern Illinois University
Carbondale *B*

Indiana

Indiana State University *B*

Kentucky

Gateway Community and Technical
College *A*

Massachusetts

Benjamin Franklin Institute of
Technology *A, B*
Massachusetts Bay Community
College *A*
Springfield Technical Community
College *C, A*

Michigan

Baker College
of Clinton Township *A*
Central Michigan University *B, M*
Ferris State University *B*
Gogebic Community College *C, A*
Grand Rapids Community College *A*
Montcalm Community College *C, A*
University of Michigan *M*

Minnesota

Hennepin Technical College *C, A*
Minnesota State University
Mankato *B*

New Jersey

Burlington County College *C, A*
Raritan Valley Community College *A*
Sussex County Community
College *C, A*

New York

City University of New York
Bronx Community College *C*
State University of New York
College of Agriculture and
Technology at
Morrisville *C, A, B*
Farmingdale *A, B*

North Dakota

North Dakota State College of
Science *A*

Ohio

Cincinnati State Technical and
Community College *C, A*
Columbus State Community
College *C, A*
Owens Community College
Toledo *C, A*

Pennsylvania

Community College of Allegheny
County *C, A*
Montgomery County Community
College *C, A*
Pennsylvania College of
Technology *C, A, B*

Puerto Rico

University of Puerto Rico
Carolina Regional College *A*

Texas

Brookhaven College *C*

Washington

Bates Technical College *C*

West Virginia

Blue Ridge Community and Technical
College *A*

Wisconsin

Mid-State Technical College *C*

Automotive technology

Alabama

Bevill State Community College *C*
Bishop State Community College *C*
Gadsden State Community College *C*
Jefferson Davis Community College *C*
Lurleen B. Wallace Community
College *C*
Northwest-Shoals Community
College *C*
Shelton State Community College *C*
Wallace State Community College at
Hanceville *C, A*

Alaska

University of Alaska
Anchorage *C, A*
Fairbanks *C*
Southeast *C, A*

Arizona

Arizona Automotive Institute *C, A*
Arizona Western College *C, A*
Central Arizona College *C, A*
Cochise College *C, A*
Eastern Arizona College *C, A*
GateWay Community College *C, A*
Glendale Community College *C, A*
Mohave Community College *A*
Northland Pioneer College *C, A*
Pima Community College *C, A*
Universal Technical Institute *C, A*

Arkansas

Arkansas Northeastern College *C*
Arkansas State University
Beebe *C*
Arkansas Tech University *C*
North Arkansas College *C*
Ouachita Technical College *C*
Ozarka College *C, A*
South Arkansas Community College *A*
Southern Arkansas University Tech *C*
University of Arkansas
Cossatot Community College of the
C, A
Fort Smith *C*
Monticello *C*
University of Arkansas Community
College at Morrilton *C, A*

California

Allan Hancock College *C, A*
American River College *A*
Antelope Valley College *C, A*
Bakersfield College *A*
Butte College *C, A*
Chabot College *C, A*
Chaffey College *C, A*
Citrus College *C, A*
College of the Canyons *C, A*
College of the Desert *C*
Columbia College *A*
Copper Mountain College *C, A*
Cypress College *C, A*
East Los Angeles College *C, A*
El Camino College *C, A*
El Camino College: Compton
Center *C, A*
Fresno City College *C, A*
Golden West College *C, A*
Hartnell College *C, A*
Imperial Valley College *C, A*
Lassen Community College *A*

Long Beach City College *C, A*
Los Angeles Harbor College *C, A*
Los Angeles Pierce College *C, A*
Merced College *C*
MiraCosta College *C, A*
Modesto Junior College *C, A*
Mount San Jacinto College *C, A*
Oxnard College *C, A*
Palo Verde College *C, A*
Rio Hondo College *C, A*
Riverside Community College *C, A*
Saddleback College *C*
San Bernardino Valley College *C, A*
San Diego Miramar College *C, A*
Santa Ana College *C, A*
Santa Barbara City College *C, A*
Santa Rosa Junior College *C*
Santiago Canyon College *A*
Shasta College *C, A*
Sierra College *C, A*
Skyline College *C, A*
Southwestern College *C, A*
Taft College *C, A*
Ventura College *C, A*
Victor Valley College *C, A*
WyoTech: Long Beach *C*
Yuba Community College
 District *C, A*

Colorado
Arapahoe Community College *C, A*
Colorado Northwestern Community
 College *C*
Front Range Community College *C, A*
Mesa State College *C, A*
Morgan Community College *C, A*
Northeastern Junior College *C, A*
Otero Junior College *C*
Pikes Peak Community College *C, A*
Pueblo Community College *C, A*
Red Rocks Community College *C, A*
Trinidad State Junior College *C, A*
Westwood College: Denver North *A*

Connecticut
Gateway Community College *A*
Naugatuck Valley Community
 College *C, A*

Delaware
Delaware Technical and Community
 College
 Owens *C, A*
 Stanton/Wilmington *C, A*

Florida
ATI Career Training Center
 Oakland Park *A*
Brevard Community College *C*
Broward College *A*
Central Florida Community
 College *C, A*
Daytona State College *A*
Florida State College at
 Jacksonville *C, A*
Hillsborough Community College *C*
Indian River State College *C, A*
Palm Beach Community College *C, A*
Pensacola Junior College *A*
Seminole Community College *C, A*
South Florida Community College *C*

Georgia
Albany Technical College *C*
Athens Technical College *C*
Central Georgia Technical College *C*
Chattahoochee Technical
 College *C, A*
Columbus Technical College *C, A*
DeKalb Technical College *A*
Gwinnett Technical College *C, A*
Middle Georgia College *A*
North Georgia Technical College *C*

Savannah Technical College *C, A*
Southwest Georgia Technical
 College *C*
Waycross College *A*
West Georgia Technical College *C*

Hawaii
University of Hawaii
 Hawaii Community College *C, A*
 Honolulu Community College *A*
 Kauai Community College *C, A*
 Maui Community College *A*

Idaho
Brigham Young University-Idaho *A*
Eastern Idaho Technical College *C, A*
Idaho State University *C, A*
Lewis-Clark State College *C, A, B*
North Idaho College *C, A*

Illinois
Black Hawk College *C, A*
Black Hawk College: East
 Campus *C, A*
City Colleges of Chicago
 Kennedy-King College *C, A*
College of DuPage *C, A*
College of Lake County *C, A*
Danville Area Community
 College *C, A*
Elgin Community College *C, A*
Highland Community College *C, A*
Illinois Eastern Community Colleges
 Frontier Community College *C, A*
John A. Logan College *C, A*
Kankakee Community College *C, A*
Kaskaskia College *C, A*
Kishwaukee College *C, A*
Lewis and Clark Community
 College *A*
Lincoln Land Community College *C, A*
McHenry County College *C, A*
Moraine Valley Community
 College *C, A*
Morton College *C, A*
Oakton Community College *C, A*
Parkland College *C, A*
Prairie State College *C, A*
Rend Lake College *C, A*
Richland Community College *A*
Rock Valley College *C, A*
Spoon River College *C, A*
Triton College *C, A*
Waubonsee Community College *C, A*

Indiana
Ivy Tech Community College
 Central Indiana *C, A*
 Columbus *C, A*
 East Central *C, A*
 Kokomo *C, A*
 Lafayette *C, A*
 North Central *C, A*
 Northeast *C, A*
 Northwest *C, A*
 Richmond *C, A*
 South Central *C, A*
 Southwest *A*
 Wabash Valley *C, A*
Vincennes University *A*

Iowa
Des Moines Area Community
 College *C, A*
Hawkeye Community College *A*
Indian Hills Community College *A*
Iowa Central Community College *A*
Iowa Lakes Community College *C*
Kirkwood Community College *C, A*
North Iowa Area Community
 College *C, A*
Northeast Iowa Community
 College *C, A*

Northwest Iowa Community
 College *C, A*
Scott Community College *C, A*
Western Iowa Tech Community
 College *C, A*

Kansas
Barton County Community
 College *C, A*
Butler Community College *C, A*
Coffeyville Community College *C*
Cowley County Community
 College *C, A*
Highland Community College *C, A*
Hutchinson Community College *C, A*
Johnson County Community
 College *C, A*
Kansas City Kansas Community
 College *C, A*
Manhattan Area Technical
 College *C, A*
McPherson College *B*
North Central Kansas Technical
 College *C, A*
Pittsburg State University *C, A, B*
Pratt Community College *A*

Kentucky
Big Sandy Community and Technical
 College *C, A*
Bluegrass Community and Technical
 College *C, A*
Elizabethtown Community and
 Technical College *C, A*
Hazard Community and Technical
 College *A*
Hopkinsville Community College *C*
Maysville Community and Technical
 College *C*
Owensboro Community and
 Technical College *C*
Somerset Community College *C, A*

Louisiana
Delgado Community College *C, A*

Maine
Central Maine Community College *A*
Eastern Maine Community
 College *C, A*
Northern Maine Community
 College *C, A*
Southern Maine Community
 College *A*
Washington County Community
 College *C*

Maryland
Allegany College of Maryland *C, A*
Community College of Baltimore
 County *C, A*
Montgomery College *C, A*

Massachusetts
Benjamin Franklin Institute of
 Technology *A, B*
Middlesex Community College *A*
Mount Wachusett Community
 College *C, A*
Quinsigamond Community
 College *C, A*

Michigan
Alpena Community College *C, A*
Baker College
 of Clinton Township *A*
 of Flint *A*
 of Owosso *A*
Bay de Noc Community College *C, A*
Delta College *C, A*
Ferris State University *A*
Glen Oaks Community College *C*
Gogebic Community College *C, A*

Grand Rapids Community College *C*
Henry Ford Community College *C, A*
Jackson Community College *C, A*
Kalamazoo Valley Community
 College *C, A*
Kirtland Community College *C, A*
Macomb Community College *C, A*
Mid Michigan Community College *C*
Mott Community College *C, A*
Northern Michigan University *C, A*
Northwestern Michigan College *C, A*
Oakland Community College *C*
Southwestern Michigan College *C, A*
Washtenaw Community College *C, A*
Wayne County Community
 College *C, A*

Minnesota
Anoka Technical College *C, A*
Central Lakes College *C, A*
Century Community and Technical
 College *C, A*
Dakota County Technical College *C, A*
Dunwoody College of
 Technology *C, A*
Hennepin Technical College *C, A*
Hibbing Community College *C*
Lake Superior College *C, A*
Mesabi Range Community and
 Technical College *C, A*
Minnesota State College - Southeast
 Technical *C*
Minnesota State Community and
 Technical College *C, A*
Minnesota State University
 Mankato *B*
Minnesota West Community and
 Technical College *C, A*
Northland Community & Technical
 College *C, A*
Northwest Technical College *C, A*
Pine Technical College *C, A*
Ridgewater College *C, A*
Riverland Community College *C, A*
Rochester Community and Technical
 College *C*
St. Cloud Technical College *C, A*
St. Paul College *C, A*
South Central College *C, A*

Mississippi
Copiah-Lincoln Community College *A*
East Mississippi Community
 College *C*
Northeast Mississippi Community
 College *C*
Southwest Mississippi Community
 College *A*

Missouri
Crowder College *C, A*
East Central College *C, A*
Jefferson College *C, A*
Linn State Technical College *C, A*
Metropolitan Community College:
 Longview *C, A*
Mineral Area College *C, A*
Ozarks Technical Community
 College *C, A*
Ranken Technical College *A*
State Fair Community College *C, A*

Montana
Dawson Community College *A*
Fort Peck Community College *C, A*
Helena College of Technology of the
 University of Montana *A*
Montana State University
 Billings *C, A*
Montana Tech of the University of
 Montana *C*

Nebraska
Central Community College *C, A*
Metropolitan Community
College *C, A*
Mid-Plains Community College
Area *A, A*
Northeast Community College *A*
Southeast Community College *A*
Western Nebraska Community
College *C, A*

Nevada
College of Southern Nevada *A*
Truckee Meadows Community
College *A*
Western Nevada College *C, A*

New Hampshire
Lakes Region Community College *A*
Manchester Community College *C, A*
Nashua Community College *A*
White Mountains Community
College *C, A*

New Jersey
Brookdale Community College *C*
Gloucester County College *A*
Mercer County Community
College *A*
Middlesex County College *A*
Sussex County Community
College *C, A*
Union County College *A*

New Mexico
Central New Mexico Community
College *C*
Clovis Community College *C, A*
Dona Ana Community College of New
Mexico State University *C, A*
Eastern New Mexico University:
Roswell Campus *C, A*
Mesalands Community College *C, A*
New Mexico Junior College *C, A*
New Mexico State University
Grants *A*
San Juan College *C, A*
Western New Mexico University *C, A*

New York
Columbia-Greene Community
College *C, A*
Corning Community College *C, A*
Erie Community College
South Campus *A*
Fulton-Montgomery Community
College *C, A*
Monroe Community College *A*
Onondaga Community College *A*
Rockland Community College *A*
State University of New York
College of Agriculture and
Technology at Morrisville *A, B*
College of Technology at Alfred *A*
College of Technology at
Canton *C, A*
College of Technology at Delhi *C, A*
Farmingdale *A*
Suffolk County Community College *A*
Westchester Community College *A*

North Carolina
Asheville-Buncombe Technical
Community College *A*
Beaufort County Community
College *C, A*
Bladen Community College *C*
Blue Ridge Community College *C*
Caldwell Community College and
Technical Institute *C*
Cape Fear Community College *A*
Catawba Valley Community
College *C, A*

Central Carolina Community
College *A*
Central Piedmont Community
College *C, A*
Coastal Carolina Community
College *C*
Davidson County Community
College *C, A*
Durham Technical Community
College *A*
Fayetteville Technical Community
College *C, A*
Forsyth Technical Community
College *A*
Guilford Technical Community
College *C, A*
Halifax Community College *C*
Haywood Community College *C, A*
James Sprunt Community College *C*
Lenoir Community College *C, A*
Martin Community College *C, A*
Pitt Community College *C, A*
Randolph Community College *A*
Rowan-Cabarrus Community
College *C*
Sandhills Community College *C, A*
Southwestern Community
College *C, A*
Surry Community College *A*
Tri-County Community College *A*
Wayne Community College *C, A*
Wilkes Community College *C, A*
Wilson Community College *C*

North Dakota
Bismarck State College *C, A*
Cankdeska Cikana Community
College *C, A*
Lake Region State College *C, A*
North Dakota State College of
Science *C, A*
Williston State College *A*

Ohio
Cincinnati State Technical and
Community College *C, A*
Columbus State Community
College *C, A*
Cuyahoga Community College
Metropolitan Campus *A*
Stark State College of Technology *A*
Terra State Community College *C, A*
University of Cincinnati
Raymond Walters College *C, A*
University of Northwestern Ohio *C, A*
Washington State Community
College *A*
Zane State College *A*

Oklahoma
Oklahoma State University
Institute of Technology:
Okmulgee *A*
Western Oklahoma State College *A*

Oregon
Central Oregon Community
College *C*
Chemeketa Community College *A*
Clackamas Community College *A*
Clatsop Community College *C*
Lane Community College *C, A*
Linn-Benton Community College *C, A*
Mt. Hood Community College *A*
Portland Community College *C, A*
Rogue Community College *C, A*
Umpqua Community College *C, A*

Pennsylvania
Commonwealth Technical Institute *C*
Harrisburg Area Community
College *C, A*
Johnson College *A*

Luzerne County Community
College *A*
Northampton Community
College *C, A*
Thaddeus Stevens College of
Technology *A*

Puerto Rico
Electronic Data Processing College:
San Sebastian *A*

South Carolina
Aiken Technical College *C*
Florence-Darlington Technical
College *C, A*
Greenville Technical College *C, A*
Midlands Technical College *C, A*
Orangeburg-Calhoun Technical
College *A*
Spartanburg Community College *C, A*
Trident Technical College *C, A*
Williamsburg Technical College *C*
York Technical College *C, A*

South Dakota
Lake Area Technical Institute *A*
Southeast Technical Institute *A*
Western Dakota Technical
Institute *C, A*

Tennessee
Nashville State Community College *A*
Northeast State Community
College *C, A*
Southern Adventist University *C, A*
Southwest Tennessee Community
College *A*

Texas
Alvin Community College *C*
Amarillo College *C, A*
Angelina College *C*
Austin Community College *C, A*
Brazosport College *C, A*
Brookhaven College *C, A*
Central Texas College *C, A*
Del Mar College *C, A*
Eastfield College *C, A*
El Paso Community College *C*
Houston Community College
System *C, A*
Kilgore College *C, A*
Lamar State College at Port
Arthur *C, A*
Laredo Community College *C*
Lone Star College System *C, A*
Midland College *C, A*
Northeast Texas Community
College *C, A*
Odessa College *C, A*
St. Philip's College *C, A*
San Jacinto College *C, A*
South Plains College *C, A*
South Texas College *C, A*
Tarrant County College *C, A*
Texarkana College *C*
Texas State Technical College
Harlingen *C*
Waco *A*
West Texas *C, A*
Trinity Valley Community College *C*
Tyler Junior College *C, A*
University of Texas
Brownsville - Texas Southmost
College *C*
Western Technical College: Diana
Drive *A*
Wharton County Junior College *C, A*

Utah
College of Eastern Utah *A*
Dixie State College of Utah *C, A*
Salt Lake Community College *A*

Utah Valley University *C, A*
Weber State University *C, A*

Vermont
Vermont Technical College *A*

Virginia
Advanced Technology Institute *C, A*
Blue Ridge Community College *C*
Danville Community College *C*
Germanna Community College *C*
J. Sargeant Reynolds Community
College *C, A*
John Tyler Community College *C*
New River Community College *A*
Northern Virginia Community
College *C, A*
Southside Virginia Community
College *C*
Southwest Virginia Community
College *C*
Thomas Nelson Community
College *C, A*
Tidewater Community College *A*

Washington
Bates Technical College *C, A*
Bellingham Technical College *C, A*
Big Bend Community College *C, A*
Clark College *C, A*
Clover Park Technical College *C, A*
Grays Harbor College *C, A*
Lake Washington Technical
College *C, A*
Lower Columbia College *A*
Olympic College *C, A*
Peninsula College *C, A*
Renton Technical College *C, A*
Shoreline Community College *C, A*
Skagit Valley College *C, A*
South Seattle Community
College *C, A*
Spokane Falls Community
College *C, A*
Walla Walla University *B*
Wenatchee Valley College *C, A*
Yakima Valley Community College *A*

West Virginia
Blue Ridge Community and Technical
College *A*
West Virginia University at
Parkersburg *A*

Wisconsin
Blackhawk Technical College *C*
Chippewa Valley Technical College *A*
Fox Valley Technical College *A*
Gateway Technical College *C, A*
Lakeshore Technical College *C*
Mid-State Technical College *C*
Milwaukee Area Technical
College *C, A*
Moraine Park Technical College *C*
Nicolet Area Technical College *C*
Northcentral Technical College *A*
Northeast Wisconsin Technical
College *C*
Southwest Wisconsin Technical
College *C*
Waukesha County Technical
College *C, A*
Western Technical College *A*
Wisconsin Indianhead Technical
College *C*

Wyoming
Casper College *C, A*
Central Wyoming College *C, A*
Laramie County Community
College *C, A*
Western Wyoming Community
College *C, A*

WyoTech: Laramie *C, A*

Aviation management

Alabama
Auburn University *B*

Alaska
University of Alaska
   Anchorage *A, B*

California
College of Alameda *C, A*
Cypress College *A*
San Bernardino Valley College *A*

Colorado
Metropolitan State College of
   Denver *B*

Delaware
Delaware State University *B*
Wilmington University *B*

Florida
Broward College *A*
Embry-Riddle Aeronautical
   University *A, B*
Embry-Riddle Aeronautical University:
   Worldwide Campus *B, M*
Everglades University: Boca Raton *B*
Florida Institute of Technology *B, M*
Florida State College at Jacksonville *A*
Jacksonville University *B*
Miami Dade College *C, A*

Hawaii
University of Hawaii
   Honolulu Community College *A*

Illinois
Lewis University *C, B, M*
Lincoln Land Community College *A*
Quincy University *B*
Southern Illinois University
   Carbondale *B*
University of Illinois
   Urbana-Champaign *B*

Indiana
Indiana State University *B*
Purdue University *B*

Iowa
University of Dubuque *B*

Kansas
Central Christian College of Kansas *A*

Louisiana
Louisiana Tech University *B*
Southern University
   Shreveport *C, A*

Massachusetts
Bridgewater State College *B*
North Shore Community College *A*

Michigan
Baker College
   of Flint *A, B*
   of Muskegon *A, B*
Eastern Michigan University *B*
Schoolcraft College *C, A*
Western Michigan University *B*

Minnesota
Academy College *A*
Anoka Technical College *C, A*
Dakota County Technical College *A*
Lake Superior College *A*
Minnesota State University
   Mankato *B*
Saint Cloud State University *B*
Vermilion Community College *A*
Winona State University *A*

Mississippi
Delta State University *M*

Missouri
Park University *A, B*
Saint Louis University *B*
University of Central Missouri *M*

Montana
Rocky Mountain College *B*

Nebraska
University of Nebraska
   Omaha *B*

New Hampshire
Daniel Webster College *A, B, M*

New Jersey
Mercer County Community College *A*

New Mexico
Eastern New Mexico University *B*
Eastern New Mexico University:
   Roswell Campus *C, A*

New York
City University of New York
   York College *B*
Dowling College *B, M*
Schenectady County Community
   College *A*
State University of New York
   Farmingdale *B*
Vaughn College of Aeronautics and
   Technology *A, B*

North Carolina
Caldwell Community College and
   Technical Institute *A*
Lenoir Community College *A*

North Dakota
University of North Dakota *B*

Ohio
Ohio University *B*

Oklahoma
National Education Center
   Spartan College of Aeronautics and
   Technology *A, B*
Southern Nazarene University *B*
Tulsa Community College *A*
Western Oklahoma State College *A*

Pennsylvania
Community College of Allegheny
   County *A*
Community College of Beaver
   County *A*
Luzerne County Community
   College *A*
Marywood University *B*

Puerto Rico
Inter American University of Puerto
   Rico
   Bayamon Campus *B*

South Carolina
Bob Jones University *B*

South Dakota
South Dakota State University *B*

Tennessee
Middle Tennessee State University *M*

Texas
LeTourneau University *B*
Mountain View College *A*
San Jacinto College *C, A*
Tarleton State University *B*
Texas Southern University *B*

Utah
Dixie State College of Utah *B*
Westminster College *B*

Virginia
Averett University *B*
Hampton University *B*

West Virginia
Fairmont State University *B*
Mountain State University *A, B*

Avionics maintenance/ technology

Alabama
Enterprise-Ozark Community
   College *C, A*

Arizona
Cochise College *C, A*
Pima Community College *C*

Arkansas
Pulaski Technical College *C*

California
Orange Coast College *C, A*

Colorado
Redstone College *C*

Connecticut
Gateway Community College *C*

Illinois
Lewis University *B*
Southern Illinois University
   Carbondale *B*
Triton College *A*

Iowa
Indian Hills Community College *A*

Kansas
Cowley County Community
   College *A*

Michigan
Lansing Community College *A*
Wayne County Community
   College *C, A*
Western Michigan University *B*

Minnesota
Northland Community & Technical
   College *A*

New Mexico
Eastern New Mexico University:
   Roswell Campus *C, A*

New York
Excelsior College *A*
Vaughn College of Aeronautics and
   Technology *A, B*

North Carolina
Guilford Technical Community
   College *C, A*
Wayne Community College *C, A*

North Dakota
Lake Region State College *A*

Oklahoma
National Education Center
   Spartan College of Aeronautics and
   Technology *C, A, B*
Tulsa Community College *A*

Pennsylvania
Lehigh Carbon Community College *A*
Pennsylvania College of
   Technology *B*

Texas
Hallmark College of Aeronautics *A*
Texas State Technical College
   Waco *A*

Utah
Salt Lake Community College *C, A*

Virginia
Aviation Institute of Maintenance:
   Virginia Beach *C, A*

Washington
Clover Park Technical College *C, A*

West Virginia
Fairmont State University *A*

Wisconsin
Fox Valley Technical College *A*

Bacteriology

Arizona
Northern Arizona University *B*
University of Arizona *B, M, D*

Arkansas
University of Arkansas *B*

California
Bakersfield College *A*
California Polytechnic State
   University: San Luis Obispo *B*
California State University
   Fresno *B, M*
   Long Beach *B, M*
   Northridge *B*
   Sacramento *B, M*
Cerritos College *A*
Crafton Hills College *A*
El Camino College: Compton
   Center *A*
Fullerton College *A*
Loma Linda University *D*
Stanford University *M, D*
University of California
   Irvine *M, D*
   Los Angeles *B, M, D*
   San Diego *B*
   Santa Barbara *B*

Colorado
Adams State College *B*

Connecticut
University of Connecticut *M, D*
Yale University *M, D*

District of Columbia
George Washington University *M, D*

Georgetown University *D*

Florida
State College of Florida,
Manatee-Sarasota *A*
University of Central Florida *B, M*
University of Florida *B, M*
University of Miami *B*
University of South Florida *B, M*

Georgia
Medical College of Georgia *M, D*

Hawaii
University of Hawaii
Manoa *M, D*

Idaho
University of Idaho *B, M, D*

Illinois
Chicago State University *B*

Indiana
Indiana University
Bloomington *B, M, D*
Indiana University-Purdue University
Indianapolis *M, D*

Kansas
Central Christian College of Kansas *A*
University of Kansas Medical
Center *M, D*

Kentucky
Eastern Kentucky University *B*
University of Kentucky: College of
Medicine *D*
University of Louisville *M, D*

Louisiana
Louisiana State University Health
Sciences Center *M, D*
Tulane University *M, D*

Maine
University of Maine *B, M, D*

Massachusetts
Boston University *M, D*
Harvard College *D*
Tufts University *M, D*

Michigan
University of Michigan *D*
University of Michigan
Dearborn *B*

Minnesota
Minnesota State University
Mankato *B, T*
University of Minnesota
Twin Cities *B, M, D*

Mississippi
Mississippi State University *B*
Mississippi University for Women *B*

Missouri
Missouri Southern State University *B*
University of Missouri
Columbia *M, D*
Washington University in St. Louis *D*

Montana
Montana State University
Bozeman *B, M, D*
University of Montana *B, M, D*

Nebraska
Creighton University *M, D*

New Hampshire
University of New Hampshire *B, M, D*

New Jersey
Rutgers, The State University of New
Jersey
New Brunswick/Piscataway
Campus *B, M, D*

New Mexico
New Mexico State University *B*

New York
Cornell University *B, M, D*
State University of New York
Buffalo *M, D*
Wagner College *B, M*
Yeshiva University *M, D*

North Carolina
Duke University *M, D*
East Carolina University *D*
University of North Carolina
Chapel Hill *M, D*
Wake Forest University *B*

North Dakota
University of North Dakota *M, D*

Ohio
Bowling Green State University *B*
Case Western Reserve University *D*
Ohio State University
Columbus Campus *M, D*
Ohio Wesleyan University *B*
University of Cincinnati *M, D*
Wilmington College *B*

Oklahoma
Eastern Oklahoma State College *A*
University of Oklahoma *M, D*

Oregon
Oregon State University *B, M, D*

Pennsylvania
Drexel University *M, D*
Penn State
Abington *B*
Altoona *B*
Beaver *B*
Berks *B*
Brandywine *B*
DuBois *B*
Erie, The Behrend College *B*
Fayette, The Eberly Campus *B*
Greater Allegheny *B*
Hazleton *B*
Lehigh Valley *B*
Mont Alto *B*
New Kensington *B*
Schuylkill *B*
Shenango *B*
University Park *B*
Wilkes-Barre *B*
Worthington Scranton *B*
York *B*
Temple University *D*
University of Pittsburgh *M, D*

Puerto Rico
Inter American University of Puerto
Rico
Arecibo Campus *B*
University of Puerto Rico
Arecibo *B*

South Carolina
Medical University of South
Carolina *D*

Tennessee
University of Tennessee
Knoxville *M, D*
University of Tennessee Health
Science Center *M, D*

Texas
Laredo Community College *A*
Texas Tech University Health Sciences
Center *M, D*
University of Texas
Health Science Center at
Houston *M, D*
Health Science Center at San
Antonio *M, D*

Utah
Snow College *A*
Weber State University *B*

Virginia
University of Virginia *D*
Virginia Commonwealth
University *M, D*

Washington
University of Washington *B, D*

West Virginia
West Liberty University *B*

Wisconsin
University of Wisconsin
Madison *B, M*
Oshkosh *B, M*

Baking/pastry arts

Alaska
University of Alaska
Fairbanks *C*

Arizona
Art Institute of Tucson *A*
Cochise College *C*

Arkansas
Pulaski Technical College *C*

California
Art Institute
of California: Orange County *C*
California Culinary Academy *C*
California School of Culinary Arts *C*
Columbia College *C*
Grossmont College *C, A*
Long Beach City College *C, A*
Orange Coast College *C, A*
Santa Rosa Junior College *C*
Shasta College *C*

Colorado
Art Institute
of Colorado *C, A*
Colorado Mountain College *C*
Johnson & Wales University:
Denver *A*

Florida
Johnson & Wales University: North
Miami *A*
Valencia Community College *C, A*

Georgia
Art Institute
of Atlanta *C, A*

Savannah Technical College *C*

Illinois
Cooking & Hospitality Institute of
Chicago *A*
Elgin Community College *C, A*
Harper College *C*
Kendall College *C, A*
Lincoln Land Community College *C*
Moraine Valley Community College *C*
Triton College *C*

Indiana
Harrison College
Indianapolis *A*

Maryland
Anne Arundel Community
College *C, A*
Baltimore International College *A*

Massachusetts
Bristol Community College *C*
Massasoit Community College *C*
Newbury College *C*

Michigan
Art Institute of Michigan *C*
Baker College
of Muskegon *C*
Bay de Noc Community College *C*
Grand Rapids Community College *C*
Henry Ford Community College *C*
Mott Community College *A*
Oakland Community College *C*
Schoolcraft College *C*
Washtenaw Community College *C*

Minnesota
Art Institutes International
Minnesota *C, A*
Le Cordon Bleu College of Culinary
Arts: Minneapolis-St. Paul *A*
Minneapolis Community and
Technical College *C*
St. Paul College *C*

Nevada
Art Institute
of Las Vegas *A*

New Hampshire
Southern New Hampshire
University *A*

New Jersey
Burlington County College *C*
Hudson County Community
College *C*

New Mexico
Central New Mexico Community
College *C*

New York
Culinary Institute of America *C, A*
Erie Community College
City Campus *C*
Niagara County Community
College *C*
Paul Smith's College *C, A*
State University of New York
College of Technology at Alfred *A*
Suffolk County Community
College *C, A*

North Carolina
Johnson & Wales University:
Charlotte *A*
Wilkes Community College *A*

North Dakota

North Dakota State College of
Science *A*

Ohio

Cincinnati State Technical and
Community College *C*
Columbus State Community
College *C*

Oklahoma

Platt College
Tulsa *C*

Pennsylvania

Bucks County Community
College *C, A*
Harrisburg Area Community
College *C*
Luzerne County Community
College *C, A*
Montgomery County Community
College *A*
Pennsylvania College of
Technology *A*
Restaurant School at Walnut Hill
College *A, B*
Westmoreland County Community
College *C, A*

Puerto Rico

Inter American University of Puerto
Rico
Aguadilla Campus *C*
Ponce Paramedical College *C*
Universal Career Community College:
Humacao *C*
Universal Career Community College:
Manati *C*
Universal Career Community College:
San Juan *C*

Rhode Island

Johnson & Wales University:
Providence *A, B*

Texas

Art Institute
of Houston *A*
Culinary Institute Alain & Marie
LeNotre *C, A*
Del Mar College *A*
El Centro College *C, A*
Houston Community College
System *C, A*
Texas Culinary Academy *C*

Virginia

J. Sargeant Reynolds Community
College *A*

Washington

Art Institute of Seattle *C*
Bellingham Technical College *C*
Clark College *C, A*
Renton Technical College *C*
South Seattle Community
College *C, A*

Wisconsin

Fox Valley Technical College *A*
Milwaukee Area Technical College *C*

Ballet

Texas

Texas Christian University *B*

Utah

Brigham Young University *B*
University of Utah *B, M*

Banking/financial services

Alabama

George C. Wallace State Community
College
Selma *C*
Jefferson State Community
College *C, A*
Wallace State Community College at
Hanceville *A*

Arizona

GateWay Community College *A*
Phoenix College *A*
Rio Salado College *A*
University of Phoenix *A*

Arkansas

Northwest Arkansas Community
College *A*

California

Cabrillo College *A*
California State University
Northridge *B*
Canada College *A*
Cerritos College *A*
Chabot College *A*
El Camino College: Compton
Center *C, A*
Fresno City College *C, A*
Hartnell College *C, A*
Imperial Valley College *C, A*
Laney College *C, A*
Los Angeles City College *C, A*
Los Angeles Pierce College *C*
Los Angeles Southwest College *C*
Los Angeles Valley College *C*
Mission College *A*
Mount San Antonio College *C, A*
Palomar College *C, A*
Pasadena City College *C, A*
Porterville College *C, A*
San Francisco State University *B*
San Joaquin Delta College *C*
San Jose City College *A*
Santa Barbara City College *A*
Shasta College *C*
Solano Community College *C, A*

Colorado

Arapahoe Community College *C, A*
Colorado Northwestern Community
College *C, A*
Community College of Aurora *C, A*
Lamar Community College *A*

Connecticut

Housatonic Community College *C*
Naugatuck Valley Community
College *C, A*
Northwestern Connecticut
Community College *A*
Sacred Heart University *A*
Three Rivers Community College *A*

Delaware

Delaware Technical and Community
College
Stanton/Wilmington *A*

Florida

Daytona State College *A*
Florida State College at
Jacksonville *C, A*
Miami Dade College *C, A*
Northwest Florida State College *A*
Northwood University
Florida *B*
Pensacola Junior College *A*
Polk State College *A*

St. Petersburg College *A*
Schiller International University *B*
Seminole Community College *A*
Tallahassee Community College *A*
University of North Florida *B*

Georgia

Central Georgia Technical College *C*
Darton College *C*
Gwinnett Technical College *C*
North Georgia Technical College *C*

Hawaii

Hawaii Pacific University *B*

Illinois

Black Hawk College *C, A*
Carl Sandburg College *A*
City Colleges of Chicago
Harold Washington College *C, A*
Harper College *C, A*
Illinois Central College *C, A*
Illinois Eastern Community Colleges
Lincoln Trail College *C, A*
Lewis and Clark Community
College *A*
Prairie State College *C*
University of Illinois
Urbana-Champaign *B, M*

Indiana

Harrison College
Anderson *A*
Columbus *A*
Evansville *A*
Fort Wayne *A*
Indianapolis *A*
Lafayette *A*
Muncie *A*
Terre Haute *A*
Manchester College *B*
University of Indianapolis *A*

Iowa

Buena Vista University *B*

Kansas

Central Christian College of Kansas *A*
Dodge City Community College *C, A*
Neosho County Community
College *A*
Seward County Community College *C*
Washburn University *A*

Kentucky

Ashland Community and Technical
College *A*
Southeast Kentucky Community and
Technical College *A*
West Kentucky Community and
Technical College *A*

Louisiana

Louisiana State University
Shreveport *B*
Southern University
Shreveport *A*

Maine

Eastern Maine Community College *A*
Husson University *B*

Maryland

Baltimore City Community College *C*
Community College of Baltimore
County *C, A*
Frederick Community College *C, A*
Hagerstown Community College *A*

Massachusetts

Bristol Community College *A*

New England College of Business and
Finance *C, A*

Michigan

Bay de Noc Community College *C*
Delta College *C*
Mid Michigan Community College *A*
Monroe County Community
College *C, A*

Minnesota

Alexandria Technical College *C, A*
Fond du Lac Tribal and Community
College *C*
Minneapolis Community and
Technical College *C*
Minnesota State Community and
Technical College *A*
Minnesota State University
Mankato *B*
North Hennepin Community
College *C*
St. Cloud Technical College *C, A*
University of Minnesota
Twin Cities *C*

Mississippi

East Mississippi Community
College *A*
Mississippi Gulf Coast Community
College *A*

Missouri

Central Methodist University *B*
Mineral Area College *A*
St. Louis Community College
St. Louis Community College at
Florissant Valley *A*
St. Louis Community College at
Meramec *A*
University of Missouri
Columbia *B*

Nebraska

Northeast Community College *A*
University of Nebraska
Omaha *B*

Nevada

College of Southern Nevada *A*

New Jersey

Bergen Community College *A*
Camden County College *A*
Saint Peter's College *B*

New Mexico

Central New Mexico Community
College *C, A*
New Mexico Junior College *A*
New Mexico State University
Alamogordo *C*
Carlsbad *C*
Santa Fe Community College *A*

New York

Erie Community College
City Campus *C*
Finger Lakes Community College *A*
Fordham University *M*
Globe Institute of Technology *C, A, B*
Hilbert College *A*
Jamestown Community College *A*
Metropolitan College of New York *M*
Mohawk Valley Community
College *C, A*
New York University *C*

North Carolina

Alamance Community College *A*
Catawba Valley Community
College *C, A*

Fayetteville Technical Community
College *A*
Forsyth Technical Community
College *A*
Isothermal Community College *A*

North Dakota

North Dakota State College of
Science *A*

Ohio

Eastern Gateway Community
College *A*
Miami University
Hamilton Campus *C*
Ohio Business College: Sandusky *A*
Owens Community College
Toledo *A*
Shawnee State University *A*
Terra State Community College *C*
Youngstown State University *B, M*

Oklahoma

Oklahoma City Community College *C*

Oregon

Southwestern Oregon Community
College *C, A*

Pennsylvania

Central Pennsylvania College *A*
Community College of Allegheny
County *C, A*
Community College of Philadelphia *A*
Harrisburg Area Community
College *C, A*
La Salle University *A, B*
Lackawanna College *A*
Luzerne County Community
College *A*
Reading Area Community
College *C, A*
Westmoreland County Community
College *C, A*

Puerto Rico

Caribbean University *A*
Universidad Metropolitana *C, B*

Rhode Island

Community College of Rhode
Island *A*

South Carolina

Trident Technical College *C*

South Dakota

Lake Area Technical Institute *A*
Northern State University *B*
Southeast Technical Institute *A*

Tennessee

Southern Adventist University *M*

Texas

Austin Community College *C, A*
College of the Mainland *A*
Houston Community College
System *C, A*
North Lake College *C*
Northeast Texas Community
College *C, A*
Palo Alto College *A*
Sam Houston State University *B*
San Antonio College *C*
South Texas College *C, A*
Texas Southern University *B*
University of North Texas *B, M, D*
University of Texas
Arlington *B, D*
University of the Incarnate Word *B*

Utah

Utah Valley University *C, A*

Virginia

Dabney S. Lancaster Community
College *C*
Germanna Community College *C*
Hampton University *B*
Southwest Virginia Community
College *C*
Tidewater Community College *A*
Virginia Western Community
College *A*

Washington

Clover Park Technical College *C*
Gonzaga University *B*
Spokane Community College *C, A*
Spokane Falls Community
College *C, A*

West Virginia

Fairmont State University *B*
New River Community and Technical
College *C, A*
West Liberty University *B*
West Virginia State Community and
Technical College *C, A*
West Virginia State University *B*

Wisconsin

Fox Valley Technical College *A*
Mid-State Technical College *C*
Milwaukee Area Technical College *A*
University of Wisconsin
Whitewater *M*

Barbering

Alabama

Bevill State Community College *C*
Calhoun Community College *C*
Jefferson Davis Community College *C*
Lawson State Community College *C*
Shelton State Community College *C*

California

Santiago Canyon College *C*

Colorado

Trinidad State Junior College *C*

Florida

Central Florida Community College *C*
Indian River State College *C*
Pensacola Junior College *C*

Georgia

Central Georgia Technical College *C*
Middle Georgia Technical College *C*

Kentucky

West Kentucky Community and
Technical College *C*

Minnesota

Minneapolis Community and
Technical College *C*
Northland Community & Technical
College *C*

New Mexico

Northern New Mexico College *C*

North Carolina

Central Carolina Community
College *C*

Utah

Snow College *C, A*

Washington

Bates Technical College *C*
Olympic College *C*

Wisconsin

Fox Valley Technical College *C*

Bartending

California

Columbia College *C*
Shasta College *C*

Georgia

Art Institute
of Atlanta *A*

Puerto Rico

Universidad del Este *C*

Behavioral sciences

Alabama

Athens State University *B*

Arizona

Glendale Community College *A*
Northern Arizona University *B*
Prescott College *B, M*
University of Phoenix *B*

California

California Baptist University *B*
California Institute of Integral
Studies *M, D*
California State Polytechnic
University: Pomona *B*
California State University
Bakersfield *M*
Dominguez Hills *B*
College of the Siskiyous *A*
Concordia University *B*
Imperial Valley College *A*
MiraCosta College *A*
Mount San Jacinto College *A*
San Diego City College *A*
San Jose State University *B*
Shasta College *A*
University of California
San Diego *B*
University of California: Merced *M, D*
University of La Verne *B*

Colorado

Metropolitan State College of
Denver *B*
United States Air Force Academy *B*
University of Colorado
Denver *D*

Connecticut

Mitchell College *B*

Delaware

Wilmington University *B*

Hawaii

Chaminade University of Honolulu *B*
Hawaii Pacific University *B*

Idaho

Lewis-Clark State College *A*

Illinois

Loyola University Chicago *B*
National-Louis University *B*
Southeastern Illinois College *A*

Indiana

Ancilla College *A*

Indiana University
Kokomo *B*
Vincennes University *A*

Iowa

Ellsworth Community College *A*

Kansas

Garden City Community College *A*
University of Kansas *B, M, D*

Maine

University of Maine
Machias *B*
Presque Isle *B*
University of Southern Maine *B*

Maryland

Garrett College *A*
Johns Hopkins University *B*

Massachusetts

Cape Cod Community College *A*

Michigan

Albion College *B*
Grand Valley State University *B*
Northern Michigan University *B*
University of Michigan
Dearborn *B*

Missouri

Evangel University *M*
University of Missouri
Columbia *B*

Nebraska

Concordia University *B*

New Hampshire

Granite State College *A, B*

New Jersey

Drew University *B*

New York

Concordia College *B*
Polytechnic Institute of New York
University *M*

North Dakota

Dickinson State University *B*

Ohio

Wright State University *M*

Oklahoma

Mid-America Christian University *B*
Murray State College *A*
Oklahoma Wesleyan University *A, B*
Seminole State College *A*
Southern Nazarene University *B*

Oregon

George Fox University *B*

Pennsylvania

Carnegie Mellon University *B, D*
Franklin & Marshall College *B*
Gettysburg College *B*
Mount Aloysius College *A, B*
Point Park University *B*
York College of Pennsylvania *B*

South Carolina

Anderson University *B*
Columbia College *B*

South Dakota

Dakota Wesleyan University *B*

Tennessee
Tennessee Wesleyan College *B*
Trevecca Nazarene University *B*

Texas
Northwest Vista College *A*
South Plains College *A*
University of Houston
Clear Lake *B, M*
University of North Texas *B, M*

Vermont
College of St. Joseph in Vermont *B*

Virginia
Bluefield College *B*

Wisconsin
Mount Mary College *B*
University of Wisconsin
Madison *B*

Bible studies

Alabama
Amridge University *B, M*
Faulkner University *B, M*
Heritage Christian University *A, B, M*
Huntsville Bible College *C, A, B*
Oakwood University *A*
Selma University *A, B, M*
Southeastern Bible College *C, A, B*

Arizona
Grand Canyon University *B*
International Baptist College *C, A, M*
Southwestern College *C, A, B*

Arkansas
Central Baptist College *B*
Ecclesia College *A, B*
Harding University *B, M*
Ouachita Baptist University *B*
Williams Baptist College *B*

California
Azusa Pacific University *B, M*
Bethany University *B*
Bethesda Christian University *B, M*
Biola University *B, M*
California Baptist University *B*
Fresno Pacific University *B*
Hope International University *C, A, B*
Horizon College of San Diego *A, B*
King's College and Seminary, The
The King's College and
Seminary *C, A, B, M, D*
Life Pacific College *A, B*
The Master's College *C, B, M*
Pacific Union College *B*
Patten University *C, A*
Point Loma Nazarene University *B*
San Diego Christian College *B*
School of Urban Missions:
Oakland *A, B*
Shasta Bible College and Graduate
School *C, A*
Simpson University *C, A, B*
Southern California Seminary *A, B, M*
Vanguard University of Southern
California *B, M*
William Jessup University *C, A*
World Mission University *B*

Colorado
Colorado Christian University *C, B*
Nazarene Bible College *A, B*

District of Columbia
Catholic University of America *M, D*

Florida
Baptist College of Florida *B*
Clearwater Christian College *C, B*
Florida Christian College *A, B*
Florida College *B*
Hobe Sound Bible College *C, A, B*
Palm Beach Atlantic University *B*
Trinity Baptist College *M*
Trinity College of Florida *C, A*
Universidad FLET *C, A, B, M*
Warner University *B*

Georgia
Atlanta Christian College *B*
Beulah Heights University *A, B, M*
Carver Bible College *C, A, B*
Covenant College *B*
Toccoa Falls College *C, B*

Idaho
Boise Bible College *C, A, B*
Northwest Nazarene University *B*

Illinois
Judson University *B*
Lincoln Christian University *A, B, M*
Moody Bible Institute *C, A, B, M*
North Park University *B*
Olivet Nazarene University *B*
Trinity International
University *B, M, D*
Wheaton College *B*

Indiana
Anderson University *B*
Bethel College *A, B*
Grace College *C, A, B*
Huntington University *B*
Indiana Wesleyan University *A, B*
Taylor University *B*
University of Evansville *B*

Iowa
Emmaus Bible College *C, A, B*
Faith Baptist Bible College and
Theological Seminary *C, A, B, M*

Kansas
Barclay College *C, A, B*
Central Christian College of
Kansas *A, B*
Tabor College *B*

Kentucky
Asbury College *B*
Campbellsville University *B*
Clear Creek Baptist Bible
College *C, A, B*
Kentucky Christian University *B*
Mid-Continent University *C, B*
St. Catharine College *C, A*

Maryland
Griggs University *B*
Washington Bible College *C, A, B, M, T*

Massachusetts
Boston Baptist College *C, A, B*
Boston College *M, D*
Boston University *M, D*
Zion Bible College *C, B*

Michigan
Andrews University *M, D*
Calvin College *B*
Cornerstone University *C, A, B*
Grace Bible College *A, B*
Great Lakes Christian College *A, B*
Kuyper College *C, A, B*
Rochester College *B*
Spring Arbor University *B*

Minnesota
Bethel University *B, M*
Crossroads College *A*
Crown College *A*
North Central University *C, A, B*
Northwestern College *C, B*
Oak Hills Christian College *C, A, B*

Mississippi
Belhaven University *C, B*
Blue Mountain College *B*
Wesley College *B*

Missouri
Baptist Bible College *C*
Calvary Bible College and Theological
Seminary *C, A, B, M*
Central Bible College *A, B*
Central Christian College of the
Bible *C, A*
Evangel University *B*
Global University *A, B, M*
Hannibal-LaGrange College *B*
Ozark Christian College *C, A, B*
St. Louis Christian College *B*
Southwest Baptist University *B*

Nebraska
Grace University *C, A, B, M*
Nebraska Christian College *B*
York College *B*

New Jersey
Drew University *M, D*
Somerset Christian College *C, A, B*

New York
Davis College *C, A*
Houghton College *B*
Roberts Wesleyan College *B*

North Carolina
Carolina Christian College *A, B*
Gardner-Webb University *M*
Mid-Atlantic Christian University *A, B*
Montreat College *B*
Piedmont Baptist
College *C, A, B, M, D*
Shepherds Theological Seminary *M*
Southeastern Baptist Theological
Seminary *A, B*

North Dakota
Trinity Bible College *C, A, B*

Ohio
Ashland University *B*
Cedarville University *C*
Cincinnati Christian University *B, M*
God's Bible School and College *A*
Malone University *B*
Mount Vernon Nazarene University *B*
Pontifical College Josephinum *M*
Rosedale Bible College *C, A*

Oklahoma
Family of Faith College *C, B*
Mid-America Christian University *B*
Oklahoma Baptist University *B*
Oklahoma Christian University *B*
Oklahoma City University *B*
Oklahoma Wesleyan University *A, B*
Oral Roberts University *B, M*
Southwestern Christian University *B*

Oregon
Corban College *C, A, B*
Eugene Bible College *C, B*
George Fox University *B*
Mount Angel Seminary *M*
Multnomah University *B, M*
Northwest Christian University *B*

Pennsylvania
Baptist Bible College of
Pennsylvania *C, D*
Eastern University *B*
Geneva College *A, B*
Lancaster Bible College *C, A, B, M*
Messiah College *B*
Philadelphia Biblical
University *C, B, M*
Valley Forge Christian College *C, A, B*

Puerto Rico
Bayamon Central University *M*
Universidad Pentecostal Mizpa *B*

Rhode Island
Providence College *M*

South Carolina
Bob Jones University *B, M, D*
Clinton Junior College *A*
Columbia International
University *C, A, B, M*
Erskine College *C, M*
North Greenville University *B, M*
Southern Methodist College *C, B*

Tennessee
American Baptist College *A, B*
Bryan College *B*
Free Will Baptist Bible College *A, B*
Freed-Hardeman University *B, M*
Johnson Bible College *C, A, B, M*
King College *B*
Lee University *B*
Lipscomb University *B, M*
Milligan College *B*
Southern Adventist University *A*
Tennessee Temple University *A, B*
Trevecca Nazarene University *M*
University of the South *M, D*

Texas
Abilene Christian University *B, M*
Arlington Baptist College *C, B*
Austin Graduate School of
Theology *B*
Baptist University of the
Americas *C, B*
College of Biblical
Studies-Houston *C, A, B*
Dallas Baptist University *A, B*
Dallas Christian College *B*
East Texas Baptist University *B*
Hardin-Simmons University *B*
Howard Payne University *B*
LeTourneau University *B*
Lubbock Christian University *B, M*
San Jacinto College *A*
Southwestern Assemblies of God
University *A, B, M*
Southwestern Baptist Theological
Seminary *C*
University of Mary Hardin-Baylor *B*

Virginia
Bluefield College *B*
Eastern Mennonite University *C, A, B*
Liberty University *C, B, M*
Regent University *A, B, M*
Virginia Baptist College *C*

Washington
Northwest University *C, B*
Trinity Lutheran College *A, B*

West Virginia
Appalachian Bible College *C, A, B, M*
Ohio Valley University *A, B*

Wisconsin
Concordia University Wisconsin *B*

Maranatha Baptist Bible College *B, M*
Marquette University *M, D*

Bilingual/bicultural education

Arizona
Northern Arizona University *M, T*
Prescott College *B, M*
University of Arizona *M*

California
Butte College *A*
California Lutheran University *M*
California Polytechnic State
    University: San Luis Obispo *T*
California State University
    Chico *M*
    Dominguez Hills *M*
    East Bay *T*
    Fullerton *M*
    Long Beach *B, M, T*
    Northridge *M*
    Sacramento *M*
    San Bernardino *M*
    San Marcos *T*
Cerritos College *A*
Chapman University *T*
Contra Costa College *A*
El Camino College: Compton
    Center *A*
Fresno City College *A*
Fresno Pacific University *M, T*
Loyola Marymount University *M*
National University *M, T*
Sacramento City College *A*
San Diego City College *A*
San Diego State University *M*
San Francisco State University *T*
University of California
    San Diego *M*
University of La Verne *T*
University of San Francisco *M, D, T*
University of the Pacific *T*

Colorado
Colorado Mountain College *A*

Connecticut
Fairfield University *M, T*
Southern Connecticut State
    University *M, T*

Delaware
Delaware Technical and Community
    College
    Terry *A*
University of Delaware *M*

Idaho
Boise State University *B, T*
Northwest Nazarene University *M*

Illinois
Aurora University *M*
Chicago State University *M, T*
Columbia College Chicago *M*
DePaul University *M, T*
Loyola University Chicago *B*
North Park University *M*
Northeastern Illinois University *B*
University of Illinois
    Urbana-Champaign *M, D*
Western Illinois University *B*

Massachusetts
Boston University *B, M, T*
Eastern Nazarene College *M, T*
Elms College *B, M, T*
Salem State College *M*

Michigan
Calvin College *B, T*
Saginaw Valley State University *T*
Wayne State University *M, T*

Minnesota
College of St. Scholastica *T*
Concordia University: St. Paul *B, T*
University of Minnesota
    Twin Cities *M*
Winona State University *B, T*

Missouri
Northwest Missouri State
    University *M, T*
Rockhurst University *T*
University of Missouri
    Kansas City *B*

Nevada
Nevada State College *B*

New Jersey
Fairleigh Dickinson University
    Metropolitan Campus *M*
Georgian Court University *T*
Montclair State University *T*
New Jersey City University *T*
Seton Hall University *M*
William Paterson University of New
    Jersey *T*

New Mexico
University of the Southwest *B*
Western New Mexico University *T*

New York
Adelphi University *M, T*
City University of New York
    Brooklyn College *B, M, T*
    City College *B, M, T*
    Hunter College *M, T*
    LaGuardia Community College *A*
    Queens College *M, T*
    York College *T*
Hofstra University *M, T*
St. John's University *M, T*
State University of New York
    Albany *M*
    Buffalo *M, T*
    College at Brockport *B, M, T*
    College at Buffalo *M*
    College at Old Westbury *B, T*

North Carolina
Greensboro College *M*

Ohio
University of Findlay *B, M, T*

Oklahoma
Oklahoma State University
    Oklahoma City *A*

Oregon
Chemeketa Community College *A*
Eastern Oregon University *T*
Treasure Valley Community College *A*
University of Oregon *T*
Western Oregon University *T*

Pennsylvania
Immaculata University *M, T*
La Salle University *B, M*

Puerto Rico
Inter American University of Puerto
    Rico
    Metropolitan Campus *B, M*
University of the Sacred Heart *B*

Texas
Del Mar College *A*
Houston Baptist University *M*
Laredo Community College *A*
McMurry University *T*
Midwestern State University *B*
Richland College *A*
Southern Methodist University *M*
Sul Ross State University *M*
Texas A&M International
    University *B, M, T*
Texas A&M University
    Commerce *M*
    Kingsville *B, M, D*
Texas Southern University *M*
Texas State University: San
    Marcos *M, T*
Texas Tech University *M*
Texas Wesleyan University *B, M, T*
University of Houston *M, T*
University of Houston
    Clear Lake *T*
    Downtown *M*
University of Texas
    Brownsville - Texas Southmost
        College *M*
    Pan American *M*
    San Antonio *M*
    of the Permian Basin *M*
West Texas A&M University *T*

Utah
Brigham Young University *D*
Weber State University *B*

Washington
University of Washington *M*
Washington State University *B, M, T*

Wisconsin
Marquette University *M*

Biochemistry

Alabama
Auburn University *B*
Oakwood University *B*
Samford University *B*
Spring Hill College *B*

Arizona
Arizona State University *B, M, D*
Grand Canyon University *B*
University of Arizona *B, M, D*

Arkansas
Harding University *B*
John Brown University *B*
Lyon College *B*

California
Azusa Pacific University *B*
Biola University *B*
California Baptist University *B*
California Institute of
    Technology *M, D*
California Lutheran University *B*
California Polytechnic State
    University: San Luis Obispo *B*
California State University
    Chico *B*
    Dominguez Hills *B*
    East Bay *B, M*
    Fullerton *B*
    Long Beach *B, M*
    Los Angeles *B*
    Northridge *B*
    San Bernardino *B*
    San Marcos *B*
Chapman University *B*
Claremont McKenna College *B*
La Sierra University *B*

Loma Linda University *D*
Loyola Marymount University *B*
Mills College *B*
Mount St. Mary's College *B*
Notre Dame de Namur University *B*
Occidental College *B*
Pacific Union College *B*
Pepperdine University *B*
Pitzer College *B*
Point Loma Nazarene University *B*
St. Mary's College of California *B*
San Francisco State University *B*
San Jose State University *B*
Santa Clara University *B*
Scripps College *B*
Sonoma State University *B*
Stanford University *D*
University of California
    Berkeley *M, D*
    Irvine *M, D*
    Los Angeles *B, M, D*
    Riverside *B, M, D*
    San Diego *B, D*
    Santa Barbara *B, M, D*
University of Redlands *B*
University of San Diego *B*
University of Southern
    California *B, M, D*
University of the Pacific *B*
Vanguard University of Southern
    California *B*

Colorado
Colorado College *B*
Colorado State University *B, M, D*
Regis University *B*
University of Colorado
    Boulder *B, D*
    Denver *D*
University of Denver *B*

Connecticut
Central Connecticut State
    University *B*
Connecticut College *B*
Eastern Connecticut State
    University *B*
Fairfield University *B*
Quinnipiac University *B*
Sacred Heart University *B*
Saint Joseph College *B, M*
Trinity College *B*
University of Connecticut *M, D*
Wesleyan University *B, D*
Yale University *B, M, D*

Delaware
University of Delaware *B, M, D*

District of Columbia
American University *B*
Catholic University of America *B*
George Washington University *M, D*
Georgetown University *B, D*
Howard University *M, D*
Trinity Washington University *B*

Florida
Eckerd College *B*
Florida Institute of Technology *B*
Florida State University *B*
New College of Florida *B*
Pensacola Junior College *A*
Stetson University *B*
University of Florida *M*
University of Miami *B, D*
University of Tampa *B*

Georgia
Agnes Scott College *B*
Emory University *D*
Georgia Institute of Technology *B*
Kennesaw State University *B*

LaGrange College *B*
Mercer University *B*
Spelman College *B*
University of Georgia *B, M, D*

Idaho

Idaho State University *B*
Northwest Nazarene University *B*
University of Idaho *B, M, D*

Illinois

Augustana College *B*
Benedictine University *B*
Blackburn College *B*
Bradley University *B, T*
Chicago State University *B*
Dominican University *B*
Illinois Institute of Technology *B*
Illinois State University *B*
Judson University *B*
Knox College *B*
Lewis University *B*
Loyola University Chicago *B, M, D*
Monmouth College *B*
North Central College *B*
Rockford College *B*
Rush University *D*
University of Chicago *B, D*
University of Illinois
   Chicago *B*
   Urbana-Champaign *B, M, D*

Indiana

Anderson University *B*
DePauw University *B*
Earlham College *B*
Indiana University
   Bloomington *B, M, D*
Indiana University-Purdue University
   Indianapolis *M, D*
Manchester College *B*
Purdue University *B, M, D*
Rose-Hulman Institute of
   Technology *B*
Saint Joseph's College *A, B*
University of Evansville *B*
University of Notre Dame *B, M, D*
Valparaiso University *B*
Vincennes University *A*

Iowa

Clarke College *B*
Coe College *B*
Cornell College *B*
Drake University *B*
Grinnell College *B*
Iowa State University *B, M, D*
Loras College *B*
Simpson College *B*
University of Iowa *B, M, D*
University of Northern Iowa *B, M*
Wartburg College *B*

Kansas

Benedictine College *B*
Kansas State University *B, M, D*
Pittsburg State University *B*
Southwestern College *B*
Tabor College *B*
University of Kansas *B*
Washburn University *B*
Wichita State University *B*

Kentucky

Asbury College *B*
Bellarmine University *B*
Bluegrass Community and Technical
   College *A*
Centre College *B*
University of Louisville *M, D*
Western Kentucky University *B*

Louisiana

Centenary College of Louisiana *B*
Louisiana State University
   Shreveport *B*
Louisiana State University Health
   Sciences Center *M, D*
Louisiana State University and
   Agricultural and Mechanical
   College *B, M, D*
Tulane University *B, M, D*
Xavier University of Louisiana *B*

Maine

Bates College *B*
Bowdoin College *B*
Colby College *B*
University of Maine *B, M, D*
University of New England *B*

Maryland

Hood College *B*
McDaniel College *B*
Montgomery College *A*
Mount St. Mary's University *B*
St. Mary's College of Maryland *B*
University of Maryland
   Baltimore County *M, D*
   College Park *B, M, D*
Washington Adventist University *B*

Massachusetts

American International College *B*
Boston College *B, M, D*
Boston University *B, M, D*
Brandeis University *B, M, D*
Bridgewater State College *B*
Clark University *B*
Eastern Nazarene College *B*
Emmanuel College *B*
Harvard College *B, M, D*
Merrimack College *B*
Mount Holyoke College *B*
Northeastern University *B*
Regis College *B*
Salem State College *B*
Simmons College *B*
Smith College *B*
Stonehill College *B*
Suffolk University *B*
Tufts University *D*
University of Massachusetts
   Boston *B*
Wellesley College *B*
Wheaton College *B*
Worcester Polytechnic Institute *B, M*

Michigan

Albion College *B*
Alma College *B*
Andrews University *B*
Calvin College *B*
Central Michigan University *B*
Eastern Michigan University *B*
Ferris State University *B*
Grand Valley State University *B*
Kettering University *B*
Lawrence Technological University *B*
Madonna University *B*
Michigan State University *B, M, D*
Northern Michigan University *B, M*
Oakland University *B*
Saginaw Valley State University *B*
Spring Arbor University *B*
University of Detroit Mercy *B*
University of Michigan *B, M, D*
University of Michigan
   Dearborn *B*
Western Michigan University *B*

Minnesota

College of St. Benedict *B*
College of St. Scholastica *B*
Gustavus Adolphus College *B*

Hamline University *B*
Minnesota State University
   Mankato *B*
Northwestern College *B*
St. Catherine University *B*
Saint Cloud State University *B*
St. John's University *B*
St. Mary's University of Minnesota *B*
University of Minnesota
   Duluth *B, M*
   Twin Cities *B, M, D*
University of St. Thomas *B*

Mississippi

Millsaps College *B*
Mississippi College *B*
Mississippi State University *B*

Missouri

Culver-Stockton College *B*
Maryville University of Saint Louis *B*
Missouri Southern State University *B*
Missouri Western State University *B*
Rockhurst University *B*
Saint Louis University *B, D*
University of Missouri
   Columbia *B, M, D*
   Missouri University of Science and
     Technology *B*
   St. Louis *B, M*
Washington University in St.
   Louis *B, D*
Westminster College *B*
William Jewell College *B*

Montana

Montana State University
   Bozeman *M, D*
University of Montana *M, D*

Nebraska

Doane College *B*
Nebraska Wesleyan University *B*
Union College *B*
University of Nebraska
   Lincoln *B, M, D*

Nevada

University of Nevada
   Reno *B, M, D*

New Hampshire

Dartmouth College *B, D*
Saint Anselm College *B*
University of New Hampshire *M, D*

New Jersey

College of St. Elizabeth *B*
Fairleigh Dickinson University
   College at Florham *B*
   Metropolitan Campus *B*
Georgian Court University *B*
Montclair State University *B*
Ramapo College of New Jersey *B*
Richard Stockton College of New
   Jersey *B*
Rider University *B*
Rowan University *B*
Rutgers, The State University of New
   Jersey
   New Brunswick/Piscataway
     Campus *B, M, D*
Saint Peter's College *B*
Seton Hall University *B*
Stevens Institute of
   Technology *B, M, D*

New Mexico

New Mexico Institute of Mining and
   Technology *B, M*
New Mexico State University *B*
University of New Mexico *B*

New York

Adelphi University *B*
Barnard College *B*
Canisius College *B*
City University of New York
   City College *B, M*
   College of Staten Island *B*
   Hunter College *M*
Colgate University *B*
College of Mount St. Vincent *B*
College of Saint Rose *B*
Columbia University *B*
Cornell University *B, M, D*
Daemen College *B*
Elmira College *B*
Hamilton College *B*
Hartwick College *B*
Hobart and William Smith Colleges *B*
Hofstra University *B*
Houghton College *B*
Iona College *B*
Ithaca College *B*
Keuka College *B*
Le Moyne College *B*
Long Island University
   Brooklyn Campus *B*
Manhattan College *B, T*
Manhattanville College *B*
Marist College *B*
Nazareth College *B*
New York University *B, M, D*
Niagara University *B*
Pace University *B*
Roberts Wesleyan College *B*
Rochester Institute of Technology *B*
Russell Sage College *B*
Saint Bonaventure University *B*
St. Lawrence University *B*
Siena College *B*
State University of New York
   Albany *B, M, D*
   Binghamton *B*
   Buffalo *B, M, D*
   College at Brockport *B*
   College at Fredonia *B*
   College at Geneseo *B*
   College at Old Westbury *B*
   College at Oneonta *B*
   College at Plattsburgh *B*
   College at Potsdam *B*
   College of Environmental Science
     and Forestry *B*
   Stony Brook *B*
   Upstate Medical University *M, D*
Syracuse University *B*
Union College *B*
University of Rochester *B, M, D*
Vassar College *B*
Wells College *B*
Yeshiva University *M, D*

North Carolina

Campbell University *B*
Duke University *M, D*
East Carolina University *B, D*
North Carolina State
   University *B, M, D*
Queens University of Charlotte *B*
University of North Carolina
   Chapel Hill *M, D*
   Greensboro *B*
Wake Forest University *D*

North Dakota

Jamestown College *B*
North Dakota State University *M, D*
University of North Dakota *M, D*

Ohio

Bowling Green State University *B*
Capital University *B*
Case Western Reserve
   University *B, M, D*

College of Mount St. Joseph *B*
College of Wooster *B*
Denison University *B*
Hiram College *B*
John Carroll University *B*
Kenyon College *B*
Marietta College *B*
Miami University
  Oxford Campus *B*
Mount Union College *B*
Notre Dame College *B*
Oberlin College *B*
Ohio Northern University *B*
Ohio State University
  Columbus Campus *B, M, D*
Ohio Wesleyan University *B*
Otterbein College *B*
University of Akron *B*
University of Cincinnati *D*
University of Dayton *B*
Wilmington College *B*
Wittenberg University *B*
Wright State University *B, M*

Oklahoma

Oklahoma Baptist University *B*
Oklahoma Christian University *B*
Oklahoma City University *B*
Oklahoma State University *B, M, D*
Oral Roberts University *B*
Southern Nazarene University *B*
University of Oklahoma *B*
University of Tulsa *B*

Oregon

Lewis & Clark College *B*
Oregon State University *B, M, D*
Pacific University *B*
Portland State University *B*
Reed College *B*
University of Oregon *B*

Pennsylvania

Albright College *B*
Allegheny College *B*
Alvernia University *B*
Bucknell University *B*
Carnegie Mellon University *D*
Cedar Crest College *B*
Chatham University *B*
Chestnut Hill College *B*
DeSales University *B*
Dickinson College *B*
Drexel University *M, D*
Duquesne University *B*
East Stroudsburg University of
  Pennsylvania *B*
Eastern University *B*
Elizabethtown College *B*
Franklin & Marshall College *B*
Gettysburg College *B*
Grove City College *B*
Holy Family University *B*
Indiana University of Pennsylvania *B*
Juniata College *B*
Keystone College *B*
Kutztown University of
  Pennsylvania *B*
La Salle University *B*
Lafayette College *B*
Lehigh University *B, D*
Mansfield University of
  Pennsylvania *B*
Mercyhurst College *B*
Messiah College *B*
Misericordia University *B*
Moravian College *B*
Muhlenberg College *B*
Penn State
  Abington *B*
  Altoona *B*
  Beaver *B*
  Berks *B*
  Brandywine *B*

DuBois *B*
Erie, The Behrend College *B*
Fayette, The Eberly Campus *B*
Greater Allegheny *B*
Hazleton *B*
Lehigh Valley *B*
Mont Alto *B*
New Kensington *B*
Schuylkill *B*
Shenango *B*
University Park *B, M, D*
Wilkes-Barre *B*
Worthington Scranton *B*
York *B*
Philadelphia University *B*
Rosemont College *B*
Saint Joseph's University *B*
St. Vincent College *B*
Seton Hill University *B*
Slippery Rock University of
  Pennsylvania *B*
Susquehanna University *B*
Swarthmore College *B*
Temple University *B, M, D*
University of Pennsylvania *B*
University of Pittsburgh *M, D*
University of Scranton *B, M*
University of the Sciences in
  Philadelphia *B, M, D*
Washington & Jefferson College *B*
West Chester University of
  Pennsylvania *B, M*
Westminster College *B*
Widener University *B*
Wilkes University *B*

Puerto Rico

University of Puerto Rico
  Medical Sciences *M, D*

Rhode Island

Brown University *B, M, D*
Providence College *B*
University of Rhode Island *M, D*

South Carolina

Charleston Southern University *B*
Claflin University *B*
Clemson University *B, M, D*
College of Charleston *B*
Converse College *B*
Medical University of South
  Carolina *D*

South Dakota

Augustana College *B*
South Dakota State University *B*
University of South Dakota *M, D*

Tennessee

Christian Brothers University *B*
Freed-Hardeman University *B*
King College *B*
Lee University *B*
Lipscomb University *B*
Maryville College *B*
Southern Adventist University *B*
Tennessee State University *B*
Tennessee Technological University *B*
University of Tennessee
  Knoxville *M, D*
University of Tennessee Health
  Science Center *M, D*
University of the South *B*
Vanderbilt University *D*

Texas

Abilene Christian University *B*
Angelo State University *B*
Austin College *B*
Baylor University *B*
McMurry University *B*
Rice University *B, M, D*

St. Edward's University *B*
St. Mary's University *B*
Schreiner University *B*
Southern Methodist University *B*
Southwestern University *B*
Stephen F. Austin State University *B*
Texas A&M University *B, M, D*
Texas Christian University *B*
Texas State University: San
  Marcos *B, M*
Texas Tech University *B*
Texas Wesleyan University *B*
Texas Woman's University *B*
Trinity University *B*
University of Dallas *B*
University of Houston *B, M, D*
University of North Texas *B, M, D*
University of St. Thomas *B*
University of Texas
  Arlington *B*
  Austin *B, M, D*
  Dallas *B*
  Health Science Center at
    Houston *M, D*
  Health Science Center at San
    Antonio *M, D*
  Southwestern Medical Center at
    Dallas *M, D*
University of the Incarnate Word *B*

Utah

Brigham Young University *B, M, D*
University of Utah *M, D*
Utah State University *M, D*

Vermont

Marlboro College *B*
Middlebury College *B*
Norwich University *B*
St. Michael's College *B*
University of Vermont *B, M, D*

Virginia

Eastern Mennonite University *B*
George Mason University *D*
Hampden-Sydney College *B*
Liberty University *B*
Old Dominion University *B*
Roanoke College *B*
University of Virginia *D*
Virginia Commonwealth
  University *M, D*
Virginia Polytechnic Institute and
  State University *B*
Washington and Lee University *B*

Washington

Gonzaga University *B*
Seattle Pacific University *B*
Seattle University *B*
University of Puget Sound *B*
University of Washington *B, M, D*
Walla Walla University *B*
Washington State University *B, M, D*
Western Washington University *B*

West Virginia

Bethany College *B*
West Virginia University *B, M*

Wisconsin

Beloit College *B*
Carroll University *B*
Lakeland College *B*
Lawrence University *B*
Marquette University *B, M*
Ripon College *B*
St. Norbert College *B*
University of Wisconsin
  La Crosse *B*
  Madison *B, M, D*
  Milwaukee *B*
  River Falls *B*

Viterbo University *B*
Wisconsin Lutheran College *B*

Biochemistry/ biophysics and molecular biology

Arkansas

Harding University *B*
Hendrix College *B*

California

University of California
  Irvine *B*
  Riverside *M, D*

Connecticut

Connecticut College *B*
Yale University *B, M, D*

Florida

Florida Southern College *B*
Florida State University *D*
Rollins College *B*
University of Central Florida *D*

Georgia

Medical College of Georgia *D*

Illinois

Illinois Institute of
  Technology *B, M, D*
Northwestern University *D*
University of Illinois
  Chicago *M, D*

Indiana

Indiana Wesleyan University *B*
Purdue University *B, M, D*

Iowa

Cornell College *B*

Kansas

Emporia State University *B*
University of Kansas *M, D*
University of Kansas Medical
  Center *M, D*

Maryland

Towson University *B*
University of Maryland
  Baltimore County *B*

Massachusetts

University of Massachusetts
  Amherst *B, M, D*

Michigan

Michigan State University *B, M, D*
Michigan Technological University *B*
University of Michigan
  Flint *B*
Wayne State University *M, D*

Nebraska

Nebraska Wesleyan University *B*
University of Nebraska
  Medical Center *M, D*

New Hampshire

Dartmouth College *B*
University of New Hampshire *B*

New Jersey

Drew University *B*

New York

Rensselaer Polytechnic
  Institute *B, M, D*

North Dakota

North Dakota State University *B*

Ohio

College of Wooster *B*

Oregon

Oregon Health & Science
University *M, D*

Pennsylvania

Lebanon Valley College *B*
University of Pennsylvania *M, D*

Tennessee

Rhodes College *B*
Vanderbilt University *D*

Texas

Hardin-Simmons University *B*

Washington

Whitman College *B*

West Virginia

West Virginia University *D*

Wisconsin

Marquette University *M, D*

Bioethics/medical ethics

California

American Jewish University *B*
Loma Linda University *M*
Loyola Marymount University *M*

Florida

University of South Florida *M*

Georgia

Emory University *M*

Illinois

Loyola University Chicago *M*
Northwestern University *M*

Missouri

Saint Louis University *D*

New Jersey

Drew University *M*

Ohio

Case Western Reserve
University *M, D*

Pennsylvania

Duquesne University *M, D*
University of Pennsylvania *M*
University of Pittsburgh *M*

Texas

University of Texas
Medical Branch at Galveston *M, D*

Bioinformatics

Arizona

Arizona State University *M, D*

Arkansas

University of Arkansas
Little Rock *M, D*

California

Coleman College: San Marcos *A*

DeVry University
Fremont *B*
Long Beach *B*
Foothill College *A*
San Diego State University *M*
Stanford University *M, D*
University of California
Irvine *B*
San Diego *B*
Santa Cruz *B, M, D*
University of Southern California *D*

Colorado

University of Denver *B*

Florida

University of South Florida *M*

Georgia

Georgia Institute of Technology *M, D*
University of Georgia *M, D*

Idaho

University of Idaho *M, D*

Illinois

Loyola University Chicago *B*
Northwestern University *M*
University of Illinois
Chicago *M, D*
Urbana-Champaign *M, D*

Indiana

Indiana University-Purdue University
Indianapolis *M*

Iowa

Iowa State University *B, M, D*
University of Northern Iowa *B*

Kansas

University of Kansas *D*

Maryland

Howard Community College *A*
Morgan State University *M*
University of Maryland
Baltimore County *B*

Massachusetts

Clark University *B*
Massachusetts Institute of
Technology *M, D*
Northeastern University *M*
Wheaton College *B*

Michigan

Davenport University *B*
Eastern Michigan University *M*
Michigan Technological University *B*
University of Michigan *M, D*

Mississippi

Mississippi Valley State University *M*

Missouri

Washington University in St. Louis *D*

Nebraska

University of Nebraska
Omaha *B*

New Jersey

New Jersey Institute of Technology *M*
Ramapo College of New Jersey *B*
Stevens Institute of Technology *B, M*
University of Medicine and Dentistry
of New Jersey
School of Health Related
Professions *M, D*

New York

Canisius College *B*
Polytechnic Institute of New York
University *M*
Rensselaer Polytechnic Institute *B*
Rochester Institute of
Technology *B, M*
Saint Bonaventure University *B*
State University of New York
Buffalo *B*

North Carolina

North Carolina State University *M, D*
University of North Carolina
Chapel Hill *D*
Charlotte *M*

Ohio

University of Toledo *M*

Oklahoma

Oklahoma City Community College *A*

Oregon

Oregon Health & Science
University *M, D*
Pacific University *B*

Pennsylvania

Gannon University *B*
St. Vincent College *B*
University of Pennsylvania *B*
University of Pittsburgh *M, D*
University of the Sciences in
Philadelphia *B, M*

South Carolina

Claflin University *B*

Tennessee

Vanderbilt University *D*

Texas

Baylor University *B*
St. Edward's University *B*
Texas Tech University *M*
University of St. Thomas *B*
University of Texas
Dallas *M*
El Paso *M*

Utah

Brigham Young University *B*

Virginia

George Mason University *M, D*
Virginia Commonwealth
University *B, M*
Virginia Polytechnic Institute and
State University *D*

Wisconsin

Marquette University *M, D*

Biological immunology

California

Stanford University *M, D*
University of California
Davis *M, D*
Los Angeles *B, M, D*

Connecticut

Yale University *M, D*

Florida

University of Miami *D*

Illinois

Loyola University Chicago *M, D*

Rush University *D*
University of Chicago *D*
University of Illinois
Chicago *M, D*

Iowa

University of Iowa *D*

Maine

University of Southern Maine *M*

Massachusetts

Harvard College *M, D*

Michigan

University of Michigan *D*
Wayne State University *M, D*

Missouri

Washington University in St. Louis *D*

New York

Cornell University *M, D*
Yeshiva University *M, D*

North Carolina

North Carolina State University *M, D*

Ohio

Ohio State University
Columbus Campus *M, D*
University of Toledo *M, D*

Pennsylvania

Penn State
University Park *M, D*
University of Pennsylvania *M, D*
University of Pittsburgh *M, D*

Texas

University of Texas
Southwestern Medical Center at
Dallas *M, D*

Washington

University of Washington *M, D*

Biological/physical sciences

Alabama

University of Alabama
Birmingham *B*
University of South Alabama *M, D*

Alaska

University of Alaska
Anchorage *B*
Fairbanks *B, M, D*

Arizona

Central Arizona College *A*
Coconino County Community
College *A*
Northern Arizona University *B, M*
Northland Pioneer College *A*
Prescott College *B, M*

Arkansas

Southern Arkansas University *B*
University of Arkansas
Little Rock *B*
Monticello *B*
University of Central Arkansas *B*

California

American River College *A*
California Lutheran University *B*
Cerro Coso Community College *A*
Citrus College *A*

College of the Canyons *A*
College of the Desert *A*
College of the Sequoias *A*
College of the Siskiyous *A*
Folsom Lake College *A*
Fresno City College *A*
Glendale Community College *A*
Golden West College *A*
Imperial Valley College *A*
Laney College *A*
Lassen Community College *A*
The Master's College *B*
National University *B*
Ohlone College *A*
Oxnard College *A*
Pitzer College *B*
Porterville College *A*
Scripps College *B*
Solano Community College *A*
University of California
  Santa Barbara *B*
University of La Verne *B*
University of the Pacific *B*
Vanguard University of Southern
  California *B*

Colorado

Colorado Christian University *B*
Colorado Mountain College *A*
Colorado State University *M*
Morgan Community College *A*
University of Colorado
  Colorado Springs *M*
  Denver *M*
University of Denver *B*

District of Columbia

American University *B, M*
Georgetown University *B*

Florida

Florida Institute of Technology *B*
Palm Beach Community College *A*
University of South Florida *B*
University of West Florida *B*

Georgia

Covenant College *B*
Spelman College *B*
University of Georgia *B*
Young Harris College *A*

Illinois

Black Hawk College *A*
College of DuPage *A*
College of Lake County *A*
DePaul University *B, M*
Elgin Community College *A*
Heartland Community College *A*
Highland Community College *A*
Illinois Eastern Community Colleges
  Lincoln Trail College *A*
John A. Logan College *A*
John Wood Community College *A*
Kaskaskia College *A*
Kishwaukee College *A*
Lincoln Land Community College *A*
McHenry County College *A*
Moraine Valley Community College *A*
Morton College *A*
National-Louis University *B*
North Central College *T*
Northwestern University *B*
Olivet Nazarene University *B, T*
Parkland College *A*
Prairie State College *A*
Rend Lake College *A*
Saint Xavier University *B*
Sauk Valley Community College *A*
Shawnee Community College *A*
Spoon River College *A*
Triton College *A*
Waubonsee Community College *A*

Indiana

Ball State University *M, D, T*
Indiana University
  Bloomington *M*
  East *A, B*
  Kokomo *B*
Purdue University *B*
St. Mary-of-the-Woods College *B*
Taylor University *B*
University of Notre Dame *B*
University of Southern Indiana *B, T*
Valparaiso University *B*
Vincennes University *A*

Iowa

Briar Cliff University *B*
Buena Vista University *B, T*
Coe College *B*
St. Ambrose University *B*
University of Northern Iowa *B, M*

Kansas

Central Christian College of Kansas *A*
Fort Hays State University *B*
Pratt Community College *A*
Seward County Community College *A*
Tabor College *B*
University of Kansas Medical
  Center *M, D*

Kentucky

Alice Lloyd College *B*
Brescia University *B*
St. Catharine College *A*
Western Kentucky University *M*

Louisiana

Delgado Community College *A*
Louisiana College *B*
Louisiana State University and
  Agricultural and Mechanical
  College *M*
Our Lady of Holy Cross College *B*

Maine

University of Maine *B, M*

Maryland

Baltimore City Community College *A*
Community College of Baltimore
  County *A*
Howard Community College *A*
Montgomery College *A*
St. Mary's College of Maryland *B*
Towson University *B*
University of Maryland
  College Park *M, D*
Wor-Wic Community College *A*

Massachusetts

American International College *B*
Eastern Nazarene College *B*
Elms College *B*
Springfield College *B*
University of Massachusetts
  Amherst *B*
  Dartmouth *D*
Wellesley College *B*
Wheaton College *B*
Worcester Polytechnic
  Institute *B, M, D*

Michigan

Albion College *B*
Alma College *B*
Andrews University *B, M*
Calvin College *B*
Eastern Michigan University *B, M*
Ferris State University *A*
Grand Valley State University *B*
Lansing Community College *A*
Michigan State University *B*

Rochester College *A*

Minnesota

College of St. Benedict *B*
Minnesota State University
  Mankato *B*
St. John's University *B*
University of Minnesota
  Twin Cities *B*
Winona State University *B, T*

Mississippi

Delta State University *B, M*
Mississippi College *M*
Mississippi State University *B*
University of Southern
  Mississippi *B, M, D*

Missouri

Avila University *B*
Maryville University of Saint Louis *B*
Missouri State University *M*
Missouri Valley College *B*
Northwest Missouri State
  University *B*
St. Louis Community College
  St. Louis Community College at
    Meramec *A*
Washington University in St.
  Louis *B, M, D*

Montana

Stone Child College *A*

New Hampshire

Keene State College *B*
Saint Anselm College *B*

New Jersey

Cumberland County College *A*
Fairleigh Dickinson University
  Metropolitan Campus *B, M*
Gloucester County College *A*
Ramapo College of New Jersey *B*
Rutgers, The State University of New
  Jersey
  Camden Regional Campus *B*
Saint Peter's College *B*
Sussex County Community College *A*

New Mexico

Northern New Mexico College *A*

New York

Adelphi University *B, M*
Alfred University *B*
City University of New York
  Baruch College *B*
  Brooklyn College *B, M*
Clarkson University *M*
Colgate University *B*
College of New Rochelle *B, T*
Corning Community College *A*
Le Moyne College *B*
North Country Community College *A*
Paul Smith's College *B*
Rensselaer Polytechnic
  Institute *B, M, D*
Roberts Wesleyan College *B*
St. Thomas Aquinas College *B, T*
State University of New York
  College at Potsdam *B*
  Empire State College *A, B*
Touro College *B*
Union College *B*

North Carolina

Brevard College *B*
East Carolina University *M, D*
Mars Hill College *B*

Ohio

Baldwin-Wallace College *B, T*
Bowling Green State University:
  Firelands College *A*
Defiance College *B, T*
Eastern Gateway Community
  College *A*
Heidelberg University *B*
Urbana University *B*
Walsh University *B*
Wilberforce University *B*
Wittenberg University *B*
Wright State University *D*

Oklahoma

Cameron University *B*
Eastern Oklahoma State College *A*
Oklahoma Christian University *B*
Oklahoma City University *B*
Oklahoma Panhandle State
  University *B*
St. Gregory's University *B*

Oregon

Linn-Benton Community College *A*
Oregon State University *B*
Portland State University *B, M*
Southern Oregon University *B*
Southwestern Oregon Community
  College *A*
University of Oregon *B*
Western Oregon University *B*

Pennsylvania

Alvernia University *B*
Arcadia University *B*
Cheyney University of
  Pennsylvania *B, T*
Clarion University of
  Pennsylvania *B, T*
Community College of Beaver
  County *A*
Drexel University *B*
East Stroudsburg University of
  Pennsylvania *B, M, T*
Edinboro University of
  Pennsylvania *B*
Gettysburg College *B*
Immaculata University *B*
Indiana University of Pennsylvania *B*
Keystone College *B*
King's College *B, T*
Kutztown University of
  Pennsylvania *B, T*
La Salle University *B*
Lehigh University *B*
Lock Haven University of
  Pennsylvania *B*
Luzerne County Community
  College *A*
Penn State
  Abington *A, B*
  Altoona *A, B*
  Beaver *A, B*
  Berks *B*
  Brandywine *B*
  DuBois *A, B*
  Erie, The Behrend College *B*
  Fayette, The Eberly Campus *A, B*
  Greater Allegheny *A, B*
  Hazleton *B*
  Lehigh Valley *B*
  Mont Alto *B*
  New Kensington *A, B*
  Schuylkill *A, B*
  Shenango *A, B*
  University Park *B*
  Wilkes-Barre *B*
  Worthington Scranton *B*
  York *B*
St. Francis University *B*
University of Pittsburgh *B*

University of Pittsburgh
  Bradford B
Ursinus College B
Villanova University A, B
West Chester University of
  Pennsylvania T

Puerto Rico
Bayamon Central University B
University of Puerto Rico
  Carolina Regional College T

Rhode Island
Brown University B
Community College of Rhode
  Island A

Tennessee
Christian Brothers University B
Middle Tennessee State University B
Tennessee State University B
Trevecca Nazarene University B

Texas
Central Texas College A
College of the Mainland A
Galveston College A
Hill College A
Navarro College A
North Central Texas College A
Palo Alto College A
Sam Houston State University B
Stephen F. Austin State University M
Texas A&M University
  Commerce B, M
  Galveston B
Texas State University: San Marcos B
Texas Tech University B
University of Houston
  Downtown B
University of Texas
  Arlington M
  Austin B, M, D
  Dallas M, T
  Health Science Center at
    Houston M, D
  Medical Branch at Galveston M
  San Antonio B
University of the Incarnate Word M
Wayland Baptist University M

Utah
Brigham Young University B, M
Snow College A

Vermont
Bennington College B
Castleton State College B
Lyndon State College B
Marlboro College B

Virginia
Averett University B
Danville Community College A
George Mason University D
J. Sargeant Reynolds Community
  College A
Jefferson College of Health
  Sciences A
Lord Fairfax Community College A
New River Community College A
Northern Virginia Community
  College A
Paul D. Camp Community College A
Piedmont Virginia Community
  College A
Southside Virginia Community
  College A
Tidewater Community College A
University of Virginia M
Virginia Commonwealth University B
Virginia Highlands Community
  College A

Virginia Western Community
  College A
Wytheville Community College A

Washington
Evergreen State College B
University of Washington M, D
Washington State University B
Western Washington University B, M
Whitworth University B

West Virginia
Bethany College B
Bluefield State College B

Wisconsin
Marquette University M
Mount Mary College B, T
St. Norbert College B
University of Wisconsin
  Green Bay B
  Madison M
  River Falls B, T
  Stevens Point B, T
  Superior B
Viterbo University B

Wyoming
Laramie County Community
  College A
Northwest College A
Sheridan College A

Biology

Alabama
Alabama Agricultural and Mechanical
  University B, M
Alabama State University B, M
Athens State University B
Auburn University B
Auburn University at Montgomery B
Birmingham-Southern College B
Calhoun Community College A
Chattahoochee Valley Community
  College A
Faulkner State Community College A
Faulkner University B, T
Gadsden State Community College A
Huntingdon College B
Jacksonville State University B, M
Judson College B
Miles College B
Oakwood University B
Samford University B
Southern Union State Community
  College A
Spring Hill College B, T
Stillman College B
Talladega College B
Troy University B, M
Tuskegee University B, M, D, T
University of Alabama B, M, D
University of Alabama
  Birmingham B, M, D
  Huntsville B, M
University of Mobile B, T
University of Montevallo B, T
University of North Alabama B
University of South Alabama B, M
University of West Alabama B, T

Alaska
University of Alaska
  Anchorage B, M
  Fairbanks B, M, D
  Southeast B

Arizona
Arizona State University B, M, D
Arizona Western College A
Central Arizona College A

Cochise College A
Dine College A
Eastern Arizona College A
Grand Canyon University B
Northern Arizona University B, M, D
Prescott College B, M
University of Arizona B

Arkansas
Arkansas State University B, M
Arkansas Tech University B
Central Baptist College B
Harding University B
Henderson State University B
Hendrix College B
John Brown University B
Lyon College B
Ouachita Baptist University B
Philander Smith College B
Phillips Community College of the
  University of Arkansas A
Southern Arkansas University B
University of Arkansas B, M, D
University of Arkansas
  Fort Smith B
  Little Rock B, M
  Monticello B
  Pine Bluff B
University of Central Arkansas B, M
University of the Ozarks B
Williams Baptist College B

California
Allan Hancock College A
American Jewish University B
Antelope Valley College A
Azusa Pacific University B
Bakersfield College A
Barstow Community College A
Biola University B
Cabrillo College A
California Baptist University B
California Institute of
  Technology B, M, D
California Lutheran University B
California Polytechnic State
  University: San Luis Obispo B, M
California State Polytechnic
  University: Pomona B, M
California State University
  Bakersfield B
  Chico B, M
  Dominguez Hills B, M
  East Bay B, M
  Fresno B, M
  Fullerton B, M
  Long Beach B, M
  Los Angeles B, M
  Monterey Bay B
  Northridge B, M
  Sacramento B, M
  San Bernardino B, M
  San Marcos B, M
  Stanislaus B, M
California State University: Channel
  Islands B, M
Canada College A
Cerritos College A
Chabot College A
Chaffey College A
Chapman University B
City College of San Francisco A
Claremont McKenna College B
College of Alameda A
College of Marin: Kentfield A
College of San Mateo A
College of the Desert A
College of the Siskiyous A
Columbia College A
Concordia University B
Contra Costa College A
Crafton Hills College A
Cuesta College A
De Anza College A

Dominican University of
  California B, M
El Camino College A
El Camino College: Compton
  Center A
Feather River College A
Folsom Lake College A
Foothill College A
Fresno Pacific University B
Fullerton College A
Gavilan College A
Glendale Community College A
Golden West College A
Grossmont College A
Hartnell College A
Harvey Mudd College B
Holy Names University B
Humboldt State University B, M
Imperial Valley College A
Irvine Valley College A
La Sierra University B
Loma Linda University M, D
Long Beach City College A
Los Angeles City College A
Los Angeles Southwest College A
Los Angeles Valley College A
Los Medanos College A
Loyola Marymount University B
The Master's College B
Mendocino College A
Merced College A
Mills College B
MiraCosta College A
Mission College A
Monterey Peninsula College A
Moorpark College A
Mount St. Mary's College B
Mount San Antonio College A
Notre Dame de Namur University B
Occidental College B, M
Ohlone College A
Orange Coast College A
Oxnard College A
Pacific Union College B
Palomar College A
Pasadena City College A
Pepperdine University B
Pitzer College B
Point Loma Nazarene University B
Pomona College B
Porterville College A
Reedley College A
Saddleback College A
St. Mary's College of California B
San Bernardino Valley College A
San Diego Christian College B
San Diego City College A
San Diego Mesa College A
San Diego Miramar College A
San Diego State University B, M, D
San Francisco State University B, M
San Joaquin Delta College A
San Jose State University B, M
Santa Ana College A
Santa Barbara City College A
Santa Clara University B
Santa Rosa Junior College A
Santiago Canyon College A
Scripps College B
Shasta College A
Sierra College A
Simpson University B
Solano Community College A
Sonoma State University B, M
Southwestern College A
Stanford University B, M, D
University of California
  Berkeley B, D
  Davis B
  Irvine B, M, D
  Los Angeles B, M, D
  Riverside B
  San Diego B, D

Santa Barbara *B, M, D*
Santa Cruz *B*
University of California: Merced *B*
University of La Verne *B*
University of Redlands *B*
University of San Diego *B*
University of San Francisco *B, M*
University of Southern
California *B, M, D*
University of the Pacific *B, M*
Vanguard University of Southern
California *B*
Ventura College *A*
West Hills College: Lemoore *A*
West Los Angeles College *A*
West Valley College *A*
Westmont College *B*
Whittier College *B*

Colorado
Adams State College *B*
Colorado Christian University *B*
Colorado College *B*
Colorado Mountain College *A*
Colorado State University *B*
Colorado State University
Pueblo *B*
Fort Lewis College *B*
Lamar Community College *A*
Mesa State College *B*
Metropolitan State College of
Denver *B, T*
Otero Junior College *A*
Pikes Peak Community College *A*
Red Rocks Community College *A*
Regis University *B*
Trinidad State Junior College *A*
United States Air Force Academy *B*
University of Colorado
Colorado Springs *B, M*
Denver *B, M*
University of Denver *B, M, D*
University of Northern
Colorado *B, M, D, T*
Western State College of Colorado *B*

Connecticut
Albertus Magnus College *B*
Central Connecticut State
University *B, M, T*
Connecticut College *B*
Eastern Connecticut State
University *B*
Fairfield University *B*
Post University *B*
Quinnipiac University *B*
Sacred Heart University *B*
Saint Joseph College *B, M*
Southern Connecticut State
University *B, M, T*
Trinity College *B*
University of Bridgeport *B*
University of Connecticut *B, M*
University of Hartford *B, M*
University of New Haven *B*
Wesleyan University *B, D*
Western Connecticut State
University *B, M*
Yale University *B*

Delaware
Delaware State University *B, M*
Delaware Technical and Community
College
Owens *A*
Stanton/Wilmington *A*
University of Delaware *B, M, D*
Wesley College *B*

District of Columbia
American University *B, M*
Catholic University of America *B*
Gallaudet University *B*

George Washington
University *B, M, D*
Georgetown University *B, M, D*
Howard University *B, M, D*
Trinity Washington University *B*
University of the District of
Columbia *B, M, T*

Florida
Ave Maria University *B*
Barry University *B, M, T*
Bethune-Cookman University *B*
Broward College *A*
Chipola College *A, B*
Clearwater Christian College *B*
Daytona State College *A*
Eckerd College *B*
Edward Waters College *B*
Florida Agricultural and Mechanical
University *B, M*
Florida Atlantic University *B, M*
Florida Gulf Coast University *B*
Florida Institute of Technology *B, D*
Florida International
University *B, M, D*
Florida Memorial University *B*
Florida Southern College *B*
Florida State University *B, M, D*
Gulf Coast Community College *B*
Indian River State College *A*
Jacksonville University *B*
Lynn University *B*
Miami Dade College *A*
New College of Florida *B*
Northwest Florida State College *A*
Nova Southeastern University *B*
Palm Beach Atlantic University *B*
Palm Beach Community College *A*
Pensacola Junior College *A*
Rollins College *B*
Saint Leo University *B*
St. Petersburg College *B*
Saint Thomas University *B*
Southeastern University *B*
State College of Florida,
Manatee-Sarasota *A*
Stetson University *B*
University of Central Florida *B, M*
University of Miami *B, M, D*
University of North Florida *B, M*
University of South Florida *B, M, D*
University of Tampa *A, B, T*
University of West Florida *B, M*
Warner University *A, B*

Georgia
Abraham Baldwin Agricultural
College *A*
Agnes Scott College *B*
Albany State University *B*
Armstrong Atlantic State
University *B, T*
Atlanta Metropolitan College *A*
Augusta State University *B*
Berry College *B*
Brenau University *B*
Brewton-Parker College *B*
Clark Atlanta University *B, M, D*
Clayton State University *B*
College of Coastal Georgia *A*
Columbus State University *B*
Covenant College *B*
Dalton State College *B*
Darton College *A*
East Georgia College *A*
Emmanuel College *B*
Emory University *B, D*
Fort Valley State University *B*
Georgia College and State
University *B, M*
Georgia Gwinnett College *B*
Georgia Highlands College *A*
Georgia Institute of
Technology *B, M, D*

Georgia Perimeter College *A*
Georgia Southern University *B, M*
Georgia Southwestern State
University *B*
Georgia State University *B, M, D*
Gordon College *A, B, T*
Kennesaw State University *B*
LaGrange College *B*
Life University *B*
Macon State College *A*
Mercer University *B*
Middle Georgia College *A*
Morehouse College *B*
North Georgia College & State
University *B*
Oglethorpe University *B*
Paine College *B*
Piedmont College *B*
Reinhardt College *B*
Savannah State University *B*
Shorter College *B*
South Georgia College *A*
Southern Polytechnic State
University *B*
Spelman College *B*
Toccoa Falls College *B*
University of Georgia *B, M, D*
University of West Georgia *B, M*
Valdosta State University *B, M*
Waycross College *A*
Wesleyan College *B*
Young Harris College *A, B*

Hawaii
Chaminade University of Honolulu *B*
Hawaii Pacific University *B*
University of Hawaii
Hilo *B*
Manoa *B*

Idaho
Boise State University *B, M, T*
Brigham Young University-Idaho *A, B*
College of Idaho *B*
Idaho State University *A, B, M, D*
Lewis-Clark State College *B*
North Idaho College *A*
Northwest Nazarene University *B*
University of Idaho *B, M, D*

Illinois
Augustana College *B*
Aurora University *B*
Benedictine University *B, T*
Black Hawk College: East Campus *A*
Blackburn College *B*
Bradley University *B, M, T*
Chicago State University *B, T*
City Colleges of Chicago
Harold Washington College *A*
Malcolm X College *A*
Olive-Harvey College *A*
Concordia University Chicago *B, T*
Danville Area Community College *A*
DePaul University *B, M, T*
Dominican University *B*
Eastern Illinois University *B, M, T*
Elmhurst College *B, T*
Eureka College *B, T*
Governors State University *B, T*
Greenville College *B, T*
Illinois College *B, T*
Illinois Institute of
Technology *B, M, D*
Illinois State University *B, M, D, T*
Illinois Valley Community College *A*
Illinois Wesleyan University *B*
John A. Logan College *A*
John Wood Community College *A*
Joliet Junior College *A*
Judson University *B*
Kankakee Community College *A*
Knox College *B*
Lake Forest College *B*

Lewis University *B, T*
Lincoln College *A*
Loyola University Chicago *B, M*
MacMurray College *B, T*
McKendree University *B, T*
Millikin University *B*
Monmouth College *B, T*
National-Louis University *B*
North Central College *B, T*
North Park University *B*
Northeastern Illinois University *B, M*
Northern Illinois University *B, M, D, T*
Northwestern University *B, M, D*
Olivet Nazarene University *B, T*
Principia College *B*
Quincy University *B, T*
Richland Community College *A*
Rockford College *B*
Roosevelt University *B, M*
Saint Xavier University *B*
South Suburban College of Cook
County *A*
Southern Illinois University
Carbondale *B, M*
Southern Illinois University
Edwardsville *B, M*
Southwestern Illinois College *A*
Trinity Christian College *B, T*
Trinity International University *B*
Triton College *A*
University of Chicago *B*
University of Illinois
Chicago *B, M, D*
Springfield *B, M*
Urbana-Champaign *B, M, D*
University of St. Francis *B*
Western Illinois University *B, M*
Wheaton College *B, T*

Indiana
Ancilla College *A*
Anderson University *B*
Ball State University *B, M, T*
Bethel College *B*
Butler University *B*
DePauw University *B*
Earlham College *B*
Franklin College *B*
Goshen College *B*
Grace College *B*
Hanover College *B*
Huntington University *B*
Indiana State University *B, M, D, T*
Indiana University
Bloomington *B, M*
East *A, B*
Kokomo *B*
Northwest *B*
South Bend *A, B*
Southeast *B*
Indiana University-Purdue University
Fort Wayne *A, B, M, T*
Indiana University-Purdue University
Indianapolis *B, M, D*
Indiana Wesleyan University *A, B*
Manchester College *B, T*
Marian University *B, T*
Oakland City University *B*
Purdue University *B, M, D*
Purdue University
Calumet *B, M*
North Central *A, B*
Rose-Hulman Institute of
Technology *B*
Saint Joseph's College *B*
Saint Mary's College *B*
St. Mary-of-the-Woods College *B*
Taylor University *B*
Trine University *B*
University of Evansville *B*
University of Indianapolis *B, M*
University of Notre Dame *B, M, D*
University of Southern Indiana *B, T*
Valparaiso University *B*

Vincennes University *A*
Wabash College *B*

Iowa

Briar Cliff University *B*
Buena Vista University *B, T*
Central College *B, T*
Clarke College *B, T*
Coe College *B*
Cornell College *B, T*
Dordt College *B*
Drake University *B*
Ellsworth Community College *A*
Graceland University *B, T*
Grand View University *B*
Grinnell College *B*
Iowa State University *B*
Iowa Wesleyan College *B*
Iowa Western Community College *A*
Loras College *B*
Luther College *B*
Marshalltown Community College *A*
Morningside College *B*
Mount Mercy College *B, T*
Northwestern College *B, T*
St. Ambrose University *B*
Simpson College *B*
University of Dubuque *B*
University of Iowa *B, M, D, T*
University of Northern Iowa *B, M*
Upper Iowa University *B*
Waldorf College *B*
Wartburg College *B, T*
William Penn University *B*

Kansas

Allen County Community College *A*
Baker University *B, T*
Barton County Community College *A*
Benedictine College *B*
Bethany College *B, T*
Bethel College *B*
Central Christian College of
    Kansas *A, B*
Coffeyville Community College *A*
Dodge City Community College *A*
Donnelly College *A*
Emporia State University *B, M, T*
Fort Hays State University *B, M*
Friends University *B*
Garden City Community College *A*
Highland Community College *A*
Hutchinson Community College *A*
Kansas State University *B, M, D*
Kansas Wesleyan University *B, T*
Labette Community College *A*
McPherson College *B, T*
MidAmerica Nazarene University *B*
Neosho County Community
    College *A*
Newman University *B*
Ottawa University *B*
Pittsburg State University *B, M*
Pratt Community College *A*
Seward County Community College *A*
Southwestern College *B*
Sterling College *B, T*
Tabor College *B*
University of Kansas *B*
University of St. Mary *B*
Washburn University *B*
Wichita State University *B, M, T*

Kentucky

Alice Lloyd College *B*
Asbury College *B, T*
Bellarmine University *B, T*
Berea College *B*
Bluegrass Community and Technical
    College *A*
Brescia University *A, B*
Campbellsville University *B*
Centre College *B*
Eastern Kentucky University *B, M*

Georgetown College *B, T*
Kentucky State University *B*
Kentucky Wesleyan College *B, T*
Lindsey Wilson College *A, B, T*
Midway College *B*
Morehead State University *B, M, T*
Murray State University *B, M, T*
Northern Kentucky University *B*
Pikeville College *B, T*
Thomas More College *A, B*
Transylvania University *B*
Union College *B*
University of Kentucky *B, M, D*
University of Louisville *B, M, D*
University of the Cumberlands *B, T*
Western Kentucky University *B, M, T*

Louisiana

Centenary College of Louisiana *B, T*
Dillard University *B*
Grambling State University *B*
Louisiana College *B*
Louisiana State University
    Alexandria *B*
    Shreveport *B, M*
Louisiana State University and
    Agricultural and Mechanical
    College *B, M, D*
Louisiana Tech University *B, M*
Loyola University New Orleans *B*
McNeese State University *B*
Nicholls State University *B*
Northwestern State University *B*
Our Lady of Holy Cross College *B, T*
Our Lady of the Lake College *B*
Southeastern Louisiana
    University *B, M*
Southern University
    New Orleans *B*
    Shreveport *A*
Southern University and Agricultural
    and Mechanical College *B, M*
Tulane University *B, M, D*
University of Louisiana at
    Lafayette *B, M*
University of Louisiana at
    Monroe *B, M*
University of New Orleans *B, M*
Xavier University of Louisiana *B*

Maine

Bates College *B, T*
Bowdoin College *B*
Colby College *B*
Husson University *B*
Kennebec Valley Community
    College *A*
Saint Joseph's College of Maine *B*
University of Maine *B, M, D*
University of Maine
    Augusta *B*
    Farmington *B*
    Fort Kent *B*
    Machias *B, T*
    Presque Isle *B*
University of New England *B*
University of Southern Maine *B*

Maryland

Allegany College of Maryland *A*
Bowie State University *B*
College of Notre Dame of Maryland *B*
Coppin State University *B*
Frederick Community College *A*
Frostburg State University *B, T*
Goucher College *B*
Harford Community College *A*
Hood College *B, T*
Johns Hopkins University *B, M, D*
Loyola University Maryland *B*
McDaniel College *B*
Morgan State University *B*
Mount St. Mary's University *B*

Prince George's Community
    College *A*
St. Mary's College of Maryland *B*
Salisbury University *B, T*
Stevenson University *B*
Towson University *B, M, T*
University of Maryland
    Baltimore County *B, M, D*
    College Park *B, M, D*
    Eastern Shore *B*
Washington Adventist University *B*
Washington College *B, T*

Massachusetts

American International College *B*
Amherst College *B*
Assumption College *B*
Atlantic Union College *B*
Bard College at Simon's Rock *B*
Bay Path College *B*
Becker College *B*
Boston College *B, M, D*
Boston University *B, M, D*
Brandeis University *B*
Bridgewater State College *B*
Bunker Hill Community College *A*
Clark University *B, M, D*
College of the Holy Cross *B*
Curry College *B*
Eastern Nazarene College *B*
Elms College *B*
Emmanuel College *B*
Fitchburg State College *B, M*
Framingham State College *B*
Gordon College *B*
Hampshire College *B*
Harvard College *B*
Lesley University *B*
Massachusetts College of Liberal
    Arts *B*
Massachusetts Institute of
    Technology *B, D*
Merrimack College *B*
Mount Holyoke College *B*
Mount Ida College *B*
Northeastern University *B, M, D*
Northern Essex Community
    College *A*
Pine Manor College *A, B*
Regis College *B*
Roxbury Community College *A*
Salem State College *B, M*
Simmons College *B*
Smith College *B, M, D*
Springfield College *B*
Springfield Technical Community
    College *A*
Stonehill College *B*
Suffolk University *B*
Tufts University *B, M, D*
University of Massachusetts
    Amherst *B, M, D*
    Boston *B, M, D*
    Dartmouth *B, M*
    Lowell *B, M*
Wellesley College *B*
Western New England College *B*
Westfield State College *B, T*
Wheaton College *B*
Williams College *B*
Worcester Polytechnic Institute *B, M*
Worcester State College *B*

Michigan

Adrian College *A, B, T*
Albion College *B, T*
Alma College *B, T*
Andrews University *B, M*
Aquinas College *B, T*
Calvin College *B, T*
Central Michigan University *B, M*
Cornerstone University *B, T*
Delta College *A*
Eastern Michigan University *B, M*

Ferris State University *B*
Gogebic Community College *A*
Grand Rapids Community College *A*
Grand Valley State University *B, M*
Hillsdale College *B*
Hope College *B*
Kalamazoo College *B*
Lake Michigan College *A*
Lake Superior State University *B, T*
Lansing Community College *A*
Macomb Community College *A*
Madonna University *B*
Marygrove College *B, T*
Michigan State University *B, M*
Michigan Technological
    University *B, M, D*
Mid Michigan Community College *A*
Northern Michigan University *B, M*
Northwestern Michigan College *A*
Oakland University *B, M, D, T*
Saginaw Valley State University *B, T*
Siena Heights University *A, B*
Spring Arbor University *B, T*
University of Detroit Mercy *B*
University of Michigan *B*
University of Michigan
    Dearborn *B*
    Flint *B, M, T*
Wayne State University *B, M, D*
Western Michigan University *B, M, D*

Minnesota

Anoka-Ramsey Community College *A*
Augsburg College *B*
Bemidji State University *B, M*
Bethel University *B*
Carleton College *B*
College of St. Benedict *B*
College of St. Scholastica *B*
Concordia College: Moorhead *B*
Concordia University: St. Paul *B*
Crown College *B*
Gustavus Adolphus College *B*
Hamline University *B*
Macalester College *B*
Mesabi Range Community and
    Technical College *A*
Metropolitan State University *B*
Minneapolis Community and
    Technical College *A*
Minnesota State Community and
    Technical College *A*
Minnesota State University
    Mankato *B, M, T*
    Moorhead *B*
Minnesota West Community and
    Technical College *A*
North Hennepin Community
    College *A*
Northland Community & Technical
    College *A*
Northwestern College *B*
Ridgewater College *A*
St. Catherine University *B*
Saint Cloud State University *B, M*
St. John's University *B*
St. Mary's University of Minnesota *B*
St. Olaf College *B*
Southwest Minnesota State
    University *B, T*
University of Minnesota
    Crookston *B*
    Duluth *B, M*
    Morris *B*
    Twin Cities *B*
University of St. Thomas *B*
Vermilion Community College *A*
Winona State University *B, T*

Mississippi

Alcorn State University *B, M*
Belhaven University *B, T*
Blue Mountain College *B*
Delta State University *B*

East Central Community College *A*
Hinds Community College *A*
Jackson State University *B, M*
Millsaps College *B*
Mississippi College *B, M*
Mississippi Delta Community
 College *A*
Mississippi Gulf Coast Community
 College *A*
Mississippi State University *B, M, D*
Mississippi University for Women *B, T*
Mississippi Valley State University *B*
Rust College *B*
Tougaloo College *B*
University of Mississippi *B, M, D, T*
University of Southern
 Mississippi *B, M, D*

Missouri

Avila University *B*
Central Methodist University *B*
College of the Ozarks *B*
Columbia College *B*
Crowder College *A*
Culver-Stockton College *B, T*
Drury University *B, T*
Evangel University *B*
Fontbonne University *B*
Hannibal-LaGrange College *B*
Lincoln University *B*
Lindenwood University *B*
Maryville University of Saint Louis *B*
Missouri Baptist University *B, T*
Missouri Southern State
 University *B, T*
Missouri State University *B, M*
Missouri Valley College *B*
Missouri Western State University *B, T*
Northwest Missouri State
 University *B, M*
Park University *B*
Rockhurst University *B*
St. Charles Community College *A*
St. Louis Community College
 St. Louis Community College at
 Florissant Valley *A*
Saint Louis University *B, M, D*
Southeast Missouri State
 University *B, M*
Southwest Baptist University *B, T*
Stephens College *B*
Three Rivers Community College *A*
Truman State University *B, M*
University of Central Missouri *B, M*
University of Missouri
 Columbia *B, M, D*
 Kansas City *B, M*
 Missouri University of Science and
 Technology *B*
 St. Louis *B, M, D*
Washington University in St.
 Louis *B, M, D*
Webster University *B*
Westminster College *B, T*
William Jewell College *B, T*
William Woods University *B, T*

Montana

Little Big Horn College *A*
Miles Community College *A*
Montana State University
 Billings *B*
 Bozeman *B, M, D*
Montana Tech of the University of
 Montana *B*
Rocky Mountain College *B, T*
University of Great Falls *B*
University of Montana *B, M, D*
University of Montana: Western *A, B*

Nebraska

Bellevue University *B*
Chadron State College *B*
College of Saint Mary *B, T*

Concordia University *B, T*
Creighton University *B*
Dana College *B*
Doane College *B*
Nebraska Wesleyan University *B*
Northeast Community College *A*
Union College *B*
University of Nebraska
 Kearney *B, M, T*
 Lincoln *B, M, D*
 Omaha *B, M*
Wayne State College *B*
Western Nebraska Community
 College *A*
York College *B*

Nevada

College of Southern Nevada *A*
Nevada State College *B*
Sierra Nevada College *B*
University of Nevada
 Las Vegas *B, M, D*
 Reno *B, M, D*

New Hampshire

Colby-Sawyer College *B*
Dartmouth College *B, M, D, T*
Franklin Pierce University *B*
Keene State College *B*
New England College *B, T*
Plymouth State University *B*
Rivier College *B, M, T*
Saint Anselm College *B, T*
Thomas More College of Liberal
 Arts *B*
University of New Hampshire *B, M*
University of New Hampshire at
 Manchester *A, B*

New Jersey

Bergen Community College *A*
Bloomfield College *B*
Caldwell College *B*
Centenary College *B*
The College of New Jersey *B, T*
College of St. Elizabeth *B, T*
Drew University *B*
Essex County College *A*
Fairleigh Dickinson University
 College at Florham *B, M*
 Metropolitan Campus *B, M*
Felician College *B*
Georgian Court University *B, M*
Gloucester County College *A*
Hudson County Community
 College *A*
Kean University *B, T*
Mercer County Community College *A*
Monmouth University *B*
Montclair State University *B, M, T*
New Jersey City University *B*
New Jersey Institute of
 Technology *B, M, D*
Ramapo College of New Jersey *B*
Richard Stockton College of New
 Jersey *B*
Rider University *B*
Rowan University *B*
Rutgers, The State University of New
 Jersey
 Camden Regional Campus *B, M, T*
 New Brunswick/Piscataway
 Campus *B, T*
 Newark Regional
 Campus *B, M, D, T*
Saint Peter's College *B*
Seton Hall University *B, M, T*
Sussex County Community College *A*
Thomas Edison State College *A, B*
Union County College *A*
Warren County Community College *A*
William Paterson University of New
 Jersey *B, M*

New Mexico

Eastern New Mexico University *B, M*
New Mexico Highlands
 University *B, M*
New Mexico Institute of Mining and
 Technology *B, M*
New Mexico Junior College *A*
New Mexico State University *B, M, D*
Northern New Mexico College *B*
San Juan College *A*
Santa Fe Community College *A*
University of New Mexico *B, M, D*
University of the Southwest *B*
Western New Mexico University *B*

New York

Adelphi University *B, M*
Alfred University *B*
Bard College *B*
Barnard College *B*
Canisius College *B*
Cayuga County Community College *A*
City University of New York
 Baruch College *B*
 Brooklyn College *B, M*
 City College *B, M*
 College of Staten Island *B, M*
 Hunter College *B, M*
 Kingsborough Community
 College *A*
 Lehman College *B, M*
 Medgar Evers College *A, B*
 Queens College *B, M*
 Queensborough Community
 College *A*
 York College *B*
Clarkson University *B*
Colgate University *B*
College of Mount St. Vincent *B, T*
College of New Rochelle *B, T*
College of Saint Rose *B*
Columbia University *B*
Columbia University
 School of General Studies *B*
Concordia College *B, T*
Cornell University *B*
D'Youville College *B*
Daemen College *B, T*
Dominican College of Blauvelt *B*
Dowling College *B*
Elmira College *B, T*
Excelsior College *B*
Fordham University *B, M, D*
Hamilton College *B*
Hartwick College *B, T*
Herkimer County Community
 College *A*
Hobart and William Smith Colleges *B*
Hofstra University *B, M*
Houghton College *B*
Iona College *B*
Ithaca College *B, T*
Keuka College *B*
Le Moyne College *B*
Long Island University
 Brooklyn Campus *B, M*
 C. W. Post Campus *B, M*
Manhattan College *B*
Manhattanville College *B*
Marist College *B*
Marymount Manhattan College *B*
Medaille College *B*
Mercy College *B*
Molloy College *B*
Monroe Community College *A*
Mount Saint Mary College *B, T*
Nazareth College *B*
New York Institute of Technology *B*
New York University *A, B, M, D*
Niagara University *B*
Pace University *B*
Paul Smith's College *B*
Rensselaer Polytechnic
 Institute *B, M, D*

Roberts Wesleyan College *B*
Rochester Institute of
 Technology *A, B*
Russell Sage College *B*
Sage College of Albany *B*
Saint Bonaventure University *B, T*
St. Francis College *B*
St. John Fisher College *B*
St. John's University *B, M, D*
St. Joseph's College *B*
St. Joseph's College: Suffolk
 Campus *B, T*
St. Lawrence University *B, T*
St. Thomas Aquinas College *B, T*
Siena College *B, T*
Skidmore College *B*
State University of New York
 Albany *B, M, D*
 Binghamton *B, M, D*
 Buffalo *B, M, D*
 College at Brockport *B, M, T*
 College at Buffalo *B, M*
 College at Cortland *B*
 College at Fredonia *B, M, T*
 College at Geneseo *B, T*
 College at Old Westbury *B, T*
 College at Oneonta *B, M*
 College at Plattsburgh *B*
 College at Potsdam *B*
 College of Agriculture and
 Technology at Morrisville *A*
 College of Technology at Alfred *A*
 Farmingdale *B*
 New Paltz *B, M*
 Oswego *B*
 Purchase *B*
 Stony Brook *B, M*
Suffolk County Community College *A*
Syracuse University *B, M, D*
Touro College *B*
Union College *B*
United States Military Academy *B*
University of Rochester *B, M, D*
Utica College *B*
Vassar College *B, M*
Wagner College *B, T*
Wells College *B*
Yeshiva University *B*

North Carolina

Appalachian State University *B, M*
Barton College *B*
Belmont Abbey College *B*
Bennett College for Women *B*
Cabarrus College of Health
 Sciences *A*
Campbell University *B, T*
Catawba College *B, T*
Chowan University *B*
Davidson College *B*
Duke University *B, D*
East Carolina University *B, M*
Elizabeth City State University *B, M*
Elon University *B*
Fayetteville State University *B, M*
Gardner-Webb University *B*
Greensboro College *B, T*
Guilford College *B*
High Point University *B*
Johnson C. Smith University *B*
Lees-McRae College *B*
Lenoir-Rhyne University *B*
Livingstone College *B*
Louisburg College *A*
Mars Hill College *B, T*
Meredith College *B*
Methodist University *A, B, T*
Montreat College *B*
Mount Olive College *A, B*
North Carolina Agricultural and
 Technical State University *B, M*
North Carolina Central
 University *B, M*
North Carolina State University *B*

North Carolina Wesleyan College *B*
Peace College *B*
Pfeiffer University *B*
Queens University of Charlotte *B*
St. Andrews Presbyterian College *B*
St. Augustine's College *B*
Salem College *B*
Sandhills Community College *A*
Shaw University *B*
Southeastern Community College *A*
University of North Carolina
    Asheville *B, T*
    Chapel Hill *B, M, D*
    Charlotte *B, M, D*
    Greensboro *B, M*
    Pembroke *B*
    Wilmington *B, M*
Wake Forest University *B, M, D*
Warren Wilson College *B*
Western Carolina University *B, M*
Wingate University *B*
Winston-Salem State University *B*

North Dakota
Dakota College at Bottineau *A*
Dickinson State University *B*
Jamestown College *B*
Mayville State University *B, T*
Minot State University *B*
North Dakota State University *B, M*
University of Mary *B*
University of North Dakota *B, M, D*

Ohio
Ashland University *B*
Baldwin-Wallace College *B*
Bluffton University *B*
Bowling Green State
    University *B, M, D*
Capital University *B*
Case Western Reserve
    University *B, M, D*
Cedarville University *B*
Central State University *B*
Cleveland State University *B*
College of Mount St. Joseph *B, T*
College of Wooster *B*
Defiance College *B, T*
Denison University *B*
Eastern Gateway Community
    College *A*
Franciscan University of
    Steubenville *B*
Heidelberg University *B*
Hiram College *B*
John Carroll University *B, M*
Kent State University *B, M, T*
Kent State University
    Trumbull *A*
Kenyon College *B*
Lourdes College *A, B*
Malone University *B*
Marietta College *B*
Mount Union College *B*
Mount Vernon Nazarene University *B*
Muskingum University *B*
Notre Dame College *B, T*
Oberlin College *B*
Ohio Dominican University *B, T*
Ohio Northern University *B*
Ohio State University
    Columbus Campus *B*
    Lima Campus *B*
Ohio University *B*
Ohio Wesleyan University *B*
Otterbein College *B*
Owens Community College
    Toledo *A*
Shawnee State University *B*
Terra State Community College *A*
University of Akron *B, M, D*
University of Cincinnati *B, M, D, T*

University of Cincinnati
    Clermont College *A*
    Raymond Walters College *A*
University of Dayton *B, M, D*
University of Findlay *B*
University of Rio Grande *A, B, T*
University of Toledo *A, B, M, D*
Ursuline College *B*
Walsh University *B*
Wilberforce University *B*
Wilmington College *B*
Wittenberg University *B*
Wright State University *A, B, M*
Wright State University: Lake
    Campus *A*
Xavier University *B*
Youngstown State University *B, M*

Oklahoma
Cameron University *B*
Carl Albert State College *A*
Connors State College *A*
East Central University *B*
Eastern Oklahoma State College *A*
Langston University *B*
Northeastern Oklahoma Agricultural
    and Mechanical College *A*
Northeastern State University *B*
Northern Oklahoma College *A*
Northwestern Oklahoma State
    University *B*
Oklahoma Baptist University *B, T*
Oklahoma Christian University *B*
Oklahoma City Community College *A*
Oklahoma City University *B*
Oklahoma Panhandle State
    University *B*
Oklahoma State University *B*
Oklahoma Wesleyan University *A, B*
Oral Roberts University *B*
Rogers State University *A, B*
Rose State College *A*
St. Gregory's University *B*
Southeastern Oklahoma State
    University *B*
Southern Nazarene University *B*
Southwestern Oklahoma State
    University *B*
University of Central Oklahoma *B, M*
University of Science and Arts of
    Oklahoma *B*
University of Tulsa *B, M, D*
Western Oklahoma State College *A*

Oregon
Central Oregon Community
    College *A*
Chemeketa Community College *A*
Concordia University *B, T*
Eastern Oregon University *B, T*
George Fox University *B*
Lewis & Clark College *B*
Linfield College *B, T*
Linn-Benton Community College *A*
Mt. Hood Community College *A*
Oregon Institute of Technology *B*
Oregon State University *B*
Pacific University *B*
Portland State University *B, M*
Reed College *B*
Southern Oregon University *B, T*
Treasure Valley Community College *A*
University of Oregon *B, M, D*
University of Portland *B, T*
Warner Pacific College *B, T*
Western Oregon University *B*
Willamette University *B*

Pennsylvania
Albright College *B, T*
Allegheny College *B*
Alvernia University *B*
Arcadia University *B*

Bloomsburg University of
    Pennsylvania *B, M, T*
Bryn Athyn College of the New
    Church *B*
Bryn Mawr College *B*
Bucknell University *B, M*
Bucks County Community College *A*
Butler County Community College *A*
Cabrini College *B*
California University of
    Pennsylvania *B, M*
Carlow University *B*
Carnegie Mellon University *B, M, D*
Cedar Crest College *B*
Chatham University *B, M*
Chestnut Hill College *A, B*
Cheyney University of
    Pennsylvania *B, M, T*
Clarion University of
    Pennsylvania *B, M*
Community College of Allegheny
    County *A*
DeSales University *B, T*
Delaware Valley College *B*
Dickinson College *B*
Drexel University *B, M, D*
Duquesne University *B, M, D*
East Stroudsburg University of
    Pennsylvania *B, M*
Eastern University *B*
Edinboro University of
    Pennsylvania *B, M, T*
Elizabethtown College *B*
Franklin & Marshall College *B*
Gannon University *B*
Geneva College *B, T*
Gettysburg College *B*
Grove City College *B*
Gwynedd-Mercy College *B*
Harrisburg Area Community
    College *A*
Haverford College *B, T*
Holy Family University *B*
Immaculata University *A, B*
Indiana University of
    Pennsylvania *B, M, T*
Juniata College *B*
Keystone College *A, B*
King's College *B, T*
Kutztown University of
    Pennsylvania *B, M, T*
La Roche College *B*
La Salle University *B, T*
Lackawanna College *A*
Lafayette College *B*
Lebanon Valley College *B, T*
Lehigh Carbon Community College *A*
Lehigh University *B*
Lincoln University *B*
Lock Haven University of
    Pennsylvania *B*
Lycoming College *B*
Mansfield University of
    Pennsylvania *B, T*
Marywood University *B*
Mercyhurst College *B*
Messiah College *B*
Millersville University of
    Pennsylvania *B, M, T*
Misericordia University *B*
Montgomery County Community
    College *A*
Moravian College *B, T*
Muhlenberg College *B*
Neumann University *B*
Northampton Community College *A*
Penn State
    Abington *B*
    Altoona *B*
    Beaver *B*
    Berks *B*
    Brandywine *B*
    DuBois *B*
    Erie, The Behrend College *B*

    Fayette, The Eberly Campus *B*
    Greater Allegheny *B*
    Hazleton *B*
    Lehigh Valley *B*
    Mont Alto *B*
    New Kensington *B*
    Schuylkill *B*
    Shenango *B*
    University Park *B, M, D*
    Wilkes-Barre *B*
    Worthington Scranton *B*
    York *B*
Philadelphia University *B*
Point Park University *B*
Reading Area Community College *A*
Robert Morris University *B*
Rosemont College *B*
St. Francis University *B*
Saint Joseph's University *A, B, M*
St. Vincent College *B*
Seton Hill University *B, T*
Shippensburg University of
    Pennsylvania *B, M, T*
Slippery Rock University of
    Pennsylvania *B*
Susquehanna University *B, T*
Swarthmore College *B*
Temple University *B, M, D*
Thiel College *B*
University of Pennsylvania *B, M, D*
University of Pittsburgh *B, M, D*
University of Pittsburgh
    Bradford *B*
    Greensburg *B*
    Johnstown *B*
University of Scranton *B, T*
University of the Sciences in
    Philadelphia *B*
Ursinus College *B, T*
Villanova University *B, M*
Washington & Jefferson College *B*
Waynesburg University *B*
West Chester University of
    Pennsylvania *B, M, T*
Westminster College *B*
Widener University *B, T*
Wilkes University *B*
Wilson College *B*
York College of Pennsylvania *A, B, T*

Puerto Rico
Bayamon Central University *B*
Caribbean University *B*
Inter American University of Puerto
    Rico
    Aguadilla Campus *B*
    Arecibo Campus *B*
    Bayamon Campus *B*
    Guayama Campus *B*
    Metropolitan Campus *B*
    Ponce Campus *B*
    San German Campus *B*
Pontifical Catholic University of
    Puerto Rico *B*
Turabo University *B*
Universidad Adventista de las
    Antillas *B*
Universidad Metropolitana *B*
Universidad del Este *B*
University of Puerto Rico
    Aguadilla *A, B*
    Bayamon University College *B*
    Cayey University College *B*
    Humacao *B*
    Medical Sciences *D*
    Ponce *B*
    Rio Piedras *B, M, D*
University of the Sacred Heart *B*

Rhode Island
Brown University *B, M, D*
Providence College *B*
Rhode Island College *B, M*
Roger Williams University *B*

Salve Regina University *B*
University of Rhode Island *B*

South Carolina
Allen University *B*
Anderson University *B*
Benedict College *B*
Bob Jones University *B*
Charleston Southern University *B*
The Citadel *B, M, T*
Claflin University *B*
Clemson University *B, M, D*
Coastal Carolina University *B*
Coker College *B*
College of Charleston *B, T*
Columbia College *B*
Converse College *B*
Erskine College *B*
Francis Marion University *B*
Furman University *B, T*
Lander University *B*
Limestone College *B*
Morris College *B*
Newberry College *B, T*
North Greenville University *B*
Presbyterian College *B, T*
South Carolina State University *B*
Southern Wesleyan University *B, T*
University of South Carolina *B, M, D*
University of South Carolina
  Aiken *B*
  Beaufort *B*
  Upstate *B*
Winthrop University *B, M*
Wofford College *B, T*

South Dakota
Augustana College *B, T*
Black Hills State University *B*
Dakota State University *B*
Dakota Wesleyan University *B*
Mount Marty College *B*
Northern State University *B*
Presentation College *A*
Sinte Gleska University *A*
South Dakota State University *B, M, D*
University of Sioux Falls *B*
University of South Dakota *B, M, D*

Tennessee
Austin Peay State University *B, M*
Belmont University *B, T*
Bethel University *B, T*
Bryan College *B, T*
Carson-Newman College *B, T*
Christian Brothers University *B*
Columbia State Community College *A*
Crichton College *B*
Cumberland University *B*
Dyersburg State Community
  College *A*
East Tennessee State
  University *B, M, T*
Fisk University *B, M*
Free Will Baptist Bible College *A*
Freed-Hardeman University *B, T*
Jackson State Community College *A*
King College *B, T*
Lambuth University *B*
Lane College *B*
LeMoyne-Owen College *B*
Lee University *B*
Lincoln Memorial University *B, T*
Lipscomb University *B*
Martin Methodist College *B*
Maryville College *B, T*
Middle Tennessee State
  University *B, M*
Milligan College *B, T*
Rhodes College *B*
Roane State Community College *A*
Southern Adventist University *B*
Tennessee State University *B, M, D*

Tennessee Technological
  University *B, M, T*
Tennessee Temple University *B*
Tennessee Wesleyan College *B*
Trevecca Nazarene University *B*
Tusculum College *B, T*
Union University *B, T*
University of Memphis *B, M, D*
University of Tennessee
  Chattanooga *B*
  Knoxville *B*
  Martin *B*
University of the South *B*
Vanderbilt University *B*

Texas
Abilene Christian University *B*
Alvin Community College *A*
Amarillo College *A*
Angelina College *A*
Angelo State University *B, M, T*
Austin College *B*
Austin Community College *A*
Baylor University *B, M, D*
Blinn College *A*
Brazosport College *A*
Central Texas College *A*
Cisco College *A*
Clarendon College *A*
Coastal Bend College *A*
College of the Mainland *A*
Concordia University Texas *B*
Dallas Baptist University *B*
Del Mar College *A*
East Texas Baptist University *B*
El Paso Community College *A*
Frank Phillips College *A*
Galveston College *A*
Grayson County College *A*
Hardin-Simmons University *B*
Hill College *A*
Houston Baptist University *B*
Howard College *A*
Howard Payne University *B, T*
Huston-Tillotson University *B*
Jarvis Christian College *B, T*
Kilgore College *A*
Lamar State College at Orange *A*
Lamar University *B, M*
Laredo Community College *A*
LeTourneau University *B*
Lon Morris College *A*
Lubbock Christian University *B*
McMurry University *B*
Midland College *A*
Midwestern State University *B, M*
Navarro College *A*
Northeast Texas Community
  College *A*
Northwest Vista College *A*
Odessa College *A*
Our Lady of the Lake University of San
  Antonio *B*
Palo Alto College *A*
Paris Junior College *A*
Prairie View A&M University *B, M*
Rice University *B, M, D*
St. Edward's University *B*
St. Mary's University *B*
St. Philip's College *A*
Sam Houston State University *B, M*
San Jacinto College *A*
Schreiner University *B*
South Plains College *A*
South Texas College *A*
Southern Methodist
  University *B, M, D*
Southwestern Adventist
  University *B, T*
Southwestern University *B, T*
Stephen F. Austin State
  University *B, M, T*
Sul Ross State University *B, M, T*
Tarleton State University *B, M*

Temple College *A*
Texarkana College *A*
Texas A&M International
  University *B, T*
Texas A&M University *B, M, D*
Texas A&M University
  Commerce *B, M*
  Corpus Christi *B, M, T*
  Galveston *B*
  Kingsville *B, M*
  Texarkana *B, T*
Texas Christian University *B, M*
Texas College *B*
Texas Lutheran University *B*
Texas Southern University *B, M*
Texas State University: San
  Marcos *B, M, T*
Texas Tech University *B, M, D*
Texas Wesleyan University *B*
Texas Woman's University *B, M*
Trinity University *B*
Trinity Valley Community College *A*
Tyler Junior College *A*
University of Dallas *B*
University of Houston *B, M, D*
University of Houston
  Clear Lake *B, M*
  Downtown *B*
  Victoria *B*
University of North Texas *B, M, D*
University of St. Thomas *B*
University of Texas
  Arlington *B, M*
  Austin *B*
  Brownsville - Texas Southmost
    College *B, M*
  Dallas *B*
  El Paso *B, M, D*
  Pan American *B, M*
  San Antonio *B, M*
  Tyler *B, M*
  of the Permian Basin *B, M*
University of the Incarnate Word *B, M*
Wayland Baptist University *B, T*
West Texas A&M University *B, M*
Western Texas College *A*
Wharton County Junior College *A*
Wiley College *B*

Utah
Brigham Young University *B, M, D*
College of Eastern Utah *T*
Dixie State College of Utah *B*
Salt Lake Community College *A*
Snow College *A*
Southern Utah University *B, T*
University of Utah *B, M, D, T*
Utah State University *B, M, D*
Utah Valley University *A, B*
Westminster College *B*

Vermont
Bennington College *B*
Castleton State College *B*
Green Mountain College *B*
Johnson State College *B*
Marlboro College *B*
Middlebury College *B*
Norwich University *B*
St. Michael's College *B*
University of Vermont *B, M, D*

Virginia
Averett University *B*
Bluefield College *B*
Bridgewater College *B*
Christopher Newport University *B*
College of William and Mary *B, M*
Eastern Mennonite University *B*
Emory & Henry College *B, T*
Ferrum College *B*
George Mason University *B, M*
Germanna Community College *A*
Hampden-Sydney College *B*

Hampton University *B, M*
Hollins University *B*
James Madison University *B, M, T*
Liberty University *B*
Longwood University *B, T*
Lynchburg College *B*
Mary Baldwin College *B*
Marymount University *B*
Mountain Empire Community
  College *A*
Norfolk State University *B*
Old Dominion University *B, M, T*
Radford University *B*
Randolph College *B*
Randolph-Macon College *B*
Roanoke College *B, T*
St. Paul's College *B*
Shenandoah University *B*
Southern Virginia University *B*
Sweet Briar College *B*
University of Mary Washington *B*
University of Richmond *B, M, T*
University of Virginia *B, M, D*
University of Virginia's College at
  Wise *B, T*
Virginia Commonwealth
  University *B, M*
Virginia Intermont College *B*
Virginia Military Institute *B*
Virginia Polytechnic Institute and
  State University *B, M, D*
Virginia State University *B, M*
Virginia Union University *B*
Virginia Wesleyan College *B*
Washington and Lee University *B*

Washington
Cascadia Community College *A*
Centralia College *A*
Eastern Washington University *B, M*
Everett Community College *A*
Evergreen State College *B*
Gonzaga University *B*
Northwest University *B*
Olympic College *A*
Pacific Lutheran University *B*
Saint Martin's University *B*
Seattle Pacific University *B*
Seattle University *B*
South Seattle Community College *A*
University of Puget Sound *B, T*
University of Washington *B*
University of Washington Bothell *B*
Walla Walla University *B, M*
Washington State University *B, M*
Western Washington University *B, M*
Whitman College *B*
Whitworth University *B, T*

West Virginia
Alderson-Broaddus College *B*
Bethany College *B*
Concord University *B*
Davis and Elkins College *B*
Fairmont State University *B*
Glenville State College *B*
Marshall University *B, M*
Mountain State University *B*
Potomac State College of West
  Virginia University *A*
Salem International University *B*
Shepherd University *B, T*
University of Charleston *B*
West Liberty University *B*
West Virginia State University *B*
West Virginia University *B, M, D, T*
West Virginia University Institute of
  Technology *B*
West Virginia Wesleyan College *B*
Wheeling Jesuit University *B*

Wisconsin
Alverno College *B*
Beloit College *B, T*

Cardinal Stritch University B, T
Carroll University B
Carthage College B
College of Menominee Nation A
Concordia University Wisconsin B
Edgewood College B
Lakeland College B
Lawrence University B, T
Maranatha Baptist Bible College B
Marian University B
Marquette University B, M, D
Mount Mary College B, T
Northland College B
Ripon College B
St. Norbert College B, T
Silver Lake College B, T
University of Wisconsin
  Eau Claire B
  Green Bay B
  La Crosse B, T
  Madison B
  Milwaukee B, M, D
  Oshkosh B
  Parkside B
  Platteville B, T
  River Falls B, T
  Stevens Point B, M
  Superior B, T
  Whitewater B, T
Viterbo University B, T
Wisconsin Lutheran College B

Wyoming
Casper College A
Central Wyoming College A
Eastern Wyoming College A
Laramie County Community
  College A
Northwest College A
Sheridan College A
University of Wyoming B
Western Wyoming Community
  College A

Biology lab technology

Alabama
Auburn University B

Arizona
Pima Community College C

California
Berkeley City College C, A
California Lutheran University B
City College of San Francisco C
College of the Canyons C
De Anza College C, A
East Los Angeles College C
Foothill College C, A
MiraCosta College C, A
San Diego City College A
Santa Barbara City College A
Skyline College A
Solano Community College C, A

Colorado
Community College of Aurora C

Connecticut
Quinnipiac University B
University of New Haven B

Delaware
Delaware State University B
Delaware Technical and Community
  College
  Owens A
  Stanton/Wilmington A

Georgia
Athens Technical College A

Indiana
Ball State University D

Iowa
Ellsworth Community College A
Indian Hills Community College A

Maine
Kennebec Valley Community
  College A

Maryland
Frederick Community College A
Hagerstown Community College C, A
Montgomery College A

Massachusetts
Massachusetts Bay Community
  College A
Middlesex Community College C, A
North Shore Community College A

Michigan
Delta College A

Minnesota
Anoka-Ramsey Community
  College C, A

Missouri
East Central College A
Jefferson College C, A

Nebraska
Southeast Community College A

New Jersey
County College of Morris A
Mercer County Community College A
Middlesex County College A
Ocean County College A

New York
Erie Community College
  North Campus C
Finger Lakes Community College A
Manhattan College M
Maria College A
Monroe Community College A
Niagara University B
State University of New York
  College at Brockport B
  College of Agriculture and
    Technology at Cobleskill A

North Carolina
Beaufort County Community
  College A
Central Carolina Community
  College A
Fayetteville Technical Community
  College A
Forsyth Technical Community
  College A
Pitt Community College A
Southeastern Community
  College C, A
Vance-Granville Community
  College A

North Dakota
North Dakota State College of
  Science A

Ohio
Cleveland State University B
University of Cincinnati
  Raymond Walters College A
Washington State Community
  College A

Oklahoma
Cameron University B

Pennsylvania
Gannon University B
Harrisburg University of Science and
  Technology B
Luzerne County Community
  College A
Northampton Community College C
Penn State
  Abington B
  Altoona B
  Beaver B
  Berks B
  Brandywine B
  DuBois B
  Erie, The Behrend College B
  Fayette, The Eberly Campus B
  Greater Allegheny B
  Hazleton B
  Lehigh Valley B
  Mont Alto B
  New Kensington B
  Schuylkill B
  Shenango B
  University Park B
  Wilkes-Barre B
  Worthington Scranton B
  York B
Thomas Jefferson University: College
  of Health Professions B
Westmoreland County Community
  College A

Texas
Austin Community College C, A
Collin County Community College
  District C, A
El Centro College C, A
Houston Community College
  System C, A
Lone Star College System C, A
Mountain View College C, A
Northwest Vista College A
Temple College C, A

Utah
Salt Lake Community College A
Weber State University C, A

Virginia
Piedmont Virginia Community
  College A

Washington
Bates Technical College C, A
Shoreline Community College C, A

West Virginia
New River Community and Technical
  College A

Wisconsin
Blackhawk Technical College C
Gateway Technical College A

Biology teacher education

Alabama
Athens State University B
Birmingham-Southern College T
Faulkner University B, M, T
Oakwood University B
Talladega College B
Tuskegee University B
University of Mobile B, T

Alaska
University of Alaska
  Fairbanks M

Arizona
Cochise College A
Grand Canyon University B
Northern Arizona University B, M, T
Prescott College B, M, T
University of Arizona B

Arkansas
Arkansas State University B, M, T
Arkansas Tech University B
Harding University B, T
Henderson State University B
John Brown University B, T
Ouachita Baptist University B, T
University of Arkansas
  Fort Smith B
University of the Ozarks B, T

California
California Polytechnic State
  University: San Luis Obispo T
California State University
  Chico B, T
  Long Beach T
  San Bernardino T
Fresno Pacific University B
Humboldt State University T
Loyola Marymount University M
The Master's College T
Pacific Union College T
Point Loma Nazarene University M
San Diego State University T
San Francisco State University T
Stanford University M, T
University of the Pacific T
Vanguard University of Southern
  California T

Colorado
Adams State College B, T
Colorado State University B, T
Colorado State University
  Pueblo T
Regis University B, T

Connecticut
Albertus Magnus College B, T
Fairfield University T
Quinnipiac University B, M
Sacred Heart University T
Saint Joseph College T
Southern Connecticut State
  University B, M, T
University of New Haven T

Delaware
Delaware State University B, M
University of Delaware B, T

District of Columbia
Catholic University of America B

Florida
Barry University T
Bethune-Cookman University B, T
Clearwater Christian College B
Daytona State College B
Florida Institute of Technology B
Gulf Coast Community College A
Palm Beach Atlantic University B, T
St. Petersburg College B
Southeastern University B, T
State College of Florida,
  Manatee-Sarasota A
Stetson University B
University of Tampa B, T

Georgia
Agnes Scott College *M, T*
Armstrong Atlantic State University *T*
Brewton-Parker College *B*
Columbus State University *B*
Kennesaw State University *B*
Macon State College *M, T*
Paine College *B*
Piedmont College *B, T*
Reinhardt College *B*
University of West Georgia *B*

Idaho
Boise State University *B, T*
Brigham Young University-Idaho *T*
Northwest Nazarene University *B*
University of Idaho *T*

Illinois
Augustana College *B, T*
Benedictine University *T*
Blackburn College *B, T*
Bradley University *B*
Chicago State University *B, T*
Concordia University Chicago *B, T*
DePaul University *M, T*
Dominican University *T*
Elmhurst College *B*
Eureka College *T*
Governors State University *B, T*
Greenville College *B, T*
Illinois College *T*
Illinois Wesleyan University *B*
Knox College *T*
Lewis University *T*
MacMurray College *B, T*
Millikin University *B, T*
North Park University *T*
Olivet Nazarene University *B, T*
Rockford College *T*
Saint Xavier University *B*
Trinity Christian College *B, T*
Trinity International University *B, T*
University of Illinois
  Chicago *B*
  Urbana-Champaign *B, M, T*

Indiana
Anderson University *B, T*
Butler University *T*
Franklin College *B, T*
Goshen College *B, T*
Huntington University *B, M*
Indiana University
  Bloomington *B, T*
  South Bend *B, T*
  Southeast *B*
Indiana University-Purdue University
  Fort Wayne *B, T*
Indiana University-Purdue University
  Indianapolis *B*
Indiana Wesleyan University *T*
Manchester College *B, T*
Oakland City University *B*
Purdue University *B, M, D*
Purdue University
  Calumet *B*
Saint Mary's College *T*
St. Mary-of-the-Woods College *B, T*
University of Evansville *B, T*
University of Indianapolis *B, T*
Valparaiso University *B*

Iowa
Briar Cliff University *B*
Buena Vista University *B, T*
Central College *T*
Cornell College *B, T*
Dordt College *B*
Drake University *M*
Ellsworth Community College *A*
Graceland University *T*
Grand View University *M, T*

Iowa State University *T*
Iowa Wesleyan College *B*
Loras College *T*
Maharishi University of
  Management *T*
Morningside College *B*
Mount Mercy College *T*
Northwestern College *T*
St. Ambrose University *B, T*
Simpson College *T*
University of Iowa *T*
Upper Iowa University *B, T*
Wartburg College *T*

Kansas
Bethany College *B*
Bethel College *T*
Central Christian College of Kansas *A*
McPherson College *B, T*
MidAmerica Nazarene University *B, T*
Pittsburg State University *B, T*
Sterling College *T*
Tabor College *B*
University of Kansas *B, T*
University of St. Mary *T*
Washburn University *B*

Kentucky
Alice Lloyd College *B*
Campbellsville University *B*
Eastern Kentucky University *B*
Kentucky Wesleyan College *B, T*
Lindsey Wilson College *B, T*
Midway College *M*

Louisiana
Centenary College of Louisiana *B, T*
Grambling State University *B*
Louisiana State University
  Shreveport *B*
McNeese State University *B, T*
Northwestern State University *B*
Southern University and Agricultural
  and Mechanical College *B*
University of Louisiana at Lafayette *B*
University of Louisiana at Monroe *B*
University of New Orleans *B*
Xavier University of Louisiana *B*

Maine
College of the Atlantic *T*
Husson University *B, T*
Saint Joseph's College of Maine *B*
University of Maine *B*
University of Maine
  Farmington *B, T*
  Machias *T*
University of Southern Maine *T*

Maryland
College of Notre Dame of Maryland *T*
Coppin State University *B, T*
Hood College *T*
Mount St. Mary's University *T*
Salisbury University *T*
University of Maryland
  Eastern Shore *B*

Massachusetts
Assumption College *T*
Bridgewater State College *B, M, T*
Eastern Nazarene College *B*
Elms College *T*
Fitchburg State College *B, M, T*
Framingham State College *M*
Merrimack College *T*
Salem State College *M*
Tufts University *T*
University of Massachusetts
  Dartmouth *T*
Western New England College *T*
Westfield State College *B, M, T*
Worcester State College *T*

Michigan
Albion College *B, T*
Alma College *T*
Andrews University *M*
Calvin College *B*
Central Michigan University *B*
Cornerstone University *B, T*
Eastern Michigan University *B, M*
Ferris State University *B*
Grand Valley State University *M, T*
Hope College *B, T*
Michigan State University *B*
Michigan Technological University *T*
Northern Michigan University *B, T*
University of Detroit Mercy *B, M, T*
University of Michigan
  Flint *B, T*
Western Michigan University *B, T*

Minnesota
Augsburg College *B, T*
Bemidji State University *T*
Bethel University *B*
College of St. Scholastica *T*
Concordia College: Moorhead *B, T*
Concordia University: St. Paul *B, T*
Gustavus Adolphus College *T*
Metropolitan State University *B*
Minnesota State University
  Mankato *B, T*
  Moorhead *B*
St. Catherine University *T*
Saint Cloud State University *B, M, T*
St. Mary's University of Minnesota *B*
Southwest Minnesota State
  University *B, T*
University of Minnesota
  Duluth *B, T*
  Morris *T*
Vermilion Community College *A*
Winona State University *B, T*

Mississippi
Blue Mountain College *B*
Millsaps College *T*
Mississippi College *B, M*
Mississippi State University *T*
Mississippi Valley State University *B, T*
Rust College *B*

Missouri
Central Methodist University *B*
College of the Ozarks *B, T*
Harris-Stowe State University *T*
Lincoln University *B*
Lindenwood University *B*
Maryville University of Saint
  Louis *M, T*
Missouri Baptist University *T*
Missouri Southern State
  University *B, T*
Missouri State University *B*
Missouri Valley College *T*
Northwest Missouri State
  University *B, T*
Southwest Baptist University *B, T*
Truman State University *M, T*
University of Central Missouri *B, T*
University of Missouri
  Columbia *B*
  Kansas City *B*
Washington University in St.
  Louis *B, M, T*
William Jewell College *B, T*
William Woods University *T*

Montana
Montana State University
  Billings *B, T*
Rocky Mountain College *B, T*
University of Great Falls *B*
University of Montana *B, M, T*
University of Montana: Western *B, T*

Nebraska
Chadron State College *B*
College of Saint Mary *B, T*
Concordia University *B, T*
Creighton University *T*
Dana College *B*
Nebraska Wesleyan University *T*
Peru State College *B, T*
Union College *T*
University of Nebraska
  Kearney *B, M, T*
  Lincoln *B*
Wayne State College *B, T*
York College *B, T*

Nevada
Great Basin College *B*
Nevada State College *B*

New Hampshire
Franklin Pierce University *M, T*
Keene State College *B, M, T*
New England College *B, T*
Rivier College *B, T*
Saint Anselm College *T*
University of New Hampshire *T*

New Jersey
Caldwell College *T*
The College of New Jersey *B, T*
County College of Morris *A*
Georgian Court University *T*
Rowan University *T*
Saint Peter's College *T*
William Paterson University of New
  Jersey *T*

New Mexico
New Mexico Highlands University *B*
New Mexico Institute of Mining and
  Technology *M*
Western New Mexico University *B*

New York
Adelphi University *M, T*
Alfred University *B, T*
City University of New York
  Brooklyn College *B, M, T*
  City College *B*
  College of Staten Island *B, M, T*
  Hunter College *B, M, T*
  Lehman College *M*
  Queens College *M, T*
Colgate University *M*
College of Mount St. Vincent *T*
College of Saint Rose *B, T*
Cornell University *B, M, T*
D'Youville College *M, T*
Dominican College of Blauvelt *B, T*
Dowling College *B, M*
Dutchess Community College *A*
Elmira College *B, T*
Fordham University *M, T*
Hobart and William Smith Colleges *T*
Hofstra University *B, M*
Houghton College *B, T*
Iona College *B, M, T*
Ithaca College *B, D, T*
Keuka College *B, T*
Le Moyne College *T*
Long Island University
  Brooklyn Campus *B, M, T*
  C. W. Post Campus *B, M, T*
Manhattan College *B, T*
Marist College *B*
Marymount Manhattan College *T*
Medaille College *B, M, T*
Molloy College *B*
Nazareth College *B, M, T*
New York Institute of
  Technology *B, T*
New York University *M*
Niagara University *B, M, T*

Pace University B, M, T
Roberts Wesleyan College B, M
St. Francis College B
St. John Fisher College B, M, T
St. John's University B, M, T
St. Joseph's College: Suffolk
   Campus B, T
St. Lawrence University T
St. Thomas Aquinas College B, M, T
State University of New York
   Albany M, T
   Binghamton M
   Buffalo M, T
   College at Brockport B, M, T
   College at Buffalo B, M
   College at Cortland B, M
   College at Fredonia B, M, T
   College at Geneseo B, M, T
   College at Old Westbury B, M, T
   College at Oneonta B, T
   College at Plattsburgh B
   College at Potsdam B, M
   College of Environmental Science
     and Forestry B, T
   New Paltz B, M, T
   Oswego B, M
   Stony Brook T
Syracuse University B, M, T
Ulster County Community College A
University of Rochester M
Vassar College T
Wagner College T
Wells College T

North Carolina

Appalachian State University B, T
Campbell University B, T
Elizabeth City State University T
Gardner-Webb University B
Greensboro College B, T
Lenoir Community College A
Lenoir-Rhyne University B
Mars Hill College T
Meredith College T
Methodist University A, B, T
North Carolina Agricultural and
   Technical State University B, T
North Carolina Central
   University B, M, T
Sandhills Community College A
University of North Carolina
   Greensboro B
   Pembroke B
   Wilmington B
Wake Forest University T
Western Carolina University M, T
Wingate University B, T

North Dakota

Dickinson State University B, T
Jamestown College B
Mayville State University B, T
Minot State University B
North Dakota State University B, T
University of Mary B
University of North Dakota T

Ohio

Antioch University McGregor M
Ashland University B
Baldwin-Wallace College T
Bluffton University B
Bowling Green State
   University B, M, T
Case Western Reserve University T
Cedarville University B
Defiance College B, T
Hiram College T
John Carroll University T
Miami University
   Oxford Campus B, M, T
Mount Union College T
Mount Vernon Nazarene
   University B, T

Ohio Dominican University B, T
Ohio Northern University B, T
Ohio Wesleyan University B
Otterbein College B
Shawnee State University B
University of Findlay B, M, T
University of Rio Grande B, T
University of Toledo M, T
Urbana University B
Wilmington College B
Xavier University B, M
Youngstown State University B, M

Oklahoma

Cameron University B
East Central University B
Eastern Oklahoma State College A
Northeastern State University B
Oklahoma Baptist University B, T
University of Central Oklahoma B
University of Tulsa T

Oregon

Concordia University B, M, T
Corban College B
Linfield College T
Oregon State University M
Portland State University T
Southern Oregon University T
Western Oregon University B, M, T

Pennsylvania

Albright College T
Alvernia University B
Arcadia University B, M, T
Bryn Athyn College of the New
   Church B
Bucks County Community College A
Cabrini College T
Chatham University M, T
DeSales University T
Dickinson College T
Duquesne University M, T
Geneva College T
Gettysburg College T
Grove City College B, T
Gwynedd-Mercy College B, T
Holy Family University B
Juniata College B, T
King's College T
La Salle University B, T
Lebanon Valley College T
Lycoming College T
Mansfield University of
   Pennsylvania B, T
Marywood University B
Mercyhurst College B, T
Messiah College B, T
Misericordia University T
Moravian College T
Point Park University B
St. Francis University B, T
St. Vincent College T
Seton Hill University B, T
Susquehanna University T
Thiel College B
University of Pittsburgh
   Johnstown B, T
Villanova University T
Washington & Jefferson College T
Waynesburg University B, T
Westminster College T
Widener University T
Wilkes University M, T
Wilson College T
York College of Pennsylvania B, T

Puerto Rico

Inter American University of Puerto
   Rico
   Arecibo Campus B
   Fajardo Campus B, T

Ponce Campus B, T
   San German Campus B
Pontifical Catholic University of
   Puerto Rico B, T
Turabo University B
University of Puerto Rico
   Arecibo B, M

Rhode Island

Rhode Island College B
Salve Regina University B

South Carolina

Coker College B, T
Furman University T
Limestone College B
Morris College B, T
North Greenville University B, T
Southern Wesleyan University B, T
Wofford College T

South Dakota

Augustana College B, T
Black Hills State University B
Dakota State University B, T
Dakota Wesleyan University B, T
Mount Marty College B
University of Sioux Falls T
University of South Dakota B, M, T

Tennessee

Belmont University B, M, T
Bryan College T
Christian Brothers University B, M, T
Crichton College B, T
Cumberland University B, T
Freed-Hardeman University B, T
King College T
Lambuth University B, T
Lee University B
Lincoln Memorial University B, T
Lipscomb University B, T
Maryville College B, T
Middle Tennessee State
   University M, T
Southern Adventist University B
Tennessee Technological University T
Tennessee Temple University B
Trevecca Nazarene University B, T
Tusculum College B, T
Union University B, T

Texas

Abilene Christian University B, T
East Texas Baptist University B
Houston Baptist University T
Howard Payne University B, T
Jarvis Christian College B, T
Kilgore College A
Lamar University T
Laredo Community College A
Lubbock Christian University B
McMurry University B, T
St. Edward's University B, T
St. Mary's University T
Sam Houston State University M, T
Schreiner University B
Tarleton State University T
Texas A&M International
   University B, T
Texas A&M University
   Commerce B
   Galveston B
   Kingsville T
Texas College B, T
Texas State University: San
   Marcos M, T
Texas Wesleyan University B, T
University of Dallas T
University of Houston T
University of Houston
   Clear Lake T
University of Mary Hardin-Baylor T

University of Texas
   Arlington T
   San Antonio T
West Texas A&M University T

Utah

Brigham Young University B
Dixie State College of Utah B
Southern Utah University B, T
Utah State University B
Utah Valley University B
Weber State University B
Western Governors University B, M, T

Vermont

Castleton State College B, T
Johnson State College B
St. Michael's College T

Virginia

Averett University B, M, T
Bluefield College B, T
Bridgewater College T
Eastern Mennonite University T
Emory & Henry College B
Hampton University M
Hollins University T
Liberty University M, T
Longwood University B, T
Old Dominion University B, M, T
Radford University T
St. Paul's College T
University of Virginia's College at
   Wise T
Virginia Intermont College B, T

Washington

Eastern Washington University B
Northwest University T
University of Washington M, T
Washington State University B, M, T
Western Washington University B
Whitworth University B, T

West Virginia

Bethany College B
Concord University B, M, T
Fairmont State University B
Shepherd University T
University of Charleston B
West Liberty University B
West Virginia Wesleyan College B

Wisconsin

Carroll University B, T
Carthage College T
Concordia University Wisconsin B
Edgewood College B
Lakeland College T
Lawrence University T
Maranatha Baptist Bible College B
Mount Mary College B, T
St. Norbert College T
Silver Lake College T
University of Wisconsin
   Green Bay T
   Parkside T
   Platteville B
   River Falls T
   Superior B, T
   Whitewater B
Viterbo University B, T

Biomedical engineering

Alabama

University of Alabama
   Birmingham B, M, D

Arizona

Arizona State University B, M, D
University of Arizona M, D

California

California Lutheran University *B*
California Polytechnic State
   University: San Luis Obispo *B, M*
California State University
   Long Beach *B*
San Diego State University *M*
Stanford University *M, D*
University of California
   Berkeley *B, D*
   Davis *B, M, D*
   Irvine *B, M, D*
   Los Angeles *M, D*
   Riverside *B, M, D*
   San Diego *B, M, D*
   Santa Cruz *B*
University of California:
   Merced *B, M, D*
University of Southern
   California *B, M, D*

Colorado

Colorado State University *M, D*
University of Denver *M*

Connecticut

Trinity College *B*
University of Connecticut *B, M, D*
Yale University *B, M, D*

Delaware

University of Delaware *B, M, D*

District of Columbia

Catholic University of
   America *B, M, D*
George Washington University *B*

Florida

Florida Agricultural and Mechanical
   University *M, D*
Florida Atlantic University *M*
Florida Gulf Coast University *B*
Florida International
   University *B, M, D*
Florida State University *M, D*
University of Florida *M*
University of Miami *B, M, D*
University of South Florida *M, D*

Georgia

Emory University *D*
Georgia Institute of
   Technology *B, M, D*
Mercer University *M*

Idaho

University of Idaho *B, M, D*

Illinois

DeVry University
   Addison *B*
   Chicago *B*
   Tinley Park *B*
Illinois Institute of Technology *B, D*
Northwestern University *B, M, D*
Southern Illinois University
   Carbondale *M*
University of Illinois
   Chicago *B, M, D*
   Urbana-Champaign *B, M, D*

Indiana

Indiana Institute of Technology *B*
Indiana University-Purdue University
   Indianapolis *B, M, D*
Purdue University *B, M, D*
Rose-Hulman Institute of
   Technology *B, M*
Vincennes University *A*

Iowa

Dordt College *B*
University of Iowa *B, M, D*

Kansas

University of Kansas *M, D*

Kentucky

University of Kentucky *M, D*
University of Louisville *B, M*

Louisiana

Louisiana State University and
   Agricultural and Mechanical
   College *B*
Louisiana Tech University *B, D*
Tulane University *B, M, D*

Maryland

Johns Hopkins University *B, M, D*
University of Maryland
   College Park *M, D*

Massachusetts

Boston University *B, M, D*
Bunker Hill Community College *A*
Massachusetts Institute of
   Technology *B, M, D*
Smith College *B*
Tufts University *B, M*
Western New England College *B*
Worcester Polytechnic
   Institute *B, M, D*

Michigan

Lawrence Technological University *B*
Michigan State University *B*
Michigan Technological
   University *B, D*
University of Michigan *B, M, D*
Wayne State University *M, D*

Minnesota

University of Minnesota
   Twin Cities *M, D*

Mississippi

Mississippi State University *B, M, D*

Missouri

Saint Louis University *B, M, D*
University of Missouri
   Columbia *B, M, D*
Washington University in St.
   Louis *B, M, D*

Nebraska

University of Nebraska
   Lincoln *B*

Nevada

University of Nevada
   Reno *M, D*

New Hampshire

Dartmouth College *B, M, D*

New Jersey

The College of New Jersey *B*
New Jersey Institute of
   Technology *B, M, D*
Rutgers, The State University of New
   Jersey
   Camden Regional Campus *B*
   New Brunswick/Piscataway
     Campus *B, M, D*
   Newark Regional Campus *B*
Stevens Institute of
   Technology *B, M, D*

New York

Alfred University *B, M*
City University of New York
   City College *B, M, D*
Columbia University *B, M, D*
Cornell University *M, D*
Hofstra University *B*
New York Institute of Technology *B*
Polytechnic Institute of New York
   University *M*
Rensselaer Polytechnic
   Institute *B, M, D*
Rochester Institute of Technology *B*
State University of New York
   Binghamton *M, D*
   Stony Brook *B, M, D*
Syracuse University *B, M, D*
Union College *B*
University of Rochester *B, M, D*

North Carolina

Duke University *B, M, D*
North Carolina State
   University *B, M, D*
University of North Carolina
   Chapel Hill *M, D*
Wake Forest University *M, D*

Ohio

Case Western Reserve
   University *B, M, D*
Cleveland State University *D*
Ohio State University
   Columbus Campus *M, D*
Ohio University *M*
University of Akron *B, M, D*
University of Toledo *B, M*
Wright State University *B, M*

Oklahoma

Oral Roberts University *B*
University of Central Oklahoma *B*
University of Oklahoma *M, D*

Oregon

Oregon Health & Science
   University *M, D*
Oregon State University *B*
Portland Community College *A*

Pennsylvania

Bucknell University *B*
Carnegie Mellon University *B, M, D*
Drexel University *B, M, D*
Gettysburg College *B*
Lehigh University *B, M, D*
Penn State
   Abington *B*
   Altoona *B*
   Beaver *B*
   Berks *B*
   Brandywine *B*
   DuBois *B*
   Erie, The Behrend College *B*
   Fayette, The Eberly Campus *B*
   Greater Allegheny *B*
   Hazleton *B*
   Lehigh Valley *B*
   Mont Alto *B*
   New Kensington *B*
   Schuylkill *B*
   Shenango *B*
   University Park *B, M, D*
   Wilkes-Barre *B*
   Worthington Scranton *B*
   York *B*
Temple University *M*
University of Pennsylvania *B, M, D*
University of Pittsburgh *B, M, D*

Rhode Island

Brown University *B, M*
University of Rhode Island *B*

South Carolina

Clemson University *B, M, D*
University of South Carolina *B, M, D*

South Dakota

South Dakota School of Mines and
   Technology *M, D*
University of South Dakota *D*

Tennessee

University of Memphis *B, M, D*
University of Tennessee
   Knoxville *B, M, D*
University of Tennessee Health
   Science Center *M, D*
Vanderbilt University *B, M, D*

Texas

Baylor University *M*
LeTourneau University *B*
Rice University *B, M, D*
Texas A&M University *B, M, D*
Texas Tech University *M*
University of Houston *M, D*
University of Texas
   Arlington *M, D*
   Austin *B, M, D*
   San Antonio *M, D*
   Southwestern Medical Center at
     Dallas *M, D*

Utah

College of Eastern Utah *A, T*
University of Utah *B, M, D*

Vermont

University of Vermont *M*

Virginia

University of Virginia *B, M, D*
Virginia Commonwealth
   University *B, M, D*
Virginia Polytechnic Institute and
   State University *M, D*

Washington

University of Washington *B, M, D*
Walla Walla University *B*
Washington State University *B*

Wisconsin

Marquette University *B, M, D*
Milwaukee School of Engineering *B*
University of Wisconsin
   Madison *B, M, D*

Biomedical sciences

Alabama

Faulkner University *B*
Oakwood University *B*
University of Alabama
   Birmingham *M*
University of South Alabama *B*

California

California State University
   East Bay *B*
Cerritos College *A*
Charles Drew University of Medicine
   and Science *B*
College of San Mateo *A*
Loma Linda University *D*
San Francisco State University *M*
University of California
   Riverside *M, D*
   San Diego *M, D*

Colorado

Colorado State University *B, D*
Community College of Denver *A*

University of Colorado
Denver *B, M*

Connecticut
Quinnipiac University *B*
University of Connecticut *M, D*

District of Columbia
George Washington University *B*
Georgetown University *B*

Florida
Barry University *M*
Florida Atlantic University *M*
Florida Institute of Technology *B*
Florida State College at Jacksonville *A*
Florida State University *D*
Nova Southeastern University *M*
Santa Fe College *A*
University of South Florida *B*

Georgia
Dalton State College *A*
Darton College *A*
Emory University *D*

Hawaii
University of Hawaii
Manoa *M, D*

Idaho
Stevens-Henager College: Boise *B*

Illinois
Chicago State University *M*
Loyola University Chicago *M, D*
National University of Health
Sciences *B*
South Suburban College of Cook
County *A*

Indiana
Indiana University-Purdue University
Indianapolis *M, D*

Iowa
University of Iowa *D*
University of Northern Iowa *B*

Kentucky
Spencerian College: Lexington *A*
University of Louisville *D*

Louisiana
Our Lady of the Lake College *B*

Maine
University of Maine *B*

Maryland
Hood College *M*
University of Maryland
Baltimore *M, D*
University College *B*

Massachusetts
Benjamin Franklin Institute of
Technology *A*
Bridgewater State College *B*
Northeastern University *D*
Suffolk University *B*
University of Massachusetts
Boston *M*
Lowell *M, D*
Worcester Polytechnic Institute *M, D*

Michigan
Central Michigan University *B*
University of Michigan
Flint *B*
Western Michigan University *B*

Minnesota
Bethany Lutheran College *B*
Rochester Community and Technical
College *A*

Mississippi
Mississippi College *B, M*

Missouri
Maryville University of Saint Louis *B*
Saint Louis University *D*
Washington University in St. Louis *M*
William Jewell College *B*

Montana
Fort Peck Community College *A*

Nebraska
Creighton University *M, D*
University of Nebraska
Lincoln *D*

New Hampshire
University of New Hampshire *B*

New Jersey
Cumberland County College *A*
Rutgers, The State University of New
Jersey
Camden Regional Campus *B*

New York
Marist College *B*
Rochester Institute of Technology *B*
St. Francis College *B*
State University of New York
Albany *M, D*
Buffalo *B, D*
College at Cortland *B*
University of Rochester *D*

North Carolina
East Carolina University *D*
Guilford College *B*
St. Augustine's College *B*

Ohio
Hiram College *B*
Hocking College *B*
University of Toledo *M, D*
Ursuline College *B*

Oklahoma
Oklahoma City University *B*
St. Gregory's University *B*

Pennsylvania
Drexel University *M, D*
Keystone College *B*
Slippery Rock University of
Pennsylvania *B*
University of Pennsylvania *B, M, D*

Puerto Rico
Inter American University of Puerto
Rico
Metropolitan Campus *B*

South Carolina
Clemson University *B*
Medical University of South
Carolina *M*
University of South Carolina *M, D*

South Dakota
Southeast Technical Institute *A*

Tennessee
Christian Brothers University *B*
Crichton College *B*

East Tennessee State University *M, D*
University of Tennessee
Knoxville *M*

Texas
Baylor University *M, D*
McMurry University *B*
St. Philip's College *A*
Texas A&M University *B, M, D*
Texas A&M University
Baylor College of Dentistry *M, D*
Corpus Christi *B*
Galveston *B*
Texas Tech University Health Sciences
Center *M, D*
University of Mary Hardin-Baylor *B, T*

Vermont
Norwich University *B*

Virginia
Jefferson College of Health
Sciences *B*
Old Dominion University *D*

Washington
Washington State University *B*

West Virginia
Ohio Valley University *A*

Biomedical technology

Arizona
DeVry University
Phoenix *B*

Arkansas
North Arkansas College *A*
Phillips Community College of the
University of Arkansas *C, A*

California
American River College *C, A*
City College of San Francisco *C*
DeVry University
Fremont *B*
Pomona *B*
Foothill College *C, A*
Los Angeles City College *C, A*
Napa Valley College *C, A*
Santa Barbara City College *C, A*

Connecticut
Gateway Community College *A*
Quinebaug Valley Community
College *A*

Delaware
Delaware Technical and Community
College
Terry *A*

Florida
DeVry University
Miramar *B*
Orlando *B*
Florida State College at Jacksonville *A*
Santa Fe College *A*
South Florida Community College *A*

Georgia
DeVry University
Decatur *B*

Illinois
DeVry University
Addison *B*
Chicago *B*
Tinley Park *B*
Illinois Institute of Technology *M*

Indiana
Indiana University-Purdue University
Indianapolis *A*

Iowa
Western Iowa Tech Community
College *C*

Louisiana
Delgado Community College *A*

Maryland
Frederick Community College *A*
Howard Community College *C*
Montgomery College *A*

Massachusetts
Benjamin Franklin Institute of
Technology *A*
Northern Essex Community
College *C, A*
Quinsigamond Community College *C*
Suffolk University *B*

Michigan
Schoolcraft College *C, A*

Minnesota
Dakota County Technical College *C, A*
Normandale Community College *C, A*
St. Paul College *A*

Missouri
DeVry University
Kansas City *B*

New Jersey
DeVry University: North Brunswick *B*
Thomas Edison State College *A, B*

New York
DeVry
College of New York *B*

North Carolina
Gaston College *C, A*
Rowan-Cabarrus Community
College *A*
Stanly Community College *A*

Ohio
Cincinnati State Technical and
Community College *A*
DeVry University
Columbus *B*
Owens Community College
Toledo *C, A*
Wright State University *B*

Oklahoma
Oklahoma State University
Institute of Technology:
Okmulgee *A*

Pennsylvania
Community College of Philadelphia *A*
DeVry University
Fort Washington *B*
Edinboro University of
Pennsylvania *A*
Johnson College *A*
Penn State
Altoona *A*
Berks *A*
DuBois *A*
Erie, The Behrend College *A*
Fayette, The Eberly Campus *A*
Hazleton *A*
New Kensington *A*
Schuylkill *A*
Shenango *A*

York A

South Carolina
York Technical College C

South Dakota
Southeast Technical Institute A

Texas
DeVry University
Irving B
St. Philip's College A
Texas State Technical College
Harlingen A

Virginia
ECPI College of Technology: Virginia
Beach C, A

Washington
Bates Technical College C, A
Bellingham Technical College A
DeVry University
Federal Way B
North Seattle Community College A

Wisconsin
Milwaukee Area Technical College A
Western Technical College A

Biometrics

California
La Sierra University B

Colorado
University of Colorado
Denver M, D

Nebraska
University of Nebraska
Lincoln M

New Jersey
Rutgers, The State University of New
Jersey
New Brunswick/Piscataway
Campus B

New York
Cornell University B, M, D
State University of New York
Albany M, D

North Carolina
Duke University M
East Carolina University D
North Carolina State University M, D

Pennsylvania
University of Pittsburgh D

South Carolina
Medical University of South
Carolina D

Texas
University of Texas
Arlington D
Health Science Center at
Houston M, D

Wisconsin
University of Wisconsin
Madison M

Biophysics

California
California Institute of
Technology M, D
La Sierra University B
Pacific Union College B
Pitzer College B
Stanford University M, D
University of California
Berkeley D
Davis D
Los Angeles B, M, D
San Diego B, M, D
University of Southern California B

Colorado
University of Colorado
Denver M, D

Connecticut
University of Connecticut B, M, D

District of Columbia
George Washington University B

Illinois
Loyola University Chicago B
University of Illinois
Urbana-Champaign B, M, D

Indiana
Indiana University-Purdue University
Indianapolis M, D
University of Notre Dame M, D
University of Southern Indiana B, T

Iowa
Iowa State University B, M, D

Louisiana
Centenary College of Louisiana B

Maryland
Johns Hopkins University B, M, D
University of Maryland
College Park M, D

Massachusetts
Boston University M, D
Brandeis University B, M, D
Harvard College D
Northeastern University B
Suffolk University B
Tufts University D

Michigan
Andrews University B
Oakland University B, D
University of Michigan B, D

Minnesota
St. Mary's University of Minnesota B
University of Minnesota
Duluth M
Twin Cities M, D

Missouri
University of Missouri
Missouri University of Science and
Technology B
Washington University in St.
Louis B, D

New York
Barnard College B
Columbia University B
Cornell University M, D
St. Lawrence University B
State University of New York
Albany D

Buffalo B, M, D
College at Geneseo B
Syracuse University D
University of Rochester M, D
Yeshiva University M, D

North Carolina
East Carolina University D
Forsyth Technical Community
College A

Ohio
Case Western Reserve University D
Ohio State University
Columbus Campus M, D

Oklahoma
Southwestern Oklahoma State
University B

Oregon
Oregon State University B, M, D

Pennsylvania
Carnegie Mellon University B, D
Penn State
University Park M, D
Temple University B
University of Pennsylvania B, D
University of Scranton B
Washington & Jefferson College B
Westminster College B

Rhode Island
Brown University B, M, D

South Carolina
Bob Jones University B

Tennessee
King College B
Southern Adventist University B
University of Tennessee Health
Science Center M, D

Texas
Texas A&M University M
University of Houston B
University of Texas
Health Science Center at
Houston M, D
Southwestern Medical Center at
Dallas M, D

Utah
Brigham Young University B

Virginia
Hampden-Sydney College B
University of Virginia D

Washington
University of Washington M, D
Walla Walla University B
Whitworth University B

Wisconsin
University of Wisconsin
Madison D

Biopsychology

Alabama
Spring Hill College B

California
Holy Names University B
Mills College B
St. Mary's College of California B

University of California
Santa Barbara B

Connecticut
Quinnipiac University B
University of Connecticut M, D

Georgia
Oglethorpe University B

Illinois
Monmouth College B
University of Chicago D

Iowa
Morningside College B

Maryland
College of Notre Dame of Maryland B

Michigan
Grand Valley State University B

Missouri
Northwest Missouri State
University B
Washington University in St. Louis B

Nebraska
Nebraska Wesleyan University B

New Jersey
Rider University B

New York
Barnard College B
Medaille College B
Skidmore College B
State University of New York
Albany D

Ohio
Wittenberg University B

Oregon
Warner Pacific College B

Pennsylvania
Carnegie Mellon University B
Franklin & Marshall College B
Immaculata University B
Messiah College B
Philadelphia University B
Westminster College B

Wisconsin
Ripon College B

Biostatistics

Alabama
University of Alabama
Birmingham M, D

California
California State University
East Bay M
Loma Linda University M
University of California
Berkeley M, D
Davis M, D
Los Angeles M, D
University of Southern
California M, D

Connecticut
Yale University M

District of Columbia
George Washington University D

Georgetown University *M*

Florida

Florida State University *M, D*

Georgia

Emory University *D*
Medical College of Georgia *M, D*

Illinois

Northwestern University *M*

Iowa

University of Iowa *M, D*

Kentucky

University of Louisville *M, D*

Louisiana

Louisiana State University Health
   Sciences Center *M, D*
Tulane University *M, D*

Massachusetts

Boston University *M, D*
Emmanuel College *B*
Harvard College *M, D*

Michigan

University of Michigan *M, D*

Minnesota

University of Minnesota
   Twin Cities *B, M, D*

New York

State University of New York
   Albany *M, D*
   Buffalo *B, M, D*
University of Rochester *M*

North Carolina

University of North Carolina
   Chapel Hill *B, M, D*

Ohio

Case Western Reserve
   University *M, D*
Ohio State University
   Columbus Campus *D*
University of Toledo *T*

Oklahoma

University of Oklahoma *M, D*

Pennsylvania

Drexel University *M*
University of Pennsylvania *M, D*
University of Pittsburgh *M, D*

Puerto Rico

University of Puerto Rico
   Medical Sciences *M*

South Carolina

University of South Carolina *M, D*

Texas

Southwestern Adventist University *B*
University of Texas
   Southwestern Medical Center at
      Dallas *M*

Utah

Brigham Young University *B*
University of Utah *M*

Vermont

University of Vermont *M*

Virginia

Virginia Commonwealth
   University *M, D*

Washington

University of Washington *M, D*

Biotechnology

Alabama

University of Alabama
   Huntsville *D*

Arizona

Glendale Community College *A*
University of Arizona *M*

Arkansas

Central Baptist College *B*
Southeast Arkansas College *A*

California

Berkeley City College *A*
California State Polytechnic
   University: Pomona *B, M*
California State University
   San Marcos *B*
California State University: Channel
   Islands *B, M*
Foothill College *A*
Southwestern College *A*
University of California
   Davis *B*
   Irvine *M*
   Los Angeles *B*
   San Diego *B*

Colorado

Red Rocks Community College *A*

Connecticut

Quinnipiac University *B*
University of Connecticut *M*

Delaware

University of Delaware *B*

Florida

Florida Gulf Coast University *B*
Miami Dade College *A*
Santa Fe College *B*
University of Central Florida *B, M*

Georgia

Athens Technical College *A*
Gwinnett Technical College *A*
Kennesaw State University *B*
Medical College of Georgia *M, D*
University of Georgia *B*

Illinois

Northwestern University *M*
Roosevelt University *B, M*
Southern Illinois University
   Edwardsville *B*
University of Illinois
   Chicago *M*
   Urbana-Champaign *B, M, D*

Indiana

Ivy Tech Community College
   Bloomington *A*
   Central Indiana *A*
   Lafayette *A*
   North Central *A*
   Southwest *A*
   Wabash Valley *A*
Vincennes University *A*

Iowa

Des Moines Area Community
   College *A*
Ellsworth Community College *A*
Grand View University *M*
Kirkwood Community College *A*
University of Northern Iowa *B, M*
Western Iowa Tech Community
   College *A*

Kansas

Hutchinson Community College *A*

Kentucky

Owensboro Community and
   Technical College *A*

Maine

Southern Maine Community
   College *A*
University of Southern Maine *B*

Maryland

Baltimore City Community College *A*
Cecil College *A*
Howard Community College *A*
Stevenson University *B*
University of Maryland
   Baltimore County *M*
   University College *M*

Massachusetts

Assumption College *B*
Bay Path College *B*
Endicott College *B*
Fitchburg State College *B*
Middlesex Community College *A*
Mount Wachusett Community
   College *A*
Northeastern University *M*
Quinsigamond Community College *A*
Springfield Technical Community
   College *A*
University of Massachusetts
   Boston *B, M*
Worcester Polytechnic
   Institute *B, M, D*
Worcester State College *B, M*

Michigan

Bay de Noc Community College *A*
Calvin College *B*
Delta College *A*
Ferris State University *B*
Mid Michigan Community College *A*
Wayne State University *M*

Minnesota

Minneapolis Community and
   Technical College *A*
Minnesota State University
   Mankato *B*
Pine Technical College *A*
Saint Cloud State University *B*

Mississippi

Alcorn State University *M*
Mississippi Gulf Coast Community
   College *A*

Missouri

Missouri Baptist University *B*
Missouri Southern State University *B*
Northwest Missouri State
   University *M*
Washington University in St. Louis *M*

Montana

Montana State University
   Bozeman *B*

Nebraska

University of Nebraska
   Omaha *B*

Nevada

University of Nevada
   Reno *B, M*

New Hampshire

Plymouth State University *B*

New Jersey

Bergen Community College *A*
Burlington County College *A*
Kean University *M*
Raritan Valley Community College *A*
Rutgers, The State University of New
   Jersey
   New Brunswick/Piscataway
      Campus *B*
Salem Community College *A*
William Paterson University of New
   Jersey *B, M*

New Mexico

Central New Mexico Community
   College *A*

New York

City University of New York
   York College *B*
Finger Lakes Community College *A*
Genesee Community College *A*
Manhattan College *M*
Polytechnic Institute of New York
   University *M*
Rochester Institute of Technology *B*
State University of New York
   Buffalo *B, M*
   College at Brockport *B*
   College at Fredonia *B*
   College of Agriculture and
      Technology at Cobleskill *B*
   College of Environmental Science
      and Forestry *B*
Tompkins Cortland Community
   College *A*

North Carolina

Alamance Community College *A*
Bladen Community College *A*
Carteret Community College *A*
Durham Technical Community
   College *A*
North Carolina State University *M*
University of North Carolina
   Pembroke *B*
Winston-Salem State University *B*

North Dakota

North Dakota State University *B*

Ohio

Kent State University *B*
Owens Community College
   Toledo *A*
Ursuline College *B*

Oklahoma

Oklahoma City Community College *A*
Southeastern Oklahoma State
   University *B*

Oregon

Oregon State University *B*
Portland Community College *A*

Pennsylvania

Duquesne University *M*
East Stroudsburg University of
   Pennsylvania *B*

Elizabethtown College *B*
Harrisburg University of Science and
   Technology *B*
Lehigh Carbon Community College *A*
Marywood University *B, M*
Montgomery County Community
   College *A*
Northampton Community College *A*
Penn State
   University Park *M*
Pennsylvania Highlands Community
   College *A*
Point Park University *B*
Thomas Jefferson University: College
   of Health Professions *B*
University of Pennsylvania *M*

Puerto Rico

Inter American University of Puerto
   Rico
   Aguadilla Campus *B*
   Bayamon Campus *B*
   Guayama Campus *B*
Turabo University *A*
Universidad del Este *B*

Rhode Island

Community College of Rhode
   Island *A*

South Carolina

Claflin University *B, M*
Clemson University *M*
Greenville Technical College *A*

Tennessee

Southwest Tennessee Community
   College *A*

Texas

San Jacinto College *A*
Stephen F. Austin State University *M*
Texas A&M University *M*
Texas Tech University *M*
Texas Tech University Health Sciences
   Center *M*
University of Texas
   Dallas *M*
   San Antonio *D*
West Texas A&M University *B*

Utah

Brigham Young University *B, M*
University of Utah *M*
Utah Valley University *B*

Virginia

James Madison University *B*

Washington

Bates Technical College *A*
Shoreline Community College *A*

West Virginia

West Liberty University *B*
West Virginia State University *M*

Wisconsin

University of Wisconsin
   Madison *M*
   River Falls *B*

Boilermaking

Indiana

Ivy Tech Community College
   Southwest *C, A*

Botany

Alabama

Auburn University *B, M, D*

Alaska

University of Alaska
   Fairbanks *M*

Arizona

Arizona State University *B, M, D*
Northern Arizona University *B*
Prescott College *B, M*

California

California State Polytechnic
   University: Pomona *B*
California State University
   Chico *B, M*
   Long Beach *B*
Cerritos College *A*
Citrus College *A*
El Camino College *A*
El Camino College: Compton
   Center *A*
Humboldt State University *B*
San Francisco State University *B*
San Joaquin Delta College *A*
University of California
   Berkeley *B, D*
   Davis *B, M, D*
   Irvine *B*
   Los Angeles *B*
   Riverside *B, M, D*

Colorado

Colorado State University *B, M, D*

Connecticut

Connecticut College *B*
University of Connecticut *M, D*

District of Columbia

George Washington University *M, D*

Florida

Daytona State College *A*
Pensacola Junior College *A*
University of Florida *B, M*

Georgia

University of Georgia *B, M, D*

Hawaii

University of Hawaii
   Manoa *B, M, D*

Idaho

Idaho State University *B*
North Idaho College *A*
University of Idaho *B, M, D*

Illinois

Saint Xavier University *B*
Southern Illinois University
   Carbondale *B, M, D*
University of Illinois
   Urbana-Champaign *B, M, D*

Indiana

Indiana University
   Bloomington *M, D*
Purdue University *B, M, D*

Iowa

Iowa State University *M, D*
Marshalltown Community College *A*

Kansas

Central Christian College of Kansas *A*

Pratt Community College *A*
University of Kansas *M, D*

Maine

University of Maine *B, M, D*

Massachusetts

University of Massachusetts
   Amherst *M, D*

Michigan

Andrews University *B*
Michigan State University *B, M, D*
Northern Michigan University *B*
University of Michigan *B*

Minnesota

Minnesota State University
   Mankato *B, T*

Missouri

Washington University in St. Louis *D*

Montana

University of Great Falls *B*
University of Montana *B*

Nebraska

University of Nebraska
   Lincoln *B*

New Hampshire

University of New Hampshire *B, M, D*

New Jersey

Rutgers, The State University of New
   Jersey
   Newark Regional Campus *B*

New Mexico

Western New Mexico University *B*

New York

Cornell University *M, D*

North Carolina

Duke University *M, D*
Mars Hill College *B*
Methodist University *B*
North Carolina State
   University *B, M, D*

North Dakota

Dakota College at Bottineau *A*
North Dakota State University *B, M, D*

Ohio

Kent State University *B, M, D*
Miami University
   Oxford Campus *B, M, D, T*
Ohio State University
   Columbus Campus *B, M, D*
Ohio University *B, M, D*
Ohio Wesleyan University *B*
University of Akron *B*

Oklahoma

Oklahoma State University *B, M, D*
University of Oklahoma *B, M, D*

Oregon

Oregon State University *B*

Pennsylvania

Juniata College *B*

South Carolina

Clemson University *B, M*

Tennessee

University of Tennessee
   Knoxville *M, D*

Texas

Hill College *A*
Laredo Community College *A*
Texas A&M University *B, M, D*
Texas A&M University
   Galveston *B*
Texas State University: San Marcos *B*
University of Texas
   Austin *M, D*

Utah

Brigham Young University *B*
Snow College *A*
Utah State University *B, M*
Weber State University *B*

Vermont

Bennington College *B*
Marlboro College *B*
University of Vermont *B, M, D*

Washington

Centralia College *A*
University of Washington *B, M, D*
Washington State University *M, D*
Western Washington University *B*

Wisconsin

University of Wisconsin
   Madison *B, M, D*
   Superior *B*

Wyoming

University of Wyoming *B, M, D*

Broadcast journalism

Arizona

Northern Arizona University *B*

Arkansas

Harding University *B*
John Brown University *A, B*
University of the Ozarks *B*

California

Bakersfield College *A*
Biola University *B*
Butte College *C, A*
California Lutheran University *B*
California State University
   East Bay *B*
   Long Beach *B*
   Northridge *B, M*
Chabot College *A*
Chaffey College *C, A*
Chapman University *B*
City College of San Francisco *C*
College of San Mateo *C, A*
College of the Siskiyous *C, A*
Cosumnes River College *A*
Cuesta College *C, A*
Foothill College *C, A*
Fullerton College *A*
Glendale Community College *A*
Golden West College *C, A*
Grossmont College *C, A*
Laney College *C, A*
Long Beach City College *C, A*
Los Angeles City College *C, A*
Los Angeles Valley College *C, A*
Modesto Junior College *C, A*
Moorpark College *C, A*
Mount San Antonio College *C, A*
National University *B, M*
Ohlone College *C, A*
Pasadena City College *C, A*
Pepperdine University *B*

Point Loma Nazarene University *B*
Saddleback College *C, A*
San Diego City College *A*
San Joaquin Delta College *A*
Santa Ana College *C, A*
Santa Rosa Junior College *C*
Southwestern College *C, A*
University of Southern
    California *B, M*

Colorado

Metropolitan State College of
    Denver *B*

Connecticut

Lincoln College of New England:
    Briarwood *A*
Middlesex Community College *C, A*
Mitchell College *B*
Quinnipiac University *B*

Delaware

Delaware State University *B*

District of Columbia

Gallaudet University *B*
Howard University *B*

Florida

Broward College *A*
City College: Fort Lauderdale *A*
Florida Southern College *B*
Gulf Coast Community College *A*
Miami Dade College *A*
Palm Beach Atlantic University *B*
Palm Beach Community College *A*
State College of Florida,
    Manatee-Sarasota *A*
University of Miami *B*

Georgia

Paine College *B*
University of Georgia *B*

Hawaii

Chaminade University of Honolulu *B*
University of Hawaii
    Leeward Community College *C, A*

Idaho

Brigham Young University-Idaho *B*

Illinois

Chicago State University *B*
City Colleges of Chicago
    Kennedy-King College *C, A*
Columbia College Chicago *B, M*
Governors State University *B, M*
Illinois Central College *A*
Illinois Eastern Community Colleges
    Wabash Valley College *A*
Lake Land College *A*
Lewis University *B*
Northwestern University *B, M*
Olivet Nazarene University *B*
University of Illinois
    Urbana-Champaign *B, M*
University of St. Francis *B*

Indiana

Franklin College *B*
Goshen College *B*
Huntington University *B*
Manchester College *A, B*
Purdue University *B*
Purdue University
    Calumet *B*

Iowa

Dordt College *B*
Drake University *B*
Grand View University *B*

Iowa Lakes Community College *C, A*
St. Ambrose University *B*
Waldorf College *B*
Wartburg College *B*

Kansas

Central Christian College of Kansas *A*
Coffeyville Community College *A*
Dodge City Community College *C, A*

Kentucky

Campbellsville University *B*
Eastern Kentucky University *B*
Northern Kentucky University *B*

Maine

New England School of
    Communications *B*

Maryland

Frederick Community College *C*
Montgomery College *A*
Washington Adventist University *B*

Massachusetts

American International College *B*
Boston University *B, M*
Emerson College *B*
New England Institute of Art *A*
Northern Essex Community
    College *A*
Suffolk University *B*

Michigan

Bay de Noc Community College *C*
Grand Valley State University *B*
Henry Ford Community College *A*
Lansing Community College *A*
Macomb Community College *C, A*
St. Clair County Community
    College *A*
Spring Arbor University *B*
University of Detroit Mercy *B*

Minnesota

Brown College *A*
Northland Community & Technical
    College *C, A*
Rochester Community and Technical
    College *C*
Saint Cloud State University *B*
Southwest Minnesota State
    University *B*
Winona State University *B*

Mississippi

Meridian Community College *A*
Northwest Mississippi Community
    College *A*
Rust College *B*

Missouri

Calvary Bible College and Theological
    Seminary *B*
College of the Ozarks *B*
Evangel University *A, B*
St. Louis Community College
    St. Louis Community College at
        Florissant Valley *A*
Stephens College *B*
University of Central Missouri *B*
University of Missouri
    Columbia *B*
Webster University *B*
William Woods University *B*

Montana

University of Montana *B, M*

Nebraska

University of Nebraska
    Kearney *B*

Lincoln *B*
Omaha *B*

New Hampshire

Rivier College *B*

New Jersey

Felician College *B*
Montclair State University *B*
Ocean County College *A*

New Mexico

Eastern New Mexico University *B*
New Mexico State University
    Carlsbad *C*

New York

Adirondack Community College *C, A*
Cayuga County Community College *A*
City University of New York
    Brooklyn College *B*
    Kingsborough Community
        College *A*
College of New Rochelle *B*
Finger Lakes Community College *A*
Five Towns College *B*
Herkimer County Community
    College *C, A*
Ithaca College *B*
Manhattan College *B*
New York Institute of Technology *B*
Onondaga Community College *A*
St. Thomas Aquinas College *B*
State University of New York
    College at Brockport *B*
    College at Buffalo *B*
    College at Fredonia *B*
    New Paltz *B*
    Oswego *B*
Suffolk County Community College *A*
Sullivan County Community
    College *A*
Tompkins Cortland Community
    College *A*

North Carolina

Campbell University *B*
East Carolina University *B*
Elon University *B*
Gardner-Webb University *B*
Gaston College *A*
North Carolina Agricultural and
    Technical State University *B*

North Dakota

Minot State University *B*

Ohio

Bowling Green State University *B*
Central State University *B*
Kent State University *B*
Marietta College *B*
Mount Vernon Nazarene University *B*
Ohio Northern University *B*
Ohio University *B*
Ohio Wesleyan University *B*
Otterbein College *B*
University of Cincinnati *M, T*
Washington State Community
    College *A*

Oklahoma

Cameron University *B*
East Central University *B*
Langston University *B*
Northern Oklahoma College *A*
Northwestern Oklahoma State
    University *B*
Oklahoma Baptist University *B*
Oklahoma Christian University *B*
Oklahoma City Community College *A*
Oklahoma City University *B*

University of Central Oklahoma *B*
University of Oklahoma *B*

Oregon

Mt. Hood Community College *A*

Pennsylvania

Bucks County Community College *C*
Chatham University *B*
Edinboro University of
    Pennsylvania *B*
Keystone College *A*
La Salle University *B*
Lincoln University *B*
Luzerne County Community
    College *A*
Mansfield University of
    Pennsylvania *B*
Point Park University *B*
Temple University *B*
Waynesburg University *B*
Westminster College *B*

Rhode Island

New England Institute of
    Technology *A*

South Carolina

Bob Jones University *B*
North Greenville University *B*
Tri-County Technical College *A*
Trident Technical College *A*
University of South Carolina *B*

Tennessee

Belmont University *B*
Southern Adventist University *B*
Union University *B*

Texas

Amarillo College *A*
Central Texas College *C, A*
Hardin-Simmons University *B*
Laredo Community College *A*
Midland College *A*
Our Lady of the Lake University of San
    Antonio *B*
South Plains College *A*
Southwestern Adventist University *B*
Texas A&M University
    Commerce *B*
Texas Christian University *B*
University of North Texas *B*
West Texas A&M University *B*

Utah

College of Eastern Utah *T*
Weber State University *B*

Vermont

Lyndon State College *B*

Virginia

Hampton University *B*
Regent University *M*
Southwest Virginia Community
    College *C*

Washington

Centralia College *A*
Gonzaga University *B*
Green River Community College *C*
Shoreline Community College *A*

West Virginia

Bethany College *B*
Concord University *B*
West Virginia University *B*

Wisconsin

Concordia University Wisconsin *B*

Marquette University *B, M*
University of Wisconsin
  Oshkosh *B*
  Superior *B*
  Whitewater *B*

Buddhist studies

California

California Institute of Integral Studies *M, D*
University of California Berkeley *D*
University of the West *C, D*

Massachusetts

Mount Holyoke College *C*
University of Massachusetts Amherst *C*

Missouri

Webster University *C*

Wisconsin

University of Wisconsin Madison *D*

Building inspection

Arizona

Scottsdale Community College *C, A*

California

Coastline Community College *C*
College of the Canyons *A*
College of the Desert *C*
Southwestern College *C, A*

Colorado

Arapahoe Community College *A*

Illinois

Harper College *C*
McHenry County College *C, A*

Maryland

Community College of Baltimore County *C, A*

Michigan

Delta College *C*

Minnesota

Inver Hills Community College *C, A*
North Hennepin Community College *C, A*

New York

Erie Community College City Campus *C*
State University of New York College of Agriculture and Technology at Morrisville *A*

Ohio

Vatterott College: Cleveland *A*

Oregon

Chemeketa Community College *A*
Portland Community College *C, A*

Pennsylvania

Harrisburg Area Community College *C, A*
Pennsylvania Highlands Community College *C*

South Carolina

Greenville Technical College *C*

Utah

Utah Valley University *C, A*

Washington

Bellingham Technical College *C*
Centralia College *A*

Building/property maintenance

Alabama

Shelton State Community College *C*

Arizona

Eastern Arizona College *C*
GateWay Community College *C, A*
Northland Pioneer College *C*
Pima Community College *C, A*

California

Allan Hancock College *C*
Butte College *C, A*
Chabot College *A*
City College of San Francisco *C*
College of San Mateo *C*
College of the Redwoods *C, A*
College of the Sequoias *C, A*
Cosumnes River College *C, A*
Diablo Valley College *C*
El Camino College *C, A*
El Camino College: Compton Center *C*
Fresno City College *C, A*
Fullerton College *A*
Laney College *C, A*
Lassen Community College *A*
Los Angeles Trade and Technical College *C, A*
Modesto Junior College *C, A*
Orange Coast College *C, A*
Palomar College *C, A*
Pasadena City College *C, A*
Porterville College *C*
Riverside Community College *C, A*
Saddleback College *C*
San Joaquin Delta College *C, A*
Santa Monica College *A*
Southwestern College *C, A*
Ventura College *C, A*
West Valley College *C, A*

Colorado

Pikes Peak Community College *C, A*

Florida

Daytona State College *C*
Florida State College at Jacksonville *A*
Miami Dade College *A*
Palm Beach Community College *C, A*
Pensacola Junior College *A*
Santa Fe College *A*
Seminole Community College *C*
Tallahassee Community College *A*

Georgia

DeKalb Technical College *C*

Illinois

College of DuPage *A*
Harper College *C, A*
Lincoln Land Community College *C, A*
Oakton Community College *A*
Parkland College *C*
Rend Lake College *C*
Sauk Valley Community College *C*
South Suburban College of Cook County *A*
Southwestern Illinois College *C, A*
Waubonsee Community College *C*

Indiana

Ivy Tech Community College
  Bloomington *C, A*
  Central Indiana *C, A*
  Columbus *C, A*
  East Central *C, A*
  Kokomo *C, A*
  Lafayette *C, A*
  North Central *C, A*
  Northeast *C, A*
  Northwest *C, A*
  Richmond *C, A*
  South Central *C, A*
  Southwest *C, A*
  Wabash Valley *C, A*
Vincennes University *C*

Iowa

Kirkwood Community College *C, A*
Southeastern Community College North Campus *A*
Western Iowa Tech Community College *C*

Kansas

Coffeyville Community College *C*
Kansas City Kansas Community College *C*

Louisiana

Delgado Community College *A*

Maine

Central Maine Community College *C, A*

Maryland

Hagerstown Community College *C*

Massachusetts

Cape Cod Community College *C*

Michigan

Bay de Noc Community College *C*
Delta College *C, A*
Henry Ford Community College *C*
Lansing Community College *C, A*
Macomb Community College *C*
Washtenaw Community College *C, A*

Minnesota

Century Community and Technical College *C, A*
Dunwoody College of Technology *C*
Hennepin Technical College *C, A*
Minnesota State University Mankato *B*
Rochester Community and Technical College *C*
University of Minnesota Twin Cities *B*

Mississippi

Mississippi Delta Community College *A*
Northeast Mississippi Community College *C*

Missouri

Linn State Technical College *A*
North Central Missouri College *A*
Park University *A*

Montana

Miles Community College *A*
University of Montana *C, A*

Nebraska

Metropolitan Community College *C, A*
Mid-Plains Community College Area *C, A*

Nevada

Truckee Meadows Community College *A*

New Hampshire

Manchester Community College *C, A*

New Mexico

Dona Ana Community College of New Mexico State University *A*
New Mexico State University Carlsbad *C*
Northern New Mexico College *C, A*
Santa Fe Community College *C*

New York

City University of New York New York City College of Technology *C, B*
Erie Community College City Campus *A*
Hudson Valley Community College *A*
Institute of Design and Construction *A*
Mohawk Valley Community College *C, A*
Orange County Community College *C*
State University of New York College of Agriculture and Technology at Morrisville *A*
College of Technology at Canton *A*
Farmingdale *B*

North Carolina

Blue Ridge Community College *C*
Guilford Technical Community College *A*
Haywood Community College *C, A*
Western Piedmont Community College *C, A*

Ohio

Eastern Gateway Community College *A*
Vatterott College: Cleveland *C*

Oklahoma

Oklahoma State University Institute of Technology: Okmulgee *A*

Pennsylvania

Commonwealth Technical Institute *C*
Community College of Allegheny County *C, A*
Luzerne County Community College *C, A*
Pennsylvania College of Technology *C*

Puerto Rico

University College of San Juan *C*

South Carolina

Aiken Technical College *C*
Denmark Technical College *C*
Technical College of the Lowcountry *C*
Trident Technical College *C*

Texas

Del Mar College *C, A*
Laredo Community College *C*
North Lake College *C*
Odessa College *C, A*
St. Philip's College *A*
Texas A&M University Commerce *B*

Texas State Technical College
  Waco *A*
Tyler Junior College *A*

Utah

Salt Lake Community College *A*
Utah Valley University *A*
Weber State University *A, B*

Vermont

Vermont Technical College *A, B*

Virginia

John Tyler Community College *C*

Washington

Bates Technical College *C, A*
Bellingham Technical College *C, A*
Centralia College *A*
Spokane Falls Community College *C*

Wisconsin

Gateway Technical College *C*
University of Wisconsin
  Platteville *B*
Waukesha County Technical
  College *C*

Business administration and management

Alabama

Alabama Agricultural and Mechanical
  University *B, M*
Alabama State University *B*
Amridge University *B*
Andrew Jackson University *M*
Athens State University *B*
Auburn University *B, M, D*
Auburn University at Montgomery *B*
Birmingham-Southern College *B, M*
Bishop State Community College *A*
Calhoun Community College *C, A*
Central Alabama Community
  College *A*
Chattahoochee Valley Community
  College *A*
Columbia Southern University *A, B, M*
Enterprise-Ozark Community
  College *C, A*
Faulkner State Community College *A*
Faulkner University *A, B*
Gadsden State Community College *A*
George C. Wallace State Community
  College
  Selma *A*
Huntingdon College *B*
Jacksonville State University *B, M*
Judson College *B*
Lawson State Community College *A*
Miles College *B*
Northeast Alabama Community
  College *A*
Oakwood University *B*
Samford University *B, M*
South University:
  Montgomery *A, B, M*
Spring Hill College *B, M*
Stillman College *B*
Talladega College *B*
Troy University *B, M*
Tuskegee University *B*
University of Alabama *B, M, D*
University of Alabama
  Birmingham *B, M*
  Huntsville *B, M*
University of Mobile *B, M*
University of Montevallo *B*
University of North Alabama *B, M*
University of South Alabama *B, M*
University of West Alabama *B*

Alaska

Alaska Pacific University *C, A, B, M*
Ilisagvik College *C, A*
University of Alaska
  Anchorage *C, A, B, M*
  Fairbanks *C, A, B, M*
  Southeast *A, M*

Arizona

Anthem College *A, B*
Argosy University: Online *B*
Argosy University: Phoenix *B*
Arizona State University *B, M, D*
Arizona Western College *A*
Brookline College
  Phoenix *C, A, B*
  Tempe *C, A*
  Tucson *C, A*
Brown Mackie College: Tucson *A, B*
Central Arizona College *C, A*
Cochise College *A*
Coconino County Community
  College *C, A*
DeVry University
  Phoenix *B, M*
Dine College *A*
Eastern Arizona College *A*
Estrella Mountain Community
  College *A*
Everest College
  Phoenix *A, B*
Grand Canyon University *B, M*
Lamson College *A*
Mesa Community College *A*
Mohave Community College *C, A*
Northcentral University *B, M, D*
Northern Arizona University *B, M*
Northland Pioneer College *C, A*
Phoenix College *C, A*
Pima Community College *C, A*
Prescott College *B, M*
Rio Salado College *C, A*
Southwestern College *A*
Tohono O'odham Community
  College *A*
University of Arizona *M, D*
University of Phoenix *C, A, B, M*
Western International
  University *A, B, M*

Arkansas

Arkansas Baptist College *A, B*
Arkansas State University *B, M*
Arkansas Tech University *B*
Black River Technical College *A*
Central Baptist College *A, B*
Crowley's Ridge College *B*
East Arkansas Community College *A*
Ecclesia College *B*
Harding University *B, M*
John Brown University *B, M*
Lyon College *B*
Northwest Arkansas Community
  College *A*
Ouachita Baptist University *B*
Ouachita Technical College *C, A*
Ozarka College *A*
Philander Smith College *B*
Phillips Community College of the
  University of Arkansas *A*
Rich Mountain Community College *A*
South Arkansas Community College *A*
Southeast Arkansas College *C*
Southern Arkansas University *M*
Southern Arkansas University Tech *A*
University of Arkansas *B, M, D*
University of Arkansas
  Community College at Batesville *A*
  Fort Smith *C, A, B*
  Little Rock *B, M*
  Monticello *B*
  Pine Bluff *B*
University of Central Arkansas *A, B, M*
University of the Ozarks *B*

Williams Baptist College *B*

California

Allan Hancock College *C, A*
Alliant International
  University *B, M, D*
Antelope Valley College *C, A*
Argosy University: Inland Empire *B*
Argosy University: Los Angeles *B*
Argosy University: Orange County *B*
Argosy University: San Diego *B*
Argosy University: San Francisco Bay
  Area *B*
Azusa Pacific University *B, M*
Bakersfield College *A*
Berkeley City College *C, A*
Bethany University *B*
Biola University *B, M*
Butte College *A*
Cabrillo College *A*
California Baptist University *B, M*
California Coast University *A, B, M*
California College San Diego *B*
California College of the Arts *M*
California Lutheran University *B, M*
California Maritime Academy *B*
California National University for
  Advanced Studies *B, M*
California Polytechnic State
  University: San Luis Obispo *B, M*
California State Polytechnic
  University: Pomona *B, M*
California State University
  Bakersfield *B, M*
  Chico *B, M*
  Dominguez Hills *B, M*
  East Bay *B, M*
  Fresno *B, M*
  Fullerton *B, M*
  Long Beach *M*
  Los Angeles *B, M*
  Monterey Bay *B, M*
  Northridge *B, M*
  Sacramento *B, M*
  San Bernardino *B, M*
  San Marcos *B, M*
  Stanislaus *B, M*
California University of Management
  and Sciences *B, M*
Canada College *C, A*
Cerritos College *A*
Cerro Coso Community College *C, A*
Chaffey College *C, A*
Chapman University *B, M*
Citrus College *C*
City College of San Francisco *A*
Coastline Community College *C, A*
Coleman University *B, M*
College of Alameda *A*
College of Marin: Kentfield *C, A*
College of the Canyons *C, A*
College of the Desert *A*
College of the Siskiyous *C, A*
Columbia College *C, A*
Concordia University *B, M*
Copper Mountain College *A*
Cosumnes River College *A*
Crafton Hills College *C, A*
Cuyamaca College *C, A*
Cypress College *A*
De Anza College *C, A*
DeVry University
  Fremont *B, M*
  Long Beach *B, M*
  Sherman Oaks *B, M*
Diablo Valley College *C, A*
Dominican University of
  California *B, M*
East Los Angeles College *A*
El Camino College *A*
El Camino College: Compton
  Center *C, A*
Evergreen Valley College *C*
Foothill College *C, A*

Fresno City College *A*
Fresno Pacific University *B*
Fullerton College *A*
Golden Gate University *C, B, M, D*
Golden West College *C, A*
Grossmont College *C, A*
Hartnell College *C, A*
Heald College
  Concord *C, A*
  Fresno *C, A*
  Hayward *A*
  Roseville *A*
  San Francisco *C, A*
  San Jose *C, A*
Holy Names University *B, M*
Hope International University *B, M*
Humboldt State University *B, M*
Humphreys College *A, B*
Imperial Valley College *A*
Irvine Valley College *C, A*
John F. Kennedy University *B, M*
Kaplan College: Panorama City *A*
Kaplan College: San Diego *C*
LA College International *C, A, B*
La Sierra University *B, M*
Lassen Community College *A*
Lincoln University *B, M*
Long Beach City College *C, A*
Los Angeles City College *C, A*
Los Angeles Harbor College *C, A*
Los Angeles Mission College *A*
Los Angeles Pierce College *C, A*
Los Angeles Southwest College *A*
Los Angeles Trade and Technical
  College *A*
Loyola Marymount University *C, B, M*
MTI College *C, A*
Marymount College *B*
The Master's College *B*
Mendocino College *C, A*
Menlo College *B*
Merced College *A*
Mills College *M*
MiraCosta College *C, A*
Mission College *A*
Modesto Junior College *A*
Monterey Peninsula College *A*
Moorpark College *C, A*
Mount St. Mary's College *B*
Mount San Antonio College *C, A*
Mount San Jacinto College *C, A*
Mt. Sierra College *B*
National Hispanic University *A, B*
National University *B, M*
Northwestern Polytechnic
  University *B, M, D*
Notre Dame de Namur
  University *B, M*
Ohlone College *C, A*
Oxnard College *C, A*
Pacific Union College *B*
Palo Verde College *C, A*
Palomar College *A*
Patten University *B, M*
Pepperdine University *B, M*
Point Loma Nazarene University *B, M*
Porterville College *A*
Remington College
  San Diego *B, M*
Riverside Community College *C, A*
Saddleback College *C, A*
St. Mary's College of California *B, M*
San Bernardino Valley College *C, A*
San Diego Christian College *B*
San Diego City College *A*
San Diego Mesa College *C, A*
San Diego Miramar College *A*
San Diego State University *B, M*
San Francisco State University *B, M*
San Joaquin Delta College *C, A*
San Joaquin Valley College *A*
San Jose City College *C*
San Jose State University *B, M*
Santa Ana College *C, A*

Santa Barbara Business College: Palm
    Desert *C, A*
Santa Barbara Business College:
    Ventura *C, A*
Santa Barbara City College *C, A*
Santa Clara University *M*
Santa Monica College *C, A*
Santa Rosa Junior College *A*
Santiago Canyon College *C, A*
Shasta College *A*
Sierra College *C, A*
Silicon Valley College
    Western Career College:
        Emeryville *C*
Silicon Valley University *B, M*
Simpson University *B*
Skyline College *C, A*
Solano Community College *C, A*
Sonoma State University *B, M*
Southern California Institute of
    Technology *A, B*
Southwestern College *A*
Stanford University *M, D*
Taft College *A*
University of California
    Berkeley *B, M, D*
    Davis *M*
    Irvine *B, M, D*
    Los Angeles *M, D*
    Riverside *B, M*
University of La Verne *B, M*
University of Redlands *B, M*
University of San Diego *B, M*
University of San Francisco *B, M*
University of Southern
    California *B, M, D*
University of the Pacific *B, M*
University of the West *M*
Vanguard University of Southern
    California *B, M*
Ventura College *A*
Victor Valley College *C, A*
West Hills College: Coalinga *C, A*
West Hills College: Lemoore *C, A*
West Los Angeles College *C, A*
West Valley College *C, A*
Westwood College of Technology
    Westwood College: Los
        Angeles *B, M*
Westwood College: Anaheim *B, M*
William Jessup University *B*
Woodbury University *B, M*
WyoTech: Long Beach *C*
Yuba Community College
    District *C, A*

Colorado

Adams State College *B, M*
American Sentinel University *A, B, M*
Argosy University: Denver *B*
Aspen University *B, M*
CollegeAmerica
    Denver *A, B*
    Fort Collins *M*
Colorado Christian University *B, M*
Colorado Mountain College *C, A*
Colorado Northwestern Community
    College *C*
Colorado State University *B, M*
Colorado Technical
    University *B, M, D*
Community College of Aurora *C, A*
Community College of Denver *C, A*
DeVry University
    Westminster *B, M*
Fort Lewis College *B*
Front Range Community College *C, A*
Institute of Business & Medical
    Careers *C, A*
Johnson & Wales University:
    Denver *B*
Jones International
    University *A, B, M, D*
Lamar Community College *A*

Metropolitan State College of
    Denver *B*
Northeastern Junior College *C*
Otero Junior College *A*
Pikes Peak Community College *C, A*
Pueblo Community College *C, A*
Red Rocks Community College *A*
Regis University *B*
Trinidad State Junior College *A*
University of Colorado
    Boulder *B, M, D*
    Colorado Springs *B, M*
University of Denver *B, M*
University of Northern Colorado *B*
Western State College of Colorado *B*
Westwood College: Denver North *B*

Connecticut

Albertus Magnus College *C, A, B, M*
Asnuntuck Community College *C, A*
Capital Community College *C, A*
Central Connecticut State
    University *B*
Eastern Connecticut State
    University *B*
Fairfield University *B, M*
Gateway Community College *A*
Goodwin College *C, A*
Housatonic Community College *A*
Lincoln College of New England:
    Briarwood *A*
Manchester Community College *A*
Middlesex Community College *A*
Mitchell College *B*
Naugatuck Valley Community
    College *C, A*
Northwestern Connecticut
    Community College *A*
Norwalk Community College *A*
Post University *A, B, M*
Quinebaug Valley Community
    College *C, A*
Quinnipiac University *B, M*
Saint Joseph College *B, M*
Southern Connecticut State
    University *B, M*
Three Rivers Community College *C, A*
Tunxis Community College *C, A*
United States Coast Guard Academy *B*
University of Bridgeport *A, M*
University of Connecticut *B*
University of Hartford *B, M*
University of New Haven *A, B, M*
Western Connecticut State
    University *B*
Yale University *M, D*

Delaware

Delaware State University *B, M*
Delaware Technical and Community
    College
    Stanton/Wilmington *C, A*
    Terry *C, A*
Goldey-Beacom College *A, B, M*
University of Delaware *B, M*
Wesley College *A, B, M*
Wilmington University *M*

District of Columbia

American University *B, M*
Gallaudet University *B*
George Washington
    University *B, M, D*
Georgetown University *B, M*
Howard University *B, M*
Potomac College *C*
Trinity Washington University *B, M*
University of the District of
    Columbia *B, M*

Florida

Angley College *A, B*
Argosy University: Sarasota *B*

Argosy University: Tampa *B*
Barry University *B, M*
Bethune-Cookman University *B*
Brevard Community College *A*
Broward College *C, A*
Brown Mackie College: Miami *A*
Carlos Albizu University *M*
Central Florida College *A*
Central Florida Community
    College *C, A*
Chipola College *A, B*
City College
    Gainesville *A, B*
    Miami *A, B*
City College: Casselberry *A*
City College: Fort Lauderdale *A, B*
Clearwater Christian College *B*
College of Business and Technology:
    Flagler *C, A*
College of Business and Technology:
    Kendall *C, A*
Daytona State College *A*
DeVry University
    Miramar *B, M*
    Orlando *B, M*
Eckerd College *B*
Edison State College *A*
Edward Waters College *B*
Embry-Riddle Aeronautical
    University *A, B, M*
Embry-Riddle Aeronautical University:
    Worldwide Campus *A, B, M*
Everglades University: Boca
    Raton *B, M*
Flagler College *B*
Florida Agricultural and Mechanical
    University *B, M*
Florida Atlantic University *B, M, D*
Florida College *B*
Florida Gulf Coast University *B, M*
Florida Institute of
    Technology *A, B, M*
Florida International
    University *B, M, D*
Florida Keys Community College *A*
Florida Memorial University *B, M*
Florida National College *A, B*
Florida Southern College *B, M*
Florida State College at Jacksonville *A*
Florida State University *M*
Gulf Coast College *C, A*
Gulf Coast Community College *A*
Herzing University *A, B*
Hillsborough Community
    College *C, A*
Hodges University *A, B, M*
Indian River State College *A*
Jacksonville University *B, M*
Johnson & Wales University: North
    Miami *B*
Jones College *A, B*
Lake City Community College *A*
Lake-Sumter Community College *C, A*
Lynn University *B, M*
Miami Dade College *C, A*
Northwest Florida State College *C, A*
Northwood University
    Florida *B*
Nova Southeastern University *B, M, D*
Palm Beach Atlantic University *B, M*
Palm Beach Community College *A*
Pasco-Hernando Community
    College *C, A*
Pensacola Junior College *A*
Polk State College *A*
Rasmussen College: Fort Myers *A, B*
Rasmussen College: Ocala *A, B*
Rasmussen College: Pasco
    County *A, B*
Rollins College *M*
Saint Johns River Community
    College *C, A*
Saint Leo University *B*
St. Petersburg College *C, A, B*

Saint Thomas University *B, M*
Santa Fe College *C, A*
Schiller International
    University *A, B, M*
Seminole Community College *A*
South Florida Community
    College *C, A*
South University: Tampa *B*
South University: West Palm
    Beach *A, B, M*
Southeastern University *M*
Southwest Florida College *B*
State College of Florida,
    Manatee-Sarasota *A*
Stetson University *B, M*
Tallahassee Community College *A*
University of Central Florida *B, M, D*
University of Miami *C, B, M, D*
University of North Florida *B, M*
University of South Florida *B, M, D*
University of Tampa *A, B, M*
University of West Florida *B, M*
Valencia Community College *C, A*
Warner University *A, B, M*
Webber International
    University *A, B, M*

Georgia

Abraham Baldwin Agricultural
    College *A*
Albany State University *B, M*
Altamaha Technical College *A*
American InterContinental
    University *A, B, M*
Argosy University: Atlanta *B*
Ashworth College *A, B, M*
Atlanta Christian College *B*
Atlanta Metropolitan College *A*
Augusta State University *B, M*
Berry College *M*
Brenau University *B*
Brewton-Parker College *B*
Brown Mackie College: Atlanta *A*
Central Georgia Technical College *C*
Clark Atlanta University *B, M*
Clayton State University *B, M*
College of Coastal Georgia *A, B*
Columbus State University *B*
Columbus Technical College *C, A*
Dalton State College *A, B*
Darton College *A*
DeKalb Technical College *A*
DeVry University
    Alpharetta *B, M*
    Decatur *B, M*
East Georgia College *A*
Emmanuel College *A, B*
Emory University *B, M, D*
Fort Valley State University *B*
Gainesville State College *A, B*
Georgia College and State
    University *B*
Georgia Gwinnett College *B*
Georgia Highlands College *A*
Georgia Institute of
    Technology *B, M, D*
Georgia Military College *A*
Georgia Perimeter College *A*
Georgia Southern University *B, M*
Georgia Southwestern State
    University *B, M*
Georgia State University *B, M, D*
Gordon College *A*
Griffin Technical College *A*
Gwinnett College *C, A*
Herzing University *A, B*
Kennesaw State University *B, M, D*
LaGrange College *B*
Macon State College *C, A, B*
Middle Georgia College *A*
Morehouse College *B*
North Georgia College & State
    University *B, M*
North Georgia Technical College *C, A*

Oglethorpe University *B*
Paine College *B*
Piedmont College *B, M*
Reinhardt College *A, B, M*
Savannah State University *B*
Shorter College *B*
South Georgia College *A*
South University: Savannah *A, B, M*
Southeastern Technical College *A*
Southwest Georgia Technical
     College *C, A*
Toccoa Falls College *B*
University of Georgia *B, M, D*
University of West Georgia *B, M*
Valdosta State University *B, M*
Waycross College *A*
Wesleyan College *B, M*
West Georgia Technical College *A*

Hawaii

Argosy University: Hawaii *B*
Chaminade University of
     Honolulu *A, B, M*
Hawaii Pacific University *A, B, M*
Heald College
     Honolulu *A*
University of Hawaii
     Hilo *B*
     Manoa *B, M*
     West Oahu *B*

Idaho

Boise State University *M*
Brigham Young University-Idaho *A*
College of Idaho *B*
Idaho State University *B, M*
Lewis-Clark State College *B*
North Idaho College *A*
Northwest Nazarene University *B*
Stevens-Henager College:
     Boise *A, B, M*
University of Idaho *B, M*

Illinois

Argosy University: Chicago *B, M, D*
Argosy University: Schaumburg *B*
Augustana College *B*
Aurora University *M*
Benedictine University *C, A, M*
Bradley University *B, M*
Carl Sandburg College *A*
Chicago State University *B*
City Colleges of Chicago
     Harold Washington College *A*
     Kennedy-King College *A*
     Malcolm X College *A*
     Olive-Harvey College *A*
College of DuPage *C, A*
College of Lake County *C, A*
Columbia College Chicago *B*
Concordia University Chicago *B, M*
DePaul University *B, M*
DeVry University
     Addison *B*
     Chicago *B*
     Tinley Park *B, M*
DeVry University: Online *B, M*
Dominican University *B, M*
East-West University *B*
Eastern Illinois University *B, M*
Elgin Community College *A*
Elmhurst College *C, B*
Eureka College *B*
Governors State University *B, M*
Greenville College *B*
Harper College *C, A*
Harry S. Truman College *A*
Illinois Central College *A*
Illinois Institute of Technology *B, M*
Illinois State University *B, M*
Illinois Wesleyan University *B*
John A. Logan College *A*
John Wood Community College *C, A*
Joliet Junior College *A*

Judson University *C, B*
Kankakee Community College *C, A*
Kaskaskia College *C*
Kendall College *B*
Lewis University *B, M*
Lewis and Clark Community
     College *A*
Lexington College *A, B*
Lincoln Christian University *B*
Lincoln College *A, B*
Lincoln Land Community College *C*
Loyola University Chicago *C, B, M*
MacCormac College *C, A*
MacMurray College *A, B*
McHenry County College *C, A*
McKendree University *B, M*
Midstate College *B*
Millikin University *B, M*
Monmouth College *B*
Moraine Valley Community College *A*
Morton College *A*
National-Louis University *C, B, M*
North Central College *B, M*
North Park University *B, M*
Northeastern Illinois University *B, M*
Northern Illinois University *M*
Northwestern College *C, A*
Northwestern University *C, M*
Oakton Community College *A*
Olivet Nazarene University *B, M*
Parkland College *A*
Principia College *B*
Quincy University *B, M*
Rasmussen College: Aurora *A*
Rasmussen College: Rockford *A*
Rend Lake College *C, A*
Robert Morris University:
     Chicago *C, A, B, M*
Rock Valley College *C, A*
Rockford Career College *A*
Rockford College *B, M*
Roosevelt University *M*
St. Augustine College *A*
Saint Xavier University *M*
Sauk Valley Community College *C, A*
Southeastern Illinois College *A*
Southern Illinois University
     Carbondale *B, M, D*
Southern Illinois University
     Edwardsville *B, M*
Southwestern Illinois College *A*
Triton College *C, A*
University of Chicago *M*
University of Illinois
     Chicago *B, M, D*
     Springfield *B, M*
     Urbana-Champaign *C, B, M*
University of St. Francis *B, M*
Waubonsee Community College *C, A*
Western Illinois University *B, M*
Westwood College: DuPage *B*
Wilbur Wright College *C, A*

Indiana

Ancilla College *A*
Anderson University *A, B, M, D*
Ball State University *A, B, M*
Bethel College *B, M*
Brown Mackie College: Fort Wayne *A*
Butler University *B*
Calumet College of St. Joseph *C, A, B*
DeVry University: Indianapolis *B, M*
Earlham College *B*
Goshen College *C, B*
Grace College *B*
Harrison College
     Anderson *A, B*
     Columbus *A, B*
     Elkhart *A*
     Evansville *A, B*
     Fort Wayne *A, B*
     Indianapolis *A, B*
     Lafayette *A*

     Muncie *A, B*
     Terre Haute *A, B*
Holy Cross College *B*
Huntington University *A, B*
Indiana Institute of
     Technology *A, B, M*
Indiana State University *B, M*
Indiana University
     Bloomington *B, M, D*
     East *A, B*
     Kokomo *A, B, M*
     South Bend *B, M*
Indiana University-Purdue University
     Fort Wayne *A, B, M*
Indiana University-Purdue University
     Indianapolis *M*
Indiana Wesleyan University *A, B, M*
Ivy Tech Community College
     Bloomington *C, A*
     Central Indiana *A*
     Columbus *C, A*
     East Central *C, A*
     Kokomo *C, A*
     Lafayette *C, A*
     North Central *C, A*
     Northeast *C, A*
     Northwest *C, A*
     Richmond *A*
     South Central *C, A*
     Southeast *C, A*
     Southwest *C, A*
     Wabash Valley *A*
Kaplan College: Indianapolis *C, A*
Manchester College *A, B*
National College: Indianapolis *C, A, B*
Oakland City University *A, B*
Purdue University *B, M, D*
Purdue University
     Calumet *B, M*
     North Central *M*
Saint Mary's College *B*
St. Mary-of-the-Woods College *B*
Taylor University *A, B, M*
Trine University *A, B*
University of Evansville *B, M*
University of Indianapolis *A, B*
University of Notre Dame *M*
University of St. Francis *B, M*
University of Southern Indiana *B*
Valparaiso University *B, M*
Vincennes University *C, A*

Iowa

AIB College of Business *A*
Briar Cliff University *B*
Central College *B, T*
Clarke College *A, B, M*
Clinton Community College *C, A*
Coe College *B*
Des Moines Area Community
     College *A*
Drake University *M*
Graceland University *B*
Indian Hills Community College *A*
Iowa Central Community College *A*
Iowa Lakes Community College *A*
Iowa State University *M*
Iowa Wesleyan College *B*
Kaplan University
     Cedar Falls *A, B*
     Cedar Rapids *A, B*
     Davenport *A, B, M*
     Des Moines *A, B*
     Mason City *A, B*
Kirkwood Community College *C, A*
Loras College *B*
Luther College *B*
Maharishi University of
     Management *B, M, D*
Marshalltown Community College *A*
Morningside College *B*
Mount Mercy College *B*
Muscatine Community College *C, A*

North Iowa Area Community
     College *C, A*
Northeast Iowa Community
     College *A*
Northwest Iowa Community
     College *A*
Northwestern College *B, T*
St. Ambrose University *B, M, D*
Simpson College *B*
Southeastern Community College
     North Campus *A*
University of Dubuque *B, M*
University of Iowa *B, M*
University of Northern Iowa *B, M*
Upper Iowa University *A, B, M*
Waldorf College *B*
Wartburg College *B*
Western Iowa Tech Community
     College *A*
William Penn University *B*

Kansas

Allen County Community College *A*
Barclay College *B*
Benedictine College *A, B, M*
Bethany College *B*
Brown Mackie College
     Salina *A*
Butler Community College *C, A*
Central Christian College of
     Kansas *A, B*
Cloud County Community
     College *C, A*
Coffeyville Community College *A*
Colby Community College *C, A*
Cowley County Community
     College *A*
Emporia State University *B, M*
Fort Hays State University *B, M*
Fort Scott Community College *C, A*
Friends University *B, M*
Highland Community College *A*
Johnson County Community
     College *A*
Kansas City Kansas Community
     College *A*
Kansas State University *B, M*
Labette Community College *A*
McPherson College *B*
MidAmerica Nazarene
     University *B, M*
Neosho County Community
     College *C, A*
Newman University *A, B, M*
Ottawa University *B*
Pittsburg State University *B, M*
Pratt Community College *C, A*
Seward County Community College *A*
Southwestern College *B, M*
Sterling College *B*
Tabor College *B, M*
University of Kansas *B, M*
University of St. Mary *B, M*
Washburn University *B, M*
Wichita State University *B, M*

Kentucky

Alice Lloyd College *B*
Ashland Community and Technical
     College *C, A*
Beckfield College *A, B*
Bellarmine University *B, M*
Bluegrass Community and Technical
     College *C, A*
Brescia University *B, M*
Campbellsville University *A, B, M*
Daymar College
     Owensboro *C, A*
Draughons Junior College *C, A*
Eastern Kentucky University *B*
Elizabethtown Community and
     Technical College *C, A*
Gateway Community and Technical
     College *A*

Henderson Community College *A*
Hopkinsville Community College *C, A*
Kentucky Christian University *B*
Kentucky State University *M*
Kentucky Wesleyan College *B*
Lindsey Wilson College *A, B*
Madisonville Community College *C, A*
Maysville Community and Technical
   College *C, A*
Mid-Continent University *B*
Morehead State University *B*
Murray State University *B*
National College
   Danville *C, A*
   Florence *A*
   Lexington *C, A, B*
   Louisville *C, A, B*
   Pikeville *C, A*
   Richmond *C, A*
Northern Kentucky University *B*
Owensboro Community and
   Technical College *A*
Pikeville College *A, B*
St. Catharine College *B*
Somerset Community College *A*
Southeast Kentucky Community and
   Technical College *A*
Southern Ohio College
   Brown Mackie College: North
      Kentucky *C, A*
Spencerian College *C, A*
Sullivan University *C, A, B, M*
Thomas More College *A*
Union College *B*
University of Louisville *B*
University of the Cumberlands *M*
West Kentucky Community and
   Technical College *C, A*
Western Kentucky University *A, B*

Louisiana

Centenary College of Louisiana *B, M*
Delgado Community College *C, A*
Dillard University *B*
Grambling State University *B*
Gretna Career College *A*
Herzing University *A, B*
ITI Technical College *A*
Louisiana College *B*
Louisiana State University
   Alexandria *B*
   Shreveport *B, M*
Louisiana State University and
   Agricultural and Mechanical
   College *B, M, D*
Louisiana Tech University *B, M, D*
Loyola University New Orleans *B*
McNeese State University *B, M*
Nicholls State University *B, M*
Northwestern State University *B*
Our Lady of Holy Cross College *B*
Southeastern Louisiana
   University *B, M*
Southern University
   Shreveport *A*
Southern University and Agricultural
   and Mechanical College *B, M*
Southwest University *A, B, M*
Tulane University *B, M, D*
University of Louisiana at
   Lafayette *B, M*
University of Louisiana at
   Monroe *B, M*
University of New Orleans *B, M*
Xavier University of Louisiana *B*

Maine

Andover College *A*
Beal College *C, A*
Central Maine Community
   College *C, A*
Eastern Maine Community College *A*
Husson University *A, B, M*
Maine Maritime Academy *B*

Northern Maine Community
   College *A*
Saint Joseph's College of
   Maine *A, B, M*
Southern Maine Community
   College *C, A*
Thomas College *B, M*
University of Maine *C, B, M*
University of Maine
   Augusta *A, B*
   Fort Kent *A, B*
   Machias *B*
   Presque Isle *B*
University of New England *B*
University of Southern Maine *C, B, M*
Washington County Community
   College *C, A*
York County Community College *A*

Maryland

Allegany College of Maryland *C, A*
Anne Arundel Community College *C*
Baltimore City Community College *A*
Bowie State University *B, M*
Capitol College *B*
Cecil College *C, A*
Chesapeake College *C*
College of Southern Maryland *C, A*
Community College of Baltimore
   County *C, A*
DeVry University: Bethesda *B, M*
Frederick Community College *A*
Frostburg State University *B, M*
Garrett College *C, A*
Goucher College *B*
Griggs University *B, M*
Hagerstown Community College *C, A*
Harford Community College *C, A*
Hood College *B, M*
Howard Community College *C, A*
Kaplan College: Hagerstown *A, B*
Loyola University Maryland *B*
McDaniel College *B*
Montgomery College *A*
Morgan State University *B, M, D*
Mount St. Mary's University *M*
Prince George's Community
   College *C, A*
Salisbury University *B, M*
Sojourner-Douglass College *B*
Stevenson University *B*
Towson University *B, M*
University of Baltimore *B, M*
University of Maryland
   College Park *M*
   Eastern Shore *B*
   University College *C, B, M*
Washington Adventist University *B*
Wor-Wic Community College *C, A*

Massachusetts

American International
   College *A, B, M*
Anna Maria College *A, B, M*
Assumption College *B, M*
Atlantic Union College *A, B*
Babson College *B, M*
Bay Path College *B, M*
Bay State College *A, B*
Becker College *B*
Bentley University *A, B, M*
Berkshire Community College *A*
Boston College *B, M*
Boston University *B, M, D*
Bridgewater State College *B*
Bristol Community College *A*
Bunker Hill Community College *A*
Cape Cod Community College *A*
Clark University *B, M*
Curry College *B, M*
Dean College *A*
Eastern Nazarene College *B*
Elms College *B*
Emmanuel College *B, M*

Endicott College *B, M*
Fisher College *A, B*
Fitchburg State College *C, B, M*
Gordon College *B*
Greenfield Community College *A*
Holyoke Community College *A*
Lasell College *B*
Lesley University *B*
Marian Court College *C, A*
Massachusetts Bay Community
   College *C, A*
Massachusetts College of Liberal
   Arts *B*
Massachusetts Maritime Academy *M*
Massasoit Community College *A*
Merrimack College *B*
Middlesex Community College *A*
Mount Ida College *B*
Mount Wachusett Community
   College *A*
New England College of Business and
   Finance *A, B*
Newbury College *A, B*
Nichols College *C, A, B, M*
North Shore Community College *A*
Northeastern University *B*
Northern Essex Community
   College *A*
Pine Manor College *B*
Quinsigamond Community College *A*
Regis College *M*
Roxbury Community College *A*
Salem State College *B, M*
Simmons College *B, M*
Springfield College *B*
Springfield Technical Community
   College *A*
Stonehill College *B*
Suffolk University *B, M*
University of Massachusetts
   Amherst *B, M, D*
   Boston *B, M*
   Dartmouth *B, M*
   Lowell *B, M*
Urban College of Boston *C*
Wentworth Institute of Technology *B*
Western New England College *B, M*
Worcester Polytechnic Institute *B, M*
Worcester State College *B, M*

Michigan

Adrian College *A, B, T*
Albion College *B*
Alma College *B*
Alpena Community College *A*
Andrews University *B, M*
Aquinas College *B, M, T*
Baker College
   of Auburn Hills *A, B*
   of Cadillac *A, B*
   of Clinton Township *A, B, M*
   of Flint *A, B, M*
   of Jackson *A, B*
   of Muskegon *A, B*
   of Owosso *A, B*
   of Port Huron *A, B, M*
Bay Mills Community College *A*
Bay de Noc Community College *C, A*
Calvin College *B*
Central Michigan University *B, M*
Cleary University *A, B, M*
Cornerstone University *B*
Davenport University *B, M*
Delta College *A*
Eastern Michigan University *B, M*
Ferris State University *A, B, M*
Finlandia University *B*
Glen Oaks Community College *C*
Gogebic Community College *A*
Grace Bible College *B*
Grand Rapids Community College *A*
Grand Valley State University *B, M*
Henry Ford Community College *A*
Hillsdale College *B*

Hope College *B*
Jackson Community College *C, A*
Kalamazoo Valley Community
   College *C, A*
Kellogg Community College *C, A*
Kettering University *B, M*
Kirtland Community College *C, A*
Kuyper College *B*
Lake Michigan College *A*
Lake Superior State University *A, B*
Lansing Community College *A*
Lawrence Technological
   University *B, M, D*
Macomb Community College *C, A*
Madonna University *A, B, M*
Marygrove College *B*
Michigan Jewish Institute *A, B*
Michigan State University *B, M, D*
Michigan Technological
   University *B, M*
Mid Michigan Community College *A*
Monroe County Community
   College *C, A*
Montcalm Community College *A*
Mott Community College *C, A*
North Central Michigan College *C, A*
Northern Michigan University *B*
Northwestern Michigan College *A*
Northwood University:
   Michigan *A, B, M*
Oakland Community College *A*
Oakland University *M*
Rochester College *B*
Saginaw Chippewa Tribal College *A*
Saginaw Valley State University *B, M*
St. Clair County Community
   College *A*
Schoolcraft College *A*
Southwestern Michigan College *A*
Spring Arbor University *B, M*
University of Detroit Mercy *B, M*
University of Michigan *B, M, D*
University of Michigan
   Dearborn *B, M*
   Flint *A, B, M*
Walsh College of Accountancy and
   Business Administration *B, M, D*
Washtenaw Community College *C, A*
Wayne County Community
   College *C, A*
Western Michigan University *M*

Minnesota

Academy College *C, A, B*
Alexandria Technical College *C, A*
Anoka-Ramsey Community
   College *C, A*
Argosy University: Twin Cities *B*
Augsburg College *B*
Bemidji State University *B*
Bethany Lutheran College *B*
Bethel University *B, M*
Capella University *C, M, D*
Central Lakes College *A*
Century Community and Technical
   College *A*
College of St. Benedict *B*
College of St. Scholastica *B, M*
Concordia College: Moorhead *B*
Concordia University: St. Paul *B, M*
Crossroads College *B*
Crown College *A, B*
Dakota County Technical College *C, A*
DeVry University
   Edina *B, M*
Duluth Business University *A, B*
Dunwoody College of Technology *B*
Globe University *C, A, B, M*
Hamline University *B, M*
Hibbing Community College *A*
Inver Hills Community College *C, A*
Itasca Community College *A*
Lake Superior College *C, A*
Leech Lake Tribal College *A*

Metropolitan State University *B, M*
Minneapolis Community and
  Technical College *A*
Minnesota School of
  Business *C, A, B, M*
Minnesota School of Business:
  Blaine *A, B*
Minnesota School of Business:
  Brooklyn Center *C, A, B*
Minnesota School of Business:
  Rochester *C, A, B*
Minnesota School of Business: St.
  Cloud *C, A, B, M*
Minnesota School of Business:
  Shakopee *A, B, M*
Minnesota State College - Southeast
  Technical *C, A*
Minnesota State Community and
  Technical College *C, A*
Minnesota State University
  Mankato *B, M*
  Moorhead *B*
Minnesota West Community and
  Technical College *A*
National American University
  Bloomington *B*
National American University:
  Roseville *A, B*
Normandale Community College *C, A*
North Central University *A, B*
North Hennepin Community
  College *C, A*
Northwest Technical College *C, A*
Northwestern College *B*
Pine Technical College *A*
Rasmussen College
  Eagan *A, B*
  Eden Prairie *A, B*
  Mankato *A, B*
  St. Cloud *A, B*
Rasmussen College: Brooklyn
  Park *A, B*
Rasmussen College: Lake
  Elmo/Woodbury *A, B*
Rochester Community and Technical
  College *C, A*
St. Catherine University *B, M*
Saint Cloud State University *B, M*
St. Cloud Technical College *A*
St. John's University *B*
St. Mary's University of
  Minnesota *B, M*
St. Paul College *B*
South Central College *A*
Southwest Minnesota State
  University *A, B, M*
University of Minnesota
  Crookston *B*
  Duluth *B, M*
  Twin Cities *C, B, M, D*
University of St. Thomas *B, M*
Vermilion Community College *A*
Walden University *B, M, D*
White Earth Tribal and Community
  College *A*
Winona State University *B*

Mississippi

Alcorn State University *B, M*
Belhaven University *C, B, M*
Blue Mountain College *B*
Copiah-Lincoln Community College *A*
Delta State University *B, M*
Holmes Community College *A*
Jackson State University *B, M, D*
Millsaps College *B, M*
Mississippi College *B, M*
Mississippi Gulf Coast Community
  College *A*
Mississippi State University *B, M, D*
Mississippi University for Women *B*
Mississippi Valley State
  University *B, M*

Northwest Mississippi Community
  College *A*
Pearl River Community College *A*
Rust College *A, B*
University of Mississippi *B, M, D*
University of Southern
  Mississippi *M*
Virginia College *A*

Missouri

Avila University *B, M*
Central Methodist University *B*
College of the Ozarks *B*
Columbia College *B*
Culver-Stockton College *B*
DeVry University
  Kansas City *B, M*
Drury University *B, M*
Evangel University *B*
Fontbonne University *B, M*
Grantham University *A, B, M*
Hannibal-LaGrange College *B*
Harris-Stowe State University *B*
Lincoln University *B, M*
Lindenwood University *B, M*
Maryville University of Saint
  Louis *B, M*
Metro Business College *C, A*
Metro Business College
  Jefferson City *C, A*
Metropolitan Community College:
  Blue River *A*
Metropolitan Community College:
  Longview *A*
Metropolitan Community College:
  Maple Woods *C, A*
Metropolitan Community College:
  Penn Valley *C, A*
Mineral Area College *A*
Missouri Baptist University *C, A, B, M*
Missouri College *A*
Missouri State University *B, M*
Missouri Valley College *B*
Missouri Western State
  University *A, B*
North Central Missouri College *C, A*
Northwest Missouri State
  University *B, M*
Ozarks Technical Community
  College *A*
Park University *A, B, M*
Patricia Stevens College *A, B*
Ranken Technical College *B*
Rockhurst University *B, M*
St. Louis Community College .
  St. Louis Community College at
    Florissant Valley *A*
Saint Louis University *B, M*
Sanford-Brown College
  St. Peters *A*
Southeast Missouri State
  University *B, M*
Southwest Baptist University *B, M*
State Fair Community College *A*
Stephens College *B, M*
Truman State University *B*
University of Central Missouri *B, M*
University of Missouri
  Columbia *B, M, D*
  Kansas City *B*
  Missouri University of Science and
    Technology *B*
  St. Louis *B, M*
Vatterott College: Kansas City *A*
Washington University in St.
  Louis *B, M, D*
Webster University *B, M, D*
Westminster College *B, T*
William Jewell College *B*
William Woods University *B, M*

Montana

Blackfeet Community College *A*

Flathead Valley Community
  College *C, A*
Fort Peck Community College *C, A*
Little Big Horn College *A*
Miles Community College *A*
Montana State University
  College of Technology: Great
    Falls *C, A*
Rocky Mountain College *B*
University of Great Falls *B*
University of Montana *B, M*
University of Montana: Western *A, B*

Nebraska

Bellevue University *B, M*
Central Community College *C, A*
Chadron State College *B, M*
Clarkson College *B, M*
College of Saint Mary *A, B, M*
Concordia University *B, T*
Creighton University *B, M*
Dana College *B*
Doane College *B*
Kaplan University
  Lincoln *A, B*
Kaplan University: Omaha *A, B, M*
Metropolitan Community College *A*
Mid-Plains Community College
  Area *C, A*
Nebraska Indian Community
  College *A*
Nebraska Wesleyan University *B*
Northeast Community College *A*
Peru State College *B*
Southeast Community College *A*
Union College *A, B*
University of Nebraska
  Kearney *B, M*
  Lincoln *B, M, D*
  Omaha *B, M*
Wayne State College *B, M*
Western Nebraska Community
  College *C, A*
York College *B*

Nevada

College of Southern Nevada *C, A*
DeVry University: Henderson *B, M*
Everest College: Las Vegas *A*
Great Basin College *C, A, B*
Morrison University *A, B, M*
Nevada State College *B*
Sierra Nevada College *B*
Truckee Meadows Community
  College *A*
University of Nevada
  Las Vegas *M*
  Reno *M*
University of Southern Nevada *M*
Western Nevada College *C, A*

New Hampshire

Colby-Sawyer College *B*
Daniel Webster College *B, M*
Dartmouth College *M*
Franklin Pierce University *M*
Keene State College *B*
Lakes Region Community
  College *C, A*
Lebanon College *A*
Manchester Community College *C, A*
NHTI-Concord's Community
  College *A*
Nashua Community College *A*
New England College *B, M*
Plymouth State University *B, M*
Rivier College *A, B, M*
Southern New Hampshire
  University *A, B, M*
University of New Hampshire *B*
University of New Hampshire at
  Manchester *A, B, M*
White Mountains Community
  College *C, A*

New Jersey

Atlantic Cape Community College *A*
Berkeley College- Garret Mountain
  Campus *A, B*
Bloomfield College *C, B*
Brookdale Community College *A*
Burlington County College *A*
Caldwell College *B, M*
Camden County College *A*
Centenary College *B, M*
The College of New Jersey *B*
College of St. Elizabeth *C, B, M*
County College of Morris *A*
Cumberland County College *A*
DeVry University: North
  Brunswick *A, B*
Drew University *B*
Essex County College *C, A*
Fairleigh Dickinson University
  College at Florham *B, M*
  Metropolitan Campus *B, M*
Felician College *B*
Georgian Court University *B, M*
Gloucester County College *A*
Hudson County Community
  College *A*
Kean University *B*
Mercer County Community
  College *C, A*
Middlesex County College *A*
Monmouth University *B, M*
Montclair State University *B, M*
New Jersey City University *B*
New Jersey Institute of
  Technology *B, M*
Ocean County College *A*
Passaic County Community College *C*
Ramapo College of New Jersey *B*
Raritan Valley Community College *A*
Richard Stockton College of New
  Jersey *B, M*
Rider University *A, B, M*
Rowan University *B, M*
Rutgers, The State University of New
  Jersey
  Camden Regional Campus *B, M*
  New Brunswick/Piscataway
    Campus *B, M, D*
  Newark Regional Campus *B, M, D*
Saint Peter's College *A, B, M*
Salem Community College *A*
Seton Hall University *B, M*
Stevens Institute of Technology *B, M*
Sussex County Community College *A*
Thomas Edison State College *A, B, M*
Union County College *A*
William Paterson University of New
  Jersey *B, M*

New Mexico

Brookline College
  Albuquerque *C, A*
Central New Mexico Community
  College *C, A*
Clovis Community College *A*
College of Santa Fe *M*
Dona Ana Community College of New
  Mexico State University *C, A*
Eastern New Mexico University *B, M*
Mesalands Community College *A*
New Mexico Highlands
  University *B, M*
New Mexico Institute of Mining and
  Technology *A, B*
New Mexico Junior College *A*
New Mexico State University *B, M, D*
Northern New Mexico College *C, A, B*
San Juan College *A*
Santa Fe Community College *A*
Southwestern Indian Polytechnic
  Institute *C, A*
University of New Mexico *B, M*
University of the Southwest *B*
Western New Mexico University *B, M*

New York

ASA Institute of Business and Computer Technology *C, A*
Adelphi University *B, M*
Adirondack Community College *A*
Alfred University *B, M*
Berkeley College *A, B*
Berkeley College of New York City *A, B*
Boricua College *B*
Bramson ORT College *A*
Briarcliffe College *A, B*
Broome Community College *A*
Bryant & Stratton Business Institute
Bryant & Stratton College: Albany *A*
Bryant & Stratton College: Buffalo *B*
Bryant & Stratton College: Rochester *A*
Bryant & Stratton College: Southtowns *C, A, B*
Bryant & Stratton College: Syracuse *A*
Canisius College *M*
Cayuga County Community College *C, A*
Cazenovia College *C, A, B*
City University of New York
Baruch College *B, M*
Borough of Manhattan Community College *A*
Brooklyn College *B*
College of Staten Island *M*
Hostos Community College *A*
Kingsborough Community College *A*
LaGuardia Community College *A*
Lehman College *B*
Medgar Evers College *A, B*
Queensborough Community College *A*
York College *B*
Clarkson University *B, M*
Clinton Community College *A*
College of Mount St. Vincent *B, M*
College of Saint Rose *B, M*
College of Westchester *C, A, B*
Columbia-Greene Community College *A*
Concordia College *A, B*
Cornell University *M, D*
Corning Community College *A*
D'Youville College *B*
Daemen College *B*
DeVry
College of New York *B, M*
Dominican College of Blauvelt *B, M*
Dowling College *B, M*
Dutchess Community College *A*
Elmira College *A, B*
Erie Community College
City Campus *A*
North Campus *A*
South Campus *A*
Excelsior College *C, A, B, M*
Finger Lakes Community College *A*
Five Towns College *A, B*
Fordham University *B, M*
Fulton-Montgomery Community College *A*
Genesee Community College *C, A*
Globe Institute of Technology *C, A, B*
Hartwick College *B*
Herkimer County Community College *A*
Hilbert College *A, B*
Hofstra University *B, M*
Houghton College *B*
Hudson Valley Community College *A*
Iona College *B, M*
Ithaca College *B, M*
Jamestown Business College *A, B*
Jamestown Community College *A*
Jefferson Community College *A*

Keuka College *B, M*
King's College *B*
Laboratory Institute of Merchandising *B*
Le Moyne College *B, M*
Long Island Business Institute *A*
Long Island University
Brooklyn Campus *A, B, M*
C. W. Post Campus *B, M*
Manhattan College *M*
Manhattanville College *B, M*
Maria College *A*
Marist College *B, M*
Marymount Manhattan College *B*
Medaille College *B, M*
Mercy College *C, A, B, M*
Metropolitan College of New York *B, M*
Mildred Elley *C, A*
Mohawk Valley Community College *A*
Molloy College *B, M*
Monroe College *A, B, M*
Mount Saint Mary College *C, B, M*
Nassau Community College *C, A*
New York Institute of Technology *A, B, M*
New York University *C, M, D*
Niagara County Community College *C, A*
Niagara University *M*
North Country Community College *A*
Nyack College *A, B, M*
Olean Business Institute *C, A*
Onondaga Community College *A*
Orange County Community College *A*
Pace University *B, M, D*
Paul Smith's College *B*
Polytechnic Institute of New York University *M, D*
Professional Business College *A*
Rensselaer Polytechnic Institute *B, M, D*
Roberts Wesleyan College *B, M*
Rochester Institute of Technology *A, B, M*
Rockland Community College *A*
Russell Sage College *B*
Sage College of Albany *B*
Saint Bonaventure University *M*
St. Francis College *A, B*
St. John Fisher College *B, M*
St. John's University *C, A, B, M*
St. Joseph's College *B, M*
St. Joseph's College: Suffolk Campus *B, M*
St. Thomas Aquinas College *A, B, M*
Siena College *B*
State University of New York
Albany *B, M*
Binghamton *B, M, D*
Buffalo *B, M, D*
College at Brockport *B*
College at Buffalo *B*
College at Fredonia *B*
College at Geneseo *B*
College at Old Westbury *B*
College at Plattsburgh *B*
College at Potsdam *B*
College of Agriculture and Technology at Cobleskill *A*
College of Agriculture and Technology at Morrisville *A*
College of Technology at Alfred *A, B*
College of Technology at Canton *A*
College of Technology at Delhi *A, B*
Empire State College *M*
Farmingdale *C, A, B*
Institute of Technology at Utica/Rome *B, M*
Maritime College *B*
New Paltz *B, M*
Oswego *B, M*
Stony Brook *B, M*

Suffolk County Community College *A*
Sullivan County Community College *A*
Syracuse University *C, B, M, D*
Tompkins Cortland Community College *C, A*
Touro College *A, B*
Trocaire College *A*
Ulster County Community College *A*
United States Military Academy *B*
University of Rochester *M, D*
Utica College *B*
Utica School of Commerce *A*
Villa Maria College of Buffalo *A*
Wagner College *B, M*
Westchester Community College *A*
Yeshiva University *B*

North Carolina

Alamance Community College *C, A*
Appalachian State University *B, M*
Asheville-Buncombe Technical Community College *A*
Barton College *B*
Beaufort County Community College *C, A*
Belmont Abbey College *B*
Bennett College for Women *B*
Bladen Community College *C, A*
Brevard College *B*
Brunswick Community College *C, A*
Caldwell Community College and Technical Institute *A*
Campbell University *B, M*
Cape Fear Community College *C, A*
Catawba College *B*
Catawba Valley Community College *C, A*
Central Carolina Community College *A*
Central Piedmont Community College *C, A*
Chowan University *B*
Cleveland Community College *C, A*
Coastal Carolina Community College *C, A*
College of the Albemarle *A*
Davidson County Community College *C, A*
DeVry University: Charlotte *B, M*
Duke University *M, D*
Durham Technical Community College *A*
East Carolina University *B, M*
Edgecombe Community College *A*
Elizabeth City State University *B*
Elon University *B, M*
Fayetteville State University *B, M*
Fayetteville Technical Community College *A*
Forsyth Technical Community College *A*
Gardner-Webb University *B, M*
Gaston College *A*
Guilford College *C, B*
Guilford Technical Community College *C, A*
Halifax Community College *A*
Haywood Community College *C, A*
High Point University *B, M*
Isothermal Community College *C, A*
James Sprunt Community College *A*
John Wesley College *B*
Johnson & Wales University: Charlotte *B*
Johnson C. Smith University *B*
Johnston Community College *A*
Lees-McRae College *B*
Lenoir Community College *C, A*
Livingstone College *B*
Mars Hill College *B*
Martin Community College *C, A*
Mayland Community College *A*
Meredith College *B, M*

Methodist University *A, B, M*
Miller-Motte Technical College *C, A, B*
Mitchell Community College *A*
Montgomery Community College *C, A*
Montreat College *C, A, B, M*
Mount Olive College *A, B*
Nash Community College *A*
North Carolina Agricultural and Technical State University *B*
North Carolina Central University *B, M*
North Carolina State University *B, M*
North Carolina Wesleyan College *B*
Pamlico Community College *A*
Peace College *B*
Pfeiffer University *B, M*
Piedmont Community College *A*
Pitt Community College *C, A*
Queens University of Charlotte *B, M*
Randolph Community College *A*
Richmond Community College *C, A*
Roanoke-Chowan Community College *A*
Robeson Community College *A*
Rockingham Community College *A*
Rowan-Cabarrus Community College *C, A*
St. Andrews Presbyterian College *B*
St. Augustine's College *B*
Salem College *B*
Sampson Community College *A*
Sandhills Community College *A*
Shaw University *A, B*
South College *B*
South Piedmont Community College *C, A*
Southeastern Community College *C, A*
Southwestern Community College *C, A*
Stanly Community College *C, A*
Surry Community College *C, A, B*
Tri-County Community College *A*
University of North Carolina
Asheville *B*
Chapel Hill *B, M, D*
Charlotte *B, M, D*
Greensboro *B, M*
Pembroke *B, M*
Wilmington *B, M*
Vance-Granville Community College *C, A*
Wake Forest University *M*
Warren Wilson College *B*
Wayne Community College *A*
Western Carolina University *B, M*
Western Piedmont Community College *C, A*
Wilkes Community College *C, A*
Wilson Community College *C, A*
Wingate University *B, M*
Winston-Salem State University *B, M*

North Dakota

Cankdeska Cikana Community College *A*
Dakota College at Bottineau *A*
Dickinson State University *B*
Jamestown College *B*
Lake Region State College *C, A*
Mayville State University *B*
Minot State University *B, M*
North Dakota State College of Science *A*
North Dakota State University *B, M*
Rasmussen College: Bismarck *A, B*
Rasmussen College: Fargo *A, B*
Sitting Bull College *A, B*
Turtle Mountain Community College *A*
United Tribes Technical College *A*
University of Mary *B, M*
University of North Dakota *B, M*

Ohio

Antioch University McGregor B, M
Ashland University C, B, M
Baldwin-Wallace College C, B, M
Bluffton University B, M
Bowling Green State University B, M
Bowling Green State University:
    Firelands College C, A, B
Bryant & Stratton College
    Eastlake B
    Parma B
Capital University B, M
Case Western Reserve
    University B, M, D
Cedarville University B
Central Ohio Technical College A
Chatfield College A
Cincinnati State Technical and
    Community College C, A
Clark State Community College C, A
Cleveland State University M, D
College of Mount St. Joseph A, B
Columbus State Community
    College C, A
Cuyahoga Community College
    Metropolitan Campus A
Davis College A
DeVry University
    Columbus B, M
Defiance College A, B, M
Eastern Gateway Community
    College C, A
Edison State Community College C
Franciscan University of
    Steubenville A, B, M
Gallipolis Career College A
Heidelberg University B, M
Hiram College B
James A. Rhodes State College C, A
John Carroll University B, M
Kent State University B, M
Lourdes College B
Malone University B, M
Marion Technical College C, A
Miami University
    Hamilton Campus A
    Oxford Campus C, B, M
Mount Union College B
Mount Vernon Nazarene
    University A, B, M
National College
    Dayton C, A
National College: Cincinnati A
National College: Stow C, A
National College: Youngstown C, A
National Institute of Technology A
North Central State College C, A
Northwest State Community
    College A
Notre Dame College C, A, B
Ohio Business College: Sandusky A
Ohio Christian University B
Ohio Dominican University A, B, M
Ohio Northern University B
Ohio State University
    Agricultural Technical Institute A
    Columbus Campus M, D
    Mansfield Campus B
    Marion Campus B
    Newark Campus B
Ohio University B, M
Ohio University
    Southern Campus at Ironton B
    Zanesville Campus M
Otterbein College B
Owens Community College
    Toledo A
Remington College: Cleveland West A
Shawnee State University A, B
Southern State Community College A
Southwestern College of Business
    Southwestern College: Franklin A
    Southwestern College:
        Tri-County A

Southwestern College: Dayton A
Stark State College of Technology A
Temple Baptist College B
Terra State Community College C, A
Tiffin University A, B, M
Trumbull Business College C, A
Union Institute & University B
University of Akron C, A, B, M
University of Akron: Wayne College A
University of Cincinnati C, A, B, M, D
University of Cincinnati
    Clermont College A
    Raymond Walters College A
University of Dayton B, M
University of Findlay B, M
University of Northwestern Ohio A, B
University of Rio Grande A, B
University of Toledo A, B, M, D
Urbana University B, M
Ursuline College B
Walsh University A, B, M
Washington State Community
    College A
Wilberforce University B
Wilmington College B
Wittenberg University B
Wright State University B, M
Wright State University: Lake
    Campus A
Xavier University A, B, M
Youngstown State
    University C, A, B, M
Zane State College C, A

Oklahoma

Bacone College A, B
Cameron University A, B, M
Carl Albert State College A
Connors State College A
DeVry University: Oklahoma City
    Center B, M
East Central University B
Eastern Oklahoma State College A
Langston University B
Mid-America Christian
    University B, M
Murray State College A
Northeastern Oklahoma Agricultural
    and Mechanical College A
Northeastern State University B, M
Northern Oklahoma College A
Northwestern Oklahoma State
    University B
Oklahoma Baptist University B, M
Oklahoma Christian University B, M
Oklahoma City University B, M
Oklahoma Panhandle State
    University A, B
Oklahoma State University B, M, D
Oklahoma State University
    Institute of Technology:
    Okmulgee A
    Oklahoma City A
Oklahoma Wesleyan
    University A, B, M
Oral Roberts University B, M
Redlands Community College A
Rogers State University A, B
Rose State College C, A
St. Gregory's University A, B, M
Seminole State College A
Southeastern Oklahoma State
    University B, M
Southern Nazarene University A, B, M
Southwestern Christian University B
Southwestern Oklahoma State
    University B, M
Tulsa Community College A
University of Central Oklahoma B, M
University of Oklahoma B, M, D
University of Science and Arts of
    Oklahoma B, T
University of Tulsa B, M
Western Oklahoma State College A

Oregon

Blue Mountain Community College A
Central Oregon Community
    College A
Chemeketa Community College A
Clackamas Community College C, A
Clatsop Community College A
Concordia University B
Corban College A, B, M
DeVry University: Portland B, M
Eastern Oregon University B, M
George Fox University B, M, D
Heald College: Portland C, A
Klamath Community College C, A
Linn-Benton Community College A
Marylhurst University B, M
Mt. Hood Community College A
Northwest Christian University B, M
Oregon Health & Science
    University M
Oregon State University B, M
Pacific University B
Portland Community College A
Portland State University B, D
Rogue Community College C, A
Southern Oregon University B, M
Southwestern Oregon Community
    College A
Treasure Valley Community College A
Umpqua Community College A
University of Oregon M, D
University of Portland B, M
Warner Pacific College B, M
Willamette University M

Pennsylvania

Albright College C, B
Arcadia University C, B, M
Bloomsburg University of
    Pennsylvania B, M
Bucknell University B
Bucks County Community
    College A
Butler County Community College A
Cabrini College B
California University of
    Pennsylvania B
Cambria-Rowe Business College:
    Indiana A
Carlow University B, M
Carnegie Mellon University B, M
Cedar Crest College B
Central Pennsylvania College A, B
Chatham University B, M
Chestnut Hill College A, B
Cheyney University of Pennsylvania B
Clarion University of
    Pennsylvania A, B, M
Community College of Allegheny
    County C, A
Community College of Beaver
    County A
Community College of
    Philadelphia C, A
Consolidated School of Business
    Lancaster A
    York A
DeSales University B, M
DeVry University
    Fort Washington B, M
Delaware Valley College B
Douglas Education Center A
Duquesne University B, M
East Stroudsburg University of
    Pennsylvania B
Eastern University B, M
Edinboro University of
    Pennsylvania A, B
Elizabethtown College C, A, B
Erie Business Center South A
Franklin & Marshall College B
Gannon University B, M
Geneva College A, B, M
Gettysburg College B

Grove City College B
Gwynedd-Mercy College A, B, M
Harcum College A
Harrisburg Area Community
    College C, A
Holy Family University B, M
Immaculata University C, A, B, M
Indiana University of
    Pennsylvania A, B, M
Juniata College B
Kaplan Career Institute: Harrisburg A
Kaplan Career Institute: Pittsburgh A
Keystone College A, B
King's College C, A, B
Kutztown University of
    Pennsylvania B, M
La Salle University A, B, M
Lackawanna College A
Laurel Business Institute A
Lebanon Valley College C, A, B, M
Lehigh Carbon Community
    College C, A
Lehigh University M
Lincoln University B
Lock Haven University of
    Pennsylvania A, B
Luzerne County Community
    College A
Lycoming College B
Manor College A
Mansfield University of
    Pennsylvania B
Marywood University B, M
Mercyhurst College A, B, T
Messiah College B
Millersville University of
    Pennsylvania B, M
Misericordia University B
Montgomery County Community
    College C, A
Moravian College B, M
Mount Aloysius College A, B
Muhlenberg College C, A, B
Neumann University C, B
Newport Business Institute: Lower
    Burrell C, A
Newport Business Institute:
    Williamsport A
Northampton Community College A
Orleans Technical Institute A
Peirce College A, B
Penn Commercial Business and
    Technical School A
Penn State
    Beaver B
    Brandywine C, B
    DuBois B, M
    Erie, The Behrend College B, M
    Fayette, The Eberly Campus B
    Greater Allegheny B
    Harrisburg B
    Hazleton B
    Lehigh Valley C, B
    Mont Alto B
    New Kensington B
    Schuylkill B
    Shenango C, B
    University Park M, D
    Wilkes-Barre B
    Worthington Scranton B
    York C, B
Pennsylvania College of
    Technology A, B
Pennsylvania Highlands Community
    College A
Pennsylvania Institute of
    Technology A
Pennsylvania School of Business C, A
Philadelphia Biblical University B
Philadelphia University A, B, M
Point Park University C, A, B, M
Reading Area Community College A
Robert Morris University C, B, M
Rosemont College B, M

St. Francis University *A, B, M*
Saint Joseph's University *C, A, B, M*
St. Vincent College *C, B, M*
Seton Hill University *B, M*
Shippensburg University of
    Pennsylvania *B, M*
Slippery Rock University of
    Pennsylvania *B*
South Hills School of Business &
    Technology: Altoona *A*
Susquehanna University *B*
Temple University *B, M, D*
Thaddeus Stevens College of
    Technology *A*
Thiel College *B*
University of Pennsylvania *B, M, D*
University of Pittsburgh *B, M, D*
University of Pittsburgh
    Bradford *B*
    Greensburg *B*
University of Scranton *A, B, M*
Valley Forge Christian College *B*
Villanova University *B, M*
Waynesburg University *B, M*
West Chester University of
    Pennsylvania *B, M*
Westminster College *B*
Westmoreland County Community
    College *C, A*
Widener University *A, B, M*
Wilkes University *B, M*
Wilson College *A, B*
YTI Career Institute: York *A*
York College of Pennsylvania *A, B, M*

Puerto Rico

American University of Puerto Rico *B*
Bayamon Central University *B, M*
Caribbean University *A, B*
Columbia Centro Universitario:
    Caguas *A, B, M*
Columbia College
    Columbia Centro Universitario:
    Yauco *A, B*
Electronic Data Processing College:
    San Sebastian *A*
Huertas Junior College *A*
Humacao Community College *A*
Inter American University of Puerto
    Rico
    Aguadilla Campus *A, B, M*
    Arecibo Campus *A, B*
    Bayamon Campus *A, B*
    Fajardo Campus *A, B*
    Guayama Campus *A, B*
    Metropolitan Campus *A, B, M*
    Ponce Campus *A, B*
    San German Campus *A, B*
National College of Business and
    Technology: Arecibo *A*
Pontifical Catholic University of
    Puerto Rico *B, M, D*
Turabo University *A, B, M, D*
Universal Career Community College:
    Humacao *C*
Universal Career Community College:
    Manati *C*
Universal Career Community College:
    San Juan *C*
Universidad Metropolitana *B, M*
Universidad Politecnica de Puerto
    Rico *B, M*
Universidad del Este *A, B, M*
University of Puerto Rico
    Arecibo *B*
    Bayamon University College *B*
    Carolina Regional College *B*
    Cayey University College *B*
    Humacao *B*
    Ponce *A, B*
    Utuado *A*
University of the Sacred Heart *B*

Rhode Island

Bryant University *B, M*
Community College of Rhode
    Island *C, A*
Johnson & Wales University:
    Providence *B*
Providence College *C, A, B, M*
Rhode Island College *B*
Roger Williams University *B*
Salve Regina University *A, B, M*
University of Rhode Island *B, M, D*

South Carolina

Aiken Technical College *C, A*
Allen University *B*
Anderson University *B, M*
Benedict College *B*
Bob Jones University *B, M*
Charleston Southern University *B, M*
The Citadel *B, M*
Claflin University *B, M*
Coastal Carolina University *B, M*
Coker College *B*
College of Charleston *B*
Columbia College *B*
Erskine College *B*
Florence-Darlington Technical
    College *C*
Forrest Junior College *A*
Francis Marion University *B, M*
Furman University *B*
Greenville Technical College *C, A*
Lander University *C, B*
Midlands Technical College *A*
Miller-Motte Technical College *A*
Morris College *B*
Newberry College *B*
North Greenville University *B, M*
Northeastern Technical College *A*
Presbyterian College *B*
South Carolina State University *B*
South University: Columbia *A, B, M*
Southern Wesleyan University *B, M*
Spartanburg Community College *A*
Technical College of the
    Lowcountry *C*
Tri-County Technical College *C, A*
Trident Technical College *A*
University of South Carolina *B, M, D*
University of South Carolina
    Beaufort *B*
    Lancaster *A*
    Upstate *B*
Winthrop University *B, M*
York Technical College *A*

South Dakota

Augustana College *B*
Black Hills State University *B, M*
Dakota State University *A, B*
Kilian Community College *A*
Lake Area Technical Institute *A*
Mitchell Technical Institute *A*
Mount Marty College *C, A, B, M*
National American University
    Rapid City *A, B, M*
Northern State University *A, B*
Oglala Lakota College *C, A, B*
Presentation College *A, B*
Sinte Gleska University *A, B*
Sisseton Wahpeton College *A*
Southeast Technical Institute *A*
University of Sioux Falls *A, B*
University of South Dakota *B, M*

Tennessee

American Baptist College *A, B*
Aquinas College *A, B*
Argosy University: Nashville *B*
Austin Peay State University *A, M*
Belmont University *M*
Bethel University *B*
Bryan College *A, B, M*

Carson-Newman College *B*
Chattanooga State Community
    College *A*
Christian Brothers University *B, M*
Cleveland State Community College *A*
Columbia State Community College *C*
Crichton College *B*
DeVry University: Memphis *B, M*
Draughons Junior College:
    Nashville *C, A*
Dyersburg State Community
    College *A*
East Tennessee State University *B, M*
Fisk University *B*
Free Will Baptist Bible College *B*
Freed-Hardeman University *B, M*
Jackson State Community College *A*
King College *B*
Lambuth University *B*
Lane College *B*
LeMoyne-Owen College *B*
Lee University *B*
Lincoln Memorial University *B, M*
Lipscomb University *B, M*
Martin Methodist College *B*
Maryville College *B*
Middle Tennessee State
    University *C, B, M*
Milligan College *B*
Motlow State Community College *A*
Nashville State Community College *A*
National College
    Knoxville *C, A*
    Nashville *C, A*
National College of Business &
    Technology
    National College: Bristol *C, A*
National College: Bartlett *A*
National College: Madison *C, A*
National College: Memphis *C, A*
Northeast State Community
    College *A*
Pellissippi State Community
    College *A*
Remington College
    Memphis *B*
Rhodes College *B*
Roane State Community College *A*
South College *A*
Southern Adventist University *A, B, M*
Southwest Tennessee Community
    College *A*
Tennessee State University *B, M*
Tennessee Temple University *A, B*
Tennessee Wesleyan College *B*
Trevecca Nazarene University *B, M*
Tusculum College *B, M*
Union University *B, M*
University of Memphis *B, M, D*
University of Tennessee
    Chattanooga *B, M*
    Knoxville *B, M, D*
    Martin *B, M*
Vanderbilt University *M, D*
Volunteer State Community College *A*
Walters State Community College *A*
West Tennessee Business College *C, A*

Texas

Abilene Christian University *B*
Alvin Community College *C, A*
Amberton University *B, M*
Angelina College *C, A*
Angelo State University *B, M*
Argosy University: Dallas *M*
Austin Community College *C, A*
Baptist University of the Americas *B*
Baylor University *B, M*
Blinn College *C*
Brazosport College *C, A*
Brookhaven College *C, A*
Cedar Valley College *C, A*
Central Texas College *C, A*
Coastal Bend College *A*

College of the Mainland *A*
Collin County Community College
    District *C, A*
Concordia University Texas *B*
Dallas Baptist University *A, B, M*
Dallas Christian College *A, B*
DeVry University
    Irving *B, M*
DeVry University: Houston *B, M*
Del Mar College *A*
Eastfield College *C, A*
El Centro College *C, A*
El Paso Community College *C, A*
Frank Phillips College *A*
Galveston College *C, A*
Hallmark College of Technology *B*
Hardin-Simmons University *B, M*
Hill College *A*
Houston Baptist University *B, M*
Houston Community College
    System *C, A*
Howard Payne University *B*
Huston-Tillotson University *B*
Jarvis Christian College *B, T*
Kilgore College *C, A*
Lamar Institute of Technology *A*
Lamar State College at Orange *C, A*
Lamar State College at Port Arthur *A*
Lamar University *B, M*
LeTourneau University *B, M*
Lee College *C, A*
Lone Star College System *C, A*
Lubbock Christian University *B*
McMurry University *B*
Midland College *A, B*
Midwestern State University *B, M*
Mountain View College *C, A*
Navarro College *C, A*
North Lake College *A*
Northeast Texas Community
    College *C, A*
Northwest Vista College *A*
Northwood University: Texas *B*
Odessa College *C, A*
Our Lady of the Lake University of San
    Antonio *B, M*
Palo Alto College *A*
Paris Junior College *A*
Prairie View A&M University *B, M*
Rice University *B, M*
Richland College *C, A*
St. Edward's University *B, M*
St. Mary's University *B, M*
St. Philip's College *C, A*
Sam Houston State University *B, M*
San Antonio College *C, A*
San Jacinto College *C, A*
Schreiner University *B*
South Plains College *A*
South Texas College *C, A*
Southern Methodist University *B, M*
Southwestern Adventist
    University *B, M*
Southwestern Assemblies of God
    University *A, B*
Stephen F. Austin State
    University *B, M*
Sul Ross State University *B, M*
Tarleton State University *B, M*
Tarrant County College *C, A*
Texarkana College *A*
Texas A&M International
    University *B, M*
Texas A&M University *M, D*
Texas A&M University
    Commerce *B, M*
    Corpus Christi *B, M*
    Galveston *B*
    Kingsville *M*
    Texarkana *B, M*
Texas Christian University *B, M*
Texas College *B*
Texas Lutheran University *B*
Texas Southern University *B, M*

Texas State University: San
    Marcos *B, M*
Texas Tech University *B, M, D*
Texas Wesleyan University *B, M*
Texas Woman's University *B, M*
Trinity University *B*
Trinity Valley Community College *A*
Tyler Junior College *C, A*
University of Dallas *B, M*
University of Houston *M, D*
University of Houston
    Clear Lake *B, M*
    Downtown *B*
    Victoria *B, M, T*
University of Mary
    Hardin-Baylor *B, M, T*
University of North Texas *M, D*
University of St. Thomas *B, M*
University of Texas
    Arlington *B, M, D*
    Austin *B, M, D*
    Brownsville - Texas Southmost
        College *B, M*
    Dallas *M, D*
    El Paso *B, M*
    Pan American *B, M*
    San Antonio *B, M*
    Tyler *B, M*
    of the Permian Basin *B, M*
University of the Incarnate
    Word *A, B, M*
Victoria College *C, A*
Wayland Baptist University *A, B, M*
West Texas A&M University *B, M*
Western Texas College *A*
Wharton County Junior College *A*
Wiley College *B*

Utah

Argosy University: Salt Lake City *B*
Brigham Young University *B, M*
College of Eastern Utah *A*
DeVry University: Sandy *B, M*
Dixie State College of Utah *A, B*
Eagle Gate College: Layton *A, B*
Eagle Gate College: Murray *A*
LDS Business College *A*
Provo College *A*
Salt Lake Community College *C, A*
Snow College *A*
Southern Utah University *B, M*
Stevens-Henager College: Logan *B*
University of Utah *B, M, D*
Utah Career College *A*
Utah State University *B, M*
Utah Valley University *C, A, B, M*
Weber State University *B, M*
Western Governors University *B, M*
Westminster College *B, M*

Vermont

Castleton State College *B*
Champlain College *B*
College of St. Joseph in
    Vermont *A, B, M*
Goddard College *B, M*
Green Mountain College *B, M*
Johnson State College *A, B*
Landmark College *A*
Lyndon State College *A, B*
Norwich University *B, M*
St. Michael's College *B*
Southern Vermont College *B*
University of Vermont *B, M*
Vermont Technical College *A, B*

Virginia

Argosy University: Washington D.C. *B*
Averett University *A, B, M*
Blue Ridge Community College *A*
Bluefield College *B*
Bridgewater College *B*
Bryant & Stratton College
    Richmond *A, B*

Bryant & Stratton College: Virginia
    Beach *A, B*
Central Virginia Community
    College *A*
Centura College: Chesapeake *A*
Centura College: Newport News *C, A*
Christopher Newport University *B*
College of William and Mary *B, M*
Dabney S. Lancaster Community
    College *A*
Danville Community College *A*
DeVry University
    Arlington *B, M*
Eastern Mennonite University *B, M*
Eastern Shore Community College *A*
Emory & Henry College *B*
Ferrum College *B*
George Mason University *B, M*
Germanna Community College *A*
Hampton University *B, M*
J. Sargeant Reynolds Community
    College *A*
James Madison University *B, M*
Liberty University *M*
Longwood University *B*
Lord Fairfax Community College *A*
Lynchburg College *B, M*
Mary Baldwin College *B*
Marymount University *B, M*
Mountain Empire Community
    College *A*
National College
    Bluefield *C, A*
    Charlottesville *C, A*
    Danville *C, A, B*
    Harrisonburg *C, A, B*
    Lynchburg *C, A, B*
    Martinsville *C, A*
    Roanoke Valley *C, A, B, M*
New River Community College *A*
Northern Virginia Community
    College *A*
Old Dominion University *B, M, D*
Patrick Henry Community College *A*
Paul D. Camp Community College *A*
Piedmont Virginia Community
    College *A*
Potomac College *A, B*
Radford University *B, M*
Rappahannock Community College *A*
Regent University *A, B, M*
Roanoke College *B*
St. Paul's College *B*
Shenandoah University *B, M*
Southern Virginia University *B*
Southside Virginia Community
    College *A*
Southwest Virginia Community
    College *A*
Stratford University: Woodbridge *B, M*
Thomas Nelson Community
    College *A*
Tidewater Community College *A*
University of Management and
    Technology *B, M*
University of Mary Washington *B, M*
University of Richmond *B, M*
University of Virginia *M, D*
University of Virginia's College at
    Wise *B*
Virginia Commonwealth University *M*
Virginia Highlands Community
    College *A*
Virginia Intermont College *B*
Virginia Polytechnic Institute and
    State University *B, M*
Virginia State University *B*
Virginia Union University *B*
Virginia University of Lynchburg *B*
Virginia Wesleyan College *B*
Virginia Western Community
    College *A*
Washington and Lee University *B*
Wytheville Community College *A*

Washington

Antioch University Seattle *M*
Argosy University: Seattle *B, M, D*
Bellevue College *C, A*
Bellingham Technical College *C*
Centralia College *A*
City University of Seattle *C, A, B, M*
Clark College *C, A*
DeVry University
    Federal Way *B, M*
Eastern Washington University *B, M*
Everett Community College *C, A*
Evergreen State College *B*
Gonzaga University *B, M*
Grays Harbor College *C, A*
Highline Community College *C, A*
Lower Columbia College *A*
Northwest University *B, M*
Olympic College *C, A*
Pacific Lutheran University *B, M*
Peninsula College *C, A, B*
Pierce College *C, A*
Saint Martin's University *B, M*
Seattle University *B, M*
Shoreline Community College *A*
Skagit Valley College *C, A*
Spokane Community College *C, A*
Spokane Falls Community
    College *C, A*
Trinity Lutheran College *B*
University of Puget Sound *B*
University of Washington *B, M, D*
University of Washington
    Bothell *B, M*
University of Washington Tacoma *B*
Walla Walla University *B*
Washington State University *B, M, D*
Wenatchee Valley College *C, A*
Western Washington University *B, M*
Whatcom Community College *C*
Whitworth University *B, M*
Yakima Valley Community College *A*

West Virginia

Alderson-Broaddus College *B*
American Public University
    System *C, A, B, M*
Blue Ridge Community and Technical
    College *A*
Bluefield State College *B*
Concord University *B*
Davis and Elkins College *A, B*
Eastern West Virginia Community and
    Technical College *C, A*
Fairmont State University *B, M*
Glenville State College *B*
Marshall University *B*
Mountain State University *A, B*
New River Community and Technical
    College *C*
Ohio Valley University *B*
Potomac State College of West
    Virginia University *A, B*
Salem International University *A, B*
Shepherd University *B, M*
Southern West Virginia Community
    and Technical College *A*
University of Charleston *B, M*
Valley College *A*
West Liberty University *B*
West Virginia Business College: Nutter
    Fort *A*
West Virginia Business College:
    Wheeling *C, A*
West Virginia Junior College *A*
West Virginia Junior College:
    Bridgeport *A*
West Virginia Northern Community
    College *A*
West Virginia State Community and
    Technical College *A*
West Virginia State University *B*
West Virginia University *B*

West Virginia University Institute of
    Technology *B*
West Virginia University at
    Parkersburg *B*
West Virginia Wesleyan College *B, M*
Wheeling Jesuit University *B, M*

Wisconsin

Alverno College *B, M*
Beloit College *B*
Cardinal Stritch University *B, M*
Carroll University *B*
Carthage College *B*
College of Menominee Nation *A*
Concordia University Wisconsin *B, M*
DeVry University: Milwaukee *B, M*
Edgewood College *B, M*
Herzing University *A, B*
Lac Courte Oreilles Ojibwa
    Community College *A*
Lakeland College *B, M*
Lakeshore Technical College *A*
Maranatha Baptist Bible College *B*
Marian University *B, M*
Marquette University *B, M*
Mid-State Technical College *A*
Milwaukee Area Technical College *A*
Milwaukee School of
    Engineering *B, M*
Mount Mary College *B, M, T*
Nicolet Area Technical College *A*
Northcentral Technical College *C, A*
Northeast Wisconsin Technical
    College *A*
Northland College *B*
Rasmussen College: Green Bay *A*
Ripon College *B*
St. Norbert College *B*
Silver Lake College *B, M*
University of Wisconsin
    Eau Claire *B, M*
    Green Bay *B*
    La Crosse *B, M*
    Madison *B, M*
    Manitowoc *C*
    Milwaukee *M*
    Oshkosh *M*
    Parkside *B, M*
    Platteville *C, B*
    River Falls *B*
    Stevens Point *B*
    Stout *B*
    Superior *B*
    Whitewater *B, M*
Viterbo University *B, M*
Western Technical College *A*
Wisconsin Indianhead Technical
    College *A*
Wisconsin Lutheran College *B*

Wyoming

Casper College *A*
Central Wyoming College *A*
Eastern Wyoming College *A*
Laramie County Community
    College *A*
Northwest College *A*
University of Wyoming *B, M*
Western Wyoming Community
    College *A*

Business/commerce

Alabama

Alabama Agricultural and Mechanical
    University *B*
Alabama Southern Community
    College *A*
Andrew Jackson University *C, A, B*
Auburn University at
    Montgomery *B, M*
Birmingham-Southern College *B*

Central Alabama Community
College *C, A*
Faulkner University *B*
Huntingdon College *B*
Jefferson Davis Community College *C*
Jefferson State Community
College *C, A*
Northeast Alabama Community
College *A*
Troy University *A, B*
University of South Alabama *B*
Wallace State Community College at
Hanceville *A*

Alaska

University of Alaska
Anchorage *C, A*
Southeast *B*

Arizona

American Indian College of the
Assemblies of God *A*
Arizona Western College *A*
Central Arizona College *C, A*
Chandler-Gilbert Community College
Pecos *A*
Cochise College *C*
Coconino County Community
College *C, A*
GateWay Community College *A*
Glendale Community College *C, A*
Northcentral University *B, M, D*
Northland Pioneer College *A*
Paradise Valley Community
College *C, A*
Penn Foster College *A, B*
Phoenix College *A*
Prescott College *B, M*
Rio Salado College *C, A*
Scottsdale Community College *C, A*
University of Arizona *B*
University of Phoenix *C*
Western International University *B*

Arkansas

Arkansas Northeastern College *C, A*
Arkansas State University
Beebe *A*
Arkansas State University: Newport *A*
Henderson State University *B, M*
North Arkansas College *A*
Ouachita Technical College *A*
Phillips Community College of the
University of Arkansas *A*
Pulaski Technical College *A*
South Arkansas Community College *A*
Southeast Arkansas College *C, A*
Southern Arkansas University *A, B*
University of Arkansas *B*
University of Arkansas
Community College at
Batesville *C, A*
Community College at Hope *A*
Cossatot Community College of the
C, A
Monticello *B*
University of Arkansas Community
College at Morrilton *C, A*
University of Central Arkansas *B*

California

Allan Hancock College *A*
American Jewish University *B*
Antelope Valley College *C, A*
Azusa Pacific University *B*
Barstow Community College *C, A*
Bethany University *B*
Butte College *C, A*
Cabrillo College *C, A*
California Coast University *A, B, M*
California Lutheran University *B*
California State University
Dominguez Hills *B, M*

East Bay *B*
Long Beach *B*
California State University: Channel
Islands *B, M*
Canada College *C, A*
Cerritos College *A*
Cerro Coso Community College *A*
Chabot College *A*
Citrus College *A*
Coastline Community College *C, A*
College of Alameda *C, A*
College of Marin: Kentfield *C, A*
College of San Mateo *C, A*
College of the Redwoods *A*
College of the Sequoias *A*
College of the Siskiyous *C, A*
Columbia College *A*
Cosumnes River College *A*
Cuesta College *C, A*
Cypress College *A*
DeVry University
Pomona *B, M*
El Camino College *C, A*
El Camino College: Compton
Center *C*
Feather River College *C, A*
Folsom Lake College *A*
Fremont College *A*
Fresno City College *C, A*
Fresno Pacific University *B*
Gavilan College *C, A*
Glendale Community College *A*
Golden West College *C, A*
Grossmont College *C, A*
Heald College
Salinas *A*
Humboldt State University *B*
Humphreys College *A, B*
Irvine Valley College *A*
Lake Tahoe Community College *A*
Laney College *C, A*
Lassen Community College *A*
Long Beach City College *C, A*
Los Angeles Harbor College *C, A*
Los Angeles Pierce College *A*
Los Angeles Southwest College *A*
Los Angeles Trade and Technical
College *A*
Los Angeles Valley College *C, A*
Loyola Marymount University *B, M*
Mendocino College *C, A*
Merced College *C, A*
Merritt College *C, A*
Mills College *B*
Mission College *C, A*
Modesto Junior College *A*
Monterey Peninsula College *A*
Mount St. Mary's College *B*
Mount San Antonio College *A*
Napa Valley College *A*
National University *B, M*
Ohlone College *A*
Orange Coast College *C, A*
Pacific Union College *B*
Palomar College *A*
Pasadena City College *A*
Porterville College *A*
Rio Hondo College *C*
Riverside Community College *C, A*
Sacramento City College *A*
Saddleback College *A*
St. Mary's College of California *B, M*
San Diego City College *C, A*
San Diego Mesa College *C, A*
San Diego State University *B, M*
San Joaquin Delta College *C, A*
San Jose City College *C*
Santa Barbara Business College *C, A*
Santa Barbara Business College
Bakersfield *C, A*
Santa Maria *C, A*
Santa Barbara City College *C, A*
Santa Monica College *C, A*
Shasta College *A*

Sierra College *C, A*
Taft College *A*
University of Redlands *B*
University of San Francisco *B*
Vanguard University of Southern
California *B*
Ventura College *C, A*
Victor Valley College *A*
West Hills College: Coalinga *C, A*
West Hills College: Lemoore *A*
West Los Angeles College *C, A*
West Valley College *A*
Westmont College *B*
Whittier College *B*

Colorado

Adams State College *A, B*
Arapahoe Community College *C*
CollegeAmerica
Fort Collins *B*
Colorado Mountain College *C, A*
Colorado State University
Pueblo *M*
Community College of Aurora *C, A*
Fort Lewis College *B*
Jones International University *B, M*
Lamar Community College *A*
Mesa State College *B, M*
Morgan Community College *A*
Pikes Peak Community College *C, A*
Regis University *B*
Trinidad State Junior College *A*
University of Colorado
Colorado Springs *B*
Denver *B, M*
University of Denver *B, M*
Westwood College: Denver North *B*

Connecticut

Goodwin College *C, A*
Housatonic Community College *C, A*
Lincoln College of New England:
Briarwood *A*
Post University *B*
Quinnipiac University *B, M*
Sacred Heart University *A, B, M*
University of Bridgeport *B, M*
University of Connecticut *B, M, D*
Western Connecticut State
University *M*

Delaware

Delaware Technical and Community
College
Owens *C, A*
Stanton/Wilmington *A*
Terry *C*
Goldey-Beacom College *B, M*

District of Columbia

Catholic University of America *B*
Gallaudet University *B*

Florida

Ave Maria University *C*
Broward College *A*
Carlos Albizu University *B*
Herzing University *A, B*
Jacksonville University *B*
Northwest Florida State College *A*
Nova Southeastern University *B*
Palm Beach Community College *A*
Pensacola Junior College *A*
Saint Leo University *A, M*
Saint Thomas University *B*
Schiller International University *B*
Southeastern University *B*
State College of Florida,
Manatee-Sarasota *A*
Tallahassee Community College *A*
Trinity College of Florida *B*
University of Central Florida *B, M*
University of Florida *B, M, D*

University of Miami *C*
University of South Florida *B, M*
Webber International University *B*

Georgia

Andrew College *A*
Atlanta Christian College *A, B*
Bainbridge College *A*
Brown Mackie College: Atlanta *C*
Chattahoochee Technical College *A*
Clayton State University *B*
Columbus State University *B, M*
Covenant College *A, B*
Dalton State College *A*
DeVry University
Alpharetta *M*
Fort Valley State University *B*
Gainesville State College *A*
Georgia College and State
University *B, M*
Life University *B*
Macon State College *C, A, B*
Mercer University *B, M*
Reinhardt College *B*
Savannah State University *M*
South Georgia College *C*
Truett-McConnell College *A, B*
University of Georgia *B*
Waycross College *C*
Young Harris College *A, B*

Hawaii

Hawaii Pacific University *A, B*
University of Hawaii
Hilo *B*
Kapiolani Community College *A*
Manoa *B*
Maui Community College *C, A*
Windward Community College *C*

Idaho

Idaho State University *A, B*
University of Idaho *B*

Illinois

Augustana College *B*
Aurora University *B*
Black Hawk College: East Campus *A*
City Colleges of Chicago
Malcolm X College *A*
Olive-Harvey College *C, A*
Concordia University Chicago *B*
DePaul University *B*
Eureka College *B*
Hebrew Theological College *B*
Illinois Central College *C, A*
John Wood Community College *A*
Kaskaskia College *A*
Kishwaukee College *A*
Lake Forest College *B*
Lake Land College *A*
Lewis University *B*
Lewis and Clark Community
College *A*
Lincoln College *A*
Lincoln Land Community College *A*
MacCormac College *C, A*
Midstate College *A*
Moraine Valley Community
College *C, A*
North Park University *B, M*
Northeastern Illinois University *B*
Northern Illinois University *B*
Northwestern University *M*
Olivet Nazarene University *A, B*
Parkland College *A*
Richard J. Daley College *C, A*
Richland Community College *A*
Rock Valley College *C, A*
Rockford Career College *A*
Roosevelt University *B*
Saint Xavier University *B*
Shawnee Community College *A*

South Suburban College of Cook
County *A*
Southwestern Illinois College *A*
Spoon River College *A*
Trinity Christian College *B*
Trinity International University *B*
University of Chicago *M, D*
University of Illinois
Urbana-Champaign *B, M, D*
University of St. Francis *B, M*

Indiana

Ball State University *B, M*
Bethel College *A*
Brown Mackie College: Fort Wayne *C*
Calumet College of St. Joseph *B, M*
Franklin College *B*
Grace College *B*
Holy Cross College *B*
Huntington University *B*
Indiana Institute of
Technology *A, B, M*
Indiana University
Bloomington *C, B, M, D*
Kokomo *A, B, M*
Northwest *A, B, M*
South Bend *A, B, M*
Southeast *A, B, M*
Indiana University-Purdue University
Indianapolis *C, B, M*
International Business College *B*
Manchester College *A, B*
Marian University *A, B*
Oakland City University *A, B*
Purdue University
Calumet *A, B*
North Central *C, A, B, M*
Saint Joseph's College *B*
St. Mary-of-the-Woods College *A, B*
University of Notre Dame *B*
University of Southern Indiana *B, M*
Valparaiso University *C*
Vincennes University *A*

Iowa

AIB College of Business *A, B*
Dordt College *A, B*
Drake University *B*
Ellsworth Community College *A*
Grand View University *B*
Iowa State University *B*
Iowa Wesleyan College *B*
Loras College *B*
Marshalltown Community College *A*
Mount Mercy College *B*
St. Ambrose University *B*
Southeastern Community College
North Campus *A*
Southwestern Community College *A*
Upper Iowa University *A, B*
Waldorf College *B*
William Penn University *M*

Kansas

Baker University *B, T*
Barclay College *B*
Barton County Community
College *C, A*
Bethel College *B*
Central Christian College of
Kansas *A, B*
Coffeyville Community College *A*
Cowley County Community
College *A*
Dodge City Community College *A*
Donnelly College *A*
Fort Hays State University *B*
Fort Scott Community College *A*
Garden City Community College *A*
Hesston College *A*
Highland Community College *C, A*
Hutchinson Community College *A*
Kansas State University *C, B*
Kansas Wesleyan University *A, B, M*

MidAmerica Nazarene
University *A, B, M*
Seward County Community
College *C, A*
University of Kansas *B, M, D*
University of St. Mary *B*
Washburn University *B*

Kentucky

Asbury College *B*
Berea College *B*
Brescia University *A, B*
Campbellsville University *A, B*
Eastern Kentucky University *B, M*
Georgetown College *B*
Kentucky State University *B*
Kentucky Wesleyan College *B*
Maysville Community and Technical
College *C, A*
Midway College *A, B, M*
Morehead State University *M*
Murray State University *A, B, M*
Northern Kentucky
University *A, B, M*
Owensboro Community and
Technical College *A*
St. Catharine College *A*
Spalding University *A, B*
Thomas More College *C, A, B, M*
Transylvania University *B*
University of Kentucky *B, M, D*
University of Louisville *M*
University of the Cumberlands *B*
Western Kentucky University *M, T*

Louisiana

Baton Rouge Community College *C, A*
Baton Rouge School of
Computers *C, A*
Bossier Parish Community College *A*
Louisiana College *B*
Louisiana State University
Eunice *A*
Loyola University New Orleans *M*
Northwestern State University *A*
Nunez Community College *A*
South Louisiana Community
College *A*
Tulane University *C, A, B, M, D*

Maine

Eastern Maine Community College *A*
Husson University *B, M*
Maine Maritime Academy *B, M*
Thomas College *A*
University of Maine *B*
University of Maine
Fort Kent *A, B*
Machias *B*
University of Southern Maine *B, M*

Maryland

Allegany College of Maryland *C, A*
Anne Arundel Community
College *C, A*
Baltimore City Community College *A*
Carroll Community College *A*
Cecil College *C, A*
Chesapeake College *A*
College of Notre Dame of Maryland *B*
College of Southern Maryland *A*
Community College of Baltimore
County *A*
Garrett College *A*
Hagerstown Community College *A*
Harford Community College *A*
Loyola University Maryland *B*
Montgomery College *A*
Mount St. Mary's University *B*
University of Baltimore *B, M*
University of Maryland
College Park *B, M, D*
University College *C, B, D*

Washington College *B*
Wor-Wic Community College *A*

Massachusetts

American International College *B*
Babson College *B*
Bay Path College *B*
Bentley University *B, M, D*
Berkshire Community College *A*
Brandeis University *B*
Cambridge College *B, M*
Clark University *B, M*
Dean College *C, A*
Eastern Nazarene College *A, B*
Endicott College *A*
Framingham State College *B, M*
Greenfield Community College *A*
Harvard College *M, D*
Massachusetts Bay Community
College *A*
Massachusetts Institute of
Technology *B, M, D*
New England College of Business and
Finance *A*
Nichols College *M, T*
Northeastern University *B, M*
Northern Essex Community
College *A*
Quincy College *C, A*
Regis College *B*
Springfield Technical Community
College *A*
Suffolk University *B*
University of Massachusetts
Lowell *A*
Western New England College *B*
Westfield State College *B, T*

Michigan

Andrews University *A*
Baker College
of Auburn Hills *B*
of Cadillac *A*
of Flint *A*
of Jackson *B*
of Muskegon *A*
of Owosso *A*
of Port Huron *A, B*
Bay de Noc Community College *C*
Calvin College *B*
Davenport University *A, B*
Delta College *A*
Eastern Michigan University *B*
Ferris State University *C, A*
Glen Oaks Community College *A*
Gogebic Community College *C, A*
Grace Bible College *A, B*
Grand Rapids Community College *A*
Henry Ford Community College *A*
Hillsdale College *B*
Jackson Community College *C, A*
Kalamazoo College *B*
Lake Superior State University *A, B*
Lansing Community College *A*
Macomb Community College *C, A*
Marygrove College *A, B*
Mott Community College *A*
North Central Michigan College *C, A*
Northern Michigan University *A, B*
Northwestern Michigan College *A*
Oakland University *B*
Saginaw Valley State University *B*
St. Clair County Community
College *C, A*
Schoolcraft College *C, A*
Siena Heights University *A, B*
University of Detroit Mercy *B*
Walsh College of Accountancy and
Business Administration *B*
Wayne State University *M, D*
West Shore Community College *A*
Western Michigan University *B*

Minnesota

Anoka-Ramsey Community
College *C, A*
Brown College *B*
Capella University *M, D*
Concordia College: Moorhead *B*
Crown College *A, B*
Gustavus Adolphus College *B*
Hamline University *B*
Inver Hills Community College *A*
Mesabi Range Community and
Technical College *A*
Minnesota State University
Mankato *B*
Minnesota West Community and
Technical College *A*
National American University
Bloomington *A, B, M*
North Hennepin Community
College *C*
Northwest Technical College *C*
Ridgewater College *A*
Saint Cloud State University *B*
St. Mary's University of Minnesota *B*
St. Paul College *C, A*
Vermilion Community College *A*
Winona State University *B, M*

Mississippi

Delta State University *B*
East Central Community College *A*
Mississippi Gulf Coast Community
College *A*
Mississippi State University *M*

Missouri

Avila University *B*
Central Methodist University *B*
Columbia College *A, B, M*
Crowder College *C, A*
Evangel University *B*
Hannibal-LaGrange College *B*
Harris-Stowe State University *B*
Jefferson College *C, A*
Lindenwood University *B, M*
Maryville University of Saint
Louis *B, M*
Metropolitan Community College:
Blue River *A*
Metropolitan Community College:
Longview *A*
Metropolitan Community College:
Maple Woods *A*
Metropolitan Community College:
Penn Valley *A*
Mineral Area College *C, A*
Missouri Southern State
University *A, B*
Missouri State University *B*
Missouri State University: West
Plains *A*
St. Louis Community College
St. Louis Community College at
Meramec *C, A*
Southwest Baptist University *A*
Stephens College *B*
University of Missouri
Columbia *B, M, D*
Kansas City *B, M, D*
Missouri University of Science and
Technology *B*
St. Louis *B, M*
Washington University in St. Louis *B*
Webster University *B, M*

Montana

Dawson Community College *A*
Fort Belknap College *A*
Fort Peck Community College *A*
Little Big Horn College *A*
Montana State University
Billings *C, A, B*
Bozeman *B*

Montana Tech of the University of
Montana *B*
Stone Child College *A*
University of Montana *B, M*
University of Montana: Western *A, B*

Nebraska

Bellevue University *B, M*
Clarkson College *B, M*
Concordia University *B*
Little Priest Tribal College *A*
Metropolitan Community College *A*
University of Nebraska
Omaha *B*
Western Nebraska Community
College *C, A*

Nevada

College of Southern Nevada *A*
Great Basin College *A*
Truckee Meadows Community
College *C, A*
University of Nevada
Reno *B*

New Hampshire

Daniel Webster College *B*
Granite State College *A*
Plymouth State University *B*
River Valley Community College *A*
Saint Anselm College *B*
University of New Hampshire *A, B, M*

New Jersey

Brookdale Community College *A*
Burlington County College *A*
Gloucester County College *A*
Mercer County Community
College *C, A*
Ocean County College *A*
Passaic County Community
College *C, A*
Raritan Valley Community College *A*
Saint Peter's College *C*
Union County College *A*
Warren County Community
College *C, A*

New Mexico

Clovis Community College *A*
Eastern New Mexico University:
Roswell Campus *C, A*
New Mexico Junior College *A*
New Mexico State University *B*
New Mexico State University
Alamogordo *A*
Carlsbad *A*
Grants *A*
Northern New Mexico College *A*
Southwestern Indian Polytechnic
Institute *A*
Western New Mexico
University *C, A, B, M*

New York

Broome Community College *C*
Bryant & Stratton Business Institute
Bryant & Stratton College:
Buffalo *A*
Bryant & Stratton College: Syracuse
North *A*
City University of New York
Baruch College *B, M*
Bronx Community College *A*
City College *B*
College of Staten Island *A, B*
Hostos Community College *A*
Medgar Evers College *B*
Queensborough Community
College *A*
City University of New York: CUNY
Online *B, M*
College of Mount St. Vincent *A, B*

College of New Rochelle *B*
Concordia College *B*
D'Youville College *B*
Excelsior College *A, B*
Finger Lakes Community College *A*
Fordham University *B, M*
Fulton-Montgomery Community
College *A*
Globe Institute of Technology *C, A, B*
Herkimer County Community
College *C, A*
Hofstra University *B*
Houghton College *B*
Hudson Valley Community College *A*
Ithaca College *B, M*
Manhattan College *B*
Maria College *A*
Medaille College *B*
Mercy College *C*
Metropolitan College of New
York *B, M*
Monroe Community College *A*
Nazareth College *B, M*
New York University *C, A, B*
Niagara University *A*
North Country Community College *A*
Olean Business Institute *C, A*
Orange County Community College *A*
Pace University *C, B*
Paul Smith's College *B*
Rochester Institute of
Technology *A, B, M*
Rockland Community College *A*
St. Joseph's College *C, B*
St. Joseph's College: Suffolk
Campus *C*
St. Thomas Aquinas College *B*
Schenectady County Community
College *A*
Skidmore College *B*
State University of New York
Albany *M*
College at Buffalo *B*
College at Geneseo *B*
College at Plattsburgh *B*
College of Agriculture and
Technology at Morrisville *A*
Empire State College *A, B*
Institute of Technology at
Utica/Rome *B, M*
Maritime College *B*
New Paltz *B, M*
Suffolk County Community College *A*
Sullivan County Community
College *A*
Touro College *A, B*
Ulster County Community
College *C, A*
Utica School of Commerce *A*
Vaughn College of Aeronautics and
Technology *B, M*
Wells College *B*
Westchester Community College *C*

North Carolina

Alamance Community College *C, A*
Blue Ridge Community College *A*
Campbell University *A, B, M*
Carteret Community College *A*
Gardner-Webb University *B, M*
Lenoir-Rhyne University *M*
Louisburg College *A*
Mars Hill College *B*
McDowell Technical Community
College *A*
North Carolina Agricultural and
Technical State University *B*
Pfeiffer University *B*
Piedmont Community College *A*
St. Andrews Presbyterian College *B*
Wake Forest University *B*
Wake Technical Community
College *A*

North Dakota

Bismarck State College *A*
Cankdeska Cikana Community
College *A*
Dickinson State University *B*
Mayville State University *A*
North Dakota State College of
Science *A*
Trinity Bible College *A, B*

Ohio

Ashland University *A, B, M*
Belmont Technical College *A*
Bowling Green State University *B*
Bowling Green State University:
Firelands College *A*
Bryant & Stratton College
Eastlake *A*
Parma *A*
Bryant & Stratton College:
Cleveland *A*
Central State University *B*
Cincinnati State Technical and
Community College *C*
Cuyahoga Community College
Metropolitan Campus *A*
Defiance College *B*
Eastern Gateway Community
College *C, A*
Edison State Community College *C, A*
Franklin University *A, B, M*
Hocking College *A*
James A. Rhodes State College *A*
Kent State University *C*
Kent State University
Ashtabula *C, A*
East Liverpool *C, A*
Salem *C, A*
Trumbull *C, A*
Tuscarawas *C, A*
Lourdes College *A*
Marion Technical College *C, A*
Mount Vernon Nazarene University *A*
Muskingum University *B*
North Central State College *A*
Northwest State Community
College *A*
Ohio Christian University *A, B*
Ohio State University
Columbus Campus *B, M, D*
Lima Campus *B*
Ohio University *M*
Ohio University
Zanesville Campus *B*
Ohio Valley College of Technology *A*
Otterbein College *B*
Owens Community College
Toledo *A*
Southern State Community College *A*
Stark State College of Technology *A*
Terra State Community College *A*
University of Akron: Wayne College *A*
University of Cincinnati
Clermont College *C, A*
Raymond Walters College *C, A*
University of Dayton *B*
University of Findlay *A, B*
University of Rio Grande *B*
University of Toledo *A*
Walsh University *A, B*
Washington State Community
College *A*
Wilmington College *C*
Wittenberg University *B*
Wright State University *M*
Wright State University: Lake
Campus *C, A*
Xavier University *B*
Youngstown State University *A, B, M*

Oklahoma

Carl Albert State College *A*
Connors State College *A*
East Central University *B*

Eastern Oklahoma State College *A*
Hillsdale Free Will Baptist College *B*
Northern Oklahoma College *A*
Oklahoma Baptist University *B*
Oklahoma Christian University *B, M*
Oklahoma City Community College *A*
Oklahoma City University *B, M*
Oklahoma State University
Institute of Technology:
Okmulgee *A*
Oklahoma Wesleyan University *B*
Rose State College *C, A*
Southern Nazarene University *B, M*
Southwestern Oklahoma State
University *A, B, M*
Tulsa Community College *A*
Western Oklahoma State College *A*

Oregon

Concordia University *B*
Corban College *B*
Eastern Oregon University *B, T*
Lane Community College *A*
Linfield College *B*
Marylhurst University *B, M*
Mt. Hood Community College *C, A*
Portland Community College *A*
Portland State University *B, M*
Rogue Community College *A*
Southern Oregon University *B*
Treasure Valley Community College *A*
Umpqua Community College *A*
University of Oregon *B, M*
Western Oregon University *B*

Pennsylvania

Alvernia University *A, B*
Arcadia University *B*
Bloomsburg University of
Pennsylvania *B, M, T*
Bryn Athyn College of the New
Church *B*
Bucks County Community College *A*
Butler County Community College *C*
Commonwealth Technical Institute *C*
Community College of Philadelphia *A*
DeSales University *B, M*
Delaware Valley College *A*
Drexel University *B, M, D*
Duquesne University *B*
Gannon University *C, A*
Harcum College *A*
Harrisburg Area Community
College *C, A*
Indiana University of
Pennsylvania *B, M*
Juniata College *B*
Keystone College *A, B*
La Salle University *B*
Lackawanna College *A*
Luzerne County Community
College *C, A*
Montgomery County Community
College *A*
Northampton Community College *A*
PJA School *A*
Penn Commercial Business and
Technical School *A*
Penn State
Abington *A, B*
Altoona *A, B*
Beaver *A*
Berks *A, B*
Brandywine *A*
DuBois *A*
Erie, The Behrend College *C, A*
Fayette, The Eberly Campus *A*
Greater Allegheny *A*
Harrisburg *A*
Hazleton *A*
Lehigh Valley *A, B*
Mont Alto *A*
New Kensington *A*
Schuylkill *A*

Shenango *C*
University Park *A*
Wilkes-Barre *A*
Worthington Scranton *A*
York *C, A*
Pennsylvania Institute of Health and
    Technology *A*
Reading Area Community
    College *C, A*
Rosemont College *B*
Saint Joseph's University *M*
Shippensburg University of
    Pennsylvania *T*
University of Pittsburgh
    Bradford *B*
    Johnstown *C, B*
    Titusville *A*
Valley Forge Military Academy &
    College *A*
Washington & Jefferson College *B*
Waynesburg University *A, B*
West Chester University of
    Pennsylvania *B*

Puerto Rico
American University of Puerto Rico *B*
Bayamon Central University *A, B, M*
Inter American University of Puerto
    Rico
    Fajardo Campus *A, B*
Pontifical Catholic University of
    Puerto Rico *A, B, M*
Universidad Adventista de las
    Antillas *A, B*
Universidad Politecnica de Puerto
    Rico *B*
University of Puerto Rico
    Aguadilla *B*
    Arecibo *A*
    Bayamon University College *A*
    Cayey University College *B*
    Humacao *B*
    Rio Piedras *B, M*

Rhode Island
Bryant University *M*
Community College of Rhode
    Island *A*
New England Institute of
    Technology *B*
Rhode Island College *B*
University of Rhode Island *B*

South Carolina
Anderson University *B*
Bob Jones University *B*
Clemson University *B, M*
Clinton Junior College *A*
Denmark Technical College *A*
Forrest Junior College *A*
Horry-Georgetown Technical
    College *C, A*
Limestone College *A*
Midlands Technical College *C*
North Greenville University *B*
Orangeburg-Calhoun Technical
    College *A*
South Carolina State University *M*
Southern Wesleyan University *A*
Technical College of the
    Lowcountry *C, A*
Trident Technical College *A*
University of South Carolina
    Aiken *B*
Williamsburg Technical College *A*
York Technical College *A*

South Dakota
Augustana College *B*
Dakota Wesleyan University *A, B*
Northern State University *B*
Sinte Gleska University *A*
University of Sioux Falls *M*

Tennessee
Austin Peay State University *B*
Belmont University *B*
Bethel University *M*
Carson-Newman College *B, T*
Christian Brothers University *B*
Columbia State Community College *A*
Cumberland University *A, B, M*
DeVry University: Memphis *M*
Free Will Baptist Bible College *A*
Lambuth University *B*
Lincoln Memorial University *B, M, T*
Lipscomb University *M*
Martin Methodist College *B*
Southwest Tennessee Community
    College *A*
Tennessee Technological
    University *B, M*
Tennessee Temple University *B*
University of Tennessee
    Knoxville *B*

Texas
Alvin Community College *A*
Amarillo College *C, A*
Amberton University *B, M*
Angelina College *C, A*
Austin College *B*
Austin Community College *A*
Baylor University *B*
Brazosport College *A*
Brookhaven College *A*
Central Texas College *C, A*
Cisco College *C, A*
Clarendon College *A*
Coastal Bend College *A*
College of the Mainland *A*
Concordia University Texas *B*
Dallas Baptist University *B*
Del Mar College *C, A*
East Texas Baptist University *B*
Eastfield College *C, A*
El Paso Community College *C, A*
Frank Phillips College *C, A*
Grayson County College *C, A*
Houston Baptist University *B*
Howard College *C, A*
Howard Payne University *B*
Kilgore College *C, A*
Lamar State College at Orange *A*
Lamar University *B, M*
Laredo Community College *A*
LeTourneau University *B*
Lon Morris College *A*
McLennan Community College *C, A*
McMurry University *B*
Midland College *A*
Midwestern State University *B*
Mountain View College *A*
Navarro College *A*
North Central Texas College *A*
Odessa College *A*
Our Lady of the Lake University of San
    Antonio *M*
Panola College *C, A*
Paris Junior College *A*
St. Mary's University *B*
Sam Houston State University *B*
San Jacinto College *C, A*
Schreiner University *B*
South Plains College *C*
Southern Methodist University *B*
Southwestern Assemblies of God
    University *A, B*
Southwestern University *B*
Stephen F. Austin State University *B*
Sul Ross State University *B*
Tarleton State University *B, T*
Tarrant County College *C, A*
Temple College *C, A*
Texarkana College *A*
Texas A&M University
    Commerce *B, M*
    Corpus Christi *B*

Kingsville *B*
Texarkana *B*
Texas Lutheran University *B*
Texas Tech University *B*
Tyler Junior College *A*
University of Houston *M, D*
University of Houston
    Clear Lake *B*
    Downtown *B*
    Victoria *B*
University of Mary Hardin-Baylor *B*
University of North Texas *B*
University of Texas
    Austin *B, M, D*
    Brownsville - Texas Southmost
        College *B*
    Dallas *B*
    El Paso *B*
    San Antonio *B*
Vernon College *C, A*
Weatherford College *C, A*
West Texas A&M University *B*
Western Texas College *A*

Utah
Brigham Young University *B*
Dixie State College of Utah *C, A*
Independence University *C, A, B*
LDS Business College *A*
Salt Lake Community College *A*
Snow College *C, A*
University of Utah *B, M*
Utah State University *B*
Westminster College *B*

Vermont
Castleton State College *A, B*
Champlain College *B*
Community College of Vermont *C, A*
Johnson State College *B*
Southern Vermont College *A*
Vermont Technical College *A, B*

Virginia
Blue Ridge Community College *C*
Central Virginia Community
    College *A*
Danville Community College *A*
Germanna Community College *A*
Hollins University *B*
J. Sargeant Reynolds Community
    College *C*
John Tyler Community College *A*
Liberty University *A, B, T*
Longwood University *B*
Lord Fairfax Community College *C*
Mountain Empire Community
    College *A*
Norfolk State University *B*
Randolph College *B*
Shenandoah University *C*
Southwest Virginia Community
    College *A*
Sweet Briar College *B*
University of Management and
    Technology *A, B, M*
University of Virginia *B, M*
Virginia Commonwealth
    University *B, M, D*
Virginia Polytechnic Institute and
    State University *D*
Virginia Western Community
    College *A*

Washington
Big Bend Community College *A*
Centralia College *A*
DeVry University
    Federal Way *B, M*
Everett Community College *C, A*
Highline Community College *C, A*
North Seattle Community College *A*
Olympic College *A*

Pierce College *C, A*
Seattle University *B*
South Puget Sound Community
    College *A*
South Seattle Community College *A*
Spokane Community College *C, A*
Spokane Falls Community
    College *C, A*
University of Washington
    Tacoma *B, M*
Walla Walla University *A*
Washington State University *B*
Whatcom Community College *A*
Yakima Valley Community College *A*

West Virginia
Alderson-Broaddus College *C, A*
Bethany College *B*
Blue Ridge Community and Technical
    College *C, A*
Concord University *B*
Davis and Elkins College *A*
Fairmont State University *B*
Glenville State College *A, B*
Huntington Junior College *A*
Marshall University *M*
New River Community and Technical
    College *A*
Potomac State College of West
    Virginia University *A*
Southern West Virginia Community
    and Technical College *A*
Valley College *A*
West Liberty University *A*
West Virginia State University *B*
West Virginia University *M*
West Virginia University Institute of
    Technology *B*

Wisconsin
Cardinal Stritch University *A, B*
Chippewa Valley Technical College *A*
Concordia University Wisconsin *B*
Edgewood College *B, M*
Fox Valley Technical College *A*
Marian University *B*
Marquette University *M*
Milwaukee School of Engineering *B*
Northeast Wisconsin Technical
    College *A*
St. Norbert College *B*
University of Wisconsin
    Madison *B, M, D*
    Parkside *B*
    Platteville *B*
    Richland *C*
    Sheboygan *C*
    Superior *B*
    Whitewater *B*

Wyoming
Central Wyoming College *A*
Laramie County Community
    College *A*
Northwest College *A*
Sheridan College *C, A*

Business communications

Arizona
University of Phoenix *B*

California
Foothill College *C*
Holy Names University *B*
Ohlone College *C*
Point Loma Nazarene University *B*
Saddleback College *C*

Colorado
Jones International University *B, M, D*

Connecticut
Quinnipiac University *B*

District of Columbia
University of the District of
Columbia *A*

Florida
Florida State College at Jacksonville *C*
Schiller International University *M*

Hawaii
Hawaii Pacific University *B*

Illinois
Dominican University *B*
Roosevelt University *B*
Trinity Christian College *B*
Waubonsee Community College *C*

Indiana
St. Mary-of-the-Woods College *B*

Iowa
Morningside College *B*

Kansas
MidAmerica Nazarene University *B*
Southwestern College *B*

Kentucky
Kentucky Wesleyan College *B*
Spalding University *M*

Maine
University of Maine
Presque Isle *B*

Maryland
Cecil College *C, A*
Stevenson University *B*
University of Baltimore *B*

Massachusetts
Babson College *B*
Bentley University *B, M*
Emerson College *B, M*
Nichols College *B*
Suffolk University *M*

Michigan
Aquinas College *B*
Calvin College *B*
Macomb Community College *C*

Minnesota
North Hennepin Community
College *C*
University of St. Thomas *M*

Missouri
Lindenwood University *B, M*
Rockhurst University *B*

Montana
Flathead Valley Community College *C*

Nebraska
Concordia University *B*
Creighton University *B*
Dana College *B*

New Jersey
College of St. Elizabeth *C*

New York
City University of New York
Baruch College *B*
Globe Institute of Technology *C*
Metropolitan College of New York *B*

Saint Bonaventure University *M*
State University of New York
College at Fredonia *B*

North Carolina
Campbell University *B*
East Carolina University *C*

North Dakota
North Dakota State University *B*
University of Mary *B*

Ohio
Edison State Community College *A*
Marietta College *B*
Ohio Dominican University *B*
Stark State College of Technology *A*
Urbana University *B*

Oregon
Corban College *B*
Marylhurst University *B, M*

Pennsylvania
Chestnut Hill College *A, B*
Community College of Beaver
County *C*
Duquesne University *B*
Grove City College *B*
La Salle University *B*
Lycoming College *B*
Montgomery County Community
College *C, A*
Penn State
Abington *B*
Rosemont College *B*
Thiel College *B*

Puerto Rico
Pontifical Catholic University of
Puerto Rico *B*

South Carolina
Forrest Junior College *A*

South Dakota
Augustana College *B*

Texas
Dallas Baptist University *C*
Houston Community College
System *C, A*
Southwestern Adventist University *B*
University of Houston *B*

Vermont
Champlain College *B*

Virginia
Dabney S. Lancaster Community
College *A*
Thomas Nelson Community
College *C*

Business machine repair

California
Yuba Community College District *C*

Georgia
Athens Technical College *C*

Idaho
Idaho State University *B*

Michigan
Bay de Noc Community College *C*

Pennsylvania
Community College of Allegheny
County *A*

Washington
Clover Park Technical College *C, A*

Business/managerial economics

Alabama
Auburn University *B, M*
Auburn University at Montgomery *B*
Jacksonville State University *B*
Samford University *B*
Talladega College *B*
University of Alabama *B, M, D*
University of Alabama
Birmingham *B*
University of North Alabama *B*

Alaska
University of Alaska
Fairbanks *B*

Arizona
Northern Arizona University *C, B*
University of Arizona *B*

Arkansas
Arkansas State University *B*
University of Arkansas *B*
University of Arkansas
Little Rock *B*

California
California Institute of Technology *B*
California Lutheran University *B*
California State University
East Bay *B, M*
Fullerton *B, M*
Long Beach *B*
Northridge *B*
San Bernardino *B*
Chapman University *B*
Claremont McKenna College *B*
College of the Desert *A*
College of the Redwoods *A*
East Los Angeles College *A*
Lincoln University *B*
Mills College *B*
San Joaquin Delta College *A*
Santa Clara University *B*
Santiago Canyon College *C, A*
University of California
Irvine *B*
Los Angeles *B*
Riverside *B*
Santa Barbara *B*
Santa Cruz *B*
University of La Verne *B*
University of Redlands *B*
University of San Diego *B*

Colorado
Colorado State University
Pueblo *B*
University of Denver *B*

Connecticut
Albertus Magnus College *B*
Quinnipiac University *B*
Sacred Heart University *B*
Southern Connecticut State
University *B*
University of New Haven *B*

Delaware
University of Delaware *M, D*

Florida
Florida Agricultural and Mechanical
University *B*
Stetson University *B*
University of Central Florida *B, M*
University of Miami *B, M, D*
University of North Florida *B*
University of South Florida *B, M*
University of Tampa *B*
University of West Florida *B*

Georgia
Clark Atlanta University *B, M*
Georgia College and State
University *B*
Georgia Highlands College *A*
Georgia Institute of Technology *B, M*
Georgia Southern University *B*
Georgia State University *B, M*
Kennesaw State University *B*
Oglethorpe University *B*
Shorter College *B*
University of Georgia *B, M, D*
University of West Georgia *B*
Valdosta State University *B*

Hawaii
Hawaii Pacific University *A, B*

Idaho
Boise State University *B*
University of Idaho *B*

Illinois
Benedictine University *B, T*
Bradley University *B*
DePaul University *B*
Illinois College *B*
Lewis University *B*
Loyola University Chicago *B*
Monmouth College *B*
Northwestern University *M, D*
Southern Illinois University
Carbondale *B*
Southern Illinois University
Edwardsville *B*
Spoon River College *A*
University of Chicago *M, D*
Western Illinois University *B*
Wheaton College *B*

Indiana
Anderson University *B*
Ball State University *B*
Huntington University *B*
Indiana University-Purdue University
Fort Wayne *B*
Indiana Wesleyan University *B*
Taylor University *B*
University of Evansville *B*
University of Indianapolis *B*

Iowa
Buena Vista University *B*
Drake University *B*
Iowa State University *B*
Northwestern College *B*
University of Iowa *B*

Kansas
Bethany College *B*
Central Christian College of
Kansas *A, B*
Pittsburg State University *B*
Washburn University *B*

Kentucky
Eastern Kentucky University *B*
Morehead State University *B*
Northern Kentucky University *B*
University of Kentucky *B*
University of Louisville *B*

Western Kentucky University *B*

Louisiana
Centenary College of Louisiana *B*
Grambling State University *B*
Louisiana State University
  Shreveport *B*
Louisiana State University and
  Agricultural and Mechanical
  College *B*
Louisiana Tech University *B*
Loyola University New Orleans *B*
Southern University and Agricultural
  and Mechanical College *B*
University of Louisiana at Lafayette *B*
University of New Orleans *B, M, D*

Maine
Husson University *B*
University of Maine *B*
University of Maine
  Farmington *B*

Maryland
Allegany College of Maryland *C, A*
University of Baltimore *B*

Massachusetts
American International College *B*
Babson College *B*
Bentley University *B, M*
Boston College *B*
Harvard College *M, D*
Nichols College *B*
Salem State College *B*

Michigan
Andrews University *B, M*
Eastern Michigan University *B*
Grand Valley State University *B*
Hope College *B*
Lake Superior State University *B*
Northwood University: Michigan *A, B*
Oakland University *B*
Saginaw Valley State University *B*
Spring Arbor University *B*

Minnesota
Winona State University *B*

Mississippi
Mississippi State University *B, M, D*
University of Mississippi *B*
University of Southern
  Mississippi *B, M*

Missouri
College of the Ozarks *B*
Lincoln University *B*
Northwest Missouri State
  University *B*
Park University *B*
Washington University in St. Louis *B*
William Jewell College *B*
William Woods University *B*

Nebraska
University of Nebraska
  Lincoln *B*
  Omaha *B, M*

Nevada
University of Nevada
  Las Vegas *B, M*
  Reno *B, M*

New Hampshire
Saint Anselm College *B*

New Jersey
Drew University *B*

Fairleigh Dickinson University
  College at Florham *B, M*
  Metropolitan Campus *B, M*
Rider University *B*
Saint Peter's College *B*
Seton Hall University *B*
William Paterson University of New
  Jersey *B*

New Mexico
Eastern New Mexico University *B*
Western New Mexico University *B*

New York
City University of New York
  Baruch College *B*
Elmira College *B*
Fordham University *B, M*
Hofstra University *B*
Ithaca College *B*
Manhattan College *B*
Metropolitan College of New York *B*
New York University *B, M, D*
Niagara University *B*
Pace University *M*
State University of New York
  College at Oneonta *B*
Touro College *B*
Ulster County Community College *A*
University of Rochester *B*
Utica College *B*
Wagner College *B*
Wells College *B*

North Carolina
Greensboro College *C, B*
North Carolina Agricultural and
  Technical State University *B*
North Carolina State University *B*
University of North Carolina
  Charlotte *B, M*
  Greensboro *B, M, D*
  Wilmington *B*
Winston-Salem State University *B*

North Dakota
Jamestown College *B*
University of North Dakota *B*

Ohio
Capital University *B*
Cleveland State University *B*
College of Wooster *B*
John Carroll University *B*
Kent State University *B, M, D*
Miami University
  Oxford Campus *B*
Muskingum University *B*
Ohio State University
  Columbus Campus *B*
Ohio University *B*
Ohio Wesleyan University *B*
Otterbein College *B*
University of Dayton *B*
Urbana University *B*
Wilberforce University *B*
Wittenberg University *B*
Wright State University *B, M*
Xavier University *B*
Youngstown State University *B*

Oklahoma
East Central University *B*
Oklahoma City University *B, M*
Oklahoma State University *B, M, D*
Tulsa Community College *A*
University of Central Oklahoma *B*
University of Oklahoma *B*

Oregon
Eastern Oregon University *B*

Pennsylvania
Allegheny College *B*
Carnegie Mellon University *B*
Chatham University *B*
Clarion University of Pennsylvania *B*
Drexel University *B*
Duquesne University *B*
Elizabethtown College *B*
Grove City College *B*
La Salle University *B*
Lehigh University *B, M, D*
Lycoming College *B*
Messiah College *B*
Penn State
  Abington *B*
  Altoona *B*
  Beaver *B*
  Berks *B*
  Brandywine *B*
  DuBois *B*
  Erie, The Behrend College *B*
  Fayette, The Eberly Campus *B*
  Greater Allegheny *B*
  Hazleton *B*
  Lehigh Valley *B*
  Mont Alto *B*
  New Kensington *B*
  Schuylkill *B*
  Shenango *B*
  University Park *B*
  Wilkes-Barre *B*
  Worthington Scranton *B*
  York *B*
Rosemont College *B*
University of Pittsburgh
  Johnstown *B*
Villanova University *B*
West Chester University of
  Pennsylvania *B*
Westminster College *B*
Widener University *B*

Puerto Rico
Inter American University of Puerto
  Rico
  Bayamon Campus *B*
  Metropolitan Campus *B, M*
Pontifical Catholic University of
  Puerto Rico *B*
Universidad Metropolitana *B*
University of Puerto Rico
  Rio Piedras *B, M*

Rhode Island
Rhode Island College *B*

South Carolina
Coastal Carolina University *B*
Converse College *B*
Forrest Junior College *A*
Francis Marion University *B*
Limestone College *B*
South Carolina State University *B*
University of South Carolina *B*
Wofford College *B*

South Dakota
Northern State University *A*
University of South Dakota *B*

Tennessee
Belmont University *B, M*
Carson-Newman College *B*
East Tennessee State University *B*
Lambuth University *B*
Lincoln Memorial University *B*
Lipscomb University *B*
Middle Tennessee State University *B*
Rhodes College *B*
Tennessee State University *B*
Tennessee Technological University *B*
Union University *B*
University of Memphis *B*

University of Tennessee
  Knoxville *B, M, D*
  Martin *B*

Texas
Baylor University *B, M*
Dallas Baptist University *B*
Houston Baptist University *B*
Lamar University *B*
Midland College *A*
Midwestern State University *B*
Sam Houston State University *B*
Stephen F. Austin State University *B*
Texas A&M International University *B*
Texas A&M University
  Commerce *B*
  Corpus Christi *B*
  Kingsville *B*
Texas State University: San Marcos *B*
Tyler Junior College *A*
University of Houston *B*
University of North Texas *B*
University of Texas
  Arlington *B*
  El Paso *B, M*
  San Antonio *B, M*
  Tyler *B*
  of the Permian Basin *B*
University of the Incarnate Word *B*
West Texas A&M University *B*

Utah
Brigham Young University *B*
Snow College *A*
Southern Utah University *B*
Weber State University *B*
Westminster College *B*

Virginia
Christopher Newport University *B*
Hampden-Sydney College *B*
Hampton University *B*
James Madison University *B*
Old Dominion University *B*
Randolph-Macon College *B*
Southwest Virginia Community
  College *A*
Virginia Commonwealth
  University *B, M*
Virginia Polytechnic Institute and
  State University *B*
Virginia State University *B, M*
Wytheville Community College *A*

Washington
Eastern Washington University *B*
Gonzaga University *B*
Seattle University *B*

West Virginia
Concord University *B*
Marshall University *B*
Potomac State College of West
  Virginia University *A*
West Liberty University *B*
West Virginia University *B, M, D*
West Virginia Wesleyan College *B*

Wisconsin
Beloit College *B*
Marquette University *B*
University of Wisconsin
  Whitewater *B*

Wyoming
Northwest College *A*
University of Wyoming *B, M, D*

Business statistics

Colorado
University of Denver *B, M*

Iowa
Iowa State University *B*

Massachusetts
Babson College *B*
Bentley University *M*

New York
Manhattan College *B*
Rochester Institute of
Technology *B, M*
Syracuse University *M*

Ohio
Bowling Green State University *M*
Cleveland State University *B*
Wright State University *B*

Oregon
University of Oregon *M, D*

Pennsylvania
La Salle University *B*

Puerto Rico
University of Puerto Rico
Rio Piedras *B, M*

Texas
University of Houston *B, M, D*
University of Texas
Arlington *D*

Utah
Brigham Young University *B*

Business teacher education

Alabama
Alabama Agricultural and Mechanical
University *B, M*
Chattahoochee Valley Community
College *A*
Faulkner State Community College *A*
Oakwood University *B*

Arizona
Eastern Arizona College *A*
Prescott College *B, T*

Arkansas
Arkansas State University *B, M, T*
Arkansas Tech University *B*
Henderson State University *B, T*
Ouachita Baptist University *B, T*
Philander Smith College *B*
Southern Arkansas University *B, T*
University of Arkansas
Pine Bluff *B, T*
University of Central Arkansas *B, M*
University of the Ozarks *B, T*

California
Azusa Pacific University *B, T*
California Baptist University *T*
California State University
Dominguez Hills *M*
Northridge *B, T*
Fresno Pacific University *B, T*
Fullerton College *A*
Humboldt State University *T*
Merritt College *A*
Mount St. Mary's College *T*

Colorado
Adams State College *B, M, T*
Colorado State University *B, T*

Connecticut
Albertus Magnus College *B, T*
Sacred Heart University *T*

Delaware
Delaware State University *B, M*

District of Columbia
University of the District of
Columbia *B*

Florida
Bethune-Cookman University *B, T*
Florida Agricultural and Mechanical
University *B, M, T*
Gulf Coast Community College *A*
St. Petersburg College *B*
University of South Florida *B, M*

Georgia
Armstrong Atlantic State
University *B, T*
Atlanta Christian College *A, B*
Darton College *A*
East Georgia College *A*
Emmanuel College *B*
University of West Georgia *B, M, T*
Valdosta State University *B, M*

Idaho
Boise State University *T*
North Idaho College *A*
University of Idaho *B, M, T*

Illinois
Benedictine University *T*
Chicago State University *B*
Illinois State University *B, T*
McKendree University *B*
Northern Illinois University *M*
Trinity Christian College *B, T*

Indiana
Ball State University *B, M, T*
Bethel College *B*
Calumet College of St. Joseph *T*
Goshen College *B, T*
Grace College *B*
Huntington University *B*
Indiana State University *B, T*
Indiana Wesleyan University *B*
Oakland City University *B*
Saint Mary's College *T*
University of Indianapolis *B, T*
University of St. Francis *B, T*
University of Southern Indiana *B*
Vincennes University *A*

Iowa
Buena Vista University *B, T*
Central College *T*
Dordt College *B*
Drake University *M, T*
Ellsworth Community College *A*
Grand View University *M, T*
Maharishi University of
Management *T*
Mount Mercy College *T*
Northwestern College *T*
St. Ambrose University *B, T*
Simpson College *T*
University of Northern Iowa *B*
Upper Iowa University *T*

Kansas
Bethany College *B*
Butler Community College *A*
Central Christian College of Kansas *A*
Emporia State University *M, T*
Fort Hays State University *B, T*
Garden City Community College *A*
Labette Community College *A*

McPherson College *B, T*
MidAmerica Nazarene University *B, T*
Southwestern College *B, T*
Tabor College *B*

Kentucky
Eastern Kentucky University *B*
Morehead State University *B*
Northern Kentucky University *B*
Thomas More College *B*
University of the Cumberlands *M, T*
Western Kentucky University *B, M, T*

Louisiana
Louisiana College *B*
Louisiana State University and
Agricultural and Mechanical
College *B*
McNeese State University *B, T*
Nicholls State University *B*
Northwestern State University *B*
Our Lady of Holy Cross College *B*
University of Louisiana at Lafayette *B*

Maine
University of Maine
Fort Kent *B*
Machias *B*

Maryland
Mount St. Mary's University *T*
Prince George's Community
College *A*
University of Maryland
Eastern Shore *B*

Massachusetts
Eastern Nazarene College *B*
Northern Essex Community
College *A*
University of Massachusetts
Dartmouth *T*
Western New England College *T*
Westfield State College *B, T*

Michigan
Central Michigan University *B*
Delta College *A*
Eastern Michigan University *B, M*
Ferris State University *B*
Grand Rapids Community College *A*
Siena Heights University *B, T*
University of Michigan
Dearborn *B*
Western Michigan University *B, T*

Minnesota
Bethel University *B*
Concordia College: Moorhead *B, T*
Minnesota State University
Mankato *B, M, T*
Minnesota West Community and
Technical College *A*
Ridgewater College *A*
St. Catherine University *B*
University of Minnesota
Twin Cities *B, M, T*
Vermilion Community College *A*
Winona State University *B, M, T*

Mississippi
Hinds Community College *A*
Millsaps College *T*
Mississippi College *B, M*
Mississippi Delta Community
College *A*
Mississippi Gulf Coast Community
College *A*
Mississippi State University *B, T*
Northwest Mississippi Community
College *A*
Rust College *B*

University of Southern Mississippi *B*

Missouri
College of the Ozarks *B*
Evangel University *B*
Hannibal-LaGrange College *B*
Lincoln University *B*
Lindenwood University *B*
Missouri Baptist University *B, T*
Missouri Southern State
University *B, T*
Missouri State University *B*
Northwest Missouri State
University *B, T*
Southeast Missouri State
University *B, T*
University of Central Missouri *B, M, T*
University of Missouri
Columbia *B*

Montana
University of Montana *B, T*
University of Montana: Western *B, T*

Nebraska
Chadron State College *B, M*
Concordia University *B, T*
Dana College *B*
Grace University *B*
Union College *T*
University of Nebraska
Kearney *B, M, T*
Lincoln *B*
Wayne State College *B, T*
York College *B, T*

Nevada
University of Nevada
Reno *B, T*

New Hampshire
Southern New Hampshire
University *B, M*

New Jersey
Montclair State University *B, M, T*
Rider University *B, M*
Rowan University *T*
Saint Peter's College *T*

New Mexico
Eastern New Mexico University *B*
Western New Mexico University *B*

New York
Alfred University *B, T*
Canisius College *M, T*
D'Youville College *M, T*
Dowling College *B, M*
Hofstra University *B, M*
Nazareth College *B, M, T*
New York Institute of
Technology *B, T*
New York University *B, M, D, T*
Niagara University *B, M, T*
State University of New York
College at Buffalo *B, M, T*
Oswego *B*

North Carolina
Appalachian State University *B, T*
East Carolina University *B*
Elizabeth City State University *B, T*
Fayetteville State University *B, T*
Lenoir-Rhyne University *T*
North Carolina Agricultural and
Technical State University *B, T*

North Dakota
Dickinson State University *B, T*
Minot State University *B*
University of Mary *B*

University of North Dakota *B, M*

Ohio

Ashland University *B, M, T*
Bluffton University *B*
Bowling Green State
    University *B, M, T*
Defiance College *B, T*
Kent State University *B*
Mount Vernon Nazarene
    University *B, T*
University of Rio Grande *B, T*
University of Toledo *B, M, T*
Wright State University *B, M, T*
Youngstown State University *B, M*

Oklahoma

East Central University *B*
Eastern Oklahoma State College *A*
Langston University *B*
Northwestern Oklahoma State
    University *B, T*
Oklahoma City University *B*
Oklahoma Panhandle State
    University *B*
Oklahoma Wesleyan University *B*
Oral Roberts University *B, T*
Southwestern Oklahoma State
    University *T*
University of Central Oklahoma *B*

Oregon

Concordia University *B, M, T*
Corban College *B*
Oregon State University *M*
Portland State University *T*

Pennsylvania

Community College of Philadelphia *A*
Gwynedd-Mercy College *B, T*
Immaculata University *B*
Mercyhurst College *B, T*
Reading Area Community College *A*
Robert Morris University *B, M*
St. Vincent College *B*
Seton Hill University *T*
Temple University *B, T*

Puerto Rico

American University of Puerto
    Rico *B, T*
Caribbean University *B, T*
Inter American University of Puerto
    Rico
    San German Campus *M*
Pontifical Catholic University of
    Puerto Rico *B, D, T*

Rhode Island

Johnson & Wales University:
    Providence *T*

South Carolina

Coker College *B*
South Carolina State University *B, T*
University of South Carolina *M*

South Dakota

Black Hills State University *B*
Dakota State University *B, T*
Dakota Wesleyan University *B, T*
Northern State University *B, T*

Tennessee

Crichton College *B, T*
Lambuth University *B, T*
Lee University *B*
Lincoln Memorial University *B, T*
Middle Tennessee State
    University *B, M, T*
Trevecca Nazarene University *B, T*
Tusculum College *B, T*

Union University *B, T*
University of Memphis *T*

Texas

Hardin-Simmons University *B, T*
Howard Payne University *B, T*
Jarvis Christian College *B, T*
Lamar University *T*
Laredo Community College *A*
LeTourneau University *B, T*
Lubbock Christian University *B*
McMurry University *T*
St. Mary's University *T*
Tarleton State University *T*
Texas A&M University
    Commerce *T*
    Kingsville *T*
Texas Christian University *B*
Texas State University: San Marcos *T*
Texas Wesleyan University *B, T*
University of Mary Hardin-Baylor *T*
Wayland Baptist University *B*
West Texas A&M University *T*

Utah

Snow College *A*
Southern Utah University *B, T*
Utah State University *B, M, D*
Utah Valley University *B*
Weber State University *B*

Virginia

Bluefield College *B, T*
Emory & Henry College *B*
Longwood University *B*
Norfolk State University *B*
St. Paul's College *B*
University of Virginia's College at
    Wise *T*
Virginia State University *B*

Washington

Eastern Washington University *B, M*
Pierce College *A*
Renton Technical College *A*
Walla Walla University *B*

West Virginia

Concord University *B, T*
Davis and Elkins College *B*
Fairmont State University *B*

Wisconsin

Concordia University Wisconsin *B, T*
Edgewood College *B, T*
Lakeland College *T*
Maranatha Baptist Bible College *B*
Mount Mary College *B, T*
University of Wisconsin
    Whitewater *B, M, T*
Viterbo University *B, T*

Wyoming

Eastern Wyoming College *A*

Cabinetmaking/
millwright

Alabama

Jefferson Davis Community College *C*
Lawson State Community College *C*
Northwest-Shoals Community
    College *C*

Arizona

Pima Community College *C*

California

Long Beach City College *C, A*

Florida

Palm Beach Community College *C*

Georgia

Central Georgia Technical College *C*
Columbus Technical College *C*
Savannah Technical College *C*

Indiana

Ivy Tech Community College
    Bloomington *C, A*
    Central Indiana *C, A*
    Lafayette *C, A*
    North Central *C, A*
    Northwest *C, A*
    South Central *C, A*
    Southwest *C, A*

Iowa

Des Moines Area Community
    College *C*

Minnesota

Minneapolis Community and
    Technical College *C, A*
Minnesota State College - Southeast
    Technical *C*
St. Cloud Technical College *C*
St. Paul College *C*
South Central College *C, A*

North Carolina

Tri-County Community College *C*

Ohio

Columbus State Community
    College *A*

Pennsylvania

Harrisburg Area Community
    College *C*
Thaddeus Stevens College of
    Technology *A*

Utah

Salt Lake Community College *C*
Southern Utah University *A*
Utah Valley University *C, A*

Washington

Bates Technical College *C, A*
Grays Harbor College *C*

Wisconsin

Milwaukee Area Technical College *C*

CAD/CADD drafting/
design technology

Alabama

Northeast Alabama Community
    College *C, A*

Arizona

Arizona Western College *C, A*
Cochise College *C*
Coconino County Community
    College *A*
Glendale Community College *C, A*

Arkansas

Arkansas Northeastern College *C*
East Arkansas Community
    College *C, A*
North Arkansas College *C*
Southern Arkansas University Tech *C*
University of Arkansas
    Fort Smith *C, A*

California

Ohlone College *A*
Orange Coast College *C, A*
Southwestern College *C, A*
Taft College *A*

Colorado

Colorado Northwestern Community
    College *C*
Front Range Community College *C, A*
Pikes Peak Community College *C, A*

Connecticut

Naugatuck Valley Community
    College *C, A*
Quinebaug Valley Community
    College *A*
Three Rivers Community College *C, A*

Delaware

Delaware Technical and Community
    College
    Stanton/Wilmington *C, A*
    Terry *C*

Florida

Gulf Coast Community College *C*
Santa Fe College *A*
Valencia Community College *C, A*

Georgia

Central Georgia Technical College *C*
Middle Georgia Technical
    College *C, A*
Savannah Technical College *C*
Southwest Georgia Technical
    College *C*

Idaho

Idaho State University *C, A*

Illinois

Black Hawk College *C*
Danville Area Community College *A*
Elgin Community College *C, A*
Heartland Community College *C, A*
Kaskaskia College *C*
Lincoln Land Community College *C*
Moraine Valley Community College *C*
Morrison Institute of Technology *A*
Morton College *C*
Sauk Valley Community College *C*
Triton College *C*
Vatterott College: Quincy *A*
Waubonsee Community College *C, A*

Indiana

Indiana University-Purdue University
    Indianapolis *A*

Iowa

Hamilton Technical College *A*

Kansas

Brown Mackie College
    Salina *A*
Kansas City Kansas Community
    College *C, A*
Manhattan Area Technical College *A*

Kentucky

Owensboro Community and
    Technical College *C, A*
Sullivan College of Technology and
    Design *C, A*

Louisiana

Bossier Parish Community
    College *C, A*
Herzing University *A*

Maine
Kennebec Valley Community
College *A*
York County Community College *C, A*

Maryland
Cecil College *C, A*
College of Southern Maryland *C*
Frederick Community College *C, A*
Harford Community College *A*
Howard Community College *C, A*

Massachusetts
Mount Wachusett Community
College *C*
Roxbury Community College *A*

Michigan
Baker College
of Muskegon *A*
Bay de Noc Community College *C, A*
Eastern Michigan University *B, M*
Ferris State University *A*
Gogebic Community College *A*
Henry Ford Community College *C, A*
Lake Michigan College *C, A*
Northern Michigan University *A*
Wayne County Community
College *C, A*
West Shore Community College *A*

Minnesota
Century Community and Technical
College *A*
Dunwoody College of Technology *C*
Lake Superior College *C, A*
Minnesota State College - Southeast
Technical *C*
Ridgewater College *C, A*
Rochester Community and Technical
College *C, A*
St. Cloud Technical College *C, A*

Mississippi
Mississippi Gulf Coast Community
College *A*

Missouri
Mineral Area College *C, A*
Missouri Southern State University *A*
Ozarks Technical Community
College *C, A*
State Fair Community College *A*
Vatterott College: Joplin *C, A*
Vatterott College: Springfield *C, A*

Nevada
College of Southern Nevada *C, A*

New Hampshire
University of New Hampshire *A*

New Jersey
Burlington County College *A*
Ocean County College *C*
Thomas Edison State College *C*

New Mexico
Navajo Technical College *A*
Southwestern Indian Polytechnic
Institute *C*

New York
Erie Community College
South Campus *A*
Jamestown Community College *C*
Niagara County Community
College *C, A*

State University of New York
College of Agriculture and
Technology at Morrisville *A*
College of Technology at Alfred *A*
Vaughn College of Aeronautics and
Technology *A*
Westchester Community College *C*

North Carolina
Edgecombe Community College *C*
Gaston College *C*

Ohio
Bryant & Stratton College:
Cleveland *A*
Central Ohio Technical College *C, A*
Edison State Community College *C*
James A. Rhodes State College *C*
Kaplan College: Columbus *A*
Marion Technical College *C*
Miami University
Hamilton Campus *C*
Owens Community College
Toledo *A*
Shawnee State University *C, A*
Southern State Community College *A*
University of Cincinnati
Clermont College *C, A*

Oklahoma
Northeastern Oklahoma Agricultural
and Mechanical College *C, A*

Oregon
Central Oregon Community
College *C, A*
Chemeketa Community College *C, A*
Clackamas Community College *C, A*

Pennsylvania
Community College of
Philadelphia *C, A*
Luzerne County Community
College *C, A*
Montgomery County Community
College *A*
Northampton Community College *A*
Thaddeus Stevens College of
Technology *A*
YTI Career Institute: York *A*

Puerto Rico
Inter American University of Puerto
Rico
San German Campus *C*

Tennessee
Pellissippi State Community
College *A*

Texas
Del Mar College *C*
Eastfield College *C, A*
San Antonio College *C*
Westwood College: Houston South *A*

Utah
College of Eastern Utah *C*
Southern Utah University *A*

Virginia
Mountain Empire Community
College *A*
Norfolk State University *B*
Southwest Virginia Community
College *C, A*
Thomas Nelson Community
College *A*
Tidewater Community College *A*

Washington
Bates Technical College *C*

Clark College *C*
Everett Community College *C, A*
Grays Harbor College *C*
Olympic College *C*
Renton Technical College *C, A*
Shoreline Community College *C, A*
South Seattle Community
College *C, A*

Wisconsin
Herzing University *A, B*
Waukesha County Technical
College *C*

Wyoming
Sheridan College *C, A*

Canadian studies

Indiana
Franklin College *B*

Kentucky
Eastern Kentucky University *B*

New York
St. Lawrence University *B*
State University of New York
College at Plattsburgh *B*

Ohio
Owens Community College
Toledo *A*

Vermont
University of Vermont *B*

Washington
University of Washington *B, M*
Western Washington University *B*

Cardiopulmonary technology

Massachusetts
Northeastern University *B, M*

North Carolina
Johnston Community College *C, A*

Cardiovascular science

Ohio
University of Toledo *D*

Wisconsin
Milwaukee School of Engineering *M*

Cardiovascular technology

California
Butte College *A*
City College of San Francisco *C*
Grossmont College *C, A*
Orange Coast College *C, A*

Connecticut
St. Vincent's College *A*

Delaware
Delaware Technical and Community
College
Stanton/Wilmington *A*

Florida
ATI College of Health *A*
Barry University *B*
Broward College *A*

Edison State College *A*
Polk State College *A*
Santa Fe College *A*
Ultrasound Diagnostic School
Sanford-Brown Institute:
Jacksonville *C, A*
Valencia Community College *A*

Georgia
Augusta Technical College *A*
Columbus Technical College *C, A*
Darton College *A*

Illinois
Harper College *C, A*

Kentucky
Draughons Junior College *C, A*
Spencerian College *A*

Louisiana
Louisiana State University Health
Sciences Center *B*

Maine
Southern Maine Community
College *A*

Maryland
Howard Community College *C, A*

Massachusetts
Bunker Hill Community College *C, A*

Michigan
Kirtland Community College *A*

Minnesota
Minneapolis Community and
Technical College *C*
Northland Community & Technical
College *A*
Rochester Community and Technical
College *A*
St. Cloud Technical College *A*

Nebraska
BryanLGH College of Health
Sciences *A*
Nebraska Methodist College of
Nursing and Allied Health *A, B*

New York
Molloy College *A*
New York University *A*

North Carolina
Caldwell Community College and
Technical Institute *C, A*
Central Piedmont Community
College *A*
Forsyth Technical Community
College *C, A*
Johnston Community College *C*
Stanly Community College *C*

Ohio
University of Toledo *A*

Oklahoma
Bacone College *A*
Oklahoma State University
Oklahoma City *A*

Pennsylvania
Community College of Allegheny
County *A*
Gwynedd-Mercy College *A, B*
Harrisburg Area Community
College *A*

Pennsylvania College of
Technology *B*
Thomas Jefferson University: College
of Health Professions *B*

Puerto Rico
Ponce Paramedical College *C*
Pontifical Catholic University of
Puerto Rico *B*

South Carolina
Medical University of South
Carolina *B*
University of South Carolina *B*

South Dakota
Southeast Technical Institute *A*

Tennessee
Chattanooga State Community
College *C*
Northeast State Community
College *A*

Texas
Alvin Community College *C, A*
El Centro College *A*
Houston Community College
System *C, A*

Virginia
Northern Virginia Community
College *C*

Washington
Spokane Community College *A*

Wisconsin
Milwaukee Area Technical College *A*

Caribbean studies

California
Pitzer College *B*

Florida
Florida State University *B*

Georgia
Emory University *B*

Illinois
University of Chicago *M*
University of Illinois
Urbana-Champaign *M*

New Hampshire
Dartmouth College *B*

New Jersey
Rutgers, The State University of New
Jersey
New Brunswick/Piscataway
Campus *B*
Newark Regional Campus *B*
William Paterson University of New
Jersey *B*

New York
City University of New York
Brooklyn College *B*
City College *B*
Hofstra University *B*
State University of New York
Albany *B, M*

Carpentry

Alabama
Bishop State Community College *C*

Central Alabama Community
College *C*
Gadsden State Community College *C*
Jefferson Davis Community College *C*
Lawson State Community College *C*
Northwest-Shoals Community
College *C*
Shelton State Community College *C*
Southern Union State Community
College *A*

Alaska
Ilisagvik College *C*
University of Alaska
Fairbanks *C, A*

Arizona
Arizona Western College *C*
Central Arizona College *C*
Cochise College *C*
Coconino County Community
College *A*
Eastern Arizona College *C*
GateWay Community College *C, A*
Mohave Community College *C*
Northland Pioneer College *C, A*
Tohono O'odham Community
College *C, A*

Arkansas
University of Arkansas
Cossatot Community College of the
A

California
Bakersfield College *A*
College of the Sequoias *C, A*
Fresno City College *C, A*
Fullerton College *A*
Hartnell College *C*
Laney College *C, A*
Long Beach City College *C, A*
Los Angeles Trade and Technical
College *C, A*
Palomar College *C, A*
Pasadena City College *C, A*
Porterville College *C, A*
San Joaquin Delta College *C, A*
Santa Rosa Junior College *C*
Santiago Canyon College *A*
Sierra College *C, A*
Victor Valley College *A*

Colorado
Community College of Aurora *A*
Pueblo Community College *A*
Red Rocks Community College *C, A*
Trinidad State Junior College *C*

Florida
Florida State College at Jacksonville *C*
Hillsborough Community College *C*
Indian River State College *C*
Palm Beach Community College *C*
Santa Fe College *C*

Georgia
Albany Technical College *C, A*
Central Georgia Technical College *C*
Columbus Technical College *C*
Gwinnett Technical College *C*
Savannah Technical College *C*
West Georgia Technical College *C*

Hawaii
University of Hawaii
Hawaii Community College *C, A*
Honolulu Community College *C, A*
Kauai Community College *C, A*
Maui Community College *A*

Idaho
Idaho State University *C, A*
North Idaho College *C, A*

Illinois
Black Hawk College *C, A*
John A. Logan College *A*
Kaskaskia College *C, A*
Southeastern Illinois College *C*
Southwestern Illinois College *C, A*

Indiana
Ivy Tech Community College
Central Indiana *C, A*
East Central *C, A*
Lafayette *C, A*
North Central *C, A*
Northwest *C, A*
Southwest *C, A*
Wabash Valley *C, A*

Iowa
Des Moines Area Community
College *C*
Ellsworth Community College *C, A*
Iowa Central Community College *C*
Iowa Lakes Community College *C*
Kirkwood Community College *C*
North Iowa Area Community
College *C*
Northeast Iowa Community
College *C, A*
Northwest Iowa Community
College *C, A*
Southeastern Community College
North Campus *C, A*
Southwestern Community
College *C, A*
Western Iowa Tech Community
College *C*

Kansas
Coffeyville Community College *C*
Hutchinson Community College *C, A*
Kansas City Kansas Community
College *C*
Manhattan Area Technical
College *C, A*

Kentucky
Bluegrass Community and Technical
College *C, A*
Elizabethtown Community and
Technical College *C*
Hopkinsville Community College *C*
Madisonville Community College *C*
Maysville Community and Technical
College *C*
Owensboro Community and
Technical College *C, A*
Somerset Community College *C, A*
West Kentucky Community and
Technical College *C*

Louisiana
Delgado Community College *C*
Nunez Community College *C*

Maine
Eastern Maine Community College *A*
Northern Maine Community
College *C, A*
Washington County Community
College *C*

Michigan
Bay de Noc Community College *C*
Delta College *A*
Gogebic Community College *A*
Kirtland Community College *C, A*
Lansing Community College *C, A*
Oakland Community College *C, A*

Minnesota
Alexandria Technical College *C*
Hennepin Technical College *C, A*
Lake Superior College *C, A*
Leech Lake Tribal College *C*
Mesabi Range Community and
Technical College *A*
Minneapolis Community and
Technical College *C*
Minnesota State College - Southeast
Technical *C, A*
Minnesota State Community and
Technical College *C, A*
Minnesota West Community and
Technical College *C*
Northland Community & Technical
College *C*
Northwest Technical College *C*
Ridgewater College *C, A*
Riverland Community College *C*
Rochester Community and Technical
College *C*
St. Cloud Technical College *C, A*
St. Paul College *C*

Mississippi
Hinds Community College *C*
Mississippi Gulf Coast Community
College *C*
Pearl River Community College *C, A*
Southwest Mississippi Community
College *C*

Missouri
Ranken Technical College *A*

Montana
Flathead Valley Community College *C*
Helena College of Technology of the
University of Montana *C, A*
Little Big Horn College *C*
Miles Community College *A*
Montana State University
College of Technology: Great
Falls *C, A*
Montana Tech of the University of
Montana *C, A*
Salish Kootenai College *C*

Nebraska
Nebraska Indian Community
College *C, A*

Nevada
Truckee Meadows Community
College *C, A*

New Mexico
Central New Mexico Community
College *C*
Navajo Technical College *C*
New Mexico State University
Carlsbad *C*
San Juan College *C, A*

New York
Hudson Valley Community College *A*
Mohawk Valley Community College *C*
State University of New York
College of Agriculture and
Technology at Morrisville *A*
College of Technology at Alfred *A*
College of Technology at Delhi *C, A*

North Carolina
Alamance Community College *C*
Asheville-Buncombe Technical
Community College *C*
Bladen Community College *C*
Blue Ridge Community College *C*
Cape Fear Community College *C*
Cleveland Community College *C*

College of the Albemarle *C*
Fayetteville Technical Community College *C*
Forsyth Technical Community College *C*
Guilford Technical Community College *C*
Martin Community College *C*
McDowell Technical Community College *C*
Piedmont Community College *C*
Rowan-Cabarrus Community College *C*
Sampson Community College *C, A*
Surry Community College *C, A*
Vance-Granville Community College *C*

North Dakota
Bismarck State College *C, A*
Sitting Bull College *C, A*

Ohio
Hocking College *A*

Oregon
Linn-Benton Community College *A*

Pennsylvania
Community College of Allegheny County *C*
Harrisburg Area Community College *C*
Johnson College *A*
Pennsylvania College of Technology *C*
Thaddeus Stevens College of Technology *A*
Triangle Tech
  DuBois *A*
  Erie *A*
  Greensburg *A*
  Pittsburgh *A*
Triangle Tech: Bethlehem *A*
Triangle Tech: Sunbury *A*
Williamson Free School of Mechanical Trades *A*

Puerto Rico
Inter American University of Puerto Rico
  San German Campus *C*

Rhode Island
New England Institute of Technology *A*

South Carolina
Bob Jones University *B*
Greenville Technical College *C*
Technical College of the Lowcountry *C*
York Technical College *C*

South Dakota
Lake Area Technical Institute *C*
Mitchell Technical Institute *A*
Oglala Lakota College *A*
Sisseton Wahpeton College *C, A*
Western Dakota Technical Institute *C*

Texas
Austin Community College *C, A*
Houston Community College System *C*
Howard College *C*
Laredo Community College *C*
North Lake College *C*
Odessa College *C, A*
Paris Junior College *A*
St. Philip's College *A*

Utah
Salt Lake Community College *C, A*
Southern Utah University *A*

Virginia
Southwest Virginia Community College *C*
Wytheville Community College *C, A*

Washington
Bates Technical College *C, A*
Grays Harbor College *C, A*
Green River Community College *A*
Peninsula College *C*
Renton Technical College *C, A*
Spokane Community College *C, A*

Wisconsin
Chippewa Valley Technical College *C*
College of Menominee Nation *C*
Gateway Technical College *C*
Lac Courte Oreilles Ojibwa Community College *C*
Lakeshore Technical College *C*
Milwaukee Area Technical College *C*
Waukesha County Technical College *C*
Western Technical College *C*
Wisconsin Indianhead Technical College *C*

Wyoming
Central Wyoming College *C, A*

Cartography

Alabama
Samford University *B*

Arizona
Coconino County Community College *C*
Northern Arizona University *B*

Arkansas
East Arkansas Community College *C*
University of Arkansas
  Fort Smith *C*

California
California State University
  Chico *C*
Riverside Community College *C, A*

Colorado
Mesa State College *C*

Georgia
Kennesaw State University *B*

Idaho
University of Idaho *B*

Illinois
DePaul University *C*

Iowa
Iowa Lakes Community College *A*

Kentucky
Western Kentucky University *C, B*

Maryland
College of Southern Maryland *C*
Montgomery College *C*

Massachusetts
Salem State College *B*
University of Massachusetts
  Boston *C*

Michigan
Michigan Technological University *C*
Northern Michigan University *A, B*

Minnesota
Alexandria Technical College *C*
Fond du Lac Tribal and Community College *C, A*
Saint Cloud State University *M*

Missouri
Missouri State University *B*

Montana
University of Montana *B, M*

Nebraska
University of Nebraska
  Omaha *C*

New Mexico
Southwestern Indian Polytechnic Institute *C, A*

New York
State University of New York
  Binghamton *B*

Ohio
University of Akron *C, A, B*

Oklahoma
East Central University *B*

South Carolina
Greenville Technical College *C, A*
Midlands Technical College *C*

Tennessee
Pellissippi State Community College *A*
Roane State Community College *C, A*

Texas
Houston Community College System *C, A*
Lone Star College System *C, A*
San Jacinto College *C*
Stephen F. Austin State University *B*
Tarrant County College *C, A*
Temple College *C, A*
Texas A&M University *B*
Texas State University: San Marcos *B, M, D*
University of Texas
  Dallas *M, D*

Utah
Brigham Young University *B, M*

Wisconsin
University of Wisconsin
  Madison *B, M*

Cell biology and histology

Alabama
University of Alabama
  Birmingham *D*

Arizona
Northern Arizona University *B*
University of Arizona *B, M, D*

California
California Institute of Technology *D*
California State University
  Dominguez Hills *B*
  Fresno *B*
  Long Beach *B*
  Northridge *B*
San Francisco State University *B, M*
Stanford University *M, D*
University of California
  Davis *B, M, D*
  Irvine *B, M, D*
  San Diego *B*
  Santa Barbara *B, M, D*
University of Southern California *M, D*

Connecticut
Quinnipiac University *M*
University of Connecticut *M, D*
University of New Haven *M*
Yale University *M, D*

District of Columbia
Catholic University of America *M, D*
Georgetown University *D*

Florida
University of Miami *D*

Georgia
University of Georgia *B, M, D*

Illinois
University of Chicago *D*
University of Illinois
  Urbana-Champaign *B, D*

Indiana
University of Indianapolis *B*

Iowa
Iowa State University *M, D*

Louisiana
Tulane University *B, M, D*

Maine
Colby College *B*
University of Maine *B, M, D*

Maryland
Johns Hopkins University *B, M, D*
University of Maryland
  Baltimore County *D*

Massachusetts
Boston University *D*
Harvard College *M, D*
Tufts University *D*

Michigan
University of Michigan *D*

Minnesota
Southwest Minnesota State University *B*
University of Minnesota
  Duluth *B, M*
  Twin Cities *B, M, D*
Winona State University *B*

Missouri
Washington University in St. Louis *D*

New Hampshire
Dartmouth College *B*

New Jersey
Rutgers, The State University of New Jersey
  New Brunswick/Piscataway Campus *B, M, D*

New York

College of Saint Rose *B*
Long Island University
  C. W. Post Campus *B*
New York University *M, D*
State University of New York
  Albany *M, D*
  College at Plattsburgh *B*
University of Rochester *B*
Yeshiva University *M, D*

North Carolina

Duke University *M, D*
East Carolina University *D*
University of North Carolina
  Chapel Hill *M, D*

Ohio

Case Western Reserve University *D*
Kent State University *M, D*
Ohio State University
  Columbus Campus *M, D*

Oklahoma

Northeastern State University *B*
Oklahoma City University *B*
University of Oklahoma *M, D*

Oregon

Oregon Health & Science
  University *D*

Pennsylvania

Juniata College *B*
Mansfield University of
  Pennsylvania *B*
Temple University *M*
University of Pittsburgh *M, D*

Rhode Island

Brown University *B, M, D*

South Carolina

Medical University of South
  Carolina *D*

Texas

Texas A&M University
  Commerce *B*
University of Texas
  Health Science Center at
    Houston *M, D*
  Health Science Center at San
    Antonio *M, D*

Utah

University of Utah *B*

Vermont

Johnson State College *B*
Marlboro College *B*

Virginia

University of Virginia *D*

Washington

University of Washington *M, D*
Western Washington University *B*

Wisconsin

Marquette University *M, D*
University of Wisconsin
  Superior *B*

Cell physiology

California

University of California
  Davis *M, D*

Ohio

Case Western Reserve University *D*

West Virginia

West Virginia University *D*

Cellular/anatomical biology

Alabama

Huntingdon College *B*

Georgia

Medical College of Georgia *M, D*

Illinois

Loyola University Chicago *M, D*
University of Illinois
  Chicago *M, D*

Iowa

University of Iowa *M, D*

Kansas

University of Kansas Medical
  Center *M, D*

Minnesota

Saint Cloud State University *B*

Nebraska

University of Nebraska
  Medical Center *M, D*

Pennsylvania

Washington & Jefferson College *B*

Texas

University of Texas
  Health Science Center at
    Houston *M, D*

Wisconsin

Marquette University *M, D*

Cellular/molecular biology

Arizona

Arizona State University *M, D*
Northern Arizona University *B*

Arkansas

Arkansas State University *D*
University of Arkansas *M, D*

California

University of California
  Berkeley *B, M, D*
  Irvine *D*
  Los Angeles *B, M, D*
  Riverside *M, D*
  Santa Cruz *B, M, D*
University of California: Merced *M, D*
University of Southern
  California *M, D*

Colorado

Colorado State University *M, D*
University of Colorado
  Boulder *B, D*
  Denver *D*

Connecticut

Connecticut College *B*
University of Connecticut *B*
Yale University *M, D*

Florida

Florida Institute of Technology *M*
University of Florida *M*

Hawaii

University of Hawaii
  Manoa *M, D*

Idaho

Northwest Nazarene University *B*

Illinois

Bradley University *B*
University of Illinois
  Urbana-Champaign *B, M, D*

Indiana

Indiana University
  Bloomington *D*
Purdue University *B, M, D*

Iowa

Drake University *B*

Kansas

Pittsburg State University *B*
University of Kansas *M, D*

Maryland

University of Maryland
  Baltimore County *M*
  College Park *M, D*

Massachusetts

Bridgewater State College *B*
Harvard College *M, D*
University of Massachusetts
  Amherst *M, D*

Michigan

Grand Valley State University *B*
Michigan State University *M, D*
University of Michigan *B, M, D*

Missouri

Missouri State University *B, M*
Washington University in St. Louis *D*

Montana

University of Montana *B*
University of Montana: Western *B*

Nevada

University of Nevada
  Reno *M, D*

New York

State University of New York
  Binghamton *B*
  College at Brockport *B*
  Stony Brook *D*

North Carolina

Methodist University *B*
Wake Forest University *M, D*

North Dakota

North Dakota State University *D*

Ohio

Cedarville University *B*
Ohio University *B, D*

Oregon

Oregon State University *D*

Pennsylvania

Bucknell University *B*
Drexel University *M, D*

Penn State

  University Park *M, D*
University of Pennsylvania *M, D*
University of the Sciences in
  Philadelphia *M, D*

Tennessee

Union University *B*

Texas

Texas A&M University *B*
Texas Tech University *B*
University of Texas
  Austin *M, D*
  Dallas *M, D*
  Health Science Center at
    Houston *M, D*
  Medical Branch at Galveston *M, D*
  San Antonio *D*
  Southwestern Medical Center at
    Dallas *M, D*

Utah

University of Utah *D*

Vermont

Bennington College *B*
University of Vermont *M, D*

Virginia

Marymount University *B*

Washington

University of Puget Sound *B*
Western Washington University *B*

Wisconsin

Beloit College *B*
Marquette University *M, D*

Wyoming

University of Wyoming *D*

Celtic languages

California

University of California
  Berkeley *B*

Massachusetts

Boston College *M*
Harvard College *M, D*

Central Asian studies

Massachusetts

Harvard College *D*

Central/Middle/Eastern European studies

California

San Diego State University *B*

Connecticut

Wesleyan University *B*

Florida

Florida State University *B*

Illinois

Illinois Wesleyan University *B*

Maine

Bowdoin College *B*

Massachusetts

Amherst College *B*
Bard College at Simon's Rock *B*

Tufts University *B, M*
Wellesley College *B*

Michigan
Michigan State University *B*

Minnesota
Augsburg College *B*

New Jersey
Rutgers, The State University of New
Jersey
New Brunswick/Piscataway
Campus *B*

New York
Columbia University *B*
State University of New York
Albany *B*

Ohio
Ohio State University
Columbus Campus *B, M*

Oregon
Portland State University *B*

Pennsylvania
La Salle University *B, M*

Tennessee
Vanderbilt University *B*

Vermont
Marlboro College *B*
Middlebury College *B*

Washington
University of Washington *B, M*

Ceramic sciences/ engineering

Illinois
University of Illinois
Urbana-Champaign *B, M, D*

Missouri
University of Missouri
Missouri University of Science and
Technology *B, M, D*

New Jersey
Rutgers, The State University of New
Jersey
Camden Regional Campus *B*
New Brunswick/Piscataway
Campus *B, M, D*
Newark Regional Campus *B*

New York
Alfred University *B, M, D*

Ohio
Ohio State University
Columbus Campus *B*

South Carolina
Clemson University *B, M, D*

Washington
University of Washington *B*

Ceramics

Arizona
Northern Arizona University *C, B*
Prescott College *B*

California
Butte College *C, A*
California College of the Arts *B, M*
California State University
East Bay *B*
Long Beach *B, M*
Northridge *B, M*
Chabot College *A*
De Anza College *C, A*
Glendale Community College *C*
Grossmont College *A*
Laney College *A*
Monterey Peninsula College *C, A*
Ohlone College *C*
Palomar College *A*
Pasadena City College *C, A*
San Francisco Art Institute *B, M*
Santa Rosa Junior College *C*
Ventura College *C, A*
West Los Angeles College *C, A*

Colorado
Adams State College *B*

Connecticut
University of Hartford *B*

District of Columbia
George Washington University *M*

Florida
University of Miami *B*

Idaho
Northwest Nazarene University *B*

Illinois
Bradley University *B*
Lincoln College *A*
Richland Community College *A*
School of the Art Institute of
Chicago *B, M*

Indiana
Indiana University-Purdue University
Indianapolis *B*
Indiana Wesleyan University *B*

Iowa
Coe College *B*
University of Iowa *B, M*

Kansas
Allen County Community College *A*
Pittsburg State University *B*
Pratt Community College *A*
Seward County Community College *A*
University of Kansas *B, M*

Kentucky
Eastern Kentucky University *B*

Maine
Maine College of Art *B*

Maryland
Hood College *M*
Maryland Institute College of Art *B*

Massachusetts
Bard College at Simon's Rock *B*
Massachusetts College of Art and
Design *B, M*
School of the Museum of Fine
Arts *B, M*
University of Massachusetts
Dartmouth *B, M*

Michigan
Andrews University *B*
College for Creative Studies *B*

Finlandia University *B*
Grand Valley State University *B*
Northern Michigan University *A, B*
Oakland Community College *C, A*
Siena Heights University *B*
University of Michigan *B*
University of Michigan
Flint *B*

Minnesota
Minnesota State University
Mankato *B, M*
Saint Cloud State University *B*

Missouri
Columbia College *B*
Kansas City Art Institute *B*
Washington University in St.
Louis *B, M*

Nevada
Sierra Nevada College *B*

New Jersey
Cumberland County College *C, A*

New York
Alfred University *B, M*
Hofstra University *B*
Rochester Institute of
Technology *A, B, M*
State University of New York
College at Fredonia *B*
New Paltz *B, M*

North Carolina
East Carolina University *B*
Elon University *B*
Gardner-Webb University *B*
Haywood Community College *A*
Methodist University *B*

Ohio
Bowling Green State University *B*
Cleveland Institute of Art *B*
Edison State Community College *C*
Ohio State University
Columbus Campus *B, M*
Ohio University *B, M*
Shawnee State University *B*
University of Akron *B*

Oregon
Mt. Hood Community College *A*
Oregon College of Art & Craft *C, B*
University of Oregon *B, M*

Pennsylvania
Arcadia University *B*
Edinboro University of
Pennsylvania *B*
Keystone College *A, B*
Marywood University *B, M*
Seton Hill University *B*
Temple University *B, M*
University of the Arts *M*

Puerto Rico
Inter American University of Puerto
Rico
San German Campus *B, M*

Rhode Island
Providence College *B*
Rhode Island School of Design *B, M*
Salve Regina University *B*

Tennessee
Tennessee Technological University *B*

Texas
Texas A&M University
Commerce *B, M*
Texas Christian University *B*
University of Dallas *B, M*
University of Houston *B, M*
University of Texas
El Paso *B, M*
Western Texas College *A*

Utah
Brigham Young University *M*

Vermont
Bennington College *B*
Marlboro College *B*

Virginia
Lord Fairfax Community College *C*

Washington
University of Washington *B, M*
Western Washington University *B*

West Virginia
West Virginia State University *B*
West Virginia Wesleyan College *B*

Wisconsin
University of Wisconsin
Madison *B*

Wyoming
Western Wyoming Community
College *A*

Chemical engineering

Alabama
Auburn University *B, M, D*
Tuskegee University *B*
University of Alabama *B, M, D*
University of Alabama
Huntsville *B*
University of South Alabama *B, M*

Arizona
Arizona State University *B, M, D*
University of Arizona *B, M, D*

Arkansas
University of Arkansas *B, M*

California
California Institute of
Technology *B, M, D*
California State Polytechnic
University: Pomona *B*
California State University
Long Beach *B*
Northridge *B, M*
San Jose State University *B, M*
Stanford University *B, M, D*
University of California
Berkeley *B, M, D*
Davis *B, M, D*
Irvine *B, M, D*
Los Angeles *B, M, D*
Riverside *B*
San Diego *B, M, D*
Santa Barbara *B, M, D*
University of Southern
California *B, M, D*

Colorado
Colorado School of Mines *B, M, D*
Colorado State University *B, M, D*
University of Colorado
Boulder *B, M, D*

Connecticut
University of Connecticut *B, M, D*
University of New Haven *B*
Yale University *B, M, D*

Delaware
University of Delaware *B, M, D*

District of Columbia
Howard University *B, M*

Florida
Florida Agricultural and Mechanical
  University *B, M, D*
Florida Institute of
  Technology *B, M, D*
Florida State University *B, M, D*
University of Florida *B, M*
University of South Florida *B, M, D*

Georgia
Georgia Institute of
  Technology *B, M, D*
University of Georgia *B, M*

Idaho
North Idaho College *A*
Northwest Nazarene University *B*
University of Idaho *B, M, D*

Illinois
Dominican University *B*
Illinois Institute of
  Technology *B, M, D*
Northwestern University *B, M, D*
University of Illinois
  Chicago *B, M, D*
  Urbana-Champaign *B, M, D*

Indiana
Purdue University *B, M, D*
Rose-Hulman Institute of
  Technology *B, M*
Trine University *B*
University of Notre Dame *B, M, D*
Vincennes University *A*

Iowa
Iowa State University *B, M, D*
University of Iowa *B, M, D*

Kansas
Kansas State University *B, M, D*
University of Kansas *B, M*

Kentucky
University of Kentucky *B, M, D*
University of Louisville *B, M, D*

Louisiana
Louisiana State University and
  Agricultural and Mechanical
  College *B, M, D*
Louisiana Tech University *B*
Tulane University *B, M, D*
University of Louisiana at
  Lafayette *B, M*

Maine
University of Maine *B, M, D*

Maryland
Johns Hopkins University *B, M, D*
University of Maryland
  Baltimore County *B, M, D*
  College Park *B, M, D*

Massachusetts
Massachusetts Institute of
  Technology *B, M, D*
Northeastern University *B, M, D*

Smith College *B*
Tufts University *B, M, D*
University of Massachusetts
  Amherst *B, M, D*
  Lowell *B, M*
Worcester Polytechnic
  Institute *B, M, D*

Michigan
Calvin College *B*
Michigan State University *B, M, D*
Michigan Technological
  University *B, M, D*
University of Michigan *B, M, D*
Wayne State University *B, M, D*
Western Michigan University *B*

Minnesota
University of Minnesota
  Duluth *B*
  Twin Cities *B, M, D*

Mississippi
Mississippi State University *B, M*
University of Mississippi *B*

Missouri
University of Missouri
  Columbia *B, M, D*
  Missouri University of Science and
    Technology *B, M, D*
Washington University in St.
  Louis *B, M, D*

Montana
Montana State University
  Bozeman *B, M*

Nebraska
University of Nebraska
  Lincoln *B, M*
  Omaha *B*

Nevada
University of Nevada
  Reno *B, M, D*

New Hampshire
University of New Hampshire *B, M, D*

New Jersey
New Jersey Institute of
  Technology *B, M, D*
Princeton University *B, M, D*
Rowan University *B*
Rutgers, The State University of New
  Jersey
  Camden Regional Campus *B*
  New Brunswick/Piscataway
    Campus *B, M, D*
  Newark Regional Campus *B*
Stevens Institute of
  Technology *B, M, D*

New Mexico
New Mexico Institute of Mining and
  Technology *B*
New Mexico State University *B, M*
University of New Mexico *B, M*

New York
City University of New York
  City College *B, M, D*
  Hostos Community College *A*
Clarkson University *B, M, D*
Columbia University *B, M, D*
Cooper Union for the Advancement of
  Science and Art *B, M*
Cornell University *B, M, D*
Manhattan College *B, M*
Polytechnic Institute of New York
  University *B, M, D*

Rensselaer Polytechnic
  Institute *B, M, D*
Rochester Institute of Technology *B*
State University of New York
  Buffalo *B, M, D*
Syracuse University *B, D*
United States Military Academy *B*
University of Rochester *B, M, D*

North Carolina
Elon University *B*
North Carolina Agricultural and
  Technical State University *B*
North Carolina State
  University *B, M, D*

North Dakota
University of North Dakota *B, M*

Ohio
Case Western Reserve
  University *B, M, D*
Cleveland State University *B, M, D*
Miami University
  Oxford Campus *B*
Ohio State University
  Columbus Campus *B, M, D*
Ohio University *B, M, D*
University of Akron *B, M, D*
University of Cincinnati *B, M, D*
University of Dayton *B, M*
University of Toledo *B, M*
Wilberforce University *B*
Youngstown State University *B, M*

Oklahoma
Oklahoma State University *B, M, D*
University of Oklahoma *B, M, D*
University of Tulsa *B, M, D*

Oregon
Oregon State University *B, M, D*

Pennsylvania
Bucknell University *B, M*
Carnegie Mellon University *B, M, D*
Drexel University *B, M, D*
Gannon University *B*
Geneva College *B*
Gettysburg College *B*
Lafayette College *B*
Lehigh University *B, M, D*
Penn State
  Abington *B*
  Altoona *B*
  Beaver *B*
  Berks *B*
  Brandywine *B*
  DuBois *B*
  Erie, The Behrend College *B*
  Fayette, The Eberly Campus *B*
  Greater Allegheny *B*
  Hazleton *B*
  Lehigh Valley *B*
  Mont Alto *B*
  New Kensington *B*
  Schuylkill *B*
  Shenango *B*
  University Park *B, M, D*
  Wilkes-Barre *B*
  Worthington Scranton *B*
  York *B*
University of Pennsylvania *B, M, D*
University of Pittsburgh *B, M, D*
University of Pittsburgh
  Bradford *B*
Villanova University *B, M*
Widener University *B, M*

Puerto Rico
Universidad Politecnica de Puerto
  Rico *B*

University of Puerto Rico
  Ponce *A*

Rhode Island
Brown University *B, M, D*
University of Rhode Island *B, M, D*

South Carolina
Clemson University *B, M, D*
University of South Carolina *B, M, D*

South Dakota
South Dakota School of Mines and
  Technology *B, M*

Tennessee
Christian Brothers University *B*
Tennessee Technological
  University *B, M, D*
University of Tennessee
  Knoxville *B, M, D*
Vanderbilt University *B, M, D*

Texas
Kilgore College *A*
Lamar University *B, M, D*
Prairie View A&M University *B*
Rice University *B, M, D*
Texas A&M University *B, M, D*
Texas A&M University
  Kingsville *B, M*
Texas Tech University *B, M, D*
University of Houston *B, M, D*
University of Texas
  Austin *B, M, D*

Utah
Brigham Young University *B, M, D*
College of Eastern Utah *A, T*
Southern Utah University *A*
University of Utah *B, M, D*

Virginia
Hampton University *B*
University of Virginia *B, M, D*
Virginia Commonwealth University *B*
Virginia Polytechnic Institute and
  State University *B, M, D*
Washington and Lee University *B*

Washington
University of Washington *B, M, D*
Washington State University *B, M, D*

West Virginia
West Virginia University *B, M, D*
West Virginia University Institute of
  Technology *B*

Wisconsin
University of Wisconsin
  Madison *B, M, D*

Wyoming
University of Wyoming *B, M, D*

Chemical physics

Arkansas
Hendrix College *B*

California
University of California
  San Diego *B*
University of Southern California *D*

Colorado
Adams State College *B*
University of Colorado
  Boulder *D*

Florida
Florida State University *M, D*

Illinois
University of Illinois
    Urbana-Champaign *M, D*

Iowa
University of Iowa *M*

Kentucky
Centre College *B*

Maine
Bowdoin College *B*

Maryland
University of Maryland
    College Park *M, D*

Michigan
Michigan State University *B, D*
Saginaw Valley State University *B*

Nevada
University of Nevada
    Reno *D*

New York
Barnard College *B*
Columbia University *B*
Hamilton College *B*

Ohio
College of Wooster *B*

Pennsylvania
Carnegie Mellon University *B*
Swarthmore College *B*

Rhode Island
Brown University *B*

Tennessee
Maryville College *B*
Union University *B*

Texas
Rice University *B*

Utah
University of Utah *D*

Wisconsin
Marquette University *M, D*

Chemical technology

Alabama
Jefferson Davis Community College *C*
Northwest-Shoals Community
    College *C*

California
Ohlone College *C*

Delaware
Delaware Technical and Community
    College
    Stanton/Wilmington *A*

Florida
Pensacola Junior College *A*

Indiana
Ball State University *A*
Indiana University-Purdue University
    Fort Wayne *A*

Iowa
Iowa Central Community College *A*

Kansas
Hutchinson Community College *C*

Massachusetts
Massachusetts Bay Community
    College *A*

Michigan
Delta College *C, A*
Ferris State University *A*
Grand Rapids Community College *A*
Lawrence Technological University *A*

Minnesota
North Hennepin Community
    College *C*
St. Paul College *A*

New Jersey
Burlington County College *A*
Essex County College *C, A*

New York
City University of New York
    New York City College of
        Technology *A*
Corning Community College *A*
Excelsior College *A*
Mohawk Valley Community College *A*
State University of New York
    College of Agriculture and
        Technology at Cobleskill *A*

North Carolina
Guilford Technical Community
    College *A*
Lenoir-Rhyne University *B*

Ohio
Miami University
    Oxford Campus *A*
University of Cincinnati
    Raymond Walters College *A*

Pennsylvania
Community College of Allegheny
    County *A*
Community College of Philadelphia *A*
Lehigh Carbon Community College *A*
Millersville University of
    Pennsylvania *A*
Northampton Community College *A*
Westmoreland County Community
    College *A*

Puerto Rico
University of Puerto Rico
    Humacao *A*

Rhode Island
Community College of Rhode
    Island *C, A*

South Carolina
Midlands Technical College *C*
York Technical College *C*

South Dakota
Dakota State University *B*

Tennessee
Chattanooga State Community
    College *C*

Texas
Alvin Community College *C, A*
Del Mar College *C, A*

Houston Community College
    System *C, A*
Lamar Institute of Technology *A*
Lamar State College at Orange *C, A*
San Jacinto College *C, A*
Texas State Technical College
    Harlingen *A*
Wharton County Junior College *A*

Utah
Salt Lake Community College *A*

Washington
Big Bend Community College *C*

Wisconsin
Milwaukee Area Technical College *A*

Chemistry

Alabama
Alabama Agricultural and Mechanical
    University *B*
Alabama State University *B*
Athens State University *B*
Auburn University *B, M, D*
Birmingham-Southern College *B*
Calhoun Community College *A*
Chattahoochee Valley Community
    College *A*
Faulkner State Community College *A*
Gadsden State Community College *A*
Huntingdon College *B*
Jacksonville State University *B*
Judson College *B*
Miles College *B*
Oakwood University *B*
Samford University *B*
Southern Union State Community
    College *A*
Spring Hill College *B, T*
Talladega College *B*
Troy University *B*
Tuskegee University *B, M*
University of Alabama *B, M, D*
University of Alabama
    Birmingham *B, M, D*
    Huntsville *B, M*
University of Montevallo *B, T*
University of North Alabama *B*
University of South Alabama *B*
University of West Alabama *B, T*

Alaska
University of Alaska
    Anchorage *B*
    Fairbanks *B, M, D*

Arizona
Arizona State University *B, M, D*
Arizona Western College *A*
Central Arizona College *A*
Cochise College *A*
Eastern Arizona College *A*
Mesa Community College *A*
Northern Arizona University *B, M*
Phoenix College *A*
University of Arizona *B, M, D*

Arkansas
Arkansas State University *B, M*
Arkansas Tech University *B*
Harding University *B*
Henderson State University *B*
Hendrix College *B*
John Brown University *B*
Lyon College *B*
Ouachita Baptist University *B*
Philander Smith College *B*
Phillips Community College of the
    University of Arkansas *A*
Southern Arkansas University *A, B*

University of Arkansas *B, M, D*
University of Arkansas
    Fort Smith *B*
    Little Rock *B, M*
    Monticello *B*
    Pine Bluff *B*
University of Central Arkansas *B*
University of the Ozarks *B*

California
Allan Hancock College *A*
Azusa Pacific University *B*
Bakersfield College *A*
Biola University *B*
Cabrillo College *A*
California Baptist University *B*
California Institute of
    Technology *B, M, D*
California Lutheran University *B*
California Polytechnic State
    University: San Luis Obispo *B*
California State Polytechnic
    University: Pomona *B, M*
California State University
    Bakersfield *B*
    Chico *C, B*
    Dominguez Hills *B*
    East Bay *B, M*
    Fresno *B, M*
    Fullerton *B, M*
    Long Beach *B, M*
    Los Angeles *B, M*
    Northridge *B, M*
    Sacramento *B, M*
    San Bernardino *B*
    San Marcos *B*
    Stanislaus *B*
California State University: Channel
    Islands *B*
Canada College *A*
Cerritos College *A*
Chaffey College *A*
Chapman University *B*
Citrus College *A*
City College of San Francisco *A*
Claremont McKenna College *B*
College of Marin: Kentfield *A*
College of San Mateo *A*
College of the Desert *A*
College of the Siskiyous *A*
Columbia College *A*
Concordia University *B*
Contra Costa College *A*
Crafton Hills College *C, A*
Cuesta College *C, A*
Cypress College *A*
De Anza College *A*
East Los Angeles College *A*
El Camino College *A*
El Camino College: Compton
    Center *A*
Foothill College *A*
Fresno City College *A*
Fresno Pacific University *B*
Fullerton College *A*
Gavilan College *A*
Glendale Community College *A*
Golden West College *A*
Grossmont College *C, A*
Hartnell College *A*
Harvey Mudd College *B*
Humboldt State University *B*
Irvine Valley College *A*
La Sierra University *B*
Los Angeles City College *A*
Los Angeles Southwest College *A*
Los Angeles Valley College *A*
Los Medanos College *A*
Loyola Marymount University *B*
Merced College *A*
Mills College *B*
MiraCosta College *A*
Mission College *A*
Monterey Peninsula College *A*

Moorpark College *A*
Mount St. Mary's College *B*
Occidental College *B*
Orange Coast College *A*
Pacific Union College *B*
Palomar College *C, A*
Pepperdine University *B*
Pitzer College *B*
Point Loma Nazarene University *B*
Pomona College *B*
Porterville College *A*
Saddleback College *A*
St. Mary's College of California *B*
San Bernardino Valley College *A*
San Diego City College *A*
San Diego Mesa College *C, A*
San Diego Miramar College *A*
San Diego State University *B, M, D*
San Francisco State University *B, M*
San Joaquin Delta College *A*
San Jose State University *B, M*
Santa Ana College *A*
Santa Barbara City College *A*
Santa Clara University *B*
Santa Monica College *A*
Santa Rosa Junior College *A*
Santiago Canyon College *A*
Scripps College *B*
Sierra College *A*
Solano Community College *A*
Sonoma State University *B*
Southwestern College *A*
Stanford University *B, M, D*
University of California
  Berkeley *B, M, D*
  Davis *B, M, D*
  Irvine *B, M, D*
  Los Angeles *B, M, D*
  Riverside *B, M, D*
  San Diego *B, D*
  Santa Barbara *B, M, D*
  Santa Cruz *B, M, D*
University of California: Merced *B*
University of La Verne *B*
University of Redlands *B*
University of San Diego *B*
University of San Francisco *B, M*
University of Southern California *B, M, D*
University of the Pacific *B, M, D*
Vanguard University of Southern California *B*
West Los Angeles College *C, A*
West Valley College *A*
Westmont College *B*
Whittier College *B*

Colorado

Adams State College *B*
Colorado College *B*
Colorado Mountain College *A*
Colorado School of Mines *B, M, D*
Colorado State University *B, M, D*
Colorado State University Pueblo *B*
Fort Lewis College *B*
Metropolitan State College of Denver *B*
Otero Junior College *A*
Pikes Peak Community College *A*
Regis University *B*
Trinidad State Junior College *A*
United States Air Force Academy *B*
University of Colorado
  Boulder *B, D*
  Colorado Springs *B, M*
  Denver *B, M*
University of Denver *B, M, D*
University of Northern Colorado *B, M, D, T*
Western State College of Colorado *B*

Connecticut

Albertus Magnus College *B*
Central Connecticut State University *B*
Connecticut College *B*
Fairfield University *B*
Quinnipiac University *B*
Sacred Heart University *B, M*
Saint Joseph College *B, M*
Southern Connecticut State University *B, M, T*
Trinity College *B*
University of Connecticut *B, M, D*
University of Hartford *B*
University of New Haven *A, B*
Wesleyan University *B, M, D*
Western Connecticut State University *B*
Yale University *B, M, D*

Delaware

Delaware State University *B, M, D*
University of Delaware *B, M, D*

District of Columbia

American University *B, M*
Catholic University of America *B, M*
Gallaudet University *B*
George Washington University *B, M, D*
Georgetown University *B, M, D*
Howard University *B, M, D*
Trinity Washington University *B*
University of the District of Columbia *B*

Florida

Barry University *B*
Bethune-Cookman University *B*
Broward College *A*
Daytona State College *A*
Eckerd College *B*
Florida Agricultural and Mechanical University *B, M*
Florida Atlantic University *B, M, D*
Florida Gulf Coast University *B*
Florida Institute of Technology *B, M, D*
Florida International University *B, M, D*
Florida Southern College *B*
Florida State University *B, M, D*
Gulf Coast Community College *A*
Indian River State College *A*
Jacksonville University *B*
Miami Dade College *A*
New College of Florida *B*
Northwest Florida State College *A*
Palm Beach Community College *A*
Pensacola Junior College *A*
Rollins College *B*
Saint Thomas University *B*
Santa Fe College *A*
State College of Florida, Manatee-Sarasota *A*
Stetson University *B*
University of Central Florida *B, M, D*
University of Florida *B, M, D*
University of Miami *B, M, D*
University of North Florida *B*
University of South Florida *B, M, D*
University of Tampa *A, B, T*
University of West Florida *B*

Georgia

Abraham Baldwin Agricultural College *A*
Agnes Scott College *B*
Albany State University *B*
Armstrong Atlantic State University *B, T*
Atlanta Metropolitan College *A*
Augusta State University *B*
Berry College *B*
Clark Atlanta University *B, M, D*
College of Coastal Georgia *A*
Columbus State University *B*
Covenant College *B*
Dalton State College *A, B*
Darton College *A*
East Georgia College *A*
Emory University *B, D*
Fort Valley State University *B*
Gainesville State College *A*
Georgia College and State University *B*
Georgia Highlands College *A*
Georgia Institute of Technology *B, M, D*
Georgia Perimeter College *A*
Georgia Southern University *B*
Georgia Southwestern State University *B*
Georgia State University *B, M, D*
Gordon College *A*
Kennesaw State University *B*
LaGrange College *B*
Macon State College *A*
Mercer University *B*
Middle Georgia College *A*
Morehouse College *B*
North Georgia College & State University *B*
Oglethorpe University *B*
Paine College *B*
Piedmont College *B*
Savannah State University *B*
Shorter College *B*
South Georgia College *A*
Southern Polytechnic State University *B*
Spelman College *B*
University of Georgia *B, M, D*
University of West Georgia *B*
Valdosta State University *B*
Waycross College *A*
Wesleyan College *B*
Young Harris College *A*

Hawaii

University of Hawaii
  Hilo *B*
  Manoa *B, M, D*

Idaho

Boise State University *B, T*
Brigham Young University-Idaho *A*
College of Idaho *B*
Idaho State University *A, B, M*
Lewis-Clark State College *B*
North Idaho College *A*
Northwest Nazarene University *B*
University of Idaho *B, M, D*

Illinois

Augustana College *B, T*
Benedictine University *B, T*
Black Hawk College: East Campus *A*
Blackburn College *B*
Bradley University *B, M, T*
Chicago State University *B, T*
City Colleges of Chicago
  Harold Washington College *A*
  Kennedy-King College *A*
  Olive-Harvey College *A*
Concordia University Chicago *B, T*
Danville Area Community College *A*
DePaul University *B, M, T*
Dominican University *B*
Eastern Illinois University *B, M*
Elmhurst College *B, T*
Eureka College *B*
Governors State University *B, T*
Greenville College *B, T*
Illinois Central College *A*
Illinois College *B*
Illinois Institute of Technology *B, M, D*
Illinois State University *B, M, T*
Illinois Valley Community College *A*
Illinois Wesleyan University *B*
John A. Logan College *A*
Joliet Junior College *A*
Judson University *B*
Kishwaukee College *A*
Knox College *B*
Lake Forest College *B*
Lewis University *B, T*
Lincoln College *A*
Loyola University Chicago *B, M, D*
MacMurray College *B*
McKendree University *B*
Millikin University *B*
Monmouth College *B, T*
North Central College *B, T*
North Park University *B*
Northeastern Illinois University *B, M*
Northern Illinois University *B, M, D, T*
Northwestern University *B, M, D*
Olivet Nazarene University *B, T*
Principia College *B*
Quincy University *B*
Rockford College *B*
Roosevelt University *B*
Saint Xavier University *B*
South Suburban College of Cook County *A*
Southern Illinois University Carbondale *B, M, D*
Southern Illinois University Edwardsville *B, M*
Southwestern Illinois College *A*
Trinity Christian College *B, T*
Trinity International University *B*
Triton College *A*
University of Chicago *B, D*
University of Illinois
  Chicago *B, M, D*
  Springfield *B*
  Urbana-Champaign *B, M, D*
Western Illinois University *B, M*
Wheaton College *B, T*

Indiana

Ancilla College *A*
Anderson University *B*
Ball State University *B, M, T*
Bethel College *B*
Butler University *B*
DePauw University *B*
Earlham College *B*
Franklin College *B*
Goshen College *B*
Hanover College *B*
Huntington University *B*
Indiana State University *B, T*
Indiana University
  Bloomington *B, M, D*
  Kokomo *B*
  Northwest *B*
  South Bend *A, B*
  Southeast *B*
Indiana University-Purdue University Fort Wayne *A, B, T*
Indiana University-Purdue University Indianapolis *A, B, M, D*
Indiana Wesleyan University *A, B*
Manchester College *B, T*
Marian University *B, T*
Purdue University *B, M, D*
Purdue University Calumet *B*
Rose-Hulman Institute of Technology *B*
Saint Joseph's College *B*
Saint Mary's College *B, T*
Taylor University *B*
Trine University *B*
University of Evansville *B*
University of Indianapolis *A, B*
University of Notre Dame *B, M, D*
University of St. Francis *B*
University of Southern Indiana *B, T*

Valparaiso University *B*
Vincennes University *A*
Wabash College *B*

Iowa

Briar Cliff University *B*
Buena Vista University *B, T*
Central College *B, T*
Clarke College *B, T*
Coe College *B*
Cornell College *B, T*
Dordt College *B*
Drake University *B*
Ellsworth Community College *A*
Graceland University *B, T*
Grinnell College *B*
Iowa State University *B, M, D*
Iowa Wesleyan College *B*
Loras College *B*
Luther College *B*
Morningside College *B*
Northwestern College *B, T*
St. Ambrose University *B*
Simpson College *B*
University of Iowa *B, M, D, T*
University of Northern Iowa *B, M*
Upper Iowa University *B*
Wartburg College *B, T*

Kansas

Allen County Community College *A*
Baker University *B, T*
Barton County Community College *A*
Benedictine College *B*
Bethany College *B, T*
Bethel College *B*
Butler Community College *A*
Central Christian College of
 Kansas *A, B*
Coffeyville Community College *A*
Cowley County Community
 College *A*
Dodge City Community College *A*
Emporia State University *B, T*
Fort Hays State University *B*
Fort Scott Community College *A*
Friends University *B*
Garden City Community College *A*
Kansas State University *B, M, D*
Kansas Wesleyan University *B, T*
McPherson College *B, T*
MidAmerica Nazarene University *B*
Neosho County Community
 College *A*
Newman University *B*
Pittsburg State University *B, M*
Pratt Community College *A*
Seward County Community College *A*
Southwestern College *B*
Sterling College *B, T*
Tabor College *B*
University of Kansas *B, M, D*
University of St. Mary *B*
Washburn University *B*
Wichita State University *B, M, D, T*

Kentucky

Asbury College *B, T*
Bellarmine University *B, T*
Berea College *B, T*
Bluegrass Community and Technical
 College *A*
Brescia University *B*
Campbellsville University *B*
Centre College *B*
Eastern Kentucky University *B, M*
Georgetown College *B, T*
Kentucky State University *B*
Kentucky Wesleyan College *B, T*
Lindsey Wilson College *A*
Morehead State University *B*
Murray State University *B, M, T*
Northern Kentucky University *B*
Pikeville College *B, T*

Thomas More College *A, B*
Transylvania University *B*
Union College *B*
University of Kentucky *B, M, D*
University of Louisville *B, M, D*
University of the Cumberlands *B*
Western Kentucky University *B, M*

Louisiana

Centenary College of Louisiana *B, T*
Dillard University *B*
Grambling State University *B*
Louisiana College *B*
Louisiana State University
 Shreveport *B*
Louisiana State University and
 Agricultural and Mechanical
 College *B, M, D*
Louisiana Tech University *B, M*
Loyola University New Orleans *B*
McNeese State University *B*
Nicholls State University *B*
Northwestern State University *B*
Our Lady of Holy Cross College *T*
Southeastern Louisiana University *B*
Southern University
 Shreveport *A*
Southern University and Agricultural
 and Mechanical College *B, M*
Tulane University *B, M, D*
University of Louisiana at Lafayette *B*
University of Louisiana at Monroe *B*
University of New Orleans *B, M, D*
Xavier University of Louisiana *B*

Maine

Bates College *B*
Bowdoin College *B*
Colby College *B*
Husson University *B*
Saint Joseph's College of Maine *B, T*
University of Maine *B, M, D*
University of New England *B*
University of Southern Maine *B*

Maryland

Allegany College of Maryland *A*
Cecil College *A*
College of Notre Dame of Maryland *B*
Coppin State University *B*
Frederick Community College *A*
Frostburg State University *B, T*
Goucher College *B*
Harford Community College *A*
Hood College *B, T*
Johns Hopkins University *B, M, D*
Loyola University Maryland *B*
McDaniel College *B*
Morgan State University *B*
Mount St. Mary's University *B*
Prince George's Community
 College *A*
St. Mary's College of Maryland *B*
Salisbury University *B, T*
Stevenson University *B*
Towson University *B*
United States Naval Academy *B*
University of Maryland
 Baltimore County *B, M, D*
 College Park *B, M, D*
 Eastern Shore *B*
Washington Adventist University *B*
Washington College *B, T*

Massachusetts

American International College *B*
Amherst College *B*
Assumption College *B*
Bard College at Simon's Rock *B*
Boston College *B, M, D*
Boston University *B, M, D*
Brandeis University *B, M, D*
Bridgewater State College *B*

Bunker Hill Community College *A*
Clark University *B; M, D*
College of the Holy Cross *B*
Eastern Nazarene College *B*
Elms College *B*
Emmanuel College *B*
Framingham State College *B*
Gordon College *B*
Hampshire College *B*
Harvard College *B, M, D*
Massachusetts College of Pharmacy
 and Health Sciences *B*
Massachusetts Institute of
 Technology *B, D*
Merrimack College *B*
Mount Holyoke College *B*
Northeastern University *B, M, D*
Regis College *B*
Salem State College *B*
Simmons College *B*
Smith College *B*
Springfield Technical Community
 College *A*
Stonehill College *B*
Suffolk University *B*
Tufts University *B*
University of Massachusetts
 Amherst *B, M, D*
 Boston *B, M, D*
 Dartmouth *B, M*
 Lowell *B, M, D*
Wellesley College *B*
Western New England College *B, T*
Westfield State College *B, T*
Wheaton College *B*
Williams College *B*
Worcester Polytechnic
 Institute *B, M, D*
Worcester State College *B*

Michigan

Adrian College *B, T*
Albion College *B, T*
Alma College *B, T*
Andrews University *B*
Aquinas College *B, T*
Calvin College *B, T*
Central Michigan University *B, M*
Delta College *A*
Eastern Michigan University *B, M*
Ferris State University *B*
Gogebic Community College *A*
Grand Rapids Community College *A*
Grand Valley State University *B*
Henry Ford Community College *A*
Hillsdale College *B*
Hope College *B*
Kalamazoo College *B*
Kettering University *B*
Lake Michigan College *A*
Lake Superior State University *A, B*
Lansing Community College *A*
Lawrence Technological University *B*
Macomb Community College *A*
Madonna University *B*
Marygrove College *B, T*
Michigan State University *B, M, D*
Michigan Technological
 University *B, M, D*
Mid Michigan Community College *A*
Northern Michigan University *B*
Oakland University *B, M, T*
Saginaw Valley State University *B, T*
Siena Heights University *A, B*
Spring Arbor University *B, T*
University of Detroit Mercy *B, M*
University of Michigan *B, M, D*
University of Michigan
 Dearborn *B*
 Flint *B*
Wayne State University *B, M, D*
Western Michigan University *B, M, D*

Minnesota

Augsburg College *B*
Bemidji State University *B, M*
Bethany Lutheran College *B*
Bethel University *B*
Carleton College *B*
College of St. Benedict *B*
College of St. Scholastica *B*
Concordia College: Moorhead *B*
Gustavus Adolphus College *B*
Hamline University *B*
Macalester College *B*
Minneapolis Community and
 Technical College *A*
Minnesota State University
 Mankato *B*
 Moorhead *B*
Minnesota West Community and
 Technical College *A*
North Hennepin Community
 College *A*
Ridgewater College *A*
St. Catherine University *B*
Saint Cloud State University *B*
St. John's University *B*
St. Mary's University of Minnesota *B*
St. Olaf College *B*
Southwest Minnesota State
 University *B*
University of Minnesota
 Duluth *B, M*
 Morris *B*
 Twin Cities *B, M, D*
University of St. Thomas *B*
Vermilion Community College *A*
Winona State University *B*

Mississippi

Alcorn State University *B*
Belhaven University *B*
Delta State University *B*
East Central Community College *A*
Hinds Community College *A*
Jackson State University *B, M, D*
Millsaps College *B*
Mississippi College *B, M*
Mississippi State University *B, M, D*
Mississippi University for Women *B, T*
Mississippi Valley State University *B*
Rust College *B*
Tougaloo College *B*
University of Mississippi *B, M, D*
University of Southern
 Mississippi *B, M, D*

Missouri

Avila University *B*
Central Methodist University *A, B*
College of the Ozarks *B*
Columbia College *B*
Crowder College *A*
Drury University *B, T*
Evangel University *B*
Lincoln University *B*
Lindenwood University *B*
Maryville University of Saint Louis *B*
Missouri Baptist University *B, T*
Missouri Southern State
 University *B, T*
Missouri State University *B, M*
Missouri Western State University *B, T*
Northwest Missouri State
 University *B*
Park University *B*
Rockhurst University *B*
St. Charles Community College *A*
St. Louis Community College
 St. Louis Community College at
  Florissant Valley *A*
Saint Louis University *B, M, D*
Southeast Missouri State
 University *B, M*
Southwest Baptist University *B, T*
Three Rivers Community College *A*

Truman State University *B*
University of Central Missouri *B*
University of Missouri
  Columbia *B, M, D*
  Kansas City *B, M, D*
  Missouri University of Science and
    Technology *B, M, D, T*
  St. Louis *B, M, D*
Washington University in St.
  Louis *B, M, D*
Westminster College *B*
William Jewell College *B, T*

Montana

Montana State University
  Billings *B, T*
  Bozeman *B, M, D*
Montana Tech of the University of
  Montana *B, M*
Rocky Mountain College *B, T*
University of Great Falls *B*
University of Montana *B, M, D*
University of Montana: Western *A, B*

Nebraska

Chadron State College *B*
College of Saint Mary *B, T*
Concordia University *B, T*
Creighton University *B*
Dana College *B*
Doane College *B*
Nebraska Wesleyan University *B*
Northeast Community College *A*
Union College *B*
University of Nebraska
  Kearney *B, T*
  Lincoln *B, M, D*
  Omaha *B*
Wayne State College *B*
Western Nebraska Community
  College *A*

Nevada

Great Basin College *A*
University of Nevada
  Las Vegas *B, M*
  Reno *B, M, D*
Western Nevada College *A*

New Hampshire

Dartmouth College *B, M, D, T*
Keene State College *B*
Plymouth State University *B*
Saint Anselm College *B, T*
University of New Hampshire *B, M, D*

New Jersey

Bergen Community College *A*
Bloomfield College *B*
Caldwell College *B*
The College of New Jersey *B, T*
College of St. Elizabeth *B*
Drew University *B*
Essex County College *C, A*
Fairleigh Dickinson University
  College at Florham *B, M*
  Metropolitan Campus *B, M*
Georgian Court University *B*
Gloucester County College *A*
Hudson County Community
  College *A*
Kean University *B, T*
Middlesex County College *A*
Monmouth University *B*
Montclair State University *B, M*
New Jersey City University *B*
New Jersey Institute of
  Technology *B, M, D*
Princeton University *B, M, D*
Ramapo College of New Jersey *B*
Richard Stockton College of New
  Jersey *B*
Rider University *B*

Rowan University *B*
Rutgers, The State University of New
  Jersey
  Camden Regional Campus *B, M, T*
  New Brunswick/Piscataway
    Campus *B, M, D*
  Newark Regional Campus *B, M, D*
Saint Peter's College *B*
Salem Community College *A*
Seton Hall University *B, M, D, T*
Stevens Institute of
  Technology *B, M, D*
Sussex County Community College *A*
Union County College *A*
Warren County Community College *A*
William Paterson University of New
  Jersey *B*

New Mexico

Eastern New Mexico University *B, M*
New Mexico Highlands
  University *B, M*
New Mexico Institute of Mining and
  Technology *B, M, D*
New Mexico Junior College *A*
New Mexico State University *B, M, D*
San Juan College *A*
University of New Mexico *B, M, D*
Western New Mexico University *B*

New York

Adelphi University *B*
Alfred University *B*
Bard College *B*
Barnard College *B*
Canisius College *B*
Cayuga County Community College *A*
City University of New York
  Brooklyn College *B, M*
  City College *B, M*
  College of Staten Island *B*
  Hunter College *B, M*
  Kingsborough Community
    College *A*
  Lehman College *B*
  Queens College *B, M, T*
  Queensborough Community
    College *A*
  York College *B*
Clarkson University *B, M, D*
Colgate University *B*
College of Mount St. Vincent *B, T*
College of New Rochelle *B, T*
College of Saint Rose *B*
Columbia University *B*
Columbia University
  School of General Studies *B*
Cornell University *B, M, D*
D'Youville College *B*
Dowling College *B*
Elmira College *B, T*
Excelsior College *B*
Finger Lakes Community College *A*
Fordham University *B, M, D*
Hamilton College *B*
Hartwick College *B, T*
Hobart and William Smith Colleges *B*
Hofstra University *B*
Houghton College *B*
Hudson Valley Community College *A*
Iona College *B*
Ithaca College *B, T*
Le Moyne College *B*
Long Island University
  Brooklyn Campus *B, M*
  C. W. Post Campus *B*
Manhattan College *B*
Manhattanville College *B*
Marist College *B*
Monroe Community College *A*
Mount Saint Mary College *B, T*
Nazareth College *B*
New York Institute of Technology *B*
New York University *B, M, D*

Niagara University *B*
Pace University *B*
Polytechnic Institute of New York
  University *B, M, D*
Rensselaer Polytechnic
  Institute *B, M, D*
Roberts Wesleyan College *B*
Rochester Institute of
  Technology *A, B, M*
Russell Sage College *B*
Saint Bonaventure University *B*
St. Francis College *B*
St. John Fisher College *B*
St. John's University *B, M*
St. Joseph's College *B*
St. Lawrence University *B, T*
St. Thomas Aquinas College *B, T*
Siena College *B, T*
Skidmore College *B*
State University of New York
  Albany *B, M, D*
  Binghamton *B, M, D*
  Buffalo *B, M, D*
  College at Brockport *B, T*
  College at Buffalo *B, M*
  College at Cortland *B*
  College at Fredonia *B, M, T*
  College at Geneseo *B, T*
  College at Old Westbury *B, T*
  College at Oneonta *B*
  College at Plattsburgh *B*
  College at Potsdam *B*
  College of Agriculture and
    Technology at Morrisville *A*
  College of Environmental Science
    and Forestry *B*
  New Paltz *B*
  Oswego *B, M*
  Purchase *B*
  Stony Brook *B, M, D*
Suffolk County Community College *A*
Syracuse University *B, M, D*
Touro College *B*
Union College *B*
United States Military Academy *B*
University of Rochester *B, M, D*
Utica College *B*
Vassar College *B, M*
Wagner College *B, T*
Wells College *B*
Yeshiva University *B*

North Carolina

Appalachian State University *B*
Barton College *B*
Bennett College for Women *B*
Campbell University *B*
Catawba College *B, T*
Davidson College *B*
Duke University *B, M, D*
East Carolina University *B, M*
Elizabeth City State University *B*
Elon University *B*
Fayetteville State University *B*
Gardner-Webb University *B*
Greensboro College *C, B*
Guilford College *B*
High Point University *B*
Johnson C. Smith University *B*
Lenoir-Rhyne University *B*
Livingstone College *B*
Mars Hill College *B, T*
Meredith College *B*
Methodist University *A, B, T*
North Carolina Agricultural and
  Technical State University *B, M*
North Carolina Central
  University *B, M*
North Carolina State
  University *B, M, D*
North Carolina Wesleyan College *B*
Pfeiffer University *B*
Queens University of Charlotte *B*
St. Andrews Presbyterian College *B*

St. Augustine's College *B*
Salem College *B*
Shaw University *B*
Southeastern Community College *A*
University of North Carolina
  Asheville *B, T*
  Chapel Hill *B, M, D*
  Charlotte *B, M*
  Greensboro *B, M*
  Pembroke *B*
  Wilmington *B, M*
Wake Forest University *B, M, D*
Warren Wilson College *B*
Western Carolina University *B, M*
Wingate University *B*
Winston-Salem State University *B*

North Dakota

Dickinson State University *B*
Jamestown College *B*
Mayville State University *B, T*
Minot State University *B*
North Dakota State
  University *B, M, D, T*
University of North Dakota *B, M, D*

Ohio

Ashland University *B*
Baldwin-Wallace College *B*
Bluffton University *B*
Bowling Green State University *B, M*
Capital University *B*
Case Western Reserve
  University *B, M, D*
Cedarville University *B*
Central State University *B*
Cleveland State University *B, M, D, T*
College of Mount St. Joseph *B, T*
College of Wooster *B*
Denison University *B*
Eastern Gateway Community
  College *A*
Franciscan University of
  Steubenville *B*
Heidelberg University *B*
Hiram College *B*
John Carroll University *B*
Kent State University *B, M, D*
Kenyon College *B*
Malone University *B*
Marietta College *B*
Miami University
  Oxford Campus *B, M, D*
Mount Union College *B*
Mount Vernon Nazarene University *B*
Muskingum University *B*
Notre Dame College *B, T*
Oberlin College *B*
Ohio Dominican University *A, B, T*
Ohio Northern University *B*
Ohio State University
  Columbus Campus *B, M, D*
Ohio University *B, M, D*
Ohio Wesleyan University *B*
Otterbein College *B*
Owens Community College
  Toledo *A*
Shawnee State University *B*
Terra State Community College *A*
University of Akron *B, M, D*
University of Cincinnati *B, M, D*
University of Cincinnati
  Clermont College *A*
  Raymond Walters College *A*
University of Dayton *B, M*
University of Rio Grande *A, B, T*
University of Toledo *B, M, D*
Walsh University *B*
Wilberforce University *B*
Wilmington College *B*
Wittenberg University *B*
Wright State University *A, B, M*
Wright State University: Lake
  Campus *A*

Xavier University *B*
Youngstown State University *B, M*

Oklahoma

Cameron University *B*
Connors State College *A*
East Central University *B, T*
Eastern Oklahoma State College *A*
Langston University *B*
Northeastern State University *B*
Northern Oklahoma College *A*
Northwestern Oklahoma State
University *B*
Oklahoma Baptist University *B, T*
Oklahoma Christian University *B*
Oklahoma City Community College *A*
Oklahoma City University *B*
Oklahoma Panhandle State
University *B*
Oklahoma State University *B, M, D*
Oklahoma Wesleyan University *A, B*
Oral Roberts University *B*
Rose State College *A*
Southeastern Oklahoma State
University *B*
Southern Nazarene University *B*
Southwestern Oklahoma State
University *B*
Tulsa Community College *A*
University of Central Oklahoma *B*
University of Oklahoma *B, M, D*
University of Science and Arts of
Oklahoma *B*
University of Tulsa *B, M, D*

Oregon

Central Oregon Community
College *A*
Chemeketa Community College *A*
Concordia University *B*
Eastern Oregon University *B, T*
George Fox University *B*
Lewis & Clark College *B*
Linfield College *B, T*
Linn-Benton Community College *A*
Mt. Hood Community College *A*
Oregon State University *B, M, D*
Pacific University *B*
Portland State University *B, M*
Reed College *B*
Southern Oregon University *B*
Treasure Valley Community College *A*
University of Oregon *B, M, D*
University of Portland *B*
Western Oregon University *B*
Willamette University *B*

Pennsylvania

Albright College *B, T*
Allegheny College *B*
Alvernia University *B*
Arcadia University *B*
Bloomsburg University of
Pennsylvania *B, T*
Bryn Mawr College *B, M, D*
Bucknell University *B, M*
Bucks County Community College *A*
Cabrini College *B*
California University of
Pennsylvania *B, M*
Carlow University *B*
Carnegie Mellon University *B, M, D*
Cedar Crest College *B*
Chatham University *B*
Chestnut Hill College *A, B*
Cheyney University of
Pennsylvania *B, T*
Clarion University of Pennsylvania *B*
Community College of Allegheny
County *A*
DeSales University *B, T*
Delaware Valley College *B*
Dickinson College *B*
Drexel University *B, M, D*

Duquesne University *B, M, D*
East Stroudsburg University of
Pennsylvania *B, T*
Eastern University *B*
Edinboro University of
Pennsylvania *B, T*
Elizabethtown College *B*
Franklin & Marshall College *B*
Gannon University *B*
Geneva College *B, T*
Gettysburg College *B*
Grove City College *B*
Harrisburg Area Community
College *A*
Harrisburg University of Science and
Technology *B*
Haverford College *B, T*
Holy Family University *B, T*
Immaculata University *A, B*
Indiana University of
Pennsylvania *B, M*
Juniata College *B*
King's College *B, T*
Kutztown University of
Pennsylvania *B, T*
La Roche College *B*
La Salle University *B*
Lafayette College *B*
Lebanon Valley College *B, T*
Lehigh University *B, M, D*
Lincoln University *B*
Lock Haven University of
Pennsylvania *B*
Lycoming College *B*
Mansfield University of
Pennsylvania *B, T*
Mercyhurst College *B*
Messiah College *B*
Millersville University of
Pennsylvania *B, T*
Misericordia University *B*
Moravian College *B, T*
Muhlenberg College *C, B*
Northampton Community College *A*
Penn State
Abington *B*
Altoona *B*
Beaver *B*
Berks *B*
Brandywine *B*
DuBois *B*
Erie, The Behrend College *B*
Fayette, The Eberly Campus *B*
Greater Allegheny *B*
Hazleton *B*
Lehigh Valley *B*
Mont Alto *B*
New Kensington *B*
Schuylkill *B*
Shenango *B*
University Park *B, M, D*
Wilkes-Barre *B*
Worthington Scranton *B*
York *B*
Philadelphia University *B*
Reading Area Community College *A*
Rosemont College *B*
St. Francis University *B*
Saint Joseph's University *A, B*
St. Vincent College *B*
Seton Hill University *B, T*
Shippensburg University of
Pennsylvania *B, T*
Slippery Rock University of
Pennsylvania *B*
Susquehanna University *B, T*
Swarthmore College *B*
Temple University *B, M, D*
Thiel College *B*
University of Pennsylvania *B, M, D*
University of Pittsburgh *B, M, D*
University of Pittsburgh
Bradford *B*

Greensburg *B*
Johnstown *B*
University of Scranton *B, M, T*
University of the Sciences in
Philadelphia *B, M, D*
Ursinus College *B, T*
Villanova University *B, M*
Washington & Jefferson College *B*
Waynesburg University *B*
West Chester University of
Pennsylvania *B, T*
Westminster College *B*
Widener University *B*
Wilkes University *B*
Wilson College *B*
York College of Pennsylvania *A, B*

Puerto Rico

Bayamon Central University *B*
Inter American University of Puerto
Rico
Arecibo Campus *B*
Bayamon Campus *B*
Metropolitan Campus *B*
San German Campus *B*
Pontifical Catholic University of
Puerto Rico *B, M*
Turabo University *B*
Universidad Adventista de las
Antillas *B*
Universidad Metropolitana *B*
University of Puerto Rico
Cayey University Collége *B*
Humacao *B*
Rio Piedras *B, M, D*
University of the Sacred Heart *B*

Rhode Island

Brown University *B, M, D*
Providence College *B*
Rhode Island College *B*
Roger Williams University *B*
Salve Regina University *B*
University of Rhode Island *B, M, D*

South Carolina

Allen University *B*
Benedict College *B*
Bob Jones University *B*
Charleston Southern University *B*
The Citadel *B, T*
Claflin University *B*
Clemson University *B, M, D*
Coastal Carolina University *B*
Coker College *B*
College of Charleston *B, T*
Columbia College *B*
Converse College *B*
Erskine College *B, T*
Francis Marion University *B*
Furman University *B, M, T*
Lander University *B*
Limestone College *B*
Newberry College *B*
Presbyterian College *B*
South Carolina State University *B*
Southern Wesleyan University *B*
University of South Carolina *B, M, D*
University of South Carolina
Aiken *B*
Upstate *B*
Winthrop University *B*
Wofford College *B, T*

South Dakota

Augustana College *B, T*
Black Hills State University *B*
Mount Marty College *B*
Northern State University *B*
South Dakota School of Mines and
Technology *B, M*
South Dakota State University *B, M, D*
University of Sioux Falls *B*

University of South Dakota *B, M*

Tennessee

Austin Peay State University *B*
Belmont University *B, T*
Bethel University *B*
Carson-Newman College *B, T*
Christian Brothers University *B*
Columbia State Community College *A*
East Tennessee State
University *B, M, T*
Fisk University *B, M*
Freed-Hardeman University *B*
Jackson State Community College *A*
King College *B, T*
Lambuth University *B*
Lane College *B*
LeMoyne-Owen College *B*
Lee University *B*
Lincoln Memorial University *B, T*
Lipscomb University *B*
Maryville College *B, T*
Middle Tennessee State
University *B, M, D*
Milligan College *B, T*
Rhodes College *B*
Southern Adventist University *B*
Tennessee State University *B, M*
Tennessee Technological
University *B, M, T*
Tennessee Wesleyan College *B*
Trevecca Nazarene University *B*
Union University *B, T*
University of Memphis *B, M, D*
University of Tennessee
Chattanooga *B*
Knoxville *B, M, D*
Martin *B*
University of the South *B*
Vanderbilt University *B, M, D*

Texas

Abilene Christian University *B*
Amarillo College *A*
Angelo State University *B*
Austin College *B*
Austin Community College *A*
Baylor University *B, M, D*
Blinn College *A*
Brazosport College *A*
Central Texas College *A*
Cisco College *A*
Clarendon College *A*
Coastal Bend College *A*
College of the Mainland *A*
Del Mar College *A*
East Texas Baptist University *B*
El Paso Community College *A*
Frank Phillips College *A*
Galveston College *A*
Grayson County College *A*
Hardin-Simmons University *B*
Hill College *A*
Houston Baptist University *B*
Howard College *A*
Howard Payne University *B, T*
Huston-Tillotson University *B*
Jarvis Christian College *B, T*
Kilgore College *A*
Lamar University *B, M*
Laredo Community College *A*
LeTourneau University *B*
Lon Morris College *A*
Lubbock Christian University *B*
McMurry University *B*
Midland College *A*
Midwestern State University *B*
Navarro College *A*
Northeast Texas Community
College *A*
Northwest Vista College *A*
Odessa College *A*
Our Lady of the Lake University of San
Antonio *B*

Palo Alto College *A*
Paris Junior College *A*
Prairie View A&M University *B, M*
Rice University *B, M, D*
St. Edward's University *B*
St. Mary's University *B*
St. Philip's College *A*
Sam Houston State University *B, M*
San Jacinto College *A*
Schreiner University *B*
South Plains College *A*
South Texas College *A*
Southern Methodist
    University *B, M, D*
Southwestern Adventist
    University *B, T*
Southwestern University *B, T*
Stephen F. Austin State
    University *B, M, T*
Sul Ross State University *B*
Tarleton State University *B, T*
Texarkana College *A*
Texas A&M International University *B*
Texas A&M University *B, M, D*
Texas A&M University
    Commerce *B, M*
    Corpus Christi *B, T*
    Kingsville *B, M*
Texas Christian University *B, M, D*
Texas Lutheran University *B*
Texas Southern University *B*
Texas State University: San
    Marcos *B, M, T*
Texas Tech University *B, M, D*
Texas Wesleyan University *B*
Texas Woman's University *B, M*
Trinity University *B*
Trinity Valley Community College *A*
Tyler Junior College *A*
University of Dallas *B*
University of Houston *B, M, D*
University of Houston
    Clear Lake *B, M*
    Downtown *B*
University of Mary Hardin-Baylor *B, T*
University of North Texas *B, M, D*
University of St. Thomas *B*
University of Texas
    Arlington *B, M, D*
    Austin *B, M, D*
    Brownsville - Texas Southmost
        College *B*
    Dallas *B, M, D*
    El Paso *B, M, D*
    Pan American *B*
    San Antonio *B, M*
    Tyler *B*
    of the Permian Basin *B*
University of the Incarnate Word *A, B*
Wayland Baptist University *B, T*
West Texas A&M University *B, M*
Western Texas College *A*
Wharton County Junior College *A*
Wiley College *B*

Utah

Brigham Young University *B, M, D*
Salt Lake Community College *A*
Snow College *A*
University of Utah *B, M, D, T*
Utah State University *B, M, D*
Utah Valley University *A, B*
Weber State University *B*
Westminster College *B*

Vermont

Bennington College *B*
Castleton State College *A*
Marlboro College *B*
Middlebury College *B*
Norwich University *B*
St. Michael's College *B*
University of Vermont *B, M, D*

Virginia

Averett University *B*
Bluefield College *B*
Bridgewater College *B*
Christopher Newport University *B*
College of William and Mary *B, M*
Eastern Mennonite University *B*
Emory & Henry College *B, T*
Ferrum College *B*
George Mason University *B, M*
Hampden-Sydney College *B*
Hampton University *B, M*
Hollins University *B*
James Madison University *B, T*
Longwood University *B, T*
Lynchburg College *B*
Mary Baldwin College *B*
Norfolk State University *B*
Old Dominion University *B, M, D, T*
Radford University *B*
Randolph College *B*
Randolph-Macon College *B*
Roanoke College *B, T*
Shenandoah University *B*
Sweet Briar College *B*
University of Mary Washington *B*
University of Richmond *B, T*
University of Virginia *B, M, D*
University of Virginia's College at
    Wise *B, T*
Virginia Commonwealth
    University *B, M, D*
Virginia Military Institute *B*
Virginia Polytechnic Institute and
    State University *B, M, D*
Virginia State University *B*
Virginia Union University *B*
Virginia Wesleyan College *B*
Washington and Lee University *B*

Washington

Cascadia Community College *A*
Centralia College *A*
Eastern Washington University *B*
Everett Community College *A*
Gonzaga University *B*
Olympic College *A*
Pacific Lutheran University *B*
Saint Martin's University *B*
Seattle Pacific University *B*
Seattle University *B*
South Seattle Community College *A*
University of Puget Sound *B*
University of Washington *B, M, D*
Walla Walla University *B*
Washington State University *B, M, D*
Western Washington University *B, M*
Whitman College *B*
Whitworth University *B, T*

West Virginia

Alderson-Broaddus College *B*
Bethany College *B*
Concord University *B*
Davis and Elkins College *B*
Fairmont State University *B*
Glenville State College *B*
Marshall University *B, M*
Potomac State College of West
    Virginia University *A*
Shepherd University *B, T*
University of Charleston *B*
West Liberty University *B*
West Virginia State University *B*
West Virginia University *B, M, D, T*
West Virginia University Institute of
    Technology *B*
West Virginia Wesleyan College *B*
Wheeling Jesuit University *B*

Wisconsin

Alverno College *B*
Beloit College *B*
Cardinal Stritch University *B, T*
Carroll University *B*
Carthage College *B*
Edgewood College *B*
Lakeland College *B*
Lawrence University *B*
Marian University *B*
Marquette University *B, M, D, T*
Mount Mary College *B, T*
Ripon College *B*
St. Norbert College *B, T*
University of Wisconsin
    Eau Claire *B*
    Green Bay *B*
    La Crosse *B, T*
    Madison *B, M, D*
    Milwaukee *B, M, D*
    Oshkosh *B*
    Parkside *B*
    Platteville *B, T*
    River Falls *B*
    Stevens Point *B, T*
    Superior *B, T*
    Whitewater *B, T*
Viterbo University *B, T*
Wisconsin Lutheran College *B*

Wyoming

Casper College *A*
Laramie County Community
    College *A*
Northwest College *A*
Sheridan College *A*
University of Wyoming *B, M, D*
Western Wyoming Community
    College *A*

Chemistry teacher education

Alabama

Athens State University *B*
Birmingham-Southern College *T*
Huntingdon College *B, T*
Oakwood University *B*
Talladega College *B*

Arizona

Cochise College *A*
Grand Canyon University *B*
Northern Arizona University *B*
Prescott College *T*
University of Arizona *B*

Arkansas

Arkansas State University *B, M, T*
Arkansas Tech University *B*
Harding University *B, T*
John Brown University *B, T*
Ouachita Baptist University *B, T*
Southern Arkansas University *B, T*
University of Arkansas
    Fort Smith *B*

California

Azusa Pacific University *T*
California Polytechnic State
    University: San Luis Obispo *T*
California State University
    Chico *B, T*
    Long Beach *T*
    San Bernardino *T*
Pepperdine University *B*
San Diego State University *T*
San Francisco State University *T*
Stanford University *M, T*
University of the Pacific *T*
Vanguard University of Southern
    California *T*

Colorado

Adams State College *B, T*
Colorado State University *B, T*
Colorado State University
    Pueblo *T*
Regis University *B, T*

Connecticut

Albertus Magnus College *B, T*
Fairfield University *T*
Quinnipiac University *B, M*
Sacred Heart University *T*
Saint Joseph College *T*
Southern Connecticut State
    University *B, M, T*
University of New Haven *T*

Delaware

Delaware State University *B*
University of Delaware *B, T*

District of Columbia

Catholic University of America *B*

Florida

Bethune-Cookman University *B, T*
Florida Institute of Technology *B*
Gulf Coast Community College *A*
State College of Florida,
    Manatee-Sarasota *A*

Georgia

Agnes Scott College *M, T*
Armstrong Atlantic State University *T*
Columbus State University *B*
Piedmont College *B, T*
University of West Georgia *B*

Idaho

Boise State University *B, T*
Brigham Young University-Idaho *T*
Northwest Nazarene University *B*
University of Idaho *T*

Illinois

Augustana College *B, T*
Benedictine University *T*
Bradley University *B*
Chicago State University *B, T*
Concordia University Chicago *B, T*
DePaul University *M, T*
Dominican University *T*
Elmhurst College *B*
Governors State University *B, T*
Greenville College *B, T*
Illinois Wesleyan University *B*
Knox College *T*
Lewis University *T*
Millikin University *B, T*
North Park University *T*
Olivet Nazarene University *B, T*
Rockford College *T*
Trinity Christian College *B, T*
University of Illinois
    Chicago *B*
    Urbana-Champaign *B, M, T*

Indiana

Anderson University *B, T*
Butler University *T*
Franklin College *B, T*
Goshen College *B, T*
Huntington University *B, M*
Indiana University
    Bloomington *B, T*
    South Bend *B, T*
Indiana University-Purdue University
    Fort Wayne *B*
Indiana University-Purdue University
    Indianapolis *B*
Indiana Wesleyan University *T*
Manchester College *B, T*
Purdue University *B, M, D*

Purdue University
  Calumet *B*
Saint Mary's College *T*
University of Evansville *B, T*
University of Indianapolis *B, T*
University of St. Francis *B, T*
Valparaiso University *B*
Vincennes University *A*

Iowa

Briar Cliff University *B*
Buena Vista University *B, T*
Central College *T*
Cornell College *B, T*
Dordt College *B*
Drake University *M, T*
Ellsworth Community College *A*
Graceland University *T*
Grand View University *T*
Iowa State University *T*
Iowa Wesleyan College *B*
Loras College *T*
Maharishi University of
  Management *T*
Morningside College *B*
Northwestern College *T*
St. Ambrose University *B, T*
Simpson College *T*
University of Iowa *T*
Upper Iowa University *B, T*
Wartburg College *T*

Kansas

Bethany College *B*
Bethel College *T*
Central Christian College of Kansas *A*
Garden City Community College *A*
McPherson College *B, T*
Pittsburg State University *B, T*
Sterling College *T*
Tabor College *B*
University of Kansas *B, T*
University of St. Mary *T*
Washburn University *B*

Kentucky

Campbellsville University *B*
Kentucky Wesleyan College *B, T*

Louisiana

Centenary College of Louisiana *B, T*
Louisiana State University
  Shreveport *B*
McNeese State University *B, T*
Northwestern State University *B*
Our Lady of Holy Cross College *T*
Southern University and Agricultural
  and Mechanical College *B*
University of Louisiana at Lafayette *B*
University of Louisiana at Monroe *B*
University of New Orleans *B*
Xavier University of Louisiana *B*

Maine

University of Maine *B*
University of Southern Maine *T*

Maryland

Anne Arundel Community College *A*
Carroll Community College *A*
College of Notre Dame of Maryland *T*
Community College of Baltimore
  County *A*
Coppin State University *B, T*
Harford Community College *A*
Hood College *T*
Howard Community College *A*
Salisbury University *T*
University of Maryland
  Eastern Shore *B*

Massachusetts

Assumption College *T*

Boston University *B*
Bridgewater State College *T*
Eastern Nazarene College *B*
Elms College *T*
Merrimack College *T*
Salem State College *M*
Tufts University *T*
University of Massachusetts
  Dartmouth *T*
Western New England College *T*
Westfield State College *M, T*
Worcester State College *T*

Michigan

Albion College *B, T*
Alma College *T*
Calvin College *B*
Central Michigan University *B, M*
Eastern Michigan University *B*
Ferris State University *B*
Grand Rapids Community College *A*
Grand Valley State University *M, T*
Hope College *T*
Michigan State University *B*
Michigan Technological University *T*
Northern Michigan University *B, T*
University of Detroit Mercy *B, M, T*
University of Michigan
  Dearborn *B*
  Flint *B*
Western Michigan University *B, T*

Minnesota

Augsburg College *T*
Bethel University *B*
College of St. Scholastica *T*
Concordia College: Moorhead *B, T*
Concordia University: St. Paul *B, T*
Gustavus Adolphus College *T*
Minnesota State University
  Mankato *B, T*
  Moorhead *B*
Saint Cloud State University *B, T*
St. Mary's University of Minnesota *B*
Southwest Minnesota State
  University *B, T*
University of Minnesota
  Duluth *B, T*
  Morris *T*
University of St. Thomas *B*
Vermilion Community College *A*
Winona State University *B, T*

Mississippi

Millsaps College *T*
Mississippi College *B, M*
Mississippi State University *T*

Missouri

Central Methodist University *B*
College of the Ozarks *B, T*
Lincoln University *B*
Lindenwood University *B*
Missouri Baptist University *T*
Missouri Southern State
  University *B, T*
Missouri State University *B*
Northwest Missouri State
  University *B, T*
Southwest Baptist University *B, T*
Truman State University *M, T*
University of Central Missouri *B, T*
University of Missouri
  Columbia *B*
  Kansas City *B*
Washington University in St.
  Louis *B, M, T*
William Jewell College *B, T*

Montana

Montana State University
  Billings *B, T*
University of Great Falls *B*

University of Montana *M, T*
University of Montana: Western *B, T*

Nebraska

Chadron State College *B*
College of Saint Mary *B, T*
Concordia University *B, T*
Creighton University *B, T*
Dana College *B*
Nebraska Wesleyan University *T*
Peru State College *T*
Union College *T*
University of Nebraska
  Kearney *B*
  Lincoln *B*
Wayne State College *B, T*

New Hampshire

Keene State College *B, M, T*
Saint Anselm College *T*
University of New Hampshire *T*

New Jersey

The College of New Jersey *B, T*
County College of Morris *A*
Rowan University *T*
Saint Peter's College *T*

New Mexico

New Mexico Institute of Mining and
  Technology *M*
Western New Mexico University *B*

New York

Adelphi University *M, T*
Alfred University *B, T*
City University of New York
  Brooklyn College *B, M, T*
  City College *B*
  College of Staten Island *B, T*
  Hunter College *B, M, T*
  Queens College *M, T*
Colgate University *M*
College of Mount St. Vincent *T*
College of Saint Rose *B, T*
Cornell University *B, M, T*
D'Youville College *M, T*
Dowling College *B, M*
Dutchess Community College *A*
Elmira College *B, T*
Fordham University *M, T*
Hofstra University *B, M*
Houghton College *B, T*
Ithaca College *B, D, T*
Le Moyne College *T*
Long Island University
  Brooklyn Campus *B, M, T*
  C. W. Post Campus *B, M, T*
Manhattan College *B, T*
Marist College *B*
Medaille College *M, T*
Nazareth College *B, M, T*
New York Institute of
  Technology *B, T*
New York University *M*
Niagara University *B, M, T*
Pace University *B, M, T*
Roberts Wesleyan College *B, M*
St. Francis College *B*
St. John Fisher College *B, M, T*
St. Lawrence University *T*
St. Thomas Aquinas College *B, M, T*
State University of New York
  Albany *M, T*
  Binghamton *M*
  Buffalo *M, T*
  College at Brockport *B, M, T*
  College at Buffalo *B, M*
  College at Cortland *B, M*
  College at Fredonia *B, M, T*
  College at Geneseo *B, T*
  College at Old Westbury *B, M, T*
  College at Oneonta *B, T*

  College at Plattsburgh *B*
  College at Potsdam *B, M*
  College of Environmental Science
    and Forestry *B, T*
  New Paltz *B, T*
  Oswego *B, M*
  Stony Brook *T*
Syracuse University *B, M, T*
Ulster County Community College *A*
University of Rochester *M*
Vassar College *T*
Wagner College *T*
Wells College *T*

North Carolina

Appalachian State University *B, T*
Catawba College *T*
Elizabeth City State University *B*
Gardner-Webb University *B*
Lenoir Community College *A*
Lenoir-Rhyne University *B*
Mars Hill College *T*
Meredith College *T*
Methodist University *A, B, T*
North Carolina Agricultural and
  Technical State University *B, T*
North Carolina Central
  University *B, M, T*
Sandhills Community College *A*
University of North Carolina
  Charlotte *B*
  Wilmington *B*
Wake Forest University *T*

North Dakota

Dickinson State University *B, T*
Jamestown College *B*
Mayville State University *B, T*
Minot State University *B*
North Dakota State University *B, T*
University of North Dakota *T*

Ohio

Ashland University *B, T*
Bluffton University *B*
Bowling Green State University *B, M*
Case Western Reserve University *T*
Cedarville University *B*
Defiance College *B, T*
Hiram College *T*
John Carroll University *T*
Kent State University *B*
Miami University
  Oxford Campus *B, M, T*
Mount Union College *T*
Mount Vernon Nazarene
  University *B, T*
Ohio Dominican University *B, T*
Ohio Northern University *B, T*
Ohio Wesleyan University *T*
Otterbein College *B*
Shawnee State University *B*
University of Findlay *T*
University of Rio Grande *B, T*
University of Toledo *T*
Wilmington College *B*
Xavier University *B, M*
Youngstown State University *B, M*

Oklahoma

Cameron University *B*
East Central University *B*
Eastern Oklahoma State College *A*
Northeastern State University *B*
Oklahoma Baptist University *B, T*
University of Central Oklahoma *B*
University of Tulsa *B, T*

Oregon

Concordia University *B, M, T*
Linfield College *T*
Oregon State University *M*
Portland State University *T*

Western Oregon University *B, M, T*

Pennsylvania

Albright College *T*
Alvernia University *B*
Arcadia University *B, M, T*
Bucks County Community College *A*
Cabrini College *T*
Chatham University *M, T*
DeSales University *T*
Dickinson College *T*
Duquesne University *M, T*
Geneva College *T*
Gettysburg College *T*
Grove City College *B, T*
Holy Family University *B*
Juniata College *B, T*
King's College *T*
La Salle University *B, T*
Lebanon Valley College *T*
Lycoming College *T*
Mansfield University of
    Pennsylvania *B, T*
Mercyhurst College *B, T*
Messiah College *B, T*
Misericordia University *T*
Moravian College *T*
St. Francis University *B, T*
St. Vincent College *T*
Seton Hill University *B, T*
Susquehanna University *T*
Thiel College *B*
University of Pittsburgh
    Johnstown *B, T*
Villanova University *T*
Washington & Jefferson College *T*
Waynesburg University *B, T*
Westminster College *T*
Widener University *T*
Wilkes University *M, T*
Wilson College *T*

Puerto Rico

Inter American University of Puerto
    Rico
    Arecibo Campus *B*
    Metropolitan Campus *B*
    San German Campus *B*
Pontifical Catholic University of
    Puerto Rico *B, T*
Turabo University *B*

Rhode Island

Rhode Island College *B*

South Carolina

Coker College *B, T*
Furman University *T*

South Dakota

Black Hills State University *B*
Mount Marty College *B*
University of Sioux Falls *T*
University of South Dakota *B, M, T*

Tennessee

Belmont University *B, M, T*
Christian Brothers University *B, M, T*
Crichton College *B, T*
King College *T*
Lambuth University *B, T*
Lincoln Memorial University *B, T*
Lipscomb University *B, T*
Maryville College *B, T*
Southern Adventist University *B*
Tennessee Technological University *T*
Trevecca Nazarene University *B, T*
Union University *B, T*

Texas

East Texas Baptist University *B*
Houston Baptist University *T*
Howard Payne University *B, T*

Kilgore College *A*
Lamar University *T*
Laredo Community College *A*
Lubbock Christian University *B*
McMurry University *B, T*
St. Edward's University *B, T*
St. Mary's University *T*
Sam Houston State University *M, T*
Tarleton State University *T*
Texas A&M University
    Commerce *B*
    Kingsville *T*
Texas State University: San Marcos *T*
Texas Wesleyan University *B, T*
University of Dallas *T*
University of Houston *T*
University of Houston
    Clear Lake *T*
University of Mary Hardin-Baylor *T*
University of Texas
    Arlington *T*
    San Antonio *T*
West Texas A&M University *T*

Utah

Brigham Young University *B*
Southern Utah University *B, T*
Utah State University *B*
Utah Valley University *B*
Weber State University *B*
Western Governors University *B, M, T*

Vermont

Castleton State College *B, T*
St. Michael's College *T*

Virginia

Averett University *B, M, T*
Bluefield College *B, T*
Bridgewater College *T*
Eastern Mennonite University *T*
Emory & Henry College *B*
Hampton University *M*
Hollins University *T*
Longwood University *B, T*
Old Dominion University *B, M, T*
Radford University *T*
University of Virginia's College at
    Wise *T*

Washington

Eastern Washington University *B*
Washington State University *B, M, T*
Western Washington University *B*
Whitworth University *B, T*

West Virginia

Bethany College *B*
Concord University *B, M, T*
Fairmont State University *B*
Shepherd University *T*
West Liberty University *B*
West Virginia Wesleyan College *B*

Wisconsin

Carroll University *B, T*
Carthage College *T*
Edgewood College *B*
Lakeland College *T*
Lawrence University *T*
Mount Mary College *B, T*
St. Norbert College *T*
University of Wisconsin
    Green Bay *T*
    Platteville *B*
    River Falls *T*
    Superior *B, T*
    Whitewater *B*
Viterbo University *B, T*

Chicano/ Hispanic-American/ Latino studies

Arizona

Arizona State University *B*
University of Arizona *B, M*

California

California State University
    Dominguez Hills *B*
    East Bay *B*
    Fresno *B*
    Fullerton *B*
    Long Beach *B*
    Los Angeles *B, M*
    Northridge *B*
    San Bernardino *B*
California State University: Channel
    Islands *B*
Cerritos College *A*
Claremont McKenna College *B*
Contra Costa College *A*
De Anza College *A*
El Camino College *A*
Fresno City College *A*
Loyola Marymount University *B*
Mills College *B*
Pitzer College *B*
Pomona College *B*
Rio Hondo College *A*
San Diego Mesa College *A*
San Diego State University *B*
San Francisco State University *B*
San Jose State University *M*
Santa Ana College *A*
Santa Barbara City College *A*
Scripps College *B*
Solano Community College *A*
Sonoma State University *B*
Southwestern College *A*
Stanford University *B*
University of California
    Berkeley *B*
    Davis *B*
    Irvine *B*
    Los Angeles *B*
    Riverside *B*
    Santa Barbara *B, M, D*
University of Southern California *B*

Colorado

Colorado College *B*
Fort Lewis College *B*
Metropolitan State College of
    Denver *B*
University of Northern Colorado *B*

Connecticut

Connecticut College *B*

Illinois

University of Illinois
    Chicago *M*

Maine

University of Southern Maine *B*

Massachusetts

Boston College *B*
Hampshire College *B*

Michigan

Michigan State University *D*
University of Michigan *B*

Minnesota

University of Minnesota
    Twin Cities *B*

New Hampshire

Dartmouth College *B*

New Jersey

Rutgers, The State University of New
    Jersey
    New Brunswick/Piscataway
        Campus *B*
    Newark Regional Campus *B*

New Mexico

Western New Mexico University *B*

New York

City University of New York
    Brooklyn College *B*
Columbia University *B*
Columbia University
    School of General Studies *B*
Hobart and William Smith Colleges *B*
Hofstra University *B*
State University of New York
    College at Oneonta *B*

Ohio

Bowling Green State University *B*
Pontifical College Josephinum *B*

Puerto Rico

Pontifical Catholic University of
    Puerto Rico *B, M*

Rhode Island

Brown University *B, M, D*

Texas

Our Lady of the Lake University of San
    Antonio *M*
Palo Alto College *A*
Rice University *B, M*
Southern Methodist University *B*
Texas A&M University *D*
University of Texas
    Austin *M*
    El Paso *B*
    Pan American *B*
    San Antonio *B, M*

Utah

Weber State University *B*

Washington

University of Washington *B*
University of Washington Tacoma *B*

Child care management

Alabama

Bevill State Community College *C, A*
Calhoun Community College *C, A*
Gadsden State Community College *C*
Jefferson State Community
    College *C, A*
Northwest-Shoals Community
    College *C*
Shelton State Community College *C*
Snead State Community College *C, A*
Wallace State Community College at
    Hanceville *A*

Alaska

University of Alaska
    Southeast *C, A*

Arizona

Glendale Community College *C*
Northland Pioneer College *C, A*
Phoenix College *C, A*
Scottsdale Community College *A*

Arkansas

Arkansas State University *M*
East Arkansas Community College *A*
Henderson State University *A*
Northwest Arkansas Community
College *A*
Ouachita Technical College *A*
Pulaski Technical College *C, A*
South Arkansas Community College *A*
University of Arkansas
Community College at Hope *A*
Cossatot Community College of the
A
Monticello *C*

California

American River College *C, A*
Antelope Valley College *C, A*
Barstow Community College *C, A*
Butte College *A*
Cabrillo College *C, A*
California State University
Northridge *B*
Canada College *C, A*
Cerro Coso Community College *C, A*
Chabot College *A*
Chaffey College *C, A*
Citrus College *C*
City College of San Francisco *C*
College of the Desert *A*
College of the Sequoias *C, A*
College of the Siskiyous *C, A*
Cuyamaca College *C*
Diablo Valley College *C*
El Camino College: Compton
Center *C, A*
Folsom Lake College *C*
Foothill College *C*
Fresno City College *C, A*
Fullerton College *C, A*
Glendale Community College *A*
Grossmont College *C, A*
Long Beach City College *C, A*
Los Angeles City College *C, A*
Los Angeles Harbor College *C, A*
Los Angeles Southwest College *C, A*
Los Medanos College *C, A*
Merritt College *C, A*
MiraCosta College *C, A*
Modesto Junior College *C, A*
Moorpark College *C, A*
Ohlone College *C, A*
Orange Coast College *C, A*
Palomar College *C, A*
Porterville College *C, A*
Reedley College *C*
Rio Hondo College *C*
Sacramento City College *C, A*
Saddleback College *C*
San Bernardino Valley College *C*
San Diego City College *C, A*
San Joaquin Delta College *A*
Santa Barbara City College *C, A*
Santa Rosa Junior College *C*
Shasta College *A*
Sierra College *A*
Southwestern College *C, A*
University of La Verne *B*
West Hills College: Lemoore *C*
West Valley College *C, A*

Colorado

Aims Community College *C, A*
Colorado Northwestern Community
College *C, A*
Community College of Aurora *C, A*
Front Range Community College *C, A*
Lamar Community College *A*
Mesa State College *C*
Trinidad State Junior College *C, A*

Connecticut

Asnuntuck Community College *C, A*
Gateway Community College *C*
Goodwin College *C, A*
Housatonic Community College *C, A*
Lincoln College of New England:
Briarwood *C, A*
Mitchell College *A, B*

Delaware

University of Delaware *B*

District of Columbia

Gallaudet University *B*

Florida

Brevard Community College *C*
Broward College *A*
Hillsborough Community College *A*
Indian River State College *C*
Miami Dade College *C*
Northwest Florida State College *C, A*
Palm Beach Community College *A*
Pensacola Junior College *A*
Polk State College *A*
Seminole Community College *A*
South Florida Community College *A*

Georgia

Abraham Baldwin Agricultural
College *A*
Albany Technical College *C*
Augusta Technical College *C*
Chattahoochee Technical
College *C, A*
Fort Valley State University *B*
Gainesville State College *C, A*
Savannah Technical College *C*
Spelman College *B*
Waycross College *A*

Hawaii

University of Hawaii
Honolulu Community College *C, A*

Idaho

Idaho State University *C, A*

Illinois

Carl Sandburg College *A*
City Colleges of Chicago
Harold Washington College *C*
Malcolm X College *C, A*
Olive-Harvey College *C, A*
College of DuPage *C, A*
Illinois Central College *A*
Illinois Eastern Community Colleges
Wabash Valley College *A*
Illinois Valley Community
College *A*
John Wood Community College *A*
Kishwaukee College *A*
Lake Land College *C, A*
Lewis and Clark Community
College *A*
Prairie State College *C, A*
Rock Valley College *C, A*
South Suburban College of Cook
County *C*
Southeastern Illinois College *A*
Southwestern Illinois College *C, A*

Indiana

Vincennes University *A*

Iowa

Iowa Western Community College *A*
Kirkwood Community College *C, A*
Marshalltown Community
College *C, A*
Southeastern Community College
North Campus *A*

Kansas

Allen County Community College *C*
Barton County Community
College *C, A*
Butler Community College *C, A*
Cloud County Community
College *C, A*
Colby Community College *A*
Cowley County Community
College *A*
Dodge City Community College *C, A*
Garden City Community College *A*
Hutchinson Community College *C, A*
Johnson County Community
College *A*
Kansas City Kansas Community
College *A*
Neosho County Community
College *C*

Kentucky

Eastern Kentucky University *A*
Somerset Community College *C, A*
Sullivan University *C, A*

Louisiana

Nicholls State University *A*

Maine

Andover College *C, A*

Maryland

Anne Arundel Community College *A*
Carroll Community College *A*
Cecil College *A*
Chesapeake College *C, A*
College of Southern Maryland *C, A*
Community College of Baltimore
County *A*
Frederick Community College *C, A*
Garrett College *C*
Hagerstown Community College *C, A*
Montgomery College *C, A*
Prince George's Community
College *C, A*
Wor-Wic Community College *C, A*

Massachusetts

Bristol Community College *A*
Holyoke Community College *C, A*
Massachusetts Bay Community
College *C, A*
Massasoit Community College *C, A*
Middlesex Community College *C*
Mount Wachusett Community
College *A*
Northern Essex Community
College *A*
Roxbury Community College *A*
Wheelock College *B, M*

Michigan

Baker College
of Muskegon *C*
of Owosso *C, A*
Bay de Noc Community College *A*
Ferris State University *A, B*
Glen Oaks Community College *C, A*
Gogebic Community College *C*
Grand Rapids Community College *A*
Kellogg Community College *C, A*
Lansing Community College *A*
Macomb Community College *A*
Mid Michigan Community
College *C, A*
Monroe County Community
College *A*
Montcalm Community College *C, A*
Oakland Community College *A*
St. Clair County Community
College *A*
Schoolcraft College *C, A*

Wayne County Community
College *C, A*

Minnesota

Alexandria Technical College *C, A*
Anoka Technical College *C, A*
Central Lakes College *C, A*
Lake Superior College *C*
Minneapolis Community and
Technical College *C, A*
Minnesota State College - Southeast
Technical *A*
Minnesota West Community and
Technical College *A*
Northwest Technical College *A*
Pine Technical College *C, A*
Rasmussen College
Eagan *C, A*
Eden Prairie *C, A*
Mankato *C, A*
St. Cloud *C, A*
Rasmussen College: Brooklyn
Park *C, A*
Rochester Community and Technical
College *C, A*
St. Cloud Technical College *C, A*
St. Paul College *C, A*
Walden University *B*

Mississippi

Hinds Community College *A*
Meridian Community College *A*
Rust College *B*

Missouri

East Central College *A*
Metropolitan Community College:
Penn Valley *C, A*
Mineral Area College *C*
Missouri State University: West
Plains *C, A*
Northwest Missouri State
University *C*
St. Charles Community College *C, A*
St. Louis Community College
St. Louis Community College at
Florissant Valley *A*
Southeast Missouri State University *A*
State Fair Community College *A*

Montana

Dawson Community College *C*
Little Big Horn College *A*

Nebraska

Central Community College *C, A*
Metropolitan Community
College *C, A*
Mid-Plains Community College
Area *C, A*
Southeast Community College *A*

Nevada

Truckee Meadows Community
College *C, A*

New Hampshire

Lakes Region Community College *C*
Nashua Community College *C*
River Valley Community College *C*

New Jersey

County College of Morris *C*
Hudson County Community
College *C, A*
Ocean County College *A*
Thomas Edison State College *A, B*

New Mexico

Central New Mexico Community
College *A*

Dona Ana Community College of New
Mexico State University *C*
Eastern New Mexico University *A*
Eastern New Mexico University:
Roswell Campus *C, A*

New York

Broome Community College *C, A*
City University of New York
LaGuardia Community College *A*
Corning Community College *C, A*
Dutchess Community College *C, A*
Erie Community College
City Campus *A*
Fulton-Montgomery Community
College *A*
Genesee Community College *C*
Hudson Valley Community College *A*
Medaille College *B*
Nassau Community College *C*
Orange County Community College *A*
Rockland Community College *C*
State University of New York
College of Agriculture and
Technology at Cobleskill *A, B*
Sullivan County Community
College *C, A*
Tompkins Cortland Community
College *A*
Trocaire College *C*
Westchester Community College *C, A*

North Carolina

Asheville-Buncombe Technical
Community College *C, A*
Beaufort County Community
College *C, A*
Blue Ridge Community College *A*
Cape Fear Community College *C, A*
Carteret Community College *C, A*
Central Carolina Community
College *C, A*
Central Piedmont Community
College *C, A*
Cleveland Community College *C, A*
Edgecombe Community College *A*
Halifax Community College *C*
Haywood Community College *C, A*
Lenoir Community College *C, A*
Mayland Community College *C*
Mid-Atlantic Christian University *A*
Nash Community College *A*
Randolph Community College *A*
Richmond Community College *C, A*
Roanoke-Chowan Community
College *A*
Sandhills Community College *A*
South Piedmont Community
College *C, A*
Southeastern Community College *A*
Southwestern Community College *A*
Vance-Granville Community
College *C, A*
Western Piedmont Community
College *C, A*

North Dakota

Lake Region State College *C, A*
Mayville State University *B*

Ohio

Cincinnati State Technical and
Community College *C, A*
Columbus State Community
College *C*
Cuyahoga Community College
Metropolitan Campus *A*
Eastern Gateway Community
College *C, A*
Edison State Community College *C, A*
Kent State University
Salem *C*

Trumbull *C*
Tuscarawas *C*
Mount Vernon Nazarene University *A*
North Central State College *C*
Youngstown State University *A*
Zane State College *A*

Oklahoma

Connors State College *C, A*
Eastern Oklahoma State College *A*
Murray State College *A*
Oklahoma City Community
College *C, A*
Oklahoma State University
Oklahoma City *A*
Redlands Community College *A*
Rose State College *A*
Tulsa Community College *C, A*
Western Oklahoma State College *A*

Oregon

Central Oregon Community
College *C*
Chemeketa Community College *C, A*
Clackamas Community College *C, A*
Clatsop Community College *C*
Linn-Benton Community College *C, A*
Portland Community College *C, A*
Rogue Community College *C, A*
Southwestern Oregon Community
College *C, A*
Umpqua Community College *A*

Pennsylvania

Central Pennsylvania College *A*
Chestnut Hill College *A, B*
Community College of Philadelphia *A*
Gannon University *M*
Keystone College *C, A, B*
Keystone Technical Institute *A*
Laurel Business Institute *A*
Montgomery County Community
College *A*
Northampton Community College *C*
Pennsylvania Highlands Community
College *C*
Reading Area Community
College *C, A*
Seton Hill University *C, B*

Puerto Rico

Inter American University of Puerto
Rico
Aguadilla Campus *C*
Ponce Paramedical College *C*

South Carolina

Bob Jones University *A*
Denmark Technical College *C*
Florence-Darlington Technical
College *C*
Forrest Junior College *C, A*
Greenville Technical College *A*
Horry-Georgetown Technical
College *A*
Midlands Technical College *C*
Northeastern Technical College *C*
Orangeburg-Calhoun Technical
College *C*
Technical College of the
Lowcountry *C, A*
Tri-County Technical College *C*
Trident Technical College *C, A*

South Dakota

Southeast Technical Institute *A*

Tennessee

Belmont University *B*
Northeast State Community College *C*
Trevecca Nazarene University *A*

Texas

Amarillo College *C, A*
Angelina College *C*
Blinn College *C, A*
Brazosport College *C, A*
Brookhaven College *A*
Central Texas College *C, A*
Coastal Bend College *C, A*
College of the Mainland *A*
Del Mar College *C, A*
El Paso Community College *C, A*
Houston Community College
System *C*
Howard College *C, A*
Kilgore College *C, A*
Lamar Institute of Technology *C*
Lamar State College at Port
Arthur *C, A*
Laredo Community College *C, A*
Lone Star College System *C, A*
McLennan Community College *C, A*
Midland College *C, A*
Navarro College *A*
Odessa College *C, A*
St. Philip's College *C, A*
San Antonio College *C*
San Jacinto College *C*
South Plains College *C, A*
Tarrant County College *C*
Temple College *C*
Trinity Valley Community
College *C, A*
Tyler Junior College *C, A*
Vernon College *C*
Victoria College *C*
Weatherford College *C, A*
Wharton County Junior College *C*

Utah

College of Eastern Utah *C*
Snow College *A*
Weber State University *A*

Virginia

Central Virginia Community
College *C*
Danville Community College *C*
J. Sargeant Reynolds Community
College *C, A*
John Tyler Community College *C, A*
Lord Fairfax Community College *C*
Southwest Virginia Community
College *C*
Thomas Nelson Community
College *C*
Virginia Western Community
College *A*
Wytheville Community College *A*

Washington

Highline Community College *C, A*
Lake Washington Technical
College *C, A*
Peninsula College *A*
Pierce College *A*
Renton Technical College *C, A*
Shoreline Community College *C*
Spokane Falls Community College *C*
Yakima Valley Community
College *C, A*

Wisconsin

Blackhawk Technical College *C*
Fox Valley Technical College *C, A*
Gateway Technical College *A*
Milwaukee Area Technical College *C*
Moraine Park Technical College *C, A*
Nicolet Area Technical College *C, A*
Northcentral Technical College *C*
Northeast Wisconsin Technical
College *C*
Southwest Wisconsin Technical
College *C, A*

Waukesha County Technical
College *A*
Western Technical College *A*

Wyoming

Central Wyoming College *A*

Child care service

Arizona

Arizona Western College *C*
Central Arizona College *C*

Arkansas

Arkansas Northeastern College *C, A*
Arkansas State University
Beebe *C*
Ouachita Technical College *C*
Rich Mountain Community College *C*
South Arkansas Community
College *C, A*
Southeast Arkansas College *C, A*
Southern Arkansas University
Tech *C, A*
University of Arkansas
Community College at Hope *C*

California

Antelope Valley College *C, A*
City College of San Francisco *C*
College of Marin: Kentfield *C, A*
College of the Siskiyous *C, A*
Feather River College *C, A*
Folsom Lake College *C*
Foothill College *C*
Merced College *C*
Monterey Peninsula College *A*
Santa Rosa Junior College *C*
Southwestern College *C, A*
Taft College *C*
West Hills College: Lemoore *C*

Colorado

Red Rocks Community College *C*

Connecticut

Naugatuck Valley Community
College *C*
Three Rivers Community College *C, A*

Florida

Daytona State College *A*
Gulf Coast Community College *C*
Hillsborough Community College *C*
Lake-Sumter Community College *A*
Palm Beach Community College *C*
Santa Fe College *C*
Tallahassee Community College *A*

Georgia

Albany Technical College *C*
Atlanta Technical College *A*
Savannah Technical College *C, A*
Southwest Georgia Technical
College *C, A*

Illinois

Black Hawk College *C, A*
Danville Area Community
College *C, A*
Elgin Community College *C*
Harper College *C, A*
Heartland Community College *C, A*
Highland Community College *C, A*
Kaskaskia College *A*
Lincoln Land Community College *C, A*
McHenry County College *C, A*
Moraine Valley Community College *A*
Morton College *C*
Parkland College *C, A*
Sauk Valley Community College *C, A*
Triton College *C, A*

Waubonsee Community College *C, A*

Indiana

St. Mary-of-the-Woods College *A*
Vincennes University *C*

Iowa

Des Moines Area Community
College *C, A*
Hawkeye Community College *C, A*
Indian Hills Community College *C, A*
Iowa Lakes Community College *C, A*
Muscatine Community College *C, A*
Northeast Iowa Community
College *C*
Scott Community College *C, A*
Western Iowa Tech Community
College *C, A*

Kansas

Kansas City Kansas Community
College *C*

Kentucky

Ashland Community and Technical
College *C*
Bluegrass Community and Technical
College *C, A*
Campbellsville University *A*
Elizabethtown Community and
Technical College *C, A*
Hopkinsville Community College *C, A*
Madisonville Community College *C, A*
Murray State University *A, B*
Owensboro Community and
Technical College *C*
St. Catharine College *C*
Somerset Community College *C, A*
Western Kentucky University *C*

Louisiana

Nunez Community College *C, A*
South Louisiana Community
College *A*
University of Louisiana at Monroe *A*

Maine

Beal College *A*

Maryland

Community College of Baltimore
County *C*

Massachusetts

Cape Cod Community College *C*
Massachusetts College of Liberal
Arts *C*
Massasoit Community College *C*
Mount Wachusett Community
College *C*
North Shore Community College *C, A*
Pine Manor College *A*
Quinsigamond Community
College *C, A*

Michigan

Baker College
of Muskegon *C*
of Port Huron *C*
Baker College of Allen Park *C*
Bay de Noc Community College *C*
Mott Community College *A*

Minnesota

Alexandria Technical College *C*
Central Lakes College *C*
Dakota County Technical College *C, A*
Fond du Lac Tribal and Community
College *C*
Inver Hills Community College *C*
Lake Superior College *C*

Minneapolis Community and
Technical College *C*
Minnesota State College - Southeast
Technical *C*
Minnesota State Community and
Technical College *C*
Minnesota West Community and
Technical College *C*
Northland Community & Technical
College *A*
Northwest Technical College *C, A*
Rasmussen College: Lake
Elmo/Woodbury *C*
Ridgewater College *C*
Rochester Community and Technical
College *C*
St. Cloud Technical College *C*
St. Paul College *C*
Walden University *B*

Missouri

North Central Missouri College *A*

Nebraska

Wayne State College *B*

New Jersey

Raritan Valley Community College *C*

New Mexico

Santa Fe Community College *C*

New York

Monroe Community College *C, A*
Onondaga Community College *C*

North Carolina

Bladen Community College *C, A*
Carteret Community College *C, A*

North Dakota

Dakota College at Bottineau *A*
Lake Region State College *A*
Mayville State University *A*
Turtle Mountain Community
College *C*

Ohio

Cincinnati State Technical and
Community College *C*
North Central State College *C*
Stark State College of Technology *A*

Oklahoma

Northeastern Oklahoma Agricultural
and Mechanical College *C*

Oregon

Lane Community College *C, A*

Pennsylvania

Harrisburg Area Community
College *C*
Keystone College *A*
Montgomery County Community
College *C*
Northampton Community College *C*
Pennsylvania College of
Technology *A*
Pennsylvania Highlands Community
College *A*
Westmoreland County Community
College *C, A*

Puerto Rico

Inter American University of Puerto
Rico
Bayamon Campus *C*

Rhode Island

Community College of Rhode
Island *C*

South Carolina

Aiken Technical College *C*
Greenville Technical College *C*
Horry-Georgetown Technical
College *C*
Midlands Technical College *C*
Spartanburg Community College *C*
Williamsburg Technical College *C*

South Dakota

Southeast Technical Institute *C*

Texas

Austin Community College *C*
Brookhaven College *A*
Collin County Community College
District *C*
Del Mar College *C*
Houston Community College
System *C*
Lamar Institute of Technology *C, A*
San Antonio College *C*
Tarrant County College *C*
University of Texas
Brownsville - Texas Southmost
College *C, A*

Washington

Bates Technical College *C*
Bellingham Technical College *C*
Centralia College *C, A*
Peninsula College *C, A*

West Virginia

American Public University System *C*
Eastern West Virginia Community and
Technical College *C, A*

Wisconsin

Chippewa Valley Technical College *A*
Fox Valley Technical College *C*
Lakeshore Technical College *C*
Northcentral Technical College *C, A*
Rasmussen College: Green Bay *C*

Wyoming

Eastern Wyoming College *C*

Child development

Alabama

Calhoun Community College *A*
Gadsden State Community College *A*
Lawson State Community College *C*

Alaska

University of Alaska
Fairbanks *B*

Arizona

Arizona State University *M*
Arizona Western College *C, A*
Central Arizona College *C, A*
Pima Community College *C, A*
Prescott College *B, M*

Arkansas

Arkansas Tech University *A*
University of Arkansas
Cossatot Community College of the
C
Fort Smith *A*
University of Arkansas Community
College at Morrilton *C, A*

California

Antelope Valley College *A*

California State University
Fresno *B*
San Bernardino *B*
City College of San Francisco *A*
College of the Canyons *C, A*
College of the Siskiyous *C, A*
Columbia College *A*
East Los Angeles College *C, A*
Foothill College *C, A*
Grossmont College *C, A*
Hartnell College *C, A*
Imperial Valley College *C, A*
Long Beach City College *C, A*
Merced College *C, A*
Mills College *B*
Monterey Peninsula College *A*
National University *B*
Oxnard College *C, A*
Palo Verde College *C, A*
Point Loma Nazarene University *B*
San Diego Mesa College *C, A*
San Diego State University *B*
Santa Barbara City College *C*
Santa Rosa Junior College *C*
Shasta College *A*
Southwestern College *C, A*
Taft College *C*
Ventura College *C, A*
West Hills College: Lemoore *C*

Colorado

Arapahoe Community College *A*
Community College of Denver *C, A*
Northeastern Junior College *A*
Pikes Peak Community College *C, A*
Pueblo Community College *C, A*
Red Rocks Community College *C, A*

Connecticut

Goodwin College *C, A, B*
Naugatuck Valley Community
College *C, A*
Saint Joseph College *B*

Florida

Florida State University *B*
Indian River State College *C*
Miami Dade College *A*
Nova Southeastern University *M, D*

Georgia

Fort Valley State University *B*
University of Georgia *B, M, D*

Idaho

Lewis-Clark State College *A, B*

Illinois

City Colleges of Chicago
Kennedy-King College *A*
Olive-Harvey College *A*
Rend Lake College *C, A*
University of Illinois
Chicago *M*
Urbana-Champaign *B, M, D*

Kansas

Kansas State University *B*
Pittsburg State University *B*
University of St. Mary *B*

Louisiana

Grambling State University *A*

Maine

Kennebec Valley Community
College *A*

Maryland

Bowie State University *B*
Howard Community College *C, A*

Massachusetts
Lesley University *B*
Mount Wachusett Community
College *A*
Wheelock College *B, M*

Michigan
Bay de Noc Community College *A*
Central Michigan University *B*
Delta College *C, A*
Grand Rapids Community College *A*
Henry Ford Community College *A*
Madonna University *A, B*
Michigan State University *B, M*
Northern Michigan University *A*
Schoolcraft College *C, A*
Western Michigan University *B*

Minnesota
Concordia University: St. Paul *C, B*
Hennepin Technical College *C, A*
South Central College *C, A*
University of Minnesota
Duluth *B*
Walden University *B*

Mississippi
Alcorn State University *B*
Mississippi Gulf Coast Community
College *C*

Missouri
Central Methodist University *B*
College of the Ozarks *B*
Mineral Area College *C, A*
Missouri State University *M*
Ozarks Technical Community
College *C, A*
Park University *B*
University of Central Missouri *A, B*

Nevada
University of Nevada
Reno *B*

New Hampshire
Southern New Hampshire
University *B, M*
University of New Hampshire *B*

New York
Sarah Lawrence College *M*
State University of New York
College at Oneonta *B*
Oswego *B*

North Carolina
Appalachian State University *B*
Beaufort County Community
College *C, A*
Campbell University *B*
Carteret Community College *C, A*
East Carolina University *B*
Isothermal Community College *C*
James Sprunt Community
College *C, A*
Lenoir-Rhyne University *B*
Meredith College *B*
Montgomery Community College *C*
Peace College *B*
University of North Carolina
Greensboro *B*
Wilson Community College *C*

Ohio
Bowling Green State University *B*
Columbus State Community
College *C, A*
Edison State Community College *C, A*
James A. Rhodes State College *C*
Northwest State Community
College *A*

Ohio University *A, B*
Ohio University
Southern Campus at Ironton *A*
Union Institute & University *B*
University of Akron *B, M*
University of Dayton *M*
Youngstown State University *A*

Oklahoma
Redlands Community College *C, A*
Rose State College *A*
University of Central Oklahoma *B*
Western Oklahoma State College *C*

Pennsylvania
Community College of Allegheny
County *C, A*
Keystone College *B*
Seton Hill University *B*

South Carolina
York Technical College *C*

Tennessee
Cleveland State Community College *A*
Dyersburg State Community
College *C, A*
East Tennessee State University *B*
Jackson State Community College *A*
Motlow State Community College *C*
Northeast State Community
College *C, A*
Pellissippi State Community
College *A*
Roane State Community College *A*
Southwest Tennessee Community
College *C, A*
Vanderbilt University *M*
Volunteer State Community College *A*
Walters State Community College *A*

Texas
Alvin Community College *A*
Angelina College *C, A*
Angelo State University *B*
Austin Community College *C, A*
Brookhaven College *C*
Collin County Community College
District *C, A*
Del Mar College *C, A*
Eastfield College *C, A*
Houston Baptist University *B*
Houston Community College
System *C, A*
San Antonio College *C, A*
San Jacinto College *C, A*
South Texas College *A*
Tarrant County College *C, A*
Temple College *C, A*
Texarkana College *C, A*
Texas Southern University *B*
Texas Tech University *B*
Texas Woman's University *B, M, D*
University of Texas
Arlington *B*
University of the Incarnate Word *B*
Victoria College *C*
Wharton County Junior College *C, A*

Utah
Southern Utah University *A*

Vermont
Bennington College *B*

Virginia
Danville Community College *A*

Washington
Eastern Washington University *B*
Lower Columbia College *C, A*
Washington State University *C*

Western Washington University *B*

West Virginia
American Public University System *B*
West Virginia University *B*

Wisconsin
Northcentral Technical College *C*

Wyoming
University of Wyoming *C*

Chinese

California
California State University
Los Angeles *B*
Claremont McKenna College *B*
Foothill College *A*
Los Angeles City College *A*
National University *B*
Pitzer College *B*
Pomona College *B*
San Francisco State University *B, M*
San Jose State University *B*
Scripps College *B*
Stanford University *B, M, D*
University of California
Berkeley *B, M, D*
Davis *B*
Irvine *B*
Los Angeles *B*
Santa Barbara *B*

Colorado
University of Colorado
Boulder *B*

Connecticut
Connecticut College *B*
Trinity College *B*
Wesleyan University *B*
Yale University *B*

District of Columbia
George Washington University *B*
Georgetown University *B*

Florida
Florida State University *B*
New College of Florida *B*

Georgia
Emory University *B*
University of Georgia *B*

Hawaii
University of Hawaii
Manoa *B, M, D*

Illinois
DePaul University *B*

Indiana
Indiana University
Bloomington *M, D*
University of Notre Dame *B*

Iowa
University of Iowa *B, T*

Maine
Bates College *B, T*

Maryland
United States Naval Academy *B*
University of Maryland
College Park *B*

Massachusetts
Bard College at Simon's Rock *B*
Tufts University *B*
University of Massachusetts
Amherst *B, M*
Wellesley College *B*
Williams College *B*

Michigan
Calvin College *B*
Michigan State University *B*

Minnesota
Concordia College: Moorhead *B*
University of Minnesota
Twin Cities *B, M, D*

Mississippi
University of Mississippi *B*

Missouri
Washington University in St.
Louis *B, M, D*

New Hampshire
Dartmouth College *B*

New Jersey
Drew University *B*
Rutgers, The State University of New
Jersey
New Brunswick/Piscataway
Campus *B*
Seton Hall University *T*

New York
Bard College *B*
City University of New York
Hunter College *B*
Queens College *B, T*
Columbia University *B*
Hamilton College *B*
Hobart and William Smith Colleges *B*
Hofstra University *B*
United States Military Academy *B*
Vassar College *B*

North Carolina
Wake Forest University *B*

Ohio
Ohio State University
Columbus Campus *B*

Oklahoma
University of Oklahoma *B*

Oregon
Pacific University *B*
Portland State University *B*
Reed College *B*
University of Oregon *B*

Pennsylvania
Carnegie Mellon University *B*
Haverford College *T*
Swarthmore College *B*
University of Pittsburgh *B*

South Carolina
Wofford College *B*

Texas
Southwestern University *B*
Trinity University *B*

Utah
Brigham Young University *B, M*
University of Utah *B*

Vermont
Bennington College *B*
Middlebury College *B, M, D*
University of Vermont *B*

Virginia
College of William and Mary *B*

Washington
Pacific Lutheran University *B*
University of Puget Sound *T*
University of Washington *B*

Wisconsin
Lawrence University *B*
University of Wisconsin
  Madison *B, M, D*

Chinese studies

California
California Institute of Integral
  Studies *M, D*
National University *B*
University of California
  Irvine *B*
  San Diego *B*

Georgia
Emory University *B*

Indiana
Valparaiso University *M*

Massachusetts
Bard College at Simon's Rock *B*

Michigan
Grand Valley State University *B*

New York
Columbia University *B*
St. John's University *M*
State University of New York
  Albany *B*

North Dakota
University of North Dakota *B*

Washington
University of Washington *B, M*

Wisconsin
Lawrence University *B*
Wisconsin Lutheran College *B*

Chiropractic (D.C.)

California
Cleveland Chiropractic College: Los
  Angeles *P*
Life Chiropractic College West *P*
Los Angeles College of Chiropractic *P*
Palmer College of
  Chiropractic-West *P*

Connecticut
University of Bridgeport College of
  Chiropractic *P*

Georgia
Life College *P*

Illinois
National University of Health
  Sciences: Professional *P*

Iowa
Palmer College of Chiropractic *P*

Minnesota
Northwestern College of
  Chiropractic *P*

Missouri
Cleveland Chiropractic College:
  Kansas City *P*
Logan University *P*

New York
New York Chiropractic College *P*

Oregon
Western States Chiropractic College *P*

South Carolina
Sherman College of Straight
  Chiropractic *P*

Texas
Parker College of Chiropractic *P*
Texas Chiropractic College *P*

Chiropractic assistant

Florida
Gulf Coast Community College *A*

Illinois
Lewis University *B*
National University of Health
  Sciences *C*

Christian studies

Alabama
Faulkner University *B, M*

Arkansas
Ouachita Baptist University *A*

California
California Baptist University *B*
Santa Clara University *M*
Simpson University *B*
Trinity Life Bible College *A*
Vanguard University of Southern
  California *B*

Florida
Bethune-Cookman University *B*

Georgia
Mercer University *B*
Truett-McConnell College *A, B*

Illinois
Loyola University Chicago *M*
Trinity International University *C, M*

Indiana
University of Notre Dame *M*

Iowa
Iowa Wesleyan College *B*
St. Ambrose University *C*

Kansas
Bethany College *B*

Kentucky
Lindsey Wilson College *B*
Mid-Continent University *B*

Louisiana
Loyola University New Orleans *B*

Massachusetts
Gordon College *B*

Stonehill College *B*

Michigan
Hillsdale College *B*
Spring Arbor University *B*

Minnesota
College of St. Scholastica *B*
North Central University *B*

Mississippi
Mississippi College *B*

Missouri
Calvary Bible College and Theological
  Seminary *M*
Lindenwood University *B*
Missouri Baptist University *C, B*

New Jersey
Seton Hall University *B*
Somerset Christian College *C, A, R*

North Carolina
Montreat College *C, B*

Ohio
Cincinnati Christian
  University *A, B, M*
Ursuline College *B*

Oklahoma
Oklahoma Baptist University *C*
Oklahoma Christian University *B*
Oklahoma Wesleyan University *B*

Oregon
Eugene Bible College *C, B*

Pennsylvania
Elizabethtown College *B*

South Carolina
Anderson University *B*

Tennessee
Bethel University *B*
Bryan College *B*
Tennessee Wesleyan College *B*
Union University *C, A, B*

Texas
Hardin-Simmons University *M*
Houston Baptist University *B*
McMurry University *B*
Southwestern Assemblies of God
  University *A, B, M*
University of Mary Hardin-Baylor *B*
Wayland Baptist University *A, B, M*

Virginia
Bluefield College *B*

Washington
Trinity Lutheran College *A, B*

West Virginia
Alderson-Broaddus College *B*

Wisconsin
Maranatha Baptist Bible College *A*

Cinematography and film/video production

Arizona
Art Institute
  of Phoenix *B*
Art Institute of Tucson *B*

Glendale Community College *A*
Prescott College *B, M*
Scottsdale Community College *C, A*

Arkansas
University of Central Arkansas *B, M*

California
Academy of Art University *C, A, B, M*
Allan Hancock College *C*
Antelope Valley College *C, A*
Art Center College of Design *B, M*
Art Institute
  of California: Los Angeles *A, B*
Art Institute of California:
  Sacramento *B*
Art Institute of California:
  Sunnyvale *B*
Biola University *B*
Brooks Institute *B*
California College of the Arts *B, M*
California Institute of the Arts *C, B, M*
California State University
  Long Beach *B*
  Sacramento *B*
Chapman University *B, M*
City College of San Francisco *A*
College of San Mateo *A*
College of the Canyons *C, A*
Cosumnes River College *A*
De Anza College *C, A*
Grossmont College *C, A*
Los Angeles City College *C, A*
Los Angeles Valley College *C*
Loyola Marymount University *B*
Modesto Junior College *A*
Moorpark College *A*
National University *M*
Orange Coast College *A*
Pacific Union College *B*
Pitzer College *B*
San Francisco Art Institute *B, M*
Southwestern College *A*
University of California
  Santa Barbara *B*
University of Southern
  California *B, M*
Vanguard University of Southern
  California *B*

Colorado
Art Institute
  of Colorado *A, B*
Red Rocks Community College *C, A*

Connecticut
University of Hartford *B*

District of Columbia
American University *B, M*

Florida
Art Institute of Fort Lauderdale *A, B*
Florida Atlantic University *C*
Florida State College at Jacksonville *A*
Florida State University *B, M*
Full Sail University *B*
Hillsborough Community
  College *C, A*
Miami Dade College *A*
Miami International University of Art
  and Design *B, M*
Palm Beach Community College *A*
Polk State College *A*
University of Central Florida *B*
University of Miami *B, M*

Georgia
Art Institute
  of Atlanta *B*
Savannah College of Art and
  Design *B, M*

Illinois

Columbia College Chicago *C, B, M*
DePaul University *B, M*
School of the Art Institute of
 Chicago *B, M*
Southern Illinois University
 Carbondale *B*
University of Illinois
 Chicago *B, M*

Iowa

University of Iowa *B, M*

Kentucky

Bluegrass Community and Technical
 College *C*

Louisiana

Baton Rouge Community College *A*
Centenary College of Louisiana *B*

Maryland

Cecil College *C*

Massachusetts

Bard College at Simon's Rock *B*
Boston University *B, M*
Emerson College *B*
Fitchburg State College *B*
Massachusetts College of Art and
 Design *B, M*
School of the Museum of Fine
 Arts *B, M*

Michigan

Calvin College *B*
College for Creative Studies *B*
Lansing Community College *A*
Northern Michigan University *B*
Wayne State University *B*

Minnesota

Art Institutes International
 Minnesota *B*
Minneapolis Community and
 Technical College *C, A*

Missouri

Kansas City Art Institute *B*
Webster University *B*

Montana

Montana State University
 Bozeman *B*
University of Montana *M*

Nevada

Art Institute
 of Las Vegas *B*

New Hampshire

Keene State College *B*

New Jersey

Cumberland County College *A*
Fairleigh Dickinson University
 College at Florham *B*
Montclair State University *B*
Raritan Valley Community College *C*

New Mexico

Central New Mexico Community
 College *C*
New Mexico State University *B*
New Mexico State University
 Carlsbad *C*

New York

Art Institute
 of New York City *A*
Bard College *B, M*

City University of New York
 Brooklyn College *C, B*
 City College *B, M*
 Hunter College *B*
Five Towns College *B*
Ithaca College *B*
Long Island University
 C. W. Post Campus *B*
New York University *B, M, D*
Pratt Institute *B*
Rochester Institute of
 Technology *A, B, M*
State University of New York
 Binghamton *B*
 Purchase *B*
Syracuse University *B, M*

North Carolina

Cape Fear Community College *A*
East Carolina University *B*
Piedmont Community College *A*
St. Augustine's College *B*
University of North Carolina
 Wilmington *B*
University of North Carolina School of
 the Arts *B, M*

Ohio

Art Institute of Ohio: Cincinnati *A*
Cincinnati State Technical and
 Community College *A*
Cleveland State University *B*
Ohio University *B, M*

Oklahoma

Oklahoma City University *B*

Oregon

Art Institute of Portland *B*
George Fox University *B*
Portland Community College *C*

Pennsylvania

Art Institute
 of Philadelphia *A, B*
 of Pittsburgh *A, B*
Bucks County Community
 College *C, A*
Drexel University *B*
La Salle University *B*
Point Park University *B*
University of the Arts *B*

Rhode Island

New England Institute of
 Technology *A*
Rhode Island School of Design *B*
University of Rhode Island *B*

South Carolina

Bob Jones University *B, M*
Trident Technical College *C*

Tennessee

Pellissippi State Community
 College *A*
Southern Adventist University *B*

Texas

El Paso Community College *C, A*
Houston Community College
 System *C, A*
North Lake College *A*
South Plains College *A*
Texas State Technical College
 Waco *A*

Vermont

Bennington College *B*
Burlington College *C*
Champlain College *B*
Marlboro College *B*

Middlebury College *B*

Virginia

George Mason University *B*
Regent University *B, M*
Virginia Commonwealth University *B*

Washington

Art Institute of Seattle *A, B*
Cornish College of the Arts *B*
Eastern Washington University *B*
Evergreen State College *B*
Shoreline Community College *A*

Wisconsin

University of Wisconsin
 Madison *B*
 Oshkosh *B*

Civil engineering

Alabama

Alabama Agricultural and Mechanical
 University *B*
Auburn University *B, M, D*
University of Alabama *B, M, D*
University of Alabama
 Birmingham *B, M, D*
 Huntsville *B, D*
University of South Alabama *B, M*

Alaska

University of Alaska
 Anchorage *B, M*
 Fairbanks *B, M*

Arizona

Arizona State University *B, M, D*
Central Arizona College *A*
Northern Arizona University *B*
University of Arizona *B, M, D*

Arkansas

Arkansas State University *B*
University of Arkansas *B, M*

California

California Baptist University *B*
California Institute of
 Technology *M, D*
California Polytechnic State
 University: San Luis Obispo *B, M*
California State Polytechnic
 University: Pomona *B*
California State University
 Chico *B*
 Fresno *B, M*
 Fullerton *B, M*
 Long Beach *B, M*
 Los Angeles *B, M*
 Northridge *B, M*
 Sacramento *B, M*
East Los Angeles College *A*
Loyola Marymount University *B, M*
San Diego State University *B, M*
San Francisco State University *B*
San Jose State University *B, M*
Santa Clara University *B, M*
Stanford University *B, M, D*
University of California
 Berkeley *B, M, D*
 Davis *B*
 Irvine *B, M, D*
 Los Angeles *B, M, D*
University of Southern
 California *B, M, D*
University of the Pacific *B*

Colorado

Colorado School of Mines *B*
Colorado State University *B, M, D*
United States Air Force Academy *B*

University of Colorado
 Boulder *B, M, D*
 Denver *B, M, D*

Connecticut

Central Connecticut State
 University *B*
United States Coast Guard Academy *B*
University of Connecticut *B, M, D*
University of Hartford *B, M*
University of New Haven *B*

Delaware

University of Delaware *B, M, D*

District of Columbia

Catholic University of
 America *B, M, D*
George Washington
 University *B, M, D*
Howard University *B, M*
University of the District of
 Columbia *A, B*

Florida

Broward College *A*
Edison State College *A*
Embry-Riddle Aeronautical
 University *B*
Florida Agricultural and Mechanical
 University *B, M, D*
Florida Atlantic University *B, M*
Florida Gulf Coast University *B*
Florida Institute of
 Technology *B, M, D*
Florida International
 University *B, M, D*
Florida State College at Jacksonville *A*
Florida State University *B, M, D*
Miami Dade College *A*
Pensacola Junior College *A*
State College of Florida,
 Manatee-Sarasota *A*
Tallahassee Community College *A*
University of Central Florida *B, M, D*
University of Florida *B, M*
University of Miami *B, M, D*
University of North Florida *B*
University of South Florida *B, M, D*

Georgia

Georgia Institute of
 Technology *B, M, D*
Georgia Southern University *B*
Middle Georgia College *A*
Southern Polytechnic State
 University *B*

Hawaii

University of Hawaii
 Manoa *B, M, D*

Idaho

Boise State University *B, M*
Brigham Young University-Idaho *A*
Idaho State University *B, M*
North Idaho College *A*
Northwest Nazarene University *B*
University of Idaho *B, M, D*

Illinois

Bradley University *B, M*
Dominican University *B*
Illinois Institute of
 Technology *B, M, D*
Lake Land College *A*
Northwestern University *B, M, D*
Southern Illinois University
 Carbondale *B, M*
Southern Illinois University
 Edwardsville *B, M*

University of Illinois
    Chicago *B, M, D*
    Urbana-Champaign *B, M, D*

Indiana

Indiana University-Purdue University
    Fort Wayne *B*
Purdue University *B, M, D*
Rose-Hulman Institute of
    Technology *B, M*
Trine University *B, M*
University of Evansville *B*
University of Notre Dame *B, M, D*
Valparaiso University *B*
Vincennes University *A*

Iowa

Dordt College *B*
Iowa State University *B, M, D*
University of Iowa *B, M, D*

Kansas

Kansas State University *B, M, D*
University of Kansas *B, M, D*

Kentucky

University of Kentucky *B, M, D*
University of Louisville *B, M, D*
Western Kentucky University *B*

Louisiana

Louisiana State University and
    Agricultural and Mechanical
    College *B, M, D*
Louisiana Tech University *B*
Southern University and Agricultural
    and Mechanical College *B*
University of Louisiana at
    Lafayette *B, M*
University of New Orleans *B*

Maine

University of Maine *B, M, D*

Maryland

Johns Hopkins University *B, M, D*
Montgomery College *A*
Morgan State University *B, M*
University of Maryland
    College Park *B, M, D*

Massachusetts

Massachusetts Institute of
    Technology *B, M, D*
Merrimack College *B*
Northeastern University *B, M, D*
Smith College *B*
Tufts University *B, M*
University of Massachusetts
    Amherst *B, M, D*
    Dartmouth *B, M*
    Lowell *B, M*
Worcester Polytechnic
    Institute *B, M, D*

Michigan

Calvin College *B*
Lawrence Technological
    University *B, M*
Michigan State University *B, M, D*
Michigan Technological
    University *B, M, D*
University of Detroit Mercy *B, M, D*
University of Michigan *B, M, D*
Wayne State University *B, M, D*
Western Michigan University *B, M*

Minnesota

Minnesota State University
    Mankato *B*

University of Minnesota
    Duluth *B*
    Twin Cities *B, M, D*
Vermilion Community College *A*

Mississippi

Jackson State University *B*
Mississippi State University *B, M*
University of Mississippi *B*

Missouri

St. Charles Community College *A*
Saint Louis University *B*
University of Missouri
    Columbia *B, M, D*
    Kansas City *B, M*
    Missouri University of Science and
        Technology *B, M, D*
    St. Louis *B*

Montana

Montana State University
    Bozeman *B, M*

Nebraska

University of Nebraska
    Lincoln *B, M*
    Omaha *B*

Nevada

University of Nevada
    Las Vegas *B, M, D*
    Reno *B, M, D*

New Hampshire

New England College *B*
University of New Hampshire *B, M, D*

New Jersey

The College of New Jersey *B*
Essex County College *A*
Middlesex County College *A*
New Jersey Institute of
    Technology *B, M, D*
Princeton University *B, M, D*
Rowan University *B*
Rutgers, The State University of New
    Jersey
    Camden Regional Campus *B*
    New Brunswick/Piscataway
        Campus *B, M, D*
    Newark Regional Campus *B*
Stevens Institute of
    Technology *B, M, D*

New Mexico

New Mexico Institute of Mining and
    Technology *B*
New Mexico State University *B, M*
University of New Mexico *B, M*

New York

City University of New York
    City College *B, M, D*
    Hostos Community College *A*
    LaGuardia Community College *A*
Clarkson University *B, M, D*
Columbia University *B, M, D*
Cooper Union for the Advancement of
    Science and Art *B, M*
Cornell University *B, M, D*
Hofstra University *B*
Manhattan College *B, M*
Polytechnic Institute of New York
    University *B, M, D*
Rensselaer Polytechnic
    Institute *B, M, D*
State University of New York
    Buffalo *B, M, D*
Syracuse University *B, D*
United States Military Academy *B*

North Carolina

Central Carolina Community
    College *A*
Duke University *B, M, D*
North Carolina Agricultural and
    Technical State University *B*
North Carolina State
    University *B, M, D*
University of North Carolina
    Charlotte *B, M*
Western Piedmont Community
    College *A*

North Dakota

North Dakota State University *B, M, D*
University of North Dakota *B, M*

Ohio

Belmont Technical College *A*
Case Western Reserve
    University *B, M, D*
Cleveland State University *B, M, D*
Ohio Northern University *B*
Ohio State University
    Columbus Campus *B, M, D*
Ohio University *B, M, D*
Stark State College of Technology *A*
University of Akron *B, M, D*
University of Cincinnati *B, M, D*
University of Dayton *B, M*
University of Toledo *B, M*
Wilberforce University *B*
Youngstown State University *B, M*

Oklahoma

Oklahoma State University *B, M, D*
Oklahoma State University
    Institute of Technology:
        Okmulgee *A, B*
University of Oklahoma *B, M, D*

Oregon

George Fox University *B*
Oregon Institute of Technology *B*
Oregon State University *B, M, D*
Portland State University *B, M, D*
University of Portland *B, M*

Pennsylvania

Bucknell University *B, M*
Carnegie Mellon University *B, M, D*
Drexel University *B, M, D*
Gettysburg College *B*
Lafayette College *B*
Lehigh University *B, M, D*
Penn State
    Abington *B*
    Altoona *B*
    Beaver *B*
    Berks *B*
    Brandywine *B*
    DuBois *B*
    Erie, The Behrend College *B*
    Fayette, The Eberly Campus *B*
    Greater Allegheny *B*
    Harrisburg *B*
    Hazleton *B*
    Lehigh Valley *B*
    Mont Alto *B*
    New Kensington *B*
    Schuylkill *B*
    Shenango *B*
    University Park *B, M, D*
    Wilkes-Barre *B*
    Worthington Scranton *B*
    York *B*
Temple University *B, M*
University of Pittsburgh *B, M, D*
University of Pittsburgh
    Bradford *B*
Villanova University *B, M*
Widener University *B, M*

Puerto Rico

Caribbean University *B*
Universidad Politecnica de Puerto
    Rico *B, M*
University of Puerto Rico
    Ponce *A*

Rhode Island

Brown University *B*
University of Rhode Island *B, M, D*

South Carolina

The Citadel *B*
Clemson University *B, M, D*
University of South Carolina *B, M, D*

South Dakota

Lake Area Technical Institute *A*
South Dakota School of Mines and
    Technology *B, M*
South Dakota State University *B*

Tennessee

Christian Brothers University *B*
Tennessee State University *B*
Tennessee Technological
    University *B, M, D*
University of Memphis *B, M*
University of Tennessee
    Knoxville *B, M, D*
Vanderbilt University *B, M, D*

Texas

Kilgore College *A*
Lamar University *B, M*
Prairie View A&M University *B*
Rice University *B, M, D*
Southern Methodist University *B, M*
Texas A&M University *B, M, D*
Texas A&M University
    Kingsville *B, M*
Texas Tech University *B, M, D*
University of Houston *B, M, D*
University of Texas
    Arlington *B, M, D*
    Austin *B, M, D*
    El Paso *B, M, D*
    San Antonio *B, M*
    Tyler *B*

Utah

Brigham Young University *B, M, D*
College of Eastern Utah *A, T*
Southern Utah University *A*
University of Utah *B, M, D*
Utah State University *B, M, D*

Vermont

Norwich University *B, M*
University of Vermont *B, M, D*

Virginia

George Mason University *B, M, D*
John Tyler Community College *A*
Lord Fairfax Community College *A*
Northern Virginia Community
    College *A*
Old Dominion University *B, M, D*
University of Virginia *B, M, D*
Virginia Military Institute *B*
Virginia Polytechnic Institute and
    State University *B, M, D*

Washington

Bates Technical College *A*
Gonzaga University *B*
Saint Martin's University *B, M*
Seattle University *B*
Shoreline Community College *A*
University of Washington *B, M, D*
Walla Walla University *B*
Washington State University *B, M, D*

West Virginia

Potomac State College of West
Virginia University *A*
West Virginia University *B, M, D*
West Virginia University Institute of
Technology *B*

Wisconsin

Chippewa Valley Technical College *A*
Marquette University *B, M, D*
Northeast Wisconsin Technical
College *A*
University of Wisconsin
Madison *B, M, D*
Milwaukee *B*
Platteville *B*

Wyoming

University of Wyoming *B, M, D*

Civil engineering drafting/CAD/CADD

Alabama

Gadsden State Community
College *C, A*

California

National University *B*
Santa Rosa Junior College *C*

Colorado

Colorado Northwestern Community
College *C*

Delaware

Delaware Technical and Community
College
Stanton/Wilmington *A*

Kentucky

Somerset Community College *C*

Minnesota

Dunwoody College of Technology *C*

North Dakota

North Dakota State College of
Science *A*

Ohio

Central Ohio Technical College *A*

Texas

Tyler Junior College *C, A*

Utah

Salt Lake Community College *A*
Southern Utah University *C*

Washington

Bates Technical College *C, A*
North Seattle Community
College *C, A*
Olympic College *C*

Wisconsin

Herzing University *A, B*

Civil engineering technology

Alabama

Alabama Agricultural and Mechanical
University *B*
Bishop State Community College *A*
Gadsden State Community
College *C, A*

Arizona

Eastern Arizona College *A*
Penn Foster College *A*
Phoenix College *A*

California

Allan Hancock College *A*
Butte College *C, A*
California State University
Long Beach *B*
Chabot College *A*
San Joaquin Delta College *C*
Santa Rosa Junior College *C, A*
Shasta College *C, A*

Colorado

Arapahoe Community College *C*
Colorado Northwestern Community
College *C, A*
Colorado State University
Pueblo *B*
Metropolitan State College of
Denver *B*
Trinidad State Junior College *C, A*

Connecticut

Central Connecticut State
University *B*
Three Rivers Community College *A*

Delaware

Delaware State University *B*
Delaware Technical and Community
College
Owens *B*
Stanton/Wilmington *C*
Terry *C, A*

Florida

Broward College *A*
Daytona State College *A*
Florida Agricultural and Mechanical
University *B*
Florida State College at Jacksonville *A*
Gulf Coast Community College *A*
Indian River State College *A*
Miami Dade College *A*
Pensacola Junior College *A*
State College of Florida,
Manatee-Sarasota *A*
Tallahassee Community College *A*
Valencia Community College *A*

Georgia

Georgia Southern University *B*
Macon State College *A*
Middle Georgia College *A*
Savannah State University *B*
Southern Polytechnic State
University *B*

Idaho

Idaho State University *C, A*

Illinois

College of Lake County *C, A*
Morrison Institute of Technology *A*

Indiana

Indiana University-Purdue University
Fort Wayne *A*
Indiana University-Purdue University
Indianapolis *A*
Purdue University
North Central *A*

Iowa

Des Moines Area Community
College *A*
Hawkeye Community College *A*
Iowa Western Community College *A*

Northeast Iowa Community
College *D*

Kansas

Johnson County Community
College *A*
Washburn University *A*

Kentucky

Bluegrass Community and Technical
College *A*
Murray State University *A, B*

Louisiana

Delgado Community College *A*
Louisiana Tech University *B*

Maine

Central Maine Community College *A*
University of Maine *B*

Maryland

Community College of Baltimore
County *C, A*
Montgomery College *A*
University of Maryland
Eastern Shore *B*

Massachusetts

Northern Essex Community
College *C*
Springfield Technical Community
College *A*
University of Massachusetts
Lowell *A, B*
Wentworth Institute of Technology *B*

Michigan

Ferris State University *A*
Lansing Community College *A*
Macomb Community College *C, A*

Minnesota

Dakota County Technical College *A*
Lake Superior College *C, A*
Minnesota School of Business *C, A*
North Hennepin Community
College *C*
St. Cloud Technical College *C, A*
South Central College *A*

Mississippi

Hinds Community College *A*
Northwest Mississippi Community
College *C, A*

Missouri

Lincoln University *B*
Linn State Technical College *A*
Mineral Area College *A*
St. Louis Community College
St. Louis Community College at
Florissant Valley *A*
Three Rivers Community College *A*

Montana

Montana Tech of the University of
Montana *A*

Nebraska

Metropolitan Community
College *C, A*
Southeast Community College *A*

New Hampshire

NHTI-Concord's Community
College *A*
University of New Hampshire *A*

New Jersey

Burlington County College *A*

Essex County College *A*
Fairleigh Dickinson University
Metropolitan Campus *B*
Gloucester County College *C, A*
Mercer County Community College *A*
Middlesex County College *A*
Ocean County College *A*
Thomas Edison State College *B*
Union County College *A*

New York

Broome Community College *A*
City University of New York
New York City College of
Technology *A*
Erie Community College
North Campus *A*
Hudson Valley Community College *A*
Mohawk Valley Community College *A*
Monroe Community College *C, A*
Nassau Community College *A*
Rochester Institute of Technology *B*
State University of New York
College of Technology at Canton *A*
Institute of Technology at
Utica/Rome *B*
United States Military Academy *B*
Westchester Community College *A*

North Carolina

Asheville-Buncombe Technical
Community College *A*
Central Carolina Community
College *A*
Central Piedmont Community
College *C, A*
Fayetteville Technical Community
College *A*
Gaston College *C, A*
Guilford Technical Community
College *C, A*
Sandhills Community College *A*
University of North Carolina
Charlotte *B*
Wake Technical Community
College *A*

North Dakota

North Dakota State College of
Science *A*

Ohio

Cincinnati State Technical and
Community College *C, A*
Columbus State Community
College *A*
James A. Rhodes State College *A*
Owens Community College
Toledo *C*
Stark State College of Technology *A*
University of Toledo *C, A, B*
Youngstown State University *A, B*

Oklahoma

Oklahoma State University
Institute of Technology:
Okmulgee *A*
Oklahoma City *A*
Tulsa Community College *C, A*

Oregon

Blue Mountain Community College *A*
Chemeketa Community College *A*
Linn-Benton Community College *C*
Mt. Hood Community College *A*
Portland Community College *C, A*
Umpqua Community College *A*

Pennsylvania

Butler County Community College *A*
Community College of Allegheny
County *A*

Harrisburg Area Community
College *C, A*
Pennsylvania College of
Technology *A, B*
Pennsylvania Institute of
Technology *A*
Point Park University *A, B*
Temple University *B*
University of Pittsburgh
Johnstown *B*

Puerto Rico

University of Puerto Rico
Bayamon University College *A*
Ponce *A*

South Carolina

Florence-Darlington Technical
College *A*
Greenville Technical College *C*
Horry-Georgetown Technical
College *A*
Midlands Technical College *A*
South Carolina State University *B*
Spartanburg Community College *A*
Trident Technical College *C, A*

South Dakota

Southeast Technical Institute *A*

Tennessee

Chattanooga State Community
College *A*
Nashville State Community College *A*
Pellissippi State Community
College *A*

Texas

Kilgore College *A*
Laredo Community College *A*
San Antonio College *C, A*
Texas Southern University *B*
University of Houston *B*
University of Houston
Downtown *B*

Vermont

Vermont Technical College *A*

Virginia

Central Virginia Community
College *A*
J. Sargeant Reynolds Community
College *A*
Northern Virginia Community
College *C, A*
Old Dominion University *B*
Tidewater Community College *A*
Virginia Western Community
College *A*

Washington

Bates Technical College *C, A*
Bellingham Technical College *A*
Centralia College *A*
Shoreline Community College *A*
South Seattle Community College *A*
Spokane Community College *A*
Yakima Valley Community College *C*

West Virginia

Bluefield State College *A, B*
Fairmont State University *B*

Wisconsin

Chippewa Valley Technical College *A*
Gateway Technical College *A*
Herzing University *A, B*
Mid-State Technical College *A*
Milwaukee Area Technical College *A*
Moraine Park Technical College *A*

Northeast Wisconsin Technical
College *A*

Wyoming

Laramie County Community
College *C, A*

Classical/ancient Mediterranean/Near Eastern studies

Alabama

Samford University *B*

California

University of California
Berkeley *B, M, D*
Davis *B*
Irvine *B*
Los Angeles *B*
University of Southern California *B*

Georgia

Emory University *B*
Georgia State University *B*

Illinois

University of Illinois
Chicago *B*

Kansas

Wichita State University *B*

Maine

Bowdoin College *B*
Colby College *B*

Massachusetts

Harvard College *B, D*
Wellesley College *B*

Michigan

Calvin College *B*
Michigan State University *B*
University of Michigan *B*

Minnesota

University of St. Thomas *B*

New Hampshire

Dartmouth College *B*

New York

Columbia University *B*
State University of New York
Albany *B*

Pennsylvania

Bryn Mawr College *B, M, D*
Lycoming College *B*

Tennessee

Vanderbilt University *B*

Texas

Rice University *B*

Classics

Alabama

Samford University *B*

Arizona

University of Arizona *B, M*

Arkansas

Hendrix College *B*
University of Arkansas *B*

California

California State University
Long Beach *B*
Claremont McKenna College *B*
Loyola Marymount University *B*
Pitzer College *B*
Pomona College *B*
St. Mary's College of California *B*
San Diego State University *B*
San Francisco State University *B, M*
Santa Clara University *B*
Scripps College *B*
Stanford University *B, M, D*
University of California
Berkeley *B, M, D*
Irvine *B, M, D*
Los Angeles *M, D*
Riverside *B, M, D*
San Diego *B*
Santa Barbara *B, M, D*
Santa Cruz *B*
University of Southern
California *B, M, D*

Colorado

Colorado College *B*
University of Colorado
Boulder *B, M, D*

Connecticut

Connecticut College *B*
Trinity College *B*
University of Connecticut *B*
Wesleyan University *B*
Yale University *B, M, D*

Delaware

University of Delaware *B*

District of Columbia

Catholic University of America *B, M*
George Washington University *B*
Georgetown University *B*
Howard University *B*

Florida

Ave Maria University *B*
Eckerd College *B*
Florida State University *D*
New College of Florida *B*
Rollins College *B*
University of Florida *B*
University of Miami *B*
University of South Florida *B, M*

Georgia

Agnes Scott College *B*
Emory University *B*
Georgia State University *B*
Mercer University *B*
University of Georgia *B, M*

Hawaii

University of Hawaii
Manoa *B*

Idaho

University of Idaho *B*

Illinois

Augustana College *B, T*
Illinois Wesleyan University *B*
Knox College *B*
Loyola University Chicago *B, M, D*
Monmouth College *B, T*
North Central College *B*
Northwestern University *B, M, D*
Rockford College *B*
Southern Illinois University
Carbondale *B*
University of Chicago *B, M, D*

University of Illinois
Chicago *B*
Urbana-Champaign *B, M*
Wheaton College *B*

Indiana

Ball State University *B*
DePauw University *B*
Earlham College *B*
Hanover College *B*
Purdue University *B*
University of Evansville *B*
University of Notre Dame *B*
Valparaiso University *B*
Wabash College *B*

Iowa

Coe College *B*
Cornell College *B*
Grinnell College *B*
Luther College *B*
University of Iowa *B, M, D*

Kansas

University of Kansas *B, M*

Kentucky

Asbury College *B*
Centre College *B*
Transylvania University *B*
University of Kentucky *B, M*

Louisiana

Centenary College of Louisiana *B*
Tulane University *B, M*

Maine

Bowdoin College *B*
Colby College *B*
University of Southern Maine *B*

Maryland

College of Notre Dame of Maryland *B*
Johns Hopkins University *B, M, D*
Loyola University Maryland *B*
University of Maryland
College Park *B, M*

Massachusetts

Amherst College *B*
Assumption College *B*
Boston College *B*
Boston University *B, M, D*
Brandeis University *B, M*
Clark University *B*
College of the Holy Cross *B*
Harvard College *B, M, D*
Hellenic College/Holy Cross *B*
Mount Holyoke College *B*
Smith College *B*
Tufts University *B, M*
University of Massachusetts
Amherst *B*
Boston *B*
Wellesley College *B*
Wheaton College *B*
Williams College *B*

Michigan

Calvin College *B*
Grand Valley State University *B*
Hillsdale College *B*
Hope College *B*
Kalamazoo College *B*
University of Michigan *B, D*
Wayne State University *B, M*

Minnesota

Carleton College *B*
College of St. Benedict *B*
Concordia College: Moorhead *B*
Gustavus Adolphus College *B*

Macalester College *B*
St. John's University *B*
St. Olaf College *B*
University of Minnesota
   Twin Cities *B, M, D*
University of St. Thomas *B*

Mississippi
Millsaps College *B*
University of Mississippi *B*

Missouri
Saint Louis University *B*
Truman State University *B*
University of Missouri
   Columbia *B, M, D*
Washington University in St.
   Louis *B, M*

Montana
University of Montana *B*

Nebraska
Creighton University *B*
University of Nebraska
   Lincoln *B, M*

New Hampshire
Dartmouth College *B*
Saint Anselm College *B*
University of New Hampshire *B*

New Jersey
Drew University *B*
Montclair State University *B*
Princeton University *B, M, D*
Rutgers, The State University of New
   Jersey
   New Brunswick/Piscataway
      Campus *B, M, D*
Saint Peter's College *B*
Seton Hall University *B*

New Mexico
University of New Mexico *B*

New York
Barnard College *B*
City University of New York
   Brooklyn College *B*
   Hunter College *B*
Colgate University *B*
College of New Rochelle *B, T*
Columbia University *B*
Columbia University
   School of General Studies *B*
Cornell University *B, M, D*
Elmira College *B*
Fordham University *B, M, D*
Hamilton College *B*
Hobart and William Smith Colleges *B*
Hofstra University *B*
New York University *B, M, D*
Saint Bonaventure University *B*
Siena College *B*
Skidmore College *B*
State University of New York
   Albany *B, M*
   Binghamton *B*
   Buffalo *B, M, D*
Syracuse University *B, M*
Union College *B*
University of Rochester *B*
Yeshiva University *B*

North Carolina
Davidson College *B*
Duke University *B, M, D*
University of North Carolina
   Asheville *B, T*
   Chapel Hill *B, M, D*
   Greensboro *B*

Wake Forest University *B*

North Dakota
North Dakota State University *B*
University of North Dakota *B*

Ohio
Bowling Green State University *B*
Case Western Reserve University *B*
College of Wooster *B*
Denison University *B*
Franciscan University of
   Steubenville *B*
Hiram College *B*
Kenyon College *B*
Miami University
   Oxford Campus *B*
Oberlin College *B*
Ohio State University
   Columbus Campus *B, M, D*
Ohio University *B*
Ohio Wesleyan University *B*
University of Akron *B*
University of Cincinnati *B, M, D*
University of Toledo *M*
Wright State University *B*
Xavier University *B*

Oklahoma
University of Oklahoma *B*

Oregon
Reed College *B*
University of Oregon *B, M*
Willamette University *B*

Pennsylvania
Bryn Mawr College *B, M, D*
Bucknell University *B*
Dickinson College *B*
Duquesne University *B*
Franklin & Marshall College *B*
Gettysburg College *B*
Haverford College *B*
La Salle University *B*
Lehigh University *B*
Moravian College *B*
Penn State
   Abington *B*
   Altoona *B*
   Beaver *B*
   Berks *B*
   Brandywine *B*
   DuBois *B*
   Erie, The Behrend College *B*
   Fayette, The Eberly Campus *B*
   Greater Allegheny *B*
   Hazleton *B*
   Lehigh Valley *B*
   Mont Alto *B*
   New Kensington *B*
   Schuylkill *B*
   Shenango *B*
   University Park *B*
   Wilkes-Barre *B*
   Worthington Scranton *B*
   York *B*
Swarthmore College *B*
Temple University *B*
University of Pennsylvania *B, M, D*
University of Pittsburgh *B, M, D*
University of Scranton *B*
Ursinus College *B, T*
Villanova University *B, M*
Westminster College *B*

Rhode Island
Brown University *B, M, D*
University of Rhode Island *B*

South Carolina
College of Charleston *B, T*
University of South Carolina *B*

Tennessee
Rhodes College *B*
University of Tennessee
   Knoxville *B*
Vanderbilt University *B, M, D*

Texas
Austin College *B*
Baylor University *B*
Rice University *B*
Southwestern University *B*
Texas A&M University *B*
Texas Tech University *B, M*
Trinity University *B*
University of Dallas *B*
University of Houston *B*
University of Texas
   Austin *B, M, D*
   San Antonio *B*

Utah
Brigham Young University *B*
University of Utah *B*

Vermont
Middlebury College *B*
St. Michael's College *B*
University of Vermont *B, M*

Virginia
Christendom College *B*
Christopher Newport University *B*
College of William and Mary *B*
Hampden-Sydney College *B*
Hollins University *B*
Randolph College *B*
Randolph-Macon College *B*
Sweet Briar College *B*
University of Mary Washington *B*
University of Virginia *B, M, D*
Washington and Lee University *B*

Washington
Evergreen State College *B*
Pacific Lutheran University *B*
Seattle Pacific University *B*
University of Puget Sound *B*
University of Washington *B, M, D*
Whitman College *B*

West Virginia
Huntington Junior College *A*

Wisconsin
Beloit College *B*
Carthage College *B*
Lawrence University *B*
Marquette University *B*
Ripon College *B*
University of Wisconsin
   Madison *B, M, D*
   Milwaukee *B*

Climatology

California
Shasta College *A*

Clinical child psychology

California
California Institute of Integral
   Studies *D*

Kansas
University of Kansas *M, D*

New York
Pace University *D*
St. John's University *D*

Ohio
Case Western Reserve University *D*

Pennsylvania
Marywood University *M*

Texas
Prairie View A&M University *D*

Clinical laboratory science

Alabama
Central Alabama Community
   College *A*
Faulkner State Community College *A*
Tuskegee University *B, M*
University of Alabama
   Birmingham *B, M*
University of South Alabama *B*

Arizona
DeVry University
   Phoenix *B*
Phoenix College *A*
University of Arizona *B, M*

Arkansas
Arkansas State University *A, B*
Arkansas Tech University *B*
Harding University *B*
Henderson State University *B*
Southern Arkansas University *B, M*
University of Central Arkansas *B*

California
California State University
   Chico *B*
   Dominguez Hills *B, M*
City College of San Francisco *A*
Fullerton College *A*
Loma Linda University *B*
San Francisco State University *B*
University of California
   Davis *M*

Colorado
Colorado State University *M, D*

Connecticut
University of Bridgeport *B*
University of Connecticut *B*
University of Hartford *B*
Western Connecticut State
   University *B*

Delaware
University of Delaware *B*
Wesley College *B*

District of Columbia
Catholic University of America *B*
Howard University *B*

Florida
Barry University *B*
Florida Gulf Coast University *B*
Florida Memorial University *B*
Gulf Coast Community College *A*
Northwest Florida State College *A*
Saint Leo University *B*
Santa Fe College *B*
State College of Florida,
   Manatee-Sarasota *A*
University of Central Florida *B*
University of South Florida *B*

Georgia
Armstrong Atlantic State University *B*
Augusta State University *B*
Darton College *A*

Medical College of Georgia *B, M*

Hawaii
University of Hawaii
  Manoa *B*

Idaho
Idaho State University *B, M*
University of Idaho *B*

Illinois
Aurora University *B*
Benedictine University *B*
Blackburn College *B*
Bradley University *B*
DePaul University *B*
DeVry University
  Chicago *B*
Eastern Illinois University *B*
Illinois State University *B*
Loyola University Chicago *B*
National-Louis University *B*
North Park University *B*
Northern Illinois University *B*
Quincy University *B*
Roosevelt University *B*
Rush University *B, M*
University of Illinois
  Springfield *B*
University of St. Francis *B*
Western Illinois University *B*

Indiana
Ball State University *B*
Harrison College
  Indianapolis East *A*
Indiana State University *B*
Indiana University
  Southeast *B*
Indiana University-Purdue University
  Fort Wayne *B*
Indiana University-Purdue University
  Indianapolis *B*
Manchester College *B*
Purdue University *B*
Purdue University
  Calumet *B*
Saint Joseph's College *B*
University of Evansville *B*
University of St. Francis *B*

Iowa
Allen College *B*
Briar Cliff University *B*
Dordt College *B*
Morningside College *B*
Mount Mercy College *B*
University of Iowa *B*
Wartburg College *B*

Kansas
Barton County Community College *A*
Pittsburg State University *B*
University of Kansas Medical
  Center *B*

Kentucky
Bellarmine University *B*
Brescia University *B*
Eastern Kentucky University *B*
Madisonville Community College *A*
Thomas More College *B*
University of Kentucky *B, M, D*
Western Kentucky University *B*

Louisiana
Louisiana State University
  Alexandria *A*
Louisiana State University Health
  Sciences Center *B*
Louisiana Tech University *B*
McNeese State University *B*

Our Lady of the Lake College *A, B*
University of Louisiana at Monroe *B*

Maine
University of Maine *B, M*

Maryland
Salisbury University *B*
Stevenson University *B*
University of Maryland
  Baltimore *B, M*

Massachusetts
Northeastern University *B*
Salem State College *B*
Springfield College *B*
University of Massachusetts
  Dartmouth *B*
  Lowell *B, M*

Michigan
Andrews University *B, M*
Baker College of Allen Park *A*
Central Michigan University *B*
Delta College *A*
Eastern Michigan University *B*
Ferris State University *A, B*
Gogebic Community College *A*
Grand Rapids Community College *A*
Grand Valley State University *B*
Lake Superior State University *B*
Lansing Community College *A*
Madonna University *B*
Michigan State University *B, M*
Michigan Technological University *B*
Northern Michigan University *A, B*
Oakland University *B*
Saginaw Valley State University *B*
University of Michigan
  Flint *B*
Wayne State University *B*

Minnesota
Argosy University: Twin Cities *B*
Augsburg College *B*
Bemidji State University *B*
Minnesota State University
  Moorhead *B*
Northland Community & Technical
  College *A*
St. Catherine University *A*
Saint Cloud State University *B*
St. Mary's University of Minnesota *B*

Mississippi
Blue Mountain College *B*
Copiah-Lincoln Community College *A*
Mississippi Gulf Coast Community
  College *A*
Mississippi State University *B*
University of Mississippi *B*
University of Southern
  Mississippi *B, M*

Missouri
Lincoln University *B*
Maryville University of Saint Louis *B*
Missouri State University *B*
Northwest Missouri State
  University *B*
Rockhurst University *B*
Saint Louis University *B*
Southeast Missouri State University *B*
Southwest Baptist University *B*
University of Missouri
  Kansas City *B*
William Jewell College *B*

Montana
University of Montana *B*

Nebraska
University of Nebraska
  Medical Center *B*

Nevada
University of Nevada
  Las Vegas *B*

New Hampshire
University of New Hampshire *B*

New Jersey
Fairleigh Dickinson University
  College at Florham *B*
  Metropolitan Campus *B, M*
Felician College *A*
Georgian Court University *B*
Kean University *B*
Monmouth University *B*
New Jersey City University *B*
Ramapo College of New Jersey *B*
Rutgers, The State University of New
  Jersey
  Newark Regional Campus *B*
Saint Peter's College *B*
Thomas Edison State College *A, B*
University of Medicine and Dentistry
  of New Jersey
  School of Health Related
    Professions *B, M*

New Mexico
Eastern New Mexico University *B*
New Mexico State University *B*
University of New Mexico *M*

New York
Albany College of Pharmacy and
  Health Sciences *B*
Canisius College *B*
City University of New York
  College of Staten Island *B*
  Hunter College *B*
  York College *B*
College of Saint Rose *B*
Elmira College *B*
Hartwick College *B*
Hudson Valley Community College *A*
Iona College *B*
Keuka College *B, M*
Long Island University
  Brooklyn Campus *B*
  C. W. Post Campus *B, M*
Marist College *B*
Mercy College *B*
Mount Saint Mary College *B*
Orange County Community College *A*
Pace University *B*
St. Francis College *B*
St. John's University *B*
State University of New York
  Buffalo *B*
  College at Plattsburgh *B*
  Stony Brook *B*
  Upstate Medical University *B, M*
Suffolk County Community College *A*

North Carolina
College of the Albemarle *A*
East Carolina University *B*
High Point University *B*
Lenoir-Rhyne University *B*
Southwestern Community College *A*
University of North Carolina
  Chapel Hill *B*
  Charlotte *B*
  Greensboro *B*
Wake Forest University *B*
Western Carolina University *B*
Winston-Salem State University *B*

North Dakota
Jamestown College *B*
Mayville State University *B*
Minot State University *B*
North Dakota State University *B*
University of Mary *B*
University of North Dakota *B, M*

Ohio
Bowling Green State University *B*
Cedarville University *B*
Kent State University *B*
Malone University *B*
Miami University
  Oxford Campus *B*
Mount Union College *B*
Mount Vernon Nazarene University *B*
Ohio State University
  Columbus Campus *B*
Shawnee State University *A*
University of Cincinnati *B*
University of Rio Grande *A, B*
Walsh University *B*
Wright State University *B*
Xavier University *B*
Youngstown State University *B*

Oklahoma
Northeastern State University *B*
Oklahoma Christian University *B*
Oral Roberts University *B*
University of Central Oklahoma *B*
University of Oklahoma *B*

Oregon
Oregon Health & Science
  University *B*
Oregon Institute of Technology *B*

Pennsylvania
Bloomsburg University of
  Pennsylvania *B*
Cheyney University of Pennsylvania *B*
DeSales University *B*
East Stroudsburg University of
  Pennsylvania *B*
Gannon University *B*
Gwynedd-Mercy College *B*
Holy Family University *B*
Indiana University of Pennsylvania *B*
Keystone College *A*
King's College *B*
Kutztown University of
  Pennsylvania *B*
Lebanon Valley College *B*
Mansfield University of
  Pennsylvania *B*
Marywood University *B*
Misericordia University *B*
Moravian College *B*
Reading Area Community College *A*
Seton Hill University *B*
Thomas Jefferson University: College
  of Health Professions *B, M*
University of Scranton *B*
University of the Sciences in
  Philadelphia *B*
Wilkes University *B*
York College of Pennsylvania *B*

Puerto Rico
Inter American University of Puerto
  Rico
  Metropolitan Campus *B, M*
  San German Campus *B*
Pontifical Catholic University of
  Puerto Rico *B*
University of Puerto Rico
  Medical Sciences *B, M*

Rhode Island
Rhode Island College *B*
University of Rhode Island *B, M*

South Carolina

Clemson University *B*
Coker College *B*
Winthrop University *B*

South Dakota

Augustana College *B*
Mount Marty College *B*
Northern State University *B*
South Dakota State University *B*
University of South Dakota *M*

Tennessee

Austin Peay State University *B*
King College *B*
Lincoln Memorial University *B*
Southern Adventist University *B*
Trevecca Nazarene University *B*
Tusculum College *B*
Union University *B*
University of Tennessee
  Chattanooga *B*
  Knoxville *B*
University of Tennessee Health
  Science Center *B, M*

Texas

Abilene Christian University *B*
Amarillo College *A*
Angelo State University *B*
Baylor University *B*
Grayson County College *A*
Lamar University *B*
Midwestern State University *B*
Odessa College *A*
Prairie View A&M University *B*
San Jacinto College *A*
Tarleton State University *A, B*
Texas A&M University
  Corpus Christi *B*
Texas Southern University *B*
Texas State Technical College
  Waco *A*
Texas State University: San Marcos *B*
Texas Tech University Health Sciences
  Center *B*
Texas Woman's University *B*
University of Houston *B*
University of Mary Hardin-Baylor *B*
University of North Texas *B*
University of Texas
  Arlington *B*
  Austin *B*
  El Paso *B*
  Health Science Center at San
    Antonio *B*
  Medical Branch at Galveston *B*
  Pan American *B*
  San Antonio *B*
  Southwestern Medical Center at
    Dallas *B*
  Tyler *B*
West Texas A&M University *B*

Utah

Brigham Young University *B*
Snow College *A*
University of Utah *B, M*
Utah State University *B*
Weber State University *B*

Vermont

University of Vermont *B*

Virginia

Averett University *B*
Bridgewater College *B*
Eastern Mennonite University *B*
Ferrum College *B*
George Mason University *B*
Mary Baldwin College *B*
Norfolk State University *B*
Old Dominion University *B*

Radford University *M*
Roanoke College *B*
University of Virginia's College at
  Wise *B*
Virginia Commonwealth
  University *B, M*

Washington

Seattle University *B*
University of Washington *B, M*

West Virginia

Concord University *B*
Marshall University *B*
West Liberty University *B*
West Virginia University *B*

Wisconsin

Carroll University *B*
University of Wisconsin
  La Crosse *B*
  Madison *B*
  Milwaukee *B, M*
  Stevens Point *B*

Clinical/medical laboratory assistant

Alabama

Gadsden State Community College *A*

Alaska

University of Alaska
  Fairbanks *C*

Arizona

Brookline College
  Phoenix *C*

California

De Anza College *C*

Delaware

Delaware Technical and Community
  College
  Owens *A*

Florida

Broward College *A*
Rasmussen College: Fort Myers *A*

Georgia

Southeastern Technical College *A*

Idaho

North Idaho College *A*

Illinois

Oakton Community College *A*
Southwestern Illinois College *A*

Kansas

Seward County Community College *A*

Kentucky

Eastern Kentucky University *B*
Madisonville Community College *C*
Somerset Community College *A*
Southeast Kentucky Community and
  Technical College *A*

Maine

University of Maine
  Augusta *A*

Massachusetts

Bunker Hill Community College *C*
Springfield Technical Community
  College *C*

Michigan

Baker College
  of Owosso *A*
Bay de Noc Community College *C, A*
Monroe County Community
  College *C*
Northern Michigan University *C*

Minnesota

Dunwoody College of Technology *A*
Rasmussen College: Brooklyn Park *A*
Rasmussen College: Lake
  Elmo/Woodbury *A*
St. Catherine University *C*

Mississippi

Hinds Community College *A*
Northeast Mississippi Community
  College *A*

Nevada

College of Southern Nevada *A*

New Mexico

New Mexico Junior College *A*
New Mexico State University
  Alamogordo *A*

New York

Elmira Business Institute *C, A*
Elmira Business Institute: Vestal *C, A*

North Carolina

Alamance Community College *A*
Carolinas College of Health
  Sciences *C*
Central Piedmont Community
  College *A*
Fayetteville Technical Community
  College *C*
Mars Hill College *B*
Stanly Community College *A*
Western Piedmont Community
  College *A*

Ohio

Cincinnati State Technical and
  Community College *C, A*
Columbus State Community
  College *A*
Eastern Gateway Community
  College *A*
Edison State Community College *C*
James A. Rhodes State College *C*
Ohio Northern University *B*
Southwestern College of Business
  Southwestern College:
    Tri-County *C*
Stark State College of Technology *A*
Washington State Community
  College *A*
Youngstown State University *A*

Oklahoma

Rose State College *A*
Tulsa Community College *A*

Oregon

Clackamas Community College *C*

Pennsylvania

Drexel University *B*
Laurel Business Institute *C*

South Carolina

Aiken Technical College *C*
Forrest Junior College *C, A*
Orangeburg-Calhoun Technical
  College *C, A*
Spartanburg Community College *C*

Tennessee

Northeast State Community
  College *A*

Texas

Central Texas College *C, A*
El Paso Community College *C*
Tyler Junior College *A*

Utah

College of Eastern Utah *C*

Virginia

Northern Virginia Community
  College *A*
Virginia Highlands Community
  College *A*

Washington

Centralia College *C*
Clover Park Technical College *A*
North Seattle Community College *C*
Pierce College *A*
Shoreline Community College *C, A*
Wenatchee Valley College *A*

Wisconsin

Blackhawk Technical College *C*
Chippewa Valley Technical College *A*
Lakeshore Technical College *C*
Northcentral Technical College *A*
Rasmussen College: Green Bay *A*

Clinical/medical laboratory technology

Alabama

Faulkner State Community College *A*
Gadsden State Community College *A*
Jefferson State Community College *A*
Wallace State Community College at
  Hanceville *A*

Arizona

Pima Community College *A*

Arkansas

Arkansas State University
  Beebe *A*
National Park Community College *A*
North Arkansas College *A*
South Arkansas Community College *A*

California

California State University
  East Bay *B*
  Sacramento *B, M*
Chabot College *A*
Fresno City College *A*
Hartnell College *A*
Los Angeles Southwest College *A*
Mount St. Mary's College *B*
Pasadena City College *A*
Southwestern College *A*

Colorado

Arapahoe Community College *A*

Connecticut

Manchester Community College *A*

Delaware

University of Delaware *B*

District of Columbia

George Washington University *A, B*

Florida

Brevard Community College *A*
Broward College *A*

Daytona State College *A*
Florida State College at Jacksonville *A*
Indian River State College *A*
Miami Dade College *A*
Palm Beach Community College *A*
St. Petersburg College *A*
State College of Florida,
 Manatee-Sarasota *A*

Georgia

Augusta Technical College *A*
Central Georgia Technical College *A*
College of Coastal Georgia *A*
Macon State College *A*
Medical College of Georgia *M*
North Georgia Technical College *A*
Southeastern Technical College *A*
Southwest Georgia Technical
 College *A*
Valdosta Technical College *A*
Waycross College *A*

Hawaii

University of Hawaii
 Kapiolani Community College *A*

Illinois

City Colleges of Chicago
 Malcolm X College *A*
Elgin Community College *A*
Illinois Central College *A*
Illinois Eastern Community Colleges
 Olney Central College *A*
John A. Logan College *A*
John Wood Community College *A*
Kankakee Community College *A*
Kaskaskia College *A*
Rend Lake College *A*
Southeastern Illinois College *A*
Southwestern Illinois College *A*

Indiana

Indiana University
 Northwest *A*
Indiana University-Purdue University
 Fort Wayne *B*
Ivy Tech Community College
 North Central *A*
 South Central *A*
 Wabash Valley *A*
Purdue University
 North Central *A*
University of Indianapolis *B*

Iowa

Des Moines Area Community
 College *A*
Dordt College *B*
Hawkeye Community College *A*
Indian Hills Community College *A*
Iowa Central Community College *A*
North Iowa Area Community
 College *A*
Northeast Iowa Community
 College *A*
Northwestern College *B*
Western Iowa Tech Community
 College *A*

Kansas

Barton County Community College *A*
Central Christian College of Kansas *A*
Seward County Community College *A*
Tabor College *B*
Washburn University *B*

Kentucky

Eastern Kentucky University *A, B*
Henderson Community College *A*
Madisonville Community College *A*
Somerset Community College *A*
Spencerian College *A*

West Kentucky Community and
 Technical College *A*

Louisiana

Delgado Community College *A*
Louisiana College *B*
Southern University
 Shreveport *A*

Maine

University of Maine
 Presque Isle *A*
University of New England *B*

Maryland

Allegany College of Maryland *A*
Anne Arundel Community College *A*
College of Southern Maryland *A*
Community College of Baltimore
 County *A*

Massachusetts

Bristol Community College *A*
Mount Wachusett Community
 College *A*
Springfield College *B*
Springfield Technical Community
 College *A*

Michigan

Baker College
 of Owosso *A*
 of Port Huron *A*
Ferris State University *A*
Kellogg Community College *A*
Madonna University *B*

Minnesota *

Alexandria Technical College *A*
Argosy University: Twin Cities *A*
Hibbing Community College *A*
Lake Superior College *A*
Minnesota State Community and
 Technical College *A*
Minnesota West Community and
 Technical College *A*
North Hennepin Community
 College *A*
Northland Community & Technical
 College *A*
Rasmussen College
 Mankato *A*
 St. Cloud *A*
St. Paul College *A*
South Central College *A*
Winona State University *B*

Mississippi

Copiah-Lincoln Community College *A*
Hinds Community College *A*
Meridian Community College *A*
Mississippi Delta Community
 College *A*
Mississippi Gulf Coast Community
 College *A*

Missouri

Evangel University *B*
Mineral Area College *A*
Missouri Southern State University *A*
Missouri Western State University *B*
Three Rivers Community College *A*

Montana

University of Montana *A*

Nebraska

Central Community College *A*
College of Saint Mary *B*
Mid-Plains Community College Area *A*
Southeast Community College *A*

Nevada

College of Southern Nevada *A*

New Hampshire

River Valley Community College *A*

New Jersey

Bergen Community College *A*
Brookdale Community College *A*
Caldwell College *B*
Camden County College *A*
County College of Morris *A*
Mercer County Community College *A*
Middlesex County College *A*
Rutgers, The State University of New
 Jersey
 New Brunswick/Piscataway
  Campus *A*
 Newark Regional Campus *B*
Sussex County Community College *A*

New Mexico

Central New Mexico Community
 College *A*
New Mexico Junior College *A*
New Mexico State University
 Alamogordo *A*
University of New Mexico *B*
Western New Mexico University *B*

New York

Broome Community College *A*
City University of New York
 Bronx Community College *A*
 Hunter College *B*
 Queensborough Community
  College *A*
 York College *B*
Dutchess Community College *A*
Erie Community College
 North Campus *A*
Hudson Valley Community College *A*
Jamestown Community College *A*
Orange County Community College *A*
State University of New York
 College at Brockport *B*
 College at Fredonia *A*
 College of Agriculture and
  Technology at Morrisville *A*
 Farmingdale *A*

North Carolina

Alamance Community College *A*
Asheville-Buncombe Technical
 Community College *A*
Beaufort County Community
 College *A*
Coastal Carolina Community
 College *A*
Davidson County Community
 College *A*
Halifax Community College *A*
Salem College *B*
Sandhills Community College *A*
Southeastern Community College *A*
Southwestern Community College *A*
Wake Technical Community
 College *A*

North Dakota

Bismarck State College *A*
Rasmussen College: Bismarck *A*
Rasmussen College: Fargo *A*

Ohio

Cincinnati State Technical and
 Community College *A*
Clark State Community College *A*
Cuyahoga Community College
 Metropolitan Campus *A*
Defiance College *B*

Eastern Gateway Community
 College *A*
Edison State Community College *A*
Marion Technical College *A*
Muskingum University *B*
Stark State College of Technology *A*
University of Rio Grande *A*
Youngstown State University *A*
Zane State College *A*

Oklahoma

Cameron University *B*
Northeastern Oklahoma Agricultural
 and Mechanical College *A*
Rose State College *A*
Seminole State College *A*
Southern Nazarene University *B*
Southwestern Oklahoma State
 University *A, B*
Tulsa Community College *A*

Oregon

Oregon State University *B*
Portland Community College *A*

Pennsylvania

California University of
 Pennsylvania *B*
Clarion University of Pennsylvania *B*
Community College of Allegheny
 County *A*
Community College of Philadelphia *A*
Edinboro University of
 Pennsylvania *B*
Harcum College *A*
Harrisburg Area Community
 College *A*
Mansfield University of
 Pennsylvania *B*
Montgomery County Community
 College *A*
Neumann University *B*
Penn State
 Hazleton *A*
 Schuylkill *A*
St. Francis University *B*
Thiel College *B*

Puerto Rico

University of Puerto Rico
 Medical Sciences *B*

Rhode Island

Community College of Rhode
 Island *A*

South Carolina

Erskine College *B*
Florence-Darlington Technical
 College *A*
Forrest Junior College *A*
Greenville Technical College *A*
Midlands Technical College *A*
Orangeburg-Calhoun Technical
 College *A*
Spartanburg Community College *A*
Tri-County Technical College *A*
Trident Technical College *A*
York Technical College *A*

South Dakota

Augustana College *B*
Lake Area Technical Institute *A*
Mitchell Technical Institute *A*
Presentation College *A*

Tennessee

Columbia State Community College *A*
Jackson State Community College *A*
Lincoln Memorial University *A*
Southwest Tennessee Community
 College *A*

Volunteer State Community College *A*

Texas
Amarillo College *A*
Angelina College *A*
Austin Community College *A*
Central Texas College *A*
Del Mar College *A*
El Centro College *A*
El Paso Community College *A*
Houston Community College
System *A*
Kilgore College *A*
Lamar State College at Orange *A*
Laredo Community College *A*
McLennan Community College *A*
Northeast Texas Community
College *A*
St. Philip's College *A*
San Jacinto College *A*
Southwestern Adventist University *B*
University of Texas
Brownsville - Texas Southmost
College *A*
Victoria College *A*
Wharton County Junior College *A*

Utah
College of Eastern Utah *A*
Weber State University *A*

Virginia
Central Virginia Community
College *A*
J. Sargeant Reynolds Community
College *A*
Northern Virginia Community
College *A*
Southside Virginia Community
College *A*
Wytheville Community College *A*

Washington
Spokane Community College *A*
Spokane Falls Community College *A*

West Virginia
Fairmont State University *A*
Marshall University *A*
Southern West Virginia Community
and Technical College *A*

Wisconsin
Chippewa Valley Technical College *A*
Gateway Technical College *A*
Lakeshore Technical College *A*
Marquette University *B*
Milwaukee Area Technical College *A*
Northcentral Technical College *A*
University of Wisconsin
Oshkosh *B*
Viterbo University *B*
Western Technical College *A*

Wyoming
Casper College *A*

Clinical/medical social work

California
Loma Linda University *D*

Indiana
University of Southern Indiana *M*

Maine
University of Southern Maine *M*

Michigan
Michigan State University *M*

Mississippi
University of Southern Mississippi *M*

Puerto Rico
Universidad del Este *M*

South Dakota
University of South Dakota *M, D*

Vermont
College of St. Joseph in Vermont *M*

Wisconsin
Concordia University Wisconsin *B*

Clinical nurse specialist

Florida
Florida Southern College *M*

Georgia
Georgia Southern University *M, T*
Mercer University *M*

Illinois
Loyola University Chicago *M*

Massachusetts
Worcester State College *M*

Michigan
Saginaw Valley State University *M*

Minnesota
College of St. Scholastica *M*

Missouri
Central Methodist University *M*
Maryville University of Saint Louis *M*

New York
Mount Saint Mary College *M*
St. John Fisher College *M, D*
State University of New York
Upstate Medical University *M*

Ohio
Case Western Reserve University *M*
Ursuline College *M*

Pennsylvania
Duquesne University *M*
Gwynedd-Mercy College *M*
Robert Morris University *D*
University of Pennsylvania *M*

South Carolina
University of South Carolina *M*

Tennessee
University of Tennessee Health
Science Center *M*

Texas
Angelo State University *M*
Texas A&M University
Corpus Christi *B*
Texas Christian University *M, D*
Texas Woman's University *M*
University of Texas
Arlington *M*
El Paso *M*
Pan American *M*

Utah
Brigham Young University *M*

Wisconsin
Marian University *M*

Clinical nutrition

Alabama
University of Alabama
Birmingham *M*

Arizona
Central Arizona College *A*
Chandler-Gilbert Community College
Pecos *A*

Florida
Gulf Coast Community College *A*

Illinois
Loyola University Chicago *B*

Indiana
Indiana University-Purdue University
Indianapolis *M*

Kentucky
University of Kentucky *M*

Minnesota
Fond du Lac Tribal and Community
College *A*
Leech Lake Tribal College *A*

New Jersey
University of Medicine and Dentistry
of New Jersey
School of Health Related
Professions *M, D*

North Carolina
East Carolina University *B*

North Dakota
University of North Dakota *B*

Ohio
University of Cincinnati
Raymond Walters College *A*

Oregon
Oregon Health & Science
University *M*

Pennsylvania
Immaculata University *M*
Marywood University *M*
Messiah College *B*

Tennessee
East Tennessee State University *M*
University of Memphis *M*

Clinical pastoral counseling

Maryland
Loyola University Maryland *M, D*

Ohio
University of Dayton *M*

Pennsylvania
Chestnut Hill College *M*

Texas
Southwestern Assemblies of God
University *B, M*

Virginia
Virginia Commonwealth University *M*

Clinical psychology

Alabama
Alabama Agricultural and Mechanical
University *M*
Auburn University *M, D*

Alaska
University of Alaska
Anchorage *M*

California
Alliant International University *M, D*
Antioch Southern California
Antioch University Los Angeles *M*
Antioch University Santa
Barbara *M, D*
Azusa Pacific University *M, D*
Bethany University *M*
Biola University *M, D*
California Institute of Integral
Studies *D*
California Lutheran University *M*
California State University
Bakersfield *M*
Chico *M*
Dominguez Hills *M*
East Bay *M*
Fullerton *M*
San Bernardino *M*
John F. Kennedy University *M*
Notre Dame de Namur University *M*
Pepperdine University *M*
San Diego State University *D*
San Jose State University *M*
Southern California Seminary *D*
University of La Verne *D*
University of Southern California *D*
Vanguard University of Southern
California *M*

Colorado
University of Denver *M, D*

Connecticut
University of Hartford *M, D*

Delaware
University of Delaware *M, D*

District of Columbia
American University *D*
Catholic University of America *M, D*
Gallaudet University *D*
George Washington University *D*
University of the District of
Columbia *M*

Florida
Barry University *M*
Carlos Albizu University *D*
Florida Institute of Technology *M, D*
Florida State University *D*
Nova Southeastern University *D*
University of Central Florida *M*

Georgia
Emory University *D*
Georgia Southern University *D*

Idaho
Idaho State University *D*

Illinois
Argosy University: Chicago *M, D*
Benedictine University *M*
DePaul University *M, D*
Eastern Illinois University *M*
Loyola University Chicago *M, D*
Northwestern University *D*
Roosevelt University *M, D*

Wheaton College *M, D*

Indiana
Ball State University *M*
Indiana State University *D*
Indiana University
Bloomington *D*
Indiana University-Purdue University
Indianapolis *M, D*
University of Indianapolis *M, D*

Iowa
Loras College *M*
University of Iowa *D*

Kansas
Emporia State University *M*
Pittsburg State University *M*
Washburn University *M*

Kentucky
Eastern Kentucky University *M*
Morehead State University *M*
Murray State University *M*
Spalding University *M, D*
University of Kentucky *M, D*
University of Louisville *M, D*

Louisiana
Northwestern State University *M*

Maine
Husson University *B*
University of Maine *D*

Maryland
Loyola University Maryland *M, D*

Massachusetts
American International College *M*
Clark University *M, D*
Eastern Nazarene College *B*
Suffolk University *M, D*
University of Massachusetts
Boston *M, D*
Dartmouth *M*

Michigan
Central Michigan University *D*
Eastern Michigan University *M, D*
Madonna University *M*
University of Detroit Mercy *M, D*
University of Michigan
Flint *B*

Minnesota
Capella University *M, D*
Minnesota State University
Mankato *M*
Saint Cloud State University *M*
Walden University *D*

Mississippi
Jackson State University *D*

Missouri
Evangel University *M*
Saint Louis University *M, D*
University of Missouri
Columbia *M, D*
Washington University in St.
Louis *M, D*

New Hampshire
Keene State College *B*

New Jersey
Fairleigh Dickinson University
College at Florham *M*
Metropolitan Campus *D*

Rutgers, The State University of New
Jersey
New Brunswick/Piscataway
Campus *D*
Seton Hall University *D*

New Mexico
New Mexico Highlands University *M*

New York
Adelphi University *D*
City University of New York
Queens College *M*
Fordham University *M, D*
Hofstra University *M, D*
Long Island University
Brooklyn Campus *D*
C. W. Post Campus *D*
New York University *D*
St. John's University *M, D*
State University of New York
Albany *D*
Binghamton *D*
Buffalo *D*
Stony Brook *D*
Syracuse University *M, D*
University of Rochester *D*
Yeshiva University *D*

North Carolina
Appalachian State University *M*
Duke University *M, D*
East Carolina University *M*
University of North Carolina
Charlotte *M*

North Dakota
University of North Dakota *D*

Ohio
Bowling Green State University *M, D*
Case Western Reserve University *D*
Kent State University *M, D*
Ohio University *M, D*
Union Institute & University *M, D*
University of Dayton *M*
Wright State University *D*
Xavier University *D*

Oklahoma
University of Tulsa *M, D*

Oregon
George Fox University *M, D*
Pacific University *D*

Pennsylvania
Bryn Mawr College *M, D*
Chestnut Hill College *M, D*
Drexel University *D*
Duquesne University *D*
Edinboro University of
Pennsylvania *M*
Immaculata University *D*
Indiana University of Pennsylvania *D*
La Salle University *D*
Marywood University *M, D*
Penn State
Harrisburg *M*
Temple University *M, D*
West Chester University of
Pennsylvania *M*
Widener University *D*

Puerto Rico
Inter American University of Puerto
Rico
Metropolitan Campus *M*
Pontifical Catholic University of
Puerto Rico *M, D*
University of Puerto Rico
Rio Piedras *M*

Rhode Island
University of Rhode Island *D*

South Carolina
Francis Marion University *M*
University of South Carolina *M, D*
University of South Carolina
Aiken *M*

South Dakota
University of South Dakota *D*

Tennessee
Vanderbilt University *M, D*

Texas
Abilene Christian University *M*
Baylor University *M, D*
Houston Baptist University *M*
Our Lady of the Lake University of San
Antonio *M*
St. Mary's University *M*
Sam Houston State University *M, D*
Southern Methodist University *M*
Southwestern Assemblies of God
University *M*
Texas A&M University *D*
Texas Tech University *D*
University of Houston *M, D*
University of Houston
Clear Lake *M*
University of North Texas *D*
University of Texas
Austin *D*
El Paso *M*
Pan American *M*
Southwestern Medical Center at
Dallas *M, D*
Tyler *M*
of the Permian Basin *M*

Utah
Brigham Young University *D*

Vermont
College of St. Joseph in Vermont *M*
St. Michael's College *M*

Virginia
Averett University *B*
College of William and Mary *D*
Norfolk State University *D*
Old Dominion University *D*
Regent University *M, D*
University of Virginia *D*
Virginia Commonwealth University *D*

Washington
Antioch University Seattle *M*
Seattle Pacific University *D*
University of Washington *D*

West Virginia
Marshall University *D*

Wisconsin
Marquette University *M, D*

Clothing, apparel and textile studies

Alabama
University of Alabama *B*

Arizona
Mesa Community College *A*

Arkansas
University of Arkansas *B*

California
Antelope Valley College *C, A*
California State Polytechnic
University: Pomona *B*
California State University
Long Beach *B*
Northridge *B*
Cerritos College *A*
Chabot College *A*
Chaffey College *C*
El Camino College *C*
El Camino College: Compton
Center *A*
Fashion Institute of Design and
Merchandising
Los Angeles *A*
San Diego *A*
San Francisco *A*
Fresno City College *C, A*
Glendale Community College *A*
Los Angeles Mission College *A*
Los Angeles Trade and Technical
College *C, A*
Mendocino College *C*
Modesto Junior College *A*
Monterey Peninsula College *A*
Mount San Antonio College *A*
Orange Coast College *C, A*
Sacramento City College *C, A*
Saddleback College *C*
San Francisco State University *B*
Santa Rosa Junior College *C*
University of California
Davis *B, M*

Colorado
Colorado State University *M*

Delaware
Delaware State University *B*

Florida
Florida State College at Jacksonville *A*
Florida State University *B, M, D*

Georgia
Georgia Southern University *B*
University of Georgia *M*

Hawaii
University of Hawaii
Manoa *B*

Idaho
University of Idaho *B*

Illinois
Joliet Junior College *A*
Northern Illinois University *B*
Southern Illinois University
Carbondale *B*

Indiana
Indiana State University *B*
Indiana University
Bloomington *B, M*
Purdue University *B, M, D*

Iowa
Ellsworth Community College *A*
Iowa State University *B, M, D*
University of Northern Iowa *B*

Kansas
Kansas State University *B, M*

Kentucky
Western Kentucky University *B*

Maryland
Baltimore City Community
College *C, A*

Massachusetts
Fisher College *A*
Framingham State College *B*

Michigan
Michigan State University *B, M*
Western Michigan University *B*

Minnesota
Minnesota State University
Mankato *B, M*
University of Minnesota
Twin Cities *B*

Mississippi
University of Southern Mississippi *B*

Missouri
Fontbonne University *B*
Missouri State University *B*
Stephens College *B*
University of Central Missouri *B*
University of Missouri
Columbia *B, M*

Nebraska
University of Nebraska
Kearney *B*
Lincoln *B, M*

New Mexico
New Mexico State University *B*

New York
Fashion Institute of Technology *A, B*
State University of New York
College at Buffalo *B*
College at Oneonta *B*

North Carolina
Appalachian State University *B*
East Carolina University *B*
North Carolina Agricultural and
Technical State University *B*
North Carolina State University *B*
University of North Carolina
Greensboro *B, M, D*

North Dakota
North Dakota State University *B*

Ohio
Bluffton University *B*
Bowling Green State University *B, M*
Ohio State University
Columbus Campus *B, M, D*
Ohio University *B, M*
University of Akron *B, M*
Youngstown State University *B*

Oklahoma
East Central University *B*
Langston University *B*

Oregon
Oregon State University *B*

Pennsylvania
Albright College *B*
Cheyney University of Pennsylvania *B*
Philadelphia University *B, M*

Rhode Island
University of Rhode Island *B, M*

South Carolina
Bob Jones University *B*
Tri-County Technical College *A*

Tennessee
Carson-Newman College *B*
Lambuth University *B*
Lipscomb University *B*
Middle Tennessee State University *B*
Tennessee State University *B*
Tennessee Technological University *B*

Texas
Lamar University *B*
Texas A&M University
Kingsville *B*
Texas Southern University *M*
Texas Tech University *B*
University of Texas
Austin *B, M*
Wade College *A*

Utah
Snow College *A*
Utah State University *B*

Virginia
Liberty University *B*

Washington
Bates Technical College *C*
Seattle Pacific University *B*
Washington State University *B, M*

West Virginia
West Virginia University *B*

Wisconsin
University of Wisconsin
Madison *B*
Stout *B*

Cognitive psychology/ psycholinguistics

Arizona
Prescott College *B*

California
California State University
Stanislaus *B*
University of California
San Diego *D*
University of Southern California *D*

Connecticut
University of Connecticut *B*

Delaware
University of Delaware *M, D*

District of Columbia
George Washington University *D*

Florida
Florida State University *D*

Georgia
Emory University *D*

Illinois
Loyola University Chicago *M, D*
Northwestern University *B*

Massachusetts
Tufts University *M, D*

Michigan
University of Michigan *B*

Missouri
University of Missouri
Columbia *M, D*

New Jersey
Kean University *M*

New York
State University of New York
Albany *D*
Binghamton *D*
Buffalo *D*

Pennsylvania
Carnegie Mellon University *B*
Temple University *D*

Rhode Island
Brown University *M, D*

Texas
Rice University *M, D*

Virginia
Averett University *B*

Cognitive science

California
Occidental College *B*
Pomona College *B*
University of California
Berkeley *B*
Irvine *D*
Los Angeles *B*
San Diego *B*
University of California: Merced *B*

Colorado
University of Colorado
Boulder *D*

Connecticut
University of Connecticut *B*
Yale University *B*

Georgia
University of Georgia *B*

Illinois
University of Chicago *D*

Indiana
University of Evansville *B*

Louisiana
University of Louisiana at Lafayette *D*

Maryland
Johns Hopkins University *B, M, D*

Massachusetts
Hampshire College *B*
Massachusetts Institute of
Technology *B, D*

Michigan
Central Michigan University *B*

New York
Rensselaer Polytechnic Institute *M, D*
State University of New York
Oswego *B*
United States Military Academy *B*
Vassar College *B*

Ohio
Case Western Reserve University *B, M*

Oregon
George Fox University *B*

Pennsylvania
Carnegie Mellon University *B*
Lehigh University *B*
University of Pennsylvania *B*

Rhode Island
Brown University *B, M, D*

Tennessee
Vanderbilt University *B*

Texas
Rice University *B*
University of Texas
Dallas *B, M*

Virginia
University of Richmond *B*

Wisconsin
Lawrence University *B*

College student counseling

Arizona
Prescott College *B*

Arkansas
Arkansas State University *M*
Arkansas Tech University *M*
University of Central Arkansas *M*

Connecticut
Southern Connecticut State
University *M, T*

Delaware
University of Delaware *M*

Florida
University of Florida *M*

Illinois
Eastern Illinois University *M*
Loyola University Chicago *M*
University of Illinois
Urbana-Champaign *M, D*
Western Illinois University *M*

Indiana
Ball State University *M*
Indiana State University *M, T*
Indiana University
Bloomington *M*

Iowa
Iowa State University *T*
University of Iowa *M, D*
University of Northern Iowa *M*

Kentucky
Eastern Kentucky University *M*
Western Kentucky University *M*

Louisiana
Northwestern State University *M*

Maine
University of Southern Maine *M*

Massachusetts
Bridgewater State College *M*
Northeastern University *M*
Springfield College *M*

Michigan

Eastern Michigan University *M*
Michigan State University *M*

Minnesota

Minnesota State University
Mankato *M*
Saint Cloud State University *M*

Mississippi

Mississippi State University *D*

Missouri

University of Missouri
Columbia *M, D*

Nebraska

Wayne State College *M*

New Hampshire

Rivier College *M*

New Jersey

Seton Hall University *M*

New York

Canisius College *M*
College of Saint Rose *M*
Fordham University *M, D*
Saint Bonaventure University *M*
State University of New York
College at Plattsburgh *M, T*
University of Rochester *M, D*

North Carolina

Appalachian State University *M*
North Carolina Central University *M*
North Carolina State University *M*
University of North Carolina
Charlotte *M*
Greensboro *M, D*
Pembroke *M*
Western Carolina University *M*

Ohio

Bowling Green State University *B, M*
Miami University
Oxford Campus *M, D*
Ohio State University
Columbus Campus *M, D*
Ohio University *M*
University of Dayton *M*
Youngstown State University *M*

Pennsylvania

Eastern University *M*
Holy Family University *M*
Indiana University of Pennsylvania *M*
Kutztown University of
Pennsylvania *M*
Penn State
University Park *M*
Shippensburg University of
Pennsylvania *M*
Villanova University *M*
Widener University *M, T*

South Carolina

Bob Jones University *B*
Clemson University *M*
University of South Carolina *M*

South Dakota

South Dakota State University *M*

Texas

Angelo State University *M*

Utah

Brigham Young University *D*

Vermont

Johnson State College *M*

Virginia

Longwood University *M*

Washington

Seattle University *M*
Walla Walla University *M*
Western Washington University *M*

Wisconsin

Marquette University *M*
University of Wisconsin
La Crosse *M*

Commercial/advertising art

Alabama

Calhoun Community College *A*
Faulkner State Community
College *C, A*
Oakwood University *A*
Shelton State Community College *C*

Arizona

Art Center Design College *A*
Art Institute
of Phoenix *B*
Collins College *A, B*
Eastern Arizona College *A*
Phoenix College *C, A*

Arkansas

Arkansas State University *B*
National Park Community College *A*
Northwest Arkansas Community
College *A*
South Arkansas Community College *A*
Southern Arkansas University Tech *C*
University of Arkansas Community
College at Morrilton *A*

California

Academy of Art University *C, A, B, M*
Allan Hancock College *A*
Art Center College of Design *B, M*
Art Institute
of California: Los Angeles *A, B*
of California: Orange County *A, B*
of California: San Diego *A, B*
Art Institute of California: San
Francisco *A, B*
Biola University *B*
Butte College *A*
California Lutheran University *B*
California State University
East Bay *B*
Long Beach *B*
Los Angeles *B*
Northridge *B*
Sacramento *B, M*
San Bernardino *B*
Cerro Coso Community College *C*
Chabot College *A*
Chaffey College *C, A*
Citrus College *C*
College of San Mateo *C, A*
College of the Redwoods *C, A*
College of the Sequoias *C, A*
Cypress College *A*
De Anza College *C, A*
El Camino College: Compton
Center *C, A*
Evergreen Valley College *A*
Foothill College *C, A*
Fullerton College *A*
Glendale Community College *C, A*
Golden West College *C, A*
Laguna College of Art and Design *C, B*
Laney College *C, A*

Long Beach City College *C, A*
Los Angeles City College *A*
Los Angeles Pierce College *C, A*
Los Angeles Southwest College *A*
Los Angeles Trade and Technical
College *A*
Los Angeles Valley College *C, A*
Los Medanos College *C, A*
MiraCosta College *C, A*
Mission College *C, A*
Modesto Junior College *C, A*
Moorpark College *C, A*
Ohlone College *C, A*
Orange Coast College *C, A*
Pacific Union College *A, B*
Palomar College *C, A*
Pasadena City College *C, A*
Platt College
Los Angeles *C, A*
Ontario *C, A, B*
San Diego *C, A, B*
Porterville College *C, A*
Rio Hondo College *A*
Riverside Community College *C, A*
Saddleback College *C, A*
San Bernardino Valley College *C, A*
San Diego City College *C, A*
Santa Ana College *A*
Santa Barbara City College *C, A*
Santa Monica College *A*
Santa Rosa Junior College *C, A*
Santiago Canyon College *A*
Shasta College *A*
Solano Community College *A*
Taft College *C*
University of San Francisco *B*
University of the Pacific *B*
Ventura College *C, A*
West Hills College: Coalinga *C, A*
Westwood College of Technology
Westwood College: Inland
Empire *A*
Woodbury University *B*

Colorado

Colorado Mountain College *C, A*
Platt College
Aurora *A, B*
Trinidad State Junior College *C, A*
Westwood College of Technology
Westwood College: Denver
South *A, B*
Westwood College: Denver
North *A, B*

Connecticut

Albertus Magnus College *B*
Asnuntuck Community College *C*
Housatonic Community College *C, A*
Manchester Community College *C, A*
Mitchell College *A*
Norwalk Community College *C, A*
Paier College of Art *C, B*
Sacred Heart University *B*
Tunxis Community College *C, A*
University of Hartford *B*

Delaware

Delaware Technical and Community
College
Terry *A*
University of Delaware *B*

District of Columbia

Gallaudet University *B*
George Washington University *M*

Florida

Brevard Community College *A*
Daytona State College *A*
Florida State College at Jacksonville *A*
Indian River State College *A*
Lake-Sumter Community College *A*

Miami Dade College *A*
Northwest Florida State College *C, A*
Palm Beach Community College *A*
Pensacola Junior College *A*
Ringling College of Art and Design *B*
Seminole Community College *A*
State College of Florida,
Manatee-Sarasota *A*
Tallahassee Community College *A*

Georgia

Art Institute
of Atlanta *C, B*
Savannah College of Art and
Design *B, M*

Hawaii

University of Hawaii
Honolulu Community College *C, A*

Idaho

Boise State University *B*
North Idaho College *A*

Illinois

Chicago State University *B*
City Colleges of Chicago
Harold Washington College *A*
Kennedy-King College *C, A*
Columbia College Chicago *B*
Dominican University *B*
Illinois Institute of Art: Schaumburg *B*
International Academy of Design and
Technology: Chicago *A, B*
Lewis University *B*
Millikin University *B*
North Park University *B*
Oakton Community College *A*
Parkland College *A*
Rend Lake College *C, A*
Robert Morris University:
Chicago *C, A*
Triton College *C, A*

Indiana

Indiana University
Bloomington *B, M*
Indiana University-Purdue University
Fort Wayne *A, B*
International Business College *C, A*
Marian University *B*
University of Indianapolis *B*
University of St. Francis *A, B*
Vincennes University *A*

Iowa

Buena Vista University *B*
Des Moines Area Community
College *C, A*
Dordt College *B*
Drake University *B*
Ellsworth Community College *A*
Graceland University *B*
Iowa Lakes Community College *A*
Iowa State University *B, M*
St. Ambrose University *B*
University of Dubuque *B*
Upper Iowa University *B*
Wartburg College *B*

Kansas

Cowley County Community
College *A*
Johnson County Community
College *A*
Labette Community College *A*
Pittsburg State University *B*
Pratt Community College *A*
Tabor College *B*
University of Kansas *B*
Wichita State University *B*

Kentucky

Bluegrass Community and Technical College *A*
Brescia University *B*
Northern Kentucky University *B*
Spencerian College: Lexington *A*

Louisiana

Delgado Community College *A*
Louisiana College *B*
Louisiana Tech University *B*
Loyola University New Orleans *B*

Maryland

Anne Arundel Community College *C, A*
Carroll Community College *A*
College of Southern Maryland *C*
Community College of Baltimore County *C, A*
Frostburg State University *B*
Hagerstown Community College *C, A*
Howard Community College *C, A*
Montgomery College *A*
Prince George's Community College *A*
University of Baltimore *M*
University of Maryland Eastern Shore *B*

Massachusetts

Art Institute of Boston at Lesley University *B*
Becker College *B*
Boston University *B, M*
Cape Cod Community College *A*
Greenfield Community College *A*
Holyoke Community College *C*
Massasoit Community College *A*
Middlesex Community College *C, A*
New England Institute of Art *B*
Northern Essex Community College *C, A*
Salem State College *B*
Simmons College *B*
Springfield Technical Community College *A*
Suffolk University *A, B*
University of Massachusetts Dartmouth *B, M*

Michigan

Andrews University *B*
Baker College
of Auburn Hills *A*
of Clinton Township *A*
of Flint *A, B*
of Muskegon *A*
of Owosso *A*
of Port Huron *A*
College for Creative Studies *B*
Ferris State University *A, B*
Finlandia University *B*
Gogebic Community College *A*
Grand Rapids Community College *A*
Grand Valley State University *B*
Henry Ford Community College *C, A*
Kalamazoo Valley Community College *C, A*
Kellogg Community College *A*
Kendall College of Art and Design of Ferris State University *B*
Lansing Community College *A*
Macomb Community College *C, A*
Mid Michigan Community College *A*
Muskegon Community College *A*
Northwestern Michigan College *A*
St. Clair County Community College *A*
Siena Heights University *B*

Minnesota

Academy College *C, A*

Alexandria Technical College *C, A*
Art Institutes International Minnesota *A, B*
Bemidji State University *B*
Central Lakes College *C, A*
College of Visual Arts *B*
Dakota County Technical College *C, A*
Mesabi Range Community and Technical College *C*
Minneapolis Business College *A*
Minnesota State University
Mankato *B*
Moorhead *B*
South Central College *C, A*
University of Minnesota
Twin Cities *C, B*
Winona State University *B*

Mississippi

Hinds Community College *A*
Mississippi Gulf Coast Community College *A*
Northwest Mississippi Community College *A*

Missouri

East Central College *C, A*
Hickey College *C*
Metropolitan Community College: Penn Valley *A*
St. Charles Community College *A*
St. Louis Community College
St. Louis Community College at Florissant Valley *A*
St. Louis Community College at Meramec *A*
Southwest Baptist University *B*
Stephens College *B*
University of Central Missouri *B*
Washington University in St. Louis *B, M*

Nebraska

Bellevue University *B*
Central Community College *C, A*
Metropolitan Community College *A*
Southeast Community College *C, A*
Union College *A, B*
University of Nebraska Kearney *B*

Nevada

College of Southern Nevada *A*

New Hampshire

Franklin Pierce University *B*
Keene State College *B*
Lakes Region Community College *A*
Manchester Community College *C, A*
Plymouth State University *B*

New Jersey

Bergen Community College *A*
Centenary College *B*
The College of New Jersey *B*
Cumberland County College *A*
Essex County College *A*
Gloucester County College *C, A*
Mercer County Community College *A*
Middlesex County College *A*
Ocean County College *C*
Seton Hall University *B*
Sussex County Community College *C, A*

New Mexico

Clovis Community College *A*
New Mexico Junior College *C, A*
New Mexico State University Alamogordo *C, A*
San Juan College *C, A*

New York

Alfred University *M*
Briarcliffe College *A*
City University of New York
Bronx Community College *A*
City College *B*
Kingsborough Community College *A*
Lehman College *B*
New York City College of Technology *A, B*
College of Saint Rose *B*
College of Westchester *C, A*
Dutchess Community College *A*
Fashion Institute of Technology *A, B*
Finger Lakes Community College *A*
Fulton-Montgomery Community College *A*
Long Island University
Brooklyn Campus *B, M*
C. W. Post Campus *B*
Mercy College *A, B*
Mohawk Valley Community College *C, A*
Monroe Community College *A*
New York Institute of Technology *B*
New York University *B, M*
Onondaga Community College *A*
Pace University *B, M*
Rochester Institute of Technology *A, B, M*
Rockland Community College *C, A*
St. Thomas Aquinas College *B*
School of Visual Arts *B, M*
State University of New York
College at Buffalo *B*
College at Cortland *B*
College at Fredonia *B*
College at Potsdam *B*
College of Agriculture and Technology at Cobleskill *A*
New Paltz *B*
Oswego *B*
Purchase *B*
Suffolk County Community College *A*
Sullivan County Community College *A*
Syracuse University *B, M*
Tompkins Cortland Community College *C, A*
Ulster County Community College *A*
Villa Maria College of Buffalo *A, B*
Westchester Community College *C*
Wood Tobe-Coburn School *C*

North Carolina

Campbell University *B*
Catawba Valley Community College *A*
Central Piedmont Community College *C, A*
Fayetteville Technical Community College *A*
Gaston College *C*
Guilford Technical Community College *C, A*
Halifax Community College *A*
Isothermal Community College *A*
James Sprunt Community College *C, A*
Johnston Community College *A*
King's College *C, A*
Lenoir Community College *C, A*
McDowell Technical Community College *A*
Pitt Community College *A*
Randolph Community College *A*
South Piedmont Community College *C, A*
Southwestern Community College *A*
Surry Community College *A*

North Dakota

Bismarck State College *C, A*

Ohio

Ashland University *B*
Bowling Green State University *B*
Bradford School *C*
Cincinnati State Technical and Community College *A*
Clark State Community College *A*
Cleveland Institute of Art *B*
Columbus College of Art and Design *B*
Cuyahoga Community College Metropolitan Campus *A*
Defiance College *B*
Edison State Community College *A*
Kent State University *B, M*
Marietta College *B*
Miami University Oxford Campus *B*
Ohio Northern University *B*
Owens Community College Toledo *C, A*
School of Advertising Art *C, A*
Terra State Community College *A*
University of Cincinnati *B*
University of Findlay *B*
Virginia Marti College of Art and Design *A*
Wilmington College *B*
Youngstown State University *B*

Oklahoma

Northeastern State University *B*
Oklahoma Christian University *B*
Oklahoma City Community College *A*
Oklahoma State University Institute of Technology: Okmulgee *A*
Oklahoma City *A*
Oral Roberts University *B*
Platt College: Oklahoma City Central *C*
Southwestern Oklahoma State University *B*

Oregon

Art Institute of Portland *B*
Lane Community College *C, A*
Linn-Benton Community College *A*
Mt. Hood Community College *A*
Portland Community College *A*
Portland State University *B*

Pennsylvania

Antonelli Institute of Art and Photography *A*
Arcadia University *B*
Art Institute
of Philadelphia *A, B*
of Pittsburgh *A, B*
Bucks County Community College *A*
California University of Pennsylvania *A, B*
Community College of Allegheny County *C, A*
Community College of Philadelphia *A*
Hussian School of Art *A*
Kutztown University of Pennsylvania *B*
Lehigh Carbon Community College *A*
Luzerne County Community College *C*
Lycoming College *B*
Marywood University *M*
Montgomery County Community College *A*
Oakbridge Academy of Arts *A*
Pennsylvania College of Technology *A, B*
Seton Hill University *C, B*
Thiel College *B*
Westmoreland County Community College *A*
York College of Pennsylvania *B*

South Carolina

Bob Jones University *B, M*
Coker College *B*
Greenville Technical College *C*
Midlands Technical College *A*
Spartanburg Community College *C*
Trident Technical College *A*
University of South Carolina
  Upstate *B*

South Dakota

Black Hills State University *B*
Northern State University *A*
Southeast Technical Institute *A*

Tennessee

Belmont University *B*
Chattanooga State Community
  College *A*
Lipscomb University *B*
Memphis College of Art *B*
Nashville State Community College *A*
Nossi College of Art *A*
O'More College of Design *B*
Pellissippi State Community
  College *A*
Southern Adventist University *A, B*
Southwest Tennessee Community
  College *A*
University of Tennessee
  Knoxville *B*

Texas

Amarillo College *C, A*
Austin Community College *C, A*
Brookhaven College *A*
Clarendon College *A*
Coastal Bend College *A*
Collin County Community College
  District *C, A*
El Paso Community College *A*
Grayson County College *A*
Hill College *A*
Kilgore College *C, A*
Lamar University *B*
Navarro College *A*
Sam Houston State University *B*
San Jacinto College *C, A*
Schreiner University *B*
South Plains College *A*
Texas A&M University
  Commerce *B, M*
Texas State Technical College
  Waco *C, A*
Tyler Junior College *C, A*
University of Houston *B, M*
University of North Texas *B*

Utah

Eagle Gate College: Salt Lake City *C, A*
Provo College *A*
Southern Utah University *B*
Weber State University *B*

Vermont

Lyndon State College *B*

Virginia

Central Virginia Community
  College *A*
Hampton University *B*
Longwood University *B*
Northern Virginia Community
  College *A*
Thomas Nelson Community
  College *A*
Tidewater Community College *A*
Virginia Intermont College *A*
Virginia Western Community
  College *A*

Washington

Art Institute of Seattle *C*
Centralia College *A*
Cornish College of the Arts *B*
Everett Community College *A*
Highline Community College *A*
Pierce College *A*
Shoreline Community College *C, A*
Skagit Valley College *C, A*
Spokane Falls Community
  College *C, A*
University of Washington *B, M*
Western Washington University *B*
Whatcom Community College *A*

West Virginia

Concord University *B*
Fairmont State University *B*
West Liberty University *B*
West Virginia State University *B*

Wisconsin

Cardinal Stritch University *B*
Carroll University *B*
Concordia University Wisconsin *B*
Mount Mary College *B*
St. Norbert College *B*
University of Wisconsin
  Madison *B*
  Platteville *B*

Wyoming

Northwest College *A*

Commercial fishing

Texas

Texas A&M University
  Galveston *B*

Commercial photography

California

Academy of Art University *C, A, B, M*
Allan Hancock College *A*
Art Center College of Design *B*
Butte College *A*
College of the Canyons *C*
Cosumnes River College *C, A*
East Los Angeles College *C*
El Camino College: Compton
  Center *C*
Lake Tahoe Community College *C*
Long Beach City College *C, A*
Modesto Junior College *A*
Orange Coast College *C, A*
Pasadena City College *C, A*
Sacramento City College *C, A*
Saddleback College *A*
Santa Monica College *A*
Solano Community College *C, A*

Colorado

Colorado Mountain College *A*

Connecticut

Paier College of Art *C, A, B*

Florida

Miami International University of Art
  and Design *B*

Georgia

Art Institute
  of Atlanta *A, B*
Gwinnett Technical College *A*
North Georgia Technical College *C*
Savannah College of Art and
  Design *M*

Illinois

College of DuPage *C, A*
Prairie State College *C, A*
Waubonsee Community College *C*

Iowa

Des Moines Area Community
  College *C*
Hawkeye Community College *A*

Kansas

Highland Community College *A*

Maryland

Cecil College *C, A*
Community College of Baltimore
  County *A*
Harford Community College *C, A*
Howard Community College *C*
Montgomery College *A*

Massachusetts

Art Institute of Boston at Lesley
  University *B*
Springfield Technical Community
  College *C, A*

Michigan

Bay de Noc Community College *C*
College for Creative Studies *B*
Washtenaw Community College *A*

Minnesota

Art Institutes International
  Minnesota *B*
Central Lakes College *C*
Minneapolis Community and
  Technical College *C, A*
Ridgewater College *C, A*

Nebraska

Metropolitan Community College *A*

Nevada

College of Southern Nevada *A*

New Jersey

Middlesex County College *A*

New York

City University of New York
  LaGuardia Community College *C, A*
Fashion Institute of Technology *A, B*
Mohawk Valley Community College *A*
Rochester Institute of
  Technology *B, M*
Rockland Community College *A*
Sullivan County Community
  College *A*

North Carolina

Alamance Community College *C*
Appalachian State University *B*
McDowell Technical Community
  College *A*
Randolph Community College *A*

Ohio

Columbus State Community
  College *C, A*
Kaplan College: Dayton *A*
Ohio University *M*
Owens Community College
  Toledo *C, A*

Pennsylvania

Antonelli Institute of Art and
  Photography *A*
Community College of Philadelphia *A*
Oakbridge Academy of Arts *A*

Tennessee

Nossi College of Art *A*

Texas

Amarillo College *A*
Austin Community College *C, A*
El Paso Community College *A*
Kilgore College *C, A*
North Central Texas College *A*
Odessa College *C, A*
Texas A&M University
  Commerce *B*

Virginia

Northern Virginia Community
  College *A*

Washington

Spokane Falls Community
  College *C, A*

Wisconsin

Milwaukee Area Technical College *A*

Wyoming

Central Wyoming College *A*
Northwest College *A*

Communication disorders

Alabama

Auburn University *B, M*

Arizona

Arizona State University *B, D*
Prescott College *B*
University of Arizona *B, M, D*

Arkansas

Harding University *B*
University of Arkansas
  Little Rock *D*

California

Biola University *B*
California State University
  Chico *B, M*
  Fresno *B, M*
  Fullerton *B, M*
  Los Angeles *B, M*
Chapman University *M*
San Diego State University *B, M, D*
San Francisco State University *B, M*
San Jose State University *B*

Colorado

University of Colorado
  Boulder *B, M, D*

District of Columbia

Howard University *M, D*

Georgia

Armstrong Atlantic State
  University *B, M*
University of Georgia *B, M, D*

Illinois

Eastern Illinois University *B, M*
Northern Illinois University *B, M*
Northwestern University *B, M, D*
Southern Illinois University
  Carbondale *B, M*
Western Illinois University *B, M*

Indiana

Butler University *B*
Saint Mary's College *B*

Kansas
Kansas State University *B*
University of Kansas *B*
Wichita State University *B, M, D*

Kentucky
Western Kentucky University *B*

Maine
University of Maine *B, M*

Maryland
University of Maryland
  College Park *B, D*

Massachusetts
Boston University *B, M*
Bridgewater State College *B*
Elms College *B*
Emerson College *B, M, D*
University of Massachusetts
  Amherst *B, M, D*
Worcester State College *B*

Michigan
Calvin College *B*
Central Michigan University *B*
Michigan State University *B, D*
Wayne State University *B, M, D*

Minnesota
Minnesota State University
  Mankato *B, M*
Saint Cloud State University *B, M*
University of Minnesota
  Duluth *B, M*
  Twin Cities *M, D*

Mississippi
Jackson State University *B, M*

Missouri
Southeast Missouri State
  University *B, M*
Truman State University *B, M*
University of Missouri
  Columbia *M, D*

New Hampshire
University of New Hampshire *M*

New Jersey
Montclair State University *M*

New York
City University of New York
  Queens College *B*
Nazareth College *B*
Pace University *B*
State University of New York
  College at Fredonia *B*
  College at Geneseo *B*
  New Paltz *B, M*
Touro College *B*

North Carolina
Appalachian State University *B*
North Carolina Central University *M*
Western Carolina University *B, M*

North Dakota
Minot State University *B, M*
University of North Dakota *B*

Ohio
Baldwin-Wallace College *B*
Bowling Green State
  University *B, M, D*
Case Western Reserve
  University *B, M, D*
University of Akron *B*

Oklahoma
University of Oklahoma *B, M, D*
University of Tulsa *B*

Oregon
University of Oregon *B, M, D*

Pennsylvania
California University of
  Pennsylvania *B, M*
Edinboro University of
  Pennsylvania *B*
Penn State
  Abington *B*
  Altoona *B*
  Beaver *B*
  Berks *B*
  Brandywine *B*
  DuBois *B*
  Erie, The Behrend College *B*
  Fayette, The Eberly Campus *B*
  Greater Allegheny *B*
  Hazleton *B*
  Lehigh Valley *B*
  Mont Alto *B*
  New Kensington *B*
  Schuylkill *B*
  Shenango *B*
  University Park *B, M, D*
  Wilkes-Barre *B*
  Worthington Scranton *B*
  York *B*

Rhode Island
University of Rhode Island *B*

South Carolina
Bob Jones University *B*
Winthrop University *B*

South Dakota
Augustana College *B*
University of South Dakota *B, M*

Tennessee
Lambuth University *B*

Texas
Baylor University *B, M*
Texas Tech University Health Sciences
  Center *B, D*
University of Houston *B*
University of Texas
  Austin *B, M, D*
  Dallas *B, M*
West Texas A&M University *B, M*

Vermont
University of Vermont *B, M*

Virginia
Hampton University *B*
Radford University *M*

Wisconsin
Marquette University *M*
University of Wisconsin
  Eau Claire *B, M*
  Madison *B, M, D*
  Milwaukee *B, M*
  River Falls *B, M*
  Whitewater *M*

Communications

Alabama
Alabama State University *B*
Andrew Jackson University *C, A, B*
Auburn University *B*
Auburn University at Montgomery *B*
Gadsden State Community College *A*

Huntingdon College *B*
Miles College *B*
Oakwood University *B*
Samford University *B*
Southern Union State Community
  College *A*
Spring Hill College *B*
University of Alabama *B, M*
University of Alabama
  Birmingham *B, M*
University of Mobile *B*
University of South Alabama *B, M*

Alaska
University of Alaska
  Fairbanks *B, M*
  Southeast *B*

Arizona
Arizona State University *B, M, D*
Arizona Western College *A*
Cochise College *A*
Grand Canyon University *B*
Northern Arizona University *B*
Phoenix College *A*
Prescott College *B, M*
University of Arizona *B, M, D*
University of Phoenix *B*

Arkansas
Harding University *B*
John Brown University *B*
University of Arkansas *B, M*
University of Arkansas
  Little Rock *B, M*

California
Azusa Pacific University *B*
Bethany University *B*
Biola University *B*
California Baptist University *B*
California Lutheran University *B*
California State Polytechnic
  University: Pomona *B*
California State University
  Bakersfield *B*
  Chico *M*
  Dominguez Hills *B*
  East Bay *B*
  Fullerton *B, M*
  Los Angeles *B, M*
  Northridge *M*
  Sacramento *B, M*
  San Bernardino *B, M, T*
  San Marcos *B*
  Stanislaus *B*
California State University: Channel
  Islands *B*
Chaffey College *A*
Chapman University *B*
City College of San Francisco *C*
College of the Desert *A*
College of the Sequoias *A*
College of the Siskiyous *C, A*
Copper Mountain College *A*
Cuesta College *C, A*
De Anza College *A*
Dominican University of California *B*
Foothill College *C, A*
Fresno City College *A*
Fresno Pacific University *B*
Fullerton College *A*
Gavilan College *A*
Grossmont College *A*
Humboldt State University *B*
Imperial Valley College *A*
La Sierra University *B*
Los Angeles Pierce College *C*
Loyola Marymount University *B*
Mendocino College *C, A*
Menlo College *B*
Merced College *A*
MiraCosta College *A*

Modesto Junior College *C, A*
Monterey Peninsula College *A*
Moorpark College *A*
Notre Dame de Namur University *B*
Pacific Union College *B*
Pasadena City College *C, A*
Pepperdine University *B, M*
Point Loma Nazarene University *B*
St. Mary's College of California *B*
San Bernardino Valley College *C, A*
San Diego Christian College *B*
San Diego Miramar College *A*
San Diego State University *M*
San Jose State University *M*
Santa Ana College *C, A*
Santa Barbara City College *A*
Santa Clara University *B*
Santa Rosa Junior College *C*
Santiago Canyon College *A*
Shasta College *A*
Simpson University *B*
Solano Community College *A*
Sonoma State University *B*
Southwestern College *A*
Stanford University *B, M, D*
University of California
  Davis *B, M*
  San Diego *B, M, D*
  Santa Barbara *B, M, D*
University of La Verne *B*
University of San Diego *B*
University of San Francisco *B*
University of Southern
  California *B, M, D*
University of the Pacific *B, M*
Vanguard University of Southern
  California *B*
Westmont College *B*

Colorado
Adams State College *B*
Colorado Christian University *B*
Colorado State University *B, M*
Jones International University *B, M*
Lamar Community College *A*
Metropolitan State College of
  Denver *B*
Regis University *B*
University of Colorado
  Boulder *B, M, D*
  Colorado Springs *B, M*
  Denver *B, M*
University of Denver *B, M, D*
University of Northern
  Colorado *B, M, T*
Western State College of Colorado *B*
Westwood College: Denver North *B*

Connecticut
Albertus Magnus College *B*
Central Connecticut State
  University *B*
Eastern Connecticut State
  University *B*
Fairfield University *B, M*
Lincoln College of New England:
  Briarwood *A*
Middlesex Community College *A*
Quinnipiac University *B, M*
Sacred Heart University *B*
Southern Connecticut State
  University *B*
Tunxis Community College *C*
University of Bridgeport *B*
University of Connecticut *B, M, D*
University of Hartford *B, M*
University of New Haven *A, B*
Western Connecticut State
  University *B*

Delaware
University of Delaware *B, M*
Wesley College *B*

District of Columbia

Catholic University of America *B*
Gallaudet University *B*
George Washington University *B*
Howard University *B, M, D*
Trinity Washington University *B*

Florida

Barry University *B*
Chipola College *A*
City College: Fort Lauderdale *A*
Clearwater Christian College *B*
Eckerd College *B*
Edward Waters College *B*
Embry-Riddle Aeronautical
   University *B*
Flagler College *B*
Florida Atlantic University *B*
Florida Institute of Technology *B*
Florida International University *B, M*
Florida State University *D*
Gulf Coast Community College *A*
Jacksonville University *B*
Nova Southeastern University *B*
Palm Beach Atlantic University *B*
Pensacola Junior College *A*
Saint Thomas University *B*
Seminole Community College *A*
Southeastern University *B*
State College of Florida,
   Manatee-Sarasota *A*
Stetson University *B*
University of Central Florida *B*
University of Florida *M, D*
University of Miami *B, M, D*
University of South Florida *B, M*
University of Tampa *B*
Warner University *B*
Webber International University *B*

Georgia

Abraham Baldwin Agricultural
   College *A*
Andrew College *A*
Atlanta Metropolitan College *A*
Augusta State University *B*
Bainbridge College *A*
Berry College *B*
Brewton-Parker College *B*
Clayton State University *B*
College of Coastal Georgia *A*
Emmanuel College *B*
Georgia Highlands College *A*
Georgia Perimeter College *A*
Georgia Southern University *B*
Georgia State University *B*
Gordon College *A*
Kennesaw State University *B*
Macon State College *B*
Mercer University *B*
Oglethorpe University *B*
Reinhardt College *B*
Shorter College *B*
South Georgia College *A*
Wesleyan College *B*
Young Harris College *A*

Hawaii

Chaminade University of Honolulu *B*
Hawaii Pacific University *B, M*
University of Hawaii
   Hilo *B*
   Manoa *B, M*

Idaho

Boise State University *B, M, T*
Brigham Young University-Idaho *B*
Idaho State University *A, B, M*
Lewis-Clark State College *B*
North Idaho College *A*
Northwest Nazarene University *B*
University of Idaho *B*

Illinois

Augustana College *B*
Aurora University *B*
Benedictine University *B*
Blackburn College *B*
Bradley University *B*
Concordia University Chicago *B*
Danville Area Community College *A*
DePaul University *B, M*
Dominican University *B*
East-West University *B*
Elmhurst College *B*
Eureka College *B*
Governors State University *B, M*
Illinois Institute of Technology *M*
Illinois State University *M*
Illinois Valley Community College *A*
John Wood Community College *A*
Judson University *B*
Kishwaukee College *A*
Lake Forest College *B*
Lewis University *B*
Lincoln College *A*
Loyola University Chicago *C, B*
McKendree University *B*
Millikin University *B*
Moody Bible Institute *B*
North Central College *B*
North Park University *B*
Northern Illinois University *B*
Northwestern University *B, M, D*
Olivet Nazarene University *B*
Quincy University *B*
Roosevelt University *B*
Saint Xavier University *B*
Southwestern Illinois College *A*
Trinity Christian College *B*
Trinity International University *B*
University of Illinois
   Chicago *B, M, D*
   Springfield *B, M*
   Urbana-Champaign *B, D*
Western Illinois University *B*
Wheaton College *B*

Indiana

Bethel College *B*
Butler University *B*
Calumet College of St. Joseph *B*
Goshen College *B*
Grace College *B*
Hanover College *B*
Holy Cross College *B*
Huntington University *B*
Indiana State University *B, M, T*
Indiana University
   Bloomington *B, M, D*
   East *B*
   Kokomo *B*
   Northwest *B*
   Southeast *B*
Indiana University-Purdue University
   Fort Wayne *B, M, T*
Indiana University-Purdue University
   Indianapolis *B*
Indiana Wesleyan University *C, A, B*
Ivy Tech Community College
   Kokomo *A*
Manchester College *B, T*
Marian University *B*
Purdue University *B, M, D*
Purdue University
   Calumet *B, M*
   North Central *C, B*
Saint Mary's College *B*
Taylor University *B*
Trine University *A, B*
University of Indianapolis *B*
University of St. Francis *B*
University of Southern Indiana *T*

Iowa

Buena Vista University *B*
Central College *B*
Clarke College *B*
Coe College *B*
Dordt College *B*
Drake University *B*
Ellsworth Community College *A*
Graceland University *B*
Iowa State University *B*
Iowa Wesleyan College *B*
Kaplan University
   Davenport *B*
Mount Mercy College *B*
St. Ambrose University *B*
University of Dubuque *B, M*
University of Iowa *B, M, D, T*
University of Northern Iowa *B, M*
Upper Iowa University *B*
Wartburg College *B*
William Penn University *B*

Kansas

Baker University *B*
Barton County Community College *A*
Bethany College *B*
Central Christian College of
   Kansas *A, B*
Coffeyville Community College *A*
Cowley County Community
   College *A*
Emporia State University *B*
Fort Hays State University *B, M*
Fort Scott Community College *A*
Friends University *B*
Garden City Community College *A*
Hutchinson Community College *A*
Kansas State University *B, M*
Kansas Wesleyan University *B, T*
McPherson College *B*
MidAmerica Nazarene University *B, T*
Neosho County Community
   College *A*
Ottawa University *B*
Pittsburg State University *B, M*
Pratt Community College *A*
Seward County Community College *A*
Southwestern College *B*
Sterling College *B*
Tabor College *B*
University of St. Mary *B*
Washburn University *B*
Wichita State University *B, M*

Kentucky

Bellarmine University *B, M*
Bluegrass Community and Technical
   College *A*
Campbellsville University *B*
Eastern Kentucky University *B*
Henderson Community College *A*
Kentucky Mountain Bible College *B*
Kentucky Wesleyan College *B*
Lindsey Wilson College *B*
Morehead State University *B, M*
Murray State University *M*
Northern Kentucky University *M*
Pikeville College *B*
Spalding University *B*
Thomas More College *A, B*
Union College *B*
University of Kentucky *B, M, D*
University of Louisville *B*
University of the Cumberlands *B, T*
West Kentucky Community and
   Technical College *A*
Western Kentucky University *C, B, M*

Louisiana

Centenary College of Louisiana *B*
Dillard University *B*
Louisiana College *B*
Louisiana State University
   Shreveport *B*
Loyola University New Orleans *B*
Southeastern Louisiana University *B*
University of Louisiana at
   Lafayette *B, M*
University of Louisiana at Monroe *M*
University of New Orleans *B*

Maine

Thomas College *B*
University of Maine *B*
University of Southern Maine *B*

Maryland

Allegany College of Maryland *A*
College of Notre Dame of
   Maryland *B, M*
Frederick Community College *A*
Frostburg State University *B*
Hood College *B*
Howard Community College *A*
Loyola University Maryland *B*
McDaniel College *B*
Mount St. Mary's University *B*
Salisbury University *B*
Towson University *B, M*
University of Maryland
   College Park *B, M, D*
   University College *B*
Washington Adventist University *B*

Massachusetts

Boston College *B*
Boston University *B, M*
Bridgewater State College *B*
Bristol Community College *A*
Bunker Hill Community College *A*
Cape Cod Community College *A*
Clark University *B, M*
Curry College *B*
Dean College *A*
Elms College *B*
Emerson College *C, B, M*
Emmanuel College *B*
Fitchburg State College *B, M*
Gordon College *B*
Hampshire College *B*
Lasell College *B*
Massachusetts Bay Community
   College *C, A*
Massachusetts College of Liberal
   Arts *B*
Merrimack College *B*
Middlesex Community College *A*
Newbury College *B*
Northeastern University *B, M*
Regis College *B*
Salem State College *B*
Simmons College *B, M*
Stonehill College *B*
Suffolk University *B, M*
University of Massachusetts
   Amherst *B, M, D*
Western New England College *B*
Westfield State College *B*
Worcester State College *B*

Michigan

Adrian College *A, B, T*
Albion College *B, T*
Andrews University *B, M*
Aquinas College *B, T*
Baker College
   of Jackson *A*
Bay de Noc Community College *C*
Calvin College *B*
Central Michigan University *B, M*
Cornerstone University *B*
Eastern Michigan University *B, M*
Ferris State University *B*
Grand Valley State University *B, M*
Hillsdale College *B*
Hope College *B*
Kuyper College *B*
Lake Superior State University *B*
Lansing Community College *A*

Lawrence Technological University *B*
Macomb Community College *C, A*
Madonna University *A, B*
Michigan State University *B, M, D*
Michigan Technological University *B*
Mid Michigan Community College *A*
Northern Michigan University *B*
Northwestern Michigan College *A*
Oakland University *B*
Rochester College *B*
Saginaw Valley State University *B, T*
Siena Heights University *B*
Spring Arbor University *B, M*
University of Detroit Mercy *B*
University of Michigan *B, M, D*
University of Michigan
  Dearborn *B*
  Flint *B, T*
Wayne State University *B, M, D*
Western Michigan University *B, M*

Minnesota

Augsburg College *B*
Bethany Lutheran College *B*
Bethel University *B, M*
Brown College *B*
College of St. Scholastica *B*
Concordia College: Moorhead *B*
Gustavus Adolphus College *B*
Hamline University *B*
Metropolitan State University *B*
Minnesota State University
  Mankato *B, M*
  Moorhead *C*
Minnesota West Community and
  Technical College *A*
Northland Community & Technical
  College *A*
Northwestern College *B*
Ridgewater College *A*
St. Catherine University *B*
Saint Cloud State University *B*
Southwest Minnesota State
  University *B*
University of Minnesota
  Crookston *B*
  Duluth *B*
  Morris *B*
University of St. Thomas *B*
Vermilion Community College *A*
Walden University *B, M*
Winona State University *B*

Mississippi

Belhaven University *B*
Meridian Community College *A*
Millsaps College *B*
Mississippi College *B, M*
Mississippi Delta Community
  College *A*
Mississippi Gulf Coast Community
  College *A*
Mississippi State University *B*
Mississippi University for Women *B*
Mississippi Valley State University *B*
University of Southern
  Mississippi *B, M, D*

Missouri

Avila University *B*
Central Methodist University *B*
College of the Ozarks *B*
Columbia College *B*
Culver-Stockton College *B*
Drury University *B, M, T*
Evangel University *A, B*
Fontbonne University *B*
Hannibal-LaGrange College *B*
Lindenwood University *B, M*
Missouri Baptist University *B*
Missouri Southern State University *B*
Missouri State University *B, M*
Missouri Western State University *B*
Park University *B, M*

Rockhurst University *B*
St. Louis Community College
  St. Louis Community College at
    Florissant Valley *A*
  St. Louis Community College at
    Meramec *A*
Saint Louis University *B, M*
Southeast Missouri State University *B*
Southwest Baptist University *B*
Stephens College *B*
Truman State University *B*
University of Central Missouri *B, M*
University of Missouri
  Columbia *B, M, D*
  Kansas City *B*
  St. Louis *B, M*
Webster University *B, M*
William Jewell College *B*
William Woods University *B*

Montana

Montana State University
  Billings *B*
Rocky Mountain College *B*
University of Montana *B, M*
University of Montana: Western *B*

Nebraska

Bellevue University *B, M*
Concordia University *B*
Creighton University *B*
Nebraska Wesleyan University *B*
University of Nebraska
  Kearney *B*
  Lincoln *B, M, D*
  Omaha *B, M*
Wayne State College *B, T*
York College *B*

Nevada

College of Southern Nevada *A*
Nevada State College *B*
University of Nevada
  Las Vegas *B, M*
  Reno *B, M*

New Hampshire

Keene State College *B*
New England College *B*
Plymouth State University *B*
Rivier College *B*
Southern New Hampshire
  University *B*
University of New Hampshire *B*
University of New Hampshire at
  Manchester *B*

New Jersey

Bergen Community College *A*
Bloomfield College *C*
Caldwell College *B*
Centenary College *B*
College of St. Elizabeth *B*
County College of Morris *C*
Fairleigh Dickinson University
  College at Florham *B, M*
Felician College *B*
Georgian Court University *B*
Gloucester County College *A*
Kean University *B*
Middlesex County College *A*
Monmouth University *B*
Montclair State University *M*
New Jersey City University *B*
Passaic County Community College *A*
Ramapo College of New Jersey *B*
Richard Stockton College of New
  Jersey *B*
Rutgers, The State University of New
  Jersey
  New Brunswick/Piscataway
    Campus *B, M, D*
Saint Peter's College *B*

Seton Hall University *B, M*
Thomas Edison State College *B*
William Paterson University of New
  Jersey *B, M*

New Mexico

Eastern New Mexico University *B, M*
New Mexico Junior College *A*
University of New Mexico *B, M, D*

New York

Alfred University *B*
Broome Community College *A*
Canisius College *B*
Cazenovia College *B*
City University of New York
  Baruch College *B, M*
  Brooklyn College *B*
  City College *B*
  College of Staten Island *B*
  Hunter College *M*
  Lehman College *B*
  York College *B*
City University of New York: CUNY
  Online *B*
Clarkson University *B*
College of Mount St. Vincent *B*
Cornell University *B, M, D*
Dutchess Community College *A*
Erie Community College
  South Campus *A*
Excelsior College *B*
Finger Lakes Community College *A*
Five Towns College *A, B*
Fordham University *B, M*
Fulton-Montgomery Community
  College *A*
Genesee Community College *A*
Hamilton College *B*
Hofstra University *B, M*
Houghton College *B*
Iona College *B*
Ithaca College *B, M*
Keuka College *B*
Le Moyne College *B*
Long Island University
  Brooklyn Campus *B, M*
Manhattan College *B*
Manhattanville College *B*
Marymount Manhattan College *B*
Metropolitan College of New
  York *A, B*
Molloy College *B*
Monroe Community College *A*
Nassau Community College *A*
Nazareth College *B*
New York Institute of Technology *B*
New York University *B, M, D*
Niagara County Community
  College *A*
Niagara University *B*
Nyack College *B*
Orange County Community College *A*
Pace University *B*
Rensselaer Polytechnic
  Institute *B, M, D*
Roberts Wesleyan College *B*
Rochester Institute of Technology *B*
Rockland Community College *A*
St. Francis College *B*
St. John Fisher College *B*
St. John's University *B*
St. Joseph's College: Suffolk
  Campus *B*
St. Thomas Aquinas College *B*
State University of New York
  Albany *B, M*
  Buffalo *B, M, D*
  College at Brockport *B, M*
  College at Buffalo *B*
  College at Cortland *B*
  College at Fredonia *B*
  College at Geneseo *B*
  College at Old Westbury *B*

  College at Oneonta *B*
  College of Agriculture and
    Technology at Cobleskill *A*
  New Paltz *B*
  Oswego *B*
Suffolk County Community College *A*
Sullivan County Community
  College *A*
Syracuse University *B*
Tompkins Cortland Community
  College *A*
Touro College *B*
Ulster County Community College *A*
Utica College *B*
Westchester Community College *A*

North Carolina

Appalachian State University *B*
Catawba College *B*
East Carolina University *B, M*
Elon University *B*
Gardner-Webb University *B*
Greensboro College *C, B*
High Point University *B*
Lees-McRae College *B*
Lenoir-Rhyne University *B*
Mars Hill College *B*
Meredith College *B, T*
Methodist University *A, B*
Mount Olive College *B*
North Carolina Agricultural and
  Technical State University *B*
North Carolina State University *B*
Peace College *B*
Pfeiffer University *B*
Queens University of Charlotte *B*
St. Augustine's College *B*
Salem College *B*
Southeastern Community College *A*
University of North Carolina
  Chapel Hill *B, M, D*
  Charlotte *B, M*
  Wilmington *B*
Wake Forest University *B, M*
Western Carolina University *B*
Wingate University *B*

North Dakota

Dickinson State University *B*
Jamestown College *B*
Mayville State University *B*
North Dakota State University *D*
University of North Dakota *B, M, D*

Ohio

Ashland University *C, B*
Baldwin-Wallace College *C, B*
Bluffton University *B*
Bowling Green State
  University *B, M, D*
Capital University *B*
Cedarville University *B*
Cincinnati Christian University *A*
Cleveland State University *B, M*
College of Mount St. Joseph *A, B*
College of Wooster *B*
Defiance College *B*
Denison University *B*
Edison State Community College *A*
Franciscan University of
  Steubenville *B*
Heidelberg University *B*
Hiram College *B*
International College of
  Broadcasting *C, A*
John Carroll University *B, M*
Kent State University *B, M, D*
Malone University *B*
Marietta College *B*
Mount Union College *B, T*
Mount Vernon Nazarene University *B*
Muskingum University *B*
Notre Dame College *B, T*
Ohio Dominican University *C, B*

Ohio Northern University *B*
Ohio State University
  Columbus Campus *B, M, D*
Ohio University *B, M, D*
Ohio University
  Southern Campus at Ironton *B*
Otterbein College *B*
Owens Community College
  Toledo *A*
Shawnee State University *A*
Terra State Community College *A*
Tiffin University *B*
University of Akron *B, M*
University of Cincinnati *B, M, T*
University of Cincinnati
  Raymond Walters College *A*
University of Dayton *B, M*
University of Findlay *B*
University of Rio Grande *A, B*
University of Toledo *B*
Urbana University *B*
Walsh University *B*
Wilmington College *B*
Wittenberg University *B*
Wright State University *A, B*
Wright State University: Lake
  Campus *A*
Youngstown State University *B*

Oklahoma

Cameron University *B*
Connors State College *A*
East Central University *B*
Langston University *B*
Northeastern State University *B, M*
Oklahoma Baptist University *B*
Oklahoma Christian University *B, T*
Oklahoma Wesleyan University *B*
Oral Roberts University *B*
Rogers State University *B*
St. Gregory's University *B*
Southeastern Oklahoma State
  University *B*
Southern Nazarene University *A, B*
Southwestern Oklahoma State
  University *B*
University of Central Oklahoma *B*
University of Oklahoma *B, M, D*
University of Science and Arts of
  Oklahoma *B*
University of Tulsa *B*

Oregon

Central Oregon Community
  College *A*
Corban College *B*
George Fox University *B*
Lewis & Clark College *B*
Linfield College *B*
Marylhurst University *B*
Multnomah University *B*
Northwest Christian University *B*
Oregon Institute of Technology *B*
Pacific University *B*
Southern Oregon University *B*
Treasure Valley Community College *A*
Warner Pacific College *B*
Western Oregon University *B*

Pennsylvania

Albright College *B*
Allegheny College *B*
Alvernia University *B*
Arcadia University *C, B*
Baptist Bible College of
  Pennsylvania *B*
Bloomsburg University of
  Pennsylvania *B, T*
Bucks County Community College *A*
Cabrini College *B*
California University of
  Pennsylvania *B, M*
Carlow University *B*
Carnegie Mellon University *B, M*

Cedar Crest College *B*
Central Pennsylvania College *A, B*
Chatham University *B*
Chestnut Hill College *B*
Cheyney University of Pennsylvania *B*
Clarion University of
  Pennsylvania *B, M*
DeSales University *B*
Duquesne University *B, M*
East Stroudsburg University of
  Pennsylvania *B, T*
Eastern University *B*
Edinboro University of
  Pennsylvania *B, M*
Geneva College *B, T*
Gettysburg College *B*
Grove City College *B*
Immaculata University *C, A, B*
Indiana University of Pennsylvania *B*
Juniata College *B*
Keystone College *A, B*
La Roche College *B*
La Salle University *A, B, M*
Lehigh Carbon Community College *A*
Lincoln University *B*
Luzerne County Community
  College *A*
Lycoming College *B*
Manor College *A*
Mansfield University of
  Pennsylvania *B*
Mercyhurst College *B*
Messiah College *B*
Millersville University of
  Pennsylvania *B*
Misericordia University *B*
Montgomery County Community
  College *A*
Muhlenberg College *C, B*
Neumann University *B*
Northampton Community College *A*
Penn State
  Abington *B*
  Altoona *B*
  Beaver *B*
  Berks *B*
  Brandywine *B*
  DuBois *B*
  Erie, The Behrend College *B*
  Fayette, The Eberly Campus *B*
  Greater Allegheny *B*
  Harrisburg *B*
  Hazleton *B*
  Lehigh Valley *B*
  Mont Alto *B*
  New Kensington *B*
  Schuylkill *B*
  Shenango *B*
  University Park *B, M, D*
  Wilkes-Barre *B*
  Worthington Scranton *B*
  York *B*
Pennsylvania Highlands Community
  College *A*
Robert Morris University *B*
Rosemont College *B, M*
St. Francis University *B*
Saint Joseph's University *C, A, B*
St. Vincent College *B*
Seton Hill University *B*
Shippensburg University of
  Pennsylvania *M*
Slippery Rock University of
  Pennsylvania *B*
Susquehanna University *A, B, T*
Thiel College *B*
University of Pennsylvania *B, M, D*
University of Pittsburgh
  Greensburg *B*
  Johnstown *B*
University of Scranton *B, T*
Ursinus College *B*
Villanova University *B, M*
Waynesburg University *B*

West Chester University of
  Pennsylvania *T*
Widener University *B*
Wilkes University *B*
York College of Pennsylvania *B*

Puerto Rico

American University of Puerto
  Rico *A, B*
Pontifical Catholic University of
  Puerto Rico *B*
Turabo University *B*
University of the Sacred Heart *B*

Rhode Island

Bryant University *B*
Rhode Island College *B*
University of Rhode Island *B, M*

South Carolina

Anderson University *B*
Bob Jones University *B*
Coastal Carolina University *B*
Coker College *B*
College of Charleston *B, M*
Columbia College *B*
Columbia International University *B*
Furman University *B*
Newberry College *B*
Southern Wesleyan University *B*
University of South Carolina
  Aiken *B*
  Upstate *B*

South Dakota

Augustana College *B*
Dakota Wesleyan University *B*
Northern State University *B, T*
Presentation College *B*
University of South Dakota *B*

Tennessee

Belmont University *B*
Bryan College *B*
Carson-Newman College *B*
East Tennessee State University *M*
Freed-Hardeman University *B*
Jackson State Community College *A*
Lambuth University *B*
Lane College *B*
Lee University *B*
Lincoln Memorial University *B*
Milligan College *B*
Tennessee State University *B*
Tennessee Technological University *B*
Trevecca Nazarene University *B*
Union University *B, T*
University of Tennessee
  Chattanooga *B*
  Knoxville *M, D*
  Martin *B*
Vanderbilt University *B*

Texas

Abilene Christian University *B, M*
Amarillo College *A*
Angelina College *A*
Angelo State University *B, M, T*
Austin College *B*
Baylor University *B, M*
Brazosport College *A*
Cisco College *A*
Clarendon College *A*
Coastal Bend College *A*
Concordia University Texas *B*
Dallas Baptist University *B*
East Texas Baptist University *B*
El Paso Community College *A*
Hardin-Simmons University *B*
Hill College *A*
Houston Baptist University *B*
Howard Payne University *B, T*
Kilgore College *A*

Lamar University *B*
Laredo Community College *A*
Lubbock Christian University *B*
McLennan Community College *A*
Midland College *A*
Navarro College *A*
North Lake College *C, A*
Northwest Vista College *A*
Our Lady of the Lake University of San
  Antonio *B*
Palo Alto College *A*
Prairie View A&M University *B*
St. Mary's University *B, M, T*
South Plains College *A*
Southwestern Adventist University *B*
Southwestern Assemblies of God
  University *A*
Southwestern University *B, T*
Stephen F. Austin State
  University *B, M, T*
Sul Ross State University *B*
Tarleton State University *B*
Texas A&M International University *B*
Texas A&M University
  Commerce *B*
  Corpus Christi *B*
  Kingsville *B*
Texas Christian University *B, M*
Texas Lutheran University *B*
Texas Southern University *B, M*
Texas Wesleyan University *B*
Trinity University *B*
Trinity Valley Community College *A*
University of Houston *B, M*
University of Houston
  Clear Lake *B*
  Victoria *B, M*
University of Mary Hardin-Baylor *B*
University of St. Thomas *B*
University of Texas
  Arlington *M*
  Austin *B*
  Brownsville - Texas Southmost
    College *B*
  El Paso *B, M*
  Pan American *B, M*
  San Antonio *B, M*
  Tyler *M*
  of the Permian Basin *B*
University of the Incarnate Word *B, M*
Wayland Baptist University *B*
Weatherford College *A*
West Texas A&M University *M*

Utah

Brigham Young University *B*
College of Eastern Utah *T*
Dixie State College of Utah *B*
Salt Lake Community College *A*
Southern Utah University *B*
University of Utah *B, M, D, T*
Utah Valley University *A, B*
Westminster College *B, M*

Vermont

Green Mountain College *B*
Lyndon State College *A, B*
Norwich University *B*
Southern Vermont College *B*

Virginia

Bluefield College *B*
Christopher Newport University *B*
Eastern Mennonite University *B*
George Mason University *B, M*
Hollins University *B*
James Madison University *B*
Liberty University *B*
Longwood University *B*
Lord Fairfax Community College *A*
Lynchburg College *B*
Mary Baldwin College *B*
Marymount University *B*

Northern Virginia Community
College *A*
Old Dominion University *B*
Radford University *B, M*
Randolph College *B*
Regent University *B, M, D*
Shenandoah University *B*
Thomas Nelson Community
College *C*
University of Virginia's College at
Wise *B*
Virginia Polytechnic Institute and
State University *B, M*
Virginia Wesleyan College *B*

Washington

City University of Seattle *B*
Eastern Washington University *B, M*
Everett Community College *A*
Evergreen State College *B*
Green River Community College *C*
Highline Community College *A*
Northwest University *B*
Olympic College *A*
Pacific Lutheran University *B*
Seattle Pacific University *B*
Skagit Valley College *A*
University of Puget Sound *B*
University of Washington *B, M, D*
University of Washington Tacoma *B*
Walla Walla University *B*
Washington State University *D*
Western Washington University *B*
Whitworth University *B*

West Virginia

Alderson-Broaddus College *B*
American Public University System *A*
Bethany College *B*
Concord University *B*
Fairmont State University *B*
Shepherd University *B*
West Liberty University *B*
West Virginia State Community and
Technical College *A*
West Virginia State University *B, M*
West Virginia University *B, M, D*
West Virginia Wesleyan College *B*

Wisconsin

Alverno College *B*
Cardinal Stritch University *B*
Carroll University *B*
Concordia University Wisconsin *B*
Edgewood College *B*
Marian University *B*
Marquette University *B, M*
Milwaukee School of Engineering *B*
Mount Mary College *B*
Ripon College *B*
St. Norbert College *B, T*
University of Wisconsin
Eau Claire *B*
Green Bay *B*
La Crosse *B*
Madison *B, M, D*
Milwaukee *B, M*
Oshkosh *B*
Parkside *B, T*
Platteville *B*
River Falls *B, T*
Stevens Point *B, M*
Superior *B, M*
Whitewater *B, M*
Wisconsin Lutheran College *B*

Wyoming

Casper College *A*
Eastern Wyoming College *A*
Laramie County Community
College *A*
Northwest College *A*
University of Wyoming *B, M*

Western Wyoming Community
College *A*

Communications systems installation/ repair

Florida
Hillsborough Community College *C*

Georgia
Gwinnett Technical College *C*

Idaho
Idaho State University *C, A*

Illinois
College of DuPage *A*
Sauk Valley Community College *C*
Triton College *C*

Iowa
Des Moines Area Community
College *C, A*

Kentucky
Big Sandy Community and Technical
College *C*

Minnesota
Lake Superior College *C*
Minnesota State College - Southeast
Technical *C*
Minnesota State Community and
Technical College *C*
Minnesota West Community and
Technical College *C*
St. Paul College *C*

New York
Erie Community College
South Campus *A*
Mohawk Valley Community College *A*
Onondaga Community College *A*
Vaughn College of Aeronautics and
Technology *A, B*

Pennsylvania
Luzerne County Community
College *C, A*

Texas
Del Mar College *C, A*
St. Philip's College *C, A*

Virginia
ECPI Technical College: Roanoke *A*

Washington
Bates Technical College *C, A*
Bellingham Technical College *A*

Wisconsin
Herzing University *A, B*
Milwaukee Area Technical College *C*
Wisconsin Indianhead Technical
College *A*

Communications technology

Alabama
Alabama Agricultural and Mechanical
University *B*
Calhoun Community College *A*
Gadsden State Community College *A*

Arizona
Northland Pioneer College *C, A*

California
Bakersfield College *A*
Barstow Community College *C*
Berkeley City College *C, A*
Butte College *C, A*
Chabot College *C, A*
City College of San Francisco *A*
College of San Mateo *C, A*
College of the Siskiyous *C, A*
Cosumnes River College *A*
Diablo Valley College *C, A*
El Camino College *A*
Laney College *C, A*
Long Beach City College *C, A*
Los Angeles City College *C, A*
Los Angeles Southwest College *A*
Los Angeles Trade and Technical
College *C, A*
Los Angeles Valley College *C*
Moorpark College *A*
Mount San Antonio College *C, A*
Napa Valley College *C, A*
Palomar College *C, A*
Pasadena City College *C, A*
Rio Hondo College *A*
San Diego City College *A*
San Diego State University *M*
San Jose City College *C, A*
Santa Barbara City College *C, A*
Santa Monica College *A*
Skyline College *C, A*
Southwestern College *C, A*

Colorado
Arapahoe Community College *C, A*
Jones International University *B, M*
Mesa State College *A*
Pueblo Community College *C, A*

Connecticut
Asnuntuck Community College *A*
Manchester Community College *C*
Naugatuck Valley Community
College *C*
Norwalk Community College *A*
Sacred Heart University *B*

Florida
Miami Dade College *A*
Pensacola Junior College *A*
Seminole Community College *A*

Georgia
DeVry University
Alpharetta *B*

Illinois
College of DuPage *C, A*
DeVry University
Tinley Park *B*
Governors State University *M*
Lewis University *B*
Southwestern Illinois College *C, A*

Indiana
Indiana University-Purdue University
Indianapolis *A*
St. Mary-of-the-Woods College *B*

Iowa
Dordt College *B*
Iowa Central Community College *A*
Kirkwood Community College *A*
Marshalltown Community College *A*
Scott Community College *A*
Waldorf College *B*

Kansas
Central Christian College of Kansas *A*
Coffeyville Community College *A*
Hutchinson Community College *A*

Louisiana
ITI Technical College *C, A*

Maine
New England School of
Communications *B*

Maryland
Allegany College of Maryland *A*
Anne Arundel Community
College *C, A*
Frederick Community College *A*

Massachusetts
Becker College *B*
Lesley University *B*
New England Institute of Art *A*
Newbury College *A*
Northern Essex Community
College *A*
Suffolk University *B*

Michigan
Andrews University *B*
Delta College *A*
Eastern Michigan University *B*
Kalamazoo Valley Community
College *C, A*
Kellogg Community College *A*
Lansing Community College *A*
Lawrence Technological
University *C, B, M*
Michigan State University *B*
Mott Community College *C, A*

Minnesota
Academy College *A*
Hennepin Technical College *C, A*
St. Mary's University of
Minnesota *B, M*
Winona State University *B*

Mississippi
Hinds Community College *A*
Meridian Community College *A*
Northwest Mississippi Community
College *A*

Missouri
Evangel University *B*
Metropolitan Community College:
Penn Valley *C*
Ranken Technical College *A*

Nebraska
Grace University *B*
University of Nebraska
Lincoln *D*

New Hampshire
NHTI-Concord's Community
College *C, A*

New Jersey
Bergen Community College *C*
Brookdale Community College *A*
County College of Morris *A*
Mercer County Community College *A*
Ocean County College *A*

New York
Cayuga County Community College *A*
City University of New York
Borough of Manhattan Community
College *A*
Queensborough Community
College *A*
York College *B*
Herkimer County Community
College *A*
Monroe Community College *A*

New York Institute of
Technology *A, M*
Suffolk County Community College *A*

North Carolina

Cleveland Community College *C, A*

North Dakota

Minot State University *B*

Ohio

Bowling Green State University:
Firelands College *A*
Cedarville University *B*
Columbus State Community
College *A*
Cuyahoga Community College
Metropolitan Campus *A*
Owens Community College
Toledo *A*

Oklahoma

Langston University *B*
Southern Nazarene University *B*
Tulsa Community College *A*

Oregon

Clackamas Community College *C, A*

Pennsylvania

Chestnut Hill College *B*
Community College of Beaver
County *A*
East Stroudsburg University of
Pennsylvania *A, B*
Philadelphia University *M*

Puerto Rico

American University of Puerto Rico *B*
Inter American University of Puerto
Rico
Bayamon Campus *B*
University of Puerto Rico
Humacao *A*

South Carolina

Trident Technical College *C, A*

Tennessee

Nashville State Community College *A*
Southern Adventist University *B*
Tennessee Technological University *B*

Texas

Amarillo College *A*
Art Institute
of Houston *A*
El Paso Community College *A*
Northwest Vista College *C, A*
Richland College *C, A*
St. Philip's College *A*
Texas A&M University
Commerce *M*
Texas State Technical College
Waco *A*
West Texas *A*
Texas State Technical College:
Marshall *C, A*

Vermont

Lyndon State College *B*

Virginia

ECPI College of Technology: Virginia
Beach *C, A*
ECPI Technical College: Roanoke *A*
Virginia Western Community
College *A*

Washington

Bates Technical College *C, A*

North Seattle Community
College *C, A*
Spokane Falls Community College *A*
University of Washington *M*
Yakima Valley Community College *C*

West Virginia

New River Community and Technical
College *A*
Southern West Virginia Community
and Technical College *A*

Wisconsin

Western Technical College *A*

Community health/ preventative medicine

California

East Los Angeles College *A*

Florida

Florida Gulf Coast University *B*
University of North Florida *M*

Illinois

Southern Illinois University
Carbondale *M*
University of Illinois
Urbana-Champaign *B, M, D*

Indiana

Indiana University-Purdue University
Indianapolis *M*

Iowa

University of Iowa *M, D*

Kentucky

Western Kentucky University *B*

Maine

University of Maine
Farmington *B*

Minnesota

Walden University *M, D*

New York

City University of New York
Hostos Community College *A*
Hofstra University *B, M*
Long Island University
Brooklyn Campus *M*
State University of New York
Buffalo *D*

Ohio

University of Cincinnati
Raymond Walters College *A*
Youngstown State University *B*

Pennsylvania

Temple University *M*

Texas

University of Texas
Health Science Center at
Houston *M, D*
Medical Branch at Galveston *M, D*

Utah

Utah Valley University *A, B*

Vermont

Goddard College *B, M*

Virginia

George Mason University *B*
Liberty University *B*

Old Dominion University *M*

Wisconsin

University of Wisconsin
Eau Claire *B*
La Crosse *B, M*
Madison *M, D*

Community health services

Alabama

Faulkner University *B*

Arizona

Cochise College *C*
Pima Community College *C*
Prescott College *B*

Arkansas

University of Arkansas *M*
University of Central Arkansas *B, M*

California

California Institute of Integral
Studies *M*
California State University
Fresno *B*
City College of San Francisco *C*

Connecticut

Quinebaug Valley Community
College *A*
Western Connecticut State
University *B*

Florida

Florida State University *M*
Hillsborough Community College *C*
State College of Florida,
Manatee-Sarasota *A*
University of Tampa *B*
University of West Florida *B, M*

Georgia

Darton College *C, A*

Illinois

McHenry County College *C*
Northeastern Illinois University *B*
Waubonsee Community College *C, A*

Indiana

Indiana State University *B*
Indiana University-Purdue University
Fort Wayne *B*
Indiana University-Purdue University
Indianapolis *M*
Indiana Wesleyan University *M*

Kansas

University of Kansas *B*

Kentucky

Northern Kentucky University *M*
University of the Cumberlands *B*

Massachusetts

Mount Wachusett Community
College *C*
Worcester State College *B, M, T*

Michigan

Michigan State University *B, M*
Mott Community College *A*
Northern Michigan University *B*
Oakland Community College *A*

Minnesota

Bethel University *B*

Inver Hills Community College *C*
Minneapolis Community and
Technical College *C*
Minnesota State University
Moorhead *B*
Rochester Community and Technical
College *C*
Saint Cloud State University *B*

Nebraska

University of Nebraska
Lincoln *B*
Omaha *B*

New York

Adelphi University *M*
City University of New York
Brooklyn College *M*
Kingsborough Community
College *A*
Erie Community College
City Campus *A*
Sarah Lawrence College *M*
State University of New York
College at Cortland *M*

North Carolina

Johnson C. Smith University *B*

Ohio

Cleveland State University *M*
Ohio University *B*
University of Dayton *M*
Youngstown State University *B*

Oklahoma

University of Oklahoma *M*

Pennsylvania

Duquesne University *M*
Messiah College *M*
Slippery Rock University of
Pennsylvania *B*
University of Pennsylvania *B*

Rhode Island

Brown University *B*

South Carolina

Morris College *B*

Texas

Texas A&M University *B*
Texas Woman's University *M*
University of Texas
Health Science Center at
Houston *M, D*
Tyler *B*

Vermont

Goddard College *B, M*

Virginia

James Madison University *B*
Old Dominion University *B*

Washington

Clark College *C*
Eastern Washington University *B*
Western Washington University *B*

West Virginia

West Virginia University *M*

Wisconsin

Marian University *M*
Marquette University *M*

Community/junior college administration

Arkansas
Arkansas State University *M, T*

California
California Lutheran University *M*

Colorado
Colorado State University *D*

Illinois
Argosy University: Chicago *D*
Chicago State University *M*
University of Illinois
   Urbana-Champaign *M, D*

Massachusetts
Springfield College *D*

Michigan
Central Michigan University *M*
Eastern Michigan University *T*

Minnesota
University of Minnesota
   Twin Cities *M*
Walden University *D*

Mississippi
Alcorn State University *M*
Mississippi State University *M, D*

New Jersey
Rowan University *M*

North Carolina
North Carolina State University *M, D*
Western Carolina University *M*

Tennessee
University of Memphis *T*

Texas
Texas A&M University
   Commerce *M, D*

Virginia
George Mason University *D*
Old Dominion University *D*

Washington
University of Washington *M, D*

Community organization/advocacy

Alaska
University of Alaska
   Fairbanks *A, B, M*

Arizona
Prescott College *B, M*

Arkansas
Southern Arkansas University *B*
University of Arkansas *D*
University of Central Arkansas *M*

California
Foothill College *C*
Humphreys College *B*
Los Angeles Trade and Technical
   College *C, A*
Merritt College *C, A*
National University *M*
University of California
   Santa Cruz *B*

Connecticut
Manchester Community College *C, A*
University of Bridgeport *B*
University of Hartford *B*

Florida
Saint Leo University *B*

Georgia
Mercer University *B*

Hawaii
University of Hawaii
   Honolulu Community College *C, A*

Illinois
DePaul University *C, B*
Lewis University *B*
North Park University *M*
Northwestern University *B, M*
Triton College *A*
University of Illinois
   Urbana-Champaign *M, D*

Iowa
Des Moines Area Community
   College *C, A*
Kirkwood Community College *A*
Marshalltown Community College *A*
Northeast Iowa Community
   College *A*

Kentucky
Henderson Community College *A*
Murray State University *M*

Maryland
College of Notre Dame of Maryland *B*

Massachusetts
Berkshire Community College *A*
Brandeis University *M*
Clark University *M*
Holyoke Community College *C*
Springfield College *B, M*
University of Massachusetts
   Boston *C, B*

Michigan
Aquinas College *B*
Central Michigan University *B*
Madonna University *C*
University of Michigan *M*

Minnesota
Bemidji State University *B*

Mississippi
Delta State University *M*

Missouri
Rockhurst University *B*

Montana
University of Montana *C*

New Hampshire
University of New Hampshire *A*
University of New Hampshire at
   Manchester *A*

New Jersey
Montclair State University *M*
Salem Community College *A*
Thomas Edison State College *A, B*

New Mexico
New Mexico State University *B*
University of New Mexico *A, B*

New York
City University of New York
   Brooklyn College *B*
   John Jay College of Criminal
      Justice *B, M*
Cornell University *B, M, D*
Erie Community College
   City Campus *C*
   North Campus *C*
   South Campus *C*
Fulton-Montgomery Community
   College *C, A*
Genesee Community College *C, A*
Hudson Valley Community College *A*
Jefferson Community College *A*
Metropolitan College of New
   York *A, B*
Mohawk Valley Community College *A*
New York University *A, B*
Pace University *B, M*
State University of New York
   College at Cortland *B*
   Empire State College *A, B*
Tompkins Cortland Community
   College *C, A*
Ulster County Community College *A*

North Carolina
University of North Carolina
   Greensboro *M*

Ohio
Cleveland State University *M*
University of Akron *C, A*
University of Cincinnati *M*
Urbana University *B*

Oklahoma
East Central University *B, M*

Oregon
Clackamas Community College *A*
Corban College *B*
Lane Community College *C, A*

Pennsylvania
Penn State
   University Park *M*
Saint Joseph's University *M*
University of Pennsylvania *M*

Rhode Island
Providence College *C, B*

South Dakota
Black Hills State University *B*
Northern State University *B*

Tennessee
Chattanooga State Community
   College *A*
Cumberland University *M*
Pellissippi State Community
   College *A*
University of Tennessee
   Chattanooga *B*
   Knoxville *M*
Vanderbilt University *M*
Volunteer State Community College *A*

Texas
Texas A&M University *B*

Utah
Westminster College *M*

Virginia
Emory & Henry College *B*
J. Sargeant Reynolds Community
   College *A*

Washington
Saint Martin's University *B*

Wisconsin
Alverno College *B*
Marquette University *M*
Northland College *B*
Western Technical College *A*

Community psychology

Alabama
Troy University *M*

Alaska
University of Alaska
   Fairbanks *M, D*

Arizona
Prescott College *B, M*

California
University of La Verne *D*

Colorado
Adams State College *M*

Connecticut
Mitchell College *B*
Southern Connecticut State
   University *M*
University of New Haven *M*

District of Columbia
George Washington University *M*

Florida
Florida Agricultural and Mechanical
   University *M*
University of Miami *B*

Georgia
Clayton State University *B*
North Georgia College & State
   University *M*
University of West Georgia *D*

Illinois
DePaul University *M, D*
Northwestern University *B*

Massachusetts
Cambridge College *B*

Michigan
Andrews University *M*

Minnesota
Saint Cloud State University *B*
University of Minnesota
   Crookston *B*

New Hampshire
New England College *M*

New Jersey
Fairleigh Dickinson University
   College at Florham *M*

New York
College of New Rochelle *M*
Hofstra University *M, D*

Ohio
Kent State University *M*
University of Akron *M*

Oklahoma
Rogers State University *B*

Pennsylvania
Penn State
  Harrisburg *M*

Puerto Rico
University of Puerto Rico
  Rio Piedras *M*

South Carolina
Clemson University *M*
Columbia College *M*
Francis Marion University *M*

Tennessee
Southern Adventist University *M*
Vanderbilt University *D*

Texas
Lamar University *M*
St. Mary's University *M, D*

Virginia
Norfolk State University *M*

Washington
University of Washington Bothell *B*

Wisconsin
Marquette University *M*
Mount Mary College *M*

Comparative/ international education

California
Stanford University *M, D*

District of Columbia
American University *M*
George Washington University *M*
Howard University *M*

Florida
Florida International University *M*
Florida State University *M, D*

Illinois
University of Illinois
  Urbana-Champaign *M, D*

Indiana
Indiana University
  Bloomington *M*

Massachusetts
Boston University *M*
Endicott College *M*
Harvard College *M, D*

New Jersey
The College of New Jersey *M*

New York
State University of New York
  Albany *M, D*

Ohio
Ohio State University
  Columbus Campus *M*

Tennessee
Vanderbilt University *M, D*

Vermont
Goddard College *M*

Virginia
University of Virginia *M, D*

Comparative literature

Arizona
Prescott College *B, M*
University of Arizona *M, D*

Arkansas
University of Arkansas *M, D*

California
California State University
  Fullerton *B, M*
  Long Beach *B*
  Northridge *B*
Mills College *B*
San Diego State University *B*
San Francisco State University *B, M*
Stanford University *B, M, D*
University of California
  Berkeley *B, M, D*
  Davis *B, M, D*
  Irvine *B, M, D*
  Los Angeles *B, M, D*
  Riverside *B, M, D*
  San Diego *M, D*
  Santa Barbara *B, M, D*
University of California: Merced *B*
University of La Verne *B*
University of San Francisco *B*
University of Southern
  California *B, M, D*
Whittier College *B*

Colorado
Colorado College *B*
University of Colorado
  Boulder *M, D*

Connecticut
Trinity College *B*
University of Connecticut *M, D*
Yale University *M, D*

Delaware
University of Delaware *B*

District of Columbia
Catholic University of America *M, D*
Georgetown University *B*

Florida
Eckerd College *B*

Georgia
Emory University *B, D*
University of Georgia *B, M, D*

Hawaii
Hawaii Pacific University *B*

Illinois
Lake Forest College *B*
Northwestern University *B, M, D*
Roosevelt University *B*
University of Chicago *B, D*
University of Illinois
  Urbana-Champaign *B, M, D*

Indiana
Earlham College *B*
Indiana University
  Bloomington *B, M, D*
Manchester College *A*
University of Notre Dame *D*

Iowa
University of Iowa *B, M, D*

Louisiana
Louisiana State University and
  Agricultural and Mechanical
  College *M, D*

Maine
University of Maine
  Fort Kent *B*

Maryland
University of Maryland
  College Park *M, D*

Massachusetts
Bard College at Simon's Rock *B*
Brandeis University *B*
Clark University *B*
College of the Holy Cross *B*
Harvard College *B, M, D*
Salem State College *B*
Simmons College *B, M*
Smith College *B*
Tufts University *B, M, D*
University of Massachusetts
  Amherst *B, M, D*
Wellesley College *B*
Williams College *B*

Michigan
Hillsdale College *B*
Michigan State University *D*
University of Michigan *B, M, D*
Wayne State University *M*

Minnesota
University of Minnesota
  Twin Cities *B, M, D*
University of St. Thomas *B*

Missouri
Washington University in St.
  Louis *B, M, D*

New Hampshire
Dartmouth College *B, M*
New England College *B*

New Jersey
Princeton University *B, M, D*
Ramapo College of New Jersey *B*
Rutgers, The State University of New
  Jersey
  New Brunswick/Piscataway
    Campus *B, M, D*

New Mexico
University of New Mexico *B, M*

New York
Bard College *B*
Barnard College *B*
City University of New York
  Baruch College *B*
  Brooklyn College *B*
  City College *B*
  Hunter College *B*
  Lehman College *B*
  Queens College *B*
Columbia University *B*
Columbia University
  School of General Studies *B*
Cornell University *B, M, D*
Eugene Lang College The New School
  for Liberal Arts *B*
Fordham University *B*
Hamilton College *B*
Hobart and William Smith Colleges *B*
Hofstra University *B*
New York University *B, M, D*
State University of New York
  Binghamton *B, M, D*
  Buffalo *M, D*

College at Geneseo *B*
College at Old Westbury *B*
Stony Brook *B, M, D*
University of Rochester *B, M*
Wells College *B*

North Carolina
Duke University *M, D*
University of North Carolina
  Chapel Hill *B, M, D*

Ohio
Case Western Reserve University *B, M*
College of Wooster *B*
John Carroll University *B*
Oberlin College *B*
Ohio State University
  Columbus Campus *B, M*
Ohio Wesleyan University *B*
Terra State Community College *A*
University of Cincinnati *B, M, D, T*
Wilberforce University *B, T*

Oklahoma
East Central University *B*
Oklahoma City University *M*

Oregon
Reed College *B*
University of Oregon *B, M, D*
Willamette University *B*

Pennsylvania
Bryn Mawr College *B*
Gettysburg College *B*
Haverford College *B, T*
La Salle University *B*
Penn State
  Abington *B*
  Altoona *B*
  Beaver *B*
  Berks *B*
  Brandywine *B*
  DuBois *B*
  Erie, The Behrend College *B*
  Fayette, The Eberly Campus *B*
  Greater Allegheny *B*
  Hazleton *B*
  Lehigh Valley *B*
  Mont Alto *B*
  New Kensington *B*
  Schuylkill *B*
  Shenango *B*
  University Park *B, M, D*
  Wilkes-Barre *B*
  Worthington Scranton *B*
  York *B*
Swarthmore College *B*
University of Pennsylvania *B, M, D*

Puerto Rico
University of Puerto Rico
  Rio Piedras *B, M*

Rhode Island
Brown University *B, M, D*
University of Rhode Island *B*

South Carolina
University of South Carolina *M, D*

Tennessee
University of Tennessee
  Knoxville *B*
University of the South *B*
Vanderbilt University *M, D*

Texas
Texas A&M University *M*
University of Texas
  Austin *M, D*
  Dallas *B*

El Paso *B, M*

Utah
Brigham Young University *B*
University of Utah *B*

Vermont
Johnson State College *B*
Marlboro College *B*

Virginia
University of Virginia *B*

Washington
Everett Community College *A*
Gonzaga University *B*
University of Washington *B, M, D*

Wisconsin
Beloit College *B*
University of Wisconsin
   Madison *B, M, D*
   Milwaukee *B*

Comparative psychology

California
California Institute of Integral
   Studies *M, D*

Washington
Western Washington University *M*

Computational mathematics

Arizona
Arizona State University *B*

California
Allan Hancock College *A*
University of California
   Davis *B*
   Los Angeles *B*

Florida
Florida State University *B, M, D*

Illinois
DePaul University *M*
Northern Illinois University *B*
University of Illinois
   Urbana-Champaign *B*

Indiana
Indiana University-Purdue University
   Fort Wayne *B*

Kentucky
Asbury College *B*

Michigan
Hillsdale College *B*
Michigan State University *B*
Michigan Technological University *D*

Missouri
Missouri Southern State University *B*

New York
City University of New York
   Brooklyn College *B*
Marist College *B*
Rochester Institute of Technology *B*

North Carolina
University of North Carolina
   Greensboro *D*

Ohio
University of Dayton *M*

Pennsylvania
Carnegie Mellon University *B, D*

Puerto Rico
University of Puerto Rico
   Humacao *B*

South Dakota
South Dakota State University *D*

Texas
North Lake College *A*
University of Texas
   El Paso *M, D*

Virginia
Old Dominion University *M, D*

Washington
Seattle Pacific University *B*

Wisconsin
Marquette University *B*

Computer education

Arizona
Northern Arizona University *M*

California
California Baptist University *M, T*
Fresno Pacific University *M*
National University *M*
San Diego State University *T*

Florida
Barry University *M*
Florida Institute of Technology *M*
St. Petersburg College *B*

Hawaii
Hawaii Pacific University *M*

Idaho
Northwest Nazarene University *B*

Illinois
Concordia University Chicago *B, M, T*
DePaul University *M, T*
Illinois Institute of Technology *M*

Indiana
Indiana Wesleyan University *T*
University of Indianapolis *T*

Iowa
Buena Vista University *B, T*
Loras College *T*

Kansas
McPherson College *B, T*
University of St. Mary *T*

Kentucky
University of the Cumberlands *B, T*

Louisiana
Southeastern Louisiana University *B*
Southern University and Agricultural
   and Mechanical College *B*

Maine
Thomas College *M*

Massachusetts
Lesley University *M*

Michigan
Alma College *T*
Eastern Michigan University *B*
Grand Valley State University *T*
Michigan State University *B*
Michigan Technological University *T*
Saginaw Valley State University *M*

Minnesota
Minnesota State University
   Mankato *B, M, T*
Vermilion Community College *A*

Mississippi
Millsaps College *T*
Mississippi College *M*
Mississippi State University *T*

Missouri
Fontbonne University *M, T*
Northwest Missouri State
   University *M, T*
Webster University *M*

Montana
Montana State University
   Billings *T*
University of Montana: Western *T*

Nebraska
College of Saint Mary *T*
Concordia University *B, T*
Peru State College *B, T*
Union College *T*
University of Nebraska
   Lincoln *B*

Nevada
University of Nevada
   Las Vegas *B*

New Hampshire
Keene State College *B, M, T*

New Jersey
Rowan University *T*
Saint Peter's College *M, T*

New Mexico
New Mexico Institute of Mining and
   Technology *M*

New York
College of Mount St. Vincent *T*
Iona College *M, T*
Manhattan College *B, T*
Nazareth College *M*
State University of New York
   College at Buffalo *M*
   College at Plattsburgh *B, M*

North Dakota
Dickinson State University *B, T*

Ohio
Ashland University *M, T*
Bowling Green State University *B, M*
University of Findlay *M, T*
Youngstown State University *B, M*

Oklahoma
Eastern Oklahoma State College *A*
Southwestern Oklahoma State
   University *T*

Oregon
Western Oregon University *T*

Pennsylvania
Alvernia University *B*

Arcadia University *M*
DeSales University *M, T*
Saint Joseph's University *M*

South Dakota
Dakota State University *B, T*

Tennessee
Bryan College *T*

Texas
Hardin-Simmons University *B, T*
Lamar University *T*
Laredo Community College *A*
LeTourneau University *B, T*
Lubbock Christian University *B*
McMurry University *B, T*
St. Mary's University *T*
Tarleton State University *B, T*
Texas A&M University
   Commerce *M, T*
Texas Christian University *B*
University of Houston *T*
University of Houston
   Clear Lake *T*
University of Mary Hardin-Baylor *T*
University of North Texas *D*
University of Texas
   San Antonio *T*
West Texas A&M University *T*

Vermont
St. Michael's College *M, T*

Virginia
Bridgewater College *T*
Hollins University *T*

Wisconsin
Cardinal Stritch University *M*
Carroll University *T*
Edgewood College *B*
Lawrence University *T*
Marian University *M*
Silver Lake College *T*
University of Wisconsin
   Whitewater *B, T*

Computer engineering

Alabama
Auburn University *B, M, D*
University of Alabama
   Birmingham *D*
   Huntsville *B, M, D*
University of South Alabama *B*

Alaska
University of Alaska
   Fairbanks *M*

Arizona
Arizona State University *B*
Embry-Riddle Aeronautical University:
   Prescott Campus *B*
Northern Arizona University *B*
University of Arizona *B*

Arkansas
Harding University *B*
University of Arkansas *B, M*

California
California Institute of Technology *B*
California Polytechnic State
   University: San Luis Obispo *B*
California State Polytechnic
   University: Pomona *B*
California State University
   Chico *B*
   Fresno *B*

Fullerton *B*
Long Beach *B, M*
Northridge *B, M*
Sacramento *B, M*
Coleman University *A, B*
De Anza College *A*
El Camino College: Compton
Center *A*
Northwestern Polytechnic
University *D*
San Diego State University *B*
San Francisco State University *B*
San Jose State University *B, M*
Santa Barbara City College *A*
Santa Clara University *B, M, D*
Sonoma State University *B, M*
University of California
Davis *B*
Irvine *B*
Los Angeles *B, M, D*
Riverside *B*
San Diego *B, M, D*
Santa Barbara *B, M, D*
Santa Cruz *B, M, D*
University of California:
Merced *B, M, D*
University of Southern
California *B, M, D*
University of the Pacific *B*
Westwood College of Technology
Westwood College: Los Angeles *A*

Colorado

Colorado State University *B*
Colorado Technical University *B, M*
Jones International University *B*
United States Air Force Academy *B*
University of Colorado
Boulder *B*
Colorado Springs *B, M*
University of Denver *B, M*
Westwood College: Denver North *A*

Connecticut

Fairfield University *B*
University of Bridgeport *B, M, D*
University of Connecticut *B, M, D*
University of Hartford *B*
University of New Haven *B*

Delaware

University of Delaware *B*

District of Columbia

George Washington
University *B, M, D*
Howard University *B*

Florida

Bethune-Cookman University *B*
Brevard Community College *A*
Broward College *A*
Chipola College *A*
Daytona State College *A*
Embry-Riddle Aeronautical
University *B*
Florida Agricultural and Mechanical
University *B*
Florida Atlantic University *B, M, D*
Florida Institute of
Technology *B, M, D*
Florida International University *B, M*
Florida State College at Jacksonville *A*
Florida State University *B*
Pensacola Junior College *A*
Southwest Florida College *A*
State College of Florida,
Manatee-Sarasota *A*
University of Central Florida *B, M, D*
University of Florida *B, M*
University of Miami *B*
University of South Florida *B, M, D*
University of West Florida *B*

Georgia

DeKalb Technical College *A*
Georgia Institute of Technology *B*
Georgia Southern University *B*
Mercer University *M*
Middle Georgia College *A*
University of Georgia *B*

Hawaii

University of Hawaii
Honolulu Community College *A*

Idaho

Brigham Young University-Idaho *B*
University of Idaho *B, M*

Illinois

Bradley University *B*
DeVry University
Tinley Park *B*
Dominican University *B*
Illinois Institute of
Technology *B, M, D*
Northwestern University *B*
Southern Illinois University
Carbondale *B*
Southern Illinois University
Edwardsville *B*
University of Illinois
Chicago *B*
Urbana-Champaign *B, M, D*

Indiana

Indiana Institute of Technology *B*
Indiana University-Purdue University
Fort Wayne *B*
Indiana University-Purdue University
Indianapolis *B*
Purdue University *B*
Purdue University
Calumet *B*
Rose-Hulman Institute of
Technology *B*
Taylor University *B*
Trine University *B*
University of Evansville *B*
University of Notre Dame *B, M, D*
Valparaiso University *B*

Iowa

Dordt College *B*
Iowa State University *B, M, D*
University of Iowa *M, D*

Kansas

Kansas State University *B*
University of Kansas *B, M*
Wichita State University *B*

Kentucky

Bellarmine University *B*
University of Louisville *B, M, D*

Louisiana

Louisiana State University and
Agricultural and Mechanical
College *B*
University of Louisiana at
Lafayette *B, M, D*
Xavier University of Louisiana *B*

Maine

University of Maine *B*

Maryland

Capitol College *A, B*
Johns Hopkins University *B*
University of Maryland
Baltimore County *B, M, D*
College Park *B*

Massachusetts

Boston University *B, M, D*
Eastern Nazarene College *B*
Merrimack College *B*
Northeastern University *B, M*
Quinsigamond Community College *A*
Smith College *B*
Suffolk University *B*
Tufts University *B, M, D*
University of Massachusetts
Amherst *B, M, D*
Dartmouth *B, M*
Lowell *M*

Michigan

Kettering University *B, M*
Kirtland Community College *A*
Lake Superior State University *B*
Lawrence Technological University *B*
Michigan State University *B, M, D*
Michigan Technological University *B*
Oakland University *B*
University of Detroit Mercy *B*
University of Michigan *B, M, D*
University of Michigan
Dearborn *B, M*
Wayne State University *M, D*
Western Michigan University *B, M*

Minnesota

Mesabi Range Community and
Technical College *A*
Minnesota State University
Mankato *B*
Saint Cloud State University *B, M*
St. Mary's University of Minnesota *B*
University of Minnesota
Duluth *B, M*
Twin Cities *B, M*

Mississippi

Jackson State University *B*
Mississippi State University *B, M, D*

Missouri

Missouri Technical School *A, B*
Saint Louis University *B*
University of Missouri
Columbia *B, M, D*
Missouri University of Science and
Technology *B, M, D*
Washington University in St.
Louis *B, M, D*

Montana

Montana State University
Bozeman *B*
Salish Kootenai College *A*

Nebraska

University of Nebraska
Lincoln *B*
Omaha *B*

Nevada

University of Nevada
Las Vegas *B*
Reno *B, M, D*

New Hampshire

University of New Hampshire *B*

New Jersey

The College of New Jersey *B*
Fairleigh Dickinson University
Metropolitan Campus *M*
New Jersey Institute of
Technology *B, M, D*
Princeton University *B, M, D*
Stevens Institute of
Technology *B, M, D*

New Mexico

New Mexico State University
Alamogordo *A*
University of New Mexico *B, M*

New York

City University of New York
City College *B, M*
Queensborough Community
College *A*
Clarkson University *B*
Columbia University *B, M, D*
Hofstra University *B*
Manhattan College *B, M*
New York Institute of Technology *B*
Polytechnic Institute of New York
University *B, M*
Rensselaer Polytechnic
Institute *B, M, D*
Rochester Institute of
Technology *B, M*
State University of New York
Binghamton *B, M*
Buffalo *B*
College of Agriculture and
Technology at Morrisville *A*
New Paltz *B, M*
Stony Brook *M*
Syracuse University *B, D*

North Carolina

Central Carolina Community
College *A*
College of the Albemarle *A*
Elon University *B*
Haywood Community College *A*
Johnson C. Smith University *B*
North Carolina State
University *B, M, D*
Southwestern Community College *A*
Surry Community College *A*
University of North Carolina
Charlotte *B*

North Dakota

North Dakota State University *B*

Ohio

Capital University *B*
Case Western Reserve
University *B, M, D*
Cedarville University *B*
Cleveland State University *B*
Miami University
Oxford Campus *B*
Ohio Northern University *B*
Ohio State University
Columbus Campus *B*
University of Akron *B, D*
University of Cincinnati *B, M, D*
University of Dayton *B*
University of Toledo *B*
Wright State University *B, M, D*
Youngstown State University *B*

Oklahoma

Oklahoma Christian University *B*
Oklahoma State University *B*
Oral Roberts University *B*
University of Oklahoma *B*

Oregon

George Fox University *B*
Oregon Health & Science
University *M, D*
Oregon State University *B, M, D*
Portland State University *B, D*
University of Portland *B*

Pennsylvania

Bucknell University *B*
Carnegie Mellon University *B, M, D*

Drexel University *B, M*
Elizabethtown College *B*
Gannon University *M*
Gettysburg College *B*
Kaplan Career Institute: Pittsburgh *A*
Lehigh University *B, M, D*
Penn State
  Abington *B*
  Altoona *B*
  Beaver *B*
  Berks *B*
  Brandywine *B*
  DuBois *B*
  Erie, The Behrend College *B*
  Fayette, The Eberly Campus *B*
  Greater Allegheny *B*
  Hazleton *B*
  Lehigh Valley *B*
  Mont Alto *B*
  New Kensington *B*
  Schuylkill *B*
  Shenango *B*
  University Park *B*
  Wilkes-Barre *B*
  Worthington Scranton *B*
  York *B*
Temple University *B*
University of Pennsylvania *B*
University of Pittsburgh *B, M*
University of Scranton *M*
Villanova University *B, M*
York College of Pennsylvania *B*

Puerto Rico

Inter American University of Puerto Rico
  Bayamon Campus *B*
Turabo University *B*
Universidad Politecnica de Puerto Rico *B, M*
University of Puerto Rico
  Ponce *A*

Rhode Island

Brown University *B*
Johnson & Wales University:
  Providence *A, B*
New England Institute of Technology *A*
University of Rhode Island *B*

South Carolina

Aiken Technical College *A*
Bob Jones University *B*
Clemson University *B, M, D*
University of South Carolina *B, M, D*

South Dakota

South Dakota School of Mines and Technology *B, M*

Tennessee

Christian Brothers University *B*
Lipscomb University *B*
Tennessee State University *M, D*
Tennessee Technological University *B, M, D*
University of Memphis *B*
University of Tennessee
  Knoxville *B, M, D*
Vanderbilt University *B*

Texas

Amarillo College *A*
LeTourneau University *B*
Prairie View A&M University *B*
Rice University *B, M, D*
St. Mary's University *B, M*
Southern Methodist University *B, M, D*
Texas A&M University *B, M, D*
Texas A&M University
  Kingsville *B, M*

Texas Tech University *B*
University of Houston *B*
University of Houston
  Clear Lake *B, M*
University of North Texas *B, M*
University of Texas
  Arlington *B, M, D*
  Dallas *B, M, D*
  El Paso *M, D*
  Pan American *B*
  San Antonio *M*
Westwood College: Houston South *A*

Utah

Brigham Young University *B*
Southern Utah University *A*
University of Utah *B*
Utah State University *B*

Virginia

Christopher Newport University *B*
George Mason University *B, M, D*
Hampton University *B*
Liberty University *B*
New River Community College *A*
Old Dominion University *B, M, D*
University of Virginia *B, M, D*
Virginia Commonwealth University *B*
Virginia Polytechnic Institute and State University *B, M, D*
Virginia State University *B*
Wytheville Community College *A*

Washington

DigiPen Institute of Technology *B*
Gonzaga University *B*
Pacific Lutheran University *B*
Seattle Pacific University *B*
University of Washington *B, M*
Walla Walla University *B*
Washington State University *B*

West Virginia

West Virginia University *B, D*

Wisconsin

Marquette University *B, M, D*
Milwaukee School of Engineering *B*
University of Wisconsin
  Madison *B*
  Milwaukee *B*
  Stout *B*

Wyoming

University of Wyoming *B*

Computer engineering technology

Arizona

Arizona State University *B*
DeVry University
  Phoenix *B*
Eastern Arizona College *C*
Glendale Community College *C*
Pima Community College *C, A*

Arkansas

Arkansas State University: Newport *A*

California

Coleman University *C, A, B*
DeVry University
  Fremont *B*
  Long Beach *B*
  Pomona *B*
  Sherman Oaks *B*
Heald College
  San Francisco *A*
Santa Barbara City College *C, A*
Southwestern College *C, A*

Colorado

Arapahoe Community College *A*
DeVry University
  Westminster *B*

Connecticut

Central Connecticut State University *B*
Naugatuck Valley Community College *C*
University of Hartford *A, B*

Delaware

Delaware Technical and Community College
  Stanton/Wilmington *A*
  Terry *A*

Florida

DeVry University
  Miramar *B*
  Orlando *B*
St. Petersburg College *A*

Georgia

DeVry University
  Alpharetta *B, M*
  Decatur *B*
Georgia Southwestern State University *B*
Middle Georgia College *A*
Savannah State University *B*
Southern Polytechnic State University *B*

Illinois

DeVry University
  Addison *B*
  Chicago *B*
  Tinley Park *B*
DeVry University: Online *B*
Lincoln Land Community College *C*
Moraine Valley Community College *C*

Indiana

Indiana State University *B*
Indiana University-Purdue University
  Fort Wayne *B*
Indiana University-Purdue University
  Indianapolis *A, B*
Purdue University *A, B*

Kansas

Kansas City Kansas Community College *A*

Kentucky

Southeast Kentucky Community and Technical College *A*
Spencerian College: Lexington *C, A*
Sullivan College of Technology and Design *A*

Maine

Southern Maine Community College *A*

Maryland

Frederick Community College *C, A*

Massachusetts

Benjamin Franklin Institute of Technology *A*
Massachusetts Bay Community College *A*
Mount Wachusett Community College *C, A*
Quinsigamond Community College *A*
Springfield Technical Community College *A*
Wentworth Institute of Technology *B*

Michigan

Eastern Michigan University *B*
Northern Michigan University *C*

Minnesota

Globe University *A, B*
Minnesota State Community and Technical College *C, A*
Minnesota State University
  Mankato *B*
Minnesota West Community and Technical College *A*
Rochester Community and Technical College *C*

Mississippi

University of Southern Mississippi *B*

Missouri

DeVry University
  Kansas City *B*
Missouri Western State University *A, B*
Vatterott College *C*

New Hampshire

NHTI-Concord's Community College *C, A*

New York

Broome Community College *A*
Cayuga County Community College *C*
DeVry
  College of New York *B*
Fulton-Montgomery Community College *C, A*
Onondaga Community College *A*
Rochester Institute of Technology *B*
State University of New York
  College of Technology at Alfred *A, B*
  Farmingdale *B*
  Institute of Technology at Utica/Rome *B*

North Carolina

Catawba Valley Community College *A*
College of the Albemarle *C*
Forsyth Technical Community College *A*
Gaston College *A*
Isothermal Community College *A*
Nash Community College *A*
Sandhills Community College *C, A*
Stanly Community College *C, A*
Wilkes Community College *A*

Ohio

Bowling Green State University:
  Firelands College *A*
Cincinnati State Technical and Community College *A*
DeVry University
  Columbus *B*
Edison State Community College *A*
Miami University
  Hamilton Campus *A*
North Central State College *A*
Owens Community College
  Toledo *C, A*
Shawnee State University *C, A, B*
University of Dayton *B*

Oregon

Oregon Institute of Technology *B*
Treasure Valley Community College *A*

Pennsylvania

California University of Pennsylvania *A, B*
Community College of Philadelphia *A*

DeVry University
Fort Washington *B*
Lehigh Carbon Community College *A*
Pennsylvania College of
Technology *A*
University of Pittsburgh
Johnstown *B*
Westmoreland County Community
College *A*

Puerto Rico

Turabo University *C, A*

Rhode Island

Community College of Rhode
Island *A*

South Carolina

Aiken Technical College *A*
York Technical College *A*

Tennessee

Southwest Tennessee Community
College *C, A*
University of Memphis *B*

Texas

DeVry University
Irving *B*
DeVry University: Houston *B*
Houston Community College
System *C, A*
LeTourneau University *B*
Mountain View College *A*
North Lake College *C*
Prairie View A&M University *B*
University of Houston
Downtown *B*

Utah

Salt Lake Community College *A*

Vermont

Vermont Technical College *A, B*

Virginia

DeVry University
Arlington *B*
National College
Roanoke Valley *C*
Norfolk State University *B*
Old Dominion University *B*

Washington

Bates Technical College *C, A*
DeVry University
Federal Way *A, B*
Eastern Washington University *B*

Wisconsin

Herzing University *A, B*
Western Technical College *A*

Computer forensics

Arizona

University of Advancing
Technology *A, B*

Florida

Santa Fe College *C*

Illinois

Harper College *C, A*
International Academy of Design and
Technology: Chicago *B*

Massachusetts

Quinsigamond Community
College *C, A*

Ohio

Defiance College *B*

Oregon

Chemeketa Community College *C*

Pennsylvania

Bloomsburg University of
Pennsylvania *B*
Chestnut Hill College *C*

South Carolina

Southern Wesleyan University *B*

Vermont

Champlain College *B*

Virginia

Stratford University: Woodbridge *B*

Computer graphics

Alabama

Calhoun Community College *A*
Faulkner State Community
College *C, A*

Arizona

Arizona Western College *A*
Estrella Mountain Community
College *C*
Glendale Community College *C*
Northland Pioneer College *C, A*
Phoenix College *A*

Arkansas

National Park Community
College *C, A*
South Arkansas Community College *A*

California

Antelope Valley College *C, A*
Art Institute
of California: Los Angeles *A, B*
of California: Orange County *A, B*
of California: San Diego *B*
Art Institute of California: San
Francisco *B*
Art Institute of California:
Sunnyvale *B*
California Lutheran University *B*
California State University
Chico *B*
Chaffey College *C*
City College of San Francisco *C*
College of the Siskiyous *C*
Cypress College *C*
Fashion Institute of Design and
Merchandising
San Francisco *A*
Foothill College *C, A*
Fullerton College *C*
Gavilan College *C, A*
Golden West College *C*
Los Angeles Southwest College *C, A*
MiraCosta College *C, A*
Modesto Junior College *C, A*
Ohlone College *C, A*
Orange Coast College *C, A*
Platt College
Los Angeles *C, A*
Ontario *C, A, B*
Saddleback College *C*
Santa Ana College *C*
Santa Barbara City College *C*
Santa Rosa Junior College *C*
Silicon Valley College
Western Career College:
Emeryville *A, B*
Western Career College: San Jose *A*
University of California
Irvine *M, D*

Colorado

Westwood College of Technology
Westwood College: Los Angeles *B*
Westwood College: Anaheim *A*

Colorado

Art Institute
of Colorado *B*
CollegeAmerica
Denver *A*
Fort Collins *A*
Colorado Mountain College *A*
Colorado Technical University *C*
Morgan Community College *C*
Rocky Mountain College of Art &
Design *B*
University of Colorado
Colorado Springs *B*
Westwood College of Technology
Westwood College: Denver
South *A, B*
Westwood College: Denver
North *A, B*

Connecticut

Norwalk Community College *C*
Quinnipiac University *B*
Tunxis Community College *C, A*

District of Columbia

American University *B*

Florida

Art Institute of Fort Lauderdale *B*
Broward College *A*
Florida State College at Jacksonville *A*
Herzing University *C*
Indian River State College *A*
Northwest Florida State College *C, A*
Polk State College *A*
Seminole Community College *A*
Tallahassee Community College *A*
University of Miami *B*
University of Tampa *B*

Georgia

Middle Georgia College *C*
Southeastern Technical College *C*

Hawaii

University of Hawaii
Honolulu Community College *A*

Idaho

Idaho State University *B*

Illinois

DePaul University *B, M*
Elgin Community College *C, A*
Lewis University *B*
Lewis and Clark Community
College *A*
Richland Community College *A*

Indiana

Indiana Institute of Technology *A*
Indiana University-Purdue University
Indianapolis *C, A, B*
Indiana Wesleyan University *B*
Purdue University *A, B*
Purdue University
Calumet *C, A, B*

Iowa

Ellsworth Community College *A*
Southeastern Community College
North Campus *A*
University of Dubuque *B*

Kansas

Seward County Community
College *C, A*

Kentucky

Spencerian College: Lexington *A*
Sullivan College of Technology and
Design *A*

Maryland

Baltimore City Community
College *C, A*
Carroll Community College *C, A*
Community College of Baltimore
County *C, A*
Frederick Community College *C*
Kaplan College: Hagerstown *A, B*
Montgomery College *A*
University of Maryland
University College *C*

Massachusetts

Hampshire College *B*
Mount Wachusett Community
College *C, A*
Newbury College *A*
Northern Essex Community
College *A*
Springfield College *B*

Michigan

Baker College
of Auburn Hills *A*
of Clinton Township *A*
of Muskegon *A*
of Owosso *A, B*
of Port Huron *C, A*
Jackson Community College *C, A*
Kalamazoo Valley Community
College *A*
Schoolcraft College *C, A*
Washtenaw Community College *C, A*

Minnesota

Academy College *C, A*
Art Institutes International
Minnesota *A, B*
Capella University *B*
Hennepin Technical College *C, A*
Minnesota School of Business *C, A*
Rochester Community and Technical
College *A*
St. Paul College *A*

Mississippi

Antonelli College
Jackson *A*
Meridian Community College *A*

Missouri

Missouri Technical School *C, B*

Montana

Fort Peck Community College *A*
Miles Community College *A*
Montana State University
College of Technology: Great
Falls *A*
University of Great Falls *B*

Nevada

Art Institute
of Las Vegas *B*
College of Southern Nevada *C, A*

New Hampshire

Lebanon College *C*

New Jersey

Bergen Community College *C, A*
Burlington County College *A*
Camden County College *A*
Cumberland County College *C*
Essex County College *C*
Gloucester County College *C, A*
Middlesex County College *A*

Salem Community College *A*

New Mexico

Clovis Community College *A*
Dona Ana Community College of New
Mexico State University *A*
New Mexico Junior College *A*
New Mexico State University
Carlsbad *C*

New York

College of Westchester *C, A*
Columbia-Greene Community
College *C*
Corning Community College *C, A*
Globe Institute of Technology *C, A, B*
Island Drafting and Technical
Institute *A*
New York Institute of
Technology *B, M*
North Country Community
College *C, A*
Pratt Institute *B, M*
Rochester Institute of
Technology *B, M*
Rockland Community College *A*
State University of New York
College at Oneonta *B*
Suffolk County Community College *A*

North Carolina

Alamance Community College *C*
Campbell University *B*
Methodist University *B*
Stanly Community College *A*
Wake Technical Community
College *C, A*
Western Piedmont Community
College *C*
Wilkes Community College *A*

Ohio

Art Institute of Cincinnati *A*
Belmont Technical College *A*
Columbus State Community
College *C, A*
James A. Rhodes State College *C*
School of Advertising Art *C, A*
Stark State College of Technology *A*
Terra State Community College *A*
University of Cincinnati
Raymond Walters College *C, A*
Washington State Community
College *A*

Oklahoma

Oklahoma State University
Institute of Technology:
Okmulgee *A*
Oklahoma City *A*
Rogers State University *B*

Oregon

Art Institute of Portland *B*

Pennsylvania

Arcadia University *C*
Bucks County Community College *A*
CHI Institute: Franklin Mills *C, A*
Erie Business Center *A*
Keystone Technical Institute *C*
La Salle University *B*
Luzerne County Community
College *A*
University of Pennsylvania *B*

South Carolina

Aiken Technical College *C*
York Technical College *C*

South Dakota

Dakota State University *B*

Tennessee

Memphis College of Art *B*
Roane State Community College *C*

Texas

Amarillo College *C, A*
Central Texas College *C*
Midland College *C, A*
North Lake College *C*
Trinity Valley Community
College *C, A*
University of Mary Hardin-Baylor *B*
Wade College *A*

Utah

College of Eastern Utah *C, A*

Vermont

Champlain College *B*

Virginia

Central Virginia Community
College *C*
New River Community College *A*
Thomas Nelson Community
College *A*

Washington

Bellevue College *C, A*
Everett Community College *A*
Olympic College *A*
South Seattle Community
College *C, A*
Spokane Falls Community College *A*
Walla Walla University *A, B*

West Virginia

Mountain State University *A*

Wisconsin

Herzing University *A, B*
Lakeshore Technical College *A*
Milwaukee Area Technical College *A*
Nicolet Area Technical College *A*
St. Norbert College *B*

Computer hardware engineering

Illinois

Illinois Institute of Technology *M*
University of Illinois
Urbana-Champaign *B, M, D*

Maryland

United States Naval Academy *B*

Massachusetts

Quinsigamond Community College *A*

Michigan

Oakland University *M*

New York

State University of New York
College of Agriculture and
Technology at Morrisville *A*
Stony Brook *B, D*

Computer hardware technology

Arkansas

Rich Mountain Community College *A*

California

Canada College *C, A*
City College of San Francisco *C*

Delaware

Delaware Technical and Community
College
Terry *C*

Florida

St. Petersburg College *C*
South Florida Community
College *C, A*

Indiana

Indiana University-Purdue University
Indianapolis *A, B*

Kentucky

Sullivan College of Technology and
Design *A*

Maryland

Frederick Community College *C, A*

Massachusetts

Benjamin Franklin Institute of
Technology *A*

Michigan

Baker College
of Muskegon *C*
Bay de Noc Community College *C*
Oakland Community College *C, A*

Minnesota

Globe University *A, B*
Lake Superior College *C, A*

Mississippi

Pearl River Community College *C*

Missouri

St. Louis Community College
St. Louis Community College at
Florissant Valley *A*

New York

Cayuga County Community College *A*
State University of New York
College of Agriculture and
Technology at Morrisville *A*
College of Technology at Alfred *A*
Farmingdale *C*

North Carolina

Forsyth Technical Community
College *C, A*

North Dakota

North Dakota State College of
Science *A*

Ohio

Edison State Community College *C*
Miami University
Hamilton Campus *C*

Pennsylvania

Bucks County Community College *C*
Temple University *B*

Rhode Island

Community College of Rhode
Island *C, A*

South Dakota

Mitchell Technical Institute *A*
Southeast Technical Institute *C, A*

Texas

North Lake College *C*
St. Philip's College *C, A*

Virginia

ECPI College of Technology: Virginia
Beach *C, A*
ECPI Technical College: Roanoke *A*
Mountain Empire Community
College *A*
Southwest Virginia Community
College *C*

Washington

Bates Technical College *C*

Wisconsin

Herzing University *A, B*

Wyoming

Laramie County Community
College *C*

Computer/information sciences, general

Alabama

Alabama Agricultural and Mechanical
University *B, M*
Alabama Southern Community
College *A*
Amridge University *B*
Athens State University *B*
Auburn University *B*
Bevill State Community College *A*
Birmingham-Southern College *B*
Bishop State Community College *A*
Calhoun Community College *C, A*
Central Alabama Community
College *C, A*
Chattahoochee Valley Community
College *A*
Enterprise-Ozark Community
College *A*
Faulkner State Community College *A*
Faulkner University *A, B*
Gadsden State Community
College *C, A*
George C. Wallace State Community
College
George C. Wallace Community
College at Dothan *C, A*
Selma *C, A*
Herzing University *A, B*
Jacksonville State University *B, M*
Jefferson State Community
College *C, A*
Lurleen B. Wallace Community
College *A*
Miles College *B*
Northeast Alabama Community
College *C, A*
Northwest-Shoals Community
College *A*
Oakwood University *A, B*
Snead State Community College *A*
Southern Union State Community
College *C, A*
Spring Hill College *C*
Stillman College *B*
Talladega College *B*
Troy University *A, B, M*
Tuskegee University *B*
University of Alabama *B, M, D*
University of Alabama
Birmingham *B, M, D*
Huntsville *B, M, D*
University of Mobile *B*
University of North Alabama *B*
University of South Alabama *B, M*

Alaska

University of Alaska
Fairbanks *B, M*
Southeast *C, A*

Arizona

Arizona State University *B*
Arizona Western College *C, A*
Central Arizona College *C, A*
Chandler-Gilbert Community College
  Pecos *A*
Dine College *A*
GateWay Community College *C, A*
Glendale Community College *C, A*
Mesa Community College *A*
Mohave Community College *A*
Northcentral University *B, M, D*
Northern Arizona University *B*
Northland Pioneer College *C, A*
Paradise Valley Community
  College *C, A*
Penn Foster College *A*
Phoenix College *A*
Pima Community College *C, A*
Prescott College *B, M*
Rio Salado College *C, A*
Scottsdale Community College *C, A*
University of Arizona *B, M, D*
University of Phoenix *C, B*
Western International
  University *A, B, M*

Arkansas

Arkansas State University *B, M*
Arkansas Tech University *B*
Henderson State University *B*
Mid-South Community College *A*
National Park Community
  College *C, A*
North Arkansas College *C, A*
Northwest Arkansas Community
  College *A*
Ouachita Technical College *C, A*
Rich Mountain Community College *A*
South Arkansas Community College *A*
Southeast Arkansas College *C*
Southern Arkansas University *B, M*
University of Arkansas *B, M, D*
University of Arkansas
  Community College at Batesville *A*
  Fort Smith *A, B*
  Little Rock *B, M*
  Pine Bluff *B*
University of Central Arkansas *B*
Williams Baptist College *B*

California

Allan Hancock College *C, A*
American River College *C, A*
Antelope Valley College *C, A*
Azusa Pacific University *B, M*
Barstow Community College *C, A*
Berkeley City College *C, A*
Butte College *C, A*
Cabrillo College *A*
California Lutheran University *B*
California State University
  East Bay *B, M*
  Long Beach *B, M*
  Los Angeles *B*
  Northridge *B, M*
  Sacramento *B, M*
  San Marcos *B*
California State University: Channel
  Islands *B, M*
California University of Management
  and Sciences *B, M*
Canada College *C, A*
Cerritos College *A*
Cerro Coso Community College *C, A*
Chabot College *A*
Chaffey College *C, A*
Chapman University *B*
Citrus College *A*
City College of San Francisco *C, A*
Coastline Community College *C, A*
Coleman University *C, A, B, M*
College of Marin: Kentfield *C, A*
College of San Mateo *C, A*

College of the Desert *C, A*
College of the Redwoods *C, A*
College of the Sequoias *C*
College of the Siskiyous *C, A*
Columbia College *C, A*
Contra Costa College *A*
Copper Mountain College *C, A*
Crafton Hills College *C, A*
Cypress College *C, A*
De Anza College *A*
DeVry University
  Pomona *B*
Diablo Valley College *C, A*
East Los Angeles College *A*
El Camino College *C, A*
El Camino College: Compton
  Center *C, A*
Evergreen Valley College *A*
Folsom Lake College *A*
Foothill College *C, A*
Fresno City College *C, A*
Fullerton College *A*
Gavilan College *C, A*
Glendale Community College *C, A*
Golden West College *A*
Grossmont College *C, A*
Harvey Mudd College *B*
Humboldt State University *B*
Humphreys College *A, B*
Imperial Valley College *C, A*
Irvine Valley College *C, A*
Kaplan College: Panorama City *C*
LA College International *C, A, B*
Lake Tahoe Community College *C*
Laney College *C, A*
Lassen Community College *C, A*
Los Angeles City College *C, A*
Los Angeles Harbor College *C, A*
Los Angeles Mission College *A*
Los Angeles Pierce College *C, A*
Los Angeles Southwest College *A*
Los Angeles Trade and Technical
  College *C, A*
Los Medanos College *C*
Loyola Marymount University *B, M*
The Master's College *B*
Mendocino College *C, A*
Merced College *A*
Merritt College *C, A*
Mills College *B, M*
MiraCosta College *C, A*
Mission College *C*
Modesto Junior College *A*
Monterey Peninsula College *C, A*
Moorpark College *A*
Mount San Jacinto College *C, A*
Mt. Sierra College *B*
Napa Valley College *A*
National Hispanic University *A, B*
National University *A, B, M*
Notre Dame de Namur University *B*
Orange Coast College *C, A*
Oxnard College *A*
Pacific States University *B*
Palo Verde College *C, A*
Palomar College *C, A*
Pepperdine University *B*
Platt College
  Los Angeles *C, A*
  Ontario *A*
Porterville College *A*
Reedley College *A*
Rio Hondo College *A*
Riverside Community College *C, A*
Sacramento City College *C, A*
Saddleback College *C, A*
San Diego City College *C, A*
San Diego Miramar College *C, A*
San Diego State University *B, M*
San Francisco State University *B*
San Joaquin Delta College *C, A*
San Jose City College *A*
Santa Ana College *C, A*
Santa Barbara City College *C, A*

Santa Monica College *C*
Shasta College *A*
Skyline College *C, A*
Solano Community College *A*
Southwestern College *C, A*
Stanford University *B, M, D*
Taft College *A*
University of California
  Irvine *B, M, D*
  Los Angeles *B*
  San Diego *B, M, D*
  Santa Barbara *B, M, D*
  Santa Cruz *B, M, D*
University of La Verne *B*
University of Redlands *B, M*
University of San Francisco *B, M*
University of the Pacific *B*
Ventura College *C, A*
West Hills College: Coalinga *C, A*
West Hills College: Lemoore *C, A*
West Valley College *C, A*
Woodbury University *B*
Yuba Community College
  District *C, A*

Colorado

Adams State College *B*
American Sentinel University *A, B, M*
Anthem College *A*
CollegeAmerica
  Fort Collins *A*
Colorado Christian University *B*
Colorado Mountain College *A*
Colorado School of Mines *B*
Colorado State University *B, M, D*
Colorado Technical
  University *B, M, D*
Community College of Aurora *C, A*
Community College of Denver *C, A*
Fort Lewis College *B*
Jones International University *B*
Lamar Community College *C*
Mesa State College *B*
Metropolitan State College of
  Denver *B*
Otero Junior College *C, A*
Pikes Peak Community College *C, A*
Pueblo Community College *C, A*
Regis University *B*
Trinidad State Junior College *A*
University of Colorado
  Colorado Springs *B, M, D*
  Denver *B, M, D*
Westwood College: Denver
  North *A, B*

Connecticut

Asnuntuck Community College *A*
Capital Community College *A*
Central Connecticut State
  University *B, M*
Eastern Connecticut State
  University *B*
Fairfield University *B*
Housatonic Community College *C, A*
Naugatuck Valley Community
  College *A*
Norwalk Community College *C, A*
Post University *B*
Quinebaug Valley Community
  College *C, A*
Quinnipiac University *B, M*
Sacred Heart University *B, M*
Southern Connecticut State
  University *B, M*
Three Rivers Community College *C, A*
Trinity College *B*
Tunxis Community College *C*
University of Bridgeport *B, M, D*
University of Hartford *B*
University of New Haven *B, M*
Wesleyan University *B, M*
Western Connecticut State
  University *B*

Yale University *B, M, D*

Delaware

Delaware State University *B, M*
Delaware Technical and Community
  College
  Owens *A*
  Stanton/Wilmington *A*
  Terry *A*
Goldey-Beacom College *A, B, M*
University of Delaware *B, M, D*
Wilmington University *B*

District of Columbia

American University *B, M*
Catholic University of
  America *B, M, D*
Gallaudet University *B*
George Washington University *B, M*
Potomac College *B*
University of the District of
  Columbia *C, A, B*

Florida

Barry University *B*
Beacon College *A, B*
Broward College *C, A*
Chipola College *A*
City College
  Gainesville *A*
City College: Casselberry *A*
Daytona State College *A*
Eckerd College *B*
Edison State College *A*
Embry-Riddle Aeronautical
  University *B*
Florida Agricultural and Mechanical
  University *B, M*
Florida Atlantic University *B, M, D*
Florida Gulf Coast University *B*
Florida International
  University *B, M, D*
Florida Keys Community College *A*
Florida Memorial University *B*
Florida National College *A*
Florida State College at Jacksonville *A*
Florida State University *B, M, D*
Gulf Coast College *C, A*
Gulf Coast Community College *A*
Indian River State College *A*
Jacksonville University *B*
Jones College *A, B*
Lake City Community College *A*
Miami Dade College *C, A*
Northwest Florida State College *A*
Northwood University
  Florida *B*
Nova Southeastern University *B, M, D*
Palm Beach Community College *A*
Pensacola Junior College *A*
Polk State College *A*
Rollins College *B*
Saint Johns River Community
  College *C*
Saint Leo University *B*
St. Petersburg College *C, A, B*
Saint Thomas University *B*
Seminole Community College *A*
State College of Florida,
  Manatee-Sarasota *A*
Stetson University *B*
University of Central Florida *B, M, D*
University of Florida *B, M*
University of North Florida *B, M*
University of South Florida *B*
University of Tampa *A, B*
University of West Florida *B, M*
Valencia Community College *A*
Webber International University *B*

Georgia

Abraham Baldwin Agricultural
  College *A*

Albany State University *B*
Armstrong Atlantic State
    University *B, M*
Atlanta Metropolitan College *A*
Atlanta Technical College *A*
Augusta State University *B*
Bainbridge College *C, A*
Chattahoochee Technical
    College *C, A*
Clark Atlanta University *B*
Clayton State University *B*
Columbus State University *B, M*
Covenant College *B*
Dalton State College *A, B*
Darton College *A*
DeKalb Technical College *C, A*
Fort Valley State University *B*
Gainesville State College *C, A*
Georgia College and State
    University *B*
Georgia Highlands College *A*
Georgia Institute of
    Technology *B, M, D*
Georgia Military College *A*
Georgia Southern University *B*
Georgia Southwestern State
    University *B*
Georgia State University *B, M, D*
Griffin Technical College *A*
Kennesaw State University *B*
LaGrange College *B*
Macon State College *A*
Middle Georgia College *A*
Morehouse College *B*
North Georgia College & State
    University *B*
Savannah State University *B*
Savannah Technical College *C, A*
Shorter College *B*
Spelman College *B*
University of West Georgia *B*
Valdosta State University *B*
Valdosta Technical College *C, A*
Waycross College *A*
Wesleyan College *B*
West Georgia Technical College *A*

Hawaii

Chaminade University of
    Honolulu *A, B*
Hawaii Pacific University *C, B*
Heald College
    Honolulu *A*
Remington College
    Honolulu *A, B*
University of Hawaii
    Hilo *B*
    Honolulu Community College *A*
    Leeward Community College *C, A*
    Manoa *B*

Idaho

Brigham Young University-Idaho *A, B*
Idaho State University *B*
Lewis-Clark State College *A, B*
North Idaho College *A*
Stevens-Henager College: Boise *B*

Illinois

Aurora University *B*
Black Hawk College: East Campus *A*
Carl Sandburg College *A*
Chicago State University *B*
City Colleges of Chicago
    Harold Washington College *A*
    Kennedy-King College *C, A*
    Olive-Harvey College *A*
Concordia University Chicago *B*
Danville Area Community College *A*
DePaul University *C, B, M, D*
Dominican University *B*
East-West University *A; B*
Eureka College *B*
Governors State University *B, M*

Greenville College *B*
Harper College *A*
Harry S. Truman College *A*
Illinois Central College *A*
Illinois Eastern Community Colleges
    Frontier Community College *C, A*
    Lincoln Trail College *A*
Illinois Institute of Technology *B*
Illinois Valley Community College *A*
Illinois Wesleyan University *B*
John A. Logan College *A*
John Wood Community College *A*
Joliet Junior College *C, A*
Lake Land College *C*
Lewis University *B*
Lewis and Clark Community
    College *A*
Loyola University Chicago *C, B*
MacCormac College *C, A*
MacMurray College *A*
McKendree University *B*
Midstate College *A*
North Central College *B*
North Park University *B*
Northern Illinois University *B, M*
Northwestern College *C, A*
Northwestern University *B*
Oakton Community College *A*
Olivet Nazarene University *B*
Principia College *B*
Richland Community College *A*
Rock Valley College *C, A*
Rockford Career College *A*
St. Augustine College *C, A*
Saint Xavier University *B*
South Suburban College of Cook
    County *C, A*
Southern Illinois University
    Edwardsville *M*
Southwestern Illinois College *C, A*
Triton College *C*
University of Chicago *B*
University of Illinois
    Urbana-Champaign *B*
Vatterott College: Quincy *C*
Western Illinois University *B, M*
Westwood College: Chicago Loop *A*
Wilbur Wright College *C, A*

Indiana

Ball State University *A, B, M*
Bethel College *A*
Brown Mackie College: Fort Wayne *A*
Brown Mackie College: South Bend *A*
Butler University *B*
Calumet College of St. Joseph *A, B*
DeVry University: Indianapolis *A*
Earlham College *B*
Franklin College *B*
Hanover College *B*
Huntington University *B*
Indiana Institute of Technology *A, B*
Indiana State University *B, M*
Indiana University
    Bloomington *B, M, D*
    East *A*
    Kokomo *B*
    South Bend *B*
    Southeast *B*
Indiana University-Purdue University
    Indianapolis *B, M, D*
Indiana Wesleyan University *B*
International Business College *C, A*
Ivy Tech Community College
    Bloomington *C, A*
    Central Indiana *C, A*
    Columbus *C, A*
    East Central *C, A*
    Kokomo *C, A*
    Lafayette *C, A*
    North Central *C, A*
    Northeast *C, A*
    Northwest *C, A*
    Richmond *C, A*

South Central *C, A*
Southeast *C, A*
Southwest *C, A*
Wabash Valley *C, A*
Kaplan College: Hammond *C, A*
Kaplan College: Indianapolis *A*
Manchester College *A, B*
Oakland City University *A, B*
Purdue University *B, M, D*
Purdue University
    Calumet *B*
    North Central *A*
Saint Joseph's College *B*
St. Mary-of-the-Woods College *B*
Taylor University *B*
Trine University *B*
University of Evansville *B, M*
University of Indianapolis *B*
University of Notre Dame *B*
University of Southern Indiana *C, B*
Vincennes University *A*

Iowa

Briar Cliff University *B*
Central College *B*
Clarke College *B*
Dordt College *B*
Drake University *B*
Ellsworth Community College *A*
Emmaus Bible College *B*
Graceland University *B*
Grand View University *B*
Hawkeye Community College *A*
Indian Hills Community College *C*
Iowa State University *B, M, D*
Iowa Wesleyan College *B*
Kaplan University
    Cedar Falls *C*
    Davenport *C*
    Mason City *C*
Marshalltown Community
    College *C, A*
Mount Mercy College *B*
Northwestern College *B*
St. Ambrose University *C, B*
University of Dubuque *B*
University of Iowa *B, M, D*
University of Northern Iowa *B, M*
Waldorf College *B*
Wartburg College *B*
William Penn University *B*

Kansas

Allen County Community College *A*
Butler Community College *C, A*
Central Christian College of Kansas *A*
Coffeyville Community College *A*
Colby Community College *A*
Dodge City Community College *A*
Emporia State University *B*
Fort Hays State University *B*
Fort Scott Community College *C, A*
Friends University *B*
Garden City Community College *A*
Hesston College *A*
Hutchinson Community College *C, A*
Kansas State University *B, M, D*
Kansas Wesleyan University *A, B*
Labette Community College *A*
Manhattan Area Technical College *A*
MidAmerica Nazarene University *B*
Neosho County Community
    College *A*
Pratt Community College *C, A*
Seward County Community
    College *C, A*
Southwestern College *B*
University of Kansas *B, M, D*
Washburn University *B*
Wichita State University *B, M*

Kentucky

Bellarmine University *B, M*
Berea College *B*

Bluegrass Community and Technical
    College *C, A*
Brescia University *B*
Campbellsville University *C, A, B*
Daymar College
    Owensboro *C, A*
Draughons Junior College *C, A*
Eastern Kentucky University *B*
Elizabethtown Community and
    Technical College *C, A*
Georgetown College *B*
Hazard Community and Technical
    College *A*
Henderson Community College *C*
Hopkinsville Community College *C, A*
Kentucky State University *B, M*
Kentucky Wesleyan College *B*
Lindsey Wilson College *A*
Madisonville Community College *C, A*
Maysville Community and Technical
    College *C, A*
Midway College *A, B*
Morehead State University *B*
Murray State University *B*
Northern Kentucky University *B*
Owensboro Community and
    Technical College *C*
Pikeville College *B*
St. Catharine College *A*
Somerset Community College *C, A*
Southeast Kentucky Community and
    Technical College *A*
Southern Ohio College
    Brown Mackie College: North
        Kentucky *A*
Sullivan University *A, B*
Thomas More College *A, B*
Transylvania University *B*
University of Kentucky *B, M, D*
West Kentucky Community and
    Technical College *C, A*
Western Kentucky University *B, M*

Louisiana

Baton Rouge Community College *A*
Baton Rouge School of
    Computers *C, A*
Camelot College *C, A*
Delta College of Arts & Technology *C*
Louisiana State University
    Eunice *A*
Our Lady of Holy Cross College *C*
Southern University
    Shreveport *A*
Xavier University of Louisiana *B*

Maine

Andover College *A*
University of Maine *C, B, M, D*
University of Maine
    Augusta *A, B*
    Fort Kent *B*
University of Southern Maine *B*

Maryland

Allegany College of Maryland *A*
Anne Arundel Community
    College *C, A*
Baltimore City Community College *A*
Cecil College *C, A*
Chesapeake College *A*
College of Notre Dame of Maryland *B*
College of Southern Maryland *A*
Community College of Baltimore
    County *A*
DeVry University: Bethesda *B*
Frederick Community College *A*
Frostburg State University *C, B, M*
Hagerstown Community College *A*
Harford Community College *A*
Hood College *M*
Johns Hopkins University *B, M, D*
Loyola University Maryland *B*
McDaniel College *B*

Montgomery College *A*
Mount St. Mary's University *B*
Prince George's Community
 College *C, A*
St. Mary's College of Maryland *B*
Salisbury University *B*
Towson University *B, M*
United States Naval Academy *B*
University of Baltimore *B, M*
University of Maryland
 Baltimore County *B, M, D*
 College Park *B, M, D*
 Eastern Shore *B, M*
 University College *C, B*
Washington Adventist University *B*
Wor-Wic Community College *A*

Massachusetts

Anna Maria College *B*
Assumption College *B*
Babson College *B*
Benjamin Franklin Institute of
 Technology *A*
Bentley University *B, M*
Berkshire Community College *A*
Boston College *B*
Boston University *B, M, D*
Bristol Community College *A*
Cape Cod Community College *A*
Clark University *B*
College of the Holy Cross *B*
Curry College *B*
Dean College *A*
Elms College *C, B*
Fisher College *A, B*
Fitchburg State College *C, B*
Framingham State College *B*
Greenfield Community College *C, A*
Massachusetts Bay Community
 College *A*
Massachusetts College of Liberal
 Arts *B*
Massachusetts Institute of
 Technology *M*
Massasoit Community College *A*
Merrimack College *A*
Mount Wachusett Community
 College *A*
Newbury College *B*
North Shore Community College *A*
Northeastern University *B, M, D*
Northern Essex Community
 College *C, A*
Quinsigamond Community
 College *C, A*
Regis College *B*
Roxbury Community College *C, A*
Salem State College *B*
Simmons College *B*
Springfield College *B*
Suffolk University *B, M*
Tufts University *B*
University of Massachusetts
 Boston *B*
 Dartmouth *B, M*
Urban College of Boston *C*
Wellesley College *B*
Wentworth Institute of Technology *B*
Wheaton College *B*
Worcester State College *B*

Michigan

Albion College *B, T*
Alpena Community College *C, A*
Andrews University *B*
Aquinas College *B*
Baker College
 of Auburn Hills *A*
 of Cadillac *B*
 of Clinton Township *A, B*
 of Flint *B, M*
 of Jackson *A*
 of Muskegon *B*
 of Owosso *A, B*
 of Port Huron *A, B*
Bay Mills Community College *A*
Calvin College *B*
Delta College *C, A*
Eastern Michigan University *B*
Gogebic Community College *A*
Grace Bible College *B*
Grand Rapids Community
 College *C, A*
Grand Valley State University *B*
Henry Ford Community College *A*
Hope College *B*
Kalamazoo College *B*
Lake Superior State University *A, B*
Lansing Community College *A*
Macomb Community College *C, A*
Marygrove College *C, B*
Michigan Jewish Institute *B*
Michigan State University *B, M, D*
Michigan Technological
 University *B, M, D*
Mid Michigan Community
 College *C, A*
Monroe County Community
 College *C, A*
Montcalm Community College *A*
Muskegon Community College *C, A*
North Central Michigan College *C, A*
Northern Michigan University *B*
Northwood University: Michigan *B*
Oakland University *B, M*
Rochester College *B*
Saginaw Valley State University *B*
Schoolcraft College *A*
Siena Heights University *A, B*
University of Detroit Mercy *B, M*
University of Michigan *B*
University of Michigan
 Dearborn *B*
 Flint *B, M*
Walsh College of Accountancy and
 Business Administration *B*
Washtenaw Community College *C, A*
Wayne County Community College *A*
Wayne State University *B, M, D*
Western Michigan University *B*

Minnesota

Academy College *C, A, B*
Alexandria Technical College *A*
Bemidji State University *B, M*
Bethel University *B*
Century Community and Technical
 College *A*
College of St. Scholastica *B, M*
Globe University *C, A, B*
Gustavus Adolphus College *B*
Hennepin Technical College *C, A*
Hibbing Community College *A*
Lake Superior College *A*
Macalester College *B*
Mesabi Range Community and
 Technical College *C, A*
Minnesota School of Business *C, A*
Minnesota State Community and
 Technical College *C*
Minnesota State University
 Mankato *B, M*
 Moorhead *B*
Minnesota West Community and
 Technical College *A*
National American University
 Bloomington *A, B*
National American University:
 Roseville *A, B*
Normandale Community College *A*
Ridgewater College *C, A*
Riverland Community College *A*
Rochester Community and Technical
 College *A*
St. Catherine University *B*
Saint Cloud State University *B*
St. Mary's University of Minnesota *B*
Southwest Minnesota State
 University *B*
University of Minnesota
 Duluth *B*
 Twin Cities *M, D*
Walden University *B*
White Earth Tribal and Community
 College *A*
Winona State University *B*

Mississippi

Alcorn State University *B, M*
Antonelli College
 Hattiesburg *C, A*
Belhaven University *B*
East Central Community College *A*
East Mississippi Community
 College *C, A*
Hinds Community College *A*
Holmes Community College *C, A*
Jackson State University *B, M*
Meridian Community College *A*
Millsaps College *B*
Mississippi College *B*
Mississippi Gulf Coast Community
 College *A*
Mississippi State University *B, M, D*
Mississippi Valley State University *B*
Northwest Mississippi Community
 College *A*
University of Mississippi *B*
University of Southern
 Mississippi *B, M*

Missouri

Avila University *B*
College of the Ozarks *B*
Columbia College *A, B*
Crowder College *A*
Drury University *B*
Evangel University *B*
Fontbonne University *B*
Hannibal-LaGrange College *B*
Harris-Stowe State University *B*
Hickey College *C, A*
Jefferson College *C, A*
Lincoln University *A*
Lindenwood University *B*
Metropolitan Community College:
 Longview *A*
Metropolitan Community College:
 Maple Woods *A*
Metropolitan Community College:
 Penn Valley *C, A*
Missouri Baptist University *B*
Missouri Southern State University *B*
Missouri State University: West
 Plains *A*
Missouri Valley College *B*
Missouri Western State University *B*
North Central Missouri College *C, A*
Northwest Missouri State
 University *B, M*
Park University *B*
Ranken Technical College *A*
St. Louis Community College
 St. Louis Community College at
 Florissant Valley *A*
 St. Louis Community College at
 Meramec *C, A*
Saint Louis University *C, B*
Southeast Missouri State University *B*
Southwest Baptist University *B*
University of Central Missouri *B*
University of Missouri
 Columbia *B, M, D*
 Missouri University of Science and
 Technology *B, M, D*
 St. Louis *B, M*
Vatterott College: Joplin *C, A*
Vatterott College: Kansas City *A*
Vatterott College: Sunset Hills *A, B*
Washington University in St.
 Louis *B, M, D*
Webster University *M*
Westminster College *B*
William Woods University *B*

Montana

Blackfeet Community College *A*
Dawson Community College *A*
Miles Community College *A*
Montana State University
 Billings *A*
Salish Kootenai College *C, A, B*
University of Great Falls *B, M*
University of Montana: Western *A*

Nebraska

Bellevue University *B, M*
Central Community College *C, A*
College of Saint Mary *A, B*
Doane College *B*
Grace University *B*
Little Priest Tribal College *C, A*
Metropolitan Community
 College *C, A*
Nebraska Indian Community
 College *A*
Northeast Community College *A*
Peru State College *B*
University of Nebraska
 Kearney *B*
 Lincoln *B, M, D*
Wayne State College *B*
Western Nebraska Community
 College *C, A*

Nevada

Career College of Northern Nevada *C*
Great Basin College *C, A*
Morrison University *A*
Nevada State College *B*
Sierra Nevada College *B*
Truckee Meadows Community
 College *A*
University of Nevada
 Reno *B, M*
Western Nevada College *A*

New Hampshire

Daniel Webster College *B*
Keene State College *A, B*
Lakes Region Community
 College *C, A*
Manchester Community College *A*
NHTI-Concord's Community
 College *C, A*
Nashua Community College *C, A*
New England College *B*
Southern New Hampshire
 University *A, B, M*
University of New Hampshire *B, M, D*
University of New Hampshire at
 Manchester *B*
White Mountains Community
 College *C, A*

New Jersey

Bergen Community College *C, A*
Bloomfield College *B*
Brookdale Community College *A*
Caldwell College *C, B*
Camden County College *C, A*
Centenary College *B*
The College of New Jersey *B*
College of St. Elizabeth *C*
County College of Morris *A*
Cumberland County College *A*
Essex County College *C, A*
Fairleigh Dickinson University
 College at Florham *B*
Felician College *B*
Gloucester County College *C, A*
Hudson County Community
 College *C*
Kean University *B*

Mercer County Community College *C*
Middlesex County College *A*
Monmouth University *C, B, M*
Montclair State University *B, M*
New Jersey City University *B*
New Jersey Institute of
　Technology *B, M, D*
Ocean County College *A*
Passaic County Community College *A*
Ramapo College of New Jersey *B*
Rider University *B*
Saint Peter's College *B*
Seton Hall University *B*
Stevens Institute of
　Technology *B, M, D*
Sussex County Community
　College *C, A*
Warren County Community
　College *C, A*
William Paterson University of New
　Jersey *B*

New Mexico

Clovis Community College *A*
Eastern New Mexico University *B*
Eastern New Mexico University:
　Roswell Campus *A*
Navajo Technical College *A*
New Mexico Institute of Mining and
　Technology *B, M, D*
New Mexico Junior College *C, A*
New Mexico State University *B, M, D*
Northern New Mexico College *A*
Santa Fe Community College *A*
University of New Mexico *B, M, D*
Western New Mexico University *B*

New York

ASA Institute of Business and
　Computer Technology *C*
Adelphi University *B*
Adirondack Community College *A*
Barnard College *B*
Bramson ORT College *C, A*
Broome Community College *A*
Bryant & Stratton Business Institute
　Bryant & Stratton College: Albany *A*
　Bryant & Stratton College:
　　Buffalo *A*
　Bryant & Stratton College:
　　Southtowns *A*
　Bryant & Stratton College:
　　Syracuse *A*
Cayuga County Community College *A*
City University of New York
　Baruch College *B, M*
　Brooklyn College *B, M*
　Hunter College *B*
　John Jay College of Criminal
　　Justice *B*
　LaGuardia Community College *A*
　Lehman College *B, M*
　New York City College of
　　Technology *A, B*
　Queensborough Community
　　College *A*
　York College *B*
Clinton Community College *A*
Colgate University *B*
College of Saint Rose *B, M*
College of Westchester *C, A*
Columbia University
　School of General Studies *B*
Columbia-Greene Community
　College *A*
Cornell University *D*
Corning Community College *C, A*
Dominican College of Blauvelt *B*
Dowling College *B*
Dutchess Community College *C, A*
Erie Community College
　North Campus *C, A*
Excelsior College *B*
Finger Lakes Community College *C, A*

Fordham University *B*
Fulton-Montgomery Community
　College *A*
Globe Institute of Technology *C, A, B*
Hamilton College *B*
Hartwick College *B*
Hobart and William Smith Colleges *B*
Ithaca College *B*
Jamestown Business College *A*
Jefferson Community College *A*
Le Moyne College *B*
Long Island University
　Brooklyn Campus *B, M*
Manhattan College *B*
Manhattanville College *B*
Maria College *A*
Medaille College *B*
Mercy College *C, B*
Mildred Elley *C, A*
Mohawk Valley Community College *A*
Monroe College *A, B*
Nassau Community College *C, A*
New York Institute of
　Technology *B, M*
New York University *C, B, M, D*
Niagara County Community
　College *A*
Niagara University *C, B*
Nyack College *A*
Onondaga Community College *A*
Orange County Community College *A*
Pace University *B, D*
Roberts Wesleyan College *B*
Rochester Institute of
　Technology *A, B, M, D*
Sage College of Albany *B*
Saint Bonaventure University *B*
St. John Fisher College *B*
St. John's University *C, A, B*
St. Thomas Aquinas College *B*
Schenectady County Community
　College *A*
Siena College *C, B*
Skidmore College *B*
State University of New York
　Albany *B, M, D*
　Binghamton *B*
　Buffalo *M, D*
　College at Brockport *B, M*
　College at Buffalo *B*
　College at Fredonia *B*
　College at Geneseo *B*
　College at Old Westbury *B*
　College at Oneonta *B*
　College at Plattsburgh *B*
　College at Potsdam *B*
　College of Agriculture and
　　Technology at Cobleskill *A, B*
　College of Agriculture and
　　Technology at Morrisville *A, B*
　College of Technology at Alfred *A*
　Farmingdale *C*
　Institute of Technology at
　　Utica/Rome *B, M*
　New Paltz *B, M*
Suffolk County Community
　College *C, A*
Sullivan County Community
　College *A*
Syracuse University *B, M, D*
Technical Career Institutes *A*
Tompkins Cortland Community
　College *A*
Touro College *B*
Ulster County Community College *A*
Union College *B*
United States Military Academy *B*
Utica College *B*
Utica School of Commerce *A*
Vassar College *B*
Westchester Community College *A*
Yeshiva University *B*

North Carolina

Barton College *B*
Bennett College for Women *B*
Bladen Community College *C, A*
Carteret Community College *C, A*
College of the Albemarle *A*
DeVry University: Charlotte *B*
Duke University *B, M, D*
Edgecombe Community College *A*
Elon University *B*
Fayetteville State University *B*
Forsyth Technical Community
　College *A*
Gardner-Webb University *B*
Gaston College *C*
Guilford College *B*
Halifax Community College *C, A*
High Point University *B*
Johnson C. Smith University *B*
King's College *C*
Lenoir-Rhyne University *B*
Livingstone College *B*
Meredith College *B*
Methodist University *A, B*
Miller-Motte Technical College *C, A*
Montreat College *C, B*
Mount Olive College *B*
North Carolina Agricultural and
　Technical State University *B, M*
Pfeiffer University *B*
St. Augustine's College *B*
Sampson Community College *A*
Sandhills Community College *C, A*
Shaw University *B*
South College *A*
South Piedmont Community
　College *A*
Southeastern Community
　College *C, A*
Southwestern Community
　College *C, A*
University of North Carolina
　Wilmington *M*
Wake Technical Community
　College *C, A*
Winston-Salem State University *M*

North Dakota

Cankdeska Cikana Community
　College *C, A*
Lake Region State College *C, A*
Mayville State University *B*
Minot State University *B*
University of Mary *B*
University of North Dakota *B, M*

Ohio

Belmont Technical College *A*
Bowling Green State University *B, M*
Bryant & Stratton College
　Eastlake *A*
Case Western Reserve
　University *B, M, D*
Cedarville University *B*
Cincinnati State Technical and
　Community College *A*
Cleveland State University *B, M*
College of Mount St. Joseph *A, B*
College of Wooster *B*
Columbus State Community
　College *C, A*
Cuyahoga Community College
　Metropolitan Campus *A*
Denison University *B*
Eastern Gateway Community
　College *C, A*
Edison State Community College *C, A*
Franciscan University of
　Steubenville *B*
Franklin University *A, B, M*
Gallipolis Career College *A*
Heidelberg University *B*
Hiram College *B*
James A. Rhodes State College *A*

John Carroll University *B*
Kaplan College: Columbus *C*
Marietta College *B*
Marion Technical College *A*
Miami University
　Hamilton Campus *A*
　Oxford Campus *B, M*
Mount Vernon Nazarene University *B*
Muskingum University *B*
National College
　Dayton *C, A*
North Central State College *C, A*
Oberlin College *B*
Ohio State University
　Columbus Campus *B, M, D*
Ohio University *B*
Ohio Valley College of Technology *A*
Ohio Wesleyan University *B*
RETS College *A*
Southwestern College of Business
　Southwestern College:
　　Franklin *C, A*
　Southwestern College:
　　Tri-County *C*
Southwestern College: Dayton *A*
Stark State College of Technology *A*
Terra State Community College *A*
Tiffin University *B*
Trumbull Business College *C, A*
University of Cincinnati *B, M*
University of Cincinnati
　Clermont College *C, A*
　Raymond Walters College *C, A*
University of Dayton *B*
University of Findlay *A, B*
University of Northwestern Ohio *A*
University of Rio Grande *A, B*
University of Toledo *A*
Walsh University *A, B*
Wilberforce University *B*
Wilmington College *B*
Wright State University *B, M, D*
Youngstown State University *A, B, M*
Zane State College *A*

Oklahoma

Bacone College *A*
Cameron University *A, B*
Connors State College *A*
East Central University *B*
Eastern Oklahoma State College *C, A*
Langston University *B*
Murray State College *A*
Northeastern Oklahoma Agricultural
　and Mechanical College *A*
Northern Oklahoma College *A*
Northwestern Oklahoma State
　University *B*
Oklahoma Baptist University *B*
Oklahoma Christian University *B*
Oklahoma City Community College *A*
Oklahoma City University *B, M*
Oklahoma Panhandle State
　University *B*
Oklahoma State University *B, M, D*
Oklahoma State University
　Institute of Technology:
　　Okmulgee *A*
Oklahoma Wesleyan University *A, B*
Oral Roberts University *B*
Redlands Community College *A*
Rogers State University *A, B*
Rose State College *A*
Southeastern Oklahoma State
　University *B*
Southern Nazarene University *B*
Southwestern Oklahoma State
　University *B*
Tulsa Community College *C, A*
University of Central Oklahoma *B*
University of Tulsa *B*
Vatterott College *A*
Western Oklahoma State College *A*

Oregon

Central Oregon Community College *C, A*
Chemeketa Community College *A*
Eastern Oregon University *B*
George Fox University *B*
Heald College: Portland *C, A*
Linn-Benton Community College *A*
Mt. Hood Community College *C, A*
Oregon State University *B, M, D*
Pacific University *B*
Southern Oregon University *B*
Treasure Valley Community College *A*
University of Oregon *B, M, D*
Western Oregon University *B*
Willamette University *B*

Pennsylvania

Albright College *B*
Alvernia University *A, B*
Arcadia University *C, B*
Bloomsburg University of Pennsylvania *B*
Bryn Athyn College of the New Church *B*
Bucknell University *B*
Bucks County Community College *A*
Cabrini College *B*
California University of Pennsylvania *A, B*
Cedar Crest College *C, B*
Chestnut Hill College *B*
Cheyney University of Pennsylvania *B*
Clarion University of Pennsylvania *B*
Community College of Philadelphia *A*
DeSales University *B, M*
Delaware Valley College *A, B*
Dickinson College *B*
East Stroudsburg University of Pennsylvania *B, M*
Edinboro University of Pennsylvania *A, B*
Elizabethtown College *B*
Erie Business Center South *A*
Gannon University *B, M*
Geneva College *B*
Gettysburg College *B*
Grove City College *B*
Gwynedd-Mercy College *B*
Harrisburg Area Community College *C, A*
Harrisburg University of Science and Technology *C, B*
Haverford College *B*
Indiana University of Pennsylvania *B*
Juniata College *B*
Kaplan Career Institute: Pittsburgh *A*
Keystone College *B*
Keystone Technical Institute *C*
King's College *C, A, B*
La Roche College *B*
La Salle University *B, M*
Lackawanna College *A*
Lafayette College *B*
Lincoln University *B*
Lock Haven University of Pennsylvania *B*
Luzerne County Community College *A*
Mansfield University of Pennsylvania *A, B*
McCann School of Business and Technology: Dickson City *A*
Mercyhurst College *C, A, B*
Millersville University of Pennsylvania *A, B*
Misericordia University *B*
Montgomery County Community College *A*
Mount Aloysius College *B*
Muhlenberg College *C, A, B*
Neumann University *B*
Newport Business Institute: Lower Burrell *C*

PJA School *C*
Penn State
    Abington *B*
    Altoona *B*
    Beaver *B*
    Berks *B*
    Brandywine *B*
    DuBois *B*
    Erie, The Behrend College *B*
    Fayette, The Eberly Campus *B*
    Greater Allegheny *B*
    Harrisburg *B, M*
    Hazleton *B*
    Lehigh Valley *B*
    Mont Alto *B*
    New Kensington *B*
    Schuylkill *C, B*
    Shenango *B*
    University Park *B*
    Wilkes-Barre *B*
    Worthington Scranton *B*
    York *B*
Pennsylvania School of Business *C, A*
St. Francis University *B*
Saint Joseph's University *B, M*
St. Vincent College *C, B*
Shippensburg University of Pennsylvania *B, M*
Swarthmore College *B*
Temple University *B, M, D*
Thiel College *B*
University of Pennsylvania *B, M, D*
University of Pittsburgh Johnstown *B*
University of Scranton *A, B*
Villanova University *B, M*
Waynesburg University *B*
West Chester University of Pennsylvania *B, M*
Westminster College *B*
Widener University *A, B, M*
Wilkes University *B*

Puerto Rico

Bayamon Central University *A*
Caribbean University *A, B*
Electronic Data Processing College: San Sebastian *A*
Inter American University of Puerto Rico
    Arecibo Campus *A, B*
    Fajardo Campus *A, M*
    Metropolitan Campus
    San German Campus *B, M*
National College of Business and Technology: Arecibo *A, B*
Universidad Adventista de las Antillas *A, B*
University College of San Juan *C, A, B*
University of Puerto Rico
    Arecibo *A*
    Bayamon University College *A, B*
    Ponce *A, B*

Rhode Island

Bryant University *B, M*
Community College of Rhode Island *C, A*
New England Institute of Technology *A, B*
Rhode Island College *B*
Roger Williams University *B*
University of Rhode Island *B, M, D*

South Carolina

Benedict College *B*
The Citadel *B*
Clemson University *B, M, D*
Coastal Carolina University *B*
College of Charleston *B*
Columbia College *B*
Denmark Technical College *C*
Forrest Junior College *C, A*
Francis Marion University *B*

Greenville Technical College *C*
Horry-Georgetown Technical College *C*
Lander University *B*
South Carolina State University *B*
Southern Wesleyan University *B*
Spartanburg Community College *C, A*
Technical College of the Lowcountry *C, A*
Tri-County Technical College *C, A*
University of South Carolina *B, M, D*
University of South Carolina Upstate *B*
Williamsburg Technical College *A*
Winthrop University *B*
Wofford College *B*
York Technical College *C*

South Dakota

Black Hills State University *A*
Dakota State University *C, B*
Lake Area Technical Institute *A*
Mitchell Technical Institute *A*
National American University Rapid City *A, B*
Northern State University *B, M*
Oglala Lakota College *B*
Sisseton Wahpeton College *C, A*
South Dakota State University *C, B*
Southeast Technical Institute *A*
University of Sioux Falls *B*
University of South Dakota *B, M, D*

Tennessee

Austin Peay State University *B*
Carson-Newman College *B*
Columbia State Community College *A*
East Tennessee State University *B, M*
Freed-Hardeman University *B*
Lambuth University *B*
Lane College *B*
Lee University *B*
Lincoln Memorial University *B*
Maryville College *B*
Middle Tennessee State University *B*
Milligan College *B*
Nashville State Community College *A*
National College Nashville *A*
Northeast State Community College *C, A*
Tennessee Technological University *B*
Tennessee Wesleyan College *B*
University of the South *B*

Texas

Amarillo College *C, A*
Angelina College *A*
Angelo State University *B, T*
Austin Community College *C, A*
Brazosport College *A*
Central Texas College *C, A*
Cisco College *C, A*
Clarendon College *A*
Coastal Bend College *C, A*
College of the Mainland *A*
Collin County Community College District *C, A*
Dallas Baptist University *B*
Eastfield College *C, A*
El Paso Community College *C, A*
Frank Phillips College *C, A*
Galveston College *A*
Grayson County College *C, A*
Hill College *C, A*
Howard College *C, A*
Huston-Tillotson University *B*
Jarvis Christian College *B*
Kilgore College *A*
Lamar Institute of Technology *C, A*
Lamar State College at Orange *C, A*
Lamar State College at Port Arthur *C, A*
Lamar University *B*

Laredo Community College *A*
LeTourneau University *B*
Lee College *C, A*
Lone Star College System *C, A*
Lubbock Christian University *B*
McLennan Community College *C, A*
McMurry University *B, T*
Midland College *A*
Midwestern State University *B, M*
Navarro College *C, A*
North Central Texas College *A*
North Lake College *C, A*
Northwest Vista College *A*
Our Lady of the Lake University of San Antonio *B*
Palo Alto College *C, A*
Panola College *C, A*
Prairie View A&M University *B, M*
Ranger College *C, A*
Richland College *C, A*
St. Edward's University *B*
St. Mary's University *B, M*
Sam Houston State University *B, M*
San Jacinto College *C*
South Plains College *A*
South Texas College *A*
Southern Methodist University *C*
Southwest Texas Junior College *A*
Southwestern Adventist University *B*
Southwestern University *B, T*
Stephen F. Austin State University *B, M, T*
Sul Ross State University *B*
Tarleton State University *B, T*
Tarrant County College *C, A*
Temple College *C, A*
Texarkana College *C, A*
Texas A&M University
    Commerce *B*
    Corpus Christi *B, M*
    Texarkana *B*
Texas Christian University *B*
Texas College *B*
Texas Lutheran University *B*
Texas Southern University *B, M*
Texas State Technical College Waco *A*
Texas State University: San Marcos *B, M*
Texas Tech University *B, M, D*
Texas Wesleyan University *B*
Texas Woman's University *B, T*
Trinity University *B*
Trinity Valley Community College *C, A*
Tyler Junior College *C, A*
University of Houston *B, M, D*
University of Houston
    Clear Lake *B, M*
    Downtown *B*
    Victoria *B, T*
University of Mary Hardin-Baylor *B*
University of North Texas *B, M, D*
University of Texas
    Arlington *M, D*
    Austin *B, M, D*
    Brownsville - Texas Southmost College *C, A, B*
    Dallas *B, M, D*
    El Paso *B, M*
    Pan American *B*
    San Antonio *B, M*
    Tyler *B, M*
    of the Permian Basin *B, M*
Victoria College *C, A*
Weatherford College *C, A*
Western Technical College: Diana Drive *C, A*
Western Texas College *A*
Wharton County Junior College *C, A*

Utah

College of Eastern Utah *C*
Dixie State College of Utah *B*

Eagle Gate College: Murray *A*
LDS Business College *C, A*
Provo College *A*
Salt Lake Community College *C, A*
Snow College *A*
Southern Utah University *B*
University of Utah *M, D*
Utah State University *B, M*
Utah Valley University *A, B*
Weber State University *A, B*
Western Governors University *B*

Vermont
Bennington College *B*
Castleton State College *B*
Champlain College *B*
Lyndon State College *A, B*
Marlboro College *B, M*
Vermont Technical College *A, B*

Virginia
Blue Ridge Community College *C, A*
Bryant & Stratton College: Virginia
  Beach *A*
College of William and Mary *B, M, D*
Dabney S. Lancaster Community
  College *A*
Danville Community College *A*
ECPI College of Technology: Virginia
  Beach *C, A, B*
ECPI Technical College: Roanoke *A*
Eastern Shore Community
  College *C, A*
Emory & Henry College *B*
George Mason University *B, M, D*
Hampton University *B*
J. Sargeant Reynolds Community
  College *A*
James Madison University *B, M*
John Tyler Community College *A*
Liberty University *B, T*
Longwood University *B*
Lord Fairfax Community College *A*
Lynchburg College *B*
Mary Baldwin College *B*
Mountain Empire Community
  College *A*
National College
  Lynchburg *A*
Norfolk State University *B, M*
Northern Virginia Community
  College *A*
Old Dominion University *B, M, D*
Patrick Henry Community College *A*
Paul D. Camp Community
  College *C, A*
Piedmont Virginia Community
  College *C, A*
Potomac College *A, B*
Randolph-Macon College *B*
Roanoke College *B*
St. Paul's College *B*
Southern Virginia University *B*
Southside Virginia Community
  College *C, A*
Southwest Virginia Community
  College *A*
Thomas Nelson Community
  College *C, A*
Tidewater Community College *A*
University of Management and
  Technology *C, A, B, M*
University of Mary Washington *B*
University of Richmond *B*
University of Virginia *B, M, D*
Virginia Commonwealth
  University *B, M*
Virginia Highlands Community
  College *A*
Virginia Polytechnic Institute and
  State University *B, M, D*
Virginia Union University *B*
Virginia Western Community
  College *C, A*

Washington and Lee University *B*

Washington
Bellevue College *C, A*
Big Bend Community College *A*
Cascadia Community College *A*
Centralia College *C, A*
City University of Seattle *M*
Eastern Washington University *B, M*
Everett Community College *C, A*
Evergreen State College *B*
Highline Community College *A*
Lower Columbia College *A*
Olympic College *A*
Peninsula College *A*
Renton Technical College *C*
Shoreline Community College *C, A*
Skagit Valley College *C, A*
South Seattle Community
  College *C, A*
Spokane Falls Community
  College *C, A*
University of Puget Sound *B*
University of Washington *B, M, D*
University of Washington
  Bothell *B, M*
University of Washington Tacoma *B*
Walla Walla University *B*
Washington State University *B*
Western Washington University *B, M*
Whitworth University *B*
Yakima Valley Community College *A*

West Virginia
Alderson-Broaddus College *C*
American Public University
  System *A, B*
Bethany College *B*
Bluefield State College *B*
Concord University *B*
Fairmont State University *B*
Huntington Junior College *A*
Marshall University *B*
Mountain State College *A*
New River Community and Technical
  College *A*
Potomac State College of West
  Virginia University *A*
Salem International University *A, B*
Shepherd University *B*
Southern West Virginia Community
  and Technical College *A*
West Virginia Business College: Nutter
  Fort *C, A*
West Virginia Business College:
  Wheeling *C, A*
West Virginia University Institute of
  Technology *B*
West Virginia Wesleyan College *B*

Wisconsin
Alverno College *B*
Carroll University *B*
Chippewa Valley Technical College *A*
College of Menominee Nation *A*
Concordia University Wisconsin *B*
DeVry University: Milwaukee *B*
Edgewood College *B*
Fox Valley Technical College *C*
Herzing University *A, B*
Lac Courte Oreilles Ojibwa
  Community College *C*
Lawrence University *B*
Nicolet Area Technical College *A*
Northeast Wisconsin Technical
  College *C, A*
University of Wisconsin
  Eau Claire *B*
  La Crosse *B, T*
  Madison *B, M, D*
  Milwaukee *B, M*
  Parkside *M*
  River Falls *B*

Stevens Point *B*
Whitewater *B, T*
Viterbo University *B*

Wyoming
Laramie County Community
  College *A*
Northwest College *A*
Sheridan College *A*
Western Wyoming Community
  College *A*

Computer installation and repair

Alabama
Northeast Alabama Community
  College *C, A*

Alaska
University of Alaska
  Fairbanks *C, A*

Arizona
Cochise College *C*

Arkansas
Mid-South Community College *C*
Ouachita Technical College *C*
South Arkansas Community College *C*
Southern Arkansas University Tech *C*
University of Arkansas
  Fort Smith *C*

California
Diablo Valley College *C*
Orange Coast College *C*
Solano Community College *C, A*

Florida
Daytona State College *C*
Miami Dade College *C*
Polk State College *A*

Georgia
Albany Technical College *C*
Dalton State College *C, A*
Gwinnett Technical College *C*
Savannah Technical College *C*

Illinois
Black Hawk College *C*
College of Lake County *C, A*
Highland Community College *C*
Illinois Eastern Community Colleges
  Frontier Community College *C*
  Lincoln Trail College *C*
  Olney Central College *C*
  Wabash Valley College *C*
Morton College *C*
Sauk Valley Community College *C*
Spoon River College *C*
Triton College *C*
Waubonsee Community College *C*

Kansas
Coffeyville Community College *C*
Kansas City Kansas Community
  College *C*

Kentucky
Bluegrass Community and Technical
  College *C*
Eastern Kentucky University *A*
Sullivan College of Technology and
  Design *A*

Louisiana
Delgado Community College *C, A*

Massachusetts
Cape Cod Community College *C*

Michigan
Baker College
  of Muskegon *C*
Montcalm Community College *C, A*
Schoolcraft College *C*

New York
Corning Community College *A*

North Carolina
Beaufort County Community
  College *C*

Ohio
Cincinnati State Technical and
  Community College *C, A*
University of Akron: Wayne College *C*
University of Cincinnati
  Raymond Walters College *C, A*

Oklahoma
Vatterott College
  Tulsa *C, A*

Pennsylvania
Harrisburg Area Community
  College *C, A*
Northampton Community
  College *C, A*
Westmoreland County Community
  College *C*

Puerto Rico
Inter American University of Puerto
  Rico
  Aguadilla Campus *A, B*
  Bayamon Campus *A, B*
  Guayama Campus *A, B*
Universal Career Community College:
  Humacao *C*
Universal Career Community College:
  Manati *C*
Universal Career Community College:
  San Juan *C*
Universidad Metropolitana *C, A*
Universidad del Este *C*

South Carolina
Midlands Technical College *C*
York Technical College *C*

Texas
Temple College *C, A*
Western Texas College *C*

Virginia
ECPI College of Technology: Virginia
  Beach *C, A*
ECPI Technical College: Roanoke *A*

Wisconsin
Blackhawk Technical College *C*
Herzing University *A, B*
Waukesha County Technical
  College *A*
Wisconsin Indianhead Technical
  College *C, A*

Computer networking/ telecommunications

Alabama
Gadsden State Community College *A*
Herzing University *A*

Alaska

University of Alaska
  Anchorage *C, A*
  Southeast *B*

Arizona

Arizona State University *M*
Arizona Western College *C*
Brown Mackie College: Tucson *C, A*
Chandler-Gilbert Community College
  Pecos *A*
Cochise College *C, A*
DeVry University
  Phoenix *A, B, M*
GateWay Community College *C, A*
Glendale Community College *C, A*
Mesa Community College *A*
Northland Pioneer College *A*
Pima Community College *C, A*
University of Advancing
    Technology *A, B, M*
University of Phoenix *B*

Arkansas

Arkansas Northeastern College *C*
Arkansas State University
  Mountain Home *C*
East Arkansas Community College *C*
Mid-South Community College *C*
North Arkansas College *C*
Southeast Arkansas College *C, A*
Southern Arkansas University
  Tech *C, A*

California

Allan Hancock College *C*
American River College *C, A*
Butte College *C, A*
California College San Diego *A*
California State University
  East Bay *C, B, M*
  Monterey Bay *B*
Chaffey College *C*
City College of San Francisco *C*
Coastline Community College *C*
College of the Canyons *C, A*
College of the Siskiyous *C*
DeVry University
  Fremont *B, M*
  Long Beach *A, B, M*
  Pomona *B, M*
  Sherman Oaks *B, M*
Diablo Valley College *C, A*
Foothill College *C*
Heald College
  Rancho Cordova *C, A*
Irvine Valley College *C, A*
Mt. Sierra College *B*
Oxnard College *C, A*
Platt College
  Ontario *A*
Remington College
  San Diego *A*
Saddleback College *C*
San Jose City College *C, A*
Shasta College *C, A*
Sierra College *C, A*
Silicon Valley University *C*
Southwestern College *C, A*
University of Southern California *M*
Westwood College of Technology
  Westwood College: Los Angeles *B*
Westwood College: Anaheim *A, B*

Colorado

Arapahoe Community College *C, A*
CollegeAmerica
  Denver *A*
Colorado Mountain College *A*
Colorado Technical University *C*
Community College of Denver *C*
DeVry University
  Westminster *A, B, M*

Front Range Community College *C*
Pikes Peak Community College *A*
Red Rocks Community College *C*
University of Colorado
  Boulder *M*
Westwood College of Technology
  Westwood College: Denver
    South *A, B*
Westwood College: Denver
    North *A, B*

Connecticut

Gateway Community College *C, A*
Manchester Community College *A*
Naugatuck Valley Community
  College *A*

Delaware

Delaware Technical and Community
  College
  Stanton/Wilmington *A*
  Terry *C, A*

Florida

College of Business and Technology:
  Flagler *C, A*
DeVry University
  Miramar *A, B, M*
  Orlando *A, B, M*
Edison State College *C*
Florida State College at
  Jacksonville *A, B*
Gulf Coast Community College *A*
Pasco-Hernando Community
  College *A*
St. Petersburg College *C, A*
Seminole Community College *C, A*
Southwest Florida College *A*
State College of Florida,
  Manatee-Sarasota *A*
Tallahassee Community College *C, A*

Georgia

Albany Technical College *C, A*
Altamaha Technical College *A*
Ashworth College *C*
Athens Technical College *C, A*
Central Georgia Technical
  College *C, A*
Clayton State University *C, A*
Darton College *C, A*
DeVry University
  Alpharetta *A, B, M*
  Decatur *A, B, M*
North Georgia Technical College *C, A*
Savannah Technical College *C, A*
Southeastern Technical College *A*
Southwest Georgia Technical
  College *C, A*
University of Georgia *M*
West Georgia Technical College *C, A*

Hawaii

Remington College
  Honolulu *A*

Idaho

Eastern Idaho Technical College *C, A*
Idaho State University *C, A*

Illinois

Black Hawk College *C*
College of Office Technology *C*
Danville Area Community
  College *C, A*
DePaul University *B, M*
DeVry University
  Addison *A, B*
  Chicago *A, B*
  Tinley Park *A, B, M*
DeVry University: Online *A, B, M*
Elgin Community College *C*
Harper College *C*

Heartland Community College *C, A*
Illinois Institute of Technology *M*
Illinois State University *B*
Kaskaskia College *C*
Lake Land College *A*
Lincoln Land Community College *C, A*
McHenry County College *C*
Moraine Valley Community College *C*
Morton College *C*
Parkland College *C, A*
Robert Morris University:
  Chicago *C, A*
Roosevelt University *B, M*
Sauk Valley Community College *C*
Spoon River College *C*
Triton College *A*
Waubonsee Community College *C*
Western Illinois University *B*

Indiana

DeVry University:
  Indianapolis *A, B, M*
Harrison College
  Indianapolis *A*
Indiana Institute of Technology *A, B*
Indiana University-Purdue University
  Fort Wayne *C*
Indiana University-Purdue University
  Indianapolis *A*
Purdue University *A, B*
Purdue University
  Calumet *B*
Vincennes University *C, A*

Iowa

Hawkeye Community College *C, A*
Indian Hills Community College *A*
Iowa Central Community College *C*
Iowa Lakes Community College *A*
Kaplan University
  Davenport *B*
Marshalltown Community College *A*
Northwest Iowa Community
  College *A*
Southeastern Community College
  North Campus *A*
University of Northern Iowa *B*
Vatterott College *C, A*

Kansas

Brown Mackie College
  Salina *A*
Coffeyville Community College *C, A*
Cowley County Community
  College *A*
Garden City Community College *A*
Hutchinson Community College *A*
Johnson County Community
  College *A*
Kansas City Kansas Community
  College *C, A*
Kansas State University *B*
Labette Community College *C, A*
Wichita State University *M*

Kentucky

Big Sandy Community and Technical
  College *C, A*
Daymar College
  Owensboro *A*

Maine

Washington County Community
  College *C*

Maryland

Anne Arundel Community College *C*
Community College of Baltimore
  County *C*
DeVry University: Bethesda *M*
Howard Community College *C, A*
Morgan State University *B*

TESST College of Technology
  Beltsville *C*
University of Maryland
  University College *C, M*

Massachusetts

Becker College *B*
Bristol Community College *C*
Bunker Hill Community College *C, A*
Cape Cod Community College *C, A*
Holyoke Community College *C*
Massasoit Community College *C*
Middlesex Community College *C, A*
Mount Wachusett Community
  College *C*
Northeastern University *M*
Quinsigamond Community College *C*
Roxbury Community College *C*

Michigan

Alpena Community College *A*
Baker College
  of Cadillac *A*
  of Clinton Township *A*
  of Muskegon *C, A*
  of Owosso *A*
  of Port Huron *C, A*
Baker College of Allen Park *A*
Bay de Noc Community College *A*
Calvin College *B*
Davenport University *A, B*
Delta College *C, A*
Grand Rapids Community
  College *C, A*
Henry Ford Community College *C*
Kirtland Community College *C*
Lake Michigan College *C, A*
Lansing Community College *A*
Macomb Community College *C, A*
Michigan Technological University *B*
Mott Community College *A*
Northern Michigan University *B*
Oakland Community College *C*
Schoolcraft College *C*
Southwestern Michigan College *A*
Walsh College of Accountancy and
  Business Administration *M*
Washtenaw Community College *C, A*
Wayne County Community College *A*

Minnesota

Alexandria Technical College *C, A*
Anoka-Ramsey Community
  College *C, A*
Capella University *M, D*
Central Lakes College *A*
Century Community and Technical
  College *C, A*
Dakota County Technical College *C, A*
DeVry University
  Edina *A, B, M*
Dunwoody College of
  Technology *C, A*
High-Tech Institute *A*
Inver Hills Community College *C, A*
Lake Superior College *C, A*
Minneapolis Community and
  Technical College *C, A*
Minnesota School of Business *C*
Minnesota State College - Southeast
  Technical *C, A*
Minnesota State Community and
  Technical College *C, A*
Northland Community & Technical
  College *A*
Ridgewater College *C, A*
Rochester Community and Technical
  College *C*
Saint Cloud State University *B*
St. Cloud Technical College *C, A*
St. Paul College *C, A*
University of Minnesota
  Twin Cities *B*

Mississippi

Antonelli College
  Jackson *A*
Copiah-Lincoln Community College *A*
Northwest Mississippi Community
  College *A*

Missouri

DeVry University
  Kansas City *A, B, M*
East Central College *C, A*
Harris-Stowe State University *B*
Linn State Technical College *C, A*
Mineral Area College *C, A*
Missouri Southern State University *A*
State Fair Community College *A*
Vatterott College: Sunset Hills *A, B*

Montana

Blackfeet Community College *A*
Montana State University
  Billings *A*
  College of Technology: Great
    Falls *C, A*
Montana Tech of the University of
  Montana *C, A, B*
University of Great Falls *B*
University of Montana: Western *B*

Nebraska

Metropolitan Community
  College *C, A*

Nevada

College of Southern Nevada *C, A*
Great Basin College *A*

New Hampshire

Nashua Community College *C, A*

New Jersey

Berkeley College- Garret Mountain
  Campus *A*
Bloomfield College *C, B*
Cumberland County College *C, A*
DeVry University: North
  Brunswick *A, B*
Kean University *B*
Mercer County Community
  College *C, A*
New Jersey Institute of Technology *M*
Ocean County College *C*
Raritan Valley Community College *C*
Stevens Institute of
  Technology *B, M, D*

New Mexico

Clovis Community College *A*

New York

ASA Institute of Business and
  Computer Technology *C, A*
Briarcliffe College *A, B*
City University of New York
  Borough of Manhattan Community
    College *A*
Clinton Community College *A*
DeVry
  College of New York *A, B*
Genesee Community College *C, A*
Globe Institute of Technology *C, A, B*
Herkimer County Community
  College *A*
Hudson Valley Community College *A*
Iona College *B, M*
Monroe Community College *A*
New York Institute of
  Technology *B, M*
Pace University *C, A, M*
Polytechnic Institute of New York
  University *M*

Rochester Institute of
  Technology *B, M*
Sage College of Albany *B*
State University of New York
  College of Technology at Alfred *B*
Syracuse University *M*
Wood Tobe-Coburn School *A*

North Carolina

Beaufort County Community
  College *C, A*
Central Carolina Community
  College *A*
Cleveland Community College *C, A*
College of the Albemarle *A*
Davidson County Community
  College *C, A*
DeVry University: Charlotte *M*
Durham Technical Community
  College *C, A*
Edgecombe Community College *A*
Fayetteville Technical Community
  College *C, A*
Forsyth Technical Community
  College *C, A*
Haywood Community College *C, A*
Isothermal Community College *C, A*
Montgomery Community College *C*
North Carolina State University *M*
Randolph Community College *A*
Richmond Community College *C, A*
South Piedmont Community
  College *C, A*
Southeastern Community
  College *C, A*
Southwestern Community College *A*
Stanly Community College *C, A*
University of North Carolina
  Greensboro *B, M*
Vance-Granville Community
  College *A*
Wayne Community College *C, A, B*
Wilson Community College *C, A*

North Dakota

Bismarck State College *A*
Lake Region State College *C, A*

Ohio

Baldwin-Wallace College *C, B*
Cincinnati State Technical and
  Community College *A*
Clark State Community College *A*
Davis College *A*
DeVry University
  Columbus *A, B, M*
Edison State Community College *C, A*
Hocking College *C, A*
James A. Rhodes State College *A*
Kent State University
  Trumbull *C*
Marion Technical College *A*
Miami University
  Hamilton Campus *A*
Ohio University *B, M*
Owens Community College
  Toledo *C*
Remington College: Cleveland West *A*
Stark State College of Technology *A*
University of Akron *C, A, B*
University of Akron: Wayne College *A*
University of Cincinnati
  Clermont College *C, A*

Oklahoma

DeVry University: Oklahoma City
  Center *A, B, M*
Oklahoma State University *M*
Oklahoma State University
  Institute of Technology:
    Okmulgee *A*
Rose State College *A*
Southern Nazarene University *B*

University of Oklahoma *M*

Oregon

Central Oregon Community
  College *A*
Chemeketa Community College *C*
Clackamas Community College *C, A*
Clatsop Community College *A*
DeVry University: Portland *A, B, M*
Lane Community College *A*

Pennsylvania

Bucks County Community
  College *C, A*
CHI Institute: Broomall *C*
Community College of Beaver
  County *A*
Community College of Philadelphia *A*
DeVry University
  Fort Washington *A, B, M*
Erie Business Center *A*
Harrisburg Area Community
  College *C, A*
Johnson College *A*
Kaplan Career Institute: Harrisburg *A*
Keystone College *B*
Laurel Business Institute *A*
Lehigh Carbon Community
  College *A*
McCann School of Business and
  Technology: Dickson City *A*
Montgomery County Community
  College *A*
Northampton Community College *A*
Penn Commercial Business and
  Technical School *A*
Pennsylvania College of
  Technology *A, B*
Pennsylvania Highlands Community
  College *A*
Pennsylvania Institute of
  Technology *A*
Reading Area Community College *A*
Thaddeus Stevens College of
  Technology *A*
University of Pennsylvania *B, M*
University of Pittsburgh *M*
Waynesburg University *B*
Westmoreland County Community
  College *C, A*

Puerto Rico

Inter American University of Puerto
  Rico
  Metropolitan Campus *C*

Rhode Island

Community College of Rhode
  Island *C, A*

South Carolina

Midlands Technical College *C*
York Technical College *C*

South Dakota

Northern State University *A*
Southeast Technical Institute *A*

Tennessee

DeVry University: Memphis *A, M*
Draughons Junior College:
  Nashville *C, A*
University of Tennessee
  Chattanooga *C*

Texas

Austin Community College *C, A*
Brookhaven College *C*
Cedar Valley College *C, A*
Central Texas College *C, A*
Collin County Community College
  District *C, A*

DeVry University
  Irving *A, B*
DeVry University: Houston *A, B*
Eastfield College *C, A*
Hallmark College of Technology *C, A*
Houston Community College
  System *C, A*
Mountain View College *C, A*
North Lake College *C, A*
Northwest Vista College *C, A*
South Texas College *A*
Tarrant County College *C, A*
Texas State Technical College
  Harlingen *C, A*
  West Texas *C, A*
Texas State Technical College:
  Marshall *C, A*
Texas Tech University *M*
University of the Incarnate Word *B*
Victoria College *C, A*
Wharton County Junior College *C, A*

Utah

DeVry University: Sandy *A, B, M*
Southern Utah University *A*
Stevens-Henager College: Logan *A*
Utah Valley University *C*
Weber State University *C, A, B*

Vermont

Champlain College *B*

Virginia

Centura College: Newport News *A*
DeVry University
  Arlington *A, B, M*
ECPI College of Technology: Virginia
  Beach *C, A*
ECPI Technical College: Roanoke *A, B*
Germanna Community College *C*
Hampton University *B*
J. Sargeant Reynolds Community
  College *C*
Lord Fairfax Community College *C, A*
Mountain Empire Community
  College *A*
Thomas Nelson Community
  College *A*
Tidewater Community College *A*
University of Management and
  Technology *A, B, M*

Washington

Bates Technical College *C, A*
Bellevue College *C, A*
Bellingham Technical College *C, A*
Cascadia Community College *C*
Centralia College *C, A*
Clark College *C, A*
Clover Park Technical College *C, A*
DeVry University
  Federal Way *A, B, M*
Everett Community College *A*
Green River Community College *C, A*
Lower Columbia College *A*
North Seattle Community
  College *C, A*
Northwest Indian College *C*
Olympic College *C, A*
Peninsula College *A*
Renton Technical College *C, A*
Shoreline Community College *C, A*
Spokane Falls Community College *C*
Wenatchee Valley College *C, A*
Yakima Valley Community College *C*

West Virginia

Blue Ridge Community and Technical
  College *C*

Wisconsin

DeVry University: Milwaukee *M*
Gateway Technical College *A*

Herzing University *A, B*
Lakeshore Technical College *A*
Mid-State Technical College *A*
Milwaukee Area Technical College *A*
Nicolet Area Technical College *A*
Northcentral Technical College *A*
Northeast Wisconsin Technical
College *A*
Southwest Wisconsin Technical
College *A*
University of Wisconsin
Stout *B*
Waukesha County Technical
College *C, A*
Western Technical College *A*
Wisconsin Indianhead Technical
College *A*

Wyoming

Eastern Wyoming College *A*

Computer programming, general

Alabama

Calhoun Community College *A*
Enterprise-Ozark Community
College *C*
Gadsden State Community College *A*
Northwest-Shoals Community
College *A*
Wallace State Community College at
Hanceville *A*

Alaska

University of Alaska
Southeast *C*

Arizona

Central Arizona College *C, A*
Cochise College *C, A*
Eastern Arizona College *C*
GateWay Community College *C*
Mohave Community College *C*
University of Phoenix *B*

Arkansas

North Arkansas College *C*
Northwest Arkansas Community
College *A*
Rich Mountain Community College *A*
South Arkansas Community College *A*
Southern Arkansas University
Tech *C, A*
University of Arkansas
Little Rock *A*

California

American River College *A*
Antelope Valley College *C, A*
Barstow Community College *C, A*
California College San Diego *A*
California Lutheran University *B*
Canada College *A*
Cerritos College *A*
Chabot College *A*
City College of San Francisco *C*
Coleman College: San Marcos *A*
College of the Redwoods *C*
College of the Siskiyous *C, A*
Columbia College *A*
Cosumnes River College *C, A*
Crafton Hills College *C, A*
Cypress College *C*
De Anza College *A*
East Los Angeles College *A*
Evergreen Valley College *C*
Folsom Lake College *C*
Foothill College *C, A*
Fresno City College *A*
Gavilan College *C*
Grossmont College *C, A*

Hartnell College *C, A*
Irvine Valley College *C, A*
Los Angeles Mission College *C*
Los Angeles Pierce College *C, A*
Los Angeles Southwest College *A*
MiraCosta College *A*
Modesto Junior College *A*
Monterey Peninsula College *A*
Ohlone College *A*
Orange Coast College *C, A*
Pasadena City College *C, A*
Riverside Community College *C, A*
Saddleback College *C, A*
San Diego Mesa College *C, A*
San Joaquin Delta College *C, A*
San Jose City College *C, A*
Santa Barbara City College *C*
Santa Monica College *C, A*
Santa Rosa Junior College *C*
Sierra College *C, A*
Solano Community College *C, A*
Sonoma State University *B*
Southwestern College *C, A*
Victor Valley College *C*
West Valley College *C, A*
Westwood College of Technology
Westwood College: Los Angeles *A*
Westwood College: Anaheim *A*

Colorado

CollegeAmerica
Denver *A*
Colorado Mountain College *A*
Colorado Technical University *C*
Community College of Denver *A*
Jones International University *B*
Red Rocks Community College *C*
Trinidad State Junior College *A*
Westwood College: Denver North *A*

Connecticut

Capital Community College *C*
Gateway Community College *A*
Northwestern Connecticut
Community College *C*
Norwalk Community College *A*
Tunxis Community College *C*
University of New Haven *C*

Delaware

Wilmington University *B*

Florida

Art Institute of Fort Lauderdale *A, B*
Brevard Community College *A*
Broward College *C, A*
Edison State College *A*
Florida Keys Community College *A*
Florida National College *A*
Florida State College at
Jacksonville *C, A*
Gulf Coast Community College *A*
Herzing University *A*
Indian River State College *A*
Lake City Community College *A*
Northwest Florida State College *C, A*
Palm Beach Community College *A*
Pasco-Hernando Community
College *C, A*
Pensacola Junior College *A*
Polk State College *A*
Saint Johns River Community
College *A*
St. Petersburg College *A*
Seminole Community College *A*
South Florida Community
College *A*
Southwest Florida College *A*
State College of Florida,
Manatee-Sarasota *C, A*
Tallahassee Community College *C, A*
Valencia Community College *C, A*

Georgia

Abraham Baldwin Agricultural
College *C*
Ashworth College *C*
Athens Technical College *C, A*
Clayton State University *B*
DeKalb Technical College *A*
Gwinnett Technical College *A*
Herzing University *A, B*
Macon State College *A, B*
Middle Georgia College *A*
Savannah Technical College *A*
Waycross College *A*

Idaho

North Idaho College *A*

Illinois

Black Hawk College *C, A*
Black Hawk College: East Campus *A*
City Colleges of Chicago
Olive-Harvey College *C, A*
Danville Area Community
College *C, A*
DePaul University *B, M*
Harper College *C, A*
Heartland Community College *C*
Illinois Central College *A*
Illinois Valley Community College *C*
Joliet Junior College *A*
Lincoln Land Community College *C, A*
Morton College *C*
Northwestern College *A*
Olivet Nazarene University *B*
Prairie State College *A*
Richland Community College *A*
Rock Valley College *C*
Sauk Valley Community College *C, A*
South Suburban College of Cook
County *C*
Southwestern Illinois College *A*
Triton College *C*
University of Illinois
Urbana-Champaign *B, M, D*
Waubonsee Community College *C, A*

Indiana

Indiana University
East *A*
South Bend *A*
Southeast *A*
Purdue University
Calumet *B*
Valparaiso University *C*
Vincennes University *A*

Iowa

Ellsworth Community College *A*
Grand View University *B*
Iowa Western Community College *A*
Kaplan University
Davenport *C*
Morningside College *B*
Southeastern Community College
North Campus *A*
Vatterott College *C, A*

Kansas

Donnelly College *C, A*
Kansas State University *A, M*
Labette Community College *A*
Seward County Community
College *C, A*
Southwestern College *B*

Kentucky

Big Sandy Community and Technical
College *C, A*

Louisiana

Herzing University *A, B*

Maine

Andover College *C, A*
Eastern Maine Community College *C*
Husson University *A, B*
Northern Maine Community
College *A*
University of Southern Maine *B*

Maryland

Cecil College *C, A*
College of Southern Maryland *A*
Hagerstown Community College *C*
Montgomery College *C, A*
Prince George's Community
College *C, A*
Stevenson University *B, M*
University of Maryland
University College *C, M*

Massachusetts

Benjamin Franklin Institute of
Technology *A*
Berkshire Community College *C*
Bristol Community College *C, A*
Bunker Hill Community College *C*
Fitchburg State College *C*
Massasoit Community College *A*
North Shore Community College *C, A*
Northern Essex Community
College *C, A*
Quinsigamond Community College *A*
Tufts University *B*

Michigan

Baker College
of Auburn Hills *A*
of Cadillac *A*
of Clinton Township *A*
of Flint *A*
of Jackson *A*
of Muskegon *A*
of Owosso *A*
of Port Huron *A*
Calvin College *B*
Delta College *A*
Gogebic Community College *A*
Grand Rapids Community
College *C, A*
Grand Valley State University *B*
Jackson Community College *C, A*
Kalamazoo Valley Community
College *A*
Kellogg Community College *C, A*
Lake Michigan College *C, A*
Lansing Community College *A*
Macomb Community College *C, A*
Monroe County Community
College *A*
Mott Community College *C*
Oakland Community College *C, A*
Schoolcraft College *C, A*
Southwestern Michigan College *A*
University of Michigan
Dearborn *B*
Washtenaw Community College *C, A*

Minnesota

Academy College *A*
Alexandria Technical College *C, A*
Anoka-Ramsey Community College *C*
Central Lakes College *A*
Dakota County Technical College *C, A*
Globe University *C, A*
Hennepin Technical College *C, A*
Inver Hills Community College *A*
Lake Superior College *C, A*
Mesabi Range Community and
Technical College *C, A*
Minneapolis Community and
Technical College *C, A*
Minnesota School of Business *C, A*
Minnesota School of Business:
Blaine *C, A*

Minnesota State College - Southeast
Technical *A*
Minnesota State Community and
Technical College *C, A*
National American University
Bloomington *A, B*
Pine Technical College *A*
St. Cloud Technical College *A*
St. Paul College *A*
Winona State University *B*

Mississippi
East Central Community College *A*
East Mississippi Community
College *A*
Holmes Community College *A*
Meridian Community College *A*
Mississippi Delta Community
College *A*
Northwest Mississippi Community
College *A*

Missouri
Hickey College *A*
Linn State Technical College *A*
Mineral Area College *A*
Missouri Southern State
University *A, B*
Missouri Technical School *C, A, B*
St. Charles Community College *C, A*
St. Louis Community College
St. Louis Community College at
Florissant Valley *A*
Southeast Missouri State University *B*
State Fair Community College *A*
Vatterott College *C, A*

Montana
Helena College of Technology of the
University of Montana *C, A*
University of Great Falls *B*

Nebraska
Northeast Community College *A*
Peru State College *B*
Western Nebraska Community
College *A*

Nevada
College of Southern Nevada *A*
Truckee Meadows Community
College *A*

New Hampshire
Daniel Webster College *C*
Lakes Region Community
College *C, A*

New Jersey
Atlantic Cape Community College *A*
Bloomfield College *C*
Essex County College *A*
Fairleigh Dickinson University
Metropolitan Campus *C*
Middlesex County College *A*
Ocean County College *C*
Saint Peter's College *C, A, B*

New Mexico
Clovis Community College *A*
New Mexico Junior College *A*
New Mexico State University
Grants *A*

New York
ASA Institute of Business and
Computer Technology *C, A*
Adirondack Community College *A*
Bramson ORT College *A*
Briarcliffe College *A, B*
Cayuga County Community College *C*

City University of New York
Borough of Manhattan Community
College *A*
College of Staten Island *A*
LaGuardia Community College *A*
Medgar Evers College *A*
Queensborough Community
College *C, A*
College of Westchester *C, A*
Corning Community College *A*
Dutchess Community College *C*
Excelsior College *A*
Finger Lakes Community College *A*
Globe Institute of Technology *C, A, B*
Ithaca College *B*
Jamestown Community College *A*
Marist College *C, B*
Mohawk Valley Community College *A*
Monroe Community College *A*
Nassau Community College *A*
Pace University *C*
Rockland Community College *A*
Schenectady County Community
College *A*
State University of New York
College at Buffalo *B*
College of Agriculture and
Technology at Morrisville *A*
Farmingdale *C, A, B*
Utica School of Commerce *A*
Wood Tobe-Coburn School *A*

North Carolina
Beaufort County Community
College *C, A*
Belmont Abbey College *B*
Bladen Community College *C, A*
Blue Ridge Community College *A*
Brunswick Community College *C, A*
Caldwell Community College and
Technical Institute *A*
Catawba Valley Community College *A*
Central Carolina Community
College *A*
Central Piedmont Community
College *C, A*
Cleveland Community College *C, A*
College of the Albemarle *A*
Davidson County Community
College *A*
Durham Technical Community
College *C, A*
Fayetteville Technical Community
College *C, A*
Gaston College *C, A*
Isothermal Community College *C, A*
Johnston Community College *A*
Lenoir Community College *A*
Mayland Community College *C*
McDowell Technical Community
College *A*
Mitchell Community College *C, A*
Piedmont Community College *A*
Rowan-Cabarrus Community
College *C, A*
Sandhills Community College *C, A*
South Piedmont Community
College *C*
Southwestern Community
College *C, A*
Wake Technical Community
College *C, A*
Wilkes Community College *C, A*
Wilson Community College *C, A*

North Dakota
Minot State University *C*

Ohio
Belmont Technical College *A*
Bowling Green State University:
Firelands College *A*
Bradford School *C, A*
Cincinnati Christian University *B*

Cleveland Institute of Electronics *C, A*
Columbus State Community
College *C, A*
Edison State Community College *C, A*
Hocking College *A*
James A. Rhodes State College *C, A*
Marion Technical College *A*
Mount Union College *B*
North Central State College *A*
Northwest State Community
College *A*
Ohio Business College: Sandusky *A*
Southern State Community College *A*
Stark State College of Technology *A*
Terra State Community College *A*
Tiffin University *A*
University of Cincinnati
Clermont College *A*
University of Toledo *A*
Washington State Community
College *A*
Youngstown State University *A, B, M*

Oklahoma
Eastern Oklahoma State College *A*
Northeastern Oklahoma Agricultural
and Mechanical College *C, A*
Northwestern Oklahoma State
University *A*
Oklahoma Christian University *B*
Oklahoma City Community College *A*
Oklahoma State University
Institute of Technology:
Okmulgee *A*
Tulsa Community College *C, A*
Vatterott College *A*
Vatterott College
Tulsa *C*
Western Oklahoma State College *A*

Oregon
Chemeketa Community College *C*
Eastern Oregon University *C*
Lane Community College *C, A*
Southern Oregon University *B*

Pennsylvania
Arcadia University *B*
Bucks County Community
College *C, A*
CHI Institute: Broomall *C*
CHI Institute: Franklin Mills *C, A*
Community College of Philadelphia *A*
Delaware Valley College *C, A*
Duquesne University *B*
Erie Business Center *A*
Gannon University *B*
Gwynedd-Mercy College *A*
Kaplan Career Institute: Pittsburgh *A*
Keystone College *A*
Keystone Technical Institute *C*
La Salle University *A, B*
Lehigh Carbon Community
College *C, A*
Metropolitan Career Center Computer
Technology Institute *A*
Montgomery County Community
College *C*
Northampton Community
College *C, A*
Reading Area Community College *A*
St. Francis University *B*
Westminster College *B*
Westmoreland County Community
College *A*

Puerto Rico
American University of Puerto Rico *A*
Columbia College
Columbia Centro Universitario:
Yauco *A*
National College of Business and
Technology: Bayamon *A, B*

Pontifical Catholic University of
Puerto Rico *A*
Universidad Metropolitana *C*

Rhode Island
Johnson & Wales University:
Providence *A*
New England Institute of
Technology *A*

South Carolina
Aiken Technical College *C*
Central Carolina Technical College *A*
Clemson University *M*
Greenville Technical College *C*
Limestone College *A, B*
Orangeburg-Calhoun Technical
College *A*
Technical College of the
Lowcountry *C, A*
Tri-County Technical College *A*
Trident Technical College *A*
York Technical College *A*

South Dakota
Dakota State University *C, A*
Lake Area Technical Institute *A*
Mount Marty College *B*
National American University
Rapid City *A, B*
Southeast Technical Institute *A*

Tennessee
Northeast State Community College *C*
Southern Adventist University *B*

Texas
Alvin Community College *C, A*
Amarillo College *C, A*
Austin Community College *C, A*
Brazosport College *C, A*
Brookhaven College *C, A*
Cedar Valley College *C, A*
Central Texas College *C, A*
Coastal Bend College *C, A*
College of the Mainland *A*
Collin County Community College
District *C, A*
Eastfield College *C, A*
El Centro College *C, A*
El Paso Community College *A*
Galveston College *C, A*
Grayson County College *A*
Hardin-Simmons University *B*
Hill College *A*
Houston Community College
System *A*
Kilgore College *A*
Lamar State College at Orange *A*
Laredo Community College *A*
Lee College *A*
McLennan Community College *A*
Midland College *A*
Mountain View College *C, A*
North Lake College *C, A*
Northeast Texas Community
College *C, A*
Northwest Vista College *C, A*
Odessa College *C, A*
Palo Alto College *A*
St. Philip's College *C, A*
San Antonio College *C, A*
San Jacinto College *C, A*
Tarrant County College *C, A*
Temple College *C, A*
Texas State Technical College
Harlingen *A*
Waco *A*
West Texas *A*
Texas State University: San Marcos *M*
Trinity Valley Community
College *C, A*
Victoria College *C, A*

Weatherford College A
Western Texas College A
Wharton County Junior College C

Utah

Provo College A
Stevens-Henager College: Logan A
Utah Valley University C

Vermont

Vermont Technical College A, B

Virginia

Blue Ridge Community College A
Danville Community College A
ECPI College of Technology: Virginia
    Beach C, A
ECPI Technical College: Roanoke A
J. Sargeant Reynolds Community
    College C, A
John Tyler Community College A
New River Community College A
Northern Virginia Community
    College A
Patrick Henry Community College A
Thomas Nelson Community
    College C, A

Washington

Bates Technical College C, A
Bellevue College C, A
Big Bend Community College A
Cascadia Community College C
Centralia College A
City University of Seattle C, B
Clark College A
Clover Park Technical College C, A
DigiPen Institute of Technology B, M
Everett Community College C, A
Lower Columbia College A
Olympic College A
Pierce College C, A
Renton Technical College A
Skagit Valley College A
South Seattle Community
    College C, A
Walla Walla University A

West Virginia

Huntington Junior College A
Potomac State College of West
    Virginia University A
West Virginia Northern Community
    College A
West Virginia University Institute of
    Technology B

Wisconsin

Chippewa Valley Technical College A
Gateway Technical College A
Herzing University A, B
Mid-State Technical College A
Milwaukee Area Technical College A
Nicolet Area Technical College A
Northcentral Technical College A
Northeast Wisconsin Technical
    College A
Southwest Wisconsin Technical
    College A
Waukesha County Technical
    College C, A
Wisconsin Indianhead Technical
    College A

Wyoming

Casper College A
Laramie County Community
    College C, A

Computer programming, specific applications

Alabama

Calhoun Community College A
Gadsden State Community College C
Northwest-Shoals Community
    College C, A

Alaska

University of Alaska
    Southeast C

Arizona

Central Arizona College C, A
Collins College A
Estrella Mountain Community
    College C, A
GateWay Community College C
Mesa Community College A

Arkansas

National Park Community
    College C, A
South Arkansas Community College A

California

Bakersfield College A
Barstow Community College A
Butte College C, A
Canada College A
Cerritos College A
Chabot College A
Chaffey College C, A
City College of San Francisco C
College of the Siskiyous C, A
Contra Costa College A
De Anza College C, A
El Camino College: Compton
    Center A
Evergreen Valley College A
Fullerton College A
Grossmont College C, A
Irvine Valley College C, A
Lassen Community College A
Long Beach City College C, A
Los Angeles City College A
Los Angeles Harbor College C, A
Los Angeles Pierce College A
Los Angeles Southwest College A
Los Angeles Valley College C, A
Mission College A
Moorpark College A
Mount San Antonio College C
Pasadena City College A
Saddleback College C
San Diego City College C, A
San Jose City College C, A
Southwestern College C, A
West Hills College: Coalinga C, A
Westwood College of Technology
    Westwood College: Inland
        Empire A

Colorado

Colorado Mountain College A
Community College of Denver C, A
Westwood College: Denver North A

Connecticut

Asnuntuck Community College C
Capital Community College C
Norwalk Community College C, A
Quinnipiac University B
Three Rivers Community College C, A
Tunxis Community College C, A

Delaware

Delaware Technical and Community
    College
    Terry C

Florida

Daytona State College A
Edison State College C
Florida State College at Jacksonville A
Gulf Coast Community College A
Hillsborough Community
    College C, A
Indian River State College A
Lake-Sumter Community College A
Miami Dade College C, A
Palm Beach Community College A
Seminole Community College A

Georgia

Abraham Baldwin Agricultural
    College A
Athens Technical College C, A
Augusta Technical College C, A
Chattahoochee Technical
    College C, A
Dalton State College C, A
Macon State College A, B
Middle Georgia College A
Southern Polytechnic State
    University B

Idaho

Idaho State University C, A
North Idaho College A

Illinois

College of DuPage C, A
Danville Area Community College A
DePaul University B, M
Harper College C, A
Illinois Central College C, A
Illinois Valley Community College A
John Wood Community College C, A
Judson University C
Kishwaukee College A
Lincoln Land Community College A
McHenry County College C, A
Moraine Valley Community College C
National-Louis University C
Northwestern College A
Parkland College C, A
Prairie State College C, A
Rend Lake College A
Southwestern Illinois College C, A
Waubonsee Community College C
Wilbur Wright College C, A

Indiana

Indiana Wesleyan University B
Kaplan College: Indianapolis A
Purdue University
    North Central A, B

Iowa

Clinton Community College C, A
Des Moines Area Community
    College C
Indian Hills Community College C, A
Iowa Lakes Community College A
Kirkwood Community College A
Muscatine Community College C, A
Northeast Iowa Community
    College A
Scott Community College C, A
Southeastern Community College
    North Campus C
Southwestern Community College A

Kansas

Central Christian College of Kansas A
Johnson County Community
    College C, A
Seward County Community
    College C, A

Kentucky

Sullivan University C, A, B, M

Louisiana

West Kentucky Community and
    Technical College A

Louisiana

Southern University
    Shreveport A

Maine

Husson University B
Northern Maine Community
    College A
University of Southern Maine B

Maryland

Cecil College C, A
Community College of Baltimore
    County C
Frederick Community College C, A
Harford Community College C
University of Maryland
    University College C

Massachusetts

Bristol Community College C
Bunker Hill Community College C, A
Cape Cod Community College A
Holyoke Community College A
Quinsigamond Community College A
Roxbury Community College A
Springfield Technical Community
    College C, A

Michigan

Baker College
    of Cadillac A
    of Muskegon A
    of Port Huron A
Bay de Noc Community College A
Jackson Community College C, A
Lansing Community College A
Mid Michigan Community College A
Monroe County Community
    College C, A
Mott Community College C
Schoolcraft College A
Washtenaw Community College C, A
Wayne County Community College A

Minnesota

Dunwoody College of
    Technology C, A
Globe University C, A
Hennepin Technical College C, A
Minneapolis Business College A
Minneapolis Community and
    Technical College C
Minnesota State College - Southeast
    Technical C
North Hennepin Community
    College C
Ridgewater College C
St. Paul College A
Winona State University B

Mississippi

East Central Community College A
Northwest Mississippi Community
    College A
Pearl River Community College A

Missouri

Metropolitan Community College:
    Longview C, A
Metropolitan Community College:
    Maple Woods C, A
St. Louis Community College
    St. Louis Community College at
        Florissant Valley A
    St. Louis Community College at
        Meramec C, A
State Fair Community College A
Vatterott College: Sunset Hills C

Montana

University of Great Falls *B*

New Hampshire

Daniel Webster College *C*
Nashua Community College *A*

New Jersey

Bergen Community College *A*
Burlington County College *C*
Camden County College *C*
Middlesex County College *C*
Passaic County Community
   College *C, A*
Sussex County Community College *A*

New Mexico

New Mexico Junior College *A*
New Mexico State University
   Carlsbad *C*
Northern New Mexico College *C*

New York

Bramson ORT College *A*
College of Westchester *C, A*
Columbia-Greene Community
   College *C, A*
Globe Institute of Technology *C, A, B*
State University of New York
   College of Agriculture and
      Technology at Morrisville *A*
   Farmingdale *C*

North Carolina

Asheville-Buncombe Technical
   Community College *A*
Beaufort County Community
   College *C, A*
Bladen Community College *C, A*
Caldwell Community College and
   Technical Institute *C, A*
Campbell University *A*
Central Carolina Community
   College *A*
Cleveland Community College *C, A*
College of the Albemarle *A*
Durham Technical Community
   College *C, A*
Forsyth Technical Community
   College *A*
Gaston College *A*
Haywood Community College *C, A*
Isothermal Community College *C, A*
King's College *A*
McDowell Technical Community
   College *A*
Piedmont Community College *A*
Pitt Community College *C, A*
Sampson Community College *A*
Sandhills Community College *A*
South Piedmont Community
   College *C*
Surry Community College *C*
Wake Technical Community
   College *C, A*

North Dakota

Cankdeska Cikana Community
   College *C, A*
North Dakota State College of
   Science *A*
Sitting Bull College *A*

Ohio

Central Ohio Technical College *A*
Cincinnati State Technical and
   Community College *A*
Clark State Community College *C, A*
Columbus State Community
   College *A*
Eastern Gateway Community
   College *C, A*

James A. Rhodes State College *C*
Kent State University *C*
Kent State University
   Ashtabula *A*
   East Liverpool *A*
   Salem *A*
   Trumbull *C, A*
   Tuscarawas *A*
Marion Technical College *A*
North Central State College *A*
Owens Community College
   Toledo *C, A*
Southern State Community College *A*
Stark State College of Technology *A*
University of Akron: Wayne College *A*
University of Cincinnati
   Clermont College *A*
University of Northwestern Ohio *C, A*
University of Rio Grande *B*

Oklahoma

Oklahoma Baptist University *B*
Oklahoma State University
   Institute of Technology:
      Okmulgee *A*
   Oklahoma City *A*
Tulsa Community College *A*

Oregon

Art Institute of Portland *B*
Chemeketa Community College *C*
Clackamas Community College *C, A*
Clatsop Community College *A*
Lane Community College *A*
Linn-Benton Community College *A*
Portland Community College *C, A*
Southwestern Oregon Community
   College *C, A*

Pennsylvania

Butler County Community College *A*
Community College of Beaver
   County *A*
Community College of Philadelphia *A*
Grove City College *B*
Kaplan Career Institute: Pittsburgh *A*
La Salle University *B, M*
Luzerne County Community
   College *C, A*
Manor College *A*
Mount Aloysius College *A*
University of Pittsburgh
   Bradford *B*
Westmoreland County Community
   College *C*

Puerto Rico

Universidad del Este *A*

Rhode Island

Community College of Rhode
   Island *C, A*

South Carolina

York Technical College *A*

South Dakota

Southeast Technical Institute *A*

Tennessee

Southwest Tennessee Community
   College *C*

Texas

Blinn College *C*
Eastfield College *A*
Hill College *A*
Houston Community College
   System *A*
North Lake College *A*
Richland College *C, A*
South Texas College *A*

Tyler Junior College *A*

Utah

Weber State University *C*

Virginia

ECPI College of Technology: Virginia
   Beach *C, A*
ECPI Technical College: Roanoke *A*

Washington

Olympic College *C*
Peninsula College *A*
Renton Technical College *C, A*
Skagit Valley College *A*
South Puget Sound Community
   College *C, A*
Spokane Community College *C, A*
Spokane Falls Community College *C*
University of Washington Bothell *B*

West Virginia

Mountain State College *A*
New River Community and Technical
   College *C*
Potomac State College of West
   Virginia University *A*
Shepherd University *B*

Wisconsin

Chippewa Valley Technical College *A*
Fox Valley Technical College *A*
Herzing University *A, B*
Moraine Park Technical College *C, A*
Western Technical College *A*

Wyoming

Casper College *A*

Computer science

Alabama

Alabama State University *B*
Bevill State Community College *A*
Birmingham-Southern College *B*
Faulkner University *B*
Gadsden State Community College *A*
Lawson State Community
   College *C, A*
Northeast Alabama Community
   College *C, A*
Oakwood University *B*
Samford University *B*

Alaska

University of Alaska
   Anchorage *B*
   Fairbanks *B, M*

Arizona

Arizona State University *B, M, D*
Brown Mackie College: Tucson *B*
Chandler-Gilbert Community College
   Pecos *A*
Cochise College *A*
Dine College *A*
GateWay Community College *A*
Mesa Community College *A*
Mohave Community College *C*
Northern Arizona University *B, M*
Paradise Valley Community College *C*

Arkansas

Harding University *B*
Hendrix College *B*
John Brown University *B*
Lyon College *B*
Ouachita Baptist University *B*
Philander Smith College *B*
Phillips Community College of the
   University of Arkansas *A*

South Arkansas Community
   College *C, A*
Southern Arkansas University
   Tech *C, A*
University of Central Arkansas *M*

California

Allan Hancock College *A*
Antelope Valley College *C, A*
Azusa Pacific University *B*
Bakersfield College *C*
Biola University *B*
California College San Diego *B*
California Institute of
   Technology *B, M, D*
California Lutheran University *B*
California National University for
   Advanced Studies *B*
California Polytechnic State
   University: San Luis Obispo *B, M*
California State Polytechnic
   University: Pomona *B, M*
California State University
   Bakersfield *B*
   Chico *B, M*
   Dominguez Hills *B, M*
   East Bay *B, M*
   Fresno *B, M*
   Fullerton *B, M*
   Long Beach *B, M*
   Monterey Bay *B*
   San Bernardino *B, M*
   San Marcos *B, M*
   Stanislaus *B*
Chabot College *A*
Chapman University *B*
City College of San Francisco *A*
Claremont McKenna College *B*
College of Marin: Kentfield *A*
College of the Canyons *A*
College of the Desert *A*
College of the Sequoias *C, A*
College of the Siskiyous *C, A*
Columbia College *C*
Copper Mountain College *C, A*
Cuesta College *C, A*
De Anza College *A*
Diablo Valley College *C, A*
El Camino College *C, A*
Foothill College *C, A*
Fresno City College *C, A*
Fresno Pacific University *B*
Golden West College *C*
Grossmont College *C, A*
Imperial Valley College *A*
La Sierra University *B*
Lake Tahoe Community College *C*
Los Angeles Pierce College *C, A*
Los Angeles Southwest College *C, A*
Los Angeles Trade and Technical
   College *C, A*
Los Medanos College *C*
Loyola Marymount University *M*
Mills College *B, M*
MiraCosta College *A*
Mission College *A*
Modesto Junior College *A*
Napa Valley College *C*
National University *B, M*
Pacific States University *M*
Pacific Union College *B*
Palomar College *C, A*
Point Loma Nazarene University *B*
Pomona College *B*
Reedley College *A*
Saddleback College *A*
San Bernardino Valley College *C, A*
San Diego State University *B, M*
San Francisco State University *B, M*
San Joaquin Delta College *C, A*
San Jose State University *B, M*
Santa Ana College *C, A*
Santa Barbara City College *C, A*
Santa Monica College *C*

Santa Rosa Junior College *C, A*
Santiago Canyon College *A*
Scripps College *B*
Silicon Valley University *B, M*
Skyline College *A*
Sonoma State University *B*
Southwestern College *C, A*
Stanford University *B, M, D*
Taft College *A*
University of California
  Berkeley *B, M, D*
  Davis *B, M, D*
  Irvine *B, M, D*
  Riverside *B, M, D*
  San Diego *B, M, D*
University of San Diego *B*
University of Southern
  California *B, M, D*
University of the Pacific *B*
Westmont College *B*
Yuba Community College
  District *C, A*

Colorado

American Sentinel University *A, B, M*
CollegeAmerica
  Denver *B*
Colorado College *B*
Colorado School of Mines *B*
Colorado Technical
  University *B, M, D*
Jones International University *B*
Lamar Community College *A*
Metropolitan State College of
  Denver *B*
Pikes Peak Community College *A*
Regis University *B*
Trinidad State Junior College *A*
United States Air Force Academy *B*
University of Colorado
  Boulder *B, M, D*
University of Denver *B, M, D*

Connecticut

Connecticut College *B*
Gateway Community College *C, A*
Quinnipiac University *B, M*
Sacred Heart University *B, M*
Trinity College *B*
University of Connecticut *B*
University of New Haven *A*

Delaware

Delaware State University *B*

District of Columbia

American University *B, M*
Gallaudet University *B*
Georgetown University *B*
Howard University *M*
University of the District of
  Columbia *B, M*

Florida

Barry University *B*
Bethune-Cookman University *B*
Broward College *A*
Chipola College *A*
Edward Waters College *B*
Embry-Riddle Aeronautical
  University *B*
Florida Institute of
  Technology *B, M, D*
Florida Memorial University *B*
Florida State University *B, M, D*
Gulf Coast Community College *A*
Nova Southeastern University *B, M, D*
Pensacola Junior College *A*
Saint Thomas University *B*
Seminole Community College *A*
Stetson University *B*
University of Miami *B, M, D*
Valencia Community College *A*

Georgia

Abraham Baldwin Agricultural
  College *A*
Andrew College *A*
Atlanta Metropolitan College *A*
Berry College *B*
Clark Atlanta University *B, M*
College of Coastal Georgia *A*
Darton College *A*
East Georgia College *A*
Emory University *B, D*
Georgia Institute of Technology *D*
Georgia Perimeter College *A*
Georgia Southwestern State
  University *B, M*
Georgia State University *B, M, D*
Gordon College *A*
Kennesaw State University *M*
LaGrange College *B*
Macon State College *A*
Mercer University *B*
Middle Georgia College *A*
Savannah State University *B*
South Georgia College *A*
Southern Polytechnic State
  University *B, M*
University of Georgia *B, M, D*
University of West Georgia *M*

Hawaii

Chaminade University of Honolulu *B*
Hawaii Pacific University *B*
University of Hawaii
  Manoa *B, M, D*

Idaho

Boise State University *B, M*
Brigham Young University-Idaho *B*
Lewis-Clark State College *B*
Northwest Nazarene University *B*
University of Idaho *B, M, D*

Illinois

Augustana College *B*
Aurora University *B*
Benedictine University *B*
Blackburn College *B*
Bradley University *B, M*
Concordia University Chicago *B*
DePaul University *B, M, D*
Dominican University *B*
Elmhurst College *B*
Eureka College *B*
Governors State University *B, M*
Harper College *A*
Illinois College *B*
Illinois Institute of
  Technology *B, M, D*
Illinois State University *B*
Knox College *B*
Lake Forest College *B*
Lewis University *B*
Lewis and Clark Community
  College *A*
Lincoln College *A*
Loyola University Chicago *M*
MacCormac College *C, A*
MacMurray College *B*
McKendree University *B*
Monmouth College *B*
Northeastern Illinois University *B, M*
Northern Illinois University *B, M*
Northwestern University *B, M, D*
Olivet Nazarene University *B*
Principia College *B*
Quincy University *B*
Richland Community College *A*
Rockford College *B*
Roosevelt University *C, B, M*
Saint Xavier University *B*
Southern Illinois University
  Carbondale *B, M*

Southern Illinois University
  Edwardsville *B, M*
Southwestern Illinois College *C, A*
Trinity Christian College *B*
University of Chicago *M, D*
University of Illinois
  Chicago *B, M, D*
  Springfield *B, M*
  Urbana-Champaign *B, M, D*
University of St. Francis *B*
Vatterott College: Quincy *A*
Wheaton College *B*

Indiana

Anderson University *B*
DePauw University *B*
Franklin College *B*
Goshen College *B*
Huntington University *B*
Indiana Institute of Technology *B*
Indiana University-Purdue University
  Fort Wayne *B*
Indiana Wesleyan University *B*
Manchester College *A, B*
Purdue University *C, B, M, D*
Purdue University
  Calumet *B*
Rose-Hulman Institute of
  Technology *B*
Trine University *B*
University of Indianapolis *B*
Valparaiso University *B*
Vincennes University *A*

Iowa

Briar Cliff University *B*
Buena Vista University *B*
Coe College *B*
Cornell College *B*
Dordt College *B*
Drake University *B*
Ellsworth Community College *A*
Grinnell College *B*
Iowa Wesleyan College *B*
Loras College *B*
Luther College *B*
Maharishi University of
  Management *B, M*
Mount Mercy College *B*
Northwestern College *B*
St. Ambrose University *B*
Simpson College *B*
University of Iowa *B*
University of Northern Iowa *B, M*

Kansas

Allen County Community College *A*
Baker University *B*
Barton County Community College *A*
Benedictine College *B*
Butler Community College *A*
Dodge City Community College *A*
Garden City Community College *A*
Kansas Wesleyan University *A, B*
MidAmerica Nazarene University *B*
Seward County Community College *A*
Southwestern College *B*
Wichita State University *B, M*

Kentucky

Bellarmine University *B*
Centre College *B*
Eastern Kentucky University *B, M*
National College
  Danville *A*
  Florence *A*
  Lexington *A*
  Louisville *A*
  Richmond *A*
Northern Kentucky University *M*

Louisiana

Dillard University *B*

Grambling State University *B*
Louisiana State University
  Shreveport *B*
Louisiana State University and
  Agricultural and Mechanical
  College *B, D*
Louisiana Tech University *B, M*
McNeese State University *B*
Nicholls State University *B*
Nunez Community College *A*
Southeastern Louisiana University *B*
Southern University
  Shreveport *A*
Southern University and Agricultural
  and Mechanical College *B, M*
University of Louisiana at
  Lafayette *B, M, D*
University of Louisiana at Monroe *B*
University of New Orleans *B, M*
Xavier University of Louisiana *B*

Maine

Andover College *A*
Bowdoin College *B*
Colby College *B*
Thomas College *B*
University of Maine
  Farmington *B*
  Fort Kent *A*
University of Southern Maine *B, M*

Maryland

Allegany College of Maryland *A*
Baltimore City Community College *A*
Bowie State University *B, M*
Capitol College *B, M*
College of Notre Dame of Maryland *B*
Coppin State University *B*
Frederick Community College *A*
Goucher College *B*
Harford Community College *A*
Hood College *B, M*
Howard Community College *A*
Loyola University Maryland *M*
Montgomery College *A*
Morgan State University *B*
Prince George's Community
  College *A*
Towson University *B, M*
Washington Adventist University *A, B*
Washington College *B*

Massachusetts

American International College *B*
Amherst College *B*
Bard College at Simon's Rock *B*
Boston College *B*
Brandeis University *B, M, D*
Bridgewater State College *B, M*
Bristol Community College *A*
Bunker Hill Community College *A*
Cape Cod Community College *A*
Clark University *B*
Endicott College *B*
Fitchburg State College *B, M*
Gordon College *B*
Hampshire College *B*
Harvard College *B, M, D*
Massachusetts Bay Community
  College *A*
Massachusetts Institute of
  Technology *B, M, D*
Merrimack College *B*
Middlesex Community College *A*
Mount Holyoke College *B*
Newbury College *B*
North Shore Community College *A*
Northeastern University *B*
Northern Essex Community
  College *C, A*
Quincy College *C, A*
Regis College *B*
Smith College *B*

Springfield Technical Community
College *A*
Stonehill College *B*
Suffolk University *B, M*
Tufts University *B*
University of Massachusetts
Amherst *B, M, D*
Boston *M, D*
Lowell *B, M, D*
Wellesley College *B*
Wentworth Institute of Technology *B*
Western New England College *B*
Westfield State College *B*
Wheaton College *B*
Williams College *B*
Worcester Polytechnic
Institute *B, M, D*

Michigan

Albion College *B*
Alma College *B*
Baker College
of Cadillac *A*
of Clinton Township *A*
of Flint *A*
of Muskegon *B*
of Owosso *A, B*
of Port Huron *A, B*
Bay Mills Community College *A*
Calvin College *B*
Central Michigan University *B, M*
Delta College *A*
Eastern Michigan University *B, M*
Grand Valley State University *B*
Hillsdale College *B*
Kettering University *B*
Lawrence Technological
University *B, M*
Madonna University *C, A, B*
Mid Michigan Community College *A*
Mott Community College *C*
Spring Arbor University *B*
University of Detroit Mercy *B, M*
University of Michigan
Flint *B, M*
Washtenaw Community College *C, A*
Western Michigan University *B, M, D*

Minnesota

Academy College *B*
Anoka-Ramsey Community College *A*
Augsburg College *B*
Bemidji State University *B*
Carleton College *B*
Century Community and Technical
College *A*
College of St. Benedict *B*
Concordia College: Moorhead *B*
Gustavus Adolphus College *B*
Inver Hills Community College *A*
Metropolitan State University *B*
Minnesota State University
Mankato *B, M*
Moorhead *B*
Normandale Community College *A*
North Hennepin Community
College *A*
Ridgewater College *A*
Rochester Community and Technical
College *A*
Saint Cloud State University *B, M*
St. John's University *B*
St. Mary's University of Minnesota *B*
St. Olaf College *B*
St. Paul College *A*
University of Minnesota
Duluth *B, M*
Morris *B*
Twin Cities *C, B*
University of St. Thomas *B*
Walden University *M*
Winona State University *B*

Mississippi

Belhaven University *B*
Holmes Community College *A*
Millsaps College *B*
Mississippi College *B, M*
Rust College *B*

Missouri

Central Methodist University *A, B*
College of the Ozarks *B*
Columbia College *B*
Drury University *B*
Grantham University *A, B*
Lindenwood University *B*
Maryville University of Saint
Louis *C, B*
Metropolitan Community College:
Blue River *A*
Missouri Southern State University *B*
Missouri State University *B, M*
Missouri Technical School *C, B*
Park University *A, B*
Southwest Baptist University *A, B*
Truman State University *B*
University of Missouri
Columbia *B, M, D*
Kansas City *B, M*
Missouri University of Science and
Technology *B, M, D*
Washington University in St.
Louis *B, M, D*
Webster University *B*

Montana

Montana State University
Bozeman *B, M, D*
Montana Tech of the University of
Montana *B*
Rocky Mountain College *B*
University of Great Falls *B*
University of Montana *B, M*

Nebraska

Concordia University *B*
Creighton University *A, B*
Doane College *B*
Nebraska Wesleyan University *B*
Northeast Community College *A*
Peru State College *B*
Union College *B*
University of Nebraska
Omaha *B, M*
Western Nebraska Community
College *A*

Nevada

Nevada State College *B*
Sierra Nevada College *B*
University of Nevada
Las Vegas *B, M, D*
Reno *B, M*

New Hampshire

Daniel Webster College *B*
Dartmouth College *B, M, D*
Lebanon College *A*
Nashua Community College *C, A*
Plymouth State University *B*
Rivier College *C, A, B, M*
Saint Anselm College *B*
University of New Hampshire *M, D*

New Jersey

Burlington County College *A*
Caldwell College *B*
College of St. Elizabeth *B*
Cumberland County College *A*
Drew University *B*
Fairleigh Dickinson University
Metropolitan Campus *B, M*
Felician College *B*
Gloucester County College *A*

Hudson County Community
College *A*
Montclair State University *B, M*
New Jersey Institute of Technology *D*
Ocean County College *A*
Rowan University *B*
Rutgers, The State University of New
Jersey
Camden Regional Campus *B*
New Brunswick/Piscataway
Campus *B*
Newark Regional Campus *B*
Saint Peter's College *B*
Salem Community College *A*
Thomas Edison State College *C, A, B*
Union County College *A*
William Paterson University of New
Jersey *B*

New Mexico

Clovis Community College *A*
Dona Ana Community College of New
Mexico State University *A*
Eastern New Mexico University *B*
New Mexico Highlands
University *B, M*
New Mexico Institute of Mining and
Technology *B, M, D*
New Mexico State University
Alamogordo *C*

New York

Adirondack Community College *A*
Bard College *B*
Barnard College *B*
Canisius College *B*
Cayuga County Community College *A*
City University of New York
Baruch College *B, M*
Bronx Community College *A*
City College *B, M*
College of Staten Island *B, M*
Kingsborough Community
College *A*
LaGuardia Community College *A*
New York City College of
Technology *A*
Queens College *B, M*
York College *B*
Clarkson University *B, M*
Colgate University *B*
College of Westchester *C, A*
Columbia University *B, M, D*
Columbia University
School of General Studies *B*
Columbia-Greene Community
College *A*
Cornell University *B, M, D*
Corning Community College *A*
Dowling College *B*
Dutchess Community College *A*
Finger Lakes Community College *A*
Globe Institute of Technology *C, A, B*
Hobart and William Smith Colleges *B*
Hofstra University *B, M*
Houghton College *B*
Iona College *B, M*
Ithaca College *B*
Jefferson Community College *A*
Long Island University
C. W. Post Campus *B*
Manhattan College *B*
Marist College *B*
Molloy College *B*
Monroe Community College *A*
Nassau Community College *A*
New York Institute of Technology *B*
New York University *B*
Niagara County Community
College *A*
Niagara University *C, B*
Pace University *C, B, M*
Polytechnic Institute of New York
University *B, M, D*

Rensselaer Polytechnic
Institute *B, M, D*
Roberts Wesleyan College *B*
Rochester Institute of
Technology *A, B, M*
Saint Bonaventure University *B*
St. John Fisher College *B*
St. Joseph's College: Suffolk
Campus *B*
St. Lawrence University *B*
Schenectady County Community
College *A*
State University of New York
Binghamton *B, M, D*
Buffalo *B*
College at Brockport *B*
College at Oneonta *B*
College of Agriculture and
Technology at Morrisville *A*
College of Technology at Alfred *A*
Farmingdale *A*
Oswego *B*
Stony Brook *B, M, D*
Suffolk County Community College *A*
Syracuse University *M, D*
Ulster County Community College *A*
University of Rochester *B, M, D*
Wagner College *B*
Wells College *B*
Westchester Community College *A*
Yeshiva University *B*

North Carolina

Appalachian State University *B, M*
Campbell University *B*
East Carolina University *B, M*
Elizabeth City State University *B*
Elon University *B*
Gardner-Webb University *B*
High Point University *B*
Lees-McRae College *B*
Mars Hill College *B*
Meredith College *B*
Methodist University *A, B*
North Carolina Central University *B*
North Carolina State
University *B, M, D*
St. Augustine's College *B*
Sandhills Community College *A*
Shaw University *B*
University of North Carolina
Asheville *B*
Chapel Hill *B, M, D*
Charlotte *B, M*
Greensboro *B, M*
Pembroke *B*
Wilmington *B*
Wake Forest University *B, M*
Western Carolina University *B*
Western Piedmont Community
College *A*
Wingate University *B*
Winston-Salem State University *B*

North Dakota

Dickinson State University *B*
Jamestown College *B*
Lake Region State College *A*
North Dakota State University *B, M, D*
Turtle Mountain Community
College *C, A*
University of North Dakota *D*

Ohio

Ashland University *B*
Baldwin-Wallace College *B*
Capital University *B*
Case Western Reserve University *B*
Cedarville University *B*
Central State University *B*
Eastern Gateway Community
College *A*
Franciscan University of
Steubenville *B*

Franklin University *A, B, M*
Heidelberg University *B*
Hiram College *B*
John Carroll University *B*
Malone University *B*
Marietta College *B*
Mount Vernon Nazarene University *B*
Muskingum University *B*
Ohio Northern University *B*
Ohio State University
    Columbus Campus *B, M, D*
Ohio University *B, M*
Ohio University
    Southern Campus at Ironton *A*
Ohio Wesleyan University *B*
Otterbein College *B*
RETS College *A*
Stark State College of Technology *A*
University of Akron *C, B, M*
University of Dayton *B, M*
University of Findlay *A, B*
University of Rio Grande *A, B*
Virginia Marti College of Art and
    Design *A*
Wilmington College *B*
Wittenberg University *B*
Wright State University *B*
Xavier University *B*
Youngstown State University *C, B*
Zane State College *C, A*

Oklahoma

Cameron University *B*
Carl Albert State College *A*
Eastern Oklahoma State College *A*
Murray State College *A*
Northeastern State University *B*
Oklahoma Baptist University *B*
Oklahoma Christian University *B*
Oklahoma City Community College *A*
Oklahoma City University *B, M*
Oklahoma Wesleyan University *B*
Oral Roberts University *B*
Seminole State College *A*
Southwestern Oklahoma State
    University *B*
University of Oklahoma *B, M, D*
University of Science and Arts of
    Oklahoma *B*
University of Tulsa *B, M, D*
Western Oklahoma State College *A*

Oregon

Central Oregon Community
    College *A*
Eastern Oregon University *B*
Lewis & Clark College *B*
Linfield College *B*
Mt. Hood Community College *A*
Portland State University *B, M, D*
Southern Oregon University *B*
Southwestern Oregon Community
    College *A*
Treasure Valley Community College *A*
University of Portland *B*

Pennsylvania

Allegheny College *B*
Arcadia University *B*
Bloomsburg University of
    Pennsylvania *B*
Bryn Mawr College *B*
Bucks County Community College *A*
CHI Institute: Franklin Mills *C, A*
Carnegie Mellon University *B, D*
Central Pennsylvania College *A, B*
DeSales University *B*
Drexel University *B, M, D*
Duquesne University *B*
Gettysburg College *B*
Harrisburg Area Community
    College *A*
King's College *B*
La Roche College *B*

La Salle University *B, M*
Laurel Business Institute *A*
Lebanon Valley College *B*
Lehigh University *B, M, D*
Lock Haven University of
    Pennsylvania *B*
Mansfield University of
    Pennsylvania *B*
Messiah College *B*
Moravian College *B*
Mount Aloysius College *A*
Northampton Community College *A*
Penn State
    Erie, The Behrend College *B*
    University Park *M, D*
Pennsylvania Institute of
    Technology *A*
St. Francis University *B*
Seton Hill University *C, B*
Slippery Rock University of
    Pennsylvania *B*
South Hills School of Business &
    Technology *C, A*
South Hills School of Business &
    Technology: Altoona *A*
Susquehanna University *B*
University of Pittsburgh *B, M, D*
University of Pittsburgh
    Bradford *B*
University of the Sciences in
    Philadelphia *B*
Ursinus College *B*
Waynesburg University *A, B*
Westminster College *B*
Widener University *B*
York College of Pennsylvania *B*

Puerto Rico

Huertas Junior College *A*
Inter American University of Puerto
    Rico
    Aguadilla Campus *C, A, B*
    Arecibo Campus *A, B*
    Bayamon Campus *C, A, B*
    Ponce Campus *A, B*
    San German Campus *A, B*
Universidad Adventista de las
    Antillas *A, B*
Universidad Metropolitana *A, B*
Universidad Politecnica de Puerto
    Rico *B*
University of Puerto Rico
    Arecibo *A*
    Rio Piedras *B*
University of the Sacred Heart *B*

Rhode Island

Brown University *B, M, D*
New England Institute of
    Technology *A, B*
Providence College *B*
Rhode Island College *B*
Roger Williams University *B*

South Carolina

Benedict College *B*
Bob Jones University *B*
Charleston Southern University *B*
The Citadel *M*
Claflin University *B*
Coker College *B*
College of Charleston *M*
Furman University *B*
Midlands Technical College *C, A*
Presbyterian College *B*
University of South Carolina
    Aiken *B*
Wofford College *B*

South Dakota

Augustana College *B*
Mount Marty College *B*
Sinte Gleska University *B*

South Dakota School of Mines and
    Technology *B, M*
University of Sioux Falls *B*

Tennessee

Belmont University *B*
Bryan College *B*
Christian Brothers University *B*
Fisk University *B*
LeMoyne-Owen College *B*
Lipscomb University *B*
Middle Tennessee State
    University *B, M*
National College of Business &
    Technology
    National College: Bristol *C, A*
Pellissippi State Community
    College *A*
Rhodes College *B*
Southern Adventist University *B*
Tennessee State University *B*
Tennessee Technological University *B*
Tennessee Temple University *B*
Union University *B*
University of Memphis *B, M, D*
University of Tennessee
    Chattanooga *B, M*
    Knoxville *B, M, D*
    Martin *B*
University of the South *B*
Vanderbilt University *B, M, D*

Texas

Abilene Christian University *B*
Austin College *B*
Baylor University *B, M*
Central Texas College *C, A*
Coastal Bend College *A*
Concordia University Texas *B*
Dallas Baptist University *B*
Eastfield College *C, A*
El Paso Community College *A*
Galveston College *A*
Hill College *C, A*
Huston-Tillotson University *B*
Laredo Community College *A*
LeTourneau University *B*
Lon Morris College *A*
Mountain View College *A*
North Lake College *C, A*
Northwest Vista College *A*
Odessa College *A*
Palo Alto College *A*
Rice University *B, M, D*
St. Edward's University *B*
St. Mary's University *B*
South Plains College *A*
South Texas College *A*
Southern Methodist
    University *B, M, D*
Southwestern Adventist University *B*
Texas A&M University *B, M, D*
Texas A&M University
    Commerce *B, M*
Texas Lutheran University *B*
Texas State Technical College
    Waco *A*
Texas Wesleyan University *B*
University of Houston
    Clear Lake *B, M*
University of Mary Hardin-Baylor *B*
University of Texas
    Arlington *B, M*
    El Paso *D*
    Pan American *B, M*
    San Antonio *D*
West Texas A&M University *B*
Western Texas College *A*
Wiley College *B*

Utah

Brigham Young University *B, M, D*
Neumont University *A, B, M*
Salt Lake Community College *A*

Snow College *A*
Southern Utah University *B*
Stevens-Henager College: Logan *B*
University of Utah *B, M, D*
Utah Valley University *A, B*
Weber State University *B*
Westminster College *B*

Vermont

Bennington College *B*
Champlain College *B*
Lyndon State College *A*
Marlboro College *B, M*
Middlebury College *B*
Norwich University *B*
St. Michael's College *B*
University of Vermont *B, M, D*

Virginia

Bridgewater College *B*
Christopher Newport University *B*
Danville Community College *A*
ECPI College of Technology: Virginia
    Beach *C, A*
ECPI Technical College: Roanoke *A*
Eastern Mennonite University *B*
Emory & Henry College *B*
Hampden-Sydney College *B*
Hampton University *B, M*
J. Sargeant Reynolds Community
    College *A*
Longwood University *B*
National College
    Bluefield *C, A*
    Charlottesville *C, A*
    Danville *C, A*
    Harrisonburg *C, A*
    Lynchburg *C, A*
    Martinsville *C, A*
Northern Virginia Community
    College *A*
Radford University *B*
Roanoke College *B*
Thomas Nelson Community
    College *A*
University of Management and
    Technology *A, B, M*
University of Virginia's College at
    Wise *B*
Virginia Military Institute *B*
Virginia State University *B, M*
Virginia Wesleyan College *B*
Virginia Western Community
    College *A*

Washington

Centralia College *A*
Everett Community College *A*
Gonzaga University *B*
Lower Columbia College *A*
Olympic College *A*
Pacific Lutheran University *B*
Renton Technical College *C, A*
Saint Martin's University *B*
Seattle Pacific University *B*
Seattle University *B*
Spokane Falls Community College *A*
University of Puget Sound *B*
University of Washington *B, M, D*
Walla Walla University *B*
Washington State University *B, M, D*
Whatcom Community College *A*
Whitworth University *B*

West Virginia

Alderson-Broaddus College *A, B*
Bethany College *B*
Concord University *B*
Davis and Elkins College *B*
Fairmont State University *B*
Mountain State University *A, B*
Salem International University *B*

West Virginia State Community and
Technical College *A*
West Virginia State University *B*
West Virginia University *B, M, D*
West Virginia University Institute of
Technology *B*
West Virginia Wesleyan College *B*
Wheeling Jesuit University *B*

Wisconsin
Beloit College *B*
Cardinal Stritch University *A, B*
Carthage College *B*
Herzing University *A, B*
Lakeland College *B*
Marquette University *B, M*
Mid-State Technical College *C*
Nicolet Area Technical College *A*
Ripon College *B*
St. Norbert College *B*
Silver Lake College *C, B*
University of Wisconsin
Green Bay *B*
Milwaukee *B*
Oshkosh *B*
Parkside *B*
Platteville *B*
Superior *B*

Wyoming
Central Wyoming College *A*
Laramie County Community
College *A*
University of Wyoming *B, M, D*
Western Wyoming Community
College *A*

Computer software technology

Arizona
Coconino County Community
College *A*

California
San Joaquin Delta College *C, A*

Connecticut
Three Rivers Community College *C*

Delaware
Delaware Technical and Community
College
Owens *C*
Wilmington University *B*

Florida
Brown Mackie College: Miami *C, A*
Palm Beach Community College *C*

Indiana
Indiana University-Purdue University
Indianapolis *A, B*

Kansas
Kansas City Kansas Community
College *C, A*

Maryland
Frederick Community College *C, A*

Massachusetts
Bunker Hill Community College *C*

Minnesota
Globe University *A, B*

Missouri
Grantham University *A, B*
Metropolitan Community College:
Blue River *A*

Nebraska
Metropolitan Community College *A*

North Dakota
North Dakota State College of
Science *C, A*

Ohio
Cleveland State University *M*

Oregon
Oregon Institute of Technology *B*
Rogue Community College *A*

Puerto Rico
Universidad del Este *A*

South Dakota
Mitchell Technical Institute *A*

Texas
North Lake College *C*

Virginia
Southwest Virginia Community
College *C, A*
University of Virginia's College at
Wise *B*

Washington
Bates Technical College *C*

Wisconsin
Herzing University *A, B*

Computer support specialist

California
San Joaquin Valley College *A*
Shasta College *C*

Florida
Pasco-Hernando Community
College *C*
Santa Fe College *C*
Valencia Community College *C*

Georgia
Altamaha Technical College *A*
Middle Georgia Technical
College *C, A*
Southeastern Technical College *A*

Kansas
Colby Community College *C*

Maryland
Howard Community College *C*

Massachusetts
Bristol Community College *C*

Michigan
Baker College of Allen Park *C*
Cleary University *C*
Lake Superior State University *C*
Mott Community College *C*
Wayne County Community College *A*

Nebraska
Northeast Community College *A*

Nevada
Kaplan College: Las Vegas *C*

New York
Genesee Community College *C*
Onondaga Community College *C*

Tompkins Cortland Community
College *A*

Ohio
Kaplan College: Dayton *C*
Miami University
Hamilton Campus *A*

Oregon
Central Oregon Community
College *A*
Chemeketa Community College *C*

Pennsylvania
Cambria-Rowe Business College:
Indiana *A*

Puerto Rico
Ponce Paramedical College *C*

South Carolina
York Technical College *C*

Texas
South Texas College *C, A*

Washington
Bates Technical College *C, A*
Grays Harbor College *C*
Olympic College *C*

West Virginia
New River Community and Technical
College *C*
West Virginia Business College:
Wheeling *C, A*

Wisconsin
Gateway Technical College *A*
Lakeshore Technical College *A*
Milwaukee Area Technical College *A*
Northcentral Technical College *A*
Wisconsin Indianhead Technical
College *A*

Computer systems analysis

Alabama
Faulkner State Community
College *C, A*

Arizona
Arizona State University *B, M*
DeVry University
Phoenix *B*
GateWay Community College *C, A*
Glendale Community College *C, A*
Mohave Community College *C*
Paradise Valley Community College *C*
Pima Community College *C, A*
University of Phoenix *B*

Arkansas
Arkansas Tech University *B*
Rich Mountain Community
College *C, A*
University of Arkansas *M*

California
California Polytechnic State
University: San Luis Obispo *B*
California State University
San Bernardino *B*
Cerritos College *A*
De Anza College *C, A*
DeVry University
Fremont *B*
Long Beach *B*
Foothill College *C*
Glendale Community College *C*

Irvine Valley College *C, A*
MTI College *C, A*
National University *B*
Platt College
Ontario *A*
San Bernardino Valley College *C, A*
San Diego City College *A*
San Jose State University *B*
University of California
San Diego *B, M, D*

Colorado
Colorado Technical
University *B, M, D*
DeVry University
Westminster *B*
Jones International University *B*
University of Denver *B*
Westwood College: Denver North *A*

Connecticut
Northwestern Connecticut
Community College *A*
Norwalk Community College *A*

Delaware
Delaware State University *B*

District of Columbia
Howard University *B*

Florida
Brevard Community College *A*
Broward College *A*
Central Florida Community College *C*
Daytona State College *C, A*
DeVry University
Miramar *B*
Orlando *B*
Florida State College at Jacksonville *A*
Gulf Coast Community College *A*
Hillsborough Community
College *C, A*
Indian River State College *A*
Lake-Sumter Community College *A*
Palm Beach Community College *A*
Pasco-Hernando Community
College *A*
Saint Johns River Community
College *C, A*
Seminole Community College *A*
State College of Florida,
Manatee-Sarasota *C, A*
Valencia Community College *C, A*

Georgia
Clayton State University *B*
DeVry University
Alpharetta *B*
Decatur *B*

Illinois
DePaul University *M*
DeVry University
Addison *B*
Chicago *B*
Tinley Park *B*
DeVry University: Online *B*
Harper College *A*

Indiana
DeVry University: Indianapolis *B*
Valparaiso University *C*

Iowa
Kaplan University
Cedar Falls *C*
Cedar Rapids *C*
Marshalltown Community College *A*
St. Ambrose University *B*

Kansas

Hutchinson Community College *A*
Kansas State University *A*
Washburn University *A, B*

Kentucky

Bellarmine University *B*
Daymar College
   Owensboro *A*

Maine

Husson University *B*

Maryland

Baltimore City Community College *A*
Frederick Community College *A*
Prince George's Community
   College *A*
Wor-Wic Community College *C, A*

Michigan

Baker College
   of Muskegon *B*
Davenport University *A*
Kirtland Community College *C, A*
Lansing Community College *A*
Oakland Community College *C, A*
Saginaw Valley State University *B*
University of Detroit Mercy *B*

Minnesota

Capella University *M*
DeVry University
   Edina *B*
Hennepin Technical College *C, A*
Mesabi Range Community and
   Technical College *A*

Missouri

DeVry University
   Kansas City *B*
Linn State Technical College *A*
Missouri Southern State University *A*
Missouri Technical School *B*
Northwest Missouri State
   University *M*
St. Louis Community College
   St. Louis Community College at
     Florissant Valley *A*

Montana

University of Great Falls *B*

Nebraska

Union College *A, B*

Nevada

College of Southern Nevada *A*

New Jersey

DeVry University: North
   Brunswick *A, B*

New Mexico

Central New Mexico Community
   College *C, A*
Clovis Community College *A*

New York

City University of New York
   Baruch College *M*
College of Westchester *C, A*
DeVry
   College of New York *B*
Globe Institute of Technology *C, A, B*
Monroe Community College *A*
Pace University *C, B, M*
Rochester Institute of
   Technology *B, M*

North Carolina

Durham Technical Community
   College *C, A*
Mayland Community College *A*
Western Piedmont Community
   College *C, A*

North Dakota

University of North Dakota *B*
Williston State College *A*

Ohio

Baldwin-Wallace College *C, B*
DeVry University
   Columbus *B*
Eastern Gateway Community
   College *A*
Kent State University *C, B, M, D*
Kent State University
   Tuscarawas *C*
Miami University
   Oxford Campus *B*
Southern State Community College *A*
Stark State College of Technology *A*
University of Akron *C, A, M*
University of Cincinnati *M*
University of Findlay *B*

Oklahoma

DeVry University: Oklahoma City
   Center *B*
Eastern Oklahoma State College *A*
Oklahoma Baptist University *B*
Oklahoma City Community College *A*

Oregon

DeVry University: Portland *B*

Pennsylvania

CHI Institute: Franklin Mills *C, A*
DeVry University
   Fort Washington *B*
Grove City College *B*
Kaplan Career Institute: Pittsburgh *A*
Keystone College *B*
Keystone Technical Institute *C*
Lehigh Carbon Community
   College *C, A*
Robert Morris University *M*
Shippensburg University of
   Pennsylvania *B*
YTI Career Institute: York *A*

Rhode Island

Johnson & Wales University:
   Providence *A, B*
New England Institute of
   Technology *A, B*

South Dakota

National American University
   Rapid City *A, B*

Texas

DeVry University
   Irving *B*
DeVry University: Houston *B*
El Paso Community College *A*
Kilgore College *C, A*
North Lake College *C, A*
University of Houston *B*

Utah

College of Eastern Utah *C, A*
DeVry University: Sandy *B*

Vermont

Champlain College *B*
University of Vermont *B*

Virginia

Blue Ridge Community College *C, A*
DeVry University
   Arlington *B*
ECPI College of Technology: Virginia
   Beach *C, A*
ECPI Technical College: Roanoke *A*
John Tyler Community College *A*
Tidewater Community College *A*
University of Management and
   Technology *A, B, M*
Virginia Western Community
   College *C*

Washington

DeVry University
   Federal Way *B*
Renton Technical College *C*
University of Washington Bothell *B*
University of Washington
   Tacoma *B, M*
Whatcom Community College *A*

Wisconsin

DeVry University: Milwaukee *B*
Lac Courte Oreilles Ojibwa
   Community College *A*
Milwaukee Area Technical College *A*
Southwest Wisconsin Technical
   College *A*
University of Wisconsin
   Whitewater *B*
Waukesha County Technical
   College *A*

Wyoming

Laramie County Community
   College *C, A*

Computer/systems security

Arizona

Anthem College *A*
Cochise College *C, A*
Glendale Community College *C, A*
University of Advancing
   Technology *A, B, M*
University of Phoenix *C, B*

California

Foothill College *C*
Heald College
   Hayward *A*
   Roseville *A*
Mt. Sierra College *B*
National University *B*
Santa Rosa Junior College *C*
University of San Francisco *M*
Westwood College of Technology
   Westwood College: Los Angeles *B*
Westwood College: Anaheim *B*
Westwood College: South Bay *B*

Colorado

American Sentinel University *B*
Aspen University *M*
Colorado Technical University *M*
University of Colorado
   Colorado Springs *B*
Westwood College of Technology
   Westwood College: Denver South *B*
Westwood College: Denver North *B*

District of Columbia

Howard University *C*
Trinity Washington University *M*

Florida

Florida State University *M*
Gulf Coast Community College *C*
Nova Southeastern University *M*
Pasco-Hernando Community
   College *A*
University of Miami *B*
Valencia Community College *C*

Georgia

Ashworth College *C*
Gwinnett Technical College *C, A*
Kennesaw State University *B*

Illinois

Black Hawk College *C*
DePaul University *B, M*
Heartland Community College *C*
Lewis University *D*
Lincoln Land Community College *C*
Loyola University Chicago *B*
Moraine Valley Community
   College *C, A*
University of Illinois
   Urbana-Champaign *B, M, D*
Westwood College: Chicago Loop *B*
Westwood College: DuPage *B*

Indiana

DeVry University: Indianapolis *B*
Indiana Institute of Technology *B*
Ivy Tech Community College
   Bloomington *C*
   Central Indiana *C*
   Columbus *C*
   East Central *C*
   Kokomo *C*
   Lafayette *C*
   North Central *C*
   Northeast *C*
   Northwest *C*
   Richmond *C*
   South Central *C*

Iowa

Indian Hills Community College *A*
Iowa Lakes Community College *C*
Iowa State University *M*
St. Ambrose University *B*

Kansas

Emporia State University *B*

Kentucky

Sullivan College of Technology and
   Design *A*

Maryland

Anne Arundel Community
   College *C, A*
College of Southern Maryland *A*
Harford Community College *A*
Howard Community College *C, A*
Johns Hopkins University *M*
University of Maryland
   University College *C, B*

Massachusetts

Holyoke Community College *C*
Springfield Technical Community
   College *A*

Michigan

Baker College
   of Port Huron *M*
Cleary University *B*
Davenport University *A, B, M*
Eastern Michigan University *M*
Ferris State University *C*
Henry Ford Community College *A*
Oakland Community College *C, A*
Washtenaw Community College *C, A*
Wayne County Community College *C*

Minnesota

Alexandria Technical College *C*

Anoka-Ramsey Community College *C*
Capella University *B, M, D*
Century Community and Technical College *C, A*
DeVry University
  Edina *B*
Fond du Lac Tribal and Community College *C, A*
Globe University *C, A, B*
Hennepin Technical College *C, A*
Hibbing Community College *A*
Inver Hills Community College *C*
Metropolitan State University *B*
Minneapolis Community and Technical College *C, A*
Minnesota State Community and Technical College *A*
Rochester Community and Technical College *C*
Saint Cloud State University *B*
University of St. Thomas *B*
Walden University *B, M*

Mississippi
Antonelli College
  Jackson *A*

Missouri
Jefferson College *C, A*

Montana
University of Great Falls *B*

New Jersey
Atlantic Cape Community College *C*
Stevens Institute of Technology *B, M*

New York
Erie Community College
  North Campus *C*
Globe Institute of Technology *C, A, B*
Mercy College *B*
Mohawk Valley Community College *C*
Pace University *C*
Rochester Institute of Technology *B, M*
St. John's University *C, A, B*
State University of New York College of Technology at Alfred *B*
Westchester Community College *C, A*

North Carolina
Durham Technical Community College *C, A*
Fayetteville Technical Community College *A*
High Point University *B*
Isothermal Community College *A*
Stanly Community College *C, A*
Vance-Granville Community College *A*
Wilson Community College *C, A*

Ohio
Edison State Community College *A*
James A. Rhodes State College *C, A*
Stark State College of Technology *A*

Oklahoma
Oklahoma City Community College *A*
Platt College
  Tulsa *A*

Oregon
Chemeketa Community College *C*
Southern Oregon University *B*

Pennsylvania
Butler County Community College *A*
Carnegie Mellon University *M*
Community College of Philadelphia *A*
Drexel University *B*

East Stroudsburg University of Pennsylvania *B*
Harrisburg Area Community College *C, A*
Kaplan Career Institute: Pittsburgh *A*
Lehigh Carbon Community College *A*
Luzerne County Community College *C, A*
Northampton Community College *A*
Peirce College *C, A*
Pennsylvania College of Technology *B*
Pennsylvania Highlands Community College *C, A*
Robert Morris University *M*
Westmoreland County Community College *C, A*

Puerto Rico
Inter American University of Puerto Rico
  Guayama Campus *M*
Universidad del Este *M*

Rhode Island
Community College of Rhode Island *C*

South Carolina
Limestone College *B*
York Technical College *C*

South Dakota
Dakota State University *B, M*

Tennessee
Chattanooga State Community College *C*
Fountainhead College of Technology *B*

Texas
North Lake College *C, A*
Sam Houston State University *M*
San Antonio College *C, A*
South Texas College *A*
University of Dallas *M*
University of Texas
  San Antonio *B*

Utah
LDS Business College *C*
Western Governors University *B*

Vermont
Champlain College *B*
Norwich University *B, M*

Virginia
ECPI College of Technology: Virginia Beach *C, A*
ECPI Technical College: Roanoke *A, B*
George Mason University *M*
Lord Fairfax Community College *C*
University of Management and Technology *A, B, M*
Virginia Polytechnic Institute and State University *M*
World College *B*

Washington
Bellevue College *C, A*
Clover Park Technical College *C, A*
DeVry University
  Federal Way *B*
Green River Community College *C, A*
Olympic College *C*
South Seattle Community College *C, A*
University of Washington Tacoma *B*

West Virginia
American Public University System *C, B*

Wisconsin
Blackhawk Technical College *A*
Milwaukee Area Technical College *A*
Nicolet Area Technical College *C*
Northcentral Technical College *C*

Computer systems technology

Alabama
Gadsden State Community College *A*
Herzing University *A, B*

Arizona
Coconino County Community College *C, A*
Northern Arizona University *B*

Arkansas
Arkansas State University
  Beebe *C, A*
Ouachita Technical College *C*
Southeast Arkansas College *C*
Southern Arkansas University Tech *A*
University of Arkansas
  Monticello *C*
University of Arkansas Community College at Morrilton *C, A*

California
Cuyamaca College *C, A*
Los Angeles Harbor College *A*
Westwood College of Technology
  Westwood College: Inland Empire *A*

Colorado
Colorado State University *B*

Delaware
Delaware Technical and Community College
  Owens *C, A*
  Terry *C, A*

Florida
Chipola College *C, A*
Daytona State College *C, A*
Florida Atlantic University *B*
Hillsborough Community College *C, A*
Lake-Sumter Community College *A*

Illinois
Harper College *C*
Heartland Community College *C*
Illinois Central College *C*
Lincoln Land Community College *C*
Morton College *C*
Parkland College *C, A*
Triton College *C*
Waubonsee Community College *C*

Indiana
Harrison College
  Indianapolis *A*
Indiana University-Purdue University Fort Wayne *C*
Indiana University-Purdue University Indianapolis *A, B*
National College: Indianapolis *A*

Kansas
Barton County Community College *C, A*
Neosho County Community College *A*

Southwestern College *B*

Kentucky
Spencerian College: Lexington *A*

Louisiana
Nunez Community College *C*

Maryland
Community College of Baltimore County *C, A*
Frederick Community College *C, A*

Massachusetts
Benjamin Franklin Institute of Technology *A*
Newbury College *B*

Michigan
Bay de Noc Community College *A*
Central Michigan University *B*
Oakland Community College *A*
Wayne State University *B*

Minnesota
Alexandria Technical College *C*
Anoka-Ramsey Community College *C*
Central Lakes College *C, A*
Century Community and Technical College *C, A*
Globe University *A, B*
Inver Hills Community College *C, A*
Lake Superior College *A*
Minnesota State College - Southeast Technical *A*
Minnesota State Community and Technical College *C, A*
Normandale Community College *A*
Rochester Community and Technical College *C, A*
St. Paul College *C*

Missouri
Metropolitan Community College: Blue River *C*
Southeast Missouri State University *A*

Nevada
DeVry University: Henderson *A*

New Hampshire
River Valley Community College *A*
White Mountains Community College *C, A*

New Jersey
Hudson County Community College *A*

New York
Erie Community College
  South Campus *A*
Genesee Community College *C*
Nassau Community College *C, A*
State University of New York College of Agriculture and Technology at Morrisville *A, B*
  Farmingdale *C, B*

North Carolina
Cape Fear Community College *C, A*

Ohio
Cincinnati State Technical and Community College *A*
Kent State University *C*
Kent State University: Geauga *A*
Miami University
  Hamilton Campus *A*
  Oxford Campus *C, A*
National College: Cincinnati *A*

National College: Stow *A*
National College: Youngstown *A*
Ohio Business College: Sandusky *C*
Southern State Community College *A*
University of Cincinnati
    Clermont College *C, A*
University of Rio Grande *A*

Oregon
Portland Community College *A*

Pennsylvania
Butler County Community College *A*
Commonwealth Technical Institute *A*
Community College of Philadelphia *A*
Luzerne County Community
    College *A*
Penn Commercial Business and
    Technical School *A*

South Carolina
Bob Jones University *B*
York Technical College *A*

South Dakota
Mitchell Technical Institute *A*

Tennessee
National College
    Knoxville *C*
National College: Bartlett *A*
National College: Madison *A*
National College: Memphis *A*

Texas
Clarendon College *C, A*
Kilgore College *C*
Lamar Institute of Technology *C, A*
Tarrant County College *C, A*
Texas State Technical College
    Harlingen *C, A*

Utah
Salt Lake Community College *C, A*

Virginia
ECPI College of Technology: Virginia
    Beach *C, A*
ECPI Technical College: Roanoke *A*
National College
    Roanoke Valley *C, A*

Washington
Bates Technical College *C*
Bellingham Technical College *A*

West Virginia
West Virginia Junior College:
    Bridgeport *C, A*

Wisconsin
Herzing University *A, B*
Mid-State Technical College *A*
Milwaukee Area Technical College *A*
Waukesha County Technical
    College *C*
Western Technical College *C*
Wisconsin Indianhead Technical
    College *A*

Wyoming
Central Wyoming College *C, A*

Computer typography

California
City College of San Francisco *C*
Santa Barbara City College *A*

Illinois
Triton College *C*

Nevada
College of Southern Nevada *C, A*

Pennsylvania
Luzerne County Community
    College *C*

Concrete finishing

Illinois
Black Hawk College *C, A*

Indiana
Ivy Tech Community College
    Lafayette *C*

Wisconsin
Milwaukee Area Technical College *C*

Conducting

Alabama
Alabama Agricultural and Mechanical
    University *B*

Alaska
University of Alaska
    Fairbanks *M*

Arizona
Northern Arizona University *M*

California
Azusa Pacific University *M*
Bethesda Christian University *B, M*
California State University
    Long Beach *B, M*
Chapman University *B*
San Francisco Conservatory of
    Music *M*
University of Southern California *M*

Colorado
Colorado State University *B, M*

Connecticut
University of Hartford *M*

District of Columbia
Catholic University of America *M, D*
Howard University *B*

Florida
Florida State University *M*
University of Miami *M, D*

Georgia
Mercer University *M*

Illinois
Northwestern University *M, D*
University of Illinois
    Urbana-Champaign *M, D*

Indiana
Butler University *M*
Indiana University
    Bloomington *B*
Indiana University-Purdue University
    Fort Wayne *T*

Iowa
University of Northern Iowa *M*

Kansas
Central Christian College of Kansas *A*
Pittsburg State University *M*
University of Kansas *M, D*

Kentucky
Campbellsville University *B*

Maine
University of Maine *M*

Maryland
Johns Hopkins University: Peabody
    Conservatory of Music *M, D*

Massachusetts
Boston Conservatory *M*
New England Conservatory of
    Music *M, D*

Michigan
Calvin College *B*
Central Michigan University *M*
Michigan State University *M, D*
Oakland University *M*
University of Michigan *M, D*

Minnesota
Saint Cloud State University *M*

Mississippi
Mississippi College *M*

New Jersey
Rider University *M*

New York
Bard College *B, M*
Eastman School of Music of the
    University of Rochester *M, D*
Houghton College *M*
Ithaca College *M*
Juilliard School *M*
Mannes College The New School for
    Music *B, M*
University of Rochester *M*

Ohio
Cleveland Institute of Music *M*
Oberlin College *B, M*
University of Cincinnati *B, M, D*

Oklahoma
Oklahoma City University *M*

Oregon
Portland State University *M*
University of Oregon *M*

Pennsylvania
Carnegie Mellon University *M*
Penn State
    University Park *M*
Temple University *M*

South Carolina
University of South Carolina *M, D*

Texas
Baylor University *M*
Concordia University Texas *B*
Rice University *M*
Southern Methodist University *M*
Stephen F. Austin State University *M*
Texas Christian University *M*
Texas Tech University *D*
University of Houston *D*

Utah
Brigham Young University *M*

Virginia
Shenandoah University *M*

Washington
University of Washington *M, D*

Wisconsin
University of Wisconsin
    Madison *B, M*

Conservation biology

Arizona
Arizona State University *B*
Prescott College *B, M*

California
San Francisco State University *M*
San Jose State University *B, M*

Colorado
Colorado State University *M*

Florida
University of Central Florida *D*

Idaho
University of Idaho *B*

Louisiana
University of Louisiana at Lafayette *B*
University of New Orleans *D*

Maryland
University of Maryland
    College Park *M*

Michigan
Central Michigan University *M*

Minnesota
Ridgewater College *A*

Missouri
Missouri Southern State University *B*
University of Missouri
    Columbia *B, M, D*

New York
St. Lawrence University *B*
State University of New York
    Albany *M*
    College of Agriculture and
        Technology at Morrisville *A*
    College of Environmental Science
        and Forestry *B*

North Carolina
Methodist University *A, B*

Ohio
Muskingum University *B*

Pennsylvania
Gettysburg College *B*

Rhode Island
University of Rhode Island *M*

Tennessee
Union University *B*

Utah
Brigham Young University *B*

Vermont
Sterling College *B*

Wisconsin
University of Wisconsin
    Madison *B*
    Milwaukee *B*

Construction engineering

Alabama
University of Alabama *B*

California
National University *B*
University of Southern
California *B, M*

Georgia
Southern Polytechnic State
University *B*

Illinois
Bradley University *B*
University of Illinois
Urbana-Champaign *B, M, D*

Indiana
Purdue University *B*

Iowa
Iowa State University *B*

Massachusetts
Worcester Polytechnic Institute *M*

Michigan
Baker College
of Flint *A*
Lawrence Technological University *M*

Missouri
Washington University in St. Louis *M*

New Jersey
Stevens Institute of Technology *M*

New Mexico
University of New Mexico *M*

New York
State University of New York
College of Agriculture and
Technology at Morrisville *A*

North Carolina
North Carolina State University *B*

North Dakota
North Dakota State University *B*

Oregon
Oregon State University *B*

Pennsylvania
Drexel University *B*

Texas
Southern Methodist University *M*
Texas Tech University *B*

Virginia
Virginia Polytechnic Institute and
State University *B*

Wisconsin
Marquette University *B, M, D*

Construction management

Alabama
Gadsden State Community College *C*

Alaska
University of Alaska
Anchorage *A, B*

Arizona
Arizona State University *B, M, D*
Coconino County Community
College *C, A*
Northern Arizona University *B*
Prescott College *B*

Arkansas
John Brown University *B*

California
Cabrillo College *C, A*
College of the Desert *C, A*
Diablo Valley College *C*
Heald College
Hayward *A*
National University *B*
San Joaquin Valley College *A*
Southwestern College *C, A*

Colorado
Colorado State University *B, M*
University of Denver *M*

Connecticut
Central Connecticut State
University *B*
Three Rivers Community College *C, A*

Delaware
Delaware Technical and Community
College
Owens *C, A*
Stanton/Wilmington *C, A*
Terry *C, A*

Florida
Everglades University: Boca Raton *B*
University of Florida *M*

Georgia
Gwinnett Technical College *A*
Savannah Technical College *C, A*
Southern Polytechnic State
University *C, B, M*

Idaho
Boise State University *B*

Illinois
Kankakee Community College *C, A*
Triton College *C, A*
Waubonsee Community College *A*
Western Illinois University *B*

Indiana
Purdue University *C*

Iowa
Southeastern Community College
North Campus *A*
University of Northern Iowa *B*

Kansas
Pittsburg State University *B*
University of Kansas *M*

Louisiana
Baton Rouge Community College *A*
Louisiana State University and
Agricultural and Mechanical
College *B*

Maryland
Community College of Baltimore
County *C, A*

Montgomery College *C, A*

Massachusetts
Wentworth Institute of Technology *B*

Michigan
Delta College *A*
Eastern Michigan University *B*
Ferris State University *C, B*
Lawrence Technological University *B*
Michigan State University *B, M, D*
Michigan Technological University *B*
Montcalm Community College *C, A*
Oakland Community College *C, A*
Southwestern Michigan College *C*

Minnesota
Inver Hills Community College *C, A*

Mississippi
Mississippi State University *B*

Missouri
Missouri State University *B*

New York
Erie Community College
North Campus *A*
Nassau Community College *C*
Polytechnic Institute of New York
University *B, M*
Pratt Institute *A, B*
State University of New York
College of Environmental Science
and Forestry *B, M, D*

North Carolina
Appalachian State University *B*

North Dakota
North Dakota State University *B, M*

Ohio
Stark State College of Technology *A*

Oklahoma
Oklahoma State University
Oklahoma City *A*
University of Oklahoma *B, M*

Pennsylvania
Lehigh Carbon Community College *A*
Northampton Community College *A*
Philadelphia University *M*

South Carolina
Clemson University *B, M*
York Technical College *C*

Texas
North Lake College *C*
St. Philip's College *A*
University of Texas
San Antonio *M*
Tyler *B*
Westwood College: Fort Worth *A, B*

Utah
Brigham Young University *B, M*

Virginia
Virginia Polytechnic Institute and
State University *B, M*

Washington
University of Washington *B, M*
Washington State University *B*

Wisconsin
Milwaukee School of Engineering *B*

Wyoming
Casper College *A*

Construction site management

Arizona
Tohono O'odham Community
College *C, A*

Arkansas
John Brown University *B*

California
City College of San Francisco *A*
College of the Canyons *C, A*
College of the Sequoias *C*
Diablo Valley College *C*
Hartnell College *C, A*
Heald College
Roseville *A*

Connecticut
Three Rivers Community College *C*

Georgia
Ashworth College *A*
Gwinnett Technical College *A*

Hawaii
Heald College
Honolulu *A*

Illinois
Westwood College: DuPage *A, B*

Indiana
Ivy Tech Community College
Kokomo *A*
Northeast *A*
Northwest *A*
Southwest *A*

Maine
University of Southern Maine *B*

Maryland
Community College of Baltimore
County *C, A*

Massachusetts
Springfield Technical Community
College *C, A*

Minnesota
Dunwoody College of
Technology *C, A*
Inver Hills Community College *C, A*
Minnesota State Community and
Technical College *A*
North Hennepin Community
College *C, A*
St. Paul College *A*
South Central College *A*

Missouri
State Fair Community College *A*

Nevada
Western Nevada College *B*

New Hampshire
University of New Hampshire *A*

New Jersey
Cumberland County College *C, A*

New York
Pratt Institute *A, B*

North Carolina
Cape Fear Community College *A*
Surry Community College *C, A*

Ohio
Ohio Northern University *B*

Oregon
Portland Community College *A*

Pennsylvania
Community College of Philadelphia *A*
Harrisburg Area Community
College *C*

Rhode Island
Roger Williams University *B*

South Carolina
York Technical College *C*

South Dakota
Southeast Technical Institute *A*

Texas
University of Texas
Brownsville - Texas Southmost
College *C*
San Antonio *B*
Westwood College: Houston
South *A, B*

Utah
Salt Lake Community College *A*
Southern Utah University *B*

Washington
Centralia College *A*
Pierce College *C, A*

Construction technology

Alabama
Jefferson State Community
College *C, A*
Lawson State Community
College *C, A*
Tuskegee University *B*

Arizona
Coconino County Community
College *A*
Northern Arizona University *B*
Pima Community College *A*

Arkansas
University of Arkansas
Little Rock *B*

California
Antelope Valley College *C, A*
Barstow Community College *C, A*
Butte College *C, A*
California State Polytechnic
University: Pomona *B*
California State University
Chico *B*
Fresno *B*
Long Beach *B*
Sacramento *B, M*
College of the Desert *C*
College of the Redwoods *A*
College of the Sequoias *C, A*
El Camino College *C, A*
El Camino College: Compton
Center *C, A*
Los Angeles Pierce College *A*
Riverside Community College *C, A*
Saddleback College *C*

San Bernardino Valley College *C*
San Diego Mesa College *C, A*
San Diego State University *B*
San Joaquin Delta College *C*
Santa Rosa Junior College *C*
Shasta College *C, A*

Colorado
Colorado State University *B, M*
Trinidad State Junior College *A*

Connecticut
Norwalk Community College *A*
Quinebaug Valley Community
College *C, A*

Florida
Daytona State College *A*
Florida Agricultural and Mechanical
University *B*
Florida Institute of Technology *B*
Florida International University *B, M*
Florida State College at Jacksonville *A*
Gulf Coast Community College *A*
Indian River State College *A*
Palm Beach Community College *A*
Pensacola Junior College *A*
Santa Fe College *A*
Seminole Community College *A*
State College of Florida,
Manatee-Sarasota *A*
Tallahassee Community College *A*
University of Florida *B*
University of North Florida *B*

Georgia
Georgia Southern University *B*

Idaho
Brigham Young University-Idaho *A*

Illinois
College of Lake County *C, A*
Danville Area Community College *C*
Joliet Junior College *C, A*
Lincoln Land Community College *A*
Morrison Institute of Technology *A*
Oakton Community College *A*
Rock Valley College *C, A*
South Suburban College of Cook
County *C, A*
Southern Illinois University
Edwardsville *B*
Southwestern Illinois College *C, A*
Triton College *C, A*

Indiana
Indiana University-Purdue University
Fort Wayne *B*
Indiana University-Purdue University
Indianapolis *B*
Purdue University *A, B*
Purdue University
Calumet *C, A, B*

Iowa
Southeastern Community College
North Campus *A*

Kansas
Kansas State University *B*
Pittsburg State University *B, M*

Kentucky
Maysville Community and Technical
College *C*
Western Kentucky University *B*

Louisiana
Bossier Parish Community College *C*
University of Louisiana at Monroe *B*

Maine
Eastern Maine Community
College *C, A*

Massachusetts
Cape Cod Community College *C*
Fitchburg State College *B*

Michigan
Alpena Community College *A*
Baker College of Allen Park *C, A*
Central Michigan University *B*
Eastern Michigan University *M*
Ferris State University *A*
Gogebic Community College *C, A*
Kalamazoo Valley Community
College *C*
Lawrence Technological University *A*
Macomb Community College *C, A*
Michigan State University *B, M, D*
Northern Michigan University *B*
Washtenaw Community College *A*
Wayne State University *B*

Minnesota
Hennepin Technical College *C, A*
Minnesota State University
Moorhead *B*

Missouri
Mineral Area College *C, A*
Missouri Western State
University *A, B*
Ozarks Technical Community
College *C, A*
University of Central Missouri *B*

Montana
Montana State University
Bozeman *B*

Nebraska
University of Nebraska
Lincoln *B*
Omaha *B*

Nevada
University of Nevada
Las Vegas *B*
Reno *B*

New Hampshire
University of New Hampshire *A*

New Jersey
Burlington County College *A*
Cumberland County College *C, A*
Essex County College *A*
Fairleigh Dickinson University
Metropolitan Campus *B*
Ocean County College *C*
Raritan Valley Community College *A*
Thomas Edison State College *B*

New Mexico
Santa Fe Community College *C, A*
Western New Mexico University *C, A*

New York
City University of New York
College of Staten Island *A*
New York City College of
Technology *C, A*
Dutchess Community College *A*
Herkimer County Community
College *A*
Monroe Community College *A*
Onondaga Community College *A*
State University of New York
College of Agriculture and
Technology at Morrisville *A*

College of Technology at
Alfred *A, B*
College of Technology at
Canton *C, A*
College of Technology at Delhi *A*
Suffolk County Community College *A*
Technical Career Institutes *A*

North Carolina
College of the Albemarle *C*
East Carolina University *B, M*
Mitchell Community College *C, A*
Vance-Granville Community
College *C*
Western Carolina University *B, M*
Western Piedmont Community
College *C, A*

North Dakota
North Dakota State College of
Science *A*

Ohio
Bowling Green State University *B*
Cincinnati State Technical and
Community College *A*
Columbus State Community
College *C, A*
Eastern Gateway Community
College *A*
Hocking College *A*
Ohio State University
Agricultural Technical Institute *A*
Columbus Campus *B*
Owens Community College
Toledo *C, A*
Stark State College of Technology *A*
Terra State Community College *C, A*
University of Akron *C, A, B*
Wright State University *A*
Youngstown State University *C*

Oklahoma
Oklahoma State University *B*
Oklahoma State University
Institute of Technology:
Okmulgee *A*
Oklahoma City *A*
Western Oklahoma State College *A*

Oregon
Clackamas Community College *C, A*
Lane Community College *C, A*
Portland Community College *C, A*
Rogue Community College *C, A*

Pennsylvania
Community College of Allegheny
County *C*
Community College of Philadelphia *A*
Harrisburg Area Community
College *C, A*
Lehigh Carbon Community
College *C, A*
Penn State
Fayette, The Eberly Campus *A*
Worthington Scranton *A, B*
Pennsylvania College of
Technology *C, A, B*
Temple University *B*

Rhode Island
New England Institute of
Technology *A*

South Carolina
Aiken Technical College *C*
Greenville Technical College *C, A*
Horry-Georgetown Technical
College *A*
Midlands Technical College *C*

Technical College of the
Lowcountry *C, A*
Trident Technical College *C*

South Dakota
South Dakota State University *B*
Southeast Technical Institute *A*

Tennessee
Nashville State Community College *A*

Texas
Brazosport College *C, A*
Houston Community College
System *C, A*
Howard College *C*
Midland College *C*
Prairie View A&M University *B*
St. Philip's College *C, A*
Sam Houston State University *B*
San Jacinto College *A*
Texas A&M University *B*
Texas A&M University
Commerce *B*
Texas State Technical College
Harlingen *C, A*
West Texas *C, A*
Texas State University: San Marcos *B*
University of Houston *B*
University of North Texas *B*

Vermont
Vermont Technical College *A, B*

Virginia
J. Sargeant Reynolds Community
College *A*
Lord Fairfax Community College *C*
Norfolk State University *B*

Washington
Clark College *C, A*
Spokane Community College *C, A*
Yakima Valley Community College *C*

West Virginia
Fairmont State University *B*

Wisconsin
Northeast Wisconsin Technical
College *C*
University of Wisconsin
Stout *B*

Wyoming
Casper College *C, A*

Construction trades

Alabama
Lawson State Community
College *C, A*

Alaska
University of Alaska
Southeast *A*

Arizona
Cochise College *A*
Mohave Community College *C*
Northland Pioneer College *C, A*
Tohono O'odham Community
College *C*

Arkansas
North Arkansas College *C*
Pulaski Technical College *C, A*
Southern Arkansas University Tech *C*

California
City College of San Francisco *C*

Diablo Valley College *C*
Foothill College *C*
Hartnell College *C*
National Polytechnic College of
Science *A*
Orange Coast College *C, A*
Palo Verde College *C, A*
San Jose City College *C, A*
Shasta College *C, A*
Sierra College *C*
Westwood College: South Bay *B*

Colorado
Arapahoe Community College *C, A*
Mesa State College *C, A*
Red Rocks Community College *C, A*

Connecticut
Central Connecticut State
University *B*
Quinebaug Valley Community
College *A*

Florida
South Florida Community College *A*
Valencia Community College *C, A*

Georgia
Gwinnett Technical College *A*

Illinois
Kaskaskia College *C*
Parkland College *C, A*

Indiana
Ivy Tech Community College
Northeast *C*
Northwest *C*
Oakland City University *A*
Vincennes University *C, A*

Iowa
Indian Hills Community College *C, A*
Iowa Central Community College *C, A*
Northeast Iowa Community
College *A*

Kansas
Highland Community College *A*
Neosho County Community
College *C*

Kentucky
Maysville Community and Technical
College *C*

Maine
Southern Maine Community
College *A*

Maryland
Cecil College *C*
Frederick Community College *C, A*

Michigan
Bay Mills Community College *A*
Delta College *C, A*
Gogebic Community College *C, A*
Henry Ford Community College *A*
Northern Michigan University *A*

Minnesota
Bemidji State University *B*
Minnesota West Community and
Technical College *C, A*
Northland Community & Technical
College *C, A*
Northwest Technical College *C*
South Central College *C, A*

Missouri
East Central College *C, A*

Montana
Blackfeet Community College *C*
Flathead Valley Community
College *C, A*
Montana State University
Billings *A*
Salish Kootenai College *C*
Stone Child College *C*

Nebraska
Central Community College *C, A*
Southeast Community College *A*

New Mexico
Mesalands Community College *C, A*
Navajo Technical College *C*

New York
Fulton-Montgomery Community
College *A*
Monroe Community College *A*
Nassau Community College *C*
Onondaga Community College *A*
State University of New York
College of Agriculture and
Technology at Morrisville *A*
Tompkins Cortland Community
College *C, A*

North Carolina
Edgecombe Community College *C*
Fayetteville Technical Community
College *C*
Isothermal Community College *C, A*
Wilkes Community College *C, A*

North Dakota
North Dakota State College of
Science *A*
Turtle Mountain Community
College *C, A*

Oregon
Clackamas Community College *C, A*
Portland Community College *C, A*
Rogue Community College *C, A*
Umpqua Community College *C*

Pennsylvania
Community College of Allegheny
County *C, A*
Harrisburg Area Community
College *C, A*
Penn Commercial Business and
Technical School *C*
Triangle Tech: Bethlehem *A*
Triangle Tech: Sunbury *A*

South Carolina
York Technical College *A*

South Dakota
Oglala Lakota College *C*

Tennessee
Southern Adventist University *A*

Texas
Midland College *C*

Utah
Snow College *C, A*
Utah Valley University *C, A*

Virginia
Piedmont Virginia Community
College *C*

Southwest Virginia Community
College *C*

Washington
Bates Technical College *C, A*
Clover Park Technical College *C*

Wisconsin
Fox Valley Technical College *A*
Northcentral Technical College *A*
Southwest Wisconsin Technical
College *C*
Waukesha County Technical
College *C*

Wyoming
Eastern Wyoming College *C*
Laramie County Community
College *C, A*
Sheridan College *C*

Consumer economics

Arizona
University of Arizona *B*

California
Long Beach City College *C, A*

Delaware
Delaware State University *B*

Georgia
University of Georgia *B*

Illinois
University of Illinois
Urbana-Champaign *B, M, D*

New York
Cornell University *B, M, D*
Rochester Institute of Technology *B*

Pennsylvania
Indiana University of Pennsylvania *B*

South Dakota
South Dakota State University *B*

Tennessee
University of Memphis *M*
University of Tennessee
Knoxville *B, M*

Utah
University of Utah *B*

Wisconsin
University of Wisconsin
Madison *B*

Consumer merchandising

California
Fashion Institute of Design and
Merchandising
Los Angeles *A*
San Diego *A*
San Francisco *A*

Florida
Florida State University *B*

Illinois
Bradley University *B*

Michigan
Madonna University *C, A, B*

Oregon

Oregon State University *B*

Wisconsin

University of Wisconsin
   Madison *B*

Consumer services/advocacy

Florida

Pensacola Junior College *A*

Correctional facilities administration

California

Diablo Valley College *C*

Connecticut

Asnuntuck Community College *C*

Illinois

Lewis University *B, M*
Triton College *C*

Massachusetts

Bunker Hill Community College *C*

Michigan

Baker College
   of Muskegon *C, A*
Kirtland Community College *C, A*

Montana

University of Great Falls *M*

New York

Excelsior College *B*

Ohio

Union Institute & University *B*

Pennsylvania

Bucks County Community College *A*

Puerto Rico

Inter American University of Puerto
   Rico
   Bayamon Campus *B*
   Metropolitan Campus *B*

West Virginia

American Public University
   System *C, B, M*
Potomac State College of West
   Virginia University *A*

Wisconsin

Carthage College *B*

Wyoming

Eastern Wyoming College *A*

Corrections

Arizona

Central Arizona College *C, A*
Coconino County Community
   College *C*
Prescott College *M*

Arkansas

Arkansas State University
   Beebe *C*

California

California State University
   East Bay *B*
   Fresno *B*
   Sacramento *B*
College of the Redwoods *C*
College of the Siskiyous *C*
East Los Angeles College *C*
Fresno City College *C, A*
Gavilan College *C, A*
Grossmont College *C, A*
Hartnell College *C, A*
Heald College
   Roseville *A*
Imperial Valley College *C, A*
Lassen Community College *A*
Sacramento City College *C, A*
San Diego Miramar College *C, A*
San Joaquin Valley College *A*
Taft College *C, A*

Delaware

Wilmington University *M*

District of Columbia

University of the District of
   Columbia *A*

Florida

Central Florida Community College *C*
Chipola College *C*
Daytona State College *C*
Florida Keys Community College *C*
Gulf Coast Community College *C*
Hillsborough Community College *C*
Lake City Community College *C*
Palm Beach Community College *C*
Pasco-Hernando Community
   College *C*
Seminole Community College *C*
South Florida Community College *C*
Tallahassee Community College *C*
Valencia Community College *C*

Idaho

Lewis-Clark State College *B*

Illinois

City Colleges of Chicago
   Harold Washington College *A*
Danville Area Community
   College *C, A*
Heartland Community College *C*
John A. Logan College *A*
Rend Lake College *C, A*
Sauk Valley Community College *A*

Iowa

Kaplan University
   Davenport *C*

Kansas

Cowley County Community
   College *A*
Kansas City Kansas Community
   College *C, A*
Labette Community College *A*
Washburn University *B*

Kentucky

Eastern Kentucky University *A, B*

Maryland

Baltimore City Community
   College *A*
Hagerstown Community College *C*

Massachusetts

Bridgewater State College *M*
Bunker Hill Community College *A*
Mount Wachusett Community
   College *A*

Michigan

Alpena Community College *C, A*
Baker College
   of Flint *C, A*
   of Port Huron *C, A*
Bay de Noc Community College *C, A*
Delta College *C, A*
Glen Oaks Community College *C*
Gogebic Community College *C*
Grand Rapids Community College *A*
Henry Ford Community College *C*
Kellogg Community College *C, A*
Kirtland Community College *C, A*
Lake Michigan College *A*
Northwestern Michigan College *C*
Oakland Community College *C, A*
St. Clair County Community
   College *C*
Schoolcraft College *A*
Washtenaw Community College *A*
Wayne County Community College *A*

Minnesota

Fond du Lac Tribal and Community
   College *A*
Lake Superior College *C*
Minnesota State Community and
   Technical College *C*
Minnesota State University
   Mankato *B*
Minnesota West Community and
   Technical College *A*
Northland Community & Technical
   College *A*
St. Mary's University of Minnesota *B*
University of Minnesota
   Crookston *B*
Walden University *M*
Winona State University *B*

Missouri

College of the Ozarks *B*
Metropolitan Community College:
   Longview *C, A*
Metropolitan Community College:
   Penn Valley *C, A*
Saint Louis University *B*
Sanford-Brown College
   St. Peters *A*
Southeast Missouri State University *B*

Montana

University of Great Falls *B*

Nebraska

Northeast Community College *A*
Western Nebraska Community
   College *C*

Nevada

College of Southern Nevada *A*
Truckee Meadows Community
   College *A*
Western Nevada College *C, A*

New Jersey

Bergen Community College *A*
Burlington County College *C*
Cumberland County College *A*
Middlesex County College *A*
Raritan Valley Community College *C*

New Mexico

New Mexico Junior College *C*
University of New Mexico *B*

New York

Adirondack Community College *A*
Broome Community College *A*
Cayuga County Community
   College *C, A*
Corning Community College *A*

Erie Community College
   City Campus *C*
   North Campus *C*
Herkimer County Community
   College *C*
Monroe Community College *C, A*
Westchester Community College *A*

North Carolina

Central Piedmont Community
   College *A*

Ohio

Bowling Green State University *B*
Clark State Community College *A*
Columbus State Community
   College *A*
Cuyahoga Community College
   Metropolitan Campus *A*
Hocking College *C, A*
James A. Rhodes State College *A*
Northwest State Community
   College *A*
Owens Community College
   Toledo *A*
Southern State Community College *A*
Tiffin University *B*
University of Cincinnati
   Clermont College *A*
Washington State Community
   College *A*
Youngstown State University *A, B, M*

Oklahoma

Langston University *B*
Oklahoma City University *B*
University of Central Oklahoma *B*
Western Oklahoma State College *A*

Oregon

Clackamas Community College *C, A*
Clatsop Community College *C*
Lane Community College *C*
Southwestern Oregon Community
   College *A*
Treasure Valley Community College *C*
Western Oregon University *B*

Pennsylvania

Bucks County Community College *A*
Butler County Community College *C*
Community College of Allegheny
   County *A*
Harrisburg Area Community
   College *C*
Kaplan Career Institute: Harrisburg *A*
Kaplan Career Institute: Pittsburgh *A*
Lehigh Carbon Community College *C*
Pennsylvania Highlands Community
   College *A*
University of Pittsburgh *B*
University of Pittsburgh
   Bradford *B*
Westmoreland County Community
   College *C*

Puerto Rico

Universidad del Este *A*

South Carolina

Trident Technical College *C*

Texas

Alvin Community College *C, A*
Amarillo College *A*
Austin Community College *A*
Central Texas College *C*
Coastal Bend College *C, A*
El Paso Community College *C, A*
Howard College *C, A*
Lamar State College at Orange *C, A*
Sam Houston State University *B*

San Antonio College *A*
San Jacinto College *C*
Stephen F. Austin State University *B*
Texas State University: San Marcos *B*
University of Texas
    Brownsville - Texas Southmost
        College *B*
Weatherford College *A*
Western Texas College *C, A*

Utah

Weber State University *B*

Virginia

Mountain Empire Community
    College *A*
Southwest Virginia Community
    College *A*

Washington

Centralia College *C*
Everett Community College *A*
Peninsula College *C, A*
Spokane Community College *C, A*
Yakima Valley Community College *C*

West Virginia

Glenville State College *A*
New River Community and Technical
    College *A*

Wisconsin

Mid-State Technical College *A*
Moraine Park Technical College *A*
Wisconsin Indianhead Technical
    College *A*

Wyoming

Eastern Wyoming College *C*
Laramie County Community
    College *A*

Cosmetic services

Alabama

Alabama Southern Community
    College *A*
Bevill State Community College *C, A*
Bishop State Community College *C*
Calhoun Community College *C*
Gadsden State Community College *C*
George C. Wallace State Community
    College
    George C. Wallace Community
        College at Dothan *C*
Lurleen B. Wallace Community
    College *C*
Northeast Alabama Community
    College *C*
Northwest-Shoals Community
    College *C*
Shelton State Community College *C*
Snead State Community College *C, A*
Wallace State Community College at
    Hanceville *C*

Arizona

Eastern Arizona College *C, A*
Northland Pioneer College *C, A*

Arkansas

Arkansas Tech University *C*
Ouachita Technical College *C*
Pulaski Technical College *C*
Southern Arkansas University Tech *C*

California

Allan Hancock College *C, A*
Butte College *C, A*
Citrus College *C, A*
College of the Sequoias *C, A*
Contra Costa College *A*

El Camino College *C, A*
El Camino College: Compton
    Center *C, A*
Fullerton College *A*
Gavilan College *C, A*
Golden West College *C, A*
Laney College *C, A*
Los Medanos College *C*
MTI College *C*
MiraCosta College *C, A*
Napa Valley College *C*
Riverside Community College *C, A*
Sacramento City College *C, A*
Saddleback College *C*
San Jose City College *C, A*
Santa Barbara City College *C, A*
Santiago Canyon College *A*
Skyline College *C*
Solano Community College *C, A*

Colorado

Colorado Northwestern Community
    College *C*
Lamar Community College *C*
Northeastern Junior College *C*
Otero Junior College *C*
Pueblo Community College *C, A*
Red Rocks Community College *C, A*
Trinidad State Junior College *C, A*

Florida

Brevard Community College *C*
Central Florida College *C, A*
Central Florida Community College *C*
Daytona State College *C*
Florida State College at Jacksonville *C*
Indian River State College *C*
Lake City Community College *C*
Palm Beach Community College *C*
Pensacola Junior College *C*
South Florida Community College *C*

Georgia

Albany Technical College *C*
Athens Technical College *C*
Augusta Technical College *C*
Central Georgia Technical College *C*
Chattahoochee Technical College *C*
Columbus Technical College *C*
DeKalb Technical College *C*
Middle Georgia Technical College *C*
North Georgia Technical College *C*
Savannah Technical College *C*
Southeastern Technical College *C*
Southwest Georgia Technical
    College *C*
Valdosta Technical College *C*
Waycross College *A*

Hawaii

University of Hawaii
    Honolulu Community College *C, A*

Idaho

Idaho State University *C*

Illinois

College of DuPage *C, A*
Danville Area Community College *C*
Harry S. Truman College *C*
Highland Community College *C*
Illinois Eastern Community Colleges
    Olney Central College *C*
John A. Logan College *C, A*
Kaskaskia College *C*
Lake Land College *C*
Rend Lake College *C*

Indiana

Vincennes University *A*

Iowa

Iowa Central Community College *A*
Northeast Iowa Community
    College *C, A*

Kansas

Cowley County Community
    College *C, A*
Garden City Community College *C*
Johnson County Community
    College *C*
Kansas City Kansas Community
    College *C*

Kentucky

Owensboro Community and
    Technical College *C*
Southeast Kentucky Community and
    Technical College *C*
West Kentucky Community and
    Technical College *C*

Massachusetts

Greenfield Community College *C, A*
North Shore Community College *C*
Springfield Technical Community
    College *C*

Michigan

Gogebic Community College *C*
Kirtland Community College *C, A*
Lansing Community College *A*
Montcalm Community College *C, A*
Mott Community College *C*
Northern Michigan University *C*
Oakland Community College *A*

Minnesota

Century Community and Technical
    College *C, A*
Minnesota State College - Southeast
    Technical *C, A*
Minnesota State Community and
    Technical College *C*
Northland Community & Technical
    College *C*
Ridgewater College *A*
St. Paul College *C, A*

Mississippi

Blue Cliff College: Gulfport *C*
Holmes Community College *C*
Mississippi Gulf Coast Community
    College *A*
Pearl River Community College *C*
Southwest Mississippi Community
    College *C*
Virginia College *C*

Missouri

Vatterott College: Joplin *C*

Montana

University of Montana *C*

Nebraska

Western Nebraska Community
    College *C, A*

New Mexico

Central New Mexico Community
    College *A*
Clovis Community College *A*
New Mexico Junior College *C, A*
Northern New Mexico College *C, A*
San Juan College *C, A*

New York

Sullivan County Community
    College *A*

North Carolina

Alamance Community College *C*
Beaufort County Community
    College *C*
Bladen Community College *C, A*
Blue Ridge Community College *C*
Brunswick Community College *C, A*
Caldwell Community College and
    Technical Institute *C*
Cape Fear Community College *C, A*
Carteret Community College *C*
Catawba Valley Community College *C*
Central Carolina Community
    College *A*
Cleveland Community College *C*
Coastal Carolina Community
    College *C*
College of the Albemarle *C*
Davidson County Community
    College *C*
Edgecombe Community College *C*
Fayetteville Technical Community
    College *C*
Gaston College *A*
Guilford Technical Community
    College *C, A*
Haywood Community College *C, A*
Isothermal Community College *C, A*
James Sprunt Community
    College *C, A*
Johnston Community College *C*
Martin Community College *C, A*
Mayland Community College *C, A*
Miller-Motte Technical College *C, A*
Mitchell Community College *C*
Nash Community College *C*
Piedmont Community College *C, A*
Pitt Community College *C, A*
Roanoke-Chowan Community
    College *C*
Robeson Community College *C*
Rockingham Community College *C*
Sampson Community College *A*
Sandhills Community College *C, A*
Southeastern Community
    College *C, A*
Southwestern Community
    College *C, A*
Stanly Community College *C, A*
Surry Community College *A*
Vance-Granville Community
    College *C*
Wayne Community College *C*
Wilson Community College *C*

Oregon

Mt. Hood Community College *A*
Umpqua Community College *A*

Pennsylvania

Butler County Community College *A*
Laurel Business Institute *C, A*

Puerto Rico

Inter American University of Puerto
    Rico
    Bayamon Campus *C*

South Carolina

Bob Jones University *A*
Denmark Technical College *C*
Florence-Darlington Technical
    College *C*
Greenville Technical College *C*
Horry-Georgetown Technical
    College *C*
Technical College of the
    Lowcountry *C, A*
Trident Technical College *C*
Williamsburg Technical College *C*

Texas

Central Texas College *C*

Del Mar College *C*
Frank Phillips College *C*
Grayson County College *C*
Houston Community College
    System *C, A*
Howard College *C*
Kilgore College *C*
Lamar State College at Port
    Arthur *C, A*
Lee College *C*
Lone Star College System *C, A*
McLennan Community College *C*
Northeast Texas Community
    College *C, A*
Odessa College *C, A*
Panola College *C*
Ranger College *C*
San Jacinto College *C*
Texarkana College *C*
Trinity Valley Community College *C*
Vernon College *C*
Weatherford College *C, A*
Wharton County Junior College *C*

Utah
College of Eastern Utah *A*
Salt Lake Community College *C, A*
Snow College *C, A*

Washington
Bates Technical College *C, A*
Clover Park Technical College *C*
Lake Washington Technical College *C*
Olympic College *C, A*
Renton Technical College *C*
Shoreline Community College *C, A*
Spokane Community College *C, A*

Wisconsin
Chippewa Valley Technical College *C*
Gateway Technical College *C*
Mid-State Technical College *C*
Moraine Park Technical College *C*
Nicolet Area Technical College *C*
Southwest Wisconsin Technical
    College *C*

Wyoming
Eastern Wyoming College *A*

Cosmetology

Alabama
Lawson State Community College *C*

Arkansas
Pulaski Technical College *C*

California
Santiago Canyon College *C*
Yuba Community College
    District *C, A*

Florida
Chipola College *C*

Georgia
Middle Georgia Technical College *C*
Savannah Technical College *C*
Southeastern Technical College *C*
West Georgia Technical College *C*

Illinois
Kaskaskia College *C*

Kansas
Seward County Community
    College *C, A*

Kentucky
Somerset Community College *A*

Michigan
Kirtland Community College *C, A*
Mott Community College *C*
Northern Michigan University *C*

Mississippi
Copiah-Lincoln Community College *C*

North Carolina
Brunswick Community College *C*
Cape Fear Community College *C*
Central Carolina Community
    College *A*
Isothermal Community College *C*
James Sprunt Community College *C*
Miller-Motte Technical College *C*
Pamlico Community College *C*

Tennessee
West Tennessee Business College *C*

Texas
Houston Community College
    System *C*
Lone Star College System *C*
Northeast Texas Community
    College *C*
Panola College *C*

Utah
Snow College *C, A*

Washington
Everett Community College *C, A*
Olympic College *C*

Counseling psychology

Alabama
Alabama Agricultural and Mechanical
    University *M*
Auburn University *D*
Samford University *B*
South University: Montgomery *M*
Troy University *M*
University of Alabama *M*
University of North Alabama *M*

Alaska
Alaska Pacific University *M*

Arizona
Northern Arizona University *M*
Prescott College *B, M*
University of Phoenix *M*

Arkansas
John Brown University *M*
University of Central Arkansas *M*

California
Alliant International University *M*
California Baptist University *M*
California Institute of Integral
    Studies *M*
California State University
    Bakersfield *M*
    Chico *T*
    East Bay *M*
    Long Beach *M*
    San Bernardino *M*
Dominican University of California *M*
Golden Gate University *M*
Holy Names University *M*
Hope International University *M*
John F. Kennedy University *M*
Loyola Marymount University *M*
Mount St. Mary's College *M*
National University *M, T*
Santa Clara University *M*
Southern California Seminary *M*

University of California
    Santa Barbara *M, D*
University of La Verne *M*
University of San Francisco *M*

Colorado
Adams State College *M*
Colorado Christian University *M*
Fort Lewis College *B*
Naropa University *M*
University of Denver *M, D*
University of Northern Colorado *M, D*

Connecticut
Saint Joseph College *M*
Southern Connecticut State
    University *M*
University of Hartford *M*

Delaware
Wilmington University *M*

District of Columbia
George Washington University *M*
Howard University *M, D*

Florida
Carlos Albizu University *M*
Nova Southeastern University *M*
Palm Beach Atlantic University *M*
Rollins College *M*
Saint Thomas University *M*
Southeastern University *M*
Trinity College of Florida *B*
University of Florida *D*
University of Miami *D*
University of North Florida *M*

Georgia
Georgia State University *D*
Mercer University *M*
Paine College *B*
University of Georgia *D*

Hawaii
Chaminade University of Honolulu *M*

Illinois
Argosy University: Chicago *M, D*
Chicago State University *M*
Governors State University *M*
Illinois State University *M*
Lewis University *M*
Loyola University Chicago *M, D*
McKendree University *M*
Northeastern Illinois University *M*
Northwestern University *M, D*
Olivet Nazarene University *M*
Saint Xavier University *M*
Trinity International University *M*
University of Illinois
    Springfield *M*

Indiana
Ball State University *M, D*
Grace College *M*
Indiana State University *M*
Indiana Wesleyan University *M*
University of St. Francis *M*
Valparaiso University *M*

Iowa
Morningside College *B*
University of Iowa *D*
University of Northern Iowa *M*

Kansas
MidAmerica Nazarene University *M*
Newman University *B*
University of Kansas *M, D*

Kentucky
Kentucky Christian University *B*
Lindsey Wilson College *M*
Mid-Continent University *B*
University of the Cumberlands *M*
Western Kentucky University *M*

Louisiana
Louisiana State University
    Shreveport *M*
Louisiana Tech University *D*
Nicholls State University *M*

Maine
University of Maine *M, D*

Maryland
Bowie State University *M*
Coppin State University *M*
Frostburg State University *M*
Loyola University Maryland *M*
Towson University *T*
University of Baltimore *M*
Washington Adventist University *B, M*
Washington Bible College *B, M*

Massachusetts
Anna Maria College *M*
Assumption College *M*
Boston University *D*
Cambridge College *M*
Eastern Nazarene College *B, M*
Emmanuel College *B*
Framingham State College *M*
Lesley University *M*
Northeastern University *M, D*
Salem State College *M*
Springfield College *M*
Tufts University *M*
Westfield State College *M*

Michigan
Andrews University *D*
Spring Arbor University *M*
Western Michigan University *M, D*

Minnesota
Bethel University *M*
Capella University *M, D*
Crossroads College *B*
Minnesota State University
    Mankato *M*
Saint Cloud State University *M*
St. Mary's University of Minnesota *M*
University of St. Thomas *M, D*
Walden University *D*

Mississippi
University of Southern
    Mississippi *M, D*

Missouri
Avila University *M*
Central Methodist University *M*
Lindenwood University *M*
Northwest Missouri State
    University *M*
University of Central Missouri *M*
University of Missouri
    Columbia *M, D*
    Kansas City *D*
Webster University *M*

Montana
University of Great Falls *M*

Nebraska
Chadron State College *M*
Doane College *M*

Nevada

University of Nevada
Las Vegas *M*

New Hampshire

Rivier College *M*

New Jersey

Caldwell College *M*
Centenary College *M*
College of St. Elizabeth *M*
Fairleigh Dickinson University
College at Florham *M*
Felician College *M*
Georgian Court University *M*
Monmouth University *M*
New Jersey City University *M*
Rider University *M*
Seton Hall University *M, D*

New Mexico

New Mexico State University *M*

New York

College of New Rochelle *M*
Fordham University *M, D*
Marist College *M*
Mercy College *M*
New York University *D*
Saint Bonaventure University *M*
State University of New York
Albany *D*
Buffalo *D*
Oswego *M*

North Carolina

Campbell University *M*
Gardner-Webb University *M*

North Dakota

University of North Dakota *D*

Ohio

Cleveland State University *D*
Franciscan University of
Steubenville *M*
Heidelberg University *M*
John Carroll University *M*
Kent State University *M*
Union Institute & University *M*
University of Akron *D*
Walsh University *M*
Wright State University *M*

Oklahoma

East Central University *M*
Mid-America Christian University *M*
Northeastern State University *M*
Northwestern Oklahoma State
University *M*
Southeastern Oklahoma State
University *M*
Southern Nazarene University *M*
University of Central Oklahoma *M*
University of Oklahoma *D*

Oregon

George Fox University *M*
Lewis & Clark College *M*
Northwest Christian University *M*
Oregon State University *M, D*
Pacific University *M*
University of Oregon *D*

Pennsylvania

Arcadia University *M*
Baptist Bible College of
Pennsylvania *M*
Carlow University *M, D*
Chatham University *M*
Chestnut Hill College *M*
Delaware Valley College *B*

Gannon University *M, D*
Geneva College *M*
Holy Family University *M*
Immaculata University *M*
Indiana University of Pennsylvania *M*
Kutztown University of
Pennsylvania *M*
La Salle University *M*
Lehigh University *D*
Marywood University *M*
Penn State
University Park *D*
Rosemont College *M*
Slippery Rock University of
Pennsylvania *M*
Temple University *M, D*
University of Pennsylvania *M*
University of Scranton *M*
Villanova University *M*
Waynesburg University *M*

Puerto Rico

Inter American University of Puerto
Rico
Aguadilla Campus *M*
Metropolitan Campus *M, D*
San German Campus *M, D*
Turabo University *M, D*

Rhode Island

Rhode Island College *M*
Salve Regina University *M*

South Carolina

Bob Jones University *B, M*
Columbia International University *M*
South University: Columbia *M*

South Dakota

South Dakota State University *M*

Tennessee

Freed-Hardeman University *M*
Johnson Bible College *M*
Lee University *M*
Lipscomb University *M*
Southern Adventist University *M*
Tennessee Technological
University *M*
Trevecca Nazarene University *M, D*
University of Memphis *D*
University of Tennessee
Knoxville *M*

Texas

Abilene Christian University *M*
Amberton University *M*
Angelo State University *M*
Arlington Baptist College *B*
Dallas Baptist University *M*
Lamar University *M*
Lubbock Christian University *M*
Midwestern State University *M*
St. Mary's University *M, D*
Sam Houston State University *M*
Southern Methodist University *M*
Southwestern Assemblies of God
University *M*
Stephen F. Austin State University *M*
Tarleton State University *M*
Texas A&M International
University *M*
Texas A&M University *D*
Texas A&M University
Commerce *M, D*
Kingsville *M*
Texarkana *M*
Texas State University: San
Marcos *M, T*
Texas Tech University *M, D*
Texas Woman's University *M, D*
University of Houston *D*

University of Houston
Victoria *M*
University of North Texas *M, D*
University of Texas
Pan American *M*
Tyler *M*
Wayland Baptist University *M*
West Texas A&M University *M*

Utah

Westminster College *M*

Vermont

College of St. Joseph in Vermont *M*
Johnson State College *M*

Virginia

Eastern Mennonite University *M*
Liberty University *M, D*
Marymount University *M*
Regent University *M, D*
Virginia Commonwealth University *D*

Washington

City University of Seattle *M*
Eastern Washington University *M*
Gonzaga University *M*
Northwest University *M*
Saint Martin's University *M*
Western Washington University *M*

West Virginia

West Virginia University *D*

Wisconsin

Concordia University Wisconsin *M*
Lakeland College *M*
Marquette University *D*
University of Wisconsin
Madison *M, D*
Stout *M*
Whitewater *M*

Counselor education

Alabama

Alabama Agricultural and Mechanical
University *B, M*
Alabama State University *M*
Auburn University *M, D, T*
Auburn University at Montgomery *M*
Jacksonville State University *M, T*
Troy University *T*
University of Alabama *M, D*
University of Alabama
Birmingham *M*
University of Montevallo *M*
University of North Alabama *M*
University of South Alabama *M, T*
University of West Alabama *M*

Alaska

University of Alaska
Anchorage *M*
Fairbanks *M*

Arizona

Arizona State University *M, D*
Northern Arizona University *M*
Prescott College *B, M, T*
University of Arizona *M*
University of Phoenix *M*

Arkansas

Arkansas State University *M, T*
Arkansas Tech University *M*
Harding University *M*
Henderson State University *M*
John Brown University *M*
Southern Arkansas University *M*
University of Arkansas *M, D*

University of Arkansas
Little Rock *M*
University of Central Arkansas *M*

California

Azusa Pacific University *M*
California Baptist University *M*
California Lutheran University *M*
California State University
Bakersfield *M*
Chico *T*
Dominguez Hills *M, T*
East Bay *M, T*
Fullerton *M, T*
Long Beach *M*
Los Angeles *M*
Northridge *M*
Sacramento *M*
San Bernardino *M*
Chapman University *M, T*
Fresno Pacific University *M, T*
Humboldt State University *T*
La Sierra University *M*
Loma Linda University *M*
Loyola Marymount University *M*
Mount St. Mary's College *M*
National University *M, T*
St. Mary's College of California *M*
San Diego State University *M*
San Francisco State University *M, T*
San Jose State University *M*
Sonoma State University *M*
University of California
Santa Barbara *M, D*
University of La Verne *M*
University of Redlands *M, T*
University of San Diego *M, T*
University of San Francisco *T*
University of Southern California *M, T*
Whittier College *M*

Colorado

Adams State College *M*
Colorado State University *M*
University of Colorado
Colorado Springs *M, T*
Denver *M*
University of Northern Colorado *M, D*

Connecticut

Central Connecticut State
University *M*
Fairfield University *M*
Saint Joseph College *M*
Southern Connecticut State
University *M, T*
University of Bridgeport *M*
University of Hartford *M, T*
Western Connecticut State
University *M*

Delaware

University of Delaware *M*
Wilmington University *M*

District of Columbia

Gallaudet University *M*
George Washington University *M, D*
Howard University *M*
Trinity Washington University *M*
University of the District of
Columbia *M*

Florida

Barry University *M*
Carlos Albizu University *M*
Florida Atlantic University *M*
Florida Gulf Coast University *M*
Florida International University *M*
Florida State University *T*
Nova Southeastern University *M*
Saint Thomas University *M*
Southeastern University *M*

Stetson University M
University of Central Florida M
University of Florida M
University of North Florida M
University of South Florida M

Georgia
Albany State University M
Augusta State University M
Clark Atlanta University M
Columbus State University M
Fort Valley State University M
Georgia Southern University M, T
Georgia State University M, D, T
Mercer University M
University of Georgia M, D, T
University of West Georgia M, D, T
Valdosta State University M

Hawaii
University of Hawaii
  Manoa M

Idaho
Boise State University M
Idaho State University M, D
University of Idaho M

Illinois
Bradley University M
Chicago State University M
Concordia University Chicago M
DePaul University M
Eastern Illinois University M
Governors State University M
Lewis University M
Loyola University Chicago M
Northeastern Illinois University M
Northern Illinois University M, D
Roosevelt University M
Western Illinois University M

Indiana
Butler University M
Indiana State University M, D, T
Indiana University
  Bloomington M, D
  South Bend M
  Southeast M
Indiana University-Purdue University
  Fort Wayne M
Indiana University-Purdue University
  Indianapolis M
Indiana Wesleyan University M
Purdue University
  Calumet M
University of St. Francis M

Iowa
Buena Vista University M
Drake University M
Iowa State University M, T
University of Iowa M, D
University of Northern Iowa M

Kansas
Emporia State University M
Fort Hays State University M
Kansas State University M, D
Wichita State University M

Kentucky
Eastern Kentucky University M
Morehead State University M
Murray State University M, T
Northern Kentucky University M
University of Kentucky M, D
University of Louisville M, D
University of the Cumberlands M, T

Louisiana
Louisiana State University and
  Agricultural and Mechanical
  College M
Louisiana Tech University M
Loyola University New Orleans M
McNeese State University M, T
Nicholls State University M
Northwestern State University M
Our Lady of Holy Cross College M
Southeastern Louisiana University M
Southern University and Agricultural
  and Mechanical College M
University of Louisiana at Lafayette M
University of Louisiana at Monroe M
University of New Orleans M, D
Xavier University of Louisiana M

Maine
Husson University M
University of Maine M, D
University of Southern Maine M

Maryland
Bowie State University M
Frostburg State University M
Loyola University Maryland M
McDaniel College M
University of Maryland
  College Park M, D
  Eastern Shore M
Washington Bible College B, M, T

Massachusetts
Assumption College M
Boston College M, D
Boston University M, D, T
Bridgewater State College M, T
Fitchburg State College M, T
Lesley University M
Salem State College M
Springfield College M
Suffolk University M
University of Massachusetts
  Boston M

Michigan
Andrews University M, D
Central Michigan University M
Eastern Michigan University M
Michigan State University M
Northern Michigan University M
Oakland University M, D
Siena Heights University M
University of Detroit Mercy M
Wayne State University M, D
Western Michigan University M, D

Minnesota
Capella University M, D
Minnesota State University
  Mankato M
  Moorhead M
Saint Cloud State University M
Winona State University M

Mississippi
Delta State University M
Jackson State University M
Mississippi College M
Mississippi State University M, D, T
University of Mississippi M, D
University of Southern Mississippi M

Missouri
Evangel University M
Lincoln University M
Lindenwood University M
Missouri Baptist University M, T
Missouri State University B, M
Northwest Missouri State
  University M, T

Saint Louis University M, D
Southeast Missouri State
  University M, T
Stephens College M
University of Central Missouri M
University of Missouri
  Columbia M, D
  Kansas City M
  St. Louis M

Montana
Montana State University
  Billings M
University of Montana M, D

Nebraska
Chadron State College M
Creighton University M
University of Nebraska
  Kearney M, T
  Omaha M
Wayne State College M

Nevada
University of Nevada
  Las Vegas M
  Reno M, D

New Hampshire
Keene State College M, T
Plymouth State University M, T
Rivier College M
University of New Hampshire M

New Jersey
Caldwell College M
The College of New Jersey M
Kean University M, T
Monmouth University M
Montclair State University M
Rider University M
Rowan University M
Seton Hall University M
William Paterson University of New
  Jersey M

New Mexico
Eastern New Mexico University M
New Mexico Highlands University M
New Mexico State University M, D
University of New Mexico M, D
University of the Southwest M
Western New Mexico University M

New York
Alfred University M
Canisius College M
City University of New York
  Brooklyn College M
  Hunter College M
  Lehman College M
  Queens College M
College of New Rochelle M, T
College of Saint Rose M
Hofstra University M, T
Long Island University
  Brooklyn Campus M
  C. W. Post Campus M
Manhattan College M
Mercy College M
New York Institute of Technology M
New York University M, D, T
Niagara University M
Roberts Wesleyan College M
St. John's University M, T
St. Lawrence University M
State University of New York
  Albany M
  Buffalo M, D, T
  College at Brockport M
  College at Buffalo M
  College at Oneonta M

College at Plattsburgh M, T
Oswego M
Syracuse University M, D, T
University of Rochester M, D

North Carolina
Appalachian State University M, T
Campbell University M
East Carolina University M, D
Gardner-Webb University M
Lenoir-Rhyne University M
North Carolina Agricultural and
  Technical State University M
North Carolina Central University M
North Carolina State University M, D
University of North Carolina
  Chapel Hill M
  Charlotte M, D
  Greensboro M, D
  Pembroke M
Wake Forest University M, T
Western Carolina University M

North Dakota
North Dakota State University M
University of Mary M
University of North Dakota M

Ohio
Bowling Green State University M, T
Cleveland State University D
Heidelberg University M
John Carroll University M
Kent State University M, D
Malone University M
Ohio State University
  Columbus Campus M, D
Ohio University M, D
Ohio University
  Zanesville Campus M
Union Institute & University M
University of Akron M, D
University of Cincinnati M, D
University of Dayton M, T
Wright State University M
Xavier University M
Youngstown State University M

Oklahoma
East Central University M, T
Northeastern State University M, T
Northwestern Oklahoma State
  University M, T
Oklahoma State University M
Southeastern Oklahoma State
  University M, T
Southwestern Oklahoma State
  University M, T
University of Central Oklahoma M
University of Oklahoma M

Oregon
George Fox University M
Lewis & Clark College M
Northwest Christian University M
Oregon State University M, D
Portland State University M, D, T

Pennsylvania
Arcadia University M
Baptist Bible College of
  Pennsylvania M
Bloomsburg University of
  Pennsylvania M
Bucknell University M
California University of
  Pennsylvania M
Carlow University M, T
Chatham University T
Duquesne University M, D, T
Eastern University M
Edinboro University of
  Pennsylvania M

Gwynedd-Mercy College *M*
Holy Family University *M*
Indiana University of Pennsylvania *M*
Kutztown University of
Pennsylvania *M, T*
Lancaster Bible College *M*
Lehigh University *M*
Marywood University *M*
Millersville University of
Pennsylvania *M*
Penn State
University Park *M, D*
Philadelphia Biblical University *M*
Shippensburg University of
Pennsylvania *M, T*
Slippery Rock University of
Pennsylvania *M*
University of Pennsylvania *M*
University of Scranton *M*
Villanova University *M*
West Chester University of
Pennsylvania *M, T*
Westminster College *M*
Widener University *M, D, T*

Puerto Rico

Bayamon Central University *M*
Inter American University of Puerto
Rico
Metropolitan Campus *M*
San German Campus *M, D*
Pontifical Catholic University of
Puerto Rico *D*
Turabo University *M*
University of Puerto Rico
Arecibo *M*
Rio Piedras *M, D*

Rhode Island

Providence College *M*
Rhode Island College *M*

South Carolina

The Citadel *M*
Clemson University *M*
South Carolina State University *M*
University of South Carolina *M, D*
Winthrop University *M, T*

South Dakota

Northern State University *M*
University of South Dakota *M, D*

Tennessee

Austin Peay State University *M*
Carson-Newman College *M*
East Tennessee State University *M, T*
Freed-Hardeman University *M*
Lincoln Memorial University *M*
Middle Tennessee State University *M*
Tennessee State University *M*
Tennessee Technological
University *M*
University of Memphis *M, D*
University of Tennessee
Chattanooga *M*
Knoxville *M*
Martin *M*
Vanderbilt University *M, D*

Texas

Angelo State University *M*
Dallas Baptist University *M*
Hardin-Simmons University *M*
Houston Baptist University *M*
Lamar University *B, M, T*
Lubbock Christian University *M*
Midwestern State University *M*
Our Lady of the Lake University of San
Antonio *M*
Prairie View A&M University *M*
St. Edward's University *M*
Sam Houston State University *M, D*

Sul Ross State University *M*
Tarleton State University *M*
Texas A&M International
University *M, T*
Texas A&M University
Corpus Christi *M, D, T*
Kingsville *M*
Texas Christian University *M*
Texas Southern University *M, D*
Texas State University: San
Marcos *M, T*
Texas Tech University *M, D*
Texas Wesleyan University *M*
Texas Woman's University *M*
University of Houston *M*
University of Houston
Clear Lake *M*
Victoria *M*
University of Mary Hardin-Baylor *M*
University of North Texas *M, D, T*
University of Texas
Brownsville - Texas Southmost
College *M*
El Paso *M*
Pan American *M*
San Antonio *M, D*
of the Permian Basin *M*
West Texas A&M University *M, T*

Utah

Brigham Young University *M*

Vermont

College of St. Joseph in Vermont *M*
Goddard College *M*
Johnson State College *M*
Lyndon State College *M*
University of Vermont *M*

Virginia

College of William and Mary *M, D*
George Mason University *M*
Hampton University *M*
James Madison University *M, T*
Liberty University *M, T*
Longwood University *M*
Lynchburg College *M*
Marymount University *M*
Old Dominion University *M, D*
Radford University *M, T*
Virginia Commonwealth University *M*
Virginia Polytechnic Institute and
State University *M, D*
Virginia State University *M*

Washington

City University of Seattle *M*
Eastern Washington University *M*
Gonzaga University *M*
Seattle Pacific University *M*
Seattle University *M*
University of Puget Sound *M*
Washington State University *M, D, T*
Western Washington University *M*
Whitworth University *M, T*

West Virginia

American Public University System *M*
Marshall University *B, M*
West Virginia University *M, T*

Wisconsin

Carthage College *M, T*
Concordia University Wisconsin *M*
Marquette University *M*
University of Wisconsin
Madison *M, D*
Oshkosh *M*
Platteville *M*
River Falls *M*
Stout *M*
Superior *M*
Whitewater *M*

Wyoming

University of Wyoming *M, D*

Court reporting

Alabama

Faulkner State Community College *A*
Gadsden State Community College *A*
Prince Institute of Professional
Studies *A*

Arizona

GateWay Community College *C, A*

California

Bryan College: Los Angeles *C, A*
Bryan College: Sacramento *A*
Butte College *C, A*
Cerritos College *C, A*
Chabot College *A*
College of Marin: Kentfield *C, A*
College of the Redwoods *C*
Cypress College *C, A*
Humphreys College *C, A, B*
Kaplan College: Panorama City *A*
Sage College *C, A*
Shasta College *C*
Taft College *C, A*
West Valley College *A*

Colorado

Denver Academy of Court
Reporting *A*

Florida

Brevard Community College *A*
Broward College *A*
Key College *A*
Miami Dade College *A*

Illinois

Illinois Central College *C, A*
Illinois Eastern Community Colleges
Wabash Valley College *C*
MacCormac College *A*
Midstate College *A, B*
South Suburban College of Cook
County *C, A*

Indiana

College of Court Reporting *A*

Iowa

AIB College of Business *A, B*

Kentucky

West Kentucky Community and
Technical College *A*

Maryland

Community College of Baltimore
County *A*

Michigan

Lansing Community College *A*
Oakland Community College *C, A*

Minnesota

Anoka Technical College *C*

Mississippi

Mississippi Gulf Coast Community
College *A*
Northwest Mississippi Community
College *A*

Missouri

St. Louis Community College
St. Louis Community College at
Meramec *A*

Nevada

Everest College: Las Vegas *A*
Truckee Meadows Community
College *C*

New Mexico

Central New Mexico Community
College *C*

New York

Business Informatics Center *A*
Erie Community College
City Campus *C*
Long Island Business Institute *C, A*
Monroe Community College *C*
New York Career Institute *A*
State University of New York
College of Technology at
Alfred *C, A*

North Carolina

Lenoir Community College *A*

Ohio

Clark State Community College *A*
Cuyahoga Community College
Metropolitan Campus *A*
Stark State College of Technology *A*

Pennsylvania

Harrisburg Area Community
College *C, A*
Luzerne County Community
College *A*

South Carolina

Midlands Technical College *C, A*

Tennessee

Chattanooga State Community
College *A*

Texas

Amarillo College *C, A*
Court Reporting Institute of Dallas *A*
Court Reporting Institute of
Houston *A*
Del Mar College *C, A*
El Paso Community College *A*
Kilgore College *C, A*
San Antonio College *C*

Washington

Green River Community College *A*

West Virginia

Huntington Junior College *A*

Wisconsin

Gateway Technical College *A*
Lakeshore Technical College *A*
Wisconsin Indianhead Technical
College *A*

Crafts/folk art/artisanry

Alaska

Ilisagvik College *C*

Arizona

Prescott College *B, M*

California

California College of the Arts *B, M*
California State University
Northridge *B*
College of the Siskiyous *C*
Fresno City College *C, A*
Palomar College *A*
Pasadena City College *A*

San Joaquin Delta College *A*
Santiago Canyon College *A*

Illinois
University of Illinois
   Urbana-Champaign *B, M*

Indiana
Indiana University-Purdue University
   Fort Wayne *B*

Kansas
Allen County Community College *A*

Massachusetts
Bridgewater State College *B*

Michigan
College for Creative Studies *B*

Montana
Miles Community College *A*

New York
Rochester Institute of
   Technology *A, B, M*

North Carolina
Montgomery Community College *C, A*

Ohio
Bowling Green State University *B*
Kent State University *B, M*

Oregon
Pacific Northwest College of Art *M*

Pennsylvania
Harrisburg Area Community
   College *A*
Kutztown University of
   Pennsylvania *B*
University of the Arts *B*

Virginia
Southwest Virginia Community
   College *C*
Virginia Commonwealth University *B*

Creative writing

Alabama
Faulkner University *B*
University of Alabama *M*

Alaska
University of Alaska
   Fairbanks *M*

Arizona
Arizona State University *M*
Northern Arizona University *M*
Prescott College *B, M*
University of Arizona *B, M*

Arkansas
Arkansas Tech University *B*
University of Arkansas *M*

California
Antioch Southern California
   Antioch University Los Angeles *M*
Berkeley City College *C*
Biola University *B*
California College of the Arts *B, M*
California State University
   Fresno *M*
   Long Beach *B, M*
   Northridge *B*

Sacramento *M*
San Bernardino *B*
Chapman University *B, M*
College of the Siskiyous *C*
Dominican University of California *B*
Foothill College *A*
Fresno Pacific University *B*
Grossmont College *C, A*
Holy Names University *M*
Loyola Marymount University *M*
Mills College *B, M*
National University *M*
Otis College of Art and Design *M*
Pepperdine University *B*
Pitzer College *B*
Point Loma Nazarene University *B*
St. Mary's College of California *M*
San Diego State University *M*
San Francisco State University *M*
San Jose State University *M*
University of California
   Irvine *M*
   Riverside *B, M*
University of La Verne *C*
University of Redlands *B*
University of San Francisco *M*
University of Southern
   California *B, M, D*

Colorado
Adams State College *B*
Colorado College *B*
Colorado State University *B, M*
Naropa University *M*
University of Colorado
   Boulder *M*

Connecticut
Albertus Magnus College *B*
Fairfield University *M*
Trinity College *B*
University of Bridgeport *B*
Western Connecticut State
   University *B, M*

District of Columbia
American University *M*
Corcoran College of Art and Design *B*

Florida
Eckerd College *B*
Florida Atlantic University *M*
Florida International University *M*
Florida State University *B, D*
Saint Leo University *B*
University of Central Florida *M*
University of Florida *M*
University of Miami *B, M*
University of Tampa *A, B*

Georgia
Agnes Scott College *B*
Emory University *B*
Georgia College and State
   University *M*
Georgia State University *M*
Kennesaw State University *M*
Savannah College of Art and
   Design *B, M*
University of Georgia *M*

Idaho
Boise State University *M*
College of Idaho *B*
Lewis-Clark State College *B*
University of Idaho *B, M*

Illinois
Columbia College Chicago *B, M*
DePaul University *M*
Eureka College *B*
Knox College *B*
Lewis University *B*

Millikin University *B*
North Central College *B*
Northwestern University *B, M*
Roosevelt University *M*
School of the Art Institute of
   Chicago *B, M*
Southern Illinois University
   Carbondale *M*
University of Illinois
   Urbana-Champaign *M*

Indiana
Butler University *B, M*
Indiana University
   Bloomington *M*
Indiana Wesleyan University *B*
Manchester College *A*
Purdue University *B, M, D*
Saint Joseph's College *B*
Saint Mary's College *B*
St. Mary-of-the-Woods College *B*
University of Evansville *B*
Valparaiso University *B*

Iowa
Briar Cliff University *B*
Coe College *B*
Loras College *B*
Northwestern College *B*
University of Iowa *M*
Waldorf College *B*

Kansas
Central Christian College of Kansas *A*
Pittsburg State University *B, M*
University of Kansas *M*
Wichita State University *M*

Kentucky
Asbury College *B*
Berea College *B*
Murray State University *M*
Spalding University *B, M*

Louisiana
Louisiana State University and
   Agricultural and Mechanical
   College *M*
McNeese State University *M*

Maine
Colby College *B*
University of Maine
   Farmington *B*
University of Southern Maine *M*

Maryland
Goucher College *M*
Johns Hopkins University *B, M*
Loyola University Maryland *B*
University of Maryland
   College Park *M*

Massachusetts
Boston University *M*
Brandeis University *B*
Bridgewater State College *B, M*
Eastern Nazarene College *B*
Emerson College *B, M*
Hampshire College *B*
Lesley University *M*
Massachusetts Institute of
   Technology *B*
Salem State College *B*
Suffolk University *B*
University of Massachusetts
   Amherst *M*
   Boston *M*
Western New England College *B*

Michigan
Adrian College *A, B*

Albion College *B*
Central Michigan University *B, M*
Eastern Michigan University *B, M*
Grand Valley State University *B*
Kalamazoo College *B*
Northern Michigan University *B, M*
Siena Heights University *B*
Spring Arbor University *B*
University of Detroit Mercy *C, B*
University of Michigan *B, M*

Minnesota
Augsburg College *B*
Concordia College: Moorhead *B*
Hamline University *M*
Minnesota State University
   Mankato *B, M*
   Moorhead *M*
Saint Cloud State University *B*
Southwest Minnesota State
   University *B*
University of Minnesota
   Twin Cities *M*
University of St. Thomas *B*

Mississippi
Belhaven University *B*
University of Mississippi *M*

Missouri
Drury University *B*
Kansas City Art Institute *B*
Lindenwood University *B, M*
Missouri Southern State University *B*
Missouri State University *M*
Rockhurst University *C*
Saint Louis University *C*
Stephens College *B*
University of Missouri
   St. Louis *M*
Washington University in St.
   Louis *C, M*

Montana
University of Montana *M*
University of Montana: Western *B*

Nebraska
Creighton University *B*
Union College *B*
University of Nebraska
   Omaha *C, B*

Nevada
University of Nevada
   Las Vegas *M*
   Reno *B*

New Hampshire
Chester College of New England *B*
Lebanon College *A*
New England College *B, M*
Southern New Hampshire
   University *B*
University of New Hampshire *M*

New Jersey
Fairleigh Dickinson University
   College at Florham *B, M*
Seton Hall University *B*

New Mexico
College of Santa Fe *B*
Institute of American Indian Arts *A, B*
New Mexico Highlands University *M*
New Mexico State University *M*
Santa Fe Community College *C*
University of New Mexico *M*

New York
Adelphi University *M*
Bard College *B, M*

City University of New York
  Baruch College *B*
  Brooklyn College *B, M*
  City College *M*
  Hunter College *B, M*
  Lehman College *M*
  Queens College *M*
Columbia University *B*
Columbia University
  School of General Studies *B*
Cornell University *M*
D'Youville College *B*
Hamilton College *B*
Hofstra University *B, M*
Ithaca College *B*
Manhattanville College *M*
New York University *M*
Pratt Institute *B*
St. Lawrence University *B*
Sarah Lawrence College *M*
State University of New York
  Albany *D*
  Binghamton *B*
  College at Brockport *B, M*
  Purchase *B*
  Stony Brook *M*
Syracuse University *B, M*

North Carolina

Elon University *B*
Gardner-Webb University *B*
North Carolina State University *M*
Queens University of Charlotte *B, M*
St. Andrews Presbyterian College *B*
Salem College *B*
University of North Carolina
  Greensboro *M*
  Wilmington *B, M*
Warren Wilson College *M*

North Dakota

Dickinson State University *B*

Ohio

Antioch University McGregor *M*
Ashland University *B*
Baldwin-Wallace College *B*
Bowling Green State University *B, M*
Capital University *B*
Cleveland State University *M*
Hiram College *B*
Miami University
  Oxford Campus *M*
Mount Union College *B*
Oberlin College *B*
Ohio Northern University *B*
Ohio University *B*
Ohio Wesleyan University *B*
Otterbein College *B*
Owens Community College
  Toledo *A*
University of Akron *M*
University of Cincinnati *M, D*
University of Findlay *B*
Youngstown State University *M*

Oklahoma

Oklahoma Christian University *B*
Oklahoma City University *M*
Oklahoma State University *M*
University of Central Oklahoma *M*
University of Oklahoma *M*

Oregon

Linfield College *B*
Oregon State University *M*
Pacific University *B, M*
Portland State University *M*
Reed College *B*
University of Oregon *M*

Pennsylvania

Allegheny College *B*

Arcadia University *B*
Bucknell University *B*
Carlow University *B, M*
Carnegie Mellon University *B*
Chatham University *B, M*
Franklin & Marshall College *B*
Gettysburg College *B*
Lycoming College *B*
Moravian College *B*
Penn State
  Erie, The Behrend College *B*
Rosemont College *M*
Saint Joseph's University *M*
Seton Hill University *B, M*
Slippery Rock University of
  Pennsylvania *B*
Susquehanna University *B*
Temple University *M*
University of Pittsburgh *C, B*
University of Pittsburgh
  Bradford *B*
  Johnstown *B*
Waynesburg University *B*
Westminster College *B, T*
Widener University *B, T*
Wilkes University *M*

Rhode Island

Brown University *M*
Rhode Island College *M*
Roger Williams University *B*

South Carolina

Bob Jones University *B*
Converse College *B, M*
Presbyterian College *B*
University of South Carolina *M*

South Dakota

Dakota Wesleyan University *B*

Tennessee

University of Memphis *M*
Vanderbilt University *M*

Texas

Houston Baptist University *B*
McMurry University *B*
Southern Methodist University *B*
Stephen F. Austin State University *B*
Texas State University: San Marcos *M*
University of Houston *M, D*
University of North Texas *M*
University of Texas
  Austin *M*
  El Paso *B, M*
  Pan American *M*

Utah

University of Utah *M*

Vermont

Bennington College *B, M*
Champlain College *B*
Goddard College *B, M*
Green Mountain College *B*
Marlboro College *B*
Southern Vermont College *B*

Virginia

Emory & Henry College *B*
George Mason University *M*
Hollins University *B, M*
Longwood University *B*
Old Dominion University *M*
Randolph College *B*
Sweet Briar College *B*
University of Virginia *M*
Virginia Commonwealth University *M*
Virginia Polytechnic Institute and
  State University *M*

Washington

Eastern Washington University *M*
Everett Community College *A*
Olympic College *C*
Pacific Lutheran University *M*
Seattle Pacific University *M*
Seattle University *B*
University of Washington *M*
Western Washington University *B*

West Virginia

Alderson-Broaddus College *B*
West Virginia University *M*
West Virginia Wesleyan College *B*
Wheeling Jesuit University *B*

Wisconsin

Beloit College *B*
Cardinal Stritch University *B*
Carroll University *B*
Marquette University *B*
St. Norbert College *B*
University of Wisconsin
  Madison *M*
  Whitewater *B*

Wyoming

University of Wyoming *M*

Credit management

Illinois

Harper College *C*

New York

Globe Institute of Technology *C*

Criminal justice and law enforcement

Alabama

Bishop State Community College *A*
Columbia Southern University *A, B, M*
Gadsden State Community College *A*
George C. Wallace State Community
  College
  Selma *C*
Judson College *B*
Northeast Alabama Community
  College *C, A*
Remington College
  Mobile *A*
South University: Montgomery *B*
Troy University *M*
University of North Alabama *B, M*

Alaska

University of Alaska
  Fairbanks *M*
  Southeast *C*

Arizona

Arizona State University *B, M*
Arizona Western College *A*
Brookline College
  Phoenix *A*
  Tempe *A*
  Tucson *A*
Eastern Arizona College *A*
Northcentral University *B, M, D*
Northern Arizona University *B, M*
Pima Community College *C*
Prescott College *M*
Rio Salado College *C, A*
Scottsdale Community College *C, A*
University of Arizona *B*
University of Phoenix *A, B*

Arkansas

Arkansas State University *A*

Arkansas State University
  Beebe *C, A*
  Mountain Home *C, A*
Arkansas Tech University *C*
Mid-South Community College *C, A*
North Arkansas College *C, A*
Northwest Arkansas Community
  College *A*
Ouachita Technical College *C*
Ozarka College *A*
Pulaski Technical College *C, A*
Southeast Arkansas College *C, A*
Southern Arkansas University *C, A*
Southern Arkansas University Tech *C*
University of Arkansas
  Community College at Hope *C, A*
  Cossatot Community College of the
    C, A
  Fort Smith *C, A, B*
  Monticello *C, A*
  Pine Bluff *C, A*
University of Arkansas Community
  College at Morrilton *C, A*

California

Alliant International University *B*
California Baptist University *B*
California State University
  East Bay *B*
  Los Angeles *B, M*
  Sacramento *B, M*
  San Bernardino *C, B, M*
Citrus College *C, A*
College of the Desert *C, A*
College of the Redwoods *C, A*
College of the Sequoias *C, A*
College of the Siskiyous *C, A*
Copper Mountain College *C, A*
Cosumnes River College *A*
Crafton Hills College *C, A*
Cuesta College *C, A*
De Anza College *A*
Diablo Valley College *C*
El Camino College *C, A*
Folsom Lake College *A*
Fresno City College *C, A*
Gavilan College *C*
Glendale Community College *A*
Golden West College *C, A*
Hartnell College *C, A*
Heald College
  Hayward *A*
  Roseville *A*
  Salinas *A*
  Stockton *C, A*
Imperial Valley College *C, A*
Irvine Valley College *C, A*
Lake Tahoe Community College *C, A*
Lassen Community College *A*
Long Beach City College *C, A*
Mendocino College *C, A*
Modesto Junior College *A*
Monterey Peninsula College *C, A*
National University *B*
Ohlone College *C, A*
Palo Verde College *C, A*
Palomar College *C, A*
San Bernardino Valley College *C, A*
San Diego Miramar College *C, A*
San Diego State University *B, M*
San Jose City College *A*
Santa Barbara City College *C, A*
Santa Monica College *C, A*
Shasta College *A*
Skyline College *C, A*
Sonoma State University *B*
Southwestern College *C, A*
Victor Valley College *C, A*
West Hills College: Lemoore *A*
Western Career College: Antioch *A*
Western Career College: Citrus
  Heights *A*
Westwood College of Technology
  Westwood College: Los Angeles *B*

Colorado

Aims Community College *A*
American Sentinel University *A, B*
Arapahoe Community College *C, A*
Aspen University *B, M*
Colorado Northwestern Community
   College *C, A*
Community College of Aurora *A*
Johnson & Wales University:
   Denver *B*
Kaplan College: Denver *A*
Mesa State College *A*
Metropolitan State College of
   Denver *B*
Northeastern Junior College *C, A*
Pikes Peak Community College *C, A*
Pueblo Community College *C, A*
Red Rocks Community College *C, A*
Trinidad State Junior College *A*
University of Colorado
   Colorado Springs *B, M*
   Denver *M*
Westwood College of Technology
   Westwood College: Denver South *B*
Westwood College: Denver North *B*

Connecticut

Goodwin College *C*
Northwestern Connecticut
   Community College *A*
Norwalk Community College *A*
Post University *B*
Quinebaug Valley Community
   College *C*
Sacred Heart University *B, M*
Three Rivers Community College *A*
Tunxis Community College *C*
University of New Haven *B*
Western Connecticut State
   University *M*

Delaware

Delaware Technical and Community
   College
   Owens *A*
   Stanton/Wilmington *A*
   Terry *C, A*

District of Columbia

George Washington University *M*
Trinity Washington University *B*
University of the District of
   Columbia *A*

Florida

Bethune-Cookman University *B*
Brown Mackie College: Miami *A*
Central Florida Community College *A*
Chipola College *C, A*
Daytona State College *A*
Edison State College *A*
Edward Waters College *B*
Florida Atlantic University *M*
Florida Keys Community College *C*
Florida State College at Jacksonville *A*
Gulf Coast Community College *A*
Hillsborough Community College *A*
Hodges University *M*
Johnson & Wales University: North
   Miami *B*
Lake City Community College *C*
Lake-Sumter Community College *A*
Lynn University *B*
Northwest Florida State College *A*
Pasco-Hernando Community
   College *A*
Pensacola Junior College *A*
Rasmussen College: Ocala *A, B*
St. Petersburg College *C, A*
Seminole Community College *C, A*
South Florida Community College *A*
Southeastern University *B*
Southwest Florida College *C, A, B*

Tallahassee Community College *A*
Valencia Community College *A*

Georgia

American InterContinental
   University *A, B*
Athens Technical College *C, A*
Atlanta Metropolitan College *A*
Bainbridge College *A*
College of Coastal Georgia *C, A*
Georgia College and State
   University *B, M*
Georgia Military College *A*
Georgia Northwestern Technical
   College *C, A*
Georgia Perimeter College *A*
Griffin Technical College *A*
Middle Georgia Technical
   College *C, A*
North Georgia College & State
   University *B*
North Georgia Technical College *C, A*
Savannah State University *B*
South University: Savannah *B, M*
Southeastern Technical College *A*

Hawaii

Chaminade University of Honolulu *M*
Hawaii Pacific University *A, B*
Heald College
   Honolulu *A*
University of Hawaii
   Hawaii Community College *A*
   Honolulu Community College *A*
   West Oahu *B*

Idaho

Boise State University *A, B, M*

Illinois

Bradley University *B*
Carl Sandburg College *A*
City Colleges of Chicago
   Harold Washington College *C, A*
Concordia University Chicago *B*
Danville Area Community College *A*
Elmhurst College *B*
Eureka College *B*
Greenville College *B*
Illinois Valley Community
   College *C, A*
Joliet Junior College *C, A*
Judson University *C*
Kaskaskia College *C, A*
Lewis University *B, M*
Lincoln College *A, B*
North Park University *B*
Rasmussen College: Aurora *A*
Rasmussen College: Rockford *A*
Rock Valley College *A*
Southeastern Illinois College *C*
Southern Illinois University
   Carbondale *B, M*
Spoon River College *A*
Taylor Business Institute *A*
Triton College *C, A*
University of St. Francis *B*
Western Illinois University *B, M*

Indiana

Ancilla College *A*
Calumet College of St. Joseph *M*
Grace College *B*
Harrison College
   Anderson *A*
   Elkhart *A*
   Evansville *A*
   Fort Wayne *A, B*
   Indianapolis *A, B*
   Muncie *A*
Indiana Institute of Technology *B*
Indiana University-Purdue University
   Fort Wayne *A, B, M*

Purdue University *B*
Purdue University
   Calumet *B*
University of Indianapolis *A, B*

Iowa

Briar Cliff University *B*
Ellsworth Community College *A*
Kaplan University
   Cedar Falls *A*
   Davenport *M*
   Des Moines *A, B*
Marshalltown Community College *A*
Mount Mercy College *B*
Southeastern Community College
   North Campus *A*

Kansas

Brown Mackie College
   Salina *A*
Central Christian College of
   Kansas *A, B*
Cowley County Community
   College *C, A*
Fort Scott Community College *A*
Garden City Community College *A*
Highland Community College *A*
Labette Community College *A*
MidAmerica Nazarene University *B*
Newman University *B*
Seward County Community College *A*
Washburn University *A, B, M*

Kentucky

Beckfield College *A, B*
Bellarmine University *B*
Campbellsville University *B*
Draughons Junior College *C, A*
Eastern Kentucky University *B*
Elizabethtown Community and
   Technical College *A*
Hopkinsville Community College *C, A*
Madisonville Community College *A*
Somerset Community College *C, A*
Thomas More College *A, B*
Union College *B*
University of Louisville *C, B, M*

Louisiana

Louisiana College *B*
Southern University
   Shreveport *A*
Southwest University *A, B, M*

Maine

Andover College *A*
Central Maine Community College *A*
Husson University *A, B, M*
Thomas College *B*
University of Maine
   Augusta *B*
   Fort Kent *A*
   Presque Isle *A, B*
York County Community College *A*

Maryland

Anne Arundel Community
   College *C, A*
Baltimore City Community College *A*
College of Southern Maryland *C, A*
Frostburg State University *B*
Kaplan College: Hagerstown *A*
Montgomery College *A*
Stevenson University *B*
University of Maryland
   University College *C*

Massachusetts

American International College *B*
Anna Maria College *M*
Bay State College *A*
Boston University *M*
Bridgewater State College *M*

Bunker Hill Community College *C, A*
Cape Cod Community College *C, A*
Curry College *M*
Dean College *A*
Eastern Nazarene College *B*
Lasell College *B*
Marian Court College *A*
Massachusetts Bay Community
   College *A*
Middlesex Community College *C, A*
Mount Wachusett Community
   College *C, A*
Newbury College *B*
Quinsigamond Community
   College *C, A*
Roxbury Community College *A*
Salem State College *B, M*
Springfield College *B*
Suffolk University *B*
University of Massachusetts
   Lowell *A, B*

Michigan

Alpena Community College *A*
Bay de Noc Community College *A*
Delta College *A*
Ferris State University *M*
Finlandia University *A*
Gogebic Community College *A*
Grand Rapids Community College *A*
Grand Valley State University *B, M*
Henry Ford Community College *A*
Kalamazoo Valley Community
   College *A*
Kirtland Community College *A*
Lake Superior State University *A, B*
Lansing Community College *A*
Michigan State University *B, M, D*
Muskegon Community College *C, A*
Northern Michigan University *A*
Northwestern Michigan College *A*
Oakland Community College *C*
St. Clair County Community
   College *C, A*
University of Detroit Mercy *B, M*
University of Michigan
   Flint *B, M*
Washtenaw Community College *A*
Wayne County Community College *A*
West Shore Community College *A*

Minnesota

Concordia University: St. Paul *B*
Fond du Lac Tribal and Community
   College *C, A*
Globe University *A*
Minnesota School of Business:
   Blaine *A*
Minnesota State University
   Mankato *C, B*
Minnesota West Community and
   Technical College *A*
Northland Community & Technical
   College *A*
Saint Cloud State University *M*
St. Mary's University of Minnesota *B*
Southwest Minnesota State
   University *B*
University of Minnesota
   Crookston *B*
University of St. Thomas *M*
Vermilion Community College *A*
Walden University *B, D*
Winona State University *B*

Mississippi

Mississippi College *B, M*
Mississippi Delta Community
   College *A*
Mississippi Valley State University *M*
University of Mississippi *B, M*

Missouri

Central Methodist University *B*
Columbia College *A, B, M*
Culver-Stockton College *B*
Grantham University *A, B*
Hannibal-LaGrange College *A, B*
Harris-Stowe State University *B*
Jefferson College *A*
Lincoln University *A, B*
Lindenwood University *M*
Metropolitan Community College:
　Blue River *A*
Metropolitan Community College:
　Maple Woods *C, A*
Metropolitan Community College:
　Penn Valley *C, A*
Missouri Southern State
　University *A, B*
Missouri Valley College *B*
Park University *A, B*
Saint Louis University *B*
Southwest Baptist University *B*
University of Central Missouri *B, M*
University of Missouri
　Kansas City *B, M*

Montana

University of Great Falls *M*

Nebraska

Bellevue University *B, M*
Peru State College *B*

Nevada

Great Basin College *A*
High-Tech Institute *A*
Kaplan College: Las Vegas *C, A*
Nevada State College *B*
Truckee Meadows Community
　College *A*

New Hampshire

Granite State College *B*
NHTI-Concord's Community
　College *A*
White Mountains Community
　College *A*

New Jersey

Berkeley College- Garret Mountain
　Campus *B*
The College of New Jersey *B*
Essex County College *A*
Fairleigh Dickinson University
　Metropolitan Campus *B*
Felician College *B*
Kean University *B, M*
Middlesex County College *A*
Raritan Valley Community College *A*
Rutgers, The State University of New
　Jersey
　New Brunswick/Piscataway
　　Campus *B*
Thomas Edison State College *A, B*
Union County College *C, A*

New Mexico

Brookline College
　Albuquerque *A*
Mesalands Community College *C, A*
New Mexico State University
　Grants *A*
Western New Mexico University *C, B*

New York

Adelphi University *B*
Berkeley College *B*
Berkeley College of New York City *B*
Briarcliffe College *B*
Bryant & Stratton Business Institute
　Bryant & Stratton College: Albany *A*
Cayuga County Community College *C*

City University of New York
　John Jay College of Criminal
　　Justice *B, M*
Clinton Community College *A*
College of Saint Rose *B*
Columbia-Greene Community
　College *A*
Corning Community College *A*
Erie Community College
　City Campus *C, A*
　North Campus *A*
Excelsior College *B*
Genesee Community College *C, A*
Herkimer County Community
　College *A*
Iona College *B, M*
Jefferson Community College *C, A*
Keuka College *B*
Long Island University
　C. W. Post Campus *B, M*
Marist College *B*
Mercy College *B*
Mohawk Valley Community College *A*
Molloy College *B, M*
Monroe College *B*
Monroe Community College *C*
Nassau Community College *A*
New York Institute of Technology *B*
Niagara County Community
　College *A*
Onondaga Community College *C*
Orange County Community College *C*
Pace University *B*
Roberts Wesleyan College *B*
Rochester Institute of Technology *B*
Sage College of Albany *B*
St. John's University *C, A, B, M*
St. Thomas Aquinas College *B*
State University of New York
　College at Potsdam *B*
　College of Technology at Canton *B*
　Farmingdale *C, A*
Tompkins Cortland Community
　College *C*
Ulster County Community College *A*

North Carolina

Alamance Community College *A*
Bladen Community College *A*
Brevard College *B*
Catawba College *B*
Chowan University *B*
College of the Albemarle *A*
Johnston Community College *A*
Methodist University *B, M*
Miller-Motte Technical College *A, B*
North Carolina Central University *B*
Rockingham Community College *A*
South College *A*
Southeastern Community
　College *C, A*
Surry Community College *A*
Vance-Granville Community
　College *A*

North Dakota

United Tribes Technical College *C, A*
University of Mary *B*

Ohio

Ashland University *A, B*
Bowling Green State University *B*
Bryant & Stratton College
　Eastlake *A*
Bryant & Stratton College:
　Cleveland *C*
Cedarville University *B*
Central Ohio Technical College *A*
Clark State Community College *A*
Columbus State Community
　College *A*
Heidelberg University *B*
James A. Rhodes State College *A*
Kaplan College: Dayton *A*

Marion Technical College *A*
Miami University
　Hamilton Campus *A*
Mount Vernon Nazarene University *B*
North Central State College *A*
Northwest State Community
　College *A*
Ohio Northern University *B*
Ohio University
　Southern Campus at Ironton *A*
Owens Community College
　Toledo *A*
Remington College: Cleveland West *A*
Southwestern College of Business
　Southwestern College: Franklin *A*
　Southwestern College:
　　Tri-County *A*
Southwestern College: Dayton *A*
Terra State Community College *C*
Tiffin University *A, B, M*
Union Institute & University *B*
University of Cincinnati
　Clermont College *A*
University of Findlay *B*
Urbana University *B*
Washington State Community
　College *A*
Youngstown State University *A, B, M*

Oklahoma

Eastern Oklahoma State College *A*
Mid-America Christian University *B*
Northeastern State University *B, M*
Northern Oklahoma College *A*
Oklahoma City University *B, M*
Rogers State University *B*
University of Central Oklahoma *M*

Oregon

Chemeketa Community College *A*
Portland State University *B*
Southern Oregon University *B*
Treasure Valley Community College *A*
Western Oregon University *B, M*

Pennsylvania

Alvernia University *B*
Butler County Community College *A*
Chestnut Hill College *A, B*
Clarion University of Pennsylvania *A*
Delaware Valley College *B*
Drexel University *B*
Gwynedd-Mercy College *B*
Harcum College *A*
Harrisburg Area Community
　College *A*
Kaplan Career Institute: Harrisburg *A*
Kaplan Career Institute: Pittsburgh *A*
Keystone College *B*
Lehigh Carbon Community
　College *C, A*
Lock Haven University of
　Pennsylvania *A, B*
Mansfield University of
　Pennsylvania *A, B*
Marywood University *M*
Mercyhurst College *M*
Penn State
　Abington *B*
　Altoona *B*
　Beaver *B*
　Berks *B*
　Brandywine *B*
　DuBois *B*
　Erie, The Behrend College *B*
　Fayette, The Eberly Campus *B*
　Greater Allegheny *B*
　Hazleton *B*
　Lehigh Valley *B*
　Mont Alto *B*
　New Kensington *B*
　Schuylkill *B*
　Shenango *B*
　University Park *B*

　Wilkes-Barre *B*
　Worthington Scranton *B*
　York *B*
Pennsylvania Highlands Community
　College *A*
Point Park University *A, B*
Reading Area Community College *A*
University of Pittsburgh
　Bradford *B*
　Greensburg *B*
　Titusville *C*
Villanova University *B, M*
Waynesburg University *B*
Widener University *B, M*
YTI Career Institute: Lancaster *A*
YTI Career Institute: York *A*
York College of Pennsylvania *A, B*

Puerto Rico

Inter American University of Puerto
　Rico
　Guayama Campus *B*
　Ponce Campus *B, M*
Turabo University *M*
Universidad del Este *B, M*
University of Puerto Rico
　Aguadilla *A*
　Carolina Regional College *B*

Rhode Island

Johnson & Wales University:
　Providence *B*
Roger Williams University *A, B, M*
Salve Regina University *A, B, M*

South Carolina

Anderson University *B*
Bob Jones University *B*
The Citadel *B*
Claflin University *B*
Lander University *B*
Limestone College *B*
Morris College *B*
South Carolina State University *B*
Spartanburg Methodist College *A*
Technical College of the
　Lowcountry *C, A*
Trident Technical College *C, A*
University of South Carolina *B, M, D*

South Dakota

Kilian Community College *A*
Southeast Technical Institute *A*

Tennessee

Austin Peay State University *B*
East Tennessee State University *B, M*
Lambuth University *B*
Middle Tennessee State
　University *B, M*
Tennessee State University *M*
Trevecca Nazarene University *B*
University of Memphis *B, M*
University of Tennessee
　Chattanooga *B, M*
　Martin *B*

Texas

Abilene Christian University *B*
Cedar Valley College *C, A*
Central Texas College *A*
Concordia University Texas *B*
East Texas Baptist University *B*
Grayson County College *A*
Hill College *C, A*
Howard College *C, A*
Kilgore College *A*
Lubbock Christian University *B*
McLennan Community College *C, A*
Midland College *A*
Palo Alto College *A*
St. Philip's College *A*
Sam Houston State University *M*

South Plains College *A*
South Texas College *A*
Sul Ross State University *M*
Texarkana College *C, A*
Texas A&M University
 Commerce *B*
Texas College *B*
Texas Southern University *B, M, D*
Texas State University: San Marcos *M*
Trinity Valley Community
 College *C, A*
University of Houston
 Victoria *B*
University of Mary Hardin-Baylor *B*
University of Texas
 Brownsville - Texas Southmost
  College *B*
 Pan American *B, M*
 of the Permian Basin *M*
Wayland Baptist University *A, B*
West Texas A&M University *B*
Western Texas College *A*
Wiley College *A, B*

Utah

Eagle Gate College: Layton *A, B*
Eagle Gate College: Murray *A*
Snow College *A*
Utah Valley University *A, B*

Vermont

Champlain College *B*
College of St. Joseph in Vermont *A, B*

Virginia

Averett University *B*
Blue Ridge Community College *C*
Bluefield College *B*
Bryant & Stratton College: Virginia
 Beach *A, B*
Central Virginia Community
 College *A*
Danville Community College *A*
George Mason University *M, D*
Hampton University *B*
Mountain Empire Community
 College *A*
New River Community College *A*
Northern Virginia Community
 College *C, A*
Rappahannock Community College *C*
Shenandoah University *B*
Thomas Nelson Community
 College *A*
Virginia Commonwealth
 University *B, M*
Virginia Intermont College *B*

Washington

Bellevue College *A*
Centralia College *A*
Everett Community College *A*
Lower Columbia College *A*
Peninsula College *C, A*
Shoreline Community College *A*
Spokane Community College *A*
Spokane Falls Community
 College *C, A*
Washington State University *B, M, D*
Yakima Valley Community
 College *C, A*

West Virginia

American Public University
 System *B, M*
Fairmont State University *B*
New River Community and Technical
 College *A*
Potomac State College of West
 Virginia University *A, B*
West Virginia Wesleyan College *B*

Wisconsin

Lakeland College *B*
Marian University *M*
University of Wisconsin
 Platteville *B*

Wyoming

Central Wyoming College *A*
Eastern Wyoming College *A*
Laramie County Community
 College *A*
Western Wyoming Community
 College *A*

Criminal justice studies

Alabama

Alabama State University *B*
Andrew Jackson University *C, A, B, M*
Athens State University *B*
Auburn University at
 Montgomery *B, M*
Central Alabama Community
 College *C, A*
Chattahoochee Valley Community
 College *C, A*
Faulkner University *A, B, M*
Jacksonville State University *B, M*
Lawson State Community College *A*
Troy University *B*
University of Alabama *B, M*
University of Alabama
 Birmingham *B, M*
University of South Alabama *B*

Alaska

University of Alaska
 Fairbanks *B*

Arizona

Arizona State University *B, M, D*
Central Arizona College *A*
Chandler-Gilbert Community College
 Pecos *C*
Coconino County Community
 College *A*
Estrella Mountain Community
 College *C, A*
Everest College
 Phoenix *A, B*
Glendale Community College *A*
Grand Canyon University *B*
Northern Arizona University *B, M*
Northland Pioneer College *A*
Pima Community College *A*
Scottsdale Community College *A*

Arkansas

Arkansas State University *M*
Arkansas Tech University *A*
Black River Technical College *A*
Harding University *B*
Northwest Arkansas Community
 College *A*
Ouachita Technical College *A*
Southeast Arkansas College *C, A*
Southern Arkansas University *B*
University of Arkansas *B*
University of Arkansas
 Community College at Batesville *A*
 Little Rock *B, M*
 Monticello *B*
 Pine Bluff *B*

California

California State University
 Bakersfield *B*
 Chico *B*
 Dominguez Hills *B*
 Fresno *B*
 Fullerton *B*

 Long Beach *B, M*
 Stanislaus *B, M*
Citrus College *A*
College of the Redwoods *C*
College of the Siskiyous *C, A*
Golden West College *C, A*
Kaplan College: Vista *A*
Loma Linda University *M*
Los Angeles Mission College *C, A*
National University *B, M*
Remington College
 San Diego *A, B*
Saddleback College *C*
San Francisco State University *B*
San Jose State University *B, M*
Santa Barbara Business College *A*
Santa Barbara Business College
 Bakersfield *A*
 Santa Maria *C, A*
Santa Barbara Business College: Palm
 Desert *A*
Santa Barbara Business College:
 Ventura *A*
Shasta College *A*
Sierra College *A*
Southwestern College *A*
Taft College *A*
Ventura College *C, A*
West Valley College *A*
Westwood College: South Bay *B*
Yuba Community College District *A*

Colorado

Colorado Mountain College *A*
Community College of Aurora *A*
Mesa State College *B*
Metropolitan State College of
 Denver *B*
Remington College
 Colorado Springs *A, B*
Trinidad State Junior College *A*
University of Northern Colorado *B*
Western State College of Colorado *B*

Connecticut

Albertus Magnus College *B*
Central Connecticut State
 University *M*
Lincoln College of New England:
 Briarwood *A, B*
Mitchell College *B*
Quinnipiac University *B*
Three Rivers Community College *C, A*
University of New Haven *M*

Delaware

Delaware State University *B*
University of Delaware *B*
Wilmington University *B*

District of Columbia

American University *B, M*
George Washington University *B, M*

Florida

Broward College *A*
Edison State College *A, B*
Florida Agricultural and Mechanical
 University *B*
Florida Atlantic University *B*
Florida Gulf Coast University *B*
Florida International University *B, M*
Florida National College *A, B*
Florida State College at Jacksonville *A*
Florida State University *M*
Gulf Coast Community College *A*
Hodges University *A, B*
Indian River State College *A*
Lake City Community College *A*
Miami Dade College *C, A, B*
Northwest Florida State College *A*
Nova Southeastern University *B, M*
Polk State College *A*

Saint Leo University *B, M*
Saint Thomas University *C, B*
State College of Florida,
 Manatee-Sarasota *A*
Tallahassee Community College *A*
University of Central Florida *B*
University of North Florida *B, M*
University of South Florida *B, M, D*
University of West Florida *B*

Georgia

Albany State University *B, M*
Albany Technical College *C, A*
Ashworth College *A, B, M*
Augusta State University *A, B*
Central Georgia Technical
 College *C, A*
Chattahoochee Technical
 College *C, A*
Clark Atlanta University *B, M*
Clayton State University *B*
Columbus State University *C, A, B*
Darton College *A*
East Georgia College *A*
Gainesville State College *A*
Georgia Southern University *B*
Georgia State University *B, M, D*
Gordon College *A*
Kennesaw State University *B*
Macon State College *A*
Mercer University *B*
Middle Georgia College *C, A*
Piedmont College *B*
Savannah Technical College *C, A*
Southwest Georgia Technical
 College *C, A*
University of Georgia *B*
Valdosta State University *B, M*
West Georgia Technical College *C, A*
Young Harris College *A*

Hawaii

Remington College
 Honolulu *A, B*
University of Hawaii
 Hawaii Community College *A*
 Honolulu Community College *A*

Idaho

Idaho State University *A*
Lewis-Clark State College *B*
North Idaho College *A*
University of Idaho *B*

Illinois

Aurora University *B*
Blackburn College *B*
Carl Sandburg College *C*
Concordia University Chicago *B*
Elmhurst College *B*
Governors State University *B, M*
Heartland Community College *A*
Illinois Central College *A*
Illinois State University *B, M*
John A. Logan College *C, A*
Judson University *B*
Lewis University *B, M*
Lewis and Clark Community
 College *A*
Lincoln Land Community College *C*
Loyola University Chicago *B, M*
Northeastern Illinois University *B*
Olivet Nazarene University *B*
Quincy University *B*
Richland Community College *A*
Roosevelt University *B*
Saint Xavier University *B*
South Suburban College of Cook
 County *C, A*
Southern Illinois University
 Edwardsville *B*

University of Illinois
  Chicago *B, M, D*
  Springfield *B*
  Westwood College: DuPage *B*

Indiana

Anderson University *A, B*
Ball State University *A, B*
Butler University *B*
Grace College *B*
Indiana Institute of Technology *A, B*
Indiana University
  Bloomington *B, M, D*
  East *A, B*
  Kokomo *A, B*
  Northwest *A, B*
  South Bend *A, B*
Indiana University-Purdue University
  Indianapolis *A, B, M*
Indiana Wesleyan University *A, B*
Ivy Tech Community College
  Bloomington *A*
  Central Indiana *A*
  Columbus *A*
  East Central *A*
  Kokomo *A*
  Lafayette *A*
  North Central *A*
  Northeast *A*
  Northwest *A*
  Richmond *A*
  South Central *A*
  Southeast *A*
  Southwest *A*
  Wabash Valley *A*
Manchester College *A*
Oakland City University *A, B*
Saint Joseph's College *B*
Trine University *A, B*
University of Southern Indiana *B*

Iowa

Buena Vista University *B*
Ellsworth Community College *A*
Grand View University *B*
Iowa Wesleyan College *B*
Kaplan University
  Cedar Rapids *B*
  Davenport *A, B*
  Mason City *A*
Loras College *B*
St. Ambrose University *B, M, T*
Simpson College *B*
University of Dubuque *B*
Upper Iowa University *B*

Kansas

Bethany College *B*
Butler Community College *A*
Central Christian College of Kansas *A*
Fort Hays State University *B*
Kansas Wesleyan University *A, B*
Southwestern College *B*
Washburn University *A, B*
Wichita State University *C, B, M*

Kentucky

Campbellsville University *A*
Eastern Kentucky University *M*
Gateway Community and Technical
  College *A*
Kentucky State University *B*
Kentucky Wesleyan College *B*
Lindsey Wilson College *B*
Murray State University *B*
Northern Kentucky University *B*
Pikeville College *A, B*
University of the Cumberlands *B*

Louisiana

Blue Cliff College: Houma *A*
Bossier Parish Community College *A*
Grambling State University *B, M*

Louisiana State University
  Alexandria *B*
  Eunice *A*
  Shreveport *B*
Loyola University New Orleans *B, M*
McNeese State University *B*
Northwestern State University *B*
South Louisiana Community
  College *A*
Southeastern Louisiana University *B*
Southern University
  New Orleans *B, M*
Southern University and Agricultural
  and Mechanical College *B, M*
University of Louisiana at Lafayette *B*
University of Louisiana at
  Monroe *B, M*

Maine

Andover College *A*
Husson University *A, B*
Saint Joseph's College of Maine *B*
Thomas College *B*
University of Maine
  Augusta *A*
  Fort Kent *A*

Maryland

Chesapeake College *A*
Coppin State University *B, M*
Frederick Community College *A*
Howard Community College *A*
Kaplan College: Hagerstown *A*
Mount St. Mary's University *B*
Prince George's Community
  College *C, A*
University of Baltimore *B, M*
University of Maryland
  University College *C, B*

Massachusetts

American International College *B*
Anna Maria College *B, M*
Bay Path College *B*
Becker College *B*
Berkshire Community College *A*
Bridgewater State College *B, M*
Bristol Community College *A*
Cape Cod Community College *A*
Curry College *B*
Dean College *A*
Eastern Nazarene College *B*
Endicott College *B*
Fitchburg State College *B*
Holyoke Community College *C, A*
Mount Ida College *B*
Mount Wachusett Community
  College *A*
Nichols College *B*
North Shore Community College *C, A*
Northeastern University *B, M, D*
Northern Essex Community
  College *C, A*
Quincy College *A*
Suffolk University *M*
University of Massachusetts
  Boston *B*
  Lowell *M*
Western New England College *B*
Westfield State College *B, M*
Worcester State College *B*

Michigan

Adrian College *A, B*
Bay de Noc Community College *A*
Davenport University *C*
Jackson Community College *C, A*
Lansing Community College *A*
Madonna University *C, A, B, M*
Michigan State University *B, M, D*
Montcalm Community College *C, A*
Northern Michigan University *A, B, M*
Saginaw Valley State University *B*

Siena Heights University *A, B*
University of Detroit Mercy *B, M*
Wayne State University *B, M*
Western Michigan University *B*

Minnesota

Bemidji State University *A, B*
Brown College *A, B*
Capella University *M, D*
Central Lakes College *C, A*
Century Community and Technical
  College *A*
Concordia University: St. Paul *B*
Gustavus Adolphus College *B*
Hamline University *B*
Inver Hills Community College *C, A*
Metropolitan State University *B*
Minneapolis Community and
  Technical College *A*
Minnesota State College - Southeast
  Technical *A*
Minnesota State Community and
  Technical College *A*
Minnesota State University
  Moorhead *B*
Normandale Community College *A*
North Hennepin Community
  College *A*
Northland Community & Technical
  College *A*
Northwestern College *B*
Ridgewater College *A*
Rochester Community and Technical
  College *A*
Saint Cloud State University *B, M*
St. Mary's University of Minnesota *B*
Southwest Minnesota State
  University *B*
Vermilion Community College *A*
Walden University *B, M, D*
Winona State University *B*

Mississippi

Alcorn State University *B*
Delta State University *B, M*
Hinds Community College *A*
Jackson State University *B, M*
Mississippi Gulf Coast Community
  College *A*
Mississippi Valley State University *B*
University of Southern
  Mississippi *B, M, D*
Virginia College Gulf Coast *A*

Missouri

Drury University *M*
Evangel University *B*
Lindenwood University *B*
Metropolitan Community College:
  Longview *A*
Metropolitan Community College:
  Maple Woods *A*
Metropolitan Community College:
  Penn Valley *A*
Missouri Baptist University *B*
Missouri Western State University *B*
North Central Missouri College *C, A*
St. Louis Community College
  St. Louis Community College at
    Meramec *A*
Saint Louis University *B*
Southeast Missouri State University *M*
Truman State University *B*
University of Missouri
  Kansas City *B*

Montana

Flathead Valley Community College *A*
Montana State University
  Billings *B*
University of Great Falls *A, B*

Nebraska

Central Community College *C, A*
Dana College *B*
Kaplan University
  Lincoln *A*
Kaplan University: Omaha *A, B*
Southeast Community College *A*
University of Nebraska
  Kearney *B*
  Omaha *B, M, D*
Wayne State College *B*

Nevada

College of Southern Nevada *C, A*
Truckee Meadows Community
  College *C, A*

New Hampshire

Franklin Pierce University *A, B*
Granite State College *B*
Lebanon College *C, A*
New England College *B, M*
Plymouth State University *B*
Saint Anselm College *B*

New Jersey

Caldwell College *B*
Centenary College *B*
College of St. Elizabeth *M*
Cumberland County College *A*
Essex County College *A*
Georgian Court University *B*
Hudson County Community
  College *A*
Monmouth University *B, M*
New Jersey City University *M*
Richard Stockton College of New
  Jersey *M*
Rowan University *B, M*
Rutgers, The State University of New
  Jersey
  Camden Regional Campus *B*
  Newark Regional Campus *B, M, D*
Seton Hall University *B*
Sussex County Community College *A*
Thomas Edison State College *A, B*
Warren County Community College *A*

New Mexico

Central New Mexico Community
  College *A*
Clovis Community College *A*
Eastern New Mexico University *B*
Eastern New Mexico University:
  Roswell Campus *A*
New Mexico Highlands University *B*
New Mexico Junior College *A*
New Mexico State University *A, B, M*
New Mexico State University
  Alamogordo *A*
  Carlsbad *A*
Northern New Mexico College *A*
Santa Fe Community College *A*
University of the Southwest *B*
Western New Mexico University *B*

New York

ASA Institute of Business and
  Computer Technology *A*
Alfred University *B*
Canisius College *B*
Cazenovia College *A, B*
City University of New York
  Hostos Community College *A*
Columbia-Greene Community
  College *A*
Corning Community College *A*
Dutchess Community College *C, A*
Elmira College *B*
Finger Lakes Community College *C, A*
Fordham University *B, M, D*
Fulton-Montgomery Community
  College *C, A*

Herkimer County Community College *A*
Hilbert College *A, B*
Jamestown Community College *A*
Monroe Community College *A*
Niagara University *B, M*
North Country Community College *A*
Onondaga Community College *A*
Orange County Community College *A*
Rockland Community College *A*
Russell Sage College *B*
St. Francis College *A, B*
Schenectady County Community College *A*
State University of New York
Albany *B, M, D*
College at Buffalo *B, M*
College at Fredonia *B*
College at Oneonta *B*
College at Plattsburgh *B*
Institute of Technology at Utica/Rome *B*
Sullivan County Community College *A*
Utica College *B, M*

North Carolina

Alamance Community College *A*
Appalachian State University *B, M*
Barton College *B*
Beaufort County Community College *C, A*
Belmont Abbey College *B*
Campbell University *B*
Carteret Community College *A*
Catawba Valley Community College *A*
Central Carolina Community College *A*
Cleveland Community College *C, A*
Davidson County Community College *A*
East Carolina University *B, M*
Edgecombe Community College *A*
Elizabeth City State University *B*
Elon University *B*
Fayetteville State University *B, M*
Fayetteville Technical Community College *A*
Forsyth Technical Community College *C, A*
Guilford College *B*
Guilford Technical Community College *A*
Haywood Community College *A*
High Point University *B*
Isothermal Community College *C, A*
Lees-McRae College *B*
Livingstone College *B*
Methodist University *A, B*
Montgomery Community College *A*
Mount Olive College *B*
North Carolina Central University *M*
North Carolina Wesleyan College *B*
Pfeiffer University *B*
Piedmont Community College *A*
Pitt Community College *A*
Roanoke-Chowan Community College *A*
Robeson Community College *C, A*
Rowan-Cabarrus Community College *A*
St. Augustine's College *B*
Sandhills Community College *A*
Shaw University *A, B*
South Piedmont Community College *C, A*
Southwestern Community College *A*
Stanly Community College *C, A*
University of North Carolina
Charlotte *B, M*
Pembroke *B*
Wilmington *B*
Wayne Community College *A*
Western Carolina University *B*

Western Piedmont Community College *A*
Wilkes Community College *C, A*
Wilson Community College *A*
Winston-Salem State University *B*

North Dakota

Bismarck State College *A*
Jamestown College *B*
Minot State University *B, M*
North Dakota State University *B, M, D*
Rasmussen College: Fargo *C, A, B*
University of Mary *B*
University of North Dakota *B, D*

Ohio

Baldwin-Wallace College *B*
Bluffton University *B*
Bowling Green State University *B, M*
Bowling Green State University: Firelands College *A*
Central Ohio Technical College *A*
Central State University *B*
Kent State University *B, M*
Kent State University
Ashtabula *A*
East Liverpool *A*
Salem *A*
Stark *A*
Trumbull *A*
Tuscarawas *A*
Lourdes College *A, B*
Mount Vernon Nazarene University *B*
North Central State College *A*
Northwest State Community College *A*
Ohio Dominican University *B*
Ohio Northern University *B*
Ohio University
Southern Campus at Ironton *B*
Remington College: Cleveland West *A*
Union Institute & University *B*
University of Akron *B*
University of Cincinnati *B, M, D*
University of Cincinnati
Clermont College *A*
Raymond Walters College *A*
University of Dayton *B*
University of Toledo *B, M*
Urbana University *B*
Wilmington College *B*
Xavier University *A, B, M*
Youngstown State University *A, B, M*

Oklahoma

Bacone College *A, B*
Cameron University *A, B*
Carl Albert State College *A*
East Central University *B*
Eastern Oklahoma State College *A*
Northeastern Oklahoma Agricultural and Mechanical College *A*
St. Gregory's University *B*
Southeastern Oklahoma State University *B*
Southern Nazarene University *B*
Southwestern Oklahoma State University *B*
Tulsa Community College *A*
University of Central Oklahoma *B*

Oregon

Central Oregon Community College *A*
Chemeketa Community College *C, A*
Clatsop Community College *A*
Lane Community College *A*
Linn-Benton Community College *A*
Portland Community College *C, A*
Portland State University *B, M*
Southern Oregon University *B*
Southwestern Oregon Community College *A*

Treasure Valley Community College *A*

Pennsylvania

Bloomsburg University of Pennsylvania *B*
Bucks County Community College *A*
CHI Institute: Franklin Mills *A*
California University of Pennsylvania *A, B*
Central Pennsylvania College *C, A, B*
DeSales University *B, M, T*
Edinboro University of Pennsylvania *B*
Gannon University *C, A, B*
Holy Family University *B*
Immaculata University *B*
Kaplan Career Institute: Harrisburg *A*
Kaplan Career Institute: Pittsburgh *A*
Keystone College *A, B*
King's College *A, B*
Kutztown University of Pennsylvania *B*
La Roche College *B*
La Salle University *A, B*
Lackawanna College *A*
Lehigh Carbon Community College *A*
Lincoln University *B*
Luzerne County Community College *A*
Lycoming College *B*
Marywood University *B*
Mercyhurst College *C, A, B, M*
Messiah College *B*
Moravian College *B*
Mount Aloysius College *A, B, M*
Neumann University *B*
Northampton Community College *A*
Penn State
Abington *B*
Altoona *A, B*
Fayette, The Eberly Campus *B*
Harrisburg *B, M*
Schuylkill *B*
University Park *B, M, D*
Wilkes-Barre *B*
Point Park University *C, A, B, M*
Rosemont College *B*
Seton Hill University *B*
Shippensburg University of Pennsylvania *B, M*
South Hills School of Business & Technology *C*
Temple University *B, M, D*
Thiel College *B*
University of Scranton *A, B*
Valley Forge Military Academy & College *A*
West Chester University of Pennsylvania *B, M*
Westminster College *B*
Westmoreland County Community College *A*
Wilkes University *B*

Puerto Rico

American University of Puerto Rico *M*
Inter American University of Puerto Rico
Aguadilla Campus *B, M*
Arecibo Campus *B*
Bayamon Campus *B*
Fajardo Campus *B*
Metropolitan Campus *B, M*
Universidad Metropolitana *C, A, B*

Rhode Island

Rhode Island College *B*

South Carolina

Aiken Technical College *C, A*
Charleston Southern University *B, M*

Florence-Darlington Technical College *A*
Greenville Technical College *C, A*
Horry-Georgetown Technical College *C, A*
Midlands Technical College *C, A*
Northeastern Technical College *C*
Orangeburg-Calhoun Technical College *A*
Southern Wesleyan University *B*
Technical College of the Lowcountry *C, A*
University of South Carolina
Lancaster *A*
Upstate *B*

South Dakota

Dakota Wesleyan University *A, B*
Mount Marty College *A, B*
University of Sioux Falls *B*
University of South Dakota *B*

Tennessee

Cumberland University *A, B*
Draughons Junior College: Nashville *C, A*
Freed-Hardeman University *B*
Lane College *B*
Remington College
Memphis *A*
Tennessee State University *B, M*

Texas

Alvin Community College *C, A*
Angelina College *C, A*
Angelo State University *B*
Blinn College *C, A*
Clarendon College *A*
Coastal Bend College *A*
Dallas Baptist University *C, B*
Del Mar College *C, A*
Eastfield College *C, A*
El Paso Community College *A*
Galveston College *C, A*
Hardin-Simmons University *B*
Hill College *A*
Huston-Tillotson University *B*
Jarvis Christian College *B*
Kilgore College *C, A*
Lamar State College at Orange *A*
Lamar State College at Port Arthur *A*
Lamar University *B, M*
Laredo Community College *A*
Lon Morris College *A*
Midwestern State University *B*
Mountain View College *C, A*
Navarro College *A*
North Central Texas College *A*
Our Lady of the Lake University of San Antonio *B, M*
Prairie View A&M University *B*
St. Edward's University *B*
St. Mary's University *B*
Sam Houston State University *B, M, D*
San Antonio College *A*
Southwestern Adventist University *B*
Stephen F. Austin State University *B*
Sul Ross State University *B*
Tarleton State University *B, M*
Tarrant County College *A*
Temple College *C, A*
Texarkana College *A*
Texas A&M International University *B, M*
Texas A&M University
Commerce *B*
Corpus Christi *B*
Texarkana *B*
Texas Christian University *B*
Texas State University: San Marcos *B*
Texas Woman's University *B*
Tyler Junior College *A*
University of Houston
Downtown *B, M*

University of North Texas *B, M*
University of Texas
    Arlington *B, M*
    Brownsville - Texas Southmost
        College *C, A, B*
    El Paso *B*
    San Antonio *B, M*
    Tyler *B, M*
    of the Permian Basin *B*
Vernon College *C, A*
West Texas A&M University *M*

Utah

Argosy University: Salt Lake City *B*
College of Eastern Utah *A, T*
Dixie State College of Utah *A*
Salt Lake Community College *A*
Weber State University *A, B, M*
Westminster College *B*

Vermont

Castleton State College *A, B*
Champlain College *B*
Norwich University *B*

Virginia

Bryant & Stratton College
    Richmond *A, B*
Dabney S. Lancaster Community
    College *A*
Ferrum College *B*
J. Sargeant Reynolds Community
    College *C, A*
Liberty University *B*
Longwood University *B*
Marymount University *C, B*
Mountain Empire Community
    College *A*
Norfolk State University *M*
Radford University *B, M*
Rappahannock Community College *A*
Roanoke College *B*
St. Paul's College *B*
University of Richmond *B*
University of Virginia's College at
    Wise *B*
Virginia State University *B, M*
Virginia Wesleyan College *B*
Virginia Western Community
    College *A*

Washington

Gonzaga University *B*
Pierce College *A*
Saint Martin's University *B*
Seattle University *B*
Yakima Valley Community College *A*

West Virginia

Blue Ridge Community and Technical
    College *C, A*
Bluefield State College *B*
Fairmont State University *B, M*
Marshall University *B, M*
Mountain State University *A, B, M*
Potomac State College of West
    Virginia University *C, A*
Salem International University *B*
West Liberty University *B*
West Virginia State University *B*
West Virginia University at
    Parkersburg *C, A, B*
Wheeling Jesuit University *B*

Wisconsin

Carroll University *B*
Concordia University Wisconsin *B*
Edgewood College *B*
Fox Valley Technical College *A*
Mount Mary College *B*
University of Wisconsin
    Eau Claire *B*
    Madison *B, M*

Milwaukee *B, M*
    Parkside *B*
    Superior *B*
Viterbo University *B*

Wyoming

Casper College *A*
Eastern Wyoming College *A*
Sheridan College *C, A*
University of Wyoming *B*

Criminalistics/criminal science

California

Diablo Valley College *C*
Fresno Pacific University *B*

Florida

Florida Gulf Coast University *B*
University of Florida *B*

Hawaii

Chaminade University of
    Honolulu *A, B*

Iowa

St. Ambrose University *B*

Michigan

Ferris State University *C*
Oakland Community College *C, A*

Minnesota

Central Lakes College *A*
Century Community and Technical
    College *A*

New York

Niagara County Community
    College *A*

Ohio

Mount Union College *B*

Pennsylvania

Gannon University *C*
Harrisburg Area Community
    College *C, A*
Keystone College *A, B*
Penn State
    Erie, The Behrend College *C*

Washington

Seattle University *B*

West Virginia

West Virginia University *B*

Criminology

Alabama

Enterprise-Ozark Community
    College *C*

Arizona

Arizona State University *M, D*
Central Arizona College *A*

Arkansas

Arkansas State University *B*

California

Bakersfield College *A*
California Coast University *A, B*
California Lutheran University *B*
California State University
    Bakersfield *B*
    Fresno *B, M*
Chabot College *A*

Fresno City College *A*
Holy Names University *B*
Los Angeles Pierce College *A*
Porterville College *A*
San Diego State University *M*
San Jose State University *M*
University of California
    Irvine *B, M, D*
University of La Verne *B*
West Hills College: Coalinga *A*

Colorado

Adams State College *B*
Regis University *B*
Trinidad State Junior College *A*
University of Denver *B*

Connecticut

Central Connecticut State
    University *B*
Mitchell College *B*
Quinnipiac University *B*
University of Bridgeport *B*

Delaware

Delaware State University *B*
University of Delaware *M, D*

District of Columbia

Gallaudet University *B*

Florida

Barry University *B*
Florida Southern College *B*
Florida State University *B, M, D*
Lake City Community College *A*
University of Miami *B*
University of South Florida *B, M, D*
University of Tampa *B*

Georgia

Dalton State College *A*
East Georgia College *A*
Paine College *B*
University of West Georgia *B, M*

Illinois

Dominican University *B*
Elmhurst College *B*
Kishwaukee College *A*

Indiana

Butler University *B*
Indiana State University *B, M*
Indiana Wesleyan University *B*
St. Mary-of-the-Woods College *B*
Valparaiso University *B*

Iowa

Ellsworth Community College *A*
North Iowa Area Community
    College *A*
University of Northern Iowa *B, M*
Upper Iowa University *B*

Kansas

Central Christian College of Kansas *A*
Fort Scott Community College *A*
University of St. Mary *B*

Louisiana

Dillard University *B*
Loyola University New Orleans *B, M*

Maine

Husson University *B, M*
University of Southern Maine *B*

Maryland

College of Notre Dame of Maryland *B*

University of Maryland
    College Park *B, M, D*
    Eastern Shore *M*

Massachusetts

American International College *B*
Stonehill College *B*
Suffolk University *B, M*
University of Massachusetts
    Dartmouth *B*

Michigan

Eastern Michigan University *B, M*

Minnesota

Ridgewater College *A*
University of Minnesota
    Duluth *B, M*
    Twin Cities *B*
University of St. Thomas *B*
Vermilion Community College *A*
Walden University *B*

Missouri

Drury University *B, M*
Evangel University *B*
Lindenwood University *B, M*
Maryville University of Saint Louis *B*
Missouri State University *B, M*
University of Missouri
    Kansas City *B*
    St. Louis *B, M, D*

Montana

University of Montana *B, M*

Nebraska

York College *B*

Nevada

University of Nevada
    Reno *B, M*

New Hampshire

University of New Hampshire *B, M*

New Jersey

Richard Stockton College of New
    Jersey *B*
Salem Community College *A*

New Mexico

New Mexico Highlands University *B*

New York

City University of New York
    John Jay College of Criminal
        Justice *B*
Dominican College of Blauvelt *B*
Keuka College *B, M*
Le Moyne College *B*
Niagara University *B*
St. John's University *M*
St. Joseph's College: Suffolk
    Campus *B*
State University of New York
    College at Cortland *B*
    College at Old Westbury *B*

North Carolina

Belmont Abbey College *B*
Johnson C. Smith University *B*
North Carolina State University *B*

Ohio

Capital University *B*
Cleveland State University *B*
College of Mount St. Joseph *B*
Defiance College *B*
Mount Union College *B*
Notre Dame College *B*

Ohio State University
Columbus Campus *B*
Ohio University *B*
Tiffin University *B, M*
University of Akron *B*
Wright State University *B*

Oklahoma
East Central University *B, M*

Oregon
Central Oregon Community
College *A*
Southern Oregon University *B*

Pennsylvania
Albright College *B*
Arcadia University *B*
Cabrini College *B*
Cedar Crest College *B*
Elizabethtown College *A, B*
Indiana University of
Pennsylvania *B, M, D*
Juniata College *B*
La Salle University *B*
Lebanon Valley College *B*
Lycoming College *B*
Mount Aloysius College *B*
Reading Area Community College *A*
Saint Joseph's University *C, A, B, M*
Slippery Rock University of
Pennsylvania *B*
University of Pennsylvania *M, D*
University of Pittsburgh
Greensburg *B*

Puerto Rico
Caribbean University *B*
Pontifical Catholic University of
Puerto Rico *B, M*
Turabo University *B*
Universidad del Este *A*

South Carolina
Coker College *B*

South Dakota
Northern State University *B*

Texas
North Central Texas College *A*
St. Edward's University *B*
South Plains College *A*
Texas A&M University
Commerce *B*
University of Houston
Clear Lake *B, M*
University of Texas
Dallas *B, M, D*
of the Permian Basin *B*
Wharton County Junior College *A*

Vermont
Castleton State College *B*

Virginia
Longwood University *B*
Marymount University *B*
Old Dominion University *B, D*

Washington
Eastern Washington University *B*

West Virginia
Alderson-Broaddus College *B*
Davis and Elkins College *A, B*

Wisconsin
Marquette University *B*

Wyoming
Western Wyoming Community
College *A*

Critical care nursing

Florida
Florida State College at Jacksonville *B*
University of Miami *M*

Illinois
Loyola University Chicago *M*

Iowa
Allen College *M*

Massachusetts
Northeastern University *M*

New York
State University of New York
Buffalo *M*
University of Rochester *M*

Ohio
Case Western Reserve University *M*

Pennsylvania
University of Pennsylvania *M*

Puerto Rico
Universidad Metropolitana *M*
Universidad del Este *B*

Crop production

Illinois
Black Hawk College *A*

Iowa
Des Moines Area Community
College *C*
Indian Hills Community College *C*
Iowa State University *M, D*
Northeast Iowa Community
College *C, A*

Massachusetts
University of Massachusetts
Amherst *A*

Michigan
Northwestern Michigan College *A*

Minnesota
University of Minnesota
Crookston *B*

North Carolina
North Carolina State University *A*

North Dakota
North Dakota State University *B*

Ohio
Ohio State University
Agricultural Technical Institute *A*

Oregon
Blue Mountain Community College *A*

Pennsylvania
Delaware Valley College *B*

Utah
Brigham Young University *B, M*

Washington
Washington State University *B*

Wenatchee Valley College *C*
Yakima Valley Community College *C*

Wisconsin
University of Wisconsin
River Falls *B*

Culinary arts and chef training

Alabama
Shelton State Community College *C*

Alaska
University of Alaska
Anchorage *A*
Fairbanks *C, A*

Arizona
Cochise College *A*
Estrella Mountain Community
College *C, A*
Mohave Community College *C*

Arkansas
Pulaski Technical College *C, A*

California
Allan Hancock College *C, A*
Art Institute
of California: Los Angeles *A, B*
of California: Orange County *A*
of California: San Diego *A*
Art Institute of California:
Hollywood *A, B*
Art Institute of California: Inland
Empire *A*
Art Institute of California: San
Francisco *A, B*
Art Institute of California:
Sunnyvale *A*
California School of Culinary Arts *A*
City College of San Francisco *A*
College of the Desert *C*
Diablo Valley College *C*
Lake Tahoe Community College *C*
Los Angeles Harbor College *C*
Santa Rosa Junior College *C*
Shasta College *C, A*

Colorado
Art Institute
of Colorado *C, A*
Colorado Mountain College *A*
Johnson & Wales University:
Denver *A, B*
Red Rocks Community College *C, A*
Westwood College: Denver North *A*

Connecticut
Gateway Community College *A*
University of New Haven *C*

Delaware
Delaware Technical and Community
College
Stanton/Wilmington *A*
Terry *A*

Florida
Art Institute of Fort Lauderdale *C, A*
Central Florida Community College *A*
Johnson & Wales University: North
Miami *A, B*

Georgia
Albany Technical College *C, A*
Art Institute
of Atlanta *A, B*
Athens Technical College *C*
College of Coastal Georgia *C*

North Georgia Technical College *C, A*
Savannah Technical College *C, A*

Idaho
Idaho State University *C, A*

Illinois
Black Hawk College *C*
City Colleges of Chicago
Kennedy-King College *C*
College of DuPage *C, A*
College of Lake County *C*
Cooking & Hospitality Institute of
Chicago *C, A*
Danville Area Community College *C*
Elgin Community College *C, A*
Harper College *C*
John Wood Community College *C*
Kaskaskia College *C, A*
Rend Lake College *C, A*
Robert Morris University Chicago *A*
St. Augustine College *C, A*
Triton College *C, A*

Indiana
Purdue University
Calumet *A*
Vincennes University *C, A*

Iowa
Des Moines Area Community
College *C, A*
Indian Hills Community College *C, A*
Scott Community College *C, A*

Kentucky
Elizabethtown Community and
Technical College *C*
Maysville Community and Technical
College *C*
Owensboro Community and
Technical College *C, A*

Louisiana
Bossier Parish Community College *C*
Nicholls State University *A, B*
Nunez Community College *C, A*

Maine
Southern Maine Community
College *A*

Maryland
Allegany College of Maryland *A*
Anne Arundel Community
College *C, A*

Massachusetts
Berkshire Community College *C*
Bunker Hill Community College *C*
Holyoke Community College *C*
Massasoit Community College *C, A*
Newbury College *A, B*
North Shore Community College *C, A*

Michigan
Art Institute of Michigan *A*
Baker College
of Muskegon *A*
Grand Rapids Community College *A*
Henry Ford Community College *C, A*
Mott Community College *A*
Northwestern Michigan College *A*
Oakland Community College *A*
Schoolcraft College *C, A*

Minnesota
Art Institutes International
Minnesota *C, A*
Hennepin Technical College *C, A*
Minneapolis Community and
Technical College *C, A*

St. Cloud Technical College C
St. Paul College C, A

Missouri
College of the Ozarks B
East Central College C, A
Jefferson College C, A

Montana
Flathead Valley Community College A

Nebraska
Northeast Community College A

Nevada
Art Institute
of Las Vegas A
College of Southern Nevada C, A
Le Cordon Bleu College of Culinary
Arts: Las Vegas C, A

New Hampshire
Southern New Hampshire
University A
White Mountains Community
College C, A

New Jersey
Atlantic Cape Community College A
Bergen Community College C, A
Hudson County Community
College A

New Mexico
Central New Mexico Community
College C, A
Santa Fe Community College C, A

New York
Culinary Institute of America C, A
Erie Community College
City Campus A
North Campus A
Mohawk Valley Community College C
Niagara County Community
College A
Onondaga Community College C
Paul Smith's College A, B
Schenectady County Community
College C
State University of New York
College of Agriculture and
Technology at Cobleskill A
College of Technology at Delhi A
Suffolk County Community
College C, A

North Carolina
Central Piedmont Community
College C, A
Fayetteville Technical Community
College C, A
Johnson & Wales University:
Charlotte A, B
Montgomery Community College C
Wilkes Community College C, A

Ohio
Art Institute of Ohio: Cincinnati A
Cincinnati State Technical and
Community College C, A
Columbus State Community
College A
Hocking College C, A
University of Akron C, A

Oregon
Linn-Benton Community College A
Umpqua Community College C

Pennsylvania
Art Institute
of Philadelphia A, B
of Pittsburgh A, B
Bucks County Community
College C, A
Commonwealth Technical Institute A
Community College of Allegheny
County C, A
Community College of Beaver
County C, A
Community College of Philadelphia A
Delaware Valley College C, A
Drexel University B
Harrisburg Area Community
College C, A
Indiana University of Pennsylvania C
Keystone College A
Keystone Technical Institute A
Mercyhurst College C
Montgomery County Community
College A
Northampton Community
College C, A
Pennsylvania College of
Technology A
Restaurant School at Walnut Hill
College A, B
Westmoreland County Community
College C, A

Puerto Rico
Ponce Paramedical College C
Universal Career Community College:
Humacao C
Universal Career Community College:
Manati C
Universal Career Community College:
San Juan C
Universidad del Este C, A

Rhode Island
Johnson & Wales University:
Providence A, B

South Carolina
Bob Jones University A
Greenville Technical College A
Horry-Georgetown Technical
College A
Spartanburg Community College C

South Dakota
Mitchell Technical Institute C, A

Tennessee
Walters State Community College C

Texas
Austin Community College C, A
Culinary Institute Alain & Marie
LeNotre A
Del Mar College C, A
El Centro College C, A
Houston Community College
System C, A
Howard College C
Odessa College C, A
St. Philip's College C, A
San Jacinto College C, A
Tarrant County College C, A
Texas Culinary Academy C, A
Texas State Technical College
West Texas C, A

Utah
Salt Lake Community College A
Snow College C, A
Utah Valley University A

Virginia
J. Sargeant Reynolds Community
College A

Washington
Art Institute of Seattle A
Bellingham Technical College C, A
Clark College C, A
Olympic College C, A
South Seattle Community
College C, A

West Virginia
Mountain State University A, B

Wisconsin
Fox Valley Technical College A
Milwaukee Area Technical College C

Wyoming
Central Wyoming College A
Sheridan College C, A

Culinary arts/related services

Alabama
Bishop State Community College C, A
Faulkner State Community
College C, A

Alaska
University of Alaska
Fairbanks C, A

Arizona
Art Institute
of Phoenix A, B
Art Institute of Tucson A, B
Central Arizona College C, A
Estrella Mountain Community
College C, A
Scottsdale Community College C, A
Scottsdale Culinary Institute C, A, B

Arkansas
Ozarka College C, A

California
American River College C, A
Art Institute
of California: Los Angeles C, A
of California: Orange
County C, A, B
Bakersfield College A
California Culinary Academy A
Chaffey College C
City College of San Francisco C
College of the Canyons C
Columbia College A
Cypress College C, A
Diablo Valley College C
Glendale Community College C, A
Grossmont College C, A
Lake Tahoe Community College C, A
Laney College C, A
Long Beach City College C, A
Los Angeles Mission College C, A
Los Angeles Trade and Technical
College C, A
Modesto Junior College C, A
Orange Coast College C, A
Oxnard College C, A
Saddleback College C
San Diego Mesa College C, A
San Joaquin Delta College C, A
Santa Barbara City College C, A
Santa Rosa Junior College C
Shasta College C, A

Colorado
Colorado Mountain College A
Community College of Aurora A
Johnson & Wales University:
Denver A, B
Mesa State College C, A
Pikes Peak Community College C, A

Connecticut
Lincoln College of New England:
Suffield C, A
Manchester Community College C
Norwalk Community College C

District of Columbia
University of the District of
Columbia A

Florida
Brevard Community College C
Chipola College A
Florida State College at Jacksonville A
Gulf Coast Community College A
Indian River State College C
Johnson & Wales University: North
Miami A, B
Palm Beach Community College C
Pensacola Junior College C, A
Valencia Community College C, A

Georgia
Art Institute
of Atlanta C, A, B
Chattahoochee Technical
College C, A
Gwinnett Technical College C, A
Savannah Technical College C
West Georgia Technical College C

Hawaii
University of Hawaii
Kapiolani Community College A
Kauai Community College C, A

Idaho
Brigham Young University-Idaho A
North Idaho College C

Illinois
City Colleges of Chicago
Malcolm X College A
College of DuPage C, A
Joliet Junior College C, A
Kendall College C, A, B
Southwestern Illinois College C, A
Triton College A

Indiana
Harrison College
Indianapolis A
Oakland City University A

Iowa
Iowa Central Community College A
Iowa Western Community College A
Kirkwood Community College C, A
Scott Community College C, A

Kentucky
Sullivan University C, A, B
West Kentucky Community and
Technical College A

Maine
Central Maine Community College C
Eastern Maine Community
College C, A
Washington County Community
College C
York County Community College C, A

Maryland

Anne Arundel Community
College *C, A*
Baltimore City Community College *C*
Baltimore International College *C, A*
Frederick Community College *C, A*

Massachusetts

Cape Cod Community College *C*
Newbury College *C, A, B*

Michigan

Baker College
of Muskegon *A, B*
Lansing Community College *A*
Macomb Community College *C, A*
Monroe County Community
College *C, A*
Northwestern Michigan College *A*
Washtenaw Community College *C, A*

Minnesota

Art Institutes International
Minnesota *C, A*
Hennepin Technical College *C, A*
Hibbing Community College *A*
Minnesota State Community and
Technical College *C*
South Central College *C, A*

Mississippi

Hinds Community College *C, A*
Mississippi University for Women *B*

Missouri

Jefferson College *C, A*
Ozarks Technical Community
College *A*
St. Louis Community College
St. Louis Community College at
Florissant Valley *A*

Montana

University of Montana *C, A*

Nebraska

Metropolitan Community
College *C, A*

Nevada

University of Nevada
Las Vegas *B*

New Hampshire

Lakes Region Community
College *C, A*

New Jersey

Brookdale Community College *C, A*
Hudson County Community
College *C, A*
Mercer County Community
College *C, A*
Middlesex County College *C*

New Mexico

Dona Ana Community College of New
Mexico State University *C*

New York

Adirondack Community College *C, A*
New York Institute of Technology *A*
Paul Smith's College *C, A, B*
Rockland Community College *C*
Schenectady County Community
College *C*
State University of New York
College of Technology at Alfred *A*
College of Technology at Delhi *A*
Suffolk County Community
College *C, A*

Westchester Community College *A*

North Carolina

Alamance Community College *C, A*
Art Institute
of Charlotte *C, A, B*
Cape Fear Community College *C, A*
College of the Albemarle *C*
Lenoir Community College *C, A*
Nash Community College *A*
Piedmont Community College *C*
Robeson Community College *C, A*
Sandhills Community College *A*
Southwestern Community College *A*
Vance-Granville Community
College *A*
Wake Technical Community
College *C, A*

North Dakota

North Dakota State College of
Science *C, A*

Ohio

Columbus State Community
College *C, A*
Cuyahoga Community College
Metropolitan Campus *A*
Zane State College *A*

Oklahoma

Oklahoma State University
Institute of Technology:
Okmulgee *A*
Platt College
Tulsa *C, A*

Oregon

Central Oregon Community
College *C*
Portland Community College *C*
Southwestern Oregon Community
College *A*

Pennsylvania

Bucks County Community
College *C, A*
Butler County Community College *C*
JNA Institute of Culinary Arts *C, A*
Keystone College *A*
Keystone Technical Institute *A*
Lehigh Carbon Community
College *C, A*
Reading Area Community College *A*
YTI Career Institute: York *A*

Rhode Island

Johnson & Wales University:
Providence *A, B*

South Carolina

Denmark Technical College *C*
Technical College of the
Lowcountry *C*
Trident Technical College *C, A*

Tennessee

Nashville State Community College *A*

Texas

Central Texas College *C, A*
Culinary Institute Alain & Marie
LeNotre *C*
El Paso Community College *C, A*
Galveston College *C, A*
Odessa College *A*
St. Philip's College *C, A*
Trinity Valley Community College *C*

Utah

Snow College *C, A*

Vermont

New England Culinary Institute
Essex Junction *A*

Virginia

J. Sargeant Reynolds Community
College *A*
Northern Virginia Community
College *C*
Tidewater Community College *C, A*

Washington

Bates Technical College *C, A*
Lake Washington Technical
College *C, A*
Olympic College *C*
Renton Technical College *C, A*
Skagit Valley College *C, A*
South Puget Sound Community
College *C, A*
South Seattle Community
College *A*
Spokane Community College *A*

West Virginia

West Virginia Northern Community
College *C, A*

Wisconsin

Blackhawk Technical College *A*
Fox Valley Technical College *A*
Moraine Park Technical College *C, A*
Nicolet Area Technical College *C, A*
Southwest Wisconsin Technical
College *C, A*

Cultural resource management

California

California State University
Dominguez Hills *B*

Georgia

University of Georgia *M*

Louisiana

Northwestern State University *B, M*

Massachusetts

Brandeis University *M*

Michigan

Eastern Michigan University *M*

Nevada

Great Basin College *B*

Utah

College of Eastern Utah *A*

Curriculum/instruction

Alabama

Spring Hill College *M*

Alaska

University of Alaska
Fairbanks *M*

Arizona

Arizona State University *M, D*
Northcentral University *M, D*
Northern Arizona University *M, D*
Prescott College *B, M*
University of Phoenix *M, D*

Arkansas

Arkansas State University *M, T*
Henderson State University *M*

University of Arkansas *D*

California

Azusa Pacific University *M*
California Coast University *M*
California Lutheran University *M*
California State University
Chico *M*
Dominguez Hills *M*
East Bay *M*
Fresno *M*
Northridge *M*
Sacramento *M*
San Bernardino *M*
Chapman University *M, D*
Concordia University *M*
Dominican University of California *M*
Fresno Pacific University *M*
Holy Names University *M*
La Sierra University *M, D*
Mills College *M*
National University *M*
St. Mary's College of California *M*
San Diego State University *D*
Sonoma State University *M*
Stanford University *M, D*
University of California
San Diego *M*
University of Redlands *M*
University of San Diego *M*
University of San Francisco *D*
University of the Pacific *M, D*

Colorado

Colorado Christian University *M*
Jones International University *M*
University of Colorado
Boulder *M, D*
Colorado Springs *M*
Denver *M*
University of Denver *M, D*

Connecticut

University of Connecticut *M, D, T*
Western Connecticut State
University *M*

Delaware

Delaware State University *M*
University of Delaware *M, D*
Wilmington University *M*

District of Columbia

George Washington University *M, D*
Howard University *M*
Trinity Washington University *M*

Florida

Barry University *M, D*
Florida Atlantic University *M, D*
Florida Gulf Coast University *M*
Florida International University *M, D*
University of Central Florida *M, D*
University of Florida *M*
University of South Florida *M, D*
University of Tampa *M*
University of West Florida *M, D, T*
Warner University *M*

Georgia

Armstrong Atlantic State University *M*
Berry College *T*
Covenant College *M*
Georgia Southern University *D*
Georgia Southwestern State
University *M*
LaGrange College *M*
Mercer University *D*
Piedmont College *D, T*
Valdosta State University *D*

Hawaii

University of Hawaii
Manoa *M*

Idaho

Boise State University *M, D*
Northwest Nazarene University *M*
University of Idaho *M*

Illinois

Aurora University *M, D*
Benedictine University *M*
Bradley University *M*
Chicago State University *M, T*
Concordia University Chicago *M*
DePaul University *M, D*
Governors State University *M*
Illinois State University *M, D*
Loyola University Chicago *M, D*
National-Louis University *M*
North Central College *M*
Northeastern Illinois University *M*
Northern Illinois University *M, D*
Olivet Nazarene University *M*
Saint Xavier University *M*
Southern Illinois University
Carbondale *M, D*
University of Illinois
Chicago *D*
Urbana-Champaign *M, D*
University of St. Francis *M*

Indiana

Anderson University *M*
Ball State University *M, T*
Huntington University *M*
Indiana State University *M, D, T*
Indiana University
Bloomington *D*
Indiana Wesleyan University *M*
University of Indianapolis *M*

Iowa

Buena Vista University *M*
Dordt College *M*
Drake University *B*
Iowa State University *M, D*
University of Iowa *M, D*
University of Northern Iowa *D*

Kansas

Emporia State University *M*
Kansas State University *D*
Newman University *M*
Southwestern College *M*
University of Kansas *M, D*
University of St. Mary *M*
Washburn University *M*
Wichita State University *M*

Kentucky

Brescia University *M*
Campbellsville University *M*
Georgetown College *M*
Morehead State University *M*
Spalding University *M*
University of Kentucky *M*
University of Louisville *D*

Louisiana

Grambling State University *M, D*
Louisiana State University and
Agricultural and Mechanical
College *M, D*
Louisiana Tech University *M, D*
McNeese State University *M*
Nicholls State University *M*
Northwestern State University *M*
Our Lady of Holy Cross College *M*
Southeastern Louisiana University *M*
University of Louisiana at Lafayette *M*

University of Louisiana at
Monroe *M, D*
University of New Orleans *M, D*
Xavier University of Louisiana *M*

Maine

University of Southern Maine *M*

Maryland

Coppin State University *M*
Frostburg State University *M*
Hood College *M*
Loyola University Maryland *M*
McDaniel College *M*
University of Maryland
Baltimore County *T*
College Park *M, D*

Massachusetts

Atlantic Union College *M*
Boston College *M, D*
Boston University *M, D*
Cambridge College *T*
Curry College *M*
Eastern Nazarene College *M, T*
Fitchburg State College *M*
Framingham State College *M*
Gordon College *M*
Harvard College *M, D*
Lesley University *M*
Tufts University *M*
University of Massachusetts
Lowell *M*

Michigan

Andrews University *M, D*
Calvin College *M, T*
Eastern Michigan University *M*
Ferris State University *M*
Michigan State University *M, D*
Oakland University *M*
University of Detroit Mercy *M*
Wayne State University *D*

Minnesota

Bemidji State University *M*
Capella University *M, D*
Concordia University: St. Paul *M*
Minnesota State University
Mankato *B, M, T*
Moorhead *M*
Saint Cloud State University *M*
University of Minnesota
Twin Cities *M*
University of St. Thomas *M, D*
Walden University *M, D*
Winona State University *B, M, T*

Mississippi

Mississippi State University *D*
Mississippi University for Women *M*
University of Mississippi *M*
University of Southern Mississippi *M*

Missouri

Columbia College *M*
Maryville University of Saint
Louis *M, T*
Northwest Missouri State
University *B*
University of Central Missouri *M, T*
University of Missouri
Columbia *M, D*
Kansas City *M*
St. Louis *M*
William Woods University *M*

Montana

Montana State University
Billings *B, M*
University of Great Falls *M*
University of Montana *M, D*

Nebraska

Concordia University *M*
Doane College *M*
University of Nebraska
Kearney *M*
Lincoln *M, D*
Wayne State College *M*

Nevada

University of Nevada
Las Vegas *M, D, T*
Reno *D*

New Hampshire

Keene State College *M*
Rivier College *M*
Southern New Hampshire
University *M*

New Jersey

Caldwell College *M*
Rider University *M*
Rowan University *M*
Seton Hall University *M*

New Mexico

New Mexico Highlands University *M*
New Mexico State University *D*
University of New Mexico *D, T*
University of the Southwest *M*

New York

Fordham University *M, D*
Hofstra University *M*
Jewish Theological Seminary of
America *M, D*
New York University *D*
St. John's University *D*
State University of New York
Albany *M, D*
College at Fredonia *M*
College at Potsdam *M*
Syracuse University *M, D*
University of Rochester *M, D*

North Carolina

Appalachian State University *M, T*
Campbell University *M*
Elon University *B, T*
North Carolina Central University *M*
North Carolina State University *M, D*
Shaw University *M*
University of North Carolina
Chapel Hill *D*
Charlotte *M, D*
Greensboro *M, D*
Wilmington *M*

Ohio

Ashland University *M, T*
Baldwin-Wallace College *M*
Bowling Green State University *M*
Cleveland State University *M*
John Carroll University *M*
Kent State University *M, D*
Malone University *M*
Miami University
Oxford Campus *M*
Mount Vernon Nazarene University *M*
Ohio Dominican University *M*
Ohio State University
Columbus Campus *M, D*
Ohio University *M, D*
Otterbein College *M*
Shawnee State University *M*
Union Institute & University *M*
University of Cincinnati *M, D*
University of Findlay *B, M*
University of Toledo *M, D*
Urbana University *M*
Ursuline College *M*
Wright State University *M*

Youngstown State University *M*

Oklahoma

Northeastern State University *M*
Oklahoma State University *M*
Oral Roberts University *M*
Southern Nazarene University *M*
University of Central Oklahoma *B*

Oregon

Concordia University *M*
George Fox University *M*
Portland State University *M, D*

Pennsylvania

Bloomsburg University of
Pennsylvania *M*
Bucknell University *M*
Gannon University *M*
King's College *M*
Lock Haven University of
Pennsylvania *M*
Neumann University *M, T*
Penn State
Beaver *M*
DuBois *M*
Harrisburg *M*
Hazleton *M*
New Kensington *M*
University Park *M, D*
York *M*
Point Park University *M*
Robert Morris University *M, D, T*
Rosemont College *M, T*
St. Vincent College *M*
Shippensburg University of
Pennsylvania *M, T*
University of Pennsylvania *M, D*
Westminster College *M*
Widener University *D*

Puerto Rico

Inter American University of Puerto
Rico
Metropolitan Campus *D*
San German Campus *D*
Pontifical Catholic University of
Puerto Rico *M, D*
Turabo University *M*
Universidad Adventista de las
Antillas *M*
Universidad Metropolitana *M*
Universidad del Este *M*
University of Puerto Rico
Rio Piedras *M, D*

South Carolina

Bob Jones University *D*
Clemson University *D*
Columbia International University *M*
University of South Carolina *D*
Winthrop University *T*

South Dakota

Black Hills State University *M*
Dakota Wesleyan University *M*
South Dakota State University *M*
University of South Dakota *M, D, T*

Tennessee

Austin Peay State University *M*
Carson-Newman College *M*
Freed-Hardeman University *B, M, T*
Lincoln Memorial University *M*
Lipscomb University *M, T*
Middle Tennessee State
University *M, T*
Southern Adventist University *M*
Tennessee State University *M, D*
Tennessee Technological
University *M*
Tennessee Temple University *M*
Trevecca Nazarene University *M*

Union University *D*
University of Memphis *M, D*
University of Tennessee
  Knoxville *M, D*
Vanderbilt University *M, D*

Texas

Angelo State University *M*
Baylor University *M, D*
Houston Baptist University *M*
Midwestern State University *M*
Our Lady of the Lake University of San
  Antonio *M*
Prairie View A&M University *M*
Sam Houston State University *M*
Southwestern Assemblies of God
  University *M*
Texas A&M University *M, D*
Texas A&M University
  Commerce *D*
  Corpus Christi *M, D, T*
  Texarkana *M*
Texas Christian University *M, D*
Texas Southern University *M, D*
Texas Tech University *M, D*
Texas Wesleyan University *D*
University of Houston *M, D, T*
University of Houston
  Clear Lake *M*
  Downtown *M*
University of Mary Hardin-Baylor *M*
University of North Texas *M, D*
University of Texas
  Arlington *M, T*
  Austin *M, D*
  Brownsville - Texas Southmost
    College *M, D*
  El Paso *M, D*
  San Antonio *M*
  Tyler *M*
Wayland Baptist University *M*
West Texas A&M University *M*

Utah

Brigham Young University *D*
Southern Utah University *M*
Utah State University *M, D*

Vermont

Castleton State College *M, T*
Goddard College *M*
Johnson State College *M*
Lyndon State College *M*
St. Michael's College *M*
Sterling College *B*
University of Vermont *M, T*

Virginia

Averett University *M*
College of William and Mary *D*
Eastern Mennonite University *M*
George Mason University *M*
Liberty University *M*
Longwood University *M*
Lynchburg College *M*
Sweet Briar College *M*
University of Virginia *M, D*
Virginia Commonwealth University *M*
Virginia Polytechnic Institute and
  State University *M, D*
Virginia State University *M*

Washington

City University of Seattle *M*
Eastern Washington University *M*
Gonzaga University *M*
Seattle Pacific University *M*
Seattle University *M*
University of Puget Sound *M*
University of Washington *D*
Walla Walla University *M*
Washington State University *M, D*
Western Washington University *M*

West Virginia

Ohio Valley University *M*
Shepherd University *M*
West Virginia University *D*

Wisconsin

Alverno College *M*
Carroll University *M*
Concordia University Wisconsin *M*
Marian University *D*
Marquette University *M, D*
University of Wisconsin
  Madison *M, D*
  Milwaukee *M*
  Whitewater *M*

Customer service management

Arizona

Northern Arizona University *C*

California

Santa Rosa Junior College *C*

Delaware

Delaware Technical and Community
  College
  Stanton/Wilmington *C, A*

Florida

Valencia Community College *C*

Maryland

University of Maryland
  University College *C*

Michigan

Henry Ford Community College *C*

Minnesota

Alexandria Technical College *C*
Art Institutes International
  Minnesota *B*
Inver Hills Community College *C*
Minnesota School of Business:
  Brooklyn Center *B*
Rochester Community and Technical
  College *C*

Missouri

Metropolitan Community College:
  Penn Valley *C*
Southwest Baptist University *B*

New York

Bryant & Stratton Business Institute
  Bryant & Stratton College:
    Rochester *A*
Genesee Community College *A*
Globe Institute of Technology *C, A, B*
Trocaire College *C*

North Carolina

Catawba Valley Community College *A*

Ohio

Edison State Community College *C*

Oregon

Central Oregon Community
  College *A*

Pennsylvania

Newport Business Institute: Lower
  Burrell *A*

Rhode Island

Community College of Rhode
  Island *C, A*

South Carolina

Trident Technical College *C, A*
York Technical College *C*

Washington

Bellingham Technical College *C*
North Seattle Community College *C*

Wisconsin

University of Wisconsin
  Stout *B*

Cytogenetics/clinical genetics technology

Alabama

Calhoun Community College *A*

Michigan

Northern Michigan University *B*

Minnesota

St. Mary's University of Minnesota *B*

Cytotechnology

Alabama

Oakwood University *B*
University of Alabama
  Birmingham *B*

California

Loma Linda University *B*

Connecticut

University of Connecticut *B*

District of Columbia

George Washington University *B*

Florida

Barry University *B*

Indiana

Indiana University
  Bloomington *B*
Indiana University-Purdue University
  Indianapolis *B*

Kansas

University of Kansas Medical
  Center *B*

Michigan

Oakland University *B*

Minnesota

Minnesota State University
  Mankato *B, M*
St. Mary's University of Minnesota *B*
Winona State University *B*

Missouri

Saint Louis University *B*

New Jersey

Felician College *B*
Saint Peter's College *B*
Thomas Edison State College *B*
University of Medicine and Dentistry
  of New Jersey
  School of Health Related
    Professions *B*

New York

Albany College of Pharmacy and
  Health Sciences *B*

Long Island University

  Brooklyn Campus *B*
  C. W. Post Campus *B*
Sage College of Albany *B*
State University of New York
  College at Plattsburgh *B*
  Stony Brook *B*

North Carolina

Central Piedmont Community
  College *A*

North Dakota

University of North Dakota *B*

Ohio

University of Rio Grande *M*

Pennsylvania

Keystone College *A*
Slippery Rock University of
  Pennsylvania *B*
Thiel College *B*
Thomas Jefferson University: College
  of Health Professions *B, M*

Tennessee

University of Tennessee
  Knoxville *M*
University of Tennessee Health
  Science Center *B, M*

Texas

University of North Texas *B*

Virginia

Old Dominion University *B*

West Virginia

Marshall University *B*

Wisconsin

Edgewood College *B*
Marian University *B*

Czech

Texas

University of Texas
  Austin *B*

Dairy husbandry

Iowa

Northeast Iowa Community
  College *C, A*

Michigan

Michigan State University *C*

New York

State University of New York
  College of Agriculture and
    Technology at Morrisville *A, B*

Vermont

Vermont Technical College *A, B*

Wisconsin

University of Wisconsin
  River Falls *B*
Wisconsin Indianhead Technical
  College *C*

Dairy science

California

California Polytechnic State
  University: San Luis Obispo *B*

California State University
Fresno *B*
College of the Sequoias *C*
Modesto Junior College *A*

Florida
University of Florida *B, M*

Georgia
University of Georgia *B, M*

Idaho
University of Idaho *B*

Iowa
Iowa State University *B*

Michigan
Michigan State University *C*

Minnesota
Ridgewater College *C, A*

Mississippi
Northwest Mississippi Community
College *A*

Nebraska
Northeast Community College *C*

New Hampshire
University of New Hampshire *A, B*

New Mexico
Eastern New Mexico University *B*

New York
State University of New York
College of Agriculture and
Technology at Morrisville *A, B*
College of Technology at Alfred *A*

Ohio
Ohio State University
Agricultural Technical Institute *A*

Oregon
Linn-Benton Community College *A*

Pennsylvania
Delaware Valley College *B*

South Carolina
Clemson University *M*

South Dakota
South Dakota State University *B*

Texas
Texas A&M University *B, M, D*

Utah
Utah State University *C, B, M*

Vermont
Vermont Technical College *A*

Virginia
Virginia Polytechnic Institute and
State University *B, M*

Washington
Skagit Valley College *A*

Wisconsin
Lakeshore Technical College *C*
Northcentral Technical College *C, A*
Southwest Wisconsin Technical
College *C*

University of Wisconsin
Madison *B, M, D*
River Falls *B*

Dance

Alabama
Birmingham-Southern College *B*
University of Alabama *B*

Arizona
Arizona State University *B, M*
Prescott College *B, M*
Scottsdale Community College *A*
University of Arizona *B*

California
Allan Hancock College *C, A*
Cabrillo College *A*
California Institute of the Arts *C, B, M*
California State University
East Bay *B*
Fullerton *B*
Long Beach *B, M*
Northridge *B*
Chabot College *A*
Chaffey College *A*
Chapman University *B*
City College of San Francisco *C*
Claremont McKenna College *B*
College of Marin: Kentfield *A*
College of the Desert *A*
Cypress College *A*
Dominican University of California *B*
El Camino College *A*
El Camino College: Compton
Center *A*
Fresno City College *C, A*
Fullerton College *A*
Glendale Community College *C, A*
Golden West College *A*
Grossmont College *C, A*
Humboldt State University *B*
Irvine Valley College *A*
Lake Tahoe Community College *A*
Laney College *A*
Long Beach City College *A*
Loyola Marymount University *B*
Mills College *B, M*
MiraCosta College *A*
Monterey Peninsula College *A*
Mount San Jacinto College *A*
Orange Coast College *C, A*
Palomar College *C, A*
Pitzer College *B*
Pomona College *B*
Rio Hondo College *A*
Saddleback College *A*
St. Mary's College of California *B*
San Diego State University *B*
San Francisco State University *B*
San Jose State University *B*
Santa Ana College *C, A*
Santa Monica College *A*
Santa Rosa Junior College *C*
Santiago Canyon College *A*
Scripps College *B*
Skyline College *A*
Southwestern College *A*
University of California
Berkeley *B*
Irvine *B, M*
Los Angeles *M*
San Diego *B*
Santa Barbara *B, M*

Colorado
Colorado College *B*
Colorado State University *B*
Pikes Peak Community College *A*
University of Colorado
Boulder *B, M*

Connecticut
Connecticut College *B*
Naugatuck Valley Community
College *C, A*
Trinity College *B*
University of Hartford *B*
Wesleyan University *B*

District of Columbia
George Washington University *B*
Howard University *B*

Florida
Daytona State College *A*
Florida State University *B, M*
Indian River State College *A*
Jacksonville University *B*
Miami Dade College *A*
Northwest Florida State College *A*
Nova Southeastern University *B*
Palm Beach Atlantic University *B*
Palm Beach Community College *A*
University of Florida *B*
University of South Florida *B*
Valencia Community College *A*

Georgia
Agnes Scott College *B*
Brenau University *B*
Darton College *A*
Emory University *B*
Kennesaw State University *B*
University of Georgia *B*
Valdosta State University *B*

Hawaii
University of Hawaii
Manoa *B, M*

Idaho
University of Idaho *B*

Illinois
Columbia College Chicago *B*
Illinois Central College *A*
Lincoln College *A*
Northwestern University *B*
University of Illinois
Urbana-Champaign *B, M*

Indiana
Ball State University *B*
Butler University *B*
Indiana University
Bloomington *B, M*

Iowa
University of Iowa *B, M*

Kansas
Barton County Community College *A*
Friends University *B*
University of Kansas *B*

Kentucky
Western Kentucky University *B*

Louisiana
Centenary College of Louisiana *B, T*
Tulane University *B*

Maryland
Goucher College *B*
Howard Community College *A*
Montgomery College *A*
Towson University *B, T*
University of Maryland
Baltimore County *B*
College Park *B, M*

Massachusetts
Amherst College *B*
Bard College at Simon's Rock *B*
Boston Conservatory *B*
Cape Cod Community College *A*
Dean College *A, B*
Hampshire College *B*
Mount Holyoke College *B*
Smith College *B, M*
Springfield College *B*
University of Massachusetts
Amherst *B*

Michigan
Alma College *B*
Eastern Michigan University *B*
Grand Valley State University *B*
Hope College *B*
Lansing Community College *A*
Marygrove College *B, T*
Oakland University *B*
University of Michigan *B, M*
Wayne State University *B, T*
Western Michigan University *B*

Minnesota
Gustavus Adolphus College *B*
St. Olaf College *B*
University of Minnesota
Twin Cities *B*
Winona State University *A*

Mississippi
Belhaven University *C, B*
University of Southern Mississippi *B*

Missouri
Lindenwood University *B*
Missouri State University *B*
Missouri Valley College *B*
Stephens College *B*
University of Missouri
Kansas City *B*
Washington University in St. Louis *B*
Webster University *B*

Montana
University of Montana *B*

Nebraska
University of Nebraska
Lincoln *B*

Nevada
University of Nevada
Las Vegas *B*

New Hampshire
Franklin Pierce University *B*
Keene State College *B*

New Jersey
Georgian Court University *B*
Middlesex County College *A*
Montclair State University *B*
Raritan Valley Community College *A*
Rowan University *B*
Rutgers, The State University of New
Jersey
New Brunswick/Piscataway
Campus *B*

New Mexico
New Mexico State University *B*
University of New Mexico *B, M*

New York
Adelphi University *B*
Bard College *B*
Barnard College *B*

City University of New York
  Hunter College *B*
  Queensborough Community
    College *A*
Columbia University *B*
Columbia University
  School of General Studies *B*
Cornell University *B*
Fordham University *B*
Hamilton College *B*
Hobart and William Smith Colleges *B*
Hofstra University *B*
Ithaca College *B*
Juilliard School *B*
Long Island University
  Brooklyn Campus *B*
  C. W. Post Campus *B*
Manhattanville College *B*
Marymount Manhattan College *B*
New York University *B, M, D*
Sarah Lawrence College *M*
Skidmore College *B*
State University of New York
  Buffalo *B*
  College at Brockport *B, M*
  College at Fredonia *B*
  College at Potsdam *B*
  Purchase *B, M*
Wells College *B*

North Carolina

Appalachian State University *B*
East Carolina University *B*
Elon University *B*
Meredith College *B*
University of North Carolina
  Charlotte *B*
  Greensboro *B, M*
University of North Carolina School of
  the Arts *C, B*

Ohio

Case Western Reserve University *M*
College of Wooster *B*
Denison University *B*
Kent State University *B*
Kenyon College *B*
Oberlin College *B*
Ohio State University
  Columbus Campus *B, M*
Ohio University *B*
Ohio Wesleyan University *B*
University of Akron *B*
University of Cincinnati *B*
Wright State University *B*

Oklahoma

Oklahoma City University *B*
Oral Roberts University *B*
St. Gregory's University *B*
University of Central Oklahoma *B*
University of Oklahoma *B, M*

Oregon

University of Oregon *B, M*
Western Oregon University *B*

Pennsylvania

Cedar Crest College *B*
DeSales University *B*
Drexel University *B*
Eastern University *B*
Franklin & Marshall College *B*
La Roche College *B*
Mercyhurst College *B*
Muhlenberg College *C, B*
Point Park University *B*
Slippery Rock University of
  Pennsylvania *B*
Swarthmore College *B*
Temple University *B, M, D*
University of the Arts *C, B*
Ursinus College *B*

West Chester University of
  Pennsylvania *B*

Rhode Island

Rhode Island College *B*
Roger Williams University *B*

South Carolina

Coker College *B*
Columbia College *B*
University of South Carolina *B*
Winthrop University *B*

Tennessee

Columbia State Community College *C*

Texas

Austin Community College *A*
Kilgore College *A*
Lamar University *B*
Sam Houston State University *B, M*
Southern Methodist University *B, M*
Stephen F. Austin State University *B, T*
Texas Christian University *B*
Texas State University: San
  Marcos *B, T*
Texas Tech University *B*
Texas Woman's University *B, M, D*
Tyler Junior College *A*
University of Houston *B*
University of North Texas *B*
University of Texas
  Austin *B, M*
  El Paso *B*
  Pan American *B*
West Texas A&M University *B*

Utah

Brigham Young University *B, M*
College of Eastern Utah *T*
Snow College *A*
Southern Utah University *B, T*
University of Utah *B, M, T*
Utah State University *B*
Utah Valley University *A, B*
Weber State University *B*

Vermont

Bennington College *B, M*
Johnson State College *B*
Marlboro College *B*
Middlebury College *B*

Virginia

George Mason University *B, M*
Hollins University *B, M*
Old Dominion University *B, T*
Radford University *B*
Randolph College *B*
Shenandoah University *B, M*
Sweet Briar College *B*
Virginia Commonwealth University *B*
Virginia Intermont College *B*

Washington

Cornish College of the Arts *B*
University of Washington *B, M*
Western Washington University *B*

Wisconsin

Beloit College *B*
University of Wisconsin
  Madison *B, M*
  Milwaukee *B*
  Stevens Point *B*
  Whitewater *B, T*

Wyoming

Casper College *A*
Western Wyoming Community
  College *A*

Dance therapy

Arizona

Prescott College *B*

California

California Institute of Integral
  Studies *M*

Illinois

Columbia College Chicago *M*

Massachusetts

Lesley University *M, D*

New York

Pratt Institute *M*

South Carolina

Coker College *B*

Vermont

Goddard College *M*

Danish

Washington

University of Washington *B*

Data entry/applications

Alabama

Gadsden State Community College *C*

Arizona

Arizona Western College *C, A*
Chandler-Gilbert Community College
  Pecos *A*
Cochise College *C*
Estrella Mountain Community
  College *C, A*
GateWay Community College *C*
Glendale Community College *A*

California

College of the Siskiyous *C*
Glendale Community College *C*
Heald College
  Stockton *C, A*
Kaplan College: Panorama City *C*
Los Angeles Harbor College *C, A*
MTI College *C*
Orange Coast College *C, A*
San Diego City College *A*
San Jose City College *C, A*
Santa Rosa Junior College *C*
Sierra College *C, A*

Colorado

Arapahoe Community College *A*
Community College of Denver *C*

Connecticut

Manchester Community College *C, A*
Three Rivers Community College *C*

Florida

Central Florida Community College *C*
Herzing University *C*

Georgia

Albany Technical College *C*
Central Georgia Technical College *C*
Gwinnett College *C*
Macon State College *A*
Middle Georgia College *A*
Southwest Georgia Technical
  College *C, A*
West Georgia Technical College *C, A*

Illinois

College of Office Technology *C, A*
Elgin Community College *A*
Heartland Community College *A*
John A. Logan College *A*
Kankakee Community College *C*
Richland Community College *A*
Sauk Valley Community College *A*

Indiana

Kaplan College: Indianapolis *A*

Kansas

Central Christian College of Kansas *A*
Highland Community College *A*
Kansas City Kansas Community
  College *A*
Seward County Community
  College *C, A*

Maine

Central Maine Community
  College *C, A*

Maryland

Howard Community College *C, A*
TESST College of Technology
  Beltsville *A*
University of Maryland
  University College *C*

Massachusetts

Bristol Community College *C*
Bunker Hill Community College *A*
Fitchburg State College *C*
Marian Court College *C, A*
Roxbury Community College *C*
Springfield Technical Community
  College *C*

Michigan

Baker College
  of Muskegon *A*
Bay de Noc Community College *C*
Macomb Community College *C, A*
Mott Community College *C*

Minnesota

Central Lakes College *C*
Fond du Lac Tribal and Community
  College *C*
Lake Superior College *C*
North Hennepin Community
  College *C*
Riverland Community College *C*
Rochester Community and Technical
  College *C*

Mississippi

Antonelli College
  Jackson *C, A*

Missouri

Metro Business College
  Jefferson City *C*
St. Louis Community College
  St. Louis Community College at
    Meramec *C*

Montana

Montana State University
  Billings *A*

Nebraska

Nebraska Indian Community
  College *C, A*

New Hampshire

Nashua Community College *A*

New Jersey
Mercer County Community College *C*

New York
Globe Institute of Technology *C*
Olean Business Institute *A*
Pace University *C*
Westchester Community College *C*

North Carolina
Beaufort County Community
College *C*

North Dakota
North Dakota State College of
Science *C, A*

Ohio
Central Ohio Technical College *A*
Marion Technical College *C, A*
Ohio Business College: Sandusky *A*
Stark State College of Technology *A*
University of Akron *A*
University of Cincinnati
Clermont College *C, A*

Oregon
Lane Community College *C*
Portland Community College *C*

Pennsylvania
Consolidated School of Business
Lancaster *A*
Gannon University *C*
Harrisburg Area Community
College *C*
Keystone Technical Institute *C, A*
Newport Business Institute: Lower
Burrell *A*
PJA School *C*
Pennsylvania Highlands Community
College *C*
Westmoreland County Community
College *C*

South Carolina
Williamsburg Technical College *C*
York Technical College *C*

Tennessee
South College *C, A*

Texas
Palo Alto College *C*
St. Philip's College *C, A*
Temple College *C, A*

Utah
Utah Valley University *C, A*

Virginia
ECPI College of Technology: Virginia
Beach *C, A*
ECPI Technical College: Roanoke *A*
Germanna Community College *C*

Washington
Bellingham Technical College *C, A*
Centralia College *C*
Clark College *C, A*
Grays Harbor College *C*
Lower Columbia College *A*
Peninsula College *C*
Yakima Valley Community College *C*

West Virginia
Valley College *C*

Wisconsin
Northcentral Technical College *A*
Western Technical College *A*

Wyoming
Western Wyoming Community
College *C*

Data processing technology

Alabama
Chattahoochee Valley Community
College *A*
Gadsden State Community College *C*
Wallace State Community College at
Hanceville *A*

Arizona
Central Arizona College *A*
Cochise College *C, A*
Eastern Arizona College *C*
GateWay Community College *C*
Mohave Community College *C*
Northland Pioneer College *C, A*
Tohono O'odham Community
College *C*

Arkansas
Arkansas State University *B*
Central Baptist College *B*
University of Arkansas *B*
University of Arkansas
Fort Smith *C*

California
Antelope Valley College *A*
Bakersfield College *A*
Barstow Community College *C*
Cabrillo College *A*
Cerritos College *A*
Chabot College *C, A*
Citrus College *A*
College of the Redwoods *C*
College of the Siskiyous *C*
Cypress College *C, A*
El Camino College: Compton
Center *C, A*
Foothill College *C*
Fresno City College *C, A*
Fullerton College *C, A*
Gavilan College *C*
Heald College
Fresno *C, A*
LA College International *C*
Long Beach City College *C, A*
Los Angeles Mission College *C*
Los Angeles Pierce College *C, A*
Los Angeles Valley College *C, A*
Monterey Peninsula College *C, A*
Mount San Antonio College *C, A*
Orange Coast College *C*
Pasadena City College *C, A*
Porterville College *C*
San Diego City College *C, A*
San Joaquin Delta College *A*
Santa Ana College *C, A*
Santa Barbara City College *C, A*
Santa Monica College *C, A*
Shasta College *A*
Skyline College *C, A*
Taft College *C*
Victor Valley College *C*
Yuba Community College District *C*

Colorado
Colorado Mountain College *C*

Connecticut
Gateway Community College *C, A*
Norwalk Community College *A*
Three Rivers Community College *C*

Delaware
Delaware State University *B*

Florida
Broward College *A*
Florida Keys Community College *C*
Florida State College at
Jacksonville *C, A*
Gulf Coast Community College *C*
Indian River State College *C*
Miami Dade College *C*
Seminole Community College *C, A*
Tallahassee Community College *C*
University of Miami *B*

Georgia
Abraham Baldwin Agricultural
College *A*
Albany Technical College *C, A*
Athens Technical College *C, A*
Central Georgia Technical
College *C, A*
Clayton State University *B*
Dalton State College *C, A*
Darton College *C*
Savannah Technical College *C, A*
Southwest Georgia Technical
College *C, A*

Hawaii
Hawaii Pacific University *A*
University of Hawaii
Kapiolani Community College *C, A*

Illinois
Black Hawk College *C*
Black Hawk College: East Campus *A*
Chicago State University *B*
City Colleges of Chicago
Harold Washington College *C, A*
Olive-Harvey College *C, A*
College of Office Technology *C*
Danville Area Community College *A*
Harper College *C, A*
Kishwaukee College *C*
Lewis and Clark Community
College *A*
Oakton Community College *C, A*
Rockford Career College *A*
Southwestern Illinois College *A*

Indiana
Indiana University
Kokomo *C*
Northwest *C, A, B*
Purdue University
North Central *A, B*
University of Southern Indiana *B*
Vincennes University *C*

Iowa
Dordt College *A*
Ellsworth Community College *A*
Kaplan University
Cedar Falls *A*
Southeastern Community College
North Campus *C, A*

Kansas
Barton County Community
College *C, A*
Dodge City Community College *C, A*
Donnelly College *C, A*
Labette Community College *A*
Seward County Community
College *C, A*

Kentucky
Bluegrass Community and Technical
College *A*
Daymar College
Owensboro *C, A*
Eastern Kentucky University *A*
Henderson Community College *A*
Southeast Kentucky Community and
Technical College *A*
Western Kentucky University *A*

Louisiana
Delgado Community College *A*
ITI Technical College *A*
Louisiana State University
Alexandria *A*

Maine
Andover College *C, A*
Husson University *A*
Northern Maine Community
College *A*

Maryland
Allegany College of Maryland *C*
Hagerstown Community College *C*
Kaplan College: Hagerstown *A, B*

Massachusetts
Bristol Community College *A*
Holyoke Community College *C*
Springfield Technical Community
College *A*

Michigan
Baker College
of Auburn Hills *A*
of Clinton Township *A*
of Flint *A*
of Jackson *A*
of Muskegon *A*
of Port Huron *A*
Bay de Noc Community College *C, A*
Glen Oaks Community College *C*
Gogebic Community College *A*
Jackson Community College *C, A*
Kalamazoo Valley Community
College *A*
Lansing Community College *A*
Montcalm Community College *C, A*
Muskegon Community College *C, A*
Oakland Community College *C, A*
St. Clair County Community
College *C, A*
Washtenaw Community College *C, A*
West Shore Community College *C, A*

Minnesota
Central Lakes College *A*
Hennepin Technical College *C, A*
Pine Technical College *C, A*
South Central College *A*

Mississippi
Copiah-Lincoln Community College *A*
East Central Community College *A*
Hinds Community College *C, A*
Northwest Mississippi Community
College *A*
Pearl River Community College *A*
Southwest Mississippi Community
College *C, A*
University of Southern Mississippi *B*

Missouri
St. Louis Community College
St. Louis Community College at
Florissant Valley *C, A*
St. Louis Community College at
Meramec *C, A*
Texas County Technical Institute *C, A*
University of Central Missouri *B*
Washington University in St. Louis *B*

Montana
Fort Belknap College *A*
Fort Peck Community College *C, A*
Little Big Horn College *A*
Miles Community College *A*

Montana Tech of the University of
    Montana *C*
University of Great Falls *B*
University of Montana *A*

Nebraska
Kaplan University: Omaha *C, A, B*

Nevada
College of Southern Nevada *A*
Truckee Meadows Community
    College *A*

New Hampshire
Lakes Region Community
    College *C, A*
Nashua Community College *C, A*
River Valley Community College *C*

New Jersey
Atlantic Cape Community College *A*
Burlington County College *C, A*
Essex County College *C*
Gloucester County College *C, A*
Hudson County Community
    College *C, A*
Ocean County College *C*
Raritan Valley Community College *A*
Saint Peter's College *A*

New Mexico
Central New Mexico Community
    College *C, A*
Dona Ana Community College of New
    Mexico State University *A*
New Mexico State University
    Alamogordo *C, A*
    Carlsbad *C*
San Juan College *C, A*

New York
Adirondack Community College *C, A*
Bramson ORT College *A*
Broome Community College *A*
Cayuga County Community College *C*
City University of New York
    Borough of Manhattan Community
        College *A*
    Bronx Community College *A*
    Brooklyn College *C*
    Hostos Community College *A*
    Kingsborough Community
        College *A*
    LaGuardia Community College *A*
    New York City College of
        Technology *A*
    Queensborough Community
        College *A*
College of Westchester *C, A*
Globe Institute of Technology *C*
Herkimer County Community
    College *A*
Hudson Valley Community
    College *C, A*
Jamestown Business College *A*
Jamestown Community College *C, A*
Olean Business Institute *A*
Orange County Community College *A*
Pace University *A*
Rockland Community College *C, A*
State University of New York
    College of Agriculture and
        Technology at Morrisville *C*
    College of Technology at
        Delhi *C, A, B*
    Farmingdale *C, A*
Sullivan County Community
    College *C, A*
Utica School of Commerce *A*

North Carolina
Caldwell Community College and
    Technical Institute *A*

Durham Technical Community
    College *C, A*
Lenoir Community College *C, A*
Stanly Community College *C*
Western Piedmont Community
    College *C, A*

North Dakota
Lake Region State College *C, A*
Mayville State University *C*
Williston State College *C, A*

Ohio
Belmont Technical College *C*
Cincinnati Christian University *B*
Eastern Gateway Community
    College *C, A*
Miami University
    Oxford Campus *A*
Mount Vernon Nazarene University *A*
Northwest State Community
    College *C*
Ohio Valley College of Technology *A*
RETS College *C*
Stark State College of Technology *A*
University of Akron: Wayne College *A*
University of Cincinnati
    Clermont College *C, A*
Washington State Community
    College *A*
Wright State University *A*

Oklahoma
Connors State College *A*
Oklahoma City Community College *A*

Pennsylvania
Bucks County Community College *A*
CHI Institute: Franklin Mills *C*
Community College of Philadelphia *A*
Consolidated School of Business
    Lancaster *A*
    York *A*
Keystone College *A*
Keystone Technical Institute *C, A*
Newport Business Institute: Lower
    Burrell *A*
Peirce College *A*
Reading Area Community College *A*
University of Pittsburgh
    Titusville *C*
Westmoreland County Community
    College *C*

South Carolina
Aiken Technical College *A*
Florence-Darlington Technical
    College *A*
Greenville Technical College *C, A*
Horry-Georgetown Technical
    College *C, A*
Midlands Technical College *C, A*
Northeastern Technical College *C, A*
Orangeburg-Calhoun Technical
    College *C, A*
Technical College of the
    Lowcountry *C, A*
Tri-County Technical College *A*
Trident Technical College *C, A*

South Dakota
Lake Area Technical Institute *A*
Sinte Gleska University *A*
Southeast Technical Institute *C*

Texas
Angelina College *C, A*
Cedar Valley College *C, A*
Central Texas College *C, A*
Coastal Bend College *A*
Eastfield College *A*
El Centro College *C, A*
El Paso Community College *C*

Frank Phillips College *C*
Galveston College *C*
Hill College *C, A*
Howard College *C*
Lamar State College at Orange *C, A*
Lee College *C, A*
McLennan Community College *C, A*
Midland College *A*
Mountain View College *C, A*
North Central Texas College *A*
Paris Junior College *C, A*
St. Philip's College *A*
South Plains College *A*
Southwest Texas Junior College *A*
Stephen F. Austin State University *B*
Texas State Technical College
    Waco *C, A*
Trinity Valley Community College *A*
Tyler Junior College *C*
Vernon College *C, A*
Weatherford College *C, A*
Western Texas College *C, A*

Utah
Utah Valley University *A, B*

Virginia
ECPI College of Technology: Virginia
    Beach *C, A*
ECPI Technical College: Roanoke *A*
J. Sargeant Reynolds Community
    College *C*
Mountain Empire Community
    College *C*
Virginia Highlands Community
    College *A*

Washington
Bellevue College *C*
Centralia College *A*
Clover Park Technical College *C*
Grays Harbor College *A*
Lake Washington Technical
    College *C, A*
Lower Columbia College *C, A*
Peninsula College *A*
Pierce College *C, A*
Renton Technical College *C*
Shoreline Community College *C, A*
South Puget Sound Community
    College *C, A*
Spokane Community College *C, A*
Walla Walla University *B*
Whatcom Community College *C, A*
Yakima Valley Community College *C*

West Virginia
Potomac State College of West
    Virginia University *A*

Wisconsin
Fox Valley Technical College *A*
Moraine Park Technical College *C, A*
Nicolet Area Technical College *A*
Northeast Wisconsin Technical
    College *A*
Southwest Wisconsin Technical
    College *C*
Waukesha County Technical
    College *C*
Western Technical College *A*

Wyoming
Western Wyoming Community
    College *C, A*

Database design/management

Arizona
University of Phoenix *B*

California
American River College *C, A*
Foothill College *C, A*
Golden Gate University *C*
San Joaquin Delta College *A*

Colorado
Colorado Technical University *C*
Jones International University *B*
Red Rocks Community College *C*

Connecticut
Norwalk Community College *C*

Florida
St. Petersburg College *C*

Indiana
Ivy Tech Community College
    Bloomington *C*
    Central Indiana *C*
    Columbus *C*
    East Central *C*
    Kokomo *C*
    Lafayette *C*
    North Central *C*
    Northeast *C*
    Northwest *C*
    Richmond *C*
    South Central *C*
Purdue University
    Calumet *B*

Kentucky
University of Louisville *C*

Maryland
University of Maryland
    University College *C*

Massachusetts
Fitchburg State College *C*

Michigan
Central Michigan University *M*
Oakland Community College *C*
Wayne County Community College *A*

Minnesota
Dakota County Technical College *C, A*
Lake Superior College *C, A*
Minneapolis Community and
    Technical College *C*

Nevada
College of Southern Nevada *C, A*

New York
Globe Institute of Technology *C, A, B*
Rochester Institute of
    Technology *B, M*
State University of New York
    College of Agriculture and
        Technology at Morrisville *B*

North Carolina
Central Piedmont Community
    College *C, A*
College of the Albemarle *C*

Ohio
Clark State Community College *A*
Stark State College of Technology *A*
University of Akron *C*

Oregon
Chemeketa Community College *C*
Mt. Hood Community College *C, A*

Pennsylvania
La Salle University *B, M*
Newport Business Institute: Lower
  Burrell *A*
Pennsylvania Highlands Community
  College *A*

Puerto Rico
Inter American University of Puerto
  Rico
  Metropolitan Campus *M*

Virginia
Lord Fairfax Community College *C, A*

Washington
Bates Technical College *C, A*
Bellevue College *A*
Clark College *C*
Clover Park Technical College *C*
Green River Community College *A*
Shoreline Community College *C, A*
Yakima Valley Community College *C*

West Virginia
Huntington Junior College *A*

Wisconsin
Northcentral Technical College *C*

Wyoming
Laramie County Community
  College *C*

Demography/ population studies

California
University of California
  Berkeley *M, D*

Florida
Florida State University *M*

Ohio
Bowling Green State University *M*

Pennsylvania
University of Pennsylvania *M, D*
University of Pittsburgh
  Bradford *B*

Puerto Rico
University of Puerto Rico
  Medical Sciences *M*

Texas
University of Texas
  San Antonio *D*

Wisconsin
University of Wisconsin
  Madison *M, D*

Dental assistant

Alabama
Calhoun Community College *C, A*
Faulkner State Community
  College *C, A*
Lawson State Community College *C*
Northeast Alabama Community
  College *C*
University of Alabama
  Birmingham *C*
Wallace State Community College at
  Hanceville *C, A*

Alaska
University of Alaska
  Anchorage *C, A*
  Fairbanks *C, A*

Arizona
Mohave Community College *C*
Phoenix College *A*
Pima Community College *C*
Rio Salado College *C*

Arkansas
Arkansas Northeastern College *C*
Northwest Arkansas Community
  College *C*
Pulaski Technical College *C*

California
Allan Hancock College *C, A*
Bakersfield College *A*
Cerritos College *C, A*
Chaffey College *C, A*
Citrus College *C, A*
City College of San Francisco *C, A*
College of Alameda *A*
College of Marin: Kentfield *C, A*
College of San Mateo *C, A*
College of the Redwoods *C*
Concorde Career College
  Garden Grove *C*
Concorde Career College: North
  Hollywood *C*
Concorde Career College: San
  Bernardino *C*
Concorde Career College: San
  Diego *C*
Contra Costa College *A*
Cypress College *C, A*
Diablo Valley College *C*
Foothill College *C, A*
Heald College
  Concord *C, A*
  Hayward *A*
  Stockton *C, A*
Kaplan College: Salida *C*
Modesto Junior College *A*
Monterey Peninsula College *C, A*
Orange Coast College *C, A*
Oxnard College *C*
Palomar College *C, A*
Pasadena City College *C, A*
Reedley College *C, A*
Sacramento City College *C, A*
San Diego Mesa College *C, A*
San Joaquin Valley College *A*
San Jose City College *C, A*
Santa Rosa Junior College *C, A*
Silicon Valley College
  Western Career College: San Jose *A*
Western Career College
  Pleasant Hill *A*
Western Career College: Citrus
  Heights *C, A*
Western Career College:
  Sacramento *C, A*

Colorado
Front Range Community College *C*
Pikes Peak Community College *C, A*
Pueblo Community College *C, A*

Connecticut
Lincoln College of New England:
  Briarwood *C, A*
Tunxis Community College *C*

Florida
Angley College *C*
Brevard Community College *C*
Broward College *C*
Central Florida Community College *C*
Daytona State College *C*
Edison State College *C*

Florida National College *C*
Florida State College at Jacksonville *C*
Gulf Coast Community College *C*
Hillsborough Community College *C*
Indian River State College *C*
Palm Beach Community College *C*
Pasco-Hernando Community
  College *C*
Pensacola Junior College *C*
Santa Fe College *C*
South Florida Community College *C*
Tallahassee Community College *C*

Georgia
Albany Technical College *C*
Athens Technical College *A*
Augusta Technical College *C*
Clayton State University *B*
Gwinnett Technical College *C*
Middle Georgia College *A*
Middle Georgia Technical College *C*
Savannah Technical College *C, A*

Hawaii
Heald College
  Honolulu *A*
University of Hawaii
  Kapiolani Community College *C, A*
  Maui Community College *C*

Idaho
Eastern Idaho Technical College *C*

Illinois
Black Hawk College *C*
Elgin Community College *C*
Illinois Central College *C*
Illinois Valley Community College *C*
John A. Logan College *C*
Kaskaskia College *C*
Lewis and Clark Community
  College *C*
Rock Valley College *C*

Indiana
Indiana University
  Northwest *C*
  South Bend *C*
Indiana University-Purdue University
  Fort Wayne *C*
Indiana University-Purdue University
  Indianapolis *C*
Ivy Tech Community College
  Columbus *C*
  East Central *C*
  Kokomo *C*
  Lafayette *C*
Kaplan College: Indianapolis *C, A*
University of Southern Indiana *C, A*

Iowa
Clinton Community College *C*
Des Moines Area Community
  College *C*
Hawkeye Community College *C*
Iowa Western Community College *C*
Kirkwood Community College *C, A*
Marshalltown Community College *C*
Northeast Iowa Community
  College *C*
Scott Community College *C*
Vatterott College *C*
Western Iowa Tech Community
  College *C*

Kentucky
West Kentucky Community and
  Technical College *C*

Maine
University of Maine
  Augusta *C*

Maryland
Community College of Baltimore
  County *C, A*
Hagerstown Community College *C*

Massachusetts
Massasoit Community College *C*
Middlesex Community College *C, A*
Northern Essex Community
  College *C*
Quinsigamond Community College *C*
Springfield Technical Community
  College *C*

Michigan
Baker College
  of Auburn Hills *A*
  of Port Huron *A*
Bay de Noc Community College *C*
Delta College *C, A*
Grand Rapids Community
  College *C, A*
Lake Michigan College *C, A*
Mott Community College *C, A*
Northwestern Michigan College *C, A*
Washtenaw Community College *C*
Wayne County Community College *C*

Minnesota
Central Lakes College *C*
Century Community and Technical
  College *C, A*
Dakota County Technical College *C, A*
Hennepin Technical College *C, A*
Hibbing Community College *A*
Minneapolis Community and
  Technical College *C*
Minnesota State Community and
  Technical College *C*
Minnesota West Community and
  Technical College *A*
Northwest Technical College *C*
Rochester Community and Technical
  College *C, A*
St. Cloud Technical College *C, A*
South Central College *C, A*

Mississippi
Hinds Community College *C, A*

Missouri
High-Tech Institute *A*
Metropolitan Community College:
  Penn Valley *C, A*
Missouri College *C, A*
Ozarks Technical Community
  College *C*
Vatterott College: Springfield *C*

Montana
Montana State University
  College of Technology: Great
    Falls *C*
Salish Kootenai College *C, A*

Nebraska
Central Community College *C, A*
Kaplan University: Omaha *C*
Metropolitan Community College *C*
Mid-Plains Community College
  Area *C, A*
Southeast Community College *C*

Nevada
High-Tech Institute *A*
Truckee Meadows Community
  College *C, A*

New Hampshire
NHTI-Concord's Community
  College *C*

New Jersey
Camden County College *C, A*
Essex County College *C*
Raritan Valley Community College *C*
Thomas Edison State College *C*
Union County College *C*
University of Medicine and Dentistry
of New Jersey
School of Health Related
Professions *C*

New Mexico
Central New Mexico Community
College *C*
Eastern New Mexico University:
Roswell Campus *C*
Santa Fe Community College *C, A*

New York
Erie Community College
North Campus *C*
Monroe Community College *C*
State University of New York
Farmingdale *A*

North Carolina
Alamance Community College *C*
Asheville-Buncombe Technical
Community College *C*
Cape Fear Community College *C*
Central Piedmont Community
College *C*
Coastal Carolina Community
College *C*
Fayetteville Technical Community
College *C*
Guilford Technical Community
College *C*
Martin Community College *C*
Miller-Motte Technical College *C*
Montgomery Community College *C*
Rowan-Cabarrus Community
College *C*
University of North Carolina
Chapel Hill *C*
Wake Technical Community
College *C*
Western Piedmont Community
College *C*
Wilkes Community College *C*

North Dakota
North Dakota State College of
Science *C*

Ohio
Cuyahoga Community College
Metropolitan Campus *C, A*
Eastern Gateway Community
College *C, A*
James A. Rhodes State College *A*
National Institute of Technology *C*
Ohio Business College: Columbus *C*
Ohio Valley College of Technology *A*
Remington College: Cleveland West *C*

Oklahoma
Platt College
Tulsa *C*
Platt College: Oklahoma City
Central *C*
Rose State College *C, A*

Oregon
Blue Mountain Community College *C*
Central Oregon Community
College *C*
Chemeketa Community College *C, A*
Clackamas Community College *C*
Lane Community College *C*
Linn-Benton Community College *C*
Portland Community College *C*

Rogue Community College *C*
Umpqua Community College *C*

Pennsylvania
Commonwealth Technical Institute *C*
Community College of Philadelphia *C*
Harcum College *C, A*
Harrisburg Area Community
College *C*
Keystone Technical Institute *C*
Luzerne County Community
College *C, A*
Manor College *A*
Westmoreland County Community
College *C*

Puerto Rico
Huertas Junior College *A*
Humacao Community College *A*
National College of Business and
Technology: Arecibo *A*
National College of Business and
Technology: Bayamon *A*
National College of Business and
Technology: Rio Grande *A*
Ponce Paramedical College *C*
University of Puerto Rico
Medical Sciences *A*

Rhode Island
Community College of Rhode
Island *C*

South Carolina
Aiken Technical College *C*
Florence-Darlington Technical
College *C*
Greenville Technical College *C*
Horry-Georgetown Technical
College *C*
Midlands Technical College *C, A*
Spartanburg Community College *C*
Tri-County Technical College *C*
Trident Technical College *C*
York Technical College *C*

South Dakota
Lake Area Technical Institute *C*

Tennessee
Chattanooga State Community
College *C*
Draughons Junior College:
Nashville *C, A*
Northeast State Community College *C*
Volunteer State Community College *C*

Texas
Amarillo College *C*
Del Mar College *C, A*
El Paso Community College *C, A*
Grayson County College *C*
Houston Community College
System *C*
Lamar State College at Orange *C*
San Antonio College *C*
Tarrant County College *C*
Texas State Technical College
Harlingen *C*
Waco *C*

Utah
Eagle Gate College: Murray *A*
Provo College *C, A*

Virginia
Centura College: Norfolk *C*
J. Sargeant Reynolds Community
College *C*
Wytheville Community College *C*

Washington
Bates Technical College *C, A*
Bellingham Technical College *C, A*
Centralia College *C*
Clover Park Technical College *C, A*
Highline Community College *A*
Lake Washington Technical
College *C, A*
Renton Technical College *C, A*
South Puget Sound Community
College *C, A*
Spokane Community College *C, A*
Yakima Valley Community College *C*

West Virginia
Huntington Junior College *C, A*
West Virginia Junior College:
Bridgeport *A*

Wisconsin
Blackhawk Technical College *C*
Chippewa Valley Technical College *C*
Fox Valley Technical College *C*
Gateway Technical College *C*
Lakeshore Technical College *C*
Milwaukee Area Technical College *C*
Northcentral Technical College *A*
Northeast Wisconsin Technical
College *C*
Waukesha County Technical
College *C*
Western Technical College *C*
Wisconsin Indianhead Technical
College *C*

Wyoming
Central Wyoming College *C*

Dental clinical services

Alabama
University of Alabama
Birmingham *M*

California
University of California
Los Angeles *M, D*
University of Southern
California *M, D*

Connecticut
University of Connecticut *M*

Florida
Nova Southeastern University *M*

Illinois
Northwestern University *M, D*

Indiana
Indiana University-Purdue University
Indianapolis *M, D*

Iowa
University of Iowa *M*

Kentucky
University of Louisville *M*

Louisiana
Louisiana State University Health
Sciences Center *M, D*

Michigan
University of Michigan *M, D*

Minnesota
Metropolitan State University *M*

Missouri
University of Missouri
Kansas City *M, D*

Nebraska
University of Nebraska
Medical Center *M, D*

New York
State University of New York
Buffalo *M*
University of Rochester *M*

North Carolina
University of North Carolina
Chapel Hill *M, D*

Ohio
Case Western Reserve University *M*

Oregon
Oregon Health & Science
University *M*

Pennsylvania
University of Pittsburgh *M*

Tennessee
University of Tennessee
Knoxville *D*

Texas
Texas A&M University
Baylor College of Dentistry *M, D*

Virginia
Virginia Commonwealth University *M*

West Virginia
West Virginia University *M*

Dental hygiene

Alabama
Wallace State Community College at
Hanceville *A*

Alaska
University of Alaska
Anchorage *A*
Fairbanks *A*

Arizona
Mohave Community College *A*
Northern Arizona University *B*
Phoenix College *A*
Pima Community College *A*
Rio Salado College *A*

Arkansas
University of Arkansas
Fort Smith *A*

California
Cabrillo College *C, A*
Cerritos College *C, A*
Chabot College *C, A*
Cypress College *C, A*
Diablo Valley College *C*
Foothill College *A*
Fresno City College *A*
Hartnell College *A*
Loma Linda University *B*
Oxnard College *A*
Pasadena City College *C, A*
Sacramento City College *C, A*
San Joaquin Valley College *A*
Santa Rosa Junior College *C, A*
Shasta College *A*

Silicon Valley College
   Western Career College: San Jose A
Southwestern College A
Taft College A
University of Southern California B
University of the Pacific B
West Los Angeles College C, A

Colorado
Colorado Northwestern Community
   College A
Community College of Denver A
Pueblo Community College A
University of Colorado
   Denver B

Connecticut
Tunxis Community College A
University of Bridgeport A, B, M
University of New Haven A, B

Delaware
Delaware Technical and Community
   College
   Stanton/Wilmington A

District of Columbia
Howard University C

Florida
Brevard Community College A
Broward College A
Daytona State College A
Edison State College A
Florida National College A
Florida State College at Jacksonville A
Gulf Coast Community College A
Hillsborough Community College A
Indian River State College A
Miami Dade College A
Palm Beach Community College A
Pasco-Hernando Community
   College A
Pensacola Junior College A
St. Petersburg College A, B
Santa Fe College A
South Florida Community College A
State College of Florida,
   Manatee-Sarasota A
Tallahassee Community College A
Valencia Community College A

Georgia
Abraham Baldwin Agricultural
   College A
Armstrong Atlantic State
   University A, B
Athens Technical College A
Central Georgia Technical College A
Clayton State University B
Columbus Technical College A
Dalton State College A
Darton College A
Gainesville State College A
Georgia Highlands College A
Georgia Perimeter College A
Gordon College A
Medical College of Georgia B
Middle Georgia College A
Middle Georgia Technical College A
Southeastern Technical College A
Valdosta State University A
Waycross College A

Hawaii
University of Hawaii
   Kapiolani Community College A
   Manoa B

Idaho
Idaho State University B, M

Illinois
City Colleges of Chicago
   Kennedy-King College A
College of DuPage A
College of Lake County A
Harper College A
Illinois Central College A
John A. Logan College A
Lake Land College A
Lewis and Clark Community
   College A
Parkland College A
Prairie State College A
Southern Illinois University
   Carbondale B

Indiana
Indiana University
   Bloomington A, B
   Northwest A
   South Bend A
Indiana University-Purdue University
   Fort Wayne A
Indiana University-Purdue University
   Indianapolis A, B
University of Southern Indiana A, B

Iowa
Clinton Community College A
Des Moines Area Community
   College A
Hawkeye Community College A
Iowa Western Community College A
Kirkwood Community College A
Muscatine Community College A
Scott Community College A
Western Iowa Tech Community
   College A

Kansas
Colby Community College A
Johnson County Community
   College A
Seward County Community College A
Wichita State University A, B

Kentucky
Big Sandy Community and Technical
   College A
Bluegrass Community and Technical
   College C, A
Elizabethtown Community and
   Technical College A
Henderson Community College C
University of Louisville A, B
Western Kentucky University A, B

Louisiana
Delgado Community College A
Louisiana State University Health
   Sciences Center B
Southern University
   Shreveport A
University of Louisiana at Lafayette B
University of Louisiana at Monroe B

Maine
University of Maine
   Augusta A, B
University of New England A, B

Maryland
Allegany College of Maryland A
Baltimore City Community College A
Carroll Community College A
Community College of Baltimore
   County A
University of Maryland
   Baltimore B, M

Massachusetts
Bristol Community College A

Cape Cod Community College A
Massachusetts College of Pharmacy
   and Health Sciences B
Middlesex Community College A
Mount Ida College A
Mount Wachusett Community
   College A
Quinsigamond Community College A
Springfield Technical Community
   College A

Michigan
Baker College
   of Auburn Hills A
   of Port Huron A
Delta College A
Ferris State University A, B
Grand Rapids Community College A
Kalamazoo Valley Community
   College A
Kellogg Community College A
Lansing Community College A
Mott Community College A
Oakland Community College A
University of Detroit Mercy B
University of Michigan B, M
Wayne County Community College A

Minnesota
Argosy University: Twin Cities A
Century Community and Technical
   College A
Lake Superior College A
Metropolitan State University B
Minnesota State Community and
   Technical College A
Minnesota State University
   Mankato B
Normandale Community College A
Rochester Community and Technical
   College A
St. Cloud Technical College A
University of Minnesota
   Twin Cities C, B

Mississippi
Meridian Community College A
Mississippi Delta Community
   College A

Missouri
Missouri Southern State University A
Ozarks Technical Community
   College A
State Fair Community College A
University of Missouri
   Kansas City B, M

Montana
Montana State University
   College of Technology: Great
   Falls A

Nebraska
Central Community College C, A
University of Nebraska
   Medical Center B

Nevada
College of Southern Nevada A, B
Truckee Meadows Community
   College A

New Hampshire
NHTI-Concord's Community
   College A

New Jersey
Bergen Community College A
Brookdale Community College A
Burlington County College A
Camden County College A

Essex County College A
Middlesex County College A
Raritan Valley Community College A
Thomas Edison State College A, B
Union County College A
University of Medicine and Dentistry
   of New Jersey
   School of Health Related
   Professions A, B

New Mexico
San Juan College A
University of New Mexico B, M

New York
Broome Community College A
City University of New York
   Hostos Community College A
   New York City College of
   Technology A
Erie Community College
   North Campus A
Hudson Valley Community College A
Monroe Community College A
New York University A, B
Orange County Community College A
State University of New York
   College of Technology at
   Canton A, B
   Farmingdale B

North Carolina
Asheville-Buncombe Technical
   Community College A
Cape Fear Community College A
Catawba Valley Community College A
Central Piedmont Community
   College A
Coastal Carolina Community
   College A
Fayetteville Technical Community
   College A
Forsyth Technical Community
   College A
Guilford Technical Community
   College A
University of North Carolina
   Chapel Hill C, B, M
Wake Technical Community
   College A
Wayne Community College A

North Dakota
North Dakota State College of
   Science A

Ohio
Columbus State Community
   College A
Cuyahoga Community College
   Metropolitan Campus A
Ohio State University
   Columbus Campus B
Owens Community College
   Toledo A
Shawnee State University A
Stark State College of Technology A
University of Cincinnati
   Raymond Walters College A
Youngstown State University A

Oklahoma
Rose State College A
Tulsa Community College A
University of Oklahoma B

Oregon
Chemeketa Community College A
Lane Community College A
Mt. Hood Community College A
Oregon Institute of Technology A, B
Portland Community College A

Pennsylvania

Community College of Philadelphia A
Harcum College A
Harrisburg Area Community
College A
Luzerne County Community
College A
Manor College A
Montgomery County Community
College A
Northampton Community College A
Pennsylvania College of
Technology A, B
University of Pittsburgh C, B
Westmoreland County Community
College A

Puerto Rico

University of Puerto Rico
Medical Sciences A

Rhode Island

Community College of Rhode
Island A

South Carolina

Aiken Technical College C
Central Carolina Technical College C
Florence-Darlington Technical
College A
Greenville Technical College A
Horry-Georgetown Technical
College C, A
Midlands Technical College A
Orangeburg-Calhoun Technical
College C
Spartanburg Community College C
Tri-County Technical College C
Trident Technical College C, A
York Technical College A

South Dakota

University of South Dakota A, B

Tennessee

Chattanooga State Community
College A
Columbia State Community College A
East Tennessee State University B
Roane State Community College A
Southern Adventist University A
Tennessee State University A, B
University of Tennessee
Knoxville M
University of Tennessee Health
Science Center B

Texas

Amarillo College A
Austin Community College A
Coastal Bend College A
Collin County Community College
District A
Del Mar College A
El Paso Community College A
Houston Community College
System A
Howard College A
Lamar Institute of Technology A
Lone Star College System A
Midwestern State University B
Northeast Texas Community
College A
Tarrant County College A
Temple College A
Texas A&M University
Baylor College of Dentistry B, M
Texas State Technical College
Harlingen A
Texas Woman's University B
Tyler Junior College A

University of Texas
Health Science Center at
Houston C, B
Health Science Center at San
Antonio B
Wharton County Junior College A

Utah

Careers Unlimited B
Dixie State College of Utah A, B
Salt Lake Community College A
Utah Valley University A
Weber State University A, B

Vermont

Vermont Technical College A, B

Virginia

Danville Community College A
Germanna Community College A
Lord Fairfax Community College A
Northern Virginia Community
College A
Old Dominion University B, M
Virginia Commonwealth University B
Virginia Highlands Community
College A
Virginia Western Community
College A
Wytheville Community College A

Washington

Bellingham Technical College A
Clark College A
Eastern Washington University B, M
Everett Community College A
Lake Washington Technical College A
Pierce College A
Shoreline Community College A
University of Washington B
Yakima Valley Community College A

West Virginia

West Liberty University A, B
West Virginia University B, M

Wisconsin

Chippewa Valley Technical College A
Fox Valley Technical College A
Gateway Technical College A
Milwaukee Area Technical College A
Northcentral Technical College A
Northeast Wisconsin Technical
College A
Waukesha County Technical
College A
Western Technical College A

Wyoming

Laramie County Community
College A
Sheridan College A
University of Wyoming B

Dental laboratory technology

Arizona

Pima Community College C, A

California

Cypress College A
Diablo Valley College C
Los Angeles City College C, A
Pasadena City College C, A
Riverside Community College C, A
San Diego Mesa College A

Florida

Florida National College A
Indian River State College A

Georgia

Gwinnett Technical College A

Idaho

Idaho State University A

Indiana

Indiana University-Purdue University
Fort Wayne A

Iowa

Kirkwood Community College A

Kentucky

Bluegrass Community and Technical
College C, A

Louisiana

Delgado Community College A
Louisiana State University Health
Sciences Center A, B

Massachusetts

Boston University B
Middlesex Community College A

Michigan

Bay de Noc Community College C
Wayne County Community College C

New York

City University of New York
New York City College of
Technology A
Erie Community College
South Campus A
New York University M

North Carolina

Durham Technical Community
College C, A

Ohio

Columbus State Community
College C, A
Cuyahoga Community College
Metropolitan Campus C, A

Oregon

Portland Community College C, A

Pennsylvania

Commonwealth Technical Institute A

Tennessee

Northeast State Community
College C, A

Texas

Howard College C, A
Texas State Technical College
Harlingen C, A
University of Texas
Health Science Center at San
Antonio B

Virginia

J. Sargeant Reynolds Community
College C, A

Washington

Bates Technical College C, A

Wisconsin

Milwaukee Area Technical
College C, A

Dentistry (D.D.S., D.M.D.)

Alabama

University of Alabama at Birmingham:
School of Dentistry P

California

Loma Linda University: School of
Dentistry P
University of California Los Angeles:
School of Dentistry P
University of California San Francisco:
School of Dentistry P
University of Southern California:
School of Dentistry P
University of the Pacific: School of
Dentistry P

Colorado

University of Colorado Health
Sciences Center: School of
Dentistry P

Connecticut

University of Connecticut: School of
Dentistry P

District of Columbia

Howard University: College of
Dentistry P

Florida

University of Florida: College of
Dentistry P

Georgia

Medical College of Georgia: School of
Dentistry P

Illinois

Northwestern University: Dental
School P
Southern Illinois University: School of
Dentistry P
University of Illinois at Chicago:
College of Dentistry P

Indiana

Indiana University School of
Dentistry P

Iowa

University of Iowa College of
Dentistry P

Kentucky

University of Kentucky: College of
Dentistry P
University of Louisville: School of
Dentistry P

Louisiana

Louisiana State University Health
Sciences Center: School of
Dentistry P

Maryland

University of Maryland at Baltimore:
School of Dentistry P

Massachusetts

Boston University: Goldman School of
Dental Medicine P
Harvard University: School of Dental
Medicine P
Tufts University: School of Dental
Medicine P

Michigan

University of Detroit Mercy: School of Dentistry *P*
University of Michigan: School of Dentistry *P*

Minnesota

University of Minnesota Twin Cities: School of Dentistry *P*

Mississippi

University of Mississippi Medical Center: School of Dentistry *P*

Missouri

University of Missouri Kansas City: School of Dentistry *P*

Nebraska

Creighton University: School of Dentistry *P*
University of Nebraska Medical Center: College of Dentistry *P*

New Jersey

University of Medicine and Dentistry of New Jersey
New Jersey Dental School *P*

New York

Columbia University College of Dental Medicine *P*
New York University: College of Dentistry *P*
State University of New York Health Sciences Center at Stony Brook: School of Dentistry *P*
State University of New York at Buffalo: School of Dentistry *P*

North Carolina

University of North Carolina at Chapel Hill: School of Dentistry *P*

Ohio

Case Western Reserve University: School of Dentistry *P*
Ohio State University Columbus Campus: College of Dentistry *P*

Oklahoma

University of Oklahoma Health Sciences Center: College of Dentistry *P*

Oregon

Oregon Health Sciences University: School of Dentistry *P*

Pennsylvania

Temple University: School of Dentistry *P*
University of Pennsylvania: School of Dental Medicine *P*
University of Pittsburgh: School of Dental Medicine *P*

Puerto Rico

University of Puerto Rico Medical Sciences Campus: School of Dentistry *P*

South Carolina

Medical University of South Carolina: College of Dental Medicine *P*

Tennessee

Meharry Medical College: School of Dentistry *P*
University of Tennessee Memphis: College of Dentistry *P*

Texas

University of Texas Health Science Center: Dental School *P*
University of Texas Health Sciences Center-Dental Branch *P*

Virginia

Virginia Commonwealth University: School of Dentistry *P*

Washington

University of Washington: School of Dentistry *P*

West Virginia

West Virginia University: School of Dentistry *P*

Wisconsin

Marquette University: School of Dentistry *P*

Design/visual communications

Alabama

Auburn University *B*

Arizona

Collins College *A*
Northern Arizona University *B*
Pima Community College *A*

California

Academy of Art University *C, A, B, M*
Allan Hancock College *A*
Art Institute
 of California: Los Angeles *A, B*
 of California: San Diego *A*
Bethesda Christian University *B*
California Institute of the Arts *C, B, M*
California State University
 Chico *B*
 Long Beach *B*
Chaffey College *C, A*
Fashion Institute of Design and Merchandising
 Los Angeles *A*
 San Diego *A*
 San Francisco *A*
Fullerton College *A*
Laney College *C, A*
Long Beach City College *A*
Loyola Marymount University *B, M*
Mount San Antonio College *A*
Otis College of Art and Design *B*
Platt College
 Los Angeles *B*
 Ontario *C, A, B*
Saddleback College *C, A*
San Diego State University *B*
University of California
 Davis *B*
 Los Angeles *B, M*
Westwood College of Technology
 Westwood College: Inland Empire *B*
 Westwood College: Los Angeles *B*
Westwood College: Anaheim *A, B*

Colorado

Colorado Mountain College *A*
Colorado State University *M*
Rocky Mountain College of Art & Design *B*
Westwood College of Technology
 Westwood College: Denver South *B*
 Westwood College: Denver North *B*

Connecticut

Central Connecticut State University *B, M*
Paier College of Art *C, B*
Sacred Heart University *B*
University of Hartford *B*

District of Columbia

American University *B*
Howard University *B*

Florida

Florida State College at Jacksonville *A*
Jacksonville University *B*
University of Miami *B*

Georgia

American InterContinental University *B*
Art Institute of Atlanta *C*
DeKalb Technical College *C*
Georgia State University *B*

Idaho

University of Idaho *B*

Illinois

Black Hawk College *C, A*
City Colleges of Chicago Harold Washington College *A*
College of DuPage *C, A*
Columbia College Chicago *C, B*
Elgin Community College *C, A*
Heartland Community College *A*
Illinois Institute of Art: Schaumburg *C, A, B*
Prairie State College *A*
Sauk Valley Community College *C*
School of the Art Institute of Chicago *B, M*
Southern Illinois University Carbondale *B*
Triton College *C, A*
Westwood College: Chicago Loop *B*
Wilbur Wright College *C, A*

Indiana

Anderson University *B*
Bethel College *B*
Indiana University-Purdue University Indianapolis *B, M*
International Business College *C, A*
Ivy Tech Community College
 Central Indiana *A*
 Columbus *A*
 Kokomo *A*
 North Central *A*
 South Central *A*
 Southwest *A*
 Wabash Valley *A*
Purdue University *B*
St. Mary-of-the-Woods College *B*
University of Evansville *B*
University of Indianapolis *B*
University of Notre Dame *B, M*

Iowa

Dordt College *B*
Iowa State University *B, M*
Iowa Wesleyan College *B*

Kansas

University of Kansas *B, M*

Kentucky

Gateway Community and Technical College *A*

Louisiana

Delgado Community College *A*

Maine

York County Community College *A*

Maryland

Cecil College *C, A*
Harford Community College *C, A*
Stevenson University *B*

Massachusetts

Bunker Hill Community College *A*
Endicott College *B*
Hampshire College *B*
Massachusetts College of Art and Design *B, M*
Montserrat College of Art *B*
Northern Essex Community College *A*
University of Massachusetts Dartmouth *B, M*

Michigan

Alma College *B*
Andrews University *B*
College for Creative Studies *B*
Ferris State University *B*
Finlandia University *B*
Kendall College of Art and Design of Ferris State University *B*
Lawrence Technological University *B*
Madonna University *B*
Michigan State University *B, M*
Spring Arbor University *B*

Minnesota

Art Institutes International Minnesota *A, B*
Brown College *A, B*
College of Visual Arts *B*
Minneapolis Community and Technical College *C, A*
University of Minnesota Twin Cities *B*
Winona State University *B*

Missouri

Drury University *B*
Missouri State University *B*
Washington University in St. Louis *B, M*
William Woods University *B*

Nevada

Art Institute of Las Vegas *B*
Truckee Meadows Community College *A*

New Hampshire

Rivier College *B*

New Jersey

Kean University *B*

New Mexico

New Mexico State University Alamogordo *A*
Northern New Mexico College *A*
Santa Fe Community College *C, A*

New York

Bryant & Stratton Business Institute Bryant & Stratton College: Rochester *A*
Cazenovia College *B*
City University of New York Baruch College *B*
Mildred Elley *C, A*
Parsons The New School for Design *A, B, M*
Pratt Institute *B, M*
Rochester Institute of Technology *B*

North Carolina
Duke University *B*
Mount Olive College *B*
North Carolina State University *B, M*
Peace College *B*

Ohio
Art Academy of Cincinnati *B*
Art Institute of Cincinnati *A*
Bowling Green State University *B*
Edison State Community College *C, A*
Northwest State Community
  College *A*
Ohio State University
  Columbus Campus *B, M*
University of Cincinnati *M*
University of Cincinnati
  Raymond Walters College *C, A*
University of Dayton *B*
Virginia Marti College of Art and
  Design *A*

Oklahoma
Northeastern State University *B*
Oklahoma Christian University *B*
Oral Roberts University *B*
University of Central Oklahoma *M*

Oregon
Art Institute of Portland *B*
Chemeketa Community College *A*
Linfield College *B*
Mt. Hood Community College *A*
Pacific Northwest College of Art *B*
Portland Community College *C, A*
Portland State University *B*

Pennsylvania
Antonelli Institute of Art and
  Photography *A*
Art Institute
  of Philadelphia *A, B*
  of Pittsburgh *A, B*
Carnegie Mellon University *D*
Drexel University *B*
Harrisburg Area Community
  College *A*
La Roche College *B*
Lehigh University *B*
Oakbridge Academy of Arts *A*
Penn State
  Abington *B*
  Altoona *B*
  Beaver *B*
  Berks *B*
  Brandywine *B*
  DuBois *B*
  Erie, The Behrend College *B*
  Fayette, The Eberly Campus *B*
  Greater Allegheny *B*
  Hazleton *B*
  Lehigh Valley *B*
  Mont Alto *B*
  New Kensington *B*
  Schuylkill *B*
  Shenango *B*
  University Park *B*
  Wilkes-Barre *B*
  Worthington Scranton *B*
  York *B*
Robert Morris University *B*

Puerto Rico
Escuela de Artes Plasticas de Puerto
  Rico *B*

South Carolina
Clemson University *M*
Horry-Georgetown Technical
  College *A*
University of South Carolina
  Upstate *B*
Winthrop University *M*

South Dakota
Dakota State University *C*

Tennessee
Freed-Hardeman University *B*
Lambuth University *B*
Memphis College of Art *B*
O'More College of Design *B*

Texas
Amarillo College *C, A*
Angelina College *C, A*
Blinn College *C*
Brookhaven College *C, A*
Cedar Valley College *C, A*
Lubbock Christian University *B*
San Jacinto College *C*
South Plains College *A*
Texas A&M University
  Commerce *B*
Texas State Technical College
  West Texas *A*
Texas State University: San Marcos *M*
University of North Texas *M*
University of Texas
  Austin *B, M*
Wade College *A*
Westwood College: Fort Worth *B*

Utah
Brigham Young University *B*
Salt Lake Community College *A*
Utah Valley University *C, A, B*
Weber State University *B*

Vermont
Bennington College *B*
Champlain College *B*
Lyndon State College *B*

Virginia
Bluefield College *B*
Liberty University *B*
Radford University *B*
Virginia Commonwealth University *M*

Washington
Cornish College of the Arts *B*
DigiPen Institute of Technology *B*
Lake Washington Technical College *B*
Northwest College of Art *B*
Shoreline Community College *C, A*
Western Washington University *B*
Yakima Valley Community College *A*

West Virginia
Bethany College *B*
Fairmont State University *A*
West Virginia University *B*

Wisconsin
University of Wisconsin
  Madison *B*
Viterbo University *B*
Western Technical College *A*

Wyoming
Northwest College *A*

Desktop publishing

Arizona
Chandler-Gilbert Community College
  Pecos *C*
Coconino County Community
  College *C*

Arkansas
South Arkansas Community College *A*

California
Academy of Art University *C, A, B*
Antelope Valley College *C*
California State University
  Chico *C*
City College of San Francisco *C*
East Los Angeles College *C, A*
Long Beach City College *C, A*
Ohlone College *A*
Platt College
  Ontario *A*
Silicon Valley College
  Western Career College:
    Emeryville *C, A, B*

Colorado
Westwood College of Technology
  Westwood College: Denver
    South *A, B*

Connecticut
Manchester Community College *C*

Illinois
Elgin Community College *C*
Harper College *C*
Highland Community College *C*
Kankakee Community College *C, A*
Moraine Valley Community College *C*
Morton College *C*
Sauk Valley Community College *A*
School of the Art Institute of
  Chicago *B, M*
South Suburban College of Cook
  County *C*
Spoon River College *C*
Triton College *C*

Iowa
Des Moines Area Community
  College *C, A*
Graceland University *B*
Iowa Central Community College *C, A*
Southeastern Community College
  North Campus *A*
Western Iowa Tech Community
  College *A*

Kansas
Kansas City Kansas Community
  College *C, A*

Kentucky
Murray State University *B*
Sullivan College of Technology and
  Design *A, B*

Maryland
Howard Community College *A*
Montgomery College *C, A*
University of Maryland
  University College *C*

Massachusetts
Bristol Community College *C*
Middlesex Community College *C, A*
Springfield Technical Community
  College *C*

Michigan
Baker College
  of Muskegon *A*
Ferris State University *A*
International Academy of Design and
  Technology: Detroit *B*
Wayne County Community College *C*

Minnesota
Dakota County Technical College *C*
Hennepin Technical College *C, A*
Minneapolis Community and
  Technical College *C, A*

North Hennepin Community
  College *C*
Ridgewater College *C, A*
Riverland Community College *C*

Nevada
College of Southern Nevada *C*

New Hampshire
Manchester Community College *C, A*

New Jersey
Bergen Community College *C*

New York
Rochester Institute of Technology *B*
Touro College *A*

Ohio
Central Ohio Technical College *A*
Cincinnati State Technical and
  Community College *C, A*
Columbus State Community
  College *C*
Owens Community College
  Toledo *C, A*
University of Cincinnati
  Raymond Walters College *C*
Wright State University *C*

Oklahoma
Oklahoma City Community College *A*

Oregon
Linn-Benton Community College *C*

Pennsylvania
La Salle University *B*

Rhode Island
New England Institute of
  Technology *A*

Tennessee
Volunteer State Community College *C*

Texas
Blinn College *C*
Eastfield College *C*
Houston Community College
  System *C*
Tarrant County College *C*
Texas State University: San Marcos *B*
Wharton County Junior College *C*

Utah
Salt Lake Community College *C*

Washington
Clark College *C*

Wisconsin
Western Technical College *A*

Development economics

Alabama
Alabama Agricultural and Mechanical
  University *M*

Arizona
Prescott College *B*

California
Hope International University *M*
University of California
  Los Angeles *B*

Colorado
University of Denver *M*

Connecticut
Mitchell College *B*
Yale University *M*

Georgia
Georgia Southern University *B*

Indiana
Taylor University *B*

Massachusetts
Brandeis University *M*
Northeastern University *B*

Michigan
Andrews University *B, M*
Calvin College *B*

Mississippi
University of Southern Mississippi *D*

New Hampshire
Southern New Hampshire
   University *M, D*

New York
Colgate University *B*

North Dakota
North Dakota State University *M*

Ohio
University of Akron *C*

Pennsylvania
Penn State
   Abington *B*
   Altoona *B*
   Beaver *B*
   Berks *B*
   Brandywine *B*
   DuBois *B*
   Erie, The Behrend College *B*
   Fayette, The Eberly Campus *B*
   Greater Allegheny *B*
   Hazleton *B*
   Lehigh Valley *B*
   Mont Alto *B*
   New Kensington *B*
   Schuylkill *B*
   Shenango *B*
   University Park *B*
   Wilkes-Barre *B*
   Worthington Scranton *B*
   York *B*

Rhode Island
Brown University *B*

Tennessee
Vanderbilt University *B, M, D*

Texas
University of St. Thomas *B*

Vermont
University of Vermont *B, M*

Virginia
Eastern Mennonite University *B*

Wisconsin
University of Wisconsin
   Madison *D*

Developmental biology/ embryology

Illinois
Northwestern University *M*

Iowa
University of Iowa *M, D*

Missouri
Washington University in St. Louis *D*

New York
University of Rochester *B*

Ohio
Case Western Reserve University *D*

Wisconsin
Marquette University *M, D*

Developmental/child psychology

Arizona
Prescott College *B*

California
California Institute of Integral
   Studies *D*
California State University
   East Bay *M*
   San Bernardino *M*
St. Mary's College of California *B*

Connecticut
Mitchell College *B*

District of Columbia
George Washington University *D*

Florida
Eckerd College *B*

Georgia
University of Georgia *D*

Illinois
Loyola University Chicago *M, D*
University of Chicago *D*

Iowa
University of Iowa *D*

Kansas
Pittsburg State University *B*
University of Kansas *B*

Maryland
University of Maryland
   Baltimore County *M, D*

Massachusetts
Bridgewater State College *M*
Clark University *M, D*
Eastern Nazarene College *B*
Emmanuel College *B*
Fitchburg State College *B*
Tufts University *M, D*
Wheelock College *M*

Michigan
Northern Michigan University *B, M*
University of Detroit Mercy *B*

Minnesota
Metropolitan State University *B*
University of Minnesota
   Twin Cities *M, D*

Missouri
University of Missouri
   Columbia *M, D*

Montana
University of Montana *M, D*

New Hampshire
Colby-Sawyer College *B*
Keene State College *B*

New Jersey
Rowan University *B*

New York
Cornell University *M, D*
University of Rochester *D*
Yeshiva University *D*

Ohio
Bowling Green State University *M, D*
Case Western Reserve University *D*
Union Institute & University *M*

Oklahoma
Northeastern State University *B*

Oregon
Warner Pacific College *B*

Pennsylvania
Duquesne University *M*
Temple University *D*
University of Pennsylvania *M*

Tennessee
Vanderbilt University *M, D*

Texas
University of Houston *M, D*
University of Texas
   Dallas *M*

Washington
Eastern Washington University *B, M*
Western Washington University *B*

Wisconsin
Marquette University *M*

Diagnostic medical sonography

Alabama
Lurleen B. Wallace Community
   College *A*
Wallace State Community College at
   Hanceville *A*

Arizona
GateWay Community College *A*

California
Charles Drew University of Medicine
   and Science *B*
Foothill College *A*
Lincoln University *A*
Orange Coast College *A*
Santa Barbara City College *A*
Western Career College: Citrus
   Heights *A*

Colorado
Pueblo Community College *A*
Red Rocks Community College *A*

Connecticut
Gateway Community College *A*

Delaware
Delaware Technical and Community
   College
   Owens *A*
   Stanton/Wilmington *A*

District of Columbia
George Washington University *B*

Florida
Barry University *B*
Broward College *A*
Florida National College *A*
Florida State College at Jacksonville *A*
Gulf Coast Community College *A*
Hillsborough Community College *A*
Nova Southeastern University *B*
Pensacola Junior College *A*
Polk State College *A*
Valencia Community College *A*

Georgia
Armstrong Atlantic State University *B*
Athens Technical College *A*
Darton College *A*
Gordon College *A*
Medical College of Georgia *B*

Hawaii
University of Hawaii
   Kapiolani Community College *A*

Illinois
Benedictine University *B*
Harper College *A*
John A. Logan College *A*
Triton College *A*
Wilbur Wright College *A*

Indiana
Indiana University
   Bloomington *B*

Iowa
Clinton Community College *A*
Mercy College of Health Sciences *A*
Muscatine Community College *A*
Scott Community College *A*

Kansas
Fort Hays State University *B*
Newman University *B*
Washburn University *B*

Kentucky
Owensboro Community and
   Technical College *A*
St. Catharine College *A*
West Kentucky Community and
   Technical College *A*

Maryland
Carroll Community College *A*
Community College of Baltimore
   County *A*
Montgomery College *A*

Massachusetts
Bunker Hill Community College *A*
Middlesex Community College *A*
Springfield Technical Community
   College *A*

Michigan
Baker College
   of Owosso *A*
   of Port Huron *A*
Bay de Noc Community College *A*
Delta College *A*
Ferris State University *A*
Jackson Community College *A*

Lake Michigan College *A*
Lansing Community College *A*
Oakland Community College *A*

Minnesota

Argosy University: Twin Cities *A*
Lake Superior College *A*
St. Catherine University *A*
St. Cloud Technical College *A*

Missouri

University of Missouri
  Columbia *B, M*

Nebraska

BryanLGH College of Health
  Sciences *A*
Nebraska Methodist College of
  Nursing and Allied Health *A, B*
University of Nebraska
  Medical Center *B*

New Jersey

Bergen Community College *A*
Burlington County College *A*
Gloucester County College *A*
Union County College *A*
University of Medicine and Dentistry
  of New Jersey
  School of Health Related
    Professions *B*

New Mexico

Central New Mexico Community
  College *A*

New York

Rochester Institute of Technology *B*
State University of New York
  Upstate Medical University *B*

North Carolina

Caldwell Community College and
  Technical Institute *A*
Cape Fear Community College *A*
Forsyth Technical Community
  College *A*
Pitt Community College *A*
South Piedmont Community
  College *A*
Southwestern Community College *A*

Ohio

Central Ohio Technical College *A*
Cincinnati State Technical and
  Community College *A*
Kettering College of Medical Arts *A, B*
Owens Community College
  Toledo *A*
University of Rio Grande *A*

Oklahoma

Bacone College *A*
Oklahoma State University
  Oklahoma City *A*
University of Oklahoma *B*

Oregon

Oregon Institute of Technology *B*

Pennsylvania

Community College of Allegheny
  County *A*
Harrisburg Area Community
  College *A*
Keystone College *A*
Lackawanna College *A*
Northampton Community College *A*
South Hills School of Business &
  Technology *A*
Thomas Jefferson University: College
  of Health Professions *B*

Puerto Rico

EDIC College *A*
Universidad del Este *A, B*

Rhode Island

Community College of Rhode
  Island *A*

South Carolina

Greenville Technical College *A*

South Dakota

Southeast Technical Institute *A*

Tennessee

Baptist College of Health Sciences *B*

Texas

Austin Community College *A*
Del Mar College *A*
El Centro College *A*
Lamar Institute of Technology *A*
Lone Star College System *A*
Temple College *A*
Tyler Junior College *A*
University of Texas
  Brownsville - Texas Southmost
    College *A*
Weatherford College *A*

Utah

Weber State University *B*

Washington

Bellevue College *A*
Centralia College *A*
Seattle University *B*
Wenatchee Valley College *A*

West Virginia

Mountain State University *A, B*

Wisconsin

Blackhawk Technical College *A*
Chippewa Valley Technical College *A*
Mount Mary College *B*

Wyoming

Laramie County Community
  College *A*

Diesel mechanics

Alabama

Bevill State Community College *C*
Bishop State Community College *C*
Gadsden State Community College *C*
Lawson State Community College *C*
Lurleen B. Wallace Community
  College *C*
Shelton State Community College *C*
Wallace State Community College at
  Hanceville *C, A*

Alaska

University of Alaska
  Fairbanks *C*
  Southeast *C, A*

Arizona

Arizona Automotive Institute *C, A*
Central Arizona College *C, A*
Eastern Arizona College *C*
Universal Technical Institute *C, A*

Arkansas

Arkansas State University
  Beebe *C*
Arkansas State University: Newport *C*
Mid-South Community College *C*

Pulaski Technical College *C*
University of Arkansas
  Community College at Hope *C*

California

Allan Hancock College *C, A*
Cerritos College *C*
Citrus College *C, A*
Golden West College *A*
Hartnell College *C, A*
Long Beach City College *C, A*
Los Angeles Trade and Technical
  College *C, A*
Merced College *C, A*
Palomar College *C, A*
San Bernardino Valley College *C, A*
San Diego Miramar College *C, A*
Santa Ana College *C, A*
Santa Rosa Junior College *C*
Shasta College *C, A*
Yuba Community College District *C*

Colorado

Colorado Northwestern Community
  College *C*
Northeastern Junior College *C, A*
Pueblo Community College *C*
Trinidad State Junior College *C, A*

Florida

Florida State College at Jacksonville *C*

Georgia

Albany Technical College *C*
DeKalb Technical College *C*
Gwinnett Technical College *C*
North Georgia Technical College *C*

Hawaii

University of Hawaii
  Hawaii Community College *C, A*
  Honolulu Community College *C, A*

Idaho

Eastern Idaho Technical College *C, A*
Idaho State University *C, A*
Lewis-Clark State College *C, A, B*
North Idaho College *C, A*

Illinois

Black Hawk College *C, A*
Black Hawk College: East Campus *C*
Illinois Eastern Community Colleges
  Wabash Valley College *A*
Kishwaukee College *C, A*
Parkland College *A*
Rend Lake College *C, A*
Southeastern Illinois College *C, A*

Indiana

Oakland City University *A*
Vincennes University *A*

Iowa

Des Moines Area Community
  College *C, A*
Hawkeye Community College *A*
Indian Hills Community College *A*
Iowa Central Community College *A*
Kirkwood Community College *C, A*
Northeast Iowa Community
  College *C*
Northwest Iowa Community
  College *A*
Scott Community College *A*
Vatterott College *A*
Western Iowa Tech Community
  College *C*

Kansas

Highland Community College *C, A*

North Central Kansas Technical
  College *C, A*
Pittsburg State University *B*

Kentucky

Big Sandy Community and Technical
  College *C*
Bluegrass Community and Technical
  College *C*
Elizabethtown Community and
  Technical College *C, A*
Maysville Community and Technical
  College *C*
Owensboro Community and
  Technical College *C*
Somerset Community College *C, A*
West Kentucky Community and
  Technical College *C*

Maine

Northern Maine Community
  College *C, A*
Washington County Community
  College *C*

Maryland

Community College of Baltimore
  County *A*

Massachusetts

Massasoit Community College *C, A*

Michigan

Baker College
  of Owosso *C, A*

Minnesota

Alexandria Technical College *C, A*
Central Lakes College *C*
Hennepin Technical College *C, A*
Hibbing Community College *C*
Minnesota State Community and
  Technical College *C, A*
Minnesota West Community and
  Technical College *C, A*
Riverland Community College *C*

Mississippi

Copiah-Lincoln Community College *A*
Northeast Mississippi Community
  College *C*
Southwest Mississippi Community
  College *A*

Missouri

Crowder College *C, A*
Ozarks Technical Community
  College *C, A*

Montana

Helena College of Technology of the
  University of Montana *A*
Montana State University
  Billings *C, A*
University of Montana *A*

Nebraska

Central Community College *C, A*
Mid-Plains Community College
  Area *C, A*
Northeast Community College *A*
Southeast Community College *A*

Nevada

Great Basin College *C, A*
Truckee Meadows Community
  College *A*

New Hampshire

White Mountains Community
  College *C, A*

New Jersey

Raritan Valley Community College *A*

New Mexico

Central New Mexico Community
    College *C*
Mesalands Community College *C, A*
San Juan College *C, A*

New York

State University of New York
    College of Agriculture and
        Technology at Cobleskill *A*
    College of Agriculture and
        Technology at Morrisville *A*
    College of Technology at Alfred *A*

North Carolina

Beaufort County Community
    College *C, A*
Cape Fear Community College *C*
Central Piedmont Community
    College *C, A*
Forsyth Technical Community
    College *C*
Johnston Community College *C, A*
Wilkes Community College *C, A*
Wilson Community College *C*

North Dakota

Lake Region State College *C, A*
North Dakota State College of
    Science *C, A*
Williston State College *A*

Ohio

University of Northwestern Ohio *C, A*
Washington State Community
    College *A*

Oklahoma

Oklahoma State University
    Institute of Technology:
        Okmulgee *A*
Western Oklahoma State College *A*

Oregon

Lane Community College *C, A*
Linn-Benton Community College *C, A*
Portland Community College *C, A*
Rogue Community College *C, A*

Pennsylvania

Johnson College *A*
Pennsylvania College of
    Technology *C, A*

South Carolina

Greenville Technical College *C*

South Dakota

Lake Area Technical Institute *A*
Southeast Technical Institute *A*
Western Dakota Technical Institute *C*

Texas

Angelina College *C*
Cedar Valley College *C*
Central Texas College *C, A*
College of the Mainland *C, A*
Del Mar College *C, A*
Houston Community College
    System *C*
Kilgore College *C, A*
Lamar Institute of Technology *C, A*
North Central Texas College *A*
Odessa College *C, A*
St. Philip's College *C, A*
San Jacinto College *C*
South Plains College *C, A*
South Texas College *C, A*

Texarkana College *C*
Texas State Technical College
    Waco *A*
    West Texas *C, A*
University of Texas
    Brownsville - Texas Southmost
        College *C*

Utah

College of Eastern Utah *A*
Salt Lake Community College *C, A*
Utah Valley University *C, A*
Weber State University *A*

Vermont

Vermont Technical College *A*

Virginia

Advanced Technology Institute *C, A*
J. Sargeant Reynolds Community
    College *C*
Southside Virginia Community
    College *C*
Southwest Virginia Community
    College *C*

Washington

Bates Technical College *C, A*
Bellingham Technical College *C, A*
Centralia College *A*
Clark College *C, A*
Grays Harbor College *C, A*
Lake Washington Technical
    College *C, A*
Lower Columbia College *A*
Peninsula College *C, A*
Skagit Valley College *C, A*
South Seattle Community
    College *C, A*
Spokane Community College *A*

Wisconsin

Blackhawk Technical College *C*
Chippewa Valley Technical College *A*
Mid-State Technical College *C*
Milwaukee Area Technical College *C*
Northeast Wisconsin Technical
    College *C*
Western Technical College *A*

Wyoming

Casper College *C, A*
Laramie County Community
    College *C, A*
Sheridan College *C, A*
Western Wyoming Community
    College *C, A*
WyoTech: Laramie *C, A*

Dietetic technician

Arizona

Central Arizona College *A*
Chandler-Gilbert Community College
    Pecos *A*

California

College of the Desert *A*
Long Beach City College *A*
Orange Coast College *A*

Illinois

Harper College *A*

Indiana

Purdue University *B*

Maine

Southern Maine Community
    College *A*

Massachusetts

North Shore Community College *A*

Michigan

Wayne County Community College *A*

New York

Suffolk County Community College *A*

North Carolina

Gaston College *A*

Ohio

Cincinnati State Technical and
    Community College *A*
Youngstown State University *A*

Pennsylvania

Westmoreland County Community
    College *A*

Wisconsin

Milwaukee Area Technical College *A*

Dietetics

Alabama

University of Alabama *B*

Arkansas

Harding University *B*
Ouachita Baptist University *B*

California

California Polytechnic State
    University: San Luis Obispo *B*
California State Polytechnic
    University: Pomona *B*
California State University
    Chico *B, M*
Loma Linda University *B*
Point Loma Nazarene University *B*
San Francisco State University *B*
San Jose State University *B, M*

Colorado

Colorado State University *M*
University of Northern Colorado *B*

Connecticut

Lincoln College of New England:
    Briarwood *A*
University of Connecticut *B*
University of New Haven *B, M*

Florida

Florida State University *B*
Palm Beach Community College *A*

Georgia

Georgia State University *B, M*
Life University *B*
University of Georgia *B*

Idaho

Idaho State University *B*

Illinois

Bradley University *B*
Dominican University *B*
Loyola University Chicago *M*
University of Illinois
    Chicago *B, M, D*
    Urbana-Champaign *B*

Indiana

Ball State University *B, M*
Indiana University-Purdue University
    Indianapolis *M*
Purdue University *B*

Vincennes University *A*

Iowa

Iowa State University *B*

Kansas

Kansas State University *B*

Louisiana

Louisiana State University and
    Agricultural and Mechanical
    College *B*
Nicholls State University *B*
University of Louisiana at Lafayette *B*

Maryland

University of Maryland
    College Park *B*

Massachusetts

Laboure College *A*

Michigan

Andrews University *B*
Central Michigan University *B*
Delta College *A*
Eastern Michigan University *B, M*
Michigan State University *B*
Wayne State University *B*
Western Michigan University *B*

Minnesota

College of St. Benedict *B*
Normandale Community College *A*
St. Catherine University *B*
St. John's University *B*

Mississippi

University of Mississippi *B*
University of Southern Mississippi *B*

Missouri

College of the Ozarks *B*
Fontbonne University *B*
Missouri State University *B*
Northwest Missouri State
    University *B*
University of Missouri
    Columbia *B*

Nebraska

Northeast Community College *A*

New Hampshire

Keene State College *B*

New Jersey

College of St. Elizabeth *B*

North Carolina

East Carolina University *B*
Meredith College *B*
Western Carolina University *B*

North Dakota

North Dakota State University *B*
University of North Dakota *B*

Ohio

Bowling Green State University *B*
Case Western Reserve
    University *B, M, D*
Ohio State University
    Columbus Campus *B*
Ohio University *B*
Owens Community College
    Toledo *A*
University of Akron *B*
University of Cincinnati
    Raymond Walters College *A*
University of Dayton *B*

Youngstown State University *B*

Oklahoma
University of Oklahoma *M*

Oregon
Oregon Health & Science
University *M*

Pennsylvania
Gannon University *B*
Harrisburg Area Community
College *A*
Immaculata University *B*
Marywood University *B*
Seton Hill University *B*
University of Pittsburgh *B*
West Chester University of
Pennsylvania *B*

Rhode Island
University of Rhode Island *B*

Tennessee
Lipscomb University *B*
Southern Adventist University *A*

Texas
Abilene Christian University *B*
El Paso Community College *A*
Sam Houston State University *M*
Texas Christian University *B*
Texas Southern University *B*
Texas Tech University *B*
Texas Woman's University *B*
University of Texas
Pan American *B*
Southwestern Medical Center at
Dallas *B*

Utah
Brigham Young University *B*

Vermont
University of Vermont *B, M*

Washington
Shoreline Community College *A*

West Virginia
Marshall University *B, M*

Wisconsin
Mount Mary College *B, M*
University of Wisconsin
Stout *B*
Viterbo University *B*

Dietician assistant

Arizona
Arizona Western College *C*

Arkansas
University of Arkansas Community
College at Morrilton *C*

Colorado
Front Range Community College *C, A*

Florida
Hillsborough Community College *A*

Illinois
Harper College *C*

Iowa
Des Moines Area Community
College *C*

Kansas
Barton County Community
College *C, A*
Coffeyville Community College *C*
Colby Community College *C*

Michigan
Bay de Noc Community College *C*

Missouri
Missouri College *C, A*

New York
Broome Community College *C*
Erie Community College
North Campus *A*

Oregon
Central Oregon Community
College *C*

Pennsylvania
Harrisburg Area Community
College *C*
Penn State
University Park *A*

Tennessee
Southwest Tennessee Community
College *A*

Texas
San Jacinto College *C, A*
Tarrant County College *C, A*

Digital art

California
College of the Siskiyous *C, A*
Diablo Valley College *C, A*
Dominican University of California *B*
Fashion Institute of Design and
Merchandising
Los Angeles *A*
San Francisco *A*
Grossmont College *A*
Mt. Sierra College *B*

Colorado
Colorado Mountain College *C*

Connecticut
Quinnipiac University *B*

District of Columbia
Corcoran College of Art and Design *C*

Florida
International Academy of Design and
Technology: Tampa *A, B*
Stetson University *B*

Illinois
School of the Art Institute of
Chicago *B, M*

Michigan
Kendall College of Art and Design of
Ferris State University *B*
Northern Michigan University *A, B*

Minnesota
University of Minnesota
Duluth *B*

New York
City University of New York
Hostos Community College *A*
Genesee Community College *A*

Long Island University
C. W. Post Campus *B*
Mohawk Valley Community College *A*
Nassau Community College *A*
Pace University *C*
Pratt Institute *A, B, M*
State University of New York
College at Oneonta *B*
College of Technology at
Alfred *A, B*

North Carolina
Elon University *B*

Ohio
Art Academy of Cincinnati *B*
Cleveland Institute of Art *B, M*

Oregon
University of Oregon *B, M*

Pennsylvania
Pennsylvania College of Art and
Design *C*

Rhode Island
Providence College *B*

Tennessee
Memphis College of Art *B*

Vermont
Lyndon State College *B*

Washington
Art Institute of Seattle *C, A*

Digital media

Arizona
Arizona State University *D*
Northern Arizona University *B*
Pima Community College *A*

Arkansas
Arkansas State University *B*
Harding University *B*
John Brown University *B*
South Arkansas Community College *A*

California
Academy of Art University *M*
Art Institute
of California: Orange County *A, B*
California Baptist University *B*
California State University
Dominguez Hills *B*
City College of San Francisco *C*
College of the Canyons *C, A*
College of the Siskiyous *C, A*
Diablo Valley College *C, A*
Grossmont College *C, A*
Hartnell College *C, A*
Holy Names University *B*
Long Beach City College *C*
Marymount College *B*
National University *B, M*
Ohlone College *C, A*
Oxnard College *C, A*
Pacific Union College *B*
Santa Barbara City College *C, A*
Sierra College *C, A*
University of California
San Diego *B*
University of Southern California *M*
Vanguard University of Southern
California *B*
Westwood College of Technology
Westwood College: Inland
Empire *A, B*

Colorado
Colorado Technical University *C*
Jones International University *A, B*
University of Denver *B, M*

Connecticut
Manchester Community College *A*
Mitchell College *B*
Quinnipiac University *B*

Delaware
Delaware Technical and Community
College
Terry *A*

Florida
Florida Atlantic University *B*
Lynn University *B*
State College of Florida,
Manatee-Sarasota *A*
University of Miami *B*
University of Tampa *B*
Valencia Community College *C, A*

Georgia
Art Institute
of Atlanta *C, A, B*
Georgia Institute of
Technology *B, M, D*
Georgia Southern University *B*
Savannah College of Art and
Design *B, M*

Idaho
University of Idaho *B*

Illinois
Harper College *C*
Lewis University *B*
Northwestern University *M, D*
School of the Art Institute of
Chicago *B, M*
Triton College *A*

Indiana
Huntington University *B*
Indiana University
Bloomington *B, M*
Valparaiso University *M*

Iowa
Briar Cliff University *B*
Dordt College *B*
Mount Mercy College *B*
Northwestern College *B*
Southeastern Community College
North Campus *A*
University of Northern Iowa *B*

Kansas
Southwestern College *B*

Louisiana
Centenary College of Louisiana *B*

Maine
New England School of
Communications *B*
Saint Joseph's College of Maine *B*
Southern Maine Community
College *A*

Maryland
Frederick Community College *C*
Howard Community College *C*

Massachusetts
Fitchburg State College *B*
Lasell College *B*
Massachusetts Institute of
Technology *M, D*

New England Institute of Art *B*

Michigan
Calvin College *B*
College for Creative Studies *B*
Cornerstone Universtory *B*
Northern Michigan University *B*
Oakland Community College *C*
Saginaw Valley State University *M*

Minnesota
Art Institutes International
    Minnesota *A, B*
Century Community and Technical
    College *C, A*
Dakota County Technical College *A*
Hennepin Technical College *C, A*
Minneapolis Community and
    Technical College *C, A*
Ridgewater College *C*
Rochester Community and Technical
    College *C, A*

Missouri
Lindenwood University *B*
Ozarks Technical Community
    College *A*
Webster University *B*

Nebraska
Central Community College *C, A*

New Hampshire
Chester College of New England *B*
Southern New Hampshire
    University *B*
University of New Hampshire *B*

New Jersey
Felician College *B*
Raritan Valley Community
    College *C, A*
Sussex County Community College *C*

New York
Canisius College *B*
Clarkson University *B*
Dominican College of Blauvelt *M*
Hilbert College *B*
Houghton College *B*
Monroe Community College *C*
Niagara County Community
    College *C, A*
Pace University *C*
Rensselaer Polytechnic Institute *B*
Rochester Institute of
    Technology *B, M*
Sage College of Albany *B*
St. Francis College *B*
State University of New York
    College of Technology at
      Alfred *A, B*

North Carolina
High Point University *B*

Ohio
Denison University *B*
Franklin University *B*
Kent State University *B*
Miami University
    Oxford Campus *B*
Muskingum University *B*
North Central State College *A*
Notre Dame College *B*
Ohio University *B*
Ohio University
    Zanesville Campus *A*
Tiffin University *B*
University of Cincinnati
    Raymond Walters College *C, A*
University of Dayton *B*

Pennsylvania
Bucks County Community College *A*
Butler County Community College *A*
Community College of Beaver
    County *A*
Juniata College *B*
Kutztown University of
    Pennsylvania *B, M*
La Salle University *B*
Lebanon Valley College *B*
Lycoming College *B*
Marywood University *B*
Montgomery County Community
    College *A*
Philadelphia University *B, M*
Slippery Rock University of
    Pennsylvania *B*
University of the Arts *B*
Valley Forge Christian College *B*
Waynesburg University *B*
Wilkes University *B*

Puerto Rico
Inter American University of Puerto
    Rico
    Bayamon Campus *B*
Universidad Metropolitana *B*
University of Puerto Rico
    Rio Piedras *B*

South Dakota
Mount Marty College *B*

Tennessee
King College *B*
Lee University *B*
Union University *B*
Visible School - Music and Worship
    Arts College *B*

Texas
Abilene Christian University *B*
Baylor University *B*
North Lake College *C*
Northwest Vista College *C*
St. Edward's University *B*
Texas A&M University *B*
Texas A&M University
    Commerce *B*
University of Texas
    Arlington *B*
    Dallas *B, M*
    El Paso *B*

Utah
Salt Lake Community College *C, A*

Vermont
Castleton State College *B*
Champlain College *B*

Virginia
Eastern Mennonite University *B*
George Mason University *M*

Washington
Olympic College *A*
Washington State University *B*

Wisconsin
Concordia University Wisconsin *B*

Wyoming
Laramie County Community
    College *A*

Directing/theatrical production

California
California Institute of the Arts *M*

College of the Siskiyous *C, A*
Monterey Peninsula College *C, A*
University of Southern California *M*

Florida
Florida State University *M*

Illinois
Bradley University *B*
Columbia College Chicago *C, B*
DePaul University *M*
Roosevelt University *M*
University of Illinois
    Urbana-Champaign *B*

Indiana
Saint Joseph's College *B*

Iowa
Coe College *B*
Drake University *B*
University of Iowa *M*

Maine
University of Southern Maine *B*

Massachusetts
Boston University *B, M*
Emerson College *B*

Michigan
Wayne County Community College *A*

Missouri
Lindenwood University *B*
Webster University *B*

New Hampshire
Keene State College *B*

New York
Bard College *B*
Hofstra University *B*
Pace University *M*
State University of New York
    Binghamton *B*

North Carolina
East Carolina University *B*

Ohio
Ohio University *M*

Oklahoma
University of Oklahoma *M*

Pennsylvania
Carnegie Mellon University *M*
Lycoming College *B*
Temple University *M*
University of the Arts *B*

Texas
Baylor University *M*
Lubbock Christian University *B*
Texas Christian University *B*

Vermont
Bennington College *B, M*

Virginia
Emory & Henry College *B*
Regent University *M*

Washington
Cornish College of the Arts *B*

Divinity/ministry (B.Div., M.Div.)

Alabama
Beeson Divinity School at Samford
    University *P*
Southern Christian University:
    Professional *P*

California
American Baptist Seminary of the
    West *P*
Azusa Pacific University: School of
    Theology *P*
Church Divinity School of the
    Pacific *P*
Claremont School of Theology *P*
Dominican School of Philosophy and
    Theology *P*
Franciscan School of Theology *P*
Fuller Theological Seminary *P*
Golden Gate Baptist Theological
    Seminary *P*
International School of Theology *P*
Jesuit School of Theology at Berkeley:
    Professional *P*
Mennonite Brethren Biblical
    Seminary *P*
Pacific Lutheran Theological
    Seminary *P*
Pacific School of Religion *P*
St. John's Seminary *P*
St. Patrick's Seminary *P*
San Francisco Theological Seminary *P*
Starr King School for the Ministry *P*
Talbot School of Theology of Biola
    University *P*
Westminster Theological Seminary in
    California *P*

Colorado
Denver Conservative Baptist
    Seminary *P*
Iliff School of Theology *P*

Connecticut
Holy Apostles College and
    Seminary *P*
Yale University: Divinity School *P*

District of Columbia
Catholic University of America: School
    of Theology *P*
Dominican House of Studies *P*
Howard University: Divinity School *P*
Washington Theological Union *P*
Wesley Theological Seminary *P*

Florida
St. Vincent De Paul Regional
    Seminary *P*

Georgia
Candler School of Theology *P*
Columbia Theological Seminary *P*
Interdenominational Theological
    Center *P*

Illinois
Catholic Theological Union *P*
Chicago Theological Seminary *P*
Garrett-Evangelical Theological
    Seminary *P*
Lincoln Christian Seminary *P*
Lutheran School of Theology at
    Chicago *P*
McCormick Theological Seminary *P*
Meadville-Lombard Theological
    School *P*
North Park Theological Seminary *P*
Northern Baptist Theological
    Seminary *P*

Seabury-Western Theological
Seminary P
Trinity Evangelical Divinity School P
University of Chicago: Divinity
School P
University of St. Mary of the
Lake–Mundelein Seminary P

Indiana

Anderson University: School of
Theology P
Associated Mennonite Biblical
Seminary P
Bethany Theological Seminary P
Bethel College P
Christian Theological Seminary P
Concordia Theological Seminary P
Earlham School of Religion P
St. Meinrad School of Theology P
University of Notre Dame: School of
Theology P

Iowa

Faith Baptist Bible College and
Theological Seminary:
Theological Professions P
University of Dubuque: School of
Theology P
Wartburg Theological Seminary P

Kansas

Central Baptist Theological
Seminary P

Kentucky

Asbury Theological Seminary P
Lexington Theological Seminary P
Louisville Presbyterian Theological
Seminary P
Southern Baptist Theological
Seminary P

Louisiana

New Orleans Baptist Theological
Seminary P
Notre Dame Seminary School of
Theology P

Maine

Bangor Theological Seminary P

Maryland

Mount St. Mary's College: Seminary P

Massachusetts

Andover Newton Theological
School P
Boston University: School of
Theology P
Episcopal Divinity School P
Gordon-Conwell Theological
Seminary P
Harvard University: Divinity School P
Holy Cross Greek Orthodox School of
Theology P
Pope John XXIII National Seminary P
St. John's Seminary P
Weston Jesuit School of Theology P

Michigan

Andrews University Seminary P
Calvin Theological Seminary P
Grand Rapids Baptist Seminary P
Sacred Heart Major Seminary P
Western Theological Seminary P

Minnesota

Bethel Theological Seminary P
St. John's University: School of
Theology P
University of St. Thomas: School of
Divinity P

Mississippi

Reformed Theological Seminary P
Wesley Biblical Seminary P

Missouri

Assemblies of God Theological
Seminary P
Concordia Seminary P
Eden Theological Seminary P
Kenrick-Glennon Seminary P
Midwestern Baptist Theological
Seminary P
Nazarene Theological Seminary P
St. Paul School of Theology P

New Jersey

Drew University: School of
Theology P
Immaculate Conception Seminary of
Seton Hall University P
New Brunswick Theological
Seminary P
Princeton Theological Seminary P

New York

Alliance Theological Seminary P
Christ The King Seminary P
Colgate Rochester Divinity
School-Bexley Crozer Theological
Seminary P
General Theological Seminary P
New York Theological Seminary P
St. Bernard's Institute P
St. John's University: Graduate School
of Arts and Sciences P
St. Joseph's Seminary and College P
St. Vladimir's Orthodox Theological
Seminary P
Seminary of the Immaculate
Conception P
Union Theological Seminary:
Theological Professions P

North Carolina

Duke University: Divinity School P
Hood Theological Seminary P
Southeastern Baptist Theological
Seminary: Theological
Professions P

Ohio

Ashland Theological Seminary P
Athenaeum of Ohio P
Methodist Theological School in
Ohio P
Pontifical College Josephinum:
Professional P
St. Mary Seminary P
Trinity Lutheran Seminary P
United Theological Seminary P
Winebrenner Seminary P

Oklahoma

Phillips Theological Seminary P

Oregon

Western Conservative Baptist
Seminary P

Pennsylvania

Academy of the New Church P
Biblical Theological Seminary P
Lancaster Theological Seminary P
Lutheran Theological Seminary at
Gettysburg P
Lutheran Theological Seminary at
Philadelphia P
Moravian Theological Seminary P
Palmer Theological Seminary P
Pittsburgh Theological Seminary P
Reformed Presbyterian Theological
Seminary P

St. Charles Borromeo
Seminary-Overbrook P
St. Vincent Seminary P
Trinity Episcopal School for
Ministry P
Westminster Theological Seminary P

Puerto Rico

Evangelical Seminary of Puerto
Rico P

South Carolina

Columbia Biblical Seminary and
Graduate School of Missions P
Erskine Theological Seminary P
Lutheran Theological Southern
Seminary P

South Dakota

North American Baptist Seminary P

Tennessee

Church of God Theological
Seminary P
Emmanuel School of Religion P
Harding University Graduate School of
Religion P
Memphis Theological Seminary P
Mid-America Baptist Theological
Seminary P
Temple Baptist Seminary: Theological
Professions P
University of the South: School of
Theology P
Vanderbilt University: The Divinity
School P

Texas

Abilene Christian University: College
of Biblical Studies P
Austin Presbyterian Theological
Seminary P
Baptist Missionary Association
Theological Seminary:
Theological Professions P
Episcopal Theological Seminary of the
Southwest P
Houston Graduate School of
Theology P
Oblate School of Theology P
Southern Methodist University:
Perkins School of Theology P
Southwestern Baptist Theological
Seminary: Theological
Professions P
Texas Christian University: Brite
Divinity School P
University of St. Thomas: School of
Theology P

Virginia

Eastern Mennonite Seminary P
Liberty Baptist Theological
Seminary P
Regent University: School of
Divinity P
Union Theological Seminary in
Virginia P
Virginia Theological Seminary P
Virginia Union University: The Samuel
DeWitt Proctor School of
Theology P

Washington

Gonzaga University: Department of
Religious Studies P
Seattle University: School of Theology
and Ministry P

Wisconsin

Sacred Heart School of Theology P
St. Francis Seminary P

Drafting and design technology

Alabama

Bevill State Community College A
Bishop State Community College A
Calhoun Community College C, A
Central Alabama Community
College A
Gadsden State Community College C
George C. Wallace State Community
College
George C. Wallace Community
College at Dothan C, A
Selma A
Jefferson Davis Community
College C, A
Lawson State Community
College C, A
Lurleen B. Wallace Community
College A
Northwest-Shoals Community
College C, A
Remington College
Mobile C
Shelton State Community
College C, A
Southern Union State Community
College C, A
Wallace State Community College at
Hanceville C, A

Alaska

University of Alaska
Anchorage C, A
Fairbanks C

Arizona

Anthem College A
Central Arizona College C
Eastern Arizona College C, A
Mesa Community College C
Northland Pioneer College C
Pima Community College C

Arkansas

Arkansas State University
Beebe C, A
North Arkansas College C
Northwest Arkansas Community
College C, A
Phillips Community College of the
University of Arkansas C, A
Pulaski Technical College C, A
Southeast Arkansas College C, A
University of Arkansas
Cossatot Community College of the
C
University of Arkansas Community
College at Morrilton C, A

California

American River College A
Antelope Valley College C, A
Bakersfield College A
Barstow Community College C
Butte College C, A
Cabrillo College A
Cerritos College A
Cerro Coso Community College C, A
Chabot College C, A
Chaffey College C, A
Citrus College C, A
City College of San Francisco C
College of San Mateo C, A
College of the Desert C, A
College of the Redwoods C, A
College of the Sequoias C, A
Contra Costa College C, A
Cosumnes River College C, A
Cuyamaca College A
De Anza College C, A
Diablo Valley College C

East Los Angeles College *C*
El Camino College *C, A*
El Camino College: Compton
 Center *C, A*
Evergreen Valley College *A*
Fresno City College *C, A*
Fullerton College *C, A*
Glendale Community College *C, A*
Golden West College *C, A*
Hartnell College *A*
Irvine Valley College *C, A*
Long Beach City College *C, A*
Los Angeles City College *A*
Los Angeles Harbor College *C, A*
Los Angeles Pierce College *C, A*
Los Angeles Southwest College *C, A*
Los Angeles Trade and Technical
 College *C, A*
Los Angeles Valley College *C*
Merced College *C, A*
MiraCosta College *C, A*
Mission College *C, A*
Modesto Junior College *A*
Monterey Peninsula College *C, A*
Mount San Antonio College *C, A*
Napa Valley College *C, A*
Orange Coast College *C, A*
Palomar College *C, A*
Pasadena City College *C, A*
Porterville College *C, A*
Rio Hondo College *A*
Riverside Community College *C, A*
Sacramento City College *C, A*
Saddleback College *C, A*
San Diego City College *C, A*
San Joaquin Delta College *A*
San Jose City College *A*
Santa Ana College *C, A*
Santa Barbara City College *C, A*
Santa Monica College *C, A*
Santiago Canyon College *A*
Solano Community College *C, A*
Southwestern College *C, A*
Ventura College *C, A*
West Valley College *C, A*
Westwood College of Technology
 Westwood College: Inland
  Empire *A*

Colorado

Aims Community College *C*
Community College of Aurora *A*
Community College of Denver *C, A*
Otero Junior College *C*
Pikes Peak Community College *C, A*
Red Rocks Community College *C, A*
Trinidad State Junior College *A*
Westwood College: Denver North *A*

Connecticut

Gateway Community College *C*
Three Rivers Community College *C, A*

Delaware

Delaware State University *B*
Delaware Technical and Community
 College
 Owens *A*
 Stanton/Wilmington *A*
 Terry *A*

Florida

Brevard Community College *A*
Daytona State College *C, A*
Florida State College at Jacksonville *A*
Gulf Coast Community College *A*
Hillsborough Community College *C*
Key College *A*
North Florida Community College *C*
Northwest Florida State College *C*
Palm Beach Community College *A*
St. Petersburg College *C, A*
Seminole Community College *C*

South Florida Community
 College *C, A*
Southwest Florida College *A*
State College of Florida,
 Manatee-Sarasota *A*
Tallahassee Community College *C, A*
Valencia Community College *C, A*

Georgia

Albany Technical College *C, A*
Altamaha Technical College *A*
Athens Technical College *C*
Augusta Technical College *C*
Bainbridge College *C, A*
Central Georgia Technical
 College *C, A*
Chattahoochee Technical College *C*
Dalton State College *C, A*
DeKalb Technical College *C*
Georgia Highlands College *A*
Griffin Technical College *C*
Gwinnett Technical College *A*
Macon State College *A*
Middle Georgia College *A*
North Georgia Technical College *C*
Savannah Technical College *C*
Southwest Georgia Technical
 College *C*
Valdosta Technical College *C, A*
West Georgia Technical College *C*

Hawaii

University of Hawaii
 Hawaii Community College *A*
 Honolulu Community College *A*
 Maui Community College *A*

Idaho

Brigham Young University-Idaho *A*
Lewis-Clark State College *A, B*
North Idaho College *C, A*

Illinois

Carl Sandburg College *C, A*
City Colleges of Chicago
 Harold Washington College *C*
College of DuPage *C, A*
Heartland Community College *C*
Illinois Central College *C*
Illinois Eastern Community Colleges
 Lincoln Trail College *A*
Illinois Valley Community College *A*
John A. Logan College *C, A*
Joliet Junior College *C, A*
Kankakee Community College *C, A*
Kishwaukee College *A*
Lake Land College *C*
Lewis and Clark Community
 College *A*
Oakton Community College *A*
Prairie State College *C*
Rend Lake College *C*
Richland Community College *A*
Robert Morris University:
 Chicago *C, A*
Sauk Valley Community College *C*
Shawnee Community College *C, A*
South Suburban College of Cook
 County *C, A*
Southwestern Illinois College *C, A*
Spoon River College *C*
Triton College *C, A*

Indiana

Indiana University-Purdue University
 Indianapolis *A*
Ivy Tech Community College
 Bloomington *A*
 Central Indiana *C*
 Columbus *A*
 East Central *A*
 Kokomo *C, A*
 Lafayette *C, A*

North Central *A*
Northeast *C, A*
Northwest *C, A*
Richmond *A*
South Central *C, A*
Southeast *A*
Southwest *A*
Wabash Valley *A*
Oakland City University *A*
Trine University *B*

Iowa

Clinton Community College *A*
Iowa Lakes Community College *A*
Kirkwood Community College *C, A*
Marshalltown Community College *A*
Southeastern Community College
 North Campus *A*
Southwestern Community
 College *C, A*
Vatterott College *C, A*

Kansas

Allen County Community College *A*
Butler Community College *C, A*
Garden City Community College *A*
Hutchinson Community College *A*
Johnson County Community
 College *C, A*
Neosho County Community
 College *A*

Kentucky

Bluegrass Community and Technical
 College *C*
Eastern Kentucky University *A*
Elizabethtown Community and
 Technical College *C*
Hopkinsville Community College *C*
Kentucky State University *A*
Madisonville Community College *A*
Murray State University *A, B*
Spencerian College: Lexington *C, A*
Sullivan College of Technology and
 Design *C, A*

Louisiana

Grambling State University *B*
ITI Technical College *C, A*

Maine

Kennebec Valley Community
 College *C, A*
Northern Maine Community
 College *A*

Maryland

Anne Arundel Community College *A*
Baltimore City Community
 College *C, A*
Chesapeake College *C, A*
Community College of Baltimore
 County *C, A*
Montgomery College *A*
Prince George's Community
 College *C, A*
Wor-Wic Community College *C, A*

Massachusetts

Bristol Community College *C*
Greenfield Community College *C*
Massachusetts Bay Community
 College *C*
Middlesex Community College *C, A*
Northern Essex Community
 College *C*
Roxbury Community College *A*

Michigan

Alpena Community College *A*
Baker College
 of Auburn Hills *A*

 of Clinton Township *A*
 of Flint *A*
 of Muskegon *A*
 of Owosso *A*
 of Port Huron *A*
Bay de Noc Community College *C, A*
Delta College *C, A*
Glen Oaks Community College *C*
Henry Ford Community College *A*
Kalamazoo Valley Community
 College *C, A*
Kellogg Community College *A*
Kirtland Community College *C, A*
Lansing Community College *A*
Macomb Community College *C, A*
Michigan Technological University *C*
Mid Michigan Community College *C*
Monroe County Community
 College *C, A*
Montcalm Community College *C, A*
Mott Community College *C, A*
Muskegon Community College *C, A*
North Central Michigan College *C*
Northwestern Michigan College *A*
Oakland Community College *C, A*
St. Clair County Community
 College *C, A*
Schoolcraft College *C, A*
Southwestern Michigan College *C, A*
Washtenaw Community College *C, A*

Minnesota

Anoka Technical College *C, A*
Hennepin Technical College *C, A*
Herzing University *A*
Minnesota State College - Southeast
 Technical *C*
Northland Community & Technical
 College *C, A*
Northwest Technical Institute *A*
Ridgewater College *C, A*
South Central College *C, A*

Mississippi

Copiah-Lincoln Community College *A*
East Central Community College *A*
East Mississippi Community
 College *A*
Hinds Community College *C, A*
Holmes Community College *A*
Meridian Community College *A*
Mississippi Gulf Coast Community
 College *A*
Northwest Mississippi Community
 College *A*
Pearl River Community College *A*

Missouri

East Central College *C, A*
Jefferson College *C, A*
Lincoln University *A*
Linn State Technical College *A*
Missouri Southern State
 University *C, A*
St. Charles Community College *C, A*
St. Louis Community College
 St. Louis Community College at
  Florissant Valley *C, A*
Three Rivers Community College *A*
University of Central Missouri *B*
Vatterott College *C, A*
Vatterott College: Kansas City *A*
Vatterott College: Sunset Hills *A*

Montana

Montana State University
 Billings *C, A*
 College of Technology: Great
  Falls *A*
Montana Tech of the University of
 Montana *C, A*

Nebraska
Central Community College C, A
Metropolitan Community
    College C, A
Southeast Community College A

Nevada
College of Southern Nevada C, A
Truckee Meadows Community
    College C, A
Western Nevada College C, A

New Hampshire
Manchester Community College C, A
Nashua Community College C, A
University of New Hampshire A

New Jersey
Bergen Community College A
Brookdale Community College C
Camden County College C, A
County College of Morris C
Gloucester County College C, A
Mercer County Community College C
Middlesex County College C
Ocean County College C

New Mexico
Clovis Community College A
Dona Ana Community College of New
    Mexico State University C, A
Eastern New Mexico University:
    Roswell Campus C, A
New Mexico Junior College C, A
New Mexico State University
    Alamogordo C
Northern New Mexico College C, A
San Juan College C, A
Santa Fe Community College C, A
Western New Mexico University C, A

New York
Adirondack Community College C, A
Cayuga County Community College C
City University of New York
    New York City College of
        Technology A
    Queensborough Community
        College A
Corning Community College C
Dutchess Community College C
Genesee Community College C, A
Hudson Valley Community College A
Institute of Design and
    Construction A
Island Drafting and Technical
    Institute A
Mohawk Valley Community College A
Orange County Community College C
State University of New York
    College of Technology at Delhi C, A
Suffolk County Community College A
Ulster County Community
    College C, A

North Carolina
Alamance Community College C, A
Asheville-Buncombe Technical
    Community College A
Beaufort County Community
    College C, A
Blue Ridge Community College C, A
Caldwell Community College and
    Technical Institute C, A
Central Carolina Community
    College A
College of the Albemarle C
Durham Technical Community
    College C, A
East Carolina University B
Forsyth Technical Community
    College A
Gaston College C

Mitchell Community College C, A
Piedmont Community College C
Richmond Community College C
Rowan-Cabarrus Community
    College A
Sandhills Community College C, A
South Piedmont Community
    College C
Surry Community College C, A
Wake Technical Community
    College C, A

Ohio
Belmont Technical College C
Clark State Community College C, A
Cuyahoga Community College
    Metropolitan Campus C, A
Eastern Gateway Community
    College A
Hocking College C, A
James A. Rhodes State College C
Marion Technical College C
North Central State College C, A
Northwest State Community
    College A
Southern State Community College A
Terra State Community College C, A
University of Akron C, A
University of Rio Grande C, A
Washington State Community
    College A
Wright State University A
Wright State University: Lake
    Campus A
Youngstown State University A
Zane State College A

Oklahoma
Langston University A
Northern Oklahoma College A
Oklahoma City Community College A
Oklahoma State University
    Institute of Technology:
        Okmulgee A
Platt College: Oklahoma City
    Central C
Tulsa Community College A
Western Oklahoma State College A

Oregon
Blue Mountain Community College A
Central Oregon Community
    College C, A
Chemeketa Community College C, A
Clackamas Community College A
Clatsop Community College C
Lane Community College C, A
Linn-Benton Community College A
Portland Community College A
Treasure Valley Community
    College C, A

Pennsylvania
Lehigh Carbon Community
    College C, A
Penn Commercial Business and
    Technical School A
Pennsylvania College of
    Technology A
Thaddeus Stevens College of
    Technology A
Triangle Tech
    Pittsburgh A

Puerto Rico
Inter American University of Puerto
    Rico
    Aguadilla Campus C
Universidad Metropolitana C, A

Rhode Island
Johnson & Wales University:
    Providence A, B

New England Institute of
    Technology A

South Carolina
Aiken Technical College C
Central Carolina Technical College A
Florence-Darlington Technical
    College C, A
Northeastern Technical College C
Orangeburg-Calhoun Technical
    College A
Technical College of the
    Lowcountry C
Tri-County Technical College C, A
Trident Technical College C
Williamsburg Technical College C, A
York Technical College A

South Dakota
Black Hills State University A
Lake Area Technical Institute A
Southeast Technical Institute A

Tennessee
Chattanooga State Community
    College C, A
Northeast State Community
    College C, A

Texas
Amarillo College C, A
Angelina College C, A
Austin Community College C, A
Brazosport College C, A
Central Texas College C, A
Cisco College C, A
Coastal Bend College A
College of the Mainland A
Collin County Community College
    District C, A
El Paso Community College C, A
Grayson County College C, A
Hill College C, A
Houston Community College
    System C, A
Howard College C
Kilgore College C, A
Lamar Institute of Technology C, A
LeTourneau University A
Lee College C, A
Midland College A
Mountain View College C, A
Navarro College A
North Central Texas College A
North Lake College C
Odessa College C, A
Paris Junior College A
Prairie View A&M University B
St. Philip's College C, A
Sam Houston State University B
San Jacinto College C, A
South Plains College C, A
South Texas College C, A
Tarrant County College C, A
Temple College C, A
Texarkana College C, A
Texas State Technical College
    Harlingen A
    Waco C, A
    West Texas C, A
Trinity Valley Community
    College C, A
Tyler Junior College C, A
University of Texas
    Brownsville - Texas Southmost
        College C, A
Vernon College C, A
Wharton County Junior College C, A

Utah
Salt Lake Community College C, A
Snow College A
Southern Utah University A

Utah State University A
Utah Valley University A
Weber State University A

Virginia
Blue Ridge Community College C
Central Virginia Community
    College C
Danville Community College A
Eastern Shore Community College C
J. Sargeant Reynolds Community
    College C
Lord Fairfax Community College C
New River Community College A
Northern Virginia Community
    College C, A
Patrick Henry Community College A
Paul D. Camp Community
    College C, A
Southside Virginia Community
    College C, A
Tidewater Community College A
Virginia Highlands Community
    College C, A
Virginia Western Community
    College C
Wytheville Community College C, A

Washington
Bates Technical College C
Green River Community College A
Highline Community College A
Lake Washington Technical
    College C, A
Olympic College C, A
Renton Technical College C, A
Shoreline Community College C, A
South Puget Sound Community
    College C, A
South Seattle Community
    College C, A
Spokane Community College C
Spokane Falls Community
    College C, A
Wenatchee Valley College C
Yakima Valley Community
    College C, A

West Virginia
Fairmont State University B
Southern West Virginia Community
    and Technical College A
West Virginia State Community and
    Technical College A

Wisconsin
Blackhawk Technical College A
Chippewa Valley Technical College A
Fox Valley Technical College A
Herzing University A, B
Moraine Park Technical College A
Northcentral Technical College A
Northeast Wisconsin Technical
    College A
Southwest Wisconsin Technical
    College A

Wyoming
Casper College A
Northwest College A

Drama and theater arts

Alabama
Alabama State University B
Auburn University B
Birmingham-Southern College B
Chattahoochee Valley Community
    College A
Faulkner University B
Jacksonville State University B
Samford University B
Spring Hill College B

University of Alabama *B, M*
University of Alabama
   Birmingham *B*
University of Mobile *B*
University of Montevallo *B, T*
University of South Alabama *B*

Alaska

University of Alaska
   Anchorage *B*
   Fairbanks *B*

Arizona

Arizona State University *B, M, D*
Arizona Western College *A*
Central Arizona College *A*
Eastern Arizona College *A*
Northern Arizona University *B*
Pima Community College *A*
Prescott College *B, M*
Scottsdale Community College *A*
University of Arizona *B, M*

Arkansas

Arkansas State University *B*
Harding University *B*
Henderson State University *B*
Hendrix College *B*
Lyon College *B*
Ouachita Baptist University *B*
Southern Arkansas University *B*
University of Arkansas *B, M*
University of Arkansas
   Little Rock *B*
University of Central Arkansas *B*
University of the Ozarks *B*

California

Allan Hancock College *C*
American River College *A*
Azusa Pacific University *B*
Bethany University *B*
Biola University *B*
California Lutheran University *B*
California Polytechnic State
   University: San Luis Obispo *B*
California State Polytechnic
   University: Pomona *B*
California State University
   Bakersfield *B*
   Chico *B*
   Dominguez Hills *B*
   East Bay *B*
   Fresno *B*
   Fullerton *B, M*
   Long Beach *B, M*
   Los Angeles *B, M*
   Northridge *B, M*
   Sacramento *B, M*
   San Bernardino *B*
   Stanislaus *B*
Canada College *A*
Cerritos College *A*
Chabot College *A*
Chaffey College *A*
Chapman University *B*
Claremont McKenna College *B*
College of Marin: Kentfield *A*
College of the Canyons *A*
College of the Desert *A*
College of the Sequoias *A*
College of the Siskiyous *C, A*
Concordia University *B*
Contra Costa College *A*
Cosumnes River College *A*
Crafton Hills College *A*
Cypress College *C, A*
East Los Angeles College *A*
El Camino College *A*
El Camino College: Compton
   Center *A*
Foothill College *A*
Fresno City College *A*

Fresno Pacific University *B*
Fullerton College *A*
Gavilan College *A*
Glendale Community College *C*
Golden West College *A*
Hartnell College *C, A*
Humboldt State University *B, M*
Irvine Valley College *A*
Lake Tahoe Community College *C, A*
Laney College *C, A*
Long Beach City College *A*
Los Angeles City College *C, A*
Los Angeles Pierce College *A*
Los Angeles Southwest College *A*
Loyola Marymount University *B*
Mendocino College *A*
Merced College *A*
MiraCosta College *A*
Modesto Junior College *A*
Monterey Peninsula College *C, A*
Moorpark College *A*
Mount San Jacinto College *A*
Notre Dame de Namur University *B*
Occidental College *B*
Orange Coast College *A*
Palomar College *A*
Pepperdine University *B*
Pitzer College *B*
Point Loma Nazarene University *B*
Pomona College *B*
Reedley College *A*
Rio Hondo College *A*
Sacramento City College *A*
Saddleback College *A*
St. Mary's College of California *B*
San Diego Christian College *B*
San Diego City College *A*
San Diego Mesa College *A*
San Diego State University *B, M*
San Francisco State University *B, M*
San Jose State University *B, M*
Santa Ana College *A*
Santa Barbara City College *A*
Santa Clara University *B*
Santa Monica College *A*
Santa Rosa Junior College *C, A*
Scripps College *B*
Shasta College *C, A*
Sierra College *A*
Solano Community College *A*
Sonoma State University *B*
Southwestern College *A*
Stanford University *B, M, D*
University of California
   Berkeley *B, M, D*
   Davis *B, M, D*
   Irvine *B, M, D*
   Los Angeles *B, M, D*
   Riverside *B*
   San Diego *B, M*
   Santa Barbara *B, M, D*
   Santa Cruz *B*
University of La Verne *B*
University of Redlands *B*
University of San Diego *B, M*
University of Southern
   California *B, M*
University of the Pacific *B*
Vanguard University of Southern
   California *B*
Ventura College *C, A*
West Valley College *A*
Westmont College *B*
Whittier College *B*
Yuba Community College District *A*

Colorado

Adams State College *A, B*
Colorado College *B*
Colorado Mountain College *A*
Colorado State University *B*
Fort Lewis College *B*
Mesa State College *B*
Otero Junior College *A*

Pikes Peak Community College *A*
University of Colorado
   Boulder *B, M, D*
   Denver *B*
University of Denver *B*
University of Northern Colorado *B, T*

Connecticut

Albertus Magnus College *B*
Central Connecticut State
   University *B*
Connecticut College *B*
Fairfield University *B*
Naugatuck Valley Community
   College *A*
Quinnipiac University *B*
Southern Connecticut State
   University *B*
Trinity College *B*
University of Connecticut *B, M*
University of Hartford *B*
Wesleyan University *B*
Western Connecticut State
   University *B*
Yale University *B, M, D*

Delaware

University of Delaware *M*

District of Columbia

American University *B*
Catholic University of America *B, M*
Gallaudet University *B*
George Washington University *B, M*
University of the District of
   Columbia *B*

Florida

Barry University *B*
Broward College *A*
Eckerd College *B*
Flagler College *B*
Florida Agricultural and Mechanical
   University *B, T*
Florida Atlantic University *B, M*
Florida Gulf Coast University *B*
Florida International University *B*
Florida Southern College *B*
Florida State College at Jacksonville *A*
Florida State University *B, M*
Gulf Coast Community College *A*
Indian River State College *A*
Jacksonville University *B*
Lynn University *B*
Miami Dade College *A*
Northwest Florida State College *A*
Palm Beach Atlantic University *B*
Palm Beach Community College *A*
Pensacola Junior College *A*
Rollins College *B*
Southeastern University *B*
State College of Florida,
   Manatee-Sarasota *A*
Stetson University *B*
University of Central Florida *B, M*
University of Florida *B, M*
University of Miami *B*
University of South Florida *B*
University of Tampa *B*
University of West Florida *B*

Georgia

Agnes Scott College *B*
Andrew College *A*
Armstrong Atlantic State University *B*
Brenau University *B*
Clayton State University *B*
Columbus State University *B*
Covenant College *B*
Darton College *A*
Emory University *B*
Gainesville State College *A*

Georgia College and State
   University *B*
Georgia Perimeter College *A*
Georgia Southern University *B*
Georgia Southwestern State
   University *B*
Gordon College *A*
Kennesaw State University *B*
LaGrange College *B*
Macon State College *A*
Mercer University *B*
Middle Georgia College *A*
Morehouse College *B*
Paine College *B*
Piedmont College *B*
Savannah College of Art and
   Design *B, M*
Shorter College *B*
South Georgia College *A*
Spelman College *B*
University of Georgia *B, M, D*
University of West Georgia *B*
Wesleyan College *B*
Young Harris College *A*

Hawaii

University of Hawaii
   Manoa *B, M, D*

Idaho

Boise State University *B*
College of Idaho *B*
Idaho State University *B, M*
University of Idaho *B, M*

Illinois

Augustana College *B*
Aurora University *B*
Bradley University *B, T*
City Colleges of Chicago
   Harold Washington College *A*
   Kennedy-King College *C, A*
Columbia College Chicago *B*
DePaul University *B*
Dominican University *B*
Eastern Illinois University *B, T*
Elmhurst College *B*
Eureka College *B*
Greenville College *B*
Illinois Central College *A*
Illinois College *B*
Illinois State University *B, M, T*
Illinois Valley Community College *A*
Illinois Wesleyan University *B*
John A. Logan College *A*
Kishwaukee College *A*
Knox College *B*
Lewis University *B, T*
Lincoln College *A*
Loyola University Chicago *C, B*
MacMurray College *B*
Millikin University *B*
Monmouth College *B, T*
National-Louis University *B*
North Central College *B*
Northern Illinois University *B, M*
Northwestern University *B, M, D*
Principia College *B*
Rockford College *B*
Roosevelt University *B, M*
South Suburban College of Cook
   County *A*
Southern Illinois University
   Carbondale *B, M*
Southern Illinois University
   Edwardsville *B*
Southwestern Illinois College *A*
Triton College *A*
University of Illinois
   Chicago *B, M*
   Urbana-Champaign *B, M, D*
Western Illinois University *B, M*

Indiana

Anderson University *B*
Ball State University *B, T*
Bethel College *B*
Butler University *B*
DePauw University *B*
Earlham College *B*
Franklin College *B*
Goshen College *B*
Grace College *B*
Hanover College *B*
Huntington University *B*
Indiana State University *B*
Indiana University
  Bloomington *B, M, D*
  Northwest *B*
  South Bend *B*
Indiana University-Purdue University
  Fort Wayne *B, T*
Indiana Wesleyan University *B*
Purdue University *B*
Saint Mary's College *B*
St. Mary-of-the-Woods College *B*
Taylor University *B*
University of Evansville *B*
University of Indianapolis *B*
University of Notre Dame *B*
University of Southern Indiana *B*
Valparaiso University *B*
Vincennes University *A*
Wabash College *B*

Iowa

Briar Cliff University *B*
Central College *B*
Clarke College *A, B, T*
Coe College *B*
Cornell College *B, T*
Dordt College *B*
Drake University *B, T*
Ellsworth Community College *A*
Graceland University *B, T*
Grand View University *B*
Grinnell College *B*
Luther College *B*
Morningside College *B*
Northwestern College *B, T*
St. Ambrose University *B*
Simpson College *B*
University of Iowa *B, M*
University of Northern Iowa *B*
Waldorf College *B*
Wartburg College *B*

Kansas

Baker University *B, T*
Barton County Community College *A*
Benedictine College *B*
Butler Community College *A*
Central Christian College of
  Kansas *A, B*
Coffeyville Community College *A*
Emporia State University *B*
Friends University *B*
Garden City Community College *A*
Highland Community College *A*
Kansas State University *B*
Kansas Wesleyan University *B, T*
McPherson College *B, T*
Neosho County Community
  College *A*
Ottawa University *B, T*
Pratt Community College *A*
Seward County Community College *A*
Southwestern College *B*
Sterling College *B, T*
University of Kansas *B, M, D*
University of St. Mary *B*
Washburn University *B*
Wichita State University *B*

Kentucky

Asbury College *B*

Berea College *B*
Bluegrass Community and Technical
  College *A*
Campbellsville University *B*
Centre College *B*
Eastern Kentucky University *B*
Georgetown College *B*
Morehead State University *B*
Murray State University *B*
Northern Kentucky University *B*
Thomas More College *A, B*
Transylvania University *B*
University of Kentucky *B, M*
University of Louisville *B, M*
University of the Cumberlands *B*
Western Kentucky University *B*

Louisiana

Bossier Parish Community College *A*
Centenary College of Louisiana *B*
Dillard University *B*
Grambling State University *B*
Louisiana College *B*
Louisiana State University and
  Agricultural and Mechanical
  College *B, M, D*
Loyola University New Orleans *B*
McNeese State University *B*
Northwestern State University *B*
Southern University and Agricultural
  and Mechanical College *B*
Tulane University *B, M*
University of New Orleans *M*

Maine

Bates College *B*
Colby College *B*
University of Maine *B, M*
University of Maine
  Farmington *B*
University of Southern Maine *B*

Maryland

Bowie State University *B*
Frederick Community College *A*
Frostburg State University *B*
Goucher College *B*
Howard Community College *A*
McDaniel College *B*
Morgan State University *B, M*
Prince George's Community
  College *C*
St. Mary's College of Maryland *B*
Salisbury University *B*
Towson University *B, M*
University of Maryland
  Baltimore County *B*
  College Park *B*
Washington College *B, T*

Massachusetts

Amherst College *B*
Bard College at Simon's Rock *B*
Boston College *B*
Brandeis University *B*
Bridgewater State College *B*
Bristol Community College *A*
Bunker Hill Community College *A*
Cape Cod Community College *A*
Clark University *B*
College of the Holy Cross *B*
Dean College *A*
Eastern Nazarene College *B*
Emerson College *B, M*
Fitchburg State College *B*
Gordon College *B*
Hampshire College *B*
Massasoit Community College *A*
Middlesex Community College *A*
Mount Holyoke College *B*
Northeastern University *B*
Regis College *B*
Salem State College *B*

Smith College *B*
Suffolk University *B*
University of Massachusetts
  Amherst *B, M*
  Boston *B*
Wellesley College *B*
Westfield State College *B*
Williams College *B*

Michigan

Adrian College *A, B*
Albion College *B, T*
Alma College *B*
Calvin College *B*
Central Michigan University *B, M*
Delta College *A*
Eastern Michigan University *B, M*
Grand Rapids Community College *A*
Grand Valley State University *B*
Henry Ford Community College *A*
Hillsdale College *B*
Hope College *B*
Kalamazoo College *B, T*
Kuyper College *B*
Lake Michigan College *A*
Lansing Community College *A*
Michigan State University *B, M*
Mid Michigan Community College *A*
Northern Michigan University *B*
Northwestern Michigan College *A*
Oakland Community College *A*
Oakland University *B*
Saginaw Valley State University *B*
Siena Heights University *B*
University of Detroit Mercy *B*
University of Michigan *B*
University of Michigan
  Flint *B*
Wayne County Community College *A*
Wayne State University *B, M, D*

Minnesota

Anoka-Ramsey Community College *A*
Augsburg College *B*
Bemidji State University *B*
Bethany Lutheran College *B*
Bethel University *B*
College of St. Benedict *B*
Concordia College: Moorhead *B*
Concordia University: St. Paul *B*
Crown College *B*
Gustavus Adolphus College *B*
Hamline University *B*
Macalester College *B*
Metropolitan State University *B*
Minneapolis Community and
  Technical College *A*
Minnesota State University
  Mankato *B, M*
  Moorhead *B*
Normandale Community College *A*
North Central University *A, B*
Northwestern College *B*
St. Catherine University *B*
Saint Cloud State University *B*
St. John's University *B*
St. Mary's University of Minnesota *B*
St. Olaf College *B*
Southwest Minnesota State
  University *B*
University of Minnesota
  Duluth *B*
  Morris *B*
  Twin Cities *B, M, D*
Vermilion Community College *A*
Winona State University *B*

Mississippi

Belhaven University *B*
Hinds Community College *A*
Millsaps College *B*
University of Mississippi *B*
University of Southern
  Mississippi *B, M*

Missouri

Avila University *B*
Central Methodist University *B*
College of the Ozarks *B*
Culver-Stockton College *B*
Drury University *B*
Evangel University *A, B*
Fontbonne University *B*
Hannibal-LaGrange College *B*
Lindenwood University *B, M*
Missouri Southern State
  University *B, T*
Missouri State University *B, M*
Missouri Valley College *B*
Northwest Missouri State
  University *B*
Park University *B*
St. Charles Community College *A*
St. Louis Community College
  St. Louis Community College at
    Florissant Valley *A*
Saint Louis University *B*
Southeast Missouri State University *B*
Southwest Baptist University *B*
Stephens College *B*
Truman State University *B*
University of Central Missouri *B, M*
University of Missouri
  Columbia *B, M, D*
  Kansas City *B, M*
  St. Louis *B*
Washington University in St.
  Louis *B, M*
Webster University *B*
William Jewell College *B*
William Woods University *B, T*

Montana

Miles Community College *A*
Montana State University
  Billings *B*
Rocky Mountain College *B*
University of Montana *B, M*
University of Montana: Western *B*

Nebraska

Chadron State College *B*
Concordia University *B, T*
Creighton University *B*
Doane College *B*
Nebraska Wesleyan University *B*
Northeast Community College *A*
University of Nebraska
  Kearney *B, T*
  Lincoln *B, M*
  Omaha *B, M*
Wayne State College *B*

Nevada

Truckee Meadows Community
  College *C, A*
University of Nevada
  Las Vegas *B, M*
  Reno *B, M*

New Hampshire

Dartmouth College *B*
Franklin Pierce University *B*
New England College *B*
Plymouth State University *B*
University of New Hampshire *B*

New Jersey

Centenary College *B*
Cumberland County College *A*
Drew University *B*
Essex County College *A*
Fairleigh Dickinson University
  College at Florham *B*
Gloucester County College *A*
Kean University *B, T*
Middlesex County College *A*
Monmouth University *B*

Montclair State University *B, M*
Ramapo College of New Jersey *B*
Rowan University *B*
Rutgers, The State University of New Jersey
  Camden Regional Campus *B, T*
  New Brunswick/Piscataway Campus *B, M*
  Newark Regional Campus *B*
Seton Hall University *B*
Thomas Edison State College *B*

New Mexico

College of Santa Fe *B*
Eastern New Mexico University *B*
New Mexico State University *B*
San Juan College *A*
University of New Mexico *B, M*

New York

Adelphi University *B*
Alfred University *B*
Bard College *B*
Barnard College *B*
City University of New York
  Brooklyn College *B, M*
  City College *B*
  College of Staten Island *B*
  Hunter College *B, M*
  Queens College *B*
  Queensborough Community College *A*
  York College *B*
Colgate University *B*
Columbia University *B*
Columbia University
  School of General Studies *B*
Cornell University *B, M, D*
Dowling College *B*
Dutchess Community College *A*
Elmira College *B*
Finger Lakes Community College *A*
Five Towns College *B*
Fordham University *B*
Genesee Community College *A*
Hamilton College *B*
Hartwick College *B*
Hobart and William Smith Colleges *B*
Hofstra University *B*
Iona College *B*
Ithaca College *B*
Juilliard School *B*
Le Moyne College *B*
Long Island University
  C. W. Post Campus *B, M*
Manhattanville College *B*
Marymount Manhattan College *B*
Mohawk Valley Community College *A*
Nazareth College *B*
New York University *B, M, D*
Niagara County Community College *A*
Niagara University *B*
Pace University *B*
Rockland Community College *A*
Russell Sage College *B*
Saint Bonaventure University *B*
St. Lawrence University *B*
Sarah Lawrence College *M*
Siena College *C*
Skidmore College *B*
State University of New York
  Albany *B, M*
  Binghamton *B, M*
  Buffalo *B*
  College at Brockport *B*
  College at Buffalo *B*
  College at Fredonia *B*
  College at Geneseo *B*
  College at Oneonta *B*
  College at Plattsburgh *B*
  College at Potsdam *B*
  New Paltz *B*
  Oswego *B*

  Purchase *B*
  Stony Brook *B, M*
Suffolk County Community College *A*
Syracuse University *B, M*
Ulster County Community College *A*
Vassar College *B*
Wagner College *B*
Wells College *B*
Westchester Community College *A*

North Carolina

Appalachian State University *B*
Barton College *B*
Brevard College *B*
Campbell University *B*
Catawba College *B*
College of the Albemarle *A*
Davidson College *B*
Duke University *B*
East Carolina University *B*
Elon University *B*
Fayetteville State University *B*
Gardner-Webb University *B*
Greensboro College *C, B, T*
Guilford College *B*
High Point University *B*
Lees-McRae College *B, T*
Lenoir-Rhyne University *B, T*
Livingstone College *B*
Mars Hill College *B*
Meredith College *B*
North Carolina Agricultural and Technical State University *B*
North Carolina Central University *B*
North Carolina Wesleyan College *B*
Pfeiffer University *B*
Queens University of Charlotte *B*
Shaw University *B*
University of North Carolina
  Asheville *B, T*
  Chapel Hill *B, M*
  Charlotte *B*
  Greensboro *B, M*
  Pembroke *B*
  Wilmington *B*
University of North Carolina School of the Arts *C, B*
Wake Forest University *B*
Western Carolina University *B*

North Dakota

Dickinson State University *B*
Jamestown College *B*
Minot State University *B*
North Dakota State University *B*
Trinity Bible College *B*
University of North Dakota *B, M*

Ohio

Ashland University *B*
Bowling Green State University *B, M, D*
Capital University *B*
Case Western Reserve University *B, M*
Cedarville University *B*
Cleveland State University *B*
College of Wooster *B*
Denison University *B*
Edison State Community College *A*
Franciscan University of Steubenville *B*
Hiram College *B, T*
Kent State University *C, B, M*
Kenyon College *B*
Malone University *B*
Marietta College *B*
Miami University
  Oxford Campus *B, M*
Mount Union College *B*
Mount Vernon Nazarene University *B*
Muskingum University *B*
Oberlin College *B*
Ohio Northern University *B*

Ohio State University
  Columbus Campus *B, M, D*
Ohio University *B, M*
Ohio Wesleyan University *B*
Otterbein College *B*
Owens Community College
  Toledo *A*
Shawnee State University *A*
University of Akron *B, M*
University of Cincinnati *B, M*
University of Dayton *B*
University of Findlay *B*
University of Toledo *B*
Wilmington College *B*
Wright State University *B*
Youngstown State University *B*

Oklahoma

Cameron University *B*
Carl Albert State College *A*
East Central University *B*
Eastern Oklahoma State College *A*
Northeastern Oklahoma Agricultural and Mechanical College *A*
Northeastern State University *B*
Northwestern Oklahoma State University *B*
Oklahoma Baptist University *B, T*
Oklahoma Christian University *B*
Oklahoma City University *B, M*
Oklahoma State University *B, M*
Oral Roberts University *B*
Southeastern Oklahoma State University *B*
Tulsa Community College *A*
University of Central Oklahoma *B*
University of Oklahoma *B, M*
University of Science and Arts of Oklahoma *B, T*
University of Tulsa *B*

Oregon

Chemeketa Community College *A*
Eastern Oregon University *B*
George Fox University *B*
Lewis & Clark College *B*
Linfield College *B*
Linn-Benton Community College *A*
Mt. Hood Community College *A*
Pacific University *B*
Portland State University *B, M*
Reed College *B*
Southern Oregon University *B, T*
University of Oregon *B, M, D*
University of Portland *B, M*
Western Oregon University *B*
Willamette University *B*

Pennsylvania

Albright College *B*
Allegheny College *B*
Arcadia University *B*
Bloomsburg University of Pennsylvania *B*
Bucknell University *B*
Bucks County Community College *A*
California University of Pennsylvania *B*
Carnegie Mellon University *B*
Cedar Crest College *B*
Cheyney University of Pennsylvania *B*
Clarion University of Pennsylvania *B*
Community College of Philadelphia *A*
DeSales University *B, T*
Dickinson College *B*
Duquesne University *B*
East Stroudsburg University of Pennsylvania *B*
Edinboro University of Pennsylvania *B*
Elizabethtown College *B*
Franklin & Marshall College *B*
Gannon University *B*
Gettysburg College *B*

Harrisburg Area Community College *A*
Indiana University of Pennsylvania *B*
Juniata College *B*
King's College *B*
Kutztown University of Pennsylvania *B*
Lehigh University *B*
Lock Haven University of Pennsylvania *B*
Lycoming College *B*
Mansfield University of Pennsylvania *B*
Marywood University *B*
Messiah College *B*
Moravian College *B*
Muhlenberg College *C, B*
Penn State
  University Park *M*
Point Park University *B*
St. Vincent College *B*
Seton Hill University *B*
Susquehanna University *B*
Swarthmore College *B*
Temple University *B*
University of Pennsylvania *B*
University of Pittsburgh *B, M, D*
University of Pittsburgh
  Johnstown *B*
University of Scranton *B*
Ursinus College *B*
Villanova University *M*
West Chester University of Pennsylvania *B*
Westminster College *B, T*
Wilkes University *B*
York College of Pennsylvania *B*

Puerto Rico

University of Puerto Rico
  Aguadilla *A*
  Rio Piedras *A*
University of the Sacred Heart *B*

Rhode Island

Brown University *B, M, D*
Community College of Rhode Island *A*
Rhode Island College *B, M*
Roger Williams University *B*
Salve Regina University *B*
University of Rhode Island *B*

South Carolina

Anderson University *B*
Bob Jones University *B, M*
Coastal Carolina University *B*
Coker College *B*
College of Charleston *B*
Converse College *B*
Francis Marion University *B*
Furman University *B, T*
Greenville Technical College *C*
Limestone College *B*
Newberry College *B*
North Greenville University *B*
Presbyterian College *B*
South Carolina State University *B*
University of South Carolina *B, M*
Winthrop University *B*

South Dakota

Augustana College *B*
Dakota Wesleyan University *B*
Mount Marty College *B*
University of Sioux Falls *B*
University of South Dakota *B, M*

Tennessee

Belmont University *B, T*
Bethel University *B*
Bryan College *B*
Freed-Hardeman University *T*

Lambuth University *B*
Lee University *B*
Lipscomb University *B*
Maryville College *B*
Middle Tennessee State University *B*
Milligan College *T*
Rhodes College *B*
Tennessee State University *B*
Trevecca Nazarene University *B*
Union University *B, T*
University of Memphis *B, M*
University of Tennessee
   Chattanooga *B*
   Knoxville *B, M*
Vanderbilt University *B*

Texas

Abilene Christian University *B*
Alvin Community College *A*
Amarillo College *A*
Angelina College *A*
Angelo State University *B, T*
Austin Community College *A*
Baylor University *B, M*
Blinn College *A*
Brazosport College *A*
Cisco College *A*
Clarendon College *A*
College of the Mainland *A*
Del Mar College *A*
East Texas Baptist University *B*
El Paso Community College *A*
Galveston College *A*
Grayson County College *A*
Hardin-Simmons University *B*
Howard College *A*
Howard Payne University *B, T*
Kilgore College *A*
Lamar University *B, M*
Laredo Community College *A*
Lee College *A*
Lon Morris College *A*
Lubbock Christian University *T*
McMurry University *B, T*
Midland College *A*
Midwestern State University *B*
Navarro College *A*
Northeast Texas Community
   College *A*
Our Lady of the Lake University of San
   Antonio *B*
Paris Junior College *A*
Prairie View A&M University *B*
St. Edward's University *B*
St. Philip's College *A*
Sam Houston State University *B*
San Jacinto College *A*
Schreiner University *B*
South Plains College *A*
Southern Methodist University *B, M*
Southwestern University *B, T*
Stephen F. Austin State University *B, T*
Sul Ross State University *B*
Tarleton State University *B*
Texarkana College *A*
Texas A&M University *B*
Texas A&M University
   Commerce *B, M*
   Corpus Christi *T*
   Kingsville *B, T*
Texas Christian University *B*
Texas Lutheran University *B*
Texas Southern University *B*
Texas State University: San
   Marcos *B, M, T*
Texas Tech University *B, M, D*
Texas Wesleyan University *B*
Texas Woman's University *B, M*
Trinity University *B*
Trinity Valley Community College *A*
Tyler Junior College *A*
University of Dallas *B, T*
University of Houston *B, M*
University of Mary Hardin-Baylor *B*

University of North Texas *B, M*
University of St. Thomas *B*
University of Texas
   Arlington *B*
   Austin *B, M, D*
   El Paso *B*
   Pan American *B, M*
University of the Incarnate Word *B*
Wayland Baptist University *B, T*
West Texas A&M University *B*
Western Texas College *A*
Wharton County Junior College *A*

Utah

Brigham Young University *B*
Southern Utah University *B, T*
University of Utah *B, M, D, T*
Utah State University *B, M*
Utah Valley University *A, B*
Weber State University *B*

Vermont

Bennington College *B, M*
Castleton State College *B*
Johnson State College *B*
Marlboro College *B*
Middlebury College *B*
St. Michael's College *B*
University of Vermont *B*

Virginia

Averett University *B*
Bluefield College *B*
Christopher Newport University *B*
College of William and Mary *B*
Eastern Mennonite University *B*
Emory & Henry College *B*
Ferrum College *B*
George Mason University *B*
Hampton University *B*
Hollins University *B*
James Madison University *B, T*
Liberty University *B*
Longwood University *B, T*
Lynchburg College *B*
Mary Baldwin College *B, M*
Old Dominion University *B, T*
Radford University *B*
Randolph College *B*
Randolph-Macon College *B*
Regent University *M*
Roanoke College *B, T*
Shenandoah University *B*
Southern Virginia University *B*
Sweet Briar College *B*
University of Richmond *B*
University of Virginia *B, M*
University of Virginia's College at
   Wise *B, T*
Virginia Commonwealth
   University *B, M*
Virginia Intermont College *B*
Virginia Polytechnic Institute and
   State University *B, M*
Virginia Union University *B*
Virginia Wesleyan College *B*
Washington and Lee University *B*

Washington

Centralia College *A*
Cornish College of the Arts *B*
Eastern Washington University *B*
Everett Community College *A*
Evergreen State College *B*
Gonzaga University *B*
Highline Community College *A*
North Seattle Community
   College *C, A*
Olympic College *A*
Saint Martin's University *B*
Seattle Pacific University *B*
Seattle University *B*
University of Puget Sound *B*

University of Washington *B, M, D*
Western Washington University *B, M*
Whitman College *B*

West Virginia

Bethany College *B*
Concord University *B*
Davis and Elkins College *B*
Fairmont State University *B*
West Virginia University *B, M*
West Virginia Wesleyan College *B*

Wisconsin

Beloit College *B*
Cardinal Stritch University *B*
Carroll University *B*
Carthage College *B, T*
Lawrence University *B*
Marquette University *B, T*
Ripon College *B, T*
St. Norbert College *B*
University of Wisconsin
   Eau Claire *B*
   Green Bay *B, T*
   La Crosse *B*
   Madison *B, M, D*
   Milwaukee *B*
   Oshkosh *B*
   Parkside *B, T*
   Platteville *B*
   Stevens Point *B*
   Superior *B, M*
   Whitewater *B*
Viterbo University *B, T*
Wisconsin Lutheran College *B*

Wyoming

Casper College *A*
Central Wyoming College *A*
Sheridan College *A*
University of Wyoming *B*
Western Wyoming Community
   College *A*

Drama/dance teacher education

Alabama

Birmingham-Southern College *T*
Faulkner University *B, T*

Arizona

Northern Arizona University *B, T*
Prescott College *B, T*
University of Arizona *B*

Arkansas

Ouachita Baptist University *B, T*

California

California State University
   Long Beach *T*
Orange Coast College *A*
San Diego State University *T*
San Francisco State University *T*
University of the Pacific *T*

District of Columbia

Catholic University of America *B*
George Washington University *T*

Florida

Flagler College *B, T*
Jacksonville University *B*
Palm Beach Atlantic University *B, T*
University of South Florida *B*

Georgia

Brenau University *B*
Columbus State University *B*
Piedmont College *B, T*

Savannah College of Art and
   Design *M*

Idaho

Brigham Young University-Idaho *T*

Illinois

Bradley University *B*
North Park University *T*
Rockford College *T*

Indiana

Anderson University *B, T*
University of Evansville *B, T*
Valparaiso University *B*

Iowa

Central College *T*
Dordt College *B*
Drake University *T*
Graceland University *T*
Simpson College *T*
University of Iowa *T*
Waldorf College *B*

Kansas

Bethel College *T*
Southwestern College *B, T*
Sterling College *T*
University of St. Mary *T*

Louisiana

Centenary College of Louisiana *B, T*

Massachusetts

Boston University *B, M*
Bridgewater State College *B, T*
Emerson College *B, M*
Tufts University *T*

Michigan

Hope College *B, T*

Minnesota

Minnesota State University
   Mankato *B, T*
Saint Cloud State University *B, T*
Southwest Minnesota State
   University *B, T*
University of Minnesota
   Morris *T*
Winona State University *B, T*

Mississippi

Millsaps College *T*

Missouri

Missouri State University *B*
Washington University in St.
   Louis *B, M, T*
William Jewell College *B, T*

Montana

Montana State University
   Billings *T*
Rocky Mountain College *B, T*
University of Montana *T*
University of Montana: Western *T*

Nebraska

Chadron State College *B*
Wayne State College *B, T*
York College *B, T*

New Jersey

County College of Morris *A*
Montclair State University *B*
Rowan University *T*

New York

City University of New York
  Hunter College B, T

North Carolina

Appalachian State University B, T
Brevard College B
East Carolina University B
Greensboro College B, T
Lees-McRae College B, T
Meredith College B, T
North Carolina Central
    University B, M, T
University of North Carolina
    Charlotte B
    Greensboro B, M

North Dakota

Dickinson State University B, T

Ohio

Ashland University B, T
Bowling Green State University B, M
Ohio State University
    Columbus Campus M
Ohio Wesleyan University B
University of Akron B, M
University of Findlay B, M, T

Oklahoma

East Central University B, T
Eastern Oklahoma State College A
University of Central Oklahoma B

Oregon

Portland State University T

Pennsylvania

Point Park University B
University of the Arts B

Rhode Island

Salve Regina University B

South Carolina

Columbia College B, T
Furman University T

South Dakota

University of Sioux Falls T
University of South Dakota B, M, T

Tennessee

Lipscomb University B, T
Trevecca Nazarene University B, T

Texas

Austin College M
East Texas Baptist University B
Hardin-Simmons University B, T
Howard Payne University B, T
Lamar University T
St. Edward's University B, T
Sam Houston State University M, T
Tarleton State University T
Texas A&M University
    Commerce T
    Kingsville T
Texas Christian University B
University of Dallas T
University of Houston T
West Texas A&M University T

Utah

Brigham Young University B
Southern Utah University B, T
Utah Valley University B
Weber State University B

Vermont

Castleton State College B, T

Johnson State College B
St. Michael's College T

Virginia

Longwood University T
Old Dominion University B, T
Shenandoah University B
Virginia Highlands Community
    College A

Washington

Western Washington University B
Whitworth University T

West Virginia

Davis and Elkins College B

Wisconsin

Carroll University T
Edgewood College B
University of Wisconsin
    Green Bay T
    Whitewater B
Viterbo University B, T

Drawing

Alabama

Birmingham-Southern College B

California

Academy of Art University C, A, B, M
Biola University B
California College of the Arts B, M
California State University
    East Bay B
    Long Beach B, M
    Northridge B, M
Chabot College A
College of the Desert A
Grossmont College A
Hartnell College C
Laguna College of Art and
    Design C, B, M
Long Beach City College A
Monterey Peninsula College C, A
Ohlone College C
Oxnard College A
Pasadena City College A
Santa Rosa Junior College C
Solano Community College A

Colorado

Adams State College B

Connecticut

Lyme Academy College of Fine Arts B
University of Hartford B

Georgia

Albany State University B
Georgia State University B, M

Idaho

Northwest Nazarene University B

Illinois

Bradley University B
City Colleges of Chicago
    Olive-Harvey College A
Lewis University B
Lincoln College A
Richland Community College A
School of the Art Institute of
    Chicago B, M

Indiana

Grace College B
Indiana University-Purdue University
    Fort Wayne B
Indiana Wesleyan University B

Iowa

Drake University B
University of Iowa B, M

Kansas

Allen County Community College A
Central Christian College of Kansas A
Pratt Community College A

Kentucky

Eastern Kentucky University B

Maine

University of Southern Maine B

Maryland

Cecil College A
Maryland Institute College of Art B

Massachusetts

Art Institute of Boston at Lesley
    University B
Bard College at Simon's Rock B
Boston University B
Montserrat College of Art B
Salem State College B
School of the Museum of Fine
    Arts B, M
University of Massachusetts
    Dartmouth M

Michigan

College for Creative Studies B
Finlandia University B
Kendall College of Art and Design of
    Ferris State University B, M
Lansing Community College A
Northern Michigan University A, B
Oakland University B
Siena Heights University B
University of Michigan B

Minnesota

College of Visual Arts B
Minneapolis College of Art and
    Design B
Minnesota State University
    Mankato B, M
Saint Cloud State University B

Missouri

Washington University in St.
    Louis B, M

Nevada

Sierra Nevada College B

New York

Pratt Institute A
State University of New York
    College at Fredonia B
    Purchase B

North Carolina

East Carolina University B
Gardner-Webb University B

Ohio

Art Academy of Cincinnati B
Bowling Green State University B
Cleveland Institute of Art B
Ohio State University
    Columbus Campus B, M
Shawnee State University B
Wright State University B

Oregon

Mt. Hood Community College A
Oregon College of Art & Craft C, B
Portland State University B

Pennsylvania

Edinboro University of
    Pennsylvania B
Keystone College A, B
Oakbridge Academy of Arts A
Seton Hill University B

Puerto Rico

Inter American University of Puerto
    Rico
    San German Campus B, M
University of Puerto Rico
    Rio Piedras B

Rhode Island

Providence College B

Tennessee

Memphis College of Art B, M
Tennessee Technological University B

Texas

University of Texas
    El Paso B, M
Western Texas College A

Vermont

Bennington College B
Marlboro College B

Washington

Cornish College of the Arts B
North Seattle Community College C
Western Washington University B

West Virginia

Marshall University M
West Virginia State University B
West Virginia Wesleyan College B

Driver/safety education

Iowa

Grand View University T
Iowa State University T

Minnesota

Saint Cloud State University B

Mississippi

Mississippi State University T

Missouri

Missouri Baptist University T
Missouri Western State University T

Nebraska

Peru State College T

North Carolina

North Carolina Agricultural and
    Technical State University B, M, T

Ohio

University of Findlay B, M, T

Oklahoma

Northeastern State University T
Southwestern Oklahoma State
    University T

South Dakota

Northern State University T

Texas

Lamar University T
Texas A&M University
    Commerce B
Texas State University: San Marcos T

Virginia

Radford University *T*
University of Virginia's College at
    Wise *T*

West Virginia

Marshall University *M*
West Virginia University *T*

Drywall installation

Indiana

Ivy Tech Community College
    Lafayette *C*

Kentucky

Big Sandy Community and Technical
    College *C*

Wisconsin

Milwaukee Area Technical College *C*

Dutch/Flemish

California

University of California
    Berkeley *B*

Iowa

Dordt College *B*

Michigan

Calvin College *B*

E-commerce

Alabama

University of South Alabama *B*

Arizona

Northcentral University *B, M, D*
University of Phoenix *B, M*

California

California State University
    Fullerton *B*
College of the Siskiyous *C*
Foothill College *C*
National University *M*
San Francisco State University *B*
San Jose City College *C*
University of La Verne *B*
University of San Francisco *M*
Westwood College of Technology
    Westwood College: Inland
        Empire *B*
    Westwood College: Los Angeles *B*

Colorado

American Sentinel University *B*
CollegeAmerica
    Fort Collins *A*
Colorado Technical University *C, A, B*
Jones International University *B, M*
Pueblo Community College *C*
Westwood College of Technology
    Westwood College: Denver South *B*
Westwood College: Denver North *B*

Delaware

Delaware Technical and Community
    College
    Owens *A*
    Stanton/Wilmington *C*
    Terry *A*

Florida

Florida Institute of Technology *B, M*
Gulf Coast Community College *A*

Pasco-Hernando Community
    College *C, A*
Santa Fe College *C*

Georgia

Ashworth College *B*
Central Georgia Technical College *C*

Illinois

Danville Area Community College *C*
DePaul University *B, M*
DeVry University
    Addison *B*
DeVry University: Online *B*
Lewis University *C*
Lincoln Land Community College *C*
Moraine Valley Community College *C*
Northwestern University *M*

Indiana

St. Mary-of-the-Woods College *B*

Kentucky

Maysville Community and Technical
    College *A*

Louisiana

Southern University and Agricultural
    and Mechanical College *B*

Maine

University of Maine
    Fort Kent *B*

Maryland

Howard Community College *C*
University of Maryland
    University College *M*

Massachusetts

Bunker Hill Community College *C*
Holyoke Community College *C*
North Shore Community College *C*

Michigan

Cleary University *B*
Eastern Michigan University *M*
Ferris State University *B*
Madonna University *C, M*
Wayne County Community
    College *C, A*
Western Michigan University *B*

Minnesota

North Hennepin Community
    College *C*
Walden University *M*

Missouri

Maryville University of Saint
    Louis *B, M*

Nebraska

Bellevue University *B*
Creighton University *B, M*

New Jersey

Bergen Community College *C*
Bloomfield College *B*
Fairleigh Dickinson University
    Metropolitan Campus *M*

New York

Finger Lakes Community College *A*
Globe Institute of Technology *C*
Orange County Community
    College *C, A*
Pace University *B*
Rochester Institute of Technology *C*
Westchester Community College *C*

North Carolina

Brunswick Community College *C*
Catawba Valley Community
    College *C, A*
Cleveland Community College *A*
Fayetteville Technical Community
    College *A*
Isothermal Community College *C, A*
Lenoir Community College *A*
Piedmont Community College *C*
Pitt Community College *A*
Sandhills Community College *A*

Ohio

Eastern Gateway Community
    College *C, A*
Marion Technical College *A*
Stark State College of Technology *A*
Tiffin University *B*
University of Akron *B*
Urbana University *B*
Washington State Community
    College *A*

Oklahoma

Northwestern Oklahoma State
    University *B*

Oregon

Clackamas Community College *C, A*
Lane Community College *C*
Portland Community College *C*

Pennsylvania

Bucks County Community College *C*
Carnegie Mellon University *M*
DeSales University *B*
Harrisburg University of Science and
    Technology *B*
La Salle University *C*
Messiah College *B*
Penn State
    Erie, The Behrend College *C*
Temple University *B*
University of Pennsylvania *B, M*
University of Pittsburgh
    Titusville *C*

Puerto Rico

Inter American University of Puerto
    Rico
    Bayamon Campus *M*
Universidad del Este *M*

Rhode Island

Bryant University *M*

South Carolina

Clemson University *M*
Trident Technical College *C, A*
Winthrop University *B*

Tennessee

Chattanooga State Community
    College *C*
Pellissippi State Community
    College *A*
Trevecca Nazarene University *B*
Vanderbilt University *M*

Texas

Brookhaven College *C, A*
Kilgore College *C, A*
Mountain View College *C, A*
North Lake College *C*
Texas Christian University *B*
Texas State Technical College:
    Marshall *C, A*
University of Dallas *M*
University of North Texas *B*

Vermont

Champlain College *B*

Virginia

Germanna Community College *C*

Washington

Seattle University *B*
Yakima Valley Community College *A*

Wisconsin

Marquette University *B, M*
Milwaukee Area Technical College *A*

Early childhood education

Alabama

Alabama Agricultural and Mechanical
    University *B, M, T*
Alabama State University *B, M*
Athens State University *B*
Auburn University *B, M, D, T*
Birmingham-Southern College *B, T*
Bishop State Community College *C*
Faulkner State Community College *A*
Gadsden State Community College *A*
Samford University *C, M, T*
Shelton State Community College *C*
Spring Hill College *B, M, T*
Troy University *B, M, T*
Tuskegee University *B, T*
University of Alabama *B, M*
University of Alabama
    Birmingham *B, M, D, T*
University of Mobile *B, M*
University of South Alabama *B, M, T*
University of West Alabama *B, M, T*

Alaska

University of Alaska
    Anchorage *C, A, B, M*
    Fairbanks *C, A*
    Southeast *C, A, M, T*

Arizona

Arizona State University *B*
Central Arizona College *C, A*
Cochise College *C, A*
Coconino County Community
    College *A*
Glendale Community College *C, A*
Northcentral University *M, D*
Northern Arizona University *M, T*
Northland Pioneer College *C, A*
Penn Foster College *A*
Pima Community College *C, A*
Prescott College *B, M*
Scottsdale Community College *C, A*
University of Phoenix *M*

Arkansas

Arkansas State University *B, M, T*
Arkansas State University
    Beebe *C, A*
Arkansas Tech University *B*
Black River Technical College *A*
Harding University *B, M, T*
Henderson State University *B*
John Brown University *B, T*
Lyon College *B*
Northwest Arkansas Community
    College *A*
Ouachita Baptist University *B, T*
Ouachita Technical College *A*
Ozarka College *C*
Phillips Community College of the
    University of Arkansas *C, A*
Pulaski Technical College *A*
Southern Arkansas University *B, T*
University of Arkansas
    Community College at Batesville *A*

Fort Smith *A, B*
Little Rock *B, M*
Pine Bluff *B, M*
University of Central Arkansas *M*
University of the Ozarks *B, T*
Williams Baptist College *B*

California
Allan Hancock College *C, A*
Bethany University *A, B*
Bethesda Christian University *C, B*
Butte College *C, A*
California Baptist University *B, M*
California College San Diego *A*
California Lutheran University *B, M*
California State University
  Bakersfield *B*
  Chico *B*
  Dominguez Hills *M*
  Fullerton *B, T*
  Long Beach *M, T*
  Northridge *M*
  Stanislaus *B*
California State University: Channel
  Islands *B*
Canada College *C, A*
Cerritos College *A*
Cerro Coso Community College *C, A*
Chabot College *C, A*
Chaffey College *C, A*
City College of San Francisco *C*
College of the Desert *C*
College of the Redwoods *C, A*
College of the Sequoias *C*
College of the Siskiyous *C, A*
Copper Mountain College *C*
Cosumnes River College *C, A*
Crafton Hills College *C, A*
Cuesta College *C, A*
De Anza College *C, A*
Diablo Valley College *C, A*
East Los Angeles College *C*
El Camino College *C, A*
Folsom Lake College *C, A*
Foothill College *C, A*
Fresno City College *C, A*
Gavilan College *C*
Glendale Community College *C, A*
Humboldt State University *B*
Imperial Valley College *C, A*
Irvine Valley College *C, A*
Lake Tahoe Community College *C, A*
Lassen Community College *A*
Long Beach City College *C*
Los Angeles Pierce College *C, A*
Los Angeles Southwest College *A*
Merced College *C, A*
Merritt College *C, A*
Mills College *M, T*
MiraCosta College *C, A*
Mount St. Mary's College *A*
Mount San Jacinto College *C, A*
Napa Valley College *C, A*
National University *B, M*
Ohlone College *C, A*
Orange Coast College *C, A*
Pacific Oaks College *T*
Pacific Union College *A, B*
Palomar College *C, A*
Pasadena City College *C, A*
Patten University *A, B*
Reedley College *C, A*
Riverside Community College *C, A*
Saddleback College *C, A*
St. Mary's College of California *M*
San Diego Christian College *B, T*
San Diego Miramar College *C, A*
San Diego State University *B, M*
San Francisco State University *B, T*
San Joaquin Delta College *C*
San Jose City College *C, A*
San Jose State University *B, M*
Santa Ana College *C, A*
Santa Barbara City College *C, A*

Santa Rosa Junior College *C, A*
Shasta Bible College and Graduate
  School *C, A*
Shasta College *A*
Sierra College *C, A*
Skyline College *C, A*
Solano Community College *C, A*
Sonoma State University *M, T*
Southwestern College *C, A*
Taft College *C, A*
University of California
  Santa Barbara *M*
University of La Verne *B, M, T*
Vanguard University of Southern
  California *C, T*
Ventura College *C, A*
West Hills College: Coalinga *C, A*
West Valley College *A*
Whittier College *B, T*
World Mission University *C*
Yuba Community College
  District *C, A*

Colorado
Adams State College *A*
Aspen University *A, B*
Colorado Christian University *C, B*
Colorado State University *B, T*
Community College of Aurora *A*
Metropolitan State College of
  Denver *T*
Morgan Community College *C*
Naropa University *B*
Northeastern Junior College *C, A*
Otero Junior College *C, A*
University of Colorado
  Denver *M*
University of Northern Colorado *M, T*

Connecticut
Asnuntuck Community College *C, A*
Capital Community College *C, A*
Eastern Connecticut State
  University *B, M, T*
Gateway Community College *C, A*
Goodwin College *C, A*
Housatonic Community College *A*
Manchester Community College *A*
Middlesex Community College *C, A*
Mitchell College *A, B*
Northwestern Connecticut
  Community College *C, A*
Norwalk Community College *C, A*
Post University *C, A*
Quinebaug Valley Community
  College *C, A*
Saint Joseph College *T*
Three Rivers Community College *C, A*
Tunxis Community College *C, A*
University of Hartford *B, M*

Delaware
Delaware State University *B*
Delaware Technical and Community
  College
  Owens *C, A*
  Stanton/Wilmington *C, A*
  Terry *C, A*
University of Delaware *B, T*
Wilmington University *A, B*

District of Columbia
Catholic University of America *B*
Gallaudet University *B, T*
George Washington University *M*
Howard University *M*
Trinity Washington University *M, T*
University of the District of
  Columbia *A, B, T*

Florida
Barry University *B, M, T*
Brevard Community College *A*

Broward College *A*
Central Florida Community
  College *C, A*
Florida Agricultural and Mechanical
  University *B, T*
Florida Atlantic University *M*
Florida Gulf Coast University *B*
Florida International University *B, M*
Florida State College at
  Jacksonville *C, B*
Florida State University *B, M, D*
Gulf Coast Community College *A*
Indian River State College *A*
Lake City Community College *A*
Lake-Sumter Community College *A*
Miami Dade College *C, A*
Northwest Florida State College *A*
Nova Southeastern University *A, B*
Palm Beach Community College *A*
Pensacola Junior College *A*
St. Petersburg College *A*
Santa Fe College *C, A*
Southwest Florida College *C, A, B*
State College of Florida,
  Manatee-Sarasota *A*
Tallahassee Community College *A*
University of Central Florida *B, M*
University of Florida *M*
University of North Florida *B*
University of South Florida *B, M*
University of West Florida *B, T*

Georgia
Abraham Baldwin Agricultural
  College *A*
Agnes Scott College *T*
Albany State University *B, M*
Albany Technical College *C, A*
Altamaha Technical College *A*
Armstrong Atlantic State University *B*
Ashworth College *A*
Athens Technical College *C, A*
Atlanta Christian College *B*
Bainbridge College *C, A*
Berry College *B, M*
Brewton-Parker College *B*
Central Georgia Technical
  College *C, A*
Clark Atlanta University *B*
Columbus State University *B, M*
Columbus Technical College *C, A*
Darton College *A*
DeKalb Technical College *C*
Gainesville State College *A, B*
Georgia College and State
  University *B, M, T*
Georgia Military College *A*
Georgia State University *M, D, T*
Gordon College *B*
Macon State College *A, B*
Middle Georgia College *A*
Middle Georgia Technical College *C*
North Georgia College & State
  University *B, M*
Oglethorpe University *M*
Piedmont College *B, M, T*
Reinhardt College *B, M*
Savannah State University *B*
Savannah Technical College *C, A*
South Georgia College *A*
Southeastern Technical College *A*
Southwest Georgia Technical
  College *C, A*
Spelman College *B, T*
Toccoa Falls College *B, T*
Truett-McConnell College *B*
University of Georgia *M*
Valdosta State University *B, M*
Valdosta Technical College *C, A*
Wesleyan College *B, M, T*
West Georgia Technical College *C, A*

Hawaii
Chaminade University of
  Honolulu *B, M, T*
University of Hawaii
  Hawaii Community College *C, A*
  Honolulu Community College *C, A*
  Kauai Community College *C, A*
  Maui Community College *C, A*
  West Oahu *B*

Idaho
Boise State University *A, M, T*
Brigham Young University-Idaho *A*
Idaho State University *B*
North Idaho College *A*
University of Idaho *B, T*

Illinois
Black Hawk College *A*
Bradley University *B, T*
Chicago State University *B, M, T*
City Colleges of Chicago
  Harold Washington College *C, A*
  Kennedy-King College *A*
Columbia College Chicago *B*
Concordia University
  Chicago *B, M, D, T*
DePaul University *B, M, T*
Dominican University *B, T*
Elmhurst College *B*
Governors State University *B, M, T*
Greenville College *B, T*
Illinois College *B, T*
Illinois State University *B, T*
John A. Logan College *C, A*
John Wood Community College *A*
Joliet Junior College *A*
Judson University *B*
Kankakee Community College *C, A*
Kendall College *B, T*
Kishwaukee College *A*
Lewis and Clark Community
  College *C, A*
Lincoln Christian University *A*
Loyola University Chicago *B, M*
Millikin University *B, T*
Morton College *A*
National-Louis University *B, M, T*
North Park University *B, M, T*
Northeastern Illinois University *B*
Northern Illinois University *M, T*
Oakton Community College *A*
Olivet Nazarene University *B, T*
Roosevelt University *B, M*
St. Augustine College *C, A*
Saint Xavier University *M*
South Suburban College of Cook
  County *A*
Southern Illinois University
  Carbondale *M*
Southern Illinois University
  Edwardsville *B, T*
Southwestern Illinois College *A*
Spoon River College *A*
Triton College *C, A*
University of Illinois
  Urbana-Champaign *B, M, D, T*

Indiana
Ancilla College *C, A*
Bethel College *A, B*
Butler University *B, T*
Indiana University
  Bloomington *B, T*
  Kokomo *C*
  South Bend *A*
Indiana University-Purdue University
  Fort Wayne *A*
Indiana Wesleyan University *T*
Ivy Tech Community College
  Bloomington *C, A*
  Central Indiana *C, A*
  Columbus *C, A*

East Central *C, A*
Kokomo *C, A*
Lafayette *C, A*
North Central *C, A*
Northeast *C, A*
Northwest *C, A*
Richmond *C, A*
South Central *C, A*
Southeast *C, A*
Southwest *C, A*
Wabash Valley *C, A*
Manchester College *A*
Oakland City University *C, A, B*
Purdue University *B*
Purdue University
Calumet *A, B*
North Central *B*
St. Mary-of-the-Woods College *A, B, T*
Taylor University *A, T*
University of Southern Indiana *B*
Vincennes University *A*

Iowa

Central College *T*
Drake University *M, T*
Graceland University *T*
Iowa State University *B, T*
Iowa Wesleyan College *B*
Loras College *B*
Mount Mercy College *T*
North Iowa Area Community
College *A*
Northwestern College *T*
St. Ambrose University *B, T*
Simpson College *T*
University of Iowa *M*
Upper Iowa University *B, T*
Wartburg College *T*

Kansas

Butler Community College *A*
Central Christian College of Kansas *A*
Coffeyville Community College *A*
Friends University *B*
Garden City Community College *A*
Hesston College *A*
Highland Community College *C, A*
Kansas Wesleyan University *A*
Labette Community College *A*
McPherson College *B, T*
Pittsburg State University *B, T*
Pratt Community College *A*
Southwestern College *B, T*
University of Kansas *B, T*
Washburn University *A, B*
Wichita State University *B*

Kentucky

Campbellsville University *B*
Elizabethtown Community and
Technical College *A*
Gateway Community and Technical
College *A*
Hazard Community and Technical
College *A*
Henderson Community College *A*
Lindsey Wilson College *A*
Madisonville Community College *A*
Maysville Community and Technical
College *C, A*
Morehead State University *B*
Murray State University *B, T*
Owensboro Community and
Technical College *A*
St. Catharine College *A*
University of Kentucky *B*
University of Louisville *M*
Western Kentucky
University *A, B, M, T*

Louisiana

Delgado Community College *A*
Dillard University *B, T*

Grambling State University *B*
Louisiana State University
Alexandria *A*
Eunice *A*
Shreveport *B*
Louisiana State University and
Agricultural and Mechanical
College *B*
Louisiana Tech University *B*
McNeese State University *B, T*
Nicholls State University *B*
Northwestern State University *B, M*
Southeastern Louisiana University *B*
Southern University
New Orleans *B*
Shreveport *A*
Southern University and Agricultural
and Mechanical College *B*
University of Louisiana at Lafayette *B*
University of New Orleans *B*
Xavier University of Louisiana *B*

Maine

Andover College *A*
Beal College *A*
Central Maine Community
College *C, A*
Eastern Maine Community
College *C, A*
Northern Maine Community
College *C, A*
Southern Maine Community
College *C, A*
Thomas College *B*
University of Maine
Farmington *B, T*
Washington County Community
College *C, A*

Maryland

Allegany College of Maryland *A*
Baltimore City Community
College *C, A*
Carroll Community College *A*
Cecil College *A*
Chesapeake College *C*
College of Notre Dame of Maryland *B*
College of Southern Maryland *A*
Community College of Baltimore
County *A*
Coppin State University *B*
Frederick Community College *A*
Frostburg State University *B, T*
Hagerstown Community College *A*
Harford Community College *A*
Hood College *B, T*
Howard Community College *C, A*
Montgomery College *C, A*
Prince George's Community
College *C, A*
Salisbury University *B, T*
Towson University *B, M, T*
Washington Adventist University *A*
Washington Bible College *B, T*
Wor-Wic Community College *A*

Massachusetts

American International
College *B, M, T*
Atlantic Union College *C, B*
Bay Path College *B*
Bay State College *A*
Becker College *B*
Berkshire Community College *C*
Boston College *B, M, T*
Boston University *B, M, T*
Bridgewater State College *B, M, T*
Bristol Community College *C, A*
Bunker Hill Community College *C*
Cambridge College *M*
Cape Cod Community College *C, A*
Curry College *B*
Dean College *C, A*
Eastern Nazarene College *A, B, M, T*

Elms College *B, M, T*
Endicott College *B*
Fisher College *A*
Fitchburg State College *B, M, T*
Framingham State College *B, M*
Gordon College *B*
Greenfield Community College *C, A*
Lasell College *B, T*
Lesley University *B, M*
Massachusetts College of Liberal
Arts *T*
Middlesex Community College *C, A*
Mount Ida College *B, T*
North Shore Community College *A*
Northern Essex Community
College *C, A*
Pine Manor College *T*
Quincy College *C, A*
Quinsigamond Community
College *C, A*
Roxbury Community College *A*
Salem State College *B, M*
Simmons College *B, M*
Springfield College *B, M, T*
Springfield Technical Community
College *A*
Stonehill College *B*
Tufts University *B, M, T*
Urban College of Boston *C, A*
Wellesley College *T*
Wheaton College *T*
Wheelock College *B, M*
Worcester State College *B, M, T*

Michigan

Adrian College *A, T*
Alma College *T*
Baker College
of Cadillac *A*
of Clinton Township *A*
of Muskegon *C, A*
of Owosso *A*
of Port Huron *C, A*
Bay Mills Community College *A*
Calvin College *B, T*
Central Michigan University *B, M*
Cornerstone University *A, B*
Eastern Michigan University *M*
Glen Oaks Community College *C, A*
Gogebic Community College *A*
Grace Bible College *B*
Grand Valley State University *M*
Henry Ford Community College *A*
Hillsdale College *B*
Jackson Community College *A*
Lake Michigan College *C, A*
Lake Superior State University *A, B*
Madonna University *B*
Marygrove College *C, B, M, T*
Michigan State University *B*
Monroe County Community
College *C, A*
Mott Community College *A*
Muskegon Community College *C, A*
North Central Michigan College *C, A*
Oakland University *M, D*
Rochester College *B*
Saginaw Valley State University *M*
Southwestern Michigan College *A*
University of Detroit Mercy *M*
University of Michigan
Dearborn *B*
Flint *T*
Washtenaw Community College *C, A*
Wayne State University *M*
Western Michigan University *B*

Minnesota

Augsburg College *B, T*
Bethel University *B*
Capella University *M*
Concordia University: St. Paul *B, M, T*
Crown College *A, B, T*
Itasca Community College *A*

Leech Lake Tribal College *A*
Martin Luther College *B*
Minnesota State University
Mankato *B, M*
Northland Community & Technical
College *A*
Northwestern College *B*
Rasmussen College: Lake
Elmo/Woodbury *A*
St. Catherine University *B, T*
Saint Cloud State University *B, T*
Southwest Minnesota State
University *B, T*
University of Minnesota
Duluth *B, T*
Morris *T*
Twin Cities *B, M*
University of St. Thomas *M*
Walden University *M, D*
Winona State University *B, M, T*

Mississippi

Jackson State University *M, D*
Mississippi State University *T*
Mississippi Valley State University *B, T*
Rust College *A*
Tougaloo College *A*

Missouri

Central Methodist University *B*
College of the Ozarks *B, T*
Culver-Stockton College *T*
Evangel University *A, B, T*
Fontbonne University *B, T*
Hannibal-LaGrange College *B*
Harris-Stowe State University *B, T*
Jefferson College *C, A*
Lincoln University *A*
Lindenwood University *B*
Maryville University of Saint
Louis *B, M, T*
Missouri Baptist University *B, T*
Missouri Southern State
University *B, M, T*
Missouri State University *B*
Missouri Valley College *T*
Northwest Missouri State
University *M, T*
Park University *B*
St. Louis Community College
St. Louis Community College at
Florissant Valley *A*
Southwest Baptist University *T*
Stephens College *B, T*
Truman State University *M, T*
University of Central Missouri *T*
University of Missouri
Columbia *B, M, D*
Kansas City *B*
St. Louis *B, M*
Washington University in St. Louis *M*
Webster University *M*
William Woods University *T*

Montana

Blackfeet Community College *A*
Dawson Community College *C, A*
Flathead Valley Community College *A*
Fort Belknap College *C*
Montana State University
Billings *A, M*
University of Great Falls *A, B*
University of Montana:
Western *C, A, B*

Nebraska

College of Saint Mary *A, B, T*
Concordia University *M, T*
Little Priest Tribal College *C*
Nebraska Indian Community
College *C, A*
Northeast Community College *C, A*
Peru State College *B, T*

University of Nebraska
  Kearney *B, T*
Wayne State College *B, T*
Western Nebraska Community
  College *C, A*

Nevada

College of Southern Nevada *A*
Great Basin College *C, A*
Truckee Meadows Community
  College *C, A*
University of Nevada
  Las Vegas *B*
Western Nevada College *C, A*

New Hampshire

Colby-Sawyer College *B, T*
Granite State College *A, B, T*
Keene State College *B, M, T*
Lakes Region Community
  College *C, A*
Manchester Community College *C, A*
NHTI-Concord's Community
  College *C, A*
Nashua Community College *C, A*
Plymouth State University *B, T*
Rivier College *C, A, B, M, T*
Southern New Hampshire
  University *B, M*
University of New Hampshire *M*
White Mountains Community
  College *C, A*

New Jersey

Bergen Community College *A*
Brookdale Community College *C*
Caldwell College *T*
The College of New Jersey *B, T*
College of St. Elizabeth *C, T*
County College of Morris *A*
Cumberland County College *C, A*
Felician College *B*
Gloucester County College *A*
Hudson County Community
  College *C, A*
New Jersey City University *B, M*
Passaic County Community College *A*
Raritan Valley Community
  College *C, A*
Rowan University *B*
Rutgers, The State University of New
  Jersey
  Camden Regional Campus *T*
  New Brunswick/Piscataway
    Campus *T*
  Newark Regional Campus *T*
Salem Community College *C, A*
Seton Hall University *B, T*
Sussex County Community
  College *C, A*
Warren County Community
  College *C, A*
William Paterson University of New
  Jersey *B, T*

New Mexico

Clovis Community College *A*
Dona Ana Community College of New
  Mexico State University *A*
Eastern New Mexico University *B*
Navajo Technical College *C, A*
New Mexico Highlands University *B*
New Mexico Junior College *A*
New Mexico State University *B*
New Mexico State University
  Alamogordo *A*
  Carlsbad *A*
Northern New Mexico College *A*
San Juan College *C, A*
Southwestern Indian Polytechnic
  Institute *C, A*
University of New Mexico *B*
Western New Mexico University *C, A*

New York

Adelphi University *M, T*
Adirondack Community College *C*
Barnard College *T*
Canisius College *B, T*
Cayuga County Community
  College *C, A*
Cazenovia College *B*
City University of New York
  Borough of Manhattan Community
    College *A*
  Brooklyn College *B, M, T*
  City College *B, M, T*
  Hostos Community College *A*
  Hunter College *B, M, T*
  Kingsborough Community
    College *A*
  Queens College *B, M, T*
College of Mount St. Vincent *T*
College of Saint Rose *B, M, T*
Corning Community College *C, A*
D'Youville College *M, T*
Daemen College *B, M, T*
Dominican College of Blauvelt *M*
Dowling College *B, M*
Dutchess Community College *C, A*
Herkimer County Community
  College *A*
Hofstra University *B, M*
Iona College *B, M, T*
Jamestown Community College *C*
Keuka College *B, M, T*
Manhattan College *B, T*
Manhattanville College *M, T*
Maria College *A*
Marymount Manhattan College *T*
Monroe Community College *C*
Mount Saint Mary College *B, M*
Nassau Community College *A*
Nazareth College *M, T*
Niagara University *B, T*
Orange County Community College *C*
Pace University *B, M, T*
Roberts Wesleyan College *B*
St. John's University *M, T*
St. Joseph's College *B, T*
St. Joseph's College: Suffolk
  Campus *B, M, T*
Sarah Lawrence College *M*
Schenectady County Community
  College *C, A*
State University of New York
  Buffalo *M*
  College at Brockport *M, T*
  College at Buffalo *B, T*
  College at Fredonia *B, T*
  College at Geneseo *B, M, T*
  College at Oneonta *B, M, T*
  College at Plattsburgh *B*
  College at Potsdam *B*
  College of Technology at
    Canton *A, T*
  College of Technology at Delhi *A*
  New Paltz *B, M, T*
Suffolk County Community College *A*
Sullivan County Community
  College *A*
Tompkins Cortland Community
  College *A*
Trocaire College *A*
University of Rochester *M*
Utica College *B*
Vassar College *T*
Villa Maria College of Buffalo *A*
Wagner College *B, M, T*
Westchester Community College *C, A*

North Carolina

Alamance Community College *C, A*
Beaufort County Community
  College *C, A*
Bladen Community College *C*
Brunswick Community College *C, A*
Caldwell Community College and
  Technical Institute *A*
Campbell University *B, M*
Catawba Valley Community
  College *C, A*
Central Carolina Community
  College *C, A*
Central Piedmont Community
  College *C, A*
Coastal Carolina Community
  College *C, A*
College of the Albemarle *C, A*
Davidson County Community
  College *C, A*
Durham Technical Community
  College *C, A*
Edgecombe Community College *C, A*
Fayetteville Technical Community
  College *C, A*
Forsyth Technical Community
  College *A*
Gaston College *C, A*
Greensboro College *C, B, T*
Guilford Technical Community
  College *C, A*
Halifax Community College *A*
High Point University *B, T*
Isothermal Community College *C, A*
James Sprunt Community
  College *C, A*
Johnston Community College *C, A*
Lenoir Community College *C, A*
Lenoir-Rhyne University *B, M, T*
Martin Community College *C, A*
Mayland Community College *C, A*
Meredith College *T*
Mitchell Community College *A*
Montgomery Community College *C, A*
Nash Community College *A*
North Carolina Agricultural and
  Technical State University *B, T*
Pamlico Community College *C, A*
Peace College *B*
Piedmont Baptist College *A*
Pitt Community College *A*
Roanoke-Chowan Community
  College *A*
Rockingham Community College *C, A*
Rowan-Cabarrus Community
  College *A*
Sampson Community College *C, A*
Sandhills Community College *A*
Southeastern Community College *A*
Southwestern Community
  College *C, A*
Stanly Community College *C, A*
Surry Community College *C, A, B*
University of North Carolina
  Chapel Hill *B*
  · Greensboro *B, M*
Vance-Granville Community
  College *C, A*
Wake Technical Community
  College *C, A*
Warren Wilson College *B, T*
Wayne Community College *C, A*
Western Piedmont Community
  College *C, A*
Wilkes Community College *C, A*
Wilson Community College *C, A*
Winston-Salem State University *B*

North Dakota

Cankdeska Cikana Community
  College *A*
Dickinson State University *B, T*
Jamestown College *B*
Mayville State University *B, T*
Sitting Bull College *A, B*
Turtle Mountain Community
  College *A*
University of Mary *B, M*
University of North Dakota *B, M*

Ohio

Antioch University McGregor *B, M*
Ashland University *B, M, T*
Baldwin-Wallace College *B, T*
Belmont Technical College *A*
Bluffton University *B*
Bowling Green State University:
  Firelands College *B*
Capital University *B*
Cedarville University *B*
Central Ohio Technical College *A*
Central State University *B*
Chatfield College *A*
Cincinnati Christian University *B, T*
Cincinnati State Technical and
  Community College *C, A*
Clark State Community College *A*
Cleveland State University *B*
College of Mount St. Joseph *B, T*
Columbus State Community
  College *C, A*
Cuyahoga Community College
  Metropolitan Campus *A*
Davis College *A*
Defiance College *B*
Eastern Gateway Community
  College *C, A*
Franciscan University of
  Steubenville *A*
Hiram College *T*
James A. Rhodes State College *C, A*
John Carroll University *M, T*
Kent State University *B, M*
Kent State University
  Ashtabula *A*
  Tuscarawas *A*
Lourdes College *B*
Malone University *B*
Marietta College *B*
Miami University
  Oxford Campus *B*
Mount Union College *B, T*
Mount Vernon Nazarene
  University *B, T*
Muskingum University *B, T*
North Central State College *A*
Notre Dame College *B, T*
Ohio Christian University *A, B*
Ohio Northern University *B, T*
Ohio State University
  Columbus Campus *M, D*
Ohio University *B, T*
Ohio University
  Southern Campus at Ironton *M*
  Zanesville Campus *B*
Ohio Wesleyan University *B*
Otterbein College *B*
Owens Community College
  Toledo *A*
Shawnee State University *B*
Southern State Community College *A*
Stark State College of Technology *A*
Terra State Community College *C, A*
Union Institute & University *B*
University of Akron *C, B*
University of Cincinnati *B, M, T*
University of Cincinnati
  Clermont College *A*
  Raymond Walters College *A*
University of Dayton *B, M*
University of Findlay *B, M, T*
University of Rio Grande *A, B*
University of Toledo *T*
Ursuline College *B, M, T*
Walsh University *B*
Wilmington College *B*
Wright State University *B, M, T*
Xavier University *A, B*
Youngstown State University *B, M*

Oklahoma

Bacone College *B*
Cameron University *A, B*
Carl Albert State College *C*

Connors State College *A*
East Central University *B, T*
Northeastern Oklahoma Agricultural and Mechanical College *A*
Northeastern State University *B, M*
Northwestern Oklahoma State University *B, T*
Oklahoma Baptist University *B, T*
Oklahoma Christian University *B, T*
Oklahoma City University *B*
Oral Roberts University *B, T*
Seminole State College *C*
Southern Nazarene University *B, M*
Southwestern Oklahoma State University *B, M, T*
University of Central Oklahoma *B, M*
University of Oklahoma *B*
University of Science and Arts of Oklahoma *B, T*
University of Tulsa *B, T*

Oregon
Blue Mountain Community College *A*
Chemeketa Community College *A*
Clackamas Community College *A*
Concordia University *B, M, T*
Eastern Oregon University *B, M*
Klamath Community College *C, A*
Linfield College *T*
Mt. Hood Community College *A*
Oregon State University *M*
Portland Community College *C, A*
Portland State University *T*
Umpqua Community College *C, A*
Warner Pacific College *M, T*
Western Oregon University *M, T*
Willamette University *M*

Pennsylvania
Albright College *B, M, T*
Alvernia University *B*
Arcadia University *B, M, T*
Baptist Bible College of Pennsylvania *A, B*
Bloomsburg University of Pennsylvania *B, M, T*
Bucknell University *B, T*
Bucks County Community College *A*
Carlow University *B*
Chatham University *B, M, T*
Chestnut Hill College *B, M, T*
Cheyney University of Pennsylvania *T*
Clarion University of Pennsylvania *A, B, T*
DeSales University *C, T*
Duquesne University *B, M, T*
East Stroudsburg University of Pennsylvania *B, T*
Elizabethtown College *B*
Gannon University *A, B*
Grove City College *B*
Gwynedd-Mercy College *T*
Harcum College *A*
Harrisburg Area Community College *A*
Holy Family University *B, M, T*
Indiana University of Pennsylvania *B, M*
Juniata College *B, T*
Keystone College *C, A, B, T*
King's College *B, T*
La Salle University *B, M, T*
Lackawanna College *A*
Lebanon Valley College *B*
Lehigh Carbon Community College *C, A*
Lincoln University *B, M, T*
Manor College *A*
Mansfield University of Pennsylvania *B, T*
Marywood University *B*
McCann School of Business and Technology: Dickson City *A*

Mercyhurst College *A, B, T*
Messiah College *B, T*
Millersville University of Pennsylvania *M*
Misericordia University *T*
Mount Aloysius College *A, B*
Neumann University *B, T*
Northampton Community College *C, A*
Philadelphia Biblical University *B, T*
Point Park University *C, A, B*
Reading Area Community College *A*
Rosemont College *T*
St. Vincent College *T*
Seton Hill University *T*
Shippensburg University of Pennsylvania *B, T*
Susquehanna University *B, T*
University of Pennsylvania *M*
University of Pittsburgh *T*
University of Scranton *B*
Valley Forge Christian College *A, B*
West Chester University of Pennsylvania *B, M, T*
Widener University *B, M, T*

Puerto Rico
Bayamon Central University *B, M*
Inter American University of Puerto Rico
Aguadilla Campus *B*
Arecibo Campus *B*
Fajardo Campus *B, T*
Ponce Campus *B*
San German Campus *B*
Pontifical Catholic University of Puerto Rico *B, M*
Turabo University *B*
Universidad Metropolitana *B, M*
Universidad del Este *B*
University of Puerto Rico
Rio Piedras *M*

Rhode Island
Community College of Rhode Island *C*
Rhode Island College *B, M*
Salve Regina University *B*
University of Rhode Island *T*

South Carolina
Anderson University *B, T*
Benedict College *B*
Bob Jones University *B*
Charleston Southern University *B*
Claflin University *B*
Clemson University *B, M*
Clinton Junior College *A*
Coastal Carolina University *B, M, T*
Coker College *B, T*
College of Charleston *B, M, T*
Columbia College *B, T*
Converse College *B, M, T*
Erskine College *B, T*
Forrest Junior College *A*
Francis Marion University *B, M, T*
Furman University *M, T*
Lander University *B, T*
Morris College *B, T*
Newberry College *B, T*
North Greenville University *B, T*
Presbyterian College *B, T*
South Carolina State University *B, M, T*
Southern Wesleyan University *B, T*
University of South Carolina *B, M, D*
University of South Carolina
Aiken *B, T*
Beaufort *B*
Upstate *B, M, T*
Williamsburg Technical College *C, A*
Winthrop University *B, M, T*
York Technical College *C, A*

South Dakota
Kilian Community College *A*
Northern State University *B, T*
Oglala Lakota College *C, A*
Sisseton Wahpeton College *A*
South Dakota State University *B*
University of South Dakota *B*

Tennessee
Belmont University *B, M, T*
Carson-Newman College *B*
Christian Brothers University *B*
Columbia State Community College *C, A*
Cumberland University *B, T*
East Tennessee State University *M, T*
Free Will Baptist Bible College *A, B*
Freed-Hardeman University *B, T*
LeMoyne-Owen College *B*
Lee University *B, T*
Lincoln Memorial University *B, T*
Middle Tennessee State University *B, T*
Milligan College *B, M, T*
Nashville State Community College *A*
Tennessee State University *B*
Tennessee Technological University *B, M, D, T*
Tennessee Temple University *T*
Tennessee Wesleyan College *B, T*
Tusculum College *B, T*
University of Tennessee
Chattanooga *B*
Knoxville *T*
Vanderbilt University *B, M, D, T*

Texas
Alvin Community College *C, A*
Austin Community College *A*
Baylor University *B, T*
Brookhaven College *C, A*
Dallas Baptist University *B, M, T*
Dallas Christian College *B, T*
Del Mar College *A*
Hardin-Simmons University *B, T*
Houston Baptist University *B, M*
Howard Payne University *T*
Jarvis Christian College *B*
Lamar University *B, M, T*
Laredo Community College *A*
Lubbock Christian University *B*
McMurry University *B*
Midwestern State University *B*
Mountain View College *A*
Our Lady of the Lake University of San Antonio *M*
Panola College *C, A*
Schreiner University *B*
South Texas College *C, A*
Southwestern Assemblies of God University *A, B, M*
Southwestern University *T*
Stephen F. Austin State University *M*
Tarleton State University *T*
Tarrant County College *A*
Texas A&M International University *B, M, T*
Texas A&M University
Commerce *B, M*
Corpus Christi *M, T*
Kingsville *M*
Texarkana *T*
Texas Christian University *B*
Texas College *A, T*
Texas Southern University *M*
Texas State University: San Marcos *M, T*
Texas Wesleyan University *B, M, T*
Texas Woman's University *M*
Trinity Valley Community College *C, A*
University of Houston *M, T*
University of Houston
Clear Lake *M, T*

University of Mary Hardin-Baylor *T*
University of North Texas *M, D, T*
University of Texas
Arlington *T*
Brownsville - Texas Southmost College *M*
Pan American *M*
San Antonio *T*
Tyler *M*
of the Permian Basin *M*
West Texas A&M University *T*
Western Texas College *C, A*
Wharton County Junior College *A*

Utah
Brigham Young University *B*
College of Eastern Utah *A*
Dixie State College of Utah *A*
Independence University *A*
Snow College *A*
Southern Utah University *T*
Utah State University *B*
Utah Valley University *A, B*
Weber State University *B*
Westminster College *B*

Vermont
Bennington College *B, M*
Champlain College *B*
Goddard College *B, M*
Johnson State College *M*
Lyndon State College *B*
University of Vermont *B, T*

Virginia
Dabney S. Lancaster Community College *C*
Eastern Mennonite University *T*
Germanna Community College *C*
Hollins University *T*
J. Sargeant Reynolds Community College *C, A*
James Madison University *T*
Liberty University *M, T*
Longwood University *B, T*
Lord Fairfax Community College *C*
New River Community College *C, A*
Northern Virginia Community College *C, A*
Old Dominion University *M, D, T*
Paul D. Camp Community College *C*
Piedmont Virginia Community College *C*
Radford University *T*
Southwest Virginia Community College *C, A*
Thomas Nelson Community College *C, A*
Tidewater Community College *C, A*
University of Richmond *T*
Virginia Western Community College *C, A*

Washington
Bates Technical College *C, A*
Bellevue College *C, A*
Bellingham Technical College *C*
Big Bend Community College *C, A*
Centralia College *C, A*
Clark College *C, A*
Clover Park Technical College *C, A*
Eastern Washington University *B, M*
Everett Community College *C, A*
Grays Harbor College *C*
Green River Community College *C, A*
North Seattle Community College *C, A*
Northwest Indian College *A*
Olympic College *C, A*
Peninsula College *C, A*
Pierce College *C, A*
Renton Technical College *C, A*
Shoreline Community College *A*

Skagit Valley College C, A
South Puget Sound Community
    College C, A
Spokane Falls Community College A
Trinity Lutheran College B
University of Washington Tacoma T
Walla Walla University A
Washington State University B, T
Wenatchee Valley College C, A
Whatcom Community College C, A
Yakima Valley Community
    College C, A

West Virginia
American Public University System M
Concord University B, T
Fairmont State University B
Marshall University M
Shepherd University T
West Liberty University B
West Virginia State University B
West Virginia University T

Wisconsin
Beloit College T
Carroll University B
College of Menominee Nation A
Concordia University Wisconsin B, T
Edgewood College B, T
Gateway Technical College A
Lakeshore Technical College A
Maranatha Baptist Bible College A, B
Marian University B, T
Mid-State Technical College A
Milwaukee Area Technical
    College C, A
Mount Mary College B, T
Nicolet Area Technical College A
Northcentral Technical College C, A
Rasmussen College: Green Bay A
Ripon College T
St. Norbert College B, T
Silver Lake College B, T
University of Wisconsin
    Green Bay T
    Oshkosh M
    Parkside T
    Platteville B, T
    River Falls T
    Stevens Point B, T
    Stout B, T
    Superior T
    Whitewater B, T
Viterbo University T
Waukesha County Technical
    College A
Wisconsin Indianhead Technical
    College A
Wisconsin Lutheran College B

Wyoming
Central Wyoming College A
Eastern Wyoming College A
Laramie County Community
    College A
Northwest College A
Sheridan College C
University of Wyoming C

Early childhood special education

Arizona
Prescott College B, T
Tohono O'odham Community
    College A

Arkansas
Harding University B, M, T
Henderson State University M

California
College of the Siskiyous A
Mills College M, T
National University M
University of San Diego T

Florida
University of Miami M

Georgia
Georgia State University D, T
South Georgia College A

Illinois
University of Illinois
    Urbana-Champaign B, M, T

Indiana
Purdue University B

Iowa
Upper Iowa University T

Louisiana
Dillard University B
Southeastern Louisiana University M
University of Louisiana at Lafayette B

Maine
University of Maine
    Farmington B, T

Massachusetts
Lesley University B, M

Minnesota
Saint Cloud State University M

Missouri
Lindenwood University B

New Jersey
Felician College B
Georgian Court University T

New York
Adelphi University M, T
Canisius College B, M, T
City University of New York
    Queens College M
Hofstra University M, T
Roberts Wesleyan College B
St. John's University M, T
St. Joseph's College: Suffolk
    Campus M
State University of New York
    College at Brockport M
    New Paltz B, M, T
University of Rochester M

North Carolina
Surry Community College A

North Dakota
University of North Dakota M

Ohio
University of Akron B, M
University of Findlay B, M, T

Oregon
Portland State University D

Pennsylvania
Juniata College B, T
La Salle University B, M, T

Puerto Rico
Inter American University of Puerto
    Rico
    Guayama Campus B, M

Tennessee
Union University B, T

Texas
Del Mar College A
Texas Christian University B, M

Utah
Salt Lake Community College A

Vermont
University of Vermont B, T

Virginia
Radford University T

Washington
Eastern Washington University B
University of Washington Tacoma T

Wisconsin
Edgewood College B
University of Wisconsin
    Superior M

East Asian languages

Arizona
Arizona State University B, M, D

California
University of California
    Irvine M, D
    Los Angeles B, M, D
University of Southern
    California B, M, D

Colorado
University of Colorado
    Boulder M

Connecticut
Wesleyan University B
Yale University M, D

Illinois
Northwestern University B
University of Chicago B, D
University of Illinois
    Urbana-Champaign B

Indiana
Indiana University
    Bloomington B
Purdue University B

Iowa
Grinnell College B

Kansas
University of Kansas B, M

Massachusetts
Northeastern University B
Smith College B

Michigan
Michigan State University B
University of Michigan M, D

Missouri
University of Missouri
    Columbia B

New York
Columbia University B
Cornell University M, D

North Carolina
Duke University B

Oregon
University of Oregon M, D

Pennsylvania
University of Pennsylvania B, M, D

Texas
University of Texas
    Austin B, M, D

Virginia
Washington and Lee University B

Washington
University of Washington B

Wisconsin
Beloit College B
Lawrence University B

East Asian studies

Arizona
University of Arizona B, M, D

California
Stanford University B, M
University of California
    Davis B
    Irvine B
    Los Angeles B, M
University of Southern
    California B, M

Connecticut
Connecticut College B
University of Bridgeport B
Wesleyan University B
Yale University B, M

Florida
Eckerd College B

Georgia
Emory University B

Illinois
DePaul University B
North Central College B
University of Chicago B, D
University of Illinois
    Urbana-Champaign B, D

Indiana
DePauw University B
Indiana University
    Bloomington B, M
Valparaiso University B

Maine
Bates College B
Colby College B

Maryland
Johns Hopkins University B

Massachusetts
Bard College at Simon's Rock B
Boston University B
Brandeis University B
Hampshire College B
Harvard College B, M, D
Simmons College B

Tufts University *B, M*
Wellesley College *B*

Michigan
Oakland University *B*
University of Michigan *B, M*
Wayne State University *B*

Minnesota
Augsburg College *B*
Hamline University *B*
Minnesota State University
   Moorhead *B*
University of Minnesota
   Twin Cities *B, M*

Missouri
University of Missouri
   Columbia *B*
Washington University in St.
   Louis *B, M*

New Jersey
Princeton University *B, M, D*
Rutgers, The State University of New
   Jersey
    New Brunswick/Piscataway
     Campus *B*

New York
City University of New York
   Queens College *B*
Columbia University *B*
Columbia University
   School of General Studies *B*
New York University *B, M, D*
St. John's University *M*
State University of New York
   Albany *B*
   Binghamton *B*
United States Military Academy *B*

Ohio
College of Wooster *B*
Denison University *B*
Miami University
   Oxford Campus *B*
Oberlin College *B*
Ohio State University
   Columbus Campus *B, M*
Ohio Wesleyan University *B*
Wittenberg University *B*

Oregon
Lewis & Clark College *B*
Portland State University *B*

Pennsylvania
Bryn Mawr College *B*
Bucknell University *B*
Dickinson College *B*
Gettysburg College *B*
Haverford College *B, T*
Penn State
   Abington *B*
   Altoona *B*
   Beaver *B*
   Berks *B*
   Brandywine *B*
   DuBois *B*
   Erie, The Behrend College *B*
   Fayette, The Eberly Campus *B*
   Greater Allegheny *B*
   Hazleton *B*
   Lehigh Valley *B*
   Mont Alto *B*
   New Kensington *B*
   Schuylkill *B*
   Shenango *B*
   University Park *B*
   Wilkes-Barre *B*

Worthington Scranton *B*
   York *B*
University of Pennsylvania *B, M, D*
University of Pittsburgh *M*
Ursinus College *B*

Rhode Island
Brown University *B*

Tennessee
Vanderbilt University *B*

Vermont
Marlboro College *B*
Middlebury College *B*

Virginia
Emory & Henry College *B*
University of Virginia *M*
Washington and Lee University *B*

Washington
University of Washington *M*
Western Washington University *B*

Wisconsin
Lawrence University *B*

Ecology

Alabama
Tuskegee University *B, M*

Arizona
Northern Arizona University *B*
Prescott College *B, M*
University of Arizona *B, M, D*

California
California State University
   Chico *B*
   Dominguez Hills *B*
   Fresno *B*
   Stanislaus *M*
Gavilan College *A*
Irvine Valley College *A*
Orange Coast College *A*
San Diego State University *M, D*
San Francisco State University *B, M*
University of California
   Davis *M, D*
   Irvine *B, M, D*
   Los Angeles *B*
   San Diego *B*
   Santa Barbara *B, M, D*
   Santa Cruz *B*

Colorado
Colorado State University *M, D*
Fort Lewis College *B*
University of Denver *B*

Connecticut
University of Connecticut *B, M, D*
University of New Haven *B, M*

Florida
Florida Institute of Technology *B, M*

Georgia
University of Georgia *B, M, D*

Idaho
Idaho State University *B*
Northwest Nazarene University *B*

Illinois
Northwestern University *B*
University of Chicago *D*

Indiana
Indiana University
   Bloomington *M, D*

Iowa
Cornell College *B*
Iowa State University *M, D*
University of Dubuque *B*
University of Northern Iowa *B, M*

Kentucky
Eastern Kentucky University *B*
Georgetown College *B*
Midway College *M*

Louisiana
Tulane University *B, M, D*

Maine
College of the Atlantic *B, M*
Unity College *B*
University of Maine *B, M, D*
University of Maine
   Machias *B*

Maryland
Frostburg State University *M*
Towson University *B, M*
University of Maryland
   College Park *B, M, D*
   Eastern Shore *B*

Massachusetts
Bard College at Simon's Rock *B*
Boston University *B*
Salem State College *B*
Tufts University *B, M*

Michigan
Michigan Technological University *M*
Northern Michigan University *B*
University of Michigan *B, M, D*
University of Michigan
   Dearborn *B*
   Flint *B*

Minnesota
Minnesota State University
   Mankato *B, M, T*
Saint Cloud State University *B, M*
Southwest Minnesota State
   University *B*
University of Minnesota
   Twin Cities *B, M, D*

Missouri
Missouri Southern State University *B*
Washington University in St.
   Louis *B, D*

Montana
University of Montana *M, D*

Nebraska
Western Nebraska Community
   College *A*

Nevada
Sierra Nevada College *B*

New Hampshire
Dartmouth College *B*

New Jersey
Princeton University *B, M, D*
Rutgers, The State University of New
   Jersey
    New Brunswick/Piscataway
     Campus *M, D*

New Mexico
New Mexico State University *B*

New York
Columbia University *B*
Concordia College *B*
Cornell University *B, M, D*
Le Moyne College *B*
Long Island University
   C. W. Post Campus *M*
Molloy College *B*
State University of New York
   Buffalo *M, D*
   College at Plattsburgh *B*
   Purchase *B*
   Stony Brook *D*
University of Rochester *B*

North Carolina
Appalachian State University *B*
Brevard College *B*
Gardner-Webb University *B*
Methodist University *A, B*
University of North Carolina
   Chapel Hill *M, D*

Ohio
Kent State University *M, D*
Ohio State University
   Columbus Campus *B, M, D*
University of Akron *B*

Oklahoma
Oklahoma State University *M, D*

Pennsylvania
East Stroudsburg University of
   Pennsylvania *B*
Juniata College *B*
Lycoming College *B*
Penn State
   University Park *M, D*
Susquehanna University *B*
University of Pittsburgh *B*
Westminster College *B*

South Dakota
Northern State University *B*

Tennessee
University of Tennessee
   Knoxville *M, D*

Texas
Angelo State University *B*
Rice University *B, M, D*
Texas State University: San Marcos *M*

Utah
Utah State University *B, M, D*

Vermont
Bennington College *B*
Marlboro College *B*
Sterling College *B*

Virginia
Averett University *B*
Old Dominion University *D*

Washington
University of Washington *B, M, D*
Western Washington University *B*

West Virginia
New River Community and Technical
   College *A*

Wisconsin
University of Wisconsin
   Superior *B*

Wyoming

University of Wyoming *D*
Western Wyoming Community
College *A*

Econometrics/ quantitative economics

California

Scripps College *B*
University of California
Irvine *B*
University of San Francisco *M*

Colorado

Colorado College *B*

Illinois

Triton College *A*

Iowa

University of Northern Iowa *B*

Maine

Bowdoin College *B*
Colby College *B*

Maryland

United States Naval Academy *B*

Minnesota

Saint Cloud State University *B*
University of Minnesota
Twin Cities *B*
University of St. Thomas *B*

New York

Hofstra University *B*
Ithaca College *B*
State University of New York
Oswego *B*

North Carolina

Wake Forest University *B*

Ohio

Baldwin-Wallace College *B*
University of Dayton *B*
Youngstown State University *B*

Pennsylvania

Bucknell University *B*
Lafayette College *B*
Lycoming College *B*

Rhode Island

University of Rhode Island *B*

Texas

Southern Methodist University *B*

Utah

University of Utah *M*

Virginia

Hampden-Sydney College *B*

Economics

Alabama

Auburn University *B*
Birmingham-Southern College *B*
Jacksonville State University *B*
Talladega College *B*
Tuskegee University *B*

Alaska

University of Alaska
Anchorage *B*

Fairbanks *B*

Arizona

Arizona State University *B, D*
Cochise College *A*
Northern Arizona University *B*
University of Arizona *B, M, D*

Arkansas

Arkansas State University *B*
Arkansas Tech University *B*
Black River Technical College *A*
Harding University *B*
Hendrix College *B*
Lyon College *B*
University of Arkansas *B, M, D*
University of Arkansas
Little Rock *B*
University of Central Arkansas *B*

California

Bakersfield College *A*
Cabrillo College *A*
California Institute of Technology *B*
California Lutheran University *B*
California Polytechnic State
University: San Luis Obispo *B, M*
California State Polytechnic
University: Pomona *B, M*
California State University
Bakersfield *B*
Chico *B*
East Bay *B, M*
Fresno *B, M*
Fullerton *B, M*
Long Beach *B, M*
Los Angeles *B, M*
Northridge *B*
Sacramento *B, M*
San Bernardino *B*
San Marcos *B*
Stanislaus *B*
California State University: Channel
Islands *B*
Cerritos College *A*
Chaffey College *A*
Claremont McKenna College *B*
College of Alameda *A*
College of the Desert *A*
Copper Mountain College *A*
Crafton Hills College *A*
Cypress College *A*
De Anza College *A*
East Los Angeles College *A*
El Camino College *A*
Foothill College *A*
Fullerton College *A*
Gavilan College *A*
Glendale Community College *A*
Golden West College *A*
Grossmont College *A*
Humboldt State University *B*
Irvine Valley College *A*
La Sierra University *B*
Los Angeles Valley College *A*
Loyola Marymount University *B*
Mills College *B*
MiraCosta College *A*
Monterey Peninsula College *A*
National University *B*
Occidental College *B*
Orange Coast College *A*
Oxnard College *A*
Palomar College *C, A*
Pepperdine University *B*
Pitzer College *B*
Pomona College *B*
Saddleback College *A*
St. Mary's College of California *B*
San Diego State University *B, M*
San Francisco State University *B, M*
San Jose State University *B, M*
Santa Ana College *A*
Santa Barbara City College *A*

Santa Clara University *B*
Santa Rosa Junior College *A*
Santiago Canyon College *A*
Scripps College *B*
Sonoma State University *B*
Southwestern College *A*
Stanford University *B, M, D*
University of California
Berkeley *B, D*
Davis *B, M, D*
Irvine *B, M, D*
Los Angeles *B, M, D*
Riverside *B, M, D*
San Diego *B, D*
Santa Barbara *B, M, D*
Santa Cruz *B, M*
University of California: Merced *B*
University of La Verne *B*
University of Redlands *B*
University of San Diego *B*
University of San Francisco *B, M*
University of Southern
California *B, M, D*
University of the Pacific *B*
West Los Angeles College *C, A*
Westmont College *B*

Colorado

Adams State College *B*
Colorado College *B*
Colorado School of Mines *B, M, D*
Colorado State University *B, M, D*
Fort Lewis College *B*
Metropolitan State College of
Denver *B, T*
Regis University *B*
United States Air Force Academy *B*
University of Colorado
Boulder *B, D*
Colorado Springs *B*
Denver *B, M*
University of Denver *B, M*
University of Northern Colorado *B*
Western State College of Colorado *B*

Connecticut

Albertus Magnus College *B*
Central Connecticut State
University *B*
Connecticut College *B*
Eastern Connecticut State
University *B*
Fairfield University *B*
Quinnipiac University *B*
Sacred Heart University *B*
Trinity College *B, M*
University of Connecticut *B, M, D*
University of Hartford *B*
Wesleyan University *B, M*
Western Connecticut State
University *B*
Yale University *B, M, D*

Delaware

Goldey-Beacom College *B*
University of Delaware *B*
Wesley College *B*

District of Columbia

American University *B, M, D*
Catholic University of America *B*
Gallaudet University *B*
George Washington
University *B, M, D*
Georgetown University *B, D*
Howard University *C, B, M, D*
Trinity Washington University *B*
University of the District of
Columbia *B*

Florida

Ave Maria University *B*
Broward College *A*

Daytona State College *A*
Eckerd College *B*
Flagler College *B*
Florida Agricultural and Mechanical
University *B*
Florida Atlantic University *B, M*
Florida International
University *B, M, D*
Florida Southern College *B*
Florida State University *B, M, D*
Gulf Coast Community College *A*
Indian River State College *A*
Jacksonville University *B*
Miami Dade College *A*
New College of Florida *B*
Nova Southeastern University *B*
Rollins College *B*
State College of Florida,
Manatee-Sarasota *A*
Stetson University *B*
University of Central Florida *B, D*
University of Florida *B, M, D*
University of Miami *B*
University of North Florida *B*
University of South Florida *B*
University of Tampa *A, B*

Georgia

Agnes Scott College *B*
Armstrong Atlantic State University *B*
Berry College *B*
Dalton State College *A*
Darton College *A*
Emory University *B, D*
Fort Valley State University *B*
Georgia Southern University *B*
Georgia State University *B, M, D*
Mercer University *B*
Middle Georgia College *A*
Morehouse College *B*
Oglethorpe University *B*
Spelman College *B*
University of Georgia *B*
University of West Georgia *B*
Wesleyan College *B*

Hawaii

Hawaii Pacific University *B*
University of Hawaii
Hilo *B*
Manoa *B, M, D*
West Oahu *B*

Idaho

Boise State University *B, T*
Brigham Young University-Idaho *B*
College of Idaho *B*
Idaho State University *B*
University of Idaho *B, M*

Illinois

Augustana College *B*
Benedictine University *B*
Black Hawk College: East Campus *A*
Bradley University *B*
Chicago State University *B*
DePaul University *B, M*
Dominican University *B*
Eastern Illinois University *B, M*
Elmhurst College *B*
Illinois College *B*
Illinois State University *B, M*
Illinois Wesleyan University *B*
John A. Logan College *A*
John Wood Community College *A*
Kishwaukee College *A*
Knox College *B*
Lake Forest College *B*
Lake Land College *A*
Lewis University *B*
Lincoln College *A*
McKendree University *B*
Monmouth College *B*

National-Louis University *B*
North Central College *B*
Northeastern Illinois University *B*
Northern Illinois University *B, M, D*
Northwestern University *B, M, D*
Olivet Nazarene University *B*
Principia College *B*
Richland Community College *A*
Rockford College *B*
Roosevelt University *B, M*
South Suburban College of Cook
    County *A*
Southern Illinois University
    Carbondale *B, M, D*
Southern Illinois University
    Edwardsville *B, M*
Southwestern Illinois College *A*
Triton College *A*
University of Chicago *B, D*
University of Illinois
    Chicago *B, M, D*
    Springfield *B*
    Urbana-Champaign *B, M, D*
Western Illinois University *B, M*
Wheaton College *B*

Indiana

Ball State University *B, T*
Butler University *B*
DePauw University *B*
Earlham College *B*
Franklin College *B*
Hanover College *B*
Indiana State University *B*
Indiana University
    Bloomington *B, M, D*
    Northwest *B*
    South Bend *B*
    Southeast *B*
Indiana University-Purdue University
    Fort Wayne *B*
Indiana University-Purdue University
    Indianapolis *B, M*
Indiana Wesleyan University *A, B*
Manchester College *B*
Marian University *B*
Purdue University *M, D*
Rose-Hulman Institute of
    Technology *B*
Saint Joseph's College *B*
Saint Mary's College *B*
Taylor University *B*
University of Evansville *B*
University of Indianapolis *B*
University of Notre Dame *B, M, D*
University of Southern Indiana *B, T*
Valparaiso University *B*
Vincennes University *A*
Wabash College *B*

Iowa

Central College *B, T*
Coe College *B*
Cornell College *B, T*
Drake University *B*
Graceland University *B, T*
Grinnell College *B*
Iowa State University *B, M, D*
Loras College *B*
Luther College *B*
Northwestern College *B*
St. Ambrose University *B, T*
Simpson College *B*
University of Iowa *B, D, T*
University of Northern Iowa *B*
Wartburg College *B, T*

Kansas

Allen County Community College *A*
Baker University *B*
Barton County Community College *A*
Benedictine College *B*
Bethany College *B*
Butler Community College *A*

Central Christian College of Kansas *A*
Coffeyville Community College *A*
Dodge City Community College *A*
Emporia State University *B, T*
Fort Hays State University *B*
Kansas State University *B, M, D*
Seward County Community College *A*
University of Kansas *B, M, D*
Washburn University *B*
Wichita State University *B, M*

Kentucky

Bellarmine University *B*
Berea College *B*
Campbellsville University *B*
Centre College *B*
Eastern Kentucky University *B*
Georgetown College *B*
Murray State University *B, M, T*
Thomas More College *A, B*
Transylvania University *B*
University of Kentucky *B, M, D*
University of Louisville *B*
Western Kentucky University *B*

Louisiana

Centenary College of Louisiana *B*
Dillard University *B*
Louisiana College *B*
Louisiana State University and
    Agricultural and Mechanical
    College *B, M, D*
Loyola University New Orleans *B*
Tulane University *B, M*

Maine

Bates College *B*
Bowdoin College *B*
Colby College *B*
University of Maine *B, M*
University of Southern Maine *B*

Maryland

Allegany College of Maryland *A*
College of Notre Dame of Maryland *B*
Frederick Community College *A*
Frostburg State University *B*
Goucher College *B*
Hood College *B*
Johns Hopkins University *B, D*
Loyola University Maryland *B*
McDaniel College *B*
Morgan State University *B, M*
Mount St. Mary's University *B*
St. Mary's College of Maryland *B*
Salisbury University *B*
Towson University *B*
United States Naval Academy *B*
University of Maryland
    Baltimore County *B, M*
    College Park *B, M, D*
Washington College *B*

Massachusetts

American International College *B*
Amherst College *B*
Assumption College *B*
Boston College *B, M, D*
Boston University *B, M, D*
Brandeis University *B, D*
Bridgewater State College *B*
Clark University *B, M, D*
College of the Holy Cross *B*
Fitchburg State College *B*
Framingham State College *B*
Gordon College *B*
Hampshire College *B*
Harvard College *B, M, D*
Massachusetts Institute of
    Technology *B, M, D*
Merrimack College *B*
Mount Holyoke College *B*
Nichols College *B*

Northeastern University *B, M, D*
Salem State College *B*
Simmons College *B*
Smith College *B*
Stonehill College *B*
Suffolk University *B, M, D*
Tufts University *B, M*
University of Massachusetts
    Amherst *B, M, D*
    Boston *B*
    Dartmouth *B*
    Lowell *B*
Wellesley College *B*
Western New England College *B*
Westfield State College *B*
Wheaton College *B*
Williams College *B, M*
Worcester Polytechnic Institute *B*
Worcester State College *B*

Michigan

Adrian College *A, B, T*
Albion College *B*
Alma College *B, T*
Andrews University *B*
Aquinas College *B, T*
Calvin College *B*
Central Michigan University *B, M*
Delta College *A*
Eastern Michigan University *B, M*
Grand Rapids Community College *A*
Grand Valley State University *B*
Hillsdale College *B*
Hope College *B*
Kalamazoo College *B*
Michigan State University *B, M, D*
Michigan Technological University *B*
Northern Michigan University *B*
Oakland University *B*
Saginaw Valley State University *B*
University of Detroit Mercy *B, M*
University of Michigan *B, M, D*
University of Michigan
    Dearborn *B*
    Flint *B*
Wayne State University *B, M, D*
Western Michigan University *B*

Minnesota

Augsburg College *B*
Bemidji State University *B*
Bethel University *B*
Carleton College *B*
College of St. Benedict *B*
Concordia College: Moorhead *B*
Gustavus Adolphus College *B*
Hamline University *B*
Macalester College *B*
Metropolitan State University *B*
Minnesota State University
    Mankato *B*
    Moorhead *B*
Minnesota West Community and
    Technical College *A*
Ridgewater College *A*
St. Catherine University *B*
Saint Cloud State University *B*
St. John's University *B*
St. Olaf College *B*
University of Minnesota
    Duluth *B*
    Morris *B*
    Twin Cities *B, M, D*
University of St. Thomas *B*
Winona State University *B*

Mississippi

Alcorn State University *B*
Millsaps College *B*
Mississippi State University *B*
Tougaloo College *B*
University of Mississippi *B, M, D*

Missouri

Drury University *B*
Missouri State University *B*
Missouri Valley College *B*
Missouri Western State University *B*
Northwest Missouri State
    University *B*
Park University *B*
Rockhurst University *B*
St. Charles Community College *A*
Saint Louis University *B*
Southeast Missouri State University *B*
Three Rivers Community College *A*
Truman State University *B*
University of Central Missouri *B, M*
University of Missouri
    Columbia *B, M, D*
    Kansas City *B, M, D*
    Missouri University of Science and
        Technology *B, T*
    St. Louis *B, M*
Washington University in St.
    Louis *B, M, D*
Webster University *B*
Westminster College *B*

Montana

Miles Community College *A*
Montana State University
    Bozeman *B, M*
Rocky Mountain College *B*
University of Montana *B, M*

Nebraska

Creighton University *B*
Doane College *B*
Nebraska Wesleyan University *B*
University of Nebraska
    Kearney *B*
    Lincoln *B, M, D*
Western Nebraska Community
    College *A*

Nevada

Nevada State College *B*

New Hampshire

Dartmouth College *B*
Keene State College *B*
Saint Anselm College *B*
Southern New Hampshire
    University *B*
University of New Hampshire *B, M, D*

New Jersey

Bergen Community College *A*
The College of New Jersey *B*
College of St. Elizabeth *B*
Drew University *B*
Fairleigh Dickinson University
    College at Florham *B*
    Metropolitan Campus *B*
Kean University *B, T*
Montclair State University *B*
New Jersey City University *B*
Princeton University *B, M, D*
Ramapo College of New Jersey *B*
Richard Stockton College of New
    Jersey *B*
Rider University *B*
Rowan University *B*
Rutgers, The State University of New
    Jersey
    Camden Regional Campus *B*
    New Brunswick/Piscataway
        Campus *B, M, D*
    Newark Regional Campus *B*
Saint Peter's College *B*
Seton Hall University *B*
Thomas Edison State College *B*
William Paterson University of New
    Jersey *B*

New Mexico

New Mexico State University *B, M*
University of New Mexico *B, M, D*

New York

Adelphi University *B*
Alfred University *B*
Bard College *B*
Barnard College *B*
Canisius College *B*
City University of New York
  Baruch College *B, M*
  Brooklyn College *B, M*
  City College *B, M*
  College of Staten Island *B*
  Hunter College *B, M*
  John Jay College of Criminal
    Justice *B*
  Lehman College *B*
  Queens College *B, T*
  York College *B*
Colgate University *B*
College of Mount St. Vincent *B*
College of New Rochelle *B*
Columbia University *B*
Columbia University
  School of General Studies *B*
Cornell University *B, M, D*
Dominican College of Blauvelt *B*
Dowling College *B*
Elmira College *B*
Eugene Lang College The New School
  for Liberal Arts *B*
Excelsior College *B*
Fordham University *B, M, D*
Hamilton College *B*
Hartwick College *B*
Hobart and William Smith Colleges *B*
Hofstra University *B*
Iona College *B*
Ithaca College *B*
Le Moyne College *B*
Long Island University
  Brooklyn Campus *B*
  C. W. Post Campus *B*
Manhattan College *B*
Manhattanville College *B*
Marist College *B*
Nazareth College *B*
New York University *B, M, D*
Pace University *B*
Rensselaer Polytechnic
  Institute *B, M, D*
Rochester Institute of Technology *B*
St. Francis College *B*
St. John Fisher College *B*
St. John's University *B*
St. Joseph's College: Suffolk
  Campus *B*
St. Lawrence University *B*
Siena College *B, T*
Skidmore College *B*
State University of New York
  Albany *B, M, D*
  Binghamton *B, M, D*
  Buffalo *B, M, D*
  College at Buffalo *B, M*
  College at Cortland *B*
  College at Fredonia *B*
  College at Geneseo *B*
  College at Oneonta *B*
  College at Plattsburgh *B*
  College at Potsdam *B*
  Empire State College *A, B*
  New Paltz *B*
  Oswego *B*
  Purchase *B*
  Stony Brook *B, M, D*
Suffolk County Community College *A*
Syracuse University *B, M, D*
Touro College *B*
Union College *B*
United States Military Academy *B*
University of Rochester *B, M, D*

Utica College *B*
Vassar College *B*
Wagner College *B*
Wells College *B*
Yeshiva University *B*

North Carolina

Appalachian State University *B*
Belmont Abbey College *B*
Campbell University *B*
Davidson College *B*
Duke University *B, M, D*
East Carolina University *B*
Elon University *B*
Guilford College *B*
Johnson C. Smith University *B*
Lenoir-Rhyne University *B, T*
Meredith College *B*
North Carolina State University *M, D*
Pfeiffer University *B*
Salem College *B*
University of North Carolina
  Asheville *B, T*
  Chapel Hill *B, M, D*
  Charlotte *B*
  Greensboro *B*
  Wilmington *B*
Wake Forest University *B*
Warren Wilson College *B*

North Dakota

Minot State University *B*
North Dakota State University *B*
University of North Dakota *B*

Ohio

Ashland University *B*
Baldwin-Wallace College *B*
Bluffton University *B*
Bowling Green State University *B, M*
Capital University *B*
Case Western Reserve University *B*
Central State University *B*
Cleveland State University *B, M*
College of Wooster *B*
Denison University *B*
Franciscan University of
  Steubenville *B*
Heidelberg University *B*
Hiram College *B, T*
John Carroll University *B*
Kent State University *D*
Kenyon College *B*
Marietta College *B*
Miami University
  Oxford Campus *B, M*
Mount Union College *B*
Muskingum University *B*
Notre Dame College *T*
Oberlin College *B*
Ohio Dominican University *B*
Ohio State University
  Columbus Campus *B, M, D*
Ohio University *B, M*
Ohio Wesleyan University *B*
Otterbein College *B*
University of Akron *B, M*
University of Cincinnati *C, B, M, D, T*
University of Cincinnati
  Raymond Walters College *A*
University of Dayton *B*
University of Findlay *B*
University of Rio Grande *B*
University of Toledo *B, M*
Wilberforce University *B*
Wilmington College *B*
Wittenberg University *B*
Wright State University *B, M*
Xavier University *B*
Youngstown State University *B, M*

Oklahoma

Langston University *B*

Oklahoma City University *B*
Oklahoma State University *B*
Tulsa Community College *A*
University of Central Oklahoma *B, M*
University of Oklahoma *B, M, D*
University of Science and Arts of
  Oklahoma *B*
University of Tulsa *B*

Oregon

Central Oregon Community
  College *A*
Chemeketa Community College *A*
George Fox University *B*
Lewis & Clark College *B*
Linfield College *B*
Linn-Benton Community College *A*
Mt. Hood Community College *A*
Oregon State University *B, M, D*
Pacific University *B*
Portland State University *B, M, D*
Reed College *B*
Southern Oregon University *B*
University of Oregon *B, M, D*
Western Oregon University *B*
Willamette University *B*

Pennsylvania

Albright College *B*
Allegheny College *B*
Bloomsburg University of
  Pennsylvania *B*
Bryn Mawr College *B*
Bucknell University *B*
Carnegie Mellon University *B, M, D*
Chatham University *B*
Cheyney University of Pennsylvania *B*
Clarion University of Pennsylvania *B*
Dickinson College *B*
Duquesne University *B*
East Stroudsburg University of
  Pennsylvania *B*
Edinboro University of
  Pennsylvania *B*
Elizabethtown College *B*
Franklin & Marshall College *B*
Gettysburg College *B*
Grove City College *B*
Haverford College *B, T*
Holy Family University *B*
Immaculata University *A, B*
Indiana University of Pennsylvania *B*
King's College *B*
La Salle University *B*
Lafayette College *B*
Lebanon Valley College *B*
Lincoln University *B*
Lock Haven University of
  Pennsylvania *B*
Lycoming College *B*
Mansfield University of
  Pennsylvania *B, T*
Messiah College *B*
Millersville University of
  Pennsylvania *B*
Moravian College *B*
Muhlenberg College *C, B*
Penn State
  Abington *B*
  Altoona *B*
  Beaver *B*
  Berks *B*
  Brandywine *B*
  DuBois *B*
  Erie, The Behrend College *B*
  Fayette, The Eberly Campus *B*
  Greater Allegheny *B*
  Hazleton *B*
  Lehigh Valley *B*
  Mont Alto *B*
  New Kensington *B*
  Schuylkill *B*
  Shenango *B*
  University Park *B, M, D*

Wilkes-Barre *B*
Worthington Scranton *B*
York *B*
Robert Morris University *B*
Rosemont College *B*
St. Francis University *B*
Saint Joseph's University *B*
St. Vincent College *B*
Seton Hill University *B*
Shippensburg University of
  Pennsylvania *B, T*
Slippery Rock University of
  Pennsylvania *B*
Susquehanna University *B*
Swarthmore College *B*
Temple University *B, M, D*
University of Pennsylvania *B, M, D*
University of Pittsburgh *B, M, D*
University of Pittsburgh
  Bradford *B*
  Johnstown *B*
University of Scranton *B*
Ursinus College *B*
Villanova University *B*
Washington & Jefferson College *B*
Westminster College *B*
Widener University *B*
Wilson College *B*
York College of Pennsylvania *B*

Puerto Rico

University of Puerto Rico
  Aguadilla *A*
  Cayey University College *B*
  Rio Piedras *B, M*

Rhode Island

Brown University *B, M, D*
Bryant University *B*
Providence College *B*
Rhode Island College *B*
Roger Williams University *B*
Salve Regina University *B*
University of Rhode Island *B*

South Carolina

Benedict College *B*
Charleston Southern University *B*
Clemson University *B, M*
College of Charleston *B*
Converse College *B*
Francis Marion University *B*
Furman University *B*
Presbyterian College *B*
University of South Carolina *B, M, D*
Wofford College *B*

South Dakota

Augustana College *B, T*
Northern State University *B*
South Dakota State University *B, M*
University of South Dakota *B*

Tennessee

Belmont University *B*
Carson-Newman College *B*
Columbia State Community College *A*
East Tennessee State University *B, T*
King College *B*
Maryville College *B, T*
Middle Tennessee State
  University *B, M, D*
Rhodes College *B*
Tennessee Technological University *B*
Union University *B, T*
University of Memphis *B, M*
University of Tennessee
  Chattanooga *B*
  Knoxville *B*
University of the South *B*
Vanderbilt University *B, M, D*

Texas

Austin College *B*
Austin Community College *A*
Brazosport College *A*
Cisco College *A*
Clarendon College *A*
College of the Mainland *A*
Galveston College *A*
Hardin-Simmons University *B*
Houston Baptist University *B*
Lamar University *B*
Laredo Community College *A*
Lon Morris College *A*
Midland College *A*
Midwestern State University *B*
Northwest Vista College *A*
Palo Alto College *A*
Rice University *B, M, D*
St. Edward's University *B*
St. Mary's University *B*
St. Philip's College *A*
Southern Methodist
    University *B, M, D*
Southwestern University *B*
Stephen F. Austin State University *B*
Tarleton State University *B, T*
Texas A&M University *B, M, D*
Texas A&M University
    Commerce *B, M*
    Corpus Christi *B*
Texas Christian University *B*
Texas Lutheran University *B*
Texas Southern University *B*
Texas State University: San
    Marcos *B, T*
Texas Tech University *B, M, D*
Trinity University *B*
University of Dallas *B*
University of Houston *B, M, D*
University of North Texas *B, M*
University of Texas
    Arlington *B, M*
    Austin *B, M, D*
    Dallas *B, M, D*
    Pan American *B*
    San Antonio *M*
West Texas A&M University *B*
Western Texas College *A*

Utah

Brigham Young University *B*
Salt Lake Community College *A*
Snow College *A*
Southern Utah University *B*
University of Utah *B, M, D, T*
Utah State University *B, M, D*
Utah Valley University *B*
Weber State University *B*
Westminster College *B*

Vermont

Marlboro College *B*
Middlebury College *B*
Norwich University *B*
St. Michael's College *B*
University of Vermont *B*

Virginia

Bridgewater College *B*
College of William and Mary *B*
Eastern Mennonite University *B*
Emory & Henry College *B*
George Mason University *B, M, D*
Hampden-Sydney College *B*
Hollins University *B*
James Madison University *B*
Longwood University *B*
Lynchburg College *B*
Mary Baldwin College *B*
Marymount University *B*
Old Dominion University *B, M*
Radford University *B*
Randolph College *B*

Randolph-Macon College *B*
Roanoke College *B, T*
Sweet Briar College *B*
University of Mary Washington *B*
University of Richmond *B, M*
University of Virginia *B, M, D*
University of Virginia's College at
    Wise *B, T*
Virginia Military Institute *B*
Virginia Polytechnic Institute and
    State University *B, M, D*
Washington and Lee University *B*

Washington

Centralia College *A*
Eastern Washington University *B*
Everett Community College *A*
Gonzaga University *B*
Highline Community College *A*
Olympic College *A*
Pacific Lutheran University *B*
Seattle Pacific University *B*
Seattle University *B*
University of Puget Sound *B*
University of Washington *B, M, D*
Washington State University *B, D*
Western Washington University *B*
Whitman College *B*
Whitworth University *B*

West Virginia

Bethany College *B*
Davis and Elkins College *B*
Marshall University *B*
Potomac State College of West
    Virginia University *A*
Shepherd University *B*
West Virginia State University *B*
West Virginia University *B*
West Virginia Wesleyan College *B*

Wisconsin

Beloit College *B*
Carthage College *B, T*
Concordia University Wisconsin *B*
Edgewood College *B*
Lawrence University *B*
Marquette University *B, M*
Ripon College *B*
St. Norbert College *B, T*
University of Wisconsin
    Eau Claire *B*
    Green Bay *B, T*
    La Crosse *B, T*
    Madison *B, M, D*
    Milwaukee *B, M, D*
    Oshkosh *B*
    Parkside *B, T*
    Platteville *B*
    River Falls *B, T*
    Stevens Point *B, T*
    Superior *B*
    Whitewater *B, T*

Wyoming

Casper College *A*
Eastern Wyoming College *A*
Laramie County Community
    College *A*
Western Wyoming Community
    College *A*

Education, general

Alabama

Alabama Agricultural and Mechanical
    University *B, M*
Athens State University *B*
Auburn University *M*
Birmingham-Southern College *B*
Bishop State Community College *A*
Calhoun Community College *A*

Central Alabama Community
    College *A*
Gadsden State Community College *A*
Jacksonville State University *T*
Shelton State Community College *A*
Troy University *M, T*
Tuskegee University *B, T*
University of Alabama
    Birmingham *D, T*
University of Montevallo *M, T*
Wallace State Community College at
    Hanceville *A*

Alaska

University of Alaska
    Fairbanks *M, T*
    Southeast *M*

Arizona

Arizona State University *D*
Arizona Western College *A*
Central Arizona College *A*
Coconino County Community
    College *A*
College of the Humanities and
    Sciences *M, D*
Dine College *A*
Estrella Mountain Community
    College *A*
Grand Canyon University *B, M*
Mohave Community College *A*
Northern Arizona University *B*
Northland Pioneer College *A*
Phoenix College *A*
Pima Community College *A*
Prescott College *B, M, D, T*
University of Arizona *M, D*

Arkansas

Central Baptist College *A*
Crowley's Ridge College *A*
Harding University *M*
Ozarka College *A*
Phillips Community College of the
    University of Arkansas *A*
Rich Mountain Community College *A*
South Arkansas Community College *A*
University of Arkansas *M*
University of Central Arkansas *M*
Williams Baptist College *B*

California

Alliant International University *M, D*
American Jewish University *M*
Antioch Southern California
    Antioch University Santa
    Barbara *M, T*
Azusa Pacific University *M, D*
Barstow Community College *A*
Bethany University *M*
Biola University *B, M, T*
Butte College *A*
California Baptist University *B, M*
California Coast University *M*
California Lutheran University *B, M*
California Polytechnic State
    University: San Luis Obispo *M*
California State Polytechnic
    University: Pomona *M*
California State University
    Bakersfield *M, T*
    Chico *M*
    Dominguez Hills *M*
    East Bay *M*
    Fresno *B, M*
    Los Angeles *M*
    Monterey Bay *M*
    Sacramento *B, M*
    San Bernardino *M*
    San Marcos *M*
    Stanislaus *M*
California State University: Channel
    Islands *M*

Chaffey College *A*
Chapman University *B, M*
College of the Siskiyous *A*
Cypress College *A*
Dominican University of California *M*
Holy Names University *M*
Humboldt State University *M*
Humphreys College *A, B, M*
John F. Kennedy University *M*
Laney College *A*
Lassen Community College *A*
Los Angeles Southwest College *A*
Loyola Marymount University *M*
The Master's College *B, M*
Merritt College *A*
Napa Valley College *A*
National Hispanic University *T*
National University *M, T*
Notre Dame de Namur
    University *M, T*
Pacific Union College *M*
Patten University *M*
Pepperdine University *B, M*
Point Loma Nazarene University *M*
Porterville College *A*
St. Mary's College of California *M*
San Diego Christian College *B*
San Diego State University *M, D, T*
San Francisco State University *M*
Santa Rosa Junior College *A*
Simpson University *T*
Sonoma State University *M*
Southwestern College *A*
Stanford University *M, D*
Taft College *A*
University of California
    Berkeley *M, D, T*
    Davis *M, D, T*
    Irvine *M, D, T*
    Los Angeles *M, D*
    Riverside *M, D, T*
    Santa Barbara *M, D*
    Santa Cruz *M, D*
University of La Verne *B, M, T*
University of Redlands *M, T*
University of Southern
    California *M, D*
University of the Pacific *B*
Vanguard University of Southern
    California *M, T*
Westmont College *B*
Whittier College *B, M, T*

Colorado

Adams State College *B, M, T*
Aspen University *M, D*
Colorado Christian University *B*
Colorado Mountain College *A*
Colorado State University *B, T*
Colorado State University
    Pueblo *M*
Jones International University *M*
Lamar Community College *A*
Mesa State College *M*
Morgan Community College *A*
Otero Junior College *A*
Regis University *B, M, T*
Trinidad State Junior College *A*

Connecticut

Albertus Magnus College *B, T*
Fairfield University *M*
Sacred Heart University *M*
Saint Joseph College *M*
Southern Connecticut State
    University *B, T*
Trinity College *B, T*
University of Connecticut *M, T*
University of New Haven *M*
Western Connecticut State
    University *M*

Delaware

Delaware State University *B, M, D*

University of Delaware *B, T*
Wesley College *B, M*
Wilmington University *D*

District of Columbia
American University *M, D*
Catholic University of America *B, M*
Gallaudet University *B*
Howard University *M, D*
Trinity Washington University *M*

Florida
Bethune-Cookman University *B*
Broward College *A*
Chipola College *A*
Daytona State College *A*
Edward Waters College *B*
Florida Atlantic University *B*
Florida Gulf Coast University *B, M*
Florida National College *A*
Florida Southern College *B, M*
Indian River State College *A*
Jacksonville University *B, M, T*
Northwest Florida State College *A*
Nova Southeastern University *M*
Palm Beach Atlantic University *B*
Pensacola Junior College *A*
Polk State College *A*
Rollins College *B, M, T*
State College of Florida,
    Manatee-Sarasota *A*
Stetson University *M*
University of Central Florida *M, D*
University of Miami *B, M*
University of South Florida *B, M, D*

Georgia
Abraham Baldwin Agricultural
    College *A*
Andrew College *A*
Bainbridge College *A*
Brewton-Parker College *B*
Clark Atlanta University *B*
College of Coastal Georgia *A*
Dalton State College *A*
East Georgia College *A*
Emory University *B, M, D*
Gainesville State College *A, B*
Georgia Gwinnett College *B*
Georgia Highlands College *A*
Georgia Military College *A*
Georgia Perimeter College *A*
Georgia Southern University *T*
Georgia State University *D*
Macon State College *A*
Morehouse College *B*
Reinhardt College *A*
South Georgia College *A*
University of Georgia *M*
Waycross College *A*
Young Harris College *A*

Hawaii
University of Hawaii
    Hilo *T*
    Manoa *D*

Idaho
Boise State University *B, M*
College of Idaho *M, T*
Idaho State University *M*
North Idaho College *A*
Northwest Nazarene University *B, M*
University of Idaho *B, M, D, T*

Illinois
Augustana College *B*
Aurora University *M*
Chicago State University *B*
City Colleges of Chicago
    Kennedy-King College *A*
Columbia College Chicago *M*
Concordia University Chicago *B, T*

Danville Area Community College *A*
DePaul University *M*
Dominican University *M*
Elgin Community College *A*
Elmhurst College *B*
Eureka College *B*
Governors State University *M*
Illinois Valley Community College *A*
Illinois Wesleyan University *B*
John Wood Community College *A*
Judson University *M*
Kankakee Community College *A*
Kishwaukee College *A*
Knox College *B*
Lake Forest College *B*
Lake Land College *A*
Lewis University *B*
Lewis and Clark Community
    College *A*
Lincoln College *A*
McKendree University *B, M*
Monmouth College *B, T*
Moody Bible Institute *B*
National-Louis University *M*
North Central College *B*
North Park University *M*
Northern Illinois University *B*
Northwestern University *B*
Olivet Nazarene University *M*
Quincy University *M, T*
Richland Community College *A*
Rockford College *B, M*
Saint Xavier University *B, M*
South Suburban College of Cook
    County *A*
Southeastern Illinois College *A*
Trinity Christian College *B, T*
Trinity International University *D*
Triton College *A*
University of Chicago *M, D*
University of Illinois
    Urbana-Champaign *M, D*

Indiana
Anderson University *B*
Butler University *M*
Calumet College of St. Joseph *B, T*
Earlham College *M*
Goshen College *B*
Huntington University *B, M*
Indiana University
    Bloomington *B, M, D, T*
    East *M*
    Southeast *B, T*
Ivy Tech Community College
    Bloomington *A*
    Central Indiana *A*
    Columbus *A*
    East Central *A*
    Kokomo *A*
    Lafayette *A*
    North Central *A*
    Northeast *A*
    Northwest *A*
    Richmond *A*
    South Central *A*
    Southeast *A*
    Southwest *A*
    Wabash Valley *A*
Manchester College *B, T*
Purdue University *B, M, D, T*
Purdue University
    Calumet *B, T*
St. Mary-of-the-Woods College *B, M*
University of Evansville *B*
University of Indianapolis *B*
Valparaiso University *M*

Iowa
Briar Cliff University *B, M*
Coe College *B, M*
Cornell College *B, T*
Dordt College *B*
Drake University *D*

Ellsworth Community College *A*
Graceland University *M*
Iowa State University *B, M, D*
Iowa Wesleyan College *B*
Iowa Western Community College *A*
Kaplan University
    Davenport *M*
Loras College *B, M*
Marshalltown Community College *A*
North Iowa Area Community
    College *A*
Northwestern College *B, T*
St. Ambrose University *B, M, T*
Simpson College *B, M*
Southwestern Community College *A*
University of Dubuque *M*
University of Northern Iowa *M, D*
Upper Iowa University *B*

Kansas
Barton County Community College *A*
Bethany College *B, T*
Central Christian College of Kansas *A*
Coffeyville Community College *A*
Cowley County Community
    College *A*
Dodge City Community College *A*
Fort Scott Community College *A*
Friends University *M*
Garden City Community College *A*
Highland Community College *A*
Hutchinson Community College *A*
Labette Community College *A*
McPherson College *B, T*
MidAmerica Nazarene University *M*
Neosho County Community
    College *A*
Newman University *B*
Pratt Community College *A*
Seward County Community College *A*
Southwestern College *B, M*
Tabor College *B*
University of St. Mary *M*
Washburn University *B*

Kentucky
Berea College *B*
Campbellsville University *A, B*
Eastern Kentucky University *D*
Madisonville Community College *A*
Morehead State University *M*
Northern Kentucky University *M*
Owensboro Community and
    Technical College *A*
Somerset Community College *A*
Spalding University *B, M, T*
Western Kentucky University *M*

Louisiana
Baton Rouge Community College *A*
Louisiana College *B, M*
Louisiana State University
    Alexandria *B*
    Shreveport *M*
Louisiana State University and
    Agricultural and Mechanical
    College *M*
Northwestern State University *M*
Nunez Community College *A*
Our Lady of Holy Cross College *M*
Xavier University of Louisiana *B*

Maine
Thomas College *M*
Unity College *B*
University of Maine *B, M*
University of Maine
    Farmington *M*
    Fort Kent *B*
    Presque Isle *B*
University of New England *B, M*

Maryland
Anne Arundel Community College *A*
Baltimore City Community College *A*
Carroll Community College *A*
Cecil College *A*
Chesapeake College *A*
College of Notre Dame of
    Maryland *M, D*
College of Southern Maryland *A*
Community College of Baltimore
    County *A*
Frederick Community College *A*
Frostburg State University *M*
Garrett College *A*
Hagerstown Community College *A*
Harford Community College *A*
McDaniel College *M, T*
Montgomery College *A*
St. Mary's College of Maryland *M*
Salisbury University *M*
Towson University *M*
University of Maryland
    Baltimore County *M, T*
    College Park *M*
Washington Adventist University *B*
Washington Bible College *B, T*
Washington College *B*
Wor-Wic Community College *A*

Massachusetts
Boston University *B, M, D, T*
Brandeis University *B*
Bunker Hill Community College *A*
Cambridge College *M*
Cape Cod Community College *A*
Clark University *M*
Curry College *B*
Eastern Nazarene College *B, M, T*
Elms College *B, M*
Fitchburg State College *B, M, T*
Hampshire College *B*
Harvard College *M, D*
Lesley University *B, M, D*
Massachusetts College of Liberal
    Arts *B, M, T*
Mount Holyoke College *B*
Salem State College *B, M*
Simmons College *B, M, D*
Smith College *B, M*
Springfield College *M*
Suffolk University *B, M*
Tufts University *B*
University of Massachusetts
    Amherst *M, D*
    Boston *D*
Western New England College *T*
Westfield State College *M*
Worcester State College *M, T*

Michigan
Adrian College *B*
Alma College *B*
Alpena Community College *A*
Aquinas College *B, M*
Baker College
    of Auburn Hills *B*
Calvin College *B, M, T*
Central Michigan University *M*
Cornerstone University *M*
Eastern Michigan University *T*
Gogebic Community College *A*
Grand Valley State University *M, T*
Hillsdale College *B*
Kalamazoo Valley Community
    College *A*
Lansing Community College *A*
Marygrove College *B*
Michigan State University *B, M*
Northwestern Michigan College *A*
Rochester College *B*
St. Clair County Community
    College *A*
Schoolcraft College *A*
Spring Arbor University *M*

University of Detroit Mercy *B, M*
University of Michigan *M, D*
University of Michigan
   Dearborn *B, M, D, T*
   Flint *B, M*
West Shore Community College *A*

Minnesota

Augsburg College *B*
Bemidji State University *B, M*
Bethel University *B, M, T*
Capella University *M, D*
College of St. Benedict *B*
Gustavus Adolphus College *B*
Hamline University *B, M, D*
Inver Hills Community College *A*
Itasca Community College *A*
Macalester College *B*
Martin Luther College *M*
Mesabi Range Community and
   Technical College *A*
Minnesota State University
   Mankato *B, M*
Minnesota West Community and
   Technical College *A*
Normandale Community College *A*
Northland Community & Technical
   College *A*
Ridgewater College *A*
St. Catherine University *B*
St. John's University *B*
St. Mary's University of
   Minnesota *M, D*
Southwest Minnesota State
   University *M*
University of Minnesota
   Duluth *M*
   Twin Cities *M, D*
Vermilion Community College *A*
Walden University *M, D*
White Earth Tribal and Community
   College *A*
Winona State University *B, M, T*

Mississippi

Belhaven University *M*
Delta State University *D*
East Central Community College *A*
Millsaps College *T*
Mississippi Delta Community
   College *A*
Mississippi Gulf Coast Community
   College *A*
Mississippi State University *D*
Northwest Mississippi Community
   College *A*
University of Mississippi *D*
University of Southern Mississippi *D*

Missouri

Central Methodist University *M, T*
Culver-Stockton College *B*
Drury University *B, M*
East Central College *A*
Evangel University *A*
Fontbonne University *M, T*
Hannibal-LaGrange College *B*
Maryville University of Saint
   Louis *M, T*
Metropolitan Community College:
   Blue River *A*
Metropolitan Community College:
   Longview *A*
Metropolitan Community College:
   Maple Woods *A*
Metropolitan Community College:
   Penn Valley *A*
Missouri Southern State University *B*
North Central Missouri College *A*
Park University *M*
Rockhurst University *M*
St. Charles Community College *A*
St. Louis Christian College *B*

St. Louis Community College
   St. Louis Community College at
      Meramec *A*
Saint Louis University *M*
Southwest Baptist University *M*
State Fair Community College *A*
Stephens College *B*
Three Rivers Community College *A*
University of Missouri
   Columbia *B*
   Kansas City *B, M, D*
   Missouri University of Science and
      Technology *T*
   St. Louis *B, M, D*
Washington University in St.
   Louis *B, M, D, T*
Webster University *B, M, T*
William Woods University *B, T*

Montana

Fort Peck Community College *A*
Miles Community College *A*
Montana State University
   Billings *B, M, T*
   Bozeman *M, D*
Rocky Mountain College *B, T*
University of Montana *B, M, D*
University of Montana:
   Western *A, B, T*

Nebraska

Concordia University *B, M, T*
Dana College *B*
Grace University *A*
Little Priest Tribal College *A*
Peru State College *B, M, T*
Union College *B*
University of Nebraska
   Kearney *B, M, T*
Western Nebraska Community
   College *A*
York College *B, T*

Nevada

Nevada State College *B*

New Hampshire

Franklin Pierce University *B*
Lebanon College *A*
NHTI-Concord's Community
   College *A*
Rivier College *A, B, M, T*
Southern New Hampshire
   University *B, M*

New Jersey

Bergen Community College *A*
Bloomfield College *B*
Brookdale Community College *A*
Centenary College *B*
College of St. Elizabeth *M*
Essex County College *A*
Felician College *M*
Georgian Court University *M*
Gloucester County College *A*
Middlesex County College *A*
Monmouth University *B, M*
Montclair State University *M, D*
Raritan Valley Community College *A*
Richard Stockton College of New
   Jersey *T*
Rowan University *B, M*
Rutgers, The State University of New
   Jersey
   New Brunswick/Piscataway
      Campus *M, D*
Saint Peter's College *M*
Salem Community College *A*
Seton Hall University *M*
Warren County Community College *A*
William Paterson University of New
   Jersey *B, M*

New Mexico

Clovis Community College *A*
College of Santa Fe *M*
Dona Ana Community College of New
   Mexico State University *A*
Eastern New Mexico University *M*
Eastern New Mexico University:
   Roswell Campus *A*
Mesalands Community College *A*
New Mexico Junior College *A*
New Mexico State University *B, M, D*
New Mexico State University
   Alamogordo *A*
   Carlsbad *A*
   Grants *A*
Santa Fe Community College *A*
Western New Mexico University *B, M*

New York

Adelphi University *M*
Barnard College *T*
Canisius College *M*
City University of New York
   Brooklyn College *B*
   Hunter College *B, M, T*
   Queens College *T*
Colgate University *B, M*
College of New Rochelle *B, M, T*
Columbia University *B*
Concordia College *B, T*
Cornell University *B, M, D*
D'Youville College *D, T*
Dominican College of Blauvelt *B*
Dowling College *B*
Eugene Lang College The New School
   for Liberal Arts *B*
Fordham University *T*
Hofstra University *D*
Houghton College *B*
Jewish Theological Seminary of
   America *M, D*
Le Moyne College *M*
Manhattan College *B*
Manhattanville College *B, M*
Medaille College *B, M, T*
Metropolitan College of New
   York *A, B*
Molloy College *B, M, T*
Nazareth College *M, T*
New York Institute of Technology *A*
New York University *M, T*
Niagara University *B, M, T*
Orange County Community College *A*
St. John Fisher College *B, M*
St. Joseph's College *B*
St. Joseph's College: Suffolk
   Campus *B, T*
St. Lawrence University *M*
St. Thomas Aquinas College *B, M, T*
Siena College *T*
State University of New York
   Binghamton *M, D*
   Buffalo *M*
   College at Brockport *B, M, T*
   College at Buffalo *B*
   College at Fredonia *B, M, T*
   Empire State College *A, B, M*
   Oswego *M*
Touro College *M*
University of Rochester *M, D*
Villa Maria College of Buffalo *A*
Wagner College *B, M*
Yeshiva University *D*

North Carolina

Beaufort County Community
   College *A*
Belmont Abbey College *B*
Bladen Community College *A*
Brevard College *B*
Campbell University *A, B, M, T*
Cape Fear Community College *A*
Carteret Community College *A*

Central Carolina Community
   College *A*
Chowan University *B*
College of the Albemarle *A*
East Carolina University *M*
Elon University *B*
Fayetteville Technical Community
   College *A*
Gardner-Webb University *B, M*
Greensboro College *B, T*
Guilford Technical Community
   College *A*
Lenoir Community College *A*
Mars Hill College *B, T*
Martin Community College *A*
Mayland Community College *A*
McDowell Technical Community
   College *A*
Methodist University *A, B*
Montreat College *A*
Mount Olive College *A*
Nash Community College *A*
North Carolina Agricultural and
   Technical State University *B, T*
North Carolina State University *B*
Pamlico Community College *A*
Queens University of Charlotte *B, M*
Sampson Community College *A*
South Piedmont Community
   College *A*
Southwestern Community College *A*
University of North Carolina
   Asheville *T*
   Chapel Hill *M, D*
Vance-Granville Community
   College *A*
Warren Wilson College *B, T*
Western Carolina University *M*
Wingate University *D*

North Dakota

Dakota College at Bottineau *A*
Minot State University *A*
United Tribes Technical College *A, T*
University of North Dakota *M*

Ohio

Antioch University McGregor *B, M*
Baldwin-Wallace College *B, M*
Bluffton University *B, M*
Bowling Green State University *B, M*
Cedarville University *M*
Clark State Community College *A*
Cleveland State University *B, D*
College of Mount St. Joseph *M, T*
Defiance College *B, M, T*
Denison University *B*
Edison State Community College *A*
Heidelberg University *M*
Hiram College *B*
Kent State University *B, M*
Lourdes College *M*
Marietta College *B, M*
Mount Vernon Nazarene University *B*
Muskingum University *M*
Northwest State Community
   College *A*
Ohio Christian University *B*
Ohio Northern University *B*
Ohio State University
   Columbus Campus *M, D*
   Lima Campus *B, M, T*
   Newark Campus *B, M, T*
Ohio Wesleyan University *B*
Otterbein College *B*
Owens Community College
   Toledo *A*
Shawnee State University *B*
Temple Baptist College *B*
Terra State Community College *A*
Tiffin University *B, M*
Union Institute & University *B, M*
University of Cincinnati
   Raymond Walters College *A*

University of Findlay *B, M*
University of Rio Grande *B, M, T*
University of Toledo *B*
Urbana University *B*
Walsh University *M*
Washington State Community
College *A*
Wilmington College *B*
Wittenberg University *B, M*
Wright State University *M*
Xavier University *B*
Youngstown State University *B, M*

Oklahoma

Cameron University *B, M, T*
Connors State College *A*
Langston University *B*
Northeastern State University *T*
Northwestern Oklahoma State
University *B, M*
Oklahoma City Community College *A*
Oklahoma City University *B, M*
Oklahoma State University *B, D*
Oklahoma State University
Institute of Technology:
Okmulgee *A*
Oral Roberts University *M*
Redlands Community College *A*
St. Gregory's University *A, B*
Seminole State College *A*
Southern Nazarene University *B*
Southwestern Oklahoma State
University *M, T*
Tulsa Community College *A*
University of Central Oklahoma *B, M*
University of Oklahoma *B*
University of Tulsa *M, T*
Western Oklahoma State College *A*

Oregon

Central Oregon Community
College *A*
Concordia University *B, M, T*
Corban College *B*
Eastern Oregon University *M*
George Fox University *M*
Lewis & Clark College *M*
Linfield College *T*
Linn-Benton Community College *A*
Oregon State University *M, D*
Pacific University *B, M, T*
Portland State University *M*
Southern Oregon University *B, M, T*
Umpqua Community College *A*
University of Oregon *B*
University of Portland *M*
Warner Pacific College *M, T*
Western Oregon University *B, M*

Pennsylvania

Allegheny College *B*
Alvernia University *B*
Arcadia University *B, M*
Bryn Athyn College of the New
Church *B*
Bucknell University *B, M*
Bucks County Community College *A*
Butler County Community College *A*
Cabrini College *B, M*
California University of
Pennsylvania *B*
Chatham University *M*
Community College of Philadelphia *A*
Duquesne University *B*
Geneva College *B*
Holy Family University *M, T*
Indiana University of Pennsylvania *T*
Juniata College *B, T*
Keystone College *A*
La Salle University *B, M, T*
Lackawanna College *A*
Lehigh Carbon Community College *A*
Luzerne County Community
College *A*

Mansfield University of
Pennsylvania *M*
Misericordia University *M*
Moravian College *M*
Neumann University *M, D, T*
Pennsylvania Highlands Community
College *A*
Philadelphia Biblical University *M*
Reading Area Community College *A*
St. Francis University *B, M*
Saint Joseph's University *M*
St. Vincent College *T*
Swarthmore College *B*
University of Pennsylvania *B, M, D*
University of Pittsburgh *M, D*
University of Pittsburgh
Bradford *B*
Villanova University *M*
Washington & Jefferson College *B*
Westminster College *B, M*
Widener University *M, D*

Puerto Rico

American University of Puerto Rico *B*
Caribbean University *M*
Inter American University of Puerto
Rico
Fajardo Campus *B, M*
San German Campus *B*
University of Puerto Rico
Aguadilla *T*
Arecibo *B*
Carolina Regional College *T*
Ponce *A*
University of the Sacred Heart *B*

Rhode Island

Brown University *B, M, T*
Johnson & Wales University:
Providence *D, T*
Rhode Island College *M, D*
University of Rhode Island *M, D*

South Carolina

Anderson University *M*
Claflin University *M*
Coker College *B*
Converse College *B, T*
Furman University *B*
Newberry College *B*
Northeastern Technical College *A*
Southern Wesleyan University *M*
University of South Carolina *D*
University of South Carolina
Aiken *B*

South Dakota

Dakota Wesleyan University *B, T*
Kilian Community College *A*
Northern State University *B*
Oglala Lakota College *A*
Sinte Gleska University *A, B, M*

Tennessee

American Baptist College *B*
Austin Peay State University *M*
Belmont University *B, M*
Bethel University *M*
Bryan College *B*
Chattanooga State Community
College *A*
Cleveland State Community College *A*
Crichton College *B, T*
Cumberland University *B, M*
Dyersburg State Community
College *A*
Jackson State Community College *A*
Lambuth University *B*
Lee University *B, M*
Lincoln Memorial University *B, T*
Maryville College *B, T*
Milligan College *B, M*
Motlow State Community College *A*

Roane State Community College *A*
Southwest Tennessee Community
College *A*
Tennessee State University *B*
Tennessee Technological University *B*
Tusculum College *M*
Union University *B, M, T*
University of Memphis *T*
University of Tennessee
Knoxville *M, D*
Vanderbilt University *B*
Walters State Community College *A*

Texas

Abilene Christian University *M*
Amarillo College *A*
Angelina College *A*
Arlington Baptist College *B*
Baylor University *B, M*
Brazosport College *A*
Central Texas College *A*
Cisco College *A*
Clarendon College *A*
Coastal Bend College *A*
Concordia University Texas *M*
Dallas Baptist University *B, M, T*
Dallas Christian College *B, T*
East Texas Baptist University *B*
Frank Phillips College *A*
Grayson County College *A*
Hill College *A*
Howard College *A*
Howard Payne University *B*
Huston-Tillotson University *B*
Jarvis Christian College *B*
Kilgore College *A*
Lamar State College at Orange *A*
Laredo Community College *A*
Lon Morris College *A*
Navarro College *A*
Northwest Vista College *A*
Odessa College *A*
Our Lady of the Lake University of San
Antonio *M*
Palo Alto College *A*
Panola College *A*
Paris Junior College *A*
St. Edward's University *M*
St. Mary's University *B*
St. Philip's College *A*
Schreiner University *B*
South Plains College *A*
Southern Methodist University *M*
Southwest Texas Junior College *A*
Southwestern Assemblies of God
University *A*
Southwestern University *B, T*
Texas A&M University
Commerce *M, D*
Kingsville *B, M*
Texarkana *M*
Texas State University: San
Marcos *M, D, T*
Texas Wesleyan University *B, T*
Texas Woman's University *M*
Trinity Valley Community College *A*
Tyler Junior College *A*
University of Dallas *B, T*
University of Houston
Clear Lake *B, M, T*
Victoria *B*
University of St. Thomas *B, M*
University of Texas
Arlington *M, T*
El Paso *B*
San Antonio *M*
University of the Incarnate
Word *M, D*
West Texas A&M University *M*
Western Texas College *A*

Utah

Snow College *A*
Southern Utah University *B, M*

University of Utah *B, M*
Utah Valley University *M*
Westminster College *B, M*

Vermont

Bennington College *B, M*
Castleton State College *M, T*
Champlain College *B*
College of St. Joseph in Vermont *M*
Community College of Vermont *A*
Goddard College *B, M*
Johnson State College *B, M*
Lyndon State College *B, M*
Norwich University *M*
University of Vermont *B, M, T*

Virginia

Bluefield College *B, T*
Central Virginia Community
College *A*
Christopher Newport University *M*
Eastern Mennonite University *T*
Eastern Shore Community College *A*
Ferrum College *B*
George Mason University *D*
Germanna Community College *A*
Hampton University *B*
Hollins University *M, T*
James Madison University *M, T*
Longwood University *B, T*
Lord Fairfax Community College *A*
Mary Baldwin College *M, T*
Mountain Empire Community
College *A*
New River Community College *A*
Norfolk State University *M*
Old Dominion University *D*
Paul D. Camp Community College *A*
Piedmont Virginia Community
College *A*
Radford University *M*
Randolph College *M*
Rappahannock Community College *A*
Regent University *B, M, D*
Shenandoah University *M*
Southside Virginia Community
College *A*
Southwest Virginia Community
College *A*
Tidewater Community College *A*
University of Mary Washington *M*
University of Richmond *T*
University of Virginia *M, D*
Virginia Commonwealth
University *M, D*
Virginia Highlands Community
College *A*
Virginia Intermont College *B*
Virginia Western Community
College *A*
Wytheville Community College *A*

Washington

Centralia College *A*
Everett Community College *A*
Evergreen State College *B*
Gonzaga University *M*
Highline Community College *A*
North Seattle Community College *A*
Northwest University *M*
Olympic College *A*
Spokane Falls Community College *A*
University of Washington *M, D, T*
University of Washington
Bothell *B, M*
University of Washington
Tacoma *M, T*
Walla Walla University *B*
Washington State
University *B, M, D, T*
Whatcom Community College *A*
Whitworth University *B, M, T*
Yakima Valley Community College *A*

West Virginia

American Public University System *M*
Bethany College *B*
Concord University *B, M, T*
Fairmont State University *B*
Marshall University *M, D*
New River Community and Technical
College *A*
Ohio Valley University *B*
Potomac State College of West
Virginia University *A*
Salem International University *B, M*
University of Charleston *B*
West Liberty University *M*
West Virginia State University *B*
West Virginia University *D*
West Virginia Wesleyan College *B*

Wisconsin

Alverno College *B, M, T*
Beloit College *B*
Cardinal Stritch University *B, M*
Carroll University *B, M*
Concordia University Wisconsin *B*
Edgewood College *M*
Lakeland College *M*
Maranatha Baptist Bible College *B*
Marquette University *M, D*
Mount Mary College *B, M, T*
Ripon College *B*
St. Norbert College *M, T*
Silver Lake College *M*
University of Wisconsin
Green Bay *M*
La Crosse *M*
Madison *M, D*
Milwaukee *B*
Platteville *M*
Stevens Point *M*
Stout *M*
Superior *M*
Whitewater *B, M, T*
Viterbo University *M, T*
Wisconsin Lutheran College *B*

Wyoming

Laramie County Community
College *A*
Northwest College *A*
University of Wyoming *M, D*
Western Wyoming Community
College *A*

Education of autistic

Arizona

Prescott College *M*

Illinois

University of Illinois
Urbana-Champaign *M*

Kansas

University of Kansas *M, D*

Massachusetts

Emerson College *B, M*

Michigan

Central Michigan University *M*
Madonna University *M, T*

Minnesota

University of St. Thomas *M*

Ohio

Youngstown State University *B, M*

Puerto Rico

Bayamon Central University *M*

Wisconsin

University of Wisconsin
Whitewater *T*

Education of blind/
visually handicapped

Arizona

Prescott College *T*

California

San Francisco State University *T*

Florida

Florida State University *M, T*

Georgia

Georgia State University *D, T*

Illinois

University of Illinois
Urbana-Champaign *M*

Iowa

University of Northern Iowa *M*

Massachusetts

Boston College *M*

Michigan

Eastern Michigan University *B, M*
Western Michigan University *M, T*

New Jersey

The College of New Jersey *M, T*

New York

City University of New York
Hunter College *M, T*
Dominican College of Blauvelt *M, T*
St. Francis College *B*

North Carolina

North Carolina Central University *M*

North Dakota

University of North Dakota *M*

Ohio

Ohio State University
Columbus Campus *M, D*
University of Toledo *T*

Oklahoma

Northeastern State University *T*

Oregon

Portland State University *T*

Pennsylvania

Kutztown University of
Pennsylvania *B, T*
University of Pittsburgh *T*

West Virginia

West Virginia University *T*

Wisconsin

Silver Lake College *T*

Education of brain
injured

Illinois

University of Illinois
Urbana-Champaign *M*

Louisiana

Dillard University *B*

Education of Deaf/
hearing impaired

Arizona

Prescott College *T*

California

California State University
Northridge *M*
San Francisco State University *T*

District of Columbia

Gallaudet University *B, M, D*

Florida

Daytona State College *A*
Flagler College *B, T*
Hillsborough Community College *A*

Georgia

Georgia State University *T*
Valdosta State University *B, M*

Idaho

Idaho State University *M*

Illinois

MacMurray College *B, T*
University of Illinois
Urbana-Champaign *M, D*

Kansas

University of Kansas *M, D*

Kentucky

Eastern Kentucky University *B*

Maryland

McDaniel College *M*

Massachusetts

Boston College *M*
Boston University *B, M, T*
Elms College *B, M, T*
Emerson College *B, M*
Smith College *M*

Michigan

Calvin College *B, T*
Eastern Michigan University *B, M*
Grand Valley State University *M, T*
Michigan State University *B*

Mississippi

University of Southern Mississippi *B*

Missouri

Fontbonne University *B, M, T*
Washington University in St. Louis *M*

Nebraska

University of Nebraska
Lincoln *B*

Nevada

College of Southern Nevada *A*

New Jersey

The College of New Jersey *B, M, T*
William Paterson University of New
Jersey *M*

New York

Adelphi University *M*
Canisius College *M*

City University of New York
Hunter College *M, T*
Ithaca College *B, M, T*
Marymount Manhattan College *T*
Nazareth College *T*
Rochester Institute of Technology *M*

North Carolina

Barton College *B*
Lenoir-Rhyne University *B, T*
University of North Carolina
Greensboro *B*

North Dakota

Minot State University *B*

Ohio

Bowling Green State University *B, T*
Cincinnati State Technical and
Community College *A*
Ohio State University
Columbus Campus *M, D*
University of Cincinnati *M, D*
University of Toledo *T*

Oklahoma

University of Science and Arts of
Oklahoma *B, T*
University of Tulsa *B, T*

Oregon

Lewis & Clark College *M*
Western Oregon University *M, T*

Pennsylvania

Bloomsburg University of
Pennsylvania *M*
Indiana University of Pennsylvania *B*
Rosemont College *T*
University of Pittsburgh *T*

South Carolina

Converse College *B, T*

South Dakota

Augustana College *B, M, T*

Tennessee

Lambuth University *B, T*
Tennessee Temple University *B*
University of Tennessee
Knoxville *B, T*
Vanderbilt University *M*

Texas

Lamar University *B, M, D*
Texas Christian University *B*
Texas Woman's University *M*

Virginia

Hampton University *M*
Longwood University *M*
Radford University *T*

Wisconsin

University of Wisconsin
Milwaukee *T*

Education of
developmentally
delayed

Illinois

University of Illinois
Urbana-Champaign *M*

Iowa

Upper Iowa University *T*

Kansas
Tabor College *B*

New Jersey
William Paterson University of New
    Jersey *T*

New York
College of New Rochelle *M, T*
St. Joseph's College: Suffolk
    Campus *M*
State University of New York
    College at Brockport *B, M*

Ohio
University of Findlay *B, M, T*

Pennsylvania
La Salle University *B, M, T*

Tennessee
Lambuth University *B, T*

Texas
Del Mar College *A*

Wisconsin
University of Wisconsin
    Superior *M*

Education of emotionally handicapped

Arizona
Prescott College *B, T*

Arkansas
Arkansas State University *M, T*

California
California Lutheran University *M*
California State University
    Northridge *M*
Sonoma State University *M*

District of Columbia
George Washington University *M, D*
Trinity Washington University *M*

Florida
Daytona State College *B*
University of South Florida *B, M*

Georgia
Columbus State University *B, M*
Georgia State University *D, T*

Illinois
Chicago State University *M*
DePaul University *M*
MacMurray College *B, T*
National-Louis University *M*
University of Illinois
    Urbana-Champaign *M, D*

Indiana
University of St. Francis *T*

Iowa
Loras College *B*
Morningside College *M*

Kansas
Tabor College *B*
University of Kansas *M, D*

Michigan
Central Michigan University *B*

Eastern Michigan University *B, M*
Grand Valley State University *M, T*
Hope College *B, T*
Northern Michigan University *B, T*
Saginaw Valley State University *T*
University of Detroit Mercy *B, M*
Western Michigan University *B, T*

Minnesota
Augsburg College *B*
Concordia University: St. Paul *T*
Minnesota State University
    Mankato *M*
University of St. Thomas *M*
Walden University *M*
Winona State University *B, T*

Mississippi
Mississippi State University *T*

Missouri
Harris-Stowe State University *T*

Nebraska
University of Nebraska
    Omaha *M*

New Hampshire
Rivier College *M*

New York
City University of New York
    City College *M, T*
Fordham University *M*
Manhattan College *M*
Nazareth College *T*
New York University *M*
State University of New York
    College at Buffalo *B, M*

North Carolina
Greensboro College *B, T*
North Carolina Central University *M*
North Carolina State University *M, T*
University of North Carolina
    Charlotte *M*
    Wilmington *B*

North Dakota
University of Mary *M*
University of North Dakota *M*

Ohio
University of Cincinnati *M, D*
University of Findlay *B, M, T*
University of Toledo *T*
Walsh University *B*
Wright State University *M*
Youngstown State University *B, M*

Pennsylvania
La Salle University *B, T*
Marywood University *B*

South Carolina
Converse College *T*
Furman University *M, T*

South Dakota
Augustana College *B, T*

Texas
West Texas A&M University *T*

Virginia
Eastern Mennonite University *T*
Longwood University *M*
University of Virginia's College at
    Wise *T*

West Virginia
Fairmont State University *B*

Wisconsin
Silver Lake College *T*
University of Wisconsin
    Oshkosh *B, M, T*

Education of gifted/talented

Alabama
Samford University *M, T*

Arizona
Northcentral University *M, D*

Arkansas
Arkansas State University *M, T*
Arkansas Tech University *M*
University of Arkansas
    Little Rock *M*

California
California State University
    Northridge *M*

Delaware
Delaware State University *B*

Florida
Daytona State College *B*
University of South Florida *M*

Georgia
University of Georgia *D*

Illinois
Chicago State University *M*
Northeastern Illinois University *M*
University of Illinois
    Urbana-Champaign *M, D*

Iowa
University of Northern Iowa *M*

Louisiana
Louisiana State University and
    Agricultural and Mechanical
    College *M*
University of Louisiana at Lafayette *M*

Michigan
Grand Valley State University *M*

Minnesota
Minnesota State University
    Mankato *M*
University of St. Thomas *M*

Mississippi
Mississippi State University *T*
Mississippi University for Women *M*

Missouri
Drury University *M*
Harris-Stowe State University *T*
Maryville University of Saint
    Louis *M, T*
University of Missouri
    Columbia *M, D*

Montana
University of Great Falls *B*

Nebraska
University of Nebraska
    Kearney *M, T*

New Jersey
Montclair State University *M*

New York
Canisius College *M*
College of New Rochelle *M, T*
Hofstra University *T*
Manhattanville College *M, T*
Saint Bonaventure University *M*

North Carolina
Catawba College *B, T*
Elon University *M*
University of North Carolina
    Charlotte *M, T*

Ohio
Ashland University *M, T*
Muskingum University *T*
University of Toledo *D*
Wright State University *M*
Youngstown State University *M*

Oklahoma
Oklahoma City University *M*

Pennsylvania
Chatham University *T*
Millersville University of
    Pennsylvania *M*

South Carolina
Converse College *T*

Texas
Hardin-Simmons University *M, T*
Texas A&M International
    University *M, T*
University of Houston *M, T*
University of Texas
    Arlington *T*
    Pan American *M*

Vermont
Johnson State College *M*

Virginia
College of William and Mary *M*
Liberty University *M, T*

Washington
Whitworth University *M*

West Virginia
Fairmont State University *B*
West Virginia State University *B*
West Virginia University *T*

Wisconsin
Carthage College *M, T*

Education of learning disabled

Arizona
Northern Arizona University *M*
Prescott College *B, M, T*
University of Phoenix *M*

California
California Lutheran University *M*
California State University
    Long Beach *T*
    Northridge *M*
Holy Names University *M, T*
San Jose State University *M*
Sonoma State University *M, T*
University of San Francisco *T*

District of Columbia

American University *M*
Trinity Washington University *M*

Florida

Bethune-Cookman University *B, T*
Florida Atlantic University *D*
Florida State University *M, T*
University of South Florida *B, M*

Georgia

Armstrong Atlantic State
   University *B, M, T*
Augusta State University *M*
Columbus State University *B, M*
Georgia State University *M, D, T*

Illinois

Bradley University *B, M*
Chicago State University *M*
DePaul University *M*
Highland Community College *A*
MacMurray College *B, T*
National-Louis University *M*
Northwestern University *B, M, D*
Rockford College *M, T*
Saint Xavier University *M*
University of Illinois
   Urbana-Champaign *M*

Indiana

Ball State University *M*
University of Indianapolis *T*
University of St. Francis *T*

Iowa

Iowa State University *T*
Northwestern College *T*

Kansas

Bethany College *T*
Tabor College *B*
University of Kansas *M, D*
Washburn University *M*

Massachusetts

Cambridge College *M*

Michigan

Aquinas College *B*
Calvin College *M, T*
Eastern Michigan University *M*
Grand Valley State University *M, T*
Hope College *B, T*
Madonna University *M, T*
Michigan State University *B*
Northern Michigan University *M*
Saginaw Valley State University *M, T*
University of Detroit Mercy *M*

Minnesota

Concordia University: St. Paul *T*
Minnesota State University
   Mankato *M*
University of Minnesota
   Duluth *T*
University of St. Thomas *M*
Walden University *M*
Winona State University *B, M, T*

Mississippi

Mississippi College *M*

Missouri

Harris-Stowe State University *T*
Northwest Missouri State University *T*
University of Missouri
   Columbia *M, D*
William Woods University *T*

Nebraska

University of Nebraska
   Kearney *B, M, T*
   Omaha *M*

New Hampshire

New England College *B, T*
Rivier College *M*

New Jersey

Fairleigh Dickinson University
   Metropolitan Campus *M*
Georgian Court University *M*
Montclair State University *M*
Rowan University *M*
William Paterson University of New
   Jersey *M*

New York

City University of New York
   Hunter College *M, T*
Fordham University *M*
Manhattanville College *M, T*
Nazareth College *T*
State University of New York
   New Paltz *M, T*

North Carolina

Appalachian State University *B, T*
Barton College *B*
East Carolina University *B, M*
Elizabeth City State University *B, T*
Fayetteville State University *M*
Greensboro College *B, T*
North Carolina Central University *M*
North Carolina State University *M, T*
Salem College *M, T*
University of North Carolina
   Charlotte *M*
   Wilmington *B*

North Dakota

Minot State University *M*
University of Mary *M*
University of North Dakota *M*

Ohio

Ashland University *M, T*
Baldwin-Wallace College *B, M, T*
Bowling Green State University *B*
Hiram College *T*
Malone University *B, M*
Muskingum University *T*
Notre Dame College *M, T*
University of Cincinnati *M, D*
University of Findlay *B, M, T*
University of Toledo *T*
Wright State University *B, M, T*
Youngstown State University *B, M*

Oklahoma

Northeastern State University *B*
Northwestern Oklahoma State
   University *B, T*
Oklahoma Baptist University *B, T*
Southwestern Oklahoma State
   University *B*

Oregon

Western Oregon University *M, T*

Pennsylvania

Immaculata University *T*
Lebanon Valley College *T*

South Carolina

Francis Marion University *M*
Furman University *M, T*

South Dakota

Augustana College *B, T*

Texas

West Texas A&M University *T*

Utah

Southern Utah University *B, T*

Vermont

St. Michael's College *M, T*

Virginia

Eastern Mennonite University *T*
Hampton University *M*
Longwood University *M*
Lynchburg College *M*
Marymount University *M*
Radford University *T*
University of Virginia's College at
   Wise *T*
Virginia Wesleyan College *T*

West Virginia

Bethany College *B*
Concord University *B, T*
West Virginia University *T*
West Virginia Wesleyan College *B*

Wisconsin

Silver Lake College *B, T*
University of Wisconsin
   Oshkosh *B, M, T*
   Superior *M*
   Whitewater *B, T*

Education of mentally handicapped

Alabama

Tuskegee University *B, T*

Arizona

Prescott College *B, T*
University of Phoenix *M*

California

California Lutheran University *M*
California State University
   Northridge *M*
San Francisco State University *T*
Sonoma State University *M*

Florida

Florida State University *M, T*
University of South Florida *B, M*
University of West Florida *B*

Georgia

Augusta State University *B*
Brenau University *B*
Columbus State University *B, M*
Georgia State University *D, T*

Illinois

Bradley University *B, T*
Chicago State University *B, M*
University of Illinois
   Urbana-Champaign *M, D*

Indiana

Manchester College *B, T*

Iowa

Iowa State University *T*
Loras College *B*
Morningside College *M*
Northwestern College *T*

Kansas

Tabor College *B*
University of Kansas *M, D*

Michigan

Calvin College *B, T*
Central Michigan University *B*
Eastern Michigan University *B, M*
Grand Valley State University *M, T*
Northern Michigan University *B, T*
University of Detroit Mercy *B, M*
Western Michigan University *B, T*

Minnesota

Minnesota State University
   Mankato *M*
University of St. Thomas *M*
Winona State University *B, T*

Mississippi

Mississippi State University *T*

Missouri

Harris-Stowe State University *T*
Northwest Missouri State University *T*
University of Missouri
   Columbia *M, D*
William Woods University *T*

Nebraska

University of Nebraska
   Kearney *B, M, T*
   Omaha *M*

New Jersey

William Paterson University of New
   Jersey *M*

New York

City University of New York
   City College *M, T*
Fordham University *M*
Manhattan College *M*
Nazareth College *T*
State University of New York
   College at Buffalo *B, M*

North Carolina

Bennett College for Women *B*
East Carolina University *M*
Greensboro College *B, T*
North Carolina Central University *M*
North Carolina State University *M, T*
University of North Carolina
   Charlotte *B, M*
   Wilmington *B*

North Dakota

Minot State University *B*
University of Mary *B*
University of North Dakota *M*

Ohio

Bluffton University *B*
Bowling Green State University *B*
Hiram College *T*
University of Cincinnati *M, D*
University of Findlay *B, M, T*
University of Toledo *T*
Walsh University *B*
Wright State University *B, M*
Youngstown State University *B*

Oklahoma

East Central University *B, T*
Northwestern Oklahoma State
   University *B, T*
Oklahoma Baptist University *B, T*
Southwestern Oklahoma State
   University *B*

Oregon

Western Oregon University *M, T*

Pennsylvania

La Salle University *B, T*
University of Pittsburgh *T*

South Carolina

Converse College *M, T*
Furman University *M, T*

South Dakota

Augustana College *B, T*

Tennessee

Lambuth University *B, T*

Texas

Texas A&M University
Kingsville *M*
Texas Woman's University *M*
West Texas A&M University *T*

Virginia

Eastern Mennonite University *T*
Longwood University *M*
Lynchburg College *M*
Radford University *T*
University of Virginia's College at
Wise *T*

West Virginia

Concord University *B, T*
Fairmont State University *T*
West Liberty University *B*
West Virginia State University *B*
West Virginia University *T*

Wisconsin

Silver Lake College *B, T*
University of Wisconsin
Oshkosh *B, M, T*
Stout *B*

Education of multiple handicapped

California

California State University
Long Beach *T*
San Francisco State University *T*
Sonoma State University *M*

District of Columbia

Gallaudet University *B, M, T*

Georgia

Georgia State University *M, T*

Illinois

Bradley University *T*
National-Louis University *M*
University of Illinois
Urbana-Champaign *B, M, D, T*

Indiana

Ball State University *B, T*

Iowa

Iowa State University *T*
Northwestern College *T*
St. Ambrose University *M, T*

Kansas

Tabor College *B*
University of Kansas *M, D*

Maine

University of Maine *M*

Massachusetts

Boston College *M*
Endicott College *M*

Westfield State College *M, T*

Minnesota

Minnesota State University
Mankato *M*
Winona State University *B, T*

Mississippi

Mississippi State University *T*

Missouri

Missouri Valley College *B, T*
Northwest Missouri State
University *B, M, T*
University of Missouri
Columbia *B*

Nebraska

University of Nebraska
Kearney *B, M, T*

New York

City University of New York
Hunter College *M, T*
Dominican College of Blauvelt *B, M, T*
Hofstra University *T*
Nazareth College *T*
State University of New York
Binghamton *M*
College at Cortland *M*

North Carolina

Greensboro College *B, T*
University of North Carolina
Charlotte *M*
Wilmington *B*

North Dakota

Minot State University *M*

Ohio

Ashland University *M, T*
Bowling Green State University *B*
Muskingum University *T*
Ohio Dominican University *B, T*
Ohio State University
Columbus Campus *M, D*
University of Findlay *B, M, T*
University of Toledo *T*
Walsh University *B*
Wright State University *B, M, T*
Youngstown State University *B*

Oregon

Portland State University *T*
Western Oregon University *M, T*

Tennessee

Lambuth University *B, T*

Virginia

Norfolk State University *M*

West Virginia

Bethany College *B*
West Virginia University *T*

Education of physically handicapped

California

California State University
Northridge *M*
Fresno Pacific University *M, T*
San Francisco State University *T*

Georgia

Georgia State University *D, T*

Illinois

University of Illinois
Urbana-Champaign *M*

Louisiana

Louisiana College *B*

Massachusetts

Springfield College *M, T*

Michigan

Eastern Michigan University *B, M*

Minnesota

Winona State University *B, T*

Nebraska

University of Nebraska
Kearney *B, M, T*

New Jersey

William Paterson University of New
Jersey *M*

New York

City University of New York
Hunter College *T*
State University of New York
College at Buffalo *B, M*

Ohio

Ohio State University
Columbus Campus *M, D*
University of Cincinnati *M, D*
University of Toledo *T*
Wright State University *M*

Oklahoma

East Central University *B, T*

Oregon

Western Oregon University *M, T*

Pennsylvania

Cheyney University of Pennsylvania *T*
Indiana University of Pennsylvania *B*
La Salle University *B, T*
University of Pittsburgh *T*

Puerto Rico

University of Puerto Rico
Bayamon University College *B*

South Dakota

Augustana College *B, T*

Texas

Texas Woman's University *M*
West Texas A&M University *T*

Education of speech impaired

Alabama

Alabama Agricultural and Mechanical
University *B*

Arizona

Prescott College *T*

California

California Baptist University *M*
California State University
Chico *T*
Long Beach *T*
Northridge *B, M*
San Francisco State University *T*
University of Redlands *B, M*
University of San Francisco *M*

Georgia

Armstrong Atlantic State
University *B, M, T*
Georgia State University *M*
South Georgia College *A*

Illinois

University of Illinois
Urbana-Champaign *M, T*

Kentucky

Eastern Kentucky University *B, M*

Louisiana

Louisiana Tech University *B*

Massachusetts

Emerson College *B, M, D*

Michigan

Calvin College *B, T*
Eastern Michigan University *B, M*
Wayne State University *B, T*

Minnesota

Minnesota State University
Mankato *M*

Nebraska

University of Nebraska
Kearney *B, M, T*
Omaha *B, M, T*

New Jersey

Kean University *M*
William Paterson University of New
Jersey *M*

New York

City University of New York
Hunter College *M, T*
College of New Rochelle *M, T*
Elmira College *B, T*
Hofstra University *M, T*
Ithaca College *B, M, T*
Long Island University
Brooklyn Campus *B, T*
Nazareth College *B, M, T*
New York University *B, M*
Pace University *B*
State University of New York
College at Buffalo *B, M*
College at Cortland *B*
College at Fredonia *B, M, T*
College at Geneseo *B, T*
New Paltz *M, T*
Syracuse University *M*

North Dakota

Minot State University *B, M*

Ohio

University of Toledo *B, M, T*

Oregon

Portland State University *T*

Pennsylvania

Indiana University of Pennsylvania *B*
Kutztown University of
Pennsylvania *B*
West Chester University of
Pennsylvania *T*

South Dakota

Augustana College *B, T*

Tennessee

Lambuth University *B, T*

Texas
Our Lady of the Lake University of San
    Antonio *B, M*

Virginia
Hampton University *M*
Longwood University *B, M*
Radford University *T*

West Virginia
West Virginia University *T*

Wisconsin
University of Wisconsin
    River Falls *B, T*
    Whitewater *M*

Educational assessment/testing

Arizona
Prescott College *M*

Arkansas
University of Arkansas *D*

California
California State University
    Northridge *M*
Stanford University *M, D*

Colorado
Jones International University *M*

Connecticut
Fairfield University *M*

Delaware
University of Delaware *M, D*

Illinois
University of Illinois
    Chicago *M*
    Urbana-Champaign *M, D*

Indiana
Indiana University
    Bloomington *D*

Iowa
Iowa State University *M*
University of Iowa *M, D*

Maryland
University of Maryland
    College Park *M, D*

Massachusetts
Tufts University *M*

Michigan
Eastern Michigan University *T*
Michigan State University *D*

New Mexico
University of the Southwest *M*

New York
Fordham University *M, D*
State University of New York
    Albany *M, D*

North Carolina
University of North Carolina
    Greensboro *M, D*

Ohio
Kent State University *M, D*

Ohio State University
    Columbus Campus *M, D*
University of Findlay *B, M*

Pennsylvania
Penn State
    Abington *B*
    Altoona *B*
    Beaver *B*
    Berks *B*
    Brandywine *B*
    DuBois *B*
    Erie, The Behrend College *B, M*
    Fayette, The Eberly Campus *B*
    Greater Allegheny *B*
    Hazleton *B*
    Lehigh Valley *B*
    Mont Alto *B*
    New Kensington *B*
    Schuylkill *B*
    Shenango *B*
    University Park *B*
    Wilkes-Barre *B*
    Worthington Scranton *B*
    York *B*
University of Pennsylvania *M*

Texas
Sul Ross State University *M*
Wayland Baptist University *M*

Utah
Western Governors University *M*

Washington
University of Washington *M, D*
Washington State University *M, D*

Educational evaluation/research

Arkansas
University of Arkansas *D*

Colorado
Jones International University *M*
University of Colorado
    Boulder *D*
    Colorado Springs *D*

Florida
University of Miami *M, D*

Georgia
Georgia State University *D, T*

Illinois
University of Illinois
    Urbana-Champaign *M, D*

Kentucky
University of Kentucky *M, D*

Massachusetts
Boston College *M, D*

Michigan
Michigan State University *D*
Wayne State University *M, D*
Western Michigan University *M, D*

Missouri
University of Missouri
    Columbia *M, D*
    Kansas City *M*

New Jersey
Rowan University *M*

North Carolina
North Carolina State University *D*

North Dakota
North Dakota State University *D*

Ohio
Ohio University *M, D*
University of Findlay *B, M*

Pennsylvania
Penn State
    Beaver *B*
    New Kensington *B*
    Shenango *B*
    University Park *M*

Puerto Rico
University of Puerto Rico
    Rio Piedras *M*

South Carolina
University of South Carolina *M, D*

South Dakota
University of South Dakota *M, D*

Tennessee
Vanderbilt University *M, D*

Texas
Texas Tech University *M, D*

Utah
Brigham Young University *D*

Vermont
Goddard College *M*

Washington
Washington State University *M, D*

Educational leadership/adminstration

Alabama
Alabama Agricultural and Mechanical
    University *M*
Alabama State University *M, D*
Auburn University *M, D, T*
Auburn University at Montgomery *M*
Jacksonville State University *M, T*
Samford University *M, D, T*
Troy University *M, T*
University of Alabama *M, D*
University of Alabama
    Birmingham *M, D, T*
University of Montevallo *M, T*
University of North Alabama *M*
University of South Alabama *M, T*
University of West Alabama *M*

Alaska
University of Alaska
    Anchorage *M*
    Fairbanks *T*

Arizona
Arizona State University *M, D*
Grand Canyon University *D*
Northcentral University *M, D*
Northern Arizona University *M, D*
Prescott College *M, T*
University of Arizona *M, D*
University of Phoenix *M, D*

Arkansas
Arkansas State University *M, D, T*
Arkansas Tech University *M*
Harding University *M, D*

Southern Arkansas University *M*
University of Arkansas *M, D*
University of Arkansas
    Little Rock *M, D*
    Monticello *M*

California
Alliant International
    University *M, D, T*
Azusa Pacific University *M, D*
Bethany University *M*
California Baptist University *M, T*
California Coast University *M, D*
California Lutheran University *M, D*
California State University
    Chico *T*
    Dominguez Hills *M*
    East Bay *M, T*
    Fresno *M, D*
    Fullerton *M, D, T*
    Long Beach *M, D, T*
    Los Angeles *M*
    Northridge *M*
    Sacramento *M, D*
    San Bernardino *M, D*
    San Marcos *M*
    Stanislaus *D*
Chapman University *M, T*
Concordia University *M*
Fresno Pacific University *M, T*
La Sierra University *M, D*
Loyola Marymount University *M, D, T*
Mills College *M, D*
Mount St. Mary's College *M*
National University *M, T*
Notre Dame de Namur
    University *M, T*
Pepperdine University *M, D*
Point Loma Nazarene University *M*
St. Mary's College of California *M, D*
San Diego State University *M, D*
San Francisco State University *D, T*
San Jose State University *M*
Santa Clara University *M*
Simpson University *M*
Sonoma State University *M*
Stanford University *M, D*
University of California
    Berkeley *T*
    Irvine *M, D*
    Los Angeles *M*
University of La Verne *M, D*
University of Redlands *M, D, T*
University of San Diego *M, D, T*
University of San Francisco *M, D, T*
University of Southern
    California *M, D*
University of the Pacific *M, D, T*
Whittier College *T*

Colorado
Colorado State University *M, D*
Jones International University *M, D*
University of Colorado
    Colorado Springs *M*
    Denver *M, D, T*
University of Denver *M, D*
University of Northern
    Colorado *M, D, T*

Connecticut
Central Connecticut State
    University *M, D*
Sacred Heart University *M, T*
Southern Connecticut State
    University *D, T*
University of Bridgeport *D*
University of Connecticut *M, D*
University of Hartford *M, D, T*
University of New Haven *M*
Western Connecticut State
    University *D*

Delaware

Delaware State University *D*
University of Delaware *M, D*
Wilmington University *M*

District of Columbia

American University *M, D*
Catholic University of America *M, D*
Gallaudet University *M*
George Washington University *M*
Howard University *M*
Trinity Washington University *M*
University of the District of
    Columbia *M*

Florida

Barry University *M, D, T*
Clearwater Christian College *M*
Florida Agricultural and Mechanical
    University *M, D, T*
Florida Atlantic University *M, D*
Florida Gulf Coast University *M*
Florida International University *M, D*
Florida State University *M, D, T*
Nova Southeastern University *D*
Saint Leo University *M*
Saint Thomas University *M, D*
Southeastern University *M*
Stetson University *M*
University of Central Florida *M, D*
University of Florida *M, D*
University of North Florida *M, D*
University of South Florida *M, D*
University of West Florida *M, T*

Georgia

Albany State University *M*
Augusta State University *M*
Clark Atlanta University *M, D, T*
Columbus State University *M*
Covenant College *M*
Georgia College and State
    University *M, T*
Georgia Southern University *M, D, T*
Georgia State University *M, T*
Kennesaw State University *M*
Mercer University *M, D*
University of Georgia *M, D, T*
University of West Georgia *M, T*
Valdosta State University *M, D*

Hawaii

University of Hawaii
    Manoa *M*

Idaho

Boise State University *M*
Idaho State University *M, D, T*
Northwest Nazarene University *M*
University of Idaho *M*

Illinois

Argosy University: Chicago *M, D*
Aurora University *M, D*
Benedictine University *M*
Bradley University *M*
Chicago State University *M, D*
Concordia University Chicago *M, D*
DePaul University *M, D, T*
Dominican University *M*
Eastern Illinois University *M*
Governors State University *M*
Illinois State University *M, D*
Lewis University *M, D*
Loyola University Chicago *M, D*
National-Louis University *M*
North Central College *M*
Northeastern Illinois University *M*
Northern Illinois University *M, D*
Northwestern University *D*
Olivet Nazarene University *D*
Roosevelt University *M, D*
Saint Xavier University *M*

Southern Illinois University
    Carbondale *M, D*
Southern Illinois University
    Edwardsville *M*
University of Illinois
    Springfield *M*
    Urbana-Champaign *M, D, T*
University of St. Francis *M*
Western Illinois University *M, D*

Indiana

Anderson University *M*
Ball State University *M, D, T*
Butler University *M*
Indiana State University *M, D, T*
Indiana University
    Bloomington *M, D*
Indiana University-Purdue University
    Fort Wayne *M*
Indiana University-Purdue University
    Indianapolis *M*
Indiana Wesleyan University *D*
Oakland City University *D*
University of Notre Dame *M*
University of St. Francis *M*

Iowa

Drake University *M, D*
Iowa State University *M, D*
Loras College *M*
St. Ambrose University *M*
University of Iowa *M, D*
University of Northern Iowa *D*

Kansas

Benedictine College *M*
Emporia State University *M*
Friends University *M*
Kansas State University *M, D*
Newman University *M*
Pittsburg State University *M*
University of Kansas *D*
Washburn University *M*
Wichita State University *M, D*

Kentucky

Asbury College *M*
Bellarmine University *M*
Northern Kentucky University *D*
Spalding University *M, D, T*
University of Louisville *M, D*
Western Kentucky University *D*

Louisiana

Centenary College of Louisiana *M*
Grambling State University *M, D*
Louisiana State University and
    Agricultural and Mechanical
    College *M*
Louisiana Tech University *D*
McNeese State University *M, T*
Nicholls State University *M*
Northwestern State University *M, T*
Our Lady of Holy Cross College *M*
Southeastern Louisiana
    University *M, D*
Southern University and Agricultural
    and Mechanical College *M*
University of Louisiana at
    Lafayette *M*
University of Louisiana at
    Monroe *M, D*
University of New Orleans *M, D*
Xavier University of Louisiana *M*

Maine

University of Maine *M, D*
University of Southern Maine *M*

Maryland

Bowie State University *M*
College of Notre Dame of
    Maryland *M*

Frostburg State University *M*
Hood College *M*
Loyola University Maryland *M*
McDaniel College *M*
Morgan State University *M, D, T*
Salisbury University *M*
University of Maryland
    College Park *M, D*
    Eastern Shore *D*

Massachusetts

Atlantic Union College *M*
Boston College *M, D*
Boston University *M, D*
Bridgewater State College *M, T*
Cambridge College *M, D, T*
Eastern Nazarene College *M, T*
Emmanuel College *M*
Fitchburg State College *M*
Framingham State College *M*
Lesley University *M, D*
Salem State College *M*
Springfield College *M*
University of Massachusetts
    Boston *M*
    Lowell *M, D*
Westfield State College *M*
Wheelock College *M*
Worcester State College *M*

Michigan

Andrews University *M, D*
Central Michigan University *M, D*
Eastern Michigan University *M, D*
Grand Valley State University *M*
Madonna University *M*
Marygrove College *M*
Michigan State University *M, D*
Northern Michigan University *M*
Oakland University *M, D*
Saginaw Valley State University *M*
University of Detroit Mercy *M*
University of Michigan
    Flint *M*
Wayne State University *D*
Western Michigan University *M, D*

Minnesota

Bemidji State University *M*
Capella University *M, D*
Concordia University: St. Paul *M*
Minnesota State University
    Mankato *M*
    Moorhead *M*
Saint Cloud State University *M, T*
St. Mary's University of Minnesota *M*
University of Minnesota
    Twin Cities *M, D*
University of St. Thomas *M, D*
Walden University *M, D*
Winona State University *M, T*

Mississippi

Delta State University *M*
Jackson State University *M, D*
Mississippi College *M, D*
Mississippi State University *M*
University of Mississippi *M*
University of Southern Mississippi *M*

Missouri

Lincoln University *M*
Lindenwood University *M, D*
Maryville University of Saint
    Louis *M, T*
Missouri Baptist University *D*
Missouri State University *M*
Northwest Missouri State
    University *M*
Saint Louis University *M, D*
Southeast Missouri State University *M*
Southwest Baptist University *M*
University of Central Missouri *M*

University of Missouri
    Columbia *M, D*
    Kansas City *M*
    St. Louis *M*
Webster University *T*
William Woods University *M*

Montana

Rocky Mountain College *M*
University of Great Falls *M*
University of Montana *M, D*

Nebraska

Doane College *M*
University of Nebraska
    Kearney *M*
    Lincoln *M, D*
    Omaha *M, D*
Wayne State College *M*

Nevada

University of Nevada
    Las Vegas *M, D*
    Reno *M, D*

New Hampshire

Franklin Pierce University *T*
Keene State College *M*
New England College *M*
Plymouth State University *M, D, T*
Rivier College *M*
University of New Hampshire at
    Manchester *M*

New Jersey

Caldwell College *M*
Centenary College *M*
The College of New Jersey *M*
College of St. Elizabeth *M, D*
Fairleigh Dickinson University
    College at Florham
    Metropolitan Campus *M*
Georgian Court University *T*
Kean University *M, T*
Monmouth University *M*
Montclair State University *M*
New Jersey City University *M*
Rider University *M*
Rowan University *D*
Saint Peter's College *M*
Seton Hall University *M, D*
Thomas Edison State College *M*

New Mexico

New Mexico Highlands University *M*
New Mexico State University *M, D*
University of New Mexico *M, D, T*
University of the Southwest *M*
Western New Mexico University *M*

New York

Adelphi University *M, T*
Canisius College *M*
City University of New York
    Baruch College *M*
    Brooklyn College *M*
    City College *M*
    Lehman College *M*
College of New Rochelle *M, T*
College of Saint Rose *M*
Dowling College *D*
Fordham University *M, D*
Hofstra University *M, D, T*
Iona College *M*
Le Moyne College *M*
Manhattan College *M*
New York Institute of Technology *T*
New York University *M, D, T*
Niagara University *M*
Pace University *M*
Saint Bonaventure University *M*
St. John Fisher College *M*
St. John's University *M, D*

St. Lawrence University M
St. Thomas Aquinas College M
State University of New York
    Albany M, D
    Buffalo M, D, T
    College at Brockport M
    College at Fredonia T
    New Paltz M
    Oswego M
Syracuse University M, D, T
Touro College M
University of Rochester M, D

North Carolina

Appalachian State University D, T
Campbell University M
East Carolina University M, D
Fayetteville State University M, D
Gardner-Webb University M, D
High Point University M
North Carolina Agricultural and
    Technical State University M
North Carolina State University M, D
Queens University of Charlotte M
University of North Carolina
    Chapel Hill D
    Charlotte M, D, T
    Greensboro M, D, T
    Wilmington M
Western Carolina University M, D

North Dakota

North Dakota State University M
University of North Dakota M, D

Ohio

Antioch University McGregor M
Ashland University M, D, T
Baldwin-Wallace College M
Bowling Green State
    University M, D, T
Cleveland State University M, D
Franciscan University of
    Steubenville M
John Carroll University M
Malone University M
Miami University
    Oxford Campus M, D
Muskingum University M
Ohio State University
    Columbus Campus M, D
Ohio University M, D
Ohio University
    Zanesville Campus M
Union Institute & University M
University of Akron M, D
University of Cincinnati M, D
University of Dayton M, D, T
University of Findlay M
University of Toledo M, D, T
Wright State University M
Xavier University M
Youngstown State University M, D

Oklahoma

East Central University M, T
Northeastern State University M, T
Northwestern Oklahoma State
    University M
Oklahoma State University M, D
Oral Roberts University M, D
Southeastern Oklahoma State
    University M
Southwestern Oklahoma State
    University M, T
University of Central Oklahoma M
University of Oklahoma M, D, T

Oregon

Concordia University M
George Fox University M, D
Lewis & Clark College M, D
Portland State University D, T

University of Oregon M, D, T

Pennsylvania

Alvernia University D
Arcadia University M
Bucknell University M
Cabrini College T
California University of
    Pennsylvania M
Carlow University M, T
Chestnut Hill College M, T
Cheyney University of
    Pennsylvania M
Delaware Valley College M
Duquesne University M, D
Edinboro University of
    Pennsylvania M
Gannon University M, D
Holy Family University M
Immaculata University M, D, T
Indiana University of
    Pennsylvania D, T
Lehigh University M, D
Marywood University M
Millersville University of
    Pennsylvania M
Penn State
    University Park M, D
Philadelphia Biblical University M
Point Park University M
St. Francis University M
Saint Joseph's University M, D
St. Vincent College M
Shippensburg University of
    Pennsylvania T
Slippery Rock University of
    Pennsylvania M
Temple University M, D
University of Pennsylvania M, D
University of Pittsburgh M, D
University of Scranton M
Westminster College M
Widener University M, D, T
Wilkes University D
York College of Pennsylvania M

Puerto Rico

Bayamon Central University M
Caribbean University M
Inter American University of Puerto
    Rico
    Aguadilla Campus M
    Metropolitan Campus M, D
    San German Campus M, D
Pontifical Catholic University of
    Puerto Rico M
Turabo University M
Universidad Adventista de las
    Antillas M
Universidad Metropolitana M
Universidad del Este M
University of Puerto Rico
    Arecibo M
    Rio Piedras M, D

Rhode Island

Johnson & Wales University:
    Providence D
Rhode Island College M

South Carolina

Anderson University M
Bob Jones University M, D
The Citadel M
Clemson University M, D
Columbia International
    University M, D
Furman University M
South Carolina State University D
University of South Carolina M, D
Winthrop University M, T

South Dakota

Oglala Lakota College M
South Dakota State University M
University of South Dakota M, D

Tennessee

Austin Peay State University M
East Tennessee State
    University M, D, T
Freed-Hardeman University M
Lee University M
Lincoln Memorial University M
Lipscomb University M, T
Middle Tennessee State
    University M, T
Southern Adventist University M
Tennessee Technological
    University M
Tennessee Temple University M
Trevecca Nazarene University M
Union University D
University of Memphis M, D
University of Tennessee
    Chattanooga M, D
    Knoxville M, D
    Martin M
Vanderbilt University M, D

Texas

Abilene Christian University M
Angelo State University M
Baylor University M
Houston Baptist University M
Lamar University M, D, T
Lubbock Christian University M
Midwestern State University M
Prairie View A&M University M, D
St. Mary's University M
Sam Houston State University M, D
Schreiner University M
Southwestern Assemblies of God
    University M
Stephen F. Austin State
    University M, D
Sul Ross State University M
Tarleton State University M, D
Texas A&M International
    University M, T
Texas A&M University M, D
Texas A&M University
    Commerce M, D
    Corpus Christi M, D, T
    Kingsville M
    Texarkana M
Texas Christian University M, D
Texas Southern University M, D
Texas State University: San
    Marcos M, D, T
Texas Tech University M, D
Texas Wesleyan University D
Texas Woman's University M
Trinity University M
University of Houston M, D
University of Houston
    Clear Lake M, D
    Victoria M
University of Mary
    Hardin-Baylor M, D
University of North Texas D
University of Texas
    Arlington M, T
    Austin M, D
    Brownsville - Texas Southmost
        College M
    El Paso M, D
    Pan American M, D
    San Antonio M, D
    Tyler M
    of the Permian Basin M
University of the Incarnate Word T
West Texas A&M University M, T

Utah

Brigham Young University M, D
University of Utah M, D
Western Governors University M

Vermont

Castleton State College M
Goddard College M
Johnson State College M
St. Michael's College M
University of Vermont M, D, T

Virginia

College of William and Mary M, D
George Mason University M
Liberty University M, D
Longwood University M
Lynchburg College M
Old Dominion University M, D
Radford University M, T
Regent University M
Shenandoah University D
University of Virginia M, D
Virginia Commonwealth University M
Virginia State University M, D

Washington

City University of Seattle M
Eastern Washington University M
Gonzaga University M, D
Pacific Lutheran University M
Saint Martin's University T
Seattle Pacific University M
Seattle University M, D
University of Washington M, D
University of Washington Bothell M
Walla Walla University M
Washington State University M, D
Whitworth University M

West Virginia

American Public University System M
Concord University M
West Virginia University M, D

Wisconsin

Alverno College M, T
Carthage College M, T
Concordia University Wisconsin M
Edgewood College D, T
Marian University M, D
Marquette University M, D
University of Wisconsin
    Madison M, D
    Milwaukee M, T
    Superior M
    Whitewater M
Viterbo University M

Educational psychology

Alabama

University of Alabama M, D

Arizona

Arizona State University M, D
Northern Arizona University M, D
Prescott College B, M
University of Arizona M, D

California

Alliant International University D
Azusa Pacific University M
California Lutheran University M
California State University
    East Bay M, T
    Long Beach M
    Northridge M
    Sacramento M
Fresno Pacific University M, T
La Sierra University M
Loyola Marymount University M

University of California
  Santa Barbara *M, D*
University of San Francisco *M, D*
University of Southern California *D*
University of the Pacific *M, D, T*

Colorado

University of Colorado
  Boulder *M, D*
  Denver *M*
University of Northern Colorado *M, D*

Connecticut

University of Connecticut *M, D, T*

Delaware

University of Delaware *M, T*

District of Columbia

Catholic University of America *D*
Howard University *M, D*

Florida

Florida State University *M, D*
University of Florida *M, D*

Georgia

Georgia State University *M, D*
University of Georgia *B, M, D*
Valdosta State University *M*

Hawaii

University of Hawaii
  Manoa *M, D*

Idaho

Idaho State University *D*

Illinois

DePaul University *B*
Loyola University Chicago *M, D*
National-Louis University *M, D*
Northern Illinois University *M, D*
Southern Illinois University
  Carbondale *M, D*
University of Illinois
  Chicago *D*
  Urbana-Champaign *M, D*

Indiana

Ball State University *M, D, T*
Indiana University
  Bloomington *M, D*

Iowa

Iowa State University *T*
University of Iowa *M, D*

Kansas

Fort Hays State University *M*
University of Kansas *M, D*
Wichita State University *M*

Kentucky

University of Kentucky *M, D*

Louisiana

Louisiana Tech University *M*
Nicholls State University *M*
University of Louisiana at Monroe *B*

Maryland

University of Maryland
  College Park *M, D*

Massachusetts

American International College *M, D*
Boston College *M, D*
Harvard College *M, D*
Tufts University *M, T*

Michigan

Andrews University *M, D*
Eastern Michigan University *M*
Michigan State University *D*
Wayne State University *M, D*

Minnesota

Capella University *M, D*
University of Minnesota
  Twin Cities *M, D*

Mississippi

Alcorn State University *B*
Mississippi State University *B, M, D*

Missouri

Lindenwood University *M*
University of Missouri
  Columbia *M, D*

Nebraska

University of Nebraska
  Kearney *M*
  Lincoln *D*

Nevada

University of Nevada
  Las Vegas *M, D*

New Jersey

Kean University *M*
Montclair State University *M*
New Jersey City University *M*
Rowan University *M*
Rutgers, The State University of New Jersey
  New Brunswick/Piscataway Campus *D*

New Mexico

University of New Mexico *M, D*

New York

College of Saint Rose *M*
Marist College *M*
New York University *M, D*
State University of New York
  Albany *D*
  Buffalo *M, D*
Touro College *M*

Ohio

Bowling Green State University *M, T*
John Carroll University *M*
Kent State University *M, D*
Miami University
  Oxford Campus *M*
Ohio State University
  Columbus Campus *M, D*
University of Toledo *M*

Oklahoma

Northwestern Oklahoma State University *M*
University of Oklahoma *D*

Pennsylvania

Edinboro University of Pennsylvania *M*
Indiana University of Pennsylvania *M*
Penn State
  University Park *M, D*
St. Vincent College *B*
Temple University *M, D*
University of Pittsburgh *B, M, D*
Widener University *M*

Puerto Rico

Pontifical Catholic University of Puerto Rico *M*

Rhode Island

Rhode Island College *M*

Tennessee

Tennessee State University *D*
Tennessee Technological University *M, D*
University of Memphis *M, D*
University of Tennessee
  Knoxville *M, D*
Vanderbilt University *M, D*

Texas

Baylor University *M, D*
Tarleton State University *M*
Texas A&M University *M, D*
Texas A&M University
  Commerce *M, D*
Texas Tech University *M, D*
University of Houston *M, D*
University of Mary Hardin-Baylor *M*
University of North Texas *M*
University of Texas
  Austin *M, D*
  Tyler *M*

Utah

University of Utah *M, D*

Virginia

George Mason University *M*
University of Virginia *M, D*

West Virginia

West Virginia University *M, D*

Wisconsin

Marquette University *M*
University of Wisconsin
  Eau Claire *M*
  Madison *M, D*
  Milwaukee *M*
  Whitewater *M*

Educational statistics/research methods

Alabama

University of Alabama *D*

Arkansas

University of Arkansas *D*

California

San Diego State University *M*
Stanford University *M, D*

Colorado

Jones International University *M*
University of Denver *M, D*
University of Northern Colorado *M, D*

Connecticut

University of Connecticut *M*

Florida

University of Florida *M*

Georgia

Georgia State University *M*

Illinois

Loyola University Chicago *M, D*
University of Illinois
  Urbana-Champaign *M, D*

Michigan

Michigan State University *D*

Nebraska

University of Nebraska
  Lincoln *M*

New York

Fordham University *M, D*
Hofstra University *M*
State University of New York
  Albany *M, D*

Ohio

Ohio State University
  Columbus Campus *M, D*
University of Toledo *M*

Pennsylvania

University of Pennsylvania *M*

Texas

University of North Texas *D*

Utah

Brigham Young University *D*

Virginia

Virginia Polytechnic Institute and State University *D*

Educational superintendency

Connecticut

Central Connecticut State University *T*

Illinois

Aurora University *D*
Concordia University Chicago *M*
Lewis University *D*
University of Illinois
  Urbana-Champaign *D, T*
Western Illinois University *M*

Maryland

Bowie State University *D*

Michigan

Michigan State University *M, D*

Missouri

Lindenwood University *M*
Maryville University of Saint Louis *D, T*
Northwest Missouri State University *M*
Southwest Baptist University *M*
University of Missouri
  Columbia *M, D*
Webster University *M*

Nebraska

Wayne State College *M*

New Hampshire

Plymouth State University *T*

New Jersey

William Paterson University of New Jersey *M*

New York

City University of New York
  City College *M, T*
Le Moyne College *M*
Saint Bonaventure University *M*
State University of New York
  New Paltz *M*

Ohio

University of Akron *M*

University of Findlay *M, T*
Youngstown State University *D*

Oregon

University of Oregon *T*

Pennsylvania

Edinboro University of
Pennsylvania *M*
Gannon University *T*

South Dakota

University of South Dakota *M, D*

Vermont

St. Michael's College *T*

Washington

City University of Seattle *T*
University of Washington *D, T*
Washington State University *D, T*

Wisconsin

Edgewood College *T*
Marian University *D*
University of Wisconsin
Superior *M*
Whitewater *M*

Educational supervision

Alabama

University of Alabama *D*

Arizona

Northcentral University *M, D*

Arkansas

Arkansas State University *M*

California

California Coast University *M*
California Lutheran University *M*
Mills College *M*
National University *M, T*
St. Mary's College of California *M*

Colorado

Jones International University *M*

Delaware

University of Delaware *M, D*

District of Columbia

George Washington University *M*
Howard University *M*
University of the District of
Columbia *M*

Florida

University of Central Florida *M*
University of Miami *D*

Georgia

Georgia State University *D, T*
Kennesaw State University *D*
Valdosta State University *M*

Illinois

Argosy University: Chicago *M, D*
Loyola University Chicago *M, D*
National-Louis University *D*
University of Illinois
Chicago *M, D*
Springfield *M*
Urbana-Champaign *M, D*

Indiana

Ball State University *D*

Kentucky

Eastern Kentucky University *M*

Louisiana

Centenary College of Louisiana *M*

Maine

University of Maine *M*

Massachusetts

Eastern Nazarene College *M*
Springfield College *M*

Michigan

Central Michigan University *M*
Northern Michigan University *M*
Wayne State University *M*

Minnesota

Bethel University *M, T*
Minnesota State University
Mankato *M*
Saint Cloud State University *T*
Winona State University *M, T*

Missouri

Northwest Missouri State
University *M*

Montana

University of Great Falls *M*

Nebraska

University of Nebraska
Kearney *M*

New Hampshire

New England College *M*
Plymouth State University *T*
University of New Hampshire *M*

New Jersey

Georgian Court University *M*

New York

City University of New York
Baruch College *M*
Fordham University *M, D*
Le Moyne College *M*
Long Island University
C. W. Post Campus *M*
Mercy College *M*
New York Institute of Technology *T*
New York University *M*
St. John's University *M*
State University of New York
Albany *D*
College at Plattsburgh *M, T*

North Carolina

Fayetteville State University *M*
North Carolina Agricultural and
Technical State University *M*
University of North Carolina
Greensboro *M*
Western Carolina University *M*

North Dakota

University of Mary *M*

Ohio

John Carroll University *M*
Kent State University *M*
Otterbein College *M*
University of Cincinnati *M, D*
University of Toledo *T*
Wright State University *M*

Oklahoma

University of Oklahoma *M, D*

Pennsylvania

Carlow University *M*
Kutztown University of
Pennsylvania *T*
Marywood University *M*
St. Francis University *M*
Saint Joseph's University *M*
Shippensburg University of
Pennsylvania *T*
Villanova University *M*
Widener University *M, D*

South Carolina

Furman University *M*
Winthrop University *T*

Tennessee

Tennessee State University *M*
Tennessee Technological
University *M*
Vanderbilt University *M, D*

Texas

Lamar University *M*
Prairie View A&M University *M*
Sam Houston State University *M*
Stephen F. Austin State University *M*
Sul Ross State University *M*
Texas A&M International University *T*
Texas A&M University
Commerce *D*
Kingsville *M*
Texas Southern University *M*
Texas Woman's University *M*
University of Houston
Victoria *M*
University of Texas
Brownsville - Texas Southmost
College *M*

Vermont

Johnson State College *M*
St. Michael's College *M*

Virginia

Longwood University *M*

Washington

Eastern Washington University *M*
Washington State University *M, D*
Western Washington University *M*

Wisconsin

University of Wisconsin
Oshkosh *M, T*
River Falls *M*
Superior *M*

Electrical and communications engineering

Alabama

Alabama Southern Community
College *A*
Auburn University *B, M, D*
Lawson State Community College *A*
Tuskegee University *B, M*
University of Alabama *B, M, D*
University of Alabama
Birmingham *B, M, D*
Huntsville *B, D*
University of South Alabama *B, M*
Wallace State Community College at
Hanceville *A*

Alaska

University of Alaska
Fairbanks *B, M*

Arizona

Anthem College *A*
Arizona State University *B, M, D*
Embry-Riddle Aeronautical University:
Prescott Campus *B*
Northern Arizona University *B, M*
University of Arizona *B, M, D*

Arkansas

Arkansas State University *B*
Arkansas Tech University *B*
Harding University *B*
University of Arkansas *B, M*

California

California Baptist University *B*
California Institute of
Technology *B, M, D*
California Polytechnic State
University: San Luis Obispo *B, M*
California State Polytechnic
University: Pomona *B, M*
California State University
Fresno *B, M*
Fullerton *B, M*
Long Beach *B, M*
Los Angeles *B, M*
Northridge *B, M*
Sacramento *B, M*
College of the Redwoods *A*
Cuesta College *A*
De Anza College *A*
East Los Angeles College *A*
Los Angeles Harbor College *A*
Los Angeles Southwest College *A*
Loyola Marymount University *B, M*
Merritt College *A*
Modesto Junior College *A*
Northwestern Polytechnic
University *B, M*
San Diego State University *B, M*
San Francisco State University *B*
San Jose State University *B, M*
Santa Clara University *B, M, D*
Southern California Institute of
Technology *A, B*
Stanford University *B, M, D*
University of California
Berkeley *B, M, D*
Davis *B, M, D*
Irvine *B, M, D*
Los Angeles *B, M, D*
Riverside *B, M, D*
San Diego *B, M, D*
Santa Barbara *B, M, D*
Santa Cruz *B, M, D*
University of San Diego *B*
University of Southern
California *B, M, D*
University of the Pacific *B*

Colorado

Colorado School of Mines *B*
Colorado State University *B, M, D*
Colorado Technical University *B, M*
United States Air Force Academy *B*
University of Colorado
Boulder *B, M, D*
Colorado Springs *B, M, D*
Denver *B, M*
University of Denver *B, M*
Westwood College: Denver
North *A, B*

Connecticut

Capital Community College *A*
Central Connecticut State
University *B*
Fairfield University *A, B, M*
Trinity College *B*
United States Coast Guard Academy *B*
University of Bridgeport *M*
University of Connecticut *B, M, D*

University of Hartford *B, M*
University of New Haven *B, M*
Yale University *B, M, D*

Delaware

Delaware State University *B*
University of Delaware *B, M, D*

District of Columbia

Catholic University of
America *B, M, D*
George Washington
University *B, M, D*
Howard University *B, M, D*
University of the District of
Columbia *B*

Florida

Broward College *A*
Embry-Riddle Aeronautical
University *B*
Florida Agricultural and Mechanical
University *B, M, D*
Florida Atlantic University *B, M, D*
Florida Institute of
Technology *B, M, D*
Florida International
University *B, M, D*
Florida State University *B, M, D*
Gulf Coast Community College *A*
Jacksonville University *B*
Miami Dade College *A*
Northwest Florida State College *A*
Palm Beach Community College *A*
Pensacola Junior College *A*
Seminole Community College *A*
University of Central Florida *B, M, D*
University of Florida *B, M*
University of Miami *B, M, D*
University of North Florida *B*
University of South Florida *B, M, D*
University of West Florida *B*

Georgia

DeKalb Technical College *A*
Georgia Institute of
Technology *B, M, D*
Georgia Southern University *B*
Mercer University *M*
Middle Georgia College *A*
Southern Polytechnic State
University *B*

Hawaii

University of Hawaii
Manoa *B, M, D*

Idaho

Boise State University *B, M, D*
Brigham Young University-Idaho *A*
Idaho State University *B*
North Idaho College *A*
Northwest Nazarene University *B*
University of Idaho *B, M, D*

Illinois

Bradley University *B, M*
City Colleges of Chicago
Olive-Harvey College *A*
DeVry University
Addison *B*
Chicago *B*
DeVry University: Online *M*
Dominican University *B*
Illinois Central College *A*
Illinois Institute of
Technology *B, M, D*
Joliet Junior College *A*
Northern Illinois University *B, M*
Northwestern University *B, M, D*
Southern Illinois University
Carbondale *B, M*

Southern Illinois University
Edwardsville *B, M*
University of Illinois
Chicago *B, M, D*
Urbana-Champaign *B, M, D*
Western Illinois University *B*

Indiana

Indiana Institute of Technology *B*
Indiana University-Purdue University
Fort Wayne *B*
Indiana University-Purdue University
Indianapolis *B, M, D*
Purdue University *B, M, D*
Purdue University
Calumet *B*
Rose-Hulman Institute of
Technology *B, M*
Trine University *B*
University of Evansville *B, M*
University of Notre Dame *B, M, D*
Valparaiso University *B*
Vincennes University *A*

Iowa

Dordt College *B*
Iowa State University *B, M, D*
Loras College *B*
Southeastern Community College
North Campus *A*
University of Iowa *B*

Kansas

Allen County Community College *A*
Kansas State University *B, M, D*
University of Kansas *B, M, D*
Wichita State University *B, M, D*

Kentucky

Daymar College: Paducah *A*
Murray State University *B*
Spencerian College: Lexington *A*
University of Kentucky *B, M, D*
University of Louisville *B, M, D*
Western Kentucky University *B*

Louisiana

Louisiana State University and
Agricultural and Mechanical
College *B, M, D*
Louisiana Tech University *B*
Southern University and Agricultural
and Mechanical College *B*
University of Louisiana at Lafayette *B*
University of New Orleans *B*

Maine

University of Maine *B, M*
University of Southern Maine *B*

Maryland

Capitol College *A, B*
Johns Hopkins University *B, M, D*
Loyola University Maryland *B*
Morgan State University *B, M*
United States Naval Academy *B*
University of Maryland
Baltimore County *M, D*
College Park *B, M, D*

Massachusetts

Boston University *B, M, D*
Eastern Nazarene College *B*
Franklin W. Olin College of
Engineering *B*
Massachusetts Institute of
Technology *B, M, D*
Merrimack College *B*
Northeastern University *B, M, D*
Quinsigamond Community College *A*
Smith College *B*
Suffolk University *B*

Tufts University *B, M, D*
University of Massachusetts
Amherst *D*
Dartmouth *B, M, D*
Lowell *B, M, D*
Western New England College *B, M*
Worcester Polytechnic
Institute *B, M, D*

Michigan

Andrews University *B*
Baker College
of Muskegon *A*
Calvin College *B*
Central Michigan University *B*
Grand Valley State University *B*
Kettering University *B, M*
Lake Superior State University *B*
Lawrence Technological
University *B, M*
Michigan State University *B, M, D*
Michigan Technological
University *B, M, D, T*
Monroe County Community
College *A*
Oakland University *B, M, D*
Saginaw Valley State University *B*
University of Detroit Mercy *B, M, D*
University of Michigan *B, M, D*
University of Michigan
Dearborn *B, M*
Wayne State University *B, M, D*
Western Michigan University *B, M, D*

Minnesota

Minnesota State University
Mankato *B, M*
Northland Community & Technical
College *A*
Saint Cloud State University *B, M*
University of Minnesota
Duluth *B, M*
Twin Cities *B, M, D*
University of St. Thomas *B*

Mississippi

Holmes Community College *A*
Jackson State University *B*
Mississippi State University *B, M, D*
University of Mississippi *B*

Missouri

Missouri Technical School *A, B*
Ozarks Technical Community
College *A*
Saint Louis University *B*
University of Missouri
Columbia *B, M, D*
Kansas City *B, M*
Missouri University of Science and
Technology *B, M, D*
St. Louis *B*
Washington University in St.
Louis *B, M, D*

Montana

Montana State University
Bozeman *B, M*
Montana Tech of the University of
Montana *B, M*
Salish Kootenai College *A*

Nebraska

University of Nebraska
Lincoln *B, M*
Omaha *B*

Nevada

College of Southern Nevada *A*
University of Nevada
Las Vegas *B, M, D*
Reno *B, M, D*

New Hampshire

Nashua Community College *A*
University of New Hampshire *B, M, D*

New Jersey

The College of New Jersey *B*
Essex County College *A*
Fairleigh Dickinson University
Metropolitan Campus *B, M*
New Jersey Institute of
Technology *B, M, D*
Princeton University *B, M, D*
Rowan University *B*
Rutgers, The State University of New
Jersey
Camden Regional Campus *B*
New Brunswick/Piscataway
Campus *B, M, D*
Newark Regional Campus *B*
Stevens Institute of
Technology *B, M, D*

New Mexico

Clovis Community College *A*
Dona Ana Community College of New
Mexico State University *A*
New Mexico Institute of Mining and
Technology *A, B*
New Mexico State University *B, M*
University of New Mexico *B, M*

New York

Alfred University *B, M*
Bramson ORT College *A*
City University of New York
City College *B, M, D*
Hostos Community College *A*
LaGuardia Community College *A*
Clarkson University *B, M, D*
Columbia University *B, M, D*
Cooper Union for the Advancement of
Science and Art *B, M*
Cornell University *B, M, D*
Dutchess Community College *A*
Hofstra University *B*
Island Drafting and Technical
Institute *A*
Manhattan College *B, M*
Nassau Community College *A*
New York Institute of
Technology *B, M*
Polytechnic Institute of New York
University *B, M, D*
Rensselaer Polytechnic
Institute *B, M, D*
Rochester Institute of
Technology *B, M*
State University of New York
Binghamton *B, M, D*
Buffalo *B, M, D*
College of Agriculture and
Technology at Morrisville *A*
Institute of Technology at
Utica/Rome *B*
Maritime College *B*
New Paltz *B, M*
Stony Brook *B, M, D*
Suffolk County Community College *A*
Syracuse University *B, M, D*
Union College *B*
United States Military Academy *B*
University of Rochester *B, M, D*

North Carolina

Alamance Community College *A*
Blue Ridge Community College *A*
Duke University *B, M, D*
Durham Technical Community
College *A*
Mayland Community College *A*
Mitchell Community College *A*
Nash Community College *A*

North Carolina Agricultural and
 Technical State
 University *B, M, D*
North Carolina State
 University *B, M, D*
Pamlico Community College *A*
Richmond Community College *A*
Rockingham Community College *A*
Southwestern Community College *A*
Surry Community College *A*
University of North Carolina
 Charlotte *B, M, D*
Vance-Granville Community
 College *A*
Western Carolina University *B*
Western Piedmont Community
 College *A*

North Dakota

Lake Region State College *A*
North Dakota State University *B, M, D*
University of North Dakota *B, M*

Ohio

Belmont Technical College *A*
Bowling Green State University:
 Firelands College *A*
Case Western Reserve
 University *B, M, D*
Cedarville University *B*
Cleveland State University *B, M, D*
Miami University
 Oxford Campus *B*
Ohio Northern University *B*
Ohio State University
 Columbus Campus *B, M, D*
Ohio University *B, M, D*
RETS College *A*
Stark State College of Technology *A*
University of Akron *B, M, D*
University of Cincinnati *B, M, D*
University of Dayton *B, M, D*
University of Toledo *B, M*
Washington State Community
 College *A*
Wilberforce University *B*
Wright State University *B, M*
Youngstown State University *B, M*

Oklahoma

Oklahoma Christian University *B*
Oklahoma State University *B, M, D*
Oklahoma State University
 Institute of Technology:
 Okmulgee *A*
Oral Roberts University *B*
University of Oklahoma *B, M, D*
University of Tulsa *B, M*

Oregon

Chemeketa Community College *A*
George Fox University *B*
Oregon Health & Science
 University *M, D*
Oregon Institute of Technology *B*
Oregon State University *B*
Portland State University *B, M, D*
University of Portland *B, M*

Pennsylvania

Bloomsburg University of
 Pennsylvania *B*
Bucknell University *B, M*
Carnegie Mellon University *B, M, D*
Drexel University *B, M, D*
Gannon University *B, M*
Gettysburg College *B*
Grove City College *B*
Lafayette College *B*
Lehigh University *B, M, D*
Penn State
 Abington *B*
 Altoona *B*

Beaver *B*
Berks *B*
Brandywine *B*
DuBois *B*
Erie, The Behrend College *B*
Fayette, The Eberly Campus *B*
Greater Allegheny *B*
Harrisburg *B, M*
Hazleton *B*
Lehigh Valley *B*
Mont Alto *B*
New Kensington *B*
Schuylkill *B*
Shenango *B*
University Park *B, M, D*
Wilkes-Barre *B*
Worthington Scranton *B*
York *B*
Pittsburgh Institute of Aeronautics *A*
Reading Area Community College *A*
Temple University *B, M*
University of Pennsylvania *B, M, D*
University of Pittsburgh *B, M, D*
University of Pittsburgh
 Bradford *B*
University of Scranton *A, B*
Villanova University *B, M*
Widener University *B, M*
Wilkes University *B, M*
York College of Pennsylvania *B*

Puerto Rico

Columbia Centro Universitario:
 Caguas *A*
Inter American University of Puerto
 Rico
 Bayamon Campus *B*
Turabo University *B*
Universidad Politecnica de Puerto
 Rico *B, M*

Rhode Island

Brown University *B, M, D*
University of Rhode Island *B, M, D*

South Carolina

Aiken Technical College *A*
Bob Jones University *B, M*
The Citadel *B*
Clemson University *B, M, D*
Horry-Georgetown Technical
 College *A*
Technical College of the
 Lowcountry *A*
University of South Carolina *B, M, D*
Williamsburg Technical College *A*

South Dakota

South Dakota School of Mines and
 Technology *B, M*
South Dakota State University *B, D*

Tennessee

Christian Brothers University *B*
Tennessee State University *B*
Tennessee Technological
 University *B, M, D*
Union University *B*
University of Memphis *B, M*
University of Tennessee
 Chattanooga *B*
 Knoxville *B, M, D*

Texas

Baylor University *B, M*
Lamar University *B, M*
Laredo Community College *A*
LeTourneau University *B*
Prairie View A&M University *B, M, D*
Rice University *B, M, D*
St. Mary's University *B, M*
Southern Methodist
 University *B, M, D*

Texas A&M University *B, M, D*
Texas A&M University
 Kingsville *B, M*
 Texarkana *B*
Texas Christian University *B*
Texas State University: San Marcos *B*
Texas Tech University *B, M, D*
University of Houston *B, M, D*
University of North Texas *B, M*
University of Texas
 Arlington *B, M, D*
 Austin *B, M, D*
 Dallas *B, M, D*
 El Paso *B, M*
 Pan American *B, M*
 San Antonio *B, M, D*
 Tyler *B*

Utah

Brigham Young University *B, M, D*
College of Eastern Utah *A, T*
Salt Lake Community College *A*
Southern Utah University *A*
University of Utah *B, M, D*
Utah State University *B, M, D*

Vermont

Norwich University *B*
University of Vermont *B, M, D*

Virginia

ECPI College of Technology: Virginia
 Beach *A*
ECPI Technical College: Roanoke *A*
Eastern Shore Community College *A*
George Mason University *B, M, D*
Hampton University *B*
John Tyler Community College *A*
Liberty University *B*
Lord Fairfax Community College *A*
Mountain Empire Community
 College *A*
Norfolk State University *B*
Old Dominion University *B, M, D*
Southwest Virginia Community
 College *A*
Thomas Nelson Community
 College *A*
University of Virginia *B, M, D*
Virginia Commonwealth University *B*
Virginia Military Institute *B*
Virginia Polytechnic Institute and
 State University *B, M, D*

Washington

Bates Technical College *A*
Eastern Washington University *B*
Gonzaga University *B*
Renton Technical College *A*
Seattle Pacific University *B*
Seattle University *B*
Skagit Valley College *A*
University of Washington *B, M, D*
University of Washington Bothell *B*
Walla Walla University *B*
Washington State University *B, M, D*

West Virginia

Potomac State College of West
 Virginia University *A*
West Virginia University *B, M, D*
West Virginia University Institute of
 Technology *B*

Wisconsin

Blackhawk Technical College *A*
Marquette University *B, M, D*
Milwaukee School of Engineering *B*
Northcentral Technical College *A*
University of Wisconsin
 Madison *B, M, D*
 Milwaukee *B*
 Platteville *B*

Wyoming

University of Wyoming *B, M, D*

Electrical drafting/ CAD/CADD

Alaska

University of Alaska
 Anchorage *C*

Arizona

Pima Community College *C*

Florida

Chipola College *C*
Miami Dade College *C, A*
Palm Beach Community College *C*

Illinois

Kaskaskia College *C*
Oakton Community College *C, A*

Minnesota

Dunwoody College of Technology *A*

Nevada

DeVry University: Henderson *A*

New Mexico

Central New Mexico Community
 College *A*

Oregon

Chemeketa Community College *C*
Clackamas Community College *A*

Texas

Collin County Community College
 District *C, A*

Washington

Bates Technical College *C, A*

Wisconsin

Herzing University *A, B*

Electrical engineering technology

Alabama

Alabama Southern Community
 College *A*
Central Alabama Community
 College *A*
Faulkner State Community College *C*
Gadsden State Community
 College *C, A*
Jacksonville State University *B*
Lawson State Community
 College *C, A*
Northeast Alabama Community
 College *C, A*
Troy University *B*

Alaska

Prince William Sound Community
 College *C, A*
University of Alaska
 Anchorage *C, A, B*

Arizona

Arizona State University *B, M*
Central Arizona College *C, A*
Cochise College *A*
DeVry University
 Phoenix *A, B*
Northland Pioneer College *C, A*
Penn Foster College *A*

Arkansas

Arkansas State University
  Beebe *A*
Arkansas Tech University *C*
East Arkansas Community College *C*
National Park Community College *A*
North Arkansas College *C, A*
Northwest Arkansas Community
  College *A*
Phillips Community College of the
  University of Arkansas *C*
Southern Arkansas University Tech *C*
University of Arkansas
  Little Rock *A*

California

Allan Hancock College *C, A*
American River College *A*
Barstow Community College *C*
Butte College *C, A*
California State Polytechnic
  University: Pomona *B*
California State University
  Long Beach *B*
Cerritos College *C, A*
Cerro Coso Community College *C, A*
Chabot College *A*
College of San Mateo *C, A*
College of the Redwoods *C*
College of the Sequoias *C, A*
Cuyamaca College *A*
DeVry University
  Fremont *A, B*
  Long Beach *A, B*
  Pomona *A, B*
  Sherman Oaks *A, B*
Diablo Valley College *C, A*
El Camino College: Compton
  Center *C, A*
Evergreen Valley College *C*
Foothill College *C, A*
Fullerton College *C, A*
Irvine Valley College *C, A*
Los Angeles City College *C, A*
Los Angeles Harbor College *C, A*
Los Angeles Pierce College *C, A*
Los Angeles Southwest College *C, A*
Los Angeles Trade and Technical
  College *C, A*
Los Angeles Valley College *C, A*
Merced College *C, A*
Moorpark College *C, A*
Mount San Antonio College *C, A*
Napa Valley College *C, A*
Ohlone College *A*
Orange Coast College *C, A*
Riverside Community College *C, A*
Saddleback College *C*
San Bernardino Valley College *C, A*
San Diego City College *A*
San Joaquin Delta College *C, A*
San Jose City College *C, A*
Santa Barbara City College *C, A*
Santa Monica College *C, A*
Santa Rosa Junior College *C, A*
Shasta College *A*
Solano Community College *C, A*
Taft College *A*
West Valley College *C, A*
Yuba Community College
  District *C, A*

Colorado

Aims Community College *A*
Arapahoe Community College *C, A*
Colorado Technical University *A, B*
Community College of Aurora *A*
DeVry University
  Westminster *A, B*
Front Range Community College *C, A*
Metropolitan State College of
  Denver *B*
Pikes Peak Community College *C, A*
Pueblo Community College *C, A*

Westwood College: Denver
  North *A, B*

Connecticut

Gateway Community College *A*
Naugatuck Valley Community
  College *A*
Three Rivers Community College *A*
University of Hartford *A, B*

Delaware

Delaware State University *B*
Delaware Technical and Community
  College
  Owens *C, A*
  Stanton/Wilmington *C, A*
  Terry *A*

District of Columbia

University of the District of
  Columbia *A*

Florida

Brevard Community College *C, A*
Daytona State College *A*
DeVry University
  Miramar *A, B*
  Orlando *A, B*
Embry-Riddle Aeronautical
  University *B*
Florida Agricultural and Mechanical
  University *B*
Florida State College at Jacksonville *A*
Gulf Coast Community College *A*
Hillsborough Community
  College *C, A*
Indian River State College *A*
Lake-Sumter Community College *C, A*
Miami Dade College *C, A*
Northwest Florida State College *C, A*
Palm Beach Community College *A*
Pensacola Junior College *A*
Polk State College *A*
Saint Johns River Community
  College *A*
St. Petersburg College *C, A*
Santa Fe College *C*
Seminole Community College *A*
South Florida Community
  College *C, A*
State College of Florida,
  Manatee-Sarasota *A*
Valencia Community College *A*

Georgia

Augusta Technical College *C, A*
Bainbridge College *C, A*
Chattahoochee Technical College *A*
Columbus Technical College *A*
DeKalb Technical College *C, A*
DeVry University
  Alpharetta *A, B*
  Decatur *A, B*
Fort Valley State University *A, B*
Gainesville State College *C, A*
Georgia Southern University *B*
Griffin Technical College *A*
Herzing University *A*
Macon State College *A*
Middle Georgia Technical
  College *C, A*
Savannah State University *B*
Savannah Technical College *A*
Southern Polytechnic State
  University *B*

Hawaii

Heald College
  Honolulu *A*
University of Hawaii
  Hawaii Community College *A*
  Honolulu Community College *C, A*
  Kauai Community College *C, A*

Idaho

Brigham Young University-Idaho *A*
Idaho State University *C, A*

Illinois

College of DuPage *C, A*
College of Lake County *C, A*
Coyne American Institute *C, A*
DeVry University
  Addison *A, B*
  Chicago *A, B*
  Tinley Park *A, B*
DeVry University: Online *A, B*
East-West University *A, B*
Harper College *A*
Heartland Community College *C, A*
Illinois Eastern Community Colleges
  Wabash Valley College *A*
John A. Logan College *C*
Joliet Junior College *C, A*
Kaskaskia College *C, A*
Kishwaukee College *C, A*
Lincoln Land Community College *C, A*
McHenry County College *C, A*
Moraine Valley Community College *C*
Oakton Community College *C, A*
Parkland College *C*
Prairie State College *C, A*
Rend Lake College *C*
Rock Valley College *C, A*
Roosevelt University *B*
Sauk Valley Community College *A*
Shawnee Community College *A*
South Suburban College of Cook
  County *C, A*
Southern Illinois University
  Carbondale *B*
Spoon River College *C*
Taylor Business Institute *A*
Triton College *A*
Waubonsee Community College *C, A*

Indiana

DeVry University: Indianapolis *A*
Indiana State University *A, B, M*
Indiana University-Purdue University
  Fort Wayne *C, A, B*
Indiana University-Purdue University
  Indianapolis *A, B*
Ivy Tech Community College
  Bloomington *A*
  Central Indiana *A*
  Columbus *A*
  East Central *A*
  Lafayette *A*
  North Central *A*
  Northwest *A*
  Richmond *A*
  South Central *A*
  Southeast *A*
  Southwest *A*
  Wabash Valley *A*
Oakland City University *A*
Purdue University *A, B*
Purdue University
  Calumet *C, A, B*
  North Central *A, B*
Vincennes University *C, A*

Iowa

Clinton Community College *C, A*
Des Moines Area Community
  College *A*
Hamilton Technical College *A, B*
Hawkeye Community College *C, A*
Indian Hills Community College *A*
Iowa Central Community College *A*
Iowa Western Community College *A*
Kirkwood Community College *C, A*
North Iowa Area Community
  College *A*
Northeast Iowa Community
  College *A*

Northwest Iowa Community
  College *A*
Southeastern Community College
  North Campus *A*
Southwestern Community College *A*
Western Iowa Tech Community
  College *C*

Kansas

Allen County Community College *C*
Johnson County Community
  College *A*
Kansas State University *B*
North Central Kansas Technical
  College *A*
Pittsburg State University *B*
Washburn University *A*

Kentucky

Bluegrass Community and Technical
  College *A*
Daymar College: Paducah *A*
Gateway Community and Technical
  College *A*
Henderson Community College *A*
Kentucky State University *A*
Maysville Community and Technical
  College *C, A*
Northern Kentucky University *B*
Owensboro Community and
  Technical College *A*
Spencerian College: Lexington *C, A*
Sullivan College of Technology and
  Design *A*

Louisiana

Delgado Community College *A*
Grambling State University *B*
ITI Technical College *C, A*
Louisiana Tech University *B*
Northwestern State University *A, B*
Southern University
  Shreveport *A*
Southern University and Agricultural
  and Mechanical College *B*

Maine

Eastern Maine Community College *A*
Kennebec Valley Community
  College *C, A*
Northern Maine Community
  College *A*
Southern Maine Community
  College *C, A*
University of Maine *B*
University of Southern Maine *B*

Maryland

Anne Arundel Community
  College *C, A*
Baltimore City Community
  College *C, A*
Capitol College *A, B*
Cecil College *C, A*
Chesapeake College *C*
College of Southern Maryland *C, A*
Community College of Baltimore
  County *C, A*
Howard Community College *C*
Montgomery College *A*
Prince George's Community
  College *C, A*
Wor-Wic Community College *C, A*

Massachusetts

Benjamin Franklin Institute of
  Technology *C, A*
Berkshire Community College *A*
Fitchburg State College *B*
Massachusetts Bay Community
  College *A*
Massasoit Community College *A*

Northern Essex Community
College *C, A*
Quinsigamond Community College *A*
Springfield Technical Community
College *C, A*
University of Massachusetts
Lowell *A, B*
Wentworth Institute of Technology *B*

Michigan
Baker College
of Flint *A, B*
of Muskegon *A*
of Owosso *A*
of Port Huron *C*
Bay de Noc Community College *C, A*
Central Michigan University *B*
Delta College *C, A*
Eastern Michigan University *B*
Ferris State University *B*
Glen Oaks Community College *C*
Grand Rapids Community College *A*
Henry Ford Community College *C, A*
Jackson Community College *C, A*
Kalamazoo Valley Community
College *C, A*
Kellogg Community College *C, A*
Kirtland Community College *C, A*
Lake Michigan College *A*
Lake Superior State University *A, B*
Lansing Community College *A*
Lawrence Technological University *A*
Macomb Community College *C, A*
Michigan Technological University *B*
Monroe County Community
College *A*
Montcalm Community College *C, A*
Mott Community College *A*
Muskegon Community College *C, A*
Northern Michigan University *A, B*
Northwestern Michigan College *C, A*
Oakland Community College *C, A*
St. Clair County Community
College *C, A*
Schoolcraft College *A*
Southwestern Michigan College *C, A*
Washtenaw Community College *A*
Wayne County Community
College *C, A*
Wayne State University *B*
West Shore Community College *A*

Minnesota
Anoka Technical College *C, A*
DeVry University
Edina *A*
Dunwoody College of Technology *A*
Hennepin Technical College *C, A*
Lake Superior College *C, A*
Minnesota State College - Southeast
Technical *C, A*
Minnesota State Community and
Technical College *C, A*
Minnesota State University
Mankato *B, M*
Ridgewater College *C, A*
St. Cloud Technical College *C, A*
St. Paul College *C, A*

Mississippi
Copiah-Lincoln Community
College *C, A*
East Central Community College *A*
Hinds Community College *A*
Mississippi Delta Community
College *A*
Mississippi Gulf Coast Community
College *T*
Northwest Mississippi Community
College *A*
Pearl River Community College *C, A*
University of Southern Mississippi *B*

Missouri
Crowder College *C, A*
DeVry University
Kansas City *A, B*
Grantham University *A, B*
Jefferson College *C, A*
Linn State Technical College *A*
Mineral Area College *C, A*
Missouri Technical School *C, A, B*
Missouri Western State
University *A, B*
Ozarks Technical Community
College *C, A*
Pinnacle Career Institute: Kansas
City *C, A*
Ranken Technical College *A*
St. Louis Community College
St. Louis Community College at
Florissant Valley *A*
St. Louis Community College at
Meramec *A*
Saint Louis University *B*
Southeast Missouri State University *C*
University of Central Missouri *B*

Montana
University of Montana *A*

Nebraska
Central Community College *C, A*
Metropolitan Community
College *C, A*
Mid-Plains Community College
Area *C, A*
Northeast Community College *A*
Southeast Community College *A*
University of Nebraska
Lincoln *B*

Nevada
Career College of Northern
Nevada *C, A*
College of Southern Nevada *A*
Great Basin College *C*
Western Nevada College *C, A*

New Hampshire
NHTI-Concord's Community
College *C, A*
Nashua Community College *A*
University of New Hampshire *B*
University of New Hampshire at
Manchester *B*

New Jersey
Bergen Community College *A*
Brookdale Community College *C, A*
Burlington County College *A*
Camden County College *A*
County College of Morris *A*
Cumberland County College *C, A*
DeVry University: North
Brunswick *A, B*
Essex County College *A*
Fairleigh Dickinson University
Metropolitan Campus *B*
Hudson County Community
College *C, A*
Kean University *B*
Mercer County Community
College *C, A*
Middlesex County College *A*
Passaic County Community College *A*
Thomas Edison State College *C, A, B*

New Mexico
Central New Mexico Community
College *C, A*
Dona Ana Community College of New
Mexico State University *C, A*
New Mexico State University
Alamogordo *A*
Grants *A*

Northern New Mexico College *C, A*
Santa Fe Community College *C*

New York
Adirondack Community College *A*
Briarcliffe College *A*
Broome Community College *A*
Cayuga County Community
College *C, A*
City University of New York
Bronx Community College *A*
New York City College of
Technology *A*
Queensborough Community
College *A*
Clinton Community College *A*
Corning Community College *A*
DeVry
College of New York *A, B*
Dutchess Community College *A*
Erie Community College
North Campus *A*
Excelsior College *A*
Fulton-Montgomery Community
College *A*
Hudson Valley Community College *A*
Island Drafting and Technical
Institute *A*
Jamestown Community College *A*
Mohawk Valley Community College *A*
Monroe Community College *C, A*
Nassau Community College *A*
New York Institute of
Technology *A, B, M*
Onondaga Community College *A*
Orange County Community College *A*
Rochester Institute of
Technology *A, B, M*
Rockland Community College *A*
State University of New York
College at Buffalo *B*
College of Agriculture and
Technology at Morrisville *A*
College of Technology at
Alfred *A, B*
College of Technology at Canton *A*
Farmingdale *B*
Institute of Technology at
Utica/Rome *B*
Suffolk County Community College *A*
Technical Career Institutes *A*
Tompkins Cortland Community
College *C, A*
Vaughn College of Aeronautics and
Technology *A, B*
Westchester Community College *A*

North Carolina
Asheville-Buncombe Technical
Community College *A*
Beaufort County Community
College *C, A*
Bladen Community College *C, A*
Blue Ridge Community College *C, A*
Caldwell Community College and
Technical Institute *A*
Cape Fear Community College *C, A*
Catawba Valley Community College *A*
Central Carolina Community
College *A*
Central Piedmont Community
College *C, A*
Cleveland Community College *C, A*
College of the Albemarle *C, A*
Davidson County Community
College *C, A*
Durham Technical Community
College *C, A*
Edgecombe Community College *C, A*
Fayetteville Technical Community
College *C, A*
Gaston College *C, A*
Guilford Technical Community
College *C, A*

Halifax Community College *A*
Haywood Community College *A*
Isothermal Community College *A*
James Sprunt Community College *C*
Lenoir Community College *A*
Mitchell Community College *C, A*
Nash Community College *A*
Pamlico Community College *C, A*
Pitt Community College *C, A*
Randolph Community College *A*
Richmond Community College *A*
Robeson Community College *A*
Rowan-Cabarrus Community
College *A*
Southeastern Community College *A*
Southwestern Community College *A*
Stanly Community College *C, A*
Surry Community College *C*
University of North Carolina
Charlotte *B*
Vance-Granville Community
College *C, A*
Wake Technical Community
College *C, A*
Wayne Community College *A*
Western Carolina University *B*
Wilkes Community College *C, A*

North Dakota
Bismarck State College *C, A*
North Dakota State College of
Science *A*

Ohio
Bowling Green State University *B*
Bowling Green State University:
Firelands College *A*
Bryant & Stratton College:
Cleveland *A, B*
Central Ohio Technical College *A*
Cincinnati State Technical and
Community College *A*
Cleveland Institute of Electronics *C, A*
Cleveland State University *B*
Columbus State Community
College *A*
Cuyahoga Community College
Metropolitan Campus *A*
DeVry University
Columbus *A, B*
ETI Technical College of Niles *C, A*
Eastern Gateway Community
College *C, A*
Edison State Community College *C, A*
Hocking College *C, A*
James A. Rhodes State College *A*
Kent State University
Ashtabula *A*
Trumbull *A*
Marion Technical College *A*
Miami University
Hamilton Campus *A*
Oxford Campus *A*
North Central State College *A*
Northwest State Community
College *C, A*
Owens Community College
Toledo *C, A*
Shawnee State University *A, B*
Southern State Community College *A*
Stark State College of Technology *A*
Terra State Community College *A*
University of Akron *C, A, B*
University of Dayton *B*
University of Toledo *A*
Washington State Community
College *A*
Wright State University *A*
Youngstown State University *A, B*
Zane State College *A*

Oklahoma
Cameron University *A, B*
Oklahoma City Community College *A*

Oklahoma State University *B*
Oklahoma State University
    Institute of Technology:
    Okmulgee *A*
    Oklahoma City *A*
Tulsa Community College *C, A*

Oregon

Blue Mountain Community College *A*
Chemeketa Community College *A*
Clackamas Community College *C, A*
Lane Community College *A*
Linn-Benton Community College *A*
Oregon Institute of Technology *B*
Portland Community College *C, A*
Rogue Community College *C, A*

Pennsylvania

Butler County Community College *A*
CHI Institute: Broomall *A*
CHI Institute: Franklin Mills *C, A*
California University of
    Pennsylvania *A, B*
Community College of Allegheny
    County *C, A*
Community College of
    Philadelphia *C, A*
DeVry University
    Fort Washington *A, B*
Harrisburg Area Community
    College *C, A*
Johnson College *A*
Lehigh Carbon Community College *A*
Luzerne County Community
    College *C, A*
Montgomery County Community
    College *A*
Northampton Community College *A*
Penn State
    Abington *B*
    Altoona *A, B*
    Beaver *B*
    Berks *A, B*
    Brandywine *B*
    DuBois *B*
    Erie, The Behrend College *A, B*
    Fayette, The Eberly Campus *A, B*
    Greater Allegheny *B*
    Hazleton *A*
    Lehigh Valley *B*
    Mont Alto *B*
    New Kensington *B*
    Schuylkill *B*
    Shenango *B*
    Wilkes-Barre *A, B*
    York *A, B*
Pennsylvania College of
    Technology *A, B*
Pennsylvania Highlands Community
    College *A*
Pennsylvania Institute of
    Technology *A*
Pittsburgh Institute of Aeronautics *A*
Reading Area Community College *A*
Triangle Tech: Sunbury *A*
University of Pittsburgh
    Johnstown *B*
Westmoreland County Community
    College *A*
YTI Career Institute: York *A*

Puerto Rico

Humacao Community College *C, A*
Inter American University of Puerto
    Rico
    Aguadilla Campus *A, B*
    Bayamon Campus *B*
    San German Campus *B*
National College of Business and
    Technology: Arecibo *A*
National College of Business and
    Technology: Bayamon *A*
Turabo University *A*
Universidad del Este *A*

University College of San Juan *A*
University of Puerto Rico
    Aguadilla *A, B*
    Bayamon University College *A, B*
    Humacao *A*

Rhode Island

Community College of Rhode
    Island *A*
New England Institute of
    Technology *A, B*

South Carolina

Aiken Technical College *C, A*
Benedict College *B*
Florence-Darlington Technical
    College *A*
Greenville Technical College *A*
Horry-Georgetown Technical
    College *A*
Midlands Technical College *C, A*
Northeastern Technical College *C, A*
Orangeburg-Calhoun Technical
    College *A*
South Carolina State University *B*
Spartanburg Community College *C, A*
Technical College of the
    Lowcountry *C*
Tri-County Technical College *A*
Trident Technical College *A*
York Technical College *A*

South Dakota

South Dakota State University *B*
Southeast Technical Institute *A*

Tennessee

Chattanooga State Community
    College *A*
Columbia State Community College *A*
Dyersburg State Community
    College *C, A*
Fountainhead College of
    Technology *A, B*
Nashville State Community College *A*
Northeast State Community
    College *C, A*
Pellissippi State Community
    College *A*
Remington College
    Memphis *A*
Southwest Tennessee Community
    College *A*
University of Memphis *B*

Texas

Alvin Community College *C, A*
Amarillo College *C, A*
Angelina College *C, A*
Austin Community College *C, A*
Brazosport College *C, A*
Brookhaven College *C, A*
College of the Mainland *A*
Collin County Community College
    District *C, A*
DeVry University
    Irving *A, B*
DeVry University: Houston *A, B*
Eastfield College *C, A*
El Paso Community College *C, A*
Grayson County College *C, A*
Hill College *C, A*
Kilgore College *C, A*
Lamar State College at Orange *C, A*
Lamar State College at Port
    Arthur *C, A*
LeTourneau University *B*
Lee College *A*
Lone Star College System *C, A*
Midland College *C, A*
Mountain View College *A*
North Central Texas College *A*
North Lake College *A*

Panola College *C*
Paris Junior College *A*
Prairie View A&M University *B*
Richland College *C, A*
St. Philip's College *A*
Sam Houston State University *B*
San Antonio College *C, A*
San Jacinto College *C*
Tarrant County College *C, A*
Texarkana College *C, A*
Texas A&M University *B*
Texas A&M University
    Corpus Christi *B*
Texas Southern University *B*
Texas State Technical College
    Harlingen *A*
    Waco *C, A*
    West Texas *C, A*
Texas Tech University *B*
Tyler Junior College *A*
University of Houston *B, M*
University of North Texas *B*
University of Texas
    Brownsville - Texas Southmost
    College *C, A, B*
Victoria College *C, A*
Weatherford College *C, A*
Western Technical College: Diana
    Drive *C, A*
Wharton County Junior College *A*

Utah

College of Eastern Utah *T*
Salt Lake Community College *C*
Southern Utah University *A*
Utah State University *B*
Utah Valley University *C, A*
Weber State University *A, B*

Vermont

Vermont Technical College *A, B*

Virginia

Blue Ridge Community College *A*
Central Virginia Community
    College *A*
Dabney S. Lancaster Community
    College *C, A*
Danville Community College *C*
ECPI College of Technology: Virginia
    Beach *C, A*
ECPI Technical College: Roanoke *A*
J. Sargeant Reynolds Community
    College *C, A*
John Tyler Community College *A*
Lord Fairfax Community College *C, A*
Mountain Empire Community
    College *A*
New River Community College *A*
Norfolk State University *B*
Northern Virginia Community
    College *C, A*
Old Dominion University *B*
Paul D. Camp Community College *A*
Rappahannock Community
    College *C, A*
Southside Virginia Community
    College *C, A*
Southwest Virginia Community
    College *A*
Thomas Nelson Community
    College *A*
Virginia Highlands Community
    College *A*
Virginia State University *B*
Virginia Western Community
    College *C, A*
World College *B*
Wytheville Community College *A*

Washington

Bates Technical College *C, A*
Centralia College *A*

DeVry University
    Federal Way *A, B*
Green River Community College *A*
Lake Washington Technical
    College *C, A*
Lower Columbia College *A*
North Seattle Community
    College *C, A*
Olympic College *C, A*
Pierce College *C, A*
Skagit Valley College *A*
South Puget Sound Community
    College *C, A*
Spokane Community College *C, A*
Spokane Falls Community
    College *C, A*
Western Washington University *B*

West Virginia

Bluefield State College *A, B*
Fairmont State University *A, B*
Southern West Virginia Community
    and Technical College *A*
West Virginia State Community and
    Technical College *A*

Wisconsin

Chippewa Valley Technical College *A*
Fox Valley Technical College *A*
Gateway Technical College *A*
Herzing University *A, B*
Mid-State Technical College *A*
Milwaukee Area Technical College *A*
Milwaukee School of Engineering *B*
Moraine Park Technical College *C*
Northcentral Technical College *A*
Northeast Wisconsin Technical
    College *A*
Southwest Wisconsin Technical
    College *A*
Waukesha County Technical
    College *A*
Western Technical College *A*

Wyoming

Casper College *C, A*

Electrician

Alabama

Bevill State Community College *C, A*
Bishop State Community College *C*
Calhoun Community College *A*
George C. Wallace State Community
    College
    George C. Wallace Community
        College at Dothan *C, A*
Jefferson Davis Community College *C*
Lawson State Community College *C*
Northwest-Shoals Community
    College *C*
Shelton State Community
    College *C, A*

Alaska

Ilisagvik College *C*

Arizona

Cochise College *C*
GateWay Community College *C, A*
Mohave Community College *C*
Northland Pioneer College *C, A*
Refrigeration School *C*
Tohono O'odham Community
    College *C, A*

Arkansas

University of Arkansas
    Cossatot Community College of the
        C

California

Allan Hancock College *C*
Foothill College *C,A*
Fresno City College *C,A*
Hartnell College *C*
Los Angeles Trade and Technical
    College *C,A*
Merced College *C*
Modesto Junior College *C,A*
Santiago Canyon College *A*
Southern California Institute of
    Technology *C*
WyoTech: Fremont *C*
WyoTech: Long Beach *C,A*

Colorado

Red Rocks Community College *C,A*

Florida

Brevard Community College *C*
Daytona State College *A*
Florida State College at Jacksonville *C*
Gulf Coast Community College *C*
Hillsborough Community College *C*
Indian River State College *C*
Palm Beach Community College *C*
Santa Fe College *C*
Seminole Community College *C*
South Florida Community College *C*

Georgia

Albany Technical College *C*
Athens Technical College *C*
Bainbridge College *C,A*
Central Georgia Technical College *C*
Chattahoochee Technical College *C*
Savannah Technical College *C,A*
Southeastern Technical College *A*
Southwest Georgia Technical
    College *C*
West Georgia Technical College *C*

Hawaii

University of Hawaii
    Honolulu Community College *C,A*
    Kauai Community College *C,A*

Idaho

Idaho State University *C*

Illinois

Black Hawk College *C,A*
College of Lake County *A*
Heartland Community College *A*
John Wood Community College *C,A*
Kaskaskia College *C*
Parkland College *A*
Prairie State College *C,A*
Rend Lake College *C*
Richland Community College *A*
Southwestern Illinois College *C,A*
Waubonsee Community College *C,A*

Indiana

Ivy Tech Community College
    Bloomington *C,A*
    Central Indiana *C,A*
    East Central *C,A*
    Kokomo *C,A*
    Lafayette *C,A*
    North Central *C,A*
    Northeast *C,A*
    Northwest *C,A*
    Richmond *C,A*
    South Central *C,A*
    Southwest *C,A*
    Wabash Valley *C,A*

Iowa

Des Moines Area Community
    College *C*
Muscatine Community College *A*

Northeast Iowa Community
    College *C,A*
Western Iowa Tech Community
    College *C*

Kansas

Coffeyville Community College *C*
Highland Community College *A*
Kansas City Kansas Community
    College *C*

Kentucky

Big Sandy Community and Technical
    College *C*
Bluegrass Community and Technical
    College *C,A*
Elizabethtown Community and
    Technical College *C,A*
Hazard Community and Technical
    College *C*
Hopkinsville Community College *C*
Madisonville Community College *C,A*
Owensboro Community and
    Technical College *C,A*
Somerset Community College *C,A*
West Kentucky Community and
    Technical College *C,A*

Louisiana

Nunez Community College *C*

Maine

Eastern Maine Community College *C*
Kennebec Valley Community
    College *C,A*
Northern Maine Community
    College *C,A*
Washington County Community
    College *C*

Maryland

College of Southern Maryland *A*

Massachusetts

Benjamin Franklin Institute of
    Technology *A*

Michigan

Delta College *C,A*
Jackson Community College *C,A*
Kellogg Community College *C,A*
Macomb Community College *C*
Michigan State University *C*
Oakland Community College *C,A*

Minnesota

Anoka Technical College *C*
Dakota County Technical College *C,A*
Dunwoody College of
    Technology *C,A*
Hennepin Technical College *C,A*
Hibbing Community College *C*
Lake Superior College *C,A*
Leech Lake Tribal College *C*
Minneapolis Community and
    Technical College *C*
Minnesota State Community and
    Technical College *C*
Minnesota West Community and
    Technical College *A*
Northland Community & Technical
    College *C*
Northwest Technical College *C*
Ridgewater College *C,A*
Riverland Community College *C*
St. Cloud Technical College *C,A*
St. Paul College *C*

Missouri

Linn State Technical College *C,A*
Vatterott College *A*

Montana

Flathead Valley Community
    College *C,A*

Nebraska

Central Community College *C,A*
Mid-Plains Community College
    Area *C,A*
Northeast Community College *A*

Nevada

Great Basin College *C,A*

New Hampshire

Lakes Region Community
    College *C,A*

New Mexico

Central New Mexico Community
    College *C*
Dona Ana Community College of New
    Mexico State University *A*
Navajo Technical College *C*
Northern New Mexico College *C,A*

New York

Onondaga Community College *A*
State University of New York
    College of Technology at Alfred *A*
    College of Technology at Delhi *C,A*

North Carolina

Beaufort County Community
    College *C,A*
Bladen Community College *C*
Blue Ridge Community College *C*
Cape Fear Community College *C,A*
Catawba Valley Community College *C*
Central Piedmont Community
    College *C,A*
Cleveland Community College *C*
Coastal Carolina Community
    College *C*
Fayetteville Technical Community
    College *C*
Forsyth Technical Community
    College *C*
Guilford Technical Community
    College *C,A*
Haywood Community College *C,A*
Isothermal Community College *C,A*
James Sprunt Community College *C*
Johnston Community College *C*
Martin Community College *C,A*
Montgomery Community College *C,A*
Pitt Community College *C,A*
Randolph Community College *C,A*
Rockingham Community College *C*
Southwestern Community College *C*
Stanly Community College *C*
Surry Community College *C*
Tri-County Community College *A*
Vance-Granville Community
    College *C*
Wilkes Community College *A*
Wilson Community College *C*

North Dakota

North Dakota State College of
    Science *A*

Ohio

Hocking College *A*
Kaplan College: Dayton *C*
Vatterott College: Cleveland *C*

Oklahoma

Oklahoma State University
    Institute of Technology:
    Okmulgee *A*

Oregon

Chemeketa Community College *C,A*
Lane Community College *C,A*
Linn-Benton Community College *A*

Pennsylvania

CHI Institute: Franklin Mills *C*
Community College of Allegheny
    County *A*
Harrisburg Area Community
    College *C,A*
Lehigh Carbon Community College *C*
Luzerne County Community
    College *C,A*
Northampton Community College *A*
Pennsylvania College of
    Technology *C,A*
Thaddeus Stevens College of
    Technology *C*
Triangle Tech
    DuBois *A*
    Erie *A*
    Greensburg *A*
    Pittsburgh *A*
Triangle Tech: Bethlehem *C,A*

Puerto Rico

Inter American University of Puerto
    Rico
    San German Campus *C*

South Carolina

Aiken Technical College *C*
Greenville Technical College *C*
Technical College of the
    Lowcountry *C*
Trident Technical College *A*
York Technical College *C*

South Dakota

Mitchell Technical Institute *A*
Oglala Lakota College *C*
Western Dakota Technical Institute *A*

Tennessee

Northeast State Community
    College *C,A*
Southwest Tennessee Community
    College *C*

Texas

Brazosport College *C,A*
Houston Community College
    System *C*
Laredo Community College *C*
St. Philip's College *C,A*
South Plains College *C*
Texarkana College *C*
Texas State Technical College
    Waco *C*
Tyler Junior College *C,A*

Utah

College of Eastern Utah *T*
Salt Lake Community College *A*

Virginia

Central Virginia Community
    College *C*
Paul D. Camp Community College *C*
Rappahannock Community College *C*
Southside Virginia Community
    College *C*
Southwest Virginia Community
    College *C*
Thomas Nelson Community
    College *C*
Virginia Highlands Community
    College *C*
Wytheville Community College *C,A*

Washington
Bates Technical College C, A
Bellingham Technical College A
Big Bend Community College C, A
Olympic College A
South Seattle Community College A
Yakima Valley Community College A

Wisconsin
Blackhawk Technical College C
Gateway Technical College C
Milwaukee Area Technical College C
Northeast Wisconsin Technical College C
Waukesha County Technical College C
Western Technical College C

Wyoming
Western Wyoming Community College C

Electrocardiograph technology

California
City College of San Francisco C
De Anza College C
East Los Angeles College A
Orange Coast College C

Delaware
Delaware Technical and Community College
Stanton/Wilmington A

Florida
Florida National College C

Illinois
Harper College C

Maryland
Anne Arundel Community College C

Michigan
Baker College
of Auburn Hills A
of Muskegon C
of Port Huron C
Monroe County Community College C

Ohio
University of Toledo C

Virginia
Southwest Virginia Community College C

Electroencephalograph technology

Arizona
Phoenix College C

California
Orange Coast College C, A

Colorado
Community College of Denver C, A

Illinois
Black Hawk College A
East-West University C
Northwestern College C
Parkland College C
Triton College C

Iowa
Clinton Community College A
Kirkwood Community College A
Muscatine Community College A
Scott Community College A

Maryland
Harford Community College A

Minnesota
Minneapolis Community and Technical College C, A
Rochester Community and Technical College A

Pennsylvania
Community College of Allegheny County C

South Dakota
Southeast Technical Institute A

Utah
Independence University A

Wisconsin
Milwaukee Area Technical College A
Western Technical College A

Electromechanical technology

Arizona
Arizona State University M
Refrigeration School C

Arkansas
John Brown University A
University of Arkansas
Monticello C

California
Allan Hancock College C, A
Ohlone College A

Delaware
Delaware State University B
Delaware Technical and Community College
Terry A

Idaho
Idaho State University C, A

Illinois
Black Hawk College C

Kentucky
Hopkinsville Community College C
Madisonville Community College A
Maysville Community and Technical College C, A
Murray State University B
Owensboro Community and Technical College C

Maryland
Hagerstown Community College C, A

Massachusetts
Quinsigamond Community College A
Springfield Technical Community College A

Michigan
Northern Michigan University A
Oakland Community College A
Wayne State University B

Minnesota
Dunwoody College of Technology A
Minnesota State College - Southeast Technical C, A

Nebraska
Northeast Community College A

New Jersey
Union County College A

New Mexico
Mesalands Community College C, A

New York
City University of New York
New York City College of Technology A, B
Excelsior College A
Rochester Institute of Technology B
State University of New York
College at Buffalo B
College of Technology at Alfred A, B

North Carolina
Cape Fear Community College C
Catawba Valley Community College A
Guilford Technical Community College C
Wayne Community College A

Ohio
Bowling Green State University B
Central Ohio Technical College A
Cincinnati State Technical and Community College A
Columbus State Community College C, A
Edison State Community College C
Marion Technical College A
Miami University
Hamilton Campus A
Owens Community College
Toledo C, A
Shawnee State University A
University of Toledo B
Wright State University A

Pennsylvania
Northampton Community College C, A
Pennsylvania College of Technology A
Temple University B

South Carolina
Aiken Technical College A

South Dakota
Western Dakota Technical Institute A

Texas
Angelina College C, A
Texas State Technical College
Harlingen C, A

Virginia
Rappahannock Community College C, A
Tidewater Community College A

Washington
Bates Technical College C, A

West Virginia
Blue Ridge Community and Technical College A

Wisconsin
Gateway Technical College A

Lakeshore Technical College A
Western Technical College A

Electronics/electrical equipment repair

Alabama
Alabama Southern Community College C, A
Bishop State Community College A
Gadsden State Community College A
George C. Wallace State Community College
George C. Wallace Community College at Dothan C, A
Jefferson Davis Community College C
Lawson State Community College C
Northeast Alabama Community College C, A
Wallace State Community College at Hanceville C, A

Arizona
Arizona Western College A
GateWay Community College A
Northland Pioneer College C
Refrigeration School C

Arkansas
Ouachita Technical College C
Pulaski Technical College C, A
South Arkansas Community College C
Southeast Arkansas College C, A
University of Arkansas
Community College at Batesville A
Fort Smith A

California
Allan Hancock College C, A
Antelope Valley College C, A
Cerritos College A
Chabot College A
Chaffey College C, A
Citrus College C, A
Coastline Community College C, A
College of the Redwoods C
College of the Sequoias C, A
Cypress College C, A
East Los Angeles College C
El Camino College C, A
Fresno City College C, A
Hartnell College C, A
Long Beach City College C, A
Los Angeles City College A
Los Angeles Harbor College C, A
Los Angeles Mission College C, A
Los Angeles Trade and Technical College C, A
Los Medanos College C, A
Mendocino College C, A
Merced College C, A
Modesto Junior College C, A
Mount San Antonio College C, A
Ohlone College C, A
Orange Coast College C, A
Oxnard College C, A
Palomar College C, A
Sacramento City College C, A
Saddleback College C
San Bernardino Valley College C, A
San Jose City College A
Santa Barbara City College C, A
Sierra College C
Southwestern College C, A
Victor Valley College C, A
Yuba Community College District C, A

Colorado
Redstone College A
Westwood College: Denver
North A, B

Connecticut

Gateway Community College *C*

Florida

Brevard Community College *C*
Florida State College at Jacksonville *C*
Indian River State College *C*
Seminole Community College *C*

Georgia

Albany Technical College *C, A*
Athens Technical College *C*
Augusta Technical College *C*
Central Georgia Technical College *C*
Chattahoochee Technical College *C*
Dalton State College *C, A*
DeKalb Technical College *C*
Middle Georgia College *A*
Southwest Georgia Technical College *C*
Waycross College *A*
West Georgia Technical College *A*

Hawaii

University of Hawaii
    Hawaii Community College *A*
    Honolulu Community College *A*

Idaho

Lewis-Clark State College *C, A, B*

Illinois

College of DuPage *C, A*
Harper College *C*
Illinois Eastern Community Colleges
    Frontier Community College *C*
    Lincoln Trail College *C, A*
    Olney Central College *C*
    Wabash Valley College *C*
John A. Logan College *C, A*
Joliet Junior College *C*
Kankakee Community College *C, A*
Prairie State College *C*
Richland Community College *A*
Sauk Valley Community College *C*
Southwestern Illinois College *C, A*
Wilbur Wright College *C, A*

Indiana

Ivy Tech Community College
    Central Indiana *A*

Iowa

Kirkwood Community College *C, A*
Southwestern Community College *C, A*

Kansas

Allen County Community College *A*
Butler Community College *A*
Dodge City Community College *C, A*
Hutchinson Community College *A*
Johnson County Community College *C, A*
North Central Kansas Technical College *A*
Pittsburg State University *C, A*

Kentucky

Spencerian College: Lexington *C, A*

Louisiana

Delgado Community College *A*
ITI Technical College *C*
Nunez Community College *C*

Maine

Central Maine Community College *C, A*
Northern Maine Community College *A*

Maryland

Anne Arundel Community College *C, A*
Howard Community College *C, A*

Massachusetts

Quinsigamond Community College *C, A*

Michigan

Baker College of Cadillac *A*
Bay de Noc Community College *C*
Delta College *C, A*
Glen Oaks Community College *C*
Grand Rapids Community College *C, A*
Jackson Community College *C, A*
Lansing Community College *A*
Macomb Community College *C, A*
Montcalm Community College *C, A*
Northwestern Michigan College *A*
Schoolcraft College *C*
Washtenaw Community College *A*

Minnesota

Hennepin Technical College *C, A*
Northland Community & Technical College *C, A*
Riverland Community College *C*
St. Paul College *C*

Mississippi

Copiah-Lincoln Community College *A*
East Mississippi Community College *C*
Hinds Community College *C, A*
Meridian Community College *A*
Mississippi Delta Community College *C*
Mississippi Gulf Coast Community College *A*
Pearl River Community College *C*

Missouri

Linn State Technical College *A*
North Central Missouri College *A*
Ranken Technical College *A*
Vatterott College: Kansas City *A*
Vatterott College: Sunset Hills *C, A*

Nebraska

Metropolitan Community College *C*
Mid-Plains Community College Area *C, A*

New Hampshire

Manchester Community College *C*
Nashua Community College *A*

New Mexico

Dona Ana Community College of New Mexico State University *C, A*
Eastern New Mexico University: Roswell Campus *C, A*
Western New Mexico University *A*

New York

Erie Community College South Campus *C*
Hudson Valley Community College *A*
Island Drafting and Technical Institute *A*
State University of New York
    College of Agriculture and Technology at Morrisville *A*
    College of Technology at Alfred *A*
Technical Career Institutes *C, A*

North Carolina

Alamance Community College *A*

Asheville-Buncombe Technical Community College *C*
Beaufort County Community College *C*
Bladen Community College *C, A*
Coastal Carolina Community College *C, A*
College of the Albemarle *C*
Durham Technical Community College *C, A*
Forsyth Technical Community College *C*
Gaston College *C*
Johnston Community College *C*
Lenoir Community College *C, A*
McDowell Technical Community College *A*
Piedmont Community College *C, A*
Pitt Community College *C, A*
Richmond Community College *C*
Rockingham Community College *A*
South Piedmont Community College *C, A*
Tri-County Community College *A*
Vance-Granville Community College *C, A*
Wake Technical Community College *C, A*

North Dakota

Lake Region State College *A*
North Dakota State College of Science *C, A*

Ohio

Cleveland Institute of Electronics *C, A*
Columbus State Community College *A*
Eastern Gateway Community College *A*
North Central State College *A*
Owens Community College Toledo *C*
Stark State College of Technology *A*

Oklahoma

Tulsa Community College *A*
Vatterott College Tulsa *C, A*
Western Oklahoma State College *A*

Oregon

Clackamas Community College *C, A*
Linn-Benton Community College *A*
Mt. Hood Community College *A*
Umpqua Community College *A*

Pennsylvania

Johnson College *A*
Pennsylvania College of Technology *B*
Pittsburgh Institute of Aeronautics *A*

Puerto Rico

Electronic Data Processing College: San Sebastian *C*
Huertas Junior College *C, A*
University College of San Juan *C*

Rhode Island

New England Institute of Technology *A*

South Carolina

Aiken Technical College *C*
Central Carolina Technical College *C*
Denmark Technical College *A*
Florence-Darlington Technical College *C*
Midlands Technical College *C*
Northeastern Technical College *C*

Orangeburg-Calhoun Technical College *A*
Technical College of the Lowcountry *C*
Tri-County Technical College *C*
Trident Technical College *C*
York Technical College *C, A*

South Dakota

Lake Area Technical Institute *A*
Mitchell Technical Institute *A*
Southeast Technical Institute *A*
Western Dakota Technical Institute *A*

Tennessee

Southwest Tennessee Community College *A*

Texas

Amarillo College *C, A*
Central Texas College *C, A*
Collin County Community College District *A*
El Paso Community College *C, A*
Grayson County College *C, A*
Kilgore College *C, A*
Laredo Community College *C, A*
Lee College *C, A*
Midland College *A*
Odessa College *C, A*
St. Philip's College *C, A*
South Plains College *C, A*
Temple College *C, A*
Texas State Technical College Waco *C, A*
Vernon College *C, A*

Utah

College of Eastern Utah *C*
Salt Lake Community College *A*
Southern Utah University *A*

Virginia

Danville Community College *C*
ECPI College of Technology: Virginia Beach *C, A*
ECPI Technical College: Roanoke *A*
Eastern Shore Community College *C, A*
Mountain Empire Community College *A*
Northern Virginia Community College *C, A*
Paul D. Camp Community College *A*
Southwest Virginia Community College *C*
Virginia Highlands Community College *C*

Washington

Bates Technical College *C, A*
Centralia College *C, A*
Peninsula College *C, A*
Renton Technical College *C, A*
Skagit Valley College *C, A*
Spokane Community College *A*

Wisconsin

Chippewa Valley Technical College *C, A*
Herzing University *A, B*
Mid-State Technical College *A*
Moraine Park Technical College *C, A*
Southwest Wisconsin Technical College *A*
Western Technical College *C*

Wyoming

Western Wyoming Community College *C, A*

Elementary education

Alabama

Alabama Agricultural and Mechanical University *B, M*
Alabama State University *B*
Athens State University *B*
Auburn University *B, M, D, T*
Auburn University at Montgomery *B, M*
Birmingham-Southern College *B, T*
Chattahoochee Valley Community College *A*
Faulkner State Community College *A*
Faulkner University *B, M, T*
Gadsden State Community College *A*
Huntingdon College *B, T*
Jacksonville State University *B, M, T*
Judson College *B*
Miles College *B*
Oakwood University *B*
Samford University *M, T*
Spring Hill College *B, M, T*
Stillman College *B, T*
Troy University *B, M, T*
Tuskegee University *B, T*
University of Alabama *B, M, D*
University of Alabama
    Birmingham *B, M*
    Huntsville *B*
University of Mobile *B, M, T*
University of Montevallo *B, M, T*
University of North Alabama *B, M*
University of South Alabama *B, M, T*
University of West Alabama *B, M, T*

Alaska

Alaska Pacific University *A, B, M, T*
University of Alaska
    Anchorage *B*
    Fairbanks *B, M, T*
    Southeast *B, M, T*

Arizona

American Indian College of the Assemblies of God *B*
Arizona State University *B, M*
Central Arizona College *A*
Chandler-Gilbert Community College
    Pecos *A*
Coconino County Community College *A*
Eastern Arizona College *A*
Grand Canyon University *B, M*
Northern Arizona University *B, M*
Northland Pioneer College *A*
Prescott College *B, M, T*
Southwestern College *B*
Tohono O'odham Community College *A*
University of Arizona *B*
University of Phoenix *B, M*

Arkansas

Arkansas Baptist College *B*
Arkansas State University *M, T*
Arkansas Tech University *B, M*
Black River Technical College *A*
Harding University *B, M, T*
Ozarka College *A*
Phillips Community College of the University of Arkansas *A*
Southern Arkansas University *M, T*
University of Arkansas *B, M, D*
University of Arkansas
    Cossatot Community College of the *A*
    Little Rock *B, M, T*
    Pine Bluff *M*
University of the Ozarks *B*
Williams Baptist College *B*

California

Allan Hancock College *A*
Alliant International University *T*
Azusa Pacific University *B, T*
Barstow Community College *A*
Biola University *B, T*
California Baptist University *M, T*
California Lutheran University *B, M*
California State University
    Chico *T*
    East Bay *T*
    Fullerton *M, T*
    Long Beach *B, M, T*
    Los Angeles *M*
    Northridge *M*
    San Bernardino *M, T*
    San Marcos *T*
California State University: Channel Islands *T*
Chapman University *M, T*
Concordia University *B, T*
Cypress College *A*
Dominican University of California *T*
Fresno Pacific University *B, T*
Holy Names University *T*
Hope International University *B, M*
Humboldt State University *B, T*
Imperial Valley College *A*
La Sierra University *M, T*
Loyola Marymount University *M, T*
The Master's College *B, T*
Mills College *T*
Mount St. Mary's College *B*
National University *T*
Notre Dame de Namur University *T*
Occidental College *T*
Pacific Union College *B*
Patten University *T*
St. Mary's College of California *M*
San Diego Christian College *B, T*
San Diego State University *M, T*
San Francisco State University *T*
San Jose State University *M*
Shasta College *A*
Simpson University *B, T*
Sonoma State University *M, T*
Southwestern College *A*
Stanford University *M, T*
University of California
    Santa Barbara *T*
University of La Verne *B, M, T*
University of Redlands *B, T*
University of San Diego *T*
University of San Francisco *T*
University of Southern California *M, T*
University of the Pacific *B, T*
Vanguard University of Southern California *M, T*
Westmont College *T*
Whittier College *T*
William Jessup University *B*

Colorado

Adams State College *A, B, M, T*
Colorado Christian University *B*
Colorado College *M*
Colorado State University
    Pueblo *T*
Metropolitan State College of Denver *T*
Otero Junior College *A*
Regis University *B, T*
University of Colorado
    Boulder *T*
University of Northern Colorado *M, D, T*
Western State College of Colorado *B, T*

Connecticut

Eastern Connecticut State University *B, M, T*
Fairfield University *M, T*
Quinnipiac University *B, M*
Sacred Heart University *M, T*
Saint Joseph College *T*
Southern Connecticut State University *B, M, T*
University of Bridgeport *M, T*
University of Connecticut *B, T*
University of Hartford *B, M*
University of New Haven *T*
Western Connecticut State University *B, M*

Delaware

Delaware State University *B*
Delaware Technical and Community College
    Owens *A*
    Stanton/Wilmington *A*
    Terry *A*
University of Delaware *B, T*
Wesley College *B*
Wilmington University *B, M*

District of Columbia

American University *B, M, T*
Catholic University of America *B*
Gallaudet University *B, T*
George Washington University *M*
Trinity Washington University *M, T*
University of the District of Columbia *B, T*

Florida

Baptist College of Florida *B*
Barry University *B, M, T*
Bethune-Cookman University *B, T*
Broward College *A*
Carlos Albizu University *B, M*
Central Florida Community College *A*
Chipola College *B*
Clearwater Christian College *B*
Daytona State College *B*
Flagler College *B, T*
Florida Agricultural and Mechanical University *B, M, T*
Florida Atlantic University *B, M*
Florida Christian College *B*
Florida College *B*
Florida Gulf Coast University *B, M*
Florida International University *B*
Florida Memorial University *B, M, T*
Florida Southern College *B, T*
Florida State College at Jacksonville *A*
Florida State University *B, M, D*
Gulf Coast Community College *A*
Hobe Sound Bible College *B, T*
Indian River State College *A*
Jacksonville University *B, M, T*
Jones College *B*
Lynn University *B*
Miami Dade College *A*
Northwest Florida State College *A, B*
Nova Southeastern University *B*
Palm Beach Atlantic University *M*
Palm Beach Community College *A*
Pensacola Junior College *A*
Saint Leo University *B, M*
St. Petersburg College *B*
Saint Thomas University *B, T*
Southeastern University *B, M, T*
State College of Florida, Manatee-Sarasota *A*
Stetson University *B*
Trinity Baptist College *B*
Trinity College of Florida *B*
University of Central Florida *B, M*
University of Florida *B*
University of Miami *B*
University of North Florida *B, M*
University of South Florida *B, M*
University of Tampa *B, T*
University of West Florida *B, T*
Warner University *B*

Georgia

Agnes Scott College *T*
Albany State University *B*
Armstrong Atlantic State University *B, M, T*
Atlanta Christian College *B*
Augusta State University *B*
Brenau University *B*
College of Coastal Georgia *A, B*
Covenant College *B, T*
Dalton State College *A, B*
Emmanuel College *B*
Fort Valley State University *B, M, T*
Gainesville State College *A*
Georgia Southern University *B*
Georgia Southwestern State University *B*
Kennesaw State University *B, M*
LaGrange College *B*
Macon State College *A*
Mercer University *B, M, T*
Middle Georgia College *A*
Oglethorpe University *M*
Paine College *B*
Reinhardt College *B, M*
Shorter College *B, T*
University of Georgia *D*
University of West Georgia *B, M, T*

Hawaii

Chaminade University of Honolulu *B, M, T*
University of Hawaii
    Hilo *T*
    Manoa *B*
    West Oahu *B*

Idaho

Boise State University *B, M, T*
Brigham Young University-Idaho *B*
Idaho State University *B*
Lewis-Clark State College *B, T*
North Idaho College *A*
Northwest Nazarene University *B*
University of Idaho *B, M, T*

Illinois

Augustana College *B, T*
Aurora University *B*
Benedictine University *B, M, T*
Black Hawk College: East Campus *A*
Blackburn College *B, T*
Bradley University *B*
Chicago State University *B, M, T*
City Colleges of Chicago
    Harold Washington College *A*
    Kennedy-King College *A*
Columbia College Chicago *M*
Concordia University Chicago *B, T*
DePaul University *B, M, T*
Dominican University *T*
Eastern Illinois University *B, M, T*
Elmhurst College *B*
Eureka College *B*
Governors State University *B, T*
Greenville College *B, M, T*
Hebrew Theological College *B*
Illinois Central College *A*
Illinois College *B, T*
Illinois State University *B, T*
Illinois Wesleyan University *B*
John A. Logan College *A*
Joliet Junior College *A*
Judson University *B*
Kankakee Community College *A*
Kishwaukee College *A*
Knox College *T*
Lewis University *B, M*
Lincoln College *A*
Loyola University Chicago *B, M*
MacMurray College *B, T*
McKendree University *B*
Millikin University *B, T*

Monmouth College B, T
National-Louis University B, M, T
North Central College B, T
North Park University B, M
Northeastern Illinois University B
Northern Illinois University B, M, T
Olivet Nazarene University B, M, T
Principia College B, T
Quincy University B, T
Rockford College B, M, T
Roosevelt University B, M
Saint Xavier University M
Southern Illinois University
  Carbondale B
Southern Illinois University
  Edwardsville B, M, T
Southwestern Illinois College A
Trinity Christian College B, T
Trinity International
  University B, M, T
University of Illinois
  Chicago B
  Urbana-Champaign B, M, D, T
University of St. Francis B, M
Western Illinois University B, M
Wheaton College B, M, T

Indiana
Ancilla College A
Anderson University B, T
Ball State University B, M, D, T
Bethel College B
Butler University B, M
Calumet College of St. Joseph B, T
DePauw University T
Franklin College B, T
Goshen College B, T
Grace College B
Hanover College B
Holy Cross College B
Huntington University B, M
Indiana Institute of Technology B
Indiana State University B, M, T
Indiana University
  Bloomington B, M, D, T
  East B
  Kokomo B, M
  Northwest B, M, T
  South Behd B, M, T
  Southeast B, M
Indiana University-Purdue University
  Fort Wayne B, M, T
Indiana University-Purdue University
  Indianapolis B, M, D, T
Indiana Wesleyan University B, T
Manchester College B, T
Marian University B
Oakland City University A, B, M
Purdue University B, M
Purdue University
  Calumet B, M, T
  North Central B, M, T
Saint Joseph's College B
Saint Mary's College B, T
St. Mary-of-the-Woods College B, T
Taylor University B, T
Trine University B, T
University of Evansville B, T
University of Indianapolis B, M, T
University of St. Francis B, T
University of Southern Indiana B, M
Valparaiso University B, M, T
Vincennes University A

Iowa
Briar Cliff University B
Buena Vista University B, T
Central College B, T
Clarke College B, T
Coe College B
Cornell College B, T
Dordt College B, T
Drake University B, M
Ellsworth Community College A

Emmaus Bible College B
Faith Baptist Bible College and
  Theological Seminary B, T
Graceland University B, T
Grand View University B, T
Grinnell College T
Iowa State University B, M, T
Iowa Wesleyan College B
Loras College B
Luther College B
Maharishi University of
  Management B, M
Marshalltown Community College A
Morningside College B
Mount Mercy College B, T
Northwestern College B, T
St. Ambrose University B, T
Simpson College B, T
University of Dubuque B, T
University of Iowa B, M, D, T
University of Northern Iowa B, M
Upper Iowa University B, T
Waldorf College B
Wartburg College B, T
William Penn University B

Kansas
Baker University B, T
Barclay College B
Benedictine College B
Bethany College B, T
Bethel College B, T
Butler Community College A
Central Christian College of
  Kansas A, B
Coffeyville Community College A
Dodge City Community College A
Donnelly College A
Emporia State University B, M
Fort Hays State University B, M, T
Friends University B, T
Garden City Community College A
Highland Community College A
Kansas State University B, M, T
Kansas Wesleyan University B, T
Labette Community College A
McPherson College B, T
MidAmerica Nazarene University B, T
Newman University B, T
Ottawa University B, T
Pittsburg State University B, M
Pratt Community College A
Southwestern College B, M, T
Sterling College B
Tabor College B
University of Kansas B, T
University of St. Mary B, T
Washburn University B
Wichita State University B, M, T

Kentucky
Alice Lloyd College B
Asbury College B, T
Bellarmine University B, M, T
Berea College B, T
Brescia University B, T
Campbellsville University B
Centre College B, T
Eastern Kentucky University B, M
Georgetown College B, M
Kentucky Christian University B, T
Kentucky Mountain Bible College B
Kentucky State University B
Kentucky Wesleyan College B, T
Lindsey Wilson College B, T
Mid-Continent University B
Midway College B
Morehead State University B, M, T
Murray State University B, M, T
Northern Kentucky University B, M
Pikeville College B, T
St. Catharine College B
Spalding University B, M, T
Thomas More College B

Transylvania University B, T
Union College B, M
University of Kentucky B, M
University of Louisville B, M
University of the Cumberlands B, M, T
Western Kentucky University B, M, T

Louisiana
Centenary College of
  Louisiana B, M, T
Dillard University B, T
Grambling State University B
Louisiana College B
Louisiana State University
  Alexandria B
  Shreveport B
Louisiana State University and
  Agricultural and Mechanical
  College B
Louisiana Tech University B
McNeese State University B, M, T
Nicholls State University B, M
Northwestern State University B, M
Our Lady of Holy Cross College B
Southeastern Louisiana
  University B, M
Southern University
  New Orleans B
Southern University and Agricultural
  and Mechanical College B, M
University of Louisiana at Lafayette B
University of Louisiana at
  Monroe B, M
University of New Orleans B
Xavier University of Louisiana B, M

Maine
College of the Atlantic T
Husson University B, T
Saint Joseph's College of Maine B
Thomas College B
University of Maine B, M
University of Maine
  Farmington B, T
  Fort Kent B
  Machias B
  Presque Isle B
University of New England B
University of Southern Maine B, T

Maryland
Allegany College of Maryland A
Anne Arundel Community College A
Bowie State University B, M
Carroll Community College A
Cecil College A
Chesapeake College A
College of Notre Dame of Maryland B
College of Southern Maryland A
Community College of Baltimore
  County A
Coppin State University B
Frostburg State University B, M, T
Garrett College A
Goucher College B, M, T
Hagerstown Community College A
Harford Community College A
Hood College T
Howard Community College A
Loyola University Maryland B, T
McDaniel College M, T
Morgan State University B, M
Mount St. Mary's University B, M, T
Prince George's Community
  College A
Salisbury University B, T
Stevenson University B
Towson University B, M, T
University of Maryland
  College Park B
Washington Adventist University B, T
Washington Bible College B, T
Wor-Wic Community College A

Massachusetts
American International
  College B, M, T
Anna Maria College B, M
Assumption College T
Atlantic Union College B
Bay Path College B
Becker College B
Boston College B, M, T
Boston University B, M, T
Bridgewater State College B, M, T
Bristol Community College A
Cambridge College M
Clark University M
Curry College B
Eastern Nazarene College B, M, T
Elms College B, M, T
Emmanuel College B, M
Endicott College B, M
Fitchburg State College B, M, T
Framingham State College B, M
Gordon College B
Hellenic College/Holy Cross B
Lasell College B, T
Lesley University B, M
Massachusetts College of Liberal
  Arts T
Merrimack College M, T
North Shore Community College A
Northeastern University M
Pine Manor College T
Regis College M
Salem State College B, M
Simmons College B, M
Smith College M
Springfield College B, M, T
Springfield Technical Community
  College A
Stonehill College B
Suffolk University M
Tufts University M
University of Massachusetts
  Dartmouth B
Wellesley College T
Western New England College B, M, T
Westfield State College B, M, T
Wheaton College T
Wheelock College B, M
Worcester State College B, M, T

Michigan
Adrian College B, T
Albion College T
Alma College B, T
Andrews University B, M
Baker College
  of Auburn Hills B
  of Clinton Township B
  of Flint B
  of Jackson B
  of Muskegon B
  of Owosso B
Baker College of Allen Park B
Calvin College B, T
Central Michigan University B, M
Cornerstone University B
Delta College A
Eastern Michigan University B, M, T
Ferris State University A, B
Finlandia University B
Gogebic Community College A
Grace Bible College B
Grand Rapids Community College A
Grand Valley State University M, T
Henry Ford Community College A
Hillsdale College B
Kuyper College B
Lake Michigan College A
Lake Superior State University B, T
Lansing Community College A
Madonna University T
Marygrove College T
Michigan State University B
Mid Michigan Community College A

Northern Michigan University *B, M, T*
Oakland University *B, M*
Rochester College *B*
Saginaw Valley State University *B, M*
Siena Heights University *B, M, T*
Spring Arbor University *B*
University of Detroit Mercy *B, M, T*
University of Michigan *B*
University of Michigan
    Dearborn *T*
    Flint *B, M*
Washtenaw Community College *A*
Wayne County Community College *A*
Wayne State University *B, M, T*
Western Michigan University *B, T*

Minnesota

Augsburg College *B, T*
Bemidji State University *B, M, T*
Bethany Lutheran College *B*
Bethel University *B*
College of St. Benedict *B*
College of St. Scholastica *B, T*
Concordia College: Moorhead *B, T*
Concordia University: St. Paul *B, T*
Crown College *B, T*
Gustavus Adolphus College *B*
Hamline University *B, M, T*
Martin Luther College *B*
Metropolitan State University *B*
Minnesota State University
    Mankato *B, M, T*
    Moorhead *B*
Minnesota West Community and
    Technical College *A*
Normandale Community College *A*
North Central University *B*
Northwestern College *B*
Ridgewater College *A*
St. Catherine University *B, M, T*
Saint Cloud State University *B, T*
St. John's University *B*
St. Mary's University of
    Minnesota *B, M*
Southwest Minnesota State
    University *B, T*
University of Minnesota
    Duluth *B, T*
    Morris *B*
    Twin Cities *B, M, T*
University of St. Thomas *B, M*
Vermilion Community College *A*
Walden University *M*
Winona State University *B, M, T*

Mississippi

Alcorn State University *B, M*
Belhaven University *B, M, T*
Blue Mountain College *B, M*
Delta State University *B, M*
Hinds Community College *A*
Holmes Community College *A*
Jackson State University *B, M*
Millsaps College *B, T*
Mississippi College *B, M*
Mississippi Delta Community
    College *A*
Mississippi Gulf Coast Community
    College *A*
Mississippi State University *B, M, D, T*
Mississippi University for Women *B, T*
Mississippi Valley State
    University *B, M, T*
Northwest Mississippi Community
    College *A*
Rust College *B*
Tougaloo College *B, T*
University of Mississippi *B, T*
University of Southern Mississippi *B*

Missouri

Avila University *B, T*
Baptist Bible College *B*

Calvary Bible College and Theological
    Seminary *B*
Central Methodist University *B*
College of the Ozarks *B, T*
Crowder College *A*
Culver-Stockton College *B, T*
Drury University *B, T*
Evangel University *B, T*
Fontbonne University *B, T*
Hannibal-LaGrange College *B*
Harris-Stowe State University *B, T*
Lincoln University *B, M*
Lindenwood University *B, M*
Maryville University of Saint
    Louis *B, M, T*
Missouri Baptist University *B, T*
Missouri Southern State
    University *B, T*
Missouri State University *B, M*
Missouri Valley College *B, T*
Missouri Western State University *B*
Northwest Missouri State
    University *B, M, T*
Ozark Christian College *A*
Park University *B*
Rockhurst University *B*
St. Louis Community College
    St. Louis Community College at
        Meramec *A*
Southeast Missouri State
    University *B, M, T*
Southwest Baptist University *B, T*
Stephens College *B, T*
Truman State University *M, T*
University of Central Missouri *B, M, T*
University of Missouri
    Columbia *B, M, D*
    Kansas City *B*
    St. Louis *B, M*
Washington University in St.
    Louis *B, M, T*
Westminster College *B, T*
William Jewell College *B, T*
William Woods University *B, T*

Montana

Blackfeet Community College *A*
Fort Belknap College *A*
Montana State University
    Billings *B, T*
    Bozeman *B*
Rocky Mountain College *B, T*
Salish Kootenai College *A*
Stone Child College *A*
University of Great Falls *B*
University of Montana *B, M*
University of Montana: Western *B, T*

Nebraska

Chadron State College *B, M*
College of Saint Mary *B, T*
Concordia University *B, T*
Creighton University *B*
Dana College *B*
Doane College *B*
Grace University *A, B*
Nebraska Wesleyan University *B*
Northeast Community College *A*
Peru State College *B, T*
Union College *B, T*
University of Nebraska
    Kearney *B, M, T*
    Lincoln *B*
    Omaha *B, M, T*
Wayne State College *B, T*
Western Nebraska Community
    College *A*
York College *B, T*

Nevada

Great Basin College *A, B*
Nevada State College *B*
Sierra Nevada College *M*

Truckee Meadows Community
    College *A*
University of Nevada
    Las Vegas *B, T*
    Reno *B, M, T*

New Hampshire

Dartmouth College *T*
Franklin Pierce University *M, T*
Granite State College *T*
Keene State College *B, M, T*
New England College *B, T*
Plymouth State University *B, M, T*
Rivier College *B, M, T*
Southern New Hampshire
    University *B, M*
University of New Hampshire *M, T*
University of New Hampshire at
    Manchester *M, T*

New Jersey

Caldwell College *B, T*
Centenary College *T*
The College of New Jersey *B, M, T*
College of St. Elizabeth *B, T*
Essex County College *A*
Felician College *B*
Georgian Court University *B, T*
Kean University *B, M, T*
Monmouth University *M*
New Jersey City University *B, T*
Raritan Valley Community College *A*
Rider University *B*
Rowan University *B, M*
Rutgers, The State University of New
    Jersey
    Camden Regional Campus *T*
    New Brunswick/Piscataway
        Campus *T*
    Newark Regional Campus *T*
Saint Peter's College *B, T*
Seton Hall University *B, M, T*
Sussex County Community College *A*
William Paterson University of New
    Jersey *B, M, T*

New Mexico

Central New Mexico Community
    College *A*
Eastern New Mexico University *B*
New Mexico Highlands
    University *B, M*
New Mexico Junior College *A*
New Mexico State University *B*
Northern New Mexico College *A*
San Juan College *A, T*
University of New Mexico *B, M*
University of the Southwest *B*
Western New Mexico
    University *B, M, T*

New York

Adelphi University *M, T*
Alfred University *B, T*
Barnard College *T*
Boricua College *B, M*
Canisius College *B, M, T*
City University of New York
    Brooklyn College *B, M*
    City College *B, M, T*
    College of Staten Island *M, T*
    Hunter College *B, M, T*
    Kingsborough Community
        College *A*
    Lehman College *T*
    Medgar Evers College *B*
    Queens College *B, M, T*
    York College *T*
Colgate University *T*
College of Mount St. Vincent *T*
College of New Rochelle *B, M, T*
College of Saint Rose *B, M, T*

Columbia University
    School of General Studies *B, T*
Concordia College *T*
Corning Community College *A*
D'Youville College *M, T*
Daemen College *B, M, T*
Dominican College of Blauvelt *B, T*
Dowling College *B, M*
Dutchess Community College *A*
Elmira College *B, M, T*
Finger Lakes Community College *A*
Five Towns College *B, M, T*
Fordham University *M, T*
Hobart and William Smith
    Colleges *M, T*
Hofstra University *B, M*
Houghton College *B, T*
Iona College *B, M, T*
Ithaca College *M*
Le Moyne College *M, T*
Long Island University
    Brooklyn Campus *B, M, T*
    C. W. Post Campus *B, M, T*
Manhattan College *B, T*
Manhattanville College *M, T*
Marymount Manhattan College *T*
Medaille College *B, M, T*
Mercy College *M, T*
Mohawk Valley Community College *A*
Molloy College *B, M, T*
Nassau Community College *A*
Nazareth College *B, M, T*
New York Institute of
    Technology *B, M, T*
New York University *B, M, D, T*
Niagara County Community
    College *A*
Niagara University *B, M, T*
Nyack College *B, M*
Onondaga Community College *A*
Orange County Community College *A*
Pace University *B, M, T*
Roberts Wesleyan College *M*
Rockland Community College *A*
Russell Sage College *B, T*
Saint Bonaventure University *B, M*
St. Francis College *B*
St. John Fisher College *B, M, T*
St. John's University *B, M, T*
St. Joseph's College *B, T*
St. Joseph's College: Suffolk
    Campus *B, T*
St. Thomas Aquinas College *B, M, T*
Sarah Lawrence College *M*
Skidmore College *B, T*
State University of New York
    Binghamton *M*
    Buffalo *M, D, T*
    College at Brockport *B, M, T*
    College at Buffalo *B, M, T*
    College at Cortland *B, M*
    College at Fredonia *B, M, T*
    College at Geneseo *B, M, T*
    College at Old Westbury *B, T*
    College at Oneonta *B, M, T*
    College at Plattsburgh *B, M*
    College at Potsdam *B, M*
    College of Technology at Delhi *A*
    New Paltz *B, M, T*
    Oswego *B, M, T*
Sullivan County Community
    College *A*
Syracuse University *B, T*
Ulster County Community College *A*
University of Rochester *M*
Utica College *B, M*
Vassar College *T*
Wagner College *M, T*
Wells College *T*
Yeshiva University *B, M*

North Carolina

Appalachian State University *B, M, T*
Barton College *B*

Belmont Abbey College B
Bennett College for Women B
Brevard College B
Campbell University B, M, T
Catawba College B, M, T
Chowan University B, M, T
East Carolina University B, M
Elizabeth City State University B, M, T
Elon University B, M, T
Fayetteville State University M
Fayetteville Technical Community
  College A
Gardner-Webb University B, M
Greensboro College B, T
Guilford College B, T
High Point University B, M, T
Isothermal Community College A
James Sprunt Community College A
John Wesley College B
Johnson C. Smith University B, T
Lees-McRae College B, T
Lenoir Community College A
Lenoir-Rhyne University B, T
Livingstone College B
Mars Hill College B, T
Martin Community College A
Meredith College M, T
Methodist University A, B, T
Montreat College B, M
North Carolina Agricultural and
  Technical State University B, M, T
North Carolina Central
  University B, M, T
North Carolina State
  University B, M, T
North Carolina Wesleyan College B
Pfeiffer University B, T
Piedmont Baptist College B
Queens University of Charlotte B, M
St. Andrews Presbyterian College B, T
St. Augustine's College B
Salem College B, M, T
Sandhills Community College A
Shaw University B, T
Southeastern Community College A
Stanly Community College A
University of North Carolina
  Asheville T
  Chapel Hill B
  Charlotte B, M
  Greensboro B
  Pembroke B, M
  Wilmington B, M
Wake Forest University B, T
Warren Wilson College B, T
Wayne Community College A
Western Carolina University B, T
Wilkes Community College A
Wilson Community College A
Wingate University B, M, T
Winston-Salem State University B, M

North Dakota

Dickinson State University B, T
Jamestown College B
Mayville State University B, T
Minot State University B, M
North Dakota State University B
Sitting Bull College A, B
Trinity Bible College B, T
Turtle Mountain Community
  College B
University of Mary B, M
University of North Dakota B, M

Ohio

Bluffton University B
Bowling Green State University B
Cedarville University B
Cincinnati Christian University B
Cleveland State University B, M, T
College of Wooster T
Defiance College B, T

Franciscan University of
  Steubenville B, M
God's Bible School and College A, B
Heidelberg University T
Hiram College B, T
John Carroll University B, M, T
Kent State University M
Kent State University
  Salem A
Marietta College B
Miami University
  Oxford Campus M
Mount Vernon Nazarene
  University B, T
Muskingum University B, M, T
Notre Dame College B, T
Ohio Christian University B
Ohio Dominican University B, T
Ohio Northern University B, T
Ohio State University
  Columbus Campus M, T
  Mansfield Campus B, M, T
  Marion Campus B, M, T
Ohio University M, T
Ohio Wesleyan University B
Otterbein College B
Temple Baptist College B
Union Institute & University B, M
University of Akron B, M
University of Akron: Wayne College M
University of Cincinnati B, M, D, T
University of Cincinnati
  Clermont College A
  Raymond Walters College A
University of Rio Grande B, T
University of Toledo M, T
Urbana University B
Walsh University B
Washington State Community
  College A
Wilmington College B
Wright State University B, M, T
Xavier University B, M
Youngstown State University B, M

Oklahoma

Bacone College B
Cameron University B, T
Carl Albert State College A
Connors State College A
East Central University B, M, T
Eastern Oklahoma State College A
Langston University B, M
Mid-America Christian University B
Murray State College A
Northeastern State University B, T
Northern Oklahoma College A
Northwestern Oklahoma State
  University B, M, T
Oklahoma Baptist University B, T
Oklahoma Christian University B, T
Oklahoma City University B, M
Oklahoma Panhandle State
  University B
Oklahoma State University B
Oklahoma Wesleyan University B, T
Oral Roberts University B, T
Rogers State University A
St. Gregory's University B
Seminole State College A
Southeastern Oklahoma State
  University B, T
Southern Nazarene University B, M
Southwestern Oklahoma State
  University B, M, T
University of Central Oklahoma B, M
University of Oklahoma B, T
University of Science and Arts of
  Oklahoma B, T
University of Tulsa B, T

Oregon

Chemeketa Community College A
Concordia University B, M, T

Corban College B, M
Eastern Oregon University B, M
George Fox University B, M, T
Lewis & Clark College M
Linfield College B, T
Linn-Benton Community College A
Multnomah University B
Oregon State University M
Portland State University T
Southern Oregon University M, T
Treasure Valley Community College A
University of Oregon M, T
University of Portland B, M, T
Warner Pacific College B, T
Western Oregon University B, T
Willamette University M

Pennsylvania

Albright College B, M, T
Alvernia University B
Arcadia University B, M, T
Baptist Bible College of
  Pennsylvania B, M
Bloomsburg University of
  Pennsylvania M
Bucknell University B, T
Cabrini College B, T
California University of
  Pennsylvania B, M
Carlow University B, M
Cedar Crest College B, T
Chatham University B, M, T
Chestnut Hill College B, M, T
Cheyney University of
  Pennsylvania B, M, T
Clarion University of
  Pennsylvania B, M, T
Community College of Allegheny
  County A
DeSales University B, M, T
Duquesne University B, M, T
East Stroudsburg University of
  Pennsylvania B, M, T
Eastern University B, M, T
Edinboro University of
  Pennsylvania B, M, T
Elizabethtown College B
Gannon University B
Geneva College B, T
Grove City College B, T
Gwynedd-Mercy College B, T
Harrisburg Area Community
  College A
Holy Family University B, M, T
Immaculata University B
Indiana University of
  Pennsylvania B, D
Juniata College B, T
Keystone College B, T
King's College B, T
Kutztown University of
  Pennsylvania B, M, T
La Roche College B
La Salle University B, M, T
Lancaster Bible College B
Lebanon Valley College B, T
Lehigh University M
Lincoln University B, M, T
Lock Haven University of
  Pennsylvania B
Lycoming College T
Manor College A
Mansfield University of
  Pennsylvania B, M, T
Marywood University B
Mercyhurst College B, T
Messiah College B, T
Millersville University of
  Pennsylvania B, M, T
Misericordia University B, T
Montgomery County Community
  College A
Moravian College T
Mount Aloysius College B

Muhlenberg College T
Neumann University B, T
Penn State
  Abington B
  Altoona B
  Beaver B
  Berks B
  Brandywine B
  DuBois B
  Erie, The Behrend College B
  Fayette, The Eberly Campus B
  Greater Allegheny B
  Harrisburg B
  Hazleton B
  Lehigh Valley B
  Mont Alto B
  New Kensington B
  Schuylkill B
  Shenango B
  University Park B
  Wilkes-Barre B
  Worthington Scranton B
  York B
Philadelphia Biblical University B, T
Point Park University B
Reading Area Community College A
Robert Morris University B, T
Rosemont College B, T
St. Francis University B, T
Saint Joseph's University B, M, T
St. Vincent College B, T
Seton Hill University M, T
Shippensburg University of
  Pennsylvania B, T
Slippery Rock University of
  Pennsylvania B, M, T
Susquehanna University B, T
Temple University B, M
Thiel College B
University of Pennsylvania B, M, T
University of Pittsburgh T
University of Pittsburgh
  Bradford B
  Johnstown B, T
University of Scranton B, M
Valley Forge Christian College B
Villanova University B
Washington & Jefferson College T
Waynesburg University B, T
West Chester University of
  Pennsylvania B, M, T
Westminster College B, M, T
Widener University B, M, T
Wilkes University B, T
Wilson College A, B, M, T
York College of Pennsylvania B, T

Puerto Rico

American University of Puerto
  Rico B, T
Bayamon Central University B, M
Caribbean University B, T
Inter American University of Puerto
  Rico
  Aguadilla Campus B, M
  Arecibo Campus B
  Fajardo Campus B, T
  Guayama Campus B
  Metropolitan Campus B, M
  Ponce Campus B, M
  San German Campus B
Pontifical Catholic University of
  Puerto Rico B, D
Turabo University B, M
Universidad Adventista de las
  Antillas B
Universidad Metropolitana B
University of Puerto Rico
  Aguadilla B
  Arecibo B, M
  Humacao B
  Ponce B
  Rio Piedras B
  Utuado B

University of the Sacred Heart B

Rhode Island

Rhode Island College B, M, T
Roger Williams University B, M
Salve Regina University B
University of Rhode Island B

South Carolina

Anderson University B, T
Benedict College B
Bob Jones University B, M
Charleston Southern University B, M
Claflin University B
Clemson University B, M
Coastal Carolina University B, M, T
Coker College B, T
College of Charleston B, M, T
Columbia College B, T
Converse College B, M, T
Erskine College B, T
Francis Marion University B, M, T
Furman University T
Lander University B, M, T
Limestone College B
Morris College B, T
Newberry College B, T
North Greenville University B, T
South Carolina State
    University B, M, T
Southern Wesleyan University B, T
University of South Carolina M, D
University of South Carolina
    Aiken B, M, T
    Upstate B, M, T
Winthrop University B, M, T

South Dakota

Augustana College B, M, T
Black Hills State University B, T
Dakota State University B, T
Dakota Wesleyan University B, T
Mount Marty College B
Northern State University B, M, T
Oglala Lakota College B
Sinte Gleska University B
University of Sioux Falls B, M, T
University of South Dakota B, M, T

Tennessee

Aquinas College B, T
Belmont University B, M, T
Bethel University B, T
Bryan College T
Carson-Newman College B, M, T
Christian Brothers University B, M, T
Columbia State Community College A
Crichton College B, T
Cumberland University B, T
East Tennessee State University M, T
Fisk University T
Free Will Baptist Bible College B
Freed-Hardeman University B, T
Johnson Bible College T
King College T
Lambuth University B, T
Lee University B, T
Lincoln Memorial University B, T
Lipscomb University B, T
Martin Methodist College B
Motlow State Community College A
Southern Adventist University B
Tennessee State University M, T
Tennessee Technological
    University M, T
Tennessee Temple University B, M, T
Tennessee Wesleyan College B, T
Trevecca Nazarene University B, M, T
Tusculum College B, T
Union University B, T
University of Tennessee
    Chattanooga M
    Knoxville B

Vanderbilt University B, M, D, T

Texas

Abilene Christian University B, T
Amarillo College A
Angelina College A
Arlington Baptist College B, T
Austin College M
Baylor University B, T
Brazosport College A
Clarendon College A
Coastal Bend College A
College of the Mainland A
Concordia University Texas B
Dallas Baptist University B, M
Dallas Christian College B, T
Del Mar College A
East Texas Baptist University B
El Paso Community College A
Frank Phillips College A
Galveston College A
Grayson County College A
Howard Payne University B, T
Huston-Tillotson University T
Jarvis Christian College B, T
Lamar University B, M, T
Laredo Community College A
LeTourneau University B, T
Lubbock Christian University B, M
McMurry University B, T
Midwestern State University M
Navarro College A
North Lake College A
Our Lady of the Lake University of San
    Antonio M
Prairie View A&M University M
St. Edward's University T
St. Mary's University T
Schreiner University B
South Texas College A
Southwestern Adventist
    University B, M, T
Southwestern Assemblies of God
    University B, M
Southwestern University B, T
Stephen F. Austin State University M, T
Sul Ross State University B, M, T
Temple College A
Texas A&M International
    University B, M, T
Texas A&M University
    Commerce B, M, D, T
    Corpus Christi M, T
    Kingsville B, M
    Texarkana T
Texas Christian University B, M
Texas College B, T
Texas Lutheran University B, T
Texas State University: San
    Marcos M, T
Texas Tech University M
Texas Wesleyan University B, M, T
Texas Woman's University M
Trinity University B, M
Trinity Valley Community College A
University of Dallas B, T
University of Houston M, T
University of Houston
    Downtown M
    Victoria M
University of Mary Hardin-Baylor B, T
University of St. Thomas B
University of Texas
    Brownsville - Texas Southmost
        College M
    Pan American M
    San Antonio M, T
University of the Incarnate Word B, T
Wayland Baptist University B, T
West Texas A&M University M, T
Wharton County Junior College A
Wiley College B

Utah

Brigham Young University B
Dixie State College of Utah B
Snow College A
Southern Utah University B, M, T
University of Utah B
Utah State University B, M, D
Utah Valley University B
Weber State University B, M
Western Governors University B, M, T
Westminster College B

Vermont

Bennington College B, M
Castleton State College B, M
Champlain College B
College of St. Joseph in Vermont B, M
Goddard College B
Green Mountain College B, T
Johnson State College B, M
Lyndon State College B
Middlebury College D, T
Norwich University T
St. Michael's College B, T
University of Vermont B, T

Virginia

Averett University M, T
Bluefield College B, T
Bridgewater College T
College of William and Mary M, T
Germanna Community College A
Hampton University M
Hollins University T
James Madison University T
Liberty University M, T
Longwood University B, T
Lynchburg College B
Mary Baldwin College T
Marymount University M
Old Dominion University M, T
Radford University T
Randolph College T
Randolph-Macon College T
Regent University M
St. Paul's College T
University of Mary Washington M
University of Richmond M
University of Virginia's College at
    Wise T
Virginia Intermont College B, T
Virginia Wesleyan College T

Washington

Cascadia Community College A
City University of Seattle B, M, T
Eastern Washington University M
Gonzaga University T
Lower Columbia College A
Northwest University B
Pacific Lutheran University B
Saint Martin's University B
Trinity Lutheran College B, T
University of Puget Sound T
University of Washington M, T
Walla Walla University B, T
Washington State University B, M, T
Western Washington University B, M
Whitworth University B, M, T

West Virginia

Alderson-Broaddus College B
Bethany College B
Bluefield State College B
Concord University B, M, T
Davis and Elkins College B
Fairmont State University B
Glenville State College B
Marshall University B, M
Mountain State University A
Ohio Valley University B
Potomac State College of West
    Virginia University A

Shepherd University B, T
University of Charleston B
West Liberty University B
West Virginia State University B
West Virginia University M, T
West Virginia University at
    Parkersburg A, B
West Virginia Wesleyan College B

Wisconsin

Alverno College B, M, T
Beloit College T
Carroll University B, T
Carthage College B, T
Concordia University Wisconsin B, T
Edgewood College B, T
Lakeland College B
Lawrence University T
Maranatha Baptist Bible College B
Marian University B, M, T
Marquette University B
Mount Mary College B, T
Ripon College T
St. Norbert College B, T
Silver Lake College B, T
University of Wisconsin
    Eau Claire B, M
    Green Bay B, T
    La Crosse B, M, T
    Madison B
    Oshkosh B, M, T
    Parkside T
    Platteville B, T
    River Falls B, M, T
    Stevens Point B, M, T
    Superior B, M, T
    Whitewater B, T
Viterbo University B, M, T
Wisconsin Lutheran College B

Wyoming

Central Wyoming College A
Eastern Wyoming College A
Northwest College A
Sheridan College A
University of Wyoming B
Western Wyoming Community
    College A

Elementary/middle school administration

Alabama

University of Alabama D

Arkansas

Arkansas State University M, T
Henderson State University M

California

California State University: Channel
    Islands M

Illinois

Concordia University Chicago M
Lewis University D
University of Illinois
    Urbana-Champaign M, D, T

Iowa

University of Northern Iowa M

Louisiana

Xavier University of Louisiana M

Massachusetts

Lesley University M
Westfield State College M

Michigan

Marygrove College M

Michigan State University *M, D*

Minnesota
Bethel University *D*

Mississippi
Mississippi State University *D*

Missouri
Lincoln University *M*
Lindenwood University *M*
Northwest Missouri State
  University *M*
Southeast Missouri State
  University *M, T*
Southwest Baptist University *M*
University of Missouri
  Columbia *M, D*

Montana
University of Great Falls *M*

Nebraska
Concordia University *M, T*
Creighton University *M*
Wayne State College *M*

New Jersey
College of St. Elizabeth *T*
William Paterson University of New
  Jersey *M*

New York
Le Moyne College *M*
Saint Bonaventure University *M*
St. John Fisher College *M, T*
State University of New York
  New Paltz *M*

North Carolina
Wingate University *M, T*

North Dakota
University of Mary *M*

Ohio
Antioch University McGregor *M*
University of Findlay *M, T*
Youngstown State University *M*

Oklahoma
University of Oklahoma *T*

Pennsylvania
East Stroudsburg University of
  Pennsylvania *T*
St. Francis University *M*
Shippensburg University of
  Pennsylvania *M, T*
Widener University *M, T*
Wilkes University *M*
York College of Pennsylvania *M*

Rhode Island
Providence College *M*

South Carolina
Charleston Southern University *M*

South Dakota
University of South Dakota *M, D*

Texas
University of North Texas *M*
University of Texas
  Arlington *T*

Vermont
St. Michael's College *T*

Washington
City University of Seattle *M, T*
University of Washington *M, D, T*
Washington State University *M, T*
Western Washington University *M*
Whitworth University *M*

Wisconsin
Cardinal Stritch University *M, D*
Edgewood College *T*
University of Wisconsin
  Superior *M*

Emergency care attendant (EMT ambulance)

Arizona
Mohave Community College *C*

Arkansas
University of Arkansas
  Community College at Hope *C*

California
Copper Mountain College *C*
San Jose City College *C*
Santa Rosa Junior College *C*

Colorado
Colorado Mountain College *C*
Colorado Northwestern Community
  College *C*

Delaware
Delaware Technical and Community
  College
  Stanton/Wilmington *A*

Florida
Pasco-Hernando Community
  College *C*
Pensacola Junior College *C*
South Florida Community College *C*
Valencia Community College *C*

Georgia
Gwinnett Technical College *C*
Southeastern Technical College *C*

Illinois
Harper College *C*
Heartland Community College *C*
Kankakee Community College *C*
Lincoln Land Community College *C*
Loyola University Chicago *C*
Sauk Valley Community College *C*
Southeastern Illinois College *C*
Trinity College of Nursing and Health
  Sciences *C, A*
Waubonsee Community College *C, A*

Iowa
Kirkwood Community College *A*

Kansas
Cloud County Community College *C*
Colby Community College *C*
Kansas City Kansas Community
  College *C*

Kentucky
St. Catharine College *C, A*

Maryland
Carroll Community College *C, A*
Howard Community College *A*

Massachusetts
Mount Wachusett Community
  College *C*
Quinsigamond Community College *C*

Michigan
Baker College
  of Muskegon *C, A*
Kirtland Community College *C*

Minnesota
Central Lakes College *C*
Lake Superior College *C*
Northland Community & Technical
  College *C, A*

Montana
Montana State University
  College of Technology: Great
  Falls *C, A*

North Carolina
Carteret Community College *A*
Sandhills Community College *A*

Ohio
University of Cincinnati
  Clermont College *C, A*

Oregon
Chemeketa Community College *A*
Clackamas Community College *C*
Klamath Community College *C*

Pennsylvania
Pennsylvania College of
  Technology *C*

Texas
Howard College *C, A*
Midland College *A*
Tyler Junior College *C, A*

Utah
Dixie State College of Utah *C*

Virginia
Virginia Western Community
  College *C*

Washington
Clark College *C*

Wisconsin
Fox Valley Technical College *C*
Mid-State Technical College *C*
Milwaukee Area Technical College *C*

Emergency management/homeland security

Arizona
Chandler-Gilbert Community College
  Pecos *C*
Northcentral University *B, M, D*

Arkansas
Arkansas Tech University *B, M*
Northwest Arkansas Community
  College *C, A*

California
National Polytechnic College of
  Science *A*

Colorado
Pikes Peak Community College *C, A*
Red Rocks Community College *C, A*

Connecticut
Goodwin College *C, A*
Mitchell College *B*
University of Connecticut *M*
University of New Haven *M*

Florida
Embry-Riddle Aeronautical
  University *B*
Herzing University *B*
Lynn University *C*

Georgia
Georgia Military College *A*
Savannah State University *B*

Hawaii
University of Hawaii
  West Oahu *C*

Illinois
Harper College *C, A*
John Wood Community College *A*
Kankakee Community College *C, A*
Western Illinois University *B*

Indiana
Ivy Tech Community College
  Central Indiana *A*
Vincennes University *B*

Kentucky
Midway College *B*

Louisiana
Baton Rouge Community College *C*

Maryland
Frederick Community College *C, A*

Massachusetts
Anna Maria College *M*

Michigan
Wayne County Community College *C*

New Hampshire
Daniel Webster College *B*

New Jersey
Cumberland County College *C, A*
Salem Community College *C*
Union County College *C, A*

New York
Excelsior College *C, B*
Onondaga Community College *A*
State University of New York
  College of Technology at Canton *B*
Ulster County Community College *A*
Utica College *C*

North Carolina
Fayetteville Technical Community
  College *A*
Methodist University *B*
Wayne Community College *A*

North Dakota
North Dakota State University *B, M, D*

Ohio
Tiffin University *B*
Union Institute & University *B*

Pennsylvania
Central Pennsylvania College *B*
La Roche College *B*

Rhode Island
Community College of Rhode
    Island *C*

Tennessee
Roane State Community College *C*

Virginia
Virginia Commonwealth
    University *B, M*

West Virginia
Blue Ridge Community and Technical
    College *C*

Wisconsin
Herzing University *B*
Marian University *B*

Wyoming
Central Wyoming College *A*
Laramie County Community
    College *C, A*

Emergency medical technology (EMT paramedic)

Alabama
Bevill State Community College *C, A*
Bishop State Community College *C*
Calhoun Community College *C, A*
Central Alabama Community
    College *A*
Enterprise-Ozark Community
    College *A*
Faulkner State Community College *A*
Gadsden State Community College *A*
George C. Wallace State Community
    College
    George C. Wallace Community
        College at Dothan *C, A*
Jefferson Davis Community College *C*
Jefferson State Community
    College *C, A*
Lawson State Community College *C*
Lurleen B. Wallace Community
    College *C, A*
Northeast Alabama Community
    College *C, A*
Northwest-Shoals Community
    College *C, A*
Shelton State Community College *C*
Southern Union State Community
    College *C, A*
University of Alabama
    Birmingham *C*
University of South Alabama *C, B*
Wallace State Community College at
    Hanceville *C, A*

Arizona
Arizona Western College *C, A*
Central Arizona College *C, A*
Cochise College *C, A*
Eastern Arizona College *C, A*
Glendale Community College *C, A*
Northland Pioneer College *A*
Phoenix College *C, A*
Pima Community College *C, A*
Scottsdale Community College *C, A*

Arkansas
Arkansas Northeastern College *C*
Arkansas State University
    Beebe *C, A*
    Mountain Home *C, A*
Arkansas State University: Newport *A*
Arkansas Tech University *C*
East Arkansas Community
    College *C, A*

National Park Community
    College *C, A*
North Arkansas College *C, A*
Northwest Arkansas Community
    College *C, A*
Ozarka College *C*
South Arkansas Community
    College *C, A*
Southeast Arkansas College *C, A*
University of Arkansas
    Community College at Batesville *A*
    Cossatot Community College of the
        C
    Monticello *C*
University of Arkansas Community
    College at Morrilton *C*

California
Allan Hancock College *C*
Bakersfield College *A*
Barstow Community College *C*
Butte College *A*
California State University
    Chico *C*
City College of San Francisco *A*
College of the Desert *C*
College of the Sequoias *C*
College of the Siskiyous *C, A*
Columbia College *C*
Cosumnes River College *C*
Crafton Hills College *C, A*
East Los Angeles College *C*
El Camino College: Compton
    Center *C, A*
Foothill College *C*
Imperial Valley College *C, A*
Loma Linda University *B*
Long Beach City College *C*
Los Angeles Harbor College *C*
Los Medanos College *C, A*
Modesto Junior College *C*
Mount San Antonio College *C, A*
Pacific Union College *A*
Palo Verde College *C*
Palomar College *C, A*
Saddleback College *C*
San Joaquin Delta College *C, A*
San Joaquin Valley College *A*
San Jose City College *C*
Santa Barbara City College *C*
Santa Rosa Junior College *C, A*
Shasta College *A*
Skyline College *C*
Southwestern College *C, A*
Ventura College *C, A*
Victor Valley College *C, A*

Colorado
Aims Community College *C*
Arapahoe Community College *C*
Colorado Northwestern Community
    College *C, A*
Community College of Denver *C*
Front Range Community College *C, A*
Mesa State College *C, A*
Morgan Community College *C*
Northeastern Junior College *C, A*
Pikes Peak Community College *C, A*
Pueblo Community College *C, A*
Red Rocks Community College *C, A*

Connecticut
Capital Community College *C, A*
Goodwin College *C*
Norwalk Community College *C*

Delaware
Delaware Technical and Community
    College
    Owens *A*
    Stanton/Wilmington *A*
    Terry *A*

Florida
Brevard Community College *C, A*
Broward College *C, A*
Central Florida Community
    College *C, A*
City College: Fort Lauderdale *A*
Daytona State College *C, A*
Edison State College *C, A*
Florida Keys Community College *C*
Florida State College at
    Jacksonville *C, A*
Gulf Coast Community College *C, A*
Hillsborough Community
    College *C, A*
Indian River State College *C, A*
Lake City Community College *C, A*
Lake-Sumter Community College *A*
Miami Dade College *C, A*
Palm Beach Community College *C, A*
Pensacola Junior College *C, A*
Polk State College *C, A*
Saint Johns River Community
    College *A*
St. Petersburg College *C, A*
Santa Fe College *C, A*
Seminole Community College *C, A*
South Florida Community
    College *C, A*
Tallahassee Community College *C, A*
Valencia Community College *C, A*

Georgia
Albany Technical College *C*
Athens Technical College *C*
Augusta Technical College *C, A*
Bainbridge College *C*
Central Georgia Technical College *C*
Dalton State College *C, A*
Darton College *C, A*
DeKalb Technical College *C*
Gainesville State College *A*
Gwinnett Technical College *C, A*
Macon State College *A*
North Georgia Technical College *C*
Savannah Technical College *C, A*
Southeastern Technical College *C*
Southwest Georgia Technical
    College *C*
Waycross College *A*
West Georgia Technical College *C*

Hawaii
University of Hawaii
    Kapiolani Community College *C, A*

Idaho
Brigham Young University-Idaho *A*
Idaho State University *C, A*

Illinois
Black Hawk College *C, A*
City Colleges of Chicago
    Malcolm X College *C, A*
College of DuPage *C, A*
College of Lake County *C*
Elgin Community College *C*
Harper College *C, A*
Heartland Community College *C*
Illinois Central College *C*
Illinois Eastern Community Colleges
    Frontier Community College *C*
John A. Logan College *C*
John Wood Community College *A*
Kankakee Community College *A*
Kaskaskia College *C, A*
Lincoln Land Community College *C*
McHenry County College *C, A*
Moraine Valley Community College *C*
Parkland College *C*
Prairie State College *C*
Rend Lake College *C, A*
Richland Community College *C, A*
Sauk Valley Community College *C, A*

South Suburban College of Cook
    County *C*
Southeastern Illinois College *C*
Southwestern Illinois College *C, A*
Triton College *C, A*

Indiana
Indiana University
    Bloomington *A*
Indiana University-Purdue University
    Indianapolis *A*
Ivy Tech Community College
    Bloomington *A*
    Central Indiana *A*
    Columbus *A*
    Kokomo *A*
    North Central *A*
    Northeast *A*
    Northwest *A*
    Richmond *A*
    Southwest *A*
    Wabash Valley *A*
Vincennes University *C, A*

Iowa
Clinton Community College *C, A*
Des Moines Area Community
    College *C*
Indian Hills Community College *C, A*
Iowa Central Community College *C, A*
Iowa Lakes Community College *C, A*
Kirkwood Community College *A*
Mercy College of Health Sciences *C, A*
Muscatine Community College *C, A*
North Iowa Area Community
    College *A*
Northeast Iowa Community
    College *A*
Northwest Iowa Community
    College *A*
Scott Community College *C, A*
Southeastern Community College
    North Campus *A*
Southwestern Community College *C*
Western Iowa Tech Community
    College *C, A*

Kansas
Allen County Community College *A*
Barton County Community
    College *C, A*
Coffeyville Community College *A*
Cowley County Community
    College *A*
Dodge City Community College *C*
Hutchinson Community College *A*
Johnson County Community
    College *C, A*
Kansas City Kansas Community
    College *A*
Neosho County Community
    College *C*

Kentucky
Eastern Kentucky University *C, A, B*
Owensboro Community and
    Technical College *C*
St. Catharine College *A*
Spalding University *A*
Western Kentucky University *A*

Louisiana
Bossier Parish Community College *A*
Delgado Community College *A*
Nunez Community College *C*
South Louisiana Community
    College *C, A*

Maine
Eastern Maine Community College *C*
Kennebec Valley Community
    College *C, A*

Southern Maine Community
College *A*

Maryland

Anne Arundel Community College *C*
Baltimore City Community
College *C, A*
Cecil College *C*
Chesapeake College *C*
College of Southern Maryland *C, A*
Community College of Baltimore
County *C, A*
Hagerstown Community College *C, A*
Howard Community College *C, A*
Prince George's Community
College *C, A*
University of Maryland
Baltimore County *B, M*
Wor-Wic Community College *C, A*

Massachusetts

Cape Cod Community College *C, A*
Greenfield Community College *C*
Massachusetts Bay Community
College *C*
North Shore Community College *C*
Northern Essex Community
College *A*
Quinsigamond Community
College *C, A*
Springfield College *B*

Michigan

Baker College
of Cadillac *C*
of Clinton Township *C*
of Muskegon *C, A*
Glen Oaks Community College *C*
Gogebic Community College *A*
Henry Ford Community College *A*
Jackson Community College *C, A*
Kalamazoo Valley Community
College *C*
Kellogg Community College *C, A*
Kirtland Community College *C, A*
Lake Michigan College *A*
Lake Superior State University *C*
Lansing Community College *A*
Macomb Community College *C, A*
Mid Michigan Community College *A*
Montcalm Community College *C*
Mott Community College *A*
North Central Michigan College *A*
Oakland Community College *C, A*
Schoolcraft College *C, A*
Southwestern Michigan College *C, A*
Wayne County Community
College *C, A*
West Shore Community College *A*

Minnesota

Anoka Technical College *C*
Century Community and Technical
College *C, A*
Hennepin Technical College *A*
Inver Hills Community College *C, A*
Mesabi Range Community and
Technical College *C*
Northland Community & Technical
College *A*
Northwest Technical College *C*
Rochester Community and Technical
College *A*
St. Cloud Technical College *A*
South Central College *C, A*

Mississippi

Copiah-Lincoln Community College *C*
East Mississippi Community
College *C*
Hinds Community College *C, A*
Mississippi Delta Community
College *A*

Mississippi Gulf Coast Community
College *A*

Missouri

Bolivar Technical College *C, A*
Crowder College *C*
East Central College *C, A*
Jefferson College *C, A*
Metropolitan Community College:
Penn Valley *A*
Mineral Area College *C*
Missouri Southern State University *C*
Ozarks Technical Community
College *A*
St. Charles Community College *A*
St. Louis Community College
St. Louis Community College at
Meramec *A*
Southwest Baptist University *A*
Texas County Technical Institute *C, A*
Three Rivers Community College *C*

Montana

Flathead Valley Community College *A*
Montana State University
Billings
College of Technology: Great
Falls *C, A*

Nebraska

Creighton University *C, A, B*
Northeast Community College *A*
Western Nebraska Community
College *C*

Nevada

College of Southern Nevada *A*

New Hampshire

NHTI-Concord's Community
College *A*

New Jersey

Essex County College *A*
Hudson County Community
College *C*
Union County College *C, A*

New Mexico

Dona Ana Community College of New
Mexico State University *C, A*
Eastern New Mexico University:
Roswell Campus *C, A*
New Mexico Junior College *A*
New Mexico State University
Alamogordo *C*
Carlsbad *C*
Santa Fe Community College *C*
University of New Mexico *B*

New York

Broome Community College *A*
City University of New York
Borough of Manhattan Community
College *A*
LaGuardia Community College *A*
Corning Community College *A*
Dutchess Community College *C, A*
Erie Community College
North Campus *C*
South Campus *C, A*
Finger Lakes Community College *C, A*
Herkimer County Community
College *A*
Hudson Valley Community College *C*
Jefferson Community College *C, A*
Mohawk Valley Community College *A*
Rockland Community College *A*
State University of New York
College of Agriculture and
Technology at Cobleskill *A*
Suffolk County Community College *A*

Ulster County Community
College *C, A*
Westchester Community College *C, A*

North Carolina

Asheville-Buncombe Technical
Community College *A*
Catawba Valley Community College *A*
Coastal Carolina Community
College *A*
Davidson County Community
College *A*
Durham Technical Community
College *C*
Fayetteville Technical Community
College *C*
Forsyth Technical Community
College *A*
Gaston College *C, A*
Guilford Technical Community
College *A*
Randolph Community College *A*
Robeson Community College *A*
Sandhills Community College *A*
Southwestern Community College *A*
Stanly Community College *A*
Tri-County Community College *C, A*
Wake Technical Community
College *C, A*
Western Carolina University *B*

North Dakota

Bismarck State College *C, A*
Dakota College at Bottineau *C, A*
Turtle Mountain Community
College *C*

Ohio

Belmont Technical College *C, A*
Central Ohio Technical College *C*
Cincinnati State Technical and
Community College *C, A*
Clark State Community College *C, A*
Columbus State Community
College *C, A*
Cuyahoga Community College
Metropolitan Campus *A*
Eastern Gateway Community
College *C, A*
Hocking College *C, A*
James A. Rhodes State College *A*
Kent State University: Geauga *A*
Owens Community College
Toledo *C*
Shawnee State University *C, A*
Southern State Community
College *C, A*
Stark State College of Technology *C*
University of Cincinnati
Clermont College *C, A*
Raymond Walters College *C, A*
University of Toledo *C, A*
Youngstown State University *C, A*

Oklahoma

Oklahoma City Community
College *C, A*
Oklahoma State University
Oklahoma City *C, A*
Redlands Community College *C, A*
Rogers State University *A*
Rose State College *A*
Western Oklahoma State College *A*

Oregon

Central Oregon Community
College *A*
Chemeketa Community College *A*
Clackamas Community College *C*
Clatsop Community College *C*
Lane Community College *C, A*
Linn-Benton Community College *C*

Oregon Health & Science
University *B*
Oregon Institute of Technology *A*
Portland Community College *C, A*
Rogue Community College *C, A*
Southwestern Oregon Community
College *C*
Treasure Valley Community College *C*
Umpqua Community College *A*

Pennsylvania

Harrisburg Area Community
College *C, A*
Lackawanna College *C, A*
Luzerne County Community
College *C, A*
Northampton Community College *C*
Pennsylvania College of
Technology *A, B*
University of Pittsburgh
Johnstown *A*

Puerto Rico

Electronic Data Processing College:
San Sebastian *A*
Inter American University of Puerto
Rico
Aguadilla Campus *C*
Metropolitan Campus *C, A*
Ponce Paramedical College *C*

South Carolina

Greenville Technical College *C, A*
Horry-Georgetown Technical
College *A*
Midlands Technical College *C*

Tennessee

Chattanooga State Community
College *C*
Cleveland State Community College *C*
Jackson State Community College *C*
Northeast State Community College *C*
Roane State Community College *C*
Southwest Tennessee Community
College *C*
Volunteer State Community College *C*
Walters State Community College *C, A*

Texas

Alvin Community College *C, A*
Amarillo College *C, A*
Angelina College *C, A*
Austin Community College *C, A*
Blinn College *C*
Brookhaven College *C*
Clarendon College *A*
Collin County Community College
District *C, A*
Del Mar College *C, A*
El Centro College *C*
El Paso Community College *C*
Galveston College *C, A*
Grayson County College *C, A*
Houston Community College
System *C, A*
Kilgore College *C, A*
Lamar Institute of Technology *C, A*
Lamar State College at Orange *C, A*
Laredo Community College *A*
Lee College *C, A*
Lone Star College System *C, A*
McLennan Community College *A*
Midland College *C, A*
Navarro College *C*
North Central Texas College *A*
Northeast Texas Community
College *C, A*
Odessa College *C, A*
San Antonio College *C*
San Jacinto College *C, A*
South Plains College *C, A*
South Texas College *C, A*

Tarrant County College *C, A*
Temple College *C, A*
Texarkana College *C, A*
Texas State Technical College
 Harlingen *C, A*
 West Texas *C, A*
Trinity Valley Community College *C*
Tyler Junior College *C, A*
University of Texas
 Brownsville - Texas Southmost
  College *C, A*
 Health Science Center at San
  Antonio *C*
Victoria College *C, A*
Weatherford College *C, A*
Western Texas College *C, A*
Wharton County Junior College *C, A*

Utah
Dixie State College of Utah *C, A*
Snow College *C, A*
Utah Valley University *C*
Weber State University *A*

Virginia
Jefferson College of Health
 Sciences *B*
Mountain Empire Community
 College *C, A*
Northern Virginia Community
 College *A*
Piedmont Virginia Community
 College *C, A*
Southwest Virginia Community
 College *C, A*
Tidewater Community College *A*

Washington
Bellingham Technical College *A*
Clark College *A*
North Seattle Community College *C*
Spokane Community College *C, A*
Spokane Falls Community College *C*

West Virginia
Blue Ridge Community and Technical
 College *C, A*
Fairmont State University *A*
Mountain State University *A*
New River Community and Technical
 College *C*
West Virginia State Community and
 Technical College *A*

Wisconsin
Blackhawk Technical College *C*
Chippewa Valley Technical College *C*
Fox Valley Technical College *C*
Gateway Technical College *C*
Lakeshore Technical College *C, A*
Mid-State Technical College *C, A*
Milwaukee Area Technical College *C*
Moraine Park Technical College *C, A*
Nicolet Area Technical College *C*
Northcentral Technical College *C, A*
Waukesha County Technical
 College *C*
Western Technical College *C*
Wisconsin Indianhead Technical
 College *C, A*

Wyoming
Casper College *A*
Central Wyoming College *C*
Laramie County Community
 College *C*

Endocrinology

California
University of California
 Berkeley *M, D*

Wisconsin
University of Wisconsin
 Madison *M, D*

Energy systems technology

Alabama
Northwest-Shoals Community
 College *C*

Arizona
Glendale Community College *A*
Refrigeration School *A*

Colorado
Colorado Northwestern Community
 College *C, A*
Pueblo Community College *C, A*
Red Rocks Community College *C, A*

Connecticut
Naugatuck Valley Community
 College *C, A*

Idaho
Idaho State University *A, B*

Illinois
Black Hawk College *C*
Illinois State University *B*
Sauk Valley Community College *C*

Iowa
Iowa Central Community College *A*
Iowa Lakes Community College *C, A*

Kentucky
Maysville Community and Technical
 College *C, A*

Massachusetts
North Shore Community College *C*
University of Massachusetts
 Lowell *M*

Michigan
Alpena Community College *C*
Ferris State University *B*
Henry Ford Community College *C, A*
Lake Michigan College *A*
Lawrence Technological University *C*
Mott Community College *C*
Schoolcraft College *C*

Minnesota
Alexandria Technical College *A*
Century Community and Technical
 College *C, A*
St. Cloud Technical College *A*

Nebraska
Northeast Community College *A*

New Jersey
Salem Community College *A*

New York
New York Institute of
 Technology *B, M*
State University of New York
 College of Technology at Canton *B*

Ohio
Hocking College *A*

Oklahoma
University of Tulsa *B*

Oregon
Lane Community College *A*
Oregon Institute of Technology *B*

Pennsylvania
Pennsylvania College of
 Technology *B*
Temple University *B*
Williamson Free School of Mechanical
 Trades *A*

Wisconsin
Wisconsin Indianhead Technical
 College *A*

Wyoming
Casper College *C, A*
Laramie County Community
 College *C, A*

Engine machinist

Arkansas
Pulaski Technical College *C*

Minnesota
Northwest Technical College *C, A*
Pine Technical College *C*

Engineering, general

Alabama
Central Alabama Community
 College *A*
Chattahoochee Valley Community
 College *A*
Gadsden State Community College *A*
Shelton State Community College *A*
Snead State Community College *A*
Spring Hill College *B*
University of Alabama
 Birmingham *M*
 Huntsville *M*
Wallace State Community College at
 Hanceville *A*

Alaska
University of Alaska
 Anchorage *B*
 Fairbanks *M, D*

Arizona
Anthem College *A*
Arizona State University *B, M*
Arizona Western College *A*
Central Arizona College *A*
Cochise College *A*
Coconino County Community
 College *A*
Embry-Riddle Aeronautical University:
 Prescott Campus *B*
GateWay Community College *A*
Mesa Community College *A*
Northern Arizona University *B, M*
Phoenix College *A*
University of Arizona *B, M*

Arkansas
Arkansas State University *B*
Arkansas Tech University *M*
John Brown University *B*
Phillips Community College of the
 University of Arkansas *A*
University of Arkansas *M, D*

California
Allan Hancock College *A*
Antelope Valley College *A*
Biola University *B*
California Baptist University *B*
California Institute of Technology *B*

California National University for
 Advanced Studies *B, M*
California Polytechnic State
 University: San Luis Obispo *M*
California State Polytechnic
 University: Pomona *B, M*
California State University
 Fullerton *B*
 Long Beach *B, M*
 Los Angeles *B*
 Northridge *B, M*
Chabot College *A*
Chaffey College *A*
Citrus College *A*
City College of San Francisco *A*
Claremont McKenna College *B*
College of San Mateo *A*
College of the Canyons *A*
College of the Sequoias *A*
College of the Siskiyous *A*
Contra Costa College *A*
Cypress College *A*
De Anza College *A*
East Los Angeles College *A*
El Camino College *A*
Foothill College *A*
Fresno City College *A*
Fullerton College *A*
Hartnell College *A*
Harvey Mudd College *B*
Imperial Valley College *A*
Long Beach City College *A*
Los Angeles City College *A*
Los Angeles Pierce College *A*
Los Angeles Southwest College *A*
Los Angeles Trade and Technical
 College *A*
Loyola Marymount University *B*
Merced College *A*
Mills College *B*
Mission College *A*
Modesto Junior College *A*
Mount San Antonio College *A*
National University *M*
Orange Coast College *A*
Palomar College *A*
Pepperdine University *B*
Riverside Community College *A*
Saddleback College *A*
San Diego City College *A*
San Diego Mesa College *A*
San Diego State University *B*
San Francisco State University *M*
San Joaquin Delta College *A*
San Jose State University *B, M*
Santa Ana College *A*
Santa Barbara City College *A*
Santa Clara University *B, M*
Santa Rosa Junior College *A*
Santiago Canyon College *A*
Scripps College *B*
Shasta College *A*
Sierra College *A*
Southwestern College *A*
Stanford University *B, M*
University of California
 Davis *M, D*
 Irvine *B, M, D*
 Los Angeles *M*
University of the Pacific *B*
Ventura College *A*
West Hills College: Lemoore *A*
West Los Angeles College *A*
West Valley College *A*

Colorado
Colorado Mountain College *A*
Colorado School of Mines *B*
Colorado State University *M*
Colorado State University
 Pueblo *B*
Trinidad State Junior College *A*
United States Air Force Academy *B*

University of Colorado
Boulder *M*
Colorado Springs *B, M, D*
Denver *M*
University of Denver *B, D*

Connecticut
Norwalk Community College *A*
Trinity College *B*
University of Connecticut *M*
University of Hartford *B*
University of New Haven *B*

District of Columbia
George Washington
University *B, M, D*

Florida
Brevard Community College *A*
Broward College *A*
Chipola College *A*
Daytona State College *A*
Edison State College *A*
Embry-Riddle Aeronautical
University *B*
Florida Gulf Coast University *B*
Florida Institute of Technology *B*
Florida State College at Jacksonville *A*
Gulf Coast Community College *A*
Indian River State College *A*
Northwest Florida State College *A*
Palm Beach Community College *A*
Pensacola Junior College *A*
State College of Florida,
Manatee-Sarasota *A*
Tallahassee Community College *A*
University of Miami *B*
University of South Florida *B, M, D*
Valencia Community College *A*

Georgia
Abraham Baldwin Agricultural
College *A*
Andrew College *A*
College of Coastal Georgia *A*
Dalton State College *A*
Gainesville State College *A*
Georgia Perimeter College *A*
Georgia Southern University *B*
Mercer University *B*
Middle Georgia College *A*
Morehouse College *B*
Spelman College *B*
University of Georgia *B*
Young Harris College *A*

Idaho
Brigham Young University-Idaho *A*
College of Idaho *B*
North Idaho College *A*

Illinois
City Colleges of Chicago
Harold Washington College *A*
Olive-Harvey College *A*
College of DuPage *A*
College of Lake County *A*
Danville Area Community College *A*
Eastern Illinois University *B*
Elgin Community College *A*
Eureka College *B*
Harper College *A*
Heartland Community College *A*
Highland Community College *A*
Illinois Central College *A*
Illinois Valley Community College *A*
John A. Logan College *A*
John Wood Community College *A*
Kankakee Community College *A*
Kishwaukee College *A*
Lake Land College *A*
Lincoln Land Community College *A*
MacMurray College *B*

McHenry County College *A*
Northwestern University *B*
Oakton Community College *A*
Olivet Nazarene University *B*
Parkland College *A*
Rend Lake College *A*
Richland Community College *A*
Sauk Valley Community College *A*
South Suburban College of Cook
County *A*
Southern Illinois University
Carbondale *D*
Southwestern Illinois College *A*
Triton College *A*
University of Illinois
Chicago *M*
Urbana-Champaign *B*
Waubonsee Community College *A*
Wheaton College *B*

Indiana
Ball State University *B*
Bethel College *B*
Indiana University Purdue University
Fort Wayne *M*
Indiana University-Purdue University
Indianapolis *B, M*
Ivy Tech Community College
Northwest *A*
Southwest *A*
Purdue University
Calumet *B, M*
University of Notre Dame *M*
University of Southern Indiana *B*

Iowa
Dordt College *B*
Ellsworth Community College *A*
Iowa State University *B*
Iowa Wesleyan College *B*
Kirkwood Community College *A*
Marshalltown Community College *A*
University of Iowa *B*

Kansas
Barton County Community College *A*
Butler Community College *A*
Coffeyville Community College *A*
Cowley County Community
College *A*
Dodge City Community College *A*
Donnelly College *A*
Garden City Community College *A*
Hutchinson Community College *A*
Pratt Community College *A*
Seward County Community College *A*

Kentucky
University of Louisville *B*

Louisiana
Louisiana Tech University *M, D*
McNeese State University *B, M*
Southern University and Agricultural
and Mechanical College *M*

Maine
Bates College *B*
University of Maine *B, M*

Maryland
Allegany College of Maryland *A*
Anne Arundel Community College *A*
Baltimore City Community College *A*
College of Notre Dame of Maryland *B*
College of Southern Maryland *A*
Community College of Baltimore
County *A*
Frederick Community College *A*
Frostburg State University *B*
Hagerstown Community College *A*
Harford Community College *A*
Howard Community College *A*

Johns Hopkins University *B*
Loyola University Maryland *B, M*
Montgomery College *A*
Morgan State University *B, M, D*
Prince George's Community
College *A*
United States Naval Academy *B*
University of Maryland
Baltimore County *B*
College Park *B, M*
Eastern Shore *B*
Washington Adventist University *A*

Massachusetts
Bard College at Simon's Rock *B*
Berkshire Community College *A*
Boston University *B, M*
Bristol Community College *A*
Bunker Hill Community College *A*
Cape Cod Community College *A*
Eastern Nazarene College *B*
Franklin W. Olin College of
Engineering *B*
Holyoke Community College *A*
Massachusetts Maritime Academy *B*
Merrimack College *B*
North Shore Community College *A*
Northeastern University *B, M, D*
Quinsigamond Community College *A*
Smith College *B*
Springfield Technical Community
College *A*
Tufts University *B*
Wellesley College *B*
Western New England College *M*

Michigan
Alpena Community College *A*
Andrews University *B*
Calvin College *B*
Delta College *A*
Ferris State University *A*
Gogebic Community College *A*
Grand Rapids Community College *A*
Henry Ford Community College *A*
Hope College *B*
Kalamazoo Valley Community
College *A*
Lake Michigan College *A*
Lake Superior State University *A*
Lansing Community College *A*
Michigan State University *B*
Michigan Technological
University *B, M*
Mid Michigan Community College *A*
Northwestern Michigan College *A*
Oakland Community College *A*
St. Clair County Community
College *A*
Schoolcraft College *A*
University of Detroit Mercy *B, M*
University of Michigan *B, M, D*
University of Michigan
Dearborn *B*
Washtenaw Community College *A*

Minnesota
Anoka-Ramsey Community College *A*
Augsburg College *B*
Central Lakes College *A*
Century Community and Technical
College *A*
Itasca Community College *A*
Minnesota State University
Mankato *B, M*
Minnesota West Community and
Technical College *A*
Normandale Community College *A*
North Hennepin Community
College *A*
Northland Community & Technical
College *A*
Northwest Technical Institute *A*

Rochester Community and Technical
College *A*
University of Minnesota
Duluth *M*
University of St. Thomas *B*

Mississippi
East Central Community College *A*
Hinds Community College *A*
Holmes Community College *A*
Jackson State University *M*
Mississippi Delta Community
College *A*
Mississippi Gulf Coast Community
College *A*
Mississippi State University *M, D*
University of Mississippi *B*

Missouri
Crowder College *A*
East Central College *A*
Jefferson College *A*
Metropolitan Community College:
Blue River *A*
Metropolitan Community College:
Longview *A*
Metropolitan Community College:
Maple Woods *A*
Metropolitan Community College:
Penn Valley *A*
Missouri Southern State University *A*
St. Charles Community College *A*
St. Louis Community College
St. Louis Community College at
Florissant Valley *A*
St. Louis Community College at
Meramec *A*
University of Missouri
Columbia *M*
Kansas City *D*

Montana
Miles Community College *A*
Montana State University
Bozeman *B*
Montana Tech of the University of
Montana *B, M*

Nebraska
Northeast Community College *A*
Union College *A*
University of Nebraska
Lincoln *M, D*
Western Nebraska Community
College *A*

Nevada
Great Basin College *A*
University of Nevada
Reno *D*
Western Nevada College *A*

New Hampshire
Dartmouth College *M, D*
Saint Anselm College *B*
University of New Hampshire *B*

New Jersey
Bergen Community College *A*
Brookdale Community College *A*
Cumberland County College *A*
Essex County College *A*
Gloucester County College *A*
New Jersey Institute of Technology *M*
Ocean County College *A*
Stevens Institute of
Technology *B, M, D*
Sussex County Community College *A*
Union County College *A*

New Mexico

Central New Mexico Community College *A*
Mesalands Community College *A*
New Mexico Institute of Mining and Technology *B*
New Mexico Junior College *A*
New Mexico State University *D*
New Mexico State University
 Alamogordo *A*
 Carlsbad *A*
San Juan College *A*
Santa Fe Community College *A*
Southwestern Indian Polytechnic Institute *A*
University of New Mexico *D*

New York

Adirondack Community College *A*
City University of New York
 Borough of Manhattan Community College *A*
 College of Staten Island *A, B*
 Kingsborough Community College *A*
 LaGuardia Community College *A*
Clarkson University *B*
Cooper Union for the Advancement of Science and Art *B*
Cornell University *B*
Erie Community College
 North Campus *A*
Finger Lakes Community College *A*
Fulton-Montgomery Community College *A*
Hudson Valley Community College *A*
Jamestown Community College *A*
Jefferson Community College *A*
Mohawk Valley Community College *A*
Nassau Community College *A*
Onondaga Community College *A*
Orange County Community College *A*
Rensselaer Polytechnic Institute *B, D*
St. Thomas Aquinas College *A*
State University of New York
 Binghamton *B*
 Buffalo *B, M*
 College of Agriculture and Technology at Morrisville *A*
 College of Environmental Science and Forestry *B*
 College of Technology at Alfred *A*
 College of Technology at Canton *A, T*
 Maritime College *B*
 Stony Brook *B*
Sullivan County Community College *A*
Syracuse University *B, D*
Tompkins Cortland Community College *A*
Ulster County Community College *A*
University of Rochester *B*
Westchester Community College *A*
Yeshiva University *B*

North Carolina

Cleveland Community College *A*
East Carolina University *B*
Elon University *B*
Lenoir Community College *A*
Livingstone College *B*
North Carolina Agricultural and Technical State University *M*
North Carolina State University *B, M*
Pfeiffer University *B*
St. Augustine's College *B*
University of North Carolina
 Asheville *B*
 Charlotte *M*
Western Piedmont Community College *A*

North Dakota

North Dakota State University *D*
University of Mary *B*
University of North Dakota *D*

Ohio

Case Western Reserve University *B, M*
Cleveland State University *D*
Eastern Gateway Community College *A*
Kent State University *B, M*
Miami University
 Oxford Campus *B*
Muskingum University *B*
Ohio Northern University *B*
Owens Community College
 Toledo *A*
University of Akron *B, M, D*
University of Cincinnati *B, M, D*
University of Dayton *M*
University of Toledo *B*
Washington State Community College *A*
Wright State University *B, M, D*
Youngstown State University *B, M*

Oklahoma

Connors State College *A*
Eastern Oklahoma State College *A*
Oklahoma Christian University *M*
Oklahoma City Community College *A*
Oral Roberts University *B*
Rose State College *A*
Southwestern Oklahoma State University *B*
Tulsa Community College *A*
University of Oklahoma *B, M, D*
Western Oklahoma State College *A*

Oregon

Central Oregon Community College *A*
Chemeketa Community College *A*
George Fox University *B*
Linn-Benton Community College *A*
Southwestern Oregon Community College *A*
Treasure Valley Community College *A*

Pennsylvania

Arcadia University *B*
Bucks County Community College *A*
Butler County Community College *A*
Carnegie Mellon University *B, M, D*
Chatham University *B*
Community College of Philadelphia *A*
Drexel University *M*
Elizabethtown College *B*
Geneva College *A, B*
Gettysburg College *B*
Harrisburg Area Community College *A*
Juniata College *B*
Lafayette College *B*
Lehigh Carbon Community College *A*
Lincoln University *B*
Messiah College *B*
Northampton Community College *A*
Philadelphia University *B*
Reading Area Community College *A*
Robert Morris University *D*
St. Francis University *B*
St. Vincent College *B*
Seton Hill University *B*
Swarthmore College *B*
Temple University *D*
University of Pittsburgh
 Bradford *B*
Valley Forge Military Academy & College *A*
Westminster College *B*
Widener University *B, M*

Puerto Rico

University of Puerto Rico
 Ponce *A*

Rhode Island

Community College of Rhode Island *A*
Roger Williams University *B*

South Dakota

South Dakota State University *M*

Tennessee

Columbia State Community College *A*
Jackson State Community College *A*
Maryville College *B*
Southern Adventist University *A*
Tennessee State University *B, M*
University of Memphis *D*
University of Tennessee
 Chattanooga *B, M*
 Martin *B*

Texas

Amarillo College *A*
Angelina College *A*
Austin Community College *A*
Baylor University *B, M*
Brazosport College *A*
Central Texas College *A*
Cisco College *A*
Clarendon College *A*
Coastal Bend College *A*
College of the Mainland *A*
El Paso Community College *A*
Galveston College *A*
Grayson County College *A*
Hill College *A*
Kilgore College *A*
Lamar University *B, M, D*
Laredo Community College *A*
LeTourneau University *B*
Lubbock Christian University *B*
Midwestern State University *B*
Navarro College *A*
Palo Alto College *A*
Prairie View A&M University *M*
St. Mary's University *M*
St. Philip's College *A*
San Antonio College *A*
Schreiner University *B*
South Plains College *A*
South Texas College *A*
Temple College *A*
Texarkana College *A*
Texas A&M University *M, D*
Texas A&M University
 Kingsville *M*
Texas Christian University *B*
Texas Tech University *B, M*
Trinity Valley Community College *A*
Tyler Junior College *A*
University of Houston *M, D*
University of Texas
 Arlington *B, T*
 El Paso *M*
 Tyler *M*
Western Texas College *A*

Utah

College of Eastern Utah *A, T*
Dixie State College of Utah *A*
Snow College *A*
Southern Utah University *A, B*
University of Utah *B*
Utah State University *B*
Utah Valley University *A*

Vermont

St. Michael's College *B*
University of Vermont *B*

Virginia

Danville Community College *A*
Hampton University *B*
J. Sargeant Reynolds Community College *A*
James Madison University *B*
Lord Fairfax Community College *A*
New River Community College *A*
Old Dominion University *M, D*
Piedmont Virginia Community College *A*
Southwest Virginia Community College *A*
Thomas Nelson Community College *A*
Tidewater Community College *A*
University of Virginia *B*
Virginia Commonwealth University *M, D*
Virginia Western Community College *A*

Washington

Centralia College *A*
Everett Community College *A*
Gonzaga University *B*
Highline Community College *A*
Lower Columbia College *A*
Olympic College *A*
Shoreline Community College *A*
South Seattle Community College *A*
Spokane Falls Community College *A*
University of Washington *B, M*
Walla Walla University *B*
Washington State University *M*
Whitworth University *B*
Yakima Valley Community College *A*

West Virginia

Marshall University *B, M*
Mountain State University *A*
Potomac State College of West Virginia University *A*
West Virginia University *M, D*
West Virginia Wesleyan College *B*

Wisconsin

Beloit College *B*
Marquette University *B*
Milwaukee School of Engineering *B, M*
Northland College *B*
University of Wisconsin
 Madison *M*
 Milwaukee *M, D*

Wyoming

Casper College *A*
Central Wyoming College *A*
Laramie County Community College *A*
Northwest College *A*
Sheridan College *A*
Western Wyoming Community College *A*

Engineering/industrial management

Alaska

University of Alaska
 Fairbanks *M*

Arizona

Central Arizona College *A*
GateWay Community College *C*
University of Arizona *B*

California

California Polytechnic State University: San Luis Obispo *M*

California State Polytechnic
University: Pomona *M*
California State University
East Bay *B, M*
Loyola Marymount University *M*
National University *B, M*
Santa Clara University *M*
Stanford University *B, M, D*
University of Southern California *M*
University of the Pacific *B*

Colorado

University of Denver *M*

Connecticut

Naugatuck Valley Community
College *A*
University of Bridgeport *M*
University of New Haven *M*

Delaware

Delaware Technical and Community
College
Stanton/Wilmington *A*

District of Columbia

Catholic University of America *C, M*
George Washington University *M, D*

Florida

Florida Institute of Technology *M*
Palm Beach Community College *A*
Tallahassee Community College *A*
University of Miami *M*
University of South Florida *M*

Georgia

Georgia Southern University *B, T*

Illinois

Illinois Institute of Technology *B*
Northern Illinois University *M*
Northwestern University *M*
University of Illinois
Chicago *B*

Indiana

Indiana University-Purdue University
Fort Wayne *M*
Purdue University *A, B*
Purdue University
Calumet *A, B*
Rose-Hulman Institute of
Technology *M*

Kansas

Kansas State University *B, M*
University of Kansas *M*
Wichita State University *M*

Kentucky

University of Louisville *M*
Western Kentucky University *M*

Louisiana

Louisiana Tech University *M*
University of New Orleans *M*

Massachusetts

Massachusetts Maritime Academy *B*
University of Massachusetts
Amherst *M*
Western New England College *M*
Worcester Polytechnic Institute *B*

Michigan

Baker College
of Muskegon *B*
Central Michigan University *M*
Eastern Michigan University *B, M*
Lake Superior State University *B*

Lawrence Technological
University *B, M*
Oakland University *M*
University of Detroit Mercy *M*
University of Michigan
Dearborn *M*
Wayne State University *M*
Western Michigan University *B, M*

Minnesota

Herzing University *B*
Saint Cloud State University *M*
University of Minnesota
Duluth *M*
University of St. Thomas *M*

Missouri

Missouri State University *B*
Saint Louis University *B*
University of Missouri
Missouri University of Science and
Technology *B, M, D*
Washington University in St. Louis *M*

Montana

Montana State University
Bozeman *M*

New Jersey

New Jersey Institute of Technology *M*
Stevens Institute of
Technology *B, M, D*

New Mexico

New Mexico Institute of Mining and
Technology *M*

New York

Clarkson University *B, M*
Columbia University *B*
Cornell University *M*
Polytechnic Institute of New York
University *B, M, D*
Rensselaer Polytechnic Institute *B, M*
Rochester Institute of Technology *M*
State University of New York
College of Technology at Canton *B*
United States Merchant Marine
Academy *B*
United States Military Academy *B*

North Carolina

Central Piedmont Community
College *C, A*
Haywood Community College *A*
Mitchell Community College *A*
North Carolina Agricultural and
Technical State University *B*
Pitt Community College *C, A*
University of North Carolina
Charlotte *M*

Ohio

Bowling Green State University *M*
Case Western Reserve University *M*
Miami University
Oxford Campus *B*
Northwest State Community
College *A*
Terra State Community College *C*
University of Dayton *M*

Oklahoma

Northeastern State University *M*
University of Tulsa *M*

Oregon

Portland State University *M, D*

Pennsylvania

Drexel University *M*
Gannon University *M*

Grove City College *B*
Philadelphia University *M*
Point Park University *M*
Robert Morris University *M*
Wilkes University *B, M*
York College of Pennsylvania *B*

Puerto Rico

Turabo University *B*

South Carolina

The Citadel *M*
University of South Carolina
Upstate *B*

South Dakota

South Dakota School of Mines and
Technology *M*
South Dakota State University *B, M*

Tennessee

Christian Brothers University *M*
Middle Tennessee State University *B*
University of Tennessee
Chattanooga *C, B, M*
Vanderbilt University *M*

Texas

Lamar University *B, M*
St. Mary's University *B, M*
Southern Methodist
University *B, M, D*
Texas A&M University
Kingsville *B, M*
University of Houston *B, M*
University of the Incarnate Word *B*

Virginia

Sweet Briar College *B*

Washington

Saint Martin's University *M*
Washington State University *M*

West Virginia

West Virginia University at
Parkersburg *A, B*

Wisconsin

Marquette University *M*
Northeast Wisconsin Technical
College *A*

Engineering mechanics

Alabama

University of Alabama *M, D*

Arizona

Central Arizona College *A*
University of Arizona *M, D*

California

California State University
Northridge *B, M*
East Los Angeles College *A*
University of California
San Diego *B, M, D*

Colorado

Colorado School of Mines *M*
United States Air Force Academy *B*

Georgia

Georgia Institute of Technology *M, D*

Illinois

Northwestern University *M, D*
University of Illinois
Urbana-Champaign *B, M, D*

Indiana

Purdue University
Calumet *B*

Iowa

Iowa State University *M, D*
Morningside College *B*
Southeastern Community College
North Campus *A*

Maryland

Johns Hopkins University *B*

Massachusetts

Boston University *M*
Smith College *B*

Michigan

Michigan State University *M, D*
Michigan Technological University *M*
Washtenaw Community College *A*

Missouri

University of Missouri
Missouri University of Science and
Technology *B, M, D*

Nebraska

University of Nebraska
Lincoln *M*

New Mexico

New Mexico Institute of Mining and
Technology *M*

New York

Columbia University *B, M, D*
Cornell University *M, D*
Rensselaer Polytechnic Institute *M, D*
State University of New York
College of Agriculture and
Technology at Morrisville *A*

Ohio

Case Western Reserve University *M*
Cleveland State University *M*
Ohio State University
Columbus Campus *M, D*
University of Cincinnati *B, M, D*
University of Dayton *M*

Pennsylvania

Gettysburg College *B*
Lehigh University *B*
Penn State
University Park *M*

South Carolina

Clemson University *M, D*

Tennessee

Lipscomb University *B*

Texas

San Jacinto College *A*
University of Texas
Austin *M, D*

Utah

University of Utah *M*

Virginia

Virginia Polytechnic Institute and
State University *B, M, D*

Wisconsin

Northcentral Technical College *A*
University of Wisconsin
Madison *B, M, D*

Waukesha County Technical
College *A*

Engineering physics

Alabama
Samford University *B*

Arizona
Northern Arizona University *B*
University of Arizona *B*

Arkansas
Arkansas Tech University *B*

California
California Institute of Technology *B*
Loyola Marymount University *B*
Point Loma Nazarene University *B*
Santa Clara University *B*
University of California
  Berkeley *B*
  San Diego *B, M, D*
University of the Pacific *B*
Westmont College *B*

Colorado
Colorado School of Mines *B, M, D*
Colorado State University *B*
University of Colorado
  Boulder *B*

Connecticut
Connecticut College *B*
University of Connecticut *B*
Yale University *B, M, D*

Florida
Embry-Riddle Aeronautical
  University *B, M*
Jacksonville University *B*

Idaho
Northwest Nazarene University *B*

Illinois
Augustana College *B*
Bradley University *B*
University of Illinois
  Chicago *B*
  Urbana-Champaign *B, M, D*

Indiana
Butler University *B*
Rose-Hulman Institute of
  Technology *B*
Taylor University *B*

Iowa
Loras College *B*
Morningside College *B*
St. Ambrose University *B*
University of Northern Iowa *B*

Kansas
Southwestern College *B*
University of Kansas *B*

Kentucky
Murray State University *B, T*

Louisiana
Tulane University *B, M, D*

Maine
University of Maine *B*

Maryland
Morgan State University *B*

Massachusetts
Eastern Nazarene College *B*
Gordon College *B*
Tufts University *B*
University of Massachusetts
  Boston *B*
Worcester Polytechnic Institute *B*

Michigan
Eastern Michigan University *B*
Michigan Technological University *D*
Oakland University *B*
University of Michigan *B*

Minnesota
Bemidji State University *B*
St. Mary's University of Minnesota *B*

Mississippi
Mississippi College *B*

Missouri
Saint Louis University *B*
Southeast Missouri State University *B*

Nebraska
University of Nebraska
  Omaha *B*

Nevada
University of Nevada
  Reno *B*

New Hampshire
Dartmouth College *B*
Saint Anselm College *B*

New Jersey
Stevens Institute of Technology *B, M*

New Mexico
New Mexico State University *B*

New York
Barnard College *B*
Columbia University *M, D*
Cornell University *B, M, D*
Houghton College *B*
Polytechnic Institute of New York
  University *M*
Rensselaer Polytechnic
  Institute *B, M, D*
State University of New York
  Buffalo *B*

North Carolina
Elon University *B*

Ohio
Case Western Reserve University *B*
John Carroll University *B*
Miami University
  Oxford Campus *B*
Ohio State University
  Columbus Campus *B*
Wright State University *B*

Oklahoma
Oral Roberts University *B*
Southwestern Oklahoma State
  University *B*
University of Central Oklahoma *B, M*
University of Oklahoma *B, M, D*
University of Tulsa *B, M*

Oregon
Oregon State University *B*

Pennsylvania
Gettysburg College *B*

Juniata College *B*
Lehigh University *B*
University of Pittsburgh *B*

Rhode Island
Brown University *B*
Providence College *B*

South Dakota
Augustana College *B*
South Dakota State University *B*

Tennessee
Christian Brothers University *B*
Union University *B*
University of Tennessee
  Knoxville *B*

Texas
Northeast Texas Community
  College *A*
Tarleton State University *B*
Texas Tech University *B*
University of Texas
  Brownsville - Texas Southmost
    College *B*

Virginia
Randolph College *B*
University of Virginia *M, D*
Washington and Lee University *B*

Wisconsin
Carroll University *B*
University of Wisconsin
  Madison *B*
  Platteville *B*

Engineering science

Arizona
Arizona State University *M, D*

California
California Institute of
  Technology *M, D*
California Polytechnic State
  University: San Luis Obispo *B*
California State University
  Fullerton *B, M*
Humboldt State University *B*
San Diego State University *D*
University of California
  Berkeley *B*
  San Diego *B*

Colorado
Colorado State University *B*

Connecticut
Asnuntuck Community College *A*
Gateway Community College *A*
Manchester Community College *A*
Norwalk Community College *A*
Tunxis Community College *A*
Yale University *B*

District of Columbia
George Washington University *M, D*

Florida
State College of Florida,
  Manatee-Sarasota *A*
University of Central Florida *M, D*
University of Florida *B*
University of Miami *B*

Idaho
Idaho State University *D*

Illinois
Benedictine University *B*
Northwestern University *B, M*
Principia College *B*
South Suburban College of Cook
  County *A*

Indiana
Manchester College *B*

Iowa
Wartburg College *B*

Kansas
Garden City Community College *A*
University of Kansas *M, D*

Kentucky
Eastern Kentucky University *B*

Louisiana
Louisiana State University and
  Agricultural and Mechanical
  College *M, D*
University of New Orleans *M, D*

Massachusetts
Boston University *D*
Bristol Community College *A*
Greenfield Community College *A*
Harvard College *B, M, D*
Merrimack College *A*
Middlesex Community College *A*
Northern Essex Community
  College *A*
Smith College *B*
Tufts University *B*

Michigan
Glen Oaks Community College *A*
University of Michigan *B*
University of Michigan
  Flint *B*
Washtenaw Community College *A*

Minnesota
Bethel University *B*

Mississippi
University of Mississippi *M, D*

New Hampshire
Daniel Webster College *A*
Dartmouth College *B*

New Jersey
Camden County College *A*
The College of New Jersey *B*
County College of Morris *A*
Gloucester County College *A*
Hudson County Community
  College *A*
Middlesex County College *A*
New Jersey Institute of
  Technology *B, M*
Passaic County Community College *A*
Raritan Valley Community College *A*
Rutgers, The State University of New
  Jersey
  Camden Regional Campus *B*
  New Brunswick/Piscataway
    Campus *B*

New Mexico
University of New Mexico *B*

New York
Broome Community College *A*
City University of New York
  Borough of Manhattan Community
    College *A*

Clarkson University *M, D*
Corning Community College *A*
Dutchess Community College *A*
Finger Lakes Community College *A*
Genesee Community College *A*
Hofstra University *B*
Hudson Valley Community College *A*
Monroe Community College *A*
Rensselaer Polytechnic
   Institute *B, M, D*
Rochester Institute of Technology *A*
State University of New York
   College of Agriculture and
      Technology at Morrisville *A*
Suffolk County Community College *A*
Sullivan County Community
   College *A*
University of Rochester *B*
Westchester Community College *A*

Ohio

Cleveland State University *B*
Eastern Gateway Community
   College *A*
Muskingum University *B*
University of Cincinnati *M, D*
University of Toledo *M, D*
Wright State University *B, M*

Pennsylvania

Gettysburg College *B*
Montgomery County Community
   College *A*
Penn State
   Abington *B*
   Altoona *B*
   Beaver *B*
   Berks *B*
   Brandywine *B*
   DuBois *B*
   Erie, The Behrend College *B*
   Fayette, The Eberly Campus *B*
   Greater Allegheny *B*
   Harrisburg *B*
   Hazleton *B*
   Lehigh Valley *B*
   Mont Alto *B*
   New Kensington *B*
   Schuylkill *B*
   Shenango *B*
   University Park *B, M, D*
   Wilkes-Barre *B*
   Worthington Scranton *B*
   York *B*
University of Pittsburgh
   Bradford *B*
Valley Forge Military Academy &
   College *A*

South Carolina

Bob Jones University *B*

Tennessee

Lipscomb University *B*
University of Tennessee
   Knoxville *B, M, D*

Texas

Abilene Christian University *B*
St. Mary's University *B*
Southern Methodist University *M*
Texas Tech University *D*
Trinity University *B*
University of Houston *M, D*

Utah

Southern Utah University *B*

Virginia

Sweet Briar College *B*

Washington

Pacific Lutheran University *B*
Seattle Pacific University *B*
Washington State University *D*

Engineering technology, general

Alabama

Jefferson State Community
   College *C, A*
Snead State Community College *A*

Arkansas

Arkansas State University *A, B, M*
East Arkansas Community College *C*
Ozarka College *A*

California

Allan Hancock College *A*
American River College *A*
California Maritime Academy *B*
California State Polytechnic
   University: Pomona *B*
Cerro Coso Community College *C, A*
City College of San Francisco *A*
Hartnell College *A*
Ohlone College *C*
Santa Barbara City College *C, A*

Colorado

Arapahoe Community College *C, A*
Pueblo Community College *C, A*

Connecticut

Central Connecticut State
   University *M*
Naugatuck Valley Community
   College *C, A*
Northwestern Connecticut
   Community College *A*
Three Rivers Community College *A*
University of Hartford *B*

Florida

St. Petersburg College *C, A*
University of West Florida *B*
Valencia Community College *A*

Georgia

Atlanta Metropolitan College *A*
Berry College *B*
Darton College *A*
Macon State College *C, A*
Southern Polytechnic State
   University *C, M*

Illinois

Southern Illinois University
   Carbondale *B*

Indiana

Indiana University-Purdue University
   Fort Wayne *M*
Purdue University
   North Central *B*
Trine University *M*
Vincennes University *A*

Iowa

Dordt College *B*

Kansas

Kansas State University *A, B*
Pittsburg State University *M*

Kentucky

Bluegrass Community and Technical
   College *C, A*
Elizabethtown Community and
   Technical College *C, A*
Hopkinsville Community College *C, A*
Lindsey Wilson College *A*
Madisonville Community College *C, A*
Murray State University *M*

Louisiana

McNeese State University *A, B*
Southeastern Louisiana University *B*

Maine

Maine Maritime Academy *B*

Maryland

Community College of Baltimore
   County *C*
Harford Community College *A*
University of Maryland
   Eastern Shore *B*

Massachusetts

Wentworth Institute of Technology *B*

Michigan

Bay de Noc Community College *A*
Eastern Michigan University *M, D*
Glen Oaks Community College *C*
Grand Rapids Community College *A*
Lawrence Technological University *B*
Michigan Technological University *A*
Saginaw Valley State University *B*
Spring Arbor University *B*
Wayne State University *M*

Minnesota

Itasca Community College *A*
Northwest Technical Institute *A*
Ridgewater College *C, A*
Saint Cloud State University *C*

Mississippi

University of Southern Mississippi *M*

Missouri

Drury University *B*
Lincoln University *A*
Southeast Missouri State University *B*

Montana

Stone Child College *C*

Nebraska

Wayne State College *B*

Nevada

College of Southern Nevada *A*

New Jersey

Bergen Community College *A*
Cumberland County College *C, A*
New Jersey Institute of Technology *B*
Rowan University *C*

New Mexico

Eastern New Mexico University *B*

New York

State University of New York
   College of Agriculture and
      Technology at Morrisville *A*
   Maritime College *A*

North Carolina

Cleveland Community College *A*
Lenoir-Rhyne University *B*
Western Carolina University *B*
Wilson Community College *A*

North Dakota

Bismarck State College *A*
Lake Region State College *C, A*

Ohio

Bowling Green State University:
   Firelands College *A*
Cleveland State University *B*
James A. Rhodes State College *A*
Miami University
   Hamilton Campus *B*
   Oxford Campus *B*
Ohio Northern University *B*
University of Dayton *B*
Wright State University: Lake
   Campus *A*
Youngstown State University *A, B*

Oklahoma

Oklahoma State University
   Oklahoma City *A*
University of Central Oklahoma *B*

Pennsylvania

California University of
   Pennsylvania *B, M*
Carnegie Mellon University *M*
Drexel University *B*
Montgomery County Community
   College *A*
South Hills School of Business &
   Technology: Altoona *A*
Temple University *B*

Puerto Rico

University of Puerto Rico
   Arecibo *A*

South Carolina

Spartanburg Community College *C, A*

Tennessee

Austin Peay State University *B*
Chattanooga State Community
   College *A*
East Tennessee State University *B, M*
Middle Tennessee State University *B*
University of Memphis *M*

Texas

North Lake College *C, A*
Southern Methodist University *M*
Tarleton State University *B*
Texas A&M University *B*
Texas State University: San Marcos *B*
Texas Tech University *B*
University of North Texas *M*
University of Texas
   Tyler *B*

Utah

Brigham Young University *M*
Southern Utah University *B*

Virginia

Germanna Community College *C*
Old Dominion University *B*
Rappahannock Community College *A*
Southwest Virginia Community
   College *A*
Virginia State University *B*

Washington

Bates Technical College *C, A*
Everett Community College *A*
Northwest Indian College *C*
Olympic College *A*

West Virginia

West Virginia University at
   Parkersburg *C, A*

Wisconsin

University of Wisconsin
   Stout *B*

English composition

Arizona
Central Arizona College *A*
Grand Canyon University *B*
Prescott College *B, M*

Arkansas
University of Central Arkansas *B*

California
California State University
  Chico *C*
  Dominguez Hills *M*
  Fresno *M*
  Long Beach *B*
  San Bernardino *M*
College of the Desert *A*
College of the Siskiyous *C, A*
Dominican University of California *B*
Glendale Community College *A*
Humboldt State University *B, M*
Irvine Valley College *A*
San Diego State University *M*
Stanford University *B, M, D*
University of California
  San Diego *B*

Colorado
University of Colorado
  Denver *B*

Connecticut
Quinnipiac University *B*
Southern Connecticut State
  University *B, M*
Western Connecticut State
  University *B*

Delaware
Delaware State University *B, M*

Florida
Florida Southern College *B*

Georgia
Georgia Southern University *B*

Idaho
Brigham Young University-Idaho *B*

Illinois
Eureka College *B*
Illinois State University *M*
Illinois Valley Community College *A*
Lewis University *B*
Lincoln College *A*
National-Louis University *M*
Northwestern University *C*
Richland Community College *A*
University of Illinois
  Urbana-Champaign *B*

Indiana
DePauw University *B*
Indiana University
  Bloomington *B*
  South Bend *A, B*
Indiana University-Purdue University
  Fort Wayne *B*
Purdue University
  Calumet *B*
University of Evansville *B*

Iowa
Briar Cliff University *B*
Dordt College *B*
Drake University *B*
Waldorf College *B*
Wartburg College *B*

Kansas
Butler Community College *A*
Central Christian College of Kansas *A*

Kentucky
University of Louisville *D*

Maine
University of Southern Maine *B*

Massachusetts
Emerson College *M*
Salem State College *B*
Wheaton College *B*

Michigan
Central Michigan University *M*
Eastern Michigan University *B, M*
Ferris State University *B*
Oakland University *B*
University of Michigan
  Flint *B, M*

Minnesota
Concordia College: Moorhead *B*
Metropolitan State University *B*
Saint Cloud State University *B*
Winona State University *B*

Mississippi
East Central Community College *A*

Missouri
William Woods University *B*

Nebraska
Creighton University *B*

Nevada
University of Nevada
  Reno *B*

New Jersey
Rowan University *B*

New Mexico
New Mexico Highlands University *M*

New York
Ithaca College *B*
Manhattan College *B*
Marist College *B*

North Carolina
Gardner-Webb University *B*
High Point University *B*
Salem College *B*

North Dakota
Jamestown College *B*

Ohio
Ohio Northern University *B*
Ohio State University
  Columbus Campus *B*
Ohio Wesleyan University *B*
Otterbein College *B*
University of Akron *M*

Oklahoma
Oklahoma Christian University *B*
Oral Roberts University *B*
University of Central Oklahoma *B, M*

Pennsylvania
Geneva College *B*
La Roche College *B*
La Salle University *B*
University of Pittsburgh
  Greensburg *B*

Texas
Austin Community College *A*
Baylor University *B*
Huston-Tillotson University *B*
Lamar State College at Orange *A*
St. Edward's University *B*
St. Philip's College *A*
Texas A&M University
  Commerce *B*
University of Texas
  Austin *B*

Utah
Snow College *A*

Vermont
Bennington College *B*
Champlain College *B*
Marlboro College *B*

Washington
Everett Community College *A*
Olympic College *C*

West Virginia
Concord University *B*

Wisconsin
Lakeland College *B*
Marian University *B*

English language and literature

Alabama
Alabama Agricultural and Mechanical
  University *B, M*
Alabama State University *B*
Athens State University *B*
Auburn University *B, M, D, T*
Auburn University at Montgomery *B*
Birmingham-Southern College *B*
Calhoun Community College *A*
Faulkner State Community College *A*
Faulkner University *B, T*
Gadsden State Community College *A*
Huntingdon College *B*
Jacksonville State University *B, M*
Judson College *B*
Miles College *B*
Northeast Alabama Community
  College *A*
Oakwood University *B*
Samford University *B*
Spring Hill College *B, T*
Stillman College *B*
Talladega College *B*
Troy University *B*
Tuskegee University *B*
University of Alabama *B, M, D*
University of Alabama
  Birmingham *B, M*
  Huntsville *B, M*
University of Mobile *B, T*
University of Montevallo *B, M, T*
University of North Alabama *B, M*
University of South Alabama *B, M*
University of West Alabama *B, T*

Alaska
University of Alaska
  Anchorage *B, M*
  Fairbanks *B, M*
  Southeast *B*

Arizona
Arizona State University *B, M, D*
Arizona Western College *A*
Central Arizona College *A*
Cochise College *A*
Eastern Arizona College *A*
Grand Canyon University *B*
Mohave Community College *A*
Northern Arizona University *B, M*
Prescott College *B*
University of Arizona *B, M, D*

Arkansas
Arkansas State University *B, M*
Arkansas Tech University *B, M*
Black River Technical College *A*
Harding University *B*
Henderson State University *B*
Hendrix College *B*
John Brown University *B*
Lyon College *B*
Ouachita Baptist University *B*
Philander Smith College *B*
Phillips Community College of the
  University of Arkansas *A*
Southern Arkansas University *B*
University of Arkansas *B, M, D*
University of Arkansas
  Fort Smith *B*
  Little Rock *B*
  Monticello *B*
  Pine Bluff *B*
University of Central Arkansas *B, M*
University of the Ozarks *B, T*
Williams Baptist College *B*

California
Allan Hancock College *A*
Azusa Pacific University *B*
Bakersfield College *A*
Berkeley City College *A*
Bethany University *B*
Biola University *B*
Butte College *A*
Cabrillo College *A*
California Baptist University *B*
California Institute of Technology *B*
California Lutheran University *B*
California Polytechnic State
  University: San Luis Obispo *B, M*
California State Polytechnic
  University: Pomona *B, M*
California State University
  Bakersfield *B, M*
  Chico *B, M*
  Dominguez Hills *B*
  East Bay *B, M*
  Fresno *B, M*
  Fullerton *B, M*
  Long Beach *B, M, T*
  Los Angeles *B, M*
  Northridge *B, M*
  Sacramento *B, M*
  San Bernardino *B*
  San Marcos *B, M*
  Stanislaus *B, M*
California State University: Channel
  Islands *B, M*
Canada College *A*
Cerritos College *A*
Chabot College *A*
Chaffey College *A*
Chapman University *B, M*
Citrus College *A*
Claremont McKenna College *B*
College of Alameda *A*
College of Marin: Kentfield *A*
College of San Mateo *A*
College of the Canyons *A*
College of the Desert *A*
College of the Sequoias *A*
College of the Siskiyous *A*
Columbia College *A*
Concordia University *B*
Contra Costa College *A*
Copper Mountain College *A*
Crafton Hills College *A*
Cypress College *A*
De Anza College *A*
Dominican University of California *B*
El Camino College *A*

El Camino College: Compton
  Center *A*
Feather River College *A*
Folsom Lake College *A*
Foothill College *A*
Fresno City College *A*
Fullerton College *A*
Gavilan College *A*
Glendale Community College *A*
Golden West College *A*
Grossmont College *A*
Hartnell College *A*
Holy Names University *B*
Humboldt State University *B, M*
Imperial Valley College *A*
La Sierra University *B*
Lake Tahoe Community College *A*
Laney College *A*
Long Beach City College *A*
Los Angeles City College *A*
Los Angeles Mission College *A*
Los Angeles Southwest College *A*
Los Angeles Valley College *A*
Loyola Marymount University *B*
The Master's College *B*
Mendocino College *A*
Merced College *A*
Merritt College *A*
Mills College *B, M*
MiraCosta College *A*
Modesto Junior College *A*
Monterey Peninsula College *A*
Mount St. Mary's College *B*
Napa Valley College *A*
National University *B, M*
Notre Dame de Namur
  University *B, M*
Occidental College *B*
Orange Coast College *A*
Oxnard College *A*
Pacific Union College *B*
Palo Verde College *A*
Pepperdine University *B*
Pitzer College *B*
Point Loma Nazarene University *B*
Pomona College *B*
Porterville College *A*
Reedley College *A*
Saddleback College *A*
St. Mary's College of California *B*
San Diego Christian College *B*
San Diego City College *A*
San Diego Miramar College *A*
San Diego State University *B, M*
San Francisco State University *B, M*
San Joaquin Delta College *A*
San Jose State University *B, M*
Santa Ana College *A*
Santa Barbara City College *A*
Santa Clara University *B*
Santa Monica College *A*
Santa Rosa Junior College *A*
Santiago Canyon College *A*
Scripps College *B*
Sierra College *A*
Simpson University *B*
Skyline College *A*
Solano Community College *A*
Sonoma State University *B, M*
Southwestern College *A*
Stanford University *B, M, D*
Taft College *A*
University of California
  Berkeley *B, D*
  Davis *B, M, D*
  Irvine *B, M, D*
  Los Angeles *B, M, D*
  Riverside *B, M, D*
  San Diego *B*
  Santa Barbara *B, M, D*
  Santa Cruz *B, M, D*
University of La Verne *B*
University of Redlands *B*
University of San Diego *B*

University of San Francisco *B*
University of Southern
  California *B, M, D*
University of the Pacific *B*
University of the West *B*
Vanguard University of Southern
  California *B*
West Los Angeles College *A*
West Valley College *A*
Westmont College *B*
Whittier College *B*
William Jessup University *B*
Yuba Community College District *A*

Colorado

Adams State College *B*
Colorado Christian University *B*
Colorado College *B*
Colorado Mountain College *A*
Colorado State University *B, M*
Colorado State University
  Pueblo *B*
Fort Lewis College *B*
Lamar Community College *A*
Mesa State College *B*
Metropolitan State College of
  Denver *B, T*
Naropa University *B*
Pikes Peak Community College *A*
Red Rocks Community College *A*
Regis University *B*
United States Air Force Academy *B*
University of Colorado
  Boulder *B, M, D*
  Colorado Springs *B*
  Denver *B, M*
University of Denver *B, M, D*
University of Northern
  Colorado *B, M, T*
Western State College of Colorado *B*

Connecticut

Albertus Magnus College *B*
Central Connecticut State
  University *B, M*
Connecticut College *B*
Eastern Connecticut State
  University *B*
Fairfield University *B*
Quinnipiac University *B*
Sacred Heart University *B*
Saint Joseph College *B*
Southern Connecticut State
  University *B, M, T*
Trinity College *B, M*
University of Bridgeport *B*
University of Connecticut *B, M, D*
University of Hartford *B*
University of New Haven *B*
Wesleyan University *B*
Western Connecticut State
  University *B, M*
Yale University *B, M, D*

Delaware

Delaware State University *B, M*
University of Delaware *B, M, D*
Wesley College *B*

District of Columbia

American University *B*
Catholic University of
  America *B, M, D*
Gallaudet University *B*
George Washington University *B*
Georgetown University *B, M*
Howard University *B, M, D*
Trinity Washington University *B*
University of the District of
  Columbia *B, M*

Florida

Ave Maria University *B*

Barry University *B*
Bethune-Cookman University *B*
Broward College *A*
Clearwater Christian College *B*
Eckerd College *B*
Flagler College *B*
Florida Agricultural and Mechanical
  University *B*
Florida Atlantic University *B, M*
Florida Gulf Coast University *B, M*
Florida International University *B, M*
Florida Memorial University *B*
Florida Southern College *B*
Florida State University *B, M, D*
Gulf Coast Community College *A*
Indian River State College *A*
Jacksonville University *B*
Lynn University *B*
Miami Dade College *A*
New College of Florida *B*
Nova Southeastern University *B*
Palm Beach Atlantic University *B*
Palm Beach Community College *A*
Pensacola Junior College *A*
Rollins College *B*
Saint Leo University *B*
Saint Thomas University *B*
South Florida Community College *A*
Southeastern University *B*
State College of Florida,
  Manatee-Sarasota *A*
Stetson University *B, M*
University of Central Florida *B, M*
University of Florida *B, M, D*
University of Miami *B, M, D*
University of North Florida *B, M*
University of South Florida *B, M, D*
University of Tampa *A, B, T*
University of West Florida *B, M*
Warner University *B*

Georgia

Abraham Baldwin Agricultural
  College *A*
Agnes Scott College *B*
Albany State University *B*
Armstrong Atlantic State University *B*
Atlanta Christian College *B*
Atlanta Metropolitan College *A*
Augusta State University *B*
Bainbridge College *A*
Berry College *B*
Brenau University *B*
Brewton-Parker College *B*
Clark Atlanta University *B, M, D*
Clayton State University *B*
College of Coastal Georgia *A*
Columbus State University *B*
Covenant College *B*
Dalton State College *A, B*
Darton College *A*
East Georgia College *A*
Emmanuel College *B*
Emory University *B, D*
Fort Valley State University *B*
Gainesville State College *A*
Georgia College and State
  University *B, M*
Georgia Gwinnett College *B*
Georgia Highlands College *A*
Georgia Perimeter College *A*
Georgia Southern University *B, M*
Georgia Southwestern State
  University *B, T*
Georgia State University *B, M, D*
Gordon College *A*
Kennesaw State University *B*
LaGrange College *B*
Macon State College *A*
Mercer University *B*
Middle Georgia College *A*
Morehouse College *B*
North Georgia College & State
  University *B*

Oglethorpe University *B*
Paine College *B*
Piedmont College *B*
Reinhardt College *B*
Savannah State University *B*
Shorter College *B, T*
South Georgia College *A*
Spelman College *B*
Toccoa Falls College *B*
Truett-McConnell College *B*
University of Georgia *B, M, D*
University of West Georgia *B, M*
Valdosta State University *B, M*
Waycross College *A*
Wesleyan College *B*
Young Harris College *A, B*

Hawaii

Chaminade University of Honolulu *B*
Hawaii Pacific University *B*
University of Hawaii
  Hilo *B*
  Manoa *B, M, D*
  West Oahu *B*

Idaho

Boise State University *B, M*
Brigham Young University-Idaho *B*
College of Idaho *B*
Idaho State University *A, B, M, D*
Lewis-Clark State College *B*
North Idaho College *A*
Northwest Nazarene University *B*
University of Idaho *B, M*

Illinois

Augustana College *B*
Aurora University *B*
Benedictine University *B, T*
Black Hawk College: East Campus *A*
Blackburn College *B*
Bradley University *B, M, T*
Chicago State University *B, M, T*
City Colleges of Chicago
  Harold Washington College *A*
  Kennedy-King College *A*
Concordia University Chicago *B*
DePaul University *B, M*
Dominican University *B*
Eastern Illinois University *B, M, T*
Elmhurst College *B*
Eureka College *B*
Governors State University *B, M, T*
Greenville College *B, T*
Harper College *A*
Hebrew Theological College *B*
Illinois Central College *A*
Illinois College *B, T*
Illinois State University *D*
Illinois Valley Community College *A*
Illinois Wesleyan University *B*
John A. Logan College *A*
Joliet Junior College *A*
Judson University *B*
Kishwaukee College *A*
Knox College *B*
Lake Forest College *B*
Lewis University *B, T*
Lincoln College *A*
Loyola University Chicago *B, M, D*
MacMurray College *B, T*
McKendree University *B*
Millikin University *B*
Monmouth College *B, T*
Morton College *A*
National-Louis University *B*
North Central College *B, T*
North Park University *B*
Northeastern Illinois University *B, M*
Northern Illinois University *B*
Northwestern University *B, M, D*
Olivet Nazarene University *B, T*
Principia College *B*
Quincy University *B, T*

Richland Community College *A*
Rockford College *B*
Roosevelt University *B, M*
Saint Xavier University *B*
South Suburban College of Cook
   County *A*
Southern Illinois University
   Carbondale *B, M, D*
Southern Illinois University
   Edwardsville *B, M*
Southwestern Illinois College *A*
Spoon River College *A*
Trinity Christian College *B, T*
Trinity International University *B*
Triton College *A*
University of Chicago *B, M, D*
University of Illinois
   Chicago *B, M, D*
   Springfield *B, M*
   Urbana-Champaign *B, M, D*
University of St. Francis *B*
Western Illinois University *B, M*
Wheaton College *B, T*

Indiana

Anderson University *B*
Ball State University *B, M, D, T*
Bethel College *B*
Butler University *B, M*
Calumet College of St. Joseph *A, B*
DePauw University *B*
Earlham College *B*
Franklin College *B*
Goshen College *B*
Grace College *B*
Hanover College *B*
Holy Cross College *B*
Huntington University *B*
Indiana State University *B, M, T*
Indiana University
   Bloomington *B, M, D*
   East *A, B*
   Kokomo *B*
   Northwest *A, B*
   South Bend *B*
   Southeast *B*
Indiana University-Purdue University
   Fort Wayne *A, B, T*
Indiana University-Purdue University
   Indianapolis *B, M*
Indiana Wesleyan University *B*
Manchester College *B, T*
Marian University *B, T*
Oakland City University *B*
Purdue University *B, M, D*
Purdue University
   Calumet *B*
   North Central *B*
Saint Joseph's College *B*
St. Mary-of-the-Woods College *B*
Taylor University *B*
University of Evansville *B*
University of Indianapolis *B*
University of Notre Dame *B, M, D*
University of St. Francis *B*
University of Southern Indiana *B, T*
Valparaiso University *B, M*
Vincennes University *A*
Wabash College *B*

Iowa

Briar Cliff University *B*
Buena Vista University *B, T*
Central College *B, T*
Clarke College *A, B, T*
Coe College *B*
Cornell College *B, T*
Dordt College *B*
Drake University *B*
Ellsworth Community College *A*
Graceland University *B, T*
Grand View University *B*
Grinnell College *B*
Iowa State University *B*

Iowa Wesleyan College *B*
Loras College *B, M*
Luther College *B*
Maharishi University of
   Management *B*
Marshalltown Community College *A*
Morningside College *B*
Mount Mercy College *B, T*
Northwestern College *B, T*
St. Ambrose University *B, T*
Simpson College *B*
University of Dubuque *B*
University of Iowa *B*
University of Northern Iowa *B, M*
Upper Iowa University *B*
Waldorf College *B*
Wartburg College *B, T*

Kansas

Baker University *B, T*
Barton County Community College *A*
Benedictine College *B*
Bethany College *B*
Bethel College *B*
Central Christian College of
   Kansas *A, B*
Coffeyville Community College *A*
Cowley County Community
   College *A*
Donnelly College *A*
Emporia State University *B, M, T*
Fort Hays State University *B, M*
Friends University *B*
Garden City Community College *A*
Hutchinson Community College *A*
Kansas State University *B, M*
Kansas Wesleyan University *B, T*
Labette Community College *A*
McPherson College *B, T*
MidAmerica Nazarene University *B*
Neosho County Community
   College *A*
Newman University *B*
Ottawa University *B*
Pittsburg State University *B, M*
Pratt Community College *A*
Seward County Community College *A*
Southwestern College *B*
Sterling College *B, T*
Tabor College *B*
University of Kansas *B, M, D*
University of St. Mary *B*
Washburn University *B*
Wichita State University *B, M, T*

Kentucky

Alice Lloyd College *B*
Asbury College *B, T*
Bellarmine University *B, T*
Berea College *B*
Bluegrass Community and Technical
   College *A*
Brescia University *B*
Campbellsville University *B*
Centre College *B*
Eastern Kentucky University *B, M*
Georgetown College *B, T*
Kentucky State University *B*
Kentucky Wesleyan College *B*
Lindsey Wilson College *B, T*
Mid-Continent University *B*
Midway College *B*
Morehead State University *B, M*
Murray State University *B, M, T*
Northern Kentucky University *B, M*
Pikeville College *B, T*
Thomas More College *A, B*
Transylvania University *B*
Union College *B*
University of Kentucky *B, M, D*
University of Louisville *B, M*
University of the Cumberlands *B, T*
Western Kentucky University *B, M, T*

Louisiana

Centenary College of Louisiana *B, T*
Dillard University *B*
Grambling State University *B*
Louisiana College *B, T*
Louisiana State University
   Shreveport *B*
Louisiana State University and
   Agricultural and Mechanical
   College *B, M, D*
Louisiana Tech University *B, M*
Loyola University New Orleans *B*
McNeese State University *B, M*
Nicholls State University *B*
Northwestern State University *B, M*
Our Lady of Holy Cross College *B*
Southeastern Louisiana
   University *B, M*
Southern University
   New Orleans *B*
Southern University and Agricultural
   and Mechanical College *B*
Tulane University *B, M, D*
University of Louisiana at
   Lafayette *M, D, T*
University of Louisiana at
   Monroe *B, M*
University of New Orleans *B, M*
Xavier University of Louisiana *B*

Maine

Bates College *B, T*
Bowdoin College *B*
Colby College *B*
Husson University *B*
Saint Joseph's College of Maine *B*
University of Maine *B, M*
University of Maine
   Augusta *B*
   Farmington *B*
   Fort Kent *B*
   Machias *B, T*
   Presque Isle *B*
University of New England *B*
University of Southern Maine *B*

Maryland

Allegany College of Maryland *A*
Bowie State University *B, M*
College of Notre Dame of
   Maryland *B, M*
Community College of Baltimore
   County *A*
Coppin State University *B*
Frederick Community College *A*
Frostburg State University *B, T*
Goucher College *B*
Harford Community College *A*
Hood College *B, T*
Howard Community College *A*
Johns Hopkins University *B, M, D*
Loyola University Maryland *B*
McDaniel College *B*
Morgan State University *B, M, D*
Mount St. Mary's University *B, T*
St. Mary's College of Maryland *B*
Salisbury University *B, M, T*
Stevenson University *B*
Towson University *B*
United States Naval Academy *B*
University of Baltimore *B*
University of Maryland
   Baltimore County *B*
   College Park *B, M, D*
   Eastern Shore *B*
   University College *B*
Washington Adventist University *B*
Washington College *B, M, T*

Massachusetts

American International College *B*
Amherst College *B*
Anna Maria College *B*

Assumption College *B*
Bard College at Simon's Rock *B*
Boston College *B, M, D*
Boston University *B, M, D*
Brandeis University *B, M, D*
Bridgewater State College *B, M*
Bunker Hill Community College *A*
Cape Cod Community College *A*
Clark University *B, M*
College of the Holy Cross *B*
Curry College *B*
Eastern Nazarene College *B*
Elms College *B*
Emmanuel College *B*
Endicott College *B*
Fitchburg State College *B*
Framingham State College *B*
Gordon College *B*
Hampshire College *B*
Harvard College *B, M, D*
Lasell College *B*
Lesley University *B*
Massachusetts College of Liberal
   Arts *B*
Massachusetts Institute of
   Technology *B*
Merrimack College *B*
Mount Holyoke College *B*
Mount Ida College *B*
Nichols College *B*
Northeastern University *B, M, D*
Pine Manor College *B*
Regis College *B*
Roxbury Community College *A*
Salem State College *B, M*
Simmons College *B, M*
Smith College *B*
Springfield College *B*
Stonehill College *B*
Suffolk University *B*
Tufts University *B, M, D*
University of Massachusetts
   Amherst *B, M, D*
   Boston *B, M*
   Dartmouth *B*
   Lowell *B*
Wellesley College *B*
Western New England College *B*
Westfield State College *B, M, T*
Wheaton College *B*
Williams College *B*
Worcester State College *B, M*

Michigan

Adrian College *A, B, T*
Albion College *B*
Alma College *B, T*
Andrews University *B, M*
Aquinas College *B*
Calvin College *B, T*
Central Michigan University *B, M*
Cornerstone University *B*
Delta College *A*
Eastern Michigan University *B, M*
Finlandia University *B*
Grand Rapids Community College *A*
Grand Valley State University *B*
Hillsdale College *B*
Hope College *B*
Kalamazoo College *B*
Kellogg Community College *A*
Lake Michigan College *A*
Lake Superior State University *B*
Lansing Community College *A*
Lawrence Technological University *B*
Madonna University *A, B*
Marygrove College *B, M*
Michigan State University *B, M, D*
Northern Michigan University *B, M*
Northwestern Michigan College *A*
Oakland University *B, M, T*
Rochester College *B*
Saginaw Valley State University *B, T*
Siena Heights University *B*

Spring Arbor University *B, T*
University of Detroit Mercy *B*
University of Michigan *B, M, D*
University of Michigan
 Dearborn *B*
 Flint *B, M, T*
Wayne State University *B, M, D*
Western Michigan University *B, M, D*

Minnesota

Augsburg College *B*
Bemidji State University *B, M*
Bethany Lutheran College *B*
Bethel University *B*
Carleton College *B*
College of St. Benedict *B*
College of St. Scholastica *B*
Concordia College: Moorhead *B, T*
Concordia University: St. Paul *B*
Crown College *B*
Gustavus Adolphus College *B*
Hamline University *B*
Macalester College *B*
Metropolitan State University *B*
Minnesota State University
 Mankato *B, M*
 Moorhead *B*
Minnesota West Community and
 Technical College *A*
North Central University *B*
Northland Community & Technical
 College *A*
Northwestern College *B*
Ridgewater College *A*
St. Catherine University *B*
Saint Cloud State University *B, M*
St. John's University *B*
St. Mary's University of Minnesota *B*
St. Olaf College *B*
Southwest Minnesota State
 University *B, T*
University of Minnesota
 Duluth *B, M*
 Morris *B*
 Twin Cities *B, M, D*
University of St. Thomas *B, M*
Vermilion Community College *A*
Winona State University *B, M*

Mississippi

Alcorn State University *B*
Belhaven University *B*
Blue Mountain College *B*
Delta State University *B*
Hinds Community College *A*
Jackson State University *B, M*
Millsaps College *B*
Mississippi College *B, M*
Mississippi Delta Community
 College *A*
Mississippi State University *B, M*
Mississippi University for Women *B, T*
Mississippi Valley State University *B*
Rust College *B*
Tougaloo College *B*
University of Mississippi *B, M, D*
University of Southern
 Mississippi *B, M, D*

Missouri

Avila University *B*
Central Methodist University *B*
College of the Ozarks *B*
Columbia College *B*
Culver-Stockton College *B, T*
Drury University *B, T*
Evangel University *B, T*
Fontbonne University *B, T*
Hannibal-LaGrange College *A, B*
Lincoln University *B*
Lindenwood University *B*
Maryville University of Saint Louis *B*
Mineral Area College *A*
Missouri Baptist University *B*

Missouri Southern State University *B*
Missouri State University *B, M*
Missouri Valley College *B*
Missouri Western State University *B*
Northwest Missouri State
 University *B, M*
Park University *B*
Rockhurst University *B*
St. Charles Community College *A*
Saint Louis University *B, M, D*
Southeast Missouri State
 University *B, M*
Southwest Baptist University *B, T*
Stephens College *B*
Three Rivers Community College *A*
Truman State University *B, M*
University of Central Missouri *B, M*
University of Missouri
 Columbia *B, M, D*
 Kansas City *B, M, D*
 Missouri University of Science and
  Technology *B, T*
 St. Louis *B, M*
Washington University in St.
 Louis *B, M, D*
Webster University *B*
Westminster College *B, T*
William Jewell College *B, T*
William Woods University *B, T*

Montana

Miles Community College *A*
Montana State University
 Billings *B, T*
 Bozeman *B, M*
Rocky Mountain College *B, T*
University of Great Falls *B*
University of Montana *B, M*
University of Montana: Western *B*

Nebraska

Bellevue University *B*
Chadron State College *B*
College of Saint Mary *B*
Concordia University *B*
Creighton University *B, M*
Dana College *B*
Doane College *B*
Little Priest Tribal College *A*
Nebraska Wesleyan University *B*
Northeast Community College *A*
Peru State College *B, T*
Union College *B*
University of Nebraska
 Kearney *B, M, T*
 Lincoln *B, M, D*
 Omaha *B, M*
Wayne State College *B*
Western Nebraska Community
 College *A*
York College *B*

Nevada

College of Southern Nevada *A*
Great Basin College *A*
Nevada State College *B*
Sierra Nevada College *B*
University of Nevada
 Las Vegas *B, M, D*
 Reno *B, M, D*

New Hampshire

Colby-Sawyer College *B*
Dartmouth College *B, T*
Franklin Pierce University *B*
Keene State College *B*
NHTI-Concord's Community
 College *A*
New England College *B*
Plymouth State University *B*
Rivier College *M*
Saint Anselm College *B, T*

Southern New Hampshire
 University *B*
Thomas More College of Liberal
 Arts *B*
University of New Hampshire *B, M, D*
University of New Hampshire at
 Manchester *B*

New Jersey

Bergen Community College *A*
Bloomfield College *B*
Caldwell College *B*
Centenary College *B, M*
The College of New Jersey *B, M*
College of St. Elizabeth *B*
Drew University *B*
Fairleigh Dickinson University
 College at Florham *B, M*
 Metropolitan Campus *B, M*
Felician College *B*
Georgian Court University *B*
Gloucester County College *A*
Kean University *B, M, T*
Monmouth University *B, M*
Montclair State University *B, M*
New Jersey City University *B*
Passaic County Community College *A*
Princeton University *B, M, D*
Raritan Valley Community College *A*
Richard Stockton College of New
 Jersey *B*
Rider University *B*
Rowan University *B*
Rutgers, The State University of New
 Jersey
 Camden Regional Campus *B, M, T*
 New Brunswick/Piscataway
  Campus *B, M, D, T*
 Newark Regional Campus *B, M, T*
Saint Peter's College *B*
Salem Community College *A*
Seton Hall University *B, M, T*
Stevens Institute of Technology *B*
Sussex County Community College *A*
Thomas Edison State College *B*
Warren County Community College *A*
William Paterson University of New
 Jersey *B, M*

New Mexico

Eastern New Mexico University *B, M*
New Mexico Highlands
 University *B, M*
New Mexico State University *B, M*
University of New Mexico *M, D*
University of the Southwest *B*
Western New Mexico University *B*

New York

Adelphi University *B*
Alfred University *B*
Bard College *B*
Barnard College *B*
Canisius College *B*
Cazenovia College *B*
City University of New York
 Baruch College *B*
 Brooklyn College *B, M*
 City College *B, M, T*
 College of Staten Island *B, M*
 Hunter College *B, M*
 John Jay College of Criminal
  Justice *B*
 Lehman College *B, M*
 Medgar Evers College *B*
 Queens College *B, M, T*
 York College *B*
Colgate University *B*
College of Mount St. Vincent *B*
College of New Rochelle *B, T*
College of Saint Rose *B, M*
Columbia University *B*
Columbia University
 School of General Studies *B*

Concordia College *B, T*
Cornell University *B, M, D*
D'Youville College *B*
Daemen College *B, T*
Dominican College of Blauvelt *B*
Dowling College *B*
Elmira College *B, T*
Fordham University *B, M, D*
Fulton-Montgomery Community
 College *A*
Hamilton College *B*
Hartwick College *B*
Hilbert College *B*
Hobart and William Smith Colleges *B*
Hofstra University *B, M*
Houghton College *B*
Iona College *B, M*
Ithaca College *B, T*
Keuka College *B*
Le Moyne College *B*
Long Island University
 Brooklyn Campus *B, M*
 C. W. Post Campus *B, M*
Manhattanville College *B*
Marist College *B*
Marymount Manhattan College *B*
Medaille College *B*
Mercy College *B*
Molloy College *B*
Mount Saint Mary College *B, T*
Nazareth College *B*
New York Institute of Technology *B*
New York University *B, M, D, T*
Niagara University *B*
Nyack College *B*
Pace University *B*
Roberts Wesleyan College *B*
Russell Sage College *B*
Saint Bonaventure University *B, T*
St. Francis College *B*
St. John Fisher College *B*
St. John's University *B, M, D*
St. Joseph's College *B, T*
St. Joseph's College: Suffolk
 Campus *B, T*
St. Thomas Aquinas College *B*
Siena College *B, T*
Skidmore College *B*
State University of New York
 Albany *B, M, D*
 Binghamton *B, M, D*
 Buffalo *B, M, D*
 College at Brockport *B, M*
 College at Buffalo *B, M*
 College at Cortland *B, M*
 College at Fredonia *B, M, T*
 College at Geneseo *B, T*
 College at Old Westbury *B*
 College at Oneonta *B*
 College at Plattsburgh *B*
 College at Potsdam *B, M*
 College of Agriculture and
  Technology at Morrisville *A*
 New Paltz *B, M*
 Oswego *B, M*
 Stony Brook *B, M, D*
Syracuse University *B, M, D*
Tompkins Cortland Community
 College *A*
Touro College *B*
Union College *B*
University of Rochester *B, M, D*
Utica College *B*
Vassar College *B*
Wagner College *B*
Wells College *B*
Yeshiva University *B, T*

North Carolina

Appalachian State University *B, M*
Barton College *B*
Belmont Abbey College *B*
Bennett College for Women *B*
Brevard College *B*

Campbell University B, T
Catawba College B
Chowan University B
Davidson College B
Duke University B, D
East Carolina University B, M
Elizabeth City State University B
Elon University B, T
Fayetteville State University B, M
Gardner-Webb University B
Greensboro College B
Guilford College B, T
High Point University B
Johnson C. Smith University B
Lees-McRae College B
Lenoir-Rhyne University B
Livingstone College B
Mars Hill College B, T
Meredith College B
Methodist University A, B
Montreat College B
Mount Olive College B
North Carolina Agricultural and
    Technical State University B, M, T
North Carolina Central
    University B, M
North Carolina State University B, M
North Carolina Wesleyan College B
Peace College B
Pfeiffer University B
Queens University of Charlotte B
St. Andrews Presbyterian College B
St. Augustine's College B
Salem College B
Shaw University B
Southeastern Community College A
University of North Carolina
    Asheville B
    Chapel Hill B, M, D
    Charlotte B, M
    Greensboro B, M, D
    Pembroke B
    Wilmington B, M
Wake Forest University B, M
Warren Wilson College B
Western Carolina University B, M
Wingate University B
Winston-Salem State University B

North Dakota

Dakota College at Bottineau A
Dickinson State University B, T
Jamestown College B
Mayville State University B, T
Minot State University B
North Dakota State University B, M, D
University of Mary B
University of North Dakota B, M, D

Ohio

Ashland University B
Baldwin-Wallace College B
Bluffton University B
Bowling Green State
    University B, M, D
Capital University B
Case Western Reserve
    University B, M, D
Cedarville University B
Central State University B
Cleveland State University B, M, T
College of Mount St. Joseph B, T
College of Wooster B
Defiance College B, T
Denison University B
Eastern Gateway Community
    College A
Franciscan University of
    Steubenville B
Heidelberg University B
Hiram College B
John Carroll University B, M
Kent State University B, M, D
Kenyon College B

Lourdes College A, B
Malone University B
Marietta College B
Miami University
    Oxford Campus B, M, D, T
Mount Union College B
Mount Vernon Nazarene University B
Muskingum University B
Notre Dame College B
Oberlin College B
Ohio Dominican University B
Ohio Northern University B
Ohio State University
    Columbus Campus B, M, D
    Lima Campus B
    Mansfield Campus B
    Marion Campus B
    Newark Campus B
Ohio University B, M, D
Ohio Wesleyan University B
Otterbein College B
Owens Community College
    Toledo A
Pontifical College Josephinum B
Shawnee State University B
Terra State Community College A
Tiffin University B
University of Akron B, M
University of Cincinnati B, M, D, T
University of Dayton B, M
University of Findlay B
University of Rio Grande A, B
University of Toledo B, M, D
Urbana University B
Ursuline College B
Walsh University B
Wilberforce University B
Wilmington College B
Wittenberg University B
Wright State University B, M
Wright State University: Lake
    Campus A
Xavier University A, B, M
Youngstown State University B, M

Oklahoma

Cameron University B
Carl Albert State College A
Connors State College A
East Central University B
Eastern Oklahoma State College A
Langston University B
Mid-America Christian University B
Murray State College A
Northeastern Oklahoma Agricultural
    and Mechanical College A
Northeastern State University B, M
Northern Oklahoma College A
Northwestern Oklahoma State
    University B
Oklahoma Baptist University B, T
Oklahoma Christian University B
Oklahoma City University B, M
Oklahoma Panhandle State
    University B
Oklahoma State University B, M, D
Oklahoma Wesleyan University B
Oral Roberts University B
Redlands Community College A
Rose State College A
St. Gregory's University A, B
Southeastern Oklahoma State
    University B
Southern Nazarene University B
Southwestern Oklahoma State
    University B
Tulsa Community College A
University of Central Oklahoma B, M
University of Oklahoma B, M, D
University of Science and Arts of
    Oklahoma B, T
University of Tulsa B, M, D
Western Oklahoma State College A

Oregon

Central Oregon Community
    College A
Chemeketa Community College A
Concordia University B
Corban College B
Eastern Oregon University B, T
George Fox University B
Lewis & Clark College B
Linfield College B
Linn-Benton Community College A
Northwest Christian University B
Oregon State University B, M
Pacific University B
Portland State University B, M
Reed College B
Southern Oregon University B, T
University of Oregon B, M, D
University of Portland B
Warner Pacific College B, T
Western Oregon University B
Willamette University B

Pennsylvania

Albright College B, T
Allegheny College B
Alvernia University B
Arcadia University B, M
Bloomsburg University of
    Pennsylvania B, T
Bryn Athyn College of the New
    Church B
Bryn Mawr College B
Bucknell University B, M
Butler County Community College A
Cabrini College B
California University of
    Pennsylvania B, M
Carlow University B
Carnegie Mellon University B
Cedar Crest College B
Chatham University B
Chestnut Hill College B
Cheyney University of Pennsylvania B
Clarion University of
    Pennsylvania B, M
DeSales University B, T
Delaware Valley College B
Dickinson College B
Drexel University B
Duquesne University B, M, D
East Stroudsburg University of
    Pennsylvania B, T
Eastern University B
Edinboro University of
    Pennsylvania B, T
Elizabethtown College B
Franklin & Marshall College B
Gannon University B, M
Geneva College B
Gettysburg College B
Grove City College B
Gwynedd-Mercy College B
Haverford College B, T
Holy Family University B, T
Immaculata University A, B
Indiana University of
    Pennsylvania B, M, D
Juniata College B
King's College B, T
Kutztown University of
    Pennsylvania B, M, T
La Roche College B
La Salle University B, T
Lafayette College B
Lebanon Valley College B
Lehigh University B, M, D
Lincoln University B
Lock Haven University of
    Pennsylvania B
Lycoming College B
Mansfield University of
    Pennsylvania A, B, T
Marywood University B

Mercyhurst College B, T
Messiah College B
Millersville University of
    Pennsylvania B, M, T
Misericordia University B
Moravian College B
Mount Aloysius College B
Muhlenberg College C, B
Neumann University B, T
Penn State
    Abington B
    Altoona B
    Beaver B
    Berks B
    Brandywine B
    DuBois B
    Erie, The Behrend College B
    Fayette, The Eberly Campus B
    Greater Allegheny B
    Harrisburg B
    Hazleton B
    Lehigh Valley B
    Mont Alto B
    New Kensington B
    Schuylkill B
    Shenango B
    University Park B, M, D
    Wilkes-Barre B
    Worthington Scranton B
    York B
Point Park University B
Robert Morris University B
Rosemont College B, M
St. Francis University B
Saint Joseph's University A, B
St. Vincent College B
Seton Hill University B, T
Shippensburg University of
    Pennsylvania B, T
Slippery Rock University of
    Pennsylvania B, M, T
Susquehanna University B
Swarthmore College B
Temple University B, M, D
Thiel College B
University of Pennsylvania B, M, D
University of Pittsburgh M, D
University of Pittsburgh
    Bradford B
    Greensburg B
University of Scranton B, M
Ursinus College B, T
Villanova University B, M
Washington & Jefferson College B
Waynesburg University B
West Chester University of
    Pennsylvania B, M, T
Westminster College B, M, T
Widener University B, T
Wilkes University B
Wilson College B
York College of Pennsylvania B

Puerto Rico

Bayamon Central University B
Inter American University of Puerto
    Rico
    San German Campus B
Pontifical Catholic University of
    Puerto Rico B
University of Puerto Rico
    Cayey University College B
    Rio Piedras B, M, D

Rhode Island

Brown University B, M, D
Bryant University B
Providence College B
Rhode Island College B, M
Salve Regina University B
University of Rhode Island B, M, D

South Carolina

Allen University B

Anderson University *B*
Benedict College *B*
Bob Jones University *B, M*
Charleston Southern University *B*
The Citadel *B, M*
Claflin University *B*
Clemson University *B, M*
Coastal Carolina University *B*
Coker College *B*
College of Charleston *B, M, T*
Columbia College *B, T*
Columbia International University *B*
Converse College *B*
Erskine College *B, T*
Francis Marion University *B*
Furman University *B, T*
Lander University *B, T*
Limestone College *B*
Morris College *B*
Newberry College *B*
North Greenville University *B, T*
Presbyterian College *B, T*
South Carolina State University *B*
Southern Wesleyan University *B*
University of South Carolina *B, M, D*
University of South Carolina
  Aiken *B*
  Beaufort *B*
  Upstate *B*
Winthrop University *B, M*
Wofford College *B, T*

South Dakota
Augustana College *B, T*
Black Hills State University *B*
Dakota State University *B*
Dakota Wesleyan University *B*
Mount Marty College *B*
Northern State University *B*
Presentation College *A*
South Dakota State University *B, M*
University of Sioux Falls *B*
University of South Dakota *B, M, D*

Tennessee
Austin Peay State University *B, M*
Belmont University *B, M, T*
Bethel University *B*
Bryan College *B*
Carson-Newman College *B, T*
Christian Brothers University *B*
Crichton College *B*
Cumberland University *B*
East Tennessee State
  University *B, M, T*
Fisk University *B*
Free Will Baptist Bible College *B*
Freed-Hardeman University *B, T*
Jackson State Community College *A*
King College *B*
Lambuth University *B*
Lane College *B*
LeMoyne-Owen College *B*
Lee University *B*
Lincoln Memorial University *B, T*
Lipscomb University *B*
Martin Methodist College *B*
Maryville College *B, T*
Middle Tennessee State
  University *B, M, D*
Milligan College *B*
Rhodes College *B*
Roane State Community College *A*
Southern Adventist University *B*
Tennessee State University *B, M*
Tennessee Technological
  University *B, M, T*
Tennessee Temple University *B*
Tennessee Wesleyan College *B*
Trevecca Nazarene University *B*
Tusculum College *B*
Union University *B, T*
University of Memphis *B, M, D*

University of Tennessee
  Chattanooga *B, M*
  Knoxville *B, M, D*
  Martin *B*
University of the South *B*
Vanderbilt University *B, M, D*
Walters State Community College *A*

Texas
Abilene Christian University *B, M*
Amarillo College *A*
Angelo State University *B, M, T*
Austin College *B*
Baylor University *B, M, D*
Blinn College *A*
Brazosport College *A*
Clarendon College *A*
Coastal Bend College *A*
Concordia University Texas *B*
Dallas Baptist University *B*
Del Mar College *A*
East Texas Baptist University *B*
El Paso Community College *A*
Frank Phillips College *A*
Galveston College *A*
Hardin-Simmons University *B, M*
Hill College *A*
Houston Baptist University *B*
Howard College *A*
Howard Payne University *B*
Jarvis Christian College *B*
Kilgore College *A*
Lamar University *B, M*
Laredo Community College *A*
LeTourneau University *B*
Lee College *A*
Lon Morris College *A*
Lubbock Christian University *B*
McMurry University *B, T*
Midland College *A*
Midwestern State University *B, M*
Navarro College *A*
North Lake College *A*
Northeast Texas Community
  College *A*
Northwest Vista College *A*
Our Lady of the Lake University of San
  Antonio *B, M*
Palo Alto College *A*
Paris Junior College *A*
Prairie View A&M University *B, M*
Rice University *B, M, D*
St. Edward's University *B*
St. Mary's University *B, M*
Sam Houston State University *B, M*
San Jacinto College *A*
Schreiner University *B*
South Plains College *A*
South Texas College *A*
Southern Methodist
  University *B, M, D*
Southwestern Adventist
  University *B, T*
Southwestern Assemblies of God
  University *A, B*
Southwestern University *B*
Stephen F. Austin State
  University *B, M*
Sul Ross State University *B, M, T*
Tarleton State University *B, M*
Texas A&M International
  University *B, M, T*
Texas A&M University *B, M, D*
Texas A&M University
  Commerce *B, M*
  Corpus Christi *B, M, T*
  Kingsville *B, M*
  Texarkana *B, M*
Texas Christian University *B, M, D*
Texas College *B*
Texas Lutheran University *B, T*
Texas Southern University *B, M*
Texas State University: San
  Marcos *B, M, T*

Texas Tech University *B, M, D*
Texas Wesleyan University *B*
Texas Woman's University *B, M*
Trinity University *B*
Trinity Valley Community College *A*
Tyler Junior College *A*
University of Dallas *B, M, D*
University of Houston *B, M, D*
University of Houston
  Clear Lake *B, M*
  Downtown *B*
  Victoria *B, T*
University of Mary Hardin-Baylor *B, T*
University of North Texas *B, M, D*
University of St. Thomas *B*
University of Texas
  Arlington *B, M, D*
  Austin *B, M, D*
  Brownsville - Texas Southmost
    College *B, M*
  El Paso *B, M*
  Pan American *B, M*
  San Antonio *B, M, D*
  Tyler *B, M*
  of the Permian Basin *B, M*
University of the Incarnate Word *B*
Wayland Baptist University *B, T*
West Texas A&M University *B, M*
Western Texas College *A*
Wharton County Junior College *A*
Wiley College *B*

Utah
Brigham Young University *B, M*
College of Eastern Utah *T*
Dixie State College of Utah *B*
Salt Lake Community College *A*
Snow College *A*
Southern Utah University *B, T*
University of Utah *B, M, D, T*
Utah State University *B, M*
Utah Valley University *A, B*
Weber State University *M*
Westminster College *B*

Vermont
Bennington College *B, M*
Castleton State College *B*
College of St. Joseph in Vermont *B*
Goddard College *B, M*
Green Mountain College *B*
Johnson State College *B*
Lyndon State College *B*
Marlboro College *B*
Middlebury College *B, M*
Norwich University *B*
St. Michael's College *B*
Southern Vermont College *B*
University of Vermont *B, M*

Virginia
Averett University *B*
Bluefield College *B*
Bridgewater College *B*
Christendom College *B*
Christopher Newport University *B*
College of William and Mary *B*
Eastern Mennonite University *B*
Emory & Henry College *B*
Ferrum College *B*
George Mason University *B*
Hampden-Sydney College *B*
Hampton University *B*
Hollins University *B*
James Madison University *B, M, T*
Liberty University *B, M, T*
Longwood University *B, M, T*
Lynchburg College *B, M*
Mary Baldwin College *B*
Marymount University *B, M*
Norfolk State University *B*
Old Dominion University *B, M, D, T*
Patrick Henry College *B*
Radford University *B, M*

Randolph College *B*
Randolph-Macon College *B*
Regent University *B*
Roanoke College *B, T*
St. Paul's College *B*
Shenandoah University *B*
Southern Virginia University *B*
Sweet Briar College *B*
University of Mary Washington *B*
University of Richmond *B*
University of Virginia *B, M, D*
University of Virginia's College at
  Wise *B, T*
Virginia Commonwealth
  University *B, M*
Virginia Intermont College *B*
Virginia Military Institute *B*
Virginia Polytechnic Institute and
  State University *B, M, D*
Virginia State University *B, M*
Virginia Union University *B*
Virginia Wesleyan College *B, T*
Washington and Lee University *B*

Washington
Centralia College *A*
Eastern Washington University *B, M*
Everett Community College *A*
Evergreen State College *B*
Gonzaga University *B, M*
Highline Community College *A*
Lower Columbia College *A*
Northwest University *B*
Olympic College *A*
Pacific Lutheran University *B*
Saint Martin's University *B*
Seattle Pacific University *B*
Seattle University *B*
Spokane Falls Community College *A*
University of Puget Sound *B, T*
University of Washington *B*
Walla Walla University *B*
Washington State University *B, M, D*
Western Washington University *B, M*
Whitman College *B*
Whitworth University *B, T*

West Virginia
Alderson-Broaddus College *B*
American Public University System *B*
Bethany College *B*
Concord University *B*
Davis and Elkins College *B*
Fairmont State University *B*
Glenville State College *B*
Marshall University *B, M*
Potomac State College of West
  Virginia University *A*
Shepherd University *B, T*
West Liberty University *B*
West Virginia State University *B*
West Virginia University *B, M, D*
West Virginia Wesleyan College *B*
Wheeling Jesuit University *B*

Wisconsin
Alverno College *B*
Beloit College *B*
Cardinal Stritch University *B, T*
Carroll University *B*
Carthage College *B, T*
Concordia University Wisconsin *B*
Edgewood College *B*
Lakeland College *B*
Lawrence University *B*
Maranatha Baptist Bible College *B*
Marian University *B*
Marquette University *B, M, D*
Mount Mary College *B, M, T*
Ripon College *B, T*
St. Norbert College *B, T*
Silver Lake College *B, T*
University of Wisconsin
  Eau Claire *B, M*

Green Bay *B*
La Crosse *B, T*
Madison *B, M, D*
Milwaukee *B, M, D*
Oshkosh *B*
Parkside *B, T*
Platteville *B*
River Falls *B, M*
Stevens Point *B, M, T*
Superior *B*
Whitewater *B*
Viterbo University *B, T*
Wisconsin Lutheran College *B*

Wyoming
Casper College *A*
Central Wyoming College *A*
Eastern Wyoming College *A*
Laramie County Community
   College *A*
Northwest College *A*
Sheridan College *A*
University of Wyoming *B, M*
Western Wyoming Community
   College *A*

English literature (British)

Arizona
Prescott College *B*

California
California State University
   East Bay *B*
   Northridge *B*
Irvine Valley College *A*
Mills College *B*
Saddleback College *A*
Stanford University *B*
University of California
   San Diego *B, M, D*
University of Redlands *B*
Whittier College *B*

Connecticut
Albertus Magnus College *B*

District of Columbia
Gallaudet University *B*
George Washington University *M, D*

Indiana
Indiana University-Purdue University
   Fort Wayne *B*
Saint Mary's College *B*

Iowa
Waldorf College *B*

Kentucky
Berea College *B*

Maine
University of Maine
   Fort Kent *B*

Maryland
Johns Hopkins University *D*

Massachusetts
Simmons College *B, M*
Tufts University *B, M, D*

Michigan
Ferris State University *B*
University of Michigan *B*

Missouri
University of Missouri
   St. Louis *M*

Washington University in St.
   Louis *B, M, D*

Nebraska
Creighton University *B*

New York
Bard College *B*
City University of New York
   Baruch College *B*
   Hunter College *B*
Columbia University *B*
Columbia University
   School of General Studies *B*
Elmira College *B, T*
Excelsior College *B*
Hofstra University *B, M*
Mercy College *M*
New York University *B, M, D*
Saint Bonaventure University *B, M*
St. Lawrence University *B*
State University of New York
   Purchase *B*
Syracuse University *B*

North Carolina
Campbell University *B, T*
Duke University *B*
Elon University *B*
Fayetteville State University *B*
Queens University of Charlotte *B*

Ohio
College of Wooster *B*
Denison University *B*
Ohio Wesleyan University *B*
University of Cincinnati *B, M, D, T*

Pennsylvania
Gannon University *B, M*
Gettysburg College *B*
La Salle University *B*
University of Pittsburgh *B*
University of Pittsburgh
   Johnstown *B*
Waynesburg University *B*
Westminster College *B, T*

Rhode Island
Brown University *B, M, D*
Roger Williams University *B*

Texas
Texas A&M University
   Commerce *B*

Vermont
Bennington College *B*
Marlboro College *B*

Virginia
George Mason University *M*
Randolph College *B*

West Virginia
Concord University *B*

Wisconsin
Marian University *B*
Marquette University *M, D*

English teacher education

Alabama
Athens State University *B*
Auburn University *B, M, D, T*
Birmingham-Southern College *T*
Faulkner University *B, M, T*
Huntingdon College *B, T*
Judson College *B*

Miles College *B*
Oakwood University *B*
Samford University *B*
Talladega College *B*
University of Mobile *B, T*

Arizona
Cochise College *A*
Grand Canyon University *B*
Northern Arizona University *B, M, T*
Prescott College *B, M, T*
University of Arizona *B, D*

Arkansas
Arkansas State University *B, M, T*
Arkansas Tech University *B, M*
Harding University *B, T*
John Brown University *B, T*
Ouachita Baptist University *B, T*
Southern Arkansas University *B, T*
University of Arkansas
   Fort Smith *B*
   Pine Bluff *B, M, T*
University of the Ozarks *T*
Williams Baptist College *B*

California
Azusa Pacific University *T*
California Baptist University *T*
California Lutheran University *B, T*
California Polytechnic State
   University: San Luis Obispo *T*
California State University
   Chico *B, T*
   Long Beach *B, M, T*
   Northridge *B, T*
   San Bernardino *T*
Fresno Pacific University *B, T*
Humboldt State University *T*
Loyola Marymount University *M*
The Master's College *T*
Mills College *B*
Mount St. Mary's College *T*
Pacific Union College *B*
Pepperdine University *B*
San Diego Christian College *B, T*
San Diego State University *T*
San Francisco State University *T*
Simpson University *B, T*
Sonoma State University *T*
Stanford University *M, T*
University of San Francisco *T*
University of the Pacific *T*
Vanguard University of Southern
   California *T*
Westmont College *T*

Colorado
Adams State College *B, M, T*
Colorado Christian University *B*
Colorado State University *B, T*
Colorado State University
   Pueblo *T*
Metropolitan State College of
   Denver *T*
Regis University *B, T*
University of Colorado
   Boulder *T*
   Colorado Springs *T*
Western State College of
   Colorado *B, T*

Connecticut
Albertus Magnus College *B, T*
Fairfield University *T*
Quinnipiac University *B, M*
Sacred Heart University *T*
Saint Joseph College *T*
Southern Connecticut State
   University *B, M, T*

Delaware
Delaware State University *B*

University of Delaware *B, T*

District of Columbia
Catholic University of America *B*
George Washington University *M, T*
Howard University *B*
Trinity Washington University *M*

Florida
Barry University *T*
Bethune-Cookman University *B, T*
Clearwater Christian College *B*
Flagler College *B, T*
Florida Agricultural and Mechanical
   University *B, M, T*
Florida Atlantic University *B*
Florida State University *B, M, D*
Hobe Sound Bible College *B, T*
Palm Beach Atlantic University *B, T*
Southeastern University *B, T*
Stetson University *B*
University of Central Florida *B, M*
University of South Florida *B, M*
University of Tampa *B, T*
University of West Florida *B*
Warner University *B*

Georgia
Agnes Scott College *M, T*
Armstrong Atlantic State
   University *B, M, T*
Brewton-Parker College *B*
Clayton State University *M*
Columbus State University *B, M*
Covenant College *B, T*
Darton College *A*
Emmanuel College *B*
Fort Valley State University *B, T*
Georgia State University *M, T*
Kennesaw State University *B*
Macon State College *M, T*
North Georgia College & State
   University *M*
Paine College *B*
Piedmont College *B, M, T*
Reinhardt College *B*
Shorter College *T*
Toccoa Falls College *B, T*
University of Georgia *B, M, T*

Hawaii
Hawaii Pacific University *M*

Idaho
Boise State University *M, T*
Brigham Young University-Idaho *T*
Lewis-Clark State College *B, T*
Northwest Nazarene University *B*
University of Idaho *B, T*

Illinois
Augustana College *B, T*
Benedictine University *T*
Blackburn College *B, T*
Bradley University *B, M*
Chicago State University *B*
Columbia College Chicago *M*
Concordia University Chicago *B, T*
DePaul University *M, T*
Dominican University *T*
Elmhurst College *B*
Eureka College *T*
Governors State University *B, M, T*
Greenville College *B, T*
Illinois College *T*
Illinois Wesleyan University *B*
Lewis University *T*
MacMurray College *B, T*
Millikin University *B, T*
National-Louis University *M*
North Park University *T*
Northeastern Illinois University *M*
Olivet Nazarene University *B, T*

Rockford College T
Saint Xavier University M
Trinity Christian College B, T
Trinity International University B, T
University of Illinois
   Chicago B
   Urbana-Champaign B, M, T
University of St. Francis B, M

Indiana

Anderson University B, T
Bethel College B
Butler University T
Franklin College B, T
Goshen College B, T
Grace College B
Huntington University B, M
Indiana University
   Bloomington B, T
   Kokomo T
   Northwest B
   Southeast B
Indiana University-Purdue University
   Fort Wayne B, M
Indiana University-Purdue University
   Indianapolis B, T
Indiana Wesleyan University B, T
Manchester College B, T
Oakland City University B
Purdue University
   Calumet B
Saint Mary's College T
St. Mary-of-the-Woods College B, T
Taylor University B, T
Trine University B, T
University of Evansville B, T
University of Indianapolis B, M, T
University of St. Francis B, T
Valparaiso University B
Vincennes University A

Iowa

Briar Cliff University B
Buena Vista University B, T
Central College T
Cornell College B, T
Dordt College B
Drake University T
Faith Baptist Bible College and
   Theological Seminary B, T
Graceland University T
Grand View University M, T
Iowa State University T
Iowa Wesleyan College B
Loras College T
Maharishi University of
   Management T
Morningside College B
Mount Mercy College T
Northwestern College T
St. Ambrose University B, T
Simpson College T
University of Iowa M, D, T
Upper Iowa University T
Waldorf College B
Wartburg College T

Kansas

Bethany College B
Bethel College T
Friends University B
Kansas Wesleyan University B, T
McPherson College B, T
MidAmerica Nazarene University B, T
Newman University T
Pittsburg State University B, T
Southwestern College B, T
Sterling College T
Tabor College B
University of Kansas B, T
University of St. Mary T
Washburn University B

Kentucky

Alice Lloyd College B
Campbellsville University B
Kentucky Christian University B, T
Kentucky Wesleyan College B, T
Lindsey Wilson College B, T
Midway College M

Louisiana

Centenary College of Louisiana B, T
Grambling State University B
Louisiana College B
Louisiana State University
   Shreveport B
McNeese State University B, T
Nicholls State University B
Northwestern State University B
Our Lady of Holy Cross College B
Southeastern Louisiana University B
Southern University and Agricultural
   and Mechanical College B
University of Louisiana at Lafayette B
University of Louisiana at Monroe B
University of New Orleans B, M
Xavier University of Louisiana B

Maine

Husson University B
Saint Joseph's College of Maine B
University of Maine B, M
University of Maine
   Farmington B, T
   Fort Kent B
   Machias T
University of Southern Maine T

Maryland

Anne Arundel Community College A
Carroll Community College A
College of Notre Dame of Maryland T
Frostburg State University B, T
Hood College T
Howard Community College A
Mount St. Mary's University T
Salisbury University B
University of Maryland
   College Park B
   Eastern Shore B
Washington Adventist University B

Massachusetts

Anna Maria College B, M, T
Assumption College T
Boston University B, M, T
Bridgewater State College B, M, T
Eastern Nazarene College B
Elms College B, M, T
Fitchburg State College B, M, T
Framingham State College M
Lasell College B, T
Lesley University B, M
Merrimack College T
Smith College M
Springfield College T
Tufts University M, T
University of Massachusetts
   Dartmouth T
Western New England College M, T
Westfield State College B, T

Michigan

Albion College B, T
Alma College T
Andrews University M
Aquinas College B, T
Calvin College B
Central Michigan University B
Cornerstone University B
Eastern Michigan University B, T
Ferris State University B
Grand Rapids Community College A
Grand Valley State University M, T
Hope College B, T

Michigan State University M
Michigan Technological University T
Northern Michigan University B, M, T
Rochester College B
Siena Heights University T
University of Michigan D
University of Michigan
   Flint B, T
Wayne State University B, M, T
Western Michigan University B, T

Minnesota

Augsburg College T
Bemidji State University M, T
Bethel University B
College of St. Benedict T
College of St. Scholastica T
Concordia College: Moorhead B, T
Concordia University: St. Paul B, T
Crown College B, T
Gustavus Adolphus College T
Metropolitan State University B
Minnesota State University
   Mankato B, M, T
   Moorhead T
Northwestern College B
St. Catherine University B, T
Saint Cloud State University B, M, T
St. John's University T
St. Mary's University of Minnesota B
University of Minnesota
   Duluth B, T
   Morris T
   Twin Cities T
University of St. Thomas B
Winona State University B, M, T

Mississippi

Blue Mountain College B
Delta State University B
Millsaps College T
Mississippi College B, M
Mississippi State University T
Mississippi Valley State University B, T
Rust College B
University of Mississippi B, T

Missouri

College of the Ozarks B, T
Culver-Stockton College T
Evangel University B, T
Hannibal-LaGrange College B
Harris-Stowe State University T
Lincoln University B
Maryville University of Saint
   Louis M, T
Missouri Baptist University T
Missouri Southern State
   University B, T
Missouri State University B
Missouri Valley College T
Missouri Western State University B
Northwest Missouri State
   University B, M, T
Park University T
Southeast Missouri State
   University B, T
Southwest Baptist University B, T
Truman State University M, T
University of Central Missouri B, M, T
University of Missouri
   Columbia B
   Kansas City B
Washington University in St. Louis B
William Jewell College B, T
William Woods University B, T

Montana

Montana State University
   Billings B, T
Rocky Mountain College B, T
University of Great Falls B
University of Montana B, T

University of Montana: Western B, T

Nebraska

Chadron State College B, M
College of Saint Mary B
Concordia University B, T
Creighton University T
Dana College B
Grace University B
Nebraska Wesleyan University B
Peru State College B, T
Union College T
University of Nebraska
   Kearney B, M, T
   Lincoln B
Wayne State College B, T
York College B, T

Nevada

Nevada State College B
University of Nevada
   Reno B, M, T

New Hampshire

Colby-Sawyer College B, T
Franklin Pierce University M, T
Keene State College B, M, T
New England College B, T
Plymouth State University M, T
Rivier College B, M, T
Saint Anselm College T
Southern New Hampshire
   University B
University of New Hampshire T
University of New Hampshire at
   Manchester M

New Jersey

Caldwell College T
Centenary College T
The College of New Jersey B, M, T
College of St. Elizabeth T
Georgian Court University T
Rowan University T
Rutgers, The State University of New
   Jersey
   New Brunswick/Piscataway
      Campus T
Saint Peter's College T
William Paterson University of New
   Jersey T

New Mexico

University of the Southwest B, T

New York

Adelphi University M
Alfred University B, T
Bard College M
City University of New York
   Brooklyn College B, M, T
   City College B, M
   College of Staten Island B, M, T
   Hunter College B, M, T
   Lehman College M, T
   Queens College M, T
Colgate University M
College of Saint Rose B, T
Cornell University M, T
D'Youville College M, T
Dominican College of Blauvelt B, T
Dowling College B, M
Dutchess Community College A
Elmira College B, T
Fordham University M, T
Hobart and William Smith Colleges T
Hofstra University B, M
Houghton College B, T
Iona College B, M, T
Ithaca College B, D, T
Keuka College B, T
Le Moyne College T

Long Island University
  Brooklyn Campus *B, M, T*
  C. W. Post Campus *B, M, T*
Manhattan College *B, T*
Manhattanville College *M, T*
Marist College *B*
Marymount Manhattan College *T*
Medaille College *B, M, T*
Molloy College *B*
Nazareth College *B, M, T*
New York Institute of
    Technology *B, T*
New York University *M*
Niagara University *B, M, T*
Pace University *B, M, T*
Roberts Wesleyan College *B, M*
Saint Bonaventure University *M*
St. Francis College *B*
St. John Fisher College *B, M, T*
St. John's University *B, M, T*
St. Joseph's College: Suffolk
    Campus *B, T*
St. Lawrence University *T*
St. Thomas Aquinas College *B, T*
State University of New York
  Albany *M, T*
  Binghamton *M*
  Buffalo *M, D, T*
  College at Brockport *B, M, T*
  College at Buffalo *B, M*
  College at Cortland *B, M*
  College at Fredonia *B, M, T*
  College at Geneseo *B, M, T*
  College at Oneonta *B, T*
  College at Plattsburgh *B, M*
  College at Potsdam *B, M*
  New Paltz *B, M, T*
  Oswego *B, M*
  Stony Brook *T*
Syracuse University *B, M, T*
Ulster County Community College *A*
University of Rochester *M*
Vassar College *T*
Wells College *T*

North Carolina
Appalachian State University *B, M, T*
Belmont Abbey College *T*
Bennett College for Women *B*
Brevard College *B*
Campbell University *B, T*
Catawba College *T*
Chowan University *B, T*
Davidson College *T*
East Carolina University *B, M*
Elizabeth City State University *B, T*
Elon University *T*
Fayetteville State University *B, T*
Gardner-Webb University *B, M*
Greensboro College *B, T*
Lenoir-Rhyne University *B, T*
Livingstone College *T*
Mars Hill College *B, T*
Meredith College *T*
Methodist University *B, T*
North Carolina Agricultural and
    Technical State University *B, M, T*
North Carolina Central
    University *B, M, T*
North Carolina State
    University *B, M, T*
Piedmont Baptist College *B*
Queens University of Charlotte *B*
Shaw University *B, T*
University of North Carolina
  Charlotte *B, M*
  Greensboro *B, M*
  Pembroke *B, M*
  Wilmington *B*
Wake Forest University *T*
Western Carolina University *B, M, T*
Wingate University *B, T*
Winston-Salem State University *B*

North Dakota
Dickinson State University *B, T*
Jamestown College *B*
Mayville State University *B, T*
Minot State University *B, M*
North Dakota State University *B, T*
University of Mary *B*

Ohio
Antioch University McGregor *M*
Ashland University *B, T*
Baldwin-Wallace College *T*
Bluffton University *B*
Bowling Green State
    University *B, M, T*
Capital University *T*
Case Western Reserve University *T*
Cedarville University *B*
Defiance College *B, T*
God's Bible School and College *B*
Hiram College *T*
John Carroll University *T*
Malone University *B*
Miami University
  Oxford Campus *B, M, T*
Mount Union College *T*
Mount Vernon Nazarene
    University *B, T*
Ohio Dominican University *B, T*
Ohio Northern University *B, T*
Ohio University *D, T*
Otterbein College *B*
Tiffin University *B*
University of Akron *B, M*
University of Findlay *B, M, T*
University of Rio Grande *B, T*
University of Toledo *B, M, T*
Urbana University *B*
Ursuline College *B, M, T*
Walsh University *B*
Wilberforce University *T*
Wilmington College *B*
Wright State University *B, M, T*
Youngstown State University *B, M*

Oklahoma
Cameron University *B, T*
East Central University *B, T*
Mid-America Christian University *B*
Northeastern State University *B*
Northwestern Oklahoma State
    University *B, T*
Oklahoma Baptist University *B, T*
Oklahoma Christian University *B, T*
Oklahoma City University *B*
Oklahoma Wesleyan University *B*
Oral Roberts University *B, T*
Southeastern Oklahoma State
    University *B, T*
Southern Nazarene University *B, M*
Southwestern Oklahoma State
    University *B, M, T*
University of Oklahoma *B, T*
University of Tulsa *T*

Oregon
Concordia University *B, M, T*
Corban College *B*
Linfield College *T*
Oregon State University *M*
Portland State University *T*
Southern Oregon University *T*
Warner Pacific College *T*

Pennsylvania
Albright College *T*
Alvernia University *T*
Arcadia University *B, M, T*
Bryn Athyn College of the New
    Church *B*
Cabrini College *T*
Chatham University *M, T*
DeSales University *M, T*

Dickinson College *T*
Duquesne University *B, M, T*
Geneva College *T*
Gettysburg College *T*
Grove City College *B, T*
Gwynedd-Mercy College *T*
Holy Family University *B*
Juniata College *B, T*
King's College *T*
La Roche College *B*
La Salle University *B, T*
Lebanon Valley College *T*
Lincoln University *B, T*
Lycoming College *T*
Mansfield University of
    Pennsylvania *B, T*
Mercyhurst College *B, T*
Messiah College *B, T*
Misericordia University *T*
Moravian College *T*
Philadelphia Biblical University *B, T*
Point Park University *B*
St. Francis University *B, T*
Saint Joseph's University *B, M*
St. Vincent College *T*
Seton Hill University *B, T*
Susquehanna University *T*
Temple University *B, M, D*
Thiel College *B*
University of Pennsylvania *M, T*
University of Pittsburgh
    Johnstown *B, T*
Villanova University *T*
Washington & Jefferson College *T*
Waynesburg University *B, T*
Westminster College *B, T*
Widener University *M, D, T*
Wilkes University *M, T*
Wilson College *T*
York College of Pennsylvania *B, T*

Puerto Rico
Bayamon Central University *B*
Caribbean University *B, T*
Inter American University of Puerto
    Rico
  San German Campus *B*
Pontifical Catholic University of
    Puerto Rico *B, T*
Turabo University *B*
Universidad del Este *B*
University of Puerto Rico
  Aguadilla *B*
  Cayey University College *B*

Rhode Island
Rhode Island College *B, M*
Salve Regina University *B*

South Carolina
Anderson University *B, T*
Bob Jones University *B, M*
Charleston Southern University *B*
Claflin University *B*
Coker College *B, T*
Francis Marion University *B, T*
Furman University *T*
Limestone College *B*
Morris College *B, T*
North Greenville University *B, T*
Southern Wesleyan University *B, T*
University of South Carolina
  Aiken *B, T*
Wofford College *T*

South Dakota
Augustana College *B, T*
Black Hills State University *B*
Dakota State University *B, T*
Dakota Wesleyan University *B, T*
Mount Marty College *B*
Northern State University *B, T*
Presentation College *A*

University of Sioux Falls *B, T*
University of South Dakota *B, T*

Tennessee
Belmont University *B, M, T*
Bethel University *T*
Bryan College *T*
Christian Brothers University *B, M, T*
Crichton College *B, T*
Cumberland University *B*
Freed-Hardeman University *B, T*
King College *T*
Lambuth University *B, T*
LeMoyne-Owen College *B*
Lee University *B*
Lincoln Memorial University *B, T*
Lipscomb University *B, T*
Maryville College *B, T*
Southern Adventist University *B*
Tennessee Technological
    University *B, T*
Tennessee Temple University *T*
Trevecca Nazarene University *B, T*
Tusculum College *B, T*
Union University *B, T*
University of Memphis *T*
University of Tennessee
  Chattanooga *B*
  Knoxville *T*
Vanderbilt University *M, D*

Texas
Abilene Christian University *B, T*
Arlington Baptist College *B, T*
Baylor University *B, T*
Dallas Christian College *B, T*
East Texas Baptist University *B*
Hardin-Simmons University *B, T*
Houston Baptist University *B*
Howard Payne University *B, T*
Jarvis Christian College *B, T*
Lamar University *T*
Laredo Community College *A*
LeTourneau University *B, T*
Lubbock Christian University *B*
McMurry University *B, T*
Midwestern State University *B*
Prairie View A&M University *M*
St. Mary's University *T*
Sam Houston State University *M, T*
Schreiner University *B*
Southwestern Assemblies of God
    University *B*
Tarleton State University *T*
Texas A&M International
    University *B, M, T*
Texas A&M University
  Commerce *D, T*
Texas Christian University *B*
Texas Lutheran University *B, T*
Texas State University: San Marcos *T*
Texas Wesleyan University *B, M, T*
University of Dallas *T*
University of Houston *T*
University of Houston
  Clear Lake *T*
University of Mary Hardin-Baylor *B, T*
University of Texas
  Arlington *T*
  El Paso *M*
  San Antonio *T*
Wayland Baptist University *B*
West Texas A&M University *T*

Utah
Brigham Young University *B*
Dixie State College of Utah *B*
Southern Utah University *B, T*
Utah Valley University *B*
Weber State University *B*

Vermont
Castleton State College *B, T*

College of St. Joseph in
Vermont *B, M, T*
Goddard College *B, M*
Green Mountain College *B, T*
Johnson State College *B*
Lyndon State College *B*
St. Michael's College *T*
University of Vermont *B, T*

Virginia
Averett University *B, M, T*
Bluefield College *B, T*
Bridgewater College *T*
Eastern Mennonite University *T*
Emory & Henry College *B, M*
Hampton University *M*
Hollins University *T*
Longwood University *B, T*
Lynchburg College *M*
Old Dominion University *B, T*
Radford University *T*
St. Paul's College *T*
University of Virginia's College at
Wise *T*
Virginia Intermont College *B, T*

Washington
Eastern Washington University *B*
Northwest University *T*
Seattle Pacific University *B, T*
Washington State University *B, M, T*
Western Washington University *B*
Whitworth University *M, T*

West Virginia
Bethany College *B*
Concord University *B, M, T*
Fairmont State University *B*
Ohio Valley University *B*
Shepherd University *T*
University of Charleston *B*
West Liberty University *B*
West Virginia State University *B*
West Virginia University *T*
West Virginia Wesleyan College *B*

Wisconsin
Alverno College *B, T*
Carroll University *B, T*
Carthage College *M, T*
Concordia University Wisconsin *B*
Edgewood College *B, T*
Lakeland College *B*
Lawrence University *T*
Maranatha Baptist Bible College *B*
Marian University *B, T*
Marquette University *B*
Mount Mary College *B, T*
St. Norbert College *T*
Silver Lake College *T*
University of Wisconsin
Green Bay *T*
Parkside *T*
Platteville *B, T*
River Falls *T*
Superior *B, T*
Whitewater *B*
Viterbo University *B, T*

Entomology

Alabama
Auburn University *M, D*

Arizona
University of Arizona *M, D*

Arkansas
University of Arkansas *M, D*

California
University of California
Davis *B, M, D*
Riverside *B, M, D*

Colorado
Colorado State University *M, D*

Connecticut
University of Connecticut *M, D*

Delaware
University of Delaware *B, M*

Florida
Florida Agricultural and Mechanical
University *D*
Gulf Coast Community College *A*
University of Florida *B, M*

Georgia
University of Georgia *B, M, D*

Hawaii
University of Hawaii
Manoa *M, D*

Idaho
University of Idaho *B, M, D*

Illinois
University of Illinois
Urbana-Champaign *B, M, D*

Indiana
Purdue University *B, M, D*

Iowa
Iowa State University *B, M, D*

Kansas
Kansas State University *M, D*
University of Kansas *M, D*

Kentucky
University of Kentucky *M, D*

Louisiana
Louisiana State University and
Agricultural and Mechanical
College *M, D*

Maine
University of Maine *B, M*

Maryland
University of Maryland
College Park *M, D*

Massachusetts
University of Massachusetts
Amherst *M, D*

Michigan
Michigan State University *B, M, D*

Minnesota
University of Minnesota
Twin Cities *M, D*

Mississippi
Mississippi State University *M*

Missouri
University of Missouri
Columbia *M, D*

Montana
Montana State University
Bozeman *M*

Nebraska
University of Nebraska
Lincoln *M, D*

New Jersey
Rutgers, The State University of New
Jersey
New Brunswick/Piscataway
Campus *M, D*

New York
Cornell University *B, M, D*

North Carolina
North Carolina State University *M, D*

North Dakota
North Dakota State University *M, D*

Ohio
Ohio State University
Columbus Campus *B, M, D*

Oklahoma
Eastern Oklahoma State College *A*
Oklahoma State University *B, M, D*

Oregon
Oregon State University *B, M, D*

Pennsylvania
Penn State
University Park *M, D*

South Carolina
Clemson University *B, M, D*

Tennessee
University of Tennessee
Knoxville *M, D*

Texas
Texas A&M University *B, M, D*
Texas Tech University *M*

Utah
Utah State University *B, M*

Virginia
Virginia Polytechnic Institute and
State University *D*

Washington
Washington State University *M, D*

Wisconsin
University of Wisconsin
Madison *B, M, D*

Wyoming
University of Wyoming *M, D*

Entrepreneurial studies

Alabama
Samford University *B*

Alaska
University of Alaska
Anchorage *C, A, B*

Arizona
Central Arizona College *C*
Eastern Arizona College *C, A*
GateWay Community College *C*

Glendale Community College *C*
Grand Canyon University *C, B*
Northern Arizona University *C*
Northland Pioneer College *C*
Rio Salado College *C*
University of Arizona *B*
University of Phoenix *B*

Arkansas
Arkansas State University
Beebe *C*
East Arkansas Community College *C*
North Arkansas College *C*
Northwest Arkansas Community
College *C*
Southeast Arkansas College *C*
Southern Arkansas University Tech *C*

California
Azusa Pacific University *M*
Cabrillo College *C, A*
California State University
Dominguez Hills *B*
East Bay *B, M*
Fullerton *B, M*
Coastline Community College *A*
College of Alameda *C, A*
College of San Mateo *C, A*
Cosumnes River College *A*
Diablo Valley College *C*
El Camino College: Compton
Center *C, A*
Fullerton College *C*
Lake Tahoe Community College *C, A*
Lincoln University *M*
Los Angeles City College *C, A*
Los Angeles Pierce College *C*
Los Angeles Trade and Technical
College *A*
Los Medanos College *C, A*
Marymount College *B*
Mendocino College *C, A*
Mount San Antonio College *C, A*
Mount San Jacinto College *C*
Mt. Sierra College *B*
Pasadena City College *A*
San Diego State University *M*
San Jose City College *C, A*
Santa Ana College *C, A*
Santa Monica College *C, A*
Shasta College *A*
Southwestern College *C, A*
University of San Francisco *B*
Yuba Community College
District *C, A*

Colorado
Colorado Northwestern Community
College *A*
Johnson & Wales University:
Denver *B*
Mesa State College *C*
Pueblo Community College *A*

Connecticut
Asnuntuck Community College *C*
Goodwin College *C, A*
Quinebaug Valley Community
College *C*
Quinnipiac University *B*
University of Hartford *B*

Delaware
Delaware Technical and Community
College
Owens *C, A*
Stanton/Wilmington *C*
Terry *C, A*

District of Columbia
Gallaudet University *B*

Florida

Central Florida Community College *C*
Daytona State College *C*
Florida Keys Community College *C*
Hillsborough Community College *C*
Lake-Sumter Community College *C*
Palm Beach Atlantic University *B*
Saint Johns River Community
  College *C*
Saint Leo University *B*
Santa Fe College *C*
Stetson University *B*
University of Miami *B*
University of Tampa *B*
Valencia Community College *C, A*

Georgia

Albany Technical College *C*
Darton College *A*
Gwinnett Technical College *C*
Southern Polytechnic State
  University *B, M*

Illinois

Black Hawk College *C, A*
Bradley University *B*
College of Lake County *C*
Elgin Community College *C, A*
Heartland Community College *C*
Kaskaskia College *C*
Kishwaukee College *C*
McHenry County College *C*
Millikin University *B*
Moraine Valley Community College *A*
Northwestern College *A*
Northwestern University *M*
Parkland College *C*
Prairie State College *C*
Triton College *C*
University of Illinois
  Chicago *B*
  Urbana-Champaign *B, M, D, T*

Indiana

Anderson University *B*
Ball State University *B*
Huntington University *B*
Purdue University
  Calumet *B*
Trine University *B*
University of Southern Indiana *B*
Vincennes University *C*

Iowa

Buena Vista University *B*
Grand View University *C, B*
North Iowa Area Community
  College *C, A*

Kansas

Central Christian College of Kansas *A*
Coffeyville Community College *A*
Cowley County Community
  College *A*
Pratt Community College *C, A*
Southwestern College *B*
Washburn University *C*

Kentucky

Northern Kentucky University *B*
St. Catharine College *A*
University of Louisville *D*
Western Kentucky University *B*

Louisiana

Southern University
  New Orleans *B*
University of New Orleans *B*

Maine

Husson University *B*
Maine Maritime Academy *B*

Washington County Community
  College *C*

Maryland

Anne Arundel Community
  College *C, A*
Howard Community College *C, A*
University of Baltimore *B*

Massachusetts

Babson College *B*
Bentley University *M*
Boston University *B*
Holyoke Community College *C*
Lasell College *B*
Middlesex Community College *C*
Mount Wachusett Community
  College *C*
Northeastern University *B, M*
Salem State College *B*
Suffolk University *B*
Tufts University *M*
University of Massachusetts
  Lowell *B*

Michigan

Andrews University *B*
Central Michigan University *B*
Cleary University *B*
Eastern Michigan University *B, M*
Ferris State University *C, B*
Gogebic Community College *A*
Kirtland Community College *C*
Lansing Community College *C*
Lawrence Technological University *C*
Mid Michigan Community College *A*
Montcalm Community College *C, A*
Mott Community College *C, A*
North Central Michigan College *C*
Northern Michigan University *B*
Northwood University: Michigan *A, B*
Oakland Community College *A*
Schoolcraft College *A*
Wayne County Community College *C*

Minnesota

Dakota County Technical College *C*
Fond du Lac Tribal and Community
  College *C*
Lake Superior College *C*
Minnesota State Community and
  Technical College *C*
Saint Cloud State University *B*
St. Mary's University of Minnesota *B*
St. Paul College *C, A*
University of Minnesota
  Crookston *B*
University of St. Thomas *B*
Walden University *M, D*

Missouri

Avila University *B*
Central Methodist University *B*
Harris-Stowe State University *B*
Lindenwood University *B, M*
Missouri State University *B*
Missouri State University: West
  Plains *C, A*
Missouri Valley College *A*
Three Rivers Community College *A*
University of Missouri
  Kansas City *B, M, D*
Washington University in St. Louis *B*

Montana

Chief Dull Knife College *C*
Flathead Valley Community College *C*

Nebraska

Creighton University *B*
Northeast Community College *A*

Nevada

University of Nevada
  Reno *B*

New Hampshire

New England College *B*

New Jersey

Bergen Community College *C*
Berkeley College- Garret Mountain
  Campus *B*
Burlington County College *C*
Fairleigh Dickinson University
  College at Florham *B, M*
  Metropolitan Campus *B, M*
Mercer County Community College *C*
Rider University *B*
Thomas Edison State College *B*
Warren County Community
  College *C, A*

New Mexico

Santa Fe Community College *C*

New York

Canisius College *B*
City University of New York
  Kingsborough Community
    College *C*
Clarkson University *B*
Erie Community College
  City Campus *C*
Excelsior College *C*
Herkimer County Community
  College *C, A*
Hofstra University *B*
Mohawk Valley Community
  College *C, A*
Pace University *B, M*
Paul Smith's College *B*
State University of New York
  Binghamton *B*
  College at Plattsburgh *B*
  College of Technology at
    Alfred *C, A*
Syracuse University *B*
Tompkins Cortland Community
  College *C*
Ulster County Community College *A*
University of Rochester *M*

North Carolina

Elon University *B*
High Point University *B*
University of North Carolina
  Pembroke *C*
Western Carolina University *B, M*

North Dakota

Sitting Bull College *A*
University of North Dakota *B*
Williston State College *C, A*

Ohio

Bowling Green State University:
  Firelands College *C*
Case Western Reserve University *M*
Columbus State Community
  College *C, A*
Cuyahoga Community College
  Metropolitan Campus *A*
University of Akron *C, M*
University of Dayton *B*
University of Findlay *B*
University of Rio Grande *B*
University of Toledo *B*
Xavier University *B, M*
Youngstown State University *C*

Oklahoma

Cameron University *M*
Northeastern State University *B*

Oklahoma State University *B*

Oregon

Portland Community College *C*
Southwestern Oregon Community
  College *A*

Pennsylvania

Bucks County Community College *C*
Carnegie Mellon University *D*
Central Pennsylvania College *A*
Community College of Allegheny
  County *C, A*
Duquesne University *B*
Eastern University *B*
Elizabethtown College *B*
Gannon University *B*
Grove City College *B*
Juniata College *B*
Lehigh University *M*
Messiah College *B*
Northampton Community College *C*
Peirce College *A*
Reading Area Community
  College *C, A*
Seton Hill University *C, B*
Temple University *B*
University of Pittsburgh
  Bradford *B*
  Titusville *C*
Wilkes University *B*
York College of Pennsylvania *B*

Puerto Rico

Inter American University of Puerto
  Rico
  Bayamon Campus *B*
  Metropolitan Campus *B*
  San German Campus *D*
National College of Business and
  Technology: Bayamon *A*
National College of Business and
  Technology: Rio Grande *A*
Pontifical Catholic University of
  Puerto Rico *B*
Universidad Metropolitana *C*
Universidad del Este *C*

Rhode Island

Community College of Rhode
  Island *C*
Johnson & Wales University:
  Providence *B*
University of Rhode Island *B*

South Carolina

Florence-Darlington Technical
  College *A*
Greenville Technical College *C*
Horry-Georgetown Technical
  College *C*
Trident Technical College *C, A*
York Technical College *C*

South Dakota

Black Hills State University *B*
South Dakota State University *C, B*

Tennessee

Belmont University *B*
Southern Adventist University *M*
Tusculum College *B*

Texas

Baylor University *B*
Brookhaven College *A*
Galveston College *C, A*
Houston Baptist University *B*
Midland College *C, A*
Palo Alto College *A*
Richland College *A*
St. Edward's University *B*

St. Mary's University *B*
Southern Methodist University *M*
Texas Christian University *B, M*
University of Dallas *M*
University of Houston *B*
University of Houston
  Victoria *M*
University of Texas
  Brownsville - Texas Southmost
  College *B*

Utah
Brigham Young University *B*
LDS Business College *C, A*
Neumont University *B*
University of Utah *B*
Westminster College *B*

Vermont
Lyndon State College *A, B*
Southern Vermont College *B*
University of Vermont *B*

Virginia
J. Sargeant Reynolds Community
  College *C*
Northern Virginia Community
  College *C*

Washington
Grays Harbor College *C*
Lake Washington Technical College *C*
North Seattle Community College *C*
Washington State University *B*
Yakima Valley Community College *A*

West Virginia
Potomac State College of West
  Virginia University *A*
Southern West Virginia Community
  and Technical College *A*
West Virginia Northern Community
  College *C*

Wisconsin
Fox Valley Technical College *C*
Moraine Park Technical College *C*
University of Wisconsin
  Platteville *B*
  Stout *C*

Wyoming
Casper College *A*
Laramie County Community
  College *C, A*

Environmental biology

Arizona
Arizona State University *D*
Eastern Arizona College *A*
Prescott College *B*

California
California State Polytechnic
  University: Pomona *B*
College of Marin: Kentfield *A*
The Master's College *B*
University of La Verne *B*

Connecticut
Mitchell College *B*

District of Columbia
American University *B, M*

Florida
Eckerd College *B*
Florida Southern College *B*

Illinois
Blackburn College *B*
Chicago State University *B*
Eureka College *B*
Governors State University *M*
Greenville College *B*
Illinois College *B*
Lewis University *B*

Indiana
Grace College *B*
Manchester College *M*

Louisiana
University of Louisiana at Lafayette *D*

Maine
Colby College *B*
Unity College *B*

Maryland
Hood College *M*
McDaniel College *B*
Morgan State University *D*

Massachusetts
Bridgewater State College *B*
Fitchburg State College *B*
Suffolk University *B*

Michigan
Cornerstone University *B*
Ferris State University *B*
Michigan State University *B*

Minnesota
St. Mary's University of Minnesota *B*

Missouri
Lindenwood University *B*

Nebraska
Concordia University *B*

New Hampshire
Plymouth State University *B*

New Jersey
Monmouth University *B*

New York
Barnard College *B*
Columbia University *B*
Houghton College *B*
Iona College *B*
State University of New York
  Albany *B*
  College at Brockport *B*
  College of Environmental Science
    and Forestry *B, M, D*

North Carolina
Queens University of Charlotte *B*
Wingate University *B*

North Dakota
North Dakota State University *M, D*

Ohio
Cedarville University *M*
Heidelberg University *B*
Notre Dame College *B*
University of Dayton *B*
Ursuline College *B*
Wilmington College *B*

Pennsylvania
Carlow University *B*
Cedar Crest College *B*
Elizabethtown College *B*

Keystone College *B*
Philadelphia University *B*
University of Pennsylvania *M*
Waynesburg University *B*

Tennessee
Belmont University *B*
Lee University *B*

Texas
Baylor University *M*
Texas A&M University *B*

Vermont
Bennington College *B*
Sterling College *B*

Virginia
Hollins University *B*

Wisconsin
Beloit College *B*
University of Wisconsin
  Superior *B*

Wyoming
Eastern Wyoming College *A*

Environmental design

Alabama
Auburn University *B*

Arizona
Arizona State University *M*
Prescott College *B, M*
Scottsdale Community College *C, A*

California
Art Center College of Design *B, M*
City College of San Francisco *A*
College of Marin: Kentfield *A*
Cosumnes River College *C, A*
Otis College of Art and Design *B*
Rio Hondo College *A*

Colorado
University of Colorado
  Boulder *B*
  Denver *D*

Connecticut
Yale University *M*

Florida
Florida State College at Jacksonville *A*

Georgia
Middle Georgia College *A*

Indiana
Ball State University *B*

Kansas
Kansas State University *D*

Maryland
Morgan State University *B, M*

Massachusetts
Boston Architectural College *B*
Massachusetts College of Art and
  Design *M*
University of Massachusetts
  Amherst *B*

Michigan
Lawrence Technological University *B*
Michigan State University *M*

Minnesota
Dunwoody College of Technology *C*
University of Minnesota
  Twin Cities *B*

Missouri
Ranken Technical College *A, B*

Montana
Montana State University
  Bozeman *B, M*

New Jersey
Rutgers, The State University of New
  Jersey
  New Brunswick/Piscataway
    Campus *B*

New Mexico
University of New Mexico *B*

New York
Cornell University *M, D*
Parsons The New School for Design *B*
Pratt Institute *M*
State University of New York
  Buffalo *B*
Suffolk County Community College *A*

North Carolina
North Carolina State University *B, D*

North Dakota
North Dakota State University *B*

Ohio
Bowling Green State University *B*
Ohio State University
  Columbus Campus *B*
Stark State College of Technology *A*

Oklahoma
University of Oklahoma *B*

Oregon
Portland Community College *C*

Pennsylvania
Marywood University *B*
University of Pennsylvania *B*

Puerto Rico
University of Puerto Rico
  Rio Piedras *B*

Tennessee
University of Memphis *B*

Texas
Texas A&M University *B*
Texas Tech University *D*
University of Houston *B*
University of Texas
  Austin *M*

Virginia
Virginia Polytechnic Institute and
  State University *D*

Environmental engineering

Alabama
University of Alabama *M*
University of Alabama
  Birmingham *D*

Alaska

University of Alaska
 Fairbanks *M*

Arizona

Arizona State University *B*
Northern Arizona University *B, M*
University of Arizona *M, D*

Arkansas

Northwest Arkansas Community
 College *A*
University of Arkansas *M*

California

California Institute of
 Technology *B, M, D*
California Polytechnic State
 University: San Luis Obispo *B*
California State University
 Fresno *B*
Loyola Marymount University *M*
National University *M*
San Diego State University *B, M*
Stanford University *B*
University of California
 Berkeley *B*
 Irvine *B, M, D*
 Riverside *B*
University of California: Merced *B*
University of Southern
 California *B, M, D*

Colorado

Colorado School of Mines *B*
Colorado State University *B*
United States Air Force Academy *B*
University of Colorado
 Boulder *B*

Connecticut

University of Connecticut *B, M, D*
University of Hartford *M*
University of New Haven *M*
Yale University *B, M, D*

Delaware

University of Delaware *B*

Florida

Florida Gulf Coast University *B*
Florida International University *B, M*
Florida State University *B*
University of Central Florida *B, M, D*
University of Florida *B, M*
University of Miami *B, M*
University of South Florida *M*

Georgia

Georgia Institute of
 Technology *B, M, D*
Mercer University *M*
University of Georgia *B, M*

Idaho

Idaho State University *M*
University of Idaho *B, M*

Illinois

Illinois Institute of Technology *M, D*
Moraine Valley Community College *C*
Northwestern University *B*
University of Illinois
 Urbana-Champaign *B, M, D*

Indiana

Rose-Hulman Institute of
 Technology *M*
Taylor University *B*
University of Notre Dame *B*

Kansas

University of Kansas *M, D*

Louisiana

Louisiana State University and
 Agricultural and Mechanical
 College *B*
University of New Orleans *M*

Maryland

Johns Hopkins University *B, M, D*
University of Maryland
 Baltimore County *M, D*

Massachusetts

Bristol Community College *A*
Massachusetts Institute of
 Technology *B, M, D*
Smith College *B*
Suffolk University *B*
Tufts University *B, M*
University of Massachusetts
 Amherst *M*
Worcester Polytechnic Institute *B, M*

Michigan

Michigan State University *M, D*
Michigan Technological
 University *B, M, D, T*
University of Michigan *M, D*

Missouri

University of Missouri
Missouri University of Science and
 Technology *B, M*
Washington University in St.
 Louis *M, D*

Montana

Montana State University
 Bozeman *M*
Montana Tech of the University of
 Montana *B, M*

Nebraska

University of Nebraska
 Lincoln *M*

Nevada

University of Nevada
 Reno *B, M, D*

New Hampshire

University of New Hampshire *B*

New Jersey

New Jersey Institute of
 Technology *B, M, D*
Rutgers, The State University of New
 Jersey
 New Brunswick/Piscataway
 Campus *B, M*
Stevens Institute of
 Technology *B, M, D*

New Mexico

Central New Mexico Community
 College *A*
New Mexico Institute of Mining and
 Technology *B, M*
New Mexico State University *M*
University of New Mexico *M*

New York

Clarkson University *B, M, D*
Columbia University *B, M, D*
Cornell University *B*
Hofstra University *B*
Manhattan College *M*
Polytechnic Institute of New York
 University *M*

Rensselaer Polytechnic
 Institute *B, M, D*
State University of New York
 Buffalo *B*
 College of Environmental Science
  and Forestry *B, M*
Syracuse University *B, M*
United States Military Academy *B*

North Carolina

Elon University *B*
North Carolina State University *B*

North Dakota

North Dakota State University *M*
University of North Dakota *B*

Ohio

Central State University *B*
Stark State College of Technology *A*

Oklahoma

Northeastern State University *B*
Oklahoma State University *M*
University of Oklahoma *B, M, D*

Oregon

Oregon State University *B*
University of Portland *B*

Pennsylvania

Carnegie Mellon University *B, M, D*
Drexel University *B, M, D*
Gannon University *B*
Gettysburg College *B*
Lehigh University *B, M, D*
Penn State
 Abington *B*
 Altoona *B*
 Beaver *B*
 Berks *B*
 Brandywine *B*
 DuBois *B*
 Erie, The Behrend College *B*
 Fayette, The Eberly Campus *B*
 Greater Allegheny *B*
 Harrisburg *B, M*
 Hazleton *B*
 Lehigh Valley *B*
 Mont Alto *B*
 New Kensington *B*
 Schuylkill *B*
 Shenango *B*
 University Park *B, M, D*
 Wilkes-Barre *B*
 Worthington Scranton *B*
 York *B*
St. Francis University *B*
University of Pennsylvania *B*
Villanova University *M*
Wilkes University *B*

South Carolina

Clemson University *M, D*

South Dakota

South Dakota School of Mines and
 Technology *B*

Tennessee

University of Tennessee
 Knoxville *M, D*

Texas

Lamar University *B, M*
Palo Alto College *A*
Rice University *B, M, D*
Southern Methodist
 University *B, M, D*
Tarleton State University *B*
Texas Tech University *B, M*
University of Houston *M, D*

University of Texas
 Arlington *M, D*
 Austin *M*
 El Paso *M, D*
 San Antonio *D*

Utah

Southern Utah University *A*
University of Utah *M, D*
Utah State University *B*

Vermont

Norwich University *B*
University of Vermont *B*

Virginia

John Tyler Community College *A*
Old Dominion University *B, M, D*
Virginia Polytechnic Institute and
 State University *M*

Washington

University of Washington *B*
Washington State University *M*

West Virginia

West Virginia University *M, D*

Wisconsin

Marquette University *B, M, D*
Milwaukee School of Engineering *M*
University of Wisconsin
 Madison *M*

Wyoming

Central Wyoming College *A*
University of Wyoming *M*

Environmental engineering technology

Alabama

Northwest-Shoals Community
 College *C, A*

Arizona

Pima Community College *C, A*
University of Phoenix *A*

Arkansas

East Arkansas Community
 College *C, A*
Northwest Arkansas Community
 College *C, A*
Pulaski Technical College *A*
Southern Arkansas University Tech *A*

California

Allan Hancock College *C, A*
Rio Hondo College *C*

Connecticut

Naugatuck Valley Community
 College *C, A*
Three Rivers Community College *C, A*
University of Hartford *B*

Delaware

Delaware Technical and Community
 College
 Stanton/Wilmington *C*

Georgia

North Georgia Technical College *C, A*

Illinois

Black Hawk College *C, A*

Iowa

Clinton Community College *C, A*

Iowa Lakes Community College *A*
Muscatine Community College *C, A*
Scott Community College *C, A*

Kentucky
Bluegrass Community and Technical
College *C, A*

Maryland
College of Southern Maryland *C, A*
Community College of Baltimore
County *C, A*

Massachusetts
Bristol Community College *A*
Holyoke Community College *A*
University of Massachusetts
Lowell *M*

Michigan
Bay de Noc Community College *A*
Ferris State University *B*
Lansing Community College *A*
Schoolcraft College *A*

Nevada
College of Southern Nevada *A*

New Jersey
Ocean County College *A*

New York
New York Institute of
Technology *B, M*
Rochester Institute of
Technology *B, M*
United States Military Academy *B*

North Carolina
Elon University *B*
North Carolina State University *B*

North Dakota
Dakota College at Bottineau *A*

Ohio
Bowling Green State University *B*
Cincinnati State Technical and
Community College *C, A*
James A. Rhodes State College *A*
Owens Community College
Toledo *C, A*
Shawnee State University *B*
University of Toledo *A*
Wright State University *B*

Pennsylvania
Bucknell University *M*
Community College of Allegheny
County *A*
Community College of Philadelphia *A*
Penn State
Harrisburg *M*
University Park *B, M*
Pennsylvania Highlands Community
College *A*
Temple University *B*

Puerto Rico
University of Puerto Rico
Aguadilla *B*

South Carolina
York Technical College *C*

Tennessee
Chattanooga State Community
College *A*
Middle Tennessee State University *B*

Texas
Angelina College *C, A*
Austin Community College *C, A*
Lamar State College at Orange *A*
Palo Alto College *C, A*
Panola College *C*

Utah
Salt Lake Community College *C, A*

Virginia
Danville Community College *C*

Washington
Clover Park Technical College *A*

West Virginia
Glenville State College *A*
Southern West Virginia Community
and Technical College *A*

Environmental health

Alabama
University of Alabama
Birmingham *D*

Arkansas
University of Arkansas
Little Rock *B*

California
California State University
East Bay *B*
Fresno *B*
San Bernardino *B*
Loma Linda University *M*
University of California
Berkeley *M, D*
Los Angeles *M, D*

Colorado
Colorado State University *B, M, D*

Georgia
University of Georgia *B, M*

Idaho
Boise State University *B*

Illinois
Illinois State University *B*
University of Illinois
Urbana-Champaign *B*

Indiana
Vincennes University *A*

Iowa
Iowa Wesleyan College *B*
University of Iowa *M, D*
University of Northern Iowa *M*

Kentucky
Western Kentucky University *B*

Louisiana
Tulane University *M, D*

Maine
University of Southern Maine *B*

Maryland
Salisbury University *B*

Massachusetts
Boston University *M, D*

Michigan
Oakland University *B*
University of Michigan *M, D*

Minnesota
University of Minnesota
Twin Cities *M, D*
Vermilion Community College *A*

Mississippi
Mississippi Valley State
University *B, M*

Missouri
Crowder College *A*
Drury University *B*
Missouri Southern State University *B*

New Mexico
New Mexico State University *B*

New York
City University of New York
Queensborough Community
College *A*
York College *B*
Polytechnic Institute of New York
University *M*
State University of New York
Albany *M, D*
University of Rochester *M*

North Carolina
Durham Technical Community
College *A*
East Carolina University *B, M*
University of North Carolina
Chapel Hill *B*
Western Carolina University *B*

Ohio
Bowling Green State University *B*
Case Western Reserve
University *M, D*
Ohio University *B*
University of Akron: Wayne College *A*
University of Findlay *B*
Wright State University *B*

Oklahoma
East Central University *B*
Oklahoma State University
Oklahoma City *A*
University of Oklahoma *M, D*

Oregon
Oregon State University *B, M*

Pennsylvania
Indiana University of Pennsylvania *B*
Temple University *M*
University of Pennsylvania *M*
University of Pittsburgh *D*

Puerto Rico
Universidad Metropolitana *B*
University of Puerto Rico
Medical Sciences *M*

South Carolina
University of South Carolina *M, D*

Tennessee
Chattanooga State Community
College *A*
East Tennessee State
University *B, M, D*
Roane State Community College *A*

Texas
Texas Southern University *B*

Texas State Technical College:
Marshall *A*

Vermont
Goddard College *B, M*

Virginia
Old Dominion University *B*

Washington
University of Washington *B, M*

Environmental psychology

Arizona
Prescott College *B, M*

Florida
Embry-Riddle Aeronautical
University *M*

New York
Polytechnic Institute of New York
University *M*

Environmental science

Alabama
Auburn University *B*
Miles College *B*
Samford University *B*
Troy University *B*
University of Alabama *B*
University of Mobile *B*

Alaska
Alaska Pacific University *B, M*
University of Alaska
Southeast *B*

Arizona
Arizona Western College *A*
Coconino County Community
College *A*
Dine College *A*
Northern Arizona University *B*
Prescott College *B*

Arkansas
Northwest Arkansas Community
College *C*
University of Arkansas *B*

California
California Lutheran University *B*
California State University
Chico *B, M*
Dominguez Hills *M*
Monterey Bay *B*
California State University: Channel
Islands *B*
Claremont McKenna College *B*
College of the Desert *A*
Fresno Pacific University *B*
Loma Linda University *B*
Loyola Marymount University *M*
Mills College *B*
National University *B*
Pitzer College *B*
Point Loma Nazarene University *B*
Santa Clara University *B*
Scripps College *B*
Stanford University *B, M, D*
University of California
Berkeley *B*
Los Angeles *B, D*
Riverside *B, M, D*
San Diego *B*
University of California: Merced *M, D*
University of La Verne *B*

University of Redlands *B*
University of San Francisco *B*
University of Southern California *B*
University of the Pacific *B*

Colorado

Colorado College *B*
Mesa State College *B*
University of Colorado
    Denver *M*
University of Denver *B*

Connecticut

Eastern Connecticut State
    University *B*
Gateway Community College *A*
Three Rivers Community College *C, A*
Trinity College *B*
Wesleyan University *B*
Yale University *M, D*

Delaware

Delaware State University *B*

District of Columbia

American University *M*
Trinity Washington University *B*

Florida

Bethune-Cookman University *B*
Broward College *A*
Florida Agricultural and Mechanical
    University *B, M, D*
Florida Atlantic University *C, M*
Florida Gulf Coast University *M*
Florida Institute of
    Technology *B, M, D*
Miami Dade College *A*
Nova Southeastern University *B, M*
Stetson University *B*
University of Miami *D*
University of Tampa *B*
University of West Florida *B, M*

Georgia

Berry College *B*
Columbus State University *M*
Georgia College and State
    University *B*
Gordon College *A*
Mercer University *B, M*
North Georgia Technical College *A*
Paine College *B*
Piedmont College *B*
Spelman College *B*
University of Georgia *B*
University of West Georgia *B*
Valdosta State University *B*
Waycross College *A*

Hawaii

Hawaii Pacific University *B*
University of Hawaii
    Manoa *B*

Idaho

Idaho State University *B*
University of Idaho *B, M, D*

Illinois

Benedictine University *B*
Bradley University *B*
DePaul University *B*
Dominican University *B*
Loyola University Chicago *C, B*
Monmouth College *B*
Northwestern University *B*
University of Illinois
    Springfield *M*
    Urbana-Champaign *B, M, D*
University of St. Francis *B*

Indiana

DePauw University *B*
Goshen College *B, M*
Indiana University
    Bloomington *B, M, D*
Indiana University-Purdue University
    Indianapolis *B*
Purdue University *B*
Taylor University *B, M*
University of Evansville *B*
University of Notre Dame *B*
University of St. Francis *M*
Valparaiso University *B*

Iowa

Briar Cliff University *B*
Buena Vista University *B*
Coe College *B*
Drake University *B*
Iowa State University *B, M, D*
Simpson College *B*
University of Iowa *B*
University of Northern Iowa *B, M*
Upper Iowa University *B*

Kentucky

Midway College *B*
Northern Kentucky University *B*
Thomas More College *B*

Louisiana

Centenary College of Louisiana *B*
Louisiana State University
    Shreveport *B, M*
Louisiana State University and
    Agricultural and Mechanical
    College *B, M*
Tulane University *B*

Maine

Colby College *B*
Saint Joseph's College of Maine *B*
Unity College *A, B*
University of Maine
    Farmington *B*
    Fort Kent *B*
University of New England *B*
University of Southern Maine *B*

Maryland

Anne Arundel Community College *A*
Harford Community College *A*
Hood College *B*
Howard Community College *A*
McDaniel College *B*
Salisbury University *B*
University of Maryland
    Baltimore County *B*
    College Park *B, M, D*

Massachusetts

Anna Maria College *B*
Assumption College *B*
Bard College at Simon's Rock *B*
Berkshire Community College *A*
Boston University *B*
Cape Cod Community College *A*
Clark University *B, M*
Curry College *B*
Eastern Nazarene College *B*
Greenfield Community College *A*
Simmons College *B*
Suffolk University *B*
University of Massachusetts
    Amherst *B*
Westfield State College *B*
Wheaton College *B*

Michigan

Adrian College *B*
Albion College *B*
Andrews University *B*
Aquinas College *B*
Calvin College *B*
Central Michigan University *B*
Delta College *A*
Hope College *B*
Lake Michigan College *A*
Lake Superior State University *B*
Madonna University *B*
Marygrove College *B*
Michigan State University *B*
Michigan Technological University *B*
Northern Michigan University *B*
University of Michigan
    Flint *B*
Wayne State University *B*

Minnesota

Anoka-Ramsey Community College *A*
Bethel University *B*
Fond du Lac Tribal and Community
    College *A*
Northland Community & Technical
    College *A*
Rochester Community and Technical
    College *A*
Saint Cloud State University *B*
St. John's University *B*
Southwest Minnesota State
    University *B*
University of Minnesota
    Duluth *B*
University of St. Thomas *B*

Missouri

Central Methodist University *B*
Columbia College *B*
Drury University *B*
Lincoln University *B*
Lindenwood University *B*
Maryville University of Saint Louis *B*
Saint Louis University *B*
University of Missouri
    Kansas City *B*
Westminster College *B*

Montana

Blackfeet Community College *A*
Rocky Mountain College *B*
University of Montana: Western *A, B*

Nevada

Nevada State College *B*
Sierra Nevada College *B*
University of Nevada
    Reno *B*

New Hampshire

Franklin Pierce University *B*
New England College *B*
Saint Anselm College *B*
University of New Hampshire *B*

New Jersey

Bergen Community College *A*
Fairleigh Dickinson University
    Metropolitan Campus *B, M*
Kean University *B*
New Jersey Institute of
    Technology *B, M, D*
Ocean County College *A*
Ramapo College of New Jersey *B*
Richard Stockton College of New
    Jersey *M*
Rider University *B*
Thomas Edison State College *A, B*
William Paterson University of New
    Jersey *B*

New Mexico

Eastern New Mexico University *B*
Navajo Technical College *C*
New Mexico State University *B*
University of New Mexico *B*

New York

Barnard College *B*
Canisius College *B*
City University of New York
    College of Staten Island *M*
    Queens College *B*
Clarkson University *B*
Columbia University *B*
Columbia-Greene Community
    College *A*
Dowling College *B*
Keuka College *B*
Long Island University
    C. W. Post Campus *B*
Marist College *B*
Nazareth College *B*
Pace University *B, M*
Paul Smith's College *A, B*
Polytechnic Institute of New York
    University *M*
Rensselaer Polytechnic Institute *B*
Rochester Institute of
    Technology *B, M*
Rockland Community College *A*
Russell Sage College *B*
State University of New York
    Albany *B*
    College at Brockport *B, M*
    College at Oneonta *B*
    College at Plattsburgh *B*
    College of Agriculture and
        Technology at Morrisville *A*
    College of Environmental Science
        and Forestry *B, M, D*
    College of Technology at Alfred *A*
    Purchase *B*
Suffolk County Community College *A*
United States Military Academy *B*
University of Rochester *B*
Wells College *B*

North Carolina

Appalachian State University *B*
Barton College *B*
Brevard College *B*
Catawba College *B*
Meredith College *B*
North Carolina Central University *B*
North Carolina State University *B*
Queens University of Charlotte *B*
Roanoke-Chowan Community
    College *A*
Southeastern Community College *A*
University of North Carolina
    Chapel Hill *B, M, D*
    Pembroke *B*
    Wilmington *B*
Western Carolina University *B*

North Dakota

Sitting Bull College *A*

Ohio

Ashland University *B*
Capital University *B*
Cedarville University *B*
Cleveland State University *B, M*
John Carroll University *B*
Lourdes College *B*
Marietta College *B*
Miami University
    Oxford Campus *B, M*
Mount Union College *B*
Muskingum University *B*
Ohio State University
    Columbus Campus *M, D*
University of Dayton *B*
Wright State University *M*
Youngstown State University *B, M*

Oklahoma

Northeastern State University *B*
Oklahoma State University *B, M, D*

Rose State College A
University of Oklahoma B, M, D

Oregon
Klamath Community College A
Oregon Health & Science University M, D
Oregon Institute of Technology B
Oregon State University B, M, D
Pacific University B
University of Oregon B, D
University of Portland B
Willamette University B

Pennsylvania
Albright College B
Allegheny College B
Bucks County Community College A
California University of Pennsylvania B, M
Carlow University B
Chatham University B
Chestnut Hill College B
Clarion University of Pennsylvania B, T
Dickinson College B
Drexel University B, M, D
Duquesne University B, M
Edinboro University of Pennsylvania B
Franklin & Marshall College B
Gannon University B
Gettysburg College B
Harrisburg Area Community College A
Harrisburg University of Science and Technology B
Juniata College B
Keystone College A
King's College B
Kutztown University of Pennsylvania B
La Salle University B
Lehigh University B, M, D
Lincoln University B
Marywood University B
Messiah College B
Montgomery County Community College A
Moravian College B
Muhlenberg College B
Point Park University B
Robert Morris University B
St. Francis University B
St. Vincent College B
Susquehanna University B, T
Temple University B
University of Pennsylvania M
University of the Sciences in Philadelphia B
Wilson College B

Puerto Rico
Inter American University of Puerto Rico
 Bayamon Campus B
 San German Campus M
Turabo University D
Universidad Metropolitana B
Universidad del Este B
University of Puerto Rico Rio Piedras B, M

Rhode Island
Brown University B
Bryant University B

South Carolina
Benedict College B
Claflin University B
Lander University B
University of South Carolina B
York Technical College C

South Dakota
South Dakota State University D

Tennessee
Lambuth University B
Lincoln Memorial University B
Lipscomb University B, M
University of Tennessee Chattanooga B, M

Texas
Abilene Christian University B
Baylor University B, M, D
Clarendon College A
Hardin-Simmons University B
Midland College A
Midwestern State University B
Palo Alto College A
Rice University M
Sam Houston State University B
Southern Methodist University B
Stephen F. Austin State University B, M
Tarleton State University M
Texas A&M University B
Texas Christian University B, M
Texas State Technical College West Texas A
Texas State University: San Marcos B, M, T
University of Houston Clear Lake B, M
University of North Texas M, D
University of St. Thomas B
University of Texas
 Arlington M
 Brownsville - Texas Southmost College B
 El Paso B, M
 Pan American B
 San Antonio B, M
 of the Permian Basin B
University of the Incarnate Word B
West Texas A&M University B, M

Utah
Brigham Young University B
University of Utah B, T

Vermont
Bennington College B
Castleton State College B
Lyndon State College B
St. Michael's College B
University of Vermont B

Virginia
Averett University B
Bridgewater College B
Eastern Mennonite University B
Emory & Henry College B
Ferrum College B
Hampton University B
Lynchburg College B
Mountain Empire Community College A
Roanoke College B, T
Sweet Briar College B
University of Virginia B, M, D
Virginia Polytechnic Institute and State University B
Washington and Lee University B

Washington
Cascadia Community College A
Eastern Washington University C, B
Everett Community College A
Evergreen State College B
Northwest University B
Olympic College C, A
Pacific Lutheran University B
University of Washington Bothell B
University of Washington Tacoma B

Washington State University B, M, D
Western Washington University B, M

West Virginia
Alderson-Broaddus College B
Davis and Elkins College B
Marshall University B, M
New River Community and Technical College A
West Virginia Wesleyan College B

Wisconsin
Alverno College B
Beloit College B
Carroll University B
Carthage College B
Milwaukee Area Technical College A
St. Norbert College B
University of Wisconsin
 Green Bay B
 Milwaukee B
 River Falls B
Wisconsin Lutheran College B

Wyoming
Casper College A
Central Wyoming College A

Environmental studies

Alabama
Birmingham-Southern College B
Northwest-Shoals Community College A
Samford University B

Alaska
Alaska Pacific University B
University of Alaska Southeast C, A

Arizona
Arizona State University D
Northern Arizona University B
Prescott College B, M
University of Arizona B

Arkansas
Arkansas State University M, D
Hendrix College B
University of Central Arkansas B
University of the Ozarks B

California
Allan Hancock College A
Alliant International University B
California State University
 East Bay B
 Fresno B
 Fullerton M
 Sacramento B, M
 San Bernardino B
Chaffey College A
Claremont McKenna College B
College of the Desert C, A
Feather River College C, A
Fresno Pacific University B
Humboldt State University B, M
Mills College B
Pitzer College B
Pomona College B
Saddleback College A
San Diego State University B
San Francisco State University B
San Jose State University B, M
Santa Barbara City College C, A
Santa Clara University B
Santa Rosa Junior College A
Scripps College B
Sonoma State University B
Southwestern College C, A

University of California
 Berkeley B, M, D
 Davis B
 Irvine B
 San Diego B
 Santa Barbara B
 Santa Cruz B
University of Redlands B
University of San Francisco B, M
University of Southern California B, M
University of the Pacific B

Colorado
Fort Lewis College B
Metropolitan State College of Denver B
Naropa University B
University of Colorado Boulder B, M, D
Western State College of Colorado B

Connecticut
Connecticut College B
Goodwin College A
Mitchell College B
Post University B
University of Connecticut B
Yale University B, M

Delaware
Wesley College B, M

District of Columbia
American University B
George Washington University B, M

Florida
Eckerd College B
Florida Gulf Coast University B
Florida State University B
Indian River State College A
New College of Florida B
Nova Southeastern University B
Rollins College B
Saint Leo University B
Saint Thomas University B

Georgia
Darton College A
Emory University B
Mercer University B
Savannah State University B
Shorter College B
University of Georgia B
University of West Georgia B

Hawaii
Chaminade University of Honolulu B
Hawaii Pacific University B

Idaho
Boise State University B
College of Idaho B

Illinois
DePaul University B
Dominican University B
Illinois Wesleyan University B
Judson University B
Knox College B
Lake Forest College B
Lincoln College A
Northeastern Illinois University B
Northwestern University B
Olivet Nazarene University B
University of Chicago B
University of Illinois Springfield M
Wheaton College B

Indiana

Earlham College *B*
Indiana University-Purdue University
  Indianapolis *M*
Manchester College *B*
University of Evansville *B*
University of St. Francis *A, B*

Iowa

Central College *B*
Cornell College *B*
Dordt College *B*
Iowa Lakes Community College *A*
Iowa State University *B*
Luther College *B*
University of Dubuque *B*
University of Iowa *B*

Kansas

Friends University *M*
Tabor College *B*
University of Kansas *B*

Kentucky

University of Kentucky *C*

Louisiana

Tulane University *B, M*
University of New Orleans *B*

Maine

Bates College *B*
Bowdoin College *B*
Colby College *B*
Saint Joseph's College of Maine *B*
Unity College *B*
University of Maine *B, M, D*
University of Maine
  Machias *B*
  Presque Isle *B*
University of New England *B*
University of Southern Maine *B*

Maryland

Frostburg State University *B*
Harford Community College *C, A*
Johns Hopkins University *B*
Mount St. Mary's University *B*
Towson University *B, M*
University of Maryland
  Baltimore County *B*
Washington College *B*

Massachusetts

Bard College at Simon's Rock *B*
Boston University *B, M*
Brandeis University *B*
Cape Cod Community College *C, A*
Clark University *B, M*
College of the Holy Cross *B*
Eastern Nazarene College *B*
Emmanuel College *B*
Endicott College *B*
Framingham State College *B*
Hampshire College *B*
Harvard College *B*
Lasell College *B*
Lesley University *B, M*
Massachusetts College of Liberal
  Arts *B*
Mount Holyoke College *B*
Mount Wachusett Community
  College *A*
Northeastern University *B*
Springfield College *B*
Stonehill College *B*
University of Massachusetts
  Boston *C, M, D*
Wellesley College *B*
Worcester Polytechnic Institute *B*

Michigan

Adrian College *B*
Albion College *B*
Aquinas College *B*
Central Michigan University *B, T*
Henry Ford Community College *A*
Madonna University *C*
Michigan State University *B*
University of Michigan *B*
University of Michigan
  Dearborn *B*
Western Michigan University *B*

Minnesota

Bethel University *B*
College of St. Benedict *B*
Concordia College: Moorhead *B*
Gustavus Adolphus College *B*
Hamline University *B*
Macalester College *B*
Minnesota State University
  Mankato *B, M*
Saint Cloud State University *B*
St. Olaf College *B*
University of Minnesota
  Duluth *B*
  Morris *B*
University of St. Thomas *B*
Vermilion Community College *A*
White Earth Tribal and Community
  College *A*
Winona State University *B*

Missouri

Columbia College *A*
Drury University *B*
Maryville University of Saint
  Louis *B, T*
Southeast Missouri State University *B*
University of Missouri
  Kansas City *B*
Washington University in St.
  Louis *B, M*
Westminster College *B*

Montana

Montana State University
  Billings *B*
Rocky Mountain College *B*

Nebraska

Dana College *B*
Doane College *B*
University of Nebraska
  Lincoln *B*
  Omaha *B*

Nevada

Truckee Meadows Community
  College *A*
University of Nevada
  Las Vegas *B*

New Hampshire

Colby-Sawyer College *B*
Dartmouth College *B*
Keene State College *B*
Plymouth State University *B*
Southern New Hampshire
  University *B*
University of New Hampshire *B, M, D*
White Mountains Community
  College *A*

New Jersey

Drew University *B*
Montclair State University *M*
Ramapo College of New Jersey *B*
Richard Stockton College of New
  Jersey *B*

Rutgers, The State University of New
  Jersey
  New Brunswick/Piscataway
    Campus *B*
Seton Hall University *B*
Sussex County Community College *A*
Thomas Edison State College *B*
Warren County Community College *A*

New Mexico

New Mexico Institute of Mining and
  Technology *B*
Santa Fe Community College *C, A*

New York

Adelphi University *B, M*
Alfred University *B*
Bard College *M*
Barnard College *B*
Cazenovia College *B*
City University of New York
  Brooklyn College *B*
  Medgar Evers College *B*
  Queens College *B*
Colgate University *B*
College of New Rochelle *B*
Columbia University
  School of General Studies *B*
Elmira College *B*
Finger Lakes Community College *A*
Genesee Community College *A*
Hamilton College *B*
Hobart and William Smith Colleges *B*
Hofstra University *B*
Hudson Valley Community College *A*
Ithaca College *B*
Le Moyne College *B*
Niagara County Community
  College *A*
Pace University *B*
Parsons The New School for Design *B*
St. John's University *B*
St. Lawrence University *B*
Siena College *C, B*
Skidmore College *B*
State University of New York
  Binghamton *B*
  College at Brockport *B*
  College at Fredonia *B*
  College at Potsdam *B*
  College of Agriculture and
    Technology at Morrisville *A*
  College of Environmental Science
    and Forestry *B, M, D*
  Purchase *B*
  Stony Brook *B*
Suffolk County Community College *A*
Ulster County Community College *A*
United States Military Academy *B*
University of Rochester *B*
Vassar College *B*
Wells College *B*

North Carolina

Appalachian State University *B*
Brevard College *B*
Catawba College *B*
Elon University *B*
Guilford College *B*
Lenoir-Rhyne University *B*
Meredith College *B*
Montreat College *B*
Pfeiffer University *B*
Queens University of Charlotte *B*
University of North Carolina
  Asheville *B*
  Chapel Hill *B*
  Wilmington *B*

North Dakota

Dakota College at Bottineau *A*
University of North Dakota *M, D*

Ohio

Case Western Reserve University *B*
Cleveland State University *B, M*
Columbus State Community
  College *C, A*
Defiance College *B*
Hiram College *B*
John Carroll University *B*
Marietta College *B*
Miami University
  Oxford Campus *B*
Oberlin College *B*
Ohio Northern University *B*
Ohio State University
  Agricultural Technical Institute *A*
Ohio University *M*
Ohio Wesleyan University *B*
Otterbein College *B*
Owens Community College
  Toledo *C*
Stark State College of Technology *A*
University of Rio Grande *B*
University of Toledo *B*
Wittenberg University *B*

Oklahoma

Eastern Oklahoma State College *A*
University of Tulsa *B*

Oregon

Lane Community College *A*
Lewis & Clark College *B*
Linfield College *B*
Marylhurst University *B*
Pacific University *B*
Southern Oregon University *B, M*
Southwestern Oregon Community
  College *A*
University of Oregon *B, M*
University of Portland *B*

Pennsylvania

Albright College *B*
Allegheny College *B*
Arcadia University *B, M*
Bucknell University *B*
Chatham University *B, T*
Delaware Valley College *C*
Dickinson College *B*
Drexel University *B*
Franklin & Marshall College *B*
Gannon University *M*
Gettysburg College *B*
Grove City College *T*
Harrisburg Area Community
  College *A*
Immaculata University *B*
Juniata College *B*
Keystone College *A*
King's College *B*
Lackawanna College *A*
Mansfield University of
  Pennsylvania *B*
Messiah College *B*
Moravian College *B*
Neumann University *B*
Penn State
  Altoona *B*
Philadelphia University *B*
St. Francis University *B*
Saint Joseph's University *B*
Shippensburg University of
  Pennsylvania *B, M*
Temple University *B*
Thiel College *B*
University of Pennsylvania *B, M*
University of Pittsburgh
  Bradford *B*
  Johnstown *B*
Ursinus College *B*
Washington & Jefferson College *B*
Wilson College *B*

Puerto Rico

Pontifical Catholic University of Puerto Rico *B*
Turabo University *M*
Universidad Politecnica de Puerto Rico *M*

Rhode Island

Brown University *B, M*
University of Rhode Island *B*

South Carolina

Wofford College *B*

Tennessee

Maryville College *B*
Tennessee Wesleyan College *B*
Tusculum College *B*
University of the South *B*

Texas

Austin College *B*
Baylor University *B, M*
Concordia University Texas *B*
Lamar University *B*
Panola College *C*
St. Edward's University *B*
Southern Methodist University *M*
Southwestern University *B*
Texas A&M University *B*
Texas A&M University Commerce *B*
Texas Southern University *B*
University of Houston Clear Lake *B, M*
University of St. Thomas *B*

Utah

University of Utah *B*
Utah State University *M*
Westminster College *B*

Vermont

Bennington College *B*
Goddard College *B, M*
Green Mountain College *B, M*
Johnson State College *B*
Marlboro College *B*
Middlebury College *B*
Southern Vermont College *C*
Sterling College *B*
University of Vermont *B*

Virginia

Christopher Newport University *B, M*
College of William and Mary *B*
Emory & Henry College *B*
Hollins University *B*
Randolph College *B*
Randolph-Macon College *B*
Shenandoah University *B*
Southwest Virginia Community College *A*
Sweet Briar College *B*
Tidewater Community College *A*
University of Richmond *B*
University of Virginia's College at Wise *B*
Virginia Commonwealth University *B, M*
Virginia Intermont College *B*
Virginia Polytechnic Institute and State University *B*
Virginia Wesleyan College *B*

Washington

Evergreen State College *B, M*
University of Washington Bothell *B*
University of Washington Tacoma *B*
Western Washington University *B*
Whitman College *B*

West Virginia

American Public University System *B, M*
Bethany College *B*
Mountain State University *A*
Shepherd University *B*

Wisconsin

Concordia University Wisconsin *B*
Lawrence University *B*
Northland College *B*
Ripon College *B*
University of Wisconsin
Green Bay *B, T*
Madison *M*
Richland *C*
Wisconsin Lutheran College *B*

Wyoming

University of Wyoming *B, M*
Western Wyoming Community College *A*

Environmental toxicology

California

University of California
Davis *B*
Irvine *M, D*
Riverside *M, D*
Santa Cruz *M, D*

Louisiana

Southern University and Agricultural and Mechanical College *D*

Michigan

Michigan State University *D*

Nebraska

University of Nebraska Medical Center *M, D*

New York

Clarkson University *B*
Cornell University *M, D*

Wisconsin

University of Wisconsin Madison *M, D*

Epidemiology

Alabama

University of Alabama Birmingham *D*

Arizona

University of Arizona *M, D*

California

Loma Linda University *M, D*
Stanford University *M, D*
University of California
Berkeley *M, D*
Davis *M, D*
Los Angeles *M, D*
University of Southern California *M, D*

Colorado

Colorado State University *M, D*

District of Columbia

George Washington University *D*

Florida

University of Miami *M, D*

Georgia

Emory University *M, D*

Hawaii

University of Hawaii Manoa *D*

Iowa

University of Iowa *M, D*

Kentucky

University of Louisville *M, D*

Louisiana

Tulane University *M, D*

Maryland

University of Maryland
Baltimore *M, D*
College Park *D*

Massachusetts

Boston University *M, D*

Michigan

Michigan State University *M, D*
University of Michigan *M, D*

Minnesota

University of Minnesota
Twin Cities *M, D*
Walden University *D*

Missouri

Washington University in St. Louis *M*

New York

State University of New York
Albany *M, D*
Buffalo *M, D*
University of Rochester *D*

North Carolina

University of North Carolina
Chapel Hill *M, D*
Wake Forest University *M*

Ohio

Case Western Reserve University *M, D*

Oklahoma

University of Oklahoma *M, D*

Pennsylvania

Drexel University *D*
Temple University *M*
University of Pennsylvania *M, D*
University of Pittsburgh *M, D*

Puerto Rico

University of Puerto Rico Medical Sciences *M*

South Carolina

University of South Carolina *M, D*

Tennessee

University of Tennessee Knoxville *M*

Texas

University of Texas Health Science Center at Houston *M, D*

Virginia

George Mason University *M*
Virginia Commonwealth University *D*

Washington

University of Washington *M*

Equestrian studies

Arizona

Cochise College *C*
Scottsdale Community College *C, A*

California

Cosumnes River College *A*
Los Angeles Pierce College *C, A*
Mount San Antonio College *C*
Santa Rosa Junior College *C, A*
Shasta College *C, A*
Sierra College *C, A*

Colorado

Colorado Northwestern Community College *C, A*
Colorado State University *B*
Lamar Community College *C, A*

Connecticut

Post University *C, B*

Florida

Central Florida Community College *C, A*

Georgia

Savannah College of Art and Design *B*

Illinois

Black Hawk College *A*
Black Hawk College: East Campus *C, A*
South Suburban College of Cook County *C*

Indiana

St. Mary-of-the-Woods College *A, B*

Iowa

Ellsworth Community College *A*
Kirkwood Community College *A*

Kansas

Colby Community College *A*
Dodge City Community College *C, A*

Kentucky

Asbury College *B*
Bluegrass Community and Technical College *C, A*
Midway College *A, B*

Maine

University of Maine *C*

Maryland

Harford Community College *A*

Massachusetts

Mount Ida College *B*
University of Massachusetts Amherst *A*

Minnesota

Minnesota State Community and Technical College *C*
University of Minnesota Crookston *B*

Missouri

William Woods University *B*

Montana

Dawson Community College *A*
Rocky Mountain College *B*

University of Montana: Western *A, B*

Nebraska

Nebraska College of Technical
    Agriculture *A*

New Hampshire

University of New Hampshire *B*

New Jersey

Centenary College *B*

New York

Cazenovia College *C*
Houghton College *B*
State University of New York
    College of Agriculture and
        Technology at Morrisville *A, B*

North Carolina

Martin Community College *C, A*
St. Andrews Presbyterian College *B*

North Dakota

North Dakota State University *B*

Ohio

Hocking College *C, A*
Ohio University
    Southern Campus at Ironton *A*
Otterbein College *B*
University of Findlay *A, B*

Oklahoma

Connors State College *C, A*
Northeastern Oklahoma Agricultural
    and Mechanical College *C, A*
Redlands Community College *A*

Oregon

Linn-Benton Community College *A*

Pennsylvania

Delaware Valley College *A*
Wilson College *B*

Rhode Island

Johnson & Wales University:
    Providence *B*

Texas

Central Texas College *C*
Clarendon College *A*
Frank Phillips College *C, A*
North Central Texas College *A*
Sul Ross State University *B*
West Texas A&M University *B*

Vermont

Vermont Technical College *B*

Virginia

Averett University *B*
J. Sargeant Reynolds Community
    College *C*
Lord Fairfax Community College *C*
Virginia Intermont College *B*

West Virginia

Bethany College *B*

Wisconsin

University of Wisconsin
    River Falls *B*

Wyoming

Central Wyoming College *C, A*
Laramie County Community
    College *A*
Northwest College *C, A*

ESL teacher education

Alabama

University of Alabama *M*

Arizona

Arizona State University *M*
Northcentral University *M, D*
Northern Arizona University *M*
University of Arizona *M, D*

Arkansas

Arkansas State University *B, T*
Arkansas Tech University *M*
Henderson State University *T*
University of Arkansas
    Little Rock *M*

California

Alliant International
    University *B, M, D*
Azusa Pacific University *M*
California Polytechnic State
    University: San Luis Obispo *T*
California State University
    Chico *B*
    East Bay *M*
    Fresno *M*
    Fullerton *M, T*
    Long Beach *T*
    Los Angeles *M*
    Sacramento *M*
Fresno Pacific University *M*
Holy Names University *M, T*
Loyola Marymount University *M*
The Master's College *B*
San Jose State University *M*
Soka University of America *M*
University of California
    Los Angeles *M*
    San Diego *M*
University of San Francisco *M*
University of Southern California *T*
University of the Pacific *T*

Connecticut

Central Connecticut State
    University *M, T*
Fairfield University *M, T*

Delaware

University of Delaware *B, M, T*

District of Columbia

American University *M*
Catholic University of America *B*
George Washington University *A*
Georgetown University *M*
Trinity Washington University *M*

Florida

Barry University *T*
Carlos Albizu University *D*
Florida Atlantic University *M*
University of Central Florida *M*
University of South Florida *D*

Georgia

Georgia State University *M, D, T*
University of Georgia *M*

Hawaii

Hawaii Pacific University *B, M*
University of Hawaii
    Manoa *B*

Idaho

Boise State University *T*
University of Idaho *M, T*

Illinois

Moody Bible Institute *B*
Southern Illinois University
    Carbondale *M*
Southern Illinois University
    Edwardsville *M*
Spoon River College *A*
University of Illinois
    Urbana-Champaign *M, T*
Wheaton College *M*

Indiana

Ball State University *M, T*
Goshen College *B, T*
Indiana State University *M, T*
Indiana University-Purdue University
    Indianapolis *B*
University of Evansville *T*

Iowa

Buena Vista University *M*
Iowa State University *M, T*
Northwestern College *T*
University of Iowa *T*
University of Northern Iowa *B, M*

Kansas

Emporia State University *M*
McPherson College *T*
Newman University *M*
Pittsburg State University *M*

Kentucky

Asbury College *M, T*
Murray State University *M*

Maryland

College of Notre Dame of
    Maryland *M*
McDaniel College *B*
Salisbury University *B, T*
University of Maryland
    Baltimore County *M*

Massachusetts

Boston University *M, T*
Clark University *T*
Elms College *B, M, T*
Framingham State College *M*
Salem State College *M*
Simmons College *B, M*

Michigan

Andrews University *M*
Central Michigan University *M*
Cornerstone University *A*
Eastern Michigan University *M, T*
Madonna University *M, T*
Michigan State University *M*

Minnesota

Bethel University *B*
Concordia University: St. Paul *B, T*
Crown College *A, B*
Hamline University *B, M, T*
Minnesota State University
    Mankato *M, T*
North Central University *B*
Northwestern College *B*
Saint Cloud State University *M*
University of Minnesota
    Duluth *T*
    Twin Cities *M, T*

Mississippi

Mississippi College *M*

Missouri

Missouri Southern State University *B*
University of Central Missouri *M, T*
Webster University *M*

Montana

University of Montana *T*

Nebraska

Concordia University *B, T*
Doane College *B*
Grace University *B*
University of Nebraska
    Kearney *B, T*
    Lincoln *B*

New Hampshire

Southern New Hampshire
    University *M*

New Jersey

The College of New Jersey *M, T*
Georgian Court University *T*
Montclair State University *T*
New Jersey City University *T*
Rutgers, The State University of New
    Jersey
    Camden Regional Campus *T*
Seton Hall University *M*
William Paterson University of New
    Jersey *T*

New Mexico

Western New Mexico University *B*

New York

Adelphi University *M, T*
City University of New York
    Hunter College *M, T*
    Lehman College *M, T*
    Queens College *B, M, T*
College of New Rochelle *M, T*
Cornell University *M, T*
D'Youville College *M*
Hofstra University *M, T*
Houghton College *B, T*
Le Moyne College *T*
Long Island University
    Brooklyn Campus *M, T*
    C. W. Post Campus *M*
Manhattanville College *M*
Mercy College *M, T*
Nazareth College *M*
New York University *B, M, D, T*
Nyack College *B*
St. John's University *M, T*
State University of New York
    Albany *M*
    Buffalo *M*
    College at Cortland *B, M*
    College at Fredonia *M*
    New Paltz *M*
    Stony Brook *M, T*
University of Rochester *M*
Utica College *B*

North Carolina

Lenoir-Rhyne University *B*
Meredith College *M, T*
University of North Carolina
    Charlotte *M*
Western Carolina University *M*
Winston-Salem State University *M*

Ohio

Cedarville University *T*
Kent State University *T*
Ohio Dominican University *M, T*
Ohio State University
    Columbus Campus *M*
Union Institute & University *B, M*
University of Findlay *B, M, T*
University of Toledo *M, T*

Oklahoma

Langston University *M*
Oklahoma Christian University *B, T*

Oklahoma City University *M*
Oral Roberts University *M*
University of Central Oklahoma *B*

Oregon
Concordia University *M*
Eastern Oregon University *B, T*
George Fox University *M*
Northwest Christian University *T*
Portland State University *M, T*
Southern Oregon University *T*
University of Oregon *T*
Western Oregon University *M, T*

Pennsylvania
Bloomsburg University of
    Pennsylvania *T*
DeSales University *T*
Duquesne University *M, T*
Gannon University *T*
Holy Family University *M, T*
King's College *T*
Marywood University *B*
Penn State
    University Park *M*
Temple University *M*
University of Pennsylvania *M*
University of Pittsburgh *T*
West Chester University of
    Pennsylvania *M*
Widener University *T*

Puerto Rico
American University of Puerto
    Rico *B, T*
Inter American University of Puerto
    Rico
    Fajardo Campus *B, T*
    Guayama Campus *B*
    Metropolitan Campus *B, M*
    Ponce Campus *B, M, T*
    San German Campus *B, M*
Pontifical Catholic University of
    Puerto Rico *B, M, T*
Turabo University *M*
Universidad Adventista de las
    Antillas *M*
University of Puerto Rico
    Arecibo *B, M*
    Humacao *B*
    Rio Piedras *M*

Rhode Island
Rhode Island College *M*

South Carolina
Columbia International University *M*

Tennessee
Carson-Newman College *M*
Lipscomb University *B, M, T*
Maryville College *B, T*
Tennessee Technological University *T*
Trevecca Nazarene University *M, T*
Union University *B, T*
University of Memphis *T*
Vanderbilt University *M*

Texas
Houston Baptist University *T*
Lamar University *T*
McMurry University *T*
North Lake College *A*
Sam Houston State University *M, T*
Texas A&M University
    Commerce *T*
Texas Wesleyan University *M*
University of North Texas *M*
University of Texas
    Arlington *M, T*
    Brownsville - Texas Southmost
        College *M*

Pan American *M*
San Antonio *M, T*
West Texas A&M University *T*

Utah
Brigham Young University *M, T*
Snow College *A*
Utah State University *M*

Vermont
St. Michael's College *T*

Virginia
Bridgewater College *T*
Eastern Mennonite University *M, T*
Liberty University *B, D, T*
Marymount University *M*
Regent University *M, T*

Washington
Eastern Washington University *M*
Evergreen State College *M*
Gonzaga University *M*
Northwest University *T*
Seattle Pacific University *M*
Seattle University *M*
University of Washington *T*
Washington State
    University *B, M, D, T*
Whitworth University *B, M, T*

Wisconsin
St. Norbert College *T*
University of Wisconsin
    Green Bay *T*
    River Falls *B, T*

Ethics

Alaska
University of Alaska
    Anchorage *C*

Arizona
Arizona State University *M*

California
University of Southern
    California *B, M, D*

District of Columbia
American University *M*

Florida
University of North Florida *M*

Indiana
Valparaiso University *M*

Iowa
Drake University *B*

Maryland
University of Maryland
    Baltimore County *M*

Massachusetts
Bridgewater State College *B*

Michigan
University of Michigan
    Flint *B*

Missouri
Webster University *B*

Nevada
University of Nevada
    Las Vegas *M*

New York
Wells College *B*

North Carolina
University of North Carolina
    Charlotte *M*

Oregon
Oregon State University *C, M*

Pennsylvania
Carnegie Mellon University *B*
Duquesne University *M*

Tennessee
Union University *B*

Washington
University of Washington Bothell *B*

Wisconsin
Marquette University *D*

Ethnic studies, general

California
College of Marin: Kentfield *A*
Mills College *B*
San Francisco State University *M*
Santa Ana College *A*
University of California
    Riverside *B*

Colorado
Colorado State University *B, M*
University of Colorado
    Boulder *B*
    Colorado Springs *B*

Georgia
Columbus State University *C*

Idaho
Boise State University *B*

Kansas
Wichita State University *B*

Massachusetts
Bard College at Simon's Rock *B*
Hampshire College *B*
Stonehill College *B*

Minnesota
Metropolitan State University *B*

Nebraska
University of Nebraska
    Lincoln *B*

Nevada
Nevada State College *B*

Oregon
Oregon State University *B*
University of Oregon *B*

Texas
Baptist University of the Americas *A*
University of Texas
    Austin *B*

Vermont
Goddard College *B, M*

Virginia
College of William and Mary *B*

Washington
Green River Community College *C*

European history

California
Pitzer College *B*

Massachusetts
Elms College *B*
Salem State College *B*
Suffolk University *B*

Michigan
Calvin College *B*
Central Michigan University *M*

New Hampshire
Keene State College *B*

New York
Bard College *B*
United States Military Academy *B*

Pennsylvania
Carnegie Mellon University *B*
Gettysburg College *B*
Lycoming College *B*

Puerto Rico
University of Puerto Rico
    Aguadilla *A*
    Rio Piedras *B*

Rhode Island
Salve Regina University *B*

South Carolina
Charleston Southern University *B*

Tennessee
Southern Adventist University *B*

Vermont
Bennington College *B*

Wisconsin
Carroll University *B*
Marquette University *M, D*

European studies

California
California State University
    Fullerton *B*
Claremont McKenna College *B*
Loyola Marymount University *B*
Pepperdine University *B*
Pitzer College *B*
St. Mary's College of California *B*
San Diego State University *B*
Scripps College *B*
University of California
    Irvine *B*
    Los Angeles *B*
Westmont College *B*

Connecticut
Yale University *B, M, D*

District of Columbia
George Washington University *B*

Florida
New College of Florida *B*

Georgia
Georgia Southern University *T*

Illinois
Northwestern University *B*

Kansas
University of Kansas *B*

Kentucky
Georgetown College *B*

Massachusetts
Amherst College *B*
Bard College at Simon's Rock *B*
Brandeis University *B*
Hampshire College *B*
Mount Holyoke College *B*
Tufts University *B, M*
Wellesley College *B*

Michigan
Central Michigan University *B*
Hillsdale College *B*

Minnesota
University of Minnesota
Morris *B*
Twin Cities *B*

Mississippi
Millsaps College *B*

Missouri
University of Missouri
Columbia *B*
Washington University in St.
Louis *B, M*

New Hampshire
University of New Hampshire *B*

New Mexico
University of New Mexico *B*

New York
Barnard College *B*
Canisius College *B*
Columbia University *B*
Hobart and William Smith Colleges *B*
New York University *B, M*
State University of New York
Stony Brook *B*
United States Military Academy *B*

North Carolina
Queens University of Charlotte *B*
University of North Carolina
Chapel Hill *B*

Ohio
Bowling Green State University *B*
Ohio University *B*
University of Toledo *B*
Wittenberg University *B*

Oregon
Portland State University *B*

Pennsylvania
Carnegie Mellon University *B*
Saint Joseph's University *B*

Rhode Island
Brown University *B*

South Carolina
University of South Carolina *B*

Tennessee
Vanderbilt University *B*

Texas
Southern Methodist University *B*
Texas State University: San Marcos *B*
Trinity University *B*
University of Texas
Austin *B*

Utah
Brigham Young University *B*

Vermont
Bennington College *B*
Goddard College *B*
Marlboro College *B*
Middlebury College *B*
University of Vermont *B*

Virginia
Emory & Henry College *B*
University of Richmond *B*

Washington
Gonzaga University *B*
Seattle Pacific University *B*
University of Washington *B, M*

Wisconsin
Carroll University *B*

Evolutionary biology

California
San Diego State University *M*
University of California
Davis *B*
Irvine *B, M, D*
San Diego *B*
University of Southern California *D*

Connecticut
Yale University *M, D*

Illinois
University of Chicago *D*

Indiana
Indiana University
Bloomington *M, D*

Louisiana
Tulane University *B, M, D*

Massachusetts
Harvard College *B, D*
University of Massachusetts
Amherst *M, D*

Missouri
Washington University in St. Louis *D*

New Hampshire
Dartmouth College *B*

New York
Columbia University *B*
Columbia University
School of General Studies *B*
Cornell University *M, D*
University of Rochester *B*

Ohio
Case Western Reserve University *B*

Oklahoma
University of Oklahoma *D*

Texas
Angelo State University *B*
Rice University *B, M, D*

Vermont
Bennington College *B*

Washington
Western Washington University *B*

Executive assistant

Arkansas
University of Arkansas
Fort Smith *C, A*

California
Grossmont College *C, A*
Shasta College *A*

Colorado
Pikes Peak Community College *A*

Florida
Central Florida Community
College *C, A*
Daytona State College *C, A*
Hillsborough Community
College *C, A*
Lake-Sumter Community College *C, A*

Georgia
West Georgia Technical College *A*

Illinois
Danville Area Community College *A*
Elgin Community College *A*
Harper College *C, A*
John A. Logan College *A*
John Wood Community College *A*
Kaskaskia College *A*
Moraine Valley Community College *C*
Parkland College *A*
Triton College *A*
Waubonsee Community College *C, A*

Indiana
Ivy Tech Community College
Bloomington *C, A*
Central Indiana *C, A*
Columbus *C, A*
East Central *C, A*
Kokomo *C, A*
Lafayette *C, A*
North Central *C, A*
Northeast *C, A*
Northwest *C, A*
Richmond *C, A*
South Central *C, A*
Southeast *C, A*
Southwest *C, A*
Wabash Valley *C, A*

Iowa
Hawkeye Community College *A*
Southeastern Community College
North Campus *A*

Kansas
Central Christian College of Kansas *A*
Manhattan Area Technical
College *C, A*

Kentucky
Bluegrass Community and Technical
College *C, A*
Elizabethtown Community and
Technical College *C, A*
Hopkinsville Community College *C, A*
Maysville Community and Technical
College *C, A*
Murray State University *C*
Owensboro Community and
Technical College *C*
Somerset Community College *A*

Spencerian College *C*
West Kentucky Community and
Technical College *C*
Western Kentucky University *A*

Louisiana
ITI Technical College *A*

Maryland
Hagerstown Community College *C*

Massachusetts
Cape Cod Community College *C, A*
Mount Wachusett Community
College *A*
North Shore Community College *A*
Springfield Technical Community
College *A*

Michigan
Davenport University *A*
Grand Rapids Community College *A*
Henry Ford Community College *C, A*
Kuyper College *A*
Montcalm Community College *A*
Mott Community College *C, A*
Northwestern Michigan College *C*
Schoolcraft College *A*
Southwestern Michigan College *A*

Minnesota
Dakota County Technical College *A*
Minnesota West Community and
Technical College *A*
St. Cloud Technical College *A*

Missouri
Pinnacle Career Institute: Kansas
City *A*

Montana
Flathead Valley Community College *A*

New York
Broome Community College *A*
Globe Institute of Technology *C*
Utica School of Commerce *A*

North Carolina
Cape Fear Community College *A*
Forsyth Technical Community
College *C, A*
Guilford Technical Community
College *A*
Lenoir Community College *C, A*
Martin Community College *C, A*
Wilson Community College *C*

North Dakota
Lake Region State College *C, A*
North Dakota State College of
Science *A*

Ohio
Bowling Green State University *B*
Cincinnati State Technical and
Community College *A*
Edison State Community College *C, A*
Marion Technical College *C, A*
Owens Community College
Toledo *C, A*
Stark State College of Technology *A*
University of Akron *C*
University of Cincinnati
Raymond Walters College *A*

Oregon
Umpqua Community College *A*

Pennsylvania

Consolidated School of Business
  Lancaster *A*
  York *A*
Newport Business Institute: Lower
  Burrell *A*
Westmoreland County Community
  College *A*

Puerto Rico

Universidad del Este *A*
University of Puerto Rico
  Aguadilla *A*
  Bayamon University College *B*

South Dakota

Kilian Community College *A*

Texas

Alvin Community College *A*
Brookhaven College *A*
El Centro College *A*
Kilgore College *C, A*
Mountain View College *C, A*

Utah

LDS Business College *C, A*
Utah Valley University *A*

Virginia

Danville Community College *A*

Washington

Bellingham Technical College *C, A*
Clark College *C, A*

West Virginia

West Virginia University at
  Parkersburg *C, A*

Exercise physiology

California

Bryan College: Sacramento *A*
University of California
  Davis *B, M*

Colorado

Colorado State University *D*

Florida

University of Miami *M, D*

Kansas

Central Christian College of
  Kansas *A, B*

Massachusetts

Fitchburg State College *B*
Gordon College *B*
University of Massachusetts
  Amherst *B, M, D*

Michigan

Eastern Michigan University *M*

Minnesota

College of St. Scholastica *B, M*

Missouri

Drury University *B*
University of Missouri
  Columbia *M, D*

New York

State University of New York
  Buffalo *B, M, D*
  College at Brockport *B*

North Carolina

East Carolina University *B*
Methodist University *B*

Ohio

Baldwin-Wallace College *B*
Ohio Northern University *B*

Oklahoma

Hillsdale Free Will Baptist College *B*

Oregon

Northwest Christian University *B*

Pennsylvania

Temple University *M, D*

Puerto Rico

University of Puerto Rico
  Rio Piedras *M*

Texas

Baylor University *B*

Utah

Brigham Young University *B*

Virginia

Bluefield College *B*
Lynchburg College *B*
Virginia Commonwealth University *D*

Washington

Washington State University *M*

West Virginia

West Virginia University *B, M, D*

Wisconsin

Concordia University Wisconsin *B*
Marquette University *M, D*

Exercise sciences

Alabama

Auburn University *B, M, D*
Huntingdon College *B*
Samford University *B*
University of Alabama *D*

Arizona

Arizona State University *B, M, D*
Central Arizona College *C, A*
Glendale Community College *C, A*
Northern Arizona University *B, M*
Scottsdale Community College *C*

Arkansas

Arkansas State University *B, M*
Harding University *B*
Hendrix College *B*
John Brown University *B*
Ouachita Baptist University *B*
Southern Arkansas University *B*
University of Arkansas *M, D*
University of Central Arkansas *B, M*

California

Biola University *B*
California Baptist University *B, M*
California State University
  Chico *B*
  East Bay *B, M*
  Fresno *A, B*
  San Bernardino *B, M*
Concordia University *B*
Diablo Valley College *C*
Fremont College *A*
Grossmont College *C, A*
La Sierra University *B*

MiraCosta College *C*
Notre Dame de Namur University *B*
Occidental College *B*
Pacific Union College *B*
Pepperdine University *B*
Point Loma Nazarene University *B*
St. Mary's College of California *B*
San Diego State University *M*
San Francisco State University *B, M*
Santa Ana College *A*
Santa Barbara City College *A*
University of San Francisco *B*
University of Southern
  California *B, M, D*
Vanguard University of Southern
  California *B*
Westmont College *B*

Colorado

Adams State College *B, M*
Colorado State University *B, M*
Colorado State University
  Pueblo *B*
Fort Lewis College *B*
Mesa State College *B*
Metropolitan State College of
  Denver *B*
University of Northern
  Colorado *B, M, D, T*
Western State College of
  Colorado *B, T*

Connecticut

Manchester Community College *A*
Southern Connecticut State
  University *B, M, T*

Delaware

Delaware Technical and Community
  College
  Stanton/Wilmington *A*
University of Delaware *B, M, D*

District of Columbia

George Washington University *B, M*

Florida

Barry University *B, M*
Clearwater Christian College *B*
Florida Atlantic University *B, M*
Florida Gulf Coast University *B*
Florida State University *B*
Jacksonville University *B*
Miami Dade College *A*
University of Florida *B, M, D*
University of Miami *B*
University of Tampa *B*
Warner University *B*

Georgia

Berry College *B*
Columbus State University *B*
Darton College *A*
East Georgia College *A*
Emmanuel College *B*
Georgia Southern University *B, M*
Georgia State University *B, M*
Kennesaw State University *B, M*
Life University *B, M*
Morehouse College *B*
University of Georgia *M, D*

Hawaii

University of Hawaii
  Manoa *B, M*

Idaho

Boise State University *B, M*
College of Idaho *B*
Lewis-Clark State College *B*
Northwest Nazarene University *B*
University of Idaho *B*

Illinois

Benedictine University *M*
Concordia University Chicago *B*
Eastern Illinois University *B, M, T*
Elgin Community College *C*
Elmhurst College *B*
Greenville College *B*
Illinois State University *B*
Moraine Valley Community College *C*
North Central College *B*
Northeastern Illinois University *M*
Olivet Nazarene University *B*
Southern Illinois University
  Carbondale *B, M*
Southern Illinois University
  Edwardsville *B*
Trinity Christian College *B*
Triton College *C*
University of Illinois
  Chicago *B, M, D*
  Urbana-Champaign *B, M, D*
Waubonsee Community College *C*
Western Illinois University *B, M*

Indiana

Anderson University *B*
DePauw University *B*
Hanover College *B*
Huntington University *B*
Indiana University
  Bloomington *D*
Indiana University-Purdue University
  Indianapolis *B*
Indiana Wesleyan University *B*
Ivy Tech Community College
  Bloomington *A*
Purdue University *B, M, D*
Taylor University *B*
University of Evansville *B*
University of Indianapolis *B*
University of Southern Indiana *B*
Valparaiso University *B*

Iowa

Briar Cliff University *B*
Buena Vista University *B*
Central College *B, T*
Cornell College *B*
Dordt College *B*
Iowa State University *B, M, D*
Iowa Wesleyan College *B*
Loras College *B*
Northwestern College *B*
St. Ambrose University *B*
Simpson College *B*
University of Iowa *B, M, D*

Kansas

Baker University *B*
Barton County Community College *A*
Central Christian College of
  Kansas *A, B*
Kansas State University *B, M*
MidAmerica Nazarene University *B*
Neosho County Community
  College *A*
Seward County Community College *A*
Washburn University *B*
Wichita State University *B*

Kentucky

Bellarmine University *B*
Berea College *B*
Campbellsville University *B*
Georgetown College *B*
Morehead State University *B*
Murray State University *B*
Thomas More College *A*
Transylvania University *B, T*
University of Louisville *M*
Western Kentucky University *B*

Louisiana

Centenary College of Louisiana *B*
McNeese State University *B, M*
University of Louisiana at
Monroe *B, M*

Maine

Saint Joseph's College of Maine *B*
University of New England *B*
University of Southern Maine *B*

Maryland

Carroll Community College *A*
Frostburg State University *B*
Howard Community College *C, A*
McDaniel College *B*
Montgomery College *A*
Salisbury University *B*
Towson University *B, M*
University of Maryland
College Park *B, M, D*
Eastern Shore *B*

Massachusetts

Boston University *B, M*
Bridgewater State College *B*
Fitchburg State College *B*
Lasell College *B*
Northeastern University *M*
Salem State College *B*
Smith College *M*
Springfield College *B, M*

Michigan

Adrian College *B*
Alma College *B*
Calvin College *B*
Central Michigan University *B, M*
Cornerstone University *B*
Henry Ford Community College *A*
Hope College *B*
Kuyper College *B*
Lake Superior State University *B*
Michigan State University *B, M, D*
Michigan Technological University *B*
Northern Michigan University *B, M*
Oakland Community College *C, A*
Oakland University *M*
Saginaw Valley State University *B*
University of Michigan *B, M, D*
Wayne State University *D*
Western Michigan University *B, M*

Minnesota

Bethel University *B*
Concordia College: Moorhead *B*
Concordia University: St. Paul *B*
Dakota County Technical College *C, A*
Globe University *C, A, B*
Hamline University *B*
Mesabi Range Community and
Technical College *A*
Minnesota State University
Mankato *B, M, T*
Moorhead *B*
Northwestern College *B*
St. Catherine University *B*
Saint Cloud State University *M*
St. Olaf College *B*
University of Minnesota
Duluth *B*
Winona State University *B*

Mississippi

Belhaven University *B*
Mississippi College *B*
University of Mississippi *B, M, D*

Missouri

Drury University *B*
Lindenwood University *B*
Missouri State University *B*

Missouri Valley College *B*
Pinnacle Career Institute: Kansas
City *C*
Rockhurst University *B*
Saint Louis University *B*
Truman State University *B*
University of Missouri
Columbia *B, M, D*

Montana

Rocky Mountain College *B*
University of Montana *B, M*

Nebraska

Concordia University *B*
Creighton University *B*
Nebraska Wesleyan University *B*
University of Nebraska
Lincoln *B*
Omaha *B*
Wayne State College *B*

Nevada

University of Nevada
Las Vegas *B, M*

New Hampshire

Colby-Sawyer College *B*
Manchester Community College *C, A*
New England College *B*
University of New Hampshire *B, M*

New Jersey

Bergen Community College *C*
Georgian Court University *B*
Gloucester County College *A*
Kean University *M*
Ocean County College *C*
Raritan Valley Community College *A*
Rutgers, The State University of New
Jersey
New Brunswick/Piscataway
Campus *B*
William Paterson University of New
Jersey *B, T*

New York

City University of New York
Brooklyn College *B, M*
Kingsborough Community
College *C, A*
Queens College *B, M*
Dutchess Community College *A*
Ithaca College *B, M*
Long Island University
Brooklyn Campus *B, M*
Orange County Community College *A*
Skidmore College *B*
State University of New York
College at Cortland *B, M*
College of Agriculture and
Technology at Morrisville *A*
Syracuse University *B, M*
United States Military Academy *B*

North Carolina

Appalachian State University *B, M*
Brevard College *B*
Campbell University *B, T*
Chowan University *B*
East Carolina University *B, M*
Elon University *B*
Greensboro College *C, B*
Guilford College *B*
High Point University *B*
Meredith College *B*
Methodist University *B*
Shaw University *B*
University of North Carolina
Greensboro *B, M, D*
Wake Forest University *B, M*
Winston-Salem State University *B*

North Dakota

University of Mary *B*
University of North Dakota *M*

Ohio

Capital University *B*
Cedarville University *B*
Cincinnati State Technical and
Community College *C*
Cleveland State University *M*
Columbus State Community
College *A*
Malone University *B*
Miami University
Oxford Campus *B, M*
Mount Union College *B*
Mount Vernon Nazarene University *B*
Ohio State University
Columbus Campus *B*
Ohio University *B, M*
University of Akron *B*
University of Dayton *B, M*
University of Findlay *B*
University of Toledo *B, M, D*
Urbana University *B*
Youngstown State University *B*

Oklahoma

Bacone College *B*
East Central University *B*
Northeastern State University *B, M*
Oklahoma Baptist University *B*
Oklahoma Wesleyan University *B*
Oral Roberts University *B*
Redlands Community College *A*
St. Gregory's University *B*
Southern Nazarene University *B*
University of Central Oklahoma *B, M*
University of Oklahoma *B, M, D*
University of Tulsa *B*

Oregon

Linfield College *B*
Mt. Hood Community College *C, A*
Oregon State University *M*
Pacific University *B*
Warner Pacific College *B*
Willamette University *B*

Pennsylvania

Bloomsburg University of
Pennsylvania *M*
Cabrini College *B*
Chatham University *B*
DeSales University *B*
East Stroudsburg University of
Pennsylvania *B*
Eastern University *B*
Gannon University *B*
Gettysburg College *B*
Immaculata University *B*
Marywood University *M*
Messiah College *B*
Penn State
Abington *B*
Altoona *B*
Beaver *B*
Berks *B*
Brandywine *B*
DuBois *B*
Erie, The Behrend College *B*
Fayette, The Eberly Campus *B*
Greater Allegheny *B*
Hazleton *B*
Lehigh Valley *B*
Mont Alto *B*
New Kensington *B*
Schuylkill *B*
Shenango *B*
University Park *B, M, D*
Wilkes-Barre *B*
Worthington Scranton *B*
York *B*

Pennsylvania College of
Technology *B*
Shippensburg University of
Pennsylvania *B*
Slippery Rock University of
Pennsylvania *B*
Temple University *B, M, D*
Waynesburg University *B*
Wilson College *B*

Puerto Rico

Inter American University of Puerto
Rico
San German Campus *M*

South Carolina

Anderson University *B*
The Citadel *M*
Coastal Carolina University *B*
Coker College *B*
Furman University *B*
Lander University *B*
University of South Carolina *B, M, D*
University of South Carolina
Aiken *B*

South Dakota

Augustana College *B*
Black Hills State University *B*
Dakota State University *B*
Dakota Wesleyan University *B*
University of Sioux Falls *B*

Tennessee

Belmont University *B*
Bryan College *B, T*
Carson-Newman College *B*
Free Will Baptist Bible College *B*
Freed-Hardeman University *B*
Lipscomb University *B, M*
Middle Tennessee State University *M*
Southern Adventist University *B*
Trevecca Nazarene University *B*
Union University *B*
University of Memphis *B, M*
University of Tennessee
Chattanooga *B, M*
Knoxville *B, M, D*

Texas

Baylor University *D*
Blinn College *A*
Clarendon College *A*
Concordia University Texas *B*
Hardin-Simmons University *B*
Houston Baptist University *B*
Howard Payne University *B*
LeTourneau University *B*
Lubbock Christian University *B*
McMurry University *B*
Midland College *A*
Midwestern State University *B*
Northwest Vista College *A*
Palo Alto College *A*
Rice University *B*
St. Edward's University *B*
St. Mary's University *B, T*
Schreiner University *B*
South Texas College *A*
Texas A&M University *D*
Texas Christian University *M*
Texas Lutheran University *B*
Tyler Junior College *A*
University of Houston *B*
University of Texas
Arlington *M*
Austin *M, D*
San Antonio *M*
Tyler *M*
University of the Incarnate Word *B, M*

Utah

Brigham Young University *M, D*

University of Utah *B, M, D, T*
Utah Career College *A, B*
Weber State University *B*

Vermont
Castleton State College *B*
Johnson State College *B*
Lyndon State College *B*
University of Vermont *B*

Virginia
Bluefield College *B*
College of William and Mary *B*
Jefferson College of Health
Sciences *B*
Liberty University *B*
Longwood University *B*
Marymount University *B*
Norfolk State University *B*
Old Dominion University *B, M, D*
University of Virginia *B, M, D*

Washington
Bastyr University *B*
Eastern Washington University *B*
Seattle Pacific University *B*
University of Puget Sound *B*
Washington State University *B, M*

West Virginia
Davis and Elkins College *B*
Fairmont State University *B*
Marshall University *B, M*
West Liberty University *B*
West Virginia University *B, M, D*
West Virginia Wesleyan College *B*

Wisconsin
Carroll University *B*
Carthage College *B*
Marquette University *B*
Ripon College *B*
University of Wisconsin
Eau Claire *B*
La Crosse *B, M*
Madison *B, M, D*
Milwaukee *B, M*
Viterbo University *B*
Wisconsin Lutheran College *B*

Wyoming
University of Wyoming *B, M*
Western Wyoming Community
College *C, A*

Experimental psychology

California
California State University
San Bernardino *M*
St. Mary's College of California *B*

Connecticut
University of Hartford *M*

District of Columbia
American University *D*
Catholic University of America *M, D*

Florida
Florida Atlantic University *D*

Georgia
Paine College *B*

Illinois
DePaul University *M, D*
Loyola University Chicago *D*

Iowa
University of Iowa *D*

Kansas
Wichita State University *D*

Kentucky
University of Kentucky *M, D*
University of Louisville *M, D*

Maine
University of Maine *M, D*

Massachusetts
Tufts University *M, D*

Michigan
Central Michigan University *D*
Northern Michigan University *B, M*

Missouri
Saint Louis University *M, D*
University of Missouri
Columbia *M, D*

New Hampshire
Keene State College *B*

New Jersey
Fairleigh Dickinson University
College at Florham *M*
Seton Hall University *M*

New York
City University of New York
Brooklyn College *M*
Fordham University *D*
New York University *D*
St. John's University *M*
State University of New York
Stony Brook *D*
Syracuse University *M, D*
University of Rochester *B, M, D*

North Carolina
Duke University *M, D*

Ohio
Bowling Green State University *M, D*
Case Western Reserve University *D*
Kent State University *M, D*
Ohio University *M, D*
Tiffin University *B*
University of Dayton *M*

Oklahoma
University of Central Oklahoma *M*

Pennsylvania
Temple University *D*

Rhode Island
University of Rhode Island *D*

South Carolina
University of South Carolina *B, M, D*

Texas
Texas Tech University *M, D*
University of Houston *M*
University of North Texas *M, D*
University of Texas
Arlington *D*
El Paso *M*
Pan American *M*
of the Permian Basin *M*

Wisconsin
Marquette University *M*

University of Wisconsin
Madison *M, D*
Oshkosh *M*

Facial treatment

Florida
Central Florida Community College *C*
Palm Beach Community College *C*

North Carolina
Cape Fear Community College *C*

Texas
Houston Community College
System *C*
Lone Star College System *C*
San Jacinto College *C*

Facilities/event planning

California
California State University
East Bay *C*

Connecticut
Naugatuck Valley Community
College *A*

Michigan
Eastern Michigan University *B*

Puerto Rico
Universidad del Este *C, B*

Texas
Southern Methodist University *M*

Utah
Brigham Young University *B*

Family and consumer sciences

Alabama
Alabama Agricultural and Mechanical
University *B, M*
Faulkner State Community College *A*
Jacksonville State University *B*
Oakwood University *B*
University of Alabama *B, M*
University of Montevallo *B, T*
University of North Alabama *B*

Alaska
University of Alaska
Anchorage *A, B*

Arizona
Arizona Western College *C, A*
Phoenix College *A*

Arkansas
Harding University *B, T*
Henderson State University *B*
University of Arkansas *M*
University of Arkansas
Pine Bluff *B*
University of Central Arkansas *B, M*

California
Allan Hancock College *A*
American River College *C, A*
Antelope Valley College *A*
Bakersfield College *A*
Butte College *C, A*
Cabrillo College *C, A*
California State University
Fresno *B*

Long Beach *B, M*
Northridge *B, M*
Sacramento *B, M*
Canada College *A*
Cerritos College *A*
Chaffey College *C, A*
College of the Sequoias *A*
El Camino College *A*
El Camino College: Compton
Center *A*
Fresno City College *A*
Fullerton College *A*
Glendale Community College *A*
Long Beach City College *C, A*
Los Angeles City College *A*
Los Angeles Valley College *A*
The Master's College *B*
Merced College *A*
Modesto Junior College *A*
Monterey Peninsula College *A*
Moorpark College *A*
Mount San Antonio College *A*
Orange Coast College *A*
Point Loma Nazarene University *B*
Riverside Community College *C, A*
Sacramento City College *C, A*
Saddleback College *C, A*
San Francisco State University *B, M*
San Joaquin Delta College *A*
Santa Monica College *C, A*
Santiago Canyon College *A*
Shasta College *A*
Sierra College *A*
Skyline College *C, A*
Solano Community College *C, A*
Ventura College *C, A*

Colorado
Colorado State University *B*

Connecticut
Saint Joseph College *B*

Delaware
University of Delaware *B*

District of Columbia
Gallaudet University *B*
University of the District of
Columbia *B*

Florida
Florida State University *B*
Northwest Florida State College *A*
Palm Beach Community College *A*

Georgia
Abraham Baldwin Agricultural
College *A*
Dalton State College *A*
East Georgia College *A*
Fort Valley State University *B*
University of Georgia *M*

Hawaii
University of Hawaii
Manoa *B*

Idaho
Idaho State University *B*
University of Idaho *B, M*

Illinois
Bradley University *B*
Eastern Illinois University *B, M, T*
Illinois Central College *A*
Illinois State University *B, M, T*
Kishwaukee College *A*
Lake Land College *A*
Olivet Nazarene University *B, T*
Western Illinois University *B*

Indiana
Ball State University *B, M*
Indiana State University *B, M, T*
Purdue University *B, M, D*
Vincennes University *A*

Iowa
Ellsworth Community College *A*
Iowa State University *B, M*
Marshalltown Community College *A*
North Iowa Area Community
    College *A*

Kansas
Coffeyville Community College *A*
Garden City Community College *A*
Hutchinson Community College *A*
Kansas State University *B, D*
Neosho County Community
    College *A*
Pittsburg State University *B*

Kentucky
Berea College *B*
University of Kentucky *B*

Louisiana
Louisiana State University and
    Agricultural and Mechanical
    College *B, M, D*
Louisiana Tech University *M*
McNeese State University *B*
Nicholls State University *B*
Northwestern State University *B*
Southeastern Louisiana University *B*
Southern University and Agricultural
    and Mechanical College *B*
University of Louisiana at Lafayette *M*

Maine
York County Community College *A*

Maryland
University of Maryland
    Eastern Shore *B*

Massachusetts
Framingham State College *B*

Michigan
Lansing Community College *A*
Madonna University *B*
Michigan State University *B, D*

Minnesota
Minnesota State University
    Mankato *B, M, T*
St. Catherine University *B*
University of Minnesota
    Twin Cities *B, M, D*
Vermilion Community College *A*

Mississippi
Delta State University *B*
Hinds Community College *A*
Mississippi Delta Community
    College *A*
Mississippi State University *B*

Missouri
College of the Ozarks *B*
Missouri State University *B*
Southeast Missouri State University *B*
University of Central Missouri *B*
University of Missouri
    Columbia *D*

Montana
Little Big Horn College *A*
Miles Community College *A*

Montana State University
    Bozeman *B, M*

Nebraska
Central Community College *C, A*
Chadron State College *B*
University of Nebraska
    Kearney *B*
    Lincoln *B, M, D*
    Omaha *B*
Wayne State College *B*

New Jersey
Montclair State University *B, M, T*

New Mexico
Eastern New Mexico University *B*
University of New Mexico *B, M, D*

New York
City University of New York
    Queens College *B, T*
Cornell University *B*
State University of New York
    College at Oneonta *B*

North Carolina
Appalachian State University *M*
Meredith College *B*
North Carolina Agricultural and
    Technical State University *B, T*
North Carolina Central
    University *B, M*
North Carolina State University *M*

Ohio
Bowling Green State University *B*
Mount Vernon Nazarene
    University *A, B*
Ohio State University
    Columbus Campus *B, M, D*
Youngstown State University *B*

Oklahoma
Cameron University *B*
Connors State College *A*
East Central University *B*
Langston University *B*
Northeastern State University *B*
Oklahoma State University *M, D*
Rose State College *A*
University of Central Oklahoma *B*

Oregon
Chemeketa Community College *A*
George Fox University *B*
Linn-Benton Community College *A*

Pennsylvania
Indiana University of Pennsylvania *B*
Keystone College *B*
Seton Hill University *B*
University of Pittsburgh
    Titusville *A*

Puerto Rico
Pontifical Catholic University of
    Puerto Rico *B*
University of Puerto Rico
    Rio Piedras *B, M*

South Carolina
Bob Jones University *B*
South Carolina State University *B*

Tennessee
East Tennessee State University *B, T*
Lambuth University *B*
Lipscomb University *B*
Middle Tennessee State University *M*
Tennessee State University *B, M*

Tennessee Technological
    University *B, T*
University of Tennessee
    Chattanooga *B*
    Knoxville *M, D*
    Martin *B, M*

Texas
Baylor University *B*
Brazosport College *A*
Coastal Bend College *A*
Lamar State College at Port Arthur *A*
Lamar University *B, M*
Laredo Community College *A*
Prairie View A&M University *M*
Sam Houston State University *B, M*
South Plains College *A*
Stephen F. Austin State
    University *B, M*
Tarleton State University *B, T*
Texas A&M University
    Kingsville *B, M*
Texas Southern University *B, M*
Texas State University: San
    Marcos *B, T*
Texas Tech University *B*
Texas Woman's University *B*
Tyler Junior College *A*
University of Houston *B*
University of Texas
    Austin *B*

Utah
Brigham Young University *B, M, D*
Snow College *A*
Southern Utah University *B, T*
Utah State University *M*

Virginia
Bridgewater College *B*
Liberty University *B, T*

Washington
Highline Community College *A*
Washington State University *B*

West Virginia
Fairmont State University *B*
Marshall University *B, M*
Shepherd University *B*
West Virginia University *B, M, T*

Wisconsin
University of Wisconsin
    Madison *B, M, D*

Wyoming
University of Wyoming *B, M*
Western Wyoming Community
    College *A*

Family/community services

Alabama
Faulkner University *B*

Arizona
Arizona State University *M*
Glendale Community College *A*
Prescott College *B*
University of Phoenix *A*

Arkansas
John Brown University *B*

California
California State University
    Northridge *B*
College of the Siskiyous *C, A*
Fresno City College *C*

Loma Linda University *M, D*
Merritt College *C, A*
Modesto Junior College *A*
Monterey Peninsula College *A*
Sacramento City College *C, A*
Santa Ana College *A*
Southwestern College *C*
Yuba Community College
    District *C, A*

Delaware
University of Delaware *B, M, D*

Florida
University of Florida *B, M*
University of Miami *B*

Illinois
Olivet Nazarene University *B, T*
Shawnee Community College *A*

Indiana
Purdue University *B, M, D*

Iowa
Ellsworth Community College *A*
Iowa State University *B*
University of Northern Iowa *B*

Maine
Beal College *A*
University of Maine *C, B*

Maryland
Stevenson University *B*
University of Maryland
    College Park *B, M, D*

Michigan
Michigan State University *B, M*

Minnesota
Capella University *M, D*
Minnesota State University
    Mankato *B, M, T*

New Hampshire
University of New Hampshire *A, B*

New York
Iona College *M*

North Carolina
East Carolina University *B, M*
North Carolina Agricultural and
    Technical State University *B*

Ohio
Bowling Green State University *B*
Columbus State Community
    College *C*
James A. Rhodes State College *A*
Ohio State University
    Columbus Campus *B, M, D*
Youngstown State University *B*

Oregon
Blue Mountain Community College *A*

Pennsylvania
Community College of Philadelphia *C*
Messiah College *B*

South Carolina
Clemson University *D*

Tennessee
Carson-Newman College *B, T*
Tennessee Technological University *B*

University of Tennessee
Knoxville M

Texas

Lamar University B
Texas Tech University B

Utah

Snow College C, A
University of Utah M

Vermont

Champlain College B

Washington

Washington State University C

West Virginia

West Virginia University B

Wisconsin

University of Wisconsin
Stevens Point M

Family/consumer business sciences

California

California State University
Northridge B
Skyline College C, A

Illinois

Northern Illinois University M

Nebraska

University of Nebraska
Kearney B

Oklahoma

Connors State College A

Texas

Our Lady of the Lake University of San
Antonio B, M
University of Houston B

Virginia

Virginia Polytechnic Institute and
State University B, M, D

Family/consumer sciences education

Alabama

Oakwood University B

Arizona

Phoenix College A
University of Arizona B

Arkansas

Harding University B, T
University of Arkansas
Pine Bluff B
University of Central Arkansas B

California

California State University
Long Beach B, T
Northridge B, T
The Master's College T
Saddleback College A
San Francisco State University T

Colorado

Colorado State University B, T

Connecticut

Saint Joseph College T

Delaware

University of Delaware B, T

District of Columbia

Gallaudet University B, T

Georgia

Fort Valley State University B, T
University of Georgia B

Idaho

Brigham Young University-Idaho T
University of Idaho B, T

Illinois

Bradley University B, M
Northern Illinois University B
Olivet Nazarene University B, T

Indiana

Purdue University B, M, D
Vincennes University A

Iowa

Ellsworth Community College A
Grand View University T
Iowa State University B, M, D, T

Kansas

Kansas State University B
Pittsburg State University B, T

Kentucky

Berea College B, T
Eastern Kentucky University B
Western Kentucky University B, T

Louisiana

Louisiana State University and
Agricultural and Mechanical
College B
McNeese State University B, T
Northwestern State University B
Southeastern Louisiana University B
University of Louisiana at Lafayette B
University of Louisiana at Monroe B

Michigan

Central Michigan University B
Ferris State University B
Michigan State University B
Western Michigan University B, M, T

Minnesota

Minnesota State University
Mankato B, M, T
St. Catherine University B, T
University of Minnesota
Twin Cities M, T

Mississippi

Mississippi State University T
Northwest Mississippi Community
College A

Missouri

College of the Ozarks B, T
Fontbonne University B, M, T
Missouri State University B
Northwest Missouri State
University B, T
Southeast Missouri State
University B, M, T
University of Central Missouri B

Nebraska

Chadron State College B

Concordia University B, T
University of Nebraska
Kearney B, T
Wayne State College B, T

Nevada

University of Nevada
Reno B, T

New Jersey

Saint Peter's College T

New Mexico

New Mexico State University B

New York

City University of New York
Queens College B, M, T
Cornell University B, M, T
State University of New York
College at Oneonta B, T

North Carolina

Appalachian State University B, M, T
East Carolina University B
Meredith College T
North Carolina Agricultural and
Technical State University B, T
North Carolina Central
University B, M, T

North Dakota

North Dakota State University B, M, T

Ohio

Ashland University B, T
Bowling Green State University B
Mount Vernon Nazarene
University B, T
Ohio State University
Columbus Campus M, D
Ohio University B
University of Akron B
Youngstown State University B, M

Oklahoma

East Central University B
Langston University B
University of Central Oklahoma B

Oregon

Oregon State University M

Pennsylvania

Immaculata University B
Marywood University B
Mercyhurst College B, T
Messiah College B, T
Seton Hill University B, T

Puerto Rico

Pontifical Catholic University of
Puerto Rico B, T
University of Puerto Rico
Rio Piedras B, M

South Carolina

South Carolina State University B, T

Tennessee

Carson-Newman College B
Tennessee Technological University T
University of Tennessee
Knoxville M, D

Texas

Lamar University B, M, T
Laredo Community College A
Prairie View A&M University M
Sam Houston State University M, T

Texas A&M University
Kingsville B
Texas Tech University M, D

Utah

Brigham Young University B
Snow College A
Southern Utah University B, T
Utah State University B

Vermont

University of Vermont B, T

Virginia

Bridgewater College T

Washington

Washington State University B, M, T

West Virginia

Fairmont State University B
Shepherd University T

Wisconsin

University of Wisconsin
Madison B
Stevens Point B, T
Stout B, M, T

Family practice nurse/ nurse practitioner

Alabama

Samford University M

Arizona

Northern Arizona University M
University of Phoenix M

California

Azusa Pacific University B
Holy Names University M
Samuel Merritt University M

Connecticut

Fairfield University M
Quinnipiac University M
Sacred Heart University M

Delaware

Wilmington University M

Florida

Florida Southern College M
University of Miami M

Georgia

Emory University D
Georgia College and State
University M
Georgia Southern University M, T
Georgia State University M
Kennesaw State University M
Medical College of Georgia M
North Georgia College & State
University M

Illinois

DePaul University M
Illinois State University M
Lewis University M
Loyola University Chicago M
Southern Illinois University
Edwardsville M

Indiana

Goshen College M
Indiana University-Purdue University
Indianapolis M
Indiana Wesleyan University M

University of St. Francis *M*

Iowa

Allen College *M*
Clarke College *M*
Graceland University *M*

Kansas

Pittsburg State University *M*

Kentucky

Bellarmine University *M, D*

Louisiana

Grambling State University *M*
Louisiana State University Health
  Sciences Center *M*
Loyola University New Orleans *M, D*
Southern University and Agricultural
  and Mechanical College *M*

Maine

Husson University *M*
University of Southern Maine *M*

Michigan

Grand Valley State University *M*
Madonna University *M*
Michigan State University *B, M*
Oakland University *M, D*
Saginaw Valley State University *M*
University of Detroit Mercy *M*

Minnesota

College of St. Scholastica *M*
Minnesota State University
  Moorhead *B, D*

Missouri

Maryville University of Saint Louis *M*
Research College of Nursing *M*

Nebraska

Clarkson College *M*

New Hampshire

Rivier College *M*

New Jersey

Felician College *M*

New York

City University of New York
  College of Staten Island *M*
  Hunter College *B, M*
College of New Rochelle *M*
Dominican College of Blauvelt *M*
Long Island University
  C. W. Post Campus *M*
Pace University *M, D*
St. John Fisher College *M, D*
State University of New York
  Binghamton *M*
  Buffalo *M*
  Stony Brook *M*
  Upstate Medical University *M*
University of Rochester *M*

North Carolina

University of North Carolina
  Wilmington *M*
Winston-Salem State University *M*

North Dakota

North Dakota State University *D*
University of Mary *M*

Ohio

Case Western Reserve University *M*
University of Toledo *M, T*
Ursuline College *M*

Oklahoma

University of Oklahoma *M*

Oregon

Oregon Health & Science
  University *M*

Pennsylvania

Carlow University *M*
DeSales University *M*
Duquesne University *M*
Gwynedd-Mercy College *M*
Millersville University of
  Pennsylvania *M*
University of Pennsylvania *M*
Widener University *D*

Puerto Rico

Turabo University *M*

South Dakota

South Dakota State University *T*

Tennessee

Southern Adventist University *M*
University of Tennessee
  Knoxville *M*
University of Tennessee Health
  Science Center *M*

Texas

Abilene Christian University *M*
Baylor University *M*
Hardin-Simmons University *M*
Midwestern State University *M*
Prairie View A&M University *M*
Texas A&M University
  Corpus Christi *B*
Texas Tech University Health Sciences
  Center *M*
Texas Woman's University *M*
University of Texas
  Arlington *M*
  El Paso *M*
  Medical Branch at Galveston *M*
  Pan American *M*
  Tyler *M*
West Texas A&M University *M*

Utah

Brigham Young University *M*
Westminster College *M*

Virginia

Marymount University *M*
Old Dominion University *D*

Washington

Seattle University *B, M*

West Virginia

Mountain State University *M*
West Virginia University *D*

Wisconsin

Concordia University Wisconsin *M*
Viterbo University *M*

Family psychology

Arizona

Northcentral University *M, D*
Southwestern College *B*

California

California Institute of Integral
  Studies *M, D*
Golden Gate University *M*

Michigan

Cornerstone University *B*
Wayne State University *M*

New Jersey

Seton Hall University *D*

Ohio

Union Institute & University *D*

Texas

Hardin-Simmons University *M*
University of Houston
  Clear Lake *M*

Family resource management studies

Alabama

University of Alabama *B*

Arizona

Arizona State University *B, M*
University of Arizona *M, D*

California

Antelope Valley College *C, A*
Long Beach City College *C, A*

Georgia

University of Georgia *B*

Idaho

University of Idaho *B, M*

Illinois

Black Hawk College *C*
Harper College *C*
Triton College *C*

Iowa

Iowa State University *B*

Kansas

Pittsburg State University *B*

Massachusetts

University of Massachusetts
  Amherst *B*

Missouri

University of Missouri
  Columbia *B, M*

Nebraska

University of Nebraska
  Omaha *B*

New Mexico

New Mexico State University *M*

Ohio

Ohio State University
  Columbus Campus *B, M, D*
Ohio University *B*

Oregon

Oregon State University *M, D*

South Dakota

South Dakota State University *B, M*

Tennessee

Middle Tennessee State University *B*

Texas

Texas Tech University *B, M*

Family systems

California

Azusa Pacific University *D*

Connecticut

University of Connecticut *D*

Florida

Florida State University *D*

Illinois

Black Hawk College *C*
Harper College *C*
Triton College *C*

Indiana

Anderson University *B*

Maryland

Towson University *B, M*

Michigan

Central Michigan University *B*
Cornerstone University *B*
Michigan State University *M*
Western Michigan University *B*

Mississippi

Mississippi University for Women *B, T*
University of Southern
  Mississippi *B, M*

Nebraska

Concordia University *M*

Ohio

Ashland University *B*
Bowling Green State University *B*
University of Akron *C, B*

Oklahoma

University of Central Oklahoma *B*

Pennsylvania

Keystone College *B*

Tennessee

Lipscomb University *B*
Southern Adventist University *B*
Union University *B*

Texas

Lubbock Christian University *B*
Texas Tech University *B*

Utah

Brigham Young University *B*

Virginia

Southern Virginia University *B*

West Virginia

Alderson-Broaddus College *B*

Farm and ranch management

Arizona

Central Arizona College *C*

Colorado

Colorado Mountain College *C*
Colorado Northwestern Community
  College *C*
Lamar Community College *C*
Northeastern Junior College *C, A*
Otero Junior College *C*
Pueblo Community College *A*

Trinidad State Junior College *C*

Georgia

Fort Valley State University *B*

Indiana

Purdue University *B*

Iowa

Ellsworth Community College *C, A*
Iowa State University *B*
North Iowa Area Community
 College *A*

Kansas

Allen County Community College *A*
Butler Community College *A*
Colby Community College *A*
Cowley County Community
 College *A*
Dodge City Community College *C, A*
Garden City Community College *A*
Highland Community College *A*
Hutchinson Community College *A*
Pratt Community College *C, A*
Seward County Community College *A*

Minnesota

Alexandria Technical College *C*
Central Lakes College *C*
Minnesota West Community and
 Technical College *C, A*
Northland Community & Technical
 College *C, A*
Ridgewater College *C, A*
Riverland Community College *C*
St. Cloud Technical College *C*

Mississippi

Mississippi Delta Community
 College *A*

Missouri

Crowder College *A*
North Central Missouri College *C, A*
Northwest Missouri State
 University *C*

Montana

Dawson Community College *A*

Nebraska

Northeast Community College *A*

Nevada

Great Basin College *A*

New York

State University of New York
 College of Agriculture and
  Technology at Morrisville *A, B*

North Dakota

Bismarck State College *A*
Dickinson State University *C*
Williston State College *A*

Ohio

University of Findlay *B*
Wilmington College *B*

Oklahoma

Eastern Oklahoma State College *A*
Langston University *B*
Northeastern Oklahoma Agricultural
 and Mechanical College *C, A*

Oregon

Blue Mountain Community College *A*
Treasure Valley Community College *A*

Rhode Island

Johnson & Wales University:
 Providence *B*

South Dakota

Mitchell Technical Institute *C*
Western Dakota Technical Institute *A*

Texas

Central Texas College *C, A*
Clarendon College *C, A*
Frank Phillips College *A*
Navarro College *A*
North Central Texas College *A*
Northeast Texas Community
 College *C*
Southwest Texas Junior College *C, A*
Texas A&M University *B*
Texas Christian University *C*
Trinity Valley Community
 College *C, A*
Tyler Junior College *C, A*
Vernon College *C, A*
Weatherford College *C, A*

Utah

Snow College *A*

Vermont

Vermont Technical College *A*

Virginia

Virginia Highlands Community
 College *C, A*

Wisconsin

Chippewa Valley Technical College *C*
Lakeshore Technical College *C*
Moraine Park Technical College *C*
Northeast Wisconsin Technical
 College *A*
Southwest Wisconsin Technical
 College *A*
Western Technical College *C*
Wisconsin Indianhead Technical
 College *C*

Wyoming

Eastern Wyoming College *C, A*

Fashion and apparel design

Alabama

Wallace State Community College at
 Hanceville *A*

Arizona

Art Institute of Tucson *B*

California

Academy of Art University *C, A, B, M*
Allan Hancock College *C, A*
Art Institute
 of California: Orange County *B*
 of California: San Diego *B*
Art Institute of California:
 Hollywood *A, B*
Art Institute of California: Inland
 Empire *B*
Art Institute of California: San
 Francisco *A, B*
Bethesda Christian University *B*
Butte College *C, A*
California College of the Arts *B*
Chaffey College *C, A*
City College of San Francisco *C*
Fashion Careers College *C, A*
Fashion Institute of Design and
 Merchandising
  Los Angeles *A*

San Diego *A*
San Francisco *A*
Fullerton College *A*
International Academy of Design and
 Technology
  Sacramento *C, A, B*
Long Beach City College *C, A*
Los Angeles Southwest College *A*
Los Angeles Trade and Technical
 College *A*
Modesto Junior College *C, A*
Orange Coast College *C, A*
Otis College of Art and Design *B*
Palomar College *C, A*
Point Loma Nazarene University *B*
Saddleback College *C, A*
San Joaquin Delta College *C, A*
Santa Ana College *A*
Santa Rosa Junior College *C, A*
Santiago Canyon College *A*
Ventura College *C, A*
West Valley College *C, A*
Westwood College of Technology
 Westwood College. Los
  Angeles *A, B*
Woodbury University *B*

Connecticut

Sacred Heart University *B*

Delaware

University of Delaware *B*

Florida

Art Institute of Fort Lauderdale *A, B*
International Academy of Design and
 Technology: Tampa *A, B*
Miami International University of Art
 and Design *A, B*
State College of Florida,
 Manatee-Sarasota *A*

Georgia

American InterContinental
 University *B*
Art Institute
 of Atlanta *B*
Brenau University *B*
Clark Atlanta University *B*
Savannah College of Art and
 Design *B, M*

Hawaii

University of Hawaii
 Honolulu Community College *C, A*

Illinois

Columbia College Chicago *B*
Dominican University *B*
International Academy of Design and
 Technology: Chicago *A, B*
International Academy of Design and
 Technology: Schaumburg *A, B*
School of the Art Institute of
 Chicago *B, M*

Indiana

Purdue University *B*

Iowa

Iowa State University *B*

Maryland

Baltimore City Community
 College *C, A*

Massachusetts

Bay State College *A, B*
Lasell College *B*
Massachusetts College of Art and
 Design *C, B*
Mount Ida College *B*

New England Institute of Art *B*

Michigan

Finlandia University *B*
International Academy of Design and
 Technology: Detroit *A, B*
Michigan State University *B, M*

Minnesota

St. Catherine University *B*
University of Minnesota
 Twin Cities *B*

Missouri

Lindenwood University *B*
Metropolitan Community College:
 Penn Valley *A*
Stephens College *B*
Washington University in St.
 Louis *B, M*

Nevada

Art Institute
 of Las Vegas *B*
International Academy of Design and
 Technology: Henderson *A, B*

New Jersey

Burlington County College *C, A*
Centenary College *B*
Montclair State University *B*

New Mexico

Santa Fe Community College *C*

New York

Art Institute
 of New York City *A*
Cazenovia College *B*
Cornell University *D*
Fashion Institute of Technology *A, B*
Marist College *B*
Parsons The New School for
 Design *A, B*
Pratt Institute *B*
State University of New York
 College at Buffalo *B*
Villa Maria College of Buffalo *B*
Wood Tobe-Coburn School *A*

North Carolina

Mars Hill College *B*
Meredith College *B*

Ohio

Bowling Green State University *B*
Columbus College of Art and
 Design *B*
Kent State University *B*
University of Cincinnati *B*
Ursuline College *B*
Virginia Marti College of Art and
 Design *A*

Oregon

Art Institute of Portland *A, B*
Oregon State University *B*

Pennsylvania

Art Institute
 of Philadelphia *A, B*
Drexel University *B, M*
Harcum College *A*
Lehigh Carbon Community College *A*
Moore College of Art and Design *B*
Philadelphia University *B*

Puerto Rico

Escuela de Artes Plasticas de Puerto
 Rico *B*

Pontifical Catholic University of
   Puerto Rico *A*
Turabo University *A*

Rhode Island
Rhode Island School of Design *B*

Tennessee
International Academy of Design and
   Technology: Nashville *A, B*
O'More College of Design *B*

Texas
Baylor University *B*
El Centro College *C, A*
El Paso Community College *A*
Houston Community College
   System *A*
Texas Southern University *B*
Texas Tech University *B*
Texas Woman's University *B*
University of North Texas *B*
University of the Incarnate Word *B*
Wade College *A*

Utah
Salt Lake Community College *C*

Virginia
Marymount University *B*
Virginia Commonwealth University *B*

Washington
Art Institute of Seattle *A, B*
Bates Technical College *C*

Wisconsin
Mount Mary College *B*
University of Wisconsin
   Madison *B, M*

Fashion/fabric consultant

California
Allan Hancock College *C, A*
City College of San Francisco *C*
Fashion Institute of Design and
   Merchandising
   Los Angeles *A*
   San Diego *A*
   San Francisco *A*
Monterey Peninsula College *A*

Illinois
Harper College *C, A*

Massachusetts
Fisher College *A*
Lasell College *B*

Fashion merchandising

Alabama
Lawson State Community College *C*
Wallace State Community College at
   Hanceville *A*

Arizona
Art Institute of Tucson *B*
Mesa Community College *A*
Northern Arizona University *B*
Phoenix College *C*
Pima Community College *C, A*
Scottsdale Community College *C, A*

Arkansas
Harding University *B*

California
American River College *C, A*
Art Institute of California:
   Hollywood *A, B*
Art Institute of California: San
   Francisco *A, B*
Art Institute of California:
   Sunnyvale *A*
Butte College *C, A*
California State University
   Long Beach *B*
Canada College *C, A*
Chaffey College *C, A*
City College of San Francisco *C, A*
College of Alameda *C, A*
College of San Mateo *C, A*
Evergreen Valley College *A*
Fashion Careers College *C, A*
Fashion Institute of Design and
   Merchandising
   Los Angeles *A*
   San Diego *A*
   San Francisco *A*
Fresno City College *C, A*
Fullerton College *A*
Long Beach City College *C, A*
Los Angeles Trade and Technical
   College *C, A*
Los Angeles Valley College *C, A*
Modesto Junior College *C, A*
Mount San Antonio College *C, A*
Orange Coast College *C, A*
Palomar College *C, A*
Pasadena City College *C, A*
Saddleback College *C, A*
San Diego Mesa College *C, A*
San Joaquin Delta College *C, A*
Santa Ana College *C, A*
Santa Rosa Junior College *C*
Ventura College *C, A*
West Valley College *C, A*
Westwood College of Technology
   Westwood College: Los
      Angeles *A, B*
Woodbury University *B*

Colorado
Johnson & Wales University:
   Denver *B*
Westwood College of Technology
   Westwood College: Denver South *B*

Connecticut
Gateway Community College *A*
Lincoln College of New England:
   Briarwood *A*
Sacred Heart University *B*
Tunxis Community College *C, A*
University of Bridgeport *A, B*

Delaware
University of Delaware *B*

District of Columbia
Howard University *B*

Florida
Art Institute of Fort Lauderdale *B*
Florida State College at Jacksonville *A*
Johnson & Wales University: North
   Miami *B*
Miami International University of Art
   and Design *A, B*
Northwest Florida State College *A*

Georgia
Abraham Baldwin Agricultural
   College *A*
American InterContinental
   University *A, B*
Brenau University *B*
Gwinnett Technical College *A*
Middle Georgia College *C*

University of Georgia *B*

Hawaii
University of Hawaii
   Honolulu Community College *C, A*

Illinois
Chicago State University *B*
College of DuPage *A*
Columbia College Chicago *B*
Dominican University *B*
Harper College *A*
Illinois Institute of Art: Schaumburg *B*
International Academy of Design and
   Technology: Chicago *A, B*
Joliet Junior College *A*
Olivet Nazarene University *B*
South Suburban College of Cook
   County *C, A*
Triton College *C*

Indiana
Harrison College
   Indianapolis *A*
Purdue University *B, M, D*
Vincennes University *A*

Iowa
Ellsworth Community College *C, A*
Kirkwood Community College *C, A*

Kansas
Pittsburg State University *B*
Seward County Community
   College *C, A*

Kentucky
Eastern Kentucky University *B*

Louisiana
Louisiana State University and
   Agricultural and Mechanical
   College *B*
University of Louisiana at Lafayette *B*

Maryland
Baltimore City Community College *A*

Massachusetts
Bay State College *A, B*
Fisher College *A, B*
Lasell College *B*
Massasoit Community College *C*
Middlesex Community College *A*
Mount Ida College *B*
New England Institute of Art *B*
Newbury College *B*

Michigan
Art Institute of Michigan *A, B*
Central Michigan University *B*
Eastern Michigan University *B, M*
Grand Rapids Community College *A*
Lansing Community College *A*
Michigan State University *B, M*
Northwood University: Michigan *A, B*

Minnesota
Alexandria Technical College *C, A*
Art Institutes International
   Minnesota *B*
Minnesota State Community and
   Technical College *C, A*
Ridgewater College *C*
St. Catherine University *B*

Mississippi
Hinds Community College *A*
Holmes Community College *A*
Mississippi Gulf Coast Community
   College *A*

Northwest Mississippi Community
   College *A*

Missouri
Metropolitan Community College:
   Penn Valley *A*
Patricia Stevens College *A, B*
St. Louis Community College
   St. Louis Community College at
      Florissant Valley *A*
Stephens College *B*
University of Central Missouri *A*

New Hampshire
Southern New Hampshire
   University *A*

New Jersey
Berkeley College- Garret Mountain
   Campus *A, B*
Brookdale Community College *A*
Middlesex County College *A*

New Mexico
Dona Ana Community College of New
   Mexico State University *A*

New York
Berkeley College *A, B*
Berkeley College of New York
   City *A, B*
Cazenovia College *B*
City University of New York
   Kingsborough Community
      College *A*
Fashion Institute of
   Technology *C, A, B*
Genesee Community College *A*
Herkimer County Community
   College *A*
Laboratory Institute of
   Merchandising *A, B, M*
Marist College *B*
Nassau Community College *A*
Parsons The New School for
   Design *A, B*
State University of New York
   College at Buffalo *B*
   College at Oneonta *B*
Wood Tobe-Coburn School *A*

North Carolina
Johnson & Wales University:
   Charlotte *B*
Meredith College *B*

North Dakota
Lake Region State College *C, A*

Ohio
Art Institute of Ohio: Cincinnati *A*
Bowling Green State University *B*
Davis College *A*
Kent State University *B*
Ohio State University
   Columbus Campus *B*
University of Akron *A*
Ursuline College *B*
Virginia Marti College of Art and
   Design *A*
Youngstown State University *B*

Oklahoma
Tulsa Community College *C, A*

Oregon
Art Institute of Portland *B*

Pennsylvania
Art Institute
   of Philadelphia *A*
   of Pittsburgh *B*

Community College of
    Philadelphia *C, A*
Harcum College *A*
Immaculata University *A, B*
Indiana University of Pennsylvania *B*
Kaplan Career Institute: Pittsburgh *A*
Mercyhurst College *B*
Philadelphia University *B*

Rhode Island
Johnson & Wales University:
    Providence *B*

Tennessee
International Academy of Design and
    Technology: Nashville *A, B*
Lambuth University *B*
Lipscomb University *B*
O'More College of Design *B*

Texas
Baylor University *B*
Brookhaven College *A*
El Paso Community College *C, A*
Houston Community College
    System *C, A*
Laredo Community College *A*
Palo Alto College *C, A*
Sam Houston State University *B*
San Jacinto College *C, A*
South Plains College *A*
Stephen F. Austin State University *B*
Tarrant County College *C*
Texas Christian University *B*
Texas State University: San Marcos *B*
Texas Tech University *B*
Texas Woman's University *B*
University of North Texas *B*
Wade College *A*

Utah
Utah State University *B*
Weber State University *A*

Virginia
Marymount University *B*

Washington
Art Institute of Seattle *A*
Highline Community College *A*
Pierce College *C*
Shoreline Community College *A*
Spokane Falls Community College *A*

Wisconsin
Mount Mary College *B*

Fashion modeling

Illinois
Harper College *A*

New York
Fashion Institute of Technology *A*

Fiber/textile arts

California
Academy of Art University *C, A, B, M*
California College of the Arts *B, M*
California State University
    Long Beach *B, M*
Fashion Institute of Design and
    Merchandising
      Los Angeles *A*
      San Diego *A*
      San Francisco *A*
University of California
    Davis *M*

Georgia
Savannah College of Art and
    Design *B, M*

Illinois
School of the Art Institute of
    Chicago *B, M*

Kansas
University of Kansas *B, M*

Maryland
Maryland Institute College of Art *B*

Massachusetts
Massachusetts College of Art and
    Design *B, M*
University of Massachusetts
    Dartmouth *B, M*

Michigan
College for Creative Studies *B*
Finlandia University *B*
University of Michigan *B*

Minnesota
Minnesota State University
    Mankato *B, M*

Missouri
Kansas City Art Institute *B*

New Mexico
Northern New Mexico College *C, A*

New York
Cornell University *B, M, D*
State University of New York
    College at Buffalo *B*

North Carolina
East Carolina University *B*
Haywood Community College *A*

Ohio
Bowling Green State University *B*
Cleveland Institute of Art *B*

Oregon
Oregon College of Art & Craft *C, B*
University of Oregon *B, M*

Pennsylvania
Edinboro University of
    Pennsylvania *B*
Marywood University *M*
Philadelphia University *B, M*
Temple University *B, M*

Rhode Island
Rhode Island School of Design *B, M*

Tennessee
Tennessee Technological University *B*

Washington
University of Washington *B, M*
Western Washington University *B*

West Virginia
West Virginia State University *B*

Wisconsin
University of Wisconsin
    Madison *B*

Filipino/Tagalog

Hawaii
University of Hawaii
    Manoa *B*

Film/cinema studies

Arizona
Prescott College *B, M*
Scottsdale Community College *C*

California
Allan Hancock College *A*
Art Institute of California: San
    Francisco *A*
Chapman University *B, M*
Long Beach City College *A*
Los Angeles City College *A*
Los Angeles Pierce College *C*
Loyola Marymount University *B*
Orange Coast College *C, A*
Palomar College *C, A*
Pitzer College *B*
San Francisco Art Institute *B, M*
San Francisco State University *B, M*
Santa Barbara City College *C, A*
Scripps College *B*
University of California
    Berkeley *B*
    Davis *B*
    Irvine *B*
    Los Angeles *B, M, D*
    Santa Barbara *B, M, D*
University of Southern
    California *B, M, D*

Colorado
Colorado College *B*
University of Colorado
    Boulder *B*

Connecticut
Connecticut College *B*
Trinity College *B*
University of Hartford *B*
Wesleyan University *B*
Yale University *B, D*

District of Columbia
American University *B, M*
Howard University *M*

Florida
Southeastern University *B*
Tallahassee Community College *A*
University of Central Florida *M*
University of Miami *M*
University of Tampa *B*

Georgia
Emory University *B, M*
Georgia Perimeter College *A*
Georgia State University *B*
Savannah College of Art and
    Design *M*
University of Georgia *B*

Illinois
Columbia College Chicago *B*
Governors State University *M*
Northwestern University *D*
University of Chicago *B, D*
University of Illinois
    Urbana-Champaign *B*

Indiana
DePauw University *B*
Grace College *B*
Huntington University *B*
Purdue University *B*

Iowa
Briar Cliff University *B*
University of Iowa *B, M, D*

Kansas
Southwestern College *B*
University of Kansas *B, M, D*

Maryland
Howard Community College *A*
Johns Hopkins University *B*
Stevenson University *B*

Massachusetts
Boston College *B*
Brandeis University *B*
Clark University *B*
Emerson College *B*
Hampshire College *B*
Massachusetts College of Art and
    Design *B, M*
Mount Holyoke College *B*
Northeastern University *B*
Smith College *B*
Suffolk University *B*

Michigan
Calvin College *B*
Eastern Michigan University *B*
Grand Valley State University *B*
Oakland University *B*
Spring Arbor University *B*
University of Michigan *B, D*
Wayne State University *B*

Minnesota
Art Institutes International
    Minnesota *B*
Augsburg College *B*
Minneapolis Community and
    Technical College *C*
Saint Cloud State University *B*
University of Minnesota
    Twin Cities *B*

Missouri
Stephens College *B*
Washington University in St. Louis *B*
Webster University *B*

Nebraska
University of Nebraska
    Lincoln *B*

Nevada
University of Nevada
    Las Vegas *B*

New Hampshire
Dartmouth College *B*
Keene State College *B*

New Jersey
Bergen Community College *A*
Kean University *B*
Rowan University *B*

New Mexico
College of Santa Fe *B*
University of New Mexico *B*

New York
Bard College *B, M*
Barnard College *B*
City University of New York
    City College *B, M*
    College of Staten Island *B, M*
    Hunter College *B*
    Queens College *B*
Columbia University *B*

Columbia University
    School of General Studies *B*
Cornell University *B*
Five Towns College *B*
Fordham University *B*
Ithaca College *B*
Pace University *B*
State University of New York
    Buffalo *B*
University of Rochester *B*
Vassar College *B*

Ohio

Baldwin-Wallace College *B*
Bowling Green State University *B*
Denison University *B*
Oberlin College *B*
University of Toledo *B*
Wright State University *B*

Oklahoma

Oklahoma City University *B*
University of Oklahoma *B*
University of Tulsa *B*

Oregon

Chemeketa Community College *A*
Willamette University *B*

Pennsylvania

DeSales University *B*
Gettysburg College *B*
La Salle University *B*
Muhlenberg College *C, B*
Penn State
    Abington *B*
    Altoona *B*
    Beaver *B*
    Berks *B*
    Brandywine *B*
    DuBois *B*
    Erie, The Behrend College *B*
    Fayette, The Eberly Campus *B*
    Greater Allegheny *B*
    Hazleton *B*
    Lehigh Valley *B*
    Mont Alto *B*
    New Kensington *B*
    Schuylkill *B*
    Shenango *B*
    University Park *B, M*
    Wilkes-Barre *B*
    Worthington Scranton *B*
    York *B*
Swarthmore College *B*
Temple University *B, M*
University of Pennsylvania *B*
University of Pittsburgh *C, B*

Rhode Island

Rhode Island College *B*

South Carolina

University of South Carolina *B*

Tennessee

Vanderbilt University *B*
Watkins College of Art, Design and
    Film *B*

Texas

San Jacinto College *A*
Southern Methodist University *B*
Texas Christian University *B*

Utah

Brigham Young University *B, M, D*
University of Utah *B, M*

Vermont

Bennington College *B*
Burlington College *A, B*

Lyndon State College *A*
Marlboro College *B*
University of Vermont *B*

Virginia

Regent University *M*

Washington

Evergreen State College *B*
Whitman College *B*

Wisconsin

University of Wisconsin
    Madison *B*
    Milwaukee *B*

Finance

Alabama

Alabama Agricultural and Mechanical
    University *B*
Alabama State University *B*
Auburn University *B*
Auburn University at Montgomery *B*
Birmingham-Southern College *B*
Faulkner State Community College *A*
Jacksonville State University *B*
Oakwood University *B*
Samford University *B*
Talladega College *B*
Troy University *B*
Tuskegee University *B*
University of Alabama *B, M, D*
University of Alabama
    Birmingham *B*
    Huntsville *B*
University of Montevallo *B*
University of North Alabama *B*
University of South Alabama *B*

Alaska

University of Alaska
    Anchorage *B*

Arizona

Arizona State University *B*
Coconino County Community
    College *A*
Mohave Community College *C*
Northcentral University *M, D*
Northern Arizona University *B*
Penn Foster College *A*
Scottsdale Community College *C*
University of Arizona *B*
University of Phoenix *B*
Western International University *B, M*

Arkansas

Arkansas State University *B*
East Arkansas Community College *A*
Harding University *B*
University of Arkansas *B*
University of Arkansas
    Little Rock *B*
University of Central Arkansas *B*
Williams Baptist College *B*

California

Azusa Pacific University *B, M*
California Lutheran University *B*
California State University
    Chico *B*
    Dominguez Hills *M*
    East Bay *B, M*
    Fresno *B*
    Fullerton *B, M*
    Long Beach *B*
    Northridge *M*
    Sacramento *B, M*
    San Bernardino *B, M*
    Stanislaus *M*
Claremont McKenna College *M*

Cosumnes River College *C, A*
Golden Gate University *C, B, M*
La Sierra University *B, M*
Lake Tahoe Community College *A*
Lincoln University *M*
Los Angeles Pierce College *C*
The Master's College *B*
Modesto Junior College *A*
National University *C, B, M*
Pacific States University *M*
Pacific Union College *B*
Pepperdine University *B*
St. Mary's College of California *B*
San Diego State University *B, M*
San Francisco State University *B*
San Joaquin Delta College *C*
San Jose State University *B*
Santa Barbara City College *C, A*
Santa Clara University *B*
Southwestern College *A*
University of San Diego *B*
University of San Francisco *B*
University of the West *M*
Vanguard University of Southern
    California *B*

Colorado

Adams State College *B*
Colorado State University *B*
Jones International University *M*
Metropolitan State College of
    Denver *B*
University of Colorado
    Boulder *B*
    Denver *M*
University of Denver *B, M*

Connecticut

Albertus Magnus College *B*
Central Connecticut State
    University *B*
Fairfield University *B, M*
Norwalk Community College *A*
Post University *C, B*
Quinnipiac University *B, M*
Sacred Heart University *B*
Southern Connecticut State
    University *B*
Tunxis Community College *A*
University of Bridgeport *B, M*
University of Connecticut *B*
University of Hartford *B*
University of New Haven *B*
Western Connecticut State
    University *B*

Delaware

Delaware State University *B*
University of Delaware *B*
Wilmington University *B*

District of Columbia

American University *B, M*
Catholic University of America *B*
George Washington University *B, M*
Georgetown University *B*
Howard University *B*
University of the District of
    Columbia *B*

Florida

Barry University *B*
Broward College *A*
Edison State College *A*
Florida Atlantic University *B, M*
Florida Gulf Coast University *B*
Florida International University *B, M*
Florida Southern College *B*
Florida State University *B, M, D*
Jacksonville University *B*
Nova Southeastern University *B*
Palm Beach Community College *A*
St. Petersburg College *B*

Saint Thomas University *B*
Schiller International University *B*
Southeastern University *B*
Stetson University *B*
University of Central Florida *B*
University of Florida *B, M*
University of Miami *B*
University of North Florida *B*
University of South Florida *B*
University of Tampa *B*
University of West Florida *B*
Webber International University *A, B*

Georgia

Ashworth College *A*
Augusta State University *B*
Berry College *B*
Columbus State University *B*
Emory University *B, D*
Georgia Southern University *B*
Georgia State University *B, M, D*
Kennesaw State University *B*
North Georgia College & State
    University *B*
University of Georgia *B*
University of West Georgia *B*
Valdosta State University *B*

Hawaii

Hawaii Pacific University *A, B*
University of Hawaii
    Hilo *B*
    Manoa *B*

Idaho

Boise State University *B*
Idaho State University *B*
University of Idaho *B, M*

Illinois

Augustana College *B*
Aurora University *B*
Benedictine University *B*
Bradley University *B*
Chicago State University *B*
DePaul University *B, M*
Eastern Illinois University *B*
Elmhurst College *B*
Eureka College *B*
Illinois College *B*
Illinois Institute of Technology *M*
Illinois State University *B*
Lewis University *B*
Loyola University Chicago *C, B*
MacMurray College *B*
Millikin University *B*
North Central College *B*
Northeastern Illinois University *B*
Northern Illinois University *B, M*
Northwestern University *M, D*
Olivet Nazarene University *B*
Quincy University *B*
Roosevelt University *B*
Saint Xavier University *M*
South Suburban College of Cook
    County *C, A*
Southern Illinois University
    Carbondale *B*
University of Illinois
    Chicago *B, M*
    Urbana-Champaign *B, M, D*
University of St. Francis *B*
Western Illinois University *B*

Indiana

Anderson University *B, D*
Ball State University *B*
Butler University *B*
Franklin College *B*
Grace College *B*
Indiana State University *B*

Indiana University
Bloomington B, M, D
South Bend A, B
Indiana University-Purdue University Fort Wayne B
Indiana University-Purdue University Indianapolis B
Indiana Wesleyan University B
Marian University A, B
Purdue University
Calumet B
Taylor University B
Trine University B
University of Evansville B
University of Notre Dame B
University of Southern Indiana B
Valparaiso University B

Iowa

Drake University B
Grand View University B
Iowa State University B
Kirkwood Community College A
Loras College B
Mount Mercy College B
Northwestern College B
St. Ambrose University B
University of Iowa B, D
University of Northern Iowa B
Waldorf College B
Wartburg College B
Western Iowa Tech Community College A

Kansas

Benedictine College B
Bethany College B
Central Christian College of Kansas A
Kansas State University B
McPherson College B
Pittsburg State University B
Seward County Community College A
Southwestern College B
University of Kansas B
University of St. Mary M
Washburn University B
Wichita State University B

Kentucky

Bellarmine University B
Berea College B
Eastern Kentucky University B
Madisonville Community College A
Morehead State University B
Murray State University B
Northern Kentucky University B
Southeast Kentucky Community and Technical College A
University of Kentucky B
University of Louisville B
Western Kentucky University B

Louisiana

Centenary College of Louisiana B
Dillard University B
Louisiana College B
Louisiana State University and Agricultural and Mechanical College B, M, D
Louisiana Tech University B
Loyola University New Orleans B
McNeese State University B
Nicholls State University B
Southeastern Louisiana University B
Southern University and Agricultural and Mechanical College B
Tulane University B, M
University of Louisiana at Lafayette B
University of Louisiana at Monroe B
University of New Orleans B
Xavier University of Louisiana B

Maine

Husson University B
Kennebec Valley Community College A
Saint Joseph's College of Maine B
Thomas College B
University of Maine B
University of Southern Maine B, M

Maryland

College of Notre Dame of Maryland B
Loyola University Maryland M
Morgan State University B, M
Salisbury University B
University of Baltimore B
University of Maryland
College Park B
University College B
Washington Adventist University M

Massachusetts

American International College B, M
Babson College B
Bentley University B, M
Boston College B, M, D
Boston University B, M
Brandeis University M
Bridgewater State College B
Bunker Hill Community College A
Clark University M
Fitchburg State College B
Gordon College B
Lasell College B
New England College of Business and Finance M
Newbury College B
Nichols College B
Northeastern University B, M
Northern Essex Community College C, A
Salem State College B
Simmons College B
Springfield Technical Community College A
Stonehill College B
Suffolk University B, M
University of Massachusetts
Amherst B
Boston M
Dartmouth B
Western New England College B

Michigan

Alma College B
Andrews University B
Central Michigan University B
Davenport University A, B
Eastern Michigan University B, M
Ferris State University B
Glen Oaks Community College C
Grand Valley State University B
Hillsdale College B
Jackson Community College C, A
Michigan State University B, M, D
Northern Michigan University B
Northwood University: Michigan B
Oakland University B
Saginaw Valley State University B
Spring Arbor University B
University of Michigan
Flint B, M
Walsh College of Accountancy and Business Administration B, M
Wayne State University B
Western Michigan University B

Minnesota

Academy College A
Augsburg College B
Capella University B, M
College of St. Scholastica B
Concordia University: St. Paul B
Fond du Lac Tribal and Community College A
Hamline University B
Metropolitan State University B
Minnesota State University
Mankato B
Moorhead B
North Hennepin Community College A
Northwestern College B
Saint Cloud State University B
Southwest Minnesota State University B
University of Minnesota
Duluth B
University of St. Thomas B
Walden University B, M, D
Winona State University B

Mississippi

Delta State University B
Hinds Community College A
Jackson State University B
Mississippi College M
Mississippi State University B
University of Mississippi B
University of Southern Mississippi B

Missouri

Avila University B
Columbia College B
Culver-Stockton College B
Drury University B
Hannibal-LaGrange College B
Lindenwood University B, M
Missouri Southern State University B
Missouri State University B
Missouri Western State University B
Northwest Missouri State University B
Saint Louis University M
Southeast Missouri State University B
Southwest Baptist University B
University of Central Missouri B
University of Missouri
Kansas City B
St. Louis B, M
Washington University in St. Louis B, M
Webster University B, M

Montana

University of Montana B

Nebraska

Chadron State College B
Creighton University B
Union College B
University of Nebraska
Lincoln B
Omaha B
York College B

Nevada

University of Nevada
Las Vegas B
Reno B, M

New Hampshire

New England College B
Saint Anselm College B
Southern New Hampshire University M

New Jersey

Fairleigh Dickinson University
College at Florham M
Metropolitan Campus M
Gloucester County College A
Kean University B
Passaic County Community College C
Rider University B
Rowan University B, M

Rutgers, The State University of New Jersey
Camden Regional Campus B
New Brunswick/Piscataway Campus B
Newark Regional Campus B
Saint Peter's College A
Seton Hall University B
Thomas Edison State College C, B
William Paterson University of New Jersey B

New Mexico

Eastern New Mexico University B
New Mexico Highlands University B
New Mexico State University B

New York

Adelphi University B, M
Alfred University B
Canisius College B
City University of New York
Baruch College B, M
Queens College B
Clinton Community College C
Concordia College B
Dominican College of Blauvelt B
Dowling College B, M
Excelsior College B
Fordham University B, M
Globe Institute of Technology C, A, B
Hilbert College A
Hofstra University B, M
Hudson Valley Community College A
Iona College B, M
Ithaca College B
Le Moyne College B
Long Island University
Brooklyn Campus B
C. W. Post Campus B
Manhattan College B
Manhattanville College B, M
Marist College B
Mercy College M
Molloy College M
New York Institute of Technology B, M
New York University C, B, M, D
Niagara University B
Orange County Community College A
Pace University B, M
Rochester Institute of Technology B, M
Saint Bonaventure University B, M
St. John Fisher College B
St. John's University B, M
St. Thomas Aquinas College B
Siena College B, T
State University of New York
Albany M
Binghamton B
Buffalo M
College at Brockport B
College at Fredonia B
College at Old Westbury B
College at Plattsburgh B
College of Technology at Alfred A
College of Technology at Canton B
Institute of Technology at Utica/Rome B
New Paltz B, M
Oswego B
Suffolk County Community College A
Syracuse University B, M
Wagner College B

North Carolina

Appalachian State University B
East Carolina University B
Elon University B
Gardner-Webb University B
Lenoir-Rhyne University B
Mars Hill College B
Methodist University B

North Carolina Agricultural and
Technical State University *B*
University of North Carolina
Charlotte *B*
Greensboro *B*
Wilmington *B*
Wake Forest University *B*
Western Carolina University *B*
Wingate University *B*

North Dakota
Dickinson State University *B*
Jamestown College *B*
Minot State University *B*
North Dakota State College of
Science *A*
North Dakota State University *B*
University of Mary *B*
University of North Dakota *B*

Ohio
Ashland University *B*
Baldwin-Wallace College *B*
Bowling Green State University *B*
Case Western Reserve University *M*
Cedarville University *B*
Cincinnati State Technical and
Community College *A*
Cleveland State University *B, D*
Eastern Gateway Community
College *C*
Franklin University *B*
James A. Rhodes State College *C, A*
John Carroll University *B*
Kent State University *B, D*
Marietta College *B*
Miami University
Oxford Campus *B*
Mount Vernon Nazarene
University *B, M*
North Central State College *C*
Northwest State Community
College *A*
Ohio Dominican University *B*
Ohio Northern University *B*
Ohio State University
Columbus Campus *B*
Ohio University *B*
Otterbein College *B*
Shawnee State University *A*
Terra State Community College *C, A*
Tiffin University *B*
University of Akron *M*
University of Cincinnati *B, M, D*
University of Dayton *B*
University of Findlay *A, B*
University of Toledo *B, M*
Walsh University *A, B*
Wilberforce University *B*
Wright State University *M*
Xavier University *B, M*
Youngstown State University *A, B, M*

Oklahoma
East Central University *B*
Northeastern State University *B*
Oklahoma Baptist University *B*
Oklahoma City Community
College *C, A*
Oklahoma City University *B, M*
Oklahoma State University *B*
Oral Roberts University *B*
Southeastern Oklahoma State
University *B*
Southern Nazarene University *B*
Tulsa Community College *A*
University of Central Oklahoma *B*
University of Oklahoma *B*
University of Tulsa *B, M*

Oregon
Corban College *B*
Linfield College *B*

Portland State University *B, M*
University of Oregon *M, D*
University of Portland *B*

Pennsylvania
Albright College *B*
Arcadia University *B*
Cabrini College *B*
Carnegie Mellon University *M, D*
Clarion University of Pennsylvania *B*
DeSales University *B*
Drexel University *M*
Duquesne University *B*
Elizabethtown College *B*
Gannon University *B*
Gettysburg College *B*
Holy Family University *B*
Immaculata University *B*
Indiana University of Pennsylvania *B*
Juniata College *B*
King's College *B*
Kutztown University of
Pennsylvania *B*
La Roche College *B*
La Salle University *B*
Lehigh University *B, M*
Lincoln University *B*
Lycoming College *B*
Mercyhurst College *B*
Muhlenberg College *C, A, B*
Penn State
Abington *B*
Altoona *B*
Beaver *B*
Berks *B*
Brandywine *B*
DuBois *B*
Erie, The Behrend College *B*
Fayette, The Eberly Campus *B*
Greater Allegheny *B*
Harrisburg *B*
Hazleton *B*
Lehigh Valley *B*
Mont Alto *B*
New Kensington *B*
Schuylkill *B*
Shenango *B*
University Park *B*
Wilkes-Barre *B*
Worthington Scranton *B*
York *B*
Philadelphia University *B*
Robert Morris University *B*
St. Francis University *B*
Saint Joseph's University *C, A, B, M*
St. Vincent College *B*
Seton Hill University *B*
Shippensburg University of
Pennsylvania *B*
Slippery Rock University of
Pennsylvania *B*
Temple University *B, M*
University of Pennsylvania *B, M, D*
University of Pittsburgh *B*
University of Pittsburgh
Johnstown *B*
University of Scranton *B, M*
Villanova University *B, M*
Waynesburg University *B*
West Chester University of
Pennsylvania *B*
Westminster College *B*
Widener University *B*
York College of Pennsylvania *B, M*

Puerto Rico
Bayamon Central University *B, M*
Inter American University of Puerto
Rico
Bayamon Campus *B*
Metropolitan Campus *B, M*
Ponce Campus *B, M*
San German Campus *B, M*

Pontifical Catholic University of
Puerto Rico *B, M*
Universidad Metropolitana *M*
University of Puerto Rico
Aguadilla *B*
Arecibo *B*
Bayamon University College *B*
Carolina Regional College *B*
Ponce *B*
Rio Piedras *B, M, D*

Rhode Island
Bryant University *B, M*
Johnson & Wales University:
Providence *B*
Providence College *B*
Rhode Island College *B*
Roger Williams University *B*
Salve Regina University *B*
University of Rhode Island *B*

South Carolina
Anderson University *B*
Charleston Southern University *B*
Clemson University *B*
Coastal Carolina University *B*
Converse College *B*
Francis Marion University *B*
University of South Carolina *B*
Wofford College *B*

South Dakota
Dakota State University *B*
Lake Area Technical Institute *A*
Northern State University *B*
University of South Dakota *B, M*

Tennessee
Belmont University *B*
Cleveland State Community College *C*
East Tennessee State University *B*
Freed-Hardeman University *B*
Lipscomb University *M*
Middle Tennessee State University *B*
Southern Adventist University *B*
Tennessee Technological University *B*
Tennessee Wesleyan College *B*
University of Memphis *B*
University of Tennessee
Knoxville *B, M, D*
Martin *B*
Vanderbilt University *M*

Texas
Abilene Christian University *B*
Amarillo College *A*
Angelo State University *B*
Baylor University *B*
Brazosport College *A*
Clarendon College *A*
Dallas Baptist University *B*
Del Mar College *C, A*
El Paso Community College *A*
Hardin-Simmons University *B*
Houston Baptist University *B*
Howard Payne University *B*
Lamar University *B*
Laredo Community College *C, A*
LeTourneau University *B*
Lubbock Christian University *B*
McMurry University *B*
Midwestern State University *B*
Our Lady of the Lake University of San
Antonio *M*
Prairie View A&M University *B*
St. Edward's University *B*
St. Mary's University *B*
Sam Houston State University *B, M*
Schreiner University *B*
Southern Methodist University *B, M*
Stephen F. Austin State University *B*
Sul Ross State University *B*
Tarleton State University *B*

Texas A&M International University *B*
Texas A&M University *B, M, D*
Texas A&M University
Corpus Christi *B*
Kingsville *B*
Texarkana *B*
Texas Christian University *B, M*
Texas State University: San Marcos *B*
Texas Tech University *B*
Texas Wesleyan University *B*
Texas Woman's University *B*
Trinity University *B*
University of Houston *B, M, D*
University of Houston
Clear Lake *B, M*
Downtown *B*
University of Mary Hardin-Baylor *B*
University of North Texas *M*
University of St. Thomas *B*
University of Texas
Arlington *M*
Austin *B, M, D*
Brownsville - Texas Southmost
College *B*
Dallas *B*
El Paso *B*
Pan American *B*
San Antonio *B, M, D*
Tyler *B*
of the Permian Basin *B*
West Texas A&M University *B, M*

Utah
Brigham Young University *B*
Salt Lake Community College *C, A*
Southern Utah University *B*
University of Utah *B, M*
Utah State University *B*
Weber State University *B*
Western Governors University *B*
Westminster College *B*

Vermont
Lyndon State College *B*

Virginia
Averett University *B*
Central Virginia Community
College *A*
Christopher Newport University *B*
Dabney S. Lancaster Community
College *C*
Ferrum College *B*
George Mason University *B*
Hampton University *B*
James Madison University *B*
Longwood University *B*
Old Dominion University *B*
Radford University *B*
Virginia Highlands Community
College *C*
Virginia Polytechnic Institute and
State University *B*
Virginia Union University *B*

Washington
City University of Seattle *M*
Eastern Washington University *B*
Seattle University *B, M*
University of Washington *B*
University of Washington Tacoma *B*
Walla Walla University *B*
Washington State University *B, D*
Western Washington University *B*

West Virginia
Bethany College *B*
Concord University *B*
Marshall University *B*
University of Charleston *B*
West Virginia State Community and
Technical College *A*
West Virginia University *B, M*

West Virginia Wesleyan College *B*

Wisconsin
Carroll University *B*
Concordia University Wisconsin *B*
Herzing University *B*
Marian University *B*
Marquette University *B, M*
St. Norbert College *B*
University of Wisconsin
  Eau Claire *B*
  La Crosse *B*
  Madison *B, M*
  Milwaukee *B*
  Oshkosh *B*
  Parkside *B*
  Platteville *B*
  Superior *B*
  Whitewater *B*
Western Technical College *A*
Wisconsin Indianhead Technical
  College *A*

Wyoming
University of Wyoming *B, M*

Financial planning

Arizona
Arizona State University *M*

California
Golden Gate University *M*
San Diego State University *B, M*
Southwestern College *C, A*

Colorado
Pikes Peak Community College *C, A*

Connecticut
Manchester Community College *C*

Florida
Florida State College at
  Jacksonville *C, A*
Schiller International University *M*

Georgia
Georgia State University *M*

Illinois
DePaul University *M*
Roosevelt University *B*
Saint Xavier University *M*
Triton College *A*
University of Illinois
  Urbana-Champaign *B, M, D*

Indiana
Purdue University *B*

Kentucky
Western Kentucky University *C*

Louisiana
Louisiana State University
  Shreveport *B*

Maine
University of Maine
  Augusta *A, B*

Maryland
Cecil College *C, A*
Howard Community College *C*

Massachusetts
Bentley University *M*
New England College of Business and
  Finance *C*

Salem State College *M*

Michigan
Central Michigan University *B*
Cleary University *B*
Cornerstone University *B*
Northern Michigan University *B*
Western Michigan University *B*

Minnesota
Minnesota State University
  Mankato *B*

Missouri
Missouri Southern State University *B*

New Jersey
Berkeley College- Garret Mountain
  Campus *A, B*
Raritan Valley Community College *C*

New York
Berkeley College *A, B*
Berkeley College of New York
  City *A, B*
Bramson ORT College *A*
Broome Community College *A*
Globe Institute of Technology *C*
Metropolitan College of New York *M*
Pace University *M*
State University of New York
  College of Technology at Alfred *B*

North Carolina
Campbell University *B*

North Dakota
Jamestown College *B*

Ohio
Ohio State University
  Lima Campus *B*
University of Akron *C, B*
University of Cincinnati
  Clermont College *C*
  Raymond Walters College *C, A*
Youngstown State University *B*

Pennsylvania
Marywood University *B, M*
Penn State
  Erie, The Behrend College *C*
Saint Joseph's University *M*
Slippery Rock University of
  Pennsylvania *C*
Widener University *B, M*

Rhode Island
Bryant University *B*
Community College of Rhode
  Island *C*
University of Rhode Island *B*

South Carolina
York Technical College *C*

South Dakota
Kilian Community College *A*

Texas
Baylor University *B*
Lamar State College at Orange *C*
Lubbock Christian University *B*
Southern Methodist University *B, M*
Texas Tech University *D*
University of Dallas *M*
University of North Texas *B*

Utah
Brigham Young University *B*

Washington
City University of Seattle *C*

Wisconsin
Fox Valley Technical College *C*
Waukesha County Technical
  College *A*

Fine/studio arts

Alabama
Auburn University *B*
Faulkner State Community College *A*
Huntingdon College *B*
Shelton State Community College *A*
Spring Hill College *B*
Talladega College *B*
University of Alabama *B, M*
University of North Alabama *B*

Alaska
University of Alaska
  Anchorage *B*

Arizona
Arizona Western College *A*
Art Center Design College *B*
Dine College *A*
Eastern Arizona College *A*
Northern Arizona University *B*
Prescott College *B, M*
Scottsdale Community College *A*
University of Arizona *B*

Arkansas
Harding University *B*
Ouachita Baptist University *B, T*
Southern Arkansas University *B*
Williams Baptist College *B*

California
Academy of Art University *C, A, B, M*
Art Center College of Design *B, M*
Azusa Pacific University *B, M*
Biola University *B*
Butte College *A*
Cabrillo College *A*
California College of the Arts *B, M*
California Institute of the Arts *C, B, M*
California Polytechnic State
  University: San Luis Obispo *B*
California State University
  Chico *B, M*
  East Bay *B*
  Fullerton *B, M*
  Long Beach *B, M*
  San Bernardino *B*
  Stanislaus *B*
Chabot College *A*
Chaffey College *A*
Chapman University *B*
Citrus College *A*
College of Alameda *A*
College of Marin: Kentfield *A*
College of San Mateo *A*
College of the Desert *A*
College of the Sequoias *A*
College of the Siskiyous *C, A*
Cosumnes River College *A*
El Camino College *A*
Foothill College *C, A*
Gavilan College *A*
Golden West College *A*
Irvine Valley College *A*
John F. Kennedy University *B, M*
La Sierra University *B*
Lake Tahoe Community College *A*
Los Angeles Pierce College *A*
Los Medanos College *A*
Loyola Marymount University *B*
Mills College *B, M*
Modesto Junior College *A*

Monterey Peninsula College *C, A*
Moorpark College *A*
Mount St. Mary's College *B*
Notre Dame de Namur University *B*
Ohlone College *A*
Orange Coast College *A*
Otis College of Art and Design *B, M*
Pacific Union College *B*
Pasadena City College *A*
Pepperdine University *B*
Pitzer College *B*
Point Loma Nazarene University *B*
Pomona College *B*
Porterville College *C, A*
Sacramento City College *A*
Saddleback College *A*
San Diego City College *A*
San Diego Mesa College *A*
San Diego Miramar College *A*
San Diego State University *B, M*
San Francisco Art Institute *B, M*
San Francisco State University *M*
San Joaquin Delta College *A*
San Jose City College *A*
San Jose State University *B, M*
Santa Barbara City College *C, A*
Santa Clara University *B*
Santa Monica College *A*
Scripps College *B*
Shasta College *A*
Sierra College *A*
Solano Community College *A*
Sonoma State University *B*
Stanford University *B*
University of California
  Davis *B*
  Irvine *B, M*
  Riverside *B*
  San Diego *B*
  Santa Barbara *B, M*
  Santa Cruz *M*
University of San Diego *B*
University of San Francisco *B*
University of Southern
  California *B, M*
University of the Pacific *B*
Ventura College *C, A*
West Hills College: Coalinga *A*
Yuba Community College District *A*

Colorado
Adams State College *B*
Colorado Christian University *B*
Colorado College *B*
Colorado State University *B, M*
Colorado State University
  Pueblo *B*
Fort Lewis College *B*
Naropa University *B*
Pikes Peak Community College *A*
Rocky Mountain College of Art &
  Design *B*
University of Colorado
  Boulder *B, M*
  Denver *B*
University of Northern
  Colorado *B, M, T*
Western State College of Colorado *B*

Connecticut
Albertus Magnus College *B*
Capital Community College *C*
Connecticut College *B*
Eastern Connecticut State
  University *B*
Fairfield University *B*
Gateway Community College *A*
Housatonic Community College *A*
Middlesex Community College *A*
Mitchell College *A*
Naugatuck Valley Community
  College *C*
Northwestern Connecticut
  Community College *C*

Norwalk Community College *A*
Paier College of Art *C, B*
Quinebaug Valley Community
  College *C, A*
Trinity College *B*
University of Connecticut *B, M*
University of New Haven *B*
Wesleyan University *B*
Western Connecticut State
  University *M*
Yale University *M*

Delaware
Delaware College of Art and Design *A*
Delaware State University *B*
University of Delaware *B, M*

District of Columbia
American University *B*
Corcoran College of Art and
  Design *A, B*
Gallaudet University *B*
George Washington University *B*
Georgetown University *B*
University of the District of
  Columbia *B*

Florida
Daytona State College *A*
Eckerd College *B*
Flagler College *B*
Florida Agricultural and Mechanical
  University *B*
Florida Atlantic University *M*
Florida International University *B, M*
Florida Southern College *B*
Florida State University *B, M*
Jacksonville University *B*
Miami Dade College *A*
New College of Florida *B*
Nova Southeastern University *B*
Palm Beach Atlantic University *B*
Palm Beach Community College *A*
Ringling College of Art and Design *B*
State College of Florida,
  Manatee-Sarasota *A*
University of Central Florida *B, M*
University of Florida *B, M*
University of Miami *B*
University of North Florida *B*
University of South Florida *B, M*
University of West Florida *B*

Georgia
Abraham Baldwin Agricultural
  College *A*
Agnes Scott College *B*
Brenau University *B*
Gainesville State College *A*
Georgia Southern University *M*
Oglethorpe University *B*
Piedmont College *B*
Reinhardt College *B*
Shorter College *B*
Spelman College *B*
University of Georgia *B*
Wesleyan College *B*
Young Harris College *A*

Idaho
North Idaho College *A*
University of Idaho *B*

Illinois
Augustana College *B*
Benedictine University *B*
Bradley University *B, M, T*
City Colleges of Chicago
  Kennedy-King College *A*
  Olive-Harvey College *A*
Columbia College Chicago *C, B*
Dominican University *B*
Elgin Community College *C*

Harper College *A*
Illinois Central College *A*
Illinois College *B*
Illinois State University *B, M*
Illinois Valley Community College *A*
Judson University *B*
Kankakee Community College *A*
Knox College *B*
Lake Land College *A*
Lewis University *B*
Lewis and Clark Community
  College *A*
Lincoln College *A*
Lincoln Land Community College *A*
Loyola University Chicago *C, B*
McKendree University *B*
Millikin University *B*
Monmouth College *B*
Morton College *A*
Northern Illinois University *B, M*
Principia College *B*
Saint Xavier University *B*
Sauk Valley Community College *A*
School of the Art Institute of
  Chicago *B, M*
South Suburban College of Cook
  County *A*
Southern Illinois University
  Carbondale *B, M*
Southern Illinois University
  Edwardsville *B, M*
Southwestern Illinois College *A*
Trinity Christian College *B*
Triton College *A*
University of Illinois
  Chicago *B, M*
  Springfield *B*
  Urbana-Champaign *B, M*
Waubonsee Community College *A*
Western Illinois University *B*

Indiana
Anderson University *B*
Calumet College of St. Joseph *C, B*
DePauw University *B*
Hanover College *B*
Huntington University *B*
Indiana State University *B, M*
Indiana University
  Bloomington *B, M*
  South Bend *B*
  Southeast *B*
Indiana University-Purdue University
  Fort Wayne *B*
Indiana University-Purdue University
  Indianapolis *B*
Indiana Wesleyan University *B*
Purdue University *B, M*
Saint Joseph's College *B*
Saint Mary's College *B*
University of Notre Dame *B, M*
University of St. Francis *B*

Iowa
Clarke College *B*
Coe College *B*
Cornell College *B*
Ellsworth Community College *A*
Graceland University *B, T*
Grand View University *B*
Iowa Wesleyan College *B*
Maharishi University of
  Management *B*
Marshalltown Community College *A*
Morningside College *B*
St. Ambrose University *B*
University of Iowa *B*
University of Northern Iowa *B*
Upper Iowa University *B*

Kansas
Allen County Community College *A*
Baker University *B, T*
Bethel College *B*

Coffeyville Community College *A*
Fort Hays State University *M*
Highland Community College *A*
Kansas State University *B, M*
Kansas Wesleyan University *B, T*
Labette Community College *A*
Neosho County Community
  College *A*
Pratt Community College *A*
Seward County Community College *A*
University of Kansas *B, M*
Washburn University *B*
Wichita State University *B, M*

Kentucky
Asbury College *B*
Berea College *B, T*
Bluegrass Community and Technical
  College *A*
Campbellsville University *B*
Eastern Kentucky University *B*
Georgetown College *B*
Kentucky State University *B*
Kentucky Wesleyan College *B*
Lindsey Wilson College *A, B, T*
Morehead State University *B, M*
Murray State University *B, T*
Northern Kentucky University *B*
St. Catharine College *A*
Thomas More College *A, B*
Transylvania University *B, T*
University of Louisville *B*
University of the Cumberlands *B*
Western Kentucky University *B*

Louisiana
Centenary College of Louisiana *B*
Louisiana College *B*
Louisiana State University and
  Agricultural and Mechanical
  College *B, M*
Loyola University New Orleans *B*
Northwestern State University *B*
Southern University and Agricultural
  and Mechanical College *B*
Tulane University *B, M*
University of Louisiana at Monroe *B*
University of New Orleans *B, M*

Maine
Bowdoin College *B*
Colby College *B*
Maine College of Art *B, M*
University of Maine *B*
University of Maine
  Augusta *A, B*
  Presque Isle *B*
University of Southern Maine *B*

Maryland
Cecil College *A*
College of Notre Dame of Maryland *B*
Frostburg State University *B, T*
Goucher College *M*
Harford Community College *A*
Howard Community College *A*
Montgomery College *A*
Morgan State University *B*
Prince George's Community
  College *A*
Salisbury University *B*
Towson University *B, M*
University of Maryland
  College Park *B, M*

Massachusetts
Amherst College *B*
Art Institute of Boston at Lesley
  University *B, M*
Atlantic Union College *B*
Bard College at Simon's Rock *B*
Boston College *B*
Boston University *M*

Brandeis University *B*
Bridgewater State College *B*
Bristol Community College *C*
Clark University *B*
College of the Holy Cross *B*
Curry College *B*
Elms College *B*
Emmanuel College *B*
Endicott College *B*
Hampshire College *B*
Lesley University *B, M*
Massachusetts College of Art and
  Design *B, M*
Massasoit Community College *A*
Merrimack College *B*
Middlesex Community College *C, A*
Montserrat College of Art *B*
Mount Holyoke College *B*
Northeastern University *B, M*
School of the Museum of Fine
  Arts *C, B, M, T*
Smith College *B*
Springfield Technical Community
  College *A*
Stonehill College *B*
Suffolk University *C, B*
Tufts University *B*
University of Massachusetts
  Amherst *B, M*
  Dartmouth *B, M*
  Lowell *B*
Wellesley College *B*
Wheaton College *B*
Williams College *B*

Michigan
Albion College *B*
Alma College *B*
Andrews University *B*
Calvin College *B*
Central Michigan University *B, M*
College for Creative Studies *B*
Eastern Michigan University *M*
Ferris State University *B, M*
Finlandia University *B*
Grand Rapids Community College *A*
Grand Valley State University *B*
Henry Ford Community College *A*
Hope College *B*
Kendall College of Art and Design of
  Ferris State University *B, M*
Lake Superior State University *B*
Madonna University *A, B*
Marygrove College *B*
Monroe County Community
  College *A*
Northwestern Michigan College *A*
Oakland University *B, T*
Saginaw Valley State University *B*
St. Clair County Community
  College *A*
Siena Heights University *B*
University of Michigan
  Flint *B*
Western Michigan University *B, M*

Minnesota
Anoka-Ramsey Community College *A*
Augsburg College *B*
Bethany Lutheran College *B*
Carleton College *B*
College of Visual Arts *B*
Concordia University: St. Paul *B*
Hamline University *B*
Inver Hills Community College *A*
Lake Superior College *A*
Minneapolis College of Art and
  Design *B, M*
Minneapolis Community and
  Technical College *A*
Minnesota State University
  Mankato *B, M*
Normandale Community College *A*

North Hennepin Community
College *A*
Northland Community & Technical
College *A*
Northwestern College *B*
Ridgewater College *A*
St. Catherine University *B*
Saint Cloud State University *B*
St. Mary's University of Minnesota *B*
University of Minnesota
Duluth *B*
Morris *B*
Winona State University *B*

Mississippi

East Central Community College *A*
Millsaps College *B*
Mississippi College *B, M*
Mississippi Delta Community
College *A*
Mississippi Valley State University *B*
University of Southern Mississippi *M*

Missouri

Avila University *B*
College of the Ozarks *B*
Drury University *A, B, T*
Evangel University *B*
Fontbonne University *B, M, T*
Lincoln University *B*
Lindenwood University *B, M*
Maryville University of Saint Louis *B*
Missouri Southern State
University *B, T*
Missouri State University *B*
Northwest Missouri State
University *B*
Park University *B*
St. Louis Community College
St. Louis Community College at
Florissant Valley *A*
St. Louis Community College at
Meramec *A*
Saint Louis University *B*
Three Rivers Community College *A*
University of Central Missouri *B*
University of Missouri
Kansas City *B, M*
Washington University in St.
Louis *B, M*
Webster University *B*
William Woods University *B, T*

Montana

Fort Peck Community College *C, A*
University of Montana: Western *B*

Nebraska

Bellevue University *B*
College of Saint Mary *B, T*
Concordia University *B*
Creighton University *B*
Metropolitan Community College *A*
Nebraska Wesleyan University *B*
Union College *B*
University of Nebraska
Kearney *B, M, T*
Lincoln *B, M*
Omaha *B*

Nevada

College of Southern Nevada *A*
Sierra Nevada College *B*
University of Nevada
Las Vegas *B, M*

New Hampshire

Chester College of New England *B*
Colby-Sawyer College *B*
Dartmouth College *B*
Franklin Pierce University *B*
Keene State College *B*
Lakes Region Community College *A*

Plymouth State University *B*
Rivier College *B*
Southern New Hampshire
University *M*
University of New Hampshire *B*
University of New Hampshire at
Manchester *A*

New Jersey

Brookdale Community College *A*
Caldwell College *B*
The College of New Jersey *B, T*
Cumberland County College *A*
Essex County College *A*
Felician College *B*
Hudson County Community
College *A*
Kean University *A*
Middlesex County College *A*
Monmouth University *B*
Montclair State University *M*
New Jersey City University *B, M*
Raritan Valley Community College *A*
Rider University *B*
Rowan University *B*
Rutgers, The State University of New
Jersey
New Brunswick/Piscataway
Campus *M*
Saint Peter's College *B*
Sussex County Community College *A*
Warren County Community College *A*

New Mexico

Art Center Design College *B*
Clovis Community College *A*
College of Santa Fe *B*
Institute of American Indian Arts *A, B*
New Mexico Highlands University *B*
New Mexico Junior College *A*
New Mexico State University *B, M*
Northern New Mexico College *A*
Western New Mexico University *B*

New York

Adelphi University *B, M*
Alfred University *B*
Bard College *B, M*
Cayuga County Community College *A*
Cazenovia College *B*
City University of New York
Brooklyn College *B, M*
City College *B*
College of Staten Island *B*
Hunter College *B*
Kingsborough Community
College *A*
LaGuardia Community College *A*
Queens College *B, M, T*
Colgate University *B*
College of New Rochelle *B, M, T*
Columbia University *B*
Columbia-Greene Community
College *A*
Cooper Union for the Advancement of
Science and Art *C, B*
Cornell University *B*
Daemen College *B*
Fashion Institute of Technology *A, B*
Finger Lakes Community College *A*
Fordham University *B*
Hamilton College *B*
Herkimer County Community
College *A*
Hobart and William Smith Colleges *B*
Hofstra University *B*
Houghton College *B*
Ithaca College *B*
Jamestown Community College *A*
Long Island University
Brooklyn Campus *B*
C. W. Post Campus *B, M*
Mannes College The New School for
Music *B, M*

Marist College *C, B*
Marymount Manhattan College *B*
Monroe Community College *A*
Nazareth College *B, T*
New York Institute of Technology *B*
New York University *B, M, D, T*
Niagara County Community
College *A*
Pace University *B, M*
Parsons The New School for
Design *B, M*
Pratt Institute *B, M*
Rensselaer Polytechnic
Institute *B, M, D*
Roberts Wesleyan College *B*
Rochester Institute of
Technology *A, B, M*
Rockland Community College *A*
Sage College of Albany *B*
St. John's University *B*
St. Lawrence University *B*
St. Thomas Aquinas College *B*
School of Visual Arts *B, M*
State University of New York
Albany *B, M*
Buffalo *B*
College at Brockport *B, M*
College at Buffalo *B*
College at Cortland *B*
College at Fredonia *B*
College at Geneseo *B*
College at Oneonta *B*
College at Potsdam *B*
Empire State College *A, B*
New Paltz *B*
Oswego *M*
Stony Brook *B, M*
Suffolk County Community College *A*
Syracuse University *B, M*
University of Rochester *B*
Villa Maria College of Buffalo *A*
Wagner College *B*
Wells College *B*

North Carolina

Appalachian State University *B*
Barton College *B*
Campbell University *B*
Chowan University *B*
East Carolina University *B, M*
Elizabeth City State University *B*
Gardner-Webb University *B*
Greensboro College *C, B*
Lenoir Community College *A*
Meredith College *B*
Methodist University *B*
Mitchell Community College *A*
Mount Olive College *A, B*
Piedmont Community College *A*
Queens University of Charlotte *B*
Randolph Community College *A*
Rockingham Community College *A*
Salem College *B*
Southeastern Community College *A*
University of North Carolina
Asheville *B*
Chapel Hill *B, M*
Charlotte *B*
Greensboro *B, M*
Pembroke *B*
Wilmington *B*
Wake Forest University *B*
Western Carolina University *B, M*
Western Piedmont Community
College *A*
Wingate University *B*

North Dakota

Dickinson State University *B*
Jamestown College *B*

Ohio

Art Academy of Cincinnati *B*
Ashland University *B*

Baldwin-Wallace College *B*
Bowling Green State University *B*
Cedarville University *B*
College of Mount St. Joseph *B*
College of Wooster *B*
Columbus College of Art and
Design *B*
Denison University *B*
Hiram College *B, T*
Kenyon College *B*
Malone University *B*
Marietta College *B*
Mount Union College *B*
Notre Dame College *B*
Oberlin College *B*
Ohio Northern University *B*
Ohio State University
Columbus Campus *B, M*
Ohio University *B*
Ohio Wesleyan University *B*
Shawnee State University *B*
University of Akron *B*
University of Cincinnati *C, B, M*
University of Dayton *B*
University of Toledo *B*
Ursuline College *B*
Wilberforce University *B*
Xavier University *B*
Youngstown State University *B*

Oklahoma

Cameron University *B*
East Central University *B*
Northeastern State University *B*
Oklahoma Baptist University *B*
Oklahoma Christian University *B*
Oklahoma City Community College *A*
Oklahoma City University *B, M*
Oral Roberts University *B*
University of Oklahoma *B, M*
University of Science and Arts of
Oklahoma *B, T*
University of Tulsa *M*

Oregon

Central Oregon Community
College *A*
Eastern Oregon University *B*
Lewis & Clark College *B*
Linfield College *B*
Marylhurst University *B*
Mt. Hood Community College *A*
Pacific Northwest College of Art *B, M*
Portland State University *B*
University of Oregon *B, M*
Western Oregon University *B, M*
Willamette University *B*

Pennsylvania

Albright College *B*
Allegheny College *B*
Arcadia University *B*
Bloomsburg University of
Pennsylvania *B*
Bryn Mawr College *B*
Bucknell University *B*
Bucks County Community College *A*
Carlow University *B*
Cedar Crest College *B*
Chatham University *B*
Community College of Beaver
County *A*
Dickinson College *B*
Elizabethtown College *B*
Franklin & Marshall College *B*
Gettysburg College *B*
Haverford College *B*
Holy Family University *B*
Indiana University of Pennsylvania *B*
Juniata College *B*
Keystone College *A, B*
Kutztown University of
Pennsylvania *B*
La Salle University *B*

Lafayette College *B*
Lebanon Valley College *B, T*
Lincoln University *B*
Lock Haven University of
 Pennsylvania *B*
Lycoming College *B*
Mansfield University of
 Pennsylvania *B*
Marywood University *M*
Mercyhurst College *B*
Messiah College *B*
Moore College of Art and Design *B, M*
Moravian College *B*
Northampton Community College *A*
Pennsylvania College of Art and
 Design *B*
Pennsylvania College of
 Technology *A*
Rosemont College *B*
St. Vincent College *B*
Seton Hill University *B*
Slippery Rock University of
 Pennsylvania *B, T*
Swarthmore College *B*
University of Pennsylvania *B, M*
University of Pittsburgh *B*
University of the Arts *B*
West Chester University of
 Pennsylvania *B*
Westminster College *B*
Widener University *B*
York College of Pennsylvania *A, B*

Puerto Rico

Pontifical Catholic University of
 Puerto Rico *B*
University of Puerto Rico
 Aguadilla *A*
 Rio Piedras *B*

Rhode Island

Brown University *B*
Providence College *B*
Rhode Island College *B*
Rhode Island School of Design *B, M*
Roger Williams University *B*
Salve Regina University *B*
University of Rhode Island *B*

South Carolina

Claflin University *B*
Coastal Carolina University *B*
Coker College *B*
College of Charleston *B*
Columbia College *B, T*
Converse College *B, M*
Limestone College *B*
North Greenville University *B*
Presbyterian College *B*
South Carolina State University *B*
University of South Carolina *B, M*
University of South Carolina
 Aiken *B*
Winthrop University *B*

South Dakota

University of South Dakota *B, M*

Tennessee

Christian Brothers University *B*
Cumberland University *B*
Lambuth University *B*
Lipscomb University *B*
Maryville College *B*
Memphis College of Art *B, M*
Tennessee Technological University *B*
Union University *B*
University of Tennessee
 Knoxville *B, M*
University of the South *B*
Vanderbilt University *B*
Watkins College of Art, Design and
 Film *B*

Texas

Abilene Christian University *B*
Angelo State University *B*
Baylor University *B*
Coastal Bend College *A*
College of the Mainland *A*
El Paso Community College *C*
Hardin-Simmons University *B*
Houston Baptist University *B*
Howard Payne University *B*
Lon Morris College *A*
McMurry University *B*
Midwestern State University *B*
Mountain View College *A*
Palo Alto College *A*
Paris Junior College *A*
Rice University *B, M*
St. Philip's College *A*
Sam Houston State University *B*
South Texas College *A*
Southern Methodist University *B, M*
Tarleton State University *B*
Texas A&M University
 Commerce *M*
 Corpus Christi *B*
 Kingsville *B, M, T*
Texas Christian University *B, M*
Texas College *B*
Texas Southern University *B, M*
Texas State University: San
 Marcos *B, T*
Texas Tech University *B*
Tyler Junior College *A*
University of Houston *B, M*
University of Mary Hardin-Baylor *B, T*
University of North Texas *B, M*
University of St. Thomas *B*
University of Texas
 Arlington *B*
 Austin *B, M*
 Dallas *B, M*
 El Paso *B, M*
 Pan American *B, M*
 San Antonio *B*
 Tyler *M*
West Texas A&M University *B, M*

Utah

Brigham Young University *B, M*
Southern Utah University *B*
Utah State University *M*
Weber State University *B*

Vermont

Bennington College *B*
Burlington College *B*
Green Mountain College *B*
Johnson State College *B, M*
Marlboro College *B*
Middlebury College *B*
St. Michael's College *B*
University of Vermont *B*

Virginia

Blue Ridge Community College *C*
Bridgewater College *B*
Christopher Newport University *B*
Germanna Community College *C*
Hampden-Sydney College *B*
Hollins University *B*
John Tyler Community College *C, A*
Longwood University *B, T*
Lord Fairfax Community College *C*
Marymount University *B*
Northern Virginia Community
 College *A*
Old Dominion University *B, T*
Radford University *B, M*
Randolph College *B*
Randolph-Macon College *B*
Regent University *M*
Sweet Briar College *B*

Thomas Nelson Community
 College *A*
Tidewater Community College *A*
University of Richmond *B, T*
Virginia Commonwealth University *M*
Virginia Western Community
 College *A*
Washington and Lee University *B*

Washington

Centralia College *A*
Cornish College of the Arts *B*
Eastern Washington University *B*
Everett Community College *A*
Evergreen State College *B*
Gonzaga University *B*
North Seattle Community
 College *C, A*
Northwest College of Art *B*
Pacific Lutheran University *B*
Washington State University *B, M*
Whitman College *B*

West Virginia

Alderson-Broaddus College *B*
Bethany College *B*
Concord University *B*
West Virginia State University *B*
West Virginia Wesleyan College *B*

Wisconsin

Cardinal Stritch University *B, T*
Carroll University *B*
Carthage College *B*
Lawrence University *B, T*
Marian University *B*
University of Wisconsin
 Madison *M*
 Oshkosh *B*
 River Falls *B*
 Stout *B*
 Superior *B, M, T*
Viterbo University *B*

Wyoming

Casper College *A*
Western Wyoming Community
 College *A*

Fire protection and safety technology

Alabama

Lawson State Community College *C*

Alaska

University of Alaska
 Fairbanks *C, A*

Arizona

Central Arizona College *C, A*
Cochise College *C, A*

California

Allan Hancock College *C, A*
American River College *A*
Antelope Valley College *C, A*
Bakersfield College *A*
Barstow Community College *C, A*
Butte College *C, A*
Cerro Coso Community College *C, A*
City College of San Francisco *C, A*
Cogswell Polytechnical College *B*
College of San Mateo *C, A*
College of the Desert *C, A*
College of the Sequoias *C, A*
College of the Siskiyous *C, A*
Columbia College *C, A*
Copper Mountain College *C, A*
Cosumnes River College *C, A*
El Camino College *C, A*

El Camino College: Compton
 Center *C*
Fresno City College *C*
Glendale Community College *C, A*
Long Beach City College *C, A*
Mission College *C, A*
Monterey Peninsula College *C, A*
Rio Hondo College *A*
Riverside Community College *C, A*
San Joaquin Delta College *C, A*
Santa Ana College *A*
Santa Rosa Junior College *C*
Santiago Canyon College *A*
Shasta College *C, A*
Sierra College *C, A*
Victor Valley College *C, A*
Yuba Community College
 District *C, A*

Colorado

Aims Community College *A*
Colorado Mountain College *C*
Pikes Peak Community College *A*
Red Rocks Community College *C, A*

Connecticut

Capital Community College *A*
Naugatuck Valley Community
 College *A*
Norwalk Community College *A*
Three Rivers Community College *A*
University of New Haven *C, A, B*

Delaware

Delaware State University *B*
Delaware Technical and Community
 College
 Stanton/Wilmington *C, A*

Florida

Central Florida Community College *A*
Daytona State College *A*
Florida State College at Jacksonville *A*
Hillsborough Community
 College *A*
Indian River State College *A*
Lake-Sumter Community College *A*
Saint Johns River Community
 College *A*
St. Petersburg College *C, A*
Seminole Community College *C, A*
Valencia Community College *A*

Hawaii

University of Hawaii
 Honolulu Community College *C, A*

Illinois

College of DuPage *C, A*
College of Lake County *C, A*
Illinois Central College *A*
John Wood Community College *A*
Kishwaukee College *C, A*
Lincoln Land Community College *C*
Parkland College *C, A*
Prairie State College *C, A*

Iowa

Des Moines Area Community
 College *C, A*

Kansas

Hutchinson Community College *A*
Kansas City Kansas Community
 College *C, A*

Kentucky

Bluegrass Community and Technical
 College *A*
Eastern Kentucky University *C, A, B*

Louisiana
Delgado Community College *A*
Louisiana State University
  Eunice *C, A*

Maryland
Anne Arundel Community College *A*
Community College of Baltimore
  County *C*
University of Maryland
  University College *C*

Massachusetts
Cape Cod Community College *A*
Massasoit Community College *C*
Middlesex Community College *A*
Mount Wachusett Community
  College *A*
North Shore Community College *A*
Springfield Technical Community
  College *A*

Michigan
Delta College *A*
Kellogg Community College *C, A*
Lake Superior State University *A, B*
Macomb Community College *C, A*
Mott Community College *A*
Wayne County Community
  College *C, A*

Minnesota
Lake Superior College *A*

Mississippi
Hinds Community College *A*
Mississippi Gulf Coast Community
  College *A*

Missouri
Jefferson College *C, A*
Ozarks Technical Community
  College *A*
St. Louis Community College
  St. Louis Community College at
    Florissant Valley *A*

Montana
Montana State University
  Billings *A*

Nebraska
Southeast Community College *A*
University of Nebraska
  Lincoln *A*

Nevada
College of Southern Nevada *A*

New Hampshire
Lakes Region Community College *A*

New Jersey
Camden County College *A*
Mercer County Community
  College *C, A*
Ocean County College *C, A*
Thomas Edison State College *A, B*
Union County College *A*

New Mexico
Central New Mexico Community
  College *A*
Eastern New Mexico University:
  Roswell Campus *A*

New York
Corning Community College *A*
Erie Community College
  City Campus *A*
Monroe Community College *A*

Onondaga Community College *C, A*
Rockland Community College *A*

North Carolina
Blue Ridge Community College *A*
Catawba Valley Community College *A*
Central Piedmont Community
  College *A*
Cleveland Community College *C, A*
Coastal Carolina Community
  College *C, A*
Davidson County Community
  College *C, A*
Fayetteville Technical Community
  College *A*
Forsyth Technical Community
  College *A*
Gaston College *A*
Guilford Technical Community
  College *A*
Rowan-Cabarrus Community
  College *A*
Wilson Community College *C, A*

Ohio
Columbus State Community
  College *A*
Cuyahoga Community College
  Metropolitan Campus *A*
Owens Community College
  Toledo *A*
University of Akron *C, A, B*

Oklahoma
Oklahoma State University *B*
Oklahoma State University
  Oklahoma City *C*
Tulsa Community College *A*

Oregon
Chemeketa Community College *A*
Portland Community College *C, A*
Rogue Community College *C, A*
Treasure Valley Community
  College *C, A*

Pennsylvania
Community College of Allegheny
  County *A*
Community College of Philadelphia *A*
Luzerne County Community
  College *A*
Montgomery County Community
  College *C, A*
Westmoreland County Community
  College *C, A*

Texas
Amarillo College *C, A*
Austin Community College *A*
College of the Mainland *A*
Collin County Community College
  District *C, A*
El Paso Community College *A*
Galveston College *C, A*
Houston Community College
  System *C, A*
Lamar Institute of Technology *A*
Laredo Community College *A*
Midland College *A*
Navarro College *C, A*
Odessa College *C, A*
San Antonio College *C, A*
San Jacinto College *C, A*
South Plains College *C, A*
Tarrant County College *C, A*
Tyler Junior College *A*

Virginia
Northern Virginia Community
  College *C, A*

Washington
Bates Technical College *C, A*
Bellevue College *C, A*
Pierce College *A*
Spokane Falls Community College *C*

West Virginia
American Public University
  System *A, B, M*
Blue Ridge Community and Technical
  College *C, A*

Wisconsin
Blackhawk Technical College *A*
Fox Valley Technical College *A*
Moraine Park Technical College *C, A*
Northcentral Technical College *C*
Northeast Wisconsin Technical
  College *A*
Western Technical College *A*

Fire services administration

Alabama
Bishop State Community College *A*
Calhoun Community College *C*
Jefferson Davis Community College *C*
Jefferson State Community
  College *C, A*
Northwest-Shoals Community
  College *C*
Shelton State Community College *C*

Alaska
University of Alaska
  Anchorage *A*

Arizona
Central Arizona College *C, A*

Arkansas
Southern Arkansas University Tech *A*

California
California State University
  Los Angeles *B*
Cogswell Polytechnical College *B*
College of the Siskiyous *C, A*
Fresno City College *C*
Santa Ana College *A*
Shasta College *C, A*

Colorado
Colorado Mountain College *C*
Colorado State University *B*

Connecticut
Gateway Community College *A*
Norwalk Community College *A*

Delaware
Delaware Technical and Community
  College
  Stanton/Wilmington *C, A*

District of Columbia
University of the District of
  Columbia *A, B*

Florida
Florida State College at Jacksonville *A*
Miami Dade College *A*
Palm Beach Community College *A*

Georgia
Georgia Perimeter College *C, A*

Hawaii
University of Hawaii
  Honolulu Community College *A*

Illinois
Black Hawk College *A*
College of DuPage *C*
Elgin Community College *C, A*
Lewis University *B*
Lincoln Land Community College *C*
Moraine Valley Community College *C*
Rend Lake College *C, A*
Southern Illinois University
  Carbondale *B*
Waubonsee Community College *C*

Iowa
Kirkwood Community College *C, A*
North Iowa Area Community
  College *A*

Kansas
Kansas City Kansas Community
  College *C*

Maryland
Frederick Community College *C, A*
University of Maryland
  University College *C, B*

Massachusetts
Cape Cod Community College *C*
Salem State College *B*

Michigan
Delta College *A*
Kirtland Community College *A*

Minnesota
Southwest Minnesota State
  University *B*

Missouri
Columbia College *A*
Lindenwood University *B*
Park University *B*

Nebraska
Metropolitan Community College *A*

New Hampshire
Lakes Region Community College *A*

New Jersey
Burlington County College *C*

New York
Erie Community College
  South Campus *A*
Jefferson Community College *A*
Mohawk Valley Community College *A*

North Carolina
University of North Carolina
  Charlotte *B*

Oklahoma
Oklahoma State University *M, D*

Oregon
Chemeketa Community College *C*
Eastern Oregon University *B*
Western Oregon University *B*

Pennsylvania
Holy Family University *B*
Northampton Community College *A*

South Carolina
Trident Technical College *A*

York Technical College *A*

Texas
Hill College *C, A*

Utah
Utah Valley University *B*

Virginia
Hampton University *B*
Northern Virginia Community
     College *C, A*
Thomas Nelson Community
     College *A*

Washington
Bates Technical College *C, A*
Bellevue College *A*
Olympic College *C, A*
Spokane Community College *A*
Yakima Valley Community College *A*

West Virginia
American Public University
     System *B, M*

Firefighting/fire science

Alabama
Alabama Southern Community
     College *C, A*
Central Alabama Community
     College *C, A*
Chattahoochee Valley Community
     College *C, A*
Columbia Southern University *A, B*

Alaska
University of Alaska
     Fairbanks *C, A*

Arizona
Arizona Western College *C, A*
Coconino County Community
     College *A*
Eastern Arizona College *C*
Glendale Community College *C, A*
Grand Canyon University *B*
Mohave Community College *C, A*
Northland Pioneer College *C, A*
Phoenix College *C, A*
Pima Community College *C, A*
Scottsdale Community College *C, A*

Arkansas
Northwest Arkansas Community
     College *A*
Southeast Arkansas College *A*
Southern Arkansas University
     Tech *C, A*

California
Allan Hancock College *C*
Cabrillo College *C, A*
Chabot College *C, A*
College of the Canyons *C, A*
College of the Sequoias *C*
College of the Siskiyous *C, A*
Crafton Hills College *C, A*
East Los Angeles College *C, A*
El Camino College *A*
El Camino College: Compton
     Center *A*
Folsom Lake College *A*
Fresno City College *C, A*
Hartnell College *C, A*
Imperial Valley College *C, A*
Lake Tahoe Community College *C, A*
Los Angeles Harbor College *C, A*
Los Medanos College *C, A*
Merced College *C, A*
Modesto Junior College *C, A*

Mount San Antonio College *C, A*
Oxnard College *C, A*
Palo Verde College *C, A*
Palomar College *C, A*
Pasadena City College *A*
Porterville College *C*
San Diego Miramar College *C, A*
Santa Ana College *A*
Santa Monica College *C, A*
Santa Rosa Junior College *C, A*
Shasta College *C, A*
Sierra College *C, A*
Solano Community College *C, A*
Southwestern College *C, A*
Yuba Community College District *C*

Colorado
Aims Community College *C*
Colorado Mountain College *A*
Pikes Peak Community College *C, A*
Pueblo Community College *C, A*

Connecticut
University of New Haven *C, B, M*

Delaware
Delaware Technical and Community
     College
     Stanton/Wilmington *A*

District of Columbia
University of the District of
     Columbia *A*

Florida
Brevard Community College *C, A*
Broward College *A*
Chipola College *C, A*
Daytona State College *C*
Edison State College *A*
Florida State College at
     Jacksonville *C, A, B*
Gulf Coast Community College *C, A*
Hillsborough Community College *C*
Indian River State College *C*
Lake-Sumter Community College *A*
Miami Dade College *C*
Palm Beach Community College *C, A*
Pensacola Junior College *C, A*
Polk State College *A*
St. Petersburg College *C, A*
Santa Fe College *A*
Seminole Community College *C, A*
South Florida Community College *A*
State College of Florida,
     Manatee-Sarasota *C, A*

Georgia
Albany Technical College *C*
Gwinnett Technical College *A*
Valdosta Technical College *C, A*
West Georgia Technical College *C, A*

Hawaii
University of Hawaii
     Honolulu Community College *C, A*

Idaho
Eastern Idaho Technical College *C, A*
Idaho State University *A, B*
Lewis-Clark State College *A, B*

Illinois
Carl Sandburg College *C, A*
City Colleges of Chicago
     Harold Washington College *A*
College of DuPage *C*
Danville Area Community
     College *C, A*
Harper College *C, A*
Illinois Eastern Community Colleges
     Frontier Community College *C*

Joliet Junior College *C*
Kishwaukee College *C, A*
Lewis and Clark Community
     College *A*
Lincoln Land Community College *C, A*
McHenry County College *C, A*
Moraine Valley Community
     College *A*
Oakton Community College *C, A*
Rend Lake College *C*
Richland Community College *A*
Rock Valley College *A*
Southeastern Illinois College *C*
Southwestern Illinois College *C, A*
Triton College *C, A*
Waubonsee Community College *C, A*

Indiana
Vincennes University *C, A*

Iowa
Clinton Community College *A*
Iowa Central Community College *A*
Iowa Western Community College *A*
Kirkwood Community College *C, A*
Muscatine Community College *A*
Western Iowa Tech Community
     College *C, A*

Kansas
Barton County Community
     College *C, A*
Butler Community College *C, A*
Dodge City Community College *A*
Garden City Community College *C, A*
Johnson County Community
     College *A*
Kansas City Kansas Community
     College *A*
Labette Community College *C, A*

Kentucky
Bluegrass Community and Technical
     College *C, A*
Elizabethtown Community and
     Technical College *C, A*
Somerset Community College *C*

Maine
Eastern Maine Community College *A*
Southern Maine Community
     College *C, A*

Maryland
Cecil College *A*
College of Southern Maryland *A*
Montgomery College *A*
University of Maryland
     University College *B*

Massachusetts
Anna Maria College *B, M*
Berkshire Community College *A*
Bristol Community College *A*
Cape Cod Community College *A*
Massasoit Community College *A*
Quinsigamond Community College *A*
Springfield Technical Community
     College *C*

Michigan
Delta College *A*
Grand Rapids Community College *A*
Henry Ford Community College *A*
Kalamazoo Valley Community
     College *C, A*
Kellogg Community College *C*
Kirtland Community College *C*
Lansing Community College *A*
Macomb Community College *C, A*
Madonna University *C, A, B*
Mid Michigan Community College *A*

Oakland Community College *C, A*
Schoolcraft College *C, A*
Southwestern Michigan College *C, A*

Minnesota
Lake Superior College *C*
Minnesota State Community and
     Technical College *C*
Northwest Technical College *C*

Mississippi
Meridian Community College *A*

Missouri
East Central College *C, A*
Metropolitan Community College:
     Blue River *C, A*
Mineral Area College *C, A*
Missouri Southern State University *C*
St. Charles Community College *A*
State Fair Community College *A*
Three Rivers Community College *C*

Montana
Helena College of Technology of the
     University of Montana *A*
Montana State University
     College of Technology: Great
     Falls *A*

Nebraska
Mid-Plains Community College
     Area *C, A*

Nevada
College of Southern Nevada *A*
Great Basin College *A*
Truckee Meadows Community
     College *C, A*

New Hampshire
Lakes Region Community College *A*

New Jersey
Burlington County College *C, A*
Essex County College *A*
Middlesex County College *A*
New Jersey City University *B*
Sussex County Community
     College *C, A*

New Mexico
Dona Ana Community College of New
     Mexico State University *A*
New Mexico Junior College *C*
New Mexico State University
     Alamogordo *A*
     Carlsbad *C*
San Juan College *C, A*

New York
Broome Community College *A*
Finger Lakes Community College *C*
Suffolk County Community College *A*

North Carolina
Alamance Community College *A*
Tri-County Community College *C*

Ohio
Cincinnati State Technical and
     Community College *C, A*
Columbus State Community
     College *A*
Hocking College *C, A*
Owens Community College
     Toledo *C, A*
Stark State College of Technology *A*

Oklahoma

Oklahoma State University
  Oklahoma City *A*
Western Oklahoma State College *A*

Oregon

Central Oregon Community
  College *C, A*
Chemeketa Community College *A*
Clackamas Community College *C, A*
Clatsop Community College *A*
Mt. Hood Community College *C, A*
Southwestern Oregon Community
  College *C, A*
Treasure Valley Community College *A*
Umpqua Community College *A*

Pennsylvania

Bucks County Community
  College *C, A*
Butler County Community College *C*
Harrisburg Area Community
  College *C, A*
Northampton Community
  College *C, A*

Rhode Island

Community College of Rhode
  Island *A*
Providence College *A*

South Carolina

Greenville Technical College *C*
Horry-Georgetown Technical
  College *C*

Tennessee

Chattanooga State Community
  College *A*
Volunteer State Community
  College *C, A*

Texas

Austin Community College *C*
Blinn College *C, A*
Collin County Community College
  District *C*
Del Mar College *C, A*
Houston Community College
  System *C*
Lamar Institute of Technology *C*
Lone Star College System *C, A*
Midland College *A*
Northeast Texas Community
  College *C*
Odessa College *C, A*
San Jacinto College *C, A*
South Plains College *A*
Temple College *C*
Trinity Valley Community
  College *C, A*
Vernon College *C*
Victoria College *C*
Wharton County Junior College *C*

Utah

Utah Valley University *C, A*

Virginia

Germanna Community College *C*
J. Sargeant Reynolds Community
  College *C, A*
Southside Virginia Community
  College *C*
Southwest Virginia Community
  College *C*
Tidewater Community College *A*
Virginia Highlands Community
  College *C*
Virginia Western Community
  College *C*

Washington

Bates Technical College *C, A*
Bellevue College *A*
Everett Community College *C, A*
Olympic College *A*
Skagit Valley College *A*
South Puget Sound Community
  College *C, A*
Spokane Falls Community
  College *C, A*
Yakima Valley Community
  College *C, A*

West Virginia

American Public University
  System *C, A*
Blue Ridge Community and Technical
  College *A*
Mountain State University *A*

Wisconsin

Chippewa Valley Technical College *A*
Gateway Technical College *A*
Mid-State Technical College *A*
Milwaukee Area Technical College *A*
Northcentral Technical College *A*
Waukesha County Technical
  College *C*

Wyoming

Casper College *C, A*
Central Wyoming College *C, A*

Fishing and fisheries

Alaska

University of Alaska
  Fairbanks *B, M, D*
  Southeast *M*

Arkansas

University of Arkansas
  Pine Bluff *B, M*

California

College of the Redwoods *C, A*
Fullerton College *A*
Humboldt State University *B*

Colorado

Colorado State University *M, D*
Trinidad State Junior College *C, A*

Delaware

Delaware State University *B*

Florida

University of Florida *M, D*

Georgia

University of Georgia *B*

Idaho

North Idaho College *A*
University of Idaho *B, M*

Indiana

Purdue University *B*

Iowa

Iowa State University *M, D*

Kentucky

Kentucky State University *M*

Louisiana

Louisiana State University and
  Agricultural and Mechanical
  College *M*

Maryland

Frostburg State University *B, M*
Garrett College *A*

Massachusetts

Bristol Community College *C*

Michigan

Grand Rapids Community College *A*
Lake Superior State University *B*
Michigan State University *B, M, D*
Mid Michigan Community College *A*

Minnesota

University of Minnesota
  Twin Cities *B, M, D*
Vermilion Community College *A*

Mississippi

Mississippi Gulf Coast Community
  College *A*

Missouri

University of Missouri
  Columbia *B, M, D*

New York

Finger Lakes Community College *A*
Paul Smith's College *B*
State University of New York
  College of Agriculture and
    Technology at Cobleskill *A, B*
  College of Agriculture and
    Technology at Morrisville *A*
  College of Environmental Science
    and Forestry *B, M, D*

North Carolina

College of the Albemarle *C, A*
Haywood Community College *A*

Ohio

Hocking College *A*
Ohio State University
  Columbus Campus *B*

Oregon

Mt. Hood Community College *A*
Oregon State University *B, M, D*

Pennsylvania

Mansfield University of
  Pennsylvania *B*

Rhode Island

University of Rhode Island *B, M*

Tennessee

Tennessee Technological University *B*

Texas

Texas A&M University *M*
Texas A&M University
  Galveston *B*
Texas Tech University *B, M, D*

Virginia

Virginia Polytechnic Institute and
  State University *M, D*

Washington

Bellingham Technical College *C, A*
Grays Harbor College *C*
Peninsula College *A*
University of Washington *B, M, D*

Wisconsin

University of Wisconsin
  Stevens Point *B*

Flight attendant

California

Chabot College *A*
Cypress College *C, A*
Mount San Antonio College *A*
Orange Coast College *C, A*
San Bernardino Valley College *C*

New Jersey

Mercer County Community College *A*

North Carolina

Asheville-Buncombe Technical
  Community College *C, A*

Washington

Spokane Falls Community College *C*

Flight instructor

Illinois

University of Illinois
  Urbana-Champaign *C*

Iowa

University of Dubuque *B*

Kansas

Central Christian College of Kansas *A*

Minnesota

Central Lakes College *C*
Saint Cloud State University *B*

North Dakota

University of North Dakota *B*

Ohio

University of Cincinnati
  Clermont College *A*

South Dakota

South Dakota State University *B*

Floriculture

California

City College of San Francisco *A*
MiraCosta College *C, A*
Santa Rosa Junior College *C*
Southwestern College *C, A*

Georgia

Albany Technical College *C*

Illinois

Danville Area Community
  College *C, A*
Harper College *C*

Massachusetts

North Shore Community College *A*

Minnesota

Hennepin Technical College *C, A*

Nebraska

University of Nebraska
  Lincoln *D*

New York

State University of New York
  College of Agriculture and
    Technology at Morrisville *A*

North Dakota

Dakota College at Bottineau *A*

Ohio

Ohio State University
  Agricultural Technical Institute A

Pennsylvania

Westmoreland County Community
  College A

Washington

Clover Park Technical College C

Food and nutrition studies

Alabama

Auburn University B
Lawson State Community College C
Oakwood University B
Tuskegee University B, M
Wallace State Community College at
  Hanceville C, A

Arizona

Arizona State University B, M
Central Arizona College C
Glendale Community College C
Mesa Community College A

Arkansas

University of Arkansas B
University of Central Arkansas B

California

Antelope Valley College A
Bakersfield College A
California State University
  Long Beach B, M
  Los Angeles B, M
  Northridge B
  San Bernardino B
College of the Desert A
College of the Sequoias C
Feather River College A
Fresno City College C, A
Glendale Community College A
Los Angeles Mission College A
The Master's College B
Merritt College C
Modesto Junior College A
Ohlone College C, A
Orange Coast College C, A
Pepperdine University B
Point Loma Nazarene University B
Reedley College C
Riverside Community College C, A
Saddleback College C, A
San Joaquin Delta College C, A
Santa Ana College C, A
Santa Rosa Junior College C

Colorado

Colorado State University B, M, D
Johnson & Wales University:
  Denver B

Connecticut

Gateway Community College A
Naugatuck Valley Community
  College C
Saint Joseph College B, M

Delaware

Delaware State University B
University of Delaware B, M

District of Columbia

Gallaudet University B
University of the District of
  Columbia B

Florida

Broward College A
Florida State University B
Miami Dade College A
Pensacola Junior College C, A

Georgia

Fort Valley State University B
Georgia Southern University B
University of Georgia B, M, D

Hawaii

University of Hawaii
  Hawaii Community College C, A
  Maui Community College A

Idaho

Brigham Young University-Idaho A
University of Idaho B

Illinois

Benedictine University B, M
Dominican University B
Illinois Central College A
Northern Illinois University B, M
Rush University M
Shawnee Community College C, A
Southern Illinois University
  Carbondale B, M

Indiana

Indiana State University B
Purdue University B, M, D
Purdue University
  North Central C

Iowa

Graceland University B
Iowa State University B
Waldorf College B

Kansas

Kansas State University M

Kentucky

Eastern Kentucky University B
Murray State University B
University of Kentucky B, M

Maine

University of Maine B, M, D
University of Maine
  Presque Isle T
Washington County Community
  College A

Maryland

Morgan State University B
University of Maryland
  College Park B

Massachusetts

Framingham State College B, M

Michigan

Andrews University B, M
Eastern Michigan University M
Madonna University A, B
Wayne State University B, M, D

Minnesota

Fond du Lac Tribal and Community
  College A
Minnesota State University
  Mankato B, M, T
St. Catherine University B
University of Minnesota
  Twin Cities B

Mississippi

Alcorn State University B

Mississippi State University M, D
University of Mississippi M
University of Southern
  Mississippi M, D

Missouri

College of the Ozarks B
Saint Louis University B, M
University of Missouri
  Columbia B, M, D

Nebraska

University of Nebraska
  Lincoln B, M
Wayne State College B
Western Nebraska Community
  College A

Nevada

University of Nevada
  Reno B, M

New Jersey

College of St. Elizabeth M
Montclair State University B, M, T

New Mexico

New Mexico State University B
Santa Fe Community College C
University of New Mexico B, M

New York

City University of New York
  Brooklyn College B, M
  Hunter College B, M
  Lehman College B, M
Cornell University B
Nassau Community College A
New York University B, M, D
Rochester Institute of Technology B
Rockland Community College A
State University of New York
  College at Buffalo B
  College at Oneonta B, M
  College at Plattsburgh B
  College of Agriculture and
    Technology at Morrisville A, B
Suffolk County Community College A
Syracuse University B, M, D
Westchester Community College A

North Carolina

Appalachian State University B
East Carolina University M
North Carolina Agricultural and
  Technical State University B, M
University of North Carolina
  Chapel Hill B

North Dakota

North Dakota State University M
University of North Dakota B

Ohio

Ashland University B
Bluffton University B
Bowling Green State University B, M
Kent State University B, M
Kent State University
  East Liverpool C
Ohio State University
  Columbus Campus B, M, D
Ohio University B, M
University of Akron M
University of Cincinnati B, M
University of Cincinnati
  Raymond Walters College A
University of Dayton B
Youngstown State University A, B

Oklahoma

Eastern Oklahoma State College C

Langston University B
Northeastern State University B
Oklahoma State University B, M
University of Central Oklahoma B, M

Oregon

Oregon State University B, M, D

Pennsylvania

Cedar Crest College B
Chatham University M
Indiana University of
  Pennsylvania B, M
Mansfield University of
  Pennsylvania A

Puerto Rico

University of Puerto Rico
  Rio Piedras B

Rhode Island

University of Rhode Island B, M, D

South Carolina

Bob Jones University B
South Carolina State University B, M
Winthrop University B, M

South Dakota

Sisseton Wahpeton College C, A
South Dakota State University B

Tennessee

Carson-Newman College B
Chattanooga State Community
  College C, A
Middle Tennessee State University B
Southern Adventist University A
Tennessee State University B
Tennessee Technological University B
University of Tennessee
  Knoxville B, M

Texas

Lamar University B
Palo Alto College C, A
Prairie View A&M University B
Sam Houston State University B
Stephen F. Austin State University B
Texas A&M University B
Texas A&M University
  Kingsville B
Texas Southern University B, M
Texas State University: San Marcos B
Texas Tech University B, M, D
Texas Woman's University B
University of Houston B
University of Texas
  Austin B

Utah

Snow College A
University of Utah M
Utah State University B, M, D

Virginia

Bridgewater College B
James Madison University B
Radford University B
Virginia Polytechnic Institute and
  State University B, M, D

Washington

Highline Community College A
Seattle Pacific University B
Shoreline Community College A
Washington State University B

West Virginia

West Virginia University B

Wisconsin
College of Menominee Nation *A*
Northeast Wisconsin Technical
College *C*
University of Wisconsin
Stevens Point *M*

Food preparation

Alabama
Shelton State Community College *C*

Arizona
Cochise College *C*

California
Art Institute
of California: Los Angeles *A, B*
Diablo Valley College *C*
Long Beach City College *C*
Santa Rosa Junior College *C*
Shasta College *C*

Colorado
Colorado Mountain College *A*

Connecticut
Gateway Community College *A*

Florida
South Florida Community College *C*

Georgia
Albany Technical College *C*
Art Institute
of Atlanta *C*
Savannah Technical College *C*

Illinois
City Colleges of Chicago
Kennedy-King College *C*
Elgin Community College *C*
Harper College *C*
Kaskaskia College *C*

Indiana
Vincennes University *C*

Kansas
Kansas City Kansas Community
College *C*

Kentucky
Owensboro Community and
Technical College *C*

Maryland
Anne Arundel Community College *C*

Massachusetts
Massasoit Community College *C*

Minnesota
Hennepin Technical College *A*
Minneapolis Community and
Technical College *C*
St. Paul College *C*

Missouri
Jefferson College *C, A*

New Mexico
Eastern New Mexico University:
Roswell Campus *C*
Southwestern Indian Polytechnic
Institute *C*

New York
Monroe Community College *C*
Paul Smith's College *A*

North Carolina
Cape Fear Community College *C*

Oregon
Lane Community College *C*

Pennsylvania
Commonwealth Technical Institute *C*

Puerto Rico
Inter American University of Puerto
Rico
Aguadilla Campus *C*

Texas
San Jacinto College *C, A*
South Texas College *C*

Virginia
Dabney S. Lancaster Community
College *A*

Washington
Art Institute of Seattle *C*
Bates Technical College *C*
Olympic College *C*
South Seattle Community
College *C, A*

Wisconsin
Waukesha County Technical
College *C*
Western Technical College *C*

Food science

Alabama
Alabama Agricultural and Mechanical
University *D*

Arizona
Prescott College *B, M*

Arkansas
Arkansas Northeastern College *A*
University of Arkansas *B, M, D*

California
California Polytechnic State
University: San Luis Obispo *B*
California State Polytechnic
University: Pomona *B*
California State University
Fresno *B, M*
Fresno City College *C, A*
Mission College *C, A*
Modesto Junior College *C, A*
Reedley College *C*
San Joaquin Delta College *A*
San Jose State University *T*
University of California
Davis *B, M, D*

Colorado
Colorado Mountain College *A*

Delaware
Delaware State University *B, M*
University of Delaware *B, M*

Florida
University of Florida *B, M, D*

Georgia
University of Georgia *B, M, D*

Hawaii
University of Hawaii
Manoa *M*

Idaho
University of Idaho *B, M, D*

Illinois
City Colleges of Chicago
Malcolm X College *C, A*
University of Illinois
Urbana-Champaign *B, M, D*

Indiana
Purdue University *B, M, D*
Vincennes University *A*

Iowa
Iowa State University *M, D*

Kansas
Kansas State University *C, B, M, D*

Kentucky
University of Kentucky *B*

Louisiana
Louisiana State University and
Agricultural and Mechanical
College *B, M, D*

Maine
Eastern Maine Community
College *C, A*
University of Maine *B, M, D*

Maryland
University of Maryland
College Park *B, M, D*
Eastern Shore *M, D*

Massachusetts
Framingham State College *B, M*
University of Massachusetts
Amherst *B, M, D*

Michigan
Michigan State University *C, B, M, D*

Minnesota
Minnesota State University
Mankato *B*
Southwest Minnesota State
University *B*
University of Minnesota
Twin Cities *B, M, D*

Mississippi
Hinds Community College *A*
Mississippi Gulf Coast Community
College *C, A*
Mississippi State University *B*
Northwest Mississippi Community
College *A*

Missouri
Missouri State University: West
Plains *C, A*
University of Missouri
Columbia *B, M, D*

Nebraska
University of Nebraska
Lincoln *B, M, D*

New Jersey
Rutgers, The State University of New
Jersey
New Brunswick/Piscataway
Campus *B*

New York
Cornell University *B, M, D*

North Carolina
North Carolina State
University *B, M, D*

North Dakota
North Dakota State University *B*

Ohio
Ohio State University
Columbus Campus *B, M, D*

Oklahoma
Eastern Oklahoma State College *A*
Oklahoma State University *B, M, D*

Oregon
Oregon State University *B, M, D*

Pennsylvania
Delaware Valley College *C, B*
Penn State
Abington *B*
Altoona *B*
Beaver *B*
Berks *B*
Brandywine *B*
DuBois *B*
Erie, The Behrend College *B*
Fayette, The Eberly Campus *B*
Greater Allegheny *B*
Hazleton *B*
Lehigh Valley *B*
Mont Alto *B*
New Kensington *B*
Schuylkill *B*
Shenango *B*
University Park *B, M, D*
Wilkes-Barre *B*
Worthington Scranton *B*
York *B*

South Carolina
Clemson University *B, D*

Tennessee
University of Tennessee
Knoxville *B, M, D*

Texas
North Lake College *C*
Sul Ross State University *B*
Texas A&M University *B, M, D*
Texas A&M University
Commerce *B*
Kingsville *B, M*
Texas Tech University *B, M*

Utah
Brigham Young University *B, M*
Utah State University *B, M, D*

Virginia
Virginia Polytechnic Institute and
State University *B*

Washington
Pierce College *C*
Washington State University *M, D*

Wisconsin
Northeast Wisconsin Technical
College *A*
University of Wisconsin
Madison *B, M, D*
River Falls *B*

Wyoming
Sheridan College *A*
University of Wyoming *M*

Food service

California
City College of San Francisco *C*
Columbia College *C*
Diablo Valley College *C*
Santa Rosa Junior College *C*
Shasta College *C*

Colorado
Johnson & Wales University:
  Denver *B*

Connecticut
Three Rivers Community College *C, A*

Florida
Central Florida Community College *C*
Johnson & Wales University: North
  Miami *B*

Georgia
Art Institute
  of Atlanta *B*

Hawaii
University of Hawaii
  Hawaii Community College *C, A*
  Maui Community College *C, A*

Illinois
Harper College *C*
Kaskaskia College *C*

Indiana
Indiana University-Purdue University
  Indianapolis *A*

Maryland
Montgomery College *C, A*

Massachusetts
Newbury College *A, B*
Quinsigamond Community
  College *C, A*

Michigan
Henry Ford Community College *C*

Mississippi
Copiah-Lincoln Community
  College *C, A*

Missouri
Jefferson College *C, A*

New York
Nassau Community College *A*
Paul Smith's College *A*
Schenectady County Community
  College *A*
State University of New York
  College of Agriculture and
    Technology at Morrisville *A, B*

Ohio
Columbus State Community
  College *C*

Pennsylvania
Northampton Community College *C*
Westmoreland County Community
  College *C*

Puerto Rico
Inter American University of Puerto
  Rico
  Aguadilla Campus *C, A*

Rhode Island
Johnson & Wales University:
  Providence *B*

Texas
Del Mar College *C*

Vermont
New England Culinary Institute
  Essex Junction *A, B*

Washington
Clark College *C*
Olympic College *C*

Food technology/ processing

Arkansas
Arkansas State University *A*

Colorado
Colorado Mountain College *A*

Illinois
Illinois Institute of Technology *M*
University of Illinois
  Urbana-Champaign *B*

Indiana
Vincennes University *A*

Ohio
Ohio State University
  Columbus Campus *B*

Puerto Rico
Inter American University of Puerto
  Rico
  Bayamon Campus *B*
University of Puerto Rico
  Utuado *A*

Utah
Brigham Young University *B*

Washington
Yakima Valley Community College *A*

Foreign language teacher education

Alabama
Auburn University *B, M, T*
Birmingham-Southern College *T*

Arizona
Cochise College *A*
Northern Arizona University *T*
Prescott College *B, M, T*
University of Arizona *B, M*

Arkansas
Arkansas State University *B, T*
Arkansas Tech University *B*
Harding University *B, T*
Ouachita Baptist University *B, T*

California
Azusa Pacific University *T*
California Lutheran University *B, T*
California State University
  Chico *M*
  Long Beach *B, T*
  Northridge *B, T*
  San Bernardino *T*
Humboldt State University *T*
Los Angeles Southwest College *A*
Mount St. Mary's College *T*

San Diego State University *T*
San Francisco State University *T*
Soka University of America *M*
Sonoma State University *T*
Stanford University *M, T*
University of the Pacific *T*
Vanguard University of Southern
  California *T*

Colorado
Colorado State University
  Pueblo *T*
Metropolitan State College of
  Denver *T*
University of Colorado
  Boulder *T*
Western State College of
  Colorado *B, T*

Connecticut
Central Connecticut State
  University *T*
Fairfield University *T*
Quinnipiac University *B, M*

Delaware
University of Delaware *B, T*

District of Columbia
George Washington University *M, T*

Florida
Florida International University *M*
Florida State University *B, M*
State College of Florida,
  Manatee-Sarasota *A*
Stetson University *B*
University of Central Florida *B*
University of South Florida *B, M*

Georgia
Darton College *A*
Fort Valley State University *B, T*
University of Georgia *B, M, T*

Idaho
University of Idaho *T*

Illinois
Augustana College *B, T*
DePaul University *M, T*
Dominican University *T*
North Park University *T*
Olivet Nazarene University *B, T*
University of Illinois
  Urbana-Champaign *B, M, T*

Indiana
Bethel College *B*
Butler University *T*
Indiana University
  Bloomington *M, D, T*
Indiana University-Purdue University
  Indianapolis *M*
Manchester College *B, T*
Purdue University *B, M, D*
Saint Mary's College *T*
St. Mary-of-the-Woods College *B, T*
University of Indianapolis *B, T*
Valparaiso University *B*

Iowa
Central College *T*
Dordt College *B*
Graceland University *T*
Iowa State University *T*
St. Ambrose University *B, T*
Simpson College *T*
University of Iowa *D, T*
University of Northern Iowa *B*

Kansas
McPherson College *B, T*
MidAmerica Nazarene University *B, T*
University of Kansas *B, T*

Louisiana
Centenary College of Louisiana *B, T*
Louisiana College *B*
McNeese State University *B, T*
Xavier University of Louisiana *B*

Maine
University of Maine *B*
University of Southern Maine *T*

Maryland
College of Notre Dame of Maryland *T*
University of Maryland
  College Park *B*

Massachusetts
Boston University *M, T*
Brandeis University *M*
Tufts University *M, T*
University of Massachusetts
  Dartmouth *T*

Michigan
Albion College *B, T*
Andrews University *M*
Eastern Michigan University *B*
University of Michigan
  Dearborn *B*
  Flint *B, T*
Wayne State University *M, T*

Minnesota
College of St. Benedict *T*
Gustavus Adolphus College *T*
Minnesota State University
  Mankato *B, M, T*
St. Catherine University *B*
Saint Cloud State University *B*
St. John's University *T*
St. Mary's University of Minnesota *B*
University of Minnesota
  Morris *T*
  Twin Cities *M*
Winona State University *B, T*

Mississippi
Millsaps College *T*
Mississippi State University *B, T*
University of Mississippi *B, T*
University of Southern Mississippi *M*

Missouri
Central Methodist University *B*
Evangel University *B*
Missouri Southern State
  University *B, T*
Northwest Missouri State University *T*
Southeast Missouri State
  University *B, T*
Truman State University *M, T*
University of Central Missouri *B, T*
University of Missouri
  Columbia *B, M, D*
  Kansas City *B*
William Jewell College *B, T*

Montana
Montana State University
  Billings *B, T*
University of Montana *T*

Nebraska
Creighton University *T*
Union College *T*
University of Nebraska
  Kearney *B, M, T*
  Lincoln *B*

Wayne State College *B, T*

Nevada

University of Nevada
  Reno *B, T*

New Hampshire

Rivier College *B, M, T*
University of New Hampshire *T*

New Jersey

The College of New Jersey *B, T*
Rowan University *T*
Rutgers, The State University of New
  Jersey
  New Brunswick/Piscataway
    Campus *T*
Saint Peter's College *T*

New York

City University of New York
  City College *B, T*
  Hunter College *B, M, T*
  Queens College *M, T*
College of Mount St. Vincent *T*
D'Youville College *M, T*
Dowling College *B, M*
Elmira College *B, T*
Fordham University *T*
Hobart and William Smith Colleges *T*
Hofstra University *B, M*
Houghton College *B, T*
Ithaca College *B, T*
Long Island University
  C. W. Post Campus *B, T*
Manhattan College *B, T*
Manhattanville College *M, T*
Nazareth College *B, M, T*
New York University *M*
Pace University *M, T*
St. Lawrence University *T*
St. Thomas Aquinas College *B, T*
State University of New York
  Albany *M, T*
  Buffalo *M, D*
  College at Buffalo *B, T*
  College at Fredonia *B, T*
  College at Oneonta *B, T*
  College at Plattsburgh *B*
  College at Potsdam *B, M*
  New Paltz *B, T*
Vassar College *T*
Wells College *T*
Yeshiva University *B*

North Carolina

Davidson College *T*
Gardner-Webb University *B*
Lenoir-Rhyne University *T*
Meredith College *T*
Methodist University *A, B, T*
North Carolina Agricultural and
    Technical State University *B, T*
Queens University of Charlotte *B*

North Dakota

Dickinson State University *B, T*
Minot State University *B*

Ohio

Bowling Green State University *B, T*
Hiram College *T*
Miami University
  Oxford Campus *B, M*
Mount Union College *T*
Ohio Northern University *B, T*
Ohio State University
  Columbus Campus *M, D*
Ohio Wesleyan University *B*
Otterbein College *B*
University of Dayton *B*
University of Findlay *B, M, T*
University of Toledo *T*

Wright State University *B, T*
Youngstown State University *B, M*

Oklahoma

Oklahoma Baptist University *B, T*
Oklahoma City University *B, M*
Oral Roberts University *B, T*
University of Oklahoma *B, T*
University of Tulsa *T*

Oregon

Linfield College *T*
Western Oregon University *T*

Pennsylvania

Dickinson College *T*
Gannon University *B*
King's College *T*
La Salle University *B, T*
Lincoln University *T*
Lycoming College *T*
Mansfield University of
    Pennsylvania *B, T*
Mercyhurst College *B, T*
Moravian College *T*
Penn State
  Abington *B*
  Altoona *B*
  Beaver *B*
  Berks *B*
  Brandywine *B*
  DuBois *B*
  Erie, The Behrend College *B*
  Fayette, The Eberly Campus *B*
  Greater Allegheny *B*
  Hazleton *B*
  Lehigh Valley *B*
  Mont Alto *B*
  New Kensington *B*
  Schuylkill *B*
  Shenango *B*
  University Park *B*
  Wilkes-Barre *B*
  Worthington Scranton *B*
  York *B*
Rosemont College *T*
St. Francis University *B, T*
Saint Joseph's University *B, M, T*
St. Vincent College *T*
Seton Hill University *B, T*
Susquehanna University *T*
Temple University *B*
University of Pennsylvania *M, T*
Westminster College *B, T*
Widener University *M*

Rhode Island

Rhode Island College *B, M*

South Carolina

College of Charleston *M, T*
Converse College *T*
Furman University *T*

South Dakota

Black Hills State University *B*
Northern State University *B, T*
University of South Dakota *B, T*

Tennessee

Lee University *B*
Middle Tennessee State
    University *M, T*
Tennessee Technological University *T*
Union University *B, T*
University of Memphis *T*
University of Tennessee
  Chattanooga *B*
  Knoxville *T*

Texas

Baylor University *T*

Lamar University *T*
Laredo Community College *A*
Sam Houston State University *M, T*
Texas Christian University *B*
University of Houston *M, T*
University of Texas
  Austin *M, D*
West Texas A&M University *T*

Utah

Southern Utah University *B*

Vermont

Bennington College *M*
Castleton State College *B, T*
St. Michael's College *T*
University of Vermont *B, T*

Virginia

Longwood University *T*
Old Dominion University *B, T*
University of Virginia's College at
    Wise *T*
Virginia Wesleyan College *T*

Washington

Washington State University *B, M, T*
Western Washington University *M*
Whitworth University *T*

West Virginia

Bethany College *B*
West Virginia University *T*

Wisconsin

Carroll University *B*
Carthage College *M, T*
Lawrence University *T*
Marquette University *B, M*
Mount Mary College *B, T*
St. Norbert College *T*
University of Wisconsin
  Parkside *T*

Foreign languages, general

Alabama

Auburn University at Montgomery *B*
Jacksonville State University *B*
Judson College *B*
Samford University *B*
Troy University *B*
University of Alabama *B*
University of Alabama
  Birmingham *B*
  Huntsville *B*
University of Montevallo *B*
University of North Alabama *B*
University of South Alabama *B*

Alaska

University of Alaska
  Anchorage *B*
  Fairbanks *B*

Arizona

Cochise College *A*
Eastern Arizona College *A*
Northern Arizona University *B*

Arkansas

Arkansas Tech University *B*

California

Cabrillo College *A*
California Lutheran University *B*
California Polytechnic State
    University: San Luis Obispo *B*
College of Marin: Kentfield *A*
College of the Sequoias *A*

Crafton Hills College *A*
Fresno City College *A*
Fullerton College *A*
Glendale Community College *A*
Golden West College *A*
Imperial Valley College *A*
Long Beach City College *A*
Los Angeles Southwest College *A*
MiraCosta College *A*
Modesto Junior College *A*
Monterey Peninsula College *A*
Occidental College *B*
Pitzer College *B*
Pomona College *B*
Reedley College *A*
Saddleback College *A*
St. Mary's College of California *B*
San Diego City College *A*
Santa Ana College *A*
Santiago Canyon College *A*
Scripps College *B*
Shasta College *A*
Solano Community College *A*
University of California
  Riverside *B*
  San Diego *B*
  Santa Cruz *B*
West Valley College *A*
Whittier College *B*

Colorado

Colorado State University *B, M*
Colorado State University
  Pueblo *B*
Metropolitan State College of
    Denver *B, T*
Pikes Peak Community College *A*
University of Northern
    Colorado *B, M, T*

Connecticut

Central Connecticut State
    University *M*
Southern Connecticut State
    University *B, M, T*
Trinity College *B*
University of Hartford *B*

Delaware

University of Delaware *B, M*

District of Columbia

George Washington University *B*
Howard University *M*
Trinity Washington University *B*

Florida

Broward College *A*
Gulf Coast Community College *A*
Indian River State College *A*
Miami Dade College *A*
New College of Florida *B*
University of Central Florida *B*
University of Tampa *A*

Georgia

Abraham Baldwin Agricultural
    College *A*
Atlanta Metropolitan College *A*
Bainbridge College *A*
College of Coastal Georgia *A*
Dalton State College *A*
Darton College *A*
Georgia Highlands College *A*
Georgia Perimeter College *A*
Georgia State University *B*
Gordon College *A*
Macon State College *A*
Middle Georgia College *A*
South Georgia College *A*
University of West Georgia *B*
Young Harris College *A*

Idaho

North Idaho College *A*
University of Idaho *B*

Illinois

City Colleges of Chicago
  Harold Washington College *A*
  Kennedy-King College *A*
  Olive-Harvey College *A*
DePaul University *T*
Eastern Illinois University *B, T*
Illinois Central College *A*
Illinois State University *B, M*
Illinois Valley Community College *A*
Kishwaukee College *A*
Knox College *B*
Olivet Nazarene University *B*
Principia College *B*
Roosevelt University *B*
Southern Illinois University
  Carbondale *M*
Southern Illinois University
  Edwardsville *B*
Southwestern Illinois College *A*
Triton College *A*

Indiana

Grace College *B*
Indiana University
  Bloomington *B, M, D*
Manchester College *B, T*
Purdue University *B, M, D*
Purdue University
  Calumet *B*
Vincennes University *A*

Iowa

Cornell College *B*
Iowa State University *B*
University of Northern Iowa *B, M*

Kansas

Barton County Community College *A*
Butler Community College *A*
Coffeyville Community College *A*
Cowley County Community
  College *A*
Emporia State University *B, T*
Fort Hays State University *B*
Hutchinson Community College *A*
Kansas State University *B, M*
Kansas Wesleyan University *B*
McPherson College *B, T*
Neosho County Community
  College *A*

Kentucky

Eastern Kentucky University *B*

Louisiana

Centenary College of Louisiana *B, T*
Dillard University *B*
Louisiana College *B*
Loyola University New Orleans *B*
University of Louisiana at Lafayette *B*

Maine

University of Maine *B*
University of Maine
  Fort Kent *B*
University of Southern Maine *B*

Maryland

College of Notre Dame of Maryland *B*
Frostburg State University *B*
St. Mary's College of Maryland *B*
Towson University *B*
University of Maryland
  Baltimore County *B, M, D*

Massachusetts

Assumption College *B*

Bard College at Simon's Rock *B*
Boston University *B*
Bunker Hill Community College *A*
Cape Cod Community College *A*
Clark University *B*
Framingham State College *B*
Gordon College *B*
Massachusetts Institute of
  Technology *B*
Stonehill College *B*
Suffolk University *B*
Tufts University *B, M*
University of Massachusetts
  Lowell *B*
Wellesley College *B*

Michigan

Delta College *A*
Grand Rapids Community College *A*
Lake Michigan College *A*
Lansing Community College *A*
Oakland University *B*
Wayne State University *B, M, D*

Minnesota

Northland Community & Technical
  College *A*
University of Minnesota
  Twin Cities *B*
Winona State University *B*

Mississippi

Delta State University *B*
Jackson State University *B*
Mississippi State University *B, M*
University of Southern Mississippi *B*

Missouri

St. Charles Community College *A*
Saint Louis University *B*
Three Rivers Community College *A*
University of Missouri
  Columbia *D*
  Kansas City *M*
Washington University in St.
  Louis *B, M, D*
Webster University *B*

Montana

Miles Community College *A*
Montana State University
  Bozeman *B*
University of Montana *M*

Nebraska

University of Nebraska
  Lincoln *M, D*
Wayne State College *B*

Nevada

University of Nevada
  Las Vegas *M*
  Reno *M*

New Jersey

Bergen Community College *A*
Monmouth University *B*
Richard Stockton College of New
  Jersey *B*
Saint Peter's College *B*
Seton Hall University *B*
Thomas Edison State College *B*

New Mexico

New Mexico State University *B*
University of New Mexico *B*

New York

Bard College *B*
City University of New York
  City College *B, M*
  Hunter College *B*

College of Mount St. Vincent *B*
Elmira College *B, T*
Eugene Lang College The New School
  for Liberal Arts *B*
Excelsior College *B*
Hamilton College *B*
Ithaca College *B*
Jewish Theological Seminary of
  America *B, M, D*
Long Island University
  Brooklyn Campus *B*
  C. W. Post Campus *B*
New York University *B, M, D, T*
Orange County Community College *A*
Pace University *B*
St. Joseph's College *B, T*
St. Lawrence University *B, T*
St. Thomas Aquinas College *B, T*
State University of New York
  College at Brockport *B*
  Purchase *B*
  Stony Brook *D*
Syracuse University *B*
Touro College *B*
Union College *B*
University of Rochester *B*
Utica College *B*
Wells College *B*

North Carolina

Elon University *B*
Gardner-Webb University *B*
High Point University *B*
Queens University of Charlotte *B*
Warren Wilson College *B*

North Dakota

Minot State University *B*
University of North Dakota *B*

Ohio

College of Wooster *B*
Kenyon College *B*
Owens Community College
  Toledo *A*
Wright State University *B*
Youngstown State University *B*

Oklahoma

Cameron University *B*
Oklahoma Baptist University *B, T*
Rose State College *A*

Oregon

Central Oregon Community
  College *A*
Lewis & Clark College *B*
Pacific University *B*
Portland State University *M*
Southern Oregon University *B*
Treasure Valley Community College *A*

Pennsylvania

California University of
  Pennsylvania *B*
Carnegie Mellon University *B*
Community College of Allegheny
  County *A*
Duquesne University *B*
Elizabethtown College *B*
Gannon University *B*
Juniata College *B*
La Salle University *B, T*
Mercyhurst College *B, T*
Muhlenberg College *B*
Penn State
  Berks *B*
  Lehigh Valley *B*
Rosemont College *B*
St. Francis University *B*
West Chester University of
  Pennsylvania *T*
Westminster College *B*

Puerto Rico

University of Puerto Rico
  Aguadilla *A*
  Rio Piedras *B*

Rhode Island

Roger Williams University *B*

South Carolina

The Citadel *B, T*
Clemson University *B*
Converse College *B*
Presbyterian College *B*
South Carolina State University *B*
University of South Carolina *M*
Winthrop University *B*

South Dakota

Augustana College *B*

Tennessee

Austin Peay State University *B*
East Tennessee State University *B, T*
King College *B*
Lambuth University *B*
Middle Tennessee State University *B*
Southern Adventist University *B*
University of Memphis *B*
University of Tennessee
  Chattanooga *B*
  Knoxville *M, D*

Texas

Austin Community College *A*
Blinn College *A*
Brazosport College *A*
Central Texas College *A*
Clarendon College *A*
Del Mar College *A*
El Paso Community College *A*
Hill College *A*
Howard College *A*
Laredo Community College *A*
Lee College *A*
Midland College *A*
Northwest Vista College *A*
Odessa College *A*
Palo Alto College *A*
Paris Junior College *A*
St. Philip's College *A*
San Jacinto College *A*
Southern Methodist University *B*
Southwestern Assemblies of God
  University *A*
Texarkana College *A*
Texas A&M University *M*
Texas Tech University *M*
Tyler Junior College *A*
University of Texas
  Arlington *B, M*
  Austin *M, D*
  Tyler *B*
Western Texas College *A*

Utah

Brigham Young University *B*
Snow College *A*
University of Utah *M, D*

Vermont

Bennington College *B*
Marlboro College *B*
St. Michael's College *B*

Virginia

George Mason University *B, M*
James Madison University *B, T*
Old Dominion University *B*
Radford University *B*
Sweet Briar College *B*
University of Mary Washington *B*

University of Virginia's College at
Wise *B*
Virginia Commonwealth University *B*
Virginia Military Institute *B*
Virginia Polytechnic Institute and
State University *B, M*
Virginia Wesleyan College *B*
Washington and Lee University *B*

Washington
Centralia College *A*
Everett Community College *A*
Evergreen State College *B*
Highline Community College *A*
Olympic College *A*
Seattle University *B*
Spokane Falls Community College *A*
Washington State University *B*
Western Washington University *B*

West Virginia
Marshall University *B*
West Virginia University *B, M*

Wisconsin
Beloit College *B*
Marquette University *M*
Ripon College *B, T*
University of Wisconsin
Milwaukee *M*

Wyoming
Casper College *A*
Eastern Wyoming College *A*
Northwest College *A*
Sheridan College *A*

Forensic chemistry

Delaware
Delaware State University *B*

Florida
University of Tampa *B*

Illinois
Western Illinois University *B*

Indiana
University of St. Francis *B*

Massachusetts
Emmanuel College *B*

Michigan
Lake Superior State University *B*
Northern Michigan University *B*

Nebraska
Concordia University *B*

New Mexico
New Mexico Highlands University *B*

New York
City University of New York
Hostos Community College *A*
Syracuse University *M*

North Carolina
Methodist University *B*

Pennsylvania
Slippery Rock University of
Pennsylvania *B*

Rhode Island
University of Rhode Island *B*

Forensic psychology

Arizona
Prescott College *M*

California
Alliant International University *B, D*
California Baptist University *M*
Holy Names University *M, T*

Colorado
University of Denver *M*

Florida
Florida Institute of Technology *B*

Iowa
St. Ambrose University *B*

Maine
Thomas College *B*

Massachusetts
American International College *M*

Minnesota
Walden University *M*

New Jersey
College of St. Elizabeth *M*
Fairleigh Dickinson University
Metropolitan Campus *M*

North Dakota
University of North Dakota *M*

Ohio
Tiffin University *B, M*

Rhode Island
Roger Williams University *M*

Texas
Prairie View A&M University *M*
Sam Houston State University *D*

Virginia
Marymount University *M*

Forensic science

Alabama
University of Alabama
Birmingham *M*

Arizona
Pima Community College *C*
Scottsdale Community College *C*

Arkansas
Arkansas State University *A, B*
Arkansas State University
Beebe *C, A*
Mountain Home *C, A*
Mid-South Community College *C, A*
North Arkansas College *C, A*
Northwest Arkansas Community
College *C, A*
Ouachita Technical College *C, A*
Pulaski Technical College *C, A*
Southeast Arkansas College *C, A*
Southern Arkansas University *C, A*
University of Arkansas
Community College at Hope *C, A*
Cossatot Community College of the
C, A
Fort Smith *C, A*
Monticello *C, A*
Pine Bluff *C, A*

University of Arkansas Community
College at Morrilton *C, A*

California
California State University
Chico *C*
East Los Angeles College *C*
Grossmont College *C, A*
National University *M*
San Jose State University *B*
Southwestern College *C, A*
University of California
Davis *M*

Connecticut
Tunxis Community College *C*
University of New Haven *C, B, M*

Florida
Edison State College *A*
Florida International University *M*
Gulf Coast Community College *C, A*
Hillsborough Community College *C*
St. Petersburg College *C, A*
Tallahassee Community College *C*
University of Central Florida *B, M*

Georgia
Albany State University *B*
Armstrong Atlantic State University *C*
Darton College *A*

Hawaii
Chaminade University of Honolulu *B*

Illinois
Lewis University *B*
Loyola University Chicago *B*
University of Illinois
Chicago *M*

Indiana
Indiana University
Bloomington *M*
Indiana University-Purdue University
Indianapolis *B*
Trine University *B*

Iowa
Iowa Western Community
College *C, A*
Simpson College *B*

Kansas
Newman University *B*
Washburn University *B*

Kentucky
Eastern Kentucky University *B*
Thomas More College *B*

Louisiana
Loyola University New Orleans *B*

Maryland
Carroll Community College *A*
Kaplan College: Hagerstown *A*
Prince George's Community
College *C, A*
Stevenson University *M*
Towson University *B, M*
University of Baltimore *B*
University of Maryland
University College *B*

Massachusetts
Bunker Hill Community College *C*
Eastern Nazarene College *B*
Holyoke Community College *C*
Massachusetts Bay Community
College *A*

Mount Ida College *B*
Quinsigamond Community
College *C, A*

Michigan
Macomb Community College *A*
Madonna University *C, B*
Michigan State University *M*
Wayne County Community College *C*

Minnesota
Fond du Lac Tribal and Community
College *C, A*

Mississippi
University of Mississippi *B*
University of Southern
Mississippi *B, M*

Missouri
Columbia College *B*
Missouri Southern State University *B*

Montana
University of Great Falls *B*

Nebraska
Nebraska Wesleyan University *C, M*
University of Nebraska
Lincoln *B*

New Jersey
Cumberland County College *A*
Salem Community College *A*

New Mexico
Eastern New Mexico University *B*
New Mexico Highlands University *B*
New Mexico State University
Alamogordo *A*

New York
College of Saint Rose *B*
Erie Community College
City Campus *C*
North Campus *C*
Herkimer County Community
College *A*
Hilbert College *B*
Hofstra University *B*
Hudson Valley Community College *A*
Long Island University
C. W. Post Campus *B*
Pace University *B, M*
Roberts Wesleyan College *B*
Russell Sage College *B*
St. Thomas Aquinas College *B*
State University of New York
College at Buffalo *B*
College of Technology at Alfred *B*
Tompkins Cortland Community
College *A*
Touro College *M*

North Carolina
Catawba Valley Community College *A*
Fayetteville Technical Community
College *C, A*
Forsyth Technical Community
College *A*
Guilford College *B*
Methodist University *B*
St. Augustine's College *B*
Wayne Community College *A*
Western Carolina University *B*

North Dakota
University of North Dakota *B*

Ohio
Cedarville University *B*

Central Ohio Technical College *A*
Defiance College *B*
Ohio Northern University *B*
Tiffin University *B*
University of Akron *C*
University of Cincinnati
Clermont College *C, A*
Youngstown State University *B*

Oklahoma
University of Central Oklahoma *B, M*

Pennsylvania
Alvernia University *B*
Arcadia University *M*
Chatham University *B*
Chestnut Hill College *B*
Community College of Philadelphia *A*
Drexel University *M*
Duquesne University *M*
Keystone College *B*
Mercyhurst College *B, M*
Penn State
Abington *B*
Altoona *B*
Beaver *B*
Berks *B*
Brandywine *B*
DuBois *B*
Erie, The Behrend College *B*
Fayette, The Eberly Campus *B*
Greater Allegheny *B*
Hazleton *B*
Lehigh Valley *B*
Mont Alto *B*
New Kensington *B*
Schuylkill *B*
Shenango *B*
University Park *B, M*
Wilkes-Barre *B*
Worthington Scranton *B*
York *B*
Seton Hill University *B*
University of Scranton *B*
Waynesburg University *B*
York College of Pennsylvania *B*

Puerto Rico
Inter American University of Puerto
Rico
Bayamon Campus *B*
Turabo University *M*
University of Puerto Rico
Carolina Regional College *B*
Ponce *B*

South Carolina
Southern Wesleyan University *B*
Trident Technical College *C*

South Dakota
Mount Marty College *B*

Texas
Howard College *C, A*
Lamar Institute of Technology *A*
St. Edward's University *B*
Sam Houston State University *M*
Texas A&M University *B*

Utah
Southern Utah University *M*
Utah Valley University *B*

Vermont
Champlain College *B*

Virginia
Bluefield College *B*
New River Community College *A*
Virginia Commonwealth
University *B, M*

Washington
Bellevue College *C*
Centralia College *A*

West Virginia
American Public University System *C*
Fairmont State University *B*
Marshall University *M*
Mountain State University *B*
Southern West Virginia Community
and Technical College *C, A*
West Virginia University *B*

Wisconsin
Carroll University *B*
Marian University *B*

Wyoming
Casper College *A*

Forest engineering

Maine
University of Maine *B*

Oregon
Oregon State University *B, M, D*

Washington
University of Washington *B*

Forest management

Arkansas
University of Arkansas
Monticello *M*

California
University of California
Berkeley *B*

Connecticut
Yale University *M*

Georgia
Abraham Baldwin Agricultural
College *A*

Idaho
University of Idaho *B*

Louisiana
Louisiana State University and
Agricultural and Mechanical
College *B*

Maine
University of Maine *B, M, D*
University of Maine
Presque Isle *A*

Maryland
Allegany College of Maryland *C, A*

Michigan
Michigan Technological
University *C, B, M*

New Hampshire
University of New Hampshire *A*

New Mexico
New Mexico Highlands University *B*

New York
Paul Smith's College *B*
State University of New York
College of Agriculture and
Technology at Morrisville *A*

College of Environmental Science
and Forestry *B, M, D*

North Carolina
North Carolina State University *B*

Ohio
Hocking College *A*

Oregon
Oregon State University *B*

Pennsylvania
Elizabethtown College *B*
Keystone College *A*
St. Francis University *B*

South Carolina
Clemson University *A, B*

Texas
Stephen F. Austin State
University *B, M*
Texas A&M University *B*

West Virginia
Potomac State College of West
Virginia University *A*
West Virginia University *B*

Forest resources production

Alabama
Lurleen B. Wallace Community
College *A*

Florida
Pensacola Junior College *A*

Idaho
University of Idaho *B, M, D*

Louisiana
Louisiana Tech University *B*

Maine
University of Maine *B*

Minnesota
University of Minnesota
Twin Cities *B*
Vermilion Community College *A*

New York
Paul Smith's College *A, B*
State University of New York
College of Environmental Science
and Forestry *B, M, D*

North Carolina
Haywood Community College *C, A*
Wayne Community College *A*

Oregon
Oregon State University *B, M, D*

Pennsylvania
Keystone College *A*

South Carolina
Orangeburg-Calhoun Technical
College *A*

Virginia
Mountain Empire Community
College *C*
Virginia Polytechnic Institute and
State University *M, D*

Washington
Spokane Community College *A*
University of Washington *B*

West Virginia
Potomac State College of West
Virginia University *A*

Forest sciences/biology

Alabama
Auburn University *B, M*

Arizona
Northern Arizona University *B, D*

Colorado
Colorado State University *B, M, D*

Florida
Chipola College *A*

Georgia
University of Georgia *M, D*

Idaho
University of Idaho *B, M, D*

Illinois
University of Illinois
Urbana-Champaign *B, M, D*

Kentucky
Bluegrass Community and Technical
College *A*
University of Kentucky *B, M*

Massachusetts
Harvard College *M*

Michigan
Michigan Technological University *D*

New York
Paul Smith's College *B*
State University of New York
College of Agriculture and
Technology at Morrisville *A*
College of Environmental Science
and Forestry *B*

Oregon
Oregon State University *M, D*

Pennsylvania
Keystone College *A*
Penn State
Abington *B*
Altoona *B*
Beaver *B*
Berks *B*
Brandywine *B*
DuBois *B*
Erie, The Behrend College *B*
Fayette, The Eberly Campus *B*
Greater Allegheny *B*
Hazleton *B*
Lehigh Valley *B*
Mont Alto *B*
New Kensington *B*
Schuylkill *B*
Shenango *B*
University Park *B*
Wilkes-Barre *B*
Worthington Scranton *B*
York *B*

South Carolina
Clemson University *B, M*

West Virginia
West Virginia University D

Wisconsin
University of Wisconsin
Madison B

Forest technology

California
Columbia College C, A
Shasta College C

Colorado
Red Rocks Community College C, A

Georgia
Abraham Baldwin Agricultural
College A

Illinois
Harper College C

Maine
Kennebec Valley Community
College C, A

Mississippi
Mississippi State University D

New Hampshire
University of New Hampshire A

New York
Paul Smith's College A
State University of New York
College of Agriculture and
Technology at Morrisville A
College of Environmental Science
and Forestry A

North Carolina
Montgomery Community College A
Southeastern Community College A

Ohio
Hocking College C

Oregon
Central Oregon Community
College C, A

Pennsylvania
Penn State
Abington B
Altoona B
Beaver B
Berks B
Brandywine B
DuBois B
Erie, The Behrend College B
Fayette, The Eberly Campus B
Greater Allegheny B
Hazleton B
Lehigh Valley B
Mont Alto A, B
New Kensington B
Schuylkill B
Shenango B
University Park B
Wilkes-Barre B
Worthington Scranton B
York B
Pennsylvania College of
Technology A

South Carolina
Clemson University M, D
Horry-Georgetown Technical
College A

Washington
Green River Community College C

West Virginia
Glenville State College A
Potomac State College of West
Virginia University A

Forestry

Alabama
Faulkner State Community College A
Gadsden State Community College A
Northwest-Shoals Community
College A
Tuskegee University B

Alaska
University of Alaska
Fairbanks B

Arizona
Eastern Arizona College A
Northern Arizona University B, M, D

Arkansas
University of Arkansas
Monticello B

California
Bakersfield College A
California Polytechnic State
University: San Luis Obispo B, M
Citrus College C, A
College of the Redwoods C, A
Columbia College C, A
Feather River College A
Fullerton College A
Humboldt State University B
Modesto Junior College C, A
Mount San Antonio College C, A
Reedley College A
Shasta College C
University of California
Berkeley B, M

Colorado
Colorado Mountain College A

Connecticut
Yale University M, D

Delaware
Delaware State University B

Florida
Gulf Coast Community College A
Lake City Community College C
Miami Dade College A
Pensacola Junior College A
University of Florida B, M, D

Georgia
Abraham Baldwin Agricultural
College A
Albany Technical College C, A
Andrew College A
Dalton State College A
Darton College A
Gainesville State College A
Georgia Southern University B
Gordon College A
Middle Georgia College A
Southeastern Technical College C, A
University of Georgia B
Young Harris College A

Idaho
North Idaho College A

Illinois
Joliet Junior College C
Shawnee Community College A
Southern Illinois University
Carbondale B, M

Indiana
Purdue University B, M, D

Iowa
Iowa State University B, M, D
Iowa Wesleyan College B
Marshalltown Community College A
Upper Iowa University B

Kansas
Barton County Community College A
Colby Community College A
Garden City Community College A
Seward County Community College A

Louisiana
Louisiana State University and
Agricultural and Mechanical
College M, D
Louisiana Tech University B

Maine
Unity College B
University of Maine B, M, D
University of Maine
Fort Kent A

Michigan
Delta College A
Gogebic Community College A
Grand Rapids Community College A
Michigan State University B, M, D
Michigan Technological
University B, M
University of Michigan M

Minnesota
Itasca Community College A
Northwest Technical College C
University of Minnesota
Twin Cities B, M, D
Vermilion Community College A

Mississippi
Holmes Community College A
Mississippi Delta Community
College A
Mississippi Gulf Coast Community
College A
Mississippi State University B, M

Missouri
University of Missouri
Columbia B, M, D

Montana
Blackfeet Community College A
Miles Community College A
Salish Kootenai College A
University of Montana B, M, D

Nebraska
Western Nebraska Community
College A

Nevada
University of Nevada
Reno B

New Hampshire
University of New Hampshire B, M
White Mountains Community
College A

New Jersey
Thomas Edison State College A, B

New Mexico
Northern New Mexico College A

New York
Jamestown Community College A
Paul Smith's College A, B
State University of New York
College of Agriculture and
Technology at Morrisville A
College of Environmental Science
and Forestry B, M, D
Sullivan County Community
College A

North Carolina
Duke University M, D
Haywood Community College C, A
High Point University B
Lenoir-Rhyne University B
North Carolina State University M, D

North Dakota
Dakota College at Bottineau C, A

Ohio
Ohio State University
Columbus Campus B, M

Oklahoma
Eastern Oklahoma State College A
Northeastern Oklahoma Agricultural
and Mechanical College A
Oklahoma State University B

Oregon
Central Oregon Community
College A
Chemeketa Community College A
Mt. Hood Community College C, A
Oregon State University M, D

Pennsylvania
Gettysburg College B
Keystone College A
Penn State
University Park M, D
St. Francis University B

Tennessee
University of Tennessee
Knoxville B, M
University of the South B

Texas
Baylor University B
Stephen F. Austin State
University B, M, D
Texas A&M University B, M, D

Utah
College of Eastern Utah T
Snow College A
Southern Utah University B
Utah State University B, M, D

Vermont
University of Vermont B

Virginia
Dabney S. Lancaster Community
College A
Mountain Empire Community
College C, A
Virginia Polytechnic Institute and
State University B

Washington
Spokane Community College A

University of Washington *B, M, D*

West Virginia

Potomac State College of West
    Virginia University *A*
West Virginia University *M*

Wisconsin

Beloit College *B*
University of Wisconsin
    Madison *M, D*
    Stevens Point *B*

Wyoming

Northwest College *A*

Franchise operations

Ohio

Ashland University *B*

French

Alabama

Auburn University *B*
Birmingham-Southern College *B*
Oakwood University *B*
Samford University *B*
Talladega College *B*

Alaska

University of Alaska
    Anchorage *B*

Arizona

Arizona State University *B, M*
Northern Arizona University *B*
University of Arizona *B, M, D*

Arkansas

Harding University *B*
Hendrix College *B*
Ouachita Baptist University *B*
University of Arkansas *B, M*
University of Arkansas
    Little Rock *B*
University of Central Arkansas *B*

California

Cabrillo College *A*
California Lutheran University *B*
California State University
    Chico *B*
    East Bay *B*
    Fresno *B*
    Fullerton *B, M*
    Long Beach *B, M*
    Los Angeles *B, M*
    Northridge *B*
    Sacramento *B, M*
    San Bernardino *B, T*
Canada College *A*
Cerritos College *A*
Chabot College *A*
Chaffey College *A*
Chapman University *B*
Citrus College *A*
Claremont McKenna College *B*
College of Marin: Kentfield *A*
College of San Mateo *A*
College of the Canyons *A*
College of the Desert *A*
College of the Sequoias *A*
Crafton Hills College *A*
Cypress College *A*
De Anza College *A*
El Camino College *A*
El Camino College: Compton
    Center *A*
Foothill College *A*
Glendale Community College *A*
Golden West College *A*

Grossmont College *A*
Humboldt State University *B*
Imperial Valley College *A*
Irvine Valley College *A*
Los Angeles City College *A*
Los Angeles Pierce College *A*
Los Angeles Southwest College *A*
Los Angeles Valley College *A*
Loyola Marymount University *B*
Mendocino College *A*
Merced College *A*
Merritt College *A*
Mills College *B*
MiraCosta College *A*
Mount St. Mary's College *B*
Occidental College *B*
Orange Coast College *A*
Pacific Union College *B*
Pepperdine University *B*
Pitzer College *B*
Pomona College *B*
St. Mary's College of California *B*
San Diego City College *A*
San Diego Mesa College *A*
San Diego State University *B, M*
San Francisco State University *B, M*
San Joaquin Delta College *A*
San Jose State University *B, M*
Santa Barbara City College *A*
Santa Clara University *B*
Santiago Canyon College *A*
Scripps College *B*
Solano Community College *A*
Sonoma State University *B*
Southwestern College *A*
Stanford University *B, M, D*
University of California
    Berkeley *B, M, D*
    Davis *B, D*
    Irvine *B, M, D*
    Los Angeles *B, M, D*
    Riverside *B*
    San Diego *B, M*
    Santa Barbara *B, M, D*
University of La Verne *B*
University of Redlands *B*
University of San Diego *B*
University of San Francisco *B*
University of Southern
    California *B, M, D*
University of the Pacific *B*
West Los Angeles College *A*
Westmont College *B*
Whittier College *B*

Colorado

Colorado College *B*
Colorado State University *B, M*
Red Rocks Community College *A*
Regis University *B*
University of Colorado
    Boulder *B, M, D*
    Denver *B*
University of Denver *B*

Connecticut

Central Connecticut State
    University *B*
Connecticut College *B*
Fairfield University *B*
Southern Connecticut State
    University *B, M, T*
Trinity College *B*
University of Connecticut *B, M, D*
Wesleyan University *B*
Yale University *B, M, D*

Delaware

Delaware State University *B, M*
University of Delaware *B, M, T*

District of Columbia

American University *B*

Catholic University of America *B*
Gallaudet University *B*
George Washington University *B*
Georgetown University *B*
Howard University *B, M, D*
University of the District of
    Columbia *B*

Florida

Barry University *B*
Eckerd College *B*
Florida Agricultural and Mechanical
    University *B*
Florida Atlantic University *B, M*
Florida International University *B*
Florida State University *B, M, D*
Jacksonville University *B*
New College of Florida *B*
Northwest Florida State College *A*
Rollins College *B*
Schiller International University *B*
State College of Florida,
    Manatee-Sarasota *A*
Stetson University *B*
University of Central Florida *B*
University of Florida *B, M, D*
University of Miami *B, D*
University of South Florida *B, M*
University of Tampa *A*

Georgia

Agnes Scott College *B*
Augusta State University *B*
Berry College *B*
Clark Atlanta University *B, M*
Columbus State University *B*
Emory University *B, D*
Georgia College and State
    University *B*
Georgia Southern University *B*
Georgia State University *B, M*
Mercer University *B*
North Georgia College & State
    University *B*
Oglethorpe University *B*
Shorter College *B*
Spelman College *B*
University of Georgia *B, M*
University of West Georgia *B*
Valdosta State University *B*
Wesleyan College *B*
Young Harris College *A*

Hawaii

University of Hawaii
    Manoa *B, M*

Idaho

Boise State University *B*
Idaho State University *A, B*
University of Idaho *B*

Illinois

Augustana College *B, T*
Bradley University *B, T*
City Colleges of Chicago
    Harold Washington College *A*
DePaul University *B*
Dominican University *B*
Elmhurst College *B, T*
Illinois College *B, T*
Illinois State University *B, T*
Illinois Wesleyan University *B*
Kishwaukee College *A*
Knox College *B*
Lake Forest College *B*
Loyola University Chicago *B*
MacMurray College *B*
Monmouth College *B, T*
North Central College *B, T*
North Park University *B*
Northeastern Illinois University *B*
Northern Illinois University *B, M, T*

Northwestern University *B, M, D*
Principia College *B*
Richland Community College *A*
Rockford College *B*
Southern Illinois University
    Carbondale *B*
Triton College *A*
University of Chicago *B, D*
University of Illinois
    Chicago *B, M*
    Urbana-Champaign *B, M, D*
Western Illinois University *B*
Wheaton College *B, T*

Indiana

Anderson University *B*
Ball State University *B, T*
Butler University *B*
DePauw University *B*
Earlham College *B*
Franklin College *B*
Grace College *B*
Hanover College *B*
Indiana University
    Bloomington *B, M, D*
    Northwest *A, B*
    South Bend *B*
    Southeast *B*
Indiana University-Purdue University
    Fort Wayne *A, B, T*
Indiana University-Purdue University
    Indianapolis *B*
Manchester College *B, T*
Marian University *B, T*
Purdue University
    Calumet *B*
Saint Mary's College *B*
Taylor University *B*
University of Evansville *B*
University of Indianapolis *B*
University of Notre Dame *B, M*
University of Southern Indiana *B, T*
Valparaiso University *B*
Wabash College *B*

Iowa

Central College *B, T*
Coe College *B*
Cornell College *B, T*
Grinnell College *B*
Luther College *B*
St. Ambrose University *B, T*
Simpson College *B*
University of Iowa *B, M, D, T*
University of Northern Iowa *B, M*
Wartburg College *B, T*

Kansas

Baker University *B, T*
Benedictine College *B*
Pittsburg State University *B*
University of Kansas *B, M, D*
Washburn University *B*
Wichita State University *B, T*

Kentucky

Asbury College *B, T*
Berea College *B, T*
Bluegrass Community and Technical
    College *A*
Centre College *B*
Eastern Kentucky University *B*
Georgetown College *B*
Morehead State University *B*
Murray State University *B, T*
Northern Kentucky University *B*
Thomas More College *A*
Transylvania University *B, T*
University of Kentucky *B, M*
University of Louisville *B, M*
Western Kentucky University *B, T*

Louisiana

Centenary College of Louisiana *B, T*
Dillard University *B*
Grambling State University *B*
Louisiana College *B, T*
Louisiana State University
   Shreveport *B*
Louisiana State University and
   Agricultural and Mechanical
   College *B, M, D*
Louisiana Tech University *B*
Loyola University New Orleans *B*
McNeese State University *B*
Southeastern Louisiana University *B*
Southern University and Agricultural
   and Mechanical College *B*
Tulane University *B, M, D*
University of Louisiana at
   Lafayette *M, D*
University of Louisiana at Monroe *B*
University of New Orleans *B*
Xavier University of Louisiana *B*

Maine

Bates College *B, T*
Bowdoin College *B*
Colby College *B*
University of Maine *B, M*
University of Maine
   Fort Kent *B*
University of Southern Maine *B*

Maryland

College of Notre Dame of Maryland *B*
Frostburg State University *T*
Goucher College *B*
Hood College *B, T*
Johns Hopkins University *B, M, D*
Loyola University Maryland *B*
McDaniel College *B*
Mount St. Mary's University *B*
Salisbury University *B, T*
Towson University *T*
University of Maryland
   College Park *B, M, D*
Washington College *B, T*

Massachusetts

Amherst College *B*
Assumption College *B*
Bard College at Simon's Rock *B*
Boston College *B, M, D*
Boston University *B, M, D*
Brandeis University *B*
Clark University *B*
College of the Holy Cross *B*
Gordon College *B*
Merrimack College *B*
Mount Holyoke College *B*
Northeastern University *B*
Roxbury Community College *A*
Simmons College *B, M*
Smith College *B*
Stonehill College *B*
Suffolk University *B*
Tufts University *B, M*
University of Massachusetts
   Amherst *B, M*
   Boston *B*
   Dartmouth *B*
Wellesley College *B*
Wheaton College *B*
Williams College *B*

Michigan

Adrian College *A, B, T*
Albion College *B, T*
Alma College *B, T*
Andrews University *B*
Aquinas College *B, T*
Calvin College *B, T*
Central Michigan University *B*
Eastern Michigan University *B, M*

Grand Valley State University *B*
Hillsdale College *B*
Hope College *B*
Kalamazoo College *B*
Lake Superior State University *B*
Lansing Community College *A*
Michigan State University *B, M, D*
Michigan Technological University *T*
Northern Michigan University *B*
Oakland University *B, T*
Saginaw Valley State University *B, T*
University of Michigan *B, M, D*
University of Michigan
   Dearborn *B*
   Flint *B, T*
Western Michigan University *B*

Minnesota

Augsburg College *B*
Bethel University *B*
Carleton College *B*
College of St. Benedict *B*
Concordia College: Moorhead *B, T*
Gustavus Adolphus College *B*
Hamline University *B*
Macalester College *B*
Minnesota State University
   Mankato *B, M, T*
St. Catherine University *B*
Saint Cloud State University *B*
St. John's University *B*
St. Mary's University of Minnesota *B*
St. Olaf College *B*
University of Minnesota
   Morris *B*
   Twin Cities *B, M, D*
University of St. Thomas *B*
Winona State University *B*

Mississippi

Millsaps College *B*
Mississippi College *B*
University of Mississippi *B*

Missouri

Drury University *B, T*
Lindenwood University *B*
Missouri Southern State University *B*
Missouri State University *B*
Missouri Western State University *B, T*
Rockhurst University *B*
St. Charles Community College *A*
Saint Louis University *B, M*
Southeast Missouri State University *B*
Truman State University *B*
University of Central Missouri *B*
University of Missouri
   Columbia *B, M*
   Kansas City *B*
   St. Louis *B*
Washington University in St.
   Louis *B, M, D*
Webster University *B*
Westminster College *B*
William Jewell College *B*

Montana

University of Montana *B, M*

Nebraska

Creighton University *B*
Doane College *B*
Nebraska Wesleyan University *B*
Union College *B*
University of Nebraska
   Kearney *B, M, T*
   Lincoln *B*
   Omaha *B*
Western Nebraska Community
   College *A*

Nevada

University of Nevada
   Las Vegas *B*
   Reno *B*

New Hampshire

Dartmouth College *B, T*
Keene State College *B*
Plymouth State University *B*
Saint Anselm College *B, T*
University of New Hampshire *B*

New Jersey

Caldwell College *B*
Drew University *B*
Fairleigh Dickinson University
   College at Florham *B*
   Metropolitan Campus *B*
Montclair State University *B, M, T*
Rider University *B*
Rutgers, The State University of New
   Jersey
   Camden Regional Campus *B, T*
   New Brunswick/Piscataway
      Campus *B, M, D, T*
   Newark Regional Campus *B, T*
Seton Hall University *B, T*
William Paterson University of New
   Jersey *B*

New Mexico

University of New Mexico *B, M, D*

New York

Adelphi University *B*
Alfred University *B*
Bard College *B*
Barnard College *B*
Canisius College *B*
City University of New York
   Brooklyn College *B, M*
   City College *B*
   Hunter College *B, M*
   Lehman College *B*
   Queens College *B, M, T*
   York College *B*
Colgate University *B*
College of Mount St. Vincent *B, T*
College of New Rochelle *B, T*
Columbia University *B*
Columbia University
   School of General Studies *B*
Cornell University *B*
Daemen College *B, T*
Elmira College *B, T*
Fordham University *B, M, D*
Hamilton College *B*
Hartwick College *B, T*
Hobart and William Smith Colleges *B*
Hofstra University *B*
Iona College *B*
Ithaca College *B, T*
Le Moyne College *B*
Long Island University
   C. W. Post Campus *B*
Manhattan College *B*
Marist College *B*
Nazareth College *B*
New York University *B, M, D*
Niagara University *B*
Orange County Community College *A*
Saint Bonaventure University *B*
St. John Fisher College *B*
St. John's University *B*
St. Lawrence University *B, T*
St. Thomas Aquinas College *B*
Siena College *B, T*
Skidmore College *B*
State University of New York
   Albany *B, M, D*
   Binghamton *B, M*
   Buffalo *B, M, D*
   College at Brockport *B, T*

College at Buffalo *B*
College at Cortland *B*
College at Fredonia *B, T*
College at Geneseo *B, T*
College at Oneonta *B*
College at Plattsburgh *B*
College at Potsdam *B*
New Paltz *B*
Oswego *B*
Stony Brook *B*
Syracuse University *B, M*
Union College *B*
United States Military Academy *B*
University of Rochester *B, M*
Vassar College *B*
Wagner College *B*
Wells College *B*
Yeshiva University *B*

North Carolina

Appalachian State University *B*
Campbell University *B*
Catawba College *B*
Davidson College *B*
Duke University *B, M, D*
East Carolina University *B*
Elon University *B*
Gardner-Webb University *B*
Greensboro College *B*
Guilford College *B, T*
High Point University *B*
Johnson C. Smith University *B*
Lenoir-Rhyne University *B*
Methodist University *A, B, T*
North Carolina Agricultural and
   Technical State University *B, T*
North Carolina Central University *B*
North Carolina State University *B, M*
Salem College *B*
University of North Carolina
   Asheville *B, T*
   Chapel Hill *B, M, D*
   Charlotte *B*
   Greensboro *B*
   Wilmington *B*
Wake Forest University *B*
Western Carolina University *B*

North Dakota

Jamestown College *B*
Minot State University *B*
North Dakota State University *B, T*
University of North Dakota *B*

Ohio

Ashland University *B, T*
Baldwin-Wallace College *B*
Bowling Green State University *B, M*
Capital University *B*
Case Western Reserve University *B, M*
Cleveland State University *B*
College of Wooster *B*
Denison University *B*
Franciscan University of
   Steubenville *B*
Hiram College *B, T*
John Carroll University *B*
Kent State University *B, M*
Kenyon College *B*
Miami University
   Oxford Campus *B, M*
Mount Union College *B*
Muskingum University *B*
Oberlin College *B*
Ohio Northern University *B*
Ohio State University
   Columbus Campus *B, M, D*
Ohio University *B, M*
Ohio Wesleyan University *B*
Otterbein College *B*
University of Akron *B*
University of Cincinnati *B, M, D, T*
University of Dayton *B*
University of Toledo *B, M*

Walsh University *B*
Wittenberg University *B*
Wright State University *R*
Xavier University *A, B*
Youngstown State University *B*

Oklahoma

Oklahoma Baptist University *B, T*
Oklahoma City Community College *A*
Oklahoma City University *B*
Oklahoma State University *B*
Oral Roberts University *B*
Tulsa Community College *A*
University of Central Oklahoma *B*
University of Oklahoma *B, M, D*
University of Tulsa *B*

Oregon

Lewis & Clark College *B*
Linfield College *B, T*
Oregon State University *B*
Pacific University *B*
Portland State University *B, M*
Reed College *B*
University of Oregon *B, M*
University of Portland *B, T*
Western Oregon University *T*
Willamette University *B*

Pennsylvania

Albright College *B, T*
Allegheny College *B*
Arcadia University *B*
Bloomsburg University of
   Pennsylvania *B, T*
Bryn Mawr College *B, M*
Bucknell University *B*
Cabrini College *B*
California University of
   Pennsylvania *B*
Carnegie Mellon University *B*
Chatham University *B*
Chestnut Hill College *A, B*
Cheyney University of
   Pennsylvania *B, T*
Clarion University of Pennsylvania *B*
Dickinson College *B*
East Stroudsburg University of
   Pennsylvania *B, T*
Elizabethtown College *B*
Franklin & Marshall College *B*
Gettysburg College *B*
Grove City College *B, T*
Haverford College *B, T*
Holy Family University *B*
Immaculata University *B, T*
Indiana University of Pennsylvania *B*
Juniata College *B*
King's College *B, T*
Kutztown University of
   Pennsylvania *B, T*
La Salle University *B, T*
Lafayette College *B*
Lebanon Valley College *B*
Lehigh University *B*
Lincoln University *B*
Lock Haven University of
   Pennsylvania *B*
Lycoming College *B*
Mansfield University of
   Pennsylvania *B, T*
Marywood University *B*
Messiah College *B*
Millersville University of
   Pennsylvania *B, T*
Moravian College *B, T*
Muhlenberg College *B*
Penn State
   Abington *B*
   Altoona *B*
   Beaver *B*
   Berks *B*
   Brandywine *B*
   DuBois *B*

Erie, The Behrend College *B*
Fayette, The Eberly Campus *B*
Greater Allegheny *D*
Hazleton *B*
Lehigh Valley *B*
Mont Alto *B*
New Kensington *B*
Schuylkill *B*
Shenango *B*
University Park *B, M, D*
Wilkes-Barre *B*
Worthington Scranton *B*
York *B*
Rosemont College *B*
St. Francis University *B*
Saint Joseph's University *B*
St. Vincent College *B*
Seton Hill University *T*
Shippensburg University of
   Pennsylvania *B, T*
Slippery Rock University of
   Pennsylvania *B, T*
Susquehanna University *B, T*
Swarthmore College *B*
Temple University *B*
University of Pennsylvania *B*
University of Pittsburgh *B, M, D*
University of Scranton *B, T*
Ursinus College *B, T*
Villanova University *B*
Washington & Jefferson College *B*
West Chester University of
   Pennsylvania *B, M, D*
Westminster College *B*
Widener University *B, T*
Wilson College *B*

Puerto Rico

University of Puerto Rico
   Aguadilla *A*
   Rio Piedras *B*

Rhode Island

Brown University *B, M, D*
Providence College *B*
Rhode Island College *B*
Salve Regina University *B*
University of Rhode Island *B*

South Carolina

Bob Jones University *B*
Coker College *B*
College of Charleston *B, T*
Columbia College *B*
Erskine College *B*
Francis Marion University *B*
Furman University *B, T*
Presbyterian College *B*
University of South Carolina *B, M*
Wofford College *B, T*

South Dakota

Augustana College *B, T*
Northern State University *B*
South Dakota State University *B*
University of South Dakota *B*

Tennessee

Belmont University *B, T*
Carson-Newman College *B, T*
King College *B, T*
Lambuth University *B*
Lane College *B*
Lee University *B*
Lipscomb University *B*
Milligan College *T*
Rhodes College *B*
Southern Adventist University *B*
Tennessee State University *B*
Tennessee Technological
   University *B, T*
Union University *B, T*

University of Tennessee
   Knoxville *B, M*
   Martin *B*
University of the South *B*
Vanderbilt University *B, M, D*

Texas

Angelo State University *B, T*
Austin College *B*
Austin Community College *A*
Baylor University *B*
Blinn College *A*
Cisco College *A*
Houston Baptist University *B*
Lamar University *B*
Midland College *A*
Paris Junior College *A*
Rice University *B, M, D*
St. Mary's University *B*
Sam Houston State University *B*
South Plains College *A*
Southern Methodist University *B*
Southwestern University *B, T*
Stephen F. Austin State University *B, T*
Texas A&M University *B*
Texas Christian University *B*
Texas Southern University *B*
Texas State University: San
   Marcos *B, T*
Texas Tech University *B, M*
Trinity University *B*
Tyler Junior College *A*
University of Dallas *B*
University of Houston *B, M*
University of North Texas *B, M*
University of St. Thomas *B*
University of Texas
   Arlington *B, M*
   Austin *B, M, D*
   El Paso *B*
   Pan American *B*
   San Antonio *B*

Utah

Brigham Young University *B, M*
Snow College *A*
Southern Utah University *B*
University of Utah *B, T*
Utah State University *B*
Weber State University *B*

Vermont

Bennington College *B*
Middlebury College *B, M, D*
St. Michael's College *B*
University of Vermont *B, M*

Virginia

Bridgewater College *B*
Christopher Newport University *B*
College of William and Mary *B*
Eastern Mennonite University *B*
Emory & Henry College *B, T*
Hampden-Sydney College *B*
Hollins University *B*
Longwood University *B, T*
Lynchburg College *B*
Mary Baldwin College *B*
Old Dominion University *B, T*
Randolph College *B*
Randolph-Macon College *B*
Roanoke College *B, T*
Sweet Briar College *B*
University of Richmond *B, T*
University of Virginia *B, M, D*
University of Virginia's College at
   Wise *B, T*
Virginia Wesleyan College *B*
Washington and Lee University *B*

Washington

Centralia College *A*
Eastern Washington University *B*

Everett Community College *A*
Gonzaga University *B*
Highline Community College *A*
Pacific Lutheran University *B*
Seattle Pacific University *B*
Seattle University *B*
University of Puget Sound *B, T*
University of Washington *B*
Walla Walla University *B*
Washington State University *B*
Western Washington University *B*
Whitman College *B*
Whitworth University *B, T*

West Virginia

Bethany College *B*
Fairmont State University *B*
West Virginia University *T*
Wheeling Jesuit University *B*

Wisconsin

Beloit College *B*
Carthage College *B*
Edgewood College *B*
Lawrence University *B*
Marquette University *B*
Ripon College *B, T*
St. Norbert College *B, T*
University of Wisconsin
   Eau Claire *B*
   Green Bay *B, T*
   La Crosse *B, T*
   Madison *B, M, D*
   Milwaukee *B*
   Oshkosh *B*
   Parkside *B, T*
   River Falls *B*
   Stevens Point *B, T*
   Whitewater *B, T*

Wyoming

University of Wyoming *B, M*

French studies

California

Mills College *B*
Scripps College *B*

Colorado

Colorado College *B*

Connecticut

Wesleyan University *B*

District of Columbia

American University *B*

Florida

New College of Florida *B*
University of North Florida *B*

Georgia

Emory University *B, D*

Indiana

Purdue University *B*

Iowa

Coe College *B*

Louisiana

University of Louisiana at Lafayette *D*

Maine

University of Southern Maine *B*

Massachusetts

Bard College at Simon's Rock *B*
Suffolk University *B*
Wellesley College *B*

Wheaton College B

Minnesota
Concordia College: Moorhead B, T
Minnesota State University
  Mankato B, M

New Hampshire
University of New Hampshire B

New Jersey
William Paterson University of New
  Jersey B

New York
Bard College B
Barnard College B
Columbia University B
Manhattanville College B
Skidmore College B

Ohio
Case Western Reserve University B
University of Cincinnati B

Pennsylvania
St. Francis University B
Saint Joseph's University B

Rhode Island
Brown University B, M, D

Tennessee
University of the South B

Virginia
Emory & Henry College B

Washington
University of Washington B, M

Wisconsin
University of Wisconsin
  Parkside B

French teacher education

Alabama
Birmingham-Southern College T
Talladega College B

Arizona
Northern Arizona University B
Prescott College T
University of Arizona B

Arkansas
Harding University B, T
Ouachita Baptist University B, T

California
California State University
  Chico B, T
  Long Beach T
  San Bernardino T
Humboldt State University T
Pacific Union College T
San Diego State University T
San Francisco State University T
Stanford University M, T
University of the Pacific T

Colorado
Colorado State University B, T

Connecticut
Fairfield University T

Delaware
Delaware State University B
University of Delaware B, T

District of Columbia
Catholic University of America B

Florida
Stetson University B

Georgia
Fort Valley State University B, T
University of West Georgia M
Valdosta State University B

Idaho
Boise State University B, T
University of Idaho T

Illinois
Augustana College B, T
Bradley University B
DePaul University M, T
Dominican University T
Elmhurst College B
Illinois College T
Illinois Wesleyan University B
Knox College T
North Park University T
Rockford College T
University of Illinois
  Chicago B
  Urbana-Champaign B, M, T

Indiana
Anderson University B, T
Franklin College B, T
Grace College B
Indiana University
  Bloomington B, T
Indiana University-Purdue University
  Fort Wayne B, T
Indiana University-Purdue University
  Indianapolis B, T
Indiana Wesleyan University T
Manchester College B, T
Purdue University B, M, D
Purdue University
  Calumet B
Saint Mary's College T
Taylor University B, T
University of Evansville B, T
University of Indianapolis B, T
Valparaiso University B

Iowa
Central College T
Cornell College B, T
Graceland University T
Iowa State University T
Loras College T
Northwestern College T
St. Ambrose University B, T
Simpson College T
University of Iowa T
Wartburg College T

Kansas
Pittsburg State University B, T
Washburn University B

Louisiana
Centenary College of Louisiana B, T
Grambling State University B
Louisiana College B
Louisiana Tech University B
Nicholls State University B
Southeastern Louisiana University B
Southern University and Agricultural
  and Mechanical College B
University of Louisiana at Lafayette B
University of Louisiana at Monroe B

Xavier University of Louisiana B

Maine
University of Maine B
University of Southern Maine T

Maryland
College of Notre Dame of Maryland T
Hood College T
Mount St. Mary's University T
Salisbury University T
Towson University T

Massachusetts
Assumption College T
Elms College T
Tufts University T
University of Massachusetts
  Dartmouth T

Michigan
Albion College B, T
Alma College T
Calvin College B
Central Michigan University B
Eastern Michigan University B
Grand Valley State University T
Hope College B, T
Michigan State University B
Northern Michigan University B, T
University of Michigan
  Flint B, T
Western Michigan University B, T

Minnesota
Augsburg College T
Bemidji State University T
Bethel University B
College of St. Benedict T
Concordia College: Moorhead B, T
Gustavus Adolphus College T
Minnesota State University
  Mankato B, M, T
St. Catherine University T
Saint Cloud State University B, T
St. John's University T
St. Mary's University of Minnesota B
University of Minnesota
  Duluth B, T
  Morris T
University of St. Thomas B
Winona State University B, T

Mississippi
Millsaps College T
Mississippi College B
Mississippi State University T

Missouri
Lindenwood University B
Missouri Southern State
  University B, T
Missouri State University B
Missouri Western State University B
Northwest Missouri State University T
Truman State University M, T
University of Central Missouri B, T
University of Missouri
  Columbia M
  Kansas City B
Washington University in St.
  Louis B, M, T
William Jewell College B, T

Montana
University of Montana T

Nebraska
Creighton University T
Nebraska Wesleyan University T
University of Nebraska
  Kearney B, T

Lincoln B

New Hampshire
Keene State College B, M, T
Saint Anselm College T
University of New Hampshire T

New Jersey
Caldwell College T
County College of Morris A
Rowan University T

New York
Alfred University B, T
City University of New York
  Brooklyn College B, M, T
  City College B
  Hunter College B, M, T
  Queens College M, T
College of Mount St. Vincent T
D'Youville College M, T
Dutchess Community College A
Elmira College B, T
Fordham University M, T
Hobart and William Smith Colleges T
Hofstra University B, M
Iona College B
Ithaca College B, D, T
Le Moyne College T
Long Island University
  C. W. Post Campus B, M, T
Manhattan College B, T
Marist College B
Medaille College M, T
Niagara University B, M, T
Saint Bonaventure University M
St. John Fisher College B, M, T
St. Lawrence University T
State University of New York
  Albany M, T
  Buffalo M, T
  College at Brockport T
  College at Buffalo B
  College at Cortland B
  College at Fredonia B, T
  College at Geneseo B, M, T
  College at Oneonta B, T
  College at Plattsburgh B
  College at Potsdam B, M
  New Paltz B, T
  Oswego B, M
  Stony Brook T
University of Rochester M
Vassar College T
Wells College T

North Carolina
Appalachian State University B, T
Campbell University B, T
Davidson College T
East Carolina University B
Elon University T
Gardner-Webb University B
Meredith College T
North Carolina Agricultural and
  Technical State University B, T
North Carolina Central University B, T
North Carolina State University B, T
Salem College T
University of North Carolina
  Charlotte B
  Greensboro B
  Wilmington B
Wake Forest University T

North Dakota
Minot State University B
North Dakota State University B, T

Ohio
Ashland University B, T
Baldwin-Wallace College T
Bowling Green State University M

Case Western Reserve University T
Hiram College T
Kent State University T
Miami University
   Oxford Campus B
Mount Union College T
Ohio Northern University B, T
Ohio University B, T
Ohio Wesleyan University B
Otterbein College B
University of Akron B, M
University of Dayton B
University of Toledo B, M, T
Youngstown State University B

Oklahoma
Oklahoma Baptist University B, T
Oklahoma City University B
University of Central Oklahoma B
University of Tulsa T

Oregon
Linfield College T
Oregon State University M
Portland State University T
Western Oregon University T

Pennsylvania
Albright College T
Cabrini College T
Dickinson College T
Gettysburg College T
Grove City College B, T
Holy Family University B
Juniata College B, T
King's College T
La Salle University B, T
Lebanon Valley College T
Lycoming College T
Mansfield University of
   Pennsylvania B, T
Marywood University B
Messiah College B, T
Moravian College T
Rosemont College T
St. Francis University B, T
St. Vincent College T
Seton Hill University T
Susquehanna University T
Villanova University T
Washington & Jefferson College T
Westminster College T
Widener University T

Rhode Island
Rhode Island College B, M
Salve Regina University B

South Carolina
Furman University T
Wofford College T

South Dakota
Augustana College B, T
University of South Dakota B, M, T

Tennessee
Belmont University B, M, T
Christian Brothers University T
King College T
Lipscomb University B, T
Southern Adventist University B
Tennessee Technological University T
Union University B, T

Texas
Houston Baptist University T
Lamar University T
St. Mary's University T
Texas A&M University
   Commerce T
   Kingsville T

Texas Christian University B
Texas State University: San Marcos T
University of Dallas T
University of Houston T
University of Texas
   Arlington T
   San Antonio T

Utah
Brigham Young University B
Southern Utah University B, T
Weber State University B

Vermont
Bennington College M
St. Michael's College T

Virginia
Bridgewater College T
Eastern Mennonite University T
Emory & Henry College B
Hollins University T
Longwood University B, T
Old Dominion University B, T
University of Virginia's College at
   Wise T

Washington
Eastern Washington University B, M
Washington State University B, M, T
Whitworth University B, T

West Virginia
Bethany College B

Wisconsin
Carthage College T
Edgewood College B
Lawrence University T
St. Norbert College T
University of Wisconsin
   Green Bay T
   Parkside T
   River Falls T
   Whitewater B

Funeral direction

Georgia
Gupton Jones College of Funeral
   Service A

Michigan
Wayne State University B

Mississippi
Mississippi Gulf Coast Community
   College A

Missouri
Lindenwood University B

North Carolina
Rowan-Cabarrus Community
   College C

Tennessee
John A. Gupton College A

Texas
San Antonio College C

Funeral services/ mortuary science

Alabama
Bishop State Community College A
Jefferson State Community
   College C, A

Arkansas
Arkansas State University
   Mountain Home A
University of Arkansas
   Community College at Hope A

California
American River College A
Cypress College C, A

Colorado
Arapahoe Community College A

Connecticut
Lincoln College of New England:
   Briarwood A, B

District of Columbia
University of the District of
   Columbia A

Florida
Florida State College at Jacksonville A
Miami Dade College C, A
St. Petersburg College A

Georgia
Gupton Jones College of Funeral
   Service A

Illinois
Carl Sandburg College A
City Colleges of Chicago
   Malcolm X College A
Southern Illinois University
   Carbondale B

Indiana
Ivy Tech Community College
   Central Indiana A
   Northwest A
Mid-America College of Funeral
   Service C, A
Vincennes University A

Iowa
Des Moines Area Community
   College C
Marshalltown Community College A
North Iowa Area Community
   College A
Upper Iowa University B

Kansas
Barton County Community College A
Kansas City Kansas Community
   College A

Louisiana
Delgado Community College A

Maryland
Community College of Baltimore
   County C, A

Massachusetts
Bristol Community College C
Mount Ida College A, B

Michigan
Delta College A
Eastern Michigan University B
Ferris State University A
Gogebic Community College A
Grand Rapids Community College A

Minnesota
University of Minnesota
   Twin Cities B

Mississippi
University of Southern Mississippi B

Missouri
Lindenwood University B

New Jersey
Hudson County Community
   College A
Mercer County Community
   College C, A

New York
American Academy McAllister
   Institute of Funeral Service A
City University of New York
   LaGuardia Community College A
Hudson Valley Community College A
Nassau Community College A
St. John's University B

North Carolina
Edgecombe Community College A
Fayetteville Technical Community
   College C, A
Forsyth Technical Community
   College C
Pitt Community College A

Ohio
Cincinnati College of Mortuary
   Science A, B
University of Cincinnati
   Raymond Walters College A

Oklahoma
University of Central Oklahoma C, B

Oregon
Mt. Hood Community College A

Pennsylvania
Gannon University B
Luzerne County Community
   College A
Northampton Community College A
Pittsburgh Institute of Mortuary
   Science A
Point Park University A, B
Thiel College B

South Carolina
Florence-Darlington Technical
   College A

Tennessee
John A. Gupton College C, A

Texas
Amarillo College A
Commonwealth Institute of Funeral
   Service C, A
Dallas Institute of Funeral Service C, A
San Antonio College A

Virginia
John Tyler Community College A

Wisconsin
Milwaukee Area Technical College A

Furniture design/ manufacturing

Michigan
College for Creative Studies B
Kendall College of Art and Design of
   Ferris State University B

Minnesota

Minneapolis College of Art and
Design *B*

New Mexico

Northern New Mexico College *C, A*

New York

Rochester Institute of
Technology *A, B, M*
State University of New York
College of Agriculture and
Technology at Morrisville *A*

North Carolina

Catawba Valley Community
College *C, A*

Ohio

University of Rio Grande *C*

Oregon

Oregon College of Art & Craft *C, B*

Pennsylvania

Thaddeus Stevens College of
Technology *A*

Vermont

Burlington College *C*

Game design

Arizona

University of Advancing
Technology *A, B, M*

California

Academy of Art University *A, B*
Art Institute
of California: Los Angeles *B*
of California: San Diego *B*
Art Institute of California: Inland
Empire *B*
Art Institute of California:
Sacramento *B*
College of the Siskiyous *C*
DeVry University
Fremont *B*
Long Beach *B*
Pomona *B*
Foothill College *C*
Mt. Sierra College *B*
National University *B*
University of California
Santa Cruz *B*

Colorado

American Sentinel University *B*
University of Colorado
Colorado Springs *B*

Connecticut

Sacred Heart University *B, M*

Florida

Full Sail University *B, M*
Rasmussen College: Fort Myers *B*

Georgia

American InterContinental
University *B*
DeVry University
Alpharetta *B*
Gwinnett Technical College *C, A*
Savannah College of Art and
Design *B, M*

Illinois

Columbia College Chicago *B*

DeVry University
Addison *B*
Tinley Park *B*
DeVry University: Online *B*
Illinois Institute of Art: Schaumburg *B*
International Academy of Design and
Technology: Chicago *B*
Westwood College: DuPage *B*

Indiana

Indiana Institute of Technology *B*

Maryland

Howard Community College *C*
Montgomery College *A*
University of Baltimore *B*

Massachusetts

Worcester Polytechnic Institute *B*

Michigan

International Academy of Design and
Technology: Detroit *B*
Wayne County Community College *C*

Minnesota

DeVry University
Edina *B*
Minnesota School of Business: St.
Cloud *A*

Nevada

Art Institute
of Las Vegas *B*
International Academy of Design and
Technology: Henderson *B*

New Hampshire

Daniel Webster College *B*

New Jersey

Union County College *A*

New York

Marist College *B*
Mildred Elley *C, A*
Rochester Institute of
Technology *B, M*

North Carolina

Blue Ridge Community College *A*
Stanly Community College *A*
Surry Community College *A*

Ohio

Edison State Community College *A*

Oklahoma

Oklahoma Christian University *B*

Texas

Panola College *C*
San Antonio College *C*

Virginia

New River Community College *A*

Washington

Art Institute of Seattle *B*
Cascadia Community College *C*
DeVry University
Federal Way *B*
Olympic College *C, A*

Wisconsin

Herzing University *B*
Northcentral Technical College *C*
University of Wisconsin
Stout *B*

Gay/lesbian studies

California

Claremont McKenna College *B*

Connecticut

Trinity College *B*
Wesleyan University *B*

Massachusetts

Bard College at Simon's Rock *B*
Hampshire College *B*

New York

Cornell University *B*
Hobart and William Smith Colleges *B*

Ohio

Denison University *B*

Vermont

Bennington College *B*
Goddard College *B, M*

Gene therapy

Connecticut

University of Connecticut *B*

Genetic counseling

California

California State University
Stanislaus *M*
University of California
Irvine *M*

Illinois

Northwestern University *M*

Maryland

University of Maryland
Baltimore *M*

Michigan

Wayne State University *M*

New York

Long Island University
C. W. Post Campus *M*

Ohio

Case Western Reserve University *M*

Oklahoma

University of Oklahoma *M*

Pennsylvania

Arcadia University *M*

South Carolina

University of South Carolina *M*

Utah

University of Utah *M, D*

Virginia

Virginia Commonwealth University *M*

Genetics

California

Stanford University *M, D*
University of California
Davis *B, M, D*
Irvine *B*
Riverside *M, D*

Connecticut

Yale University *M, D*

District of Columbia

George Washington University *M, D*
Howard University *M, D*

Georgia

University of Georgia *B, M, D*

Illinois

University of Chicago *D*

Indiana

Indiana University
Bloomington *D*

Iowa

Iowa State University *B, M, D*
University of Iowa *D*

Kansas

Kansas State University *M, D*

Louisiana

Tulane University *M, D*

Massachusetts

Harvard College *D*
Tufts University *M, D*

Michigan

Michigan State University *M, D*

Minnesota

Minnesota State University
Mankato *B*
University of Minnesota
Twin Cities *M, D*

Missouri

Missouri Southern State University *B*
University of Missouri
Columbia *D*
Washington University in St. Louis *D*

New Hampshire

Dartmouth College *B, D*
University of New Hampshire *B, M, D*

New Jersey

Rutgers, The State University of New
Jersey
New Brunswick/Piscataway
Campus *B*

New York

State University of New York
Stony Brook *D*
University of Rochester *M, D*
Yeshiva University *M, D*

North Carolina

North Carolina State University *M, D*
University of North Carolina
Chapel Hill *M, D*

North Dakota

North Dakota State University *M, D*

Ohio

Ohio State University
Columbus Campus *B, M, D*
Ohio Wesleyan University *B*

Oregon

Oregon State University *M, D*

Pennsylvania

Cedar Crest College *B*
Penn State
    University Park *M, D*

South Carolina

Clemson University *B, M, D*

Vermont

Marlboro College *B*

Washington

University of Washington *M, D*
Washington State University *B*

West Virginia

Concord University *B*
West Virginia University *M, D*

Wisconsin

Marquette University *M, D*
University of Wisconsin
    Madison *B, M, D*

Geochemistry

Arizona

Northern Arizona University *B*

California

California Institute of
    Technology *B, M, D*
California State University
    Fullerton *M*
University of California
    Los Angeles *M, D*

Colorado

Colorado School of Mines *M, D*

Maine

Bowdoin College *B*
University of Maine
    Farmington *B*

Massachusetts

Bridgewater State College *B*

Michigan

Grand Valley State University *B*
Western Michigan University *B*

Missouri

University of Missouri
    Missouri University of Science and
        Technology *B, M, D*

Nevada

University of Nevada
    Reno *M, D*

New Mexico

New Mexico Institute of Mining and
    Technology *M, D*

New York

College of Saint Rose *B*
Columbia University *B*
Columbia University
    School of General Studies *B*
State University of New York
    Albany *M, D*
    College at Fredonia *B*
    College at Geneseo *B*
    Oswego *B*

Ohio

Bowling Green State University *B*

Rhode Island

Brown University *B*

Geography

Alabama

Auburn University *B, M*
Jacksonville State University *B*
Samford University *B*
University of Alabama *B, M*
University of North Alabama *B*
University of South Alabama *C, B*

Alaska

University of Alaska
    Fairbanks *B, M*

Arizona

Arizona State University *B, M, D*
Cochise College *A*
Northern Arizona University *B, M*
Prescott College *B, M*
University of Arizona *B, M, D*

Arkansas

Arkansas State University *B*
University of Arkansas *B, M*
University of Central Arkansas *B*

California

Bakersfield College *A*
Cabrillo College *A*
California State Polytechnic
    University: Pomona *B*
California State University
    Chico *B, M*
    Dominguez Hills *B*
    East Bay *B, M*
    Fresno *B, M*
    Fullerton *B, M*
    Long Beach *B, M*
    Los Angeles *B, M*
    Northridge *B*
    Sacramento *B*
    San Bernardino *B*
    Stanislaus *B*
Canada College *A*
Cerritos College *A*
Chabot College *A*
Chaffey College *A*
College of Alameda *A*
College of Marin: Kentfield *A*
College of the Desert *A*
Contra Costa College *A*
Crafton Hills College *A*
Cypress College *A*
De Anza College *A*
Diablo Valley College *A*
East Los Angeles College *A*
El Camino College *A*
El Camino College: Compton
    Center *A*
Foothill College *A*
Fresno City College *A*
Fullerton College *A*
Gavilan College *A*
Grossmont College *A*
Humboldt State University *B*
Irvine Valley College *A*
Los Angeles Southwest College *A*
Los Angeles Valley College *A*
MiraCosta College *A*
Ohlone College *C*
Orange Coast College *A*
Rio Hondo College *A*
Saddleback College *A*
San Bernardino Valley College *A*
San Diego City College *A*
San Diego State University *B, M, D*
San Francisco State University *B, M*
San Jose State University *B, M*
Santa Ana College *A*
Santa Barbara City College *A*

Santa Rosa Junior College *A*
Santiago Canyon College *A*
Sierra College *C*
Sonoma State University *B*
Southwestern College *A*
University of California
    Berkeley *B, D*
    Davis *M, D*
    Los Angeles *B, M, D*
    Santa Barbara *B, M, D*
University of Southern
    California *B, M, D*
West Hills College: Coalinga *A*
West Los Angeles College *C, A*

Colorado

Pikes Peak Community College *A*
United States Air Force Academy *B*
University of Colorado
    Boulder *B, M, D*
    Colorado Springs *B, M, T*
    Denver *B*
University of Denver *B, M, D*
University of Northern Colorado *B, T*

Connecticut

Central Connecticut State
    University *B, M*
Southern Connecticut State
    University *B, T*
University of Connecticut *B, M, D*

Delaware

University of Delaware *B, M*

District of Columbia

George Washington University *B, M*
University of the District of
    Columbia *B*

Florida

Broward College *A*
Daytona State College *A*
Florida Atlantic University *B, M*
Florida International University *B*
Florida State University *B, M, D*
Jacksonville University *B*
Palm Beach Community College *A*
Stetson University *B*
University of Florida *B, M, D*
University of Miami *B, M*
University of South Florida *B, M*

Georgia

Dalton State College *A*
Darton College *A*
Georgia Southern University *B*
Georgia State University *B, M*
Kennesaw State University *B*
University of Georgia *B, M, D*
University of West Georgia *B, M*

Hawaii

University of Hawaii
    Hilo *B*
    Manoa *B, M, D*

Idaho

University of Idaho *B, M, D*

Illinois

Augustana College *B, T*
Chicago State University *B, M, T*
Concordia University Chicago *B*
DePaul University *B, T*
Eastern Illinois University *B*
Elmhurst College *B, T*
Illinois State University *B, T*
Lincoln College *A*
Northeastern Illinois University *B, M*
Northern Illinois University *B, M*
Northwestern University *B*

Richland Community College *A*
South Suburban College of Cook
    County *A*
Southern Illinois University
    Carbondale *B, M*
Southern Illinois University
    Edwardsville *B, M*
Southwestern Illinois College *A*
Triton College *A*
University of Chicago *B, D*
University of Illinois
    Chicago *M*
    Urbana-Champaign *B, M, D*
Western Illinois University *B, M*

Indiana

Ball State University *B, M, T*
Indiana State University *C, B, M, D, T*
Indiana University
    Bloomington *B, M, D*
    Southeast *B*
Indiana University-Purdue University
    Indianapolis *C, B, M*
Taylor University *B*
Valparaiso University *B*
Vincennes University *A*

Iowa

North Iowa Area Community
    College *A*
University of Iowa *B, M, D, T*
University of Northern Iowa *B, M*

Kansas

Allen County Community College *A*
Kansas State University *C, B, M, D*
Pittsburg State University *B*
University of Kansas *B, M, D*
Wichita State University *B*

Kentucky

Eastern Kentucky University *B*
Morehead State University *B*
Northern Kentucky University *B*
University of Kentucky *B, M, D*
University of Louisville *B*
Western Kentucky University *B, M*

Louisiana

Louisiana State University
    Shreveport *B*
Louisiana State University and
    Agricultural and Mechanical
    College *B, M, D*
Louisiana Tech University *B*
University of New Orleans *B, M*

Maine

University of Maine
    Farmington *B*
University of Southern Maine *B*

Maryland

Community College of Baltimore
    County *A*
Frostburg State University *B*
Johns Hopkins University *B, M, D*
Salisbury University *B, M, T*
Towson University *B, M*
University of Maryland
    Baltimore County *B*
    College Park *B, M, D*

Massachusetts

Boston University *B, M, D*
Bridgewater State College *B*
Clark University *B, M, D*
Fitchburg State College *B*
Framingham State College *B*
Holyoke Community College *C, A*
Mount Holyoke College *B*
Salem State College *B, M*

Springfield Technical Community
College *C*
University of Massachusetts
Amherst *B, M*
Worcester State College *B*

Michigan
Aquinas College *B, T*
Calvin College *B, T*
Central Michigan University *B*
Delta College *A*
Eastern Michigan University *B, M*
Grand Valley State University *B*
Lake Michigan College *A*
Lansing Community College *A*
Michigan State University *B, M, D*
Northern Michigan University *B*
Western Michigan University *B, M*

Minnesota
Bemidji State University *B*
Gustavus Adolphus College *B*
Itasca Community College *A*
Macalester College *B*
Minnesota State University
Mankato *B, M, T*
Minnesota West Community and
Technical College *A*
Saint Cloud State University *B, M*
University of Minnesota
Duluth *B*
Twin Cities *B, M, D*
University of St. Thomas *B*
Vermilion Community College *A*

Mississippi
University of Southern
Mississippi *B, M, D*

Missouri
Metropolitan Community College:
Longview *C*
Metropolitan Community College:
Maple Woods *C*
Missouri State University *B*
Northwest Missouri State
University *B*
Park University *B*
Three Rivers Community College *A*
University of Central Missouri *B*
University of Missouri
Columbia *B, M*
Kansas City *B*

Montana
Montana State University
Billings *T*
University of Montana *B, M*

Nebraska
Concordia University *B, T*
University of Nebraska
Kearney *B, T*
Lincoln *B, M, D*
Omaha *B, M*
Wayne State College *B*
Western Nebraska Community
College *A*

Nevada
University of Nevada
Reno *B, M, D*

New Hampshire
Dartmouth College *B*
Keene State College *B*
Plymouth State University *B*
University of New Hampshire *B*

New Jersey
Montclair State University *B*
Rowan University *B*

Rutgers, The State University of New
Jersey
New Brunswick/Piscataway
Campus *B, M, D*
William Paterson University of New
Jersey *B*

New Mexico
New Mexico State University *B, M*
University of New Mexico *B, M*

New York
Barnard College *B*
City University of New York
Hunter College *B, M*
Lehman College *B*
Colgate University *B*
Erie Community College
North Campus *C*
Excelsior College *B*
Hofstra University *B*
Long Island University
C. W. Post Campus *B*
State University of New York
Albany *B, M*
Binghamton *B, M*
Buffalo *B, M, D*
College at Buffalo *B*
College at Cortland *B*
College at Geneseo *B*
College at Oneonta *B*
College at Plattsburgh *B*
New Paltz *B*
Syracuse University *B, M, D*
United States Military Academy *B*
Vassar College *B*

North Carolina
Appalachian State University *B, M*
East Carolina University *B, M*
Fayetteville State University *B*
North Carolina Central University *B*
North Carolina State University *B*
University of North Carolina
Chapel Hill *B, M, D*
Charlotte *B, M, T*
Greensboro *B, M, D*
Wilmington *B*
Western Carolina University *B*

North Dakota
Minot State University *B*
University of North Dakota *B, M*

Ohio
Bowling Green State University *B*
Kent State University *B, M, D*
Miami University
Oxford Campus *B, M*
Ohio State University
Columbus Campus *B, M, D*
Ohio University *B, M*
Ohio Wesleyan University *B*
University of Akron *B, M*
University of Cincinnati *B, M, D, T*
University of Toledo *B, M*
Wittenberg University *B*
Wright State University *A, B*
Youngstown State University *B*

Oklahoma
Langston University *B*
Northeastern State University *B*
Oklahoma State University *B, M, D*
Tulsa Community College *A*
University of Central Oklahoma *B*
University of Oklahoma *B, M, D*

Oregon
Chemeketa Community College *A*
Linn-Benton Community College *A*
Mt. Hood Community College *A*
Oregon State University *B, M, D*

Portland State University *B, M*
Southern Oregon University *B*
University of Oregon *B, M, D*
Western Oregon University *B*

Pennsylvania
Bloomsburg University of
Pennsylvania *B*
Bucknell University *B*
California University of
Pennsylvania *B, M*
Community College of Philadelphia *A*
East Stroudsburg University of
Pennsylvania *B*
Edinboro University of
Pennsylvania *B*
Harrisburg University of Science and
Technology *B*
Indiana University of
Pennsylvania *B, M*
Kutztown University of
Pennsylvania *B*
Lock Haven University of
Pennsylvania *B*
Mansfield University of
Pennsylvania *A, B, T*
Millersville University of
Pennsylvania *B*
Penn State
Abington *B*
Altoona *B*
Beaver *B*
Berks *B*
Brandywine *B*
DuBois *B*
Erie, The Behrend College *B*
Fayette, The Eberly Campus *B*
Greater Allegheny *B*
Hazleton *B*
Lehigh Valley *B*
Mont Alto *B*
New Kensington *B*
Schuylkill *B*
Shenango *B*
University Park *B, M, D*
Wilkes-Barre *B*
Worthington Scranton *B*
York *B*
Shippensburg University of
Pennsylvania *B, T*
Slippery Rock University of
Pennsylvania *B*
Temple University *M*
University of Pittsburgh *C, M*
University of Pittsburgh
Johnstown *B*
Villanova University *B*
West Chester University of
Pennsylvania *B, M, T*

Puerto Rico
University of Puerto Rico
Aguadilla *A*
Rio Piedras *B*

Rhode Island
Rhode Island College *B*

South Carolina
University of South Carolina *B, M, D*

South Dakota
South Dakota State University *B, M*

Tennessee
Columbia State Community College *A*
East Tennessee State University *B, T*
University of Memphis *B*
University of Tennessee
Knoxville *B, M, D*

Texas
Austin Community College *A*

Baylor University *B*
Galveston College *A*
Sam Houston State University *B*
Stephen F. Austin State University *B, T*
Texas A&M University *B, M, D*
Texas A&M University
Commerce *B*
Texas Christian University *B*
Texas State University: San
Marcos *B, M, D, T*
Texas Tech University *B*
University of Houston
Clear Lake *B*
University of North Texas *B, M*
University of Texas
Austin *B, M, D*
Dallas *B*
San Antonio *B*
West Texas A&M University *B*
Western Texas College *A*

Utah
Brigham Young University *B, M*
Salt Lake Community College *A*
Snow College *A*
University of Utah *B, M, D, T*
Utah State University *B, M*
Weber State University *B*

Vermont
Middlebury College *B*
University of Vermont *B*

Virginia
Emory & Henry College *B*
George Mason University *B, M*
James Madison University *B*
Longwood University *T*
Old Dominion University *B, T*
Radford University *B*
University of Mary Washington *B*
Virginia Polytechnic Institute and
State University *B, M, D*

Washington
Eastern Washington University *C, B*
Everett Community College *A*
Highline Community College *A*
Olympic College *A*
University of Washington *B, M, D*
Western Washington University *B, M*

West Virginia
Concord University *B*
Marshall University *B, M*
West Virginia University *B, M, D*

Wisconsin
Carthage College *B*
University of Wisconsin
Eau Claire *B*
La Crosse *B, T*
Madison *B, M, D*
Milwaukee *B, M, D*
Oshkosh *B*
Parkside *B, T*
Platteville *B, T*
River Falls *B, T*
Stevens Point *B, T*
Whitewater *B, T*

Wyoming
University of Wyoming *B, M*

Geography teacher
education

Arizona
Arizona State University *M*
Prescott College *T*

California
Stanford University *M, T*

Delaware
University of Delaware *B, T*

Idaho
University of Idaho *T*

Illinois
DePaul University *M, T*
University of Illinois
   Urbana-Champaign *M*

Indiana
Valparaiso University *B*

Iowa
University of Iowa *T*

Kentucky
Eastern Kentucky University *B*

Massachusetts
Fitchburg State College *B, T*

Michigan
Central Michigan University *B*
Eastern Michigan University *M*
Michigan State University *B*
Northern Michigan University *B, T*
Western Michigan University *B, T*

Minnesota
University of Minnesota
   Morris *T*
Vermilion Community College *A*

Missouri
Missouri State University *B*
University of Missouri
   Kansas City *B*

Nebraska
Concordia University *B, T*
Wayne State College *B, T*

New York
City University of New York
   Hunter College *B, T*

North Dakota
Mayville State University *B, T*

Ohio
Kent State University *T*
University of Findlay *B, M, T*

Rhode Island
Rhode Island College *B*

Texas
West Texas A&M University *T*

Virginia
Old Dominion University *B, T*

Wisconsin
Carroll University *B, T*
Carthage College *T*

Geological engineering

Alaska
University of Alaska
   Fairbanks *B, M*

Arizona
University of Arizona *B*

California
University of California
   Berkeley *B*
   Los Angeles *B*

Colorado
Colorado School of Mines *B, M, D*

Idaho
University of Idaho *B, M*

Michigan
Michigan Technological
   University *B, M, D*
University of Michigan *B*

Minnesota
University of Minnesota
   Twin Cities *B, M, D*

Mississippi
University of Mississippi *B*

Missouri
University of Missouri
   Missouri University of Science and
   Technology *B, M, D*

Montana
Montana Tech of the University of
   Montana *B, M*

Nevada
University of Nevada
   Reno *B, M, D*

New Jersey
New Jersey Institute of Technology *B*

New York
Columbia University *B, M, D*
Cornell University *M*
University of Rochester *B*

North Dakota
University of North Dakota *B, M*

Oklahoma
University of Oklahoma *M, D*

Pennsylvania
Drexel University *M*
University of Pennsylvania *M*

South Dakota
South Dakota School of Mines and
   Technology *B, M, D*

Texas
Texas A&M University *B*

Utah
University of Utah *B, M, D*

Wisconsin
University of Wisconsin
   Madison *B, M, D*

Geology/earth science

Alabama
Auburn University *B, M*
University of Alabama *B, M, D*
University of North Alabama *B*
University of South Alabama *B*

Alaska
Alaska Pacific University *B*

University of Alaska
   Fairbanks *B, M, D*

Arizona
Arizona State University *B, M, D*
Eastern Arizona College *A*
Northern Arizona University *B, M*
Prescott College *B, M*
University of Arizona *B, M, D*

Arkansas
Arkansas Tech University *B*
University of Arkansas *B, M*
University of Arkansas
   Little Rock *B*

California
Bakersfield College *A*
California Institute of
   Technology *B, M, D*
California Lutheran University *B*
California Polytechnic State
   University: San Luis Obispo *B*
California State Polytechnic
   University: Pomona *B*
California State University
   Bakersfield *B, M*
   Chico *B, M*
   Dominguez Hills *B*
   East Bay *B, M*
   Fresno *B, M*
   Fullerton *B, M*
   Long Beach *B, M*
   Los Angeles *B, M*
   Northridge *B, M*
   Sacramento *B, M*
   San Bernardino *B*
   Stanislaus *B*
Cerritos College *A*
Chaffey College *A*
College of San Mateo *A*
College of the Desert *A*
College of the Siskiyous *A*
Crafton Hills College *C, A*
Cypress College *A*
De Anza College *A*
East Los Angeles College *A*
El Camino College *A*
El Camino College: Compton
   Center *A*
Folsom Lake College *A*
Foothill College *A*
Fullerton College *A*
Gavilan College *A*
Golden West College *A*
Grossmont College *A*
Hartnell College *A*
Humboldt State University *B, M*
Irvine Valley College *A*
Loma Linda University *B, M, D*
Los Angeles Southwest College *A*
Los Angeles Valley College *A*
Merced College *A*
MiraCosta College *A*
Moorpark College *A*
National University *B*
Occidental College *B*
Orange Coast College *A*
Palomar College *A*
Pomona College *B*
Saddleback College *A*
San Bernardino Valley College *A*
San Diego City College *A*
San Diego State University *B, M*
San Francisco State University *B, M*
San Joaquin Delta College *A*
San Jose State University *B, M*
Santa Ana College *A*
Santa Barbara City College *A*
Santa Monica College *A*
Santiago Canyon College *A*
Scripps College *B*
Shasta College *A*
Sierra College *A*

Sonoma State University *B*
Southwestern College *A*
Stanford University *B, M, D*
University of California
   Berkeley *B, M, D*
   Davis *B, M, D*
   Irvine *B, M, D*
   Los Angeles *B, M, D*
   Riverside *B, M, D*
   Santa Barbara *B, M, D*
   Santa Cruz *B, M, D*
University of California: Merced *B*
University of Southern
   California *B, M, D*
University of the Pacific *B*
West Los Angeles College *C, A*
West Valley College *A*

Colorado
Adams State College *A, B*
Colorado College *B*
Colorado Mountain College *A*
Colorado School of Mines *B, M, D*
Colorado State University *B, M, D, T*
Fort Lewis College *B*
Pikes Peak Community College *A*
University of Colorado
   Boulder *B, M, D*
University of Northern
   Colorado *B, M, T*
Western State College of
   Colorado *B, T*

Connecticut
Central Connecticut State
   University *B*
Southern Connecticut State
   University *B, T*
University of Connecticut *B, M, D*
Wesleyan University *B*
Western Connecticut State
   University *B, M*
Yale University *B, M, D*

Delaware
University of Delaware *B, M, D*

District of Columbia
George Washington
   University *B, M, D*

Florida
Florida Atlantic University *B, M*
Florida International
   University *B, M, D*
Florida State University *M, D*
Gulf Coast Community College *A*
Miami Dade College *A*
Northwest Florida State College *A*
Pensacola Junior College *A*
University of Florida *B, M, D*
University of Miami *B, M, D*
University of South Florida *B, M, D*

Georgia
Columbus State University *B*
East Georgia College *A*
Gainesville State College *A*
Georgia Highlands College *A*
Georgia Institute of
   Technology *B, M, D*
Georgia Perimeter College *A*
Georgia Southern University *B*
Georgia Southwestern State
   University *B*
Georgia State University *B, M*
Middle Georgia College *A*
University of Georgia *B, M, D*
University of West Georgia *B*

Hawaii
University of Hawaii
   Hilo *B*

Manoa *B, M, D*

Idaho

Boise State University *B, M, D*
Brigham Young University-Idaho *B*
Idaho State University *A, B, M*
North Idaho College *A*
University of Idaho *B, M, D*

Illinois

Augustana College *B, T*
Eastern Illinois University *B*
Illinois Central College *A*
Illinois State University *B*
Illinois Valley Community College *A*
Northeastern Illinois University *B, M*
Northern Illinois University *B, M, D*
Northwestern University *B, M, D*
Olivet Nazarene University *B*
South Suburban College of Cook
   County *A*
Southern Illinois University
   Carbondale *B, M*
Triton College *A*
University of Illinois
   Chicago *B, M, D*
   Urbana-Champaign *B, M, D, T*
Western Illinois University *B*
Wheaton College *B, T*

Indiana

Ball State University *B, M*
DePauw University *B*
Hanover College *B*
Indiana State University *B, M, T*
Indiana University
   Bloomington *B, M, D*
   Northwest *A, B*
Indiana University-Purdue University
   Fort Wayne *B*
Indiana University-Purdue University
   Indianapolis *B, M*
Purdue University *B, M, D*
Taylor University *B*
University of Indianapolis *B*
University of Southern Indiana *B*
Valparaiso University *B*
Vincennes University *A*

Iowa

Cornell College *B, T*
Iowa State University *B, M, D*
University of Iowa *B, M, D, T*
University of Northern Iowa *B*

Kansas

Emporia State University *B, T*
Fort Hays State University *B, M*
Kansas State University *B, M*
University of Kansas *B, M, D*
Wichita State University *B*

Kentucky

Bluegrass Community and Technical
   College *A*
Eastern Kentucky University *B, M*
Morehead State University *B*
Murray State University *B, T*
Northern Kentucky University *B*
University of Kentucky *B, M, D*
Western Kentucky University *B*

Louisiana

Centenary College of Louisiana *B*
Louisiana State University and
   Agricultural and Mechanical
   College *B, M, D*
Louisiana Tech University *B*
Tulane University *B, M, D*
University of Louisiana at
   Lafayette *B, M*
University of New Orleans *B, M*

Maine

Bates College *B*
Bowdoin College *B*
Colby College *B*
University of Maine *B, M, D*
University of Maine
   Farmington *B*
   Presque Isle *B*
University of Southern Maine *B*

Maryland

Johns Hopkins University *B, M, D*
Towson University *B*
University of Maryland
   College Park *B, M, D*

Massachusetts

Amherst College *B*
Boston College *B, M*
Boston University *B, M, D*
Bridgewater State College *B*
Hampshire College *B*
Harvard College *B, M, D*
Massachusetts Institute of
   Technology *B, M, D*
Mount Holyoke College *B*
Northeastern University *B*
Salem State College *B*
Smith College *B*
Tufts University *B*
University of Massachusetts
   Amherst *B, M, D*
   Boston *C, B*
Wellesley College *B*
Williams College *B*

Michigan

Adrian College *A, B*
Albion College *B, T*
Calvin College *B, T*
Central Michigan University *B, M*
Delta College *A*
Eastern Michigan University *B*
Grand Rapids Community College *A*
Grand Valley State University *B*
Lake Michigan College *A*
Lake Superior State University *B, T*
Michigan State University *B, M, D*
Michigan Technological
   University *B, M, D*
Northern Michigan University *B*
University of Michigan *B, M, D*
Wayne State University *B, M*
Western Michigan University *B, M*

Minnesota

Bemidji State University *B*
Carleton College *B*
Gustavus Adolphus College *B*
Macalester College *B*
Ridgewater College *A*
Saint Cloud State University *B*
University of Minnesota
   Duluth *B, M*
   Morris *B*
   Twin Cities *B, M, D*
University of St. Thomas *B*
Vermilion Community College *A*
Winona State University *B*

Mississippi

Hinds Community College *A*
Jackson State University *B*
Millsaps College *B*
Mississippi State University *B, M*
University of Mississippi *B*
University of Southern
   Mississippi *B, M*

Missouri

Missouri State University *B*
Northwest Missouri State
   University *B*

Saint Louis University *B, M*
University of Central Missouri *B*
University of Missouri
   Columbia *B, M, D*
   Kansas City *B*
   Missouri University of Science and
     Technology *B, M, D*
Washington University in St.
   Louis *B, M, D*

Montana

Montana Tech of the University of
   Montana *M*
Rocky Mountain College *B*
University of Montana *B, M, D*
University of Montana: Western *A, B*

Nebraska

University of Nebraska
   Lincoln *B, M, D*
   Omaha *B*

Nevada

Great Basin College *A*
University of Nevada
   Las Vegas *B, M, D*
   Reno *B, M, D*

New Hampshire

Dartmouth College *M, D*
Keene State College *B*
University of New Hampshire *B, M, D*

New Jersey

Kean University *B, T*
Montclair State University *B, M, T*
New Jersey City University *B*
Princeton University *B, M, D*
Richard Stockton College of New
   Jersey *B*
Rider University *B*
Rutgers, The State University of New
   Jersey
   New Brunswick/Piscataway
     Campus *B, M, D*
   Newark Regional Campus *B*

New Mexico

Eastern New Mexico University *B*
Mesalands Community College *A*
New Mexico Highlands University *B*
New Mexico Institute of Mining and
   Technology *B, M, D*
New Mexico State University *B, M*
San Juan College *A*
University of New Mexico *B, M, D*

New York

Alfred University *B*
Barnard College *B*
Cayuga County Community College *A*
City University of New York
   Brooklyn College *B, M*
   City College *B, M*
   Lehman College *B*
   Queens College *B, M, T*
   York College *B*
Colgate University *B*
Columbia University *B*
Columbia University
   School of General Studies *B*
Concordia College *B*
Cornell University *B, M, D*
Excelsior College *B*
Hamilton College *B*
Hartwick College *B*
Hobart and William Smith Colleges *B*
Hofstra University *B*
Long Island University
   C. W. Post Campus *B, M*
Rensselaer Polytechnic
   Institute *B, M, D*
St. Lawrence University *B, T*

Skidmore College *B*
State University of New York
   Albany *M, D*
   Binghamton *B, M, D*
   Buffalo *B, M, D*
   College at Brockport *B*
   College at Buffalo *B*
   College at Cortland *B*
   College at Fredonia *B, T*
   College at Geneseo *B, T*
   College at Oneonta *B, M*
   College at Plattsburgh *B*
   College at Potsdam *B*
   New Paltz *B*
   Oswego *B*
   Stony Brook *B, M, D*
Suffolk County Community College *A*
Syracuse University *B, M, D*
Union College *B*
University of Rochester *B, M, D*
Vassar College *B*

North Carolina

Appalachian State University *B*
Duke University *B, M, D*
East Carolina University *B, M*
Elizabeth City State University *B*
Guilford College *B*
North Carolina Central University *M*
North Carolina State University *B*
University of North Carolina
   Chapel Hill *B, M, D*
   Charlotte *B, M*
   Wilmington *B, M*
Western Carolina University *B*

North Dakota

Minot State University *B*
North Dakota State University *B, T*
University of North Dakota *B, M, D*

Ohio

Ashland University *B*
Bowling Green State University *B, M*
Case Western Reserve
   University *B, M, D*
Cedarville University *B*
Central State University *B*
Cleveland State University *B*
College of Wooster *B*
Denison University *B*
Kent State University *B, M, D*
Marietta College *B*
Miami University
   Oxford Campus *B, M, D*
Mount Union College *B*
Muskingum University *B*
Oberlin College *B*
Ohio State University
   Columbus Campus *B, M, D*
Ohio University *B, M*
Ohio Wesleyan University *B*
University of Akron *B, M*
University of Cincinnati *B, M, D, T*
University of Dayton *B*
University of Toledo *B, M*
Wilmington College *B*
Wittenberg University *B*
Wright State University *B, M*
Youngstown State University *B*

Oklahoma

Oklahoma State University *B, M, D*
Rose State College *A*
Tulsa Community College *A*
University of Oklahoma *B, M, D*
University of Tulsa *B, M, D*

Oregon

Central Oregon Community
   College *A*
Chemeketa Community College *A*
Mt. Hood Community College *A*

Oregon State University *B, M, D*
Portland State University *B, M*
Southern Oregon University *B*
Treasure Valley Community College *A*
University of Oregon *B, M, D*
Western Oregon University *B*

Pennsylvania

Allegheny College *B*
Bloomsburg University of
    Pennsylvania *B, T*
Bryn Mawr College *B*
Bucknell University *B*
California University of
    Pennsylvania *B, M*
Clarion University of Pennsylvania *B*
Dickinson College *B*
East Stroudsburg University of
    Pennsylvania *B, T*
Edinboro University of
    Pennsylvania *B*
Franklin & Marshall College *B*
Haverford College *B*
Indiana University of Pennsylvania *B*
Juniata College *B*
Kutztown University of
    Pennsylvania *B, T*
La Salle University *B*
Lafayette College *B*
Lehigh University *B, M, D*
Lock Haven University of
    Pennsylvania *B*
Mansfield University of
    Pennsylvania *B*
Mercyhurst College *B*
Millersville University of
    Pennsylvania *B, T*
Moravian College *B*
Penn State
    Abington *B*
    Altoona *B*
    Beaver *B*
    Berks *B*
    Brandywine *B*
    DuBois *B*
    Erie, The Behrend College *B*
    Fayette, The Eberly Campus *B*
    Greater Allegheny *B*
    Hazleton *B*
    Lehigh Valley *B*
    Mont Alto *B*
    New Kensington *B*
    Schuylkill *B*
    Shenango *B*
    University Park *B, M, D*
    Wilkes-Barre *B*
    Worthington Scranton *B*
    York *B*
Shippensburg University of
    Pennsylvania *B, T*
Slippery Rock University of
    Pennsylvania *B*
Temple University *B, M*
University of Pennsylvania *B, M, D*
University of Pittsburgh *B, M, D*
University of Pittsburgh
    Johnstown *B*
West Chester University of
    Pennsylvania *B, M, T*
Wilkes University *B*

Rhode Island

Brown University *B, M, D*
University of Rhode Island *B*

South Carolina

Clemson University *B, M*
College of Charleston *B*
Furman University *B*
University of South Carolina *B, M, D*

South Dakota

South Dakota School of Mines and
    Technology *B, M, D*
University of South Dakota *B, M*

Tennessee

Austin Peay State University *B*
Middle Tennessee State
    University *C, B*
Tennessee Technological University *B*
University of Memphis *B, M, D*
University of Tennessee
    Chattanooga *B*
    Knoxville *B, M, D*
    Martin *B*
University of the South *B*
Vanderbilt University *B, M*

Texas

Amarillo College *A*
Austin Community College *A*
Baylor University *B, M, D*
Central Texas College *A*
Clarendon College *A*
Coastal Bend College *A*
Del Mar College *A*
El Paso Community College *A*
Galveston College *A*
Grayson County College *A*
Hardin-Simmons University *B*
Hill College *A*
Lamar University *B*
Laredo Community College *A*
Midland College *A*
Midwestern State University *B*
Odessa College *A*
Rice University *B, M, D*
St. Mary's University *B, T*
St. Philip's College *A*
Sam Houston State University *B*
San Jacinto College *A*
South Plains College *A*
Southern Methodist
    University *B, M, D*
Stephen F. Austin State
    University *B, M*
Sul Ross State University *B, M*
Tarleton State University *B*
Texas A&M University *B, M, D, D*
Texas A&M University
    Commerce *B*
    Corpus Christi *B, T*
    Galveston *B*
    Kingsville *B, M, D*
Texas Christian University *B, M*
Texas Tech University *B, M, D*
Trinity University *B*
Tyler Junior College *A*
University of Houston *B, M, D*
University of Texas
    Arlington *B, M*
    Austin *B, M, D*
    Dallas *B, M, D*
    El Paso *B, M, D*
    San Antonio *B, M*
    of the Permian Basin *B, M*
West Texas A&M University *B*
Western Texas College *A*

Utah

Brigham Young University *B, M*
Salt Lake Community College *A*
Snow College *A*
Southern Utah University *B*
University of Utah *B, M, D, T*
Utah State University *B, M*
Weber State University *B*

Vermont

Castleton State College *B*
Middlebury College *B*
Norwich University *B*
University of Vermont *B, M*

Virginia

College of William and Mary *B*
George Mason University *B, M*
James Madison University *B, T*
Old Dominion University *B, M, T*
Radford University *B*
Virginia Polytechnic Institute and
    State University *B, M, D*
Washington and Lee University *B*

Washington

Cascadia Community College *A*
Centralia College *A*
Eastern Washington University *B*
Everett Community College *A*
Highline Community College *A*
Olympic College *A*
Pacific Lutheran University *B*
University of Puget Sound *B, T*
University of Washington *B, M, D*
Washington State University *B, M, D*
Western Washington University *B, M*
Whitman College *B*

West Virginia

Concord University *B*
Marshall University *B*
Potomac State College of West
    Virginia University *A*
West Virginia University *B, M, D*

Wisconsin

Beloit College *B*
Lawrence University *B, T*
St. Norbert College *B, T*
University of Wisconsin
    Eau Claire *B*
    Madison *B, M, D*
    Milwaukee *B, M, D*
    Oshkosh *B*
    Parkside *B, T*
    River Falls *B*

Wyoming

Casper College *A*
Central Wyoming College *A*
University of Wyoming *B, M, D*
Western Wyoming Community
    College *A*

Geophysics/seismology

Alaska

University of Alaska
    Fairbanks *M, D*

California

California Institute of
    Technology *B, M, D*
California State University
    Northridge *B*
Occidental College *B*
Stanford University *B, M, D*
University of California
    Berkeley *B*
    Los Angeles *B, M, D*
    Riverside *B*
    Santa Barbara *B, M*

Colorado

Colorado School of Mines *B, M, D*
University of Colorado
    Boulder *D*

Delaware

University of Delaware *B*

Florida

Florida Institute of Technology *M*

Idaho

Boise State University *B, M, D*
Idaho State University *M*
University of Idaho *M*

Illinois

University of Chicago *B, D*

Maine

Bowdoin College *B*

Massachusetts

Boston College *B, M*
Boston University *B*
Massachusetts Institute of
    Technology *M, D*

Michigan

Eastern Michigan University *B*
Michigan State University *B*
Michigan Technological
    University *B, M*
Western Michigan University *B*

Minnesota

University of Minnesota
    Twin Cities *B, M, D*

Missouri

Saint Louis University *B, M, D*
University of Missouri
    Missouri University of Science and
        Technology *B, M, D*

Nevada

University of Nevada
    Reno *B, M, D*

New Mexico

New Mexico Institute of Mining and
    Technology *B, M, D*

New York

Columbia University *B*
Columbia University
    School of General Studies *B*
St. Lawrence University *B*
State University of New York
    College at Fredonia *B*
    College at Geneseo *B*

Ohio

Bowling Green State University *B, M*
Ohio State University
    Columbus Campus *B, M, D*
University of Akron *B, M*
Wright State University *M*

Oklahoma

University of Oklahoma *B, M, D*
University of Tulsa *B, M, D*

Oregon

Oregon State University *M, D*

Rhode Island

Brown University *B*

South Carolina

University of South Carolina *B*

Tennessee

University of Memphis *M, D*

Texas

Baylor University *B*
Rice University *B, M*
Southern Methodist
    University *B, M, D*
Texas A&M University *B, M, D*

Texas Tech University *B*
University of Houston *B*
University of Texas
Austin *B*
El Paso *B, M*

Utah

University of Utah *B, M, D*

Washington

University of Washington *M, D*
Western Washington University *B*

Wisconsin

University of Wisconsin
Madison *B, M, D*

Wyoming

University of Wyoming *M, D*

Geotechnical engineering

California

University of Southern California *M*

Delaware

Delaware State University *B*

Illinois

Illinois Institute of Technology *M*
University of Illinois
Urbana-Champaign *B, M, D*

New Jersey

Stevens Institute of Technology *M*

South Dakota

Western Dakota Technical Institute *A*

German

Alabama

Auburn University *B*
Birmingham-Southern College *B*
Samford University *B*
University of Alabama *M*

Alaska

University of Alaska
Anchorage *B*

Arizona

Arizona State University *B, M*
Northern Arizona University *B*
University of Arizona *B, M*

Arkansas

Hendrix College *B*
University of Arkansas *B, M*
University of Arkansas
Little Rock *B*

California

Bakersfield College *A*
Cabrillo College *A*
California Lutheran University *B*
California State University
Chico *B*
Fullerton *B, M*
Long Beach *B, M*
Northridge *B*
Cerritos College *A*
Chabot College *A*
Chaffey College *A*
Citrus College *A*
Claremont McKenna College *B*
College of San Mateo *A*
College of the Desert *A*
Cypress College *A*

De Anza College *A*
El Camino College *A*
El Camino College: Compton
Center *A*
Golden West College *A*
Grossmont College *A*
Los Angeles City College *A*
Los Angeles Valley College *A*
Loyola Marymount University *B*
Merced College *A*
MiraCosta College *A*
Orange Coast College *A*
Pepperdine University *B*
Pitzer College *B*
Pomona College *B*
St. Mary's College of California *B*
San Diego State University *B*
San Francisco State University *B, M*
San Joaquin Delta College *A*
San Jose State University *B*
Santa Clara University *B*
Scripps College *B*
Solano Community College *A*
Sonoma State University *B*
Stanford University *B, M, D*
University of California
Berkeley *B, M, D*
Davis *B, M, D*
Irvine *M, D*
Los Angeles *B*
San Diego *B, M*
Santa Barbara *B, M, D*
University of La Verne *B*
University of Redlands *B*
University of the Pacific *B*

Colorado

Colorado College *B*
Colorado State University *B, M*
Red Rocks Community College *A*
University of Colorado
Boulder *M*
University of Denver *B*

Connecticut

Central Connecticut State
University *B*
Connecticut College *B*
Fairfield University *B*
Southern Connecticut State
University *B, T*
Trinity College *B*
University of Connecticut *B, M, D*
Wesleyan University *B*
Yale University *B, M, D*

Delaware

Delaware State University *B*
University of Delaware *B, M, T*

District of Columbia

American University *B*
Catholic University of America *B*
George Washington University *B*
Georgetown University *B, M, D*
Howard University *B*

Florida

Florida Atlantic University *B, M*
Florida State University *B, M*
New College of Florida *B*
Schiller International University *B*
State College of Florida,
Manatee-Sarasota *A*
Stetson University *B*
University of Florida *B, M*
University of Miami *B*
University of South Florida *B*

Georgia

Agnes Scott College *B*
Berry College *B*
Emory University *B*

Georgia Southern University *B*
Georgia State University *B, M*
Mercer University *B*
North Georgia College & State
University *B*
University of Georgia *B, M*
University of West Georgia *B*

Hawaii

University of Hawaii
Manoa *B*

Idaho

Boise State University *B*
Idaho State University *A, B*
University of Idaho *B*

Illinois

Augustana College *B, T*
Bradley University *B, T*
City Colleges of Chicago
Harold Washington College *A*
DePaul University *B*
Elmhurst College *B, T*
Illinois College *B, T*
Illinois State University *B, T*
Illinois Wesleyan University *B*
Knox College *B*
North Central College *B*
Northern Illinois University *B, M, T*
Northwestern University *B, M, D*
Richland Community College *A*
Rockford College *B*
Southern Illinois University
Carbondale *B*
University of Chicago *B, D*
University of Illinois
Urbana-Champaign *B, M, D*
Wheaton College *B, T*

Indiana

Ball State University *B, T*
Butler University *B*
DePauw University *B*
Earlham College *B*
Grace College *B*
Hanover College *B*
Indiana University
Bloomington *B, M, D*
South Bend *B*
Southeast *B*
Indiana University-Purdue University
Fort Wayne *A, B, T*
Indiana University-Purdue University
Indianapolis *B*
Manchester College *B, T*
University of Evansville *B*
University of Indianapolis *B*
University of Notre Dame *B, M*
University of Southern Indiana *B, T*
Valparaiso University *B*
Wabash College *B*

Iowa

Central College *B, T*
Coe College *B*
Cornell College *B, T*
Grinnell College *B*
Luther College *B*
St. Ambrose University *B, T*
Simpson College *B*
University of Iowa *B, M, D, T*
University of Northern Iowa *B, M*
Wartburg College *B, T*

Kansas

Baker University *B, T*
Kansas Wesleyan University *B*
Washburn University *B*

Kentucky

Berea College *B, T*

Bluegrass Community and Technical
College *A*
Centre College *B*
Eastern Kentucky University *B*
Georgetown College *B*
Murray State University *B, T*
Northern Kentucky University *B*
University of Kentucky *B, M*
Western Kentucky University *B, T*

Louisiana

Centenary College of Louisiana *B, T*
Dillard University *B*
Louisiana State University and
Agricultural and Mechanical
College *B*
Loyola University New Orleans *B*
Tulane University *B*

Maine

Bates College *B, T*
Bowdoin College *B*
Colby College *B*
University of Maine *B*

Maryland

Hood College *B*
Johns Hopkins University *B, M, D*
Loyola University Maryland *B*
McDaniel College *B*
Mount St. Mary's University *B*
Towson University *T*
University of Maryland
College Park *B, M, D*
Washington College *B, T*

Massachusetts

Amherst College *B*
Bard College at Simon's Rock *B*
Boston College *B*
Boston University *B*
Brandeis University *B*
College of the Holy Cross *B*
Gordon College *B*
Harvard College *B, M, D*
Smith College *B*
Suffolk University *B*
Tufts University *B, M*
University of Massachusetts
Amherst *B, M, D*
Wellesley College *B*
Wheaton College *B*
Williams College *B*

Michigan

Adrian College *A, B, T*
Albion College *B, T*
Alma College *B, T*
Aquinas College *B, T*
Calvin College *B, T*
Central Michigan University *B*
Eastern Michigan University *B, M*
Grand Valley State University *B*
Hillsdale College *B*
Hope College *B*
Kalamazoo College *B*
Lansing Community College *A*
Michigan State University *B, M, D*
Michigan Technological University *T*
Oakland University *B, T*
University of Michigan *B, D*
Wayne State University *B, M*
Western Michigan University *B*

Minnesota

Augsburg College *B*
Bemidji State University *B*
Carleton College *B*
College of St. Benedict *B*
Concordia College: Moorhead *B, T*
Gustavus Adolphus College *B*
Hamline University *B*
Macalester College *B*

Minnesota State University
   Mankato *B, M, T*
Saint Cloud State University *B*
St. John's University *B*
St. Olaf College *B*
University of Minnesota
   Duluth *B*
   Morris *B*
   Twin Cities *B, M, D*
University of St. Thomas *B*
Winona State University *B*

Mississippi
University of Mississippi *B*

Missouri
Drury University *B, T*
Missouri Southern State University *B*
Missouri State University *B*
Missouri Western State University *T*
Saint Louis University *B*
Southeast Missouri State University *B*
Truman State University *B*
University of Central Missouri *B*
University of Missouri
   Columbia *B, M*
   Kansas City *B*
   St. Louis *B*
Washington University in St.
   Louis *B, M, D*
Webster University *B*

Montana
University of Montana *B, M*

Nebraska
Creighton University *B*
Doane College *B*
Nebraska Wesleyan University *B*
Union College *B*
University of Nebraska
   Kearney *B, M, T*
   Lincoln *B*
   Omaha *B*

Nevada
University of Nevada
   Las Vegas *B*
   Reno *B*

New Hampshire
Dartmouth College *B*
University of New Hampshire *B*

New Jersey
Drew University *B*
Princeton University *B, M, D*
Rider University *B*
Rutgers, The State University of New
   Jersey
   Camden Regional Campus *B, T*
   New Brunswick/Piscataway
   Campus *B, M, D, T*
Seton Hall University *T*

New Mexico
University of New Mexico *B, M*

New York
Alfred University *B*
Bard College *B*
Barnard College *B*
City University of New York
   Hunter College *B*
   Queens College *B, T*
Colgate University *B*
Columbia University *B*
Columbia University
   School of General Studies *B*
Cornell University *B*
Fordham University *B*
Hartwick College *B, T*

Hofstra University *B*
Ithaca College *B, T*
Nazareth College *B*
New York University *B, M, D*
St. Lawrence University *B, T*
Skidmore College *B*
State University of New York
   Binghamton *B*
   Buffalo *B, M, D*
   Oswego *B*
   Stony Brook *B, M*
Syracuse University *B, M*
Union College *B*
United States Military Academy *B*
University of Rochester *B, M*
Vassar College *B*
Wells College *B*

North Carolina
Davidson College *B*
Duke University *B, M, D*
East Carolina University *B*
Guilford College *B, T*
Lenoir-Rhyne University *B*
Methodist University *A*
University of North Carolina
   Asheville *B, T*
   Chapel Hill *B, M, D*
   Charlotte *B*
   Greensboro *B*
   Wilmington *B*
Wake Forest University *B*
Western Carolina University *B*

North Dakota
Jamestown College *B*
Minot State University *B*
University of North Dakota *B*

Ohio
Baldwin-Wallace College *B*
Bowling Green State University *B, M*
Case Western Reserve University *B*
College of Wooster *B*
Denison University *B*
Franciscan University of
   Steubenville *B*
Heidelberg University *B*
Hiram College *B, T*
John Carroll University *B*
Kent State University *B, M*
Kenyon College *B*
Miami University
   Oxford Campus *B*
Mount Union College *B*
Muskingum University *B*
Oberlin College *B*
Ohio Northern University *B*
Ohio State University
   Columbus Campus *B, M, D*
Ohio University *B, M*
Ohio Wesleyan University *B*
University of Cincinnati *B, T*
University of Dayton *B*
University of Toledo *B, M*
Wittenberg University *B*
Wright State University *B*
Xavier University *A, B*
Youngstown State University *B*

Oklahoma
Oklahoma Baptist University *B, T*
Oklahoma City University *B*
Oklahoma State University *B*
Oral Roberts University *B*
Tulsa Community College *A*
University of Central Oklahoma *B*
University of Tulsa *B*

Oregon
Lewis & Clark College *B*
Linfield College *B, T*
Oregon State University *B*

Pacific University *B*
Portland State University *B, M*
Reed College *B*
University of Oregon *B, M, D*
University of Portland *B, T*
Western Oregon University *T*
Willamette University *B*

Pennsylvania
Allegheny College *B*
Bloomsburg University of
   Pennsylvania *B, T*
Bryn Mawr College *B*
Bucknell University *B*
California University of
   Pennsylvania *B*
Carnegie Mellon University *B*
Dickinson College *B*
Edinboro University of
   Pennsylvania *B, T*
Elizabethtown College *B*
Franklin & Marshall College *B*
Gettysburg College *B*
Haverford College *B, T*
Immaculata University *B*
Indiana University of Pennsylvania *B*
Juniata College *B*
Kutztown University of
   Pennsylvania *B*
La Salle University *B*
Lafayette College *B*
Lebanon Valley College *B*
Lehigh University *B*
Lock Haven University of
   Pennsylvania *B*
Lycoming College *B*
Mansfield University of
   Pennsylvania *B, T*
Messiah College *B*
Millersville University of
   Pennsylvania *B, M, T*
Moravian College *B, T*
Muhlenberg College *B*
Penn State
   Abington *B*
   Altoona *B*
   Beaver *B*
   Berks *B*
   Brandywine *B*
   DuBois *B*
   Erie, The Behrend College *B*
   Fayette, The Eberly Campus *B*
   Greater Allegheny *B*
   Hazleton *B*
   Lehigh Valley *B*
   Mont Alto *B*
   New Kensington *B*
   Schuylkill *B*
   Shenango *B*
   University Park *B, M, D*
   Wilkes-Barre *B*
   Worthington Scranton *B*
   York *B*
Rosemont College *B*
Saint Joseph's University *B*
Susquehanna University *B, T*
Swarthmore College *B*
Temple University *B*
University of Pennsylvania *B, M, D*
University of Pittsburgh *B, M, D*
University of Scranton *B, T*
Ursinus College *B, T*
Villanova University *B*
Washington & Jefferson College *B*
West Chester University of
   Pennsylvania *B, M, T*
Westminster College *B*

Rhode Island
Brown University *B, M, D*
University of Rhode Island *B*

South Carolina
Bob Jones University *B*

College of Charleston *B, T*
Francis Marion University *B*
Furman University *B, T*
Presbyterian College *B*
University of South Carolina *B, M*
Wofford College *B*

South Dakota
Augustana College *B, T*
Northern State University *B*
South Dakota State University *B*
University of South Dakota *B*

Tennessee
Belmont University *B*
Lipscomb University *B*
Rhodes College *B*
Tennessee Technological
   University *B, T*
University of Tennessee
   Knoxville *B*
University of the South *B*
Vanderbilt University *B, M, D*

Texas
Angelo State University *B, T*
Austin College *B*
Austin Community College *A*
Baylor University *B*
Blinn College *A*
Paris Junior College *A*
Rice University *B*
Southern Methodist University *B*
Southwestern University *B*
Texas A&M University *B*
Texas A&M University
   Commerce *B*
Texas Christian University *B*
Texas State University: San
   Marcos *B, T*
Texas Tech University *B, M*
Trinity University *B*
University of Dallas *B*
University of Houston *B, M*
University of North Texas *B*
University of Texas
   Arlington *B*
   Austin *B*
   San Antonio *B*

Utah
Brigham Young University *B, M*
Southern Utah University *B*
University of Utah *B, T*
Utah State University *B*
Weber State University *B*

Vermont
Middlebury College *B, M, D*
University of Vermont *B, M*

Virginia
Christopher Newport University *B*
College of William and Mary *B*
Hampden-Sydney College *B*
Hollins University *B*
Longwood University *B, T*
Old Dominion University *B, T*
Randolph-Macon College *B*
Sweet Briar College *B*
University of Virginia *B, M, D*
Virginia Wesleyan College *B*
Washington and Lee University *B*

Washington
Centralia College *A*
Everett Community College *A*
Highline Community College *A*
Pacific Lutheran University *B*
Seattle Pacific University *B*
University of Puget Sound *B, T*
University of Washington *B, M, D*
Walla Walla University *B*

Western Washington University *B*
Whitman College *B*

West Virginia
Bethany College *B*
West Virginia University *T*

Wisconsin
Beloit College *B*
Carthage College *B*
Concordia University Wisconsin *B*
Lakeland College *B*
Lawrence University *B, T*
Marquette University *B*
Ripon College *B, T*
St. Norbert College *B, T*
University of Wisconsin
  Green Bay *B, T*
  La Crosse *B, T*
  Milwaukee *B*
  Oshkosh *B*
  Parkside *B, T*
  Platteville *B*
  River Falls *B*
  Stevens Point *B, T*
  Whitewater *B, T*
Wisconsin Lutheran College *B*

Wyoming
University of Wyoming *B, M*

German studies

California
Pomona College *B*
Scripps College *B*
Stanford University *B, M, D*
University of California
  Irvine *B*
  Riverside *B, M, D*
  San Diego *B*
  Santa Cruz *B*

Connecticut
Wesleyan University *B*

District of Columbia
American University *B*

Florida
New College of Florida *B*

Georgia
Emory University *B*

Illinois
University of Chicago *B, D*
University of Illinois
  Chicago *B, M, D*

Indiana
Purdue University *B*

Iowa
Coe College *B*

Louisiana
Tulane University *B*

Massachusetts
Bard College at Simon's Rock *B*
College of the Holy Cross *B*
Mount Holyoke College *B*
Suffolk University *B*
Wellesley College *B*
Wheaton College *B*

Minnesota
Concordia College: Moorhead *B, T*
Minnesota State University
  Mankato *B*

Missouri
Washington University in St. Louis *B*

New Hampshire
Dartmouth College *B*

New York
Bard College *B*
Barnard College *B*
Columbia University *B*
Cornell University *B, M, D*
Hamilton College *B*

North Carolina
Guilford College *B*

Ohio
Case Western Reserve University *B*
University of Cincinnati *B*

Oregon
Linfield College *B*

Pennsylvania
Kutztown University of
  Pennsylvania *B*
Moravian College *B*
Muhlenberg College *B*
Swarthmore College *B*

Rhode Island
Brown University *B, M, D*

Tennessee
University of the South *B*
Vanderbilt University *B*

Texas
Rice University *B*
Southern Methodist University *B*
University of Houston *B*

Utah
Brigham Young University *B, M*

Virginia
Sweet Briar College *B*
University of Richmond *B*

Washington
University of Washington *B, M*

Wisconsin
University of Wisconsin
  Parkside *B*

German teacher
education

Alabama
Birmingham-Southern College *T*

Arizona
Northern Arizona University *B*
Prescott College *T*
University of Arizona *B*

California
California State University
  Chico *B, T*
  Long Beach *T*
Humboldt State University *T*
San Diego State University *T*
San Francisco State University *T*
Stanford University *M, T*
University of the Pacific *T*

Colorado
Colorado State University *B, T*

Connecticut
Fairfield University *T*

Delaware
University of Delaware *B, T*

Florida
Stetson University *B*

Georgia
University of West Georgia *M*

Idaho
Boise State University *B, T*

Illinois
Augustana College *B, T*
Bradley University *B*
DePaul University *M, T*
Elmhurst College *B*
Illinois College *T*
Knox College *T*
North Park University *T*
Rockford College *T*
University of Illinois
  Chicago *B*
  Urbana-Champaign *B, M, T*

Indiana
Indiana University
  Bloomington *B, T*
Indiana University-Purdue University
  Fort Wayne *B, T*
Indiana University-Purdue University
  Indianapolis *B, T*
Manchester College *B, T*
Purdue University *B, M, D*
University of Evansville *B, T*
University of Indianapolis *T*
Valparaiso University *B*

Iowa
Central College *T*
Cornell College *B, T*
Graceland University *T*
Iowa State University *T*
Loras College *T*
St. Ambrose University *B, T*
Simpson College *T*
University of Iowa *T*
Wartburg College *T*

Kansas
Bethel College *T*
Washburn University *B*

Louisiana
Centenary College of Louisiana *B, T*
University of Louisiana at Lafayette *B*

Maryland
Mount St. Mary's University *T*
Towson University *T*

Massachusetts
Tufts University *T*

Michigan
Albion College *B, T*
Alma College *T*
Calvin College *B*
Central Michigan University *B*
Eastern Michigan University *B*
Grand Valley State University *T*
Hope College *B, T*
Michigan State University *B*
Western Michigan University *B, T*

Minnesota
Augsburg College *T*
Bemidji State University *T*
College of St. Benedict *T*
Concordia College: Moorhead *B, T*
Gustavus Adolphus College *T*
Minnesota State University
  Mankato *B, M, T*
Saint Cloud State University *B, T*
St. John's University *T*
University of Minnesota
  Duluth *B, T*
  Morris *T*
University of St. Thomas *B*
Winona State University *B, T*

Mississippi
Mississippi State University *T*

Missouri
Missouri Southern State
  University *B*
Missouri State University *B*
University of Central Missouri *B, T*
University of Missouri
  Columbia *M*
  Kansas City *B*
Washington University in St.
  Louis *B, M, T*

Montana
University of Montana *T*

Nebraska
Creighton University *T*
Nebraska Wesleyan University *T*
University of Nebraska
  Kearney *B, T*
  Lincoln *B*

New Hampshire
University of New Hampshire *T*

New Jersey
County College of Morris *A*

New York
City University of New York
  Hunter College *B, T*
Dutchess Community College *A*
Fordham University *M, T*
Hofstra University *B, M*
Ithaca College *B, T*
St. Lawrence University *T*
State University of New York
  Buffalo *M, T*
  Oswego *T*
  Stony Brook *T*
University of Rochester *M*
Vassar College *T*
Wells College *T*

North Carolina
East Carolina University *B*
University of North Carolina
  Charlotte *B*
  Wilmington *B*
Wake Forest University *T*
Western Carolina University *B, T*

North Dakota
Minot State University *B*

Ohio
Baldwin-Wallace College *T*
Bowling Green State University *M*
Hiram College *T*
Kent State University *T*
Miami University
  Oxford Campus *B*
Mount Union College *T*
Ohio University *B, T*

Ohio Wesleyan University B
University of Dayton B
University of Toledo B, M, T

Oklahoma
Oklahoma Baptist University B, T
Oklahoma City University B
University of Central Oklahoma B
University of Tulsa T

Oregon
Eastern Oregon University B, T
Linfield College T
Oregon State University M
Portland State University T
Western Oregon University T

Pennsylvania
Dickinson College T
Gettysburg College T
Juniata College B, T
La Salle University B, T
Lebanon Valley College T
Lycoming College T
Mansfield University of
    Pennsylvania B, T
Messiah College B, T
Moravian College T
Susquehanna University T
Villanova University T
Washington & Jefferson College T
Westminster College T

South Carolina
Furman University T

South Dakota
Augustana College B, T
University of South Dakota B, M, T

Tennessee
Lipscomb University B, T
Tennessee Technological University T

Texas
Texas State University: San Marcos T
University of Dallas T
University of Houston T
University of Texas
    Arlington T
    San Antonio T

Utah
Brigham Young University B
Southern Utah University B, T
Weber State University B

Vermont
St. Michael's College T

Virginia
Eastern Mennonite University T
Hollins University T
Longwood University B, T
Old Dominion University B, T

Washington
Washington State University B, M, T
Western Washington University B
Whitworth University T

West Virginia
Bethany College B

Wisconsin
Carthage College T
Lawrence University T
St. Norbert College T
University of Wisconsin
    Green Bay T
    Madison M

Parkside T
Platteville B, T
River Falls T
Whitewater B

Germanic languages

California
University of California
    Los Angeles M, D

Colorado
University of Colorado
    Boulder B

Kansas
University of Kansas B, M, D

Massachusetts
Bard College at Simon's Rock B

Michigan
Eastern Michigan University B

Missouri
Washington University in St.
    Louis B, M, D

New York
Canisius College B
Columbia University B

North Carolina
Guilford College B

Ohio
Cleveland State University B
Ohio Northern University B

Oklahoma
University of Oklahoma B, M

Tennessee
Lambuth University B

Texas
University of Texas
    Austin M, D

Utah
Brigham Young University B

Vermont
Bennington College B

Washington
University of Washington B

Wisconsin
University of Wisconsin
    Eau Claire B
    Madison B, M, D

Gerontology

Arizona
University of Arizona M

Arkansas
Arkansas State University M

California
American River College A
California State University
    Chico B
    Fullerton M
    Long Beach M
    Sacramento B, M
Chaffey College A

Cosumnes River College A
Folsom Lake College A
Loma Linda University M
MiraCosta College A
San Diego State University B, M
San Francisco State University M
University of La Verne M
University of Southern
    California B, M, D

Connecticut
Quinnipiac University B
Saint Joseph College M

Delaware
Wilmington University M

Florida
Bethune-Cookman University B
University of South Florida B, M, D

Georgia
Georgia State University B, M

Illinois
Concordia University Chicago M
Dominican University B
Eastern Illinois University M
Northeastern Illinois University M
Western Illinois University M
Wilbur Wright College A

Indiana
Indiana University
    Kokomo B
Manchester College A
Purdue University
    Calumet B
Valparaiso University M

Iowa
University of Northern Iowa B

Kansas
Central Christian College of Kansas A
University of Kansas M, D
Washburn University A, B
Wichita State University B, M

Kentucky
Thomas More College A
University of Kentucky D

Louisiana
University of Louisiana at
    Monroe M, T

Maryland
Anne Arundel Community College A
McDaniel College M
Sojourner-Douglass College B
Towson University B, M
University of Maryland
    Baltimore M, D
    Baltimore County D
    University College B

Massachusetts
University of Massachusetts
    Boston B, M, D

Michigan
Alma College B
Central Michigan University M
Lansing Community College A
Madonna University A, B
Siena Heights University A
Wayne County Community College A

Minnesota
Bethel University M

College of St. Scholastica C
Minnesota State University
    Mankato B, M
    Moorhead B
Saint Cloud State University B, M

Mississippi
East Central Community College A

Missouri
Lindenwood University B, M
Missouri State University B
University of Central Missouri M
University of Missouri
    St. Louis M
Webster University M

Nebraska
University of Nebraska
    Omaha B, M

Nevada
Nevada State College B

New Hampshire
Lakes Region Community
    College C, A

New Jersey
Thomas Edison State College A, B

New York
Alfred University B
City University of New York
    Hostos Community College A
    LaGuardia Community College A
    York College B
College of New Rochelle M
Dowling College M
Excelsior College B
Hofstra University M
Ithaca College B
New York Institute of Technology M
Saint Bonaventure University B
State University of New York
    College at Oneonta B
Touro College M

North Carolina
Appalachian State University M
Barton College B
University of North Carolina
    Charlotte M
    Greensboro M
Winston-Salem State University B

Ohio
Bowling Green State University B
Case Western Reserve University B
Columbus State Community
    College A
John Carroll University B
Miami University
    Oxford Campus B, M
Ohio Dominican University A
University of Akron: Wayne College C
University of Toledo T
Youngstown State University B

Oregon
Marylhurst University M
Portland Community College A

Pennsylvania
California University of
    Pennsylvania B
Marywood University M
Reading Area Community College A

Puerto Rico

Pontifical Catholic University of
Puerto Rico *B*
University of Puerto Rico
Medical Sciences *M*

Texas

Abilene Christian University *M*
McLennan Community College *A*
Stephen F. Austin State University *B*
University of North Texas *B, M, D*
University of Texas
Health Science Center at
Houston *M*

Utah

University of Utah *M*
Weber State University *B*

Virginia

New River Community College *A*
Northern Virginia Community
College *A*

West Virginia

West Virginia State Community and
Technical College *A*

Geropsychology

Arizona

Prescott College *B*

Ohio

University of Akron *D*

GIS technology

Alaska

University of Alaska
Anchorage *C*

California

American River College *A*
Los Angeles Pierce College *C*
Palo Verde College *C*

Colorado

Colorado Northwestern Community
College *C, A*

Idaho

Idaho State University *M*

Illinois

Morrison Institute of Technology *C*

Louisiana

Louisiana Tech University *M*

Michigan

Northern Michigan University *C*

Missouri

Northwest Missouri State
University *B, M*

New Jersey

Burlington County College *C, A*

New Mexico

Navajo Technical College *A*

New York

Cayuga County Community College *A*

North Carolina

Southeastern Community College *C*

University of North Carolina
Wilmington *C*

North Dakota

Bismarck State College *C, A*

Ohio

James A. Rhodes State College *A*
Miami University
Hamilton Campus *C*

Oregon

Central Oregon Community
College *C, A*
Clackamas Community College *C, A*

Pennsylvania

Shippensburg University of
Pennsylvania *C*

Texas

Lamar Institute of Technology *C, A*

Utah

Southern Utah University *C*

Washington

Olympic College *C*

Wyoming

Casper College *C, A*

Glazier

Indiana

Ivy Tech Community College
Central Indiana *C, A*

Michigan

Bay de Noc Community College *C*

Wisconsin

Milwaukee Area Technical College *C*

Global studies

Alabama

University of Alabama
Birmingham *B*

Arizona

Arizona State University *B*
Prescott College *B*

Arkansas

Arkansas Tech University *B*
Harding University *B*
John Brown University *B*
University of Central Arkansas *B*

California

California Maritime Academy *B*
Chapman University *M*
Concordia University *B, M*
Humboldt State University *B*
La Sierra University *B*
National University *B*
Pepperdine University *B*
Pitzer College *B*
Point Loma Nazarene University *B*
Pomona College *B*
Skyline College *A*
Sonoma State University *B, M*
Stanford University *B*
University of California
Berkeley *M*
Irvine *B*
Los Angeles *B*
Riverside *B*
Santa Barbara *B, M*

University of Southern California *B*

Colorado

Colorado Christian University *B*
Colorado State University *B*
University of Colorado
Boulder *B*
Denver *B*
University of Denver *B*

Connecticut

Central Connecticut State
University *B, M*
Mitchell College *B*
Saint Joseph College *B*
University of Connecticut *M*
University of New Haven *B*

District of Columbia

American University *B, M*

Florida

Barry University *B*
Eckerd College *B*
New College of Florida *B*
Schiller International University *B, M*
University of Central Florida *B*
University of North Florida *B*

Georgia

Agnes Scott College *M*
Georgia Institute of Technology *B*
Georgia State University *B*
Shorter College *B*
Spelman College *B*

Illinois

Benedictine University *B*
Greenville College *B*
Illinois College *B*
Knox College *B*
Lewis University *B*
Millikin University *B*
Monmouth College *B*
North Central College *B*
Northwestern University *D*
Principia College *B*
University of Illinois
Springfield *B*
Urbana-Champaign *B*

Indiana

Manchester College *B*

Iowa

Central College *B*
Graceland University *B*
University of Iowa *B*

Kansas

Baker University *B*
University of Kansas *B, M*
Wichita State University *B*

Louisiana

Louisiana State University and
Agricultural and Mechanical
College *B*
University of New Orleans *B*

Maine

Colby College *B*
University of Maine
Farmington *B*
University of Southern Maine *B*

Maryland

Howard Community College *A*
Salisbury University *B*

Massachusetts

Assumption College *B*
Brandeis University *B, M*
Cape Cod Community College *A*
Clark University *B*
Emmanuel College *B*
Endicott College *B*
Lesley University *B*
Western New England College *B*
Worcester Polytechnic Institute *B*

Michigan

Adrian College *B*
Hope College *B*
Michigan State University *B, M*
Michigan Technological University *T*
Saginaw Valley State University *B*
Spring Arbor University *B*
University of Michigan *B*
Western Michigan University *B*

Minnesota

College of St. Scholastica *B*
Concordia College: Moorhead *B*
Macalester College *B*
Saint Cloud State University *B*
St. Mary's University of Minnesota *B*
University of Minnesota
Duluth *B*

Mississippi

Belhaven University *B*
Mississippi College *B*

Missouri

Rockhurst University *B*
Southeast Missouri State University *B*
Webster University *B*

Nebraska

Dana College *B*
Doane College *B*
Nebraska Wesleyan University *B*
University of Nebraska
Omaha *B*

Nevada

Sierra Nevada College *B*

New Jersey

Burlington County College *A*
College of St. Elizabeth *B*
Ramapo College of New Jersey *B*

New York

Adelphi University *B*
Bard College *B*
City University of New York
City College *B, M*
College of New Rochelle *B*
D'Youville College *B*
Iona College *B*
Nazareth College *B*
Orange County Community College *A*
Russell Sage College *B*
Saint Bonaventure University *B*
St. Lawrence University *B*
State University of New York
Albany *B*
College at Fredonia *B*
Oswego *B*
United States Military Academy *B*
Wells College *B*

North Carolina

Appalachian State University *B*
High Point University *B*
Meredith College *B*
North Carolina State University *B*
Queens University of Charlotte *B*
Roanoke-Chowan Community
College *A*

University of North Carolina
Chapel Hill *B*
Charlotte *B*
Wake Technical Community
College *A*

North Dakota
North Dakota State University *B*
University of North Dakota *B*

Ohio
Baldwin-Wallace College *B*
Cedarville University *B*
University of Dayton *B*
Wittenberg University *B*

Oklahoma
Oklahoma State University *M*
University of Oklahoma *B, M*
University of Tulsa *B*

Oregon
George Fox University *B*
Northwest Christian University *B*
Oregon State University *B*
University of Oregon *B, M*
Willamette University *B*

Pennsylvania
Gannon University *B*
Gettysburg College *B*
Juniata College *B*
Lehigh University *B*
Mercyhurst College *B*
Penn State
University Park *M*
Susquehanna University *B*
University of Pennsylvania *B, M*
Washington & Jefferson College *B*

Rhode Island
Providence College *B*

South Carolina
Newberry College *B*

South Dakota
Augustana College *B*
South Dakota State University *B*
University of South Dakota *B*

Tennessee
Lambuth University *B*
Tennessee Wesleyan College *B*
University of the South *B*

Texas
Abilene Christian University *B*
East Texas Baptist University *B*
Midwestern State University *B*
St. Edward's University *B*
San Antonio College *A*
Texas A&M University *B*
Texas State University: San
Marcos *B, M*
University of North Texas *B*

Utah
Salt Lake Community College *A*
University of Utah *B, M*

Vermont
Bennington College *B*
Lyndon State College *B*
Marlboro College *B*
University of Vermont *B*

Virginia
George Mason University *M*
Hollins University *B*
Randolph College *B*

Randolph-Macon College *B*
Virginia Commonwealth University *B*
Virginia Military Institute *B*
Virginia Wesleyan College *B*

Washington
Evergreen State College *B*
Pacific Lutheran University *B*
Seattle University *B*
University of Washington Bothell *B*

West Virginia
American Public University
System *B, M*
Bethany College *B*
Concord University *B*

Wisconsin
Carroll University *B*
Lawrence University *B*
Marquette University *B*
Ripon College *B*
University of Wisconsin
Madison *B, M*
Milwaukee *B*
River Falls *B*
Whitewater *B*

Wyoming
Central Wyoming College *A*

Golf management

California
College of the Desert *C, A*

Florida
University of Central Florida *B*

Maryland
Harford Community College *A*
University of Maryland
Eastern Shore *B*

Michigan
Ferris State University *B*

North Carolina
Methodist University *B, M*
Queens University of Charlotte *B*

Pennsylvania
YTI Career Institute: York *A*

Wisconsin
University of Wisconsin
Stout *B*

Graphic communications

Alabama
Gadsden State Community College *A*

Arizona
Arizona State University *B*
Chandler-Gilbert Community College
Pecos *C*
Pima Community College *C, A*

California
Allan Hancock College *A*
Art Center College of Design *B, M*
California Polytechnic State
University: San Luis Obispo *B*
College of the Siskiyous *C, A*
El Camino College: Compton
Center *A*
Ex'pression College for Digital Arts *B*
Folsom Lake College *C*

Platt College
Ontario *C, A, B*
Santa Rosa Junior College *C*
Santiago Canyon College *A*
Westwood College: South Bay *B*

Colorado
Colorado Mountain College *A*
Pikes Peak Community College *C, A*
Westwood College of Technology
Westwood College: Denver
South *A, B*

Connecticut
Mitchell College *A, B*
Northwestern Connecticut
Community College *A*
Paier College of Art *C*
Three Rivers Community College *C*

Florida
Miami Dade College *A*

Georgia
Art Institute
of Atlanta *A, B*

Illinois
City Colleges of Chicago
Kennedy-King College *C, A*
Heartland Community College *C*
Illinois Institute of Art:
Schaumburg *C, A, B*
School of the Art Institute of
Chicago *B, M*

Indiana
Holy Cross College *B*
St. Mary-of-the-Woods College *B*

Iowa
Briar Cliff University *B*
Clinton Community College *C, A*
Dordt College *B*
Grand View University *B*
Hawkeye Community College *A*
Southeastern Community College
North Campus *A*
University of Northern Iowa *B*

Kansas
Pittsburg State University *M*

Kentucky
Somerset Community College *C, A*
Sullivan College of Technology and
Design *A, B*

Maryland
Anne Arundel Community
College *C, A*
Montgomery College *C, A*

Massachusetts
New England Institute of Art *B*
Newbury College *A*
Quinsigamond Community College *A*

Michigan
Baker College
of Muskegon *A*
of Owosso *A, B*
Gogebic Community College *A*
International Academy of Design and
Technology: Detroit *B*

Minnesota
Academy College *B*
Art Institutes International
Minnesota *A, B*
Brown College *A, B*

Hennepin Technical College *C, A*
St. Cloud Technical College *C*

Nevada
Western Nevada College *C, A*

New Hampshire
Manchester Community College *C, A*

New Mexico
Clovis Community College *A*

New York
Rochester Institute of
Technology *B, M*
State University of New York
College of Technology at Canton *B*

North Carolina
Chowan University *B*

North Dakota
University of North Dakota *B*

Ohio
Notre Dame College *B*
University of Cincinnati
Raymond Walters College *C, A*

Oklahoma
Oklahoma City Community College *A*

Pennsylvania
Keystone College *A, B*
Philadelphia University *B*

Rhode Island
New England Institute of
Technology *A*
Roger Williams University *B*

Texas
Howard Payne University *B*
North Lake College *C, A*
Wharton County Junior College *C, A*

Utah
Snow College *C*

Vermont
Champlain College *B*

Virginia
Bluefield College *B*

Washington
Centralia College *A*
Clark College *A*
Eastern Washington University *B*

West Virginia
Bethany College *B*

Wisconsin
Carroll University *B*
Carthage College *B*
Milwaukee Area Technical College *A*
Nicolet Area Technical College *A*
Waukesha County Technical
College *A*

Graphic design

Alabama
Samford University *B*
Spring Hill College *B*

Arizona
Arizona State University *B*

Art Center Design College *B*
Art Institute
    of Phoenix *A, B*
Art Institute of Tucson *A, B*
Eastern Arizona College *C*
Glendale Community College *C, A*

Arkansas

Harding University *B*
John Brown University *B*
Ouachita Baptist University *B*
University of Arkansas
    Fort Smith *C, A, B*

California

Academy of Art University *C, A, B, M*
Art Center College of Design *B*
Art Institute
    of California: Los Angeles *A, B*
    of California: Orange County *A, B*
    of California: San Diego *A, B*
Art Institute of California:
    Hollywood *A, B*
Art Institute of California: Inland
    Empire *A*
Art Institute of California:
    Sacramento *A, B*
Art Institute of California: San
    Francisco *A, B*
Art Institute of California:
    Sunnyvale *A, B*
Brooks Institute *B*
California Baptist University *B*
California College of the Arts *B*
California State Polytechnic
    University: Pomona *B*
California State University
    Chico *B*
    Dominguez Hills *B*
Chaffey College *C, A*
Chapman University *B*
City College of San Francisco *A*
Coleman College: San Marcos *A*
Coleman University *C, A, B*
College of the Canyons *C, A*
College of the Desert *A*
College of the Siskiyous *C, A*
Ex'pression College for Digital Arts *B*
Fashion Institute of Design and
    Merchandising
    Los Angeles *A*
    San Diego *A*
    San Francisco *A*
Hartnell College *C*
LA College International *A*
Monterey Peninsula College *C, A*
Mt. Sierra College *B*
Notre Dame de Namur University *B*
Ohlone College *C, A*
Otis College of Art and Design *B, M*
Platt College
    Ontario *A*
Point Loma Nazarene University *B*
San Diego State University *B*
San Jose State University *B*
Santa Barbara City College *C*
Southwestern College *A*
Westwood College of Technology
    Westwood College: Inland
        Empire *A*
    Westwood College: Los Angeles *A*
Westwood College: South Bay *A*
Woodbury University *B*

Colorado

Arapahoe Community College *C, A*
Art Institute
    of Colorado *A, B*
Colorado Mountain College *A*
Colorado State University *B*
Community College of Denver *C, A*
Mesa State College *B*
Rocky Mountain College of Art &
    Design *B*

University of Denver *B, M*
Westwood College of Technology
    Westwood College: Denver
        South *A, B*
    Westwood College: Denver
        North *A, B*

Connecticut

Gateway Community College *A*
Mitchell College *A, B*
Northwestern Connecticut
    Community College *C*
Paier College of Art *C, B*
Quinebaug Valley Community
    College *C, A*
University of Bridgeport *B*
University of New Haven *C, A, B*

Delaware

Delaware College of Art and
    Design *C, A*

District of Columbia

American University *B*
Corcoran College of Art and
    Design *C, A, B*

Florida

Art Institute of Fort Lauderdale *A, B*
College of Business and Technology:
    Kendall *A*
Daytona State College *A*
Florida Agricultural and Mechanical
    University *B*
Florida Southern College *B*
Lake City Community College *C, A*
Lynn University *B*
Miami International University of Art
    and Design *B, M*
Palm Beach Atlantic University *B*
Ringling College of Art and Design *B*
Santa Fe College *A*
University of Miami *C, B*
University of Tampa *B*
Valencia Community College *C, A*

Georgia

Art Institute
    of Atlanta *A, B*
Brenau University *B*
Darton College *C*
Savannah College of Art and
    Design *C, B, M*

Idaho

Northwest Nazarene University *B*
Stevens-Henager College: Boise *A, B*

Illinois

Bradley University *B*
Columbia College Chicago *C, B*
Elgin Community College *A*
Fox College *C*
Harrington College of Design *B*
Highland Community College *C, A*
International Academy of Design and
    Technology: Chicago *A, B*
John Wood Community College *A*
Judson University *B*
Lewis University *B*
Lincoln Land Community College *A*
Moraine Valley Community College *A*
Quincy University *B*
Robert Morris University: Chicago *B*
School of the Art Institute of
    Chicago *B, M*
University of Illinois
    Chicago *B, M*
    Urbana-Champaign *B, M*
Waubonsee Community College *C, A*
Westwood College: Chicago Loop *A*
Westwood College: DuPage *A*

Indiana

Grace College *B*
Huntington University *B*
Indiana University-Purdue University
    Fort Wayne *B*
Indiana Wesleyan University *B*
Oakland City University *B*
St. Mary-of-the-Woods College *B*
University of St. Francis *B*

Iowa

Briar Cliff University *B*
Grand View University *B*
Iowa State University *B, M*
Morningside College *B*
Mount Mercy College *B*
St. Ambrose University *B*
University of Dubuque *B*

Kansas

Barton County Community
    College *C, A*
Cloud County Community
    College *C, A*
University of Kansas *B, M*

Kentucky

Sullivan College of Technology and
    Design *A, B*

Maine

Maine College of Art *B*

Maryland

Anne Arundel Community
    College *C, A*
Cecil College *C*
Howard Community College *C*
Maryland Institute College of Art *B, M*

Massachusetts

Anna Maria College *B*
Art Institute of Boston at Lesley
    University *B*
Bridgewater State College *B*
Cape Cod Community College *A*
Curry College *B*
Emmanuel College *B*
Fitchburg State College *B*
Lasell College *B*
Massachusetts College of Art and
    Design *C, B*
Montserrat College of Art *B*
Mount Ida College *B*
New England Institute of Art *C, B*
Newbury College *B*
North Shore Community College *C, A*
Northeastern University *B*
Regis College *B*
Simmons College *B*
Stonehill College *B*
Suffolk University *M*
University of Massachusetts
    Lowell *B*

Michigan

Alma College *B*
Andrews University *B*
Art Institute of Michigan *A*
Baker College
    of Muskegon *A*
    of Port Huron *A*
Central Michigan University *B*
College for Creative Studies *B*
Delta College *A*
Ferris State University *A, B*
Finlandia University *B*
International Academy of Design and
    Technology: Detroit *A, B*
Jackson Community College *C, A*
Kendall College of Art and Design of
    Ferris State University *B*

Kirtland Community College *C, A*
Lake Michigan College *A*
Madonna University *A, B*
Mott Community College *A*
Northern Michigan University *A, B*
Oakland Community College *A*
Saginaw Valley State University *B*
Spring Arbor University *B*
University of Michigan *B*
University of Michigan
    Flint *B*
Western Michigan University *B*

Minnesota

Art Institutes International
    Minnesota *A, B*
Concordia University: St. Paul *B*
Dakota County Technical College *C, A*
Dunwoody College of
    Technology *C, A*
Minneapolis College of Art and
    Design *B*
Minnesota State Community and
    Technical College *C, A*
North Hennepin Community
    College *A*
Northwestern College *B*
Rochester Community and Technical
    College *C, A*
St. Mary's University of Minnesota *B*
South Central College *C, A*
University of Minnesota
    Duluth *B, M*

Mississippi

Antonelli College
    Jackson *A*
Mississippi College *B*

Missouri

Columbia College *B*
Kansas City Art Institute *B*
Maryville University of Saint Louis *B*
Metropolitan Community College:
    Penn Valley *C, A*
Missouri Western State University *B*
Ozarks Technical Community
    College *C, A*
Park University *B*
Stephens College *B*
Washington University in St. Louis *B*
William Woods University *B*

Montana

Flathead Valley Community
    College *C, A*
Montana State University
    College of Technology: Great
        Falls *A*

Nebraska

Concordia University *B*
Creative Center *A, B*
Creighton University *B*
Dana College *B*
Doane College *B*
Mid-Plains Community College Area *A*
Wayne State College *B*

Nevada

Art Institute
    of Las Vegas *B*
International Academy of Design and
    Technology: Henderson *A, B*

New Hampshire

Chester College of New England *B*
Colby-Sawyer College *B*
Southern New Hampshire
    University *B*

New Jersey
Burlington County College *A*
Cumberland County College *A*
Montclair State University *B*

New Mexico
Art Center Design College *B*
College of Santa Fe *B*

New York
Art Institute
  of New York City *A*
Bryant & Stratton College: Syracuse
  North *A*
City University of New York
  City College *B*
  Queens College *B*
Cooper Union for the Advancement of
  Science and Art *C, B*
Daemen College *B*
Dowling College *B*
Fashion Institute of Technology *B*
Marymount Manhattan College *B*
Nassau Community College *C, A*
Parsons The New School for Design *A*
Pratt Institute *A*
Rochester Institute of
  Technology *A, B, M*
Sage College of Albany *B*
St. John's University *B*
St. Thomas Aquinas College *B*
State University of New York
  Purchase *B*

North Carolina
Appalachian State University *B*
Art Institute
  of Charlotte *A, B*
Chowan University *B*
East Carolina University *B*
Forsyth Technical Community
  College *A*
Lenoir-Rhyne University *B*
Meredith College *B*
Methodist University *B*
North Carolina State University *B, M*

North Dakota
University of North Dakota *B*

Ohio
Art Academy of Cincinnati *A*
Art Institute of Ohio: Cincinnati *A*
Cedarville University *B*
College of Mount St. Joseph *A, B*
Davis College *C, A*
Defiance College *B*
Kaplan College: Dayton *A*
Mount Vernon Nazarene University *B*
Notre Dame College *B*
Ohio Dominican University *B*
Ohio University *B, M*
University of Akron *B*
University of Cincinnati
  Raymond Walters College *C, A*
University of Rio Grande *B*
Ursuline College *B*

Oklahoma
Oklahoma Christian University *B*
Oklahoma City University *B, M*
Southeastern Oklahoma State
  University *B*
Southern Nazarene University *B*
University of Central Oklahoma *B*

Oregon
Art Institute of Portland *A, B*

Pennsylvania
Arcadia University *B*
Bucks County Community College *A*

Butler County Community College *A*
Cabrini College *B*
California University of
  Pennsylvania *B*
Douglas Education Center *A*
Drexel University *B*
East Stroudsburg University of
  Pennsylvania *B*
Edinboro University of
  Pennsylvania *B*
Harrisburg Area Community
  College *C, A*
Hussian School of Art *A*
Immaculata University *C*
Keystone College *A, B*
Luzerne County Community
  College *C, A*
Mansfield University of
  Pennsylvania *B*
Marywood University *B, M*
Moore College of Art and Design *B*
Moravian College *B*
Northampton Community College *A*
Oakbridge Academy of Arts *A*
Penn State
  Abington *B*
  Altoona *B*
  Beaver *B*
  Berks *B*
  Brandywine *B*
  DuBois *B*
  Erie, The Behrend College *B*
  Fayette, The Eberly Campus *B*
  Greater Allegheny *B*
  Hazleton *B*
  Lehigh Valley *B*
  Mont Alto *B*
  New Kensington *B*
  Schuylkill *B*
  Shenango *B*
  University Park *B*
  Wilkes-Barre *B*
  Worthington Scranton *B*
  York *B*
Pennsylvania College of Art and
  Design *B*
Philadelphia University *B*
St. Vincent College *B*
South Hills School of Business &
  Technology *A*
Susquehanna University *B*
Temple University *B, M*
University of the Arts *B*
Westmoreland County Community
  College *C*

Puerto Rico
Turabo University *C, B*
Universidad del Este *A*

Rhode Island
Rhode Island School of Design *B, M*
Roger Williams University *B*
Salve Regina University *B*

South Carolina
Coastal Carolina University *B*
Limestone College *B*
South University: Columbia *A, B*
Trident Technical College *C, A*

South Dakota
South Dakota State University *B*

Tennessee
International Academy of Design and
  Technology: Nashville *A, B*
Memphis College of Art *B*
Nossi College of Art *B*
Watkins College of Art, Design and
  Film *B*

Texas
Abilene Christian University *B*
Art Institute
  of Houston *B*
Hardin-Simmons University *B*
McMurry University *B*
St. Edward's University *B*
San Antonio College *A*
Schreiner University *B*
Texas Christian University *B*
Texas State University: San Marcos *B*
Texas Tech University *B*
University of Houston *B, M*
University of Texas
  El Paso *B, M*
University of the Incarnate Word *B*
West Texas A&M University *B*
Westwood College: Fort Worth *A*
Westwood College: Houston South *A*

Utah
Brigham Young University *B*
College of Eastern Utah *A, T*
Eagle Gate College: Layton *A*
Eagle Gate College: Murray *A*
Stevens-Henager College: Logan *A*

Vermont
Champlain College *B*
Lyndon State College *A, B*

Virginia
Emory & Henry College *B*
Germanna Community College *C*
Marymount University *B*
Old Dominion University *B*
Piedmont Virginia Community
  College *C*
Tidewater Community College *A*
Virginia Commonwealth University *B*

Washington
Art Institute of Seattle *C, A, B*
Centralia College *A*
Cornish College of the Arts *B*
Eastern Washington University *B*
Western Washington University *B*

West Virginia
Concord University *B*
Mountain State University *A, B*
West Virginia Wesleyan College *B*

Wisconsin
Concordia University Wisconsin *B*
Edgewood College *B*
Gateway Technical College *A*
Herzing University *A, B*
Marian University *B*
Milwaukee Area Technical College *A*
Nicolet Area Technical College *A*
St. Norbert College *B*
Viterbo University *B*
Waukesha County Technical
  College *A*
Western Technical College *A*
Wisconsin Indianhead Technical
  College *C*
Wisconsin Lutheran College *B*

Wyoming
Casper College *A*
Central Wyoming College *A*

Graphic/printing production

Alabama
Alabama Agricultural and Mechanical
  University *B*
Bishop State Community College *C*
Lawson State Community College *C*

Arkansas
Arkansas State University *B*
Phillips Community College of the
  University of Arkansas *A*

California
Allan Hancock College *A*
American River College *A*
Antelope Valley College *C, A*
Bakersfield College *A*
Butte College *A*
City College of San Francisco *A*
Fresno City College *C, A*
Fullerton College *A*
Laney College *A*
Long Beach City College *A*
Los Angeles Trade and Technical
  College *C, A*
Mission College *C, A*
Modesto Junior College *C, A*
Moorpark College *A*
National University *M*
Palomar College *C, A*
Rio Hondo College *A*
Riverside Community College *C, A*
Sacramento City College *C, A*
Saddleback College *C*
San Joaquin Delta College *A*
Santa Barbara City College *C*

Colorado
Aims Community College *C, A*
Colorado Mountain College *A*
Community College of Aurora *A*
Westwood College: Denver
  North *A, B*

Connecticut
Gateway Community College *C*

District of Columbia
University of the District of
  Columbia *A, B*

Florida
Florida State College at Jacksonville *A*
Indian River State College *A*
Miami Dade College *A*
Palm Beach Community College *A*
Tallahassee Community College *C*

Georgia
Albany Technical College *C*
Art Institute
  of Atlanta *A, B*
Augusta Technical College *C*
Chattahoochee Technical College *C*
Columbus Technical College *C*
DeKalb Technical College *C*
Georgia Southern University *B*
Valdosta Technical College *C, A*
West Georgia Technical College *C*

Hawaii
University of Hawaii
  Honolulu Community College *A*

Idaho
Idaho State University *C, A*
Lewis-Clark State College *A, B*

Illinois
College of DuPage *C, A*
Elgin Community College *C*
Harper College *C, A*
Kaskaskia College *C*
Prairie State College *C*
Western Illinois University *B*

Indiana
Vincennes University *A*

Iowa

Clinton Community College *A*
Iowa Western Community College *A*
Kirkwood Community College *A*

Kansas

Coffeyville Community College *C*
Fort Scott Community College *C, A*
Pittsburg State University *M*

Kentucky

Eastern Kentucky University *A*

Maine

Central Maine Community College *A*

Maryland

Community College of Baltimore
  County *C, A*
Montgomery College *A*

Massachusetts

Northern Essex Community
  College *C*
Springfield Technical Community
  College *C*

Michigan

Alpena Community College *C, A*
Baker College
  of Muskegon *A*
Bay de Noc Community College *C*
Delta College *C, A*
Ferris State University *B*
Lansing Community College *A*
Macomb Community College *C, A*
Muskegon Community College *A*
Southwestern Michigan College *A*
Washtenaw Community College *A*

Minnesota

Dunwoody College of
  Technology *C, A*
Hennepin Technical College *C, A*
Mesabi Range Community and
  Technical College *C, A*
South Central College *C, A*

Mississippi

Hinds Community College *C, A*
Mississippi Delta Community
  College *C*
Northwest Mississippi Community
  College *C, A*

Missouri

Mineral Area College *C, A*
Ozarks Technical Community
  College *C, A*
St. Louis Community College
  St. Louis Community College at
    Florissant Valley *A*
Southeast Missouri State University *C*
University of Central Missouri *A, B*

Nebraska

Metropolitan Community
  College *C, A*

Nevada

College of Southern Nevada *C, A*
Truckee Meadows Community
  College *C*

New Hampshire

Lakes Region Community
  College *C, A*

New Jersey

Bergen Community College *C*
Brookdale Community College *C, A*

New York

City University of New York
  New York City College of
    Technology *C, A, B*
Erie Community College
  South Campus *A*
Fulton-Montgomery Community
  College *A*
Rochester Institute of
  Technology *C, A*

North Carolina

Alamance Community College *C*
Central Piedmont Community
  College *C, A*
Chowan University *A*
McDowell Technical Community
  College *A*

Ohio

Columbus State Community
  College *C, A*

Oklahoma

Oklahoma State University
  Institute of Technology:
    Okmulgee *A*

Oregon

Chemeketa Community College *A*
Mt. Hood Community College *C, A*

Pennsylvania

Bucks County Community College *A*
Pennsylvania College of
  Technology *B*
Thaddeus Stevens College of
  Technology *A*

Puerto Rico

University of Puerto Rico
  Carolina Regional College *B*

Rhode Island

New England Institute of
  Technology *A*

South Carolina

Midlands Technical College *C*
Trident Technical College *C*

South Dakota

Northern State University *A*
Southeast Technical Institute *A*

Texas

Central Texas College *C, A*
College of the Mainland *C*
Eastfield College *C, A*
Houston Community College
  System *C, A*
Lee College *C, A*
Midland College *A*
Navarro College *A*
North Lake College *C*
San Jacinto College *A*
South Plains College *A*
Tarrant County College *A*
Texas A&M University
  Commerce *B*
Texas State Technical College
  Waco *C, A*
Tyler Junior College *C, A*

Virginia

Dabney S. Lancaster Community
  College *C, A*
Danville Community College *A*
J. Sargeant Reynolds Community
  College *C*
John Tyler Community College *C*

Virginia Intermont College *A*

Washington

Clover Park Technical College *C, A*
Lake Washington Technical College *C*
Shoreline Community College *C, A*
Spokane Falls Community College *C*
Walla Walla University *A, B*
Yakima Valley Community College *A*

West Virginia

Fairmont State University *B*

Wisconsin

Fox Valley Technical College *C, A*
Milwaukee Area Technical College *A*
Moraine Park Technical College *C, A*
Northcentral Technical College *A*
Northeast Wisconsin Technical
  College *A*
Waukesha County Technical
  College *C*

Wyoming

Northwest College *A*

Greenhouse operations

California

Los Angeles Pierce College *C, A*
Southwestern College *C, A*
Yuba Community College District *C*

Georgia

Albany Technical College *C*

Illinois

College of DuPage *C*
Joliet Junior College *C, A*
Kishwaukee College *C, A*
Southwestern Illinois College *A*
Triton College *C, A*

Maine

University of Maine *B*

Michigan

Bay de Noc Community College *C*

Minnesota

Century Community and Technical
  College *C, A*
Rochester Community and Technical
  College *C, A*
University of Minnesota
  Crookston *B*

Nebraska

Nebraska College of Technical
  Agriculture *A*

New York

State University of New York
  College of Agriculture and
    Technology at Morrisville *A, B*

North Carolina

Alamance Community College *C*
Carteret Community College *C, A*
Johnston Community College *C*
Pitt Community College *C*

North Dakota

Dakota College at Bottineau *C, A*

Ohio

Ohio State University
  Agricultural Technical Institute *A*

Pennsylvania

Community College of Allegheny
  County *C*

South Dakota

Southeast Technical Institute *A*

Texas

Western Texas College *C, A*

Vermont

Vermont Technical College *A*

Washington

South Seattle Community
  College *C, A*
Spokane Community College *A*

Wisconsin

Fox Valley Technical College *C*
University of Wisconsin
  River Falls *B*

Gunsmithing

Alabama

Jefferson Davis Community College *C*

California

Lassen Community College *C*

Colorado

Trinidad State Junior College *C, A*

Minnesota

Pine Technical College *C, A*

North Carolina

Montgomery Community College *C, A*
Piedmont Community College *A*

Hair styling

Alabama

Calhoun Community College *C*

California

San Jose City College *C, A*

Colorado

Pueblo Community College *C*
Red Rocks Community College *C*
Trinidad State Junior College *C*

Michigan

Kirtland Community College *C*

North Carolina

Cape Fear Community College *C*
Lenoir Community College *C*

Wisconsin

Gateway Technical College *C*
Milwaukee Area Technical College *C*
Wisconsin Indianhead Technical
  College *C*

Wyoming

Eastern Wyoming College *C*

Hazardous materials information systems

New Mexico

New Mexico State University
  Carlsbad *C*

Virginia

Southwest Virginia Community
College *C*

West Virginia

American Public University
System *C, A*

Hazardous materials technology

Alabama

Central Alabama Community
College *C*
Faulkner State Community College *A*

Arizona

Cochise College *C*
GateWay Community College *C, A*
Paradise Valley Community
College *C, A*

Arkansas

Southern Arkansas University Tech *C*

California

Allan Hancock College *C*
Cabrillo College *C, A*
Hartnell College *C, A*
Oxnard College *C, A*

Connecticut

Three Rivers Community College *C, A*
University of New Haven *C*

Florida

Pensacola Junior College *A*

Indiana

Vincennes University *C*

Kansas

Barton County Community
College *C, A*
Kansas City Kansas Community
College *A*

Michigan

Wayne State University *M*

Mississippi

Jackson State University *M*

New Mexico

New Mexico Junior College *C, A*

Ohio

University of Findlay *C, A, B, M*

Washington

Green River Community College *C, A*

West Virginia

American Public University System *C*

Health aide

California

College of Alameda *C, A*
National University *A*

Colorado

Community College of Denver *C, A*

Illinois

McHenry County College *C*

Kansas

Barton County Community College *C*

Cloud County Community College *C*
Coffeyville Community College *C*

Massachusetts

North Shore Community College *C*

Michigan

Bay de Noc Community College *C*
Delta College *C*

Minnesota

Minnesota West Community and
Technical College *C*
Northland Community & Technical
College *C*
St. Cloud Technical College *C*

Pennsylvania

Community College of Beaver
County *A*

Texas

Howard College *C*

Virginia

Southwest Virginia Community
College *C*

Wyoming

Casper College *C*

Health care administration

Alabama

Auburn University *B*
Columbia Southern University *B, M*
South University: Montgomery *B, M*
University of Alabama
Birmingham *M, D*

Alaska

Alaska Pacific University *B, M*
University of Alaska
Southeast *A*

Arizona

Arizona State University *M*
Brookline College
Phoenix *A*
Tempe *A*
GateWay Community College *C, A*
Northcentral University *B, M, D*
Northern Arizona University *B*
Prescott College *B*
University of Arizona *B*
University of Phoenix *B, M, D*

Arkansas

Arkansas State University *M*
Harding University *B*
University of Arkansas
Little Rock *M*
University of Central Arkansas *M*

California

Barstow Community College *C*
California Coast University *A, B*
California College San Diego *B*
California State University
Bakersfield *M*
Chico *M*
Dominguez Hills *B*
East Bay *M*
Los Angeles *M*
Northridge *M*
California University of Management
and Sciences *A*
Concorde Career College: San
Diego *C*
Loma Linda University *B, M*

Mount St. Mary's College *B*
National University *C, B, M*
St. Mary's College of California *B*
San Joaquin Valley College *A*
San Jose State University *B*
Simpson University *B*
University of California
Berkeley *D*
University of La Verne *B, M*
University of San Francisco *M*
University of Southern California *M*
Western Career College: Citrus
Heights *C, A*
Western Career College:
Sacramento *C, A*
Western Career College:
Stockton *C, A*

Colorado

Adams State College *B*
CollegeAmerica
Denver *B*
Community College of Denver *C*
Metropolitan State College of
Denver *B*
University of Colorado
Denver *M*
University of Northern Colorado *B*

Connecticut

Quinnipiac University *B, M*
Sacred Heart University *M*
St. Vincent's College *C*
University of Connecticut *B*
University of New Haven *M*
Western Connecticut State
University *M*

District of Columbia

George Washington University *M*
Georgetown University *B, M*

Florida

Barry University *C, B, M*
Broward College *A*
Florida Agricultural and Mechanical
University *B, M*
Florida Atlantic University *C, B, M*
Florida Gulf Coast University *B*
Florida Institute of
Technology *A, B, M*
Florida International University *B, M*
Florida State University *M*
Hodges University *B*
Pensacola Junior College *A*
Rasmussen College: Fort Myers *B*
Rasmussen College: Pasco County *B*
Saint Leo University *B*
Saint Thomas University *B*
South University: Tampa *B*
South University: West Palm
Beach *B, M*
Southwest Florida College *B*
State College of Florida,
Manatee-Sarasota *A*
University of Central Florida *B*
University of Florida *M, D*
University of Miami *M*
University of North Florida *M*
University of South Florida *M*

Georgia

Armstrong Atlantic State University *M*
Ashworth College *A, M*
Clayton State University *B, M*
Georgia Institute of Technology *M*
Georgia Southern University *M*
Georgia State University *M*
Macon State College *B*
South University: Savannah *B, M*
Southeastern Technical College *C*

Hawaii

University of Hawaii
Hawaii Community College *C*
West Oahu *C*

Idaho

Idaho State University *B*
Stevens-Henager College: Boise *B, M*

Illinois

Benedictine University *B*
DePaul University *C*
Governors State University *B, M*
Illinois Central College *C, A*
Lewis University *B, M*
Lincoln College *B*
Loyola University Chicago *B, M*
National-Louis University *B*
Northwestern University *M*
Roosevelt University *C*
Rush University *M, D*
Southern Illinois University
Carbondale *B*
Spoon River College *A*
University of St. Francis *B, M*
Western Illinois University *B*

Indiana

Calumet College of St. Joseph *B*
Harrison College
Evansville *B*
Fort Wayne *B*
Indianapolis *B*
Muncie *A, B*
Terre Haute *B*
Indiana University
Bloomington *B*
Northwest *B*
South Bend *B*
Indiana University-Purdue University
Fort Wayne *B*
Purdue University
North Central *A*
University of Evansville *B, M*
University of St. Francis *M*
University of Southern Indiana *B, M*
Vincennes University *A*

Iowa

Des Moines Area Community
College *C, A*
Graceland University *M*
Iowa Lakes Community College *A*
Mercy College of Health Sciences *B*
Mount Mercy College *B*
St. Ambrose University *M*
University of Iowa *M, D*
Upper Iowa University *B*

Kansas

Friends University *B*
Neosho County Community
College *A*
University of St. Mary *C*
Wichita State University *B*

Kentucky

Eastern Kentucky University *B*
Midway College *B*
University of Kentucky *B, M*
Western Kentucky University *B, M*

Louisiana

Our Lady of the Lake College *B*
Tulane University *M, D*
University of Louisiana at Lafayette *M*
University of Louisiana at Monroe *B*
University of New Orleans *M*

Maine

University of Southern Maine *M*

Maryland
Baltimore City Community
College *C, A*
Howard Community College *A*
Sojourner-Douglass College *B*
Towson University *B*
University of Baltimore *B, M*
University of Maryland
University College *C*
Washington Adventist University *B*

Massachusetts
Boston University *M*
Brandeis University *B, M*
Elms College *B*
Framingham State College *M*
Newbury College *B*
Simmons College *M, D*
Springfield College *B, M*
Stonehill College *B*
Suffolk University *M*
University of Massachusetts
Lowell *M*
Worcester State College *M*

Michigan
Baker College
of Clinton Township *B*
of Flint *B, M*
of Muskegon *B*
of Owosso *B*
of Port Huron *B*
Central Michigan University *B, M, D*
Davenport University *B*
Eastern Michigan University *B, M*
Ferris State University *B*
Lansing Community College *A*
Madonna University *B*
Oakland Community College *C, A*
Spring Arbor University *B*
University of Detroit Mercy *B, M*
University of Michigan *M, D*
University of Michigan
Dearborn *B*
Flint *B, M*

Minnesota
Capella University *M, D*
Concordia College: Moorhead *B*
High-Tech Institute *A*
Minnesota School of Business: St.
Cloud *B*
Minnesota State University
Mankato *B, M*
Moorhead *B*
Rasmussen College: Lake
Elmo/Woodbury *A*
Ridgewater College *C, A*
St. Mary's University of Minnesota *M*
University of Minnesota
Crookston *B*
Duluth *B*
Twin Cities *M*
Walden University *B, M, D*
Winona State University *B*

Mississippi
Belhaven University *B*
Jackson State University *B*

Missouri
Lindenwood University *B, M*
Missouri College *B*
Saint Louis University *D*
University of Missouri
Columbia *M*
St. Louis *M*
Washington University in St. Louis *B*
Webster University *M*

Montana
Montana State University
Billings *B, M*

Nebraska
Bellevue University *B*
Clarkson College *C, A, B, M*
Creighton University *B, M*
University of Nebraska
Omaha *B*

Nevada
University of Nevada
Las Vegas *B*

New Hampshire
New England College *B, M*
Rivier College *M*
University of New Hampshire *B, M*

New Jersey
Berkeley College- Garret Mountain
Campus *A, B*
College of St. Elizabeth *C, M*
Essex County College *A*
Seton Hall University *M*
University of Medicine and Dentistry
of New Jersey
School of Health Related
Professions *D*

New Mexico
Brookline College
Albuquerque *A*

New York
Berkeley College *A, B*
Berkeley College of New York
City *A, B*
City University of New York
Baruch College *M*
Borough of Manhattan Community
College *A*
Brooklyn College *M*
Cornell University *M*
D'Youville College *B, M*
Dowling College *M*
Excelsior College *C, B*
Globe Institute of Technology *C, A, B*
Herkimer County Community
College *A*
Hofstra University *M*
Iona College *B, M*
Pace University *M*
Roberts Wesleyan College *B, M*
Rochester Institute of Technology *M*
St. John's University *C, B*
St. Joseph's College *C, B*
State University of New York
College at Brockport *B, M*
Institute of Technology at
Utica/Rome *B, M*
Stony Brook *M*
Utica School of Commerce *A*

North Carolina
Appalachian State University *B*
Cabarrus College of Health
Sciences *B*
Duke University *M*
Gardner-Webb University *B*
Methodist University *B*
Pfeiffer University *B, M*
University of North Carolina
Chapel Hill *B, M, D*
Charlotte *M*
Greensboro *M*
Western Carolina University *B, M*

North Dakota
Minot State University *B*
University of Mary *M*

Ohio
Baldwin-Wallace College *B*
Bowling Green State University *B*

Franklin University *B*
Heidelberg University *B*
Kent State University
Ashtabula *A*
Salem *A*
Lourdes College *B*
Mercy College of Northwest Ohio *B*
Ohio State University
Columbus Campus *M, D*
Ohio University *B, M*
Owens Community College
Toledo *C, A*
University of Akron: Wayne College *A*
University of Cincinnati *B, M*
University of Findlay *B*
University of Northwestern Ohio *B*
University of Rio Grande *B*
University of Toledo *M*
Ursuline College *B*
Wilberforce University *B*
Wright State University *M*
Xavier University *M*
Youngstown State University *M*

Oklahoma
Langston University *B*
Oklahoma State University
Oklahoma City *A*
Southwestern Oklahoma State
University *B*
University of Oklahoma *M, D*

Oregon
Chemeketa Community College *A*
Concordia University *B*
Oregon Health & Science
University *M*
Oregon Institute of Technology *B*
Oregon State University *B, M*
Portland State University *M*

Pennsylvania
Arcadia University *C, B*
Butler County Community College *A*
Carnegie Mellon University *M*
Chestnut Hill College *A, B*
Drexel University *B*
Duquesne University *B, M*
Eastern University *M*
Harrisburg Area Community
College *A*
Immaculata University *C, B*
King's College *M*
Lebanon Valley College *B*
Marywood University *B*
Misericordia University *B*
Neumann University *C*
Penn State
Abington *B*
Altoona *B*
Beaver *B*
Berks *B*
Brandywine *B*
DuBois *B*
Erie, The Behrend College *B*
Fayette, The Eberly Campus *B*
Greater Allegheny *B*
Harrisburg *M*
Hazleton *B*
Lehigh Valley *B*
Mont Alto *B*
New Kensington *B*
Schuylkill *B*
Shenango *B*
University Park *B, M, D*
Wilkes-Barre *B*
Worthington Scranton *B*
York *B*
Philadelphia University *C, B*
Saint Joseph's University *M*
Shippensburg University of
Pennsylvania *B*
Temple University *M*
University of Pennsylvania *B, M, D*

University of Pittsburgh *M*
University of Scranton *C, A, B, M*
West Chester University of
Pennsylvania *B*

Puerto Rico
Inter American University of Puerto
Rico
Metropolitan Campus *C, B*
Universidad del Este *B*

Rhode Island
Providence College *C, B*
Salve Regina University *M*
University of Rhode Island *B*

South Carolina
Clemson University *M*
Medical University of South
Carolina *M, D*
South University: Columbia *B, M*
Tri-County Technical College *C*
University of South Carolina *M*

South Dakota
Presentation College *B*

Tennessee
Baptist College of Health Sciences *B*
Carson-Newman College *B*
Freed-Hardeman University *B*
Lipscomb University *M*
Middle Tennessee State University *C*
Southern Adventist University *B, M*
Tennessee State University *B*
University of Tennessee
Knoxville *M, D*

Texas
Baylor University *M*
Concordia University Texas *B*
Dallas Baptist University *C, B*
Galveston College *A*
Houston Baptist University *M*
LeTourneau University *M*
Midwestern State University *M*
Our Lady of the Lake University of San
Antonio *M*
Texas A&M University
Commerce *B*
Texas Southern University *B*
Texas State University: San
Marcos *B, M*
Texas Tech University Health Sciences
Center *B, M*
Texas Wesleyan University *M*
Texas Woman's University *M*
Trinity University *M*
University of Houston
Clear Lake *B, M*
University of Texas
Arlington *M*
Dallas *M*
Health Science Center at
Houston *M, D*
University of the Incarnate Word *M*
West Texas A&M University *M*
Western Technical College: Diana
Drive *C*

Utah
Independence University *B*
Stevens-Henager College: Logan *B*
Weber State University *B*
Western Governors University *M*

Virginia
ECPI Technical College: Roanoke *A*
George Mason University *B*
James Madison University *B*
Jefferson College of Health
Sciences *B*

Mary Baldwin College *B*
Marymount University *M*
Norfolk State University *B*
Virginia Commonwealth
  University *M, D*

Washington
Eastern Washington University *B*
Highline Community College *A*
University of Washington *M*
Washington State University *M*

West Virginia
Fairmont State University *B*
Marshall University *M*
Wheeling Jesuit University *B*

Wisconsin
Herzing University *B*
Marian University *B*
Marquette University *M*
Northeast Wisconsin Technical
  College *A*
University of Wisconsin
  Eau Claire *B*
  Madison *M*

Health communications

California
Chapman University *M*

Massachusetts
Emerson College *M*

Michigan
Michigan State University *M*

North Dakota
North Dakota State University *B*

Ohio
Ohio University *M, D*
Ohio University
  Southern Campus at Ironton *B*
  Zanesville Campus *B*

Pennsylvania
Juniata College *B*

South Carolina
Clemson University *M*

Virginia
George Mason University *D*

Health management/ clinical assistant

Alaska
University of Alaska
  Southeast *C, A*

Arizona
Central Arizona College *C*
Pima Community College *C*

California
California College San Diego *A*
Concorde Career College: San
  Diego *C*
Ohlone College *C*
Platt College
  Ontario *A*

Connecticut
Northwestern Connecticut
  Community College *C*

Georgia
Georgia Northwestern Technical
  College *C, A*
Southwest Georgia Technical
  College *C*

Idaho
Lewis-Clark State College *C, A, B*

Kansas
Neosho County Community
  College *C*

Maryland
Hagerstown Community College *C*

Michigan
Davenport University *C, B*
Henry Ford Community College *A*
Mott Community College *C*
Oakland Community College *C*

Minnesota
Minnesota School of Business: St.
  Cloud *C, A*
Rasmussen College: Lake
  Elmo/Woodbury *A*

Nevada
Career College of Northern Nevada *C*

New York
Globe Institute of Technology *C*

North Carolina
Fayetteville Technical Community
  College *C, A*
Pitt Community College *C*

Ohio
Owens Community College
  Toledo *A*

Oregon
Clackamas Community College *C*

Pennsylvania
Bucks County Community
  College *C, A*
Consolidated School of Business
  Lancaster *A*
  York *A*

Washington
Centralia College *C*

Health/medical psychology

Alabama
University of South Alabama *D*

Arizona
Northcentral University *M, D*
Northern Arizona University *M*
Prescott College *B*

California
University of California
  Irvine *D*

Indiana
Indiana University-Purdue University
  Indianapolis *D*

Massachusetts
Bridgewater State College *M*
Massachusetts College of Pharmacy
  and Health Sciences *B*

Minnesota
Walden University *M, D*

New York
State University of New York
  Stony Brook *D*
Yeshiva University *D*

North Carolina
University of North Carolina
  Charlotte *D*

Pennsylvania
University of the Sciences in
  Philadelphia *B, M*

Texas
Texas State University: San Marcos *M*
University of Texas
  El Paso *D*

Virginia
Jefferson College of Health
  Sciences *B*
Virginia Commonwealth University *D*
Virginia State University *D*

Health occupations teacher education

California
Crafton Hills College *A*

Florida
Palm Beach Community College *A*

Illinois
North Park University *T*
University of Illinois
  Chicago *M*
  Urbana-Champaign *M*

Indiana
Indiana University-Purdue University
  Indianapolis *B, M*

Massachusetts
Bridgewater State College *B*

Minnesota
Gustavus Adolphus College *T*
Minnesota State University
  Mankato *B*
Winona State University *B, M, T*

New York
Daemen College *M*
New York Institute of
  Technology *A, B, T*
State University of New York
  College at Brockport *M, T*
  College at Buffalo *B, M*
  Oswego *B*

North Carolina
North Carolina State University *B, T*

Oklahoma
University of Central Oklahoma *B*

Tennessee
Belmont University *B, M, T*

Texas
Baylor University *B, T*
Kilgore College *A*
Midwestern State University *M*
Texas A&M University
  Commerce *M*
Texas State University: San Marcos *T*

University of Houston *M, D*

Health/physical fitness

Alabama
Calhoun Community College *A*
Chattahoochee Valley Community
  College *A*
Faulkner University *B, M, T*
Gadsden State Community College *A*
Oakwood University *B*
Samford University *B*
University of Mobile *B, T*
University of Montevallo *B, T*

Alaska
University of Alaska
  Anchorage *B*

Arizona
Arizona Western College *A*
Cochise College *A*
Eastern Arizona College *A*
Northern Arizona University *B, M*
Pima Community College *C*
University of Arizona *M*

Arkansas
Arkansas State University *B*
Southern Arkansas University *M*
University of Arkansas *B*
University of Arkansas
  Monticello *B*
University of the Ozarks *B*

California
Antelope Valley College *A*
Biola University *B*
California Polytechnic State
  University: San Luis Obispo *B, M*
California State Polytechnic
  University: Pomona *B, M*
California State University
  Chico *B*
  Dominguez Hills *B*
  East Bay *B, M*
  Fresno *A*
  Fullerton *B, M*
  Long Beach *M*
  Monterey Bay *B*
  Sacramento *B, M*
  Stanislaus *B*
Chaffey College *C*
Citrus College *A*
College of the Canyons *A*
College of the Siskiyous *A*
Columbia College *A*
Cypress College *C*
Diablo Valley College *C*
East Los Angeles College *A*
El Camino College *A*
Feather River College *C, A*
Foothill College *C*
Fremont College *C*
Fresno Pacific University *B*
Humboldt State University *B*
Imperial Valley College *A*
Irvine Valley College *C, A*
La Sierra University *B*
Lake Tahoe Community College *A*
Long Beach City College *A*
The Master's College *B*
Merced College *A*
Modesto Junior College *A*
Orange Coast College *A*
Pacific Union College *B*
Palomar College *A*
Point Loma Nazarene University *B*
Saddleback College *A*
St. Mary's College of California *B, M*
San Diego City College *C, A*
San Diego Miramar College *A*
San Diego State University *B, M*

San Jose State University B, M
Santa Barbara City College C, A
Shasta College A
Sierra College A
Solano Community College A
Southwestern College A
University of the Pacific B, M, T
Vanguard University of Southern
   California B
West Los Angeles College C, A

Colorado

Adams State College B, M
Arapahoe Community College C, A
Community College of Denver A
Trinidad State Junior College A

Delaware

Delaware State University B
University of Delaware B, M
Wesley College B, M

District of Columbia

American University B

Florida

Barry University B
Florida State University B
Gulf Coast Community College A
Palm Beach Community College A
University of Miami C, B
University of West Florida B, M.

Georgia

Abraham Baldwin Agricultural
   College A
Albany State University B
Andrew College A
Atlanta Metropolitan College A
Brewton-Parker College B
Darton College A
East Georgia College A
Georgia Southern University B
Georgia State University B, M, T
Gordon College A
Middle Georgia College A
Morehouse College B
North Georgia College & State
   University B, M
South Georgia College A
Valdosta State University B
Waycross College A
Young Harris College A

Hawaii

University of Hawaii
   Hilo B

Idaho

Boise State University B, M
College of Idaho B
North Idaho College A
Northwest Nazarene University B

Illinois

Blackburn College B
Chicago State University B, M, T
DePaul University B
Elmhurst College B
Illinois State University M
Illinois Valley Community College A
John Wood Community College A
Kishwaukee College A
Lincoln College A
McHenry County College C
North Central College B, T
Quincy University B
Robert Morris University: Chicago A
South Suburban College of Cook
   County A
Southern Illinois University
   Edwardsville B, M, T

Southwestern Illinois College A
Trinity Christian College B
Trinity International University B
University of Illinois
   Urbana-Champaign M, D
Waubonsee Community College A

Indiana

Goshen College C, B
Grace College B
Indiana Wesleyan University B
Oakland City University B
Purdue University B, M, D
Saint Joseph's College B
Trine University B
Valparaiso University B
Vincennes University A

Iowa

Briar Cliff University B
Coe College B
Cornell College B, T
Dordt College B
Ellsworth Community College A
Graceland University B, T
Grand View University B
Iowa Wesleyan College B
Loras College M
Luther College B
Northwestern College B, T
St. Ambrose University B
University of Northern Iowa B, M
Upper Iowa University B
William Penn University B

Kansas

Baker University B, T
Barton County Community College A
Bethel College B
Central Christian College of Kansas A
Coffeyville Community College A
Dodge City Community College A
Friends University B
Garden City Community College A
Highland Community College A
Kansas Wesleyan University B, T
McPherson College B, T
Ottawa University B
Seward County Community College A
Southwestern College B
Sterling College B, T
Tabor College B
University of Kansas B
Washburn University B

Kentucky

Asbury College B
Berea College B, T
Campbellsville University B
Georgetown College B
Lindsey Wilson College B
Murray State University B, T
University of Kentucky M, D
University of Louisville B
University of the Cumberlands B

Louisiana

Centenary College of Louisiana B, T
Louisiana College B
Louisiana State University
   Shreveport B
Louisiana Tech University B
Northwestern State University B, M
Xavier University of Louisiana B

Maine

Husson University B, T

Maryland

Anne Arundel Community College A
Chesapeake College C
College of Southern Maryland C, A
Frostburg State University B

Hagerstown Community College C
Howard Community College A
Washington Adventist University B

Massachusetts

Becker College B
Berkshire Community College C
Bridgewater State College M
Dean College A
Eastern Nazarene College B
Greenfield Community College C
Holyoke Community College C, A
Roxbury Community College C
Salem State College B
Springfield College B, M
University of Massachusetts
   Boston B
Westfield State College B

Michigan

Adrian College A, B, T
Alma College T
Aquinas College B
Bay Mills Community College A
Calvin College B, T
Central Michigan University B
Delta College C, A
Eastern Michigan University B, M
Grand Valley State University B
Lake Michigan College A
Lake Superior State University A
Michigan Technological University B
Northern Michigan University B
Spring Arbor University B, T

Minnesota

Alexandria Technical College C, A
Anoka-Ramsey Community College C
Bemidji State University B
Bethel University B
Concordia College: Moorhead B
Concordia University: St. Paul B
Gustavus Adolphus College B
Hamline University B
Minnesota State University
   Mankato B, M, T
   Moorhead B
Northwestern College B
Rainy River Community College C
Ridgewater College A
Saint Cloud State University B, M
Southwest Minnesota State
   University B
Winona State University B, T

Mississippi

Blue Mountain College B
Mississippi University for Women B, T
University of Mississippi T

Missouri

College of the Ozarks B
Missouri Southern State
   University B, T
Missouri Western State University B, T
Southeast Missouri State University B
Southwest Baptist University B, T
Three Rivers Community College A
Truman State University B

Montana

Miles Community College A
Montana State University
   Billings B, T
Rocky Mountain College B, T
University of Great Falls B
University of Montana B, M

Nebraska

Concordia University B, T
Nebraska Wesleyan University B
Northeast Community College A
Union College B

University of Nebraska
   Omaha M
Wayne State College B
Western Nebraska Community
   College A

Nevada

University of Nevada
   Las Vegas B

New Hampshire

Colby-Sawyer College C
Keene State College B
Plymouth State University B

New Jersey

Camden County College C
County College of Morris A
Gloucester County College A
Middlesex County College A
Monmouth University B
Raritan Valley Community
   College C, A
Rowan University B
Salem Community College A

New Mexico

Central New Mexico Community
   College C
Clovis Community College A
Eastern New Mexico University B
New Mexico Highlands University B
Santa Fe Community College C, A

New York

Adelphi University B
City University of New York
   Brooklyn College B, M
Corning Community College A
Fulton-Montgomery Community
   College A
Genesee Community College A
Herkimer County Community
   College A
Houghton College B
Ithaca College B, M, T
Monroe Community College A
Niagara County Community
   College A
State University of New York
   College at Buffalo B
   College of Agriculture and
      Technology at Morrisville A

North Carolina

Barton College B
Campbell University B
Catawba College B
Chowan University B, T
Gardner-Webb University B
Greensboro College C, B, T
Guilford College B
Mars Hill College B
Meredith College B
Methodist University B
North Carolina Agricultural and
   Technical State University B, T
North Carolina Central
   University B, M
St. Andrews Presbyterian College B
St. Augustine's College B
University of North Carolina
   Chapel Hill B, M
   Charlotte B
   Pembroke B
   Wilmington B

North Dakota

Dakota College at Bottineau A
Dickinson State University B, T
Mayville State University B, T
University of Mary B

Ohio

Baldwin-Wallace College *B*
Bluffton University *B*
Bowling Green State University *M*
Capital University *B*
Cedarville University *B*
Cincinnati State Technical and
　Community College *C*
Cleveland State University *M*
Defiance College *B, T*
Kent State University *M, D*
Miami University
　Oxford Campus *B*
Mount Vernon Nazarene
　University *B, T*
Ohio Northern University *B*
Ohio State University
　Columbus Campus *B, M, D*
Ohio University *B, M*
Otterbein College *B*
Shawnee State University *B*
University of Akron *M*
University of Findlay *B, T*
University of Rio Grande *A*
University of Toledo *B, M*
Youngstown State University *B*

Oklahoma

Cameron University *B*
Carl Albert State College *A*
East Central University *B, T*
Eastern Oklahoma State College *A*
Northeastern Oklahoma Agricultural
　and Mechanical College *A*
Northwestern Oklahoma State
　University *B*
Oklahoma Baptist University *B, T*
Oklahoma Christian University *B*
Oklahoma City University *B*
Oklahoma Panhandle State
　University *B*
Oklahoma State University *M, D*
Oral Roberts University *B*
Redlands Community College *A*
Rose State College *A*
Seminole State College *A*
University of Science and Arts of
　Oklahoma *B, T*
Western Oklahoma State College *A*

Oregon

Blue Mountain Community College *A*
Central Oregon Community
　College *A*
Chemeketa Community College *A*
Concordia University *B*
Corban College *B*
Eastern Oregon University *B*
George Fox University *B*
Linfield College *B, T*
Oregon State University *B, M, D*
Portland Community College *C, A*
Southern Oregon University *B, T*
Warner Pacific College *B, T*

Pennsylvania

Baptist Bible College of
　Pennsylvania *B*
Bucks County Community College *A*
Community College of Allegheny
　County *A*
Edinboro University of
　Pennsylvania *B, T*
Gettysburg College *B*
Indiana University of
　Pennsylvania *B, M*
Lincoln University *B*
Luzerne County Community
　College *A*
Marywood University *B*
Neumann University *B*
Philadelphia Biblical University *B*

Slippery Rock University of
　Pennsylvania *B, M, T*
Ursinus College *B, T*
West Chester University of
　Pennsylvania *B, M, T*

Puerto Rico

Inter American University of Puerto
　Rico
　San German Campus *B*
University of the Sacred Heart *B*

South Carolina

Benedict College *B*
Bob Jones University *B*
Charleston Southern University *B*
Claflin University *B*
Erskine College *B, T*
Furman University *B, T*
South Carolina State University *B*

South Dakota

Augustana College *B, T*
Northern State University *B*
South Dakota State University *B, M*

Tennessee

Austin Peay State University *B, M*
Belmont University *B, T*
Carson-Newman College *B, T*
Columbia State Community College *A*
Cumberland University *B*
East Tennessee State
　University *B, M, T*
Jackson State Community College *A*
King College *B*
Lambuth University *B*
Lee University *B*
Lincoln Memorial University *B, T*
Maryville College *B, T*
Middle Tennessee State
　University *B, M, D*
Milligan College *B, T*
Tennessee Technological University *B*
Tennessee Wesleyan College *B*
Tusculum College *B*
University of Tennessee
　Knoxville *M, D*
　Martin *B*

Texas

Abilene Christian University *B*
Alvin Community College *A*
Amarillo College *A*
Angelo State University *B, M, T*
Austin Community College *C, A*
Baylor University *B*
Clarendon College *A*
Del Mar College *A*
East Texas Baptist University *B*
El Paso Community College *A*
Hardin-Simmons University *B*
Hill College *A*
Houston Baptist University *B*
Houston Community College
　System *C, A*
Howard College *A*
Howard Payne University *B*
Kilgore College *A*
Lamar State College at Orange *C*
Lamar University *B, M*
Lee College *A*
Lubbock Christian University *B*
Midwestern State University *B, M*
Northeast Texas Community
　College *A*
Northwest Vista College *A*
Prairie View A&M University *B*
St. Philip's College *A*
Sam Houston State University *B*
San Jacinto College *A*
South Plains College *A*

Southwestern Adventist
　University *A, B, T*
Stephen F. Austin State University *B, T*
Sul Ross State University *B, T*
Tarleton State University *B, D*
Texas A&M International
　University *B, T*
Texas A&M University *B, M*
Texas A&M University
　Commerce *B*
　Corpus Christi *B*
Texas Christian University *B*
Texas College *B*
Texas Lutheran University *B, T*
Texas Southern University *B, M*
Texas State University: San
　Marcos *B, T*
Texas Tech University *B, M*
Texas Wesleyan University *B, M*
Texas Woman's University *B, M, D*
Trinity Valley Community College *A*
Tyler Junior College *A*
University of Houston *B, M*
University of Houston
　Clear Lake *B, M*
University of North Texas *B, M, T*
University of Texas
　Arlington *B*
　Austin *B*
　Brownsville - Texas Southmost
　　College *B*
　El Paso *B, M*
　Pan American *B, M*
　San Antonio *B*
　Tyler *B, M*
　of the Permian Basin *B, M*
West Texas A&M University *B, M*
Western Texas College *A*

Utah

Brigham Young University *B, M, D*
Snow College *A*
University of Utah *B*
Utah Valley University *A, B*
Weber State University *B*

Vermont

Castleton State College *B*
Johnson State College *B*
Lyndon State College *B*
Norwich University *B*

Virginia

Averett University *B*
Bridgewater College *B, T*
Emory & Henry College *B, T*
Ferrum College *B*
James Madison University *B, M, T*
Liberty University *B*
Longwood University *B, T*
Lynchburg College *B*
Northern Virginia Community
　College *C*
Roanoke College *B, T*
University of Virginia's College at
　Wise *T*
Virginia Intermont College *B, T*

Washington

Centralia College *A*
Eastern Washington
　University *C, B, M*
Highline Community College *A*
Olympic College *A*
Pacific Lutheran University *B*
University of Puget Sound *T*
Western Washington University *B, M*
Whitworth University *B, T*

West Virginia

Bethany College *B*
Concord University *B, T*
Fairmont State University *B*

West Virginia University *B*
West Virginia Wesleyan College *B*

Wisconsin

Carroll University *B*
University of Wisconsin
　Platteville *B, T*
　Stevens Point *B, T*

Wyoming

Sheridan College *A*

Health physics/radiologic health

California

California State University
　Dominguez Hills *B*

Georgia

Georgia Institute of Technology *M*

Illinois

Illinois Institute of Technology *M*

Kentucky

University of Kentucky *M*
West Kentucky Community and
　Technical College *A*

Louisiana

Louisiana State University and
　Agricultural and Mechanical
　College *M*

Michigan

Delta College *A*
Wayne State University *M, D*

Nevada

University of Nevada
　Las Vegas *B, M*

New York

Monroe Community College *A*

Oregon

Oregon State University *B, M, D*

Pennsylvania

Bloomsburg University of
　Pennsylvania *B*

Virginia

Central Virginia Community
　College *A*

Health services

Alabama

Central Alabama Community
　College *A*
South University: Montgomery *A, B*
Wallace State Community College at
　Hanceville *A*

Alaska

Ilisagvik College *C, A*
University of Alaska
　Anchorage *B*

Arizona

Arizona Western College *C, A*
Bryman School *C*
Cochise College *A*
Kaplan College: Phoenix *C*
Prescott College *B*

Arkansas

Arkansas State University *M*
Arkansas State University
  Beebe *A*
Central Baptist College *B*
East Arkansas Community College *C*
Hendrix College *B*
North Arkansas College *C*
Southeast Arkansas College *C*
Southern Arkansas University Tech *C*
University of Central Arkansas *B*

California

Allan Hancock College *C, A*
American River College *A*
California Baptist University *B*
California State University
  Chico *B*
  Dominguez Hills *B, M*
  Fullerton *B*
Charles Drew University of Medicine
  and Science *B*
Cypress College *A*
Dominican University of California *B*
Heald College
  Roseville *A*
Kaplan College: Panorama City *C*
Loma Linda University *B, D*
Los Angeles City College *A*
Los Angeles Trade and Technical
  College *A*
Merced College *A*
Mission College *A*
Mount San Antonio College *C, A*
Napa Valley College *C, A*
Platt College
  Ontario *A*
Rio Hondo College *A*
San Diego State University *B*
San Jose State University *B*
Shasta College *A*
West Hills College: Coalinga *A*

Colorado

Adams State College *B*
CollegeAmerica
  Denver *A*
  Fort Collins *B*
Colorado Mountain College *C*
Community College of Aurora *C*
University of Colorado
  Colorado Springs *B*
University of Northern Colorado *B*

Connecticut

Goodwin College *A, B*
Northwestern Connecticut
  Community College *C, A*
Norwalk Community College *C*
Sacred Heart University *B*
University of Connecticut *B*
University of Hartford *A, B*

Florida

City College: Casselberry *A*
Florida Agricultural and Mechanical
  University *B*
Florida Atlantic University *B*
Florida College of Natural Health
  Miami *C*
Florida Gulf Coast University *B, M*
Gulf Coast Community College *A*
Nova Southeastern University *B, M, D*
Palm Beach Community College *A*
South University: Tampa *B*
South University: West Palm Beach *B*
Stetson University *B*
University of Central Florida *B, M*
University of Florida *B*
University of Miami *B*
University of North Florida *B, M*

Georgia

Armstrong Atlantic State University *B*
Brenau University *B*
Brewton-Parker College *A*
Central Georgia Technical College *C*
Columbus State University *B*
Emory University *M, D*
Georgia Highlands College *A*
Georgia Military College *A*
Gwinnett Technical College *C, A*
Macon State College *A, B*
Middle Georgia Technical College *C*
South Georgia College *A*
South University: Savannah *A, B*

Idaho

Idaho State University *B*
North Idaho College *A*

Illinois

Benedictine University *B*
Bradley University *B*
City Colleges of Chicago
  Kennedy-King College *A*
Lewis University *B*
Loyola University Chicago *C*
National University of Health
  Sciences *D*
Rasmussen College: Aurora *A*
Rush University *D*
South Suburban College of Cook
  County *C*
Wheaton College *B*

Indiana

Harrison College
  Indianapolis East *C*
Purdue University *B, M*

Iowa

Dordt College *B*
Drake University *B*
Grand View University *B*
Marshalltown Community
  College *C, A*

Kansas

Barton County Community College *A*
Bethel College *C*
Central Christian College of
  Kansas *A, B*
Highland Community College *C, A*
Washburn University *C, A, B*

Kentucky

Asbury College *B*
Lindsey Wilson College *A*
Northern Kentucky University *B*
St. Catharine College *B*
Southern Ohio College
  Brown Mackie College: North
  Kentucky *A*
Spencerian College: Lexington *C, A*
Western Kentucky University *B*

Louisiana

Louisiana State University Health
  Sciences Center *M*
Nicholls State University *B*
Our Lady of the Lake College *B*
Southern University
  Shreveport *A*
University of Louisiana at Monroe *B*

Maine

Kennebec Valley Community
  College *C*

Maryland

Allegany College of Maryland *A*
Baltimore City Community
  College *C, A*
Cecil College *A*
Howard Community College *A*
Towson University *B, M*
University of Maryland
  Baltimore County *B*

Massachusetts

Anna Maria College *B*
Berkshire Community College *A*
Curry College *B*
Dean College *A*
Lesley University *B*
Massachusetts College of Pharmacy
  and Health Sciences *B*
Merrimack College *B*
Middlesex Community College *A*
Mount Wachusett Community
  College *C, A*
Northeastern University *B, M*
Roxbury Community College *C*
Worcester State College *C, B*

Michigan

Baker College of Allen Park *B*
Bay de Noc Community College *A*
Cornerstone University *A, B*
Ferris State University *A*
Kellogg Community College *A*
Macomb Community College *C, A*
Oakland University *B*
Saginaw Valley State University *B*
Schoolcraft College *A*
University of Michigan *M*
University of Michigan
  Flint *B*
Wayne State University *B*
Western Michigan University *D*

Minnesota

Anoka-Ramsey Community College *C*
College of St. Scholastica *B*
Minnesota West Community and
  Technical College *A*
Northland Community & Technical
  College *C, A*
Rochester Community and Technical
  College *A*
University of Minnesota
  Crookston *B*
  Rochester *B*
Walden University *D*

Mississippi

University of Southern Mississippi *B*

Missouri

College of the Ozarks *B*
Grantham University *A*
Mineral Area College *A*
Texas County Technical Institute *C, A*

Montana

Blackfeet Community College *A*

Nebraska

College of Saint Mary *D*
Little Priest Tribal College *A*
Southeast Community College *A*

New Hampshire

Colby-Sawyer College *B*

New Jersey

Bergen Community College *A*
Burlington County College *A*
Cumberland County College *A*
Essex County College *A*
Fairleigh Dickinson University
  College at Florham *B*
Felician College *B*
Monmouth University *B*
Montclair State University *B*
New Jersey City University *B, M*
Ramapo College of New Jersey *B*
Raritan Valley Community College *A*
Salem Community College *A*
Seton Hall University *B*
Sussex County Community College *A*
Thomas Edison State College *B*
University of Medicine and Dentistry
  of New Jersey
  School of Health Related
    Professions *C, B, M, D*
Warren County Community College *A*

New York

Albany College of Pharmacy and
  Health Sciences *B*
Canisius College *M*
City University of New York
  LaGuardia Community College *A*
  York College *B*
Dominican College of Blauvelt *B*
Dutchess Community College *A*
Excelsior College *B*
Hilbert College *B*
Hofstra University *B*
Mercy College *C, B*
Mohawk Valley Community College *C*
North Country Community
  College *C, A*
Orange County Community College *A*
Russell Sage College *B*
State University of New York
  College at Cortland *B*
  College at Potsdam *B*
  Farmingdale *C*
University of Rochester *D*
Utica College *B*

North Carolina

Brevard College *B*
Catawba Valley Community
  College *C, A*
East Carolina University *B, D*
Miller-Motte Technical College *B*
Pitt Community College *A*
Wilkes Community College *C, A*

North Dakota

Dakota College at Bottineau *A*

Ohio

Antioch University McGregor *B*
Belmont Technical College *A*
Columbus State Community
  College *C, A*
Cuyahoga Community College
  Metropolitan Campus *A*
Defiance College *B*
North Central State College *A*
Ohio State University
  Lima Campus *B*
Ohio University
  Southern Campus at Ironton *B*
University of Cincinnati
  Raymond Walters College *A*
Urbana University *B*
Ursuline College *B*
Zane State College *A*

Oklahoma

Oklahoma State University
  Oklahoma City *A*
Redlands Community College *A*
University of Oklahoma *M, D*

Oregon

Chemeketa Community College *A*
Linfield College *B*
Mt. Hood Community College *A*
Oregon Institute of Technology *B*
Warner Pacific College *A*

Pennsylvania
Bucks County Community College *A*
Community College of Philadelphia *C*
Drexel University *M*
Edinboro University of
    Pennsylvania *A*
Gettysburg College *B*
Harcum College *A*
Immaculata University *A, B*
Keystone College *A*
King's College *B*
La Roche College *M*
Lebanon Valley College *B*
Manor College *A*
Marywood University *B*
Mercyhurst College *B*
Mount Aloysius College *B*
Reading Area Community College *A*
Saint Joseph's University *B*
University of the Sciences in
    Philadelphia *B*
Widener University *A, B*

Puerto Rico
Pontifical Catholic University of
    Puerto Rico *B, M*

South Carolina
Aiken Technical College *C*
Horry-Georgetown Technical
    College *C*
Medical University of South
    Carolina *M*
South University: Columbia *B*

Tennessee
East Tennessee State University *B*
Lee University *B*

Texas
Clarendon College *A*
Howard Payne University *A*
Northwest Vista College *A*
Palo Alto College *C, A*
Prairie View A&M University *B*
Sam Houston State University *B*
South Plains College *A*
Stephen F. Austin State University *B*
Texas A&M University
    Corpus Christi *B*
Texas Southern University *B*
Texas State University: San Marcos *B*
Texas Tech University *B*
Texas Tech University Health Sciences
    Center *B*
Texas Woman's University *B*
University of North Texas *B, M*
University of Texas
    Austin *B*
    Brownsville - Texas Southmost
        College *B*
    El Paso *B*
    Pan American *B*
    San Antonio *B*
    Tyler *M*
Vernon College *C*
Westwood College: Houston South *C*

Utah
University of Utah *B, M*

Vermont
Community College of Vermont *C*
Goddard College *B, M*

Virginia
Blue Ridge Community College *A*
Ferrum College *B*
Germanna Community College *C*
Old Dominion University *B, D*
Randolph College *B*

Southside Virginia Community
    College *C*
Southwest Virginia Community
    College *C, A*
Virginia Western Community
    College *A*

Washington
Clover Park Technical College *C, A*
Evergreen State College *B*
Spokane Falls Community College *A*

West Virginia
Alderson-Broaddus College *B*
Mountain State College *A*
Mountain State University *B, M*
Southern West Virginia Community
    and Technical College *C, A*

Wisconsin
Concordia University Wisconsin *B*
Moraine Park Technical College *C, A*

Wyoming
Casper College *A*
Central Wyoming College *A*
Sheridan College *A*
University of Wyoming *B*

Health services administration

Arizona
Arizona State University *D*
Prescott College *B*

California
California Institute of Integral
    Studies *M*
Chapman University *B*
Charles Drew University of Medicine
    and Science *B*
University of California
    Los Angeles *M, D*

Colorado
Jones International University *M*

Florida
Florida National College *A*
Nova Southeastern University *M*
St. Petersburg College *B*
Santa Fe College *B*

Illinois
University of Illinois
    Chicago *M*
    Urbana-Champaign *B, M, D*

Indiana
Indiana University-Purdue University
    Fort Wayne *B*

Iowa
University of Iowa *M, D*

Louisiana
Our Lady of the Lake College *B*

Maine
Saint Joseph's College of Maine *M*
University of New England *B*

Maryland
Howard Community College *A*
University of Maryland
    College Park *M, D*

Massachusetts
Elms College *B*

Mississippi
Mississippi College *M*

Missouri
Harris-Stowe State University *B*
University of Missouri
    Columbia *B*
Washington University in St. Louis *M*

New Jersey
University of Medicine and Dentistry
    of New Jersey
    School of Health Related
        Professions *D*

New York
City University of New York
    New York City College of
        Technology *B*
Molloy College *B*
Monroe College *B*
Rochester Institute of Technology *M*
State University of New York
    Albany *M*

North Carolina
Cabarrus College of Health
    Sciences *B*

Ohio
Ohio University *M*

Oregon
Northwest Christian University *B*

Pennsylvania
Arcadia University *B*
Community College of Philadelphia *A*
East Stroudsburg University of
    Pennsylvania *B*
Harrisburg Area Community
    College *A*
Marywood University *M*
Robert Morris University *B*
Slippery Rock University of
    Pennsylvania *B*
Temple University *M*
University of the Sciences in
    Philadelphia *M, D*

Puerto Rico
University of Puerto Rico
    Medical Sciences *M*

South Dakota
University of South Dakota *B*

Texas
University of Houston
    Clear Lake *B*
University of Texas
    Health Science Center at
        Houston *M, D*

Utah
Weber State University *M*

Wisconsin
Marquette University *M*

Health teacher education

Alabama
Auburn University *B*
Jacksonville State University *B, T*
Stillman College *B*
University of Alabama
    Birmingham *B, M, T*
University of South Alabama *B, M, T*

Arizona
Northern Arizona University *B*
Prescott College *T*

Arkansas
Harding University *B, T*
Ouachita Baptist University *B, T*

California
Azusa Pacific University *T*
California State University
    Chico *B, T*
    Long Beach *T*
    Northridge *B, T*
    San Bernardino *M, T*
San Francisco State University *T*
Vanguard University of Southern
    California *T*

Connecticut
Southern Connecticut State
    University *M, T*
Western Connecticut State
    University *B*

Delaware
Delaware State University *B*
University of Delaware *B, T*

District of Columbia
Howard University *B*
University of the District of
    Columbia *B*

Florida
Gulf Coast Community College *A*
Palm Beach Community College *A*
State College of Florida,
    Manatee-Sarasota *A*
Tallahassee Community College *A*

Georgia
Armstrong Atlantic State
    University *B, M, T*
Bainbridge College *A*
Georgia College and State
    University *B*
Georgia Perimeter College *A*
Middle Georgia College *A*
South Georgia College *A*
University of Georgia *B*

Idaho
Brigham Young University-Idaho *T*
Idaho State University *B, M*
Northwest Nazarene University *B*
University of Idaho *B, T*

Illinois
Chicago State University *B*
DePaul University *B, M, T*
Eastern Illinois University *B, T*
Eureka College *T*
Illinois State University *B, T*
McKendree University *B*
North Park University *T*
Northern Illinois University *B, T*
Olivet Nazarene University *B, T*
Southern Illinois University
    Carbondale *B, M, D*
Southern Illinois University
    Edwardsville *B, T*
Western Illinois University *B, M*

Indiana
Ball State University *B, T*
Butler University *T*
Indiana State University *M, T*
Indiana University
    Bloomington *B, M, D, T*
Indiana Wesleyan University *T*
Manchester College *B, T*

Oakland City University *B*
Purdue University *B, M, D*
Trine University *B, T*
University of Indianapolis *T*
University of St. Francis *B, T*
Vincennes University *A*

Iowa

Central College *T*
Dordt College *B*
Drake University *T*
Graceland University *T*
Grand View University *T*
Iowa State University *B, T*
Iowa Wesleyan College *B*
Luther College *B*
Northwestern College *T*
St. Ambrose University *B, T*
Simpson College *T*
University of Northern Iowa *B, M*
Upper Iowa University *B, T*
Wartburg College *T*

Kansas

Bethany College *B*
Bethel College *T*
Garden City Community College *A*
McPherson College *T*
MidAmerica Nazarene University *B, T*
Tabor College *B*

Kentucky

Campbellsville University *B*
Kentucky Wesleyan College *T*
Morehead State University *B*
Murray State University *B, T*
Union College *B*
University of Kentucky *B*
University of the Cumberlands *B, M, T*

Louisiana

Centenary College of Louisiana *B, T*
Louisiana College *B*
Southeastern Louisiana University *B*

Maine

University of Maine
  Farmington *B, T*
  Presque Isle *B*

Maryland

Allegany College of Maryland *A*
Morgan State University *B*
Prince George's Community
  College *A*
Salisbury University *B, T*
University of Maryland
  College Park *B, D*

Massachusetts

Boston University *M, T*
Bridgewater State College *B*
Cambridge College *M*
Springfield College *B, M, T*
University of Massachusetts
  Lowell *B*
Worcester State College *T*

Michigan

Adrian College *B, T*
Alma College *T*
Central Michigan University *B*
Eastern Michigan University *M, T*
Michigan State University *B*
Michigan Technological University *T*
Northern Michigan University *B, T*
Wayne State University *B, M, T*
Western Michigan University *B, T*

Minnesota

Augsburg College *B, T*
Bemidji State University *T*

Bethel University *B*
Concordia College: Moorhead *B, T*
Concordia University: St. Paul *B, T*
Gustavus Adolphus College *T*
Hamline University *B, T*
Minnesota State University
  Mankato *B, M, T*
  Moorhead *B*
Ridgewater College *A*
Saint Cloud State University *B*
Southwest Minnesota State
  University *B, T*
University of Minnesota
  Duluth *B, T*
University of St. Thomas *B*
Vermilion Community College *A*
Winona State University *B, M, T*

Mississippi

Mississippi Delta Community
  College *A*
Mississippi State University *T*
Mississippi University for Women *M*
Tougaloo College *B*

Missouri

Culver-Stockton College *T*
Missouri Baptist University *B, T*
Missouri Southern State
  University *B, T*
Northwest Missouri State University *T*
Southwest Baptist University *B, T*
Truman State University *M, T*
Webster University *M*

Montana

Montana State University
  Billings *B, T*
University of Great Falls *B*
University of Montana *T*
University of Montana: Western *B, T*

Nebraska

Concordia University *B, T*
University of Nebraska
  Kearney *B, T*
  Lincoln *B*

Nevada

University of Nevada
  Las Vegas *B*
  Reno *B, T*

New Hampshire

Keene State College *B, T*
Plymouth State University *M, T*

New Jersey

Caldwell College *T*
The College of New Jersey *B, M*
Montclair State University *B, M, T*
Rowan University *T*
Seton Hall University *M*
William Paterson University of New
  Jersey *B, T*

New Mexico

University of New Mexico *B, M*
Western New Mexico University *B*

New York

Adelphi University *B, M, T*
City University of New York
  Hunter College *B, T*
  Lehman College *B, M*
  York College *B, T*
Corning Community College *A*
Hofstra University *B, M*
Ithaca College *B, T*
Long Island University
  C. W. Post Campus *B, T*
Manhattan College *B, T*

Monroe Community College *A*
New York University *M, D*
State University of New York
  College at Brockport *B, M, T*
  College at Cortland *B, M*
  Oswego *T*

North Carolina

Appalachian State University *B, T*
East Carolina University *B, M*
Fayetteville State University *B, T*
Gardner-Webb University *B*
Johnson C. Smith University *B*
Lenoir Community College *A*
North Carolina Central University *B, T*

North Dakota

Dickinson State University *B, T*
Mayville State University *B, T*
North Dakota State University *B, T*

Ohio

Ashland University *T*
Baldwin-Wallace College *T*
Bluffton University *B*
Bowling Green State University *B, M*
Capital University *T*
Defiance College *B, T*
Kent State University *B, M, D*
Malone University *B*
Miami University
  Oxford Campus *B*
Mount Union College *B, T*
Mount Vernon Nazarene
  University *B, T*
Ohio Northern University *B, T*
Ohio State University
  Columbus Campus *M, D*
Ohio Wesleyan University *B*
Otterbein College *B*
University of Cincinnati *B, M, T*
University of Findlay *B, M, T*
University of Rio Grande *B, T*
University of Toledo *B, M, T*
Wilmington College *B*
Youngstown State University *B, M*

Oklahoma

Bacone College *B*
East Central University *T*
Eastern Oklahoma State College *A*
Northwestern Oklahoma State
  University *B, T*
Oklahoma Baptist University *B, T*
Oklahoma City University *B*
Oral Roberts University *B, T*
Southwestern Oklahoma State
  University *B, M, T*

Oregon

Concordia University *B, M, T*
George Fox University *M, T*
Linfield College *T*
Oregon State University *M*
Portland State University *B, M, T*
Western Oregon University *B, T*

Pennsylvania

Arcadia University *M*
Baptist Bible College of
  Pennsylvania *B*
Bucks County Community College *A*
Chatham University *M*
East Stroudsburg University of
  Pennsylvania *B, M, T*
Lincoln University *T*
Penn State
  Harrisburg *M*
Saint Joseph's University *M*
Temple University *M*
West Chester University of
  Pennsylvania *M*

Puerto Rico

Universidad del Este *B*

Rhode Island

Rhode Island College *B, M*

South Carolina

University of South Carolina *M*

South Dakota

Mount Marty College *B*
University of Sioux Falls *B*
University of South Dakota *M, T*

Tennessee

Austin Peay State University *B*
Belmont University *B, M, T*
Lambuth University *B, T*
Lee University *B*
Lincoln Memorial University *B, T*
Maryville College *B, T*
Middle Tennessee State University *B*
Tennessee Technological
  University *B, M, T*
Tusculum College *B, T*
Union University *T*
University of Tennessee
  Knoxville *M, T*

Texas

Angelina College *A*
Austin Community College *A*
Baylor University *M*
Brazosport College *A*
Del Mar College *A*
Kilgore College *A*
Lamar University *B, M, T*
Laredo Community College *A*
Prairie View A&M University *M*
Texas A&M University *M, D*
Texas A&M University
  Commerce *M, T*
  Kingsville *B*
Texas Southern University *B, M*
Texas State University: San
  Marcos *M, T*
University of Houston *B, M*
University of Houston
  Clear Lake *T*
University of Texas
  Austin *M, D*
  El Paso *M*
  San Antonio *T*
  Tyler *M*

Utah

Brigham Young University *B*
Snow College *A*
Utah State University *B*
Utah Valley University *B*

Virginia

Averett University *B, M, T*
Bluefield College *B, T*
Eastern Mennonite University *T*
George Mason University *B*
Hampton University *B*
James Madison University *M, T*
Longwood University *B, T*
Lynchburg College *B*
Radford University *B, T*
University of Virginia's College at
  Wise *T*
Virginia Commonwealth University *B*

Washington

Eastern Washington University *B*
Northwest University *T*
Washington State University *B, M, T*
Whitworth University *T*

West Virginia

Concord University B
Shepherd University T
University of Charleston B
West Liberty University B
West Virginia State University B
West Virginia University T
West Virginia Wesleyan College B

Wisconsin

Carroll University B
Carthage College T
Concordia University Wisconsin B
Ripon College T
University of Wisconsin
  La Crosse B, M, T
  Platteville T
  River Falls T
  Superior T

Health unit coordinator

California

City College of San Francisco A
East Los Angeles College C
Hartnell College C

Florida

Pasco-Hernando Community
  College C
Pensacola Junior College C

Georgia

Middle Georgia Technical College C
Southwest Georgia Technical
  College C

Iowa

Indian Hills Community College C

Kentucky

Spencerian College C

Michigan

Delta College C

Minnesota

Hennepin Technical College C, A
Minnesota State College - Southeast
  Technical C
Rochester Community and Technical
  College C
St. Paul College C

Missouri

Cox College C

New Mexico

Central New Mexico Community
  College C

New York

Globe Institute of Technology C

North Carolina

Pitt Community College C
Roanoke-Chowan Community
  College C

Ohio

Cincinnati State Technical and
  Community College C, A
Eastern Gateway Community
  College C, A

Pennsylvania

Community College of Allegheny
  County C
Consolidated School of Business
  Lancaster A

York A

South Dakota

Western Dakota Technical Institute C

Utah

Salt Lake Community College C

Washington

Centralia College C
Clover Park Technical College C
Spokane Community College C, A
Whatcom Community College C

Wisconsin

Gateway Technical College C
Lakeshore Technical College C
Mid-State Technical College C
Milwaukee Area Technical College C
Waukesha County Technical
  College C
Western Technical College C

Health unit manager

Illinois

Southern Illinois University
  Carbondale M

Wisconsin

Herzing University B

Heating/air conditioning/ refrigeration maintenance

Alabama

Calhoun Community College C, A
Gadsden State Community
  College C, A
Lawson State Community College C
Southern Union State Community
  College C, A
Wallace State Community College at
  Hanceville C, A

Alaska

University of Alaska
  Anchorage C, A

Arizona

Arizona Western College C, A
Cochise College C
Eastern Arizona College C
GateWay Community College C, A
Mohave Community College C, A
Northland Pioneer College C, A
Refrigeration School C, A

Arkansas

Arkansas Northeastern College C
Arkansas State University
  Beebe C
Arkansas Tech University C
North Arkansas College C
Ouachita Technical College C
Pulaski Technical College C, A
Southeast Arkansas College C
University of Arkansas
  Community College at Hope C
University of Arkansas Community
  College at Morrilton C, A

California

Cerro Coso Community College C, A
Citrus College C, A
College of San Mateo C, A
College of the Desert C, A
Cypress College C, A

El Camino College C, A
Foothill College C
Fresno City College C, A
Imperial Valley College C, A
Laney College C
Los Angeles Trade and Technical
  College C, A
Merced College C, A
Modesto Junior College C, A
Mount San Antonio College C, A
Orange Coast College C, A
Riverside Community College C, A
Sacramento City College C, A
San Bernardino Valley College C, A
San Diego City College C, A
San Joaquin Valley College A
San Jose City College C, A
Santa Rosa Junior College C
Southwestern College C
WyoTech: Fremont C, A
WyoTech: Long Beach C

Colorado

Community College of Aurora A
Redstone College C
Westwood College: Denver North A

Delaware

Delaware Technical and Community
  College
  Owens C, A

District of Columbia

University of the District of
  Columbia C

Florida

ATI Career Training Center
  Oakland Park A
Brevard Community College C
Central Florida Community College C
College of Business and Technology:
  Flagler C
College of Business and Technology:
  Kendall A
Daytona State College C
Florida State College at Jacksonville C
Hillsborough Community College C
Indian River State College C, A
Lake City Community College C
Miami Dade College C, A
Palm Beach Community College C
Santa Fe College C
Seminole Community College C
South Florida Community College C

Georgia

Albany Technical College C
Athens Technical College C
Augusta Technical College C
Central Georgia Technical College C
Chattahoochee Technical College C
Columbus Technical College C
DeKalb Technical College C
Gwinnett Technical College C
Middle Georgia College A
Middle Georgia Technical College C
North Georgia Technical College C, A
Savannah Technical College C, A
Southeastern Technical College C
Southwest Georgia Technical
  College C
Waycross College A

Hawaii

University of Hawaii
  Honolulu Community College C, A

Idaho

Lewis-Clark State College C, A, B
North Idaho College C, A

Illinois

Black Hawk College C, A
City Colleges of Chicago
  Kennedy-King College C, A
College of DuPage C
College of Lake County C, A
Danville Area Community College C
Elgin Community College C, A
Harper College C, A
Heartland Community College C
Illinois Eastern Community Colleges
  Lincoln Trail College C, A
John A. Logan College C
Joliet Junior College C
Kankakee Community College C, A
Kaskaskia College C
Lake Land College C
Lincoln Land Community College C
Moraine Valley Community
  College C, A
Morton College C, A
Oakton Community College C
Prairie State College C
Rend Lake College C
Richland Community College C, A
Sauk Valley Community College C, A
Southwestern Illinois College C, A
Triton College C, A
Vatterott College: Quincy A
Waubonsee Community College C, A

Indiana

Ivy Tech Community College
  Bloomington C, A
  Central Indiana C, A
  Columbus C, A
  East Central C, A
  Kokomo C, A
  Lafayette C, A
  North Central C, A
  Northeast C, A
  Northwest C, A
  Richmond C, A
  South Central C, A
  Southwest C, A
  Wabash Valley C, A
Oakland City University A

Iowa

Des Moines Area Community
  College C, A
Hawkeye Community College C
Indian Hills Community College C
Kirkwood Community College C
Marshalltown Community College A
North Iowa Area Community
  College C, A
Northeast Iowa Community
  College C
Scott Community College C, A
Vatterott College C
Western Iowa Tech Community
  College C

Kansas

Highland Community College C, A
Kansas City Kansas Community
  College C
Manhattan Area Technical
  College C, A

Kentucky

Big Sandy Community and Technical
  College C, A
Bluegrass Community and Technical
  College C, A
Elizabethtown Community and
  Technical College C
Madisonville Community College C
Owensboro Community and
  Technical College C
Somerset Community College C

Sullivan College of Technology and
Design *A*
West Kentucky Community and
Technical College *C*

Louisiana
ITI Technical College *C*
Nunez Community College *C, A*

Maine
Eastern Maine Community
College *C, A*
Northern Maine Community
College *A*
Southern Maine Community
College *C, A*
Washington County Community
College *C*

Maryland
Chesapeake College *C*
Community College of Baltimore
County *C, A*

Massachusetts
Benjamin Franklin Institute of
Technology *C*
Springfield Technical Community
College *C*

Michigan
Baker College
of Owosso *C*
Delta College *C, A*
Grand Rapids Community
College *C, A*
Jackson Community College *C, A*
Kellogg Community College *C, A*
Kirtland Community College *C, A*
Lansing Community College *A*
Macomb Community College *C, A*
Mid Michigan Community
College *C, A*
Northern Michigan University *C*
Washtenaw Community College *A*
Wayne County Community
College *C, A*

Minnesota
Century Community and Technical
College *C, A*
Dunwoody College of
Technology *C, A*
Hennepin Technical College *C, A*
Hibbing Community College *C*
Minneapolis Community and
Technical College *C, A*
Minnesota State College - Southeast
Technical *C, A*
Minnesota State Community and
Technical College *C*
Minnesota West Community and
Technical College *A*
Rochester Community and Technical
College *C*
St. Cloud Technical College *C, A*
South Central College *C, A*

Mississippi
East Central Community College *C*
Hinds Community College *C*
Holmes Community College *A*
Mississippi Delta Community
College *A*
Mississippi Gulf Coast Community
College *C*
Northwest Mississippi Community
College *C, A*
Pearl River Community College *C, A*
Southwest Mississippi Community
College *C*

Missouri
East Central College *C, A*
Jefferson College *C, A*
Linn State Technical College *A*
Metropolitan Community College:
Penn Valley *C, A*
Mineral Area College *C, A*
Ozarks Technical Community
College *C, A*
Ranken Technical College *A*
Vatterott College *C, A, B*
Vatterott College: Kansas City *A*
Vatterott College: Springfield *C*
Vatterott College: Sunset Hills *A*

Montana
Flathead Valley Community College *C*
Montana State University
Billings *A*

Nebraska
Central Community College *C, A*
Metropolitan Community
College *C, A*
Mid-Plains Community College
Area *C, A*
Northeast Community College *A*
Southeast Community College *A*

Nevada
College of Southern Nevada *C, A*
Truckee Meadows Community
College *C, A*

New Hampshire
Manchester Community College *C, A*

New Mexico
Central New Mexico Community
College *C*
Clovis Community College *C, A*
Dona Ana Community College of New
Mexico State University *C, A*
New Mexico State University
Carlsbad *C*
Santa Fe Community College *C*

New York
Dutchess Community College *C*
Erie Community College
North Campus *C*
Hudson Valley Community College *A*
Mohawk Valley Community College *C*
Monroe Community College *C, A*
State University of New York
College of Technology at Alfred *A*
College of Technology at Canton *C*
College of Technology at Delhi *C, A*
Technical Career Institutes *C, A*

North Carolina
Alamance Community College *C, A*
Asheville-Buncombe Technical
Community College *C, A*
Blue Ridge Community College *C*
Brunswick Community College *C*
Caldwell Community College and
Technical Institute *C*
Cape Fear Community College *C*
Catawba Valley Community College *C*
Central Piedmont Community
College *C, A*
Cleveland Community College *C*
Coastal Carolina Community
College *C, A*
College of the Albemarle *C*
Davidson County Community
College *C*
Fayetteville Technical Community
College *C, A*
Forsyth Technical Community
College *C*

Gaston College *C*
Guilford Technical Community
College *C, A*
Johnston Community College *C, A*
Martin Community College *C, A*
McDowell Technical Community
College *C*
Mitchell Community College *C*
Piedmont Community College *C*
Pitt Community College *C, A*
Roanoke-Chowan Community
College *C*
Rockingham Community College *C*
Rowan-Cabarrus Community
College *C*
South Piedmont Community
College *C, A*
Southwestern Community College *C*
Stanly Community College *C*
Surry Community College *C, A*
Tri-County Community College *C*
Vance-Granville Community
College *C*
Wake Technical Community
College *C, A*
Wilson Community College *C*

North Dakota
Bismarck State College *C, A*
North Dakota State College of
Science *C, A*

Ohio
Belmont Technical College *C, A*
Cincinnati State Technical and
Community College *C*
Columbus State Community
College *C, A*
ETI Technical College of Niles *C*
Owens Community College
Toledo *C*
RETS College *C*
Stark State College of Technology *A*
Terra State Community College *C, A*
University of Northwestern Ohio *C, A*
Vatterott College: Cleveland *C*
Washington State Community
College *A*

Oklahoma
Oklahoma State University
Institute of Technology:
Okmulgee *A*
Tulsa Community College *A*
Vatterott College *A*
Vatterott College
Tulsa *C, A*

Oregon
Linn-Benton Community College *C*
Portland Community College *C, A*

Pennsylvania
Butler County Community College *A*
CHI Institute: Broomall *C*
CHI Institute: Franklin Mills *C*
Community College of Allegheny
County *C, A*
Harrisburg Area Community
College *C, A*
Johnson College *A*
Lehigh Carbon Community
College *C, A*
Luzerne County Community
College *C, A*
Northampton Community
College *C, A*
Pennsylvania College of
Technology *B*
Reading Area Community College *C*
Thaddeus Stevens College of
Technology *A*

Triangle Tech
Pittsburgh *A*
Westmoreland County Community
College *C, A*

Puerto Rico
Huertas Junior College *C, A*

Rhode Island
New England Institute of
Technology *A*

South Carolina
Aiken Technical College *C*
Central Carolina Technical College *C*
Florence-Darlington Technical
College *C, A*
Greenville Technical College *C*
Horry-Georgetown Technical
College *C, A*
Midlands Technical College *C, A*
Spartanburg Community College *C*
Technical College of the
Lowcountry *C, A*
Tri-County Technical College *A*
Trident Technical College *C*
Williamsburg Technical College *C, A*
York Technical College *C, A*

South Dakota
Mitchell Technical Institute *A*
Oglala Lakota College *C*
Southeast Technical Institute *A*

Tennessee
Chattanooga State Community
College *C*
Northeast State Community College *C*

Texas
Brazosport College *C, A*
Cedar Valley College *C, A*
Central Texas College *C, A*
College of the Mainland *C, A*
Del Mar College *C, A*
Eastfield College *C, A*
El Paso Community College *C, A*
Frank Phillips College *C*
Grayson County College *C, A*
Hill College *C, A*
Houston Community College
System *C*
Lamar State College at Port
Arthur *C, A*
Laredo Community College *C*
Lee College *C, A*
Lone Star College System *C, A*
Midland College *C, A*
Odessa College *C, A*
Panola College *C*
Paris Junior College *A*
St. Philip's College *C, A*
San Jacinto College *C, A*
South Plains College *C, A*
South Texas College *C, A*
Texarkana College *C*
Texas State Technical College
Harlingen *C, A*
Waco *C, A*
West Texas *C*
Trinity Valley Community College *C*
Tyler Junior College *C, A*
University of Texas
Brownsville - Texas Southmost
College *C*
Western Technical College: Diana
Drive *A*
Western Texas College *C*
Wharton County Junior College *C*

Utah
Salt Lake Community College *C, A*
Utah Valley University *C, A*

Virginia

Advanced Technology Institute *C, A*
Central Virginia Community
  College *C*
Danville Community College *A*
John Tyler Community College *C*
Mountain Empire Community
  College *C*
New River Community College *C*
Northern Virginia Community
  College *C, A*
Patrick Henry Community College *C*
Southside Virginia Community
  College *C*
Southwest Virginia Community
  College *C*
Thomas Nelson Community
  College *C*
Tidewater Community College *C*
Virginia Highlands Community
  College *C*
Virginia Western Community
  College *C, A*

Washington

Bates Technical College *C, A*
Bellingham Technical College *A*
Clover Park Technical College *C, A*
North Seattle Community
  College *C, A*
Renton Technical College *C, A*
Spokane Community College *A*
Spokane Falls Community College *C*
Wenatchee Valley College *C, A*

West Virginia

Blue Ridge Community and Technical
  College *A*
West Virginia Northern Community
  College *A*

Wisconsin

Blackhawk Technical College *A*
Chippewa Valley Technical
  College *C, A*
Milwaukee Area Technical College *C*
Moraine Park Technical College *C, A*
Northeast Wisconsin Technical
  College *A*
Western Technical College *C*

Heating/air conditioning/ refrigeration technology

Alabama

Bevill State Community College *C, A*
Calhoun Community College *A*
Gadsden State Community
  College *C, A*
Lurleen B. Wallace Community
  College *C*
Northwest-Shoals Community
  College *C*
Shelton State Community
  College *C, A*

Arizona

Refrigeration School *C*

California

Citrus College *C*
City College of San Francisco *C*
College of the Desert *C, A*
Imperial Valley College *C, A*
Long Beach City College *C, A*
Orange Coast College *C, A*
Oxnard College *C, A*
San Jose City College *C, A*

Colorado

Community College of Denver *A*
Front Range Community College *C, A*
Red Rocks Community College *C, A*

Delaware

Delaware Technical and Community
  College
  Stanton/Wilmington *A*

Florida

Palm Beach Community College *C*
Santa Fe College *C*

Georgia

North Georgia Technical College *C, A*
Southeastern Technical College *C*

Illinois

City Colleges of Chicago
  Kennedy-King College *C, A*
Coyne American Institute *C, A*
Oakton Community College *C*

Kentucky

Sullivan College of Technology and
  Design *A*

Maryland

Cecil College *A*

Massachusetts

Massasoit Community College *A*
Springfield Technical Community
  College *A*

Michigan

Delta College *C, A*
Ferris State University *A*
Grand Rapids Community College *A*
Henry Ford Community College *C*
Jackson Community College *C, A*
Mott Community College *C, A*
Northern Michigan University *A*
Oakland Community College *C, A*

Minnesota

Dunwoody College of
  Technology *C, A*
Hennepin Technical College *C, A*
Hibbing Community College *C*
Minnesota West Community and
  Technical College *A*
South Central College *C, A*

Nebraska

Northeast Community College *A*

New Jersey

Raritan Valley Community College *A*

New York

City University of New York
  New York City College of
    Technology *A*
Mohawk Valley Community College *A*
Monroe Community College *A*
State University of New York
  College of Technology at Alfred *A*
  College of Technology at
    Canton *C, A*
Suffolk County Community College *A*

North Carolina

College of the Albemarle *C, A*
Gaston College *C*
Roanoke-Chowan Community
  College *C*
Robeson Community College *C*
Southeastern Community College *C*

North Dakota

North Dakota State College of
  Science *A*

Ohio

North Central State College *C, A*
Owens Community College
  Toledo *C*
RETS College *C*

Oregon

Chemeketa Community College *C, A*

Pennsylvania

Community College of Beaver
  County *A*
Penn Commercial Business and
  Technical School *A*
Pennsylvania College of
  Technology *A, B*
Thaddeus Stevens College of
  Technology *A*
Triangle Tech
  Greensburg *A*

Puerto Rico

Humacao Community College *C, A*

South Carolina

York Technical College *C, A*

South Dakota

Mitchell Technical Institute *C, A*
Southeast Technical Institute *C, A*

Tennessee

Northeast State Community College *C*

Texas

Austin Community College *C, A*
Lamar Institute of Technology *C, A*
St. Philip's College *C, A*
Tarrant County College *C, A*
Western Technical College *C, A*

Virginia

Lord Fairfax Community College *C*
Southwest Virginia Community
  College *C*

Wisconsin

Gateway Technical College *A*
Milwaukee Area Technical College *A*
Western Technical College *A*
Wisconsin Indianhead Technical
  College *C*

Heavy/earthmoving equipment operation

Alabama

Jefferson Davis Community College *C*
Shelton State Community College *C*

Alaska

University of Alaska
  Anchorage *A*

Arizona

Northland Pioneer College *C, A*

Arkansas

North Arkansas College *C*

Florida

Indian River State College *C*

Indiana

Ivy Tech Community College
  Southwest *C, A*

Wabash Valley *C, A*

Iowa

Northwest Iowa Community
  College *C*

Maine

Southern Maine Community
  College *C*

Michigan

Wayne County Community College *C*

Minnesota

Central Lakes College *C*

Missouri

Linn State Technical College *C*

Montana

Flathead Valley Community College *C*
Miles Community College *C*

North Carolina

Wilson Community College *C*

Pennsylvania

Pittsburgh Institute of Aeronautics *C*

South Dakota

Southeast Technical Institute *C*

Utah

College of Eastern Utah *C*

Virginia

Southside Virginia Community
  College *C*
Southwest Virginia Community
  College *C*

Heavy equipment maintenance

Alaska

University of Alaska
  Anchorage *C, A*

Arkansas

University of Arkansas
  Monticello *C*

California

Rio Hondo College *C*
San Diego Miramar College *C, A*
San Joaquin Delta College *C, A*
Shasta College *C*

Georgia

Albany Technical College *C*
Gwinnett Technical College *C*
Southwest Georgia Technical
  College *A*

Illinois

Highland Community College *C, A*
Rend Lake College *C, A*

Kentucky

Bluegrass Community and Technical
  College *C, A*

Michigan

Ferris State University *A, B*

Minnesota

Central Lakes College *A*
Dakota County Technical College *C, A*

Missouri
Linn State Technical College *A*

New York
State University of New York
    College of Agriculture and
        Technology at Morrisville *A*
    College of Technology at Alfred *A*

North Carolina
Asheville-Buncombe Technical
    Community College *C*
Beaufort County Community
    College *C, A*
Wilson Community College *C*

Oregon
Linn-Benton Community College *A*

Pennsylvania
Pennsylvania College of
    Technology *A*

Virginia
Advanced Technology Institute *C, A*

Washington
Bates Technical College *C, A*
Clover Park Technical College *C, A*
Lower Columbia College *A*
South Seattle Community
    College *C, A*

Wisconsin
Blackhawk Technical College *C*

Wyoming
Western Wyoming Community
    College *C, A*

Hebrew

California
University of California
    Los Angeles *B*

District of Columbia
Catholic University of America *M, D*
George Washington University *B*

Illinois
Concordia University Chicago *B*
Moody Bible Institute *B*
Trinity International University *M*
University of Chicago *B*
University of Illinois
    Urbana-Champaign *B*

Maryland
Washington Bible College *M*

Massachusetts
Brandeis University *B*

Michigan
University of Michigan *B*

Minnesota
Carleton College *B*
University of Minnesota
    Twin Cities *B*

Missouri
Washington University in St.
    Louis *B, M*

New Hampshire
Dartmouth College *B*

New York
Bard College *B*
City University of New York
    Hunter College *B*
    Queens College *B*
Hofstra University *B*
Jewish Theological Seminary of
    America *M, D*
New York University *B, M, D*
State University of New York
    Binghamton *B*
Touro College *B*
Yeshiva University *B*

Ohio
Ohio State University
    Columbus Campus *B*

Oregon
Multnomah University *B*

Pennsylvania
Temple University *B*

Texas
University of Texas
    Austin *B, M, D*

Utah
University of Utah *B, M, D*

Washington
University of Washington *B*

Wisconsin
University of Wisconsin
    Madison *B, M, D*
    Milwaukee *B*

Herbalism

Vermont
Goddard College *B, M*

Washington
Bastyr University *B*

Higher education administration

Alabama
University of Alabama *M, D*

Arizona
Arizona State University *M, D*
Grand Canyon University *M*
Northcentral University *M, D*
University of Arizona *M, D*
University of Phoenix *D*

Arkansas
University of Arkansas *M, D*
University of Arkansas
    Little Rock *M, D*

California
Azusa Pacific University *M, D*
California Coast University *M*
San Jose State University *M*
Stanford University *D*
University of Southern California *M*

Colorado
Colorado State University *M*
Jones International University *M, D*
University of Denver *M, D*
University of Northern Colorado *D*

Connecticut
University of Connecticut *M, D, T*

District of Columbia
George Washington University *M, D*

Florida
Barry University *M*
Florida International University *M, D*
Florida State University *M, D*
Nova Southeastern University *D*
University of Florida *D*
University of Miami *M, D*
University of South Florida *M*

Georgia
Georgia Southern University *M*
University of Georgia *D*

Illinois
Benedictine University *D*
Loyola University Chicago *M, D*
Southern Illinois University
    Carbondale *M*
University of Illinois
    Urbana-Champaign *M, D*

Indiana
Indiana University
    Bloomington *D*
Indiana University-Purdue University
    Indianapolis *M*
Taylor University *M*

Iowa
Iowa State University *M, D*
Kaplan University
    Davenport *M*
University of Iowa *M, D*

Kansas
University of Kansas *M*

Kentucky
University of Kentucky *M*
University of Louisville *M*

Maine
University of Maine *M, D*
University of Southern Maine *M*

Maryland
Morgan State University *M, D*

Massachusetts
Boston College *M, D*
Harvard College *M, D*
Salem State College *M*
Springfield College *D*
Suffolk University *M*

Michigan
Eastern Michigan University *M*
Grand Valley State University *M*
Michigan State University *M, D*

Minnesota
Capella University *M, D*
Minnesota State University
    Mankato *M*
Saint Cloud State University *M, D*
University of St. Thomas *M*
Walden University *D*

Mississippi
Mississippi College *M*
University of Mississippi *M, D*
University of Southern Mississippi *D*

Missouri
Northwest Missouri State
    University *M*
Saint Louis University *M, D*
Southeast Missouri State University *M*

University of Central Missouri *M*
University of Missouri
    Columbia *D*

New Jersey
Rowan University *M*
Seton Hall University *D*

New York
City University of New York
    Baruch College *M*
Fordham University *M, D*
Saint Bonaventure University *M*
State University of New York
    Albany *M, D*
    Binghamton *M*
    Buffalo *M, D*
    College at Buffalo *M*
Syracuse University *M, D*
University of Rochester *M, D*

North Carolina
Appalachian State University *M*
Fayetteville State University *M*
North Carolina State University *M, D*

Ohio
Baldwin-Wallace College *M*
Bowling Green State University *D*
Kent State University *M, D*
Ohio State University
    Columbus Campus *M, D*
Ohio University *M, D*
Union Institute & University *D*
University of Akron *M*
University of Dayton *M*
University of Findlay *M, T*
University of Toledo *M, D, T*
Wright State University *M*
Youngstown State University *M*

Oklahoma
Northeastern State University *M*
Oklahoma State University *D*

Oregon
George Fox University *M*
Portland State University *D*

Pennsylvania
Drexel University *M*
Geneva College *M*
Marywood University *M*
Penn State
    University Park *M, D*
Slippery Rock University of
    Pennsylvania *M*
University of Pennsylvania *M, D*
Villanova University *M*
Widener University *M, D*

Puerto Rico
Inter American University of Puerto
    Rico
    Metropolitan Campus *M*

South Dakota
Dakota Wesleyan University *M*
University of South Dakota *M, D*

Tennessee
Union University *D*
University of Memphis *D*
Vanderbilt University *M, D*

Texas
Abilene Christian University *M*
Baylor University *M*
Dallas Baptist University *M, D*
Texas A&M University
    Commerce *M, D*
    Kingsville *M, D*

University of Houston *M, D*
University of North Texas *M, D*
University of Texas
    San Antonio *M*

Vermont
University of Vermont *M*

Virginia
College of William and Mary *M, D*
Old Dominion University *M, D*
University of Virginia *D*

Washington
City University of Seattle *M*
Seattle University *M*
University of Washington *M, D*
Washington State University *M, D*
Western Washington University *M*

Wisconsin
Concordia University Wisconsin *M*

Hindu studies

California
California Institute of Integral
    Studies *M, D*

West Virginia
Alderson-Broaddus College *T*

Histologic assistant

Arizona
Pima Community College *A*

Georgia
Darton College *A*

Michigan
Mott Community College *A*

New Jersey
Ocean County College *A*

Ohio
University of Akron *A*
Youngstown State University *A*

Rhode Island
Community College of Rhode
    Island *A*

Texas
Houston Community College
    System *A*
Tarleton State University *A*

Histologic technology

Delaware
Delaware Technical and Community
    College
    Stanton/Wilmington *A*

Florida
Miami Dade College *A*

Michigan
Northern Michigan University *A*
Oakland Community College *A*
Oakland University *B*

Minnesota
North Hennepin Community
    College *A*

Historic preservation

California
University of Southern California *M*

Delaware
Delaware State University *B, M*
University of Delaware *B, M*

District of Columbia
George Washington University *M*

Georgia
Georgia State University *M*
Savannah College of Art and
    Design *B, M*
University of Georgia *M*

Illinois
School of the Art Institute of
    Chicago *M*

Indiana
Ball State University *M*

Kentucky
University of Kentucky *M*

Maryland
Harford Community College *A*
University of Maryland
    College Park *M*

Massachusetts
Boston University *M*

Michigan
Eastern Michigan University *M*

New York
Cornell University *M*

North Carolina
Randolph Community College *A*

Ohio
Belmont Technical College *A*
Ursuline College *B*

Oregon
University of Oregon *M*

Pennsylvania
University of Pennsylvania *M*

Rhode Island
Roger Williams University *B*
Salve Regina University *B*

South Carolina
Clemson University *M*
College of Charleston *B, M*

Texas
Texas Tech University *M*
University of Texas
    Austin *M, D*

Vermont
University of Vermont *M*

Virginia
University of Mary Washington *B*

History

Alabama
Alabama State University *B*
Athens State University *B*

Auburn University *B, M, D*
Auburn University at Montgomery *B*
Birmingham-Southern College *B*
Calhoun Community College *A*
Faulkner University *B, T*
Gadsden State Community College *A*
Huntingdon College *B*
Jacksonville State University *B, M*
Judson College *B*
Miles College *B*
Oakwood University *B*
Samford University *B*
Spring Hill College *B, T*
Stillman College *B*
Talladega College *B*
Troy University *B*
Tuskegee University *B*
University of Alabama *B, M, D*
University of Alabama
    Birmingham *B, M*
    Huntsville *B, M*
University of Mobile *B, T*
University of Montevallo *B, T*
University of North Alabama *B*
University of South Alabama *B, M*
University of West Alabama *B, T*

Alaska
University of Alaska
    Anchorage *B*
    Fairbanks *B, M*

Arizona
Arizona State University *B, M, D*
Arizona Western College *A*
Cochise College *A*
Eastern Arizona College *A*
Grand Canyon University *B*
Northern Arizona University *B, M, D*
Prescott College *B, M*
University of Arizona *B, M, D*

Arkansas
Arkansas State University *B, M*
Arkansas Tech University *B, M*
Harding University *B*
Henderson State University *B*
Hendrix College *B*
John Brown University *B*
Lyon College *B*
Ouachita Baptist University *B*
Southern Arkansas University *B*
University of Arkansas *B, M, D*
University of Arkansas
    Fort Smith *B*
    Little Rock *B, M*
    Monticello *B*
    Pine Bluff *B*
University of Central Arkansas *B, M*
University of the Ozarks *B*
Williams Baptist College *B*

California
Azusa Pacific University *B*
Bakersfield College *A*
Biola University *B*
Cabrillo College *A*
California Baptist University *B*
California Institute of Technology *B*
California Lutheran University *B*
California Polytechnic State
    University: San Luis Obispo *B, M*
California State Polytechnic
    University: Pomona *B, M*
California State University
    Bakersfield *B, M*
    Chico *B, M*
    Dominguez Hills *B*
    East Bay *B, M*
    Fresno *B, M*
    Fullerton *B, M*
    Long Beach *B, M*
    Los Angeles *B, M*

    Northridge *B*
    Sacramento *B, M*
    San Bernardino *B, T*
    San Marcos *B, M*
    Stanislaus *B, M*
California State University: Channel
    Islands *B*
Canada College *A*
Cerritos College *A*
Chabot College *A*
Chaffey College *A*
Chapman University *B*
Claremont McKenna College *B*
College of Alameda *A*
College of Marin: Kentfield *A*
College of the Desert *A*
College of the Siskiyous *A*
Concordia University *B*
Contra Costa College *A*
Copper Mountain College *A*
Crafton Hills College *A*
Cypress College *A*
De Anza College *A*
Dominican University of California *B*
East Los Angeles College *A*
El Camino College *A*
El Camino College: Compton
    Center *A*
Feather River College *A*
Foothill College *A*
Fresno City College *A*
Fresno Pacific University *B*
Fullerton College *A*
Gavilan College *A*
Glendale Community College *A*
Golden West College *A*
Grossmont College *A*
Hartnell College *A*
Holy Names University *B*
Humboldt State University *B*
Imperial Valley College *A*
Irvine Valley College *A*
La Sierra University *B*
Los Angeles Southwest College *A*
Los Angeles Valley College *A*
Loyola Marymount University *B, M*
The Master's College *A*
Merced College *A*
Mills College *B*
MiraCosta College *A*
Monterey Peninsula College *A*
Mount St. Mary's College *B*
National University *B*
Notre Dame de Namur University *B*
Occidental College *B*
Orange Coast College *A*
Oxnard College *A*
Pacific Union College *B*
Palo Verde College *A*
Pepperdine University *B, M*
Pitzer College *B*
Point Loma Nazarene University *B*
Pomona College *B*
Saddleback College *A*
St. Mary's College of California *B*
San Diego Christian College *B*
San Diego City College *A*
San Diego State University *B, M*
San Francisco State University *B, M*
San Jose State University *B, M*
Santa Ana College *A*
Santa Barbara City College *A*
Santa Clara University *B*
Santa Monica College *A*
Santa Rosa Junior College *A*
Santiago Canyon College *A*
Scripps College *B*
Sierra College *A*
Simpson University *B*
Solano Community College *A*
Sonoma State University *B, M*
Southwestern College *A*
Stanford University *B, M, D*

University of California
  Berkeley *B, M, D*
  Davis *B, M, D*
  Irvine *B, M, D*
  Los Angeles *B, M, D*
  Riverside *B, M, D*
  San Diego *B, M, D*
  Santa Barbara *B, M, D*
  Santa Cruz *B, M, D*
University of California:
  Merced *B, M, D*
University of La Verne *B*
University of Redlands *B*
University of San Diego *B, M*
University of San Francisco *B*
University of Southern
  California *B, M, D*
University of the Pacific *B*
University of the West *B*
Vanguard University of Southern
  California *B*
West Los Angeles College *A*
West Valley College *A*
Westmont College *B*
Whittier College *B*
William Jessup University *B*
Yuba Community College District *A*

Colorado

Adams State College *B, M*
Colorado Christian University *B*
Colorado College *B*
Colorado State University *B, M*
Colorado State University
  Pueblo *B*
Fort Lewis College *B*
Lamar Community College *A*
Mesa State College *B*
Metropolitan State College of
  Denver *B, T*
Otero Junior College *A*
Pikes Peak Community College *A*
Regis University *B*
United States Air Force Academy *B*
University of Colorado
  Boulder *B, M, D*
  Colorado Springs *B, M*
  Denver *B, M*
University of Denver *B*
University of Northern
  Colorado *B, M, T*
Western State College of Colorado *B*

Connecticut

Albertus Magnus College *B*
Central Connecticut State
  University *B, M, T*
Connecticut College *B*
Eastern Connecticut State
  University *B*
Fairfield University *B*
Quinnipiac University *B*
Sacred Heart University *B*
Saint Joseph College *B*
Southern Connecticut State
  University *B, M, T*
Trinity College *B, M*
University of Connecticut *B, M, D*
University of Hartford *B*
University of New Haven *B*
Wesleyan University *B*
Western Connecticut State
  University *B, M*
Yale University *B, M, D*

Delaware

Delaware State University *B*
University of Delaware *B, M, D*
Wesley College *B*

District of Columbia

American University *B, M, D*

Catholic University of
  America *B, M, D*
Gallaudet University *B*
George Washington
  University *B, M, D*
Georgetown University *B, D*
Howard University *B, M, D*
Trinity Washington University *B*
University of the District of
  Columbia *B*

Florida

Ave Maria University *B*
Barry University *B*
Bethune-Cookman University *B*
Broward College *A*
Chipola College *A*
Clearwater Christian College *B*
Eckerd College *B*
Flagler College *B*
Florida Agricultural and Mechanical
  University *B*
Florida Atlantic University *B, M*
Florida Gulf Coast University *B, M*
Florida International
  University *B, M, D*
Florida Southern College *B*
Florida State University *B, M, D*
Gulf Coast Community College *A*
Indian River State College *A*
Jacksonville University *B*
Miami Dade College *A*
New College of Florida *B*
Nova Southeastern University *B*
Palm Beach Atlantic University *B*
Palm Beach Community College *A*
Pensacola Junior College *A*
Rollins College *B*
Saint Leo University *B*
Saint Thomas University *B*
Southeastern University *B*
State College of Florida,
  Manatee-Sarasota *A*
Stetson University *B*
University of Central Florida *B, M*
University of Florida *B, M, D*
University of Miami *B, M, D*
University of North Florida *B, M*
University of South Florida *B, M*
University of Tampa *A, B*
University of West Florida *B, M*
Warner University *B*

Georgia

Abraham Baldwin Agricultural
  College *A*
Agnes Scott College *B*
Albany State University *B*
Andrew College *A*
Armstrong Atlantic State
  University *B, M, T*
Atlanta Metropolitan College *A*
Augusta State University *B*
Bainbridge College *A*
Berry College *B*
Brenau University *B*
Brewton-Parker College *B*
Clark Atlanta University *B, M, D*
Clayton State University *B*
College of Coastal Georgia *A*
Columbus State University *B*
Covenant College *B*
Dalton State College *A, B*
Darton College *A*
East Georgia College *A*
Emmanuel College *B*
Emory University *B, D*
Gainesville State College *A*
Georgia College and State
  University *B*
Georgia Gwinnett College *B*
Georgia Military College *A*
Georgia Perimeter College *A*
Georgia Southern University *B, M*

Georgia Southwestern State
  University *B, T*
Georgia State University *B, M, D*
Gordon College *A*
Kennesaw State University *B*
LaGrange College *B*
Macon State College *A*
Mercer University *B*
Middle Georgia College *A*
Morehouse College *B*
North Georgia College & State
  University *B*
Oglethorpe University *B*
Paine College *B*
Piedmont College *B*
Reinhardt College *B*
Savannah State University *B*
Shorter College *B, T*
South Georgia College *A*
Spelman College *B*
Toccoa Falls College *B*
Truett-McConnell College *B*
University of Georgia *B, M, D*
University of West Georgia *B, M*
Valdosta State University *B, M*
Waycross College *A*
Wesleyan College *B*
Young Harris College *A*

Hawaii

Chaminade University of Honolulu *B*
Hawaii Pacific University *B*
University of Hawaii
  Hilo *B*
  Manoa *B, M, D*
  West Oahu *B*

Idaho

Boise State University *B, M*
Brigham Young University-Idaho *B*
College of Idaho *B*
Idaho State University *A, B, M*
North Idaho College *A*
Northwest Nazarene University *B*
University of Idaho *B, M, D*

Illinois

Augustana College *B, T*
Aurora University *B*
Benedictine University *B, T*
Black Hawk College: East Campus *A*
Blackburn College *B*
Bradley University *B, T*
Chicago State University *B, M*
City Colleges of Chicago
  Kennedy-King College *A*
Concordia University Chicago *B*
Danville Area Community College *A*
DePaul University *B, M, T*
Dominican University *B*
Eastern Illinois University *B, M, T*
Elmhurst College *B, T*
Eureka College *B, T*
Greenville College *B*
Illinois College *B, T*
Illinois State University *B, M, T*
Illinois Valley Community College *A*
Illinois Wesleyan University *B*
John Wood Community College *A*
Joliet Junior College *A*
Judson University *B*
Kishwaukee College *A*
Knox College *B*
Lake Forest College *B*
Lewis University *B, T*
Lincoln College *A*
Loyola University Chicago *B, M, D*
MacMurray College *B*
McKendree University *B*
Millikin University *B*
Monmouth College *B, T*
North Central College *B, T*
North Park University *B*
Northeastern Illinois University *B, M*

Northern Illinois University *B, M, D*
Northwestern University *B, M, D*
Olivet Nazarene University *B, T*
Principia College *B*
Quincy University *B, T*
Richland Community College *A*
Rockford College *B*
Roosevelt University *B, M*
Saint Xavier University *B*
South Suburban College of Cook
  County *A*
Southern Illinois University
  Carbondale *B, M, D*
Southern Illinois University
  Edwardsville *B, M, T*
Southwestern Illinois College *A*
Spoon River College *A*
Trinity Christian College *B, T*
Trinity International University *B*
Triton College *A*
University of Chicago *B, D*
University of Illinois
  Chicago *B, M, D*
  Springfield *B, M*
  Urbana-Champaign *B, M, D*
University of St. Francis *B*
Western Illinois University *B, M*
Wheaton College *B, T*

Indiana

Ancilla College *A*
Anderson University *B*
Ball State University *B, M, T*
Bethel College *B*
Butler University *B, M*
DePauw University *B*
Earlham College *B*
Franklin College *B*
Goshen College *B*
Grace College *B*
Hanover College *B*
Holy Cross College *B*
Huntington University *B*
Indiana State University *B, M*
Indiana University
  Bloomington *B, M, D*
  East *A*
  Northwest *A, B*
  South Bend *A, B*
  Southeast *B*
Indiana University-Purdue University
  Fort Wayne *A, B*
Indiana University-Purdue University
  Indianapolis *B, M*
Indiana Wesleyan University *A, B*
Manchester College *B, T*
Marian University *B, T*
Oakland City University *B*
Purdue University *B, M, D*
Purdue University
  Calumet *B*
Saint Joseph's College *B*
Saint Mary's College *B*
Taylor University *B*
University of Evansville *B*
University of Indianapolis *B, M*
University of Notre Dame *B, M, D*
University of St. Francis *B*
University of Southern Indiana *B*
Valparaiso University *B, M*
Vincennes University *A*
Wabash College *B*

Iowa

Briar Cliff University *B*
Buena Vista University *B, T*
Central College *B, T*
Clarke College *A, B, T*
Coe College *B*
Cornell College *B, T*
Dordt College *B*
Drake University *B*
Ellsworth Community College *A*
Graceland University *B, T*

Grand View University *B*
Grinnell College *B*
Iowa State University *B, M*
Iowa Wesleyan College *B*
Loras College *B*
Luther College *B*
Morningside College *B*
Mount Mercy College *B, T*
Northwestern College *B, T*
St. Ambrose University *B, T*
Simpson College *B*
University of Iowa *B, M, D, T*
University of Northern Iowa *B, M*
Waldorf College *B*
Wartburg College *B, T*
William Penn University *B*

Kansas

Allen County Community College *A*
Baker University *B, T*
Barton County Community College *A*
Benedictine College *B*
Bethany College *B, T*
Bethel College *B*
Butler Community College *A*
Central Christian College of
    Kansas *A, B*
Coffeyville Community College *A*
Cowley County Community
    College *A*
Emporia State University *B, M, T*
Fort Hays State University *B, M*
Fort Scott Community College *A*
Friends University *B*
Highland Community College *A*
Kansas State University *B, M, D*
Kansas Wesleyan University *B, T*
Labette Community College *A*
McPherson College *B, T*
MidAmerica Nazarene University *B*
Newman University *B*
Ottawa University *B, T*
Pittsburg State University *B, M*
Pratt Community College *A*
Seward County Community College *A*
Southwestern College *B*
Sterling College *B, T*
Tabor College *B*
University of Kansas *B, M, D*
University of St. Mary *B*
Washburn University *B*
Wichita State University *B, M, T*

Kentucky

Alice Lloyd College *B*
Asbury College *B*
Bellarmine University *B*
Berea College *B, T*
Brescia University *B*
Campbellsville University *B*
Centre College *B*
Eastern Kentucky University *B, M*
Georgetown College *B, T*
Kentucky Christian University *B*
Kentucky Wesleyan College *B*
Lindsey Wilson College *A, B*
Morehead State University *B*
Murray State University *B, M, T*
Pikeville College *B*
Thomas More College *A, B*
Transylvania University *B*
Union College *B*
University of Kentucky *B, M, D*
University of Louisville *B, M*
University of the Cumberlands *B*
Western Kentucky University *B, M*

Louisiana

Centenary College of Louisiana *B, T*
Dillard University *B*
Grambling State University *B*
Louisiana College *B*

Louisiana State University
  Alexandria *B*
  Shreveport *B*
Louisiana State University and
    Agricultural and Mechanical
    College *B, M, D*
Louisiana Tech University *B, M*
Loyola University New Orleans *B*
McNeese State University *B*
Nicholls State University *B*
Northwestern State University *B*
Our Lady of Holy Cross College *B*
Southeastern Louisiana
    University *B, M*
Southern University and Agricultural
    and Mechanical College *B*
Tulane University *B, M, D*
University of Louisiana at
    Lafayette *B, M*
University of Louisiana at
    Monroe *B, M*
University of New Orleans *B, M*
Xavier University of Louisiana *B*

Maine

Bates College *B*
Bowdoin College *B*
Colby College *B*
Saint Joseph's College of Maine *B*
University of Maine *B, M, D*
University of Maine
  Farmington *B*
  Machias *B, T*
University of New England *B*
University of Southern Maine *B*

Maryland

Allegany College of Maryland *A*
Bowie State University *B*
College of Notre Dame of Maryland *B*
Coppin State University *B*
Frederick Community College *A*
Frostburg State University *B*
Goucher College *B*
Harford Community College *A*
Hood College *B, T*
Howard Community College *A*
Johns Hopkins University *B, M, D*
Loyola University Maryland *B*
McDaniel College *B*
Morgan State University *B, M, D*
Mount St. Mary's University *B*
St. Mary's College of Maryland *B*
Salisbury University *B, M, T*
Towson University *B*
United States Naval Academy *B*
University of Baltimore *B*
University of Maryland
  Baltimore County *B, M*
  College Park *B, M, D*
  Eastern Shore *B*
  University College *B*
Washington Adventist University *B*
Washington College *B, M, T*

Massachusetts

American International College *B*
Amherst College *B*
Anna Maria College *B*
Assumption College *B*
Bentley University *B*
Boston College *B, M, D*
Boston University *B, M, D*
Brandeis University *B, M, D*
Bridgewater State College *B*
Bunker Hill Community College *A*
Cape Cod Community College *A*
Clark University *B, M, D*
College of the Holy Cross *B*
Dean College *B*
Eastern Nazarene College *B*
Elms College *B*
Emmanuel College *B*
Endicott College *B*

Fitchburg State College *B, M*
Framingham State College *B*
Gordon College *B*
Hampshire College *B*
Harvard College *B, M, D*
Lasell College *B*
Massachusetts College of Liberal
    Arts *B*
Massachusetts Institute of
    Technology *B*
Merrimack College *B*
Mount Holyoke College *B*
Nichols College *B, T*
Northeastern University *B, M, D*
Pine Manor College *B*
Regis College *B*
Salem State College *B, M*
Simmons College *B, M*
Smith College *B*
Springfield College *B*
Stonehill College *B*
Suffolk University *B*
Tufts University *B, M, D, T*
University of Massachusetts
  Amherst *B, M, D*
  Boston *B, M*
  Dartmouth *B*
  Lowell *B*
Wellesley College *B*
Western New England College *B*
Westfield State College *B, M, T*
Wheaton College *B*
Williams College *B*
Worcester State College *B, M, T*

Michigan

Adrian College *A, B, T*
Albion College *B, T*
Alma College *B, T*
Andrews University *B, M*
Aquinas College *B, T*
Calvin College *B, T*
Central Michigan University *B, M, D*
Cornerstone University *B, T*
Eastern Michigan University *B, M*
Ferris State University *B*
Gogebic Community College *A*
Grand Valley State University *B*
Great Lakes Christian College *B*
Hillsdale College *B*
Hope College *B*
Kalamazoo College *B*
Lake Michigan College *A*
Lake Superior State University *B, T*
Lansing Community College *A*
Madonna University *B, M*
Marygrove College *B, T*
Michigan State University *B, M, D*
Michigan Technological University *B*
Northern Michigan University *B*
Oakland University *B, M, T*
Rochester College *B*
Saginaw Valley State University *B, T*
Siena Heights University *B*
Spring Arbor University *B, T*
University of Detroit Mercy *B*
University of Michigan *B, M, D*
University of Michigan
  Dearborn *B*
  Flint *B, T*
Wayne State University *B, M, D*
Western Michigan University *B, M, D*

Minnesota

Augsburg College *B*
Bemidji State University *B*
Bethany Lutheran College *B*
Bethel University *B*
Carleton College *B*
College of St. Benedict *B*
College of St. Scholastica *B*
Concordia College: Moorhead *B*
Concordia University: St. Paul *B*
Crown College *B*

Gustavus Adolphus College *B*
Hamline University *B*
Macalester College *B*
Metropolitan State University *B*
Minnesota State University
  Mankato *B, M*
  Moorhead *B*
Minnesota West Community and
    Technical College *A*
North Hennepin Community
    College *A*
Northwestern College *B*
Ridgewater College *A*
St. Catherine University *B*
Saint Cloud State University *B, M*
St. John's University *B*
St. Mary's University of Minnesota *B*
St. Olaf College *B*
Southwest Minnesota State
    University *B*
University of Minnesota
  Duluth *B*
  Morris *B*
  Twin Cities *B, M, D*
University of St. Thomas *B*
Vermilion Community College *A*
Winona State University *B*

Mississippi

Alcorn State University *B*
Belhaven University *B*
Blue Mountain College *B*
Delta State University *B*
Hinds Community College *A*
Jackson State University *B, M*
Millsaps College *B*
Mississippi College *B, M*
Mississippi Delta Community
    College *A*
Mississippi State University *B, M, D*
Mississippi University for Women *B, T*
Mississippi Valley State University *B*
Tougaloo College *B*
University of Mississippi *B, M, D, T*
University of Southern
    Mississippi *B, M, D*

Missouri

Avila University *B*
Central Methodist University *B*
College of the Ozarks *B*
Columbia College *B*
Crowder College *A*
Culver-Stockton College *B, T*
Drury University *B, T*
Evangel University *B*
Fontbonne University *B, T*
Hannibal-LaGrange College *B*
Lincoln University *B, M*
Lindenwood University *B*
Maryville University of Saint Louis *B*
Missouri Baptist University *B, T*
Missouri Southern State
    University *B, T*
Missouri State University *B, M*
Missouri Valley College *B*
Missouri Western State University *B, T*
Northwest Missouri State
    University *B, M*
Park University *B*
Rockhurst University *B*
St. Charles Community College *A*
Saint Louis University *B, M, D*
Southeast Missouri State
    University *B, M*
Southwest Baptist University *B*
Three Rivers Community College *A*
Truman State University *B*
University of Central Missouri *B, M*
University of Missouri
  Columbia *B, M, D*
  Kansas City *B, M, D*

Missouri University of Science and
Technology *B*
St. Louis *B, M*
Washington University in St.
Louis *B, M, D*
Webster University *B*
Westminster College *B, T*
William Jewell College *B*
William Woods University *B*

Montana
Montana State University
Billings *B, T*
Bozeman *B, M*
Rocky Mountain College *B, T*
University of Great Falls *B*
University of Montana *B, M*
University of Montana: Western *B, T*

Nebraska
Bellevue University *B*
Chadron State College *B, M*
Concordia University *B, T*
Creighton University *B*
Dana College *B*
Doane College *B*
Nebraska Wesleyan University *B*
Union College *B*
University of Nebraska
Kearney *B, M, T*
Lincoln *B, M, D*
Omaha *B, M*
Wayne State College *B*
Western Nebraska Community
College *A*
York College *B*

Nevada
Great Basin College *A*
Nevada State College *B*
University of Nevada
Las Vegas *B, M, D*
Reno *B, M, D*

New Hampshire
Dartmouth College *B*
Franklin Pierce University *B*
Keene State College *B*
New England College *B*
Plymouth State University *B*
Rivier College *B*
Saint Anselm College *B, T*
Southern New Hampshire
University *B*
University of New Hampshire *B, M, D*
University of New Hampshire at
Manchester *B*

New Jersey
Bergen Community College *A*
Bloomfield College *B*
Caldwell College *B*
Centenary College *B*
The College of New Jersey *B, T*
College of St. Elizabeth *B*
Drew University *B, D*
Fairleigh Dickinson University
College at Florham *B*
Metropolitan Campus *B, M*
Felician College *B*
Georgian Court University *B*
Gloucester County College *A*
Hudson County Community
College *A*
Kean University *B, T*
Monmouth University *B, M*
Montclair State University *B, M*
New Jersey City University *B*
New Jersey Institute of
Technology *B, M*
Princeton University *B, M, D*
Ramapo College of New Jersey *B*

Richard Stockton College of New
Jersey *B*
Rider University *B*
Rowan University *B*
Rutgers, The State University of New
Jersey
Camden Regional Campus *B*
New Brunswick/Piscataway
Campus *B, M, D*
Newark Regional Campus *B*
Saint Peter's College *B*
Salem Community College *A*
Seton Hall University *B, M, T*
Stevens Institute of Technology *B*
Thomas Edison State College *B*
William Paterson University of New
Jersey *B*

New Mexico
Eastern New Mexico University *B*
New Mexico Highlands
University *B, M*
New Mexico State University *B, M*
University of New Mexico *B, M, D*
University of the Southwest *B*
Western New Mexico University *B*

New York
Adelphi University *B*
Alfred University *B*
Bard College *B*
Barnard College *B*
Canisius College *B*
City University of New York
Baruch College *B*
Brooklyn College *B, M*
City College *B, M*
College of Staten Island *B, M*
Hunter College *B, M*
Lehman College *B, M*
Queens College *B, M, T*
Queensborough Community
College *A*
York College *B*
Clarkson University *B*
Colgate University *B*
College of Mount St. Vincent *A, B, T*
College of New Rochelle *B, T*
Columbia University *B*
Columbia University
School of General Studies *B*
Concordia College *B, T*
Cornell University *B, M, D*
D'Youville College *B*
Daemen College *B*
Dominican College of Blauvelt *B*
Dowling College *B*
Elmira College *B, T*
Eugene Lang College The New School
for Liberal Arts *B*
Excelsior College *B*
Fordham University *B, M, D*
Hamilton College *B*
Hartwick College *B, T*
Hobart and William Smith Colleges *B*
Hofstra University *B*
Houghton College *B*
Iona College *B, M*
Ithaca College *B*
Jewish Theological Seminary of
America *M, D*
Le Moyne College *B*
Long Island University
Brooklyn Campus *B*
C. W. Post Campus *B, M*
Manhattan College *B*
Manhattanville College *B*
Marist College *B*
Marymount Manhattan College *B*
Mercy College *B*
Molloy College *B*
Monroe Community College *A*
Mount Saint Mary College *B, T*
Nazareth College *B, T*

New York University *B, M, D*
Niagara University *B*
Nyack College *B*
Pace University *B*
Roberts Wesleyan College *B*
Russell Sage College *B*
Saint Bonaventure University *B*
St. Francis College *B*
St. John Fisher College *B*
St. John's University *B, M, D*
St. Joseph's College *B*
St. Joseph's College: Suffolk
Campus *B, T*
St. Lawrence University *B*
St. Thomas Aquinas College *B, T*
Siena College *B, T*
Skidmore College *B*
State University of New York
Albany *B, M, D*
Binghamton *B, M, D*
Buffalo *B, M, D*
College at Brockport *B, M, T*
College at Buffalo *B, M*
College at Cortland *B, M*
College at Fredonia *B*
College at Geneseo *B, T*
College at Oneonta *B*
College at Plattsburgh *B*
College at Potsdam *B*
Empire State College *A, B*
New Paltz *B*
Oswego *B, M*
Purchase *B*
Stony Brook *B, M, D*
Suffolk County Community College *A*
Sullivan County Community
College *A*
Syracuse University *B, M, D*
Touro College *B*
Union College *B*
University of Rochester *B, M, D*
Utica College *B*
Vassar College *B*
Wagner College *B*
Wells College *B*
Yeshiva University *B*

North Carolina
Appalachian State University *B, M*
Barton College *B*
Belmont Abbey College *B*
Brevard College *B*
Campbell University *B*
Catawba College *B, T*
Chowan University *B*
Davidson College *B*
Duke University *B, D*
East Carolina University *B, M*
Elizabeth City State University *B*
Elon University *B, T*
Fayetteville State University *B*
Gardner-Webb University *B*
Greensboro College *C, B, T*
Guilford College *B, T*
High Point University *B*
Johnson C. Smith University *B*
Lenoir-Rhyne University *B, T*
Livingstone College *B*
Mars Hill College *B, T*
Meredith College *B*
Methodist University *A, B, T*
Montreat College *B*
Mount Olive College *B*
North Carolina Agricultural and
Technical State University *B, M, T*
North Carolina Central
University *B, M*
North Carolina State University *B, M*
North Carolina Wesleyan College *B*
Peace College *B*
Pfeiffer University *B*
Queens University of Charlotte *B*
St. Andrews Presbyterian College *B*
St. Augustine's College *B*

Salem College *B*
Southeastern Community College *A*
University of North Carolina
Asheville *B, T*
Chapel Hill *B, M, D*
Charlotte *B, M*
Greensboro *B, M, D*
Pembroke *B*
Wilmington *B, M*
Wake Forest University *B*
Warren Wilson College *B*
Western Carolina University *B, M*
Wingate University *B*
Winston-Salem State University *B*

North Dakota
Dakota College at Bottineau *A*
Dickinson State University *B*
Jamestown College *B*
Minot State University *B*
North Dakota State
University *B, M, D, T*
University of North Dakota *B, M, D*

Ohio
Ashland University *B, M*
Baldwin-Wallace College *B*
Bluffton University *B*
Bowling Green State
University *B, M, D*
Capital University *B*
Case Western Reserve
University *B, M, D*
Cedarville University *B*
Central State University *B*
Cleveland State University *B, M, T*
College of Mount St. Joseph *B, T*
College of Wooster *B*
Defiance College *B, T*
Denison University *B*
Franciscan University of
Steubenville *B*
Heidelberg University *B*
Hiram College *B, T*
John Carroll University *B, M*
Kent State University *B, M, D*
Kenyon College *B*
Lourdes College *A, B*
Malone University *B*
Marietta College *B*
Miami University
Oxford Campus *B, M*
Mount Union College *B*
Mount Vernon Nazarene University *B*
Muskingum University *B*
Notre Dame College *B, T*
Oberlin College *B*
Ohio Dominican University *B, T*
Ohio Northern University *B*
Ohio State University
Columbus Campus *B, M, D*
Lima Campus *B*
Mansfield Campus *B*
Marion Campus *B*
Ohio University *B, M*
Ohio University
Southern Campus at Ironton *B*
Ohio Wesleyan University *B*
Otterbein College *B*
Owens Community College
Toledo *A*
Pontifical College Josephinum *B*
Shawnee State University *B*
Tiffin University *B*
University of Akron *B, M, D*
University of Cincinnati *B, M, D, T*
University of Dayton *B*
University of Findlay *B, T*
University of Rio Grande *A, B*
University of Toledo *B, M, D*
Urbana University *B*
Ursuline College *B*
Walsh University *B*
Wilmington College *B*

Wittenberg University *B*
Wright State University *A, B*
Wright State University: Lake
    Campus *A*
Xavier University *A, B*
Youngstown State University *B, M*

Oklahoma
Cameron University *B, M*
Connors State College *A*
East Central University *B*
Eastern Oklahoma State College *A*
Langston University *B*
Murray State College *A*
Northeastern State University *B*
Northwestern Oklahoma State
    University *B*
Oklahoma Baptist University *B*
Oklahoma Christian University *B*
Oklahoma City Community College *A*
Oklahoma City University *B*
Oklahoma Panhandle State
    University *B*
Oklahoma State University *B, M, D*
Oklahoma Wesleyan University *B*
Oral Roberts University *B*
Rogers State University *A*
Rose State College *A*
St. Gregory's University *B*
Southeastern Oklahoma State
    University *B*
Southern Nazarene University *B*
Southwestern Oklahoma State
    University *B*
Tulsa Community College *A*
University of Central Oklahoma *B, M*
University of Oklahoma *B, M, D*
University of Science and Arts of
    Oklahoma *B*
University of Tulsa *B, M*
Western Oklahoma State College *A*

Oregon
Central Oregon Community
    College *A*
Chemeketa Community College *A*
Concordia University *B*
Corban College *B*
Eastern Oregon University *B, T*
George Fox University *B*
Lewis & Clark College *B*
Linfield College *B, T*
Linn-Benton Community College *A*
Mt. Hood Community College *A*
Multnomah University *B*
Northwest Christian University *B*
Oregon State University *B*
Pacific University *B*
Portland State University *B, M*
Reed College *B*
Southern Oregon University *B*
Treasure Valley Community College *A*
University of Oregon *B, M, D*
University of Portland *B*
Warner Pacific College *B*
Western Oregon University *B*
Willamette University *B*

Pennsylvania
Albright College *B, T*
Allegheny College *B*
Alvernia University *B*
Arcadia University *B*
Bloomsburg University of
    Pennsylvania *B*
Bryn Athyn College of the New
    Church *B*
Bryn Mawr College *B*
Bucknell University *B*
Cabrini College *B*
California University of
    Pennsylvania *B*
Carlow University *B*
Carnegie Mellon University *B, M, D*

Cedar Crest College *B*
Chatham University *B*
Chestnut Hill College *B*
Clarion University of Pennsylvania *B*
DeSales University *B, T*
Dickinson College *B*
Drexel University *B*
Duquesne University *B, M*
East Stroudsburg University of
    Pennsylvania *B, M*
Eastern University *B*
Edinboro University of
    Pennsylvania *B*
Elizabethtown College *B*
Franklin & Marshall College *B*
Gannon University *B*
Geneva College *B, T*
Gettysburg College *B*
Grove City College *B*
Gwynedd-Mercy College *B*
Haverford College *B, T*
Holy Family University *B*
Immaculata University *B*
Indiana University of
    Pennsylvania *B, M*
Juniata College *B*
King's College *B*
Kutztown University of
    Pennsylvania *B*
La Roche College *B*
La Salle University *B, T*
Lafayette College *B*
Lebanon Valley College *B*
Lehigh University *B, M, D*
Lincoln University *B*
Lock Haven University of
    Pennsylvania *B*
Lycoming College *B*
Mansfield University of
    Pennsylvania *B, T*
Marywood University *B*
Mercyhurst College *B*
Messiah College *B*
Millersville University of
    Pennsylvania *B, M*
Misericordia University *B*
Moravian College *B, T*
Mount Aloysius College *B*
Muhlenberg College *B*
Penn State
    Abington *B*
    Altoona *B*
    Beaver *B*
    Berks *B*
    Brandywine *B*
    DuBois *B*
    Erie, The Behrend College *B*
    Fayette, The Eberly Campus *B*
    Greater Allegheny *B*
    Hazleton *B*
    Lehigh Valley *B*
    Mont Alto *B*
    New Kensington *B*
    Schuylkill *B*
    Shenango *B*
    University Park *B, M, D*
    Wilkes-Barre *B*
    Worthington Scranton *B*
    York *B*
Point Park University *B*
Rosemont College *B*
St. Francis University *B*
Saint Joseph's University *B*
St. Vincent College *B*
Seton Hill University *B, T*
Shippensburg University of
    Pennsylvania *B, M, T*
Slippery Rock University of
    Pennsylvania *B, M, T*
Susquehanna University *B*
Swarthmore College *B*
Temple University *B, M, D*
Thiel College *B*
University of Pennsylvania *B, M, D*

University of Pittsburgh *B, M, D*
University of Pittsburgh
    Greensburg *B*
    Johnstown *B*
University of Scranton *B*
Ursinus College *B, T*
Villanova University *B, M*
Washington & Jefferson College *B*
Waynesburg University *B*
West Chester University of
    Pennsylvania *B, M, T*
Westminster College *B, M*
Widener University *B, T*
Wilkes University *B*
York College of Pennsylvania *B*

Puerto Rico
Inter American University of Puerto
    Rico
    Metropolitan Campus *B, M, D*
Pontifical Catholic University of
    Puerto Rico *B, M*
Universidad Adventista de las
    Antillas *B*
University of Puerto Rico
    Aguadilla *A*
    Cayey University College *B*
    Rio Piedras *M, D*

Rhode Island
Brown University *B, M, D*
Bryant University *B*
Providence College *B, M, D*
Rhode Island College *B, M*
Roger Williams University *B*
University of Rhode Island *B, M*

South Carolina
Anderson University *B*
Benedict College *B*
Bob Jones University *B, M*
Charleston Southern University *B*
The Citadel *B, M*
Claflin University *B*
Clemson University *B, M*
Coastal Carolina University *B*
Coker College *B*
College of Charleston *B, M, T*
Columbia College *B*
Converse College *B*
Erskine College *B*
Francis Marion University *B*
Furman University *B, T*
Lander University *B, T*
Limestone College *B*
Morris College *B*
Newberry College *B, T*
North Greenville University *B, T*
Presbyterian College *B*
South Carolina State University *B*
Southern Wesleyan University *B*
University of South Carolina *B, M, D*
University of South Carolina
    Aiken *B*
    Beaufort *B*
    Upstate *B*
Winthrop University *B, M*
Wofford College *B*

South Dakota
Augustana College *B, T*
Black Hills State University *B*
Dakota Wesleyan University *B*
Kilian Community College *A*
Mount Marty College *B*
Northern State University *B*
Oglala Lakota College *B*
South Dakota State University *B*
University of Sioux Falls *B*
University of South Dakota *B, M, D*

Tennessee
Austin Peay State University *B*

Belmont University *B, T*
Bethel University *B*
Bryan College *B, T*
Carson-Newman College *B, T*
Christian Brothers University *B*
Columbia State Community College *A*
Crichton College *B*
Cumberland University *B*
Dyersburg State Community
    College *A*
East Tennessee State
    University *B, M, T*
Fisk University *B*
Free Will Baptist Bible College *B*
Freed-Hardeman University *B, T*
Jackson State Community College *A*
King College *B, T*
Lambuth University *B*
Lane College *B*
LeMoyne-Owen College *B*
Lee University *B*
Lincoln Memorial University *B, T*
Lipscomb University *B*
Martin Methodist College *B*
Maryville College *B, T*
Middle Tennessee State
    University *B, M, D*
Milligan College *B, T*
Rhodes College *B*
Southern Adventist University *B*
Tennessee State University *B, M*
Tennessee Technological
    University *B, T*
Tennessee Temple University *B*
Tennessee Wesleyan College *B*
Trevecca Nazarene University *B*
Tusculum College *B*
Union University *B, T*
University of Memphis *B, M, D*
University of Tennessee
    Chattanooga *B*
    Knoxville *B, M, D*
    Martin *B*
University of the South *B*
Vanderbilt University *B, M, D*

Texas
Abilene Christian University *B*
Angelo State University *B, M, T*
Austin College *B*
Austin Community College *A*
Baylor University *B, M*
Blinn College *A*
Brazosport College *A*
Cisco College *A*
Clarendon College *A*
Coastal Bend College *A*
College of the Mainland *A*
Concordia University Texas *B*
Dallas Baptist University *B*
Del Mar College *A*
East Texas Baptist University *B*
El Paso Community College *A*
Frank Phillips College *A*
Galveston College *A*
Hardin-Simmons University *B, M*
Houston Baptist University *B*
Howard Payne University *B, T*
Huston-Tillotson University *B*
Jarvis Christian College *B, T*
Kilgore College *A*
Lamar University *B, M*
Laredo Community College *A*
LeTourneau University *B*
Lon Morris College *A*
Lubbock Christian University *T*
McMurry University *B, T*
Midland College *A*
Midwestern State University *B, M*
Northeast Texas Community
    College *A*
Northwest Vista College *A*
Our Lady of the Lake University of San
    Antonio *B*

Palo Alto College *A*
Paris Junior College *A*
Prairie View A&M University *B*
Rice University *B, M, D*
St. Edward's University *B*
St. Mary's University *B, T*
St. Philip's College *A*
Sam Houston State University *B, M*
San Jacinto College *A*
Schreiner University *B*
South Plains College *A*
South Texas College *A*
Southern Methodist
　University *B, M, D*
Southwestern Adventist
　University *B, T*
Southwestern Assemblies of God
　University *B*
Southwestern University *B, T*
Stephen F. Austin State
　University *B, M, T*
Sul Ross State University *B, M, T*
Tarleton State University *B, M, T*
Texarkana College *A*
Texas A&M International
　University *B, M, T*
Texas A&M University *B, M, D*
Texas A&M University
　Commerce *B, M*
　Corpus Christi *B, T*
　Kingsville *B, M*
　Texarkana *B, T*
Texas Christian University *B, M, D*
Texas College *B*
Texas Lutheran University *B, T*
Texas Southern University *B, M*
Texas State University: San
　Marcos *B, M, T*
Texas Tech University *B, M, D*
Texas Wesleyan University *B*
Texas Woman's University *B, M*
Trinity University *B*
Tyler Junior College *A*
University of Dallas *B*
University of Houston *B, M, D*
University of Houston
　Clear Lake *B, M*
　Downtown *B*
　Victoria *B, T*
University of Mary Hardin-Baylor *B, T*
University of North Texas *B, M, D*
University of St. Thomas *B*
University of Texas
　Arlington *B, M*
　Austin *B, M, D*
　Brownsville - Texas Southmost
　　College *B, M*
　Dallas *B, M*
　El Paso *B, M, D*
　Pan American *B, M*
　San Antonio *B, M*
　Tyler *B, M*
　of the Permian Basin *B, M*
University of the Incarnate Word *B*
Wayland Baptist University *B, T*
West Texas A&M University *B, M*
Western Texas College *A*
Wharton County Junior College *A*
Wiley College *B*

Utah

Brigham Young University *B, M*
Salt Lake Community College *A*
Snow College *A*
Southern Utah University *B, T*
University of Utah *B, M, D, T*
Utah State University *B, M*
Utah Valley University *A, B*
Weber State University *B*
Westminster College *B*

Vermont

Bennington College *B*
Castleton State College *B*

College of St. Joseph in Vermont *B*
Goddard College *B, M*
Green Mountain College *B*
Johnson State College *B*
Marlboro College *B*
Middlebury College *B*
Norwich University *B*
St. Michael's College *B*
University of Vermont *B, M*

Virginia

Averett University *B*
Bluefield College *B*
Bridgewater College *B*
Christendom College *B*
Christopher Newport University *B*
College of William and Mary *B, M, D*
Eastern Mennonite University *B*
Emory & Henry College *B, T*
Ferrum College *B*
George Mason University *B, M, D*
Hampden-Sydney College *B*
Hampton University *B*
Hollins University *B*
James Madison University *B, M, T*
Liberty University *B, M, T*
Longwood University *B, T*
Lynchburg College *B*
Mary Baldwin College *B*
Marymount University *B*
Norfolk State University *B*
Old Dominion University *B, M, T*
Patrick Henry College *B*
Radford University *B*
Randolph College *B*
Randolph-Macon College *B*
Regent University *A, B*
Roanoke College *B, T*
Shenandoah University *C, B*
Southern Virginia University *B*
Sweet Briar College *B*
University of Mary Washington *B*
University of Richmond *B, M, T*
University of Virginia *B, M, D*
University of Virginia's College at
　Wise *B, T*
Virginia Commonwealth
　University *B, M*
Virginia Intermont College *B*
Virginia Military Institute *B*
Virginia Polytechnic Institute and
　State University *B, M*
Virginia State University *B, M*
Virginia Union University *B*
Virginia Wesleyan College *B*
Washington and Lee University *B*

Washington

Centralia College *A*
Eastern Washington
　University *C, B, M*
Everett Community College *A*
Evergreen State College *B*
Gonzaga University *B*
Highline Community College *A*
Northwest University *B*
Pacific Lutheran University *B*
Saint Martin's University *B*
Seattle Pacific University *B*
Seattle University *B*
University of Puget Sound *B, T*
University of Washington *B, M, D*
Walla Walla University *B*
Washington State University *B, M, D*
Western Washington University *B, M*
Whitman College *B*
Whitworth University *B, T*

West Virginia

Alderson-Broaddus College *B*
American Public University
　System *A, B, M*
Bethany College *B*
Concord University *B*

Davis and Elkins College *B*
Fairmont State University *B*
Glenville State College *B*
Marshall University *B, M*
Potomac State College of West
　Virginia University *A*
Shepherd University *B*
University of Charleston *B*
West Liberty University *B*
West Virginia State University *B*
West Virginia University *B, M, D*
West Virginia University Institute of
　Technology *B*
West Virginia Wesleyan College *B*
Wheeling Jesuit University *B*

Wisconsin

Alverno College *B*
Beloit College *B*
Cardinal Stritch University *B, M, T*
Carroll University *B*
Carthage College *B*
Concordia University Wisconsin *B, T*
Edgewood College *B*
Lakeland College *B*
Lawrence University *B*
Marian University *B*
Marquette University *B, M, D, T*
Mount Mary College *B, T*
Ripon College *B, T*
St. Norbert College *B, T*
Silver Lake College *B, T*
University of Wisconsin
　Eau Claire *B, M*
　Green Bay *B, T*
　La Crosse *B, T*
　Madison *B, M, D*
　Milwaukee *B, M*
　Oshkosh *B*
　Parkside *B*
　Platteville *B, T*
　River Falls *B*
　Stevens Point *B, M, T*
　Superior *B, T*
　Whitewater *B, T*
Wisconsin Lutheran College *B*

Wyoming

Casper College *A*
Eastern Wyoming College *A*
Laramie County Community
　College *A*
Northwest College *A*
Sheridan College *A*
University of Wyoming *B, M*
Western Wyoming Community
　College *A*

History of science/
technology

California

California Institute of Technology *B*

Connecticut

Yale University *B, M, D*

Georgia

Georgia Institute of
　Technology *B, M, D*

Indiana

Indiana University
　Bloomington *M, D*

Iowa

Iowa State University *M, D*

Maryland

Johns Hopkins University *B, M, D*

Massachusetts

Harvard College *B, M, D*

New York

Cornell University *M, D*
Polytechnic Institute of New York
　University *B, M*

Ohio

Case Western Reserve University *B*

Oklahoma

University of Oklahoma *M, D*

Oregon

Oregon State University *M, D*

Pennsylvania

University of Pennsylvania *B, M, D*
University of Pittsburgh *B, M, D*

Wisconsin

University of Wisconsin
　Madison *B, M, D*

History teacher
education

Alabama

Athens State University *B*
Birmingham-Southern College *T*
Faulkner University *B, M, T*
Huntingdon College *B, T*
Oakwood University *B*
Samford University *B*
Talladega College *B*
University of Mobile *B, T*

Arizona

Cochise College *A*
Northern Arizona University *B, T*
Prescott College *B, T*
University of Arizona *B*

Arkansas

Ouachita Baptist University *B, T*
University of Arkansas
　Fort Smith *B*

California

Azusa Pacific University *T*
California State University
　San Bernardino *T*
Loyola Marymount University *M*
The Master's College *T*
Pacific Union College *T*
San Diego Christian College *B, T*
Stanford University *M, T*
University of the Pacific *T*
Vanguard University of Southern
　California *T*

Colorado

Adams State College *B, M, T*
Colorado Christian University *B*
Colorado State University
　Pueblo *T*
Regis University *B, T*

Connecticut

Albertus Magnus College *B, T*
Fairfield University *T*
Quinnipiac University *B, M*
Sacred Heart University *T*
Saint Joseph College *T*
Southern Connecticut State
　University *B, M, T*
University of New Haven *T*

Delaware

University of Delaware *B, T*

District of Columbia

Catholic University of America *B*

Florida

Baptist College of Florida *B*
Barry University *T*
Palm Beach Atlantic University *B, T*

Georgia

Agnes Scott College *T*
Armstrong Atlantic State
     University *M, T*
Brewton-Parker College *B*
Covenant College *B, T*
Emmanuel College *B*
Macon State College *M, T*
Paine College *B*
Piedmont College *B, M, T*
Shorter College *T*
Toccoa Falls College *B, T*

Idaho

Boise State University *B, T*
Brigham Young University-Idaho *T*
Northwest Nazarene University *B*
University of Idaho *T*

Illinois

Augustana College *B, T*
Blackburn College *T*
Bradley University *B*
Chicago State University *B, T*
Concordia University Chicago *B, T*
DePaul University *M, T*
Dominican University *B*
Elmhurst College *B*
Eureka College *T*
Greenville College *B, T*
Illinois College *T*
Illinois Wesleyan University *B*
John A. Logan College *A*
Lewis University *T*
MacMurray College *B, T*
McKendree University *B*
Monmouth College *T*
North Park University *T*
Olivet Nazarene University *B, T*
Rockford College *T*
Saint Xavier University *B*
Trinity Christian College *B, T*
Trinity International University *B, T*
University of Illinois
     Chicago *B, M*
     Urbana-Champaign *B, M, T*

Indiana

Butler University *T*
Indiana University-Purdue University
     Fort Wayne *B*
Manchester College *B, T*
Oakland City University *B*
University of Indianapolis *B, M, T*
Valparaiso University *B*

Iowa

Briar Cliff University *B*
Buena Vista University *B, T*
Central College *T*
Cornell College *B, T*
Dordt College *B*
Drake University *M, T*
Ellsworth Community College *A*
Graceland University *T*
Grand View University *T*
Iowa State University *T*
Iowa Wesleyan College *B*
Loras College *T*
Morningside College *B*
Mount Mercy College *T*

Northwestern College *T*
St. Ambrose University *B, T*
Simpson College *T*
University of Iowa *T*
Upper Iowa University *B, T*
Waldorf College *B*
Wartburg College *B, T*

Kansas

Bethany College *B*
Bethel College *T*
Central Christian College of
     Kansas *A, B*
Garden City Community College *A*
McPherson College *B, T*
Sterling College *T*
Tabor College *B, T*
University of Kansas *B, T*
University of St. Mary *T*
Washburn University *B*

Kentucky

Campbellsville University *B*

Louisiana

Centenary College of Louisiana *B, T*
University of New Orleans *M*
Xavier University of Louisiana *B*

Maine

Saint Joseph's College of Maine *B*
University of Maine *B*
University of Maine
     Machias *T*
University of Southern Maine *T*

Maryland

College of Notre Dame of Maryland *T*
Hood College *T*
Mount St. Mary's University *T*
Salisbury University *T*

Massachusetts

Anna Maria College *B*
Assumption College *T*
Bridgewater State College *M, T*
Eastern Nazarene College *B*
Elms College *M, T*
Fitchburg State College *B, M, T*
Framingham State College *M*
Lasell College *B, T*
Merrimack College *T*
Salem State College *M*
Tufts University *T*
University of Massachusetts
     Dartmouth *T*
Western New England College *T*
Westfield State College *B, M, T*

Michigan

Albion College *B, T*
Alma College *T*
Andrews University *M*
Calvin College *B*
Central Michigan University *B*
Cornerstone University *B, T*
Eastern Michigan University *B, T*
Ferris State University *B*
Grand Valley State University *M, T*
Hope College *B, T*
Michigan State University *B, M*
Northern Michigan University *B, T*
Rochester College *B*
University of Detroit Mercy *B, M, T*
University of Michigan
     Flint *B, T*
Western Michigan University *B, T*

Minnesota

Bemidji State University *T*
Concordia College: Moorhead *B, T*
Concordia University: St. Paul *B, T*

Crown College *B*
Minnesota State University
     Mankato *B, M, T*
Saint Cloud State University *B, M, T*
University of Minnesota
     Morris *T*
Vermilion Community College *A*
Winona State University *B, T*

Mississippi

Millsaps College *T*

Missouri

College of the Ozarks *B, T*
Culver-Stockton College *T*
Lindenwood University *B*
Maryville University of Saint
     Louis *M, T*
Missouri Baptist University *T*
Missouri Southern State
     University *B, T*
Missouri State University *B*
Northwest Missouri State
     University *M, T*
Truman State University *M, T*
University of Missouri
     Kansas City *B*
Washington University in St.
     Louis *B, M, T*

Montana

Montana State University
     Billings *B, T*
Rocky Mountain College *B, T*
University of Great Falls *B*
University of Montana *T*
University of Montana: Western *B, T*

Nebraska

Chadron State College *B*
Concordia University *B, T*
Creighton University *T*
Dana College *B*
Grace University *B*
Nebraska Wesleyan University *T*
Peru State College *B, T*
Union College *T*
University of Nebraska
     Kearney *B, T*
     Lincoln *B*
Wayne State College *B, T*
York College *B, T*

Nevada

Great Basin College *B*
Nevada State College *B*

New Hampshire

Franklin Pierce University *M, T*
Keene State College *B, M, T*
Rivier College *B, T*
Saint Anselm College *T*

New Jersey

Caldwell College *T*
The College of New Jersey *B, T*
County College of Morris *A*
Rowan University *T*
Saint Peter's College *T*

New York

Bard College *M*
City University of New York
     City College *B, M*
     College of Staten Island *B, T*
     Hunter College *B, T*
College of Mount St. Vincent *T*
D'Youville College *M, T*
Elmira College *B, T*
Fordham University *M, T*
Hobart and William Smith Colleges *T*
Houghton College *B, T*

Ithaca College *B, T*
Manhattan College *B, T*
Molloy College *B*
Nazareth College *B, M, T*
Pace University *B, T*
Roberts Wesleyan College *B, M*
St. John Fisher College *B, M, T*
St. Joseph's College: Suffolk
     Campus *B, T*
St. Lawrence University *T*
St. Thomas Aquinas College *B, T*
State University of New York
     College at Brockport *B, M, T*
     College at Oneonta *B, T*
     College at Plattsburgh *B*
     New Paltz *B, M, T*
     Oswego *B, M*
Vassar College *T*
Wells College *T*

North Carolina

Appalachian State University *B, M, T*
Campbell University *B, T*
Chowan University *B*
East Carolina University *M*
Elizabeth City State University *B*
Elon University *T*
Gardner-Webb University *B*
Greensboro College *B, T*
Lenoir Community College *A*
Lenoir-Rhyne University *B*
Mars Hill College *T*
Meredith College *T*
North Carolina Agricultural and
     Technical State University *B, T*
North Carolina Central
     University *B, M, T*
Queens University of Charlotte *M*
Sandhills Community College *A*
University of North Carolina
     Charlotte *B*
     Wilmington *B*
Wake Forest University *T*

North Dakota

Dickinson State University *B, T*
Jamestown College *B*
Mayville State University *B, T*
Minot State University *B*
North Dakota State University *B, T*
University of Mary *B*

Ohio

Bluffton University *B*
Bowling Green State University *B, M*
Case Western Reserve University *T*
Cedarville University *T*
Defiance College *B, T*
Hiram College *T*
John Carroll University *T*
Kent State University *T*
Mount Union College *T*
Mount Vernon Nazarene
     University *T*
Ohio Northern University *B, T*
Otterbein College *B*
Shawnee State University *B*
Tiffin University *B*
University of Findlay *B, M, T*
University of Rio Grande *B, T*
University of Toledo *M, T*
Wilmington College *B*
Youngstown State University *B, M*

Oklahoma

Cameron University *B*
East Central University *B, T*
Eastern Oklahoma State College *A*
Oklahoma Baptist University *B, T*
Oklahoma City University *B*
Southern Nazarene University *B*
Southwestern Oklahoma State
     University *B, M, T*

University of Central Oklahoma *B*
University of Tulsa *T*

Oregon
Concordia University *B, M, T*
Corban College *B*
Linfield College *T*
Warner Pacific College *T*
Western Oregon University *M, T*

Pennsylvania
Albright College *T*
Arcadia University *M*
Bryn Athyn College of the New
Church *B*
DeSales University *T*
Gettysburg College *T*
Grove City College *B, T*
Holy Family University *B*
King's College *T*
La Salle University *B, T*
Lycoming College *T*
Mansfield University of
Pennsylvania *B, T*
Misericordia University *T*
Moravian College *T*
Rosemont College *T*
St. Francis University *B, T*
St. Vincent College *T*
Susquehanna University *T*
Thiel College *B*
Villanova University *T*
Washington & Jefferson College *T*
Waynesburg University *B, T*
Westminster College *T*
Widener University *T*
Wilkes University *M, T*

Puerto Rico
Inter American University of Puerto
Rico
Metropolitan Campus *B*
San German Campus *B*
Pontifical Catholic University of
Puerto Rico *B, T*
Turabo University *B*
University of Puerto Rico
Arecibo *M*
Cayey University College *B*

Rhode Island
Rhode Island College *B, M*
Salve Regina University *B*

South Carolina
Anderson University *B, T*
Bob Jones University *M*
Coker College *B, T*
Francis Marion University *B, T*

South Dakota
Augustana College *B, T*
Black Hills State University *B*
Mount Marty College *B*
Northern State University *B, T*
University of Sioux Falls *T*
University of South Dakota *B, T*

Tennessee
American Baptist College *B*
Belmont University *B, M, T*
Bethel University *T*
Bryan College *T*
Christian Brothers University *B, M, T*
Crichton College *B, T*
Cumberland University *B, T*
Freed-Hardeman University *B, T*
King College *T*
Lambuth University *B, T*
Lee University *B*
Lincoln Memorial University *B, T*
Lipscomb University *B, T*
Maryville College *B, T*

Southern Adventist University *B*
Tennessee Technological University *T*
Tennessee Temple University *B*
Trevecca Nazarene University *B, T*
Tusculum College *B, T*
Union University *B, T*

Texas
Abilene Christian University *B, T*
Dallas Christian College *B, T*
East Texas Baptist University *B*
Hardin-Simmons University *B, T*
Houston Baptist University *T*
Howard Payne University *B, T*
Jarvis Christian College *B, T*
Kilgore College *A*
Lamar University *T*
Laredo Community College *A*
LeTourneau University *B, T*
Lubbock Christian University *B*
McMurry University *B, T*
St. Edward's University *B, T*
St. Mary's University *T*
Schreiner University *B*
Tarleton State University *T*
Texas A&M International
University *B, T*
Texas A&M University
Commerce *T*
Kingsville *T*
Texas Christian University *B*
Texas College *B, T*
Texas Lutheran University *B, T*
Texas State University: San
Marcos *M, T*
Texas Wesleyan University *B, T*
University of Dallas *T*
University of Houston *T*
University of Houston
Clear Lake *T*
University of Mary Hardin-Baylor *T*
University of Texas
Arlington *T*
San Antonio *T*
West Texas A&M University *T*

Utah
Brigham Young University *B*
Southern Utah University *B, T*
Utah Valley University *B*
Weber State University *B*

Vermont
Castleton State College *B, T*
College of St. Joseph in
Vermont *B, M, T*
Goddard College *B, M*
Johnson State College *B*

Virginia
Averett University *M, T*
Bluefield College *B, T*
Bridgewater College *T*
Hampton University *M*
Hollins University *T*
Liberty University *M, T*
Longwood University *B, T*
Old Dominion University *B, T*
University of Virginia's College at
Wise *T*

Washington
Northwest University *T*
Washington State University *B, M, T*
Western Washington University *B*
Whitworth University *B, T*

West Virginia
Bethany College *B*
Fairmont State University *B*
West Virginia Wesleyan College *B*

Wisconsin
Carroll University *B, T*
Carthage College *T*
Concordia University Wisconsin *B*
Lakeland College *T*
Lawrence University *T*
Maranatha Baptist Bible College *B*
Mount Mary College *B, T*
St. Norbert College *T*
University of Wisconsin
Green Bay *T*
Parkside *T*
Platteville *B*
River Falls *T*
Superior *B*
Whitewater *B*

Holocaust studies

New Jersey
Kean University *M*
Richard Stockton College of New
Jersey *M*

Home furnishings

California
Antelope Valley College *A*

Illinois
Harper College *A*

Michigan
Bay de Noc Community College *C*

Home health attendant

Alabama
Jefferson Davis Community College *C*
Lawson State Community College *C*

Arizona
Coconino County Community
College *C*
Eastern Arizona College *C*
Pima Community College *C*

California
College of the Desert *C*
Copper Mountain College *C*
Palo Verde College *C*
Santa Barbara City College *C*

Florida
Central Florida College *C*
Seminole Community College *C*

Georgia
Albany Technical College *C*

Kansas
Barton County Community College *C*
Cloud County Community College *C*
Coffeyville Community College *C*
Colby Community College *C*
Kansas City Kansas Community
College *C*

Maryland
Anne Arundel Community College *C*

Massachusetts
Cape Cod Community College *C*
Springfield Technical Community
College *C*

Michigan
Baker College
of Flint *C*
Bay de Noc Community College *C*

Minnesota
Anoka Technical College *C*
Itasca Community College *C*
Lake Superior College *C*
Pine Technical College *C*
Ridgewater College *C*

Pennsylvania
Drexel University *C*
Erie Business Center *C*

Virginia
Eastern Shore Community College *C*

Washington
Peninsula College *C, A*

Homeopathic medicine

Minnesota
Minneapolis Community and
Technical College *A*

Vermont
Goddard College *B, M*

Horse husbandry/
equine science

California
Feather River College *C, A*
Los Angeles Pierce College *C, A*
Santa Rosa Junior College *C, A*

Indiana
St. Mary-of-the-Woods College *B*

Iowa
Clinton Community College *C, A*
Scott Community College *C, A*

Kansas
Cloud County Community
College *C, A*
Colby Community College *A*

Maryland
Cecil College *C, A*

Michigan
Michigan State University *C*

Minnesota
Rochester Community and Technical
College *C, A*
University of Minnesota
Crookston *B*

Missouri
Stephens College *B*

New Mexico
Navajo Technical College *C*

New York
Cazenovia College *B*
State University of New York
College of Agriculture and
Technology at Morrisville *A, B*

Ohio
Ohio State University
Agricultural Technical Institute *A*
Tiffin University *B*
Wilmington College *B*

Oklahoma
Oklahoma Panhandle State
University *B*

Oregon
Linn-Benton Community College *A*

Rhode Island
Johnson & Wales University:
Providence *B*

Texas
Weatherford College *C*

Utah
Southern Utah University *A*

Vermont
Vermont Technical College *B*

Wisconsin
University of Wisconsin
River Falls *B*

Horticultural science

Alabama
Auburn University *B, M*

Arizona
Eastern Arizona College *C*

Arkansas
University of Arkansas *M*

California
California Polytechnic State
University: San Luis Obispo *B*
California State University
Fresno *B*
Cosumnes River College *C, A*
Golden West College *C, A*
Los Angeles Pierce College *C, A*
Merritt College *C, A*
Reedley College *C*

Colorado
Colorado State University *B, M, D*

Connecticut
University of Connecticut *B*

Delaware
Delaware Technical and Community
College
Owens *C*

Florida
Florida Southern College *B*
Lake City Community College *C*
South Florida Community College *C*
University of Florida *B, M, D*
Valencia Community College *A*

Georgia
Columbus Technical College *C, A*
Fort Valley State University *A, B*
Valdosta Technical College *C*

Hawaii
University of Hawaii
Hilo *B*

Idaho
University of Idaho *B*

Illinois
Black Hawk College: East Campus *C*
Kishwaukee College *A*
Lake Land College *C*
Richland Community College *A*
University of Illinois
Urbana-Champaign *B, M, D*

Indiana
Purdue University *B, M, D*

Iowa
Northeast Iowa Community
College *A*

Kansas
Kansas State University *B, M, D*

Kentucky
Maysville Community and Technical
College *C*

Maine
University of Maine *C, B, M*

Maryland
Howard Community College *A*

Massachusetts
Cape Cod Community College *C*

Michigan
Michigan State University *C, B, M, D*
St. Clair County Community
College *C, A*

Minnesota
Century Community and Technical
College *A*
Rochester Community and Technical
College *A*
University of Minnesota
Crookston *B*
Twin Cities *M, D*

Mississippi
Mississippi State University *B*

Missouri
College of the Ozarks *B*
Missouri State University *B*
Missouri State University: West
Plains *C, A*
Northwest Missouri State
University *B*
St. Louis Community College
St. Louis Community College at
Meramec *C, A*
Southeast Missouri State University *B*
University of Missouri
Columbia *M, D*

Montana
Montana State University
Bozeman *B*

Nebraska
Nebraska College of Technical
Agriculture *C, A*
Northeast Community College *A*
University of Nebraska
Lincoln *B, M*

New Hampshire
University of New Hampshire *A, B*

New Mexico
New Mexico State University *B, M*

New York
City University of New York
Bronx Community College *A*
Cornell University *B, M, D*
State University of New York
College of Agriculture and
Technology at Morrisville *A, B*
College of Technology at Delhi *A*

North Carolina
Alamance Community College *C, A*
Brunswick Community College *C, A*
Carteret Community College *C, A*
Catawba Valley Community
College *C, A*
North Carolina State
University *B, M, D*
Rockingham Community College *C, A*

North Dakota
North Dakota State University *B, M*

Ohio
Kent State University: Geauga *A*
Ohio State University
Agricultural Technical Institute *A*
Southern State Community College *C*

Oklahoma
Cameron University *B*
Eastern Oklahoma State College *A*
Oklahoma State University *B, M*
Tulsa Community College *A*

Oregon
Central Oregon Community
College *A*
Chemeketa Community College *A*
Linn-Benton Community College *C, A*
Oregon State University *B, M, D*

Pennsylvania
Delaware Valley College *B*
Lehigh Carbon Community College *A*
Penn State
Abington *B*
Altoona *B*
Beaver *B*
Berks *B*
Brandywine *B*
DuBois *B*
Erie, The Behrend College *B*
Fayette, The Eberly Campus *B*
Greater Allegheny *B*
Hazleton *B*
Lehigh Valley *B*
Mont Alto *B*
New Kensington *B*
Schuylkill *B*
Shenango *B*
University Park *B, M, D*
Wilkes-Barre *B*
Worthington Scranton *B*
York *B*
Temple University *B*

South Carolina
Clemson University *B, M*
Trident Technical College *A*

Tennessee
Tennessee Technological University *B*

Texas
Palo Alto College *C, A*
Richland College *A*
Sam Houston State University *B*
Stephen F. Austin State University *B*
Texas A&M University *B, M, D*

Utah
Utah State University *B, M, D*

Vermont
University of Vermont *B*
Vermont Technical College *A*

Virginia
Ferrum College *B*
Germanna Community College *C*

Northern Virginia Community
College *A*
Virginia Polytechnic Institute and
State University *B, M, D*
Virginia Western Community
College *A*

Washington
South Seattle Community
College *C, A*
Washington State University *B, M, D*

West Virginia
Potomac State College of West
Virginia University *A*
West Virginia University *B*

Wisconsin
Blackhawk Technical College *C*
Chippewa Valley Technical College *A*
University of Wisconsin
Madison *B, M, D*
River Falls *B*

Wyoming
Sheridan College *A*

Horticulture

Alabama
Calhoun Community College *C*
Faulkner State Community College *C*
Jefferson Davis Community College *C*
Wallace State Community College at
Hanceville *C*

Arizona
Mesa Community College *A*

Arkansas
Arkansas Northeastern College *C, A*

California
Bakersfield College *A*
Butte College *C, A*
College of San Mateo *C, A*
Diablo Valley College *C*
Fullerton College *A*
Los Angeles Pierce College *C, A*
Merced College *C, A*
Mount San Antonio College *C, A*
San Joaquin Delta College *A*
Santa Barbara City College *C, A*
Shasta College *C*
Sierra College *C, A*

Colorado
Colorado State University *B*
Front Range Community College *C, A*
Northeastern Junior College *C, A*

Connecticut
Naugatuck Valley Community
College *C, A*
University of Connecticut *A*

Delaware
Delaware Technical and Community
College
Owens *A*

Florida
Central Florida Community
College *C, A*

Georgia
Albany Technical College *C*
Augusta Technical College *C*
Central Georgia Technical College *C*
University of Georgia *B, M, D*

Idaho

Brigham Young University-Idaho *B*

Illinois

Black Hawk College *C, A*
Black Hawk College: East
    Campus *C, A*
College of DuPage *C, A*
Harper College *C, A*
Illinois Central College *C, A*
Illinois Eastern Community Colleges
    Lincoln Trail College *C, A*
    Wabash Valley College *A*
John Wood Community College *C, A*
Joliet Junior College *C, A*
Kaskaskia College *C*
Kishwaukee College *C, A*
McHenry County College *C, A*
Rend Lake College *C, A*
Richland Community College *A*
Shawnee Community College *C, A*
Southwestern Illinois College *C, A*
Triton College *C, A*
University of Illinois
    Urbana-Champaign *B, M, D*

Indiana

Oakland City University *A*
Purdue University *B, M, D*
Vincennes University *A*

Iowa

Hawkeye Community College *C, A*
Indian Hills Community College *C*
Iowa State University *B, M, D*
Muscatine Community College *A*

Kansas

Coffeyville Community College *A*
Dodge City Community College *A*

Kentucky

Bluegrass Community and Technical
    College *C*
St. Catharine College *A*

Louisiana

Delgado Community College *C, A*

Maine

Southern Maine Community
    College *A*

Maryland

Cecil College *C*
Community College of Baltimore
    County *C, A*
Harford Community College *A*

Massachusetts

Cape Cod Community College *C*
North Shore Community College *A*
University of Massachusetts
    Amherst *A*

Michigan

Andrews University *B*
Michigan State University *C*

Minnesota

Anoka Technical College *C, A*
Central Lakes College *C, A*
Century Community and Technical
    College *C*

Mississippi

Meridian Community College *A*
Mississippi Delta Community
    College *A*
Northwest Mississippi Community
    College *A*

Missouri

College of the Ozarks *B*
Mineral Area College *C, A*
State Fair Community College *A*

Nebraska

Central Community College *C, A*
Metropolitan Community
    College *C, A*
Nebraska College of Technical
    Agriculture *A*
Nebraska Indian Community
    College *C*
Northeast Community College *A*

New Hampshire

University of New Hampshire *A*

New Jersey

Bergen Community College *A*
Ocean County College *A*
Thomas Edison State College *A, B*

New York

Paul Smith's College *A*
State University of New York
    College of Agriculture and
        Technology at Morrisville *A*
    College of Technology at Delhi *A*
    Farmingdale *B*

North Carolina

Alamance Community College *C, A*
Blue Ridge Community College *A*
Carteret Community College *C, A*
Central Piedmont Community
    College *C, A*
Fayetteville Technical Community
    College *C, A*
Forsyth Technical Community
    College *A*
Haywood Community College *C, A*
Johnston Community College *C*
Lenoir Community College *C, A*
Mayland Community College *C, A*
Sampson Community College *A*
Surry Community College *A*
Western Piedmont Community
    College *C, A*
Wilkes Community College *C, A*

Ohio

Clark State Community College *A*
Cuyahoga Community College
    Metropolitan Campus *A*
Kent State University
    Salem *A*
Ohio State University
    Agricultural Technical Institute *A*
    Columbus Campus *M, D*

Oklahoma

Eastern Oklahoma State College *A*
Oklahoma State University
    Oklahoma City *C, A*

Oregon

Clackamas Community College *A*

Pennsylvania

Community College of Allegheny
    County *A*
Luzerne County Community
    College *C*
Pennsylvania College of
    Technology *A*
Temple University *C, A*
Westmoreland County Community
    College *C, A*
Williamson Free School of Mechanical
    Trades *A*

Puerto Rico

University of Puerto Rico
    Utuado *A*

South Carolina

Clemson University *B*
Horry-Georgetown Technical
    College *A*
Spartanburg Community College *A*
Technical College of the
    Lowcountry *C, A*
Trident Technical College *C, A*

South Dakota

Mount Marty College *A*
South Dakota State University *B*
Southeast Technical Institute *A*

Tennessee

Southwest Tennessee Community
    College *C, A*
Tennessee Technological University *B*

Texas

Central Texas College *C*
Houston Community College
    System *A*
Richland College *C, A*
Stephen F. Austin State University *B*
Tarrant County College *C, A*
Texas A&M University *B, M, D*
Texas Tech University *B, M*
Trinity Valley Community
    College *C, A*
Western Texas College *C, A*

Vermont

Vermont Technical College *A*

Virginia

J. Sargeant Reynolds Community
    College *A*
Tidewater Community College *A*
Virginia Western Community
    College *A*

Washington

Clark College *A*
Lake Washington Technical
    College *C, A*
Skagit Valley College *A*
South Puget Sound Community
    College *C, A*
Spokane Community College *A*

Wisconsin

Fox Valley Technical College *A*
Gateway Technical College *A*
Northeast Wisconsin Technical
    College *C*
University of Wisconsin
    River Falls *B*

Hospital/health care facilities administration

Alabama

University of Alabama *B*

Arizona

University of Phoenix *B*

California

Loma Linda University *M*

Colorado

Jones International University *M*

Connecticut

Quinnipiac University *M*

Florida

Nova Southeastern University *M*
Saint Leo University *B*

Georgia

Clayton State University *B*

Iowa

Upper Iowa University *B*

Kansas

University of Kansas Medical
    Center *M, D*

Louisiana

Our Lady of the Lake College *B*

Maine

Husson University *M*

Massachusetts

Elms College *B*

Missouri

Avila University *B*
Missouri State University *M*
Saint Louis University *M, D*
Washington University in St. Louis *M*

New Jersey

Thomas Edison State College *B*
University of Medicine and Dentistry
    of New Jersey
    School of Health Related
        Professions *D*

New York

City University of New York
    Lehman College *B*
Globe Institute of Technology *B*
Ithaca College *B*
Long Island University
    Brooklyn Campus *M*
    C. W. Post Campus *B, M*
Mercy College *M*
New York University *M*
Pace University *M*
St. Joseph's College: Suffolk
    Campus *B*
State University of New York
    College of Technology at Canton *B*
University of Rochester *M*
Utica College *B*

North Carolina

Methodist University *B*

Ohio

University of Toledo *B*
Ursuline College *B*
Youngstown State University *B, M*

Oklahoma

Northeastern State University *B*

Pennsylvania

Arcadia University *B*
Saint Joseph's University *B, M*
Temple University *M*

South Dakota

Black Hills State University *B*
National American University
    Rapid City *B*

Tennessee

University of Memphis *M*
University of Tennessee
    Knoxville *M*

Texas

University of Houston
    Clear Lake *M*
University of North Texas *M*

Utah

University of Utah *M*

Wisconsin

Herzing University *B*
Marquette University *M*
University of Wisconsin
    Milwaukee *B*

Hospitality administration and management

Alabama

Columbia Southern University *B, M*
Faulkner State Community
    College *C, A*
Jefferson State Community
    College *C, A*
Tuskegee University *B*

Alaska

University of Alaska
    Anchorage *B*

Arizona

Arizona Western College *A*
Cochise College *C, A*
Coconino County Community
    College *C, A*
Northern Arizona University *C, B*
Penn Foster College *A*
Pima Community College *C, A*
Scottsdale Community College *C, A*
University of Phoenix *A, B*

Arkansas

Arkansas State University
    Beebe *C, A*
Arkansas Tech University *B*
East Arkansas Community College *C*
National Park Community
    College *C, A*
Northwest Arkansas Community
    College *C*
Pulaski Technical College *A*
University of Arkansas
    Monticello *C*

California

California State Polytechnic
    University: Pomona *B*
Chaffey College *C*
College of the Canyons *A*
College of the Redwoods *C, A*
Columbia College *C, A*
Diablo Valley College *C*
Empire College *C*
Grossmont College *C, A*
Heald College
    Rancho Cordova *C, A*
MiraCosta College *C, A*
Monterey Peninsula College *A*
National University *C, A, B, M*
Orange Coast College *C*
San Diego State University *B*
San Francisco State University *B*
San Jose State University *B*
Santa Rosa Junior College *C*
Skyline College *C, A*
West Hills College: Lemoore *C*

Colorado

Arapahoe Community College *A*
Colorado Mountain College *A*
Front Range Community College *C, A*

Johnson & Wales University:
    Denver *B*
Metropolitan State College of
    Denver *B*
University of Denver *B*
Westwood College: Denver North *A*

Connecticut

Lincoln College of New England:
    Suffield *C, A*
Mitchell College *B*
Northwestern Connecticut
    Community College *A*
Norwalk Community College *A*
Three Rivers Community College *C, A*
University of New Haven *B*

Delaware

Delaware State University *B*

District of Columbia

Howard University *B*

Florida

Broward College *A*
Daytona State College *A*
Edison State College *A*
Florida Atlantic University *B*
Florida International University *B, M*
Florida National College *A*
Florida State College at Jacksonville *A*
Florida State University *B*
Gulf Coast Community College *A*
Hillsborough Community College *A*
Indian River State College *A*
Johnson & Wales University: North
    Miami *B*
Lynn University *B, M*
Palm Beach Community College *A*
Saint Leo University *B*
St. Petersburg College *A*
Saint Thomas University *B*
South Florida Community College *A*
University of Central Florida *B, M*
University of South Florida *B*
University of West Florida *B*
Valencia Community College *C, A*
Webber International University *A, B*

Georgia

Abraham Baldwin Agricultural
    College *A*
Albany Technical College *C*
Savannah Technical College *C*
Young Harris College *A*

Hawaii

Heald College
    Honolulu *A*
University of Hawaii
    Kauai Community College *C, A*

Idaho

Lewis-Clark State College *C, A, B*

Illinois

City Colleges of Chicago
    Harold Washington College *C, A*
DePaul University *B*
Elgin Community College *C*
Fox College *A*
Harper College *A*
Kendall College *B*
Lincoln Land Community College *A*
MacCormac College *C, A*
Moraine Valley Community
    College *C, A*
Northwestern College *A*
Richland Community College *C, A*
Roosevelt University *C, B, M*
Southern Illinois University
    Carbondale *B*

Southwestern Illinois College *C, A*
Triton College *C, A*
University of Illinois
    Urbana-Champaign *B*

Indiana

Indiana University-Purdue University
    Fort Wayne *B*
International Business College *C, A*
Ivy Tech Community College
    Bloomington *C, A*
    Central Indiana *A*
    East Central *C, A*
    North Central *A*
    Northeast *C, A*
    Northwest *C, A*
    Southwest *C, A*
Purdue University *B, M, D*
Vincennes University *C, A*

Iowa

Des Moines Area Community
    College *C, A*
Grand View University *B*
Iowa State University *B*
North Iowa Area Community
    College *A*
Scott Community College *A*

Kansas

Butler Community College *A*
Colby Community College *C*
Seward County Community
    College *C, A*

Kentucky

University of Kentucky *B*
Western Kentucky University *A, B*

Louisiana

Delgado Community College *A*
Northwestern State University *B*
Southern University
    Shreveport *C*
University of Louisiana at Lafayette *B*
University of New Orleans *B, M*

Maine

Andover College *C, A*
Central Maine Community College *A*
Husson University *B*
Thomas College *B*
University of Maine
    Machias *B*

Maryland

Allegany College of Maryland *A*
Baltimore City Community College *A*
Baltimore International College *M*
College of Southern Maryland *A*
Frederick Community College *C, A*
Montgomery College *C, A*
Morgan State University *B*
Sojourner-Douglass College *B*
University of Maryland
    Eastern Shore *B*
Wor-Wic Community College *C, A*

Massachusetts

Bay State College *B*
Becker College *B*
Berkshire Community College *A*
Boston University *B*
Bunker Hill Community College *A*
Endicott College *B*
Fisher College *A, B*
Holyoke Community College *C, A*
Lasell College *B*
Marian Court College *C, A*
Massachusetts Bay Community
    College *C, A*
Massasoit Community College *A*

Middlesex Community College *C, A*
Mount Ida College *B*
Newbury College *B*
North Shore Community College *A*
Quinsigamond Community College *C*
Salem State College *B*
University of Massachusetts
    Amherst *B, M*

Michigan

Baker College
    of Clinton Township *A*
Bay de Noc Community College *C, A*
Central Michigan University *B*
Eastern Michigan University *B, M*
Ferris State University *B*
Henry Ford Community College *A*
Lake Michigan College *C, A*
Madonna University *B*
Michigan State University *B, M*
Northern Michigan University *B*

Minnesota

Alexandria Technical College *C, A*
Art Institutes International
    Minnesota *B*
Central Lakes College *C*
Metropolitan State University *B*
Minneapolis Business College *A*
National American University
    Bloomington *B*
Normandale Community College *C, A*
St. Paul College *C, A*
Southwest Minnesota State
    University *B*
University of Minnesota
    Crookston *B*

Mississippi

Copiah-Lincoln Community College *A*
Delta State University *B*
University of Mississippi *B*

Missouri

College of the Ozarks *B*
Harris-Stowe State University *B*
Lindenwood University *B, M*
Missouri State University *B*
Ozarks Technical Community
    College *A*
Patricia Stevens College *A*

Montana

Blackfeet Community College *C, A*

Nebraska

University of Nebraska
    Lincoln *B*

Nevada

College of Southern Nevada *A*
Sierra Nevada College *B*
University of Nevada
    Las Vegas *B, M, D*
    Reno *B*

New Hampshire

NHTI-Concord's Community
    College *A*
Southern New Hampshire
    University *B, M*
University of New Hampshire *B*

New Jersey

Bergen Community College *C*
Essex County College *A*
Fairleigh Dickinson University
    College at Florham *B, M*
    Metropolitan Campus *B, M*
Georgian Court University *B*
Gloucester County College *C, A*

Hudson County Community
College C, A
Richard Stockton College of New
Jersey B
Rutgers, The State University of New
Jersey
Camden Regional Campus B
Thomas Edison State College B
Union County College A

New Mexico

Central New Mexico Community
College C, A
Dona Ana Community College of New
Mexico State University A
New Mexico State University B
Southwestern Indian Polytechnic
Institute A

New York

City University of New York
New York City College of
Technology A, B
Excelsior College B
Globe Institute of Technology C, A, B
Monroe College A, B
Niagara County Community
College C, A
Niagara University B
Paul Smith's College A, B
Rochester Institute of
Technology A, B, M
Rockland Community College A
St. John's University B
State University of New York
College at Buffalo B
College of Agriculture and
Technology at Morrisville B

North Carolina

Appalachian State University B
Cape Fear Community College A
Central Piedmont Community
College C, A
Methodist University B, M
North Carolina Central University B
University of North Carolina
Greensboro B
Western Carolina University B

North Dakota

Jamestown College B
North Dakota State University B

Ohio

Ashland University C
Bowling Green State University B
Columbus State Community
College C, A
Cuyahoga Community College
Metropolitan Campus A
Kent State University: Geauga C
Ohio State University
Columbus Campus B
Lima Campus B
Stark State College of Technology A
Tiffin University B
University of Akron C, A
University of Findlay B
Youngstown State University A, B

Oklahoma

Oklahoma State University B, M
Tulsa Community College A

Oregon

Chemeketa Community College C, A
Clackamas Community College C
Mt. Hood Community College C, A
Southern Oregon University B

Pennsylvania

Bucks County Community
College C, A
Cheyney University of Pennsylvania B
East Stroudsburg University of
Pennsylvania B
Harrisburg Area Community
College A
Indiana University of Pennsylvania B
Marywood University B
Mercyhurst College A, B
Newport Business Institute: Lower
Burrell A
Northampton Community College C
Penn State
Abington B
Altoona B
Beaver B
Berks B
Brandywine B
DuBois B
Erie, The Behrend College B
Fayette, The Eberly Campus B
Greater Allegheny B
Hazleton B
Lehigh Valley B
Mont Alto B
New Kensington B
Schuylkill B
Shenango B
University Park A, B, M, D
Wilkes-Barre B
Worthington Scranton B
York B
Robert Morris University B
Rosemont College B
Seton Hill University B
Temple University B, M
University of Pittsburgh
Bradford B
Widener University B, M, D
YTI Career Institute: York A

Rhode Island

Community College of Rhode
Island C
Johnson & Wales University:
Providence B

South Carolina

College of Charleston B
Spartanburg Community College A
Technical College of the
Lowcountry C
Trident Technical College C, A
University of South Carolina B, M
University of South Carolina
Beaufort B

South Dakota

Sisseton Wahpeton College C, A
University of Sioux Falls B

Tennessee

Belmont University B
National College: Madison A

Texas

Austin Community College C, A
Central Texas College C, A
Collin County Community College
District C, A
Galveston College C
Lamar State College at Port Arthur C
Lone Star College System C, A
St. Philip's College A
Stephen F. Austin State University B
Texas Tech University D
University of North Texas B, M
Westwood College: Fort Worth A

Utah

Southern Utah University B

Utah Valley University A, B

Vermont

Champlain College B
Green Mountain College B
Johnson State College B

Virginia

J. Sargeant Reynolds Community
College A
James Madison University B
Norfolk State University B
Stratford University: Woodbridge A
Tidewater Community College A
Virginia Polytechnic Institute and
State University B, M, D
Virginia State University B

Washington

South Puget Sound Community
College C, A
South Seattle Community
College A, B
Washington State University B, D

West Virginia

American Public University
System A, B
Concord University B
Davis and Elkins College A, B
New River Community and Technical
College A
Southern West Virginia Community
and Technical College A
West Virginia Northern Community
College A

Wisconsin

Fox Valley Technical College A
University of Wisconsin
Stout B, M
Waukesha County Technical
College A

Wyoming

Casper College A
Sheridan College C, A

Hospitality/recreation marketing

Alaska

University of Alaska
Anchorage B

Arizona

Central Arizona College A
Northland Pioneer College C

Arkansas

National Park Community
College C, A

California

Alliant International University B
American River College A
City College of San Francisco A
Cypress College C, A
Glendale Community College A
Los Angeles Trade and Technical
College A
Los Angeles Valley College A
Monterey Peninsula College A
Orange Coast College C, A
Pasadena City College A
Santa Barbara City College C, A

Colorado

Community College of Aurora C
Metropolitan State College of
Denver B

Pueblo Community College C, A
Westwood College: Denver North A

Connecticut

Manchester Community College C, A

District of Columbia

Howard University B

Florida

City College: Fort Lauderdale A
Pensacola Junior College A
Valencia Community College C

Hawaii

University of Hawaii
Kapiolani Community College C, A

Illinois

Harper College C, A

Kansas

Butler Community College C, A

Maine

Andover College C, A
Husson University B
University of Maine
Machias B

Maryland

Allegany College of Maryland A

Massachusetts

Bay State College A, B
Roxbury Community College A

Michigan

Ferris State University B
Lansing Community College A
Siena Heights University A, B

Minnesota

Art Institutes International
Minnesota B

Mississippi

Northwest Mississippi Community
College A

Nevada

College of Southern Nevada A

New Hampshire

Lakes Region Community
College C, A
NHTI-Concord's Community
College C, A

New Jersey

Cumberland County College A

New York

Adirondack Community College A
Finger Lakes Community College A
Paul Smith's College B
Rochester Institute of Technology M
State University of New York
College at Buffalo B

North Carolina

Methodist University B
Wake Technical Community
College A

Ohio

Columbus State Community
College C, A
Ohio State University
Columbus Campus B

University of Findlay *B*
Youngstown State University *A, B*

Oklahoma
Oklahoma State University
  Institute of Technology:
    Okmulgee *A*
Tulsa Community College *A*

Oregon
Central Oregon Community
  College *A*

Pennsylvania
Montgomery County Community
  College *A*
Newport Business Institute: Lower
  Burrell *A*

South Carolina
Technical College of the
  Lowcountry *C, A*

South Dakota
Sinte Gleska University *B*

Texas
Central Texas College *C*
El Paso Community College *C, A*
San Jacinto College *A*

Utah
Provo College *A*

Vermont
Champlain College *B*
Green Mountain College *B*

Washington
Highline Community College *A*
Lake Washington Technical
  College *C, A*
Skagit Valley College *A*

West Virginia
Concord University *B*
Mountain State College *A*

Wisconsin
Chippewa Valley Technical College *A*
Fox Valley Technical College *A*
Northeast Wisconsin Technical
  College *A*

Hotel/motel administration/ management

Arizona
Arizona Western College *C*
Estrella Mountain Community
  College *C, A*
Northern Arizona University *B*

Arkansas
East Arkansas Community College *C*

California
College of the Canyons *A, T*
College of the Desert *A*
Long Beach City College *C, A*
Orange Coast College *A*
Oxnard College *C, A*
San Diego Mesa College *C, A*
Shasta College *A*
University of San Francisco *B*
West Hills College: Lemoore *C*

Colorado
Colorado Mountain College *A*

Johnson & Wales University:
  Denver *B*

Connecticut
Gateway Community College *A*
Mitchell College *B*
University of New Haven *C, A, B*

Delaware
Delaware Technical and Community
  College
    Stanton/Wilmington *C, A*
    Terry *A*

Florida
Bethune-Cookman University *B*
Johnson & Wales University: North
  Miami *B*
Northwood University
  Florida *B*
St. Petersburg College *C*
Schiller International
  University *A, B, M*

Georgia
Georgia Southern University *B*

Illinois
Elgin Community College *C, A*
Harper College *C*
Lexington College *A, B*
Lincoln Land Community College *C*
Parkland College *C, A*
Triton College *C, A*

Indiana
Indiana University-Purdue University
  Indianapolis *C*
Purdue University *B, M, D*
Vincennes University *A*

Iowa
Iowa Lakes Community College *C, A*

Louisiana
Grambling State University *B*

Maine
Husson University *B*
Southern Maine Community
  College *A*

Maryland
Anne Arundel Community
  College *C, A*
Community College of Baltimore
  County *A*
Montgomery College *A*
University of Maryland
  Eastern Shore *B*

Massachusetts
Bay State College *B*
Cape Cod Community College *C, A*
Lasell College *B*
North Shore Community College *A*
Quinsigamond Community
  College *C, A*

Michigan
Bay de Noc Community College *C*
Central Michigan University *B*
Ferris State University *C, B*
Henry Ford Community College *C*
Northwood University: Michigan *A, B*
Oakland Community College *A*
Wayne County Community College *C*

Minnesota
Art Institutes International
  Minnesota *B*

Normandale Community College *C*
University of Minnesota
  Crookston *C, B*

Mississippi
University of Southern Mississippi *B*

Missouri
Ozarks Technical Community
  College *A*
University of Central Missouri *B*
University of Missouri
  Columbia *B, M*

New Jersey
Atlantic Cape Community College *A*
Bergen Community College *A*

New York
Broome Community College *A*
Bryant & Stratton Business Institute
  Bryant & Stratton College:
    Syracuse *A*
Cornell University *B, M, D*
Finger Lakes Community College *A*
Globe Institute of Technology *C, A, B*
Mohawk Valley Community
  College *C, A*
Monroe College *A*
New York Institute of Technology *B*
New York University *C, B, M*
Niagara University *B*
Onondaga Community College *A*
Pace University *B*
Paul Smith's College *A, B*
Rochester Institute of
  Technology *A, B, M*
State University of New York
  College at Plattsburgh *B*
  College of Agriculture and
    Technology at Cobleskill *A*
Tompkins Cortland Community
  College *A*

North Carolina
Cape Fear Community College *C, A*
Carteret Community College *C, A*
East Carolina University *B*
Fayetteville Technical Community
  College *C, A*
Johnson & Wales University:
  Charlotte *B*
Nash Community College *A*
Sandhills Community College *A*
Southwestern Community College *C*

Ohio
Cincinnati State Technical and
  Community College *A*
Hocking College *C, A*
University of Akron *C, A, B*

Oregon
Lane Community College *C, A*

Pennsylvania
Bucks County Community
  College *C, A*
Central Pennsylvania College *A*
Drexel University *B*
Erie Business Center *C*
Harrisburg Area Community
  College *A*
Luzerne County Community
  College *C, A*
Newport Business Institute: Lower
  Burrell *A*
Northampton Community College *A*
Restaurant School at Walnut Hill
  College *A, B*
Westmoreland County Community
  College *C, A*

Puerto Rico
Inter American University of Puerto
  Rico
    Aguadilla Campus *B*
    Ponce Campus *B*
    San German Campus *C*
Universidad del Este *C, A, B*
University of Puerto Rico
  Aguadilla *T*
  Carolina Regional College *A, B*

Rhode Island
Johnson & Wales University:
  Providence *B*

South Carolina
Horry-Georgetown Technical
  College *A*
Spartanburg Community College *A*
Trident Technical College *A*

South Dakota
South Dakota State University *B*

Tennessee
Southwest Tennessee Community
  College *A*
University of Memphis *B*
University of Tennessee
  Knoxville *B*

Texas
Del Mar College *C, A*
Houston Community College
  System *C, A*
Texas Tech University *B, M*

Vermont
Champlain College *B*

West Virginia
Concord University *B*

Wisconsin
Gateway Technical College *A*
Milwaukee Area Technical College *A*

Wyoming
Central Wyoming College *C, A*

Housing and human environments

Arkansas
Harding University *B*
University of Arkansas *B*

California
Allan Hancock College *C, A*
California State University
  Northridge *B*

Florida
Northwest Florida State College *A*

Georgia
University of Georgia *B, M, D*

Illinois
Olivet Nazarene University *B*

Iowa
Iowa State University *B*

Kentucky
Eastern Kentucky University *B*

Minnesota

Minnesota State University
Mankato *B, M, T*
University of Minnesota
Twin Cities *B*

Missouri

Missouri State University *B*
University of Missouri
Columbia *B, M*

Nebraska

University of Nebraska
Kearney *B*
Lincoln *B*

New York

Cornell University *M, D*

Ohio

Ohio University *B*
University of Akron *B*

Oklahoma

Oklahoma State University *B, M*

Oregon

Oregon State University *B*

Tennessee

Tennessee Technological University *B*
University of Tennessee
Knoxville *M*

Texas

Texas Tech University *M*

Utah

Utah State University *B*

Human development and family studies

Alabama

Auburn University *B, M, D*
Oakwood University *B*
Samford University *B*
University of Alabama *B*

Arizona

Central Arizona College *C, A*
Cochise College *A*
Prescott College *B*
University of Arizona *B*

Arkansas

University of Arkansas *B*

California

Azusa Pacific University *M*
California State University
Northridge *B, M*
San Bernardino *B*
San Marcos *B*
City College of San Francisco *C*
College of the Siskiyous *C, A*
Folsom Lake College *C, A*
Fullerton College *A*
Hope International University *B*
Loyola Marymount University *M*
Merced College *A*
Moorpark College *A*
Pacific Oaks College *B, M*
San Diego Christian College *B*
San Diego Miramar College *A*
Shasta College *A*
Solano Community College *C*
Sonoma State University *B*

University of California
Davis *B, M, D*
San Diego *B*
University of La Verne *M*
Vanguard University of Southern
California *B*

Colorado

Colorado State University *B, M, D*

Connecticut

Connecticut College *B*
Mitchell College *B, T*
Three Rivers Community College *C, A*
University of Connecticut *B, M*

Delaware

University of Delaware *B*

District of Columbia

University of the District of
Columbia *B*

Florida

Florida State University *B, M*
University of Florida *M, D*

Georgia

Fort Valley State University *B*
Georgia Military College *A*
Georgia Southern University *B*
Middle Georgia College *A*

Hawaii

Hawaii Pacific University *B*

Idaho

University of Idaho *B*

Illinois

City Colleges of Chicago
Harold Washington College *A*
North Park University *B*
Northern Illinois University *B, M*
University of Illinois
Urbana-Champaign *B, M, D*

Indiana

Indiana State University *B*
Purdue University *B, M, D*

Iowa

Iowa State University *M, D*

Kansas

Friends University *M*
Kansas State University *C, B, M*

Kentucky

Eastern Kentucky University *B*
Kentucky State University *B*
University of Kentucky *M*

Louisiana

Louisiana Tech University *B*
Southern University
New Orleans *B*
University of Louisiana at Lafayette *B*

Maine

University of Maine *M*

Maryland

University of Maryland
University College *C*

Massachusetts

Hellenic College/Holy Cross *B*
Lesley University *B*
Springfield College *M*

Wheelock College *B*

Michigan

Andrews University *B*
Central Michigan University *M*
Kalamazoo College *B*
Kalamazoo Valley Community
College *C, A*
Kellogg Community College *C*
Michigan State University *M, D*
Spring Arbor University *B, M*

Minnesota

Concordia University: St. Paul *C, B, M*
Crown College *T*
Minnesota State University
Mankato *B, M, T*
Ridgewater College *A*
St. Mary's University of Minnesota *M*
University of Minnesota
Twin Cities *B*

Mississippi

University of Southern Mississippi *B*

Missouri

Missouri Baptist University *B*
Missouri State University *B*
Northwest Missouri State
University *B*
Stephens College *B*
University of Central Missouri *B*
University of Missouri
Columbia *B, M*

Nebraska

University of Nebraska
Kearney *B*
Lincoln *M, D*

Nevada

University of Nevada
Reno *B, M*

New Hampshire

University of New Hampshire *B, M, D*

New Jersey

Seton Hall University *M, D*

New Mexico

New Mexico State University *B*
University of New Mexico *B*

New York

Cornell University *B, M, D*
Mercy College *M*
New York Institute of Technology *M*
Nyack College *M*
State University of New York
College at Oneonta *B*
College at Plattsburgh *B*
Syracuse University *A, B, M, D*

North Carolina

Campbell University *B*
North Carolina Agricultural and
Technical State University *B*
University of North Carolina
Charlotte *B*
Greensboro *B, M, D*

North Dakota

North Dakota State University *B, M*

Ohio

Bowling Green State University *B, M*
Kent State University *B, M*
Miami University
Oxford Campus *B, M*

Northwest State Community
College *A*
Ohio State University
Columbus Campus *B, M, D*
Ohio University *B, M*
University of Dayton *M*
Youngstown State University *B*

Oklahoma

Langston University *B*
Oklahoma Christian University *B*
Oklahoma State University *B, M*
University of Central Oklahoma *M*

Oregon

Clackamas Community College *C*
Oregon State University *B, M, D*
Portland State University *B*
Southwestern Oregon Community
College *A*
Warner Pacific College *B*

Pennsylvania

Indiana University of Pennsylvania *B*
Penn State
Abington *A, B*
Altoona *A, B*
Beaver *A, B*
Berks *A, B*
Brandywine *A, B*
DuBois *A, B*
Erie, The Behrend College *A, B*
Fayette, The Eberly Campus *A, B*
Greater Allegheny *A, B*
Harrisburg *B*
Hazleton *A, B*
Lehigh Valley *A, B*
Mont Alto *A, B*
New Kensington *A, B*
Schuylkill *A, B*
Shenango *A, B*
University Park *A, B, M, D*
Wilkes-Barre *A, B*
Worthington Scranton *A, B*
York *A, B*
Waynesburg University *B*

Rhode Island

University of Rhode Island *B, M, T*

South Carolina

Benedict College *B*
Columbia College *B*
South Carolina State University *M*

South Dakota

South Dakota State University *B*

Tennessee

East Tennessee State University *B, T*
Freed-Hardeman University *B*
Lee University *B*
Northeast State Community
College *C, A*
Tennessee State University *B*
University of Tennessee
Knoxville *B, M*

Texas

Abilene Christian University *B*
Baylor University *B*
El Paso Community College *A*
Galveston College *A*
Lubbock Christian University *M*
Stephen F. Austin State University *B*
Texas A&M University
Kingsville *B*
Texas State University: San
Marcos *B*
Texas Tech University *B, M, D*
Texas Woman's University *B, M, D*
University of Houston *B*

University of North Texas *B, M*
University of Texas
    Austin *B, M, D*
    of the Permian Basin *B*

Utah
Brigham Young University *B*
Salt Lake Community College *A*
University of Utah *B*
Utah State University *B, M, D*
Weber State University *B*

Vermont
University of Vermont *B*

Virginia
Virginia Polytechnic Institute and
    State University *B, M, D*

Washington
Washington State University *B, M*

West Virginia
American Public University System *B*

Wisconsin
Moraine Park Technical College *C, A*
University of Wisconsin
    Madison *B*
    Stout *B*

Human/medical genetics

Alabama
University of Alabama
    Birmingham *D*

California
University of California
    Los Angeles *M, D*

Florida
University of Miami *M, D*

Louisiana
Louisiana State University Health
    Sciences Center *M, D*

Michigan
University of Michigan *M, D*

New York
Sarah Lawrence College *M*
State University of New York
    College at Fredonia *B*

North Carolina
University of North Carolina
    Greensboro *M*

Ohio
Case Western Reserve University *D*

Pennsylvania
Arcadia University *M*

South Carolina
Clemson University *D*
University of South Carolina *M*

Tennessee
Vanderbilt University *D*

Texas
University of Texas
    Southwestern Medical Center at
        Dallas *M, D*

Utah
University of Utah *M, D*

Virginia
Virginia Commonwealth
    University *M, D*

Wisconsin
University of Wisconsin
    Madison *M*

Human nutrition

California
City College of San Francisco *A*
College of the Desert *A*
University of California
    Davis *M*

Colorado
Colorado State University *B*

Connecticut
University of Bridgeport *M*

District of Columbia
Howard University *M, D*

Illinois
University of Illinois
    Urbana-Champaign *B, M, D*

Iowa
Iowa State University *B, M, D*

Kansas
Kansas State University *B, M, D*

Kentucky
Murray State University *M*

Massachusetts
University of Massachusetts
    Amherst *B*

Michigan
Central Michigan University *M*
Michigan State University *M, D*

Missouri
University of Missouri
    Columbia *B, M*

New York
Rochester Institute of Technology *B*
Russell Sage College *B*

North Carolina
Meredith College *M*

Ohio
Case Western Reserve
    University *B, M, D*

Pennsylvania
Mansfield University of
    Pennsylvania *A*
Penn State
    Abington *B*
    Altoona *B*
    Beaver *B*
    Berks *B*
    Brandywine *B*
    DuBois *B*
    Erie, The Behrend College *B*
    Fayette, The Eberly Campus *B*
    Greater Allegheny *B*
    Hazleton *B*
    Lehigh Valley *B*
    Mont Alto *B*

New Kensington *B*
    Schuylkill *B*
    Shenango *B*
    University Park *B, M, D*
    Wilkes-Barre *B*
    Worthington Scranton *B*
    York *B*

Tennessee
University of Memphis *M*

Texas
Baylor University *B*
Texas State University: San Marcos *M*

Utah
Southern Utah University *B*

Washington
Washington State University *B, M*

Wisconsin
University of Wisconsin
    Stout *M*

Human resources development

Alabama
Samford University *B*

Arizona
Northcentral University *M, D*

California
University of San Francisco *M*

Colorado
Colorado Technical University *C*

Florida
Barry University *M*

Georgia
Gwinnett Technical College *C*
Oglethorpe University *B*
West Georgia Technical College *C*

Illinois
Roosevelt University *M*
Trinity International University *B*
University of Illinois
    Urbana-Champaign *M, D*

Indiana
DeVry University: Indianapolis *M*

Kansas
Central Christian College of Kansas *A*
Southwestern College *B*

Maryland
Bowie State University *M*
McDaniel College *M*

Massachusetts
Dean College *C*
Fisher College *B*
Lasell College *M*
Nichols College *B*

Michigan
Andrews University *B*
Northern Michigan University *M*
Oakland University *B, M*
Western Michigan University *M*

Minnesota
Academy College *A*

Alexandria Technical College *C*
Dakota County Technical College *C*
DeVry University
    Edina *M*
Lake Superior College *C*
Rochester Community and Technical
    College *C*
St. Cloud Technical College *C*
Walden University *B*

Mississippi
University of Southern Mississippi *D*

Missouri
Webster University *M*

Montana
Montana State University
    Billings *A*

Nebraska
University of Nebraska
    Omaha *C*

New Jersey
Seton Hall University *M*

New York
Niagara University *B*
St. John Fisher College *M*

North Carolina
Pitt Community College *C, A*

Oklahoma
University of Oklahoma *C*

Pennsylvania
Central Pennsylvania College *C*

Puerto Rico
Inter American University of Puerto
    Rico
    Ponce Campus *B*

South Carolina
Converse College *B*
Limestone College *B*

Tennessee
Vanderbilt University *M*

Texas
Brookhaven College *C*
Concordia University Texas *B*
Midwestern State University *M*
University of Dallas *B*
University of North Texas *M, D*
University of Texas
    Tyler *B, M, D*

Washington
DeVry University
    Federal Way *M*

Wisconsin
Blackhawk Technical College *A*
Fox Valley Technical College *A*
Northcentral Technical College *C*
University of Wisconsin
    Milwaukee *B*
    Stout *M*

Human resources management

Alabama
Athens State University *B*
Auburn University *B*
Auburn University at Montgomery *B*

Columbia Southern University *B, M*
Faulkner University *B, M*
Troy University *M*
Tuskegee University *M*

Arizona

DeVry University
   Phoenix *M*
Northcentral University *M, D*
Prescott College *B*
University of Arizona *B*
University of Phoenix *M*

Arkansas

Harding University *B*

California

Antioch Southern California
   Antioch University Santa Barbara *M*
Azusa Pacific University *M*
California National University for
   Advanced Studies *M*
California State University
   Chico *B*
   Dominguez Hills *M*
   East Bay *B, M*
   Fresno *B*
   Long Beach *B*
   Northridge *B, M*
   Sacramento *B, M*
   San Bernardino *B, M*
Cerritos College *A*
City College of San Francisco *A*
DeVry University
   Fremont *M*
   Long Beach *M*
   Pomona *M*
   Sherman Oaks *M*
Fresno Pacific University *B*
Golden Gate University *B, M*
Holy Names University *B*
La Sierra University *B, M*
Lincoln University *M*
National University *B, M*
San Diego State University *M*
San Joaquin Valley College *A*
San Jose State University *B*
Yuba Community College District *A*

Colorado

American Sentinel University *B*
Colorado Christian University *B*
Colorado Technical University *B, M*
DeVry University
   Westminster *M*
University of Colorado
   Denver *B*
University of Denver *M*

Connecticut

Goodwin College *A*
Post University *A*
Quinnipiac University *B*

Delaware

Delaware Technical and Community
   College
   Terry *A*
Wilmington University *B, M*

District of Columbia

Catholic University of America *B, M*
George Washington University *D*
Trinity Washington University *M*

Florida

DeVry University
   Miramar *M*
   Orlando *M*
Florida Atlantic University *B*
Florida Institute of Technology *M*
Florida International University *B, M*

Florida State University *B*
Nova Southeastern University *M*
Rollins College *M*
Saint Leo University *B*
Saint Thomas University *M*
University of Miami *B*
Valencia Community College *A*

Georgia

Ashworth College *A, M*
DeVry University
   Alpharetta *M*
   Decatur *M*
Georgia Southwestern State
   University *B*
Georgia State University *M*
Gwinnett Technical College *A*
Macon State College *A*
Middle Georgia College *A*
University of Georgia *M*

Hawaii

Hawaii Pacific University *B, M*
University of Hawaii
   Manoa *B, M*

Idaho

Boise State University *B*
Idaho State University *B, M*
University of Idaho *B*

Illinois

Bradley University *B*
DePaul University *B, M*
DeVry University
   Tinley Park *M*
DeVry University: Online *M*
Illinois Institute of Technology *M*
Judson University *B*
Kishwaukee College *A*
Lake Land College *A*
Lewis University *B*
Loyola University Chicago *B, M*
Moraine Valley Community
   College *C, A*
National-Louis University *M*
North Central College *B*
Northwestern University *M*
Roosevelt University *B, M*
Saint Xavier University *M*
Trinity International University *B, M*
Triton College *A*
University of Illinois
   Urbana-Champaign *B*
University of St. Francis *B*
Waubonsee Community College *A*
Western Illinois University *B*

Indiana

Ball State University *B*
Bethel College *B*
Harrison College
   Anderson *A*
   Elkhart *A*
   Indianapolis *A*
   Lafayette *A*
   Muncie *A*
   Terre Haute *A*
Indiana Institute of Technology *B, M*
Indiana State University *B, M*
Indiana University-Purdue University
   Indianapolis *B*
Oakland City University *B*
Purdue University *B, M, D*
Purdue University
   Calumet *B*
   North Central *A, B*
St. Mary-of-the-Woods College *B*

Iowa

Briar Cliff University *B, M*
Buena Vista University *B*
Grand View University *B*

Iowa Wesleyan College *B*
Northwestern College *B*
University of Iowa *B, D*
Western Iowa Tech Community
   College *A*

Kansas

Barton County Community College *A*
Central Christian College of Kansas *A*
Emporia State University *B*
Friends University *B, M*
MidAmerica Nazarene University *B*
Pittsburg State University *B*
University of St. Mary *M*
Wichita State University *B*

Kentucky

Mid-Continent University *M*
Midway College *B*

Louisiana

Louisiana Tech University *B*

Maine

Saint Joseph's College of Maine *B*
Thomas College *B*

Maryland

DeVry University: Bethesda *M*
Towson University *M*
University of Baltimore *B*
University of Maryland
   University College *B, M*

Massachusetts

Becker College *B*
Boston College *B*
Emerson College *M*
Emmanuel College *M*
Fisher College *B*
Fitchburg State College *M*
Framingham State College *M*
Holyoke Community College *A*
Marian Court College *A*
Nichols College *B*
Northeastern University *B*
Salem State College *B*
Springfield College *M*
Suffolk University *M*

Michigan

Baker College
   of Cadillac *A, B*
   of Clinton Township *A, B*
   of Flint *M*
   of Muskegon *A, B*
   of Owosso *A, B*
   of Port Huron *A, B*
Baker College of Allen Park *B*
Central Michigan University *B, M*
Cleary University *B*
Davenport University *B, M*
Eastern Michigan University *M*
Ferris State University *B*
Grand Valley State University *B*
Lansing Community College *A*
Madonna University *B*
Marygrove College *M*
Michigan State University *B, M, D*
Northern Michigan University *M*
Oakland University *B*

Minnesota

Anoka-Ramsey Community College *A*
Bethel University *B*
Capella University *B, M, D*
DeVry University
   Edina *M*
Metropolitan State University *B*
Minnesota State Community and
   Technical College *A*

Minnesota State University
   Mankato *B*
Saint Cloud State University *B*
St. Mary's University of
   Minnesota *B, M*
St. Paul College *A*
University of Minnesota
   Duluth *B*
   Twin Cities *B, M, D*
University of St. Thomas *B*
Walden University *B, M*
Winona State University *B*

Mississippi

University of Southern Mississippi *B*
Virginia College Gulf Coast *A*

Missouri

Avila University *B*
Columbia College *B*
DeVry University
   Kansas City *B*
Fontbonne University *M*
Lindenwood University *B, M*
Saint Louis University *B*
University of Central Missouri *B*
Washington University in St.
   Louis *B, M*
Webster University *M*

Montana

Montana State University
   Billings *A*
University of Montana *A*

Nebraska

Bellevue University *B, D*
Doane College *B*
York College *B*

Nevada

University of Nevada
   Las Vegas *B*
   Reno *B*

New Hampshire

New England College *B*
Rivier College *M*

New Jersey

Berkeley College- Garret Mountain
   Campus *B*
Fairleigh Dickinson University
   College at Florham *M*
   Metropolitan Campus *M*
Rider University *A, B*
Rowan University *B*
Rutgers, The State University of New
   Jersey
   New Brunswick/Piscataway
    Campus *M*
Stevens Institute of Technology *M*
Thomas Edison State College *B, M*

New Mexico

Eastern New Mexico University *B*

New York

Adelphi University *M*
Bryant & Stratton Business Institute
   Bryant & Stratton College: Albany *A*
City University of New York
   Baruch College *B, M*
Dominican College of Blauvelt *B*
Excelsior College *B*
Herkimer County Community
   College *A*
Hofstra University *M*
Iona College *M*
Long Island University
   Brooklyn Campus *M*
Manhattanville College *M*

Marist College *B*
Mercy College *M*
Nazareth College *B, M*
New York Institute of
    Technology *B, M*
New York University *M*
Niagara University *B*
Pace University *B, M*
Roberts Wesleyan College *B*
Rochester Institute of
    Technology *A, M*
St. Joseph's College *B*
State University of New York
    Albany *M*
    Oswego *B*
Suffolk County Community College *A*

North Carolina
Barton College *B*
Davidson County Community
    College *A*
DeVry University: Charlotte *M*
Fayetteville Technical Community
    College *A*
Guilford Technical Community
    College *A*
High Point University *B*
Mount Olive College *B*
Peace College *B*
Pitt Community College *A*
Stanly Community College *A*
University of North Carolina
    Chapel Hill *B*
Western Carolina University *M*

North Dakota
University of North Dakota *B*

Ohio
Antioch University McGregor *B*
Baldwin-Wallace College *B, M*
Bowling Green State University *B*
Bryant & Stratton College
    Eastlake *A*
Central Ohio Technical College *A*
Clark State Community College *A*
Columbus State Community
    College *A*
Davis College *A*
DeVry University
    Columbus *M*
Edison State Community College *A*
Franklin University *B*
Lourdes College *B*
Marietta College *B*
Marion Technical College *A*
Mount Vernon Nazarene University *M*
Notre Dame College *B*
Ohio Business College: Sandusky *A*
Ohio State University
    Columbus Campus *B, M, D*
Ohio University *B*
Tiffin University *B*
University of Akron *B, M*
University of Cincinnati *M*
University of Findlay *B*
University of Toledo *B, M*
Urbana University *B*
Ursuline College *B*
Wright State University *B*
Xavier University *B, M*
Youngstown State University *B*

Oklahoma
DeVry University: Oklahoma City
    Center *M*
Langston University *B*
Northeastern State University *B*
Southwestern Oklahoma State
    University *B*
Tulsa Community College *A*
University of Central Oklahoma *B*

Oregon
DeVry University: Portland *M*
Portland State University *B*

Pennsylvania
Alvernia University *B*
Arcadia University *B*
Butler County Community College *A*
Cabrini College *A*
Carlow University *B*
Chestnut Hill College *A, B*
Community College of Allegheny
    County *A*
Community College of Beaver
    County *A*
DeSales University *B*
DeVry University
    Fort Washington *M*
Drexel University *M*
Geneva College *B*
Holy Family University *B, M*
Immaculata University *B*
Indiana University of Pennsylvania *B*
Juniata College *B*
King's College *A, B*
Kutztown University of
    Pennsylvania *B*
La Roche College *M*
La Salle University *B*
Lehigh Carbon Community College *A*
Lincoln University *B*
Mansfield University of
    Pennsylvania *B*
Messiah College *B*
Muhlenberg College *B*
Peirce College *A*
Point Park University *B*
Reading Area Community College *A*
Robert Morris University *M*
Rosemont College *B*
St. Francis University *M*
Saint Joseph's University *M*
Seton Hill University *B*
University of Pennsylvania *B, M*
University of Scranton *B, M*
Villanova University *M*
Westmoreland County Community
    College *A*
Widener University *B, M*
York College of Pennsylvania *M*

Puerto Rico
Bayamon Central University *B*
Inter American University of Puerto
    Rico
    Bayamon Campus *B*
    Guayama Campus *B*
    Metropolitan Campus *B, M, D*
    Ponce Campus *B, M*
    San German Campus *B, M*
Pontifical Catholic University of
    Puerto Rico *B, M*
Turabo University *M*
Universidad Metropolitana *M*
Universidad del Este *M*
University of Puerto Rico
    Aguadilla *B*
    Humacao *B*
    Rio Piedras *B, M*
University of the Sacred Heart *M*

Rhode Island
University of Rhode Island *T*

South Carolina
Anderson University *B*
Bob Jones University *B*
Clemson University *M*
Forrest Junior College *A*
University of South Carolina *M*
York Technical College *A*

South Dakota
Black Hills State University *B*

Tennessee
DeVry University: Memphis *M*
Freed-Hardeman University *B*
Lipscomb University *B*
Southern Adventist University *B*
Tennessee Wesleyan College *B*
University of Tennessee
    Knoxville *B, M, D*

Texas
Amberton University *M*
Baylor University *B*
DeVry University
    Irving *M*
Houston Baptist University *M*
Lamar University *B*
LeTourneau University *B*
Our Lady of the Lake University of San
    Antonio *B, M*
St. Mary's University *B*
Sam Houston State University *B*
Tarleton State University *B, M*
Texas A&M University
    Commerce *B*
    Texarkana *B*
University of Dallas *M*
University of Houston *B*
University of Houston
    Clear Lake *M*
University of Texas
    Arlington *M*
    San Antonio *B, M*
University of the Incarnate Word *B*
Vernon College *A*
Weatherford College *A*

Utah
DeVry University: Sandy *M*
University of Utah *M*
Utah State University *B*
Weber State University *B*
Western Governors University *B*
Westminster College *B*

Vermont
Champlain College *B*

Virginia
Bryant & Stratton College
    Richmond *A*
Bryant & Stratton College: Virginia
    Beach *A*
Marymount University *B, M*
Regent University *A*
University of Richmond *A, B, M*

Washington
Bellingham Technical College *A*
Clark College *A*
DeVry University
    Federal Way *M*
University of Washington *B*
Walla Walla University *B*
Western Washington University *B*

West Virginia
Alderson-Broaddus College *B*
American Public University System *A*
Concord University *B*
Mountain State University *A*
Ohio Valley University *B*

Wisconsin
Carroll University *B*
Concordia University Wisconsin *M*
DeVry University: Milwaukee *M*
Fox Valley Technical College *A*
Herzing University *B*
Lakeshore Technical College *A*

Marian University *B*
Marquette University *B, M*
Mid-State Technical College *A*
St. Norbert College *B*
Silver Lake College *B*
University of Wisconsin
    Milwaukee *B*
    Oshkosh *B*
    Parkside *B*
    Platteville *B*
    Whitewater *B, T*
Western Technical College *A*

Human sciences communication

Alabama
Faulkner University *B*

California
Antelope Valley College *A*

Georgia
University of Georgia *B*

Nebraska
University of Nebraska
    Omaha *B*

Virginia
Virginia State University *B*

Wisconsin
University of Wisconsin
    Madison *B, M*

Human services

Alabama
Troy University *B*

Alaska
Alaska Pacific University *B*
University of Alaska
    Fairbanks *A*

Arizona
Arizona Western College *C, A*
Cochise College *A*
Northland Pioneer College *C*
Prescott College *B, M*
University of Phoenix *B*

California
Allan Hancock College *C, A*
California State University
    Dominguez Hills *B*
    Fullerton *B*
    Monterey Bay *B*
Canada College *A*
City College of San Francisco *C*
College of the Sequoias *C, A*
College of the Siskiyous *C, A*
Columbia College *C*
Cypress College *C, A*
Folsom Lake College *A*
Gavilan College *C*
Holy Names University *B*
Hope International University *B*
Long Beach City College *C, A*
Mendocino College *C, A*
Merced College *A*
Modesto Junior College *C, A*
Mount St. Mary's College *M*
Notre Dame de Namur University *B*
Oxnard College *A*
Riverside Community College *C, A*
Saddleback College *C*
Santa Rosa Junior College *C*
Shasta College *C, A*
Solano Community College *C, A*

Colorado

Community College of Denver *C, A*
Metropolitan State College of
Denver *B*
University of Northern Colorado *B*

Connecticut

Albertus Magnus College *B*
Asnuntuck Community College *C, A*
Goodwin College *C, A*
Housatonic Community College *A*
Middlesex Community College *C, A*
Mitchell College *B*
Naugatuck Valley Community
College *A*
Northwestern Connecticut
Community College *C, A*
Norwalk Community College *A*
Post University *B, M*
Quinebaug Valley Community
College *A*
St. Vincent's College *C*
Three Rivers Community College *C, A*
Tunxis Community College *C, A*

Delaware

Delaware Technical and Community
College
Owens *C, A*
Stanton/Wilmington *C, A*
Terry *C, A*

District of Columbia

George Washington University *B, M*
Trinity Washington University *B*

Florida

Beacon College *A, B*
Central Florida Community
College *C, A*
Daytona State College *A*
Florida State College at Jacksonville *A*
Indian River State College *A*
Lynn University *B*
Miami Dade College *A*
Palm Beach Community College *A*
Pasco-Hernando Community
College *C, A*
St. Petersburg College *C, A*
Saint Thomas University *B*
Southeastern University *B, M*

Georgia

Abraham Baldwin Agricultural
College *A*
Darton College *A*
Fort Valley State University *B*
Georgia Highlands College *A*
Kennesaw State University *B*
Macon State College *B*
Spelman College *B*

Hawaii

Hawaii Pacific University *B*
University of Hawaii
Honolulu Community College *A*
Maui Community College *A*

Idaho

North Idaho College *A*

Illinois

Carl Sandburg College *C*
Danville Area Community College *A*
DePaul University *M*
Harper College *C, A*
Judson University *B*
Lewis University *B*
Loyola University Chicago *B*
Millikin University *B*
National-Louis University *B, M*
North Park University *B*

Oakton Community College *C*
Quincy University *B*
Rock Valley College *C, A*
Roosevelt University *M*
South Suburban College of Cook
County *A*
Southeastern Illinois College *A*
University of Illinois
Springfield *M*

Indiana

Bethel College *A, B*
Calumet College of St. Joseph *B*
Indiana Institute of Technology *B*
Indiana Wesleyan University *C*
St. Mary-of-the-Woods College *B*
Vincennes University *C*

Iowa

Ellsworth Community College *C, A*
Grand View University *B*
Iowa Wesleyan College *B*
Iowa Western Community College *A*
Southeastern Community College
North Campus *A*
Upper Iowa University *B*
William Penn University *B*

Kansas

Ottawa University *B*

Kentucky

Big Sandy Community and Technical
College *A*
Elizabethtown Community and
Technical College *A*
Hazard Community and Technical
College *A*
Kentucky Wesleyan College *B*
University of the Cumberlands *B*

Louisiana

Southern University
Shreveport *A*

Maine

University of Maine
Fort Kent *A*
Machias *B*

Maryland

Anne Arundel Community
College *C, A*
Chesapeake College *C*
Coppin State University *M*
Frederick Community College *A*
Howard Community College *C, A*
McDaniel College *M*
University of Baltimore *B, M*

Massachusetts

Anna Maria College *B*
Becker College *B*
Berkshire Community College *C*
Bridgewater State College *M*
Bunker Hill Community College *C, A*
Cape Cod Community College *C, A*
Endicott College *B*
Fitchburg State College *B*
Framingham State College *M*
Holyoke Community College *C*
Lasell College *B*
Massachusetts Bay Community
College *C, A*
Massasoit Community College *A*
Merrimack College *A, B*
Mount Ida College *B*
Mount Wachusett Community
College *C, A*
Northeastern University *B*
Quinsigamond Community
College *C, A*

Springfield College *B, M*
University of Massachusetts
Boston *B, M*
Urban College of Boston *C, A*

Michigan

Baker College
of Auburn Hills *A*
of Cadillac *A, B*
of Clinton Township *A, B*
of Jackson *A, B*
of Muskegon *A, B*
of Owosso *A, B*
Baker College of Allen Park *B*
Bay Mills Community College *C*
Delta College *A*
Finlandia University *B*
Grace Bible College *B*

Minnesota

Alexandria Technical College *C, A*
Capella University *M, D*
Century Community and Technical
College *A*
Fond du Lac Tribal and Community
College *A*
Inver Hills Community College *C, A*
Itasca College *A, B*
Mesabi Range Community and
Technical College *A*
Metropolitan State University *B*
Minneapolis Community and
Technical College *C, A*
Minnesota State University
Mankato *B, M*
Minnesota West Community and
Technical College *A*
Northland Community & Technical
College *A*
Pine Technical College *C, A*
Riverland Community College *A*
St. Mary's University of Minnesota *B*
South Central College *C, A*
Walden University *D*

Missouri

Columbia College *B*
Fontbonne University *B*
Hannibal-LaGrange College *B*
Lindenwood University *B, M*
Missouri Baptist University *B*
North Central Missouri College *A*
St. Charles Community College *A*
Southwest Baptist University *B*

Montana

Blackfeet Community College *A*
Flathead Valley Community College *A*
Fort Belknap College *A*
Fort Peck Community College *A*
Miles Community College *A*
Montana State University
Billings *B*
Stone Child College *A*
University of Great Falls *M*

Nebraska

Bellevue University *B, M*

New Hampshire

Lakes Region Community
College *C, A*
Manchester Community College *C*
NHTI-Concord's Community
College *C, A*
Nashua Community College *C, A*
River Valley Community College *A*
White Mountains Community
College *C, A*

New Jersey

Atlantic Cape Community
College *C, A*

Burlington County College *C, A*
Essex County College *A*
Mercer County Community College *A*
Ocean County College *A*
Passaic County Community College *A*
Thomas Edison State College *A, B*
Union County College *A*

New Mexico

New Mexico State University
Carlsbad *A*
Grants *A*
Northern New Mexico College *A*
Santa Fe Community College *A*

New York

Boricua College *B, M*
Cazenovia College *A, B*
City University of New York
Borough of Manhattan Community
College *A*
New York City College of
Technology *A, B*
Clinton Community College *A*
Columbia University
School of General Studies *B*
Corning Community College *A*
Elmira College *A, B*
Erie Community College
South Campus *A*
Finger Lakes Community College *A*
Herkimer County Community
College *A*
Hilbert College *A, B*
Jamestown Community College *A*
Mercy College *A*
Metropolitan College of New
York *A, B*
Monroe Community College *C, A*
Mount Saint Mary College *B*
Niagara County Community
College *A*
Onondaga Community College *A*
Orange County Community College *A*
Rockland Community College *A*
St. John's University *B*
State University of New York
College of Technology at Alfred *A*
Oswego *M*
Suffolk County Community College *A*
Sullivan County Community
College *A*
Touro College *A*
Westchester Community College *C*

North Carolina

Beaufort County Community
College *C, A*
Central Carolina Community
College *A*
Edgecombe Community College *A*
Elon University *B*
Halifax Community College *A*
Lenoir-Rhyne University *B*
Mitchell Community College *A*
Montreat College *B*
South Piedmont Community
College *C, A*
Vance-Granville Community
College *A*
Wake Technical Community
College *C, A*
Wingate University *B*

North Dakota

Bismarck State College *A*
Sitting Bull College *A*

Ohio

Antioch University McGregor *B*
Bowling Green State University:
Firelands College *A*
Central Ohio Technical College *A*

Chatfield College *A*
Cincinnati State Technical and
  Community College *C*
Cleveland State University *M*
Hocking College *A*
James A. Rhodes State College *C, A*
John Carroll University *M*
Marion Technical College *A*
Mount Vernon Nazarene University *A*
Ohio University
  Southern Campus at Ironton *A*
  Zanesville Campus *B*
Southern State Community College *A*
Stark State College of Technology *A*
Tiffin University *B*
Washington State Community
  College *A*

Oklahoma
East Central University *B*

Oregon
Blue Mountain Community College *A*
Chemeketa Community College *C, A*
Umpqua Community College *A*
University of Oregon *B, M*

Pennsylvania
Chestnut Hill College *A, B, M*
Community College of Philadelphia *A*
Geneva College *B*
Harrisburg Area Community
  College *C, A*
La Roche College *B*
Lackawanna College *A*
Lehigh Carbon Community
  College *C, A*
Lincoln University *B, M*
Luzerne County Community
  College *A*
Pennsylvania Highlands Community
  College *A*
Seton Hill University *B*
University of Scranton *C, A, B*
Villanova University *B*
Waynesburg University *B*
Westmoreland County Community
  College *A*

Rhode Island
Community College of Rhode
  Island *C*

South Carolina
Aiken Technical College *A*
Anderson University *B*
Denmark Technical College *A*
Southern Wesleyan University *B*
Trident Technical College *C, A*
Williamsburg Technical College *C*

South Dakota
Dakota Wesleyan University *B*
Oglala Lakota College *B*
Sinte Gléska University *B*

Tennessee
Bethel University *B*
Martin Methodist College *B*
Milligan College *B*
Tennessee Wesleyan College *B*

Texas
Angelina College *C, A*
Austin Community College *A*
Laredo Community College *C, A*
St. Edward's University *M*
South Plains College *A*
Tyler Junior College *C, A*
Wayland Baptist University *A, B*

Vermont
Burlington College *B*
Champlain College *B*
College of St. Joseph in Vermont *A*
Lyndon State College *B*
Southern Vermont College *A*

Virginia
Blue Ridge Community College *A*
Central Virginia Community
  College *C*
John Tyler Community College *A*
Liberty University *M*
New River Community College *C, A*
Northern Virginia Community
  College *A*
Shenandoah University *D*
Southside Virginia Community
  College *C, A*
Southwest Virginia Community
  College *C, A*
Thomas Nelson Community
  College *A*
University of Richmond *C, A, B, M*
Virginia Wesleyan College *B*
Virginia Western Community
  College *A*

Washington
Everett Community College *A*
Grays Harbor College *C, A*
Highline Community College *A*
Olympic College *C, A*
Skagit Valley College *A*
Western Washington University *B*

Wisconsin
College of Menominee Nation *A*
Fox Valley Technical College *A*
Gateway Technical College *A*
Lac Courte Oreilles Ojibwa
  Community College *A*
Marian University *B*
Milwaukee Area Technical College *A*
Southwest Wisconsin Technical
  College *A*
University of Wisconsin
  Oshkosh *B*
  Superior *M*
Waukesha County Technical
  College *A*
Wisconsin Lutheran College *B*

Wyoming
Central Wyoming College *A*
Laramie County Community
  College *A*

Humanities

Alabama
Faulkner University *B*
Spring Hill College *B*
University of Mobile *B*

Arizona
Arizona State University *B*
Central Arizona College *A*
Cochise College *A*
College of the Humanities and
  Sciences *A, B, M, D*
Mesa Community College *A*
Northern Arizona University *B*
Prescott College *B, M*

Arkansas
Harding University *B*

California
Berkeley City College *A*
California Institute of Integral
  Studies *B, M, D*

California State Polytechnic
  University; Pomona *B*
California State University
  Chico *B*
  Dominguez Hills *M*
  Monterey Bay *B*
  Sacramento *B, M*
  San Bernardino *B*
College of the Canyons *A*
College of the Siskiyous *A*
Concordia University *B*
Dominican University of
  California *B, M*
Feather River College *A*
Glendale Community College *A*
Holy Names University *B*
Imperial Valley College *A*
Lake Tahoe Community College *A*
Loyola Marymount University *B*
Orange Coast College *A*
Oxnard College *C, A*
Pepperdine University *B*
San Diego Miramar College *A*
San Diego State University *B*
San Francisco State University *B, M*
San Jose State University *B*
Scripps College *B*
Shasta College *A*
Southwestern College *A*
Stanford University *B, M*
University of California
  Riverside *B*
University of San Diego *B*
West Hills College: Lemoore *A*

Colorado
Fort Lewis College *B*
Pikes Peak Community College *A*
United States Air Force Academy *B*
University of Colorado
  Boulder *B*
  Denver *M*

Connecticut
Holy Apostles College and
  Seminary *B*
Mitchell College *B*
University of Bridgeport *B*
Yale University *B*

Florida
Clearwater Christian College *B*
Eckerd College *B*
Florida Institute of Technology *B*
Florida Southern College *B*
Florida State University *B*
Jacksonville University *B*
New College of Florida *B*
Nova Southeastern University *B*
State College of Florida,
  Manatee-Sarasota *A*
Stetson University *B*
University of Central Florida *B*
University of South Florida *B*
University of West Florida *B, M*

Georgia
Atlanta Christian College *B*
Truett-McConnell College *B*

Illinois
Black Hawk College *C*
Bradley University *B*
DePaul University *B*
Principia College *B*
Quincy University *B*
Rockford College *B*
Shimer College *B*
Trinity International University *B*
University of Illinois
  Urbana-Champaign *B*

Indiana
Bethel College *B*
Indiana University
  East *B*
  Kokomo *B*
  South Bend *A*
Indiana University-Purdue University
  Indianapolis *A*
Oakland City University *B*
Purdue University *B*
Saint Mary's College *B*
St. Mary-of-the-Woods College *A, B*
Valparaiso University *A, B*

Iowa
University of Northern Iowa *B*
Waldorf College *B*

Kansas
Kansas State University *B*
Tabor College *B*
University of Kansas *B*
Washburn University *A*

Kentucky
Kentucky Christian University *B*
Lindsey Wilson College *B*
Spalding University *B*
Thomas More College *A, B*
University of Louisville *B*

Louisiana
Our Lady of the Lake College *B*

Maine
University of Southern Maine *B*

Maryland
Hood College *M*
St. John's College *B, M*
St. Mary's College of Maryland *B*
Towson University *M*
University of Maryland
  University College *A, B*
Washington College *B*

Massachusetts
Hampshire College *B*
Lasell College *B*
Roxbury Community College *A*
Suffolk University *B*
Wheelock College *B*
Worcester Polytechnic Institute *B*

Michigan
Alma College *B*
Aquinas College *B*
Central Michigan University *M*
Kirtland Community College *A*
Lake Michigan College *A*
Lawrence Technological University *B*
Madonna University *B*
Michigan State University *B*
Michigan Technological University *A*
University of Michigan *B*

Minnesota
College of St. Benedict *B*
College of St. Scholastica *B*
Macalester College *B*
North Central University *A*
St. John's University *B*
University of Minnesota
  Morris *B*
White Earth Tribal and Community
  College *A*

Mississippi
Belhaven University *B*

Missouri

Missouri State University *B*
Northwest Missouri State
 University *B*
Saint Louis University *B*
Southeast Missouri State University *B*
Washington University in St. Louis *B*
Webster University *B*

Montana

Flathead Valley Community College *A*

Nebraska

University of Nebraska
 Lincoln *B*

New Hampshire

Plymouth State University *B*
University of New Hampshire *B*
University of New Hampshire at
 Manchester *B*

New Jersey

Cumberland County College *A*
Fairleigh Dickinson University
 College at Florham *B*
 Metropolitan Campus *B*
Felician College *B*
Georgian Court University *B*
Montclair State University *B*
Ramapo College of New Jersey *B*
Salem Community College *A*
Seton Hall University *B*
Thomas Edison State College *B*

New Mexico

University of New Mexico *B*
University of the Southwest *B*

New York

Adelphi University *B*
Canisius College *A, B*
City University of New York
 Hunter College *B*
Clarkson University *B*
Corning Community College *A*
Dominican College of Blauvelt *B*
Dowling College *B*
Dutchess Community College *A*
Erie Community College
 City Campus *A*
 North Campus *A*
 South Campus *A*
Fulton-Montgomery Community
 College *A*
Genesee Community College *A*
Hofstra University *B, M*
Houghton College *A, B*
Jamestown Community College *A*
Long Island University
 Brooklyn Campus *B*
Marymount Manhattan College *B*
Mohawk Valley Community College *A*
New York University *B, M, D, T*
Niagara County Community
 College *A*
Onondaga Community College *A*
Roberts Wesleyan College *B, T*
State University of New York
 Buffalo *M*
 College at Buffalo *B*
 College at Old Westbury *B*
 College at Potsdam *B*
 College of Agriculture and
  Technology at Cobleskill *A*
 College of Agriculture and
  Technology at Morrisville *A*
 College of Technology at Alfred *A*
 Stony Brook *B*
Syracuse University *B*
Tompkins Cortland Community
 College *A*
Ulster County Community College *A*

Union College *B*
United States Military Academy *B*
Villa Maria College of Buffalo *A*
Wells College *B*

North Dakota

North Dakota State University *B*

Ohio

Antioch University McGregor *B*
Franciscan University of
 Steubenville *B*
John Carroll University *M*
Kent State University *B*
Muskingum University *B*
Ohio State University
 Columbus Campus *M*
Ohio University *A*
Pontifical College Josephinum *B*
Tiffin University *M*
University of Akron *B*
University of Rio Grande *B*
University of Toledo *B*
Ursuline College *B*
Wright State University *M*

Oklahoma

Oklahoma City University *B*
St. Gregory's University *B*
University of Oklahoma *B*

Oregon

Central Oregon Community
 College *A*
Chemeketa Community College *A*
Corban College *B*
University of Oregon *B*
Willamette University *B*

Pennsylvania

Arcadia University *M*
Bucknell University *B*
Bucks County Community College *A*
Community College of Allegheny
 County *A*
Community College of Beaver
 County *A*
Drexel University *B, M*
East Stroudsburg University of
 Pennsylvania *B*
Edinboro University of
 Pennsylvania *B*
Holy Family University *B*
Juniata College *B*
Keystone College *A, B*
Lackawanna College *A*
Lehigh Carbon Community College *A*
Luzerne County Community
 College *A*
Messiah College *B*
Montgomery County Community
 College *A*
Mount Aloysius College *B*
Penn State
 Harrisburg *B, M*
 Schuylkill *B*
Rosemont College *B*
Saint Joseph's University *B*
University of Pennsylvania *B*
University of Pittsburgh *B*
University of Pittsburgh
 Bradford *B*

Puerto Rico

Turabo University *B*
University of Puerto Rico
 Aguadilla *T*
 Bayamon University College *A*
 Carolina Regional College *T*
 Cayey University College *B*
 Utuado *A*

Rhode Island

Providence College *B*
Salve Regina University *M, D*

South Carolina

Bob Jones University *B*
Charleston Southern University *B*
Columbia International University *B*
Lander University *B*
Newberry College *B*

Tennessee

LeMoyne-Owen College *B*
Lincoln Memorial University *B*
Milligan College *B*
University of Tennessee
 Chattanooga *B*

Texas

Baylor University *B*
Lubbock Christian University *B*
Midwestern State University *B*
Schreiner University *B*
Southern Methodist University *B*
Southwestern Baptist Theological
 Seminary *B*
Stephen F. Austin State University *B*
Texarkana College *A*
University of Dallas *M*
University of Houston
 Clear Lake *B, M*
 Downtown *B*
University of Texas
 Arlington *M*
 Austin *M*
 San Antonio *B*
 of the Permian Basin *B*

Utah

Brigham Young University *B*
Salt Lake Community College *A*
University of Utah *B, M*
Utah Valley University *A*

Vermont

Bennington College *B*
Goddard College *B, M*

Virginia

Danville Community College *A*
George Mason University *D*
Hampden-Sydney College *B*
Marymount University *M*
Old Dominion University *M*
University of Richmond *B*
Virginia Wesleyan College *B*

Washington

Eastern Washington University *B*
Evergreen State College *B*
Saint Martin's University *B*
Seattle University *B*
University of Washington Bothell *B*
Washington State University *B*
Western Washington University *B*

West Virginia

American Public University System *M*
Bluefield State College *B*
Marshall University *B, M*

Wisconsin

Carthage College *B*
Concordia University Wisconsin *B*
Maranatha Baptist Bible College *B*
Northland College *B*
St. Norbert College *B*
University of Wisconsin
 Green Bay *B*

Wyoming

Laramie County Community
 College *A*
Sheridan College *A*
University of Wyoming *B*

Hydraulics technology

Iowa

Des Moines Area Community
 College *C, A*

Maryland

Community College of Baltimore
 County *C, A*

Michigan

Lansing Community College *A*

Minnesota

Alexandria Technical College *C, A*
Hennepin Technical College *C, A*

Ohio

Ohio State University
 Agricultural Technical Institute *C, A*
Owens Community College
 Toledo *C, A*

Pennsylvania

Community College of Allegheny
 County *C, A*

Washington

Spokane Community College *A*

Wisconsin

Milwaukee Area Technical College *C*

Hydrology/water resources science

Arizona

Northern Arizona University *B*
University of Arizona *B, M, D*

California

California State University
 Chico *C, B, M*
Santiago Canyon College *A*
University of California
 Davis *B, M, D*

Illinois

Illinois State University *M*

Kansas

University of Kansas *M*

Michigan

Western Michigan University *B*

Minnesota

Saint Cloud State University *B*

Nebraska

University of Nebraska
 Lincoln *B*

New Hampshire

University of New Hampshire *B, M*

New Mexico

New Mexico Institute of Mining and
 Technology *M, D*

New York

Rensselaer Polytechnic Institute *B, M*

State University of New York
  College at Brockport *B*
  College at Oneonta *B*

Pennsylvania

University of Pennsylvania *M*

Texas

Tarleton State University *B*
Texas A&M University *M, D*
Texas A&M University
  Galveston *B*
University of Texas
  Austin *B*

Utah

Brigham Young University *B, M*
Utah State University *B, M, D*

Illustration

Arizona

Art Center Design College *B*

Arkansas

John Brown University *B*

California

Academy of Art University *C, A, B, M*
Art Center College of Design *B*
California College of the Arts *B*
Orange Coast College *C*
Otis College of Art and Design *B*

Colorado

Rocky Mountain College of Art &
  Design *B*

Connecticut

Lyme Academy College of Fine Arts *B*
Paier College of Art *C, B*
University of Bridgeport *B*

Delaware

Delaware College of Art and Design *A*

Florida

Art Institute of Fort Lauderdale *B*
Ringling College of Art and Design *B*

Georgia

Art Institute
  of Atlanta *B*
Savannah College of Art and
  Design *B, M*

Illinois

Columbia College Chicago *C, B*
Lewis University *B*

Indiana

Grace College *B*
Indiana Wesleyan University *B*

Kansas

University of Kansas *B, M*

Maine

Maine College of Art *B*

Maryland

Maryland Institute College of Art *B*

Massachusetts

Art Institute of Boston at Lesley
  University *B*
Montserrat College of Art *B*
New England Institute of Art *B*
Northeastern University *B*

School of the Museum of Fine
  Arts *B, M*

Michigan

College for Creative Studies *B*
Ferris State University *B*
Finlandia University *B*
Henry Ford Community College *C*
Kendall College of Art and Design of
  Ferris State University *B*
Lawrence Technological University *B*
Northern Michigan University *A, B*
University of Michigan *B*

Minnesota

College of Visual Arts *B*
Minneapolis College of Art and
  Design *B*

Missouri

Washington University in St. Louis *B*

Montana

University of Montana: Western *B*

New Jersey

Montclair State University *B*

New Mexico

Art Center Design College *B*

New York

Fashion Institute of
  Technology *A, B, M*
Parsons The New School for Design *B*
Pratt Institute *A*
Rochester Institute of
  Technology *A, B*
St. John's University *B*

North Carolina

East Carolina University *B*

Ohio

Art Academy of Cincinnati *B*
Cleveland Institute of Art *B*
Columbus College of Art and
  Design *B*
Edison State Community College *C*
Virginia Marti College of Art and
  Design *A*

Oregon

Pacific Northwest College of Art *B*

Pennsylvania

Arcadia University *B*
Douglas Education Center *A*
Keystone College *A, B*
Luzerne County Community
  College *C, A*
Marywood University *B, M*
Moore College of Art and Design *B*
Pennsylvania College of Art and
  Design *B*
University of the Arts *B*

Rhode Island

Rhode Island School of Design *B*

Tennessee

Memphis College of Art *B*

Utah

Brigham Young University *B*

Vermont

Lyndon State College *B*

Virginia

Virginia Commonwealth University *B*

Washington

Cornish College of the Arts *B*

Wisconsin

Concordia University Wisconsin *B*

Industrial design

Alabama

Auburn University *B, M*

Arizona

Arizona State University *B*

California

Academy of Art University *C, A, B, M*
Art Center College of Design *B, M*
Art Institute
  of California: Orange County *B*
Art Institute of California:
  Hollywood *B*
California College of the Arts *B*
California State University
  Long Beach *B, M*
Los Angeles Pierce College *C, A*
Otis College of Art and Design *B*
San Francisco State University *B, M*
San Jose State University *B*

Colorado

Art Institute
  of Colorado *B*
Metropolitan State College of
  Denver *B*

Connecticut

University of Bridgeport *B*

Florida

Art Institute of Fort Lauderdale *B*

Georgia

Georgia Institute of Technology *B, M*
Savannah College of Art and
  Design *B, M*

Illinois

Columbia College Chicago *C, B*
School of the Art Institute of
  Chicago *B, M*
University of Illinois
  Chicago *B, M*

Indiana

Oakland City University *A, B*

Kansas

University of Kansas *B, M*

Louisiana

University of Louisiana at Lafayette *B*

Massachusetts

Massachusetts College of Art and
  Design *C, B*
Wentworth Institute of Technology *B*

Michigan

College for Creative Studies *B*
Ferris State University *B*
Kendall College of Art and Design of
  Ferris State University *B*
Kirtland Community College *A*
University of Michigan *B*

New Jersey

Kean University *B*

Montclair State University *B*
Salem Community College *C, A*

New York

Fashion Institute of Technology *B*
Parsons The New School for Design *B*
Pratt Institute *B, M*
Rochester Institute of
  Technology *A, B, M*

North Carolina

Appalachian State University *B*
North Carolina State University *B, M*

Ohio

Cleveland Institute of Art *B*
Columbus College of Art and
  Design *B*
Ohio State University
  Columbus Campus *B, M*
University of Cincinnati *B*

Oregon

Art Institute of Portland *B*

Pennsylvania

Art Institute
  of Philadelphia *A, B*
  of Pittsburgh *A, B*
Carnegie Mellon University *B*
Philadelphia University *B*
University of the Arts *B, M*

Puerto Rico

Escuela de Artes Plasticas de Puerto
  Rico *B*
Turabo University *B*

Rhode Island

Rhode Island School of Design *B, M*

South Carolina

Clemson University *B, M*

Texas

Texas A&M University
  Commerce *B*
University of Houston *B*

Utah

Brigham Young University *B, M*

Virginia

Lord Fairfax Community College *C*
Virginia Polytechnic Institute and
  State University *B*

Washington

Art Institute of Seattle *A*
University of Washington *B, M*
Western Washington University *B*

Industrial electronics technology

Alabama

Bevill State Community College *C, A*
Lawson State Community College *C*
Lurleen B. Wallace Community
  College *A*
Northeast Alabama Community
  College *C, A*
Shelton State Community
  College *C, A*

Arizona

Eastern Arizona College *C*
Pima Community College *C, A*

Arkansas

Arkansas Northeastern College *C*
Arkansas State University
    Beebe *C*
East Arkansas Community College *C*
Southeast Arkansas College *C, A*
Southern Arkansas University Tech *C*
University of Arkansas
    Community College at Hope *C*
    Fort Smith *C*

California

Irvine Valley College *C*
Victor Valley College *A*

Georgia

Dalton State College *C, A*
Southeastern Technical College *C*

Idaho

Lewis-Clark State College *C, A, B*

Illinois

College of DuPage *C, A*
College of Lake County *C, A*
Danville Area Community College *A*
Harper College *C*
John Wood Community College *C*
Kankakee Community College *C, A*
Lincoln Land Community College *C, A*
Moraine Valley Community College *A*
Parkland College *C*
Sauk Valley Community College *C*
Spoon River College *C*

Indiana

Ivy Tech Community College
    Central Indiana *A*

Iowa

Indian Hills Community College *C*
Iowa Central Community College *C, A*
North Iowa Area Community
    College *A*
Northwest Iowa Community
    College *A*

Kentucky

Bluegrass Community and Technical
    College *C, A*
Somerset Community College *C, A*

Michigan

Ferris State University *A*
Oakland Community College *C*

Minnesota

Central Lakes College *A*
Mesabi Range Community and
    Technical College *A*

Missouri

Crowder College *A*

New Mexico

Clovis Community College *C, A*

North Carolina

Beaufort County Community
    College *C*
Cleveland Community College *C*
Surry Community College *A*

Pennsylvania

Lackawanna College *A*
Lehigh Carbon Community
    College *C, A*
Northampton Community
    College *C, A*
Pennsylvania College of
    Technology *B*

South Carolina

Aiken Technical College *C*
Greenville Technical College *C*
Horry-Georgetown Technical
    College *A*
Midlands Technical College *C*
Spartanburg Community College *C, A*
York Technical College *C*

Utah

Salt Lake Community College *C*

Virginia

Danville Community College *C*
ECPI Technical College: Roanoke *A*

Washington

Bates Technical College *C, A*
Lower Columbia College *A*
North Seattle Community
    College *C, A*
Wenatchee Valley College *C, A*

Wisconsin

Gateway Technical College *C*
Herzing University *A, B*
Lakeshore Technical College *C*
Milwaukee Area Technical College *C*
Western Technical College *C*
Wisconsin Indianhead Technical
    College *C*

Wyoming

Western Wyoming Community
    College *C, A*

Industrial engineering

Alabama

University of Alabama
    Huntsville *B, D*

Arizona

Arizona State University *B, M, D*
University of Arizona *B, M*

Arkansas

University of Arkansas *B, M*

California

California Polytechnic State
    University: San Luis Obispo *B, M*
California State Polytechnic
    University: Pomona *B*
National University *M*
San Jose State University *B, M*
Stanford University *M, D*
University of San Diego *B*
University of Southern
    California *B, M, D*

Colorado

Colorado State University
    Pueblo *B, M*

Connecticut

University of Connecticut *B*
University of New Haven *M*

Florida

Florida Agricultural and Mechanical
    University *B, M, D*
Florida State University *B, M, D*
University of Central Florida *B, M, D*
University of Miami *B, M, D*

Georgia

Georgia Institute of
    Technology *B, M, D*

Illinois

Bradley University *B, M*
Northern Illinois University *B*
Northwestern University *B, M, D*
Southern Illinois University
    Edwardsville *B, M*
University of Illinois
    Chicago *B, M, D*
    Urbana-Champaign *B, M, D*

Indiana

Indiana Institute of Technology *A, B*
Indiana University
    East *A*
Purdue University *B, M, D*

Iowa

Iowa State University *B, M, D*
St. Ambrose University *B*
University of Iowa *B, M, D*

Kansas

Kansas State University *B, M, D*
Wichita State University *B, M, D*

Kentucky

Maysville Community and Technical
    College *A*
University of Louisville *B, M, D*

Louisiana

Louisiana State University and
    Agricultural and Mechanical
    College *B, M*

Maryland

Morgan State University *B, M*

Massachusetts

Northeastern University *B, M, D*
University of Massachusetts
    Amherst *B, M, D*
Western New England College *B*
Worcester Polytechnic Institute *B*

Michigan

Andrews University *B*
Kettering University *B, M*
Lawrence Technological University *B*
Oakland University *B, M*
University of Michigan *B, M, D*
Wayne State University *B, M, D*
Western Michigan University *B, M, D*

Minnesota

University of Minnesota
    Crookston *B*
    Duluth *B*

Mississippi

Mississippi State University *B, M*

Missouri

Missouri Southern State University *B*
University of Missouri
    Columbia *B, M, D*

Nebraska

University of Nebraska
    Lincoln *B, M*

New Jersey

New Jersey Institute of
    Technology *B, M, D*

New Mexico

New Mexico State University *B, M*

New York

Hofstra University *B*
Polytechnic Institute of New York
    University *M*
Rochester Institute of
    Technology *B, M*
State University of New York
    Binghamton *B, M, D*
    Buffalo *B, M, D*
    Maritime College *B*

North Carolina

Catawba Valley Community College *A*
North Carolina State
    University *B, M, D*

North Dakota

North Dakota State University *B, M, D*

Ohio

Cleveland State University *B, M*
Kent State University *B*
Ohio State University
    Columbus Campus *B, M, D*
Ohio University *B, M*
University of Toledo *B, M*
Youngstown State University *B, M*

Oklahoma

Oklahoma State University *B, M, D*
University of Oklahoma *B, M, D*

Oregon

Clackamas Community College *A*
Oregon State University *B, M, D*

Pennsylvania

Drexel University *B*
Elizabethtown College *B*
Lehigh University *B, M, D*
Penn State
    Abington *B*
    Altoona *B*
    Beaver *B*
    Berks *B*
    Brandywine *B*
    DuBois *B*
    Erie, The Behrend College *B*
    Fayette, The Eberly Campus *B*
    Greater Allegheny *B*
    Hazleton *B*
    Lehigh Valley *B*
    Mont Alto *B*
    New Kensington *B*
    Schuylkill *B*
    Shenango *B*
    University Park *B, M, D*
    Wilkes-Barre *B*
    Worthington Scranton *B*
    York *B*
Philadelphia University *B*
University of Pittsburgh *B, M, D*
University of Pittsburgh
    Bradford *B*

Puerto Rico

Inter American University of Puerto
    Rico
    Bayamon Campus *B*
Universidad Politecnica de Puerto
    Rico *B*

Rhode Island

University of Rhode Island *B, M, D*

South Carolina

Clemson University *B, M, D*

South Dakota

South Dakota School of Mines and
    Technology *B*

Tennessee
Tennessee Technological
    University *B, M, D*
University of Tennessee
    Knoxville *B, M, D*

Texas
Lamar University *B, M*
St. Mary's University *B, M*
Texas A&M University *B, M, D*
Texas State University: San Marcos *B*
Texas Tech University *B, M, D*
University of Texas
    Arlington *B, M, D*
    Austin *M, D*
    El Paso *B, M*
    Pan American *B*

Vermont
University of Vermont *B*

Virginia
Liberty University *B*
Tidewater Community College *A*
Virginia Polytechnic Institute and
    State University *B, M, D*

Washington
University of Washington *B*

West Virginia
West Virginia University *B, M*

Wisconsin
Milwaukee School of Engineering *B*
University of Wisconsin
    Madison *B, M, D*

Industrial equipment maintenance/repair

Alabama
Alabama Southern Community
    College *C, A*
Gadsden State Community
    College *C, A*
Lawson State Community College *C*
Northeast Alabama Community
    College *C, A*
Shelton State Community College *C*
Snead State Community College *C*
University of West Alabama *A*

Alaska
University of Alaska
    Anchorage *C, A*

Arizona
Central Arizona College *A*
Eastern Arizona College *C*
Northland Pioneer College *C, A*

Arkansas
Arkansas Northeastern College *C, A*
Arkansas State University
    Beebe *A*
East Arkansas Community
    College *C, A*
Mid-South Community College *C*
Ouachita Technical College *C*
Phillips Community College of the
    University of Arkansas *A*
Pulaski Technical College *C*
South Arkansas Community
    College *C, A*
Southeast Arkansas College *C, A*
Southern Arkansas University Tech *C*
University of Arkansas
    Community College at Batesville *A*
    Community College at Hope *C*
    Fort Smith *C*

Monticello *C, A*

California
Allan Hancock College *C*
Cabrillo College *C, A*
Fresno City College *C, A*
Merced College *C, A*
Taft College *A*

Florida
Hillsborough Community College *C*
Miami Dade College *A*

Georgia
Albany Technical College *C, A*
Athens Technical College *C*
Augusta Technical College *C*
Bainbridge College *C, A*
Central Georgia Technical College *C*
Chattahoochee Technical College *C*
Columbus Technical College *C, A*
Middle Georgia College *A*
Savannah Technical College *C, A*
Waycross College *A*
West Georgia Technical College *A*

Hawaii
University of Hawaii
    Hawaii Community College *C*

Idaho
North Idaho College *A*

Illinois
Black Hawk College *C*
College of Lake County *C, A*
Danville Area Community
    College *C, A*
Elgin Community College *C, A*
Heartland Community College *C, A*
Highland Community College *C*
Illinois Eastern Community Colleges
    Olney Central College *C, A*
    Wabash Valley College *C, A*
John A. Logan College *A*
John Wood Community College *C, A*
Kaskaskia College *C, A*
Lake Land College *C*
Moraine Valley Community College *C*
Prairie State College *C*
Rend Lake College *C, A*
Richland Community College *A*
Southwestern Illinois College *C, A*
Triton College *C, A*
Waubonsee Community College *C, A*

Iowa
Des Moines Area Community
    College *A*
Hawkeye Community College *C*
Iowa Central Community College *C*
Marshalltown Community College *A*
Muscatine Community College *A*
Western Iowa Tech Community
    College *C, A*

Kentucky
Big Sandy Community and Technical
    College *C*
Hopkinsville Community College *C*
Madisonville Community College *C*
Maysville Community and Technical
    College *C*
Somerset Community College *C, A*
West Kentucky Community and
    Technical College *C, A*

Louisiana
Bossier Parish Community College *A*

Maine
Northern Maine Community
    College *A*
Washington County Community
    College *C*

Michigan
Grand Rapids Community College *C*
Henry Ford Community College *C, A*
Kellogg Community College *C, A*
Kirtland Community College *C, A*
Lake Michigan College *A*
Lansing Community College *A*
Macomb Community College *C*
Muskegon Community College *C, A*
Northern Michigan University *A*
Southwestern Michigan College *C, A*

Minnesota
Central Lakes College *C*
Hennepin Technical College *C, A*
Mesabi Range Community and
    Technical College *C*
Minnesota State College - Southeast
    Technical *C, A*
Minnesota State Community and
    Technical College *C, A*
Rainy River Community College *C, A*
Riverland Community College *C*
St. Paul College *C, A*

Mississippi
East Central Community College *C*
Hinds Community College *C*
Meridian Community College *C*
Mississippi Delta Community
    College *C*

Missouri
Jefferson College *A*
Mineral Area College *C, A*
Ozarks Technical Community
    College *C, A*
Ranken Technical College *A*

Montana
University of Montana *C*

Nebraska
Central Community College *C, A*
Metropolitan Community College *A*

Nevada
Great Basin College *C, A*

New Hampshire
Nashua Community College *A*

New Mexico
Clovis Community College *C, A*
San Juan College *C, A*

North Carolina
Alamance Community College *C, A*
Beaufort County Community
    College *C*
Bladen Community College *C*
Blue Ridge Community College *C*
Caldwell Community College and
    Technical Institute *A*
Central Carolina Community
    College *A*
Durham Technical Community
    College *C*
Halifax Community College *C, A*
Mayland Community College *C*
McDowell Technical Community
    College *A*
Mitchell Community College *A*
Nash Community College *C*
Richmond Community College *C*

Roanoke-Chowan Community
    College *C*
Rockingham Community College *C*
Rowan-Cabarrus Community
    College *C, A*
Sampson Community College *C, A*
Surry Community College *A*
Vance-Granville Community
    College *C*

North Dakota
Bismarck State College *C, A*

Ohio
Eastern Gateway Community
    College *A*
Stark State College of Technology *A*

Oregon
Blue Mountain Community College *A*
Chemeketa Community College *A*
Linn-Benton Community College *A*
Portland Community College *C, A*
Rogue Community College *C*

Pennsylvania
Harrisburg Area Community
    College *C, A*
Johnson College *A*
Pennsylvania College of
    Technology *A*
Reading Area Community College *A*
Westmoreland County Community
    College *A*

South Carolina
Aiken Technical College *C, A*
Central Carolina Technical College *C*
Greenville Technical College *C, A*
Midlands Technical College *C*
Spartanburg Community College *C*
Tri-County Technical College *A*
Trident Technical College *C, A*
York Technical College *C, A*

South Dakota
Western Dakota Technical Institute *A*

Tennessee
Northeast State Community
    College *C, A*
Walters State Community College *C*

Texas
Amarillo College *C, A*
Lamar Institute of Technology *C, A*
San Jacinto College *C*
Texas State Technical College
    Waco *C, A*

Utah
Weber State University *A*

Virginia
Germanna Community College *C*
John Tyler Community College *C*
New River Community College *C*
Southside Virginia Community
    College *C*
Southwest Virginia Community
    College *C*
Thomas Nelson Community
    College *C*
Tidewater Community College *A*
Virginia Highlands Community
    College *C*

Washington
Bellingham Technical College *A*
Big Bend Community College *C, A*
Lake Washington Technical College *C*
Lower Columbia College *A*

Renton Technical College *C, A*
Spokane Community College *A*

West Virginia

Blue Ridge Community and Technical
College *C*
Eastern West Virginia Community and
Technical College *C, A*
West Virginia Northern Community
College *C*

Wisconsin

Blackhawk Technical College *C*
Chippewa Valley Technical College *A*
Gateway Technical College *C, A*
Lakeshore Technical College *C*
Milwaukee Area Technical College *C*
Moraine Park Technical College *C*
Northeast Wisconsin Technical
College *A*
Waukesha County Technical
College *C*
Wisconsin Indianhead Technical
College *C*

Wyoming

Casper College *C, A*
Western Wyoming Community
College *C, A*

Industrial/ organizational psychology

Alabama

Alabama Agricultural and Mechanical
University *M*

Arizona

Northcentral University *M, D*
Prescott College *B*
University of Phoenix *M, D*

Arkansas

University of Arkansas
Little Rock *M*

California

Alliant International University *M, D*
Antioch Southern California
Antioch University Santa Barbara *M*
California State University
Long Beach *M*
San Bernardino *M*
Golden Gate University *M*
John F. Kennedy University *M*
Point Loma Nazarene University *B*
St. Mary's College of California *B*
San Jose State University *M*

Colorado

Colorado State University *M*
Fort Lewis College *B*

Connecticut

University of New Haven *M*

District of Columbia

George Washington University *D*

Florida

Carlos Albizu University *M*
Florida Institute of Technology *M, D*
University of Central Florida *M*

Georgia

Georgia Institute of
Technology *B, M, D*

Idaho

Northwest Nazarene University *B*

Illinois

Argosy University: Chicago *M*
DePaul University *M, D*
Roosevelt University *M*
Saint Xavier University *B*
University of Illinois
Urbana-Champaign *M, D*

Iowa

Morningside College *B*

Kentucky

Eastern Kentucky University *M*
Northern Kentucky University *M*

Louisiana

Louisiana Tech University *M*

Maryland

University of Baltimore *M*
University of Maryland
Baltimore County *M*

Massachusetts

Bridgewater State College *M*
Fitchburg State College *B*
Salem State College *M*
Springfield College *M*

Michigan

Central Michigan University *M, D*
Madonna University *B*
University of Detroit Mercy *M*
Wayne State University *M*

Minnesota

Capella University *M, D*
Minnesota State University
Mankato *M*
Saint Cloud State University *M*
University of Minnesota
Crookston *B*
Walden University *M, D*

Missouri

Maryville University of Saint Louis *B*
Northwest Missouri State
University *B*
Saint Louis University *M, D*
Washington University in St. Louis *B*

Nebraska

Nebraska Wesleyan University *B*
University of Nebraska
Omaha *M*

New Jersey

Fairleigh Dickinson University
College at Florham *M*
Rutgers, The State University of New
Jersey
New Brunswick/Piscataway
Campus *D*

New York

City University of New York
Baruch College *M*
Brooklyn College *M*
Hofstra University *M, D*
Ithaca College *B*
New York University *M, D*
State University of New York
Albany *M, D*
Farmingdale *B*

North Carolina

Appalachian State University *M*

University of North Carolina
Charlotte *M*

Ohio

Bowling Green State University *M, D*
Ohio State University
Columbus Campus *M, D*
Ohio University *M, D*
Tiffin University *B*
Union Institute & University *M*
University of Akron *D*
Wright State University *M, D*

Oklahoma

University of Tulsa *M, D*

Pennsylvania

Holy Family University *B*
Lincoln University *B*
Marywood University *B*
Saint Joseph's University *B*

Puerto Rico

Inter American University of Puerto
Rico
Metropolitan Campus *M, D*
University of Puerto Rico
Arecibo *B*
Rio Piedras *M*

South Carolina

Clemson University *D*

Tennessee

Southern Adventist University *M*
University of Tennessee
Knoxville *M, D*

Texas

Angelo State University *M*
Lamar University *M*
Rice University *M, D*
St. Mary's University *M*
Texas A&M University *M*
University of Houston *M, D*
University of Texas
El Paso *D*

Virginia

Averett University *B*
Old Dominion University *D*

Washington

Seattle Pacific University *M, D*

Wisconsin

University of Wisconsin
Oshkosh *M*

Industrial radiologic technology

Alabama

Northwest-Shoals Community
College *C*

Kansas

Cowley County Community
College *A*

Utah

Salt Lake Community College *A*

Industrial safety technology

Alaska

University of Alaska
Fairbanks *C*

New Mexico

Eastern New Mexico University:
Roswell Campus *C*

North Carolina

Nash Community College *A*

Ohio

James A. Rhodes State College *C, A*

Oklahoma

Northeastern State University *B*
University of Central Oklahoma *B*

South Dakota

South Dakota State University *B*

Texas

University of Houston
Downtown *B*

Virginia

Southwest Virginia Community
College *C*

Washington

Bates Technical College *C, A*

Industrial technology

Alabama

Gadsden State Community
College *C, A*

Alaska

University of Alaska
Fairbanks *A*

Arizona

Arizona State University *B*
Arizona Western College *A*
Penn Foster College *A*

Arkansas

Arkansas Tech University *A*
Pulaski Technical College *A*
Southern Arkansas University *A, B*
Southern Arkansas University Tech *A*
University of Arkansas
Pine Bluff *A, B*

California

California State University
Fresno *B, M*
Los Angeles *B*
College of the Sequoias *C, A*
San Francisco State University *B*
San Joaquin Valley College *C*

Colorado

Red Rocks Community College *C, A*

Connecticut

Asnuntuck Community College *A*
Central Connecticut State
University *B*
Northwestern Connecticut
Community College *A*

Delaware

Delaware State University *B*

Florida

St. Petersburg College *A*
South Florida Community College *A*

Georgia

Macon State College *A*
Middle Georgia Technical College *C*
North Georgia Technical College *C, A*

Illinois
Eastern Illinois University *B, M*
Highland Community College *C, A*
Illinois Institute of Technology *M*
Illinois State University *B, M*
Northern Illinois University *B*
Parkland College *C, A*
Southern Illinois University
   Carbondale *B*

Indiana
Ball State University *B*
Indiana State University *B, M, D*
Indiana University-Purdue University
   Fort Wayne *A, B*
Ivy Tech Community College
   Bloomington *C*
   Central Indiana *C, A*
   Columbus *C*
   East Central *C*
   Kokomo *C*
   Lafayette *C*
   North Central *C*
   Northeast *C*
   Northwest *C*
   Richmond *C, A*
   South Central *C*
Purdue University *A, B, M, D*
Purdue University
   North Central *C, A*
Vincennes University *B*

Iowa
University of Northern Iowa *B, M, D*
William Penn University *B*

Kansas
Kansas State University *A*
Manhattan Area Technical College *A*
Neosho County Community
   College *C, A*

Kentucky
Bluegrass Community and Technical
   College *C*
Maysville Community and Technical
   College *C*
Northern Kentucky University *B*
Western Kentucky University *B*

Louisiana
Baton Rouge Community College *A*
Bossier Parish Community College *A*
Northwestern State University *B*
Nunez Community College *A*
South Louisiana Community
   College *A*
Southeastern Louisiana
   University *A, B*
University of Louisiana at Lafayette *B*

Maryland
Community College of Baltimore
   County *C, A*
Hagerstown Community College *C, A*

Massachusetts
Bristol Community College *C*
Fitchburg State College *B*
University of Massachusetts
   Lowell *B*

Michigan
Delta College *A*
Eastern Michigan University *B*
Ferris State University *B*
Kirtland Community College *C, A*
Lawrence Technological University *B*
Michigan Technological University *B*
Montcalm Community College *A*
Mott Community College *C*
Northern Michigan University *B*

Oakland Community College *C, A*
Wayne State University *B*

Minnesota
Alexandria Technical College *A*
Dunwoody College of Technology *C*
Hennepin Technical College *C, A*
Minnesota State University
   Moorhead *B*
Northwest Technical College *A*
St. Mary's University of Minnesota *B*

Mississippi
Jackson State University *B*
Mississippi State University *B*
Mississippi Valley State University *B*
University of Southern
   Mississippi *B, M*

Missouri
Ozarks Technical Community
   College *C, A*
St. Charles Community College *A*
Southeast Missouri State University *B*
University of Central Missouri *B, M*

Nebraska
University of Nebraska
   Lincoln *B*
   Omaha *B*

New Jersey
Salem Community College *A*

New Mexico
San Juan College *A*

New York
Broome Community College *C, A*
Clinton Community College *A*
Erie Community College
   North Campus *A*
   South Campus *A*
State University of New York
   College at Buffalo *B*
   Farmingdale *B*
   Institute of Technology at
     Utica/Rome *B*
Ulster County Community College *A*

North Carolina
Appalachian State University *M*
Bladen Community College *C, A*
Davidson County Community
   College *C*
East Carolina University *B, M*
Elizabeth City State University *B*
Gaston College *C, A*
Roanoke-Chowan Community
   College *A*
Rowan-Cabarrus Community
   College *A*
Western Carolina University *B, M*
Wilkes Community College *C, A*

North Dakota
Bismarck State College *C, A*
University of North Dakota *B, M*

Ohio
Bowling Green State University *B*
Central State University *B*
Cincinnati State Technical and
   Community College *A*
Clark State Community College *C, A*
Columbus State Community
   College *A*
Edison State Community College *C, A*
James A. Rhodes State College *A*
Kent State University
   Salem *A*

   Trumbull *A*
   Tuscarawas *A*
Kent State University: Geauga *A*
Ohio University *B*
Owens Community College
   Toledo *C, A*
University of Dayton *B*
University of Rio Grande *C*
University of Toledo *A*
Wright State University *A*

Oklahoma
Oklahoma Panhandle State
   University *A, B*

Oregon
Central Oregon Community
   College *A*
Clackamas Community College *C, A*
Lane Community College *C, A*
Linn-Benton Community College *C*
Umpqua Community College *A*

Pennsylvania
Lackawanna College *A*
Millersville University of
   Pennsylvania *A, B*
Pennsylvania College of
   Technology *B*
South Hills School of Business &
   Technology *A*

Puerto Rico
University of Puerto Rico
   Arecibo *B*
   Bayamon University College *A*

South Carolina
South Carolina State University *B*

South Dakota
Black Hills State University *B*

Tennessee
Chattanooga State Community
   College *A*
Cleveland State Community College *A*
Jackson State Community College *A*
Middle Tennessee State
   University *B, M*
Walters State Community College *C, A*

Texas
Lamar University *B*
Lone Star College System *C, A*
Panola College *C, A*
Prairie View A&M University *B*
Sam Houston State University *B, M*
Tarleton State University *B*
Texas Southern University *B, M*
Texas State Technical College:
   Marshall *C, A*
Texas State University: San
   Marcos *B, M*
University of Houston *B*
University of Texas
   Brownsville - Texas Southmost
     College *C, A, B*
   Tyler *B, M*
   of the Permian Basin *B*
West Texas A&M University *B, M*

Virginia
Piedmont Virginia Community
   College *A*

Washington
Olympic College *C, A*
Shoreline Community College *A*
Western Washington University *B*

West Virginia
Fairmont State University *A*

Wisconsin
Mid-State Technical College *A*
Milwaukee Area Technical College *A*

Information resources management

Alabama
Athens State University *B*

Alaska
Alaska Pacific University *M*

Arkansas
Ozarka College *A*

California
Golden Gate University *B, M*
Santa Clara University *M*
University of San Diego *M*

Colorado
Colorado Technical University *B*

Delaware
Wilmington University *B*

Florida
Florida Institute of Technology *B*

Illinois
DePaul University *M*

Iowa
Dordt College *B*

Maryland
Mount St. Mary's University *B*

Michigan
Michigan State University *B, M, D*
Montcalm Community College *A*
Western Michigan University *B*

Minnesota
Capella University *M, D*
Metropolitan State University *B*

Missouri
Grantham University *A*

New Jersey
Seton Hall University *B*

North Carolina
Chowan University *B*
Coastal Carolina Community
   College *A*

Oregon
Corban College *B*

Pennsylvania
Duquesne University *M*
Juniata College *B*

Puerto Rico
Turabo University *D*

South Carolina
Williamsburg Technical College *A*

Texas
Abilene Christian University *B*
Houston Baptist University *B*

Lubbock Christian University *B*
St. Edward's University *M*
University of Dallas *M*

Utah

Brigham Young University *B, M*
Westminster College *B*

Vermont

Champlain College *M*

Virginia

University of Management and
Technology *M*

Wisconsin

University of Wisconsin
Eau Claire *B*

Information systems

Alabama

Alabama State University *B*
Faulkner University *B*
Gadsden State Community College *A*
Herzing University *A, B*
Northwest-Shoals Community
College *A*
Prince Institute of Professional
Studies *A*

Arizona

Cochise College *A*
Collins College *A*
Eastern Arizona College *C, A*
GateWay Community College *C, A*
Phoenix College *A*
Prescott College *B, M*
Scottsdale Community College *C, A*
Western International University *M*

Arkansas

Arkansas State University
Mountain Home *C, A*
Ozarka College *C*
Rich Mountain Community
College *C, A*
University of Arkansas
Little Rock *B*

California

Antelope Valley College *C, A*
California Lutheran University *B*
California State University
East Bay *B, M*
Long Beach *B, M*
Los Angeles *M*
Sacramento *B, M*
Chabot College *A*
Coleman University *M*
Cosumnes River College *A*
Cypress College *C, A*
El Camino College: Compton
Center *C*
Empire College *C, A*
Fresno City College *C, A*
Humboldt State University *B*
LA College International *C*
La Sierra University *B*
Laney College *A*
Los Angeles Harbor College *A*
Merced College *A*
Mission College *C, A*
Moorpark College *C, A*
National University *B*
Ohlone College *C, A*
Orange Coast College *C, A*
Palomar College *C, A*
Platt College
Ontario *A*
Reedley College *C, A*

Remington College
San Diego *A*
San Diego City College *A*
San Diego State University *B, M*
San Joaquin Delta College *C*
San Jose State University *B*
Santa Monica College *C, A*
Santa Rosa Junior College *C*
Santiago Canyon College *A*
Skyline College *C, A*
Southwestern College *A*
Taft College *C, A*
University of California
Berkeley *M, D*
Irvine *B*
Los Angeles *M, D*
San Diego *B*
University of Redlands *M*
University of San Francisco *B*
University of the Pacific *B*
West Hills College: Coalinga *C*

Colorado

American Sentinel University *B, M*
Colorado State University *B*
Colorado State University
Pueblo *B*
Colorado Technical University *A, B, M*
Community College of Aurora *C, A*
Front Range Community College *C*
Lamar Community College *A*
University of Colorado
Denver *M*
University of Denver *M*
Westwood College: Denver
North *A, B*

Connecticut

Albertus Magnus College *C, A, B*
Central Connecticut State
University *M*
Gateway Community College *C, A*
Manchester Community College *C, A*
Middlesex Community College *C, A*
Norwalk Community College *C, A*
Three Rivers Community College *A*
University of Hartford *B*
University of New Haven *B*

District of Columbia

American University *M*
Gallaudet University *B*
George Washington University *B, M*
Howard University *B*

Florida

Bethune-Cookman University *B*
Broward College *A*
Chipola College *A*
Clearwater Christian College *B*
Florida Institute of
Technology *A, B, M*
Florida State College at Jacksonville *A*
Florida State University *M, D*
Lake City Community College *A*
Miami Dade College *C, A*
Nova Southeastern University *D*
Palm Beach Community College *A*
Pensacola Junior College *A*
Polk State College *A*
Seminole Community College *A*
State College of Florida,
Manatee-Sarasota *A*
University of Miami *C, B, M*
University of South Florida *B*

Georgia

Albany State University *B*
American InterContinental
University *M*
Brewton-Parker College *B*
Clayton State University *C, A, B*
Columbus Technical College *C*

Darton College *A*
DeVry University
Alpharetta *B*
Decatur *B*
Fort Valley State University *B*
Georgia Institute of Technology *M*
Georgia Southern University *B*
Gordon College *A*
Griffin Technical College *A*
Herzing University *A, B*
Kennesaw State University *B, M*
Macon State College *B*
Mercer University *B*
Reinhardt College *B*
Savannah State University *B*
Valdosta State University *B*

Hawaii

Hawaii Pacific University *M*
University of Hawaii
Honolulu Community College *A*
Maui Community College *B*

Idaho

Boise State University *B*
Idaho State University *B, M*

Illinois

Benedictine University *B*
Bradley University *B, M*
Chicago State University *B*
City Colleges of Chicago
Harold Washington College *C, A*
DePaul University *C, B, M*
DeVry University
Addison *B*
Tinley Park *B, M*
Dominican University *B, M*
Elmhurst College *B*
Harper College *C, A*
Illinois Valley Community College *A*
John A. Logan College *C*
Joliet Junior College *A*
Kaskaskia College *A*
Lewis University *B*
MacCormac College *C, A*
McKendree University *B*
Midstate College *B*
National-Louis University *C, B*
Northwestern University *B, M*
Olivet Nazarene University *B*
Quincy University *B*
Rockford Career College *A*
Roosevelt University *C, M*
Southeastern Illinois College *A*
Southern Illinois University
Carbondale *B*
Southwestern Illinois College *A*
Trinity Christian College *B*
Triton College *C, A*
University of Illinois
Chicago *B*

Indiana

Anderson University *B*
Bethel College *B*
Butler University *B*
Goshen College *B*
Indiana Institute of Technology *A, B*
Indiana University-Purdue University
Fort Wayne *A, B*
Indiana University-Purdue University
Indianapolis *B*
Purdue University
Calumet *A, B*
Taylor University *A*
University of Indianapolis *A, B*

Iowa

Central College *B*
Dordt College *B*
Ellsworth Community College *C, A*
St. Ambrose University *B*

Simpson College *B*
Southwestern Community College *A*
Waldorf College *B*
Wartburg College *B*

Kansas

Baker University *B*
Barton County Community College *A*
Central Christian College of Kansas *A*
Emporia State University *B*
Kansas State University *B*
MidAmerica Nazarene University *B*
Newman University *A, B*
Pittsburg State University *B*

Kentucky

Ashland Community and Technical
College *A*
Daymar College
Owensboro *A*
Murray State University *A, B, M*
Northern Kentucky University *B*
Owensboro Community and
Technical College *A*
Sullivan College of Technology and
Design *A*

Louisiana

Bossier Parish Community College *A*
Grambling State University *B*
ITI Technical College *A*
Louisiana State University
Shreveport *B*
Louisiana State University and
Agricultural and Mechanical
College *M*
Northwestern State University *B*
Nunez Community College *C, A*

Maine

Eastern Maine Community College *C*
Husson University *A*
University of Maine *M*

Maryland

Allegany College of Maryland *A*
Baltimore City Community College *A*
Chesapeake College *C*
Frederick Community College *A*
Frostburg State University *C*
Garrett College *C, A*
Montgomery College *A*
Morgan State University *B*
Prince George's Community
College *C, A*
Salisbury University *B*
TESST College of Technology
Beltsville *C, A*
Towson University *M, D*
University of Maryland
Baltimore County *B, M, D*
College Park *B, M*
University College *C, B, M*
Washington Adventist University *A, B*

Massachusetts

American International College *B*
Babson College *B*
Boston College *B*
Bristol Community College *A*
Cape Cod Community College *A*
Massachusetts Bay Community
College *C, A*
North Shore Community College *C*
Northeastern University *B, M*
Northern Essex Community
College *A*
Springfield College *B*
Suffolk University *B*
Tufts University *B*
University of Massachusetts
Lowell *A, B*
Western New England College *B*

Westfield State College *B*

Michigan

Alpena Community College *C, A*
Andrews University *B*
Baker College
  of Auburn Hills *A*
  of Jackson *C*
  of Muskegon *B*
  of Owosso *A*
  of Port Huron *A, B*
Calvin College *B*
Delta College *C, A*
Eastern Michigan University *M*
Grand Valley State University *B, M*
Lawrence Technological University *M*
Michigan State University *B*
Northwestern Michigan College *A*
University of Michigan *M, D*
University of Michigan
  Flint *B, M*
Washtenaw Community College *C, A*
Wayne State University *B*

Minnesota

Anoka Technical College *C, A*
Augsburg College *C*
Brown College *B*
Hennepin Technical College *C, A*
Metropolitan State University *B*
National American University
  Bloomington *A*
Pine Technical College *A*
St. Catherine University *B*
St. Mary's University of Minnesota *B*
University of Minnesota
  Duluth *B*
  Twin Cities *C*
University of St. Thomas *B*

Missouri

Grantham University *A, B*
Harris-Stowe State University *B*
Lincoln University *B*
Missouri Southern State
  University *A, B*
Missouri Technical School *B*
Missouri Western State University *B*
Northwest Missouri State
  University *C*
University of Central Missouri *M*
University of Missouri
  Missouri University of Science and
    Technology *B, M*
Vatterott College: Kansas City *A*
Washington University in St.
  Louis *B, M*

Montana

Little Big Horn College *A*
Stone Child College *A*
University of Great Falls *M*

Nebraska

Bellevue University *B*
Chadron State College *B*
Doane College *B*
Southeast Community College *C, A*
Union College *A, B*
University of Nebraska
  Kearney *B*
Wayne State College *B*

Nevada

College of Southern Nevada *A*

New Hampshire

Daniel Webster College *A, B*
Nashua Community College *A*

New Jersey

Burlington County College *C, A*
Essex County College *C*
Mercer County Community College *C*
New Jersey Institute of
  Technology *B, M, D*
Ocean County College *C*
Ramapo College of New Jersey *B*
Richard Stockton College of New
  Jersey *B*
Rutgers, The State University of New
  Jersey
  Newark Regional Campus *B*
Saint Peter's College *C, A, B*

New Mexico

Central New Mexico Community
  College *C, A*
New Mexico State University *B*
New Mexico State University
  Alamogordo *A*

New York

Adelphi University *B*
Adirondack Community College *A*
Broome Community College *A*
Cayuga County Community College *C*
City University of New York
  Baruch College *B*
  Brooklyn College *B, M*
  College of Staten Island *B*
  Lehman College *B*
  Medgar Evers College *B*
  Queensborough Community
    College *A*
College of Westchester *C, A*
Columbia University *M, D*
Excelsior College *B*
Finger Lakes Community College *C, A*
Fulton-Montgomery Community
  College *A*
Genesee Community College *A*
Globe Institute of Technology *C*
Hartwick College *B*
Ithaca College *B*
Jefferson Community College *A*
Long Island University
  C. W. Post Campus *B, M, D*
Manhattan College *B*
Marist College *B, M*
Mercy College *B*
Mildred Elley *C, A*
Molloy College *B*
Nazareth College *B*
New York University *M*
Niagara University *C, B*
Onondaga Community College *A*
Pace University *A, B, M*
Siena College *C*
State University of New York
  Albany *B, M, D*
  Buffalo *B, M*
  College at Buffalo *B*
  College at Old Westbury *B*
  College of Agriculture and
    Technology at Cobleskill *A*
  College of Technology at Canton *A*
  Farmingdale *C, A*
  Institute of Technology at
    Utica/Rome *B, M*
  Oswego *B*
  Stony Brook *B*
Suffolk County Community
  College *C, A*
Syracuse University *B, M, D*
Tompkins Cortland Community
  College *A*
United States Military Academy *B*
Westchester Community College *C, A*

North Carolina

Alamance Community College *A*
Beaufort County Community
  College *C, A*
Blue Ridge Community College *A*
Brunswick Community College *A*
Campbell University *B*
Catawba Valley Community College *A*
Central Carolina Community
  College *C, A*
Cleveland Community College *C, A*
Coastal Carolina Community
  College *A*
College of the Albemarle *C, A*
Edgecombe Community College *A*
Elon University *B*
Fayetteville Technical Community
  College *C, A*
Guilford College *B*
Guilford Technical Community
  College *A*
Isothermal Community College *A*
Lees-McRae College *B*
Lenoir-Rhyne University *B*
Martin Community College *C, A*
Mitchell Community College *C, A*
Nash Community College *A*
North Carolina Central
  University *B, M*
North Carolina Wesleyan College *B*
Pitt Community College *C, A*
Queens University of Charlotte *B*
Richmond Community College *C, A*
Roanoke-Chowan Community
  College *A*
Rockingham Community College *C, A*
Rowan-Cabarrus Community
  College *C, A*
Sampson Community College *A*
Sandhills Community College *C, A*
South Piedmont Community
  College *A*
Stanly Community College *C, A*
Surry Community College *C, A*
Tri-County Community College *A*
University of North Carolina
  Chapel Hill *B, M*
Western Piedmont Community
  College *C, A*
Wilkes Community College *C, A*

North Dakota

North Dakota State College of
  Science *A*
University of Mary *B*

Ohio

Bryant & Stratton College
  Parma *A*
Case Western Reserve
  University *M, D*
Clark State Community College *A*
Columbus State Community
  College *A*
Eastern Gateway Community
  College *C, A*
Marietta College *B*
Ohio Dominican University *B*
Ohio State University
  Columbus Campus *B*
Stark State College of Technology *A*
Terra State Community College *A*
Tiffin University *B*
University of Cincinnati *M, D*
University of Toledo *B, M*
Urbana University *B*
Wilberforce University *B*
Wright State University *B*
Wright State University: Lake
  Campus *A*
Youngstown State University *A, B*
Zane State College *A*

Oklahoma

Northwestern Oklahoma State
  University *B*
Oklahoma Baptist University *B*
Oklahoma Christian University *B*
Oklahoma City University *M*
Southeastern Oklahoma State
  University *B*
Southwestern Oklahoma State
  University *B*
University of Oklahoma *B*
Western Oklahoma State College *A*

Oregon

George Fox University *B*
Lane Community College *C*
Southwestern Oregon Community
  College *A*
Umpqua Community College *A*

Pennsylvania

Albright College *B*
Bucks County Community College *A*
Carnegie Mellon University *B, M*
Clarion University of Pennsylvania *B*
Drexel University *B, M, D*
Elizabethtown College *C, A, B*
Immaculata University *C, A, B*
Keystone College *A, B*
Keystone Technical Institute *C*
La Salle University *A, B, M*
Lehigh Carbon Community
  College *C, A*
Lehigh University *B, M*
Mansfield University of
  Pennsylvania *A, B*
Marywood University *M*
Messiah College *B*
Montgomery County Community
  College *A*
Peirce College *B*
Penn State
  Abington *A, B*
  Altoona *A, B*
  Beaver *A, B*
  Berks *A, B*
  Brandywine *A, B*
  DuBois *A, B*
  Erie, The Behrend College *A, B*
  Fayette, The Eberly Campus *A, B*
  Greater Allegheny *C, B*
  Harrisburg *B*
  Hazleton *A, B*
  Lehigh Valley *A, B*
  Mont Alto *B*
  New Kensington *A, B*
  Schuylkill *A, B*
  Shenango *A, B*
  University Park *A, B, M, D*
  Wilkes-Barre *A, B*
  Worthington Scranton *B*
  York *A, B*
Robert Morris University *B, D*
St. Francis University *B*
Saint Joseph's University *A, B*
Slippery Rock University of
  Pennsylvania *B*
Susquehanna University *B*
Thiel College *A, B*
University of Pittsburgh *B, M, D*
University of Pittsburgh
  Bradford *A*
  Greensburg *B*
University of Scranton *C, B*
Villanova University *B*
Widener University *B*
Wilkes University *B*

Puerto Rico

Humacao Community College *A*
Inter American University of Puerto
  Rico
  Metropolitan Campus *M*
  Ponce Campus *B*
National College of Business and
  Technology: Bayamon *A, B*
Universidad Adventista de las
  Antillas *B*
University of the Sacred Heart *B*

Rhode Island
Bryant University *M*
Johnson & Wales University:
 Providence *B*
Salve Regina University *B*

South Carolina
Clemson University *B*
Coastal Carolina University *B*
College of Charleston *B*
Forrest Junior College *C, A*
Midlands Technical College *C, A*
Orangeburg-Calhoun Technical
 College *C*
Trident Technical College *A*
University of South Carolina
 Upstate *B*

South Dakota
Dakota State University *B, M, D*
Kilian Community College *A*
Southeast Technical Institute *C*

Tennessee
Belmont University *B, M*
Dyersburg State Community
 College *C, A*
Pellissippi State Community
 College *A*

Texas
Amarillo College *C, A*
Baylor University *M, D*
Brookhaven College *A*
Central Texas College *C, A*
El Centro College *C, A*
El Paso Community College *C, A*
Frank Phillips College *C*
Galveston College *A*
Howard Payne University *B*
Lamar University *M*
Laredo Community College *A*
LeTourneau University *B*
Lee College *C, A*
Midland College *C, A*
North Lake College *C, A*
Odessa College *A*
Palo Alto College *A*
Panola College *C*
Prairie View A&M University *M*
St. Philip's College *A*
Southern Methodist University *B, M*
Southwestern Adventist
 University *A, B, T*
Tarleton State University *M*
Texas A&M University
 Commerce *B*
Texas Lutheran University *B*
Texas State Technical College
 Waco *C, A*
Texas Wesleyan University *B*
Tyler Junior College *C, A*
University of Houston *B*
University of Houston
 Victoria *B, M*
University of Mary Hardin-Baylor *B, M*
University of North Texas *B, M, D*
University of Texas
 Brownsville - Texas Southmost
  College *B*
 Dallas *M*
 El Paso *M*
 Pan American *M*
 San Antonio *M*
 of the Permian Basin *B*
Victoria College *C, A*

Utah
College of Eastern Utah *C*
Snow College *A*
Utah State University *B, M*
Weber State University *B*

Vermont
Champlain College *B*
St. Michael's College *B*

Virginia
Averett University *B*
Blue Ridge Community College *A*
Central Virginia Community
 College *A*
Christopher Newport University *B*
Danville Community College *C*
ECPI College of Technology: Virginia
 Beach *C, A*
ECPI Technical College: Roanoke *C, A*
Ferrum College *B*
George Mason University *M*
J. Sargeant Reynolds Community
 College *A*
James Madison University *B*
Marymount University *B, M*
Mountain Empire Community
 College *A*
Radford University *B*
Rappahannock Community College *A*
Roanoke College *B*
Stratford University: Woodbridge *B, M*
Thomas Nelson Community
 College *C, A*
University of Management and
 Technology *A, B, M*
University of Richmond *C, A*
Virginia Commonwealth
 University *B, M*
Virginia Polytechnic Institute and
 State University *M*
Wytheville Community College *C, A*

Washington
Centralia College *A*
City University of Seattle *C*
Everett Community College *C, A*
Renton Technical College *C*
Skagit Valley College *A*
South Puget Sound Community
 College *C, A*
South Seattle Community
 College *C, A*
Spokane Community College *A*
Spokane Falls Community College *A*
University of Washington *B, M, D*
University of Washington Bothell *B*
Walla Walla University *B*
Yakima Valley Community College *A*

West Virginia
Blue Ridge Community and Technical
 College *C, A*
Davis and Elkins College *B*
Eastern West Virginia Community and
 Technical College *A*
Marshall University *M*
West Liberty University *B*
West Virginia Junior College *A*
West Virginia State Community and
 Technical College *A*
West Virginia University at
 Parkersburg *C, A*
West Virginia Wesleyan College *B*

Wisconsin
Carroll University *B*
Fox Valley Technical College *A*
Herzing University *A, B*
Marquette University *B*
Silver Lake College *B*
University of Wisconsin
 Green Bay *B*

Wyoming
Northwest College *A*
Sheridan College *A*
Western Wyoming Community
 College *A*

Information technology

Alabama
Columbia Southern University *B*
Gadsden State Community College *A*
Northwest-Shoals Community
 College *A*
Oakwood University *B*
South University: Montgomery *A, B*

Alaska
Ilisagvik College *C*

Arizona
Chandler-Gilbert Community College
 Pecos *A*
GateWay Community College *C*
University of Phoenix *A, B*

Arkansas
Arkansas Tech University *A, B, M*
Harding University *B*
Phillips Community College of the
 University of Arkansas *A*
South Arkansas Community College *A*

California
Allan Hancock College *C, A*
Bethesda Christian University *B*
California State University
 Chico *A*
 Dominguez Hills *B*
 Fullerton *B, M*
 Stanislaus *B*
College of the Siskiyous *C*
DeVry University
 Long Beach *B*
Foothill College *C, A*
Golden Gate University *C, B, M*
Hartnell College *C, A*
Kaplan College: Panorama City *A*
Mt. Sierra College *B*
National University *B, M*
Oxnard College *C, A*
Pacific States University *M*
Platt College
 Ontario *A*
San Diego State University *B, M*
San Jose State University *B*
Sierra College *A*
Silicon Valley College
 Western Career College:
  Emeryville *C, A*
Southwestern College *C, A*
Vanguard University of Southern
 California *B*

Colorado
American Sentinel University *B, M*
Aspen University *M*
Colorado Mountain College *A*
Colorado State University *B*
Colorado Technical
 University *C, A, B, M*
Jones International University *M*
University of Denver *C, B*

Connecticut
Sacred Heart University *B, M*

Florida
Barry University *B*
Florida Atlantic University *M*
Florida International University *B*
Florida State University *B*
Gulf Coast Community College *A*
Herzing University *C, A, B*
Hodges University *A, B, M*
Indian River State College *A*
Miami Dade College *C, A*
Pasco-Hernando Community
 College *A*

St. Petersburg College *C*
Santa Fe College *C*
South University: West Palm
 Beach *A, B*
Southwest Florida College *A*
University of Central Florida *B*
University of South Florida *B*
University of West Florida *B*
Valencia Community College *A*

Georgia
Abraham Baldwin Agricultural
 College *A*
American InterContinental
 University *B*
Armstrong Atlantic State University *B*
Clayton State University *B*
Columbus State University *B*
DeVry University
 Alpharetta *M*
Georgia Gwinnett College *B*
Gwinnett College *A*
Macon State College *C, A*
Middle Georgia College *A*
South Georgia College *A*
South University: Savannah *A, B, M*
Southern Polytechnic State
 University *B, M*

Hawaii
University of Hawaii
 Maui Community College *B*

Illinois
DePaul University *B*
DeVry University
 Addison *B*
Heartland Community College *A*
Highland Community College *A*
Illinois Institute of Technology *B, M*
Illinois State University *B, M*
International Academy of Design and
 Technology: Chicago *A, B*
John A. Logan College *A*
Kankakee Community College *A*
Lewis and Clark Community
 College *A*
Loyola University Chicago *B, M*
McKendree University *B*
Morton College *A*
Rasmussen College: Aurora *A*
Rasmussen College: Rockford *A*
Robert Morris University: Chicago *B*
Spoon River College *A*
University of St. Francis *B*

Indiana
Harrison College
 Evansville *A*
 Fort Wayne *A*
 Indianapolis *B*
 Terre Haute *A*
Indiana State University *B*
Ivy Tech Community College
 Bloomington *A*
 Central Indiana *A*
 Columbus *A*
 East Central *C, A*
 Kokomo *C, A*
 Lafayette *A*
 North Central *C, A*
 Northeast *C, A*
 Northwest *C, A*
 Richmond *C, A*
 South Central *C, A*
 Southeast *C, A*
 Southwest *A*
 Wabash Valley *A*
Kaplan College: Indianapolis *A*
Valparaiso University *M*

Iowa
AIB College of Business *A*

Des Moines Area Community
   College *A*
Drake University *B*
Grand View University *B*
Kaplan University
   Cedar Rapids *A*
   Davenport *A, B, M*
   Des Moines *A, B*
   Mason City *A, B*
Upper Iowa University *C*
William Penn University *B*

Kansas

Brown Mackie College
   Salina *A*
Central Christian College of Kansas *A*
Colby Community College *C*
Ottawa University *B*
Seward County Community
   College *C, A*
University of Kansas *M*
University of St. Mary *B*

Kentucky

Big Sandy Community and Technical
   College *A*
Bluegrass Community and Technical
   College *A*
Gateway Community and Technical
   College *A*
Kentucky State University *B*
Northern Kentucky University *B*
Sullivan College of Technology and
   Design *A*
Western Kentucky University *B*

Louisiana

Herzing University *A, B*
McNeese State University *A*

Maine

Husson University *A*
Thomas College *B*
University of Maine
   Fort Kent *B*

Maryland

College of Southern Maryland *C, A*
Frederick Community College *C, A*
Frostburg State University *B*
Howard Community College *C, A*
Towson University *B, M*
United States Naval Academy *B*

Massachusetts

Bristol Community College *C*
Bunker Hill Community College *C*
Cape Cod Community College *C, A*
Endicott College *M*
Mount Wachusett Community
   College *C*
University of Massachusetts
   Boston *B, M*

Michigan

Baker College of Allen Park *B*
Central Michigan University *B*
Cleary University *A*
Delta College *A*
Ferris State University *A, B, M*
Grace Bible College *B*
Lake Michigan College *C, A*
Lawrence Technological
   University *B, D*
Oakland Community College *C, A*
Oakland University *B, M, D*
Walsh College of Accountancy and
   Business Administration *B*

Minnesota

Brown College *A, B*
Capella University *B, M, D*

Fond du Lac Tribal and Community
   College *A*
Globe University *B*
Inver Hills Community College *C*
Minnesota School of Business *C, A, B*
Minnesota School of Business:
   Blaine *C, A, B*
Minnesota School of Business:
   Brooklyn Center *B*
Minnesota School of Business: St.
   Cloud *A, B*
South Central College *C, A*
Southwest Minnesota State
   University *B*
University of St. Thomas *B, M*
Walden University *B*
Winona State University *B*

Missouri

Grantham University *A*
Lindenwood University *B, M*
Ozarks Technical Community
   College *C, A*
Saint Louis University *M*
University of Missouri
   Columbia *B*
   Kansas City *B*
   Missouri University of Science and
      Technology *B, M*

Montana

Flathead Valley Community College *A*
Montana State University
   College of Technology: Great
      Falls *C, A*
University of Montana: Western *C, A*

Nebraska

Bellevue University *B, M*
Kaplan University
   Lincoln *A*
Mid-Plains Community College
   Area *C, A*
Nebraska Wesleyan University *B*
University of Nebraska
   Lincoln *D*
   Omaha *D*

New Hampshire

Franklin Pierce University *B*
Plymouth State University *B*
University of New Hampshire *B*

New Jersey

Bergen Community College *A*
Cumberland County College *A*
Fairleigh Dickinson University
   Metropolitan Campus *B*
Montclair State University *B*
New Jersey Institute of
   Technology *B, M*
Raritan Valley Community College *A*
Union County College *A*

New Mexico

Clovis Community College *C, A*
New Mexico Institute of Mining and
   Technology *B*
New Mexico State University *B*

New York

Briarcliffe College *B*
Bryant & Stratton Business Institute
   Bryant & Stratton College:
      Rochester *A*
Bryant & Stratton College: Syracuse
   North *A*
Clarkson University *M*
Cornell University *B, D*
D'Youville College *B*
Erie Community College
   City Campus *A*

North Campus *A*
South Campus *A*
Excelsior College *B*
Globe Institute of Technology *C, A, B*
Houghton College *B*
Ithaca College *B*
Long Island University
   C. W. Post Campus *B*
Marist College *B*
Mercy College *A*
Monroe Community College *A*
Mount Saint Mary College *C, B*
Pace University *C, M*
Polytechnic Institute of New York
   University *M*
Rensselaer Polytechnic Institute *B, M*
Rochester Institute of
   Technology *A, B, M*
St. Joseph's College: Suffolk
   Campus *B*
State University of New York
   College of Agriculture and
      Technology at Cobleskill *B*
   College of Agriculture and
      Technology at Morrisville *A, B*
   College of Technology at Alfred *B*
   College of Technology at Canton *B*
Suffolk County Community
   College *C, A*
United States Military Academy *B*

North Carolina

Cape Fear Community College *C, A*
Carteret Community College *C, A*
Catawba Valley Community College *A*
Central Piedmont Community
   College *C, A*
Davidson County Community
   College *C, A*
Durham Technical Community
   College *C, A*
East Carolina University *B*
Fayetteville Technical Community
   College *C, A*
Forsyth Technical Community
   College *C, A*
Gaston College *A*
Guilford College *B*
Isothermal Community College *C, A*
James Sprunt Community
   College *C, A*
Johnson C. Smith University *B*
Montgomery Community College *C, A*
Robeson Community College *A*
Southeastern Community
   College *C, A*
Stanly Community College *C, A*
University of North Carolina
   Charlotte *M, D*
   Pembroke *B*
Vance-Granville Community
   College *A*
Wayne Community College *A*
Wilkes Community College *C, A*
Wilson Community College *C, A*
Winston-Salem State University *B*

North Dakota

Dakota College at Bottineau *A*
Jamestown College *B*

Ohio

Bluffton University *B*
Bryant & Stratton College:
   Cleveland *A*
Cincinnati Christian University *B*
ETI Technical College of Niles *A*
Edison State Community College *C, A*
Franklin University *A, B*
Marion Technical College *A*
Ohio University *B*
Owens Community College
   Toledo *A*
Stark State College of Technology *A*

Tiffin University *B*
University of Cincinnati
   Clermont College *C, A*
   Raymond Walters College *C, A*
University of Toledo *B*
Vatterott College: Cleveland *C*
Youngstown State University *A, B*

Oklahoma

University of Central Oklahoma *B*
University of Tulsa *B*
Vatterott College *A*

Oregon

Mt. Hood Community College *C, A*
Oregon Institute of Technology *B*

Pennsylvania

Bucks County Community College *A*
Cabrini College *B*
Carnegie Mellon University *M, D*
Chestnut Hill College *B*
Edinboro University of
   Pennsylvania *M*
Harrisburg Area Community
   College *C, A*
Harrisburg University of Science and
   Technology *B, M*
Indiana University of Pennsylvania *M*
Juniata College *B*
Kaplan Career Institute: Pittsburgh *A*
Keystone College *A, B*
Kutztown University of
   Pennsylvania *B, M*
La Roche College *B*
La Salle University *B*
Lincoln University *B*
Misericordia University *B*
Mount Aloysius College *B*
Penn Commercial Business and
   Technical School *A*
Pennsylvania College of
   Technology *A*
Point Park University *C, A, B*
Slippery Rock University of
   Pennsylvania *B*
Temple University *B*
Washington & Jefferson College *B*
Waynesburg University *A, B*
West Chester University of
   Pennsylvania *M*

Puerto Rico

National College of Business and
   Technology: Arecibo *B*
National College of Business and
   Technology: Rio Grande *A, B*
Universal Career Community College:
   Humacao *A*
Universal Career Community College:
   Manati *A*
Universal Career Community College:
   San Juan *A*

Rhode Island

Bryant University *B*
New England Institute of
   Technology *A, B*

South Carolina

Bob Jones University *B*
South University: Columbia *A, B*
University of South Carolina
   Upstate *B*

South Dakota

Dakota State University *C*
Mount Marty College *B*
Northern State University *C*
Oglala Lakota College *C*

Tennessee
King College *B*
LeMoyne-Owen College *B*
Lipscomb University *B*
Trevecca Nazarene University *A, B*

Texas
Abilene Christian University *B, M*
Baylor University *B*
Dallas Baptist University *C*
North Lake College *C, A*
Southern Methodist University *M*
Stephen F. Austin State University *B*
Texas Christian University *B*
Westwood College: Fort Worth *A, B*
Westwood College: Houston South *B*

Utah
Brigham Young University *B, M*
Neumont University *B*
Southern Utah University *A*
Utah Career College *A, B*
Western Governors University *B*

Vermont
Champlain College *M*
Southern Vermont College *C*
Vermont Technical College *A, B*

Virginia
Bluefield College *B*
Bryant & Stratton College
    Richmond *A*
ECPI Technical College: Roanoke *A*
George Mason University *M*
Germanna Community College *A*
Mountain Empire Community
    College *A*
New River Community College *A*
Potomac College *A, B*
Regent University *A, B*
University of Management and
    Technology *A, B, M*
University of Richmond *B*
Virginia State University *B*

Washington
Bates Technical College *C, A*
DeVry University
    Federal Way *B*
Northwest Indian College *A*
Shoreline Community College *C*
University of Washington *B, M, D*
Yakima Valley Community College *C*

West Virginia
American Public University
    System *C, B*
Mountain State University *B*
New River Community and Technical
    College *A*
Ohio Valley University *B*
Potomac State College of West
    Virginia University *A*
Southern West Virginia Community
    and Technical College *A*
West Virginia Junior College *A*
West Virginia Junior College:
    Bridgeport *A*

Wisconsin
Concordia University Wisconsin *M*
Herzing University *A, B*
Marian University *B*
Nicolet Area Technical College *A*
University of Wisconsin
    Stout *B, M*
    Whitewater *B, M*
Waukesha County Technical
    College *C*

Wyoming
Casper College *C, A*
Laramie County Community
    College *A*

Inorganic chemistry

Florida
Florida State University *M, D*

Iowa
Iowa State University *M, D*

Massachusetts
Tufts University *M, D*

Montana
University of Montana *M, D*

New York
Fordham University *M*
State University of New York
    Albany *D*

Wisconsin
Marquette University *M, D*

Institutional food production

Alabama
Jefferson Davis Community College *C*
Shelton State Community College *C*
Wallace State Community College at
    Hanceville *C, A*

Arizona
Central Arizona College *C*
Phoenix College *C, A*

California
American River College *A*
Bakersfield College *A*
Cerritos College *A*
Chaffey College *C*
College of the Redwoods *C*
College of the Sequoias *C*
Contra Costa College *A*
Cypress College *C, A*
Fresno City College *C, A*
Long Beach City College *C, A*
Los Angeles Mission College *A*
Los Angeles Trade and Technical
    College *C, A*
Modesto Junior College *C*
Monterey Peninsula College *A*
Ohlone College *C, A*
Orange Coast College *C, A*
Palomar College *C, A*
San Joaquin Delta College *A*
Santa Barbara City College *C, A*
Santa Rosa Junior College *C*
Shasta College *A*

Connecticut
Gateway Community College *C, A*
Manchester Community College *A*
Naugatuck Valley Community
    College *A*
University of New Haven *A*

Delaware
Delaware Technical and Community
    College
    Stanton/Wilmington *C*

Florida
Brevard Community College *C*
Indian River State College *C*

Johnson & Wales University: North
    Miami *B*
Pensacola Junior College *A*
Valencia Community College *A*

Georgia
Augusta Technical College *C*

Hawaii
University of Hawaii
    Honolulu Community College *C, A*
    Kapiolani Community College *C, A*

Illinois
City Colleges of Chicago
    Malcolm X College *A*
Dominican University *B*
Harper College *C, A*
Lexington College *A, B*

Iowa
Iowa State University *B*
Iowa Western Community College *A*
Kirkwood Community College *C, A*

Kansas
Coffeyville Community College *A*
Johnson County Community
    College *C, A*

Kentucky
Eastern Kentucky University *A*

Louisiana
Delgado Community College *A*

Maine
Eastern Maine Community College *C*
Washington County Community
    College *C, A*

Maryland
Anne Arundel Community College *C*
Montgomery College *C, A*

Massachusetts
Quinsigamond Community College *A*

Michigan
Bay de Noc Community College *C*
Central Michigan University *B*
Lansing Community College *A*
Mott Community College *A*
Northern Michigan University *A*
Wayne County Community
    College *C, A*
Western Michigan University *B*

Mississippi
Hinds Community College *C, A*
Mississippi Gulf Coast Community
    College *C*

Missouri
Metropolitan Community College:
    Penn Valley *C*
Northwest Missouri State
    University *B*
Saint Louis University *C*

Nebraska
Metropolitan Community College *A*

Nevada
Truckee Meadows Community
    College *C, A*

New Hampshire
University of New Hampshire *A*

New Mexico
Central New Mexico Community
    College *C*

New York
City University of New York
    LaGuardia Community College *A*
Mohawk Valley Community College *A*
Monroe Community College *C, A*
Rockland Community College *A*
State University of New York
    College of Agriculture and
        Technology at Cobleskill *A*
    College of Technology at Delhi *A*
Sullivan County Community
    College *C, A*
Syracuse University *B*
Westchester Community College *A*

North Carolina
Asheville-Buncombe Technical
    Community College *A*
Cape Fear Community College *C, A*
James Sprunt Community College *C*
Johnston Community College *C*

North Dakota
North Dakota State College of
    Science *A*

Ohio
Cincinnati State Technical and
    Community College *C, A*
Ohio University *B*
Owens Community College
    Toledo *C*

Pennsylvania
Bucks County Community
    College *C, A*
Butler County Community
    College *C, A*
Community College of
    Philadelphia *C, A*
Harrisburg Area Community
    College *C, A*
Luzerne County Community
    College *A*
Pennsylvania College of
    Technology *A*

Puerto Rico
Inter American University of Puerto
    Rico
    Bayamon Campus *C*

Tennessee
Lipscomb University *B*
Southwest Tennessee Community
    College *A*

Texas
El Paso Community College *A*
Hill College *A*
St. Philip's College *A*
Sam Houston State University *B*
San Jacinto College *C, A*
Texas State Technical College
    Waco *C, A*
Texas Woman's University *M*

Virginia
J. Sargeant Reynolds Community
    College *A*
Northern Virginia Community
    College *A*

Washington
Bates Technical College *C, A*

Wisconsin

Blackhawk Technical College *A*
Fox Valley Technical College *C, A*
Milwaukee Area Technical College *C*
Northeast Wisconsin Technical
College *C*
University of Wisconsin
Stout *B*
Waukesha County Technical
College *C*
Wisconsin Indianhead Technical
College *C*

Institutional food service

California

Santa Barbara City College *C, A*
Shasta College *C*

New Jersey

Atlantic Cape Community College *A*

New Mexico

Southwestern Indian Polytechnic
Institute *A*

Pennsylvania

Immaculata University *A, B*
Montgomery County Community
College *C*

South Carolina

Greenville Technical College *C*

Texas

Lamar Institute of Technology *C, A*
San Jacinto College *A*
Texas State Technical College
, Harlingen *C, A*

Washington

Bates Technical College *C*

West Virginia

Fairmont State University *A*

Instructional media

Alabama

Alabama State University *M*
Auburn University *M, T*
Jacksonville State University *M, T*
Miles College *B*
University of South Alabama *M, D, T*

Arizona

Arizona State University *M, D*
Grand Canyon University *M*
Paradise Valley Community College *A*
University of Phoenix *M, D*

Arkansas

Arkansas Tech University *M*
Southern Arkansas University *M*
University of Arkansas *M*
University of Arkansas
Little Rock *M*
University of Central Arkansas *M*

California

California State University
Chico *B, M*
Dominguez Hills *M*
Fullerton *M, T*
Sacramento *M*
San Bernardino *M*
Fresno Pacific University *M, T*
National University *M*
San Diego State University *M, D*

San Jose State University *M*
Stanford University *M, D*
University of San Francisco *M*

Colorado

Jones International University *M*
University of Northern Colorado *M, T*

Connecticut

Central Connecticut State
University *M*
Fairfield University *M, T*
University of Connecticut *M, D, T*

Delaware

Wilmington University *M*

District of Columbia

American University *M*
Gallaudet University *M*

Florida

Full Sail University *M*
Nova Southeastern University *M, D*
Saint Leo University *M*
University of Central Florida *M*
University of West Florida *D*

Georgia

Columbus State University *M*
Georgia College and State
University *M, T*
Georgia Southern University *M*
Georgia State University *M, D*
Southern Polytechnic State
University *M*
University of Georgia *M, D, T*
University of West Georgia *M, T*

Hawaii

University of Hawaii
Manoa *M*

Idaho

Boise State University *M*
Idaho State University *M, D*

Illinois

DeVry University: Online *M*
Illinois State University *M*
National-Louis University *M*
Northern Illinois University *M, D*
Southern Illinois University
Edwardsville *M*
University of Illinois
Urbana-Champaign *M, D*
University of St. Francis *M*
Western Illinois University *B, M*

Indiana

Indiana State University *M, T*
Indiana University
Bloomington *M, D, T*

Iowa

Iowa State University *T*
University of Northern Iowa *M*

Kansas

Emporia State University *M*

Louisiana

McNeese State University *M*

Maryland

Community College of Baltimore
County *T*
McDaniel College *M*
Towson University *M, D*
University of Maryland
University College *M*

Massachusetts

Boston University *M, T*
Bridgewater State College *M, T*
Cambridge College *M*
Lesley University *M*
Salem State College *M*
University of Massachusetts
Boston *M*

Michigan

Eastern Michigan University *M, T*
Lawrence Technological University *M*
Michigan State University *M*
Wayne State University *M, D*
Western Michigan University *M*

Minnesota

Capella University *M, D*
Inver Hills Community College *A*
Minnesota State University
Mankato *M*
Ridgewater College *A*
Saint Cloud State University *B, M*
Walden University *B, M, D*

Mississippi

Jackson State University *B*
University of Southern Mississippi *M*

Missouri

Missouri State University *M*
Webster University *M*

New Jersey

Georgian Court University *T*
Kean University *M*
Richard Stockton College of New
Jersey *M*
William Paterson University of New
Jersey *T*

New York

Dominican College of Blauvelt *M*
Long Island University
C. W. Post Campus *M, T*
Rochester Institute of Technology *M*
State University of New York
Albany *M*
Buffalo *M*
College at Oneonta *M*
College at Potsdam *M*
Syracuse University *M*

North Carolina

Appalachian State University *M, T*
East Carolina University *M*
North Carolina Agricultural and
Technical State University *M*
North Carolina Central University *M*
North Carolina State University *M*
University of North Carolina
Charlotte *M*
Wilmington *M*

North Dakota

University of North Dakota *M*

Ohio

Bowling Green State University *B, M*
John Carroll University *M*
Kent State University *M*
Malone University *M*
Ohio State University
Columbus Campus *M, D*
Ohio University *M, D*
University of Toledo *M*

Oklahoma

Northwestern Oklahoma State
University *M*
Oklahoma State University *M*
University of Central Oklahoma *B, M*

University of Oklahoma *M*

Oregon

Portland State University *M, T*
Western Oregon University *B*

Pennsylvania

Bloomsburg University of
Pennsylvania *M*
Cabrini College *M*
Carlow University *T*
Chestnut Hill College *M, T*
Drexel University *M*
Duquesne University *M, D, T*
East Stroudsburg University of
Pennsylvania *M, T*
Kutztown University of
Pennsylvania *M, T*
Lehigh University *D*
Penn State
University Park *M, D*
Philadelphia University *M*
Saint Joseph's University *M*
Seton Hill University *M*
University of Pittsburgh *T*
Widener University *M*

Puerto Rico

Bayamon Central University *B*
University of the Sacred Heart *M*

South Carolina

University of South Carolina
Aiken *M*

South Dakota

Dakota State University *M*
University of South Dakota *M*

Tennessee

East Tennessee State University *M, T*
University of Memphis *T*

Texas

Angelo State University *M*
Lone Star College System *A*
Midwestern State University *M*
Prairie View A&M University *M*
Texas A&M University *M*
Texas A&M University
Corpus Christi *M, T*
Texarkana *M*
Texas State University: San
Marcos *M, T*
Texas Tech University *M, D*
University of Houston *M, T*
University of Houston
Clear Lake *M*
University of North Texas *M*
University of Texas
Brownsville - Texas Southmost
College *M*
Southwestern Medical Center at
Dallas *M*
Tyler *M*
West Texas A&M University *M*

Utah

Brigham Young University *M, D*
Southern Utah University *M, T*
Utah State University *M, D*
Western Governors University *M*

Virginia

Longwood University *M*
Old Dominion University *M, D, T*

Washington

Eastern Washington University *M*
Walla Walla University *M*
Washington State University *T*

West Virginia
American Public University System *M*
West Virginia University *M, D*

Wisconsin
University of Wisconsin
  La Crosse *M*

Instrumentation technology

Alabama
Athens State University *B*

Alaska
University of Alaska
  Fairbanks *C*

Arkansas
University of Arkansas
  Monticello *C*

Colorado
Colorado Northwestern Community
  College *C, A*

Georgia
Central Georgia Technical College *C*
DeKalb Technical College *A*

Idaho
Idaho State University *C, A*

Illinois
Kaskaskia College *C*
Moraine Valley Community
  College *C, A*

Kentucky
Owensboro Community and
  Technical College *C*

Louisiana
ITI Technical College *A*

Maryland
Community College of Baltimore
  County *A*

Minnesota
Ridgewater College *C, A*
St. Cloud Technical College *C, A*

New Mexico
San Juan College *A*
Southwestern Indian Polytechnic
  Institute *A*

New York
Excelsior College *A*
Monroe Community College *C, A*

North Carolina
Cape Fear Community College *A*

Ohio
Cincinnati State Technical and
  Community College *C*

Pennsylvania
Butler County Community College *A*
Pennsylvania College of
  Technology *A*

Puerto Rico
University College of San Juan *A*
University of Puerto Rico
  Bayamon University College *A*

Texas
Houston Community College
  System *C, A*
Lamar Institute of Technology *C, A*
Lamar State College at Port Arthur *A*
St. Philip's College *A*
San Jacinto College *C, A*
Texas A&M University
  Corpus Christi *B*
Victoria College *C, A*

Utah
Salt Lake Community College *A*

Virginia
New River Community College *A*

Washington
Bellingham Technical College *A*
Yakima Valley Community College *A*

Wisconsin
Mid-State Technical College *A*

Wyoming
Western Wyoming Community
  College *C, A*

Insurance

Alabama
Wallace State Community College at
  Hanceville *A*

Arizona
Pima Community College *C*

Arkansas
University of Central Arkansas *B*

California
California State University
  Sacramento *B*
Fresno City College *C, A*
Los Angeles Southwest College *A*
Santa Ana College *C, A*

Colorado
Community College of Aurora *C*

Connecticut
University of Connecticut *B*
University of Hartford *B*

District of Columbia
Howard University *B*

Florida
Daytona State College *C*
Florida State College at
  Jacksonville *C, A*
Florida State University *B, M, D*
Miami Dade College *C*
Northwest Florida State College *A*
University of Florida *B, M*

Georgia
Central Georgia Technical College *C*
Georgia State University *B, M, D*
University of Georgia *B*

Idaho
Idaho State University *B*

Illinois
Bradley University *B*
Harper College *C*
Heartland Community College *C, A*
Illinois State University *B*
Illinois Wesleyan University *B*

Roosevelt University *B*
University of Illinois
  Urbana-Champaign *B, M, D*

Indiana
Harrison College
  Indianapolis East *A*
Indiana State University *B*

Iowa
Ellsworth Community College *A*

Kentucky
Eastern Kentucky University *B*

Louisiana
University of Louisiana at Lafayette *B*
University of Louisiana at Monroe *B*

Michigan
Delta College *C*
Lansing Community College *A*
Mott Community College *C*

Minnesota
Fond du Lac Tribal and Community
  College *C*
Saint Cloud State University *B*
University of Minnesota
  Twin Cities *B*

Mississippi
Delta State University *B*
Mississippi State University *B*
University of Mississippi *B*

Missouri
Missouri State University *B*

New York
Excelsior College *B*
Hudson Valley Community College *A*
St. John's University *B, M*
Sullivan County Community
  College *A*

North Carolina
Appalachian State University *B*
Isothermal Community College *C*
Pitt Community College *C*

Ohio
Bowling Green State University *B*
Davis College *A*
Hondros College *C*
Ohio State University
  Columbus Campus *B*

Oklahoma
Oklahoma City Community College *C*
Tulsa Community College *C, A*
University of Central Oklahoma *B*

Pennsylvania
Gannon University *C, B*
La Salle University *B*
Temple University *B*
University of Pennsylvania *B, M, D*

Puerto Rico
Universidad del Este *B*

South Carolina
University of South Carolina *B*

Texas
Baylor University *B*
University of Houston
  Downtown *B*
University of North Texas *B*

Wisconsin
Chippewa Valley Technical College *C*
University of Wisconsin
  Madison *B, M*

Intercultural/diversity studies

Arizona
Prescott College *M*

California
Biola University *B*
California Baptist University *B*
California Institute of Integral
  Studies *M, D*
Foothill College *A*
Humboldt State University *B*
National University *B*
Pitzer College *B*
Shasta College *A*
Stanford University *B*
University of California
  Berkeley *M*
University of San Diego *B*
Vanguard University of Southern
  California *B*

Colorado
Colorado Heights University *A, B*

Georgia
Atlanta Christian College *B*

Illinois
Judson University *B*
Trinity International University *D*
Triton College *A*

Indiana
Anderson University *M*

Iowa
Divine Word College *A, B*

Kentucky
Midway College *B*

Massachusetts
Lesley University *M*

Minnesota
Macalester College *B*
North Central University *B*
St. Catherine University *B*

New York
Alfred University *B*
Columbia University *B*
Fordham University *B*
Ithaca College *B*

Ohio
Antioch University McGregor *M*

Oregon
Northwest Christian University *B*

Puerto Rico
University of Puerto Rico
  Rio Piedras *B*

South Carolina
Columbia International University *B*

Tennessee
Christian Brothers University *B*
Tennessee Wesleyan College *B*
Union University *B, M*

Texas

Dallas Christian College *B*
Howard Payne University *B*
South Texas College *A*
University of Houston
  Clear Lake *M*
University of Texas
  San Antonio *M*
University of the Incarnate Word *B*

Washington

Evergreen State College *B*
University of Washington
  Tacoma *B, M*
Western Washington University *M*

Wisconsin

Marquette University *B*

Interior architecture

Alabama

Auburn University *B*

Arizona

Arizona State University *B*
Phoenix College *A*

California

California State University
  Long Beach *B*
  Sacramento *B, M*
City College of San Francisco *A*
Cosumnes River College *C, A*
Otis College of Art and Design *B*
Woodbury University *B*

Colorado

Westwood College of Technology
  Westwood College: Denver South *B*
Westwood College: Denver North *B*

Connecticut

University of New Haven *A, B*

Florida

Daytona State College *A*
Florida State College at Jacksonville *A*
Palm Beach Community College *A*
Seminole Community College *A*

Idaho

University of Idaho *B*

Illinois

Columbia College Chicago *B, M*
Illinois Central College *A*
School of the Art Institute of
  Chicago *B, M*
Triton College *C, A*

Indiana

Indiana State University *B*

Kansas

Kansas State University *M*

Kentucky

Sullivan College of Technology and
  Design *C, A*

Louisiana

Delgado Community College *A*
Louisiana State University and
  Agricultural and Mechanical
  College *B*
Louisiana Tech University *B*
University of Louisiana at Lafayette *B*

Maryland

Anne Arundel Community
  College *C, A*

Massachusetts

Boston Architectural College *B, M*
Newbury College *B*
University of Massachusetts
  Amherst *B, M*

Michigan

Central Michigan University *B*
Ferris State University *B*
Lansing Community College *A*
Lawrence Technological University *B*

Mississippi

Mississippi State University *B*
University of Southern Mississippi *B*

Missouri

St. Louis Community College
  St. Louis Community College at
    Meramec *A*

Nebraska

Metropolitan Community College *A*
University of Nebraska
  Lincoln *B*

Nevada

University of Nevada
  Las Vegas *B*

New York

Onondaga Community College *A*
Parsons The New School for Design *B*
Suffolk County Community College *A*
Syracuse University *B, M*

North Carolina

Cape Fear Community College *A*

Ohio

Bowling Green State University *B*
Miami University
  Oxford Campus *B*
Ohio State University
  Columbus Campus *B*

Oregon

University of Oregon *B, M*

Pennsylvania

Chatham University *B, M*
La Roche College *B*
Philadelphia University *B*

Rhode Island

Rhode Island School of Design *B, M*

Texas

Lamar University *B*
St. Philip's College *C, A*
Sam Houston State University *B*
Stephen F. Austin State University *B*
Texas A&M University
  Kingsville *B, M*
Texas Tech University *B*
University of Houston *B, M*
University of North Texas *B*
University of Texas
  Arlington *B*
  San Antonio *B*

Wisconsin

University of Wisconsin
  Stevens Point *B*

Interior design

Alabama

Samford University *B*
University of Alabama *B*
Wallace State Community College at
  Hanceville *A*

Arizona

Art Center Design College *A, B*
Art Institute
  of Phoenix *B*
Art Institute of Tucson *B*
Glendale Community College *C*
Mesa Community College *A*
Northern Arizona University *B*
Phoenix College *A*
Prescott College *B*
Scottsdale Community College *C, A*

Arkansas

Harding University *B*
University of Central Arkansas *B*

California

Academy of Art University *C, A, B, M*
Allan Hancock College *A*
American River College *A*
Antelope Valley College *C, A*
Art Center College of Design *B, M*
Art Institute
  of California: Los Angeles *B*
  of California: Orange County *A, B*
  of California: San Diego *B*
Art Institute of California:
  Hollywood *B*
Art Institute of California: Inland
  Empire *B*
Art Institute of California:
  Sacramento *B*
Art Institute of California: San
  Francisco *B*
Art Institute of California:
  Sunnyvale *B*
Bakersfield College *A*
California College of the Arts *B*
California State University
  Chico *B*
  Fresno *B*
  Long Beach *B, M*
Canada College *C, A*
Cerritos College *A*
Chaffey College *C, A*
City College of San Francisco *A*
College of the Canyons *C, A*
Contra Costa College *A*
Cosumnes River College *C, A*
Cuesta College *C, A*
Design Institute of San Diego *B*
Fashion Institute of Design and
  Merchandising
  Los Angeles *A*
  San Francisco *A*
Interior Designers Institute *A, B, M*
International Academy of Design and
  Technology
  Sacramento *C, A, B*
Long Beach City College *C, A*
Los Angeles Harbor College *A*
Los Angeles Mission College *C, A*
Modesto Junior College *C, A*
Monterey Peninsula College *C, A*
Moorpark College *C, A*
Mount San Antonio College *C, A*
Ohlone College *A*
Orange Coast College *C, A*
Otis College of Art and Design *B*
Palomar College *C, A*
Point Loma Nazarene University *B*
Saddleback College *C, A*
San Diego Mesa College *C, A*
San Diego State University *B*
San Francisco State University *B*

San Joaquin Delta College *C, A*
San Jose State University *B*
Santa Barbara City College *C, A*
Santa Rosa Junior College *C*
Solano Community College *C, A*
West Valley College *C, A*
Westwood College of Technology
  Westwood College: Inland
    Empire *B*
  Westwood College: Los Angeles *B*
Westwood College: South Bay *B*

Colorado

Arapahoe Community College *C, A*
Art Institute
  of Colorado *A, B*
Colorado State University *B, M*
Front Range Community College *C, A*
Pikes Peak Community College *A*
Rocky Mountain College of Art &
  Design *B*
Westwood College of Technology
  Westwood College: Denver South *B*

Connecticut

Paier College of Art *C, B*
University of Bridgeport *B*
University of New Haven *C, A, B*

Delaware

Delaware College of Art and
  Design *C, A*
Delaware Technical and Community
  College
  Terry *A*

District of Columbia

Corcoran College of Art and
  Design *C, B, M*
George Washington University *B, M*
Howard University *B*

Florida

Art Institute of Fort
  Lauderdale *C, A, B*
Broward College *A*
Daytona State College *A*
Florida International University *M*
Florida State College at Jacksonville *A*
Florida State University *B, M*
Indian River State College *A*
International Academy of Design and
  Technology: Tampa *A, B*
Miami International University of Art
  and Design *B, M*
Northwest Florida State College *A*
Palm Beach Community College *A*
Ringling College of Art and Design *B*
Seminole Community College *A, B*
Southwest Florida College *A, B*
University of Florida *B*

Georgia

American InterContinental
  University *B*
Art Institute
  of Atlanta *B*
Athens Technical College *C, A*
Brenau University *B*
Georgia Southern University *B*
Gwinnett Technical College *A*
Savannah College of Art and
  Design *B, M*
Valdosta State University *B*

Hawaii

Chaminade University of
  Honolulu *A, B*

Idaho

Brigham Young University-Idaho *B*
University of Idaho *B*

Illinois

Black Hawk College *A*
Columbia College Chicago *B, M*
Harrington College of Design *A, B, M*
Illinois Institute of Art:
  Schaumburg *C, B*
International Academy of Design and
  Technology: Chicago *B*
International Academy of Design and
  Technology: Schaumburg *A, B*
Joliet Junior College *A*
Judson University *B*
Prairie State College *A*
Robert Morris University: Chicago *A*
School of the Art Institute of
  Chicago *B, M*
Southern Illinois University
  Carbondale *B*
Triton College *C, A*
Westwood College: Chicago Loop *A*
Westwood College: DuPage *B*

Indiana

Indiana University
  Bloomington *B, M*
Indiana University-Purdue University
  Fort Wayne *A, B*
Indiana University-Purdue University
  Indianapolis *A, B*
Indiana Wesleyan University *B*
Ivy Tech Community College
  Columbus *A*
  North Central *A*
  Southwest *A*
Purdue University *B, M*

Iowa

Hawkeye Community College *A*
Iowa State University *B, M*
Scott Community College *A*
University of Northern Iowa *B*
Western Iowa Tech Community
  College *C, A*

Kansas

Kansas State University *B*
Pittsburg State University *B*
University of Kansas *B, M*

Kentucky

Bluegrass Community and Technical
  College *A*
Eastern Kentucky University *B*
Sullivan College of Technology and
  Design *C, A, B*
University of Kentucky *B*

Maryland

Anne Arundel Community
  College *C, A*
Harford Community College *C, A*
Howard Community College *A*
Maryland Institute College of Art *B*
Montgomery College *A*

Massachusetts

Bay Path College *B*
Becker College *B*
Endicott College *B*
Massachusetts Bay Community
  College *C*
Mount Ida College *B*
Newbury College *B*
Suffolk University *C, B, M*
University of Massachusetts
  Amherst *M*
Wentworth Institute of Technology *B*

Michigan

Adrian College *B*
Art Institute of Michigan *B*
Baker College
  of Auburn Hills *A*
  of Cadillac *A*
  of Clinton Township *A*
  of Flint *A, B*
  of Muskegon *A*
  of Owosso *A*
Baker College of Allen Park *A*
Bay de Noc Community College *C*
College for Creative Studies *B*
Delta College *A*
Eastern Michigan University *B, M*
Ferris State University *B*
Finlandia University *B*
Grand Rapids Community College *A*
Henry Ford Community College *A*
International Academy of Design and
  Technology: Detroit *A, B*
Kendall College of Art and Design of
  Ferris State University *B*
Lawrence Technological University *M*
Michigan State University *B, M*
Oakland Community College *A*
Western Michigan University *B*

Minnesota

Alexandria Technical College *C, A*
Art Institutes International
  Minnesota *A, B*
Century Community and Technical
  College *C, A*
Dakota County Technical College *C, A*
Dunwoody College of Technology *B*
University of Minnesota
  Twin Cities *B*

Mississippi

Antonelli College
  Jackson *A*
Mississippi College *B*
Mississippi Gulf Coast Community
  College *A*

Missouri

Maryville University of Saint Louis *B*
Park University *B*
Patricia Stevens College *C, A, B*
Stephens College *B*
University of Central Missouri *B*

Montana

Montana State University
  College of Technology: Great
  Falls *A*

Nevada

Art Institute
  of Las Vegas *B*
International Academy of Design and
  Technology: Henderson *A, B*

New Hampshire

Manchester Community College *C, A*

New Jersey

Berkeley College- Garret Mountain
  Campus *A*
Brookdale Community College *A*
Kean University *B*
Raritan Valley Community College *A*

New Mexico

Art Center Design College *B*
Santa Fe Community College *C, A*

New York

Art Institute
  of New York City *A*
Cazenovia College *B*
Fashion Institute of Technology *A, B*
Institute of Design and
  Construction *A*
Monroe Community College *C, A*
Nassau Community College *C, A*
New York Institute of Technology *B*
New York School of Interior
  Design *C, A, B, M*
Parsons The New School for
  Design *A, B, M*
Pratt Institute *B, M*
Rochester Institute of
  Technology *A, B, M*
Sage College of Albany *B*
School of Visual Arts *B*
State University of New York
  College at Buffalo *B*
  College of Technology at Alfred *A*
Suffolk County Community College *A*
Villa Maria College of Buffalo *A, B*

North Carolina

Appalachian State University *B*
Art Institute
  of Charlotte *A, B*
Cape Fear Community College *A*
Carteret Community College *C, A*
Central Piedmont Community
  College *C, A*
East Carolina University *B*
Forsyth Technical Community
  College *A*
Halifax Community College *C, A*
High Point University *B*
Meredith College *B*
Randolph Community College *C, A*
Salem College *B*
University of North Carolina
  Greensboro *B, M*
Western Carolina University *B*
Western Piedmont Community
  College *C, A*

North Dakota

North Dakota State University *B*

Ohio

Art Institute of Ohio: Cincinnati *A*
Cleveland Institute of Art *B*
College of Mount St. Joseph *A, B*
Columbus College of Art and
  Design *B*
Davis College *A*
Kent State University *B*
Ohio State University
  Columbus Campus *B, M*
Owens Community College
  Toledo *C*
University of Cincinnati *B*
Ursuline College *B*
Virginia Marti College of Art and
  Design *A*

Oklahoma

Oklahoma Christian University *B*
Tulsa Community College *C, A*
University of Central Oklahoma *B, M*
University of Oklahoma *B*

Oregon

Art Institute of Portland *A, B*
Marylhurst University *B*
Oregon State University *B*
Portland Community College *C, A*

Pennsylvania

Arcadia University *B*
Art Institute
  of Philadelphia *A, B*
  of Pittsburgh *A, B*
Drexel University *B, M*
Harcum College *A*
Lehigh Carbon Community College *A*
Marywood University *B, M*
Mercyhurst College *B*
Moore College of Art and Design *B, M*
Northampton Community
  College *C, A*
Pennsylvania College of Art and
  Design *C*
Philadelphia University *B*

Puerto Rico

Turabo University *B*
University of Puerto Rico
  Carolina Regional College *A*

Rhode Island

New England Institute of
  Technology *A, B*
Rhode Island School of Design *C*

South Carolina

Anderson University *B*
Converse College *B*

South Dakota

South Dakota State University *B*

Tennessee

Carson-Newman College *B*
Freed-Hardeman University *B*
International Academy of Design and
  Technology: Nashville *A, B*
Lambuth University *B*
Middle Tennessee State University *B*
O'More College of Design *B*
Pellissippi State Community
  College *A*
University of Tennessee
  Chattanooga *B*
  Knoxville *B, M*
Watkins College of Art, Design and
  Film *A, B*

Texas

Abilene Christian University *B*
Amarillo College *C, A*
Art Institute
  of Houston *B*
Baylor University *B*
Collin County Community College
  District *C, A*
El Centro College *C, A*
El Paso Community College *C, A*
Houston Community College
  System *C, A*
Lone Star College System *C, A*
St. Philip's College *C*
San Jacinto College *C, A*
Texas A&M University
  Kingsville *B*
Texas Christian University *B*
Texas State University: San Marcos *B*
Tyler Junior College *A*
University of Houston *B*
University of Texas
  Austin *B*
University of the Incarnate Word *B*
Wade College *A*

Utah

LDS Business College *C, A*
Salt Lake Community College *C*
Utah State University *B*
Weber State University *A*

Virginia

Lord Fairfax Community College *C*
Marymount University *B, M*
Northern Virginia Community
  College *A*
Tidewater Community College *A*
Virginia Commonwealth University *B*
Virginia Polytechnic Institute and
  State University *B*

Washington

Art Institute of Seattle C, A, B
Bellevue College A, B
Clover Park Technical College A
Cornish College of the Arts B
Seattle Pacific University B
Spokane Falls Community
    College C, A
Washington State University B, M

West Virginia

University of Charleston B

Wisconsin

Concordia University Wisconsin B
Fox Valley Technical College A
Gateway Technical College A
Milwaukee Area Technical College A
Mount Mary College B
University of Wisconsin
    Madison B
    Stevens Point B
Waukesha County Technical
    College A
Western Technical College A

International agriculture

California

University of California
    Davis B, M

Florida

Florida Agricultural and Mechanical
    University B

Illinois

University of Illinois
    Urbana-Champaign B

Iowa

Iowa State University B

New York

Cornell University B, M

North Dakota

North Dakota State University M

International business

Alabama

Auburn University B
Birmingham-Southern College B
Samford University B

Arizona

Arizona State University B
Dunlap-Stone University B
GateWay Community College A
Northcentral University B, M, D
Paradise Valley Community College A
Pima Community College A
Rio Salado College A
Scottsdale Community College A
University of Phoenix B, M
Western International University M

Arkansas

Arkansas State University B
Harding University B
John Brown University B
University of Arkansas B
University of Arkansas
    Little Rock B

California

Alliant International
    University B, M, D
Antioch Southern California
    Antioch University Santa Barbara M

Azusa Pacific University M
Biola University B
California State University
    Dominguez Hills B
    East Bay M
    Fresno B
    Fullerton B, M
    Long Beach B
    Sacramento B, M
    San Bernardino B
Dominican University of California M
Foothill College A
Fresno Pacific University B
Fullerton College A
Golden Gate University B, M
Grossmont College A
Holy Names University B
Lincoln University B, M
Marymount College B
Monterey Peninsula College A
Mount St. Mary's College B
National University M
Orange Coast College A
Pacific States University M, D
Pacific Union College B
Palomar College A
Pepperdine University B, M
St. Mary's College of California B
San Diego State University B, M
San Francisco State University B
San Jose State University B
Santa Ana College A
Santa Barbara City College A
Southwestern College A
University of La Verne B
University of San Diego M
University of San Francisco B
University of Southern
    California B, M
University of the West B, M
Vanguard University of Southern
    California B

Colorado

Arapahoe Community College A
Colorado Heights University A, B, M
Johnson & Wales University:
    Denver B
Jones International University B, M
Pikes Peak Community College A
University of Colorado
    Boulder B
    Denver M
University of Denver B, M

Connecticut

Albertus Magnus College B
Fairfield University B
Goodwin College A
Quinnipiac University B
University of Bridgeport B, M
University of New Haven B
Yale University M

Delaware

Goldey-Beacom College B, M

District of Columbia

Catholic University of America B
George Washington University B, M
Georgetown University B
Howard University B

Florida

Barry University B
Bethune-Cookman University B
Broward College A
Eckerd College B
Edison State College A
Florida Atlantic University B, M
Florida Institute of Technology B
Florida International University B, M
Florida Southern College B, M

Florida State University B
Jacksonville University B
Northwood University
    Florida B
Nova Southeastern University M
Palm Beach Atlantic University B
Rollins College B
Saint Leo University B
St. Petersburg College B
Saint Thomas University B, M
Schiller International
    University A, B, M
Southeastern University B
Stetson University B
University of Miami B
University of North Florida B
University of South Florida B
University of Tampa B

Georgia

Georgia Southern University B
Georgia State University B, M
Kennesaw State University B
Mercer University M
Paine College B
Toccoa Falls College B
University of Georgia B
Wesleyan College B

Hawaii

Hawaii Pacific University B
Remington College
    Honolulu A
University of Hawaii
    Manoa B, D

Idaho

Boise State University B
College of Idaho B

Illinois

Augustana College B
Benedictine University B
Bradley University B
City Colleges of Chicago
    Harold Washington College A
Dominican University B
Elmhurst College B
Harper College A
Illinois Central College A
Illinois State University B
Illinois Wesleyan University B
Lewis University B
Loyola University Chicago B, M
MacCormac College A
Millikin University B
Monmouth College B
North Central College B
Northwestern University M
Oakton Community College A
Olivet Nazarene University B
Roosevelt University M
Saint Xavier University B, M
Triton College A

Indiana

Anderson University B
Butler University B
Grace College B
Indiana University-Purdue University
    Indianapolis B
Taylor University B
University of Evansville B
University of Indianapolis B
Valparaiso University B, M

Iowa

Buena Vista University B
Central College B
Drake University B
Iowa State University B
St. Ambrose University B
Simpson College B

Wartburg College B

Kansas

Baker University B
Benedictine College B
Friends University B
McPherson College B
Pittsburg State University B, M
University of St. Mary B
Wichita State University B

Kentucky

Murray State University B

Louisiana

Louisiana State University and
    Agricultural and Mechanical
    College B
Loyola University New Orleans B

Maine

Husson University B
Maine Maritime Academy B, M
Saint Joseph's College of Maine B
Thomas College B

Maryland

Carroll Community College A
College of Notre Dame of Maryland B
Frederick Community College A
Howard Community College A
Montgomery College A
University of Baltimore B, M
University of Maryland
    College Park B
    University College M

Massachusetts

American International College B, M
Assumption College B
Babson College B, M
Bentley University M
Boston University B
Brandeis University M
Bridgewater State College B
Bunker Hill Community College A
Elms College B
Emerson College M
Fitchburg State College B
Lasell College B
Newbury College B
Nichols College B
Northeastern University B, M
Northern Essex Community
    College A
Salem State College B
Stonehill College B
Suffolk University B, M
University of Massachusetts
    Boston M

Michigan

Adrian College B
Alma College B
Aquinas College B
Baker College
    of Flint M
    of Port Huron B
Central Michigan University B, M
Cornerstone University B
Davenport University B
Delta College A
Eastern Michigan University B, M
Ferris State University B
Finlandia University B
Grace Bible College B
Grand Valley State University B
Kuyper College B
Lansing Community College A
Lawrence Technological
    University B, M
Madonna University B, M
Marygrove College B

Michigan Technological University *T*
Mott Community College *A*
Muskegon Community College *A*
Northwood University: Michigan *B*
Oakland Community College *A*
Saginaw Valley State University *B*
University of Michigan
Flint *B, M*
Wayne State University *B*

Minnesota

Augsburg College *B*
Concordia College: Moorhead *B*
Gustavus Adolphus College *B*
Hamline University *B*
Metropolitan State University *B*
Minnesota State University
Mankato *B*
Moorhead *B*
National American University
Bloomington *B*
Northwestern College *B*
St. Catherine University *B*
Saint Cloud State University *B*
St. Mary's University of
Minnesota *B, M*
University of Minnesota
Twin Cities *B*
University of St. Thomas *B*
Walden University *B, M, D*
Winona State University *A*

Mississippi

University of Southern Mississippi *B*

Missouri

Avila University *B*
Central Methodist University *B*
College of the Ozarks *B*
Columbia College *B*
Lindenwood University *B, M*
Missouri Southern State University *B*
Northwest Missouri State
University *B*
Saint Louis University *M, D*
Southwest Baptist University *B*
University of Missouri
Columbia *B*
St. Louis *B, M*
Washington University in St. Louis *B*
Webster University *B, M*
William Jewell College *B*
William Woods University *B*

Montana

University of Montana *B*

Nebraska

Creighton University *B*
Nebraska Wesleyan University *B*
Northeast Community College *A*
University of Nebraska
Lincoln *B*

Nevada

University of Nevada
Reno *B*

New Hampshire

Southern New Hampshire
University *B, M, D*

New Jersey

Berkeley College- Garret Mountain
Campus *A, B*
Caldwell College *B*
Fairleigh Dickinson University
College at Florham *M*
Metropolitan Campus *M*
Felician College *B*
Monmouth University *B*
Ramapo College of New Jersey *B*

Rider University *B*
Saint Peter's College *A, B, M*
Seton Hall University *M*
Thomas Edison State College *B*

New Mexico

New Mexico Highlands University *B*
New Mexico State University *B*

New York

Berkeley College *A, B*
Berkeley College of New York
City *A, B*
Canisius College *B*
City University of New York
Baruch College *M*
Queens College *B*
Concordia College *B*
D'Youville College *B, M*
Daemen College *M*
Dominican College of Blauvelt *B*
Elmira College *B*
Excelsior College *B*
Fashion Institute of Technology *M*
Fordham University *B, M*
Herkimer County Community
College *A*
Hofstra University *B, M*
Hudson Valley Community College *A*
Iona College *B*
Ithaca College *B*
Manhattan College *B*
Manhattanville College *M*
Marist College *B*
Monroe Community College *A*
Nazareth College *B*
New York Institute of Technology *M*
New York University *B, M, D*
Niagara University *B*
Pace University *B, M*
Rochester Institute of
Technology *B, M*
St. John's University *M*
State University of New York
Binghamton *B*
College at Brockport *B*
College at Plattsburgh *B*
New Paltz *B, M*
Syracuse University *M*
Tompkins Cortland Community
College *A*
Touro College *M*
Wagner College *B*
Westchester Community College *A*

North Carolina

Appalachian State University *B*
Campbell University *B*
Central Piedmont Community
College *A*
Elon University *B*
Forsyth Technical Community
College *A*
Gardner-Webb University *B, M*
High Point University *B*
Lenoir-Rhyne University *B*
Mars Hill College *B*
Montreat College *B*
Piedmont Community College *A*
Queens University of Charlotte *B*
St. Andrews Presbyterian College *B*
Salem College *B*
Shaw University *B*
University of North Carolina
Charlotte *B*
Greensboro *B*
Western Carolina University *B*

North Dakota

Jamestown College *B*
Minot State University *B*

Ohio

Baldwin-Wallace College *B, M*
Bowling Green State University *B*
Cedarville University *B*
Cincinnati State Technical and
Community College *A*
Cleveland State University *B*
Marietta College *B*
Mount Union College *B*
Mount Vernon Nazarene University *B*
Notre Dame College *B*
Ohio Dominican University *B*
Ohio Northern University *B*
Ohio State University
Columbus Campus *B*
Ohio University *B*
Ohio Wesleyan University *B*
Owens Community College
Toledo *B*
Stark State College of Technology *A*
Tiffin University *B*
University of Akron *B, M*
University of Cincinnati *M, D*
University of Dayton *B*
University of Findlay *B*
University of Toledo *B, M*
Wright State University *M*
Xavier University *B, M*

Oklahoma

Northeastern State University *B*
Oklahoma Baptist University *B*
Oklahoma City University *B, M*
Oklahoma State University *B*
Oral Roberts University *B*
University of Tulsa *B*

Oregon

Concordia University *B*
Linfield College *B*
Portland State University *M*
University of Portland *B*
Warner Pacific College *B*

Pennsylvania

Albright College *B*
Arcadia University *B*
Chatham University *B*
Chestnut Hill College *B, M*
Clarion University of Pennsylvania *B*
Dickinson College *B*
Duquesne University *B*
Eastern University *B*
Elizabethtown College *B*
Gannon University *B*
Gettysburg College *B*
Grove City College *B*
Holy Family University *B*
Indiana University of Pennsylvania *B*
Juniata College *B*
King's College *B*
Kutztown University of
Pennsylvania *B*
La Roche College *B*
La Salle University *B*
Lehigh University *M*
Manor College *A*
Mansfield University of
Pennsylvania *B*
Marywood University *B*
Mercyhurst College *B*
Messiah College *B*
Moravian College *B*
Neumann University *B*
Penn State
Erie, The Behrend College *B*
Harrisburg *B*
Philadelphia University *B*
Saint Joseph's University *B, M*
St. Vincent College *B*
Seton Hill University *B*
Slippery Rock University of
Pennsylvania *B*

Temple University *B, M*
Thiel College *B*
University of Pennsylvania *B, M*
University of Pittsburgh *M*
University of Scranton *B, M*
Washington & Jefferson College *B*
Waynesburg University *B*
Westminster College *B*
Widener University *B*

Puerto Rico

Inter American University of Puerto
Rico
Metropolitan Campus *M, D*
Ponce Campus *B, M*
San German Campus *D*
Pontifical Catholic University of
Puerto Rico *B, M*
Universidad Metropolitana *M*
University of Puerto Rico
Humacao *B*
Rio Piedras *M, D*

Rhode Island

Bryant University *B*
Johnson & Wales University:
Providence *B, M*
Roger Williams University *B*
University of Rhode Island *B*

South Carolina

Bob Jones University *B*
College of Charleston *B*
Converse College *B*
North Greenville University *B*
University of South Carolina *M*
Wofford College *B*

South Dakota

Northern State University *B*

Tennessee

Lambuth University *B*
Lipscomb University *B*
Maryville College *B*
Southern Adventist University *B*
Union University *B*
University of Memphis *B, M*

Texas

Angelo State University *B*
Austin Community College *A*
Baylor University *B, M*
El Paso Community College *A*
Houston Community College
System *A*
Huston-Tillotson University *B*
LeTourneau University *B*
Our Lady of the Lake University of San
Antonio *M*
St. Edward's University *B*
St. Mary's University *B*
Sam Houston State University *B*
San Jacinto College *A*
Schreiner University *B*
Southwestern Adventist University *B*
Stephen F. Austin State University *B*
Sul Ross State University *M*
Texas A&M International
University *M, D*
Texas A&M University
Galveston *B*
Kingsville *B*
Texarkana *B*
Texas Christian University *B, M*
Texas Tech University *B, M*
Trinity University *B*
University of Dallas *M*
University of Houston *M*
University of Houston
Downtown *B*
University of Texas
Arlington *B, M*

Brownsville - Texas Southmost
College B
Dallas M, D
El Paso D
Pan American B, D
San Antonio B, M
University of the Incarnate Word B

Utah
Utah Valley University A
Westminster College B

Vermont
Champlain College B

Virginia
Eastern Mennonite University B
Emory & Henry College B
James Madison University B
Lynchburg College B
Northern Virginia Community
College A
Old Dominion University B
Regent University A, B, M
Virginia Intermont College B

Washington
City University of Seattle B
Gonzaga University B
Highline Community College A
Seattle University B, M
Shoreline Community College A
Spokane Falls Community College A
University of Washington B
University of Washington Tacoma B
Walla Walla University B
Washington State University B
Western Washington University B
Whitworth University B, M

West Virginia
Bethany College B
Davis and Elkins College B
Marshall University B
Salem International University M
West Virginia Wesleyan College B
Wheeling Jesuit University B

Wisconsin
Alverno College B
Cardinal Stritch University B
Lakeland College B
Marquette University B, M
Milwaukee School of
Engineering B, M
St. Norbert College B
University of Wisconsin
La Crosse B
Madison B, M
Superior B

International economics

California
California State University
Chico B
University of California
Los Angeles B
Santa Cruz D
University of San Francisco B

Colorado
Colorado College B

Connecticut
University of Hartford B

District of Columbia
American University M
Catholic University of America M

Florida
Schiller International University B

Georgia
Georgia State University B
University of West Georgia B

Indiana
Valparaiso University B

Louisiana
Tulane University B

Maryland
Howard Community College A

Massachusetts
Brandeis University M, D
Fitchburg State College B
Hampshire College B
Suffolk University B, M

Michigan
Eastern Michigan University M

Minnesota
University of St. Thomas B

New York
Pace University M

Ohio
Youngstown State University B

Pennsylvania
Eastern University M
La Salle University B
Lafayette College B

Texas
Austin College B
Baylor University M
Texas Christian University B

Virginia
University of Richmond B

Washington
University of Puget Sound B

Wisconsin
Carthage College B
Marquette University M

International finance

Colorado
University of Denver M

District of Columbia
Catholic University of America B

Hawaii
Hawaii Pacific University B

Illinois
University of Illinois
Urbana-Champaign M, D

Massachusetts
Babson College B
Bentley University M
Boston University B, M
Brandeis University M

Missouri
Washington University in St. Louis B

Nebraska
Union College B

New Jersey
William Paterson University of New
Jersey B

New York
Broome Community College A
Pace University M

Ohio
University of Akron M

Oklahoma
Oklahoma Baptist University B

Pennsylvania
Lycoming College B
Westminster College B

Rhode Island
Bryant University B

Texas
Texas A&M University
Galveston B
Texas Christian University B

West Virginia
Bethany College B

Wisconsin
Concordia University Wisconsin B

International marketing

Arizona
Northern Arizona University C

California
Allan Hancock College C, A
Antioch Southern California
Antioch University Santa Barbara M
East Los Angeles College A
Sacramento City College C, A

Connecticut
Quinnipiac University B, M

Florida
Broward College A
Schiller International University B

Illinois
MacCormac College A

Maine
Husson University B

Maryland
University of Maryland
University College C

Massachusetts
Babson College B

Michigan
Adrian College B
Hillsdale College B

Minnesota
St. Paul College C, A

Nevada
University of Nevada
Las Vegas B

New York
Fashion Institute of Technology B
Pace University C, B
St. Thomas Aquinas College B
State University of New York
College at Brockport B
Farmingdale C

Ohio
Muskingum University B

Oklahoma
Oral Roberts University B

Pennsylvania
Community College of Philadelphia A
La Salle University B
Philadelphia University M
Saint Joseph's University B, M
Waynesburg University B

Texas
Texas Christian University B
Texas Wesleyan University B
University of Texas
Brownsville - Texas Southmost
College C, A

Virginia
University of Management and
Technology B

West Virginia
Davis and Elkins College B

Wisconsin
Marquette University M
Milwaukee Area Technical College A
Waukesha County Technical
College A

International public health

Arizona
Prescott College M

District of Columbia
Georgetown University B

Michigan
University of Michigan M

Texas
University of Texas
Health Science Center at
Houston M, D

Utah
Brigham Young University M

Virginia
George Mason University M

International relations

Alabama
Samford University B
Spring Hill College B
Troy University M
University of Alabama B

Arizona
Embry-Riddle Aeronautical University:
Prescott Campus B
Northern Arizona University B
Prescott College B, M

Arkansas

Hendrix College *B*
University of Arkansas *B*
University of Arkansas
  Little Rock *B*

California

Allan Hancock College *A*
Alliant International University *B, M*
Azusa Pacific University *B*
California Lutheran University *B*
California State University
  Chico *B*
  Fresno *M*
  Monterey Bay *B*
  Sacramento *M*
Claremont McKenna College *B*
Holy Names University *B*
Mills College *B*
Occidental College *B*
Pitzer College *B*
Pomona College *B*
Saddleback College *A*
San Diego State University *B*
San Francisco State University *B, M*
San Jose State University *B*
Solano Community College *A*
Stanford University *B, M*
University of California
  Davis *B*
  San Diego *D*
University of La Verne *B*
University of Redlands *B*
University of San Diego *B, M*
University of Southern
  California *B, M, D*
University of the Pacific *B*
Ventura College *C, A*
Whittier College *B*

Colorado

University of Denver *B, M, D*

Connecticut

Connecticut College *B*
Fairfield University *B*
Trinity College *B*
University of Bridgeport *B, M*
Yale University *M*

Delaware

University of Delaware *B, M*

District of Columbia

American University *B, M, D*
Catholic University of America *M*
George Washington University *B, M*
Georgetown University *B, M*
Trinity Washington University *B*

Florida

Bethune-Cookman University *B*
Eckerd College *B*
Florida International
  University *B, M, D*
Florida State University *B, M*
Lynn University *B*
Miami Dade College *A*
New College of Florida *B*
Nova Southeastern University *B*
Palm Beach Community College *A*
Rollins College *B*
Saint Leo University *B*
Schiller International University *B, M*
Stetson University *B*
University of Florida *M, D*
University of Miami *B, M, D*
University of South Florida *B*
University of West Florida *B*

Georgia

Agnes Scott College *B*

Berry College *B*
Brenau University *B*
Emory University *B*
Georgia Institute of
  Technology *B, M, D*
Georgia Military College *A*
Georgia Southern University *B*
Kennesaw State University *B*
Mercer University *B*
Morehouse College *B*
North Georgia College & State
  University *B, M*
Oglethorpe University *B*
Southern Polytechnic State
  University *B*
University of Georgia *B, M*
University of West Georgia *B*
Wesleyan College *B*

Hawaii

Chaminade University of Honolulu *B*
Hawaii Pacific University *B*

Idaho

Brigham Young University-Idaho *A*
College of Idaho *B*
Idaho State University *B*
Northwest Nazarene University *B*
University of Idaho *B*

Illinois

Benedictine University *B*
Bradley University *B*
DePaul University *B, M*
Dominican University *B*
John A. Logan College *A*
Knox College *B*
Lake Forest College *B*
Loyola University Chicago *C, B*
MacMurray College *B*
McKendree University *B*
Monmouth College *B*
Northwestern University *B*
Rockford College *B*
Roosevelt University *B*
Saint Xavier University *B*
University of Chicago *B, M*
Wheaton College *B*

Indiana

Butler University *B*
Indiana University
  Southeast *B*
Indiana Wesleyan University *B*
Saint Joseph's College *B*
Taylor University *B*
University of Evansville *B*
University of Indianapolis *B*
University of Southern Indiana *B*
Valparaiso University *B*

Iowa

Cornell College *B*
Drake University *B*
Iowa State University *B*
Loras College *B*
Morningside College *B*
Mount Mercy College *B*
Simpson College *B*
Wartburg College *B*

Kansas

Kansas State University *M, D*
Pittsburg State University *B*

Kentucky

Centre College *B*
Murray State University *B*
Northern Kentucky University *B*
Thomas More College *A, B*

Maine

Colby College *B*
University of Maine *B*
University of Maine
  Presque Isle *B*
University of Southern Maine *B*

Maryland

College of Notre Dame of Maryland *B*
Frostburg State University *C, B*
Goucher College *B*
Harford Community College *A*
Johns Hopkins University *B, M, D*
Mount St. Mary's University *B*
Towson University *B*
Washington College *B*

Massachusetts

American International College *B*
Boston University *B, M*
Bridgewater State College *B*
Clark University *B, M*
Elms College *B*
Gordon College *B*
Hampshire College *B*
Mount Holyoke College *C, B*
Northeastern University *B*
Regis College *B*
Simmons College *B*
Stonehill College *B*
Suffolk University *B, M*
Tufts University *B, M, D*
University of Massachusetts
  Boston *C*
Wellesley College *B*
Wheaton College *B*

Michigan

Albion College *B*
Aquinas College *B*
Calvin College *B*
Central Michigan University *B*
Grand Valley State University *B*
Lake Superior State University *C*
Michigan State University *B*
Northern Michigan University *B*
Oakland University *B*

Minnesota

Augsburg College *B*
Bethel University *B*
Carleton College *B*
Hamline University *B*
Minnesota State University
  Mankato *B*
St. Catherine University *B*
Saint Cloud State University *B*
University of Minnesota
  Twin Cities *B*
University of St. Thomas *B*

Mississippi

University of Mississippi *B*
University of Southern Mississippi *B*

Missouri

Drury University *B*
Lindenwood University *B*
Missouri Southern State University *B*
Missouri State University *M*
Saint Louis University *B*
Washington University in St.
  Louis *B, M*
Webster University *B, M*
Westminster College *B*
William Jewell College *B*

Montana

University of Montana *B*

Nebraska

Creighton University *B, M*

Doane College *B*
University of Nebraska
  Kearney *B*
  Lincoln *B*

Nevada

University of Nevada
  Reno *B*

New Hampshire

Saint Anselm College *B*

New Jersey

The College of New Jersey *B*
Fairleigh Dickinson University
  Metropolitan Campus *B, M*
Rider University *B*
Seton Hall University *B, M*
William Paterson University of New
  Jersey *M*

New York

Canisius College *B*
City University of New York
  City College *B, M*
  College of Staten Island *B*
  Hunter College *B*
Colgate University *B*
Elmira College *B*
Hamilton College *B*
Hobart and William Smith Colleges *B*
Houghton College *B*
Long Island University
  C. W. Post Campus *B, M*
Marymount Manhattan College *B*
New York University *B, M*
Rochester Institute of Technology *B*
St. John Fisher College *B, M*
Skidmore College *B*
State University of New York
  Binghamton *B*
  College at Brockport *B*
  College at Cortland *B*
  College at Geneseo *B*
  New Paltz *B*
Syracuse University *B, M*
United States Military Academy *B*
University of Rochester *B*
Utica College *B*
Vassar College *B*
Wells College *B*

North Carolina

Campbell University *B*
Duke University *M*
Elon University *B*
Guilford College *B*
Lees-McRae College *B*
Lenoir-Rhyne University *B*
Mars Hill College *B*
Meredith College *B*
North Carolina State University *M*
Salem College *B*
Shaw University *B*

Ohio

Bowling Green State University *B*
Capital University *B*
Case Western Reserve University *B*
Cleveland State University *B, M*
College of Wooster *B*
Kent State University *B*
Kenyon College *B*
Miami University
  Oxford Campus *B*
Mount Union College *B*
Muskingum University *B*
Ohio Northern University *B*
Ohio State University
  Columbus Campus *B*
Ohio University *M*
Ohio Wesleyan University *B*
Otterbein College *B*

Shawnee State University *B*
Tiffin University *B*
University of Akron *C, B*
University of Cincinnati *B*
University of Toledo *B*
Wright State University *B*
Xavier University *B*

Oklahoma

Oral Roberts University *B*
University of Central Oklahoma *M*

Oregon

Lewis & Clark College *B*
Pacific University *B*
Portland State University *B*
Reed College *B*

Pennsylvania

Allegheny College *B*
Arcadia University *B*
Bucknell University *B*
Chatham University *B*
Dickinson College *B*
Drexel University *B*
Duquesne University *B*
Gettysburg College *B*
Harrisburg Area Community
 College *A*
Immaculata University *C, A, B*
Indiana University of Pennsylvania *B*
Juniata College *B*
La Roche College *B*
La Salle University *B*
Lafayette College *B*
Lehigh University *B*
Lincoln University *B*
Lock Haven University of
 Pennsylvania *B*
Millersville University of
 Pennsylvania *B*
Muhlenberg College *C, B*
Penn State
 Abington *B*
 Altoona *B*
 Beaver *B*
 Berks *B*
 Brandywine *B*
 DuBois *B*
 Erie, The Behrend College *B*
 Fayette, The Eberly Campus *B*
 Greater Allegheny *B*
 Hazleton *B*
 Lehigh Valley *B*
 Mont Alto *B*
 New Kensington *B*
 Schuylkill *B*
 Shenango *B*
 University Park *B*
 Wilkes-Barre *B*
 Worthington Scranton *B*
 York *B*
Point Park University *B*
Saint Joseph's University *B*
Seton Hill University *B*
Temple University *B*
University of Pennsylvania *B*
University of Pittsburgh *M*
University of Scranton *B*
Ursinus College *B*
Westminster College *B*
Widener University *B*
Wilkes University *B*
Wilson College *B*
York College of Pennsylvania *B*

Rhode Island

Brown University *B*
Bryant University *B*
Salve Regina University *M*

South Carolina

Bob Jones University *B*

Francis Marion University *B*
Newberry College *B*
University of South Carolina *B, M, D*

Tennessee

Lambuth University *B*
Maryville College *B*
Middle Tennessee State University *B*
Rhodes College *B*
University of Memphis *B*
University of Tennessee
 Martin *B*

Texas

Austin College *B*
Baylor University *B, M*
St. Mary's University *B, M*
Southern Methodist University *B*
Southwestern Adventist University *B*
Southwestern University *B*
Texas A&M University *M*
Texas Christian University *B*
Texas State University: San Marcos *B*
University of St. Thomas *B*
University of Texas
 Austin *M*
University of the Incarnate Word *B*
Western Texas College *A*

Utah

Brigham Young University *B*

Vermont

Bennington College *B*
Middlebury College *B*
Norwich University *B*

Virginia

Bridgewater College *B*
College of William and Mary *B*
Ferrum College *B*
George Mason University *B, M*
Hampden-Sydney College *B*
James Madison University *B*
Lynchburg College *B*
Mary Baldwin College *B*
Old Dominion University *B, M, D*
Regent University *M*
Roanoke College *B*
Sweet Briar College *B*
University of Mary Washington *B*
University of Richmond *B*
University of Virginia *B, M, D*
Virginia Polytechnic Institute and
 State University *B*
Virginia Wesleyan College *B*

Washington

Eastern Washington University *B*
Gonzaga University *B*
University of Washington *B, M*
University of Washington Tacoma *B*
Whitworth University *B*

West Virginia

American Public University
 System *A, B, M*
Bethany College *B*
Marshall University *B*
West Virginia Wesleyan College *B*
Wheeling Jesuit University *B*

Wisconsin

Alverno College *B*
Beloit College *B*
Edgewood College *B*
Marquette University *B, M*
Mount Mary College *B*
St. Norbert College *B*
University of Wisconsin
 Madison *M*

Wyoming

Casper College *A*
University of Wyoming *B, M*
Western Wyoming Community
 College *A*

Investments/securities

Arizona

Northern Arizona University *C*

California

Golden Gate University *M*

Illinois

Saint Xavier University *M*

Massachusetts

Babson College *B*

Missouri

Lindenwood University *M*

Nebraska

University of Nebraska
 Omaha *B*

New York

City University of New York
 Baruch College *M*
Globe Institute of Technology *C*
Pace University *M*
State University of New York
 Albany *M*

Pennsylvania

Duquesne University *B*

Rhode Island

Johnson & Wales University:
 Providence *B*

Wisconsin

University of Wisconsin
 Platteville *B*

Iranian/Persian languages

California

National University *B*

Maryland

University of Maryland
 College Park *B*

Texas

University of Texas
 Austin *B, M, D*

Utah

University of Utah *B, M, D*

Ironworking

California

Foothill College *C*

Indiana

Ivy Tech Community College
 Central Indiana *C, A*
 Lafayette *C, A*
 North Central *C, A*
 Northeast *C, A*
 Northwest *C, A*
 Southwest *C, A*
 Wabash Valley *C, A*

Minnesota

Hennepin Technical College *C, A*
St. Paul College *C*

Utah

Salt Lake Community College *A*

Islamic studies

California

University of California
 Los Angeles *M, D*

District of Columbia

Georgetown University *D*

Illinois

DePaul University *B*

Missouri

Washington University in St.
 Louis *B, M*

Ohio

Ohio State University
 Columbus Campus *B*

Pennsylvania

Swarthmore College *B*

Texas

University of Texas
 Austin *B*

Italian

Arizona

Arizona State University *B*
University of Arizona *B*

California

Cabrillo College *A*
Chabot College *A*
Claremont McKenna College *B*
College of the Desert *A*
Los Angeles City College *A*
Los Angeles Pierce College *A*
Los Angeles Valley College *A*
Orange Coast College *A*
Pitzer College *B*
St. Mary's College of California *B*
San Diego City College *A*
San Francisco State University *B, M*
Santa Clara University *B*
Santiago Canyon College *A*
Scripps College *B*
Stanford University *B, M, D*
University of California
 Berkeley *B, M, D*
 Davis *B*
 Los Angeles *B, M, D*
 San Diego *B*
 Santa Barbara *B*
University of Southern California *B*

Colorado

Colorado College *B*
University of Colorado
 Boulder *B*
University of Denver *B*

Connecticut

Central Connecticut State
 University *B*
Connecticut College *B*
Fairfield University *B*
Southern Connecticut State
 University *B, M, T*
Trinity College *B*
University of Connecticut *B, M, D*
Wesleyan University *B*

Yale University *B, M, D*

Delaware
University of Delaware *B, M, T*

District of Columbia
George Washington University *B*
Georgetown University *B*

Florida
Florida State University *B*
University of South Florida *B*

Georgia
Emory University *B*
University of Georgia *B*

Illinois
DePaul University *B*
Dominican University *B*
Loyola University Chicago *B*
Northwestern University *B*
Triton College *A*
University of Chicago *B, D*
University of Illinois
    Chicago *B*
    Urbana-Champaign *B, M, D*

Indiana
Indiana University
    Bloomington *B, M, D*
Saint Mary's College *B*
University of Notre Dame *B, M*

Iowa
University of Iowa *B, T*

Kentucky
Bluegrass Community and Technical
    College *A*

Louisiana
Tulane University *B*

Maryland
Johns Hopkins University *B, M, D*
University of Maryland
    College Park *B*

Massachusetts
Assumption College *B*
Boston College *B, M*
Boston University *B*
College of the Holy Cross *B*
Mount Holyoke College *B*
Smith College *B, M*
Tufts University *B*
University of Massachusetts
    Amherst *B, M*
    Boston *B*
Wellesley College *B*
Wheaton College *B*

Michigan
University of Michigan *B, M, D*

Minnesota
University of Minnesota
    Twin Cities *B, M*

Missouri
Saint Louis University *B*
Washington University in St. Louis *B*

New Hampshire
Dartmouth College *B*

New Jersey
Montclair State University *B, T*
Princeton University *B, M, D*

Rutgers, The State University of New
    Jersey
    New Brunswick/Piscataway
        Campus *B, M, D, T*
Seton Hall University *B, T*

New York
Bard College *B*
Barnard College *B*
City University of New York
    Brooklyn College *B*
    Hunter College *B, M*
    Lehman College *B*
    Queens College *B, M, T*
Columbia University *B*
Columbia University
    School of General Studies *B*
Cornell University *B*
Fordham University *B*
Hofstra University *B*
Iona College *B, M*
Ithaca College *B*
Long Island University
    C. W. Post Campus *B*
Nazareth College *B*
New York University *B, M, D*
St. John's University *B*
State University of New York
    Albany *B*
    Binghamton *B, M*
    Buffalo *B*
    Stony Brook *B*
Syracuse University *B*
Vassar College *B*

North Carolina
Duke University *B, M, D*
University of North Carolina
    Chapel Hill *B, M, D*

Ohio
Ohio State University
    Columbus Campus *B, M, D*
Youngstown State University *B*

Oklahoma
Tulsa Community College *A*
University of Oklahoma *B*

Oregon
University of Oregon *B, M*

Pennsylvania
Bryn Mawr College *B*
Cabrini College *B*
Dickinson College *B*
Haverford College *B*
La Salle University *B, T*
Penn State
    Abington *B*
    Altoona *B*
    Beaver *B*
    Berks *B*
    Brandywine *B*
    DuBois *B*
    Erie, The Behrend College *B*
    Fayette, The Eberly Campus *B*
    Greater Allegheny *B*
    Hazleton *B*
    Lehigh Valley *B*
    Mont Alto *B*
    New Kensington *B*
    Schuylkill *B*
    Shenango *B*
    University Park *B*
    Wilkes-Barre *B*
    Worthington Scranton *B*
    York *B*
Rosemont College *B*
Saint Joseph's University *B*
Temple University *B*
University of Pennsylvania *B*
University of Pittsburgh *B, M*

Villanova University *B*

Rhode Island
Brown University *B, M, D*
Providence College *B*
University of Rhode Island *B*

South Carolina
University of South Carolina *B*

Tennessee
University of Tennessee
    Knoxville *B*

Texas
Southern Methodist University *B*
University of Houston *B*
University of Texas
    Austin *B*

Utah
Brigham Young University *B*

Vermont
Bennington College *B*
Middlebury College *B, M, D*

Virginia
University of Virginia *B, M*

Washington
Gonzaga University *B*
University of Washington *B*

Wisconsin
University of Wisconsin
    Madison *B, M, D*
    Milwaukee *B*

Italian studies

California
Scripps College *B*
University of California
    San Diego *B*
    Santa Cruz *B*

Colorado
Colorado College *B*

Florida
Florida State University *M*

Georgia
Emory University *B, D*

Massachusetts
Boston University *B*
Brandeis University *B*
College of the Holy Cross *B*
Wheaton College *B*

New York
Bard College *B*
Columbia University *B*

Ohio
Miami University
    Oxford Campus *B*

Pennsylvania
Arcadia University *B*
Dickinson College *B*

Rhode Island
Brown University *B, M, D*

Texas
Southern Methodist University *B*

University of Texas
    Austin *M, D*

Vermont
University of Vermont *B*

Virginia
Sweet Briar College *B*

Washington
University of Washington *B, M*

Japanese

Alaska
University of Alaska
    Anchorage *B*
    Fairbanks *B*

California
Cabrillo College *A*
California State University
    Fullerton *B*
    Long Beach *B*
    Los Angeles *B*
Citrus College *A*
Claremont McKenna College *B*
El Camino College *A*
Foothill College *A*
Grossmont College *A*
Los Angeles City College *A*
MiraCosta College *A*
Orange Coast College *A*
Pitzer College *B*
Pomona College *B*
St. Mary's College of California *B*
San Diego State University *B*
San Francisco State University *B, M*
San Jose State University *B*
Scripps College *B*
Stanford University *B, M, D*
University of California
    Berkeley *B, M, D*
    Davis *B*
    Irvine *B*
    Los Angeles *B*
    San Diego *B*
    Santa Barbara *B*
University of San Francisco *B*
University of Southern California *M*
University of the Pacific *B*

Colorado
University of Colorado
    Boulder *B*

Connecticut
Connecticut College *B*
Trinity College *B*
Wesleyan University *B*
Yale University *B*

District of Columbia
George Washington University *B*
Georgetown University *B*

Florida
Florida State University *B*

Georgia
Emory University *B*
Oglethorpe University *B*
University of Georgia *B*

Hawaii
University of Hawaii
    Hilo *B*
    Manoa *B, M, D*

Illinois

City Colleges of Chicago
  Harold Washington College *A*
North Central College *B*

Indiana

Ball State University *B, T*
Indiana University
  Bloomington *M, D*
Purdue University *B*
University of Notre Dame *B*

Iowa

University of Iowa *B, T*

Maine

Bates College *B, T*

Maryland

University of Maryland
  College Park *B*

Massachusetts

Tufts University *B*
University of Massachusetts
  Amherst *B, M*
Wellesley College *B*
Williams College *B*

Michigan

Aquinas College *B*
Calvin College *B*
Eastern Michigan University *B*
Michigan State University *B*
Oakland University *B*

Minnesota

Gustavus Adolphus College *B*
Macalester College *B*
University of Minnesota
  Twin Cities *B, M, D*

Missouri

Washington University in St.
  Louis *B, M, D*

Montana

University of Montana *B*

New Hampshire

Dartmouth College *B*

New Jersey

Seton Hall University *T*

New York

Bard College *B*
Colgate University *B*
Columbia University *B*
Hobart and William Smith Colleges *B*
University of Rochester *B*
Vassar College *B*

North Carolina

Wake Forest University *B*

Ohio

Mount Union College *B, T*
Ohio State University
  Columbus Campus *B, M, D*
University of Findlay *B*

Oklahoma

Tulsa Community College *A*

Oregon

Linfield College *B*
Pacific University *B*
Portland State University *B, T*
University of Oregon *B*

Pennsylvania

Carnegie Mellon University *B*
Elizabethtown College *B*
Gettysburg College *B*
Penn State
  Abington *B*
  Altoona *B*
  Beaver *B*
  Berks *B*
  Brandywine *B*
  DuBois *B*
  Erie, The Behrend College *B*
  Fayette, The Eberly Campus *B*
  Greater Allegheny *B*
  Hazleton *B*
  Lehigh Valley *B*
  Mont Alto *B*
  New Kensington *B*
  Schuylkill *B*
  Shenango *B*
  University Park *B*
  Wilkes-Barre *B*
  Worthington Scranton *B*
  York *B*
Swarthmore College *B*
University of Pittsburgh *B*
Ursinus College *T*

Texas

Austin Community College *A*

Utah

Brigham Young University *B, M*
Snow College *A*
University of Utah *B*

Vermont

Bennington College *B*
Middlebury College *B, M, D*
University of Vermont *B*

Washington

Everett Community College *A*
University of Puget Sound *T*
University of Washington *B*

Wisconsin

Lawrence University *B*
University of Wisconsin
  Madison *B, M, D*

Japanese studies

California

University of California
  San Diego *B*

Georgia

Emory University *B*

Indiana

Earlham College *B*
Purdue University *B*

Michigan

Adrian College *A, B*
Hope College *B*

Minnesota

Gustavus Adolphus College *B*

New York

Columbia University *B*
State University of New York
  Albany *B*

Ohio

Case Western Reserve University *B*

Oregon

Willamette University *B*

Pennsylvania

Gettysburg College *B*

Washington

University of Washington *B, M*

Wisconsin

Lawrence University *B*

Jazz studies

California

California State University
  Long Beach *B, M*
Grossmont College *A*
University of Southern
  California *M, D*

Connecticut

University of Hartford *B*

District of Columbia

Howard University *B*

Florida

Florida Agricultural and Mechanical
  University *B*
Florida State University *B, M*
Palm Beach Community College *A*
State College of Florida,
  Manatee-Sarasota *A*
University of Miami *B, M, D*
University of North Florida *B*

Illinois

Augustana College *B*
Columbia College Chicago *B*
DePaul University *B, M*
Lincoln College *A*
North Central College *B*
Northwestern University *B, M*
Roosevelt University *B*
University of Illinois
  Urbana-Champaign *B*

Indiana

Indiana University
  Bloomington *B*

Iowa

University of Iowa *B, T*
University of Northern Iowa *M*

Louisiana

Loyola University New Orleans *B, M*

Maine

University of Southern Maine *B, M*

Massachusetts

Berklee College of Music *B*
New England Conservatory of
  Music *B, M, D*

Michigan

Hope College *B*
Michigan State University *B, M*
University of Michigan *B*
Western Michigan University *B, M*

Minnesota

Saint Cloud State University *B*
University of Minnesota
  Duluth *B*

Missouri

Webster University *M*

Nevada

University of Nevada
  Las Vegas *B*

New Jersey

Rowan University *B*
Rutgers, The State University of New
  Jersey
  Newark Regional Campus *M*
William Paterson University of New
  Jersey *B*

New York

Bard College *B*
Barnard College *B*
City University of New York
  City College *B*
Columbia University *B*
Eastman School of Music of the
  University of Rochester *B, M, D*
Five Towns College *A, B, M*
Hofstra University *B*
Ithaca College *B*
Juilliard School *B, M, D*
Long Island University
  Brooklyn Campus *B, T*
University of Rochester *B, M, D*
Villa Maria College of Buffalo *A*

North Carolina

East Carolina University *B*
North Carolina Central University *B*

Ohio

Bowling Green State University *B, M*
Capital University *B*
Central State University *B*
Oberlin College *B, M*
Ohio State University
  Columbus Campus *B*
University of Akron *B*
University of Cincinnati *B*
Youngstown State University *B, M*

Oregon

University of Oregon *B, M*

Pennsylvania

Carnegie Mellon University *B, M*
Temple University *B*
University of the Arts *M*

Puerto Rico

Conservatory of Music of Puerto
  Rico *B*

Rhode Island

Community College of Rhode
  Island *A*

South Carolina

University of South Carolina *M*

Texas

Texas State University: San Marcos *B*
University of North Texas *B, M*
University of Texas
  Austin *B*

Utah

Brigham Young University *B*

Vermont

Bennington College *B*
Johnson State College *B*

Washington

Cornish College of the Arts *B*
Whitworth University *B*

Wisconsin

University of Wisconsin
  Madison *B, M*

Journalism

Alabama

Alabama Agricultural and Mechanical
  University *B*
Auburn University *B*
Faulkner State Community College *A*
Faulkner University *B*
Samford University *B*
Talladega College *B*
Troy University *B*
University of Alabama *B, M*

Alaska

University of Alaska
  Anchorage *B*
  Fairbanks *B*

Arizona

Central Arizona College *A*
Cochise College *A*
Glendale Community College *C*
Mesa Community College *A*
Northern Arizona University *B*
Prescott College *B*
University of Arizona *B, M*

Arkansas

Arkansas State University *B, M*
Arkansas Tech University *B*
Harding University *B*
Henderson State University *B*
John Brown University *A, B*
Southern Arkansas University *B*
University of Arkansas *B, M*
University of Arkansas
  Little Rock *B, M*
  Pine Bluff *B*
University of Central Arkansas *B*

California

Alliant International University *B*
American River College *A*
Azusa Pacific University *B*
Bakersfield College *A*
Biola University *B*
Butte College *C, A*
Cabrillo College *A*
California Baptist University *B*
California Lutheran University *B*
California Polytechnic State
  University: San Luis Obispo *B*
California State University
  Chico *B*
  Dominguez Hills *B*
  East Bay *B*
  Fullerton *B, M*
  Long Beach *B*
  Northridge *B, M*
  Sacramento *B, M*
Canada College *A*
Cerritos College *A*
Chabot College *A*
Chaffey College *C*
City College of San Francisco *A*
College of the Canyons *C, A*
College of the Desert *A*
College of the Redwoods *C, A*
College of the Sequoias *A*
Cosumnes River College *A*
Cuesta College *C, A*
Cypress College *A*
Diablo Valley College *C*
East Los Angeles College *A*
El Camino College *C, A*
El Camino College: Compton
  Center *A*
Fresno City College *A*
Fullerton College *A*

Gavilan College *A*
Glendale Community College *A*
Golden West College *C, A*
Grossmont College *C, A*
Humboldt State University *B*
Imperial Valley College *A*
Laney College *A*
Lassen Community College *C, A*
Long Beach City College *C, A*
Los Angeles City College *A*
Los Angeles Pierce College *A*
Los Angeles Southwest College *A*
Los Angeles Trade and Technical
  College *C, A*
Los Angeles Valley College *C, A*
Los Medanos College *A*
Merced College *A*
Modesto Junior College *C, A*
Mount San Antonio College *A*
National University *B*
Ohlone College *C, A*
Orange Coast College *A*
Oxnard College *A*
Pacific Union College *B*
Palo Verde College *C*
Palomar College *C, A*
Pasadena City College *C, A*
Pepperdine University *B*
Point Loma Nazarene University *B*
Rio Hondo College *C, A*
Sacramento City College *C, A*
Saddleback College *C, A*
San Diego State University *B*
San Francisco State University *B*
San Joaquin Delta College *A*
San Jose State University *B*
Santa Ana College *C, A*
Santa Monica College *A*
Santa Rosa Junior College *C*
Shasta College *C, A*
Solano Community College *A*
Southwestern College *A*
Taft College *A*
University of California
  Berkeley *M*
  Irvine *B*
University of La Verne *B*
University of Southern
  California *B, M*
Yuba Community College
  District *C, A*

Colorado

Adams State College *A*
Colorado State University *B, M*
Jones International University *B, M*
Metropolitan State College of
  Denver *B*
Trinidad State Junior College *A*
University of Colorado
  Boulder *B, M*
University of Denver *B*
University of Northern Colorado *B*

Connecticut

Central Connecticut State
  University *B*
Manchester Community College *A*
Mitchell College *B*
Norwalk Community College *A*
Quinnipiac University *B, M*
Southern Connecticut State
  University *B*
University of Bridgeport *B*
University of Connecticut *B*
University of New Haven *C*

Delaware

Delaware State University *B*
University of Delaware *B*

District of Columbia

American University *B, M*

George Washington University *B*
Georgetown University *M*
Howard University *B*

Florida

Bethune-Cookman University *B*
Broward College *A*
Chipola College *A*
Florida Agricultural and Mechanical
  University *B, M*
Florida Southern College *B*
Gulf Coast Community College *A*
Lynn University *B*
Miami Dade College *A*
Palm Beach Atlantic University *B*
Palm Beach Community College *A*
Pensacola Junior College *A*
Southeastern University *B*
State College of Florida,
  Manatee-Sarasota *A*
University of Central Florida *B*
University of Florida *B*
University of Miami *B, M*
Warner University *B*

Georgia

Abraham Baldwin Agricultural
  College *A*
Albany State University *B*
Andrew College *A*
Darton College *A*
Emory University *B*
Fort Valley State University *B*
Gainesville State College *A*
Georgia College and State
  University *B*
Georgia Highlands College *A*
Georgia Perimeter College *A*
Georgia Southern University *B*
Georgia State University *B*
Macon State College *A*
Mercer University *B*
Middle Georgia College *A*
Paine College *B*
South Georgia College *A*
University of Georgia *B*
University of West Georgia *B*

Hawaii

Hawaii Pacific University *B*
University of Hawaii
  Manoa *B*

Idaho

Boise State University *B, T*
Brigham Young University-Idaho *B*
North Idaho College *A*
Northwest Nazarene University *B*
University of Idaho *B*

Illinois

Black Hawk College: East Campus *A*
Bradley University *B*
City Colleges of Chicago
  Harold Washington College *A*
  Kennedy-King College *A*
College of DuPage *C*
Columbia College Chicago *B, M*
Danville Area Community College *A*
DePaul University *M*
Dominican University *B*
Eastern Illinois University *B*
Governors State University *B, M*
Harper College *C*
Illinois Central College *A*
Illinois Institute of Technology *B*
Illinois State University *B*
Illinois Valley Community College *A*
John A. Logan College *A*
Kishwaukee College *A*
Lake Land College *A*
Lewis University *B*
Lincoln College *A*

Loyola University Chicago *B*
MacMurray College *B*
North Central College *B*
Northern Illinois University *B*
Northwestern University *B, M*
Olivet Nazarene University *B*
Richland Community College *A*
Roosevelt University *B, M*
Southern Illinois University
  Carbondale *B*
University of Illinois
  Springfield *M*
  Urbana-Champaign *B, M*
Western Illinois University *B*

Indiana

Ball State University *B, M, T*
Bethel College *A*
Butler University *B*
Franklin College *B*
Goshen College *B*
Grace College *B*
Huntington University *B*
Indiana University
  Bloomington *B, M, D, T*
  Southeast *A, B*
Indiana University-Purdue University
  Indianapolis *B*
Indiana Wesleyan University *B*
Manchester College *B*
Purdue University *B*
Purdue University
  Calumet *B*
St. Mary-of-the-Woods College *B*
University of Southern Indiana *B*
Valparaiso University *B*
Vincennes University *A*

Iowa

Dordt College *B*
Drake University *B*
Grand View University *B*
Iowa Lakes Community College *C, A*
Iowa State University *B, M*
Loras College *B*
Marshalltown Community College *A*
Mount Mercy College *B*
Northwestern College *B*
St. Ambrose University *B*
Southeastern Community College
  North Campus *A*
University of Iowa *B, M, D, T*
Waldorf College *B*
Wartburg College *B, T*

Kansas

Baker University *T*
Barton County Community College *A*
Butler Community College *A*
Central Christian College of Kansas *A*
Cloud County Community
  College *C, A*
Coffeyville Community College *A*
Cowley County Community
  College *A*
Dodge City Community College *A*
Emporia State University *T*
Garden City Community College *A*
Kansas State University *B, M*
Labette Community College *A*
Pittsburg State University *B*
Pratt Community College *A*
Seward County Community College *A*
Tabor College *B*
University of Kansas *B, M*

Kentucky

Asbury College *B*
Bluegrass Community and Technical
  College *A*
Campbellsville University *B*
Eastern Kentucky University *B*
Kentucky State University *B*

Lindsey Wilson College *B*
Murray State University *B*
Northern Kentucky University *B*
University of Kentucky *B*
Western Kentucky University *B*

Louisiana

Louisiana College *B*
Louisiana Tech University *B*
Northwestern State University *B*

Maine

Saint Joseph's College of Maine *B*
University of Maine *B*

Maryland

Howard Community College *A*
Towson University *B, M*
University of Maryland
   College Park *B, M, D*
Washington Adventist University *B*

Massachusetts

American International College *B*
Boston University *B, M*
Cape Cod Community College *A*
Eastern Nazarene College *B*
Emerson College *B, M*
Lasell College *B*
Newbury College *B*
Northeastern University *B, M*
Northern Essex Community
   College *A*
Salem State College *B*
Suffolk University *B*
University of Massachusetts
   Amherst *B*
Western New England College *B*

Michigan

Adrian College *B*
Andrews University *B*
Bay de Noc Community College *C*
Central Michigan University *B*
Delta College *A*
Eastern Michigan University *B*
Grand Rapids Community College *A*
Grand Valley State University *B*
Hillsdale College *B*
Hope College *B*
Kuyper College *B*
Lansing Community College *A*
Madonna University *A, B*
Michigan State University *B, M*
Oakland University *B*
St. Clair County Community
   College *A*
University of Detroit Mercy *B*
University of Michigan
   Flint *B*
Wayne State University *B*
Western Michigan University *B*

Minnesota

Bemidji State University *B*
Bethel University *B*
College of St. Scholastica *B*
Minnesota State University
   Mankato *B*
   Moorhead *C*
North Central University *B*
Northland Community & Technical
   College *A*
Northwestern College *B*
Ridgewater College *A*
Rochester Community and Technical
   College *C*
Saint Cloud State University *B*
St. Mary's University of Minnesota *B*
University of Minnesota
   Twin Cities *B, M, D*
University of St. Thomas *B*
Vermilion Community College *A*

Winona State University *B*

Mississippi

Delta State University *B*
Hinds Community College *A*
Mississippi College *B*
Northwest Mississippi Community
   College *A*
Rust College *B*
University of Mississippi *B, M*
University of Southern Mississippi *B*

Missouri

College of the Ozarks *B*
Crowder College *A*
Evangel University *A, B*
Lincoln University *B*
Lindenwood University *B*
Missouri State University *B*
Northwest Missouri State
   University *B*
Rockhurst University *C*
St. Louis Community College
   St. Louis Community College at
      Florissant Valley *A*
Stephens College *B*
University of Central Missouri *B, M*
University of Missouri
   Columbia *B, M, D*
Washington University in St. Louis *B*
Webster University *B*
Westminster College *B*
William Woods University *B*

Montana

Miles Community College *A*
University of Montana *B, M*

Nebraska

Concordia University *B*
Creighton University *B*
Dana College *B*
Doane College *B*
Northeast Community College *A*
Union College *B*
University of Nebraska
   Kearney *B*
   Lincoln *B, M*
   Omaha *B*
Wayne State College *B, T*
Western Nebraska Community
   College *A*

Nevada

University of Nevada
   Reno *B, M*

New Hampshire

Keene State College *B*
Rivier College *B*

New Jersey

Bergen Community College *A*
County College of Morris *A*
Cumberland County College *A*
Essex County College *A*
Felician College *B*
Gloucester County College *A*
Middlesex County College *A*
Ocean County College *A*
Rider University *B*
Rowan University *B*
Rutgers, The State University of New
   Jersey
   New Brunswick/Piscataway
      Campus *B*
   Newark Regional Campus *B*
Salem Community College *A*
Seton Hall University *B*
Sussex County Community College *A*
Thomas Edison State College *B*

New Mexico

Eastern New Mexico University *B*
New Mexico State University *B*
University of New Mexico *B*

New York

Adelphi University *B*
City University of New York
   Baruch College *B, M*
   Brooklyn College *B*
   City College *B*
   Kingsborough Community
      College *A*
Five Towns College *B*
Fulton-Montgomery Community
   College *C, A*
Hofstra University *B, M*
Iona College *B, M*
Ithaca College *B*
Long Island University
   Brooklyn Campus *B*
   C. W. Post Campus *B*
Manhattan College *B*
Marist College *B*
New York Institute of Technology *M*
New York University *B, M*
Rochester Institute of Technology *B*
Saint Bonaventure University *B*
St. John's University *B*
St. Thomas Aquinas College *B*
State University of New York
   College at Brockport *B*
   College at Buffalo *B*
   College at Plattsburgh *B*
   College of Agriculture and
      Technology at Morrisville *A, B*
   New Paltz *B*
   Oswego *B*
   Purchase *B*
   Stony Brook *B*
Syracuse University *B, M*
Utica College *B*

North Carolina

Appalachian State University *B*
Campbell University *B*
Elon University *B*
Gardner-Webb University *B*
High Point University *B*
Methodist University *B*
North Carolina Agricultural and
   Technical State University *B*
Queens University of Charlotte *B*
Wingate University *B*

North Dakota

North Dakota State University *B*

Ohio

Ashland University *B*
Bowling Green State University *B*
Cedarville University *B*
Central State University *B*
Defiance College *B*
Kent State University *B, M*
Malone University *B*
Marietta College *B*
Miami University
   Oxford Campus *B*
Mount Vernon Nazarene University *B*
Muskingum University *B*
Ohio Northern University *B*
Ohio State University
   Columbus Campus *B, M*
Ohio University *B, M, D*
Ohio Wesleyan University *B*
Otterbein College *B*
Tiffin University *B*
University of Cincinnati
   Raymond Walters College *C*
University of Dayton *B*
University of Findlay *B*
University of Rio Grande *B*

Urbana University *B*
Wilberforce University *B*
Wilmington College *B*
Youngstown State University *B*

Oklahoma

Bacone College *A*
Cameron University *B*
Carl Albert State College *A*
Connors State College *A*
East Central University *B*
Eastern Oklahoma State College *A*
Langston University *B*
Northeastern State University *B*
Northern Oklahoma College *A*
Northwestern Oklahoma State
   University *B*
Oklahoma Baptist University *B*
Oklahoma Christian University *B*
Oklahoma City Community College *A*
Oklahoma City University *B*
Oklahoma State University *B*
Southern Nazarene University *B*
Tulsa Community College *A*
University of Central Oklahoma *B*
University of Oklahoma *B, M*

Oregon

Chemeketa Community College *A*
Corban College *B*
George Fox University *B*
Linn-Benton Community College *A*
Mt. Hood Community College *A*
Multnomah University *B*
Pacific University *B*
Southern Oregon University *B*
Umpqua Community College *C*
University of Oregon *B, M*

Pennsylvania

Allegheny College *B*
Bucks County Community College *A*
Chatham University *B*
Community College of Allegheny
   County *A*
Duquesne University *B*
Edinboro University of
   Pennsylvania *B*
Gannon University *B*
Gettysburg College *B*
Indiana University of Pennsylvania *B*
Keystone College *A, B*
La Salle University *B*
Lehigh University *B*
Lincoln University *B*
Lock Haven University of
   Pennsylvania *B*
Luzerne County Community
   College *A*
Mansfield University of
   Pennsylvania *A, B*
Messiah College *B*
Northampton Community College *A*
Penn State
   Abington *B*
   Altoona *B*
   Beaver *B*
   Berks *B*
   Brandywine *B*
   DuBois *B*
   Erie, The Behrend College *B*
   Fayette, The Eberly Campus *B*
   Greater Allegheny *B*
   Hazleton *B*
   Lehigh Valley *B*
   Mont Alto *B*
   New Kensington *B*
   Schuylkill *B*
   Shenango *B*
   University Park *B, M*
   Wilkes-Barre *B*
   Worthington Scranton *B*
   York *B*
Point Park University *B, M*

Seton Hill University *B*
Shippensburg University of
   Pennsylvania *B*
Slippery Rock University of
   Pennsylvania *B*
Temple University *B, M*
University of Pittsburgh
   Greensburg *B*
   Johnstown *B*
Waynesburg University *B*

Puerto Rico

Bayamon Central University *B*
Inter American University of Puerto
   Rico
   Ponce Campus *B*
University of Puerto Rico
   Rio Piedras *B, M*
University of the Sacred Heart *B, M*

Rhode Island

Roger Williams University *B*
University of Rhode Island *B*

South Carolina

Bob Jones University *B*
Columbia College *B*
North Greenville University *B*
University of South Carolina *B, M, D*
Winthrop University *B*

South Dakota

Augustana College *B*
Dakota Wesleyan University *B*
South Dakota State University *B*
University of Sioux Falls *B*
University of South Dakota *B, M*

Tennessee

Belmont University *B*
Carson-Newman College *B*
Columbia State Community College *A*
Freed-Hardeman University *B*
Lee University *B*
Lipscomb University *B*
Southern Adventist University *B*
Tennessee State University *B*
Tennessee Technological University *B*
Tusculum College *B*
Union University *B*
University of Memphis *B, M*
University of Tennessee
   Knoxville *B*

Texas

Abilene Christian University *B*
Amarillo College *A*
Angelo State University *B, T*
Baylor University *B, M, T*
College of the Mainland *A*
Del Mar College *A*
El Paso Community College *A*
Hill College *C, A*
Howard College *A*
Jarvis Christian College *B*
Kilgore College *A*
Midland College *A*
North Lake College *C*
Northwest Vista College *A*
Our Lady of the Lake University of San
   Antonio *B*
Palo Alto College *A*
Paris Junior College *A*
Sam Houston State University *B*
San Antonio College *A*
San Jacinto College *A*
South Plains College *A*
Southern Methodist University *B*
Southwestern Adventist University *B*
Stephen F. Austin State
   University *B, M, T*
Texarkana College *A*
Texas A&M University *B*

Texas A&M University
   Commerce *B*
Texas Christian University *B, M*
Texas Southern University *B*
Texas State University: San Marcos *B*
Texas Tech University *B, M*
Texas Wesleyan University *B*
Trinity Valley Community College *A*
Tyler Junior College *A*
University of Houston *B, M*
University of North Texas *B, M*
University of Texas
   Arlington *B*
   Austin *B, M, D*
   El Paso *B*
   Pan American *B*
   Tyler *B*
University of the Incarnate Word *B*
West Texas A&M University *B*
Western Texas College *A*
Wiley College *B*

Utah

Brigham Young University *B*
College of Eastern Utah *T*
Snow College *A*
Utah State University *B, M*
Weber State University *B*

Vermont

Bennington College *B*
Castleton State College *B*
Champlain College *B*
Green Mountain College *B*
Johnson State College *B*
Lyndon State College *B*
St. Michael's College *B*

Virginia

Averett University *B*
Hampton University *B*
Norfolk State University *B*
Patrick Henry College *B*
Radford University *B*
Regent University *B, M*
Southwest Virginia Community
   College *C*
University of Richmond *B*
Virginia Union University *B*
Washington and Lee University *B*

Washington

Centralia College *A*
Eastern Washington University *B*
Everett Community College *A*
Evergreen State College *B*
Gonzaga University *B*
Highline Community College *A*
Olympic College *A*
Peninsula College *A*
Seattle University *B*
Spokane Falls Community College *A*
Walla Walla University *B*
Western Washington University *B*
Whitworth University *B*

West Virginia

Bethany College *B*
Concord University *B*
Marshall University *B, M*
Potomac State College of West
   Virginia University *A*
West Virginia University *B, M, T*
West Virginia University at
   Parkersburg *A*

Wisconsin

Carroll University *B*
Marquette University *B, M*
University of Wisconsin
   Eau Claire *B*
   Madison *B, M, D*
   Milwaukee *B, M*

   Oshkosh *B*
   River Falls *B, T*
   Superior *B*
   Whitewater *B*

Wyoming

Northwest College *A*
University of Wyoming *B*
Western Wyoming Community
   College *A*

Judaic studies

Arizona

University of Arizona *B*

California

American Jewish University *B*
California State University
   Chico *B*
San Diego State University *B*
San Francisco State University *B*
Scripps College *B*
University of California
   Berkeley *D*
   San Diego *B, M*
University of Southern California *B*

Connecticut

Trinity College *B*
University of Connecticut *M*
University of Hartford *B*
Yale University *B*

District of Columbia

American University *B*
George Washington University *B*

Florida

Florida Atlantic University *B*
University of Florida *B*
University of Miami *B*

Georgia

Emory University *B, M*

Illinois

DePaul University *B*
Hebrew Theological College *B*
Moody Bible Institute *B*
University of Chicago *B*

Indiana

Indiana University
   Bloomington *B*

Louisiana

Tulane University *B*

Maryland

Towson University *B, M*
University of Maryland
   College Park *B, M*

Massachusetts

Brandeis University *B, M, D*
Northeastern University *B*
University of Massachusetts
   Amherst *B*
Wellesley College *B*

Michigan

Michigan Jewish Institute *B*
University of Michigan *B, M*

Minnesota

University of Minnesota
   Twin Cities *B*

Missouri

Washington University in St.
   Louis *B, M*

New Jersey

Rutgers, The State University of New
   Jersey
   New Brunswick/Piscataway
      Campus *B*
Seton Hall University *M*

New York

Bard College *B*
Beth Hamedrash Shaarei Yosher
   Institute *B, D*
Beth Hatalmud Rabbinical College *B*
Central Yeshiva Tomchei
   Tmimim-Lubavitch *B, M*
City University of New York
   Brooklyn College *B, M*
   City College *R*
   Hunter College *B*
   Queens College *B*
Eugene Lang College The New School
   for Liberal Arts *B*
Hofstra University *B*
Jewish Theological Seminary of
   America *B, M, D*
Kehilath Yakov Rabbinical
   Seminary *B*
Ohr Somayach Tanenbaum Education
   Center *B*
State University of New York
   Albany *B*
   Binghamton *B*
Talmudical Institute of Upstate New
   York *B*
Touro College *B, M*
Vassar College *B*
Yeshiva University *A, B, M, D, T*
Yeshivat Mikdash Melech *B, M*

Ohio

Oberlin College *B*
Ohio State University
   Columbus Campus *B*
University of Cincinnati *B*

Oklahoma

University of Oklahoma *B*

Oregon

University of Oregon *B*

Pennsylvania

Dickinson College *B*
Penn State
   Abington *B*
   Altoona *B*
   Beaver *B*
   Berks *B*
   Brandywine *B*
   DuBois *B*
   Erie, The Behrend College *B*
   Fayette, The Eberly Campus *B*
   Greater Allegheny *B*
   Hazleton *B*
   Lehigh Valley *B*
   Mont Alto *B*
   New Kensington *B*
   Schuylkill *B*
   Shenango *B*
   University Park *B*
   Wilkes-Barre *B*
   Worthington Scranton *B*
   York *B*
Temple University *B*
University of Pennsylvania *B*
West Chester University of
   Pennsylvania *M*

Rhode Island
Brown University *B*

Tennessee
Vanderbilt University *B*

Texas
University of Texas
Austin *B*

Vermont
Bennington College *B*

Washington
University of Washington *B*

Wisconsin
University of Wisconsin
Madison *M, D*
Milwaukee *B*

Juvenile corrections

Arizona
Arizona Western College *C*
Pima Community College *C*

California
Diablo Valley College *C*
Santa Rosa Junior College *C*

Connecticut
Mitchell College *B*

Illinois
Danville Area Community College *A*
Kaskaskia College *A*
Moraine Valley Community College *A*

Iowa
Western Iowa Tech Community
College *A*

Missouri
Harris-Stowe State University *B*

Montana
University of Great Falls *B*

Nevada
Truckee Meadows Community
College *A*

Oklahoma
University of Central Oklahoma *B*

Oregon
Central Oregon Community
College *C*
Chemeketa Community College *C, A*
Clackamas Community College *C*
Clatsop Community College *C*
Linn-Benton Community College *C*
Portland Community College *C*
Rogue Community College *C*
Southwestern Oregon Community
College *C*

Pennsylvania
Gannon University *C*

Texas
Prairie View A&M University *M, D*

Kindergarten/preschool education

Alabama
Gadsden State Community College *A*

Arizona
University of Arizona *B*

Arkansas
Ozarka College *C*
University of Arkansas *B*
University of Arkansas
Monticello *B*
University of Central Arkansas *B*

California
California Polytechnic State
University: San Luis Obispo *B*
California State University
Los Angeles *B, M*
Sacramento *B, M*
Los Angeles Pierce College *C, A*
Orange Coast College *C, A*
Santa Barbara City College *C, A*
Southwestern College *C, A*

Connecticut
Central Connecticut State
University *M*
Mitchell College *B*
Saint Joseph College *T*

Delaware
Delaware Technical and Community
College
Owens *A*
Stanton/Wilmington *A*
Terry *A*

Florida
Nova Southeastern University *B*
Seminole Community College *C, A*
State College of Florida,
Manatee-Sarasota *C, A*

Georgia
Dalton State College *C*
Georgia Military College *A*
Georgia State University *M, D*
University of Georgia *B, M, D, T*
University of West Georgia *B*

Illinois
Columbia College Chicago *B*
Eastern Illinois University *B, T*
Elmhurst College *B*
University of Illinois
Urbana-Champaign *B, M, D, T*

Indiana
Ball State University *B, T*
Butler University *B*
Indiana University
South Bend *A*
Purdue University *B*
St. Mary-of-the-Woods College *B, T*

Iowa
Grand View University *T*
Iowa State University *B*
University of Northern Iowa *B, M*
Upper Iowa University *B*

Kansas
Emporia State University *M*
Tabor College *B*

Kentucky
Berea College *B, T*
Northern Kentucky University *B*
Western Kentucky University *A*

Louisiana
South Louisiana Community
College *A*

Maine
University of Maine
Farmington *B, T*

Maryland
Bowie State University *B, M*
Hood College *T*
Stevenson University *B*
University of Maryland
College Park *B*

Massachusetts
Anna Maria College *B, M*
Bridgewater State College *B*
Bristol Community College *A*
Cape Cod Community College *A*
Eastern Nazarene College *A, B, M, T*
Lesley University *B, M*
North Shore Community College *A*
Salem State College *M*
Westfield State College *B, M, T*
Wheelock College *M*

Michigan
Alma College *T*
Baker College
of Muskegon *A*
Bay de Noc Community College *A*
Delta College *A*
Kuyper College *A, B*
Michigan State University *B*

Minnesota
Bethel University *B*
Concordia University: St. Paul *B, T*
Metropolitan State University *B*
Minnesota State University
Moorhead *B*
Saint Cloud State University *B*
University of Minnesota
Crookston *B*
Vermilion Community College *A*
White Earth Tribal and Community
College *A*

Mississippi
Tougaloo College *A, B*

Missouri
Southeast Missouri State
University *B, T*
University of Missouri
Kansas City *B*

Montana
University of Great Falls *A, B*

Nebraska
Dana College *B*

Nevada
College of Southern Nevada *A*

New Jersey
Caldwell College *T*
Essex County College *A*
Kean University *B, M, T*
Raritan Valley Community
College *C, A*
William Paterson University of New
Jersey *B, T*

New Mexico
Santa Fe Community College *A*

New York
Adelphi University *M, T*
City University of New York
Brooklyn College *B, M*
Hunter College *M, T*
Lehman College *M*

College of Saint Rose *B, M, T*
Dutchess Community College *A*
Long Island University
C. W. Post Campus *B, M, T*
New York University *B, M*
St. Joseph's College: Suffolk
Campus *B, T*
Sarah Lawrence College *M*
State University of New York
College at Buffalo *B*
College at Cortland *B*
Tompkins Cortland Community
College *A*
Ulster County Community College *A*
University of Rochester *M*

North Carolina
Appalachian State University *B, M, T*
East Carolina University *B, M*
Meredith College *T*
North Carolina Central University *B, T*
University of North Carolina
Chapel Hill *M*
Charlotte *B, M*
Pembroke *B*
Wilmington *B*
Western Carolina University *B*

Ohio
Ashland University *B, M, T*
Bluffton University *B*
Bowling Green State University *B, T*
Clark State Community College *C, A*
Cleveland State University *B*
John Carroll University *T*
Miami University
Hamilton Campus *A*
Ohio Wesleyan University *B*
Shawnee State University *B*
University of Cincinnati
Clermont College *A*
University of Findlay *B, M, T*
University of Toledo *B*
Youngstown State University *B*

Pennsylvania
Butler County Community College *A*
Cabrini College *B, T*
California University of
Pennsylvania *A, B*
Kutztown University of
Pennsylvania *B, T*
Lock Haven University of
Pennsylvania *B*
Seton Hill University *T*
Temple University *M*

Puerto Rico
Inter American University of Puerto
Rico
Guayama Campus *B, M*
San German Campus *B*
National College of Business and
Technology: Arecibo *B*
National College of Business and
Technology: Bayamon *B*
Universidad Metropolitana *B*

Rhode Island
Community College of Rhode
Island *A*

South Dakota
Black Hills State University *B*
University of South Dakota *B*

Tennessee
Middle Tennessee State University *B*
Union University *B, T*

Texas
Arlington Baptist College *B, T*

Lone Star College System *A*
Mountain View College *A*
North Lake College *A*
Our Lady of the Lake University of San
Antonio *B*
San Jacinto College *C*
South Texas College *C*

Utah
Salt Lake Community College *A*
Utah Valley University *C, B*
Western Governors University *B, M, T*

Vermont
Champlain College *B*

Virginia
Norfolk State University *B, M*

Washington
University of Washington Tacoma *T*
Washington State University *B, M, T*
Yakima Valley Community College *C*

West Virginia
Glenville State College *B*
Marshall University *B*
West Virginia Wesleyan College *B*

Wisconsin
College of Menominee Nation *A*
Concordia University Wisconsin *B*
Lakeland College *B*
Northcentral Technical College *C*
University of Wisconsin
Superior *T*

Wyoming
Casper College *A*

Kinesiotherapy

California
California State University
San Bernardino *B, M*
Humboldt State University *B, M*

Connecticut
Sacred Heart University *B, M*

Massachusetts
Bridgewater State College *B, M*

North Carolina
University of North Carolina
Charlotte *M*

Texas
University of Houston *B*

Knowledge management

Colorado
University of Denver *M*

Illinois
Dominican University *M*

Massachusetts
Framingham State College *B*

Minnesota
Walden University *B, M, D*

New York
Rochester Institute of Technology *D*

Ohio
Kent State University *M*

Oklahoma
University of Oklahoma *M*

Texas
University of Texas
San Antonio *M*

Korean

California
University of California
Irvine *B*
Los Angeles *B*

Hawaii
University of Hawaii
Manoa *B, M, D*

New York
Columbia University *B*

Utah
Brigham Young University *B*

Washington
University of Washington *B*

Korean studies

New York
Columbia University *B*

Washington
University of Washington *B, M*

Labor/industrial relations

Alabama
Wallace State Community College at
Hanceville *A*

California
California State University
San Bernardino *M*
Los Angeles Trade and Technical
College *C, A*
Los Medanos College *C, A*
San Diego City College *A*

Connecticut
University of Bridgeport *B, M*
University of New Haven *M*

Florida
Nova Southeastern University *M*

Illinois
Kankakee Community College *C*
Northwestern University *M*
University of Illinois
Urbana-Champaign *M, D*

Indiana
Indiana University
Bloomington *C, A, B*
Kokomo *C, A, B*
Northwest *C, A, B*
South Bend *C, A, B*
Southeast *A, B*
Indiana University-Purdue University
Indianapolis *A, B*
Purdue University
North Central *A, B*

Iowa
University of Iowa *B*

Maine
University of Maine *B*

Maryland
Community College of Baltimore
County *C, A*

Massachusetts
University of Massachusetts
Amherst *M*
Boston *C*

Michigan
Michigan State University *M*
Wayne County Community College *A*
Wayne State University *M*

Minnesota
University of Minnesota
Twin Cities *C, B, M, D*

New Jersey
Rutgers, The State University of New
Jersey
New Brunswick/Piscataway
Campus *B, M, D*
Seton Hall University *B*
Thomas Edison State College *C, B*

New York
City University of New York
Baruch College *B, M*
Cornell University *B, M, D*
New York University *B*
Onondaga Community College *A*
State University of New York
College at Old Westbury *B*
College at Potsdam *B*
Empire State College *A, B, M*
Stony Brook *M*
Tompkins Cortland Community
College *A*

Ohio
Bowling Green State University *B*
Case Western Reserve University *M*
Cincinnati State Technical and
Community College *C*
Cleveland State University *B, M, D*
Edison State Community College *C, A*
Youngstown State University *A*

Pennsylvania
Clarion University of Pennsylvania *B*
Indiana University of Pennsylvania *M*
La Salle University *B*
Penn State
Abington *B*
Altoona *B*
Beaver *B*
Berks *B*
Brandywine *B*
DuBois *B*
Erie, The Behrend College *B*
Fayette, The Eberly Campus *B*
Greater Allegheny *B*
Hazleton *B*
Lehigh Valley *B*
Mont Alto *B*
New Kensington *B*
Schuylkill *B*
Shenango *B*
University Park *B, M*
Wilkes-Barre *B*
Worthington Scranton *B*
York *B*
St. Francis University *M*
Temple University *B, M*

Puerto Rico
Inter American University of Puerto
Rico
Metropolitan Campus *M*
San German Campus *M, D*
University of Puerto Rico
Rio Piedras *B*

Rhode Island
Providence College *C, A, B*
University of Rhode Island *M*

Tennessee
Tennessee Technological University *B*

Texas
College of the Mainland *A*
Southern Methodist University *M*
University of North Texas *M*

West Virginia
Marshall University *M*
West Virginia University *M*

Wisconsin
University of Wisconsin
Milwaukee *M*

Labor studies

Arizona
Prescott College *M*

California
California State University
Dominguez Hills *B*
San Francisco State University *B*
San Jose City College *C, A*

Indiana
Indiana University
South Bend *C, A, B*
Indiana University-Purdue University
Fort Wayne *C, A, B*
Indiana University-Purdue University
Indianapolis *C, A, B*

Maryland
National Labor College *B*

Michigan
Eastern Michigan University *B*
Michigan State University *D*
Wayne State University *B*

New York
City University of New York
Queens College *B*
Hofstra University *B*
Le Moyne College *B*

Pennsylvania
Penn State
Lehigh Valley *C*

Rhode Island
Rhode Island College *B*
University of Rhode Island *T*

Wisconsin
University of Wisconsin
Madison *M*

LAN/WAN management

Alabama
Gadsden State Community College *A*
Herzing University *A, B*

Alaska
University of Alaska
Southeast *C*

Arizona
Cochise College *C*
Collins College *A, B*
Estrella Mountain Community
College *C, A*
GateWay Community College *C, A*
Glendale Community College *C*
University of Advancing
Technology *A, B*

Arkansas
Northwest Arkansas Community
College *A*
Phillips Community College of the
University of Arkansas *C, A*
Rich Mountain Community College *A*
Southern Arkansas University Tech *C*
University of Arkansas Community
College at Morrilton *C*

California
Allan Hancock College *C*
College of the Siskiyous *C*
DeVry University
Fremont *A*
Pomona *A*
Foothill College *C, A*
Golden Gate University *M*
Grossmont College *C, A*
Kaplan College: Panorama City *A*
Kaplan College: Vista *A*
Los Angeles Harbor College *C*
MiraCosta College *C, A*
Monterey Peninsula College *C, A*
Ohlone College *C, A*
Orange Coast College *C*
Platt College
Ontario *A*
San Diego Mesa College *C*
Santa Barbara Business College
Bakersfield *C, A*
Santa Barbara City College *C*
Santa Rosa Junior College *C*
Shasta College *C*
Southwestern College *C*
Westwood College of Technology
Westwood College: Inland
Empire *B*
Westwood College: South Bay *A, B*

Colorado
Arapahoe Community College *C, A*
Colorado Technical University *C*
Pikes Peak Community College *C, A*
Red Rocks Community College *C*
Westwood College of Technology
Westwood College: Denver South *B*

Florida
College of Business and Technology:
Kendall *A*
Herzing University *C, A*
Santa Fe College *A*
South Florida Community
College *C, A*

Georgia
Gwinnett Technical College *C, A*
Middle Georgia Technical
College *C, A*
Southeastern Technical College *A*

Hawaii
University of Hawaii
West Oahu *B*

Illinois
DeVry University
Addison *A*
Harper College *C*
Lake Land College *A*
Lewis and Clark Community
College *A*
Moraine Valley Community
College *C, A*
Morrison Institute of Technology *A*
Oakton Community College *C*
Rend Lake College *C, A*
Sauk Valley Community College *A*
Southeastern Illinois College *A*
Waubonsee Community College *A*
Westwood College: Chicago Loop *A*

Indiana
Indiana University-Purdue University
Indianapolis *A*
International Business College *A*
Ivy Tech Community College
Bloomington *C*
Central Indiana *C*
Columbus *C*
East Central *C*
Kokomo *C*
Lafayette *C*
North Central *C*
Northeast *C*
Northwest *C*
Richmond *C*
South Central *C*

Iowa
Dordt College *B*
Ellsworth Community College *C, A*
Kirkwood Community College *C*
St. Ambrose University *B*

Kansas
Cloud County Community
College *C, A*
Colby Community College *C*
Labette Community College *C, A*

Kentucky
Sullivan College of Technology and
Design *A*

Louisiana
Herzing University *A, B*

Maine
Central Maine Community College *A*

Maryland
Howard Community College *C*
Kaplan College: Hagerstown *A, B*

Massachusetts
Cape Cod Community College *A*
North Shore Community College *C*

Michigan
Alpena Community College *C, A*
Baker College
of Muskegon *C, A*
Grand Rapids Community College *A*
Northern Michigan University *B*
Oakland Community College *C*
Washtenaw Community College *C, A*

Minnesota
Capella University *B*
Globe University *C, A, B*
Riverland Community College *C, A*
South Central College *C, A*

Mississippi
Alcorn State University *B*

Missouri
Missouri Technical School *C, A, B*
Ozarks Technical Community
College *A*
Ranken Technical College *A*
Vatterott College *B*

Montana
Montana State University
Billings *C*
University of Great Falls *B*

Nevada
College of Southern Nevada *A*
DeVry University: Henderson *M*
Great Basin College *A*
Western Nevada College *C, A*

New Hampshire
Daniel Webster College *C, B*

New Jersey
Cumberland County College *A*
Gloucester County College *C, A*
Ocean County College *A*

New Mexico
New Mexico State University
Alamogordo *C*
Southwestern Indian Polytechnic
Institute *C, A*

New York
College of Westchester *A*
Columbia-Greene Community
College *A*
Globe Institute of Technology *C, A, B*
Rochester Institute of
Technology *B, M*
State University of New York
College of Agriculture and
Technology at Cobleskill *B*
College of Agriculture and
Technology at Morrisville *B*
College of Technology at Alfred *B*
Technical Career Institutes *A*
Westchester Community College *C, A*

North Carolina
Carteret Community College *C, A*
Catawba Valley Community College *A*
Central Piedmont Community
College *C, A*
Miller-Motte Technical College *C, A*
Stanly Community College *C, A*
Surry Community College *C*
Wilkes Community College *C, A*

North Dakota
North Dakota State College of
Science *C, A*

Ohio
Bradford School *A*
Cincinnati Christian University *B*
James A. Rhodes State College *A*
Marion Technical College *C, A*
Northwest State Community
College *A*
University of Akron: Wayne College *C*
Youngstown State University *C*

Oklahoma
Rose State College *A*
Vatterott College *A*
Vatterott College
Tulsa *A*

Oregon
Klamath Community College *C, A*
Lane Community College *C*
Mt. Hood Community College *C, A*
Southwestern Oregon Community
College *C*

Pennsylvania
Consolidated School of Business
York *A*
Kaplan Career Institute: Harrisburg *A*
Kaplan Career Institute: Pittsburgh *A*
Keystone College *C, A, B*

Rhode Island
Community College of Rhode
Island *C*

South Carolina
York Technical College *C, A*

South Dakota
Kilian Community College *A*
National American University
Rapid City *B*
Southeast Technical Institute *A*

Tennessee
Northeast State Community College *C*
Pellissippi State Community
College *C*
Remington College
Memphis *A*
South College *A*

Texas
Houston Community College
System *C*
Mountain View College *C, A*
North Lake College *C*
St. Philip's College *C, A*
San Antonio College *C*
San Jacinto College *C, A*
Temple College *C, A*
Texas State Technical College:
Marshall *C, A*
Western Texas College *C, A*

Utah
Salt Lake Community College *C*
Western Governors University *B*

Vermont
Champlain College *B*

Virginia
Centura College: Chesapeake *A*
Centura College: Richmond *A*
ECPI College of Technology: Virginia
Beach *C, A*
ECPI Technical College: Roanoke *A, B*
Rappahannock Community College *C*
Southwest Virginia Community
College *C*
University of Management and
Technology *A, B, M*

Washington
Centralia College *C, A*
Clover Park Technical College *C, A*
Green River Community College *C*
South Seattle Community
College *C, A*
Yakima Valley Community College *C*

West Virginia
New River Community and Technical
College *A*

Wisconsin
Blackhawk Technical College *A*
Herzing University *A, B*
Mid-State Technical College *A*
Nicolet Area Technical College *A*

Western Technical College *A*

Land use planning

Arizona
Arizona State University *M*

California
California State University
  Bakersfield *B*
  Chico *M*

Colorado
Metropolitan State College of
  Denver *B*

Idaho
University of Idaho *M*

Louisiana
University of Louisiana at Lafayette *B*

Maine
University of Maine
  Farmington *B*

Maryland
University of Maryland
  College Park *M*

Pennsylvania
Keystone College *A*

Texas
Texas State University: San Marcos *M*
Texas Tech University *D*

Utah
Brigham Young University *M*

Wisconsin
University of Wisconsin
  Madison *M, D*

Landscape architecture

Alabama
Auburn University *M*

Arizona
Arizona State University *B, M*
Art Center Design College *B*
University of Arizona *M*

Arkansas
University of Arkansas *B*

California
American River College *C, A*
California Polytechnic State
  University: San Luis Obispo *B*
California State Polytechnic
  University: Pomona *B, M*
Cosumnes River College *C, A*
Diablo Valley College *C*
East Los Angeles College *A*
Fullerton College *A*
MiraCosta College *C, A*
Modesto Junior College *A*
Otis College of Art and Design *B*
San Diego Mesa College *C, A*
San Joaquin Delta College *C, A*
Santa Rosa Junior College *C*
Southwestern College *C, A*
University of California
  Berkeley *B, M*
  Davis *B*
University of Southern
  California *B, M*
West Valley College *A*

Colorado
Colorado State University *B, M*
University of Colorado
  Denver *M*

Connecticut
University of Connecticut *B*

Florida
Broward College *A*
Florida Agricultural and Mechanical
  University *M*
Florida International University *M*
University of Florida *B, M*

Georgia
University of Georgia *B, M*

Idaho
University of Idaho *B, M*

Illinois
Illinois Institute of Technology *M*
Kishwaukee College *A*
University of Illinois
  Urbana-Champaign *B, D*

Indiana
Ball State University *B, M*
Purdue University *B*

Iowa
Iowa State University *B, M*

Kansas
Kansas State University *M*

Kentucky
Bluegrass Community and Technical
  College *A*
University of Kentucky *B*

Louisiana
Louisiana State University and
  Agricultural and Mechanical
  College *B, M*

Maryland
Anne Arundel Community College *C*
Morgan State University *M*
University of Maryland
  College Park *B*

Massachusetts
Boston Architectural College *B*
Harvard College *M*
University of Massachusetts
  Amherst *B, M*

Michigan
Bay de Noc Community College *A*
Lansing Community College *A*
Michigan State University *B*
University of Michigan *M, D*

Minnesota
University of Minnesota
  Twin Cities *B, M*

Mississippi
Mississippi State University *B, M*

Nebraska
University of Nebraska
  Lincoln *B*

Nevada
Truckee Meadows Community
  College *A*

University of Nevada
  Las Vegas *B*

New Jersey
Cumberland County College *C*

New Mexico
University of New Mexico *M*

New York
City University of New York
  City College *M*
Cornell University *B, M*
Monroe Community College *A*
Parsons The New School for Design *B*
State University of New York
  College of Agriculture and
    Technology at Morrisville *A*
  College of Environmental Science
    and Forestry *B, M*
  College of Technology at Delhi *A*

North Carolina
Cape Fear Community College *A*
North Carolina Agricultural and
  Technical State University *B*
North Carolina State University *B, M*
Wake Technical Community
  College *C, A*

North Dakota
North Dakota State University *B*

Ohio
Columbus State Community
  College *A*
Hocking College *A*
Ohio State University
  Columbus Campus *B, M*

Oklahoma
Oklahoma State University *B*
University of Oklahoma *M*

Oregon
Central Oregon Community
  College *A*
University of Oregon *B, M, D*

Pennsylvania
Chatham University *M*
Keystone College *A*
Penn State
  University Park *B, M*
Philadelphia University *B*
Temple University *B*
University of Pennsylvania *M*

Puerto Rico
Universidad Politecnica de Puerto
  Rico *M*

Rhode Island
Rhode Island School of Design *B, M*
University of Rhode Island *B*

South Carolina
Clemson University *B, M*

Texas
Howard College *C*
Texas A&M University *B, M*
Texas Tech University *B, M*
University of Texas
  Arlington *M*
  Austin *M*

Utah
Utah State University *B, M*

Virginia
University of Virginia *M*
Virginia Polytechnic Institute and
  State University *B, M*

Washington
South Seattle Community
  College *C, A*
University of Washington *B, M*
Washington State University *B, M*

West Virginia
West Virginia University *B*

Wisconsin
University of Wisconsin
  Madison *M*

Landscaping/ groundskeeping

Alabama
Faulkner State Community
  College *C, A*

Arizona
Mesa Community College *A*

Arkansas
University of Arkansas
  Little Rock *A*

California
Antelope Valley College *C, A*
City College of San Francisco *A*
College of Marin: Kentfield *C, A*
College of the Canyons *C, A*
College of the Redwoods *C*
College of the Sequoias *C, A*
Cosumnes River College *C*
Diablo Valley College *C*
Foothill College *C, A*
Los Angeles Pierce College *C, A*
Merritt College *C, A*
MiraCosta College *C, A*
Modesto Junior College *C, A*
Mount San Antonio College *C*
San Joaquin Delta College *C*
Santa Barbara City College *C, A*
Santa Rosa Junior College *C*
Shasta College *C*
Solano Community College *C, A*
Southwestern College *C, A*
Victor Valley College *C*
Yuba Community College
  District *C, A*

Colorado
Colorado State University *B*

Delaware
Delaware Technical and Community
  College
  Owens *C*

Florida
Central Florida Community
  College *C, A*
Florida Agricultural and Mechanical
  University *B*
Gulf Coast Community College *A*
Hillsborough Community
  College *C, A*
Lake City Community College *C, A*
Miami Dade College *A*
Valencia Community College *C, A*

Georgia
Albany Technical College *C*
Gainesville State College *C*
West Georgia Technical College *C*

Idaho
Brigham Young University-Idaho *A*

Illinois
College of DuPage *C*
College of Lake County *C, A*
Danville Area Community College *C*
Harper College *C*
Joliet Junior College *C, A*
Kishwaukee College *C, A*
Lincoln Land Community College *C, A*
McHenry County College *C*
Parkland College *A*
Southwestern Illinois College *A*
Triton College *C, A*

Iowa
Iowa Lakes Community College *A*

Maine
Unity College *A*
University of Maine *C, B*

Maryland
Harford Community College *A*
Wor-Wic Community College *C*

Massachusetts
Springfield Technical Community College *C, A*
University of Massachusetts Amherst *A*

Michigan
Bay de Noc Community College *C*
Grand Rapids Community College *A*
Michigan State University *C*
Northwestern Michigan College *A*
Oakland Community College *C, A*

Minnesota
Anoka Technical College *C, A*
Century Community and Technical College *C, A*
Dakota County Technical College *C, A*
Hennepin Technical College *C, A*
Minnesota State Community and Technical College *C*
Northwest Technical College *A*
University of Minnesota Crookston *B*

Mississippi
Hinds Community College *A*
Mississippi Gulf Coast Community College *C, A*
Mississippi State University *B*

Nebraska
Nebraska College of Technical Agriculture *A*
University of Nebraska Lincoln *B*

Nevada
College of Southern Nevada *A*

New Hampshire
NHTI-Concord's Community College *C*

New Jersey
Bergen Community College *C*

New Mexico
Central New Mexico Community College *C*
Dona Ana Community College of New Mexico State University *A*

New York
State University of New York
College of Agriculture and Technology at Cobleskill *B*
College of Agriculture and Technology at Morrisville *A*
College of Technology at Delhi *A*

North Carolina
Alamance Community College *C*
Blue Ridge Community College *C*
Cape Fear Community College *A*
Johnston Community College *C*
North Carolina State University *A*
Sampson Community College *C*
Sandhills Community College *A*

North Dakota
Dakota College at Bottineau *A*

Ohio
Cincinnati State Technical and Community College *C, A*
Ohio State University
Agricultural Technical Institute *A*
Columbus Campus *B*
Owens Community College Toledo *A*

Oklahoma
Oklahoma State University *B*

Oregon
Clackamas Community College *A*
Portland Community College *C, A*
Rogue Community College *C*

Pennsylvania
Chatham University *M*
Community College of Allegheny County *C, A*
Community College of Beaver County *A*
Delaware Valley College *C*
Harrisburg Area Community College *C, A*
Luzerne County Community College *A*
Penn State
Abington *B*
Altoona *B*
Beaver *B*
Berks *B*
Brandywine *B*
DuBois *B*
Erie, The Behrend College *B*
Fayette, The Eberly Campus *B*
Greater Allegheny *B*
Hazleton *B*
Lehigh Valley *B*
Mont Alto *B*
New Kensington *B*
Schuylkill *B*
Shenango *B*
University Park *B*
Wilkes-Barre *B*
Worthington Scranton *B*
York *B*
Pennsylvania College of Technology *A*
Temple University *C, A*
Williamson Free School of Mechanical Trades *A*

South Carolina
Spartanburg Community College *C*
Technical College of the Lowcountry *C*
Trident Technical College *C*

South Dakota
South Dakota State University *B*

Southeast Technical Institute *A*

Tennessee
Chattanooga State Community College *C*
Tennessee Technological University *B*

Texas
Houston Community College System *C*
Palo Alto College *C, A*
Western Texas College *C, A*

Utah
Brigham Young University *B*

Vermont
Vermont Technical College *A*

Virginia
J. Sargeant Reynolds Community College *A*
Mountain Empire Community College *C*
Virginia Western Community College *A*

Washington
Clark College *C, A*
Clover Park Technical College *A*
Pierce College *A*
South Seattle Community College *C, A*

Wisconsin
Chippewa Valley Technical College *A*
Milwaukee Area Technical College *A*
University of Wisconsin River Falls *B*

Language interpretation/ translation

Alabama
Troy University *B*

Arizona
Cochise College *A*

California
Bethesda Christian University *B, M*
Santa Ana College *T*

District of Columbia
American University *C*

Florida
Miami Dade College *A*

Georgia
East Georgia College *A*
Georgia State University *T*

Iowa
Des Moines Area Community College *A*

Massachusetts
Salem State College *B*

Minnesota
Century Community and Technical College *A*

Mississippi
Mississippi College *B*

Nebraska
University of Nebraska Kearney *B*

Nevada
Great Basin College *A*

New Jersey
Union County College *A*

New York
Bard College *B*
State University of New York Binghamton *D*

North Carolina
Fayetteville Technical Community College *A*
Surry Community College *A*
Wilson Community College *A*

Ohio
Kent State University *M*

Oklahoma
Oklahoma City Community College *A*

Pennsylvania
Valley Forge Christian College *B*

Puerto Rico
University of Puerto Rico Rio Piedras *M*

South Carolina
College of Charleston *M*

Texas
University of Texas
Brownsville - Texas Southmost College *B*

Utah
Brigham Young University *B*

Vermont
Marlboro College *B*

Virginia
Shenandoah University *T*

Washington
Pierce College *A*

Laser/optical technology

Arizona
Pima Community College *C, A*

California
San Jose City College *C, A*
Sierra College *C*
University of California Davis *B*

Connecticut
Three Rivers Community College *C, A*

Delaware
Delaware Technical and Community College Stanton/Wilmington *C*

Idaho
Idaho State University *C, A*

Indiana
Vincennes University *C*

Iowa
Indian Hills Community College *A*

Maryland
Howard Community College *C, A*

Massachusetts
Massachusetts Bay Community
   College *A*
Springfield Technical Community
   College *A*

Michigan
Schoolcraft College *C*

New Mexico
Central New Mexico Community
   College *C, A*

New York
Monroe Community College *C, A*

Ohio
Cincinnati State Technical and
   Community College *A*

Latin

Alabama
Samford University *B*

California
Loyola Marymount University *B, M*
Santa Clara University *B*
University of California
   Berkeley *B, M*
   Irvine *B*
   Los Angeles *B, M*

Connecticut
Yale University *B*

Delaware
University of Delaware *B, M, T*

District of Columbia
Catholic University of
   America *B, M, D*
George Washington University *B*

Florida
Florida State University *B, M*
University of Miami *B*

Georgia
Emory University *B*
Mercer University *B*
University of Georgia *B, M*

Idaho
Idaho State University *A*
University of Idaho *B*

Illinois
Augustana College *B, T*
Concordia University Chicago *B*
Loyola University Chicago *B*
Monmouth College *B, T*
Rockford College *B*
University of Chicago *B, M*

Indiana
Ball State University *B*
Butler University *B*
DePauw University *B*
Indiana University
   Bloomington *B, M, D*
Wabash College *B*

Iowa
Cornell College *T*
Luther College *B*
University of Iowa *B, M, T*

Kansas
Wichita State University *B*

Kentucky
Berea College *B, T*

Louisiana
Centenary College of Louisiana *B*
Louisiana State University and
   Agricultural and Mechanical
   College *B*

Maine
University of Maine *B*

Maryland
Loyola University Maryland *B*

Massachusetts
Amherst College *B*
Bard College at Simon's Rock *B*
Boston College *B, M*
Boston University *B*
Harvard College *B*
Mount Holyoke College *B*
Smith College *B*
Tufts University *B*
Wellesley College *B*
Wheaton College *B*

Michigan
Calvin College *B, T*
Grand Valley State University *B*
University of Michigan *B, M*
Western Michigan University *B*

Minnesota
Carleton College *B*
Concordia College: Moorhead *B, T*
St. Olaf College *B*
University of Minnesota
   Twin Cities *B, M, D*
University of St. Thomas *B*

Missouri
Missouri State University *B*
Washington University in St.
   Louis *B, M*

Montana
University of Montana *B*

Nebraska
Creighton University *B*
University of Nebraska
   Lincoln *B*

New Hampshire
Saint Anselm College *T*
University of New Hampshire *B*

New Jersey
Montclair State University *B, T*
Seton Hall University *T*

New York
Bard College *B*
Barnard College *B*
City University of New York
   Hunter College *B*
   Queens College *B, T*
Colgate University *B*
College of New Rochelle *B, T*
Columbia University *B*
Elmira College *B*
Fordham University *B, M, D*

Hobart and William Smith Colleges *B*
Hofstra University *B*
Saint Bonaventure University *B*
State University of New York
   Binghamton *B*
Vassar College *B*

North Carolina
Duke University *B*
Lenoir-Rhyne University *B*
Wake Forest University *B*

Ohio
Bowling Green State University *B*
John Carroll University *B*
Kent State University *B, M*
Kenyon College *B*
Oberlin College *B*
Ohio State University
   Columbus Campus *B, M, D*
Ohio University *B*
Ohio Wesleyan University *B*
University of Cincinnati *B, T*
Wright State University *B*

Oregon
University of Oregon *B*

Pennsylvania
Bryn Mawr College *B, M, D*
Duquesne University *B*
Franklin & Marshall College *B*
Gettysburg College *B*
Haverford College *B, T*
La Salle University *B*
Saint Joseph's University *B*
Swarthmore College *B*
University of Scranton *B, T*
West Chester University of
   Pennsylvania *B, M, T*
Westminster College *B, T*

Rhode Island
Brown University *B*

South Carolina
Furman University *B, T*

Tennessee
University of Tennessee
   Knoxville *B*
University of the South *B*

Texas
Austin College *B*
Austin Community College *A*
Baylor University *B*
Rice University *B*
Southwestern University *B, T*
University of Houston *B*
University of Texas
   Austin *B*

Utah
Brigham Young University *B*

Vermont
St. Michael's College *B*
University of Vermont *B*

Virginia
Hampden-Sydney College *B*
Randolph College *B*
Randolph-Macon College *B*
University of Richmond *B, T*

Washington
Seattle Pacific University *B*
University of Washington *B*

West Virginia
Marshall University *M*

Wisconsin
Lawrence University *B*
University of Wisconsin
   Madison *B*

Latin American studies

Alabama
Samford University *B*
University of Alabama *B, M*

Arizona
Prescott College *B, M*
University of Arizona *B, M*

California
Alliant International University *B*
California State University
   Chico *B*
   East Bay *B*
   Fullerton *B*
   Los Angeles *B, M*
Claremont McKenna College *B*
Cypress College *A*
De Anza College *A*
Fullerton College *A*
Laney College *A*
Los Angeles Pierce College *A*
Mills College *B*
Pepperdine University *B*
Pitzer College *B*
Pomona College *B*
St. Mary's College of California *B*
San Diego City College *A*
San Diego State University *B, M*
Santa Rosa Junior College *A*
Scripps College *B*
University of California
   Berkeley *B, M, D*
   Los Angeles *B, M*
   Riverside *B*
   San Diego *B, M*
   Santa Barbara *B, M*
University of Redlands *B*
University of San Francisco *M*
Whittier College *B*

Connecticut
Connecticut College *B*
Trinity College *B*
University of Connecticut *B*
Wesleyan University *B*
Yale University *B*

Delaware
University of Delaware *B*

District of Columbia
American University *B, M*
George Washington University *B, M*
Georgetown University *M*

Florida
Flagler College *B*
Florida International University *M*
Florida State University *B*
Miami Dade College *A*
New College of Florida *B*
Rollins College *B*
State College of Florida,
   Manatee-Sarasota *A*
Stetson University *B*
University of Miami *B, M*
University of South Florida *M*

Georgia
Emory University *B*
University of Georgia *B*

Idaho
University of Idaho *B*

Illinois
Blackburn College *B*
DePaul University *B*
Illinois Wesleyan University *B*
Lake Forest College *B*
University of Chicago *B, M*
University of Illinois
   Chicago *B, M*
   Urbana-Champaign *B, M*

Indiana
Earlham College *B*
Indiana University
   Bloomington *M*

Iowa
Cornell College *B*
University of Northern Iowa *B*

Kansas
University of Kansas *B, M*

Kentucky
Bluegrass Community and Technical
   College *A*
University of Kentucky *B*

Louisiana
Tulane University *B, M*

Maine
Bowdoin College *B*
Colby College *B*

Maryland
Hood College *B*
Johns Hopkins University *B*

Massachusetts
Assumption College *B*
Bard College at Simon's Rock *B*
Boston University *B*
Brandeis University *B*
Hampshire College *B*
Mount Holyoke College *B*
Smith College *B*
Tufts University *B, M*
Wellesley College *B*
Wheaton College *B*

Michigan
Oakland University *B*
University of Michigan *B, D*

Minnesota
Carleton College *B*
Hamline University *B*
Macalester College *B*
Saint Cloud State University *B*
St. Olaf College *B*
University of Minnesota
   Morris *B*
   Twin Cities *B*

Mississippi
Millsaps College *B*

Missouri
Saint Louis University *B*
University of Missouri
   Columbia *B*
Washington University in St. Louis *B*

Nebraska
University of Nebraska
   Lincoln *B*
   Omaha *B*

Nevada
University of Nevada
   Las Vegas *B*

New Hampshire
Dartmouth College *B*

New Jersey
Rutgers, The State University of New
   Jersey
   New Brunswick/Piscataway
      Campus *B*
Seton Hall University *B*
William Paterson University of New
   Jersey *B*

New Mexico
University of New Mexico *B, M, D*

New York
Adelphi University *B*
Bard College *B*
Barnard College *B*
Boricua College *B, M*
City University of New York
   Brooklyn College *B*
   City College *B*
   Hunter College *B*
   Lehman College *B*
   Queens College *B, T*
Colgate University *B*
Columbia University *B*
Columbia University
   School of General Studies *B*
Fordham University *B*
Hobart and William Smith Colleges *B*
Hofstra University *B*
New York University *B*
State University of New York
   Albany *B, M*
   Binghamton *B*
   College at Plattsburgh *B*
   New Paltz *B*
Syracuse University *B*
Union College *B*
United States Military Academy *B*
Vassar College *B*

North Carolina
University of North Carolina
   Chapel Hill *B*
   Charlotte *B, M*

Ohio
Bowling Green State University *B*
College of Wooster *B*
Denison University *B*
Kent State University *B*
Miami University
   Oxford Campus *B*
Oberlin College *B*
Ohio State University
   Columbus Campus *B*
Ohio University *B, M*
Pontifical College Josephinum *B*
University of Cincinnati *B*
University of Toledo *B*

Oregon
Pacific University *B*
Portland State University *B*
Willamette University *B*

Pennsylvania
Albright College *B*
Bucknell University *B*
Carnegie Mellon University *B*
Edinboro University of
   Pennsylvania *B*
Gettysburg College *B*
Penn State
   Abington *B*

Altoona *B*
Beaver *B*
Berks *B*
Brandywine *B*
DuBois *B*
Erie, The Behrend College *B*
Fayette, The Eberly Campus *B*
Greater Allegheny *B*
Hazleton *B*
Lehigh Valley *B*
Mont Alto *B*
New Kensington *B*
Schuylkill *B*
Shenango *B*
University Park *B*
Wilkes-Barre *B*
Worthington Scranton *B*
York *B*
Temple University *B*
University of Pennsylvania *M*

Rhode Island
Brown University *B, M, D*
Rhode Island College *B*
University of Rhode Island *B*

South Carolina
College of Charleston *B*
University of South Carolina *B*

Tennessee
Rhodes College *B*
University of Tennessee
   Knoxville *B*
Vanderbilt University *B, M*

Texas
Austin College *B*
Baylor University *B*
Palo Alto College *A*
Rice University *B*
St. Edward's University *B*
Southern Methodist University *B*
Southwestern University *B*
Texas A&M International University *B*
Texas Tech University *B*
Trinity University *B*
University of Texas
   Austin *B, M, D*
   Dallas *M*
   El Paso *B*

Utah
Brigham Young University *B*

Vermont
Bennington College *B*
Burlington College *B*
Goddard College *B*
Marlboro College *B*
Middlebury College *B*
University of Vermont *B*

Virginia
George Mason University *B*
University of Richmond *B*
University of Virginia *B*

Washington
Gonzaga University *B*
Seattle Pacific University *B*
University of Washington *B, M*
Whitman College *B*

Wisconsin
Ripon College *B*
University of Wisconsin
   Eau Claire *B*
   Madison *B, M*

Latin teacher education

Idaho
University of Idaho *T*

Illinois
Knox College *T*
University of Illinois
   Urbana-Champaign *B, M, T*

Indiana
Indiana University
   Bloomington *B, T*

Iowa
Cornell College *T*
University of Iowa *T*

Maryland
Mount St. Mary's University *T*

Massachusetts
Assumption College *T*

Michigan
Western Michigan University *B, T*

Minnesota
Concordia College: Moorhead *B, T*

Mississippi
Millsaps College *T*

Missouri
Missouri State University *B*

Nebraska
Creighton University *B*

New York
City University of New York
   Hunter College *B, M, T*
Hobart and William Smith Colleges *T*
State University of New York
   Buffalo *M, T*
University of Rochester *M*

Ohio
Case Western Reserve University *T*
Kent State University *T*
Miami University
   Oxford Campus *T*
Ohio Wesleyan University *B*

Pennsylvania
Albright College *T*
Duquesne University *B, M, T*
Gettysburg College *T*

Texas
University of Dallas *T*

Utah
Brigham Young University *B*

Vermont
St. Michael's College *T*

Wisconsin
Lawrence University *T*

Law (J.D.)

Alabama
Samford University: Cumberland
   School of Law *P*
Thomas Goode Jones School of
   Law–Faulkner University *P*

University of Alabama: School of
    Law *P*

Arizona

Arizona State University: College of
    Law *P*
University of Arizona: College of
    Law *P*

Arkansas

University of Arkansas at Little Rock:
    School of Law *P*
University of Arkansas: School of
    Law *P*

California

California Western School of Law *P*
Golden Gate University: School of
    Law *P*
Humphreys College: School of Law *P*
John F. Kennedy University: School of
    Law *P*
Loyola Marymount University: School
    of Law *P*
McGeorge School of Law: University
    of the Pacific *P*
Pepperdine University: School of
    Law *P*
Santa Clara University: School of
    Law *P*
Southwestern University School of
    Law *P*
Stanford University: School of Law *P*
Thomas Jefferson School of Law *P*
University of California
    Hastings College of the Law *P*
University of California Berkeley:
    School of Law *P*
University of California Davis: School
    of Law *P*
University of California Los Angeles:
    School of Law *P*
University of La Verne College of Law
    at San Fernando Valley *P*
University of La Verne: School of
    Law *P*
University of San Diego: School of
    Law *P*
University of San Francisco: School of
    Law *P*
University of Southern California: Law
    School *P*
University of West Los Angeles: School
    of Law *P*
Western State University College of
    Law *P*
Whittier Law School *P*

Colorado

University of Colorado at Boulder:
    School of Law *P*
University of Denver: College of
    Law *P*

Connecticut

Quinnipiac College: School of Law *P*
University of Connecticut: School of
    Law *P*
Yale Law School *P*

Delaware

Widener University School of Law *P*

District of Columbia

American University: Washington
    College of Law *P*
Catholic University of America: School
    of Law *P*
George Washington University Law
    School *P*
Georgetown University: Law Center *P*
Howard University: School of Law *P*

University of the District of Columbia:
    School of Law *P*

Florida

Florida Coastal School of Law *P*
Florida State University: School of
    Law *P*
Nova Southeastern University:
    Shepard Broad Law Center *P*
St. Thomas University: School of
    Law *P*
Stetson University: College of Law *P*
University of Florida: College of
    Law *P*
University of Miami: School of Law *P*

Georgia

Emory University: School of Law *P*
Georgia State University: College of
    Law *P*
Mercer University: Walter F. George
    School of Law *P*
University of Georgia: School of
    Law *P*

Hawaii

University of Hawaii William S.
    Richardson: School of Law *P*

Idaho

University of Idaho: College of Law *P*

Illinois

Chicago-Kent College of Law, Illinois
    Institute of Technology *P*
De Paul University: College of Law *P*
Loyola University Chicago: School of
    Law *P*
Northern Illinois University: College
    of Law *P*
Northwestern University: School of
    Law *P*
Southern Illinois University at
    Carbondale: School of Law *P*
University of Chicago: School of
    Law *P*
University of Illinois at
    Urbana-Champaign: College of
    Law *P*

Indiana

Indiana University Bloomington:
    School of Law *P*
Indiana University Indianapolis:
    School of Law *P*
University of Notre Dame: School of
    Law *P*
Valparaiso University: School of
    Law *P*

Iowa

Drake University Law School *P*
University of Iowa: College of Law *P*

Kansas

University of Kansas: School of Law *P*
Washburn University: School of
    Law *P*

Kentucky

Northern Kentucky University:
    Salmon P. Chase School of Law *P*
University of Kentucky: College of
    Law *P*
University of Louisville: School of
    Law *P*

Louisiana

Louisiana State University and
    Agricultural and Mechanical
    College: School of Law *P*
Loyola University: School of Law *P*

Southern University: Law Center *P*
Tulane University: School of Law *P*

Maine

University of Maine: School of Law *P*

Maryland

University of Baltimore: School of
    Law *P*
University of Maryland at Baltimore:
    School of Law *P*

Massachusetts

Boston College: Law School *P*
Boston University: School of Law *P*
Harvard University Law School *P*
New England School of Law *P*
Northeastern University: School of
    Law *P*
Suffolk University: Law School *P*
Western New England College: School
    of Law *P*

Michigan

Detroit College of Law *P*
Thomas M. Cooley Law School *P*
University of Detroit Mercy: School of
    Law *P*
University of Michigan: School of
    Law *P*
Wayne State University: School of
    Law *P*

Minnesota

Hamline University: School of Law *P*
University of Minnesota Twin Cities:
    School of Law *P*
William Mitchell College of Law: Law
    Professions *P*

Mississippi

Mississippi College: School of Law *P*
University of Mississippi: School of
    Law *P*

Missouri

St. Louis University: School of Law *P*
University of Missouri Columbia:
    School of Law *P*
University of Missouri Kansas City:
    School of Law *P*
Washington University: School of
    Law *P*

Montana

University of Montana: School of
    Law *P*

Nebraska

Creighton University: School of Law *P*
University of Nebraska Lincoln:
    College of Law *P*

New Hampshire

Franklin Pierce Law Center *P*

New Jersey

Rutgers, The State University of New
    Jersey
    Camden School of Law *P*
    Newark School of Law *P*
Seton Hall University: School of
    Law *P*

New Mexico

University of New Mexico: School of
    Law *P*

New York

Albany Law School of Union
    University *P*

Benjamin N. Cardozo School of Law *P*
Brooklyn Law School *P*
City University of New York
    School of Law at Queens College *P*
Columbia University
    School of Law *P*
Cornell University: School of Law *P*
Fordham University: School of Law *P*
Hofstra University: School of Law *P*
New York Law School *P*
New York University: School of Law *P*
Pace University Westchester: School
    of Law *P*
St. John's University: School of Law *P*
State University of New York at
    Buffalo: School of Law *P*
Syracuse University: College of Law *P*
Touro College: Jacob D. Fuchsberg
    Law Center *P*

North Carolina

Campbell University: Norman Adrian
    Wiggins School of Law *P*
Duke University: School of Law *P*
North Carolina Central University:
    School of Law *P*
University of North Carolina at Chapel
    Hill: School of Law *P*
Wake Forest University: School of
    Law *P*

North Dakota

University of North Dakota: School of
    Law *P*

Ohio

Capital University: School of Law *P*
Case Western Reserve University:
    School of Law *P*
Cleveland State University: College of
    Law *P*
Ohio Northern University: College of
    Law *P*
Ohio State University: College of
    Law *P*
University of Akron: School of Law *P*
University of Cincinnati: College of
    Law *P*
University of Dayton: School of Law *P*
University of Toledo: College of
    Law *P*

Oklahoma

Oklahoma City University: School of
    Law *P*
University of Oklahoma: College of
    Law *P*
University of Tulsa: College of Law *P*

Oregon

Lewis and Clark College:
    Northwestern School of Law *P*
University of Oregon: School of
    Law *P*
Willamette University: College of
    Law *P*

Pennsylvania

Dickinson School of Law *P*
Duquesne University: School of
    Law *P*
Temple University: School of Law *P*
University of Pennsylvania Law
    School *P*
University of Pittsburgh: School of
    Law *P*
Villanova University: School of Law *P*
Widener University School of Law *P*

Puerto Rico

Inter American University of Puerto
    Rico: School of Law *P*

Pontifical Catholic University of
Puerto Rico: School of Law P
University of Puerto Rico Rio Piedras
Campus: School of Law P

South Carolina

University of South Carolina: School
of Law P

South Dakota

University of South Dakota: School of
Law P

Tennessee

University of Memphis: School of
Law P
University of Tennessee College of
Law P
Vanderbilt University: School of
Law P

Texas

Baylor University: School of Law P
St. Mary's University: School of Law P
South Texas College of Law P
Southern Methodist University: School
of Law P
Texas Southern University: Thurgood
Marshall School of Law P
Texas Tech University: School of
Law P
University of Houston: Law Center P
University of Texas at Austin: School
of Law P

Utah

Brigham Young University: School of
Law P
University of Utah: College of Law P

Vermont

Vermont Law School P

Virginia

College of William and Mary: School
of Law P
George Mason University: School of
Law P
Regent University: School of Law P
University of Richmond: The T.C.
Williams School of Law P
University of Virginia: School of
Law P
Washington and Lee University:
School of Law P

Washington

Gonzaga University: School of Law P
Seattle University: School of Law P
University of Washington: School of
Law P

West Virginia

West Virginia University: College of
Law P

Wisconsin

Marquette University: School of
Law P
University of Wisconsin Madison:
School of Law P

Wyoming

University of Wyoming: College of
Law P

Legal administrative assistance

Alabama

Faulkner State Community College A

Lawson State Community College A
Wallace State Community College at
Hanceville A

Arizona

Brookline College
Phoenix C
Tempe C
Tucson C
Coconino County Community
College C
Phoenix College C, A

Arkansas

National Park Community College C
Pulaski Technical College C

California

Allan Hancock College C, A
Butte College C, A
Chabot College A
Chaffey College C
City College of San Francisco C, A
Coastline Community College C
College of San Mateo C, A
College of the Redwoods C, A
Columbia College C
East Los Angeles College A
Empire College C
Fresno City College C, A
Fullerton College A
Glendale Community College C, A
Golden West College C, A
Heald College
Fresno C, A
Rancho Cordova C, A
San Jose A
Humphreys College C, A, B
Kaplan College: Panorama City C
Lassen Community College C
Long Beach City College C, A
Los Angeles City College C, A
Los Angeles Harbor College C, A
MTI College A
Merced College C, A
Palomar College C, A
Pasadena City College A
Platt College
Ontario C, A, B
Porterville College C
Riverside Community College C, A
Sacramento City College C, A
Saddleback College C, A
San Bernardino Valley College C
Santa Rosa Junior College C
Shasta College A
Skyline College C, A
Solano Community College C, A
South Coast College C
Southwestern College C, A

Colorado

Community College of Aurora A
Lamar Community College A
Otero Junior College A

Connecticut

Gateway Community College A
Lincoln College of New England:
Briarwood C, A
Middlesex Community College A
Naugatuck Valley Community
College A
Norwalk Community College C, A
Tunxis Community College C, A

Delaware

Delaware Technical and Community
College
Owens C, A
Terry C, A

Florida

Brevard Community College A
Broward College C, A
Indian River State College A
Miami Dade College C, A
Northwest Florida State College A
Pensacola Junior College A
Santa Fe College A
Seminole Community College A

Georgia

Augusta Technical College C
Central Georgia Technical College C
DeKalb Technical College C
Gwinnett College C

Hawaii

Heald College
Honolulu A
University of Hawaii
Kapiolani Community College A

Idaho

Lewis-Clark State College C, A, B
North Idaho College A

Illinois

Black Hawk College C, A
College of DuPage C, A
Elgin Community College C, A
Harper College C, A
John Wood Community College A
Joliet Junior College A
Kaskaskia College C
Kishwaukee College C
Lake Land College A
Lewis and Clark Community
College A
Lincoln Land Community College C, A
MacCormac College C, A
McHenry County College C
Midstate College C, A
Moraine Valley Community College C
Rockford Career College A
Sauk Valley Community College C, A
Shawnee Community College A

Indiana

Brown Mackie College: South Bend A
Kaplan College: Hammond C, A
Kaplan College: Indianapolis A

Iowa

Ellsworth Community College A
Iowa Western Community College A
Kaplan University
Davenport C
Kirkwood Community College C, A
Southeastern Community College
North Campus A
Western Iowa Tech Community
College C, A

Kansas

Dodge City Community College C, A
Labette Community College A
Pratt Community College C, A
Seward County Community
College C, A
Washburn University C, A

Kentucky

Ashland Community and Technical
College A
Daymar College
Owensboro A
National College
Lexington A
Louisville A
Pikeville A
Sullivan University C, A

Louisiana

Bossier Parish Community College C

Maine

Andover College C, A
Beal College A
Northern Maine Community
College A

Maryland

Allegany College of Maryland C
Baltimore City Community College A
Community College of Baltimore
County C
Frederick Community College C, A
Howard Community College C
Kaplan College: Hagerstown C
Prince George's Community
College C, A

Massachusetts

Boston University B
Bristol Community College C
Cape Cod Community College C, A
Marian Court College C, A
Massasoit Community College A
North Shore Community College C, A
Roxbury Community College A

Michigan

Baker College
of Auburn Hills A
of Cadillac A
of Flint A
of Jackson A
of Owosso A
of Port Huron A
Bay de Noc Community College A
Delta College A
Henry Ford Community College A
Kalamazoo Valley Community
College C, A
Kellogg Community College A
Kirtland Community College A
Lake Michigan College A
Lansing Community College A
Mid Michigan Community College A
Monroe County Community
College C, A
Muskegon Community College A
Northwestern Michigan College C
St. Clair County Community
College A

Minnesota

Academy College C
Alexandria Technical College C, A
Anoka Technical College C
Dakota County Technical College C, A
Globe University C, A
Hibbing Community College A
Inver Hills Community College C, A
Lake Superior College C, A
Minneapolis Business College C, A
Minneapolis Community and
Technical College C
Minnesota School of Business C
Minnesota School of Business: St.
Cloud C
Minnesota State College - Southeast
Technical C, A
Minnesota State Community and
Technical College C, A
Ridgewater College C, A
Riverland Community College C, A
St. Cloud Technical College C, A
South Central College C, A

Mississippi

Hinds Community College A
Northwest Mississippi Community
College A
Pearl River Community College C, A

Missouri
East Central College C, A
Hickey College C, A
Metropolitan Community College:
  Penn Valley C
St. Louis Community College
  St. Louis Community College at
    Meramec A

Montana
Flathead Valley Community College A
Helena College of Technology of the
  University of Montana C
University of Montana A

Nebraska
Northeast Community College A

Nevada
Career College of Northern Nevada C
College of Southern Nevada C, A
Great Basin College C
Truckee Meadows Community
  College A

New Hampshire
Nashua Community College C

New Jersey
Gloucester County College A
Warren County Community College C

New Mexico
Brookline College
  Albuquerque C
Clovis Community College A
Dona Ana Community College of New
  Mexico State University A
New Mexico Junior College C, A
Western New Mexico University C, A

New York
ASA Institute of Business and
  Computer Technology C
Briarcliffe College A
Bryant & Stratton Business Institute
  Bryant & Stratton College:
    Rochester A
  Bryant & Stratton College:
    Syracuse A
City University of New York
  Kingsborough Community
    College A
  LaGuardia Community College A
Dutchess Community College C, A
Elmira Business Institute C, A
Globe Institute of Technology C, A, B
Herkimer County Community
  College A
Nassau Community College C, A
New York Career Institute A
Olean Business Institute C
Trocaire College A
Ulster County Community
  College C, A
Utica School of Commerce C, A

North Carolina
Alamance Community College C, A
Carteret Community College A
Central Carolina Community
  College A
Central Piedmont Community
  College A
Cleveland Community College A
Gaston College A
King's College C, A
Nash Community College A
Piedmont Community College A

North Dakota
Bismarck State College C, A

Dickinson State University A
Lake Region State College C, A

Ohio
Bradford School C, A
Bryant & Stratton College
  Parma A
Cincinnati State Technical and
  Community College A
Clark State Community College A
Columbus State Community
  College A
Davis College A
ETI Technical College of Niles A
Eastern Gateway Community
  College A
Edison State Community College C, A
James A. Rhodes State College A
North Central State College A
Northwest State Community
  College A
Ohio Business College: Sandusky A
Ohio University
  Southern Campus at Ironton C
Shawnee State University A
Stark State College of Technology A
University of Akron: Wayne
  College C, A
University of Cincinnati
  Clermont College C, A
  Raymond Walters College A
University of Northwestern Ohio A
University of Rio Grande A
Wright State University A

Oklahoma
Eastern Oklahoma State College A
Oklahoma City Community
  College C
Oklahoma State University
  Institute of Technology:
    Okmulgee A
Tulsa Community College C, A

Oregon
Clatsop Community College A
Lane Community College C
Linn-Benton Community College A
Mt. Hood Community College A
Southwestern Oregon Community
  College C
Treasure Valley Community College A
Umpqua Community College A

Pennsylvania
Bucks County Community
  College C, A
Butler County Community College A
Clarion University of Pennsylvania A
Consolidated School of Business
  Lancaster A
  York A
Erie Business Center C, A
Erie Business Center South A
Kaplan Career Institute: Pittsburgh A
Laurel Business Institute A
Newport Business Institute:
  Williamsport A
Northampton Community
  College A
PJA School C
Penn Commercial Business and
  Technical School A
Reading Area Community
  College C, A
South Hills School of Business &
  Technology A
South Hills School of Business &
  Technology: Altoona A

Puerto Rico
Caribbean University A

National College of Business and
  Technology: Arecibo A
National College of Business and
  Technology: Bayamon A
National College of Business and
  Technology: Rio Grande A
Ponce Paramedical College C
Universidad del Este C, A

Rhode Island
Community College of Rhode
  Island C, A

South Carolina
Forrest Junior College A
Greenville Technical College C
York Technical College C

South Dakota
Western Dakota Technical Institute C

Tennessee
Nashville State Community College A
South College C

Texas
Blinn College C
Brookhaven College A
El Centro College C
El Paso Community College C
Frank Phillips College C, A
Kilgore College C
Lamar State College at Port Arthur A
Laredo Community College C
McLennan Community College A
Midland College C, A
North Central Texas College A
Northeast Texas Community
  College C, A
Odessa College C, A
Panola College A
St. Philip's College C
San Antonio College C
South Plains College A
South Texas College C, A
Texas A&M University
  Commerce B
Texas State Technical College
  Harlingen A
Trinity Valley Community
  College C, A
Tyler Junior College A
University of Texas
  Brownsville - Texas Southmost
    College C, A

Utah
LDS Business College A
Salt Lake Community College C

Virginia
Blue Ridge Community College C
Danville Community College C
J. Sargeant Reynolds Community
  College A
Mountain Empire Community
  College A
New River Community College C, A
Rappahannock Community College C
Southwest Virginia Community
  College C
Virginia Highlands Community
  College A
Virginia Western Community
  College A

Washington
Bates Technical College C, A
Bellingham Technical College C, A
Centralia College C, A
Clark College C, A
Clover Park Technical College C, A

Everett Community College C
Green River Community College A
Lake Washington Technical
  College C, A
Lower Columbia College C, A
North Seattle Community College C
Olympic College C, A
Peninsula College C
Pierce College C, A
Renton Technical College C, A
South Puget Sound Community
  College C, A
Spokane Community College C, A
Wenatchee Valley College C
Yakima Valley Community College C

West Virginia
Huntington Junior College C, A
Mountain State College A
New River Community and Technical
  College C, A
Valley College C
West Virginia Business College: Nutter
  Fort C, A
West Virginia Junior College C
West Virginia State Community and
  Technical College C

Wisconsin
Blackhawk Technical College A
Fox Valley Technical College A
Milwaukee Area Technical College A
Moraine Park Technical College C, A
Southwest Wisconsin Technical
  College A

Legal studies

Alabama
Faulkner University A, B, D
South University: Montgomery B
University of Alabama M

Arkansas
University of Arkansas M

California
Claremont McKenna College B
John F. Kennedy University B
Mills College B
National University B
Pepperdine University M
Santa Barbara City College A
Scripps College B
Southwestern College A
Stanford University M, D
Thomas Jefferson School of Law D
University of California
  Berkeley B, M, D
  Los Angeles M, D
  Santa Barbara B
  Santa Cruz B
University of La Verne B, D
University of San Diego M
University of Southern
  California M, D
University of the Pacific M, D
Western State University College of
  Law D

Colorado
United States Air Force Academy B
University of Denver B

Connecticut
Mitchell College A, B
Quinnipiac University B
University of Connecticut M, D
University of Hartford A, B
University of New Haven A, B
Yale University M, D

District of Columbia
American University *B, M, D*
Catholic University of America *M, D*
George Washington University *M, D*
Howard University *M*

Florida
Barry University *B, M, D*
City College
  Gainesville *A*
Florida National College *B*
Gulf Coast Community College *A*
Nova Southeastern University *B, M*
Saint Thomas University *D*
South University: West Palm Beach *B*
State College of Florida,
  Manatee-Sarasota *A*
Stetson University *D*
University of Miami *B*

Georgia
Brenau University *B*
Emory University *D*
Georgia State University *D*
Mercer University *D*
South University: Savannah *B*

Idaho
University of Idaho *D*

Illinois
City Colleges of Chicago
  Harold Washington College *A*
  Olive-Harvey College *A*
Illinois Institute of Technology *M*
Illinois Valley Community College *A*
Northwestern University *B, M*
Southern Illinois University
  Carbondale *M*
University of Illinois
  Springfield *B, M*
  Urbana-Champaign *M, D*

Indiana
Indiana University
  Bloomington *M, D*

Iowa
Drake University *B*
Kaplan University
  Davenport *B*

Louisiana
Tulane University *A, B*

Maine
University of Southern Maine *M*

Maryland
Carroll Community College *A*
Harford Community College *A*
Hood College *A*
Towson University *B*
University of Baltimore *M*
University of Maryland
  Baltimore *D*
  University College *B*

Massachusetts
Amherst College *B*
Bay Path College *B*
Becker College *B*
Boston College *D*
Boston University *M*
Bridgewater State College *B*
Elms College *B*
Hampshire College *B*
Lasell College *B*
Newbury College *B*
Nichols College *B*
Northeastern University *M, D*

University of Massachusetts
  Amherst *B*
  Boston *C, B*
Western New England College *B*

Michigan
Central Michigan University *B*
Grand Valley State University *B*

Minnesota
Crown College *B*
Hamline University *B, M*
Minnesota School of Business:
  Blaine *C, A*
Minnesota School of Business:
  Brooklyn Center *A*
Minnesota State University
  Moorhead *B*
Minnesota West Community and
  Technical College *A*

Mississippi
Antonelli College
  Jackson *A*

Missouri
Park University *B*
Saint Louis University *B*
University of Missouri
  Columbia *M*
Webster University *B, M*
William Woods University *B*

Nebraska
Chadron State College *B*

Nevada
University of Nevada
  Las Vegas *D*

New Jersey
Montclair State University *M*
Ramapo College of New Jersey *B*
Seton Hall University *M, D*
Warren County Community College *A*

New Mexico
Clovis Community College *A*

New York
ASA Institute of Business and
  Computer Technology *A*
College of Saint Rose *B*
Hofstra University *M, D*
Ithaca College *B*
Mercy College *B*
Mildred Elley *A*
Sage College of Albany *B*
St. John's University *A, B*
State University of New York
  College at Fredonia *B*
Touro College *M*
United States Military Academy *B*

North Carolina
Duke University *D*
Elon University *D*
Livingstone College *B*
South College *B*
Wake Forest University *M, D*

Ohio
Capital University *M, D*
Franciscan University of
  Steubenville *B*
RETS College *A*
University of Dayton *M*
University of Toledo *D*

Oklahoma
University of Oklahoma: College of
  Law *D*
University of Tulsa *B, D*

Oregon
Lewis & Clark College *M, D*
University of Oregon *D*

Pennsylvania
Arcadia University *B*
California University of
  Pennsylvania *M*
Central Pennsylvania College *B*
DeSales University *B*
Dickinson College *B*
Drexel University *D*
Point Park University *B*
Saint Joseph's University *C, A, B*
University of Pennsylvania *B, M, D*
University of Pittsburgh: School of
  Law *D*
Villanova University *D*
Widener University *M, D*
Widener University School of Law *D*

Puerto Rico
Pontifical Catholic University of
  Puerto Rico *B, M*
University of Puerto Rico
  Rio Piedras *M*

Rhode Island
Roger Williams University *B*

South Dakota
University of South Dakota *D*

Tennessee
Lipscomb University *B*
South College *B*
University of Tennessee
  Knoxville *D*

Texas
Baylor University *D*
Brazosport College *A*
Central Texas College *A*
Southern Methodist University *M, D*
Texas Southern University *D*
Texas Tech University *D*
University of Houston *M, D*

Vermont
Burlington College *B*
Champlain College *M*

Virginia
Bryant & Stratton College: Virginia
  Beach *A*
College of William and Mary *M*
Regent University *M*
Virginia Intermont College *B*

Washington
Gonzaga University *M, D*
Highline Community College *A*
Seattle University *D*
University of Washington *M, D*

West Virginia
American Public University System *B*
Mountain State University *B*
West Virginia Junior College *A*
West Virginia University *M*

Wisconsin
Herzing University *A, B*
University of Wisconsin
  Madison *B, M*
  Superior *B*

Liberal arts and sciences

Alabama
Alabama Southern Community
  College *A*
Amridge University *A, B, M*
Athens State University *B*
Auburn University at
  Montgomery *B, M*
Bevill State Community College *A*
Bishop State Community College *A*
Calhoun Community College *A*
Central Alabama Community
  College *A*
Chattahoochee Valley Community
  College *A*
Enterprise-Ozark Community
  College *A*
Faulkner State Community College *A*
Faulkner University *B, M*
Gadsden State Community College *A*
George C. Wallace State Community
  College
  George C. Wallace Community
    College at Dothan *A*
  Selma *A*
Jacksonville State University *B, M*
Jefferson Davis Community College *A*
Jefferson State Community College *A*
Lawson State Community College *A*
Lurleen B. Wallace Community
  College *A*
Northeast Alabama Community
  College *A*
Northwest-Shoals Community
  College *A*
Oakwood University *B*
Shelton State Community College *A*
Snead State Community College *A*
Spring Hill College *M*
Troy University *A, B*
University of South Alabama *B*
Wallace State Community College at
  Hanceville *A*

Alaska
Alaska Pacific University *B, M*
Prince William Sound Community
  College *A*
University of Alaska
  Anchorage *B*
  Fairbanks *A, B*
  Southeast *A, B*

Arizona
Argosy University: Online *B*
Argosy University: Phoenix *B*
Arizona State University *B, M*
Central Arizona College *A*
College of the Humanities and
  Sciences *B, M, D*
Dine College *A*
Eastern Arizona College *A*
Estrella Mountain Community
  College *A*
GateWay Community College *A*
Mesa Community College *A*
Mohave Community College *A*
Northern Arizona University *B, M*
Northland Pioneer College *A*
Paradise Valley Community College *A*
Phoenix College *A*
Pima Community College *C, A*
Prescott College *B, M*
Scottsdale Community College *A*
Tohono O'odham Community
  College *A*
Western International University *A, B*

Arkansas
Arkansas Northeastern College *A*

Arkansas State University
  Beebe *A*
  Mountain Home *C, A*
Arkansas State University: Newport *A*
Arkansas Tech University *M*
Crowley's Ridge College *A*
East Arkansas Community College *C*
Henderson State University *M*
Mid-South Community College *C, A*
National Park Community College *A*
North Arkansas College *C, A*
Northwest Arkansas Community
  College *A*
Ouachita Technical College *A*
Ozarka College *A*
Phillips Community College of the
  University of Arkansas *A*
Pulaski Technical College *C, A*
Rich Mountain Community College *A*
South Arkansas Community College *A*
Southeast Arkansas College *A*
Southern Arkansas University Tech *C*
University of Arkansas
  Community College at Batesville *A*
  Community College at Hope *A*
  Cossatot Community College of the
    A
  Fort Smith *A, B*
  Little Rock *B, M*
University of Arkansas Community
  College at Morrilton *C, A*
University of Central Arkansas *B*

California

Allan Hancock College *A*
American Jewish University *B*
American River College *A*
Antelope Valley College *A*
Antioch Southern California
  Antioch University Los Angeles *B*
  Antioch University Santa Barbara *B*
Argosy University: Inland Empire *B*
Argosy University: Los Angeles *B*
Argosy University: Orange County *B*
Argosy University: San Diego *B*
Argosy University: San Francisco Bay
  Area *B*
Azusa Pacific University *B*
Bakersfield College *A*
Barstow Community College *A*
Berkeley City College *A*
Bethany University *B, T*
Biola University *B*
Butte College *A*
Cabrillo College *A*
California Baptist University *B*
California Institute of Integral
  Studies *B, D*
California Lutheran University *B*
California Polytechnic State
  University: San Luis Obispo *B*
California State Polytechnic
  University: Pomona *B*
California State University
  Bakersfield *B*
  Chico *B*
  Dominguez Hills *B*
  East Bay *B*
  Fresno *B*
  Fullerton *B*
  Long Beach *B*
  Los Angeles *B*
  Monterey Bay *B*
  Northridge *B*
  Sacramento *B, M*
  San Bernardino *B*
  San Marcos *B*
  Stanislaus *B*
California State University: Channel
  Islands *B*
Canada College *A*
Cerro Coso Community College *A*
Chabot College *A*
Chaffey College *A*

Chapman University *B*
Citrus College *A*
Coastline Community College *A*
College of Alameda *A*
College of Marin: Kentfield *A*
College of San Mateo *A*
College of the Canyons *A*
College of the Desert *A*
College of the Redwoods *A*
College of the Sequoias *A*
College of the Siskiyous *A*
Columbia College *A*
Concordia University *A, B*
Contra Costa College *A*
Copper Mountain College *A*
Cosumnes River College *A*
Crafton Hills College *C, A*
Cuesta College *A*
Cuyamaca College *A*
Cypress College *A*
De Anza College *A*
Deep Springs College *A*
Dominican University of California *B*
East Los Angeles College *A*
El Camino College: Compton
  Center *A*
Evergreen Valley College *A*
Feather River College *A*
Folsom Lake College *A*
Foothill College *A*
Fresno City College *A*
Fresno Pacific University *A, B*
Fullerton College *A*
Gavilan College *A*
Glendale Community College *A*
Golden West College *A*
Grossmont College *A*
Hartnell College *A*
Holy Names University *B*
Humboldt State University *B*
Humphreys College *A, B*
Imperial Valley College *A*
Irvine Valley College *A*
John F. Kennedy University *B*
La Sierra University *B*
Lake Tahoe Community College *A*
Laney College *A*
Lassen Community College *A*
Long Beach City College *A*
Los Angeles City College *A*
Los Angeles Harbor College *A*
Los Angeles Mission College *A*
Los Angeles Pierce College *A*
Los Angeles Southwest College *A*
Los Angeles Trade and Technical
  College *A*
Los Angeles Valley College *A*
Los Medanos College *A*
Loyola Marymount University *B*
Marymount College *A, B*
The Master's College *B*
Mendocino College *A*
Menlo College *B*
Merced College *A*
Merritt College *A*
Mills College *B, M*
MiraCosta College *A*
Mission College *A*
Monterey Peninsula College *A*
Moorpark College *A*
Mount St. Mary's College *A*
Mount San Antonio College *A*
Mount San Jacinto College *A*
Napa Valley College *A*
National Hispanic University *A, B*
National University *A, B*
Notre Dame de Namur University *B*
Ohlone College *A*
Orange Coast College *A*
Oxnard College *C, A*
Palo Verde College *A*
Palomar College *A*
Pasadena City College *C, A*
Patten University *B*

Pepperdine University *B*
Point Loma Nazarene University *B*
Porterville College *A*
Reedley College *A*
Rio Hondo College *A*
Sacramento City College *A*
Saddleback College *A*
St. Mary's College of California *B, M*
San Bernardino Valley College *A*
San Diego City College *A*
San Diego Mesa College *C, A*
San Diego State University *B, M*
San Francisco State University *B*
San Joaquin Delta College *A*
San Jose City College *A*
San Jose State University *B*
Santa Ana College *A*
Santa Barbara City College *A*
Santa Clara University *B*
Santa Monica College *A*
Santa Rosa Junior College *A*
Santiago Canyon College *A*
Sierra College *A*
Simpson University *B*
Skyline College *A*
Soka University of America *B*
Solano Community College *A*
Sonoma State University *B*
Southwestern College *A*
Stanford University *M*
Taft College *A*
Thomas Aquinas College *B*
University of California
  Los Angeles *B*
  Riverside *B*
University of La Verne *B*
University of Redlands *B*
University of San Diego *B*
University of San Francisco *B*
University of Southern California *M*
University of the Pacific *B*
Vanguard University of Southern
  California *B*
Victor Valley College *A*
West Hills College: Coalinga *A*
West Hills College: Lemoore *A*
West Los Angeles College *C, A*
West Valley College *A*
Whittier College *B*
Yuba Community College District *A*

Colorado

Adams State College *A, B*
Aims Community College *A*
Arapahoe Community College *A*
Argosy University: Denver *B*
Colorado Christian University *B*
Colorado College *B*
Colorado Mountain College *A*
Colorado Northwestern Community
  College *A*
Colorado State University *B*
Colorado State University
  Pueblo *B*
Community College of Denver *A*
Fort Lewis College *B*
Front Range Community College *A*
Lamar Community College *A*
Mesa State College *A, B*
Morgan Community College *A*
Northeastern Junior College *A*
Otero Junior College *A*
Pikes Peak Community College *A*
Pueblo Community College *A*
Red Rocks Community College *A*
Regis University *B*
Trinidad State Junior College *A*
University of Denver *B, M*

Connecticut

Albertus Magnus College *A, B, M*
Asnuntuck Community College *A*
Capital Community College *A*
Charter Oak State College *A, B*

Fairfield University *A*
Gateway Community College *A*
Housatonic Community College *A*
Lincoln College of New England:
  Briarwood *A*
Manchester Community College *A*
Middlesex Community College *A*
Mitchell College *A*
Naugatuck Valley Community
  College *A*
Northwestern Connecticut
  Community College *A*
Norwalk Community College *A*
Quinebaug Valley Community
  College *A*
Quinnipiac University *A*
Sacred Heart University *A, B*
Saint Joseph College *B*
Southern Connecticut State
  University *B*
Three Rivers Community College *A*
Tunxis Community College *A*
University of Bridgeport *A, B*
University of Hartford *A, B*
University of New Haven *B*
Wesleyan University *B, M*
Western Connecticut State
  University *A, B*

Delaware

University of Delaware *A, B, M, D*
Wesley College *A, B*
Wilmington University *A, B*

District of Columbia

American University *B*
Catholic University of America *B*
George Washington University *B*
Georgetown University *B, M, D*
Trinity Washington University *B*

Florida

Argosy University: Sarasota *B*
Argosy University: Tampa *B*
Barry University *B, M*
Beacon College *A, B*
Broward College *A*
Central Florida Community College *A*
Clearwater Christian College *A, B*
Daytona State College *A*
Edison State College *A*
Edward Waters College *B*
Flagler College *A*
Florida Agricultural and Mechanical
  University *A*
Florida Atlantic University *A, B, M*
Florida College *A*
Florida Gulf Coast University *A, B*
Florida Institute of Technology *A*
Florida International University *B, M*
Florida State University *A*
Gulf Coast Community College *A*
Hillsborough Community College *A*
Indian River State College *A*
Jacksonville University *B*
Lake City Community College *A*
Lake-Sumter Community College *A*
Lynn University *B*
Miami Dade College *A*
New College of Florida *B*
North Florida Community College *A*
Nova Southeastern University *B*
Palm Beach Community College *A*
Pasco-Hernando Community
  College *A*
Pensacola Junior College *A*
Polk State College *A*
Rollins College *A*
Saint Johns River Community
  College *A*
Saint Leo University *A*
St. Petersburg College *A*
Saint Thomas University *B*
Santa Fe College *A*

Schiller International University *A*
Seminole Community College *A*
South Florida Community College *A*
State College of Florida,
    Manatee-Sarasota *A*
Tallahassee Community College *A*
University of Central Florida *B, M*
University of Florida *A*
University of Miami *C, B, M*
University of North Florida *A, B*
University of South Florida *A, B, M*
University of Tampa *B*
University of West Florida *A*
Valencia Community College *A*
Warner University *A*

Georgia

Abraham Baldwin Agricultural
    College *A*
Andrew College *A*
Argosy University: Atlanta *B*
Atlanta Christian College *B*
Augusta State University *A*
Brenau University *B*
Clayton State University *A, B, M*
College of Coastal Georgia *A*
Columbus State University *A, B*
Dalton State College *A, B*
East Georgia College *A*
Emmanuel College *A*
Emory University *A, D*
Fort Valley State University *A, B*
Gainesville State College *A*
Georgia College and State
    University *B*
Georgia Highlands College *A*
LaGrange College *A*
Macon State College *A*
Mercer University *B*
Middle Georgia College *A*
Oglethorpe University *B*
Oxford College of Emory
    University *A*
Reinhardt College *A, B*
Shorter College *B*
Southern Polytechnic State
    University *A*
Truett-McConnell College *A*
University of Georgia *B*
Valdosta State University *A, B*
Wesleyan College *B*
Young Harris College *A*

Hawaii

Argosy University: Hawaii *B*
Chaminade University of
    Honolulu *A, B*
Hawaii Pacific University *B*
Hawaii Tokai International College *A*
University of Hawaii
    Hawaii Community College *A*
    Hilo *B*
    Honolulu Community College *A*
    Kapiolani Community College *A*
    Kauai Community College *A*
    Leeward Community College *C, A*
    Manoa *B*
    Maui Community College *A*
    Windward Community College *A*

Idaho

Boise State University *B*
Brigham Young University-Idaho *A*
College of Idaho *B*
Lewis-Clark State College *A*
New Saint Andrews College *A, B*
North Idaho College *A*
Northwest Nazarene University *B*

Illinois

Argosy University: Schaumburg *B*
Augustana College *B*
Aurora University *B*

Black Hawk College *A*
Black Hawk College: East Campus *A*
Bradley University *B, M*
City Colleges of Chicago
    Harold Washington College *A*
    Kennedy-King College *A*
    Malcolm X College *A*
    Olive-Harvey College *A*
College of DuPage *A*
College of Lake County *A*
Columbia College Chicago *B*
Danville Area Community College *A*
DePaul University *M*
East-West University *A, B*
Eastern Illinois University *B*
Elgin Community College *A*
Elmhurst College *B*
Eureka College *B*
Governors State University *B*
Greenville College *B*
Harper College *A*
Heartland Community College *A*
Hebrew Theological College *B*
Highland Community College *A*
Illinois Central College *A*
Illinois Eastern Community Colleges
    Frontier Community College *A*
    Lincoln Trail College *A*
    Olney Central College *A*
    Wabash Valley College *A*
Illinois Institute of Technology *B*
Illinois State University *B*
John A. Logan College *A*
John Wood Community College *A*
Joliet Junior College *A*
Kaskaskia College *A*
Kishwaukee College *A*
Lake Forest College *M*
Lake Land College *A*
Lewis University *B*
Lewis and Clark Community
    College *A*
Lincoln College *A, B*
Lincoln Land Community College *A*
McHenry County College *A*
McKendree University *B*
Monmouth College *A*
Moraine Valley Community College *A*
Morton College *A*
National-Louis University *B*
North Central College *B, M*
Northeastern Illinois University *B*
Northern Illinois University *B*
Northwestern University *C, B, M*
Oakton Community College *A*
Olivet Nazarene University *B*
Parkland College *A*
Prairie State College *A*
Principia College *B*
Quincy University *A, B*
Rend Lake College *A*
Richard J. Daley College *C, A*
Richland Community College *A*
Rock Valley College *A*
Roosevelt University *B*
St. Augustine College *A*
Saint Xavier University *B, M*
Sauk Valley Community College *A*
Shawnee Community College *A*
Shimer College *B*
South Suburban College of Cook
    County *A*
Southeastern Illinois College *A*
Southern Illinois University
    Carbondale *B*
Southern Illinois University
    Edwardsville *B*
Southwestern Illinois College *A*
Triton College *A*
University of Chicago *B, M*
University of Illinois
    Chicago *B*
    Springfield *B, M*
    Urbana-Champaign *B*

University of St. Francis *B*
Waubonsee Community College *A*
Western Illinois University *B, M*
Wilbur Wright College *A*

Indiana

Ancilla College *A*
Ball State University *B*
Bethel College *A, B*
Butler University *A, B*
Calumet College of St. Joseph *A, B*
Holy Cross College *A, B*
Indiana State University *A, B*
Indiana University
    Bloomington *A, B*
    East *A*
    Kokomo *A*
    Northwest *A*
    South Bend *A, M*
    Southeast *A, M*
Indiana University-Purdue University
    Fort Wayne *A*
Indiana University-Purdue University
    Indianapolis *A, B*
Ivy Tech Community College
    Bloomington *A*
    Central Indiana *A*
    Columbus *A*
    East Central *A*
    Kokomo *A*
    Lafayette *A*
    North Central *A*
    Northeast *A*
    Northwest *A*
    Richmond *A*
    South Central *A*
    Southeast *A*
    Southwest *A*
    Wabash Valley *A*
Manchester College *B*
Marian University *A*
Oakland City University *A, B*
Purdue University *B, M, D*
Purdue University
    Calumet *A*
    North Central *B*
St. Mary-of-the-Woods College *A, B*
Taylor University *A*
University of Evansville *B*
University of Indianapolis *A*
University of Notre Dame *B*
University of St. Francis *A, B*
University of Southern Indiana *B, M*
Vincennes University *A*
Wabash College *B*

Iowa

Briar Cliff University *A*
Clarke College *A*
Clinton Community College *C, A*
Des Moines Area Community
    College *C, A*
Dordt College *B*
Ellsworth Community College *A*
Graceland University *B*
Grand View University *A, B*
Hawkeye Community College *A*
Indian Hills Community College *A*
Iowa Central Community College *A*
Iowa Lakes Community College *A*
Iowa State University *B*
Iowa Western Community College *A*
Kirkwood Community College *A*
Loras College *A, B*
Marshalltown Community College *A*
Muscatine Community College *C, A*
North Iowa Area Community
    College *A*
Northeast Iowa Community
    College *A*
Northwest Iowa Community
    College *A*
Northwestern College *B*
Scott Community College *C, A*

Simpson College *B, T*
Southeastern Community College
    North Campus *A*
Southwestern Community College *A*
University of Iowa *B*
University of Northern Iowa *B*
Upper Iowa University *A*
Waldorf College *A, B*
Western Iowa Tech Community
    College *A*
William Penn University *A*

Kansas

Barton County Community College *A*
Benedictine College *B*
Bethany College *B*
Butler Community College *A*
Central Christian College of
    Kansas *A, B*
Cloud County Community College *A*
Coffeyville Community College *A*
Colby Community College *A*
Cowley County Community
    College *A*
Emporia State University *B*
Fort Scott Community College *A*
Friends University *A, B*
Garden City Community College *A*
Hesston College *A*
Hutchinson Community College *A*
Johnson County Community
    College *A*
Kansas City Kansas Community
    College *A*
Kansas State University *C*
Labette Community College *A*
McPherson College *B*
MidAmerica Nazarene University *A*
Neosho County Community
    College *A*
Newman University *A, B*
Pratt Community College *A*
Seward County Community College *A*
Southwestern College *B*
Tabor College *A*
University of Kansas *B*
University of St. Mary *A, B*
Washburn University *A, B, M*
Wichita State University *A, B, M*

Kentucky

Asbury College *A*
Ashland Community and Technical
    College *A*
Bellarmine University *B*
Big Sandy Community and Technical
    College *A*
Bluegrass Community and Technical
    College *A*
Brescia University *A, B*
Campbellsville University *A*
Eastern Kentucky University *B*
Elizabethtown Community and
    Technical College *A*
Georgetown College *B*
Hazard Community and Technical
    College *A*
Henderson Community College *A*
Hopkinsville Community College *A*
Kentucky State University *A, B*
Madisonville Community College *A*
Maysville Community and Technical
    College *A*
Midway College *B*
Murray State University *A, B*
Northern Kentucky
    University *A, B, M*
Owensboro Community and
    Technical College *A*
St. Catharine College *A, B*
Somerset Community College *A*
Southeast Kentucky Community and
    Technical College *A*
Thomas More College *A, B*

Transylvania University *B*
University of Louisville *B*
West Kentucky Community and
    Technical College *A*
Western Kentucky University *C*

Louisiana

Baton Rouge Community College *A*
Bossier Parish Community College *A*
Centenary College of Louisiana *B*
Delgado Community College *A*
Grambling State University *M*
Louisiana State University
    Alexandria *A, B*
    Eunice *A*
    Shreveport *B, M*
Louisiana State University and
    Agricultural and Mechanical
    College *B, M*
Louisiana Tech University *A, B*
McNeese State University *A*
Northwestern State University *B*
Our Lady of Holy Cross College *B*
River Parishes Community College *A*
St. Joseph Seminary College *B*
South Louisiana Community
    College *A*
Southeastern Louisiana University *B*
Southern University
    Shreveport *A*

Maine

Central Maine Community College *A*
Eastern Maine Community College *A*
Husson University *B*
Kennebec Valley Community
    College *A*
Thomas College *A*
Unity College *A, B*
University of Maine *B, M*
University of Maine
    Augusta *C, A*
    Fort Kent *A, B*
    Machias *B*
    Presque Isle *A, B*
University of New England *B*
University of Southern Maine *A, B*
Washington County Community
    College *A*

Maryland

Allegany College of Maryland *A*
Anne Arundel Community College *A*
Baltimore City Community College *A*
Carroll Community College *A*
Cecil College *A*
Chesapeake College *A*
College of Notre Dame of
    Maryland *B, M*
College of Southern Maryland *C, A*
Community College of Baltimore
    County *C, A*
Coppin State University *B*
Frederick Community College *A*
Frostburg State University *B*
Garrett College *A*
Hagerstown Community College *A*
Howard Community College *A*
Johns Hopkins University *B, M*
Loyola University Maryland *M*
McDaniel College *M*
Montgomery College *A*
Mount St. Mary's University *M*
Prince George's Community
    College *A*
St. John's College *B, M*
Towson University *M*
University of Baltimore *B*
University of Maryland
    Eastern Shore *B*
    University College *A, B*
Washington Adventist University *B*
Washington College *B*

Massachusetts

American International College *A, B*
Anna Maria College *B*
Atlantic Union College *B*
Bard College at Simon's Rock *A, B*
Bay Path College *B*
Becker College *A*
Bentley University *B*
Berkshire Community College *A*
Bristol Community College *A*
Cambridge College *B*
Cape Cod Community College *A*
Clark University *B, M*
Curry College *B*
Dean College *A*
Eastern Nazarene College *B*
Elms College *B*
Emmanuel College *B*
Endicott College *B*
Fisher College *A*
Fitchburg State College *B*
Framingham State College *B*
Greenfield Community College *A*
Hampshire College *B*
Harvard College *B*
Hellenic College/Holy Cross *B*
Holyoke Community College *A*
Lesley University *A, B, M*
Marian Court College *A*
Massachusetts Bay Community
    College *C, A*
Massachusetts College of Liberal
    Arts *B*
Massachusetts Institute of
    Technology *B*
Massasoit Community College *A*
Merrimack College *A, B*
Middlesex Community College *A*
Mount Holyoke College *C*
Mount Ida College *B*
Mount Wachusett Community
    College *A*
Newbury College *A*
North Shore Community College *A*
Northeastern University *B*
Northern Essex Community
    College *A*
Pine Manor College *A, B*
Quincy College *A*
Quinsigamond Community College *A*
Regis College *B*
Roxbury Community College *A*
Salem State College *B*
Springfield College *B*
Springfield Technical Community
    College *A*
Suffolk University *A, B*
Tufts University *B*
University of Massachusetts
    Dartmouth *C, B*
    Lowell *B*
Urban College of Boston *C, A*
Western New England College *A, B*
Westfield State College *B*
Wheaton College *B*
Wheelock College *B*

Michigan

Alma College *B*
Alpena Community College *A*
Aquinas College *A, B*
Bay de Noc Community College *A*
Calvin College *B*
Central Michigan University *B*
Delta College *A*
Ferris State University *A*
Finlandia University *A, B*
Glen Oaks Community College *A*
Gogebic Community College *A*
Grace Bible College *A, B*
Grand Rapids Community College *A*
Grand Valley State University *B*
Henry Ford Community College *A*
Hillsdale College *B*

Jackson Community College *A*
Kalamazoo Valley Community
    College *A*
Kellogg Community College *A*
Kirtland Community College *A*
Kuyper College *A*
Lake Michigan College *A*
Lake Superior State University *A, B*
Lansing Community College *A*
Macomb Community College *A*
Madonna University *M*
Marygrove College *A, T*
Michigan Technological University *B*
Mid Michigan Community College *A*
Monroe County Community
    College *A*
Montcalm Community College *A*
Mott Community College *A*
North Central Michigan College *A*
Northern Michigan
    University *C, A, B, M*
Northwestern Michigan College *A*
Oakland Community College *A*
Oakland University *B, M*
Rochester College *A*
Sacred Heart Major Seminary *B*
St. Clair County Community
    College *A*
Siena Heights University *A, B*
Southwestern Michigan College *C, A*
Spring Arbor University *A*
University of Detroit Mercy *B, M*
University of Michigan
    Dearborn *B*
    Flint *B, M*
Washtenaw Community College *A*
Wayne County Community College *A*
West Shore Community College *A*

Minnesota

Anoka-Ramsey Community College *A*
Argosy University: Twin Cities *B*
Augsburg College *B*
Bemidji State University *A, B*
Bethany Lutheran College *B*
Bethel University *A*
Central Lakes College *A*
Century Community and Technical
    College *A*
College of St. Benedict *B*
Concordia College: Moorhead *B*
Crossroads College *A*
Crown College *A, B*
Fond du Lac Tribal and Community
    College *A*
Hamline University *M*
Hibbing Community College *A*
Inver Hills Community College *A*
Itasca Community College *A*
Lake Superior College *A*
Leech Lake Tribal College *A*
Mesabi Range Community and
    Technical College *A*
Metropolitan State University *B*
Minneapolis Community and
    Technical College *A*
Minnesota State Community and
    Technical College *A*
Minnesota State University
    Mankato *A*
    Moorhead *A, M*
Minnesota West Community and
    Technical College *A*
Normandale Community College *A*
North Hennepin Community
    College *A*
Northland Community & Technical
    College *A*
Northwestern College *A*
Oak Hills Christian College *A, B*
Rainy River Community College *A*
Ridgewater College *A*
Riverland Community College *A*

Rochester Community and Technical
    College *A*
Saint Cloud State University *A, B*
St. John's University *B*
St. Olaf College *B*
St. Paul College *A*
South Central College *A*
Southwest Minnesota State
    University *B*
University of Minnesota
    Duluth *M*
    Twin Cities *C, B*
University of St. Thomas *B*
Winona State University *A, B*

Mississippi

Alcorn State University *B*
Copiah-Lincoln Community College *A*
East Central Community College *A*
Hinds Community College *A*
Holmes Community College *A*
Jones County Junior College *A*
Mississippi College *M*
Mississippi Delta Community
    College *A*
Mississippi Gulf Coast Community
    College *A*
Mississippi State University *B*
Mississippi University for Women *B*
Northwest Mississippi Community
    College *A*
Pearl River Community College *A*
Southwest Mississippi Community
    College *A*
Tougaloo College *B*
University of Mississippi *B*
Wesley College *C*

Missouri

Columbia College *A*
Cottey College *A*
Crowder College *A*
Culver-Stockton College *B*
Drury University *A, B, M*
Evangel University *A*
Fontbonne University *B*
Hannibal-LaGrange College *A, B*
Jefferson College *A*
Lincoln University *B*
Maryville University of Saint Louis *B*
Metropolitan Community College:
    Blue River *A*
Metropolitan Community College:
    Longview *A*
Metropolitan Community College:
    Maple Woods *A*
Metropolitan Community College:
    Penn Valley *A*
Mineral Area College *A*
Missouri Baptist University *B*
Missouri State University: West
    Plains *A*
Missouri Valley College *A, B*
Missouri Western State University *B*
North Central Missouri College *A*
Ozarks Technical Community
    College *A*
Park University *A, B*
St. Charles Community College *C, A*
St. Louis Christian College *A*
St. Louis Community College
    St. Louis Community College at
        Florissant Valley *A*
    St. Louis Community College at
        Meramec *A*
Stephens College *A, B*
Three Rivers Community College *A*
University of Missouri
    Kansas City *B, M*
    St. Louis *B*
Washington University in St.
    Louis *B, M*
Webster University *B*

Wentworth Military Junior
College *C, A*
William Jewell College *B*

Montana

Blackfeet Community College *A*
Dawson Community College *A*
Flathead Valley Community College *A*
Fort Belknap College *A*
Helena College of Technology of the
University of Montana *A*
Little Big Horn College *A*
Miles Community College *A*
Montana State University
Billings *A, B*
Montana Tech of the University of
Montana *B*
Rocky Mountain College *A*
Salish Kootenai College *A*
Stone Child College *A*
University of Montana *A, B*
University of Montana: Western *A, B*

Nebraska

Bellevue University *B*
Central Community College *A*
Chadron State College *B, M*
College of Saint Mary *A, B*
Dana College *B*
Doane College *B*
Grace University *B*
Little Priest Tribal College *A*
Metropolitan Community College *A*
Mid-Plains Community College Area *A*
Nebraska Christian College *A*
Nebraska Indian Community
College *A*
Northeast Community College *A*
Southeast Community College *A*
University of Nebraska
Kearney *B*
Lincoln *B*
Western Nebraska Community
College *A*

Nevada

College of Southern Nevada *A*
Great Basin College *B*
Sierra Nevada College *B*
University of Nevada
Las Vegas *B, M*
Western Nevada College *A*

New Hampshire

Colby-Sawyer College *A*
Daniel Webster College *A*
Dartmouth College *M*
Franklin Pierce University *B*
Granite State College *A, B*
Lakes Region Community College *A*
Magdalen College *A, B*
Manchester Community College *A*
NHTI-Concord's Community
College *A*
Nashua Community College *C, A*
New England College *A, B*
River Valley Community College *C, A*
Rivier College *A, B*
Saint Anselm College *B*
Southern New Hampshire
University *A*
Thomas More College of Liberal
Arts *B*
University of New Hampshire *M*
University of New Hampshire at
Manchester *A, B*
White Mountains Community
College *A*

New Jersey

Assumption College for Sisters *A*
Atlantic Cape Community College *A*
Bergen Community College *A*

Brookdale Community College *A*
Burlington County College *C, A*
Caldwell College *M*
Camden County College *A*
County College of Morris *A*
Cumberland County College *A*
Essex County College *A*
Fairleigh Dickinson University
Metropolitan Campus *A*
Felician College *A*
Gloucester County College *A*
Hudson County Community
College *A*
Kean University *B, M*
Mercer County Community College *A*
Monmouth University *M*
Montclair State University *B*
Ocean County College *A*
Passaic County Community College *A*
Ramapo College of New Jersey *B, M*
Raritan Valley Community
College *C, A*
Richard Stockton College of New
Jersey *B*
Rider University *A, B*
Rowan University *B, M*
Rutgers, The State University of New
Jersey
Camden Regional Campus *B, M*
Newark Regional Campus *M*
Salem Community College *A*
Seton Hall University *B*
Stevens Institute of Technology *B*
Sussex County Community College *A*
Thomas Edison State College *A, B, M*
Union County College *A*
Warren County Community College *A*

New Mexico

Central New Mexico Community
College *A*
Clovis Community College *A*
Eastern New Mexico University *A, B*
Eastern New Mexico University:
Roswell Campus *A*
Mesalands Community College *C, A*
New Mexico Junior College *A*
New Mexico Military Institute *A*
New Mexico State University
Alamogordo *A*
Northern New Mexico College *A*
St. John's College *B, M*
San Juan College *A*
Santa Fe Community College *A*
Southwestern Indian Polytechnic
Institute *A*
University of New Mexico *B*
University of the Southwest *B*
Western New Mexico University *B*

New York

Adelphi University *A*
Adirondack Community College *A*
Alfred University *B*
Bard College *A, B*
Boricua College *A, B*
Broome Community College *A*
Canisius College *B*
Cayuga County Community College *A*
Cazenovia College *A, B*
City University of New York
Baruch College *B*
Borough of Manhattan Community
College *A*
Bronx Community College *A*
Brooklyn College *B, M*
College of Staten Island *A, B, M*
Hostos Community College *A*
Kingsborough Community
College *A*
LaGuardia Community College *A*
Lehman College *B, M*
Medgar Evers College *A, B*

New York City College of
Technology *A*
Queens College *B, M*
Queensborough Community
College *A*
York College *B*
Clarkson University *B*
Clinton Community College *A*
Colgate University *B*
College of Mount St. Vincent *A, B*
College of Saint Rose *B*
Columbia-Greene Community
College *A*
Concordia College *A, B*
Cornell University *B*
Corning Community College *A*
Dominican College of Blauvelt *A*
Dowling College *B, M*
Dutchess Community College *A*
Elmira College *A*
Erie Community College
City Campus *A*
North Campus *A*
South Campus *A*
Eugene Lang College The New School
for Liberal Arts *B*
Excelsior College *A, B, M*
Finger Lakes Community College *A*
Five Towns College *A*
Fulton-Montgomery Community
College *A*
Genesee Community College *A*
Hamilton College *B*
Hartwick College *B*
Herkimer County Community
College *A*
Hilbert College *A, B*
Hofstra University *B*
Hudson Valley Community College *C*
Iona College *B*
Ithaca College *B*
Jamestown Community College *C, A*
Jefferson Community College *A*
Keuka College *B*
Long Island University
Brooklyn Campus *A, B*
C. W. Post Campus *B, M*
Manhattanville College *B, M*
Maria College *A*
Medaille College *A, B*
Mercy College *C, A, B, T*
Mohawk Valley Community
College *C, A*
Molloy College *A, B*
Monroe Community College *A*
Nassau Community College *A*
New York University *A, B, M*
Niagara County Community
College *A*
Niagara University *A, B, T*
North Country Community College *A*
Nyack College *A, B*
Onondaga Community College *A*
Orange County Community College *A*
Pace University *A, B*
Paul Smith's College *A, B*
Polytechnic Institute of New York
University *B*
Roberts Wesleyan College *B*
Rockland Community College *A*
Russell Sage College *B*
Sage College of Albany *A*
St. Francis College *A, B*
St. John Fisher College *B*
St. John's University *A, B, M*
St. Joseph's College *B*
St. Joseph's College: Suffolk
Campus *B*
St. Thomas Aquinas College *A, B*
Sarah Lawrence College *B*
Schenectady County Community
College *C, A*
Skidmore College *B, M*

State University of New York
Albany *M*
College at Brockport *M*
College at Old Westbury *B*
College at Plattsburgh *B, M*
College at Potsdam *B*
College of Agriculture and
Technology at Cobleskill *A*
College of Agriculture and
Technology at Morrisville *A*
College of Technology at Alfred *A*
College of Technology at
Canton *C, A, T*
College of Technology at Delhi *A*
Empire State College *A, B, M*
Farmingdale *A*
Maritime College *B*
New Paltz *B*
Purchase *B*
Stony Brook *M*
Suffolk County Community College *A*
Sullivan County Community
College *A*
Syracuse University *B*
Tompkins Cortland Community
College *C, A*
Touro College *A, B*
Trocaire College *A*
Ulster County Community College *A*
Union College *B*
University of Rochester *B, M*
Utica College *B, M*
Vassar College *B*
Villa Maria College of Buffalo *A*
Wagner College *B*
Westchester Community College *A*

North Carolina

Alamance Community College *A*
Appalachian State University *B*
Asheville-Buncombe Technical
Community College *A*
Barton College *B*
Beaufort County Community
College *A*
Belmont Abbey College *B*
Bladen Community College *A*
Blue Ridge Community College *A*
Brevard College *B*
Brunswick Community College *A*
Caldwell Community College and
Technical Institute *A*
Cape Fear Community College *A*
Carteret Community College *A*
Catawba Valley Community College *A*
Central Carolina Community
College *A*
Central Piedmont Community
College *A*
Chowan University *B*
Cleveland Community College *A*
Coastal Carolina Community
College *A*
College of the Albemarle *A*
Davidson County Community
College *A*
Duke University *M*
Durham Technical Community
College *A*
East Carolina University *B*
Edgecombe Community College *A*
Fayetteville Technical Community
College *A*
Forsyth Technical Community
College *A*
Gaston College *A*
Greensboro College *C, B*
Guilford Technical Community
College *A*
Halifax Community College *A*
Haywood Community College *A*
Isothermal Community College *A*
James Sprunt Community College *A*
Johnson C. Smith University *B*

Johnston Community College *A*
Lees-McRae College *B*
Lenoir Community College *A*
Lenoir-Rhyne University *B*
Louisburg College *A*
Mars Hill College *B*
Martin Community College *A*
Mayland Community College *A*
McDowell Technical Community
  College *A*
Methodist University *A, B*
Mitchell Community College *A*
Montgomery Community College *A*
Mount Olive College *A, B*
Nash Community College *A*
North Carolina State University *B, M*
Peace College *B*
Pfeiffer University *B*
Piedmont Community College *A*
Pitt Community College *C, A*
Randolph Community College *A*
Richmond Community College *A*
Roanoke-Chowan Community
  College *A*
Rockingham Community College *A*
St. Andrews Presbyterian College *B*
Sandhills Community College *A*
Shaw University *B*
South Piedmont Community
  College *A*
Southeastern Community College *A*
Southwestern Community College *A*
Stanly Community College *A*
Surry Community College *A*
Tri-County Community College *C, A*
University of North Carolina
  Asheville *B, M*
  Chapel Hill *B*
  Charlotte *M*
  Greensboro *B, M*
  Wilmington *M*
University of North Carolina School of
  the Arts *B*
Vance-Granville Community
  College *A*
Wake Forest University *M*
Wake Technical Community
  College *C, A*
Warren Wilson College *B*
Wayne Community College *A*
Western Carolina University *B*
Western Piedmont Community
  College *A*
Wilkes Community College *A*
Wilson Community College *A*
Wingate University *B*
Winston-Salem State University *B*

North Dakota
Bismarck State College *A*
Dakota College at Bottineau *A*
Dickinson State University *A, B*
Lake Region State College *A*
Minot State University *B*
North Dakota State College of
  Science *A*
Williston State College *A*

Ohio
Antioch University McGregor *B*
Ashland University *A, B*
Bowling Green State University *B*
Bowling Green State University:
  Firelands College *A*
Chatfield College *A*
Cincinnati State Technical and
  Community College *A*
Clark State Community College *A*
Cleveland State University *B*
College of Mount St. Joseph *B*
Columbus State Community
  College *A*
Cuyahoga Community College
  Metropolitan Campus *A*

Defiance College *B*
Eastern Gateway Community
  College *A*
Edison State Community College *A*
John Carroll University *B, M*
Kent State University *C, B, M*
Kent State University
  Ashtabula *A*
  East Liverpool *A*
  Salem *A*
  Stark *A*
  Trumbull *A*
  Tuscarawas *C, A*
Kent State University: Geauga *A*
Lourdes College *A*
Malone University *B*
Marietta College *A, M*
Miami University
  Oxford Campus *A, B*
Northwest State Community
  College *A*
Ohio Dominican University *A, B, M*
Ohio Northern University *B*
Ohio State University
  Columbus Campus *B, M*
  Lima Campus *A*
  Mansfield Campus *A*
  Marion Campus *A*
  Newark Campus *A*
Ohio University *A*
Ohio University
  Zanesville Campus *A*
Ohio Wesleyan University *B*
Southern State Community College *A*
Stark State College of Technology *A*
Terra State Community College *A*
Tiffin University *B*
Union Institute & University *B*
University of Akron *A, B*
University of Akron: Wayne College *A*
University of Cincinnati *B*
University of Cincinnati
  Clermont College *A*
  Raymond Walters College *A*
University of Findlay *A, M*
University of Rio Grande *A*
University of Toledo *B, M*
Urbana University *A, B*
Ursuline College *M*
Walsh University *B*
Washington State Community
  College *A*
Wilberforce University *B*
Wilmington College *B*
Wittenberg University *B*
Wright State University *B*
Wright State University: Lake
  Campus *A*
Xavier University *A, B*
Youngstown State University *A, B*

Oklahoma
Bacone College *A*
Connors State College *A*
Mid-America Christian University *A*
Murray State College *A*
Northern Oklahoma College *A*
Oklahoma Baptist University *B*
Oklahoma Christian University *B*
Oklahoma City Community College *A*
Oklahoma City University *B, M*
Oklahoma State University *B*
Oral Roberts University *B*
Rogers State University *A, B*
Rose State College *A*
St. Gregory's University *A, B*
Seminole State College *A*
Southern Nazarene University *B*
University of Central Oklahoma *B*
University of Oklahoma *C, B, M*
University of Tulsa *B*
Western Oklahoma State College *A*

Oregon
Blue Mountain Community College *A*
Central Oregon Community
  College *A*
Chemeketa Community College *A*
Clackamas Community College *A*
Clatsop Community College *A*
Concordia University *A, B*
Corban College *B*
Eastern Oregon University *B*
Gutenberg College *B*
Klamath Community College *A*
Lane Community College *A*
Lewis & Clark College *B*
Linn-Benton Community College *A*
Marylhurst University *B*
Mount Angel Seminary *C, B, M*
Oregon State University *B*
Pacific University *B*
Portland Community College *A*
Portland State University *B*
Reed College *M*
Rogue Community College *A*
Southwestern Oregon Community
  College *A*
Treasure Valley Community College *A*
Umpqua Community College *A*
Warner Pacific College *B*
Western Oregon University *A, B*

Pennsylvania
Alvernia University *A, B, M*
Arcadia University *B*
Baptist Bible College of
  Pennsylvania *A*
Bryn Athyn College of the New
  Church *A*
Bucks County Community College *A*
Cabrini College *B*
California University of
  Pennsylvania *A, B*
Carlow University *B*
Carnegie Mellon University *B*
Chatham University *B*
Chestnut Hill College *B*
Clarion University of
  Pennsylvania *A, B*
Community College of Allegheny
  County *A*
Community College of Beaver
  County *A*
Community College of Philadelphia *A*
DeSales University *B*
Duquesne University *B, M*
East Stroudsburg University of
  Pennsylvania *B*
Eastern University *A*
Edinboro University of
  Pennsylvania *A, B*
Gannon University *A, B*
Geneva College *B*
Gettysburg College *B*
Gwynedd-Mercy College *A*
Harcum College *A*
Haverford College *B*
Immaculata University *B*
Juniata College *B*
Keystone College *A*
La Roche College *B*
La Salle University *A, B*
Lackawanna College *A*
Lebanon Valley College *C*
Lehigh Carbon Community College *A*
Lock Haven University of
  Pennsylvania *B, M*
Luzerne County Community
  College *A*
Manor College *A*
Mansfield University of
  Pennsylvania *B*
Mercyhurst College *C, A*
Misericordia University *B*
Montgomery County Community
  College *A*

Mount Aloysius College *A, B*
Neumann University *A, B*
Northampton Community College *A*
Penn State
  Abington *A, B*
  Altoona *A, B*
  Beaver *A, B*
  Berks *A, B*
  Brandywine *A, B*
  DuBois *A, B*
  Erie, The Behrend College *C, A, B*
  Fayette, The Eberly Campus *A, B*
  Greater Allegheny *A, B*
  Harrisburg *B*
  Hazleton *A, B*
  Lehigh Valley *A, B*
  Mont Alto *A, B*
  New Kensington *A, B*
  Schuylkill *A, B*
  Shenango *A, B*
  University Park *A, B*
  Wilkes-Barre *C, A, B*
  Worthington Scranton *A, B*
  York *A, B*
Pennsylvania Highlands Community
  College *A*
Reading Area Community College *A*
Rosemont College *B*
Saint Joseph's University *A, B*
St. Vincent College *B*
Susquehanna University *B*
Temple University *B*
Thiel College *A*
University of Pennsylvania *B, M*
University of Pittsburgh *B*
University of Pittsburgh
  Bradford *A*
  Greensburg *B*
  Johnstown *A*
  Titusville *A*
Valley Forge Military Academy &
  College *A*
Villanova University *A, B, M*
Waynesburg University *A*
West Chester University of
  Pennsylvania *B*
Westmoreland County Community
  College *A*
Widener University *A, B, M*
Wilkes University *B*
Wilson College *A*

Puerto Rico
Pontifical Catholic University of
  Puerto Rico *B*
University of Puerto Rico
  Arecibo *A*
  Ponce *A*
  Rio Piedras *B*

Rhode Island
Community College of Rhode
  Island *A*
Providence College *A, B*
Rhode Island College *B*
Salve Regina University *B*

South Carolina
Aiken Technical College *A*
Anderson University *B*
Central Carolina Technical College *A*
Clinton Junior College *A*
Coastal Carolina University *B*
Columbia College *B*
Converse College *M*
Denmark Technical College *A*
Florence-Darlington Technical
  College *A*
Francis Marion University *B*
Furman University *B*
Greenville Technical College *C, A*
Horry-Georgetown Technical
  College *C, A*
Lander University *B*

Limestone College *A, B*
Midlands Technical College *C, A*
Morris College *B*
Newberry College *B*
North Greenville University *B*
Northeastern Technical College *A*
Orangeburg-Calhoun Technical
   College *A*
Spartanburg Community College *A*
Spartanburg Methodist College *A*
Technical College of the
   Lowcountry *A*
Tri-County Technical College *A*
Trident Technical College *A*
University of South Carolina *A, B*
University of South Carolina
   Beaufort *A, B*
   Lancaster *A*
   Salkehatchie Regional Campus *A*
   Sumter *A*
   Union *A*
   Upstate *B*
Williamsburg Technical College *A*
Winthrop University *M*
Wofford College *B*
York Technical College *A*

South Dakota

Dakota Wesleyan University *A*
Kilian Community College *A*
Mount Marty College *B*
National American University
   Rapid City *A*
Northern State University *A*
Oglala Lakota College *A, B*
Sinte Gleska University *A*
Sisseton Wahpeton College *A*
South Dakota State University *B*
University of Sioux Falls *A*
University of South Dakota *A, B, M*

Tennessee

American Baptist College *B*
Aquinas College *A, B*
Argosy University: Nashville *B*
Austin Peay State University *B*
Belmont University *B*
Bryan College *A, B*
Carson-Newman College *B*
Chattanooga State Community
   College *A*
Christian Brothers University *B*
Cleveland State Community College *A*
Columbia State Community College *A*
Crichton College *B*
Cumberland University *B*
Dyersburg State Community
   College *A*
East Tennessee State University *B, M*
Freed-Hardeman University *B, T*
Jackson State Community College *A*
Lambuth University *B*
Martin Methodist College *A*
Middle Tennessee State University *B*
Motlow State Community College *A*
Nashville State Community College *C*
Northeast State Community
   College *A*
Pellissippi State Community
   College *A*
Southern Adventist University *A*
Southwest Tennessee Community
   College *A*
Tennessee State University *B*
Tennessee Temple University *A, B*
University of Memphis *B, M*
Vanderbilt University *M*
Volunteer State Community College *A*
Walters State Community College *A*

Texas

Abilene Christian University *M*
Alvin Community College *A*
Amarillo College *A*

Amberton University *B*
Argosy University: Dallas *B*
Blinn College *A*
Brazosport College *A*
Central Texas College *A*
Clarendon College *A*
Coastal Bend College *A*
College of Saint Thomas More *A, B*
College of the Mainland *A*
Concordia University Texas *B*
Dallas Baptist University *A, B, M*
Dallas Christian College *B*
Del Mar College *A*
East Texas Baptist University *B*
Eastfield College *A*
El Centro College *A*
El Paso Community College *A*
Frank Phillips College *A*
Galveston College *A*
Grayson County College *A*
Hill College *C, A*
Houston Baptist University *M*
Howard College *A*
Howard Payne University *B*
Huston-Tillotson University *B*
Jacksonville College *A*
Kilgore College *A*
Lamar State College at Orange *A*
Lamar University *B*
Laredo Community College *A*
Lee College *A*
Lon Morris College *A*
Lone Star College System *A*
Lubbock Christian University *B*
Mountain View College *A*
Navarro College *A*
North Lake College *A*
Northeast Texas Community
   College *A*
Northwest Vista College *A*
Odessa College *A*
Our Lady of the Lake University of San
   Antonio *B*
Palo Alto College *A*
Panola College *C, A*
Paris Junior College *A*
Ranger College *A*
Richland College *A*
St. Edward's University *B*
St. Mary's University *B*
St. Philip's College *A*
San Antonio College *C*
San Jacinto College *C*
Schreiner University *A, B*
South Plains College *A*
South Texas College *A*
Southern Methodist University *M*
Southwest Texas Junior College *A*
Stephen F. Austin State University *B*
Tarleton State University *B, M*
Temple College *A*
Texas A&M University
   Commerce *B*
   Galveston *B*
Texas Christian University *B, M*
Texas College *B*
Texas Tech University *B*
Trinity Valley Community College *A*
Tyler Junior College *A*
University of Houston
   Clear Lake *B, M*
   Downtown *B*
University of St. Thomas *B, M*
University of Texas
   Austin *B*
   Brownsville - Texas Southmost
     College *B*
   Dallas *B, M, D*
University of the Incarnate Word *A, B*
Vernon College *A*
Victoria College *A*
Weatherford College *A*
Western Texas College *A*
Wharton County Junior College *A*

Utah

Argosy University: Salt Lake City *B*
College of Eastern Utah *A*
Utah State University *A, B, M*
Weber State University *A, B*

Vermont

Bennington College *B*
Champlain College *B*
College of St. Joseph in Vermont *A, B*
Community College of Vermont *A*
Goddard College *B, M*
Green Mountain College *B*
Johnson State College *A, B*
Landmark College *A*
Lyndon State College *A, B*
Marlboro College *B*
Middlebury College *B*
Norwich University *B*
Southern Vermont College *A, B*
Sterling College *B*
University of Vermont *B*

Virginia

Argosy University: Washington D.C. *B*
Averett University *A, B*
Blue Ridge Community College *A*
Bluefield College *B*
Bridgewater College *B*
Central Virginia Community
   College *A*
Christendom College *A*
Dabney S. Lancaster Community
   College *A*
Danville Community College *A*
Eastern Mennonite University *B*
Eastern Shore Community College *A*
Ferrum College *B*
George Mason University *B*
Germanna Community College *A*
Hampton University *B*
Hollins University *M*
J. Sargeant Reynolds Community
   College *A*
James Madison University *B*
John Tyler Community College *A*
Liberty University *B, T*
Longwood University *B, T*
Lord Fairfax Community College *A*
Marymount University *B*
Mountain Empire Community
   College *A*
New River Community College *A*
Northern Virginia Community
   College *A*
Patrick Henry College *B*
Patrick Henry Community College *A*
Piedmont Virginia Community
   College *A*
Rappahannock Community College *A*
Richard Bland College *A*
Shenandoah University *B*
Southern Virginia University *B*
Southside Virginia Community
   College *A*
Southwest Virginia Community
   College *A*
Sweet Briar College *B*
Thomas Nelson Community
   College *A*
Tidewater Community College *A*
University of Mary Washington *B*
University of Richmond *M*
University of Virginia *B*
University of Virginia's College at
   Wise *B, T*
Virginia Highlands Community
   College *A*
Virginia Polytechnic Institute and
   State University *B*
Virginia State University *B*
Virginia University of Lynchburg *A*
Virginia Wesleyan College *B*

Virginia Western Community
   College *A*
Wytheville Community College *A*

Washington

Antioch University Seattle *B, M*
Argosy University: Seattle *B*
Bellevue College *A*
Big Bend Community College *A*
Centralia College *A*
City University of Seattle *A, B*
Clark College *A*
Everett Community College *A*
Evergreen State College *B*
Gonzaga University *B*
Grays Harbor College *A*
Green River Community College *A*
Highline Community College *A*
Lower Columbia College *A*
Olympic College *A*
Peninsula College *A*
Pierce College *A*
Seattle Pacific University *B*
Seattle University *B*
Shoreline Community College *C, A*
Skagit Valley College *A*
South Puget Sound Community
   College *A*
South Seattle Community College *A*
Spokane Community College *A*
Spokane Falls Community College *A*
University of Washington *B*
University of Washington Tacoma *B*
Walla Walla University *B*
Washington State University *B*
Wenatchee Valley College *A*
Whatcom Community College *A*
Whitworth University *B*
Yakima Valley Community College *A*

West Virginia

Alderson-Broaddus College *B*
Blue Ridge Community and Technical
   College *C, A*
Bluefield State College *B*
Concord University *B*
Eastern West Virginia Community and
   Technical College *A*
Fairmont State University *A*
Glenville State College *A*
Mountain State University *A*
Ohio Valley University *A, B*
Potomac State College of West
   Virginia University *A*
Salem International University *A, B*
Southern West Virginia Community
   and Technical College *A*
West Liberty University *B*
West Virginia Northern Community
   College *A*
West Virginia State Community and
   Technical College *A*
West Virginia State University *B*
West Virginia University *B, M*
West Virginia University at
   Parkersburg *A*
Wheeling Jesuit University *B*

Wisconsin

Alverno College *A, B*
Beloit College *B*
Cardinal Stritch University *A*
College of Menominee Nation *A*
Concordia University Wisconsin *B*
Lac Courte Oreilles Ojibwa
   Community College *A*
Lakeland College *A*
Marian University *B*
Milwaukee Area Technical College *A*
Moraine Park Technical College *C*
Nicolet Area Technical College *A*
Silver Lake College *A*
University of Wisconsin
   Baraboo/Sauk County *C, A*

Barron County *A*
Eau Claire *A, B*
Fond du Lac *A*
Fox Valley *A*
Green Bay *A, B*
Manitowoc *A*
Marathon County *A*
Marinette *A*
Marshfield/Wood County *A*
Milwaukee *M*
Oshkosh *B*
Parkside *B*
Platteville *A*
Richland *A*
Rock County *A*
Sheboygan *A*
Stevens Point *A, B*
Superior *A, B*
Washington County *A*
Waukesha *A*
Whitewater *A, B*
Viterbo University *B*

Wyoming
Casper College *A*
Eastern Wyoming College *A*
Northwest College *A*

Library assistance

Arizona
Mesa Community College *A*
Northland Pioneer College *C, A*

California
Cabrillo College *A*
Chabot College *A*
Citrus College *C, A*
City College of San Francisco *A*
College of the Canyons *C, A*
College of the Sequoias *C*
Cuesta College *C, A*
Foothill College *C, A*
Fresno City College *A*
Fullerton College *A*
Imperial Valley College *C*
Palomar College *A*
Pasadena City College *C, A*
Rio Hondo College *A*
Sacramento City College *C, A*
San Bernardino Valley College *C, A*
Santa Ana College *A*
Santiago Canyon College *A*
Sierra College *C, A*

Colorado
Pueblo Community College *C, A*

Connecticut
Capital Community College *A*
Three Rivers Community College *C, A*

Florida
Indian River State College *A*

Georgia
Georgia Perimeter College *A*

Illinois
College of DuPage *C, A*
College of Lake County *C, A*
Illinois Central College *A*
Wilbur Wright College *C, A*

Indiana
Ivy Tech Community College
Bloomington *A*
Central Indiana *A*
Columbus *A*
East Central *A*
Kokomo *A*
Lafayette *A*

North Central *A*
Northeast *A*
Northwest *A*
Richmond *A*
South Central *A*
Southeast *A*
Southwest *A*
Wabash Valley *A*

Kansas
Seward County Community College *A*

Kentucky
Bluegrass Community and Technical
College *C*

Maine
University of Maine
Augusta *A*

Michigan
Bay de Noc Community College *C*
Oakland Community College *C, A*

Minnesota
Minneapolis Community and
Technical College *C, A*
St. Catherine University *C*

Missouri
Three Rivers Community College *A*

Nebraska
Mid-Plains Community College Area *A*
Northeast Community College *A*

New Mexico
Clovis Community College *A*
Dona Ana Community College of New
Mexico State University *A*
Northern New Mexico College *C, A*

Ohio
Clark State Community College *A*

Oklahoma
Rose State College *C, A*
Tulsa Community College *A*

Oregon
Portland Community College *C*

Pennsylvania
Northampton Community College *C*
Westmoreland County Community
College *C*

Tennessee
Jackson State Community College *C*

Texas
Brazosport College *A*

Utah
Salt Lake Community College *C*

Washington
Highline Community College *A*
Lake Washington Technical College *C*

Library science

Alabama
University of Alabama *M*

Arizona
University of Arizona *M, D*

Arkansas
University of Central Arkansas *M*

California
Azusa Pacific University *M*
Los Angeles Harbor College *A*
San Jose State University *M*
University of California
Los Angeles *M, D*

Colorado
University of Colorado
Denver *M*
University of Denver *M*

Connecticut
Southern Connecticut State
University *B, M*

District of Columbia
Catholic University of America *M*

Florida
University of South Florida *M*

Georgia
Valdosta State University *M*

Hawaii
University of Hawaii
Manoa *M*

Illinois
Chicago State University *M*
Dominican University *M, D*
University of Illinois
Urbana-Champaign *M, D*

Indiana
Ball State University *B*
Indiana University
Bloomington *M, D*
Indiana University-Purdue University
Indianapolis *M*

Iowa
University of Iowa *M*
University of Northern Iowa *M*

Kansas
Allen County Community College *A*
Emporia State University *M, D*

Kentucky
University of Kentucky *M*
Western Kentucky University *M, T*

Louisiana
Louisiana State University and
Agricultural and Mechanical
College *M*

Maine
University of Maine
Augusta *B*

Maryland
University of Maryland
College Park *M, D*

Massachusetts
Simmons College *M, D*

Michigan
Grand Rapids Community College *A*
Wayne State University *M*

Minnesota
Minnesota State University
Mankato *M*

St. Catherine University *M*
Saint Cloud State University *B, M*

Mississippi
University of Southern
Mississippi *B, M*

Missouri
Harris-Stowe State University *T*
Lindenwood University *M*
Missouri Baptist University *T*
University of Central Missouri *M*
University of Missouri
Columbia *M*

Montana
University of Montana: Western *T*

Nebraska
Chadron State College *B*
University of Nebraska
Omaha *B*

New Jersey
Rowan University *M*
Rutgers, The State University of New
Jersey
New Brunswick/Piscataway
Campus *M, D*

New York
City University of New York
Queens College *M*
Long Island University
C. W. Post Campus *M*
Pratt Institute *M*
St. John's University *M*
State University of New York
Buffalo *M*
Syracuse University *M*

North Carolina
Appalachian State University *M, T*
East Carolina University *M*
North Carolina Central University *M*
University of North Carolina
Chapel Hill *M, D*
Greensboro *M*

Ohio
Kent State University *M*

Oklahoma
Northeastern State University *M, T*
Northwestern Oklahoma State
University *M*
University of Oklahoma *C, M*

Pennsylvania
Arcadia University *M*
Clarion University of
Pennsylvania *B, M, T*
Drexel University *M*
Kutztown University of
Pennsylvania *B, M, T*
Mansfield University of
Pennsylvania *M*
University of Pittsburgh *M, D*

Puerto Rico
Inter American University of Puerto
Rico
San German Campus *M*
Turabo University *M*
University of Puerto Rico
Rio Piedras *M*

Rhode Island
University of Rhode Island *M*

South Carolina

University of South Carolina *M, D*

Tennessee

Tennessee Technological
    University *M*
Trevecca Nazarene University *M*
Union University *T*
University of Tennessee
    Knoxville *M, D, T*

Texas

Our Lady of the Lake University of San
    Antonio *M*
Sam Houston State University *M*
Texas A&M University
    Commerce *B, M*
Texas Woman's University *M, D*
University of Houston
    Clear Lake *M*
University of North Texas *M*
University of Texas
    Austin *M, D*

Virginia

University of Virginia's College at
    Wise *T*

Washington

University of Washington *M*

West Virginia

Concord University *B, T*

Wisconsin

University of Wisconsin
    Madison *M, D*
    Milwaukee *M*

Licensed midwifery

Florida

Miami Dade College *A*

Pennsylvania

Philadelphia University *M*

Licensed practical nursing

Alabama

Alabama Southern Community
    College *C, A*
Bevill State Community College *C*
Bishop State Community College *C*
Calhoun Community College *C*
Chattahoochee Valley Community
    College *C*
Gadsden State Community College *C*
George C. Wallace State Community
    College
    Selma *C*
Jefferson State Community College *C*
Lurleen B. Wallace Community
    College *C*
Northeast Alabama Community
    College *C*
Northwest-Shoals Community
    College *C*
Shelton State Community College *C*
Snead State Community College *C*
Southern Union State Community
    College *C*
Wallace State Community College at
    Hanceville *C*

Alaska

University of Alaska
    Anchorage *C*

Arizona

Arizona Western College *C*
Central Arizona College *C*
Cochise College *C*
GateWay Community College *C*
Glendale Community College *C*
Mesa Community College *C*
Mohave Community College *C*
Northland Pioneer College *C*
Phoenix College *C*
Pima Community College *C*
Rio Salado College *C*
Scottsdale Community College *C*

Arkansas

Arkansas Northeastern College *C*
Arkansas State University
    Beebe *C*
    Mountain Home *C*
Arkansas State University: Newport *C*
Arkansas Tech University *C*
North Arkansas College *C*
Ouachita Technical College *C*
Ozarka College *C, A*
Phillips Community College of the
    University of Arkansas *C*
Pulaski Technical College *C*
Rich Mountain Community College *C*
South Arkansas Community College *C*
Southeast Arkansas College *C*
Southern Arkansas University Tech *C*
University of Arkansas
    Community College at Hope *C*
    Cossatot Community College of the
        C
    Fort Smith *C*
    Monticello *C*
University of Arkansas Community
    College at Morrilton *C*

California

Allan Hancock College *C, A*
Antelope Valley College *C*
Bakersfield College *A*
Butte College *A*
Cabrillo College *A*
Cerritos College *A*
Cerro Coso Community College *C, A*
Citrus College *C, A*
City College of San Francisco *C*
College of the Desert *C, A*
College of the Siskiyous *C, A*
Concorde Career College: North
    Hollywood *C*
Concorde Career College: San
    Bernardino *C*
Concorde Career College: San
    Diego *C*
Copper Mountain College *A*
El Camino College *A*
El Camino College: Compton
    Center *C, A*
Feather River College *C, A*
Gavilan College *C*
Glendale Community College *A*
Hartnell College *C*
Imperial Valley College *C, A*
Long Beach City College *C, A*
Los Angeles Trade and Technical
    College *A*
Los Medanos College *C*
Merced College *C, A*
Merritt College *A*
MiraCosta College *C, A*
Mission College *A*
Modesto Junior College *C*
Mount San Jacinto College *C*
Napa Valley College *C, A*
National University *A*
Palo Verde College *C*
Pasadena City College *C, A*
Porterville College *C, A*
Rio Hondo College *A*
Riverside Community College *C, A*

Sacramento City College *C, A*
San Joaquin Valley College *A*
Santa Barbara City College *C, A*
Santa Rosa Junior College *C, A*
Shasta College *C*
Southwestern College *C, A*
Western Career College
    San Leandro *C*
Western Career College: Antioch *A*
Western Career College:
    Sacramento *A*

Colorado

Arapahoe Community College *C*
Colorado Mountain College *C*
Community College of Denver *C*
Front Range Community College *C*
Lamar Community College *C*
Mesa State College *C*
Morgan Community College *C*
Northeastern Junior College *C*
Otero Junior College *C*
Pikes Peak Community College *C*

Delaware

Delaware Technical and Community
    College
    Owens *C*
    Terry *C*

Florida

Brevard Community College *C*
Central Florida Community
    College *C, A*
Daytona State College *C*
Florida National College *C*
Florida State College at Jacksonville *C*
Indian River State College *C*
Lake City Community College *C*
Palm Beach Community College *C*
Pasco-Hernando Community
    College *C*
Pensacola Junior College *C*
Rasmussen College: Pasco County *C*
Santa Fe College *C*
Seminole Community College *C*
South Florida Community College *C*

Georgia

Albany Technical College *C*
Athens Technical College *C*
Bainbridge College *C*
Central Georgia Technical College *C*
Chattahoochee Technical College *C*
Columbus Technical College *C*
Dalton State College *C*
Darton College *A*
DeKalb Technical College *C*
Gwinnett Technical College *C*
Middle Georgia College *A*
North Georgia Technical College *C*
Savannah Technical College *A*
Southeastern Technical College *C*
Southwest Georgia Technical
    College *C*
West Georgia Technical College *C*

Hawaii

University of Hawaii
    Hawaii Community College *C*
    Kapiolani Community College *C, A*
    Kauai Community College *C*

Idaho

Eastern Idaho Technical College *C*
Idaho State University *C*
Lewis-Clark State College *A*
North Idaho College *C*

Illinois

Black Hawk College *C*
Carl Sandburg College *C*

City Colleges of Chicago
    Kennedy-King College *C*
    Olive-Harvey College *C*
Danville Area Community College *C*
Elgin Community College *C*
Harper College *C*
Heartland Community College *C*
Highland Community College *C*
Illinois Eastern Community Colleges
    Olney Central College *C*
Illinois Valley Community College *C*
John A. Logan College *C*
John Wood Community College *C*
Joliet Junior College *C*
Kankakee Community College *C*
Kaskaskia College *C*
Kishwaukee College *C*
Lake Land College *C*
Lincoln Land Community College *C*
Morton College *C*
Parkland College *C*
Rend Lake College *C*
Richland Community College *G*
Sauk Valley Community College *C*
South Suburban College of Cook
    County *C*
Southeastern Illinois College *C*
Triton College *C*
Wilbur Wright College *A*

Indiana

Ivy Tech Community College
    Bloomington *C*
    Central Indiana *C*
    Columbus *C*
    East Central *C*
    Kokomo *C*
    Lafayette *C*
    North Central *C*
    Northeast *C*
    Northwest *C*
    Richmond *C*
    South Central *C*
    Southeast *C*
    Southwest *C*
    Wabash Valley *C*
Vincennes University *C*

Iowa

Clinton Community College *C*
Des Moines Area Community
    College *C*
Ellsworth Community College *C*
Hawkeye Community College *C*
Indian Hills Community College *C*
Iowa Central Community College *C*
Iowa Lakes Community College *C*
Iowa Western Community College *C*
Kaplan University
    Cedar Falls *A*
    Cedar Rapids *C*
    Des Moines *C*
    Mason City *C*
Kirkwood Community College *C*
Marshalltown Community College *C*
Muscatine Community College *C*
North Iowa Area Community
    College *C*
Northeast Iowa Community
    College *C*
Northwest Iowa Community
    College *C*
Scott Community College *C*
Southeastern Community College
    North Campus *C*
Southwestern Community College *C*
Western Iowa Tech Community
    College *C*

Kansas

Barton County Community College *C*
Butler Community College *C, A*
Cloud County Community College *C*
Colby Community College *C*

Dodge City Community College *C, A*
Fort Scott Community College *A*
Garden City Community College *C*
Highland Community College *C, A*
Hutchinson Community College *C*
Johnson County Community
College *C*
Kansas City Kansas Community
College *C*
Labette Community College *C*
Manhattan Area Technical College *C*
Neosho County Community
College *C, A*
Pratt Community College *A*
Seward County Community College *C*

Kentucky
Bluegrass Community and Technical
College *C*
Elizabethtown Community and
Technical College *C*
Hopkinsville Community College *C*
Madisonville Community College *C*
Maysville Community and Technical
College *C*
Owensboro Community and
Technical College *C*
Somerset Community College *C, A*
Spencerian College *C*

Louisiana
Delgado Community College *C*
Delta College of Arts & Technology *A*
Louisiana State University
Eunice *A*
Nunez Community College *C*
Our Lady of the Lake College *C, A*

Maine
Eastern Maine Community College *C*
Northern Maine Community
College *C*

Maryland
Allegany College of Maryland *C*
Anne Arundel Community College *C*
Baltimore City Community College *A*
Carroll Community College *C*
Cecil College *C*
College of Southern Maryland *C, A*
Community College of Baltimore
County *C*
Frederick Community College *C*
Hagerstown Community College *C*
Harford Community College *C*
Howard Community College *C, A*
Prince George's Community
College *C*
Wor-Wic Community College *C*

Massachusetts
Berkshire Community College *C*
Greenfield Community College *C*
Holyoke Community College *C*
Massachusetts Bay Community
College *C*
Mount Wachusett Community
College *C*
North Shore Community College *C*
Northern Essex Community
College *C*
Quincy College *C*
Quinsigamond Community College *C*
Roxbury Community College *C*

Michigan
Alpena Community College *C*
Baker College
of Auburn Hills *A*
Bay de Noc Community College *C*
Davenport University *C*
Delta College *C, A*
Glen Oaks Community College *C*

Gogebic Community College *C*
Grand Rapids Community
College *C, A*
Henry Ford Community College *A*
Jackson Community College *C*
Kalamazoo Valley Community
College *A*
Kellogg Community College *C*
Kirtland Community College *C*
Lake Michigan College *C*
Lake Superior State University *C*
Lansing Community College *A*
Mid Michigan Community College *C*
Montcalm Community College *C*
Mott Community College *C*
Muskegon Community College *A*
Northern Michigan University *C*
Northwestern Michigan College *C*
Oakland Community College *C*
St. Clair County Community
College *C*
Schoolcraft College *C, A*
Southwestern Michigan College *C*

Minnesota
Alexandria Technical College *C*
Anoka Technical College *A*
Central Lakes College *C*
Dakota County Technical College *C*
Fond du Lac Tribal and Community
College *C, A*
Hennepin Technical College *C, A*
Itasca Community College *C*
Lake Superior College *C*
Mesabi Range Community and
Technical College *C*
Minneapolis Community and
Technical College *C*
Minnesota State College - Southeast
Technical *C*
Minnesota State Community and
Technical College *C, A*
Minnesota West Community and
Technical College *C*
Northland Community & Technical
College *C*
Northwest Technical College *C, A*
Pine Technical College *C*
Rainy River Community College *C*
Rasmussen College
Eagan *A*
Mankato *A*
St. Cloud *A*
Rasmussen College: Brooklyn Park *A*
Rasmussen College: Lake
Elmo/Woodbury *A*
Ridgewater College *C*
Riverland Community College *C*
St. Cloud Technical College *C, A*
St. Paul College *C, A*
South Central College *C, A*

Mississippi
Copiah-Lincoln Community College *C*
East Central Community College *C*
East Mississippi Community
College *C*
Hinds Community College *A*
Meridian Community College *A*
Mississippi Gulf Coast Community
College *C*
Northeast Mississippi Community
College *A*
Pearl River Community College *C, A*
Southwest Mississippi Community
College *C*

Missouri
Bolivar Technical College *C*
Jefferson College *C*
Metropolitan Community College:
Penn Valley *C*
Mineral Area College *C*
North Central Missouri College *C*

Ozarks Technical Community
College *C, A*
St. Charles Community College *C*
Sanford-Brown College
St. Peters *C*
State Fair Community College *C*
Texas County Technical Institute *C*

Montana
Flathead Valley Community College *A*
Helena College of Technology of the
University of Montana *C*
Montana State University
Billings *A*
College of Technology: Great
Falls *A*
University of Montana *A*

Nebraska
Central Community College *C, A*
Clarkson College *C*
Grace University *A*
Kaplan University
Lincoln *C*
Kaplan University: Omaha *C*
Metropolitan Community College *C*
Mid-Plains Community College Area *C*
Northeast Community College *C*
Southeast Community College *C*
Western Nebraska Community
College *C*

Nevada
College of Southern Nevada *C*
Kaplan College: Las Vegas *C*
Western Nevada College *C*

New Hampshire
River Valley Community College *C*

New Jersey
Cumberland County College *C*
Hudson County Community
College *C*
Salem Community College *C*
Union County College *C*

New Mexico
Central New Mexico Community
College *C*
Eastern New Mexico University:
Roswell Campus *C*
New Mexico Junior College *C*
New Mexico State University
Carlsbad *C*
Northern New Mexico College *C*
Western New Mexico University *A*

New York
City University of New York
Bronx Community College *C*
Hostos Community College *C*
Medgar Evers College *C*
Maria College *C*
Mildred Elley *C*
Niagara County Community
College *C*
State University of New York
College of Technology at Canton *C*
College of Technology at Delhi *C*
Farmingdale *C*
Suffolk County Community College *C*
Touro College *C*
Westchester Community College *C*

North Carolina
Alamance Community College *C*
Asheville-Buncombe Technical
Community College *C*
Beaufort County Community
College *C*
Bladen Community College *C*

Brunswick Community College *C*
Cape Fear Community College *C*
Carteret Community College *C*
Central Carolina Community
College *A*
Cleveland Community College *C*
Coastal Carolina Community
College *C*
College of the Albemarle *C*
Davidson County Community
College *C*
Durham Technical Community
College *C*
Edgecombe Community College *C*
Fayetteville Technical Community
College *C*
Forsyth Technical Community
College *A*
Isothermal Community College *C*
James Sprunt Community College *C*
Lenoir Community College *C*
Mayland Community College *C*
McDowell Technical Community
College *C*
Montgomery Community College *C*
Nash Community College *A*
Rockingham Community College *C*
Sampson Community College *A*
Sandhills Community College *C*
South Piedmont Community
College *C*
Southeastern Community College *C*
Southwestern Community College *C*
Surry Community College *C*
Vance-Granville Community
College *C*
Wayne Community College *A*
Wilson Community College *C*

North Dakota
Bismarck State College *A*
Dakota College at Bottineau *C*
Dickinson State University *A*
Lake Region State College *C, A*
North Dakota State College of
Science *A*
Rasmussen College: Fargo *A*
Sitting Bull College *A*
United Tribes Technical College *C, A*
Williston State College *C*

Ohio
Belmont Technical College *C*
Central Ohio Technical College *C*
Clark State Community College *C*
Eastern Gateway Community
College *C*
Hocking College *C*
Hondros College *C*
James A. Rhodes State College *C*
North Central State College *C*
Northwest State Community
College *C*
Owens Community College
Toledo *C*
Southern State Community College *C*
University of Akron *B*
Washington State Community
College *C*

Oklahoma
Platt College
Tulsa *A*
Platt College: Oklahoma City
Central *A*

Oregon
Blue Mountain Community College *C*
Central Oregon Community
College *C*
Chemeketa Community College *C*
Clackamas Community College *C*
Clatsop Community College *C*

Linn-Benton Community College C
Portland Community College C
Rogue Community College C
Southwestern Oregon Community
  College C, A
Treasure Valley Community College C
Umpqua Community College C

Pennsylvania

Community College of Allegheny
  County C
Community College of Beaver
  County C
Harrisburg Area Community
  College C
Lehigh Carbon Community College C
Mercyhurst College C
Northampton Community College C
Pennsylvania College of
  Technology C
Reading Area Community
  College C, A
York College of Pennsylvania B

Puerto Rico

Inter American University of Puerto
  Rico
  Bayamon Campus B
  Metropolitan Campus A
  San German Campus A, B
Turabo University C
Universidad Metropolitana C

South Carolina

Aiken Technical College C
Central Carolina Technical College C
Denmark Technical College A
Florence-Darlington Technical
  College C
Greenville Technical College C
Horry-Georgetown Technical
  College C
Midlands Technical College C
Northeastern Technical College C, A
Orangeburg-Calhoun Technical
  College C
Spartanburg Community College C
Tri-County Technical College C
Trident Technical College C
York Technical College C

South Dakota

Lake Area Technical Institute C
Southeast Technical Institute C
Western Dakota Technical Institute C

Tennessee

Chattanooga State Community
  College C
Tennessee State University A

Texas

Alvin Community College C
Amarillo College C
Angelina College C
Austin Community College C
Brazosport College C
Central Texas College C
Clarendon College C
Coastal Bend College C
College of the Mainland A
Del Mar College C
El Centro College C
El Paso Community College C
Frank Phillips College C
Galveston College C
Grayson County College C
Hill College C, A
Houston Community College
  System C
Howard College C
Kilgore College C
Lamar State College at Orange C

Lamar State College at Port Arthur C
Lone Star College System C
McLennan Community College C
Midland College C
Navarro College C, A
Northeast Texas Community
  College C
Odessa College C
Panola College C
Paris Junior College A
Ranger College C
St. Philip's College C
San Jacinto College C
Schreiner University C
South Plains College C
South Texas College C
Southwest Texas Junior College A
Sul Ross State University C
Temple College C
Texarkana College C
Texas State Technical College
  West Texas C, A
Trinity Valley Community College C
University of Texas
  Brownsville - Texas Southmost
    College C
Vernon College C
Victoria College C
Weatherford College C, A
Western Texas College C
Wharton County Junior College C

Utah

College of Eastern Utah C
Snow College C, A
Southern Utah University A
Utah Career College A
Weber State University C

Vermont

Vermont Technical College C

Virginia

Centura College: Norfolk C
Centura College: Richmond C
Danville Community College C
ECPI College of Technology: Virginia
  Beach C, A
Germanna Community College C
J. Sargeant Reynolds Community
  College C
Lord Fairfax Community College C
Mountain Empire Community
  College C
New River Community College C
Rappahannock Community College C
Southside Virginia Community
  College C
Southwest Virginia Community
  College C
Thomas Nelson Community
  College A
Virginia Western Community
  College C
Wytheville Community College C

Washington

Bates Technical College C, A
Bellingham Technical College C
Big Bend Community College C
Centralia College C
Clover Park Technical College C, A
Everett Community College C
Grays Harbor College C
Green River Community College C
Lake Washington Technical
  College C, A
Lower Columbia College A
North Seattle Community
  College C, A
Olympic College C, A
Renton Technical College C, A
Skagit Valley College C, A

South Seattle Community
  College C, A
Spokane Community College C
Wenatchee Valley College C
Yakima Valley Community
  College C, A

West Virginia

New River Community and Technical
  College C

Wisconsin

Chippewa Valley Technical College C
Fox Valley Technical College C
Gateway Technical College C
Lakeshore Technical College C
Milwaukee Area Technical College C
Moraine Park Technical College C
Northeast Wisconsin Technical
  College C
Southwest Wisconsin Technical
  College C
Waukesha County Technical
  College C
Western Technical College C
Wisconsin Indianhead Technical
  College C

Wyoming

Laramie County Community
  College C
Sheridan College C
Western Wyoming Community
  College C, A

Lineworker

California

Santa Rosa Junior College C

Colorado

Mesa State College C

Florida

South Florida Community College C

Georgia

North Georgia Technical College C
Southeastern Technical College C

Indiana

Ivy Tech Community College
  Lafayette C, A

Iowa

Northwest Iowa Community
  College C, A

Kentucky

Hopkinsville Community College C

Maine

Kennebec Valley Community
  College C

Maryland

College of Southern Maryland A

Michigan

Alpena Community College C
Northern Michigan University C

Minnesota

Dakota County Technical College C, A
Minnesota State Community and
  Technical College C
Minnesota West Community and
  Technical College A

Mississippi

Mississippi Gulf Coast Community
  College A

Missouri

Linn State Technical College A

Nebraska

Northeast Community College A
Western Nebraska Community
  College C, A

New Jersey

Raritan Valley Community College A

New Mexico

Dona Ana Community College of New
  Mexico State University A

North Carolina

Nash Community College A

North Dakota

Bismarck State College C, A

Pennsylvania

Harrisburg Area Community
  College A
Pennsylvania College of
  Technology A
Pennsylvania Highlands Community
  College A

South Carolina

York Technical College C

South Dakota

Mitchell Technical Institute C, A

Texas

Lamar Institute of Technology C

Utah

Utah Valley University C, A

Washington

Clover Park Technical College C

Wisconsin

Milwaukee Area Technical College C
Wisconsin Indianhead Technical
  College C

Linguistics

Alaska

University of Alaska
  Fairbanks B

Arizona

Arizona State University D
Northern Arizona University M, D
Prescott College M
University of Arizona B, M, D

Arkansas

Arkansas State University B

California

California State University
  Chico B
  Fresno B, M
  Fullerton B, M
  Monterey Bay B
  Northridge B, M
Foothill College A
Pitzer College B
Pomona College B
San Diego State University B, M
San Francisco State University M

San Jose State University *B, M*
Scripps College *B*
Stanford University *B, M, D*
University of California
 Berkeley *B, M, D*
 Davis *B, M, D*
 Los Angeles *B, M, D*
 Riverside *B*
 San Diego *B, M, D*
 Santa Barbara *B, M, D*
 Santa Cruz *B, M, D*
University of Southern
 California *B, M, D*

Colorado

University of Colorado
 Boulder *B, M, D*

Connecticut

University of Connecticut *B, M, D*
Yale University *B, M, D*

Delaware

University of Delaware *M, D*

District of Columbia

Gallaudet University *M, D*
Georgetown University *B, M, D*

Florida

Florida Atlantic University *B, M*
Florida International University *M*
University of Florida *B, M*
University of South Florida *M*

Georgia

Emory University *B*
Georgia State University *B, M, D*
University of Georgia *B, M, D*

Hawaii

University of Hawaii
 Hilo *B*
 Manoa *M, D*

Illinois

Moody Bible Institute *B*
Northeastern Illinois University *B, M*
Northwestern University *B, M, D*
Southern Illinois University
 Carbondale *B, M*
University of Chicago *B, D*
University of Illinois
 Chicago *M*
 Urbana-Champaign *B, M, D*

Indiana

Ball State University *M*
Indiana University
 Bloomington *B, M, D*
Purdue University *M, D*

Iowa

Central College *B*
Iowa State University *B*
University of Iowa *B, M, D*

Kansas

University of Kansas *B, M, D*

Kentucky

Bluegrass Community and Technical
 College *A*
University of Kentucky *B*

Louisiana

Tulane University *B, M, D*

Maine

University of Southern Maine *B*

Maryland

University of Maryland
 Baltimore County *B, M, D*
 College Park *B, M, D*

Massachusetts

Bard College at Simon's Rock *B*
Boston College *B, M*
Boston University *B*
Brandeis University *B, M*
Hampshire College *B*
Harvard College *B, M, D*
Massachusetts Institute of
 Technology *B, M, D*
Northeastern University *B*
University of Massachusetts
 Amherst *B, D*
 Boston *M*
Wellesley College *B*

Michigan

Eastern Michigan University *B, M*
Michigan State University *B, M, D*
Oakland University *B, M*
University of Michigan *B, M, D*
Wayne State University *B, M*

Minnesota

Crown College *B*
Macalester College *B*
Saint Cloud State University *B*
University of Minnesota
 Twin Cities *B, M, D*

Mississippi

University of Mississippi *B*

Missouri

Truman State University *B*
University of Central Missouri *M*
University of Missouri
 Columbia *B*
Washington University in St. Louis *B*

Montana

University of Montana *M*

New Hampshire

Dartmouth College *B*
University of New Hampshire *B*

New Jersey

Montclair State University *B, M*
Rutgers, The State University of New
 Jersey
 New Brunswick/Piscataway
 Campus *B, M, D*

New Mexico

University of New Mexico *B, M, D*

New York

Barnard College *B*
City University of New York
 Brooklyn College *B*
 Lehman College *B*
 Queens College *B, M*
Columbia University *B*
Cornell University *B, M, D*
Hofstra University *B*
New York University *B, M, D*
State University of New York
 Albany *B*
 Binghamton *B*
 Buffalo *B, M, D*
 Oswego *B*
 Stony Brook *B, M, D*
Syracuse University *B, M*
University of Rochester *B, M, D*

North Carolina

Mid-Atlantic Christian University *B*
University of North Carolina
 Chapel Hill *B, M, D*

North Dakota

University of North Dakota *M*

Ohio

Cleveland State University *B*
Miami University
 Oxford Campus *B*
Ohio State University
 Columbus Campus *B, M, D*
Ohio University *B, M*
University of Cincinnati *B*
University of Toledo *B*
Wright State University *B*

Oklahoma

Cameron University *B*
University of Oklahoma *B*

Oregon

Portland State University *B, M*
Reed College *B*
University of Oregon *B, M, D*

Pennsylvania

Carnegie Mellon University *B*
Penn State
 University Park *D*
Swarthmore College *B*
Temple University *B, M*
University of Pennsylvania *B, M, D*
University of Pittsburgh *B, M, D*

Puerto Rico

University of Puerto Rico
 Aguadilla *A*
 Rio Piedras *M*

Rhode Island

Brown University *B*

South Carolina

University of South Carolina *M, D*

Texas

Baylor University *B*
Navarro College *A*
Rice University *B, M, D*
Texas Tech University *M*
University of Houston *M*
University of North Texas *M*
University of Texas
 Arlington *M, D*
 Austin *B, M, D*
 El Paso *B, M*

Utah

Brigham Young University *B, M*
University of Utah *B, M, D*

Vermont

Marlboro College *B*

Virginia

College of William and Mary *B*
George Mason University *D*
Old Dominion University *M*
University of Virginia *M*

Washington

Evergreen State College *B*
Highline Community College *A*
University of Washington *B, M, D*
Washington State University *B*
Western Washington University *B*

Wisconsin

Lawrence University *B*
University of Wisconsin
 Madison *B, M, D*
 Milwaukee *B*

Livestock management

Kansas

Colby Community College *C*
Kansas State University *C*

Michigan

Michigan State University *C*

Nebraska

Northeast Community College *A*

New Mexico

Navajo Technical College *C*

New York

State University of New York
 College of Agriculture and
 Technology at Morrisville *A, B*

Texas

Tarleton State University *B*

Locksmithing

Alabama

Jefferson Davis Community College *C*

California

San Joaquin Delta College *C, A*

Kentucky

Elizabethtown Community and
 Technical College *C, A*

Logic

California

University of California
 Berkeley *D*

Pennsylvania

Carnegie Mellon University *B, M, D*
University of Pennsylvania *B*

Logistics/materials management

Alabama

Auburn University *B*

Alaska

University of Alaska
 Anchorage *B*

Arizona

Central Arizona College *C*
Cochise College *C, A*
University of Phoenix *B*

Arkansas

Northwest Arkansas Community
 College *C*
Southern Arkansas University Tech *C*
University of Arkansas *B*

California

California Maritime Academy *B*
California State University
 Dominguez Hills *B, M*
 East Bay *M*
 Fresno *B*
Cerritos College *A*

Chabot College *A*
College of San Mateo *C, A*
Golden Gate University *M*
San Jose State University *M*
University of San Diego *M*

Colorado

Colorado Technical University *C, B, M*
United States Air Force Academy *B*

Connecticut

University of New Haven *C*

Delaware

Wilmington University *M*

Florida

Florida Institute of Technology *M*

Georgia

Albany State University *B*
Albany Technical College *C*
Athens Technical College *C*
Central Georgia Technical
   College *C, A*
Georgia College and State
   University *M*
Georgia Institute of Technology *M*
Georgia Military College *A*
Georgia Southern University *B, D*
Middle Georgia College *B*
Savannah Technical College *C*
West Georgia Technical College *C*

Illinois

Elmhurst College *B, M*
Heartland Community College *C*
Kishwaukee College *C*
Prairie State College *C*
Rock Valley College *C, A*
Sauk Valley Community College *C*
University of Illinois
   Urbana-Champaign *B*
Waubonsee Community College *C, A*
Western Illinois University *B*

Indiana

Ivy Tech Community College
   Central Indiana *A*
Vincennes University *A*

Iowa

Iowa Central Community College *A*
Iowa State University *B*
Muscatine Community College *C, A*
Scott Community College *C, A*

Kansas

University of Kansas *B*

Kentucky

University of Louisville *C*

Louisiana

Southeastern Louisiana University *B*

Maine

Maine Maritime Academy *B, M*

Maryland

University of Maryland
   College Park *B*

Massachusetts

Middlesex Community College *C*
Northeastern University *B*
Northern Essex Community
   College *C, A*

Michigan

Central Michigan University *B*

Eastern Michigan University *B, M*
Henry Ford Community College *C*
Michigan State University *B, M, D*
University of Michigan *M*
Wayne County Community College *C*

Minnesota

St. Paul College *C, A*
University of Minnesota
   Twin Cities *B*

Missouri

Fontbonne University *M*
Missouri State University *B*
Park University *A, B*
University of Missouri
   St. Louis *B, M, D*

Nevada

University of Nevada
   Reno *B*

New Jersey

Bloomfield College *C*

New York

Clarkson University *B*
Globe Institute of Technology *C*
Herkimer County Community
   College *A*
Niagara University *B*
State University of New York
   Binghamton *B*

North Carolina

Forsyth Technical Community
   College *C, A*

Ohio

Bowling Green State University *B*
Clark State Community College *A*
Columbus State Community
   College *C, A*
Edison State Community College *C, A*
John Carroll University *B*
Ohio State University
   Columbus Campus *B*
Stark State College of Technology *A*
Tiffin University *B*
University of Akron *C, A*
University of Toledo *A, B, M*
Wright State University *M*

Oklahoma

Northeastern State University *B*

Oregon

Portland State University *B*

Pennsylvania

Community College of
   Philadelphia *C, A*
Duquesne University *B*
Johnson College *A*
Lehigh University *B, M*
Luzerne County Community
   College *C*
Shippensburg University of
   Pennsylvania *B*
University of Pittsburgh *C*

Puerto Rico

Inter American University of Puerto
   Rico
   Bayamon Campus *B*
Turabo University *M*
University of Puerto Rico
   Bayamon University College *B*

South Carolina

Trident Technical College *C, A*

York Technical College *C, A*

Tennessee

University of Memphis *B*
University of Tennessee
   Knoxville *B, M, D*
Volunteer State Community College *C*

Texas

Baylor University *B*
Houston Community College
   System *C, A*
North Lake College *C*
Palo Alto College *C, A*
South Texas College *C, A*
Tarrant County College *C*
Texas A&M International
   University *M*
Texas A&M University *M*
University of Dallas *M*
University of North Texas *B*
University of Texas
   Arlington *M*
   Austin *B*
   Dallas *M*

Utah

Brigham Young University *B*
Weber State University *B*

Virginia

New River Community College *A*

Washington

Shoreline Community College *C, A*

Wisconsin

Chippewa Valley Technical College *A*
Lac Courte Oreilles Ojibwa
   Community College *A*
Lakeshore Technical College *A*
Milwaukee Area Technical College *A*
Northeast Wisconsin Technical
   College *A*

Machine shop technology

Arizona

Pima Community College *C, A*

Arkansas

University of Arkansas
   Fort Smith *C*

California

Long Beach City College *C, A*
Los Angeles Pierce College *C*
Los Angeles Valley College *C*

Colorado

Community College of Denver *C*
Front Range Community College *C, A*
Pikes Peak Community College *C, A*
Pueblo Community College *C, A*
Red Rocks Community College *C, A*

Georgia

Athens Technical College *C*
Central Georgia Technical College *C*
Savannah Technical College *A*
Southwest Georgia Technical
   College *C*

Illinois

Black Hawk College *C*
College of Lake County *C, A*
Illinois Eastern Community Colleges
   Wabash Valley College *C, A*
John A. Logan College *A*
McHenry County College *C*

Oakton Community College *C, A*
Triton College *C*

Indiana

Ivy Tech Community College
   Central Indiana *A*

Iowa

North Iowa Area Community
   College *C*
Northwest Iowa Community
   College *C*

Kansas

Cowley County Community
   College *C, A*

Kentucky

Bluegrass Community and Technical
   College *C, A*
Elizabethtown Community and
   Technical College *C, A*
Hopkinsville Community College *C*
Madisonville Community College *C, A*
Somerset Community College *C, A*
West Kentucky Community and
   Technical College *C*

Louisiana

Delgado Community College *A*

Maryland

Community College of Baltimore
   County *C, A*

Michigan

Grand Rapids Community
   College *C, A*
Montcalm Community College *C*
Northwestern Michigan College *C*

Minnesota

Central Lakes College *C*
Hennepin Technical College *C, A*
Lake Superior College *C*
Minnesota State College - Southeast
   Technical *C*
Pine Technical College *C*
St. Paul College *C*

Missouri

Ranken Technical College *A*

New Mexico

Central New Mexico Community
   College *C*
San Juan College *C, A*

New York

Adirondack Community College *C*
Mohawk Valley Community College *C*

North Carolina

Cape Fear Community College *C, A*
Catawba Valley Community College *C*
Central Piedmont Community
   College *C, A*
College of the Albemarle *A*
Fayetteville Technical Community
   College *C, A*
Forsyth Technical Community
   College *C*
Guilford Technical Community
   College *C, A*
Isothermal Community College *C, A*
Lenoir Community College *C, A*
Mitchell Community College *C, A*
Pitt Community College *C, A*
Rockingham Community College *C*
Wayne Community College *A*

Oregon

Clackamas Community College *A*
Portland Community College *A*

Pennsylvania

Butler County Community
College *C, A*
Community College of Allegheny
County *C*
Pennsylvania College of
Technology *C*
Thaddeus Stevens College of
Technology *A*
Westmoreland County Community
College *C, A*

South Dakota

Southeast Technical Institute *A*

Texas

Houston Community College
System *C, A*
St. Philip's College *C*
University of Texas
Brownsville - Texas Southmost
College *C*

Utah

Salt Lake Community College *C*

Virginia

New River Community College *C, A*

Washington

Bellingham Technical College *C*
Renton Technical College *C, A*

West Virginia

West Virginia University at
Parkersburg *C, A*

Wisconsin

Blackhawk Technical College *C*
Lakeshore Technical College *C*
Milwaukee Area Technical College *C*
Waukesha County Technical
College *C*
Western Technical College *A*
Wisconsin Indianhead Technical
College *C*

Wyoming

Eastern Wyoming College *C*

Machine tool technology

Alabama

Calhoun Community College *C, A*
Northeast Alabama Community
College *C, A*
Northwest-Shoals Community
College *C*

Arkansas

Arkansas State University
Beebe *C*
Pulaski Technical College *C*
Rich Mountain Community
College *C, A*

California

Long Beach City College *C, A*
Los Angeles Pierce College *C*
Orange Coast College *C, A*
San Jose City College *C, A*

Colorado

Mesa State College *C, A*

Connecticut

Asnuntuck Community College *C, A*

Georgia

Middle Georgia Technical College *C*
North Georgia Technical College *C*
West Georgia Technical College *C*

Idaho

Idaho State University *C, A*

Illinois

Danville Area Community College *C*
Elgin Community College *C, A*
Heartland Community College *C*
John A. Logan College *C*
Kankakee Community College *C*
Sauk Valley Community College *C*
Spoon River College *C*

Indiana

Ivy Tech Community College
Bloomington *C, A*
Central Indiana *C, A*
Columbus *C, A*
East Central *C, A*
Kokomo *C, A*
Lafayette *C, A*
North Central *C, A*
Northeast *C, A*
Northwest *C, A*
Richmond *C, A*
South Central *C, A*
Southwest *C, A*
Wabash Valley *C, A*

Iowa

Des Moines Area Community
College *A*
Hawkeye Community College *C, A*
Indian Hills Community College *A*
Iowa Central Community College *A*
North Iowa Area Community
College *A*
Northeast Iowa Community
College *C*
Scott Community College *C, A*
Southeastern Community College
North Campus *C, A*

Kansas

Hutchinson Community College *C, A*
Kansas City Kansas Community
College *C*

Kentucky

Owensboro Community and
Technical College *C, A*

Maine

Central Maine Community
College *C, A*
Eastern Maine Community
College *C, A*
Kennebec Valley Community
College *C, A*
Southern Maine Community
College *C, A*

Michigan

Delta College *A*
Glen Oaks Community College *C*
Henry Ford Community College *C*
Kirtland Community College *C, A*
Lake Michigan College *C, A*
Northern Michigan University *A*
Oakland Community College *C, A*
St. Clair County Community
College *C, A*
Southwestern Michigan College *C, A*
Wayne County Community
College *C, A*

Minnesota

Alexandria Technical College *C, A*
Central Lakes College *C*
Dunwoody College of Technology *A*
Hennepin Technical College *C, A*
Lake Superior College *C, A*
Minneapolis Community and
Technical College *C*
Minnesota State College - Southeast
Technical *C*
Minnesota West Community and
Technical College *A*
Pine Technical College *C, A*
Ridgewater College *C, A*
St. Cloud Technical College *C, A*
St. Paul College *C*
South Central College *C, A*

Mississippi

Copiah-Lincoln Community
College *C, A*

Missouri

East Central College *C, A*
Jefferson College *C, A*
Linn State Technical College *A*
Mineral Area College *C, A*
Ozarks Technical Community
College *C, A*
State Fair Community College *C, A*

Montana

Helena College of Technology of the
University of Montana *C, A*

Nebraska

Central Community College *C, A*
Southeast Community College *A*

Nevada

Western Nevada College *C, A*

New York

Corning Community College *C, A*
State University of New York
College of Technology at
Alfred *C, A*

North Carolina

Beaufort County Community
College *C*
Rowan-Cabarrus Community
College *C*
Tri-County Community College *C*

North Dakota

North Dakota State College of
Science *C, A*

Ohio

Cincinnati State Technical and
Community College *A*
Northwest State Community
College *C, A*
Terra State Community College *C, A*

Oregon

Clackamas Community College *C*
Linn-Benton Community College *C*
Mt. Hood Community College *C, A*
Portland Community College *C, A*

Pennsylvania

Butler County Community College *C*
Community College of Beaver
County *A*
Johnson College *A*
Luzerne County Community
College *C*
Pennsylvania College of
Technology *C*

Thaddeus Stevens College of
Technology *A*
Westmoreland County Community
College *C, A*
Williamson Free School of Mechanical
Trades *A*

South Carolina

Aiken Technical College *C, A*
Greenville Technical College *C, A*
Horry-Georgetown Technical
College *A*
Midlands Technical College *C*
Spartanburg Community College *C, A*
Williamsburg Technical College *C, A*
York Technical College *C, A*

South Dakota

Southeast Technical Institute *A*

Texas

Angelina College *C, A*
Del Mar College *C, A*
Kilgore College *C, A*
Lamar Institute of Technology *C, A*
Odessa College *C, A*
St. Philip's College *A*
Texas State Technical College
Harlingen *C*
West Texas *C, A*

Utah

College of Eastern Utah *C*
Salt Lake Community College *A*
Snow College *C*

Virginia

Danville Community College *C*

Washington

Bates Technical College *C, A*
Bellingham Technical College *C, A*
Clark College *C, A*
Clover Park Technical College *C, A*
Shoreline Community College *C, A*

West Virginia

New River Community and Technical
College *C*

Wisconsin

Chippewa Valley Technical College *A*
Lakeshore Technical College *C*
Mid-State Technical College *C*
Milwaukee Area Technical College *C*
Northcentral Technical College *A*
Southwest Wisconsin Technical
College *C*
Western Technical College *C*
Wisconsin Indianhead Technical
College *C*

Wyoming

Casper College *C, A*
Sheridan College *C, A*

Make-up artist

North Carolina

Carteret Community College *C*
Martin Community College *C*

Tennessee

West Tennessee Business College *C*

Management information systems

Alabama

Auburn University *M*
Auburn University at Montgomery *B*

Central Alabama Community
   College *C, A*
Enterprise-Ozark Community
   College *A*
Faulkner University *B*
Troy University *B*
University of Alabama *B*
University of Alabama
   Birmingham *B*
   Huntsville *B, M*
University of North Alabama *B*
University of West Alabama *B*

Alaska
University of Alaska
   Anchorage *B*
   Southeast *C, A*

Arizona
Arizona State University *B*
DeVry University
   Phoenix *M*
Northcentral University *M, D*
Northern Arizona University *C, B, M*
Phoenix College *C, A*
Scottsdale Community College *C, A*
University of Arizona *B, M*
University of Phoenix *B, M, D*
Western International University *B, M*

Arkansas
Arkansas Northeastern College *A*
Arkansas State University *A, M*
Arkansas State University
   Beebe *C, A*
   Mountain Home *C*
Arkansas State University:
   Newport *C, A*
Arkansas Tech University *C*
Black River Technical College *C, A*
East Arkansas Community
   College *C, A*
Henderson State University *B*
Pulaski Technical College *C, A*
Rich Mountain Community
   College *C, A*
Southeast Arkansas College *C, A*
University of Arkansas
   Cossatot Community College of the
     A
   Little Rock *B, M*
   Monticello *B*
University of Central Arkansas *B*

California
Allan Hancock College *A*
Alliant International University *B*
American River College *A*
Azusa Pacific University *B*
Bakersfield College *A*
Biola University *B*
Butte College *C, A*
California State University
   Chico *C, B*
   East Bay *B, M*
   Fresno *B*
   Northridge *B*
   Sacramento *M*
   San Bernardino *B, M*
Canada College *C, A*
Chabot College *A*
Chaffey College *C*
Citrus College *A*
City College of San Francisco *A*
College of San Mateo *C, A*
College of the Sequoias *C, A*
College of the Siskiyous *C, A*
Columbia College *C, A*
Cypress College *C, A*
DeVry University
   Fremont *M*
   Long Beach *M*

Pomona *M*
   Sherman Oaks *M*
El Camino College: Compton
   Center *A*
Evergreen Valley College *A*
Folsom Lake College *C*
Fresno Pacific University *B*
Fullerton College *A*
Gavilan College *C*
Heald College
   Fresno *C, A*
Hope International University *C*
Laney College *C, A*
Lassen Community College *A*
Lincoln University *B, M*
Los Angeles City College *C, A*
Los Angeles Harbor College *C, A*
Los Angeles Southwest College *A*
Los Angeles Valley College *C, A*
The Master's College *B*
Mission College *A*
Modesto Junior College *A*
Moorpark College *A*
Orange Coast College *C, A*
Pacific States University *B, M*
Pacific Union College *B*
Pasadena City College *A*
Point Loma Nazarene University *B*
Porterville College *C*
Sacramento City College *C, A*
San Bernardino Valley College *C*
San Diego City College *C, A*
San Joaquin Delta College *A*
Santa Clara University *B*
Shasta College *A*
Simpson University *B*
Skyline College *C, A*
Taft College *C, A*
University of La Verne *M*
University of Redlands *B*
West Hills College: Coalinga *C, A*

Colorado
Adams State College *B*
Aims Community College *A*
American Sentinel University *B*
Arapahoe Community College *A*
Colorado Christian University *B*
Colorado Mountain College *A*
Colorado Northwestern Community
   College *A*
Colorado State University *B*
Colorado Technical University *B, M*
Community College of Aurora *C, A*
Community College of Denver *C, A*
DeVry University
   Westminster *M*
Front Range Community College *C, A*
Jones International University *M*
Mesa State College *B*
Northeastern Junior College *C, A*
Pikes Peak Community College *A*
Red Rocks Community College *C, A*
University of Colorado
   Boulder *B*
University of Denver *B*
Western State College of Colorado *B*
Westwood College: Denver North *B*

Connecticut
Albertus Magnus College *C, A, B*
Central Connecticut State
   University *B*
Eastern Connecticut State
   University *B*
Fairfield University *B*
Manchester Community College *C, A*
Norwalk Community College *A*
Quinnipiac University *B, M*
University of Bridgeport *B, M*
University of Connecticut *B*
University of Hartford *B*
Western Connecticut State
   University *B*

Delaware
Delaware Technical and Community
   College
   Owens *A*
   Stanton/Wilmington *A*
   Terry *A*
Goldey-Beacom College *B*
University of Delaware *B*
Wilmington University *M*

District of Columbia
American University *B, M*
Gallaudet University *B*
George Washington University *B, M*
Howard University *B*
University of the District of
   Columbia *A*

Florida
Brevard Community College *A*
Daytona State College *C, A*
DeVry University
   Miramar *M*
   Orlando *M*
Florida Atlantic University *B, M*
Florida Gulf Coast University *B, M*
Florida Institute of Technology *B, M*
Florida International University *B, M*
Florida Memorial University *B*
Florida Southern College *B*
Florida State College at Jacksonville *A*
Florida State University *B, M, D*
Hillsborough Community
   College *C, A*
Indian River State College *A*
Northwest Florida State College *C, A*
Northwood University
   Florida *B*
Nova Southeastern University *M*
Palm Beach Community College *A*
Pensacola Junior College *A*
Rasmussen College: Fort Myers *A*
Schiller International University *B, M*
Southeastern University *B*
Stetson University *B*
Tallahassee Community College *A*
University of South Florida *B, M*
University of West Florida *B*
Valencia Community College *C, A*

Georgia
Albany State University *B*
Ashworth College *T*
Augusta State University *B*
Bainbridge College *C, A*
Columbus State University *B*
Dalton State College *B*
DeVry University
   Alpharetta *M*
   Decatur *M*
Emory University *B*
Georgia College and State
   University *M*
Georgia Southern University *B*
Life University *A, B*
Paine College *B*
University of Georgia *B*
University of West Georgia *B*
West Georgia Technical College *C*

Hawaii
Hawaii Pacific University *B*
University of Hawaii
   Manoa *B*

Idaho
Boise State University *B, M*
University of Idaho *B*

Illinois
Augustana College *B*
Aurora University *B*
Benedictine University *M*

Bradley University *B*
Chicago State University *B*
City Colleges of Chicago
   Olive-Harvey College *C, A*
DePaul University *B, M*
DeVry University
   Tinley Park *B, M*
DeVry University: Online *M*
Dominican University *M*
Eastern Illinois University *B*
Eureka College *B*
Governors State University *B, M*
Greenville College *B*
Illinois College *B*
Joliet Junior College *C*
Judson University *B*
Kishwaukee College *A*
Lewis University *B*
Loyola University Chicago *C, B, M*
MacCormac College *C, A*
MacMurray College *B*
Millikin University *B*
Moraine Valley Community College *A*
North Central College *B, M*
Northern Illinois University *M*
Northwestern University *M*
Richland Community College *A*
Robert Morris University: Chicago *M*
Saint Xavier University *M*
Sauk Valley Community College *C*
Southern Illinois University
   Edwardsville *B, M*
Southwestern Illinois College *C, A*
Trinity Christian College *B*
Triton College *C, A*
University of Illinois
   Chicago *M, D*
   Springfield *M*
   Urbana-Champaign *B, M, D*
Western Illinois University *B*

Indiana
Ball State University *B*
DeVry University: Indianapolis *M*
Grace College *B*
Indiana Institute of Technology *A, B*
Indiana State University *B*
Indiana University
   East *B*
   South Bend *M*
   Southeast *M*
Indiana University-Purdue University
   Indianapolis *B*
Indiana Wesleyan University *A, B*
Marian University *B*
Oakland City University *B*
Saint Joseph's College *A, B*
Saint Mary's College *B*
University of Evansville *B*
University of Indianapolis *B*
University of Notre Dame *B*

Iowa
Briar Cliff University *B*
Buena Vista University *B*
Drake University *B*
Iowa State University *B, M*
Kaplan University
   Davenport *C*
Loras College *B*
Luther College *B*
Mount Mercy College *B*
University of Iowa *B*
University of Northern Iowa *B*
Upper Iowa University *B*

Kansas
Central Christian College of Kansas *A*
Coffeyville Community College *A*
Dodge City Community College *A*
Fort Scott Community College *C, A*
Friends University *B, M*
Newman University *B*
Southwestern College *B*

University of Kansas *B*
Wichita State University *B*

Kentucky

Ashland Community and Technical College *A*
Big Sandy Community and Technical College *A*
Eastern Kentucky University *B*
Henderson Community College *A*
Madisonville Community College *A*
Morehead State University *A, B, M*
Murray State University *B*
Northern Kentucky University *B, M*
Owensboro Community and Technical College *A*
Southeast Kentucky Community and Technical College *A*
University of Louisville *B*
University of the Cumberlands *B*
West Kentucky Community and Technical College *A*
Western Kentucky University *B*

Louisiana

Herzing University *B*
Louisiana Tech University *B*
Nicholls State University *B*
Southern University
New Orleans *B, M*
Tulane University *B*
University of Louisiana at Lafayette *B*
University of Louisiana at Monroe *B*
University of New Orleans *B*

Maine

Husson University *B*
Kennebec Valley Community College *A*
Northern Maine Community College *A*
University of Maine *B*
University of Maine
Fort Kent *A, B*
University of Southern Maine *B*
York County Community College *A*

Maryland

Allegany College of Maryland *C, A*
Anne Arundel Community College *C, A*
Baltimore City Community College *A*
Bowie State University *M*
Capitol College *M*
Carroll Community College *C, A*
Cecil College *C, A*
Chesapeake College *C, A*
Community College of Baltimore County *C, A*
DeVry University: Bethesda *M*
Hagerstown Community College *C, A*
Harford Community College *A*
Hood College *M*
Howard Community College *A*
Montgomery College *C, A*
Sojourner-Douglass College *B*
Stevenson University *B, M*
University of Baltimore *B, M*
University of Maryland
University College *C, M*

Massachusetts

Anna Maria College *B*
Babson College *B*
Bentley University *M*
Boston College *B*
Boston University *B, M*
Bridgewater State College *B*
Fisher College *B*
Greenfield Community College *C*
Marian Court College *C, A*
New England College of Business and Finance *C*

Nichols College *B*
Northeastern University *B*
Roxbury Community College *A*
Salem State College *B, M*
Simmons College *B*
Suffolk University *B*
University of Massachusetts
Boston *C*
Dartmouth *B*
Western New England College *B*
Worcester Polytechnic Institute *B, M*

Michigan

Alpena Community College *A*
Aquinas College *B*
Baker College
of Flint *A, B*
of Muskegon *A*
of Owosso *B*
of Port Huron *B*
Calvin College *B*
Central Michigan University *B, M*
Cleary University *A, B*
Cornerstone University *B*
Eastern Michigan University *B, M*
Kalamazoo Valley Community College *A*
Kettering University *M*
Kirtland Community College *A*
Lake Superior State University *A*
Lansing Community College *A*
Madonna University *B*
Michigan State University *B, M, D*
Montcalm Community College *A*
Mott Community College *A*
Northern Michigan University *B*
Northwestern Michigan College *C, A*
Northwood University: Michigan *A, B*
Oakland University *B, M*
Rochester College *B*
Spring Arbor University *B*
Walsh College of Accountancy and Business Administration *M*
Wayne State University *B*
West Shore Community College *A*

Minnesota

Augsburg College *B*
Dakota County Technical College *C, A*
DeVry University
Edina *M*
Lake Superior College *C, A*
Metropolitan State University *B, M*
Minneapolis Business College *A*
Minnesota State University
Mankato *B*
Moorhead *B*
National American University
Bloomington *A, B*
North Hennepin Community College *C, A*
Northland Community & Technical College *A*
Northwestern College *B*
Rasmussen College: Lake Elmo/Woodbury *A*
Ridgewater College *A*
St. Catherine University *B*
Saint Cloud State University *B*
St. Paul College *C, A*
University of Minnesota
Crookston *B*
Duluth *B*
Twin Cities *B*
Walden University *B, M, D*
Winona State University *B*

Mississippi

Delta State University *B*
Hinds Community College *C, A*
Meridian Community College *A*
Mississippi College *M*
Mississippi Gulf Coast Community College *A*

Mississippi State University *B, M*
Northwest Mississippi Community College *A*
Pearl River Community College *A*
University of Mississippi *B*
University of Southern Mississippi *B*

Missouri

Grantham University *A*
Lindenwood University *B, M*
Maryville University of Saint Louis *B*
Missouri State University *B, M*
Northwest Missouri State University *B*
Park University *B*
St. Louis Community College
St. Louis Community College at Florissant Valley *C, A*
St. Louis Community College at Meramec *A*
Saint Louis University *B*
Three Rivers Community College *A*
University of Central Missouri *B*
University of Missouri
Missouri University of Science and Technology *B*
St. Louis *B, M, D*
Webster University *M*
Westminster College *B*
William Woods University *B*

Montana

Little Big Horn College *A*
Rocky Mountain College *B*
Stone Child College *A*
University of Montana *B*

Nebraska

Bellevue University *B, M*
Chadron State College *B*
Concordia University *B*
Creighton University *B, M*
Dana College *B*
Metropolitan Community College *C, A*
University of Nebraska
Omaha *C, B, M*

Nevada

College of Southern Nevada *C, A*
DeVry University: Henderson *M*
University of Nevada
Las Vegas *B, M*

New Hampshire

Daniel Webster College *B*
Franklin Pierce University *B*
Nashua Community College *C*
New England College *B*
Rivier College *A, B*

New Jersey

Atlantic Cape Community College *A*
Bergen Community College *C*
Burlington County College *A*
Camden County College *A*
County College of Morris *A*
Cumberland County College *C, A*
Fairleigh Dickinson University
Metropolitan Campus *M*
Hudson County Community College *C, A*
Kean University *M*
Mercer County Community College *C, A*
Passaic County Community College *C, A*
Raritan Valley Community College *C, A*
Rowan University *B*

Rutgers, The State University of New Jersey
New Brunswick/Piscataway Campus *B*
Saint Peter's College *A, B, M*
Seton Hall University *B*
Stevens Institute of Technology *B, M, D*

New Mexico

Clovis Community College *A*
Eastern New Mexico University *B*
New Mexico Highlands University *B*
New Mexico State University
Alamogordo *C, A*
Northern New Mexico College *A*
Southwestern Indian Polytechnic Institute *A*
University of the Southwest *B*

New York

Berkeley College *A, B*
Berkeley College of New York City *A, B*
Bramson ORT College *A*
Canisius College *B*
City University of New York
Baruch College *B, M*
Bronx Community College *A*
York College *B*
Clarkson University *B*
College of Westchester *C, A*
DeVry
College of New York *M*
Dominican College of Blauvelt *B*
Excelsior College *B*
Fordham University *B, M*
Globe Institute of Technology *C, A, B*
Hofstra University *B, M*
Iona College *B, M*
Le Moyne College *B*
Manhattan College *B*
Marist College *M*
Medaille College *B*
Mohawk Valley Community College *A*
Nassau Community College *A*
New York Institute of Technology *B, M*
Pace University *M*
Polytechnic Institute of New York University *B, M*
Rochester Institute of Technology *C, B, M*
Saint Bonaventure University *B*
St. John's University *B, M*
State University of New York
Albany *M*
Binghamton *B*
College at Fredonia *B*
College at Plattsburgh *B*
College of Technology at Canton *B*
College of Technology at Delhi *A*
Sullivan County Community College *A*
Touro College *B*
Utica School of Commerce *A*

North Carolina

Appalachian State University *B*
Asheville-Buncombe Technical Community College *A*
Campbell University *A, B*
Catawba College *B*
Catawba Valley Community College *C, A*
Central Piedmont Community College *C, A*
DeVry University: Charlotte *M*
East Carolina University *B*
Elon University *B*
Gardner-Webb University *B*
Guilford Technical Community College *C, A*
High Point University *B*

Lenoir Community College *C, A*
Lenoir-Rhyne University *B*
Martin Community College *C, A*
Methodist University *B*
Mount Olive College *B*
Nash Community College *A*
Randolph Community College *A*
Richmond Community College *C, A*
Roanoke-Chowan Community
  College *A*
University of North Carolina
  Charlotte *B*
  Greensboro *D*
  Wilmington *B*
Western Carolina University *B*

North Dakota

Dickinson State University *A, B*
Jamestown College *B*
Lake Region State College *C, A*
Minot State University *C, B*
North Dakota State University *B*
University of Mary *B*

Ohio

Ashland University *B*
Bluffton University *B*
Bowling Green State University *B*
Case Western Reserve
  University *M, D*
Cedarville University *B*
Cleveland State University *B, D*
Cuyahoga Community College
  Metropolitan Campus *A*
DeVry University
  Columbus *M*
Defiance College *B*
Eastern Gateway Community
  College *C, A*
Franklin University *B*
James A. Rhodes State College *A*
Kent State University *B, M, D*
Kent State University
  Trumbull *C*
  Tuscarawas *C*
Marietta College *B*
Miami University
  Oxford Campus *B*
Mount Vernon Nazarene University *B*
Notre Dame College *C, B*
Ohio State University
  Columbus Campus *B*
Ohio University *B*
Shawnee State University *B*
Stark State College of Technology *A*
University of Akron *B, M*
University of Akron: Wayne
  College *C, A*
University of Cincinnati *B*
University of Dayton *B*
University of Toledo *B*
Ursuline College *B*
Walsh University *B*
Wright State University *A, B, M*
Wright State University: Lake
  Campus *A*
Xavier University *B, M*
Youngstown State University *B*

Oklahoma

DeVry University: Oklahoma City
  Center *M*
Eastern Oklahoma State College *A*
Mid-America Christian University *B*
Northeastern State University *B*
Oklahoma Baptist University *B*
Oklahoma City University *B, M*
Oklahoma State University *B, M*
Oklahoma State University
  Institute of Technology:
  Okmulgee *A*
Oral Roberts University *B*
Southwestern Oklahoma State
  University *B*

Tulsa Community College *C, A*
University of Central Oklahoma *B*
University of Oklahoma *B, M*
University of Tulsa *B*

Oregon

Central Oregon Community
  College *A*
Chemeketa Community College *A*
Clatsop Community College *A*
Corban College *B*
DeVry University: Portland *M*
George Fox University *B*
Oregon Institute of Technology *B*
Portland Community College *A*
Portland State University *B*
Southwestern Oregon Community
  College *A*
Treasure Valley Community College *A*
Umpqua Community College *A*
University of Oregon *M, D*

Pennsylvania

Arcadia University *C, B*
Cabrini College *B*
Cambria-Rowe Business College:
  Indiana *A*
Carnegie Mellon University *M, D*
Community College of Allegheny
  County *C, A*
Community College of Beaver
  County *A*
DeSales University *B, M*
DeVry University
  Fort Washington *M*
Delaware Valley College *C, B*
Duquesne University *B, M*
Elizabethtown College *B*
Gannon University *B*
Holy Family University *B, M*
Indiana University of Pennsylvania *B*
Keystone College *B*
Lock Haven University of
  Pennsylvania *A*
Luzerne County Community
  College *A*
Marywood University *M*
Montgomery County Community
  College *A*
Muhlenberg College *C, B*
Peirce College *A*
Penn State
  Abington *B*
  Altoona *B*
  Beaver *B*
  Berks *B*
  Brandywine *B*
  DuBois *B*
  Erie, The Behrend College *B*
  Fayette, The Eberly Campus *B*
  Greater Allegheny *B*
  Harrisburg *B, M*
  Hazleton *B*
  Lehigh Valley *B*
  Mont Alto *B*
  New Kensington *B*
  Schuylkill *B*
  Shenango *B*
  University Park *B*
  Wilkes-Barre *B*
  Worthington Scranton *B*
  York *B*
Pennsylvania College of
  Technology *B*
Philadelphia University *B*
Reading Area Community College *A*
Robert Morris University *C, B, M*
St. Francis University *A, B*
Saint Joseph's University *C, A, B, M*
Seton Hill University *B*
South Hills School of Business &
  Technology: Altoona *A*
Temple University *B, M, D*
Thiel College *A, B*

University of Pennsylvania *B, M*
University of Pittsburgh *M*
University of Pittsburgh
  Greensburg *B*
  Titusville *A*
Villanova University *B*
Widener University *B, M*
Wilson College *A, B*
York College of Pennsylvania *B*

Puerto Rico

Bayamon Central University *A, B*
Columbia Centro Universitario:
  Caguas *C, A*
Inter American University of Puerto
  Rico
  Aguadilla Campus *B, M*
  Bayamon Campus *B*
  Metropolitan Campus *B*
  Ponce Campus *B*
  San German Campus *B, M*
Pontifical Catholic University of
  Puerto Rico *B, M*
Turabo University *A, B, M*
Universidad Metropolitana *B, M*
Universidad del Este *B, M*
University of Puerto Rico
  Aguadilla *B*
  Rio Piedras *B*
University of the Sacred Heart *M*

Rhode Island

Rhode Island College *B*
Roger Williams University *B*
University of Rhode Island *B*

South Carolina

Charleston Southern University *B*
Claflin University *B*
Francis Marion University *B*
Furman University *B*

South Dakota

Augustana College *B*
National American University
  Rapid City *B, M*
Northern State University *B*
Oglala Lakota College *B*

Tennessee

Aquinas College *B*
Belmont University *B*
Bethel University *B*
Chattanooga State Community
  College *C, A*
DeVry University: Memphis *M*
Freed-Hardeman University *B*
Jackson State Community College *A*
King College *B, M*
Lambuth University *B*
Lipscomb University *B*
Middle Tennessee State University *B*
Southern Adventist University *B*
Southwest Tennessee Community
  College *A*
Trevecca Nazarene University *B*
University of Memphis *B*
University of Tennessee
  Martin *B*
Vanderbilt University *M*
Walters State Community College *A*

Texas

Abilene Christian University *B*
Angelo State University *B*
Baylor University *B*
Brookhaven College *A*
Cedar Valley College *C, A*
Dallas Baptist University *B*
DeVry University
  Irving *M*
DeVry University: Houston *M*
Del Mar College *C, A*

Eastfield College *C, A*
El Centro College *C, A*
Hardin-Simmons University *B*
Houston Baptist University *B*
Kilgore College *C, A*
Lamar University *B, M*
LeTourneau University *B*
Lubbock Christian University *B*
McMurry University *B*
Midland College *A*
Midwestern State University *B*
Our Lady of the Lake University of San
  Antonio *M*
Prairie View A&M University *B*
Richland College *C, A*
St. Mary's University *B*
San Jacinto College *A*
Schreiner University *B*
Southern Methodist University *B, M*
Southwest Texas Junior College *A*
Southwestern Adventist University *B*
Tarleton State University *B, M*
Texas A&M International
  University *B, M*
Texas A&M University *M*
Texas A&M University
  Commerce *B*
  Corpus Christi *B*
  Kingsville *B*
  Texarkana *B*
Texas Southern University *B, M*
Texas State Technical College
  West Texas *C, A*
Texas State University: San Marcos *B*
Texas Tech University *B*
Texas Wesleyan University *B*
University of Dallas *M*
University of Houston *B, M, D*
University of Houston
  Clear Lake *B, M*
  Downtown *B*
University of Mary Hardin-Baylor *B*
University of North Texas *B, M, D*
University of Texas
  Arlington *B, M, D*
  Austin *B*
  El Paso *B*
  Pan American *B*
  San Antonio *B, M, D*
University of the Incarnate Word *B*
West Texas A&M University *B, M*

Utah

Brigham Young University *B*
DeVry University: Sandy *M*
Neumont University *B*
Southern Utah University *B*
University of Utah *B, M*
Weber State University *C, A, B*
Western Governors University *B, M*
Westminster College *B*

Vermont

Champlain College *M*

Virginia

Bridgewater College *B*
Central Virginia Community
  College *C, A*
DeVry University
  Arlington *M*
Ferrum College *B*
Hampton University *B*
Liberty University *A, B*
Longwood University *B*
Lord Fairfax Community College *A*
Northern Virginia Community
  College *A*
Old Dominion University *B*
St. Paul's College *B*
University of Management and
  Technology *B*
University of Mary Washington *M*
University of Virginia *M*

University of Virginia's College at
Wise *B*
Virginia Union University *B*
Virginia Western Community
College *A*

Washington
City University of Seattle *C, B, M*
DeVry University
Federal Way *M*
Eastern Washington University *B*
Everett Community College *A*
Gonzaga University *B*
Pacific Lutheran University *M*
Seattle Pacific University *M*
Spokane Community College *A*
Spokane Falls Community
College *C, A*
University of Washington *B*
Washington State University *B, D*
Western Washington University *B*

West Virginia
Davis and Elkins College *B*
Fairmont State University *B*
Marshall University *B*
Potomac State College of West
Virginia University *A*
West Virginia University *B*
West Virginia University at
Parkersburg *A*

Wisconsin
Cardinal Stritch University *C, B, M*
Carroll University *B*
Carthage College *B*
DeVry University: Milwaukee *M*
Edgewood College *B*
Marquette University *B, M*
Milwaukee School of Engineering *B*
Rasmussen College: Green Bay *A*
St. Norbert College *B*
University of Wisconsin
La Crosse *B*
Madison *B, M*
Milwaukee *B*
Oshkosh *B, M*
Parkside *B*
Superior *B*
Viterbo University *B*

Wyoming
Casper College *A*
Northwest College *A*

Management science

Alabama
Faulkner University *B, M*
Tuskegee University *B*
University of Alabama *B, M, D*

Alaska
Ilisagvik College *A*
University of Alaska
Anchorage *B, M*
Southeast *B*

Arizona
Arizona State University *M*
Arizona Western College *A*
Northcentral University *B, M, D*
Phoenix College *A*
University of Phoenix *B*

Arkansas
University of Arkansas *M*

California
Allan Hancock College *A*
California State University
East Bay *M*

Long Beach *B*
Northridge *B, M*
Canada College *A*
Chabot College *A*
Coastline Community College *A*
Cypress College *A*
Folsom Lake College *A*
Grossmont College *A*
Los Angeles Mission College *A*
Los Angeles Pierce College *A*
Mission College *A*
Notre Dame de Namur University *M*
Palomar College *A*
Remington College
San Diego *A*
San Diego City College *A*
San Francisco State University *B*
Santa Ana College *A*
University of California
San Diego *B*
University of California: Merced *B*

Colorado
Colorado Christian University *B*
United States Air Force Academy *B*

Connecticut
Quinnipiac University *B, M*
Southern Connecticut State
University *B*

Delaware
Delaware Technical and Community
College
Stanton/Wilmington *A*
Goldey-Beacom College *A, B, M*

District of Columbia
Catholic University of America *B, M*
Potomac College *A, B*
University of the District of
Columbia *A*

Florida
Broward College *A*
Eckerd College *B*
Florida Institute of Technology *M*
Miami Dade College *A, B*
Pensacola Junior College *A*
Saint Leo University *B*
Stetson University *B*
University of Florida *B*
University of Miami *B*

Georgia
Dalton State College *B*
Emory University *B, D*
Georgia College and State
University *B*
Griffin Technical College *A*
West Georgia Technical College *A*

Illinois
Aurora University *B*
DePaul University *B*
Eastern Illinois University *B*
Illinois Institute of Technology *D*
Illinois State University *B*
Illinois Valley Community College *A*
Judson University *B*
Lewis University *B*
McKendree University *B*
Northwestern University *M*
Quincy University *B*
Roosevelt University *B*
Shawnee Community College *A*
Southern Illinois University
Carbondale *B*
Southwestern Illinois College *A*
Trinity International University *B*
University of Illinois
Chicago *B*
Urbana-Champaign *B, M, D*

University of St. Francis *B, M*

Indiana
Indiana Wesleyan University *M*
Oakland City University *M*
Valparaiso University *B*

Iowa
Drake University *B*
St. Ambrose University *B*
University of Iowa *B*

Kansas
Southwestern College *B*

Kentucky
Big Sandy Community and Technical
College *A*
University of Kentucky *B*

Louisiana
Louisiana State University and
Agricultural and Mechanical
College *B, M, D*
Louisiana Tech University *B*
Southwest University *A, B, M*
Xavier University of Louisiana *B*

Maryland
College of Notre Dame of
Maryland *M*
Coppin State University *B*
University of Maryland
College Park *B*
University College *B*

Massachusetts
American International College *B, M*
Babson College *B*
Cape Cod Community College *A*
Fisher College *B*
Fitchburg State College *B*
Lasell College *M*
Mount Ida College *M*
Worcester Polytechnic Institute *B, M*

Michigan
Adrian College *B*
Baker College
of Auburn Hills *A, B*
of Clinton Township *A, B*
of Muskegon *A, B*
Cornerstone University *B*
Grace Bible College *B*
Grand Valley State University *B*
Henry Ford Community College *A*
University of Michigan
Dearborn *B*
Western Michigan University *B*

Minnesota
Minnesota State University
Mankato *B*
Riverland Community College *A*
University of Minnesota
Morris *B*
Winona State University *B*

Missouri
Central Methodist University *B*
Hickey College *B*
Missouri Southern State University *B*
Saint Louis University *B*

Montana
Rocky Mountain College *B*

Nebraska
Chadron State College *B*
Doane College *M*
Grace University *B*

Union College *B*
University of Nebraska
Lincoln *B*

Nevada
Nevada State College *B*
Western Nevada College *A*

New Hampshire
Franklin Pierce University *B*
Granite State College *B*
Manchester Community College *A*
Rivier College *A, B*

New Jersey
Caldwell College *B*
Rider University *B*
Rowan University *B, M*
Rutgers, The State University of New
Jersey
New Brunswick/Piscataway
Campus *B*

New York
Canisius College *B*
Laboratory Institute of
Merchandising *B*
Olean Business Institute *A*
Pace University *B, M*
Polytechnic Institute of New York
University *B*
Saint Bonaventure University *B*
State University of New York
Albany *M*
College at Fredonia *B*
Oswego *B*
Suffolk County Community College *A*

North Carolina
Alamance Community College *A*
Johnson & Wales University:
Charlotte *B*
Lenoir-Rhyne University *B*
St. Augustine's College *B*
Wake Forest University *B*

Ohio
Case Western Reserve University *M*
Franklin University *B*
Heidelberg University *B*
Kent State University *B*
Lourdes College *B*
Mount Vernon Nazarene University *M*
Ohio Northern University *B*
University of Cincinnati *B, M, D*
University of Dayton *M*
University of Toledo *B*
Wilmington College *B*
Wright State University *B, M*

Oklahoma
Mid-America Christian University *B*
Oklahoma Baptist University *B*
Oklahoma Christian University *B*
Oklahoma City University *B*
Oklahoma State University
Oklahoma City *A*
Oral Roberts University *B, M*
Southeastern Oklahoma State
University *B*
University of Oklahoma *B*
Western Oklahoma State College *A*

Oregon
Chemeketa Community College *A*

Pennsylvania
Arcadia University *B*
California University of
Pennsylvania *M*
Carnegie Mellon University *D*
DeSales University *B*

Duquesne University *B*
Gettysburg College *B*
La Roche College *B*
La Salle University *B*
Lehigh University *B*
Misericordia University *B*
Penn State
  Harrisburg *M*
Rosemont College *B, M*
Shippensburg University of
  Pennsylvania *B, T*
University of Scranton *B*
Westminster College *B*

Puerto Rico
Bayamon Central University *B, M*
Inter American University of Puerto
  Rico
  Arecibo Campus *B*
  Ponce Campus *B, M*
  San German Campus *B*

Rhode Island
Salve Regina University *B, M*

South Carolina
Central Carolina Technical College *A*
Clemson University *D*
Southern Wesleyan University *M*
University of South Carolina *B*

Tennessee
Belmont University *B*
Cumberland University *B*
Lincoln Memorial University *B*
Roane State Community College *A*
Southern Adventist University *B*
Tennessee Technological University *B*
University of Tennessee
  Knoxville *M, D*

Texas
Clarendon College *A*
El Paso Community College *A*
Hardin-Simmons University *B*
Midland College *A*
North Lake College *A*
Southern Methodist University *B*
Southwestern Adventist University *B*
Texas A&M University *B, D*
Texas A&M University
  Kingsville *B*
Texas Christian University *B*
Texas Wesleyan University *B*
Trinity University *B*
University of North Texas *M, D*
University of Texas
  San Antonio *B, M*

Utah
Westminster College *B*

Vermont
Castleton State College *B*

Virginia
Averett University *B*
Longwood University *B*
Southside Virginia Community
  College *A*
Thomas Nelson Community
  College *A*
Virginia Polytechnic Institute and
  State University *B*
Virginia University of Lynchburg *B, M*

Washington
Walla Walla University *B*

West Virginia
American Public University System *M*
Fairmont State University *B*

Wisconsin
University of Wisconsin
  Green Bay *M*
  Milwaukee *D*

Wyoming
Laramie County Community
  College *A*
University of Wyoming *B*

Manicurist

Alabama
Gadsden State Community College *C*
Lawson State Community College *C*
Lurleen B. Wallace Community
  College *C*
Northeast Alabama Community
  College *C*
Shelton State Community College *C*
Snead State Community College *C*

Arizona
Eastern Arizona College *C*

Arkansas
Pulaski Technical College *C*

Colorado
Pueblo Community College *C*
Red Rocks Community College *C, A*
Trinidad State Junior College *C*

Florida
Central Florida Community College *C*
Daytona State College *C*
Indian River State College *C*
Palm Beach Community College *C*
Pensacola Junior College *C*

Georgia
Central Georgia Technical College *C*
Savannah Technical College *C*
Southeastern Technical College *C*
West Georgia Technical College *C*

Illinois
Highland Community College *C*
Kaskaskia College *C*

Iowa
Northeast Iowa Community
  College *C*

Kansas
Kansas City Kansas Community
  College *C*

Michigan
Kirtland Community College *C, A*

Minnesota
Century Community and Technical
  College *C*
Minnesota State College - Southeast
  Technical *C*
Minnesota State Community and
  Technical College *C*
Northland Community & Technical
  College *C*
Ridgewater College *C*
St. Paul College *C*

New Mexico
Clovis Community College *C*

North Carolina
Brunswick Community College *C*
Cape Fear Community College *C*
Carteret Community College *C*

Isothermal Community College *C*
Lenoir Community College *C*
Martin Community College *C*
Miller-Motte Technical College *C*
Roanoke-Chowan Community
  College *C*
Southeastern Community College *C*
Southwestern Community College *C*
Vance-Granville Community
  College *C*

Tennessee
West Tennessee Business College *C*

Texas
Houston Community College
  System *C*
Howard College *C*
Lamar State College at Port Arthur *C*
Panola College *C*
San Jacinto College *C*

Washington
Clover Park Technical College *C*
Olympic College *C*

Wyoming
Eastern Wyoming College *C*

Manufacturing
engineering

Alabama
Auburn University *M*

Arizona
Central Arizona College *A*
Cochise College *A*

California
California Polytechnic State
  University: San Luis Obispo *B*
California State Polytechnic
  University: Pomona *B*
San Diego State University *M*
University of California
  Berkeley *B*
  Los Angeles *M*
University of Southern California *M*

Florida
University of South Florida *B, M, D*

Illinois
Bradley University *B, M*
Illinois Institute of Technology *M*
Northwestern University *B, M*
Southern Illinois University
  Edwardsville *B*
University of Illinois
  Urbana-Champaign *B, M, D*

Kansas
Wichita State University *B*

Kentucky
Maysville Community and Technical
  College *A*

Massachusetts
Bristol Community College *A*
Quinsigamond Community College *A*
University of Massachusetts
  Amherst *M*
Worcester Polytechnic Institute *M, D*

Michigan
Central Michigan University *B*
Grand Valley State University *B, M*
Lawrence Technological
  University *M, D*

University of Detroit Mercy *B*
University of Michigan *M, D*
University of Michigan
  Dearborn *B*
Wayne State University *M*
Western Michigan University *B, M*

Minnesota
Dunwoody College of Technology *A*
Saint Cloud State University *B*
University of St. Thomas *M*

Missouri
University of Missouri
  Missouri University of Science and
  Technology *M*

Nebraska
University of Nebraska
  Lincoln *M*

New Jersey
New Jersey Institute of
  Technology *B, M, D*

New Mexico
University of New Mexico *M*

New York
Hofstra University *B*
Polytechnic Institute of New York
  University *M*
Rochester Institute of
  Technology *B, M*

North Carolina
Edgecombe Community College *A*
North Carolina State University *M*

North Dakota
North Dakota State University *B, M*

Ohio
Central State University *B*
Miami University
  Oxford Campus *B*

Oregon
Oregon State University *B, M*
Portland State University *M*

Pennsylvania
Lehigh University *B*
Penn State
  Erie, The Behrend College *M*
  Fayette, The Eberly Campus *A*
  Greater Allegheny *A*
  Hazleton *A*
  Wilkes-Barre *A*
  York *A*
Robert Morris University *B*

Puerto Rico
Universidad Politecnica de Puerto
  Rico *M*

Rhode Island
New England Institute of
  Technology *A, B*

Texas
Southern Methodist University *M*
Texas State University: San Marcos *B*
Texas Tech University *M*
University of Texas
  Austin *M*
  El Paso *M*
  Pan American *B, M*
  San Antonio *M*

Utah

Brigham Young University B, M
Salt Lake Community College A

Virginia

Mountain Empire Community
College A
Virginia State University B

Washington

Washington State University B

Wisconsin

Marquette University B, M, D
University of Wisconsin
Milwaukee B
Stout B, M

Manufacturing technologies

Alabama

Jacksonville State University B
Jefferson State Community
College C, A
University of West Alabama B

Arizona

Arizona State University B, M
Cochise College C
GateWay Community College C, A

Arkansas

East Arkansas Community
College C, A
Mid-South Community College C
Phillips Community College of the
University of Arkansas C, A
Pulaski Technical College A
Southern Arkansas University Tech C

California

California State University
Long Beach B
Cerritos College C, A
College of the Canyons C, A
College of the Sequoias A
Irvine Valley College C, A
Long Beach City College C
San Diego City College C, A

Colorado

Arapahoe Community College C, A
Front Range Community College C, A
Mesa State College A
Red Rocks Community College C, A
Trinidad State Junior College C, A

Connecticut

Asnuntuck Community College C, A
Central Connecticut State
University B
Gateway Community College A
Manchester Community College A
Naugatuck Valley Community
College C, A
Quinebaug Valley Community
College C
Three Rivers Community College A
Tunxis Community College A

Delaware

Delaware Technical and Community
College
Stanton/Wilmington A

Florida

Daytona State College A
Florida Agricultural and Mechanical
University B
Hillsborough Community College A

Pensacola Junior College A

Georgia

Central Georgia Technical College C
Macon State College A
Middle Georgia College A

Idaho

Brigham Young University-Idaho A
Lewis-Clark State College A, B

Illinois

Black Hawk College C, A
Bradley University B, M
Danville Area Community College A
Heartland Community College C, A
Highland Community College C
Illinois Eastern Community Colleges
Wabash Valley College A
Kankakee Community College A
Kishwaukee College C, A
Morrison Institute of Technology A
Rend Lake College A
Rock Valley College C, A
Sauk Valley Community College A
Southern Illinois University
Carbondale M
Western Illinois University B, M

Indiana

Indiana State University B
Ivy Tech Community College
Bloomington C
Central Indiana C
Columbus C
East Central C
Kokomo C
Lafayette C
North Central C
Northeast C
Northwest C
Richmond C
South Central C
Purdue University A, B
University of Southern Indiana B
Vincennes University A

Iowa

Clinton Community College A
Hawkeye Community College A
Iowa Central Community College A
Muscatine Community College C, A
Northwest Iowa Community
College A
University of Northern Iowa B

Kansas

Hutchinson Community College C, A
Pittsburg State University B
Southwestern College B

Kentucky

Berea College B
Bluegrass Community and Technical
College C
Eastern Kentucky University B, M
Hopkinsville Community College C
Morehead State University A, B, M
Murray State University A, B
Northern Kentucky University C
St. Catharine College A
Western Kentucky University A, B

Maine

University of Southern Maine B, M

Maryland

Chesapeake College A
College of Southern Maryland C

Massachusetts

Fitchburg State College B

Quinsigamond Community
College C, A
University of Massachusetts
Lowell M

Michigan

Alpena Community College A
Baker College
of Flint A
Central Michigan University B
Delta College A
Eastern Michigan University B, M
Ferris State University B
Henry Ford Community College C, A
Kirtland Community College C, A
Lake Superior State University B
Lawrence Technological University A
Macomb Community College C, A
Mid Michigan Community College A
Monroe County Community
College C, A
Montcalm Community College C, A
Mott Community College A
Northern Michigan University A, B
Oakland Community College C, A
St. Clair County Community
College A
Schoolcraft College C, A
Southwestern Michigan College C
Wayne State University B

Minnesota

Alexandria Technical College C, A
Dakota County Technical College C, A
Hennepin Technical College C, A
Minnesota State College - Southeast
Technical C
Minnesota State Community and
Technical College C, A
Minnesota State University
Mankato B, M
Minnesota West Community and
Technical College A
Normandale Community College C, A
Northwest Technical College C, A
Pine Technical College C, A
St. Paul College A

Missouri

East Central College A
Linn State Technical College C, A
Mineral Area College A
Missouri Southern State
University C, A
Missouri State University: West
Plains C, A
Missouri Western State University A
St. Louis Community College
St. Louis Community College at
Florissant Valley A
State Fair Community College C, A

Montana

Flathead Valley Community College C

Nebraska

Southeast Community College A
University of Nebraska
Omaha B

New Hampshire

NHTI-Concord's Community
College A
Nashua Community College A
River Valley Community College A

New Jersey

Bergen Community College C, A
Essex County College A
Middlesex County College A
Raritan Valley Community
College C, A
Thomas Edison State College A, B

New Mexico

Central New Mexico Community
College C, A
Southwestern Indian Polytechnic
Institute A

New York

Corning Community College A
Dutchess Community College A
Erie Community College
North Campus C
Excelsior College A
Monroe Community College A
Rochester Institute of
Technology B, M
State University of New York
College of Agriculture and
Technology at Morrisville A
College of Technology at Alfred B
Farmingdale C, B

North Carolina

Central Carolina Community
College A
East Carolina University B
Edgecombe Community College C, A
Mitchell Community College A
Pitt Community College C, A
Randolph Community College A
Richmond Community College A
Wake Technical Community
College A
Western Carolina University B

Ohio

Bowling Green State University:
Firelands College A
Cincinnati State Technical and
Community College C, A
Eastern Gateway Community
College C, A
Edison State Community College C, A
James A. Rhodes State College C, A
Kent State University
Tuscarawas C
Marion Technical College C, A
North Central State College C
Ohio Northern University B
Owens Community College
Toledo A
Stark State College of Technology A
Terra State Community College C, A
University of Akron A, B
University of Dayton B
University of Rio Grande A, B
Wright State University: Lake
Campus A

Oklahoma

Oklahoma City Community College A
Oklahoma State University
Institute of Technology:
Okmulgee A
Southwestern Oklahoma State
University B
Western Oklahoma State College A

Oregon

Central Oregon Community
College C, A
Clackamas Community College C, A
Lane Community College A
Oregon Institute of Technology B, M
Portland Community College C, A
Rogue Community College C, A

Pennsylvania

Butler County Community College A
Edinboro University of
Pennsylvania A
Lehigh Carbon Community
College C, A

Pennsylvania College of
Technology *A, B*
Temple University *B*
Westmoreland County Community
College *A*

Rhode Island

Community College of Rhode
Island *C*
New England Institute of
Technology *A, B*

South Carolina

Trident Technical College *C, A*
York Technical College *C*

South Dakota

South Dakota State University *B*

Tennessee

Middle Tennessee State University *M*
Tennessee Technological University *B*
University of Memphis *B*

Texas

Frank Phillips College *C, A*
Houston Community College
System *C, A*
Midwestern State University *B*
Richland College *A*
Sam Houston State University *B*
Tarleton State University *B*
Texas A&M University *B*
Texas A&M University
Commerce *B*
Texas State University: San Marcos *B*
University of Houston *B*
University of North Texas *B*
University of Texas
Brownsville - Texas Southmost
College *B*

Utah

Salt Lake Community College *A*
Utah Valley University *A*

Virginia

Danville Community College *A*
John Tyler Community College *A*
Mountain Empire Community
College *A*
Thomas Nelson Community
College *C*

Washington

Bellingham Technical College *A*
Clark College *A*
Everett Community College *A*
Highline Community College *A*
Shoreline Community College *A*
Western Washington University *B*

West Virginia

West Virginia State Community and
Technical College *A*

Wisconsin

Gateway Technical College *A*
Mid-State Technical College *A*
Wisconsin Indianhead Technical
College *A*

Wyoming

Casper College *C, A*

Marine biology

Alabama

Alabama State University *B*
Auburn University *B*
Samford University *B*

Troy University *B*
University of Alabama *B, M*
University of Mobile *B*
University of North Alabama *B*
University of West Alabama *B*

Alaska

Alaska Pacific University *B*
University of Alaska
Fairbanks *M, D*
Southeast *B*

Arizona

Prescott College *B, M*

California

California State University
Fresno *M*
Monterey Bay *M*
Sacramento *M*
Stanislaus *M*
Mount San Antonio College *A*
Oxnard College *A*
San Francisco State University *B, M*
San Jose State University *B, M*
University of California
Los Angeles *B*
San Diego *D*
Santa Barbara *B*
Santa Cruz *B, M, D*
University of San Diego *B, M*
University of Southern California *M*

Connecticut

University of Connecticut *B*
University of New Haven *B*

Delaware

University of Delaware *M, D*

District of Columbia

American University *B*

Florida

Daytona State College *A*
Eckerd College *B*
Florida Institute of Technology *B, M*
Florida International University *B*
Florida Keys Community College *A*
Florida State University *M, D*
Gulf Coast Community College *A*
Jacksonville University *B*
New College of Florida *B*
Northwest Florida State College *A*
Nova Southeastern University *B, M, D*
Rollins College *B*
State College of Florida,
Manatee-Sarasota *A*
University of Miami *B, M, D*
University of Tampa *B*
University of West Florida *B*

Georgia

Savannah State University *B, M*
University of Georgia *M, D*

Hawaii

Hawaii Pacific University *B*
University of Hawaii
Hilo *B*
Manoa *B*

Kansas

Southwestern College *B*

Louisiana

Nicholls State University *M*

Maine

Maine Maritime Academy *B, T*

Southern Maine Community
College *A*
Unity College *B*
University of Maine *B, M, D*
University of Maine
Machias *B*
University of New England *B, M*

Maryland

University of Maryland
Baltimore *M, D*
Baltimore County *M, D*
Eastern Shore *M, D*

Massachusetts

Boston University *B*
Massachusetts Bay Community
College *A*
Northeastern University *M*
Salem State College *B*
Suffolk University *B*
University of Massachusetts
Amherst *M, D*
Boston *M, D*
Lowell *M, D*

Minnesota

Bemidji State University *B*
Saint Cloud State University *B*

Mississippi

University of Southern
Mississippi *B, M, D*

Missouri

Central Methodist University *B*
Missouri Southern State University *B*
Northwest Missouri State
University *B*

New Jersey

Fairleigh Dickinson University
College at Florham *B*
Metropolitan Campus *B*
Richard Stockton College of New
Jersey *B*
Rutgers, The State University of New
Jersey
New Brunswick/Piscataway
Campus *B*

New York

State University of New York
College of Agriculture and
Technology at Morrisville *A*
Stony Brook *B*

North Carolina

Duke University *D*
University of North Carolina
Wilmington *B, M, D*

Oregon

Chemeketa Community College *A*
University of Oregon *B*

Pennsylvania

East Stroudsburg University of
Pennsylvania *B*
Juniata College *B*
Mansfield University of
Pennsylvania *B*
St. Francis University *B*
Waynesburg University *B*

Puerto Rico

University of Puerto Rico
Humacao *B*

Rhode Island

Roger Williams University *B*

University of Rhode Island *B*

South Carolina

Coastal Carolina University *B, M*
College of Charleston *B, M*
University of South Carolina *B, M, D*

Texas

Galveston College *A*
Lamar University *B*
Laredo Community College *A*
Texas A&M University
Corpus Christi *M*
Galveston *B*

Utah

Utah State University *M, D*

Virginia

College of William and Mary *M, D*
Hampton University *B*
Old Dominion University *B*
St. Paul's College *B*

Washington

Olympic College *A*
University of Washington *B*
Western Washington University *B*

Marine engineering/
naval architecture

California

California Maritime Academy *B*
Santa Barbara City College *A*

Connecticut

United States Coast Guard Academy *B*

Louisiana

University of New Orleans *B*

Maine

Maine Maritime Academy *B*

Maryland

United States Naval Academy *B*

Michigan

University of Michigan *B, M, D*

New Jersey

Stevens Institute of Technology *M*

New York

State University of New York
Maritime College *B*
United States Merchant Marine
Academy *B, M*
Webb Institute *B*

Texas

Texas A&M University
Galveston *B*

Virginia

Virginia Polytechnic Institute and
State University *M*

Wisconsin

University of Wisconsin
Madison *B*

Marine maintenance/
fitter/ship repair

Florida

Florida Keys Community College *C, A*
Palm Beach Community College *A*

Georgia
Central Georgia Technical College *C*

Hawaii
University of Hawaii
  Honolulu Community College *A*

Iowa
Iowa Lakes Community College *C*

Minnesota
Alexandria Technical College *C*
Central Lakes College *C, A*
Hennepin Technical College *C, A*
Minnesota State Community and
  Technical College *C, A*

Missouri
State Fair Community College *C, A*

New Hampshire
Lakes Region Community
  College *C, A*

New York
United States Merchant Marine
  Academy *B, M*

North Carolina
Cape Fear Community College *C*
Carteret Community College *C*

Washington
Northwest School of Wooden
  Boatbuilding *C, A*
Olympic College *A*

Wisconsin
Wisconsin Indianhead Technical
  College *C*

Marine science

California
San Francisco State University *M*
University of California
  Santa Barbara *M, D*

Connecticut
University of Connecticut *M, D*

Florida
Florida Keys Community College *A*

Maine
Saint Joseph's College of Maine *B*

Maritime technology/
Merchant Marine

Florida
Florida Keys Community College *A*

Maine
Maine Maritime Academy *A, B*

Massachusetts
Massachusetts Maritime Academy *B*

Michigan
Northwestern Michigan College *A*

New York
United States Merchant Marine
  Academy *B*

Puerto Rico
Pontifical Catholic University of
  Puerto Rico *B*

Turabo University *C*

Texas
Texas A&M University
  Galveston *B*

Marketing

Alabama
Alabama Agricultural and Mechanical
  University *B*
Alabama State University *B*
Auburn University *B*
Auburn University at Montgomery *B*
Birmingham-Southern College *B*
Columbia Southern University *B, M*
Faulkner University *B*
Jacksonville State University *B*
Oakwood University *B*
Samford University *B*
Talladega College *B*
Troy University *B*
University of Alabama *B, M, D*
University of Alabama
  Birmingham *B*
  Huntsville *B*
University of North Alabama *B*
University of South Alabama *B*

Alaska
University of Alaska
  Anchorage *B*
  Southeast *B*

Arizona
Arizona State University *B*
Arizona Western College *A*
Art Center Design College *B*
Central Arizona College *A*
Coconino County Community
  College *A*
Glendale Community College *C, A*
Grand Canyon University *B*
Mesa Community College *A*
Northcentral University *B, M, D*
Northern Arizona University *C, B*
Penn Foster College *A*
Phoenix College *C, A*
University of Arizona *B*
University of Phoenix *C, B, M*
Western International University *B, M*

Arkansas
Arkansas State University *B*
Central Baptist College *B*
Harding University *B*
John Brown University *B*
University of Arkansas *B*
University of Arkansas
  Little Rock *B*
University of Central Arkansas *B*
University of the Ozarks *B*

California
Azusa Pacific University *B*
Bakersfield College *C*
Biola University *B*
Butte College *C, A*
California Baptist University *B*
California Lutheran University *B*
California State University
  Chico *B*
  Dominguez Hills *B, M*
  East Bay *B, M*
  Fresno *B*
  Fullerton *B, M*
  Sacramento *B, M*
  San Bernardino *B, M*
City College of San Francisco *A*
College of Alameda *C, A*
Crafton Hills College *C, A*
De Anza College *C, A*

El Camino College: Compton
  Center *C*
Fashion Institute of Design and
  Merchandising
  Los Angeles *A, B*
  San Diego *A*
Folsom Lake College *A*
Fresno Pacific University *B*
Golden Gate University *B, M*
Grossmont College *C, A*
Holy Names University *B, M*
Imperial Valley College *C, A*
La Sierra University *B*
Lake Tahoe Community College *C, A*
Los Angeles Pierce College *C, A*
Modesto Junior College *A*
National University *C, M*
Ohlone College *C, A*
Pacific States University *B*
Pacific Union College *B*
Pepperdine University *B*
Riverside Community College *C, A*
Saddleback College *C, A*
San Diego Miramar College *A*
San Diego State University *B, M*
San Francisco State University *B*
San Jose City College *C, A*
San Jose State University *B*
Santa Ana College *C, A*
Santa Barbara City College *C, A*
Santa Clara University *B*
Santiago Canyon College *A*
University of San Diego *B*
University of San Francisco *B*
Vanguard University of Southern
  California *B*
Westwood College of Technology
  Westwood College: Inland
    Empire *B*
Westwood College: Anaheim *B*
Woodbury University *B*
Yuba Community College District *C*

Colorado
Adams State College *B*
Aims Community College *C, A*
American Sentinel University *B*
Arapahoe Community College *C, A*
Colorado State University *B*
Community College of Aurora *A*
Community College of Denver *C*
Fort Lewis College *B*
Johnson & Wales University:
  Denver *B*
Metropolitan State College of
  Denver *B*
Pikes Peak Community College *C, A*
University of Colorado
  Boulder *B*
  Denver *M*
University of Denver *B, M*
Westwood College: Denver North *B*

Connecticut
Asnuntuck Community College *C*
Central Connecticut State
  University *B*
Fairfield University *B*
Middlesex Community College *A*
Northwestern Connecticut
  Community College *A*
Norwalk Community College *A*
Post University *A, B*
Quinnipiac University *B, M*
Sacred Heart University *B*
Southern Connecticut State
  University *B*
University of Bridgeport *B, M*
University of Connecticut *B*
University of Hartford *B*
University of New Haven *B*
Western Connecticut State
  University *B*

Delaware
Delaware Technical and Community
  College
  Owens *C, A*
  Stanton/Wilmington *C, A*
  Terry *C, A*
Goldey-Beacom College *B, M*
Wilmington University *B*

District of Columbia
Georgetown University *B*

Florida
Barry University *B*
City College: Casselberry *A*
Daytona State College *A*
Edison State College *C, A*
Florida Atlantic University *B*
Florida Gulf Coast University *B*
Florida Institute of
  Technology *A, B, M*
Florida International University *B*
Florida Southern College *B*
Florida State University *B*
Jacksonville University *B*
Johnson & Wales University: North
  Miami *B*
Northwest Florida State College *C, A*
Northwood University
  Florida *B*
Nova Southeastern University *B*
Palm Beach Atlantic University *B*
Palm Beach Community College *A*
Pasco-Hernando Community
  College *A*
Polk State College *A*
Saint Leo University *B*
St. Petersburg College *A*
Santa Fe College *C*
Schiller International University *B*
Seminole Community College *C*
Southeastern University *B*
Southwest Florida College *A*
Stetson University *B*
University of Central Florida *B*
University of Florida *B, M*
University of Miami *B*
University of North Florida *B*
University of South Florida *B*
University of Tampa *B*
University of West Florida *B*
Valencia Community College *A*
Webber International University *A, B*

Georgia
Albany State University *B*
Altamaha Technical College *A*
Ashworth College *A, B, M*
Augusta State University *B*
Bainbridge College *C, A*
Berry College *B*
Brenau University *B*
Chattahoochee Technical
  College *C, A*
Clayton State University *B*
Columbus State University *B*
Dalton State College *C, A, B*
DeKalb Technical College *A*
Emory University *B, D*
Fort Valley State University *B*
Georgia College and State
  University *B*
Georgia Northwestern Technical
  College *C, A*
Georgia Southern University *B*
Georgia Southwestern State
  University *B*
Georgia State University *B, M, D*
Gwinnett Technical College *C, A*
Kennesaw State University *B*
Macon State College *B*
Middle Georgia Technical
  College *C, A*

North Georgia College & State
University *B*
Paine College *B*
Savannah State University *B*
Southeastern Technical College *A*
University of Georgia *B*
University of West Georgia *B*
Valdosta State University *B*

Hawaii
Chaminade University of Honolulu *B*
Hawaii Pacific University *B*
University of Hawaii
Hawaii Community College *C, A*
Hilo *B*
Manoa *B*

Idaho
Boise State University *B*
Eastern Idaho Technical College *C, A*
Idaho State University *C, A, B*
University of Idaho *B*

Illinois
Augustana College *B*
Aurora University *B*
Benedictine University *C, B*
Blackburn College *B*
Bradley University *B*
College of DuPage *C*
Columbia College Chicago *C, B*
Concordia University Chicago *B*
DePaul University *B*
Eastern Illinois University *B*
Elgin Community College *C, A*
Elmhurst College *B*
Eureka College *B*
Greenville College *B*
Illinois Institute of Technology *M*
Illinois State University *B*
Lewis University *B*
Loyola University Chicago *C, B*
MacCormac College *A*
McKendree University *B*
Millikin University *B*
Moraine Valley Community College *C*
North Central College *B*
Northeastern Illinois University *B*
Northern Illinois University *B*
Northwestern University *M, D*
Olivet Nazarene University *B*
Parkland College *A*
Quincy University *B*
Rock Valley College *C, A*
Rockford Career College *A*
Roosevelt University *B*
Saint Xavier University *M*
South Suburban College of Cook
County *C, A*
Southern Illinois University
Carbondale *B*
Trinity International University *B*
Triton College *C, A*
University of Illinois
Chicago *B*
Urbana-Champaign *B, D*
University of St. Francis *B*
Western Illinois University *B*
Westwood College: Chicago Loop *B*

Indiana
Anderson University *B, D*
Ball State University *B*
Butler University *B*
Franklin College *B*
Grace College *B*
Harrison College
Anderson *A*
Columbus *A*
Elkhart *A*
Evansville *A*
Fort Wayne *A*
Indianapolis *A*

Lafayette *A*
Muncie *A*
Terre Haute *A*
Indiana Institute of Technology *B, M*
Indiana State University *B*
Indiana University
East *B*
Kokomo *B*
South Bend *B*
Indiana University-Purdue University
Fort Wayne *B*
Indiana Wesleyan University *B*
Manchester College *B*
Marian University *B*
Purdue University *B, M, D*
Purdue University
North Central *A, B*
St. Mary-of-the-Woods College *B*
Taylor University *B*
University of Evansville *B*
University of Indianapolis *B*
University of Notre Dame *B*
University of Southern Indiana *B*
Valparaiso University *B*

Iowa
AIB College of Business *A*
Buena Vista University *B*
Des Moines Area Community
College *C, A*
Dordt College *B*
Drake University *B*
Grand View University *B*
Iowa State University *B*
Loras College *B*
Mount Mercy College *B*
Northwestern College *B*
St. Ambrose University *B*
Simpson College *B*
Southwestern Community College *A*
University of Iowa *B*
University of Northern Iowa *B*
Waldorf College *B*
Wartburg College *B*

Kansas
Bethany College *B*
Central Christian College of Kansas *A*
Emporia State University *B*
Fort Hays State University *B*
Highland Community College *A*
Kansas City Kansas Community
College *A*
Pittsburg State University *B*
Southwestern College *B*
Tabor College *B*
University of Kansas *B*
Washburn University *B*
Wichita State University *B*

Kentucky
Berea College *B*
Campbellsville University *B*
Eastern Kentucky University *B*
Hazard Community and Technical
College *A*
Morehead State University *B*
Murray State University *B*
Northern Kentucky University *B*
St. Catharine College *A*
University of Kentucky *B*
University of Louisville *B*
Western Kentucky University *B*

Louisiana
Grambling State University *B*
Louisiana College *B*
Louisiana State University
Shreveport *B*
Louisiana State University and
Agricultural and Mechanical
College *B, D*
Louisiana Tech University *B*

Loyola University New Orleans *B*
McNeese State University *B*
Nicholls State University *B*
Southeastern Louisiana University *B*
Southern University and Agricultural
and Mechanical College *B*
Tulane University *B*
University of Louisiana at Lafayette *B*
University of Louisiana at Monroe *B*
University of New Orleans *B*
Xavier University of Louisiana *B*

Maine
Husson University *B*
Kennebec Valley Community
College *B*
New England School of
Communications *B*
Saint Joseph's College of Maine *B*
Thomas College *B*
University of Maine
Machias *B*
University of Southern Maine *B, M*

Maryland
Allegany College of Maryland *A*
Baltimore City Community College *A*
Cecil College *A*
Hagerstown Community College *C*
Montgomery College *C*
Morgan State University *B*
Prince George's Community
College *C, A*
Salisbury University *B*
University of Baltimore *B, M*
University of Maryland
College Park *B*
University College *C, B*
Washington Adventist University *B*

Massachusetts
American International College *B, M*
Assumption College *B*
Babson College *B*
Bay Path College *B*
Bay State College *A, B*
Becker College *B*
Bentley University *B, M*
Boston University *B*
Bridgewater State College *B, M*
Cape Cod Community College *A*
Eastern Nazarene College *B*
Elms College *B*
Emerson College *C, B, M*
Fisher College *B*
Fitchburg State College *B*
Greenfield Community College *C*
Lasell College *B, M*
Marian Court College *C, A*
Massasoit Community College *C, A*
Newbury College *B*
Nichols College *B*
North Shore Community College *A*
Northeastern University *B*
Northern Essex Community
College *A*
Salem State College *B, M*
Springfield Technical Community
College *A*
Stonehill College *B*
Suffolk University *B, M*
University of Massachusetts
Amherst *B*
Dartmouth *B*
Western New England College *B*
Worcester Polytechnic Institute *M*

Michigan
Adrian College *B*
Alma College *B*
Baker College
of Cadillac *A*
of Flint *A*

of Muskegon *A, B*
of Owosso *A, B*
of Port Huron *A, B*
Bay de Noc Community College *A*
Central Michigan University *B*
Cleary University *B*
Cornerstone University *B*
Davenport University *B*
Delta College *A*
Eastern Michigan University *B, M*
Ferris State University *C, B*
Finlandia University *B*
Glen Oaks Community College *C*
Grace Bible College *B*
Grand Valley State University *B*
Hillsdale College *B*
Kellogg Community College *C*
Lake Michigan College *A*
Lansing Community College *A*
Macomb Community College *C, A*
Madonna University *B*
Michigan State University *B, D*
Mid Michigan Community College *A*
Mott Community College *C, A*
Muskegon Community College *A*
Northern Michigan University *B*
Northwood University: Michigan *A, B*
Oakland University *B*
Rochester College *B*
Saginaw Valley State University *B*
Schoolcraft College *A*
University of Detroit Mercy *B*
University of Michigan
Flint *B*
Wayne State University *B*
West Shore Community College *A*
Western Michigan University *B*

Minnesota
Alexandria Technical College *C, A*
Anoka-Ramsey Community College *A*
Art Institutes International
Minnesota *B*
Augsburg College *B*
Capella University *B, M*
Century Community and Technical
College *C, A*
College of St. Scholastica *B*
Concordia College: Moorhead *B*
Concordia University: St. Paul *C, B*
Dakota County Technical College *C, A*
Hamline University *B*
Lake Superior College *A*
Mesabi Range Community and
Technical College *C, A*
Metropolitan State University *B*
Minnesota State University
Moorhead *B*
National American University
Bloomington *B*
Normandale Community College *C, A*
North Hennepin Community
College *C, A*
Northland Community & Technical
College *A*
Northwest Technical College *C*
Northwestern College *B*
Ridgewater College *A*
Saint Cloud State University *B*
St. Mary's University of Minnesota *B*
South Central College *C, A*
Southwest Minnesota State
University *A, B*
University of Minnesota
Crookston *B*
Duluth *B*
Twin Cities *B*
University of St. Thomas *B*
Walden University *B, M, D*

Mississippi
Delta State University *B*
Jackson State University *B*
Mississippi College *B*

Mississippi Gulf Coast Community
College *A*
Mississippi State University *B*
Southwest Mississippi Community
College *A*
University of Mississippi *B*
University of Southern Mississippi *B*

Missouri

Avila University *B*
Central Methodist University *B*
College of the Ozarks *B*
Columbia College *B*
East Central College *C, A*
Evangel University *B*
Hannibal-LaGrange College *B*
Harris-Stowe State University *B*
Lincoln University *B*
Lindenwood University *B, M*
Maryville University of Saint
Louis *B, M*
Missouri Baptist University *B*
Missouri Southern State
University *B, T*
Missouri State University *B*
Missouri Western State University *B*
Northwest Missouri State
University *B*
Park University *B*
St. Charles Community College *C, A*
Saint Louis University *B*
Southeast Missouri State University *B*
Southwest Baptist University *B*
Stephens College *B*
Three Rivers Community College *A*
University of Central Missouri *B*
University of Missouri
Columbia *B*
St. Louis *B, M*
Washington University in St.
Louis *B, M*
Webster University *C, B, M*

Montana

University of Montana *A, B*

Nebraska

Bellevue University *B*
Creighton University *B*
Northeast Community College *C, A*
Southeast Community College *A*
University of Nebraska
Lincoln *B*
Omaha *B*
Western Nebraska Community
College *C*

Nevada

University of Nevada
Las Vegas *B*
Reno *B*

New Hampshire

Daniel Webster College *B*
Franklin Pierce University *B*
Manchester Community College *C, A*
NHTI-Concord's Community
College *A*
New England College *B*
Plymouth State University *B*
Rivier College *M*
Southern New Hampshire
University *A, B, M*

New Jersey

Bergen Community College *A*
Berkeley College- Garret Mountain
Campus *A, B*
Bloomfield College *C*
Brookdale Community College *A*
Caldwell College *B*
Camden County College *A*
College of St. Elizabeth *C*

Cumberland County College *A*
Fairleigh Dickinson University
College at Florham *B*
Metropolitan Campus *B*
Felician College *B*
Gloucester County College *A*
Kean University *B*
Passaic County Community College *A*
Raritan Valley Community College *A*
Rider University *B*
Rowan University *B, M*
Rutgers, The State University of New
Jersey
Camden Regional Campus *B*
New Brunswick/Piscataway
Campus *B*
Newark Regional Campus *B*
Seton Hall University *B*
Thomas Edison State College *C, B*
Union County College *A*

New Mexico

Art Center Design College *B*
Dona Ana Community College of New
Mexico State University *C, A*
Eastern New Mexico University *B*
New Mexico Highlands University *B*
New Mexico State University *B*
University of the Southwest *B*
Western New Mexico University *B*

New York

Adirondack Community College *A*
Alfred University *B*
Berkeley College *A, B*
Berkeley College of New York
City *A, B*
Briarcliffe College *B*
Bryant & Stratton Business Institute
Bryant & Stratton College:
Syracuse *A*
Canisius College *B*
City University of New York
New York City College of
Technology *A*
York College *B*
College of Westchester *A*
Dominican College of Blauvelt *B*
Elmira College *B*
Excelsior College *B*
Finger Lakes Community College *A*
Globe Institute of Technology *C*
Herkimer County Community
College *A*
Hofstra University *B, M*
Iona College *B, M*
Ithaca College *B*
Jamestown Business College *A*
Jamestown Community College *A*
Keuka College *B*
Laboratory Institute of
Merchandising *B*
Le Moyne College *B*
Marist College *B*
Monroe Community College *A*
Nazareth College *B*
New York Institute of
Technology *B, M*
Niagara University *B*
Pace University *B, M*
Roberts Wesleyan College *B, M*
Rochester Institute of
Technology *A, B, M*
St. John's University *B, M*
St. Thomas Aquinas College *B, M*
Siena College *B, T*
State University of New York
Albany *M*
Binghamton *B*
College at Old Westbury *B*
College at Plattsburgh *B*
College of Technology at Alfred *A*
College of Technology at Delhi *A*

Farmingdale *C*
Maritime College *B*
Suffolk County Community
College *C, A*
Syracuse University *B, M*
Touro College *B*
Wagner College *B*
Westchester Community College *A*

North Carolina

Appalachian State University *B*
Chowan University *B*
East Carolina University *B*
Elon University *B*
Fayetteville Technical Community
College *C, A*
High Point University *B*
Isothermal Community College *A*
Johnson & Wales University:
Charlotte *B*
Lenoir-Rhyne University *B*
Methodist University *B*
Montreat College *B*
North Carolina Agricultural and
Technical State University *B*
Pitt Community College *C, A*
Queens University of Charlotte *B*
Southwestern Community College *A*
University of North Carolina
Charlotte *B*
Wilmington *B*
Wayne Community College *A*
Western Carolina University *B*
Wilkes Community College *C, A*
Wingate University *B*

North Dakota

Jamestown College *B*
Minot State University *B*
North Dakota State University *B*
University of Mary *B*
University of North Dakota *B*
Williston State College *C, A*

Ohio

Ashland University *B*
Baldwin-Wallace College *B*
Bowling Green State University:
Firelands College *C*
Capital University *B*
Case Western Reserve University *M*
Cedarville University *B*
Cincinnati State Technical and
Community College *C, A*
Clark State Community College *A*
Cleveland State University *B, M*
Columbus State Community
College *A*
Davis College *A*
Edison State Community College *C, A*
Franklin University *B*
James A. Rhodes State College *A*
Kent State University *B, D*
Lourdes College *B*
Marietta College *B*
Marion Technical College *A*
Miami University
Hamilton Campus *A*
Oxford Campus *A, B*
Mount Vernon Nazarene University *B*
North Central State College *C*
Northwest State Community
College *A*
Notre Dame College *C, B*
Ohio Northern University *B*
Ohio State University
Columbus Campus *B*
Ohio University *B*
Ohio University
Southern Campus at Ironton *C*
Stark State College of Technology *A*
Terra State Community College *A*
Tiffin University *B*
University of Akron *C, A, B, M*

University of Akron: Wayne College *A*
University of Cincinnati
Clermont College *C, A*
University of Dayton *B*
University of Findlay *B*
University of Northwestern Ohio *A*
University of Rio Grande *B*
University of Toledo *B, M*
Urbana University *B*
Ursuline College *B*
Walsh University *A, B*
Washington State Community
College *A*
Wilmington College *B*
Wittenberg University *B*
Wright State University *A, B, M*
Xavier University *B, M*
Youngstown State University *A, B, M*
Zane State College *A*

Oklahoma

East Central University *B*
Mid-America Christian University *B*
Northeastern Oklahoma Agricultural
and Mechanical College *C, A*
Northeastern State University *B*
Oklahoma Baptist University *B*
Oklahoma City University *B, M*
Oklahoma State University *B*
Oral Roberts University *B*
Southeastern Oklahoma State
University *B*
Southern Nazarene University *B*
University of Central Oklahoma *B*
University of Oklahoma *B*
University of Tulsa *B*

Oregon

Blue Mountain Community College *A*
Central Oregon Community
College *A*
Clackamas Community College *C, A*
Klamath Community College *C, A*
Oregon Institute of Technology *B*
Portland Community College *C, A*
Portland State University *B*
Southern Oregon University *B*
Umpqua Community College *A*
University of Oregon *M, D*
University of Portland *B*

Pennsylvania

Albright College *B*
Alvernia University *B*
Arcadia University *B*
Bucks County Community College *A*
Butler County Community College *A*
Cabrini College *C, B*
Carnegie Mellon University *D*
Cedar Crest College *B*
Central Pennsylvania College *A*
Chatham University *B*
Chestnut Hill College *A, B*
Clarion University of Pennsylvania *B*
Community College of Allegheny
County *A*
Community College of Beaver
County *A*
DeSales University *B*
Delaware Valley College *B*
Drexel University *M*
Duquesne University *B*
Eastern University *B*
Edinboro University of
Pennsylvania *B*
Elizabethtown College *B*
Erie Business Center *A*
Erie Business Center South *A*
Gannon University *B*
Gettysburg College *B*
Grove City College *B*
Immaculata University *B*
Indiana University of Pennsylvania *B*
Juniata College *B*

King's College *B*
Kutztown University of
    Pennsylvania *B*
La Roche College *B*
La Salle University *B*
Lehigh University *B, M*
Lycoming College *B*
Manor College *A*
Mansfield University of
    Pennsylvania *B*
Marywood University *B*
McCann School of Business and
    Technology: Dickson City *A*
Messiah College *B*
Misericordia University *B*
Neumann University *B*
Northampton Community College *A*
Peirce College *A*
Penn State
    Abington *B*
    Altoona *B*
    Beaver *B*
    Berks *B*
    Brandywine *B*
    DuBois *B*
    Erie, The Behrend College *B*
    Fayette, The Eberly Campus *B*
    Greater Allegheny *B*
    Harrisburg *B*
    Hazleton *B*
    Lehigh Valley *B*
    Mont Alto *B*
    New Kensington *B*
    Schuylkill *B*
    Shenango *B*
    University Park *B*
    Wilkes-Barre *B*
    Worthington Scranton *B*
    York *B*
Philadelphia University *B*
Robert Morris University *C, B*
Rosemont College *B*
St. Francis University *B*
Saint Joseph's University *C, A, B, M*
St. Vincent College *B*
Seton Hill University *C, B*
Shippensburg University of
    Pennsylvania *B*
Slippery Rock University of
    Pennsylvania *B*
South Hills School of Business &
    Technology *A*
South Hills School of Business &
    Technology: Altoona *A*
Temple University *B, M*
University of Pennsylvania *B, M, D*
University of Pittsburgh *B*
University of Pittsburgh
    Johnstown *B*
University of Scranton *B*
University of the Sciences in
    Philadelphia *B*
Villanova University *B*
Westmoreland County Community
    College *C, A*
YTI Career Institute: York *A*
York College of Pennsylvania *B*

Puerto Rico

Bayamon Central University *B, M*
Inter American University of Puerto
    Rico
    Aguadilla Campus *B, M*
    Bayamon Campus *B*
    Guayama Campus *M*
    Metropolitan Campus *B, M*
    Ponce Campus *B, M*
    San German Campus *B, M*
Pontifical Catholic University of
    Puerto Rico *B, M*
Turabo University *B, M*
Universidad Metropolitana *A, B, M*
Universidad del Este *A, B*

University of Puerto Rico
    Aguadilla *B*
    Arecibo *B*
    Bayamon University College *B*
    Ponce *B*
    Rio Piedras *B, M*
University of the Sacred Heart *M*

Rhode Island

Bryant University *B, M*
Community College of Rhode
    Island *C, A*
Johnson & Wales University:
    Providence *B, M*
Providence College *B*
Rhode Island College *B*
Roger Williams University *B*
University of Rhode Island *B*

South Carolina

Anderson University *B*
Charleston Southern University *B*
Claflin University *B*
Clemson University *B*
Coastal Carolina University *B*
Converse College *B*
Forrest Junior College *A*
Francis Marion University *B*
Limestone College *B*
North Greenville University *B*
South Carolina State University *B*
Spartanburg Community College *A*
Trident Technical College *A*
University of South Carolina *B*

South Dakota

Black Hills State University *B*
Dakota State University *B*
National American University
    Rapid City *B*
Northern State University *B*
Southeast Technical Institute *A*
Western Dakota Technical Institute *A*

Tennessee

Belmont University *B*
East Tennessee State University *B*
Freed-Hardeman University *B*
Lambuth University *B*
Lipscomb University *B*
Middle Tennessee State University *B*
Southern Adventist University *B, M*
Trevecca Nazarene University *B*
Union University *B*
University of Memphis *B*
University of Tennessee
    Knoxville *B, M, D*
    Martin *B*
Vanderbilt University *M*

Texas

Abilene Christian University *B*
Angelo State University *B*
Austin Community College *C, A*
Baylor University *B*
Brookhaven College *C, A*
Cedar Valley College *C, A*
Clarendon College *A*
College of the Mainland *A*
Dallas Baptist University *B, M*
Galveston College *C, A*
Hardin-Simmons University *B*
Houston Baptist University *B*
Houston Community College
    System *C, A*
Howard Payne University *B*
Huston-Tillotson University *B*
Lamar University *B*
Laredo Community College *A*
LeTourneau University *B*
Lubbock Christian University *B*
McMurry University *B*
Midwestern State University *B*

Northwood University: Texas *B*
Our Lady of the Lake University of San
    Antonio *B*
St. Edward's University *B*
St. Mary's University *B*
Sam Houston State University *B*
Schreiner University *B*
South Texas College *C, A*
Southern Methodist University *B, M*
Southwestern Assemblies of God
    University *B*
Stephen F. Austin State University *B*
Sul Ross State University *B*
Tarleton State University *B*
Texarkana College *C, A*
Texas A&M International University *B*
Texas A&M University *B, M, D*
Texas A&M University
    Commerce *B*
    Corpus Christi *B*
    Texarkana *B*
Texas Christian University *B*
Texas Southern University *B*
Texas State University: San Marcos *B*
Texas Tech University *B*
Texas Wesleyan University *B*
Texas Woman's University *B*
Trinity University *B*
Tyler Junior College *C, A*
University of Dallas *M*
University of Houston *B, M, D*
University of Houston
    Clear Lake *B*
    Downtown *B*
    Victoria *B*
University of Mary Hardin-Baylor *B*
University of North Texas *B, D*
University of St. Thomas *B*
University of Texas
    Arlington *B, D*
    Austin *B, M, D*
    Brownsville - Texas Southmost
        College *B*
    El Paso *B*
    Pan American *B*
    San Antonio *B, M*
    Tyler *B*
    of the Permian Basin *B*
University of the Incarnate Word *B*
Vernon College *A*
Weatherford College *C, A*
West Texas A&M University *B, M*

Utah

Brigham Young University *B*
Independence University *A, B*
Salt Lake Community College *C, A*
Southern Utah University *B*
University of Utah *B, M*
Utah State University *B*
Weber State University *B*
Western Governors University *B*
Westminster College *B*

Vermont

Castleton State College *B*
Champlain College *B*
Lyndon State College *B*

Virginia

Averett University *B*
Christopher Newport University *B*
Ferrum College *B*
George Mason University *B*
Hampton University *B*
James Madison University *B*
Longwood University *B*
Lord Fairfax Community College *A*
Lynchburg College *B*
Old Dominion University *B*
Radford University *B*
Regent University *A, M*
University of Management and
    Technology *A, B, M*

Virginia Commonwealth University *B*
Virginia Intermont College *B*
Virginia Polytechnic Institute and
    State University *B*
Virginia State University *B*

Washington

Bates Technical College *C, A*
Bellevue College *C, A*
Bellingham Technical College *C, A*
Centralia College *C, A*
City University of Seattle *C, B*
Clover Park Technical College *C, A*
Eastern Washington University *B*
Green River Community College *A*
Peninsula College *C, A*
Seattle University *B*
Shoreline Community College *C, A*
Spokane Community College *C, A*
Spokane Falls Community
    College *C, A*
University of Washington Tacoma *B*
Washington State University *B, D*
Western Washington University *B*
Whitworth University *B*
Yakima Valley Community
    College *C, A*

West Virginia

Alderson-Broaddus College *B*
American Public University System *B*
Concord University *B*
Davis and Elkins College *B*
Marshall University *B*
New River Community and Technical
    College *A*
Southern West Virginia Community
    and Technical College *A*
West Virginia University *B*
West Virginia Wesleyan College *B*

Wisconsin

Blackhawk Technical College *A*
Carroll University *B*
Carthage College *B*
Concordia University Wisconsin *B*
Gateway Technical College *A*
Lakeland College *B*
Lakeshore Technical College *A*
Maranatha Baptist Bible College *B*
Marian University *B*
Marquette University *B, M*
Mid-State Technical College *A*
Milwaukee Area Technical College *A*
Moraine Park Technical College *A*
Mount Mary College *B*
Northcentral Technical College *C, A*
St. Norbert College *B*
University of Wisconsin
    Eau Claire *B*
    La Crosse *B*
    Madison *B, M*
    Milwaukee *B*
    Superior *B*
    Whitewater *B*
Viterbo University *B*
Waukesha County Technical
    College *A*
Wisconsin Indianhead Technical
    College *A*

Wyoming

Casper College *C, A*
University of Wyoming *B*
Western Wyoming Community
    College *A*

Marketing research

California

California State University
    Northridge *M*
Los Angeles Mission College *A*

Southwestern College *C, A*

District of Columbia

Howard University *B*

Georgia

University of Georgia *M*

Hawaii

University of Hawaii
 Hawaii Community College *C, A*

Idaho

Boise State University *B*

Illinois

Harper College *C*
Southern Illinois University
 Edwardsville *M*
University of Illinois
 Urbana-Champaign *B, D*

Indiana

Indiana University-Purdue University
 Indianapolis *B*

Kansas

Fort Hays State University *B*

Maine

Husson University *B*

Massachusetts

Boston University *B*

Minnesota

Winona State University *B*

Missouri

University of Missouri
 Kansas City *B*

Nebraska

University of Nebraska
 Lincoln *M, D*

New Jersey

Fairleigh Dickinson University
 College at Florham *M*
 Metropolitan Campus *M*

New York

City University of New York
 Baruch College *M*
Fashion Institute of Technology *B*
Fordham University *B, M*
Hofstra University *M*
Ithaca College *B*
Rochester Institute of Technology *B*

North Dakota

Lake Region State College *C, A*

Ohio

Bowling Green State University *B*
Stark State College of Technology *A*
University of Toledo *B*
Wright State University *M*

Oklahoma

Oklahoma Christian University *B*

Pennsylvania

La Salle University *B*

Rhode Island

Salve Regina University *B*

Texas

University of Texas
 Arlington *M*

Virginia

University of Management and
 Technology *B*

Marriage/family therapy

Alabama

Auburn University *M*
Faulkner University *B*

Arizona

Arizona State University *D*
Prescott College *M*

Arkansas

Harding University *M*
John Brown University *M*

California

Azusa Pacific University *M*
California Institute of Integral
 Studies *M*
California State University
 Dominguez Hills *M*
 Fresno *M*
 Los Angeles *M*
Chapman University *M*
Dominican University of California *M*
Loma Linda University *M, D*
Mount St. Mary's College *M*
Notre Dame de Namur University *M*
Pacific Oaks College *M*
University of La Verne *M*
University of San Diego *M*
University of Southern California *M*

Colorado

Colorado State University *M*

Connecticut

Central Connecticut State
 University *M*
Fairfield University *M*
Saint Joseph College *M*

Florida

Nova Southeastern University *M, D*
Saint Thomas University *M*
Stetson University *M*
University of Central Florida *M*
University of Miami *M*

Georgia

Mercer University *M*
Valdosta State University *M*

Idaho

Idaho State University *M*

Illinois

Northwestern University *M*

Indiana

Indiana Wesleyan University *M*

Kansas

Central Christian College of Kansas *A*
Friends University *M*

Louisiana

University of Louisiana at
 Monroe *M, D*

Maryland

University of Maryland
 College Park *M*
Washington Bible College *M*

Massachusetts

Eastern Nazarene College *M*
University of Massachusetts
 Boston *M*

Michigan

Michigan State University *B, M*

Minnesota

Capella University *M*
Saint Cloud State University *M*
St. Mary's University of Minnesota *M*
Walden University *M*

Mississippi

Mississippi College *M*

Missouri

Saint Louis University *M, D*

New Hampshire

University of New Hampshire *M*

New Jersey

Kean University *M*
Seton Hall University *M, D*

New York

City University of New York
 Hunter College *M*
Hofstra University *M*
Iona College *M*
Mercy College *M*
New York University *M, D*
Syracuse University *M, D*
University of Rochester *M*

North Carolina

Appalachian State University *M*
East Carolina University *B, M, D*

Ohio

University of Akron *M*

Oregon

George Fox University *M*

Pennsylvania

Drexel University *M, D*
Duquesne University *M*
Lancaster Bible College *M*
Seton Hill University *M*
Thomas Jefferson University: College
 of Health Professions *M*

South Carolina

Converse College *M*

Tennessee

Trevecca Nazarene University *M*

Texas

Abilene Christian University *M*
Del Mar College *A*
Lubbock Christian University *M*
Texas Tech University *M, D*
Texas Woman's University *M, D*
University of Houston
 Clear Lake *M*
University of Texas
 Tyler *M*

Utah

Brigham Young University *M, D*

Vermont

Goddard College *M*

Washington

Pacific Lutheran University *M*
Seattle Pacific University *M*

Wisconsin

Edgewood College *M*
Marquette University *D*
University of Wisconsin
 Stout *M*

Masonry

Alabama

Bishop State Community College *C*
Central Alabama Community
 College *C*
Gadsden State Community College *C*
Jefferson Davis Community College *C*
Lawson State Community College *C*

Arizona

Central Arizona College *C*
Eastern Arizona College *C*
GateWay Community College *C, A*

California

Bakersfield College *A*
Palomar College *C, A*

Colorado

Front Range Community College *C, A*

Florida

North Florida Community College *C*
Palm Beach Community College *C*
Santa Fe College *C*
South Florida Community College *C*

Georgia

Albany Technical College *C*
Savannah Technical College *C*

Illinois

Southwestern Illinois College *C, A*

Indiana

Ivy Tech Community College
 Central Indiana *C, A*
 Columbus *C, A*
 East Central *C, A*
 Lafayette *C, A*
 North Central *C, A*
 Northeast *C, A*
 Northwest *C, A*
 South Central *C, A*
 Southwest *C, A*
 Wabash Valley *C, A*

Iowa

Ellsworth Community College *C*
Kirkwood Community College *C*

Kentucky

Big Sandy Community and Technical
 College *C*
Bluegrass Community and Technical
 College *C*
Somerset Community College *C, A*

Maryland

Cecil College *C*

Michigan

Lansing Community College *A*

Minnesota

Alexandria Technical College *C*

Dakota County Technical College C, A
Riverland Community College C
St. Paul College C

Mississippi
Hinds Community College C
Mississippi Delta Community
    College C
Pearl River Community College C, A

Nevada
Truckee Meadows Community
    College C, A

New York
State University of New York
    College of Technology at Alfred A
    College of Technology at Delhi C, A

North Carolina
Blue Ridge Community College C
James Sprunt Community College C
Johnston Community College C
Piedmont Community College C
Pitt Community College C
Southeastern Community College C
Southwestern Community College C
Tri-County Community College C

Pennsylvania
Pennsylvania College of
    Technology C, A, B
Thaddeus Stevens College of
    Technology A
Williamson Free School of Mechanical
    Trades A

South Carolina
Greenville Technical College C

Texas
Howard College C
Trinity Valley Community College C

Utah
Salt Lake Community College C

Virginia
Southwest Virginia Community
    College C

Wisconsin
Gateway Technical College C
Lakeshore Technical College C
Milwaukee Area Technical College C
Southwest Wisconsin Technical
    College C
Waukesha County Technical
    College C
Western Technical College C
Wisconsin Indianhead Technical
    College C

Massage therapy

Alabama
Gadsden State Community College C

Arizona
Arizona Western College C, A
Brookline College
    Phoenix C
    Tempe C
    Tucson C
Central Arizona College C, A
Chandler-Gilbert Community College
    Pecos C, A
Pima Community College C, A

California
Bryan College: Sacramento A

Concorde Career College: North
    Hollywood C
Concorde Career College: San
    Bernardino C
Concorde Career College: San
    Diego C
Kaplan College: Palm Springs C
Kaplan College: Vista C
LA College International C
San Joaquin Valley College A
Santa Barbara Business College: Palm
    Desert C
Santa Barbara City College C
Silicon Valley College
    Western Career College: San Jose A
Western Career College: Antioch C, A
Western Career College: Citrus
    Heights C, A
Western Career College:
    Sacramento C, A
Western Career College:
    Stockton C, A
WyoTech: Long Beach C

Colorado
Anthem College C, A
Boulder College of Massage
    Therapy C, A
Colorado School of Healing Arts C, A
Community College of Denver C
Pueblo Community College C
Trinidad State Junior College C, A

Florida
Angley College C, A
Daytona State College C
Florida College of Natural Health
    Miami A
Gulf Coast Community College C
Herzing University C
Miami Dade College C
Palm Beach Community College A
Pensacola Junior College C
Rasmussen College: Ocala A
Southwest Florida College C, A

Georgia
Gwinnett College C

Idaho
Idaho State University C, A

Illinois
Black Hawk College C
Illinois Eastern Community Colleges
    Olney Central College C
Kaskaskia College C
Kishwaukee College C
Moraine Valley Community College C
Morton College C
National University of Health
    Sciences C, A
Parkland College C
Rasmussen College: Aurora C, A
Rasmussen College: Rockford C, A
Rend Lake College C
Rockford Career College A
Waubonsee Community College C, A

Indiana
Harrison College
    Indianapolis East C, A
Ivy Tech Community College
    Northeast C, A
Kaplan College: Hammond C, A
Kaplan College: Indianapolis C, A
Kaplan College: Merrillville C, A
Vincennes University C, A

Iowa
Clinton Community College C
Indian Hills Community College C
Iowa Lakes Community College C

Muscatine Community College C
Northeast Iowa Community
    College C
Scott Community College C

Kansas
Colby Community College C

Kentucky
Spencerian College C, A
Spencerian College: Lexington C

Louisiana
Blue Cliff College: Houma C
Blue Cliff College: Lafayette C
Blue Cliff College: Metairie C, A
Delgado Community College C
Our Lady of the Lake College C

Maine
Kennebec Valley Community
    College C

Maryland
Allegany College of Maryland A
College of Southern Maryland A
Community College of Baltimore
    County C
Harford Community College A

Massachusetts
Berkshire Community College C
Mount Wachusett Community
    College C
Springfield Technical Community
    College C, A

Michigan
Baker College
    of Clinton Township A
    of Flint C, A
    of Jackson C, A
    of Muskegon C
    of Port Huron C, A
Baker College of Allen Park C
Kirtland Community College C, A
Oakland Community College C, A
Schoolcraft College C, A

Minnesota
Lake Superior College C
Minnesota School of Business C, A
Minnesota School of Business:
    Blaine C, A
Minnesota School of Business: St.
    Cloud C, A
Minnesota State College - Southeast
    Technical C, A
Minnesota State Community and
    Technical College C
Minnesota West Community and
    Technical College C
Northwest Technical College C, A
Northwestern Health Sciences
    University C
Rasmussen College
    Eagan C, A
    Eden Prairie C, A
    Mankato C, A
    St. Cloud C, A
Rasmussen College: Brooklyn
    Park C, A
Rasmussen College: Lake
    Elmo/Woodbury C, A
Ridgewater College C
St. Paul College C, A

Mississippi
Antonelli College
    Jackson A
Blue Cliff College: Gulfport C, A

Southwest Mississippi Community
    College A

Missouri
High-Tech Institute C
Missouri College C, A
Pinnacle Career Institute: Kansas
    City C
St. Charles Community College A
Sanford-Brown College
    St. Peters C, A

Nevada
High-Tech Institute A

New Hampshire
Nashua Community College C
River Valley Community College C

New York
Columbia-Greene Community
    College C
Finger Lakes Community College A
Mildred Elley C, A
North Country Community College A
State University of New York
    College of Agriculture and
        Technology at Morrisville A
Swedish Institute A
Trocaire College C, A

North Carolina
Carteret Community College C, A
Forsyth Technical Community
    College A
Gaston College C, A
Lenoir Community College C, A
Miller-Motte Technical College C, A
Miller-Motte Technical College:
    Cary A
Sandhills Community College C, A
South Piedmont Community
    College A
Southeastern Community
    College C, A
Southwestern Community College C

North Dakota
Rasmussen College: Bismarck A
Williston State College C, A

Ohio
Cincinnati State Technical and
    Community College C, A
Hocking College C, A
Ohio Business College:
    Columbus C, A
Ohio College of Massotherapy C, A
Owens Community College
    Toledo C, A
Southwestern College of Business
    Southwestern College:
        Tri-County C
Southwestern College: Dayton C
Stark State College of Technology C, A

Oklahoma
Platt College
    Tulsa C

Oregon
Central Oregon Community
    College C, A
Rogue Community College C

Pennsylvania
Butler County Community
    College C, A
Career Training Academy A
Keystone Technical Institute C, A
Laurel Business Institute A

McCann School of Business and
Technology: Dickson City A
Penn Commercial Business and
Technical School C
University of Pittsburgh
Titusville C

Puerto Rico

Ponce Paramedical College C

Rhode Island

Community College of Rhode
Island A

South Carolina

Horry-Georgetown Technical
College C
Miller-Motte Technical College C, A

Tennessee

Draughons Junior College:
Nashville C
Roane State Community College C

Texas

Houston Community College
System C
St. Philip's College C
Western Technical College: Diana
Drive C

Utah

Eagle Gate College: Salt Lake City C
Utah Career College A

Virginia

Centura College: Newport News C, A
Centura College: Richmond A

Washington

Clover Park Technical College A
Peninsula College C
Renton Technical College C, A
Whatcom Community College A

Wisconsin

Rasmussen College: Green Bay C, A
Wisconsin Indianhead Technical
College C

Wyoming

Sheridan College C, A

Materials engineering

Alabama

Auburn University B, M, D
Tuskegee University D
University of Alabama D
University of Alabama
Birmingham B, M, D

Arizona

Arizona State University B, M, D

California

California Polytechnic State
University: San Luis Obispo B
California State Polytechnic
University: Pomona B
California State University
Long Beach B
Northridge B, M
San Jose State University B, M
Stanford University B, M, D
University of California
Davis B, M, D
Irvine B, M, D
Los Angeles B, M, D
Santa Barbara M, D
University of California: Merced B

University of Southern California M

Colorado

Colorado School of Mines M

Connecticut

University of Connecticut B

Delaware

University of Delaware M, D

District of Columbia

George Washington University M
Howard University M, D

Florida

Florida International University M, D
Florida State University B
University of Central Florida M, D
University of Florida B, M

Georgia

Georgia Institute of
Technology B, M, D

Idaho

University of Idaho B, M, D

Illinois

Illinois Institute of
Technology B, M, D
Northwestern University B, M, D
University of Illinois
Chicago M, D
Urbana-Champaign B, M, D

Indiana

Purdue University B, M, D

Iowa

Iowa State University B, M, D

Kentucky

University of Kentucky B, M, D

Maryland

Johns Hopkins University B, M, D
University of Maryland
College Park B, M, D

Massachusetts

Massachusetts Institute of
Technology B, M, D
Worcester Polytechnic Institute M, D

Michigan

Michigan State University B, M, D
Michigan Technological
University B, M, D, T

Minnesota

University of Minnesota
Twin Cities B, M, D
Winona State University B

Missouri

Washington University in St. Louis M

New Jersey

New Jersey Institute of
Technology M, D
Stevens Institute of Technology M, D

New Mexico

New Mexico Institute of Mining and
Technology B, M, D

New York

Alfred University B, M, D
Columbia University B, M, D

Cornell University B, M, D
Polytechnic Institute of New York
University D
Rensselaer Polytechnic
Institute B, M, D
Rochester Institute of Technology M
State University of New York
Binghamton M, D
Stony Brook M, D
University of Rochester M, D

North Carolina

North Carolina Agricultural and
Technical State University B
North Carolina State
University B, M, D

North Dakota

North Dakota State University D

Ohio

Case Western Reserve
University B, M, D
Ohio State University
Columbus Campus B, M, D
University of Cincinnati M, D
University of Dayton M, D
Wright State University B
Youngstown State University B

Oregon

Oregon State University M

Pennsylvania

Carnegie Mellon University B, M, D
Community College of Beaver
County A
Drexel University B, M, D
Lehigh University B, M, D
Penn State
University Park M, D
University of Pennsylvania B, M, D
University of Pittsburgh B, M, D

Rhode Island

Brown University B, M, D

South Carolina

Clemson University M, D

South Dakota

South Dakota School of Mines and
Technology M, D

Tennessee

University of Tennessee
Knoxville B, M, D

Texas

Rice University B, M, D
Texas A&M University M, D
University of Houston M, D
University of Texas
Arlington M, D
Austin M, D
Dallas M, D
El Paso M, D

Utah

Salt Lake Community College A
Southern Utah University A
University of Utah B, M, D

Virginia

University of Virginia M, D
Virginia Polytechnic Institute and
State University B, M, D

Washington

University of Washington B, M, D
Washington State University B, M

Wisconsin

Milwaukee Area Technical College A
University of Wisconsin
Madison B, M, D
Milwaukee B

Materials science

Alabama

Tuskegee University D
University of Alabama
Birmingham D
Huntsville M, D

Arizona

University of Arizona B, M, D

California

California Institute of
Technology B, M, D
Stanford University B, M, D
University of California
Berkeley B, M, D
Los Angeles B
Riverside B
San Diego M, D
University of Southern
California M, D

Colorado

Colorado School of Mines M, D
University of Denver M, D

Connecticut

University of Connecticut B, M, D

Idaho

Boise State University B, M

Illinois

Northwestern University B
University of Illinois
Urbana-Champaign B, M, D

Iowa

Iowa State University B, M, D

Maryland

Johns Hopkins University B, M, D

Massachusetts

University of Massachusetts
Amherst M, D
Worcester Polytechnic Institute M, D

Michigan

Central Michigan University D
Michigan State University B, M, D
University of Michigan B, M, D
Wayne State University M, D

Minnesota

University of Minnesota
Twin Cities B, M, D
Winona State University B

Missouri

Missouri State University M
Washington University in St.
Louis M, D

New Hampshire

University of New Hampshire B, M, D

New Jersey

Stevens Institute of
Technology B, M, D

New Mexico

University of New Mexico M, D

New York

Alfred University *B, M*
Columbia University *B, M, D*
Polytechnic Institute of New York
     University *M*
Rochester Institute of Technology *M*
State University of New York
     Albany *B, M, D*
     Binghamton *M, D*

North Carolina

University of North Carolina
     Chapel Hill *M, D*

Ohio

Case Western Reserve
     University *B, M, D*
Hocking College *A*
Ohio State University
     Columbus Campus *B, M, D*
Youngstown State University *M*

Oregon

Oregon State University *M, D*

Pennsylvania

Carnegie Mellon University *B, M, D*
Penn State
     Abington *B*
     Altoona *B*
     Beaver *B*
     Berks *B*
     Brandywine *B*
     DuBois *B*
     Erie, The Behrend College *B*
     Fayette, The Eberly Campus *B*
     Greater Allegheny *B*
     Hazleton *B*
     Lehigh Valley *B*
     Mont Alto *B*
     New Kensington *B*
     Schuylkill *B*
     Shenango *B*
     University Park *B*
     Wilkes-Barre *B*
     Worthington Scranton *B*
     York *B*
University of Pennsylvania *B*

Tennessee

University of Tennessee
     Knoxville *B, M, D*
Vanderbilt University *M, D*

Texas

Southern Methodist University *M*
University of North Texas *B, M, D*

Vermont

University of Vermont *M, D*

Washington

University of Washington *B*
Washington State University *D*

Wisconsin

Marquette University *M, D*

Maternal/child health

Indiana

Indiana University-Purdue University
     Indianapolis *M*

Maryland

University of Maryland
     College Park *D*

Minnesota

University of Minnesota
     Twin Cities *M*

North Carolina

University of North Carolina
     Chapel Hill *M, D*

Ohio

Union Institute & University *B*

Puerto Rico

University of Puerto Rico
     Medical Sciences *M*

Maternal/child health nursing

Florida

St. Petersburg College *A*

Georgia

Georgia State University *M*

Indiana

Indiana University-Purdue University
     Indianapolis *M*

Michigan

University of Michigan *M*
Wayne State University *M*

New York

City University of New York
     Hunter College *B, M*
State University of New York
     Buffalo *M*
     Stony Brook *M*
     Upstate Medical University *M*
University of Rochester *M*

Ohio

Case Western Reserve University *M*

Pennsylvania

University of Pennsylvania *M*

South Carolina

Medical University of South
     Carolina *M*

Tennessee

University of Tennessee
     Knoxville *M*

Texas

Baylor University *M*
Texas Christian University *M*

Mathematical statistics/probability

Alabama

University of Alabama *M, D*

Arizona

Northern Arizona University *B*

Colorado

Colorado School of Mines *B*

Florida

University of Miami *B*

Illinois

Northern Illinois University *B*

Nebraska

University of Nebraska
     Lincoln *M, D*

New York

Rochester Institute of
     Technology *B, M*

Pennsylvania

Carnegie Mellon University *B*

Texas

University of the Incarnate Word *M*

Washington

Evergreen State College *B*

Mathematics

Alabama

Alabama Agricultural and Mechanical
     University *B*
Alabama State University *B, M*
Athens State University *B*
Auburn University *B, M, D, T*
Auburn University at Montgomery *B*
Birmingham-Southern College *B*
Calhoun Community College *A*
Chattahoochee Valley Community
     College *A*
Faulkner State Community College *A*
Faulkner University *B, T*
Gadsden State Community College *A*
Huntingdon College *B*
Jacksonville State University *B, M*
Judson College *B*
Miles College *B*
Oakwood University *B*
Samford University *B*
Shelton State Community College *A*
Spring Hill College *B, T*
Stillman College *B*
Talladega College *B*
Troy University *B*
Tuskegee University *B, T*
University of Alabama *B, M, D*
University of Alabama
     Birmingham *B, M*
     Huntsville *B, M*
University of Mobile *B, T*
University of Montevallo *B, T*
University of North Alabama *B*
University of South Alabama *M*
University of West Alabama *B, T*

Alaska

University of Alaska
     Anchorage *B*
     Fairbanks *B, M, D*
     Southeast *B*

Arizona

Arizona State University *B, M, D*
Arizona Western College *A*
Central Arizona College *A*
Cochise College *A*
Eastern Arizona College *A*
Mesa Community College *A*
Northern Arizona University *B, M*
Prescott College *B, M*
University of Arizona *B, M, D*

Arkansas

Arkansas State University *B, M*
Arkansas Tech University *B*
Harding University *B*
Henderson State University *B*
Hendrix College *B*
John Brown University *B*
Lyon College *B*
Ouachita Baptist University *B*
Philander Smith College *B*
Phillips Community College of the
     University of Arkansas *A*
Southern Arkansas University *B*
University of Arkansas *B, M, D*

University of Arkansas
     Fort Smith *B*
     Little Rock *B*
     Monticello *B*
     Pine Bluff *B*
University of Central Arkansas *B, M*
University of the Ozarks *B*

California

Allan Hancock College *A*
Antelope Valley College *A*
Azusa Pacific University *B*
Bakersfield College *A*
Barstow Community College *A*
Biola University *B*
Butte College *A*
Cabrillo College *A*
California Baptist University *B*
California Institute of
     Technology *B, M, D*
California Lutheran University *B*
California Polytechnic State
     University: San Luis Obispo *B, M*
California State Polytechnic
     University: Pomona *B, M*
California State University
     Bakersfield *B*
     Chico *B*
     Dominguez Hills *B*
     East Bay *B, M*
     Fresno *B, M*
     Fullerton *B, M*
     Long Beach *B, M*
     Los Angeles *B, M*
     Monterey Bay *B*
     Northridge *B, M*
     Sacramento *B, M*
     San Bernardino *B, M*
     San Marcos *B, M*
     Stanislaus *B*
California State University: Channel
     Islands *B*
Canada College *A*
Cerritos College *A*
Chabot College *A*
Chaffey College *A*
Chapman University *B*
Citrus College *A*
Claremont McKenna College *B*
College of Alameda *A*
College of Marin: Kentfield *A*
College of San Mateo *A*
College of the Canyons *A*
College of the Desert *A*
College of the Sequoias *A*
College of the Siskiyous *A*
Columbia College *A*
Concordia University *B*
Contra Costa College *A*
Copper Mountain College *A*
Crafton Hills College *A*
Cuesta College *A*
Cypress College *A*
De Anza College *A*
Diablo Valley College *A*
East Los Angeles College *A*
El Camino College *A*
El Camino College: Compton
     Center *A*
Feather River College *A*
Folsom Lake College *A*
Foothill College *A*
Fresno City College *A*
Fresno Pacific University *B*
Fullerton College *A*
Gavilan College *A*
Glendale Community College *A*
Golden West College *A*
Grossmont College *A*
Hartnell College *A*
Harvey Mudd College *B*
Humboldt State University *B*
Imperial Valley College *A*
Irvine Valley College *A*

La Sierra University *B*
Lake Tahoe Community College *A*
Laney College *A*
Lassen Community College *A*
Long Beach City College *A*
Los Angeles City College *A*
Los Angeles Mission College *A*
Los Angeles Southwest College *A*
Los Angeles Valley College *A*
Los Medanos College *A*
Loyola Marymount University *B, M*
The Master's College *B*
Mendocino College *A*
Merced College *A*
Merritt College *A*
Mills College *B*
MiraCosta College *A*
Mission College *A*
Monterey Peninsula College *A*
Moorpark College *A*
Mount St. Mary's College *B*
Mount San Jacinto College *A*
National University *B*
Occidental College *B*
Orange Coast College *A*
Oxnard College *A*
Pacific Union College *B*
Palomar College *A*
Pepperdine University *B*
Pitzer College *B*
Point Loma Nazarene University *B*
Pomona College *B*
Porterville College *A*
Reedley College *A*
Sacramento City College *A*
Saddleback College *A*
St. Mary's College of California *B*
San Bernardino Valley College *A*
San Diego Christian College *B*
San Diego City College *A*
San Diego Mesa College *A*
San Diego Miramar College *A*
San Diego State University *B, M*
San Francisco State University *B, M*
San Joaquin Delta College *A*
San Jose State University *B, M*
Santa Ana College *A*
Santa Barbara City College *A*
Santa Clara University *B*
Santa Rosa Junior College *A*
Santiago Canyon College *A*
Scripps College *B*
Shasta College *A*
Sierra College *A*
Simpson University *B*
Skyline College *A*
Solano Community College *A*
Sonoma State University *B*
Southwestern College *A*
Stanford University *B, M, D*
Taft College *A*
University of California
  Berkeley *B, M, D*
  Davis *B, M, D*
  Irvine *B, M, D*
  Los Angeles *B, M, D*
  Riverside *B, M, D*
  San Diego *B, M, D*
  Santa Barbara *B, M, D*
  Santa Cruz *B, M, D*
University of La Verne *B*
University of Redlands *B*
University of San Diego *B*
University of San Francisco *B*
University of Southern
  California *B, M, D*
University of the Pacific *B*
Vanguard University of Southern
  California *B*
Victor Valley College *A*
West Hills College: Lemoore *A*
West Valley College *A*
Westmont College *B*
Whittier College *B*

Yuba Community College District *A*

Colorado

Adams State College *B*
Colorado Christian University *B*
Colorado College *B*
Colorado Mountain College *A*
Colorado School of Mines *M, D*
Colorado State University *B, M, D*
Colorado State University
  Pueblo *B*
Fort Lewis College *B*
Lamar Community College *A*
Mesa State College *B*
Metropolitan State College of
  Denver *B, T*
Otero Junior College *A*
Pikes Peak Community College *A*
Regis University *B*
Trinidad State Junior College *A*
University of Colorado
  Boulder *B, M, D*
  Colorado Springs *B*
  Denver *B*
University of Denver *B, M, D*
University of Northern
  Colorado *B, M, T*
Western State College of Colorado *B*

Connecticut

Albertus Magnus College *B*
Central Connecticut State
  University *B, M, T*
Connecticut College *B*
Eastern Connecticut State
  University *B*
Fairfield University *B, M*
Gateway Community College *A*
Norwalk Community College *A*
Quinnipiac University *B*
Sacred Heart University *B*
Saint Joseph College *B*
Southern Connecticut State
  University *B, M, T*
Trinity College *B*
University of Bridgeport *B*
University of Connecticut *B, M, D*
University of Hartford *B*
University of New Haven *B*
Wesleyan University *B, M, D*
Western Connecticut State
  University *B, M*
Yale University *B, M, D*

Delaware

Delaware State University *B, M*
University of Delaware *B, M, D*
Wesley College *B*

District of Columbia

American University *B, M*
Catholic University of America *B*
Gallaudet University *B*
George Washington
  University *B, M, D*
Georgetown University *B*
Howard University *B, M, D*
Trinity Washington University *B*
University of the District of
  Columbia *B, M*

Florida

Ave Maria University *B*
Barry University *B*
Bethune-Cookman University *B*
Broward College *A*
Chipola College *A, B*
Clearwater Christian College *B*
Daytona State College *A*
Eckerd College *B*
Edward Waters College *B*
Florida Agricultural and Mechanical
  University *B*

Florida Atlantic University *B, M, D*
Florida Gulf Coast University *B*
Florida Institute of Technology *B*
Florida International University *B*
Florida Memorial University *B*
Florida Southern College *B*
Florida State University *B, M, D*
Gulf Coast Community College *A*
Indian River State College *A*
Jacksonville University *B*
Miami Dade College *A*
New College of Florida *B*
Northwest Florida State College *A*
Palm Beach Atlantic University *B*
Palm Beach Community College *A*
Pensacola Junior College *A*
Rollins College *B*
Saint Leo University *B*
Southeastern University *B*
State College of Florida,
  Manatee-Sarasota *A*
Stetson University *B*
University of Central Florida *R*
University of Florida *B, M*
University of Miami *B, M, D*
University of North Florida *B*
University of South Florida *B, M, D*
University of Tampa *A, B, T*
University of West Florida *B, M*

Georgia

Abraham Baldwin Agricultural
  College *A*
Agnes Scott College *B*
Albany State University *B*
Andrew College *A*
Atlanta Metropolitan College *A*
Augusta State University *B*
Bainbridge College *A*
Berry College *B*
Brewton-Parker College *B*
Clark Atlanta University *B, M*
Clayton State University *B*
College of Coastal Georgia *A*
Columbus State University *B*
Covenant College *B*
Dalton State College *A, B*
Darton College *A*
East Georgia College *A*
Emmanuel College *B*
Emory University *B, M, D*
Fort Valley State University *B*
Gainesville State College *A*
Georgia College and State
  University *B*
Georgia Gwinnett College *B*
Georgia Highlands College *A*
Georgia Institute of Technology *M, D*
Georgia Perimeter College *A*
Georgia Southern University *B, M*
Georgia Southwestern State
  University *B, T*
Georgia State University *B, M, D*
Gordon College *A, B, T*
Kennesaw State University *B*
LaGrange College *B*
Macon State College *A, B*
Mercer University *B*
Middle Georgia College *A*
Morehouse College *B*
North Georgia College & State
  University *B*
Oglethorpe University *B*
Paine College *B*
Piedmont College *B*
Savannah State University *B*
Shorter College *B, T*
South Georgia College *A*
Southern Polytechnic State
  University *B*
Spelman College *B*
University of Georgia *B, M, D*
University of West Georgia *B*
Valdosta State University *B*

Waycross College *A*
Wesleyan College *B, T*
Young Harris College *A*

Hawaii

Hawaii Pacific University *A*
University of Hawaii
  Hilo *B*
  Manoa *B, M, D*

Idaho

Boise State University *B, M, T*
Brigham Young University-Idaho *B*
College of Idaho *B*
Idaho State University *A, B, M, D*
Lewis-Clark State College *B*
North Idaho College *A*
Northwest Nazarene University *B*
University of Idaho *B, M, D*

Illinois

Augustana College *B, T*
Aurora University *B, M*
Benedictine University *B, T*
Black Hawk College: East Campus *A*
Blackburn College *B*
Bradley University *B, T*
Chicago State University *B, M, T*
City Colleges of Chicago
  Harold Washington College *A*
  Kennedy-King College *A*
  Olive-Harvey College *A*
Concordia University Chicago *B, T*
Danville Area Community College *A*
DePaul University *B, M, T*
Dominican University *B*
East-West University *B*
Eastern Illinois University *B, M, T*
Elmhurst College *B, T*
Eureka College *B, T*
Governors State University *B*
Greenville College *B, T*
Illinois Central College *A*
Illinois College *B, T*
Illinois State University *B, M, T*
Illinois Valley Community College *A*
Illinois Wesleyan University *B*
John A. Logan College *A*
John Wood Community College *A*
Joliet Junior College *A*
Judson University *B*
Kankakee Community College *A*
Kishwaukee College *A*
Knox College *B*
Lake Forest College *B*
Lake Land College *A*
Lewis University *B, T*
Lincoln College *A*
Loyola University Chicago *B, M*
MacMurray College *B, T*
McKendree University *B, T*
Monmouth College *B, T*
National-Louis University *B*
North Central College *B, T*
North Park University *B*
Northeastern Illinois University *B, M*
Northern Illinois University *B, M, D, T*
Northwestern University *B, M, D*
Olivet Nazarene University *B, T*
Principia College *B*
Quincy University *B, T*
Richland Community College *A*
Rockford College *B*
Roosevelt University *B, M*
Saint Xavier University *B*
South Suburban College of Cook
  County *A*
Southeastern Illinois College *A*
Southern Illinois University
  Carbondale *B, M, D*
Southern Illinois University
  Edwardsville *B, M*
Southwestern Illinois College *A*
Trinity Christian College *B, T*

Trinity International University B
Triton College A
University of Chicago B, M, D
University of Illinois
  Chicago B, M, D
  Springfield B
  Urbana-Champaign B, M, D
University of St. Francis B
Western Illinois University B, M
Wheaton College B, T

Indiana

Anderson University B
Ball State University B, M, T
Bethel College B
Butler University B
DePauw University B
Earlham College B
Franklin College B
Goshen College B
Grace College B
Hanover College B
Huntington University B
Indiana State University B, M, T
Indiana University
  Bloomington B, M, D
  East A
  Kokomo B
  Northwest B
  South Bend B
  Southeast B
Indiana University-Purdue University
  Fort Wayne A, B, M, T
Indiana University-Purdue University
  Indianapolis B, M, D
Indiana Wesleyan University B
Manchester College B, T
Marian University B, T
Purdue University B, M, D
Purdue University
  Calumet B, M
  North Central A
Rose-Hulman Institute of
  Technology B
Saint Joseph's College B
Saint Mary's College B
St. Mary-of-the-Woods College B
Taylor University B
Trine University A, B
University of Evansville B
University of Indianapolis B
University of Notre Dame B, M, D
University of St. Francis B
University of Southern Indiana B, T
Valparaiso University B
Vincennes University A
Wabash College B

Iowa

Briar Cliff University B
Buena Vista University B, T
Central College B, T
Clarke College B, T
Coe College B
Cornell College B, T
Dordt College B
Drake University B
Ellsworth Community College A
Graceland University B, T
Grinnell College B
Iowa State University B, M, D
Iowa Wesleyan College B
Iowa Western Community College A
Loras College B
Luther College B
Maharishi University of
  Management B
Marshalltown Community College A
Morningside College B
Mount Mercy College B, T
Northwestern College B, T
St. Ambrose University B
Simpson College B
University of Iowa B, M, D, T

University of Northern Iowa B, M
Upper Iowa University B
Wartburg College B, T
William Penn University B

Kansas

Allen County Community College A
Baker University B, T
Barton County Community College A
Benedictine College B
Bethany College B, T
Bethel College B
Butler Community College A
Central Christian College of
  Kansas A, B
Coffeyville Community College A
Cowley County Community
  College A
Dodge City Community College A
Donnelly College A
Emporia State University B, M, T
Fort Hays State University B, M
Friends University B
Garden City Community College A
Highland Community College A
Hutchinson Community College A
Kansas State University B, M, D
Kansas Wesleyan University B, T
McPherson College B, T
MidAmerica Nazarene University B
Neosho County Community
  College A
Newman University B
Ottawa University B
Pittsburg State University B, M
Pratt Community College A
Seward County Community College A
Southwestern College B
Sterling College B
Tabor College B
University of Kansas B, M, D
University of St. Mary B
Washburn University B
Wichita State University B, M, D, T

Kentucky

Asbury College B, T
Bellarmine University B, T
Berea College B, T
Bluegrass Community and Technical
  College A
Campbellsville University B
Centre College B
Eastern Kentucky University B, M
Georgetown College B
Kentucky State University B
Kentucky Wesleyan College B, T
Lindsey Wilson College A, B, T
Mid-Continent University B
Midway College B
Morehead State University B
Murray State University B, M, T
Northern Kentucky University B
Pikeville College B, T
St. Catharine College A
Thomas More College A, B
Transylvania University B
Union College B
University of Kentucky B, M, D
University of Louisville B, M
University of the Cumberlands B, T
Western Kentucky University B, M, T

Louisiana

Centenary College of Louisiana B, T
Dillard University B
Grambling State University B
Louisiana College B, T
Louisiana State University
  Alexandria B
  Shreveport B
Louisiana State University and
  Agricultural and Mechanical
  College B, M, D

Louisiana Tech University B, M
Loyola University New Orleans B
McNeese State University B, M
Nicholls State University B
Northwestern State University B
Southeastern Louisiana University B
Southern University and Agricultural
  and Mechanical College B, M
Tulane University B, M, D
University of Louisiana at
  Lafayette B, M, D
University of Louisiana at Monroe B
University of New Orleans B, M
Xavier University of Louisiana B

Maine

Bates College B, T
Bowdoin College B
Colby College B
Saint Joseph's College of Maine B
University of Maine B, M
University of Maine
  Farmington B
University of New England B
University of Southern Maine B

Maryland

Allegany College of Maryland A
Anne Arundel Community College A
Bowie State University B
Cecil College A
College of Notre Dame of Maryland B
Coppin State University B
Frederick Community College A
Frostburg State University B
Garrett College A
Goucher College B
Harford Community College A
Hood College B, T
Howard Community College A
Johns Hopkins University B, M, D
McDaniel College B
Montgomery College A
Morgan State University B, M
Mount St. Mary's University B, T
St. Mary's College of Maryland B
Salisbury University B, T
Towson University B, T
United States Naval Academy B
University of Maryland
  Baltimore County B
  College Park B, M, D
  Eastern Shore B
Washington Adventist University B

Massachusetts

Amherst College B
Assumption College B
Bard College at Simon's Rock B
Bentley University B
Boston College B, M
Boston University B, M, D
Brandeis University B, M, D
Bridgewater State College B
Bunker Hill Community College A
Cape Cod Community College A
Clark University B
College of the Holy Cross B
Dean College A
Eastern Nazarene College B
Elms College B
Emmanuel College B
Fitchburg State College B
Framingham State College B
Gordon College B
Hampshire College B
Harvard College B, M, D
Lesley University B
Massachusetts College of Liberal
  Arts B
Massachusetts Institute of
  Technology B, D
Merrimack College B
Mount Holyoke College B

Nichols College B, T
Northeastern University B, M, D
Roxbury Community College A
Salem State College B, M
Simmons College B
Smith College B
Springfield College B
Springfield Technical Community
  College A
Stonehill College B
Suffolk University B
Tufts University B, M, D
University of Massachusetts
  Amherst B, M, D
  Boston B
  Dartmouth B
  Lowell B
Wellesley College B
Western New England College B
Westfield State College B
Wheaton College B
Wheelock College B
Williams College B
Worcester Polytechnic
  Institute B, M, D
Worcester State College B

Michigan

Adrian College B, T
Albion College B, T
Alma College B, T
Andrews University B
Aquinas College B, T
Calvin College B, T
Central Michigan University B, M, D
Cornerstone University B, T
Delta College A
Eastern Michigan University B, M
Ferris State University B
Gogebic Community College A
Grand Rapids Community College A
Grand Valley State University B
Hillsdale College B
Hope College B
Kalamazoo College B
Lake Michigan College A
Lake Superior State University B, T
Lansing Community College A
Lawrence Technological University B
Macomb Community College A
Madonna University B
Marygrove College B, T
Michigan State University B, M, D
Michigan Technological
  University B, M, D
Mid Michigan Community College A
Northern Michigan University B
Northwestern Michigan College A
Oakland University B, M, T
Saginaw Valley State University B, T
Siena Heights University A, B
Spring Arbor University B, T
University of Detroit Mercy B
University of Michigan B, M, D
University of Michigan
  Dearborn B, M
  Flint B, T
Wayne State University B, M, D
West Shore Community College A
Western Michigan University B, M, D

Minnesota

Augsburg College B
Bemidji State University B
Bethel University B
Carleton College B
College of St. Benedict B
College of St. Scholastica B
Concordia College: Moorhead B
Concordia University: St. Paul B
Gustavus Adolphus College B
Hamline University B
Macalester College B

Minneapolis Community and
    Technical College *A*
Minnesota State University
    Mankato *B, M, T*
    Moorhead *B*
Minnesota West Community and
    Technical College *A*
North Hennepin Community
    College *A*
Northland Community & Technical
    College *A*
Northwestern College *B*
Rainy River Community College *A*
Ridgewater College *A*
St. Catherine University *B*
Saint Cloud State University *B, M*
St. John's University *B*
St. Mary's University of Minnesota *B*
St. Olaf College *B*
Southwest Minnesota State
    University *B, T*
University of Minnesota
    Duluth *B*
    Morris *B*
    Twin Cities *B, M, D*
University of St. Thomas *B*
Winona State University *B, T*

Mississippi
Alcorn State University *B*
Belhaven University *B, T*
Blue Mountain College *B*
Delta State University *B*
East Central Community College *A*
Hinds Community College *A*
Holmes Community College *A*
Jackson State University *B*
Millsaps College *B*
Mississippi College *B, M*
Mississippi Gulf Coast Community
    College *A*
Mississippi State University *B, M*
Mississippi University for Women *B, T*
Mississippi Valley State University *B*
Rust College *B*
Tougaloo College *B*
University of Mississippi *B, M, D*
University of Southern
    Mississippi *B, M*

Missouri
Central Methodist University *B*
College of the Ozarks *B*
Columbia College *B*
Crowder College *A*
Culver-Stockton College *B, T*
Drury University *B, T*
Evangel University *B, T*
Fontbonne University *B, T*
Hannibal-LaGrange College *B*
Lincoln University *B*
Lindenwood University *B*
Maryville University of Saint Louis *B*
Missouri Baptist University *B, T*
Missouri Southern State
    University *B, T*
Missouri State University *B, M*
Missouri Valley College *B*
Missouri Western State University *B, T*
Northwest Missouri State
    University *B*
Park University *B*
Rockhurst University *B*
St. Charles Community College *A*
St. Louis Community College
    St. Louis Community College at
        Florissant Valley *A*
    St. Louis Community College at
        Meramec *A*
Saint Louis University *B, M, D*
Southeast Missouri State
    University *B, M*
Southwest Baptist University *B, T*
Three Rivers Community College *A*

Truman State University *B*
University of Central Missouri *B, M*
University of Missouri
    Columbia *B, M, D*
    Kansas City *B, M, D*
    Missouri University of Science and
        Technology *M, D, T*
    St. Louis *B, M*
Washington University in St.
    Louis *B, M, D*
Webster University *B*
Westminster College *B, T*
William Jewell College *B, T*
William Woods University *B, T*

Montana
Little Big Horn College *A*
Miles Community College *A*
Montana State University
    Billings *B, T*
    Bozeman *B, M, D*
Montana Tech of the University of
    Montana *B*
Rocky Mountain College *B, T*
Stone Child College *A*
University of Great Falls *B*
University of Montana *B, M, D*
University of Montana: Western *B*

Nebraska
Chadron State College *B*
College of Saint Mary *B, T*
Concordia University *B, T*
Creighton University *A, B*
Dana College *B*
Doane College *B*
Little Priest Tribal College *A*
Nebraska Wesleyan University *B*
Northeast Community College *A*
Peru State College *B*
Union College *B*
University of Nebraska
    Kearney *B, T*
    Lincoln *B, M, D*
    Omaha *B, M*
Wayne State College *B*
Western Nebraska Community
    College *A*
York College *B*

Nevada
Great Basin College *A*
Nevada State College *B*
University of Nevada
    Las Vegas *B, M, D*
    Reno *B, M*
Western Nevada College *A*

New Hampshire
Dartmouth College *B, M, D, T*
Franklin Pierce University *B*
Keene State College *B*
New England College *B*
Plymouth State University *B*
Rivier College *B, M, T*
Saint Anselm College *B, T*
University of New Hampshire *B, M, D*

New Jersey
Bergen Community College *A*
Bloomfield College *B*
Caldwell College *B*
Centenary College *B*
The College of New Jersey *B, T*
College of St. Elizabeth *B*
County College of Morris *A*
Cumberland County College *A*
Drew University *B*
Essex County College *A*
Fairleigh Dickinson University
    College at Florham *B, M*
    Metropolitan Campus *B, M*
Felician College *B*

Georgian Court University *B, M*
Gloucester County College *A*
Hudson County Community
    College *A*
Kean University *B, T*
Mercer County Community College *A*
Monmouth University *B*
Montclair State University *B, M, T*
New Jersey City University *B, M*
New Jersey Institute of Technology *D*
Passaic County Community College *A*
Princeton University *B, M, D*
Ramapo College of New Jersey *B*
Richard Stockton College of New
    Jersey *B*
Rider University *B*
Rowan University *B, M*
Rutgers, The State University of New
    Jersey
    Camden Regional Campus *B, T*
    New Brunswick/Piscataway
        Campus *B, M, D, T*
    Newark Regional Campus *B, T*
Saint Peter's College *B*
Salem Community College *A*
Seton Hall University *B, T*
Stevens Institute of Technology *M, D*
Sussex County Community College *A*
Thomas Edison State College *A, B*
William Paterson University of New
    Jersey *B, T*

New Mexico
Clovis Community College *A*
Eastern New Mexico University *B, M*
New Mexico Highlands University *B*
New Mexico Institute of Mining and
    Technology *B, M*
New Mexico Junior College *A*
New Mexico State University *B, M, D*
San Juan College *A*
University of New Mexico *B, M, D*
Western New Mexico University *B*

New York
Adelphi University *B*
Alfred University *B*
Bard College *B*
Barnard College *B*
Canisius College *B*
Cayuga County Community College *A*
City University of New York
    Baruch College *B*
    Borough of Manhattan Community
        College *A*
    Brooklyn College *B, M*
    City College *B, M*
    College of Staten Island *B*
    Hostos Community College *A*
    Hunter College *B, M*
    Kingsborough Community
        College *A*
    Lehman College *B, M*
    Medgar Evers College *A, B*
    Queens College *B, M, T*
    York College *B*
Clarkson University *B, M, D*
Clinton Community College *A*
Colgate University *B*
College of Mount St. Vincent *B, T*
College of New Rochelle *B, T*
College of Saint Rose *B*
Columbia University *B*
Columbia University
    School of General Studies *B*
Concordia College *A, B*
Cornell University *B, M, D*
Corning Community College *A*
D'Youville College *B*
Daemen College *B, T*
Dominican College of Blauvelt *B*
Dowling College *B*
Dutchess Community College *A*
Elmira College *B, T*

Excelsior College *B*
Fordham University *B, M, D*
Hamilton College *B*
Hartwick College *B, T*
Herkimer County Community
    College *A*
Hobart and William Smith Colleges *B*
Hofstra University *B, M*
Houghton College *B*
Iona College *B*
Ithaca College *B, T*
Keuka College *B*
Le Moyne College *B*
Long Island University
    Brooklyn Campus *B*
    C. W. Post Campus *B*
Manhattan College *B*
Manhattanville College *B*
Marist College *B*
Medaille College *B*
Mercy College *B*
Molloy College *B*
Monroe Community College *A*
Mount Saint Mary College *B, T*
Nassau Community College *A*
Nazareth College *B*
New York University *B, M, D*
Niagara University *B*
Nyack College *B*
Orange County Community College *A*
Pace University *B*
Rensselaer Polytechnic
    Institute *B, M, D*
Roberts Wesleyan College *B*
Russell Sage College *B*
Saint Bonaventure University *B*
St. Francis College *B*
St. John Fisher College *B*
St. John's University *B, M*
St. Joseph's College *B*
St. Joseph's College: Suffolk
    Campus *B, T*
St. Lawrence University *B, T*
St. Thomas Aquinas College *B, T*
Siena College *B, T*
Skidmore College *B*
State University of New York
    Albany *B, M, D*
    Binghamton *B, M, D*
    Buffalo *B, M, D*
    College at Brockport *B, M, T*
    College at Buffalo *B*
    College at Cortland *B*
    College at Fredonia *B, T*
    College at Geneseo *B, T*
    College at Old Westbury *B, T*
    College at Oneonta *B*
    College at Plattsburgh *B*
    College at Potsdam *B, M*
    College of Agriculture and
        Technology at Morrisville *A*
    College of Technology at Delhi *A*
    New Paltz *B*
    Oswego *B*
    Purchase *B*
    Stony Brook *B, M, D, T*
Suffolk County Community College *A*
Sullivan County Community
    College *A*
Syracuse University *B, M, D*
Touro College *B*
Ulster County Community College *A*
Union College *B*
United States Military Academy *B*
University of Rochester *B, M, D*
Utica College *B*
Vassar College *B*
Wagner College *B, T*
Wells College *B*
Yeshiva University *B, T*

North Carolina
Appalachian State University *B, M*
Barton College *B*

Belmont Abbey College *B*
Bennett College for Women *B*
Brevard College *B*
Caldwell Community College and
    Technical Institute *A*
Campbell University *B, T*
Carteret Community College *A*
Catawba College *B*
Davidson College *B*
Duke University *B, M, D*
East Carolina University *B, M*
Elizabeth City State University *B, M*
Elon University *B, T*
Fayetteville State University *B, M*
Gardner-Webb University *B*
Greensboro College *B, T*
Guilford College *B*
High Point University *B*
Johnson C. Smith University *B*
Lees-McRae College *B*
Lenoir Community College *A*
Lenoir-Rhyne University *B, T*
Livingstone College *B*
Mars Hill College *B, T*
Meredith College *B*
Methodist University *B*
Mount Olive College *B*
North Carolina Agricultural and
    Technical State University *B, M, T*
North Carolina Central
    University *B, M*
North Carolina State
    University *B, M, D*
North Carolina Wesleyan College *B*
Pfeiffer University *B*
Queens University of Charlotte *B*
St. Andrews Presbyterian College *B*
St. Augustine's College *B*
Salem College *B*
Sandhills Community College *A*
Shaw University *B*
Southeastern Community College *A*
University of North Carolina
    Asheville *B, T*
    Chapel Hill *B, M, D*
    Charlotte *B, M*
    Greensboro *B, M*
    Pembroke *B*
    Wilmington *B, M*
Wake Forest University *B, M*
Warren Wilson College *B*
Western Carolina University *B*
Wingate University *B*
Winston-Salem State University *B*

North Dakota

Dakota College at Bottineau *A*
Dickinson State University *B*
Jamestown College *B*
Mayville State University *B, T*
Minot State University *B*
North Dakota State
    University *B, M, D, T*
University of Mary *B*
University of North Dakota *B, M*

Ohio

Antioch University McGregor *B*
Ashland University *B*
Baldwin-Wallace College *B*
Bluffton University *B*
Bowling Green State
    University *B, M, D*
Capital University *B*
Case Western Reserve
    University *B, M, D*
Cedarville University *B*
Central State University *B*
Cleveland State University *B, M, T*
College of Mount St. Joseph *B, T*
College of Wooster *B*
Defiance College *B, T*
Denison University *B*

Franciscan University of
    Steubenville *B*
Heidelberg University *B*
Hiram College *B, T*
John Carroll University *B, M, T*
Kent State University *B, M, D*
Kenyon College *B*
Malone University *B*
Marietta College *B*
Miami University
    Oxford Campus *B, M, T*
Mount Union College *B*
Mount Vernon Nazarene University *B*
Muskingum University *B*
Notre Dame College *B, T*
Oberlin College *B*
Ohio Dominican University *B, T*
Ohio Northern University *B*
Ohio State University
    Columbus Campus *B, M, D*
    Lima Campus *B*
Ohio University *B, M, D*
Ohio Wesleyan University *B*
Otterbein College *B*
Owens Community College
    Toledo *A*
Shawnee State University *A, B*
Stark State College of Technology *A*
University of Akron *B, M*
University of Cincinnati *B, M, D, T*
University of Dayton *B*
University of Findlay *B, T*
University of Rio Grande *A, B, T*
University of Toledo *B, M, D*
Urbana University *B*
Ursuline College *B*
Walsh University *B*
Washington State Community
    College *A*
Wilberforce University *B*
Wilmington College *B*
Wittenberg University *B*
Wright State University *B, M*
Xavier University *B*
Youngstown State University *B, M*

Oklahoma

Cameron University *B*
Carl Albert State College *A*
Connors State College *A*
East Central University *B, T*
Eastern Oklahoma State College *A*
Langston University *B*
Mid-America Christian University *B*
Murray State College *A*
Northeastern Oklahoma Agricultural
    and Mechanical College *A*
Northeastern State University *B*
Northern Oklahoma College *A*
Northwestern Oklahoma State
    University *B*
Oklahoma Baptist University *B, T*
Oklahoma Christian University *B, T*
Oklahoma City Community College *A*
Oklahoma City University *B*
Oklahoma Panhandle State
    University *B*
Oklahoma State University *B, M, D*
Oklahoma Wesleyan University *A, B*
Oral Roberts University *B*
Redlands Community College *A*
Rose State College *A*
St. Gregory's University *B*
Seminole State College *A*
Southeastern Oklahoma State
    University *B*
Southern Nazarene University *B*
Southwestern Oklahoma State
    University *B*
Tulsa Community College *A*
University of Central Oklahoma *B, M*
University of Oklahoma *B, M, D*
University of Science and Arts of
    Oklahoma *B, T*

University of Tulsa *B*
Western Oklahoma State College *A*

Oregon

Central Oregon Community
    College *A*
Chemeketa Community College *A*
Corban College *B*
Eastern Oregon University *B, T*
George Fox University *B*
Lewis & Clark College *B*
Linfield College *B, T*
Linn-Benton Community College *A*
Mt. Hood Community College *A*
Northwest Christian University *B*
Oregon State University *B, M, D*
Pacific University *B*
Portland State University *B, D*
Reed College *B*
Southern Oregon University *B, T*
Southwestern Oregon Community
    College *A*
Treasure Valley Community College *A*
University of Oregon *B, M, D*
University of Portland *B, T*
Warner Pacific College *T*
Western Oregon University *B*
Willamette University *B*

Pennsylvania

Albright College *B, T*
Allegheny College *B*
Alvernia University *B*
Arcadia University *B*
Bloomsburg University of
    Pennsylvania *B, T*
Bryn Athyn College of the New
    Church *B*
Bryn Mawr College *B, M, D*
Bucknell University *B, M*
Bucks County Community College *A*
Butler County Community College *A*
Cabrini College *B*
California University of
    Pennsylvania *B, M*
Carlow University *B*
Carnegie Mellon University *B, M, D*
Cedar Crest College *B*
Chatham University *B*
Chestnut Hill College *B*
Cheyney University of
    Pennsylvania *B, T*
Clarion University of
    Pennsylvania *B, T*
Community College of Allegheny
    County *A*
Community College of Philadelphia *A*
DeSales University *B, T*
Delaware Valley College *B*
Dickinson College *B*
Drexel University *B, M, D*
Duquesne University *B*
East Stroudsburg University of
    Pennsylvania *B, T*
Eastern University *B*
Edinboro University of
    Pennsylvania *B, T*
Elizabethtown College *B*
Franklin & Marshall College *B*
Gannon University *B*
Gettysburg College *B*
Grove City College *B*
Gwynedd-Mercy College *B*
Harrisburg Area Community
    College *A*
Haverford College *B, T*
Holy Family University *B, T*
Immaculata University *B*
Indiana University of
    Pennsylvania *B, M*
Juniata College *B*
King's College *B, T*
Kutztown University of
    Pennsylvania *B, M, T*

La Roche College *B*
La Salle University *B, T*
Lafayette College *B*
Lebanon Valley College *B, T*
Lehigh Carbon Community College *A*
Lehigh University *B, M, D*
Lincoln University *B, M*
Lock Haven University of
    Pennsylvania *B*
Luzerne County Community
    College *A*
Lycoming College *B*
Mansfield University of
    Pennsylvania *B, T*
Marywood University *B*
Mercyhurst College *B, T*
Messiah College *B*
Millersville University of
    Pennsylvania *B, M, T*
Misericordia University *B*
Montgomery County Community
    College *A*
Moravian College *B, T*
Muhlenberg College *B*
Northampton Community College *A*
Penn State
    Abington *B*
    Altoona *B*
    Beaver *B*
    Berks *B*
    Brandywine *B*
    DuBois *B*
    Erie, The Behrend College *B*
    Fayette, The Eberly Campus *B*
    Greater Allegheny *B*
    Hazleton *B*
    Lehigh Valley *B*
    Mont Alto *B*
    New Kensington *B*
    Schuylkill *B*
    Shenango *B*
    University Park *B, M, D*
    Wilkes-Barre *B*
    Worthington Scranton *B*
    York *B*
Rosemont College *B*
St. Francis University *B*
Saint Joseph's University *B*
St. Vincent College *B*
Seton Hill University *B, T*
Shippensburg University of
    Pennsylvania *B, T*
Slippery Rock University of
    Pennsylvania *B, T*
Susquehanna University *B, T*
Swarthmore College *B*
Temple University *B, M, D*
Thiel College *B*
University of Pennsylvania *B, M, D*
University of Pittsburgh *B, M, D*
University of Pittsburgh
    Johnstown *B*
University of Scranton *B, T*
Ursinus College *B, T*
Villanova University *B, M*
Washington & Jefferson College *B*
Waynesburg University *B*
West Chester University of
    Pennsylvania *B, M, T*
Westminster College *B*
Widener University *B, T*
Wilkes University *B, M*
Wilson College *B*
York College of Pennsylvania *B, T*

Puerto Rico

Inter American University of Puerto
    Rico
    Bayamon Campus *B*
    Metropolitan Campus *B*
    San German Campus *B, M*
Pontifical Catholic University of
    Puerto Rico *B*

University of Puerto Rico
   Cayey University College *B*
   Ponce *B*
   Rio Piedras *B, M, D*
University of the Sacred Heart *B*

Rhode Island

Brown University *B, M, D*
Providence College *B*
Rhode Island College *B, M*
Roger Williams University *B*
Salve Regina University *B*
University of Rhode Island *B, M, D*

South Carolina

Allen University *B*
Anderson University *B*
Benedict College *B*
Bob Jones University *B*
Charleston Southern University *B*
The Citadel *B*
Claflin University *B*
Clemson University *B, M, D*
Coker College *B*
College of Charleston *B, M, T*
Columbia College *B, T*
Converse College *B*
Erskine College *B, T*
Francis Marion University *B*
Furman University *B, T*
Lander University *B, T*
Limestone College *B*
Morris College *B*
Newberry College *B, T*
North Greenville University *B, T*
Presbyterian College *B, T*
South Carolina State University *B*
Southern Wesleyan University *B, T*
University of South Carolina *B, M, D*
University of South Carolina
   Upstate *B*
Winthrop University *B, M*
Wofford College *B, T*

South Dakota

Augustana College *B, T*
Black Hills State University *B*
Dakota Wesleyan University *B*
Mount Marty College *B*
Northern State University *B*
South Dakota School of Mines and
   Technology *B*
South Dakota State University *B, M*
University of Sioux Falls *B*
University of South Dakota *B, M*

Tennessee

Austin Peay State University *B*
Belmont University *B, T*
Bethel University *B*
Bryan College *B, T*
Carson-Newman College *B, T*
Christian Brothers University *B*
Columbia State Community College *A*
Cumberland University *B*
Dyersburg State Community
   College *A*
East Tennessee State
   University *B, M, T*
Fisk University *B*
Freed-Hardeman University *B, T*
Jackson State Community College *A*
King College *B, T*
Lambuth University *B*
Lane College *B*
LeMoyne-Owen College *B*
Lee University *B*
Lincoln Memorial University *B, T*
Lipscomb University *B*
Maryville College *B, T*
Middle Tennessee State
   University *B, M*
Milligan College *B, T*

Rhodes College *B*
Roane State Community College *A*
Southern Adventist University *B*
Tennessee State University *B, M*
Tennessee Technological
   University *B, M, T*
Tennessee Temple University *B*
Tennessee Wesleyan College *B*
Trevecca Nazarene University *B*
Tusculum College *B, T*
Union University *B, T*
University of Memphis *B, M, D*
University of Tennessee
   Chattanooga *B, T*
   Knoxville *B, M, D*
   Martin *B*
University of the South *B*
Vanderbilt University *B, M, D*

Texas

Abilene Christian University *B*
Alvin Community College *A*
Amarillo College *A*
Angelina College *A*
Angelo State University *B, T*
Austin College *B*
Austin Community College *A*
Baylor University *B, M, D*
Blinn College *A*
Brazosport College *A*
Central Texas College *A*
Cisco College *A*
Clarendon College *A*
Coastal Bend College *A*
College of the Mainland *A*
Concordia University Texas *B*
Dallas Baptist University *B*
Del Mar College *A*
East Texas Baptist University *B*
El Paso Community College *A*
Frank Phillips College *A*
Galveston College *A*
Grayson County College *A*
Hardin-Simmons University *B*
Hill College *A*
Houston Baptist University *B*
Howard College *A*
Howard Payne University *B, T*
Huston-Tillotson University *B*
Jarvis Christian College *B, T*
Kilgore College *A*
Lamar State College at Orange *A*
Lamar University *B, M*
Laredo Community College *A*
LeTourneau University *B*
Lee College *A*
Lon Morris College *A*
Lubbock Christian University *B*
McMurry University *B, T*
Midland College *A*
Midwestern State University *B*
Mountain View College *A*
Navarro College *A*
North Lake College *A*
Northeast Texas Community
   College *A*
Northwest Vista College *A*
Odessa College *A*
Our Lady of the Lake University of San
   Antonio *B*
Palo Alto College *A*
Paris Junior College *A*
Prairie View A&M University *B, M*
Rice University *B, M, D*
St. Edward's University *B*
St. Mary's University *B*
St. Philip's College *A*
Sam Houston State University *B, M*
San Antonio College *A*
San Jacinto College *A*
Schreiner University *B*
South Plains College *A*
South Texas College *A*
Southern Methodist University *B*

Southwestern Adventist
   University *B, T*
Southwestern University *B, T*
Stephen F. Austin State
   University *B, M, T*
Sul Ross State University *B*
Tarleton State University *B, M, T*
Temple College *A*
Texarkana College *A*
Texas A&M International
   University *B, M, T*
Texas A&M University *B, M, D*
Texas A&M University
   Commerce *B, M*
   Corpus Christi *B, M, T*
   Kingsville *B, M, T*
   Texarkana *B*
Texas Christian University *B, M, D*
Texas College *B*
Texas Lutheran University *B, T*
Texas Southern University *B, M*
Texas State University: San
   Marcos *B, M, T*
Texas Tech University *B, M, D*
Texas Wesleyan University *B*
Texas Woman's University *B, M*
Trinity University *B*
Trinity Valley Community College *A*
Tyler Junior College *A*
University of Dallas *B*
University of Houston *B, M, D*
University of Houston
   Clear Lake *B, M*
   Downtown *B*
   Victoria *B, T*
University of Mary Hardin-Baylor *B, T*
University of North Texas *B, M, D*
University of St. Thomas *B*
University of Texas
   Arlington *B, M*
   Austin *B, M, D*
   Brownsville - Texas Southmost
    College *B, M*
   Dallas *B, M*
   El Paso *B, M*
   Pan American *B, M*
   San Antonio *B, M*
   Tyler *B, M*
   of the Permian Basin *B*
University of the Incarnate Word *B, M*
Wayland Baptist University *B, T*
West Texas A&M University *B, M*
Western Texas College *A*
Wharton County Junior College *A*
Wiley College *B*

Utah

Brigham Young University *B, M, D*
College of Eastern Utah *T*
Salt Lake Community College *A*
Snow College *A*
Southern Utah University *B, T*
University of Utah *B, M, D, T*
Utah State University *B, M*
Utah Valley University *A, B*
Weber State University *B*
Westminster College *B*

Vermont

Bennington College *B*
Castleton State College *B*
Johnson State College *B*
Lyndon State College *B*
Marlboro College *B*
Middlebury College *B*
Norwich University *B*
St. Michael's College *B*
University of Vermont *B, M, D*

Virginia

Averett University *B*
Bluefield College *B*
Bridgewater College *B*
Christopher Newport University *B*

College of William and Mary *B*
Eastern Mennonite University *B*
Emory & Henry College *B, T*
Ferrum College *B*
George Mason University *B, M, D*
Hampden-Sydney College *B*
Hampton University *B, M*
Hollins University *B*
J. Sargeant Reynolds Community
   College *A*
James Madison University *B, T*
Liberty University *B, T*
Longwood University *B, T*
Lynchburg College *B*
Mary Baldwin College *B*
Marymount University *B*
Mountain Empire Community
   College *A*
Norfolk State University *B*
Northern Virginia Community
   College *A*
Old Dominion University *B, M, T*
Radford University *B*
Randolph College *B*
Randolph-Macon College *B*
Regent University *B*
Roanoke College *B, T*
St. Paul's College *B*
Shenandoah University *B*
Sweet Briar College *B*
University of Mary Washington *B*
University of Richmond *B, T*
University of Virginia *B, M, D*
University of Virginia's College at
   Wise *B, T*
Virginia Commonwealth
   University *B, M*
Virginia Military Institute *B*
Virginia Polytechnic Institute and
   State University *B, M, D*
Virginia State University *B, M*
Virginia Union University *B*
Virginia Wesleyan College *B*
Virginia Western Community
   College *A*
Washington and Lee University *B*

Washington

Centralia College *A*
Eastern Washington University *B, M*
Everett Community College *A*
Gonzaga University *B*
Highline Community College *A*
Northwest University *B*
Olympic College *A*
Pacific Lutheran University *B*
Saint Martin's University *B*
Seattle Pacific University *B*
Seattle University *B*
Spokane Falls Community College *A*
University of Puget Sound *B, T*
University of Washington *B, M, D*
Walla Walla University *B*
Washington State University *B*
Western Washington University *B, M*
Whitman College *B*
Whitworth University *B, T*

West Virginia

Bethany College *B*
Concord University *B*
Davis and Elkins College *B*
Fairmont State University *B*
Marshall University *B, M*
Potomac State College of West
   Virginia University *A*
Shepherd University *B, T*
West Liberty University *B*
West Virginia State University *B*
West Virginia University *B, M, D, T*
West Virginia University Institute of
   Technology *B*
West Virginia Wesleyan College *B*
Wheeling Jesuit University *B*

Wisconsin

Alverno College *B*
Beloit College *B*
Cardinal Stritch University *B, T*
Carroll University *B*
Carthage College *B*
College of Menominee Nation *A*
Concordia University Wisconsin *B, T*
Edgewood College *B*
Lakeland College *B*
Lawrence University *B*
Marian University *B*
Marquette University *B, M, D, T*
Mount Mary College *B, T*
Northland College *B*
Ripon College *B, T*
St. Norbert College *B, T*
Silver Lake College *B, T*
University of Wisconsin
   Eau Claire *B*
   Green Bay *B*
   La Crosse *B, T*
   Madison *B, M, D*
   Milwaukee *B, M, D*
   Oshkosh *B*
   Parkside *B, T*
   Platteville *B, T*
   River Falls *B, T*
   Stevens Point *B, T*
   Superior *B, T*
   Whitewater *B, T*
Viterbo University *B, T*
Wisconsin Lutheran College *B*

Wyoming

Casper College *A*
Central Wyoming College *A*
Eastern Wyoming College *A*
Laramie County Community
   College *A*
Northwest College *A*
Sheridan College *A*
University of Wyoming *B, M, D*
Western Wyoming Community
   College *A*

Mathematics/computer science

Alabama

Birmingham-Southern College *B*
Oakwood University *B*

Alaska

University of Alaska
   Anchorage *B*

Arkansas

Philander Smith College *B*

California

California Lutheran University *B*
California State University
   Chico *B*
Claremont McKenna College *B*
Harvey Mudd College *B*
Pepperdine University *B*
Pomona College *B*
St. Mary's College of California *B*
San Diego State University *M, D*
Santa Clara University *B*
Stanford University *B*
University of California
   San Diego *B*

Colorado

Colorado College *B*
Colorado School of Mines *B*
United States Air Force Academy *B*

Connecticut

Quinnipiac University *B*

Yale University *B*

Delaware

Delaware State University *B*

Florida

Florida Southern College *B*
University of Tampa *B*

Georgia

Emory University *B, M, D*
Paine College *B*
Piedmont College *B*

Illinois

Augustana College *B*
DePaul University *B*
Dominican University *B*
Eastern Illinois University *B*
Eureka College *B*
Loyola University Chicago *B*
Monmouth College *B*
Southeastern Illinois College *A*
University of Illinois
   Urbana-Champaign *B*
University of St. Francis *B*

Indiana

Anderson University *B*
Huntington University *B*
Indiana University
   South Bend *M*
Indiana University-Purdue University
   Fort Wayne *B*
Manchester College *B*
Purdue University
   Calumet *B*
Saint Mary's College *B, T*

Iowa

Central College *B, T*
Coe College *B*

Kansas

Central Christian College of Kansas *A*
Seward County Community College *A*
Tabor College *B*

Kentucky

Brescia University *B*

Maine

Bowdoin College *B*
University of Maine
   Fort Kent *B*
University of Southern Maine *B*

Maryland

Washington College *B, T*

Massachusetts

Amherst College *B*
Bard College at Simon's Rock *B*
Boston University *B*
Clark University *B*
Massachusetts Institute of
   Technology *B*
Salem State College *B*
Tufts University *B, M, D*
Wheaton College *B*

Michigan

Albion College *B, T*
Central Michigan University *B*
Eastern Michigan University *M*
Hillsdale College *B*
Lake Superior State University *B*
Lawrence Technological University *B*

Minnesota

Carleton College *B*

College of St. Benedict *B*
Concordia College: Moorhead *B*
Minnesota State University
   Mankato *B, M*
Northland Community & Technical
   College *A*
Ridgewater College *A*
St. John's University *B*
St. Mary's University of Minnesota *B*
University of Minnesota
   Twin Cities *M, D*

Mississippi

Mississippi College *M*
Tougaloo College *B*

Missouri

Crowder College *A*
Evangel University *B*
Park University *B*
Washington University in St.
   Louis *B, M, D*

Montana

University of Montana *B*

New Hampshire

Saint Anselm College *B*

New Jersey

Cumberland County College *A*
Gloucester County College *A*
Stevens Institute of
   Technology *B, M, D*

New York

City University of New York
   Brooklyn College *B*
Colgate University *B*
Hobart and William Smith Colleges *B*
Hofstra University *B*
Rochester Institute of Technology *B*
St. Thomas Aquinas College *B*
Schenectady County Community
   College *A*
State University of New York
   Purchase *B*

North Carolina

Gardner-Webb University *B*
Wingate University *B*

Ohio

Defiance College *B, T*
Eastern Gateway Community
   College *A*
Hiram College *B*
Wittenberg University *B*

Oklahoma

Connors State College *A*
Oklahoma Baptist University *B*
Oklahoma Christian University *B*

Oregon

Lewis & Clark College *B*
Southern Oregon University *B*
University of Oregon *B*
Western Oregon University *B*

Pennsylvania

Chestnut Hill College *B*
Duquesne University *M*
Gettysburg College *B*
Grove City College *B*
Immaculata University *A, B*
La Salle University *B*
Mount Aloysius College *A, B*
St. Francis University *B*
Westminster College *B*

Rhode Island

Brown University *B*

South Carolina

Furman University *B*
University of South Carolina
   Aiken *B*

Tennessee

Bryan College *B*
Christian Brothers University *B*
Maryville College *B*
University of the South *B*

Texas

Laredo Community College *A*
LeTourneau University *B*
University of Houston
   Clear Lake *B, M*
University of Texas
   Austin *B*

Utah

University of Utah *M*

Vermont

Bennington College *B*
Castleton State College *B*
Marlboro College *B*

Virginia

George Mason University *B, M, D*
Hampden-Sydney College *B*
J. Sargeant Reynolds Community
   College *A*
Virginia Wesleyan College *B*

West Virginia

Bethany College *B*

Wisconsin

Cardinal Stritch University *B, T*
Lawrence University *B*
Marquette University *B, M, D*
University of Wisconsin
   Parkside *B*

Mathematics teacher education

Alabama

Athens State University *B*
Auburn University *B, M, D, T*
Birmingham-Southern College *T*
Faulkner University *B, M, T*
Gadsden State Community College *A*
Huntingdon College *B, T*
Judson College *B*
Miles College *B*
Oakwood University *B*
Talladega College *B*
Tuskegee University *B*
University of Mobile *B, T*

Alaska

University of Alaska
   Fairbanks *M*

Arizona

Cochise College *A*
Grand Canyon University *B*
Northern Arizona University *B, M, T*
Prescott College *B, M, T*
University of Arizona *B*

Arkansas

Arkansas State University *B, M, T*
Arkansas Tech University *B, M*
Harding University *B, T*
John Brown University *B, T*
Ouachita Baptist University *B, T*

Southern Arkansas University *B, T*
University of Arkansas *M*
University of Arkansas
  Fort Smith *B*
  Pine Bluff *B, M, T*
University of Central Arkansas *B*
University of the Ozarks *T*

California

Azusa Pacific University *T*
California Baptist University *T*
California Lutheran University *B, T*
California Polytechnic State
  University: San Luis Obispo *T*
California State University
  Chico *B, M, T*
  Dominguez Hills *M*
  East Bay *B, M*
  Long Beach *T*
  Northridge *B, T*
  Sacramento *B*
  San Bernardino *M, T*
Cuesta College *A*
Fresno Pacific University *B, M, T*
Humboldt State University *T*
Los Angeles Southwest College *A*
Loyola Marymount University *M*
The Master's College *T*
Mills College *T*
Mount St. Mary's College *T*
National University *B*
Pacific Union College *B*
Saddleback College *A*
San Diego Christian College *B, T*
San Diego State University *M, T*
San Francisco State University *T*
Simpson University *B, T*
Sonoma State University *T*
Stanford University *M, T*
University of the Pacific *T*
Vanguard University of Southern
  California *T*
Westmont College *T*

Colorado

Adams State College *B, M, T*
Colorado Christian University *B*
Colorado State University *B, T*
Colorado State University
  Pueblo *T*
Metropolitan State College of
  Denver *T*
Regis University *B, T*
University of Colorado
  Boulder *T*
  Colorado Springs *T*
Western State College of
  Colorado *B, T*

Connecticut

Albertus Magnus College *B, T*
Central Connecticut State
  University *T*
Fairfield University *T*
Quinnipiac University *B, M*
Sacred Heart University *T*
Saint Joseph College *T*
Southern Connecticut State
  University *B, M, T*
University of New Haven *T*

Delaware

Delaware State University *B, M*
Delaware Technical and Community
  College
  Owens *A*
  Stanton/Wilmington *A*
  Terry *A*
University of Delaware *B, T*

District of Columbia

Catholic University of America *B*
George Washington University *M, T*

University of the District of
  Columbia *M*

Florida

Barry University *T*
Broward College *A*
Chipola College *B*
Clearwater Christian College *B*
Daytona State College *B*
Florida Agricultural and Mechanical
  University *B, M, T*
Florida Atlantic University *B*
Florida Institute of
  Technology *B, M, D*
Florida State University *B, M, D*
Gulf Coast Community College *A*
Hobe Sound Bible College *B, T*
Miami Dade College *A, B*
Northwest Florida State College *B*
Palm Beach Atlantic University *B, T*
St. Petersburg College *B*
Southeastern University *B, T*
State College of Florida,
  Manatee-Sarasota *A*
Stetson University *B*
University of Central Florida *B, M*
University of Miami *M*
University of North Florida *B, M*
University of South Florida *B, M*
University of Tampa *B, T*
University of West Florida *B*

Georgia

Agnes Scott College *M, T*
Albany State University *B*
Armstrong Atlantic State
  University *B, M, T*
Augusta State University *M*
Berry College *B*
Brewton-Parker College *B*
Clayton State University *M*
Columbus State University *B, M*
Covenant College *B, T*
Darton College *A*
Emmanuel College *B*
Fort Valley State University *B, T*
Gainesville State College *A*
Georgia State University *M, T*
Kennesaw State University *B*
Macon State College *M, T*
North Georgia College & State
  University *M*
Paine College *B*
Piedmont College *M, T*
Shorter College *B, T*
University of Georgia *B, M, D, T*
Valdosta State University *M*

Hawaii

Hawaii Pacific University *M*

Idaho

Boise State University *M, T*
Brigham Young University-Idaho *T*
Lewis-Clark State College *B, T*
Northwest Nazarene University *B*
University of Idaho *T*

Illinois

Augustana College *B, T*
Benedictine University *T*
Black Hawk College *A*
Blackburn College *B, T*
Bradley University *B*
Chicago State University *B*
Concordia University Chicago *M*
DePaul University *M, T*
Dominican University *T*
Elmhurst College *B*
Eureka College *T*
Governors State University *B*
Greenville College *B, T*
Heartland Community College *A*

Highland Community College *A*
Illinois College *T*
Illinois Institute of Technology *M, D*
Illinois State University *D*
Illinois Wesleyan University *B*
John A. Logan College *A*
Kankakee Community College *A*
Kaskaskia College *A*
Knox College *T*
Lake Land College *A*
Lewis University *T*
Loyola University Chicago *B, M*
MacMurray College *B, T*
Millikin University *B*
Moraine Valley Community College *A*
National-Louis University *M*
North Park University *T*
Northwestern University *B*
Olivet Nazarene University *B, T*
Rockford College *T*
Saint Xavier University *B, M, T*
Sauk Valley Community College *A*
Trinity Christian College *B, T*
Trinity International University *B, T*
Triton College *A*
University of Illinois
  Chicago *B, M*
  Urbana-Champaign *B, M, T*
University of St. Francis *B, M*
Waubonsee Community College *A*

Indiana

Anderson University *B, T*
Bethel College *B*
Butler University *T*
Franklin College *B, T*
Goshen College *B, T*
Grace College *B*
Huntington University *B, M*
Indiana University
  Bloomington *B, T*
  Northwest *B*
  South Bend *B, T*
  Southeast *B*
Indiana University-Purdue University
  Fort Wayne *B, T*
Indiana University-Purdue University
  Indianapolis *B, M*
Indiana Wesleyan University *B, T*
Manchester College *B, T*
Oakland City University *B*
Purdue University *B, M, D*
Saint Mary's College *T*
St. Mary-of-the-Woods College *B, T*
Taylor University *B, T*
Trine University *B, T*
University of Evansville *B, T*
University of Indianapolis *B, T*
Valparaiso University *B*
Vincennes University *A, B*

Iowa

Briar Cliff University *B*
Buena Vista University *B, T*
Central College *T*
Cornell College *B, T*
Dordt College *B*
Drake University *B, M, T*
Ellsworth Community College *A*
Graceland University *B*
Grand View University *M, T*
Iowa State University *M, T*
Iowa Wesleyan College *B*
Loras College *T*
Maharishi University of
  Management *T*
Morningside College *B*
Mount Mercy College *T*
Northwestern College *T*
St. Ambrose University *B, T*
Simpson College *T*
University of Iowa *M, D, T*
Upper Iowa University *T*
Wartburg College *T*

Kansas

Allen County Community College *A*
Bethany College *B*
Bethel College *T*
Fort Hays State University *M*
Friends University *B*
Garden City Community College *A*
McPherson College *B, T*
MidAmerica Nazarene University *B, T*
Newman University *T*
Pittsburg State University *B, T*
Southwestern College *B, T*
Sterling College *B*
Tabor College *B*
University of Kansas *B, T*
University of St. Mary *T*
Washburn University *B*

Kentucky

Alice Lloyd College *B*
Campbellsville University *B*
Eastern Kentucky University *B*
Kentucky Wesleyan College *B, T*
Lindsey Wilson College *B, T*
Midway College *M*
University of Kentucky *B*

Louisiana

Centenary College of Louisiana *B, T*
Grambling State University *B*
Louisiana College *B*
Louisiana State University
  Shreveport *B*
McNeese State University *B, T*
Nicholls State University *B*
Northwestern State University *B*
Our Lady of Holy Cross College *B*
Southeastern Louisiana University *B*
Southern University and Agricultural
  and Mechanical College *B*
University of Louisiana at Lafayette *B*
University of Louisiana at Monroe *B*
University of New Orleans *B*
Xavier University of Louisiana *B*

Maine

Saint Joseph's College of Maine *B*
University of Maine *B*
University of Maine
  Farmington *B, T*
University of Southern Maine *B, T*

Maryland

Anne Arundel Community College *A*
Carroll Community College *A*
College of Notre Dame of Maryland *T*
Community College of Baltimore
  County *A*
Coppin State University *B, T*
Frostburg State University *B, T*
Harford Community College *A*
Hood College *M, T*
Howard Community College *A*
Morgan State University *M, D*
Mount St. Mary's University *T*
Prince George's Community
  College *A*
Salisbury University *M, T*
Towson University *M, T*
University of Maryland
  College Park *B*
  Eastern Shore *B*
Washington Adventist University *B*

Massachusetts

Assumption College *T*
Boston University *B, M, T*
Bridgewater State College *M, T*
Cambridge College *M*
Eastern Nazarene College *B*
Elms College *M, T*
Fitchburg State College *B, T*
Framingham State College *M*

Lasell College B, T
Lesley University B, M
Merrimack College T
Regis College B
Salem State College M
Springfield College T
Tufts University M, T
University of Massachusetts
    Dartmouth T
Western New England College M, T
Westfield State College B, M, T
Worcester Polytechnic Institute M
Worcester State College T

Michigan

Albion College B, T
Alma College T
Andrews University B
Calvin College B
Central Michigan University B, M
Cornerstone University B, T
Eastern Michigan University B, M
Ferris State University T
Grand Rapids Community College A
Grand Valley State University M, T
Hope College B, T
Lansing Community College A
Madonna University B, T
Michigan State University B, M, D
Michigan Technological University T
Northern Michigan University B, M, T
Rochester College B
University of Detroit Mercy B, M, T
University of Michigan
    Dearborn B
    Flint B, T
Wayne State University B, M, T
Western Michigan
    University B, M, D, T

Minnesota

Augsburg College T
Bemidji State University M, T
Bethel University B
College of St. Benedict T
College of St. Scholastica T
Concordia College: Moorhead B, T
Concordia University: St. Paul B, T
Gustavus Adolphus College T
Metropolitan State University B
Minnesota State University
    Mankato B, M, T
    Moorhead B
Northwestern College B
Ridgewater College A
St. Catherine University B, T
Saint Cloud State University B, M, T
St. John's University T
St. Mary's University of Minnesota B
Southwest Minnesota State
    University B, T
University of Minnesota
    Duluth B, T
    Morris T
    Twin Cities B, M, T
University of St. Thomas B
Vermilion Community College A
Walden University M
Winona State University B, T

Mississippi

Blue Mountain College B
Delta State University B
Jackson State University M
Millsaps College T
Mississippi College B, M
Mississippi Gulf Coast Community
    College A
Mississippi State University T
Mississippi Valley State University B, T
Northwest Mississippi Community
    College A
Rust College B
University of Mississippi B, T

Missouri

College of the Ozarks B, T
Culver-Stockton College T
Evangel University B, T
Hannibal-LaGrange College B
Harris-Stowe State University T
Lincoln University B
Maryville University of Saint
    Louis M, T
Missouri Baptist University T
Missouri Southern State
    University B, T
Missouri State University B
Missouri Valley College T
Northwest Missouri State
    University B, M, T
Park University T
Southeast Missouri State
    University B, T
Southwest Baptist University T
Truman State University M, T
University of Central Missouri B, M, T
University of Missouri
    Columbia B, M, D
Washington University in St.
    Louis B, M, T
Webster University M
William Jewell College B, T
William Woods University B, T

Montana

Montana State University
    Billings B, T
Rocky Mountain College B, T
University of Great Falls B
University of Montana B, M, T
University of Montana: Western B, T

Nebraska

Chadron State College B, M
College of Saint Mary B, T
Concordia University B, T
Creighton University T
Dana College B
Grace University B
Nebraska Wesleyan University T
Peru State College B, T
Union College T
University of Nebraska
    Kearney B, T
    Lincoln B, M
Wayne State College B, T
York College B, T

Nevada

Great Basin College B
Nevada State College B
University of Nevada
    Reno B, T

New Hampshire

Franklin Pierce University T
Keene State College B, M, T
New England College B, T
Plymouth State University B, M, T
Rivier College B, T
Saint Anselm College T
University of New Hampshire B, D, T

New Jersey

Caldwell College T
Centenary College T
The College of New Jersey B, T
College of St. Elizabeth T
Felician College B
Georgian Court University T
Kean University M
Montclair State University M, T
Rowan University T
Rutgers, The State University of New
    Jersey
    New Brunswick/Piscataway
        Campus D, T

Saint Peter's College T
William Paterson University of New
    Jersey B, T

New Mexico

New Mexico Highlands University B
New Mexico Institute of Mining and
    Technology M
University of the Southwest B, T
Western New Mexico University B

New York

Adelphi University M, T
Alfred University B, T
Bard College M
City University of New York
    Brooklyn College B, M, T
    City College B, M, T
    College of Staten Island B, M, T
    Hunter College B, M, T
    Lehman College B, M
    Queens College M, T
Colgate University M
College of Saint Rose B, T
Cornell University B, M, T
D'Youville College M, T
Dominican College of Blauvelt B, T
Dowling College B, M
Dutchess Community College A
Elmira College B, T
Fordham University T
Hobart and William Smith Colleges T
Hofstra University B, M
Houghton College B, T
Iona College B, M, T
Ithaca College B, D, T
Keuka College B, T
Le Moyne College T
Long Island University
    Brooklyn Campus B, M, T
    C. W. Post Campus B, M, T
Manhattan College B, T
Manhattanville College M, T
Marist College B
Medaille College B, M, T
Molloy College B
Nazareth College B, M, T
New York Institute of
    Technology B, T
New York University B, M
Niagara University B, M, T
Pace University B, M, T
Roberts Wesleyan College B, M
Saint Bonaventure University M
St. Francis College B
St. John Fisher College B, M, T
St. John's University B, M, T
St. Joseph's College B, T
St. Joseph's College: Suffolk
    Campus B, T
St. Lawrence University T
St. Thomas Aquinas College B, T
State University of New York
    Albany M, T
    Binghamton M
    Buffalo M, D, T
    College at Brockport B, M
    College at Buffalo B, M, T
    College at Cortland B, M
    College at Fredonia B, M, T
    College at Geneseo B, M, T
    College at Old Westbury B, M, T
    College at Oneonta B, M, T
    College at Plattsburgh B, M
    College at Potsdam B, M
    New Paltz B, T
    Oswego B, M
    Stony Brook T
Syracuse University B, M, D, T
Ulster County Community College A
University of Rochester M
Vassar College T
Wells College T

North Carolina

Appalachian State University B, M, T
Belmont Abbey College T
Bennett College for Women B
Brevard College B
Campbell University B, T
Catawba College T
Chowan University T
Davidson College T
East Carolina University B, M
Elizabeth City State University B, T
Elon University T
Fayetteville State University B, T
Gardner-Webb University B
Greensboro College B, T
Johnson C. Smith University B
Lenoir-Rhyne University B, T
Livingstone College T
Mars Hill College T
Meredith College T
Methodist University A, B, T
North Carolina Agricultural and
    Technical State University B, M, T
North Carolina Central
    University B, M, T
North Carolina State
    University B, M, D, T
Queens University of Charlotte M
Shaw University B, T
University of North Carolina
    Charlotte B, M
    Greensboro B
    Pembroke B, M
    Wilmington B
Wake Forest University T
Western Carolina University B, M, T
Wingate University B, T
Winston-Salem State University B

North Dakota

Dickinson State University B, T
Jamestown College B
Mayville State University B, T
Minot State University B, M
North Dakota State University B, T
University of Mary B
University of North Dakota T

Ohio

Antioch University McGregor M
Ashland University B, T
Baldwin-Wallace College T
Bluffton University B
Bowling Green State
    University B, M, T
Capital University T
Case Western Reserve University T
Cedarville University B, T
Defiance College B, T
Hiram College T
John Carroll University M
Kent State University B, M
Malone University T
Miami University
    Oxford Campus B, M, T
Mount Union College T
Mount Vernon Nazarene
    University B, T
Ohio Dominican University B, T
Ohio Northern University B, T
Ohio State University
    Columbus Campus M, D
Ohio University M, D, T
Ohio Wesleyan University B
Otterbein College B
Shawnee State University B
Union Institute & University B, M
University of Akron B, M
University of Findlay B, M, T
University of Rio Grande B, T
University of Toledo B, M, T
Urbana University B
Ursuline College B, M, T
Walsh University B

Wilmington College *B*
Wright State University *B, M, T*
Youngstown State University *B, M*

Oklahoma
Cameron University *B, T*
East Central University *B, T*
Eastern Oklahoma State College *A*
Langston University *B*
Mid-America Christian University *B*
Northeastern State University *B, M*
Northwestern Oklahoma State
   University *B, T*
Oklahoma Baptist University *B, T*
Oklahoma Christian University *B, T*
Oklahoma City University *B*
Oklahoma Wesleyan University *B*
Oral Roberts University *B, T*
Southeastern Oklahoma State
   University *B, M, T*
Southern Nazarene University *B*
Southwestern Oklahoma State
   University *B, M, T*
University of Central Oklahoma *B*
University of Oklahoma *B, T*
University of Tulsa *B, T*

Oregon
Concordia University *B, M, T*
Corban College *B*
Linfield College *T*
Oregon State University *M, D*
Portland State University *D, T*
Southern Oregon University *T*
Western Oregon University *M, T*

Pennsylvania
Albright College *T*
Alvernia University *B*
Arcadia University *B, M, T*
Baptist Bible College of
   Pennsylvania *B*
Bucks County Community College *A*
Cabrini College *T*
Chatham University *M, T*
DeSales University *M, T*
Dickinson College *T*
Drexel University *M, T*
Duquesne University *B, M, T*
Geneva College *B, T*
Gettysburg College *T*
Grove City College *B, T*
Gwynedd-Mercy College *B, T*
Holy Family University *B*
Immaculata University *B, M*
Juniata College *B, T*
Keystone College *B, T*
King's College *T*
La Salle University *B, T*
Lebanon Valley College *T*
Lincoln University. *B, T*
Lycoming College *T*
Mansfield University of
   Pennsylvania *B, T*
Marywood University *B*
Mercyhurst College *B, T*
Messiah College *B, T*
Misericordia University *T*
Moravian College *T*
Philadelphia Biblical University *B, T*
Point Park University *B*
Rosemont College *T*
St. Francis University *B, T*
Saint Joseph's University *B, M, T*
St. Vincent College *T*
Seton Hill University *B, T*
Susquehanna University *T*
Temple University *B, M*
Thiel College *B*
University of Pennsylvania *M, T*
University of Pittsburgh *T*
University of Pittsburgh
   Johnstown *B, T*
Villanova University *T*

Washington & Jefferson College *T*
Waynesburg University *B, T*
Westminster College *T*
Widener University *T*
Wilkes University *M, T*
Wilson College *T*
York College of Pennsylvania *B, T*

Puerto Rico
American University of Puerto
   Rico *B, T*
Bayamon Central University *B*
Caribbean University *B, T*
Inter American University of Puerto
   Rico
   Metropolitan Campus *B, M*
   San German Campus *B*
Pontifical Catholic University of
   Puerto Rico *B, T*
Turabo University *B*
University of Puerto Rico
   Arecibo *B, M*
   Cayey University College *B*

Rhode Island
Providence College *B, M*
Rhode Island College *B, M*
Salve Regina University *B*

South Carolina
Anderson University *B, T*
Bob Jones University *B, M*
Charleston Southern University *B*
The Citadel *M*
Claflin University *B*
Clemson University *B*
Coker College *B, T*
College of Charleston *M, T*
Francis Marion University *B, T*
Furman University *T*
Limestone College *B*
Morris College *B, T*
North Greenville University *B, T*
Southern Wesleyan University *B, T*
University of South Carolina
   Aiken *B, T*
Wofford College *T*

South Dakota
Augustana College *B, T*
Black Hills State University *B*
Dakota State University *B, T*
Dakota Wesleyan University *B, T*
Mount Marty College *B*
Northern State University *B, T*
University of Sioux Falls *B*
University of South Dakota *B, M, T*

Tennessee
Belmont University *B, M, T*
Bryan College *T*
Christian Brothers University *B, M, T*
Crichton College *B, T*
Cumberland University *B, T*
Freed-Hardeman University *B, T*
King College *T*
Lambuth University *B, T*
LeMoyne-Owen College *B*
Lee University *B*
Lincoln Memorial University *B, T*
Lipscomb University *B, M, T*
Maryville College *B, T*
Middle Tennessee State
   University *M, T*
Southern Adventist University *B*
Tennessee Technological University *T*
Tennessee Temple University *B*
Trevecca Nazarene University *B, T*
Tusculum College *B, T*
Union University *B, T*
University of Memphis *T*
University of Tennessee
   Chattanooga *B*

Vanderbilt University *M, D*

Texas
Abilene Christian University *B, T*
Baylor University *B, T*
East Texas Baptist University *B*
Hardin-Simmons University *B, T*
Houston Baptist University *B, T*
Howard Payne University *B, T*
Jarvis Christian College *B, T*
Lamar University *B, M, T*
Laredo Community College *A*
LeTourneau University *B, T*
Lubbock Christian University *B*
McMurry University *B, T*
Midwestern State University *B, T*
Prairie View A&M University *M*
St. Edward's University *B, T*
St. Mary's University *T*
Sam Houston State University *M, T*
Schreiner University *B*
Stephen F. Austin State University *M*
Tarleton State University *T*
Texas A&M International
   University *B, T*
Texas A&M University
   Commerce *T*
   Kingsville *T*
Texas Christian University *B, M*
Texas College *B, T*
Texas Lutheran University *B, T*
Texas State University: San
   Marcos *M, D, T*
Texas Wesleyan University *B, T*
University of Dallas *T*
University of Houston *M, T*
University of Houston
   Clear Lake *T*
   Victoria *M*
University of Mary Hardin-Baylor *B, T*
University of Texas
   Arlington *T*
   Austin *M, D*
   Dallas *M, T*
   Pan American *M*
   San Antonio *M, T*
West Texas A&M University *T*

Utah
Brigham Young University *B, M*
Southern Utah University *B, T*
Utah State University *B*
Utah Valley University *B*
Weber State University *B*
Western Governors University *B, M, T*

Vermont
Castleton State College *B, T*
Goddard College *M*
Johnson State College *B*
St. Michael's College *T*
University of Vermont *B, T*

Virginia
Averett University *B, M, T*
Bluefield College *B, T*
Bridgewater College *T*
Eastern Mennonite University *T*
Emory & Henry College *B*
Hampton University *M*
Hollins University *T*
James Madison University *M, T*
Liberty University *M, T*
Longwood University *B, T*
Old Dominion University *B, T*
Radford University *T*
St. Paul's College *T*
University of Virginia's College at
   Wise *T*

Washington
Eastern Washington University *B, M*
Evergreen State College *M*

Northwest University *T*
Seattle Pacific University *B, T*
Washington State
   University *B, M, D, T*
Western Washington University *B*
Whitworth University *B, T*

West Virginia
Bethany College *B*
Concord University *B, M, T*
Davis and Elkins College *B*
Fairmont State University *B*
Ohio Valley University *B*
Shepherd University *T*
West Liberty University *B*
West Virginia State University *B*
West Virginia University *T*
West Virginia Wesleyan College *B*

Wisconsin
Carroll University *B, T*
Carthage College *T*
Concordia University Wisconsin *B*
Edgewood College *B*
Lakeland College *T*
Lawrence University *T*
Maranatha Baptist Bible College *B*
Marquette University *B, M*
Mount Mary College *B, T*
Northland College *B, T*
St. Norbert College *T*
Silver Lake College *T*
University of Wisconsin
   Green Bay *T*
   Oshkosh *M, T*
   Parkside *T*
   Platteville *B*
   River Falls *T*
   Superior *B, T*
   Whitewater *B*
Viterbo University *B, T*

Wyoming
Eastern Wyoming College *A*

Meat cutting

Georgia
Art Institute
   of Atlanta *C*

Michigan
Bay de Noc Community College *C*

Wisconsin
Wisconsin Indianhead Technical
   College *C*

Mechanical drafting/ CAD/CADD

Alabama
Gadsden State Community
   College *C, A*
Lawson State Community
   College *C, A*

Alaska
University of Alaska
   Anchorage *C*

California
City College of San Francisco *C*
Hartnell College *C*
Los Angeles Pierce College *C*
Ohlone College *C*
Orange Coast College *C, A*
Sierra College *C, A*

Colorado

Westwood College of Technology
  Westwood College: Denver South *A*

Connecticut

Naugatuck Valley Community
  College *C*

Delaware

Delaware Technical and Community
  College
  Owens *A*

Florida

Palm Beach Community College *C*

Georgia

Albany Technical College *C*
Southwest Georgia Technical
  College *C*

Illinois

Danville Area Community College *C*
John Wood Community College *A*
Kaskaskia College *C*
Moraine Valley Community College *C*
Morton College *C*
Parkland College *C*
Sauk Valley Community College *C*
Triton College *C*
Wilbur Wright College *C, A*

Indiana

Purdue University *A, B*
Vincennes University *A*

Iowa

Des Moines Area Community
  College *C, A*
Indian Hills Community College *A*
Iowa Central Community College *C*
Scott Community College *C, A*
Western Iowa Tech Community
  College *C, A*

Kentucky

Sullivan College of Technology and
  Design *C, A*

Massachusetts

Benjamin Franklin Institute of
  Technology *A*
North Shore Community College *C*
Springfield Technical Community
  College *C*

Michigan

Baker College
  of Muskegon *A*
Eastern Michigan University *B*
Grand Rapids Community College *A*
Mott Community College *A*
Oakland Community College *C, A*

Minnesota

Alexandria Technical College *C, A*
Central Lakes College *C*
Herzing University *A*
Lake Superior College *C, A*
Minnesota State Community and
  Technical College *C, A*
Northwest Technical Institute *A*
Rochester Community and Technical
  College *C*
St. Cloud Technical College *C, A*

New Jersey

Bergen Community College *C, A*

New York

Cayuga County Community College *C*

North Carolina

Central Piedmont Community
  College *C*
Isothermal Community College *C, A*
Piedmont Community College *C*

Ohio

Edison State Community College *C, A*

Oklahoma

Cameron University *A, B*

Oregon

Chemeketa Community College *C, A*

Pennsylvania

Butler County Community College *A*
Commonwealth Technical Institute *A*
Triangle Tech
  DuBois *A*
  Erie *A*
  Greensburg *A*
Westmoreland County Community
  College *A*

South Carolina

Aiken Technical College *A*
Greenville Technical College *C, A*
Midlands Technical College *C, A*
Spartanburg Community College *C*
York Technical College *C, A*

South Dakota

Southeast Technical Institute *A*

Tennessee

Northeast State Community
  College *C, A*

Texas

North Lake College *C*

Washington

Bates Technical College *C*
Olympic College *C*

West Virginia

Fairmont State University *A*

Wisconsin

Fox Valley Technical College *A*
Herzing University *A, B*
Lakeshore Technical College *A*
Milwaukee Area Technical
  College *C, A*
Waukesha County Technical
  College *A*
Western Technical College *A*
Wisconsin Indianhead Technical
  College *A*

Wyoming

Casper College *C*

Mechanical engineering

Alabama

Alabama Agricultural and Mechanical
  University *B*
Auburn University *B, M, D*
Tuskegee University *B, M*
University of Alabama *B, M, D*
University of Alabama
  Birmingham *B, M, D*
  Huntsville *B, D*
University of South Alabama *B, M*

Alaska

University of Alaska
  Fairbanks *B, M*

Arizona

Arizona State University *B, M, D*
Central Arizona College *A*
Northern Arizona University *B*
University of Arizona *B, M, D*

Arkansas

Arkansas State University *B*
Arkansas Tech University *B*
Harding University *B*
University of Arkansas *B, M*

California

California Baptist University *B*
California Institute of
  Technology *B, M, D*
California Maritime Academy *B*
California Polytechnic State
  University: San Luis Obispo *B, M*
California State Polytechnic
  University: Pomona *B, M*
California State University
  Chico *B*
  Fresno *B, M*
  Fullerton *B, M*
  Long Beach *B, M*
  Los Angeles *B, M*
  Northridge *B, M*
  Sacramento *B, M*
City College of San Francisco *A*
De Anza College *A*
Loyola Marymount University *B, M*
San Diego State University *B, M*
San Francisco State University *B*
San Jose State University *B, M*
Santa Clara University *B, M, D*
Stanford University *B, M, D*
University of California
  Berkeley *B, M, D*
  Davis *B, M, D*
  Irvine *B, M, D*
  Los Angeles *B, M, D*
  Riverside *B, M, D*
  San Diego *B, M, D*
  Santa Barbara *B, M, D*
University of California:
  Merced *B, M, D*
University of San Diego *B*
University of Southern
  California *B, M, D*
University of the Pacific *B*

Colorado

Colorado Mountain College *A*
Colorado School of Mines *B*
Colorado State University *B, M, D*
United States Air Force Academy *B*
University of Colorado
  Boulder *B, M, D*
  Colorado Springs *B, M*
  Denver *B, M*
University of Denver *B, M*

Connecticut

Central Connecticut State
  University *B*
Fairfield University *A, B, M*
Trinity College *B*
United States Coast Guard Academy *B*
University of Bridgeport *M*
University of Connecticut *B, M, D*
University of Hartford *B, M*
University of New Haven *B, M*
Yale University *B, M, D*

Delaware

University of Delaware *B, M, D*

District of Columbia

Catholic University of
  America *B, M, D*
George Washington University *B, M*
Howard University *B, M, D*

University of the District of
  Columbia *B*

Florida

Embry-Riddle Aeronautical
  University *B, M*
Florida Agricultural and Mechanical
  University *B, M, D*
Florida Atlantic University *B, M, D*
Florida Institute of
  Technology *B, M, D*
Florida International
  University *B, M, D*
Florida State University *B, M, D*
Jacksonville University *B*
University of Central Florida *B, M, D*
University of Florida *B, M*
University of Miami *B, M, D*
University of North Florida *B*
University of South Florida *B, M, D*

Georgia

Georgia Institute of
  Technology *B, M, D*
Georgia Southern University *B*
Mercer University *M*
Southern Polytechnic State
  University *B*

Hawaii

University of Hawaii
  Manoa *B, M, D*

Idaho

Boise State University *B, M*
Brigham Young University-Idaho *B*
Idaho State University *B, M*
University of Idaho *B, M, D*

Illinois

Bradley University *B, M*
Dominican University *B*
Illinois Institute of
  Technology *B, M, D*
Northern Illinois University *B, M*
Northwestern University *B, M, D*
Southern Illinois University
  Carbondale *B, M*
Southern Illinois University
  Edwardsville *B, M*
University of Illinois
  Chicago *B, M, D*
  Urbana-Champaign *B, M, D*

Indiana

Indiana Institute of Technology *B*
Indiana University
  East *A*
Indiana University-Purdue University
  Fort Wayne *B*
Indiana University-Purdue University
  Indianapolis *B, M, D*
Purdue University *B, M, D*
Purdue University
  Calumet *B*
  North Central *B*
Rose-Hulman Institute of
  Technology *B, M*
Trine University *B, M*
University of Evansville *B*
University of Notre Dame *B, M, D*
Valparaiso University *B*
Vincennes University *A*

Iowa

Dordt College *B*
Iowa State University *B, M, D*
University of Iowa *B, M, D*
William Penn University *B*

Kansas

Kansas State University *B, M, D*

University of Kansas *B, M, D*
Wichita State University *B, M, D*

Kentucky
University of Kentucky *B, M, D*
University of Louisville *B, M, D*
Western Kentucky University *B*

Louisiana
Louisiana State University and
 Agricultural and Mechanical
 College *B, M, D*
Louisiana Tech University *B*
Southern University and Agricultural
 and Mechanical College *B*
University of Louisiana at
 Lafayette *B, M*
University of New Orleans *B*

Maine
University of Maine *B, M, D*
University of Southern Maine *B*

Maryland
Johns Hopkins University *B, M, D*
United States Naval Academy *B*
University of Maryland
 Baltimore County *B, M, D*
 College Park *B, M, D*

Massachusetts
Boston University *B, M, D*
Bristol Community College *A*
Franklin W. Olin College of
 Engineering *B*
Massachusetts Institute of
 Technology *B, M, D*
Northeastern University *B, M, D*
Smith College *B*
Tufts University *B, M, D*
University of Massachusetts
 Amherst *B, M, D*
 Dartmouth *B, M*
 Lowell *B, M, D*
Western New England College *B, M*
Worcester Polytechnic
 Institute *B, M, D*

Michigan
Andrews University *B*
Baker College
 of Flint *B*
Calvin College *B*
Central Michigan University *B*
Delta College *A*
Grand Valley State University *B, M*
Kettering University *B, M*
Lake Superior State University *B*
Lawrence Technological
 University *B, M*
Michigan State University *B, M, D*
Michigan Technological
 University *B, M, D, T*
Oakland University *B, M, D*
Saginaw Valley State University *B*
University of Detroit Mercy *B, M, D*
University of Michigan *B, M, D*
University of Michigan
 Dearborn *B, M*
 Flint *B*
Wayne State University *B, M, D*
Western Michigan University *B, M, D*

Minnesota
Minnesota State University
 Mankato *B, M*
Northwest Technical Institute *A*
Saint Cloud State University *B, M*
University of Minnesota
 Duluth *B*
 Twin Cities *B, M, D*
University of St. Thomas *B*

Mississippi
Mississippi State University *B, M*
University of Mississippi *B*

Missouri
St. Charles Community College *A*
Saint Louis University *B*
University of Missouri
 Columbia *B, M, D*
 Kansas City *B, M*
 Missouri University of Science and
 Technology *B, M, D*
 St. Louis
Washington University in St.
 Louis *B, M, D*

Montana
Montana State University
 Bozeman *B, M*

Nebraska
University of Nebraska
 Lincoln *B, M*

Nevada
University of Nevada
 Las Vegas *B, M, D*
 Reno *B, M, D*

New Hampshire
Daniel Webster College *B*
University of New Hampshire *B, M, D*

New Jersey
The College of New Jersey *B*
New Jersey Institute of
 Technology *B, M, D*
Princeton University *B, M, D*
Rowan University *B*
Rutgers, The State University of New
 Jersey
 Camden Regional Campus *B*
 New Brunswick/Piscataway
 Campus *B, M, D*
 Newark Regional Campus *B*
Stevens Institute of
 Technology *B, M, D*

New Mexico
New Mexico Institute of Mining and
 Technology *B*
New Mexico State University *B, M*
University of New Mexico *B, M*

New York
Alfred University *B, M*
City University of New York
 City College *B, M, D*
 Hostos Community College *A*
 LaGuardia Community College *A*
Clarkson University *B, M, D*
Columbia University *B, M, D*
Cooper Union for the Advancement of
 Science and Art *B, M*
Cornell University *B, M, D*
Hofstra University *B*
Manhattan College *B, M*
New York Institute of Technology *B*
Polytechnic Institute of New York
 University *B, M, D*
Rensselaer Polytechnic
 Institute *B, M, D*
Rochester Institute of
 Technology *B, M*
State University of New York
 Binghamton *B, M, D*
 Buffalo *B, M, D*
 Maritime College *B*
 Stony Brook *B, M, D*
Syracuse University *B, M, D*
Union College *B*
United States Military Academy *B*

University of Rochester *B, M, D*

North Carolina
Duke University *B, M, D*
North Carolina Agricultural and
 Technical State
 University *B, M, D*
North Carolina State
 University *B, M, D*
University of North Carolina
 Charlotte *B, M, D*
Western Piedmont Community
 College *A*

North Dakota
North Dakota State University *B, M, D*
University of North Dakota *B, M*

Ohio
Case Western Reserve
 University *B, M, D*
Cedarville University *B*
Cleveland State University *B, M, D*
Miami University
 Oxford Campus *B*
Ohio Northern University *B*
Ohio State University
 Columbus Campus *B, M, D*
Ohio University *B, M*
Terra State Community College *A*
University of Akron *B, M, D*
University of Cincinnati *B, M, D*
University of Dayton *B, M, D*
University of Toledo *B, M*
Wilberforce University *B*
Wright State University *B*
Youngstown State University *B, M*

Oklahoma
Oklahoma Christian University *B*
Oklahoma State University *B, M, D*
Oral Roberts University *B*
University of Oklahoma *B, M, D*
University of Tulsa *B, M, D*

Oregon
George Fox University *B*
Oregon Institute of Technology *B*
Oregon State University *B, M, D*
Portland State University *B, M, D*
University of Portland *B, M*

Pennsylvania
Bucknell University *B, M*
Carnegie Mellon University *B, M, D*
Drexel University *B, M, D*
Gannon University *B, M*
Gettysburg College *B*
Grove City College *B*
Lafayette College *B*
Lehigh Carbon Community College *A*
Lehigh University *B, M, D*
Penn State
 Abington *B*
 Altoona *B*
 Beaver *B*
 Berks *B*
 Brandywine *B*
 DuBois *B*
 Erie, The Behrend College *B*
 Fayette, The Eberly Campus *B*
 Greater Allegheny *B*
 Harrisburg *B*
 Hazleton *B*
 Lehigh Valley *B*
 Mont Alto *B*
 New Kensington *B*
 Schuylkill *B*
 Shenango *B*
 University Park *B, M, D*
 Wilkes-Barre *B*
 Worthington Scranton *B*
 York *B*

Philadelphia University *B*
Temple University *B, M*
Thaddeus Stevens College of
 Technology *B*
University of Pennsylvania *B, M, D*
University of Pittsburgh *B, M, D*
University of Pittsburgh
 Bradford *B*
Villanova University *B, M*
Widener University *B, M*
Wilkes University *B*
York College of Pennsylvania *B*

Puerto Rico
Inter American University of Puerto
 Rico
 Bayamon Campus *B*
Turabo University *B*
Universidad Politecnica de Puerto
 Rico *B*
University of Puerto Rico
 Carolina Regional College *A*

Rhode Island
Brown University *B, M, D*
New England Institute of
 Technology *A, B*
University of Rhode Island *B, M, D*

South Carolina
Clemson University *B, M, D*
University of South Carolina *B, M, D*

South Dakota
Lake Area Technical Institute *A*
South Dakota School of Mines and
 Technology *B*
South Dakota State University *B*

Tennessee
Christian Brothers University *B*
Lipscomb University *B*
Tennessee Technological
 University *B, M, D*
Union University *B*
University of Memphis *B, M*
University of Tennessee
 Chattanooga *B*
 Knoxville *B, M, D*

Texas
Baylor University *B, M*
Lamar University *B, M*
LeTourneau University *B*
Midwestern State University *B*
Prairie View A&M University *B*
Rice University *B, M, D*
Southern Methodist
 University *B, M, D*
Texas A&M University *B, M, D*
Texas A&M University
 Corpus Christi *B*
 Kingsville *B, M*
Texas Christian University *B*
Texas Tech University *B, M, D*
University of Houston *B, M, D*
University of North Texas *B, M*
University of Texas
 Arlington *B, M, D*
 Austin *B, M, D*
 Dallas *B, M*
 El Paso *B, M*
 Pan American *B, M*
 San Antonio *B, M*
 Tyler *B*
 of the Permian Basin *B*
West Texas A&M University *B*

Utah
Brigham Young University *B, M, D*
College of Eastern Utah *A, T*
Salt Lake Community College *A*
Southern Utah University *A*

University of Utah *B, M, D*
Utah State University *B, M, D*

Vermont

Norwich University *B*
University of Vermont *B, M, D*

Virginia

John Tyler Community College *A*
Lord Fairfax Community College *A*
Old Dominion University *B, M, D*
University of Virginia *B, M, D*
Virginia Commonwealth University *B*
Virginia Military Institute *B*
Virginia Polytechnic Institute and
  State University *B, M, D*

Washington

Bates Technical College *A*
Gonzaga University *B*
Saint Martin's University *B*
Seattle University *B*
Shoreline Community College *A*
University of Washington *B, M, D*
Walla Walla University *B*
Washington State University *B, M, D*

West Virginia

Potomac State College of West
  Virginia University *A*
West Virginia University *B, M, D*
West Virginia University Institute of
  Technology *B*

Wisconsin

Marquette University *B, M, D*
Milwaukee School of Engineering *B*
University of Wisconsin
  Madison *B, M, D*
  Milwaukee *B*
  Platteville *B*
Waukesha County Technical
  College *A*

Wyoming

University of Wyoming *B, M, D*

Mechanical engineering technology

Alabama

Gadsden State Community
  College *C, A*

Alaska

University of Alaska
  Anchorage *C*

Arizona

Arizona State University *B, M*
Penn Foster College *A*

California

California State University
  Sacramento *B, M*
City College of San Francisco *A*
Diablo Valley College *C*
Hartnell College *C, A*

Connecticut

Central Connecticut State
  University *B*
Naugatuck Valley Community
  College *A*
University of Hartford *B*

Delaware

Delaware State University *B*
Delaware Technical and Community
  College
  Stanton/Wilmington *A*

Georgia

Georgia Southern University *B*
Macon State College *A*
Southern Polytechnic State
  University *B*

Idaho

Idaho State University *A, B*

Illinois

College of Lake County *C, A*
McHenry County College *C, A*
Moraine Valley Community College *A*
Parkland College *C*
Sauk Valley Community College *A*
Triton College *C, A*

Indiana

Indiana University-Purdue University
  Fort Wayne *A, B*
Indiana University-Purdue University
  Indianapolis *A, B*
Purdue University *A, B*
Purdue University
  North Central *C, A, B*

Kansas

Pittsburg State University *B*

Maryland

Community College of Baltimore
  County *C, A*
Hagerstown Community College *C, A*

Massachusetts

Benjamin Franklin Institute of
  Technology *A*
Springfield Technical Community
  College *C, A*
University of Massachusetts
  Lowell *C, A*
Wentworth Institute of Technology *B*

Michigan

Bay de Noc Community College *C*
Central Michigan University *B*
Eastern Michigan University *B*
Ferris State University *A, B*
Lawrence Technological University *A*
Michigan Technological University *B*
Mott Community College *A*
Northern Michigan University *B*
Wayne State University *B*

Minnesota

Hennepin Technical College *C, A*
Minnesota State University
  Mankato *B, M*
Northwest Technical Institute *A*
Rochester Community and Technical
  College *A*

Missouri

Lincoln University *B*
St. Louis Community College
  St. Louis Community College at
    Florissant Valley *A*

Nevada

College of Southern Nevada *C, A*

New Hampshire

University of New Hampshire *B*

New Jersey

Fairleigh Dickinson University
  Metropolitan Campus *B*
Thomas Edison State College *A, B*
Union County College *A*

New York

Broome Community College *A*
Cayuga County Community College *A*
City University of New York
  New York City College of
    Technology *A*
Erie Community College
  North Campus *A*
Excelsior College *B*
Finger Lakes Community College *A*
Jamestown Community College *A*
Mohawk Valley Community College *A*
Monroe Community College *A*
New York Institute of Technology *B*
Niagara County Community
  College *A*
Onondaga Community College *A*
Rochester Institute of Technology *B*
State University of New York
  College at Buffalo *B*
  College of Agriculture and
    Technology at Morrisville *A*
  College of Technology at
    Alfred *A, B*
  College of Technology at Canton *A*
  College of Technology at
    Farmingdale *A, B*
  Institute of Technology at
    Utica/Rome *B*
Tompkins Cortland Community
  College *A*
United States Military Academy *B*
Vaughn College of Aeronautics and
  Technology *A, B*

North Carolina

Cape Fear Community College *C, A*
Catawba Valley Community College *A*
Central Piedmont Community
  College *A*
Edgecombe Community College *C*
Forsyth Technical Community
  College *C, A*
Guilford Technical Community
  College *C, A*
Isothermal Community College *A*
Lenoir Community College *C, A*
University of North Carolina
  Charlotte *B*
Wayne Community College *A*
Wilson Community College *C, A*

Ohio

Bowling Green State University *B*
Cincinnati State Technical and
  Community College *C, A*
Clark State Community College *A*
Columbus State Community
  College *C, A*
Edison State Community College *C, A*
James A. Rhodes State College *A*
Kent State University
  Ashtabula *A*
  Trumbull *A*
  Tuscarawas *A*
Marion Technical College *A*
Miami University
  Hamilton Campus *A, B*
  Oxford Campus *C, A*
North Central State College *A*
Northwest State Community
  College *C, A*
Owens Community College
  Toledo *A*
University of Akron *A, B*
University of Dayton *B*
University of Toledo *C, A, B*
Youngstown State University *A, B*

Oklahoma

Oklahoma State University *B*

Oregon

Oregon Institute of Technology *B*

Portland Community College *C, A*

Pennsylvania

Harrisburg Area Community
  College *C, A*
Montgomery County Community
  College *A*
Penn State
  Altoona *A*
  Berks *A*
  DuBois *A*
  Erie, The Behrend College *A, B*
  Hazleton *A*
  New Kensington *A*
  York *A*
Pennsylvania College of
  Technology *B*
Pittsburgh Institute of Aeronautics *A*
Point Park University *A, B*
Thaddeus Stevens College of
  Technology *A*
University of Pittsburgh
  Johnstown *B*
Westmoreland County Community
  College *A*

Puerto Rico

Turabo University *A*

Rhode Island

Community College of Rhode
  Island *C, A*

South Carolina

Greenville Technical College *A*
South Carolina State University *B*
Spartanburg Community College *A*
York Technical College *A*

South Dakota

Southeast Technical Institute *A*

Tennessee

Chattanooga State Community
  College *A*
Pellissippi State Community
  College *A*
Southwest Tennessee Community
  College *C*

Texas

LeTourneau University *B*
Palo Alto College *C*
Texas A&M University
  Corpus Christi *B*
  Galveston *B*
Texas Tech University *B*
University of Houston
  Downtown *B*
University of North Texas *B*
University of Texas
  Brownsville - Texas Southmost
    College *B*

Utah

Salt Lake Community College *A*

Virginia

John Tyler Community College *C, A*
Old Dominion University *B*
Virginia State University *B*

Washington

Bates Technical College *C, A*
Bellingham Technical College *A*
Clover Park Technical College *A*
Eastern Washington University *B*
Shoreline Community College *A*
South Seattle Community College *A*

West Virginia

Bluefield State College *A, B*

...e University *A, B*

...nsin
...way Technical College *A*
...waukee School of Engineering *B*
...Western Technical College *A*

Mechanics/repairers, general

Alabama
Central Alabama Community
   College *C*
George C. Wallace State Community
   College
   Selma *A*
Lawson State Community College *C*

Arkansas
Pulaski Technical College *C*
University of Arkansas
   Community College at
    Batesville *C, A*

California
Allan Hancock College *C, A*
Cerritos College *A*
College of the Redwoods *C*
Columbia College *C*
El Camino College: Compton
   Center *C, A*
Fresno City College *C, A*
Imperial Valley College *C, A*
Long Beach City College *C, A*
Modesto Junior College *C, A*
Palomar College *C*
Riverside Community College *C, A*
San Jose City College *C*
WyoTech: Fremont *C, A*
Yuba Community College
   District *C, A*

Colorado
Colorado Northwestern Community
   College *C*
Colorado School of Trades *A*
Otero Junior College *C*
Westwood College: Denver North *A*

Connecticut
Gateway Community College *A*

Florida
Florida State College at Jacksonville *C*
Seminole Community College *C*

Georgia
Columbus Technical College *C*
Southwest Georgia Technical
   College *C*
West Georgia Technical College *A*

Hawaii
University of Hawaii
   Honolulu Community College *C, A*

Idaho
Eastern Idaho Technical College *C, A*
Idaho State University *A*
Lewis-Clark State College *C, A, B*
North Idaho College *C*

Illinois
Kankakee Community College *C, A*
Richland Community College *A*
Southwestern Illinois College *C, A*

Indiana
Ivy Tech Community College
   Bloomington *C, A*
   Central Indiana *C, A*

Northwest *C, A*
Richmond *C, A*

Iowa
Iowa Western Community College *A*
Southeastern Community College
   North Campus *A*

Kansas
Butler Community College *C, A*

Kentucky
Maysville Community and Technical
   College *C*

Louisiana
Baton Rouge School of Computers *A*
Nunez Community College *C*

Maine
Washington County Community
   College *C, A*

Massachusetts
Benjamin Franklin Institute of
   Technology *A*

Michigan
Bay de Noc Community College *C, A*
Glen Oaks Community College *C*
Lansing Community College *A*
Macomb Community College *C*
Muskegon Community College *C, A*
Oakland Community College *C, A*

Minnesota
Hennepin Technical College *C, A*
Mesabi Range Community and
   Technical College *A*

Mississippi
Northeast Mississippi Community
   College *C*
Northwest Mississippi Community
   College *C*

Missouri
North Central Missouri College *A*

Nebraska
Mid-Plains Community College
   Area *C, A*

North Carolina
Alamance Community College *C*
Forsyth Technical Community
   College *C*
Johnston Community College *C*
Mayland Community College *C*
Rockingham Community College *C*
Sandhills Community College *C*

Ohio
Ohio Technical College *C, A*

Oklahoma
Oklahoma City Community College *A*

Oregon
Linn-Benton Community College *A*
Rogue Community College *A*

Pennsylvania
Johnson College *A*
Penn Commercial Business and
   Technical School *A*
Rosedale Technical Institute *A*

Puerto Rico
Electronic Data Processing College:
   San Sebastian *A*

South Carolina
Central Carolina Technical College *C*
Tri-County Technical College *C*
Trident Technical College *C*
Williamsburg Technical College *C, A*
York Technical College *A*

South Dakota
Lake Area Technical Institute *A*
Southeast Technical Institute *A*

Tennessee
Chattanooga State Community
   College *C*
Northeast State Community
   College *C, A*

Texas
Central Texas College *C, A*
Cisco College *C, A*
Laredo Community College *C*
Texas State Technical College
   Waco *C, A*
Western Technical College *C, A*

Utah
Snow College *C, A*

Virginia
ECPI College of Technology: Virginia
   Beach *C, A*
Virginia Highlands Community
   College *C*
Virginia Western Community
   College *A*

Washington
Bates Technical College *C, A*

West Virginia
West Virginia University at
   Parkersburg *A*

Wisconsin
Nicolet Area Technical College *C*

Wyoming
Laramie County Community
   College *C*

Media studies

Alabama
Talladega College *B*
University of Alabama *D*

Arizona
Prescott College *B*

Arkansas
Arkansas Tech University *M*
Ouachita Baptist University *B*
University of the Ozarks *B*

California
Academy of Art University *B, M*
American Jewish University *B*
California Baptist University *B*
California State University
   Fresno *B, M*
Claremont McKenna College *B*
College of Marin: Kentfield *A*
College of the Desert *A*
College of the Siskiyous *C, A*
Foothill College *C, A*
Marymount College *B*

The Master's College *B*
National University *B*
Orange Coast College *A*
Point Loma Nazarene University *B*
Pomona College *B*
Rio Hondo College *A*
University of California
   Berkeley *B*
University of San Francisco *B*
Woodbury University *B*
Yuba Community College
   District *C, A*

Colorado
Colorado State University
   Pueblo *B*
Mesa State College *B*
University of Denver *M*

Connecticut
Albertus Magnus College *B*
Mitchell College *B*
Sacred Heart University *B*
University of Bridgeport *B*
University of New Haven *C*
Western Connecticut State
   University *B*

Delaware
Delaware State University *B*

District of Columbia
American University *B*

Florida
Florida Gulf Coast University *B*
Florida State University *D*
Lynn University *B, M*
Rollins College *B*
Saint Leo University *B*
Saint Thomas University *B*
State College of Florida,
   Manatee-Sarasota *A*
University of Central Florida *M*
University of Miami *B*
University of North Florida *B*
University of West Florida *B, M*

Georgia
Abraham Baldwin Agricultural
   College *A*
Brenau University *B*
Georgia State University *M, D*
Macon State College *A*
Mercer University *B*
Piedmont College *B*
Savannah State University *B*
Southern Polytechnic State
   University *B*
Toccoa Falls College *B*
University of Georgia *D*
Valdosta State University *B*

Hawaii
Chaminade University of Honolulu *B*
Hawaii Pacific University *M*

Idaho
Boise State University *B*
Idaho State University *B*
Northwest Nazarene University *B*
University of Idaho *B*

Illinois
DePaul University *M*
Eureka College *B*
Greenville College *B*
Illinois State University *B*
Judson University *B*
Principia College *B*
Southern Illinois University
   Carbondale *M, D*

Southern Illinois University
   Edwardsville *B, M*
University of Illinois
   Urbana-Champaign *B, D*
University of St. Francis *B*

Indiana

Ancilla College *A*
Anderson University *B*
Calumet College of St. Joseph *C, A, B*
DePauw University *B*
Indiana University
   Bloomington *D*
   South Bend *B*
Indiana University-Purdue University
   Fort Wayne *B*
Indiana Wesleyan University *B*
Saint Joseph's College *B*
St. Mary-of-the-Woods College *B*
Taylor University *B*
University of Southern Indiana *B*
Valparaiso University *B*

Iowa

Briar Cliff University *B*
Buena Vista University *B*
Dordt College *B*
Drake University *B*
Grand View University *C, B*
Loras College *B*
Luther College *B*
Maharishi University of
   Management *B*
Morningside College *B*
St. Ambrose University *B*
University of Iowa *B*
Waldorf College *B*

Kansas

Baker University *B*
Benedictine College *B*
Bethel College *B*
Central Christian College of
   Kansas *A, B*
Kansas State University *B*
MidAmerica Nazarene University *B*
Newman University *B*
Washburn University *B*

Kentucky

Berea College *B*
Georgetown College *B*

Louisiana

Centenary College of Louisiana *B*
Grambling State University *B, M*
Louisiana College *B*
Louisiana State University
   Shreveport *B*
Louisiana State University and
   Agricultural and Mechanical
   College *B, M, D*
McNeese State University *B*
Nicholls State University *B*
Southern University and Agricultural
   and Mechanical College *B, M*
Tulane University *A, B*
University of Louisiana at Lafayette *B*
University of Louisiana at Monroe *B*
Xavier University of Louisiana *B*

Maine

University of Southern Maine *B*

Maryland

Goucher College *B*
Harford Community College *C, A*
Howard Community College *A*
Towson University *B*
University of Maryland
   Baltimore County *B*

Massachusetts

American International College *B*
Anna Maria College *B*
Cape Cod Community College *A*
Emerson College *B*
Endicott College *B*
Fisher College *B*
Lasell College *B*
Massachusetts Institute of
   Technology *B, M*
Massasoit Community College *A*
Newbury College *B*
Pine Manor College *B*
Salem State College *B*
Suffolk University *B*
Western New England College *B*
Wheelock College *B*
Worcester State College *B*

Michigan

Adrian College *A, B, T*
Alma College *B*
Calvin College *B*
Cornerstone University *B*
Kuyper College *B*
Michigan State University *D*
University of Michigan
   Flint *B*

Minnesota

Augsburg College *B*
Bethel University *B*
Concordia University: St. Paul *B*
Itasca Community College *A*
Minnesota State University
   Mankato *B*
   Moorhead *B*
Minnesota West Community and
   Technical College *A*
North Central University *A, B*
Northland Community & Technical
   College *A*
Ridgewater College *A*
Rochester Community and Technical
   College *A*
Saint Cloud State University *B, M*
Walden University *B*
Winona State University *B*

Mississippi

Alcorn State University *B*
Jackson State University *B, M*
Mississippi College *B*
Tougaloo College *B*

Missouri

Calvary Bible College and Theological
   Seminary *B*
Lindenwood University *B*
Maryville University of Saint Louis *B*
Missouri Southern State University *B*
Missouri State University *B*
Missouri Valley College *B*
Stephens College *B*
University of Missouri
   St. Louis *B*
Westminster College *B*

Montana

Montana State University
   Billings *B*

Nebraska

Wayne State College *B, T*

New Hampshire

Chester College of New England *B*
Colby-Sawyer College *B*
Franklin Pierce University *B*
Saint Anselm College *B*

New Jersey

Essex County College *A*
Union County College *A*
William Paterson University of New
   Jersey *M*

New Mexico

New Mexico Highlands
   University *B, M*
University of New Mexico *B*

New York

Adelphi University *B*
Adirondack Community College *C, A*
City University of New York
   Brooklyn College *M*
   Hunter College *B, M*
   LaGuardia Community College *A*
   Queens College *B*
College of New Rochelle *B, M*
College of Saint Rose *B, M*
Dominican College of Blauvelt *B*
Five Towns College *B*
Herkimer County Community
   College *A*
Hobart and William Smith Colleges *B*
Hofstra University *B*
Iona College *B*
Ithaca College *B*
Marist College *B*
Medaille College *B*
Mercy College *B*
Mount Saint Mary College *B*
Nassau Community College *A*
Russell Sage College *B*
Saint Bonaventure University *B, M*
State University of New York
   Buffalo *B, M*
   College at Brockport *B*
   College at Buffalo *B*
   College at Oneonta *B*
   College at Plattsburgh *B*
   Farmingdale *B*
   Purchase *B*
Syracuse University *M, D*
Vassar College *B*

North Carolina

Barton College *B*
Bennett College for Women *B*
Johnson C. Smith University *B*
Meredith College *B*
Methodist University *A, B*
Montreat College *B*
North Carolina Central University *B*
Queens University of Charlotte *B*
St. Andrews Presbyterian College *B*
Shaw University *B*
University of North Carolina
   Asheville *B*
   Chapel Hill *B, M, D*
   Greensboro *B*
   Pembroke *B*
Winston-Salem State University *B*

Ohio

Baldwin-Wallace College *B*
Bowling Green State University *M, D*
Cedarville University *B*
Miami University
   Oxford Campus *B*
Tiffin University *B*
University of Cincinnati
   Raymond Walters College *C*
University of Dayton *B*
University of Rio Grande *B*
University of Toledo *B*
Washington State Community
   College *A*
Wilmington College *B*
Wright State University *B*

Oklahoma

Oklahoma Christian University *B*
Oklahoma City University *B, M*
Oklahoma State University *M*
University of Oklahoma *D*

Oregon

Linfield College *B*
University of Oregon *B, M*
University of Portland *B, M*

Pennsylvania

Allegheny College *B*
Arcadia University *B*
Bloomsburg University of
   Pennsylvania *B*
Carlow University *B*
Edinboro University of
   Pennsylvania *B*
Harrisburg Area Community
   College *A*
Holy Family University *B*
King's College *B*
La Roche College *B*
La Salle University *B*
Lackawanna College *A*
Penn State
   University Park *D*
Pennsylvania College of
   Technology *A*
Point Park University *B*
Temple University *D*
University of Pittsburgh *C, B*
Wilson College *A, B*
York College of Pennsylvania *A, B*

Puerto Rico

Universidad Metropolitana *B*
University of Puerto Rico
   Rio Piedras *B, M*

Rhode Island

Roger Williams University *B*

South Carolina

Aiken Technical College *C*
Claflin University *B*
Francis Marion University *B*
Morris College *B*
North Greenville University *B*
South Carolina State University *B*
University of South Carolina *B, M*

South Dakota

Black Hills State University *B*
University of South Dakota *B, M*

Tennessee

Austin Peay State University *B, M*
Belmont University *B*
East Tennessee State University *B*
Freed-Hardeman University *B*
Lipscomb University *B*
Middle Tennessee State
   University *B, M*
Southern Adventist University *B*
Trevecca Nazarene University *B*
University of Memphis *B, M, D*

Texas

East Texas Baptist University *B*
Hardin-Simmons University *B*
Houston Baptist University *B*
Midwestern State University *B*
Northwest Vista College *A*
St. Edward's University *B*
Sam Houston State University *B*
Southern Methodist University *B*
Southwestern University *B*
Texas A&M University
   Texarkana *B*

Texas State University: San
  Marcos *B, M*
Texas Tech University *D*
University of Texas
  El Paso *B*
  San Antonio *B*
University of the Incarnate Word *B*
Wayland Baptist University *B*

Utah

Brigham Young University *M*
University of Utah *B*

Vermont

Castleton State College *B*
Champlain College *B*
Community College of Vermont *A*
Lyndon State College *B*

Virginia

Bridgewater College *B*
Emory & Henry College *B*
Hampton University *B*
Norfolk State University *B, M*
Virginia Commonwealth
    University *B, M*
Virginia State University *B*

Washington

Northwest University *B*
Seattle University *B*
Trinity Lutheran College *B*
University of Washington Bothell *B*
Walla Walla University *B*
Washington State University *B, M*

West Virginia

University of Charleston *B*
West Virginia University *B, M, D*

Wisconsin

Concordia University Wisconsin *B*
Marquette University *B, M*
St. Norbert College *B*
University of Wisconsin
  Eau Claire *B*
  Milwaukee *B, M*
  Superior *B*
Western Technical College *A*

Wyoming

Laramie County Community
    College *A*

Medical administrative assistant

Alabama

Faulkner State Community College *A*
Lawson State Community
    College *C, A*

Alaska

University of Alaska
  Fairbanks *C*

Arizona

Brookline College
  Phoenix *C*
  Tempe *C*
  Tucson *C*
Central Arizona College *C, A*
Coconino County Community
    College *A*
GateWay Community College *C*

Arkansas

Arkansas Tech University *C*
National Park Community College *A*

California

Antelope Valley College *C, A*
Barstow Community College *C*
Butte College *C, A*
Chaffey College *C*
City College of San Francisco *A*
College of the Redwoods *C*
Columbia College *C*
De Anza College *C*
East Los Angeles College *C*
Empire College *C, A*
Fresno City College *C, A*
Gavilan College *C*
Glendale Community College *C, A*
Heald College
  Rancho Cordova *C, A*
  Salinas *A*
  San Francisco *A*
Humphreys College *C, A, B*
Lassen Community College *C*
Los Angeles City College *C, A*
Los Angeles Harbor College *C, A*
MTI College *C*
Merced College *C, A*
Mount San Antonio College *C, A*
Palomar College *C, A*
Pasadena City College *C, A*
Riverside Community College *C, A*
Sacramento City College *C, A*
San Joaquin Valley College *A*
Santa Rosa Junior College *C*
Shasta College *C*
Skyline College *C, A*
Solano Community College *C, A*
Ventura College *C, A*
Western Career College
  San Leandro *C, A*

Colorado

Community College of Aurora *A*
Lamar Community College *A*
Otero Junior College *A*

Connecticut

Gateway Community College *A*
Lincoln College of New England:
    Briarwood *C, A*
Middlesex Community College *A*
Quinebaug Valley Community
    College *C*
Tunxis Community College *C, A*

Florida

Broward College *C*
Brown Mackie College: Miami *A*
Florida National College *A*
Florida State College at
    Jacksonville *C, A*
Indian River State College *C*
Key College *A*
Miami Dade College *A*
Palm Beach Community College *C*
Pasco-Hernando Community
    College *C*
Rasmussen College: Ocala *A*
Rasmussen College: Pasco County *A*
Santa Fe College *A*
Seminole Community College *A*
South Florida Community
    College *C, A*
Tallahassee Community College *C*
Valencia Community College *A*

Georgia

Augusta Technical College *C*
Chattahoochee Technical College *C*
Gwinnett College *C, A*

Hawaii

Heald College
  Honolulu *A*

Idaho

North Idaho College *A*

Illinois

Black Hawk College *C*
Danville Area Community
    College *C, A*
Harper College *C, A*
Illinois Eastern Community Colleges
  Olney Central College *C, A*
John Wood Community College *A*
Joliet Junior College *A*
Kaskaskia College *C*
Lincoln Land Community College *C*
Moraine Valley Community College *C*
Northwestern College *A*
Rockford Career College *A*
Sauk Valley Community College *C, A*
Shawnee Community College *A*
Waubonsee Community College *C*

Indiana

International Business College *C, A*
Kaplan College: Hammond *C, A*
Kaplan College: Indianapolis *C, A*

Iowa

Des Moines Area Community
    College *C, A*
Dordt College *A*
Ellsworth Community College *A*
Hawkeye Community College *C, A*
Iowa Lakes Community College *C*
Iowa Western Community College *A*
Kirkwood Community College *C, A*
Mercy College of Health Sciences *C*
Southeastern Community College
    North Campus *A*
Western Iowa Tech Community
    College *C, A*

Kansas

Central Christian College of Kansas *A*
Labette Community College *A*
Pratt Community College *C, A*
Seward County Community
    College *C, A*
Washburn University *A*

Kentucky

Ashland Community and Technical
    College *A*
Bluegrass Community and Technical
    College *C, A*
Daymar College
  Owensboro *C, A*
Draughons Junior College *C, A*
Elizabethtown Community and
    Technical College *C, A*
Madisonville Community College *C, A*
Maysville Community and Technical
    College *C, A*
National College
  Danville *A*
  Florence *A*
  Lexington *A*
  Louisville *A*
  Pikeville *A*
  Richmond *A*
Owensboro Community and
    Technical College *C, A*
Somerset Community College *C, A*
Spencerian College *C*

Louisiana

Gretna Career College *A*
ITI Technical College *A*

Maine

Andover College *C, A*
Beal College *A*

Northern Maine Community
    College *A*
Washington County Community
    College *C*

Maryland

Allegany College of Maryland *A*
Anne Arundel Community
    College *C, A*
Baltimore City Community College *A*
College of Southern Maryland *C*
Community College of Baltimore
    County *C, A*
Hagerstown Community College *C, A*
Kaplan College: Hagerstown *C, A*
Prince George's Community
    College *C, A*

Massachusetts

Bristol Community College *A*
Bunker Hill Community College *C, A*
Cape Cod Community College *C, A*
Holyoke Community College *C*
Marian Court College *C, A*
Mount Wachusett Community
    College *C*
North Shore Community College *C, A*
Northern Essex Community
    College *A*
Quinsigamond Community College *A*
Roxbury Community College *A*
Springfield Technical Community
    College *A*

Michigan

Baker College
  of Auburn Hills *C, A*
  of Cadillac *A*
  of Clinton Township *A*
  of Flint *C, A*
  of Jackson *C, A*
  of Muskegon *C, A*
  of Owosso *A*
  of Port Huron *C, A*
Bay de Noc Community College *A*
Delta College *C, A*
Glen Oaks Community College *C*
Kalamazoo Valley Community
    College *C, A*
Kellogg Community College *C, A*
Kirtland Community College *C, A*
Lansing Community College *A*
Macomb Community College *C, A*
Mid Michigan Community College *A*
Monroe County Community
    College *C, A*
Montcalm Community College *C, A*
Muskegon Community College *C, A*
St. Clair County Community
    College *A*

Minnesota

Alexandria Technical College *A*
Anoka Technical College *C, A*
Central Lakes College *C, A*
Century Community and Technical
    College *C, A*
Dakota County Technical College *C, A*
Hennepin Technical College *C, A*
Hibbing Community College *A*
Lake Superior College *C, A*
Minnesota School of Business *C, A*
Minnesota School of Business:
    Blaine *C, A*
Minnesota State College - Southeast
    Technical *C, A*
Minnesota State Community and
    Technical College *C, A*
Minnesota West Community and
    Technical College *A*
Northland Community & Technical
    College *C, A*
Northwest Technical College *C, A*

Rasmussen College
  Eagan *A*
  Eden Prairie *A*
  Mankato *A*
  St. Cloud *A*
Rasmussen College: Brooklyn Park *A*
Ridgewater College *C, A*
Riverland Community College *C, A*
Rochester Community and Technical
  College *A*

Mississippi
Meridian Community College *A*
Mississippi Gulf Coast Community
  College *A*
Northwest Mississippi Community
  College *A*
Pearl River Community College *A*

Missouri
Bolivar Technical College *C, A*
East Central College *C, A*
Jefferson College *A*
Metropolitan Community College:
  Maple Woods *C*
Metropolitan Community College:
  Penn Valley *C*
Northwest Missouri State
  University *A*
State Fair Community College *C*
Texas County Technical Institute *C, A*

Montana
Flathead Valley Community College *A*
Helena College of Technology of the
  University of Montana *C, A*
Miles Community College *A*
Montana State University
  Billings *A*
University of Montana *A*

Nebraska
Northeast Community College *C, A*

Nevada
Career College of Northern Nevada *A*
Truckee Meadows Community
  College *A*

New Hampshire
Lakes Region Community College *C*
Manchester Community College *C*
River Valley Community College *C*

New Jersey
Bergen Community College *C*
Essex County College *A*
Gloucester County College *C, A*
Mercer County Community College *C*

New Mexico
Brookline College
  Albuquerque *C*
Clovis Community College *A*
Dona Ana Community College of New
  Mexico State University *A*
New Mexico State University
  Alamogordo *C*
  Carlsbad *C*
Western New Mexico University *C, A*

New York
Bryant & Stratton Business Institute
  Bryant & Stratton College:
    Syracuse *A*
City University of New York
  Hostos Community College *A*
Elmira Business Institute *C, A*
Fulton-Montgomery Community
  College *C*
Genesee Community College *C, A*
Globe Institute of Technology *C*

Herkimer County Community
  College *A*
Hudson Valley Community College *A*
Jamestown Business College *C, A*
Jefferson Community College *A*
Long Island Business Institute *C, A*
Nassau Community College *C, A*
New York Career Institute *A*
Olean Business Institute *C, A*
Trocaire College *C*
Utica School of Commerce *C, A*

North Carolina
Alamance Community College *C, A*
Asheville-Buncombe Technical
  Community College *C*
Beaufort County Community
  College *C, A*
Blue Ridge Community College *C*
Caldwell Community College and
  Technical Institute *C, A*
Central Carolina Community
  College *A*
Cleveland Community College *C, A*
College of the Albemarle *A*
Durham Technical Community
  College *A*
Gaston College *A*
Halifax Community College *A*
Johnston Community College *A*
King's College *C, A*
Lenoir Community College *A*
Martin Community College *C, A*
Mayland Community College *A*
Nash Community College *A*
Piedmont Community College *A*
Pitt Community College *C, A*
Rockingham Community College *A*
Wake Technical Community
  College *C, A*

North Dakota
Bismarck State College *C, A*
Dakota College at Bottineau *A*
Dickinson State University *A*
Lake Region State College *A*
Rasmussen College: Bismarck *A*
Rasmussen College: Fargo *A*

Ohio
Bowling Green State University:
  Firelands College *C*
Bryant & Stratton College
  Parma *A*
Clark State Community College *A*
Columbus State Community
  College *A*
Davis College *A*
ETI Technical College of Niles *A*
Eastern Gateway Community
  College *A*
Edison State Community College *C, A*
Gallipolis Career College *A*
James A. Rhodes State College *A*
Marion Technical College *A*
Northwest State Community
  College *A*
Ohio Business College: Sandusky *C, A*
Ohio Valley College of Technology *A*
Owens Community College
  Toledo *C, A*
Southwestern College of Business
  Southwestern College: Franklin *A*
Southwestern College: Dayton *A*
Terra State Community College *A*
Trumbull Business College *A*
University of Akron: Wayne College *A*
University of Cincinnati
  Raymond Walters College *C, A*
University of Northwestern Ohio *A*
University of Rio Grande *A*
Wright State University *A*

Oklahoma
Eastern Oklahoma State College *A*
Northeastern Oklahoma Agricultural
  and Mechanical College *C, A*
Oklahoma State University
  Institute of Technology:
    Okmulgee *A*
Tulsa Community College *C, A*
Western Oklahoma State College *A*

Oregon
Blue Mountain Community College *A*
Chemeketa Community College *A*
Clackamas Community College *C*
Clatsop Community College *A*
Heald College: Portland *C, A*
Lane Community College *C*
Linn-Benton Community College *C, A*
Portland Community College *C*
Southwestern Oregon Community
  College *C*
Treasure Valley Community College *A*
Umpqua Community College *A*

Pennsylvania
CHI Institute: Franklin Mills *C*
Cambria-Rowe Business College:
  Indiana *A*
Commonwealth Technical Institute *A*
Community College of Beaver
  County *A*
Consolidated School of Business
  Lancaster *A*
  York *A*
Douglas Education Center *A*
Erie Business Center *C, A*
Kaplan Career Institute: Pittsburgh *A*
Keystone Technical Institute *C, A*
McCann School of Business and
  Technology: Dickson City *A*
Mercyhurst College *C, A*
Newport Business Institute: Lower
  Burrell *A*
Newport Business Institute:
  Williamsport *A*
Northampton Community
  College *C, A*
Penn Commercial Business and
  Technical School *A*
Pennsylvania College of
  Technology *A*
Pennsylvania Institute of Health and
  Technology *A*
Pennsylvania Institute of
  Technology *A*
Reading Area Community
  College *C, A*
South Hills School of Business &
  Technology *A*
South Hills School of Business &
  Technology: Altoona *A*
University of Pittsburgh
  Titusville *A*
Westmoreland County Community
  College *A*

Puerto Rico
Caribbean University *A*
Humacao Community College *C, A*
National College of Business and
  Technology: Arecibo *A*
National College of Business and
  Technology: Rio Grande *A*
Ponce Paramedical College *C*
Turabo University *C*
Universidad del Este *C, A*

Rhode Island
Community College of Rhode
  Island *A*
New England Institute of
  Technology *A*

South Carolina
Aiken Technical College *C*
Florence-Darlington Technical
  College *C*
Forrest Junior College *A*
Greenville Technical College *C*
Orangeburg-Calhoun Technical
  College *C*
Spartanburg Community College *C*
Tri-County Technical College *C*
Trident Technical College *C*
Williamsburg Technical College *C*
York Technical College *C*

South Dakota
Kilian Community College *A*
Lake Area Technical Institute *C*
Western Dakota Technical Institute *C*

Tennessee
Nashville State Community College *A*
National College
  Nashville *A*
West Tennessee Business College *C, A*

Texas
Blinn College *C*
Central Texas College *C*
Coastal Bend College *C, A*
Del Mar College *C, A*
El Centro College *C*
El Paso Community College *C*
Frank Phillips College *C, A*
Galveston College *C, A*
Grayson County College *C*
Kilgore College *C*
Lamar State College at Orange *C, A*
Lamar State College at Port
  Arthur *C, A*
Laredo Community College *A*
Lone Star College System *C, A*
McLennan Community College *C, A*
Northeast Texas Community
  College *C, A*
Odessa College *C, A*
St. Philip's College *A*
San Jacinto College *C, A*
South Plains College *A*
Tyler Junior College *C, A*
University of Texas
  Brownsville - Texas Southmost
    College *C, A*
Vernon College *C*

Utah
LDS Business College *A*
Provo College *A*
Salt Lake Community College *C*
Southern Utah University *C*

Virginia
Bryant & Stratton College
  Richmond *A*
Centura College: Chesapeake *A*
Danville Community College *A*
ECPI College of Technology: Virginia
  Beach *C, A*
ECPI Technical College: Roanoke *A*
Mountain Empire Community
  College *A*
New River Community College *C, A*
Southwest Virginia Community
  College *A*
Virginia Western Community
  College *A*

Washington
Bates Technical College *C*
Bellingham Technical College *C*
Centralia College *C*
Clark College *A*
Everett Community College *C*
Green River Community College *A*

Lower Columbia College *A*
Peninsula College *C, A*
Pierce College *A*
Renton Technical College *C, A*
Shoreline Community College *A*
South Puget Sound Community
  College *C, A*
Spokane Community College *C, A*
Wenatchee Valley College *C*
Whatcom Community College *C*
Yakima Valley Community
  College *C, A*

West Virginia

Mountain State University *A*
Valley College *C*
West Virginia Business College: Nutter
  Fort *A*
West Virginia Junior College:
  Bridgeport *C, A*

Wisconsin

Blackhawk Technical College *A*
Chippewa Valley Technical College *C*
Fox Valley Technical College *C*
Lakeshore Technical College *A*
Milwaukee Area Technical College *A*
Moraine Park Technical College *C, A*
Northeast Wisconsin Technical
  College *A*
Wisconsin Indianhead Technical
  College *A*

Wyoming

Western Wyoming Community
  College *A*

Medical claims examiner

Puerto Rico

Inter American University of Puerto
  Rico
  Ponce Campus *C*
Universidad Metropolitana *C*

Medical/clinical assistant

Alabama

Central Alabama Community
  College *A*
Enterprise-Ozark Community
  College *A*
George C. Wallace State Community
  College
George C. Wallace Community
  College at Dothan *C, A*
Northeast Alabama Community
  College *C, A*
Remington College
  Mobile *C*
South University: Montgomery *A*
Wallace State Community College at
  Hanceville *A*

Alaska

University of Alaska
  Anchorage *A*
  Fairbanks *C, A*

Arizona

Brookline College
  Phoenix *C*
  Tempe *C*
  Tucson *C*
Central Arizona College *C, A*
Cochise College *C*
Eastern Arizona College *C*
Lamson College *C, A*
Northland Pioneer College *C, A*

Arkansas

Arkansas Tech University *A*
East Arkansas Community College *A*
National Park Community
  College *C, A*
University of Arkansas
  Cossatot Community College of the
  A

California

Allan Hancock College *C, A*
Antelope Valley College *C, A*
Barstow Community College *C, A*
Butte College *A*
Cabrillo College *C, A*
Cerritos College *C, A*
Chabot College *C, A*
Citrus College *C, A*
City College of San Francisco *C, A*
College of Marin: Kentfield *C, A*
College of San Mateo *C, A*
College of the Canyons *C*
College of the Redwoods *C*
Concorde Career College
  Garden Grove *C*
Concorde Career College: San
  Bernardino *C*
Contra Costa College *A*
Cosumnes River College *C, A*
Cypress College *A*
De Anza College *C, A*
East Los Angeles College *A*
El Camino College: Compton
  Center *A*
Empire College *C*
Fresno City College *C, A*
Glendale Community College *A*
Heald College
  Hayward *A*
  Roseville *A*
  Stockton *C, A*
Imperial Valley College *C*
Kaplan College: Sacramento *C*
Kaplan College: Salida *C*
Lake Tahoe Community College *C, A*
Long Beach City College *C, A*
MTI College *C*
Modesto Junior College *A*
Monterey Peninsula College *C, A*
Ohlone College *A*
Orange Coast College *C, A*
Palomar College *C, A*
Pasadena City College *C, A*
Platt College
  Ontario *A*
Riverside Community College *C, A*
Saddleback College *C, A*
San Diego Mesa College *C, A*
San Joaquin Valley College *C, A*
Santa Ana College *C, A*
Santa Barbara Business College: Palm
  Desert *C, A*
Santa Rosa Junior College *C*
Santiago Canyon College *A*
Shasta College *C*
Silicon Valley College
  Western Career College:
  Emeryville *A*
  Western Career College: San Jose *A*
Victor Valley College *C, A*
West Valley College *C, A*
Western Career College
  Pleasant Hill *A*
Western Career College: Antioch *C, A*
Western Career College:
  Sacramento *C, A*
Western Career College:
  Stockton *C, A*
WyoTech: Long Beach *C*

Colorado

Anthem College *C, A*
CollegeAmerica
  Fort Collins *A*

Kaplan College: Denver *C*
Morgan Community College *C*
Pueblo Community College *C*
Westwood College: Denver North *A*

Connecticut

Capital Community College *C, A*
Goodwin College *C, A*
Lincoln College of New England:
  Briarwood *C, A*
Northwestern Connecticut
  Community College *A*
Norwalk Community College *C*
Quinebaug Valley Community
  College *A*
St. Vincent's College *C, A*

Delaware

Delaware Technical and Community
  College
  Owens *C, A*
  Stanton/Wilmington *C, A*
  Terry *C, A*

Florida

ATI College of Health *C*
Angley College *C, A*
Brevard Community College *C*
Broward College *C*
Central Florida College *A*
City College
  Gainesville *C*
College of Business and Technology:
  Flagler *C, A*
College of Business and Technology:
  Kendall *A*
Daytona State College *C*
Florida National College *A*
Florida State College at Jacksonville *C*
Hodges University *A*
Indian River State College *C*
Jones College *C, A, B*
Lake City Community College *C*
Miami Dade College *C, A*
Palm Beach Community College *C*
Pasco-Hernando Community
  College *C*
Rasmussen College: Fort Myers *C, A*
Rasmussen College: Ocala *C, A*
Rasmussen College: Pasco
  County *C, A*
Seminole Community College *C*
Southwest Florida College *C, A*
Ultrasound Diagnostic School
  Sanford-Brown Institute:
  Jacksonville *C*

Georgia

Albany Technical College *C*
Athens Technical College *C*
Augusta Technical College *C*
Brown Mackie College: Atlanta *C, A*
Central Georgia Technical
  College *C, A*
Chattahoochee Technical College *C*
Clayton State University *C, A*
Columbus Technical College *C*
DeKalb Technical College *C*
Fort Valley State University *A, B*
Gwinnett College *C, A*
Macon State College *A*
Middle Georgia College *A*
Middle Georgia Technical College *C*
North Georgia Technical College *C*
Savannah Technical College *A*
South University: Savannah *A*
Southwest Georgia Technical
  College *C, A*
West Georgia Technical College *C*

Hawaii

Heald College
  Honolulu *A*

Remington College
  Honolulu *A*
University of Hawaii
  Kapiolani Community College *C, A*

Idaho

Eastern Idaho Technical College *C, A*
Idaho State University *A*
North Idaho College *A*

Illinois

Black Hawk College *C*
College of DuPage *C*
College of Office Technology *C*
Coyne American Institute *A*
Fox College *A*
Harper College *C*
Highland Community College *A*
Illinois Central College *C*
Kankakee Community College *C, A*
Midstate College *A*
Moraine Valley Community College *C*
Northwestern College *A*
Parkland College *C*
Robert Morris University:
  Chicago *C, A*
Rockford Career College *A*
South Suburban College of Cook
  County *A*
Southwestern Illinois College *C, A*
Triton College *C*
Vatterott College: Quincy *A*
Waubonsee Community College *C*

Indiana

Brown Mackie College: Fort
  Wayne *C, A*
Brown Mackie College: South Bend *A*
Harrison College
  Anderson *A*
  Columbus *A*
  Elkhart *A*
  Evansville *A*
  Fort Wayne *A*
  Indianapolis *A*
  Indianapolis East *A*
  Lafayette *A*
  Muncie *A*
  Terre Haute *A*
International Business College *C, A*
Ivy Tech Community College
  Central Indiana *C, A*
  Columbus *C, A*
  East Central *C, A*
  Kokomo *C, A*
  Lafayette *C, A*
  North Central *C, A*
  Northeast *C, A*
  Northwest *C, A*
  Richmond *C, A*
  South Central *C, A*
  Southeast *C, A*
  Southwest *C, A*
  Wabash Valley *C, A*
Kaplan College: Hammond *A*
Kaplan College: Indianapolis *C, A*
Kaplan College: Merrillville *C, A*
National College: Indianapolis *C, A*

Iowa

Des Moines Area Community
  College *C*
Hamilton Technical College *C*
Iowa Central Community College *C, A*
Iowa Lakes Community College *C*
Iowa Western Community College *C*
Kaplan University
  Cedar Falls *C*
  Cedar Rapids *A*
  Davenport *A*
  Des Moines *A*
  Mason City *A*
Kirkwood Community College *C, A*

Marshalltown Community College *C*
Mercy College of Health Sciences *C*
North Iowa Area Community
    College *C*
Southeastern Community College
    North Campus *A*
Western Iowa Tech Community
    College *C*

Kansas
Barton County Community
    College *C, A*
Kansas City Kansas Community
    College *C*

Kentucky
Beckfield College *C*
Bluegrass Community and Technical
    College *C, A*
Daymar College
    Owensboro *C, A*
Draughons Junior College *C, A*
Eastern Kentucky University *A, B*
Gateway Community and Technical
    College *A*
National College
    Danville *A*
    Florence *A*
    Lexington *A*
    Louisville *A*
    Pikeville *A*
    Richmond *A*
Somerset Community College *C, A*
Spencerian College *C*
Spencerian College: Lexington *C*
West Kentucky Community and
    Technical College *C*

Louisiana
Blue Cliff College: Houma *C, A*
Blue Cliff College: Metairie *C*
Bossier Parish Community College *A*
Gretna Career College *C*

Maine
Andover College *A*
Beal College *A*
Central Maine Community College *A*
Kennebec Valley Community
    College *A*
Southern Maine Community
    College *A*
Washington County Community
    College *C*

Maryland
Allegany College of Maryland *C, A*
Anne Arundel Community
    College *C, A*
College of Southern Maryland *C*
Community College of Baltimore
    County *A*
Harford Community College *C, A*
Kaplan College: Hagerstown *C, A*

Massachusetts
Bay State College *A*
Bristol Community College *C*
Bunker Hill Community College *C*
Cape Cod Community College *C*
Holyoke Community College *C*
Massasoit Community College *C*
Middlesex Community College *C, A*
Mount Wachusett Community
    College *A*
North Shore Community College *C*
Northern Essex Community
    College *C*
Quinsigamond Community
    College *C, A*
Springfield Technical Community
    College *C, A*

Michigan
Alpena Community College *A*
Baker College
    of Auburn Hills *A*
    of Cadillac *A*
    of Clinton Township *A*
    of Flint *A*
    of Jackson *A*
    of Muskegon *C, A*
    of Owosso *A*
    of Port Huron *A*
Bay de Noc Community College *C*
Davenport University *C, A*
Delta College *A*
Glen Oaks Community College *C*
Henry Ford Community College *C*
Jackson Community College *C, A*
Kalamazoo Valley Community
    College *A*
Kirtland Community College *C, A*
Lansing Community College *A*
Macomb Community College *C, A*
Mid Michigan Community College *A*
Montcalm Community College *C*
North Central Michigan College *C*
Northwestern Michigan College *A*
Oakland Community College *C, A*
Southwestern Michigan College *C, A*

Minnesota
Academy College *C*
Anoka Technical College *C*
Century Community and Technical
    College *C*
Dakota County Technical College *C, A*
Globe University *C, A*
High-Tech Institute *A*
Lake Superior College *C*
Minneapolis Business College *A*
Minnesota School of Business *C, A*
Minnesota School of Business:
    Blaine *C, A*
Minnesota West Community and
    Technical College *A*
Northland Community & Technical
    College *C, A*
Rasmussen College
    Eagan *A*
    Eden Prairie *A*
    Mankato *A*
    St. Cloud *A*
Rasmussen College: Brooklyn Park *A*
Ridgewater College *C, A*
Walden University *D*

Mississippi
Antonelli College
    Jackson *A*
Northeast Mississippi Community
    College *A*

Missouri
Missouri College *C, A*
Pinnacle Career Institute: Kansas
    City *C, A*
Sanford-Brown College
    St. Peters *A*
Vatterott College: Joplin *A*
Vatterott College: Springfield *C, A*

Montana
Flathead Valley Community College *A*
Montana State University
    Billings *A*
    College of Technology: Great
        Falls *A*
Montana Tech of the University of
    Montana *A*
University of Montana *A*

Nebraska
Central Community College *C, A*

Kaplan University
    Lincoln *A*
Kaplan University: Omaha *A*
Nebraska Methodist College of
    Nursing and Allied Health *C*
Southeast Community College *C*

Nevada
Career College of Northern
    Nevada *C, A*
Everest College: Las Vegas *A*
High-Tech Institute *A*

New Hampshire
Manchester Community College *C, A*
River Valley Community College *C*

New Jersey
Bergen Community College *A*
Hudson County Community
    College *A*
Raritan Valley Community College *A*

New Mexico
Brookline College
    Albuquerque *C*
Eastern New Mexico University:
    Roswell Campus *C, A*
Santa Fe Community College *C*

New York
ASA Institute of Business and
    Computer Technology *C, A*
Broome Community College *A*
Bryant & Stratton Business Institute
    Bryant & Stratton College: Albany *A*
    Bryant & Stratton College:
        Buffalo *A*
    Bryant & Stratton College:
        Syracuse *A*
City University of New York
    Bronx Community College *A*
    Queensborough Community
        College *C*
College of Westchester *C, A*
Elmira Business Institute *C, A*
Globe Institute of Technology *C*
Mildred Elley *C, A*
Mohawk Valley Community
    College *C, A*
Niagara County Community
    College *A*
Rockland Community College *C, A*
Trocaire College *A*
Wood Tobe-Coburn School *A*

North Carolina
Cabarrus College of Health
    Sciences *C, A*
Carteret Community College *C*
Central Carolina Community
    College *A*
Central Piedmont Community
    College *C, A*
College of the Albemarle *A*
Davidson County Community
    College *C, A*
Durham Technical Community
    College *C*
Edgecombe Community College *A*
Forsyth Technical Community
    College *A*
Gaston College *A*
Guilford Technical Community
    College *A*
Haywood Community College *C, A*
James Sprunt Community College *A*
Johnston Community College *A*
Lenoir Community College *A*
Martin Community College *C, A*
Miller-Motte Technical College *C, A*
Miller-Motte Technical College:
    Cary *A*

Mitchell Community College *C*
Montgomery Community College *A*
Pamlico Community College *C*
Piedmont Community College *C*
Pitt Community College *A*
Richmond Community College *A*
South College *A*
South Piedmont Community
    College *C, A*
Stanly Community College *C, A*
Surry Community College *A*
Tri-County Community College *A*
Vance-Granville Community
    College *A*
Wake Technical Community
    College *C, A*
Wayne Community College *A*
Western Piedmont Community
    College *C, A*
Wilkes Community College *C, A*

North Dakota
Dakota College at Bottineau *C, A*
Rasmussen College: Fargo *A*

Ohio
Belmont Technical College *A*
Bradford School *C*
Bryant & Stratton College
    Parma *A*
Cincinnati State Technical and
    Community College *C*
Clark State Community College *A*
Columbus State Community
    College *C*
Cuyahoga Community College
    Metropolitan Campus *C, A*
Davis College *A*
ETI Technical College of Niles *C, A*
Eastern Gateway Community
    College *C, A*
Edison State Community College *C, A*
Hocking College *C, A*
James A. Rhodes State College *A*
Kaplan College: Columbus *C, A*
Kaplan College: Dayton *C*
Marion Technical College *C*
National College: Stow *A*
National Institute of Technology *A*
Ohio Business College:
    Columbus *C, A*
Ohio Valley College of Technology *A*
RETS College *C, A*
Southern State Community College *A*
Southwestern College of Business
    Southwestern College:
        Tri-County *C, A*
Southwestern College: Dayton *C*
Stark State College of Technology *A*
Trumbull Business College *A*
University of Akron *A*
University of Akron: Wayne College *A*
University of Cincinnati
    Clermont College *C*
University of Northwestern Ohio *C, A*
Youngstown State University *C, A*
Zane State College *C, A*

Oklahoma
Tulsa Community College *A*

Oregon
Central Oregon Community
    College *C*
Clackamas Community College *C*
Clatsop Community College *A*
Heald College: Portland *C, A*
Linn-Benton Community College *A*
Mt. Hood Community College *A*
Portland Community College *C*
Southwestern Oregon Community
    College *A*
Umpqua Community College *C*

Pennsylvania

Bucks County Community
    College *C, A*
CHI Institute: Broomall *C*
CHI Institute: Franklin Mills *C*
Career Training Academy *A*
Central Pennsylvania College *A*
Community College of Allegheny
    County *C, A*
Community College of Philadelphia *A*
Erie Business Center *A*
Harrisburg Area Community
    College *C, A*
Kaplan Career Institute: Harrisburg *A*
Kaplan Career Institute: Pittsburgh *A*
Keystone Technical Institute *C, A*
Laurel Business Institute *A*
Lehigh Carbon Community College *A*
McCann School of Business and
    Technology: Dickson City *A*
Montgomery County Community
    College *C*
Mount Aloysius College *A*
Newport Business Institute: Lower
    Burrell *C*
Northampton Community College *C*
Pennsylvania Institute of
    Technology *C*
Westmoreland County Community
    College *C*
YTI Career Institute: Lancaster *A*
YTI Career Institute: York *A*

Rhode Island

New England Institute of
    Technology *A*

South Carolina

Aiken Technical College *C*
Central Carolina Technical College *C*
Forrest Junior College *C, A*
Horry-Georgetown Technical
    College *C*
Midlands Technical College *C*
Miller-Motte Technical College *A*
South University: Columbia *A*
Spartanburg Community College *C*
Technical College of the
    Lowcountry *C*
Tri-County Technical College *C*
Trident Technical College *C*

South Dakota

Lake Area Technical Institute *C*
Presentation College *A*

Tennessee

Draughons Junior College:
    Nashville *C, A*
National College
    Knoxville *A*
    Nashville *A*
National College of Business &
    Technology
    National College: Bristol *A*
National College: Bartlett *C, A*
National College: Madison *A*
National College: Memphis *A*
Northeast State Community
    College *A*
Remington College
    Memphis *C*
South College *A*
West Tennessee Business College *C*

Texas

El Centro College *C*
El Paso Community College *C, A*
Hallmark College of Technology *C, A*
Houston Community College
    System *C*
Howard College *A*
Laredo Community College *A*

Lone Star College System *C*
Northeast Texas Community
    College *C, A*
San Antonio College *C, A*
San Jacinto College *C, A*
Texas State Technical College
    Harlingen *C, A*
Western Technical College *C*
Western Technical College: Diana
    Drive *C*

Utah

Eagle Gate College: Layton *C, A*
Eagle Gate College: Murray *A*
Eagle Gate College: Salt Lake City *C, A*
LDS Business College *C*
Salt Lake Community College *C*
Utah Career College *A*

Virginia

Bryant & Stratton College
    Richmond *A*
Bryant & Stratton College: Virginia
    Beach *A*
Centura College: Chesapeake *A*
Centura College: Newport News *A*
Centura College: Norfolk *A*
Centura College: Richmond *A*
ECPI College of Technology: Virginia
    Beach *C, A*
ECPI Technical College: Roanoke *A*
National College
    Bluefield *A*
    Charlottesville *A*
    Danville *A*
    Harrisonburg *A*
    Lynchburg *A*
    Roanoke Valley *C*
Stratford University: Woodbridge *A*

Washington

Big Bend Community College *C, A*
Centralia College *C*
Clark College *C, A*
Clover Park Technical College *C*
Everett Community College *C, A*
Highline Community College *A*
Lake Washington Technical
    College *C, A*
Lower Columbia College *A*
North Seattle Community
    College *C, A*
Olympic College *C, A*
Peninsula College *C, A*
Renton Technical College *C, A*
Skagit Valley College *C*
South Puget Sound Community
    College *C, A*
Spokane Falls Community
    College *C, A*
Wenatchee Valley College *C*
Whatcom Community College *C, A*
Yakima Valley Community
    College *C, A*

West Virginia

Blue Ridge Community and Technical
    College *C, A*
Huntington Junior College *C, A*
Mountain State College *A*
Mountain State University *A*
New River Community and Technical
    College *A*
West Virginia Junior College *A*
West Virginia Junior College:
    Bridgeport *C, A*

Wisconsin

Blackhawk Technical College *C*
Concordia University Wisconsin *C*
Gateway Technical College *C*
Herzing University *C*

Lac Courte Oreilles Ojibwa
    Community College *A*
Lakeshore Technical College *C*
Mid-State Technical College *C*
Milwaukee Area Technical College *C*
Nicolet Area Technical College *C*
Northeast Wisconsin Technical
    College *C*
Rasmussen College: Green Bay *A*
Southwest Wisconsin Technical
    College *C*
Waukesha County Technical
    College *C*
Western Technical College *C*
Wisconsin Indianhead Technical
    College *C*

Wyoming

Western Wyoming Community
    College *A*

Medical illustrating

California

California State University
    Long Beach *B*

Georgia

Medical College of Georgia *M*

Illinois

University of Illinois
    Chicago *M*

Iowa

Iowa State University *B*

Michigan

Alma College *B*

New York

Rochester Institute of
    Technology *B, M*

Ohio

Cleveland Institute of Art *B*

Pennsylvania

Arcadia University *B*

Texas

University of Texas
    Southwestern Medical Center at
    Dallas *M*

Medical informatics

Arizona

University of Phoenix *M*

California

University of California
    Davis *M*

Florida

Nova Southeastern University *M*

Idaho

Idaho State University *C, A*

Illinois

Loyola University Chicago *C*
Northwestern University *M*

Indiana

Indiana University-Purdue University
    Indianapolis *B*

Kentucky

Northern Kentucky University *M*

Maryland

Community College of Baltimore
    County *A*

Massachusetts

Massachusetts Bay Community
    College *A*
Northeastern University *M*

Minnesota

Rochester Community and Technical
    College *C*
Walden University *B*

Montana

Montana Tech of the University of
    Montana *A, B*

Tennessee

University of Tennessee
    Knoxville *M*

Texas

Richland College *A*

Utah

University of Utah *M, D*
Western Governors University *B*

Wisconsin

Milwaukee School of Engineering *M*
University of Wisconsin
    Milwaukee *D*

Medical insurance coding specialist

Alabama

Remington College
    Mobile *C*
Southern Union State Community
    College *A*

Alaska

Ilisagvik College *C*

Arizona

Bryman School *A*

California

Charles Drew University of Medicine
    and Science *C*
City College of San Francisco *C*
Concorde Career College: North
    Hollywood *C*
Empire College *C*
Heald College
    Concord *C*
    Hayward *A*
    Roseville *C*
Kaplan College: Vista *C*
Loma Linda University *C*
San Joaquin Valley College *A*
Santa Barbara City College *C*
Santa Rosa Junior College *C*
Southwestern College *C, A*

Colorado

Pueblo Community College *C*
Westwood College: Denver North *A*

Connecticut

Goodwin College *C*
St. Vincent's College *C*

Delaware

Delaware Technical and Community
    College
    Stanton/Wilmington *C*

Florida

Central Florida Community College *C*
City College
   Gainesville *C*
College of Business and Technology:
   Flagler *C*
Herzing University *C, A*
Lake City Community College *C*
Miami Dade College *C*
Palm Beach Community College *C*
Pasco-Hernando Community
   College *C*
Polk State College *C*
Rasmussen College: Fort Myers *C*
Rasmussen College: Ocala *C*
Rasmussen College: Pasco County *C*
Saint Johns River Community
   College *C*
St. Petersburg College *C*
Santa Fe College *C*
Southwest Florida College *C*
Valencia Community College *C, A*

Georgia

Albany Technical College *C*
Central Georgia Technical College *C*
Middle Georgia Technical College *C*
Savannah Technical College *C*
Southwest Georgia Technical
   College *C*

Illinois

Coyne American Institute *C*
Harper College *C*
Highland Community College *C*
Illinois Valley Community College *C*
Kankakee Community College *C*
Lincoln Land Community College *C*
Midstate College *C*
Moraine Valley Community College *C*
Rasmussen College: Aurora *C*
Rasmussen College: Rockford *C*
Spoon River College *C*
Taylor Business Institute *A*
Waubonsee Community College *C*

Indiana

Harrison College
   Anderson *A*
   Columbus *A*
   Elkhart *A*
   Evansville *A*
   Indianapolis East *A*
   Lafayette *A*
   Muncie *A*
   Terre Haute *A*

Iowa

Hamilton Technical College *C*
Indian Hills Community College *C*
Mercy College of Health Sciences *C*

Kansas

Neosho County Community
   College *C*

Kentucky

Daymar College: Paducah *A*
Draughons Junior College *C, A*
Spencerian College *C*
Spencerian College: Lexington *C*

Louisiana

Gretna Career College *C*
Herzing University *C*
ITI Technical College *A*
Nunez Community College *C*

Maine

Central Maine Community College *C*

Maryland

Hagerstown Community College *C*

Massachusetts

Bunker Hill Community College *C*
North Shore Community College *C*
Springfield Technical Community
   College *C, A*

Michigan

Baker College
   of Clinton Township *A*
   of Muskegon *C*
Davenport University *C, A*
Delta College *C*
Ferris State University *C*
Oakland Community College *C*
Southwestern Michigan College *C*
Wayne County Community College *C*

Minnesota

Academy College *C*
Alexandria Technical College *C*
Lake Superior College *C*
Minnesota State College - Southeast
   Technical *C*
Minnesota State Community and
   Technical College *C*
Minnesota West Community and
   Technical College *C*
Northland Community & Technical
   College *C, A*
Pine Technical College *C, A*
Rasmussen College
   Eagan *C*
   Eden Prairie *C*
   Mankato *C*
   St. Cloud *C*
Rasmussen College: Brooklyn Park *C*
Rasmussen College: Lake
   Elmo/Woodbury *C*
Rochester Community and Technical
   College *C*
St. Paul College *C*
South Central College *C*

Mississippi

Antonelli College
   Jackson *C*
Virginia College Gulf Coast *A*

Missouri

High-Tech Institute *A*
Pinnacle Career Institute: Kansas
   City *C*
Sanford-Brown College
   St. Peters *C*

Montana

Flathead Valley Community College *C*
Montana State University
   Billings *C*

Nebraska

Northeast Community College *C*

Nevada

Career College of Northern
   Nevada *C, A*
High-Tech Institute *A*
Kaplan College: Las Vegas *C, A*

New Hampshire

River Valley Community College *C*

New Jersey

Salem Community College *C*

New Mexico

Eastern New Mexico University:
   Roswell Campus *C*

New York

City University of New York
   Borough of Manhattan Community
      College *C*
College of Westchester *C, A*
Elmira Business Institute *A*
Elmira Business Institute: Vestal *C, A*
Globe Institute of Technology *C*
State University of New York
   College of Technology at Alfred *C*

North Dakota

Dakota College at Bottineau *C*
North Dakota State College of
   Science *A*
Rasmussen College: Bismarck *C*
Rasmussen College: Fargo *C*
Turtle Mountain Community
   College *A*
Williston State College *C*

Ohio

Cincinnati State Technical and
   Community College *C*
Davis College *A*
ETI Technical College of Niles *A*
James A. Rhodes State College *C*
Marion Technical College *C*
Mercy College of Northwest Ohio *C*
National Institute of Technology *C*
Ohio University
   Southern Campus at Ironton *C*
RETS College *C*
Southwestern College of Business
   Southwestern College: Franklin *C*
Southwestern College: Dayton *C*
Stark State College of Technology *C*
University of Cincinnati
   Clermont College *C*

Oregon

Lane Community College *C*
Umpqua Community College *C*

Pennsylvania

Butler County Community College *C*
Consolidated School of Business
   Lancaster *A*
   York *A*
Drexel University *C*
Erie Business Center *C*
Laurel Business Institute *A*
Lehigh Carbon Community College *C*
Mercyhurst College *C*
Newport Business Institute: Lower
   Burrell *A*
Northampton Community College *C*
Penn Commercial Business and
   Technical School *C*
Pennsylvania College of
   Technology *C*
Pennsylvania Highlands Community
   College *C*
University of Pittsburgh
   Titusville *C*
Westmoreland County Community
   College *C*

Puerto Rico

Ponce Paramedical College *C*

South Dakota

Dakota State University *C*
Kilian Community College *C*

Tennessee

Walters State Community College *C*

Texas

Austin Community College *C*
Hallmark College of Technology *C*

Houston Community College
   System *C*
Panola College *C*
Richland College *A*
San Jacinto College *C*
South Texas College *C*

Utah

Eagle Gate College: Layton *C, A*
Eagle Gate College: Murray *A*
LDS Business College *C*
Salt Lake Community College *C*

Virginia

Lord Fairfax Community College *C*
Virginia Western Community
   College *C*

Washington

Bellingham Technical College *C, A*
Centralia College *C*
Clark College *C*
Clover Park Technical College *C*
Everett Community College *C*
Grays Harbor College *C*
Olympic College *C*
Renton Technical College *C, A*
Shoreline Community College *C*
Whatcom Community College *C*
Yakima Valley Community
   College *C, A*

West Virginia

Huntington Junior College *C, A*
Mountain State University *C*
West Virginia Junior College *A*

Wisconsin

Blackhawk Technical College *C*
Herzing University *C, A*
Lakeshore Technical College *C*
Milwaukee Area Technical College *C*
Northcentral Technical College *C*
Rasmussen College: Green Bay *C*
Waukesha County Technical
   College *C*

Medical insurance specialist

Arizona

Anthem College *A*
Brookline College
   Phoenix *C*
   Tempe *C*
   Tucson *C*
Bryman School *A*
Lamson College *C*

California

City College of San Francisco *C*
Kaplan College: Palm Springs *C*
Long Beach City College *C*
MTI College *C*
National University *C*
Santa Barbara City College *C*

Colorado

Westwood College: Denver North *A*

Florida

Central Florida College *A*
City College
   Gainesville *C*
Herzing University *C, A*
Palm Beach Community College *C*
Santa Fe College *C*

Georgia

Middle Georgia Technical College *C*
Savannah Technical College *C*

Illinois
College of Lake County C

Indiana
Harrison College
  Anderson A
  Columbus A
  Fort Wayne A
  Indianapolis East A
  Lafayette A

Kansas
Brown Mackie College
  Salina C

Kentucky
Daymar College: Paducah A
Spencerian College A

Louisiana
ITI Technical College A

Michigan
Baker College
  of Flint C, A
  of Muskegon C
  of Owosso C, A
  of Port Huron C, A
Baker College of Allen Park C
Davenport University C
Delta College C
Henry Ford Community College C
Kirtland Community College C
Schoolcraft College C
Wayne County Community College A

Minnesota
Academy College C
Ridgewater College C

Mississippi
Southwest Mississippi Community
  College A

Missouri
Missouri College C

Montana
Montana State University
  College of Technology: Great
    Falls C, A

Nevada
Career College of Northern
  Nevada C, A

New Mexico
Brookline College
  Albuquerque C

New York
City University of New York
  Borough of Manhattan Community
    College C
College of Westchester C, A
Elmira Business Institute C
Globe Institute of Technology C
Westchester Community College C

North Dakota
Williston State College C

Ohio
Ohio University
  Southern Campus at Ironton C
Owens Community College
  Toledo C
Southwestern College of Business
  Southwestern College: Franklin C
University of Cincinnati
  Raymond Walters College A

Pennsylvania
Consolidated School of Business
  Lancaster A
  York A
Lehigh Carbon Community College C
Luzerne County Community
  College A
Newport Business Institute: Lower
  Burrell A

Puerto Rico
Inter American University of Puerto
  Rico
  Metropolitan Campus C
  San German Campus C
Universal Career Community College:
  Humacao C
Universal Career Community College:
  Manati C
Universal Career Community College:
  San Juan C

Rhode Island
Community College of Rhode
  Island C

Tennessee
National College
  Knoxville C

Utah
Salt Lake Community College C

Virginia
Lord Fairfax Community College C
National College
  Roanoke Valley C

West Virginia
New River Community and Technical
  College C

Wisconsin
Herzing University C, A

Medical office administration

Alabama
Northeast Alabama Community
  College C, A

Arizona
Mohave Community College C

Arkansas
Ouachita Technical College C

California
California Institute of Integral
  Studies M
City College of San Francisco A
Concorde Career College: San
  Bernardino C
Heald College
  Concord C, A
  Hayward A
  Roseville C, A
  San Jose C, A
LA College International C
MTI College C
Merced College C, A
San Joaquin Valley College C
Santa Barbara Business College
  Bakersfield C

Colorado
Arapahoe Community College C, A
Community College of Denver C
Pikes Peak Community College C, A
Pueblo Community College C

Red Rocks Community College C, A

Connecticut
Goodwin College A

Florida
College of Business and Technology:
  Flagler C, A
College of Business and Technology:
  Kendall C, A
Herzing University C
Rasmussen College: Fort Myers A

Georgia
Dalton State College A

Illinois
College of Lake County C, A
East-West University C

Indiana
Kaplan College: Indianapolis C, A
Kaplan College: Merrillville C, A

Iowa
Kaplan University
  Davenport A
  Mason City A
Western Iowa Tech Community
  College A

Kansas
Brown Mackie College
  Salina A

Kentucky
Spencerian College A

Louisiana
ITI Technical College A
Nunez Community College A

Massachusetts
Holyoke Community College C
North Shore Community College C

Michigan
Baker College
  of Clinton Township B
Henry Ford Community College A

Minnesota
Academy College C
Globe University B
Hennepin Technical College C, A
Minnesota School of Business: St.
  Cloud A

Nevada
Career College of Northern Nevada C

New York
Bryant & Stratton Business Institute
  Bryant & Stratton College:
    Rochester A
College of Westchester C, A
Erie Community College
  North Campus C, A
Fulton-Montgomery Community
  College C, A
Globe Institute of Technology C, A, B
Monroe College A
Olean Business Institute A

North Carolina
Beaufort County Community
  College C, A
Carteret Community College C, A
Catawba Valley Community
  College C, A

Central Piedmont Community
  College C
College of the Albemarle A
Durham Technical Community
  College C, A
Fayetteville Technical Community
  College C, A
Forsyth Technical Community
  College C, A
Gaston College C, A
Isothermal Community College C, A
Pitt Community College C, A
Surry Community College C, A
Wayne Community College C, A
Western Piedmont Community
  College A

North Dakota
North Dakota State College of
  Science A
Turtle Mountain Community
  College C

Ohio
Eastern Gateway Community
  College C
Edison State Community College C, A
Kaplan College: Dayton A
National Institute of Technology A
University of Akron C, A
Youngstown State University A

Oregon
Chemeketa Community College C

Pennsylvania
Consolidated School of Business
  Lancaster A
Douglas Education Center A
Luzerne County Community
  College C, A
Newport Business Institute: Lower
  Burrell A
Pennsylvania Institute of
  Technology C

Texas
Panola College C, A
Tyler Junior College C, A

Utah
LDS Business College A

Washington
Big Bend Community College C, A
North Seattle Community College C
Peninsula College C

Wisconsin
Herzing University A, B
Milwaukee Area Technical College A
Rasmussen College: Green Bay A
Western Technical College C

Medical office assistant

Alabama
Northeast Alabama Community
  College C, A

Arizona
Mohave Community College C

California
Antelope Valley College C, A
City College of San Francisco A
Heald College
  Stockton C, A
Kaplan College: Sacramento C
Kaplan College: Salida C
Kaplan College: Vista C

MTI College *C*
Ohlone College *C*
Platt College
   Ontario *A*
San Joaquin Delta College *C*
San Joaquin Valley College *A*
Santa Barbara Business College *C, A*
Santa Barbara Business College
   Bakersfield *C*
   Santa Maria *C, A*
Santa Barbara Business College: Palm
   Desert *C*
Santa Barbara Business College:
   Ventura *C, A*
Southwestern College *C*
Western Career College: Citrus
   Heights *C, A*

Colorado
Front Range Community College *C, A*
Kaplan College: Denver *C*

Connecticut
Goodwin College *C, A*

Florida
Angley College *C, A*
Pasco-Hernando Community
   College *C*

Georgia
Dalton State College *C*
Gwinnett Technical College *C*
Middle Georgia Technical College *C*
Southeastern Technical College *C*

Hawaii
Heald College
   Honolulu *A*

Idaho
Lewis-Clark State College *C, A, B*
Stevens-Henager College: Boise *A*

Illinois
College of Office Technology *C*
Elgin Community College *C*
Lincoln Land Community College *A*
Southeastern Illinois College *A*
Westwood College: DuPage *C*

Indiana
Harrison College
   Anderson *C*
   Evansville *C*
   Fort Wayne *C*
   Indianapolis *C*
   Indianapolis East *C*
   Lafayette *C*
   Muncie *C*
   Terre Haute *C*
Vincennes University *C*

Iowa
Vatterott College *C*

Kansas
Colby Community College *C*

Kentucky
Beckfield College *C*
Owensboro Community and
   Technical College *C, A*
Spencerian College: Lexington *C*

Louisiana
Bossier Parish Community College *C*
Gretna Career College *A*
Herzing University *C*
ITI Technical College *A*

Maryland
Harford Community College *C*

Massachusetts
Quinsigamond Community
   College *C, A*

Michigan
Baker College
   of Clinton Township *A*
   of Flint *A*
   of Muskegon *A*
Delta College *C, A*
Lake Michigan College *C, A*
Oakland Community College *C*
Schoolcraft College *C*
West Shore Community College *C*

Minnesota
Academy College *C*
Century Community and Technical
   College *C*
Hennepin Technical College *C*
Minneapolis Community and
   Technical College *C*
Minnesota School of Business: St.
   Cloud *C, A*
Northland Community & Technical
   College *C, A*
St. Cloud Technical College *C*
St. Paul College *A*

Mississippi
Blue Cliff College: Gulfport *C, A*
Virginia College *C, A*

Missouri
Crowder College *A*
Metro Business College
   Jefferson City *C, A*
North Central Missouri College *C, A*
Vatterott College: Springfield *C*

Montana
Flathead Valley Community College *A*

Nevada
Career College of Northern Nevada *C*
Kaplan College: Las Vegas *C, A*

New York
College of Westchester *C, A*
Globe Institute of Technology *C*

North Carolina
Pitt Community College *C*

North Dakota
North Dakota State College of
   Science *C, A*

Ohio
Bryant & Stratton College
   Eastlake *A*
James A. Rhodes State College *A*
Marion Technical College *A*
National College: Youngstown *A*
Ohio Business College: Sandusky *C*
Stark State College of Technology *A*
University of Cincinnati
   Clermont College *C*
   Raymond Walters College *A*

Oklahoma
Platt College
   Tulsa *C*
Vatterott College
   Tulsa *C, A*

Oregon
Blue Mountain Community College *C*

Chemeketa Community College *C*
Clackamas Community College *C*
Klamath Community College *C, A*
Linn-Benton Community College *C, A*

Pennsylvania
Bucks County Community
   College *C, A*
Butler County Community
   College *C, A*
Consolidated School of Business
   Lancaster *A*
Laurel Business Institute *A*
Lincoln Technical Institute: Northeast
   Philadelphia *A*
Mercyhurst College *C, A*
Newport Business Institute: Lower
   Burrell *A*
Penn Commercial Business and
   Technical School *A*
Westmoreland County Community
   College *C*

Puerto Rico
Universidad del Este *C*

Rhode Island
New England Institute of
   Technology *A*

South Carolina
Williamsburg Technical College *C*
York Technical College *C*

South Dakota
Mitchell Technical Institute *A*
Southeast Technical Institute *C*

Tennessee
National College
   Knoxville *C*

Texas
South Texas College *C, A*

Utah
LDS Business College *A*
Stevens-Henager College: Logan *A*

Virginia
Bryant & Stratton College: Virginia
   Beach *A*
Centura College: Norfolk *A*
Danville Community College *A*

Washington
Clover Park Technical College *C*
North Seattle Community
   College *C, A*
Olympic College *C*
Yakima Valley Community College *C*

Wisconsin
Herzing University *C, A*
Milwaukee Area Technical College *C*
Northcentral Technical College *C*

Wyoming
Central Wyoming College *C, A*

Medical office
computer specialist

Arizona
Anthem College *A*

California
Kaplan College: Salida *C*
MTI College *C*

Kansas
Central Christian College of Kansas *A*

Louisiana
ITI Technical College *A*

Minnesota
Hennepin Technical College *C*
Northland Community & Technical
   College *C*

Mississippi
Antonelli College
   Jackson *C*

Missouri
Mineral Area College *C*

Nevada
Career College of Northern Nevada *C*

New York
Globe Institute of Technology *C*

Ohio
University of Rio Grande *C*

Oregon
Rogue Community College *C, A*

Pennsylvania
Consolidated School of Business
   Lancaster *A*
   York *A*
Newport Business Institute: Lower
   Burrell *A*
South Hills School of Business &
   Technology: Altoona *A*

South Carolina
York Technical College *C*

West Virginia
West Virginia Junior College *C*

Wisconsin
Herzing University *C, A*

Medical radiologic
technology/radiation
therapy

Alabama
Central Alabama Community
   College *A*
Gadsden State Community College *A*
George C. Wallace State Community
   College
     George C. Wallace Community
      College at Dothan *A*
Jefferson State Community College *A*
University of Alabama
   Birmingham *B*
University of South Alabama *B*
Wallace State Community College at
   Hanceville *A*

Arizona
GateWay Community College *A*
Scottsdale Community College *A*

Arkansas
Arkansas State University *A, B*
East Arkansas Community College *A*
National Park Community College *A*
North Arkansas College *A*
South Arkansas Community College *A*
Southeast Arkansas College *A*
University of Arkansas
   Fort Smith *A*

University of Central Arkansas B

California

Bakersfield College A
Cabrillo College A
California State University
  Long Beach B
Canada College A
Chaffey College A
City College of San Francisco A
Crafton Hills College A
Cypress College A
El Camino College A
El Camino College: Compton
  Center A
Foothill College A
Fresno City College A
Loma Linda University A, B
Long Beach City College A
Los Angeles City College A
Merced College A
Merritt College A
Moorpark College A
Mount San Antonio College A
Orange Coast College A
Pasadena City College A
San Diego Mesa College A
San Joaquin Delta College A
Santa Barbara City College A
Santa Rosa Junior College A
Yuba Community College District A

Colorado

Aims Community College A

Connecticut

Capital Community College A
Gateway Community College A
Middlesex Community College A
Naugatuck Valley Community
  College A
University of Hartford B

District of Columbia

Georgetown University M
Howard University B
University of the District of
  Columbia A

Florida

Brevard Community College A
Broward College A
Daytona State College A
Edison State College A
Florida State College at Jacksonville A
Gulf Coast Community College A
Hillsborough Community College A
Indian River State College A
Miami Dade College A
Palm Beach Community College A
Pensacola Junior College A
Santa Fe College A
State College of Florida,
  Manatee-Sarasota A
Tallahassee Community College A

Georgia

Armstrong Atlantic State University B
College of Coastal Georgia A
Darton College A
Gwinnett Technical College A
Medical College of Georgia B, M
Middle Georgia College A
Southwest Georgia Technical
  College A
Waycross College A

Hawaii

University of Hawaii
  Kapiolani Community College A

Idaho

Boise State University A, B
Idaho State University A, B

Illinois

Black Hawk College A
City Colleges of Chicago
  Malcolm X College A
College of DuPage A
College of Lake County A
Illinois Central College A
Illinois Eastern Community Colleges
  Olney Central College A
John Wood Community College A
Kishwaukee College A
National-Louis University B
North Central College B
Roosevelt University B
South Suburban College of Cook
  County A
Southern Illinois University
  Carbondale B, M
Southwestern Illinois College A
Triton College A
University of St. Francis B
Wilbur Wright College A

Indiana

Ball State University A, B
Indiana University
  Bloomington B
  Kokomo A
  South Bend A
Indiana University-Purdue University
  Indianapolis A, B
Ivy Tech Community College
  Bloomington A
  Central Indiana A
  Columbus A
  East Central A
  North Central A
  Northwest A
  Richmond A
  South Central A
  Wabash Valley A
University of St. Francis A
University of Southern Indiana A
Vincennes University A

Iowa

Briar Cliff University B
Iowa Central Community College A
Mercy College of Health Sciences A
St. Luke's College A
Southeastern Community College
  North Campus A

Kansas

Fort Hays State University A
Friends University B
Hutchinson Community College A
Johnson County Community
  College A
Newman University A
Washburn University A

Kentucky

Bluegrass Community and Technical
  College A
Elizabethtown Community and
  Technical College A
Hazard Community and Technical
  College A
Madisonville Community College A
Morehead State University A, B
Northern Kentucky University A
Owensboro Community and
  Technical College A
St. Catharine College A
Southeast Kentucky Community and
  Technical College A
Spencerian College A

West Kentucky Community and
  Technical College A

Louisiana

Delgado Community College A
Louisiana State University
  Eunice A
Our Lady of Holy Cross College B
Southern University
  Shreveport A

Maine

Central Maine Community College A
Eastern Maine Community College A
Saint Joseph's College of Maine B
Southern Maine Community
  College A
University of Southern Maine B

Maryland

Allegany College of Maryland A
Anne Arundel Community College A
Chesapeake College A
College of Notre Dame of Maryland B
Community College of Baltimore
  County A
Hagerstown Community College A
Howard Community College A
Montgomery College A
Prince George's Community
  College A
Wor-Wic Community College A

Massachusetts

Bunker Hill Community College A
Holyoke Community College A
Massachusetts Bay Community
  College A
Massachusetts College of Pharmacy
  and Health Sciences B
Massasoit Community College A
Middlesex Community College A
Quinsigamond Community College A
Regis College A

Michigan

Baker College
  of Muskegon A
  of Owosso A
Delta College A
Ferris State University A
Grand Rapids Community College A
Grand Valley State University B
Kellogg Community College A
Lake Michigan College A
Lansing Community College A
Mid Michigan Community College A
Mott Community College A
Oakland Community College A
Oakland University B
University of Michigan
  Flint B
Washtenaw Community College A
Wayne State University B

Minnesota

Argosy University: Twin Cities A
Dunwoody College of Technology A
High-Tech Institute A
Ridgewater College A
Riverland Community College A
Saint Cloud State University B

Mississippi

Copiah-Lincoln Community College A
Meridian Community College A
Mississippi Delta Community
  College A
Mississippi Gulf Coast Community
  College A
Northeast Mississippi Community
  College A

Missouri

East Central College A
Metropolitan Community College:
  Penn Valley A
Missouri Southern State University A
Saint Louis University B
University of Missouri
  Columbia B

Montana

Flathead Valley Community College A

Nebraska

Clarkson College A, B
Northeast Community College A
Southeast Community College A
University of Nebraska
  Kearney B
  Medical Center B
Western Nebraska Community
  College A

Nevada

Truckee Meadows Community
  College A
University of Nevada
  Las Vegas B

New Hampshire

NHTI-Concord's Community
  College A

New Jersey

Bergen Community College A
Brookdale Community College A
Burlington County College A
Cumberland County College A
Essex County College A
Fairleigh Dickinson University
  College at Florham A
Mercer County Community College A
Passaic County Community College A
Thomas Edison State College A, B
Union County College A
University of Medicine and Dentistry
  of New Jersey
  School of Health Related
    Professions B, M

New Mexico

Central New Mexico Community
  College A
Clovis Community College A
Dona Ana Community College of New
  Mexico State University A
New Mexico Junior College A
Northern New Mexico College A
University of New Mexico B

New York

Broome Community College A
City University of New York
  Bronx Community College A
  Hostos Community College A
  New York City College of
    Technology A
Erie Community College
  City Campus A
Fulton-Montgomery Community
  College A
Hudson Valley Community College A
Long Island University
  C. W. Post Campus B
Mohawk Valley Community College A
Nassau Community College A
Niagara County Community
  College A
North Country Community College A
Orange County Community College A
St. Francis College B
State University of New York
  Oswego B

Trocaire College *A*
Westchester Community College *A*

North Carolina

Asheville-Buncombe Technical
    Community College *A*
Caldwell Community College and
    Technical Institute *A*
Cape Fear Community College *A*
Carolinas College of Health
    Sciences *A*
Carteret Community College *A*
Catawba Valley Community College *A*
Cleveland Community College *A*
Edgecombe Community College *A*
Fayetteville Technical Community
    College *A*
Forsyth Technical Community
    College *A*
Johnston Community College *A*
Pitt Community College *A*
Sandhills Community College *A*
Southwestern Community College *A*
University of North Carolina
    Chapel Hill *B*
Vance-Granville Community
    College *A*
Wake Technical Community
    College *A*

North Dakota

Minot State University *B*

Ohio

Bowling Green State University:
    Firelands College *A*
Central Ohio Technical College *A*
Columbus State Community
    College *A*
Eastern Gateway Community
    College *A*
James A. Rhodes State College *A*
Kent State University
    Salem *A, B*
Kettering College of Medical Arts *A*
Marion Technical College *A*
North Central State College *A*
Ohio State University
    Columbus Campus *B*
Owens Community College
    Toledo *A*
Shawnee State University *A*
University of Akron *A*
University of Akron: Wayne College *A*
University of Cincinnati
    Raymond Walters College *A*
Washington State Community
    College *A*
Xavier University *A*
Zane State College *A*

Oklahoma

Bacone College *A, B*
Northern Oklahoma College *A*
Tulsa Community College *A*
University of Oklahoma *B*
Western Oklahoma State College *A*

Oregon

Oregon Health & Science
    University *B*
Portland Community College *A*

Pennsylvania

Bloomsburg University of
    Pennsylvania *B*
Clarion University of Pennsylvania *B*
Community College of Allegheny
    County *A*
Community College of Philadelphia *A*
Drexel University *A*
Gannon University *A*
Gwynedd-Mercy College *A, B*

Keystone College *A*
La Roche College *A, B*
Mansfield University of
    Pennsylvania *A*
Misericordia University *B*
Montgomery County Community
    College *A*
Penn State
    New Kensington *A*
    Schuylkill *A*
Pennsylvania College of
    Technology *A*
Reading Area Community College *A*
Robert Morris University *B*

Puerto Rico

Inter American University of Puerto
    Rico
    Ponce Campus *A*
    San German Campus *A*
Universidad del Este *B*
University of Puerto Rico
    Medical Sciences *A*

South Carolina

Aiken Technical College *A*
Florence-Darlington Technical
    College *A*
Greenville Technical College *A*
Horry-Georgetown Technical
    College *A*
Midlands Technical College *A*
Orangeburg-Calhoun Technical
    College *A*
Southern Wesleyan University *B*
Spartanburg Community College *A*
Trident Technical College *A*
York Technical College *A*

South Dakota

Mitchell Technical Institute *A*
Mount Marty College *B*
Presentation College *A, B*

Tennessee

Austin Peay State University *B*
Baptist College of Health Sciences *B*
Chattanooga State Community
    College *A*
Columbia State Community College *A*
Jackson State Community College *A*
Roane State Community College *A*
Southwest Tennessee Community
    College *A*
Volunteer State Community College *A*

Texas

Amarillo College *A*
Blinn College *A*
El Centro College *A*
El Paso Community College *A*
Galveston College *A*
Kilgore College *A*
Lamar Institute of Technology *A*
Laredo Community College *A*
Lone Star College System *A*
McLennan Community College *A*
Midland College *A*
Northeast Texas Community
    College *A*
Odessa College *A*
St. Philip's College *A*
San Jacinto College *A*
South Plains College *A*
Texas State University: San Marcos *B*
Tyler Junior College *A*
Weatherford College *A*

Utah

Salt Lake Community College *A*
Weber State University *A, B*

Vermont

University of Vermont *B*

Virginia

Averett University *B*
Northern Virginia Community
    College *A*
Tidewater Community College *A*
Virginia Highlands Community
    College *A*
Virginia Western Community
    College *A*

Washington

Bellevue College *A, B*
Bellingham Technical College *A*
Yakima Valley Community College *A*

West Virginia

Alderson-Broaddus College *B*
Bluefield State College *A*
Southern West Virginia Community
    and Technical College *A*
West Virginia Northern Community
    College *A*

Wisconsin

Blackhawk Technical College *A*
Chippewa Valley Technical College *A*
Concordia University Wisconsin *B*
Gateway Technical College *A*
Lakeshore Technical College *A*
Milwaukee Area Technical College *A*
Mount Mary College *B*
Western Technical College *A*

Wyoming

Laramie County Community
    College *A*

Medical receptionist

Arizona

Mohave Community College *C*

California

City College of San Francisco *C*
Platt College
    Ontario *A*
Santa Rosa Junior College *C*

Colorado

Morgan Community College *C*

Georgia

Central Georgia Technical College *C*

Iowa

Dordt College *A*

Louisiana

ITI Technical College *A*

Michigan

Baker College
    of Muskegon *C*
Delta College *C*
Henry Ford Community College *C*
Jackson Community College *C*

Minnesota

Academy College *C*
Alexandria Technical College *C*
Dakota County Technical College *C*
Lake Superior College *C*
St. Paul College *C*

Montana

Flathead Valley Community College *A*

Nevada

Career College of Northern Nevada *C*

New York

Globe Institute of Technology *C*
Utica School of Commerce *C*

Ohio

Edison State Community College *C, A*

Oregon

Linn-Benton Community College *C*

Pennsylvania

Consolidated School of Business
    Lancaster *A*
    York *A*
McCann School of Business and
    Technology: Dickson City *A*
Newport Business Institute: Lower
    Burrell *A*

Washington

Clark College *C*
Everett Community College *C*
North Seattle Community College *C*
Olympic College *C*
Peninsula College *C*
Whatcom Community College *C*

Wisconsin

Herzing University *C, A*

Medical records administration

Alabama

Alabama State University *B*
University of Alabama
    Birmingham *B*

Arizona

Pima Community College *A*
University of Phoenix *M*

Arkansas

Arkansas Tech University *B*

California

Allan Hancock College *C, A*
Barstow Community College *C*
Chabot College *C, A*
Chaffey College *C*
City College of San Francisco *C, A*
Cypress College *C, A*
Lake Tahoe Community College *C, A*
Loma Linda University *C, B*
Palomar College *C, A*
San Bernardino Valley College *C*
San Joaquin Valley College *A*
Santa Rosa Junior College *C*
Southwestern College *C, A*

Colorado

Regis University *B*
Westwood College: Denver North *A*

Florida

Broward College *A*
Florida Agricultural and Mechanical
    University *B*
Gulf Coast Community College *A*
Indian River State College *A*
Miami Dade College *A*
Pensacola Junior College *A*
Polk State College *A*
Rasmussen College: Fort Myers *A*
St. Petersburg College *C, A*
University of Central Florida *B*
Valencia Community College *A*

Georgia

Atlanta Metropolitan College *A*
Dalton State College *A*
Darton College *A*
Gordon College *A*
Macon State College *B*
Medical College of Georgia *B*
Middle Georgia College *A*

Idaho

Boise State University *B*

Illinois

Chicago State University *B*
Illinois State University *B*
Spoon River College *C*
University of Illinois
　Chicago *B, M*

Indiana

Indiana University
　Northwest *B*
Indiana University-Purdue University
　Indianapolis *B*

Kansas

Barton County Community College *A*
Labette Community College *C*
Seward County Community College *C*
University of Kansas Medical
　Center *B*

Kentucky

Beckfield College *A*
Eastern Kentucky University *C, B*

Louisiana

ITI Technical College *A*
Louisiana Tech University *B*
Southern University
　New Orleans *B*
University of Louisiana at Lafayette *B*

Maine

Andover College *A*

Maryland

Baltimore City Community College *A*
Coppin State University *B*
Prince George's Community
　College *C, A*

Massachusetts

Cape Cod Community College *C*
Northern Essex Community
　College *C, A*
Springfield College *B*

Michigan

Baker College
　of Auburn Hills *A*
　of Flint *B*
　of Jackson *A*
Davenport University *B*
Ferris State University *B*
Washtenaw Community College *A*

Minnesota

Anoka-Ramsey Community College *C*
College of St. Scholastica *B, M*
Dunwoody College of Technology *B*
Globe University *C, A*
Hennepin Technical College *C*
St. Catherine University *A, B*
Walden University *M*

Mississippi

Mississippi Delta Community
　College *A*
Mississippi Gulf Coast Community
　College *A*

Southwest Mississippi Community
　College *A*

Missouri

Park University *A*
Saint Louis University *B*
Stephens College *B*

Montana

Montana State University
　College of Technology: Great
　Falls *C*

New Jersey

Cumberland County College *C, A*
Kean University *B*

New Mexico

Central New Mexico Community
　College *A*

New York

Elmira Business Institute *C, A*
Globe Institute of Technology *C*
Long Island University
　C. W. Post Campus *B*
Monroe College *A*
Olean Business Institute *C, A*
State University of New York
　Institute of Technology at
　Utica/Rome *B*

North Carolina

Alamance Community College *A*
Durham Technical Community
　College *C, A*
East Carolina University *B*
Sandhills Community College *A*
Western Carolina University *B*

Ohio

Bowling Green State University *B*
Columbus State Community
　College *C, A*
Cuyahoga Community College
　Metropolitan Campus *C, A*
Edison State Community College *C, A*
Ohio Business College: Sandusky *A*
Ohio State University
　Columbus Campus *B*
University of Akron: Wayne College *C*
University of Toledo *B*

Oklahoma

Southwestern Oklahoma State
　University *B*
Western Oklahoma State College *A*

Oregon

Chemeketa Community College *A*
Linn-Benton Community College *C, A*
Mt. Hood Community College *A*
Oregon Institute of Technology *B*

Pennsylvania

Consolidated School of Business
　Lancaster *A*
Drexel University *M*
Erie Business Center South *A*
Gwynedd-Mercy College *B*
Keystone Technical Institute *C, A*
Mercyhurst College *C, A*
Newport Business Institute: Lower
　Burrell *A*
Pennsylvania College of
　Technology *B*
Temple University *B*
University of Pittsburgh *B*

Puerto Rico

Huertas Junior College *A*

Inter American University of Puerto
　Rico
　Aguadilla Campus *C*

South Carolina

Forrest Junior College *C, A*
Midlands Technical College *C*

South Dakota

Dakota State University *B*

Tennessee

Draughons Junior College:
　Nashville *C, A*
Fountainhead College of
　Technology *C, A*
National College
　Knoxville *A*
Southern Adventist University *A*
Tennessee State University *B*
University of Tennessee
　Chattanooga *C*
University of Tennessee Health
　Science Center *B, M*

Texas

El Centro College *A*
Howard College *C, A*
Laredo Community College *C*
St. Philip's College *A*
Texas A&M University
　Commerce *B*
Texas Southern University *B*
Texas State University: San Marcos *B*

Utah

LDS Business College *A*
Utah Career College *A*

Virginia

ECPI College of Technology: Virginia
　Beach *C, A*
ECPI Technical College: Roanoke *A*
Mountain Empire Community
　College *C*
Norfolk State University *B*

Washington

Renton Technical College *C, A*
Seattle University *B*

Wisconsin

Herzing University *A, B*
Northeast Wisconsin Technical
　College *A*
University of Wisconsin
　Milwaukee *M*

Medical records technology

Alabama

Bishop State Community College *A*
Central Alabama Community
　College *A*
Chattahoochee Valley Community
　College *A*
Enterprise-Ozark Community
　College *A*
Gadsden State Community College *A*
Wallace State Community College at
　Hanceville *A*

Arizona

Penn Foster College *A*
Phoenix College *A*
Pima Community College *A*
University of Phoenix *B*

Arkansas

Arkansas State University
　Beebe *C*
National Park Community
　College *C, A*
North Arkansas College *C*
Ouachita Technical College *C*
University of Arkansas
　Monticello *C*

California

Allan Hancock College *C, A*
Cerritos College *A*
Chabot College *C, A*
City College of San Francisco *C, A*
College of San Mateo *C*
Cosumnes River College *A*
Cypress College *A*
DeVry University
　Fremont *A*
　Long Beach *A*
　Pomona *A*
　Sherman Oaks *A*
East Los Angeles College *C*
Fresno City College *C, A*
Los Angeles City College *A*
National Polytechnic College of
　Science *A*
Orange Coast College *C, A*
Oxnard College *C, A*
Santa Barbara City College *C*
Santa Rosa Junior College *C*
Silicon Valley College
　Western Career College: San Jose *A*
Southwestern College *C, A*
Western Career College: Antioch *C, A*
Western Career College:
　Sacramento *C, A*

Colorado

American Sentinel University *A, B, M*
Arapahoe Community College *C, A*
Front Range Community College *A*

Connecticut

Lincoln College of New England:
　Briarwood *C, A*
Quinebaug Valley Community
　College *C*

Florida

Brevard Community College *C*
Central Florida College *A*
Central Florida Community
　College *C, A*
Daytona State College *C, A*
Florida State College at Jacksonville *A*
Hillsborough Community College *C*
Hodges University *A*
Indian River State College *A*
Lake-Sumter Community College *A*
Miami Dade College *C*
Polk State College *A*
Rasmussen College: Ocala *A*
Rasmussen College: Pasco County *A*
Seminole Community College *C*
Southwest Florida College *A*
Tallahassee Community College *C*
Valencia Community College *A*

Georgia

Abraham Baldwin Agricultural
　College *A*
Augusta Technical College *C*
Bainbridge College *C*
Darton College *A*
DeVry University
　Alpharetta *A*
　Decatur *A*
Macon State College *A*
Middle Georgia College *A*
Southwest Georgia Technical
　College *C*

West Georgia Technical College *C, A*

Hawaii
Heald College
  Honolulu *A*

Idaho
Boise State University *A*
Idaho State University *C, A*

Illinois
Black Hawk College *C, A*
College of DuPage *A*
Danville Area Community
  College *C, A*
DeVry University
  Chicago *A*
DeVry University: Online *A*
Highland Community College *A*
Illinois Central College *A*
John A. Logan College *A*
Kaskaskia College *A*
Midstate College *A, B*
Moraine Valley Community College *A*
Morton College *C*
Northwestern College *A*
Oakton Community College *A*
Rasmussen College: Rockford *A*
Rend Lake College *C, A*
Rock Valley College *C, A*
Shawnee Community College *C, A*
South Suburban College of Cook
  County *C*
Southeastern Illinois College *A*
Southwestern Illinois College *A*
Spoon River College *C*
Triton College *C*

Indiana
Harrison College
  Anderson *A*
  Columbus *A*
  Evansville *A*
  Fort Wayne *A*
  Indianapolis East *A*
  Lafayette *A*
  Terre Haute *A*
Indiana University
  Bloomington *B*
  Northwest *A*
  Southeast *A*
Ivy Tech Community College
  Bloomington *A*
  Central Indiana *A*
  Lafayette *A*
National College: Indianapolis *A*
Vincennes University *A*

Iowa
Indian Hills Community College *A*
Kirkwood Community College *A*
Northeast Iowa Community
  College *C, A*
Northwest Iowa Community
  College *A*
Scott Community College *C, A*

Kansas
Central Christian College of Kansas *A*
Dodge City Community College *C, A*
Highland Community College *A*
Hutchinson Community College *C, A*
Johnson County Community
  College *A*
Washburn University *C, A*

Kentucky
Eastern Kentucky University *A, B*
Henderson Community College *C*
National College
  Danville *C*
  Florence *C*
  Lexington *C*
  Louisville *C*
  Pikeville *C*
  Richmond *C*
Western Kentucky University *A*

Louisiana
Delgado Community College *A*
ITI Technical College *A*
Louisiana Tech University *A*
Southern University
  Shreveport *A*

Maine
Andover College *A*
Kennebec Valley Community
  College *C, A*

Maryland
Anne Arundel Community College *A*
Baltimore City Community
  College *C, A*
Carroll Community College *C*
Chesapeake College *A*
College of Southern Maryland *C*
Community College of Baltimore
  County *A*
Kaplan College: Hagerstown *C, A*
Montgomery College *C, A*
Prince George's Community
  College *C, A*

Massachusetts
Bristol Community College *A*
Holyoke Community College *C*
Laboure College *C, A*
Massasoit Community College *C*
Northern Essex Community
  College *C*

Michigan
Baker College
  of Auburn Hills *A*
  of Clinton Township *A*
  of Flint *A*
  of Jackson *A*
  of Owosso *A*
  of Port Huron *A*
Bay de Noc Community College *C*
Davenport University *A*
Delta College *C*
Ferris State University *A*
Gogebic Community College *C*
Henry Ford Community College *A*
Northern Michigan University *A*
Schoolcraft College *C, A*
Southwestern Michigan College *C, A*

Minnesota
Hennepin Technical College *C*
Minnesota State Community and
  Technical College *C, A*
Northwest Technical College *C*
Rasmussen College
  Eagan *A*
  Eden Prairie *A*
  Mankato *A*
  St. Cloud *A*
Rasmussen College: Brooklyn Park *A*
Rasmussen College: Lake
  Elmo/Woodbury *A*
Ridgewater College *C, A*
Riverland Community College *C*
Rochester Community and Technical
  College *A*
St. Catherine University *C, A*
St. Cloud Technical College *A*
St. Paul College *A*
Walden University *B*

Mississippi
Hinds Community College *A*
Meridian Community College *A*

Southwest Mississippi Community
  College *A*

Missouri
Missouri Western State
  University *C, A*
Ozarks Technical Community
  College *C, A*
St. Charles Community College *A*
Sanford-Brown College
  St. Peters *A*
State Fair Community College *A*

Montana
Montana State University
  College of Technology: Great
  Falls *A*

Nebraska
Central Community College *C, A*
Northeast Community College *A*
Western Nebraska Community
  College *C, A*

Nevada
Career College of Northern Nevada *C*
College of Southern Nevada *A*
Truckee Meadows Community
  College *C*

New Hampshire
Manchester Community College *C, A*
NHTI-Concord's Community
  College *C*

New Jersey
Berkeley College- Garret Mountain
  Campus *A*
Burlington County College *C, A*
Hudson County Community
  College *C, A*
Passaic County Community College *C*
Raritan Valley Community
  College *C, A*

New Mexico
Central New Mexico Community
  College *C*
Eastern New Mexico University:
  Roswell Campus *C, A*
San Juan College *C, A*

New York
ASA Institute of Business and
  Computer Technology *A*
Berkeley College *A*
Berkeley College of New York City *A*
Broome Community College *A*
Elmira Business Institute *C, A*
Erie Community College
  North Campus *A*
Fulton-Montgomery Community
  College *C*
Globe Institute of Technology *C*
Molloy College *A*
Monroe Community College *A*
Onondaga Community College *A*
Rockland Community College *A*
St. John's University *B*
State University of New York
  College of Technology at Alfred *A*
Suffolk County Community College *A*
Touro College *C, B*
Trocaire College *A*
Utica School of Commerce *A*

North Carolina
Brunswick Community College *A*
Catawba Valley Community
  College *C, A*
Central Piedmont Community
  College *C, A*

Davidson County Community
  College *A*
Edgecombe Community College *A*
Fayetteville Technical Community
  College *A*
Pitt Community College *C, A*
South Piedmont Community
  College *C, A*
Southwestern Community
  College *C, A*
Wake Technical Community
  College *C, A*

North Dakota
North Dakota State College of
  Science *A*
Rasmussen College: Bismarck *A*
Rasmussen College: Fargo *A*
Williston State College *C, A*

Ohio
Bowling Green State University:
  Firelands College *A*
Cincinnati State Technical and
  Community College *C, A*
Columbus State Community
  College *C, A*
Cuyahoga Community College
  Metropolitan Campus *A*
DeVry University
  Columbus *A*
Franklin University *B*
Hocking College *A*
Mercy College of Northwest Ohio *A*
National College: Stow *A*
National College: Youngstown *A*
Owens Community College
  Toledo *C, A*
Stark State College of Technology *A*
University of Cincinnati
  Clermont College *C*

Oklahoma
East Central University *B*
Rose State College *A*

Oregon
Central Oregon Community
  College *C, A*
Chemeketa Community College *C*
Lane Community College *C*
Linn-Benton Community College *C*
Portland Community College *A*

Pennsylvania
Community College of Allegheny
  County *C, A*
Community College of Philadelphia *A*
DeVry University
  Fort Washington *A*
Gwynedd-Mercy College *A*
Harrisburg Area Community
  College *A*
Keystone Technical Institute *C, A*
Lehigh Carbon Community College *A*
Mercyhurst College *C, A, B*
Pennsylvania College of
  Technology *A*
South Hills School of Business &
  Technology *A*
South Hills School of Business &
  Technology: Altoona *A*

Puerto Rico
Huertas Junior College *A*
Humacao Community College *A*
Inter American University of Puerto
  Rico
  Guayama Campus *C*
  San German Campus *A*
Universidad Adventista de las
  Antillas *A*

South Carolina

Aiken Technical College *C*
Florence-Darlington Technical
College *A*
Forrest Junior College *C, A*
Greenville Technical College *A*
Midlands Technical College *C, A*
Spartanburg Community College *C*

South Dakota

Dakota State University *A*
Presentation College *A*

Tennessee

Chattanooga State Community
College *A*
Dyersburg State Community
College *C, A*
National College
Nashville *C*
National College of Business &
Technology
National College: Bristol *C*
National College: Bartlett *A*
National College: Madison *A*
National College: Memphis *A*
Roane State Community College *A*
Tennessee State University *A*
Volunteer State Community College *A*
Walters State Community College *C, A*

Texas

Amarillo College *A*
Central Texas College *C*
Cisco College *C, A*
Coastal Bend College *C, A*
DeVry University
Irving *A*
DeVry University: Houston *A*
Del Mar College *C, A*
El Centro College *A*
El Paso Community College *C, A*
Galveston College *C, A*
Houston Community College
System *C, A*
Howard College *C, A*
Lamar Institute of Technology *A*
Lee College *C, A*
Lone Star College System *C, A*
McLennan Community College *A*
Midland College *C, A*
Mountain View College *C, A*
Panola College *C, A*
Paris Junior College *A*
Richland College *A*
St. Philip's College *C, A*
San Jacinto College *C, A*
South Plains College *A*
South Texas College *C, A*
Tarrant County College *A*
Texas State Technical College
Harlingen *A*
West Texas *C, A*
Tyler Junior College *A*
Wharton County Junior College *A*

Utah

LDS Business College *C*
Salt Lake Community College *C*
Weber State University *A*

Virginia

ECPI College of Technology: Virginia
Beach *C, A*
ECPI Technical College: Roanoke *A*
J. Sargeant Reynolds Community
College *C*
National College
Bluefield *C*
Charlottesville *C*
Danville *C*
Harrisonburg *C*

Lynchburg *C*
Martinsville *C*
Northern Virginia Community
College *A*
Piedmont Virginia Community
College *C*
Southwest Virginia Community
College *C*
Tidewater Community College *A*
Wytheville Community College *C*

Washington

Centralia College *C*
Clark College *C*
Grays Harbor College *C*
North Seattle Community College *C*
Shoreline Community College *A*
Spokane Falls Community
College *C, A*
Yakima Valley Community College *C*

West Virginia

Fairmont State University *A*
Mountain State University *C*

Wisconsin

Chippewa Valley Technical College *A*
Gateway Technical College *A*
Herzing University *C, B*
Moraine Park Technical College *C, A*
Rasmussen College: Green Bay *A*
Western Technical College *A*

Medical scientist

California

University of California
Los Angeles *M*
University of Southern California *M*

Colorado

University of Colorado
Denver *M, D*

Connecticut

Yale University *D*

Georgia

Medical College of Georgia *M*

Illinois

Northwestern University *M, D*
Rush University *M, D*

Maine

University of Southern Maine *M*

Michigan

University of Michigan *D*
Wayne State University *M*

Missouri

Washington University in St. Louis *M*

New Mexico

University of New Mexico *M, D*

New York

State University of New York
Upstate Medical University *D*
University of Rochester *M*

Ohio

Case Western Reserve University *M*

Pennsylvania

University of Pennsylvania *M*
University of Pittsburgh *M*

South Carolina

Medical University of South
Carolina *M*

Texas

University of Texas
Medical Branch at Galveston *M, D*

Virginia

University of Virginia *M, D*

Medical staff services technology

Kansas

Central Christian College of Kansas *A*
Wichita State University *B*

Maryland

Morgan State University *B*

Minnesota

Minnesota School of Business *A*

Missouri

Missouri Southern State University *A*

New York

Globe Institute of Technology *C*

North Carolina

Elon University *B*

Oregon

Umpqua Community College *A*

Wisconsin

Western Technical College *C*

Medical transcription

Alabama

Gadsden State Community College *C*
George C. Wallace State Community
College
George C. Wallace Community
College at Dothan *C*
Prince Institute of Professional
Studies *C, A*
Snead State Community College *C*
Wallace State Community College at
Hanceville *C*

Arizona

Central Arizona College *C, A*
Eastern Arizona College *C*
GateWay Community College *C, A*
Mohave Community College *C*
Northland Pioneer College *C, A*
Phoenix College *A*

Arkansas

Arkansas Tech University *C*
Mid-South Community College *C*
National Park Community College *C*
North Arkansas College *C*
Ozarka College *A*
Pulaski Technical College *C*
South Arkansas Community College *C*
Southeast Arkansas College *C*
University of Arkansas
Cossatot Community College of the
C

California

Chabot College *C*
Chaffey College *C*
City College of San Francisco *C*
Columbia College *C*
Cosumnes River College *C*

De Anza College *C*
Empire College *C*
Fresno City College *C, A*
Modesto Junior College *C*
Ohlone College *C*
Orange Coast College *C*
Riverside Community College *C, A*
Santa Rosa Junior College *C*
Shasta College *C*
Skyline College *C, A*
South Coast College *A*
Southwestern College *C, A*
Yuba Community College
District *C, A*

Colorado

Pikes Peak Community College *C*
Westwood College: Denver North *A*

Connecticut

Lincoln College of New England:
Briarwood *C*

Delaware

Delaware Technical and Community
College
Owens *C*
Stanton/Wilmington *C*

Florida

Brevard Community College *C*
Florida State College at Jacksonville *C*
Indian River State College *C*
Lake City Community College *C*
Miami Dade College *C*
Palm Beach Community College *C*
Pasco-Hernando Community
College *C*
Polk State College *C*
Seminole Community College *C*

Georgia

Albany Technical College *C*
Augusta Technical College *C*
Central Georgia Technical College *C*
Chattahoochee Technical College *C*
Clayton State University *C*
Dalton State College *C, A*
Darton College *C*
Gwinnett Technical College *C*
Middle Georgia Technical College *C*
Southeastern Technical College *C*
Southwest Georgia Technical
College *C*
West Georgia Technical College *C*

Idaho

North Idaho College *A*

Illinois

Black Hawk College *C*
College of DuPage *C*
College of Lake County *C*
Harper College *C*
Heartland Community College *C*
Highland Community College *C*
Illinois Eastern Community Colleges
Olney Central College *C*
Illinois Valley Community College *C*
John A. Logan College *C*
Kaskaskia College *C*
Kishwaukee College *C*
Lincoln Land Community College *C*
MacCormac College *C, A*
McHenry County College *C*
Midstate College *C*
Moraine Valley Community College *C*
Oakton Community College *C*
Parkland College *C*
Rasmussen College: Aurora *C, A*
Rasmussen College: Rockford *C, A*
Rend Lake College *C*

South Suburban College of Cook
County *C*
Southeastern Illinois College *C*
Spoon River College *C*
Waubonsee Community College *C*

Indiana
Brown Mackie College: South Bend *A*
College of Court Reporting *A*
Indiana University
Southeast *C*
Kaplan College: Hammond *C*

Iowa
Indian Hills Community College *C*
Iowa Central Community College *C*
Kaplan University
Davenport *A*
Des Moines *C*
Northeast Iowa Community
College *C*
Southwestern Community College *A*

Kansas
Neosho County Community
College *C*

Kentucky
National College
Danville *C*
Florence *C*
Lexington *C*
Louisville *C*
Pikeville *C*
Richmond *C*
Owensboro Community and
Technical College *C, A*
Spencerian College *C*

Louisiana
ITI Technical College *A*

Maine
Andover College *A*
Beal College *C*
Central Maine Community College *C*

Maryland
Allegany College of Maryland *A*
Howard Community College *C*
Kaplan College: Hagerstown *C, A*
Prince George's Community
College *C*

Massachusetts
Bristol Community College *C*
Marian Court College *C, A*

Michigan
Baker College
of Cadillac *A*
of Clinton Township *A*
of Flint *A*
of Jackson *A*
of Muskegon *A*
of Port Huron *A*
Davenport University *C*
Delta College *C*
Henry Ford Community College *C*
Jackson Community College *C*
Kirtland Community College *C, A*
Mid Michigan Community College *A*
North Central Michigan College *C*
Oakland Community College *C, A*
Schoolcraft College *C*
Southwestern Michigan College *C*

Minnesota
Academy College *C*
Alexandria Technical College *C*
Anoka Technical College *C*
Dakota County Technical College *C*

Hennepin Technical College *C*
Lake Superior College *C*
Minnesota State College - Southeast
Technical *C*
Minnesota State Community and
Technical College *C*
Northland Community & Technical
College *C, A*
Rasmussen College
Eagan *C, A*
Eden Prairie *C, A*
Mankato *C, A*
St. Cloud *C, A*
Rasmussen College: Brooklyn
Park *C, A*
Rasmussen College: Lake
Elmo/Woodbury *C, A*
Rochester Community and Technical
College *C*
St. Catherine University *C*
St. Paul College *C*
South Central College *C*

Mississippi
Antonelli College
Jackson *A*

Missouri
Cox College *C*
Metropolitan Community College:
Penn Valley *C*

Montana
Dawson Community College *A*
Flathead Valley Community College *C*
Montana State University
College of Technology: Great
Falls *C, A*
University of Montana *A*

Nebraska
Metropolitan Community College *C*
Western Nebraska Community
College *C*

New Hampshire
Manchester Community College *C*
NHTI-Concord's Community
College *C*

New Jersey
Gloucester County College *C*
Hudson County Community
College *C*
Passaic County Community College *C*
Sussex County Community College *C*

New Mexico
Eastern New Mexico University:
Roswell Campus *C*

New York
Broome Community College *C*
Elmira Business Institute *C, A*
Globe Institute of Technology *C*
Herkimer County Community
College *C*
Trocaire College *C*

North Carolina
Alamance Community College *C*
Carteret Community College *C*
College of the Albemarle *C*
Durham Technical Community
College *C*
Edgecombe Community College *C*
Forsyth Technical Community
College *C*
Guilford Technical Community
College *C*
Sandhills Community College *C*

South Piedmont Community
College *C*
Western Piedmont Community
College *C*

North Dakota
Dakota College at Bottineau *C*
North Dakota State College of
Science *C, A*
Rasmussen College: Bismarck *C, A*
Rasmussen College: Fargo *C, A*
Williston State College *C, A*

Ohio
Belmont Technical College *C*
Cincinnati State Technical and
Community College *C*
Columbus State Community
College *C*
Davis College *A*
ETI Technical College of Niles *A*
Eastern Gateway Community
College *C*
Edison State Community College *C, A*
Mercy College of Northwest Ohio *C*
Owens Community College
Toledo *C*
Southern State Community College *C*
Stark State College of Technology *C*
University of Akron *C*
University of Akron: Wayne College *C*
University of Cincinnati
Raymond Walters College *C, A*
Washington State Community
College *A*

Oklahoma
Oklahoma State University
Institute of Technology:
Okmulgee *A*

Oregon
Central Oregon Community
College *C*
Chemeketa Community College *A*
Lane Community College *C*
Linn-Benton Community College *C*
Southwestern Oregon Community
College *C*
Treasure Valley Community College *A*

Pennsylvania
Bucks County Community College *C*
Consolidated School of Business
Lancaster *A*
York *A*
Erie Business Center *A*
Erie Business Center South *A*
Keystone Technical Institute *C, A*
Laurel Business Institute *A*
Lehigh Carbon Community College *C*
Luzerne County Community
College *A*
Mercyhurst College *C*
Newport Business Institute: Lower
Burrell *A*
Northampton Community College *C*
Penn Commercial Business and
Technical School *C*
Pennsylvania Highlands Community
College *A*
Westmoreland County Community
College *C*

Rhode Island
Community College of Rhode
Island *C*

South Carolina
Aiken Technical College *C*
Florence-Darlington Technical
College *C*
Forrest Junior College *C, A*

Tri-County Technical College *C*
York Technical College *C*

South Dakota
Mitchell Technical Institute *A*
Presentation College *C*
Western Dakota Technical Institute *A*

Tennessee
Dyersburg State Community
College *C*
National College
Knoxville *C*
Nashville *C*
National College of Business &
Technology
National College: Bristol *C*
Roane State Community College *C*
South College *C*
Walters State Community College *C*

Texas
Central Texas College *C*
El Centro College *C*
Galveston College *C*
Howard College *C*
Laredo Community College *C*
Lee College *C*
Lone Star College System *C*
North Central Texas College *C*
St. Philip's College *C*
San Antonio College *C*
South Plains College *C*
South Texas College *C*
Texas State Technical College
Harlingen *C*
West Texas *C*
Tyler Junior College *C*

Utah
Independence University *A*
LDS Business College *C*
Southern Utah University *C*

Virginia
ECPI College of Technology: Virginia
Beach *C, A*
ECPI Technical College: Roanoke *A*
J. Sargeant Reynolds Community
College *C*
Lord Fairfax Community College *C*
Mountain Empire Community
College *A*
National College
Bluefield *C*
Charlottesville *C*
Danville *C*
Harrisonburg *C*
Lynchburg *C*
Martinsville *C*
Roanoke Valley *C*
Northern Virginia Community
College *C*
Tidewater Community College *C*
Virginia Western Community
College *C*

Washington
Bates Technical College *C*
Bellingham Technical College *C*
Centralia College *C*
Clark College *C*
Clover Park Technical College *C*
Everett Community College *C*
Grays Harbor College *C*
Green River Community College *C*
Highline Community College *C, A*
Lake Washington Technical College *C*
North Seattle Community College *C*
Peninsula College *C*
Pierce College *C*
Shoreline Community College *C*
Skagit Valley College *C*

South Puget Sound Community
College *C*
Spokane Community College *C*
Yakima Valley Community College *C*

West Virginia

Mountain State College *A*

Wisconsin

Chippewa Valley Technical College *C*
Fox Valley Technical College *C*
Gateway Technical College *C*
Lac Courte Oreilles Ojibwa
Community College *C*
Lakeshore Technical College *C*
Mid-State Technical College *C*
Moraine Park Technical College *C*
Northcentral Technical College *C*
Rasmussen College: Green Bay *C, A*
Southwest Wisconsin Technical
College *C*
Waukesha County Technical
College *C*

Wyoming

Sheridan College *C*

Medication aide

Arkansas

East Arkansas Community College *C*
Southeast Arkansas College *C*

Kansas

Barton County Community College *C*
Cloud County Community College *C*
Colby Community College *C*
Kansas City Kansas Community
College *C*

Kentucky

Maysville Community and Technical
College *C*
Owensboro Community and
Technical College *C*
Somerset Community College *C*

Louisiana

Our Lady of the Lake College *C*

Minnesota

Minnesota State College - Southeast
Technical *C*

Texas

Tyler Junior College *C*

Wisconsin

Mid-State Technical College *C*

Medicinal/ pharmaceutical chemistry

Arizona

University of Arizona *M, D*

California

Loma Linda University *D*
University of California
San Diego *B*

Colorado

University of Colorado
Denver *D*

Connecticut

University of Connecticut *M, D*

Georgia

Mercer University *D*

Illinois

Illinois Institute of Technology *B*
University of Illinois
Chicago *M, D*

Kansas

University of Kansas *M, D*

Maryland

Towson University *B*

Massachusetts

Massachusetts College of Pharmacy
and Health Sciences *M, D*

Michigan

Michigan Technological University *B*
University of Michigan *B, M, D*

Minnesota

University of Minnesota
Twin Cities *M, D*

Nebraska

Chadron State College *B*
University of Nebraska
Medical Center *M, D*

New Jersey

New Jersey Institute of Technology *M*
Rutgers, The State University of New
Jersey
New Brunswick/Piscataway
Campus *M, D*

New York

State University of New York
Buffalo *M, D*

North Carolina

Campbell University *B*
East Carolina University *D*
Livingstone College *B*

Ohio

Cleveland State University *B*
Ohio Northern University *B*
Ohio State University
Columbus Campus *M, D*

Pennsylvania

Duquesne University *M, D*
Temple University *M, D*
University of the Sciences in
Philadelphia *B*

Rhode Island

University of Rhode Island *M, D*

Tennessee

University of Tennessee
Knoxville *M, D*
University of Tennessee Health
Science Center *M, D*

Texas

Texas Tech University Health Sciences
Center *M, D*
University of Houston *M*

Utah

University of Utah *M, D*

Washington

University of Washington *M, D*

West Virginia

West Virginia University *M, D*

Medicine (M.D.)

Alabama

University of Alabama at Birmingham:
School of Medicine *P*
University of South Alabama: School
of Medicine *P*

Arizona

University of Arizona: College of
Medicine *P*

Arkansas

University of Arkansas for Medical
Sciences: College of Medicine *P*

California

Loma Linda University: School of
Medicine *P*
Stanford University: School of
Medicine *P*
University of California Davis: School
of Medicine *P*
University of California Irvine: College
of Medicine *P*
University of California Los Angeles:
School of Medicine *P*
University of California San Diego:
School of Medicine *P*
University of California San Francisco:
School of Medicine *P*
University of Southern California:
School of Medicine *P*

Colorado

University of Colorado Health
Sciences Center: School of
Medicine *P*

Connecticut

University of Connecticut: School of
Medicine *P*
Yale University: School of Medicine *P*

District of Columbia

George Washington University: School
of Medicine and Health
Sciences *P*
Georgetown University: School of
Medicine *P*
Howard University: School of
Medicine *P*

Florida

University of Florida: School of
Medicine *P*
University of Miami: School of
Medicine *P*
University of South Florida: College of
Medicine *P*

Georgia

Emory University: School of
Medicine *P*
Medical College of Georgia: School of
Medicine *P*
Mercer University: School of
Medicine *P*
Morehouse School of Medicine *P*

Hawaii

University of Hawaii at Manoa: John A.
Burns School of Medicine *P*

Illinois

Loyola University Chicago: Stritch
School of Medicine *P*

Northwestern University: School of
Medicine *P*
Rosalind Franklin University of
Medicine and Science:
Professional *P*
Rush University: Rush Medical
College *P*
Southern Illinois University: School of
Medicine *P*
University of Chicago: Pritzker School
of Medicine *P*
University of Illinois at Chicago:
College of Medicine *P*

Indiana

Indiana University: School of
Medicine *P*

Iowa

University of Iowa: College of
Medicine *P*

Kansas

University of Kansas Medical Center:
School of Medicine *P*

Kentucky

University of Kentucky: College of
Medicine *P*
University of Louisville: School of
Medicine *P*

Louisiana

Louisiana State University Health
Sciences Center: School of
Medicine *P*
Louisiana State University: School of
Medicine *P*
Tulane University: School of
Medicine *P*

Maryland

Johns Hopkins University: School of
Medicine *P*
Uniformed Services University of the
Health Sciences: School of
Medicine *P*
University of Maryland at Baltimore:
School of Medicine *P*

Massachusetts

Boston University: School of
Medicine *P*
Harvard University: Harvard Medical
School *P*
Tufts University: School of
Medicine *P*
University of Massachusetts Medical
School *P*

Michigan

Michigan State University: College of
Human Medicine *P*
University of Michigan: School of
Medicine *P*
Wayne State University: School of
Medicine *P*

Minnesota

Mayo Medical School *P*
University of Minnesota Medical
School *P*

Mississippi

University of Mississippi Medical
Center: School of Medicine *P*

Missouri

St. Louis University: School of
Medicine *P*
University of Missouri Columbia:
School of Medicine *P*

University of Missouri Kansas City:
    School of Medicine *P*
Washington University: School of
    Medicine *P*

Nebraska
Creighton University: School of
    Medicine *P*
University of Nebraska Medical
    Center: College of Medicine *P*

Nevada
University of Nevada: School of
    Medicine *P*

New Hampshire
Dartmouth College: School of
    Medicine *P*

New Jersey
University of Medicine and Dentistry
    of New Jersey
    New Jersey Medical School *P*
    Robert Wood Johnson Medical
        School *P*
    Robert Wood Johnson Medical
        School at Camden *P*

New Mexico
University of New Mexico: School of
    Medicine *P*

New York
Albany Medical College: School of
    Medicine *P*
Albert Einstein College of Medicine *P*
Columbia University
    College of Physicians and
        Surgeons *P*
Cornell University Medical College *P*
Mount Sinai School of Medicine of
    City University of New York *P*
New York Medical College *P*
New York University: School of
    Medicine *P*
State University of New York Health
    Science Center at Brooklyn:
    School of Medicine *P*
State University of New York Health
    Science Center at Syracuse:
    School of Medicine *P*
State University of New York Health
    Sciences Center at Stony Brook:
    School of Medicine *P*
State University of New York at
    Buffalo: School of Medicine *P*
University of Rochester: School of
    Medicine and Dentistry *P*

North Carolina
Duke University: School of
    Medicine *P*
East Carolina University: School of
    Medicine *P*
University of North Carolina at Chapel
    Hill: School of Medicine *P*
Wake Forest University: Bowman Gray
    School of Medicine *P*

North Dakota
University of North Dakota: School of
    Medicine *P*

Ohio
Case Western Reserve University:
    School of Medicine *P*
Medical College of Ohio *P*
Northeastern Ohio Universities
    College of Medicine *P*
Ohio State University Columbus
    Campus: College of Medicine *P*

University of Cincinnati: College of
    Medicine *P*
Wright State University: School of
    Medicine *P*

Oklahoma
University of Oklahoma Health
    Sciences Center: College of
    Medicine *P*

Oregon
Oregon Health Sciences University:
    School of Medicine *P*

Pennsylvania
Jefferson Medical College of Thomas
    Jefferson University *P*
Medical College of Pennsylvania and
    Hahnemann University School of
    Medicine *P*
Pennsylvania State University College
    of Medicine *P*
Temple University: School of
    Medicine *P*
University of Pennsylvania: School of
    Medicine *P*
University of Pittsburgh: School of
    Medicine *P*

Puerto Rico
Ponce School of Medicine *P*
Universidad Central del Caribe:
    Medical School *P*
University of Puerto Rico Medical
    Sciences Campus: School of
    Medicine *P*

Rhode Island
Brown University: School of
    Medicine *P*

South Carolina
Medical University of South Carolina:
    College of Medicine *P*
University of South Carolina: School
    of Medicine *P*

South Dakota
University of South Dakota: School of
    Medicine *P*

Tennessee
East Tennessee State University: James
    H. Quillen College of Medicine *P*
Meharry Medical College: School of
    Medicine *P*
University of Tennessee Memphis:
    College of Medicine *P*
Vanderbilt University: School of
    Medicine *P*

Texas
Baylor College of Medicine *P*
Texas A&M University: Health Science
    Center College of Medicine *P*
Texas Tech University Health Sciences
    Center: School of Medicine *P*
University of Texas
    Medical Branch at Galveston:
        School of Medicine *P*
University of Texas Health Science
    Center: Medical School *P*
University of Texas Southwestern
    Medical Center at Dallas
    Southwestern Medical School *P*
University of Texas-Houston Health
    Science Center *P*

Utah
University of Utah: School of
    Medicine *P*

Vermont
University of Vermont: College of
    Medicine *P*

Virginia
Eastern Virginia Medical School of the
    Medical College of Hampton
    Roads: Medical Professions *P*
University of Virginia: School of
    Medicine *P*
Virginia Commonwealth University:
    School of Medicine *P*

Washington
University of Washington: School of
    Medicine *P*

West Virginia
Marshall University: School of
    Medicine *P*
West Virginia University: School of
    Medicine *P*

Wisconsin
Medical College of Wisconsin: School
    of Medicine *P*
University of Wisconsin Madison:
    School of Medicine *P*

Medieval and Renaissance studies

California
University of California
    Davis *B*
    Santa Barbara *B*

Connecticut
University of Connecticut *M, D*
Wesleyan University *B*
Yale University *B, M, D*

District of Columbia
Catholic University of
    America *B, M, D*
Georgetown University *B*

Florida
New College of Florida *B*

Georgia
Emory University *B*

Indiana
Hanover College *B*
University of Notre Dame *B, M, D*

Louisiana
Tulane University *B*

Massachusetts
Boston College *D*
College of the Holy Cross *B*
Mount Holyoke College *B*
Smith College *B*
Wellesley College *B*

Michigan
University of Michigan *B*
Western Michigan University *M*

Minnesota
Augsburg College *B*
St. Olaf College *B*

Nebraska
University of Nebraska
    Lincoln *B*

New Jersey
Rutgers, The State University of New
    Jersey
    New Brunswick/Piscataway
        Campus *B*

New York
Bard College *B*
Barnard College *B*
Columbia University *B*
Cornell University *M, D*
State University of New York
    Albany *B*
    Binghamton *B*
Vassar College *B*

North Carolina
Duke University *B*

Ohio
Ohio State University
    Columbus Campus *B*
Ohio Wesleyan University *B*
University of Toledo *B*

Oregon
University of Oregon *B*

Pennsylvania
Dickinson College *B*
Gettysburg College *B*
Penn State
    Abington *B*
    Altoona *B*
    Beaver *B*
    Berks *B*
    Brandywine *B*
    DuBois *B*
    Erie, The Behrend College *B*
    Fayette, The Eberly Campus *B*
    Greater Allegheny *B*
    Hazleton *B*
    Lehigh Valley *B*
    Mont Alto *B*
    New Kensington *B*
    Schuylkill *B*
    Shenango *B*
    University Park *B*
    Wilkes-Barre *B*
    Worthington Scranton *B*
    York *B*
Swarthmore College *B*

Rhode Island
Brown University *B*

Tennessee
University of Tennessee
    Knoxville *B*
University of the South *B*

Texas
Rice University *B*
Southern Methodist University *B, M*
University of Texas
    Austin *D*

Virginia
College of William and Mary *B*
Washington and Lee University *B*

Wisconsin
University of Wisconsin
    Madison *M, D*

Medium/heavy vehicle technology

Arkansas
Mid-South Community College *C*
Pulaski Technical College *C*

California

Merced College *C*

Maine

Washington County Community
    College *C*

Michigan

Oakland Community College *A*

Minnesota

Dakota County Technical College *C, A*
Hennepin Technical College *C, A*
St. Cloud Technical College *C, A*
St. Paul College *C*

Missouri

Linn State Technical College *A*

Nebraska

Northeast Community College *A*

Ohio

Edison State Community College *C, A*

Wisconsin

Milwaukee Area Technical College *C*

Mental health counseling

Alabama

Faulkner University *B*

Arizona

Prescott College *B*
University of Phoenix *M*

California

California Institute of Integral
    Studies *M*
University of San Diego *M*

Florida

Barry University *M*
Nova Southeastern University *M*
South University: West Palm Beach *M*
Stetson University *M*
University of Miami *M*
University of North Florida *M*

Georgia

Fort Valley State University *M*
South University: Savannah *M*

Idaho

Idaho State University *M*

Illinois

Roosevelt University *M*

Kansas

Emporia State University *M*

Louisiana

Xavier University of Louisiana *M*

Maryland

Bowie State University *M*

Massachusetts

Bridgewater State College *M*
Fitchburg State College *M*
Lesley University *M*
Suffolk University *M*
University of Massachusetts
    Boston *M*

Minnesota

Capella University *M*
Saint Cloud State University *M*
Walden University *M*

Mississippi

Mississippi College *M*

New Hampshire

Southern New Hampshire
    University *M*

New Jersey

Seton Hall University *M, D*

New York

Adelphi University *M*
City University of New York
    Brooklyn College *M*
Hofstra University *M*
Iona College *M*
Medaille College *M*
New York Institute of Technology *M*
Pace University *M*
St. John Fisher College *M*
St. John's University *M*
State University of New York
    Buffalo *M*
    New Paltz *M*

North Carolina

Gardner-Webb University *M*

North Dakota

University of Mary *M*

Ohio

Malone University *M*
Xavier University *M*

Pennsylvania

Alvernia University *M*
Lancaster Bible College *M*

Texas

St. Edward's University *M*
Southern Methodist University *M*

Vermont

College of St. Joseph in Vermont *M*
Goddard College *M*

Wisconsin

Marquette University *M*

Mental health services technology

California

San Joaquin Delta College *A*
Santa Rosa Junior College *C, A*

Colorado

Pikes Peak Community College *C, A*
Pueblo Community College *C*

Connecticut

Asnuntuck Community College *C, A*
Capital Community College *A*
Housatonic Community College *C, A*
Naugatuck Valley Community
    College *C, A*

Florida

Daytona State College *A*
Hillsborough Community College *A*

Georgia

Darton College *A*

Idaho

North Idaho College *A*

Illinois

College of DuPage *C*
Elgin Community College *C*
Illinois Eastern Community Colleges
    Frontier Community College *A*
    Lincoln Trail College *C*
    Olney Central College *C*
    Wabash Valley College *C*
Moraine Valley Community College *C*
Prairie State College *A*

Indiana

Indiana University-Purdue University
    Fort Wayne *B*
Ivy Tech Community College
    Bloomington *C, A*
    Central Indiana *A*
    Columbus *C, A*
    East Central *C, A*
    Kokomo *A*
    Lafayette *C, A*
    North Central *C, A*
    Northeast *C, A*
    Northwest *C, A*
    Richmond *A*
    South Central *C, A*
    Southeast *C, A*
    Southwest *A*
    Wabash Valley *A*

Kentucky

Northern Kentucky University *B*

Louisiana

Southern University and Agricultural
    and Mechanical College *M*

Maine

University of Maine
    Machias *B*

Maryland

Allegany College of Maryland *A*
Anne Arundel Community
    College *C, A*
Chesapeake College *C, A*
College of Southern Maryland *C*
Community College of Baltimore
    County *C, A*
Hagerstown Community College *A*
Howard Community College *A*
University of Maryland
    University College *C*

Massachusetts

Berkshire Community College *C*
Bunker Hill Community College *C*
Massasoit Community College *C*
Mount Wachusett Community
    College *C, A*
North Shore Community College *C, A*
Northern Essex Community
    College *C, A*

Michigan

Wayne County Community
    College *C, A*

Minnesota

Rochester Community and Technical
    College *C, A*

Missouri

Metropolitan Community College:
    Penn Valley *A*

New Hampshire

NHTI-Concord's Community
    College *A*

New York

City University of New York
    Kingsborough Community
    College *A*
Dutchess Community College *A*

North Carolina

Central Piedmont Community
    College *A*
Guilford Technical Community
    College *A*
Pitt Community College *A*
Richmond Community College *A*
Roanoke-Chowan Community
    College *A*
Southwestern Community College *A*
Wayne Community College *A*

North Dakota

North Dakota State College of
    Science *A*

Ohio

Columbus State Community
    College *C, A*
Franciscan University of
    Steubenville *B*
North Central State College *A*
University of Toledo *A*

Pennsylvania

Community College of Allegheny
    County *C, A*
Community College of Philadelphia *A*
Montgomery County Community
    College *C, A*
Northampton Community College *C*
Pennsylvania College of
    Technology *A*

Texas

Alvin Community College *A*
Del Mar College *A*
Eastfield College *C, A*
El Paso Community College *A*
Houston Community College
    System *C, A*
Laredo Community College *A*
McLennan Community College *C, A*
San Jacinto College *C*
Tarrant County College *C, A*
Wharton County Junior College *C, A*

Virginia

Virginia Western Community
    College *A*

Washington

Pierce College *C, A*

West Virginia

Mountain State College *A*
West Virginia State Community and
    Technical College *C, A*

Merchandising/buying operations

California

Fashion Institute of Design and
    Merchandising
    Los Angeles *A*
Merced College *C, A*

Connecticut

Naugatuck Valley Community
    College *C, A*

Florida

International Academy of Design and
    Technology: Tampa *B*

Georgia

Gwinnett Technical College *C*
Middle Georgia College *A*

Michigan

Delta College *A*

Minnesota

Art Institutes International
    Minnesota *B*

Nebraska

Northeast Community College *A*

New York

Westchester Community College *A*

Ohio

University of Akron *A*
Youngstown State University *A, B, M*

Pennsylvania

Saint Joseph's University *B, M*

Texas

University of Houston *B*
University of North Texas *M*

Metal building assembly

Washington

Bates Technical College *C, A*

Wisconsin

Gateway Technical College *C*
Lakeshore Technical College *C*
Milwaukee Area Technical College *C*

Metal/jewelry arts

Arizona

Northern Arizona University *B*

California

Academy of Art University *C, A, B, M*
Bethesda Christian University *B*
California College of the Arts *B, M*
California State University
    Long Beach *B, M*
    Northridge *B, M*
El Camino College *C*
Fashion Institute of Design and
    Merchandising
    Los Angeles *A*
    San Francisco *A*
Monterey Peninsula College *C, A*
Orange Coast College *C*
Palomar College *A*
Santa Rosa Junior College *C*
Santiago Canyon College *A*

Colorado

Adams State College *B*

Connecticut

Middlesex Community College *A*

District of Columbia

Corcoran College of Art and Design *C*

Georgia

Savannah College of Art and
    Design *B, M*

Iowa

University of Iowa *B, M*

Kansas

Pittsburg State University *B*
University of Kansas *B, M*

Maine

Maine College of Art *B*

Massachusetts

Massachusetts College of Art and
    Design *B, M*
School of the Museum of Fine
    Arts *B, M*
University of Massachusetts
    Dartmouth *B, M*

Michigan

College for Creative Studies *B*
Ferris State University *B*
Grand Valley State University *B*
Kendall College of Art and Design of
    Ferris State University *B*
Northern Michigan University *A, B*
Siena Heights University *B*
University of Michigan *B*

Montana

Flathead Valley Community
    College *C, A*

New York

Fashion Institute of Technology *A*
Hofstra University *B*
Rochester Institute of
    Technology *A, B, M*
State University of New York
    College at Buffalo *B*
    New Paltz *B, M*

North Carolina

East Carolina University *B*
Haywood Community College *A*

Ohio

Bowling Green State University *B*
Cleveland Institute of Art *B*
University of Akron *B*

Oregon

Oregon College of Art & Craft *C, B*
University of Oregon *B, M*

Pennsylvania

Arcadia University *B*
Seton Hill University *B*
Temple University *B, M*

Rhode Island

Rhode Island School of Design *B, M*

Tennessee

Memphis College of Art *B, M*

Texas

Paris Junior College *A*
Texas A&M University
    Commerce *B*
University of Houston *B, M*
University of Texas
    El Paso *B, M*
Western Texas College *A*

Washington

University of Washington *B, M*

Wisconsin

Northeast Wisconsin Technical
    College *C*

University of Wisconsin
    Madison *B*

Metallurgical engineering

Alabama

University of Alabama *B, M*

Colorado

Colorado School of Mines *B, M, D*

Connecticut

University of Connecticut *M, D*

Idaho

University of Idaho *B, M*

Illinois

University of Illinois
    Urbana-Champaign *B, M, D*

Missouri

University of Missouri
    Missouri University of Science and
    Technology *B, M, D*

Montana

Montana Tech of the University of
    Montana *B, M*

Nevada

University of Nevada
    Reno *B, M, D*

New Mexico

New Mexico Institute of Mining and
    Technology *B*

New York

Columbia University *B, M, D*

Ohio

Cleveland State University *B, M*
Ohio State University
    Columbus Campus *B*
University of Cincinnati *B, M, D*

South Dakota

South Dakota School of Mines and
    Technology *B, M*

Tennessee

University of Tennessee
    Knoxville *M, D*

Texas

University of Texas
    El Paso *B*

Utah

University of Utah *B, M, D*

Washington

University of Washington *B*

Wisconsin

University of Wisconsin
    Madison *D*

Metallurgical technology

Arkansas

Arkansas Northeastern College *C, A*

California

City College of San Francisco *C*

Michigan

Mott Community College *C*
Schoolcraft College *C, A*

Minnesota

Ridgewater College *A*

Oregon

Linn-Benton Community College *C*

Pennsylvania

Penn State
    Altoona *A*
    Berks *A*
    DuBois *A*
    Erie, The Behrend College *A*
    Fayette, The Eberly Campus *A*
    Hazleton *A*
    New Kensington *A*
    Schuylkill *A*
    Shenango *A*
    Wilkes-Barre *A*
    York *A*

Texas

Kilgore College *C, A*

Meteorology

Florida

Daytona State College *A*
Florida Institute of Technology *B, M*
University of Miami *B*

Hawaii

University of Hawaii
    Manoa *B, M, D*

Illinois

Western Illinois University *B*

Indiana

Purdue University *B*

Iowa

Iowa State University *M, D*

Kentucky

Western Kentucky University *A, B*

Massachusetts

Massachusetts Institute of
    Technology *M, D*

Michigan

Central Michigan University *B*

Minnesota

Saint Cloud State University *B*

New York

State University of New York
    College at Brockport *B*
    Oswego *B*
Suffolk County Community College *A*

North Carolina

University of North Carolina
    Charlotte *B*

Oklahoma

University of Oklahoma *B, M, D*

Texas

University of the Incarnate Word *B*

Utah

University of Utah *B, M, D*

Vermont

Lyndon State College *B*

West Virginia

West Virginia State Community and
Technical College *A*

Microbiology

Alabama

Alabama State University *D*
University of Alabama *B*
University of Alabama
Birmingham *D*

Arizona

Arizona State University *B, M, D*
Northern Arizona University *B*

California

California State Polytechnic
University: Pomona *B*
California State University
Chico *B*
Dominguez Hills *B*
Los Angeles *B*
Loma Linda University *D*
Pitzer College *B*
San Diego State University *B, M*
San Francisco State University *B, M*
San Jose State University *B, M*
University of California
Berkeley *B, D*
Davis *B, M, D*
Riverside *M, D*
University of Southern
California *M, D*

Colorado

Colorado State University *B, M, D*

District of Columbia

Howard University *M, D*

Florida

Daytona State College *A*

Georgia

University of Georgia *B, M, D*

Hawaii

University of Hawaii
Manoa *B, M, D*

Idaho

Idaho State University *B, M*
University of Idaho *B*

Illinois

Southern Illinois University
Carbondale *B*
University of Illinois
Urbana-Champaign *B, M, D*

Indiana

Purdue University *B, M, D*

Iowa

Iowa State University *B, M, D*
University of Iowa *B, M, D*
University of Northern Iowa *B*

Kansas

Central Christian College of Kansas *A*
Kansas State University *B, D*
University of Kansas *B, M, D*

Louisiana

Louisiana State University and
Agricultural and Mechanical
College *B*
University of Louisiana at Lafayette *B*
Xavier University of Louisiana *B*

Maryland

University of Maryland
Baltimore *M, D*
College Park *B*

Massachusetts

University of Massachusetts
Amherst *B, M, D*

Michigan

Michigan State University *B, M, D*
Northern Michigan University *B*
University of Michigan *B, D*

Missouri

Saint Louis University *M, D*
University of Missouri
Columbia *B*

New Hampshire

University of New Hampshire *B, M, D*

New Jersey

Seton Hall University *M*

New York

State University of New York
Stony Brook *D*
Upstate Medical University *M, D*
University of Rochester *B, M*

North Carolina

Methodist University *A, B*
North Carolina State
University *B, M, D*

North Dakota

North Dakota State University *B, M*

Ohio

Ohio State University
Columbus Campus *B, M, D*
Ohio University *B, M, D*
Ohio Wesleyan University *B*
University of Akron *B*

Oklahoma

Oklahoma State University *B, M, D*
University of Oklahoma *B, M, D*

Oregon

Oregon Health & Science
University *D*

Pennsylvania

Juniata College *B*
University of Pittsburgh *B*
University of the Sciences in
Philadelphia *B*

Puerto Rico

Inter American University of Puerto
Rico
Aguadilla Campus *B*
Universidad del Este *B*
University of Puerto Rico
Humacao *B*
Medical Sciences *M, D*

Rhode Island

University of Rhode Island *B, M, D*

South Carolina

Clemson University *B, M, D*

South Dakota

South Dakota State University *B*

Tennessee

University of Tennessee
Knoxville *M, D*
Vanderbilt University *D*

Texas

Texas A&M University *B, M, D*
Texas State University: San Marcos *B*
Texas Tech University *B, M*
University of Houston
Downtown *B*
University of Texas
Arlington *B*
Austin *M, D*
El Paso *B*
Health Science Center at
Houston *M, D*
Medical Branch at Galveston *M, D*
Southwestern Medical Center at
Dallas *M, D*

Utah

Brigham Young University *B, M, D*

Vermont

University of Vermont *B*

Washington

University of Washington *B*
Washington State University *B, M, D*

West Virginia

West Virginia University *M, D*

Wisconsin

Marquette University *M, D*
University of Wisconsin
La Crosse *B*
Madison *B, M, D*
Milwaukee *B*

Wyoming

University of Wyoming *B*

Middle school education

Alabama

Athens State University *B*
Birmingham-Southern College *T*

Alaska

Alaska Pacific University *A, B, M*

Arizona

University of Phoenix *M*

Arkansas

Arkansas Northeastern College *A*
Arkansas State University *B, T*
Arkansas State University
Mountain Home *A*
Arkansas State University: Newport *A*
Arkansas Tech University *B*
East Arkansas Community College *A*
Harding University *B, T*
Henderson State University *B, M, T*
John Brown University *B, T*
Mid-South Community College *A*
Northwest Arkansas Community
College *A*
Ouachita Baptist University *B, T*
Ozarka College *A*
Southern Arkansas University *B*

University of Arkansas *B, M*
University of Arkansas
Community College at Hope *A*
Cossatot Community College of the
A
Fort Smith *B*
Little Rock *B, M*
Monticello *B*
Pine Bluff *B*
University of Central Arkansas *B*
University of the Ozarks *B*

California

Alliant International University *T*
Azusa Pacific University *B, T*
California Baptist University *M, T*
California Lutheran University *B, M*
California State University
East Bay *T*
Long Beach *T*
Northridge *M*
San Bernardino *M, T*
San Marcos *T*
The Master's College *B, T*
Mills College *T*
Mount St. Mary's College *B*
National University *T*
Occidental College *T*
St. Mary's College of California *T*
San Diego Christian College *B, T*
San Francisco State University *T*
Sonoma State University *M*
University of Redlands *B, T*
University of Southern California *M, T*
Whittier College *T*

Colorado

Adams State College *B, T*
Regis University *B, T*

Connecticut

Albertus Magnus College *B, T*
Eastern Connecticut State
University *B, T*
Quinnipiac University *B, M*
University of New Haven *T*

Delaware

Delaware State University *B*
Delaware Technical and Community
College
Owens *A*
Stanton/Wilmington *A*
Terry *A*
University of Delaware *B, T*

Florida

Chipola College *B*
Florida Institute of Technology *B*
Gulf Coast Community College *A*
Saint Leo University *B*
University of Florida *B*
University of North Florida *B*
University of West Florida *B*

Georgia

Albany State University *B, M*
Armstrong Atlantic State
University *B, M, T*
Augusta State University *B*
Bainbridge College *A*
Berry College *B, M*
Brenau University *B*
Brewton-Parker College *B*
Clayton State University *B*
College of Coastal Georgia *A, B*
Columbus State University *B, M*
Dalton State College *A*
Darton College *A*
Emmanuel College *B*
Fort Valley State University *B, M, T*
Georgia College and State
University *B, M, T*

Georgia Southern University *B*
Georgia Southwestern State
  University *B*
Georgia State University *M, T*
Kennesaw State University *B, M*
Mercer University *B, M, T*
Middle Georgia College *A*
North Georgia College & State
  University *B, M*
Oglethorpe University *M*
Paine College *B*
Piedmont College *B, M, T*
Reinhardt College *B*
Shorter College *B, T*
South Georgia College *A*
Toccoa Falls College *B, T*
University of Georgia *M, D, T*
University of West Georgia *B, M, T*
Valdosta State University *B, M*

Idaho

Boise State University *T*

Illinois

Augustana College *B, T*
City Colleges of Chicago
  Kennedy-King College *A*
Dominican University *T*
Eureka College *B*
Illinois State University *B, T*
Monmouth College *T*
North Park University *B, M, T*
Southwestern Illinois College *A*
Trinity Christian College *T*

Indiana

Ball State University *M*
Butler University *B, M*
Earlham College *M*
Huntington University *M*
Indiana University
  Kokomo *T*
  Northwest *T*
Indiana Wesleyan University *B, T*
Manchester College *B, T*
Trine University *B, T*
University of Evansville *T*
University of Indianapolis *T*
Valparaiso University *B, M, T*

Iowa

Buena Vista University *T*
Central College *T*
Coe College *B*
Cornell College *B, T*
Dordt College *B, T*
Ellsworth Community College *A*
Faith Baptist Bible College and
  Theological Seminary *B, T*
Graceland University *T*
Grinnell College *T*
Iowa Wesleyan College *B*
Mount Mercy College *T*
Northwestern College *T*
Simpson College *T*
University of Northern Iowa *B, M*
Upper Iowa University *B, T*
Waldorf College *B*

Kansas

Baker University *B, T*
Bethel College *T*
Central Christian College of
  Kansas *A, B*
Friends University *B, T*
Garden City Community College *A*
McPherson College *B, T*
MidAmerica Nazarene University *B, T*
Newman University *B, T*
Tabor College *B*
University of Kansas *B, T*

Kentucky

Alice Lloyd College *B*
Asbury College *B, T*
Bellarmine University *B, M, T*
Berea College *B, T*
Brescia University *B, T*
Campbellsville University *B*
Eastern Kentucky University *B, M*
Georgetown College *B, M*
Kentucky Christian University *B, T*
Kentucky Wesleyan College *B, T*
Lindsey Wilson College *B, T*
Midway College *T*
Morehead State University *B, M, T*
Murray State University *B, M, T*
Northern Kentucky University *B, M*
Pikeville College *B, T*
St. Catharine College *B*
Spalding University *B, M, T*
Thomas More College *B, M*
Transylvania University *B, T*
Union College *B, M*
University of Kentucky *B, M*
University of Louisville *M*
University of the Cumberlands *B, M, T*
Western Kentucky University *B, M, T*

Louisiana

Centenary College of Louisiana *B, T*
Grambling State University *B*
Louisiana College *B*
Nicholls State University *B*
Northwestern State University *B, M*
Southeastern Louisiana University *B*
Southern University and Agricultural
  and Mechanical College *B*
University of Louisiana at Lafayette *B*

Maine

University of Maine
  Machias *B*
University of Southern Maine *T*

Maryland

Goucher College *M*
Hood College *T*
Morgan State University *M*
Stevenson University *B*

Massachusetts

American International
  College *B, M, T*
Assumption College *T*
Clark University *M*
Eastern Nazarene College *B, M, T*
Fitchburg State College *B, M, T*
Gordon College *B*
Lesley University *B, M*
Massachusetts College of Liberal
  Arts *T*
Merrimack College *T*
Salem State College *B, M*
Simmons College *B, M*
Tufts University *M, T*
Wellesley College *T*
Westfield State College *M, T*
Worcester State College *M, T*

Michigan

Adrian College *T*
Baker College
  of Auburn Hills *B*
  of Clinton Township *B*
  of Flint *B*
  of Jackson *B*
  of Muskegon *B*
  of Owosso *B*
Baker College of Allen Park *B*
Calvin College *B, T*
Central Michigan University *M*
Eastern Michigan University *M*
Grand Valley State University *T*
Michigan State University *B*

Rochester College *B*
Saginaw Valley State University *M*
University of Detroit Mercy *B, M, T*

Minnesota

Bethel University *B*
College of St. Scholastica *T*
Concordia University: St. Paul *B, T*
Minnesota State University
  Mankato *B*
Ridgewater College *A*
St. Catherine University *B*
University of Minnesota
  Duluth *B, T*
University of St. Thomas *B*
Vermilion Community College *A*
Walden University *M*
Winona State University *B, M, T*

Missouri

Avila University *B, T*
Central Methodist University *B*
College of the Ozarks *T*
Culver-Stockton College *T*
Evangel University *B, T*
Fontbonne University *B, T*
Harris-Stowe State University *B, T*
Lindenwood University *B, M*
Maryville University of Saint
  Louis *B, M, T*
Missouri Baptist University *B, T*
Missouri Southern State
  University *B, T*
Missouri State University *B*
Missouri Valley College *T*
Missouri Western State University *B*
Northwest Missouri State
  University *B, M, T*
Ozark Christian College *A*
Southeast Missouri State
  University *B, T*
Southwest Baptist University *B, T*
Truman State University *M, T*
University of Central Missouri *B, T*
University of Missouri
  Columbia *B, M, D*
  Kansas City *B*
Washington University in St.
  Louis *B, M, T*
Westminster College *B, T*
William Jewell College *T*
William Woods University *B, T*

Montana

Rocky Mountain College *B, T*
University of Great Falls *B, M*

Nebraska

Chadron State College *B*
College of Saint Mary *B, T*
Concordia University *B, T*
Grace University *B*
Nebraska Wesleyan University *B*
Peru State College *B, T*
University of Nebraska
  Kearney *B, M, T*
  Lincoln *B*
Wayne State College *B, T*
York College *B, T*

Nevada

Sierra Nevada College *M*

New Hampshire

Franklin Pierce University *M, T*

New Jersey

Caldwell College *T*
Centenary College *T*
The College of New Jersey *B, M, T*
Rutgers, The State University of New
  Jersey
  Camden Regional Campus *T*

New Brunswick/Piscataway
  Campus *T*
Newark Regional Campus *T*

New Mexico

New Mexico Junior College *A*
Western New Mexico University *B, M*

New York

Alfred University *B, T*
Barnard College *T*
City University of New York
  Brooklyn College *M*
College of Mount St. Vincent *T*
D'Youville College *M*
Dowling College *B, M*
Dutchess Community College *A*
Elmira College *B, T*
Iona College *T*
Le Moyne College *M, T*
Long Island University
  C. W. Post Campus *M, T*
Manhattan College *T*
Manhattanville College *M, T*
Medaille College *B*
Mercy College *M, T*
Mount Saint Mary College *M*
Nassau Community College *A*
Nazareth College *T*
New York Institute of
  Technology *B, T*
St. Joseph's College *B, T*
St. Joseph's College: Suffolk
  Campus *B, T*
State University of New York
  College at Fredonia *T*
  College at Old Westbury *B, M, T*
  New Paltz *B, M, T*
Ulster County Community College *A*
University of Rochester *M*
Vassar College *T*
Wagner College *B, M, T*

North Carolina

Appalachian State University *B, M, T*
Barton College *B*
Bennett College for Women *B*
Campbell University *B, M, T*
Catawba College *B, M, T*
East Carolina University *B, M*
Elizabeth City State University *B, T*
Elon University *B, T*
Fayetteville State University *B, M*
Gardner-Webb University *B*
Greensboro College *B, T*
High Point University *B, T*
Lenoir-Rhyne University *B, T*
Mars Hill College *B, T*
Meredith College *T*
Methodist University *A, B, T*
North Carolina Central
  University *B, M, T*
North Carolina State
  University *B, M, T*
North Carolina Wesleyan College *B*
University of North Carolina
  Asheville *T*
  Chapel Hill *B*
  Charlotte *B*
  Greensboro *B*
  Pembroke *B, M*
  Wilmington *B, M*
Warren Wilson College *B, T*
Western Carolina University *B, T*
Wingate University *B, T*
Winston-Salem State University *B*

North Dakota

Dickinson State University *B, T*
University of North Dakota *B*

Ohio

Antioch University McGregor *M*

Ashland University *B, T*
Baldwin-Wallace College *B, T*
Bluffton University *B*
Bowling Green State University *B, T*
Capital University *B*
Cedarville University *B*
Central State University *B*
Cincinnati Christian University *B*
Cleveland State University *B*
College of Mount St. Joseph *B, T*
College of Wooster *T*
Defiance College *B, T*
Hiram College *T*
Kent State University *B*
Lourdes College *B*
Malone University *B*
Marietta College *B*
Miami University
   Oxford Campus *B*
Mount Union College *B, T*
Mount Vernon Nazarene
   University *B, T*
Muskingum University *B, M, T*
Notre Dame College *T*
Ohio Dominican University *B, T*
Ohio Northern University *B, T*
Ohio State University
   Columbus Campus *M*
Ohio University *M, D, T*
Ohio University
   Southern Campus at Ironton *M*
   Zanesville Campus *B*
Ohio Wesleyan University *B*
Otterbein College *B*
University of Akron *B*
University of Cincinnati
   Clermont College *A*
   Raymond Walters College *A*
University of Dayton *B, M, T*
University of Findlay *B, M, T*
University of Rio Grande *B, T*
Urbana University *B*
Ursuline College *B, M, T*
Walsh University *B*
Wilmington College *B*
Wright State University *M*
Xavier University *B, M*
Youngstown State University *B, M*

Oklahoma
Northwestern Oklahoma State
   University *T*
Oklahoma Christian University *B, T*
Southeastern Oklahoma State
   University *T*
Southwestern Oklahoma State
   University *M, T*

Oregon
Concordia University *B, M, T*
Corban College *B*
Eastern Oregon University *B, M*
Lewis & Clark College *M*
Linfield College *T*
Portland State University *T*
University of Oregon *M, T*
Warner Pacific College *T*
Western Oregon University *B, M, T*
Willamette University *M*

Pennsylvania
Bloomsburg University of
   Pennsylvania *B, T*
Carlow University *B*
DeSales University *T*
Elizabethtown College *B*
Gettysburg College *T*
La Salle University *B, T*
Mansfield University of
   Pennsylvania *B, T*
Northampton Community College *A*
Reading Area Community College *A*
St. Vincent College *T*

Shippensburg University of
   Pennsylvania *B, T*
West Chester University of
   Pennsylvania *B*
Westminster College *B, T*

South Carolina
Bob Jones University *B*
Claflin University *B*
Clemson University *B, M*
Coastal Carolina University *B, T*
College of Charleston *B, T*
Columbia College *B, T*
Presbyterian College *B, T*
South Carolina State University *B, T*
University of South Carolina *M*
University of South Carolina
   Aiken *B, T*
   Upstate *M*
Winthrop University *B, M*

South Dakota
Black Hills State University *B*
Mount Marty College *B*

Tennessee
Belmont University *B, M, T*
Carson-Newman College *B, M*
Crichton College *B, T*
Cumberland University *B, T*
Freed-Hardeman University *B, T*
King College *T*
Lambuth University *B, T*
Lincoln Memorial University *B, T*
Martin Methodist College *B*
Milligan College *M, T*
Tennessee Technological University *T*
Tusculum College *B, T*
Union University *B, T*
University of Tennessee
   Chattanooga *B*
   Knoxville *B*

Texas
Abilene Christian University *B, T*
Arlington Baptist College *B, T*
Austin College *M*
Austin Community College *A*
Dallas Christian College *T*
Del Mar College *A*
Houston Baptist University *B, M*
Howard Payne University *T*
Jarvis Christian College *B, T*
LeTourneau University *B, T*
Lone Star College System *A*
Lubbock Christian University *B*
McMurry University *B, T*
Mountain View College *A*
Our Lady of the Lake University of San
   Antonio *M*
St. Edward's University *T*
Schreiner University *B*
South Texas College *A*
Tarrant County College *A*
Texas A&M University
   Commerce *B*
   Kingsville *M*
Texas Christian University *B, M*
Texas College *B, T*
Texas Lutheran University *B, T*
Trinity Valley Community College *A*
University of Dallas *T*
Wayland Baptist University *B, T*
West Texas A&M University *T*

Vermont
Bennington College *B, M*
Castleton State College *B, M, T*
Champlain College *B*
Goddard College *B, M*
Green Mountain College *B, T*
Johnson State College *B, M*
St. Michael's College *T*

University of Vermont *B, T*

Virginia
Bluefield College *B, T*
Hollins University *T*
Longwood University *B, T*
Mary Baldwin College *T*
Radford University *T*
University of Richmond *T*
Virginia Wesleyan College *T*

Washington
City University of Seattle *B, M, T*
Northwest University *B*
University of Puget Sound *T*
University of Washington *M, T*
Whitworth University *B, M, T*

West Virginia
Fairmont State University *B, M*
Salem International University *T*
West Virginia State University *B*

Wisconsin
Alverno College *B, M, T*
Beloit College *T*
Carroll University *B, T*
Concordia University Wisconsin *B, T*
Lakeland College *B*
Marquette University *B*
Ripon College *T*
St. Norbert College *T*
Silver Lake College *T*
University of Wisconsin
   Green Bay *T*
   Parkside *T*
   Platteville *T*
   River Falls *T*
   Superior *M, T*

Military technologies

Arizona
Cochise College *A*

Arkansas
Pulaski Technical College *A*

Florida
Florida State College at Jacksonville *A*

Kansas
Barton County Community College *A*
Seward County Community College *A*

Missouri
University of Missouri
   Columbia *B*

Nevada
Truckee Meadows Community
   College *A*

New Jersey
Fairleigh Dickinson University
   College at Florham *M*
   Metropolitan Campus *M*
Thomas Edison State College *A*

New York
United States Military Academy *B*

Ohio
Owens Community College
   Toledo *A*
Wright State University *B*

Utah
Weber State University *B*

Washington
Eastern Washington University *B*

West Virginia
American Public University
   System *B, M*

Mining and mineral
engineering

Alaska
University of Alaska
   Fairbanks *B, M*

Arizona
University of Arizona *B, M, D*

Colorado
Colorado School of Mines *B, M, D*

Idaho
University of Idaho *B, M, D*

Illinois
Southern Illinois University
   Carbondale *B, M*

Kentucky
University of Kentucky *B, M, D*

Michigan
Michigan Technological
   University *M, D, T*

Missouri
University of Missouri
   Missouri University of Science and
     Technology *B, M, D*

Montana
Montana Tech of the University of
   Montana *B, M*

Nevada
University of Nevada
   Reno *B, M*

New Mexico
New Mexico Institute of Mining and
   Technology *B, M*

New York
Columbia University *B, M, D*

Oregon
Oregon State University *B*

Pennsylvania
Penn State
   Abington *B*
   Altoona *B*
   Beaver *B*
   Berks *B*
   Brandywine *B*
   DuBois *B*
   Erie, The Behrend College *B*
   Fayette, The Eberly Campus *B*
   Greater Allegheny *B*
   Hazleton *B*
   Lehigh Valley *B*
   Mont Alto *B*
   New Kensington *B*
   Schuylkill *B*
   Shenango *B*
   University Park *B*
   Wilkes-Barre *B*
   Worthington Scranton *B*
   York *B*

South Dakota
South Dakota School of Mines and
Technology *B*

Utah
University of Utah *B, M, D*

Virginia
Virginia Polytechnic Institute and
State University *B, M, D*

West Virginia
West Virginia University *B, M, D*

Mining technology

Alaska
University of Alaska
Fairbanks *C*

Arizona
Eastern Arizona College *A*

Colorado
Colorado Northwestern Community
College *C*

Illinois
Illinois Eastern Community Colleges
Wabash Valley College *C*

Indiana
Vincennes University *A*

Kentucky
Madisonville Community College *C*

Pennsylvania
Penn State
Fayette, The Eberly Campus *A*

Virginia
Southwest Virginia Community
College *A*

West Virginia
Bluefield State College *B*
Mountain State University *A*

Wyoming
Casper College *C, A*
Western Wyoming Community
College *C, A*

Missionary studies

Alabama
Faulkner University *B, M*

Arizona
International Baptist College *B*
Southwestern College *C, A, B*

Arkansas
Ecclesia College *B*
Harding University *B, M*
John Brown University *B*
Ouachita Baptist University *B*
Williams Baptist College *B*

California
Bethany University *B*
Bethesda Christian University *B*
Biola University *D*
California Baptist University *B*
Hope International University *A, B, M*
Salvation Army College for Officer
Training at Crestmont *C, A*
San Diego Christian College *B*

Simpson University *B*
Vanguard University of Southern
California *B*
William Jessup University *C, B*

Florida
Florida Christian College *B*
Hobe Sound Bible College *C, A, B*
Southeastern University *B*
Trinity Baptist College *B*
Trinity College of Florida *B*

Georgia
Toccoa Falls College *B*

Idaho
Boise Bible College *A, B*
Northwest Nazarene University *B*

Illinois
Lincoln Christian University *B, M*
Moody Bible Institute *B, M*
Trinity International University *M*
Wheaton College *M*

Indiana
Grace College *B, M, D*
Huntington University *B*
Taylor University *C*

Iowa
Dordt College *B*
Emmaus Bible College *B*
Faith Baptist Bible College and
Theological Seminary *A, B*

Kansas
Barclay College *B*
Central Christian College of
Kansas *A, B*
MidAmerica Nazarene University *B*

Kentucky
Asbury College *B*
Kentucky Mountain Bible College *B*
Mid-Continent University *B*

Maryland
Washington Bible College *B*

Michigan
Andrews University *M, D*
Grace Bible College *B*
Kuyper College *B*
Spring Arbor University *B*

Minnesota
Bethel University *M*
Concordia University: St. Paul *B, M*
Crossroads College *B*
Crown College *B, M*
North Central University *A, B*
Northwestern College *B*
Oak Hills Christian College *B*

Mississippi
Wesley College *B*

Missouri
Baptist Bible College *B, M*
Calvary Bible College and Theological
Seminary *B*
Central Bible College *A, B*
Evangel University *B*
Global University *B*
Ozark Christian College *A, B*
St. Louis Christian College *A, B*
Southwest Baptist University *B*

Nebraska
Grace University *B*

Nebraska Christian College *A, B*

North Carolina
Gardner-Webb University *B, M*
Mid-Atlantic Christian University *B*
Montreat College *B*
Pfeiffer University *B*
Piedmont Baptist College *B*

North Dakota
Trinity Bible College *B*

Ohio
Ashland University *B*
Cedarville University *B*
Cincinnati Christian University *B*
God's Bible School and College *A, B*
Mount Vernon Nazarene University *B*
Ohio Christian University *A, B*

Oklahoma
Oklahoma Baptist University *B*
Oklahoma Christian University *B*
Oklahoma Wesleyan University *C, B*
Oral Roberts University *B, M*
Southern Nazarene University *B*
Southwestern Christian University *B*

Oregon
Corban College *B*
Eugene Bible College *B*
Multnomah University *B*
Northwest Christian University *B*

Pennsylvania
Baptist Bible College of
Pennsylvania *B*
Eastern University *B*
Philadelphia Biblical University *B*
Valley Forge Christian College *B*

Puerto Rico
Universidad Pentecostal Mizpa *A*

South Carolina
Bob Jones University *B*
Columbia International University *M*
North Greenville University *B*

Tennessee
Free Will Baptist Bible College *B*
Freed-Hardeman University *B*
Lee University *B*
Lipscomb University *B*
Southern Adventist University *B*
Tennessee Temple University *B*

Texas
Abilene Christian University *C, B, M*
Arlington Baptist College *B*
Dallas Baptist University *D*
East Texas Baptist University *B*
Hardin-Simmons University *B*
Lubbock Christian University *B*
Southwestern Assemblies of God
University *B, M*

Virginia
Liberty University *B, M*
Regent University *M*

Washington
Northwest University *B*
Trinity Lutheran College *B*

Wisconsin
Concordia University Wisconsin *B*
Maranatha Baptist Bible College *B, M*

Modern Greek

California
Loyola Marymount University *B*

District of Columbia
Howard University *B*

Indiana
Butler University *B*

Kansas
Central Christian College of Kansas *A*

Louisiana
Tulane University *B*

Massachusetts
Boston University *B*
Wheaton College *B*

Michigan
Calvin College *B*
University of Michigan *B, D*

Missouri
Saint Louis University *B*

New York
Barnard College *B*
Colgate University *B*
Columbia University *B*
Fordham University *B*

Ohio
Ohio State University
Columbus Campus *B, M, D*
Wright State University *B*

Tennessee
Rhodes College *B*
University of the South *B*

Molecular biochemistry

Alabama
University of Alabama
Birmingham *D*

California
Mills College *B*
University of California
Davis *B, M, D*
Los Angeles *M, D*
Santa Cruz *B*

Connecticut
Wesleyan University *B, D*

Illinois
Southern Illinois University
Carbondale *M, D*

Iowa
Cornell College *B*

Maine
Colby College *B*

New York
Clarkson University *B*
Polytechnic Institute of New York
University *B*

Tennessee
Belmont University *B*

Texas

University of Texas
 Medical Branch at Galveston *D*

Virginia

University of Richmond *B*

Wisconsin

Marquette University *M, D*
University of Wisconsin
 Madison *D*

Molecular biology

Alabama

Auburn University *B*

Alaska

University of Alaska
 Fairbanks *M, D*

Arizona

Arizona State University *B*
Northern Arizona University *B*

California

California Baptist University *B*
California Institute of Technology *D*
California Lutheran University *B*
California State University
 Fresno *B*
 Long Beach *B*
 Northridge *B*
 Sacramento *B, M*
Claremont McKenna College *B*
Los Angeles Southwest College *A*
Pomona College *B*
San Diego State University *M*
San Jose State University *B*
Scripps College *B*
Stanford University *M, D*
University of California
 Irvine *M, D*
 Los Angeles *D*
 Riverside *M, D*
 San Diego *B*
 Santa Barbara *B, M, D*
University of Southern
 California *M, D*

Colorado

University of Denver *B*

Connecticut

Central Connecticut State
 University *B, M*
Connecticut College *B*
Quinnipiac University *B, M*
University of Connecticut *M, D*
Wesleyan University *B, D*
Yale University *B, M, D*

District of Columbia

Georgetown University *D*

Florida

Florida Institute of Technology *B*
Stetson University *B*

Georgia

Medical College of Georgia *M, D*

Idaho

University of Idaho *B, M, D*

Illinois

Benedictine University *B*
Chicago State University *B*
Loyola University Chicago *M, D*
Millikin University *B*
University of Chicago *D*

Indiana

Goshen College *B*
Indiana University
 Bloomington *D*
Purdue University *B, M, D*

Iowa

Coe College *B*
Cornell College *B*
Iowa State University *M, D*
University of Iowa *D*

Kansas

Baker University *B*
University of Kansas *B*
University of Kansas Medical
 Center *M*

Kentucky

Centre College *B*

Louisiana

Tulane University *B, M, D*

Maine

Colby College *B*
University of Maine *B, M, D*
University of Southern Maine *D*

Maryland

Johns Hopkins University *B, M, D*
University of Maryland
 Baltimore County *M*
 College Park *D*

Massachusetts

Boston University *B, M, D*
Brandeis University *M, D*
Clark University *B*
Tufts University *M, D*
Western New England College *B*

Michigan

Andrews University *B*
Eastern Michigan University *M*
Lawrence Technological University *B*
Michigan State University *B, M, D*
University of Michigan *M, D*
University of Michigan
 Flint *B*
Wayne State University *M, D*

Minnesota

University of Minnesota
 Duluth *B, M*
 Twin Cities *D*
Winona State University *B*

Mississippi

Mississippi State University *D*

Missouri

Saint Louis University *M, D*
Washington University in St. Louis *D*
William Jewell College *B*

Montana

Montana State University
 Bozeman *M, D*

New Hampshire

Dartmouth College *B*

New Jersey

Montclair State University *B*
Princeton University *B, M, D*
Rutgers, The State University of New
 Jersey
 New Brunswick/Piscataway
 Campus *B*
Seton Hall University *D*

New Mexico

New Mexico State University *M, D*

New York

Colgate University *B*
Cornell University *M, D*
Hamilton College *B*
Long Island University
 Brooklyn Campus *B*
State University of New York
 Albany *B, M, D*
 Stony Brook *D*
 Upstate Medical University *D*
Wells College *B*
Yeshiva University *M, D*

North Carolina

East Carolina University *M*
Meredith College *B*
Wake Forest University *M, D*
Winston-Salem State University *B*

Ohio

Case Western Reserve University *D*
College of Wooster *B*
Kenyon College *B*
Muskingum University *B*
Ohio Northern University *B*
Ohio State University
 Columbus Campus *M, D*
Otterbein College *B*
University of Cincinnati *M, D*
University of Toledo *M, D*
Wittenberg University *B*

Oklahoma

University of Tulsa *D*

Oregon

Oregon State University *D*
Reed College *B*

Pennsylvania

Chestnut Hill College *B*
Clarion University of Pennsylvania *B*
Gettysburg College *B*
Grove City College *B*
Juniata College *B*
Lehigh University *B, M, D*
Lycoming College *B*
Mansfield University of
 Pennsylvania *B*
Temple University *D*
University of Pittsburgh *B*
University of Scranton *B*
Westminster College *B*

Puerto Rico

Universidad Metropolitana *B*

Rhode Island

Brown University *B, M, D*
University of Rhode Island *M, D*

Tennessee

Belmont University *B*
Vanderbilt University *B, M, D*

Texas

Houston Baptist University *B*
Texas Lutheran University *B*
Texas Tech University Health Sciences
 Center *M, D*
Texas Woman's University *D*
University of North Texas *M, D*
University of Texas
 Dallas *B*
 Health Science Center at
 Houston *M, D*
Wayland Baptist University *B*

Utah

Brigham Young University *B, M, D*

Vermont

Johnson State College *B*
Marlboro College *B*
Middlebury College *B*
University of Vermont *B, M, D*

Virginia

Hampton University *B*

Washington

University of Washington *M, D*

Wisconsin

Alverno College *B*
Beloit College *B*
Marquette University *B, M, D*
University of Wisconsin
 Eau Claire *B*
 Madison *B, M, D*
 Parkside *B, M*
 Superior *B*

Wyoming

University of Wyoming *B, M, D*

Molecular biophysics

Florida

Florida State University *D*

Missouri

Washington University in St. Louis *D*

Pennsylvania

University of Pittsburgh *M, D*

Wisconsin

Marquette University *M, D*

Molecular genetics

California

University of California
 Los Angeles *B, M, D*

Georgia

Emory University *D*

Illinois

University of Chicago *D*
University of Illinois
 Chicago *D*

Indiana

Indiana University-Purdue University
 Indianapolis *M, D*

Michigan

Michigan State University *B*
Michigan Technological
 University *M, D*

Missouri

Washington University in St. Louis *D*

New York

State University of New York
 College at Fredonia *B*
University of Rochester *B*

North Carolina

Wake Forest University *D*

Ohio

Ohio State University
 Columbus Campus *B, M, D*

Oregon
Oregon Health & Science
University *D*

Texas
Texas A&M University *B, M, D*
University of Texas
Health Science Center at
Houston *M, D*

Utah
University of Utah *M, D*

Washington
Washington State University *B*

Molecular pharmacology

California
University of California
Los Angeles *M, D*

New York
State University of New York
Stony Brook *D*

Pennsylvania
University of Pittsburgh *M, D*

Molecular physiology

Alabama
University of Alabama
Birmingham *D*

California
University of California
Los Angeles *D*

Illinois
Southern Illinois University
Carbondale *M, D*

Maryland
University of Maryland
Baltimore *M, D*

Tennessee
Vanderbilt University *D*

Molecular toxicology

California
University of California
Los Angeles *D*

Michigan
Wayne State University *M, D*

Pennsylvania
Penn State
University Park *M, D*

Montessori teacher education

California
St. Mary's College of California *M*

Florida
Barry University *M*

Maryland
Loyola University Maryland *M*

Massachusetts
Endicott College *M*

Ohio
Xavier University *B, M*

Oklahoma
Oklahoma City University *B*

Pennsylvania
Chestnut Hill College *T*
Lehigh Carbon Community College *A*

South Carolina
Lander University *B, M*

Mortuary science/embalming

Georgia
Gupton Jones College of Funeral
Service *A*

Iowa
Marshalltown Community College *A*

Michigan
Wayne County Community College *A*

New York
Nassau Community College *A*

Puerto Rico
Ponce Paramedical College *C*

Motorcycle maintenance

California
WyoTech: Fremont *C*

Georgia
North Georgia Technical College *C*

Iowa
Iowa Lakes Community College *C*

Kansas
Pittsburg State University *B*

Minnesota
Hennepin Technical College *C, A*

Missouri
Linn State Technical College *A*

North Carolina
Davidson County Community
College *C*

Texas
Austin Community College *C*
Cedar Valley College *C*

Virginia
Southside Virginia Community
College *C*

Movement therapy

California
California Institute of Integral
Studies *M*
Ohlone College *C*

Illinois
Columbia College Chicago *M*

Massachusetts
Eastern Nazarene College *B*

Missouri
Washington University in St. Louis *D*

New York
City University of New York
York College *B*

North Carolina
University of North Carolina
Chapel Hill *M, D*

Pennsylvania
Keystone Technical Institute *C, A*

Texas
Texas Christian University *B*

Vermont
Goddard College *B, M*

Multicultural education

Alaska
University of Alaska
Fairbanks *M*

California
California Baptist University *M*

Colorado
Fort Lewis College *B*

District of Columbia
American University *M*

Illinois
Trinity International University *D*

New York
College of New Rochelle *M, T*
Iona College *M*
State University of New York
New Paltz *M, T*

Ohio
Bowling Green State University *M*
University of Findlay *B*

Oklahoma
Langston University *M*
University of Central Oklahoma *M*

South Dakota
Augustana College *B, M*

Texas
University of Houston
Clear Lake *M*

Washington
University of Washington *M, D*

Multimedia

Arizona
Arizona Western College *C, A*

California
Academy of Art University *C, A, B, M*
Antelope Valley College *C, A*
Art Institute
of California: San Diego *B*
Art Institute of California: Inland
Empire *B*
Art Institute of California:
Sacramento *A, B*
Canada College *C, A*
Chaffey College *A*
College of the Canyons *A*

College of the Sequoias *A*
Fashion Institute of Design and
Merchandising
Los Angeles *A*
San Francisco *A*
Long Beach City College *A*
Mills College *B*
Mt. Sierra College *B*
National University *B, M*
Ohlone College *C, A*
Otis College of Art and Design *B*
Pepperdine University *B*
Platt College
Ontario *C*
San Francisco Art Institute *B, M*
Santa Barbara City College *A*

Colorado
Art Institute
of Colorado *C, A, B*

Connecticut
Naugatuck Valley Community
College *A*

District of Columbia
American University *B*

Florida
International Academy of Design and
Technology: Tampa *M*
University of Central Florida *B, M*

Georgia
Art Institute
of Atlanta *A, B*
Augusta State University *B*

Illinois
Columbia College Chicago *C, B*
Illinois Institute of Art:
Schaumburg *C, B*
School of the Art Institute of
Chicago *B, M*

Iowa
St. Ambrose University *B*
University of Iowa *M*

Louisiana
Tulane University *C, B*

Maryland
Maryland Institute College of Art *B*

Massachusetts
Massachusetts College of Art and
Design *B, M*
New England Institute of Art *B*
Northeastern University *B*
School of the Museum of Fine
Arts *B, M*
University of Massachusetts
Dartmouth *B, M*

Michigan
Andrews University *B*
Bay de Noc Community College *C*
College for Creative Studies *B*
Kendall College of Art and Design of
Ferris State University *B*
Oakland University *B*
University of Michigan *M*

Minnesota
Art Institutes International
Minnesota *A, B*

Missouri
Lindenwood University *B*
Missouri State University *B*

Nevada

Art Institute
of Las Vegas *B*

New Jersey

The College of New Jersey *B*
Ramapo College of New Jersey *B*

New Mexico

College of Santa Fe *B*

New York

Art Institute
of New York City *A*
Bard College *B*
City University of New York
Borough of Manhattan Community
College *A*
Long Island University
C. W. Post Campus *B, M*
Medaille College *C*
Pratt Institute *A*
Rochester Institute of Technology *B*
State University of New York
College at Oneonta *B*
New Paltz *M*

Ohio

Art Institute of Ohio: Cincinnati *A*
University of Rio Grande *B*

Oregon

Art Institute of Portland *A, B*
Pacific Northwest College of Art *B*
Pacific University *B*
University of Oregon *B, M*

Pennsylvania

California University of
Pennsylvania *M*
Indiana University of
Pennsylvania *B, M*
University of the Arts *B*

Puerto Rico

University of Puerto Rico
Rio Piedras *B*

Rhode Island

Rhode Island College *M*
Rhode Island School of Design *M*

South Carolina

Benedict College *B*

Tennessee

Memphis College of Art *B, M*

Texas

Westwood College: Houston South *A*

Vermont

Bennington College *B*
Champlain College *B*

Virginia

Tidewater Community College *A*

Washington

Art Institute of Seattle *A*
DigiPen Institute of Technology *B*
Evergreen State College *B*
Highline Community College *A*
Western Washington University *B*

Wisconsin

University of Wisconsin
Milwaukee *B*

Museum studies

California

California State University
Chico *M*
San Bernardino *B*
John F. Kennedy University *M*
San Francisco Art Institute *M*
San Francisco State University *M*

Colorado

University of Colorado
Boulder *M*

District of Columbia

George Washington University *M*
Georgetown University *M*

Idaho

University of Idaho *B*

Illinois

Western Illinois University *M*

Kansas

University of Kansas *M*

Massachusetts

Regis College *B*

Nebraska

University of Nebraska
Lincoln *M*

New Jersey

Seton Hall University *M*

New Mexico

Institute of American Indian Arts *A, B*

New York

City University of New York
City College *M*
Fashion Institute of Technology *M*
State University of New York
College at Oneonta *M*
Syracuse University *M*

Pennsylvania

Juniata College *B*
Moore College of Art and Design *B*
University of the Arts *M*

Tennessee

Tusculum College *B*

Texas

Baylor University *B, M*
Texas Tech University *M*

Utah

College of Eastern Utah *T*

Virginia

Randolph College *B*

Washington

University of Washington *M*

Wisconsin

University of Wisconsin
Madison *M, D*

Wyoming

Casper College *A*

Music, general

Arizona

Cochise College *C*
Paradise Valley Community
College *C, A*

California

East Los Angeles College *C*
MTI College *C*
Santa Rosa Junior College *C*

Colorado

Colorado Technical University *A*
Pikes Peak Community College *C, A*

Connecticut

Three Rivers Community College *C*

Delaware

Delaware Technical and Community
College
Owens *A*
Stanton/Wilmington *A*

Florida

Central Florida Community College *C*

Georgia

Albany Technical College *C*
Atlanta Technical College *A*
Central Georgia Technical College *C*
Southwest Georgia Technical
College *C*

Kansas

Cowley County Community
College *C, A*

Maine

University of Maine
Augusta *C*

Michigan

Bay de Noc Community College *C*
Glen Oaks Community College *C*

Minnesota

Minneapolis Community and
Technical College *C*

Missouri

Metropolitan Community College:
Penn Valley *A*

New Jersey

Union County College *A*

New York

Globe Institute of Technology *C*
Westchester Community College *C*

North Carolina

Isothermal Community College *C, A*

Ohio

Hondros College *A*

Pennsylvania

Newport Business Institute: Lower
Burrell *A*

South Carolina

York Technical College *C*

South Dakota

Mitchell Technical Institute *C*

Texas

Northwest Vista College *C*

Washington

Clover Park Technical College *C*
Olympic College *C*

West Virginia

New River Community and Technical
College *C*

Wisconsin

Milwaukee Area Technical College *C*
Western Technical College *A*

Wyoming

Central Wyoming College *A*
Laramie County Community
College *C*

Music history/literature

Alabama

Birmingham-Southern College *B*

Arizona

Northern Arizona University *B*

Arkansas

Ouachita Baptist University *B*

California

California State University
East Bay *M*
Long Beach *B*
Northridge *B, M*
San Bernardino *B*
Foothill College *C*
Mills College *M*
Pepperdine University *B*
University of California
Los Angeles *B*
University of Redlands *B*
University of Southern
California *M, D*
University of the Pacific *B*
Vanguard University of Southern
California *B*
Whittier College *B*

Colorado

University of Colorado
Boulder *D*

Connecticut

University of Hartford *B, M*
Yale University *M, D*

District of Columbia

American University *B*
Catholic University of
America *B, M, D*
Howard University *B*

Florida

Broward College *A*
Florida State University *B*

Idaho

University of Idaho *B*

Illinois

Illinois State University *B, T*
Illinois Valley Community College *A*
Lincoln College *A*
University of Illinois
Urbana-Champaign *B, M*
Wheaton College *B*

Indiana

Butler University *M*
Saint Joseph's College *B*

Iowa

Cornell College *B*
University of Northern Iowa *M*

Kentucky

Bluegrass Community and Technical
   College *A*
University of Kentucky *B, M, D*
University of Louisville *D*

Maryland

Johns Hopkins University: Peabody
   Conservatory of Music *M*

Massachusetts

Bard College at Simon's Rock *B*
Boston University *B, M, D*
Eastern Nazarene College *B*
New England Conservatory of
   Music *B, M*
Simmons College *B*
Tufts University *B, M*
Wellesley College *B*

Michigan

Calvin College *B*
Eastern Michigan University *M*
University of Michigan *B, M, D*
Western Michigan University *M*

Minnesota

Saint Cloud State University *B*

Missouri

St. Charles Community College *A*
University of Missouri
   Kansas City *M*
   St. Louis *B*
Washington University in St.
   Louis *B, M, D*
William Jewell College *B*

New Hampshire

Keene State College *B*

New Jersey

Seton Hall University *B*

New York

Bard College *B*
City University of New York
   Hunter College *M*
   Queensborough Community
      College *A*
Cornell University *M*
Eastman School of Music of the
   University of Rochester *M, D*
Hofstra University *B*
Nazareth College *B*
Skidmore College *B*
State University of New York
   Buffalo *M*
   College at Fredonia *B*
Syracuse University *B*
University of Rochester *M*

North Carolina

Wake Forest University *B*

Ohio

Baldwin-Wallace College *B*
Bowling Green State University *B, M*
Case Western Reserve University *M*
College of Wooster *B*
Kent State University *M, D*
Oberlin College *B, M*

Ohio State University

Columbus Campus *B, M, D*
Ohio University *B, M*
Otterbein College *B*
Owens Community College
   Toledo *A*
University of Akron *B, M*
University of Cincinnati *B, M*
Wright State University *B*
Youngstown State University *B, M*

Oklahoma

Connors State College *A*

Oregon

University of Oregon *M, D*

Pennsylvania

Bucknell University *B*
La Salle University *B*
Lafayette College *B*
Lehigh University *B*
Penn State
   University Park *M*
Temple University *B, M*
West Chester University of
   Pennsylvania *M*

South Carolina

Converse College *B, M*
Furman University *B*
Newberry College *B*
University of South Carolina *M*

South Dakota

University of South Dakota *M*

Texas

Baylor University *B, M*
Hardin-Simmons University *B*
Lon Morris College *A*
Rice University *B, M*
Southern Methodist University *M*
Southwestern University *B*
Texas A&M University
   Commerce *B*
Texas Lutheran University *B*
University of Houston *M*
University of North Texas *B*
University of Texas
   Austin *B*

Utah

Brigham Young University *B*

Vermont

Bennington College *B, M*
Johnson State College *B*
Marlboro College *B*

Virginia

Bridgewater College *B*
Randolph College *B*

Washington

University of Washington *B*
Western Washington University *B*

Wisconsin

University of Wisconsin
   Madison *B, M, D*
   Stevens Point *B*

Music management

Arizona

Chandler-Gilbert Community College
   Pecos *C, A*
Glendale Community College *C, A*

California

Bethesda Christian University *B, M*
California State University
   Sacramento *B, M*
Diablo Valley College *C*
Fresno City College *A*
Los Medanos College *C*
The Master's College *B*
Orange Coast College *C, A*
Sacramento City College *C, A*
University of Southern California *B*
University of the Pacific *B*

Colorado

Western State College of Colorado *B*

Connecticut

University of Hartford *B*
University of New Haven *B*

District of Columbia

Howard University *B*

Florida

Florida Atlantic University *B, M*
Florida Southern College *B*
Jacksonville University *B*

Georgia

Berry College *B*
Georgia State University *B*

Idaho

Boise State University *B*
University of Idaho *B*

Illinois

Bradley University *B*
Columbia College Chicago *B, M*
DePaul University *B*
Elmhurst College *B*
Greenville College *B*
Lewis University *B*

Indiana

Anderson University *B*
Butler University *B*
DePauw University *B*
Grace College *B*
Huntington University *B*
Indiana University-Purdue University
   Indianapolis *M*
Saint Joseph's College *B*
University of Evansville *B*

Iowa

Drake University *B*
University of Iowa *B*
Waldorf College *B*

Kansas

Benedictine College *B*
Central Christian College of Kansas *A*
Labette Community College *A*

Kentucky

Kentucky Christian University *B*
Kentucky Wesleyan College *B*
Murray State University *B*

Louisiana

Dillard University *B*
Loyola University New Orleans *B*

Maine

University of Maine
   Farmington *B*

Massachusetts

Bay State College *A, B*
Berklee College of Music *B*

Eastern Nazarene College *B*

Michigan

Ferris State University *B*
Grand Rapids Community College *A*
University of Michigan *M*

Minnesota

Augsburg College *B*
Minnesota School of Business: St.
   Cloud *A*
Minnesota State University
   Mankato *B, M, T*
   Moorhead *B*
North Central University *B*
Rochester Community and Technical
   College *A*
St. Mary's University of Minnesota *B*
Southwest Minnesota State
   University *B*
Winona State University *B*

Mississippi

Mississippi Valley State University *B*
University of Southern Mississippi *B*

Missouri

Lindenwood University *B*

Nebraska

Northeast Community College *A*

New Jersey

William Paterson University of New
   Jersey *B*

New York

City University of New York
   Baruch College *B*
Hofstra University *B*
Nazareth College *B*
State University of New York
   College at Fredonia *B*
   College at Oneonta *B*
Syracuse University *B*
Villa Maria College of Buffalo *A, B*

North Carolina

Appalachian State University *B*
Elizabeth City State University *B*
Gardner-Webb University *B*
Guilford Technical Community
   College *A*
Montreat College *B*
Winston-Salem State University *B*

Ohio

Capital University *B*
Heidelberg University *B*
Ohio Northern University *B*
Owens Community College
   Toledo *A*
University of Rio Grande *B*

Oklahoma

Northern Oklahoma College *A*
Oklahoma City University *B*
Southwestern Oklahoma State
   University *B*

Oregon

Northwest Christian University *B*
Southern Oregon University *B*

Pennsylvania

Clarion University of Pennsylvania *B*
Geneva College *B*
Grove City College *B*
Harrisburg Area Community
   College *C, A*
Lebanon Valley College *B*

Mansfield University of
    Pennsylvania *B*

Puerto Rico
Inter American University of Puerto
    Rico
    Metropolitan Campus *A*

South Carolina
South Carolina State University *B*

South Dakota
South Dakota State University *B*

Tennessee
Belmont University *B, M*
Bethel University *B*
Lee University *B*
Middle Tennessee State University *B*
Trevecca Nazarene University *B*
Visible School - Music and Worship
    Arts College *C, B*

Texas
Angelina College *A*
Austin Community College *A*
Collin County Community College
    District *A*
Hardin-Simmons University *B*
Houston Community College
    System *C, A*
Lubbock Christian University *B*
University of Texas
    Austin *B*
    El Paso *B*
    San Antonio *B*
University of the Incarnate Word *B*

Vermont
Lyndon State College *B*

Washington
Shoreline Community College *A*
University of Puget Sound *B*

Wisconsin
Marian University *B*

Music pedagogy

Alabama
Miles College *B*
Samford University *B*

California
Holy Names University *B, M, T*

Florida
University of Miami *M*

Illinois
Trinity International University *B*

Indiana
Butler University *B, M*
Indiana University-Purdue University
    Fort Wayne *C*

Kansas
Central Christian College of Kansas *A*

Louisiana
Louisiana College *B*

Maryland
Hood College *C*

Massachusetts
Eastern Nazarene College *B*

New England Conservatory of
    Music *M*

Michigan
Central Michigan University *M*
Eastern Michigan University *M*
Madonna University *C*
Michigan State University *B, M, D*
Oakland University *M*
Spring Arbor University *A*

Minnesota
St. Catherine University *T*
Saint Cloud State University *M*
University of Minnesota
    Duluth *B*

Mississippi
Mississippi College *M*

New Jersey
Rider University *M*

New York
Ithaca College *M*

North Carolina
Meredith College *B*

Ohio
Cedarville University *B*

Oklahoma
University of Oklahoma *B*

Pennsylvania
Carnegie Mellon University *M*
Temple University *B, M*

South Carolina
Converse College *B*

Tennessee
Belmont University *B, M*

Texas
Baylor University *B*
Texas A&M University
    Commerce *B, M*
Texas Christian University *B, M*
Texas Tech University *M*
University of Houston *M*

Virginia
James Madison University *D*

Wisconsin
Maranatha Baptist Bible College *B*
University of Wisconsin
    Parkside *C*
Viterbo University *B*

Music performance

Alabama
Alabama Agricultural and Mechanical
    University *B, M*
Huntingdon College *B*
Miles College *B*
Samford University *B, M*

Alaska
University of Alaska
    Fairbanks *B, M*

Arizona
Arizona State University *B, M*
Northern Arizona University *B*
University of Arizona *B*

Arkansas
Arkansas State University *B, M*
Henderson State University *B*
John Brown University *B*
Ouachita Baptist University *B*
University of Arkansas *B, M*
University of Central Arkansas *B, M*

California
Antelope Valley College *C*
Azusa Pacific University *B*
Bethesda Christian University *B, M*
Biola University *B*
California Baptist University *B*
California Institute of the Arts *C, B, M*
California State University
    East Bay *M*
    Fresno *B*
    Fullerton *B, M*
    Long Beach *B, M*
    Los Angeles *B, M*
    Northridge *B, M*
    Sacramento *B, M*
    San Bernardino *B*
    Stanislaus *B*
Chabot College *A*
Chapman University *B*
College of the Siskiyous *C, A*
Cypress College *C, A*
Foothill College *C*
Fresno Pacific University *B*
Gavilan College *A*
Golden West College *C, A*
Holy Names University *B, M*
La Sierra University *C*
Los Angeles Harbor College *C*
Los Angeles Valley College *C*
Los Medanos College *C, A*
Mills College *M*
Mount St. Mary's College *B*
Notre Dame de Namur
    University *B, M*
Orange Coast College *C*
Pacific Union College *B*
Point Loma Nazarene University *B*
San Diego Christian College *B*
San Diego State University *B, M*
San Francisco Conservatory of
    Music *B, M*
San Francisco State University *B, M*
San Jose State University *B*
Sierra College *A*
University of California
    Irvine *B*
University of Redlands *B*
University of Southern
    California *B, M, D*
University of the Pacific *B*
Vanguard University of Southern
    California *B*

Colorado
Adams State College *B*
Colorado Christian University *B*
Colorado State University *B, M*
Metropolitan State College of
    Denver *B*
University of Colorado
    Boulder *B, M, D*
University of Denver *C, B*

Connecticut
University of Connecticut *D*
University of Hartford *B, M, D*
Yale University *M, D*

Delaware
University of Delaware *B, M*

District of Columbia
American University *B*
Catholic University of
    America *B, M, D*

George Washington University *M*

Florida
Bethune-Cookman University *B*
Florida Agricultural and Mechanical
    University *B*
Florida Gulf Coast University *B*
Florida State University *C, B, M, D*
Hobe Sound Bible College *B*
Jacksonville University *B*
Lynn University *B*
Palm Beach Atlantic University *B*
Seminole Community College *C*
Southeastern University *B*
Stetson University *B*
University of Central Florida *B*
University of Miami *B, M, D*
University of North Florida *B*
University of South Florida *B, M*
University of Tampa *B*
University of West Florida *B*

Georgia
Augusta State University *B*
Brenau University *B*
Brewton-Parker College *B*
Clayton State University *B*
Columbus State University *B, M*
Covenant College *B*
Gainesville State College *A*
Georgia Southern University *B*
Georgia State University *B, M*
Kennesaw State University *B*
Mercer University *B, M*
Toccoa Falls College *B*
University of Georgia *B*
University of West Georgia *B, M*
Valdosta State University *B, M*

Idaho
Boise State University *B, M*
Idaho State University *B*
North Idaho College *A*
Northwest Nazarene University *B*
University of Idaho *B*

Illinois
Augustana College *B*
Bradley University *B*
Columbia College Chicago *B*
Concordia University Chicago *B*
DePaul University *C, B, M*
Eureka College *B, T*
Illinois State University *B*
Illinois Valley Community College *A*
Illinois Wesleyan University *B*
Judson University *B*
Lincoln College *A*
Millikin University *B*
Moody Bible Institute *B*
North Park University *B*
Northern Illinois University *M*
Northwestern University *B, M, D*
Olivet Nazarene University *B*
Roosevelt University *B, M*
Trinity Christian College *B*
Trinity International University *B*
University of Illinois
    Urbana-Champaign *B, M, D*
University of St. Francis *B*
Western Illinois University *B*
Wheaton College *B*

Indiana
Anderson University *B*
Butler University *B, M*
DePauw University *B*
Grace College *B*
Huntington University *B*
Indiana State University *B, M*
Indiana University
    Bloomington *B, M, D*
    South Bend *B, M*

Indiana Wesleyan University *B, T*
Manchester College *B*
Oakland City University *B*
University of Evansville *B*
University of Indianapolis *B*
Valparaiso University *B*
Vincennes University *A*

Iowa

Buena Vista University *B*
Coe College *B*
Cornell College *B*
Drake University *B*
Morningside College *B*
Simpson College *B*
Southwestern Community College *A*
University of Iowa *B*
University of Northern Iowa *B, M*
Waldorf College *B*
Wartburg College *B*

Kansas

Bethany College *B*
Central Christian College of
    Kansas *A, B*
Friends University *B*
Highland Community College *A*
Kansas State University *B*
Kansas Wesleyan University *B*
McPherson College *B*
MidAmerica Nazarene University *B*
Pittsburg State University *B, M*
Seward County Community College *A*
University of Kansas *B, M, D*
Washburn University *B*
Wichita State University *B*

Kentucky

Berea College *B, T*
Bluegrass Community and Technical
    College *A*
Campbellsville University *B*
Kentucky Christian University *B*
Kentucky Wesleyan College *B*
Morehead State University *M*
Northern Kentucky University *C*
Transylvania University *B*
University of Kentucky *B, M*

Louisiana

Centenary College of Louisiana *B, T*
Grambling State University *B*
Louisiana College *B*
Louisiana State University and
    Agricultural and Mechanical
    College *B, M, D*
Louisiana Tech University *B*
Loyola University New Orleans *B, M*
McNeese State University *B*
Northwestern State University *B, M*
Southeastern Louisiana
    University *B, M*
Southern University and Agricultural
    and Mechanical College *B*
Tulane University *B*
University of Louisiana at
    Lafayette *B, M*
University of Louisiana at
    Monroe *B, M*
University of New Orleans *M*
Xavier University of Louisiana *B*

Maine

University of Maine *B, M*
University of Southern Maine *B, M*

Maryland

Hood College *C*
Johns Hopkins University: Peabody
    Conservatory of Music *B, M, D*
Towson University *M*
University of Maryland
    College Park *B*

Massachusetts

Anna Maria College *B*
Bard College at Simon's Rock *B*
Berklee College of Music *B*
Boston Conservatory *B, M*
Boston University *B, M, D*
Eastern Nazarene College *B*
Gordon College *B*
Greenfield Community College *C*
New England Conservatory of
    Music *B, M, D*
Simmons College *B*
University of Massachusetts
    Amherst *B, M, D*
    Lowell *B, M*

Michigan

Albion College *B*
Alma College *B*
Andrews University *B, M*
Aquinas College *A*
Calvin College *B*
Central Michigan University *M*
Cornerstone University *B, T*
Eastern Michigan University *B, M*
Grand Rapids Community College *A*
Hope College *B*
Lake Michigan College *A*
Lansing Community College *A*
Madonna University *B*
Marygrove College *B*
Michigan State University *B, M, D*
Oakland Community College *A*
Oakland University *B, M*
Rochester College *B*
University of Michigan *B, M, D, T*
University of Michigan
    Flint *B*
Western Michigan University *B*

Minnesota

Augsburg College *B*
Bethel University *B*
College of St. Scholastica *B*
Concordia College: Moorhead *B*
Crown College *B*
Gustavus Adolphus College *B*
Hamline University *B*
Minnesota State University
    Mankato *B, M, T*
    Moorhead *B*
North Central University *B*
Northwestern College *B*
St. Catherine University *B*
Saint Cloud State University *B*
St. Mary's University of Minnesota *B*
St. Olaf College *B*
University of Minnesota
    Duluth *B, M*
    Morris *B*
    Twin Cities *B, M, D*
University of St. Thomas *B*
Winona State University *B*

Mississippi

Alcorn State University *B*
Jackson State University *B*
Mississippi College *B, M*
University of Southern Mississippi *D*

Missouri

Avila University *B*
Calvary Bible College and Theological
    Seminary *B*
Central Methodist University *B*
Evangel University *B*
Hannibal-LaGrange College *A, B*
Lindenwood University *B*
Missouri Baptist University *B*
Missouri State University *B*

Truman State University *B*
University of Missouri
    Kansas City *B, M, D*
Webster University *M*
William Jewell College *B*

Montana

Montana State University
    Billings *B*
Rocky Mountain College *B*
University of Montana *B, M*

Nebraska

Creighton University *B*
Grace University *B*
Nebraska Wesleyan University *B*
Northeast Community College *A*
Union College *B*
University of Nebraska
    Kearney *B*
    Omaha *B*

Nevada

University of Nevada
    Reno *B*

New Hampshire

Franklin Pierce University *B*
Keene State College *B*

New Jersey

Middlesex County College *A*
Montclair State University *B*
Rowan University *B, M*
Seton Hall University *B*
William Paterson University of New
    Jersey *B*

New Mexico

College of Santa Fe *B*
New Mexico Highlands University *B*
New Mexico State University *B, M*
University of New Mexico *B, M*

New York

Bard College *B, M*
City University of New York
    Brooklyn College *B, M*
    City College *B, M*
    Hunter College *B, M*
    Lehman College *B*
    Queens College *B, M*
College of Saint Rose *B, M*
Columbia University
    School of General Studies *B*
Dutchess Community College *C*
Eastman School of Music of the
    University of Rochester *B, M, D*
Five Towns College *A, B, M, D*
Hofstra University *B*
Houghton College *B, M*
Ithaca College *B, M, T*
Jewish Theological Seminary of
    America *B*
Juilliard School *B, M, D*
Long Island University
    Brooklyn Campus *B*
    C. W. Post Campus *B, M*
Manhattan School of Music *B, M, D*
Mannes College The New School for
    Music *B, M*
Molloy College *B*
Monroe Community College *A*
Nassau Community College *A*
Nazareth College *B*
New York University *B, M, D*
Nyack College *B*
Onondaga Community College *A*
State University of New York
    Albany *B*
    Binghamton *B, M*
    Buffalo *B, M*
    College at Fredonia *B*

College at Geneseo *B*
College at Potsdam *B, M*
Purchase *B, M*
Stony Brook *M, D*
Syracuse University *B, M*
University of Rochester *B, M*
Villa Maria College of Buffalo *A, B*
Wagner College *B*
Westchester Community College *A*

North Carolina

Appalachian State University *B, M*
Brevard College *B*
Catawba College *B*
Chowan University *B*
Duke University *M*
East Carolina University *B, M*
Elon University *B*
Gardner-Webb University *B*
Greensboro College *C, B, T*
Lenoir-Rhyne University *B*
Mars Hill College *B*
Meredith College *B, M*
Methodist University *B*
Montreat College *B*
Peace College *B*
Queens University of Charlotte *B*
St. Augustine's College *B*
Salem College *B*
Southeastern Community College *A*
University of North Carolina
    Chapel Hill *B*
    Charlotte *B*
    Greensboro *B, M, D*
    Pembroke *B*
    Wilmington *B*
University of North Carolina School of
    the Arts *C, B, M*
Wake Forest University *B*
Western Carolina University *B, M*
Wingate University *B*

North Dakota

Jamestown College *B*
Minot State University *B*
University of Mary *B*
University of North Dakota *B*

Ohio

Ashland University *B*
Baldwin-Wallace College *B*
Bowling Green State University *B, M*
Capital University *B*
Cedarville University *B*
Central State University *B*
Cleveland Institute of Music *B, M, D*
College of Wooster *B*
Heidelberg University *B*
Kent State University *M*
Miami University
    Oxford Campus *B, M*
Mount Union College *B*
Mount Vernon Nazarene University *B*
Ohio Northern University *B*
Ohio State University
    Columbus Campus *B, M, D*
Ohio University *B, M*
Ohio Wesleyan University *B*
Otterbein College *B*
Owens Community College
    Toledo *A*
University of Akron *B, M*
University of Cincinnati *B, M, D*
University of Dayton *B*
University of Toledo *M*
Wright State University *B*
Youngstown State University *B, M*

Oklahoma

Langston University *B*
Mid-America Christian University *B*
Northwestern Oklahoma State
    University *B*

Oklahoma Baptist University *B*
Oklahoma Christian University *B*
Oklahoma City University *B, M*
Oral Roberts University *B*
Southeastern Oklahoma State
University *B*
Southwestern Christian University *B*
Southwestern Oklahoma State
University *B*
University of Central Oklahoma *A, B*
University of Oklahoma *B, M, D*
University of Tulsa *B*

Oregon
Corban College *B*
Lewis & Clark College *B*
Linfield College *B*
Pacific University *B*
Portland Community College *C*
Portland State University *B, M*
University of Oregon *B, M, D*
Willamette University *B*

Pennsylvania
Allegheny College *B*
Bucknell University *B*
Carnegie Mellon University *B, M*
Community College of Philadelphia *A*
Curtis Institute of Music *B*
Duquesne University *B, M*
Geneva College *B*
Gettysburg College *B*
Grove City College *B*
Immaculata University *B*
Indiana University of Pennsylvania *B*
Lebanon Valley College *B*
Mansfield University of
Pennsylvania *B*
Marywood University *B*
Mercyhurst College *B*
Messiah College *M*
Moravian College *B*
Penn State
University Park *B, M*
Philadelphia Biblical University *B*
St. Vincent College *B*
Seton Hill University *B*
Slippery Rock University of
Pennsylvania *B*
Susquehanna University *B*
Temple University *B, M, D*
University of the Arts *C, B, M*
Valley Forge Christian College *B*
West Chester University of
Pennsylvania *B, M*
Westminster College *B*
Wilkes University *B*

Puerto Rico
Conservatory of Music of Puerto
Rico *B*
Inter American University of Puerto
Rico
Metropolitan Campus *A, B, M*
San German Campus *B*

Rhode Island
Rhode Island College *B*
University of Rhode Island *B*

South Carolina
Anderson University *B*
Bob Jones University *B, M*
Charleston Southern University *B*
Coker College *B, T*
Columbia College *B*
Converse College *B, M*
Furman University *B*
Limestone College *B*
Newberry College *B*
North Greenville University *B*
Presbyterian College *B*
South Carolina State University *B*

University of South Carolina *M, D*

South Dakota
University of South Dakota *B, M*

Tennessee
Belmont University *B, M*
Carson-Newman College *B*
Fisk University *B*
Lambuth University *B*
Lee University *B*
Lipscomb University *B*
Maryville College *B, T*
Southern Adventist University *B*
Tennessee Technological University *B*
Union University *B*
Vanderbilt University *B*
Visible School - Music and Worship
Arts College *C, B*

Texas
Alvin Community College *A*
Baylor University *B, M*
Cedar Valley College *C, A*
Del Mar College *A*
Hardin-Simmons University *B, M*
Houston Baptist University *B*
Houston Community College
System *C, A*
Howard Payne University *B*
Lon Morris College *A*
Midland College *A*
Navarro College *A*
Prairie View A&M University *B*
Rice University *B, M, D*
Sam Houston State University *B*
Southern Methodist
University *C, B, M*
Southwestern Assemblies of God
University *B*
Southwestern University *B*
Stephen F. Austin State University *M*
Tarleton State University *B*
Texas A&M University
Commerce *B, M*
Texas Christian University *B, M*
Texas Lutheran University *B*
Texas State University: San Marcos *B*
Texas Tech University *B, M, D*
Trinity University *B*
Tyler Junior College *A*
University of Houston *B, M, D*
University of Mary Hardin-Baylor *B*
University of North Texas *B, M, D*
University of Texas
Arlington *B, M*
Austin *B*
El Paso *B, M*
Pan American *B*
San Antonio *B, M*
Wayland Baptist University *B*
West Texas A&M University *B, M*

Utah
Brigham Young University *B, M*
Southern Utah University *B*
Weber State University *B*

Vermont
Bennington College *B, M*
Johnson State College *B*
Lyndon State College *B*
University of Vermont *B*

Virginia
Bluefield College *B*
Christopher Newport University *B*
Emory & Henry College *B*
George Mason University *B*
Hampton University *B*
James Madison University *B, M, T*
Longwood University *B*
Norfolk State University *M*

Old Dominion University *B*
Randolph College *B*
Shenandoah University *B, M, D*
Virginia Commonwealth
University *B, M*
Virginia State University *B*

Washington
Cornish College of the Arts *B*
Everett Community College *A*
Gonzaga University *B*
Shoreline Community College *A*
University of Puget Sound *B, T*
University of Washington *B, M, D*
Walla Walla University *B*
Washington State University *B, M*
Western Washington University *B*
Whitworth University *B, T*

West Virginia
Alderson-Broaddus College *B*
Glenville State College *B*

Wisconsin
Cardinal Stritch University *B, M, T*
Concordia University Wisconsin *B*
Lawrence University *B, T*
Maranatha Baptist Bible College *B*
Milwaukee Area Technical College *A*
University of Wisconsin
Madison *B, M, D*
Parkside *T*
Stevens Point *B*
Superior *B*
Viterbo University *B*

Wyoming
Casper College *A*
University of Wyoming *B*

Music teacher education

Alabama
Alabama Agricultural and Mechanical
University *B*
Alabama State University *B*
Auburn University *B, M, D, T*
Birmingham-Southern College *B, T*
Huntingdon College *B, T*
Judson College *B*
Oakwood University *B*
Shelton State Community College *A*
Talladega College *B*
University of Alabama *B*
University of Alabama
Birmingham *T*
University of Mobile *B, T*

Alaska
University of Alaska
Fairbanks *B*

Arizona
Arizona State University *B, M*
Cochise College *A*
Northern Arizona University *B, M, T*
Prescott College *B, M, T*
Southwestern College *B*
University of Arizona *B*

Arkansas
Arkansas State University *B, M, T*
Arkansas Tech University *B*
Harding University *B, T*
John Brown University *B, T*
Ouachita Baptist University *B, T*
Southern Arkansas University *B, T*
University of Arkansas
Fort Smith *B*
Monticello *B*
Williams Baptist College *B*

California
Azusa Pacific University *T*
Biola University *B, T*
California Baptist University *T*
California Lutheran University *B, T*
California State University
Chico *B, T*
East Bay *M*
Fresno *B, M*
Fullerton *B, M*
Long Beach *M, T*
Northridge *B, T*
San Bernardino *T*
Chapman University *B*
Fresno Pacific University *B, T*
Holy Names University *M, T*
Hope International University *B*
Humboldt State University *T*
Los Angeles Southwest College *A*
The Master's College *T*
Mount St. Mary's College *T*
Orange Coast College *A*
Pacific Union College *B*
Pepperdine University *B*
Point Loma Nazarene University *B*
Saddleback College *A*
San Diego Christian College *B, T*
San Diego State University *B*
San Francisco State University *T*
Simpson University *B, T*
Sonoma State University *T*
University of Redlands *B, T*
University of Southern California *M*
University of the Pacific *B, T*
Vanguard University of Southern
California *B, T*
Westmont College *T*

Colorado
Adams State College *B, T*
Colorado Christian University *B*
Colorado State University *B, T*
Colorado State University
Pueblo *T*
Metropolitan State College of
Denver *T*
University of Colorado
Boulder *B, M, T*
University of Northern Colorado *B, T*
Western State College of
Colorado *B, T*

Connecticut
Central Connecticut State
University *B, M, T*
Fairfield University *T*
University of Connecticut *B*
University of Hartford *B, M, D*
Western Connecticut State
University *B, M*

Delaware
Delaware State University *B*
University of Delaware *B, T*

District of Columbia
Catholic University of America *B*
George Washington University *M, T*
Howard University *B, M*

Florida
Baptist College of Florida *B*
Bethune-Cookman University *B, T*
Broward College *A*
Clearwater Christian College *B*
Florida Agricultural and Mechanical
University *B, T*
Florida Atlantic University *B*
Florida International University *M*
Florida Southern College *B, T*
Florida State University *B, M, D*
Hobe Sound Bible College *B, T*
Jacksonville University *B, M, T*

Palm Beach Atlantic University *B, T*
Palm Beach Community College *A*
Pensacola Junior College *A*
Southeastern University *B, T*
State College of Florida,
    Manatee-Sarasota *A*
Stetson University *B*
University of Central Florida *B*
University of Florida *B, M*
University of Miami *B, M, D*
University of North Florida *B, M*
University of South Florida *B, M*
University of Tampa *B, T*
Warner University *B*

Georgia

Albany State University *B, M*
Armstrong Atlantic State
    University *B, M, T*
Augusta State University *B*
Berry College *B*
Brenau University *B*
Brewton-Parker College *B*
Columbus State University *B, M*
Darton College *A*
Emmanuel College *B*
Fort Valley State University *B, T*
Gainesville State College *A*
Georgia College and State
    University *B, T*
Georgia Southern University *B*
Georgia State University *M, T*
Kennesaw State University *B*
Mercer University *B*
North Georgia College & State
    University *B, M*
Piedmont College *M, T*
Reinhardt College *B, M*
Shorter College *B, T*
Toccoa Falls College *B, T*
University of Georgia *B, M, D, T*
University of West Georgia *B, M*
Valdosta State University *B, M*
Young Harris College *A*

Idaho

Boise State University *B, M, T*
Brigham Young University-Idaho *T*
Idaho State University *B*
Northwest Nazarene University *B*
University of Idaho *B, T*

Illinois

Augustana College *B, T*
Bradley University *B, M, T*
Chicago State University *B*
College of Lake County *A*
Concordia University Chicago *B, M, T*
DePaul University *B, M, T*
Elmhurst College *B*
Eureka College *T*
Greenville College *B, T*
Illinois College *T*
Illinois Eastern Community Colleges
    Lincoln Trail College *A*
    Olney Central College *A*
Illinois State University *B, M, T*
Illinois Wesleyan University *B*
Judson University *B*
Knox College *T*
MacMurray College *B, T*
McKendree University *B*
Millikin University *B, T*
Monmouth College *T*
North Central College *B, T*
North Park University *T*
Northern Illinois University *M*
Northwestern University *B, M, D*
Olivet Nazarene University *B, T*
Parkland College *A*
Quincy University *B, T*
Roosevelt University *B*
Saint Xavier University *B*
Trinity Christian College *B, T*

Trinity International University *B*
University of Illinois
    Urbana-Champaign *B, M, D, T*
University of St. Francis *B*
VanderCook College of Music *B, M, T*
Waubonsee Community College *A*
Wheaton College *B, T*

Indiana

Anderson University *B, M, T*
Bethel College *B*
Butler University *B, M, T*
DePauw University *B*
Goshen College *B, T*
Grace College *B*
Huntington University *B*
Indiana University
    Bloomington *B, M, D, T*
    South Bend *B, T*
Indiana University-Purdue University
    Fort Wayne *B, T*
Indiana Wesleyan University *B, T*
Manchester College *B, T*
Marian University *B*
Oakland City University *B*
Saint Mary's College *T*
St. Mary-of-the-Woods College *B, T*
Taylor University *B, T*
University of Evansville *B, T*
University of Indianapolis *B, T*
Valparaiso University *B*
Vincennes University *A*

Iowa

Briar Cliff University *B*
Buena Vista University *B, T*
Central College *B, T*
Clarke College *B, T*
Coe College *B*
Cornell College *B, T*
Dordt College *B*
Drake University *B*
Emmaus Bible College *B*
Faith Baptist Bible College and
    Theological Seminary *B, T*
Graceland University *T*
Grand View University *M, T*
Iowa State University *B, T*
Iowa Wesleyan College *B*
Loras College *T*
Morningside College *B*
Mount Mercy College *T*
Northwestern College *T*
St. Ambrose University *B, T*
Simpson College *B, T*
University of Iowa *M, D, T*
University of Northern Iowa *B, M*
Waldorf College *B*
Wartburg College *B, T*

Kansas

Allen County Community College *A*
Baker University *B, T*
Benedictine College *B*
Bethany College *B*
Bethel College *T*
Central Christian College of Kansas *A*
Emporia State University *B, T*
Fort Hays State University *B*
Friends University *B*
Garden City Community College *A*
Kansas State University *B, M, T*
Labette Community College *A*
McPherson College *B, T*
MidAmerica Nazarene University *B, T*
Pittsburg State University *B, M, T*
Southwestern College *B, T*
Sterling College *B*
Tabor College *B*
University of Kansas *B, M, D, T.*
Washburn University *B*
Wichita State University *B, M, T*

Kentucky

Asbury College *B, T*
Berea College *B, T*
Campbellsville University *B, M*
Eastern Kentucky University *B, M*
Georgetown College *B*
Kentucky Christian University *B, T*
Kentucky Wesleyan College *T*
Murray State University *B, M, T*
Transylvania University *B, T*
University of Kentucky *B, M*
University of Louisville *B, M*
University of the Cumberlands *B, M, T*
Western Kentucky University *M, T*

Louisiana

Centenary College of Louisiana *B, T*
Grambling State University *B*
Louisiana College *B*
Louisiana State University and
    Agricultural and Mechanical
    College *B*
Louisiana Tech University *B*
Loyola University New Orleans *B*
McNeese State University *B, T*
Nicholls State University *B*
Northwestern State University *B*
Southeastern Louisiana University *B*
Southern University and Agricultural
    and Mechanical College *B*
University of Louisiana at Lafayette *B*
University of Louisiana at Monroe *B*
University of New Orleans *B*
Xavier University of Louisiana *B*

Maine

University of Maine *B*
University of Maine
    Fort Kent *B*
University of Southern Maine *B, T*

Maryland

College of Notre Dame of Maryland *T*
Frostburg State University *B, T*
Johns Hopkins University: Peabody
    Conservatory of Music *B, M*
Mount St. Mary's University *T*
Salisbury University *T*
Towson University *B, M, T*
University of Maryland
    College Park *B*
    Eastern Shore *B*
Washington Adventist University *B*
Washington Bible College *B, T*

Massachusetts

Anna Maria College *B*
Boston Conservatory *M*
Boston University *B, M, D*
Bridgewater State College *B, M, T*
Eastern Nazarene College *B, M, T*
Gordon College *B, M*
Smith College *M*
Tufts University *M*
University of Massachusetts
    Amherst *M*
    Dartmouth *T*
    Lowell *B, M*
Westfield State College *B, M, T*

Michigan

Adrian College *B, T*
Albion College *B, T*
Alma College *T*
Andrews University *M*
Aquinas College *B, T*
Calvin College *B*
Central Michigan University *B, M*
Cornerstone University *B, T*
Delta College *A*
Eastern Michigan University *B, M*
Grace Bible College *B*
Grand Rapids Community College *A*

Grand Valley State University *B, T*
Hope College *B, T*
Lansing Community College *A*
Michigan State University *B*
Northern Michigan University *B, T*
Oakland University *B, M, D*
Rochester College *B*
University of Michigan *B, M, D, T*
University of Michigan
    Flint *B, T*
Western Michigan University *T*

Minnesota

Augsburg College *B, T*
Bemidji State University *T*
Bethel University *B*
College of St. Benedict *T*
College of St. Scholastica *T*
Concordia College: Moorhead *B, T*
Concordia University: St. Paul *B, T*
Crown College *B, T*
Gustavus Adolphus College *T*
Hamline University *B, M, T*
Minnesota State University
    Mankato *B, M, T*
    Moorhead *B, M*
Northwestern College *B*
Ridgewater College *A*
Rochester Community and Technical
    College *A*
St. Catherine University *B, T*
Saint Cloud State University *B, T*
St. John's University *T*
St. Mary's University of Minnesota *B*
St. Olaf College *B*
Southwest Minnesota State
    University *B*
University of Minnesota
    Duluth *B, T*
    Morris *T*
    Twin Cities *B, M*
University of St. Thomas *B, M*
Winona State University *B, T*

Mississippi

Blue Mountain College *B*
Delta State University *B*
Jackson State University *B, M*
Millsaps College *T*
Mississippi College *B, M*
Mississippi State University *B, M*
Mississippi University for Women *B, T*
Mississippi Valley State University *B, T*
Northwest Mississippi Community
    College *A*
University of Southern
    Mississippi *B, M, D*

Missouri

Baptist Bible College *B*
Calvary Bible College and Theological
    Seminary *B*
Central Methodist University *B*
College of the Ozarks *B, T*
Culver-Stockton College *B, T*
Drury University *B, T*
Evangel University *B, T*
Hannibal-LaGrange College *B*
Lincoln University *B*
Missouri Baptist University *B, T*
Missouri Southern State
    University *B, T*
Missouri State University *B*
Missouri Western State University *B*
Northwest Missouri State
    University *B, M, T*
Southeast Missouri State
    University *B, M, T*
Southwest Baptist University *B, T*
Truman State University *M, T*
University of Central Missouri *B, M, T*
University of Missouri
    Columbia *B, M, D*

Kansas City B, M
St. Louis B, M
Washington University in St. Louis M
Webster University B, M
William Jewell College B, T

Montana
Montana State University
  Billings B, T
  Bozeman B
Rocky Mountain College B, T
University of Montana B, M, T
University of Montana: Western B, T

Nebraska
Chadron State College B
Concordia University B, T
Dana College B
Grace University B
Nebraska Wesleyan University B
Northeast Community College A
Peru State College B, T
Union College T
University of Nebraska
  Kearney B, M, T
  Lincoln B
  Omaha B, M, T
Wayne State College B, T
Western Nebraska Community
  College A
York College B, T

Nevada
University of Nevada
  Reno B, T

New Hampshire
Keene State College B, M, T
Plymouth State University B, M, T

New Jersey
Caldwell College T
The College of New Jersey B, T
Essex County College A
Georgian Court University T
Kean University B, T
New Jersey City University M, T
Rider University B, M
Rowan University B
William Paterson University of New
  Jersey B, T

New Mexico
Eastern New Mexico University B
New Mexico Highlands University B
New Mexico State University B
University of New Mexico B
Western New Mexico University B

New York
City University of New York
  Brooklyn College B, M, T
  City College B, T
  Hunter College B, M, T
  Lehman College M
  Queens College B, M, T
College of Saint Rose B, M, T
Dowling College B
Eastman School of Music of the
  University of
  Rochester B, M, D, T
Five Towns College B, M, D, T
Fordham University T
Hartwick College B, T
Hobart and William Smith Colleges T
Hofstra University B, M, T
Houghton College B, T
Ithaca College B, M, T
Long Island University
  Brooklyn Campus B, T
  C. W. Post Campus B, M, T
Manhattanville College M, T
Molloy College B

Monroe Community College A
Nazareth College B, M, T
New York University B, M, D, T
Nyack College B
Roberts Wesleyan College B, M
State University of New York
  Buffalo M, T
  College at Buffalo B
  College at Fredonia B, M, T
  College at Potsdam B, M
  New Paltz M
Syracuse University B, M, T
University of Rochester M, D
Wagner College T

North Carolina
Appalachian State University B, M, T
Bennett College for Women B
Brevard College B
Campbell University B, T
Catawba College B, T
Chowan University B
East Carolina University B, M
Elizabeth City State University T
Elon University T
Fayetteville State University B, T
Gardner-Webb University B
Greensboro College B, T
Lenoir-Rhyne University B
Livingstone College T
Mars Hill College B
Meredith College B, T
Methodist University A, B, T
North Carolina Agricultural and
  Technical State University B, T
North Carolina Central University B, T
Pfeiffer University B, T
Piedmont Baptist College B
Salem College B
University of North Carolina
  Charlotte B
  Greensboro B, M, D
  Pembroke B, M
  Wilmington B
Western Carolina University B, T
Wingate University B, T
Winston-Salem State University B

North Dakota
Dickinson State University B, T
Jamestown College B
Minot State University B, M
North Dakota State University B, T
University of Mary B
University of North Dakota B, D

Ohio
Ashland University B, T
Baldwin-Wallace College B, T
Bluffton University B
Bowling Green State
  University B, M, T
Capital University B, M
Case Western Reserve
  University B, M, D
Cedarville University B
College of Wooster B
God's Bible School and College B
Heidelberg University B
Hiram College T
Kent State University B, M, D
Malone University B
Miami University
  Oxford Campus B, M
Mount Union College B, T
Mount Vernon Nazarene
  University B, T
Oberlin College B, M
Ohio Christian University B
Ohio Northern University B, T
Ohio State University
  Columbus Campus B
Ohio Wesleyan University B
Otterbein College B

University of Akron B, M
University of Cincinnati B, M, D, T
University of Dayton B, M
University of Rio Grande B, T
University of Toledo B, M, T
Wilberforce University T
Wright State University B, M, T
Xavier University B, M
Youngstown State University B, M

Oklahoma
Cameron University B, T
East Central University B
Eastern Oklahoma State College A
Langston University B
Mid-America Christian University B
Northeastern State University B
Northwestern Oklahoma State
  University B, T
Oklahoma Baptist University B, T
Oklahoma Christian University B, T
Oklahoma City University B
Oklahoma State University B
Oklahoma Wesleyan University B
Oral Roberts University B, T
Southeastern Oklahoma State
  University B, M, T
Southern Nazarene University B
Southwestern Oklahoma State
  University B, M, T
University of Central Oklahoma B, M
University of Oklahoma B, M, D, T
University of Tulsa B, T

Oregon
Corban College B
George Fox University B, M, T
Linfield College B, T
Oregon State University M
Portland State University T
Southern Oregon University T
University of Oregon B, M, D, T
University of Portland B, M, T
Warner Pacific College B, T
Willamette University B, M

Pennsylvania
Baptist Bible College of
  Pennsylvania B
Bucknell University B, T
Chestnut Hill College B, T
Duquesne University B, M, T
Geneva College B, T
Gettysburg College B, T
Grove City College B, T
Immaculata University B
Lebanon Valley College B, M, T
Lincoln University B, T
Lycoming College T
Mansfield University of
  Pennsylvania B, M, T
Marywood University B, M
Mercyhurst College B, T
Messiah College B, T
Moravian College B, T
Penn State
  University Park M, D
Philadelphia Biblical University B, T
Seton Hill University B, T
Susquehanna University B, T
Temple University B, M, D
University of the Arts M
Valley Forge Christian College B
Westminster College T
York College of Pennsylvania B, T

Puerto Rico
Conservatory of Music of Puerto
  Rico B, M, T
Inter American University of Puerto
  Rico
  San German Campus B, M

Pontifical Catholic University of
  Puerto Rico B, T
Universidad Adventista de las
  Antillas B

Rhode Island
Providence College B
Rhode Island College B, M
Salve Regina University B
University of Rhode Island B, T

South Carolina
Anderson University B, T
Bob Jones University B, M
Charleston Southern University B
Claflin University B
Coker College B, T
Columbia College B, T
Converse College T
Furman University B, T
Limestone College B
Newberry College B
North Greenville University B, T
Presbyterian College B, T
South Carolina State University B, T
Southern Wesleyan University B, T
University of South Carolina M, D
University of South Carolina
  Aiken B, T
Winthrop University B, M, T

South Dakota
Augustana College B, T
Black Hills State University B
Dakota Wesleyan University B, T
Mount Marty College B
Northern State University B, T
South Dakota State University B
University of Sioux Falls B
University of South Dakota B, M, T

Tennessee
Belmont University B, M, T
Bethel University B, T
Bryan College T
Carson-Newman College B
Cumberland University B, T
Fisk University B
Free Will Baptist Bible College B
Freed-Hardeman University B, T
King College B
Lambuth University B, T
Lee University B
Lipscomb University B, T
Maryville College B, T
Milligan College B, M, T
Southern Adventist University B
Tennessee Technological
  University B, T
Tennessee Temple University B
Trevecca Nazarene University B, T
Union University B, T
University of Memphis T
University of Tennessee
  Chattanooga B
  Knoxville B, T

Texas
Abilene Christian University B, T
Amarillo College A
Arlington Baptist College B, T
Austin College M
Baylor University B, M, T
Dallas Baptist University B
Dallas Christian College B, T
Del Mar College A
East Texas Baptist University B
Hardin-Simmons University B, M, T
Houston Baptist University B, M, T
Howard Payne University B, T
Lamar University B, M, T
Laredo Community College A
Lubbock Christian University B

North Lake College *A*
Prairie View A&M University *M*
Sam Houston State University *M, T*
Schreiner University *B*
Southern Methodist
   University *B, M, T*
Southwestern Assemblies of God
   University *B*
Southwestern University *B, T*
Stephen F. Austin State University *M*
Tarleton State University *T*
Texas A&M University
   Commerce *M, T*
   Kingsville *B, M, T*
Texas Christian University *B, M*
Texas College *B, T*
Texas Lutheran University *B, T*
Texas State University: San
   Marcos *M, T*
Texas Tech University *M*
Texas Wesleyan University *B, T*
University of Houston *M, D, T*
University of Mary Hardin-Baylor *B, T*
University of North Texas *M, D*
University of St. Thomas *B*
University of Texas
   Arlington *M, T*
   Austin *M, D*
   Brownsville - Texas Southmost
     College *M*
   El Paso *M*
   San Antonio *M, T*
University of the Incarnate Word *B, T*
Wayland Baptist University *B, T*
West Texas A&M University *T*

Utah

Brigham Young University *B, M*
Southern Utah University *B, T*
Utah State University *B*
Utah Valley University *B*
Weber State University *B*

Vermont

Castleton State College *B, T*
Johnson State College *B*
University of Vermont *B, T*

Virginia

Bluefield College *B, T*
Bridgewater College *T*
Eastern Mennonite University *T*
Emory & Henry College *B*
George Mason University *D*
Hampton University *M*
Hollins University *T*
James Madison University *T*
Longwood University *B, T*
Old Dominion University *B, M, T*
Radford University *T*
Shenandoah University *B, M, D*
Virginia Wesleyan College *T*

Washington

Eastern Washington University *B*
Gonzaga University *B, T*
Northwest University *T*
Seattle Pacific University *B, T*
University of Puget Sound *B, T*
University of Washington *B, M, D*
Walla Walla University *B*
Washington State University *B, M, T*
Western Washington University *B*
Whitworth University *B, T*

West Virginia

Alderson-Broaddus College *B*
Concord University *B, T*
Davis and Elkins College *B*
Fairmont State University *B*
Shepherd University *M, T*
West Liberty University *B*
West Virginia State University *B*

West Virginia University *T*
West Virginia Wesleyan College *B*

Wisconsin

Alverno College *B, T*
Carroll University *B, T*
Carthage College *T*
Concordia University Wisconsin *B, T*
Edgewood College *B*
Lakeland College *T*
Lawrence University *B, T*
Maranatha Baptist Bible College *B*
Marian University *B, T*
Mount Mary College *B, T*
St. Norbert College *B*
Silver Lake College *B, M, T*
University of Wisconsin
   Green Bay *T*
   Madison *B, M*
   Milwaukee *B, T*
   Oshkosh *B, T*
   Parkside *T*
   River Falls *B, T*
   Stevens Point *B, M, T*
   Superior *B, T*
   Whitewater *B*
Viterbo University *B, T*

Wyoming

Casper College *A*
Eastern Wyoming College *A*
University of Wyoming *B, M*

Music theory and composition

Alabama

Birmingham-Southern College *B*
Samford University *B*

Alaska

University of Alaska
   Fairbanks *M*

Arizona

Arizona State University *B, M*
Northern Arizona University *M*

Arkansas

Ouachita Baptist University *B*

California

Azusa Pacific University *B, M*
Bethesda Christian University *B, M*
Biola University *B*
California Baptist University *B*
California Institute of the
   Arts *C, B, M, D*
California State University
   Chico *B*
   East Bay *M*
   Long Beach *M*
   Northridge *B, M*
   Sacramento *B*
Chapman University *B*
Foothill College *C*
Fresno Pacific University *B*
Golden West College *C, A*
Los Angeles Harbor College *C*
Mills College *M*
Mount St. Mary's College *B*
Ohlone College *C*
Pepperdine University *B*
Point Loma Nazarene University *B*
San Francisco Conservatory of
   Music *B, M*
Solano Community College *C*
University of California
   Santa Cruz *D*
University of Redlands *B*
University of Southern
   California *B, M, D*

University of the Pacific *B*

Colorado

Adams State College *B*
Colorado State University *B*

Connecticut

University of Hartford *B, M, D*
Western Connecticut State
   University *B*
Yale University *M, D*

Delaware

University of Delaware *B*

District of Columbia

American University *B*
Catholic University of
   America *B, M, D*
Howard University *B*

Florida

Florida Southern College *B*
Florida State University *B, M, D*
Jacksonville University *B*
Palm Beach Atlantic University *B*
State College of Florida,
   Manatee-Sarasota *A*
Stetson University *B*
University of Miami *B, M, D*

Georgia

Clayton State University *B*
Georgia Southern University *B*
University of Georgia *B*
University of West Georgia *B*

Idaho

Boise State University *B*
North Idaho College *A*
Northwest Nazarene University *B*
University of Idaho *B*

Illinois

Bradley University *B*
Concordia University Chicago *B*
DePaul University *B, M*
Illinois Wesleyan University *B*
Lincoln College *A*
Moody Bible Institute *B*
Northwestern University *B, M, D*
Roosevelt University *B, M*
Trinity International University *B*
University of Illinois
   Urbana-Champaign *B, M, D*
Wheaton College *B*

Indiana

Butler University *B, M*
DePauw University *B*
Grace College *B*
Indiana University
   Bloomington *B, M, D*
Indiana Wesleyan University *B*
Valparaiso University *B*

Iowa

Coe College *B*
Cornell College *B*
University of Iowa *B*
University of Northern Iowa *B, M*
Wartburg College *B*

Kansas

Central Christian College of
   Kansas *A, B*
University of Kansas *B, M, D*
Wichita State University *B*

Kentucky

Bluegrass Community and Technical
   College *A*
Campbellsville University *B*

Louisiana

Centenary College of Louisiana *B*
Loyola University New Orleans *B*
Tulane University *B*

Maine

University of Maine *M*

Maryland

Johns Hopkins University: Peabody
   Conservatory of Music *B, M, D*

Massachusetts

Bard College at Simon's Rock *B*
Berklee College of Music *B*
Boston Conservatory *B, M*
Boston University *B, M, D*
Brandeis University *M, D*
Eastern Nazarene College *B*
New England Conservatory of
   Music *B, M, D*
Tufts University *B*

Michigan

Calvin College *B*
Central Michigan University *B, M*
Cornerstone University *B, T*
Hope College *B*
Lansing Community College *A*
Marygrove College *B*
Michigan State University *B, M, D*
Oakland Community College *A*
University of Michigan *B, M, D*
Western Michigan University *B*

Minnesota

Concordia College: Moorhead *B*
Hamline University *B*
Northwestern College *B*
Rochester Community and Technical
   College *C, A*
St. Olaf College *B*

Mississippi

Mississippi College *B, M*

Missouri

Drury University *B*
Lindenwood University *B*
University of Missouri
   Kansas City *B, M, D*
Washington University in St. Louis *B*
Webster University *M*
William Jewell College *B*

Montana

University of Montana *B, M*

Nebraska

Grace University *B*
University of Nebraska
   Omaha *B*

New Hampshire

Keene State College *B*

New Jersey

Rider University *B, M*
Rowan University *B*

New Mexico

College of Santa Fe *B*

New York

Bard College *B, M*

City University of New York
Brooklyn College B, M
City College B, M
Hunter College B, M
Cornell University M, D
Eastman School of Music of the
University of Rochester B, M, D
Five Towns College A, B, M, D
Hofstra University B
Houghton College B, M
Ithaca College B, M
Jewish Theological Seminary of
America B
Juilliard School B, M, D
Manhattan School of Music B, M, D
Mannes College The New School for
Music B, M
Nazareth College B
Nyack College B
State University of New York
Albany B
Buffalo M, D
College at Fredonia B
College at Potsdam D
Purchase B, M
Syracuse University B, M
University of Rochester B, M, D

North Carolina
Duke University M
East Carolina University B, M
Gardner-Webb University B
University of North Carolina
Greensboro B, M
University of North Carolina School of
the Arts C, M

Ohio
Ashland University B
Baldwin-Wallace College B
Bowling Green State University B, M
Capital University B
Cedarville University B
Cleveland Institute of Music B, M, D
College of Wooster B
Heidelberg University B
Kent State University M, D
Oberlin College B
Ohio Northern University B
Ohio State University
Columbus Campus B, M, D
Ohio University B, M
Otterbein College B
University of Akron B, M
University of Cincinnati B, M, D
University of Dayton B
Wright State University B
Youngstown State University B, M

Oklahoma
Oklahoma Baptist University B
Oklahoma City University B, M
Oral Roberts University B
Southwestern Oklahoma State
University B
University of Tulsa B

Oregon
Linfield College B
University of Oregon B, M, D
Willamette University B

Pennsylvania
Bucknell University B
Carnegie Mellon University B, M
Curtis Institute of Music B
Duquesne University M
Gettysburg College B
Moravian College B
Penn State
University Park M
Philadelphia Biblical University B
Temple University B, M, D

University of the Arts C, B
Westminster College B

Rhode Island
University of Rhode Island B

South Carolina
Coker College B, T
Converse College B, M
Furman University B
Newberry College B
University of South Carolina M, D

Tennessee
Belmont University B, M
Carson-Newman College B
Lipscomb University B
Southern Adventist University B
Union University B
University of Tennessee
Knoxville B
Vanderbilt University D

Texas
Baylor University B, M
Dallas Baptist University B
Del Mar College A
Hardin-Simmons University B, M
Houston Baptist University B
Houston Community College
System C, A
Lon Morris College A
Rice University B, M, D
Southern Methodist University B, M
Southwestern University B
Texas A&M University
Commerce B, M
Texas Christian University B, M
Texas Tech University B, M, D
Trinity University B
University of Houston B, M, D
University of Mary Hardin-Baylor B
University of North Texas B, M, D
University of Texas
Austin B
El Paso B
San Antonio B
West Texas A&M University B

Utah
Brigham Young University B, M

Vermont
Bennington College B, M
Johnson State College B

Virginia
Randolph College B
Shenandoah University B, M
Virginia Union University B

Washington
Centralia College A
Cornish College of the Arts B
University of Washington B, M
Washington State University B, M
Western Washington University B

Wisconsin
Lawrence University B, T
University of Wisconsin
Madison B, M
Whitewater B, T

Music therapy

Arizona
Arizona State University B, M

California
California State University
Northridge M
University of the Pacific B, M

Colorado
Colorado State University B, M

District of Columbia
Howard University B

Florida
Florida State University B, M
University of Miami B, M

Georgia
Georgia College and State
University B, M
University of Georgia B

Indiana
Indiana University-Purdue University
Fort Wayne B
St. Mary-of-the-Woods College B, M
University of Evansville B

Iowa
University of Iowa B
Wartburg College B

Kansas
Central Christian College of Kansas A
University of Kansas B, M

Kentucky
University of Louisville B

Louisiana
Loyola University New Orleans B, M

Maryland
Howard Community College A

Massachusetts
Anna Maria College B
Berklee College of Music B
Lesley University M, D

Michigan
Eastern Michigan University B
Western Michigan University B

Minnesota
Augsburg College B
University of Minnesota
Twin Cities B

Mississippi
Mississippi University for Women B

Missouri
Drury University B
Maryville University of Saint
Louis B, M
University of Missouri
Kansas City B

New Jersey
Montclair State University B

New York
Molloy College B, M
Nazareth College B, M
State University of New York
College at Fredonia B
New Paltz M

North Carolina
Appalachian State University B, M
East Carolina University B, M

Queens University of Charlotte B

North Dakota
University of North Dakota B

Ohio
Baldwin-Wallace College B
Cleveland State University B
College of Wooster B
Ohio University M
University of Dayton B

Oklahoma
Southwestern Oklahoma State
University B

Pennsylvania
Duquesne University B
Elizabethtown College B
Immaculata University B, M
Mansfield University of
Pennsylvania B
Marywood University B, M
Seton Hill University B
Slippery Rock University of
Pennsylvania B
Temple University B, M, D

South Carolina
Charleston Southern University B
Converse College B

Texas
Lubbock Christian University B
Sam Houston State University B
Southern Methodist University B, M
Texas Woman's University B
University of the Incarnate Word B
West Texas A&M University B

Utah
Utah State University B, M

Virginia
Shenandoah University C, B, M

Wisconsin
Alverno College B

Musical instrument
fabrication/repair

Indiana
Indiana University
Bloomington A

Iowa
Western Iowa Tech Community
College A

Minnesota
Minnesota State College - Southeast
Technical C

Washington
Renton Technical College C, A

Musical theater

Alabama
Samford University B

Arizona
University of Arizona B

Arkansas
Ouachita Baptist University B

California

California State University
  Chico *B*
College of the Siskiyous *C*
Grossmont College *C, A*

Idaho

University of Idaho *B*

Illinois

Illinois Wesleyan University *B*
Millikin University *B*
North Central College *B*
Rockford College *B*
Roosevelt University *B*
Southern Illinois University
  Carbondale *B*
Western Illinois University *B*

Kansas

Wichita State University *B*

Louisiana

Tulane University *B*

Michigan

Adrian College *B*
Oakland University *B*

Minnesota

University of Minnesota
  Duluth *B*

Missouri

Culver-Stockton College *B*
Lindenwood University *B*
Webster University *B*

Nebraska

Dana College *B*

New Jersey

Rider University *B*

New Mexico

College of Santa Fe *B*

New York

Genesee Community College *C*
Nazareth College *B*
Russell Sage College *B*

North Carolina

Elon University *B*
Lees-McRae College *B*

Ohio

Baldwin-Wallace College *B*
Heidelberg University *B*

Oklahoma

Oklahoma City University *M*

Pennsylvania

University of the Arts *B*

South Carolina

Anderson University *B*
Coastal Carolina University *B*

South Dakota

Northern State University *B*

Texas

Texas Christian University *B*

Utah

Brigham Young University *B*

Vermont

Johnson State College *B*

Virginia

Emory & Henry College *B*

Wyoming

Casper College *A*

Musicology/ ethnomusicology

California

California State University
  San Bernardino *B*
University of California
  Los Angeles *B, M, D*

Colorado

University of Denver *B*

Connecticut

Wesleyan University *D*

Florida

Florida State University *M, D*
University of Miami *M*

Illinois

Northwestern University *B, M, D*
University of Illinois
  Urbana-Champaign *D*

Indiana

Indiana University
  Bloomington *M, D*

Kansas

University of Kansas *B, M*

Maryland

University of Maryland
  College Park *M, D*

Massachusetts

Boston University *D*
Brandeis University *M, D*
New England Conservatory of
  Music *B, M*
Tufts University *B*

Michigan

Michigan State University *M*
University of Michigan *T*

Missouri

Washington University in St.
  Louis *M, D*

New York

Columbia University
  School of General Studies *B*
Cornell University *M*
Eastman School of Music of the
  University of Rochester *M, D*
State University of New York
  Buffalo *D*
University of Rochester *M, D*

North Carolina

Duke University *M, D*
University of North Carolina
  Chapel Hill *M, D*

Ohio

Bowling Green State University *B, M*
Case Western Reserve University *D*
Ohio State University
  Columbus Campus *M, D*
University of Cincinnati *D*

Oregon

University of Oregon *M, D*

Pennsylvania

Penn State
  University Park *M*

Rhode Island

Brown University *B, M, D*

Texas

Rice University *M*
Southwestern University *B*
Texas A&M University
  Commerce *B*
Texas Christian University *M*
Texas Tech University *M*
University of North Texas *M, D*

Utah

Brigham Young University *M*
University of Utah *M*

Vermont

Bennington College *B, M*

Virginia

Shenandoah University *C*

Washington

University of Washington *B*

Nanotechnology

California

Foothill College *C, A*

Illinois

Harper College *A*

Maryland

Allegany College of Maryland *A*

Michigan

Wayne County Community College *C*

Virginia

Virginia Commonwealth University *D*

Washington

North Seattle Community
  College *C, A*

Native American education

Minnesota

College of St. Scholastica *B, T*

Oklahoma

Northeastern State University *B*

Washington

Northwest Indian College *A*

Native American languages

Alaska

University of Alaska
  Fairbanks *A, B*

Arizona

Dine College *A*

Idaho

Idaho State University *A*

Native American studies

Alaska

Ilisagvik College *A*
University of Alaska
  Fairbanks *B*

Arizona

Arizona State University *B*
Dine College *A*
Northern Arizona University *B*
Pima Community College *A*
Prescott College *M*
Scottsdale Community College *A*
University of Arizona *M, D*

California

California State University
  East Bay *B*
De Anza College *A*
El Camino College *A*
Fresno City College *A*
Grossmont College *A*
Humboldt State University *B*
San Diego State University *B*
San Francisco State University *B*
Santa Barbara City College *A*
Solano Community College *A*
Stanford University *B*
University of California
  Berkeley *B*
  Davis *B, M, D*
  Los Angeles *B, M*
  Riverside *B*

Colorado

Fort Lewis College *B*

Hawaii

University of Hawaii
  Hilo *B*
  Manoa *B, M*

Idaho

North Idaho College *A*

Kansas

University of Kansas *M*

Massachusetts

Hampshire College *B*

Michigan

Bay Mills Community College *A*
Michigan State University *B*
Saginaw Chippewa Tribal College *A*

Minnesota

Augsburg College *B*
Bemidji State University *B*
Itasca Community College *A*
Leech Lake Tribal College *A*
Rainy River Community College *A*
University of Minnesota
  Duluth *B*
  Morris *B*
  Twin Cities *B*

Montana

Blackfeet Community College *A*
Fort Belknap College *A*
Fort Peck Community College *A*
Little Big Horn College *A*
Montana State University
  Bozeman *M*
Salish Kootenai College *A*
Stone Child College *A*
University of Montana *B*

Nebraska

Creighton University *B*
Little Priest Tribal College *A*
Nebraska Indian Community
College *A*

New Hampshire

Dartmouth College *B*

New Mexico

Institute of American Indian Arts *A*
University of New Mexico *B*

New York

Colgate University *B*

North Carolina

University of North Carolina
Pembroke *B*

North Dakota

Cankdeska Cikana Community
College *A*
Sitting Bull College *A*
University of North Dakota *B*

Oklahoma

Bacone College *A, B*
Northeastern Oklahoma Agricultural
and Mechanical College *A*
Northeastern State University *B*
Northern Oklahoma College *A*
University of Oklahoma *B, M*
University of Science and Arts of
Oklahoma *B*

South Dakota

Black Hills State University *B*
Oglala Lakota College *A, B, M*
Sisseton Wahpeton College *A*
University of South Dakota *B*

Utah

Weber State University *B*

Vermont

Goddard College *B*

Washington

Evergreen State College *B*
Northwest Indian College *A*
University of Washington *B*

Wisconsin

Lac Courte Oreilles Ojibwa
Community College *A*
Northland College *B*
University of Wisconsin
Eau Claire *B*
Green Bay *B*

Wyoming

Central Wyoming College *A*

Natural resource economics

California

California State University
Stanislaus *M*

Colorado

Colorado State University *B*

Michigan

Michigan State University *B*

New Hampshire

University of New Hampshire *B*

New York

Cornell University *B, M*

Ohio

Baldwin-Wallace College *B*

Puerto Rico

Universidad Metropolitana *M*

West Virginia

West Virginia University *D*

Natural resources and conservation

Alabama

Tuskegee University *B, M*
University of West Alabama *B*

Alaska

University of Alaska
Fairbanks *B, M*

Arizona

Prescott College *B, M*
University of Arizona *B, M, D*

Arkansas

Arkansas Tech University *B, M*
John Brown University *B*
South Arkansas Community
College *C, A*

California

American River College *C, A*
California State University
East Bay *B*
Sacramento *B, M*
College of Marin: Kentfield *C*
College of the Desert *A*
Columbia College *A*
Feather River College *C, A*
Fresno City College *C, A*
Fullerton College *A*
Humboldt State University *B*
Irvine Valley College *C, A*
Modesto Junior College *C, A*
Mount San Antonio College *A*
Ohlone College *C*
Saddleback College *A*
San Diego State University *B*
San Joaquin Delta College *A*
Santa Rosa Junior College *C, A*
Shasta College *C*
Sonoma State University *B*
University of California
Berkeley *B*
Davis *B*
Ventura College *C, A*
Whittier College *B*

Colorado

Colorado Mountain College *A*
Colorado State University *B*
Metropolitan State College of
Denver *B*
Trinidad State Junior College *A*

Connecticut

Gateway Community College *A*
Middlesex Community College *A*
Post University *B*
Sacred Heart University *B*
University of Connecticut *B, M, D*
University of New Haven *B, M*

Delaware

University of Delaware *B*

District of Columbia

George Washington University *B*

University of the District of
Columbia *B*

Florida

Florida International University *B, M*
University of South Florida *B, M*

Georgia

Shorter College *B*
University of Georgia *B, M*

Hawaii

Hawaii Pacific University *B*

Idaho

University of Idaho *B, M, D*

Illinois

Augustana College *B*
Illinois Central College *A*
Lewis University *B*
Lincoln College *A*
Principia College *B*
Southern Illinois University
Edwardsville *M*
University of Illinois
Urbana-Champaign *B, M, D*

Indiana

Ball State University *B, M*
Bethel College *B*
Indiana University
Bloomington *B, M, D*
Manchester College *B*
Purdue University *B, M*
University of St. Francis *B*
Vincennes University *A*

Iowa

Dordt College *B*
Ellsworth Community College *A*
Kirkwood Community College *A*
Mount Mercy College *B*
Muscatine Community College *A*
Northwestern College *B*
University of Dubuque *B*
Upper Iowa University *B*

Kansas

Fort Scott Community College *C, A*

Kentucky

Bluegrass Community and Technical
College *A*
University of Kentucky *B*

Louisiana

Louisiana Tech University *B*

Maine

University of Maine *B, M, D*
University of Maine
Machias *B, T*

Maryland

Frostburg State University *B, M*
Garrett College *C, A*
Howard Community College *A*
University of Maryland
College Park *B*
University College *B*

Massachusetts

Boston University *B, M*
Cape Cod Community College *C, A*
Greenfield Community College *C, A*
Quincy College *C, A*
Roxbury Community College *A*
Simmons College *B*
Springfield College *B*
Suffolk University *A*

University of Massachusetts
Amherst *B, M, D*

Michigan

Bay de Noc Community College *A*
Central Michigan University *B, T*
Delta College *A*
Gogebic Community College *A*
Lake Superior State University *A, B*
Lansing Community College *A*
Mid Michigan Community College *A*
Northern Michigan University *B*
University of Michigan *M*
University of Michigan
Dearborn *B*

Minnesota

Bemidji State University *B, M*
Central Lakes College *C, A*
Gustavus Adolphus College *B*
Itasca Community College *A*
Minnesota State University
Mankato *B*
University of Minnesota
Crookston *B*
Twin Cities *B, M, D*
Vermilion Community College *A*
White Earth Tribal and Community
College *A*
Winona State University *B*

Missouri

Missouri Southern State University *B*

Montana

Blackfeet Community College *A*
Fort Peck Community College *A*
Miles Community College *A*
Montana State University
Bozeman *B, M*
Salish Kootenai College *B*
Stone Child College *A*
University of Montana *B, M*
University of Montana: Western *B*

Nebraska

Little Priest Tribal College *A*
Nebraska Indian Community
College *A*
University of Nebraska
Lincoln *B, M, D*

Nevada

Great Basin College *A*
University of Nevada
Las Vegas *B, M, D*
Reno *B, M*
Western Nevada College *A*

New Hampshire

Dartmouth College *B*
University of New Hampshire *B, M*

New Jersey

Montclair State University *M*
Rutgers, The State University of New
Jersey
New Brunswick/Piscataway
Campus *B, M, D*
Newark Regional Campus *B, M, D*
Warren County Community College *A*
William Paterson University of New
Jersey *B*

New Mexico

Navajo Technical College *C*
New Mexico Institute of Mining and
Technology *A*
Northern New Mexico College *C, A*

New York

Colgate University *B*

Columbia University *B*
Columbia University
 School of General Studies *B*
Cornell University *B, M, D*
Finger Lakes Community College *C, A*
Ithaca College *B*
Paul Smith's College *A, B*
Saint Bonaventure University *B*
State University of New York
 College at Brockport *B*
 College at Plattsburgh *B*
 College of Agriculture and
  Technology at Cobleskill *A, B*
 College of Agriculture and
  Technology at Morrisville *A, B*
 College of Environmental Science
  and Forestry *B, M, D*
Sullivan County Community
 College *A*
Tompkins Cortland Community
 College *A*
Wells College *B*

North Carolina
Blue Ridge Community College *C, A*
Cape Fear Community College *C, A*
Duke University *B, M, D*
North Carolina State University *B, M*
North Carolina Wesleyan College *B*
Pamlico Community College *A*
Shaw University *B*
Wake Technical Community
 College *A*
Warren Wilson College *B*
Western Piedmont Community
 College *C, A*

North Dakota
Dakota College at Bottineau *A*

Ohio
Defiance College *B*
Denison University *B*
Hocking College *A*
Kent State University *B*
Ohio Northern University *B*
Ohio State University
 Agricultural Technical Institute *A*
 Columbus Campus *B, M, D*
Otterbein College *B*
University of Cincinnati *M, D*
University of Rio Grande *B*

Oklahoma
Eastern Oklahoma State College *A*
St. Gregory's University *B*
Southeastern Oklahoma State
 University *B*
Southern Nazarene University *B*

Oregon
Central Oregon Community
 College *A*
Eastern Oregon University *B*
Oregon State University *B*
Portland State University *B, D*

Pennsylvania
Albright College *B*
Arcadia University *M*
Eastern University *B*
Gettysburg College *B*
Keystone College *A, B*
La Salle University *B*
Mansfield University of
 Pennsylvania *B*
Penn State
 Abington *B*
 Altoona *B*
 Beaver *B*
 Berks *B*
 Brandywine *B*
 DuBois *B*

Erie, The Behrend College *B*
Fayette, The Eberly Campus *B*
Greater Allegheny *B*
Hazleton *B*
Lehigh Valley *B*
Mont Alto *B*
New Kensington *B*
Schuylkill *B*
Shenango *B*
University Park *B, M, D*
Wilkes-Barre *B*
Worthington Scranton *B*
York *B*
Slippery Rock University of
 Pennsylvania *M, T*
Thiel College *B*
University of Scranton *B*

Puerto Rico
Bayamon Central University *B*
Inter American University of Puerto
 Rico
 Ponce Campus *B*
Pontifical Catholic University of
 Puerto Rico *B*

Rhode Island
Roger Williams University *B*
University of Rhode Island *M, D*

South Carolina
Clemson University *B*
College of Charleston *M*

South Dakota
Oglala Lakota College *A, B*
Sinte Gleska University *A*

Tennessee
Tennessee Technological
 University *B, D*
Tusculum College *B*
University of Tennessee
 Knoxville *D*

Texas
Coastal Bend College *A*
Lamar University *B, M*
Sul Ross State University *B*
Texas A&M International University *B*
Texas A&M University *B, M, D*
Texas A&M University
 Commerce *B*
 Corpus Christi *B, M*
 Galveston *B, M*
Texas State University: San Marcos *D*
Texas Tech University *B*
University of Houston
 Clear Lake *B, M*

Utah
Snow College *A*

Vermont
Green Mountain College *B*
Johnson State College *B*
Marlboro College *B*
Norwich University *B*
Sterling College *B*
University of Vermont *B, M, D*

Virginia
Mountain Empire Community
 College *A*
St. Paul's College *B*

Washington
Everett Community College *A*
Evergreen State College *B*
Grays Harbor College *A*
Peninsula College *C*
Seattle University *B*

Skagit Valley College *A*
University of Washington *B*
Washington State University *B, M*
Wenatchee Valley College *C, A*

West Virginia
Potomac State College of West
 Virginia University *A*
Shepherd University *B*

Wisconsin
Carroll University *B*
College of Menominee Nation *A*
Fox Valley Technical College *A*
Northland College *B*
University of Wisconsin
 Madison *M, D*
 Platteville *B*
 River Falls *B*
 Stevens Point *B, T*

Wyoming
University of Wyoming *C*
Western Wyoming Community
 College *A*

Natural resources management/policy

Alaska
Alaska Pacific University *B*
University of Alaska
 Fairbanks *B, M*

Arizona
Prescott College *B, M*

California
California State University
 Chico *C, B*
California State University: Channel
 Islands *B*
College of the Redwoods *C*
Columbia College *C, A*
Humboldt State University *B, M*
Los Angeles Pierce College *C, A*
National University *B*
San Joaquin Delta College *C*
University of California
 Berkeley *B*
University of Redlands *B*

Colorado
Adams State College *B*
Colorado Mountain College *A*
Colorado State University *B*
Naropa University *M*
Pikes Peak Community College *A*
University of Denver *M*

Connecticut
University of Connecticut *D*
Yale University *M*

Delaware
Delaware State University *B, M*
University of Delaware *B*

Florida
Florida Institute of Technology *M*
Nova Southeastern University *M*
Pensacola Junior College *A*
St. Petersburg College *B*
University of Miami *B*

Hawaii
University of Hawaii
 Manoa *B, M, D*

Idaho
University of Idaho *B, M*

Illinois
College of Lake County *C, A*
Elmhurst College *B*
Illinois Institute of Technology *M*
Southern Illinois University
 Carbondale *D*
Spoon River College *C, A*
University of Illinois
 Urbana-Champaign *B, M, D*

Iowa
Drake University *B*
Hawkeye Community College *C, A*
Upper Iowa University *B*

Kansas
Garden City Community College *A*

Kentucky
Eastern Kentucky University *B*

Louisiana
Louisiana State University and
 Agricultural and Mechanical
 College *B*
University of Louisiana at Lafayette *B*

Maine
Unity College *B*
University of Maine *B, M, D*
University of Maine
 Fort Kent *B*

Massachusetts
Boston University *B*
Cape Cod Community College *C*

Michigan
Grand Rapids Community College *A*
Grand Valley State University *B*
Lake Superior State University *A, B*
Michigan State University *M, D*
University of Michigan *D*

Minnesota
Northland Community & Technical
 College *A*
St. Mary's University of Minnesota *M*
University of Minnesota
 Crookston *B*
Vermilion Community College *A*

Missouri
Missouri Southern State University *B*

Montana
Flathead Valley Community
 College *C, A*
Fort Belknap College *A*
Fort Peck Community College *A*
Montana State University
 Bozeman *B, D*
University of Montana *M*

Nebraska
Nebraska College of Technical
 Agriculture *C, A*
University of Nebraska
 Lincoln *B*

Nevada
Sierra Nevada College *B*
University of Nevada
 Las Vegas *B, M*
 Reno *B*

New Hampshire
White Mountains Community
 College *A*

New Jersey

Montclair State University *M, D*
Rutgers, The State University of New Jersey
  New Brunswick/Piscataway
    Campus *B*

New Mexico

New Mexico Highlands University *M*
Northern New Mexico College *C, A*

New York

Bard College *M*
Finger Lakes Community College *A*
Paul Smith's College *B*
State University of New York
  College of Agriculture and
    Technology at Morrisville *A, B*
  College of Environmental Science
    and Forestry *B, M, D*

North Carolina

North Carolina State University *B, M*
Western Carolina University *B*

North Dakota

Dakota College at Bottineau *A*
North Dakota State University *B, M, D*

Ohio

Bowling Green State University *B*
Heidelberg University *B*
Hocking College *A*
Ohio State University
  Columbus Campus *B, M, D*
Otterbein College *B*
Zane State College *A*

Oklahoma

Northwestern Oklahoma State
  University *B*

Oregon

Mt. Hood Community College *A*
Oregon State University *B*
Portland State University *M*
Treasure Valley Community College *A*

Pennsylvania

Carnegie Mellon University *B*
Drexel University *M*
Gettysburg College *B*
Keystone College *B*
Philadelphia University *M*
St. Vincent College *B*
University of Pennsylvania *M*

Puerto Rico

Universidad Metropolitana *M*

Rhode Island

University of Rhode Island *B, M*

South Carolina

Central Carolina Technical College *A*

South Dakota

Oglala Lakota College *A*
South Dakota State University *B*

Tennessee

University of Tennessee
  Martin *B*
University of the South *B*

Texas

Angelo State University *B*
Hardin-Simmons University *M*
Sul Ross State University *B*
Texas A&M University *B*

Utah

Snow College *A*
Utah State University *M*

Vermont

Green Mountain College *B*
Johnson State College *B*

Virginia

Roanoke College *B, T*
Virginia Polytechnic Institute and
  State University *M*

Washington

Evergreen State College *M*
University of Washington *M, D*
Washington State University *M*

West Virginia

Glenville State College *B*

Wisconsin

University of Wisconsin
  Green Bay *M*
  River Falls *B*

Wyoming

Northwest College *A*

Natural sciences

Alabama

Oakwood University *B*
University of Alabama
  Birmingham *B*

Alaska

University of Alaska
  Anchorage *B*
  Fairbanks *A*

Arizona

Arizona State University *M*
Prescott College *B, M*

California

California State University
  Dominguez Hills *B*
  Fresno *B*
  Fullerton *M*
  Los Angeles *B*
College of the Siskiyous *A*
Columbia College *A*
Lake Tahoe Community College *A*
Loma Linda University *M*
Loyola Marymount University *B*
The Master's College *B*
Ohlone College *A*
Orange Coast College *A*
Pacific Union College *B*
Pepperdine University *B*
Pitzer College *B*
Saddleback College *A*
San Joaquin Delta College *A*
San Jose State University *B, M*
Santa Rosa Junior College *A*
Shasta College *A*
University of California
  Davis *B*
University of La Verne *B*

Colorado

Colorado Mountain College *A*
Colorado State University *B*
Colorado State University
  Pueblo *M*
University of Colorado
  Colorado Springs *D*

Florida

Gulf Coast Community College *A*

New College of Florida *B*
St. Petersburg College *A*

Georgia

Reinhardt College *A*

Hawaii

University of Hawaii
  Hilo *B*

Idaho

Lewis-Clark State College *B*

Illinois

Black Hawk College: East Campus *A*
Concordia University Chicago *B, T*
Saint Xavier University *B*
Shimer College *B*
Southeastern Illinois College *A*

Indiana

Indiana University
  East *A, B*
Trine University *A*

Iowa

Central College *B, T*
Ellsworth Community College *A*
Northwestern College *T*
St. Ambrose University *B, T*

Kansas

Benedictine College *B*
Bethel College *B*
Central Christian College of
  Kansas *A, B*
Garden City Community College *A*
Neosho County Community
  College *A*
Seward County Community College *A*
Tabor College *B*
Washburn University *A*

Kentucky

Spalding University *B*

Louisiana

Louisiana State University
  Eunice *A*

Maine

University of Maine *B, M, D*
University of Southern Maine *B*

Massachusetts

Cape Cod Community College *A*
Elms College *B*
Lesley University *B*

Michigan

Albion College *B*
Calvin College *B*
Madonna University *A, B*
Marygrove College *A, B, T*
Siena Heights University *A, B*

Minnesota

College of St. Benedict *B*
Rochester Community and Technical
  College *A*
Saint Cloud State University *B*
St. John's University *B*

Mississippi

Blue Mountain College *B*

Missouri

Missouri State University *M*
Missouri Western State University *B*
Park University *B*

Nebraska

Doane College *B*
Peru State College *B*
University of Nebraska
  Omaha *B*

New Jersey

Felician College *B*
Georgian Court University *B*
Thomas Edison State College *B*
Warren County Community College *A*

New Mexico

Clovis Community College *A*
New Mexico State University
  Carlsbad *A*

New York

Colgate University *B*
Daemen College *B*
Hofstra University *B*
Mount Saint Mary College *B*
Rensselaer Polytechnic Institute *M*
Roberts Wesleyan College *B*
State University of New York
  Buffalo *M*
  College at Plattsburgh *M*

North Carolina

Johnson C. Smith University *B*
Western Piedmont Community
  College *A*

North Dakota

Dickinson State University *B*

Ohio

Case Western Reserve University *B*
Cleveland State University *T*
College of Mount St. Joseph *B*
Defiance College *B*
John Carroll University *M*
Lourdes College *A*
Shawnee State University *A*
Terra State Community College *A*
Walsh University *B*
Washington State Community
  College *A*
Xavier University *B*

Oklahoma

Cameron University *B*
Oklahoma State University *M*
St. Gregory's University *A, B*
University of Oklahoma *M*
University of Science and Arts of
  Oklahoma *B, T*

Oregon

Western Oregon University *B*

Pennsylvania

Gettysburg College *B*
Indiana University of Pennsylvania *M*
Juniata College *B*
Keystone College *B*
Muhlenberg College *B*
University of Pennsylvania *B*
University of Pittsburgh
  Titusville *A*

Puerto Rico

Bayamon Central University *B*
Turabo University *B*
Universidad Metropolitana *A, B*
Universidad del Este *A*
University of Puerto Rico
  Aguadilla *A*
  Arecibo *A*
  Cayey University College *B*
  Ponce *A*

Rio Piedras *B*
Utuado *A*
University of the Sacred Heart *B*

South Carolina
University of South Carolina *M*

South Dakota
Sisseton Wahpeton College *A*

Tennessee
Christian Brothers University *B*
Vanderbilt University *B*

Texas
Lee College *A*
Mountain View College *A*
Our Lady of the Lake University of San
Antonio *B*
Tyler Junior College *A*
University of Texas
El Paso *M*

Utah
Snow College *A*

Vermont
Castleton State College *B*
Lyndon State College *B*

Virginia
J. Sargeant Reynolds Community
College *A*
Thomas Nelson Community
College *A*
Virginia Commonwealth University *D*
Virginia Union University *B*
Virginia Wesleyan College *B*
Virginia Western Community
College *A*

Washington
Everett Community College *A*
Evergreen State College *B*
University of Puget Sound *B, T*

Wisconsin
Edgewood College *B*
Lawrence University *B*
Silver Lake College *T*
Viterbo University *B*

Wyoming
University of Wyoming *M*

Naturopathic medicine

Connecticut
University of Bridgeport *D*

Illinois
National University of Health
Sciences *D*

Puerto Rico
Turabo University *D*

Vermont
Goddard College *B, M*

Washington
Bastyr University *D*

Near and Middle Eastern studies

Arizona
University of Arizona *B, M, D*

California
National University *B*
University of California
Berkeley *B, M, D*

Connecticut
Trinity College *B*
University of Connecticut *B*

District of Columbia
George Washington University *B*
Georgetown University *M*

Georgia
Emory University *B*

Illinois
University of Chicago *B, M, D*

Maryland
Johns Hopkins University *B, M, D*

Massachusetts
Brandeis University *B, M, D*
Hampshire College *B*
Harvard College *B, M, D*
Northeastern University *B*
Tufts University *B*
University of Massachusetts
Amherst *B*
Wellesley College *B*

Michigan
University of Michigan *B, M*

Minnesota
University of Minnesota
Twin Cities *B*

Missouri
Washington University in St.
Louis *B, M*

New Hampshire
Dartmouth College *B*

New Jersey
Princeton University *B, M, D*
Rutgers, The State University of New
Jersey
New Brunswick/Piscataway
Campus *B*

New York
Bard College *B*
Barnard College *B*
City University of New York
Hunter College *B*
Columbia University *B*
Columbia University
School of General Studies *B*
Cornell University *B, M, D*
Fordham University *B*
New York University *B, M*
Syracuse University *B*
United States Military Academy *B*

Ohio
College of Wooster *B*
Ohio State University
Columbus Campus *B*
University of Toledo *B*

Oregon
Portland State University *B*

Pennsylvania
Dickinson College *B*

Rhode Island
Brown University *B*

South Carolina
Columbia International University *B*

Texas
Texas State University: San Marcos *B*
University of Texas
Austin *B, M*

Utah
University of Utah *B, M, D*

Vermont
Goddard College *B*
Marlboro College *B*
Middlebury College *B*

Virginia
Emory & Henry College *B*

Washington
University of Washington *B, M, D*

West Virginia
American Public University System *B*

Neuroanatomy

Kentucky
Berea College *B*

New York
University of Rochester *M, D*

North Carolina
Wake Forest University *D*

Neurobiology/ physiology

Alabama
University of Alabama
Birmingham *D*

California
University of California
Davis *B*
Irvine *M, D*
Los Angeles *M, D*
University of Southern California *D*

Connecticut
Yale University *M, D*

District of Columbia
Georgetown University *B*

Illinois
Northwestern University *M*

Indiana
Indiana University-Purdue University
Indianapolis *M, D*

Iowa
University of Iowa *D*

Maine
Colby College *B*

Massachusetts
Hampshire College *B*
Harvard College *B, M, D*

Michigan
Wayne State University *M*

New York
St. Lawrence University *B*
State University of New York
Upstate Medical University *D*

North Carolina
University of North Carolina
Chapel Hill *M, D*

Oklahoma
University of Oklahoma *M, D*

Pennsylvania
University of Pittsburgh *M, D*

Utah
University of Utah *M, D*

Wisconsin
Marquette University *M, D*

Neuropharmacology

New Jersey
Fairleigh Dickinson University
Metropolitan Campus *M*

Pennsylvania
Temple University *D*

Texas
Texas Tech University Health Sciences
Center *M, D*

Neuroscience

Arizona
Arizona State University *D*
University of Arizona *M, D*

California
California Institute of Technology *D*
Claremont McKenna College *B*
Pitzer College *B*
Pomona College *B*
Scripps College *B*
Stanford University *M, D*
University of California
Berkeley *D*
Davis *M, D*
Irvine *B, D*
Los Angeles *B, D*
Riverside *B, M, D*
San Diego *B, M, D*
Santa Cruz *B*
University of Southern
California *B, M, D*

Colorado
Colorado College *B*
Regis University *B*
University of Colorado
Boulder *D*
Denver *D*

Connecticut
Connecticut College *B*
Trinity College *B*
University of Hartford *M*
Wesleyan University *B, M*
Yale University *M, D*

Delaware
Delaware State University *M*
University of Delaware *D*

District of Columbia
George Washington University *D*
Georgetown University *D*

Florida
Florida State University *D*
University of Miami *B, D*

Georgia
Agnes Scott College *M*
Emory University *B, D*
Medical College of Georgia *M, D*
University of Georgia *D*

Idaho
Northwest Nazarene University *B*
University of Idaho *M, D*

Illinois
Dominican University *B*
Knox College *B*
Loyola University Chicago *M, D*
Northwestern University *B, D*
Rush University *D*
University of Chicago *D*
University of Illinois
  Chicago *B, M, D*
  Urbana-Champaign *D*

Indiana
Indiana University
  Bloomington *D*
University of Evansville *B*

Iowa
Drake University *B*
Iowa State University *M, D*
St. Ambrose University *B*

Kansas
University of Kansas *M, D*
University of Kansas Medical
  Center *M, D*

Louisiana
Centenary College of Louisiana *B*
Louisiana State University Health
  Sciences Center *M, D*
Tulane University *B, M, D*

Maine
Bates College *B*
Bowdoin College *B*
Colby College *B*

Maryland
Johns Hopkins University *B, M*
University of Maryland
  Baltimore *M, D*
  Baltimore County *M, D*
  College Park *D*
Washington College *B*

Massachusetts
Amherst College *B*
Boston University *B, M, D*
Brandeis University *B, M, D*
Emmanuel College *B*
Massachusetts Institute of
  Technology *B, M, D*
Mount Holyoke College *B*
Northeastern University *B*
Smith College *B*
Stonehill College *B*
Tufts University *M, D*
University of Massachusetts
  Amherst *M, D*
Wellesley College *B*

Michigan
Albion College *B*
Andrews University *B*
Central Michigan University *B, M*
Michigan State University *M, D*
University of Michigan *B, M, D*

Wayne State University *D*

Minnesota
Macalester College *B*
University of Minnesota
  Twin Cities *D*
University of St. Thomas *B*

Missouri
Saint Louis University *D*
University of Missouri
  Columbia *M, D*
Washington University in St.
  Louis *B, D*

Nevada
University of Nevada
  Reno *B*

New Hampshire
Dartmouth College *B*

New Jersey
Drew University *B*
Rutgers, The State University of New
  Jersey
  Newark Regional Campus *D*

New York
Bard College *B*
City University of New York
  College of Staten Island *M*
  Queens College *M*
Colgate University *B*
Columbia University *B*
Cornell University *B, M, D*
Hamilton College *B*
Manhattanville College *B*
New York University *B, M, D*
St. Lawrence University *B*
Skidmore College *B*
State University of New York
  Buffalo *M, D*
  Stony Brook *D*
Union College *B*
University of Rochester *B, M, D*
Vassar College *B*
Yeshiva University *M, D*

North Carolina
Duke University *B, M, D*
Wake Forest University *D*

Ohio
Baldwin-Wallace College *B*
Bowling Green State University *B*
Case Western Reserve University *D*
College of Wooster *B*
Kent State University *M, D*
Kenyon College *B*
Mount Union College *B*
Muskingum University *B*
Oberlin College *B*
Ohio State University
  Columbus Campus *M, D*
Ohio University *B*
Ohio Wesleyan University *B*
University of Cincinnati *B*
University of Toledo *M, D*

Oklahoma
University of Oklahoma *D*

Oregon
Oregon Health & Science
  University *D*

Pennsylvania
Allegheny College *B*
Bucknell University *B*
Carnegie Mellon University *B*
Cedar Crest College *B*

Dickinson College *B*
Drexel University *M, D*
Franklin & Marshall College *B*
Gettysburg College *B*
King's College *B*
Lafayette College *B*
Moravian College *B*
Muhlenberg College *B*
Penn State
  University Park *M, D*
Temple University *D*
Thiel College *B*
University of Pennsylvania *B, M, D*
University of Pittsburgh *B, M, D*
University of Scranton *B*
Ursinus College *B*

Rhode Island
Brown University *B, M, D*

South Carolina
Furman University *M*

Tennessee
King College *B*
University of Tennessee Health
  Science Center *D*
Vanderbilt University *B*

Texas
Baylor University *B, M*
Texas Christian University *B*
University of Texas
  Austin *M, D*
  Dallas *B, D*
  Health Science Center at
    Houston *M, D*
  Medical Branch at Galveston *D*
  San Antonio *M, D*
  Southwestern Medical Center at
    Dallas *M, D*

Utah
Brigham Young University *B, M, D*
Westminster College *B*

Vermont
Middlebury College *B*
University of Vermont *M, D*

Virginia
College of William and Mary *B*
George Mason University *B, D*
University of Virginia *B*
Washington and Lee University *B*

Washington
University of Washington *D*
Washington State University *B, M, D*

West Virginia
West Virginia University *D*

Wisconsin
Carthage College *B*
Lawrence University *B*
University of Wisconsin
  Madison *M, D*

Wyoming
University of Wyoming *M, D*

Nonprofit/public organization management

Alabama
Birmingham-Southern College *M*

Arizona
Arizona State University *B, M*
Chandler-Gilbert Community College
  Pecos *A*
DeVry University
  Phoenix *M*
Prescott College *B, M*
University of Phoenix *B, M*

California
American Jewish University *M*
California State University
  San Bernardino *M*
DeVry University
  Fremont *M*
  Long Beach *M*
  Pomona *M*
  Sherman Oaks *M*
Fresno Pacific University *B*
Hope International University *M*
University of the West *M*

Colorado
DeVry University
  Westminster *M*
University of Denver *M*

Connecticut
Goodwin College *A*
Quinnipiac University *B, M*

Delaware
Delaware State University *B*

Florida
DeVry University
  Miramar *M*
Florida Atlantic University *M*
Florida Institute of Technology *M*
Palm Beach Atlantic University *B*
University of Central Florida *M*
University of West Florida *M*

Georgia
DeVry University
  Alpharetta *M*
  Decatur *M*
University of Georgia *M*

Illinois
DePaul University *M*
DeVry University
  Tinley Park *M*
DeVry University: Online *M*
North Park University *B, M*
Northwestern University *M*
Trinity International University *B*

Indiana
DeVry University: Indianapolis *M*
Grace College *B*
Huntington University *B*
Indiana Institute of Technology *B, M*
Indiana University-Purdue University
  Indianapolis *M*
Manchester College *A, B*
St. Mary-of-the-Woods College *B, M*

Iowa
University of Northern Iowa *M*

Kansas
Central Christian College of Kansas *A*
Donnelly College *B*
Southwestern College *B*

Maryland
College of Notre Dame of
  Maryland *B, M*
DeVry University: Bethesda *M*

Massachusetts
American International College *M*
Bay Path College *M*
Boston University *M*
Lasell College *M*
Suffolk University *M*
Wheelock College *M*
Worcester State College *M*

Michigan
Andrews University *B, M*
Cleary University *B, M*
Eastern Michigan University *M*

Minnesota
Capella University *M, D*
Crossroads College *B*
DeVry University
  Edina *M*
Hamline University *M*
Saint Cloud State University *M*
Southwest Minnesota State
  University *B*
Walden University *M*

Missouri
DeVry University
  Kansas City *M*
Lindenwood University *B, M*
Rockhurst University *B*
Washington University in St. Louis *M*
William Jewell College *B*

New Jersey
Berkeley College- Garret Mountain
  Campus *B*
Caldwell College *M*

New York
City University of New York
  Baruch College *M*
Globe Institute of Technology *A, B*
Pace University *M*
St. John Fisher College *D*
State University of New York
  College at Brockport *M*
Utica School of Commerce *A*

North Carolina
Mid-Atlantic Christian University *B*
Pfeiffer University *M*
Salem College *B*

Ohio
Baldwin-Wallace College *B*
Case Western Reserve University *M*
DeVry University
  Columbus *M*
Franklin University *B*
John Carroll University *M*
Mount Vernon Nazarene University *M*
Tiffin University *B*

Oklahoma
DeVry University: Oklahoma City
  Center *M*
Northeastern State University *B*
Rogers State University *B*
University of Central Oklahoma *B*

Oregon
Corban College *M*
DeVry University: Portland *M*

Pennsylvania
Alvernia University *M*
DeVry University
  Fort Washington *M*
Duquesne University *B, M*
Eastern University *B, M, D*
Gettysburg College *B*
La Salle University *B*

Misericordia University *M*
Philadelphia Biblical University *M*
Robert Morris University *M*
University of Pennsylvania *M*
West Chester University of
  Pennsylvania *M*

Puerto Rico
University of the Sacred Heart *M*

South Carolina
Columbia International University *B*

Tennessee
Austin Peay State University *B*
DeVry University: Memphis *M*
East Tennessee State University *M*
Johnson Bible College *B*
Lipscomb University *M*
Southern Adventist University *B, M*
Williamson Christian College *A, B*

Texas
Our Lady of the Lake University of San
  Antonio *B, M, D*
University of Dallas *M*

Utah
DeVry University: Sandy *M*

Vermont
Southern Vermont College *B*

Virginia
DeVry University
  Arlington *M*
University of Management and
  Technology *M*

Washington
DeVry University
  Federal Way *M*
Seattle University *M*
Trinity Lutheran College *B*

West Virginia
Alderson-Broaddus College *B*
Mountain State University *B*
Ohio Valley University *B*

Wisconsin
DeVry University: Milwaukee *M*
Lakeland College *B*
University of Wisconsin
  Milwaukee *M*
  Whitewater *B*

Norwegian

Minnesota
St. Olaf College *B*

Washington
Pacific Lutheran University *B*
University of Washington *B*

Nuclear engineering

California
University of California
  Berkeley *B, M, D*

Colorado
Colorado School of Mines *B*

Florida
University of Florida *B, M*

Georgia
Georgia Institute of
  Technology *B, M, D*

Idaho
Idaho State University *B, M, D*
University of Idaho *M, D*

Illinois
University of Illinois
  Urbana-Champaign *B, M, D*

Indiana
Purdue University *B, M, D*

Kansas
Kansas State University *M, D*

Maryland
University of Maryland
  College Park *M, D*

Massachusetts
Massachusetts Institute of
  Technology *B, M, D*

Michigan
University of Michigan *B, M, D*

Missouri
University of Missouri
  Columbia *M, D*
Missouri University of Science and
  Technology *B, M, D*

New Mexico
University of New Mexico *B, M*

New York
Columbia University *M, D*
Cornell University *M, D*
Rensselaer Polytechnic
  Institute *B, M, D*
United States Military Academy *B*

North Carolina
North Carolina State
  University *B, M, D*

Ohio
Ohio State University
  Columbus Campus *M, D*
University of Cincinnati *B, M, D*

Oregon
Oregon State University *B, M, D*

Pennsylvania
Penn State
  Abington *B*
  Altoona *B*
  Beaver *B*
  Berks *B*
  Brandywine *B*
  DuBois *B*
  Erie, The Behrend College *B*
  Fayette, The Eberly Campus *B*
  Greater Allegheny *B*
  Hazleton *B*
  Lehigh Valley *B*
  Mont Alto *B*
  New Kensington *B, M*
  Schuylkill *B*
  Shenango *B*
  University Park *B, M, D*
  Wilkes-Barre *B*
  Worthington Scranton *B*
  York *B*

South Carolina
South Carolina State University *B*
University of South Carolina *M, D*

Tennessee
University of Tennessee
  Knoxville *B, M, D*

Texas
Texas A&M University *B, M, D*

Utah
University of Utah *M, D*

Washington
University of Washington *M, D*

Wisconsin
University of Wisconsin
  Madison *B, M, D*

Nuclear engineering technology

Arkansas
Arkansas Tech University *A*

Connecticut
Three Rivers Community College *A*

Delaware
Delaware Technical and Community
  College
  Owens *A*
  Stanton/Wilmington *A*

New Jersey
Thomas Edison State College *A, B*

New York
Excelsior College *B*
United States Military Academy *B*

North Dakota
Bismarck State College *C, A*

Pennsylvania
Luzerne County Community
  College *A*

Texas
Wharton County Junior College *A*

Virginia
Old Dominion University *B*

Nuclear medical technology

Alabama
University of Alabama
  Birmingham *B*

Arizona
GateWay Community College *A*

Arkansas
University of Central Arkansas *B*

California
Charles Drew University of Medicine
  and Science *B*

Connecticut
Gateway Community College *A*

Delaware

Delaware Technical and Community
College
Stanton/Wilmington *A*

Florida

Barry University *B*
Broward College *A*
Hillsborough Community College *A*
Santa Fe College *A*
State College of Florida,
Manatee-Sarasota *A*

Georgia

Armstrong Atlantic State University *B*
Dalton State College *A*
Darton College *A*
Gordon College *A*

Illinois

Benedictine University *B*
North Central College *B*
Roosevelt University *B*
Triton College *A*
University of St. Francis *B*

Indiana

Ball State University *A*
Indiana University
Bloomington *B*
Indiana University-Purdue University
Indianapolis *B*
Vincennes University *A*

Iowa

Allen College *B*
Clinton Community College *A*
Muscatine Community College *A*
Scott Community College *A*
University of Iowa *B*

Kentucky

Bluegrass Community and Technical
College *A*

Maryland

Carroll Community College *A*
Community College of Baltimore
County *A*
Frederick Community College *A*
Prince George's Community
College *A*

Massachusetts

Bunker Hill Community College *A*
Massachusetts College of Pharmacy
and Health Sciences *B*
Salem State College *B*
Springfield Technical Community
College *A*

Michigan

Ferris State University *A, B*
Lansing Community College *A*
Oakland Community College *A*
Oakland University *B*

Minnesota

Saint Cloud State University *B*
St. Mary's University of Minnesota *B*

Missouri

Saint Louis University *B*
University of Missouri
Columbia *B*

Nebraska

University of Nebraska
Medical Center *B*

Nevada

University of Nevada
Las Vegas *B*

New Jersey

Felician College *B*
Gloucester County College *A*
Thomas Edison State College *A, B*
Union County College *A*
University of Medicine and Dentistry
of New Jersey
School of Health Related
Professions *B*

New York

City University of New York
Bronx Community College *A*
Long Island University
Brooklyn Campus *B*
Manhattan College *B*
Molloy College *A*
State University of New York
Buffalo *B*

North Carolina

Caldwell Community College and
Technical Institute *A*
Fayetteville Technical Community
College *A*
Forsyth Technical Community
College *A*
Pitt Community College *A*

Ohio

Columbus State Community
College *A*
Kent State University
Salem *A*
Kettering College of Medical Arts *A*
Owens Community College
Toledo *A*
University of Cincinnati *B*
University of Cincinnati
Raymond Walters College *A*
University of Findlay *A, B*

Oklahoma

University of Oklahoma *B*

Oregon

Oregon Institute of Technology *B*

Pennsylvania

Cedar Crest College *B*
Community College of Allegheny
County *A*
Harrisburg Area Community
College *A*
Indiana University of Pennsylvania *B*
York College of Pennsylvania *B*

Puerto Rico

University of Puerto Rico
Medical Sciences *B*

South Carolina

Midlands Technical College *A*

South Dakota

Southeast Technical Institute *A*

Tennessee

Baptist College of Health Sciences *B*

Texas

Amarillo College *A*
Del Mar College *A*
Galveston College *A*
Houston Community College
System *A*
University of Houston *B*

University of the Incarnate Word *B*

Utah

Weber State University *B*

Vermont

University of Vermont *B*

Virginia

Old Dominion University *B*

Washington

Bellevue College *A*

West Virginia

West Virginia State Community and
Technical College *A*
Wheeling Jesuit University *B*

Wisconsin

University of Wisconsin
La Crosse *B*

Nuclear physics

Iowa

Iowa State University *M, D*

Nuclear power technology

Connecticut

Three Rivers Community College *A*

Michigan

Lake Michigan College *A*

Missouri

Linn State Technical College *A*

New York

Excelsior College *A*

South Carolina

Aiken Technical College *C, A*

Texas

Texas A&M University *M*
University of North Texas *B*

Wisconsin

Lakeshore Technical College *A*

Nurse anesthetist

Alabama

Samford University *M*
University of Alabama
Birmingham *M*

Arkansas

Arkansas State University *M*

California

California State University
Long Beach *M*
Samuel Merritt University *M*
University of Southern California *M*

Connecticut

Central Connecticut State
University *M*
Fairfield University *M*

Florida

University of Miami *M*

Georgia

Medical College of Georgia *M*
Mercer University *M*

Illinois

Bradley University *M*
DePaul University *M*
Rush University *M*
Southern Illinois University
Edwardsville *M*

Iowa

University of Iowa *M*

Kansas

Newman University *M*
University of Kansas Medical
Center *M*

Louisiana

Louisiana State University Health
Sciences Center *M*
Our Lady of the Lake College *M*

Maine

University of New England *M*

Massachusetts

Northeastern University *M*

Michigan

Oakland University *M*
University of Detroit Mercy *M*
University of Michigan
Flint *M*
Wayne State University *M*

Minnesota

St. Mary's University of Minnesota *M*
University of Minnesota
Twin Cities *B*

Missouri

Goldfarb School of Nursing at
Barnes-Jewish College *M*
Missouri State University *M*
Webster University *M*

Nebraska

BryanLGH College of Health
Sciences *M*

New York

State University of New York
Buffalo *M*

Ohio

Case Western Reserve University *M*
Ohio State University
Columbus Campus *M*
Youngstown State University *M*

Oregon

Oregon Health & Science
University *M*

Pennsylvania

Drexel University *M*
Gannon University *M*
Saint Joseph's University *M*
St. Vincent College *M*
University of Pennsylvania *M*
University of Pittsburgh *M, D*
Villanova University *M*

Puerto Rico

Inter American University of Puerto
Rico
Arecibo Campus *M*

University of Puerto Rico
  Medical Sciences *M*

South Carolina

Medical University of South
  Carolina *M*
University of South Carolina *M*

South Dakota

Mount Marty College *M*

Tennessee

Union University *M*
University of Tennessee
  Knoxville *M*
University of Tennessee Health
  Science Center *M*

Texas

Texas Christian University *M, D*
Texas Wesleyan University *M, D*
University of Texas
  Health Science Center at
    Houston *M*

Utah

Westminster College *M*

Virginia

Virginia Commonwealth
  University *M, D*

Washington

Gonzaga University *M*

West Virginia

Mountain State University *M*

Nurse midwifery

Georgia

Emory University *D*

New Jersey

University of Medicine and Dentistry
  of New Jersey
  School of Health Related
    Professions *M*
William Paterson University of New
  Jersey *M*

New York

State University of New York
  Stony Brook *M*

Ohio

Case Western Reserve University *M*

Oregon

Oregon Health & Science
  University *M*

Pennsylvania

University of Pennsylvania *M*

Puerto Rico

University of Puerto Rico
  Medical Sciences *M*

Texas

Baylor University *D*
University of Texas
  El Paso *M*

Wisconsin

Marquette University *M*
Southwest Wisconsin Technical
  College *A*

Nursery operations

California

City College of San Francisco *A*
College of Marin: Kentfield *C, A*
College of the Redwoods *C*
Cosumnes River College *C*
Foothill College *C, A*
Fullerton College *A*
Los Angeles Pierce College *C*
MiraCosta College *C, A*
Modesto Junior College *C*
Santa Rosa Junior College *C*
Southwestern College *C, A*

Colorado

Colorado State University *B*

Georgia

Albany Technical College *C*

Illinois

College of DuPage *C*
Harper College *C*
Joliet Junior College *C, A*
Kishwaukee College *C, A*
Southwestern Illinois College *A*

Iowa

Kirkwood Community College *A*

Kansas

Dodge City Community College *C*

Maine

University of Maine *B*

Michigan

Michigan State University *C*
Northwestern Michigan College *A*

Minnesota

Anoka Technical College *C, A*
Hennepin Technical College *C, A*

Nebraska

Metropolitan Community
  College *C, A*
Nebraska College of Technical
  Agriculture *A*

New York

State University of New York
  College of Agriculture and
    Technology at Morrisville *A*

Ohio

Ohio State University
  Agricultural Technical Institute *A*

Pennsylvania

Pennsylvania College of
  Technology *A*

South Dakota

Southeast Technical Institute *A*

Tennessee

Tennessee Technological University *B*

Texas

Western Texas College *C, A*

Washington

Clark College *C*
South Seattle Community
  College *C, A*
Spokane Community College *A*

Nursing (RN)

Alabama

Alabama Southern Community
  College *A*
Auburn University *B, M*
Auburn University at
  Montgomery *B, M*
Bevill State Community College *A*
Bishop State Community College *A*
Calhoun Community College *A*
Chattahoochee Valley Community
  College *A*
Gadsden State Community College *A*
George C. Wallace State Community
  College
  Selma *A*
Jacksonville State University *B, M*
Jefferson Davis Community College *A*
Jefferson State Community College *A*
Lawson State Community College *A*
Lurleen B. Wallace Community
  College *A*
Northeast Alabama Community
  College *A*
Northwest-Shoals Community
  College *A*
Samford University *B, M*
Shelton State Community College *A*
Snead State Community College *A*
South University: Montgomery *B*
Southern Union State Community
  College *A*
Spring Hill College *B, M*
Troy University *A, B, M*
University of Alabama *B*
University of Alabama
  Birmingham *B, M*
  Huntsville *B, M*
University of Mobile *A, B, M*
University of North Alabama *B, M*
University of South Alabama *B, M, D*
University of West Alabama *A*
Wallace State Community College at
  Hanceville *A*

Alaska

University of Alaska
  Anchorage *A*

Arizona

Arizona State University *B, M*
Arizona Western College *A*
Brookline College
  Phoenix *A*
Central Arizona College *A*
Cochise College *A*
Eastern Arizona College *A*
Everest College
  Phoenix *A*
GateWay Community College *A*
Glendale Community College *A*
Grand Canyon University *B, M*
Mesa Community College *A*
Mohave Community College *A*
Northern Arizona University *B, M*
Northland Pioneer College *A*
Phoenix College *A*
Pima Community College *A*
Scottsdale Community College *A*
University of Arizona *B*
University of Phoenix *B, M*

Arkansas

Arkansas Northeastern College *A*
Arkansas State University *A, B, M*
Arkansas Tech University *B*
East Arkansas Community College *A*
Harding University *B*
Henderson State University *B*
National Park Community College *A*
North Arkansas College *A*

Northwest Arkansas Community
  College *A*
Ouachita Technical College *A*
Phillips Community College of the
  University of Arkansas *A*
South Arkansas Community College *A*
Southeast Arkansas College *A*
Southern Arkansas University *A, B*
University of Arkansas *B*
University of Arkansas
  Community College at Batesville *A*
  Cossatot Community College of the
    A
  Fort Smith *A, B*
  Little Rock *A*
  Monticello *A, B*
  Pine Bluff *B*
University of Arkansas Community
  College at Morrilton *A*
University of Central Arkansas *B, M*

California

Allan Hancock College *A*
American River College *A*
Antelope Valley College *A*
Azusa Pacific University *B, M, D*
Bakersfield College *A*
Biola University *B*
Butte College *A*
Cabrillo College *A*
California Baptist University *B, M*
California State University
  Bakersfield *B*
  Chico *B, M*
  Dominguez Hills *B, M*
  Fresno *B, M*
  Fullerton *B, M*
  Long Beach *B*
  Los Angeles *B, M*
  Northridge *B*
  Sacramento *B, M*
  San Bernardino *B, M*
  Stanislaus *B, M*
Cerritos College *A*
Chabot College *A*
Chaffey College *A*
City College of San Francisco *A*
College of Marin: Kentfield *A*
College of San Mateo *A*
College of the Canyons *A*
College of the Desert *A*
College of the Sequoias *A*
College of the Siskiyous *A*
Contra Costa College *A*
Cuesta College *A*
Cypress College *A*
De Anza College *A*
Dominican University of
  California *B, M*
East Los Angeles College *A*
El Camino College *A*
El Camino College: Compton
  Center *A*
Evergreen Valley College *A*
Fresno City College *A*
Gavilan College *A*
Glendale Community College *A*
Golden West College *A*
Grossmont College *A*
Hartnell College *A*
Holy Names University *B*
Humboldt State University *B*
Imperial Valley College *A*
Lassen Community College *A*
Loma Linda University *A, B, M, D*
Long Beach City College *A*
Los Angeles County College of
  Nursing and Allied Health *A*
Los Angeles Harbor College *A*
Los Angeles Pierce College *A*
Los Angeles Southwest College *A*
Los Angeles Valley College *A*
Los Medanos College *A*
Merced College *A*

Merritt College *A*
Mission College *A*
Modesto Junior College *A*
Monterey Peninsula College *A*
Moorpark College *A*
Mount St. Mary's College *A, B*
Mount San Antonio College *A*
Mount San Jacinto College *A*
Napa Valley College *A*
National University *B, M*
Ohlone College *A*
Pacific Union College *A, B*
Palomar College *A*
Pasadena City College *A*
Point Loma Nazarene University *B, M*
Rio Hondo College *A*
Riverside Community College *A*
Sacramento City College *A*
Saddleback College *A*
St. Mary's College of California *A*
Samuel Merritt University *B*
San Diego City College *A*
San Diego State University *B, M*
San Francisco State University *B, M*
San Joaquin Delta College *A*
San Joaquin Valley College *A*
San Jose State University *B, M*
Santa Ana College *A*
Santa Barbara City College *A*
Santa Rosa Junior College *A*
Shasta College *A*
Sierra College *A*
Solano Community College *A*
Sonoma State University *B*
Southwestern College *A*
University of San Diego *B, M*
University of San Francisco *B, M*
Vanguard University of Southern
    California *B*
Ventura College *A*
Victor Valley College *A*
West Coast University *A, B*
Western Career College:
    Sacramento *A*
Yuba Community College District *A*

Colorado

Adams State College *B*
American Sentinel University *B, M*
Arapahoe Community College *A*
Aspen University *M*
Colorado Christian University *A, B*
Colorado Mountain College *A*
Colorado Northwestern Community
    College *A*
Colorado State University
    Pueblo *B, M*
Community College of Denver *A*
Front Range Community College *A*
Mesa State College *A, B*
Metropolitan State College of
    Denver *B*
Morgan Community College *A*
Northeastern Junior College *A*
Otero Junior College *A*
Pikes Peak Community College *A*
Platt College
    Aurora *B*
Pueblo Community College *A*
Red Rocks Community College *A*
University of Colorado
    Colorado Springs *B, M, D*
    Denver *B*
University of Northern
    Colorado *B, M, D*

Connecticut

Capital Community College *A*
Central Connecticut State
    University *B*
Fairfield University *B, M*
Gateway Community College *A*
Goodwin College *A*
Housatonic Community College *A*

Naugatuck Valley Community
    College *A*
Norwalk Community College *A*
Quinnipiac University *B, M*
Sacred Heart University *B, M*
Saint Joseph College *B, M*
St. Vincent's College *A*
Southern Connecticut State
    University *B*
Three Rivers Community College *A*
University of Connecticut *B*
University of Hartford *B*
Western Connecticut State
    University *B*
Yale University *M, D*

Delaware

Delaware State University *B*
Delaware Technical and Community
    College
    Owens *A*
    Stanton/Wilmington *A*
    Terry *A*
University of Delaware *B*
Wesley College *B, M*

District of Columbia

Catholic University of
    America *B, M, D*
Georgetown University *B, M*
University of the District of
    Columbia *A, B*

Florida

Barry University *B*
Bethune-Cookman University *B*
Brevard Community College *A*
Broward College *A*
Central Florida Community College *A*
Chipola College *A, B*
Daytona State College *A*
Edison State College *A*
Florida Agricultural and Mechanical
    University *B, M*
Florida Atlantic University *B, M, D*
Florida Gulf Coast University *B, M*
Florida International University *B, M*
Florida Keys Community College *A*
Florida Southern College *B, M*
Florida State College at Jacksonville *A*
Florida State University *B, M*
Gulf Coast Community College *A*
Herzing University *A*
Hillsborough Community College *A*
Indian River State College *A, B*
Jacksonville University *B, M*
Lake City Community College *A*
Lake-Sumter Community College *A*
Miami Dade College *A, B*
Nova Southeastern University *B*
Palm Beach Atlantic University *B*
Palm Beach Community College *A*
Pasco-Hernando Community
    College *A*
Pensacola Junior College *A*
Polk State College *A*
Rasmussen College: Ocala *A*
St. Petersburg College *A, B*
Santa Fe College *A*
Seminole Community College *A*
South Florida Community College *A*
South University: Tampa *B*
South University: West Palm Beach *B*
State College of Florida,
    Manatee-Sarasota *A*
Tallahassee Community College *A*
University of Central Florida *B, M, D*
University of Florida *B, M*
University of Miami *B, M*
University of North Florida *B, M, D*
University of South Florida *B, M*
University of Tampa *B*
University of West Florida *B, M*
Valencia Community College *A*

Georgia

Albany State University *B, M*
Armstrong Atlantic State
    University *B, M*
Athens Technical College *A*
Augusta State University *A*
Bainbridge College *A*
Berry College *B*
Brenau University *B, M*
Clayton State University *B*
College of Coastal Georgia *A, B*
Columbus State University *B*
Columbus Technical College *A*
Dalton State College *A*
Darton College *A*
Emory University *B, M*
Georgia College and State
    University *B*
Georgia Highlands College *A*
Georgia Perimeter College *A*
Georgia Southern University *B*
Georgia Southwestern State
    University *B*
Georgia State University *B, M, D*
Gordon College *A, B*
Kennesaw State University *B*
LaGrange College *B*
Macon State College *A, B*
Medical College of Georgia *B, M*
Mercer University *B*
Middle Georgia College *A*
North Georgia College & State
    University *A, B, M*
Piedmont College *B*
South Georgia College *A*
South University: Savannah *B, M*
Southwestern Georgia Technical
    College *A*
University of West Georgia *B, M*
Valdosta State University *B, M*

Hawaii

Hawaii Pacific University *B, M*
University of Hawaii
    Hawaii Community College *A*
    Kapiolani Community College *A*
    Kauai Community College *A*
    Manoa *B, M*

Idaho

Boise State University *A, B, M*
Brigham Young University-Idaho *A, B*
Eastern Idaho Technical College *A*
Idaho State University *A, B*
Lewis-Clark State College *B*
North Idaho College *A*
Northwest Nazarene University *B*
University of Idaho *B*

Illinois

Aurora University *B*
Benedictine University *B*
Black Hawk College *A*
Blessing-Rieman College of
    Nursing *B, M*
Bradley University *B*
Carl Sandburg College *A*
Chicago State University *B*
City Colleges of Chicago
    Kennedy-King College *A*
    Malcolm X College *A*
College of DuPage *A*
College of Lake County *A*
Danville Area Community College *A*
DePaul University *B, M*
Eastern Illinois University *B*
Elgin Community College *A*
Elmhurst College *B*
Governors State University *B*
Harper College *A*
Harry S. Truman College *A*
Heartland Community College *A*
Highland Community College *A*

Illinois Eastern Community Colleges
    Olney Central College *A*
Illinois State University *B*
Illinois Valley Community College *A*
Illinois Wesleyan University *B*
John A. Logan College *A*
John Wood Community College *A*
Joliet Junior College *A*
Kankakee Community College *A*
Kaskaskia College *A*
Kishwaukee College *A*
Lake Land College *A*
Lakeview College of Nursing *B*
Lewis University *B*
Lewis and Clark Community
    College *A*
Lincoln Land Community College *A*
Loyola University Chicago *B, M*
McKendree University *B, M*
Millikin University *B, M*
Moraine Valley Community College *A*
Morton College *A*
North Park University *B*
Northern Illinois University *B*
Oakton Community College *A*
Parkland College *A*
Prairie State College *A*
Quincy University *B*
Rend Lake College *A*
Richland Community College *A*
Robert Morris University: Chicago *A*
Rock Valley College *A*
Rockford College *B*
Rush University *M, D*
St. Francis Medical Center College of
    Nursing *B, M, D*
St. John's College *B*
Saint Xavier University *B*
Sauk Valley Community College *A*
South Suburban College of Cook
    County *A*
Southeastern Illinois College *A*
Southern Illinois University
    Edwardsville *B*
Southwestern Illinois College *A*
Trinity Christian College *B*
Trinity College of Nursing and Health
    Sciences *A, B*
Triton College *A*
University of Illinois
    Chicago *B*
University of St. Francis *B, M, D*
Waubonsee Community College *A*
West Suburban College of
    Nursing *B, M*
Western Illinois University *B*
Wheaton College *B*

Indiana

Ancilla College *A*
Anderson University *B*
Ball State University *B, M*
Bethel College *A, B, M*
Goshen College *B*
Harrison College
    Indianapolis East *A*
Huntington University *B*
Indiana State University *B, M*
Indiana University
    Bloomington *B*
    East *A, B*
    Kokomo *A, B*
    Northwest *A, B*
    South Bend *A, B*
    Southeast *A*
Indiana University-Purdue University
    Fort Wayne *B*
Indiana University-Purdue University
    Indianapolis *A, B*
Indiana Wesleyan University *B*
Ivy Tech Community College
    Bloomington *A*
    Central Indiana *A*
    Columbus *A*

East Central *A*
Kokomo *A*
Lafayette *A*
North Central *A*
Northeast *A*
Northwest *A*
Richmond *A*
South Central *A*
Southeast *A*
Southwest *A*
Wabash Valley *A*
Marian University *A, B*
Purdue University *B, M*
Purdue University
  Calumet *A, B, M*
  North Central *A, B*
Saint Joseph's College *B*
Saint Mary's College *B*
University of Evansville *B*
University of Indianapolis *A, B*
University of St. Francis *A, B*
University of Southern
  Indiana *B, M, D*
Valparaiso University *B, M*
Vincennes University *A, B*

Iowa
Allen College *B, M*
Briar Cliff University *B, M*
Clarke College *B, M*
Clinton Community College *A*
Coe College *B*
Des Moines Area Community
  College *A*
Dordt College *B*
Ellsworth Community College *A*
Graceland University *B*
Grand View University *B*
Hawkeye Community College *A*
Indian Hills Community College *A*
Iowa Central Community College *A*
Iowa Lakes Community College *A*
Iowa Wesleyan College *B*
Iowa Western Community College *A*
Kaplan University
  Davenport *A*
Kirkwood Community College *A*
Luther College *B*
Marshalltown Community College *A*
Mercy College of Health
  Sciences *A, B*
Morningside College *B*
Mount Mercy College *B*
North Iowa Area Community
  College *A*
Northeast Iowa Community
  College *A*
Northwest Iowa Community
  College *A*
Northwestern College *B*
St. Ambrose University *B, M*
St. Luke's College *A*
Scott Community College *A*
Southeastern Community College
  North Campus *A*
Southwestern Community College *A*
University of Dubuque *B*
University of Iowa *B*
Western Iowa Tech Community
  College *A*

Kansas
Barton County Community College *A*
Bethel College *B*
Butler Community College *A*
Cloud County Community College *A*
Colby Community College *A*
Dodge City Community College *A*
Emporia State University *B*
Garden City Community College *A*
Hesston College *A*
Hutchinson Community College *A*
Johnson County Community
  College *A*

Kansas City Kansas Community
  College *A*
Kansas Wesleyan University *A*
Labette Community College *A*
Manhattan Area Technical College *A*
MidAmerica Nazarene University *B*
Neosho County Community
  College *A*
Newman University *B*
North Central Kansas Technical
  College *A*
Pittsburg State University *B, M*
Pratt Community College *A*
Seward County Community College *A*
Southwestern College *B*
University of Kansas Medical
  Center *B, M, D*
University of St. Mary *B*
Washburn University *B, M*

Kentucky
Ashland Community and Technical
  College *A*
Beckfield College *B*
Bellarmine University *B, M*
Berea College *B*
Big Sandy Community and Technical
  College *A*
Bluegrass Community and Technical
  College *A*
Campbellsville University *A*
Eastern Kentucky University *A, B*
Elizabethtown Community and
  Technical College *A*
Gateway Community and Technical
  College *A*
Hazard Community and Technical
  College *A*
Hopkinsville Community College *A*
Kentucky Christian University *B*
Kentucky State University *A, B*
Madisonville Community College *A*
Maysville Community and Technical
  College *A*
Midway College *A, B*
Morehead State University *A, B*
Murray State University *B, M*
Northern Kentucky
  University *A, B, M*
Owensboro Community and
  Technical College *A*
Pikeville College *A*
St. Catharine College *A*
Somerset Community College *A*
Southeast Kentucky Community and
  Technical College *A*
Spalding University *B, M*
Spencerian College *A*
Thomas More College *B*
University of Louisville *B, M*
West Kentucky Community and
  Technical College *A*
Western Kentucky University *A, B, M*

Louisiana
Baton Rouge Community College *A*
Delgado Community College *A*
Dillard University *B*
Grambling State University *B*
Louisiana College *B*
Louisiana State University
  Alexandria *A, B*
Louisiana State University Health
  Sciences Center *B*
Louisiana Tech University *A*
Loyola University New Orleans *B, M*
McNeese State University *A, B, M*
Nicholls State University *A, B*
Northwestern State University *A, B*
Our Lady of the Lake College *A, B, M*
Southeastern Louisiana
  University *B, M*
Southern University and Agricultural
  and Mechanical College *B, M*

University of Louisiana at
  Lafayette *B, M*
University of Louisiana at Monroe *B*

Maine
Central Maine Community College *A*
Central Maine Medical Center College
  of Nursing and Health
  Professions *A*
Eastern Maine Community College *A*
Husson University *B, M*
Kennebec Valley Community
  College *A*
Northern Maine Community
  College *A*
Saint Joseph's College of Maine *B*
Southern Maine Community
  College *A*
University of Maine *B, M*
University of Maine
  Augusta *A, B*
  Fort Kent *B*
  Presque Isle *T*
University of New England *A, B*
University of Southern Maine *B, M*

Maryland
Allegany College of Maryland *A*
Anne Arundel Community College *A*
Baltimore City Community College *A*
Bowie State University *B, M*
Carroll Community College *A*
Cecil College *A*
Chesapeake College *A*
College of Southern Maryland *A*
Community College of Baltimore
  County *A*
Coppin State University *B, M, T*
Frederick Community College *A*
Frostburg State University *B*
Hagerstown Community College *A*
Harford Community College *A*
Howard Community College *A*
Montgomery College *A*
Prince George's Community
  College *A*
Salisbury University *B, M*
Stevenson University *B*
Towson University *B, M*
University of Maryland
  Baltimore *B*
  College Park *B*
Washington Adventist University *B, M*
Wor-Wic Community College *A*

Massachusetts
American International College *B, M*
Anna Maria College *A, B*
Atlantic Union College *A, B*
Becker College *A, B*
Berkshire Community College *A*
Boston College *B, M*
Bristol Community College *A*
Bunker Hill Community College *A*
Cape Cod Community College *A*
Curry College *B*
Elms College *B*
Endicott College *B*
Fitchburg State College *B*
Framingham State College *B, M*
Greenfield Community College *A*
Holyoke Community College *A*
Laboure College *A, B*
Massachusetts Bay Community
  College *A*
Massachusetts College of Pharmacy
  and Health Sciences *B, M*
Massasoit Community College *A*
Middlesex Community College *A*
Mount Wachusett Community
  College *A*
North Shore Community College *A*
Northeastern University *B, M, D*

Northern Essex Community
  College *A*
Quincy College *A*
Quinsigamond Community College *A*
Regis College *A, B, M*
Roxbury Community College *A*
Salem State College *B, M*
Simmons College *B, M*
Springfield Technical Community
  College *A*
University of Massachusetts
  Amherst *B*
  Boston *B*
  Dartmouth *B, M*
  Lowell *B, M, D*
Worcester State College *B, M*

Michigan
Alpena Community College *A*
Andrews University *B*
Baker College
  of Clinton Township *B*
  of Flint *B*
  of Muskegon *A*
  of Owosso *A*
Bay de Noc Community College *A*
Calvin College *B*
Davenport University *A, B*
Delta College *A*
Eastern Michigan University *B, M*
Ferris State University *A, B*
Finlandia University *B*
Glen Oaks Community College *A*
Gogebic Community College *A*
Grand Rapids Community College *A*
Grand Valley State University *B, M*
Henry Ford Community College *A*
Hope College *B*
Jackson Community College *A*
Kalamazoo Valley Community
  College *A*
Kellogg Community College *A*
Kirtland Community College *A*
Lake Michigan College *A*
Lake Superior State University *B*
Macomb Community College *A*
Madonna University *A, B, M*
Michigan State University *B, M*
Mid Michigan Community College *A*
Monroe County Community
  College *A*
Montcalm Community College *A*
Mott Community College *A*
Muskegon Community College *A*
North Central Michigan College *A*
Northern Michigan University *B, M*
Northwestern Michigan College *A*
Oakland Community College *A*
Oakland University *B*
Saginaw Valley State University *B, M*
St. Clair County Community
  College *A*
Schoolcraft College *A*
Southwestern Michigan College *A*
Spring Arbor University *B*
University of Detroit Mercy *B, M*
University of Michigan *B, D*
University of Michigan
  Flint *B, M, D*
Washtenaw Community College *A*
Wayne County Community College *A*
West Shore Community College *A*
Western Michigan University *B*

Minnesota
Alexandria Technical College *A*
Anoka-Ramsey Community College *A*
Augsburg College *B*
Bethel University *B, M, T*
Central Lakes College *A*
Century Community and Technical
  College *A*
College of St. Benedict *B*
College of St. Scholastica *B*

Concordia College: Moorhead *B, M*
Crown College *B*
Fond du Lac Tribal and Community
  College *A*
Gustavus Adolphus College *B*
Hibbing Community College *A*
Inver Hills Community College *A*
Lake Superior College *A*
Metropolitan State University *B*
Minneapolis Community and
  Technical College *A*
Minnesota School of Business *B*
Minnesota State College - Southeast
  Technical *A*
Minnesota State Community and
  Technical College *A*
Minnesota State University
  Mankato *B, M*
Minnesota West Community and
  Technical College *A*
Normandale Community College *A*
North Hennepin Community
  College *A*
Northland Community & Technical
  College *A*
Northwest Technical College *A*
Ridgewater College *A*
Riverland Community College *A*
Rochester Community and Technical
  College *A*
St. Catherine University *A, B, M*
Saint Cloud State University *B, M*
St. John's University *B*
St. Mary's University of Minnesota *B*
St. Olaf College *B*
South Central College *A*
University of Minnesota
  Twin Cities *B, M, D*
Walden University *B, M*
Winona State University *B, M, D*

Mississippi

Alcorn State University *A, B*
Copiah-Lincoln Community College *A*
Delta State University *B, M*
Mississippi College *B*
Mississippi Gulf Coast Community
  College *A*
Mississippi University for
  Women *A, B, M*
Southwest Mississippi Community
  College *A*
University of Southern Mississippi *B*

Missouri

Avila University *B*
Bolivar Technical College *A*
Central Methodist University *B*
College of the Ozarks *B*
Columbia College *A*
Cox College *A, B*
Crowder College *A*
Culver-Stockton College *B*
Drury University *B*
East Central College *A*
Goldfarb School of Nursing at
  Barnes-Jewish College *B, M*
Hannibal-LaGrange College *A, B*
Jefferson College *A*
Lincoln University *A, B*
Maryville University of Saint
  Louis *B, M*
Metropolitan Community College:
  Maple Woods *A*
Metropolitan Community College:
  Penn Valley *A*
Mineral Area College *A*
Missouri Southern State University *B*
Missouri State University *B*
Missouri State University: West
  Plains *A*
Missouri Valley College *B*
Missouri Western State
  University *B, M*

North Central Missouri College *A*
Northwest Missouri State
  University *B*
Park University *A*
Research College of Nursing *B*
Rockhurst University *B*
St. Charles Community College *A*
Saint Louis University *B, M, D*
St. Luke's College *B*
Sanford-Brown College
  St. Peters *A*
Southeast Missouri Hospital College of
  Nursing and Health Sciences *A*
Southeast Missouri State
  University *B, M*
Southwest Baptist University *A, B*
State Fair Community College *A*
Texas County Technical Institute *A*
Three Rivers Community College *A*
Truman State University *B*
University of Central Missouri *B, M*
University of Missouri
  Columbia *B, M, D*
  Kansas City *B, M, D*
  St. Louis *B, M, D*
Webster University *B, M*
William Jewell College *B*

Montana

Helena College of Technology of the
  University of Montana *A*
Miles Community College *A*
Montana State University
  Bozeman *B, M*
Montana Tech of the University of
  Montana *A, B*
Salish Kootenai College *A, B*

Nebraska

BryanLGH College of Health
  Sciences *B*
Central Community College *A*
Clarkson College *B*
College of Saint Mary *A, B, M*
Creighton University *B*
Grace University *B*
Metropolitan Community College *A*
Mid-Plains Community College Area *A*
Nebraska Methodist College of
  Nursing and Allied Health *B, M*
Nebraska Wesleyan University *B*
Northeast Community College *A*
Southeast Community College *A*
University of Nebraska
  Medical Center *B, M*
Western Nebraska Community
  College *A*

Nevada

College of Southern Nevada *A*
Great Basin College *A, B*
Nevada State College *B*
Truckee Meadows Community
  College *A*
University of Nevada
  Las Vegas *B, M, D*
  Reno *B*
University of Southern Nevada *B*
Western Nevada College *A*

New Hampshire

Colby-Sawyer College *B*
Manchester Community College *A*
NHTI-Concord's Community
  College *A*
Nashua Community College *A*
River Valley Community College *A*
Rivier College *A, B, M*
Saint Anselm College *B*
University of New Hampshire *B, M*
White Mountains Community
  College *A*

New Jersey

Atlantic Cape Community College *A*
Bergen Community College *A*
Bloomfield College *B*
Brookdale Community College *A*
Burlington County College *A*
Camden County College *A*
The College of New Jersey *B, M*
College of St. Elizabeth *B*
County College of Morris *A*
Cumberland County College *A*
Essex County College *A*
Fairleigh Dickinson University
  College at Florham *B*
  Metropolitan Campus *B, M*
Felician College *A, B, M*
Georgian Court University *B*
Gloucester County College *A*
Hudson County Community
  College *A*
Mercer County Community College *A*
Middlesex County College *A*
Monmouth University *B*
New Jersey City University *B*
Ocean County College *A*
Passaic County Community College *A*
Raritan Valley Community College *A*
Richard Stockton College of New
  Jersey *B, M*
Rutgers, The State University of New
  Jersey
  Camden Regional Campus *B*
  New Brunswick/Piscataway
    Campus *B*
  Newark Regional Campus *B*
Saint Peter's College *B, M*
Salem Community College *A*
Seton Hall University *B, D*
Thomas Edison State College *B, M*
Union County College *A*
Warren County Community College *A*
William Paterson University of New
  Jersey *B*

New Mexico

Central New Mexico Community
  College *A*
Dona Ana Community College of New
  Mexico State University *A*
Eastern New Mexico University *B*
New Mexico Highlands University *B*
New Mexico State University *B, M, D*
New Mexico State University
  Carlsbad *A*
San Juan College *A*
Santa Fe Community College *A*
University of New Mexico *B, M*

New York

Adelphi University *B, M*
Adirondack Community College *A*
Broome Community College *A*
Cayuga County Community College *A*
City University of New York
  Borough of Manhattan Community
    College *A*
  Bronx Community College *A*
  College of Staten Island *A, B*
  Hostos Community College *A*
  Hunter College *B, M*
  Kingsborough Community
    College *A*
  Lehman College *B*
  Medgar Evers College *A, B*
  New York City College of
    Technology *B*
  Queensborough Community
    College *A*
  York College *B*
Clinton Community College *A*
Cochran School of Nursing *A*
College of Mount St. Vincent *B, M*
College of New Rochelle *B, M*

Columbia-Greene Community
  College *A*
Concordia College *B*
Corning Community College *A*
D'Youville College *B, M*
Daemen College *B, M*
Dominican College of Blauvelt *B*
Dutchess Community College *A*
Elmira College *B*
Erie Community College
  City Campus *A*
  North Campus *A*
Excelsior College *A, B, M*
Finger Lakes Community College *A*
Fulton-Montgomery Community
  College *A*
Genesee Community College *A*
Hartwick College *B*
Helene Fuld College of Nursing *A*
Hudson Valley Community College *A*
Jamestown Community College *A*
Jefferson Community College *A*
Keuka College *B*
Le Moyne College *B, M*
Long Island University
  Brooklyn Campus *B*
  C. W. Post Campus *B, M*
Maria College *A, B*
Mercy College *M*
Mohawk Valley Community College *A*
Molloy College *B*
Monroe College *A*
Monroe Community College *A*
Mount Saint Mary College *B*
Nassau Community College *A*
Nazareth College *B*
New York Institute of Technology *B*
New York University *B, M, D, T*
Niagara County Community
  College *A*
Niagara University *B*
North Country Community College *A*
Onondaga Community College *A*
Pace University *B*
Phillips Beth Israel School of
  Nursing *A*
Roberts Wesleyan College *B*
Rockland Community College *A*
Russell Sage College *B*
Sage College of Albany *B*
St. Elizabeth College of Nursing *A*
St. Francis College *A, B*
St. John Fisher College *B*
St. Joseph's College of Nursing *A*
State University of New York
  Binghamton *B, M*
  Buffalo *B, D*
  College at Brockport *B*
  College at Plattsburgh *B*
  College of Agriculture and
    Technology at Morrisville *A, B*
  College of Technology at Alfred *A*
  College of Technology at
    Canton *A, B*
  College of Technology at Delhi *A, B*
  Empire State College *B*
  Farmingdale *B*
  Institute of Technology at
    Utica/Rome *B, M*
  Stony Brook *B*
  Upstate Medical University *B, M*
Suffolk County Community College *A*
Sullivan County Community
  College *A*
Tompkins Cortland Community
  College *A*
Touro College *B*
Trocaire College *A*
Ulster County Community College *A*
University of Rochester *B*
Utica College *B*
Wagner College *B, M*
Westchester Community College *A*

North Carolina

Alamance Community College *A*
Appalachian State University *B*
Asheville-Buncombe Technical
　Community College *A*
Barton College *B*
Beaufort County Community
　College *A*
Bladen Community College *A*
Blue Ridge Community College *A*
Brunswick Community College *A*
Cabarrus College of Health
　Sciences *A, B*
Caldwell Community College and
　Technical Institute *A*
Cape Fear Community College *A*
Carolinas College of Health
　Sciences *A*
Catawba Valley Community College *A*
Central Carolina Community
　College *A*
Central Piedmont Community
　College *A*
Cleveland Community College *A*
Coastal Carolina Community
　College *A*
College of the Albemarle *A*
Davidson County Community
　College *A*
Durham Technical Community
　College *A*
East Carolina University *B, M*
Edgecombe Community College *A*
Fayetteville Technical Community
　College *A*
Forsyth Technical Community
　College *A*
Gardner-Webb University *A, B, M*
Gaston College *A*
Guilford Technical Community
　College *A*
Halifax Community College *A*
Haywood Community College *A*
Isothermal Community College *A*
James Sprunt Community College *A*
Johnston Community College *A*
Lenoir Community College *A*
Lenoir-Rhyne University *B*
Mayland Community College *A*
McDowell Technical Community
　College *A*
Methodist University *B*
Mitchell Community College *A*
Nash Community College *A*
North Carolina Central University *B*
Piedmont Community College *A*
Pitt Community College *A*
Queens University of Charlotte *A, B*
Randolph Community College *A*
Richmond Community College *A*
Roanoke-Chowan Community
　College *A*
Robeson Community College *A*
Rockingham Community College *A*
Rowan-Cabarrus Community
　College *A*
Sampson Community College *A*
Sandhills Community College *A*
South Piedmont Community
　College *A*
Southwestern Community College *A*
Stanly Community College *A*
Surry Community College *A*
Tri-County Community College *A*
University of North Carolina
　Chapel Hill *B, M*
　Charlotte *B, M*
　Greensboro *B*
　Pembroke *B*
　Wilmington *B*
Vance-Granville Community
　College *A*
Wake Technical Community
　College *A*
Wayne Community College *A*
Western Carolina University *B, M*
Western Piedmont Community
　College *A*
Wilkes Community College *A*
Wilson Community College *A*
Winston-Salem State University *B*

North Dakota

Bismarck State College *A*
Dakota College at Bottineau *A*
Dickinson State University *B*
Jamestown College *B*
Medcenter One College of Nursing *B*
Minot State University *B*
North Dakota State University *B, M*
University of Mary *B, M*
University of North Dakota *B, M, D*
Williston State College *A*

Ohio

ATS Institute of Technology *A*
Aultman College of Nursing and
　Health Sciences *A*
Belmont Technical College *A*
Bowling Green State University *B*
Bowling Green State University:
　Firelands College *A*
Bryant & Stratton College
　Eastlake *A*
　Parma *A*
Capital University *B*
Case Western Reserve
　University *B, M, D*
Cedarville University *B*
Central Ohio Technical College *A*
Cincinnati State Technical and
　Community College *A*
Clark State Community College *A*
Cleveland State University *B, M*
College of Mount St. Joseph *B, M*
Columbus State Community
　College *A*
Cuyahoga Community College
　Metropolitan Campus *A*
Edison State Community College *A*
Franciscan University of
　Steubenville *B, M*
Good Samaritan College of Nursing
　and Health Science *A*
Hocking College *A*
Hondros College *A*
James A. Rhodes State College *A*
Kent State University *B*
Kent State University
　Ashtabula *A*
　East Liverpool *A, B*
　Tuscarawas *A*
Kettering College of Medical Arts *A, B*
Lourdes College *B, M*
Malone University *B, M*
Marion Technical College *A*
MedCentral College of Nursing *B*
Mercy College of Northwest
　Ohio *A, B*
Miami University
　Hamilton Campus *A, B*
　Oxford Campus *A, B*
Mount Carmel College of
　Nursing *B, M*
Mount Vernon Nazarene University *B*
Muskingum University *B*
North Central State College *A*
Northwest State Community
　College *A*
Notre Dame College *A, B*
Ohio Northern University *B*
Ohio University *A, B, M*
Ohio University
　Southern Campus at Ironton *A, B*
　Zanesville Campus *A*
Otterbein College *B*
Owens Community College
　Toledo *A*

RETS College *A*
Shawnee State University *A, B*
Southern State Community College *A*
Stark State College of Technology *A*
University of Akron *B, M, D*
University of Cincinnati *B*
University of Cincinnati
　Clermont College *A*
　Raymond Walters College *A*
University of Rio Grande *A, B*
University of Toledo *A, B, M*
Ursuline College *B*
Walsh University *B*
Washington State Community
　College *A*
Wright State University *B, M*
Xavier University *B, M*
Youngstown State University *B*

Oklahoma

Bacone College *A, B*
Carl Albert State College *A*
Connors State College *A*
Eastern Oklahoma State College *A*
Northeastern Oklahoma Agricultural
　and Mechanical College *A*
Northeastern State University *B*
Northern Oklahoma College *A*
Northwestern Oklahoma State
　University *B*
Oklahoma Baptist University *B, M*
Oklahoma City Community College *A*
Oklahoma City University *B*
Oklahoma Panhandle State
　University *B*
Oklahoma State University
　Oklahoma City *A*
Oklahoma Wesleyan University *A*
Oral Roberts University *B*
Platt College
　Tulsa *A, B*
Redlands Community College *A*
Rogers State University *A, B*
Rose State College *A*
Seminole State College *A*
Southwestern Oklahoma State
　University *A, B*
University of Central Oklahoma *B*
University of Oklahoma *B, M*
University of Tulsa *B*
Western Oklahoma State College *A*

Oregon

Blue Mountain Community College *A*
Central Oregon Community
　College *A*
Chemeketa Community College *A*
Clackamas Community College *A*
Clatsop Community College *A*
Concordia University *B*
Eastern Oregon University *B*
George Fox University *B*
Lane Community College *A*
Linfield College *B*
Linn-Benton Community College *A*
Oregon Health & Science
　University *B, D*
Rogue Community College *A*
Southern Oregon University *B*
Treasure Valley Community College *A*
Umpqua Community College *A*
University of Portland *B, M, D*

Pennsylvania

Alvernia University *B, M*
Bloomsburg University of
　Pennsylvania *B, M*
Bucks County Community College *A*
Butler County Community College *A*
California University of
　Pennsylvania *A, B*
Carlow University *B, M*
Chatham University *B, M, D*

Clarion University of
　Pennsylvania *A, B, M*
Community College of Allegheny
　County *A*
Community College of Beaver
　County *A*
Community College of Philadelphia *A*
DeSales University *B*
Drexel University *B, M*
Duquesne University *B*
East Stroudsburg University of
　Pennsylvania *B*
Eastern University *B*
Edinboro University of
　Pennsylvania *B, M*
Gannon University *B, M*
Gettysburg College *B*
Gwynedd-Mercy College *A, B*
Harrisburg Area Community
　College *A*
Holy Family University *B, M*
Immaculata University *B*
Indiana University of
　Pennsylvania *B, M*
Kutztown University of
　Pennsylvania *B, M, T*
La Roche College *A, B, M*
La Salle University *B*
Lehigh Carbon Community College *A*
Lock Haven University of
　Pennsylvania *A*
Luzerne County Community
　College *A*
Marywood University *B*
Mercyhurst College *A*
Messiah College *B*
Millersville University of
　Pennsylvania *B, M*
Misericordia University *B, M*
Montgomery County Community
　College *A*
Moravian College *B*
Mount Aloysius College *A, B*
Neumann University *B, M*
Northampton Community College *A*
Penn State
　Abington *B*
　Altoona *A, B*
　Beaver *A, B*
　Berks *B*
　Brandywine *A, B*
　DuBois *B*
　Erie, The Behrend College *A, B*
　Fayette, The Eberly Campus *B*
　Greater Allegheny *B*
　Harrisburg *B*
　Hazleton *A, B*
　Lehigh Valley *A, B*
　Mont Alto *A, B*
　New Kensington *A, B*
　Schuylkill *A, B*
　Shenango *B*
　University Park *A, B, M, D*
　Wilkes-Barre *A, B*
　Worthington Scranton *A, B*
　York *A, B*
Pennsylvania College of
　Technology *A*
Reading Area Community College *A*
Robert Morris University *B, M*
St. Francis University *B*
Seton Hill University *B*
Slippery Rock University of
　Pennsylvania *B*
Temple University *B, M*
Thomas Jefferson University: College
　of Health Professions *B, M*
University of Pennsylvania *B, M, D*
University of Pittsburgh *B, D*
University of Pittsburgh
　Bradford *A, B*
　Titusville *A*
University of Scranton *B, M*
Villanova University *B*

Waynesburg University *B, M*
West Chester University of
   Pennsylvania *B, M, T*
Westmoreland County Community
   College *A*
Widener University *B, M*
Wilkes University *B, M*
York College of Pennsylvania *B*

Puerto Rico

Caribbean University *B*
Columbia Centro Universitario:
   Caguas *A, B*
Columbia College
   Columbia Centro Universitario:
      Yauco *A, B*
Inter American University of Puerto
   Rico
   Aguadilla Campus *A, B*
   Arecibo Campus *A, B*
   Bayamon Campus *A, B*
   Guayama Campus *A, B*
   Metropolitan Campus *A, B*
   Ponce Campus *A, B*
   San German Campus *B*
National College of Business and
   Technology: Arecibo *A, B*
National College of Business and
   Technology: Bayamon *A, B*
National College of Business and
   Technology: Rio Grande *A, B*
Ponce Paramedical College *A*
Pontifical Catholic University of
   Puerto Rico *B*
Turabo University *B, M*
Universidad Metropolitana *A, B, M*
Universidad del Este *A, B*
University College of San Juan *A, B*
University of Puerto Rico
   Aguadilla *A*
   Arecibo *A, B*
   Humacao *A, B*
   Medical Sciences *B, M*
University of the Sacred Heart *A, B*

Rhode Island

Community College of Rhode
   Island *A*
Rhode Island College *B, M*
Salve Regina University *B*
University of Rhode Island *B*

South Carolina

Aiken Technical College *A*
Bob Jones University *B*
Central Carolina Technical College *A*
Charleston Southern University *B*
Clemson University *B, M*
Florence-Darlington Technical
   College *A*
Francis Marion University *B*
Greenville Technical College *A*
Horry-Georgetown Technical
   College *A*
Lander University *B*
Medical University of South
   Carolina *B*
Midlands Technical College *A*
Orangeburg-Calhoun Technical
   College *A*
South Carolina State University *B*
South University: Columbia *B*
Spartanburg Community College *A*
Technical College of the
   Lowcountry *A*
Tri-County Technical College *A*
Trident Technical College *A*
University of South Carolina *B*
University of South Carolina
   Aiken *B*
   Beaufort *B*
   Lancaster *A*
   Upstate *B*
York Technical College *A*

South Dakota

Augustana College *B, M*
Dakota Wesleyan University *A*
Lake Area Technical Institute *A*
Mount Marty College *B*
Presentation College *A, B*
Sisseton Wahpeton College *A*
South Dakota State University *B, M*
University of Sioux Falls *B*
University of South Dakota *A*

Tennessee

Aquinas College *A, B*
Austin Peay State University *B*
Baptist College of Health Sciences *B*
Belmont University *B, M*
Bethel University *B*
Carson-Newman College *B*
Chattanooga State Community
   College *A*
Cleveland State Community College *A*
Cumberland University *B*
Dyersburg State Community
   College *A*
East Tennessee State University *B, M*
Fisk University *B*
Freed-Hardeman University *A*
Jackson State Community College *A*
King College *B, M*
Lincoln Memorial University *A, B*
Lipscomb University *B*
Martin Methodist College *B*
Maryville College *B*
Middle Tennessee State
   University *B, M*
Milligan College *B*
Motlow State Community College *A*
Roane State Community College *A*
Southern Adventist University *A, B*
Southwest Tennessee Community
   College *A*
Tennessee Technological University *B*
Tennessee Wesleyan College *B*
Trevecca Nazarene University *B*
Union University *B*
University of Memphis *B, M*
University of Tennessee
   Chattanooga *B, M*
   Knoxville *B, M*
   Martin *B*
University of Tennessee Health
   Science Center *B, M, D*
Walters State Community College *A*

Texas

Abilene Christian University *B*
Alvin Community College *A*
Amarillo College *A*
Angelina College *A*
Angelo State University *A, B*
Austin Community College *A*
Baylor University *B*
Blinn College *A*
Brazosport College *A*
Brookhaven College *A*
Central Texas College *A*
Clarendon College *A*
Coastal Bend College *A*
Collin County Community College
   District *A*
Del Mar College *A*
East Texas Baptist University *B*
El Centro College *A*
El Paso Community College *A*
Galveston College *A*
Grayson County College *A*
Hardin-Simmons University *B, M*
Houston Baptist University *A, B, M*
Houston Community College
   System *A*
Howard College *A*
Kilgore College *A*
Lamar State College at Orange *A*
Lamar State College at Port Arthur *A*

Lamar University *A, B, M*
Laredo Community College *A*
Lone Star College System *A*
Lubbock Christian University *B*
McMurry University *B*
Midland College *A*
Midwestern State University *B*
North Central Texas College *A*
Northeast Texas Community
   College *A*
Odessa College *A*
Panola College *A*
Prairie View A&M University *B, M*
St. Philip's College *A*
San Antonio College *A*
San Jacinto College *A*
South Plains College *A*
Southwest Texas Junior College *A*
Southwestern Adventist University *B*
Stephen F. Austin State University *B*
Tarleton State University *B*
Tarrant County College *A*
Temple College *A*
Texarkana College *A*
Texas A&M International University *B*
Texas A&M University
   Corpus Christi *B*
   Texarkana *B*
Texas Christian University *B*
Texas Southern University *B*
Texas State University: San Marcos *B*
Texas Tech University Health Sciences
   Center *B*
Texas Woman's University *B*
Trinity Valley Community College *A*
Tyler Junior College *A*
University of Houston
   Victoria *B, M*
University of Mary Hardin-Baylor *B*
University of Texas
   Arlington *B*
   Austin *B, M, D*
   Brownsville - Texas Southmost
      College *A, B, M*
   El Paso *B, M*
   Health Science Center at
      Houston *B*
   Health Science Center at San
      Antonio *B*
   Medical Branch at Galveston *B, M*
   Pan American *B*
   Tyler *B*
University of the Incarnate Word *B, M*
Vernon College *A*
Victoria College *A*
Wayland Baptist University *B*
West Texas A&M University *B*
Wharton County Junior College *A*

Utah

Brigham Young University *B, M*
College of Eastern Utah *A*
Dixie State College of Utah *A, B*
Salt Lake Community College *A*
Southern Utah University *B*
University of Utah *B, M, D*
Utah Valley University *A, B, M*
Weber State University *A, B, M*
Western Governors University *B, M*
Westminster College *B*

Vermont

Castleton State College *A, B*
Southern Vermont College *A, B*
University of Vermont *B*
Vermont Technical College *A*

Virginia

Blue Ridge Community College *A*
Eastern Mennonite University *B*
George Mason University *B, M, D*
Germanna Community College *A*
Hampton University *B*

J. Sargeant Reynolds Community
   College *A*
James Madison University *B*
Jefferson College of Health
   Sciences *A, B, M*
John Tyler Community College *A*
Liberty University *B, M*
Longwood University *B*
Lord Fairfax Community College *A*
Lynchburg College *B, M*
Marymount University *B, M*
Mountain Empire Community
   College *A*
Norfolk State University *A, B*
Old Dominion University *B, M*
Paul D. Camp Community College *A*
Piedmont Virginia Community
   College *A*
Radford University *B*
Rappahannock Community College *A*
Shenandoah University *B, M, D*
Southside Virginia Community
   College *A*
Southwest Virginia Community
   College *A*
Tidewater Community College *A*
University of Virginia *B, M, D*
University of Virginia's College at
   Wise *B*
Virginia Commonwealth
   University *B, M*
Virginia Highlands Community
   College *A*
Virginia State University *A*
Virginia Western Community
   College *A*
Wytheville Community College *A*

Washington

Bellevue College *A*
Bellingham Technical College *A*
Big Bend Community College *A*
Centralia College *A*
Clark College *A*
Eastern Washington University *B, M*
Everett Community College *A*
Grays Harbor College *A*
Highline Community College *A*
Lower Columbia College *A*
North Seattle Community College *A*
Northwest University *B*
Olympic College *A, B*
Pacific Lutheran University *B, M*
Peninsula College *A*
Seattle Pacific University *B*
Seattle University *B*
Shoreline Community College *A*
Skagit Valley College *A*
Spokane Falls Community College *A*
University of Washington *B*
University of Washington
   Bothell *B, M*
University of Washington
   Tacoma *B, M*
Walla Walla University *B*
Washington State University *B, M, D*
Wenatchee Valley College *A*
Whatcom Community College *A*
Whitworth University *B*
Yakima Valley Community College *A*

West Virginia

Alderson-Broaddus College *B*
Blue Ridge Community and Technical
   College *A*
Bluefield State College *A, B*
Davis and Elkins College *A*
Fairmont State University *A, B*
Marshall University *A, B*
Mountain State University *B*
Shepherd University *B*
Southern West Virginia Community
   and Technical College *A*
University of Charleston *A, B*

West Virginia Northern Community
College A
West Virginia State Community and
Technical College A
West Virginia University B, M
West Virginia University at
Parkersburg A
West Virginia Wesleyan College B, M
Wheeling Jesuit University B, M

Wisconsin
Alverno College A, B, M
Beloit College B
Blackhawk Technical College A
Cardinal Stritch University A, B, M
Carroll University B
Chippewa Valley Technical College A
Concordia University Wisconsin B, M
Edgewood College B, M
Fox Valley Technical College A
Gateway Technical College A
Herzing University A
Lakeshore Technical College A
Maranatha Baptist Bible College B
Marian University B, M
Marquette University B, M, D
Mid-State Technical College A
Milwaukee Area Technical College A
Milwaukee School of Engineering B
Moraine Park Technical College A
Mount Mary College B
Nicolet Area Technical College A
Northcentral Technical College A
Northeast Wisconsin Technical
College A
Silver Lake College B
Southwest Wisconsin Technical
College A
University of Wisconsin
Eau Claire B, M
Green Bay B
Madison B, M, D
Milwaukee B, M, D
Oshkosh B, M
Viterbo University B, M
Waukesha County Technical
College A
Western Technical College A
Wisconsin Indianhead Technical
College A
Wisconsin Lutheran College B

Wyoming
Casper College A
Central Wyoming College A
Laramie County Community
College A
Sheridan College A
University of Wyoming B, M

Nursing administration

Alabama
Samford University M
Troy University D
University of Alabama M
University of Alabama
Huntsville D

Arizona
Arizona State University M
Arizona Western College A

Arkansas
Arkansas Tech University M

California
California College San Diego B
California State University
San Bernardino M
Holy Names University M
Samuel Merritt University M
University of San Diego M

University of San Francisco M, D

Colorado
University of Colorado
Denver M, D

Connecticut
Sacred Heart University M
Southern Connecticut State
University M
University of Connecticut M
University of Hartford M

District of Columbia
George Washington University M

Florida
Barry University M, D
Nova Southeastern University M
University of Miami D
University of Tampa M

Georgia
Clayton State University B, M
Georgia College and State
University M
Kennesaw State University M

Illinois
Bradley University M
DePaul University M
Lewis University M, D
Loyola University Chicago M
North Park University M
Saint Xavier University M
Southern Illinois University
Edwardsville M

Indiana
Anderson University M
Indiana University-Purdue University
Fort Wayne M
Indiana University-Purdue University
Indianapolis M
Indiana Wesleyan University M

Iowa
Allen College M
Clarke College M
University of Iowa M, D

Kentucky
Bellarmine University M

Louisiana
Louisiana State University Health
Sciences Center M
Northwestern State University M
Our Lady of the Lake College M

Maine
Husson University M
Saint Joseph's College of Maine M
University of Southern Maine M

Massachusetts
Curry College M
Elms College M
Northeastern University M
Regis College M
Salem State College M
University of Massachusetts
Boston M, D

Michigan
Andrews University M
Ferris State University M
Madonna University M
Saginaw Valley State University M
University of Detroit Mercy M
University of Michigan M

Western Michigan University M

Minnesota
College of St. Scholastica M
Saint Cloud State University M
Walden University M
Winona State University M

Mississippi
University of Southern Mississippi M

Missouri
Missouri State University M
Research College of Nursing M

Nebraska
Clarkson College M
Nebraska Wesleyan University M

Nevada
University of Nevada
Reno M

New Jersey
Felician College B, M
Kean University M
Seton Hall University M

New York
Adelphi University M
City University of New York
Hunter College M
College of Mount St. Vincent M
College of New Rochelle M
Le Moyne College M
Mercy College B, M
Roberts Wesleyan College M
State University of New York
Buffalo M
Institute of Technology at
Utica/Rome M
Upstate Medical University M

North Dakota
University of Mary M

Ohio
Ashland University B
Capital University B, M
Kent State University M, D
Ohio University M
Otterbein College M
Xavier University M

Oklahoma
Oklahoma City University M

Pennsylvania
Carlow University M
DeSales University M
Duquesne University M
Holy Family University M
Marywood University M
University of Pennsylvania M
Villanova University M, D
York College of Pennsylvania M

Puerto Rico
Universidad Metropolitana B, M

South Carolina
Medical University of South
Carolina M
University of South Carolina M

Tennessee
Southern Adventist University M
Union University M
University of Tennessee
Knoxville M

University of Tennessee Health
Science Center D

Texas
Abilene Christian University M
Baylor University M
Lubbock Christian University M
Midwestern State University M
Texas A&M University
Corpus Christi M
Texarkana M
Texas Tech University Health Sciences
Center M
Texas Woman's University M
University of Texas
Arlington M
Brownsville - Texas Southmost
College M
El Paso M
Medical Branch at Galveston M
Tyler M
University of the Incarnate Word M
West Texas A&M University M

Utah
Western Governors University M
Westminster College M

Virginia
Marymount University M
Stratford University: Woodbridge B

Washington
Seattle Pacific University M
University of Washington Tacoma B

West Virginia
Marshall University D
Mountain State University M
West Virginia Wesleyan College M

Wisconsin
Marquette University M
University of Wisconsin
Oshkosh M
Viterbo University M

Nursing assistant

Alabama
Alabama Southern Community
College C, A
Bevill State Community College C
Bishop State Community College C
Gadsden State Community College C
George C. Wallace State Community
College
Selma C
Jefferson Davis Community College C
Lawson State Community College C
Northeast Alabama Community
College C
Northwest-Shoals Community
College C
Shelton State Community College C

Arizona
Arizona Western College C
Brookline College
Phoenix C
Tempe C
Tucson C
Chandler-Gilbert Community College
Pecos C, A
Cochise College C
Coconino County Community
College C, A
Eastern Arizona College C
GateWay Community College C
Mesa Community College C
Northland Pioneer College C
Phoenix College C

Rio Salado College *C, A*
Scottsdale Community College *C*

Arkansas

Arkansas State University
    Beebe *C*
Arkansas Tech University *C*
Black River Technical College *C*
North Arkansas College *C*
Ouachita Technical College *C*
South Arkansas Community College *C*
Southeast Arkansas College *C*
Southern Arkansas University Tech *C*
University of Arkansas Community
    College at Morrilton *C*

California

Allan Hancock College *C*
Chaffey College *C*
City College of San Francisco *C*
College of the Desert *C*
College of the Sequoias *C*
College of the Siskiyous *C*
Copper Mountain College *C*
Gavilan College *C*
Kaplan College: Vista *C*
Lassen Community College *A*
Long Beach City College *C*
Los Angeles Harbor College *C*
Merritt College *C*
MiraCosta College *C*
Modesto Junior College *C*
Palo Verde College *C*
Santa Barbara City College *C*
Santa Rosa Junior College *C, A*
Shasta College *C*
Southwestern College *C*
Yuba Community College District *C*

Colorado

Arapahoe Community College *C*
Colorado Mountain College *C*
Community College of Denver *C*
Front Range Community College *C*
Lamar Community College *C*
Mesa State College *C*
Morgan Community College *C*
Northeastern Junior College *C*
Otero Junior College *C*
Pikes Peak Community College *C*
Pueblo Community College *C*
Red Rocks Community College *C*
Trinidad State Junior College *C*

Connecticut

Capital Community College *C*
Northwestern Connecticut
    Community College *C*

Delaware

Delaware Technical and Community
    College
    Owens *C*
    Stanton/Wilmington *C*
    Terry *C*

Florida

Angley College *C*
Brevard Community College *C*
Central Florida College *C*
Chipola College *C*
Florida National College *C*
Florida State College at Jacksonville *C*
Gulf Coast Community College *C*
Indian River State College *C*
Lake City Community College *C*
North Florida Community
    College *C, A*
Northwest Florida State College *B*
Palm Beach Community College *C*
Pasco-Hernando Community
    College *C*
Pensacola Junior College *C*

Santa Fe College *C*
Seminole Community College *C*
South Florida Community College *C*
Tallahassee Community College *C*

Georgia

Albany Technical College *C*
Athens Technical College *C*
Atlanta Technical College *C*
Bainbridge College *C*
Central Georgia Technical College *C*
Columbus Technical College *C*
Middle Georgia Technical College *C*
Savannah Technical College *C*
Southeastern Technical College *C*
Southwest Georgia Technical
    College *C*
West Georgia Technical College *C*

Hawaii

University of Hawaii
    Hawaii Community College *C*
    Kapiolani Community College *A*
    Kauai Community College *C*

Illinois

Black Hawk College *C*
City Colleges of Chicago
    Harold Washington College *C*
    Kennedy-King College *C*
    Malcolm X College *C*
College of DuPage *C*
College of Lake County *C*
College of Office Technology *C*
East-West University *C*
Elgin Community College *C*
Harper College *C*
Harry S. Truman College *C*
Heartland Community College *C*
Highland Community College *C*
Illinois Eastern Community Colleges
    Frontier Community College *C*
    Lincoln Trail College *C*
    Olney Central College *C*
    Wabash Valley College *C*
John A. Logan College *C*
John Wood Community College *C*
Kankakee Community College *C*
Kaskaskia College *C*
Kishwaukee College *C*
Lewis and Clark Community
    College *C*
Lincoln Land Community College *C*
McHenry County College *C*
Morton College *C*
Parkland College *C*
Prairie State College *C*
Rend Lake College *C*
Richland Community College *C*
Rock Valley College *C*
Rockford Career College *C*
Sauk Valley Community College *C*
South Suburban College of Cook
    County *C*
Southeastern Illinois College *C*
Southwestern Illinois College *C*
Spoon River College *C*
Triton College *C*
Waubonsee Community College *C*
Wilbur Wright College *C*

Iowa

Des Moines Area Community
    College *C*
Indian Hills Community College *C*
Iowa Lakes Community College *C*
Mercy College of Health Sciences *C*
North Iowa Area Community
    College *C*
Western Iowa Tech Community
    College *C*

Kansas

Allen County Community College *A*
Barton County Community College *A*
Brown Mackie College
    Salina *C*
Cloud County Community College *C*
Coffeyville Community College *A*
Colby Community College *C*
Cowley County Community
    College *C, A*
Dodge City Community College *C, A*
Highland Community College *C, A*
Johnson County Community
    College *C*
Kansas City Kansas Community
    College *C*
Neosho County Community
    College *C*

Kentucky

Owensboro Community and
    Technical College *C*
St. Catharine College *C*

Louisiana

Gretna Career College *C*

Maine

Central Maine Medical Center College
    of Nursing and Health
    Professions *C*

Maryland

Allegany College of Maryland *C*
College of Southern Maryland *C*

Massachusetts

Bunker Hill Community College *C*
Cape Cod Community College *C*
Middlesex Community College *C*
Northeastern University *M*

Michigan

Baker College
    of Flint *C*
Delta College *C*
Gogebic Community College *C*
Henry Ford Community College *C*
Kellogg Community College *C*
Montcalm Community College *C*
Schoolcraft College *C*
Wayne County Community College *C*
West Shore Community College *A*

Minnesota

Alexandria Technical College *C*
Anoka Technical College *C*
Dakota County Technical College *C*
Fond du Lac Tribal and Community
    College *C*
Inver Hills Community College *C*
Itasca Community College *C*
Lake Superior College *C*
Mesabi Range Community and
    Technical College *C*
Minneapolis Community and
    Technical College *C*
Minnesota State College - Southeast
    Technical *C*
Normandale Community College *C*
Northwest Technical College *C*
Ridgewater College *C*
Rochester Community and Technical
    College *C*
St. Paul College *C*
South Central College *C*

Mississippi

Copiah-Lincoln Community College *C*
Hinds Community College *A*
Mississippi Gulf Coast Community
    College *C*

Northwest Mississippi Community
    College *C*
Southwest Mississippi Community
    College *C*

Missouri

Bolivar Technical College *C*
Texas County Technical Institute *C*

Montana

Montana Tech of the University of
    Montana *C*

Nebraska

BryanLGH College of Health
    Sciences *C*
Nebraska Methodist College of
    Nursing and Allied Health *C*

New Mexico

Central New Mexico Community
    College *C*
Clovis Community College *C*
Dona Ana Community College of New
    Mexico State University *C*
Eastern New Mexico University:
    Roswell Campus *C*
Northern New Mexico College *C*

New York

Monroe College *C, A*
Westchester Community College *C, A*

North Carolina

Beaufort County Community
    College *C*
Bladen Community College *C*
Brunswick Community College *C*
Carolinas College of Health
    Sciences *C*
Carteret Community College *C*
Central Carolina Community
    College *C*
Coastal Carolina Community
    College *C*
College of the Albemarle *C*
Edgecombe Community College *C*
Gaston College *C*
Halifax Community College *C*
Haywood Community College *C*
McDowell Technical Community
    College *C*
Mitchell Community College *C*
Nash Community College *C*
Richmond Community College *C*
Robeson Community College *C*
Sampson Community College *C*
Sandhills Community College *C*
Southeastern Community
    College *C, A*
Stanly Community College *C*
Tri-County Community College *C*
Vance-Granville Community
    College *C*

North Dakota

Lake Region State College *C*

Ohio

Central Ohio Technical College *C*
Cincinnati State Technical and
    Community College *C*
Columbus State Community
    College *C*
Kent State University
    East Liverpool *C*
    Tuscarawas *C*
Marion Technical College *C*

Oregon

Central Oregon Community
    College *C*

Chemeketa Community College *C*
Klamath Community College *C, A*
Linn-Benton Community College *C*
Southwestern Oregon Community
College *C*
Umpqua Community College *C*

Pennsylvania

Commonwealth Technical Institute *C*
Community College of Allegheny
County *C*
Erie Business Center *C*
Laurel Business Institute *A*
Mercyhurst College *C, A*
Pennsylvania Institute of
Technology *C*

Puerto Rico

Inter American University of Puerto
Rico
San German Campus *C*
Universidad Metropolitana *M*
Universidad del Este *C*

South Carolina

Forrest Junior College *C*
Trident Technical College *C*
Williamsburg Technical College *C*
York Technical College *C*

South Dakota

Oglala Lakota College *A*
Western Dakota Technical Institute *C*

Texas

Cedar Valley College *C*
El Centro College *C*
El Paso Community College *C*
Galveston College *C*
Howard College *C*
Midland College *C*
Palo Alto College *A*
South Plains College *C*
South Texas College *A*
Texas State Technical College
Harlingen *C*

Utah

Dixie State College of Utah *C*
Salt Lake Community College *C*
Southern Utah University *C*

Virginia

Germanna Community College *C*
J. Sargeant Reynolds Community
College *C*
Mountain Empire Community
College *C*
Rappahannock Community College *C*
Southside Virginia Community
College *C*
Virginia Western Community
College *C*

Washington

Bellingham Technical College *C*
Big Bend Community College *C*
Centralia College *C*
Clark College *C*
Clover Park Technical College *C*
Everett Community College *C*
Grays Harbor College *C*
Lake Washington Technical College *C*
Lower Columbia College *C, A*
North Seattle Community College *C*
Olympic College *C*
Renton Technical College *C*
South Puget Sound Community
College *C, A*
South Seattle Community College *C*
Wenatchee Valley College *C*

Wisconsin

Blackhawk Technical College *C*
Chippewa Valley Technical College *C*
Fox Valley Technical College *C*
Gateway Technical College *C*
Lakeshore Technical College *C*
Mid-State Technical College *C*
Milwaukee Area Technical College *C*
Moraine Park Technical College *C*
Nicolet Area Technical College *C*
Northcentral Technical College *C*
Northeast Wisconsin Technical
College *C*
Southwest Wisconsin Technical
College *C*
Waukesha County Technical
College *C*
Western Technical College *C*
Wisconsin Indianhead Technical
College *C*

Wyoming

Laramie County Community
College *C*

Nursing science

Alabama

University of Alabama
Birmingham *D*

Alaska

University of Alaska
Anchorage *A, B*

Arizona

University of Phoenix *B, M*

California

University of California
Irvine *B, M*
Los Angeles *B, M, D*
University of San Diego *D*

Connecticut

University of Connecticut *D*
Yale University *D*

Florida

Florida Atlantic University *D*
Florida International University *D*
University of Central Florida *D*
University of Miami *D*
University of South Florida *D*

Georgia

Emory University *M, D*
Georgia Southern University *D*
Kennesaw State University *D*
Medical College of Georgia *D*
Mercer University *D*

Hawaii

University of Hawaii
Manoa *D*

Illinois

DePaul University *M*
Governors State University *M, D*
Illinois State University *D*
Lewis University *M*
Loyola University Chicago *M, D*
University of Illinois
Chicago *M, D*

Indiana

Indiana University-Purdue University
Indianapolis *D*
University of St. Francis *M*

Iowa

University of Iowa *M, D*

Kansas

University of Kansas Medical
Center *M, D*
Wichita State University *B, M*

Kentucky

University of Louisville *D*

Louisiana

Louisiana State University Health
Sciences Center *D*
Our Lady of the Lake College *M*
Southern University and Agricultural
and Mechanical College *D*

Maryland

University of Maryland
Baltimore *M, D*

Massachusetts

Elms College *M*
Regis College *D*
Salem State College *M*
Simmons College *D*
University of Massachusetts
Amherst *M, D*
Boston *M*
Dartmouth *D*

Michigan

Michigan State University *D*
Wayne State University *B, D*

Minnesota

College of St. Scholastica *D*
Metropolitan State University *M, D*
Saint Cloud State University *M*

Mississippi

University of Southern Mississippi *D*

Nebraska

Clarkson College *M*
Creighton University *M, D*
University of Nebraska
Medical Center *D*

New Jersey

College of St. Elizabeth *M*
Fairleigh Dickinson University
Metropolitan Campus *D*
Kean University *B, M, T*
Monmouth University *M*
New Jersey Institute of Technology *M*
Ramapo College of New Jersey *B, M*
Seton Hall University *M*
University of Medicine and Dentistry
of New Jersey
School of Nursing *B, M, D*
William Paterson University of New
Jersey *M*

New Mexico

New Mexico State University *D*
University of New Mexico *D*

New York

Adelphi University *D*
State University of New York
Binghamton *D*
Buffalo *M*
University of Rochester *D*

North Carolina

East Carolina University *D*
University of North Carolina
Chapel Hill *D*
Greensboro *B, M, D, T*

Ohio

Case Western Reserve
University *M, D*
Cleveland State University *M*
Kent State University *D, T*
University of Toledo *M, D*

Oklahoma

Oklahoma City University *M*

Pennsylvania

Drexel University *D*
Immaculata University *M*
Widener University *D*

Rhode Island

University of Rhode Island *M, D, T*

South Carolina

Clemson University *B, M*
Medical University of South
Carolina *D*
University of South Carolina *M, D*

South Dakota

South Dakota State University *D*

Tennessee

East Tennessee State University *D*
University of Tennessee
Knoxville *D*
University of Tennessee Health
Science Center *D*

Texas

Texas Tech University Health Sciences
Center *D, T*
Texas Woman's University *D*
University of Texas
Arlington *D*
Medical Branch at Galveston *D*
Tyler *D*

Vermont

University of Vermont *M*

Virginia

Hampton University *M, D*
Jefferson College of Health
Sciences *M*
Virginia Commonwealth
University *M, D*

West Virginia

West Virginia University *D*

Wisconsin

Marquette University *M, D*
Milwaukee School of Engineering *M*

Nutrition sciences

Alabama

Auburn University *M, D*
Samford University *B*
University of Alabama
Birmingham *D*

Arizona

University of Arizona *B, M, D*

California

Chapman University *M*
Pepperdine University *B*
University of California
Berkeley *B, M, D*
Davis *B, M, D*

Connecticut

University of Connecticut *B, M, D*

University of New Haven *B, M*

Delaware
University of Delaware *B, M*

District of Columbia
Howard University *B, M, D*

Florida
Florida State University *B*
Northwest Florida State College *A*

Georgia
Life University *A, B*
University of Georgia *B*

Hawaii
University of Hawaii
   Manoa *B, M*

Illinois
Dominican University *B*
Rush University *M*
Southern Illinois University
   Carbondale *B*
University of Illinois
   Urbana-Champaign *M, D*

Indiana
Purdue University *B, M, D*
University of Southern Indiana *B*

Kansas
University of Kansas Medical
   Center *M*

Kentucky
University of Kentucky *M, D*

Maine
University of Maine *D*

Maryland
Howard Community College *A*
University of Maryland
   College Park *M, D*

Massachusetts
Boston University *B, M, D*
Simmons College *B, M*
Tufts University *M, D*
University of Massachusetts
   Amherst *M*

Michigan
Michigan State University *B*
University of Michigan *M*

Minnesota
College of St. Benedict *B*
Concordia College: Moorhead *B*
St. John's University *B*
University of Minnesota
   Twin Cities *B, M, D*

Missouri
Southeast Missouri State University *M*
University of Missouri
   Columbia *B, M, D*

Nebraska
University of Nebraska
   Lincoln *M, D*

Nevada
University of Nevada
   Las Vegas *B*
   Reno *B*

New Hampshire
University of New Hampshire *B, M*

New Jersey
Rutgers, The State University of New
   Jersey
   New Brunswick/Piscataway
     Campus *B, M, D*

New York
City University of New York
   Brooklyn College *M*
Cornell University *M, D*
Ithaca College *B*
Long Island University
   C. W. Post Campus *B, M*
Mohawk Valley Community College *A*
New York Institute of
   Technology *B, M*
State University of New York
   Buffalo *M*
   College of Agriculture and
     Technology at Morrisville *A*

North Carolina
North Carolina State University *M, D*
University of North Carolina
   Chapel Hill *M, D*
   Greensboro *B, M, D*

Ohio
Case Western Reserve
   University *B, M, D*
Ohio State University
   Columbus Campus *B, M, D*
University of Cincinnati
   Raymond Walters College *A*

Oklahoma
University of Central Oklahoma *M*

Pennsylvania
Drexel University *B, M*
La Salle University *B*
Messiah College *B*

Puerto Rico
University of Puerto Rico
   Medical Sciences *M*

Rhode Island
Johnson & Wales University:
   Providence *B*

South Carolina
Clemson University *B, M*

Texas
Baylor University *M*
Texas A&M University *M, D*
Texas Woman's University *B, M, D*
University of Texas
   Austin *M, D*
University of the Incarnate Word *B, M*

Utah
Brigham Young University *B, M*
Utah State University *M*

Vermont
University of Vermont *B, M*

Washington
Bastyr University *B, M*
University of Washington *M, D*
Washington State University *D*

Wisconsin
University of Wisconsin
   Madison *M, D*

Wyoming
Casper College *A*

Occupational/ environmental health nursing

Arizona
Arizona State University *D*

Pennsylvania
University of Pennsylvania *M*

Tennessee
University of Tennessee
   Knoxville *B*

Occupational health/ industrial hygiene

California
California State University
   Fresno *B*
San Diego State University *M*

Connecticut
University of New Haven *M*

Hawaii
University of Hawaii
   Honolulu Community College *A*

Illinois
Illinois State University *B*

Indiana
Purdue University *B, M*

Iowa
University of Iowa *M, D*

Maryland
National Labor College *B*

Massachusetts
Anna Maria College *M*
Harvard College *M, D*
University of Massachusetts
   Lowell *M, D*

Michigan
Grand Valley State University *B*
Oakland University *B, M*
University of Michigan *M, D*
Wayne State University *M*

Missouri
University of Central Missouri *M*

Montana
Montana Tech of the University of
   Montana *B, M*

North Carolina
Durham Technical Community
   College *A*
East Carolina University *M*
North Carolina Agricultural and
   Technical State University *B*
St. Augustine's College *B*

Ohio
Ohio University *B*
University of Findlay *B*
University of Toledo *M, T*

Oklahoma
University of Oklahoma *M, D*

Pennsylvania
University of Pittsburgh *M*

Puerto Rico
Bayamon Central University *B*
University of Puerto Rico
   Medical Sciences *M*
University of the Sacred Heart *M*

Texas
Laredo Community College *A*
North Central Texas College *A*

Utah
University of Utah *M*

Occupational safety/ health technology

Alabama
Jacksonville State University *B*

Alaska
University of Alaska
   Anchorage *A*

Arizona
GateWay Community College *C, A*

California
California State University
   Fresno *B*
Southwestern College *C, A*

Colorado
Trinidad State Junior College *C, A*

Connecticut
University of Connecticut *M*
University of New Haven *C, A, B, M*

Florida
Embry-Riddle Aeronautical
   University *B*

Georgia
Georgia Southern University *B, T*

Hawaii
University of Hawaii
   Honolulu Community College *C, A*

Indiana
Indiana State University *B*
Ivy Tech Community College
   Central Indiana *A*
   East Central *C, A*
   Kokomo *C, A*
   North Central *C, A*
   Northeast *A*
   Northwest *A*
   Southwest *C, A*
   Wabash Valley *C, A*

Iowa
Clinton Community College *A*

Kentucky
Murray State University *B, M*

Louisiana
Delgado Community College *A*
Southeastern Louisiana University *B*

Maryland
Anne Arundel Community
   College *C, A*
Community College of Baltimore
   County *C, A*

Massachusetts

Anna Maria College *M*

Michigan

Grand Valley State University *B*
Madonna University *C, B*

Minnesota

South Central College *C, A*

Missouri

Mineral Area College *A*

New Hampshire

Keene State College *B*

New Jersey

New Jersey Institute of Technology *M*
Rider University *C*

New Mexico

Eastern New Mexico University:
  Roswell Campus *C*

New York

Rochester Institute of
  Technology *C, B*

North Carolina

Central Piedmont Community
  College *A*
Methodist University *B*
North Carolina Agricultural and
  Technical State University *B*

North Dakota

University of North Dakota *B*

Ohio

Cincinnati State Technical and
  Community College *C, A*
James A. Rhodes State College *C*
Owens Community College
  Toledo *C*
Wright State University *A*

Oklahoma

Southeastern Oklahoma State
  University *B, M*

Pennsylvania

Indiana University of
  Pennsylvania *B, M*
Millersville University of
  Pennsylvania *B*
Slippery Rock University of
  Pennsylvania *B*

Tennessee

Southwest Tennessee Community
  College *C*

Texas

Del Mar College *A*
Kilgore College *C, A*
Lamar Institute of Technology *A*
Odessa College *C, A*
San Antonio College *C, A*
San Jacinto College *C, A*
Tarrant County College *C, A*
University of Houston
  Downtown *B*
University of Texas
  Tyler *B, M*

Virginia

Tidewater Community College *A*

West Virginia

Blue Ridge Community and Technical
  College *C, A*
Fairmont State University *A, B*
Marshall University *B, M*

Wisconsin

University of Wisconsin
  Stout *M*
  Whitewater *B, M*

Wyoming

Central Wyoming College *A*

Occupational therapy

Alabama

Alabama State University *M*
University of Alabama
  Birmingham *M*
University of South Alabama *M*

Arkansas

University of Central Arkansas *M*

California

California State University
  Dominguez Hills *M*
Dominican University of California *M*
Loma Linda University *M, D*
Samuel Merritt University *M*
San Jose State University *M*
University of Southern
  California *M, D*

Colorado

Colorado State University *M, D*

Connecticut

Quinnipiac University *M*
Sacred Heart University *M*
University of Hartford *M*

Florida

Barry University *M*
Florida Agricultural and Mechanical
  University *M*
Florida Gulf Coast University *M*
Florida International University *M*
Nova Southeastern University *M, D*
University of Florida *M*

Georgia

Brenau University *M*
Medical College of Georgia *M*

Idaho

Idaho State University *M*

Illinois

Governors State University *M, D*
Rush University *M*
University of Illinois
  Chicago *M, D*

Indiana

Indiana University-Purdue University
  Indianapolis *M*
University of Indianapolis *M*
University of Southern Indiana *M*

Iowa

St. Ambrose University *M*

Kansas

University of Kansas Medical
  Center *M, D*

Kentucky

Eastern Kentucky University *M*

Spalding University *M*

Louisiana

Louisiana State University Health
  Sciences Center *M*

Maine

Husson University *M*
University of New England *M*
University of Southern Maine *M*

Maryland

Towson University *M, D*

Massachusetts

American International College *M*
Bay Path College *M*
Boston University *M*
Salem State College *M*
Springfield College *M*
Worcester State College *M*

Michigan

Baker College
  of Flint *D*
  of Port Huron *M*
Calvin College *M*
Eastern Michigan University *M*
Grand Valley State University *M*
Saginaw Valley State University *M*
Wayne State University *M*
Western Michigan University *M*

Minnesota

College of St. Scholastica *M*
St. Catherine University *M*

Missouri

Maryville University of Saint Louis *M*
Rockhurst University *M*
Saint Louis University *M, D*
University of Missouri
  Columbia *M*
Washington University in St.
  Louis *M, D*

Nebraska

College of Saint Mary *M*
Creighton University *D*

New Hampshire

University of New Hampshire *M*

New Jersey

Kean University *M*
Richard Stockton College of New
  Jersey *M*
Seton Hall University *M*

New Mexico

University of New Mexico *M*

New York

City University of New York
  York College *M*
D'Youville College *M*
Dominican College of Blauvelt *M*
Ithaca College *M*
Long Island University
  Brooklyn Campus *M*
Mercy College *M*
New York Institute of Technology *M*
New York University *M, D*
State University of New York
  Buffalo *M*
  Stony Brook *M*
Touro College *M*
Utica College *M*

North Carolina

East Carolina University *M*

Lenoir-Rhyne University *M*
University of North Carolina
  Chapel Hill *M, D*
Winston-Salem State University *M*

North Dakota

University of Mary *M*
University of North Dakota *M*

Ohio

Cleveland State University *M*
Ohio State University
  Columbus Campus *M*
Shawnee State University *M*
University of Findlay *M*
University of Toledo *M, D*
Xavier University *M*

Oklahoma

University of Oklahoma *M*

Oregon

Pacific University *M*

Pennsylvania

Alvernia University *M*
Chatham University *M, D*
Duquesne University *M*
Elizabethtown College *M*
Gannon University *M*
Misericordia University *M, D*
Mount Aloysius College *M*
Philadelphia University *M*
St. Francis University *M*
Temple University *M*
Thomas Jefferson University: College
  of Health Professions *M, D*
University of Pittsburgh *M*
University of Scranton *M*
University of the Sciences in
  Philadelphia *M*

Puerto Rico

University of Puerto Rico
  Medical Sciences *M*

South Dakota

University of South Dakota *M*

Tennessee

Belmont University *D*
Milligan College *M*
University of Tennessee
  Knoxville *M, D*

Texas

Texas Tech University Health Sciences
  Center *M*
Texas Woman's University *M, D*
University of Texas
  El Paso *M*
  Medical Branch at Galveston *M*
  Pan American *M*

Utah

University of Utah *M*

Virginia

James Madison University *M*
Jefferson College of Health
  Sciences *M*
Radford University *M*
Shenandoah University *M*
Virginia Commonwealth
  University *M, D*

Washington

Eastern Washington University *M*
University of Puget Sound *M*

West Virginia
West Virginia University *M*

Wisconsin
Concordia University Wisconsin *M*
Mount Mary College *M*
University of Wisconsin
La Crosse *M*
Madison *M*
Milwaukee *M*

Occupational therapy assistant

Alabama
Central Alabama Community
College *A*
Wallace State Community College at
Hanceville *A*

Arkansas
East Arkansas Community College *A*
Pulaski Technical College *A*
South Arkansas Community College *A*

California
Grossmont College *A*
Loma Linda University *A*
Mount St. Mary's College *A*
Sacramento City College *C, A*
Santa Ana College *A*

Colorado
Arapahoe Community College *A*
Morgan Community College *A*
Pueblo Community College *A*

Connecticut
Lincoln College of New England:
Briarwood *A*
Manchester Community College *A*

Delaware
Delaware Technical and Community
College
Owens *A*
Stanton/Wilmington *A*

Florida
Daytona State College *A*
Gulf Coast Community College *A*
Palm Beach Community College *A*
Polk State College *A*
State College of Florida,
Manatee-Sarasota *A*
Tallahassee Community College *C*

Georgia
Brown Mackie College: Atlanta *C, A*
Darton College *A*
Middle Georgia College *A*

Hawaii
University of Hawaii
Kapiolani Community College *A*

Illinois
College of DuPage *A*
Illinois Central College *A*
John A. Logan College *A*
Kaskaskia College *A*
Lewis and Clark Community
College *A*
Lincoln Land Community College *A*
Parkland College *A*
Rend Lake College *A*
South Suburban College of Cook
County *A*
Southeastern Illinois College *A*
Wilbur Wright College *A*

Indiana
Brown Mackie College: Fort Wayne *A*
Brown Mackie College: South Bend *A*
University of Southern Indiana *A*

Iowa
Iowa Central Community College *A*
Iowa Lakes Community College *C*
Kirkwood Community College *A*

Kansas
Johnson County Community
College *A*
Newman University *A*

Kentucky
Madisonville Community College *A*
Spalding University *B*

Louisiana
Delgado Community College *A*
University of Louisiana at Monroe *A*

Maine
Kennebec Valley Community
College *A*

Maryland
Allegany College of Maryland *A*

Massachusetts
Bristol Community College *A*
Greenfield Community College *A*
North Shore Community College *A*
Quinsigamond Community College *A*
Springfield Technical Community
College *A*

Michigan
Baker College
of Cadillac *A*
of Muskegon *A*
Grand Rapids Community College *A*
Macomb Community College *A*
Mott Community College *A*
Oakland Community College *A*
Schoolcraft College *A*
Wayne County Community College *A*

Minnesota
Anoka Technical College *A*
Lake Superior College *A*
Northland Community & Technical
College *A*
St. Catherine University *A*

Missouri
East Central College *A*
Metropolitan Community College:
Penn Valley *A*
Ozarks Technical Community
College *A*
St. Charles Community College *A*
St. Louis Community College
St. Louis Community College at
Meramec *A*
State Fair Community College *A*

New Hampshire
River Valley Community College *A*

New Mexico
Eastern New Mexico University:
Roswell Campus *A*

New York
City University of New York
LaGuardia Community College *A*
Erie Community College
North Campus *A*
Genesee Community College *A*

Herkimer County Community
College *A*
Ithaca College *B, M*
Jamestown Community College *A*
Maria College *A*
Mercy College *A*
Orange County Community College *A*
Rockland Community College *A*
Suffolk County Community College *A*
Touro College *A*

North Carolina
Cape Fear Community College *A*
Durham Technical Community
College *A*
Pitt Community College *A*

North Dakota
North Dakota State College of
Science *A*

Ohio
Cincinnati State Technical and
Community College *A*
Cuyahoga Community College
Metropolitan Campus *A*
James A. Rhodes State College *A*
Kent State University
East Liverpool *A*
Marion Technical College *A*
Owens Community College
Toledo *A*
Shawnee State University *A*
Stark State College of Technology *A*
Zane State College *A*

Oklahoma
Oklahoma City Community College *A*
Southwestern Oklahoma State
University *A*
Tulsa Community College *A*

Oregon
Mt. Hood Community College *A*

Pennsylvania
Community College of Allegheny
County *A*
Kaplan Career Institute: Pittsburgh *A*
Lehigh Carbon Community College *A*
Mount Aloysius College *A*
Penn State
Berks *A*
DuBois *A*
Mont Alto *A*
Pennsylvania College of
Technology *A*

Puerto Rico
Inter American University of Puerto
Rico
Ponce Campus *A*
University of Puerto Rico
Humacao *A*

Rhode Island
Community College of Rhode
Island *A*
New England Institute of
Technology *A*

South Carolina
Central Carolina Technical College *C*
Greenville Technical College *A*
Midlands Technical College *C*
Tri-County Technical College *C*
Trident Technical College *A*

South Dakota
Lake Area Technical Institute *A*

Tennessee
Roane State Community College *A*
South College *A*

Texas
Amarillo College *A*
Austin Community College *A*
Del Mar College *A*
Houston Community College
System *C, A*
Laredo Community College *A*
Lone Star College System *A*
North Central Texas College *A*
Panola College *A*
St. Philip's College *A*
South Texas College *A*

Utah
Salt Lake Community College *A*
University of Utah *B*

Virginia
J. Sargeant Reynolds Community
College *A*
Jefferson College of Health
Sciences *A*
Southwest Virginia Community
College *C*
Tidewater Community College *A*

Washington
Green River Community College *A*
Spokane Falls Community College *A*

West Virginia
Mountain State University *A*

Wisconsin
Fox Valley Technical College *A*
Gateway Technical College *A*
Milwaukee Area Technical College *A*
Western Technical College *A*
Wisconsin Indianhead Technical
College *A*

Wyoming
Casper College *A*

Ocean engineering

California
University of California
San Diego *M, D*

Connecticut
University of Connecticut *M*

Florida
Florida Atlantic University *B, M, D*
Florida Institute of
Technology *B, M, D*
University of Florida *M*

Hawaii
University of Hawaii
Manoa *M, D*

Maryland
United States Naval Academy *B*

New Hampshire
University of New Hampshire *B, M, D*

New Jersey
Stevens Institute of Technology *M, D*

Oregon
Oregon State University *M*

Rhode Island
University of Rhode Island *B, M, D*

Texas
Texas A&M University *B, M, D*
Texas A&M University
Galveston *B*

Oceanography

Alaska
University of Alaska
Fairbanks *M, D*

Arizona
Arizona Western College *A*

California
Humboldt State University *B*
Shasta College *A*
University of California
Berkeley *B*
San Diego *D*
Santa Cruz *M, D*
University of Southern
California *M, D*

Connecticut
United States Coast Guard Academy *B*
University of Connecticut *M, D*

Delaware
University of Delaware *M, D*

Florida
Florida Institute of
Technology *B, M, D*
Florida State University *M, D*
Gulf Coast Community College *A*
Nova Southeastern University *D*
University of Miami *B, M, D*
University of South Florida *M, D*
University of West Florida *B*

Hawaii
Hawaii Pacific University *B*
University of Hawaii
Manoa *M, D*

Illinois
Illinois Valley Community College *A*

Louisiana
Louisiana State University and
Agricultural and Mechanical
College *B, M, D*

Maine
Maine Maritime Academy *B*
University of Maine *B, M, D*

Maryland
United States Naval Academy *B*

Massachusetts
Massachusetts Institute of
Technology *M, D*

Michigan
Central Michigan University *B*
Grand Rapids Community College *A*
University of Michigan *B, M, D*

Mississippi
University of Southern
Mississippi *B, M, D*

New Hampshire
University of New Hampshire *M*

New Jersey
Rider University *B*
Rutgers, The State University of New
Jersey
New Brunswick/Piscataway
Campus *M, D*

New York
Columbia University
School of General Studies *B*
State University of New York
Stony Brook *D*

North Carolina
Cape Fear Community College *A*
Elizabeth City State University *B*
North Carolina State University *B*
University of North Carolina
Chapel Hill *M, D*
Wilmington *M*

Oregon
Oregon State University *M, D*

Pennsylvania
Kutztown University of
Pennsylvania *B*
Millersville University of
Pennsylvania *B*

Rhode Island
University of Rhode Island *B, M, D*

Texas
Texas A&M University *M, D*
Texas A&M University
Galveston *B*

Virginia
Old Dominion University *B, M, D*

Washington
Everett Community College *A*
Shoreline Community College *A*
University of Washington *B, M, D*

Wisconsin
University of Wisconsin
Madison *M, D*

Office/clerical services

Alabama
Faulkner State Community College *C*
Gadsden State Community College *C*
Lawson State Community College *C*
Wallace State Community College at
Hanceville *C, A*

Alaska
University of Alaska
Anchorage *C*
Southeast *A*

Arizona
Cochise College *C*
Coconino County Community
College *C*
Dine College *C, A*
Eastern Arizona College *C*
Mesa Community College *A*
Paradise Valley Community
College *C, A*
Phoenix College *C*

Arkansas
Arkansas State University
Beebe *C*
Arkansas State University: Newport *C*
East Arkansas Community College *C*
Mid-South Community College *C*

National Park Community College *C*
Ouachita Technical College *C*
Pulaski Technical College *C*
University of Arkansas
Community College at Hope *C*

California
Allan Hancock College *A*
American River College *A*
Bakersfield College *A*
Barstow Community College *C, A*
Berkeley City College *C, A*
Canada College *C, A*
Cerritos College *A*
Cerro Coso Community College *C, A*
Chabot College *A*
Chaffey College *C*
Citrus College *C, A*
City College of San Francisco *A*
Coastline Community College *C*
College of Alameda *A*
College of Marin: Kentfield *C*
College of San Mateo *A*
College of the Redwoods *C*
College of the Sequoias *C, A*
College of the Siskiyous *C, A*
Columbia College *C*
Contra Costa College *A*
Crafton Hills College *C, A*
Cypress College *C, A*
East Los Angeles College *A*
El Camino College: Compton
Center *C, A*
Empire College *C*
Evergreen Valley College *A*
Fresno City College *C, A*
Gavilan College *C*
Golden West College *C, A*
Heald College
Fresno *C, A*
Humphreys College *C, A, B*
Imperial Valley College *C, A*
Kaplan College: Panorama City *C*
Lake Tahoe Community College *C, A*
Laney College *C, A*
Lassen Community College *C, A*
Long Beach City College *C, A*
Los Angeles City College *C, A*
Los Angeles Harbor College *C, A*
Los Angeles Mission College *C, A*
Los Angeles Southwest College *A*
Los Angeles Trade and Technical
College *C, A*
Los Angeles Valley College *A*
MTI College *C*
MiraCosta College *C, A*
Mission College *A*
Modesto Junior College *C*
Monterey Peninsula College *C, A*
Mount St. Mary's College *A*
Mount San Antonio College *C, A*
Mount San Jacinto College *C*
Ohlone College *C, A*
Orange Coast College *C, A*
Palo Verde College *C, A*
Palomar College *C, A*
Pasadena City College *C, A*
Porterville College *A*
Reedley College *C*
Sacramento City College *C, A*
Saddleback College *C*
San Bernardino Valley College *C*
San Diego City College *C, A*
San Diego Miramar College *A*
San Joaquin Delta College *C, A*
San Jose City College *C, A*
Santa Barbara City College *C*
Santa Monica College *C, A*
Santa Rosa Junior College *C*
Shasta College *A*
Skyline College *C, A*
Southwestern College *C, A*
Taft College *C, A*
Ventura College *C, A*

West Hills College: Coalinga *C, A*
West Valley College *A*
Yuba Community College District *C*

Colorado
Lamar Community College *C*
Trinidad State Junior College *C*

Connecticut
Gateway Community College *C, A*
Lincoln College of New England:
Briarwood *C*
Quinebaug Valley Community
College *C*
Tunxis Community College *A*

Florida
Brevard Community College *C*
Broward College *A*
Central Florida Community College *C*
Gulf Coast Community College *C, A*
Herzing University *C*
Lake City Community College *C, A*
Miami Dade College *C, A*
Pasco-Hernando Community
College *C*
Pensacola Junior College *C*
Polk State College *A*
Santa Fe College *A*
Seminole Community College *C*

Georgia
Abraham Baldwin Agricultural
College *A*
Augusta Technical College *C*
Central Georgia Technical College *C*
Chattahoochee Technical College *C*
Clayton State University *C*
Dalton State College *C, A*
Darton College *C*
Gwinnett Technical College *C*
Macon State College *C, A*
Middle Georgia Technical
College *C, A*
Southeastern Technical College *C*
Southwest Georgia Technical
College *C, A*

Hawaii
University of Hawaii
Kauai Community College *C, A*
Leeward Community College *C, A*

Illinois
City Colleges of Chicago
Kennedy-King College *C*
Danville Area Community College *A*
East-West University *C*
Elgin Community College *C*
Harper College *C*
Highland Community College *C*
John A. Logan College *C*
Joliet Junior College *A*
Kankakee Community College *C*
Kaskaskia College *C*
Kishwaukee College *C, A*
Lake Land College *C*
Lewis and Clark Community
College *A*
Lincoln Land Community College *C*
MacCormac College *C, A*
Midstate College *C*
Morton College *C*
Rockford Career College *A*
Sauk Valley Community College *C*
Southeastern Illinois College *C*
Southwestern Illinois College *C, A*
Spoon River College *C*
Waubonsee Community College *C*
Wilbur Wright College *C*

Indiana
Kaplan College: Hammond *C*

Purdue University
   North Central *A*
Vincennes University *C*

Iowa

Des Moines Area Community
   College *C*
Dordt College *A*
Ellsworth Community College *C, A*
Hawkeye Community College *C*
Iowa Lakes Community College *C*
Iowa Western Community College *C*
Kaplan University
   Cedar Rapids *C*
Marshalltown Community College *C*
Southeastern Community College
   North Campus *C, A*

Kansas

Allen County Community College *C*
Butler Community College *C, A*
Central Christian College of Kansas *A*
Coffeyville Community College *A*
Cowley County Community
   College *C, A*
Donnelly College *A*
Kansas City Kansas Community
   College *C*
Labette Community College *A*
Neosho County Community
   College *C*
Pratt Community College *C, A*
Seward County Community
   College *C, A*
Washburn University *C, A*

Kentucky

Ashland Community and Technical
   College *A*
Daymar College
   Owensboro *C, A*
National College
   Lexington *A*
Owensboro Community and
   Technical College *A*
Sullivan University *C, A*

Maine

Andover College *C, A*
Northern Maine Community
   College *C*
University of Maine
   Machias *B*

Maryland

Hagerstown Community College *C*
Kaplan College: Hagerstown *C*

Massachusetts

Bristol Community College *C*
Bunker Hill Community College *A*
Cape Cod Community College *C, A*
Massasoit Community College *C*
Middlesex Community College *C*
Northern Essex Community
   College *C*
Quinsigamond Community
   College *C, A*
Springfield Technical Community
   College *C*

Michigan

Baker College
   of Auburn Hills *C*
   of Cadillac *C*
   of Clinton Township *C*
   of Flint *C*
   of Jackson *C*
   of Muskegon *C*
   of Owosso *C, A*
   of Port Huron *C*
Bay de Noc Community College *C*
Glen Oaks Community College *C*

Grand Rapids Community College *C*
Henry Ford Community College *A*
Kellogg Community College *C*
Kirtland Community College *C*
Mid Michigan Community College *C*
Monroe County Community
   College *C, A*
North Central Michigan College *C, A*
Northern Michigan University *C*
St. Clair County Community
   College *C, A*
West Shore Community College *C, A*

Minnesota

Alexandria Technical College *C*
Central Lakes College *C*
Century Community and Technical
   College *C*
Crown College *C, A*
Fond du Lac Tribal and Community
   College *C*
Hennepin Technical College *C, A*
Hibbing Community College *C, A*
Lake Superior College *C*
Minnesota State College - Southeast
   Technical *C*
Northland Community & Technical
   College *C*
Ridgewater College *C*
Rochester Community and Technical
   College *C*
St. Cloud Technical College *C*
Winona State University *B*

Mississippi

Southwest Mississippi Community
   College *C, A*

Missouri

Crowder College *C, A*
Jefferson College *C, A*
Metropolitan Community College:
   Longview *C*
Metropolitan Community College:
   Penn Valley *C*
North Central Missouri College *C, A*
St. Louis Community College
   St. Louis Community College at
      Meramec *A*
Three Rivers Community College *C*

Montana

Helena College of Technology of the
   University of Montana *C*
Little Big Horn College *C*
Miles Community College *C, A*
Stone Child College *C, A*

Nebraska

Kaplan University
   Lincoln *C*
Northeast Community College *C, A*
Southeast Community College *A*
University of Nebraska
   Kearney *B*
Western Nebraska Community
   College *C, A*

New Hampshire

River Valley Community College *C*
White Mountains Community
   College *A*

New Jersey

Berkeley College- Garret Mountain
   Campus *C*
Essex County College *C*
Gloucester County College *C, A*

New Mexico

Dona Ana Community College of New
   Mexico State University *C*

New Mexico State University
   Alamogordo *C*
   Carlsbad *C, A*

New York

Adirondack Community College *C*
Berkeley College *C*
Berkeley College of New York City *C*
Corning Community College *C*
Erie Community College
   City Campus *C*
Fulton-Montgomery Community
   College *C*
Globe Institute of Technology *C*
Herkimer County Community
   College *A*
North Country Community
   College *C, A*
Olean Business Institute *C*
Professional Business College *C*
Schenectady County Community
   College *C*
Trocaire College *C*
Ulster County Community College *A*
Utica School of Commerce *C*
Westchester Community College *C, A*

North Carolina

Asheville-Buncombe Technical
   Community College *C, A*
Bladen Community College *C, A*
Carteret Community College *A*
Central Carolina Community
   College *A*
College of the Albemarle *A*
Forsyth Technical Community
   College *C, A*
Gaston College *C*
Halifax Community College *A*
Johnston Community College *A*
Mayland Community College *C*
McDowell Technical Community
   College *A*
Pamlico Community College *A*
Rockingham Community College *A*
Sampson Community College *A*
Surry Community College *C, A*
Western Piedmont Community
   College *C, A*

North Dakota

Dakota College at Bottineau *C, A*
Lake Region State College *C, A*
North Dakota State College of
   Science *C, A*

Ohio

Belmont Technical College *C, A*
Bowling Green State University:
   Firelands College *C*
Cincinnati State Technical and
   Community College *A*
Columbus State Community
   College *C, A*
Eastern Gateway Community
   College *C*
Kent State University
   Trumbull *A*
Miami University
   Hamilton Campus *C*
Northwest State Community
   College *C*
Ohio Valley College of Technology *A*
Southern State Community College *C*
Stark State College of Technology *C*
Terra State Community College *A*
University of Akron *C*
University of Cincinnati
   Raymond Walters College *C, A*
University of Northwestern Ohio *C*
University of Toledo *C*
Wright State University *A*

Oklahoma

Carl Albert State College *C*
Eastern Oklahoma State College *A*
Northeastern Oklahoma Agricultural
   and Mechanical College *C*
Oklahoma City Community College *A*
Seminole State College *A*
Tulsa Community College *C*
Western Oklahoma State College *A*

Oregon

Central Oregon Community
   College *C*
Chemeketa Community College *C*
Clackamas Community College *C*
Clatsop Community College *C*
Lane Community College *A*
Linn-Benton Community College *C*
Portland Community College *C*
Southwestern Oregon Community
   College *C*
Treasure Valley Community College *A*
Umpqua Community College *C*

Pennsylvania

Bucks County Community
   College *C, A*
Butler County Community College *C*
Commonwealth Technical Institute *C*
Community College of
   Philadelphia *C, A*
Newport Business Institute: Lower
   Burrell *A*
Northampton Community College *C*
Pennsylvania Highlands Community
   College *C*
Reading Area Community
   College *C, A*
South Hills School of Business &
   Technology *C*
South Hills School of Business &
   Technology: Altoona *A*

Puerto Rico

American University of Puerto Rico *B*
Caribbean University *A*
Humacao Community College *C*
Inter American University of Puerto
   Rico
   Metropolitan Campus *A, B*
Pontifical Catholic University of
   Puerto Rico *A*
Universidad Adventista de las
   Antillas *A*
University of Puerto Rico
   Bayamon University College *A*
   Cayey University College *A, B*
   Utuado *A, B*

Rhode Island

Community College of Rhode
   Island *C*

South Carolina

Aiken Technical College *C*
Florence-Darlington Technical
   College *C*
Forrest Junior College *A*
Horry-Georgetown Technical
   College *C*
Northeastern Technical College *C, A*
Orangeburg-Calhoun Technical
   College *C*
Spartanburg Community College *C*
Technical College of the
   Lowcountry *C*
Tri-County Technical College *C*
Trident Technical College *C*
Williamsburg Technical College *C*
York Technical College *C*

South Dakota

Northern State University *A, B*

Sinte Gleska University *A*
Western Dakota Technical Institute *C*

Tennessee
Chattanooga State Community
College *A*
Lincoln Memorial University *A, B*
West Tennessee Business College *C*

Texas
Alvin Community College *C*
Amarillo College *A*
Blinn College *A*
Central Texas College *C*
Coastal Bend College *C, A*
College of the Mainland *A*
Del Mar College *C*
El Centro College *C*
El Paso Community College *C, A*
Galveston College *C, A*
Grayson County College *C, A*
Hill College *A*
Howard College *C, A*
Kilgore College *C*
Laredo Community College *C, A*
Lee College *C, A*
McLennan Community College *C*
Midland College *C, A*
Mountain View College *C*
North Central Texas College *A*
Panola College *C*
South Plains College *C*
Texarkana College *C*
Texas A&M University
Commerce *B*
Tyler Junior College *C*
University of Texas
Brownsville - Texas Southmost
College *C, A*
Vernon College *C*
Victoria College *C*
Weatherford College *C, A*

Utah
LDS Business College *C*
Salt Lake Community College *C*

Virginia
Central Virginia Community
College *C*
Dabney S. Lancaster Community
College *C, A*
ECPI College of Technology: Virginia
Beach *C, A*
ECPI Technical College: Roanoke *A*
Eastern Shore Community
College *C, A*
J. Sargeant Reynolds Community
College *C, A*
Lord Fairfax Community College *C*
Mountain Empire Community
College *A*
Patrick Henry Community College *C*
Paul D. Camp Community College *C*
Southside Virginia Community
College *C*
Tidewater Community College *C*
Wytheville Community College *C*

Washington
Bellingham Technical College *C*
Big Bend Community College *C*
Centralia College *C, A*
Clark College *C*
Clover Park Technical College *C*
Everett Community College *C, A*
Grays Harbor College *C*
Green River Community College *C, A*
Highline Community College *C, A*
Lake Washington Technical College *C*
Lower Columbia College *A*
North Seattle Community
College *C, A*

Olympic College *C*
Peninsula College *C*
Pierce College *C, A*
Renton Technical College *C, A*
Shoreline Community College *C*
Skagit Valley College *C*
South Puget Sound Community
College *C, A*
Spokane Community College *C*
Spokane Falls Community
College *C, A*
Wenatchee Valley College *C*
Yakima Valley Community College *C*

West Virginia
Concord University *A*
New River Community and Technical
College *C*
Valley College *C*

Wisconsin
Chippewa Valley Technical College *C*
Fox Valley Technical College *C*
Gateway Technical College *C*
Herzing University *A, B*
Mid-State Technical College *C, A*
Milwaukee Area Technical College *C*
Moraine Park Technical College *C*
Nicolet Area Technical College *C*
Southwest Wisconsin Technical
College *C*
University of Wisconsin
Whitewater *B*
Western Technical College *C*

Wyoming
Central Wyoming College *C*
Eastern Wyoming College *C*

Office management

Alabama
Alabama Agricultural and Mechanical
University *B*
Enterprise-Ozark Community
College *C, A*
Lawson State Community College *A*
Northeast Alabama Community
College *A*
Southern Union State Community
College *C, A*
Wallace State Community College at
Hanceville *A*

Alaska
Ilisagvik College *C, A*
Prince William Sound Community
College *C, A*
University of Alaska
Fairbanks *A*

Arizona
Arizona Western College *C, A*
Cochise College *C*
Everest College
Phoenix *A*
GateWay Community College *A*
Glendale Community College *C*
Mesa Community College *A*
Mohave Community College *C*
Prescott College *B*
Rio Salado College *C, A*
University of Phoenix *B*

Arkansas
East Arkansas Community College *C*
National Park Community
College *C, A*
Southern Arkansas University Tech *A*

California
Barstow Community College *C, A*

Cerritos College *A*
Cerro Coso Community College *C, A*
Chabot College *A*
Chaffey College *C, A*
Citrus College *C, A*
Coastline Community College *C*
College of the Desert *C, A*
College of the Siskiyous *C, A*
De Anza College *A*
El Camino College *C, A*
El Camino College: Compton
Center *C*
Foothill College *C*
Glendale Community College *A*
Golden West College *C, A*
Heald College
Salinas *C*
San Jose *C, A*
Irvine Valley College *C, A*
Kaplan College: Panorama City *A*
Los Angeles Harbor College *C, A*
Los Angeles Mission College *C, A*
Los Medanos College *C, A*
MiraCosta College *C, A*
Mission College *A*
Modesto Junior College *C*
Moorpark College *A*
Napa Valley College *C*
Ohlone College *C, A*
Porterville College *C*
Saddleback College *C, A*
San Jose City College *C*
Santa Barbara City College *C, A*
Santa Rosa Junior College *C*
Shasta College *C, A*
Skyline College *C*
Solano Community College *C, A*
Southwestern College *C, A*
Ventura College *C, A*
West Valley College *A*
Yuba Community College District *C*

Colorado
Arapahoe Community College *C, A*
Colorado Northwestern Community
College *C, A*
Front Range Community College *C, A*
Lamar Community College *A*
Mesa State College *C, A*

Connecticut
Norwalk Community College *C, A*
Quinnipiac University *B*

Delaware
Delaware Technical and Community
College
Owens *C, A*
Stanton/Wilmington *C, A*
Terry *C, A*

District of Columbia
University of the District of
Columbia *B*

Florida
Brevard Community College *C, A*
Clearwater Christian College *B*
Florida State College at
Jacksonville *C, A, B*
Herzing University *C*
Indian River State College *A*
Lake City Community College *C, A*
Miami Dade College *A*
Northwest Florida State College *C, A*
Pensacola Junior College *C, A*
Polk State College *A*
Rasmussen College: Fort Myers *A*
Santa Fe College *C*
Seminole Community College *C, A*
Trinity Baptist College *A*

Georgia
Atlanta Metropolitan College *C, A*
Chattahoochee Technical
College *C, A*
Clayton State University *B*
Dalton State College *C*
Darton College *C, A*
Fort Valley State University *B*
Georgia Highlands College *A*
Gwinnett Technical College *A*
Macon State College *C*
Southeastern Technical College *C*

Illinois
Black Hawk College *C*
College of DuPage *C, A*
Danville Area Community College *C*
Elgin Community College *C*
John A. Logan College *C, A*
Joliet Junior College *C, A*
Kaskaskia College *C*
Kishwaukee College *A*
Loyola University Chicago *C, B*
MacCormac College *A*
Oakton Community College *C, A*
Roosevelt University *B*
Sauk Valley Community College *C*
South Suburban College of Cook
County *C, A*
Spoon River College *C*

Indiana
Ball State University *B*
Indiana State University *B*
University of Southern Indiana *B*

Iowa
Des Moines Area Community
College *C, A*
Iowa Lakes Community College *A*
Southeastern Community College
North Campus *A*

Kansas
Allen County Community College *A*
Central Christian College of
Kansas *A, B*
Coffeyville Community College *A*
Dodge City Community College *C, A*
Fort Hays State University *B*
Neosho County Community
College *A*
Pratt Community College *C, A*
Seward County Community
College *C, A*
Tabor College *B*
Washburn University *C, A*

Kentucky
Campbellsville University *A, B*
Daymar College
Owensboro *A*
Daymar College: Paducah *C*
Eastern Kentucky University *B*
Maysville Community and Technical
College *C, A*
National College
Lexington *A*

Louisiana
ITI Technical College *A*

Maine
Andover College *A*
Beal College *A*
Eastern Maine Community College *A*
Northern Maine Community
College *A*
University of Maine
Machias *A, B*
Washington County Community
College *C, A*

Maryland
Baltimore City Community College *A*
Cecil College *C, A*
Howard Community College *C, A*
Prince George's Community
   College *C, A*

Massachusetts
Babson College *B*
Cape Cod Community College *C, A*
Fitchburg State College *C*
Massasoit Community College *A*
Middlesex Community College *A*
Northern Essex Community
   College *A*
Roxbury Community College *A*

Michigan
Baker College
   of Auburn Hills *A*
   of Cadillac *A, B*
   of Clinton Township *B*
   of Flint *B*
   of Jackson *C, A*
   of Muskegon *B*
   of Owosso *A, B*
   of Port Huron *A, B*
Delta College *A*
Eastern Michigan University *B*
Gogebic Community College *A*
Henry Ford Community College *C*
Lake Superior State University *A*
Lansing Community College *A*
Mott Community College *C, A*
Oakland Community College *C*
Wayne County Community
   College *C, A*

Minnesota
Academy College *C*
Alexandria Technical College *A*
Fond du Lac Tribal and Community
   College *C*
Minneapolis Business College *A*
Minnesota West Community and
   Technical College *C, A*
Rasmussen College: Lake
   Elmo/Woodbury *A*
St. Paul College *A*

Mississippi
Hinds Community College *A*
Mississippi Valley State University *B*
Virginia College Gulf Coast *A*

Missouri
Evangel University *A*
Metropolitan Community College:
   Longview *C, A*
Metropolitan Community College:
   Penn Valley *C, A*
Park University *A*
St. Charles Community College *C, A*
St. Louis Community College
   St. Louis Community College at
     Florissant Valley *C*
   St. Louis Community College at
     Meramec *C*
Southeast Missouri State University *B*
Southwest Baptist University *B*
University of Central Missouri *B*

Montana
Blackfeet Community College *A*
Chief Dull Knife College *C*
Miles Community College *A*
University of Montana *A*
University of Montana: Western *B*

Nebraska
Chadron State College *B*

Mid-Plains Community College
   Area *C, A*
Northeast Community College *C*
Union College *A*
University of Nebraska
   Kearney *B*

Nevada
College of Southern Nevada *C, A*
Great Basin College *A*
Truckee Meadows Community
   College *A*

New Hampshire
Lakes Region Community College *C*
Manchester Community College *C, A*

New Jersey
Cumberland County College *C, A*
Gloucester County College *C, A*
Middlesex County College *A*
Rider University *A, B*
Warren County Community College *C*

New Mexico
Clovis Community College *C, A*
Dona Ana Community College of New
   Mexico State University *C, A*
Navajo Technical College *C*
New Mexico Junior College *C, A*
New Mexico State University
   Grants *A*
Western New Mexico University *C, A*

New York
Bryant & Stratton Business Institute
   Bryant & Stratton College:
     Syracuse *A*
City University of New York
   Borough of Manhattan Community
     College *A*
   Kingsborough Community
     College *A*
   Queensborough Community
     College *A*
College of Westchester *C, A*
Columbia-Greene Community
   College *A*
Erie Community College
   City Campus *A*
   North Campus *A*
   South Campus *A*
Globe Institute of Technology *C, A, B*
Herkimer County Community
   College *A*
Jamestown Business College *C*
Jamestown Community College *A*
Long Island Business Institute *C, A*
Mohawk Valley Community College *C*
Olean Business Institute *C, A*
Rockland Community College *C*
St. Joseph's College: Suffolk
   Campus *C*
State University of New York
   College at Buffalo *B, M*
   College of Agriculture and
     Technology at Morrisville *A*
   Farmingdale *C*
Suffolk County Community College *A*
Sullivan County Community
   College *A*
Trocaire College *A*

North Carolina
Alamance Community College *A*
Catawba Valley Community
   College *C, A*
Fayetteville State University *A, B*
Fayetteville Technical Community
   College *C, A*
Halifax Community College *A*
Isothermal Community College *C, A*

James Sprunt Community
   College *C, A*
Montgomery Community College *C, A*
Pitt Community College *C, A*
Southeastern Community
   College *C, A*
Wayne Community College *C, A*
Wilkes Community College *C, A*
Wilson Community College *C, A*

North Dakota
Dickinson State University *A, B*
Lake Region State College *C, A*
North Dakota State College of
   Science *A*
University of Mary *M*

Ohio
Bowling Green State University *B*
Bradford School *C, A*
Cincinnati State Technical and
   Community College *A*
Columbus State Community
   College *C, A*
Eastern Gateway Community
   College *C, A*
Edison State Community College *C*
James A. Rhodes State College *C, A*
Marion Technical College *C, A*
Miami University
   Hamilton Campus *C, A*
   Oxford Campus *C, A*
Mount Vernon Nazarene
   University *A, B*
Owens Community College
   Toledo *A*
Shawnee State University *A*
Stark State College of Technology *A*
Terra State Community College *A*
University of Akron *C*
University of Akron: Wayne College *A*
University of Cincinnati
   Clermont College *C, A*
University of Rio Grande *B*
Youngstown State University *A*

Oklahoma
East Central University *B*
Eastern Oklahoma State College *C*
Northern Oklahoma College *A*
Seminole State College *A*

Oregon
Chemeketa Community College *A*
Clackamas Community College *C, A*
Clatsop Community College *A*
Lane Community College *A*
Linn-Benton Community College *A*
Portland Community College *C, A*
Southwestern Oregon Community
   College *C, A*
Treasure Valley Community College *A*
Umpqua Community College *C*

Pennsylvania
Bucks County Community
   College *C, A*
Community College of Beaver
   County *C*
Indiana University of Pennsylvania *B*
Lebanon Valley College *C*
Mercyhurst College *A*
Reading Area Community College *A*
South Hills School of Business &
   Technology: Altoona *A*

Puerto Rico
Electronic Data Processing College:
   San Sebastian *A*
Inter American University of Puerto
   Rico
   Bayamon Campus *A, B*
   Guayama Campus *A, B*

Metropolitan Campus *A, B*
San German Campus *A, B*
Turabo University *A, B*
Universidad Metropolitana *A, B*
University of Puerto Rico
   Cayey University College *B*

South Carolina
Bob Jones University *B*
Forrest Junior College *A*
Northeastern Technical College *C*
Technical College of the
   Lowcountry *C, A*
Trident Technical College *A*
University of South Carolina *B*
Williamsburg Technical College *A*

South Dakota
Black Hills State University *B*
Dakota State University *A*
Mitchell Technical Institute *A*
Oglala Lakota College *A*
Southeast Technical Institute *C*

Tennessee
Middle Tennessee State University *B*
National College of Business &
   Technology
   National College: Bristol *A*
Pellissippi State Community
   College *C*
Tennessee Temple University *B*

Texas
Brookhaven College *A*
Cedar Valley College *C, A*
Central Texas College *C, A*
College of the Mainland *A*
Eastfield College *C, A*
Grayson County College *C, A*
Hill College *C, A*
Lamar State College at Orange *C*
Lamar University *B*
Laredo Community College *C, A*
North Lake College *A*
Palo Alto College *C, A*
Panola College *A*
Paris Junior College *A*
South Plains College *C, A*
South Texas College *A*
Sul Ross State University *C, B*
Tarleton State University *B*
Temple College *C, A*
Texas A&M University
   Commerce *B*
Tyler Junior College *A*

Utah
LDS Business College *A*
Weber State University *B*

Virginia
Blue Ridge Community College *C*
Central Virginia Community
   College *C*
Dabney S. Lancaster Community
   College *C, A*
Germanna Community College *C*
Lord Fairfax Community College *C, A*
Mountain Empire Community
   College *A*
National College
   Bluefield *A*
   Harrisonburg *A*
Northern Virginia Community
   College *A*
Paul D. Camp Community College *A*
Thomas Nelson Community
   College *A*
Virginia Highlands Community
   College *C, A*

Washington
Bellevue College *C, A*
Big Bend Community College *C, A*
Clover Park Technical College *A*
Grays Harbor College *C, A*
North Seattle Community
College *C, A*
Peninsula College *C, A*
Pierce College *A*
Renton Technical College *C, A*
South Seattle Community
College *C, A*
Spokane Community College *A*
Spokane Falls Community College *A*
Wenatchee Valley College *A*
Whatcom Community College *C*
Yakima Valley Community College *A*

West Virginia
Concord University *A*
Fairmont State University *B*

Wisconsin
Blackhawk Technical College *A*
Herzing University *A, B*
Lac Courte Oreilles Ojibwa
Community College *A*
Maranatha Baptist Bible College *B*
Mid-State Technical College *A*
Moraine Park Technical College *C, A*
Northeast Wisconsin Technical
College *A*
Rasmussen College: Green Bay *A*

Wyoming
Eastern Wyoming College *A*
Northwest College *A*

Office technology/data entry

Alabama
Faulkner State Community
College *C, A*
Lawson State Community College *A*

Alaska
University of Alaska
Anchorage *A*

Arizona
Brown Mackie College: Tucson *C*
Central Arizona College *A*
Chandler-Gilbert Community College
Pecos *A*
Coconino County Community
College *C*
Eastern Arizona College *C, A*
GateWay Community College *C*
Glendale Community College *C*
Paradise Valley Community
College *C, A*
Phoenix College *C*
Scottsdale Community College *C*

Arkansas
Mid-South Community College *A*
National Park Community
College *C, A*
Phillips Community College of the
University of Arkansas *A*
Southern Arkansas University Tech *C*

California
Allan Hancock College *C, A*
Bakersfield College *A*
Barstow Community College *C*
Butte College *C, A*
Cabrillo College *C, A*
Canada College *C, A*
Cerro Coso Community College *A*
Chabot College *C, A*

Chaffey College *C*
City College of San Francisco *C, A*
Coastline Community College *A*
College of the Redwoods *C, A*
College of the Sequoias *C*
Columbia College *C*
Cypress College *C, A*
Diablo Valley College *C*
East Los Angeles College *C, A*
El Camino College: Compton
Center *C, A*
Evergreen Valley College *A*
Foothill College *C, A*
Fresno City College *C*
Gavilan College *C*
Golden West College *C, A*
Heald College
Fresno *A*
Hayward *C*
Rancho Cordova *C, A*
Stockton *C, A*
Humphreys College *C, A, B*
Imperial Valley College *C, A*
Irvine Valley College *C, A*
Kaplan College: Panorama City *C*
Kaplan College: Vista *C*
Laney College *C*
Lassen Community College *C, A*
Long Beach City College *C, A*
Los Angeles City College *C, A*
Los Angeles Harbor College *C, A*
Los Angeles Southwest College *A*
Los Angeles Valley College *C, A*
MTI College *C*
MiraCosta College *C*
Ohlone College *C, A*
Orange Coast College *C, A*
Reedley College *C*
Riverside Community College *C, A*
Saddleback College *C*
San Diego City College *C, A*
San Joaquin Delta College *A*
San Jose City College *A*
Santa Barbara City College *C*
Santa Rosa Junior College *C*
Shasta College *C, A*
West Hills College: Coalinga *C, A*
West Hills College: Lemoore *C*
West Valley College *C, A*

Colorado
Community College of Aurora *A*
Community College of Denver *C*
Morgan Community College *A*
Pueblo Community College *C, A*
Red Rocks Community College *C, A*

Connecticut
Asnuntuck Community College *A*
Gateway Community College *C*
Lincoln College of New England:
Briarwood *C, A*
Middlesex Community College *C*
Norwalk Community College *C, A*
Quinebaug Valley Community
College *C, A*
Three Rivers Community College *A*
Tunxis Community College *C*

Delaware
Delaware Technical and Community
College
Owens *C, A*
Stanton/Wilmington *A*
Terry *A*

District of Columbia
University of the District of
Columbia *C, A*

Florida
Central Florida Community College *C*

Florida State College at
Jacksonville *C, A*
Indian River State College *C*
Pasco-Hernando Community
College *C*
Santa Fe College *A*
Seminole Community College *C*
Tallahassee Community College *C*

Georgia
Abraham Baldwin Agricultural
College *C, A*
Dalton State College *C, A*
DeKalb Technical College *C*
Georgia Highlands College *A*
Gwinnett Technical College *A*
Macon State College *C*
Middle Georgia College *A*
Middle Georgia Technical College *A*
North Georgia Technical College *C, A*
Savannah Technical College *C, A*
Southwest Georgia Technical
College *C*
West Georgia Technical College *C*

Hawaii
University of Hawaii
Kapiolani Community College *C, A*

Illinois
Black Hawk College *C, A*
Black Hawk College: East
Campus *C, A*
City Colleges of Chicago
Malcolm X College *C, A*
College of Lake County *C, A*
Danville Area Community College *A*
Elgin Community College *C*
Heartland Community College *C*
Illinois Central College *C*
Illinois Eastern Community Colleges
Frontier Community College *C, A*
Lincoln Trail College *C, A*
Olney Central College *C, A*
Wabash Valley College *C, A*
John Wood Community College *C*
Joliet Junior College *C, A*
Kaskaskia College *C, A*
Kishwaukee College *C*
Lake Land College *C*
Lincoln Land Community College *C, A*
MacCormac College *C, A*
McHenry County College *C*
Moraine Valley Community College *C*
Morton College *C*
National-Louis University *C*
Parkland College *C*
Prairie State College *C*
Rend Lake College *C*
Sauk Valley Community College *C*
Shawnee Community College *C*
Southeastern Illinois College *A*
Spoon River College *C*
Triton College *C*
Waubonsee Community College *C, A*

Indiana
College of Court Reporting *A*
Ivy Tech Community College
Columbus *C*
Kokomo *C*
Lafayette *C*
North Central *C*
Northeast *C*
Northwest *C*
Richmond *C*

Iowa
Ellsworth Community College *C, A*
Kirkwood Community College *A*
Northeast Iowa Community
College *C, A*

Southeastern Community College
North Campus *A*
Western Iowa Tech Community
College *C, A*

Kansas
Allen County Community College *C*
Cloud County Community College *A*
Pratt Community College *C, A*
Seward County Community
College *C, A*
Washburn University *A*

Kentucky
Daymar College
Owensboro *C, A*
West Kentucky Community and
Technical College *A*

Louisiana
Baton Rouge Community College *C, A*
ITI Technical College *A*

Maine
Andover College *A*
Central Maine Community
College *C, A*
Northern Maine Community
College *A*

Maryland
Baltimore City Community
College *C, A*
Garrett College *C, A*
Kaplan College: Hagerstown *C, A, B*
Montgomery College *C*
Prince George's Community
College *C, A*

Massachusetts
Berkshire Community College *A*
Massasoit Community College *C*
Middlesex Community College *C, A*
North Shore Community College *C*
Northern Essex Community
College *A*
Quincy College *A*
Roxbury Community College *A*
Suffolk University *B*

Michigan
Baker College
of Auburn Hills *A*
of Flint *A*
of Muskegon *A*
of Port Huron *A*
Delta College *A*
Glen Oaks Community College *A*
Gogebic Community College *A*
Lake Michigan College *C*
Lake Superior State University *A*
Lansing Community College *A*
Macomb Community College *C, A*
Monroe County Community
College *C, A*
Montcalm Community College *C, A*
Mott Community College *C, A*
North Central Michigan College *C*
Northern Michigan University *A*
Northwestern Michigan College *A*
Oakland Community College *C, A*
St. Clair County Community
College *A*
Schoolcraft College *C, A*
West Shore Community College *A*

Minnesota
Anoka-Ramsey Community College *C*
Dakota County Technical College *C*
Hennepin Technical College *C, A*
Inver Hills Community College *C*

Mesabi Range Community and
Technical College *C, A*
Minneapolis Community and
Technical College *A*
Minnesota State College - Southeast
Technical *C*
Minnesota State Community and
Technical College *C, A*
Normandale Community College *C*
Northland Community & Technical
College *C*
Pine Technical College *C*
Riverland Community College *C*
Rochester Community and Technical
College *C*

Mississippi
Antonelli College
Jackson *C, A*
Copiah-Lincoln Community College *A*
Mississippi Gulf Coast Community
College *A*
Northwest Mississippi Community
College *A*
Pearl River Community College *A*

Missouri
Baptist Bible College *A*
Metropolitan Community College:
Longview *C, A*
Metropolitan Community College:
Maple Woods *C, A*
Metropolitan Community College:
Penn Valley *C, A*
North Central Missouri College *C, A*
Ozarks Technical Community
College *C, A*
St. Louis Community College
St. Louis Community College at
Florissant Valley *C, A*
St. Louis Community College at
Meramec *C, A*

Montana
Helena College of Technology of the
University of Montana *A*

Nebraska
Peru State College *B*

Nevada
Everest College: Las Vegas *C*
Great Basin College *C, A*
Truckee Meadows Community
College *A*
Western Nevada College *A*

New Hampshire
Nashua Community College *C*
River Valley Community College *A*
White Mountains Community
College *C, A*

New Jersey
Berkeley College- Garret Mountain
Campus *C*
Camden County College *C*
Essex County College *A*
Gloucester County College *A*
Warren County Community College *C*

New Mexico
Clovis Community College *A*
New Mexico Junior College *C, A*
New Mexico State University
Alamogordo *C*
Southwestern Indian Polytechnic
Institute *C, A*

New York
Berkeley College *C*
Berkeley College of New York City *C*

Bryant & Stratton Business Institute
Bryant & Stratton College:
Rochester *A*
Business Informatics Center *A*
City University of New York
Bronx Community College *A*
Hostos Community College *C, A*
Queensborough Community
College *C*
Columbia-Greene Community
College *C, A*
Dutchess Community College *C, A*
Globe Institute of Technology *C*
Herkimer County Community
College *C, A*
Hudson Valley Community
College *C, A*
Jamestown Community College *C*
Mercy College *A*
Olean Business Institute *A*
Orange County Community
College *C, A*
Professional Business College *A*
St. Joseph's College: Suffolk
Campus *C*
State University of New York
College of Agriculture and
Technology at Morrisville *C, A*
Suffolk County Community
College *C, A*
Sullivan County Community
College *C, A*
Technical Career Institutes *C, A*
Trocaire College *C*

North Carolina
Asheville-Buncombe Technical
Community College *A*
Bladen Community College *A*
Central Piedmont Community
College *C*
East Carolina University *B*
Halifax Community College *A*
Piedmont Community College *A*
Rockingham Community College *A*
Rowan-Cabarrus Community
College *C, A*
South College *A*
Vance-Granville Community
College *A*
Western Piedmont Community
College *C, A*

North Dakota
Bismarck State College *C, A*
Cankdeska Cikana Community
College *A*
Minot State University *C*
Sitting Bull College *A*

Ohio
Ashland University *C, A*
Bowling Green State University:
Firelands College *C*
Cincinnati State Technical and
Community College *C*
Kent State University
Trumbull *A*
Marion Technical College *C, A*
Northwest State Community
College *A*
Ohio University
Southern Campus at Ironton *A*
Southern State Community College *A*
Southwestern College of Business
Southwestern College: Franklin *A*
Stark State College of Technology *A*
Terra State Community College *C*
Trumbull Business College *A*
University of Akron: Wayne
College *C, A*
University of Cincinnati
Clermont College *C, A*
Raymond Walters College *C*

University of Northwestern Ohio *C, A*
University of Rio Grande *C, A, B*
University of Toledo *A*

Oklahoma
Oklahoma State University
Oklahoma City *A*
Tulsa Community College *A*
Western Oklahoma State College *A*

Oregon
Chemeketa Community College *C, A*
Clatsop Community College *C, A*
Portland Community College *C*
Rogue Community College *C*
Treasure Valley Community College *C*

Pennsylvania
Bucks County Community College *C*
Community College of Allegheny
County *C*
Consolidated School of Business
Lancaster *A*
York *A*
Douglas Education Center *A*
Newport Business Institute: Lower
Burrell *A*
Penn Commercial Business and
Technical School *C*
Reading Area Community
College *C, A*

Puerto Rico
American University of Puerto Rico *B*
Columbia College
Columbia Centro Universitario:
Yauco *A*
Huertas Junior College *C*
Inter American University of Puerto
Rico
Ponce Campus *A, B*
National College of Business and
Technology: Bayamon *A*
Universal Career Community College:
Humacao *A*
Universal Career Community College:
Manati *A*
Universal Career Community College:
San Juan *A*

South Carolina
Aiken Technical College *C*
Central Carolina Technical College *C*
Denmark Technical College *C*
Florence-Darlington Technical
College *C*
Forrest Junior College *A*
Northeastern Technical College *C, A*
Orangeburg-Calhoun Technical
College *C*
Tri-County Technical College *C*
Trident Technical College *C*
York Technical College *C*

Tennessee
Austin Peay State University *A*
Chattanooga State Community
College *C*
Remington College
Memphis *A*

Texas
Amarillo College *C*
Angelina College *C*
Brookhaven College *C, A*
Cedar Valley College *A*
Central Texas College *C*
Clarendon College *C, A*
Coastal Bend College *C, A*
College of the Mainland *C, A*
Collin County Community College
District *C, A*
Eastfield College *A*

El Centro College *C*
El Paso Community College *C*
Galveston College *C*
Grayson County College *C, A*
Hallmark College of Technology *A*
Hill College *C, A*
Houston Community College
System *C, A*
Laredo Community College *C, A*
McLennan Community College *C, A*
Midland College *A*
Navarro College *C*
North Central Texas College *A*
North Lake College *A*
Northeast Texas Community
College *C, A*
Palo Alto College *A*
Panola College *C*
Paris Junior College *A*
San Antonio College *C*
San Jacinto College *C, A*
Southwest Texas Junior College *A*
Tarrant County College *C*
Texas State Technical College
Harlingen *C*
Texas Wesleyan University *B*
Trinity Valley Community
College *C, A*
Vernon College *C, A*
Weatherford College *C*

Utah
Salt Lake Community College *C*
Utah Valley University *A*

Virginia
Blue Ridge Community College *C*
Centura College: Chesapeake *A*
Dabney S. Lancaster Community
College *C*
ECPI College of Technology: Virginia
Beach *C, A*
ECPI Technical College: Roanoke *A*
J. Sargeant Reynolds Community
College *C, A*
Mountain Empire Community
College *C*
New River Community College *A*
Northern Virginia Community
College *C*
Paul D. Camp Community College *C*
Virginia Western Community
College *A*

Washington
Centralia College *C, A*
Clark College *C, A*
Green River Community College *C, A*
Lower Columbia College *C, A*
North Seattle Community College *A*
Olympic College *C*
Peninsula College *C*
South Seattle Community
College *C, A*
Spokane Community College *C, A*

West Virginia
Blue Ridge Community and Technical
College *C, A*
New River Community and Technical
College *C*
West Virginia Junior College *C, A*
West Virginia Northern Community
College *C*

Wisconsin
Chippewa Valley Technical College *A*
Fox Valley Technical College *C, A*
Herzing University *A, B*
Milwaukee Area Technical College *C*
Moraine Park Technical College *C, A*
Northeast Wisconsin Technical
College *C, A*

Southwest Wisconsin Technical
College *C*
Wisconsin Indianhead Technical
College *C*

Wyoming

Casper College *C, A*
Central Wyoming College *C*
Western Wyoming Community
College *C, A*

Oncology

Arizona*

University of Arizona *M, D*

California

Stanford University *M, D*

District of Columbia

George Washington University *D*
Georgetown University *M, D*

Florida

University of Miami *D*
University of South Florida *D*

Illinois

University of Chicago *D*

Michigan

Wayne State University *M, D*

Nebraska

University of Nebraska
Medical Center *M, D*

North Carolina

Wake Forest University *D*

Ohio

University of Toledo *M, D*

Tennessee

Vanderbilt University *D*

Texas

University of Texas
Health Science Center at
Houston *M, D*

Utah

University of Utah *M, D*

West Virginia

West Virginia University *D*

Wisconsin

University of Wisconsin
Madison *M, D*

Operations management

Alabama

Auburn University *B*
Lawson State Community College *A*
Remington College
Mobile *B*

Arizona

Arizona State University *B*
Eastern Arizona College *C*
University of Arizona *B*
University of Phoenix *M, D*

Arkansas

East Arkansas Community College *C*

California

California State University
Dominguez Hills *B*
East Bay *M*
Long Beach *B*
Sacramento *B, M*
San Bernardino *B, M*
Citrus College *C*
City College of San Francisco *C, A*
DeVry University
Long Beach *B*
Sherman Oaks *M*
Fashion Institute of Design and
Merchandising
Los Angeles *A*
Golden Gate University *C, B, M*
Laney College *C, A*
National University *B*
Palomar College *C, A*
San Diego City College *C, A*
San Diego State University *M*

Colorado

Fort Lewis College *B*

Connecticut

Central Connecticut State
University *M*

Delaware

University of Delaware *B*

District of Columbia

George Washington University *M*

Florida

Daytona State College *A*
Florida State College at Jacksonville *C*
Hillsborough Community College *A*
Pasco-Hernando Community
College *C*

Georgia

Albany Technical College *C*
Central Georgia Technical
College *C, A*
Clayton State University *B*
Dalton State College *B*
DeVry University
Alpharetta *B*
Decatur *B*
Georgia State University *M, D*
Macon State College *B*
Savannah Technical College *C, A*
Southwest Georgia Technical
College *C, A*

Hawaii

University of Hawaii
Hawaii Community College *C, A*

Idaho

Boise State University *B*
University of Idaho *B*

Illinois

Aurora University *B*
Carl Sandburg College *A*
Kishwaukee College *C, A*
Loyola University Chicago *C, B*
McHenry County College *C, A*
Northern Illinois University *B*
Northwestern University *M*
Prairie State College *C, A*
University of Illinois
Urbana-Champaign *B, D*

Indiana

Ball State University *B*
Indiana Institute of Technology *B*
Indiana University-Purdue University
Fort Wayne *C, A, B, M*

Purdue University *A, B*
Purdue University
North Central *C, A, B*
Trine University *B*
University of Southern Indiana *B, M*

Iowa

Iowa Central Community College *A*
Iowa State University *B*

Kansas

Barton County Community College *A*
Southwestern College *B*

Kentucky

Daymar College
Owensboro *A*

Maine

Northern Maine Community
College *A*

Maryland

University of Maryland
University College *C, M*

Massachusetts

Babson College *B*
Bentley University *M*
Boston College *B*
Boston University *B*
Bridgewater State College *M*
Bunker Hill Community College *A*
Wentworth Institute of Technology *B*
Worcester Polytechnic Institute *B, M*

Michigan

Baker College
of Flint *A, B*
Central Michigan University *B*
Ferris State University *C, B*
Kettering University *M*
Lawrence Technological University *M*
Macomb Community College *C, A*
Michigan State University *D*
Oakland University *B*
Saginaw Valley State University *B*
Spring Arbor University *B, M*
University of Michigan
Flint *B*

Minnesota

Alexandria Technical College *C, A*
Crown College *B*
Dakota County Technical College *C*
Metropolitan State University *B*
Minnesota State University
Mankato *B*
University of St. Thomas *B*
Winona State University *B*

Mississippi

Hinds Community College *A*

Missouri

Missouri Baptist University *B*
Missouri Southern State University *B*
University of Missouri
St. Louis *B, M*
Washington University in St.
Louis *B, M*

Nebraska

University of Nebraska
Kearney *B*

Nevada

Truckee Meadows Community
College *C*

New Hampshire

Nashua Community College *C*
Southern New Hampshire
University *M*

New Jersey

Cumberland County College *A*
New Jersey Institute of Technology *M*
Thomas Edison State College *C, B*
Warren County Community College *C*

New Mexico

Western New Mexico University *B*

New York

City University of New York
Baruch College *B*
Excelsior College *B*
Globe Institute of Technology *C, A, B*
Le Moyne College *B*
Polytechnic Institute of New York
University *M*
State University of New York
Farmingdale *B*

North Carolina

Asheville-Buncombe Technical
Community College *A*
Catawba Valley Community College *A*
Central Piedmont Community
College *C*
Cleveland Community College *A*
Durham Technical Community
College *C, A*
Fayetteville Technical Community
College *C, A*
Isothermal Community College *C, A*
Mitchell Community College *A*
Pitt Community College *C, A*
University of North Carolina
Asheville *B*
Charlotte *B*
Wayne Community College *C, A*
Western Piedmont Community
College *C, A*

North Dakota

Bismarck State College *B*
University of Mary *M*
University of North Dakota *B*

Ohio

Bowling Green State University *B*
Bowling Green State University:
Firelands College *C, A*
Case Western Reserve University *M*
Franklin University *B*
Miami University
Oxford Campus *B*
North Central State College *C, A*
Ohio State University
Columbus Campus *B*
Owens Community College
Toledo *C, A*
Stark State College of Technology *A*
Terra State Community College *C*
Tiffin University *B*
University of Akron *B, M*
University of Cincinnati *B, M, D*
University of Dayton *B*
University of Rio Grande *B*
University of Toledo *B, M*
Wright State University *M*
Youngstown State University *B*

Oklahoma

East Central University *B*
Northeastern State University *B*
University of Central Oklahoma *B*

Oregon

Clackamas Community College *C, A*

Oregon Institute of Technology B

Pennsylvania
Bucks County Community College A
Butler County Community College C
Carnegie Mellon University M, D
Community College of Philadelphia A
Edinboro University of
   Pennsylvania B
La Salle University B
Lehigh Carbon Community College A
Reading Area Community College A
University of Pennsylvania B, M, D
University of Scranton B, M
Widener University B

Puerto Rico
Inter American University of Puerto
   Rico
   Ponce Campus B
Turabo University M
University of Puerto Rico
   Rio Piedras B, M

Rhode Island
Bryant University M

South Carolina
Clemson University B, M, D
Morris College B

Tennessee
Chattanooga State Community
   College C
Tennessee Technological University B
Vanderbilt University M

Texas
El Paso Community College A
Kilgore College C, A
Lamar University M
LeTourneau University B
Odessa College C
Sam Houston State University B
San Antonio College C
Tarrant County College C, A
Texas A&M University M
Texas A&M University
   Commerce B
Texas Southern University B
Texas State Technical College
   Waco A
University of Dallas M
University of Houston B, M, D
University of North Texas B
University of Texas
   El Paso B
   San Antonio B, M
Weatherford College C, A
Wiley College B

Utah
Utah State University B
Utah Valley University B

Vermont
College of St. Joseph in Vermont B

Virginia
St. Paul's College B

Washington
Bellingham Technical College C, A
City University of Seattle M
Washington State University B
Western Washington University B

Wisconsin
Alverno College B
Blackhawk Technical College A
Chippewa Valley Technical College A
Gateway Technical College A

Lakeshore Technical College A
Marian University B
Marquette University M
Milwaukee Area Technical College A
University of Wisconsin
   Madison B, M
   Milwaukee B
   Oshkosh B
   Stout B
   Whitewater B
Waukesha County Technical
   College C, A
Western Technical College A
Wisconsin Indianhead Technical
   College A

Operations research

Alabama
University of Alabama
   Huntsville M

Arkansas
University of Arkansas M

California
California State University
   Fullerton B, M
University of California
   Berkeley B, M, D
University of Southern California M

Colorado
United States Air Force Academy B

Delaware
Delaware Technical and Community
   College
   Stanton/Wilmington A
University of Delaware B, M, D

District of Columbia
George Washington University M, D

Florida
Florida Institute of Technology M, D

Georgia
Georgia Institute of Technology M

Illinois
University of Illinois
   Urbana-Champaign B, M, D

Iowa
Iowa State University M

Kansas
Kansas State University M

Massachusetts
Massachusetts Institute of
   Technology M, D
Northeastern University M

Missouri
University of Missouri
   Missouri University of Science and
      Technology M

New Jersey
Princeton University B, M, D
Rutgers, The State University of New
   Jersey
   New Brunswick/Piscataway
      Campus M, D

New York
City University of New York
   Baruch College B, M

Columbia University B, M, D
Cornell University B, M, D
New York University B, M, D
United States Military Academy B

North Carolina
North Carolina State University M, D

Ohio
Bowling Green State University B
Case Western Reserve
   University M, D

Oregon
Oregon State University M

Pennsylvania
Carnegie Mellon University B
University of Pennsylvania D

South Carolina
Bob Jones University B

Texas
Southern Methodist University M, D
Texas A&M University
   Commerce B

Utah
Utah State University M

Virginia
George Mason University M

Ophthalmic laboratory technology

California
Canada College A

Connecticut
Middlesex Community College A

Florida
Broward College A

Georgia
DeKalb Technical College A

Indiana
Indiana University
   Bloomington A

Minnesota
St. Catherine University A

New York
Rochester Institute of Technology A

Oregon
Eastern Oregon University B

Puerto Rico
Inter American University of Puerto
   Rico
   Ponce Campus A
University of Puerto Rico
   Medical Sciences A

Texas
Abilene Christian University B
Tyler Junior College A

Ophthalmic technology

Illinois
Triton College A

Indiana
Ivy Tech Community College
   Columbus A

New York
Rochester Institute of Technology A

Oregon
Portland Community College A

Tennessee
Volunteer State Community College A

Virginia
Old Dominion University B

Opticianry/ophthalmic dispensing

Connecticut
Middlesex Community College A

Florida
Gulf Coast Community College A
Hillsborough Community College A
Miami Dade College A

Georgia
DeKalb Technical College A

Indiana
Indiana University
   Bloomington A

Massachusetts
Holyoke Community College A

Michigan
Baker College
   of Jackson A

Mississippi
Mississippi Gulf Coast Community
   College A

Nevada
College of Southern Nevada A

New Jersey
Camden County College A
Essex County College A
Raritan Valley Community College A

New Mexico
Southwestern Indian Polytechnic
   Institute A

New York
City University of New York
   New York City College of
      Technology A
Erie Community College
   North Campus A

North Carolina
Durham Technical Community
   College A

Ohio
Cuyahoga Community College
   Metropolitan Campus A
Hocking College A

Rhode Island
Community College of Rhode
   Island A

Tennessee
Roane State Community College A

Texas
El Paso Community College *A*
University of Houston *B*

Virginia
J. Sargeant Reynolds Community
College *A*

Washington
Spokane Community College *A*

Optics

Arizona
University of Arizona *B, M, D*

California
Yuba Community College District *C*

Delaware
Delaware State University *D*

Indiana
Indiana University
Bloomington *M, D*

Massachusetts
Tufts University *M, D*

Michigan
Saginaw Valley State University *B*

New Mexico
University of New Mexico *M, D*

New York
Corning Community College *A*
Excelsior College *A, B*
Monroe Community College *A*
University of Rochester *B, M, D*

North Carolina
University of North Carolina
Charlotte *M, D*

Ohio
University of Dayton *M, D*

Oklahoma
Oklahoma State University *D*

Pennsylvania
Albright College *B*
Indiana University of Pennsylvania *A*

Puerto Rico
EDIC College *A*

Virginia
Norfolk State University *B*

Optometric assistant

Florida
Hillsborough Community College *A*

Iowa
Hawkeye Community College *C*

Michigan
Bay de Noc Community College *C*
Delta College *A*
Oakland Community College *C*

New Jersey
Raritan Valley Community College *C*

New Mexico
Southwestern Indian Polytechnic
Institute *C*

Ohio
Mercy College of Northwest Ohio *C*

Texas
San Jacinto College *C, A*

Optometry (O.D.)

Alabama
University of Alabama at Birmingham:
School of Optometry *P*

California
Southern California College of
Optometry *P*
University of California Berkeley:
School of Optometry *P*

Florida
Nova Southeastern University Health
Professions Division: College of
Optometry *P*

Illinois
Illinois College of Optometry *P*

Indiana
Indiana University Bloomington:
School of Optometry *P*

Massachusetts
New England College of Optometry *P*

Michigan
Ferris State University: College of
Optometry *P*

Missouri
University of Missouri St. Louis:
School of Optometry *P*

New York
State University of New York College
of Optometry *P*

Ohio
Ohio State University Columbus
Campus: College of Optometry *P*

Oklahoma
Northeastern State University: College
of Optometry *P*

Oregon
Pacific University: School of
Optometry *P*

Pennsylvania
Salus University *P*

Puerto Rico
Inter American University of Puerto
Rico School of Optometry *P*

Tennessee
Southern College of Optometry *P*

Texas
University of Houston: College of
Optometry *P*

Organic chemistry

Arizona
Mesa Community College *A*

California
Pitzer College *B*

Florida
Florida State University *M, D*

Iowa
Iowa State University *M, D*

Massachusetts
Tufts University *M, D*

Montana
University of Montana *M, D*

New York
Fordham University *M*
State University of New York
Albany *D*

Texas
Texas A&M University
Commerce *B*

Vermont
Marlboro College *B*

Wisconsin
Marquette University *M, D*
University of Wisconsin
River Falls *B*

Organizational behavior studies

Arizona
Estrella Mountain Community
College *C, A*
Paradise Valley Community
College *C, A*
University of Phoenix *M*

Arkansas
Central Baptist College *B*

California
Antioch Southern California
Antioch University Los Angeles *M*
Antioch University Santa Barbara *M*
California Institute of Integral
Studies *M, D*
California State University
San Bernardino *B*
Fresno Pacific University *B*
National University *B, M*
Pepperdine University *M*
Pitzer College *B*
St. Mary's College of California *M*
Santa Clara University *B*
Scripps College *B*
Simpson University *B*
University of La Verne *M*
University of San Francisco *B*
Woodbury University *B, M*

Colorado
Colorado Christian University *C, B*
Colorado Technical University *C*
University of Colorado
Denver *M*
University of Denver *B*

Connecticut
Central Connecticut State
University *B*
Eastern Connecticut State
University *M*
University of Hartford *M*

Delaware
Wilmington University *M*

District of Columbia
American University *M*
George Washington University *M*

Florida
Bethune-Cookman University *M*
Nova Southeastern University *M*
Palm Beach Atlantic University *M*
Saint Thomas University *B*

Georgia
Brenau University *B*
Emory University *B*
LaGrange College *B, M*
Oglethorpe University *B*

Illinois
Benedictine University *B, M, D*
DePaul University *B*
Dominican University *B, M*
Greenville College *B*
Loyola University Chicago *C, B, M*
North Park University *B*
Northwestern University *C, B, M, D*
Roosevelt University *C, B*
Trinity International University *B, M*
University of Illinois
Urbana-Champaign *B, D*
University of St. Francis *B*

Indiana
Anderson University *B*
Calumet College of St. Joseph *B*
Indiana University
Bloomington *D*
Oakland City University *B*

Iowa
St. Ambrose University *B*

Kansas
Central Christian College of Kansas *A*
Cowley County Community
College *C, A*
Kansas State University *C*

Kentucky
Mid-Continent University *B*
Midway College *B*
Northern Kentucky University *B, M*
University of the Cumberlands *B*

Maine
University of Southern Maine *B*

Maryland
Washington Adventist University *B*

Massachusetts
Boston College *D*
Boston University *B*
Bridgewater State College *M*
Emerson College *M*
Harvard College *M, D*
Mount Holyoke College *B*

Michigan
Central Michigan University *M*
Michigan State University *D*
University of Michigan *B*
University of Michigan
Flint *B, M*
Wayne State University *B*

Minnesota
Bethel University *B, M*
College of St. Scholastica *B*
Northwestern College *M*

Walden University D

Missouri
Calvary Bible College and Theological
    Seminary B
Fontbonne University B
Hannibal-LaGrange College B
Saint Louis University B
University of Missouri
    St. Louis B
Washington University in St. Louis M

New Jersey
Rider University B

New York
City University of New York
    Baruch College M
Polytechnic Institute of New York
    University M
United States Military Academy B

North Carolina
High Point University B
Mount Olive College B

Ohio
Baldwin-Wallace College C
Bluffton University B, M
Bowling Green State University B, M
Case Western Reserve
    University M, D
College of Mount St. Joseph M
Denison University B
Lourdes College M
Mount Vernon Nazarene University B
Owens Community College
    Toledo C
Tiffin University B, M
University of Findlay M
University of Toledo B
Urbana University B

Oklahoma
Oral Roberts University B
University of Oklahoma M
University of Tulsa B

Pennsylvania
Cabrini College M
Carnegie Mellon University D
Keystone College B
La Salle University B
Neumann University M
Penn State
    Abington B
    Altoona B
    Beaver B
    Berks B
    Brandywine B
    DuBois B
    Erie, The Behrend College B
    Fayette, The Eberly Campus B
    Greater Allegheny B
    Harrisburg B, M
    Hazleton B
    Lehigh Valley B
    Mont Alto B
    New Kensington B
    Schuylkill B
    Shenango B
    University Park B
    Wilkes-Barre B
    Worthington Scranton B
    York B
Robert Morris University B, M
Rosemont College B
Shippensburg University of
    Pennsylvania M
University of Pennsylvania M
Valley Forge Christian College M
Westminster College B

Rhode Island
Providence College B

South Carolina
Anderson University B
Claflin University B

South Dakota
University of Sioux Falls B

Tennessee
Vanderbilt University M

Texas
Lubbock Christian University M
Southern Methodist University B
University of Dallas M
University of Houston B
University of North Texas B
University of Texas
    San Antonio D
University of the Incarnate Word B

Utah
Brigham Young University B

Vermont
Champlain College B

Virginia
Eastern Mennonite University B
George Mason University M
Regent University B, D
University of Richmond C, B

Washington
University of Washington B, M

Wisconsin
Carroll University B
University of Wisconsin
    Platteville B

Organizational communication

Arizona
University of Phoenix A, B

California
Bethany University B
California State University
    Chico B
College of the Desert A
Folsom Lake College A
Ohlone College C
Pepperdine University B

Colorado
Colorado State University M
Jones International University B, M

Connecticut
Mitchell College B
Three Rivers Community College C

Florida
Barry University M
Florida Institute of Technology M
Palm Beach Atlantic University B
Southeastern University B

Georgia
Toccoa Falls College B

Idaho
University of Idaho B

Illinois
Bradley University B
North Central College B
Roosevelt University B
Saint Xavier University B
University of Illinois
    Urbana-Champaign B

Indiana
Indiana University-Purdue University
    Fort Wayne B
Valparaiso University B

Iowa
Buena Vista University B
University of Northern Iowa B

Kansas
Tabor College B

Kentucky
Murray State University B, M
Western Kentucky University B

Louisiana
Southeastern Louisiana University M

Maryland
Bowie State University M

Massachusetts
Assumption College B
Regis College M
Suffolk University B, M

Michigan
Central Michigan University B, M
Michigan Technological University C
University of Michigan
    Flint B
Western Michigan University B

Minnesota
Augsburg College B

Missouri
Lindenwood University B, M
Northwest Missouri State
    University B
Rockhurst University C
William Jewell College B

Nebraska
Creighton University A, B
Doane College B

New Jersey
Montclair State University B

New York
Canisius College M
Ithaca College B
Marist College M
State University of New York
    College at Cortland B
    College at Plattsburgh B

North Carolina
Methodist University B
North Carolina State University M
Queens University of Charlotte B, M
University of North Carolina
    Charlotte B, M

Ohio
Capital University B
Cedarville University B
Marietta College B
Ohio Northern University B
Ohio University M, D

Ohio University
    Southern Campus at Ironton B
    Zanesville Campus B
Otterbein College B
University of Akron C, B
Wright State University B
Xavier University A, B

Oregon
George Fox University B
University of Portland B, M

Pennsylvania
Butler County Community College A
Penn State
    Lehigh Valley C
Temple University B, M

South Carolina
College of Charleston M

Tennessee
Lipscomb University B
Trevecca Nazarene University B

Texas
Lubbock Christian University B

Vermont
Champlain College B

Virginia
Liberty University M

Washington
Northwest University B

Wisconsin
Carroll University B
Marian University B
Viterbo University B

Ornamental horticulture

Arkansas
University of Arkansas B

California
Antelope Valley College C, A
Bakersfield College A
Butte College C, A
Cabrillo College C, A
California Polytechnic State
    University: San Luis Obispo B
Cerritos College A
City College of San Francisco A
College of San Mateo C, A
College of the Desert C, A
College of the Sequoias C, A
Cuyamaca College A
El Camino College C, A
Foothill College C, A
Long Beach City College C, A
Los Angeles Pierce College C, A
Merced College C, A
Modesto Junior College A
Monterey Peninsula College C, A
Mount San Antonio College C
Orange Coast College C, A
Saddleback College C, A
San Joaquin Delta College C, A
Santa Barbara City College C, A
Santa Rosa Junior College C
Shasta College C, A
Solano Community College C, A
Southwestern College C, A
Victor Valley College C, A
Yuba Community College
    District C, A

Colorado

Northeastern Junior College *C, A*

Delaware

University of Delaware *B, M*

Florida

Florida Southern College *B*
Gulf Coast Community College *A*
Palm Beach Community College *A*
Pensacola Junior College *A*
South Florida Community
  College *C, A*

Georgia

Abraham Baldwin Agricultural
  College *A*
Fort Valley State University *A*

Illinois

College of DuPage *C*
College of Lake County *C, A*
Joliet Junior College *C, A*
Kishwaukee College *C, A*
McHenry County College *C*
Triton College *C, A*
University of Illinois
  Urbana-Champaign *B*

Iowa

Kirkwood Community College *C*

Kentucky

Eastern Kentucky University *B*

Maine

Unity College *B*
University of Maine *C, B*

Maryland

Prince George's Community
  College *C*

Michigan

Ferris State University *A*

Mississippi

Mississippi Gulf Coast Community
  College *C, A*

Missouri

St. Louis Community College
  St. Louis Community College at
    Meramec *C, A*

Nebraska

Nebraska College of Technical
  Agriculture *A*

Nevada

College of Southern Nevada *C, A*

New Jersey

Brookdale Community College *C*
Cumberland County College *C, A*
Mercer County Community
  College *C, A*

New York

Cornell University *B, M, D*
Finger Lakes Community College *C, A*
Niagara County Community
  College *C*
State University of New York
  College of Agriculture and
    Technology at Cobleskill *A*
  College of Agriculture and
    Technology at Morrisville *A*
  College of Technology at Delhi *A*
  Farmingdale *C, A*

North Carolina

Blue Ridge Community College *C*
Sampson Community College *A*

Ohio

Ohio State University
  Agricultural Technical Institute *A*

Oklahoma

Eastern Oklahoma State College *A*

Oregon

Clackamas Community College *C, A*

Pennsylvania

Community College of Allegheny
  County *C*
Delaware Valley College *B*

Puerto Rico

Inter American University of Puerto
  Rico
  San German Campus *C*

Tennessee

University of Tennessee
  Knoxville *B, M*
Walters State Community College *A*

Texas

Houston Community College
  System *C*
Palo Alto College *A*
Tarleton State University *B*
Texas A&M University *B, M*

Utah

Utah State University *C, A, B*

Vermont

Vermont Technical College *A*

Washington

South Puget Sound Community
  College *C, A*
South Seattle Community
  College *C, A*
Spokane Community College *C*

Wisconsin

Blackhawk Technical College *C*
Fox Valley Technical College *C*

Orthotics/prosthetics

Connecticut

University of Hartford *M*

Florida

St. Petersburg College *B*

Georgia

Georgia Institute of Technology *M*

Illinois

Northwestern University *C*

Massachusetts

Boston University *M, D*

Michigan

Baker College
  of Flint *A*
Eastern Michigan University *M*

Minnesota

Century Community and Technical
  College *C, A*

Mississippi

Mississippi Gulf Coast Community
  College *A*

Nevada

College of Southern Nevada *A*

Oklahoma

Oklahoma State University
  Institute of Technology:
    Okmulgee *A*

Pennsylvania

University of Pittsburgh *B*

Texas

University of Texas
  Southwestern Medical Center at
    Dallas *B*

Washington

Centralia College *C*
Spokane Falls Community College *A*
University of Washington *B*

Osteopathic medicine (D.O.)

California

Western University of Health
  Sciences *P*

Florida

Nova Southeastern University Health
  Professions Division: College of
  Osteopathic Medicine *P*

Illinois

Midwestern University: Chicago
  College of Osteopathic
  Medicine *P*

Iowa

Des Moines University: Osteopathic
  Medical Center *P*

Maine

University of New England: School of
  Osteopathic Medicine *P*

Michigan

Michigan State University: College of
  Osteopathic Medicine *P*

Missouri

Kirksville College of Osteopathic
  Medicine *P*
University of Health Sciences College
  of Osteopathic Medicine *P*

New Jersey

UMDNJ-School of Osteopathic
  Medicine *P*

New York

New York College of Osteopathic
  Medicine of New York Institute
  of Technology *P*

Ohio

Ohio University
  College of Osteopathic Medicine *P*

Oklahoma

Oklahoma State University: College of
  Osteopathic Medicine *P*

Pennsylvania

Lake Erie College of Osteopathic
  Medicine *P*
Philadelphia College of Osteopathic
  Medicine *P*

Texas

University of North Texas Health
  Science Center at Fort Worth:
  Osteopathic Medicine *P*

West Virginia

West Virginia School of Osteopathic
  Medicine *P*

Pacific area/rim studies

California

Claremont McKenna College *B*
University of California
  San Diego *M*

Hawaii

University of Hawaii
  Manoa *M*
  West Oahu *B*

Painting

Alabama

Birmingham-Southern College *B*

Arizona

Northern Arizona University *B*
Prescott College *B*

Arkansas

Harding University *B*

California

Academy of Art University *C, A, B, M*
Art Center College of Design *B, M*
Biola University *B*
California College of the Arts *B, M*
California State University
  East Bay *B*
  Long Beach *B, M*
  Northridge *B, M*
Chabot College *A*
College of San Mateo *A*
College of the Desert *A*
De Anza College *C, A*
Grossmont College *A*
Laguna College of Art and Design *C, B*
Monterey Peninsula College *C, A*
Ohlone College *C*
Otis College of Art and Design *B, M*
Palomar College *A*
Pasadena City College *A*
San Francisco Art Institute *B, M*
Santa Rosa Junior College *C*
Solano Community College *A*

Colorado

Adams State College *B*
Rocky Mountain College of Art &
  Design *B*

Connecticut

Lyme Academy College of Fine
  Arts *C, B*
Paier College of Art *C, B*
University of Hartford *B*

District of Columbia

American University *M*
George Washington University *M*

Florida

Ringling College of Art and Design *B*
University of Miami *B*

Georgia

Savannah College of Art and
 Design *B, M*

Idaho

Northwest Nazarene University *B*

Illinois

Bradley University *B*
City Colleges of Chicago
 Olive-Harvey College *A*
Lewis University *B*
Lincoln College *A*
Richland Community College *A*
School of the Art Institute of
 Chicago *B, M*
University of Illinois
 Urbana-Champaign *B, M*

Indiana

Indiana University-Purdue University
 Fort Wayne *B*
Indiana University-Purdue University
 Indianapolis *B*
Indiana Wesleyan University *B*

Iowa

Coe College *B*
Drake University *B*
University of Iowa *B, M*

Kansas

Allen County Community College *A*
Central Christian College of Kansas *A*
Pittsburg State University *B*
Pratt Community College *A*
Seward County Community College *A*
University of Kansas *B, M*

Kentucky

Eastern Kentucky University *B*

Louisiana

Centenary College of Louisiana *B*

Maine

Maine College of Art *B*
University of Southern Maine *B*

Maryland

Maryland Institute College of Art *B, M*

Massachusetts

Art Institute of Boston at Lesley
 University *B*
Bard College at Simon's Rock *B*
Boston University *B, M*
Massachusetts College of Art and
 Design *B, M*
Montserrat College of Art *B*
Salem State College *B*
School of the Museum of Fine
 Arts *B, M*
University of Massachusetts
 Dartmouth *B, M*

Michigan

Andrews University *B*
College for Creative Studies *B*
Ferris State University *B*
Finlandia University *B*
Grand Valley State University *B*
Kendall College of Art and Design of
 Ferris State University *B, M*
Lansing Community College *A*
Northern Michigan University *A, B*
Oakland University *B*
Siena Heights University *B*
University of Michigan
 Dearborn *B*
 Flint *B*

Minnesota

College of Visual Arts *B*
Minneapolis College of Art and
 Design *B*
Minnesota State University
 Mankato *B, M*
Saint Cloud State University *B*

Missouri

Columbia College *B*
Kansas City Art Institute *B*
Washington University in St.
 Louis *B, M*

Nevada

Sierra Nevada College *B*

New Hampshire

University of New Hampshire *M*

New Mexico

College of Santa Fe *B*

New York

Columbia University
 School of General Studies *B*
Hofstra University *B*
Pratt Institute *A*
Rochester Institute of
 Technology *A, B, M*
State University of New York
 College at Buffalo *B*
 College at Fredonia *B*
 New Paltz *B, M*
 Purchase *B, M*
Syracuse University *B, M*

North Carolina

East Carolina University *B*
Elon University *B*
Gardner-Webb University *B*
Methodist University *B*

Ohio

Art Academy of Cincinnati *B*
Bowling Green State University *B*
Cleveland Institute of Art *B*
Kent State University *B, M*
Ohio State University
 Columbus Campus *B, M*
Ohio University *B, M*
Shawnee State University *B*
Youngstown State University *B*

Oregon

Mt. Hood Community College *A*
Oregon College of Art & Craft *C, B*
Pacific Northwest College of Art *B*
Portland State University *B, M*
University of Oregon *B, M*

Pennsylvania

Arcadia University *B*
Edinboro University of
 Pennsylvania *B*
Keystone College *A, B*
Lycoming College *B*
Marywood University *B, M*
Oakbridge Academy of Arts *A*
Seton Hill University *B*
Temple University *B, M*
University of the Arts *B, M*

Puerto Rico

Escuela de Artes Plasticas de Puerto
 Rico *B*
Inter American University of Puerto
 Rico
 San German Campus *B, M*
University of Puerto Rico
 Rio Piedras *B*

Rhode Island

Providence College *B*
Rhode Island School of Design *B, M*
Salve Regina University *B*

Tennessee

Carson-Newman College *B*
Memphis College of Art *B, M*
Tennessee Technological University *B*

Texas

Texas A&M University
 Commerce *B, M*
Texas Christian University *B, M*
University of Dallas *B, M*
University of Houston *B, M*
University of Texas
 El Paso *B, M*
Western Texas College *A*

Vermont

Bennington College *B*
Marlboro College *B*

Virginia

Virginia Commonwealth University *B*

Washington

Cornish College of the Arts *B*
North Seattle Community College *C*
University of Washington *B, M*
Western Washington University *B*

West Virginia

West Virginia State University *B*
West Virginia Wesleyan College *B*

Wisconsin

University of Wisconsin
 Madison *B*

Painting/wall covering

Arizona

Tohono O'odham Community
 College *C, A*

California

Allan Hancock College *C*

Illinois

Parkland College *C*

Indiana

Ivy Tech Community College
 Central Indiana *C, A*
 East Central *C, A*
 Lafayette *C, A*
 North Central *C, A*
 Northeast *C, A*
 Northwest *C, A*
 Southwest *C, A*
 Wabash Valley *C, A*

Kentucky

Big Sandy Community and Technical
 College *C*

Minnesota

St. Paul College *C*

Oregon

Linn-Benton Community College *A*

Pennsylvania

Community College of Allegheny
 County *A*

Wisconsin

Gateway Technical College *C*

Milwaukee Area Technical College *C*

Paleontology

Arizona

Northern Arizona University *B*

Arkansas

University of Arkansas *D*

New Mexico

Mesalands Community College *A*

North Carolina

North Carolina State University *M, D*

Ohio

Bowling Green State University *B*
Ohio State University
 Columbus Campus *M, D*

South Dakota

South Dakota School of Mines and
 Technology *M*

Paralegal studies

Alabama

Bevill State Community College *C, A*
Calhoun Community College *A*
Enterprise-Ozark Community
 College *C, A*
Faulkner State Community College *A*
Faulkner University *A, B*
Gadsden State Community College *A*
Northeast Alabama Community
 College *A*
Samford University *C*
Shelton State Community College *C*
South University: Montgomery *A*
Wallace State Community College at
 Hanceville *A*

Alaska

University of Alaska
 Anchorage *C*
 Fairbanks *A*
 Southeast *A*

Arizona

Brookline College
 Phoenix *A*
 Tempe *A*
 Tucson *A*
Coconino County Community
 College *A*
Everest College
 Phoenix *A*
Lamson College *A*
Mohave Community College *C, A*
Paralegal Institute *A*
Penn Foster College *A*
Phoenix College *C, A*
Pima Community College *C, A*

Arkansas

Northwest Arkansas Community
 College *A*
Pulaski Technical College *A*
Southeast Arkansas College *A*
University of Arkansas
 Community College at Hope *A*
 Fort Smith *A*

California

American River College *A*
Butte College *C, A*
California State University
 Chico *C, B*
 East Bay *C*
 San Bernardino *C*

Canada College *A*
Cerritos College *A*
City College of San Francisco *C, A*
Coastline Community College *C*
College of the Canyons *A*
College of the Redwoods *C, A*
College of the Sequoias *A*
De Anza College *C, A*
El Camino College *C, A*
El Camino College: Compton
    Center *C, A*
Empire College *C, A*
Fremont College *A*
Fresno City College *C, A*
Fullerton College *A*
Glendale Community College *A*
Heald College
    Hayward *A*
    Roseville *A*
    Stockton *C, A*
Humphreys College *C, B*
Imperial Valley College *C, A*
John F. Kennedy University *C, B*
Kaplan College: Palm Springs *A*
Kaplan College: Panorama City *C, A*
Kaplan College: Sacramento *A*
Kaplan College: Vista *A*
Los Angeles City College *A*
Los Angeles Mission College *C, A*
Los Angeles Southwest College *A*
MTI College *C, A*
Merritt College *C, A*
Mount San Antonio College *A*
Napa Valley College *C, A*
Oxnard College *A*
Palomar College *C, A*
Pasadena City College *C, A*
Platt College
    Ontario *C, A, B*
Saddleback College *C, A*
Sage College *A*
San Diego City College *A*
San Diego Miramar College *C, A*
Santa Ana College *C, A*
Santa Barbara Business College *A*
Santa Barbara Business College
    Bakersfield *C, A*
    Santa Maria *C, A*
Santa Barbara Business College: Palm
    Desert *C, A*
Santa Barbara Business College:
    Ventura *C, A*
Santiago Canyon College *A*
Shasta College *A*
Skyline College *C, A*
South Coast College *A*
Southwestern College *C, A*
University of La Verne *C*
West Los Angeles College *C, A*
West Valley College *A*

Colorado

Arapahoe Community College *C, A*
Colorado Northwestern Community
    College *A*
Community College of Aurora *C, A*
Community College of Denver *C, A*
Front Range Community College *C, A*
Kaplan College: Denver *C, A*
Pikes Peak Community College *C, A*

Connecticut

Lincoln College of New England:
    Briarwood *A*
Manchester Community College *C, A*
Naugatuck Valley Community
    College *A*
Norwalk Community College *C, A*
Post University *C, A*
Quinnipiac University *B*
University of Hartford *C, A, B*
University of New Haven *C*

Delaware

Wesley College *C, A, B*

District of Columbia

George Washington University *C*
University of the District of
    Columbia *A*

Florida

Brevard Community College *A*
Broward College *A*
Brown Mackie College: Miami *C, A*
Central Florida Community College *A*
City College: Fort Lauderdale *A*
Daytona State College *A*
Edison State College *A*
Florida Gulf Coast University *B*
Florida National College *A*
Florida State College at Jacksonville *A*
Gulf Coast Community College *A*
Herzing University *A*
Hillsborough Community
    College *C, A*
Hodges University *A, B*
Indian River State College *A*
Jones College *A, B*
Key College *A*
Lake-Sumter Community College *A*
Miami Dade College *C, A*
Northwest Florida State College *A*
Nova Southeastern University *B*
Palm Beach Community College *A*
Pasco-Hernando Community
    College *A*
Pensacola Junior College *A*
Rasmussen College: Fort Myers *C, A*
Rasmussen College: Ocala *C, A*
St. Petersburg College *A, B*
Santa Fe College *A*
Seminole Community College *A*
South University: West Palm Beach *A*
Southwest Florida College *A*
State College of Florida,
    Manatee-Sarasota *C, A*
Tallahassee Community College *A*
University of Central Florida *B*
University of West Florida *B*
Valencia Community College *A*

Georgia

Ashworth College *A*
Athens Technical College *A*
Atlanta Technical College *A*
Augusta State University *C*
Brown Mackie College: Atlanta *C, A*
Clayton State University *C, A*
Darton College *C, A*
Gainesville State College *C, A*
Gwinnett College *C, A*
Middle Georgia Technical
    College *C, A*
Savannah Technical College *A*
South University: Savannah *A*
Valdosta State University *B*

Hawaii

Heald College
    Honolulu *A*
University of Hawaii
    Kapiolani Community College *C, A*

Idaho

Eastern Idaho Technical College *C, A*
Idaho State University *A*
Lewis-Clark State College *C, A, B*

Illinois

Black Hawk College *A*
Black Hawk College: East Campus *A*
College of Lake County *C, A*
Elgin Community College *C, A*
Harper College *C, A*
Illinois Central College *C, A*

Kankakee Community College *A*
Loyola University Chicago *C*
MacCormac College *A*
Midstate College *A*
Northwestern College *C, A*
Robert Morris University:
    Chicago *C, A*
Rock Valley College *C, A*
Rockford Career College *A*
Roosevelt University *B*
South Suburban College of Cook
    County *C, A*
Southern Illinois University
    Carbondale *B*
Southwestern Illinois College *C, A*

Indiana

Brown Mackie College: Fort
    Wayne *C, A*
Calumet College of St. Joseph *C, A, B*
Indiana University-Purdue University
    Indianapolis *C*
International Business College *C, A*
Ivy Tech Community College
    Bloomington *A*
    Central Indiana *A*
    Columbus *A*
    East Central *A*
    Kokomo *A*
    Lafayette *A*
    North Central *A*
    Northeast *A*
    Northwest *A*
    Richmond *A*
    South Central *A*
    Southeast *A*
    Southwest *A*
    Wabash Valley *A*
Kaplan College: Indianapolis *A*
St. Mary-of-the-Woods College *C, A, B*
Vincennes University *A*

Iowa

Des Moines Area Community
    College *C, A*
Grand View University *B*
Iowa Lakes Community College *A*
Iowa Western Community College *A*
Kaplan University
    Cedar Falls *A*
    Davenport *A, B*
    Des Moines *A*
    Mason City *A*
Kirkwood Community College *A*

Kansas

Brown Mackie College
    Salina *A*
Cloud County Community
    College *C, A*
Hutchinson Community College *A*
Johnson County Community
    College *C, A*
Kansas City Kansas Community
    College *A*
Newman University *A*
Washburn University *C, A, B*

Kentucky

Beckfield College *C, A, B*
Daymar College
    Owensboro *A*
Draughons Junior College *A*
Eastern Kentucky University *A, B*
Morehead State University *B*
Sullivan University *A, B*
University of Louisville *A*
Western Kentucky University *A*

Louisiana

Grambling State University *A, B*
Herzing University *C, A*

Louisiana State University
    Eunice *A*
McNeese State University *A*
Nicholls State University *A*
Nunez Community College *C, A*
Tulane University *C, A, B*

Maine

Andover College *C, A*
Beal College *C, A*
Husson University *A, B*
University of Maine
    Augusta *A*

Maryland

Anne Arundel Community
    College *C, A*
Baltimore City Community
    College *C, A*
Chesapeake College *C, A*
College of Southern Maryland *A*
Community College of Baltimore
    County *C, A*
Frederick Community College *C, A*
Hagerstown Community College *C*
Harford Community College *C*
Kaplan College: Hagerstown *A*
Montgomery College *C, A*
Prince George's Community
    College *C, A*
Stevenson University *B*
University of Maryland
    University College *C*

Massachusetts

Anna Maria College *C, A, B*
Bay Path College *C, A*
Bentley University *A*
Boston University *B*
Bristol Community College *A*
Bunker Hill Community College *C*
Cape Cod Community College *C*
Eastern Nazarene College *C*
Elms College *C, A, B*
Fisher College *A*
Marian Court College *C, A*
Massachusetts Bay Community
    College *C, A*
Massasoit Community College *A*
Merrimack College *A*
Middlesex Community College *C, A*
Mount Wachusett Community
    College *C, A*
Newbury College *B*
North Shore Community College *C, A*
Northern Essex Community
    College *C, A*
Quincy College *C, A*
Roxbury Community College *A*
Suffolk University *A, B*

Michigan

Baker College
    of Auburn Hills *A*
Bay de Noc Community College *C*
Davenport University *C, A, B*
Delta College *C, A*
Eastern Michigan University *B*
Ferris State University *A*
Grand Valley State University *B*
Henry Ford Community College *A*
Kellogg Community College *C, A*
Lake Superior State University *A, B*
Lansing Community College *A*
Macomb Community College *A*
Madonna University *A, B*
North Central Michigan College *A*
Northwestern Michigan College *C*
Oakland Community College *C, A*
University of Detroit Mercy *C, A, B*
Wayne County Community College *A*

Minnesota

Alexandria Technical College *A*
Duluth Business University *A*
Globe University *C, A, B*
Hamline University *B*
Inver Hills Community College *C, A*
Lake Superior College *C, A*
Minnesota School of Business *A, B*
Minnesota School of Business:
    Brooklyn Center *B*
Minnesota State Community and
    Technical College *A*
Minnesota State University
    Moorhead *B*
North Hennepin Community
    College *C, A*
Rasmussen College
    Eagan *C, A*
    Eden Prairie *C, A*
    Mankato *C, A*
    St. Cloud *C, A*
Rasmussen College: Brooklyn
    Park *C, A*
Rasmussen College: Lake
    Elmo/Woodbury *C, A*
St. Cloud Technical College *A*
Winona State University *B*

Mississippi

Hinds Community College *A*
Mississippi College *B*
Mississippi Gulf Coast Community
    College *A*
Mississippi University for Women *B*
Northwest Mississippi Community
    College *A*
University of Mississippi *C, B*
University of Southern Mississippi *B*
Virginia College Gulf Coast *A*

Missouri

Avila University *B*
Hickey College *C, A*
Maryville University of Saint Louis *B*
Metropolitan Community College:
    Penn Valley *C, A*
Missouri Southern State University *C*
Missouri Western State
    University *C, A*
Patricia Stevens College *A, B*
Rockhurst University *C*
St. Louis Community College
    St. Louis Community College at
    Meramec *C, A*
Sanford-Brown College
    St. Peters *A*
Vatterott College: Springfield *C, A*
Webster University *C, B*
William Woods University *A, B*

Montana

University of Great Falls *A, B*
University of Montana *A*

Nebraska

Central Community College *C, A*
College of Saint Mary *C, A, B*
Doane College *B*
Kaplan University
    Lincoln *A*
Kaplan University: Omaha *A*
Metropolitan Community College *A*
Northeast Community College *C, A*

Nevada

Career College of Northern Nevada *A*
College of Southern Nevada *C, A*
Everest College: Las Vegas *A*
Truckee Meadows Community
    College *A*
Western Nevada College *A*

New Hampshire

NHTI-Concord's Community
    College *C, A*
Nashua Community College *C, A*

New Jersey

Atlantic Cape Community College *A*
Bergen Community College *A*
Berkeley College- Garret Mountain
    Campus *A*
Brookdale Community College *A*
Burlington County College *A*
Cumberland County College *A*
Essex County College *A*
Gloucester County College *C, A*
Hudson County Community
    College *A*
Mercer County Community
    College *C, A*
Middlesex County College *A*
Ocean County College *C, A*
Raritan Valley Community
    College *C, A*
Rider University *C*
Sussex County Community
    College *C, A*
Thomas Edison State College *A, B*
Union County College *C, A*
Warren County Community
    College *A*

New Mexico

Brookline College
    Albuquerque *A*
Central New Mexico Community
    College *A*
Dona Ana Community College of New
    Mexico State University *A*
Eastern New Mexico University:
    Roswell Campus *A*
Navajo Technical College *A*
New Mexico Junior College *C, A*
New Mexico State University
    Alamogordo *C, A*
    Carlsbad *C*
    Grants *A*
San Juan College *A*
Santa Fe Community College *C, A*

New York

Berkeley College of New York City *A*
Broome Community College *C, A*
Bryant & Stratton Business Institute
    Bryant & Stratton College: Albany *A*
    Bryant & Stratton College:
    Rochester *A*
    Bryant & Stratton College: Syracuse
    North *A*
City University of New York
    Bronx Community College *C, A*
    Hostos Community College *A*
    LaGuardia Community College *A*
    New York City College of
    Technology *A, B*
Corning Community College *A*
Dutchess Community College *C, A*
Elmira Business Institute *C, A*
Erie Community College
    City Campus *A*
Finger Lakes Community College *A*
Genesee Community College *A*
Globe Institute of Technology *C, A, B*
Herkimer County Community
    College *A*
Hilbert College *A, B*
Jefferson Community College *A*
Maria College *C, A*
Marist College *C*
Mildred Elley *C, A*
Monroe Community College *C, A*
Nassau Community College *C, A*
New York Career Institute *A*
Olean Business Institute *C, A*

Rockland Community College *C, A*
State University of New York
    College of Technology at Canton *B*
Suffolk County Community
    College *C, A*
Sullivan County Community
    College *A*
Tompkins Cortland Community
    College *A*
Westchester Community College *C, A*

North Carolina

Caldwell Community College and
    Technical Institute *A*
Cape Fear Community College *A*
Carteret Community College *A*
Central Carolina Community
    College *C, A*
Central Piedmont Community
    College *C, A*
Coastal Carolina Community
    College *A*
Davidson County Community
    College *C, A*
Durham Technical Community
    College *A*
Fayetteville Technical Community
    College *C, A*
Forsyth Technical Community
    College *A*
Gaston College *A*
Guilford Technical Community
    College *C, A*
Isothermal Community College *A*
Johnston Community College *A*
King's College *A*
Miller-Motte Technical College *A*
Pitt Community College *A*
Rowan-Cabarrus Community
    College *A*
South College *A*
South Piedmont Community
    College *A*
Southwestern Community College *A*
Surry Community College *A*
Western Piedmont Community
    College *C, A*
Wilson Community College *A*

North Dakota

Lake Region State College *C, A*
Rasmussen College: Fargo *C, A*
Turtle Mountain Community
    College *C*

Ohio

Bradford School *A*
Cincinnati State Technical and
    Community College *C*
College of Mount St. Joseph *C, A, B*
Columbus State Community
    College *C, A*
Cuyahoga Community College
    Metropolitan Campus *C, A*
ETI Technical College of Niles *A*
Edison State Community College *A*
James A. Rhodes State College *C, A*
Kent State University *B*
Kent State University
    East Liverpool *A*
    Trumbull *A*
Marion Technical College *A*
North Central State College *A*
Northwest State Community
    College *A*
RETS College *A*
Shawnee State University *A*
Stautzenberger College:
    Brecksville *C, A*
University of Akron *C, A*
University of Cincinnati
    Clermont College *C, A*
University of Northwestern Ohio *C, A*
University of Rio Grande *A*

University of Toledo *C, A, B*
Ursuline College *C, B*
Zane State College *A*

Oklahoma

East Central University *B*
Oklahoma Wesleyan University *A*
Rogers State University *A*
Rose State College *A*
Tulsa Community College *A*

Oregon

Linn-Benton Community College *A*
Portland Community College *C, A*
Treasure Valley Community College *A*
Umpqua Community College *C, A*

Pennsylvania

Bucks County Community
    College *C, A*
Central Pennsylvania College *A*
Community College of Philadelphia *A*
Consolidated School of Business
    York *A*
Erie Business Center *A*
Gannon University *C, A, B*
Harrisburg Area Community
    College *C, A*
Immaculata University *C*
Keystone Technical Institute *C, A*
Lehigh Carbon Community
    College *C, A*
Lock Haven University of
    Pennsylvania *B*
Luzerne County Community
    College *A*
Manor College *C, A*
McCann School of Business and
    Technology: Dickson City *A*
Mount Aloysius College *A*
Northampton Community College *A*
PJA School *C, A*
Peirce College *C, A, B*
Pennsylvania College of
    Technology *C, A*
Westmoreland County Community
    College *C, A*
Widener University *C, A*

Puerto Rico

Ponce Paramedical College *C*
Turabo University *C*
Universidad Metropolitana *C*
Universidad del Este *A, B*

Rhode Island

Community College of Rhode
    Island *A*
Roger Williams University *C, B*

South Carolina

Central Carolina Technical College *A*
Florence-Darlington Technical
    College *A*
Forrest Junior College *C, A*
Greenville Technical College *C, A*
Horry-Georgetown Technical
    College *A*
Midlands Technical College *C, A*
Miller-Motte Technical College *A*
Orangeburg-Calhoun Technical
    College *A*
South University: Columbia *A, B*
Technical College of the
    Lowcountry *C, A*
Trident Technical College *C, A*
York Technical College *C, A*

South Dakota

National American University
    Rapid City *A, B*
Western Dakota Technical Institute *A*

Tennessee
Chattanooga State Community
    College *A*
Draughons Junior College:
    Nashville *C, A*
Pellissippi State Community
    College *A*
Roane State Community College *A*
South College *A*
Southwest Tennessee Community
    College *A*
University of Tennessee
    Chattanooga *B*
Volunteer State Community College *A*

Texas
Alvin Community College *C, A*
Angelina College *A*
Austin Community College *C, A*
Blinn College *C, A*
Brazosport College *A*
Central Texas College *A*
Collin County Community College
    District *C, A*
Del Mar College *A*
El Centro College *A*
El Paso Community College *C, A*
Houston Community College
    System *C, A*
Howard College *A*
Kilgore College *C, A*
Lee College *A*
Lone Star College System *C, A*
McLennan Community College *A*
Midland College *C, A*
Navarro College *C, A*
North Central Texas College *A*
Odessa College *C, A*
St. Philip's College *A*
San Antonio College *A*
San Jacinto College *A*
South Plains College *A*
South Texas College *A*
Stephen F. Austin State University *B*
Tarrant County College *C, A*
Texas A&M University
    Commerce *B*
Texas State University: San Marcos *M*
Texas Wesleyan University *B*
Texas Woman's University *B*
Trinity Valley Community
    College *C, A*
Tyler Junior College *A*
University of Texas
    Brownsville - Texas Southmost
      College *C, A*
Vernon College *A*
Victoria College *C, A*
Westwood College: Fort Worth *A*
Westwood College: Houston South *A*
Wharton County Junior College *C, A*

Utah
Eagle Gate College: Layton *A*
Eagle Gate College: Salt Lake City *A*
LDS Business College *A*
Salt Lake Community College *A*
Southern Utah University *A*
Utah Career College *A, B*
Utah Valley University *A, B*

Vermont
Burlington College *C*
Champlain College *B*

Virginia
Blue Ridge Community College *C*
Bryant & Stratton College
    Richmond *A*
Central Virginia Community
    College *C*
Centura College: Chesapeake *A*
Centura College: Richmond *A*

Germanna Community College *C*
Hampton University *C, B*
J. Sargeant Reynolds Community
    College *A*
Marymount University *B, M*
Mountain Empire Community
    College *A*
National College
    Roanoke Valley *A*
New River Community College *C, A*
Northern Virginia Community
    College *A*
Patrick Henry Community College *A*
Thomas Nelson Community
    College *A*
Tidewater Community College *C, A*
University of Richmond *C, A*
Virginia Highlands Community
    College *C*
Virginia Intermont College *B*
Virginia Western Community
    College *A*

Washington
Centralia College *A*
Clark College *C, A*
Highline Community College *A*
Lake Washington Technical
    College *C, A*
Lower Columbia College *C, A*
Pierce College *A*
Skagit Valley College *C, A*
South Puget Sound Community
    College *C, A*
Spokane Community College *C, A*
Spokane Falls Community
    College *C, A*
Whatcom Community College *C, A*

West Virginia
American Public University
    System *C, A*
Blue Ridge Community and Technical
    College *C, A*
Fairmont State University *A*
Mountain State College *A*
Mountain State University *A*
West Virginia Business College: Nutter
    Fort *A*
West Virginia Business College:
    Wheeling *C, A*
West Virginia Junior College *A*

Wisconsin
Carthage College *C*
Chippewa Valley Technical College *A*
College of Menominee Nation *A*
Fox Valley Technical College *A*
Herzing University *A*
Lakeshore Technical College *A*
Milwaukee Area Technical College *A*
Northeast Wisconsin Technical
    College *A*
Rasmussen College: Green Bay *C, A*
University of Wisconsin
    Superior *C*
Western Technical College *A*

Wyoming
Casper College *C, A*
Laramie County Community
    College *C, A*

Parasitology

Louisiana
Tulane University *M, D*

Ohio
Bowling Green State University *B*

Pennsylvania
University of Pennsylvania *D*

Parks, recreation, and leisure studies

Alabama
Jacksonville State University *B*
University of North Alabama *B, M*
University of South Alabama *B*

Alaska
University of Alaska
    Southeast *C*

Arizona
Arizona State University *B, M, D*
Grand Canyon University *B*
Northern Arizona University *C, B*
Northland Pioneer College *C, A*
Pima Community College *C*
Prescott College *B, M*
Scottsdale Community College *A*

Arkansas
National Park Community College *A*
University of Arkansas *B*
University of Arkansas
    Pine Bluff *B*

California
Allan Hancock College *A*
American River College *A*
Bakersfield College *A*
California Polytechnic State
    University: San Luis Obispo *B*
California State University
    Chico *B, M*
    Dominguez Hills *B*
    East Bay *B*
    Northridge *B, M*
    Sacramento *B, M*
    Stanislaus *M*
Cerritos College *A*
Chabot College *A*
College of the Canyons *A*
College of the Desert *A*
El Camino College: Compton
    Center *C, A*
Feather River College *A*
Fresno City College *A*
Fullerton College *A*
Glendale Community College *C, A*
Los Angeles Southwest College *A*
Los Angeles Valley College *A*
Merritt College *A*
Modesto Junior College *A*
Mount San Antonio College *A*
Palomar College *C, A*
Pasadena City College *A*
San Diego State University *B*
San Jose State University *B*
Santa Barbara City College *A*
Santa Monica College *C, A*
Santa Rosa Junior College *C, A*
Simpson University *B*
Southwestern College *A*

Colorado
Colorado Mountain College *A*
Community College of Denver *C, A*
Fort Lewis College *B*
Metropolitan State College of
    Denver *B*

Connecticut
Norwalk Community College *C, A*
Southern Connecticut State
    University *B, M*

District of Columbia
Gallaudet University *M*

Howard University *B*

Florida
Broward College *A*
Chipola College *A*
Gulf Coast Community College *A*
Northwest Florida State College *A*
Palm Beach Community College *A*
St. Petersburg College *A*

Georgia
College of Coastal Georgia *A*
Darton College *A*
East Georgia College *A*
Georgia College and State
    University *B*
Georgia Southern University *B*
Middle Georgia College *A*
South Georgia College *A*

Idaho
Brigham Young University-Idaho *B*
Northwest Nazarene University *B*

Illinois
Aurora University *B*
Greenville College *B*
Southern Illinois University
    Carbondale *B, M*
University of Illinois
    Urbana-Champaign *B, M, D*

Indiana
Franklin College *B*
Indiana University
    Bloomington *B, M, D*
    Southeast *A*

Iowa
Dordt College *B*
Graceland University *B*
University of Dubuque *B*
University of Iowa *B, M*
University of Northern Iowa *B, M, D*

Kansas
Central Christian College of Kansas *A*
Emporia State University *B*
Pittsburg State University *B*
Seward County Community College *A*
Tabor College *B*

Kentucky
Alice Lloyd College *B*
Campbellsville University *B*
Eastern Kentucky University *B*

Louisiana
Grambling State University *B*

Maine
Unity College *B*
University of Maine
    Machias *A, B*
    Presque Isle *A, B*
University of Southern Maine *B*

Maryland
Community College of Baltimore
    County *C, A*
Frostburg State University *B, M*
Garrett College *C, A*

Massachusetts
American International College *B*
Bridgewater State College *B*
Gordon College *B*
Salem State College *B*

Michigan
Aquinas College *B*

Calvin College B
Central Michigan University B
Grand Valley State University B
Michigan State University B
Northern Michigan University B
Spring Arbor University B
Western Michigan University B

Minnesota
Minneapolis Community and Technical College C, A
Minnesota State University Mankato B
Northland Community & Technical College A
Ridgewater College A
Saint Cloud State University B
University of Minnesota Duluth B, Twin Cities B, M
Vermilion Community College A
Winona State University B

Mississippi
Alcorn State University B
University of Southern Mississippi B, M

Missouri
Evangel University B
Metropolitan Community College: Blue River C
Missouri State University B
Southeast Missouri State University B
Southwest Baptist University B
University of Central Missouri B
University of Missouri Columbia B, M
William Jewell College B

Montana
University of Montana: Western A

Nebraska
Chadron State College B
University of Nebraska Omaha B

Nevada
University of Nevada Las Vegas B

New Hampshire
New England College B
River Valley Community College A

New Jersey
Thomas Edison State College A, B

New Mexico
Central New Mexico Community College C, A
San Juan College A

New York
City University of New York Kingsborough Community College A
Dutchess Community College A
Finger Lakes Community College C
Houghton College B
Paul Smith's College A, B
St. Joseph's College: Suffolk Campus B
State University of New York College at Brockport B, M
College at Cortland B, M
College at Plattsburgh B
College of Agriculture and Technology at Morrisville B
Ulster County Community College A

North Carolina
Catawba College B
Montreat College C, B
Mount Olive College A, B
Shaw University B
Southwestern Community College A
University of North Carolina Greensboro B
Vance-Granville Community College A
Warren Wilson College B

North Dakota
Dakota College at Bottineau A
North Dakota State University B

Ohio
Ashland University B
Bowling Green State University B, M
Central State University B
Ohio University B
University of Toledo B, M
Urbana University B

Oklahoma
East Central University B
Oklahoma State University B, M
Southeastern Oklahoma State University B
Southwestern Oklahoma State University B
University of Central Oklahoma B

Oregon
Central Oregon Community College A
Oregon State University B

Pennsylvania
Butler County Community College A
Keystone College B
Kutztown University of Pennsylvania B
Messiah College B
Penn State Abington B
York College of Pennsylvania B

Puerto Rico
Caribbean University B
University of Puerto Rico Carolina Regional College A

South Carolina
Newberry College B
North Greenville University B
Southern Wesleyan University B

South Dakota
Black Hills State University B
Presentation College B
University of South Dakota B

Tennessee
Carson-Newman College B
Maryville College B
University of Tennessee Knoxville B, M

Texas
Clarendon College A
Howard Payne University B
Texas A&M University B, M, D
Texas A&M University Galveston B
Texas State University: San Marcos M, T

Utah
Brigham Young University B
Snow College A

Southern Utah University B
University of Utah B, M, D
Utah State University B

Vermont
Green Mountain College B
Johnson State College B
Sterling College B

Virginia
Ferrum College B
Hampton University B
Radford University B
Tidewater Community College A
Virginia Commonwealth University B, M
Virginia Wesleyan College B

Washington
Bellevue College A
Eastern Washington University B
Pacific Lutheran University B
Western Washington University B

West Virginia
Concord University B
Davis and Elkins College B
Shepherd University B

Wisconsin
University of Wisconsin Milwaukee B, Parkside C

Wyoming
Central Wyoming College A

Parks/recreational/leisure facilities management

Alabama
Alabama State University B
Faulkner State Community College C, A
Wallace State Community College at Hanceville A

Alaska
Alaska Pacific University B, M

Arizona
Northern Arizona University B
Prescott College B, M

Arkansas
Arkansas Tech University B
Henderson State University B
University of Arkansas M, D

California
Butte College C, A
California State University Chico B, East Bay B, Fresno A, B, Long Beach B, M
Cerro Coso Community College C, A
College of the Desert A
College of the Sequoias A
Fresno City College A
Golf Academy of America: San Diego A
Humboldt State University B
Mount San Antonio College A
National University C
Palomar College C, A
Professional Golfers Career College A
San Francisco State University B, M
Santa Rosa Junior College C
West Valley College C, A

Colorado
Colorado Mountain College A
Colorado State University B, M, D
Johnson & Wales University: Denver B
University of Northern Colorado B

Connecticut
University of Connecticut B

Delaware
University of Delaware B

District of Columbia
Gallaudet University B

Florida
Edison State College A
Florida International University B, M
Florida State University B, M
Johnson & Wales University: North Miami B
Lake City Community College A
Professional Golfers Career College: Orlando A
Tallahassee Community College A
University of Florida B, M
Webber International University A, B, M

Georgia
Abraham Baldwin Agricultural College A
Georgia Southern University M
Georgia Southwestern State University B
University of West Georgia B

Hawaii
University of Hawaii Hilo B

Idaho
University of Idaho B, M

Illinois
Aurora University M
Eastern Illinois University B
Illinois State University B
Moraine Valley Community College A
University of St. Francis B
Western Illinois University B, M

Indiana
Bethel College B
Huntington University B
Indiana Institute of Technology A, B
Indiana State University B
Indiana University Bloomington B, M, D, Southeast A
Indiana Wesleyan University B

Iowa
Iowa Lakes Community College A
University of Iowa B, M
University of Northern Iowa M
Upper Iowa University B

Kansas
Bethany College B
Central Christian College of Kansas A, B
Friends University B
Kansas State University B
Pittsburg State University B

Kentucky
Asbury College B
Eastern Kentucky University B, M
Murray State University B, M

Union College *B*
Western Kentucky University *B, M*

Maine

Husson University *B*
Unity College *B*
University of Maine *B, M*
University of Maine
Machias *B*

Maryland

Allegany College of Maryland *A*

Massachusetts

Greenfield Community College *C*
Springfield College *B, M*

Michigan

Bay de Noc Community College *C*
Central Michigan University *B, M*
Eastern Michigan University *B*
Ferris State University *B*
Gogebic Community College *A*
Lake Superior State University *B*
Lansing Community College *A*

Minnesota

Anoka Technical College *C, A*
Minnesota State University
Mankato *B*
University of Minnesota
Crookston *B*
Vermilion Community College *A*
Winona State University *B*

Mississippi

University of Mississippi *B, M*

Missouri

Central Methodist University *B*
College of the Ozarks *B*
Hannibal-LaGrange College *B*
Missouri Valley College *B*
Missouri Western State University *B*
Northwest Missouri State
University *B*
University of Central Missouri *B*

Montana

University of Montana *B, M*

Nebraska

University of Nebraska
Kearney *B*

Nevada

Truckee Meadows Community
College *A*

New Hampshire

Franklin Pierce University *B*
New England College *B*
University of New Hampshire *B, M*

New Jersey

Kean University *B*

New Mexico

New Mexico State University *B*

New York

Dutchess Community College *A*
Erie Community College
South Campus *A*
Mohawk Valley Community College *A*
New York University *B, M, D, T*
North Country Community College *A*
Onondaga Community College *A*
Orange County Community College *A*
Paul Smith's College *A, B*
St. Thomas Aquinas College *B*

State University of New York
College at Brockport *B, M*
College at Cortland *B*
College of Agriculture and
Technology at Morrisville *A*
College of Technology at Delhi *A*
Sullivan County Community
College *A*
Tompkins Cortland Community
College *A*

North Carolina

Appalachian State University *B*
Brevard College *B*
Central Piedmont Community
College *A*
East Carolina University *B, M*
Elon University *B*
High Point University *B*
Johnson & Wales University:
Charlotte *B*
Mars Hill College *B*
Methodist University *B*
North Carolina Agricultural and
Technical State University *B*
North Carolina Central
University *B, M*
North Carolina State
University *B, M, D*
Pfeiffer University *B*
University of North Carolina
Chapel Hill *B, M*
Greensboro *M*
Pembroke *B*
Wilmington *B*
Western Carolina University *B*
Wingate University *B*

North Dakota

Dakota College at Bottineau *A*
University of North Dakota *B*

Ohio

Ashland University *B*
Bluffton University *B*
Kent State University *B*
Ohio State University
Columbus Campus *B*
University of Dayton *B*

Oklahoma

Bacone College *B*
Eastern Oklahoma State College *A*
Oklahoma Baptist University *B*
Oral Roberts University *B*
Southwestern Oklahoma State
University *B*

Oregon

Mt. Hood Community College *C, A*

Pennsylvania

California University of
Pennsylvania *B*
Cheyney University of Pennsylvania *B*
East Stroudsburg University of
Pennsylvania *B*
Keystone College *A, B*
Lock Haven University of
Pennsylvania *B*
Penn State
Altoona *B*
Beaver *B*
Berks *B*
Brandywine *B*
DuBois *B*
Erie, The Behrend College *B*
Fayette, The Eberly Campus *B*
Greater Allegheny *B*
Hazleton *B*
Lehigh Valley *B*
Mont Alto *B*
New Kensington *B*

Schuylkill *B*
Shenango *B*
University Park *B, M, D*
Wilkes-Barre *B*
Worthington Scranton *B*
York *B*
Slippery Rock University of
Pennsylvania *B, M*
Temple University *B, M, D*

Puerto Rico

Universidad Metropolitana *M*
Universidad del Este *C*

Rhode Island

Johnson & Wales University:
Providence *B*

South Carolina

Clemson University *B, M, D*
Morris College *B*
Technical College of the
Lowcountry *C*

South Dakota

Mount Marty College *B*
South Dakota State University *B*

Tennessee

Lambuth University *B*
Middle Tennessee State University *B*
University of Tennessee
Knoxville *M*

Texas

Midwestern State University *B*
Stephen F. Austin State University *B*
Texas A&M University *B*
Texas State University: San
Marcos *B, M, T*
Texas Wesleyan University *B*
University of North Texas *B, M*
Wayland Baptist University *B*
Western Texas College *A*

Utah

Utah State University *B, M, D*

Vermont

Green Mountain College *B*
Lyndon State College *B*
University of Vermont *B*

Virginia

Hampton University *B*
Northern Virginia Community
College *A*
Old Dominion University *B, M*
Tidewater Community College *A*

Washington

Eastern Washington University *B*
Skagit Valley College *C*
Spokane Community College *A*

West Virginia

Alderson-Broaddus College *B*
Concord University *B*
Marshall University *B*
Potomac State College of West
Virginia University *A*
West Virginia State University *B*
West Virginia University *B, M*

Wisconsin

Carroll University *B*
Fox Valley Technical College *A*
University of Wisconsin
La Crosse *B, M*
Madison *B*

Wyoming

Central Wyoming College *A*
Northwest College *A*

Particle physics

Massachusetts

Tufts University *M, D*

Wisconsin

University of Wisconsin
Madison *M, D*

Parts/warehousing operations

Arkansas

Pulaski Technical College *C*

Pastoral counseling

Alabama

Amridge University *M, D*
Spring Hill College *M*

Arizona

International Baptist College *B*

Arkansas

Ecclesia College *B*
Harding University *M*
Ouachita Baptist University *B*

California

Bethany University *B*
Biola University *M, D*
Holy Names University *M*
Horizon College of San Diego *C*
Life Pacific College *B*
Loyola Marymount University *M*
The Master's College *B, M, D*
Shasta Bible College and Graduate
School *M*
Simpson University *B*
Vanguard University of Southern
California *B*
William Jessup University *C, A, B*

Colorado

Nazarene Bible College *C, B*

Florida

Baptist College of Florida *B*
Barry University *M*
Clearwater Christian College *B*
Florida Christian College *B*
Trinity Baptist College *B*
Trinity College of Florida *B*

Georgia

Emmanuel College *B*
Emory University *D*
Toccoa Falls College *B*

Hawaii

Chaminade University of Honolulu *M*

Idaho

Boise Bible College *B*
Northwest Nazarene University *B*

Illinois

Dominican University *C, B*
Greenville College *B*
Lewis University *M*
Lincoln Christian University *M*
Loyola University Chicago *M*
Moody Bible Institute *B, M*
North Park University *M*
Olivet Nazarene University *M*

Trinity International University *B, M*

Indiana
Huntington University *M*
Marian University *C*
Saint Joseph's College *B*

Iowa
St. Ambrose University *M*
Wartburg College *B*

Kansas
Barclay College *B*
Central Christian College of
  Kansas *A, B*
Newman University *B*
Southwestern College *B*
University of St. Mary *B*

Kentucky
Brescia University *A, B*
Kentucky Christian University *B*

Maryland
Griggs University *C*
Loyola University Maryland *M, D*
Washington Bible College *B, M, T*

Massachusetts
Boston College *M*
Eastern Nazarene College *B*
Elms College *M*

Michigan
Andrews University *M, D*
Grace Bible College *B*
Marygrove College *M*
Spring Arbor University *B*

Minnesota
Bethel University *M*
Crown College *B*
North Central University *B*
St. Mary's University of Minnesota *M*
University of St. Thomas *M*

Mississippi
Wesley College *B*

Missouri
Baptist Bible College *B, M*
Calvary Bible College and Theological
  Seminary *B, M*
Central Bible College *B*
Central Christian College of the
  Bible *B*
Lindenwood University *B*

Nebraska
Grace University *M*
Union College *B*

New Jersey
College of St. Elizabeth *C*
Seton Hall University *M*

New Mexico
University of the Southwest *B*

New York
Iona College *M*

North Carolina
Gardner-Webb University *M*
John Wesley College *B*
Mid-Atlantic Christian University *B*
Shepherds Theological Seminary *M*
Southeastern Baptist Theological
  Seminary *M, D*

Ohio
Ashland University *M, D*
Cedarville University *B*
College of Mount St. Joseph *B*
God's Bible School and College *B*
Malone University *B*
Mount Vernon Nazarene University *B*
Ohio Christian University *A, B*
University of Dayton *M*

Oklahoma
Mid-America Christian University *B*
Oral Roberts University *B, M*
Southwestern Christian University *B*

Oregon
Corban College *B*
Eugene Bible College *B*
George Fox University *B, M, D*
Multnomah University *B*
Northwest Christian University *B*

Pennsylvania
Duquesne University *M*
Eastern University *D*
Gannon University *M*
La Salle University *M*
Moravian College *M*
Neumann University *M*
Philadelphia Biblical University *B*
Valley Forge Christian College *B*

Puerto Rico
Bayamon Central University *M*
Inter American University of Puerto
  Rico
  Metropolitan Campus *D*
Universidad Pentecostal Mizpa *A, B*

South Carolina
Columbia International
  University *B, M*
Erskine College *M*
Southern Methodist College *C*

South Dakota
Mount Marty College *M*

Tennessee
American Baptist College *B*
Lee University *B*
Southern Adventist University *B*

Texas
Arlington Baptist College *B*
Dallas Baptist University *B*
East Texas Baptist University *B*
Hardin-Simmons University *M*
Houston Baptist University *B*
St. Mary's University *M*
Southwestern Assemblies of God
  University *B*
University of Dallas *M*
University of Mary Hardin-Baylor *B*
University of St. Thomas *B, M*

Vermont
St. Michael's College *M*

Virginia
Eastern Mennonite University *M*
Liberty University *B, M, D*

Washington
Northwest University *B*
Seattle University *M*
University of Puget Sound *M*

Wisconsin
Cardinal Stritch University *B*
Concordia University Wisconsin *B*

Maranatha Baptist Bible College *B, M*

Pathology assistant

Connecticut
Quinnipiac University *M*

Massachusetts
Boston University *M, D*

Michigan
Wayne State University *B*

New York
St. John's University *B*

Pennsylvania
Drexel University *M*

Pathology, human/ animal

Alabama
Auburn University *M*
University of Alabama
  Birmingham *D*

Arizona
University of Arizona *M, D*

California
University of California
  Davis *M, D*
  Irvine *D*
  Los Angeles *M, D*
University of Southern
  California *M, D*

Colorado
Colorado State University *D*
University of Colorado
  Denver *D*

Connecticut
University of Connecticut *B, M, D*
Yale University *M, D*

District of Columbia
Georgetown University *D*

Illinois
University of Chicago *D*
University of Illinois
  Chicago *M, D*

Indiana
Indiana University
  Bloomington *M, D*
Indiana University-Purdue University
  Indianapolis *M, D*

Kansas
Kansas State University *M, D*
University of Kansas Medical
  Center *M, D*

Louisiana
Louisiana State University Health
  Sciences Center *M, D*

Maine
University of Maine *B, M*

Maryland
University of Maryland
  Baltimore *M*

Massachusetts
Boston University *D*

Harvard College *D*
Tufts University *M, D*

Michigan
Michigan State University *M, D*
University of Michigan *D*
Wayne State University *D*

Missouri
Saint Louis University *D*
University of Missouri
  Columbia *M, D*

Nebraska
University of Nebraska
  Medical Center *M, D*

New York
New York University *M, D*
State University of New York
  Buffalo *M, D*
  Stony Brook *D*
University of Rochester *M, D*
Yeshiva University *M, D*

North Carolina
Duke University *M, D*
University of North Carolina
  Chapel Hill *B, M, D*

North Dakota
North Dakota State University *D*

Ohio
Case Western Reserve University *D*
Ohio State University
  Columbus Campus *D*
University of Cincinnati *M, D*
University of Toledo *T*

Oklahoma
University of Oklahoma *M, D*

Pennsylvania
Drexel University *M, D*
Penn State
  Abington *B*
  Altoona *B*
  Beaver *B*
  Berks *B*
  Brandywine *B*
  DuBois *B*
  Erie, The Behrend College *B*
  Fayette, The Eberly Campus *B*
  Greater Allegheny *B*
  Hazleton *B*
  Lehigh Valley *B*
  Mont Alto *B*
  New Kensington *B*
  Schuylkill *B*
  Shenango *B*
  University Park *B, M, D*
  Wilkes-Barre *B*
  Worthington Scranton *B*
  York *B*
University of Pennsylvania *D*
University of Pittsburgh *M, D*

South Carolina
Medical University of South
  Carolina *D*

Tennessee
University of Tennessee
  Knoxville *M, D*
University of Tennessee Health
  Science Center *M, D*
Vanderbilt University *D*

Texas

University of Texas
El Paso *D*
Health Science Center at
Houston *M, D*
Medical Branch at Galveston *M, D*

Utah

University of Utah *M, D*

Vermont

University of Vermont *M*

Virginia

Virginia Commonwealth University *D*

Washington

University of Washington *M, D*

Wisconsin

University of Wisconsin
Madison *M, D*

Peace and conflict studies

Arizona

Prescott College *B, M*

California

California State University
Dominguez Hills *B, M*
San Bernardino *M*
Chapman University *B*
University of California
Berkeley *B*
University of San Diego *M*

Colorado

Naropa University *B*
University of Denver *M*

District of Columbia

American University *M*
Georgetown University *B*

Florida

Nova Southeastern University *M, D*

Georgia

Kennesaw State University *M*
Middle Georgia College *T*

Indiana

DePauw University *B*
Earlham College *B*
Goshen College *B*
Manchester College *B*
University of Notre Dame *M*

Maryland

Goucher College *B*
Howard Community College *A*
Salisbury University *B, M*
University of Baltimore *M*

Massachusetts

Brandeis University *M*
Hampshire College *B*
Tufts University *B*
University of Massachusetts
Boston *M*
Wellesley College *B*

Michigan

Wayne State University *M*

Minnesota

Bethel University *B*
College of St. Benedict *B*

Hamline University *B*
St. John's University *B*
University of St. Thomas *B*

Missouri

Missouri State University *M*
University of Missouri
Columbia *B*

Nebraska

Creighton University *B, M*

New Jersey

Montclair State University *B*

New York

Colgate University *B*
Le Moyne College *B*
Manhattan College *B*
Nazareth College *B*

North Carolina

Guilford College *B*
University of North Carolina
Chapel Hill *B*

Ohio

Antioch University McGregor *M*
Kent State University *B*
Ohio State University
Columbus Campus *B*

Pennsylvania

Arcadia University *M*
Gettysburg College *B*
Juniata College *B*
La Salle University *B*
University of Pennsylvania *D*

Puerto Rico

Turabo University *M*

Tennessee

Lipscomb University *B, M*

Texas

Abilene Christian University *M*

Vermont

Bennington College *B*
Marlboro College *B*
Norwich University *B*

Virginia

Eastern Mennonite University *B, M*
George Mason University *B, M, D*

Washington

University of Washington *B*
Whitworth University *B*

Pediatric nursing

Georgia

Emory University *D*
Georgia State University *M*
Medical College of Georgia *M*

Illinois

DePaul University *M*

Indiana

Indiana University-Purdue University
Indianapolis *M*
Purdue University
North Central *A*

Iowa

University of Iowa *M*

Maine

University of Southern Maine *B, M*

Massachusetts

Elms College *B*

New Jersey

Seton Hall University *M*

New York

City University of New York
Hunter College *B, M*
State University of New York
Upstate Medical University *M*
University of Rochester *M*

Ohio

Case Western Reserve University *M*
University of Toledo *M, T*
Youngstown State University *M*

Pennsylvania

University of Pennsylvania *M*

Texas

Texas Christian University *M*

Wisconsin

Marquette University *M*

Perfusion technology

Illinois

Rush University *B, M*

Nebraska

University of Nebraska
Medical Center *M*

New Jersey

Thomas Edison State College *B*

New York

State University of New York
Oswego *B*
Upstate Medical University *B*

Ohio

Ohio State University
Columbus Campus *B*

Pennsylvania

Carlow University *B*
Keystone College *A*

Wisconsin

Milwaukee School of Engineering *M*

Permanent cosmetics/tattooing

North Carolina

Johnston Community College *C*

Personal/culinary services

Arizona

Mesa Community College *A*

Arkansas

Northwest Arkansas Community
College *C*

California

Art Institute
of California: Los Angeles *B*

Art Institute of California:
Sacramento *A*
Chabot College *A*
College of San Mateo *C, A*
MiraCosta College *C*
WyoTech: Long Beach *C*

Colorado

Colorado Mountain College *A*

Florida

Broward College *A*
Florida College of Natural Health
Miami *C*
Florida State College at Jacksonville *C*
Palm Beach Community College *C*
State College of Florida,
Manatee-Sarasota *A*

Maryland

Allegany College of Maryland *A*

Michigan

Baker College
of Muskegon *A, B*

Minnesota

Le Cordon Bleu College of Culinary
Arts: Minneapolis-St. Paul *C, A*

New Mexico

Northern New Mexico College *C*

New York

Monroe Community College *A*

North Carolina

Cape Fear Community College *C, A*
College of the Albemarle *C*
Piedmont Community College *A*

Pennsylvania

Thiel College *B*

South Carolina

Denmark Technical College *C*
Forrest Junior College *A*

Texas

Art Institute
of Houston *A*
South Texas College *A*

Virginia

Stratford University:
Woodbridge *C, A, B*
Virginia Western Community
College *A*

Washington

Bates Technical College *C, A*

West Virginia

Potomac State College of West
Virginia University *A*

Personal/financial services marketing

Alabama

Jefferson Davis Community College *C*

Arizona

University of Phoenix *C*

Kansas

Hutchinson Community College *A*

New York

Mohawk Valley Community College *C*

South Dakota

National American University
Rapid City *B*

Texas

University of Houston *B*

Personality psychology

Massachusetts

Clark University *M, D*

New York

State University of New York
Albany *D*

Petroleum engineering

Alaska

University of Alaska
Fairbanks *B, M*

California

Stanford University *B, M, D*
University of Southern
California *B, M, D*

Colorado

Colorado School of Mines *B, M, D*

Illinois

Illinois Institute of Technology *M*

Kansas

University of Kansas *B, M*

Louisiana

Louisiana State University and
Agricultural and Mechanical
College *B, M, D*
University of Louisiana at
Lafayette *B, M*

Michigan

Wayne State University *M*

Missouri

University of Missouri
Missouri University of Science and
Technology *B, M, D*

Montana

Montana Tech of the University of
Montana *B, M*

New Mexico

New Mexico Institute of Mining and
Technology *B, M, D*

Ohio

Marietta College *B*

Oklahoma

University of Oklahoma *B, M, D*
University of Tulsa *B, M, D*

Pennsylvania

Penn State
Abington *B*
Altoona *B*
Beaver *B*
Berks *B*
Brandywine *B*
DuBois *B*
Erie, The Behrend College *B*
Fayette, The Eberly Campus *B*

Greater Allegheny *B*
Hazleton *B*
Lehigh Valley *B*
Mont Alto *B*
New Kensington *B*
Schuylkill *B*
Shenango *B*
University Park *B, M, D*
Wilkes-Barre *B*
Worthington Scranton *B*
York *B*
University of Pittsburgh *M*

Puerto Rico

Caribbean University *B*

Texas

Laredo Community College *A*
Midland College *A*
Texas A&M University *B, M, D*
Texas A&M University
Kingsville *B, M*
Texas Tech University *B, M, D*
University of Houston *M*
University of Texas
Austin *B, M, D*

West Virginia

West Virginia University *B, M, D*

Wyoming

University of Wyoming *B, M, D*

Petroleum technology

Arkansas

Arkansas State University
Beebe *C*
University of Arkansas Community
College at Morrilton *C, A*

California

Taft College *C, A*

Colorado

Colorado Northwestern Community
College *C, A*

Louisiana

Nicholls State University *A, B*

Mississippi

Southwest Mississippi Community
College *A*

Montana

Montana State University
Billings *A*

New Jersey

DeVry University: North Brunswick *A*

Pennsylvania

University of Pittsburgh
Bradford *B*

Texas

Houston Community College
System *C, A*
Odessa College *C, A*
Panola College *C, A*

Pharmaceutical sciences

California

Charles Drew University of Medicine
and Science *A*
University of California
Irvine *B*

Connecticut

University of Connecticut *M*

Georgia

South University: Savannah *D*

Hawaii

Heald College
Honolulu *A*

Idaho

Idaho State University *M, D*

Indiana

Butler University *B, M*

Iowa

Drake University *B*

Louisiana

University of Louisiana at
Monroe *M, D*

Maryland

University of Maryland
Baltimore *M, D*

Massachusetts

Massachusetts College of Pharmacy
and Health Sciences *B, M, D*

Michigan

University of Michigan *B, M, D*

Mississippi

University of Mississippi *B, M, D*

Missouri

University of Missouri
Kansas City *B, M, D*

Nebraska

Creighton University *D*

New York

Albany College of Pharmacy and
Health Sciences *B, M*
St. John's University *M, D*

North Carolina

University of North Carolina
Chapel Hill *B, M, D*

Ohio

University of Findlay *D*
University of Toledo *B*

Pennsylvania

Lehigh University *B*
Wilkes University *B*

Rhode Island

University of Rhode Island *M, D*

South Dakota

South Dakota State University *B*

Texas

University of Texas
Austin *M, D*

Virginia

Virginia Commonwealth
University *M, D*

Pharmacology

Alabama

Auburn University *M*

Arizona

University of Arizona *M, D*

California

Loma Linda University *D*
Stanford University *M, D*
University of California
Irvine *D*
Santa Barbara *B*

Colorado

University of Colorado
Denver *D*

Connecticut

Yale University *M, D*

District of Columbia

George Washington
University *B, M, D*
Georgetown University *D*
Howard University *M, D*

Florida

University of Miami *D*

Georgia

Emory University *D*
Georgia Southern University *B*
Medical College of Georgia *M, D*

Illinois

Loyola University Chicago *M, D*
Rush University *M, D*
Southern Illinois University
Carbondale *M, D*
University of Chicago *D*
University of Illinois
Chicago *M, D*

Indiana

Indiana University
Bloomington *M, D*
Indiana University-Purdue University
Indianapolis *M, D*

Iowa

Drake University *B, M*
University of Iowa *M, D*

Kansas

University of Kansas Medical
Center *M, D*

Kentucky

University of Kentucky *D*

Louisiana

Louisiana State University Health
Sciences Center *M, D*
Tulane University *M, D*

Massachusetts

Boston University *M, D*
Massachusetts College of Pharmacy
and Health Sciences *M, D*
Tufts University *M*

Michigan

University of Michigan *D*

Minnesota

University of Minnesota
Duluth *M*
Twin Cities *M, D*

Missouri

Saint Louis University *M, D*
University of Missouri
Columbia *M, D*

Montana

University of Montana *D*

Nebraska

Creighton University *M, D*
University of Nebraska
   Medical Center *M, D*

Nevada

University of Nevada
   Reno *D*

New Hampshire

Dartmouth College *D*

New York

City University of New York
   Hunter College *B, M*
Cornell University *M, D*
Long Island University
   Brooklyn Campus *M*
New York University *M, D*
State University of New York
   Buffalo *M, D*
   Stony Brook *B*
   Upstate Medical University *D*
University of Rochester *M, D*
Yeshiva University *M, D*

North Carolina

University of North Carolina
   Chapel Hill *M, D*
Wake Forest University *D*

North Dakota

University of North Dakota *M, D*

Ohio

Case Western Reserve University *D*
Kent State University *M, D*
Ohio State University
   Columbus Campus *M, D*
University of Cincinnati *D*

Oregon

Chemeketa Community College *A*
Oregon Health & Science
   University *D*

Pennsylvania

Drexel University *M, D*
Temple University *D*
University of Pennsylvania *M, D*

Puerto Rico

Turabo University *A*
University of Puerto Rico
   Medical Sciences *M, D*

South Carolina

Medical University of South
   Carolina *D*

Tennessee

University of Tennessee
   Knoxville *M, D*
University of Tennessee Health
   Science Center *M, D*
Vanderbilt University *D*

Texas

University of Texas
   Health Science Center at
      Houston *M, D*
   Health Science Center at San
      Antonio *M, D*
   Medical Branch at Galveston *M, D*

Vermont

University of Vermont *M, D*

Virginia

University of Virginia *D*
Virginia Commonwealth
   University *M, D*

Washington

University of Washington *M, D*

Wisconsin

University of Wisconsin
   Madison *D*

Pharmacology/ toxicology

Alabama

University of Alabama
   Birmingham *D*

California

University of California
   Davis *M, D*
   Irvine *M, D*
University of Southern
   California *M, D*

Kansas

University of Kansas *M, D*

Kentucky

University of Louisville *M, D*

Massachusetts

Massachusetts College of Pharmacy
   and Health Sciences *B*

Michigan

Michigan State University *M, D*

New York

State University of New York
   Buffalo *B, M*

Ohio

Wright State University *B*

Pennsylvania

Duquesne University *M, D*
University of the Sciences in
   Philadelphia *B, M, D*

Rhode Island

University of Rhode Island *M, D*

Texas

University of Texas
   Health Science Center at
      Houston *M, D*

Washington

Washington State University *M, D*

West Virginia

West Virginia University *M*

Wisconsin

University of Wisconsin
   Madison *B*

Pharmacy (Pharm.D.)

Alabama

Auburn University: School of
   Pharmacy *P*
Samford University: McWhorter
   School of Pharmacy *P*

Arizona

University of Arizona: College of
   Pharmacy *P*

Arkansas

University of Arkansas for Medical
   Sciences: College of Pharmacy *P*

California

University of California San Francisco:
   School of Pharmacy *P*
University of Southern California:
   School of Pharmacy *P*
University of the Pacific: School of
   Pharmacy *P*

Colorado

University of Colorado Health
   Sciences Center: College of
   Pharmacy *P*

Connecticut

University of Connecticut: School of
   Pharmacy *P*

District of Columbia

Howard University: School of
   Pharmacy *P*

Florida

Florida Agricultural and Mechanical
   University: School of Pharmacy *P*
Nova Southeastern University of the
   Health Sciences: College of
   Pharmacy *P*
University of Florida: College of
   Pharmacy *P*

Georgia

Mercer University Southern School of
   Pharmacy *P*
University of Georgia: College of
   Pharmacy *P*

Idaho

Idaho State University: College of
   Pharmacy *P*

Illinois

Midwestern University: Chicago
   College of Pharmacy *P*
University of Illinois at Chicago:
   College of Pharmacy *P*

Indiana

Butler University: College of
   Pharmacy *P*
Purdue University: School of
   Pharmacy *P*

Iowa

Drake University: College of
   Pharmacy *P*
University of Iowa: College of
   Pharmacy *P*

Louisiana

Northeast Louisiana University School
   of Pharmacy *P*
Xavier University of Louisiana: College
   of Pharmacy *P*

Maryland

University of Maryland at Baltimore:
   School of Pharmacy *P*

Massachusetts

Northeastern University: Bouve
   College of Pharmacy and Health
   Sciences *P*

Michigan

Ferris State University College of
   Pharmacy *P*
University of Michigan: College of
   Pharmacy *P*
Wayne State University: College of
   Pharmacy and Allied Health *P*

Mississippi

University of Mississippi: School of
   Pharmacy *P*

Missouri

St. Louis College of Pharmacy *P*

Montana

University of Montana School of
   Pharmacy and Allied Health
   Sciences *P*

Nebraska

University of Nebraska Medical
   Center: College of Pharmacy *P*

New Jersey

Rutgers, The State University of New
   Jersey
   College of Pharmacy *P*

New Mexico

University of New Mexico College of
   Pharmacy *P*

New York

Long Island University:Arnold and
   Marie Schwartz College of
   Pharmacy and Health Sciences *P*
St. John's University: College of
   Pharmacy and Allied Health
   Professions *P*
State University of New York at
   Buffalo: School of Pharmacy *P*

North Carolina

Campbell University: School of
   Pharmacy *P*
University of North Carolina at Chapel
   Hill: School of Pharmacy *P*

North Dakota

North Dakota State University: College
   of Pharmacy *P*

Ohio

Ohio Northern University: College of
   Pharmacy *P*
Ohio State University Columbus
   Campus: College of Pharmacy *P*
University of Cincinnati: College of
   Pharmacy *P*
University of Toledo: College of
   Pharmacy *P*

Oklahoma

Southwestern Oklahoma State
   University School of Pharmacy *P*
University of Oklahoma College of
   Pharmacy *P*

Oregon

Oregon State University: College of
   Pharmacy *P*

Pennsylvania

Philadelphia College of Pharmacy and
   Science: School of Pharmacy *P*
Temple University: School of
   Pharmacy *P*
University of Pittsburgh: School of
   Pharmacy *P*

Puerto Rico

University of Puerto Rico Medical Sciences Campus: School of Pharmacy *P*

Rhode Island

University of Rhode Island: College of Pharmacy *P*

South Carolina

Medical University of South Carolina: College of Pharmacy *P*
University of South Carolina: School of Pharmacy *P*

South Dakota

South Dakota State University: College of Pharmacy *P*

Tennessee

University of Tennessee Memphis: College of Pharmacy *P*

Texas

Texas Southern University: College of Pharmacy and Health Sciences *P*
University of Houston: College of Pharmacy *P*
University of Texas at Austin: College of Pharmacy *P*

Utah

University of Utah: College of Pharmacy *P*

Washington

Washington State University: College of Pharmacy *P*

West Virginia

West Virginia University: School of Pharmacy *P*

Wisconsin

University of Wisconsin Madison: School of Pharmacy *P*

Wyoming

University of Wyoming: School of Pharmacy *P*

Pharmacy assistant

Alabama

Northeast Alabama Community College *C*
Remington College
  Mobile *C*

Arizona

Brookline College
  Phoenix *C*
  Tempe *C*
  Tucson *C*
Central Arizona College *A*
Eastern Arizona College *C, A*
Mohave Community College *C, A*
Pima Community College *C, A*

Arkansas

Arkansas State University
  Beebe *C, A*

California

Charles Drew University of Medicine and Science *A*
City College of San Francisco *C*
Foothill College *C, A*

Heald College
  Hayward *A*
  Roseville *A*
Kaplan College: Palm Springs *C*
Kaplan College: Vista *C*
National University *C*
Palo Verde College *C*
San Joaquin Valley College *A*
Santa Ana College *C, A*
Santa Barbara Business College *C, A*
Santa Barbara Business College
  Bakersfield *C, A*
  Santa Maria *C, A*
Santa Rosa Junior College *C, A*
Silicon Valley College
  Western Career College:
    Emeryville *A*
  Western Career College: San Jose *A*
Western Career College
  San Leandro *A*
Western Career College: Antioch *C, A*
Western Career College: Citrus
  Heights *A*
Western Career College:
  Sacramento *A*
Western Career College: Stockton *A*

Colorado

Arapahoe Community College *C*
Front Range Community College *C*
Kaplan College: Denver *C*
Otero Junior College *A*
Pikes Peak Community College *C*
Pueblo Community College *C*

Connecticut

Gateway Community College *C, A*
Manchester Community College *A*

Florida

Rasmussen College: Ocala *A*
Rasmussen College: Pasco County *A*

Georgia

Albany Technical College *C, A*
Augusta Technical College *C, A*
Central Georgia Technical College *C*
Macon State College *A*
Middle Georgia College *A*
North Georgia Technical College *C*
Southeastern Technical College *C*
Southwest Georgia Technical
  College *C, A*
West Georgia Technical College *C, A*

Idaho

North Idaho College *A*

Illinois

City Colleges of Chicago
  Malcolm X College *C*
Coyne American Institute *C*
Lewis University *B*
Rasmussen College: Aurora *A*
Rasmussen College: Rockford *A*
Richland Community College *C*
Robert Morris University: Chicago *A*
Rock Valley College *C*
Rockford Career College *A*
South Suburban College of Cook
  County *C, A*

Indiana

National College: Indianapolis *A*
Vincennes University *C, A*

Iowa

Clinton Community College *C*
Indian Hills Community College *C*
Mercy College of Health Sciences *C*
Western Iowa Tech Community
  College *C*

Kansas

Hutchinson Community College *C*
Labette Community College *C*

Kentucky

Daymar College
  Owensboro *A*
Daymar College: Paducah *A*
Draughons Junior College *C, A*
National College
  Florence *C*
  Richmond *C*
Owensboro Community and
  Technical College *C*
St. Catharine College *C, A*
West Kentucky Community and
  Technical College *C*

Louisiana

Bossier Parish Community
  College *C, A*
Delgado Community College *C*
Louisiana State University
  Alexandria *C*

Maryland

Allegany College of Maryland *C*
Anne Arundel Community College *C*
College of Southern Maryland *C*
Hagerstown Community College *C*

Massachusetts

Benjamin Franklin Institute of
  Technology *C*
North Shore Community College *C*

Michigan

Baker College
  of Flint *C, A*
  of Jackson *C, A*
  of Muskegon *C, A*
Bay de Noc Community College *C*
Delta College *A*
Henry Ford Community College *C*
Madonna University *A*
Oakland Community College *C, A*
St. Clair County Community
  College *C*
Washtenaw Community College *C*
Wayne County Community
  College *C, A*

Minnesota

Minnesota State Community and
  Technical College *C, A*
Northland Community & Technical
  College *A*
Rasmussen College
  Eagan *A*
  Eden Prairie *A*
  Mankato *A*
  St. Cloud *A*
Rasmussen College: Brooklyn Park *A*
Rasmussen College: Lake
  Elmo/Woodbury *A*

Mississippi

Northeast Mississippi Community
  College *A*

Missouri

State Fair Community College *C*
Vatterott College: Joplin *A*
Vatterott College: Springfield *C, A*

Montana

Flathead Valley Community College *C*
University of Montana *C*

Nebraska

Southeast Community College *C*

Nevada

Career College of Northern Nevada *C*
High-Tech Institute *A*
Kaplan College: Las Vegas *C, A*

New Jersey

Middlesex County College *A*

New Mexico

Brookline College
  Albuquerque *C*
Central New Mexico Community
  College *C*
Eastern New Mexico University:
  Roswell Campus *C*

New York

ASA Institute of Business and
  Computer Technology *A*

North Carolina

Cape Fear Community College *C*
Davidson County Community
  College *C*
Durham Technical Community
  College *C*
Fayetteville Technical Community
  College *C*
Southeastern Community College *C*

North Dakota

North Dakota State College of
  Science *C, A*

Ohio

Cuyahoga Community College
  Metropolitan Campus *C, A*
Kaplan College: Dayton *C*
Marion Technical College *C*
National College: Cincinnati *A*
National College: Stow *A*
Southern State Community College *C*
University of Northwestern Ohio *C, A*

Oklahoma

Platt College
  Tulsa *C*

Oregon

Linn-Benton Community College *C*

Pennsylvania

Community College of Allegheny
  County *C, A*
Laurel Business Institute *C, A*
Pennsylvania Highlands Community
  College *C*
Pennsylvania Institute of
  Technology *C*

Puerto Rico

Electronic Data Processing College:
  San Sebastian *C*
Huertas Junior College *A*
Humacao Community College *A*
Inter American University of Puerto
  Rico
  Aguadilla Campus *C, A*
  Guayama Campus *A*
  Ponce Campus *C*
  San German Campus *C*
National College of Business and
  Technology: Arecibo *A*
National College of Business and
  Technology: Bayamon *A*
National College of Business and
  Technology: Rio Grande *A*
Ponce Paramedical College *C*
Turabo University *C*
Universidad Metropolitana *C*
Universidad del Este *A*

South Carolina
Aiken Technical College *C*
Central Carolina Technical College *C*
Greenville Technical College *C*
Horry-Georgetown Technical
College *A*
Midlands Technical College *C, A*
Spartanburg Community College *C*
Tri-County Technical College *C*
Trident Technical College *C*

South Dakota
Southeast Technical Institute *C*
Western Dakota Technical Institute *C*

Tennessee
Chattanooga State Community
College *C*
Draughons Junior College:
Nashville *C, A*
National College
Knoxville *C, A*
Nashville *C*
National College: Bartlett *A*
National College: Madison *A*
National College: Memphis *A*
Remington College
Memphis *C*
Roane State Community College *C*
Southwest Tennessee Community
College *C*
Walters State Community College *C*

Texas
Amarillo College *C*
Angelina College *C*
Austin Community College *C*
Del Mar College *A*
El Paso Community College *C*
Houston Community College
System *C*
Lamar State College at Orange *C*
Lone Star College System *C, A*
Northwest Vista College *C*
San Jacinto College *C*
South Texas College *C, A*
Tarrant County College *C*
Weatherford College *C, A*

Utah
Eagle Gate College: Layton *C, A*
Eagle Gate College: Murray *A*
Eagle Gate College: Salt Lake City *C*
Salt Lake Community College *C*
Snow College *A*
Utah Career College *A*

Virginia
J. Sargeant Reynolds Community
College *C*
Mountain Empire Community
College *C*
National College
Roanoke Valley *C*
Southwest Virginia Community
College *C*
Virginia Western Community
College *C*
Wytheville Community College *C*

Washington
Centralia College *C*
Clark College *C*
Clover Park Technical College *C, A*
Grays Harbor College *C*
North Seattle Community
College *C, A*
Renton Technical College *C, A*
Spokane Community College *C, A*
Spokane Falls Community College *C*
Yakima Valley Community
College *C, A*

Wisconsin
Chippewa Valley Technical College *A*
Gateway Technical College *C*
Lakeshore Technical College *C*
Mid-State Technical College *C*
Milwaukee Area Technical College *C*
Rasmussen College: Green Bay *A*

Wyoming
Casper College *C, A*
Sheridan College *A*

Philosophy

Alabama
Auburn University *B*
Birmingham-Southern College *B*
Samford University *B*
Spring Hill College *B*
University of Alabama *B*
University of Alabama
Birmingham *B*
Huntsville *B*
University of South Alabama *B*

Alaska
University of Alaska
Anchorage *B*
Fairbanks *B*

Arizona
Arizona State University *B, M, D*
Arizona Western College *A*
Cochise College *A*
College of the Humanities and
Sciences *M, D*
Mesa Community College *A*
Northern Arizona University *B*
Prescott College *M*
University of Arizona *B, M, D*

Arkansas
Arkansas State University *B*
Hendrix College *B*
Lyon College *B*
Ouachita Baptist University *B*
Philander Smith College *B*
University of Arkansas *B, M, D*
University of Arkansas
Little Rock *B*
University of Central Arkansas *B*
University of the Ozarks *B*

California
Azusa Pacific University *B*
Bakersfield College *A*
Biola University *B, M, D*
California Baptist University *B*
California Institute of Integral
Studies *M, D*
California Institute of Technology *B*
California Lutheran University *B*
California Polytechnic State
University: San Luis Obispo *B*
California State Polytechnic
University: Pomona *B*
California State University
Bakersfield *B*
Chico *B*
Dominguez Hills *B*
East Bay *B*
Fresno *B*
Fullerton *B*
Long Beach *B, M*
Los Angeles *B, M*
Northridge *B*
Sacramento *B, M*
San Bernardino *B*
Stanislaus *B*
Canada College *A*
Cerritos College *A*
Chabot College *A*

Chaffey College *A*
Chapman University *B*
Claremont McKenna College *B*
College of Alameda *A*
College of the Desert *A*
College of the Siskiyous *C, A*
Copper Mountain College *A*
Cypress College *A*
De Anza College *A*
East Los Angeles College *A*
El Camino College *A*
El Camino College: Compton
Center *A*
Foothill College *A*
Fresno Pacific University *B*
Fullerton College *A*
Gavilan College *A*
Glendale Community College *A*
Golden West College *A*
Grossmont College *A*
Holy Names University *B*
Humboldt State University *B*
Irvine Valley College *A*
Loma Linda University *M*
Los Angeles Mission College *A*
Los Angeles Southwest College *A*
Los Angeles Valley College *A*
Loyola Marymount University *B*
Merced College *A*
Mills College *B*
MiraCosta College *A*
Monterey Peninsula College *A*
Mount St. Mary's College *B*
Notre Dame de Namur University *B*
Occidental College *B*
Orange Coast College *A*
Oxnard College *C, A*
Pepperdine University *B*
Pitzer College *B*
Point Loma Nazarene University *B*
Pomona College *B*
Saddleback College *A*
St. Mary's College of California *B*
San Diego City College *A*
San Diego Mesa College *A*
San Diego State University *B, M*
San Francisco State University *B, M*
San Jose State University *B, M*
Santa Ana College *A*
Santa Barbara City College *A*
Santa Clara University *B*
Santa Rosa Junior College *A*
Santiago Canyon College *A*
Scripps College *B*
Sierra College *A*
Sonoma State University *B*
Southwestern College *A*
Stanford University *B, M, D*
University of California
Berkeley *B, D*
Davis *B, M, D*
Irvine *B, M, D*
Los Angeles *B, M, D*
Riverside *B, M, D*
San Diego *B, M, D*
Santa Barbara *B, M, D*
Santa Cruz *B, M, D*
University of La Verne *B*
University of Redlands *B*
University of San Diego *B*
University of San Francisco *B*
University of Southern
California *B, M, D*
University of the Pacific *B*
West Los Angeles College *A*
Westmont College *B*
Whittier College *B*

Colorado
Colorado College *B*
Colorado State University *B, M*
Fort Lewis College *B*
Metropolitan State College of
Denver *B*
Pikes Peak Community College *A*
Regis University *B*
Trinidad State Junior College *A*
University of Colorado
Boulder *B, M, D*
Colorado Springs *B*
Denver *B*
University of Denver *B, M*
University of Northern Colorado *B*

Connecticut
Albertus Magnus College *B*
Central Connecticut State
University *B*
Connecticut College *B*
Fairfield University *B*
Holy Apostles College and
Seminary *B, M*
Sacred Heart University *B*
Saint Joseph College *B*
Southern Connecticut State
University *B*
Trinity College *B*
University of Connecticut *B, M, D*
University of Hartford *B*
Wesleyan University *B*
Yale University *B, M, D*

Delaware
Delaware State University *B*
University of Delaware *B*

District of Columbia
American University *B, M*
Catholic University of
America *B, M, D*
Gallaudet University *B*
George Washington University *B*
Georgetown University *B, M, D*
Howard University *B, M*
University of the District of
Columbia *A, B*

Florida
Ave Maria University *B*
Barry University *B*
Daytona State College *A*
Eckerd College *B*
Flagler College *B*
Florida Atlantic University *B*
Florida Christian College *B*
Florida Gulf Coast University *B*
Florida International University *B*
Florida Southern College *B*
Florida State University *B, M, D*
Gulf Coast Community College *A*
Indian River State College *A*
Jacksonville University *B*
Miami Dade College *A*
New College of Florida *B*
Palm Beach Atlantic University *B*
Palm Beach Community College *A*
Pensacola Junior College *A*
Rollins College *B*
St. John Vianney College Seminary *B*
State College of Florida,
Manatee-Sarasota *A*
Stetson University *B*
University of Central Florida *B*
University of Florida *B, M, D*
University of Miami *B, M, D*
University of North Florida *B*
University of South Florida *B, M, D*
University of Tampa *A, B*
University of West Florida *B*

Georgia
Agnes Scott College *B*
Clark Atlanta University *B*
Covenant College *B*
Dalton State College *A*
Darton College *A*
Emory University *B, D*

Georgia College and State
University *B*
Georgia Highlands College *A*
Georgia Perimeter College *A*
Georgia Southern University *B*
Georgia State University *B, M*
Mercer University *B*
Morehouse College *B*
Oglethorpe University *B*
Paine College *B*
Piedmont College *B*
South Georgia College *A*
Spelman College *B*
Toccoa Falls College *B*
University of Georgia *B, M, D*
University of West Georgia *B*
Valdosta State University *B*
Wesleyan College *B*

Hawaii
University of Hawaii
Hilo *R*
Manoa *B, M, D*
West Oahu *B*

Idaho
Boise State University *B*
College of Idaho *B*
Idaho State University *B*
North Idaho College *A*
Northwest Nazarene University *B*
University of Idaho *B, M*

Illinois
Augustana College *B*
Benedictine University *B*
Bradley University *B*
City Colleges of Chicago
Harold Washington College *A*
Olive-Harvey College *A*
Concordia University Chicago *B*
DePaul University *B, M, D*
Dominican University *B*
Eastern Illinois University *B*
Elmhurst College *B*
Eureka College *B*
Greenville College *B*
Harper College *A*
Illinois College *B*
Illinois State University *B*
Illinois Wesleyan University *B*
Knox College *B*
Lake Forest College *B*
Lewis University *B*
Lincoln College *A*
Loyola University Chicago *B, M, D*
MacMurray College *B*
McKendree University *B*
Millikin University *B*
Monmouth College *B*
North Central College *B*
North Park University *B*
Northeastern Illinois University *B*
Northern Illinois University *B, M*
Northwestern University *B, M, D*
Principia College *B*
Richland Community College *A*
Rockford College *B*
Roosevelt University *B*
Saint Xavier University *B*
South Suburban College of Cook
County *A*
Southern Illinois University
Carbondale *B, M, D*
Southern Illinois University
Edwardsville *B*
Southwestern Illinois College *A*
Trinity Christian College *B*
Trinity International University *B, M*
Triton College *A*
University of Chicago *B, D*
University of Illinois
Chicago *B, M, D*

Springfield *B*
Urbana-Champaign *B, M, D*
Western Illinois University *B*
Wheaton College *B*

Indiana
Anderson University *B*
Ball State University *B*
Bethel College *B*
Butler University *B*
DePauw University *B*
Earlham College *B*
Franklin College *B*
Hanover College *B*
Huntington University *B*
Indiana State University *B*
Indiana University
Bloomington *B, M, D*
Northwest *B*
South Bend *B*
Southeast *B*
Indiana University-Purdue University
Fort Wayne *B*
Indiana University-Purdue University
Indianapolis *B, M*
Indiana Wesleyan University *A, B*
Manchester College *B*
Marian University *B*
Purdue University *B, M, D*
Purdue University
Calumet *B*
Saint Joseph's College *B*
Saint Mary's College *B*
Taylor University *B*
University of Evansville *B*
University of Indianapolis *B*
University of Notre Dame *B, M, D*
University of St. Francis *B*
University of Southern Indiana *B*
Valparaiso University *B*
Vincennes University *A*
Wabash College *B*

Iowa
Buena Vista University *B*
Central College *B*
Clarke College *A, B*
Coe College *B*
Cornell College *B*
Divine Word College *B*
Dordt College *B*
Drake University *B*
Grinnell College *B*
Iowa State University *B*
Iowa Wesleyan College *B*
Loras College *B*
Luther College *B*
Morningside College *B*
Mount Mercy College *B*
Northwestern College *B*
St. Ambrose University *B*
Simpson College *B*
University of Dubuque *B*
University of Iowa *B, M, D*
University of Northern Iowa *B*
Wartburg College *B*

Kansas
Baker University *B*
Barton County Community College *A*
Benedictine College *B*
Cowley County Community
College *A*
Fort Hays State University *B*
Kansas State University *B*
Newman University *B*
Southwestern College *B*
Tabor College *B*
University of Kansas *B, M, D*
Washburn University *B*
Wichita State University *B*

Kentucky
Asbury College *B*
Bellarmine University *B*
Berea College *B*
Bluegrass Community and Technical
College *A*
Centre College *B*
Eastern Kentucky University *B*
Georgetown College *B*
Morehead State University *B*
Murray State University *B*
Northern Kentucky University *B*
Thomas More College *A, B*
Transylvania University *B*
University of Kentucky *B, M, D*
University of Louisville *B*
Western Kentucky University *B*

Louisiana
Centenary College of Louisiana *B*
Dillard University *B*
Louisiana State University and
Agricultural and Mechanical
College *B, M*
Loyola University New Orleans *B*
Tulane University *B, M, D*
University of Louisiana at Lafayette *B*
University of New Orleans *B*
Xavier University of Louisiana *B*

Maine
Bates College *B*
Bowdoin College *B*
Colby College *B*
Saint Joseph's College of Maine *B*
University of Maine *B*
University of Southern Maine *B*

Maryland
College of Notre Dame of Maryland *B*
Frederick Community College *A*
Frostburg State University *B*
Goucher College *B*
Harford Community College *A*
Hood College *B*
Howard Community College *A*
Johns Hopkins University *B, M, D*
Loyola University Maryland *B*
McDaniel College *B*
Mount St. Mary's University *B, M*
St. Mary's College of Maryland *B*
Salisbury University *B*
Towson University *B*
University of Maryland
Baltimore County *B*
College Park *B, M, D*
Washington College *B*

Massachusetts
Amherst College *B*
Assumption College *B*
Bard College at Simon's Rock *B*
Bentley University *B*
Boston College *B, M, D*
Boston University *B, M, D*
Brandeis University *B, M*
Bridgewater State College *B*
Cape Cod Community College *A*
Clark University *B*
College of the Holy Cross *B*
Curry College *B*
Gordon College *B*
Hampshire College *B*
Harvard College *B, M, D*
Massachusetts College of Liberal
Arts *B*
Massachusetts Institute of
Technology *B, D*
Merrimack College *B*
Mount Holyoke College *B*
Northeastern University *B*
Simmons College *B*
Smith College *B, D*

Stonehill College *B*
Suffolk University *B*
Tufts University *B, M*
University of Massachusetts
Amherst *B, M, D*
Boston *B*
Dartmouth *B*
Lowell *B*
Wellesley College *B*
Western New England College *B*
Wheaton College *B*
Williams College *B*

Michigan
Adrian College *B*
Albion College *B*
Alma College *B*
Aquinas College *B*
Calvin College *B*
Central Michigan University *B*
Eastern Michigan University *B*
Grand Valley State University *B*
Hillsdale College *B*
Hope College *B*
Kalamazoo College *B*
Lake Michigan College *A*
Lansing Community College *A*
Madonna University *B*
Michigan State University *B, M, D*
Northern Michigan University *B*
Oakland University *B*
Sacred Heart Major Seminary *B*
Siena Heights University *B*
Spring Arbor University *B*
University of Detroit Mercy *B*
University of Michigan *B, M, D*
University of Michigan
Dearborn *B*
Flint *B*
Wayne State University *B, M, D*
Western Michigan University *B, M*

Minnesota
Augsburg College *B*
Bemidji State University *B*
Bethel University *B*
Carleton College *B*
College of St. Benedict *B*
Concordia College: Moorhead *B*
Gustavus Adolphus College *B*
Hamline University *B*
Macalester College *B*
Metropolitan State University *B*
Minnesota State University
Mankato *B*
Moorhead *B*
Minnesota West Community and
Technical College *A*
St. Catherine University *B*
Saint Cloud State University *B*
St. John's University *B*
St. Mary's University of Minnesota *B*
St. Olaf College *B*
Southwest Minnesota State
University *B*
University of Minnesota
Duluth *B*
Morris *B*
Twin Cities *B, M, D*
University of St. Thomas *B*

Mississippi
Belhaven University *B*
Millsaps College *B*
Mississippi State University *B*
University of Mississippi *B, M*
University of Southern
Mississippi *B, M*

Missouri
Central Methodist University *B*
College of the Ozarks *B*
Conception Seminary College *B*

Drury University R
Lindenwood University B
Missouri State University B
Missouri Valley College B
Northwest Missouri State
  University B
Rockhurst University B
St. Charles Community College A
Saint Louis University B, M, D
Southeast Missouri State University B
Three Rivers Community College A
University of Missouri
  Columbia B, M, D
  Kansas City B
  Missouri University of Science and
    Technology B
  St. Louis B, M
Washington University in St.
  Louis B, M, D
Webster University B
Westminster College B
William Jewell College B

Montana

Montana State University
  Bozeman B
University of Montana B, M

Nebraska

Creighton University B
Doane College B
Nebraska Wesleyan University B
University of Nebraska
  Kearney B
  Lincoln B, M, D
  Omaha B

Nevada

University of Nevada
  Las Vegas B
  Reno B, M

New Hampshire

Dartmouth College B
New England College B
Plymouth State University B
Saint Anselm College B
Thomas More College of Liberal
  Arts B
University of New Hampshire B

New Jersey

Bergen Community College A
Bloomfield College B
The College of New Jersey B
College of St. Elizabeth B
Drew University B
Fairleigh Dickinson University
  College at Florham B
  Metropolitan Campus B
Felician College B
Montclair State University B
New Jersey City University B
Princeton University B, M, D
Rider University B
Rutgers, The State University of New
  Jersey
  Camden Regional Campus B
  New Brunswick/Piscataway
    Campus B, M, D
  Newark Regional Campus B
Saint Peter's College B
Seton Hall University B
Stevens Institute of Technology B
Thomas Edison State College B
William Paterson University of New
  Jersey B

New Mexico

New Mexico State University B
University of New Mexico B, M, D

New York

Adelphi University B
Alfred University B
Bard College B
Barnard College B
Canisius College B
City University of New York
  Baruch College B
  Brooklyn College B
  City College B
  College of Staten Island B
  Hunter College B
  Lehman College B
  Queens College B, M
  York College B
Colgate University B
College of Mount St. Vincent B
College of New Rochelle B
College of Saint Rose B
Columbia University B
Columbia University
  School of General Studies B
Cornell University B, M, D
D'Youville College B
Dowling College B
Elmira College B
Eugene Lang College The New School
  for Liberal Arts B
Excelsior College B
Fordham University B, M, D
Hamilton College B
Hartwick College B
Hobart and William Smith Colleges B
Hofstra University B
Houghton College B
Iona College B
Ithaca College B
Le Moyne College B
Long Island University
  Brooklyn Campus B
  C. W. Post Campus B
Manhattan College B
Manhattanville College B
Marist College B
Marymount Manhattan College B
Molloy College B
Nazareth College B
New York University B, M, D
Niagara University B
Nyack College B
Pace University B
Rensselaer Polytechnic Institute B
Rochester Institute of Technology B
Saint Bonaventure University B
St. Francis College B
St. John Fisher College B
St. John's University B
St. Lawrence University B
St. Thomas Aquinas College B
Siena College B
Skidmore College B
State University of New York
  Albany B, M, D
  Binghamton B, M, D
  Buffalo B, M, D
  College at Brockport B
  College at Buffalo B
  College at Cortland B
  College at Fredonia B
  College at Geneseo B
  College at Old Westbury B
  College at Oneonta B
  College at Plattsburgh B
  College at Potsdam B
  New Paltz B
  Oswego B
  Purchase B
  Stony Brook B, M, D
Sullivan County Community
  College A
Syracuse University B, M, D
Touro College B
Union College B

Union Theological Seminary:
  Theological Professions D
University of Rochester B, M, D
Utica College B
Vassar College B
Wagner College B
Wells College B
Yeshiva University B

North Carolina

Appalachian State University B
Belmont Abbey College B
Davidson College B
Duke University B, M, D
East Carolina University B
Elon University B
Gardner-Webb University B
Guilford College B
High Point University B
Lenoir-Rhyne University B
Methodist University A, B
North Carolina State University B
St. Andrews Presbyterian College B
Salem College B
Southeastern Baptist Theological
  Seminary M
University of North Carolina
  Asheville B
  Chapel Hill B, M, D
  Charlotte B
  Greensboro B
  Wilmington B
Wake Forest University B
Warren Wilson College B
Western Carolina University B
Wingate University B

North Dakota

North Dakota State University B
University of North Dakota B

Ohio

Ashland University B
Baldwin-Wallace College B
Bowling Green State
  University B, M, D
Capital University B
Case Western Reserve University B
Cedarville University B
Cleveland State University B, M
College of Wooster B
Denison University B
Franciscan University of
  Steubenville B, M
Hiram College B
John Carroll University B
Kent State University B, M
Kenyon College B
Malone University B
Miami University
  Oxford Campus B, M
Mount Union College B
Mount Vernon Nazarene University B
Muskingum University B
Oberlin College B
Ohio Dominican University B
Ohio Northern University B
Ohio State University
  Columbus Campus B, M, D
Ohio University B, M
Ohio Wesleyan University B
Otterbein College B
Pontifical College Josephinum B
University of Akron B
University of Cincinnati B, M, D
University of Dayton B
University of Findlay B
University of Toledo B, M
Urbana University B
Ursuline College B
Walsh University B
Wittenberg University B
Wright State University B
Xavier University B

Youngstown State University B

Oklahoma

Oklahoma Baptist University B
Oklahoma City University B, M
Oklahoma State University B, M
Southern Nazarene University B
Tulsa Community College A
University of Central Oklahoma B
University of Oklahoma B, M, D
University of Tulsa B

Oregon

Chemeketa Community College A
George Fox University B
Lewis & Clark College B
Linfield College B
Marylhurst University B
Mount Angel Seminary B, M
Mt. Hood Community College A
Oregon State University B
Pacific University B
Portland State University B
Reed College B
University of Oregon B, M, D
University of Portland B
Western Oregon University B
Willamette University B

Pennsylvania

Albright College B
Allegheny College B
Arcadia University B
Bloomsburg University of
  Pennsylvania B
Bryn Mawr College B
Bucknell University B
Cabrini College B
California University of
  Pennsylvania B
Carlow University B
Carnegie Mellon University B, M
Clarion University of Pennsylvania B
DeSales University B
Dickinson College B
Duquesne University B, M, D
East Stroudsburg University of
  Pennsylvania B
Edinboro University of
  Pennsylvania B
Elizabethtown College B
Franklin & Marshall College B
Gannon University B
Geneva College B
Gettysburg College B
Grove City College B
Haverford College B
Indiana University of Pennsylvania B
Juniata College B
King's College B
Kutztown University of
  Pennsylvania B
La Salle University B
Lafayette College B
Lebanon Valley College B
Lehigh University B
Lincoln University B
Lock Haven University of
  Pennsylvania B
Lycoming College B
Mansfield University of
  Pennsylvania B
Marywood University B
Mercyhurst College B
Messiah College B
Millersville University of
  Pennsylvania B
Misericordia University B
Moravian College B
Muhlenberg College B
Penn State
  Abington B
  Altoona B
  Beaver B

Berks *B*
Brandywine *B*
DuBois *B*
Erie, The Behrend College *B*
Fayette, The Eberly Campus *B*
Greater Allegheny *B*
Hazleton *B*
Lehigh Valley *B*
Mont Alto *B*
New Kensington *B*
Schuylkill *B*
Shenango *B*
University Park *B, M, D*
Wilkes-Barre *B*
Worthington Scranton *B*
York *B*
Rosemont College *B*
St. Charles Borromeo Seminary -
    Overbrook *B*
St. Francis University *B*
Saint Joseph's University *B*
St. Vincent College *B*
Slippery Rock University of
    Pennsylvania *B*
Susquehanna University *B*
Swarthmore College *B*
Temple University *B, M, D*
Thiel College *B*
University of Pennsylvania *B, M, D*
University of Pittsburgh *B, M, D*
University of Scranton *B*
Ursinus College *B*
Villanova University *B, M, D*
Washington & Jefferson College *B*
West Chester University of
    Pennsylvania *B, M*
Westminster College *B*
Wilkes University *B*
Wilson College *B*
York College of Pennsylvania *B*

Puerto Rico

Bayamon Central University *B*
Pontifical Catholic University of
    Puerto Rico *B*
University of Puerto Rico
    Aguadilla *A*
    Rio Piedras *B, M*

Rhode Island

Brown University *B, M, D*
Providence College *B*
Rhode Island College *B*
Roger Williams University *B*
Salve Regina University *B*
University of Rhode Island *B*

South Carolina

Claflin University *B*
Clemson University *B*
Coastal Carolina University *B*
College of Charleston *B*
Erskine College *B*
Furman University *B*
Newberry College *B*
Presbyterian College *B*
University of South Carolina *B, M, D*
Winthrop University *B*
Wofford College *B*

South Dakota

Augustana College *B*
University of South Dakota *B*

Tennessee

Austin Peay State University *B*
Belmont University *B*
Carson-Newman College *B*
Christian Brothers University *B*
East Tennessee State University *B, T*
Freed-Hardeman University *B*
Jackson State Community College *A*
Lambuth University *B*

Lipscomb University *B*
Maryville College *B*
Middle Tennessee State University *B*
Rhodes College *B*
Union University *B*
University of Memphis *B, M, D*
University of Tennessee
    Knoxville *B, M, D*
    Martin *B*
University of the South *B*
Vanderbilt University *B, M, D*

Texas

Austin College *B*
Austin Community College *A*
Baylor University *B, M, D*
Blinn College *A*
Dallas Baptist University *B*
Frank Phillips College *A*
Hardin-Simmons University *B*
Houston Baptist University *B*
Howard Payne University *B*
Laredo Community College *A*
Lon Morris College *A*
Our Lady of the Lake University of San
    Antonio *B*
Palo Alto College *A*
Rice University *B, M, D*
St. Edward's University *B*
St. Mary's University *B*
St. Philip's College *A*
Sam Houston State University *B*
San Jacinto College *A*
South Texas College *A*
Southern Methodist University *B*
Southwestern Baptist Theological
    Seminary: Theological
    Professions *D*
Southwestern University *B*
Stephen F. Austin State University *B*
Texas A&M University *B, M, D*
Texas Christian University *B*
Texas Lutheran University *B*
Texas State University: San Marcos *B*
Texas Tech University *B, M*
Trinity University *B*
University of Dallas *B, M, D*
University of Houston *B, M*
University of Houston
    Downtown *B*
University of North Texas *B, M, D*
University of St. Thomas *B, M, D*
University of Texas
    Arlington *B*
    Austin *B, M, D*
    El Paso *B*
    Pan American *B*
    San Antonio *B*
University of the Incarnate Word *B*
Western Texas College *A*

Utah

Brigham Young University *B*
Snow College *A*
Southern Utah University *B*
University of Utah *B, M, D, T*
Utah State University *B*
Utah Valley University *A, B*
Westminster College *B*

Vermont

Bennington College *B*
Castleton State College *B*
Green Mountain College *B*
Lyndon State College *B*
Marlboro College *B*
Middlebury College *B*
St. Michael's College *B*
University of Vermont *B*

Virginia

Christendom College *B*
Christopher Newport University *B*

College of William and Mary *B*
Emory & Henry College *B*
Ferrum College *B*
George Mason University *B, M*
Hampden-Sydney College *B*
Hollins University *B*
Liberty University *B*
Lord Fairfax Community College *A*
Lynchburg College *B*
Mary Baldwin College *B*
Marymount University *B*
Old Dominion University *B*
Randolph College *B*
Randolph-Macon College *B*
Roanoke College *B, T*
St. Paul's College *B*
Southern Virginia University *B*
Sweet Briar College *B*
University of Mary Washington *B*
University of Richmond *B*
University of Virginia *B, M, D*
Virginia Commonwealth University *B*
Virginia Polytechnic Institute and
    State University *B, M*
Virginia Wesleyan College *B*
Washington and Lee University *B*

Washington

Eastern Washington University *B*
Everett Community College *A*
Evergreen State College *B*
Gonzaga University *B, M*
Northwest University *B*
Pacific Lutheran University *B*
Saint Martin's University *B*
Seattle Pacific University *B*
Seattle University *B*
University of Puget Sound *B*
University of Washington *B, M, D*
Washington State University *B, M*
Western Washington University *B*
Whitman College *B*
Whitworth University *B*

West Virginia

American Public University System *B*
Bethany College *B*
West Virginia University *B*
West Virginia Wesleyan College *B*
Wheeling Jesuit University *B*

Wisconsin

Alverno College *B*
Beloit College *B*
Carthage College *B*
Lawrence University *B*
Marquette University *B, M, D, T*
Mount Mary College *B*
Ripon College *B*
St. Norbert College *B*
University of Wisconsin
    Eau Claire *B*
    Green Bay *B*
    La Crosse *B*
    Madison *B, M, D*
    Milwaukee *B, M*
    Oshkosh *B*
    Parkside *B*
    Platteville *B*
    Stevens Point *B, T*
Viterbo University *B*
Wisconsin Lutheran College *B*

Wyoming

University of Wyoming *B, M*

Phlebotomy

Alabama

Bevill State Community College *C*

Arizona

Brookline College
    Phoenix *C*
    Tempe *C*
    Tucson *C*

Arkansas

North Arkansas College *C*
Phillips Community College of the
    University of Arkansas *A*

California

Charles Drew University of Medicine
    and Science *C*
MTI College *C*
Palo Verde College *C*

Colorado

Front Range Community College *C*
Pikes Peak Community College *C*
Pueblo Community College *C*
Red Rocks Community College *C*

Connecticut

Goodwin College *C*

Florida

City College
    Gainesville *C*
College of Business and Technology:
    Flagler *C*
Lake City Community College *C*
Pasco-Hernando Community
    College *C*

Georgia

Atlanta Technical College *C*
Dalton State College *C*
Darton College *C*
Southeastern Technical College *C*

Illinois

College of Office Technology *C*
Harper College *C*
Kankakee Community College *C*
Moraine Valley Community College *C*
Waubonsee Community College *C*

Iowa

Des Moines Area Community
    College *C*
St. Luke's College *C*

Kansas

Colby Community College *C*
Kansas City Kansas Community
    College *C*

Kentucky

Bluegrass Community and Technical
    College *C*
Somerset Community College *C*
Spencerian College *C*
Spencerian College: Lexington *C*
West Kentucky Community and
    Technical College *C*

Louisiana

Bossier Parish Community College *C*

Maryland

Hagerstown Community College *C*

Massachusetts

Bunker Hill Community College *C*
Mount Wachusett Community
    College *C*

Michigan

Davenport University *C*
Ferris State University *C*

Oakland Community College *C*
Schoolcraft College *C*
Southwestern Michigan College *C*
Wayne County Community College *C*

Minnesota
Alexandria Technical College *C*
Lake Superior College *C*
Minneapolis Community and
  Technical College *C*
Minnesota State Community and
  Technical College *C*
Minnesota West Community and
  Technical College *C*
Northland Community & Technical
  College *C*
St. Catherine University *C*
South Central College *C*

Mississippi
University of Southern Mississippi *C*

New Hampshire
Manchester Community College *C*

New Mexico
Eastern New Mexico University:
  Roswell Campus *A*

New York
Broome Community College *C*
Niagara County Community
  College *C*

North Carolina
Brunswick Community College *C*
College of the Albemarle *C*
Fayetteville Technical Community
  College *C*
Halifax Community College *A*
Southeastern Community College *C*

North Dakota
Bismarck State College *C*

Ohio
Eastern Gateway Community
  College *C*
Edison State Community College *C*
James A. Rhodes State College *A*
Marion Technical College *C*
Mercy College of Northwest Ohio *C*
Southern State Community College *C*
Southwestern College of Business
  Southwestern College: Franklin *C*
  Southwestern College:
    Tri-County *C*
  Southwestern College: Dayton *C*

Oklahoma
Platt College
  Tulsa *C*

Pennsylvania
Harrisburg Area Community
  College *C*
Lackawanna College *C*
Penn Commercial Business and
  Technical School *C*
Westmoreland County Community
  College *C*

Rhode Island
Community College of Rhode
  Island *C*

South Carolina
York Technical College *C*

South Dakota
Southeast Technical Institute *C*

Western Dakota Technical Institute *C*

Texas
Howard College *C*
Weatherford College *A*

Utah
Dixie State College of Utah *C*

Virginia
Southwest Virginia Community
  College *C*
Stratford University: Woodbridge *A*
Wytheville Community College *C*

Washington
Centralia College *C*
Clark College *C*
Olympic College *C*
Yakima Valley Community College *C*

West Virginia
Mountain State University *C*
New River Community and Technical
  College *C*

Wisconsin
Blackhawk Technical College *C*
Mid-State Technical College *C*
Milwaukee Area Technical College *C*
Waukesha County Technical
  College *C*

Wyoming
Casper College *C*

Photographic/film/video technology

Alabama
Calhoun Community College *A*
Lawson State Community College *C*

California
Allan Hancock College *C, A*
Cypress College *C*
Ex'pression College for Digital Arts *B*
National University *M*
Santiago Canyon College *A*

Colorado
Colorado Mountain College *A*

Florida
Daytona State College *C, A*

Georgia
Art Institute
  of Atlanta *A, B*

Illinois
Illinois Institute of Art: Schaumburg *B*
School of the Art Institute of
  Chicago *B, M*

Kansas
Central Christian College of Kansas *A*

Maine
New England School of
  Communications *B*

Maryland
Anne Arundel Community
  College *C, A*
Frederick Community College *C*

Massachusetts
Bard College at Simon's Rock *B*
New England Institute of Art *A, B*

Michigan
Bay de Noc Community College *C*
Grace Bible College *B*
Lawrence Technological University *C*
Oakland Community College *A*

Minnesota
Central Lakes College *C, A*
Hennepin Technical College *C, A*
Minneapolis Community and
  Technical College *A*

New Jersey
Burlington County College *A*
Ocean County College *A*

New Mexico
New Mexico State University
  Alamogordo *C, A*

New York
Cayuga County Community College *A*
Hilbert College *B*
Mohawk Valley Community College *C*
Rochester Institute of Technology *B*
St. John's University *A, B*

North Carolina
Carteret Community College *C, A*
Catawba Valley Community College *A*
Randolph Community College *A*

Oklahoma
Oklahoma City Community
  College *C, A*

Oregon
Mt. Hood Community College *A*

Pennsylvania
Westmoreland County Community
  College *C, A*

Texas
Austin Community College *C*
North Lake College *C, A*

Utah
Salt Lake Community College *A*

Washington
Bates Technical College *C*

Photography

Alabama
Birmingham-Southern College *B*
Calhoun Community College *A*

Arizona
Art Center Design College *B*
Art Institute of Tucson *B*
Northern Arizona University *B*
Prescott College *B, M*

Arkansas
John Brown University *B*

California
Academy of Art University *C, A, B, M*
Allan Hancock College *A*
Antelope Valley College *C, A*
Art Center College of Design *B*
Art Institute of California:
  Hollywood *A, B*
Bakersfield College *A*
Brooks Institute *B, M*
Butte College *A*
California College of the Arts *B, M*
California Institute of the Arts *C, B, M*

California State University
  East Bay *B*
  Long Beach *B*
  Sacramento *B, M*
Cerritos College *A*
Chabot College *A*
Chaffey College *C, A*
Citrus College *C, A*
City College of San Francisco *A*
College of San Mateo *A*
College of the Canyons *C, A*
College of the Desert *A*
College of the Siskiyous *C*
Columbia College *A*
Cosumnes River College *C, A*
Cypress College *C*
De Anza College *A*
East Los Angeles College *A*
El Camino College *C, A*
Foothill College *C, A*
Fresno City College *C, A*
Glendale Community College *C*
Golden West College *A*
Grossmont College *A*
Hartnell College *C, A*
Irvine Valley College *A*
Los Angeles City College *A*
Los Angeles Southwest College *A*
Los Angeles Trade and Technical
  College *C, A*
Merced College *C, A*
Modesto Junior College *A*
Monterey Peninsula College *C, A*
Moorpark College *A*
Mount San Antonio College *C, A*
Mount San Jacinto College *A*
Ohlone College *C*
Orange Coast College *C, A*
Otis College of Art and Design *B, M*
Pacific Union College *A, B*
Palomar College *C, A*
Rio Hondo College *A*
Riverside Community College *C, A*
Saddleback College *A*
San Diego City College *C, A*
San Francisco Art Institute *B, M*
San Joaquin Delta College *A*
Santa Ana College *C, A*
Santa Monica College *A*
Santa Rosa Junior College *C*
Sierra College *C, A*
Southwestern College *A*
Ventura College *C, A*
Yuba Community College
  District *C, A*

Colorado
Adams State College *B*
Art Institute
  of Colorado *C, A, B*
Colorado Mountain College *C, A*
Red Rocks Community College *C, A*
Rocky Mountain College of Art &
  Design *B*

Connecticut
Albertus Magnus College *B*
Paier College of Art *C, A, B*
Quinebaug Valley Community
  College *C, A*
University of Hartford *B*

Delaware
Delaware College of Art and Design *A*
Delaware Technical and Community
  College
  Terry *A*

District of Columbia
Corcoran College of Art and
  Design *A, B*
George Washington University *M*

Florida
Art Institute of Fort Lauderdale A, B
Barry University C, B, M
Daytona State College A
International Academy of Design and Technology: Tampa A
Palm Beach Community College A
Ringling College of Art and Design B
St. Petersburg College A
University of Central Florida B
University of Miami B

Georgia
Art Institute of Atlanta A, B
Gwinnett Technical College A
Savannah College of Art and Design B, M

Idaho
Brigham Young University-Idaho A
University of Idaho B

Illinois
Bradley University B
City Colleges of Chicago Olive-Harvey College A
Columbia College Chicago C, B, M
Dominican University B
Harrington College of Design A
Lincoln College A
Prairie State College C, A
School of the Art Institute of Chicago B, M
Southwestern Illinois College A
University of Illinois Chicago B, M
Urbana-Champaign B, M

Indiana
Indiana University-Purdue University Fort Wayne B
Indiana University-Purdue University Indianapolis B
Indiana Wesleyan University B
Purdue University B
St. Mary-of-the-Woods College B

Iowa
Coe College B
Iowa Lakes Community College A
Morningside College B
University of Iowa B, M

Kansas
Highland Community College A

Louisiana
Louisiana Tech University B

Maine
Maine College of Art B
University of Maine Augusta A

Maryland
Cecil College A
College of Notre Dame of Maryland B
Howard Community College C
Maryland Institute College of Art B, M
Montgomery College A

Massachusetts
Art Institute of Boston at Lesley University B
Bard College at Simon's Rock B
Bridgewater State College B
Fitchburg State College B
Hampshire College B
Massachusetts College of Art and Design B, M
Massasoit Community College C

Montserrat College of Art B
Salem State College B
School of the Museum of Fine Arts B, M
University of Massachusetts Dartmouth B, M

Michigan
Andrews University B
College for Creative Studies B
Delta College A
Ferris State University B
Grand Rapids Community College A
Grand Valley State University B
Kendall College of Art and Design of Ferris State University B, M
Lansing Community College A
Mott Community College A
Northern Michigan University A, B
Oakland Community College C, A
Oakland University B
Siena Heights University B
University of Michigan B
University of Michigan Flint B
Washtenaw Community College A

Minnesota
Art Institutes International Minnesota B
College of Visual Arts B
Dakota County Technical College C, A
Minneapolis College of Art and Design B
Ridgewater College C, A
Rochester Community and Technical College C

Missouri
Columbia College B
Kansas City Art Institute B
St. Louis Community College St. Louis Community College at Meramec A
University of Central Missouri B
Washington University in St. Louis B, M
Webster University B

Montana
Miles Community College A

Nevada
Art Institute of Las Vegas B

New Hampshire
Chester College of New England B
Lebanon College A
New England College B
Rivier College B

New Jersey
Brookdale Community College A
Burlington County College C, A
Camden County College A
Thomas Edison State College B

New Mexico
Art Center Design College B
College of Santa Fe B
New Mexico State University Alamogordo C

New York
Bard College B, M
Briarcliffe College A
Cazenovia College B
City University of New York Queensborough Community College C, A
Fordham University B

Herkimer County Community College A
Hofstra University B
Ithaca College B
Long Island University C. W. Post Campus B
Monroe Community College A
Nassau Community College C, A
New York University B
Onondaga Community College A
Parsons The New School for Design B, M
Pratt Institute B
Rochester Institute of Technology A, B, M
Rockland Community College A
St. John's University B
School of Visual Arts B, M
State University of New York College at Buffalo B
New Paltz B, M
Purchase B
Syracuse University B, M
Tompkins Cortland Community College A
Villa Maria College of Buffalo A, B

North Carolina
Carteret Community College C, A
East Carolina University B
Elon University B
Gardner-Webb University B
Randolph Community College A

Ohio
Art Academy of Cincinnati B
Bowling Green State University B
Clark State Community College C
Cleveland Institute of Art B
Columbus College of Art and Design B
Cuyahoga Community College Metropolitan Campus A
Kaplan College: Dayton A
Ohio State University Columbus Campus B
Ohio University B, M
Shawnee State University B
University of Akron B
University of Dayton B
Virginia Marti College of Art and Design A
Wright State University B
Youngstown State University B

Oklahoma
Northeastern State University B
Oklahoma City University B
Oklahoma State University Institute of Technology: Okmulgee A

Oregon
Linn-Benton Community College A
Mt. Hood Community College A
Oregon College of Art & Craft C, B
Pacific Northwest College of Art B
University of Oregon B, M

Pennsylvania
Antonelli Institute of Art and Photography A
Arcadia University B
Art Institute of Philadelphia A, B
of Pittsburgh A, B
Chatham University B
Drexel University B
Edinboro University of Pennsylvania B
Harrisburg Area Community College A
Keystone College A, B

Luzerne County Community College A
Lycoming College B
Marywood University B, M
Moore College of Art and Design B
Oakbridge Academy of Arts A
Pennsylvania College of Art and Design B
Point Park University B
Temple University B, M
University of the Arts B

Puerto Rico
Inter American University of Puerto Rico Bayamon Campus A
San German Campus B, M
University of Puerto Rico Rio Piedras B
University of the Sacred Heart A, B

Rhode Island
Providence College B
Rhode Island School of Design B, M
Salve Regina University B

South Carolina
Coker College B
Trident Technical College C

Tennessee
Carson-Newman College B
Memphis College of Art B, M
Nashville State Community College C, A
Pellissippi State Community College C
Southern Adventist University B
Watkins College of Art, Design and Film B

Texas
Amarillo College A
El Paso Community College A
St. Edward's University B
Sam Houston State University B
Texas A&M University Commerce B
Texas Christian University B
Texas State University: San Marcos B
Tyler Junior College C
University of Houston B, M
Western Texas College A

Utah
Brigham Young University B
Salt Lake Community College A
Weber State University B

Vermont
Bennington College B
Burlington College B
Marlboro College B

Virginia
Central Virginia Community College C
Eastern Mennonite University B
Lord Fairfax Community College C
Northern Virginia Community College A
Southwest Virginia Community College C
Thomas Nelson Community College A
Tidewater Community College C, A
Virginia Commonwealth University B
Virginia Intermont College B

Washington
Art Institute of Seattle A
Cornish College of the Arts B

Everett Community College *A*
Shoreline Community College *A*
University of Washington *B, M*
Western Washington University *B*

West Virginia
West Virginia State University *B*

Wisconsin
Cardinal Stritch University *B*
Carroll University *B*
Concordia University Wisconsin *B*

Wyoming
Casper College *A*
Northwest College *A*

Photojournalism

Arizona
Prescott College *B*

California
Brooks Institute *B, M*
Long Beach City College *C*
Los Angeles Pierce College *C, A*

Colorado
Colorado Mountain College *A*

Florida
University of Miami *B*

Illinois
Bradley University *B*

Indiana
Vincennes University *A*

Kansas
Central Christian College of Kansas *A*
Pittsburg State University *B*

Kentucky
Western Kentucky University *B*

Maine
New England School of
    Communications *B*

Michigan
Central Michigan University *B*

Minnesota
Art Institutes International
    Minnesota *B*
Winona State University *B*

Missouri
University of Missouri
    Columbia *B*

New York
Rochester Institute of Technology *B*

North Carolina
Carteret Community College *A*

Ohio
Kent State University *B*
Ohio University *B*

Oklahoma
Oklahoma City University *M*
University of Central Oklahoma *B*

Pennsylvania
Point Park University *B*

Texas
North Lake College *C*
Texas Tech University *B*

Vermont
Lyndon State College *B*

Physical anthropology

California
Merced College *A*

New York
State University of New York
    Binghamton *M*

Pennsylvania
Mercyhurst College *M*

Physical education

Alabama
Alabama Agricultural and Mechanical
    University *B, M*
Alabama State University *B*
Athens State University *B*
Auburn University *B, M, D*
Chattahoochee Valley Community
    College *A*
Faulkner State Community College *A*
Faulkner University *B, M, T*
Jacksonville State University *B, M, T*
Oakwood University *B*
Samford University *B*
Southern Union State Community
    College *A*
Tuskegee University *B*
University of Alabama *B, M*
University of Alabama
    Birmingham *B, M, T*
University of Mobile *B, T*
University of South Alabama *B, M, T*
University of West Alabama *B, M, T*

Arizona
Arizona State University *M*
Cochise College *A*
Grand Canyon University *B*
Northern Arizona University *B, T*
Prescott College *B, M, T*
University of Arizona *B*

Arkansas
Arkansas State University *B, M, T*
Arkansas Tech University *B, M*
Harding University *B, T*
Henderson State University *M, T*
Hendrix College *T*
Ouachita Baptist University *B, T*
Southern Arkansas University *B, T*
University of Arkansas
    Monticello *B*
    Pine Bluff *B, M, T*
University of Central Arkansas *B*
University of the Ozarks *B, T*
Williams Baptist College *B*

California
Allan Hancock College *A*
Azusa Pacific University *B, M, T*
Biola University *B, T*
Butte College *A*
California Baptist University *B, M, T*
California Lutheran University *B, T*
California State University
    Chico *B, M, T*
    East Bay *B, M, T*
    Long Beach *B, M, T*
    Los Angeles *B, M*
    Northridge *B, T*
    San Bernardino *B, M, T*
Chaffey College *A*

College of the Sequoias *A*
Cuesta College *A*
Cypress College *A*
Diablo Valley College *A*
El Camino College: Compton
    Center *A*
Fresno Pacific University *B, T*
Golden West College *A*
Humboldt State University *B, M, T*
Irvine Valley College *A*
Lassen Community College *A*
The Master's College *B, T*
Mount San Jacinto College *A*
Pacific Union College *B*
Pepperdine University *B*
Reedley College *A*
Saddleback College *A*
San Diego Christian College *B, T*
San Diego Mesa College *A*
San Francisco State University *T*
Santa Barbara City College *A*
Sonoma State University *M, T*
Southwestern College *A*
Taft College *A*
University of La Verne *B*
University of the Pacific *T*
Vanguard University of Southern
    California *B, T*
Westmont College *T*
Yuba Community College District *A*

Colorado
Adams State College *B, M, T*
Colorado State University
    Pueblo *T*
Metropolitan State College of
    Denver *T*
Regis University *B, T*
Trinidad State Junior College *A*
University of Northern
    Colorado *M, D, T*
Western State College of
    Colorado *B, T*

Connecticut
Central Connecticut State
    University *M, T*
Eastern Connecticut State
    University *B, M, T*
Southern Connecticut State
    University *B, M, T*
University of Connecticut *B, M, D, T*

Delaware
Delaware State University *B*
University of Delaware *B, M, T*
Wesley College *B*

District of Columbia
Gallaudet University *B, T*
George Washington
    University *A, B, M*
Howard University *B, M, T*
University of the District of
    Columbia *B*

Florida
Barry University *B*
Bethune-Cookman University *B, T*
Clearwater Christian College *B*
Edward Waters College *B*
Florida Agricultural and Mechanical
    University *B, M, T*
Florida International University *B, M*
Florida Memorial University *B, T*
Florida Southern College *B, T*
Florida State University *B, M, D*
Gulf Coast Community College *A*
Jacksonville University *B, T*
Miami Dade College *A*
Palm Beach Atlantic University *B, T*
Palm Beach Community College *A*
Pensacola Junior College *A*

University of Central Florida *B, M*
University of North Florida *B*
University of South Florida *B, M*
Warner University *B*

Georgia
Albany State University *B, M*
Armstrong Atlantic State
    University *B, T*
Augusta State University *B, M*
Bainbridge College *A*
Berry College *B*
Brewton-Parker College *B*
Columbus State University *B*
Fort Valley State University *B, T*
Gainesville State College *A*
Georgia College and State
    University *M, T*
Georgia Perimeter College *A*
Georgia Southern University *B*
Georgia Southwestern State
    University *B*
Georgia State University *B, M, D*
Kennesaw State University *B*
North Georgia College & State
    University *B, M*
Reinhardt College *B*
South Georgia College *A*
University of Georgia *B, M, D*
University of West Georgia *B, M, T*
Valdosta State University *B, M*
Waycross College *A*

Idaho
Boise State University *B, M, T*
College of Idaho *B*
Idaho State University *B, M*
Lewis-Clark State College *B, T*
Northwest Nazarene University *B*
University of Idaho *B, M, T*

Illinois
Augustana College *B, T*
Aurora University *B*
Blackburn College *B, T*
Chicago State University *B, M*
Concordia University Chicago *B, T*
DePaul University *B, T*
Elgin Community College *A*
Elmhurst College *B*
Eureka College *T*
Greenville College *B, T*
Illinois Central College *A*
Illinois College *B, T*
Illinois State University *B, M, T*
John A. Logan College *A*
Judson University *B*
Kishwaukee College *A*
Lewis University *T*
MacMurray College *B, T*
McKendree University *B*
Millikin University *B, T*
Monmouth College *B, T*
North Central College *B, T*
North Park University *T*
Northeastern Illinois University *B*
Northern Illinois University *B, M, T*
Olivet Nazarene University *B, T*
Quincy University *B, T*
Rockford College *B, T*
Southern Illinois University
    Carbondale *B, M*
Trinity Christian College *B, T*
Trinity International University *B*
University of Illinois
    Urbana-Champaign *B, M, T*

Indiana
Anderson University *B, T*
Ball State University *B, M, T*
Bethel College *B*
Butler University *T*
Franklin College *B, T*

Goshen College *B, T*
Huntington University *B*
Indiana Institute of Technology *B*
Indiana State University *B, M, T*
Indiana University
    Bloomington *B, M, D, T*
Indiana University-Purdue University
    Indianapolis *B, M*
Indiana Wesleyan University *B, T*
Manchester College *B, T*
Marian University *B, T*
Oakland City University *B*
Purdue University *B, M, D*
Saint Joseph's College *B*
Taylor University *B, T*
Trine University *B, T*
University of Evansville *B, T*
University of Indianapolis *B, T*
University of Southern Indiana *B*
Valparaiso University *B*
Vincennes University *A*

Iowa
Briar Cliff University *B*
Buena Vista University *B, T*
Central College *T*
Clarke College *B, T*
Coe College *B*
Cornell College *B, T*
Dordt College *B*
Ellsworth Community College *A*
Graceland University *T*
Grand View University *T*
Iowa State University *T*
Iowa Wesleyan College *B*
Loras College *B*
Luther College *B*
Marshalltown Community College *A*
North Iowa Area Community
    College *A*
Northwestern College *T*
St. Ambrose University *B, T*
Simpson College *B, T*
University of Dubuque *B, T*
University of Northern Iowa *B, M*
Upper Iowa University *B, T*
Wartburg College *B, T*

Kansas
Benedictine College *B*
Bethany College *B, T*
Bethel College *T*
Butler Community College *A*
Central Christian College of
    Kansas *A, B*
Coffeyville Community College *A*
Emporia State University *M, T*
Fort Hays State University *B, M, T*
Friends University *B*
Garden City Community College *A*
Highland Community College *B*
McPherson College *B, T*
MidAmerica Nazarene University *B, T*
Pittsburg State University *B, M, T*
Southwestern College *B, T*
Sterling College *T*
Tabor College *B*
University of Kansas *B, M, D, T*
Washburn University *B*
Wichita State University *B, M, T*

Kentucky
Alice Lloyd College *B*
Asbury College *B, T*
Campbellsville University *B*
Eastern Kentucky University *B, M*
Kentucky State University *B*
Kentucky Wesleyan College *B, T*
Lindsey Wilson College *B, T*
Morehead State University *B, M*
Northern Kentucky University *B*
Transylvania University *B, T*
Union College *B*
University of Kentucky *B*

University of Louisville *M*
University of the Cumberlands *B, M, T*
Western Kentucky University *B, M, T*

Louisiana
Centenary College of Louisiana *B, T*
Dillard University *B*
Grambling State University *B*
Louisiana College *B*
Louisiana State University
    Shreveport *B*
Louisiana State University and
        Agricultural and Mechanical
        College *B, M, D*
Louisiana Tech University *B, M*
McNeese State University *B, T*
Nicholls State University *B*
Northwestern State University *B, M*
Southeastern Louisiana
    University *B, M*
Southern University and Agricultural
        and Mechanical College *B*
University of Louisiana at Lafayette *B*
University of Louisiana at Monroe *B*
University of New Orleans *M*
Xavier University of Louisiana *B*

Maine
Husson University *B, T*
Saint Joseph's College of Maine *B*
University of Maine *B, M*
University of Maine
    Presque Isle *B*

Maryland
Allegany College of Maryland *A*
Frederick Community College *A*
Frostburg State University *B, M, T*
Garrett College *A*
McDaniel College *M*
Morgan State University *B, M*
Prince George's Community
    College *A*
Salisbury University *B, T*
Towson University *B, T*
University of Maryland
    College Park *B*
    Eastern Shore *B*
Washington Adventist University *B, T*
Washington Bible College *B*

Massachusetts
Boston University *B, M, T*
Bridgewater State College *B, T*
Dean College *A*
Eastern Nazarene College *B, M, T*
Endicott College *B*
Salem State College *B, M*
Springfield College *B, M, D, T*
Westfield State College *B, M, T*

Michigan
Adrian College *B, T*
Albion College *B, T*
Alma College *T*
Aquinas College *B, T*
Calvin College *B, T*
Central Michigan University *B, M*
Cornerstone University *B, T*
Delta College *A*
Eastern Michigan University *B, M, T*
Grand Rapids Community College *A*
Grand Valley State University *B, T*
Hillsdale College *B*
Hope College *B, T*
Lansing Community College *A*
Madonna University *B*
Michigan State University *B*
Michigan Technological University *T*
Northern Michigan University *B, T*
Saginaw Valley State University *B, T*
University of Michigan *B*
Wayne State University *B, M, T*

Western Michigan University *B, T*

Minnesota
Augsburg College *B, T*
Bemidji State University *M, T*
Bethel University *B*
Concordia College: Moorhead *B, T*
Concordia University: St. Paul *B, T*
Crown College *B, T*
Gustavus Adolphus College *T*
Hamline University *B, M, T*
Inver Hills Community College *A*
Minnesota State University
    Mankato *B, M, T*
    Moorhead *B*
Minnesota West Community and
    Technical College *A*
North Hennepin Community
    College *A*
Northwestern College *B*
Ridgewater College *A*
St. Catherine University *B, T*
Saint Cloud State University *B, M, T*
Southwest Minnesota State
    University *B, T*
University of Minnesota
    Duluth *B, T*
    Twin Cities *B, M, D, T*
University of St. Thomas *B*
Winona State University *B, M, T*

Mississippi
Blue Mountain College *B*
Delta State University *B, M*
Hinds Community College *A*
Jackson State University *B, M*
Mississippi College *B*
Mississippi Delta Community
    College *A*
Mississippi State University *B, M, T*
Mississippi Valley State University *B, T*
Northwest Mississippi Community
    College *A*
University of Southern
    Mississippi *B, M, D*

Missouri
Central Methodist University *B*
College of the Ozarks *B, T*
Crowder College *A*
Culver-Stockton College *B, T*
Drury University *B, T*
Evangel University *B, T*
Hannibal-LaGrange College *B*
Lincoln University *B*
Lindenwood University *B*
Missouri Baptist University *B, T*
Missouri Southern State
    University *B, T*
Missouri State University *B*
Missouri Valley College *B*
Northwest Missouri State
    University *B, M, T*
Southeast Missouri State
    University *B, T*
Southwest Baptist University *B, T*
Truman State University *M, T*
University of Central Missouri *B, M, T*
University of Missouri
    St. Louis *B*
Westminster College *B, T*
William Jewell College *B, T*
William Woods University *B, T*

Montana
Montana State University
    Billings *B, T*
Rocky Mountain College *B, T*
University of Great Falls *B*
University of Montana *B, M, T*
University of Montana: Western *B, T*

Nebraska
Bellevue University *B*
Chadron State College *B, M*
Concordia University *B, T*
Doane College *B*
Nebraska Wesleyan University *B*
Peru State College *B, T*
Union College *T*
University of Nebraska
    Kearney *B, M, T*
    Lincoln *B, M, D*
    Omaha *B, T*
Wayne State College *B, T*
Western Nebraska Community
    College *A*
York College *B, T*

Nevada
University of Nevada
    Las Vegas *B*
    Reno *B, T*

New Hampshire
Keene State College *B, M, T*
New England College *B, T*

New Jersey
The College of New Jersey *B, M, T*
Essex County College *A*
Gloucester County College *A*
Kean University *B, T*
Montclair State University *B, M, T*
Rowan University *T*
William Paterson University of New
    Jersey *B, T*

New Mexico
Eastern New Mexico University *B, M*
New Mexico Junior College *A*
New Mexico State University *B*
University of New Mexico *B, M, D*
University of the Southwest *B, T*
Western New Mexico University *B*

New York
Adelphi University *B, M, T*
Canisius College *B, M, T*
City University of New York
    Brooklyn College *B, M, T*
    Hunter College *B, T*
    Lehman College *B, M*
    Queens College *B, M, T*
    York College *B, T*
College of Mount St. Vincent *T*
Columbia-Greene Community
    College *A*
Corning Community College *A*
Dowling College *B*
Erie Community College
    City Campus *A*
    North Campus *A*
    South Campus *A*
Finger Lakes Community College *A*
Herkimer County Community
    College *A*
Hofstra University *B, M*
Houghton College *B, T*
Hudson Valley Community College *A*
Ithaca College *B, M, T*
Long Island University
    Brooklyn Campus *B, T*
    C. W. Post Campus *B, T*
Manhattan College *B, T*
Monroe Community College *A*
Roberts Wesleyan College *B*
Rockland Community College *A*
Sage College of Albany *B*
Saint Bonaventure University *B*
St. Francis College *B*
State University of New York
    College at Brockport *B, M, T*
    College at Buffalo *B*

College at Cortland *B, M*
College of Technology at Delhi *A*
Syracuse University *B, M, T*

North Carolina

Appalachian State University *B, T*
Barton College *B, T*
Brevard College *B*
Campbell University *B, M, T*
Catawba College *B, T*
Chowan University *B, T*
East Carolina University *B, M*
Elizabeth City State University *B*
Elon University *T*
Fayetteville State University *B, T*
Gardner-Webb University *B, M*
Greensboro College *B, T*
Guilford College *B, T*
High Point University *B, T*
Johnson C. Smith University *B*
Lees-McRae College *B, T*
Lenoir Community College *A*
Lenoir-Rhyne University *B, T*
Livingstone College *T*
Mars Hill College *B, T*
Meredith College *B*
Methodist University *A, B, T*
North Carolina Agricultural and
Technical State University *B, M, T*
North Carolina Central
University *B, M, T*
North Carolina Wesleyan College *B*
Pfeiffer University *B*
Piedmont Baptist College *B*
St. Andrews Presbyterian College *B, T*
University of North Carolina
Greensboro *B*
Pembroke *B, M*
Wilmington *B*
Western Carolina University *B, M, T*
Wingate University *B, T*
Winston-Salem State University *B*

North Dakota

Dickinson State University *B, T*
Jamestown College *B*
Mayville State University *B, T*
Minot State University *B*
North Dakota State University *B, T*
University of Mary *B*
University of North Dakota *B*

Ohio

Ashland University *B, M, T*
Baldwin-Wallace College *T*
Bluffton University *B*
Bowling Green State University *B, T*
Capital University *B*
Cedarville University *B*
Cleveland State University *B, M, T*
Defiance College *B, T*
Denison University *B*
Heidelberg University *B*
John Carroll University *B*
Kent State University *B*
Malone University *B*
Miami University
Oxford Campus *B*
Mount Union College *B, T*
Mount Vernon Nazarene
University *B, T*
Ohio Northern University *B, T*
Ohio State University
Columbus Campus *B, M, D*
Ohio University *B, M, T*
Ohio Wesleyan University *B*
Otterbein College *B*
Union Institute & University *B*
University of Akron *B, M*
University of Dayton *B, M, T*
University of Findlay *B, M, T*
University of Rio Grande *A, B, T*
University of Toledo *B, M, T*
Walsh University *B*

Wilmington College *B*
Wright State University *B, M, T*
Youngstown State University *B*

Oklahoma

Bacone College *B*
Cameron University *B, T*
Connors State College *A*
East Central University *B, T*
Eastern Oklahoma State College *A*
Langston University *B*
Northeastern State University *B*
Northern Oklahoma College *A*
Northwestern Oklahoma State
University *B, T*
Oklahoma Baptist University *B, T*
Oklahoma Christian University *B, T*
Oklahoma City University *B*
Oklahoma State University *B*
Oklahoma Wesleyan University *B*
Oral Roberts University *B, T*
Southeastern Oklahoma State
University *B, M, T*
Southern Nazarene University *B*
Southwestern Oklahoma State
University *B, M, T*
Tulsa Community College *A*
University of Central Oklahoma *B*
Western Oklahoma State College *A*

Oregon

Concordia University *B, M, T*
Corban College *B*
George Fox University *M, T*
Linfield College *T*
Linn-Benton Community College *A*
Oregon State University *M*
Warner Pacific College *B, T*
Western Oregon University *B, M, T*

Pennsylvania

Baptist Bible College of
Pennsylvania *B*
Bucks County Community College *A*
East Stroudsburg University of
Pennsylvania *B, M, T*
Lancaster Bible College *B*
Lincoln University *T*
Messiah College *B, T*
Montgomery County Community
College *A*
Philadelphia Biblical University *B, T*
University of Pittsburgh *B, M, D, T*
University of Pittsburgh
Bradford *B*

Puerto Rico

American University of Puerto
Rico *B, T*
Bayamon Central University *B*
Inter American University of Puerto
Rico
Guayama Campus *B*
Metropolitan Campus *B, M*
San German Campus *B, M*
Pontifical Catholic University of
Puerto Rico *B, T*
Turabo University *B, M*
Universidad Metropolitana *B*
Universidad del Este *B*
University of Puerto Rico
Arecibo *B*
Cayey University College *B*

Rhode Island

Rhode Island College *B, T*
University of Rhode Island *B, M, T*

South Carolina

Anderson University *B, T*
Charleston Southern University *B*
The Citadel *B, M, T*
Coastal Carolina University *B, T*

Coker College *B, T*
College of Charleston *B, T*
Erskine College *B, T*
Furman University *T*
Lander University *B*
Limestone College *B, T*
Newberry College *B, T*
South Carolina State University *B, T*
Southern Wesleyan University *B, T*
University of South Carolina *B, M, D*
University of South Carolina
Upstate *B, T*
Winthrop University *B, M, T*

South Dakota

Augustana College *B, T*
Black Hills State University *B*
Dakota State University *B, T*
Dakota Wesleyan University *B, T*
Mount Marty College *B*
Northern State University *B, T*
University of Sioux Falls *T*
University of South Dakota *B, M, T*

Tennessee

Belmont University *B, M, T*
Bethel University *B, T*
Bryan College *T*
Carson-Newman College *B*
Cumberland University *B, T*
Free Will Baptist Bible College *B*
Freed-Hardeman University *B, T*
King College *B*
Lambuth University *B, T*
Lane College *B*
Lee University *B, T*
Lincoln Memorial University *B, T*
Lipscomb University *B, T*
Maryville College *B, T*
Southern Adventist University *B*
Tennessee State University *B*
Tennessee Technological
University *B, M, T*
Trevecca Nazarene University *B, T*
Tusculum College *B, T*
Union University *B, T*
University of Memphis *B*
University of Tennessee
Knoxville *M, D*

Texas

Abilene Christian University *B, T*
Alvin Community College *A*
Amarillo College *A*
Austin College *M*
Baylor University *B, T*
Dallas Baptist University *B, T*
East Texas Baptist University *B*
El Paso Community College *A*
Galveston College *A*
Hardin-Simmons University *B, T*
Houston Baptist University *B, M*
Howard Payne University *B, T*
Huston-Tillotson University *B*
Jarvis Christian College *B, T*
Lamar University *B, M, T*
Laredo Community College *A*
LeTourneau University *B, T*
Lubbock Christian University *B*
McMurry University *B, T*
Midland College *A*
Navarro College *A*
Prairie View A&M University *M*
St. Edward's University *B, T*
Sam Houston State University *M, T*
Schreiner University *B*
Southwestern Adventist
University *B, T*
Southwestern University *B, T*
Stephen F. Austin State University *M*
Sul Ross State University *M*
Tarleton State University *M, T*
Texas A&M International University *T*
Texas A&M University *M, D*

Texas A&M University
Commerce *B, T*
Kingsville *B, M*
Texas Christian University *B*
Texas College *B, T*
Texas Lutheran University *B, T*
Texas Southern University *B, M*
Texas State University: San
Marcos *M, T*
Texas Wesleyan University *B, M, T*
University of Houston *B, M, D, T*
University of Mary
Hardin-Baylor *B, M, T*
University of Texas
Arlington *T*
Austin *M, D*
San Antonio *T*
University of the Incarnate Word *B, T*
Wayland Baptist University *B, T*
West Texas A&M University *T*
Wiley College *B*

Utah

Brigham Young University *B*
Snow College *A*
Southern Utah University *B, T*
Utah State University *B*
Utah Valley University *B*
Weber State University *B*

Vermont

Castleton State College *B, T*
Johnson State College *B*
Lyndon State College *B*
Norwich University *B, T*
University of Vermont *B, T*

Virginia

Bluefield College *B, T*
Bridgewater College *B, T*
Eastern Mennonite University *B, T*
Emory & Henry College *B*
George Mason University *B, M*
Hampton University *B*
Longwood University *B, T*
Lynchburg College *B*
Old Dominion University *B, M, D, T*
Radford University *B, T*
Randolph College *T*
Roanoke College *B, T*
Shenandoah University *B*
University of Richmond *T*
University of Virginia's College at
Wise *T*
Virginia Commonwealth University *M*
Virginia Intermont College *B, T*
Virginia Polytechnic Institute and
State University *M*
Virginia State University *B*

Washington

Gonzaga University *B, M, T*
Northwest University *T*
Walla Walla University *B*
Washington State University *B, M, T*
Western Washington University *B*
Whitworth University *B, T*

West Virginia

Alderson-Broaddus College *B*
Bethany College *B*
Concord University *B, T*
Davis and Elkins College *B*
Fairmont State University *B*
Marshall University *B, M*
Ohio Valley University *B*
Potomac State College of West
Virginia University *A*
Shepherd University *T*
University of Charleston *B*
West Liberty University *B*
West Virginia State University *B*
West Virginia University *B, M, D, T*

West Virginia University Institute of
Technology *B*
West Virginia Wesleyan College *B*

Wisconsin
Carroll University *B, T*
Carthage College *B, T*
Concordia University Wisconsin *B, T*
Maranatha Baptist Bible College *B*
Ripon College *T*
University of Wisconsin
Oshkosh *B, T*
Parkside *T*
River Falls *B, T*
Stevens Point *B, T*
Superior *B, T*
Whitewater *B, M, T*

Wyoming
Casper College *A*
Eastern Wyoming College *A*
Laramie County Community
College *A*
University of Wyoming *B*

Physical sciences

Alabama
Auburn University at Montgomery *B*
Troy University *B*

Arizona
Mesa Community College *A*
Northern Arizona University *B*
Scottsdale Community College *A*

Arkansas
Arkansas Tech University *B*

California
Azusa Pacific University *B*
California State University
Chico *B*
Sacramento *B*
Stanislaus *B*
Cerro Coso Community College *C, A*
College of Marin: Kentfield *A*
College of the Siskiyous *A*
Feather River College *A*
Humboldt State University *B*
Imperial Valley College *A*
La Sierra University *B*
Long Beach City College *A*
The Master's College *B*
Merced College *A*
National University *B*
San Diego State University *B*
Shasta College *A*
Taft College *A*
University of California
Berkeley *B*
Riverside *B*
University of Southern California *B*

Colorado
Colorado Mountain College *C*
Colorado State University *B*
Mesa State College *B*
University of Denver *B*

Connecticut
Mitchell College *A*
Three Rivers Community College *A*
University of Bridgeport *B*

District of Columbia
Trinity Washington University *B*
University of the District of
Columbia *A*

Florida
Daytona State College *A*

Georgia
Andrew College *A*
Covenant College *B*

Illinois
Harper College *A*
John Wood Community College *A*

Indiana
Grace College *B*

Iowa
Coe College *B*
Dordt College *B*
Loras College *B*

Kansas
Barton County Community College *A*
Cowley County Community
College *A*
Donnelly College *A*
Emporia State University *B, M, T*
Garden City Community College *A*
Highland Community College *A*
Hutchinson Community College *A*
Kansas State University *B*
Washburn University *B*

Kentucky
Asbury College *B*
Bluegrass Community and Technical
College *A*

Maine
Bates College *T*

Maryland
Howard Community College *A*
United States Naval Academy *B*
University of Maryland
College Park *B*

Massachusetts
Cape Cod Community College *A*
Dean College *A*
Roxbury Community College *A*
Suffolk University *B*
Westfield State College *B, T*
Worcester State College *B*

Michigan
Delta College *C, A*
Gogebic Community College *A*
Kalamazoo Valley Community
College *A*
Lake Michigan College *A*
Michigan State University *B, M*
Northwestern Michigan College *A*

Minnesota
Bethany Lutheran College *B*
Crown College *A, B*
Saint Cloud State University *B*
Vermilion Community College *A*

Mississippi
Mississippi University for Women *B, T*

Missouri
Crowder College *A*
Metropolitan Community College:
Maple Woods *C, A*
William Woods University *B*

Montana
Miles Community College *A*
Montana Tech of the University of
Montana *A*

Nebraska
College of Saint Mary *B*

Concordia University *B, T*

New Hampshire
Keene State College *B*

New Jersey
Bergen Community College *A*
Burlington County College *A*
Gloucester County College *C, A*

New Mexico
Northern New Mexico College *A*
San Juan College *A*
Santa Fe Community College *A*

New York
City University of New York
John Jay College of Criminal
Justice *B, M*
Corning Community College *A*
Dutchess Community College *A*
Roberts Wesleyan College *A*
St. John's University *B*
Schenectady County Community
College *A*
Union College *B*
United States Military Academy *B*
Westchester Community College *A*

North Carolina
Chowan University *B*

North Dakota
Dakota College at Bottineau *A*
Minot State University *B*
University of North Dakota *B*

Ohio
Bowling Green State University *M*
Mount Vernon Nazarene University *B*
University of Dayton *B*
University of Rio Grande *B*
Wittenberg University *B*
Youngstown State University *B, M*

Oklahoma
Northeastern Oklahoma Agricultural
and Mechanical College *A*
Redlands Community College *A*

Oregon
Central Oregon Community
College *A*
Linfield College *B*
Warner Pacific College *B*

Pennsylvania
Butler County Community College *A*
California University of
Pennsylvania *B*
Clarion University of Pennsylvania *M*
Community College of Philadelphia *A*
East Stroudsburg University of
Pennsylvania *B*
Harrisburg Area Community
College *A*
Harrisburg University of Science and
Technology *B*
Indiana University of Pennsylvania *B*
Juniata College *B*
Lehigh Carbon Community College *A*
Lincoln University *B*
Montgomery County Community
College *A*
Muhlenberg College *C, B*
Penn State
Erie, The Behrend College *B*
University of Pittsburgh *B*
University of Pittsburgh
Bradford *B*

Puerto Rico
Universidad Metropolitana *B*

South Carolina
Aiken Technical College *C*
Clinton Junior College *A*
Florence-Darlington Technical
College *A*
Midlands Technical College *C*
Trident Technical College *A*
University of South Carolina *M*

South Dakota
Black Hills State University *B*
Dakota State University *B, T*

Tennessee
Christian Brothers University *B*
Freed-Hardeman University *B*
Jackson State Community College *A*
Tennessee Temple University *B*
Union University *B*

Texas
Alvin Community College *A*
Amarillo College *A*
Angelo State University *T*
Austin Community College *A*
Brazosport College *C, A*
Lee College *A*
McMurry University *T*
Midwestern State University *B*
Palo Alto College *A*
San Jacinto College *A*
Southwestern University *B*
Texas A&M University *M*
Texas A&M University
Galveston *B*
Texas State Technical College
Waco *A*
University of Texas
San Antonio *B*
Wayland Baptist University *B, T*

Utah
University of Utah *B*
Utah Valley University *A*
Weber State University *C, A*

Vermont
Bennington College *B*
St. Michael's College *B*

Virginia
George Mason University *D*

Washington
Big Bend Community College *A*
Centralia College *A*
Evergreen State College *B*
Grays Harbor College *A*
Seattle University *B*
Shoreline Community College *A*
Washington State University *B*

West Virginia
Marshall University *M*

Wisconsin
Ripon College *B*
St. Norbert College *T*

Wyoming
Central Wyoming College *A*
Sheridan College *A*
University of Wyoming *B*

Physical/theoretical chemistry

Florida
Florida State University *M, D*

Iowa
Iowa State University *M, D*

Montana
University of Montana *M, D*

New Jersey
New Jersey Institute of Technology *M*

New York
Fordham University *M*
State University of New York
  Albany *D*

Puerto Rico
University of Puerto Rico
  Rio Piedras *D*

Texas
LeTourneau University *B*
Rice University *B, M, D*

Wisconsin
Marquette University *M, D*

Physical therapy

Alabama
Alabama State University *D*
University of Alabama
  Birmingham *D*
University of South Alabama *M*

Arizona
Northern Arizona University *D*

Arkansas
Arkansas State University *M, D*
University of Central Arkansas *D*

California
Azusa Pacific University *D*
California State University
  Fresno *M, D*
  Long Beach *M*
  Sacramento *D*
Chapman University *D*
Loma Linda University *M, D*
Mount St. Mary's College *D*
Samuel Merritt University *D*
San Francisco State University *M, D*
University of Southern
  California *M, D*
University of the Pacific *M, D*

Colorado
Regis University *D*
University of Colorado
  Denver *M*

Connecticut
Quinnipiac University *D*
Sacred Heart University *D*
University of Connecticut *M, D*
University of Hartford *M, D*

Delaware
University of Delaware *D*

District of Columbia
George Washington University *D*
Howard University *M*

Florida
Florida Agricultural and Mechanical
  University *M, D*
Florida Gulf Coast University *M, D*
Florida International University *D*
Nova Southeastern University *D*
University of Central Florida *M, D*
University of Florida *D*
University of Miami *D*
University of North Florida *D*
University of South Florida *M, D*

Georgia
Armstrong Atlantic State University *D*
Emory University *D*
Georgia State University *D*
Medical College of Georgia *D*
North Georgia College & State
  University *M, D*

Idaho
Idaho State University *D*

Illinois
Bradley University *D*
Governors State University *M, D*
Northern Illinois University *M*
Northwestern University *M, D*
University of Illinois
  Chicago *M, D*

Indiana
Indiana University-Purdue University
  Indianapolis *D*
University of Evansville *D*
University of Indianapolis *M, D*

Iowa
Clarke College *M, D*
St. Ambrose University *D*
University of Iowa *M, D*

Kansas
University of Kansas Medical
  Center *D*
Wichita State University *M, D*

Kentucky
Bellarmine University *D*
University of Kentucky *M*

Louisiana
Louisiana State University Health
  Sciences Center *M*

Maine
Husson University *D*
University of New England *M*

Maryland
University of Maryland
  Baltimore *M, D*
  Eastern Shore *D*

Massachusetts
American International College *D*
Boston University *M, D*
Northeastern University *M, D*
Simmons College *D*
Springfield College *M*
University of Massachusetts
  Lowell *M, D*

Michigan
Andrews University *M, D*
Baker College
  of Flint *M*
Central Michigan University *M, D*
Grand Valley State University *D*
Oakland University *M, D*

University of Michigan
  Flint *D*
Wayne State University *D*

Minnesota
College of St. Scholastica *D*
St. Catherine University *D*
University of Minnesota
  Twin Cities *M*

Missouri
Maryville University of Saint
  Louis *M, D*
Missouri State University *M, D*
Rockhurst University *D*
Saint Louis University *M, D, T*
Southwest Baptist University *D*
University of Missouri
  Columbia *M*
Washington University in St.
  Louis *M, D*

Montana
University of Montana *M, D*

Nebraska
Creighton University *D*
University of Nebraska
  Medical Center *D*

Nevada
University of Nevada
  Las Vegas *M, D*

New Hampshire
Franklin Pierce University *D*

New Jersey
Richard Stockton College of New
  Jersey *D*
Rutgers, The State University of New
  Jersey
  Camden Regional Campus *M*
Seton Hall University *D*
University of Medicine and Dentistry
  of New Jersey
  School of Health Related
    Professions *D*

New Mexico
University of New Mexico *D*

New York
City University of New York
  Hunter College *M*
Clarkson University *D*
D'Youville College *M, D*
Daemen College *D*
Dominican College of Blauvelt *M, D*
Ithaca College *D*
Long Island University
  Brooklyn Campus *M*
Mercy College *M, D*
Nazareth College *D*
New York Institute of
  Technology *M, D*
New York University *M, D*
State University of New York
  Buffalo *D*
  Stony Brook *M, D*
  Upstate Medical University *D*
Touro College *M, D*
Utica College *D*

North Carolina
Duke University *M*
East Carolina University *D*
Elon University *D*
University of North Carolina
  Chapel Hill *M, D*
Western Carolina University *M*
Winston-Salem State University *M*

North Dakota
University of Mary *D*
University of North Dakota *M, D*

Ohio
Cleveland State University *M, D*
College of Mount St. Joseph *D*
Ohio State University
  Columbus Campus *M*
Ohio University *D*
University of Dayton *D*
University of Findlay *D*
University of Toledo *M, D*
Walsh University *D*
Youngstown State University *D*

Oklahoma
Langston University *D*
University of Oklahoma *M*

Oregon
Pacific University *D*

Pennsylvania
Arcadia University *D*
Chatham University *D*
Drexel University *M, D*
Duquesne University *D*
Gannon University *D*
Lebanon Valley College *D*
Misericordia University *M, D*
Mount Aloysius College *M*
Neumann University *D*
St. Francis University *D*
Slippery Rock University of
  Pennsylvania *D*
Temple University *M, D*
Thomas Jefferson University: College
  of Health Professions *D*
University of Pittsburgh *D*
University of Scranton *D*
University of the Sciences in
  Philadelphia *M, D*
Widener University *D*

Puerto Rico
University of Puerto Rico
  Medical Sciences *M*

Rhode Island
University of Rhode Island *M, D*

South Carolina
Medical University of South
  Carolina *D*
University of South Carolina *D*

South Dakota
University of South Dakota *D*

Tennessee
Belmont University *D*
Carson-Newman College *T*
East Tennessee State University *D*
University of Tennessee
  Chattanooga *D*
  Knoxville *M, D*
University of Tennessee Health
  Science Center *M, D*

Texas
Angelo State University *M, D*
Baylor University *D*
Hardin-Simmons University *D*
Texas State University: San Marcos *D*
Texas Tech University Health Sciences
  Center *M, D*
Texas Woman's University *M, D*
University of Texas
  El Paso *M*
  Health Science Center at San
    Antonio *M*

Medical Branch at Galveston *M, D*
Southwestern Medical Center at
  Dallas *D*

Utah

University of Utah *M, D*

Vermont

University of Vermont *D*

Virginia

Marymount University *D*
Old Dominion University *D*
Radford University *D*
Shenandoah University *D*
Virginia Commonwealth University *D*

Washington

Eastern Washington University *D*
University of Puget Sound *D*
University of Washington *M*

West Virginia

Wheeling Jesuit University *D*

Wisconsin

Carroll University *M, D*
Concordia University Wisconsin *M*
Marquette University *D*
University of Wisconsin
  La Crosse *M, D*
  Madison *M*

Physical therapy assistant

Alabama

Bishop State Community College *A*
Central Alabama Community
  College *A*
Jefferson State Community College *A*
South University: Montgomery *A*
Wallace State Community College at
  Hanceville *A*

Arizona

GateWay Community College *C, A*
Mohave Community College *A*

Arkansas

Arkansas State University *A*
Arkansas Tech University *A*
Northwest Arkansas Community
  College *A*
South Arkansas Community College *A*

California

Allan Hancock College *A*
Cerritos College *A*
De Anza College *C*
Loma Linda University *A*
Mount St. Mary's College *A*
Ohlone College *A*
Sacramento City College *C, A*
San Diego Mesa College *A*

Colorado

Arapahoe Community College *A*
Morgan Community College *A*
Pueblo Community College *A*

Connecticut

Capital Community College *A*
Housatonic Community College *A*
Manchester Community College *A*
Naugatuck Valley Community
  College *A*
Northwestern Connecticut
  Community College *A*

Delaware

Delaware Technical and Community
  College
  Owens *A*
  Stanton/Wilmington *A*

Florida

Broward College *C, A*
Central Florida Community College *A*
Daytona State College *A*
Florida State College at Jacksonville *A*
Gulf Coast Community College *A*
Indian River State College *A*
Lake City Community College *A*
Pensacola Junior College *A*
Polk State College *A*
St. Petersburg College *A*
Seminole Community College *A*
South University: Tampa *A*
South University: West Palm Beach *A*
State College of Florida,
  Manatee-Sarasota *A*

Georgia

Athens Technical College *A*
Darton College *A*
Macon State College *A*
Middle Georgia College *A*
South University: Savannah *A*

Hawaii

University of Hawaii
  Kapiolani Community College *A*

Idaho

Idaho State University *A*
North Idaho College *A*

Illinois

Black Hawk College *A*
College of DuPage *A*
Elgin Community College *A*
Fox College *A*
Illinois Central College *A*
Kankakee Community College *A*
Kaskaskia College *A*
Lake Land College *A*
Morton College *A*
Oakton Community College *A*
Southern Illinois University
  Carbondale *A*
Southwestern Illinois College *A*

Indiana

Brown Mackie College: South Bend *A*
Ivy Tech Community College
  East Central *A*
  Northwest *A*
University of Evansville *A*
University of Indianapolis *A*
University of St. Francis *A*
Vincennes University *A*

Iowa

Clinton Community College *A*
Indian Hills Community College *A*
Iowa Central Community College *A*
Iowa Lakes Community College *C*
Kirkwood Community College *A*
Mercy College of Health Sciences *A*
Muscatine Community College *A*
North Iowa Area Community
  College *A*
Scott Community College *A*
Upper Iowa University *B*
Western Iowa Tech Community
  College *A*

Kansas

Central Christian College of Kansas *A*
Colby Community College *A*
Fort Hays State University *B*

Hutchinson Community College *A*
Johnson County Community
  College *A*
Kansas City Kansas Community
  College *A*
Washburn University *A*

Kentucky

Ashland Community and Technical
  College *A*
Hazard Community and Technical
  College *A*
Madisonville Community College *A*
Somerset Community College *A*
Southeast Kentucky Community and
  Technical College *A*
West Kentucky Community and
  Technical College *A*

Louisiana

Bossier Parish Community College *A*
Delgado Community College *A*
Louisiana College *B*
Our Lady of the Lake College *A*

Maine

Kennebec Valley Community
  College *A*

Maryland

Allegany College of Maryland *A*
Anne Arundel Community College *A*
Baltimore City Community College *A*
Carroll Community College *A*
Chesapeake College *A*
College of Southern Maryland *A*
Howard Community College *A*
Montgomery College *A*

Massachusetts

Bay State College *A*
Berkshire Community College *A*
Massachusetts Bay Community
  College *A*
Mount Wachusett Community
  College *A*
North Shore Community College *A*
Springfield Technical Community
  College *A*

Michigan

Baker College
  of Cadillac *A*
  of Flint *A*
  of Muskegon *A*
Baker College of Allen Park *A*
Bay de Noc Community College *C*
Delta College *A*
Finlandia University *A*
Henry Ford Community College *A*
Kellogg Community College *A*
Macomb Community College *A*
Mott Community College *A*
Oakland Community College *A*

Minnesota

Anoka Technical College *A*
Anoka-Ramsey Community College *A*
Dunwoody College of Technology *A*
Lake Superior College *A*
Northland Community & Technical
  College *A*
St. Catherine University *A*

Mississippi

Meridian Community College *A*

Missouri

Linn State Technical College *A*
Metropolitan Community College:
  Penn Valley *A*
Missouri Western State University *A*

Ozarks Technical Community
  College *A*
St. Louis Community College
  St. Louis Community College at
    Meramec *A*
State Fair Community College *A*

Montana

Montana State University
  College of Technology: Great
    Falls *A*

Nebraska

Clarkson College *A*
Nebraska Methodist College of
  Nursing and Allied Health *A*
Northeast Community College *A*

Nevada

College of Southern Nevada *A*

New Hampshire

River Valley Community College *A*

New Jersey

Bergen Community College *A*
Essex County College *A*
Mercer County Community College *A*
Union County College *A*

New Mexico

San Juan College *A*

New York

Broome Community College *A*
City University of New York
  Kingsborough Community
    College *A*
  LaGuardia Community College *A*
Dutchess Community College *A*
Genesee Community College *A*
Herkimer County Community
  College *A*
Nassau Community College *A*
Niagara County Community
  College *A*
Onondaga Community College *A*
Orange County Community College *A*
State University of New York
  College of Technology at Canton *A*
Suffolk County Community College *A*
Touro College *A*
Villa Maria College of Buffalo *A*

North Carolina

Caldwell Community College and
  Technical Institute *A*
Central Piedmont Community
  College *A*
Fayetteville Technical Community
  College *A*
Guilford Technical Community
  College *A*
Martin Community College *A*
Southwestern Community College *A*
Surry Community College *A*

North Dakota

Williston State College *A*

Ohio

Clark State Community College *A*
Cuyahoga Community College
  Metropolitan Campus *A*
Edison State Community College *A*
Hocking College *A*
James A. Rhodes State College *A*
Kent State University
  Ashtabula *A*
  East Liverpool *A, B*
Marion Technical College *A*
National College: Youngstown *A*

North Central State College *A*
Owens Community College
   Toledo *A*
Remington College: Cleveland West *A*
Shawnee State University *A*
Stark State College of Technology *A*
University of Cincinnati
   Clermont College *A*
Washington State Community
   College *A*
Zane State College *A*

Oklahoma
Carl Albert State College *A*
Northeastern Oklahoma Agricultural
   and Mechanical College *A*
Oklahoma City Community College *A*
Southwestern Oklahoma State
   University *A*
Tulsa Community College *A*

Oregon
Lane Community College *A*
Mt. Hood Community College *A*

Pennsylvania
Butler County Community College *A*
California University of
   Pennsylvania *A*
Central Pennsylvania College *A*
Community College of Allegheny
   County *A*
Erie Business Center *C*
Harcum College *A*
Lehigh Carbon Community College *A*
Mercyhurst College *A*
Mount Aloysius College *A*
Penn State
   DuBois *A*
   Hazleton *A*
   Mont Alto *A*
   Shenango *A*
University of Pittsburgh
   Titusville *A*

Puerto Rico
Inter American University of Puerto
   Rico
   Ponce Campus *A*
University of Puerto Rico
   Humacao *A*
   Ponce *A*

Rhode Island
Community College of Rhode
   Island *A*
New England Institute of
   Technology *A*

South Carolina
Aiken Technical College *C*
Central Carolina Technical College *C*
Florence-Darlington Technical
   College *C, A*
Greenville Technical College *C, A*
Horry-Georgetown Technical
   College *C*
Midlands Technical College *C, A*
Orangeburg-Calhoun Technical
   College *C*
Spartanburg Community College *C*
Trident Technical College *A*

South Dakota
Lake Area Technical Institute *A*

Tennessee
Chattanooga State Community
   College *A*
Jackson State Community College *A*
Roane State Community College *A*
South College *A*

Southwest Tennessee Community
   College *A*
Volunteer State Community College *A*
Walters State Community College *A*

Texas
Amarillo College *A*
Austin Community College *A*
Del Mar College *A*
El Paso Community College *A*
Houston Community College
   System *C*
Howard College *A*
Kilgore College *A*
Laredo Community College *A*
Lone Star College System *A*
Northeast Texas Community
   College *A*
Odessa College *A*
St. Philip's College *A*
San Jacinto College *A*
South Texas College *A*
Tarrant County College *A*
Western Technical College: Diana
   Drive *A*
Wharton County Junior College *A*

Utah
Dixie State College of Utah *A*
Provo College *A*
Salt Lake Community College *A*

Virginia
Jefferson College of Health
   Sciences *A*
Northern Virginia Community
   College *A*
Tidewater Community College *A*
Virginia Highlands Community
   College *A*
Wytheville Community College *A*

Washington
Green River Community College *A*
Olympic College *A*
Spokane Falls Community College *A*
Whatcom Community College *A*

West Virginia
Fairmont State University *A*
Mountain State University *A*

Wisconsin
Blackhawk Technical College *A*
Chippewa Valley Technical College *A*
Gateway Technical College *A*
Milwaukee Area Technical College *A*
Northeast Wisconsin Technical
   College *A*
Western Technical College *A*

Wyoming
Laramie County Community
   College *A*

Physician assistant

Alabama
Oakwood University *A*
University of Alabama
   Birmingham *M*

California
Charles Drew University of Medicine
   and Science *B*
City College of San Francisco *A*
Foothill College *A*
Hartnell College *A*
Loma Linda University *M*
Samuel Merritt University *M*
San Joaquin Valley College *A*
University of Southern California *M*

Colorado
University of Colorado
   Denver *M*

Connecticut
Quinnipiac University *B, M*
Yale University *M*

District of Columbia
George Washington University *B, M*
Howard University *B*

Florida
Barry University *M*
Miami Dade College *A, B*
Nova Southeastern University *M*
South University: Tampa *M*

Georgia
Brenau University *B*
Dalton State College *A*
Georgia Highlands College *A*
Gordon College *A*
Medical College of Georgia *B, M*
Mercer University *M*
South University: Savannah *M*

Hawaii
University of Hawaii
   Kapiolani Community College *A*

Idaho
Idaho State University *M*
Northwest Nazarene University *B*

Illinois
Southern Illinois University
   Carbondale *B, M*
University of St. Francis *M*

Indiana
Butler University *B, M*
University of St. Francis *B, M*

Iowa
University of Iowa *M*

Kansas
Central Christian College of Kansas *A*
Wichita State University *B, M*

Kentucky
National College
   Danville *A*
   Lexington *A*
University of Kentucky *M*

Louisiana
Our Lady of the Lake College *M*

Maine
University of New England *M*

Maryland
Towson University *M*
University of Maryland
   Eastern Shore *B*

Massachusetts
Massachusetts College of Pharmacy
   and Health Sciences *M*
Northeastern University *M*
Simmons College *M, D*
Springfield College *B*

Michigan
Central Michigan University *M*
Grand Valley State University *M*
Lansing Community College *A*
University of Detroit Mercy *M*

Wayne State University *M*
Western Michigan University *M*

Minnesota
Augsburg College *M*
Lake Superior College *A*

Missouri
Drury University *B*
Missouri State University *M*
Saint Louis University *M*

Montana
Rocky Mountain College *M*

Nebraska
Union College *M*
University of Nebraska
   Medical Center *M*

New Jersey
Rutgers, The State University of New
   Jersey
   New Brunswick/Piscataway
    Campus *B*
Seton Hall University *M*
University of Medicine and Dentistry
   of New Jersey
   School of Health Related
    Professions *M*

New Mexico
University of New Mexico *B*

New York
City University of New York
   City College *B*
   York College *B*
D'Youville College *B*
Daemen College *M*
Hofstra University *B, M*
Hudson Valley Community College *A*
Le Moyne College *M*
Long Island University
   Brooklyn Campus *B*
Mercy College *M*
New York Institute of Technology *B*
Pace University *M*
Rochester Institute of Technology *B*
St. Francis College *B*
St. John's University *B*
State University of New York
   Stony Brook *M*
   Upstate Medical University *M*
Touro College *B*
Wagner College *B, M*

North Carolina
Duke University *M*
East Carolina University *M*
Mars Hill College *B*
Methodist University *B, M*
Wake Forest University *M*

North Dakota
University of North Dakota *M*

Ohio
Cleveland State University *B*
Kettering College of Medical Arts *M*
Marietta College *M*
Mount Union College *M*
Ohio Northern University *B*
University of Findlay *M*
University of Toledo *M*

Oklahoma
University of Oklahoma *M*

Oregon

Oregon Health & Science
    University M
Pacific University M

Pennsylvania

Arcadia University M
Chatham University M
DeSales University M
Drexel University B, M
Duquesne University M
Gannon University M
King's College M
Lock Haven University of
    Pennsylvania M
Marywood University M
Mount Aloysius College B, M
Philadelphia University M
St. Francis University B, M
Seton Hill University B, M
University of the Sciences in
    Philadelphia B, M

South Carolina

Medical University of South
    Carolina M

South Dakota

University of South Dakota M

Tennessee

Bethel University M
Carson-Newman College T
Trevecca Nazarene University M

Texas

Baylor University D
Texas Tech University Health Sciences
    Center M
University of Texas
    Health Science Center at San
        Antonio B
    Medical Branch at Galveston M
    Pan American B
    Southwestern Medical Center at
        Dallas M

Utah

University of Utah M

Virginia

James Madison University M
Jefferson College of Health
    Sciences M
Shenandoah University M

Washington

University of Washington B

West Virginia

Alderson-Broaddus College M
Mountain State University M

Wisconsin

Marquette University M
University of Wisconsin
    La Crosse B, M
    Madison B

Physics

Alabama

Alabama Agricultural and Mechanical
    University B, M, D
Alabama State University B
Athens State University B
Auburn University B, M, D, T
Birmingham-Southern College B
Chattahoochee Valley Community
    College A
Jacksonville State University B

Samford University B
Talladega College B
Tuskegee University B
University of Alabama B, M, D
University of Alabama
    Birmingham B, M, D
    Huntsville B, M, D
University of North Alabama B
University of South Alabama B

Alaska

University of Alaska
    Fairbanks B, M, D

Arizona

Arizona State University B, M, D
Arizona Western College A
Cochise College A
Eastern Arizona College A
Embry-Riddle Aeronautical University:
    Prescott Campus B
Mesa Community College A
Northern Arizona University B, M
University of Arizona B, M, D

Arkansas

Arkansas State University B
Harding University B
Henderson State University B
Hendrix College B
Ouachita Baptist University B
Phillips Community College of the
    University of Arkansas A
Southern Arkansas University B
University of Arkansas B, M, D
University of Arkansas
    Little Rock B
    Pine Bluff B
University of Central Arkansas B
University of the Ozarks B

California

Allan Hancock College A
Azusa Pacific University B
Bakersfield College A
Biola University B
Cabrillo College A
California Institute of
    Technology B, M, D
California Lutheran University B
California Polytechnic State
    University: San Luis Obispo B
California State Polytechnic
    University: Pomona B
California State University
    Bakersfield B
    Chico B
    Dominguez Hills B
    East Bay B
    Fresno B, M
    Fullerton B, M
    Long Beach B, M
    Los Angeles B, M
    Northridge B, M
    Sacramento B, M
    San Bernardino B
    San Marcos B
    Stanislaus B
Canada College A
Cerritos College A
Chabot College A
Chaffey College A
Citrus College A
Claremont McKenna College B
College of Marin: Kentfield A
College of San Mateo A
College of the Desert A
College of the Siskiyous A
Columbia College A
Contra Costa College A
Crafton Hills College A
Cuesta College A
Cypress College A

De Anza College A
East Los Angeles College A
El Camino College A
El Camino College: Compton
    Center A
Foothill College A
Fullerton College A
Glendale Community College A
Grossmont College A
Hartnell College A
Harvey Mudd College B
Humboldt State University B
Los Angeles City College A
Los Angeles Southwest College A
Los Angeles Valley College A
Loyola Marymount University B
Merced College A
MiraCosta College A
Mission College A
Monterey Peninsula College A
Moorpark College A
Occidental College B
Orange Coast College A
Pacific Union College B
Pepperdine University B
Pitzer College B
Point Loma Nazarene University B
Pomona College B
Saddleback College A
St. Mary's College of California B
San Bernardino Valley College A
San Diego City College A
San Diego Mesa College A
San Diego Miramar College A
San Diego State University B, M
San Francisco State University B, M
San Joaquin Delta College A
San Jose State University B, M
Santa Ana College A
Santa Barbara City College A
Santa Clara University B
Santa Monica College A
Santa Rosa Junior College A
Santiago Canyon College A
Scripps College B
Sierra College A
Solano Community College A
Sonoma State University B
Southwestern College A
Stanford University B, M, D
University of California
    Berkeley B, D
    Davis B, M, D
    Irvine B, M, D
    Los Angeles B, M, D
    Riverside B, M, D
    San Diego B, M, D
    Santa Barbara B, M, D
    Santa Cruz B, M, D
University of California: Merced B
University of La Verne B
University of Redlands B
University of San Diego B
University of San Francisco B
University of Southern
    California B, M, D
University of the Pacific B
West Los Angeles College A
West Valley College A
Westmont College B
Whittier College B

Colorado

Adams State College B
Colorado College B
Colorado School of Mines B, M, D
Colorado State University B, M, D
Colorado State University
    Pueblo B
Fort Lewis College B
Metropolitan State College of
    Denver B
Pikes Peak Community College A
United States Air Force Academy B

University of Colorado
    Boulder B, M, D
    Colorado Springs B, M
    Denver B
University of Denver B, M, D
University of Northern Colorado B, T

Connecticut

Central Connecticut State
    University B
Connecticut College B
Fairfield University B
Southern Connecticut State
    University B, T
Trinity College B
University of Connecticut B, M, D
University of Hartford B
Wesleyan University B, M, D
Yale University B, M, D

Delaware

Delaware State University B, M, D
University of Delaware B, M, D

District of Columbia

American University B
Catholic University of
    America B, M, D
Gallaudet University B
George Washington
    University B, M, D
Georgetown University B, D
Howard University B, M, D
University of the District of
    Columbia B

Florida

Bethune-Cookman University B
Broward College A
Eckerd College B
Embry-Riddle Aeronautical
    University B
Florida Agricultural and Mechanical
    University B, M, D
Florida Atlantic University B, M, D
Florida Institute of
    Technology B, M, D
Florida International
    University B, M, D
Florida State University B, M, D
Gulf Coast Community College A
Indian River State College A
Jacksonville University B
Miami Dade College A
New College of Florida B
Northwest Florida State College A
Palm Beach Community College A
Pensacola Junior College A
Rollins College B
State College of Florida,
    Manatee-Sarasota A
Stetson University B
University of Central Florida B, M, D
University of Florida B, M, D
University of Miami B, M, D
University of North Florida B
University of South Florida B, M, D
University of West Florida B

Georgia

Abraham Baldwin Agricultural
    College A
Agnes Scott College B
Armstrong Atlantic State University B
Atlanta Metropolitan College A
Augusta State University B
Berry College B
Clark Atlanta University B, M
College of Coastal Georgia A
Covenant College B
Dalton State College A
Darton College A
Emory University B, M, D

Gainesville State College A
Georgia Highlands College A
Georgia Institute of
    Technology B, M, D
Georgia Perimeter College A
Georgia Southern University B
Georgia State University B, M, D
Gordon College A
Macon State College A
Mercer University B
Middle Georgia College A
Morehouse College B
North Georgia College & State
    University B
Oglethorpe University B
South Georgia College A
Southern Polytechnic State
    University B
Spelman College B
University of Georgia B, M, D
University of West Georgia B
Valdosta State University B
Wesleyan College B
Young Harris College A

Hawaii

University of Hawaii
    Hilo B
    Manoa B, M, D

Idaho

Boise State University B, T
Brigham Young University-Idaho B
Idaho State University A, B, M, D
North Idaho College A
Northwest Nazarene University B
University of Idaho B, M, D

Illinois

Augustana College B, T
Benedictine University B, T
Bradley University B, T
Chicago State University B
City Colleges of Chicago
    Harold Washington College A
    Kennedy-King College A
    Olive-Harvey College A
DePaul University B, M, T
Eastern Illinois University B
Elmhurst College B, T
Greenville College B, T
Illinois Central College A
Illinois College B
Illinois Institute of
    Technology B, M, D
Illinois State University B, T
Illinois Valley Community College A
Illinois Wesleyan University B
John A. Logan College A
John Wood Community College A
Kishwaukee College A
Knox College B
Lake Forest College B
Lewis University B, T
Lincoln College A
Loyola University Chicago B
MacMurray College B
Millikin University B
Monmouth College B, T
North Central College B, T
North Park University B
Northeastern Illinois University B
Northern Illinois University B, M, T
Northwestern University B
Principia College B
South Suburban College of Cook
    County A
Southern Illinois University
    Carbondale B, M, D
Southern Illinois University
    Edwardsville B, M
Southwestern Illinois College A
Triton College A
University of Chicago B, D

University of Illinois
    Chicago B, M, D
    Urbana-Champaign B, M, D
Western Illinois University B, M
Wheaton College B, T

Indiana

Anderson University B
Ball State University B, M, T
Butler University B
DePauw University B
Earlham College B
Goshen College B
Hanover College B
Indiana University
    Bloomington B, M, D
    South Bend B
    Southeast B
Indiana University-Purdue University
    Fort Wayne B, T
Indiana University-Purdue University
    Indianapolis B, M, D
Manchester College B, T
Marian University T
Purdue University B, M, D
Purdue University
    Calumet B
Rose-Hulman Institute of
    Technology B
Taylor University B
University of Evansville B
University of Indianapolis B
University of Notre Dame B, M, D
University of Southern Indiana T
Valparaiso University B
Vincennes University A
Wabash College B

Iowa

Buena Vista University B, T
Central College B, T
Coe College B
Cornell College B, T
Dordt College B
Drake University B
Ellsworth Community College A
Grinnell College B
Iowa State University B, M, D
Luther College B
Morningside College B
Northwestern College T
St. Ambrose University B
Simpson College B
University of Iowa B, M, D, T
University of Northern Iowa B, M
Wartburg College B, T

Kansas

Allen County Community College A
Baker University B
Barton County Community College A
Benedictine College B
Butler Community College A
Central Christian College of Kansas A
Coffeyville Community College A
Emporia State University B, T
Fort Hays State University B
Fort Scott Community College A
Kansas State University B, M, D
Kansas Wesleyan University B, T
MidAmerica Nazarene University B
Pittsburg State University B, M
Seward County Community College A
Southwestern College B
University of Kansas B, M, D
Washburn University B
Wichita State University B, M, T

Kentucky

Bellarmine University B
Berea College B, T
Bluegrass Community and Technical
    College A

Campbellsville University B
Centre College B
Eastern Kentucky University B
Georgetown College B, T
Kentucky Wesleyan College B
Morehead State University B
Murray State University B, T
Northern Kentucky University B
Thomas More College A, B
Transylvania University B
University of Kentucky B, M, D
University of Louisville B, M, D
University of the Cumberlands B
Western Kentucky University B

Louisiana

Centenary College of Louisiana B, T
Dillard University B
Grambling State University B
Louisiana State University
    Shreveport B
Louisiana State University and
    Agricultural and Mechanical
    College B, M, D
Louisiana Tech University B, M
Loyola University New Orleans B
McNeese State University B
Northwestern State University B
Southeastern Louisiana University B
Southern University
    New Orleans B
Southern University and Agricultural
    and Mechanical College B, M
Tulane University B, M, D
University of Louisiana at
    Lafayette B, M
University of New Orleans B, M
Xavier University of Louisiana B

Maine

Bates College B
Bowdoin College B
Colby College B
University of Maine B, M, D
University of Southern Maine B

Maryland

Allegany College of Maryland A
Cecil College A
College of Notre Dame of Maryland B
Frostburg State University B, T
Goucher College B
Harford Community College A
Johns Hopkins University B, D
Loyola University Maryland B
McDaniel College B
Montgomery College A
Morgan State University B
St. Mary's College of Maryland B
Salisbury University B, T
Towson University B
United States Naval Academy B
University of Maryland
    Baltimore County B, M, D
    College Park B, M, D
Washington College B, T

Massachusetts

Amherst College B
Bard College at Simon's Rock B
Boston College B, M, D
Boston University B, M, D
Brandeis University B, M, D
Bridgewater State College B
Bunker Hill Community College A
Clark University B, M, D
College of the Holy Cross B
Eastern Nazarene College B
Gordon College B
Hampshire College B
Harvard College B, M, D
Massachusetts College of Liberal
    Arts B

Massachusetts Institute of
    Technology B, M, D
Merrimack College B
Mount Holyoke College B
Northeastern University B, M, D
Simmons College B
Smith College B
Springfield Technical Community
    College A
Stonehill College B
Suffolk University B
Tufts University B, M, D
University of Massachusetts
    Amherst B, M, D
    Boston B, M
    Dartmouth B, M
    Lowell B, M, D
Wellesley College B
Wheaton College B
Williams College B
Worcester Polytechnic
    Institute B, M, D

Michigan

Adrian College A, B, T
Albion College B, T
Alma College B, T
Andrews University B
Calvin College B, T
Central Michigan University B, M
Eastern Michigan University B, M
Gogebic Community College A
Grand Rapids Community College A
Grand Valley State University B
Hillsdale College B
Hope College B
Kalamazoo College B
Lake Michigan College A
Lawrence Technological University B
Madonna University B
Michigan State University B, M, D
Michigan Technological
    University B, M, D
Northern Michigan University B
Oakland University B
Saginaw Valley State University B, T
University of Michigan B, M, D
University of Michigan
    Dearborn B
    Flint B, T
Wayne State University B, M, D
Western Michigan University B, M, D

Minnesota

Augsburg College B
Bemidji State University B
Bethel University B
Carleton College B
College of St. Benedict B
Concordia College: Moorhead B
Gustavus Adolphus College B
Hamline University B
Macalester College B
Minnesota State University
    Mankato B, M, T
    Moorhead B
Minnesota West Community and
    Technical College A
St. Catherine University B
Saint Cloud State University B
St. John's University B
St. Olaf College B
University of Minnesota
    Duluth B, M
    Morris B
    Twin Cities B, M, D
University of St. Thomas B
Vermilion Community College A
Winona State University B

Mississippi

Hinds Community College A
Jackson State University B
Millsaps College B

Mississippi College *B*
Mississippi State University *B, M*
Tougaloo College *B*
University of Mississippi *B, M, D*
University of Southern
   Mississippi *B, M*

Missouri

Central Methodist University *B*
Crowder College *A*
Lincoln University *B*
Missouri Southern State
   University *B, T*
Missouri State University *B*
Northwest Missouri State
   University *B*
Rockhurst University *B*
St. Louis Community College
   St. Louis Community College at
     Florissant Valley *A*
Saint Louis University *B*
Southeast Missouri State University *B*
Truman State University *B*
University of Central Missouri *B*
University of Missouri
   Columbia *B, M, D*
   Kansas City *B, M, D*
   Missouri University of Science and
     Technology *B, M, D, T*
   St. Louis *B, M, D*
Washington University in St.
   Louis *B, M, D*
Westminster College *B, T*
William Jewell College *B, T*

Montana

Montana State University
   Billings *T*
   Bozeman *B, M, D*
University of Montana *B, M*

Nebraska

Creighton University *B, M*
Doane College *B*
Nebraska Wesleyan University *B*
Northeast Community College *A*
Union College *B*
University of Nebraska
   Kearney *B, T*
   Lincoln *B, M, D*
   Omaha *B*
Western Nebraska Community
   College *A*

Nevada

Great Basin College *A*
University of Nevada
   Las Vegas *B, M, D*
   Reno *B, M, D*
Western Nevada College *A*

New Hampshire

Dartmouth College *B, M, D, T*
Saint Anselm College *B*
University of New Hampshire *B, M, D*

New Jersey

Bergen Community College *A*
The College of New Jersey *B, T*
Drew University *B*
Fairleigh Dickinson University
   Metropolitan Campus *B, M*
Middlesex County College *A*
Montclair State University *B*
New Jersey City University *B*
New Jersey Institute of
   Technology *B, M, D*
Princeton University *B, M, D*
Ramapo College of New Jersey *B*
Richard Stockton College of New
   Jersey *B*
Rider University *B*
Rowan University *B*

Rutgers, The State University of New
   Jersey
   Camden Regional Campus *B, T*
   New Brunswick/Piscataway
     Campus *B, M, D*
   Newark Regional Campus *B*
Saint Peter's College *B*
Salem Community College *A*
Seton Hall University *B, T*
Stevens Institute of
   Technology *B, M, D*

New Mexico

New Mexico Institute of Mining and
   Technology *B, M, D*
New Mexico Junior College *A*
New Mexico State University *B, M, D*
San Juan College *A*
University of New Mexico *B, M, D*

New York

Adelphi University *B*
Alfred University *B*
Bard College *B*
Barnard College *B*
Canisius College *B*
City University of New York
   Brooklyn College *B, M*
   City College *B, M*
   College of Staten Island *B*
   Hunter College *B, M*
   Kingsborough Community
     College *A*
   Lehman College *B*
   Queens College *B, M, T*
   York College *B*
Clarkson University *B, M, D*
Colgate University *B*
Columbia University *B*
Columbia University
   School of General Studies *B*
Cornell University *B, M, D*
Excelsior College *B*
Fordham University *B, M, D*
Hamilton College *B*
Hartwick College *B, T*
Hobart and William Smith Colleges *B*
Hofstra University *B*
Houghton College *B*
Iona College *B*
Ithaca College *B, T*
Le Moyne College *B*
Long Island University
   C. W. Post Campus *B*
Manhattan College *B*
Manhattanville College *B*
Monroe Community College *A*
New York University *B, M, D*
Polytechnic Institute of New York
   University *B*
Rensselaer Polytechnic
   Institute *B, M, D*
Roberts Wesleyan College *B*
Rochester Institute of
   Technology *A, B*
Saint Bonaventure University *B*
St. John Fisher College *B*
St. John's University *B*
St. Lawrence University *B, T*
St. Thomas Aquinas College *B, T*
Siena College *B, T*
Skidmore College *B*
State University of New York
   Albany *B, M, D*
   Binghamton *B, M, D*
   Buffalo *B, M, D*
   College at Brockport *B, T*
   College at Buffalo *B*
   College at Cortland *B*
   College at Fredonia *B, T*
   College at Geneseo *B, T*
   College at Oneonta *B*
   College at Plattsburgh *B*
   College at Potsdam *B*

   College of Agriculture and
     Technology at Morrisville *A*
   New Paltz *B*
   Oswego *B*
   Stony Brook *B, M, D*
Suffolk County Community College *A*
Syracuse University *B, M, D*
Union College *B*
United States Military Academy *B*
University of Rochester *B, M, D*
Utica College *B*
Vassar College *B*
Wagner College *B, T*
Wells College *B*
Yeshiva University *B*

North Carolina

Appalachian State University *B, M*
Davidson College *B*
Duke University *B, M, D*
East Carolina University *B, M*
Elizabeth City State University *B*
Elon University *B*
Guilford College *B*
Lenoir-Rhyne University *B*
North Carolina Agricultural and
   Technical State University *B, M, T*
North Carolina Central University *B*
North Carolina State
   University *B, M, D*
Shaw University *B*
University of North Carolina
   Asheville *B, T*
   Chapel Hill *B, M, D*
   Charlotte *B, M*
   Greensboro *B*
   Pembroke *B*
   Wilmington *B*
Wake Forest University *B, M, D*

North Dakota

Minot State University *B*
North Dakota State
   University *B, M, D, T*
University of North Dakota *B, M, D*

Ohio

Ashland University *B*
Baldwin-Wallace College *B*
Bluffton University *B*
Bowling Green State University *B, M*
Case Western Reserve
   University *B, M, D*
Cedarville University *B*
Cleveland State University *B, M, T*
College of Wooster *B*
Denison University *B*
Eastern Gateway Community
   College *A*
Heidelberg University *B*
Hiram College *B*
John Carroll University *B*
Kent State University *B, M, D*
Kenyon College *B*
Marietta College *B*
Miami University
   Oxford Campus *B, M*
Mount Union College *B*
Mount Vernon Nazarene University *B*
Muskingum University *B*
Oberlin College *B*
Ohio Northern University *B*
Ohio State University
   Columbus Campus *B, M, D*
Ohio University *B, M, D*
Ohio Wesleyan University *B*
Otterbein College *B*
Terra State Community College *A*
University of Akron *B, M*
University of Cincinnati *B, M, D, T*
University of Dayton *B*
University of Toledo *B, M, D*
Wittenberg University *B*
Wright State University *B, M*

Xavier University *B*
Youngstown State University *B*

Oklahoma

Cameron University *B*
Connors State College *A*
East Central University *B, T*
Eastern Oklahoma State College *A*
Northern Oklahoma College *A*
Oklahoma Baptist University *B, T*
Oklahoma Christian University *B*
Oklahoma City Community College *A*
Oklahoma City University *B*
Oklahoma State University *B, M, D*
Oral Roberts University *B*
Rogers State University *A*
Rose State College *A*
Southern Nazarene University *B*
Southwestern Oklahoma State
   University *B*
Tulsa Community College *A*
University of Central Oklahoma *B, M*
University of Oklahoma *B, M, D*
University of Science and Arts of
   Oklahoma *B*
University of Tulsa *B, M*

Oregon

Central Oregon Community
   College *A*
Chemeketa Community College *A*
Eastern Oregon University *B, T*
Lewis & Clark College *B*
Linfield College *B, T*
Linn-Benton Community College *A*
Mt. Hood Community College *A*
Oregon State University *B, M, D*
Pacific University *B*
Portland State University *B, M*
Reed College *B*
Southern Oregon University *B*
Treasure Valley Community College *A*
University of Oregon *B, M, D*
University of Portland *B*
Willamette University *B*

Pennsylvania

Albright College *B, T*
Allegheny College *B*
Arcadia University *B*
Bloomsburg University of
   Pennsylvania *B, T*
Bryn Mawr College *B, M, D*
Bucknell University *B*
California University of
   Pennsylvania *B, M*
Carnegie Mellon University *B, M, D*
Chatham University *B*
Clarion University of Pennsylvania *B*
Community College of Allegheny
   County *A*
Dickinson College *B*
Drexel University *B, M, D*
Duquesne University *B*
East Stroudsburg University of
   Pennsylvania *B, T*
Edinboro University of
   Pennsylvania *B, T*
Elizabethtown College *B*
Franklin & Marshall College *B*
Geneva College *B, T*
Gettysburg College *B*
Grove City College *B*
Haverford College *B, T*
Indiana University of
   Pennsylvania *B, M*
Juniata College *B*
Kutztown University of
   Pennsylvania *B, T*
Lafayette College *B*
Lebanon Valley College *B, T*
Lehigh University *B, M, D*
Lincoln University *B*

Lock Haven University of
Pennsylvania *B*
Lycoming College *B*
Mansfield University of
Pennsylvania *B, T*
Messiah College *B*
Millersville University of
Pennsylvania *B, T*
Moravian College *B, T*
Muhlenberg College *B*
Northampton Community College *A*
Penn State
Abington *B*
Altoona *B*
Beaver *B*
Berks *B*
Brandywine *B*
DuBois *B*
Erie, The Behrend College *B*
Fayette, The Eberly Campus *B*
Greater Allegheny *B*
Hazleton *B*
Lehigh Valley *B*
Mont Alto *B*
New Kensington *B*
Schuylkill *B*
Shenango *B*
University Park *B, M, D*
Wilkes-Barre *B*
Worthington Scranton *B*
York *B*
Saint Joseph's University *B*
St. Vincent College *B*
Shippensburg University of
Pennsylvania *B, T*
Slippery Rock University of
Pennsylvania *B*
Susquehanna University *B, T*
Swarthmore College *B*
Temple University *B, M, D*
Thiel College *B*
University of Pennsylvania *B, M, D*
University of Pittsburgh *B, M, D*
University of Scranton *B, T*
University of the Sciences in
Philadelphia *B*
Ursinus College *B, T*
Villanova University *B*
Washington & Jefferson College *B*
West Chester University of
Pennsylvania *B, T*
Westminster College *B*
Widener University *B*
York College of Pennsylvania *A*

Puerto Rico

Pontifical Catholic University of
Puerto Rico *B*
University of Puerto Rico
Humacao *B*
Ponce *A*
Rio Piedras *B, M*

Rhode Island

Brown University *B, M, D*
Rhode Island College *B*
University of Rhode Island *B, M, D*

South Carolina

Benedict College *B*
Bob Jones University *B*
The Citadel *B*
Clemson University *B, M, D*
Coastal Carolina University *B*
College of Charleston *B, T*
Erskine College *B*
Francis Marion University *B*
Furman University *B, T*
Presbyterian College *B*
South Carolina State University *B*
University of South Carolina *B, M, D*
Wofford College *B*

South Dakota

Augustana College *B, T*
South Dakota School of Mines and
Technology *B*
South Dakota State University *B*
University of South Dakota *B, M*

Tennessee

Austin Peay State University *B*
Belmont University *B, T*
Carson-Newman College *B*
Christian Brothers University *B*
Columbia State Community College *A*
East Tennessee State University *B, T*
Fisk University *B, M*
King College *B, T*
Lane College *B*
Lipscomb University *B*
Middle Tennessee State University *B*
Rhodes College *B*
Southern Adventist University *B*
Tennessee State University *B*
Tennessee Technological
University *B, T*
Trevecca Nazarene University *B*
Union University *B*
University of Memphis *B, M*
University of Tennessee
Chattanooga *B*
Knoxville *B, M, D*
University of the South *B*
Vanderbilt University *B, M, D*

Texas

Abilene Christian University *B*
Amarillo College *A*
Angelina College *A*
Angelo State University *B*
Austin College *B*
Austin Community College *A*
Baylor University *B, M, D*
Blinn College *A*
Brazosport College *A*
Central Texas College *A*
Clarendon College *A*
Coastal Bend College *A*
Del Mar College *A*
El Paso Community College *A*
Frank Phillips College *A*
Galveston College *A*
Grayson County College *A*
Hardin-Simmons University *B*
Hill College *A*
Houston Baptist University *B*
Howard College *A*
Kilgore College *A*
Lamar University *B*
Laredo Community College *A*
Lon Morris College *A*
McMurry University *B*
Midland College *A*
Midwestern State University *B*
Navarro College *A*
Palo Alto College *A*
Paris Junior College *A*
Prairie View A&M University *B*
Rice University *B, M, D*
St. Mary's University *B*
Sam Houston State University *B*
San Jacinto College *A*
South Plains College *A*
South Texas College *A*
Southern Methodist
University *B, M, D*
Southwestern University *B, T*
Stephen F. Austin State
University *B, M, T*
Tarleton State University *B*
Texarkana College *A*
Texas A&M University *B, M, D*
Texas A&M University
Commerce *B, M*
Kingsville *B, M*
Texas Christian University *B, M, D*

Texas Lutheran University *B*
Texas Southern University *B*
Texas State University: San
Marcos *B, M, T*
Texas Tech University *B, M, D*
Trinity University *B*
Trinity Valley Community College *A*
Tyler Junior College *A*
University of Dallas *B*
University of Houston *B, M, D*
University of Houston
Clear Lake *B, M*
University of North Texas *B, M, D*
University of Texas
Arlington *B, M*
Austin *B, M, D*
Brownsville - Texas Southmost
College *B, M*
Dallas *B, M, D*
El Paso *B, M*
Pan American *B*
San Antonio *B*
West Texas A&M University *B*
Western Texas College *A*
Wharton County Junior College *A*

Utah

Brigham Young University *B, M, D*
Salt Lake Community College *A*
Snow College *A*
University of Utah *B, M, D, T*
Utah State University *B, M, D*
Utah Valley University *A, B*
Weber State University *B*
Westminster College *B*

Vermont

Bennington College *B*
Marlboro College *B*
Middlebury College *B*
Norwich University *B*
St. Michael's College *B*
University of Vermont *B, M*

Virginia

Bridgewater College *B*
Christopher Newport University *B*
College of William and Mary *B, M, D*
Emory & Henry College *B, T*
George Mason University *B, D*
Hampden-Sydney College *B*
Hampton University *B, M, D*
Hollins University *B*
James Madison University *B, T*
Longwood University *B, T*
Lynchburg College *B*
Mary Baldwin College *B*
Norfolk State University *B*
Old Dominion University *B, M, D, T*
Radford University *B*
Randolph College *B*
Randolph-Macon College *B*
Roanoke College *B, T*
Sweet Briar College *B*
University of Mary Washington *B*
University of Richmond *B, T*
University of Virginia *B, M, D*
Virginia Commonwealth
University *B, M*
Virginia Military Institute *B*
Virginia Polytechnic Institute and
State University *B, M, D*
Virginia State University *B, M*
Washington and Lee University *B*

Washington

Cascadia Community College *A*
Centralia College *A*
Eastern Washington University *B*
Everett Community College *A*
Gonzaga University *B*
Olympic College *A*
Pacific Lutheran University *B*

Seattle Pacific University *B*
Seattle University *B*
University of Puget Sound *B, T*
University of Washington *B, M, D*
Walla Walla University *B*
Washington State University *B, M, D*
Western Washington University *B*
Whitman College *B*
Whitworth University *B, T*

West Virginia

Bethany College *B*
Marshall University *B*
Potomac State College of West
Virginia University *A*
West Virginia State University *B*
West Virginia University *B, M, D, T*
West Virginia Wesleyan College *B*
Wheeling Jesuit University *B*

Wisconsin

Beloit College *B*
Carthage College *B*
Lawrence University *B, T*
Marquette University *B*
Ripon College *B*
St. Norbert College *B, T*
University of Wisconsin
Eau Claire *B*
Green Bay *B*
La Crosse *B, T*
Madison *B, M, D*
Milwaukee *B, M, D*
Oshkosh *B, M*
Parkside *B*
River Falls *B*
Stevens Point *B, T*
Whitewater *B, T*

Wyoming

Casper College *A*
Northwest College *A*
University of Wyoming *B, M, D*

Physics teacher education

Alabama

Athens State University *B*
Birmingham-Southern College *T*

Alaska

University of Alaska
Fairbanks *M*

Arizona

Northern Arizona University *B, T*
Prescott College *T*
University of Arizona *B*

Arkansas

Arkansas State University *B, T*
Ouachita Baptist University *B, T*

California

Azusa Pacific University *T*
California Polytechnic State
University: San Luis Obispo *T*
California State University
Chico *T*
San Bernardino *T*
San Francisco State University *T*
Stanford University *M, T*
University of the Pacific *T*
Vanguard University of Southern
California *T*

Colorado

Colorado State University *B, T*
Colorado State University
Pueblo *T*

Connecticut
Southern Connecticut State University B, T
University of New Haven T

Delaware
Delaware State University B, M
University of Delaware B, T

Florida
Florida Institute of Technology B
Florida State University B, M
Gulf Coast Community College A
State College of Florida, Manatee-Sarasota A

Georgia
Agnes Scott College M, T
University of West Georgia B

Idaho
Boise State University B, T
Brigham Young University-Idaho T
Northwest Nazarene University B
University of Idaho T

Illinois
Augustana College B, T
Benedictine University T
Bradley University B
DePaul University M, T
Elmhurst College B
Greenville College B, T
Illinois Wesleyan University B
Knox College T
Lewis University T
North Park University T
University of Illinois
 Chicago B
 Urbana-Champaign B, M, T

Indiana
Anderson University B, T
Butler University T
Goshen College B, T
Indiana University
 Bloomington B, T
 South Bend B, T
Indiana University-Purdue University Fort Wayne B, T
Indiana University-Purdue University Indianapolis B
Manchester College B, T
Purdue University B, M, D
Purdue University Calumet B
University of Evansville B, T
University of Indianapolis B, T
Valparaiso University B

Iowa
Buena Vista University B, T
Central College T
Cornell College B, T
Dordt College B
Drake University T
Ellsworth Community College A
Graceland University T
Iowa State University T
Iowa Wesleyan College B
Loras College T
Maharishi University of Management T
Morningside College B
Northwestern College T
St. Ambrose University B, T
Simpson College T
University of Iowa T
Wartburg College T

Kansas
Bethel College T
Garden City Community College A
Pittsburg State University B, T
University of Kansas B, T

Kentucky
Campbellsville University B

Louisiana
Grambling State University B
Louisiana State University Shreveport B
Northwestern State University B
Southern University and Agricultural and Mechanical College B
University of Louisiana at Lafayette B

Maine
University of Southern Maine T

Maryland
Anne Arundel Community College A
Community College of Baltimore County A
Harford Community College A
Howard Community College A
University of Maryland Baltimore County B

Massachusetts
Bridgewater State College M, T
Eastern Nazarene College B
Tufts University T
University of Massachusetts Dartmouth T
Worcester State College T

Michigan
Albion College B, T
Alma College T
Calvin College B
Central Michigan University B
Eastern Michigan University B, M
Grand Valley State University M, T
Hope College B, T
Michigan State University B
Michigan Technological University T
Northern Michigan University B, T
University of Michigan Flint B, T
Western Michigan University B, T

Minnesota
Augsburg College T
Bethel University B
Concordia College: Moorhead B, T
Gustavus Adolphus College T
Minnesota State University
 Mankato B, M, T
 Moorhead B
St. Catherine University T
Saint Cloud State University B, T
St. Mary's University of Minnesota B
University of Minnesota
 Duluth B, T
 Morris T
University of St. Thomas B
Vermilion Community College A
Winona State University B, T

Mississippi
Millsaps College T
Mississippi State University T

Missouri
Central Methodist University B
Lincoln University B
Missouri Southern State University B, T
Missouri State University B
Northwest Missouri State University B, T
Truman State University M, T
University of Central Missouri B, T
University of Missouri
 Columbia B
 Kansas City B
Washington University in St. Louis B, M, T
William Jewell College B, T

Montana
Montana State University Billings B, T
University of Montana T

Nebraska
Chadron State College B
Concordia University B, T
Creighton University B
Nebraska Wesleyan University T
Peru State College B, T
Union College T
University of Nebraska
 Kearney B, T
 Lincoln B

New Hampshire
University of New Hampshire T

New Jersey
The College of New Jersey B, T
County College of Morris A
Saint Peter's College T

New Mexico
New Mexico Institute of Mining and Technology M

New York
Adelphi University M, T
Alfred University B, T
Bard College M
City University of New York
 Brooklyn College B, M, T
 City College B, M
 Hunter College B, D, T
 Queens College B, M, T
Colgate University M
Cornell University B, M, T
D'Youville College M, T
Fordham University M, T
Hobart and William Smith Colleges T
Hofstra University B, M
Houghton College B, T
Ithaca College B, M, T
Le Moyne College T
Manhattan College B, T
New York Institute of Technology B, T
Roberts Wesleyan College B, M
St. John Fisher College B, M, T
St. John's University B, T
St. Lawrence University T
St. Thomas Aquinas College B, T
State University of New York
 Albany M, T
 Binghamton M
 Buffalo M, T
 College at Brockport B, M, T
 College at Buffalo B
 College at Cortland B, M
 College at Fredonia B, T
 College at Geneseo B, T
 College at Oneonta B, T
 College at Plattsburgh B
 College at Potsdam B, M
 New Paltz B, T
 Oswego B, M
 Stony Brook T
Syracuse University B, M, T
University of Rochester M
Vassar College T
Wagner College T
Wells College T

North Carolina
Appalachian State University B, T
North Carolina Agricultural and Technical State University B
North Carolina Central University B, T
Wake Forest University T

North Dakota
Minot State University B
North Dakota State University B, T
University of North Dakota T

Ohio
Bluffton University B
Bowling Green State University B, M
Case Western Reserve University T
Cedarville University B
Hiram College T
John Carroll University T
Kent State University T
Miami University Oxford Campus B, T
Mount Union College T
Mount Vernon Nazarene University B, T
Ohio Dominican University B, T
Ohio Northern University B, T
Ohio Wesleyan University B
Otterbein College B
University of Rio Grande B, T
University of Toledo M, T
Xavier University B, M
Youngstown State University B, M

Oklahoma
East Central University T
Eastern Oklahoma State College A
Northeastern State University B
Oklahoma Baptist University B, T
University of Central Oklahoma B
University of Tulsa T

Oregon
Linfield College T
Oregon State University M
Portland State University T

Pennsylvania
Albright College T
Chatham University M, T
Dickinson College T
Duquesne University M, T
Geneva College T
Gettysburg College T
Grove City College B, T
Juniata College B, T
Lebanon Valley College T
Lycoming College T
Mansfield University of Pennsylvania B, T
Moravian College T
St. Vincent College B, T
Susquehanna University T
Thiel College T
Villanova University T
Westminster College T
Widener University T

Rhode Island
Rhode Island College B

South Carolina
Furman University T

South Dakota
Augustana College B, T
University of South Dakota B, M, T

Tennessee
Belmont University B, M, T
Christian Brothers University B, M, T
King College T

Lipscomb University *B, T*
Southern Adventist University *B*
Tennessee Technological University *T*
Trevecca Nazarene University *B, T*

Texas

Houston Baptist University *T*
Lamar University *T*
Laredo Community College *A*
McMurry University *T*
St. Mary's University *T*
Tarleton State University *T*
Texas A&M University
   Commerce *T*
   Kingsville *T*
University of Dallas *T*
University of Houston *T*
University of Houston
   Clear Lake *T*
University of Texas
   Arlington *T*
   San Antonio *T*
West Texas A&M University *T*

Utah

Brigham Young University *B*
Utah State University *B*
Weber State University *B*

Vermont

Castleton State College *B, T*

Virginia

Averett University *M*
Bridgewater College *T*
Hampton University *M*
Hollins University *T*
Longwood University *B, T*
Old Dominion University *B, T*

Washington

Eastern Washington University *B*
Washington State University *B, M, T*
Whitworth University *B, T*

West Virginia

Fairmont State University *B*

Wisconsin

Carthage College *T*
Lawrence University *T*
St. Norbert College *T*
University of Wisconsin
   Green Bay *T*
   Parkside *T*
   River Falls *T*

Physiology

Arizona

Northern Arizona University *B*

California

Loma Linda University *D*
San Diego State University *M*
San Francisco State University *B, M*
San Jose State University *B, M*
Santa Rosa Junior College *A*
University of California
   Irvine *M, D*
   Los Angeles *B, M*
University of Southern
   California *M, D*

Colorado

University of Colorado
   Boulder *B, M, D*
   Denver *D*

Connecticut

Yale University *M, D*

District of Columbia

Georgetown University *M, D*
Howard University *M, D*

Florida

University of Miami *D*

Georgia

Medical College of Georgia *M, D*

Hawaii

University of Hawaii
   Manoa *M, D*

Illinois

Loyola University Chicago *M, D*
Southern Illinois University
   Carbondale *B*
University of Illinois
   Chicago *M, D*
   Urbana-Champaign *B, M, D*

Indiana

Indiana University
   Bloomington *M, D*
Indiana University-Purdue University
   Indianapolis *M, D*

Iowa

Iowa State University *M, D*
University of Iowa *M, D*

Kansas

University of Kansas Medical
   Center *M, D*

Kentucky

University of Louisville *M, D*

Louisiana

Louisiana State University Health
   Sciences Center *M, D*

Michigan

Eastern Michigan University *M*
Michigan State University *B, M, D*
Northern Michigan University *B*
University of Michigan *D*
Wayne State University *M, D*

Missouri

University of Missouri
   Columbia *M, D*

Nebraska

University of Nebraska
   Medical Center *M, D*

New York

State University of New York
   Buffalo *M, D*
   Stony Brook *D*
   Upstate Medical University *M, D*
University of Rochester *M, D*

North Carolina

East Carolina University *D*
North Carolina State University *M, D*
University of North Carolina
   Chapel Hill *M, D*

North Dakota

University of North Dakota *M, D*

Oklahoma

Oklahoma State University *B*
University of Oklahoma *M, D*

Oregon

University of Oregon *B, M, D*

Pennsylvania

Temple University *M, D*

Texas

Texas Tech University Health Sciences
   Center *M, D*
University of Texas
   Health Science Center at
      Houston *M, D*
   Southwestern Medical Center at
      Dallas *M, D*

Utah

Brigham Young University *B, M, D*
Snow College *A*
University of Utah *M, D*

Vermont

University of Vermont *M, D*

Virginia

University of Virginia *D*
Virginia Commonwealth
   University *M, D*

West Virginia

West Virginia University *M*

Wisconsin

University of Wisconsin
   Madison *M, D*

Wyoming

University of Wyoming *B*

Piano/organ

Alabama

Birmingham-Southern College *B*
Samford University *B, M*
Talladega College *B*

Arkansas

Ouachita Baptist University *B*

California

Bethesda Christian University *B, M*
California Baptist University *B*
California State University
   Chico *C, B*
   Long Beach *B, M*
Chapman University *B*
Fresno City College *A*
The Master's College *B*
Ohlone College *C*
Point Loma Nazarene University *B*
San Francisco Conservatory of
   Music *B, M*
University of Southern
   California *B*
University of the Pacific *B*

Delaware

University of Delaware *B*

District of Columbia

Catholic University of
   America *B, M, D*
Howard University *B*

Florida

Florida State University *B, M, D*
Hobe Sound Bible College *B*
Palm Beach Atlantic University *B*
Southeastern University *B*
Stetson University *B*
University of Miami *B, M, D*

Georgia

Mercer University *M*

Shorter College *B*

Idaho

Brigham Young University-Idaho *A*
Northwest Nazarene University *B*

Illinois

Augustana College *B*
Illinois Wesleyan University *B*
Lincoln College *A*
Millikin University *B*
Moody Bible Institute *B*
Northwestern University *B, M, D*
Olivet Nazarene University *B*
Roosevelt University *B, M*
Trinity International University *B*

Indiana

Ancilla College *C*
Butler University *B, M*
Grace College *B*
Huntington University *B*
Indiana University
   Bloomington *B*
Indiana University-Purdue University
   Fort Wayne *B*
Valparaiso University *B*

Iowa

Dordt College *B*
University of Iowa *B, T*
University of Northern Iowa *M*
Waldorf College *B*

Kansas

Central Christian College of
   Kansas *A, B*
MidAmerica Nazarene University *T*
University of Kansas *B, M, D*

Kentucky

Campbellsville University *B*

Louisiana

Centenary College of Louisiana *B, T*
Louisiana College *B*
Xavier University of Louisiana *B*

Maine

University of Southern Maine *B, M*

Maryland

Hood College *C*
Johns Hopkins University: Peabody
   Conservatory of Music *B, M, D*
Washington Bible College *B, T*

Massachusetts

Berklee College of Music *B*
Boston Conservatory *B, M*
Boston University *B, M, D*
Eastern Nazarene College *B*
New England Conservatory of
   Music *B, M, D*

Michigan

Calvin College *B*
Grand Rapids Community College *A*
Hope College *B*
Northwestern Michigan College *A*
Oakland University *B, M*
University of Michigan *M, T*

Minnesota

Northwestern College *B*
Saint Cloud State University *B*

Mississippi

Mississippi College *B, M*

Missouri
Calvary Bible College and Theological
Seminary *B*
Drury University *B*
University of Missouri
Kansas City *B*

Nebraska
Concordia University *B, T*
Grace University *B*
University of Nebraska
Omaha *B*

New Jersey
Rider University *A, B, M*

New York
Bard College *B*
Eastman School of Music of the
University of Rochester *B, M, D*
Five Towns College *A, B, M*
Houghton College *B, M*
Juilliard School *B, M, D*
Mannes College The New School for
Music *B, M*
Roberts Wesleyan College *B*
State University of New York
College at Fredonia *B*
University of Rochester *M, D*

North Carolina
Campbell University *B*
East Carolina University *B*
Gardner-Webb University *B*

Ohio
Baldwin-Wallace College *B*
Bowling Green State University *B*
Capital University *B*
Oberlin College *B, M*
Ohio State University
Columbus Campus *B*
Ohio University *B*
University of Akron *C, B, M*
University of Cincinnati *B, M, D*
Youngstown State University *B, M*

Oklahoma
East Central University *B, T*
Northwestern Oklahoma State
University *B*
Oklahoma Baptist University *B*
Oklahoma Christian University *B*
Oklahoma City University *B*
Oral Roberts University *B*
Southwestern Oklahoma State
University *B*
University of Central Oklahoma *B*
University of Tulsa *B*

Oregon
Corban College *B*
University of Oregon *M*
Willamette University *B*

Pennsylvania
Carnegie Mellon University *B, M*
Gettysburg College *B*
Mansfield University of
Pennsylvania *B*
Penn State
University Park *M*
Temple University *M*
Westminster College *B*

Puerto Rico
Conservatory of Music of Puerto
Rico *B*

South Carolina
Bob Jones University *B, M*
Coker College *B*

Columbia College *B*
Converse College *B, M*
North Greenville University *B*
University of South Carolina *M, D*

Tennessee
Belmont University *B, M*
Lambuth University *B*
Lipscomb University *B*
University of Tennessee
Knoxville *B*
Vanderbilt University *B*

Texas
Abilene Christian University *B*
Angelina College *A*
Baylor University *M*
Concordia University Texas *B*
Dallas Baptist University *B*
East Texas Baptist University *B*
Hardin-Simmons University *B, M*
Howard Payne University *B*
Lon Morris College *A*
Southern Methodist University *B, M*
Southwestern Assemblies of God
University *B*
Texas A&M University
Commerce *B, M*
Texas Christian University *C, B, M*
Texas Tech University *D*
University of Texas
El Paso *B*

Utah
Brigham Young University *B*
Weber State University *B*

Vermont
Bennington College *B*
Johnson State College *B*

Virginia
Bluefield College *B*
Shenandoah University *B, M*
Virginia Union University *B*

Washington
Cornish College of the Arts *B*
University of Washington *B, M, D*
Whitworth University *B*

Wisconsin
Concordia University Wisconsin *B*
Maranatha Baptist Bible College *B*
University of Wisconsin
Madison *B, M*

Pipefitting

Alabama
Bishop State Community College *C*
Lawson State Community College *C*

Alaska
Ilisagvik College *C*

Arizona
Central Arizona College *C*
GateWay Community College *C, A*

California
Allan Hancock College *C*
Bakersfield College *A*
College of San Mateo *A*
Foothill College *C*
Fresno City College *A*
Los Angeles Trade and Technical
College *C, A*
Modesto Junior College *C, A*
Orange Coast College *C, A*
Palomar College *C, A*

San Diego City College *C, A*
Santa Rosa Junior College *C*

Florida
Florida State College at Jacksonville *C*
Hillsborough Community College *C*
Palm Beach Community College *C*
Seminole Community College *C*
Tallahassee Community College *C*

Indiana
Ivy Tech Community College
Central Indiana *C, A*
East Central *C, A*
North Central *C, A*
Northeast *C, A*
Northwest *C, A*
South Central *C, A*
Southwest *C, A*
Wabash Valley *C, A*

Iowa
Kirkwood Community College *C*

Kentucky
Somerset Community College *C, A*

Maine
Eastern Maine Community
College *C, A*
Northern Maine Community
College *C, A*

Michigan
Bay de Noc Community College *C*
Delta College *A*
Kellogg Community College *C, A*
Lansing Community College *A*
Macomb Community College *C*
Oakland Community College *C, A*

Minnesota
Dunwoody College of Technology *C*
St. Paul College *C*

Mississippi
Mississippi Gulf Coast Community
College *C, A*
Northeast Mississippi Community
College *C*

Missouri
Ranken Technical College *C*

Nevada
Truckee Meadows Community
College *C, A*

New Mexico
Central New Mexico Community
College *C*
New Mexico State University
Grants *C*
Northern New Mexico College *C, A*

North Carolina
Blue Ridge Community College *C*
Cleveland Community College *C*
Tri-County Community College *C*
Wake Technical Community
College *C*

North Dakota
North Dakota State College of
Science *C*

Oklahoma
Oklahoma State University
Institute of Technology:
Okmulgee *A*

Oregon
Linn-Benton Community College *A*

Pennsylvania
Community College of Allegheny
County *C*

Rhode Island
New England Institute of
Technology *A*

South Carolina
Denmark Technical College *C*

Texas
Brazosport College *C, A*
Frank Phillips College *C, A*
Howard College *C*
Lee College *A*
North Lake College *C*
St. Philip's College *C*

Utah
Salt Lake Community College *A*

Virginia
Central Virginia Community
College *C*

Wisconsin
Blackhawk Technical College *C*
Chippewa Valley Technical College *C*
Gateway Technical College *C*
Milwaukee Area Technical College *C*

Planetary sciences

Arizona
Mesa Community College *A*
Northern Arizona University *B*
Prescott College *B, M*

Arkansas
University of Arkansas *D*

California
California Institute of
Technology *B, M, D*
California State University
Northridge *B*
Cerritos College *A*
Chaffey College *A*
College of the Redwoods *A*
Columbia College *A*
Los Angeles Valley College *A*
University of California
San Diego *B, D*

Connecticut
Wesleyan University *B, M*

Delaware
University of Delaware *B, T*

Florida
Florida Institute of Technology *B*

Illinois
Augustana College *B, T*
Black Hawk College: East Campus *A*
City Colleges of Chicago
Olive-Harvey College *A*
Illinois Central College *A*
Illinois Valley Community College *A*
Richland Community College *A*

Iowa
Iowa State University *B, M, D*
University of Dubuque *B*

Maryland

Towson University *B*

Massachusetts

Boston University *B*
Massachusetts Institute of
   Technology *M, D*
Tufts University *T*

Michigan

University of Michigan *D*

Minnesota

Saint Cloud State University *B*
Winona State University *B, T*

Missouri

University of Central Missouri *B*
Washington University in St.
   Louis *B, M, D*

Montana

Montana State University
   Bozeman *B, M*

New Hampshire

Dartmouth College *B, M, D*

New Jersey

Rutgers, The State University of New
   Jersey
   Newark Regional Campus *T*
William Paterson University of New
   Jersey *T*

New York

City University of New York
   City College *B*
Columbia University *B*
State University of New York
   College at Brockport *B*
   College at Buffalo *B*
   College at Fredonia *B*
Suffolk County Community College *A*

Ohio

Ashland University *B, T*
Muskingum University *B*
Wilmington College *B*
Youngstown State University *B*

Oregon

Western Oregon University *B*

Pennsylvania

Edinboro University of
   Pennsylvania *B, T*
La Salle University *B*
Mansfield University of
   Pennsylvania *T*

South Dakota

Sisseton Wahpeton College *A*

Texas

Brazosport College *A*
College of the Mainland *A*
Lamar University *B*
Stephen F. Austin State University *T*
Texas A&M University
   Commerce *B, M*
   Corpus Christi *T*
University of Houston *B*

Washington

Centralia College *A*
University of Washington *B*

Wisconsin

University of Wisconsin
   Madison *B*
   River Falls *B, T*

Plant breeding

Arizona

Prescott College *B, M*

Georgia

University of Georgia *M, D*

Iowa

Iowa State University *M, D*

Minnesota

University of Minnesota
   Twin Cities *M, D*

Texas

Texas A&M University *M, D*
Texas Tech University *M*

Plant genetics

California

University of California
   Riverside *D*

Indiana

Purdue University *B, M, D*

Michigan

Michigan State University *M, D*

Wisconsin

University of Wisconsin
   Madison *M, D*

Plant molecular biology

Illinois

University of Illinois
   Urbana-Champaign *B, M, D*

Kansas

Pittsburg State University *B*

Washington

Washington State University *M, D*

Plant pathology

Alabama

Auburn University *M, D*

Arizona

University of Arizona *M, D*

Arkansas

University of Arkansas *M*

California

University of California
   Davis *M, D*
   Riverside *M, D*

Colorado

Colorado State University *M, D*

Delaware

University of Delaware *B*

Florida

University of Florida *B, M*

Georgia

University of Georgia *M, D*

Hawaii

University of Hawaii
   Manoa *M, D*

Illinois

University of Illinois
   Urbana-Champaign *M, D*

Iowa

Iowa State University *M, D*

Kansas

Kansas State University *M, D*
Pittsburg State University *B*

Kentucky

University of Kentucky *M, D*

Louisiana

Louisiana State University and
   Agricultural and Mechanical
   College *M, D*

Michigan

Michigan State University *B, M, D*

Minnesota

University of Minnesota
   Twin Cities *M, D*

Missouri

University of Missouri
   Columbia *M, D*

Montana

Montana State University
   Bozeman *M*

New Mexico

New Mexico State University *B, M*

New York

Cornell University *B, M, D*

North Carolina

North Carolina State University *M, D*

North Dakota

North Dakota State University *M, D*

Ohio

Ohio State University
   Columbus Campus *M, D*

Oklahoma

Oklahoma State University *D*

Oregon

Oregon State University *M, D*

Pennsylvania

Penn State
   University Park *M, D*

South Carolina

Clemson University *B, M, D*

Texas

Texas A&M University *M, D*

Virginia

Virginia Polytechnic Institute and
   State University *D*

Washington

Washington State University *M, D*

Wisconsin

University of Wisconsin
   Madison *B, M, D*

Plant physiology

Iowa

Iowa State University *M, D*

Kansas

Pittsburg State University *B*

Kentucky

University of Kentucky *D*

Missouri

Washington University in St. Louis *D*

Nebraska

Peru State College *B*

Oregon

Oregon State University *M, D*

South Carolina

Clemson University *D*

Texas

Texas A&M University *M, D*

Vermont

Marlboro College *B*

Washington

Washington State University *M, D*

Plant protection/pest management

California

California State Polytechnic
   University: Pomona *B*
California State University
   Fresno *B*
College of the Sequoias *C*
San Joaquin Delta College *A*
University of California
   Davis *M*

Colorado

Colorado State University *M, D*

Florida

Hillsborough Community College *C*

Georgia

University of Georgia *M*

Hawaii

University of Hawaii
   Hilo *B*
   Manoa *B*

Idaho

University of Idaho *B*

Iowa

Iowa State University *B*

Michigan

Michigan State University *M*

Minnesota

South Central College *C*

Mississippi

Mississippi State University *B*

Nebraska
University of Nebraska
Lincoln *B*

New York
Cornell University *B*
State University of New York
College of Environmental Science
and Forestry *B, M, D*

North Carolina
North Carolina State University *A*

North Dakota
North Dakota State University *B*

Ohio
Ohio State University
Columbus Campus *B*

Puerto Rico
University of Puerto Rico
Utuado *A*

Tennessee
University of Tennessee
Knoxville *M, D*

Texas
Texas A&M University *B, M*
West Texas A&M University *B*

Washington
Washington State University *B*

Plant sciences

Alabama
Alabama Agricultural and Mechanical
University *D*
Tuskegee University *B, M*

Arizona
Arizona Western College *A*
University of Arizona *B, M, D*

Arkansas
Arkansas State University *B*
University of Arkansas *D*

California
California State University
Fresno *B, M*
College of the Desert *A*
College of the Redwoods *C, A*
College of the Sequoias *C*
Cosumnes River College *A*
Mendocino College *C, A*
Modesto Junior College *A*
Reedley College *A*
San Joaquin Delta College *C, A*
Santa Rosa Junior College *C*
University of California
Santa Cruz *B*
Ventura College *C, A*
Yuba Community College District *C*

Connecticut
University of Connecticut *M, D*

Delaware
Delaware State University *B, M*
University of Delaware *B, M, D*

Florida
University of Florida *B, D*

Georgia
Abraham Baldwin Agricultural
College *A*

Fort Valley State University *B*

Idaho
University of Idaho *B, M, D*

Illinois
Southern Illinois University
Carbondale *B, M*

Iowa
Dordt College *B*
Iowa State University *B*

Louisiana
Louisiana State University and
Agricultural and Mechanical
College *B*

Maine
University of Maine *B, M, D*

Maryland
Community College of Baltimore
County *C, A*

Massachusetts
University of Massachusetts
Amherst *B, M, D*

Minnesota
Minnesota State University
Mankato *B, M, T*
Minnesota West Community and
Technical College *A*

Mississippi
Northwest Mississippi Community
College *A*

Missouri
Missouri State University *M*
Southeast Missouri State University *B*
University of Missouri
Columbia *B*

Montana
Montana State University
Bozeman *B, M, D*

New Jersey
Mercer County Community College *A*
Rutgers, The State University of New
Jersey
New Brunswick/Piscataway
Campus *B*

New York
Cornell University *B, M, D*
State University of New York
College of Agriculture and
Technology at Cobleskill *B*
College of Environmental Science
and Forestry *M, D*

North Carolina
North Carolina Agricultural and
Technical State University *B*

Ohio
Ohio State University
Agricultural Technical Institute *A*
Columbus Campus *B, M*

Oregon
Oregon State University *B, M*

Pennsylvania
Penn State
University Park *M, D*

South Carolina
Clemson University *B, M, D*

South Dakota
South Dakota State University *M*

Tennessee
Middle Tennessee State University *B*
University of Tennessee
Knoxville *B, M*

Texas
Lubbock Christian University *B*
Texas A&M University *B, M*
Texas A&M University
Commerce *B*
Kingsville *B, M*

Utah
Utah State University *M, D*

Vermont
University of Vermont *M, D*
Vermont Technical College *A*

Virginia
Virginia State University *M*

Washington
Washington State University *B*

West Virginia
West Virginia University *B, M*

Plasma/ high-temperature physics

Texas
Rice University *M, D*

Wisconsin
University of Wisconsin
Madison *M, D*

Plastics engineering technology

California
Cerritos College *C, A*

Connecticut
Naugatuck Valley Community
College *A*
Quinebaug Valley Community
College *C, A*

Illinois
College of DuPage *C, A*
Elgin Community College *C*

Kansas
Pittsburg State University *B*

Kentucky
Maysville Community and Technical
College *C*

Massachusetts
Fitchburg State College *C*
Mount Wachusett Community
College *A*

Michigan
Eastern Michigan University *B, M*
Ferris State University *A, B*
Grand Rapids Community
College *C, A*

Minnesota
Hennepin Technical College *C, A*

New York
State University of New York
College of Agriculture and
Technology at Morrisville *A*

North Carolina
Edgecombe Community College *C, A*
Guilford Technical Community
College *A*
Isothermal Community College *C, A*

Ohio
Cincinnati State Technical and
Community College *A*
Edison State Community College *C, A*
Kent State University *C*
Kent State University
Trumbull *A*
Tuscarawas *A*
Northwest State Community
College *A*
Shawnee State University *C, A, B*
Terra State Community College *C, A*

Pennsylvania
Penn State
Erie, The Behrend College *A*
Pennsylvania College of
Technology *A, B*

Texas
St. Philip's College *C*

Washington
Peninsula College *C*
Western Washington University *B*

Wisconsin
Milwaukee Area Technical College *A*

Platemaker/imager

Illinois
Triton College *C*

Ohio
Cincinnati State Technical and
Community College *C*

Pennsylvania
Pennsylvania College of
Technology *A*

Playwriting/ screenwriting

Arizona
Prescott College *B*
Scottsdale Community College *C*

California
Chapman University *B, M*
Loyola Marymount University *B*
Otis College of Art and Design *M*
University of Southern
California *B, M*

Florida
Palm Beach Atlantic University *B*
University of South Florida *M*

Illinois
Columbia College Chicago *B*
DePaul University *B*
Northwestern University *M*

Iowa
University of Iowa M

Kansas
Central Christian College of Kansas A

Massachusetts
Bard College at Simon's Rock B
Emerson College B, M
Smith College M

Minnesota
Metropolitan State University B
Minneapolis Community and
Technical College A

New Mexico
University of New Mexico M

New York
Bard College B
Sarah Lawrence College M
State University of New York
Purchase B

Ohio
Ohio University B, M

Pennsylvania
Drexel University B
Slippery Rock University of
Pennsylvania B
University of the Arts B

Texas
Texas Tech University M

Vermont
Bennington College B, M
Burlington College C
Marlboro College B

Virginia
Hollins University M
Regent University M

Washington
Cornish College of the Arts B

Plumbing

Alabama
Lawson State Community College C

Alaska
Ilisagvik College C

Arizona
Arizona Western College C
Mohave Community College C
Northland Pioneer College C, A
Tohono O'odham Community
College C, A

California
City College of San Francisco C
Foothill College C
WyoTech: Fremont C
WyoTech: Long Beach C

Colorado
Red Rocks Community College C, A

Florida
Daytona State College A
Hillsborough Community College C
Indian River State College C
Santa Fe College C
South Florida Community College C

Georgia
Athens Technical College C
Savannah Technical College C

Indiana
Ivy Tech Community College
Bloomington C, A
Central Indiana C, A
North Central C, A
Richmond C, A

Iowa
Northeast Iowa Community
College A

Kentucky
Elizabethtown Community and
Technical College C
Somerset Community College C, A

Maine
Southern Maine Community
College C
Washington County Community
College C

Michigan
Delta College A

Minnesota
Minnesota State Community and
Technical College C
Minnesota West Community and
Technical College A
Northland Community & Technical
College C
Northwest Technical College C
St. Cloud Technical College C, A
St. Paul College C

Montana
Flathead Valley Community College C

New Mexico
Dona Ana Community College of New
Mexico State University C

New York
State University of New York
College of Technology at Alfred A

North Carolina
Fayetteville Technical Community
College C
Forsyth Technical Community
College C
Johnston Community College C
Southeastern Community College C
Southwestern Community College C

North Dakota
North Dakota State College of
Science C

Oregon
Chemeketa Community College C, A

Pennsylvania
Community College of Allegheny
County C
Luzerne County Community
College C
Pennsylvania College of
Technology C
Thaddeus Stevens College of
Technology A

South Carolina
York Technical College C

Utah
Salt Lake Community College A

Virginia
Southwest Virginia Community
College C
Wytheville Community College C, A

Washington
Olympic College A

Wisconsin
Blackhawk Technical College C
Gateway Technical College C
Lakeshore Technical College C
Milwaukee Area Technical College C
Waukesha County Technical
College C
Western Technical College C
Wisconsin Indianhead Technical
College C

Podiatry (D.P.M.)

California
California College of Podiatric
Medicine P

Florida
Barry University: School of Graduate
Medical Sciences P

Illinois
Dr. William M. Scholl College of
Podiatric Medicine P

Iowa
University of Osteopathic Medicine
and Health Sciences: College of
Podiatric Medicine and
Surgery P

New York
New York College of Podiatric
Medicine P

Ohio
Ohio College of Podiatric Medicine P

Pennsylvania
Pennsylvania College of Podiatric
Medicine P

Polarity therapy

Vermont
Goddard College B, M

Washington
Centralia College A

Police science

Alabama
Central Alabama Community
College C, A
Enterprise-Ozark Community
College C
Jefferson State Community
College C, A
Northeast Alabama Community
College C, A
Northwest-Shoals Community
College A
Shelton State Community College C
Wallace State Community College at
Hanceville A

Arizona
Anthem College A, B

Argosy University: Online B
Argosy University: Phoenix B
Arizona Western College A
Central Arizona College C
Cochise College C
Eastern Arizona College C, A
Glendale Community College C
Mohave Community College C, A
Penn Foster College A, B
Phoenix College A
Pima Community College C, A
Scottsdale Community College C

Arkansas
Arkansas Northeastern College C, A
Arkansas State University A
Arkansas State University
Beebe C, A
East Arkansas Community
College C, A
Northwest Arkansas Community
College C
South Arkansas Community College A
Southern Arkansas University Tech C
University of Arkansas
Community College at Hope A
Little Rock A

California
Allan Hancock College C
American River College A
Argosy University: Inland Empire B
Argosy University: Los Angeles B
Argosy University: Orange County B
Argosy University: San Diego B
Argosy University: San Francisco Bay
Area B
Bakersfield College A
Barstow Community College C, A
Butte College C, A
Cabrillo College C, A
California Baptist University B
California Lutheran University B
Cerritos College A
Cerro Coso Community College C, A
Chabot College A
Citrus College C
City College of San Francisco C, A
College of the Canyons A
College of the Redwoods C
College of the Siskiyous C, A
Contra Costa College A
East Los Angeles College C, A
El Camino College A
El Camino College: Compton
Center A
Evergreen Valley College A
Feather River College C, A
Fresno City College C, A
Fullerton College A
Glendale Community College A
Grossmont College C, A
Irvine Valley College C, A
Lassen Community College C, A
Los Angeles City College C, A
Los Angeles Harbor College C, A
Los Angeles Valley College C, A
Merced College C, A
MiraCosta College C, A
Moorpark College C, A
Mount San Antonio College C, A
Mount San Jacinto College C, A
Napa Valley College C, A
Palomar College C, A
Pasadena City College C, A
Porterville College C, A
Rio Hondo College A
Sacramento City College C, A
San Bernardino Valley College C
San Joaquin Delta College A
Santa Ana College C, A
Santa Monica College A
Santa Rosa Junior College C, A
Shasta College A

Sierra College *A*
Solano Community College *C, A*
Southwestern College *C*
West Hills College: Coalinga *A*
Western Career College: Stockton *A*
Westwood College of Technology
   Westwood College: Inland
     Empire *B*
Yuba Community College District *A*

Colorado

Aims Community College *C*
Arapahoe Community College *C*
Argosy University: Denver *B*
Colorado Mountain College *C*
Mesa State College *C*
Red Rocks Community College *C*
Trinidad State Junior College *A*
Western State College of Colorado *B*

Connecticut

Asnuntuck Community College *A*
Housatonic Community College *C, A*
Naugatuck Valley Community
   College *C, A*
Three Rivers Community College *A*
University of Hartford *B*
University of New Haven *C, A*
Western Connecticut State
   University *B*

Delaware

Delaware Technical and Community
   College
   Owens *A*
   Stanton/Wilmington *A*
   Terry *A*

District of Columbia

American University *B, M, D*
George Washington University *A, B*

Florida

Argosy University: Sarasota *B*
Argosy University: Tampa *B*
Brevard Community College *C, A*
Central Florida College *A*
Central Florida Community College *C*
Daytona State College *C*
Florida State College at Jacksonville *C*
Hillsborough Community College *C*
Indian River State College *C*
Lake City Community College *C*
Miami Dade College *C*
Northwest Florida State College *C*
Palm Beach Community College *C*
Polk State College *C, A*
Rasmussen College: Fort Myers *A, B*
Santa Fe College *A*
Seminole Community College *C*
South Florida Community College *C*
South University: West Palm Beach *B*
Tallahassee Community College *C*
Valencia Community College *C, A*

Georgia

Abraham Baldwin Agricultural
   College *A*
Altamaha Technical College *A*
Argosy University: Atlanta *B*
Armstrong Atlantic State
   University *A, B, M*
Bainbridge College *C, A*
Dalton State College *A, B*
Georgia Gwinnett College *B*
Georgia Highlands College *A*
Gwinnett Technical College *A*
Middle Georgia College *C, A*
South Georgia College *A*
Southwest Georgia Technical
   College *C, A*

Hawaii

Argosy University: Hawaii *B*
University of Hawaii
   Honolulu Community College *A*

Idaho

Idaho State University *C, A*
North Idaho College *A*

Illinois

Argosy University: Schaumburg *B*
Black Hawk College *C, A*
City Colleges of Chicago
   Harold Washington College *C, A*
   Olive-Harvey College *C*
College of DuPage *C, A*
College of Lake County *C, A*
Concordia University Chicago *B*
Danville Area Community College *A*
Elgin Community College *A*
Harper College *C, A*
Illinois Eastern Community Colleges
   Frontier Community College *C*
   Olney Central College *A*
Illinois Valley Community College *A*
John Wood Community College *A*
Kankakee Community College *A*
Kishwaukee College *C, A*
Lake Land College *A*
Lewis University *B, M*
Lincoln College *A*
Lincoln Land Community College *C, A*
McHenry County College *A*
Moraine Valley Community College *A*
Morton College *A*
Oakton Community College *C, A*
Parkland College *A*
Prairie State College *C, A*
Rend Lake College *C, A*
Richland Community College *A*
Sauk Valley Community College *A*
Southeastern Illinois College *C, A*
Southwestern Illinois College *C, A*
Triton College *A*
Waubonsee Community College *A*
Westwood College: Chicago Loop *B*

Indiana

Calumet College of St. Joseph *A, B*
Indiana Wesleyan University *A*
Vincennes University *A*

Iowa

Clinton Community College *C, A*
Des Moines Area Community
   College *C, A*
Dordt College *B*
Hawkeye Community College *A*
Indian Hills Community College *A*
Iowa Central Community College *C, A*
Iowa Lakes Community College *A*
Kirkwood Community College *C, A*
Marshalltown Community College *A*
Muscatine Community College *C, A*
North Iowa Area Community
   College *A*
Scott Community College *C, A*
Western Iowa Tech Community
   College *C, A*

Kansas

Allen County Community College *A*
Barton County Community
   College *C, A*
Bethany College *B*
Butler Community College *C, A*
Central Christian College of
   Kansas *A, B*
Cloud County Community
   College *C, A*
Colby Community College *A*
Cowley County Community
   College *A*

Garden City Community College *A*
Hutchinson Community College *C, A*
Johnson County Community
   College *C, A*
Kansas City Kansas Community
   College *C, A*
Seward County Community
   College *C, A*
Washburn University *B*

Kentucky

Ashland Community and Technical
   College *A*
Big Sandy Community and Technical
   College *A*
Eastern Kentucky University *B, M*
Northern Kentucky University *A*
Owensboro Community and
   Technical College *A*
Somerset Community College *C, A*
Southeast Kentucky Community and
   Technical College *A*

Louisiana

Baton Rouge Community College *A*
Delgado Community College *A*
Grambling State University *A*
Louisiana State University
   Alexandria *A*
Nicholls State University *A, B*
Northwestern State University *A*
Southeastern Louisiana University *A*
University of Louisiana at Monroe *A*

Maine

Andover College *A*
Beal College *A*
Southern Maine Community
   College *A*

Maryland

Allegany College of Maryland *C, A*
Anne Arundel Community
   College *C, A*
Baltimore City Community College *A*
Carroll Community College *A*
Cecil College *C, A*
Chesapeake College *C, A*
Community College of Baltimore
   County *C, A*
Frederick Community College *A*
Frostburg State University *B*
Garrett College *C, A*
Hagerstown Community College *C, A*
Harford Community College *A*
Howard Community College *A*
University of Maryland
   Eastern Shore *B*
Wor-Wic Community College *C, A*

Massachusetts

American International College *B*
Eastern Nazarene College *B*
Greenfield Community College *A*
Massasoit Community College *C, A*
Springfield Technical Community
   College *C, A*

Michigan

Delta College *C, A*
Ferris State University *A, B*
Grand Rapids Community College *A*
Kalamazoo Valley Community
   College *C, A*
Kellogg Community College *A*
Kirtland Community College *C, A*
Lake Michigan College *A*
Lansing Community College *A*
Macomb Community College *C, A*
Mid Michigan Community College *A*
Mott Community College *C, A*
North Central Michigan College *C*
Northwestern Michigan College *A*

Minnesota

Alexandria Technical College *C, A*
Argosy University: Twin Cities *B*
Central Lakes College *A*
Century Community and Technical
   College *A*
Fond du Lac Tribal and Community
   College *C, A*
Hibbing Community College *A*
Inver Hills Community College *A*
Leech Lake Tribal College *A*
Metropolitan State University *C, B*
Minneapolis Community and
   Technical College *C, A*
Minnesota School of Business: St.
   Cloud *A*
Minnesota State University
   Mankato *B*
Minnesota West Community and
   Technical College *A*
Normandale Community College *C, A*
North Hennepin Community
   College *A*
Northland Community & Technical
   College *A*
Rasmussen College: Lake
   Elmo/Woodbury *A*
Ridgewater College *A*
Riverland Community College *C, A*
Rochester Community and Technical
   College *C, A*
St. Mary's University of Minnesota *B*
University of Minnesota
   Crookston *B*
Vermilion Community College *A*
Walden University *B*
Winona State University *B*

Mississippi

Virginia College Gulf Coast *A*

Missouri

College of the Ozarks *B*
East Central College *A*
Jefferson College *A*
Metropolitan Community College:
   Blue River *C, A*
Mineral Area College *C, A*
Missouri Southern State University *C*
Missouri State University: West
   Plains *A*
Missouri Western State University *A*
St. Charles Community College *C, A*
St. Louis Community College
   St. Louis Community College at
     Florissant Valley *A*
   St. Louis Community College at
     Meramec *C, A*
State Fair Community College *A*
Three Rivers Community College *A*
University of Missouri
   Kansas City *B*

Montana

Dawson Community College *C, A*
University of Great Falls *B*

Nebraska

Metropolitan Community College *A*
Mid-Plains Community College Area *A*
Nebraska Indian Community
   College *A*
Northeast Community College *C*
University of Nebraska
   Kearney *B*
Western Nebraska Community
   College *C, A*

Oakland Community College *C, A*
Schoolcraft College *A*
University of Detroit Mercy *B, M*
Washtenaw Community College *A*

Nevada
College of Southern Nevada C, A
Great Basin College A
Truckee Meadows Community
    College A
Western Nevada College C, A

New Jersey
Atlantic Cape Community College A
Bergen Community College A
Berkeley College- Garret Mountain
    Campus A
Brookdale Community College A
Burlington County College C, A
Camden County College A
County College of Morris A
Cumberland County College C, A
Essex County College A
Gloucester County College A
Mercer County Community College A
Ocean County College C, A
Passaic County Community
    College C, A
Raritan Valley Community College A

New Mexico
Eastern New Mexico University:
    Roswell Campus A
New Mexico Junior College A
San Juan College C, A
Santa Fe Community College A

New York
Adirondack Community College A
Berkeley College of New York City A
Broome Community College A
Bryant & Stratton Business Institute
    Bryant & Stratton College:
        Syracuse A
Cayuga County Community College A
City University of New York
    John Jay College of Criminal
        Justice C, A
Erie Community College
    City Campus C, A
    North Campus C, A
    South Campus A
Excelsior College B
Hilbert College B
Jamestown Community College A
Medaille College B
Mercy College C
Monroe College A
Monroe Community College A
Orange County Community College A
State University of New York
    College at Brockport B
    College of Technology at
        Canton A, B
    Farmingdale A
Sullivan County Community
    College A
Tompkins Cortland Community
    College A
Ulster County Community College C
Westchester Community College A

North Carolina
Asheville-Buncombe Technical
    Community College C, A
Bladen Community College C
Brunswick Community College C
Cape Fear Community College C, A
Carteret Community College C, A
Catawba Valley Community College C
Central Piedmont Community
    College C
Cleveland Community College C
Coastal Carolina Community
    College C, A
College of the Albemarle C
Davidson County Community
    College C

Durham Technical Community
    College C
Fayetteville Technical Community
    College C
Gaston College C
Halifax Community College C
Isothermal Community College C
James Sprunt Community
    College C, A
Johnston Community College C, A
Lenoir Community College C
Mayland Community College C
Mitchell Community College C, A
Montgomery Community College C
Nash Community College A
Pfeiffer University B
Pitt Community College C, A
Randolph Community College C
Rockingham Community College C
Sampson Community College C
Sandhills Community College C
Southwestern Community College C
Stanly Community College C
Vance-Granville Community
    College C
Wake Technical Community
    College A
Wayne Community College C
Western Piedmont Community
    College C
Wilkes Community College C
Wilson Community College C

North Dakota
Lake Region State College C, A

Ohio
Bowling Green State University B
Cincinnati State Technical and
    Community College C
Columbus State Community
    College C, A
Cuyahoga Community College
    Metropolitan Campus A
Eastern Gateway Community
    College A
Edison State Community College A
Hocking College C, A
James A. Rhodes State College A
Kaplan College: Columbus A
Miami University
    Oxford Campus A
Muskingum University B
North Central State College C, A
Northwest State Community
    College A
Ohio Northern University B
Ohio University
    Zanesville Campus A
Owens Community College
    Toledo A
Remington College: Cleveland West A
Southern State Community College A
Terra State Community College C, A
University of Akron C, A
Wright State University B
Youngstown State University C, A

Oklahoma
Connors State College A
East Central University B
Langston University B
Northwestern Oklahoma State
    University B
Oklahoma City University B
Oklahoma State University
    Oklahoma City A
Redlands Community College A
Rogers State University A
Rose State College A
Tulsa Community College A
University of Central Oklahoma B
Western Oklahoma State College A

Oregon
Chemeketa Community College A
Clackamas Community College A
Linn-Benton Community College A
Rogue Community College A
Southern Oregon University B
Southwestern Oregon Community
    College A
Treasure Valley Community College A
Umpqua Community College C, A
Western Oregon University M

Pennsylvania
Bucks County Community College A
Butler County Community College A
Community College of Allegheny
    County A
Community College of Beaver
    County C, A
Community College of
    Philadelphia C, A
Edinboro University of
    Pennsylvania A
Harrisburg Area Community
    College C, A
Kaplan Career Institute: Pittsburgh A
Lackawanna College C, A
Montgomery County Community
    College A
Reading Area Community College A
YTI Career Institute: York A

Puerto Rico
Caribbean University A
Universidad del Este A
University College of San Juan A, B

Rhode Island
Community College of Rhode
    Island A

South Carolina
South University: Columbia B
Williamsburg Technical College C
York Technical College C, A

South Dakota
University of Sioux Falls B
Western Dakota Technical Institute A

Tennessee
Argosy University: Nashville B
Cleveland State Community College C
Dyersburg State Community
    College A
Jackson State Community College A
LeMoyne-Owen College B
Nashville State Community College A
Roane State Community College C, A
Southwest Tennessee Community
    College A
Walters State Community College C, A

Texas
Amarillo College C, A
Argosy University: Dallas B
Austin Community College C, A
Brazosport College C, A
Central Texas College C
Coastal Bend College A
College of the Mainland A
Collin County Community College
    District A
Del Mar College C, A
Eastfield College C
El Centro College C
Grayson County College A
Hill College C, A
Houston Community College
    System C, A
Howard Payne University B
Kilgore College C, A

Lamar Institute of Technology C
Lee College A
Midland College A
Navarro College A
North Central Texas College A
Northeast Texas Community
    College C, A
Odessa College C, A
San Antonio College C, A
San Jacinto College C, A
Stephen F. Austin State University B
Tarrant County College C
Texas State University: San Marcos B
Tyler Junior College C, A
Vernon College C
Weatherford College C, A
Western Texas College A
Wharton County Junior College C, A

Utah
Southern Utah University A, B
Weber State University B

Vermont
Southern Vermont College A, B

Virginia
Argosy University: Washington D.C. B
Bluefield College B
Dabney S. Lancaster Community
    College C, A
George Mason University B
Germanna Community College C, A
Lord Fairfax Community College C
Mountain Empire Community
    College C
Paul D. Camp Community College A
Piedmont Virginia Community
    College C, A
Southside Virginia Community
    College C, A
Southwest Virginia Community
    College C, A
Virginia Highlands Community
    College A
Virginia Western Community
    College A
Wytheville Community College C, A

Washington
Argosy University: Seattle B
Centralia College A
Grays Harbor College C, A
Green River Community College A
Olympic College C, A
Spokane Community College A
Wenatchee Valley College C, A
Whatcom Community College A

West Virginia
Fairmont State University A
West Virginia Northern Community
    College A
West Virginia State Community and
    Technical College A
West Virginia State University B

Wisconsin
Blackhawk Technical College C, A
Carthage College B
Chippewa Valley Technical College A
Fox Valley Technical College A
Gateway Technical College A
Lakeshore Technical College C, A
Marian University B
Mid-State Technical College A
Milwaukee Area Technical College A
Moraine Park Technical College A
Nicolet Area Technical College A
Northcentral Technical College A
Northeast Wisconsin Technical
    College A
Rasmussen College: Green Bay A

University of Wisconsin
   Superior *B*
Waukesha County Technical
   College *A*
Western Technical College *A*
Wisconsin Indianhead Technical
   College *C, A*

Wyoming

Eastern Wyoming College *A*

Polish

Illinois

University of Illinois
   Chicago *B*

Pennsylvania

University of Pittsburgh *B*

Wisconsin

University of Wisconsin
   Madison *B*

Polish studies

New York

Columbia University *B*

Political communications

District of Columbia

George Washington University *B*

Massachusetts

Emerson College *B, M*
Suffolk University *B*

Missouri

Missouri State University *B*

Nebraska

Nebraska Wesleyan University *B*

Ohio

Cedarville University *B*
Ohio University
   Southern Campus at Ironton *B*

Political science

Alabama

Alabama Agricultural and Mechanical
   University *B*
Alabama State University *B*
Athens State University *B*
Auburn University *B*
Auburn University at
   Montgomery *B, M*
Birmingham-Southern College *B*
Huntingdon College *B*
Jacksonville State University *B*
Miles College *B*
Samford University *B*
Spring Hill College *B*
Troy University *B*
Tuskegee University *B*
University of Alabama *B, M, D*
University of Alabama
   Birmingham *B*
   Huntsville *B*
University of Mobile *B*
University of Montevallo *B, T*
University of North Alabama *B*
University of South Alabama *B*

Alaska

University of Alaska
   Anchorage *B*

Fairbanks *B, M*
Southeast *B*

Arizona

Arizona State University *B, M, D*
Arizona Western College *A*
Cochise College *A*
Eastern Arizona College *A*
Northern Arizona University *B, M, D*
Pima Community College *A*
Prescott College *B, T*
University of Arizona *B, M, D*

Arkansas

Arkansas State University *B, M*
Harding University *B*
Henderson State University *B*
Hendrix College *B*
John Brown University *B*
Lyon College *B*
Ouachita Baptist University *B*
Philander Smith College *B*
Southern Arkansas University *B*
University of Arkansas *B, M*
University of Arkansas
   Little Rock *B*
   Monticello *B*
   Pine Bluff *B*
University of Central Arkansas *B*
University of the Ozarks *B*

California

American Jewish University *B*
Azusa Pacific University *B*
Bakersfield College *A*
Cabrillo College *A*
California Baptist University *B*
California Institute of Technology *B*
California Lutheran University *B*
California Maritime Academy *B*
California Polytechnic State
   University: San Luis Obispo *B*
California State Polytechnic
   University: Pomona *B*
California State University
   Bakersfield *B*
   Chico *B, M*
   Dominguez Hills *B*
   East Bay *B*
   Fresno *B*
   Fullerton *B, M*
   Los Angeles *B, M*
   Northridge *B*
   Sacramento *B, M*
   San Bernardino *B, T*
   San Marcos *B*
   Stanislaus *B*
California State University: Channel
   Islands *B*
Canada College *A*
Cerritos College *A*
Chabot College *A*
Chaffey College *A*
Chapman University *B*
Claremont McKenna College *B*
College of Alameda *A*
College of the Desert *A*
Concordia University *B*
Copper Mountain College *A*
Crafton Hills College *A*
Cypress College *A*
De Anza College *A*
Diablo Valley College *A*
Dominican University of California *B*
East Los Angeles College *A*
El Camino College *A*
El Camino College: Compton
   Center *A*
Foothill College *A*
Fresno Pacific University *B*
Fullerton College *A*
Gavilan College *A*
Golden West College *A*
Grossmont College *A*

Humboldt State University *B*
Irvine Valley College *A*
Los Angeles Southwest College *A*
Los Angeles Valley College *A*
Loyola Marymount University *B*
The Master's College *B*
Mills College *B*
MiraCosta College *A*
Monterey Peninsula College *A*
Mount St. Mary's College *B*
Notre Dame de Namur University *B*
Occidental College *B*
Orange Coast College *A*
Oxnard College *A*
Pepperdine University *B*
Pitzer College *B*
Point Loma Nazarene University *B*
Pomona College *B*
Saddleback College *A*
St. Mary's College of California *B*
San Diego City College *A*
San Diego State University *B, M*
San Francisco State University *B, M*
San Jose State University *B*
Santa Ana College *A*
Santa Barbara City College *A*
Santa Clara University *B*
Santa Monica College *A*
Santa Rosa Junior College *A*
Santiago Canyon College *A*
Scripps College *B*
Solano Community College *A*
Sonoma State University *B*
Southwestern College *A*
Stanford University *B, M, D*
University of California
   Berkeley *B, D*
   Davis *B, M, D*
   Irvine *B, M, D*
   Los Angeles *B, M, D*
   Riverside *B, M, D*
   San Diego *B, M, D*
   Santa Barbara *B, M, D*
   Santa Cruz *B, D*
University of California: Merced *B*
University of La Verne *B*
University of Redlands *B*
University of San Diego *B*
University of San Francisco *B*
University of Southern California *B, D*
University of the Pacific *B*
Vanguard University of Southern
   California *B*
West Los Angeles College *A*
Westmont College *B*
Whittier College *B*

Colorado

Colorado College *B*
Colorado State University *B, M, D*
Colorado State University
   Pueblo *B*
Fort Lewis College *B*
Mesa State College *B*
Metropolitan State College of
   Denver *B, T*
Otero Junior College *A*
Pikes Peak Community College *A*
Regis University *B*
United States Air Force Academy *B*
University of Colorado
   Boulder *B, M, D*
   Colorado Springs *B*
   Denver *B, M*
University of Denver *B*
University of Northern Colorado *B*
Western State College of Colorado *B*

Connecticut

Albertus Magnus College *B*
Central Connecticut State
   University *B*
Connecticut College *B*

Eastern Connecticut State
   University *B*
Fairfield University *B*
Quinnipiac University *B*
Sacred Heart University *B*
Southern Connecticut State
   University *B, M, T*
Trinity College *B*
United States Coast Guard Academy *B*
University of Bridgeport *B*
University of Connecticut *B, M, D*
University of Hartford *B*
University of New Haven *B*
Wesleyan University *B*
Western Connecticut State
   University *B*
Yale University *B, M, D*

Delaware

Delaware State University *B*
University of Delaware *B, M, D*
Wesley College *B*

District of Columbia

American University *B, M, D*
Catholic University of
   America *B, M, D*
Gallaudet University *B*
George Washington
   University *B, M, D*
Georgetown University *B, M, D*
Howard University *B, M, D*
Trinity Washington University *B*
University of the District of
   Columbia *B*

Florida

Ave Maria University *B*
Barry University *B*
Bethune-Cookman University *B*
Broward College *A*
Daytona State College *A*
Eckerd College *B*
Flagler College *B*
Florida Agricultural and Mechanical
   University *B*
Florida Atlantic University *B, M*
Florida Gulf Coast University *B*
Florida International
   University *B, M, D*
Florida Southern College *B*
Florida State University *B, D*
Gulf Coast Community College *A*
Indian River State College *A*
Jacksonville University *B*
Miami Dade College *A*
New College of Florida *B*
Palm Beach Atlantic University *B*
Palm Beach Community College *A*
Rollins College *B*
Saint Leo University *B*
Saint Thomas University *B*
Stetson University *B*
University of Central Florida *B, M*
University of Florida *B, M, D*
University of Miami *B*
University of North Florida *B*
University of South Florida *B, M*
University of Tampa *A, B*
University of West Florida *B, M*

Georgia

Agnes Scott College *B*
Albany State University *B*
Armstrong Atlantic State
   University *B, T*
Atlanta Metropolitan College *A*
Augusta State University *B*
Bainbridge College *A*
Berry College *B*
Brewton-Parker College *B*
Clark Atlanta University *B, M, D*
Clayton State University *B*

Columbus State University *B*
Dalton State College *A*
Darton College *A*
East Georgia College *A*
Emory University *B, D*
Fort Valley State University *B*
Gainesville State College *A*
Georgia College and State
    University *B*
Georgia Gwinnett College *B*
Georgia Highlands College *A*
Georgia Perimeter College *A*
Georgia Southern University *B, M*
Georgia Southwestern State
    University *B*
Georgia State University *B, M, D*
Gordon College *A*
Kennesaw State University *B*
LaGrange College *B*
Macon State College *A*
Mercer University *B*
Middle Georgia College *A*
Morehouse College *B*
North Georgia College & State
    University *B*
Oglethorpe University *B*
Piedmont College *B*
Savannah State University *B*
South Georgia College *A*
Southern Polytechnic State
    University *B*
Spelman College *B*
University of Georgia *B, M, D*
University of West Georgia *B*
Valdosta State University *B*
Waycross College *A*

Hawaii

Chaminade University of Honolulu *B*
Hawaii Pacific University *B*
University of Hawaii
    Hilo *B*
    Manoa *B, M, D*
    West Oahu *B*

Idaho

Boise State University *B, T*
Brigham Young University-Idaho *B*
College of Idaho *B*
Idaho State University *A, B, M, D*
North Idaho College *A*
Northwest Nazarene University *B*
University of Idaho *B, M, D*

Illinois

Augustana College *B, T*
Aurora University *B*
Benedictine University *B*
Black Hawk College: East Campus *A*
Blackburn College *B*
Bradley University *B*
Chicago State University *B*
Concordia University Chicago *B*
Danville Area Community College *A*
DePaul University *B*
Dominican University *B*
Eastern Illinois University *B, M*
Elmhurst College *B, T*
Eureka College *B*
Governors State University *M*
Illinois College *B*
Illinois Institute of Technology *B*
Illinois State University *B, M*
Illinois Valley Community College *A*
Illinois Wesleyan University *B*
John A. Logan College *A*
Joliet Junior College *A*
Kankakee Community College *A*
Kishwaukee College *A*
Knox College *B*
Lake Forest College *B*
Lewis University *B*
Loyola University Chicago *B, M, D*
MacMurray College *B*

McKendree University *B*
Millikin University *B*
Monmouth College *B, T*
North Central College *B*
North Park University *B*
Northeastern Illinois University *B, M*
Northern Illinois University *B, M, D*
Northwestern University *B, M, D*
Olivet Nazarene University *B*
Principia College *B*
Quincy University *B*
Richland Community College *A*
Rockford College *B*
Roosevelt University *B*
Saint Xavier University *B*
South Suburban College of Cook
    County *A*
Southern Illinois University
    Carbondale *B, M, D*
Southern Illinois University
    Edwardsville *B*
Southwestern Illinois College *A*
Trinity Christian College *B*
Triton College *A*
University of Chicago *B, D*
University of Illinois
    Chicago *B, M, D*
    Springfield *B, M*
    Urbana-Champaign *B, M, D*
University of St. Francis *B*
Western Illinois University *B, M*
Wheaton College *B*

Indiana

Anderson University *B*
Ball State University *B, M, T*
Butler University *B*
DePauw University *B*
Earlham College *B*
Franklin College *B*
Hanover College *B*
Indiana State University *B, M, T*
Indiana University
    Bloomington *B, M, D*
    Northwest *B*
    South Bend *B*
    Southeast *B*
Indiana University-Purdue University
    Fort Wayne *A, B*
Indiana University-Purdue University
    Indianapolis *B*
Indiana Wesleyan University *A, B*
Manchester College *B*
Marian University *B, T*
Purdue University *B, M, D*
Purdue University
    Calumet *B*
Saint Joseph's College *B*
Saint Mary's College *B*
Taylor University *B*
University of Evansville *B*
University of Indianapolis *B*
University of Notre Dame *B, M, D*
University of St. Francis *B*
University of Southern Indiana *B*
Valparaiso University *B*
Vincennes University *A*
Wabash College *B*

Iowa

Briar Cliff University *B*
Buena Vista University *B, T*
Central College *B, T*
Coe College *B*
Cornell College *B, T*
Dordt College *B*
Drake University *B*
Graceland University *T*
Grand View University *B*
Grinnell College *B*
Iowa State University *B, M*
Loras College *B*
Luther College *B*
Morningside College *B*

Mount Mercy College *B*
North Iowa Area Community
    College *A*
Northwestern College *B*
St. Ambrose University *B, T*
Simpson College *B*
University of Iowa *B, M, D, T*
University of Northern Iowa *B*
Waldorf College *B*
Wartburg College *B, T*

Kansas

Baker University *B, T*
Barton County Community College *A*
Benedictine College *B*
Butler Community College *A*
Central Christian College of Kansas *A*
Coffeyville Community College *A*
Emporia State University *B, T*
Fort Hays State University *B, M*
Friends University *B*
Kansas State University *C, B, M*
Labette Community College *A*
Pittsburg State University *B*
Pratt Community College *A*
University of Kansas *B, M, D*
University of St. Mary *B*
Washburn University *B*
Wichita State University *B*

Kentucky

Asbury College *B*
Bellarmine University *B*
Berea College *B*
Brescia University *B*
Campbellsville University *B*
Centre College *B*
Eastern Kentucky University *B, M*
Georgetown College *B, T*
Kentucky State University *B*
Kentucky Wesleyan College *B, T*
Morehead State University *B*
Murray State University *B, T*
Northern Kentucky University *B*
Thomas More College *A, B*
Transylvania University *B*
University of Kentucky *B, M, D*
University of Louisville *B, M*
University of the Cumberlands *B*
Western Kentucky University *B*

Louisiana

Centenary College of Louisiana *B, T*
Dillard University *B*
Grambling State University *B*
Louisiana College *B*
Louisiana State University
    Shreveport *B*
Louisiana State University and
    Agricultural and Mechanical
    College *B, M, D*
Louisiana Tech University *B*
Loyola University New Orleans *B*
McNeese State University *B*
Nicholls State University *B*
Northwestern State University *B*
Southeastern Louisiana University *B*
Southern University and Agricultural
    and Mechanical College *B*
Tulane University *B, M*
University of Louisiana at Lafayette *B*
University of Louisiana at Monroe *B*
University of New Orleans *B, M, D*
Xavier University of Louisiana *B*

Maine

Bates College *B*
Bowdoin College *B*
Colby College *B*
Saint Joseph's College of Maine *B*
Thomas College *B*
University of Maine *B*

University of Maine
    Farmington *B*
    Presque Isle *B*
University of New England *B*
University of Southern Maine *B*

Maryland

Allegany College of Maryland *A*
College of Notre Dame of Maryland *B*
Coppin State University *B*
Frederick Community College *A*
Frostburg State University *B*
Goucher College *B*
Harford Community College *A*
Hood College *B*
Johns Hopkins University *B, M, D*
Loyola University Maryland *B*
McDaniel College *B*
Morgan State University *B*
Mount St. Mary's University *B*
St. Mary's College of Maryland *B*
Salisbury University *B, T*
Towson University *B*
United States Naval Academy *B*
University of Baltimore *B*
University of Maryland
    Baltimore County *B*
    College Park *B, M, D*
    University College *C, B*
Washington Adventist University *B*
Washington College *B*

Massachusetts

American International College *B*
Amherst College *B*
Anna Maria College *B*
Assumption College *B*
Bard College at Simon's Rock *B*
Boston College *B, M, D*
Boston University *B, M, D*
Brandeis University *B, M, D*
Bridgewater State College *B*
Clark University *B*
College of the Holy Cross *B*
Emmanuel College *B*
Fitchburg State College *B*
Framingham State College *B*
Gordon College *B*
Hampshire College *B*
Harvard College *B, M, D*
Massachusetts College of Liberal
    Arts *B*
Massachusetts Institute of
    Technology *B, M, D*
Merrimack College *B*
Mount Holyoke College *B*
Northeastern University *B, M, D*
Pine Manor College *B*
Regis College *B*
Salem State College *B*
Simmons College *B*
Smith College *B*
Springfield College *B*
Stonehill College *B*
Suffolk University *B, M*
Tufts University *B*
University of Massachusetts
    Amherst *B, M, D*
    Boston *B*
    Dartmouth *B*
    Lowell *B*
Wellesley College *B*
Western New England College *B*
Westfield State College *B*
Wheaton College *B*
Williams College *B*

Michigan

Adrian College *A, B, T*
Albion College *B, T*
Alma College *B, T*
Andrews University *B*
Aquinas College *B, T*
Calvin College *B, T*

Central Michigan University *B, M*
Eastern Michigan University *B*
Ferris State University *B*
Grand Rapids Community College *A*
Grand Valley State University *B*
Hillsdale College *B*
Hope College *B*
Kalamazoo College *B*
Lake Michigan College *A*
Lake Superior State University *B*
Lansing Community College *A*
Madonna University *B*
Marygrove College *B, T*
Michigan State University *B, M, D*
Northern Michigan University *B*
Oakland University *B*
Saginaw Valley State University *B*
Spring Arbor University *B*
University of Detroit Mercy *B*
University of Michigan *B, M, D*
University of Michigan
  Dearborn *B*
  Flint *B, M*
Wayne State University *B, M, D*
Western Michigan University *B, M, D*

Minnesota
Augsburg College *B*
Bemidji State University *B*
Bethel University *B*
Carleton College *B*
College of St. Benedict *B*
Concordia College: Moorhead *B*
Gustavus Adolphus College *B*
Hamline University *B*
Macalester College *B*
Minnesota State University
  Mankato *B, M*
  Moorhead *B*
Minnesota West Community and
  Technical College *A*
Ridgewater College *A*
St. Catherine University *B*
Saint Cloud State University *B*
St. John's University *B*
St. Mary's University of Minnesota *B*
St. Olaf College *B*
Southwest Minnesota State
  University *B*
University of Minnesota
  Duluth *B*
  Morris *B*
  Twin Cities *B, M, D*
University of St. Thomas *B*
Vermilion Community College *A*
Winona State University *B*

Mississippi
Alcorn State University *B*
Belhaven University *B*
Delta State University *B*
Hinds Community College *A*
Jackson State University *B, M*
Millsaps College *B*
Mississippi College *B, M*
Mississippi State University *B, M*
Mississippi University for Women *B*
Mississippi Valley State University *B*
Rust College *B*
Tougaloo College *B*
University of Mississippi *B, M, D*
University of Southern
  Mississippi *B, M*

Missouri
Avila University *B*
Central Methodist University *B*
Columbia College *B*
Culver-Stockton College *B*
Drury University *B, T*
Evangel University *B*
Lincoln University *B*
Lindenwood University *B*

Missouri Southern State
  University *B, T*
Missouri State University *B*
Missouri Valley College *B*
Missouri Western State University *B, T*
Northwest Missouri State
  University *B*
Park University *B*
Rockhurst University *B*
St. Charles Community College *A*
Saint Louis University *B, M*
Southeast Missouri State University *B*
Southwest Baptist University *B*
Three Rivers Community College *A*
Truman State University *B*
University of Central Missouri *B*
University of Missouri
  Columbia *B, M, D*
  Kansas City *B, M*
  St. Louis *B, M, D*
Washington University in St.
  Louis *B, M, D*
Webster University *B*
Westminster College *B*
William Jewell College *B*
William Woods University *B*

Montana
Miles Community College *A*
Montana State University
  Billings *B, T*
  Bozeman *B*
Rocky Mountain College *B, T*
University of Great Falls *B*
University of Montana *B, M*
University of Montana: Western *B*

Nebraska
Creighton University *B*
Doane College *B*
Nebraska Wesleyan University *B*
University of Nebraska
  Kearney *B, T*
  Lincoln *B, M, D*
  Omaha *B, M*
Wayne State College *B*
Western Nebraska Community
  College *A*

Nevada
University of Nevada
  Las Vegas *B, M*
  Reno *B, M, D*

New Hampshire
Dartmouth College *B*
Franklin Pierce University *B*
Keene State College *B*
New England College *B, M*
Plymouth State University *B*
Rivier College *B*
Saint Anselm College *B, T*
Southern New Hampshire
  University *B*
Thomas More College of Liberal
  Arts *B*
University of New Hampshire *B, M*
University of New Hampshire at
  Manchester *B*

New Jersey
Bloomfield College *B*
Caldwell College *B*
Centenary College *B*
The College of New Jersey *B*
Drew University *B*
Fairleigh Dickinson University
  College at Florham *B*
  Metropolitan Campus *B, M*
Felician College *B*
Gloucester County College *A*
Kean University *B, M, T*
Middlesex County College *A*

Monmouth University *B*
Montclair State University *B*
New Jersey City University *B*
Princeton University *B, M, D*
Ramapo College of New Jersey *B*
Richard Stockton College of New
  Jersey *B*
Rider University *B*
Rowan University *B*
Rutgers, The State University of New
  Jersey
  Camden Regional Campus *B*
  New Brunswick/Piscataway
    Campus *B*
  Newark Regional Campus *B, M*
Saint Peter's College *B*
Salem Community College *A*
Seton Hall University *B, T*
Thomas Edison State College *B*
William Paterson University of New
  Jersey *B*

New Mexico
Eastern New Mexico University *B*
New Mexico Highlands
  University *B, M*
New Mexico State University *B, M*
University of New Mexico *B, M, D*

New York
Adelphi University *B*
Alfred University *B*
Bard College *B*
Barnard College *B*
Canisius College *B*
City University of New York
  Baruch College *B*
  Brooklyn College *B, M*
  City College *B*
  College of Staten Island *B*
  Hunter College *B*
  John Jay College of Criminal
    Justice *B*
  Lehman College *B*
  Queens College *B, T*
  Queensborough Community
    College *A*
  York College *B*
Clarkson University *B*
Colgate University *B*
College of New Rochelle *B*
College of Saint Rose *B, M*
Columbia University *B*
Columbia University
  School of General Studies *B*
Cornell University *B, M, D*
Daemen College *B, T*
Dowling College *B*
Elmira College *B*
Excelsior College *B*
Fordham University *B, M, D*
Hamilton College *B*
Hartwick College *B*
Hilbert College *B*
Hobart and William Smith Colleges *B*
Hofstra University *B*
Houghton College *B*
Iona College *B*
Ithaca College *B*
Le Moyne College *B*
Long Island University
  Brooklyn Campus *B, M*
  C. W. Post Campus *B, M*
Manhattanville College *B*
Marist College *B*
Marymount Manhattan College *B*
Mercy College *B*
Molloy College *B*
Monroe Community College *A*
Nazareth College *B*
New York Institute of Technology *B*
New York University *B, M, D*
Niagara University *B*
Pace University *C, B*

Russell Sage College *B*
Saint Bonaventure University *B*
St. Francis College *B*
St. John Fisher College *B*
St. John's University *B, M*
St. Joseph's College: Suffolk
  Campus *B*
St. Lawrence University *B*
Siena College *B, T*
Skidmore College *B*
State University of New York
  Albany *B, M, D*
  Binghamton *B, M, D*
  Buffalo *B, M, D*
  College at Brockport *B*
  College at Buffalo *B*
  College at Cortland *B*
  College at Fredonia *B*
  College at Geneseo *B*
  College at Oneonta *B*
  College at Plattsburgh *B*
  College at Potsdam *B*
  New Paltz *B*
  Oswego *B*
  Purchase *B*
  Stony Brook *B, M, D*
Suffolk County Community College *A*
Syracuse University *B, M*
Touro College *B*
Union College *B*
United States Military Academy *B*
University of Rochester *B, M, D*
Utica College *B*
Vassar College *B*
Wagner College *B*
Wells College *B*
Yeshiva University *B*

North Carolina
Appalachian State University *B, M*
Barton College *B*
Belmont Abbey College *B*
Bennett College for Women *B*
Campbell University *B*
Catawba College *B*
Davidson College *B*
Duke University *B, M, D*
East Carolina University *B*
Elizabeth City State University *B*
Elon University *B*
Fayetteville State University *B, M*
Gardner-Webb University *B*
Greensboro College *B*
Guilford College *B*
High Point University *B*
Johnson C. Smith University *B*
Lenoir-Rhyne University *B, T*
Livingstone College *B*
Mars Hill College *B*
Meredith College *B*
Methodist University *A, B*
North Carolina Agricultural and
  Technical State University *B*
North Carolina Central University *B*
North Carolina State University *B*
North Carolina Wesleyan College *B*
Peace College *B*
Queens University of Charlotte *B*
St. Andrews Presbyterian College *B*
St. Augustine's College *B*
Shaw University *B*
University of North Carolina
  Asheville *B, T*
  Chapel Hill *B, M, D*
  Charlotte *B*
  Greensboro *B, M*
  Pembroke *B*
  Wilmington *B*
Wake Forest University *B*
Warren Wilson College *B*
Western Carolina University *B*
Winston-Salem State University *B*

North Dakota
Dickinson State University *B*
Jamestown College *B*
North Dakota State University *B*
University of North Dakota *B*

Ohio
Ashland University *B*
Baldwin-Wallace College *B*
Bowling Green State University *B*
Capital University *B*
Case Western Reserve
 University *B, M, D*
Cedarville University *B*
Central State University *B*
Cleveland State University *B*
College of Wooster *B*
Denison University *B*
Franciscan University of
 Steubenville *B*
Heidelberg University *B*
Hiram College *B*
John Carroll University *B*
Kent State University *B, M, D*
Kenyon College *B*
Malone University *B*
Marietta College *B*
Miami University
 Oxford Campus *B, M*
Mount Union College *B*
Muskingum University *B*
Notre Dame College *B, T*
Oberlin College *B*
Ohio Dominican University *B*
Ohio Northern University *B*
Ohio State University
 Columbus Campus *B, M, D*
Ohio University *B, M*
Ohio Wesleyan University *B*
Otterbein College *B*
University of Akron *M*
University of Cincinnati *B, M, D*
University of Dayton *B*
University of Findlay *B*
University of Toledo *B, M*
Urbana University *B*
Walsh University *B*
Wilberforce University *B*
Wilmington College *B*
Wittenberg University *B*
Wright State University *B*
Xavier University *A, B*
Youngstown State University *B*

Oklahoma
Cameron University *B*
East Central University *B*
Northeastern State University *B*
Northwestern Oklahoma State
 University *B*
Oklahoma Baptist University *B*
Oklahoma Christian University *B*
Oklahoma City University *B*
Oklahoma State University *B, M*
Oklahoma Wesleyan University *B*
Oral Roberts University *B*
Rose State College *A*
St. Gregory's University *B*
Southeastern Oklahoma State
 University *B*
Southern Nazarene University *B*
Southwestern Oklahoma State
 University *B*
Tulsa Community College *A*
University of Central Oklahoma *B, M*
University of Oklahoma *B, M, D*
University of Science and Arts of
 Oklahoma *B*
University of Tulsa *B*
Western Oklahoma State College *A*

Oregon
Central Oregon Community
 College *A*
Chemeketa Community College *A*
Eastern Oregon University *B*
George Fox University *B*
Lewis & Clark College *B*
Linfield College *B, T*
Linn-Benton Community College *A*
Mt. Hood Community College *A*
Oregon State University *B*
Pacific University *B*
Portland State University *B, M*
Reed College *B*
Southern Oregon University *B*
Treasure Valley Community College *A*
University of Oregon *B, M, D*
University of Portland *B*
Western Oregon University *B*
Willamette University *B*

Pennsylvania
Albright College *B*
Allegheny College *B*
Alvernia University *B*
Arcadia University *B*
Bloomsburg University of
 Pennsylvania *B*
Bryn Mawr College *B*
Bucknell University *B*
Cabrini College *B*
California University of
 Pennsylvania *B, M*
Carlow University *B*
Cedar Crest College *B*
Chatham University *B*
Chestnut Hill College *B*
Cheyney University of Pennsylvania *B*
Clarion University of Pennsylvania *B*
DeSales University *B, T*
Dickinson College *B*
Drexel University *B*
Duquesne University *B*
East Stroudsburg University of
 Pennsylvania *B, M*
Eastern University *B*
Edinboro University of
 Pennsylvania *B*
Elizabethtown College *B*
Franklin & Marshall College *B*
Gannon University *B*
Geneva College *B, T*
Gettysburg College *B*
Grove City College *B*
Haverford College *B, T*
Immaculata University *C, A, B*
Indiana University of Pennsylvania *B*
Juniata College *B*
King's College *B*
Kutztown University of
 Pennsylvania *B*
La Roche College *B*
La Salle University *B*
Lafayette College *B*
Lebanon Valley College *B*
Lehigh University *B, M*
Lincoln University *B*
Lock Haven University of
 Pennsylvania *B*
Lycoming College *B*
Mansfield University of
 Pennsylvania *B, T*
Mercyhurst College *B*
Messiah College *B*
Millersville University of
 Pennsylvania *B*
Moravian College *B*
Mount Aloysius College *B*
Muhlenberg College *B*
Neumann University *B, T*
Penn State
 Abington *B*
 Altoona *B*
 Beaver *B*

Berks *B*
Brandywine *B*
DuBois *B*
Erie, The Behrend College *B*
Fayette, The Eberly Campus *B*
Greater Allegheny *B*
Hazleton *B*
Lehigh Valley *B*
Mont Alto *B*
New Kensington *B*
Schuylkill *B*
Shenango *B*
University Park *B, M, D*
Wilkes-Barre *B*
Worthington Scranton *B*
York *B*
Point Park University *B*
Rosemont College *B*
St. Francis University *B*
Saint Joseph's University *B*
St. Vincent College *B*
Seton Hill University *B*
Shippensburg University of
 Pennsylvania *B, T*
Slippery Rock University of
 Pennsylvania *B*
Susquehanna University *B*
Swarthmore College *B*
Temple University *B, M, D*
Thiel College *B*
University of Pennsylvania *B, M, D*
University of Pittsburgh *B, M, D*
University of Pittsburgh
 Bradford *B*
 Greensburg *B*
 Johnstown *B*
University of Scranton *A, B*
Ursinus College *B, T*
Villanova University *B, M*
Washington & Jefferson College *B*
Waynesburg University *B*
West Chester University of
 Pennsylvania *B, T*
Westminster College *B, T*
Widener University *B*
Wilkes University *B*
York College of Pennsylvania *A, B*

Puerto Rico
Caribbean University *A*
Inter American University of Puerto
 Rico
 Metropolitan Campus *B*
 San German Campus *B*
Pontifical Catholic University of
 Puerto Rico *B*
University of Puerto Rico
 Aguadilla *A*
 Rio Piedras *B*

Rhode Island
Brown University *B, M, D*
Providence College *B*
Rhode Island College *B*
Roger Williams University *B*
Salve Regina University *B*
University of Rhode Island *B, M*

South Carolina
Benedict College *B*
Bob Jones University *B*
Charleston Southern University *B*
The Citadel *B*
Claflin University *B*
Clemson University *B*
Coastal Carolina University *B*
Coker College *B*
College of Charleston *B, T*
Columbia College *B*
Converse College *B*
Erskine College *B*
Francis Marion University *B*
Furman University *B*
Lander University *B*

Morris College *B*
Newberry College *B*
Presbyterian College *B*
South Carolina State University *B*
University of South Carolina *B, M, D*
University of South Carolina
 Aiken *B*
 Upstate *B*
Winthrop University *B*

South Dakota
Augustana College *B, T*
Black Hills State University *B*
Northern State University *B*
South Dakota State University *B*
University of Sioux Falls *B*
University of South Dakota *B, M*

Tennessee
Austin Peay State University *B*
Belmont University *B, T*
Bryan College *B*
Carson-Newman College *B, T*
Cumberland University *B*
East Tennessee State University *B, T*
Fisk University *B*
Jackson State Community College *A*
King College *B, T*
Lambuth University *B*
LeMoyne-Owen College *B*
Lee University *B*
Lipscomb University *B*
Maryville College *B, T*
Middle Tennessee State University *B*
Rhodes College *B*
Tennessee State University *B*
Tennessee Technological University *B*
Tennessee Temple University *B*
Tusculum College *B*
Union University *B, T*
University of Memphis *B, M*
University of Tennessee
 Chattanooga *B*
 Knoxville *B, M, D*
 Martin *B*
University of the South *B*
Vanderbilt University *B, M, D*

Texas
Abilene Christian University *B*
Angelo State University *B, T*
Austin College *B*
Austin Community College *A*
Baylor University *B, M, D*
Brazosport College *A*
Clarendon College *A*
Coastal Bend College *A*
College of the Mainland *A*
Dallas Baptist University *B*
Del Mar College *A*
East Texas Baptist University *B*
El Paso Community College *A*
Frank Phillips College *A*
Galveston College *A*
Hardin-Simmons University *B*
Houston Baptist University *B*
Howard Payne University *B*
Huston-Tillotson University *B*
Lamar University *B, M*
Laredo Community College *A*
LeTourneau University *B*
Lon Morris College *A*
McMurry University *B*
Midland College *A*
Midwestern State University *B, M*
Northeast Texas Community
 College *A*
Northwest Vista College *A*
Our Lady of the Lake University of San
 Antonio *B*
Palo Alto College *A*
Paris Junior College *A*
Prairie View A&M University *B*
Rice University *B, M, D*

St. Edward's University *B*
St. Mary's University *B, M, T*
St. Philip's College *A*
Sam Houston State University *B, M*
Schreiner University *B*
South Plains College *A*
South Texas College *A*
Southern Methodist University *B*
Southwestern University *B, T*
Stephen F. Austin State University *B, T*
Sul Ross State University *B, M*
Tarleton State University *B, M, T*
Texarkana College *A*
Texas A&M International
   University *B, M, T*
Texas A&M University *B, M, D*
Texas A&M University
   Commerce *B, M*
   Corpus Christi *B, T*
   Kingsville *B, M, T*
   Texarkana *B*
Texas Christian University *B*
Texas College *B*
Texas Lutheran University *B*
Texas Southern University *B*
Texas State University: San
   Marcos *B, M, T*
Texas Tech University *B, M, D*
Texas Wesleyan University *B, T*
Texas Woman's University *B, M*
Trinity University *B*
University of Dallas *B, M, D*
University of Houston *B, M, D*
University of Houston
   Clear Lake *B*
   Downtown *B*
University of Mary Hardin-Baylor *B*
University of North Texas *B, M, D*
University of St. Thomas *B*
University of Texas
   Arlington *B, M*
   Austin *B, M, D*
   Brownsville - Texas Southmost
     College *B*
   Dallas *B, D*
   El Paso *B, M*
   Pan American *B*
   San Antonio *B, M*
   Tyler *B, M*
   of the Permian Basin *B*
University of the Incarnate Word *B*
West Texas A&M University *B, M*
Western Texas College *A*

Utah

Brigham Young University *B*
Salt Lake Community College *A*
Snow College *A*
Southern Utah University *B*
University of Utah *B, M, D, T*
Utah State University *B, M*
Utah Valley University *B*
Weber State University *B*
Westminster College *B*

Vermont

Bennington College *B*
Johnson State College *B*
Marlboro College *B*
Middlebury College *B*
Norwich University *B*
St. Michael's College *B*
University of Vermont *B*

Virginia

Averett University *B*
Bridgewater College *B*
Christendom College *B*
Christopher Newport University *B*
College of William and Mary *B*
Emory & Henry College *B*
Ferrum College *B*
George Mason University *M, D*
Hampden-Sydney College *B*

Hampton University *B*
Hollins University *B*
James Madison University *B, M*
Liberty University *B*
Longwood University *B, T*
Lynchburg College *B*
Mary Baldwin College *B*
Marymount University *B*
Norfolk State University *B*
Old Dominion University *B, T*
Patrick Henry College *B*
Radford University *B*
Randolph College *B*
Randolph-Macon College *B*
Regent University *B, M*
Roanoke College *B, T*
St. Paul's College *B*
Sweet Briar College *B*
University of Mary Washington *B*
University of Richmond *B*
University of Virginia *B, M, D*
University of Virginia's College at
   Wise *B, T*
Virginia Commonwealth University *B*
Virginia Intermont College *B*
Virginia Polytechnic Institute and
   State University *B, M, D*
Virginia State University *B*
Virginia Union University *B*
Virginia Wesleyan College *B*
Washington and Lee University *B*

Washington

Centralia College *A*
Eastern Washington University *C, B*
Everett Community College *A*
Evergreen State College *B*
Gonzaga University *B*
Northwest University *B*
Olympic College *A*
Pacific Lutheran University *B*
Saint Martin's University *B*
Seattle Pacific University *B*
Seattle University *B*
University of Puget Sound *B, T*
University of Washington *B, M, D*
University of Washington Tacoma *B*
Washington State University *B, M, D*
Western Washington University *B, M*
Whitman College *B*
Whitworth University *B*

West Virginia

Alderson-Broaddus College *B*
American Public University
   System *B, M*
Bethany College *B*
Concord University *B*
Davis and Elkins College *B*
Fairmont State University *B*
Marshall University *B, M*
Potomac State College of West
   Virginia University *A*
Shepherd University *B*
University of Charleston *B*
West Liberty University *B*
West Virginia State University *B*
West Virginia University *B, M, D*
West Virginia Wesleyan College *B*
Wheeling Jesuit University *B*

Wisconsin

Alverno College *B*
Beloit College *B*
Cardinal Stritch University *B*
Carroll University *B*
Carthage College *B*
Edgewood College *B*
Lawrence University *B*
Marian University *B*
Marquette University *B, M*
Ripon College *B*
St. Norbert College *B, T*

University of Wisconsin
   Eau Claire *B*
   Green Bay *B, T*
   La Crosse *B, T*
   Madison *B, M, D*
   Milwaukee *B, M, D*
   Oshkosh *B*
   Parkside *B, T*
   Platteville *B, T*
   River Falls *B, T*
   Stevens Point *B*
   Superior *B*
   Whitewater *B*

Wyoming

Casper College *A*
Eastern Wyoming College *A*
Laramie County Community
   College *A*
Northwest College *A*
University of Wyoming *B, M*
Western Wyoming Community
   College *A*

Polymer chemistry

California

California Polytechnic State
   University: San Luis Obispo *M*

Connecticut

University of Connecticut *M, D*

Georgia

Georgia Institute of Technology *B*

Kansas

Pittsburg State University *B*

Massachusetts

University of Massachusetts
   Lowell *M, D*

Michigan

University of Michigan *M, D*

Minnesota

Winona State University *B*

New York

Polytechnic Institute of New York
   University *D*
Rochester Institute of Technology *B*

North Carolina

North Carolina State
   University *B, M, D*

North Dakota

North Dakota State University *M, D*

Ohio

University of Akron *B, M, D*

Pennsylvania

Carnegie Mellon University *M*

Wisconsin

University of Wisconsin
   River Falls *B*

Polymer/plastics engineering

California

University of Southern California *B*

Connecticut

Quinebaug Valley Community
   College *A*

Georgia

Georgia Institute of Technology *M*

Hawaii

University of Hawaii
   Honolulu Community College *A*

Illinois

University of Illinois
   Urbana-Champaign *B, M, D*

Massachusetts

University of Massachusetts
   Lowell *B, M, D*

Michigan

University of Michigan *M*

Minnesota

Winona State University *B*

Mississippi

University of Southern
   Mississippi *M, D*

Missouri

University of Missouri
   Missouri University of Science and
     Technology *B*

New Jersey

Stevens Institute of Technology *M*

New York

Polytechnic Institute of New York
   University *M*
Rochester Institute of Technology *B*
State University of New York
   College of Agriculture and
     Technology at Morrisville *A*

Ohio

Case Western Reserve
   University *B, M, D*
Terra State Community College *A*
University of Akron *B, M, D*

Pennsylvania

Lehigh University *M, D*
Penn State
   Erie, The Behrend College *B*

Tennessee

University of Tennessee
   Knoxville *M, D*

Texas

Trinity Valley Community College *A*

Virginia

Virginia Polytechnic Institute and
   State University *M, D*

Wisconsin

University of Wisconsin
   Stout *B*

Population biology

California

University of California
   Davis *M, D*
   Riverside *D*

Missouri

Washington University in St. Louis *D*

Texas

Texas State University: San Marcos *M*

University of Texas
Austin *M, D*

Portuguese

California
Chabot College *A*
University of California
Los Angeles *B, M*
Santa Barbara *B, M*

Connecticut
Yale University *B, M, D*

District of Columbia
George Washington University *B*
Georgetown University *B*

Florida
Florida International University *B*
University of Florida *B*

Illinois
University of Chicago *B, D*
University of Illinois
Urbana-Champaign *B, M, D*

Indiana
Indiana University
Bloomington *B, M, D*

Iowa
University of Iowa *B, T*

Louisiana
Tulane University *B, M*

Massachusetts
Smith College *B*
University of Massachusetts
Amherst *B*
Dartmouth *B, M, D*

Minnesota
University of Minnesota
Twin Cities *B, M*

New Jersey
Rutgers, The State University of New Jersey
New Brunswick/Piscataway
Campus *B*

New Mexico
University of New Mexico *B, M*

New York
Columbia University
School of General Studies *B*
United States Military Academy *B*

North Carolina
University of North Carolina
Chapel Hill *B, M, D*

Ohio
Ohio State University
Columbus Campus *B*

Rhode Island
Brown University *B, M, D*

Tennessee
University of Tennessee
Knoxville *B*
Vanderbilt University *M, D*

Texas
University of Texas
Austin *B, M, D*

Utah
Brigham Young University *B, M*

Wisconsin
University of Wisconsin
Madison *B, M, D*

Poultry science

Alabama
Auburn University *B*
Tuskegee University *B, M*

Arkansas
University of Arkansas *B, M, D*

California
Modesto Junior College *A*

Delaware
Delaware State University *B, M*
Delaware Technical and Community
College
Owens *C, A*

Florida
University of Florida *B, M*

Georgia
Abraham Baldwin Agricultural
College *A*
University of Georgia *B, M, D*

Minnesota
Ridgewater College *C*

Mississippi
Mississippi State University *B*
Northwest Mississippi Community
College *A*

Missouri
Crowder College *A*

New York
State University of New York
College of Agriculture and
Technology at Cobleskill *A*

North Carolina
North Carolina State University *B, M*
Wayne Community College *A*

Ohio
Ohio State University
Columbus Campus *M, D*

Oregon
Oregon State University *M, D*

South Carolina
Clemson University *M*

Texas
Stephen F. Austin State University *B*
Texas A&M University *B, M, D*

Wisconsin
University of Wisconsin
Madison *B, M, D*

Power/electrical transmission

Alabama
Alabama Southern Community
College *C*
Lawson State Community College *C*

Arizona
Coconino County Community
College *C*
GateWay Community College *C, A*

Arkansas
Phillips Community College of the
University of Arkansas *C*

California
Bakersfield College *A*
Chabot College *A*
Coastline Community College *C*
College of the Redwoods *C*
Foothill College *C*
Fresno City College *C, A*
Los Angeles Trade and Technical
College *A*
Orange Coast College *C, A*
Palomar College *C, A*
San Diego City College *C, A*
San Joaquin Delta College *C, A*
San Jose City College *A*

Colorado
Colorado Northwestern Community
College *C, A*
Community College of Aurora *A*

Florida
Florida State College at Jacksonville *C*
Palm Beach Community College *C*
Polk State College *A*
South Florida Community
College *C, A*

Georgia
Augusta Technical College *C*
Chattahoochee Technical College *C*

Hawaii
University of Hawaii
Hawaii Community College *C, A*

Illinois
Illinois Eastern Community Colleges
Lincoln Trail College *C*
Kishwaukee College *C*
Southwestern Illinois College *C, A*

Iowa
Kirkwood Community College *A*

Kansas
Allen County Community College *C*
Johnson County Community
College *C, A*
Manhattan Area Technical
College *C, A*

Maine
Eastern Maine Community College *A*
Northern Maine Community
College *A*

Michigan
Lansing Community College *A*
Macomb Community College *C*

Minnesota
Fond du Lac Tribal and Community
College *A*
Minnesota West Community and
Technical College *A*

Mississippi
Hinds Community College *C*
Mississippi Delta Community
College *C*
Mississippi Gulf Coast Community
College *C, A*
Pearl River Community College *A*

Montana
Miles Community College *A*

Nebraska
Metropolitan Community
College *C, A*

Nevada
Truckee Meadows Community
College *C, A*

New York
Mohawk Valley Community College *C*

North Carolina
Durham Technical Community
College *C*
Mayland Community College *C*
Randolph Community College *C*
Richmond Community College *C*
Robeson Community College *C*
Wake Technical Community
College *C, A*

Ohio
Eastern Gateway Community
College *A*
Ohio State University
Agricultural Technical Institute *A*

Oklahoma
Oklahoma State University
Institute of Technology:
Okmulgee *A*

Oregon
Portland Community College *C, A*

Pennsylvania
Community College of Allegheny
County *A*
Thaddeus Stevens College of
Technology *A*
Triangle Tech
Pittsburgh *A*

South Carolina
Aiken Technical College *C*
Technical College of the
Lowcountry *C*

South Dakota
Mitchell Technical Institute *A*
Western Dakota Technical
Institute *C, A*

Tennessee
Northeast State Community
College *A*

Texas
Amarillo College *C, A*
Frank Phillips College *C, A*
Houston Community College
System *C*
Laredo Community College *A*
North Lake College *A*
San Jacinto College *C, A*
South Plains College *C, A*
Texas State Technical College
Waco *A*
Western Texas College *C, A*

Virginia
Tidewater Community College *C*

Washington
Clark College *C*
Clover Park Technical College *C*

Spokane Community College *A*

Wisconsin

Chippewa Valley Technical College *C*
Milwaukee Area Technical College *C*
Northeast Wisconsin Technical
College *C*
Western Technical College *C*

Precision production trades, general

Alabama

Shelton State Community
College *C, A*

Arkansas

Ouachita Technical College *A*

California

Yuba Community College
District *C, A*

Connecticut

Naugatuck Valley Community
College *C*

Iowa

Southeastern Community College
North Campus *C, A*

Michigan

Grand Rapids Community College *A*

Minnesota

Ridgewater College *C*

Missouri

Mineral Area College *A*
St. Charles Community College *A*

Nebraska

Central Community College *C, A*

Texas

South Texas College *C, A*

Washington

Clover Park Technical College *C*

Predental

Alabama

Calhoun Community College *A*
Faulkner State Community College *A*
Faulkner University *B*
Gadsden State Community College *A*

Arkansas

Harding University *B*
Ouachita Baptist University *B*
University of the Ozarks *B*

California

Azusa Pacific University *B*
Bakersfield College *A*
California Lutheran University *B*
California State University
Chico *B*
Chabot College *A*
Chapman University *B*
College of the Siskiyous *A*
Cypress College *A*
El Camino College *A*
Foothill College *A*
Golden West College *A*
Monterey Peninsula College *A*
Mount St. Mary's College *B*
Notre Dame de Namur University *B*
Westmont College *B*

Whittier College *B*

Colorado

Adams State College *B*
Lamar Community College *A*
Otero Junior College *A*
Regis University *B*

Connecticut

Quinnipiac University *B*
Sacred Heart University *B*
Southern Connecticut State
University *B*

Delaware

University of Delaware *B*

District of Columbia

American University *B*

Florida

Barry University *B*
Broward College *A*
Florida Southern College *B*
Florida State University *B*
Gulf Coast Community College *A*
Indian River State College *A*
Jacksonville University *B*
Miami Dade College *A*
Northwest Florida State College *A*
Pensacola Junior College *A*
University of Central Florida *B*
University of Miami *B*

Georgia

Abraham Baldwin Agricultural
College *A*
Andrew College *A*
Darton College *A*
Georgia Perimeter College *A*
Georgia Southern University *B*
Macon State College *A*
Mercer University *B*
Middle Georgia College *A*
Oglethorpe University *B*
Young Harris College *A*

Idaho

Boise State University *B*
Brigham Young University-Idaho *B*
North Idaho College *A*
Northwest Nazarene University *B*
University of Idaho *B*

Illinois

Augustana College *B*
Black Hawk College: East Campus *A*
City Colleges of Chicago
Harold Washington College *A*
Kennedy-King College *A*
Dominican University *B*
Elmhurst College *B*
Eureka College *B*
Greenville College *B*
Illinois Central College *A*
Kankakee Community College *A*
Kishwaukee College *A*
Lewis University *B*
Lewis and Clark Community
College *A*
MacMurray College *B*
Millikin University *B*
Triton College *A*
University of Illinois
Chicago *B*
University of St. Francis *B*

Indiana

Ball State University *B*
Bethel College *B*
Indiana University-Purdue University
Fort Wayne *B*

Indiana University-Purdue University
Indianapolis *B*
Indiana Wesleyan University *B*
Manchester College *B*
Purdue University *B*
Saint Joseph's College *B*
St. Mary-of-the-Woods College *B*
University of Evansville *B*
University of St. Francis *B*
Vincennes University *A*

Iowa

Clarke College *B*
Coe College *B*
Dordt College *B*
Ellsworth Community College *A*
Iowa Wesleyan College *B*
Marshalltown Community College *A*
Simpson College *B*
University of Iowa *B*
Upper Iowa University *B*

Kansas

Barton County Community College *A*
Coffeyville Community College *A*
McPherson College *B*
Pittsburg State University *B*
Pratt Community College *A*
Seward County Community College *A*
Tabor College *B*
Washburn University *B*

Kentucky

Campbellsville University *B*
Eastern Kentucky University *B*
Georgetown College *B*

Louisiana

Centenary College of Louisiana *B*
Louisiana College *B*
Loyola University New Orleans *B*
Xavier University of Louisiana *B*

Maine

University of Southern Maine *B*

Maryland

Frostburg State University *B*
Howard Community College *A*
Montgomery College *A*
University of Maryland
College Park *B*
Washington Adventist University *B*

Massachusetts

American International College *B*
Cape Cod Community College *A*
Eastern Nazarene College *B*
Elms College *B*
Simmons College *B*
Springfield College *B*
University of Massachusetts
Amherst *B*
Worcester Polytechnic Institute *B*

Michigan

Adrian College *B*
Alma College *B*
Calvin College *B*
Cornerstone University *B*
Delta College *A*
Eastern Michigan University *B*
Gogebic Community College *A*
Grand Rapids Community College *A*
Grand Valley State University *B*
Hillsdale College *B*
Kalamazoo College *B*
Kirtland Community College *A*
Lake Michigan College *A*
Lansing Community College *A*
Madonna University *B*
Northern Michigan University *B*

Siena Heights University *A, B*
University of Detroit Mercy *B*

Minnesota

College of St. Benedict *B*
Gustavus Adolphus College *B*
Hamline University *B*
Minnesota State University
Mankato *B*
Moorhead *B*
Minnesota West Community and
Technical College *A*
St. Catherine University *B*
Saint Cloud State University *B*
St. John's University *B*
University of Minnesota
Twin Cities *B*
University of St. Thomas *B*
Vermilion Community College *A*
Winona State University *B*

Mississippi

East Central Community College *A*
Holmes Community College *A*
Jackson State University *B*
Mississippi Delta Community
College *A*

Missouri

Drury University *B*
Evangel University *B*
Maryville University of Saint Louis *B*
Missouri Southern State University *B*
St. Louis Community College
St. Louis Community College at
Florissant Valley *A*
University of Missouri
Kansas City *B*
Missouri University of Science and
Technology *B*
Washington University in St. Louis *B*

Montana

University of Great Falls *B*

Nebraska

College of Saint Mary *B*
Concordia University *B*
Northeast Community College *A*
University of Nebraska
Lincoln *B*
Western Nebraska Community
College *A*
York College *A*

New Hampshire

Rivier College *B*
Saint Anselm College *B*

New Jersey

Rutgers, The State University of New
Jersey
Camden Regional Campus *B*
New Brunswick/Piscataway
Campus *B*
Newark Regional Campus *B*
Sussex County Community College *A*

New Mexico

New Mexico Junior College *A*

New York

Alfred University *B*
Colgate University *B*
D'Youville College *B*
Elmira College *B*
Fordham University *B*
Hobart and William Smith Colleges *B*
Hofstra University *B*
Houghton College *B*
Ithaca College *B*
Le Moyne College *B*

Manhattan College *B*
Niagara University *B*
Paul Smith's College *B*
Rochester Institute of Technology *B*
St. Joseph's College: Suffolk
Campus *B*
St. Thomas Aquinas College *B*
State University of New York
Albany *B*
College at Brockport *B*
Sullivan County Community
College *A*
Syracuse University *B*
Touro College *B*
Wagner College *B*
Wells College *B*

North Carolina
Belmont Abbey College *B*
Brevard College *B*
Campbell University *B*
Carteret Community College *A*
Chowan University *B*
Elon University *B*
Gardner-Webb University *B*
Lees-McRae College *B*
Livingstone College *B*
Mars Hill College *B*
Methodist University *B*
Mitchell Community College *A*
Pfeiffer University *B*
Queens University of Charlotte *B*
Sandhills Community College *A*
Wingate University *B*

North Dakota
Dickinson State University *B*
Mayville State University *B*

Ohio
Baldwin-Wallace College *B*
Bowling Green State University *B*
Cedarville University *B*
Defiance College *B*
Heidelberg University *B*
John Carroll University *B*
Kent State University *B*
Kettering College of Medical Arts *B*
Muskingum University *B*
Oberlin College *B*
Ohio Northern University *B*
Ohio Wesleyan University *B*
Otterbein College *B*
University of Cincinnati *B*
University of Cincinnati
Clermont College *A*
Raymond Walters College *A*
University of Dayton *B*
University of Toledo *B*
Urbana University *B*
Walsh University *B*
Wright State University *B*
Youngstown State University *B*

Oklahoma
Connors State College *A*
East Central University *B*
Eastern Oklahoma State College *A*
Northeastern Oklahoma Agricultural
and Mechanical College *A*
Oklahoma Christian University *B*
Oklahoma City University *B*
Rose State College *A*

Oregon
Chemeketa Community College *A*
Corban College *B*
Eastern Oregon University *B*
Linn-Benton Community College *A*
Southern Oregon University *B*
Treasure Valley Community College *A*

Pennsylvania
Albright College *B*
Allegheny College *B*
Edinboro University of
Pennsylvania *B*
Gettysburg College *B*
Grove City College *B*
Juniata College *B*
Keystone College *B*
La Salle University *B*
Lehigh University *B*
Mansfield University of
Pennsylvania *B*
Reading Area Community College *A*
St. Vincent College *B*
University of Pittsburgh
Greensburg *B*
Johnstown *B*
Villanova University *B*
Waynesburg University *B*
Westminster College *B*
Widener University *B*

Rhode Island
Rhode Island College *B*

South Carolina
Clemson University *B*
College of Charleston *B*
Furman University *B*
Limestone College *B*
North Greenville University *B*
Southern Wesleyan University *B*
Spartanburg Community College *A*

South Dakota
Augustana College *B*
Dakota Wesleyan University *B*

Tennessee
Carson-Newman College *B*
Columbia State Community College *A*
Cumberland University *B*
Lincoln Memorial University *B*
Lipscomb University *B*
Maryville College *B*
Tennessee Technological University *B*
Tennessee Wesleyan College *B*
University of Tennessee
Knoxville *B*

Texas
Abilene Christian University *B*
Amarillo College *A*
Angelina College *A*
Austin Community College *A*
Baylor University *B*
Clarendon College *A*
Coastal Bend College *A*
El Paso Community College *A*
Galveston College *A*
Hardin-Simmons University *B*
Howard College *A*
Laredo Community College *A*
LeTourneau University *B*
Lon Morris College *A*
Lubbock Christian University *B*
Midland College *A*
Midwestern State University *B*
Navarro College *A*
Paris Junior College *A*
St. Philip's College *A*
South Plains College *A*
Texas A&M University
Commerce *B*
Texas Wesleyan University *B*
Trinity Valley Community College *A*
Tyler Junior College *A*
Weatherford College *A*
Western Texas College *A*

Utah
Snow College *A*

University of Utah *B*
Utah State University *B*

Virginia
Eastern Mennonite University *B*
Longwood University *B*
Mountain Empire Community
College *A*
Virginia Wesleyan College *B*

Washington
Everett Community College *A*
Saint Martin's University *B*

West Virginia
Concord University *B*
Potomac State College of West
Virginia University *A*
University of Charleston *B*
West Virginia Wesleyan College *B*

Wisconsin
Carroll University *B*
Marquette University *B*
Mount Mary College *B*
Ripon College *B*
St. Norbert College *B*
University of Wisconsin
Milwaukee *B*
Oshkosh *B*
Parkside *B*

Wyoming
Casper College *A*
Eastern Wyoming College *A*
Laramie County Community
College *A*
Northwest College *A*
Western Wyoming Community
College *A*

Prelaw

Alabama
Calhoun Community College *A*
Faulkner University *B*
Gadsden State Community College *A*
Lawson State Community College *A*
Talladega College *B*
Wallace State Community College at
Hanceville *A*

Alaska
University of Alaska
Southeast *A*

Arizona
Eastern Arizona College *A*
Northern Arizona University *B*

Arkansas
Harding University *B*
Phillips Community College of the
University of Arkansas *A*
University of the Ozarks *B*

California
Bakersfield College *A*
Biola University *B*
Butte College *A*
California Lutheran University *B*
California State University
Dominguez Hills *B*
Chabot College *A*
Claremont McKenna College *B*
College of the Siskiyous *A*
Foothill College *A*
Golden West College *A*
The Master's College *B*
MiraCosta College *A*
Mount St. Mary's College *B*
Notre Dame de Namur University *B*

San Diego City College *A*
San Joaquin Delta College *A*
Vanguard University of Southern
California *B*
Westmont College *B*
Whittier College *B*

Colorado
Adams State College *B*
Colorado Mountain College *A*
Lamar Community College *A*
Otero Junior College *A*
Regis University *B*
Trinidad State Junior College *A*
Western State College of Colorado *B*

Connecticut
Albertus Magnus College *B*
Mitchell College *B*
Post University *B*
Quinnipiac University *B*
Southern Connecticut State
University *B*
Trinity College *B*

Delaware
University of Delaware *B*
Wilmington University *B*

District of Columbia
American University *B*

Florida
Barry University *B*
Broward College *A*
Chipola College *A*
Clearwater Christian College *B*
Florida State University *B*
Gulf Coast Community College *A*
Indian River State College *A*
Jacksonville University *B*
Miami Dade College *A*
Nova Southeastern University *B*
Palm Beach Atlantic University *B*
Pensacola Junior College *A*
Saint Thomas University *B*
State College of Florida,
Manatee-Sarasota *A*
University of Miami *B*
Webber International University *B*

Georgia
Abraham Baldwin Agricultural
College *A*
Andrew College *A*
College of Coastal Georgia *A*
Darton College *A*
Emmanuel College *B*
Middle Georgia College *A*
Oglethorpe University *B*
Young Harris College *A*

Idaho
Brigham Young University-Idaho *A*
North Idaho College *A*
Northwest Nazarene University *B*

Illinois
Augustana College *B*
Aurora University *B*
Black Hawk College: East Campus *A*
City Colleges of Chicago
Harold Washington College *A*
Kennedy-King College *A*
Danville Area Community College *A*
Elmhurst College *B*
Eureka College *B*
Illinois Central College *A*
John Wood Community College *A*
Kishwaukee College *A*
Lake Land College *A*
Lewis University *B*

Lewis and Clark Community
College *A*
Millikin University *B*
Richland Community College *A*
Saint Xavier University *B*
Southeastern Illinois College *A*
Southwestern Illinois College *A*
Spoon River College *A*
Trinity International University *B*
Triton College *A*
University of Illinois
Urbana-Champaign *B*

Indiana

Anderson University *B*
Huntington University *B*
Indiana University-Purdue University
Indianapolis *B*
Indiana Wesleyan University *B*
Manchester College *B*
Purdue University
Calumet *B*
Saint Joseph's College *B*
St. Mary-of-the-Woods College *B*
University of St. Francis *B*

Iowa

Coe College *B*
Dordt College *B*
Ellsworth Community College *A*
Grand View University *B*
Iowa Central Community College *A*
Iowa Wesleyan College *B*
Loras College *B*
Marshalltown Community College *A*
Simpson College *B*
University of Iowa *B*
Upper Iowa University *B*
Waldorf College *B*

Kansas

Barton County Community College *A*
Butler Community College *A*
Central Christian College of
Kansas *A, B*
Coffeyville Community College *A*
Dodge City Community College *A*
Garden City Community College *A*
Labette Community College *A*
McPherson College *B*
Pittsburg State University *B*
Pratt Community College *A*
Seward County Community College *A*
Tabor College *B*
Washburn University *B*
Wichita State University *B*

Kentucky

Lindsey Wilson College *A, B*
Northern Kentucky University *A*
Thomas More College *A*

Louisiana

Centenary College of Louisiana *B*
Grambling State University *B*
Louisiana College *B*
Xavier University of Louisiana *B*

Maine

University of Southern Maine *B*

Maryland

Anne Arundel Community College *A*
College of Notre Dame of Maryland *B*
University of Baltimore *B*
University of Maryland
College Park *B*
Washington Adventist University *B*

Massachusetts

American International College *B*
Babson College *B*
Bay Path College *B*
Becker College *B*
Eastern Nazarene College *B*
Elms College *B*
Hampshire College *B*
Lasell College *B*
Newbury College *B*
Springfield College *B*
Suffolk University *B*
Worcester Polytechnic Institute *B*

Michigan

Adrian College *B*
Alma College *B*
Bay de Noc Community College *A*
Calvin College *B*
Delta College *A*
Eastern Michigan University *B*
Ferris State University *A*
Gogebic Community College *A*
Grand Rapids Community College *A*
Hillsdale College *B*
Kalamazoo College *B*
Lansing Community College *A*
Madonna University *B*
Michigan State University *B*
Northern Michigan University *B*
Siena Heights University *B*
University of Detroit Mercy *B*
West Shore Community College *A*

Minnesota

College of St. Benedict *B*
Gustavus Adolphus College *B*
Minnesota State University
Mankato *B*
Northland Community & Technical
College *A*
Ridgewater College *A*
St. Catherine University *B*
Saint Cloud State University *B*
St. John's University *B*
University of Minnesota
Twin Cities *B*
University of St. Thomas *B*
Vermilion Community College *A*
Winona State University *B*

Mississippi

Hinds Community College *A*
Meridian Community College *A*
Mississippi College *B*
Mississippi Delta Community
College *A*
Mississippi Gulf Coast Community
College *A*

Missouri

Evangel University *B*
Fontbonne University *B*
Stephens College *B*
Three Rivers Community College *A*
University of Missouri
Kansas City *B*
Missouri University of Science and
Technology *B*

Montana

University of Montana: Western *B*

Nebraska

Bellevue University *B*
Chadron State College *B*
Concordia University *B*
Northeast Community College *A*
Western Nebraska Community
College *A*

New Hampshire

New England College *B*
Rivier College *B*
Saint Anselm College *B*

New Jersey

Rutgers, The State University of New
Jersey
Camden Regional Campus *B*
New Brunswick/Piscataway
Campus *B*
Newark Regional Campus *B*
Warren County Community College *A*

New Mexico

New Mexico Junior College *A*

New York

Bard College *B*
City University of New York
City College *B*
College of New Rochelle *B*
College of Saint Rose *B*
Concordia College *B*
D'Youville College *B*
Dominican College of Blauvelt *B*
Elmira College *B*
Fordham University *B*
Hofstra University *B*
Ithaca College *B*
Keuka College *B*
Le Moyne College *B*
Manhattan College *B*
Metropolitan College of New
York *A, B*
Niagara University *B*
Rensselaer Polytechnic Institute *B*
Rochester Institute of Technology *B*
St. Thomas Aquinas College *B*
State University of New York
Binghamton *B*
College at Fredonia *B*
Oswego *B*
Sullivan County Community
College *A*
Syracuse University *B*
Wells College *B*

North Carolina

Belmont Abbey College *B*
Campbell University *B*
Catawba College *B*
Chowan University *B*
College of the Albemarle *A*
Elon University *B*
Gardner-Webb University *B*
Lenoir-Rhyne University *B*
Mars Hill College *B*
Methodist University *B*
Mitchell Community College *A*
Pfeiffer University *B*
Queens University of Charlotte *B*
St. Andrews Presbyterian College *B*
St. Augustine's College *B*
Sandhills Community College *A*
Wingate University *B*

North Dakota

Dickinson State University *B*
Mayville State University *B*
North Dakota State University *B*

Ohio

Ashland University *B*
Bowling Green State University *B*
Cedarville University *B*
Defiance College *B*
Heidelberg University *B*
Hiram College *B*
John Carroll University *B*
Muskingum University *B*
Oberlin College *B*
Ohio Wesleyan University *B*
Otterbein College *B*
University of Cincinnati
Clermont College *A*
Raymond Walters College *A*
University of Dayton *B*

University of Findlay *B*
University of Rio Grande *B*
University of Toledo *B*
Urbana University *B*
Wilmington College *B*
Wright State University *B*
Youngstown State University *B*

Oklahoma

Carl Albert State College *A*
Connors State College *A*
East Central University *B*
Eastern Oklahoma State College *A*
Langston University *B*
Northern Oklahoma College *A*
Northwestern Oklahoma State
University *B*
Oklahoma Christian University *B*
Oklahoma City Community College *A*
Oklahoma City University *B*
Southern Nazarene University *B*
University of Tulsa *B*

Oregon

Central Oregon Community
College *A*
Chemeketa Community College *A*
Corban College *B*
Eastern Oregon University *B*
Linn-Benton Community College *A*
Southern Oregon University *B*
Treasure Valley Community College *A*

Pennsylvania

Allegheny College *B*
Chatham University *B*
Dickinson College *B*
Gannon University *B*
Gettysburg College *B*
Grove City College *B*
Immaculata University *A*
Juniata College *B*
Keystone College *B*
La Salle University *B*
Mansfield University of
Pennsylvania *B*
Mount Aloysius College *B*
Peirce College *A*
Philadelphia University *B*
Reading Area Community College *A*
Seton Hill University *B*
University of Pittsburgh
Johnstown *B*
Waynesburg University *B*
Westminster College *B*
Widener University *B*

Puerto Rico

Caribbean University *B*
Pontifical Catholic University of
Puerto Rico *B*
University of Puerto Rico
Rio Piedras *B*

Rhode Island

Rhode Island College *B*

South Carolina

Furman University *B*
Limestone College *B*
Newberry College *B*
North Greenville University *B*

South Dakota

Dakota Wesleyan University *B*
National American University
Rapid City *B*

Tennessee

Columbia State Community College *A*
Crichton College *B*
Cumberland University *B*

Jackson State Community College *A*
Lambuth University *B*
Lincoln Memorial University *B*
Lipscomb University *B*
Tennessee Temple University *B*
Tennessee Wesleyan College *B*
Tusculum College *B*
University of Tennessee
    Knoxville *B*

Texas

Abilene Christian University *B*
Amarillo College *A*
Angelina College *A*
Central Texas College *A*
Cisco College *A*
Clarendon College *A*
Coastal Bend College *A*
Concordia University Texas *B*
Galveston College *A*
Hardin-Simmons University *B*
Hill College *A*
Howard Payne University *B*
Kilgore College *A*
LeTourneau University *B*
Lon Morris College *A*
Midland College *A*
Midwestern State University *B*
Northwest Vista College *A*
Paris Junior College *A*
St. Philip's College *A*
Texas A&M University
    Commerce *B*
Texas Wesleyan University *B*
Trinity Valley Community College *A*
Tyler Junior College *A*
University of Houston
    Clear Lake *B*
University of Texas
    Pan American *B*
Wayland Baptist University *B*
West Texas A&M University *B*
Western Texas College *A*

Utah

Snow College *A*
Southern Utah University *B*
University of Utah *B*
Utah State University *B*

Vermont

Bennington College *B*
Champlain College *B*
Marlboro College *B*
Southern Vermont College *B*

Virginia

Averett University *B*
Emory & Henry College *B*
Hampton University *B*
Longwood University *B*
Mountain Empire Community
    College *A*
Virginia Intermont College *B*

Washington

Everett Community College *A*
Highline Community College *A*
Olympic College *A*
Seattle Pacific University *B*
Spokane Community College *A*

West Virginia

Concord University *B*
Potomac State College of West
    Virginia University *A*
West Virginia Wesleyan College *B*

Wisconsin

Cardinal Stritch University *B*
Concordia University Wisconsin *B*
Marquette University *B*
Mount Mary College *B*

Ripon College *B*
St. Norbert College *B*
University of Wisconsin
    Milwaukee *B*
    Oshkosh *B*
    Parkside *B*
    Superior *B*
    Whitewater *B*

Wyoming

Casper College *A*
Central Wyoming College *A*
Laramie County Community
    College *A*
Northwest College *A*
Western Wyoming Community
    College *A*

Premedicine

Alabama

Auburn University *B*
Calhoun Community College *A*
Faulkner State Community College *A*
Faulkner University *B*
Gadsden State Community College *A*

Arizona

Eastern Arizona College *A*
Northern Arizona University *B*
Phoenix College *A*

Arkansas

Harding University *B*
Ouachita Baptist University *B*
University of the Ozarks *B*

California

Azusa Pacific University *B*
Bakersfield College *A*
California Lutheran University *B*
California State University
    Chico *B*
    San Bernardino *B*
Chabot College *A*
Chapman University *B*
Charles Drew University of Medicine
    and Science *B*
Claremont McKenna College *B*
College of the Siskiyous *A*
Cypress College *A*
El Camino College *A*
El Camino College: Compton
    Center *A*
Foothill College *A*
Fresno Pacific University *B*
Golden West College *A*
The Master's College *B*
MiraCosta College *A*
Monterey Peninsula College *A*
Mount St. Mary's College *B*
Notre Dame de Namur University *B*
Vanguard University of Southern
    California *B*
Westmont College *B*
Whittier College *B*

Colorado

Adams State College *B*
Otero Junior College *A*
Pikes Peak Community College *A*
Regis University *B*

Connecticut

Albertus Magnus College *B*
Quinnipiac University *B*
Sacred Heart University *B*
Southern Connecticut State
    University *B*
Trinity College *B*

Delaware

University of Delaware *B*

District of Columbia

American University *B*

Florida

Barry University *B*
Broward College *A*
Clearwater Christian College *B*
Florida Southern College *B*
Florida State University *B*
Gulf Coast Community College *A*
Indian River State College *A*
Jacksonville University *B*
Miami Dade College *A*
Northwest Florida State College *A*
Nova Southeastern University *B*
Palm Beach Community College *A*
Pensacola Junior College *A*
Saint Thomas University *B*
Southeastern University *B*
University of Central Florida *B*
University of Miami *B*

Georgia

Abraham Baldwin Agricultural
    College *A*
Andrew College *A*
Darton College *A*
Emmanuel College *B*
Georgia Highlands College *A*
Georgia Perimeter College *A*
Georgia Southern University *B*
Macon State College *A*
Mercer University *B*
Middle Georgia College *A*
Oglethorpe University *B*
Young Harris College *A*

Hawaii

Hawaii Pacific University *B*
University of Hawaii
    Hilo *B*

Idaho

Boise State University *B*
Brigham Young University-Idaho *B*
North Idaho College *A*
Northwest Nazarene University *B*
University of Idaho *B*

Illinois

Augustana College *B*
Black Hawk College: East Campus *A*
City Colleges of Chicago
    Harold Washington College *A*
    Kennedy-King College *A*
Dominican University *B*
Elmhurst College *B*
Eureka College *B*
Greenville College *B*
Illinois Central College *A*
Kankakee Community College *A*
Kishwaukee College *A*
Lake Land College *A*
Lewis University *B*
Lewis and Clark Community
    College *A*
MacMurray College *B*
Millikin University *B*
Northwestern University *B*
Saint Xavier University *B*
Southwestern Illinois College *A*
Trinity International University *B*
Triton College *A*
University of St. Francis *B*

Indiana

Ball State University *B*
Bethel College *B*
Earlham College *B*

Huntington University *B*
Indiana University-Purdue University
    Fort Wayne *B*
Indiana University-Purdue University
    Indianapolis *B*
Indiana Wesleyan University *B*
Manchester College *B*
Purdue University *B*
Purdue University
    Calumet *B*
Saint Joseph's College *B*
St. Mary-of-the-Woods College *B*
Trine University *B*
University of Evansville *B*
University of Notre Dame *B*
University of St. Francis *B*
Vincennes University *A*

Iowa

Clarke College *B*
Coe College *B*
Dordt College *B*
Ellsworth Community College *A*
Grand View University *B*
Iowa Central Community College *A*
Iowa State University *B*
Iowa Wesleyan College *B*
Maharishi University of
    Management *B*
Marshalltown Community College *A*
Mercy College of Health Sciences *B*
Simpson College *B*
University of Iowa *B*
Upper Iowa University *B*

Kansas

Barton County Community College *A*
Butler Community College *A*
Central Christian College of Kansas *A*
Coffeyville Community College *A*
Dodge City Community College *A*
McPherson College *B*
Pittsburg State University *B*
Pratt Community College *A*
Seward County Community College *A*
Tabor College *B*
Washburn University *B*

Kentucky

Campbellsville University *B*
Eastern Kentucky University *B*

Louisiana

Centenary College of Louisiana *B*
Dillard University *B*
Louisiana College *B*
Loyola University New Orleans *B*
Our Lady of the Lake College *B*
Xavier University of Louisiana *B*

Maine

University of Southern Maine *B*

Maryland

Frostburg State University *B*
Howard Community College *A*
Montgomery College *A*
Prince George's Community
    College *A*
Washington Adventist University *B*

Massachusetts

American International College *B*
Eastern Nazarene College *B*
Elms College *B*
Hampshire College *B*
Massachusetts College of Pharmacy
    and Health Sciences *B*
Simmons College *B*
Springfield Technical Community
    College *A*
University of Massachusetts
    Amherst *B*

Worcester Polytechnic Institute *B*

Michigan

Adrian College *B*
Alma College *B*
Calvin College *B*
Cornerstone University *B*
Delta College *A*
Eastern Michigan University *B*
Gogebic Community College *A*
Grand Rapids Community College *A*
Grand Valley State University *B*
Hillsdale College *B*
Kalamazoo College *B*
Kirtland Community College *A*
Lake Michigan College *A*
Madonna University *B*
Michigan State University *B*
Northern Michigan University *B*
Siena Heights University *B*
University of Detroit Mercy *B*
Washtenaw Community College *A*

Minnesota

College of St. Benedict *B*
Gustavus Adolphus College *B*
Hamline University *B*
Minnesota State University
 Mankato *B*
 Moorhead *B*
Minnesota West Community and
 Technical College *A*
St. Catherine University *B*
Saint Cloud State University *B*
St. John's University *B*
University of Minnesota
 Twin Cities *B*
Vermilion Community College *A*
Winona State University *B*

Mississippi

East Central Community College *A*
Holmes Community College *A*

Missouri

Drury University *B*
Evangel University *B*
Missouri Southern State University *B*
St. Louis Community College
 St. Louis Community College at
 Florissant Valley *A*
Three Rivers Community College *A*
University of Missouri
 Columbia *B*
 Kansas City *B*
 Missouri University of Science and
 Technology *B*
Washington University in St. Louis *B*

Montana

University of Great Falls *B*

Nebraska

Bellevue University *B*
College of Saint Mary *B*
Concordia University *B*
Northeast Community College *A*
University of Nebraska
 Lincoln *B*
 Omaha *B*
Western Nebraska Community
 College *A*
York College *A*

Nevada

Sierra Nevada College *B*

New Hampshire

New England College *B*
Rivier College *B*
Saint Anselm College *B*

New Jersey

Essex County College *A*
Rutgers, The State University of New
 Jersey
 Camden Regional Campus *B*
 New Brunswick/Piscataway
 Campus *B*
 Newark Regional Campus *B*
Sussex County Community College *A*

New Mexico

New Mexico Junior College *A*
San Juan College *A*

New York

Alfred University *B*
Bard College *B*
City University of New York
 City College *B*
Colgate University *B*
Columbia University
 School of General Studies *B*
Concordia College *B*
Cornell University *B*
D'Youville College *B*
Elmira College *B*
Fordham University *B*
Hobart and William Smith Colleges *B*
Hofstra University *B*
Houghton College *B*
Ithaca College *B*
Le Moyne College *B*
Manhattan College *B*
New York Institute of Technology *B*
Niagara University *B*
Paul Smith's College *B*
Rensselaer Polytechnic Institute *B*
Rochester Institute of Technology *B*
St. Joseph's College: Suffolk
 Campus *B*
St. Thomas Aquinas College *B*
State University of New York
 Albany *B*
 Binghamton *B*
 College at Brockport *B*
Sullivan County Community
 College *A*
Syracuse University *B*
Touro College *B*
Wagner College *B*
Wells College *B*
Yeshiva University *B*

North Carolina

Belmont Abbey College *B*
Brevard College *B*
Campbell University *B*
Carteret Community College *A*
Chowan University *B*
Elon University *B*
Gardner-Webb University *B*
Lees-McRae College *B*
Lenoir-Rhyne University *B*
Mars Hill College *B*
Methodist University *B*
Mitchell Community College *A*
North Carolina Wesleyan College *B*
Pfeiffer University *B*
Queens University of Charlotte *B*
St. Andrews Presbyterian College *B*
St. Augustine's College *B*
Sandhills Community College *A*
Warren Wilson College *B*
Wingate University *B*

North Dakota

Dakota College at Bottineau *A*
Dickinson State University *B*
Mayville State University *B*

Ohio

Baldwin-Wallace College *B*
Bluffton University *B*
Bowling Green State University *B*
Cedarville University *B*
Defiance College *B*
Heidelberg University *B*
John Carroll University *B*
Kent State University *B*
Kettering College of Medical Arts *B*
Muskingum University *B*
Oberlin College *B*
Ohio Northern University *B*
Ohio Wesleyan University *B*
Otterbein College *B*
Shawnee State University *B*
University of Cincinnati *B*
University of Cincinnati
 Clermont College *A*
 Raymond Walters College *A*
University of Dayton *B*
University of Rio Grande *B*
University of Toledo *A, B*
Urbana University *B*
Walsh University *B*
Wright State University *B*
Youngstown State University *B*

Oklahoma

Carl Albert State College *A*
Connors State College *A*
East Central University *B*
Eastern Oklahoma State College *A*
Northeastern Oklahoma Agricultural
 and Mechanical College *A*
Northern Oklahoma College *A*
Oklahoma Christian University *B*
Oklahoma City University *B*
Rose State College *A*

Oregon

Central Oregon Community
 College *A*
Chemeketa Community College *A*
Concordia University *B*
Corban College *B*
Eastern Oregon University *B*
Linn-Benton Community College *A*
Southern Oregon University *B*
Treasure Valley Community College *A*

Pennsylvania

Albright College *B*
Allegheny College *B*
Cabrini College *B*
Duquesne University *B*
Edinboro University of
 Pennsylvania *B*
Gannon University *B*
Gettysburg College *B*
Grove City College *B*
Gwynedd-Mercy College *B*
Immaculata University *B*
Juniata College *B*
Keystone College *B*
La Salle University *B*
Lehigh University *B*
Mansfield University of
 Pennsylvania *B*
Penn State
 Abington *B*
 Altoona *B*
 Beaver *B*
 Berks *B*
 Brandywine *B*
 DuBois *B*
 Erie, The Behrend College *B*
 Fayette, The Eberly Campus *B*
 Greater Allegheny *B*
 Hazleton *B*
 Lehigh Valley *B*
 Mont Alto *B*
 New Kensington *B*
 Schuylkill *B*
 Shenango *B*
 University Park *B*
 Wilkes-Barre *B*
 Worthington Scranton *B*
 York *B*
Philadelphia University *B*
Reading Area Community College *A*
St. Vincent College *B*
University of Pittsburgh
 Greensburg *B*
 Johnstown *B*
Villanova University *B*
Waynesburg University *B*
West Chester University of
 Pennsylvania *B*
Westminster College *B*
Widener University *B*

Puerto Rico

Caribbean University *B*
Pontifical Catholic University of
 Puerto Rico *B*
University of Puerto Rico
 Ponce *A*

Rhode Island

Rhode Island College *B*

South Carolina

Bob Jones University *B*
Clemson University *B*
College of Charleston *B*
Furman University *B*
Limestone College *B*
North Greenville University *B*
Southern Wesleyan University *B*

South Dakota

Augustana College *B*
Dakota Wesleyan University *B*

Tennessee

Bethel University *B*
Carson-Newman College *B*
Columbia State Community College *A*
Cumberland University *B*
Jackson State Community College *A*
Lincoln Memorial University *B*
Lipscomb University *B*
Maryville College *B*
Tennessee Technological University *B*
Tennessee Temple University *B*
Tennessee Wesleyan College *B*
Tusculum College *B*
University of Tennessee
 Knoxville *B*

Texas

Abilene Christian University *B*
Amarillo College *A*
Angelina College *A*
Austin Community College *A*
Baylor University *B*
Central Texas College *A*
Clarendon College *A*
Coastal Bend College *A*
El Paso Community College *A*
Galveston College *A*
Hardin-Simmons University *B*
Howard College *A*
Howard Payne University *B*
Jarvis Christian College *B*
Laredo Community College *A*
LeTourneau University *B*
Lon Morris College *A*
Lubbock Christian University *B*
Midland College *A*
Midwestern State University *B*
Navarro College *A*
Paris Junior College *A*
St. Philip's College *A*
South Plains College *A*
Texas A&M University
 Commerce *B*
Texas Christian University *B*
Texas Wesleyan University *B*

Trinity Valley Community College *A*
Tyler Junior College *A*
Weatherford College *A*
Western Texas College *A*

Utah
Snow College *A*
Southern Utah University *B*
University of Utah *B*
Utah State University *B*

Vermont
Bennington College *B*
Johnson State College *B*

Virginia
Averett University *B*
Eastern Mennonite University *B*
Jefferson College of Health
  Sciences *B*
Longwood University *B*
Mountain Empire Community
  College *A*
Virginia Intermont College *B*
Virginia Wesleyan College *B*

Washington
Everett Community College *A*
Northwest University *B*
Saint Martin's University *B*
South Seattle Community College *A*
Washington State University *B*

West Virginia
Concord University *B*
Potomac State College of West
  Virginia University *A*
University of Charleston *B*
West Virginia Wesleyan College *B*

Wisconsin
Carroll University *B*
Marquette University *B*
Mount Mary College *B*
Ripon College *B*
St. Norbert College *B*
University of Wisconsin
  Madison *M*
  Milwaukee *B*
  Oshkosh *B*
  Parkside *B*

Wyoming
Casper College *A*
Eastern Wyoming College *A*
Laramie County Community
  College *A*
Northwest College *A*
Western Wyoming Community
  College *A*

Preministerial studies

Arkansas
Ecclesia College *B*

California
Point Loma Nazarene University *B*
Trinity Life Bible College *C, A, B*

Florida
Southeastern University *B*
Trinity College of Florida *B*

Georgia
Wesleyan College *B*

Illinois
Elmhurst College *B*
Trinity International University *B*

Iowa
Simpson College *B*

Maryland
Washington Bible College *B*

Massachusetts
Eastern Nazarene College *B*

Michigan
Adrian College *B*
Alma College *B*
Hillsdale College *B*
Kuyper College *B*

Minnesota
Northwestern College *B*
St. John's University *B*
St. Mary's University of Minnesota *B*
University of St. Thomas *B, D*

Missouri
Calvary Bible College and Theological
  Seminary *B*

Nebraska
Concordia University *B*

New York
Houghton College *B*
Roberts Wesleyan College *B*
St. John's University *M*

Ohio
Ohio Wesleyan University *B*
University of Rio Grande *B*

Oregon
Corban College *B*
Warner Pacific College *B*

Pennsylvania
Baptist Bible College of
  Pennsylvania *B*
Gettysburg College *B*

Tennessee
Crichton College *C, A, B*
Lee University *B*
Tennessee Wesleyan College *B*

Texas
Abilene Christian University *B*
College of Biblical Studies-Houston *B*
Hardin-Simmons University *B*
Southern Methodist University *B*
Texas A&M University
  Commerce *B*
Texas Lutheran University *B*
University of Dallas *B*

Virginia
Bluefield College *B*
Eastern Mennonite University *A, B*
Liberty University *M*
Shenandoah University *C*

Wisconsin
Concordia University Wisconsin *B*

Prenursing

Alabama
Calhoun Community College *A*
Faulkner State Community College *A*
Faulkner University *B*
Gadsden State Community College *A*

Arkansas
Ouachita Baptist University *B*

California
California State University
  East Bay *B*
  Fresno *B*
  Fullerton *B*
  Sacramento *B, M*
College of the Siskiyous *A*
Fullerton College *A*
Southwestern College *A*
Westmont College *B*

Colorado
Adams State College *B*
Colorado Mountain College *A*

Delaware
Delaware State University *B*

District of Columbia
American University *B*

Florida
Broward College *A*
Jacksonville University *B*
Pensacola Junior College *A*

Georgia
Andrew College *A*
East Georgia College *A*
Emmanuel College *A*
Georgia Highlands College *A*
Georgia Military College *A*
Middle Georgia College *A*
Reinhardt College *A*
Young Harris College *A*

Idaho
College of Idaho *B*

Illinois
Concordia University Chicago *B*
Dominican University *B*
Eureka College *B*
Greenville College *B*
Kishwaukee College *A*
Lewis University *B*
Lewis and Clark Community
  College *A*
Trinity International University *A*
Triton College *A*

Indiana
Ancilla College *A*
Indiana University-Purdue University
  Indianapolis *B*
Manchester College *A*

Iowa
Marshalltown Community College *A*
University of Iowa *B*

Kansas
Barton County Community College *A*
Central Christian College of Kansas *A*
Coffeyville Community College *A*
Donnelly College *A*
Seward County Community College *A*
Tabor College *A*

Kentucky
Georgetown College *B*

Maryland
Carroll Community College *A*
Frederick Community College *A*
Frostburg State University *B*

Massachusetts
Cape Cod Community College *A*
Eastern Nazarene College *B*
Roxbury Community College *A*

Michigan
Bay de Noc Community College *A*
Delta College *A*
Gogebic Community College *A*
Hillsdale College *B*
Kuyper College *B*
Lake Michigan College *A*
Madonna University *B*
Southwestern Michigan College *A*

Minnesota
Fond du Lac Tribal and Community
  College *A*
Itasca Community College *A*
Minnesota West Community and
  Technical College *A*
Walden University *M*

Missouri
Drury University *B*
University of Missouri
  Kansas City *B*

Montana
Blackfeet Community College *A*
Miles Community College *A*

Nebraska
Concordia University *B*
Northeast Community College *A*
Western Nebraska Community
  College *A*

Nevada
Sierra Nevada College *B*

New Hampshire
Manchester Community College *A*

New Mexico
New Mexico State University
  Carlsbad *A*

New York
City University of New York
  Kingsborough Community
  College *A*
St. Joseph's College *B*
St. Thomas Aquinas College *B*
State University of New York
  College of Agriculture and
  Technology at Morrisville *A*

North Carolina
Brevard College *B*
Carteret Community College *A*
Chowan University *B*
Methodist University *B*
Sandhills Community College *A*
Southeastern Community College *A*

North Dakota
Cankdeska Cikana Community
  College *A*
Dakota College at Bottineau *A*
Mayville State University *B*

Ohio
Edison State Community College *A*
Heidelberg University *B*
Notre Dame College *B*
University of Cincinnati
  Clermont College *A*
University of Findlay *B*
Ursuline College *B*

Oklahoma
Eastern Oklahoma State College *A*
Northeastern Oklahoma Agricultural
  and Mechanical College *A*
Oklahoma Christian University *B*

Rose State College *A*

Oregon

Chemeketa Community College *A*
Corban College *B*
Linn-Benton Community College *A*

Pennsylvania

Allegheny College *B*
Juniata College *B*
Keystone College *A*
Manor College *A*
Mount Aloysius College *A*
Widener University *B*

South Carolina

Furman University *B*
Limestone College *B*

Tennessee

Jackson State Community College *A*
Lipscomb University *B*
Maryville College *B*
Tennessee Wesleyan College *B*

Texas

Baylor University *B*
Del Mar College *A*
Lon Morris College *A*
Lubbock Christian University *B*
McMurry University *B*
St. Philip's College *A*
South Plains College *A*
Trinity Valley Community College *A*
Tyler Junior College *A*
Weatherford College *A*
Western Texas College *A*

Utah

Snow College *A*
University of Utah *B*

Vermont

Lyndon State College *B*

Virginia

Jefferson College of Health
  Sciences *B*

Washington

Skagit Valley College *A*
South Seattle Community College *A*
Spokane Falls Community College *A*

West Virginia

West Virginia University *B*

Wisconsin

College of Menominee Nation *A*
Ripon College *B*
St. Norbert College *B*

Wyoming

Eastern Wyoming College *A*
Western Wyoming Community
  College *A*

Preoperative/surgical nursing

California

El Camino College: Compton
  Center *A*
Loma Linda University *M*
National University *B, M*
Sonoma State University *M*

Connecticut

Sacred Heart University *B*

Delaware

Wilmington University *B*

Georgia

Medical College of Georgia *B, M*

Illinois

Lewis University *M*
Saint Xavier University *M*
Southern Illinois University
  Edwardsville *M*

Indiana

Purdue University
  Calumet *B*

Kansas

Kansas Wesleyan University *B*
Tabor College *B*

Kentucky

Eastern Kentucky University *B, M*

Maine

Eastern Maine Community College *A*
Husson University *M*
University of Maine *M*
University of Southern Maine *B*

Massachusetts

Elms College *B*

Michigan

University of Michigan *M*

Minnesota

Bemidji State University *B*
Minnesota State University
  Mankato *B, M*
Winona State University *B, M*

Missouri

Missouri State University *B*

Nebraska

Clarkson College *B*

New Hampshire

Rivier College *B, M*

New York

College of Mount St. Vincent *B*
D'Youville College *B, M*
Roberts Wesleyan College *B*

North Carolina

Queens University of Charlotte *B*

Ohio

Case Western Reserve University *M*
Kent State University
  Ashtabula *A*
Ursuline College *B*

Oregon

Eastern Oregon University *B*
Southern Oregon University *B*

Pennsylvania

La Salle University *M*
Mansfield University of
  Pennsylvania *B*
Mount Aloysius College *A*
Thomas Jefferson University: College
  of Health Professions *B, M*
University of Pennsylvania *M*

Puerto Rico

Pontifical Catholic University of
  Puerto Rico *M*

Texas

South Plains College *A*
Texas A&M International University *B*
University of Texas
  Health Science Center at
    Houston *M, D*
  Health Science Center at San
    Antonio *M, D*

Washington

Gonzaga University *B, M*

Prepharmacy

Alabama

Calhoun Community College *A*
Faulkner State Community College *A*
Faulkner University *B*
Gadsden State Community College *A*

Arizona

Eastern Arizona College *A*

Arkansas

Harding University *B*
Ouachita Baptist University *B*
University of the Ozarks *B*

California

Bakersfield College *A*
California Lutheran University *B*
California State University
  Chico *B*
Chabot College *A*
College of the Siskiyous *A*
Cypress College *A*
El Camino College *A*
Foothill College *A*
Golden West College *A*
Monterey Peninsula College *A*
Notre Dame de Namur University *B*
Westmont College *B*
Whittier College *B*

Colorado

Adams State College *B*
Lamar Community College *A*
Otero Junior College *A*

Connecticut

Sacred Heart University *B*
Southern Connecticut State
  University *B*
University of Connecticut *B*

Delaware

University of Delaware *B*

District of Columbia

American University *B*

Florida

Barry University *B*
Broward College *A*
Florida State University *B*
Gulf Coast Community College *A*
Indian River State College *A*
Miami Dade College *A*
Northwest Florida State College *A*
Pensacola Junior College *A*
University of Central Florida *B*

Georgia

Abraham Baldwin Agricultural
  College *A*
Andrew College *A*
Dalton State College *A*
Darton College *A*
Emmanuel College *A*
Georgia Highlands College *A*
Georgia Perimeter College *A*

Georgia Southern University *B*
Gordon College *A*
Macon State College *A*
Mercer University *B*
Middle Georgia College *A*
Oglethorpe University *B*
Young Harris College *A*

Idaho

Brigham Young University-Idaho *B*
North Idaho College *A*
Northwest Nazarene University *B*

Illinois

Black Hawk College: East Campus *A*
City Colleges of Chicago
  Harold Washington College *A*
  Kennedy-King College *A*
Dominican University *B*
Elmhurst College *B*
Illinois Central College *A*
John A. Logan College *A*
Kankakee Community College *A*
Kishwaukee College *A*
Lake Land College *A*
Lewis University *B*
Lewis and Clark Community
  College *A*
Millikin University *B*
Saint Xavier University *B*
Southwestern Illinois College *A*
Triton College *A*
University of St. Francis *B*

Indiana

Indiana University-Purdue University
  Indianapolis *B*
Indiana Wesleyan University *B*
Manchester College *B*
Purdue University
  Calumet *B*
St. Mary-of-the-Woods College *B*
University of St. Francis *B*
Vincennes University *A*

Iowa

Clarke College *B*
Dordt College *B*
Ellsworth Community College *A*
Grand View University *B*
Iowa Central Community College *A*
Iowa Wesleyan College *B*
Marshalltown Community College *A*
Simpson College *B*
University of Iowa *B*
Upper Iowa University *B*

Kansas

Barton County Community College *A*
Coffeyville Community College *A*
Dodge City Community College *A*
McPherson College *B*
Pittsburg State University *B*
Pratt Community College *A*
Seward County Community College *A*
Tabor College *B*
Washburn University *B*

Kentucky

Campbellsville University *B*
Eastern Kentucky University *B*
Georgetown College *B*

Louisiana

Centenary College of Louisiana *B*
Louisiana College *B*
Xavier University of Louisiana *B*

Maine

Husson University *B*

Maryland

Allegany College of Maryland *A*
Frederick Community College *A*
Frostburg State University *B*
Howard Community College *A*
Montgomery College *A*
Prince George's Community
    College *A*
Washington Adventist University *B*

Massachusetts

Eastern Nazarene College *B*
Simmons College *B*
Western New England College *B*

Michigan

Adrian College *B*
Calvin College *B*
Delta College *A*
Eastern Michigan University *B*
Ferris State University *A*
Gogebic Community College *A*
Grand Rapids Community College *A*
Grand Valley State University *B*
Henry Ford Community College *A*
Hillsdale College *B*
Kirtland Community College *A*
Lake Michigan College *A*
Madonna University *A, B*
Mid Michigan Community College *A*
Northern Michigan University *B*
Siena Heights University *A, B*
West Shore Community College *A*

Minnesota

College of St. Benedict *B*
Minnesota State University
    Mankato *B*
    Moorhead *B*
Minnesota West Community and
    Technical College *A*
St. Catherine University *B*
Saint Cloud State University *B*
St. John's University *B*
University of Minnesota
    Twin Cities *B*
Winona State University *B*

Mississippi

East Central Community College *A*
Holmes Community College *A*
Mississippi Delta Community
    College *A*
Mississippi Gulf Coast Community
    College *A*

Missouri

Drury University *B*
Missouri Southern State University *B*
St. Louis Community College
    St. Louis Community College at
        Florissant Valley *A*
Three Rivers Community College *A*
University of Missouri
    Columbia *B*
    Kansas City *B*
Washington University in St. Louis *B*

Nebraska

College of Saint Mary *B*
Concordia University *B*
Northeast Community College *A*
University of Nebraska
    Lincoln *B*
Western Nebraska Community
    College *A*

Nevada

Sierra Nevada College *B*

New Jersey

Sussex County Community College *A*

New Mexico

New Mexico Junior College *A*

New York

City University of New York
    City College *B*
D'Youville College *B*
Fordham University *B*
Houghton College *B*
Le Moyne College *B*
Long Island University
    C. W. Post Campus *B*
Rochester Institute of Technology *B*
St. Thomas Aquinas College *B*
State University of New York
    Albany *B*
Sullivan County Community
    College *A*
Touro College *B*

North Carolina

Belmont Abbey College *B*
Campbell University *B*
Carteret Community College *A*
Chowan University *B*
Gardner-Webb University *B*
Livingstone College *B*
Mars Hill College *B*
Methodist University *B*
Mitchell Community College *A*
Queens University of Charlotte *B*
Sandhills Community College *A*
Wingate University *B*

North Dakota

Dakota College at Bottineau *A*
Dickinson State University *A*
Mayville State University *B*

Ohio

Baldwin-Wallace College *B*
Muskingum University *B*
Otterbein College *B*
Shawnee State University *B*
University of Cincinnati *B*
University of Cincinnati
    Clermont College *A*
    Raymond Walters College *A*
Wright State University *B*
Youngstown State University *B*

Oklahoma

Carl Albert State College *A*
Connors State College *A*
East Central University *B*
Eastern Oklahoma State College *A*
Northeastern Oklahoma Agricultural
    and Mechanical College *A*
Northern Oklahoma College *A*
Oklahoma Christian University *B*
Oklahoma City University *B*
Rose State College *A*

Oregon

Central Oregon Community
    College *A*
Chemeketa Community College *A*
Corban College *B*
Eastern Oregon University *B*
Linn-Benton Community College *A*
Southern Oregon University *B*

Pennsylvania

Allegheny College *B*
Gettysburg College *B*
Juniata College *B*
Keystone College *B*
Luzerne County Community
    College *A*
Mansfield University of
    Pennsylvania *B*
Reading Area Community College *A*

St. Vincent College *B*
University of Pittsburgh
    Greensburg *B*
Westminster College *B*

South Carolina

Clemson University *B*
Furman University *B*
Limestone College *B*
North Greenville University *B*

South Dakota

Augustana College *B*
Dakota Wesleyan University *B*

Tennessee

Bethel University *B*
Carson-Newman College *B*
Columbia State Community College *A*
Cumberland University *B*
Lincoln Memorial University *B*
Lipscomb University *B*
Maryville College *B*
Tennessee Technological University *B*
Tennessee Wesleyan College *B*
Tusculum College *B*
University of Tennessee
    Knoxville *B*

Texas

Abilene Christian University *B*
Amarillo College *A*
Angelina College *A*
Austin Community College *A*
Clarendon College *A*
Coastal Bend College *A*
El Paso Community College *A*
Laredo Community College *A*
LeTourneau University *B*
Lon Morris College *A*
Lubbock Christian University *B*
Midland College *A*
Midwestern State University *B*
Navarro College *A*
Paris Junior College *A*
South Plains College *A*
Texas A&M University
    Commerce *B*
Texas Southern University *B*
Trinity Valley Community College *A*
Tyler Junior College *A*
University of Houston *B*
Weatherford College *A*
Western Texas College *A*

Utah

Snow College *A*
Southern Utah University *B*
University of Utah *B*

Virginia

Emory & Henry College *B*
Jefferson College of Health
    Sciences *B*
Longwood University *B*
Mountain Empire Community
    College *A*
Virginia Wesleyan College *B*

Washington

Everett Community College *A*
Saint Martin's University *B*
South Seattle Community College *A*

West Virginia

Concord University *B*
Potomac State College of West
    Virginia University *A*
University of Charleston *A, B*
West Virginia University *B*
West Virginia Wesleyan College *B*

Wisconsin

Carroll University *B*
Ripon College *B*
St. Norbert College *B*
University of Wisconsin
    Milwaukee *B*
    Oshkosh *B*

Wyoming

Casper College *A*
Eastern Wyoming College *A*
Laramie County Community
    College *A*
Northwest College *A*
Western Wyoming Community
    College *A*

Prephysical therapy

Arkansas

Ouachita Baptist University *B*

Connecticut

Sacred Heart University *B*

Georgia

Gordon College *A*

Illinois

University of St. Francis *B*

Iowa

Iowa Wesleyan College *B*
Simpson College *B*

Kansas

Pittsburg State University *B*

Kentucky

Asbury College *B*

Michigan

Calvin College *B*
Northern Michigan University *B*

Minnesota

St. Mary's University of Minnesota *B*
University of St. Thomas *B*

Missouri

Drury University *B*

North Carolina

Gardner-Webb University *B*

Ohio

Baldwin-Wallace College *B*

Pennsylvania

Keystone College *B*

South Dakota

Augustana College *B*

Tennessee

Tennessee Wesleyan College *B*

Utah

Southern Utah University *B*
University of Utah *B*

Preveterinary

Alabama

Calhoun Community College *A*
Faulkner State Community College *A*
Faulkner University *B*
Gadsden State Community College *A*

Arizona

Central Arizona College *A*
Northern Arizona University *B*
University of Arizona *B*

Arkansas

Harding University *B*
Ouachita Baptist University *B*
University of the Ozarks *B*

California

Bakersfield College *A*
California Lutheran University *B*
California State University
  Chico *B*
Chabot College *A*
Chapman University *B*
College of the Siskiyous *A*
Cypress College *A*
Foothill College *A*
Golden West College *A*
Los Angeles Pierce College *A*
MiraCosta College *A*
Monterey Peninsula College *A*
Mount St. Mary's College *B*
Notre Dame de Namur University *B*
Westmont College *B*
Whittier College *B*

Colorado

Adams State College *B*
Lamar Community College *A*
Otero Junior College *A*
Regis University *B*

Connecticut

Quinnipiac University *B*
Sacred Heart University *B*
Southern Connecticut State
  University *B*

Delaware

Delaware State University *B*
University of Delaware *B*

District of Columbia

American University *B*

Florida

Barry University *B*
Broward College *A*
Florida Southern College *B*
Florida State University *B*
Gulf Coast Community College *A*
Indian River State College *A*
Jacksonville University *B*
Miami Dade College *A*
Northwest Florida State College *A*
Pensacola Junior College *A*
Saint Thomas University *B*
University of Central Florida *B*
University of Miami *B*

Georgia

Andrew College *A*
Darton College *A*
Georgia Highlands College *A*
Georgia Southern University *B*
Macon State College *A*
Middle Georgia College *A*
Oglethorpe University *B*
Young Harris College *A*

Idaho

Boise State University *B*
Brigham Young University-Idaho *B*
North Idaho College *A*
Northwest Nazarene University *B*

Illinois

Dominican University *B*
Elmhurst College *B*
Eureka College *B*
Greenville College *B*
Illinois Central College *A*
Kankakee Community College *A*
Kishwaukee College *A*
Lake Land College *A*
Lewis University *B*
MacMurray College *B*
Millikin University *B*
Southwestern Illinois College *A*
Triton College *A*
University of Illinois
  Urbana-Champaign *B*
University of St. Francis *B*

Indiana

Indiana University-Purdue University
  Fort Wayne *B*
Indiana University-Purdue University
  Indianapolis *B*
Indiana Wesleyan University *B*
Manchester College *B*
Purdue University
  Calumet *B*
Saint Joseph's College *B*
St. Mary-of-the-Woods College *B*
University of Evansville *B*
Vincennes University *A*

Iowa

Clarke College *B*
Coe College *B*
Dordt College *B*
Ellsworth Community College *A*
Iowa Central Community College *A*
Iowa State University *B*
Iowa Wesleyan College *B*
Marshalltown Community College *A*
Simpson College *B*
University of Iowa *B*
Upper Iowa University *B*

Kansas

Barton County Community College *A*
Central Christian College of
  Kansas *A, B*
Coffeyville Community College *A*
Dodge City Community College *A*
Kansas State University *B*
McPherson College *B*
Pittsburg State University *B*
Pratt Community College *A*
Seward County Community College *A*
Tabor College *B*
Washburn University *B*

Kentucky

Campbellsville University *B*
Georgetown College *B*

Louisiana

Centenary College of Louisiana *B*
Louisiana College *B*
Loyola University New Orleans *B*
Xavier University of Louisiana *B*

Maine

University of Southern Maine *B*

Maryland

Frostburg State University *B*
Howard Community College *A*
University of Maryland
  College Park *B*
Washington Adventist University *B*

Massachusetts

American International College *B*
Becker College *B*
Eastern Nazarene College *B*
Elms College *B*
Massachusetts College of Pharmacy
  and Health Sciences *B*
University of Massachusetts
  Amherst *B*
Worcester Polytechnic Institute *B*

Michigan

Adrian College *B*
Alma College *B*
Calvin College *B*
Cornerstone University *B*
Delta College *A*
Eastern Michigan University *B*
Gogebic Community College *A*
Grand Rapids Community College *A*
Grand Valley State University *B*
Hillsdale College *B*
Kalamazoo College *B*
Kirtland Community College *A*
Lake Michigan College *A*
Madonna University *B*
Northern Michigan University *B*
Siena Heights University *A*

Minnesota

College of St. Benedict *B*
Gustavus Adolphus College *B*
Hamline University *B*
Minnesota State University
  Mankato *B*
  Moorhead *B*
Minnesota West Community and
  Technical College *A*
St. Catherine University *B*
Saint Cloud State University *B*
St. John's University *B*
University of Minnesota
  Twin Cities *B*
University of St. Thomas *B*
Vermilion Community College *A*
Winona State University *B*

Mississippi

East Central Community College *A*
Holmes Community College *A*
Mississippi Delta Community
  College *A*

Missouri

Drury University *B*
Evangel University *B*
Missouri Southern State University *B*
Northwest Missouri State
  University *B*
Three Rivers Community College *A*
University of Missouri
  Columbia *B*
Washington University in St. Louis *B*

Montana

University of Great Falls *B*

Nebraska

College of Saint Mary *B*
Concordia University *B*
Northeast Community College *A*
University of Nebraska
  Lincoln *B*
Western Nebraska Community
  College *A*
York College *B*

Nevada

University of Nevada
  Reno *B*

New Hampshire

Rivier College *B*

New York

Alfred University *B*
City University of New York
  City College *B*
Colgate University *B*
D'Youville College *B*
Elmira College *B*
Fordham University *B*
Hobart and William Smith Colleges *B*
Hofstra University *B*
Houghton College *B*
Ithaca College *B*
Le Moyne College *B*
Manhattan College *B*
Niagara University *B*
Paul Smith's College *B*
Rochester Institute of Technology *B*
St. Joseph's College: Suffolk
  Campus *B*
St. Thomas Aquinas College *B*
State University of New York
  Albany *B*
  Binghamton *B*
  College at Brockport *B*
Sullivan County Community
  College *A*
Syracuse University *B*
Touro College *B*
Wells College *B*

North Carolina

Belmont Abbey College *B*
Brevard College *B*
Campbell University *B*
Carteret Community College *A*
Chowan University *B*
Gardner-Webb University *B*
Lees-McRae College *B*
Mars Hill College *B*
Methodist University *B*
Mitchell Community College *A*
Pfeiffer University *B*
Queens University of Charlotte *B*
St. Andrews Presbyterian College *B*
Sandhills Community College *A*
Warren Wilson College *B*
Wingate University *B*

North Dakota

Dakota College at Bottineau *A*
Dickinson State University *B*
Mayville State University *B*
North Dakota State University *B*

Ohio

Baldwin-Wallace College *B*
Cedarville University *B*
Defiance College *B*
Heidelberg University *B*
John Carroll University *B*
Kent State University *B*
Muskingum University *B*
Oberlin College *B*
Ohio Northern University *B*
Ohio Wesleyan University *B*
Otterbein College *B*
Shawnee State University *B*
University of Cincinnati *B*
University of Cincinnati
  Clermont College *A*
  Raymond Walters College *A*
University of Findlay *B*
University of Toledo *B*
Walsh University *B*
Wright State University *B*
Youngstown State University *B*

Oklahoma

Carl Albert State College *A*
Connors State College *A*
East Central University *B*
Eastern Oklahoma State College *A*
Langston University *B*
Murray State College *A*

Northeastern Oklahoma Agricultural
and Mechanical College A
Oklahoma Christian University B
Oklahoma City University B

Oregon

Corban College B
Eastern Oregon University B
Linn-Benton Community College A
Southern Oregon University B
Treasure Valley Community College A

Pennsylvania

Albright College B
Allegheny College B
Edinboro University of
Pennsylvania B
Gettysburg College B
Grove City College B
Gwynedd-Mercy College B
Juniata College B
Keystone College B
La Salle University B
Manor College A
Mansfield University of
Pennsylvania B
St. Vincent College B
University of Pittsburgh
Greensburg B
Johnstown B
Waynesburg University B
Westminster College B
Widener University B

Rhode Island

Rhode Island College B

South Carolina

Bob Jones University B
Clemson University B
Furman University B
Limestone College B

South Dakota

Augustana College B
Dakota Wesleyan University B

Tennessee

Cumberland University B
Lincoln Memorial University B
Lipscomb University B
Maryville College B
Tennessee Technological University B
Tennessee Wesleyan College B
University of Tennessee
Knoxville B

Texas

Abilene Christian University B
Amarillo College A
Angelina College A
Austin Community College A
Clarendon College A
Coastal Bend College A
El Paso Community College A
Galveston College A
Laredo Community College A
LeTourneau University B
Lon Morris College A
Lubbock Christian University B
Midwestern State University B
Navarro College A
Paris Junior College A
South Plains College A
Sul Ross State University A
Texas A&M University B
Texas A&M University
Commerce B
Trinity Valley Community College A
Tyler Junior College A
Western Texas College A

Utah

Snow College A
Southern Utah University B
Utah State University B, M

Virginia

Eastern Mennonite University B
Emory & Henry College B
Longwood University B
Mountain Empire Community
College A
Virginia Intermont College B
Virginia Wesleyan College B

Washington

Everett Community College A
Saint Martin's University B

West Virginia

Concord University B
Potomac State College of West
Virginia University A
University of Charleston B
West Virginia Wesleyan College B

Wisconsin

Carroll University B
Mount Mary College B
Ripon College B
St. Norbert College B
University of Wisconsin
Milwaukee B
Oshkosh B
Parkside B

Wyoming

Casper College A
Eastern Wyoming College A
Laramie County Community
College A
Northwest College A
Western Wyoming Community
College A

Printing management

Kansas

Pittsburg State University M

Kentucky

Murray State University B
Somerset Community College C, A

Maryland

Montgomery College C

Michigan

Ferris State University B

New Jersey

Kean University B, M

New York

Rochester Institute of
Technology B, M

Ohio

Cincinnati State Technical and
Community College C

Wisconsin

Carroll University B
University of Wisconsin
Stout B

Printing press operator

California

City College of San Francisco C

Georgia

Albany Technical College C

Illinois

City Colleges of Chicago
Kennedy-King College A

Minnesota

Dunwoody College of
Technology C, A
Hennepin Technical College A

Pennsylvania

Commonwealth Technical Institute C

Printmaking

Arizona

Northern Arizona University B

Arkansas

Phillips Community College of the
University of Arkansas C, A

California

Academy of Art University C, A, B, M
California College of the Arts B, M
California State University
East Bay B
Long Beach B, M
Northridge B, M
City College of San Francisco C, A
College of the Desert A
De Anza College C, A
Fresno City College C, A
Long Beach City College A
Monterey Peninsula College C, A
Ohlone College C
Palomar College A
Pasadena City College C, A
San Francisco Art Institute B, M
Santa Rosa Junior College C

Colorado

Adams State College B

Connecticut

Capital Community College C
University of Hartford B

District of Columbia

American University M
Corcoran College of Art and Design C
George Washington University M

Florida

Ringling College of Art and Design B
University of Miami B

Georgia

Savannah College of Art and
Design B, M

Idaho

Northwest Nazarene University B

Illinois

Bradley University B
School of the Art Institute of
Chicago B, M

Indiana

Indiana University-Purdue University
Fort Wayne B
Indiana University-Purdue University
Indianapolis B
Indiana Wesleyan University B

Iowa

Drake University B

University of Iowa B, M

Kansas

University of Kansas B, M

Kentucky

Eastern Kentucky University B

Maine

Maine College of Art B

Maryland

Maryland Institute College of Art B

Massachusetts

Art Institute of Boston at Lesley
University B
Bard College at Simon's Rock B
Massachusetts College of Art and
Design B, M
Montserrat College of Art B
Salem State College B
School of the Museum of Fine
Arts B, M
University of Massachusetts
Dartmouth M

Michigan

Andrews University B
College for Creative Studies B
Grand Valley State University B
Kendall College of Art and Design of
Ferris State University B, M
Northern Michigan University A, B
University of Michigan B
University of Michigan
Flint B

Minnesota

College of Visual Arts B
Minneapolis College of Art and
Design B
Saint Cloud State University B

Missouri

Columbia College B
Kansas City Art Institute B
Washington University in St.
Louis B, M

Nevada

Sierra Nevada College B

New York

Daemen College B
Rochester Institute of
Technology A, B, M
State University of New York
College at Buffalo B
College at Fredonia B
New Paltz B, M
Purchase B, M

North Carolina

East Carolina University B
Gardner-Webb University B
Methodist University B

Ohio

Art Academy of Cincinnati B
Bowling Green State University B
Cleveland Institute of Art B
Ohio State University
Columbus Campus B, M
Ohio University B, M
University of Akron B
Youngstown State University B

Oregon

Mt. Hood Community College A
Pacific Northwest College of Art B

Portland State University *B*
University of Oregon *B, M*

Pennsylvania
Arcadia University *B*
Edinboro University of
Pennsylvania *B*
Keystone College *A, B*
Lycoming College *B*
Marywood University *M*
Seton Hill University *B*
Temple University *B, M*
University of the Arts *B, M*

Puerto Rico
Escuela de Artes Plasticas de Puerto
Rico *B*
Inter American University of Puerto
Rico
San German Campus *M*

Rhode Island
Rhode Island School of Design *B, M*

Tennessee
Memphis College of Art *B, M*

Texas
Texas A&M University
Commerce *B*
Texas Christian University *B, M*
University of Dallas *B, M*
University of Houston *B, M*
University of Texas
El Paso *B, M*

Vermont
Bennington College *B*

Washington
Cornish College of the Arts *B*
University of Washington *B, M*
Western Washington University *B*

West Virginia
West Virginia State University *B*

Wisconsin
University of Wisconsin
Madison *B*

Psychiatric nursing

Georgia
Georgia State University *M*

Illinois
Southern Illinois University
Edwardsville *M*

Indiana
Indiana University-Purdue University
Indianapolis *M*

Iowa
Allen College *M*
University of Iowa *M*

Louisiana
Louisiana State University Health
Sciences Center *M*

Maine
Husson University *M*
University of Southern Maine *B, M*

Massachusetts
Northeastern University *M*

Michigan
University of Michigan *M*
Wayne State University *M*

Minnesota
College of St. Scholastica *M*

New Hampshire
Rivier College *M*

New York
City University of New York
Hunter College *B, M*
State University of New York
Buffalo *M*
Stony Brook *M*
Upstate Medical University *M*
University of Rochester *M*

Ohio
Case Western Reserve University *M*
University of Toledo *M, T*

Oregon
Oregon Health & Science
University *M*

Pennsylvania
University of Pennsylvania *M*

Puerto Rico
Pontifical Catholic University of
Puerto Rico *M*

Tennessee
University of Tennessee
Knoxville *M*
University of Tennessee Health
Science Center *D*

Psychoanalysis

California
California Institute of Integral
Studies *M*

Vermont
Goddard College *M*

Psychobiology/ physiological psychology

California
Holy Names University *B*
La Sierra University *B*
University of California
Los Angeles *B*

District of Columbia
American University *D*

Florida
Florida Atlantic University *B, D*
Florida State University *D*

Georgia
Emory University *D*

Indiana
Earlham College *B*

Maine
University of New England *B*

Massachusetts
Simmons College *B*
Wheaton College *B*

Missouri
Northwest Missouri State
University *B*

New York
State University of New York
Albany *D*
Binghamton *B, D*
Buffalo *D*
Stony Brook *D*

Pennsylvania
Arcadia University *M*
Carnegie Mellon University *B*
Lebanon Valley College *B*
Lincoln University *B*
Swarthmore College *B*
Temple University *D*
Wilson College *B*

Tennessee
Southern Adventist University *M*

Texas
Baylor University *D*
University of Houston *M, D*
University of Texas
Dallas *M, D*
Tyler *M*

Virginia
Averett University *B*

Psychology

Alabama
Alabama Agricultural and Mechanical
University *B*
Alabama State University *B*
Athens State University *B*
Auburn University *B, M, D*
Auburn University at
Montgomery *B, M*
Birmingham-Southern College *B*
Columbia Southern University *B*
Faulkner University *B*
Gadsden State Community College *A*
Huntingdon College *B*
Jacksonville State University *B, M*
Judson College *B*
Oakwood University *B*
Samford University *B*
South University: Montgomery *B*
Spring Hill College *B*
Talladega College *B*
Troy University *B*
Tuskegee University *B*
University of Alabama *B, M, D*
University of Alabama
Birmingham *B, M, D*
Huntsville *B, M*
University of Mobile *B*
University of Montevallo *B*
University of North Alabama *B*
University of South Alabama *B, M*
University of West Alabama *B*

Alaska
Alaska Pacific University *B*
University of Alaska
Anchorage *B*
Fairbanks *B*

Arizona
Argosy University: Online *B*
Argosy University: Phoenix *B*
Arizona State University *B, D*
Central Arizona College *A*
Cochise College *A*
Coconino County Community
College *A*
Dine College *A*

Eastern Arizona College *A*
Estrella Mountain Community
College *A*
Grand Canyon University *B*
Mesa Community College *A*
Northcentral University *B, M, D*
Northern Arizona University *B, M*
Prescott College *B, M*
University of Arizona *B, M, D*
University of Phoenix *A, M*

Arkansas
Arkansas State University *B*
Arkansas Tech University *B, M*
Harding University *B*
Henderson State University *B*
Hendrix College *B*
John Brown University *B*
Lyon College *B*
Ouachita Baptist University *B*
Philander Smith College *B*
Phillips Community College of the
University of Arkansas *A*
Southern Arkansas University *B*
University of Arkansas *B, M, D*
University of Arkansas
Fort Smith *B*
Little Rock *B*
Monticello *B*
Pine Bluff *B*
University of Central Arkansas *B*
University of the Ozarks *B*
Williams Baptist College *B*

California
Allan Hancock College *A*
Alliant International
University *B, M, D*
American Jewish University *M*
Antioch Southern California
Antioch University Los Angeles *M*
Antioch University Santa Barbara *M*
Argosy University: Inland Empire *B*
Argosy University: Los Angeles *B*
Argosy University: Orange County *B*
Argosy University: San Diego *B*
Argosy University: San Francisco Bay
Area *B*
Azusa Pacific University *B*
Bakersfield College *A*
Bethany University *B*
Biola University *B, M, D*
Cabrillo College *A*
California Baptist University *B*
California Coast University *A, B, M*
California Institute of Integral
Studies *M, D*
California Lutheran University *B*
California Polytechnic State
University: San Luis Obispo *B, M*
California State Polytechnic
University: Pomona *B, M*
California State University
Bakersfield *B, M*
Chico *B, M*
Dominguez Hills *B*
East Bay *B*
Fresno *B, M*
Fullerton *B, M*
Long Beach *B, M*
Los Angeles *B, M*
Monterey Bay *B*
Northridge *B*
Sacramento *B, M*
San Bernardino *B, M*
San Marcos *B, M*
Stanislaus *B, M*
California State University: Channel
Islands *B*
Canada College *A*
Cerritos College *A*
Chabot College *A*
Chaffey College *A*
Chapman University *B*

Citrus College *A*
Claremont McKenna College *B*
College of Alameda *A*
College of Marin: Kentfield *A*
College of the Canyons *A*
College of the Desert *A*
College of the Siskiyous *A*
Concordia University *B*
Contra Costa College *A*
Copper Mountain College *A*
Crafton Hills College *C, A*
Cypress College *A*
De Anza College *A*
Diablo Valley College *A*
Dominican University of California *B*
East Los Angeles College *A*
El Camino College *A*
El Camino College: Compton
    Center *A*
Folsom Lake College *A*
Foothill College *A*
Fresno City College *A*
Fresno Pacific University *B*
Fullerton College *A*
Gavilan College *A*
Glendale Community College *A*
Golden West College *A*
Hartnell College *A*
Holy Names University *B*
Hope International University *B*
Humboldt State University *B, M*
Imperial Valley College *A*
Irvine Valley College *A*
John F. Kennedy University *B, D*
La Sierra University *B*
Lake Tahoe Community College *A*
Loma Linda University *M, D*
Los Angeles City College *A*
Los Angeles Harbor College *A*
Los Angeles Mission College *A*
Los Angeles Southwest College *A*
Los Angeles Valley College *A*
Los Medanos College *A*
Loyola Marymount University *B*
Mendocino College *A*
Merced College *A*
Mills College *B*
MiraCosta College *A*
Monterey Peninsula College *A*
Mount St. Mary's College *B*
National University *B*
Notre Dame de Namur University *B*
Occidental College *B*
Orange Coast College *A*
Oxnard College *A*
Pacific Union College *B*
Pasadena City College *A*
Patten University *B*
Pepperdine University *B, M, D*
Pitzer College *B*
Point Loma Nazarene University *B*
Pomona College *B*
Remington College
    San Diego *B, M*
Saddleback College *A*
St. Mary's College of California *B*
San Bernardino Valley College *A*
San Diego Christian College *B*
San Diego City College *A*
San Diego Mesa College *A*
San Diego Miramar College *A*
San Diego State University *B, M*
San Francisco State University *B, M*
San Joaquin Delta College *A*
San Jose City College *A*
San Jose State University *B, M*
Santa Ana College *A*
Santa Barbara City College *A*
Santa Clara University *B*
Santa Rosa Junior College *A*
Santiago Canyon College *A*
Scripps College *B*
Sierra College *A*
Simpson University *B, M*

Skyline College *A*
Solano Community College *A*
Sonoma State University *B, M*
Southwestern College *A*
Stanford University *B, M, D*
University of California
    Berkeley *B, D*
    Davis *B, D*
    Irvine *B, M, D*
    Los Angeles *B, M, D*
    Riverside *B, M, D*
    San Diego *B, M, D*
    Santa Barbara *B, M, D*
    Santa Cruz *B, D*
University of California: Merced *B*
University of La Verne *B*
University of Redlands *B*
University of San Diego *B*
University of San Francisco *B*
University of Southern
    California *B, M, D*
University of the Pacific *B, M*
University of the West *B, M*
Vanguard University of Southern
    California *B*
West Hills College: Coalinga *A*
West Hills College: Lemoore *A*
West Los Angeles College *A*
West Valley College *A*
Westmont College *B*
Whittier College *B*
William Jessup University *B*
Woodbury University *B*

Colorado

Adams State College *B*
Argosy University: Denver *B*
Colorado Christian University *B*
Colorado College *B*
Colorado Mountain College *C*
Colorado State University *B, M, D*
Colorado State University
    Pueblo *B*
Fort Lewis College *B*
Lamar Community College *A*
Mesa State College *B*
Metropolitan State College of
    Denver *B*
Naropa University *B, M*
Otero Junior College *A*
Regis University *B*
Trinidad State Junior College *A*
University of Colorado
    Boulder *B, D*
    Colorado Springs *B, M, D*
    Denver *B, M*
University of Denver *B, M, D*
University of Northern Colorado *B, M*
Western State College of Colorado *B*

Connecticut

Albertus Magnus College *B*
Central Connecticut State
    University *B, M*
Connecticut College *B, M*
Eastern Connecticut State
    University *B*
Fairfield University *B*
Mitchell College *B*
Naugatuck Valley Community
    College *A*
Post University *B*
Quinnipiac University *B*
Sacred Heart University *B*
Saint Joseph College *B*
Southern Connecticut State
    University *B, M*
Trinity College *B*
University of Bridgeport *B*
University of Connecticut *B, M, D*
University of Hartford *B, M*
University of New Haven *B*
Wesleyan University *B, M*

Western Connecticut State
    University *B*
Yale University *B, M, D*

Delaware

Delaware State University *B*
Goldey-Beacom College *B*
University of Delaware *B, M, D*
Wesley College *B*
Wilmington University *B*

District of Columbia

American University *B, M*
Catholic University of America *B, M*
Gallaudet University *B*
George Washington
    University *B, M, D*
Georgetown University *B, D*
Howard University *B, M, D*
Trinity Washington University *B*
University of the District of
    Columbia *B*

Florida

Argosy University: Sarasota *B*
Argosy University: Tampa *B*
Barry University *B, M*
Bethune-Cookman University *B*
Broward College *A*
Carlos Albizu University *B, M, D*
Clearwater Christian College *B*
Daytona State College *A*
Eckerd College *B*
Edward Waters College *B*
Flagler College *B*
Florida Agricultural and Mechanical
    University *B*
Florida Atlantic University *B, M*
Florida Gulf Coast University *B*
Florida Institute of Technology *B*
Florida International
    University *B, M, D*
Florida Memorial University *B*
Florida Southern College *B*
Florida State University *B, M*
Gulf Coast Community College *A*
Indian River State College *A*
Jacksonville University *B*
Lynn University *B*
Miami Dade College *A*
New College of Florida *B*
Nova Southeastern University *B*
Palm Beach Atlantic University *B*
Palm Beach Community College *A*
Pensacola Junior College *A*
Rollins College *B*
Saint Leo University *B*
Saint Thomas University *B*
South University: Tampa *B*
South University: West Palm Beach *B*
Southeastern University *B*
State College of Florida,
    Manatee-Sarasota *A*
Stetson University *B*
University of Central Florida *B, M, D*
University of Florida *B, M, D*
University of Miami *B, M, D*
University of North Florida *B, M*
University of South Florida *B, M, D*
University of Tampa *A, B*
University of West Florida *B, M*
Warner University *A, B*

Georgia

Abraham Baldwin Agricultural
    College *A*
Agnes Scott College *B*
Albany State University *B*
Andrew College *A*
Argosy University: Atlanta *B*
Armstrong Atlantic State University *B*
Ashworth College *A*
Atlanta Christian College *B*

Atlanta Metropolitan College *A*
Augusta State University *B, M*
Bainbridge College *A*
Berry College *B*
Brenau University *B*
Brewton-Parker College *B*
Clark Atlanta University *B*
College of Coastal Georgia *A*
Columbus State University *B*
Covenant College *B*
Dalton State College *A*
Darton College *A*
East Georgia College *A*
Emmanuel College *B*
Emory University *B, D*
Fort Valley State University *B*
Gainesville State College *A*
Georgia College and State
    University *B*
Georgia Gwinnett College *B*
Georgia Highlands College *A*
Georgia Military College *A*
Georgia Perimeter College *A*
Georgia Southern University *B, M*
Georgia Southwestern State
    University *B*
Georgia State University *B, M, D*
Gordon College *A*
Kennesaw State University *B*
LaGrange College *B*
Macon State College *A*
Mercer University *B*
Middle Georgia College *A*
Morehouse College *B*
North Georgia College & State
    University *B*
Oglethorpe University *B*
Paine College *B*
Piedmont College *B*
Reinhardt College *B*
Shorter College *B*
South Georgia College *A*
South University: Savannah *B*
Southern Polytechnic State
    University *B*
Spelman College *B*
Toccoa Falls College *B*
University of Georgia *B, M, D*
University of West Georgia *B, M*
Valdosta State University *B, M*
Waycross College *A*
Wesleyan College *B*
Young Harris College *A*

Hawaii

Argosy University: Hawaii *B*
Chaminade University of Honolulu *B*
Hawaii Pacific University *B*
University of Hawaii
    Hilo *B*
    Manoa *B, M, D*
    West Oahu *B*

Idaho

Boise State University *B*
Brigham Young University-Idaho *B*
College of Idaho *B*
Idaho State University *B, M*
Lewis-Clark State College *B*
North Idaho College *A*
Northwest Nazarene University *B*
University of Idaho *B, M*

Illinois

Argosy University: Chicago *B*
Argosy University: Schaumburg *B*
Augustana College *B, T*
Aurora University *B*
Benedictine University *B*
Black Hawk College: East Campus *A*
Blackburn College *B*
Bradley University *B, T*
Chicago State University *B*

City Colleges of Chicago
   Kennedy-King College *A*
Concordia University Chicago *B, M*
Danville Area Community College *A*
DePaul University *B, M*
Dominican University *B*
Eastern Illinois University *B*
Elmhurst College *B, T*
Eureka College *B*
Governors State University *B, M*
Greenville College *B*
Hebrew Theological College *B*
Illinois College *B*
Illinois Institute of
   Technology *B, M, D*
Illinois State University *B, M*
Illinois Valley Community College *A*
Illinois Wesleyan University *B*
John A. Logan College *A*
John Wood Community College *A*
Joliet Junior College *A*
Judson University *B*
Kankakee Community College *A*
Kendall College *B*
Kishwaukee College *A*
Knox College *B*
Lake Forest College *B*
Lake Land College *A*
Lewis University *B, T*
Lincoln Christian University *B*
Lincoln College *A*
Loyola University Chicago *B*
MacMurray College *B*
McKendree University *B*
Millikin University *B*
Monmouth College *B*
National-Louis University *B, M*
North Central College *B*
North Park University *B*
Northeastern Illinois University *B*
Northern Illinois University *B, M, D*
Northwestern University *B, M, D*
Olivet Nazarene University *B, M*
Quincy University *B*
Richland Community College *A*
Rockford College *B*
Roosevelt University *B*
Saint Xavier University *B*
South Suburban College of Cook
   County *A*
Southern Illinois University
   Carbondale *B, M, D*
Southern Illinois University
   Edwardsville *B, M*
Southwestern Illinois College *A*
Trinity Christian College *B*
Trinity International University *B, M*
Triton College *A*
University of Chicago *B, D*
University of Illinois
   Chicago *B, M, D*
   Springfield *B*
   Urbana-Champaign *B, M, D*
University of St. Francis *B*
Western Illinois University *B, M*
Wheaton College *B, M*

Indiana

Anderson University *B*
Ball State University *B, M, T*
Bethel College *B*
Butler University *B*
Calumet College of St. Joseph *B*
DePauw University *B*
Earlham College *B*
Franklin College *B*
Goshen College *B*
Grace College *B*
Hanover College *B*
Holy Cross College *B*
Huntington University *B*
Indiana Institute of Technology *B*
Indiana State University *B, M*

Indiana University
   Bloomington *B, M, D*
   East *B*
   Kokomo *B*
   Northwest *B*
   South Bend *B, M*
   Southeast *B*
Indiana University-Purdue University
   Fort Wayne *A, B*
Indiana University-Purdue University
   Indianapolis *B, M*
Indiana Wesleyan University *B, T*
Manchester College *B*
Marian University *B, T*
Oakland City University *B*
Purdue University *B, M, D*
Purdue University
   Calumet *B*
Saint Joseph's College *B*
Saint Mary's College *B*
St. Mary-of-the-Woods College *B*
Taylor University *B*
Trine University *B*
University of Evansville *B*
University of Indianapolis *B*
University of Notre Dame *B, M, D*
University of St. Francis *B, M*
University of Southern Indiana *B*
Valparaiso University *B, M*
Vincennes University *A*
Wabash College *B*

Iowa

Briar Cliff University *B*
Buena Vista University *B*
Central College *B*
Clarke College *B, T*
Coe College *B*
Cornell College *B, T*
Dordt College *B*
Drake University *B*
Ellsworth Community College *A*
Graceland University *B, T*
Grand View University *B*
Grinnell College *B*
Iowa State University *B, M, D*
Iowa Wesleyan College *B*
Iowa Western Community College *A*
Kaplan University
   Davenport *B*
Loras College *B*
Luther College *B*
Marshalltown Community College *A*
Morningside College *B*
Mount Mercy College *B*
Northwestern College *B, T*
St. Ambrose University *B, T*
Simpson College *B*
University of Dubuque *B*
University of Iowa *B, D, T*
University of Northern Iowa *B, M*
Upper Iowa University *B*
Waldorf College *B*
Wartburg College *B, T*
William Penn University *B*

Kansas

Baker University *B, T*
Barclay College *B*
Barton County Community College *A*
Benedictine College *B*
Bethany College *B, T*
Bethel College *B*
Butler Community College *A*
Central Christian College of
   Kansas *A, B*
Coffeyville Community College *A*
Cowley County Community
   College *A*
Donnelly College *A*
Emporia State University *B, M, T*
Fort Hays State University *B, M*
Fort Scott Community College *A*
Friends University *B*

Garden City Community College *A*
Highland Community College *A*
Hutchinson Community College *A*
Kansas State University *B, M, D*
Kansas Wesleyan University *B*
Labette Community College *A*
McPherson College *B, T*
MidAmerica Nazarene University *B, T*
Neosho County Community
   College *A*
Newman University *B*
Ottawa University *B*
Pittsburg State University *B, M*
Pratt Community College *A*
Seward County Community College *A*
Southwestern College *B*
Sterling College *B*
Tabor College *B*
University of Kansas *B, M, D*
University of St. Mary *B, M*
Washburn University *B*
Wichita State University *B, M, D*

Kentucky

Asbury College *B*
Bellarmine University *B*
Berea College *B*
Bluegrass Community and Technical
   College *A*
Brescia University *B*
Campbellsville University *B*
Centre College *B*
Eastern Kentucky University *B, M*
Georgetown College *B*
Kentucky State University *B*
Kentucky Wesleyan College *B*
Lindsey Wilson College *B*
Mid-Continent University *B*
Midway College *B*
Morehead State University *B, M*
Murray State University *B, M*
Northern Kentucky University *B*
Pikeville College *B*
St. Catharine College *B*
Spalding University *B*
Thomas More College *A, B*
Transylvania University *B*
Union College *B, M*
University of Kentucky *B*
University of Louisville *B, M*
University of the Cumberlands *B*
Western Kentucky University *B, M*

Louisiana

Centenary College of Louisiana *B, T*
Dillard University *B*
Grambling State University *B*
Louisiana College *B*
Louisiana State University
   Alexandria *B*
   Shreveport *B*
Louisiana State University and
   Agricultural and Mechanical
   College *B, M, D*
Louisiana Tech University *B*
Loyola University New Orleans *B*
McNeese State University *B, M*
Nicholls State University *B*
Northwestern State University *B*
Our Lady of the Lake College *B*
Southeastern Louisiana
   University *B, M*
Southern University
   New Orleans *B*
Southern University and Agricultural
   and Mechanical College *B*
Tulane University *B, M, D*
University of Louisiana at
   Lafayette *B, M*
University of Louisiana at
   Monroe *B, M*
University of New Orleans *B, M*
Xavier University of Louisiana *B*

Maine

Bates College *B*
Bowdoin College *B*
Colby College *B*
Husson University *B*
Saint Joseph's College of Maine *B*
Thomas College *B*
University of Maine *B, M, D*
University of Maine
   Farmington *B*
   Fort Kent *B*
   Machias *B*
   Presque Isle *B*
University of New England *B*
University of Southern Maine *B*

Maryland

Allegany College of Maryland *A*
Bowie State University *B*
Carroll Community College *A*
Chesapeake College *A*
College of Notre Dame of Maryland *B*
Coppin State University *B*
Frederick Community College *A*
Frostburg State University *B*
Garrett College *A*
Goucher College *B*
Harford Community College *A*
Hood College *B*
Howard Community College *A*
Johns Hopkins University *B, M, D*
Loyola University Maryland *B, M*
McDaniel College *B*
Morgan State University *B*
Mount St. Mary's University *B*
Prince George's Community
   College *A*
St. Mary's College of Maryland *B*
Salisbury University *B*
Stevenson University *B*
Towson University *B, M*
University of Baltimore *B, M, D*
University of Maryland
   Baltimore County *B, M*
   College Park *B, M, D*
   University College *B*
Washington Adventist University *B*
Washington College *B, M, T*

Massachusetts

American International College *B*
Amherst College *B*
Anna Maria College *B*
Assumption College *B*
Atlantic Union College *B*
Bard College at Simon's Rock *B*
Bay Path College *B*
Becker College *B*
Boston College *B, M, D*
Boston University *B, M, D*
Brandeis University *B, M, D*
Bridgewater State College *B, M*
Bunker Hill Community College *A*
Cambridge College *B*
Cape Cod Community College *A*
Clark University *B, M, D*
College of the Holy Cross *B*
Curry College *B*
Dean College *A*
Eastern Nazarene College *B*
Elms College *B*
Emmanuel College *B*
Endicott College *B*
Fisher College *A*
Fitchburg State College *B*
Framingham State College *B*
Gordon College *B*
Hampshire College *B*
Harvard College *B, M, D*
Hellenic College/Holy Cross *B*
Lasell College *B*
Massachusetts College of Liberal
   Arts *B*
Merrimack College *B*

Mount Holyoke College *B, M*
Mount Ida College *B*
Newbury College *B*
Nichols College *B, T*
Northeastern University *B, M, D*
Pine Manor College *B*
Regis College *B*
Salem State College *B*
Simmons College *B*
Smith College *B*
Springfield College *B*
Stonehill College *B*
Suffolk University *B*
Tufts University *B, M, D*
University of Massachusetts
  Amherst *B, M, D*
  Boston *B*
  Dartmouth *B, M*
  Lowell *B*
Wellesley College *B*
Western New England College *B, D*
Westfield State College *B, M*
Wheaton College *B*
Williams College *B*
Worcester State College *B*

Michigan

Adrian College *A, B, T*
Albion College *B, T*
Alma College *B, T*
Andrews University *B, M, D*
Aquinas College *B, T*
Calvin College *B, T*
Central Michigan University *B, M*
Cornerstone University *B*
Delta College *A*
Eastern Michigan University *B, M*
Ferris State University *A, B*
Finlandia University *B*
Gogebic Community College *A*
Grand Rapids Community College *A*
Grand Valley State University *B, T*
Hillsdale College *B*
Hope College *B*
Kalamazoo College *B*
Lake Michigan College *A*
Lake Superior State University *B*
Lansing Community College *A*
Lawrence Technological University *B*
Madonna University *B*
Marygrove College *B*
Michigan State University *B, M, D*
Michigan Technological University *B*
Mid Michigan Community College *A*
Northern Michigan University *B*
Oakland University *B*
Rochester College *B*
Saginaw Valley State University *B*
Siena Heights University *A, B*
Spring Arbor University *B*
University of Detroit Mercy *B, M*
University of Michigan *B, M, D*
University of Michigan
  Dearborn *B*
  Flint *B*
Wayne State University *B, M, D*
Western Michigan
  University *B, M, D, T*

Minnesota

Argosy University: Twin Cities *B*
Augsburg College *B*
Bemidji State University *B, M*
Bethany Lutheran College *B*
Bethel University *B*
Capella University *M, D*
Carleton College *B*
College of St. Benedict *B*
College of St. Scholastica *B*
Concordia College: Moorhead *B*
Concordia University: St. Paul *B*
Crown College *A, B*
Gustavus Adolphus College *B*
Hamline University *B*

Itasca Community College *A*
Macalester College *B*
Metropolitan State University *B, M*
Minnesota State University
  Mankato *B, M*
  Moorhead *B*
Minnesota West Community and
  Technical College *A*
North Central University *A, B*
Northland Community & Technical
  College *A*
Northwestern College *B*
Oak Hills Christian College *B*
Ridgewater College *A*
St. Catherine University *B*
Saint Cloud State University *B*
St. John's University *B*
St. Mary's University of Minnesota *B*
St. Olaf College *B*
Southwest Minnesota State
  University *B*
University of Minnesota
  Duluth *B*
  Morris *B*
  Twin Cities *B, M, D*
University of St. Thomas *B*
Vermilion Community College *A*
Walden University *B, M, D*
Winona State University *B*

Mississippi

Alcorn State University *B*
Belhaven University *B*
Blue Mountain College *B*
Delta State University *B*
East Central Community College *A*
Hinds Community College *A*
Jackson State University *B*
Millsaps College *B*
Mississippi College *B*
Mississippi Delta Community
  College *A*
Mississippi Gulf Coast Community
  College *A*
Mississippi State University *B, M*
Mississippi University for Women *B*
Tougaloo College *B*
University of Mississippi *B, M, D*
University of Southern
  Mississippi *B, M, D*

Missouri

Avila University *B*
Central Methodist University *B*
College of the Ozarks *B*
Columbia College *B*
Crowder College *A*
Culver-Stockton College *B*
Drury University *B*
Evangel University *B, M*
Fontbonne University *B*
Hannibal-LaGrange College *B*
Lincoln University *B*
Lindenwood University *B*
Maryville University of Saint Louis *B*
Missouri Baptist University *B*
Missouri Southern State University *B*
Missouri State University *B, M*
Missouri Valley College *B*
Missouri Western State University *B*
Northwest Missouri State
  University *B*
Park University *B*
Rockhurst University *B*
St. Charles Community College *A*
St. Louis Community College
  St. Louis Community College at
    Florissant Valley *A*
Saint Louis University *B*
Southeast Missouri State University *B*
Southwest Baptist University *B*
Stephens College *B*
Three Rivers Community College *A*
Truman State University *B*

University of Central Missouri *B, M*
University of Missouri
  Columbia *B, M, D*
  Kansas City *B, M, D*
  Missouri University of Science and
    Technology *B, T*
  St. Louis *B, M, D*
Washington University in St.
  Louis *B, M, D*
Webster University *B*
Westminster College *B*
William Jewell College *B*
William Woods University *B*

Montana

Blackfeet Community College *A*
Little Big Horn College *A*
Miles Community College *A*
Montana State University
  Billings *A, B, M, T*
  Bozeman *B, M*
Rocky Mountain College *B, T*
Salish Kootenai College *A*
University of Great Falls *B*
University of Montana *B, M, D*
University of Montana: Western *B*

Nebraska

Bellevue University *B*
Chadron State College *B*
College of Saint Mary *B*
Concordia University *B*
Creighton University *B*
Dana College *B*
Doane College *B*
Grace University *B*
Nebraska Wesleyan University *B*
Northeast Community College *A*
Peru State College *B, T*
Union College *B*
University of Nebraska
  Kearney *B, T*
  Lincoln *B, M, D*
  Omaha *B, M*
Wayne State College *B*
Western Nebraska Community
  College *A*
York College *B*

Nevada

College of Southern Nevada *A*
Great Basin College *A*
Nevada State College *B*
Sierra Nevada College *B*
University of Nevada
  Las Vegas *B, M, D*
  Reno *B, M, D*

New Hampshire

Colby-Sawyer College *B*
Daniel Webster College *B*
Dartmouth College *B, M, D*
Franklin Pierce University *B*
Keene State College *B*
New England College *B*
Plymouth State University *B*
Rivier College *B*
Saint Anselm College *B*
Southern New Hampshire
  University *B*
University of New Hampshire *B, M, D*
University of New Hampshire at
  Manchester *B*

New Jersey

Bergen Community College *A*
Bloomfield College *C, B*
Caldwell College *B*
Centenary College *B*
The College of New Jersey *B*
College of St. Elizabeth *B*
Drew University *B*

Fairleigh Dickinson University
  College at Florham *B, M*
  Metropolitan Campus *B, M*
Felician College *B*
Georgian Court University *B*
Gloucester County College *A*
Hudson County Community
  College *A*
Kean University *B, M*
Monmouth University *B*
Montclair State University *B, M, T*
New Jersey City University *B, M*
Passaic County Community College *A*
Princeton University *B, M, D*
Ramapo College of New Jersey *B*
Richard Stockton College of New
  Jersey *B*
Rider University *B*
Rowan University *B*
Rutgers, The State University of New
  Jersey
  Camden Regional Campus *B*
  New Brunswick/Piscataway
    Campus *B, M, D*
  Newark Regional Campus *B, D*
Saint Peter's College *B*
Salem Community College *A*
Seton Hall University *B, M, T*
Sussex County Community College *A*
Thomas Edison State College *B*
William Paterson University of New
  Jersey *B*

New Mexico

Clovis Community College *A*
Eastern New Mexico
  University *A, B, M*
New Mexico Highlands
  University *B, M*
New Mexico Institute of Mining and
  Technology *B*
New Mexico Junior College *A*
New Mexico State University *B, M, D*
Santa Fe Community College *A*
University of New Mexico *B, M, D*
University of the Southwest *B*
Western New Mexico University *B*

New York

Adelphi University *B, M*
Alfred University *B*
Bard College *B*
Barnard College *B*
Canisius College *B*
Cazenovia College *B*
City University of New York
  Baruch College *B*
  Brooklyn College *B*
  City College *B, M*
  College of Staten Island *B*
  Hunter College *B, M*
  John Jay College of Criminal
    Justice *B, M*
  Lehman College *B*
  Medgar Evers College *B*
  Queens College *B, M*
  Queensborough Community
    College *A*
  York College *B*
Clarkson University *B*
Colgate University *B*
College of Mount St. Vincent *A, B*
College of New Rochelle *B*
College of Saint Rose *B*
Columbia University *B*
Columbia University
  School of General Studies *B*
Concordia College *B*
Cornell University *B, M, D*
D'Youville College *B*
Daemen College *B*
Dominican College of Blauvelt *B*
Dowling College *B*
Elmira College *B*

Eugene Lang College The New School
for Liberal Arts *B*
Excelsior College *B*
Fordham University *B, M, D*
Hamilton College *B*
Hartwick College *B*
Hilbert College *B*
Hobart and William Smith Colleges *B*
Hofstra University *B*
Houghton College *B*
Iona College *B, M*
Ithaca College *B*
Keuka College *B*
Le Moyne College *B*
Long Island University
Brooklyn Campus *B, M*
C. W. Post Campus *B, M*
Manhattan College *B*
Manhattanville College *B*
Marist College *B, M*
Marymount Manhattan College *B*
Medaille College *B, M*
Mercy College *B, M*
Molloy College *B*
Mount Saint Mary College *B, T*
Nazareth College *B*
New York Institute of Technology *B*
New York University *B, M*
Niagara University *B*
Nyack College *B*
Pace University *B, M*
Rensselaer Polytechnic Institute *B*
Roberts Wesleyan College *B*
Rochester Institute of Technology *B*
Russell Sage College *B*
Sage College of Albany *B*
Saint Bonaventure University *B*
St. Francis College *B*
St. John Fisher College *B*
St. John's University *B, M*
St. Joseph's College *B*
St. Joseph's College: Suffolk
Campus *B*
St. Lawrence University *B*
St. Thomas Aquinas College *B*
Siena College *B*
Skidmore College *B*
State University of New York
Albany *B, D*
Binghamton *B, M*
Buffalo *B, M*
College at Brockport *B, M*
College at Buffalo *B*
College at Cortland *B*
College at Fredonia *B*
College at Geneseo *B, T*
College at Old Westbury *B*
College at Oneonta *B*
College at Plattsburgh *B*
College at Potsdam *B*
College of Agriculture and
Technology at Morrisville *A*
Empire State College *A, B*
Institute of Technology at
Utica/Rome *B*
New Paltz *B, M*
Oswego *B*
Purchase *B*
Stony Brook *B, M*
Suffolk County Community College *A*
Sullivan County Community
College *A*
Syracuse University *B, M*
Touro College *B*
Union College *B*
United States Military Academy *B*
University of Rochester *B, M*
Utica College *B*
Vassar College *B*
Wagner College *B*
Wells College *B*
Yeshiva University *B, M, D*

North Carolina

Appalachian State University *B, M*
Barton College *B*
Belmont Abbey College *B*
Bennett College for Women *B*
Brevard College *B*
Campbell University *B*
Carteret Community College *A*
Catawba College *B*
Chowan University *B*
Davidson College *B*
Duke University *B*
East Carolina University *B, M*
Elizabeth City State University *B*
Elon University *B*
Fayetteville State University *B, M*
Gardner-Webb University *B*
Greensboro College *B*
Guilford College *B*
High Point University *B*
Johnson C. Smith University *B*
Lees-McRae College *B*
Lenoir Community College *A*
Lenoir-Rhyne University *B*
Livingstone College *B*
Mars Hill College *B*
Meredith College *B*
Methodist University *A, B*
Montreat College *B*
Mount Olive College *B*
North Carolina Agricultural and
Technical State University *B*
North Carolina Central
University *B, M*
North Carolina State
University *B, M, D*
North Carolina Wesleyan College *B*
Peace College *B*
Pfeiffer University *B*
Queens University of Charlotte *B*
St. Andrews Presbyterian College *B*
St. Augustine's College *B*
Salem College *B*
Sandhills Community College *A*
Shaw University *B*
Southeastern Community College *A*
University of North Carolina
Asheville *B, T*
Chapel Hill *B, M, D*
Charlotte *B*
Greensboro *B, M, D*
Pembroke *B*
Wilmington *B, M*
Wake Forest University *B, M*
Warren Wilson College *B*
Western Carolina University *B, M*
Wingate University *B*
Winston-Salem State University *B*

North Dakota

Dakota College at Bottineau *A*
Dickinson State University *B*
Jamestown College *B*
Mayville State University *B*
Minot State University *B, T*
North Dakota State University *B, M, D*
University of Mary *B*
University of North Dakota *B, M, D*

Ohio

Antioch University McGregor *M*
Ashland University *B*
Baldwin-Wallace College *B*
Bluffton University *B*
Bowling Green State
University *B, M, D*
Capital University *B*
Case Western Reserve
University *B, M, D*
Cedarville University *B*
Central State University *B*
Cincinnati Christian University *A, B*
Cleveland State University *B, M*
College of Mount St. Joseph *B*

College of Wooster *B*
Defiance College *B*
Denison University *B*
Eastern Gateway Community
College *A*
Franciscan University of
Steubenville *B*
Heidelberg University *B, M*
Hiram College *B, T*
John Carroll University *B*
Kent State University *B*
Kenyon College *B*
Lourdes College *B*
Malone University *B*
Marietta College *B, M*
Miami University
Oxford Campus *B, M, D*
Mount Union College *B*
Mount Vernon Nazarene University *B*
Muskingum University *B*
Notre Dame College *B*
Oberlin College *B*
Ohio Christian University *A, B*
Ohio Dominican University *B*
Ohio Northern University *B*
Ohio State University
Columbus Campus *B, M, D*
Lima Campus *B*
Mansfield Campus *B*
Marion Campus *B*
Newark Campus *B*
Ohio University *B*
Ohio Wesleyan University *B*
Otterbein College *B*
Owens Community College
Toledo *A*
Shawnee State University *B*
Tiffin University *B*
Union Institute & University *B, M*
University of Akron *B, M*
University of Cincinnati *B, M, D*
University of Cincinnati
Clermont College *A*
University of Dayton *B, M*
University of Findlay *B*
University of Rio Grande *A, B*
University of Toledo *B, M, D*
Urbana University *B*
Ursuline College *B*
Walsh University *B*
Wilberforce University *B*
Wilmington College *B*
Wittenberg University *B*
Wright State University *A, B*
Wright State University: Lake
Campus *A*
Xavier University *A, B, M*
Youngstown State University *B*

Oklahoma

Cameron University *B, M*
Carl Albert State College *A*
Connors State College *A*
East Central University *B*
Eastern Oklahoma State College *A*
Hillsdale Free Will Baptist College *B*
Langston University *B*
Northeastern Oklahoma Agricultural
and Mechanical College *A*
Northeastern State University *B*
Northwestern Oklahoma State
University *B*
Oklahoma Baptist University *B*
Oklahoma Christian University *B*
Oklahoma City Community College *A*
Oklahoma City University *B*
Oklahoma Panhandle State
University *B*
Oklahoma State University *B, M, D*
Oklahoma Wesleyan University *B*
Oral Roberts University *B*
Redlands Community College *A*
Rose State College *A*
St. Gregory's University *B*

Southeastern Oklahoma State
University *B*
Southern Nazarene University *B*
Southwestern Oklahoma State
University *B, M*
Tulsa Community College *A*
University of Central Oklahoma *B*
University of Oklahoma *B, M, D*
University of Science and Arts of
Oklahoma *B*
University of Tulsa *B*
Western Oklahoma State College *A*

Oregon

Central Oregon Community
College *A*
Chemeketa Community College *A*
Concordia University *B*
Corban College *B*
Eastern Oregon University *B, T*
George Fox University *B*
Lewis & Clark College *B*
Linfield College *B, T*
Linn-Benton Community College *A*
Marylhurst University *B*
Mt. Hood Community College *A*
Multnomah University *B*
Northwest Christian University *B*
Oregon Institute of Technology *B*
Oregon State University *B*
Pacific University *B, M, D*
Portland State University *B, M, D*
Reed College *B*
Southern Oregon University *B, M*
Treasure Valley Community College *A*
University of Oregon *B, M, D*
University of Portland *B*
Warner Pacific College *A, B*
Western Oregon University *B*
Willamette University *B*

Pennsylvania

Albright College *B*
Allegheny College *B*
Alvernia University *B*
Arcadia University *B*
Bloomsburg University of
Pennsylvania *B*
Bryn Mawr College *B*
Bucknell University *B, M*
Bucks County Community College *A*
Butler County Community College *A*
Cabrini College *B*
California University of
Pennsylvania *B*
Carlow University *B*
Carnegie Mellon University *B, D*
Cedar Crest College *B*
Chatham University *B*
Chestnut Hill College *A, B*
Cheyney University of Pennsylvania *B*
Clarion University of Pennsylvania *B*
Community College of Allegheny
County *A*
DeSales University *B*
Dickinson College *B*
Drexel University *B, M*
Duquesne University *B*
East Stroudsburg University of
Pennsylvania *B*
Eastern University *B*
Edinboro University of
Pennsylvania *B*
Elizabethtown College *B*
Franklin & Marshall College *B*
Gannon University *B*
Geneva College *B*
Gettysburg College *B*
Grove City College *B*
Gwynedd-Mercy College *B*
Harcum College *A*
Harrisburg Area Community
College *A*
Haverford College *B*

Holy Family University *B*
Immaculata University *B*
Indiana University of Pennsylvania *B*
Juniata College *B*
Keystone College *B*
King's College *B*
Kutztown University of
  Pennsylvania *B*
La Roche College *B*
La Salle University *B, M, D*
Lafayette College *B*
Lebanon Valley College *B*
Lehigh Carbon Community College *A*
Lehigh University *B, M, D*
Lincoln University *B*
Lock Haven University of
  Pennsylvania *B*
Lycoming College *B*
Manor College *A*
Mansfield University of
  Pennsylvania *B*
Marywood University *B, M*
Mercyhurst College *B*
Messiah College *B*
Millersville University of
  Pennsylvania *B, M*
Misericordia University *B*
Moravian College *B*
Mount Aloysius College *B, M*
Muhlenberg College *A, B*
Neumann University *B*
Penn State
  Abington *B*
  Altoona *C, B*
  Beaver *B*
  Berks *B*
  Brandywine *B*
  DuBois *B*
  Erie, The Behrend College *B*
  Fayette, The Eberly Campus *B*
  Greater Allegheny *B*
  Harrisburg *B, M*
  Hazleton *B*
  Lehigh Valley *B*
  Mont Alto *B*
  New Kensington *B*
  Schuylkill *B*
  Shenango *B*
  University Park *B, M, D*
  Wilkes-Barre *B*
  Worthington Scranton *B*
  York *B*
Philadelphia University *B*
Point Park University *B*
Reading Area Community College *A*
Robert Morris University *B*
Rosemont College *B*
St. Francis University *B*
Saint Joseph's University *B, M*
St. Vincent College *B*
Seton Hill University *B*
Shippensburg University of
  Pennsylvania *B, M*
Slippery Rock University of
  Pennsylvania *B*
Susquehanna University *B*
Swarthmore College *B*
Temple University *B, M, D*
Thiel College *B*
University of Pennsylvania *A, B, M, D*
University of Pittsburgh *B, M, D*
University of Pittsburgh
  Bradford *B*
  Greensburg *B*
  Johnstown *B*
University of Scranton *B*
University of the Sciences in
  Philadelphia *B*
Ursinus College *B*
Villanova University *B, M*
Washington & Jefferson College *B*
Waynesburg University *B*
West Chester University of
  Pennsylvania *B, M*

Westminster College *B*
Widener University *B*
Wilkes University *B*
Wilson College *B*
York College of Pennsylvania *B*

Puerto Rico

Bayamon Central University *B, M*
Inter American University of Puerto
  Rico
  Bayamon Campus *B*
  Metropolitan Campus *B, M*
  San German Campus *B*
Pontifical Catholic University of
  Puerto Rico *B*
Universidad Adventista de las
  Antillas *B*
Universidad Metropolitana *B*
Universidad del Este *B*
University of Puerto Rico
  Aguadilla *A*
  Cayey University College *B*
  Ponce *B*
  Rio Piedras *B, M, D*
University of the Sacred Heart *B*

Rhode Island

Brown University *B, M, D*
Bryant University *B*
Providence College *B*
Rhode Island College *B, M*
Roger Williams University *B*
Salve Regina University *B, M*
University of Rhode Island *B*

South Carolina

Anderson University *B*
Charleston Southern University *B*
The Citadel *B, M*
Clemson University *B*
Coastal Carolina University *B*
Coker College *B*
College of Charleston *B*
Columbia College *B*
Columbia International University *B*
Converse College *B*
Erskine College *B*
Francis Marion University *B*
Furman University *B*
Lander University *B*
Limestone College *B*
Newberry College *B*
North Greenville University *B*
Presbyterian College *B*
South Carolina State University *B*
South University: Columbia *B*
Southern Wesleyan University *B*
University of South Carolina
  Aiken *B*
  Beaufort *B*
  Upstate *B*
Winthrop University *B*
Wofford College *B, T*

South Dakota

Augustana College *B*
Black Hills State University *B*
Dakota Wesleyan University *B*
Kilian Community College *A*
Mount Marty College *B*
Northern State University *B*
South Dakota State University *B*
University of Sioux Falls *B*
University of South Dakota *B, M, D*

Tennessee

Argosy University: Nashville *B*
Austin Peay State University *B, M*
Belmont University *B, T*
Bethel University *B*
Bryan College *B, T*
Carson-Newman College *B*
Christian Brothers University *B*

Columbia State Community College *A*
Crichton College *B*
Cumberland University *B*
Dyersburg State Community
  College *A*
East Tennessee State
  University *B, M, D, T*
Fisk University *B, M*
Free Will Baptist Bible College *B*
Freed-Hardeman University *B*
Jackson State Community College *A*
King College *B*
Lambuth University *B*
Lee University *B*
Lincoln Memorial University *B*
Lipscomb University *B*
Martin Methodist College *B*
Maryville College *B*
Middle Tennessee State
  University *B, M*
Milligan College *B, T*
Rhodes College *B*
Southern Adventist University *B*
Tennessee State University *B, M*
Tennessee Technological University *B*
Tennessee Temple University *B*
Tennessee Wesleyan College *B*
Trevecca Nazarene University *B*
Tusculum College *B*
Union University *B*
University of Memphis *B, M, D*
University of Tennessee
  Chattanooga *B, M*
  Knoxville *B, M, D*
  Martin *B*
University of the South *B*
Vanderbilt University *B, M, D*

Texas

Abilene Christian University *B, M*
Amarillo College *A*
Angelo State University *B, M*
Argosy University: Dallas *B*
Austin College *B*
Austin Community College *A*
Baylor University *B*
Blinn College *A*
Brazosport College *A*
Cisco College *A*
Clarendon College *A*
Coastal Bend College *A*
College of the Mainland *A*
Dallas Baptist University *B*
Dallas Christian College *B*
Del Mar College *A*
East Texas Baptist University *B*
El Paso Community College *A*
Frank Phillips College *A*
Galveston College *A*
Grayson County College *A*
Hardin-Simmons University *B*
Hill College *A*
Houston Baptist University *B*
Howard College *A*
Howard Payne University *B*
Huston-Tillotson University *B*
Kilgore College *A*
Lamar State College at Orange *A*
Lamar University *B, M*
Laredo Community College *A*
LeTourneau University *B*
Lon Morris College *A*
Lubbock Christian University *B*
McMurry University *B*
Midland College *A*
Midwestern State University *B, M*
Navarro College *A*
North Lake College *C, A*
Northeast Texas Community
  College *A*
Northwest Vista College *A*
Odessa College *A*
Our Lady of the Lake University of San
  Antonio *B, M, D*

Palo Alto College *A*
Paris Junior College *A*
Prairie View A&M University *B*
Rice University *B, M, D*
St. Edward's University *B*
St. Mary's University *B*
St. Philip's College *A*
Sam Houston State University *B, M*
San Antonio College *A*
San Jacinto College *A*
Schreiner University *B*
South Plains College *A*
South Texas College *A*
Southern Methodist
  University *B, M, D*
Southwestern Adventist
  University *B, T*
Southwestern Assemblies of God
  University *A*
Southwestern University *B, T*
Stephen F. Austin State
  University *B, M, T*
Sul Ross State University *B*
Tarleton State University *B*
Texas A&M International
  University *B, M, T*
Texas A&M University *B, M, D*
Texas A&M University
  Commerce *B, M*
  Corpus Christi *B, M*
  Kingsville *B, M*
  Texarkana *B*
Texas Christian University *B, M, D*
Texas Lutheran University *B*
Texas Southern University *B, M*
Texas State University: San Marcos *B*
Texas Tech University *B, M, D*
Texas Wesleyan University *B, T*
Texas Woman's University *B*
Trinity University *B*
Trinity Valley Community College *A*
Tyler Junior College *A*
University of Dallas *B, M*
University of Houston *B, M, D*
University of Houston
  Clear Lake *B, M*
  Downtown *B*
  Victoria *B*
University of Mary Hardin-Baylor *B, M*
University of North Texas *B, M*
University of St. Thomas *B*
University of Texas
  Arlington *B, M*
  Austin *B, M, D*
  Brownsville - Texas Southmost
    College *B*
  Dallas *B, M, D*
  El Paso *B, M, D*
  Pan American *B*
  San Antonio *B, M*
  Tyler *B*
  of the Permian Basin *B*
University of the Incarnate Word *B*
Wayland Baptist University *B*
West Texas A&M University *B, M*
Western Texas College *A*
Wharton County Junior College *A*

Utah

Argosy University: Salt Lake City *B*
Brigham Young University *B, M, D*
Salt Lake Community College *A*
Snow College *A*
Southern Utah University *B, T*
University of Utah *B, M, D, T*
Utah State University *B, M, D*
Utah Valley University *A, B*
Weber State University *B*
Westminster College *B*

Vermont

Bennington College *B*
Burlington College *B*
Castleton State College *B*

Champlain College *B*
College of St. Joseph in Vermont *B, M*
Green Mountain College *B*
Johnson State College *B*
Lyndon State College *B*
Marlboro College *B*
Middlebury College *B*
Norwich University *B*
St. Michael's College *B*
Southern Vermont College *B*
University of Vermont *B, M, D*

Virginia
Argosy University: Washington D.C. *B*
Bluefield College *B*
Bridgewater College *B*
Christopher Newport University *B*
College of William and Mary *B, M*
Eastern Mennonite University *B*
Emory & Henry College *B*
Ferrum College *B*
George Mason University *B, M, D*
Germanna Community College *A*
Hampden-Sydney College *B*
Hampton University *B*
Hollins University *B*
James Madison University *B, M, D*
Liberty University *A, B*
Longwood University *B, T*
Lynchburg College *B*
Mary Baldwin College *B*
Marymount University *B*
Norfolk State University *B*
Northern Virginia Community
    College *A*
Old Dominion University *B, M, D*
Radford University *B, M, D*
Randolph College *B*
Randolph-Macon College *B*
Regent University *A, B*
Roanoke College *B, T*
Shenandoah University *B*
Sweet Briar College *B*
University of Mary Washington *B*
University of Richmond *B, M*
University of Virginia *B, M, D*
University of Virginia's College at
    Wise *B, T*
Virginia Commonwealth
    University *B, D*
Virginia Intermont College *B*
Virginia Military Institute *B*
Virginia Polytechnic Institute and
    State University *B, M, D*
Virginia State University *B, M*
Virginia Union University *B*
Virginia Wesleyan College *B*
Washington and Lee University *B*

Washington
Antioch University Seattle *D*
Argosy University: Seattle *B*
Bastyr University *B*
Centralia College *A*
City University of Seattle *B*
Eastern Washington University *B, M*
Everett Community College *A*
Evergreen State College *B*
Gonzaga University *B*
Highline Community College *A*
Northwest University *B, D*
Olympic College *A*
Pacific Lutheran University *B*
Saint Martin's University *B*
Seattle Pacific University *B*
Seattle University *B, M*
Trinity Lutheran College *B*
University of Puget Sound *B*
University of Washington *B, M, D*
University of Washington Tacoma *B*
Walla Walla University *B*
Washington State University *B, M, D*
Western Washington University *B*
Whitman College *B*

Whitworth University *B*

West Virginia
Alderson-Broaddus College *B*
American Public University System *B*
Bethany College *B*
Concord University *B*
Davis and Elkins College *B*
Fairmont State University *B*
Marshall University *B, M*
Mountain State University *B*
Ohio Valley University *B*
Potomac State College of West
    Virginia University *A*
Shepherd University *B*
University of Charleston *B*
West Liberty University *B*
West Virginia State University *B*
West Virginia University *B, M, D*
West Virginia Wesleyan College *B*
Wheeling Jesuit University *B*

Wisconsin
Alverno College *B*
Beloit College *B*
Cardinal Stritch University *B, M*
Carroll University *B*
Carthage College *B*
Concordia University Wisconsin *B*
Edgewood College *B*
Lakeland College *B*
Lawrence University *B*
Marian University *B*
Marquette University *B, T*
Mount Mary College *B*
Ripon College *B*
St. Norbert College *B, T*
Silver Lake College *B, T*
University of Wisconsin
    Eau Claire *B*
    Green Bay *B*
    La Crosse *B, T*
    Madison *B, M, D*
    Milwaukee *B, M, D*
    Oshkosh *B, M*
    Parkside *B*
    Platteville *B, T*
    River Falls *B, T*
    Stevens Point *B, T*
    Stout *B, M*
    Superior *B*
    Whitewater *B, T*
Viterbo University *B*
Wisconsin Lutheran College *B*

Wyoming
Casper College *A*
Central Wyoming College *A*
Eastern Wyoming College *A*
Laramie County Community
    College *A*
Northwest College *A*
Sheridan College *A*
University of Wyoming *B, M, D*
Western Wyoming Community
    College *A*

Psychology teacher education

Arizona
University of Arizona *D*

Delaware
University of Delaware *B, T*

Idaho
Northwest Nazarene University *B*
University of Idaho *T*

Illinois
Bradley University *B*

Indiana
Valparaiso University *B*

Iowa
Buena Vista University *B, T*
St. Ambrose University *B*
Simpson College *T*

Kansas
Central Christian College of Kansas *A*
Pittsburg State University *B*

Louisiana
Centenary College of Louisiana *B, T*

Michigan
Alma College *T*

Minnesota
Saint Cloud State University *B*
University of Minnesota
    Morris *T*

Mississippi
Millsaps College *T*

Montana
University of Great Falls *B*

Nebraska
Wayne State College *B, T*

North Carolina
Lenoir-Rhyne University *B*

Ohio
University of Findlay *B, M, T*

Pennsylvania
Arcadia University *M*
DeSales University *T*
St. Francis University *B, T*
St. Vincent College *B*
Widener University *T*

South Carolina
Wofford College *T*

South Dakota
Augustana College *B, T*

Tennessee
Bryan College *T*
Crichton College *B, T*
King College *T*
Lee University *B*
Tusculum College *B, T*

Wisconsin
Carroll University *B, T*
Carthage College *T*
Lawrence University *T*
St. Norbert College *T*

Psychometrics/ quantitative psychology

Alabama
Alabama Agricultural and Mechanical
    University *M*

Arizona
University of Phoenix *M*

North Dakota
North Dakota State University *B*

Utah
University of Utah *M*

Virginia
James Madison University *D*

Psychopharmacology

California
Alliant International University *M*

Florida
Nova Southeastern University *M*

Public administration

Alabama
Andrew Jackson University *M*
Auburn University *B, M, D*
Auburn University at
    Montgomery *M, D*
Jacksonville State University *M*
Samford University *B*
Talladega College *B*
Troy University *M*
University of Alabama *M*
University of Alabama
    Birmingham *M*
    Huntsville *M*
University of South Alabama *M*

Alaska
University of Alaska
    Anchorage *B, M*
    Southeast *M*

Arizona
Arizona State University *M, D*
DeVry University
    Phoenix *M*
Northcentral University *B, M, D*
Northern Arizona University *M*
Rio Salado College *C, A*
Scottsdale Community College *C*
University of Arizona *B, M*
University of Phoenix *M*
Western International University *M*

Arkansas
Arkansas State University *M*
Harding University *B*
Henderson State University *B*
Southern Arkansas University *M*
University of Arkansas *B, M*
University of Arkansas
    Little Rock *M*
University of Central Arkansas *B*
University of the Ozarks *B*

California
California Baptist University *M*
California Lutheran University *M*
California Polytechnic State
    University: San Luis Obispo *M*
California State Polytechnic
    University: Pomona *M*
California State University
    Bakersfield *B, M*
    Chico *B, M*
    Dominguez Hills *B, M*
    East Bay *B, M*
    Fresno *B, M*
    Fullerton *B, M*
    Long Beach *M*
    Los Angeles *M*
    Monterey Bay *M*
    Northridge *M*
    Sacramento *M*
    San Bernardino *B, M*
    Stanislaus *M*
Fresno City College *C, A*
Golden Gate University *M*
Loma Linda University *D*
Long Beach City College *C, A*
Loyola Marymount University *B, M*

National University *B, M*
Notre Dame de Namur University *M*
Palomar College *C, A*
San Diego State University *B, M*
San Francisco State University *M*
San Joaquin Delta College *A*
San Jose State University *M*
Santa Barbara City College *A*
Sonoma State University *M*
University of California
  Los Angeles *M*
University of La Verne *B, M, D*
University of San Francisco *B, M*
University of Southern
  California *B, M, D*

Colorado

DeVry University
  Westminster *M*
Mesa State College *B*
University of Colorado
  Colorado Springs *M*
  Denver *M, D*
University of Denver *M*

Connecticut

University of Connecticut *M*
University of Hartford *M*
University of New Haven *B, M*

Delaware

University of Delaware *M*
Wilmington University *M*

District of Columbia

American University *M, D*
Howard University *M*
University of the District of
  Columbia *M*

Florida

Barry University *C, B*
Flagler College *B*
Florida Atlantic University *C, B, M, D*
Florida Gulf Coast University *M*
Florida International
  University *B, M, D*
Florida Keys Community College *A*
Florida Memorial University *B*
Florida National College *A*
Florida State University *M, D*
Hodges University *M*
Miami Dade College *A*
Nova Southeastern University *M, D*
State College of Florida,
  Manatee-Sarasota *A*
Tallahassee Community College *A*
University of Central Florida *B, M, D*
University of Miami *M*
University of North Florida *M*
University of South Florida *M*

Georgia

Albany State University *M*
Augusta State University *M*
Clark Atlanta University *M*
DeVry University
  Alpharetta *M*
Georgia College and State
  University *M*
Georgia Southern University *M*
Georgia State University *M*
Kennesaw State University *M*
Macon State College *A, B*
Middle Georgia College *A*
North Georgia College & State
  University *M*
Savannah State University *M*
South University: Savannah *M*
University of Georgia *M, D*
University of West Georgia *M*
Valdosta State University *M, D*

Hawaii

Hawaii Pacific University *B*
University of Hawaii
  Hilo *B*
  Manoa *B*
  West Oahu *B*

Idaho

Boise State University *M*
Idaho State University *M*
University of Idaho *M*

Illinois

Augustana College *B*
Blackburn College *B*
DePaul University *C, M*
DeVry University
  Tinley Park *M*
Governors State University *B, M*
Illinois Institute of Technology *M*
Lewis University *B*
Northern Illinois University *M*
Northwestern University *M*
Roosevelt University *M*
Southern Illinois University
  Carbondale *M*
Southern Illinois University
  Edwardsville *M*
University of Illinois
  Chicago *M, D*
  Springfield *M, D*
  Urbana-Champaign *M*

Indiana

Ball State University *M*
Indiana State University *M*
Indiana University
  Bloomington *A, B, M, D*
  Kokomo *B*
  Northwest *A, B, M*
  South Bend *A, B, M*
Indiana University-Purdue University
  Fort Wayne *C, A, B, M*
Indiana University-Purdue University
  Indianapolis *A, B, M*
University of Evansville *B*
University of Notre Dame *M*
University of Southern Indiana *M*
Vincennes University *A*

Iowa

Buena Vista University *B*
Dordt College *B*
Drake University *M*
Iowa State University *M*
St. Ambrose University *B*
University of Northern Iowa *B*

Kansas

Barton County Community College *A*
Kansas State University *M*
University of Kansas *B, M, D*
Washburn University *C, B*
Wichita State University *M*

Kentucky

Eastern Kentucky University *M*
Kentucky State University *B, M*
Morehead State University *M*
Murray State University *M*
Northern Kentucky University *M*
University of Kentucky *M, D*
University of Louisville *M*
Western Kentucky University *M*

Louisiana

Grambling State University *M*
Louisiana College *B*
Louisiana State University and
  Agricultural and Mechanical
  College *M*

Southern University
  New Orleans *B*
Southern University and Agricultural
  and Mechanical College *M*
University of New Orleans *M*

Maine

University of Maine *B, M*
University of Maine
  Augusta *A, B*
University of Southern Maine *M, D*

Maryland

Bowie State University *M*
Community College of Baltimore
  County *A*
University of Baltimore *M, D*
University of Maryland
  University College *B*

Massachusetts

American International College *M*
Anna Maria College *M*
Bridgewater State College *M*
Clark University *B, M*
Framingham State College *M*
Harvard College *M, D*
Northeastern University *M*
Regis College *M*
Stonehill College *B*
Suffolk University *B, M*
University of Massachusetts
  Boston *B, M*
Westfield State College *M*

Michigan

Calvin College *B*
Central Michigan University *M*
Eastern Michigan University *B, M*
Ferris State University *A, B*
Grand Valley State University *B, M*
Michigan State University *B*
Northern Michigan University *B, M*
Oakland University *B, M*
Saginaw Valley State University *B, M*
University of Michigan
  Dearborn *B, M*
  Flint *B, M*
Wayne State University *B, M*
Western Michigan University *M, D*

Minnesota

Hamline University *M, D*
Metropolitan State University *M*
Minneapolis Community and
  Technical College *C, A*
Minnesota State University
  Mankato *B, M*
  Moorhead *M*
Saint Cloud State University *B*
St. Mary's University of Minnesota *M*
Southwest Minnesota State
  University *B*
University of Minnesota
  Twin Cities *M*
Walden University *M, D*
Winona State University *B*

Mississippi

Belhaven University *M*
Jackson State University *M, D*
Millsaps College *B*
Mississippi State University *M, D*
Mississippi Valley State
  University *B, M*

Missouri

Harris-Stowe State University *B*
Lincoln University *B*
Lindenwood University *B, M*
Missouri State University *B, M*
Missouri Valley College *B*

Northwest Missouri State
  University *B*
Park University *C, B, M*
Saint Louis University *M*
University of Missouri
  Columbia *M*
  Kansas City *M*
  St. Louis *B, M*
Webster University *M*

Montana

Miles Community College *A*
Montana State University
  Billings *M*
  Bozeman *M*
University of Montana *M*

Nebraska

Bellevue University *B, M*
Doane College *B*
University of Nebraska
  Omaha *B, M, D*

Nevada

DeVry University: Henderson *M*
University of Nevada
  Las Vegas *M*
  Reno *M*

New Hampshire

Plymouth State University *B*
Southern New Hampshire
  University *B*
University of New Hampshire *M*

New Jersey

County College of Morris *A*
Cumberland County College *A*
Fairleigh Dickinson University
  College at Florham *M*
  Metropolitan Campus *M*
Kean University *B, M*
Princeton University *B, M, D*
Rider University *C*
Rutgers, The State University of New
  Jersey
  Camden Regional Campus *M*
  Newark Regional Campus *M, D*
Seton Hall University *M*
Thomas Edison State College *C, B*
William Paterson University of New
  Jersey *M*

New Mexico

Navajo Technical College *A*
New Mexico State University *M*
San Juan College *C, A*
University of New Mexico *M*

New York

City University of New York
  Baruch College *B, M*
  City College *M*
  Hostos Community College *A*
  John Jay College of Criminal
    Justice *B, M*
  Medgar Evers College *A, B*
Cornell University *B, M*
Dowling College *M*
Elmira College *B*
Erie Community College
  South Campus *A*
Fordham University *B, M*
Long Island University
  Brooklyn Campus *M*
  C. W. Post Campus *B, M*
Marist College *M*
Mohawk Valley Community College *A*
New York University *B, M, D*
Pace University *M*
St. John's University *B*
State University of New York
  Albany *M, D*

Binghamton *M*
College at Brockport *M*
Stony Brook *M*
Syracuse University *B, M, D*

North Carolina
Appalachian State University *M*
Campbell University *B*
Catawba College *B*
DeVry University: Charlotte *M*
East Carolina University *M*
Elon University *B*
Fayetteville State University *B*
Fayetteville Technical Community
College *A*
High Point University *M*
North Carolina Central University *M*
North Carolina State University *M, D*
Shaw University *B*
University of North Carolina
Chapel Hill *M*
Charlotte *M*
Greensboro *M*
Pembroke *M*
Wilmington *M*
Western Carolina University *B, M*

North Dakota
University of North Dakota *B, M*

Ohio
Bowling Green State University *B, M*
Capital University *B*
Cedarville University *B*
Cleveland State University *M*
Columbus State Community
College *A*
Heidelberg University *B*
Kent State University *M*
Miami University
Oxford Campus *B*
Ohio State University
Columbus Campus *M, D*
Ohio University *M*
Owens Community College
Toledo *A*
Union Institute & University *B*
University of Akron *M*
University of Cincinnati *M*
University of Dayton *M*
University of Rio Grande *B*
University of Toledo *M*
Wright State University *B, M*
Youngstown State University *B*

Oklahoma
DeVry University: Oklahoma City
Center *M*
Rogers State University *B*
University of Oklahoma *B, M*

Oregon
DeVry University: Portland *M*
Portland Community College *C, A*
Portland State University *M, D*
University of Oregon *B, M*
Western Oregon University *B*

Pennsylvania
Carnegie Mellon University *M*
Cheyney University of
Pennsylvania *M*
Gannon University *M*
Holy Family University *T*
Indiana University of Pennsylvania *M*
Juniata College *B*
Kutztown University of
Pennsylvania *B, M*
La Salle University *B*
Lincoln University *B*
Marywood University *M*
Penn State
Harrisburg *M, D*

Point Park University *A, B*
Reading Area Community College *A*
St. Francis University *B*
Saint Joseph's University *B*
Shippensburg University of
Pennsylvania *B, M*
University of Pennsylvania *M*
University of Pittsburgh *C, B, M*
Villanova University *M*
Widener University *M*

Puerto Rico
Bayamon Central University *B*
Inter American University of Puerto
Rico
Bayamon Campus *B*
San German Campus *B*
Pontifical Catholic University of
Puerto Rico *B, M*
Turabo University *A, B*
University of Puerto Rico
Rio Piedras *M*

Rhode Island
Rhode Island College *B, M*
Roger Williams University *B, M*
University of Rhode Island *M*

South Carolina
Clemson University *M*
College of Charleston *M*
University of South Carolina *M*

South Dakota
Oglala Lakota College *M*
University of South Dakota *M*

Tennessee
Cleveland State Community College *A*
Cumberland University *B*
Jackson State Community College *A*
Lipscomb University *B*
Tennessee State University *M, D*
University of Memphis *M*
University of Tennessee
Chattanooga *M*
Knoxville *B*

Texas
Angelo State University *M*
Baylor University *B, M*
Brazosport College *A*
College of the Mainland *A*
Houston Community College
System *C, A*
Lamar Institute of Technology *C, A*
Lamar University *M*
Midwestern State University *M*
St. Mary's University *M*
Sam Houston State University *M*
San Antonio College *C, A*
San Jacinto College *A*
Stephen F. Austin State
University *B, M*
Sul Ross State University *M*
Tarrant County College *C, A*
Texas A&M International
University *M*
Texas A&M University *M*
Texas A&M University
Corpus Christi *M*
Texas Southern University *B, M*
Texas State University: San
Marcos *B, M*
Texas Tech University *M*
University of Houston *M*
University of Houston
Clear Lake *M*
University of North Texas *B, M, D*
University of Texas
Arlington *M, D*
Brownsville - Texas Southmost
College *B, M*

Dallas *B, M, D*
El Paso *M*
Pan American *M*
San Antonio *M*
Tyler *M*
of the Permian Basin *M*
Wayland Baptist University *M*
West Texas A&M University *B*

Utah
Brigham Young University *M*
DeVry University: Sandy *M*
Southern Utah University *C*
University of Utah *M*

Vermont
Norwich University *M*
University of Vermont *M*

Virginia
George Mason University *B, M*
James Madison University *B, M*
Old Dominion University *M, D*
Regent University *M*
Shenandoah University *B*
Thomas Nelson Community
College *A*
Tidewater Community College *A*
University of Management and
Technology *M*
University of Virginia's College at
Wise *B*
Virginia Commonwealth
University *M, D*
Virginia Polytechnic Institute and
State University *M, D*
Virginia State University *B*

Washington
DeVry University
Federal Way *M*
Eastern Washington University *M*
Evergreen State College *B, M*
Seattle University *B, M*
University of Washington *M*

West Virginia
American Public University System *M*
Concord University *B*
West Virginia University *M*

Wisconsin
DeVry University: Milwaukee *M*
Silver Lake College *B*
University of Wisconsin
Green Bay *B*
Madison *M*
Milwaukee *M*
Oshkosh *M*
Stevens Point *B*
Superior *B*
Whitewater *B, M*

Wyoming
Laramie County Community
College *C, A*
University of Wyoming *M*

Public finance

Alabama
Alabama Agricultural and Mechanical
University *B*

California
National University *M*

Maine
Husson University *B*

Massachusetts
Boston University *M*

Michigan
Cleary University *B*

New York
City University of New York
Baruch College *M*

Ohio
Youngstown State University *B*

Rhode Island
Johnson & Wales University:
Providence *B*

Texas
Texas A&M University
Commerce *B*

Public health

Alabama
University of Alabama
Birmingham *M, D*

Alaska
University of Alaska
Fairbanks *A*

Arizona
Prescott College *B*
University of Arizona *M, D*

California
California State University
Fresno *M*
Fullerton *M*
Long Beach *M*
Northridge *M*
Charles Drew University of Medicine
and Science *M*
Loma Linda University *D*
San Diego State University *M, D*
San Francisco State University *M*
San Jose State University *M*
Santa Clara University *B*
University of California
Berkeley *M, D*
Davis *M*
Irvine *B, M*
Los Angeles *M, D*
University of Southern
California *B, M, D*

Colorado
Colorado State University *M*
University of Colorado
Denver *M*

Connecticut
Southern Connecticut State
University *B, M*
University of Connecticut *M*
Yale University *M, D*

Delaware
Delaware State University *B*

District of Columbia
George Washington University *M, D*
Trinity Washington University *B*

Florida
Barry University *M*
Florida Agricultural and Mechanical
University *M, D*
Florida International University *M, D*
Nova Southeastern University *M*

Palm Beach Community College *A*
University of South Florida *M, D*
University of West Florida *M*

Georgia

Armstrong Atlantic State University *M*
Emory University *M*
Fort Valley State University *M*
Georgia Southern University *D*
Georgia State University *M*
Mercer University *M*
University of Georgia *M, D*

Hawaii

University of Hawaii
  Manoa *M, D*

Idaho

Boise State University *M*
Idaho State University *M*

Illinois

Benedictine University *M*
DePaul University *M*
Northern Illinois University *M*
Northwestern University *M*
University of Illinois
  Chicago *M, D*
  Springfield *M*
  Urbana-Champaign *M, D*

Indiana

Indiana University
  Bloomington *B, M*
Indiana University-Purdue University
  Indianapolis *B, M*

Iowa

University of Iowa *M*

Kansas

Kansas State University *M*
University of Kansas Medical
  Center *M*

Kentucky

University of Kentucky *M*
University of Louisville *M*
Western Kentucky University *M*

Louisiana

Louisiana State University Health
  Sciences Center *M*
Tulane University *M, D*

Maine

University of New England *M*
University of Southern Maine *M*

Maryland

Howard Community College *A*
Johns Hopkins University *B*
Morgan State University *M, D*
University of Maryland
  Baltimore *M*
  College Park *M*

Massachusetts

Boston University *M, D*
Hampshire College *B*
Harvard College *M, D*
Northeastern University *B, M*
Springfield College *B, M*
University of Massachusetts
  Amherst *B, M, D*

Michigan

Michigan State University *M*
University of Michigan *M, D*
Wayne State University *M*

Minnesota

Minnesota State University
  Mankato *B, M*
University of Minnesota
  Twin Cities *M*
Walden University *M, D*

Mississippi

Jackson State University *M, D*
University of Southern
  Mississippi *B, M*

Missouri

Maryville University of Saint Louis *B*
Missouri State University *M*
Saint Louis University *M, D*
University of Missouri
  Columbia *M*

Nebraska

University of Nebraska
  Medical Center *M*
  Omaha *M*

Nevada

University of Nevada
  Reno *M*

New Hampshire

University of New Hampshire *M*

New Jersey

Montclair State University *M*
New Jersey Institute of Technology *M*
Richard Stockton College of New
  Jersey *B*
Rutgers, The State University of New
  Jersey
  New Brunswick/Piscataway
    Campus *B*

New Mexico

University of New Mexico *M*

New York

City University of New York
  Brooklyn College *M*
  Lehman College *M*
New York University *M*
State University of New York
  Albany *M, D*
  Buffalo *M*
  Upstate Medical University *M*
University of Rochester *M*

North Carolina

East Carolina University *M*
University of North Carolina
  Chapel Hill *M*
  Charlotte *D*

Ohio

Case Western Reserve University *M*
Cleveland State University *M*
Ohio State University
  Columbus Campus *M*
University of Akron *M*
Youngstown State University *M*

Oklahoma

Southwestern Oklahoma State
  University *B*
University of Central Oklahoma *M*
University of Oklahoma *M, D*

Oregon

Oregon Health & Science
  University *M*
Oregon State University *M, D*
Portland State University *B, M*

Pennsylvania

Arcadia University *M*
Drexel University *M, D*
East Stroudsburg University of
  Pennsylvania *M*
La Salle University *M*
Penn State
  University Park *M*
Slippery Rock University of
  Pennsylvania *B*
University of the Sciences in
  Philadelphia *M*
West Chester University of
  Pennsylvania *B, M*

Puerto Rico

University of Puerto Rico
  Medical Sciences *M, D*

South Carolina

University of South Carolina *M, D*

Tennessee

East Tennessee State University *B, M*
University of Memphis *M*
University of Tennessee
  Knoxville *M*

Texas

University of Texas
  El Paso *M*
  Health Science Center at
    Houston *M, D*
  Medical Branch at Galveston *M*

Utah

Brigham Young University *M*
Independence University *M*
Snow College *A*
University of Utah *M, D*
Utah State University *B*

Virginia

George Mason University *M*
Old Dominion University *M*
University of Virginia *M*
Virginia Commonwealth University *M*
Virginia Polytechnic Institute and
  State University *M*

Washington

Highline Community College *A*
University of Washington *B, M*

West Virginia

American Public University
  System *A, B, M*
West Virginia University *M*

Public health education

Arizona

Dine College *A*
Prescott College *B*

California

California Institute of Integral
  Studies *M*
California State University
  Chico *T*
  Long Beach *B, M*
Loma Linda University *M, D*
San Francisco State University *B*

Colorado

University of Northern Colorado *B, M*

Georgia

Georgia Military College *A*
Georgia Southern University *B, M*
University of Georgia *B, M, D*

Iowa

University of Northern Iowa *D*

Kansas

Emporia State University *B*

Louisiana

Dillard University *B*
Southeastern Louisiana University *B*

Maine

University of Maine
  Farmington *B*

Maryland

University of Maryland
  Baltimore *M, D*

Massachusetts

Boston University *M*
Springfield College *M*

Michigan

Central Michigan University *B, M*
Eastern Michigan University *M*
University of Michigan *M, D*
University of Michigan
  Flint *B, M*

Minnesota

Anoka-Ramsey Community College *A*
Minnesota State University
  Mankato *B, M*
Saint Cloud State University *B*
University of St. Thomas *B*
Walden University *D*
Winona State University *B*

Nebraska

Nebraska Methodist College of
  Nursing and Allied Health *M*

New Hampshire

Plymouth State University *B, M*

New Jersey

Felician College *D*
Thomas Edison State College *B*

New Mexico

New Mexico State University *B, M*

New York

City University of New York
  Hunter College *M*
  York College *B*
Ithaca College *B*
State University of New York
  Buffalo *M*
  Oswego *B*

North Carolina

Appalachian State University *B*
East Carolina University *B, M*
North Carolina Central University *B*
University of North Carolina
  Asheville *B*
  Chapel Hill *M, D*
  Charlotte *B, M*
  Greensboro *B, M, D*
  Pembroke *B*
  Wilmington *B*

Ohio

Malone University *B*
University of Toledo *B, M, D*
Youngstown State University *B*

Oklahoma

Oklahoma State University *B*

University of Central Oklahoma B
University of Oklahoma M, D

Oregon
Oregon State University B, M
Portland State University B, M

Pennsylvania
Arcadia University M
Temple University B, M, D

Puerto Rico
Turabo University M
University of Puerto Rico
Medical Sciences B, M

South Carolina
Coastal Carolina University B
University of South Carolina M, D

Tennessee
University of Tennessee
Knoxville M

Texas
University of Texas
Austin M, D

Utah
Brigham Young University B
University of Utah B, M, D, T

Vermont
Goddard College B, M

Virginia
Liberty University B
Marymount University M
Virginia Commonwealth University D

Washington
Eastern Washington University B

Wisconsin
Carroll University B

Public health nursing

Arizona
Northern Arizona University M

California
California State University
San Bernardino M

Connecticut
University of Hartford M

Delaware
Delaware State University B, M

Illinois
Northern Illinois University B
Southern Illinois University
Edwardsville M

Indiana
Indiana University-Purdue University
Indianapolis M

Iowa
University of Iowa M

Louisiana
Louisiana State University Health
Sciences Center M

Maryland
Coppin State University M

Massachusetts
Elms College B

Michigan
University of Michigan M
Wayne State University M

Minnesota
Augsburg College B, M
Crown College A, B
Metropolitan State University M

Missouri
University of Central Missouri M
Washington University in St. Louis M

New Jersey
William Paterson University of New
Jersey B, M

New York
City University of New York
Hunter College B, M
College of New Rochelle M
State University of New York
Binghamton M

North Carolina
University of North Carolina
Chapel Hill M

Ohio
Capital University M
Case Western Reserve University M
Kent State University M
Wright State University M

Oregon
Oregon Health & Science
University M

Pennsylvania
Holy Family University M

South Carolina
University of South Carolina M

Tennessee
University of Tennessee Health
Science Center D

Texas
University of Texas
Brownsville - Texas Southmost
College M
El Paso M

Washington
Seattle University B, M

Public history/archives

California
California State University
Sacramento M, D

Connecticut
Central Connecticut State
University M

District of Columbia
American University M

Illinois
Loyola University Chicago M

Maryland
Stevenson University B

Massachusetts
Salem State College B

Michigan
Western Michigan University B

New York
City University of New York
Queens College T

North Carolina
Appalachian State University M
East Carolina University B
North Carolina State University M
St. Andrews Presbyterian College B

North Dakota
North Dakota State University B

Pennsylvania
Duquesne University M

South Carolina
University of South Carolina M

Texas
McMurry University B
Texas Lutheran University B

Virginia
Emory & Henry College B
Longwood University B

Public policy analysis

Arizona
Arizona State University M
Northern Arizona University B
Prescott College B

Arkansas
University of Arkansas D

California
California State University
East Bay B
Loma Linda University D
Mills College B
Pepperdine University M
Pomona College B
Scripps College B
Stanford University B
University of California
Berkeley M, D
Los Angeles M
Riverside B
San Diego B
University of Southern
California M, D

Colorado
University of Denver B, M

Connecticut
Trinity College B, M

District of Columbia
American University M
George Washington
University B, M, D
Georgetown University M

Florida
New College of Florida B

Georgia
Georgia Institute of
Technology B, M, D
Georgia State University B, D

Illinois
DePaul University B, M
Loyola University Chicago M
Northwestern University B, M
Olivet Nazarene University B
University of Chicago B, M, D
University of Illinois
Chicago D

Indiana
Indiana University
Bloomington D
Indiana University-Purdue University
Fort Wayne B

Iowa
University of Northern Iowa M

Louisiana
Southern University and Agricultural
and Mechanical College D

Maine
University of Southern Maine M, D

Maryland
Johns Hopkins University B, M
St. Mary's College of Maryland B
University of Maryland
Baltimore County M, D
College Park M, D

Massachusetts
Anna Maria College B
Brandeis University M, D
Hampshire College B
Harvard College M, D
Massachusetts College of Liberal
Arts B
Northeastern University M, D
Simmons College B
Suffolk University B
University of Massachusetts
Amherst M
Boston M, D
Dartmouth M

Michigan
Albion College B
Michigan State University B, M
Michigan Technological University M
University of Michigan B, M, D

Minnesota
University of St. Thomas M
Walden University B, M, D

Mississippi
University of Mississippi B

Missouri
Saint Louis University D

New Hampshire
New England College M

New Jersey
Monmouth University M
New Jersey Institute of Technology M
Rutgers, The State University of New
Jersey
New Brunswick/Piscataway
Campus M, D
Saint Peter's College A, B
William Paterson University of New
Jersey M

New York
Cornell University B
Hamilton College B
Hobart and William Smith Colleges B

Rochester Institute of
  Technology *B, M*
Sage College of Albany *B*
State University of New York
  Albany *M*
  Stony Brook *M*
Wagner College *B*
Wells College *B*

North Carolina

Duke University *B, M, D*
University of North Carolina
  Chapel Hill *B, D*
  Charlotte *D*

Ohio

Ohio State University
  Columbus Campus *M, D*

Oregon

Oregon State University *M*

Pennsylvania

Carlow University *B*
Carnegie Mellon University *B, M*
Chatham University *B*
Dickinson College *B*
Duquesne University *M*
Immaculata University *A, B*
Lafayette College *B*
Penn State
  Harrisburg *B*
St. Vincent College *B*
University of Pennsylvania *B, M, D*
University of Pittsburgh *M*

Rhode Island

Brown University *B*
University of Rhode Island *B, M, D*

South Carolina

Clemson University *D*

Tennessee

Vanderbilt University *M*

Texas

Houston Baptist University *B*
Rice University *B*
Southern Methodist University *B*
University of Houston
  Clear Lake *B*
University of Texas
  Austin *M, D*
  Dallas *D*

Utah

Brigham Young University *M*
University of Utah *M*

Virginia

College of William and Mary *B, M*
George Mason University *M, D*
Regent University *M*
University of Virginia *M*
Virginia Polytechnic Institute and
  State University *B*
Washington and Lee University *B*

Washington

University of Washington *M*
University of Washington Bothell *M*
Washington State University *B, M*

West Virginia

University of Charleston *B*

Wisconsin

University of Wisconsin
  Madison *M*
  Superior *B*

Whitewater *B, T*

Public relations

Alabama

Auburn University *B*
University of Alabama *B*

Arizona

Glendale Community College *A*
Grand Canyon University *B*
Northern Arizona University *B*
Scottsdale Community College *C, A*

Arkansas

Harding University *B*
John Brown University *A, B*
University of Central Arkansas *B*

California

Bethany University *B*
Biola University *B*
California Lutheran University *B*
California State University
  Chico *B*
  Dominguez Hills *B*
  East Bay *B*
  Fullerton *B, M*
  Long Beach *B*
Chapman University *B*
Cosumnes River College *A*
Fullerton College *C*
Golden Gate University *M*
Golden West College *C, A*
Long Beach City College *C, A*
Los Angeles City College *A*
The Master's College *B*
Oxnard College *A*
Pacific Union College *B*
Pepperdine University *B*
San Diego State University *B*
San Jose State University *B*
University of Southern
  California *B, M*

Colorado

Colorado State University *B*
Jones International University *B, M*
University of Denver *M*

Connecticut

Manchester Community College *C*
Mitchell College *B*
Quinnipiac University *B*
Three Rivers Community College *A*
University of Bridgeport *B*

District of Columbia

American University *B, M*

Florida

Barry University *B, M*
Florida Agricultural and Mechanical
  University *B*
Florida Southern College *B*
Florida State University *B*
Indian River State College *A*
Lynn University *B*
State College of Florida,
  Manatee-Sarasota *A*
University of Florida *B*
University of Miami *B, M*
Valencia Community College *A*

Georgia

Fort Valley State University *B*
Georgia Southern University *B*
Paine College *B*
Shorter College *B*
University of Georgia *B*

Hawaii

Chaminade University of Honolulu *B*
Hawaii Pacific University *B*

Idaho

Brigham Young University-Idaho *B*
North Idaho College *A*
University of Idaho *B*

Illinois

Black Hawk College: East Campus *A*
Bradley University *B*
Columbia College Chicago *B*
Dominican University *B*
Eureka College *B*
Greenville College *B*
Illinois State University *B*
Lewis University *B*
Monmouth College *B*
University of St. Francis *B*

Indiana

Ball State University *M*
Goshen College *B*
Grace College *B*
Huntington University *B*
Indiana University-Purdue University
  Indianapolis *B*
Indiana Wesleyan University *B*
Purdue University *B, M, D*
Purdue University
  Calumet *B*
St. Mary-of-the-Woods College *B*
University of St. Francis *B*
Valparaiso University *B*
Vincennes University *A*

Iowa

Coe College *B*
Dordt College *B*
Drake University *B*
Grand View University *B*
Loras College *B*
Mount Mercy College *B*
Northwestern College *B*
St. Ambrose University *B*
University of Northern Iowa *B*
Wartburg College *B*

Kansas

Fort Scott Community College *A*
Kansas Wesleyan University *B*
MidAmerica Nazarene University *B*
Pittsburg State University *B*
Tabor College *B*

Kentucky

Campbellsville University *B*
Eastern Kentucky University *B*
Murray State University *B*
Northern Kentucky University *B*
Western Kentucky University *C, B*

Louisiana

University of Louisiana at Lafayette *B*

Maine

New England School of
  Communications *B*
Saint Joseph's College of Maine *B*

Maryland

Cecil College *C*
University of Baltimore *B*

Massachusetts

American International College *B*
Boston University *B, M*
Cape Cod Community College *A*
Emerson College *B, M*
Lasell College *B*
Regis College *B*

Salem State College *B*
Simmons College *B*
Suffolk University *B, M*
Western New England College *B*

Michigan

Andrews University *B*
Central Michigan University *B*
Eastern Michigan University *B*
Ferris State University *B*
Grand Valley State University *B*
Kuyper College *B*
Macomb Community College *C, A*
Michigan State University *B, M*
Northern Michigan University *B*
Spring Arbor University *B*
University of Detroit Mercy *B*
Wayne State University *B*
Western Michigan University *B*

Minnesota

Minneapolis College of Art and
  Design *B*
Minnesota State University
  Mankato *B*
Northwestern College *B*
Saint Cloud State University *B*
St. Mary's University of Minnesota *B*
Southwest Minnesota State
  University *B*
Winona State University *B*

Mississippi

Mississippi College *B, M*
Northwest Mississippi Community
  College *A*
University of Southern Mississippi *M*

Missouri

Avila University *B*
College of the Ozarks *B*
Crowder College *A*
Drury University *B*
Missouri State University *B*
Northwest Missouri State
  University *B*
St. Louis Community College
  St. Louis Community College at
    Florissant Valley *A*
Stephens College *B*
University of Central Missouri *B*
University of Missouri
  Columbia *M*
Webster University *B, M*
William Woods University *B*

Montana

Montana State University
  Billings *B, M*

Nebraska

Union College *B*

New Hampshire

New England College *B*
Rivier College *B*
Southern New Hampshire
  University *B*

New Jersey

Kean University *M*
Monmouth University *M*
Rowan University *B, M*
Seton Hall University *B*

New York

City University of New York
  City College *B*
Hofstra University *B*
Houghton College *B*
Iona College *B, M*

Long Island University
  C. W. Post Campus B
Marist College B
Monroe Community College A
Mount Saint Mary College B
New York Institute of Technology M
Rochester Institute of
  Technology C, B
St. Francis College B
St. John's University B
State University of New York
  College at Fredonia B
  Oswego B
Syracuse University M
Utica College B

North Carolina
Appalachian State University B
Campbell University B
Gardner-Webb University B
North Carolina Agricultural and
  Technical State University B
Wingate University B

North Dakota
Bismarck State College A
North Dakota State University B
University of Mary B

Ohio
Baldwin-Wallace College B
Bowling Green State University B
Capital University B
Cleveland State University B
Defiance College B
Heidelberg University B
Kent State University B
Malone University B
Marietta College B
Miami University
  Oxford Campus B
Mount Vernon Nazarene University B
Notre Dame College B
Ohio Dominican University B
Ohio Northern University B
Ohio State University
  Columbus Campus B, M
Otterbein College B
Tiffin University B
University of Akron B
University of Dayton B
University of Findlay B
University of Rio Grande A, B
Ursuline College B
Wilmington College B
Xavier University A, B
Youngstown State University B

Oklahoma
Cameron University B
Northeastern State University B
Northern Oklahoma College A
Northwestern Oklahoma State
  University B
Oklahoma Baptist University B
Oklahoma Christian University B
Oklahoma City University B
University of Central Oklahoma B

Oregon
Marylhurst University C
Southern Oregon University B
University of Oregon B

Pennsylvania
Chatham University B
Drexel University M
Duquesne University B
Elizabethtown College B
Keystone College A, B
La Salle University B
Mansfield University of
  Pennsylvania B

Marywood University M
St. Francis University B
Slippery Rock University of
  Pennsylvania B
Temple University B, M
University of Pittsburgh
  Bradford B
  Greensburg B
Waynesburg University B
Westminster College B
York College of Pennsylvania B

Puerto Rico
Inter American University of Puerto
  Rico
  Ponce Campus B
University of Puerto Rico
  Rio Piedras B
University of the Sacred Heart M

Rhode Island
University of Rhode Island B

South Carolina
Bob Jones University B
University of South Carolina B
Winthrop University B

Tennessee
Belmont University B
Freed-Hardeman University B
Lee University B
Lipscomb University B
Southern Adventist University B
Union University B
University of Tennessee
  Knoxville B

Texas
Hardin-Simmons University B
Howard Payne University B
North Lake College C
Our Lady of the Lake University of San
  Antonio B
Sam Houston State University B
Southern Methodist University B
Texas A&M University
  Commerce B
Texas State University: San Marcos B
Texas Tech University B
Texas Wesleyan University B
University of Houston B, M
University of Mary Hardin-Baylor B
University of Texas
  Arlington B
  Austin B
  El Paso B
  San Antonio B

Utah
Weber State University B

Vermont
Champlain College B
University of Vermont B

Virginia
Hampton University B

Washington
Gonzaga University B
Seattle University B

West Virginia
Bethany College B
Concord University B
West Virginia University B
West Virginia Wesleyan College B

Wisconsin
Carroll University B
Carthage College B

Marquette University B, M
Mount Mary College B

Publishing

California
California State University
  Chico C
Foothill College C
Long Beach City College C, A

Illinois
Benedictine University B

Massachusetts
Emerson College B, M

Minnesota
Hennepin Technical College C, A
Ridgewater College C, A

New York
Pace University M
State University of New York
  College of Agriculture and
    Technology at Cobleskill B

Oregon
Clackamas Community College C

Texas
North Lake College C

Virginia
Southwest Virginia Community
  College C

Purchasing/
procurement/contracts

Alabama
Athens State University C
Miles College B
University of Alabama
  Huntsville B

Arizona
Arizona State University B

Arkansas
Southern Arkansas University Tech C

California
California State University
  East Bay C, B
Coastline Community College C
De Anza College C, A
Fresno City College C, A
Fullerton College A
San Diego City College C, A

District of Columbia
Potomac College C, B

Florida
Florida Institute of Technology M

Georgia
DeVry University
  Alpharetta M
  Decatur M

Illinois
DeVry University
  Tinley Park M
Harper College C
University of Illinois
  Urbana-Champaign B, D

Iowa
St. Ambrose University C

Maryland
Cecil College C
University of Maryland
  University College C

Massachusetts
Middlesex Community College C
Northern Essex Community
  College C

Michigan
Central Michigan University B, M

Missouri
Saint Louis University B
Webster University M

New York
Cazenovia College C
Globe Institute of Technology C

Ohio
Ashland University B, M
Cincinnati State Technical and
  Community College A
Columbus State Community
  College C, A
North Central State College C
Wright State University M

Pennsylvania
Saint Joseph's University A, B

Puerto Rico
American University of Puerto Rico B

South Carolina
Greenville Technical College A

Tennessee
Middle Tennessee State University B

Texas
Brazosport College A
University of Houston
  Downtown B

Virginia
Central Virginia Community
  College C
Northern Virginia Community
  College C, A
University of Management and
  Technology M

Wisconsin
Northeast Wisconsin Technical
  College C

Quality control
technology

Arkansas
East Arkansas Community College C

California
California State University
  Dominguez Hills B, M
San Jose State University B, M

Connecticut
Naugatuck Valley Community
  College C, A

Georgia

Southern Polytechnic State
University *C, M*

Illinois

Heartland Community College *C*
Sauk Valley Community College *C*
Triton College *C*

Indiana

Indiana University-Purdue University
Fort Wayne *C*

Kentucky

Elizabethtown Community and
Technical College *A*
Hopkinsville Community College *C*

Maryland

Community College of Baltimore
County *C, A*

Michigan

Baker College
of Muskegon *C, A*
Bay de Noc Community College *C*
Eastern Michigan University *M*
Ferris State University *B*
Grand Rapids Community
College *C, A*
Mott Community College *C, A*
Schoolcraft College *C, A*

Minnesota

Dunwoody College of Technology *C*
Lake Superior College *C*
St. Cloud Technical College *C*
St. Paul College *C*
University of Minnesota
Crookston *B*

Missouri

Missouri Southern State University *C*

Nebraska

Central Community College *C, A*
Southeast Community College *A*

New York

Broome Community College *C, A*

Ohio

Bowling Green State University *B*
Columbus State Community
College *A*
Edison State Community College *C, A*
James A. Rhodes State College *A*
Marion Technical College *C, A*
Northwest State Community
College *C, A*
Owens Community College
Toledo *C, A*
University of Akron *C*

Oklahoma

National Education Center
Spartan College of Aeronautics and
Technology *A*

Oregon

Clackamas Community College *C*

Pennsylvania

Northampton Community
College *C, A*

Puerto Rico

Turabo University *A*

Tennessee

Southwest Tennessee Community
College *C*
Walters State Community College *C*

Texas

Austin Community College *C, A*

Virginia

Tidewater Community College *A*

Wisconsin

Gateway Technical College *A*
Lakeshore Technical College *A*

Rabbinical studies (M.H.L., Rav.)

California

Hebrew Union College-Jewish
Institute of Religion *P*

Colorado

Yeshiva Toras Chaim Talmudical
Seminary *P*

Connecticut

Beth Benjamin Academy of
Connecticut *P*

Illinois

Brisk Rabbinical College *P*
Hebrew Theological College:
Professional *P*

Maryland

Ner Israel Rabbinical College *P*

New York

Jewish Theological Seminary of
America: Professional *P*
Kehilath Yakov Rabbinical Seminary *P*
Kol Yaakov Torah Center *P*
Mesivta Eastern Parkway Rabbinical
Seminary *P*
Mesivta Tifereth Jerusalem of
America *P*
Mirrer Yeshiva Central Institute *P*
Ohr Hameir Theological Seminary *P*
Ohr Somayach Institutions: School of
Theology *P*
Rabbi Isaac Elchanan Theological
Seminary *P*
Rabbinical College Bobover Yeshiva
B'nei Zion *P*
Rabbinical Seminary M'Kor Chaim *P*
Sh'or Yoshuv Rabbinical College *P*
Yeshiva Karlin Stolin Beth Aron
Y'Israel Rabbinical Institute *P*
Yeshiva of Nitra Rabbinical College *P*
Yeshivat Mikdash Melech *P*

Ohio

Hebrew Union College-Jewish
Institute of Religion *P*

Radiation biology

District of Columbia

George Washington University *D*

Illinois

University of Chicago *D*

Iowa

University of Iowa *M, D*

Massachusetts

Suffolk University *B*

Ohio

University of Cincinnati *M*
University of Toledo *M*

Pennsylvania

Drexel University *M, D*

Texas

University of Texas
Health Science Center at San
Antonio *D*
Southwestern Medical Center at
Dallas *M, D*

Radiation protection/ health physics technology

New Jersey

Thomas Edison State College *A, B*

Ohio

University of Cincinnati
Raymond Walters College *C, A*

Radio and television

Alabama

Auburn University *B*
Jacksonville State University *B*
Lawson State Community College *C*
Troy University *B*
University of Alabama *B, M*
University of Montevallo *B*

Arizona

Arizona Western College *A*
Northern Arizona University *B*
Pima Community College *C, A*
Prescott College *B*
University of Arizona *B, M*

Arkansas

Arkansas State University *B, M*

California

Biola University *B*
California State University
Chico *B*
Fullerton *B, M*
Los Angeles *B, M*
Monterey Bay *B*
San Bernardino *B*
College of the Canyons *C, A*
College of the Siskiyous *C, A*
Foothill College *C, A*
Loyola Marymount University *B, M*
The Master's College *B*
National University *B, M*
Oxnard College *A*
Pepperdine University *B*
Rio Hondo College *C*
San Diego State University *B, M*
San Francisco State University *B, M*
San Jose State University *B*
University of La Verne *B*
University of Southern
California *B, M*

Colorado

Colorado State University *B*

Connecticut

Mitchell College *B*

Delaware

Delaware State University *B*

District of Columbia

American University *B*

Howard University *B*

Florida

Barry University *B, M*
Palm Beach Atlantic University *B*
Southeastern University *B*
State College of Florida,
Manatee-Sarasota *A*
University of Central Florida *B*
University of Miami *B, M*

Idaho

University of Idaho *B*

Illinois

Bradley University *B*
Columbia College Chicago *C, B*
DePaul University *M*
Lewis University *B*
Lewis and Clark Community
College *A*
North Central College *B*
Northwestern University *B, M, D*
Parkland College *A*
Southern Illinois University
Carbondale *B*.
University of St. Francis *B*
Western Illinois University *B, M*

Indiana

Ball State University *B, M*
Butler University *B*
Huntington University *B*
University of Southern Indiana *B, T*
Valparaiso University *B*

Iowa

Drake University *B*
Grand View University *B*
St. Ambrose University *B*
Waldorf College *B*

Kansas

Central Christian College of Kansas *A*
Colby Community College *C, A*
Pittsburg State University *B*
Southwestern College *B*

Kentucky

Bluegrass Community and Technical
College *A*
Murray State University *B*
University of Kentucky *B*
Western Kentucky University *B*

Maine

New England School of
Communications *B*

Massachusetts

American International College *B*
Lasell College *B*
New England Institute of Art *A*

Michigan

Lawrence Technological University *A*
Michigan State University *B, M*
Wayne State University *B*

Minnesota

Northland Community & Technical
College *A*
Northwestern College *A, B*
Saint Cloud State University *B*
Southwest Minnesota State
University *B*

Mississippi

University of Southern Mississippi *B*

Missouri

Northwest Missouri State
University *B*
University of Missouri
Columbia *B*

New Jersey

Cumberland County College *A*
Montclair State University *B*
Seton Hall University *B*

New York

Cayuga County Community College *A*
City University of New York
Brooklyn College *B, M*
Five Towns College *A, B*
Hofstra University *B*
Iona College *B*
Ithaca College *B*
Marist College *B*
New York Institute of Technology *B*
New York University *B*
St. Francis College *B*
State University of New York
College at Plattsburgh *B*
Syracuse University *B, M*

North Carolina

Appalachian State University *B*
Campbell University *B*

North Dakota

Minot State University *B*

Ohio

Ashland University *A, B*
Bowling Green State University *B*
Capital University *B*
Cedarville University *B*
Kent State University *B*
Malone University *B*
Marietta College *B*
Ohio University *B, M, D*
Ohio University
Southern Campus at Ironton *A*
University of Akron *B*
University of Cincinnati *B*
Xavier University *A, B*
Youngstown State University *B*

Oklahoma

Northeastern Oklahoma Agricultural
and Mechanical College *A*
Oklahoma City University *B*

Pennsylvania

Arcadia University *B*
Drexel University *M*
Keystone College *A*
La Salle University *B*
Messiah College *B*
Temple University *B, M*
University of Pittsburgh
Bradford *B*

Puerto Rico

University of Puerto Rico
Arecibo *B*

South Carolina

Bob Jones University *B*
North Greenville University *B*

Texas

Alvin Community College *C, A*
Austin Community College *A*
Del Mar College *A*
Hardin-Simmons University *B*
North Lake College *C*
Sam Houston State University *B*
San Antonio College *C, A*
Southern Methodist University *B, M*

Stephen F. Austin State University *B*
Texas Christian University *B*
Texas Southern University *B*
Texas State University: San Marcos *B*
Texas Tech University *B*
Texas Wesleyan University *B*
University of Houston *B*
University of North Texas *B, M*
University of Texas
Arlington *B*
Austin *B, M, D*
University of the Incarnate Word *B*

Utah

College of Eastern Utah *T*

Vermont

Lyndon State College *B*

Washington

Centralia College *A*

West Virginia

Bethany College *B*

Wisconsin

Marquette University *M*

Wyoming

Central Wyoming College *A*

Radio/television broadcasting

Alabama

Jefferson State Community
College *C, A*

Arizona

Arizona Western College *A*
Scottsdale Community College *C, A*

Arkansas

Mid-South Community College *C*
Southern Arkansas University Tech *C*

California

Chabot College *C, A*
City College of San Francisco *C*
College of the Siskiyous *C, A*
National University *M*
San Bernardino Valley College *C*
Southwestern College *C, A*

Colorado

Pikes Peak Community College *C, A*
Pueblo Community College *C*

Connecticut

Asnuntuck Community College *C, A*

Florida

Art Institute of Fort Lauderdale *A*
Miami Dade College *A*
State College of Florida,
Manatee-Sarasota *A*

Georgia

University of Georgia *B*

Illinois

Black Hawk College *A*
Lewis University *B*
Parkland College *A*
Waubonsee Community College *C, A*

Indiana

Vincennes University *A*

Iowa

Iowa Central Community College *A*

Kansas

Central Christian College of Kansas *A*
Cloud County Community
College *C, A*
Colby Community College *C*

Kentucky

Asbury College *B*

Maine

New England School of
Communications *B*

Maryland

Bowie State University *B*
Community College of Baltimore
County *C, A*
Montgomery College *C*
Towson University *B*

Massachusetts

Mount Wachusett Community
College *A*
New England Institute of Art *A*
Newbury College *A*
Roxbury Community College *A*
Springfield Technical Community
College *A*
Suffolk University *B*
Worcester State College *B*

Michigan

Eastern Michigan University *B*
Ferris State University *B*
Oakland Community College *A*
Schoolcraft College *A*

Minnesota

Lake Superior College *C*

Nebraska

Northeast Community College *A*
Southeast Community College *A*

New Jersey

Bergen Community College *A*

New York

City University of New York
Brooklyn College *B*
Long Island University
C. W. Post Campus *B, M*
Mercy College *C*
Monroe Community College *A*
New York University *C, B, M, D, T*
Syracuse University *M*
Tompkins Cortland Community
College *A*

North Carolina

Isothermal Community College *C, A*
Southeastern Community College *A*
Wilkes Community College *C, A*

Ohio

Hocking College *A*
North Central State College *A*

Oregon

Mt. Hood Community College *A*

Pennsylvania

Gannon University *B*
La Salle University *B*
Northampton Community College *A*
Thiel College *B*
Westmoreland County Community
College *C*

Puerto Rico

University of Puerto Rico
Aguadilla *T*
Arecibo *A, B*

Rhode Island

New England Institute of
Technology *A*

South Carolina

York Technical College *C*

Texas

Austin Community College *C*
Houston Community College
System *C, A*
Howard Payne University *B*
San Jacinto College *C*
Tarrant County College *C, A*
Western Texas College *C, A*

Utah

Salt Lake Community College *A*

Virginia

Southwest Virginia Community
College *C*

Washington

Bates Technical College *C, A*
Centralia College *A*
Clover Park Technical College *A*
Yakima Valley Community College *C*

Wisconsin

Gateway Technical College *A*
Milwaukee Area Technical College *A*

Radiologic technology/ medical imaging

Alabama

Southern Union State Community
College *A*

Arizona

Arizona Western College *A*
Pima Community College *A*

Arkansas

South Arkansas Community College *A*
University of Arkansas
Fort Smith *A, B*

California

Charles Drew University of Medicine
and Science *A, B*
Foothill College *A*
Fresno City College *A*
Orange Coast College *A*

Colorado

Anthem College *A*
Colorado State University *M, D*
Community College of Denver *A*
Mesa State College *A, B*
Pueblo Community College *A*
Red Rocks Community College *A*

Connecticut

Quinnipiac University *B, M*
St. Vincent's College *A*

Delaware

Delaware Technical and Community
College
Owens *A*
Stanton/Wilmington *A*

Florida

Florida National College *A*
Gulf Coast Community College *A*
Pasco-Hernando Community
    College *A*
St. Petersburg College *A*
Santa Fe College *A*
South Florida Community College *A*
Valencia Community College *A*

Georgia

Athens Technical College *A*
Dalton State College *A*
Georgia Highlands College *A*
Gordon College *A*
Griffin Technical College *A*
Gwinnett Technical College *A*
Middle Georgia Technical College *A*
Southeastern Technical College *A*
Southwest Georgia Technical
    College *A*
Valdosta Technical College *A*

Idaho

Lewis-Clark State College *A*

Illinois

Danville Area Community College *A*
Harper College *A*
Heartland Community College *A*
Kankakee Community College *A*
Kaskaskia College *A*
Lincoln Land Community College *A*
Moraine Valley Community College *A*
Parkland College *A*
Richland Community College *A*
Sauk Valley Community College *A*
Trinity College of Nursing and Health
    Sciences *A*
Triton College *A*
University of St. Francis *B*
Wilbur Wright College *A*

Indiana

Indiana University
    Northwest *A*
Indiana University-Purdue University
    Fort Wayne *A*
Indiana University-Purdue University
    Indianapolis *B*

Iowa

Allen College *A*
Clinton Community College *A*
Indian Hills Community College *A*
Iowa Central Community College *A*
Mercy College of Health Sciences *A*
Muscatine Community College *A*
Northeast Iowa Community
    College *A*
Northwest Iowa Community
    College *A*
Scott Community College *A*
University of Iowa *B*

Kansas

Labette Community College *A*
Washburn University *A*

Louisiana

Louisiana State University
    Alexandria *A*
McNeese State University *B*
Northwestern State University *B, M*
Our Lady of the Lake College *A*
Southeastern Louisiana University *B*
University of Louisiana at Monroe *B*

Maine

Kennebec Valley Community
    College *A*

Southern Maine Community
    College *A*

Maryland

Carroll Community College *A*
Howard Community College *A*

Massachusetts

Massachusetts College of Pharmacy
    and Health Sciences *B*
North Shore Community College *A*
Springfield Technical Community
    College *A*

Michigan

Baker College
    of Clinton Township *A*
    of Muskegon *A*
Bay de Noc Community College *A*
Henry Ford Community College *A*
Jackson Community College *A*
Lake Michigan College *A*
Northern Michigan University *A, B*
Oakland University *B*
Wayne State University *M*

Minnesota

Century Community and Technical
    College *A*
Lake Superior College *A*
Minnesota State College - Southeast
    Technical *A*
Minnesota State Community and
    Technical College *A*
Minnesota West Community and
    Technical College *A*
Normandale Community College *A*
Northland Community & Technical
    College *A*
Rochester Community and Technical
    College *A*
St. Catherine University *A*

Missouri

Missouri State University *B*
Southeast Missouri Hospital College of
    Nursing and Health Sciences *A*
State Fair Community College *A*
University of Missouri
    Columbia *B*

Montana

Montana State University
    Billings *A*
    College of Technology: Great
       Falls *A*
Montana Tech of the University of
    Montana *A*

Nebraska

Clarkson College *B*
Nebraska Methodist College of
    Nursing and Allied Health *A, B*
University of Nebraska
    Medical Center *B*

Nevada

Truckee Meadows Community
    College *A*

New Hampshire

Lebanon College *A*

New Jersey

Fairleigh Dickinson University
    Metropolitan Campus *A, B*
Union County College *A*

New York

Adirondack Community College *A*
St. John's University *B*

North Carolina

Carteret Community College *A*
Fayetteville Technical Community
    College *A*
Forsyth Technical Community
    College *A*
Johnston Community College *A*
Lenoir Community College *A*
Robeson Community College *A*
Rowan-Cabarrus Community
    College *A*
Stanly Community College *A*

North Dakota

Jamestown College *B*
North Dakota State University *B*
University of Mary *B*

Ohio

James A. Rhodes State College *A*
Mercy College of Northwest Ohio *A*
North Central State College *A*
Owens Community College
    Toledo *A*
University of Cincinnati
    Raymond Walters College *A, B*
University of Rio Grande *A*

Oklahoma

Oklahoma State University
    Oklahoma City *A*
Rose State College *A*
Southwestern Oklahoma State
    University *A*

Oregon

Central Oregon Community
    College *A*
Oregon Institute of Technology *B*

Pennsylvania

Bloomsburg University of
    Pennsylvania *M*
Butler County Community College *A*
Harcum College *A*
Harrisburg Area Community
    College *A*
Holy Family University *A, B*
Johnson College *A*
Keystone College *A*
Mount Aloysius College *A, B*
Northampton Community College *A*
University of Pittsburgh
    Bradford *B*
Westmoreland County Community
    College *A*
Widener University *A*

Puerto Rico

EDIC College *A*
Universidad del Este *A*

Rhode Island

Community College of Rhode
    Island *A*

South Carolina

York Technical College *A*

Tennessee

Baptist College of Health Sciences *B*

Texas

Angelina College *A*
Austin Community College *A*
Brookhaven College *A*
Del Mar College *A*
Houston Community College
    System *A*
Midwestern State University *A, B, M*
San Jacinto College *A*
South Texas College *A*

Tarrant County College *A*
Tyler Junior College *A*
University of Texas
    Brownsville - Texas Southmost
       College *A*
Weatherford College *A*
Wharton County Junior College *A*

Utah

Dixie State College of Utah *A*

Vermont

Champlain College *A*
College of St. Joseph in Vermont *A, B*
Southern Vermont College *B*

Virginia

Germanna Community College *A*
Southwest Virginia Community
    College *A*
Virginia Commonwealth University *B*
Wytheville Community College *A*

Washington

Bellingham Technical College *A*
Clark College *A*
North Seattle Community College *A*
Wenatchee Valley College *A*

West Virginia

Bluefield State College *B*
Marshall University *B*
Mountain State University *A*
University of Charleston *B*

Wisconsin

Carroll University *B*
Chippewa Valley Technical College *A*
Marian University *B*
Nicolet Area Technical College *A*
Northcentral Technical College *A*

Wyoming

Casper College *A*
Laramie County Community
    College *A*

Range science

Arizona

Prescott College *M*
University of Arizona *M, D*

California

California State University
    Chico *B*
College of the Redwoods *C*
Humboldt State University *B*
University of California
    Berkeley *M*
    Davis *B*

Colorado

Colorado State University *B, M, D*
Lamar Community College *A*

Idaho

University of Idaho *B, M*

Kansas

Pratt Community College *A*

Montana

Montana State University
    Bozeman *B*

Nebraska

Chadron State College *B*
University of Nebraska
    Lincoln *B*

New Mexico

Navajo Technical College *C*
New Mexico State University *B, M, D*

Oregon

Eastern Oregon University *B*
Oregon State University *B, M, D*

South Dakota

Sinte Gleska University *A*
South Dakota State University *B*

Texas

Frank Phillips College *A*
Sul Ross State University *B, M*
Texas A&M University *B, M, D*
Texas A&M University
  Kingsville *B, M, D*
Texas Tech University *B, M, D*

Utah

Utah State University *B, M, D*

Wyoming

Casper College *A*
Central Wyoming College *A*
Eastern Wyoming College *A*
Northwest College *A*
Sheridan College *A*
University of Wyoming *B, M, D*

Reading teacher education

Alabama

Alabama Agricultural and Mechanical
  University *D*
Jacksonville State University *M, T*
University of South Alabama *M*

Alaska

University of Alaska
  Fairbanks *M*

Arizona

Grand Canyon University *M*
University of Arizona *M, D*

Arkansas

Arkansas State University *M, T*
Harding University *M, T*
University of Arkansas *M*
University of Arkansas
  Little Rock *M, D*
University of Central Arkansas *M*

California

Azusa Pacific University *M, T*
California Baptist University *M, T*
California Lutheran University *B, T*
California State University
  Chico *M, T*
  East Bay *M, T*
  Fresno *M*
  Fullerton *M, T*
  Long Beach *T*
  Sacramento *M*
  San Bernardino *M, T*
Chapman University *M*
Fresno Pacific University *M, T*
Loyola Marymount University *M*
National University *M*
St. Mary's College of California *M*
San Diego State University *M*
Sonoma State University *M, T*
University of La Verne *M*

Colorado

University of Colorado
  Colorado Springs *T*
University of Northern Colorado *M, T*

Connecticut

Central Connecticut State
  University *M*
Eastern Connecticut State
  University *M*

District of Columbia

Howard University *M*
Trinity Washington University *M*
University of the District of
  Columbia *M*

Florida

Barry University *M*
Florida Atlantic University *M*
Florida Gulf Coast University *M*
Florida International University *M*
Florida Memorial University *M*
Florida State University *M, D*
Palm Beach Atlantic University *M*
Saint Leo University *M*
Stetson University *M*
University of Central Florida *M*
University of Miami *M*
University of South Florida *M*
University of West Florida *M*

Georgia

Berry College *M*
Georgia Southern University *M*
Georgia State University *M, T*
Mercer University *M*
University of Georgia *M, D, T*
University of West Georgia *M*
Valdosta State University *M*

Idaho

Boise State University *M*
Northwest Nazarene University *M*

Illinois

Aurora University *M*
Benedictine University *M*
Chicago State University *M, T*
Concordia University Chicago *M*
DePaul University *M*
Governors State University *M*
Greenville College *M, T*
Illinois State University *M, T*
Lewis University *M, T*
Loyola University Chicago *M*
National-Louis University *M, D*
North Central College *T*
North Park University *T*
Northeastern Illinois University *M*
Northern Illinois University *M*
Rockford College *M*
Roosevelt University *M*
Saint Xavier University *M*
University of St. Francis *M*
Western Illinois University *M*

Indiana

Butler University *M, T*
Huntington University *M*
Oakland City University *B*
University of Indianapolis *T*

Iowa

Briar Cliff University *B*
Buena Vista University *B, T*
Central College *T*
Dordt College *B*
Drake University *M, T*
Graceland University *T*
Grand View University *T*
Iowa State University *T*
Iowa Wesleyan College *T*
Mount Mercy College *M, T*
Northwestern College *T*
St. Ambrose University *T*
Simpson College *T*

University of Iowa *M*
University of Northern Iowa *B, M*
Upper Iowa University *B, T*
Wartburg College *T*

Kansas

Garden City Community College *A*
Pittsburg State University *M*
Washburn University *M*

Kentucky

Bellarmine University *M*
Campbellsville University *B*
Georgetown College *M*
Murray State University *M, T*
Spalding University *M*
Union College *M*
University of Louisville *M*
Western Kentucky University *M*

Louisiana

Centenary College of Louisiana *T*
Nicholls State University *M*

Maine

University of Maine *M*
University of Southern Maine *M, T*

Maryland

Bowie State University *M*
Coppin State University *M*
Frostburg State University *M, T*
Hood College *M*
Loyola University Maryland *M*
McDaniel College *M*
Mount St. Mary's University *T*
Salisbury University *M*
Towson University *M, T*

Massachusetts

Boston College *M*
Boston University *M, T*
Bridgewater State College *M*
Eastern Nazarene College *M, T*
Elms College *M*
Endicott College *M*
Framingham State College *M*
Lesley University *M*
Salem State College *M*
Tufts University *M*
University of Massachusetts
  Lowell *M, D*
Westfield State College *M, T*
Wheelock College *M*
Worcester State College *M, T*

Michigan

Andrews University *M*
Calvin College *B, M, T*
Central Michigan University *M*
Eastern Michigan University *B, M*
Marygrove College *M*
Michigan State University *B, M*
Northern Michigan University *M*
Oakland University *M, D*
Saginaw Valley State University *M*
University of Detroit Mercy *B, M, T*
Wayne State University *M, D*
Western Michigan University *M*

Minnesota

Capella University *M*
Minnesota State University
  Moorhead *M*
Saint Cloud State University *B, T*
St. Mary's University of Minnesota *M*
University of St. Thomas *M*
Winona State University *B, M, T*

Mississippi

Millsaps College *T*
Mississippi State University *T*

Mississippi University for Women *M*
University of Mississippi *M*

Missouri

Evangel University *M*
Harris-Stowe State University *T*
Maryville University of Saint
  Louis *M, T*
Missouri Baptist University *T*
Missouri Southern State
  University *B, T*
Missouri State University *M*
Northwest Missouri State
  University *M, T*
University of Central Missouri *M, T*
University of Missouri
  Columbia *M, D*
  Kansas City *M*

Montana

Montana State University
  Billings *M, T*
University of Great Falls *B*
University of Montana: Western *T*

Nebraska

Chadron State College *M*
College of Saint Mary *T*
Concordia University *M*
University of Nebraska
  Kearney *M, T*
  Lincoln *B*
  Omaha *M*
York College *B, T*

New Hampshire

Plymouth State University *M, T*
Rivier College *M*
University of New Hampshire *M*

New Jersey

The College of New Jersey *M, T*
Georgian Court University *T*
Kean University *M, T*
Monmouth University *M*
Montclair State University *M, T*
New Jersey City University *B*
Rider University *M*
Rowan University *T*
Saint Peter's College *M, T*
William Paterson University of New
  Jersey *T*

New Mexico

New Mexico State University *D*
Western New Mexico University *M*

New York

Adelphi University *M, T*
Canisius College *M, T*
City University of New York
  Lehman College *M*
  Queens College *M, T*
College of New Rochelle *M, T*
College of Saint Rose *M, T*
Dowling College *M*
Hofstra University *M, D, T*
Iona College *M, T*
Le Moyne College *M*
Long Island University
  Brooklyn Campus *M, T*
  C. W. Post Campus *M, T*
Manhattanville College *M, T*
Medaille College *M, T*
Mercy College *M*
Nazareth College *M*
New York University *M*
Pace University *M, T*
Roberts Wesleyan College *M*
Saint Bonaventure University *M*
St. John's University *M, D, T*
St. Thomas Aquinas College *M*

State University of New York
Albany *M, D*
Binghamton *M*
Buffalo *M, D*
College at Brockport *M*
College at Buffalo *B, M, T*
College at Cortland *M*
College at Fredonia *M, T*
College at Geneseo *M, T*
College at Oneonta *M, T*
College at Plattsburgh *M*
College at Potsdam *M*
New Paltz *M, T*
Oswego *M*
Syracuse University *D*
University of Rochester *M*

North Carolina

Appalachian State University *M, T*
Catawba College *T*
East Carolina University *M*
Mars Hill College *T*
Meredith College *M*
North Carolina Agricultural and
  Technical State University *M*
North Carolina State University *M, T*
University of North Carolina
  Asheville *T*
  Charlotte *M*
  Pembroke *M*
  Wilmington *M*
Wingate University *B, T*

North Dakota

Dickinson State University *B, T*
University of Mary *B*
University of North Dakota *M*

Ohio

Ashland University *M, T*
Baldwin-Wallace College *M*
Bowling Green State University *M, T*
Hiram College *T*
John Carroll University *M, T*
Kent State University *M*
Malone University *M*
Miami University
  Oxford Campus *M*
Notre Dame College *M, T*
Ohio Northern University *T*
Ohio State University
  Columbus Campus *M, D*
Ohio University *M*
Otterbein College *M*
Union Institute & University *B, M*
University of Akron *M*
University of Cincinnati *M*
University of Dayton *M*
University of Findlay *B, M, T*
University of Rio Grande *B, T*
Ursuline College *T*
Walsh University *B*
Wilmington College *M, T*
Wright State University *M*
Xavier University *M*
Youngstown State University *M*

Oklahoma

Northeastern State University *M, T*
Northwestern Oklahoma State
  University *M*
Southeastern Oklahoma State
  University *M, T*
Southern Nazarene University *B*
University of Central Oklahoma *B, M*
University of Oklahoma *T*

Oregon

George Fox University *M, T*
Portland State University *T*
Warner Pacific College *T*
Western Oregon University *B, M, T*

Pennsylvania

Arcadia University *M*
Bloomsburg University of
  Pennsylvania *M, T*
Bucknell University *M*
Cabrini College *T*
California University of
  Pennsylvania *M*
Chestnut Hill College *T*
Clarion University of
  Pennsylvania *M, T*
Duquesne University *M, T*
East Stroudsburg University of
  Pennsylvania *M, T*
Edinboro University of
  Pennsylvania *M*
Gannon University *M, T*
Geneva College *M*
Gwynedd-Mercy College *M*
Holy Family University *M, T*
Indiana University of
  Pennsylvania *M, T*
King's College *M*
Kutztown University of
  Pennsylvania *M, T*
Lincoln University *M, T*
Marywood University *M*
Millersville University of
  Pennsylvania *M*
Penn State
  Harrisburg *M*
Saint Joseph's University *M, T*
Shippensburg University of
  Pennsylvania *M, T*
University of Pennsylvania *M, D*
University of Scranton *M*
West Chester University of
  Pennsylvania *M, T*
Westminster College *M*
Widener University *M, D*
York College of Pennsylvania *M*

Rhode Island

Providence College *M*
Rhode Island College *M*
Roger Williams University *M*

South Carolina

The Citadel *M*
Clemson University *M*
University of South Carolina *M, D*
Winthrop University *M, T*

South Dakota

University of Sioux Falls *M*

Tennessee

Austin Peay State University *M*
East Tennessee State University *M, T*
Middle Tennessee State University *M*
Tennessee Technological
  University *M, D, T*
Trevecca Nazarene University *M, T*
Vanderbilt University *M, D*

Texas

Angelo State University *M*
Dallas Baptist University *T*
Hardin-Simmons University *B, M, T*
Houston Baptist University *M*
Jarvis Christian College *B*
Laredo Community College *A*
Midwestern State University *M*
Prairie View A&M University *M*
St. Mary's University *M, T*
Sam Houston State University *M, D, T*
Southwestern Assemblies of God
  University *B*
Southwestern University *T*
Stephen F. Austin State University *M, T*
Sul Ross State University *M*
Texas A&M International
  University *B, M, T*

Texas A&M University
  Commerce *M, T*
  Corpus Christi *M, D, T*
  Kingsville *M, T*
Texas Christian University *B*
Texas Lutheran University *B, T*
Texas State University: San
  Marcos *M, T*
Texas Tech University *M*
Texas Wesleyan University *B, M, T*
Texas Woman's University *M, D*
University of Dallas *T*
University of Houston *M, T*
University of Houston
  Clear Lake *M, T*
  Victoria *M*
University of Mary Hardin-Baylor *M, T*
University of North Texas *M, D*
University of Texas
  Brownsville - Texas Southmost
    College *M*
  El Paso *M*
  Pan American *M*
  San Antonio *M, T*
  Tyler *M*
  of the Permian Basin *M*
West Texas A&M University *M, T*

Utah

Southern Utah University *M*

Vermont

College of St. Joseph in Vermont *M*
Johnson State College *M*
St. Michael's College *M, T*
University of Vermont *M, T*

Virginia

Averett University *M*
Bluefield College *B, T*
College of William and Mary *M*
James Madison University *T*
Liberty University *M, T*
Longwood University *M, T*
Lynchburg College *M*
Old Dominion University *M, D, T*
Radford University *M, T*
Virginia Commonwealth University *M*

Washington

City University of Seattle *M*
Eastern Washington University *B, M*
Northwest University *T*
Pacific Lutheran University *M*
Seattle Pacific University *M*
Walla Walla University *M*
Washington State
  University *B, M, D, T*
Western Washington University *M*
Whitworth University *T*

West Virginia

Marshall University *M*
West Virginia University *M, T*

Wisconsin

Alverno College *M, T*
Cardinal Stritch University *M*
Carroll University *T*
Carthage College *M, T*
Concordia University Wisconsin *M, T*
Mount Mary College *T*
Silver Lake College *T*
University of Wisconsin
  La Crosse *M*
  Oshkosh *M*
  Platteville *T*
  River Falls *M, T*
  Superior *M, T*
  Whitewater *M*

Real estate

Alabama

Enterprise-Ozark Community
  College *A*
Jefferson Davis Community College *C*

Arizona

Arizona State University *B*
Coconino County Community
  College *C*
Glendale Community College *A*
Paradise Valley Community College *C*

California

American River College *C, A*
Antelope Valley College *C, A*
Bakersfield College *A*
Butte College *C, A*
Cabrillo College *A*
California State University
  Dominguez Hills *B*
  East Bay *B*
  Fresno *B*
  Long Beach *B*
  Northridge *B*
  Sacramento *B, M*
  San Bernardino *B*
Cerritos College *C, A*
Chabot College *A*
Citrus College *C*
City College of San Francisco *C, A*
Coastline Community College *C, A*
College of Marin: Kentfield *C, A*
College of San Mateo *C*
College of the Canyons *C, A*
College of the Redwoods *A*
College of the Sequoias *C, A*
Contra Costa College *C, A*
Cosumnes River College *C, A*
Cuesta College *C, A*
Cuyamaca College *A*
De Anza College *C, A*
Diablo Valley College *C*
East Los Angeles College *C, A*
El Camino College *C, A*
El Camino College: Compton
  Center *A*
Folsom Lake College *C, A*
Foothill College *C, A*
Fresno City College *C, A*
Fullerton College *C, A*
Glendale Community College *C, A*
Golden West College *C, A*
Hartnell College *C, A*
Irvine Valley College *C, A*
Lassen Community College *A*
Long Beach City College *C, A*
Los Angeles City College *C, A*
Los Angeles Harbor College *A*
Los Angeles Mission College *C, A*
Los Angeles Southwest College *C, A*
Los Angeles Trade and Technical
  College *C, A*
Los Medanos College *C, A*
Merced College *C, A*
Merritt College *C, A*
MiraCosta College *C, A*
Mission College *A*
Modesto Junior College *A*
Monterey Peninsula College *C, A*
Moorpark College *C, A*
Mount San Antonio College *C, A*
Mount San Jacinto College *C, A*
Napa Valley College *C, A*
Ohlone College *C, A*
Orange Coast College *C, A*
Pacific States University *M*
Palomar College *C, A*
Pasadena City College *C, A*
Porterville College *C, A*
Riverside Community College *C, A*
Sacramento City College *C, A*

Saddleback College *C, A*
San Bernardino Valley College *C, A*
San Diego City College *C, A*
San Diego Mesa College *C, A*
San Diego State University *B, M*
San Joaquin Delta College *C, A*
San Jose City College *C, A*
Santa Barbara City College *C, A*
Santa Monica College *C, A*
Santa Rosa Junior College *C*
Shasta College *C*
Sierra College *C, A*
Solano Community College *C, A*
Southwestern College *C, A*
University of San Diego *M*
University of Southern California *M*
Victor Valley College *C, A*
West Los Angeles College *C, A*
West Valley College *C, A*

Colorado
Arapahoe Community College *C*
Colorado Mountain College *C, A*
Colorado State University *B*
Mesa State College *C*
Pikes Peak Community College *C*
Red Rocks Community College *C, A*
University of Colorado
  Boulder *B*
University of Denver *B*

Connecticut
Manchester Community College *C*
University of Connecticut *B*

District of Columbia
George Washington University *M*

Florida
Florida Atlantic University *B*
Florida International University *B*
Florida State College at Jacksonville *C*
Florida State University *B*
Miami Dade College *C, A*
Northwest Florida State College *A*
Seminole Community College *C*
University of Central Florida *B, M*
University of Florida *B, M*
University of Miami *B*
Valencia Community College *A*

Georgia
Georgia State University *B, M, D*
University of Georgia *B*
University of West Georgia *B*

Illinois
City Colleges of Chicago
  Kennedy-King College *C*
  Olive-Harvey College *C*
College of DuPage *C, A*
Danville Area Community College *C*
DePaul University *B, M*
Harper College *C*
Illinois Central College *C, A*
Joliet Junior College *C*
Kishwaukee College *C*
Lewis and Clark Community
  College *C*
Lincoln Land Community College *C*
McHenry County College *C, A*
Northwestern University *M*
Oakton Community College *C, A*
Prairie State College *C*
Roosevelt University *M*
Southeastern Illinois College *C*
Southwestern Illinois College *C*
Triton College *C*
University of Illinois
  Chicago *M*
  Urbana-Champaign *B, M, D*
Waubonsee Community College *C*

Iowa
Grand View University *C, B*
University of Northern Iowa *B*

Kentucky
Ashland Community and Technical
  College *A*
Big Sandy Community and Technical
  College *A*
Elizabethtown Community and
  Technical College *A*
Madisonville Community College *A*
Morehead State University *B*
West Kentucky Community and
  Technical College *A*
Western Kentucky University *C*

Maine
University of Southern Maine *C*

Maryland
Community College of Baltimore
  County *C, A*
University of Baltimore *B*

Massachusetts
Greenfield Community College *C*
Massachusetts Institute of
  Technology *M*

Michigan
Central Michigan University *B*
Delta College *C*
Henry Ford Community College *A*
Lansing Community College *A*
Wayne County Community College *C*

Minnesota
Dakota County Technical College *C, A*
Fond du Lac Tribal and Community
  College *C*
Saint Cloud State University *B*
University of St. Thomas *B, M*

Mississippi
Mississippi State University *B*
University of Mississippi *B*

Missouri
St. Louis Community College
  St. Louis Community College at
    Meramec *C, A*
State Fair Community College *C*
University of Missouri
  Columbia *B*

Nebraska
Northeast Community College *A*
University of Nebraska
  Omaha *B*

Nevada
College of Southern Nevada *C, A*
Truckee Meadows Community
  College *A*
University of Nevada
  Las Vegas *B*
Western Nevada College *A*

New Hampshire
Lakes Region Community College *C*

New Jersey
Camden County College *C*
Gloucester County College *C*
Ocean County College *C*
Thomas Edison State College *B*

New Mexico
New Mexico Junior College *A*
New Mexico State University *B*

New York
City University of New York
  Baruch College *B*
Cornell University *M*
Hudson Valley Community College *A*
New York University *B, M*
Utica School of Commerce *C*

North Carolina
Asheville-Buncombe Technical
  Community College *C*
Blue Ridge Community College *C*
Cape Fear Community College *C*
Catawba Valley Community College *A*
Central Piedmont Community
  College *C, A*
Cleveland Community College *C*
College of the Albemarle *C*
Forsyth Technical Community
  College *C*
Haywood Community College *C*
Isothermal Community College *C*
Pitt Community College *C*
St. Augustine's College *B*
Sampson Community College *C*
Southwestern Community College *C*
Surry Community College *C, A*
Tri-County Community College *C*

Ohio
Bowling Green State University *B*
Cincinnati State Technical and
  Community College *A*
Columbus State Community
  College *C, A*
Cuyahoga Community College
  Metropolitan Campus *A*
Eastern Gateway Community
  College *C*
Edison State Community College *C*
Hocking College *C*
Hondros College *C, A*
Marion Technical College *A*
Miami University
  Hamilton Campus *A*
  Oxford Campus *A*
Northwest State Community
  College *C*
Ohio Business College: Sandusky *C*
Ohio State University
  Columbus Campus *B*
Ohio University
  Southern Campus at Ironton *C*
Owens Community College
  Toledo *C*
Shawnee State University *A*
Southern State Community College *A*
Terra State Community College *A*
University of Akron *C*
University of Cincinnati *B, M*
University of Cincinnati
  Raymond Walters College *C, A*
University of Rio Grande *B*

Oklahoma
Oklahoma City Community College *A*
Tulsa Community College *A*

Oregon
Marylhurst University *C, B*

Pennsylvania
Clarion University of Pennsylvania *B*
Community College of Philadelphia *A*
Harrisburg Area Community
  College *C, A*
La Roche College *B*
Luzerne County Community
  College *A*
Montgomery County Community
  College *C, A*
Northampton Community College *C*
St. Francis University *A*

Temple University *B*
University of Pennsylvania *B, M, D*
University of Pittsburgh
  Titusville *C*
Westmoreland County Community
  College *C, A*

Puerto Rico
Caribbean University *A*

Rhode Island
Community College of Rhode
  Island *A*

South Carolina
Clemson University *M*
Greenville Technical College *C*
University of South Carolina *B*

Tennessee
University of Memphis *B*

Texas
Amarillo College *C, A*
Angelina College *C*
Angelo State University *B*
Austin Community College *C, A*
Baylor University *B*
Blinn College *C*
Cedar Valley College *C, A*
Central Texas College *C, A*
College of the Mainland *A*
Collin County Community College
  District *C, A*
El Paso Community College *C, A*
Hill College *A*
Houston Community College
  System *C, A*
Kilgore College *A*
Lamar Institute of Technology *C, A*
Laredo Community College *C, A*
Lee College *C*
McLennan Community College *C, A*
North Lake College *A*
Northeast Texas Community
  College *A*
Paris Junior College *A*
Richland College *A*
San Antonio College *C*
San Jacinto College *C, A*
South Plains College *C, A*
Southern Methodist University *B*
Tarrant County College *C, A*
Texarkana College *C*
Texas A&M University *M*
Trinity Valley Community College *C*
Tyler Junior College *C*
University of North Texas *B, M*
University of Texas
  Arlington *B, M*
  San Antonio *B*

Virginia
Eastern Shore Community College *C*
George Mason University *M*
J. Sargeant Reynolds Community
  College *C*
Lord Fairfax Community College *C*
Northern Virginia Community
  College *C, A*
Southwest Virginia Community
  College *C*
Tidewater Community College *A*
Virginia Western Community
  College *C, A*

Washington
Bellevue College *C, A*
Green River Community College *C, A*
North Seattle Community
  College *C, A*
Spokane Falls Community College *C*
Washington State University *B*

West Virginia
American Public University
System *C, A*

Wisconsin
Chippewa Valley Technical College *C*
Fox Valley Technical College *C*
Milwaukee Area Technical College *A*
University of Wisconsin
Madison *B, M*
Milwaukee *B*
Stout *B*
Waukesha County Technical
College *A*

Receptionist

Arizona
Cochise College *C*

California
Empire College *C*
Kaplan College: Panorama City *C*
Ohlone College *A*

Iowa
Southeastern Community College
North Campus *A*

Kansas
Central Christian College of Kansas *A*

Maryland
Hagerstown Community College *C*

Massachusetts
Bunker Hill Community College *C*
Holyoke Community College *C*

Michigan
Baker College
of Muskegon *C*

Minnesota
Alexandria Technical College *C*
Dakota County Technical College *C*
Minnesota State College - Southeast
Technical *C*
Minnesota West Community and
Technical College *C*
St. Cloud Technical College *C*
South Central College *C*

New York
Globe Institute of Technology *C*

North Carolina
Lenoir Community College *C*

North Dakota
Dakota College at Bottineau *A*

Oregon
Clackamas Community College *C*

Pennsylvania
Newport Business Institute: Lower
Burrell *A*

South Dakota
Mitchell Technical Institute *C*

Texas
Brookhaven College *C*
Mountain View College *C*

Utah
Salt Lake Community College *C*
Utah Valley University *C*

Virginia
Danville Community College *A*

Washington
Bellingham Technical College *C*
Centralia College *C, A*
Clark College *C*
Peninsula College *C*

West Virginia
New River Community and Technical
College *A*
Valley College *C*

Recording arts

Arizona
Glendale Community College *A*

California
City College of San Francisco *C*
Loyola Marymount University *B*
Southwestern College *C, A*

District of Columbia
American University *B*

Florida
Full Sail University *A*
Miami International University of Art
and Design *B*

Georgia
Art Institute
of Atlanta *B*
Savannah College of Art and
Design *B, M*

Illinois
Columbia College Chicago *B*
School of the Art Institute of
Chicago *B, M*

Indiana
Butler University *B*
Indiana University
Bloomington *A, B*
Vincennes University *C, A*

Kansas
Central Christian College of Kansas *A*
Kansas City Kansas Community
College *A*

Louisiana
Bossier Parish Community
College *C, A*

Maine
New England School of
Communications *B*

Maryland
Johns Hopkins University: Peabody
Conservatory of Music *B, M*
Montgomery College *C*

Massachusetts
New England Institute of Art *B*

Michigan
Grace Bible College *B*
Michigan Technological University *B*
Schoolcraft College *C, A*

Minnesota
Hennepin Technical College *C, A*
Minneapolis Community and
Technical College *A*

Missouri
Webster University *B*

Nebraska
Northeast Community College *C, A*

Nevada
Art Institute
of Las Vegas *B*

New Jersey
Bergen Community College *A*
Burlington County College *A*
Union County College *C, A*

New York
Cayuga County Community College *A*
City University of New York
Queensborough Community
College *A*
Finger Lakes Community College *A*
Five Towns College *A, B*
Ithaca College *B*
State University of New York
College at Fredonia *B*

North Carolina
Guilford Technical Community
College *A*

Ohio
Cleveland Institute of Music *B*
Malone University *B*

Oregon
Clackamas Community College *C*

Pennsylvania
Community College of Philadelphia *A*
Harrisburg Area Community
College *C*
Lebanon Valley College *B*
Lehigh Carbon Community College *A*
Luzerne County Community
College *A*
Montgomery County Community
College *A*
York College of Pennsylvania *B*

Rhode Island
New England Institute of
Technology *A, B*

Texas
Cedar Valley College *C, A*
Texas Southern University *B*
Texas State University: San Marcos *B*
University of Texas
Austin *B*

Washington
Bates Technical College *C*

Recreational therapy

Arizona
Prescott College *B, M*

California
California State University
Chico *B*
East Bay *B*
Santa Barbara City College *A*
Whittier College *B*

Connecticut
Northwestern Connecticut
Community College *A*
Norwalk Community College *A*

District of Columbia
Gallaudet University *B*
Howard University *B*

Florida
Broward College *A*

Illinois
University of St. Francis *B*

Indiana
Indiana Institute of Technology *B*

Iowa
University of Iowa *B*

Kansas
Pittsburg State University *B*

Louisiana
Southern University and Agricultural
and Mechanical College *B*

Maine
Unity College *B*
University of Southern Maine *A, B*

Massachusetts
Springfield College *B, M*

Michigan
Calvin College *B*
Central Michigan University *B, M*
Eastern Michigan University *B*
Lake Superior State University *B*

Minnesota
Minnesota State University
Mankato *B*
Saint Cloud State University *B*
Winona State University *B*

Missouri
Northwest Missouri State
University *M*

New Hampshire
University of New Hampshire *B*

New York
Genesee Community College *A*
Ithaca College *B*
Onondaga Community College *A*
St. Joseph's College: Suffolk
Campus *B*
State University of New York
College at Cortland *B*
Utica College *B*

North Carolina
Carteret Community College *A*
Catawba College *B*
East Carolina University *B, M*
North Carolina Central University *M*
St. Andrews Presbyterian College *B*
Shaw University *B*
University of North Carolina
Wilmington *B*
Vance-Granville Community
College *A*
Western Carolina University *B*
Western Piedmont Community
College *A*
Winston-Salem State University *B*

Ohio
Ashland University *B*
University of Akron *B*
University of Toledo *B*

Pennsylvania

Lincoln University *B*
Slippery Rock University of
    Pennsylvania *B*
Temple University *B, M, D*

South Carolina

Coker College *B*

Texas

Austin Community College *A*
Texas State University: San Marcos *M*

Utah

Brigham Young University *B*

Virginia

Longwood University *B*

Washington

Eastern Washington University *B*
Spokane Community College *A*

West Virginia

Alderson-Broaddus College *B*
West Virginia State University *B*

Wisconsin

University of Wisconsin
    La Crosse *B*
    Milwaukee *B*

Regional studies

Arizona

Prescott College *B, M*

California

Claremont McKenna College *B*

Colorado

Colorado College *B*

Georgia

Georgia State University *B*
Mercer University *B*

Kansas

Central Christian College of Kansas *A*

Maine

University of Southern Maine *M*

Massachusetts

Bard College at Simon's Rock *B*

Nebraska

University of Nebraska
    Lincoln *B*

New Mexico

Northern New Mexico College *A*

New York

Columbia University *B*
United States Military Academy *B*

Pennsylvania

La Salle University *B*

Tennessee

Vanderbilt University *B*

Reiki

Vermont

Goddard College *B, M*

Religious education

Alabama

Huntingdon College *B*
Oakwood University *B*

Arizona

International Baptist
    College *A, B, M, D*
Southwestern College *C, A, B*

Arkansas

Ecclesia College *B*
Harding University *B*
Williams Baptist College *B*

California

Azusa Pacific University *B, M, D*
Bethesda Christian University *B*
Biola University *B, M, D*
California Lutheran University *B*
Loyola Marymount University *M*
The Master's College *B*
Mount St. Mary's College *M*
Patten University *B*
Vanguard University of Southern
    California *B*
Yeshiva Ohr Elchonon Chabad/West
    Coast Talmudical Seminary *B*

Colorado

Nazarene Bible College *C, A, B*

Connecticut

Holy Apostles College and
    Seminary *M*

District of Columbia

Catholic University of America *M, D*

Florida

Baptist College of Florida *A, B*
Saint Thomas University *B*

Georgia

LaGrange College *B*

Idaho

Boise Bible College *A, B*
Northwest Nazarene University *B*

Illinois

Concordia University Chicago *B, M, T*
Lincoln Christian University *B, M*
Loyola University Chicago *B, M*
Moody Bible Institute *B, T*
North Park University *M*
Olivet Nazarene University *B*
Trinity International University *B, M*
Wheaton College *B, M*

Indiana

Huntington University *B, M*
Indiana Wesleyan University *A, B*
Marian University *A, B*
Taylor University *B*

Iowa

Faith Baptist Bible College and
    Theological Seminary *B*
Northwestern College *B*
Wartburg College *B, T*

Kansas

Central Christian College of Kansas *A*
Kansas Wesleyan University *B*
MidAmerica Nazarene University *A, B*
Sterling College *B*

Kentucky

Asbury College *B*
Brescia University *C, A*
Campbellsville University *B, M*
Kentucky Mountain Bible College *B*
Mid-Continent University *C, B*
Union College *B*
University of the Cumberlands *B*

Louisiana

Louisiana College *B*
Loyola University New Orleans *M*

Maryland

Griggs University *B*
Washington Adventist University *B*
Washington Bible College *B, M*

Massachusetts

Boston College *M, D*

Michigan

Andrews University *B, M, D*
Grace Bible College *A, B*
Great Lakes Christian College *B*
Kuyper College *B*

Minnesota

Bethel University *M*
Concordia University: St. Paul *B*
Crossroads College *B*
Crown College *A, B, M*
North Central University *B*
St. Mary's University of Minnesota *B*
University of St. Thomas *M*

Mississippi

Wesley College *B*

Missouri

Baptist Bible College *B*
Calvary Bible College and Theological
    Seminary *A, B*
Central Bible College *A, B*
Central Christian College of the
    Bible *B*
Global University *B*
Hannibal-LaGrange College *B*
Missouri Baptist University *B*
Ozark Christian College *B*
St. Louis Christian College *B*
Southwest Baptist University *B*

Nebraska

Concordia University *B, T*
Grace University *B*
Nebraska Christian College *A, B*
Union College *B, T*
York College *B, T*

New Jersey

Felician College *M*
Georgian Court University *C*
Seton Hall University *B, T*

New York

Concordia College *B*
Davis College *B*
Jewish Theological Seminary of
    America *M*
Nyack College *B*
Yeshiva University *D*

North Carolina

Apex School of Theology *A, M, D*
Campbell University *B, M, D*
Duke University *M*
Gardner-Webb University *B, M*
John Wesley College *B*
Methodist University *A, B, T*
Mid-Atlantic Christian University *B*

Montreat College *B*
Pfeiffer University *B*
Shaw University *M*
Southeastern Baptist Theological
    Seminary *M, D*

North Dakota

Trinity Bible College *B*

Ohio

Ashland University *B, M, T*
Cedarville University *B*
Cincinnati Christian University *B, M*
College of Mount St. Joseph *B*
Defiance College *B, T*
Franciscan University of
    Steubenville *B*
God's Bible School and College *B*
Mount Vernon Nazarene University *B*
Muskingum University *B*
Notre Dame College *C*
Ohio Christian University *A, B*
Temple Baptist College *B*

Oklahoma

Oklahoma Baptist University *B*
Oklahoma Christian University *B*
Oklahoma City University *B, M*
Oral Roberts University *B, M*
Southern Nazarene University *B*
Southwestern Christian University *B*

Oregon

Concordia University *B*
Corban College *B*
Eugene Bible College *B*
Multnomah University *B*
Warner Pacific College *A*

Pennsylvania

Duquesne University *M*
Immaculata University *C*
La Roche College *B*
La Salle University *B, M*
Manor College *C*
Mercyhurst College *A, B*
Messiah College *B*
Philadelphia Biblical University *B, T*
St. Vincent College *B*
Thiel College *B*
Valley Forge Christian College *B*
Westminster College *B, T*

Puerto Rico

Inter American University of Puerto
    Rico
    Metropolitan Campus *B, D*
Pontifical Catholic University of
    Puerto Rico *M*
Universidad Pentecostal Mizpa *C, A, B*

South Carolina

Bob Jones University *B, M, D*
Columbia College *B*
Columbia International
    University *B, M*
Erskine College *B, M*
Morris College *B*
Southern Methodist College *A*

Tennessee

American Baptist College *B*
Bryan College *B*
Free Will Baptist Bible College *B*
Lee University *B*
Southern Adventist University *B*
Tennessee Temple University *B, M*

Texas

Arlington Baptist College *B*
Concordia University Texas *B*
Dallas Baptist University *A, B, M, D*

Dallas Christian College *B*
East Texas Baptist University *B*
Howard Payne University *B*
St. Edward's University *B, T*
Southern Methodist University *M*
Southwestern Assemblies of God
　University *B*
Texas Wesleyan University *B*
University of Dallas *M*
Wayland Baptist University *B*

Utah

Brigham Young University *M*

Virginia

Liberty University *M*

Washington

Seattle Pacific University *B*
Seattle University *M*

West Virginia

Davis and Elkins College *B*
West Virginia Wesleyan College *B*
Wheeling Jesuit University *M*

Wisconsin

Cardinal Stritch University *T*
Carthage College *M*
Concordia University Wisconsin *B*
Edgewood College *B*
Marquette University *D, T*
Mount Mary College *B, T*
St. Norbert College *B*

Religious studies

Alabama

Athens State University *B*
Auburn University *B*
Birmingham-Southern College *B*
Faulkner University *B, M*
Gadsden State Community College *A*
Huntingdon College *B*
Judson College *B*
Oakwood University *B*
Samford University *B*
University of Alabama *B*
University of Mobile *B, M*
Wallace State Community College at
　Hanceville *C*

Arizona

Arizona State University *B, M, D*
College of the Humanities and
　Sciences *M, D*
Grand Canyon University *B*
Mesa Community College *A*
Northern Arizona University *B*
Prescott College *B, M*
Southwestern College *C, B*
University of Arizona *B*

Arkansas

Crowley's Ridge College *A, B*
Hendrix College *B*
Lyon College *B*
Philander Smith College *B*
University of Central Arkansas *B*
University of the Ozarks *B*

California

Azusa Pacific University *B, M*
Bethesda Christian University *B, M*
Biola University *B*
California Institute of Integral
　Studies *M, D*
California Lutheran University *B*
California State University
　Bakersfield *B*
　Chico *B*
　East Bay *B*

Fresno *R*
Fullerton *B*
　Long Beach *B, M*
　Northridge *B*
　Sacramento *B, M*
Chaffey College *A*
Chapman University *B*
Claremont McKenna College *B*
Crafton Hills College *C*
Dominican University of California *B*
Holy Names University *B, M*
Hope International University *M*
Humboldt State University *B*
La Sierra University *B, M*
The Master's College *B*
Mount St. Mary's College *B, M*
Notre Dame de Namur University *B*
Occidental College *B*
Orange Coast College *A*
Pacific Union College *B*
Patten University *A, B*
Pepperdine University *B, M*
Pitzer College *B*
Point Loma Nazarene University *M*
Pomona College *B*
St. Mary's College of California *B*
San Diego State University *B*
San Jose State University *B*
Santa Clara University *B, M*
Scripps College *B*
Simpson University *B*
Stanford University *B, M, D*
University of California
　Berkeley *B*
　Davis *B*
　Irvine *B*
　Los Angeles *B*
　Riverside *B, M, D*
　San Diego *B*
　Santa Barbara *B, M, D*
University of La Verne *B*
University of Redlands *B*
University of San Diego *B, M*
University of Southern
　California *B, M, D*
University of the Pacific *B*
University of the West *B, M, D*
Vanguard University of Southern
　California *B, M*
Westmont College *B*
Whittier College *B*

Colorado

Colorado College *B*
Naropa University *B, M*
Nazarene Bible College *A*
Regis University *B*
University of Colorado
　Boulder *B, M*
University of Denver *B, M, D*

Connecticut

Albertus Magnus College *B*
Connecticut College *B*
Fairfield University *B*
Holy Apostles College and
　Seminary *C, A, B, M*
Sacred Heart University *B, M*
Saint Joseph College *B*
Trinity College *B*
University of Bridgeport *B*
Wesleyan University *B*
Yale University *B, M, D*

Delaware

Wesley College *C*

District of Columbia

Catholic University of
　America *B, M, D*
George Washington University *B, M*
Georgetown University *B*
Howard University *M, D*

Florida

Baptist College of Florida *B*
Broward College *A*
Eckerd College *B*
Florida Christian College *B*
Florida International University *B, M*
Florida Southern College *B*
Florida State University *B, M, D*
Gulf Coast Community College *A*
Hobe Sound Bible College *B*
Miami Dade College *A*
New College of Florida *B*
Palm Beach Atlantic University *B*
Pensacola Junior College *A*
Rollins College *B*
Saint Leo University *B*
Saint Thomas University *B*
State College of Florida,
　Manatee-Sarasota *A*
Stetson University *B*
University of Central Florida *B*
University of Florida *B, M*
University of Miami *B*
University of South Florida *B, M*

Georgia

Agnes Scott College *B*
Berry College *B*
Brewton-Parker College *B*
Clark Atlanta University *B*
Emory University *B, D*
Georgia State University *B, M*
LaGrange College *B*
Morehouse College *B*
Paine College *B*
Piedmont College *B*
Reinhardt College *B*
Shorter College *B*
Spelman College *B*
University of Georgia *B, M*
Wesleyan College *B*
Young Harris College *A*

Hawaii

Chaminade University of Honolulu *B*
University of Hawaii
　Hilo *B*
　Manoa *B, M*

Idaho

College of Idaho *B*
Northwest Nazarene University *B*

Illinois

Augustana College *B*
Aurora University *B*
Bradley University *B*
DePaul University *B*
Eureka College *B*
Greenville College *B*
Illinois College *B*
Illinois Wesleyan University *B*
Lake Forest College *B*
Lewis University *B*
Lincoln Christian
　University *C, A, B, M, D*
Lincoln College *A*
MacMurray College *B*
McKendree University *B*
Monmouth College *B*
North Central College *B*
Northwestern University *B, M, D*
Olivet Nazarene University *B, M*
Principia College *B*
Saint Xavier University *B*
Trinity International University *M*
University of Chicago *B, M, D*
University of Illinois
　Urbana-Champaign *B*
Western Illinois University *B*

Indiana

Anderson University *B*

Ball State University *B*
Bethel College *B*
Butler University *B*
Calumet College of St. Joseph *C, A, B*
DePauw University *B*
Earlham College *B*
Franklin College *B*
Huntington University *B*
Indiana University
　Bloomington *B, M, D*
Indiana University-Purdue University
　Indianapolis *B*
Indiana Wesleyan University *C, A, B*
Manchester College *B*
Oakland City University *C, A, B*
Purdue University *B*
Saint Mary's College *B*
Taylor University *M*
University of Indianapolis *B*
Vincennes University *C*
Wabash College *B*

Iowa

Central College *B*
Clarke College *A, B*
Coe College *B*
Cornell College *B*
Divine Word College *B*
Dordt College *B*
Drake University *B*
Faith Baptist Bible College and
　Theological Seminary *M*
Graceland University *B, M*
Grand View University *B*
Grinnell College *B*
Iowa State University *B*
Iowa Wesleyan College *B*
Loras College *B*
Luther College *B*
Morningside College *B*
Mount Mercy College *B*
Northwestern College *B*
Simpson College *B*
University of Dubuque *B, M*
University of Iowa *B, M, D*
University of Northern Iowa *B*
Wartburg College *B*

Kansas

Baker University *B*
Barclay College *B*
Benedictine College *B*
Bethel College *B*
Central Christian College of
　Kansas *A, B*
Cowley County Community
　College *A*
Kansas Wesleyan University *B*
MidAmerica Nazarene University *B, T*
Ottawa University *B*
Seward County Community College *A*
Southwestern College *B*
Tabor College *B*
University of Kansas *B, M*
Washburn University *B*
Wichita State University *B*

Kentucky

Berea College *B*
Bluegrass Community and Technical
　College *A*
Brescia University *A, B*
Campbellsville University *B*
Centre College *B*
Georgetown College *B*
Kentucky Mountain Bible College *A*
Kentucky Wesleyan College *B*
Lindsey Wilson College *A*
Pikeville College *B*
Spalding University *C*
Thomas More College *C, A, B*
Transylvania University *B*
Union College *B*
Western Kentucky University *B*

Louisiana

Centenary College of Louisiana *B*
Dillard University *B*
Louisiana College *B*
Loyola University New Orleans *B, M*

Maine

Bates College *B*
Bowdoin College *B*
Colby College *B*

Maryland

College of Notre Dame of Maryland *B*
Goucher College *B*
Griggs University *B*
Hood College *B*
Howard Community College *A*
Loyola University Maryland *B*
McDaniel College *B*
St. Mary's College of Maryland *B*
Towson University *B*
Washington Adventist University *B, M*

Massachusetts

Amherst College *B*
Atlantic Union College *B*
Boston University *B, M, D*
College of the Holy Cross *B*
Eastern Nazarene College *B*
Elms College *B, M*
Hampshire College *B*
Harvard College *B, M, D*
Merrimack College *A, B*
Mount Holyoke College *B*
Northeastern University *B*
Smith College *B*
Stonehill College *B*
Tufts University *B*
Wellesley College *B*
Wheaton College *B*
Williams College *B*

Michigan

Adrian College *B, T*
Albion College *B*
Alma College *B*
Andrews University *B, M*
Aquinas College *B*
Calvin College *B, T*
Central Michigan University *B*
Henry Ford Community College *A*
Hillsdale College *B*
Hope College *B*
Kalamazoo College *B*
Lansing Community College *A*
Madonna University *A, B*
Marygrove College *B*
Michigan State University *B*
Rochester College *B*
Siena Heights University *B*
Spring Arbor University *B, M*
University of Detroit Mercy *B, M*
University of Michigan *B*
Wayne County Community College *A*
Western Michigan University *B, M*

Minnesota

Augsburg College *B*
Carleton College *B*
College of St. Scholastica *B*
Concordia College: Moorhead *B*
Gustavus Adolphus College *B*
Hamline University *B*
Macalester College *B*
North Central University *A, B*
St. Olaf College *B*
University of Minnesota
 Twin Cities *B*
University of St. Thomas *B, M*

Mississippi

Millsaps College *B*
Tougaloo College *A*

University of Mississippi *A*
University of Southern Mississippi *B*
Wesley College *B*

Missouri

Avila University *B*
Baptist Bible College *B*
Central Christian College of the
 Bible *B*
Central Methodist University *B*
College of the Ozarks *B*
Culver-Stockton College *B*
Drury University *B*
Global University *A*
Lindenwood University *B*
Midwest University *B*
Missouri State University *B, M*
Missouri Valley College *B*
Rockhurst University *B*
Southwest Baptist University *B*
University of Missouri
 Columbia *B, M*
Washington University in St.
 Louis *B, M*
Webster University *B*
Westminster College *B*
William Jewell College *B*

Montana

University of Great Falls *B*

Nebraska

Creighton University *A, B*
Dana College *B*
Doane College *B*
Nebraska Wesleyan University *B*
Union College *B*
University of Nebraska
 Omaha *B*
York College *B, T*

New Hampshire

Dartmouth College *B*

New Jersey

Bergen Community College *A*
Bloomfield College *B*
Drew University *B*
Felician College *B*
Georgian Court University *B*
Montclair State University *B*
Princeton University *B, M, D*
Rutgers, The State University of New
 Jersey
 New Brunswick/Piscataway
 Campus *B*
Saint Peter's College *B*
Seton Hall University *B, M*
Thomas Edison State College *B*

New Mexico

Eastern New Mexico University *B*
University of New Mexico *B*
University of the Southwest *B*

New York

Bard College *B*
Barnard College *B*
Canisius College *B*
City University of New York
 Brooklyn College *B*
 Hunter College *B*
 Queens College *B*
Colgate University *B*
College of Mount St. Vincent *B*
College of New Rochelle *B*
College of Saint Rose *B*
Columbia University *B*
Columbia University
 School of General Studies *B*
Concordia College *A, B*
Cornell University *B*
Daemen College *B*

Elmira College *B*
Eugene Lang College The New School
 for Liberal Arts *B*
Fordham University *B, M, D*
Hamilton College *B*
Hartwick College *B*
Hobart and William Smith Colleges *B*
Hofstra University *B*
Houghton College *B*
Iona College *B*
Le Moyne College *B*
Manhattan College *B*
Manhattanville College *B*
Marymount Manhattan College *B*
Nazareth College *B*
New York University *B, M, D*
Niagara University *B*
Nyack College *B*
Pace University *B*
St. Francis College *B*
St. John Fisher College *B*
St. Lawrence University *B*
St. Thomas Aquinas College *B*
Siena College *B*
Skidmore College *B*
State University of New York
 Albany *B*
 Stony Brook *B*
Syracuse University *B, M, D*
Union College *B*
University of Rochester *B*
Vassar College *B*
Wells College *B*

North Carolina

Appalachian State University *B*
Barton College *B*
Belmont Abbey College *B*
Brevard College *B*
Campbell University *B, M, D*
Catawba College *B*
Chowan University *B*
Davidson College *B*
Duke University *B, M, D*
Elon University *B*
Gardner-Webb University *B*
Greensboro College *C, B*
Guilford College *B*
High Point University *B*
Lees-McRae College *B*
Lenoir-Rhyne University *B*
Mars Hill College *B*
Meredith College *B*
Methodist University *A, B, T*
Mid-Atlantic Christian
 University *C, A, B*
Mount Olive College *A, B*
North Carolina State University *B*
North Carolina Wesleyan College *B*
Pfeiffer University *B, M*
Queens University of Charlotte *B*
St. Andrews Presbyterian College *B*
St. Augustine's College *B*
Salem College *B*
Shaw University *A, B*
University of North Carolina
 Asheville *B*
 Chapel Hill *B, M, D*
 Charlotte *B, M*
 Greensboro *B*
 Wilmington *B*
Wake Forest University *B, M*
Warren Wilson College *B*
Wingate University *B*

North Dakota

Jamestown College *B*
Trinity Bible College *A, B*
University of Mary *B*
University of North Dakota *B*

Ohio

Ashland University *B*
Baldwin-Wallace College *B*

Bluffton University *B*
Capital University *B*
Case Western Reserve University *B*
Cleveland State University *B*
College of Mount St. Joseph *B, M*
College of Wooster *B*
Defiance College *B*
Denison University *B*
Heidelberg University *B*
Hiram College *B*
John Carroll University *B, M, T*
Kenyon College *B*
Lourdes College *A, B*
Miami University
 Oxford Campus *B, M*
Mount Union College *B*
Mount Vernon Nazarene
 University *B, M*
Muskingum University *B*
Oberlin College *B*
Ohio Christian University *A, B*
Ohio Northern University *B*
Ohio State University
 Columbus Campus *B*
Ohio University *B*
Ohio Wesleyan University *B*
Otterbein College *B*
Pontifical College Josephinum *B*
University of Dayton *B*
University of Findlay *A, B*
University of Toledo *B*
Urbana University *B*
Wittenberg University *B*
Wright State University *B*
Youngstown State University *B*

Oklahoma

Mid-America Christian University *B*
Oklahoma Baptist University *B*
Oklahoma Christian University *B*
Oklahoma City University *B, M*
Southern Nazarene University *B*
Southwestern Christian
 University *A, B*
University of Oklahoma *B*
University of Tulsa *B*

Oregon

Chemeketa Community College *A*
Concordia University *B*
Corban College *A, B*
Eugene Bible College *B*
George Fox University *B*
Lewis & Clark College *B*
Linfield College *B*
Marylhurst University *B*
Reed College *B*
University of Oregon *B*
Warner Pacific College *A, B, M*
Willamette University *B*

Pennsylvania

Albright College *B*
Allegheny College *B*
Alvernia University *B*
Bryn Athyn College of the New
 Church *B, M*
Bryn Mawr College *B*
Bucknell University *B*
Cabrini College *B*
Chestnut Hill College *C*
Dickinson College *B*
Elizabethtown College *B*
Franklin & Marshall College *B*
Gettysburg College *B*
Grove City College *B*
Haverford College *B*
Holy Family University *B*
Indiana University of Pennsylvania *B*
Juniata College *B*
La Roche College *B*
La Salle University *B, M*
Lafayette College *B*
Lebanon Valley College *B*

Lehigh University *B*
Lincoln University *B*
Lycoming College *B*
Marywood University *B*
Mercyhurst College *B*
Moravian College *B*
Muhlenberg College *C, B*
Neumann University *B*
Penn State
  Abington *B*
  Altoona *B*
  Beaver *B*
  Berks *B*
  Brandywine *B*
  DuBois *B*
  Erie, The Behrend College *B*
  Fayette, The Eberly Campus *B*
  Greater Allegheny *B*
  Hazleton *B*
  Lehigh Valley *B*
  Mont Alto *B*
  New Kensington *B*
  Schuylkill *B*
  Shenango *B*
  University Park *B*
  Wilkes-Barre *B*
  Worthington Scranton *B*
  York *B*
Rosemont College *B*
St. Charles Borromeo Seminary -
  Overbrook *C*
St. Francis University *B*
Saint Joseph's University *B*
Seton Hill University *C, B*
Susquehanna University *B*
Swarthmore College *B*
Temple University *B, M, D*
Thiel College *B*
University of Pennsylvania *B, M, D*
University of Pittsburgh *B, M, D*
University of Scranton *B, M*
Villanova University *B, M*
Washington & Jefferson College *B*
Waynesburg University *B*
Westminster College *B*
Wilson College *B*

Puerto Rico
Bayamon Central University *B*
Inter American University of Puerto
  Rico
  Bayamon Campus *B*
  Guayama Campus *A, B*
Universidad Adventista de las
  Antillas *M*

Rhode Island
Brown University *B, M, D*
Salve Regina University *B*

South Carolina
Allen University *B*
Bob Jones University *D*
Charleston Southern University *B*
Claflin University *B*
College of Charleston *B*
Columbia College *B*
Converse College *B*
Erskine College *B*
Furman University *B*
Newberry College *B*
Presbyterian College *B*
Southern Wesleyan University *B, M*
University of South Carolina *B, M*
Winthrop University *B*
Wofford College *B*

South Dakota
Augustana College *B*
Dakota Wesleyan University *B*
Mount Marty College *B*
Presentation College *A*
University of Sioux Falls *B*

Tennessee
Belmont University *B, T*
Carson-Newman College *B*
Christian Brothers University *B*
King College *B*
Lambuth University *B*
Lane College *B*
Martin Methodist College *B*
Maryville College *B*
Rhodes College *B*
Southern Adventist University *B, M*
Trevecca Nazarene University *B*
Union University *B*
University of Tennessee
  Knoxville *B*
University of the South *B*
Vanderbilt University *B, M, D*
Williamson Christian College *B*

Texas
Amarillo College *A*
Arlington Baptist College *B*
Austin College *B*
Baptist Missionary Association
  Theological Seminary *A, B, M*
Baylor University *B, M, D*
Clarendon College *A*
Concordia University Texas *B, T*
East Texas Baptist University *C, B*
Howard Payne University *B*
Jarvis Christian College *B*
Lon Morris College *A*
Our Lady of the Lake University of San
  Antonio *B*
Rice University *B, D*
Schreiner University *B*
Southern Methodist
  University *B, M, D*
Southwestern Adventist University *B*
Southwestern University *B*
Texas Christian University *B*
Texas College *B*
Texas Wesleyan University *B*
Trinity University *B*
University of Texas
  Austin *B*
University of the Incarnate Word *B, M*

Vermont
Marlboro College *B*
Middlebury College *B*
St. Michael's College *B*
University of Vermont *B*

Virginia
Averett University *B*
Christendom College *M*
College of William and Mary *B*
Emory & Henry College *B*
Ferrum College *B*
George Mason University *B*
Hampden-Sydney College *B*
Hollins University *B*
Liberty University *A, B, M, D*
Lord Fairfax Community College *A*
Lynchburg College *B*
Mary Baldwin College *B*
Marymount University *B*
Randolph College *B*
Randolph-Macon College *B*
Regent University *A, B, M, D*
Roanoke College *B, T*
St. Paul's College *B*
Shenandoah University *B*
Sweet Briar College *B*
University of Mary Washington *B*
University of Richmond *B*
University of Virginia *B, M, D*
Virginia Commonwealth University *B*
Virginia Intermont College *B*
Virginia Union University *B*
Virginia University of Lynchburg *B*
Virginia Wesleyan College *B*

Washington and Lee University *B*

Washington
Evergreen State College *B*
Faith Evangelical Seminary *B*
Gonzaga University *B, M*
Pacific Lutheran University *B*
Saint Martin's University *B*
Seattle University *B*
Trinity Lutheran College *A, B*
University of Puget Sound *B*
University of Washington *B, M*
Walla Walla University *B*
Washington State University *B*
Whitman College *B*

West Virginia
American Public University System *B*
Bethany College *B*
Davis and Elkins College *B*
Mountain State University *B*
Ohio Valley University *B*
West Virginia Wesleyan College *B*

Wisconsin
Alverno College *B*
Beloit College *B*
Cardinal Stritch University *B, M*
Carroll University *B*
Carthage College *B*
Concordia University Wisconsin *B*
Edgewood College *B, M*
Lakeland College *B*
Lawrence University *B*
Marian University *B*
Marquette University *B, M, D*
Mount Mary College *B*
Ripon College *B*
St. Norbert College *B, T*
University of Wisconsin
  Eau Claire *B*
  Madison *B, M*
  Milwaukee *B*
  Oshkosh *B*
Viterbo University *B, T*

Wyoming
Laramie County Community
  College *A*
University of Wyoming *B*

Renal/dialysis
technology

Illinois
City Colleges of Chicago
  Malcolm X College *A*

Pennsylvania
Drexel University *A*

Wisconsin
Chippewa Valley Technical College *A*

Reproductive biology

Texas
University of Texas
  Health Science Center at
  Houston *M, D*

West Virginia
West Virginia University *M, D*

Wisconsin
Marquette University *M, D*

Wyoming
University of Wyoming *M, D*

Resort management

California
Orange Coast College *C*

Colorado
Colorado Mountain College *A*
Western State College of Colorado *B*

Florida
Florida Gulf Coast University *B*

Massachusetts
Bay State College *B*

Minnesota
Art Institutes International
  Minnesota *B*
Central Lakes College *C*
Normandale Community College *C*
University of Minnesota
  Crookston *B*

Mississippi
Virginia College Gulf Coast *A*

Nevada
Sierra Nevada College *B*

New York
Globe Institute of Technology *C, A, B*
Paul Smith's College *B*
Rochester Institute of
  Technology *A, B, M*
State University of New York
  College of Agriculture and
  Technology at Morrisville *B*

North Carolina
Methodist University *B, M*

Pennsylvania
Lehigh Carbon Community College *A*
Newport Business Institute: Lower
  Burrell *A*
Northampton Community College *C*

South Carolina
Coastal Carolina University *B*

Utah
Eagle Gate College: Salt Lake City *C*

Vermont
Green Mountain College *C, B*
Lyndon State College *B*

Washington
Wenatchee Valley College *C*

West Virginia
Concord University *B*

Wisconsin
Lakeland College *B*

Respiratory therapy

Alabama
Central Alabama Community
  College *A*
George C. Wallace State Community
  College
  George C. Wallace Community
  College at Dothan *A*
Shelton State Community College *A*
University of Alabama
  Birmingham *B*
University of South Alabama *B*

Wallace State Community College at
   Hanceville *A*

Arizona
GateWay Community College *A*
Kaplan College: Phoenix *A*
Pima Community College *A*

Arkansas
Arkansas State University
   Mountain Home *A*
Northwest Arkansas Community
   College *A*
Pulaski Technical College *A*
Southeast Arkansas College *A*
University of Arkansas
   Community College at Hope *A*
   Fort Smith *A*

California
American River College *A*
Butte College *A*
California College San Diego *A, B*
Concorde Career College
   Garden Grove *A*
Concorde Career College: North
   Hollywood *A*
Concorde Career College: San
   Bernardino *A*
Crafton Hills College *A*
East Los Angeles College *A*
El Camino College *A*
El Camino College: Compton
   Center *A*
Foothill College *A*
Fresno City College *A*
Grossmont College *A*
Los Angeles Southwest College *A*
Los Angeles Valley College *A*
Modesto Junior College *A*
Mount San Antonio College *A*
Napa Valley College *A*
Ohlone College *A*
Orange Coast College *A*
San Joaquin Valley College *A*
Skyline College *A*
Victor Valley College *A*

Colorado
Pueblo Community College *A*

Connecticut
Goodwin College *A*
Manchester Community College *A*
Naugatuck Valley Community
   College *A*
Norwalk Community College *A*
University of Hartford *B*

District of Columbia
University of the District of
   Columbia *A*

Florida
ATI College of Health *A*
Broward College *A*
Daytona State College *A*
Edison State College *A*
Florida Agricultural and Mechanical
   University *B*
Florida National College *A*
Florida State College at Jacksonville *A*
Hillsborough Community College *A*
Indian River State College *A*
Miami Dade College *A*
Palm Beach Community College *A*
Polk State College *A*
St. Petersburg College *A*
Santa Fe College *A*
Seminole Community College *A*
State College of Florida,
   Manatee-Sarasota *A*
Tallahassee Community College *A*

Valencia Community College *A*

Georgia
Armstrong Atlantic State University *B*
Athens Technical College *A*
Augusta Technical College *A*
Darton College *A*
Georgia Highlands College *A*
Georgia State University *B, M*
Gwinnett Technical College *A*
Macon State College *A*
Medical College of Georgia *B*
Middle Georgia College *A*
Southwest Georgia Technical
   College *A*

Hawaii
University of Hawaii
   Kapiolani Community College *A*

Idaho
Boise State University *A, B*
Idaho State University *A*

Illinois
City Colleges of Chicago
   Malcolm X College *A*
College of DuPage *A*
Illinois Central College *A*
Kankakee Community College *A*
Kaskaskia College *A*
Moraine Valley Community
   College *C, A*
National-Louis University *B*
Parkland College *A*
Rock Valley College *A*
Rush University *B, M*
St. Augustine College *A*
Southern Illinois University
   Carbondale *A*
Southwestern Illinois College *A*
Trinity College of Nursing and Health
   Sciences *A*
Triton College *A*

Indiana
Ball State University *B*
Indiana University
   Bloomington *B*
   Northwest *A*
Ivy Tech Community College
   Bloomington *A*
   Central Indiana *A*
   East Central *A*
   Lafayette *A*
   North Central *A*
   Northeast *A*
   Northwest *A*
   Richmond *A*
   South Central *A*
   Wabash Valley *A*
University of Indianapolis *B*
University of Southern Indiana *A*

Iowa
Des Moines Area Community
   College *A*
Hawkeye Community College *A*
Kirkwood Community College *A*
Muscatine Community College *A*
Northeast Iowa Community
   College *A*
St. Luke's College *A*
Scott Community College *A*

Kansas
Johnson County Community
   College *A*
Kansas City Kansas Community
   College *A*
Labette Community College *A*
Newman University *A*
Seward County Community College *A*

University of Kansas Medical
   Center *B*
Washburn University *A*

Kentucky
Ashland Community and Technical
   College *A*
Bellarmine University *B*
Bluegrass Community and Technical
   College *A*
Madisonville Community College *A*
Morehead State University *A*
Northern Kentucky University *A*
Southeast Kentucky Community and
   Technical College *A*
West Kentucky Community and
   Technical College *A*

Louisiana
Bossier Parish Community College *A*
Delgado Community College *A*
Louisiana State University
   Eunice *A*
Nicholls State University *A*
Our Lady of Holy Cross College *A, B*
Our Lady of the Lake College *A*
Southern University
   Shreveport *A*

Maine
Kennebec Valley Community
   College *A*
Southern Maine Community
   College *A*

Maryland
Allegany College of Maryland *A*
Baltimore City Community College *A*
Carroll Community College *A*
Community College of Baltimore
   County *A*
Frederick Community College *A*
Howard Community College *A*
Prince George's Community
   College *A*
Salisbury University *B*
Washington Adventist University *A*

Massachusetts
Berkshire Community College *A*
Bunker Hill Community College *A*
Massachusetts Bay Community
   College *A*
Massasoit Community College *A*
North Shore Community College *A*
Northern Essex Community
   College *A*
Quinsigamond Community College *A*
Springfield Technical Community
   College *A*

Michigan
Delta College *A*
Ferris State University *A*
Henry Ford Community College *A*
Kalamazoo Valley Community
   College *A*
Lansing Community College *A*
Macomb Community College *A*
Monroe County Community
   College *A*
Mott Community College *A*
Muskegon Community College *A*
Northern Michigan University *B*
Oakland Community College *A*
Washtenaw Community College *A*

Minnesota
Lake Superior College *A*
Northland Community & Technical
   College *A*
St. Catherine University *B*
St. Paul College *A*

Mississippi
Copiah-Lincoln Community College *A*
Hinds Community College *A*
Meridian Community College *A*
Mississippi Gulf Coast Community
   College *A*
Northeast Mississippi Community
   College *A*
Northwest Mississippi Community
   College *A*
Pearl River Community College *A*

Missouri
East Central College *A*
Hannibal-LaGrange College *A*
Metropolitan Community College:
   Penn Valley *A*
Mineral Area College *A*
Missouri Southern State University *A*
Missouri State University *B*
Missouri State University: West
   Plains *A*
Ozarks Technical Community
   College *A*
University of Missouri
   Columbia *B*

Montana
Montana State University
   College of Technology: Great
   Falls *A*
University of Montana *A*

Nebraska
Metropolitan Community College *A*
Nebraska Methodist College of
   Nursing and Allied Health *A, B*
Southeast Community College *A*
University of Nebraska
   Kearney *B*

New Hampshire
River Valley Community College *A*

New Jersey
Atlantic Cape Community College *A*
Bergen Community College *A*
Brookdale Community College *A*
Burlington County College *A*
Camden County College *A*
County College of Morris *A*
Essex County College *A*
Fairleigh Dickinson University
   College at Florham *B*
Felician College *B*
Gloucester County College *A*
Hudson County Community
   College *A*
Mercer County Community College *A*
Middlesex County College *A*
Passaic County Community College *A*
Raritan Valley Community College *A*
Sussex County Community College *A*
Thomas Edison State College *A, B*
Union County College *A*
University of Medicine and Dentistry
   of New Jersey
   School of Health Related
   Professions *A, B*

New Mexico
Central New Mexico Community
   College *A*
Dona Ana Community College of New
   Mexico State University *A*
Santa Fe Community College *A*

New York
City University of New York
   Borough of Manhattan Community
   College *A*

Erie Community College
  North Campus *A*
Genesee Community College *A*
Hudson Valley Community College *A*
Mohawk Valley Community College *A*
Nassau Community College *A*
Onondaga Community College *A*
Rockland Community College *A*
State University of New York
  Stony Brook *B*
  Upstate Medical University *B*
Westchester Community College *A*

North Carolina
Carteret Community College *A*
Catawba Valley Community College *A*
Central Piedmont Community
  College *A*
Durham Technical Community
  College *A*
Edgecombe Community College *A*
Fayetteville Technical Community
  College *A*
Forsyth Technical Community
  College *A*
Pitt Community College *A*
Robeson Community College *A*
Rockingham Community College *A*
Sandhills Community College *A*
Southwestern Community College *A*
Stanly Community College *A*
University of North Carolina
  Charlotte *B*

North Dakota
North Dakota State University *B*
University of Mary *B*

Ohio
Bowling Green State University:
  Firelands College *A*
Cincinnati State Technical and
  Community College *A*
Columbus State Community
  College *A*
Eastern Gateway Community
  College *A*
Kettering College of Medical Arts *A*
North Central State College *A*
Ohio State University
  Columbus Campus *B, M*
Shawnee State University *A*
Southern State Community College *A*
Stark State College of Technology *A*
University of Akron *A, B*
University of Akron: Wayne College *A*
University of Cincinnati
  Clermont College *A*
University of Toledo *B*
Washington State Community
  College *A*
Youngstown State University *B*

Oklahoma
Northern Oklahoma College *A*
Platt College
  Tulsa *A*
Rose State College *A*
Tulsa Community College *A*

Oregon
Lane Community College *A*
Mt. Hood Community College *A*
Oregon Institute of Technology *A, B*

Pennsylvania
Community College of Allegheny
  County *A*
Community College of Philadelphia *A*
Gannon University *A, B*
Gwynedd-Mercy College *A, B*
Harrisburg Area Community
  College *A*

Indiana University of Pennsylvania *B*
Keystone College *A*
La Roche College *B*
Laurel Business Institute *A*
Luzerne County Community
  College *A*
Mansfield University of
  Pennsylvania *A*
Reading Area Community College *A*
University of Pittsburgh
  Johnstown *A*
York College of Pennsylvania *A, B*

Puerto Rico
Huertas Junior College *A*
Inter American University of Puerto
  Rico
  Guayama Campus *A, B*
Ponce Paramedical College *A*
Universidad Adventista de las
  Antillas *A, B*
Universidad Metropolitana *A, B*

Rhode Island
Community College of Rhode
  Island *A*

South Carolina
Florence-Darlington Technical
  College *A*
Greenville Technical College *A*
Midlands Technical College *A*
Spartanburg Community College *A*
Trident Technical College *A*

South Dakota
Dakota State University *A, B*

Tennessee
Baptist College of Health Sciences *B*
Chattanooga State Community
  College *A*
Columbia State Community College *A*
Jackson State Community College *A*
Roane State Community College *A*
Southern Adventist University *A*
Volunteer State Community College *A*
Walters State Community College *A*

Texas
Alvin Community College *A*
Amarillo College *A*
Angelina College *A*
Collin County Community College
  District *A*
Del Mar College *A*
El Centro College *A*
El Paso Community College *A*
Houston Community College
  System *A*
Howard College *A*
Lamar Institute of Technology *A*
Lone Star College System *A*
McLennan Community College *A*
Midland College *A*
Midwestern State University *B*
Odessa College *A*
St. Philip's College *A*
San Jacinto College *A*
South Plains College *A*
Tarrant County College *A*
Temple College *A*
Texas Southern University *B*
Texas State University: San Marcos *B*
Tyler Junior College *A*
University of Texas
  Brownsville - Texas Southmost
    College *A*
  Health Science Center at San
    Antonio *A*
  Medical Branch at Galveston *B*
Victoria College *A*
Weatherford College *A*

Utah
Dixie State College of Utah *A*
Independence University *A*
Weber State University *A, B*

Virginia
J. Sargeant Reynolds Community
  College *A*
Jefferson College of Health
  Sciences *A*
Mountain Empire Community
  College *A*
Northern Virginia Community
  College *A*
Shenandoah University *B*
Southside Virginia Community
  College *A*
Tidewater Community College *A*
Wytheville Community College *A*

Washington
Highline Community College *A*
Spokane Community College *A*

West Virginia
Fairmont State University *A*
Marshall University *B*
West Virginia Northern Community
  College *A*
Wheeling Jesuit University *B*

Wisconsin
Chippewa Valley Technical College *A*
Mid-State Technical College *A*
Milwaukee Area Technical College *A*
Northeast Wisconsin Technical
  College *A*
Western Technical College *A*

Wyoming
Casper College *A*

Respiratory therapy assistant

California
Concorde Career College
  Garden Grove *C*
Concorde Career College: San
  Diego *A*
Foothill College *C, A*
Kaplan College: Salida *A*
Santa Rosa Junior College *C*

Delaware
Delaware Technical and Community
  College
  Owens *A*
  Stanton/Wilmington *A*

Florida
Gulf Coast Community College *A*
Valencia Community College *A*

Georgia
Dalton State College *A*
Darton College *A*
Gordon College *A*

Hawaii
University of Hawaii
  West Oahu *C*

Illinois
Moraine Valley Community College *A*

Indiana
Indiana University-Purdue University
  Indianapolis *B*

Kansas
Kansas City Kansas Community
  College *A*

Louisiana
Our Lady of the Lake College *A*

Maryland
Howard Community College *A*

Michigan
Baker College
  of Auburn Hills *A*
Delta College *A*
Northern Michigan University *A*

Minnesota
Northland Community & Technical
  College *A*
University of Minnesota
  Crookston *B*

Montana
Montana State University
  College of Technology: Great
    Falls *A*

New Jersey
Cumberland County College *A*

New Mexico
Eastern New Mexico University:
  Roswell Campus *A*

New York
Long Island University
  Brooklyn Campus *B*

North Carolina
Durham Technical Community
  College *A*
Pitt Community College *A*
Southwestern Community College *A*

Ohio
James A. Rhodes State College *A*
Stark State College of Technology *A*
University of Rio Grande *A*

Oklahoma
Rose State College *A*

Pennsylvania
Clarion University of Pennsylvania *A*

Puerto Rico
Ponce Paramedical College *C*

Texas
Weatherford College *A*

Virginia
Danville Community College *A*
Southwest Virginia Community
  College *A*

Wisconsin
Chippewa Valley Technical College *A*
Gateway Technical College *A*
Mid-State Technical College *A*
Milwaukee Area Technical College *A*

Restaurant/catering management

Alabama
Shelton State Community College *C*

Arizona

Arizona Western College C, A
Pima Community College C, A

Arkansas

Arkansas Tech University A

California

American River College C, A
Art Institute
  of California: Los Angeles B
  of California: Orange County A, B
  of California: San Diego A, B
Art Institute of California: Inland
  Empire B
Art Institute of California:
  Sacramento B
Art Institute of California: San
  Francisco A, B
Art Institute of California:
  Sunnyvale B
California Culinary Academy A
California School of Culinary Arts A
City College of San Francisco A
College of the Canyons A
College of the Desert C, A
Diablo Valley College C
Grossmont College C, A
Long Beach City College C, A
Orange Coast College C, A
Oxnard College C, A
Shasta College C, A
West Hills College: Lemoore C, A

Colorado

Art Institute
  of Colorado B
Colorado Mountain College A
Johnson & Wales University:
  Denver B
Pikes Peak Community College C

Connecticut

Gateway Community College A
Three Rivers Community College C, A

Delaware

Delaware Technical and Community
  College
  Stanton/Wilmington A

Florida

Art Institute of Fort Lauderdale B
Daytona State College A
Hillsborough Community College A
Indian River State College A
Johnson & Wales University: North
  Miami B
Pensacola Junior College C
St. Petersburg College C
Valencia Community College A

Georgia

Art Institute
  of Atlanta B
College of Coastal Georgia A

Hawaii

University of Hawaii
  Hawaii Community College C, A
  West Oahu B

Illinois

Black Hawk College A
College of DuPage C, A
College of Lake County C, A
Elgin Community College C, A
John Wood Community College A
Kaskaskia College C
Lincoln Land Community College C
Moraine Valley Community
  College C, A

Parkland College C, A
Richland Community College C

Indiana

Harrison College
  Indianapolis B
Vincennes University A

Iowa

Clinton Community College C, A
Muscatine Community College C, A
Scott Community College C, A

Maryland

Anne Arundel Community
  College C, A
Baltimore International College A, B
Community College of Baltimore
  County C, A
Howard Community College C, A

Massachusetts

Massasoit Community College C
Newbury College A, B
Quinsigamond Community
  College C, A

Michigan

Art Institute of Michigan B
Baker College
  of Muskegon B
Ferris State University A
Grand Rapids Community College A
Henry Ford Community College A
Schoolcraft College C
Washtenaw Community College C

Minnesota

Art Institutes International
  Minnesota B
Hennepin Technical College C, A
South Central College C, A

Missouri

College of the Ozarks B
Jefferson College C, A

Nebraska

Central Community College C, A
Southeast Community College A

Nevada

Art Institute
  of Las Vegas B

New Hampshire

White Mountains Community
  College C, A

New Jersey

Bergen Community College C, A
County College of Morris A
Hudson County Community
  College C
Raritan Valley Community College A

New York

Erie Community College
  North Campus A
Fulton-Montgomery Community
  College A
Mohawk Valley Community College A
Monroe College A
Nassau Community College A
Paul Smith's College A, B
Rochester Institute of
  Technology A, B, M
Schenectady County Community
  College A

State University of New York
  College of Agriculture and
    Technology at Cobleskill A
  College of Technology at Delhi A
Suffolk County Community
  College C, A
Westchester Community College A

North Carolina

Cape Fear Community College C, A
Carteret Community College C, A
Johnson & Wales University:
  Charlotte B

North Dakota

North Dakota State College of
  Science A

Ohio

Bowling Green State University B
Cincinnati State Technical and
  Community College A
Ohio State University
  Agricultural Technical Institute A

Oregon

Lane Community College C, A
Linn-Benton Community College A

Pennsylvania

Art Institute
  of Pittsburgh A, B
Bucks County Community
  College C, A
Community College of Allegheny
  County C, A
Community College of Philadelphia A
Drexel University B
Harrisburg Area Community
  College C
Keystone College A
Luzerne County Community
  College C, A
Pennsylvania College of
  Technology B
Restaurant School at Walnut Hill
  College A, B
Westmoreland County Community
  College A
YTI Career Institute: Lancaster A

Puerto Rico

Universal Career Community College:
  Humacao A
Universal Career Community College:
  Manati A
Universal Career Community College:
  San Juan A
Universidad del Este B

Rhode Island

Johnson & Wales University:
  Providence B

South Carolina

Greenville Technical College C

Texas

Del Mar College A
St. Philip's College C, A
San Jacinto College C

Vermont

Champlain College B

Virginia

J. Sargeant Reynolds Community
  College A
Stratford University: Woodbridge A, B

Washington

Clover Park Technical College C
Olympic College C
South Seattle Community
  College C, A

West Virginia

Blue Ridge Community and Technical
  College A

Wisconsin

Chippewa Valley Technical College A
Gateway Technical College A
Milwaukee Area Technical College A
Waukesha County Technical
  College A
Western Technical College A

Restaurant/food
services management

Alabama

University of Alabama B

Alaska

University of Alaska
  Anchorage B

California

College of the Desert C, A
Diablo Valley College C
Long Beach City College C, A
Shasta College A
University of San Francisco B
West Hills College: Lemoore C

Colorado

Colorado State University B
Pikes Peak Community College C

Connecticut

Gateway Community College A
Mitchell College B
Three Rivers Community College C, A

Florida

Central Florida Community
  College C, A
Hillsborough Community
  College C, A
St. Petersburg College C
University of Central Florida B
Valencia Community College A

Georgia

Gwinnett Technical College C, A

Illinois

Lexington College A, B
Triton College C, A

Indiana

Vincennes University C

Iowa

Iowa Lakes Community College C, A

Kansas

Colby Community College C

Massachusetts

Holyoke Community College A
Quinsigamond Community
  College C, A

Michigan

Baker College
  of Muskegon A, B
Michigan State University M
Oakland Community College A

Minnesota
Art Institutes International
   Minnesota *B*
Normandale Community College *C*
South Central College *C, A*
Southwest Minnesota State
   University *B*
University of Minnesota
   Crookston *C, B*

Missouri
College of the Ozarks *B*
University of Missouri
   Columbia *B, M*

New Hampshire
White Mountains Community
   College *C, A*

New Jersey
Burlington County College *C, A*

New Mexico
Santa Fe Community College *C*

New York
Cornell University *B*
Culinary Institute of America *B*
Globe Institute of Technology *C, A, B*
New York University *B, M, D, T*
Niagara University *B*
Paul Smith's College *B*
Rochester Institute of
   Technology *A, B, M*
State University of New York
   College at Plattsburgh *B*
   College of Agriculture and
      Technology at Morrisville *A*

North Carolina
Cape Fear Community College *C, A*
Johnson & Wales University:
   Charlotte *B*
Sandhills Community College *A*
Southwestern Community College *C*

North Dakota
North Dakota State College of
   Science *A*

Ohio
Cincinnati State Technical and
   Community College *A*
Ohio State University
   Agricultural Technical Institute *A*
Owens Community College
   Toledo *C, A*
University of Akron *C, A*

Oklahoma
Platt College
   Tulsa *B*

Oregon
Lane Community College *C*

Pennsylvania
Bucks County Community
   College *C, A*
Harrisburg Area Community
   College *A*
Lehigh Carbon Community College *A*
Luzerne County Community
   College *C, A*
Northampton Community College *A*
Pennsylvania College of
   Technology *A*
Pennsylvania Highlands Community
   College *A*
Restaurant School at Walnut Hill
   College *A, B*

South Carolina
Spartanburg Community College *A*
Trident Technical College *A*

Texas
Houston Community College
   System *C*

Utah
Salt Lake Community College *A*

Vermont
Champlain College *B*

Washington
South Seattle Community
   College *C, A*

West Virginia
Concord University *B*

Wisconsin
Chippewa Valley Technical College *A*
Fox Valley Technical College *A*

Wyoming
Casper College *C*

Retailing

Arizona
Chandler-Gilbert Community College
   Pecos *C, A*
Eastern Arizona College *C*
Pima Community College *C*
Scottsdale Community College *C, A*
University of Phoenix *B*

Arkansas
Arkansas State University
   Beebe *C*
Northwest Arkansas Community
   College *C*

California
Bakersfield College *C*
College of the Canyons *C*
Fashion Institute of Design and
   Merchandising
   Los Angeles *A*
Los Angeles Pierce College *C*
Orange Coast College *C*
Shasta College *C*
West Hills College: Lemoore *C*

Florida
Santa Fe College *C*

Georgia
Gwinnett Technical College *C*

Illinois
Black Hawk College *C, A*
Elgin Community College *C, A*
Fox College *A*
Harper College *C*
Kaskaskia College *C*
McHenry County College *C*
Moraine Valley Community College *A*
Spoon River College *C*
Waubonsee Community College *A*

Indiana
Purdue University
   Calumet *B*

Iowa
Des Moines Area Community
   College *C*

Northeast Iowa Community
   College *C*
Western Iowa Tech Community
   College *C*

Kansas
Coffeyville Community College *A*
Colby Community College *C*
Hutchinson Community College *C, A*

Maryland
Anne Arundel Community College *C*
Howard Community College *C*

Massachusetts
Bay State College *A*
Holyoke Community College *C, A*

Michigan
Bay de Noc Community College *C*
Central Michigan University *B*

Minnesota
Anoka-Ramsey Community College *C*
Art Institutes International
   Minnesota *B*
Minnesota State College - Southeast
   Technical *C, A*
North Hennepin Community
   College *C*
Ridgewater College *A*
Rochester Community and Technical
   College *C, A*

Missouri
Lindenwood University *B*
Patricia Stevens College *A, B*

New Hampshire
Southern New Hampshire
   University *B*

New York
Genesee Community College *A*
Niagara County Community
   College *A*
Tompkins Cortland Community
   College *A*
Utica School of Commerce *A*

North Carolina
Central Piedmont Community
   College *C, A*

Ohio
Bowling Green State University *B*
Owens Community College
   Toledo *A*
University of Akron *C*
University of Rio Grande *B*
Youngstown State University *B*

Oregon
Central Oregon Community
   College *C*
Clackamas Community College *C*
Clatsop Community College *C*
Lane Community College *C, A*
Portland Community College *C, A*
Rogue Community College *C*

Pennsylvania
Bucks County Community College *A*
Commonwealth Technical Institute *C*
Harrisburg Area Community
   College *A*
Montgomery County Community
   College *C*
Newport Business Institute: Lower
   Burrell *A*

South Hills School of Business &
   Technology *C*
South Hills School of Business &
   Technology: Altoona *C, A*
University of Pittsburgh
   Titusville *C*
York College of Pennsylvania *M*

South Carolina
Anderson University *B*
University of South Carolina *B, M*

Texas
Westwood College: Fort Worth *B*

Virginia
Longwood University *B*

Washington
Bates Technical College *C, A*
Clark College *C*
Grays Harbor College *C*
Olympic College *C*

West Virginia
New River Community and Technical
   College *C*

Wisconsin
Waukesha County Technical
   College *A*
Wisconsin Indianhead Technical
   College *A*

Wyoming
Casper College *C, A*

Robotics technology

Arizona
University of Advancing
   Technology *A, B*

California
Allan Hancock College *C, A*
American River College *C*
Cerritos College *A*
Long Beach City College *C*
Orange Coast College *C*
University of California
   San Diego *M, D*

Colorado
Pikes Peak Community College *A*

Illinois
College of DuPage *C, A*
Illinois Central College *C, A*
Oakton Community College *A*

Indiana
Indiana State University *B*
Indiana University-Purdue University
   Fort Wayne *C*
Indiana University-Purdue University
   Indianapolis *A, B*
Purdue University *A, B*
Purdue University
   North Central *A*

Iowa
Indian Hills Community College *A*
Southeastern Community College
   North Campus *A*

Kentucky
Sullivan College of Technology and
   Design *A*

...mmunity College *C*

...*ege C*

...sachusetts

...ringfield Technical Community
College *C*

Michigan

Oakland Community College *C, A*

Minnesota

Central Lakes College *C, A*
Dunwoody College of Technology *A*
Mesabi Range Community and
Technical College *C, A*
Minnesota West Community and
Technical College *A*

Mississippi

Alcorn State University *B*

New Hampshire

Nashua Community College *A*

New York

State University of New York
College of Technology at Alfred *A*

North Carolina

Central Carolina Community
College *A*

Ohio

Eastern Gateway Community
College *A*
James A. Rhodes State College *C*
Terra State Community College *A*
University of Rio Grande *A*

Pennsylvania

Butler County Community College *A*
Community College of Allegheny
County *A*
Luzerne County Community
College *A*
Pennsylvania College of
Technology *A*

Puerto Rico

University of Puerto Rico
Carolina Regional College *A*

Rhode Island

Johnson & Wales University:
Providence *A*

South Carolina

Trident Technical College *A*

Texas

Hill College *A*
Tarrant County College *C, A*
Texas State Technical College
West Texas *A*

Utah

Utah Valley University *A*

Washington

Spokane Community College *A*

Wisconsin

Blackhawk Technical College *A*
Chippewa Valley Technical College *A*
Gateway Technical College *A*

Wyoming

Casper College *C, A*

Romance languages

Alabama

University of Alabama *M, D*

Arizona

Prescott College *M*

California

Point Loma Nazarene University *B*
University of California
Berkeley *D*
Los Angeles *B, M, D*

Connecticut

Wesleyan University *B*

District of Columbia

George Washington University *B*

Georgia

University of Georgia *B, M, D*

Illinois

Rockford College *B*

Indiana

DePauw University *B*
University of Notre Dame *B, M*

Louisiana

University of New Orleans *M*

Maine

Bowdoin College *B*

Maryland

University of Maryland
College Park *B*

Massachusetts

Boston College *M*
Harvard College *B, M, D*
Merrimack College *B*
Mount Holyoke College *B*

Michigan

Michigan State University *D*
University of Michigan *D*

Minnesota

Carleton College *B*

Missouri

Truman State University *B*
University of Missouri
Columbia *D*
Washington University in St. Louis *B*

New York

City University of New York
Hunter College *B*
Cornell University *M, D*
Manhattanville College *B*
State University of New York
Stony Brook *M*

North Carolina

Appalachian State University *M*
Duke University *D*
University of North Carolina
Chapel Hill *B, M, D*

Oregon

University of Oregon *B, M, D*

Puerto Rico

University of Puerto Rico
Aguadilla *A*

Tennessee

University of Memphis *M*
Vanderbilt University *B, M, D*

Virginia

Washington and Lee University *B*

Wisconsin

University of Wisconsin
Madison *B, M, D*

Romanian

Georgia

Clark Atlanta University *D*

Roofing

Indiana

Ivy Tech Community College
North Central *A*

Washington

Clover Park Technical College *C*

Wisconsin

Milwaukee Area Technical College *C*

Russian

Alaska

University of Alaska
Anchorage *B*
Fairbanks *B, M*

Arizona

Arizona State University *B*
University of Arizona *B, M*

Arkansas

Ouachita Baptist University *B*

California

Claremont McKenna College *B*
Grossmont College *A*
Pitzer College *B*
Pomona College *B*
San Diego State University *B*
Scripps College *B*
Stanford University *M*
University of California
Davis *B*
Los Angeles *B*
San Diego *B*
Santa Barbara *B*
University of Southern California *B*

Colorado

Colorado College *B*
University of Denver *B*

Connecticut

Trinity College *B*
Wesleyan University *B*
Yale University *B*

Delaware

University of Delaware *B, T*

District of Columbia

American University *B*
George Washington University *B*
Georgetown University *B*
Howard University *B*

Florida

Florida State University *B*
New College of Florida *B*
University of Florida *B*
University of South Florida *B*

Georgia

Emory University *B*
University of Georgia *B*

Hawaii

University of Hawaii
Manoa *B*

Idaho

Idaho State University *A*

Illinois

Northern Illinois University *B*
University of Chicago *B, D*
University of Illinois
Chicago *B*
Urbana-Champaign *B, T*

Indiana

Purdue University *B*
University of Notre Dame *B*

Iowa

Cornell College *B, T*
Grinnell College *B*
University of Iowa *B, T*
University of Northern Iowa *B*

Kentucky

Bluegrass Community and Technical
College *A*
University of Kentucky *B*

Louisiana

Tulane University *B*

Maine

Bates College *B*
Bowdoin College *B*

Maryland

Goucher College *B*
University of Maryland
College Park *B*

Massachusetts

Amherst College *B*
Boston College *B, M*
Boston University *B*
Brandeis University *B*
College of the Holy Cross *B*
Smith College *B*
Tufts University *B*
Wellesley College *B*
Wheaton College *B*
Williams College *B*

Michigan

Michigan State University *B*
University of Michigan *B, M, D*

Minnesota

Carleton College *B*
Concordia College: Moorhead *B, T*
Gustavus Adolphus College *B*
Macalester College *B*
St. Olaf College *B*
University of Minnesota
Twin Cities *B*

Missouri

Saint Louis University *B*
Truman State University *B*
University of Missouri
Columbia *B, M*

Montana

University of Montana *B*

Nebraska

University of Nebraska
Lincoln *B*

New Hampshire

Dartmouth College *B*
University of New Hampshire *B*

New Jersey

Montclair State University *T*
Rider University *B*
Rutgers, The State University of New
Jersey
New Brunswick/Piscataway
Campus *B, T*
Seton Hall University *T*

New Mexico

University of New Mexico *B*

New York

Bard College *B*
Barnard College *B*
City University of New York
Brooklyn College *B*
Hunter College *B*
Queens College *B*
Colgate University *B*
Columbia University *B*
Columbia University
School of General Studies *B*
Cornell University *B*
Fordham University *B, M*
Hobart and William Smith Colleges *B*
Hofstra University *B*
New York University *B, M*
State University of New York
Albany *B, M*
Stony Brook *B*
Syracuse University *B*
United States Military Academy *B*
University of Rochester *B*
Vassar College *B*

North Carolina

Duke University *B, M*
Wake Forest University *B*

Ohio

Bowling Green State University *B*
College of Wooster *B*
Kent State University *B*
Oberlin College *B*
Ohio State University
Columbus Campus *B*
Ohio University *B*

Oklahoma

Oklahoma State University *B*
Tulsa Community College *A*
University of Oklahoma *B*

Oregon

Portland State University *B, T*
Reed College *B*
University of Oregon *B, M*

Pennsylvania

Bryn Mawr College *B, M, D*
Bucknell University *B*
California University of
Pennsylvania *B*
Dickinson College *B*
Haverford College *B, T*
Juniata College *B*
Penn State
Abington *B*
Altoona *B*
Beaver *B*

Berks *B*
Brandywine *B*
DuBois *B*
Erie, The Behrend College *B*
Fayette, The Eberly Campus *B*
Greater Allegheny *B*
Hazleton *B*
Lehigh Valley *B*
Mont Alto *B*
New Kensington *B*
Schuylkill *B*
Shenango *B*
University Park *B, M*
Wilkes-Barre *B*
Worthington Scranton *B*
York *B*
Swarthmore College *B*
Temple University *B*
University of Pennsylvania *B, D*
University of Pittsburgh *B*
West Chester University of
Pennsylvania *B, T*

South Carolina

University of South Carolina *B*

Tennessee

Rhodes College *B*
University of Tennessee
Knoxville *B*
University of the South *B*
Vanderbilt University *B*

Texas

Austin Community College *A*
Baylor University *B*
Southern Methodist University *B*
Texas A&M University *B*
Trinity University *B*
University of Texas
Arlington *B*
Austin *B*

Utah

Brigham Young University *B, M*
University of Utah *B, T*

Vermont

Middlebury College *B, M, D*
University of Vermont *B*

Virginia

Ferrum College *B*

Washington

Everett Community College *A*
Seattle Pacific University *B*
University of Washington *B, M, D*

West Virginia

West Virginia University *T*

Wisconsin

Beloit College *B, T*
Lawrence University *B*
University of Wisconsin
Madison *B*
Milwaukee *B*

Wyoming

University of Wyoming *B*

Russian/Slavic studies

Alaska

University of Alaska
Fairbanks *B*

California

San Diego State University *B*
Stanford University *M*

University of California
Los Angeles *B*
Riverside *B*
San Diego *B*

Colorado

Colorado College *B*
University of Colorado
Boulder *B*

Connecticut

Trinity College *B*
Wesleyan University *B*
Yale University *B, M*

District of Columbia

American University *B*
Georgetown University *M*

Florida

Florida State University *B, M*
Stetson University *B*

Georgia

Emory University *B*

Illinois

University of Chicago *B, D*
University of Illinois
Urbana-Champaign *B, M*

Indiana

Indiana University
Bloomington *M*

Iowa

Cornell College *B*
Luther College *B*
University of Iowa *B*

Kansas

University of Kansas *B, M*

Kentucky

Bluegrass Community and Technical
College *A*

Louisiana

Tulane University *B*

Maine

Colby College *B*
University of Southern Maine *B*

Maryland

University of Maryland
College Park *B*

Massachusetts

Bard College at Simon's Rock *B*
Boston College *M*
Boston University *B*
College of the Holy Cross *B*
Mount Holyoke College *B*
Tufts University *B*
University of Massachusetts
Amherst *B*
Wellesley College *B*
Wheaton College *B*

Michigan

Grand Valley State University *B*
Michigan State University *B*
University of Michigan *B, M*

Minnesota

Carleton College *B*
Concordia College: Moorhead *B*
Gustavus Adolphus College *B*
St. Olaf College *B*

University of Minnesota
Twin Cities *B, M*

New Hampshire

Dartmouth College *B*

New Jersey

Rutgers, The State University of New
Jersey
New Brunswick/Piscataway
Campus *B*

New Mexico

University of New Mexico *B*

New York

Bard College *B*
Barnard College *B*
City University of New York
Hunter College *M*
Colgate University *B*
Columbia University *B*
Columbia University
School of General Studies *D*
Cornell University *B, M, D*
Fordham University *B*
Hamilton College *B*
Hobart and William Smith Colleges *B*
New York University *M, D*
State University of New York
Albany *B, M*
Syracuse University *B*
United States Military Academy *B*
University of Rochester *B*

North Carolina

University of North Carolina
Chapel Hill *B, M*

Ohio

Bowling Green State University *B*
College of Wooster *B*
Kent State University *B*
Oberlin College *B*
Ohio State University
Columbus Campus *B, M*
Wittenberg University *B*

Oklahoma

University of Tulsa *B*

Oregon

University of Oregon *B, M*

Pennsylvania

Carnegie Mellon University *B*
La Salle University *B*
Lafayette College *B*
Muhlenberg College *B*

Tennessee

Rhodes College *B*
University of Tennessee
Knoxville *B*
University of the South *B*
Vanderbilt University *B*

Texas

Texas Tech University *B*
University of Houston *B*
University of Texas
Austin *B, M*

Vermont

Marlboro College *B*
Middlebury College *B*
University of Vermont *B*

Virginia

George Mason University *B*
University of Richmond *B*

Washington and Lee University *B*

Washington

University of Washington *B, M*

Wisconsin

Lawrence University *B*

Sacred music

Alabama

Birmingham-Southern College *B*
Samford University *B, M*
University of Mobile *B*

Arizona

International Baptist College *B*
Southwestern College *C, A, B*

Arkansas

Central Baptist College *B*
Ecclesia College *B*
John Brown University *B*
Ouachita Baptist University *B*
Williams Baptist College *B*

California

Azusa Pacific University *B*
Bethany University *B*
Bethesda Christian University *B*
Hope International University *B, M*
The Master's College *B*
Mount St. Mary's College *B*
Patten University *B*
Point Loma Nazarene University *B*
Santa Clara University *M*

Colorado

Nazarene Bible College *A, B*

Connecticut

Holy Apostles College and
    Seminary *M*
University of Hartford *B*

District of Columbia

Catholic University of America *M, D*

Florida

Ave Maria University *B*
Baptist College of Florida *A, B*
Clearwater Christian College *B*
Florida Christian College *B*
Hobe Sound Bible College *C, B*
Jacksonville University *B*
Palm Beach Atlantic University *B*
Southeastern University *B*
Warner University *B*

Georgia

Andrew College *C*
Darton College *C*
Emmanuel College *B*
Emory University *M*
Mercer University *M*
Shorter College *B*
Toccoa Falls College *B*

Idaho

Boise Bible College *A, B*
Northwest Nazarene University *B*

Illinois

Concordia University Chicago *B, M*
Judson University *B*
Lincoln Christian University *B, M*
Moody Bible Institute *B*
Northwestern University *M, D*
Olivet Nazarene University *B*
Trinity International University *B*

Indiana

Anderson University *B*
Bethel College *B*
Goshen College *C*
Huntington University *B*
Indiana Wesleyan University *A, B*
Manchester College *B*
Saint Joseph's College *C, M*
Valparaiso University *B*

Iowa

Dordt College *B*
Faith Baptist Bible College and
    Theological Seminary *B*
Wartburg College *B*

Kansas

Barclay College *B*
Central Christian College of
    Kansas *A, B*
MidAmerica Nazarene University *A, B*

Kentucky

Asbury College *B*
Campbellsville University *B, M*
Kentucky Christian University *B*
Kentucky Mountain Bible College *B*

Louisiana

Centenary College of Louisiana *B*
Louisiana College *B*

Maryland

Washington Bible College *B*

Massachusetts

Boston University *D*
Eastern Nazarene College *B*

Michigan

Andrews University *B*
Aquinas College *B*
Calvin College *B*
Grace Bible College *B*
Great Lakes Christian College *B*
Kuyper College *B*
Madonna University *B*
Marygrove College *C*
Spring Arbor University *B*

Minnesota

Bethany Lutheran College *B*
Bethel University *B*
Concordia University: St. Paul *B*
Crossroads College *B*
Crown College *B*
Gustavus Adolphus College *B*
North Central University *C, B*
Oak Hills Christian College *B*
St. Catherine University *C*
St. John's University *M*
St. Mary's University of Minnesota *B*
St. Olaf College *B*

Mississippi

Blue Mountain College *B*
Mississippi College *B*

Missouri

Baptist Bible College *B*
Calvary Bible College and Theological
    Seminary *B*
Central Bible College *A, B*
Central Christian College of the
    Bible *B*
College of the Ozarks *B*
Evangel University *B*
Hannibal-LaGrange College *B*
Lincoln University *B*
Missouri Baptist University *B*
Ozark Christian College *A, B*
St. Louis Christian College *B*

Southwest Baptist University *B*
Webster University *M*
William Jewell College *B*

Nebraska

Concordia University *B*
Grace University *B*
Nebraska Christian College *A, B*

New Jersey

Rider University *B, M*

New York

Concordia College *B*
Holy Trinity Orthodox Seminary *C*
Jewish Theological Seminary of
    America *B, M, D*
Nyack College *B*

North Carolina

Campbell University *B, M, T*
Gardner-Webb University *B*
Lenoir-Rhyne University *B*
Pfeiffer University *B*
Southeastern Baptist Theological
    Seminary *M, D*

North Dakota

University of Mary *B*

Ohio

Ashland University *M*
Bowling Green State University *B*
Cedarville University *B*
Cincinnati Christian University *B*
Franciscan University of
    Steubenville *B*
God's Bible School and College *A, B*
Malone University *B*
Mount Vernon Nazarene
    University *A, B*
Ohio Christian University *A, B*

Oklahoma

Mid-America Christian University *B*
Oklahoma Baptist University *B*
Oklahoma City University *B*
Oklahoma Wesleyan University *B*
Oral Roberts University *B, M*
Southern Nazarene University *B*
Southwestern Christian University *B*
Southwestern Oklahoma State
    University *B*

Oregon

Corban College *B*
Eugene Bible College *B*
Multnomah University *B*
Northwest Christian University *B*

Pennsylvania

Baptist Bible College of
    Pennsylvania *B*
Duquesne University *M*
Immaculata University *C, A*
Moravian College *B*
Philadelphia Biblical University *B*
St. Charles Borromeo Seminary -
    Overbrook *C*
Seton Hill University *C, B*
Valley Forge Christian College *B*

South Carolina

Charleston Southern University *B*
Columbia International University *B*
Erskine College *M*
Furman University *B*
Newberry College *B*
North Greenville University *B*
Presbyterian College *B*

South Dakota

Augustana College *B*
Dakota Wesleyan University *B*

Tennessee

Belmont University *B*
Carson-Newman College *B*
Johnson Bible College *B*
Lambuth University *B*
Lee University *B, M*
Tennessee Temple University *B*
Union University *B*

Texas

Arlington Baptist College *B*
Baylor University *B, M*
Concordia University Texas *B*
Dallas Baptist University *B, M*
Dallas Christian College *B*
East Texas Baptist University *B*
Hardin-Simmons University *B, M*
Houston Baptist University *B*
Howard Payne University *B*
St. Mary's University *M*
Southern Methodist University *M*
Southwestern Assemblies of God
    University *A, B*
Southwestern Baptist Theological
    Seminary *B, M, D*
Southwestern Baptist Theological
    Seminary: Theological
    Professions *M*
Texas Christian University *B*
University of Mary Hardin-Baylor *B*
Wayland Baptist University *B*

Virginia

Bluefield College *B*
Liberty University *B*
Virginia Wesleyan College *C*

Washington

Northwest University *B*
Trinity Lutheran College *B*

Wisconsin

Concordia University Wisconsin *B*
Maranatha Baptist Bible College *B*

Sales/distribution

Alabama

Gadsden State Community College *A*
University of Alabama
    Birmingham *B*
Wallace State Community College at
    Hanceville *A*

Arizona

Cochise College *C*
Prescott College *M*

Arkansas

Harding University *B*

California

Chabot College *A*
Chaffey College *C, A*
Citrus College *C*
College of the Canyons *C, A*
College of the Sequoias *C, A*
Columbia College *C*
Diablo Valley College *C*
East Los Angeles College *C, A*
El Camino College *C, A*
Fashion Institute of Design and
    Merchandising
    Los Angeles *A*
Golden West College *C, A*
Grossmont College *C, A*
Heald College
    Hayward *A*

Laney College *C, A*
Long Beach City College *C, A*
Orange Coast College *C, A*
Pasadena City College *A*
Santa Barbara City College *C, A*
Shasta College *A*
Sierra College *C, A*
Skyline College *C*

Colorado

Community College of Aurora *C, A*
Community College of Denver *C*

Connecticut

Gateway Community College *A*
Middlesex Community College *C*

Delaware

Wesley College *B*

Florida

Florida State College at Jacksonville *A*
Indian River State College *A*
Palm Beach Community College *A*
Tallahassee Community College *A*

Georgia

Albany Technical College *C, A*
Athens Technical College *C, A*
Augusta Technical College *C, A*
Clayton State University *C, A*
Kennesaw State University *B*
Middle Georgia College *A*
Savannah Technical College *C, A*

Hawaii

Heald College
   Honolulu *A*
University of Hawaii
   Kapiolani Community College *C, A*

Illinois

College of DuPage *C, A*
Harper College *C, A*
Illinois Eastern Community Colleges
   Wabash Valley College *C*
John Wood Community College *C, A*
Joliet Junior College *C*
Kishwaukee College *C*
Southwestern Illinois College *A*
Spoon River College *C*
Triton College *A*
University of Illinois
   Urbana-Champaign *B*
Waubonsee Community College *C*
Wilbur Wright College *C, A*

Indiana

International Business College *C, A*
Vincennes University *C*

Iowa

Des Moines Area Community
   College *A*
Hawkeye Community College *C, A*
Iowa Lakes Community College *C, A*
Iowa Western Community College *A*
Kirkwood Community College *C, A*
Muscatine Community College *C*
Northeast Iowa Community
   College *C, A*
Western Iowa Tech Community
   College *A*

Kansas

Allen County Community College *A*
Johnson County Community
   College *A*
Seward County Community
   College *C, A*

Kentucky

Henderson Community College *C*
Madisonville Community College *A*

Maine

Beal College *A*
Husson University *B*

Maryland

Community College of Baltimore
   County *C, A*
Howard Community College *C*

Massachusetts

Babson College *B*
Middlesex Community College *A*
Simmons College *B*

Michigan

Bay de Noc Community College *C, A*
Grand Rapids Community College *A*
Lansing Community College *A*

Minnesota

Academy College *A*
Concordia University: St. Paul *B*
Dakota County Technical College *A*
Inver Hills Community College *C*
Metropolitan State University *B*
Minnesota School of Business: St.
   Cloud *A*
Minnesota State College - Southeast
   Technical *A*
Minnesota State Community and
   Technical College *C, A*
Northland Community & Technical
   College *A*
Northwest Technical College *C, A*
Ridgewater College *C, A*
St. Catherine University *B*
St. Cloud Technical College *C, A*
St. Mary's University of Minnesota *B*
University of Minnesota
   Twin Cities *B*

Mississippi

Hinds Community College *C, A*

Missouri

Metropolitan Community College:
   Longview *A*
Metropolitan Community College:
   Maple Woods *A*
Metropolitan Community College:
   Penn Valley *A*

Montana

Flathead Valley Community College *C*
University of Montana *C*

Nevada

College of Southern Nevada *A*

New Jersey

Bergen Community College *A*
Burlington County College *C, A*
Camden County College *A*
Cumberland County College *C*
Gloucester County College *C, A*
Mercer County Community College *C*
Ocean County College *C*
Passaic County Community College *A*

New York

Bryant & Stratton Business Institute
Bryant & Stratton College:
   Syracuse *A*
City University of New York
   Baruch College *B, M*
Dutchess Community College *A*
Finger Lakes Community College *C, A*

Long Island University
   Brooklyn Campus *B*
Mercy College *M*
Monroe Community College *C, A*
Nassau Community College *A*
Orange County Community College *A*
Suffolk County Community College *A*
Sullivan County Community
   College *A*
Syracuse University *B*
Trocaire College *A*
Utica School of Commerce *A*
Westchester Community College *A*

North Carolina

Alamance Community College *C, A*
Asheville-Buncombe Technical
   Community College *A*
Blue Ridge Community College *A*
Pitt Community College *C, A*
Wake Technical Community
   College *C*
Western Piedmont Community
   College *C, A*

North Dakota

Lake Region State College *C, A*

Ohio

Bowling Green State University *B*
Cincinnati State Technical and
   Community College *C*
Columbus State Community
   College *C, A*
Edison State Community College *A*
Owens Community College
   Toledo *C*
Stark State College of Technology *A*
University of Akron *B*
University of Cincinnati
   Raymond Walters College *C, A*
University of Northwestern Ohio *C*
Wilmington College *B*
Youngstown State University *A, B, M*
Zane State College *A*

Oklahoma

East Central University *B*

Oregon

Clackamas Community College *C, A*
Southwestern Oregon Community
   College *C, A*
Umpqua Community College *C*

Pennsylvania

Butler County Community College *A*
Commonwealth Technical Institute *C*
Community College of
   Philadelphia *C, A*
Harcum College *A*
Harrisburg Area Community
   College *C, A*
Lehigh University *M*
Montgomery County Community
   College *C, A*
Seton Hill University *B*
University of Pennsylvania *B, M*
West Chester University of
   Pennsylvania *B*

Puerto Rico

Inter American University of Puerto
   Rico
   San German Campus *A*
Universidad Metropolitana *A, B*
Universidad del Este *C*

South Carolina

Aiken Technical College *C, A*
Florence-Darlington Technical
   College *C, A*

Greenville Technical College *C, A*
Midlands Technical College *C*

Tennessee

Middle Tennessee State University *B*

Texas

Baylor University *B*
Collin County Community College
   District *C, A*
Lamar University *B*
Laredo Community College *A*
Tarrant County College *C, A*
Texas A&M University *B*
University of Houston *B*
University of North Texas *B*
University of Texas
   San Antonio *B*
   Tyler *B, M*
University of the Incarnate Word *B*
Wade College *A*

Utah

Weber State University *A*

Virginia

Lord Fairfax Community College *C*
Tidewater Community College *C, A*
Virginia Union University *B*

Washington

Centralia College *C, A*
Highline Community College *A*
Lake Washington Technical College *C*
Olympic College *C*
Pierce College *C*
Shoreline Community College *A*

West Virginia

West Virginia State Community and
   Technical College *A*

Wisconsin

Moraine Park Technical College *C, A*
Northeast Wisconsin Technical
   College *A*
University of Wisconsin
   Madison *M*
   Stout *B*
Western Technical College *A*

Sales/marketing education

California

San Diego Mesa College *A*
San Diego State University *T*

Colorado

Colorado State University *B, T*

Florida

Palm Beach Community College *A*

Louisiana

Louisiana State University and
   Agricultural and Mechanical
   College *B*

Michigan

Eastern Michigan University *B*
Western Michigan University *B, T*

Minnesota

University of Minnesota
   Twin Cities *B, M*

Mississippi

Northwest Mississippi Community
   College *A*

Nebraska

Jersey
University *B*

New Mexico
Eastern New Mexico University *B*
University of the Southwest *B, T*

New York
College of Saint Rose *M, T*
Nazareth College *T*
New York Institute of
Technology *B, T*
State University of New York
College at Buffalo *B, M, T*

North Carolina
East Carolina University *D*
North Carolina State University *B, T*

Ohio
Bowling Green State
University *B, M, T*
Ohio State University
Columbus Campus *M, D*
Wright State University *M*

Oregon
Oregon State University *M*

South Carolina
Forrest Junior College *A*

Tennessee
Middle Tennessee State University *B*
University of Tennessee
Knoxville *T*

Utah
Utah State University *B, M*

Virginia
Old Dominion University *B, T*

Wisconsin
University of Wisconsin
Stout *B, T*
Whitewater *B, T*

Salon management

Michigan
Kirtland Community College *C, A*
Mott Community College *C, A*
Oakland Community College *A*
Schoolcraft College *C*

North Carolina
Cape Fear Community College *C*

Texas
Houston Community College
System *C*

Sanskrit/classical Indian languages

Iowa
University of Iowa *B*

Massachusetts
Harvard College *B, D*

New York
Bard College *B*

Scandinavian languages

California
University of California
Berkeley *B, M, D*
Los Angeles *B, M*

Illinois
Augustana College *B*
North Park University *B*
University of Chicago *B, D*

Minnesota
Augsburg College *B*
Concordia College: Moorhead *B*
Gustavus Adolphus College *B*
University of Minnesota
Twin Cities *B*

North Dakota
University of North Dakota *B*

Texas
University of Texas
Austin *B*

Washington
University of Washington *B, M, D*

Scandinavian studies

Iowa
Luther College *B*

Minnesota
Augsburg College *B*
Concordia College: Moorhead *B*
Gustavus Adolphus College *B*
Minnesota State University
Mankato *B*
University of Minnesota
Twin Cities *M, D*

Washington
Pacific Lutheran University *B*
University of Washington *B, M*

Wisconsin
University of Wisconsin
Madison *B, M*

School librarian education

California
California State University
Chico *T*

Georgia
Columbus State University *M*
Georgia State University *M, T*

Illinois
University of Illinois
Urbana-Champaign *M, T*

Kentucky
Eastern Kentucky University *M*

Massachusetts
Fitchburg State College *M*

Michigan
Central Michigan University *M*

Minnesota
College of St. Scholastica *B, M, T*
Minnesota State University
Mankato *M*

Missouri
Lindenwood University *M*
University of Missouri
Columbia *M*

Montana
University of Montana: Western *B, T*

New Jersey
Seton Hall University *M*

New York
City University of New York
Queens College *M*

Oregon
George Fox University *M, T*

Pennsylvania
Arcadia University *M*
St. Vincent College *M*

Rhode Island
University of Rhode Island *T*

Virginia
Longwood University *M*

Wisconsin
University of Wisconsin
Superior *M, T*

School psychology

Alabama
Auburn University *M, D*
University of Alabama *D*

Arizona
Northern Arizona University *M, D*

Arkansas
University of Central Arkansas *M, D*

California
Alliant International University *M*
Azusa Pacific University *M*
California Baptist University *M*
California State University
Chico *M, T*
East Bay *T*
Fresno *D*
Long Beach *M*
Chapman University *M, D, T*
National University *M*
Stanford University *D*
University of the Pacific *T*

Colorado
University of Colorado
Denver *T*
University of Denver *M, D*
University of Northern Colorado *D, T*

District of Columbia
Gallaudet University *M*
Howard University *M, D*

Florida
Barry University *M*
Carlos Albizu University *M*
Florida Agricultural and Mechanical
University *M, T*
Nova Southeastern University *M*
University of Central Florida *M*
University of Florida *M, D*
University of South Florida *M, D*

Georgia
Georgia Southern University *M, T*

Georgia State University *M, D, T*
University of Georgia *M, D*

Idaho
University of Idaho *M*

Illinois
Governors State University *M*
Illinois State University *M, D*
Lewis University *M*
Loyola University Chicago *M, D*
National-Louis University *M, D*
Western Illinois University *M*

Indiana
Ball State University *M, T*
Indiana State University *M, T*
Valparaiso University *M*

Iowa
University of Iowa *D*
University of Northern Iowa *M*

Kansas
Emporia State University *M*
University of Kansas *D*
Wichita State University *B, M*

Kentucky
Eastern Kentucky University *M*

Maine
University of Southern Maine *M*

Maryland
Bowie State University *M*
Towson University *T*

Massachusetts
Northeastern University *M, D*
University of Massachusetts
Amherst *D*
Boston *M*
Worcester State College *M*

Michigan
Andrews University *M*
Central Michigan University *M, D*
Michigan State University *M, D*
University of Detroit Mercy *M*
Wayne State University *M*

Minnesota
Capella University *M*
Minnesota State University
Mankato *M*
Moorhead *M*
Saint Cloud State University *M*
Walden University *D*

Missouri
Lindenwood University *M*
University of Missouri
Columbia *M, D*

Montana
University of Great Falls *M*
University of Montana *M*

Nebraska
University of Nebraska
Kearney *M*
Omaha *M*

Nevada
University of Nevada
Las Vegas *M*

New Hampshire
Rivier College *M*

New Jersey
Fairleigh Dickinson University
  Metropolitan Campus *M, D*
Georgian Court University *M*
Kean University *M, D*
New Jersey City University *M*
Rider University *M*
Rowan University *M*
Rutgers, The State University of New
  Jersey
  New Brunswick/Piscataway
    Campus *D*
Seton Hall University *M*

New Mexico
New Mexico State University *D*

New York
Adelphi University *M*
Alfred University *M, D*
City University of New York
  Brooklyn College *M, T*
  Queens College *M, T*
College of New Rochelle *M*
Hofstra University *M, D*
Iona College *M*
Long Island University
  Brooklyn Campus *M*
Marist College *M*
Roberts Wesleyan College *M*
Rochester Institute of Technology *M*
St. John's University *M, D*
State University of New York
  Buffalo *M*
  College at Plattsburgh *M, T*
  Oswego *M*
Syracuse University *D*
Yeshiva University *D*

North Carolina
Appalachian State University *M, T*
East Carolina University *M*
North Carolina State University *M, D*
University of North Carolina
  Chapel Hill *M, D*
Western Carolina University *M*

North Dakota
Minot State University *M*

Ohio
John Carroll University *M*
Kent State University *M, D*
Miami University
  Oxford Campus *M*
Union Institute & University *M*
University of Cincinnati *M, D*
University of Dayton *M*
University of Toledo *M*

Oklahoma
Oklahoma State University *M, D*
University of Central Oklahoma *M*

Oregon
George Fox University *M*
Lewis & Clark College *M*
University of Oregon *M, D*

Pennsylvania
Bucknell University *M*
California University of
  Pennsylvania *M*
Duquesne University *D*
Eastern University *M*
Edinboro University of
  Pennsylvania *M*
Immaculata University *D*
Indiana University of Pennsylvania *D*
Lehigh University *D*
Marywood University *M*

Penn State
  University Park *M, D*
Temple University *M, D*

Puerto Rico
Inter American University of Puerto
  Rico
  Metropolitan Campus *M, D*
  San German Campus *M, D*
Turabo University *M*
University of Puerto Rico
  Rio Piedras *M*

Rhode Island
Rhode Island College *M*
University of Rhode Island *M, D*

South Carolina
The Citadel *M*
Francis Marion University *M*
University of South Carolina *M, D*
Winthrop University *M, T*

Tennessee
Lee University *M*
Southern Adventist University *M*
University of Memphis *M*

Texas
Abilene Christian University *M*
Baylor University *M*
Sam Houston State University *M*
Stephen F. Austin State University *M*
Tarleton State University *M*
Texas A&M University *D*
Texas A&M University
  Texarkana *M*
Texas State University: San Marcos *M*
Texas Woman's University *M, D*
Trinity University *M*
University of Houston
  Clear Lake *M*
University of North Texas *M*
University of Texas
  Tyler *M*

Utah
Brigham Young University *D*

Virginia
College of William and Mary *M*
James Madison University *M, T*

Washington
Eastern Washington University *M*
Seattle University *M*

West Virginia
Marshall University *T*

Wisconsin
Marquette University *M*
University of Wisconsin
  La Crosse *M*
  Madison *M, D*
  River Falls *M*
  Stout *M*
  Whitewater *M*

Science teacher education

Alabama
Athens State University *B*
Auburn University *B, M, D, T*
Birmingham-Southern College *T*
Faulkner University *B, M, T*
Judson College *B*
Miles College *B*
Oakwood University *B*
Tuskegee University *B*

Arizona
Northern Arizona University *M*
Prescott College *B, M, T*
University of Arizona *B*

Arkansas
Arkansas Tech University *B*
Harding University *B, T*
Ouachita Baptist University *B, T*
Southern Arkansas University *B, T*
University of Arkansas
  Pine Bluff *B, M, T*
University of Central Arkansas *B*
University of the Ozarks *B, T*

California
Azusa Pacific University *T*
California Lutheran University *B, T*
California State University
  Chico *B, T*
  Long Beach *B, T*
  San Bernardino *M*
Fresno Pacific University *B, M, T*
Humboldt State University *T*
The Master's College *B, T*
Mills College *T*
Mount St. Mary's College *T*
San Diego State University *M, D, T*
San Francisco State University *T*
Shasta College *A*
Sonoma State University *T*
Stanford University *M, T*
University of the Pacific *T*
Vanguard University of Southern
  California *T*

Colorado
Adams State College *B, M, T*
Colorado Christian University *B*
Colorado State University *B, T*
Colorado State University
  Pueblo *T*
Metropolitan State College of
  Denver *T*
Regis University *B, T*
University of Colorado
  Boulder *T*
  Colorado Springs *T*
Western State College of
  Colorado *B, T*

Connecticut
Albertus Magnus College *B, T*
Central Connecticut State
  University *T*
Eastern Connecticut State
  University *M*
Fairfield University *T*
Quinnipiac University *B, M*
Sacred Heart University *T*
Saint Joseph College *T*
Southern Connecticut State
  University *B, M, T*
University of New Haven *T*

Delaware
Delaware State University *B*
University of Delaware *B, T*

District of Columbia
George Washington University *M, T*

Florida
Broward College *A, B*
Chipola College *B*
Florida Agricultural and Mechanical
  University *B, M, T*
Florida Atlantic University *B*
Florida Institute of
  Technology *B, M, D*
Florida State University *B, M, D*
Gulf Coast Community College *A*

Miami Dade College *A, B*
Northwest Florida State College *B*
Palm Beach Community College *A*
St. Petersburg College *B*
Southeastern University *B, T*
State College of Florida,
  Manatee-Sarasota *A*
University of Central Florida *B, M*
University of Miami *M*
University of North Florida *B, M*
University of South Florida *B, M*
University of West Florida *M*
Warner University *B*

Georgia
Albany State University *B, M*
Armstrong Atlantic State
  University *B, M, T*
Brewton-Parker College *B*
Columbus State University *B, M*
Covenant College *B, T*
Gainesville State College *A*
Georgia State University *M, T*
North Georgia College & State
  University *M*
Piedmont College *M, T*
Shorter College *T*
Toccoa Falls College *B, T*
University of Georgia *B, M, D, T*
University of West Georgia *M*
Valdosta State University *M*

Hawaii
Hawaii Pacific University *M*

Idaho
Boise State University *B, M, T*
Brigham Young University-Idaho *T*
Lewis-Clark State College *B, T*
University of Idaho *T*

Illinois
Augustana College *B, T*
Benedictine University *M*
Bradley University *B, M*
Chicago State University *T*
Concordia University Chicago *B, T*
DePaul University *M*
Eastern Illinois University *B, M, T*
Eureka College *T*
Illinois Institute of Technology *M, D*
Lewis University *T*
Loyola University Chicago *B, M*
McKendree University *B*
Monmouth College *T*
Moraine Valley Community College *A*
National-Louis University *M*
North Park University *M*
Olivet Nazarene University *B, T*
Southern Illinois University
  Edwardsville *B, T*
Trinity Christian College *B, T*
Triton College *A*
University of Illinois
  Urbana-Champaign *B, M, T*
University of St. Francis *B, M*

Indiana
Ball State University *B, D, T*
Bethel College *B*
Butler University *T*
Calumet College of St. Joseph *B*
Goshen College *B, T*
Grace College *B*
Huntington University *B, M*
Indiana State University *B, M, T*
Indiana University
  Bloomington *B, D, T*
  Kokomo *T*
  South Bend *B, T*
  Southeast *B*
Indiana University-Purdue University
  Fort Wayne *B, T*

Indiana Wesleyan University *B, T*
Manchester College *B, T*
Oakland City University *B*
Purdue University
   Calumet *B*
Saint Mary's College *T*
St. Mary-of-the-Woods College *B, T*
Taylor University *B, T*
Trine University *B, T*
University of Indianapolis *B, T*
University of Notre Dame *B*
University of St. Francis *B, T*
Valparaiso University *B*
Vincennes University *B*

Iowa

Briar Cliff University *B*
Buena Vista University *B, T*
Central College *T*
Coe College *B*
Cornell College *B, T*
Dordt College *B*
Drake University *M, T*
Ellsworth Community College *A*
Graceland University *T*
Grand View University *T*
Iowa State University *T*
Loras College *T*
Morningside College *B*
Mount Mercy College *T*
Northwestern College *B*
St. Ambrose University *B, T*
Simpson College *T*
University of Iowa *M, D, T*
University of Northern Iowa *B*
Upper Iowa University *B*
Waldorf College *B*
Wartburg College *T*

Kansas

Bethany College *T*
Friends University *B*
Garden City Community College *A*
Kansas Wesleyan University *T*
McPherson College *B, T*
Southwestern College *B, T*
Tabor College *B*
University of Kansas *B, T*

Kentucky

Alice Lloyd College *B*
Campbellsville University *B*
Eastern Kentucky University *B*
Kentucky Wesleyan College *T*
Murray State University *M*
Union College *B*
University of Kentucky *B*

Louisiana

Centenary College of Louisiana *B, T*
Louisiana College *B*
Louisiana State University
   Shreveport *B*
Nicholls State University *B*
Our Lady of Holy Cross College *T*
Southeastern Louisiana University *B*
Southern University and Agricultural
   and Mechanical College *B*
University of Louisiana at Lafayette *B*
University of New Orleans *M*
Xavier University of Louisiana *B*

Maine

University of Maine *B, M*
University of Maine
   Farmington *B*
   Fort Kent *B*
University of Southern Maine *T*

Maryland

Bowie State University *B*
College of Notre Dame of Maryland *T*
Montgomery College *A*

Morgan State University *B, M, D*
Prince George's Community
   College *A*
Towson University *T*
University of Maryland
   College Park *B*
Washington Adventist University *B*

Massachusetts

Assumption College *T*
Boston University *B, M, T*
Bridgewater State College *M, T*
Cambridge College *M*
Eastern Nazarene College *B*
Fitchburg State College *M, T*
Lesley University *B, M*
Merrimack College *T*
Salem State College *M*
Smith College *M*
Tufts University *M, T*
Westfield State College *B, M, T*
Worcester State College *T*

Michigan

Albion College *B, T*
Alma College *T*
Andrews University *M*
Aquinas College *B, T*
Calvin College *B, T*
Central Michigan University *B*
Cornerstone University *B, T*
Eastern Michigan University *B*
Grand Rapids Community College *A*
Grand Valley State University *B, T*
Hope College *B, T*
Lansing Community College *A*
Lawrence Technological University *M*
Madonna University *B*
Michigan State University *B, M*
Michigan Technological
   University *M, T*
Northern Michigan University *B, M, T*
Rochester College *B*
Saginaw Valley State University *M*
University of Detroit Mercy *B, M, T*
University of Michigan
   Dearborn *B*
   Flint *B, T*
Wayne State University *B, M, T*
Western Michigan
   University *B, M, D, T*

Minnesota

Augsburg College *T*
Bemidji State University *T*
College of St. Benedict *T*
College of St. Scholastica *T*
Concordia University: St. Paul *B, T*
Crown College *B*
Gustavus Adolphus College *T*
Hamline University *B, M, T*
Minnesota State University
   Mankato *B, M, T*
   Moorhead *B*
Rainy River Community College *A*
Ridgewater College *A*
St. Catherine University *T*
Saint Cloud State University *B, T*
St. John's University *T*
Southwest Minnesota State
   University *B, T*
University of Minnesota
   Crookston *B*
   Duluth *B, T*
   Morris *T*
   Twin Cities *M, T*
University of St. Thomas *B*
Vermilion Community College *A*
Walden University *M*
Winona State University *B, M, T*

Mississippi

Blue Mountain College *B*

Jackson State University *M*
Millsaps College *T*
Mississippi Gulf Coast Community
   College *A*
Mississippi State University *T*
Northwest Mississippi Community
   College *A*
University of Mississippi *B*
University of Southern
   Mississippi *M, D*

Missouri

Central Methodist University *B*
College of the Ozarks *B, T*
Culver-Stockton College *T*
Evangel University *B*
Hannibal-LaGrange College *B*
Harris-Stowe State University *T*
Lindenwood University *B*
Missouri Baptist University *B, T*
Missouri Southern State
   University *B, T*
Missouri State University *B*
Missouri Valley College *T*
Northwest Missouri State
   University *B, M, T*
Southeast Missouri State
   University *B, M, T*
Southwest Baptist University *B, T*
Truman State University *M, T*
University of Central Missouri *B, T*
University of Missouri
   Columbia *B, M, D*
   Kansas City *B*
Washington University in St.
   Louis *B, M, T*
Webster University *M*
William Woods University *B*

Montana

Fort Peck Community College *A*
Montana State University
   Billings *B, T*
   Bozeman *M*
University of Great Falls *B*
University of Montana *T*
University of Montana: Western *B, T*

Nebraska

Chadron State College *B, M*
College of Saint Mary *B, T*
Concordia University *B, T*
Nebraska Wesleyan University *B*
Peru State College *B, T*
University of Nebraska
   Kearney *B, M, T*
   Lincoln *B*
Wayne State College *T*

Nevada

Great Basin College *B*
University of Nevada
   Reno *B, T*

New Hampshire

Franklin Pierce University *M, T*
Keene State College *B, M, T*
New England College *B, T*
Plymouth State University *M, T*
Rivier College *B, T*
Saint Anselm College *T*
University of New Hampshire *T*

New Jersey

Caldwell College *T*
Centenary College *T*
The College of New Jersey *M, T*
College of St. Elizabeth *T*
Ramapo College of New Jersey *M*
Rider University *T*
Rowan University *T*

Rutgers, The State University of New
   Jersey
   New Brunswick/Piscataway
     Campus *T*
   Newark Regional Campus *T*
Saint Peter's College *T*
William Paterson University of New
   Jersey *T*

New Mexico

New Mexico Highlands University *B*
New Mexico Institute of Mining and
   Technology *M*
University of the Southwest *B, T*
Western New Mexico University *B*

New York

Adelphi University *M, T*
Bard College *M*
City University of New York
   Brooklyn College *M, T*
   City College *B, M, T*
   Lehman College *M, T*
   Queens College *M, T*
College of Mount St. Vincent *T*
College of Saint Rose *B, T*
Cornell University *B, M, T*
D'Youville College *M, T*
Dowling College *B, M*
Dutchess Community College *A*
Elmira College *B, T*
Fordham University *M, T*
Hofstra University *B, M*
Iona College *M, T*
Ithaca College *B, T*
Le Moyne College *T*
Manhattan College *B, T*
Manhattanville College *M, T*
Nazareth College *T*
New York Institute of
   Technology *B, T*
Pace University *B, M, T*
Roberts Wesleyan College *B, M*
Saint Bonaventure University *M*
St. Joseph's College *B, T*
St. Joseph's College: Suffolk
   Campus *B, T*
St. Lawrence University *T*
St. Thomas Aquinas College *B, M, T*
State University of New York
   Albany *M, T*
   Binghamton *T*
   Buffalo *M, D, T*
   College at Brockport *B, M, T*
   College at Buffalo *B, M*
   College at Cortland *B, M*
   College at Fredonia *M, T*
   College at Geneseo *B, M*
   College at Old Westbury *B, M, T*
   College at Oneonta *B, T*
   College at Plattsburgh *B, M*
   College at Potsdam *B, M*
   College of Environmental Science
     and Forestry *B, T*
   New Paltz *B, T*
   Oswego *B, M*
Syracuse University *M, D*
Ulster County Community College *A*
University of Rochester *M*
Vassar College *T*
Wagner College *T*
Wells College *T*

North Carolina

Belmont Abbey College *T*
Brevard College *B*
Catawba College *T*
East Carolina University *B, M*
Elon University *T*
Forsyth Technical Community
   College *A*
Gardner-Webb University *B*
Lenoir-Rhyne University *B, T*
Livingstone College *T*

Mars Hill College *T*
Meredith College *T*
North Carolina State
    University *B, M, D, T*
Sandhills Community College *A*
University of North Carolina
    Pembroke *B, M*
Wake Forest University *T*
Western Carolina University *B*

North Dakota

Dickinson State University *B, T*
Minot State University *B, M*
North Dakota State University *B, T*
University of North Dakota *B, T*

Ohio

Antioch University McGregor *M*
Ashland University *B, T*
Baldwin-Wallace College *T*
Bluffton University *B*
Bowling Green State
    University *B, M, T*
Capital University *T*
Cedarville University *B*
Defiance College *B, T*
Hiram College *T*
Kent State University *B*
Malone University *B*
Miami University
    Oxford Campus *B, T*
Mount Union College *T*
Mount Vernon Nazarene
    University *B, T*
Ohio Dominican University *B, T*
Ohio Northern University *B, T*
Ohio State University
    Columbus Campus *M, D*
Ohio University *D, T*
Ohio Wesleyan University *B*
Otterbein College *B*
Shawnee State University *B*
University of Akron *B, M*
University of Findlay *B, M, T*
University of Rio Grande *B, T*
University of Toledo *B, T*
Urbana University *B*
Ursuline College *B, M, T*
Walsh University *B*
Wilmington College *B*
Wright State University *B, M, T*
Youngstown State University *B, M*

Oklahoma

Cameron University *B, T*
East Central University *B*
Eastern Oklahoma State College *A*
Northeastern State University *B, M*
Northwestern Oklahoma State
    University *B, T*
Oklahoma Baptist University *B, T*
Oklahoma Christian University *B, T*
Oklahoma City University *B*
Oklahoma Wesleyan University *B*
Oral Roberts University *B, T*
Southeastern Oklahoma State
    University *B, M, T*
Southern Nazarene University *B*
Southwestern Oklahoma State
    University *B, M, T*
University of Central Oklahoma *B*
University of Oklahoma *B, T*
University of Tulsa *T*

Oregon

Concordia University *B, M, T*
Corban College *B*
Eastern Oregon University *B*
Linfield College *T*
Oregon State University *M, D*
Western Oregon University *B, M, T*

Pennsylvania

Albright College *T*
Alvernia University *B*
Arcadia University *B, M, T*
Baptist Bible College of
    Pennsylvania *B*
DeSales University *M, T*
Dickinson College *T*
Elizabethtown College *B*
Gannon University *M*
Gettysburg College *T*
Grove City College *B, T*
Juniata College *B, T*
La Salle University *B, T*
Lebanon Valley College *M*
Lincoln University *T*
Lycoming College *T*
Marywood University *B*
Mercyhurst College *B, T*
Moravian College *B*
St. Francis University *T*
Saint Joseph's University *B, M, T*
St. Vincent College *T*
Susquehanna University *T*
Temple University *B, M, T*
Thiel College *B*
University of Pennsylvania *M, T*
University of Pittsburgh
    Johnstown *B, T*
University of Scranton *T*
University of the Sciences in
    Philadelphia *B*
Villanova University *T*
Waynesburg University *B*
Widener University *B, T*
York College of Pennsylvania *B, T*

Puerto Rico

Bayamon Central University *B*
Caribbean University *B, T*
Inter American University of Puerto
    Rico
    Metropolitan Campus *B, M*
    San German Campus *M*
Pontifical Catholic University of
    Puerto Rico *B, T*
Turabo University *B*
Universidad del Este *B*
University of Puerto Rico
    Cayey University College *B*

Rhode Island

Rhode Island College *B, T*

South Carolina

Bob Jones University *B*
Charleston Southern University *B*
Clemson University *B*
College of Charleston *M, T*
Converse College *T*
Furman University *T*
University of South Carolina
    Aiken *B, T*

South Dakota

Black Hills State University *B*
Dakota Wesleyan University *B, T*
Mount Marty College *B*
Northern State University *B, T*
University of South Dakota *B, M, T*

Tennessee

Belmont University *B, M, T*
Bethel University *T*
Freed-Hardeman University *B, T*
King College *T*
LeMoyne-Owen College *B*
Lincoln Memorial University *B, T*
Tennessee Technological University *T*
Tennessee Temple University *B*
Union University *B, T*

University of Tennessee
    Chattanooga *B*
    Knoxville *T*
Vanderbilt University *M, D*

Texas

Abilene Christian University *B, T*
Arlington Baptist College *B, T*
Baylor University *B, T*
Dallas Baptist University *B, T*
Hardin-Simmons University *B, T*
Houston Baptist University *B, T*
Howard Payne University *B, T*
Lamar University *B, M, T*
LeTourneau University *B, T*
Lubbock Christian University *B*
McMurry University *T*
Midwestern State University *B*
Prairie View A&M University *M*
Sam Houston State University *M, T*
Southwestern University *B, T*
Stephen F. Austin State University *T*
Tarleton State University *B, T*
Texas A&M University
    Commerce *T*
    Galveston *B*
    Kingsville *T*
Texas Christian University *B, M, D*
Texas Tech University *M*
Texas Wesleyan University *B, M*
Texas Woman's University *M*
University of Dallas *T*
University of Houston *M, T*
University of Houston
    Clear Lake *T*
University of Mary Hardin-Baylor *B, T*
University of Texas
    Arlington *T*
    Austin *M, D*
    San Antonio *T*
Wayland Baptist University *B, T*
West Texas A&M University *T*

Utah

Brigham Young University *B*
Dixie State College of Utah *B*
Southern Utah University *B*
Utah State University *B*
Utah Valley University *B*
Weber State University *B*
Western Governors University *B, M, T*

Vermont

Castleton State College *B, T*
Johnson State College *B*
Lyndon State College *B*
St. Michael's College *T*
University of Vermont *B, T*

Virginia

Eastern Shore Community College *A*
Longwood University *B, T*
University of Virginia's College at
    Wise *T*

Washington

Eastern Washington University *B, M*
Seattle Pacific University *B, T*
University of Washington *M*
University of Washington Tacoma *T*
Washington State University *B, M, T*
Western Washington University *B, M*
Whitworth University *T*

West Virginia

Concord University *B, T*
Fairmont State University *B*
Ohio Valley University *B*
Shepherd University *T*
University of Charleston *B*
West Liberty University *B*
West Virginia State University *B*
West Virginia University *T*

West Virginia Wesleyan College *B*
Wheeling Jesuit University *B*

Wisconsin

Alverno College *B, M, T*
Beloit College *B*
Carroll University *B, T*
Carthage College *M, T*
Concordia University Wisconsin *B, T*
Edgewood College *B*
Lakeland College *T*
Lawrence University *T*
Maranatha Baptist Bible College *B*
Marian University *B, T*
Marquette University *T*
Mount Mary College *B, T*
Northland College *B, T*
St. Norbert College *T*
Silver Lake College *T*
University of Wisconsin
    Eau Claire *B*
    Green Bay *T*
    La Crosse *B, T*
    Madison *M*
    Milwaukee *M*
    Oshkosh *B*
    Parkside *B*
    Platteville *B, T*
    River Falls *T*
    Stout *B*
    Superior *B, T*
    Whitewater *B, T*
Viterbo University *B, T*

Science, technology, and society

Alabama

Samford University *A, B*

Arizona

Arizona State University *B, M, D*
Embry-Riddle Aeronautical University:
    Prescott Campus *B*

California

California Institute of Technology *B*
Chaffey College *A*
Pitzer College *B*
Pomona College *B*
Scripps College *B*
Stanford University *B*
University of California
    Davis *B*

Colorado

Colorado Mountain College *A*
University of Colorado
    Boulder *D*
University of Denver *B*

Connecticut

Wesleyan University *B*

District of Columbia

George Washington University *M*
Georgetown University *B, M*

Georgia

Georgia Institute of Technology *B*

Illinois

Northwestern University *B*
University of Illinois
    Urbana-Champaign *B*

Indiana

Butler University *B*
Indiana University
    Bloomington *B, M*

...siana University *M*

...ge *B*

...nd

...versity of Maryland
    College Park *M*

Massachusetts
Clark University *B*
Massachusetts Institute of
    Technology *B, D*
Wellesley College *B*
Worcester Polytechnic Institute *B*

Michigan
Eastern Michigan University *B, M*
Michigan State University *B*

Minnesota
Saint Cloud State University *M*
University of Minnesota
    Twin Cities *M*

Missouri
Washington University in St.
    Louis *B, M, D*

Nevada
University of Nevada
    Reno *B*

New Jersey
New Jersey Institute of Technology *B*
Rutgers, The State University of New
    Jersey
    Newark Regional Campus *B*

New York
Cornell University *B, M, D*
Polytechnic Institute of New York
    University *B*
Rensselaer Polytechnic
    Institute *B, M, D*
State University of New York
    Farmingdale *B*
Union College *B*
Vassar College *B*

North Carolina
North Carolina State University *B*
Western Carolina University *M*

Pennsylvania
Drexel University *M*
Lehigh University *B*
Slippery Rock University of
    Pennsylvania *B*

South Dakota
South Dakota School of Mines and
    Technology *B*

Tennessee
Vanderbilt University *B*

Texas
Angelina College *A*

Virginia
Danville Community College *A*
George Mason University *D*
James Madison University *B, M*
University of Virginia *M*
Virginia Polytechnic Institute and
    State University *B, M, D*

Washington
University of Puget Sound *B*
University of Washington Bothell *B*

West Virginia
West Virginia State Community and
    Technical College *A*
West Virginia University *M, D*

Wisconsin
Beloit College *B*

Sculpture

Alabama
Birmingham-Southern College *B*

Arizona
Northern Arizona University *B*
Prescott College *B*

California
Academy of Art University *C, A, B, M*
Art Center College of Design *B, M*
Biola University *B*
California College of the Arts *B, M*
California State University
    East Bay *B*
    Long Beach *B, M*
    Northridge *B, M*
Chabot College *A*
De Anza College *C, A*
Grossmont College *A*
Hartnell College *C*
Long Beach City College *A*
Monterey Peninsula College *C, A*
Ohlone College *C*
Otis College of Art and Design *B, M*
Oxnard College *A*
Palomar College *A*
Pasadena City College *A*
San Francisco Art Institute *B, M*
Santa Rosa Junior College *C*
Solano Community College *A*

Colorado
Adams State College *B*
Rocky Mountain College of Art &
    Design *B*

Connecticut
Lyme Academy College of Fine
    Arts *C, B*
University of Hartford *B*

District of Columbia
American University *M*
George Washington University *M*

Florida
Ringling College of Art and Design *B*
University of Miami *B*

Georgia
Savannah College of Art and
    Design *B, M*

Idaho
Northwest Nazarene University *B*

Illinois
Bradley University *B*
Lincoln College *A*
Richland Community College *A*
School of the Art Institute of
    Chicago *B*
University of Illinois
    Urbana-Champaign *B, M*

Indiana
Indiana University-Purdue University
    Fort Wayne *B*
Indiana University-Purdue University
    Indianapolis *B*

Iowa
Drake University *B*
University of Iowa *B, M*

Kansas
University of Kansas *B, M*

Kentucky
Eastern Kentucky University *B*

Louisiana
Centenary College of Louisiana *B*

Maine
Maine College of Art *D*
University of Southern Maine *B*

Maryland
Maryland Institute College of Art *B, M*

Massachusetts
Bard College at Simon's Rock *B*
Boston University *B, M*
Massachusetts College of Art and
    Design *B, M*
Montserrat College of Art *B*
Salem State College *B*
School of the Museum of Fine
    Arts *B, M*
University of Massachusetts
    Dartmouth *B, M*

Michigan
College for Creative Studies *B*
Ferris State University *B*
Grand Valley State University *B*
Kendall College of Art and Design of
    Ferris State University *B*
Northern Michigan University *A, B*
Siena Heights University *B*
University of Michigan *B*
University of Michigan
    Flint *B*

Minnesota
College of Visual Arts *B*
Minneapolis College of Art and
    Design *B*
Minnesota State University
    Mankato *B, M*
Saint Cloud State University *B*

Mississippi
Mississippi Gulf Coast Community
    College *A*

Missouri
Kansas City Art Institute *B*
Washington University in St.
    Louis *B, M*

Nevada
Sierra Nevada College *B*

New Mexico
College of Santa Fe *B*

New York
Alfred University *M*
Columbia University
    School of General Studies *B*
Rochester Institute of
    Technology *A, B, M*
State University of New York
    College at Buffalo *B*

College at Fredonia *B*
New Paltz *B, M*
Purchase *B, M*
Syracuse University *B, M*

North Carolina
East Carolina University *B*
Gardner-Webb University *B*
Methodist University *B*

Ohio
Art Academy of Cincinnati *B*
Bowling Green State University *B*
Cleveland Institute of Art *B*
Ohio State University
    Columbus Campus *B, M*
Ohio University *B, M*
University of Akron *B*

Oregon
Pacific Northwest College of Art *B*
Portland State University *B, M*
University of Oregon *B, M*

Pennsylvania
Edinboro University of
    Pennsylvania *B*
Keystone College *A, B*
Lycoming College *B*
Marywood University *B, M*
Seton Hill University *B*
Temple University *B, M*
University of the Arts *B, M*

Puerto Rico
Escuela de Artes Plasticas de Puerto
    Rico *B*
Inter American University of Puerto
    Rico
    San German Campus *B, M*
University of Puerto Rico
    Rio Piedras *B*

Rhode Island
Providence College *B*
Rhode Island School of Design *B, M*

Tennessee
Memphis College of Art *B, M*
Tennessee Technological University *B*
University of Tennessee
    Knoxville *M*

Texas
Texas A&M University
    Commerce *B, M*
Texas Christian University *B, M*
University of Dallas *B, M*
University of Houston *B, M*
University of Texas
    El Paso *B, M*
Western Texas College *A*

Utah
Brigham Young University *M*

Vermont
Bennington College *B*
Marlboro College *B*

Virginia
Virginia Commonwealth University *B*

Washington
Cornish College of the Arts *B*
University of Washington *B, M*
Western Washington University *B*

West Virginia
West Virginia State University *B*

Wisconsin

University of Wisconsin
    Madison *B*

Secondary education

Alabama

Alabama Agricultural and Mechanical
    University *B, M*
Alabama State University *B, M*
Athens State University *B*
Auburn University *M, D, T*
Auburn University at
    Montgomery *B, M*
Birmingham-Southern College *B, T*
Calhoun Community College *A*
Chattahoochee Valley Community
    College *A*
Faulkner University *B, M, T*
Jacksonville State University *B, M, T*
Miles College *B*
Samford University *M, T*
Shelton State Community College *A*
Spring Hill College *B, M, T*
Talladega College *B*
Troy University *B, M, T*
University of Alabama *B, M, D*
University of Alabama
    Birmingham *B, M*
University of Montevallo *M, T*
University of North Alabama *B, M*
University of South Alabama *B, M, T*
University of West Alabama *B, M*

Alaska

University of Alaska
    Fairbanks *M, T*
    Southeast *M, T*

Arizona

Arizona State University *B, M*
Arizona Western College *A*
Eastern Arizona College *A*
Estrella Mountain Community
    College *A*
Grand Canyon University *B, M*
Northern Arizona University *M, T*
Prescott College *B, M, T*
Southwestern College *B*
University of Arizona *B*
University of Phoenix *B, M*

Arkansas

Harding University *M, T*
Hendrix College *T*
Ouachita Baptist University *B, T*
South Arkansas Community College *A*
Southern Arkansas University *M, T*
University of Arkansas *M*
University of Arkansas
    Little Rock *M*
    Monticello *M*
Williams Baptist College *B*

California

Alliant International University *T*
Azusa Pacific University *B, T*
Biola University *B, T*
California Baptist University *M, T*
California Lutheran University *B, M*
California State University
    East Bay *T*
    Fullerton *M, T*
    Long Beach *M, T*
    Los Angeles *M*
    Northridge *M*
    San Bernardino *M, T*
    San Marcos *T*
California State University: Channel
    Islands *T*
Chapman University *M, T*
Concordia University *T*
Cypress College *A*

Dominican University of California *T*
Holy Names University *T*
Humboldt State University *T*
La Sierra University *M, T*
Loyola Marymount University *M, T*
The Master's College *B, T*
Mills College *T*
Mount St. Mary's College *B*
National University *B, T*
Notre Dame de Namur University *T*
Occidental College *T*
Pacific Union College *T*
St. Mary's College of California *M*
San Diego Christian College *B, T*
San Diego State University *M, T*
San Francisco State University *T*
San Jose State University *M*
Sonoma State University *M*
Stanford University *M, T*
University of California
    Santa Barbara *T*
University of La Verne *B, M, T*
University of Redlands *B, T*
University of San Diego *M, T*
University of San Francisco *T*
University of Southern California *M, T*
University of the Pacific *B, T*
Vanguard University of Southern
    California *T*
Westmont College *T*
Whittier College *T*

Colorado

Adams State College *B, M, T*
Colorado Christian University *B*
Colorado College *M*
Colorado State University
    Pueblo *T*
Metropolitan State College of
    Denver *T*
Otero Junior College *A*
Regis University *B, T*
University of Colorado
    Boulder *T*

Connecticut

Albertus Magnus College *B, T*
Central Connecticut State
    University *B, M, T*
Eastern Connecticut State
    University *B, M, T*
Quinnipiac University *B, M*
Sacred Heart University *M, T*
Saint Joseph College *T*
Southern Connecticut State
    University *B, M, T*
University of Bridgeport *M, T*
University of Connecticut *T*
University of Hartford *B, M*
University of New Haven *T*
Western Connecticut State
    University *B, M*

Delaware

University of Delaware *B, M, T*

District of Columbia

American University *B, M, T*
Catholic University of America *B, M*
Gallaudet University *B, T*
George Washington University *M, T*
Howard University *M*
Trinity Washington University *M*

Florida

Chipola College *B*
Florida Agricultural and Mechanical
    University *M*
Florida Gulf Coast University *M*
Florida Institute of Technology *M*
Indian River State College *A*
Jacksonville University *B, M, T*
Miami Dade College *A, B*

Northwest Florida State College *A*
Nova Southeastern University *B*
Palm Beach Community College *A*
Saint Thomas University *B, T*
State College of Florida,
    Manatee-Sarasota *A*
Stetson University *B*
Trinity Baptist College *B*
University of North Florida *B, M*
University of Tampa *B, T*

Georgia

Agnes Scott College *T*
Armstrong Atlantic State
    University *B, M, T*
Bainbridge College *A*
Berry College *M*
Brewton-Parker College *B*
Clark Atlanta University *M*
College of Coastal Georgia *A*
Columbus State University *B, M*
Dalton State College *A*
Fort Valley State University *B, T*
Gainesville State College *A*
Georgia College and State
    University *M, T*
Georgia Military College *A*
Macon State College *A*
Mercer University *M*
Middle Georgia College *A*
Piedmont College *B, M, T*
South Georgia College *A*
University of West Georgia *B, M, T*
Valdosta State University *B, M*

Hawaii

Chaminade University of
    Honolulu *B, M, T*
Hawaii Pacific University *M*
University of Hawaii
    Hilo *T*
    Manoa *B, T*

Idaho

Boise State University *T*
Idaho State University *B*
Lewis-Clark State College *T*
North Idaho College *A*
Northwest Nazarene University *B*
University of Idaho *B, M, T*

Illinois

Augustana College *B, T*
Aurora University *B*
Benedictine University *M, T*
Black Hawk College: East Campus *A*
Bradley University *T*
Chicago State University *B, M, T*
City Colleges of Chicago
    Harold Washington College *A*
Columbia College Chicago *M*
Concordia University Chicago *B, T*
DePaul University *B, M, T*
Dominican University *T*
Elmhurst College *B*
Eureka College *B*
Greenville College *M, T*
Illinois Central College *A*
John A. Logan College *A*
Joliet Junior College *A*
Judson University *B*
Kankakee Community College *A*
Kishwaukee College *A*
Knox College *T*
Lewis University *T*
Loyola University Chicago *B, M, T*
MacMurray College *B, T*
Monmouth College *T*
National-Louis University *M, T*
North Central College *T*
North Park University *M, T*
Northern Illinois University *M*
Northwestern University *B*

Olivet Nazarene University *B, M, T*
Rockford College *M, T*
Roosevelt University *B, M*
Saint Xavier University *B*
Southern Illinois University
    Edwardsville *M, T*
Southwestern Illinois College *A*
Trinity Christian College *T*
Trinity International
    University *B, M, T*
University of Illinois
    Urbana-Champaign *B, M, D, T*
University of St. Francis *M*
Western Illinois University *M*
Wheaton College *B, M, T*

Indiana

Ancilla College *A*
Anderson University *T*
Ball State University *M, T*
Butler University *B, M*
Calumet College of St. Joseph *B, T*
Earlham College *M*
Goshen College *B, T*
Huntington University *B*
Indiana University
    Bloomington *B, M, D, T*
    East *B*
    Kokomo *M*
    Northwest *B, M, T*
    South Bend *B, M, T*
    Southeast *B, M*
Indiana University-Purdue University
    Fort Wayne *B, M, T*
Indiana University-Purdue University
    Indianapolis *M, T*
Indiana Wesleyan University *B, T*
Manchester College *B, T*
Marian University *T*
Purdue University *B*
Purdue University
    Calumet *B, M*
Saint Joseph's College *B*
Saint Mary's College *T*
St. Mary-of-the-Woods College *B, T*
Taylor University *T*
University of Evansville *T*
University of Indianapolis *A, B, T*
University of Southern Indiana *M*
Valparaiso University *B, M, T*
Vincennes University *A*
Wabash College *T*

Iowa

Briar Cliff University *B*
Buena Vista University *T*
Central College *T*
Coe College *B*
Cornell College *B, T*
Dordt College *B, T*
Drake University *B, M*
Ellsworth Community College *A*
Faith Baptist Bible College and
    Theological Seminary *B*
Graceland University *T*
Grand View University *B, T*
Grinnell College *T*
Iowa State University *T*
Iowa Wesleyan College *B*
Loras College *B*
Maharishi University of
    Management *B, M*
Marshalltown Community College *A*
Mount Mercy College *B, T*
North Iowa Area Community
    College *A*
Northwestern College *T*
St. Ambrose University *B, T*
Simpson College *T*
University of Iowa *M, D, T*
Upper Iowa University *B, T*
Waldorf College *B*
Wartburg College *T*
William Penn University *B*

Kansas

Allen County Community College A
Baker University B, T
Bethany College B, T
Bethel College T
Butler Community College A
Central Christian College of
  Kansas A, B
Coffeyville Community College A
Dodge City Community College A
Emporia State University B, M, T
Fort Hays State University M
Friends University B, T
Garden City Community College A
Highland Community College A
Kansas State University B, M, T
Kansas Wesleyan University B, T
Labette Community College A
MidAmerica Nazarene University B, T
Neosho County Community
  College A
Newman University B, T
Pittsburg State University M
Pratt Community College A
Southwestern College B, M, T
Tabor College B
University of Kansas B, T
Washburn University B
Wichita State University B, T

Kentucky

Alice Lloyd College B
Bellarmine University M, T
Berea College B, T
Brescia University B, T
Campbellsville University B
Centre College T
Eastern Kentucky University M
Georgetown College M
Kentucky Christian University B, T
Kentucky Wesleyan College T
Lindsey Wilson College B, T
Midway College B
Morehead State University M
Murray State University M, T
Northern Kentucky University M
Spalding University M, T
Thomas More College B, M
Union College B, M
University of Kentucky M
University of Louisville M
University of the Cumberlands M, T
Western Kentucky University M, T

Louisiana

Centenary College of
  Louisiana B, M, T
Dillard University B, T
Louisiana College B
Louisiana State University and
  Agricultural and Mechanical
  College B
Louisiana Tech University B
McNeese State University M, T
Northwestern State University M
Our Lady of Holy Cross College B
Southeastern Louisiana University M
Southern University and Agricultural
  and Mechanical College B, M
University of Louisiana at Lafayette B
University of Louisiana at Monroe M
University of New Orleans B
Xavier University of Louisiana M

Maine

Bowdoin College T
Husson University B
University of Maine B, M
University of Maine
  Farmington B, T
  Fort Kent B
  Machias B, T
  Presque Isle B

University of Southern Maine T

Maryland

Allegany College of Maryland A
Anne Arundel Community College A
Bowie State University M
Carroll Community College A
Cecil College A
Chesapeake College A
College of Notre Dame of
  Maryland B, M
Coppin State University B, T
Frostburg State University M, T
Garrett College A
Goucher College T
Harford Community College A
Hood College T
Howard Community College A
McDaniel College M, T
Mount St. Mary's University M, T
Prince George's Community
  College A
Salisbury University M
Towson University M, T
University of Maryland
  Eastern Shore M
  University College M
Washington Adventist University B, T

Massachusetts

American International
  College B, M, T
Amherst College T
Assumption College T
Atlantic Union College B
Boston College B, M, T
Clark University M
Eastern Nazarene College M, T
Elms College B, M, T
Emmanuel College B, M
Fitchburg State College B, M, T
Framingham State College M
Gordon College B
Lasell College B, T
Lesley University B, M
Massachusetts College of Liberal
  Arts T
Merrimack College T
Nichols College B
Salem State College B, M
Simmons College B, M
Smith College M
Springfield College B, T
Suffolk University M
Tufts University M, T
University of Massachusetts
  Dartmouth T
Wellesley College T
Western New England College B, T
Westfield State College M, T
Wheaton College T
Worcester State College M, T

Michigan

Adrian College B
Albion College T
Alma College B, T
Andrews University B, M
Baker College
  of Auburn Hills B
  of Clinton Township B
  of Flint B
  of Jackson B
  of Muskegon B
  of Owosso B
Baker College of Allen Park B
Calvin College B, T
Central Michigan University M
Cornerstone University B
Delta College A
Eastern Michigan University B, M, T
Ferris State University A
Gogebic Community College A
Grace Bible College B

Grand Valley State University M, T
Henry Ford Community College A
Hillsdale College B
Kuyper College B
Lake Michigan College A
Lake Superior State University B, T
Lansing Community College A
Madonna University T
Marygrove College T
Michigan State University B
Mid Michigan Community College A
Northern Michigan University B, M, T
Oakland University M
Rochester College B
Saginaw Valley State University M
Siena Heights University B, M, T
Spring Arbor University B
University of Detroit Mercy B, M, T
University of Michigan
  Dearborn B, T
  Flint B, T
Washtenaw Community College A
Wayne State University M, T

Minnesota

Augsburg College B, T
Bethel University B
College of St. Benedict T
College of St. Scholastica T
Concordia College: Moorhead B, T
Concordia University: St. Paul B, T
Crown College B
Gustavus Adolphus College B
Hamline University B, M, T
Minnesota State University
  Mankato B, M, T
Minnesota West Community and
  Technical College A
North Central University B
Ridgewater College A
St. Catherine University B, T
Saint Cloud State University B, T
St. John's University T
University of Minnesota
  Duluth B, T
  Morris T
University of St. Thomas M
Vermilion Community College A
Winona State University B, M, T

Mississippi

Alcorn State University M
Belhaven University T
Delta State University M
Hinds Community College A
Holmes Community College A
Jackson State University M
Millsaps College T
Mississippi College B, M
Mississippi Delta Community
  College A
Mississippi Gulf Coast Community
  College A
Mississippi State University B, M, D, T
Mississippi University for Women M
Northwest Mississippi Community
  College A
Tougaloo College B, T
University of Southern Mississippi M

Missouri

Avila University B, T
Calvary Bible College and Theological
  Seminary B
Central Methodist University B
College of the Ozarks B, T
Crowder College A
Drury University T
Evangel University B, M, T
Hannibal-LaGrange College B
Harris-Stowe State University B, T
Jefferson College A
Lincoln University M
Missouri Baptist University T

Missouri Southern State
  University B, T
Missouri State University M
Missouri Valley College B, T
Northwest Missouri State
  University M, T
Ozark Christian College A
Park University T
Rockhurst University B
St. Louis Community College
  St. Louis Community College at
    Meramec A
Southeast Missouri State
  University M, T
Truman State University M, T
University of Central Missouri B, M, T
University of Missouri
  Columbia B, M, D
  Kansas City B
  Missouri University of Science and
    Technology T
  St. Louis B, M
Washington University in St.
  Louis B, M, T
Westminster College B, T
William Jewell College B, T
William Woods University B, T

Montana

Montana State University
  Billings B, M, T
  Bozeman T
Rocky Mountain College B, T
University of Great Falls B, M
University of Montana B, M
University of Montana: Western B, T

Nebraska

Chadron State College B, M
College of Saint Mary B, T
Concordia University B, T
Creighton University B
Grace University B
Nebraska Wesleyan University T
Northeast Community College A
Peru State College B, T
Union College B, T
University of Nebraska
  Kearney B, M, T
  Omaha B, M, T
Western Nebraska Community
  College A
York College B, T

Nevada

Great Basin College B
Nevada State College B
Sierra Nevada College M
Truckee Meadows Community
  College A
University of Nevada
  Las Vegas B, T
  Reno B, M, T

New Hampshire

Dartmouth College T
Franklin Pierce University M, T
Keene State College B, T
New England College B, T
Plymouth State University M, T
Rivier College B, M, T
Saint Anselm College T
Southern New Hampshire
  University M
University of New Hampshire M
University of New Hampshire at
  Manchester T

New Jersey

Caldwell College T
Centenary College T
The College of New Jersey M, T
College of St. Elizabeth T

Drew University *M*
Essex County College *A*
Felician College *B*
Monmouth University *M*
Raritan Valley Community College *A*
Rider University *B*
Rowan University *B, M*
Rutgers, The State University of New Jersey
    Camden Regional Campus *T*
    New Brunswick/Piscataway Campus *T*
    Newark Regional Campus *T*
Saint Peter's College *T*
Seton Hall University *B, M*
Sussex County Community College *A*

New Mexico

New Mexico Highlands University *B*
New Mexico Junior College *A*
New Mexico State University *B*
San Juan College *A, T*
University of New Mexico *B, M*
University of the Southwest *B, T*
Western New Mexico University *B, M, T*

New York

Adelphi University *B, M, T*
Alfred University *T*
Bard College *M*
Barnard College *T*
Canisius College *B, M, T*
City University of New York
    City College *B, M, T*
    Hunter College *B, M, T*
    Queens College *M, T*
    York College *T*
Colgate University *M, T*
College of Mount St. Vincent *T*
College of Saint Rose *B, M, T*
Columbia University
    School of General Studies *B, T*
Cornell University *M*
D'Youville College *M, T*
Daemen College *M, T*
Dominican College of Blauvelt *B, T*
Dowling College *M, T*
Dutchess Community College *A*
Elmira College *B, M, T*
Fordham University *M, T*
Hobart and William Smith Colleges *T*
Hofstra University *B, M, T*
Houghton College *B, T*
Iona College *B, M, T*
Ithaca College *B, M, T*
Keuka College *B, T*
Le Moyne College *M, T*
Long Island University
    Brooklyn Campus *B, M, T*
    C. W. Post Campus *M, T*
Manhattan College *B, T*
Manhattanville College *M, T*
Marymount Manhattan College *T*
Medaille College *B, M, T*
Mercy College *M, T*
Mohawk Valley Community College *A*
Molloy College *B, M, T*
Mount Saint Mary College *B, M*
Nassau Community College *A*
Nazareth College *B, M, T*
Niagara University *B, M, T*
Onondaga Community College *A*
Pace University *M, T*
Saint Bonaventure University *M*
St. John Fisher College *B, M, T*
St. John's University *M, T*
St. Joseph's College *B, T*
St. Joseph's College: Suffolk Campus *B, T*
St. Thomas Aquinas College *B, M, T*
State University of New York
    Albany *M, T*
    College at Brockport *B, M, T*

College at Buffalo *B, M, T*
College at Fredonia *B, M, T*
College at Old Westbury *B, M, T*
College at Plattsburgh *M*
College of Technology at Delhi *A*
New Paltz *B, M, T*
Oswego *B, M, T*
Suffolk County Community College *A*
Syracuse University *M, T*
Tompkins Cortland Community College *A*
University of Rochester *M*
Utica College *B, M*
Vassar College *T*
Wagner College *B, M*
Wells College *T*
Yeshiva University *M*

North Carolina

Brevard College *B*
Campbell University *B, M*
Catawba College *T*
Chowan University *B*
Davidson College *T*
Duke University *M*
Elon University *B, T*
Fayetteville State University *B*
Gardner-Webb University *B, M*
Greensboro College *T*
Guilford College *B, T*
High Point University *B*
Mars Hill College *B, T*
Martin Community College *A*
Meredith College *T*
Methodist College *A, B, T*
North Carolina Wesleyan College *T*
Pfeiffer University *B, T*
Salem College *B, T*
Sandhills Community College *A*
Southeastern Community College *A*
University of North Carolina
    Asheville *T*
    Wilmington *M*
Wake Forest University *M, T*
Warren Wilson College *B, T*

North Dakota

Dickinson State University *B, T*
Jamestown College *B*
University of Mary *M*

Ohio

Bluffton University *B*
Bowling Green State University *M*
Central State University *B*
Cincinnati Christian University *B*
College of Wooster *T*
Defiance College *B, T*
Heidelberg University *T*
Hiram College *T*
John Carroll University *M, T*
Kent State University *M*
Lourdes College *B*
Malone University *T*
Marietta College *B*
Miami University
    Oxford Campus *B, M, T*
Mount Union College *T*
Mount Vernon Nazarene University *B, T*
Muskingum University *B, M, T*
Notre Dame College *B, T*
Ohio Christian University *B*
Ohio Dominican University *B, T*
Ohio Northern University *B, T*
Ohio State University
    Columbus Campus *M*
Ohio University *B, M, D, T*
Ohio Wesleyan University *B*
Otterbein College *B*
Union Institute & University *B, M*
University of Akron *M, D*
University of Cincinnati *B, M, D, T*

University of Cincinnati
    Clermont College *A*
    Raymond Walters College *A*
University of Dayton *B, M, T*
University of Findlay *B, M, T*
University of Rio Grande *B, T*
University of Toledo *B, M, T*
Urbana University *B*
Walsh University *B*
Washington State Community College *A*
Wilmington College *B*
Wright State University *M*
Xavier University *B, M*
Youngstown State University *B, M*

Oklahoma

Cameron University *B, T*
Carl Albert State College *A*
Connors State College *A*
East Central University *M, T*
Eastern Oklahoma State College *A*
Langston University *B*
Mid-America Christian University *B*
Northern Oklahoma College *A*
Northwestern Oklahoma State University *M*
Oklahoma Baptist University *B, T*
Oklahoma Christian University *B, T*
Oklahoma City Community College *A*
Oklahoma City University *B, M*
Oklahoma State University *B*
Rogers State University *A*
St. Gregory's University *B*
Southeastern Oklahoma State University *B, M, T*
Southern Nazarene University *B*
Southwestern Oklahoma State University *M, T*

Oregon

Chemeketa Community College *A*
Concordia University *B, M, T*
Corban College *B, M*
Eastern Oregon University *B, M*
George Fox University *M, T*
Lewis & Clark College *M*
Linfield College *T*
Linn-Benton Community College *A*
Oregon State University *M*
Portland State University *T*
Southern Oregon University *M, T*
Treasure Valley Community College *A*
University of Portland *B, M, T*
Warner Pacific College *B, T*
Western Oregon University *B, M, T*
Willamette University *M*

Pennsylvania

Albright College *B, M, T*
Arcadia University *B, M, T*
Baptist Bible College of Pennsylvania *B*
Bryn Mawr College *T*
Bucknell University *B, T*
California University of Pennsylvania *M*
Carlow University *M*
Cedar Crest College *B, T*
Chatham University *M, T*
Chestnut Hill College *T*
Community College of Philadelphia *A*
DeSales University *M, T*
Delaware Valley College *B*
Dickinson College *T*
Duquesne University *B, M, T*
East Stroudsburg University of Pennsylvania *M, T*
Eastern University *T*
Gannon University *B*
Gettysburg College *T*
Grove City College *B*
Harrisburg Area Community College *A*

Holy Family University *M, T*
Juniata College *B, T*
King's College *T*
Kutztown University of Pennsylvania *M*
La Salle University *B, M, T*
Lebanon Valley College *T*
Lehigh University *M*
Lincoln University *B, M, T*
Lycoming College *T*
Mansfield University of Pennsylvania *B, T*
Marywood University *M*
Mercyhurst College *B, M*
Millersville University of Pennsylvania *B*
Misericordia University *T*
Montgomery County Community College *A*
Muhlenberg College *T*
Penn State
    Abington *B*
    Altoona *B*
    Beaver *B*
    Berks *B*
    Brandywine *B*
    DuBois *B*
    Erie, The Behrend College *B*
    Fayette, The Eberly Campus *B*
    Greater Allegheny *B*
    Hazleton *B*
    Lehigh Valley *B*
    Mont Alto *B*
    New Kensington *B*
    Schuylkill *B*
    Shenango *B*
    University Park *B*
    Wilkes-Barre *B*
    Worthington Scranton *B*
    York *B*
Reading Area Community College *A*
Robert Morris University *T*
Rosemont College *B, T*
St. Francis University *B, T*
Saint Joseph's University *B, M, T*
St. Vincent College *T*
Slippery Rock University of Pennsylvania *M, T*
Susquehanna University *T*
Temple University *M*
University of Pennsylvania *M, T*
University of Pittsburgh *T*
University of Pittsburgh
    Bradford *B*
    Johnstown *B, T*
University of Scranton *B, M*
Villanova University *B, M*
Washington & Jefferson College *T*
Waynesburg University *B, T*
West Chester University of Pennsylvania *M, T*
Westminster College *B, T*
Widener University *M*
Wilson College *T*
York College of Pennsylvania *T*

Puerto Rico

American University of Puerto Rico *B, T*
Bayamon Central University *B*
Caribbean University *B, T*
Inter American University of Puerto Rico
    Aguadilla Campus *B*
    Arecibo Campus *B*
    Fajardo Campus *B, T*
    Ponce Campus *B, M*
    San German Campus *B*
Pontifical Catholic University of Puerto Rico *B*
Universidad Adventista de las Antillas *B*
Universidad Metropolitana *B*
Universidad del Este *B*

University of Puerto Rico
  Rio Piedras *B*
  Utuado *A*
University of the Sacred Heart *B*

Rhode Island

Providence College *B, M, T*
Rhode Island College *B, M, T*
Roger Williams University *B*
University of Rhode Island *B*

South Carolina

Bob Jones University *M*
Charleston Southern University *M*
The Citadel *B, M, T*
Clemson University *B, M*
Coastal Carolina University *M, T*
College of Charleston *B, T*
Converse College *M, T*
Erskine College *B, T*
Francis Marion University *B, M, T*
Furman University *T*
Lander University *B, M, T*
Presbyterian College *T*
South Carolina State University *M, T*
University of South Carolina *M, D*
University of South Carolina
  Aiken *B, T*
  Upstate *B, T*
Winthrop University *M, T*
Wofford College *T*

South Dakota

Augustana College *B, M, T*
Black Hills State University *T*
Mount Marty College *B*
South Dakota State University *B, T*
University of Sioux Falls *T*
University of South Dakota *M, T*

Tennessee

Belmont University *B, M, T*
Bethel University *T*
Carson-Newman College *B*
Christian Brothers University *B, M, T*
Cumberland University *B, T*
East Tennessee State University *M, T*
Fisk University *T*
Free Will Baptist Bible College *B*
Freed-Hardeman University *B, T*
King College *T*
Lambuth University *B, T*
Lee University *B, T*
Lincoln Memorial University *B, T*
Martin Methodist College *B*
Motlow State Community College *A*
Rhodes College *T*
Tennessee State University *B, M, T*
Tennessee Technological
  University *B, M, T*
Tennessee Temple University *B, M, T*
Tennessee Wesleyan College *B, T*
Trevecca Nazarene University *B, T*
Tusculum College *B, T*
Union University *B, T*
University of Tennessee
  Chattanooga *M*
  Knoxville *B*
  Martin *B*
University of the South *T*
Vanderbilt University *B, M, T*

Texas

Abilene Christian University *B, T*
Arlington Baptist College *B, T*
Austin College *M*
Austin Community College *A*
Baylor University *T*
Brazosport College *A*
Clarendon College *A*
Coastal Bend College *A*
College of the Mainland *A*
Concordia University Texas *B*

Dallas Baptist University *B, M*
Dallas Christian College *B, T*
Del Mar College *A*
El Paso Community College *A*
Frank Phillips College *A*
Grayson County College *A*
Houston Baptist University *B, M*
Howard Payne University *B, T*
Huston-Tillotson University *T*
Jarvis Christian College *B, T*
Lamar University *B, M, T*
LeTourneau University *B, T*
Lubbock Christian University *B, M*
McMurry University *B, T*
Navarro College *A*
Our Lady of the Lake University of San
  Antonio *M*
Rice University *M, T*
St. Edward's University *T*
Schreiner University *B*
South Texas College *A*
Southwestern Assemblies of God
  University *B*
Southwestern University *T*
Stephen F. Austin State University *M*
Sul Ross State University *M*
Tarrant County College *A*
Texas A&M International
  University *M, T*
Texas A&M University
  Commerce *M, D, T*
  Corpus Christi *M, T*
  Kingsville *B, M*
  Texarkana *T*
Texas Christian University *B, M*
Texas Lutheran University *T*
Texas State University: San
  Marcos *M, T*
Texas Tech University *M*
Texas Wesleyan University *B, M, T*
Trinity University *M*
University of Dallas *T*
University of Houston *M, T*
University of Houston
  Downtown *M*
  Victoria *M*
University of Mary Hardin-Baylor *T*
University of North Texas *M*
University of St. Thomas *B*
University of Texas
  Pan American *M*
University of the Incarnate Word *T*
Wayland Baptist University *M*
West Texas A&M University *T*
Wiley College *B*

Utah

Dixie State College of Utah *T*
Snow College *A*
Southern Utah University *B*
Utah State University *B, M, D*
Utah Valley University *A*
Weber State University *B*
Western Governors University *B, M, T*
Westminster College *B, T*

Vermont

Bennington College *B, M*
Castleton State College *B, M*
Champlain College *B*
College of St. Joseph in
  Vermont *B, M, T*
Goddard College *B, M*
Green Mountain College *B, T*
Johnson State College *B, M*
Middlebury College *D, T*
Norwich University *T*
St. Michael's College *T*
University of Vermont *B, T*

Virginia

Bluefield College *B, T*
College of William and Mary *M, T*
Eastern Mennonite University *T*

Hampton University *M*
Hollins University *T*
James Madison University *T*
Liberty University *M, T*
Longwood University *T*
Mary Baldwin College *T*
Marymount University *M*
Old Dominion University *M, T*
Radford University *T*
Randolph College *T*
Randolph-Macon College *T*
St. Paul's College *T*
University of Richmond *T*
University of Virginia's College at
  Wise *T*
Virginia Intermont College *B*
Virginia Polytechnic Institute and
  State University *B*
Virginia Wesleyan College *T*

Washington

Gonzaga University *T*
Northwest University *B*
Pacific Lutheran University *B*
Saint Martin's University *T*
Seattle Pacific University *M, T*
University of Washington *M, T*
University of Washington Bothell *M, T*
Walla Walla University *M, T*
Washington State University *B, M, T*
Western Washington University *M*
Whitworth University *B, M, T*

West Virginia

Alderson-Broaddus College *B*
Bethany College *B*
Fairmont State University *B*
Glenville State College *B*
Marshall University *B, M*
Mountain State University *A*
Ohio Valley University *B*
Potomac State College of West
  Virginia University *A*
Salem International University *B, T*
Shepherd University *B, T*
University of Charleston *B*
West Liberty University *B*
West Virginia State University *B*
West Virginia University *M*
West Virginia Wesleyan College *B*

Wisconsin

Beloit College *T*
Carthage College *T*
Concordia University Wisconsin *B, T*
Lakeland College *B*
Lawrence University *T*
Maranatha Baptist Bible College *B*
Marian University *B, T*
Marquette University *B*
Mount Mary College *B, T*
Ripon College *T*
St. Norbert College *T*
University of Wisconsin
  Green Bay *T*
  Oshkosh *B, T*
  Parkside *T*
  Platteville *T*
  River Falls *T*
  Stevens Point *B, T*
  Superior *M, T*
  Whitewater *B, T*
Viterbo University *B, M, T*
Wisconsin Lutheran College *B*

Wyoming

Central Wyoming College *A*
Eastern Wyoming College *A*
Northwest College *A*
Sheridan College *A*
University of Wyoming *B*
Western Wyoming Community
  College *A*

Secondary school administration

Alabama

University of Alabama *D*

Arkansas

Arkansas State University *M, T*

Illinois

Concordia University Chicago *M*
Lewis University *D*
University of Illinois
  Urbana-Champaign *M, D, T*

Indiana

Indiana University-Purdue University
  Indianapolis *M*

Kentucky

Morehead State University *M*
Murray State University *M, T*

Louisiana

Xavier University of Louisiana *M*

Massachusetts

Lesley University *M*
Westfield State College *M*

Michigan

Eastern Michigan University *M*
Michigan State University *M, D*

Minnesota

Capella University *M, D*

Missouri

Lincoln University *M*
Lindenwood University *M*
Northwest Missouri State
  University *M*
Southwest Baptist University *M*

Montana

University of Great Falls *M*

Nebraska

Concordia University *M, T*
Creighton University *M*
University of Nebraska
  Lincoln *D*
Wayne State College *M*

New Jersey

William Paterson University of New
  Jersey *M*

New York

Le Moyne College *M*
Saint Bonaventure University *M*
St. John Fisher College *M, T*
State University of New York
  New Paltz *M*
University of Rochester *M, D*

North Carolina

Appalachian State University *M, T*
North Carolina Central University *M*
University of North Carolina
  Chapel Hill *M*
  Pembroke *M*
Western Carolina University *M*
Wingate University *M, T*

North Dakota

University of Mary *M*

Ohio

Antioch University McGregor *M*

Kent State University *M, D*
University of Findlay *M, T*
Youngstown State University *M*

Oklahoma
University of Oklahoma *T*

Pennsylvania
East Stroudsburg University of
Pennsylvania *T*
Widener University *M, T*

South Carolina
Charleston Southern University *M*

South Dakota
University of South Dakota *M, D*

Texas
Our Lady of the Lake University of San
Antonio *M*
University of Texas
Arlington *T*

Vermont
St. Michael's College *T*

Virginia
Marymount University *M*

Washington
City University of Seattle *M, T*
University of Washington *M, D, T*
Washington State University *M, T*
Western Washington University *M*
Whitworth University *M*

Wisconsin
Concordia University Wisconsin *M*
University of Wisconsin
Superior *M*

Security/loss prevention

Arizona
Arizona Western College *C*
University of Phoenix *B*

California
De Anza College *C, A*
East Los Angeles College *C*
Grossmont College *C, A*
National University *B*
Palomar College *C, A*
Sierra College *A*

Colorado
Community College of Denver *C, A*

Connecticut
Three Rivers Community College *C*
University of New Haven *C*

Florida
Broward College *A*
Hillsborough Community College *C*
Miami Dade College *C*
St. Petersburg College *C, A, B*

Georgia
Albany Technical College *C*

Illinois
Black Hawk College *C*
Lewis University *B*
Lincoln Land Community College *C*
Moraine Valley Community College *C*
Southwestern Illinois College *C, A*
Triton College *C*

Waubonsee Community College *C*

Indiana
Vincennes University *A*

Kansas
Highland Community College *A*
Southwestern College *B*
Washburn University *B*

Kentucky
Eastern Kentucky University *B, M*

Maryland
University of Maryland
University College *C*

Massachusetts
Anna Maria College *M*
Marian Court College *C, A*

Michigan
Baker College
of Muskegon *C*
Grand Valley State University *B*
Macomb Community College *C*
Northern Michigan University *B*
Schoolcraft College *A*

Minnesota
Winona State University *B*

Missouri
University of Central Missouri *M*

Nevada
College of Southern Nevada *A*

New Jersey
Cumberland County College *C*
Essex County College *C*
New Jersey City University *B*

New York
Dutchess Community College *C*
Schenectady County Community
College *C*
State University of New York
Farmingdale *B*

Ohio
Ohio University
Zanesville Campus *A*
Owens Community College
Toledo *A*
University of Cincinnati
Clermont College *A*
Youngstown State University *B*

Oregon
Chemeketa Community College *C, A*

Pennsylvania
Kaplan Career Institute: Pittsburgh *A*
Montgomery County Community
College *C, A*
YTI Career Institute: York *A*

Texas
Hill College *A*
Tarrant County College *C*

Vermont
Champlain College *B*

Virginia
Northern Virginia Community
College *C, A*

Washington
Clover Park Technical College *C*
Spokane Community College *A*

Security services management

Arizona
University of Phoenix *M*

Colorado
University of Denver *M*

Florida
City College: Casselberry *A*
Webber International University *B, M*

Georgia
Ashworth College *A*

Illinois
Lewis University *M*

Indiana
Vincennes University *A, B*

Kansas
Barton County Community
College *C, A*
Central Christian College of
Kansas *A, B*

Kentucky
Bluegrass Community and Technical
College *C*

Maryland
Washington Adventist University *C*

Massachusetts
Bunker Hill Community College *A*
Massachusetts Maritime Academy *B*

Michigan
Davenport University *A, B*
Henry Ford Community College *A*

Minnesota
St. Mary's University of
Minnesota *C, B*

New York
St. John's University *B*
State University of New York
College at Brockport *B*
Farmingdale *B*

Pennsylvania
Duquesne University *B*
Harrisburg Area Community
College *C*
Penn State
University Park *B*

Puerto Rico
Inter American University of Puerto
Rico
Metropolitan Campus *C*

Texas
Sam Houston State University *M*
San Antonio College *C, A*
University of Houston
Downtown *M*

Vermont
Champlain College *B*

West Virginia
American Public University
System *C, B, M*

Selling/sales operations

California
Orange Coast College *A*
Santa Barbara City College *C, A*
Santiago Canyon College *A*

Colorado
Arapahoe Community College *C, A*

Georgia
Gwinnett Technical College *C*

Illinois
Bradley University *B*
Danville Area Community
College *C, A*
Harper College *C, A*
McHenry County College *C, A*
Parkland College *A*
Sauk Valley Community College *C, A*
Triton College *A*

Iowa
AIB College of Business *A*
Des Moines Area Community
College *C*

Kansas
Brown Mackie College
Salina *A*

Michigan
Ferris State University *C*

Minnesota
Alexandria Technical College *C*
Art Institutes International
Minnesota *B*
Dakota County Technical College *C*
Lake Superior College *C, A*
Minnesota State College - Southeast
Technical *C, A*
Minnesota State Community and
Technical College *A*
North Hennepin Community
College *C*
Northwest Technical College *C*

New York
Genesee Community College *C*

Ohio
Hondros College *A*
University of Akron *C, A*
University of Toledo *A*
Youngstown State University *A, B, M*

Pennsylvania
Harrisburg Area Community
College *C*

Tennessee
University of Memphis *B*

Utah
LDS Business College *C*

Washington
Spokane Community College *A*

West Virginia
West Virginia State Community and
Technical College *C*

Wyoming
Central Wyoming College *C*

Semitic languages

California
University of California
 Los Angeles *M, D*

Illinois
Trinity International University *M*

New York
Yeshiva University *M, D*

Pennsylvania
University of Pennsylvania *B, M, D*

Texas
University of Texas
 Austin *B*

Sheet metal technology

California
Foothill College *C*
Yuba Community College
 District *C, A*

Florida
Hillsborough Community College *C*

Illinois
Black Hawk College *C*

Indiana
Ivy Tech Community College
 Bloomington *C, A*
 Central Indiana *C, A*
 Lafayette *C, A*
 North Central *C, A*
 Northeast *C, A*
 Northwest *C, A*
 Richmond *C, A*
 South Central *C, A*
 Southwest *C, A*
 Wabash Valley *C, A*

Michigan
Oakland Community College *C, A*

Minnesota
Dunwoody College of Technology *C*
Hennepin Technical College *C, A*
St. Paul College *C*

Montana
Montana State University
 Billings *C*

Ohio
Columbus State Community
 College *A*
Northwest State Community
 College *C, A*

Oregon
Lane Community College *A*

Pennsylvania
Community College of Allegheny
 County *C*
Thaddeus Stevens College of
 Technology *A*

Washington
Bates Technical College *C, A*
Clover Park Technical College *C*

Wisconsin
Western Technical College *C*

Shoe/leather repair

Alabama
Jefferson Davis Community College *C*

Sign language interpretation

Arizona
Arizona Western College *C*
Cochise College *A*
Phoenix College *C, A*
Pima Community College *A*

Arkansas
University of Arkansas
 Little Rock *A, B*

California
Berkeley City College *C, A*
College of the Canyons *A*
College of the Sequoias *C*
Golden West College *C, A*
Los Angeles Pierce College *A*
Mount San Antonio College *C, A*
Oxnard College *C, A*
Palomar College *C, A*
Riverside Community College *C, A*
Saddleback College *C, A*
San Diego City College *C*

Colorado
Front Range Community College *A*
Pikes Peak Community College *A*
University of Northern Colorado *B*

Connecticut
Northwestern Connecticut
 Community College *C, A*

District of Columbia
Gallaudet University *M*

Florida
Florida State College at Jacksonville *A*
Miami Dade College *C, A*
St. Petersburg College *A*
University of North Florida *B*

Georgia
Georgia Perimeter College *C, A*
Valdosta State University *B*

Idaho
Idaho State University *B*

Illinois
Black Hawk College *A*
Columbia College Chicago *C, B*
Harper College *C*
Illinois Central College *C*
MacMurray College *A, B*
Quincy University *B*
Waubonsee Community College *C, A*

Indiana
Bethel College *A, B*
Goshen College *B*

Iowa
Iowa Western Community College *A*
Kirkwood Community College *A*
Scott Community College *A*

Kansas
Cowley County Community
 College *A*

Johnson County Community
 College *A*

Kentucky
Eastern Kentucky University *A, B*

Louisiana
Delgado Community College *C, A*

Maryland
Community College of Baltimore
 County *C, A*
Frederick Community College *C*

Massachusetts
Northern Essex Community
 College *C, A*

Michigan
Lansing Community College *A*
Mott Community College *A*
Oakland Community College *A*

Minnesota
North Central University *A, B*
North Hennepin Community
 College *C*
St. Catherine University *B*
St. Paul College *C, A*

Mississippi
Hinds Community College *A*

Missouri
Metropolitan Community College:
 Maple Woods *A*
St. Louis Community College
 St. Louis Community College at
  Florissant Valley *A*

Nebraska
Metropolitan Community
 College *C, A*

New Hampshire
Nashua Community College *C*
University of New Hampshire at
 Manchester *B*

New Jersey
Burlington County College *C, A*
Camden County College *A*
Ocean County College *C, A*
Union County College *C, A*

New Mexico
Santa Fe Community College *C, A*
University of New Mexico *B*

New York
Corning Community College *A*
Keuka College *B*
Mohawk Valley Community College *A*
Rochester Institute of
 Technology *A, B*
Suffolk County Community College *A*
Ulster County Community College *C*

North Carolina
Blue Ridge Community College *A*
Central Piedmont Community
 College *C, A*
Gardner-Webb University *B*
Randolph Community College *C, A*
Wilson Community College *C, A*

North Dakota
Lake Region State College *C*

Ohio
Cincinnati State Technical and
 Community College *A*
Columbus State Community
 College *C, A*
Cuyahoga Community College
 Metropolitan Campus *A*
Kent State University *B*
Shawnee State University *C*
Terra State Community College *A*
University of Akron *C*

Oklahoma
Oklahoma State University
 Oklahoma City *C, A*
Tulsa Community College *C, A*

Oregon
Chemeketa Community College *A*
Portland Community College *C, A*
Western Oregon University *B*

Pennsylvania
Bloomsburg University of
 Pennsylvania *B*
Community College of
 Philadelphia *C, A*
Mount Aloysius College *A, B*

Puerto Rico
Turabo University *B*

South Carolina
Spartanburg Community College *C*

South Dakota
Augustana College *B*

Tennessee
Chattanooga State Community
 College *A*
Maryville College *B*
Nashville State Community College *A*

Texas
Austin Community College *C, A*
Blinn College *A*
Collin County Community College
 District *C, A*
Del Mar College *C, A*
Eastfield College *C, A*
El Paso Community College *C, A*
Houston Community College
 System *C, A*
Howard College *C, A*
Lone Star College System *C, A*
McLennan Community College *C, A*
San Antonio College *C, A*
South Texas College *A*
Tarrant County College *C, A*
Tyler Junior College *C, A*

Utah
Salt Lake Community College *A*

Virginia
J. Sargeant Reynolds Community
 College *C*
New River Community College *C*

Washington
Olympic College *C*
Spokane Falls Community College *A*

West Virginia
Fairmont State University *A*

Wisconsin
Gateway Technical College *A*
Milwaukee Area Technical College *A*
Northcentral Technical College *A*

Sign language linguistics

Oklahoma

Oklahoma State University
  Oklahoma City *A*

Slavic languages

California

Stanford University *B, D*
University of California
  Berkeley *B, M, D*
  Los Angeles *B, M, D*
  Santa Barbara *B*
University of Southern
  California *M, D*

Connecticut

Connecticut College *B*
Yale University *M, D*

Florida

Florida State University *M*

Illinois

Northwestern University *B, M, D*
University of Chicago *B, D*
University of Illinois
  Urbana-Champaign *M, D*

Indiana

Indiana University
  Bloomington *B, M, D*

Kansas

University of Kansas *B, M, D*

Massachusetts

Harvard College *B, M, D*

Michigan

University of Michigan *M, D*
Wayne State University *B*

New Jersey

Princeton University *B, M, D*

New York

Columbia University *B*

North Carolina

Duke University *B, M*
University of North Carolina
  Chapel Hill *B, M, D*

Pennsylvania

University of Pittsburgh *B, M, D*

Rhode Island

Brown University *B, M, D*

Texas

Rice University *B*
University of Texas
  Austin *M, D*

Virginia

University of Virginia *B, M, D*

Wisconsin

University of Wisconsin
  Madison *M, D*

Slavic studies

Connecticut

Connecticut College *B*

Illinois

University of Chicago *B, D*

Michigan

Oakland University *B*

New York

Barnard College *B*
Columbia University *B*

Rhode Island

Brown University *B, M, D*

Texas

Baylor University *B*
Rice University *B*

Washington

University of Washington *B, M*

Slovak

New York

State University of New York
  Stony Brook *M*

Small business administration/ management

Alaska

University of Alaska
  Southeast *C*

California

Berkeley City College *C, A*
College of the Canyons *C, A*
Folsom Lake College *C, A*
Foothill College *C*
Ohlone College *C, A*
San Francisco State University *B*
Santa Barbara City College *C, A*
Sierra College *C, A*

Colorado

Adams State College *B*
Colorado Technical University *C*
Jones International University *B, M*
Northeastern Junior College *C*
Pueblo Community College *A*
University of Colorado
  Boulder *B*

Connecticut

Mitchell College *B*

Florida

Central Florida Community College *C*
Pasco-Hernando Community
  College *C*
Santa Fe College *C*
Valencia Community College *A*

Georgia

Athens Technical College *C*
Dalton State College *C*
Gwinnett Technical College *C*
Southeastern Technical College *C*

Idaho

Lewis-Clark State College *C, A, B*

Illinois

Bradley University *B*
Elgin Community College *C*
Harper College *C, A*
Moraine Valley Community College *A*
North Central College *B*
University of Illinois
  Urbana-Champaign *T*

Indiana

Huntington University *B*
Purdue University
  Calumet *B*

Iowa

Des Moines Area Community
  College *C*

Kansas

Central Christian College of
  Kansas *A, B*
Colby Community College *C*

Maine

Husson University *B*
Southern Maine Community
  College *C*
Washington County Community
  College *A*

Massachusetts

Babson College *B*
Mount Wachusett Community
  College *C*
Springfield Technical Community
  College *A*

Michigan

Baker College
  of Clinton Township *A*
  of Muskegon *C, A*
Bay de Noc Community College *A*
Delta College *C, A*
Henry Ford Community College *C*
Northern Michigan University *B*
Schoolcraft College *A*
Southwestern Michigan College *C*

Minnesota

Central Lakes College *C*
Inver Hills Community College *C*
Normandale Community College *C*
North Hennepin Community
  College *C, A*
South Central College *C*

Montana

Blackfeet Community College *A*
Flathead Valley Community College *A*
University of Montana: Western *B*

Nebraska

University of Nebraska
  Omaha *B*

New Jersey

Raritan Valley Community College *C*

New York

Columbia-Greene Community
  College *C*
Globe Institute of Technology *C, A, B*
Westchester Community College *C*

North Carolina

Brunswick Community College *C, A*
Chowan University *B*

North Dakota

Lake Region State College *A*

Ohio

Baldwin-Wallace College *M*
Miami University
  Hamilton Campus *C*
University of Akron *C, A*

Oregon

Oregon Institute of Technology *B*

Pennsylvania

Bucks County Community College *A*
Harrisburg Area Community
  College *C, A*
Newport Business Institute: Lower
  Burrell *A*

Puerto Rico

Inter American University of Puerto
  Rico
  Metropolitan Campus *C*

Tennessee

Carson-Newman College *B*

Texas

Blinn College *C, A*
Tarrant County College *C, A*

Vermont

Champlain College *B*
Lyndon State College *B*

Virginia

Germanna Community College *C*

Washington

Grays Harbor College *C*
Shoreline Community College *C, A*

West Virginia

Southern West Virginia Community
  and Technical College *A*
Valley College *A*

Wisconsin

Carroll University *B*
Milwaukee Area Technical College *C*

Small engine mechanics

Alabama

Gadsden State Community College *C*
Shelton State Community College *C*

Arkansas

Pulaski Technical College *C*
University of Arkansas
  Cossatot Community College of the
    C

California

College of the Desert *C*
El Camino College: Compton
  Center *C, A*
Los Medanos College *C, A*
Merced College *C*
Southwestern College *C, A*

Georgia

Central Georgia Technical College *C*
Southwest Georgia Technical
  College *C*

Kentucky

Bluegrass Community and Technical
  College *C*

Michigan

Bay de Noc Community College *C*
Kirtland Community College *C, A*

Minnesota

Alexandria Technical College *C*
Hennepin Technical College *C, A*
Minnesota State College - Southeast
  Technical *C*
Minnesota State Community and
  Technical College *C*

Nebraska

Southeast Community College *C*

New York

Jamestown Community College *A*

North Carolina

Haywood Community College *C*

North Dakota

North Dakota State College of
Science *C, A*

Pennsylvania

Commonwealth Technical Institute *C*

Texas

Austin Community College *C*
Cedar Valley College *C*
Tarrant County College *C*
Texarkana College *C*

Washington

Bates Technical College *C, A*

Wisconsin

Wisconsin Indianhead Technical
College *C*

Social/philosophical foundations of education

Arizona

Arizona State University *M*

California

California State University
Long Beach *M*
Northridge *M*
Hope International University *M*
Stanford University *M, D*

Colorado

University of Colorado
Boulder *M, D*

Connecticut

Central Connecticut State
University *M*
University of Connecticut *D, T*

Florida

Florida Atlantic University *M*
Florida State University *M, D*
University of Florida *M*

Georgia

Georgia State University *M*
University of Georgia *D*

Hawaii

University of Hawaii
Manoa *M*

Illinois

DePaul University *M*
Loyola University Chicago *M, D*
Northern Illinois University *M*
Northwestern University *M*
University of Illinois
Urbana-Champaign *M, D*
Western Illinois University *M*

Indiana

Indiana University
Bloomington *M, D*

Iowa

Iowa State University *M*
University of Iowa *M, D*
University of Northern Iowa *M*

Kansas

University of Kansas *M*

Kentucky

University of Kentucky *M*

Massachusetts

Tufts University *M*

Michigan

Eastern Michigan University *M*
Western Michigan University *M*

Minnesota

University of Minnesota
Twin Cities *B, M*

Missouri

University of Missouri
Columbia *M, D*

New Jersey

Rutgers, The State University of New
Jersey
New Brunswick/Piscataway
Campus *D*

New Mexico

University of New Mexico *M, D*

New York

Fordham University *M*
Hofstra University *M, T*
New York University *M, D*
State University of New York
Buffalo *D*

Ohio

Ohio University *M, D*
University of Akron *M*
University of Cincinnati *M, D*
University of Findlay *B, M*
University of Toledo *M, D*

Oklahoma

University of Oklahoma *M, D*

Pennsylvania

Penn State
University Park *M, D*
University of Pennsylvania *M, D*

South Carolina

University of South Carolina *D*

Texas

University of Houston *M, D*
University of Texas
San Antonio *M*

Utah

University of Utah *M, D*

Vermont

Goddard College *B, M*
University of Vermont *M*

Washington

Eastern Washington University *M*
Saint Martin's University *M*
University of Washington *M, D*

Wisconsin

University of Wisconsin
Madison *M, D*

Milwaukee *M*
Whitewater *M*

Social psychology

Arizona

Prescott College *B*

California

California Institute of Integral
Studies *D*
St. Mary's College of California *B*
University of California
Irvine *B, D*

District of Columbia

George Washington University *D*

Florida

Florida Atlantic University *B*
Florida State University *D*

Georgia

Paine College *B*

Illinois

Loyola University Chicago *M, D*
University of Illinois
Urbana-Champaign *M, D*

Indiana

Ball State University *M*

Iowa

University of Iowa *D*

Kansas

Wichita State University *B*

Maine

University of New England *B*

Massachusetts

Clark University *M, D*
Eastern Nazarene College *B*
Harvard College *M, D*
Northeastern University *M*
Tufts University *M, D*
University of Massachusetts
Lowell *M*

Michigan

Grand Valley State University *B*

Minnesota

Walden University *M*

Missouri

Maryville University of Saint Louis *B*
Northwest Missouri State
University *B*
University of Missouri
Columbia *M, D*

Nevada

University of Nevada
Reno *B, M, D*

New Hampshire

Keene State College *B*

New York

Fordham University *M, D*
State University of New York
Albany *D*
Buffalo *D*
Syracuse University *M, D*
University of Rochester *D*

North Carolina

Duke University *M, D*

Ohio

Bowling Green State University *M, D*

Oklahoma

Mid-America Christian University *B*

Pennsylvania

Clarion University of Pennsylvania *B*
Penn State
Abington *B*
Temple University *M, D*

Texas

University of Houston *M, D*

Vermont

Bennington College *B*

Social science teacher education

Alabama

Athens State University *B*
Auburn University *B, M, D, T*
Birmingham-Southern College *T*
Faulkner University *B, T*
Judson College *T*
Miles College *B*
Oakwood University *B*
Samford University *B*
University of Mobile *B, T*

Arizona

Prescott College *B, M, T*
University of Arizona *B*

Arkansas

Arkansas State University *B, M, T*
Henderson State University *B*
University of Arkansas
Pine Bluff *B, T*

California

Azusa Pacific University *T*
California Baptist University *T*
California Lutheran University *B, T*
California Polytechnic State
University: San Luis Obispo *T*
California State University
Chico *B, M, T*
Long Beach *B, T*
Northridge *B, T*
San Bernardino *T*
Fresno Pacific University *B, T*
Hope International University *B*
Humboldt State University *T*
Loyola Marymount University *M*
The Master's College *T*
Mills College *T*
Mount St. Mary's College *T*
Pacific Union College *T*
Saddleback College *A*
San Diego Christian College *B, T*
San Diego State University *T*
San Francisco State University *T*
Simpson University *B, T*
Sonoma State University *T*
Stanford University *M, T*
Taft College *A*
University of Redlands *T*
University of the Pacific *T*
Vanguard University of Southern
California *T*
Westmont College *T*

Colorado

Adams State College *B, T*

Colorado State University
    Pueblo *T*
Metropolitan State College of
    Denver *T*
Western State College of
    Colorado *B, T*

Connecticut

Southern Connecticut State
    University *B, M, T*

Delaware

University of Delaware *B, T*

District of Columbia

George Washington University *T*

Florida

Flagler College *B, T*
Florida Agricultural and Mechanical
    University *B, M, T*
Florida Atlantic University *B*
Florida State University *B, M, D, T*
Palm Beach Atlantic University *B, T*
Palm Beach Community College *A*
Southeastern University *B, T*
Stetson University *B*
University of Central Florida *B, M*
University of South Florida *B, M*
Warner University *B*

Georgia

Albany State University *B*
Armstrong Atlantic State
    University *B, M, T*
Columbus State University *B, M*
Darton College *A*
Gainesville State College *A*
North Georgia College & State
    University *M*
Shorter College *T*

Idaho

Boise State University *B, T*
Brigham Young University-Idaho *T*
Lewis-Clark State College *B, T*
Northwest Nazarene University *B*

Illinois

Augustana College *B, T*
Benedictine University *T*
Blackburn College *B, T*
Bradley University *B*
Concordia University Chicago *B, T*
DePaul University *M, T*
Dominican University *T*
Eastern Illinois University *B, T*
Knox College *B*
Lake Land College *A*
Lewis University *T*
Millikin University *B, T*
North Park University *T*
Olivet Nazarene University *B, T*
Saint Xavier University *B*
University of Illinois
    Urbana-Champaign *B, M, T*

Indiana

Butler University *T*
Manchester College *B, T*
Oakland City University *B*
Purdue University
    Calumet *B*
St. Mary-of-the-Woods College *B, T*
University of Evansville *B*
Valparaiso University *B*

Iowa

Briar Cliff University *B*
Buena Vista University *B, T*
Central College *T*
Cornell College *B, T*

Dordt College *B*
Drake University *M, T*
Ellsworth Community College *A*
Iowa State University *T*
Loras College *T*
Mount Mercy College *T*
Northwestern College *T*
St. Ambrose University *B, T*
Simpson College *T*
University of Northern Iowa *B*
Upper Iowa University *B, T*
Wartburg College *T*

Kansas

Bethany College *B*
Central Christian College of Kansas *A*
Emporia State University *M, T*
Friends University *B*
Garden City Community College *A*
Newman University *B*
Tabor College *B*

Kentucky

Campbellsville University *B*
Lindsey Wilson College *B, T*

Louisiana

Grambling State University *M*

Maine

University of Maine
    Farmington *B, T*
University of Southern Maine *T*

Maryland

Frostburg State University *B, T*

Massachusetts

Bridgewater State College *T*
Western New England College *T*
Worcester State College *T*

Michigan

Adrian College *B, T*
Alma College *T*
Andrews University *B, M*
Aquinas College *B, T*
Calvin College *B*
Cornerstone University *B, T*
Eastern Michigan University *B*
Ferris State University *B*
Grand Valley State University *T*
Michigan State University *B*
Michigan Technological University *T*
Northern Michigan University *B, T*
University of Detroit Mercy *B, M, T*
Western Michigan University *B*

Minnesota

College of St. Scholastica *B, T*
Concordia College: Moorhead *B, T*
Gustavus Adolphus College *T*
Minnesota State University
    Mankato *B, M, T*
Saint Cloud State University *B, M, T*
St. Mary's University of Minnesota *B*
University of Minnesota
    Morris *T*
Winona State University *B, T*

Mississippi

Blue Mountain College *B*
Delta State University *B*
Jackson State University *B*
Millsaps College *T*
Mississippi College *M*
Mississippi State University *T*
Mississippi Valley State University *B, T*
Northwest Mississippi Community
    College *A*
Rust College *B*

Missouri

Central Methodist University *B*
Evangel University *T*
Lincoln University *B*
Missouri Baptist University *T*
Missouri Southern State
    University *B, T*
Northwest Missouri State
    University *B, T*
Southwest Baptist University *B, T*
University of Missouri
    Kansas City *B*
Washington University in St.
    Louis *B, M, T*
Webster University *M*
William Woods University *B, T*

Montana

Montana State University
    Billings *B, T*
University of Great Falls *B*
University of Montana *T*

Nebraska

Chadron State College *B*
College of Saint Mary *B, T*
Creighton University *T*
Dana College *B*
Grace University *B*
Nebraska Wesleyan University *B*
Peru State College *B, T*
Union College *T*
University of Nebraska
    Kearney *B, M, T*
    Lincoln *B*
Wayne State College *B, T*
York College *B, T*

Nevada

Great Basin College *B*
University of Nevada
    Reno *B, T*

New Hampshire

Keene State College *M, T*
New England College *B, T*
Rivier College *B, T*
Saint Anselm College *T*

New Jersey

Georgian Court University *T*
Saint Peter's College *T*

New Mexico

University of the Southwest *B, T*
Western New Mexico University *B*

New York

Dominican College of Blauvelt *B, T*
Dowling College *B, M*
Elmira College *B, T*
Fordham University *M, T*
Manhattan College *B, T*
Manhattanville College *M, T*
New York Institute of
    Technology *B, T*
Roberts Wesleyan College *B, M*
State University of New York
    College at Oneonta *B, T*
    College at Plattsburgh *B*
    New Paltz *B, M, T*
Vassar College *T*
Wells College *T*

North Carolina

Fayetteville State University *B, T*
Gardner-Webb University *B*
Lenoir Community College *A*
Lenoir-Rhyne University *B*
Mars Hill College *T*
North Carolina Agricultural and
    Technical State University *B, M, T*

Pfeiffer University *B*
Sandhills Community College *A*
University of North Carolina
    Greensboro *B*

North Dakota

Dickinson State University *B, T*
Mayville State University *B, T*
Minot State University *B*
North Dakota State University *B, T*
University of Mary *B*
University of North Dakota *B*

Ohio

Bowling Green State University *B, M*
Defiance College *B, T*
Hiram College *T*
Ohio Wesleyan University *B*
Shawnee State University *B*
University of Findlay *B, M, T*
University of Rio Grande *B, T*
University of Toledo *M*
Walsh University *B*
Wilmington College *B*
Youngstown State University *B, M*

Oklahoma

Eastern Oklahoma State College *A*
Mid-America Christian University *B*
Northwestern Oklahoma State
    University *B, T*
Oklahoma Baptist University *B, T*
Southwestern Oklahoma State
    University *B, M, T*
University of Tulsa *T*

Oregon

Corban College *B*
Eastern Oregon University *B*
Linfield College *T*

Pennsylvania

Arcadia University *B, M, T*
Grove City College *T*
Holy Family University *B*
Indiana University of Pennsylvania *B*
La Salle University *B, T*
Lebanon Valley College *T*
Marywood University *B*
Mercyhurst College *B, T*
Moravian College *B*
St. Francis University *B, T*
St. Vincent College *T*
Susquehanna University *T*
University of Pittsburgh
    Bradford *B*
    Johnstown *B, T*
Washington & Jefferson College *T*
Wilson College *T*

Puerto Rico

Turabo University *B*
University of Puerto Rico
    Cayey University College *B*

Rhode Island

Rhode Island College *B*

South Carolina

Converse College *T*
University of South Carolina
    Aiken *B, T*
Wofford College *T*

South Dakota

Black Hills State University *B*
Dakota Wesleyan University *B, T*
Mount Marty College *B*
Northern State University *B, T*
University of Sioux Falls *T*
University of South Dakota *B, M, T*

Tennessee

American Baptist College *B*
Belmont University *B, M, T*
Cumberland University *B, T*
Lincoln Memorial University *B, T*
Maryville College *B, T*

Texas

Howard Payne University *B, T*
Kilgore College *A*
McMurry University *T*
Stephen F Austin State University *T*
Texas A&M University
  Commerce *T*
Texas Christian University *B*
Texas State University: San Marcos *T*
Texas Wesleyan University *B, M, T*
University of Mary Hardin-Baylor *T*
University of Texas
  San Antonio *T*
West Texas A&M University *T*

Utah

Brigham Young University *B*
Southern Utah University *B*
University of Utah *B*
Weber State University *B*
Western Governors University *B, M, T*

Vermont

Castleton State College *B, T*
Johnson State College *B*
Lyndon State College *B*

Virginia

Bridgewater College *T*
Eastern Mennonite University *T*
Liberty University *M, T*
Radford University *T*
University of Virginia's College at
  Wise *T*
Virginia Western Community
  College *A*

Washington

Seattle Pacific University *B*
Western Washington University *B*
Whitworth University *T*

West Virginia

West Liberty University *B*

Wisconsin

Carroll University *B, T*
Carthage College *M, T*
Concordia University Wisconsin *B*
Lawrence University *T*
Marquette University *B*
St. Norbert College *T*
Silver Lake College *T*
University of Wisconsin
  Green Bay *T*
  Oshkosh *B, T*
  Parkside *T*
  Platteville *B, T*
  River Falls *T*
  Superior *B, T*
  Whitewater *B, T*

Social sciences

Alabama

Calhoun Community College *A*
Faulkner State Community College *A*
Faulkner University *B*
Southern Union State Community
  College *A*
Spring Hill College *B, T*
Troy University *B*
University of Mobile *B, T*
University of Montevallo *B, T*

Alaska

University of Alaska
  Southeast *B*

Arizona

Arizona State University *B*
Arizona Western College *A*
Central Arizona College *A*
College of the Humanities and
  Sciences *M, D*
Dine College *A*
Northern Arizona University *B, M*
Prescott College *B, M*
Tohono O'odham Community
  College *A*

Arkansas

Arkansas Baptist College *B*
Harding University *B*
Phillips Community College of the
  University of Arkansas *A*
Southern Arkansas University *B*
University of Arkansas
  Monticello *B*
University of the Ozarks *B*

California

Allan Hancock College *A*
Azusa Pacific University *B, M*
Barstow Community College *A*
Berkeley City College *A*
Bethany University *B*
Biola University *B*
Butte College *A*
Cabrillo College *A*
California Institute of
  Technology *B, M, D*
California Polytechnic State
  University: San Luis Obispo *B*
California State Polytechnic
  University: Pomona *B*
California State University
  Chico *B, M*
  Los Angeles *M*
  Monterey Bay *B*
  Sacramento *B, M*
  San Bernardino *C, B, M*
  San Marcos *B*
  Stanislaus *B*
Canada College *A*
Cerro Coso Community College *A*
Chabot College *A*
Chaffey College *A*
Citrus College *A*
College of Alameda *A*
College of Marin: Kentfield *A*
College of San Mateo *A*
College of the Canyons *A*
College of the Desert *A*
College of the Sequoias *A*
College of the Siskiyous *A*
Columbia College *A*
Copper Mountain College *A*
Crafton Hills College *A*
East Los Angeles College *A*
El Camino College: Compton
  Center *A*
Feather River College *A*
Folsom Lake College *A*
Foothill College *A*
Fresno City College *A*
Fresno Pacific University *B*
Gavilan College *A*
Glendale Community College *A*
Golden West College *A*
Hartnell College *A*
Hope International University *B*
Humboldt State University *B, M*
Humphreys College *B*
Imperial Valley College *A*
Lake Tahoe Community College *A*
Laney College *A*
Lassen Community College *A*

Long Beach City College *A*
Mendocino College *A*
Merced College *A*
Merritt College *A*
Mills College *B*
MiraCosta College *A*
Mission College *A*
Modesto Junior College *A*
Moorpark College *A*
Mount St. Mary's College *B*
Mount San Jacinto College *A*
Napa Valley College *A*
Notre Dame de Namur University *B*
Ohlone College *A*
Orange Coast College *A*
Pacific Union College *B*
Pasadena City College *A*
Pitzer College *B*
Point Loma Nazarene University *B*
Pomona College *B*
Porterville College *A*
Reedley College *A*
Sacramento City College *C, A*
Saddleback College *A*
San Diego Christian College *B*
San Diego City College *A*
San Diego Mesa College *A*
San Diego Miramar College *A*
San Diego State University *B*
San Francisco State University *M*
San Joaquin Delta College *A*
San Jose City College *A*
San Jose State University *B, M*
Santa Ana College *A*
Santa Monica College *A*
Santiago Canyon College *A*
Shasta College *A*
Sierra College *A*
Simpson University *B*
Solano Community College *A*
Taft College *A*
University of California
  Irvine *B, M, D*
University of California: Merced *B*
University of La Verne *B*
University of the Pacific *B, T*
Vanguard University of Southern
  California *B*
West Hills College: Coalinga *A*
West Hills College: Lemoore *A*
West Valley College *A*
Westmont College *B*
Yuba Community College District *A*

Colorado

Colorado Christian University *B*
Colorado Mountain College *A*
Colorado State University *B*
Lamar Community College *A*
Mesa State College *B*
United States Air Force Academy *B*
University of Colorado
  Denver *M*
University of Denver *B*
University of Northern
  Colorado *B, M, T*

Connecticut

Albertus Magnus College *B*
Central Connecticut State
  University *B, M*
Holy Apostles College and
  Seminary *B*
Quinnipiac University *B*
Trinity College *B*
University of Bridgeport *B*
Western Connecticut State
  University *B*

Florida

Florida Agricultural and Mechanical
  University *M*
Florida Atlantic University *B*
Florida Southern College *B*

Florida State University *B*
New College of Florida *B*
Palm Beach Community College *A*
State College of Florida,
  Manatee-Sarasota *A*
Stetson University *B*
Tallahassee Community College *A*
University of Central Florida *B*
University of South Florida *B*
University of West Florida *B*
Warner University *B*

Georgia

Abraham Baldwin Agricultural
  College *A*
Andrew College *A*
Berry College *B*
Brewton-Parker College *B*
Columbus State University *M*
Covenant College *B*
Dalton State College *A*
Georgia Military College *A*
Piedmont College *B*
Shorter College *B, T*
Wesleyan College *B*
Young Harris College *A*

Hawaii

Chaminade University of Honolulu *B*
Hawaii Pacific University *B*
University of Hawaii
  West Oahu *B*
  Windward Community College *C*

Idaho

Boise State University *A, B, T*
Lewis-Clark State College *B*
North Idaho College *A*
Northwest Nazarene University *B*

Illinois

Benedictine University *B, T*
City Colleges of Chicago
  Harold Washington College *A*
  Kennedy-King College *A*
  Olive-Harvey College *A*
DePaul University *B, T*
Dominican University *B*
Governors State University *B*
Illinois College *T*
Illinois Valley Community College *A*
Kishwaukee College *A*
Lake Land College *A*
Lewis University *T*
Lincoln College *A*
McKendree University *B*
National-Louis University *B*
North Central College *B, T*
Northeastern Illinois University *B*
Northern Illinois University *T*
Olivet Nazarene University *B, T*
Principia College *B*
Richard J. Daley College *C, A*
Richland Community College *A*
Rockford College *B*
Saint Xavier University *B*
Shimer College *B*
Southern Illinois University
  Carbondale *B*
Trinity International University *B*
University of Illinois
  Springfield *B*

Indiana

Ancilla College *A*
Ball State University *B, M, T*
Bethel College *A, B*
Calumet College of St. Joseph *B*
Indiana University
  Bloomington *B, M*
  Kokomo *B*
  South Bend *A*
Indiana Wesleyan University *B*

Manchester College *B, T*
Oakland City University *B*
Purdue University *B, M*
St. Mary-of-the-Woods College *B*
Taylor University *B*
Trine University *A, B*
University of Southern Indiana *A, B, T*
Valparaiso University *A, B, M*
Vincennes University *A*

Iowa
Buena Vista University *B, T*
Central College *B, T*
Dordt College *B*
Drake University *B*
Ellsworth Community College *A*
Grand View University *B*
Marshalltown Community College *A*
Mount Mercy College *T*
North Iowa Area Community
    College *A*
Northwestern College *T*
Upper Iowa University *B*
Waldorf College *B*
Wartburg College *T*

Kansas
Benedictine College *B*
Bethany College *B, T*
Central Christian College of
    Kansas *A, B*
Coffeyville Community College *A*
Cowley County Community
    College *A*
Dodge City Community College *A*
Donnelly College *A*
Emporia State University *B, T*
Fort Scott Community College *A*
Garden City Community College *A*
Hutchinson Community College *A*
Kansas State University *B*
Labette Community College *A*
McPherson College *T*
MidAmerica Nazarene University *B*
Neosho County Community
    College *A*
Pratt Community College *A*
Seward County Community College *A*
Tabor College *B*

Kentucky
Alice Lloyd College *B*
Asbury College *B, T*
Brescia University *A, B*
Campbellsville University *A, B, M*
Kentucky State University *B*
Lindsey Wilson College *A, B, T*
Mid-Continent University *B*
Morehead State University *B*
Northern Kentucky University *B*
Spalding University *B*
University of Kentucky *B*
Western Kentucky University *B, T*

Louisiana
Louisiana College *B*
Loyola University New Orleans *B*
Our Lady of Holy Cross College *B, T*
Southern University
    Shreveport *A*
Southern University and Agricultural
    and Mechanical College *M*

Maine
Bates College *T*
Saint Joseph's College of Maine *B*
University of Maine
    Augusta *B*
    Fort Kent *B*
University of Southern Maine *B*

Maryland
Allegany College of Maryland *A*

Chesapeake College *A*
Coppin State University *B, M*
Frostburg State University *B, T*
Howard Community College *A*
Johns Hopkins University *B, M*
Mount St. Mary's University *B, T*
Sojourner-Douglass College *B, M*
Towson University *B, M*
University of Maryland
    University College *B*

Massachusetts
Bard College at Simon's Rock *B*
Boston University *M*
Cape Cod Community College *A*
Harvard College *B*
Lasell College *B*
Lesley University *B*
Massachusetts Bay Community
    College *A*
Roxbury Community College *A*
Suffolk University *B*
University of Massachusetts
    Boston *B*
Worcester Polytechnic Institute *B*

Michigan
Andrews University *B*
Aquinas College *B*
Calvin College *B*
Central Michigan University *B*
Cornerstone University *B*
Eastern Michigan University *B, M*
Finlandia University *B*
Gogebic Community College *A*
Grand Valley State University *B*
Lake Superior State University *B, T*
Lansing Community College *A*
Marygrove College *B*
Michigan State University *B*
Michigan Technological University *B*
Northwestern Michigan College *A*
Siena Heights University *B*
Spring Arbor University *B, T*
University of Michigan *B*
University of Michigan
    Flint *B, M*
Washtenaw Community College *A*
Wayne County Community College *A*

Minnesota
Augsburg College *B*
Bemidji State University *B*
Bethany Lutheran College *B*
Bethel University *B*
College of St. Benedict *B*
College of St. Scholastica *B*
Hamline University *B*
Metropolitan State University *B*
Northland Community & Technical
    College *A*
Ridgewater College *A*
St. Catherine University *B*
Saint Cloud State University *B*
St. John's University *B*
St. Mary's University of Minnesota *B*
University of St. Thomas *B*
Vermilion Community College *A*
Winona State University *B*

Mississippi
Belhaven University *B*
Blue Mountain College *B*
Delta State University *B*
Jackson State University *B*
Mississippi Delta Community
    College *A*
Mississippi University for Women *B, T*
Rust College *B*

Missouri
Crowder College *A*
Evangel University *A, B*

Lincoln University *M*
Mineral Area College *A*
Missouri Baptist University *B, T*
Missouri Southern State
    University *B, T*
Rockhurst University *B*
St. Louis Community College
    St. Louis Community College at
        Florissant Valley *A*
    St. Louis Community College at
        Meramec *A*
Washington University in St. Louis *B*
Webster University *B*

Montana
Little Big Horn College *A*
Miles Community College *A*
University of Great Falls *B*
University of Montana: Western *A, B*

Nebraska
Bellevue University *B*
Chadron State College *B*
College of Saint Mary *T*
Dana College *B*
Doane College *B*
Northeast Community College *A*
Peru State College *B, T*
Union College *B*
University of Nebraska
    Kearney *B, M, T*
Wayne State College *B*

Nevada
College of Southern Nevada *A*
Great Basin College *B*

New Hampshire
Daniel Webster College *B*
Dartmouth College *T*
Keene State College *B*
NHTI-Concord's Community
    College *A*
Plymouth State University *B*
Rivier College *B, T*
Southern New Hampshire
    University *B*

New Jersey
Brookdale Community College *A*
Caldwell College *B*
County College of Morris *A*
Cumberland County College *A*
Essex County College *A*
Felician College *B*
Montclair State University *M*
New Jersey Institute of Technology *D*
Saint Peter's College *A, B*
Salem Community College *A*
Sussex County Community College *A*
Thomas Edison State College *B*
Warren County Community College *A*

New Mexico
Eastern New Mexico University *B*
New Mexico Junior College *A*
University of the Southwest *B*
Western New Mexico University *B*

New York
Adelphi University *B*
Bard College *B*
Cazenovia College *B*
City University of New York
    Queens College *B, M, T*
Clarkson University *B*
Colgate University *B*
Concordia College *B, T*
Cornell University *B*
Corning Community College *A*
Dominican College of Blauvelt *B*
Dowling College *B*
Elmira College *B, T*

Eugene Lang College The New School
    for Liberal Arts *B*
Finger Lakes Community College *A*
Herkimer County Community
    College *A*
Hofstra University *B*
Hudson Valley Community College *A*
Ithaca College *B, T*
Jamestown Community College *A*
Keuka College *B*
Long Island University
    Brooklyn Campus *A, B, M*
Marymount Manhattan College *A*
Mercy College *B*
Metropolitan College of New
    York *A, B*
Monroe Community College *A*
Mount Saint Mary College *B, T*
Nazareth College *B*
New York University *B, M, D*
Niagara University *B*
Nyack College *B*
Pace University *B*
Roberts Wesleyan College *B*
Rockland Community College *A*
Sage College of Albany *B*
Saint Bonaventure University *B*
St. John's University *B*
St. Joseph's College *B*
St. Joseph's College: Suffolk
    Campus *B*
St. Thomas Aquinas College *B, T*
Schenectady County Community
    College *A*
State University of New York
    Binghamton *B, M*
    Buffalo *B, M*
    College at Old Westbury *B*
    College of Agriculture and
        Technology at Morrisville *A*
    College of Technology at Delhi *A*
    Empire State College *A, B*
    Stony Brook *B, T*
Suffolk County Community College *A*
Sullivan County Community
    College *A*
Syracuse University *B, M, D*
Touro College *B*
Ulster County Community College *A*
Union College *B*
Westchester Community College *A*

North Carolina
Belmont Abbey College *B*
Chowan University *B*
Elizabeth City State University *B*
Fayetteville State University *B*
Gardner-Webb University *B*
Johnson C. Smith University *B*
Livingstone College *B*
North Carolina Agricultural and
    Technical State University *B, M, T*
Sandhills Community College *A*
Southeastern Community College *A*
Western Carolina University *B*

North Dakota
Dakota College at Bottineau *A*
Dickinson State University *B*
Mayville State University *B, T*
Minot State University *B*
North Dakota State University *B, M, T*
University of Mary *B*
University of North Dakota *B*

Ohio
Bluffton University *B*
Bowling Green State University *B*
Bowling Green State University:
    Firelands College *A*
Cedarville University *B*
Cleveland State University *B*
Defiance College *B, T*
Heidelberg University *B*

Hiram College *B*
Notre Dame College *T*
Ohio Northern University *B*
Ohio State University
  Columbus Campus *B, M, D*
Ohio University *M*
Ohio University
  Southern Campus at Ironton *A*
Shawnee State University *A, B*
Stark State College of Technology *A*
University of Akron *B*
University of Findlay *A, B*
University of Rio Grande *A, B, T*
Urbana University *B*
Wilmington College *B*
Wittenberg University *B*
Youngstown State University *B, M*

Oklahoma

Carl Albert State College *A*
Connors State College *A*
East Central University *B*
Eastern Oklahoma State College *A*
Langston University *B*
Mid-America Christian University *B*
Northeastern Oklahoma Agricultural
  and Mechanical College *A*
Northern Oklahoma College *A*
Northwestern Oklahoma State
  University *B*
Oklahoma Baptist University *B, T*
Oklahoma Panhandle State
  University *B*
Oklahoma Wesleyan University *A, B*
Redlands Community College *A*
Rogers State University *B*
Rose State College *A*
St. Gregory's University *A, B*
Seminole State College *A*
Southern Nazarene University *B*
Tulsa Community College *A*
Western Oklahoma State College *A*

Oregon

Central Oregon Community
  College *A*
Concordia University *B*
Corban College *B*
Linn-Benton Community College *A*
Marylhurst University *B*
Portland State University *B, M*
Southern Oregon University *B, T*
Treasure Valley Community College *A*
University of Oregon *B*
Warner Pacific College *A, B*
Western Oregon University *B*

Pennsylvania

Alvernia University *B*
Bucks County Community College *A*
California University of
  Pennsylvania *B, M*
Carnegie Mellon University *B, D*
Cheyney University of
  Pennsylvania *B, T*
Community College of Allegheny
  County *A*
Community College of Beaver
  County *A*
East Stroudsburg University of
  Pennsylvania *B, T*
Edinboro University of
  Pennsylvania *B, M, T*
Elizabethtown College *B*
Harrisburg Area Community
  College *A*
Juniata College *B*
Keystone College *B*
Kutztown University of
  Pennsylvania *B, M, T*
La Salle University *B, T*
Lackawanna College *A*
Lehigh Carbon Community College *A*

Lock Haven University of
  Pennsylvania *B*
Luzerne County Community
  College *A*
Mansfield University of
  Pennsylvania *B*
Marywood University *B*
Montgomery County Community
  College *A*
Mount Aloysius College *B*
Point Park University *B*
Reading Area Community College *A*
Robert Morris University *B*
Rosemont College *B*
Saint Joseph's University *B*
University of Pennsylvania *A, B, D*
University of Pittsburgh *B*
University of Pittsburgh
  Bradford *B*
  Greensburg *B*
  Johnstown *B*
University of Scranton *T*
Waynesburg University *B*
Wilson College *B*

Puerto Rico

American University of Puerto Rico *B*
Caribbean University *B*
Inter American University of Puerto
  Rico
  Metropolitan Campus *B*
Turabo University *B*
Universidad Metropolitana *B*
Universidad del Este *B*
University of Puerto Rico
  Aguadilla *A*
  Bayamon University College *A*
  Carolina Regional College *T*
  Cayey University College *B*
  Humacao *B*
  Ponce *A*
  Rio Piedras *B*
  Utuado *A*
University of the Sacred Heart *B*

Rhode Island

Providence College *B*
Rhode Island College *B*

South Carolina

Allen University *B*
Charleston Southern University *B*
The Citadel *M*
South Carolina State University *B*
Southern Wesleyan University *B*
University of South Carolina *M*
University of South Carolina
  Beaufort *B*
Wofford College *T*

South Dakota

Augustana College *T*
Black Hills State University *B*
Dakota Wesleyan University *B*
Mount Marty College *B*
Sinte Gleska University *A, B*
University of Sioux Falls *A, B*

Tennessee

American Baptist College *A, B*
Cumberland University *B*
Dyersburg State Community
  College *A*
Freed-Hardeman University *B, T*
LeMoyne-Owen College *B*
Lincoln Memorial University *B, T*
Northeast State Community
  College *A*
Tennessee State University *B*
University of Tennessee
  Chattanooga *B*
Vanderbilt University *B, M, D*

Texas

Amarillo College *A*
Blinn College *A*
Central Texas College *A*
Cisco College *A*
College of the Mainland *A*
Concordia University Texas *A, B*
El Paso Community College *A*
Frank Phillips College *A*
Howard College *A*
Howard Payne University *B*
Huston-Tillotson University *B*
Laredo Community College *A*
Lon Morris College *A*
Midland College *A*
Navarro College *A*
Northwest Vista College *A*
Odessa College *A*
Our Lady of the Lake University of San
  Antonio *B*
Rice University *B*
San Jacinto College *A*
South Texas College *A*
Southern Methodist University *B*
Southwestern Adventist
  University *B, T*
Southwestern Assemblies of God
  University *A*
Stephen F. Austin State University *B*
Sul Ross State University *B, M, T*
Texarkana College *A*
Texas A&M International University *B*
Texas A&M University
  Commerce *B, M*
Texas Wesleyan University *B*
Trinity Valley Community College *A*
Tyler Junior College *A*
University of Houston
  Downtown *B*
University of North Texas *B*
University of Texas
  Pan American *B*
West Texas A&M University *B*
Western Texas College *A*

Utah

Snow College *A*
Southern Utah University *B, T*
University of Utah *B*
Utah State University *M*
Westminster College *B*

Vermont

Bennington College *B, M*
Castleton State College *B*
Johnson State College *B*
Lyndon State College *B*
Marlboro College *B*

Virginia

Bluefield College *B*
Eastern Mennonite University *B*
Ferrum College *B*
Hollins University *M*
J. Sargeant Reynolds Community
  College *A*
James Madison University *B*
Liberty University *B, T*
Radford University *B*
St. Paul's College *B*
Thomas Nelson Community
  College *A*
Tidewater Community College *A*
University of Virginia's College at
  Wise *T*
Virginia Wesleyan College *B*
Virginia Western Community
  College *A*

Washington

Centralia College *C, A*
Everett Community College *A*
Evergreen State College *B*

Highline Community College *A*
Olympic College *A*
University of Puget Sound *T*
University of Washington *B*
Washington State University *B*
Whitworth University *B, T*

West Virginia

Bluefield State College *B*
Glenville State College *B*
West Liberty University *B*

Wisconsin

Alverno College *B*
Cardinal Stritch University *B, T*
Carthage College *B*
College of Menominee Nation *A*
Edgewood College *B*
Marquette University *B*
Mount Mary College *B*
St. Norbert College *T*
Silver Lake College *T*
University of Wisconsin
  Milwaukee *B*
  Platteville *B*
  River Falls *B*
  Stevens Point *B, T*
  Superior *B, T*
  Whitewater *B*
Viterbo University *B*
Wisconsin Lutheran College *B*

Wyoming

Central Wyoming College *A*
Laramie County Community
  College *A*
Northwest College *A*
Sheridan College *A*
University of Wyoming *B*
Western Wyoming Community
  College *A*

Social studies teacher education

Alabama

Athens State University *B*
Birmingham-Southern College *T*
Faulkner University *B, T*
Miles College *B*

Arizona

Prescott College *B, M, T*
University of Arizona *B*

Arkansas

Arkansas Tech University *B, M*
Harding University *B, T*
John Brown University *B, T*
Ouachita Baptist University *B, T*
Southern Arkansas University *B, T*
University of Arkansas
  Pine Bluff *M, T*
University of Central Arkansas *B*
University of the Ozarks *T*
Williams Baptist College *B*

California

Azusa Pacific University *T*
California Lutheran University *B, T*
California State University
  Northridge *B, T*
The Master's College *T*
Mills College *T*
Mount St. Mary's College *T*
Stanford University *M, T*
University of San Francisco *T*
University of the Pacific *T*
Vanguard University of Southern
  California *T*

Colorado

Adams State College *B, M, T*
Colorado State University *B, T*
Colorado State University
  Pueblo *T*
Metropolitan State College of
  Denver *T*
Trinidad State Junior College *A*
University of Colorado
  Boulder *T*
  Colorado Springs *T*
Western State College of
  Colorado *B, T*

Connecticut

Albertus Magnus College *B, T*
Central Connecticut State
  University *T*
Fairfield University *T*
Quinnipiac University *B, M*
Sacred Heart University *T*
Saint Joseph College *T*
Southern Connecticut State
  University *B, M, T*

Delaware

University of Delaware *T*

District of Columbia

George Washington University *M, T*
Trinity Washington University *M*

Florida

Barry University *T*
Bethune-Cookman University *B, T*
Clearwater Christian College *B*
Flagler College *B, T*
Saint Thomas University *B, T*
State College of Florida,
  Manatee-Sarasota *A*

Georgia

Agnes Scott College *T*
Columbus State University *B*
Georgia State University *M, T*
Kennesaw State University *B*
University of Georgia *B, M, D, T*

Hawaii

Hawaii Pacific University *M*

Idaho

Boise State University *B, T*
Brigham Young University-Idaho *T*

Illinois

Bradley University *B*
Chicago State University *T*
Concordia University Chicago *B, T*
Eureka College *T*
Illinois College *T*
Illinois State University *B, T*
John A. Logan College *A*
Knox College *T*
Lewis University *T*
Monmouth College *T*
North Park University *T*
Olivet Nazarene University *B, T*
University of Illinois
  Urbana-Champaign *B, M*
University of St. Francis *B, M*

Indiana

Anderson University *B, T*
Bethel College *B*
Butler University *T*
Franklin College *T*
Goshen College *B, T*
Grace College *B*
Huntington University *B, M*
Indiana State University *B, M, T*

Indiana University
  Bloomington *B, M, T*
  Kokomo *T*
  Northwest *B*
  South Bend *B*
  Southeast *B*
Indiana University-Purdue University
  Fort Wayne *B, T*
Indiana University-Purdue University
  Indianapolis *B, T*
Indiana Wesleyan University *B, T*
Manchester College *B, T*
Oakland City University *B*
Purdue University *B, M, D*
Purdue University
  Calumet *B*
Saint Mary's College *T*
St. Mary-of-the-Woods College *B, T*
Taylor University *B, T*
Trine University *B, T*
University of Evansville *B, T*
University of Indianapolis *B, T*
University of St. Francis *B, T*

Iowa

Cornell College *B, T*
Dordt College *B*
Drake University *M, T*
Ellsworth Community College *A*
Graceland University *T*
Grand View University *T*
Iowa Wesleyan College *B*
Mount Mercy College *T*
Northwestern College *T*
St. Ambrose University *T*
Simpson College *T*
University of Iowa *M, D*
Upper Iowa University *B, T*
Waldorf College *B*
Wartburg College *T*

Kansas

Central Christian College of Kansas *A*
Garden City Community College *A*
Kansas Wesleyan University *T*
McPherson College *B, T*
MidAmerica Nazarene University *B, T*
Pittsburg State University *B, T*
Tabor College *B*
University of Kansas *B, T*
University of St. Mary *T*

Kentucky

Alice Lloyd College *B*
Brescia University *B, T*
Campbellsville University *B*
Kentucky Christian University *B, T*
Kentucky Wesleyan College *B, T*
Thomas More College *B*
Union College *B*
University of the Cumberlands *B, M, T*

Louisiana

Centenary College of Louisiana *B, T*
Grambling State University *B*
Louisiana College *B*
Louisiana State University
  Shreveport *B*
McNeese State University *B, T*
Nicholls State University *B*
Northwestern State University *B*
Our Lady of Holy Cross College *B, T*
Southeastern Louisiana University *B*
Southern University and Agricultural
  and Mechanical College *B*
University of Louisiana at Lafayette *B*
University of Louisiana at Monroe *B*
University of New Orleans *B*
Xavier University of Louisiana *B*

Maine

Bowdoin College *T*
College of the Atlantic *T*

University of Maine *B, M*
University of Maine
  Fort Kent *B*
University of Southern Maine *T*

Maryland

College of Notre Dame of Maryland *T*
Mount St. Mary's University *T*
University of Maryland
  College Park *B*
  Eastern Shore *B*

Massachusetts

Boston University *B, M, T*
Eastern Nazarene College *B*
Elms College *T*
Lesley University *B, M*
Merrimack College *T*
Simmons College *B*
Springfield College *T*
Tufts University *M, T*
University of Massachusetts
  Dartmouth *T*
Worcester State College *T*

Michigan

Albion College *B, T*
Alma College *T*
Andrews University *B*
Aquinas College *B, T*
Calvin College *B*
Central Michigan University *B*
Cornerstone University *B, T*
Eastern Michigan University *B*
Ferris State University *B*
Grand Valley State University *T*
Hope College *B, T*
Madonna University *B*
Michigan State University *B*
Michigan Technological University *T*
Northern Michigan University *B, T*
University of Detroit Mercy *B, M, T*
University of Michigan
  Dearborn *B*
  Flint *B, T*
Wayne State University *B, M, T*
Western Michigan University *B*

Minnesota

Augsburg College *T*
Bemidji State University *M, T*
Bethel University *B*
College of St. Benedict *T*
Concordia College: Moorhead *B, T*
Concordia University: St. Paul *B, T*
Crown College *B, T*
Gustavus Adolphus College *T*
Metropolitan State University *B*
Minnesota State University
  Mankato *B, M, T*
  Moorhead *B*
Northwestern College *B*
St. Catherine University *T*
Saint Cloud State University *B, T*
St. John's University *T*
St. Olaf College *B*
Southwest Minnesota State
  University *T*
University of Minnesota
  Duluth *B, T*
  Morris *T*
  Twin Cities *M, T*
University of St. Thomas *B*
Vermilion Community College *A*
Winona State University *B, T*

Mississippi

Millsaps College *T*
Mississippi College *B*
Mississippi State University *T*
Northwest Mississippi Community
  College *A*
University of Mississippi *B, T*

Missouri

College of the Ozarks *B, T*
Evangel University *B, T*
Hannibal-LaGrange College *B*
Harris-Stowe State University *T*
Lindenwood University *B*
Missouri Baptist University *B*
Missouri Valley College *B, T*
Park University *T*
Southeast Missouri State
  University *B, M, T*
Truman State University *M, T*
University of Central Missouri *B, M, T*
University of Missouri
  Columbia *B, M, D*
  Kansas City *T*
Washington University in St.
  Louis *B, M, T*
William Jewell College *B, T*

Montana

Montana State University
  Billings *B, T*
Rocky Mountain College *B, T*
University of Great Falls *B*
University of Montana *T*
University of Montana: Western *B, T*

Nebraska

Concordia University *B, T*
Creighton University *T*

Nevada

University of Nevada
  Reno *B, T*

New Hampshire

Colby-Sawyer College *B, T*
Franklin Pierce University *M, T*
Keene State College *B, T*
New England College *B, T*
Plymouth State University *M, T*
Rivier College *B, T*
Southern New Hampshire
  University *B*
University of New Hampshire *T*
University of New Hampshire at
  Manchester *M*

New Jersey

Caldwell College *T*
Centenary College *T*
The College of New Jersey *B, T*
College of St. Elizabeth *T*
Georgian Court University *T*
Rutgers, The State University of New
  Jersey
  Camden Regional Campus *T*
  Newark Regional Campus *T*
Saint Peter's College *T*
William Paterson University of New
  Jersey *T*

New Mexico

Western New Mexico University *B*

New York

Adelphi University *M, T*
Alfred University *B, T*
Bard College *M*
City University of New York
  Brooklyn College *B, M*
  City College *B, T*
  College of Staten Island *M, T*
  Hunter College *B, M, T*
  Lehman College *M, T*
  Queens College *M, T*
Colgate University *M*
College of Mount St. Vincent *T*
College of Saint Rose *B, T*
D'Youville College *M, T*
Dowling College *B, M*

Dutchess Community College *A*
Elmira College *B, T*
Fordham University *T*
Hobart and William Smith Colleges *T*
Hofstra University *B, M*
Houghton College *B, T*
Iona College *B, M, T*
Ithaca College *B, D, T*
Keuka College *B, T*
Le Moyne College *T*
Long Island University
    Brooklyn Campus *M, T*
    C. W. Post Campus *B, M, T*
Manhattan College *B, T*
Manhattanville College *M, T*
Marist College *B*
Marymount Manhattan College *T*
Medaille College *B, T*
Molloy College *B*
Nazareth College *T*
New York Institute of
    Technology *B, T*
New York University *B, M*
Niagara University *B, M, T*
Pace University *B, M, T*
Roberts Wesleyan College *B, M*
Saint Bonaventure University *M*
St. Francis College *B*
St. John Fisher College *B, M, T*
St. John's University *B, M, T*
St. Joseph's College *B, T*
St. Joseph's College: Suffolk
    Campus *B, T*
St. Lawrence University *T*
St. Thomas Aquinas College *B, T*
State University of New York
    Albany *M, T*
    Binghamton *M*
    Buffalo *M, T*
    College at Brockport *B, M, T*
    College at Buffalo *B, M, T*
    College at Cortland *B, M*
    College at Fredonia *B*
    College at Geneseo *B, M, T*
    College at Old Westbury *B, M, T*
    College at Plattsburgh *B, M*
    College at Potsdam *B, M*
    New Paltz *B, M, T*
    Oswego *B, M*
    Stony Brook *T*
Syracuse University *B, M, T*
Ulster County Community College *A*
University of Rochester *M*
Wagner College *T*
Wells College *T*

North Carolina
Appalachian State University *B, T*
Barton College *B, T*
Belmont Abbey College *T*
Brevard College *B*
Campbell University *B, T*
Catawba College *T*
Davidson College *T*
East Carolina University *B*
Greensboro College *B, T*
Lenoir-Rhyne University *B, T*
Livingstone College *T*
Mars Hill College *T*
Meredith College *T*
Methodist University *A, B, T*
North Carolina State
    University *B, M, T*
Sandhills Community College *A*
University of North Carolina
    Greensboro *B*
    Pembroke *B, M*
Wake Forest University *B, T*
Western Carolina University *B, T*
Wingate University *B, T*
Winston-Salem State University *B*

North Dakota
North Dakota State University *B, T*

Ohio
Antioch University McGregor *M*
Ashland University *B, T*
Baldwin-Wallace College *T*
Bluffton University *B*
Bowling Green State University *B, T*
Capital University *T*
Cedarville University *B*
Defiance College *B, T*
Hiram College *T*
John Carroll University *T*
Kent State University *B*
Malone University *B*
Miami University
    Oxford Campus *B, T*
Mount Union College *T*
Mount Vernon Nazarene
    University *B, T*
Ohio Dominican University *B, T*
Ohio Northern University *B, T*
Ohio State University
    Columbus Campus *M, D*
Ohio University *D, T*
Ohio Wesleyan University *B*
Otterbein College *B*
Union Institute & University *B*
University of Akron *B, M*
University of Findlay *B, M, T*
University of Toledo *B, T*
Urbana University *B*
Ursuline College *B, M, T*
Walsh University *B*
Wilmington College *B*
Wright State University *B, T*
Youngstown State University *B, M*

Oklahoma
Cameron University *B, T*
East Central University *B*
Eastern Oklahoma State College *A*
Langston University *B*
Mid-America Christian University *B*
Northeastern State University *B*
Oklahoma Baptist University *B, T*
Oklahoma Christian University *B, T*
Oklahoma City University *B*
Oklahoma Wesleyan University *B*
Oral Roberts University *B, T*
Southeastern Oklahoma State
    University *B, M, T*
University of Central Oklahoma *B*
University of Oklahoma *B, T*
University of Tulsa *T*
Western Oklahoma State College *A*

Oregon
Concordia University *B, M, T*
Corban College *B*
Eastern Oregon University *B*
Portland State University *T*
Southern Oregon University *T*
Warner Pacific College *T*
Western Oregon University *B, M, T*

Pennsylvania
Albright College *T*
Alvernia University *B*
Arcadia University *B, M, T*
Baptist Bible College of
    Pennsylvania *B*
Cabrini College *T*
Chatham University *M, T*
DeSales University *T*
Dickinson College *T*
Duquesne University *B, M, T*
Gannon University *B*
Geneva College *T*
Gettysburg College *T*
Grove City College *B, T*
Gwynedd-Mercy College *T*
Holy Family University *B*
Juniata College *B, T*
Keystone College *B, T*

King's College *T*
La Salle University *B, T*
Lebanon Valley College *T*
Lincoln University *T*
Lycoming College *T*
Mansfield University of
    Pennsylvania *B, T*
Messiah College *B, T*
Penn State
    Harrisburg *B*
Philadelphia Biblical University *B, T*
Rosemont College *T*
St. Francis University *B, T*
Saint Joseph's University *B, M, T*
St. Vincent College *T*
Seton Hill University *T*
Susquehanna University *T*
Temple University *B*
Thiel College *B*
University of Pennsylvania *M, T*
University of Pittsburgh
    Johnstown *T*
Villanova University *T*
Waynesburg University *B, T*
West Chester University of
    Pennsylvania *T*
Westminster College *B, T*
Widener University *M, T*
York College of Pennsylvania *B*

Puerto Rico
Inter American University of Puerto
    Rico
    Fajardo Campus *B, T*
    San German Campus *B*
Pontifical Catholic University of
    Puerto Rico *B, T*
University of Puerto Rico
    Cayey University College *B*

Rhode Island
Rhode Island College *B, M*

South Carolina
Bob Jones University *B*
Charleston Southern University *B*
Converse College *T*
Erskine College *B, T*
Francis Marion University *B, T*
Furman University *T*
Limestone College *B*
Morris College *B, T*
North Greenville University *B, T*
Presbyterian College *T*
University of South Carolina
    Aiken *B, T*

South Dakota
Augustana College *B, T*
Dakota Wesleyan University *B, T*

Tennessee
Belmont University *B, M, T*
King College *T*
LeMoyne-Owen College *B*
Lincoln Memorial University *B, T*
Maryville College *B, T*
Tennessee Technological University *T*
University of Tennessee
    Chattanooga *B*
    Knoxville *T*

Texas
Abilene Christian University *B, T*
Arlington Baptist College *B, T*
Baylor University *B, T*
Dallas Baptist University *T*
East Texas Baptist University *B*
Hardin-Simmons University *B, T*
Houston Baptist University *B*
Howard Payne University *T*
Lamar University *B, M, T*
LeTourneau University *B, T*

Lubbock Christian University *B*
McMurry University *T*
Midwestern State University *B*
St. Edward's University *B, T*
St. Mary's University *T*
Sam Houston State University *M, T*
Southwestern Assemblies of God
    University *B*
Southwestern University *B, T*
Texas A&M International
    University *B, T*
Texas A&M University
    Commerce *T*
    Kingsville *T*
Texas Christian University *B*
Texas Lutheran University *B, T*
Texas Wesleyan University *B*
University of Dallas *T*
University of Houston *M, T*
University of Houston
    Clear Lake *T*
University of Mary Hardin-Baylor *B, T*
University of Texas
    Arlington *T*
    San Antonio *T*
Wayland Baptist University *B, T*
West Texas A&M University *T*

Utah
Utah State University *B*
Weber State University *B*

Vermont
Castleton State College *B, T*
College of St. Joseph in
    Vermont *B, M, T*
Goddard College *B, M*
Green Mountain College *B, T*
Johnson State College *B*
St. Michael's College *T*
University of Vermont *B, T*

Virginia
Averett University *B, M, T*
Bluefield College *B, T*
Hollins University *T*
Longwood University *B, T*
University of Richmond *T*
University of Virginia's College at
    Wise *T*
Virginia Intermont College *B, T*
Virginia Wesleyan College *T*

Washington
Eastern Washington University *B, M*
Northwest University *T*
Washington State University *B, M, T*
Western Washington University *B*
Whitworth University *T*

West Virginia
Bethany College *B*
Concord University *B, M, T*
Fairmont State University *B*
Ohio Valley University *B*
Shepherd University *T*
University of Charleston *B*
West Virginia State University *B*
West Virginia University *T*
West Virginia Wesleyan College *B*

Wisconsin
Alverno College *B, T*
Carroll University *B*
Concordia University Wisconsin *B, T*
Maranatha Baptist Bible College *B*
Marian University *B, T*
Marquette University *B*
Mount Mary College *B, T*
Northland College *B, T*
St. Norbert College *T*
University of Wisconsin
    Eau Claire *B*

Green Bay *T*
La Crosse *B, T*
Madison *B*
Platteville *B, T*
River Falls *T*
Superior *B, T*
Whitewater *B*
Viterbo University *B, T*

Wyoming
Casper College *A*

Social work

Alabama
Alabama Agricultural and Mechanical
    University *B, M*
Alabama State University *B*
Auburn University *B*
Jacksonville State University *B*
Lawson State Community College *A*
Miles College *B*
Oakwood University *B*
Shelton State Community College *A*
Talladega College *B*
Troy University *B*
Tuskegee University *B*
University of Alabama *B, M, D*
University of Alabama
    Birmingham *B*
University of Montevallo *B*
University of North Alabama *B*
University of South Alabama *B*

Alaska
University of Alaska
    Fairbanks *B*

Arizona
Arizona State University *B, M, D*
Cochise College *C, A*
Coconino County Community
    College *A*
Estrella Mountain Community
    College *A*
Northern Arizona University *B, M*
Prescott College *B*

Arkansas
Arkansas State University *B, M*
Central Baptist College *B*
Harding University *B*
Henderson State University *B, M*
Philander Smith College *B*
Southern Arkansas University *B*
University of Arkansas *B*
University of Arkansas
    Little Rock *B, M*
    Monticello *B*
    Pine Bluff *B*

California
Azusa Pacific University *B*
California State University
    Chico *B, M*
    Dominguez Hills *M*
    East Bay *B*
    Fresno *B, M*
    Fullerton *M*
    Long Beach *B, M*
    Los Angeles *B, M*
    Sacramento *B, M*
    San Bernardino *B, M*
    Stanislaus *M*
Chapman University *B*
Fresno City College *A*
Fresno Pacific University *B*
Humboldt State University *B*
La Sierra University *B*
Loma Linda University *M, D*
Merced College *A*
Pacific Union College *B*
Point Loma Nazarene University *B*

San Bernardino Valley College *A*
San Diego State University *B, M*
San Francisco State University *B, M*
San Jose State University *B, M*
Southwestern College *A*
University of California
    Berkeley *B, M, D*
    Los Angeles *M, D*
University of Southern
    California *M, D*
Whittier College *B*

Colorado
Colorado State University *B, M*
Colorado State University
    Pueblo *B*
Lamar Community College *A*
Metropolitan State College of
    Denver *B*
University of Denver *M, D*

Connecticut
Albertus Magnus College *B*
Central Connecticut State
    University *B*
Eastern Connecticut State
    University *B*
Naugatuck Valley Community
    College *A*
Sacred Heart University *B*
Saint Joseph College *B*
Southern Connecticut State
    University *B, M*
University of Connecticut *M, D*
Western Connecticut State
    University *B*

Delaware
Delaware State University *B, M*

District of Columbia
Catholic University of
    America *B, M, D*
Gallaudet University *B, M*
Howard University *M, D*
University of the District of
    Columbia *B*

Florida
Barry University *B, M, D*
Broward College *A*
Daytona State College *A*
Florida Agricultural and Mechanical
    University *B, M*
Florida Atlantic University *B, M*
Florida Gulf Coast University *B, M*
Florida International
    University *B, M, D*
Florida State University *B, M, D*
Gulf Coast Community College *A*
Miami Dade College *A*
Palm Beach Community College *A*
Saint Leo University *B*
Southeastern University *B*
State College of Florida,
    Manatee-Sarasota *A*
University of Central Florida *B, M*
University of South Florida *B, M, D*
University of West Florida *B, M*
Warner University *B*

Georgia
Albany State University *B*
Athens Technical College *C, A*
Atlanta Metropolitan College *A*
Augusta State University *B*
Clark Atlanta University *B, M, D*
Dalton State College *A, B*
Darton College *A*
Fort Valley State University *B*
Gainesville State College *A*
Georgia State University *B, M*
Gordon College *A*

Kennesaw State University *M*
LaGrange College *B*
Middle Georgia College *A*
Oglethorpe University *B*
Savannah State University *B, M*
University of Georgia *B, M, D*
Valdosta State University *M*

Hawaii
Hawaii Pacific University *B, M*
University of Hawaii
    Honolulu Community College *A*
    Manoa *B, M, D*

Idaho
Boise State University *B, M*
Idaho State University *B*
Lewis-Clark State College *B*
Northwest Nazarene University *B, M*

Illinois
Aurora University *B, M*
Bradley University *B*
City Colleges of Chicago
    Harold Washington College *A*
    Kennedy-King College *A*
College of DuPage *A*
College of Lake County *A*
Concordia University Chicago *B*
DePaul University *M*
Dominican University *M*
Elgin Community College *C, A*
Governors State University *B, M*
Greenville College *B*
Illinois Eastern Community Colleges
    Wabash Valley College *A*
Illinois State University *B, M*
Illinois Valley Community College *A*
John A. Logan College *A*
Kishwaukee College *A*
Lewis University *B*
Loyola University Chicago *B, M, D*
MacMurray College *B*
Northeastern Illinois University *B*
Olivet Nazarene University *B*
Parkland College *A*
St. Augustine College *B*
Sauk Valley Community College *A*
Southern Illinois University
    Carbondale *B, M*
Southern Illinois University
    Edwardsville *B, M*
Southwestern Illinois College *A*
Trinity Christian College *B*
Triton College *A*
University of Illinois
    Chicago *M, D*
    Springfield *B*
    Urbana-Champaign *M, D, T*
University of St. Francis *B, M*
Waubonsee Community College *A*
Western Illinois University *B*

Indiana
Anderson University *B*
Ball State University *B*
Goshen College *B*
Grace College *B*
Huntington University *B*
Indiana State University *B*
Indiana University
    East *A, B*
Indiana University-Purdue University
    Indianapolis *B, M, D*
Indiana Wesleyan University *B*
Manchester College *B*
Purdue University *B, M, D*
Saint Mary's College *B*
Taylor University *B*
University of Indianapolis *B*
University of St. Francis *A, B*
University of Southern Indiana *B*
Valparaiso University *B*

Vincennes University *A*

Iowa
Briar Cliff University *B*
Buena Vista University *B*
Clarke College *B*
Dordt College *B*
Ellsworth Community College *A*
Iowa Central Community College *C, A*
Iowa Western Community College *A*
Loras College *B*
Luther College *B*
Mount Mercy College *B*
Northeast Iowa Community
    College *C, A*
Northwestern College *B*
St. Ambrose University *M*
Simpson College *B*
University of Iowa *B, M, D*
University of Northern Iowa *B, M*
Wartburg College *B*

Kansas
Barton County Community College *A*
Bethany College *B*
Bethel College *B*
Butler Community College *A*
Central Christian College of Kansas *A*
Coffeyville Community College *A*
Fort Hays State University *B*
Kansas State University *B*
Neosho County Community
    College *A*
Newman University *M*
Pittsburg State University *B*
Seward County Community College *A*
University of Kansas *B, M, D*
Washburn University *B, M*
Wichita State University *B*

Kentucky
Asbury College *B, M*
Bluegrass Community and Technical
    College *C, A*
Brescia University *B*
Campbellsville University *B, M*
Eastern Kentucky University *B*
Elizabethtown Community and
    Technical College *C, A*
Henderson Community College *A*
Hopkinsville Community College *C, A*
Kentucky Christian University *B*
Kentucky State University *B*
Morehead State University *B*
Murray State University *B*
Northern Kentucky University *B*
Owensboro Community and
    Technical College *A*
Pikeville College *B*
St. Catharine College *A*
Spalding University *B, M*
University of Kentucky *B, M, D*
University of Louisville *M, D*
University of the Cumberlands *B*
Western Kentucky University *B, M*

Louisiana
Dillard University *B*
Grambling State University *B, M*
Louisiana College *B*
Louisiana State University and
    Agricultural and Mechanical
    College *M, D*
Northwestern State University *B*
Southeastern Louisiana University *B*
Southern University
    New Orleans *B, M*
Southern University and Agricultural
    and Mechanical College *B*
Tulane University *M, D*
University of Louisiana at Monroe *B*

Maine

University of Maine *B, M*
University of Maine
  Fort Kent *A, B*
  Presque Isle *B*
University of New England *M*
University of Southern Maine *B, M*

Maryland

Allegany College of Maryland *A*
Baltimore City Community College *A*
Bowie State University *B*
Coppin State University *B*
Frostburg State University *B*
Harford Community College *A*
Hood College *B*
McDaniel College *B*
Salisbury University *B, M*
Sojourner-Douglass College *B*
University of Maryland
  Baltimore *M, D*
  Baltimore County *B*

Massachusetts

Anna Maria College *B*
Boston College *M, D*
Boston University *M, D*
Bridgewater State College *B, M*
Eastern Nazarene College *B*
Elms College *B*
Gordon College *B*
Holyoke Community College *C, A*
Northern Essex Community
  College *A*
Regis College *B*
Salem State College *B, M*
Simmons College *M, D*
Smith College *M, D*
Springfield College *M*
Western New England College *B*
Westfield State College *B*
Wheelock College *B, M*

Michigan

Adrian College *B*
Andrews University *B, M*
Calvin College *B*
Central Michigan University *B*
Cornerstone University *B*
Delta College *A*
Eastern Michigan University *B, M*
Ferris State University *A, B*
Gogebic Community College *A*
Grand Rapids Community College *A*
Grand Valley State University *B, M*
Hope College *B*
Kellogg Community College *A*
Kuyper College *B*
Lansing Community College *A*
Madonna University *B*
Marygrove College *B*
Michigan State University *B, M, D*
Northern Michigan University *B*
Oakland University *B*
Rochester College *B*
Saginaw Valley State University *B*
Siena Heights University *A, B*
Southwestern Michigan College *A*
Spring Arbor University *B*
University of Detroit Mercy *B*
University of Michigan *M*
University of Michigan
  Flint *B*
Wayne County Community College *A*
Wayne State University *B, M, D*
Western Michigan University *B, M*

Minnesota

Augsburg College *B, M*
Bemidji State University *B*
Bethel University *B*
College of St. Scholastica *B*
Concordia College: Moorhead *B*

Itasca Community College *A*
Metropolitan State University *B*
Minnesota State University
  Mankato *B*
  Moorhead *B*
North Central University *B*
Ridgewater College *A*
St. Catherine University *B, M*
Saint Cloud State University *B, M*
St. Olaf College *B*
Southwest Minnesota State
  University *B*
University of Minnesota
  Duluth *M*
  Morris *B*
  Twin Cities *M, D*
University of St. Thomas *B, M*
Walden University *D*
Winona State University *B*

Mississippi

Delta State University *B*
Jackson State University *B, M, D*
Mississippi College *B*
Mississippi Delta Community
  College *A*
Mississippi Gulf Coast Community
  College *A*
Mississippi State University *B*
Mississippi Valley State
  University *B, M*
Rust College *B*
University of Mississippi *B, M*
University of Southern
  Mississippi *B, M*

Missouri

Avila University *B*
College of the Ozarks *B*
Evangel University *A, B*
Fontbonne University *B*
Lincoln University *B*
Lindenwood University *B*
Missouri State University *B, M*
Missouri Western State University *B*
Park University *B*
St. Charles Community College *A*
St. Louis Community College
  St. Louis Community College at
    Meramec *A*
Saint Louis University *B, M*
Southeast Missouri State University *B*
University of Central Missouri *B*
University of Missouri
  Columbia *B, M, D*
  Kansas City *M*
  St. Louis *B, M*
Washington University in St.
  Louis *M, D*
William Woods University *B*

Montana

Blackfeet Community College *A*
Miles Community College *A*
Salish Kootenai College *B*
University of Montana *B, M*

Nebraska

Chadron State College *B*
Creighton University *B*
Dana College *B*
Metropolitan Community College *A*
Nebraska Indian Community
  College *A*
Nebraska Wesleyan University *B*
Union College *B*
University of Nebraska
  Kearney *B*
  Omaha *B, M*
Western Nebraska Community
  College *A*

Nevada

Great Basin College *A*
University of Nevada
  Las Vegas *B, M*
  Reno *B, M*

New Hampshire

Franklin Pierce University *B*
Lakes Region Community
  College *C, A*
Plymouth State University *B*
University of New Hampshire *B, M*
University of New Hampshire at
  Manchester *M*

New Jersey

Brookdale Community College *A*
Camden County College *A*
Cumberland County College *A*
Essex County College *A*
Georgian Court University *B*
Kean University *B, M*
Monmouth University *B*
Montclair State University *M, T*
Ocean County College *C, A*
Ramapo College of New Jersey *B*
Richard Stockton College of New
  Jersey *B, M*
Rutgers, The State University of New
  Jersey
  Camden Regional Campus *B, M*
  New Brunswick/Piscataway
    Campus *B, D*
  Newark Regional Campus *B*
Salem Community College *C*
Seton Hall University *B*
Sussex County Community College *A*

New Mexico

Eastern New Mexico University *B*
Eastern New Mexico University:
  Roswell Campus *A*
New Mexico Highlands
  University *B, M*
New Mexico State University *B, M*
New Mexico State University
  Alamogordo *C, A*
Northern New Mexico College *A*
San Juan College *A*
Santa Fe Community College *A*
Western New Mexico University *B*

New York

Adelphi University *B, M, D*
City University of New York
  College of Staten Island *B*
  Hunter College *M*
  Lehman College *B, M*
  York College *B*
College of New Rochelle *B*
College of Saint Rose *B*
Columbia-Greene Community
  College *A*
Concordia College *B, D*
Daemen College *B*
Dominican College of Blauvelt *B*
Fordham University *B, M, D*
Hudson Valley Community College *A*
Iona College *B*
Keuka College *B*
Long Island University
  Brooklyn Campus *B, M*
  C. W. Post Campus *B, M*
Marist College *B*
Mercy College *B*
Metropolitan College of New
  York *A, B*
Molloy College *B*
Nazareth College *B, M*
New York University *C, B, M, D*
Niagara County Community
  College *C*
Niagara University *B*

Nyack College *B*
Roberts Wesleyan College *B, M*
Siena College *B*
Skidmore College *B*
State University of New York
  Albany *B, M, D*
  Binghamton *M*
  Buffalo *M, D*
  College at Brockport *B, M*
  College at Buffalo *B*
  College at Fredonia *B*
  College at Plattsburgh *B*
  College of Agriculture and
    Technology at Cobleskill *A*
  Stony Brook *B, M*
Syracuse University *B, M*
Ulster County Community College *C*
Westchester Community College *C, A*
Yeshiva University *M, D*

North Carolina

Appalachian State University *B, M*
Asheville-Buncombe Technical
  Community College *A*
Barton College *B*
Bennett College for Women *B*
Campbell University *B*
East Carolina University *B, M*
Elizabeth City State University *B*
Gaston College *A*
Halifax Community College *A*
Johnson C. Smith University *B*
Lenoir Community College *A*
Livingstone College *B*
Mars Hill College *B*
Meredith College *B, T*
Methodist University *A, B*
North Carolina Agricultural and
  Technical State University *B, M*
North Carolina Central University *B*
North Carolina State University *B, M*
Piedmont Community College *A*
Richmond Community College *A*
Sandhills Community College *A*
Shaw University *B*
University of North Carolina
  Chapel Hill *M, D*
  Charlotte *B, M*
  Greensboro *B, M*
  Pembroke *B, M*
  Wilmington *B, M*
Warren Wilson College *B*
Western Carolina University *B, M*
Winston-Salem State University *B*

North Dakota

Minot State University *B*
University of Mary *B*
University of North Dakota *B, M*

Ohio

Ashland University *B*
Bluffton University *B*
Bowling Green State University *B*
Capital University *B*
Case Western Reserve
  University *M, D*
Cedarville University *B*
Central Ohio Technical College *A*
Central State University *B*
Clark State Community College *C, A*
Cleveland State University *B, M*
College of Mount St. Joseph *B*
College of Wooster *B*
Defiance College *B*
Edison State Community College *A*
Franciscan University of
  Steubenville *B*
Lourdes College *B*
Malone University *B*
Miami University
  Oxford Campus *B, D*
Mount Vernon Nazarene University *B*

Northwest State Community
  College A
Ohio Dominican University B
Ohio State University
  Columbus Campus B, M, D
  Lima Campus M
Ohio University B, M
Owens Community College
  Toledo C, A
Union Institute & University B
University of Akron B, M
University of Akron: Wayne College A
University of Cincinnati B, M
University of Cincinnati
  Clermont College A
  Raymond Walters College A
University of Findlay B
University of Rio Grande A, B
University of Toledo B
Ursuline College B
Wilmington College B
Wright State University A, B
Wright State University: Lake
  Campus A
Xavier University B
Youngstown State University A, B, M
Zane State College A

Oklahoma

Connors State College A
East Central University B
Northeastern State University B
Northwestern Oklahoma State
  University B
Oklahoma Baptist University B
Oklahoma City University B
Oral Roberts University B
Rose State College A
Southwestern Oklahoma State
  University B
University of Oklahoma B, M

Oregon

Chemeketa Community College A
Clackamas Community College C, A
Concordia University B
George Fox University B
Pacific University B
Portland State University B, M, D
Rogue Community College A
Southwestern Oregon Community
  College A
Treasure Valley Community College A
University of Portland B
Warner Pacific College B

Pennsylvania

Alvernia University B
Bloomsburg University of
  Pennsylvania B
Bryn Mawr College M, D
Bucks County Community College A
Cabrini College B
California University of
  Pennsylvania B, M
Carlow University B
Cedar Crest College B
Chatham University B
Community College of Allegheny
  County A
Eastern University B
Edinboro University of
  Pennsylvania A, B, M
Elizabethtown College B
Gannon University B
Harrisburg Area Community
  College A
Holy Family University B
Juniata College B
Kutztown University of
  Pennsylvania B, M
La Salle University B
Lock Haven University of
  Pennsylvania B

Mansfield University of
  Pennsylvania B
Marywood University B, M
Mercyhurst College B
Messiah College B
Millersville University of
  Pennsylvania B, M
Misericordia University B
Northampton Community College A
Philadelphia Biblical University B
Reading Area Community College A
St. Francis University B
Seton Hill University B
Shippensburg University of
  Pennsylvania B, M
Slippery Rock University of
  Pennsylvania B
Temple University B, M
University of Pennsylvania M, D
University of Pittsburgh C, B, M, D
Valley Forge Christian College B
West Chester University of
  Pennsylvania B, M
Westminster College B
Widener University B, M, D

Puerto Rico

Bayamon Central University B
Caribbean University A, B
Inter American University of Puerto
  Rico
  Arecibo Campus B
  Metropolitan Campus B, M
Pontifical Catholic University of
  Puerto Rico B
Turabo University B
Universidad Metropolitana B
Universidad del Este A, B, M
University of Puerto Rico
  Humacao B
  Rio Piedras B, M, D
University of the Sacred Heart B

Rhode Island

Community College of Rhode
  Island A
Providence College B
Rhode Island College B, M
Salve Regina University B

South Carolina

Aiken Technical College A
Benedict College B
Coker College B
Columbia College B
Florence-Darlington Technical
  College A
Greenville Technical College C, A
Horry-Georgetown Technical
  College A
Limestone College B
Midlands Technical College A
South Carolina State University B
University of South Carolina M, D
Winthrop University B

South Dakota

Kilian Community College A
Northern State University B
Oglala Lakota College B
Presentation College B
University of Sioux Falls B
University of South Dakota B, M

Tennessee

Austin Peay State University B, M
Belmont University B, T
East Tennessee State University B, M
Freed-Hardeman University B
Jackson State Community College A
Lambuth University B
LeMoyne-Owen College B
Lincoln Memorial University B

Lipscomb University B
Middle Tennessee State University B
Southern Adventist University B
Tennessee State University B
Trevecca Nazarene University B
Union University B, M, T
University of Memphis B
University of Tennessee
  Chattanooga B
  Knoxville M, D
  Martin B

Texas

Abilene Christian University B, M
Amarillo College A
Angelina College A
Austin Community College A
Baylor University B, M
Cisco College A
Clarendon College A
College of the Mainland A
Del Mar College A
Eastfield College C, A
Galveston College A
Hardin-Simmons University B
Howard Payne University B
Lamar University B
Laredo Community College A
Lubbock Christian University B
Midland College A
Midwestern State University B
Northwest Vista College A
Our Lady of the Lake University of San
  Antonio B, M
Palo Alto College A
Prairie View A&M University B
St. Edward's University B
St. Philip's College A
Stephen F. Austin State
  University B, M
Tarleton State University B
Temple College A
Texas A&M International University B
Texas A&M University
  Commerce B, M
Texas Christian University B
Texas College B
Texas Southern University B
Texas State University: San
  Marcos B, M
Texas Tech University B
Texas Woman's University B
University of Houston M, D
University of Houston
  Clear Lake B
  Downtown B
University of Mary Hardin-Baylor B
University of North Texas B
University of Texas
  Arlington B, M, D
  Austin B, M, D
  El Paso B
  Pan American B, M
  San Antonio M
  of the Permian Basin B
West Texas A&M University B

Utah

Brigham Young University B, M
Salt Lake Community College A
Snow College A
Southern Utah University M
University of Utah B, M, D
Utah State University B
Weber State University B

Vermont

Castleton State College B
Champlain College B
University of Vermont B, M

Virginia

Christopher Newport University B

Eastern Mennonite University B
Ferrum College B
George Mason University B, M
James Madison University B
Longwood University B
Mountain Empire Community
  College A
Norfolk State University B, M, D
Radford University B, M
Thomas Nelson Community
  College A
Virginia Commonwealth
  University B, M, D
Virginia Highlands Community
  College A
Virginia Intermont College B
Virginia State University B
Virginia Union University B

Washington

Eastern Washington
  University C, B, M
Pacific Lutheran University B
Seattle University B
Trinity Lutheran College B
University of Washington B, M, D
University of Washington
  Tacoma B, M
Walla Walla University B, M

West Virginia

Bethany College B
Concord University B
Marshall University B
Mountain State University B
Potomac State College of West
  Virginia University A
Shepherd University B
West Virginia State University B
West Virginia University B, M

Wisconsin

Cardinal Stritch University C
Carthage College B
Concordia University Wisconsin B
Marian University B
Mount Mary College B
University of Wisconsin
  Eau Claire B
  Green Bay B, M
  Madison B, M, D
  Milwaukee B, M
  Oshkosh B, M
  River Falls B
  Superior B
  Whitewater B, T
Viterbo University B

Wyoming

Casper College A
University of Wyoming B, M
Western Wyoming Community
  College A

Sociology

Alabama

Alabama Agricultural and Mechanical
  University B
Alabama State University B
Athens State University B
Auburn University B, M
Auburn University at Montgomery B
Birmingham-Southern College B
Gadsden State Community College A
Jacksonville State University B
Samford University B
Talladega College B
Troy University B
Tuskegee University B
University of Alabama B

University of Alabama
  Birmingham *B, M, D*
  Huntsville *B*
University of Mobile *B*
University of Montevallo *B, T*
University of North Alabama *B*
University of South Alabama *B, M*
University of West Alabama *B*

Alaska

University of Alaska
  Anchorage *B*
  Fairbanks *B*

Arizona

Arizona State University *B, M, D*
Cochise College *A*
Coconino County Community
  College *A*
Eastern Arizona College *A*
GateWay Community College *A*
Grand Canyon University *B*
Northern Arizona University *B, M*
Pima Community College *A*
Prescott College *B, M*
University of Arizona *B, M, D*

Arkansas

Arkansas State University *B, M*
Arkansas Tech University *B*
Henderson State University *B*
Hendrix College *B*
Ouachita Baptist University *B*
Philander Smith College *B*
Southern Arkansas University *B*
University of Arkansas *B, M*
University of Arkansas
  Little Rock *B*
  Pine Bluff *B*
University of Central Arkansas *B*
University of the Ozarks *B*

California

Azusa Pacific University *B*
Bakersfield College *A*
Biola University *B*
Cabrillo College *A*
California Baptist University *B*
California Lutheran University *B*
California Polytechnic State
  University: San Luis Obispo *B*
California State Polytechnic
  University: Pomona *B*
California State University
  Bakersfield *B*
  Chico *B*
  Dominguez Hills *B, M*
  East Bay *B, M*
  Fresno *B*
  Fullerton *B, M*
  Long Beach *B*
  Los Angeles *B, M*
  Northridge *B*
  Sacramento *B, M*
  San Bernardino *B*
  San Marcos *B, M*
  Stanislaus *B*
California State University: Channel
  Islands *B*
Cerritos College *A*
Chabot College *A*
Chaffey College *A*
Chapman University *B*
College of Alameda *A*
College of the Canyons *A*
College of the Desert *A*
Contra Costa College *A*
Cosumnes River College *A*
Crafton Hills College *A*
Cypress College *A*
De Anza College *A*
East Los Angeles College *A*
El Camino College *A*

El Camino College: Compton
  Center *A*
Foothill College *A*
Fresno City College *A*
Fresno Pacific University *B*
Fullerton College *A*
Gavilan College *A*
Glendale Community College *A*
Golden West College *A*
Holy Names University *B*
Humboldt State University *B, M*
Irvine Valley College *A*
La Sierra University *B*
Lake Tahoe Community College *A*
Los Angeles Southwest College *A*
Los Angeles Valley College *A*
Los Medanos College *A*
Loyola Marymount University *B*
Mills College *B*
MiraCosta College *A*
Monterey Peninsula College *A*
Mount St. Mary's College *B*
National University *B*
Notre Dame de Namur University *B*
Occidental College *B*
Ohlone College *C*
Orange Coast College *A*
Oxnard College *A*
Pepperdine University *B*
Pitzer College *B*
Point Loma Nazarene University *B*
Pomona College *B*
Saddleback College *A*
St. Mary's College of California *B*
San Diego Mesa College *A*
San Diego State University *B, M*
San Francisco State University *B*
San Jose State University *B, M*
Santa Ana College *A*
Santa Barbara City College *A*
Santa Clara University *B*
Santa Rosa Junior College *A*
Santiago Canyon College *A*
Scripps College *B*
Sonoma State University *B*
Southwestern College *A*
Stanford University *B, M, D*
University of California
  Berkeley *B, D*
  Davis *B, M, D*
  Irvine *B, M, D*
  Los Angeles *B, M, D*
  Riverside *B, D*
  San Diego *B, M, D*
  Santa Barbara *B, M, D*
  Santa Cruz *B, D*
University of La Verne *B*
University of Redlands *B*
University of San Diego *B*
University of San Francisco *B*
University of Southern
  California *B, M, D*
University of the Pacific *B*
Vanguard University of Southern
  California *B*
West Los Angeles College *C, A*
West Valley College *A*
Westmont College *B*
Whittier College *B*

Colorado

Adams State College *B*
Colorado College *B*
Colorado State University *B, M, D*
Colorado State University
  Pueblo *B*
Fort Lewis College *B*
Mesa State College *B*
Metropolitan State College of
  Denver *B, T*
Pikes Peak Community College *A*
Regis University *B*
University of Colorado
  Boulder *B, D*

Colorado Springs *B, M*
Denver *B, M*
University of Denver *B*
University of Northern Colorado *B*
Western State College of Colorado *B*

Connecticut

Albertus Magnus College *B*
Central Connecticut State
  University *B*
Connecticut College *B*
Eastern Connecticut State
  University *B*
Fairfield University *B*
Post University *B*
Quinnipiac University *B*
Sacred Heart University *B*
Southern Connecticut State
  University *B, M, T*
Trinity College *B*
University of Bridgeport *B*
University of Connecticut *B, M, D*
University of Hartford *C, B*
Wesleyan University *B*
Western Connecticut State
  University *B*
Yale University *B, M, D*

Delaware

Delaware State University *B*
University of Delaware *B, M, D*

District of Columbia

American University *B, M*
Catholic University of America *B, M*
Gallaudet University *B*
George Washington University *B, M*
Georgetown University *B*
Howard University *B, M, D*
Trinity Washington University *B*
University of the District of
  Columbia *B*

Florida

Barry University *B*
Bethune-Cookman University *B*
Broward College *A*
Daytona State College *A*
Eckerd College *B*
Edward Waters College *B*
Flagler College *B*
Florida Agricultural and Mechanical
  University *B*
Florida Atlantic University *B, M*
Florida Gulf Coast University *B*
Florida International
  University *B, M, D*
Florida Memorial University *B*
Florida Southern College *B*
Florida State University *B, M, D*
Gulf Coast Community College *A*
Indian River State College *A*
Jacksonville University *B*
Miami Dade College *A*
New College of Florida *B*
Nova Southeastern University *B*
Palm Beach Community College *A*
Pensacola Junior College *A*
Rollins College *B*
Saint Leo University *B*
Stetson University *B*
University of Central Florida *B, M, D*
University of Florida *B, M, D*
University of Miami *B, M, D*
University of North Florida *B, M*
University of South Florida *B, M*
University of Tampa *A, B*
University of West Florida *B*

Georgia

Abraham Baldwin Agricultural
  College *A*
Agnes Scott College *B*

Albany State University *B*
Andrew College *A*
Augusta State University *B*
Brewton-Parker College *B*
Clark Atlanta University *B, M*
College of Coastal Georgia *A*
Columbus State University *B*
Covenant College *B*
Dalton State College *A*
Darton College *A*
East Georgia College *A*
Emory University *B, D*
Fort Valley State University *B*
Gainesville State College *A*
Georgia College and State
  University *B*
Georgia Highlands College *A*
Georgia Perimeter College *A*
Georgia Southern University *B, M*
Georgia Southwestern State
  University *B*
Georgia State University *B, M, D*
Gordon College *A*
Kennesaw State University *B*
LaGrange College *B*
Macon State College *A*
Mercer University *B*
Middle Georgia College *A*
Morehouse College *B*
North Georgia College & State
  University *B*
Oglethorpe University *B*
Paine College *B*
Piedmont College *B*
Reinhardt College *B*
Savannah State University *B*
Shorter College *B*
South Georgia College *A*
Spelman College *B*
University of Georgia *B, M, D*
University of West Georgia *B, M*
Valdosta State University *B, M*
Waycross College *A*

Hawaii

Hawaii Pacific University *B*
University of Hawaii
  Hilo *B*
  Manoa *B, M, D*
  West Oahu *B*

Idaho

Boise State University *A, B, T*
Brigham Young University-Idaho *B*
College of Idaho *B*
Idaho State University *B, M*
North Idaho College *A*
University of Idaho *B*

Illinois

Augustana College *B, T*
Aurora University *B*
Benedictine University *B*
Black Hawk College: East Campus *A*
Bradley University *B*
Chicago State University *B*
Concordia University Chicago *B*
Danville Area Community College *A*
DePaul University *B, M*
Dominican University *B*
Eastern Illinois University *B*
Elmhurst College *B, T*
Greenville College *B*
Illinois College *B*
Illinois State University *B, M*
Illinois Valley Community College *A*
Illinois Wesleyan University *B*
John A. Logan College *A*
John Wood Community College *A*
Joliet Junior College *A*
Judson University *B*
Kishwaukee College *A*
Knox College *B*
Lewis University *B, T*

Lincoln College *A*
Loyola University Chicago *B, M, D*
McKendree University *B*
Millikin University *B*
Monmouth College *B*
North Central College *B*
North Park University *B*
Northeastern Illinois University *B*
Northern Illinois University *B, M*
Northwestern University *B, M, D*
Olivet Nazarene University *B*
Principia College *B*
Richland Community College *A*
Roosevelt University *B, M*
Saint Xavier University *B*
South Suburban College of Cook
    County *A*
Southern Illinois University
    Carbondale *B, M, D*
Southern Illinois University
    Edwardsville *B, M*
Southwestern Illinois College *A*
Trinity Christian College *B*
Triton College *A*
University of Chicago *B, D*
University of Illinois
    Chicago *B, M, D*
    Urbana-Champaign *B, M, D*
Western Illinois University *B, M*
Wheaton College *B*

Indiana
Ancilla College *A*
Anderson University *B*
Ball State University *B, M, T*
Bethel College *B*
Butler University *B*
DePauw University *B*
Earlham College *B*
Franklin College *B*
Goshen College *B*
Grace College *B*
Hanover College *B*
Huntington University *B*
Indiana University
    Bloomington *B, M, D*
    East *B*
    Kokomo *B*
    Northwest *A, B*
    South Bend *B*
    Southeast *B*
Indiana University-Purdue University
    Fort Wayne *B, M*
Indiana University-Purdue University
    Indianapolis *B, M*
Manchester College *B*
Marian University *B, T*
Oakland City University *B*
Purdue University *B, M, D*
Purdue University
    Calumet *B*
Saint Joseph's College *B*
Saint Mary's College *B*
Taylor University *B*
University of Evansville *B*
University of Indianapolis *B, M*
University of Notre Dame *B, M, D*
University of St. Francis *B*
University of Southern Indiana *B*
Valparaiso University *B*
Vincennes University *A*

Iowa
Briar Cliff University *B*
Buena Vista University *B*
Central College *B, T*
Coe College *B*
Cornell College *B, T*
Drake University *B*
Ellsworth Community College *A*
Graceland University *B, T*
Grinnell College *B*
Iowa State University *B, M, D*
Iowa Wesleyan College *B*

Loras College *B*
Luther College *B*
Mount Mercy College *B*
North Iowa Area Community
    College *A*
Northwestern College *B, T*
St. Ambrose University *B, T*
Simpson College *B*
University of Dubuque *B, T*
University of Iowa *B, M, D, T*
University of Northern Iowa *B, M*
Upper Iowa University *B*
Wartburg College *B, T*
William Penn University *B*

Kansas
Allen County Community College *A*
Baker University *B*
Barton County Community College *A*
Benedictine College *B*
Bethany College *B*
Central Christian College of Kansas *A*
Coffeyville Community College *A*
Dodge City Community College *A*
Emporia State University *B, T*
Fort Hays State University *B*
Friends University *B*
Kansas State University *B, M, D*
Kansas Wesleyan University *B*
McPherson College *B, T*
MidAmerica Nazarene University *B*
Newman University *B*
Ottawa University *B*
Pittsburg State University *B*
Pratt Community College *A*
Seward County Community College *A*
Tabor College *B*
University of Kansas *B, M, D*
Washburn University *B*
Wichita State University *B, M*

Kentucky
Asbury College *B*
Bellarmine University *B*
Berea College *B*
Brescia University *B*
Campbellsville University *B*
Centre College *B*
Eastern Kentucky University *B*
Georgetown College *B*
Kentucky Wesleyan College *B*
Morehead State University *B, M*
Murray State University *B*
Northern Kentucky University *B*
Pikeville College *B*
Thomas More College *A, B*
Transylvania University *B*
Union College *B*
University of Kentucky *B, M, D*
University of Louisville *B, M*
Western Kentucky University *B, M*

Louisiana
Centenary College of Louisiana *B*
Dillard University *B*
Grambling State University *B*
Louisiana College *B*
Louisiana State University
    Shreveport *B*
Louisiana State University and
    Agricultural and Mechanical
    College *B, M, D*
Louisiana Tech University *B*
Loyola University New Orleans *B*
McNeese State University *B*
Nicholls State University *B*
Northwestern State University *B*
Southeastern Louisiana
    University *B, M*
Southern University
    New Orleans *B*
    Shreveport *A*
Southern University and Agricultural
    and Mechanical College *B*

Tulane University *B, M, D*
University of Louisiana at Lafayette *B*
University of Louisiana at Monroe *B*
University of New Orleans *B, M*
Xavier University of Louisiana *B*

Maine
Bates College *B*
Bowdoin College *B*
Colby College *B*
Saint Joseph's College of Maine *B*
University of Maine *B*
University of Maine
    Presque Isle *B*
University of New England *B*
University of Southern Maine *B*

Maryland
Allegany College of Maryland *A*
Bowie State University *B*
Coppin State University *B*
Frederick Community College *A*
Frostburg State University *B*
Goucher College *B*
Harford Community College *A*
Hood College *B*
Howard Community College *A*
Johns Hopkins University *B, M, D*
Loyola University Maryland *B*
McDaniel College *B*
Morgan State University *B, M*
Mount St. Mary's University *B*
St. Mary's College of Maryland *B*
Salisbury University *B*
Towson University *B*
University of Maryland
    Baltimore County *B, M*
    College Park *B, M, D*
    Eastern Shore *B*
Washington College *B, T*

Massachusetts
American International College *B*
Amherst College *B*
Anna Maria College *B*
Assumption College *B*
Bard College at Simon's Rock *B*
Boston College *B, M, D*
Boston University *B, M, D*
Brandeis University *B, M, D*
Bridgewater State College *B*
Bunker Hill Community College *A*
Cape Cod Community College *A*
Clark University *B*
College of the Holy Cross *B*
Curry College *B*
Elms College *B*
Emmanuel College *B*
Fitchburg State College *B*
Framingham State College *B*
Gordon College *B*
Hampshire College *B*
Harvard College *B, M, D*
Lasell College *B*
Massachusetts College of Liberal
    Arts *B*
Merrimack College *B*
Mount Holyoke College *B*
Northeastern University *B, M, D*
Regis College *B*
Salem State College *B*
Simmons College *B*
Smith College *B*
Springfield College *B*
Stonehill College *B*
Suffolk University *B*
Tufts University *B*
University of Massachusetts
    Amherst *B, M, D*
    Boston *B, M*
    Dartmouth *B*
    Lowell *B*
Wellesley College *B*
Western New England College *B*

Westfield State College *B*
Wheaton College *B*
Williams College *B*
Worcester State College *B*

Michigan
Adrian College *A, B, T*
Albion College *B*
Alma College *B, T*
Andrews University *B*
Aquinas College *B, T*
Calvin College *B*
Central Michigan University *B, M*
Delta College *A*
Eastern Michigan University *B, M*
Ferris State University *B*
Grand Rapids Community College *A*
Grand Valley State University *B*
Hillsdale College *B*
Hope College *B*
Kalamazoo College *B*
Lake Michigan College *A*
Lake Superior State University *B*
Lansing Community College *A*
Madonna University *C, B*
Michigan State University *B, M, D*
Mid Michigan Community College *A*
Northern Michigan University *B*
Oakland University *B*
Saginaw Valley State University *B*
Spring Arbor University *B*
University of Detroit Mercy *B*
University of Michigan *B, M, D*
University of Michigan
    Dearborn *B*
    Flint *B*
Wayne State University *B, M, D*
Western Michigan University *B, M, D*

Minnesota
Augsburg College *B*
Bemidji State University *B*
Bethany Lutheran College *B*
Carleton College *B*
College of St. Benedict *B*
Concordia College: Moorhead *B*
Concordia University: St. Paul *B*
Gustavus Adolphus College *B*
Hamline University *B*
Macalester College *B*
Minnesota State University
    Mankato *B, M*
    Moorhead *B*
Minnesota West Community and
    Technical College *A*
Ridgewater College *A*
St. Catherine University *B*
Saint Cloud State University *B*
St. John's University *B*
St. Mary's University of Minnesota *B*
St. Olaf College *B*
Southwest Minnesota State
    University *B*
University of Minnesota
    Duluth *B*
    Morris *B*
    Twin Cities *B, M, D*
University of St. Thomas *B*
Winona State University *B*

Mississippi
Alcorn State University *B*
Hinds Community College *A*
Jackson State University *B, M*
Millsaps College *B*
Mississippi College *B*
Mississippi Delta Community
    College *A*
Mississippi State University *B, M, D*
Mississippi Valley State University *B*
Rust College *B*
Tougaloo College *B*
University of Mississippi *B, M*
University of Southern Mississippi *B*

Missouri

Avila University *B*
Central Methodist University *B*
College of the Ozarks *B*
Columbia College *B*
Drury University *B*
Evangel University *B*
Fontbonne University *B*
Hannibal-LaGrange College *B*
Lincoln University *B, M*
Lindenwood University *B*
Maryville University of Saint Louis *B*
Missouri Southern State
   University *B, T*
Missouri State University *B*
Missouri Valley College *B*
Northwest Missouri State
   University *B*
Park University *B*
St. Charles Community College *A*
Saint Louis University *B*
Southwest Baptist University *B*
Three Rivers Community College *A*
Truman State University *B*
University of Central Missouri *B, M*
University of Missouri
   Columbia *B, M, D*
   Kansas City *B, M*
   St. Louis *B, M*
Webster University *B*
Westminster College *B*

Montana

Montana State University
   Billings *B, T*
   Bozeman *B*
Rocky Mountain College *B, T*
University of Great Falls *B*
University of Montana *B, M*
University of Montana: Western *B*

Nebraska

Bellevue University *B*
Chadron State College *B*
Creighton University *B*
Doane College *B*
Nebraska Wesleyan University *B*
Peru State College *B, T*
University of Nebraska
   Kearney *B*
   Lincoln *B, M, D*
   Omaha *B*
Wayne State College *B*
Western Nebraska Community
   College *A*

Nevada

Great Basin College *A*
Nevada State College *B*
University of Nevada
   Las Vegas *B, M, D*
   Reno *B, M*

New Hampshire

Colby-Sawyer College *B*
Dartmouth College *B*
Keene State College *B*
New England College *B*
Rivier College *B*
Saint Anselm College *B*
University of New Hampshire *B, M, D*

New Jersey

Bergen Community College *A*
Bloomfield College *B*
Caldwell College *B*
Centenary College *B*
The College of New Jersey *B*
College of St. Elizabeth *B*
Drew University *B*
Fairleigh Dickinson University
   College at Florham *B*
   Metropolitan Campus *B*

Felician College *B*
Georgian Court University *B*
Gloucester County College *A*
Hudson County Community
   College *A*
Kean University *B, M*
Middlesex County College *A*
Monmouth University *B*
Montclair State University *B, M*
New Jersey City University *B*
Passaic County Community College *A*
Princeton University *B, M, D*
Ramapo College of New Jersey *B*
Richard Stockton College of New
   Jersey *B*
Rider University *B*
Rowan University *B*
Rutgers, The State University of New
   Jersey
   Camden Regional Campus *B*
   New Brunswick/Piscataway
     Campus *B, M, D*
   Newark Regional Campus *B*
Saint Peter's College *B*
Salem Community College *A*
Seton Hall University *B, T*
Thomas Edison State College *B*
William Paterson University of New
   Jersey *B, M*

New Mexico

Eastern New Mexico University *B*
New Mexico Highlands University *B*
New Mexico State University *B, M*
University of New Mexico *B, M, D*
Western New Mexico University *B*

New York

Adelphi University *B*
Alfred University *B*
Bard College *B*
Barnard College *B*
Canisius College *B*
City University of New York
   Baruch College *B*
   Brooklyn College *B, M*
   City College *B, M*
   Hunter College *B, M*
   Lehman College *B*
   Queens College *B, M, T*
   Queensborough Community
     College *A*
   York College *B*
Clarkson University *B*
Colgate University *B*
College of Mount St. Vincent *B*
College of New Rochelle *B*
College of Saint Rose *B*
Columbia University *B*
Columbia University
   School of General Studies *B*
Cornell University *B, M, D*
D'Youville College *B*
Dowling College *B*
Elmira College *B*
Excelsior College *B*
Fordham University *B, M, D*
Hamilton College *B*
Hartwick College *B*
Hobart and William Smith Colleges *B*
Hofstra University *B, M*
Houghton College *B*
Iona College *B*
Ithaca College *B*
Keuka College *B*
Le Moyne College *B*
Long Island University
   Brooklyn Campus *B*
   C. W. Post Campus *B*
Manhattan College *B*
Manhattanville College *B*
Marymount Manhattan College *B*
Mercy College *B*

Metropolitan College of New
   York *A, B*
Molloy College *B*
Mount Saint Mary College *B, T*
Nazareth College *B*
New York Institute of Technology *B*
New York University *B, M, D*
Niagara University *B*
Roberts Wesleyan College *B*
Russell Sage College *B*
Saint Bonaventure University *B*
St. Francis College *B*
St. John Fisher College *B*
St. John's University *B, M*
St. Joseph's College *B*
St. Joseph's College: Suffolk
   Campus *B*
St. Lawrence University *B*
Siena College *B, T*
Skidmore College *B*
State University of New York
   Albany *B, M, D*
   Binghamton *B, M, D*
   Buffalo *B, M, D*
   College at Brockport *B*
   College at Buffalo *B*
   College at Cortland *B*
   College at Fredonia *B*
   College at Geneseo *B*
   College at Old Westbury *B*
   College at Oneonta *B*
   College at Plattsburgh *B*
   College at Potsdam *B*
   Institute of Technology at
     Utica/Rome *B, M*
   New Paltz *B*
   Oswego *B*
   Purchase *B*
   Stony Brook *B, M, D*
Sullivan County Community
   College *A*
Syracuse University *B, M, D*
Touro College *B*
Union College *B*
United States Military Academy *B*
Utica College *B*
Vassar College *B*
Wagner College *B*
Wells College *B*
Yeshiva University *B*

North Carolina

Appalachian State University *B*
Belmont Abbey College *B*
Bennett College for Women *B*
Catawba College *B*
Davidson College *B*
Duke University *B, M, D*
East Carolina University *B, M*
Elizabeth City State University *B*
Elon University *B*
Fayetteville State University *B, M*
Gardner-Webb University *B*
Greensboro College *C, B*
Guilford College *B*
High Point University *B*
Lees-McRae College *B*
Lenoir-Rhyne University *B*
Livingstone College *B*
Mars Hill College *B, T*
Meredith College *B*
Methodist University *A, B*
North Carolina Agricultural and
   Technical State University *B*
North Carolina Central
   University *B, M*
North Carolina State
   University *B, M, D*
North Carolina Wesleyan College *B*
Pfeiffer University *B*
Queens University of Charlotte *B*
St. Augustine's College *B*
Salem College *B*
Shaw University *B*

University of North Carolina
   Asheville *B, T*
   Chapel Hill *B, M, D*
   Charlotte *B, M*
   Greensboro *B, M*
   Pembroke *B*
   Wilmington *B, M*
Wake Forest University *B*
Warren Wilson College *B*
Western Carolina University *B*
Wingate University *B*
Winston-Salem State University *B*

North Dakota

Minot State University *B*
North Dakota State University *B, M*
University of North Dakota *B, M*

Ohio

Ashland University *B*
Baldwin-Wallace College *B*
Bluffton University *B*
Bowling Green State
   University *B, M, D*
Capital University *B*
Case Western Reserve
   University *B, M, D*
Cedarville University *B*
Central State University *B*
Cleveland State University *B, M*
College of Mount St. Joseph *B*
College of Wooster *B*
Denison University *B*
Franciscan University of
   Steubenville *B*
Hiram College *B*
John Carroll University *B*
Kent State University *B, M, D*
Kenyon College *B*
Lourdes College *A, B*
Miami University
   Oxford Campus *B*
Mount Union College *B*
Mount Vernon Nazarene University *B*
Muskingum University *B*
Oberlin College *B*
Ohio Dominican University *B*
Ohio Northern University *B*
Ohio State University
   Columbus Campus *B, M, D*
Ohio University *B, M*
Ohio Wesleyan University *B*
Otterbein College *B*
Owens Community College
   Toledo *A*
Shawnee State University *B*
University of Akron *C, B, M, D*
University of Cincinnati *B, M, D*
University of Dayton *B*
University of Findlay *B*
University of Rio Grande *A*
University of Toledo *B, M*
Urbana University *B*
Ursuline College *B*
Walsh University *B*
Wilberforce University *B*
Wilmington College *B*
Wittenberg University *B*
Wright State University *A, B*
Wright State University: Lake
   Campus *A*
Xavier University *A, B*
Youngstown State University *B*

Oklahoma

Cameron University *B*
Carl Albert State College *A*
Connors State College *A*
East Central University *B*
Eastern Oklahoma State College *A*
Langston University *B*
Northeastern State University *B*
Northwestern Oklahoma State
   University *B*

Oklahoma Baptist University *B*
Oklahoma City Community College *A*
Oklahoma City University *B*
Oklahoma State University *B, M, D*
Rose State College *A*
St. Gregory's University *B*
Southeastern Oklahoma State
University *B*
Southern Nazarene University *B*
Southwestern Oklahoma State
University *B*
Tulsa Community College *A*
University of Central Oklahoma *B*
University of Oklahoma *B, M, D*
University of Science and Arts of
Oklahoma *B*
University of Tulsa *B*
Western Oklahoma State College *A*

Oregon

Central Oregon Community
College *A*
Chemeketa Community College *A*
Eastern Oregon University *B, T*
George Fox University *B*
Lewis & Clark College *B*
Linfield College *B, T*
Linn-Benton Community College *A*
Mt. Hood Community College *A*
Oregon State University *B*
Pacific University *B*
Portland State University *B, M, D*
Reed College *B*
Southern Oregon University *B*
University of Oregon *B, M, D*
University of Portland *B*
Western Oregon University *B*
Willamette University *B*

Pennsylvania

Albright College *B*
Arcadia University *B*
Bloomsburg University of
Pennsylvania *B*
Bryn Mawr College *B*
Bucknell University *B*
Cabrini College *B*
Carlow University *B*
Chestnut Hill College *B*
Cheyney University of Pennsylvania *B*
Clarion University of Pennsylvania *B*
Community College of Allegheny
County *A*
Dickinson College *B*
Drexel University *B*
Duquesne University *B*
East Stroudsburg University of
Pennsylvania *B*
Eastern University *B*
Edinboro University of
Pennsylvania *B*
Elizabethtown College *B*
Franklin & Marshall College *B*
Geneva College *B*
Gettysburg College *B*
Grove City College *B*
Gwynedd-Mercy College *B*
Haverford College *B, T*
Holy Family University *B*
Immaculata University *B*
Indiana University of
Pennsylvania *B, M*
Juniata College *B*
King's College *B*
Kutztown University of
Pennsylvania *B*
La Roche College *B*
La Salle University *B*
Lafayette College *B*
Lebanon Valley College *B*
Lehigh University *B, M*
Lincoln University *B*
Lock Haven University of
Pennsylvania *B*

Lycoming College *B*
Mansfield University of
Pennsylvania *B*
Mercyhurst College *B, T*
Messiah College *B*
Millersville University of
Pennsylvania *B*
Moravian College *B*
Muhlenberg College *C, B*
Penn State
Abington *B*
Altoona *B*
Beaver *B*
Berks *B*
Brandywine *B*
DuBois *B*
Erie, The Behrend College *B*
Fayette, The Eberly Campus *B*
Greater Allegheny *B*
Harrisburg *B*
Hazleton *B*
Lehigh Valley *B*
Mont Alto *B*
New Kensington *B*
Schuylkill *B*
Shenango *B*
University Park *B, M, D*
Wilkes-Barre *B*
Worthington Scranton *B*
York *B*
Rosemont College *B*
St. Francis University *B*
Saint Joseph's University *C, A, B*
St. Vincent College *B*
Seton Hill University *B*
Shippensburg University of
Pennsylvania *B*
Susquehanna University *B*
Swarthmore College *B*
Temple University *B, M, D*
Thiel College *B*
University of Pennsylvania *A, B, M, D*
University of Pittsburgh *B, M, D*
University of Pittsburgh
Bradford *B*
Johnstown *B*
University of Scranton *A, B*
Ursinus College *B*
Villanova University *B*
Washington & Jefferson College *B*
Waynesburg University *B*
West Chester University of
Pennsylvania *B*
Westminster College *B, T*
Widener University *B*
Wilkes University *B*
Wilson College *B*
York College of Pennsylvania *B*

Puerto Rico

Inter American University of Puerto
Rico
Metropolitan Campus *B*
San German Campus *B*
Pontifical Catholic University of
Puerto Rico *B*
Turabo University *B*
University of Puerto Rico
Aguadilla *A*
Cayey University College *B*
Rio Piedras *B, M*

Rhode Island

Brown University *B, M, D*
Bryant University *B*
Providence College *B*
Rhode Island College *B*
Roger Williams University *B*
Salve Regina University *B*
University of Rhode Island *B*

South Carolina

Charleston Southern University *B*
Claflin University *B*

Clemson University *B*
Coastal Carolina University *B*
Coker College *B*
College of Charleston *B, T*
Francis Marion University *B*
Furman University *B*
Lander University *B*
Morris College *B*
Newberry College *B*
Presbyterian College *B*
South Carolina State University *B*
University of South Carolina *B, M, D*
University of South Carolina
Aiken *B*
Upstate *B*
Winthrop University *B*
Wofford College *B*

South Dakota

Augustana College *B, T*
Black Hills State University *B*
Dakota Wesleyan University *B*
Kilian Community College *A*
Northern State University *B*
Oglala Lakota College *B*
South Dakota State University *B, M, D*
University of Sioux Falls *B*
University of South Dakota *B*

Tennessee

Austin Peay State University *B*
Belmont University *B, T*
Bethel University *B*
Carson-Newman College *B*
Columbia State Community College *A*
Cumberland University *B*
East Tennessee State
University *B, M, T*
Fisk University *B*
Jackson State Community College *A*
Lambuth University *B*
Lane College *B*
LeMoyne-Owen College *B*
Lee University *B*
Maryville College *B*
Middle Tennessee State
University *B, M*
Milligan College *B, T*
Rhodes College *B*
Tennessee State University *B*
Tennessee Technological University *B*
Trevecca Nazarene University *B*
Union University *B, T*
University of Memphis *B, M*
University of Tennessee
Chattanooga *B*
Knoxville *B, M, D*
Martin *B*
Vanderbilt University *B, M, D*

Texas

Abilene Christian University *B*
Angelo State University *B*
Austin College *B*
Austin Community College *A*
Baylor University *B, M, D*
Brazosport College *A*
Cisco College *A*
Clarendon College *A*
Coastal Bend College *A*
College of the Mainland *A*
Dallas Baptist University *B*
Del Mar College *A*
East Texas Baptist University *B*
El Paso Community College *A*
Frank Phillips College *A*
Galveston College *A*
Grayson County College *A*
Hardin-Simmons University *B*
Houston Baptist University *B*
Howard Payne University *B*
Huston-Tillotson University *B*
Jarvis Christian College *B*
Kilgore College *A*

Lamar State College at Orange *A*
Lamar University *B*
Laredo Community College *A*
Lon Morris College *A*
McMurry University *B*
Midland College *A*
Midwestern State University *B*
Northeast Texas Community
College *A*
Northwest Vista College *A*
Our Lady of the Lake University of San
Antonio *B*
Palo Alto College *A*
Paris Junior College *A*
Prairie View A&M University *B, M*
Rice University *B*
St. Edward's University *B*
St. Mary's University *B, T*
St. Philip's College *A*
Sam Houston State University *B, M*
San Jacinto College *A*
South Plains College *A*
Southern Methodist University *B*
Southwestern University *B*
Stephen F. Austin State University *B, T*
Tarleton State University *B*
Texas A&M International
University *B, M*
Texas A&M University *B, M, D*
Texas A&M University
Commerce *B, M*
Corpus Christi *B*
Kingsville *B, M*
Texas Christian University *B*
Texas College *B*
Texas Lutheran University *B*
Texas Southern University *B, M*
Texas State University: San
Marcos *B, M, T*
Texas Tech University *B, M*
Texas Woman's University *B, M, D*
Trinity University *B*
Trinity Valley Community College *A*
Tyler Junior College *A*
University of Houston *B, M*
University of Houston
Clear Lake *B, M*
Downtown *B*
University of Mary Hardin-Baylor *B*
University of North Texas *B, M, D*
University of Texas
Arlington *B, M*
Austin *B, M, D*
Brownsville - Texas Southmost
College *B*
Dallas *B, M*
El Paso *B, M*
Pan American *B, M*
San Antonio *B, M*
Tyler *B, M*
of the Permian Basin *B*
University of the Incarnate Word *B*
Wayland Baptist University *B*
Weatherford College *A*
West Texas A&M University *B*
Western Texas College *A*
Wharton County Junior College *A*
Wiley College *B*

Utah

Brigham Young University *B, M, D*
Salt Lake Community College *A*
Snow College *A*
Southern Utah University *B*
University of Utah *B, M, D, T*
Utah State University *B, M, D*
Weber State University *B*
Westminster College *B*

Vermont

Bennington College *B*
Castleton State College *B*
Green Mountain College *B*
Johnson State College *B*

Marlboro College *B*
Middlebury College *B*
St. Michael's College *B*
University of Vermont *B*

Virginia

Averett University *B*
Bridgewater College *B*
Christopher Newport University *B*
College of William and Mary *B*
Eastern Mennonite University *B*
Emory & Henry College *B*
George Mason University *B, M, D*
Hampton University *B*
Hollins University *B*
James Madison University *B*
Longwood University *B, M, T*
Lynchburg College *B*
Mary Baldwin College *B*
Marymount University *B*
Norfolk State University *B, M*
Old Dominion University *B, M*
Radford University *B*
Randolph College *B*
Randolph-Macon College *B*
Roanoke College *B, T*
St. Paul's College *B*
Shenandoah University *B*
Sweet Briar College *B*
University of Mary Washington *B*
University of Richmond *B*
University of Virginia *B, M, D*
University of Virginia's College at
Wise *B, T*
Virginia Commonwealth
University *B, M*
Virginia Polytechnic Institute and
State University *B, M, D*
Virginia State University *B*
Virginia Union University *B*
Virginia University of Lynchburg *B*
Virginia Wesleyan College *B*
Washington and Lee University *B*

Washington

Centralia College *A*
Eastern Washington University *B*
Everett Community College *A*
Evergreen State College *B*
Gonzaga University *B*
Highline Community College *A*
Olympic College *A*
Pacific Lutheran University *B*
Saint Martin's University *B*
Seattle Pacific University *B*
Seattle University *B*
University of Puget Sound *B, T*
University of Washington *B, M, D*
Walla Walla University *B*
Washington State University *B, M, D*
Western Washington University *B, M*
Whitman College *B*
Whitworth University *B*

West Virginia

American Public University System *B*
Concord University *B*
Davis and Elkins College *B*
Fairmont State University *B*
Marshall University *B, M*
Potomac State College of West
Virginia University *A*
Shepherd University *B*
West Liberty University *B*
West Virginia State University *B*
West Virginia University *B, M*
West Virginia Wesleyan College *B*

Wisconsin

Alverno College *B*
Beloit College *B*
Cardinal Stritch University *B*
Carroll University *B*

Carthage College *B, T*
Edgewood College *B*
Lakeland College *B*
Marquette University *B*
Northland College *B*
Ripon College *B*
St. Norbert College *B, T*
University of Wisconsin
Eau Claire *B*
Green Bay *B*
La Crosse *B, T*
Madison *B, M, D*
Milwaukee *B, M*
Oshkosh *B*
Parkside *B, T*
Platteville *B*
River Falls *B, T*
Stevens Point *B, T*
Superior *B*
Whitewater *B, T*
Viterbo University *B*

Wyoming

Casper College *A*
Eastern Wyoming College *A*
Laramie County Community
College *A*
Northwest College *A*
University of Wyoming *B, M*
Western Wyoming Community
College *A*

Software engineering

Alabama

Auburn University *B, M*

Arizona

DeVry University
Phoenix *B*
Embry-Riddle Aeronautical University:
Prescott Campus *B*
Phoenix College *A*
University of Advancing
Technology *A, B, M*
University of Phoenix *B*

California

California State University
East Bay *B*
Fullerton *M*
Cogswell Polytechnical College *B*
Foothill College *A*
Los Angeles City College *A*
National University *M*
Northwestern Polytechnic
University *B, M*
San Jose State University *B, M*
Santa Clara University *M*

Colorado

Colorado Technical
University *B, M, D*
DeVry University
Westminster *B*
University of Denver *M*

Connecticut

Fairfield University *B, M*

District of Columbia

George Washington University *M*

Florida

Broward College *A*
DeVry University
Orlando *B*
Embry-Riddle Aeronautical
University *B, M*
Florida Institute of Technology *B, M*
Florida State University *B*
Seminole Community College *A*

Tallahassee Community College *A*

Georgia

DeVry University
Alpharetta *B*
Decatur *B*
Mercer University *M*
Southern Polytechnic State
University *C, B, M*

Idaho

Boise State University *D*

Illinois

DeVry University
Addison *B*
Tinley Park *B*
DeVry University: Online *B*
Moraine Valley Community College *C*
University of Illinois
Urbana-Champaign *B, M, D*

Indiana

Indiana Institute of Technology *B*
Purdue University
Calumet *B*
Rose-Hulman Institute of
Technology *B*

Iowa

Iowa State University *B*

Maryland

Capitol College *B, M*

Massachusetts

Northeastern University *M*

Michigan

Andrews University *M*
Baker College
of Flint *M*
Michigan Technological University *B*
University of Michigan
Dearborn *M*

Minnesota

DeVry University
Edina *B*
Globe University *A, B*
Riverland Community College *A*
University of Minnesota
Crookston *B*
Walden University *M*

Missouri

Hickey College *A*
Missouri Technical School *A, B*

Montana

Montana Tech of the University of
Montana *B*

Nevada

College of Southern Nevada *A*
University of Nevada
Las Vegas *B*

New Jersey

Monmouth University *B, M*
New Jersey Institute of Technology *M*

New York

Clarkson University *B*
College of Westchester *A*
Pace University *M*
Rochester Institute of
Technology *B, M*

State University of New York
College of Agriculture and
Technology at Morrisville *A*
Oswego *B*
Wood Tobe-Coburn School *A*

North Carolina

East Carolina University *M*

North Dakota

North Dakota State University *M, D*

Ohio

Cleveland State University *M*
Ohio Business College: Sandusky *A*
Stark State College of Technology *A*

Oregon

Oregon State University *M*
Portland State University *M*

Pennsylvania

Allegheny College *B*
Carnegie Mellon University *M, D*
DeVry University
Fort Washington *B*
Drexel University *B, M*
Penn State
Erie, The Behrend College *B*
Robert Morris University *B*
Widener University *M*

South Carolina

Claflin University *B*

South Dakota

South Dakota State University *B*

Texas

DeVry University
Irving *B*
Southern Methodist University *M*
Texas Tech University *M*
University of Houston
Clear Lake *M*
University of Texas
Arlington *B*
Dallas *B, M, D*

Vermont

Champlain College *B*

Virginia

DeVry University
Arlington *B*
George Mason University *D*
Liberty University *B*

Washington

DeVry University
Federal Way *B*
Seattle University *M*
South Seattle Community College *A*

West Virginia

West Virginia University *M*

Wisconsin

Carroll University *B, M*
Herzing University *A, B*
Milwaukee School of Engineering *B*
University of Wisconsin
La Crosse *M*

Soil chemistry/physics

Tennessee

University of Tennessee
Knoxville *B, M, D*

Soil science

Alabama
Alabama Agricultural and Mechanical
    University *D*
Auburn University *B, M, D*
Tuskegee University *B, M*

Arizona
Prescott College *B, M*
University of Arizona *B, M, D*

California
California Polytechnic State
    University: San Luis Obispo *B*
Merced College *A*
Modesto Junior College *A*
San Joaquin Delta College *A*
University of California
    Davis *B*

Colorado
Colorado Mountain College *A*
Colorado State University *B, M, D*

Delaware
Delaware State University *B*
University of Delaware *B, M, D*

Florida
University of Florida *B, M, D*

Hawaii
University of Hawaii
    Hilo *B*

Idaho
University of Idaho *B, M, D*

Iowa
Iowa State University *M, D*

Kentucky
University of Kentucky *D*

Maine
University of Maine *B, M*

Michigan
Michigan State University *B, M, D*

Minnesota
Southwest Minnesota State
    University *B*
University of Minnesota
    Twin Cities *M, D*

Missouri
University of Missouri
    Columbia *B, M, D*

Nebraska
University of Nebraska
    Lincoln *B*

New Hampshire
University of New Hampshire *M*

New Mexico
New Mexico State University *B*

New York
Cornell University *M, D*
State University of New York
    College of Environmental Science
    and Forestry *M, D*

North Carolina
North Carolina State University *M, D*

North Dakota
North Dakota State University *B, M, D*

Ohio
Ohio State University
    Agricultural Technical Institute *A*
    Columbus Campus *D*

Oklahoma
Eastern Oklahoma State College *A*
Oklahoma State University *B, M*

Oregon
Eastern Oregon University *B*
Oregon State University *M, D*

Pennsylvania
Penn State
    Abington *B*
    Altoona *B*
    Beaver *B*
    Berks *B*
    Brandywine *B*
    DuBois *B*
    Erie, The Behrend College *B*
    Fayette, The Eberly Campus *B*
    Greater Allegheny *B*
    Hazleton *B*
    Lehigh Valley *B*
    Mont Alto *B*
    New Kensington *B*
    Schuylkill *B*
    Shenango *B*
    University Park *B, M, D*
    Wilkes-Barre *B*
    Worthington Scranton *B*
    York *B*

Tennessee
Middle Tennessee State University *B*
Tennessee Technological University *B*

Texas
Prairie View A&M University *M*
Texas A&M University *B, M, D*
Texas A&M University
    Commerce *B*
    Kingsville *M*
Texas Tech University *M*

Utah
Utah State University *B, M, D*

Virginia
Mountain Empire Community
    College *A*

Washington
Spokane Community College *A*
Washington State University *B, M, D*

West Virginia
West Virginia University *B*

Wisconsin
University of Wisconsin
    Madison *B, M, D*
    River Falls *B*
    Stevens Point *B*

Wyoming
Northwest College *A*
University of Wyoming *M, D*

Solar energy technology

Arizona
Coconino County Community
    College *A*

California
Cabrillo College *A*

Colorado
Red Rocks Community College *C*

Michigan
Henry Ford Community College *C*

Minnesota
Century Community and Technical
    College *C, A*

Missouri
Crowder College *A*

Nevada
Truckee Meadows Community
    College *C, A*

New Mexico
San Juan College *C, A*

North Carolina
Appalachian State University *B*

Solid-state/ low-temperature physics

Massachusetts
Tufts University *M, D*

New York
State University of New York
    Albany *M, D*

Wisconsin
University of Wisconsin
    Madison *M, D*

Somatic bodywork

California
California Institute of Integral
    Studies *M*

Vermont
Goddard College *B, M*

South Asian languages

Illinois
University of Chicago *B, D*

Minnesota
University of Minnesota
    Twin Cities *M, D*

Missouri
University of Missouri
    Columbia *B*

New Hampshire
Dartmouth College *B*

Washington
University of Washington *B*

South Asian studies

California
Claremont McKenna College *B*

Georgia
Emory University *B*

Illinois
University of Chicago *B, D*

Massachusetts
Bard College at Simon's Rock *B*
Hampshire College *B*
Wellesley College *B*

Michigan
Oakland University *B*
University of Michigan *M*

Minnesota
University of Minnesota
    Twin Cities *M, D*

Missouri
University of Missouri
    Columbia *B*

New York
State University of New York
    Binghamton *B*

Ohio
College of Wooster *B*

Pennsylvania
University of Pennsylvania *B, M, D*

Rhode Island
Brown University *B*

Vermont
Marlboro College *B*

Washington
University of Washington *B, M*

Wisconsin
University of Wisconsin
    Madison *B, M, D*

Southeast Asian languages

Washington
University of Washington *B*

Southeast Asian studies

California
Claremont McKenna College *B*
University of California
    Berkeley *B*
    Los Angeles *B*
    Riverside *D*

Massachusetts
Bard College at Simon's Rock *B*

Michigan
University of Michigan *M*

Ohio
Ohio State University
    Columbus Campus *M*
Ohio University *M*

Vermont
Marlboro College *B*
Middlebury College *B*

Washington
University of Washington *B, M*

Wisconsin
University of Wisconsin
    Madison *M*

Spanish

Alabama
Auburn University *B, M*
Birmingham-Southern College *B*
Oakwood University *B*
Samford University *B*
Spring Hill College *B, T*
Talladega College *B*
University of Alabama *B*

Alaska
University of Alaska
  Anchorage *B*

Arizona
Arizona State University *B, M, D*
Arizona Western College *A*
Northern Arizona University *B, M*
Prescott College *B, M*
University of Arizona *B, M, D*

Arkansas
Arkansas Tech University *M*
Harding University *B*
Henderson State University *B*
Hendrix College *B*
John Brown University *B*
Lyon College *B*
Ouachita Baptist University *B*
Southern Arkansas University *B*
University of Arkansas *B, M*
University of Arkansas
  Fort Smith *B*
  Little Rock *B*
University of Central Arkansas *B, M*

California
Allan Hancock College *A*
Azusa Pacific University *B*
Bakersfield College *A*
Biola University *B*
Cabrillo College *A*
California Baptist University *B*
California Lutheran University *B*
California State Polytechnic
  University: Pomona *B*
California State University
  Bakersfield *B*
  Chico *B*
  Dominguez Hills *B*
  East Bay *B*
  Fresno *B, M*
  Fullerton *B, M*
  Long Beach *B, M*
  Los Angeles *B, M*
  Northridge *B, M*
  Sacramento *B, M*
  San Bernardino *B, M, T*
  San Marcos *B, M*
  Stanislaus *B*
California State University: Channel
  Islands *B*
Canada College *A*
Cerritos College *A*
Chabot College *A*
Chaffey College *A*
Chapman University *B*
Citrus College *A*
Claremont McKenna College *B*
College of Alameda *A*
College of Marin: Kentfield *A*
College of San Mateo *A*
College of the Canyons *A*
College of the Desert *A*
College of the Siskiyous *A*
Copper Mountain College *A*
Crafton Hills College *A*
Cypress College *A*
De Anza College *A*
El Camino College *A*
El Camino College: Compton
  Center *A*

Foothill College *A*
Fresno City College *A*
Fresno Pacific University *B*
Gavilan College *A*
Glendale Community College *A*
Golden West College *A*
Grossmont College *A*
Holy Names University *B*
Humboldt State University *B*
Imperial Valley College *A*
Irvine Valley College *A*
La Sierra University *B*
Lake Tahoe Community College *A*
Long Beach City College *A*
Los Angeles City College *A*
Los Angeles Mission College *A*
Los Angeles Pierce College *A*
Los Angeles Southwest College *A*
Los Angeles Valley College *A*
Loyola Marymount University *B*
Mendocino College *A*
Merced College *A*
Merritt College *A*
Mills College *B*
MiraCosta College *A*
Modesto Junior College *A*
Mount St. Mary's College *B*
Occidental College *B*
Orange Coast College *A*
Oxnard College *A*
Pacific Union College *B*
Pepperdine University *B*
Pitzer College *B*
Point Loma Nazarene University *B*
Pomona College *B*
St. Mary's College of California *B*
San Diego City College *A*
San Diego Mesa College *A*
San Diego State University *B, M*
San Francisco State University *B, M*
San Joaquin Delta College *A*
San Jose State University *B, M*
Santa Barbara City College *A*
Santa Clara University *B*
Santa Rosa Junior College *A*
Santiago Canyon College *A*
Scripps College *B*
Skyline College *A*
Solano Community College *A*
Sonoma State University *B*
Southwestern College *A*
Stanford University *B, M, D*
University of California
  Berkeley *B, M, D*
  Davis *B, M, D*
  Irvine *B, M, D*
  Los Angeles *B, M, D*
  Riverside *B, M, D*
  San Diego *B, M*
  Santa Barbara *B, M, D*
University of La Verne *B*
University of Redlands *B*
University of San Diego *B*
University of San Francisco *B*
University of Southern
  California *B, M, D*
University of the Pacific *B*
West Los Angeles College *A*
Westmont College *B*
Whittier College *B*

Colorado
Adams State College *B, M*
Colorado College *B*
Colorado State University *B, M*
Fort Lewis College *B*
Mesa State College *B*
Metropolitan State College of
  Denver *B, T*
Red Rocks Community College *A*
Regis University *B*
Trinidad State Junior College *A*
University of Colorado
  Boulder *B, M, D*

Colorado Springs *B*
Denver *B, M*
University of Denver *B*
University of Northern Colorado *B, T*
Western State College of Colorado *B*

Connecticut
Albertus Magnus College *B*
Central Connecticut State
  University *B, M*
Connecticut College *B*
Eastern Connecticut State
  University *B*
Fairfield University *B*
Quinnipiac University *B*
Sacred Heart University *B*
Saint Joseph College *B*
Southern Connecticut State
  University *B, M, T*
Trinity College *B*
University of Connecticut *B, M, D*
Wesleyan University *B*
Western Connecticut State
  University *B*
Yale University *B, M, D*

Delaware
Delaware State University *B, M*
University of Delaware *B, M, T*

District of Columbia
American University *B, M*
Catholic University of
  America *B, M, D*
Gallaudet University *B*
George Washington University *B*
Georgetown University *B, M, D*
Howard University *B, M, D*
University of the District of
  Columbia *B*

Florida
Barry University *B*
Eckerd College *B*
Flagler College *B*
Florida Agricultural and Mechanical
  University *B*
Florida Atlantic University *B, M*
Florida Gulf Coast University *B*
Florida International
  University *B, M, D*
Florida Southern College *B*
Florida State University *B, M, D*
Jacksonville University *B*
New College of Florida *B*
Northwest Florida State College *A*
Rollins College *B*
State College of Florida,
  Manatee-Sarasota *A*
Stetson University *B*
University of Central Florida *B, M*
University of Florida *B*
University of Miami *B, D*
University of North Florida *B*
University of South Florida *B, M*
University of Tampa *A, B*

Georgia
Agnes Scott College *B*
Albany State University *B*
Armstrong Atlantic State
  University *B, T*
Augusta State University *B*
Berry College *B*
Brewton-Parker College *B*
Clark Atlanta University *B, M*
Columbus State University *B*
Emory University *B, D*
Georgia College and State
  University *B*
Georgia State University *B, M*
LaGrange College *B*
Mercer University *B*

Morehouse College *B*
North Georgia College & State
  University *B*
Oglethorpe University *B*
Piedmont College *B*
Shorter College *B*
Southern Polytechnic State
  University *C*
Spelman College *B*
University of Georgia *B, M*
University of West Georgia *B*
Valdosta State University *B*
Wesleyan College *B*
Young Harris College *A*

Hawaii
University of Hawaii
  Manoa *B, M*

Idaho
Boise State University *B*
College of Idaho *B*
Idaho State University *A, B*
Northwest Nazarene University *B*
University of Idaho *B, M*

Illinois
Augustana College *B, T*
Aurora University *B*
Benedictine University *B, T*
Blackburn College *B*
Bradley University *B, T*
Chicago State University *B*
City Colleges of Chicago
  Harold Washington College *A*
DePaul University *B*
Dominican University *B*
Elmhurst College *B, T*
Greenville College *B*
Illinois College *B, T*
Illinois State University *B, T*
Illinois Wesleyan University *B*
John Wood Community College *A*
Kishwaukee College *A*
Knox College *B*
Lake Forest College *B*
Loyola University Chicago *B, M*
MacMurray College *B, T*
Millikin University *B*
Monmouth College *B, T*
North Central College *B, T*
North Park University *B*
Northeastern Illinois University *B*
Northern Illinois University *B, M, T*
Northwestern University *B*
Olivet Nazarene University *B, T*
Principia College *B*
Richland Community College *A*
Rockford College *B*
Roosevelt University *B, M*
Saint Xavier University *B*
South Suburban College of Cook
  County *A*
Southern Illinois University
  Carbondale *B*
Trinity Christian College *B, T*
Triton College *A*
University of Chicago *B, D*
University of Illinois
  Chicago *B, M, D*
  Urbana-Champaign *B, M, D*
Western Illinois University *B*
Wheaton College *B, T*

Indiana
Anderson University *B*
Ball State University *B, T*
Bethel College *B*
Butler University *B*
DePauw University *B*
Earlham College *B*
Franklin College *B*
Goshen College *B*

Grace College B
Hanover College B
Huntington University B
Indiana University
  Bloomington B, M, D
  Northwest A, B
  South Bend B
  Southeast B
Indiana University-Purdue University
  Fort Wayne A, B, T
Indiana University-Purdue University
  Indianapolis B
Indiana Wesleyan University B
Manchester College B, T
Marian University B, T
Purdue University B, M, D
Purdue University
  Calumet B
Saint Mary's College B
Taylor University B
University of Evansville B
University of Indianapolis B
University of Notre Dame B, M
University of Southern Indiana B, T
Valparaiso University B
Wabash College B

Iowa
Briar Cliff University B
Buena Vista University B, T
Central College B, T
Clarke College B, T
Coe College B
Cornell College B, T
Dordt College B
Graceland University B, T
Grand View University A, M
Grinnell College B
Loras College B
Luther College B
Marshalltown Community College A
Morningside College B
Northwestern College B, T
St. Ambrose University B, T
Simpson College B
University of Iowa B, M, D, T
University of Northern Iowa B, M
Wartburg College B, T

Kansas
Baker University B, T
Benedictine College B
Butler Community College A
Central Christian College of Kansas A
Coffeyville Community College A
Friends University B
Kansas Wesleyan University B, T
McPherson College B, T
MidAmerica Nazarene University B
Pittsburg State University B
University of Kansas B, M, D
Washburn University B
Wichita State University B, M, T

Kentucky
Asbury College B, T
Bellarmine University B
Berea College B, T
Bluegrass Community and Technical
  College A
Brescia University B
Centre College B
Eastern Kentucky University B
Georgetown College B
Kentucky Wesleyan College B
Morehead State University B
Murray State University B, T
Northern Kentucky University B
Thomas More College A, B
Transylvania University B, T
University of Kentucky B, M, D
University of Louisville B, M
University of the Cumberlands B
Western Kentucky University B, T

Louisiana
Centenary College of Louisiana B, T
Dillard University B
Grambling State University B
Louisiana College T
Louisiana State University
  Shreveport B
Louisiana State University and
  Agricultural and Mechanical
  College B, M
Louisiana Tech University B
Loyola University New Orleans B
McNeese State University B
Southeastern Louisiana University B
Southern University and Agricultural
  and Mechanical College B
Tulane University B, M, D
University of Louisiana at Monroe B
University of New Orleans B
Xavier University of Louisiana B

Maine
Bates College B, T
Bowdoin College B
Colby College B
University of Maine B

Maryland
Allegany College of Maryland A
College of Notre Dame of Maryland B
Frostburg State University T
Goucher College B
Hood College B
Howard Community College A
Johns Hopkins University B, M, D
Loyola University Maryland B
McDaniel College B
Mount St. Mary's University B, T
Salisbury University B, T
Towson University T
University of Maryland
  College Park B, M, D
Washington College B, T

Massachusetts
Amherst College B
Anna Maria College B
Assumption College B
Bard College at Simon's Rock B
Boston College B, M, D
Boston University B, M, D
Brandeis University B
Bridgewater State College B
Clark University B
College of the Holy Cross B
Elms College B, M, T
Emmanuel College B
Gordon College B
Merrimack College B
Mount Holyoke College B
Northeastern University B
Regis College B
Salem State College B, M
Simmons College B, M
Smith College B
Stonehill College B
Suffolk University B
Tufts University B
University of Massachusetts
  Amherst B, M, D
  Boston B
  Dartmouth B
Wellesley College B
Wheaton College B
Williams College B
Worcester State College B, M, T

Michigan
Adrian College A, B, T
Albion College B, T
Alma College B, T
Andrews University B
Aquinas College B, T

Calvin College B, T
Central Michigan University B, M
Cornerstone University B
Eastern Michigan University B, M
Grand Valley State University B
Hillsdale College B
Hope College B
Kalamazoo College B
Lake Superior State University B
Lansing Community College A
Madonna University B
Michigan State University B, M, D
Michigan Technological University T
Northern Michigan University B
Oakland University B, T
Saginaw Valley State University B, T
Siena Heights University B
Spring Arbor University B, T
University of Michigan B, M, D
University of Michigan
  Dearborn B
  Flint B, T
Western Michigan University B, M, D

Minnesota
Augsburg College B
Bemidji State University B
Bethel University B
Carleton College B
College of St. Benedict B
College of St. Scholastica B
Concordia College: Moorhead B, T
Gustavus Adolphus College B
Hamline University B
Macalester College B
Minnesota State University
  Mankato B, M, T
  Moorhead B
Northwestern College B
St. Catherine University B
Saint Cloud State University B
St. John's University B
St. Mary's University of Minnesota B
St. Olaf College B
Southwest Minnesota State
  University B
University of Minnesota
  Duluth B
  Morris B
  Twin Cities B, M, D
University of St. Thomas B
Winona State University B

Mississippi
Blue Mountain College B
Millsaps College B
Mississippi College B
Mississippi University for Women B, T
University of Mississippi B

Missouri
Central Methodist University B
College of the Ozarks B
Crowder College A
Drury University B, T
Evangel University B, T
Lincoln University B
Lindenwood University B
Missouri Southern State University B
Missouri State University B
Missouri Western State University B, T
Northwest Missouri State
  University B
Park University B
Rockhurst University B
St. Charles Community College A
Saint Louis University B, M
Southeast Missouri State University B
Southwest Baptist University B
Truman State University B
University of Central Missouri B, T
University of Missouri
  Columbia B, M

Kansas City B
St. Louis B
Washington University in St.
  Louis B, M, D
Webster University B
Westminster College B
William Jewell College B
William Woods University B

Montana
Montana State University
  Billings B, T
University of Montana B, M

Nebraska
Chadron State College B
College of Saint Mary B, T
Concordia University B, T
Creighton University B
Dana College B
Doane College B
Nebraska Wesleyan University B
Union College B
University of Nebraska
  Kearney B, M, T
  Lincoln B
  Omaha B
Wayne State College B
Western Nebraska Community
  College A

Nevada
University of Nevada
  Las Vegas B, M
  Reno B

New Hampshire
Dartmouth College B, T
Keene State College B
Plymouth State University B
Rivier College B, M, T
Saint Anselm College B, T
University of New Hampshire B, M

New Jersey
Caldwell College B
The College of New Jersey B, T
College of St. Elizabeth B, T
Drew University B
Fairleigh Dickinson University
  College at Florham B
  Metropolitan Campus B
Georgian Court University B
Kean University B, T
Montclair State University B, M, T
New Jersey City University B
Princeton University B, M, D
Ramapo College of New Jersey B
Rider University B
Rowan University B
Rutgers, The State University of New
  Jersey
  Camden Regional Campus B, T
  New Brunswick/Piscataway
    Campus B, M, D, T
  Newark Regional Campus B, T
Saint Peter's College B
Seton Hall University B, T
William Paterson University of New
  Jersey B

New Mexico
Eastern New Mexico University B
New Mexico Highlands University B
New Mexico Junior College A
New Mexico State University M
Santa Fe Community College A
University of New Mexico B, M, D
Western New Mexico University B

New York
Adelphi University B
Alfred University B

Bard College *B*
Barnard College *B*
Canisius College *B*
City University of New York
  Baruch College *B*
  Brooklyn College *B, M*
  City College *B, M*
  College of Staten Island *B*
  Hunter College *B, M*
  Lehman College *B, M*
  Queens College *B, M, T*
  York College *B*
Colgate University *B*
College of Mount St. Vincent *B, T*
College of New Rochelle *B, T*
College of Saint Rose *B*
Columbia University *B*
Columbia University
  School of General Studies *B*
Cornell University *B, D*
Daemen College *B, T*
Dominican College of Blauvelt *B*
Elmira College *B, T*
Fordham University *B, M*
Hamilton College *B*
Hartwick College *B, T*
Hobart and William Smith Colleges *B*
Hofstra University *B, M*
Houghton College *B*
Iona College *B, M*
Ithaca College *B, T*
Le Moyne College *B*
Long Island University
  C. W. Post Campus *B, M*
Manhattan College *B*
Marist College *B*
Mercy College *B*
Molloy College *B*
Mount Saint Mary College *B*
Nazareth College *B*
New York University *B, M, D*
Niagara University *B*
Orange County Community College *A*
Pace University *B*
Roberts Wesleyan College *B*
Russell Sage College *B*
Saint Bonaventure University *B*
St. Francis College *B*
St. John Fisher College *B*
St. John's University *B, M*
St. Joseph's College: Suffolk
  Campus *B*
St. Lawrence University *B, T*
St. Thomas Aquinas College *B*
Siena College *B, T*
Skidmore College *B*
State University of New York
  Albany *B, M, D*
  Binghamton *B, M*
  Buffalo *B, M, D*
  College at Brockport *B, T*
  College at Buffalo *B*
  College at Cortland *B*
  College at Fredonia *B, T*
  College at Geneseo *B, T*
  College at Old Westbury *B, T*
  College at Oneonta *B*
  College at Plattsburgh *B*
  College at Potsdam *B*
  New Paltz *B*
  Oswego *B*
  Stony Brook *B, M, D*
Syracuse University *B, M*
Union College *B*
United States Military Academy *B*
University of Rochester *B, M*
Vassar College *B*
Wagner College *B*
Wells College *B*

North Carolina

Appalachian State University *B*
Barton College *B, T*
Campbell University *B*

Catawba College *B*
Davidson College *B*
Duke University *B, M, D*
East Carolina University *B*
Elon University *B*
Gardner-Webb University *B*
Greensboro College *B, T*
Guilford College *B, T*
High Point University *B*
Johnson C. Smith University *B*
Lenoir-Rhyne University *B*
Mars Hill College *B*
Meredith College *B*
Methodist University *A, B, T*
North Carolina Central University *B*
North Carolina State University *B, M*
Peace College *B*
Salem College *B*
Shaw University *B*
University of North Carolina
  Asheville *B, T*
  Chapel Hill *B, M, D*
  Charlotte *B, M*
  Greensboro *B*
  Pembroke *B*
  Wilmington *B, M*
Wake Forest University *B*
Western Carolina University *B*
Wingate University *B*
Winston-Salem State University *B*

North Dakota

Dickinson State University *B*
Jamestown College *B*
Minot State University *B*
North Dakota State University *B, T*
University of North Dakota *B*

Ohio

Ashland University *B, T*
Baldwin-Wallace College *B*
Bluffton University *B*
Bowling Green State University *B, M*
Capital University *B*
Case Western Reserve University *B*
Cedarville University *B*
Cleveland State University *B, M*
College of Wooster *B*
Denison University *B*
Franciscan University of
  Steubenville *B*
Heidelberg University *B*
Hiram College *B, T*
John Carroll University *B*
Kent State University *B, M*
Kenyon College *B*
Malone University *B*
Marietta College *B*
Miami University
  Oxford Campus *B, M*
Mount Union College *B*
Mount Vernon Nazarene University *B*
Muskingum University *B*
Notre Dame College *T*
Oberlin College *B*
Ohio Northern University *B*
Ohio State University
  Columbus Campus *B, M, D*
Ohio University *B, M*
Ohio Wesleyan University *B*
Otterbein College *B*
University of Akron *B, M*
University of Cincinnati *B, M, D, T*
University of Dayton *B*
University of Findlay *B, T*
University of Rio Grande *A, B*
University of Toledo *B, M*
Walsh University *B*
Wilmington College *B*
Wittenberg University *B*
Wright State University *B*
Xavier University *A, B*
Youngstown State University *B*

Oklahoma

Northeastern State University *B*
Oklahoma Baptist University *B, T*
Oklahoma Christian University *B*
Oklahoma City Community College *A*
Oklahoma City University *B*
Oklahoma State University *B*
Oral Roberts University *B*
Southeastern Oklahoma State
  University *B*
Southern Nazarene University *B*
Tulsa Community College *A*
University of Central Oklahoma *B*
University of Oklahoma *B, M, D*
University of Tulsa *B*
Western Oklahoma State College *A*

Oregon

George Fox University *B*
Lewis & Clark College *B*
Linfield College *B, T*
Linn-Benton Community College *A*
Oregon State University *B*
Pacific University *B*
Portland State University *B, M*
Reed College *B*
Southern Oregon University *B*
University of Oregon *B, M*
University of Portland *B, T*
Western Oregon University *B, T*
Willamette University *B*

Pennsylvania

Albright College *B, T*
Allegheny College *B*
Arcadia University *B*
Bloomsburg University of
  Pennsylvania *B, T*
Bryn Mawr College *B*
Bucknell University *B*
Cabrini College *B*
California University of
  Pennsylvania *B*
Carlow University *B*
Carnegie Mellon University *B*
Cedar Crest College *B*
Chatham University *B*
Chestnut Hill College *A, B*
Cheyney University of
  Pennsylvania *B, T*
Clarion University of Pennsylvania *B*
DeSales University *B, T*
Dickinson College *B*
Duquesne University *B*
East Stroudsburg University of
  Pennsylvania *B, T*
Eastern University *B*
Edinboro University of
  Pennsylvania *B, T*
Elizabethtown College *B*
Franklin & Marshall College *B*
Gettysburg College *B*
Grove City College *B, T*
Haverford College *B, T*
Holy Family University *B*
Immaculata University *A, B, T*
Indiana University of Pennsylvania *B*
Juniata College *B*
King's College *B, T*
Kutztown University of
  Pennsylvania *B, M, T*
La Roche College *B*
La Salle University *B, T*
Lafayette College *B*
Lebanon Valley College *B*
Lehigh University *B*
Lincoln University *B*
Lock Haven University of
  Pennsylvania *B*
Lycoming College *B*
Mansfield University of
  Pennsylvania *B, T*
Marywood University *B*
Messiah College *B*

Millersville University of
  Pennsylvania *B, M, T*
Moravian College *B, T*
Muhlenberg College *B*
Penn State
  Abington *B*
  Altoona *B*
  Beaver *B*
  Berks *B*
  Brandywine *B*
  DuBois *B*
  Erie, The Behrend College *B*
  Fayette, The Eberly Campus *B*
  Greater Allegheny *B*
  Hazleton *B*
  Lehigh Valley *B*
  Mont Alto *B*
  New Kensington *B*
  Schuylkill *B*
  Shenango *B*
  University Park *B, M, D*
  Wilkes-Barre *B*
  Worthington Scranton *B*
  York *B*
Rosemont College *B*
St. Francis University *B*
Saint Joseph's University *B*
St. Vincent College *B*
Seton Hill University *B, T*
Shippensburg University of
  Pennsylvania *B, T*
Slippery Rock University of
  Pennsylvania *B, T*
Susquehanna University *B, T*
Swarthmore College *B*
Temple University *B, M, D*
University of Pennsylvania *B*
University of Pittsburgh *B, M, D*
University of Scranton *B, T*
Ursinus College *B, T*
Villanova University *B, M*
Washington & Jefferson College *B*
West Chester University of
  Pennsylvania *B, M, T*
Westminster College *B*
Widener University *B, T*
Wilkes University *B*
Wilson College *B*
York College of Pennsylvania *B*

Puerto Rico

Bayamon Central University *B*
Caribbean University *B*
Inter American University of Puerto
  Rico
  Metropolitan Campus *B, M*
Pontifical Catholic University of
  Puerto Rico *B, M*
Universidad Adventista de las
  Antillas *B*
University of Puerto Rico
  Aguadilla *A*
  Cayey University College *B*
  Rio Piedras *B, M, D*

Rhode Island

Brown University *B, M, D*
Providence College *B*
Rhode Island College *B*
Salve Regina University *B*
University of Rhode Island *B, M*

South Carolina

Anderson University *B*
Bob Jones University *B*
Charleston Southern University *B*
Clemson University *B*
Coastal Carolina University *B*
Coker College *B*
College of Charleston *B, T*
Columbia College *B*
Converse College *B*
Erskine College *B*
Francis Marion University *B*

Furman University B, T
Lander University B, T
Presbyterian College B, T
University of South Carolina B, M
University of South Carolina
  Beaufort B
  Upstate B
Winthrop University M
Wofford College B, T

South Dakota

Augustana College B, T
Black Hills State University B
Northern State University B
South Dakota State University B
University of Sioux Falls B
University of South Dakota B

Tennessee

Austin Peay State University B
Belmont University B, T
Bryan College B
Carson-Newman College B, T
Fisk University B
King College B, T
Lambuth University B
Lee University B
Lipscomb University B
Maryville College B, T
Milligan College T
Rhodes College B
Southern Adventist University B
Tennessee State University B
Tennessee Technological
  University B, T
Union University B, T
University of Tennessee
  Knoxville B, M
  Martin B
University of the South B
Vanderbilt University B, M, D

Texas

Abilene Christian University B
Angelo State University B, T
Austin College B
Austin Community College A
Baptist University of the Americas B
Baylor University B, M, T
Blinn College A
Cisco College A
Coastal Bend College A
East Texas Baptist University B
Galveston College A
Hardin-Simmons University B
Houston Baptist University B
Howard Payne University B, T
Kilgore College A
Lamar University B
Laredo Community College A
Lon Morris College A
McMurry University B, T
Midland College A
Midwestern State University B
Northeast Texas Community
  College A
Our Lady of the Lake University of San
  Antonio B
Paris Junior College A
Prairie View A&M University B
Rice University B, M
St. Edward's University B
St. Mary's University B
St. Philip's College A
Sam Houston State University B
South Plains College A
South Texas College A
Southern Methodist University B
Southwestern University B, T
Stephen F. Austin State University B, T
Sul Ross State University B
Tarleton State University B, T
Texas A&M International
  University B, M, T

Texas A&M University B, M
Texas A&M University
  Commerce B, M
  Corpus Christi B, T
  Kingsville B, M
Texas Christian University B
Texas Lutheran University B
Texas Southern University B
Texas State University: San
  Marcos B, M, T
Texas Tech University B, M, D
Texas Wesleyan University B
Trinity University B
Trinity Valley Community College A
Tyler Junior College A
University of Dallas B
University of Houston B, M, D
University of Houston
  Downtown B
University of Mary Hardin-Baylor B, T
University of North Texas B, M
University of St. Thomas B
University of Texas
  Arlington B, M
  Austin B, M, D
  Brownsville - Texas Southmost
    College B, M
  El Paso B, M
  Pan American B, M
  San Antonio B, M
  Tyler B
  of the Permian Basin B, M
University of the Incarnate Word B
Wayland Baptist University B, T
West Texas A&M University B

Utah

Brigham Young University B, M
Snow College A
University of Utah B, T
Utah State University B
Utah Valley University B
Weber State University B

Vermont

Bennington College B, M
Castleton State College B
Marlboro College B
Middlebury College B, M, D
Norwich University B
St. Michael's College B
University of Vermont B

Virginia

Bridgewater College B
Christopher Newport University B
College of William and Mary B
Eastern Mennonite University B
Emory & Henry College B, T
Ferrum College B
Hampden-Sydney College B
Hampton University B
Hollins University B
Liberty University B, T
Longwood University B, T
Lynchburg College B
Mary Baldwin College B
Old Dominion University B, T
Randolph College B
Randolph-Macon College B
Roanoke College B, T
Shenandoah University B
Southern Virginia University B
Sweet Briar College B
University of Richmond B, T
University of Virginia B, M, D
University of Virginia's College at
  Wise B, T
Virginia Wesleyan College B
Washington and Lee University B

Washington

Centralia College A

Eastern Washington University B
Everett Community College A
Gonzaga University B
Pacific Lutheran University B
Seattle Pacific University B
Seattle University B
University of Puget Sound B, T
University of Washington B
Walla Walla University B
Washington State University B, M
Western Washington University B
Whitman College B
Whitworth University B, T

West Virginia

Bethany College B
Davis and Elkins College B
Fairmont State University B
Marshall University M
Potomac State College of West
  Virginia University A
Shepherd University B
West Virginia University T
Wheeling Jesuit University B

Wisconsin

Beloit College B
Cardinal Stritch University B
Carroll University B
Carthage College B
Concordia University Wisconsin B
Edgewood College B
Lakeland College B
Lawrence University B, T
Marian University B
Marquette University B, M
Mount Mary College B, T
Ripon College B, T
St. Norbert College B, T
Silver Lake College T
University of Wisconsin
  Eau Claire B
  Green Bay B, T
  La Crosse B, T
  Madison B, M, D
  Milwaukee B
  Oshkosh B
  Parkside B, T
  Platteville B
  River Falls B
  Stevens Point B, T
  Whitewater B, T
Viterbo University B, T
Wisconsin Lutheran College B

Wyoming

Laramie County Community
  College A
University of Wyoming B, M
Western Wyoming Community
  College A

Spanish/Iberian studies

California

Claremont McKenna College B
Scripps College B

Florida

New College of Florida B

Iowa

Coe College B

Massachusetts

Bard College at Simon's Rock B
Elms College B

Minnesota

Concordia College: Moorhead B, T

New Hampshire

Dartmouth College B

New York

Bard College B
Barnard College B
Columbia University B

Ohio

University of Cincinnati B

Pennsylvania

Arcadia University B

Tennessee

Vanderbilt University B

Virginia

Emory & Henry College B

Spanish teacher education

Alabama

Birmingham-Southern College T

Arizona

Northern Arizona University B, T
Prescott College B, M, T
University of Arizona B

Arkansas

Arkansas State University B, T
Harding University B, T
Ouachita Baptist University B, T
Southern Arkansas University B, T
University of Arkansas
  Fort Smith B

California

Azusa Pacific University T
California State University
  Chico B, T
  Long Beach T
  San Bernardino M, T
Humboldt State University T
Pacific Union College T
San Francisco State University T
Stanford University M, T
University of the Pacific T
Vanguard University of Southern
  California T

Colorado

Adams State College B, M, T
Colorado State University B, T
Colorado State University
  Pueblo T
Metropolitan State College of
  Denver T
University of Colorado
  Colorado Springs T

Connecticut

Albertus Magnus College B, T
Fairfield University T
Quinnipiac University B, M
Sacred Heart University T
Saint Joseph College T
Southern Connecticut State
  University B, M, T

Delaware

Delaware State University B
University of Delaware B, T

District of Columbia

Catholic University of America B

Florida
Barry University *T*
Stetson University *B*

Georgia
Armstrong Atlantic State University *T*
Georgia Southern University *M*
Piedmont College *M, T*
University of West Georgia *M*
Valdosta State University *B*

Idaho
Boise State University *B, T*
Brigham Young University-Idaho *T*
Northwest Nazarene University *B*
University of Idaho *M, T*

Illinois
Augustana College *B, T*
Benedictine University *T*
Bradley University *B*
DePaul University *M, T*
Dominican University *T*
Elmhurst College *B*
Greenville College *B, T*
Illinois College *T*
Illinois Wesleyan University *B*
Knox College *T*
MacMurray College *B, T*
North Park University *T*
Olivet Nazarene University *B, T*
Rockford College *T*
Saint Xavier University *B*
Trinity Christian College *B, T*
University of Illinois
  Chicago *B*
  Urbana-Champaign *B, M, T*

Indiana
Anderson University *B, T*
Butler University *T*
Franklin College *B, T*
Goshen College *B, T*
Grace College *B*
Indiana University
  Bloomington *B, T*
  Northwest *B*
  South Bend *B, T*
Indiana University-Purdue University
  Fort Wayne *B, T*
Indiana University-Purdue University
  Indianapolis *B, T*
Indiana Wesleyan University *T*
Manchester College *B, T*
Purdue University *B, M, D*
Saint Mary's College *T*
St. Mary-of-the-Woods College *B, T*
Taylor University *B, T*
University of Evansville *B, T*
University of Indianapolis *B, T*
Valparaiso University *B*

Iowa
Buena Vista University *B, T*
Central College *T*
Cornell College *B, T*
Dordt College *B*
Graceland University *T*
Grand View University *T*
Iowa State University *T*
Loras College *T*
Morningside College *B*
Northwestern College *T*
St. Ambrose University *B, T*
Simpson College *T*
University of Iowa *T*
Wartburg College *T*

Kansas
Bethel College *T*
Central Christian College of Kansas *A*
Friends University *B*
McPherson College *B, T*

MidAmerica Nazarene University *B, T*
Pittsburg State University *B, T*
University of St. Mary *T*
Washburn University *B*

Kentucky
Brescia University *B, T*
Eastern Kentucky University *B*
Kentucky Wesleyan College *B, T*
University of the Cumberlands *B, T*

Louisiana
Centenary College of Louisiana *B, T*
Louisiana College *B*
Southeastern Louisiana University *B*
Southern University and Agricultural
  and Mechanical College *B*
University of Louisiana at Lafayette *B*
University of Louisiana at Monroe *B*
Xavier University of Louisiana *B*

Maine
University of Maine *B*

Maryland
Anne Arundel Community College *A*
Carroll Community College *A*
College of Notre Dame of Maryland *T*
Community College of Baltimore
  County *A*
Frederick Community College *A*
Hood College *T*
Howard Community College *A*
Mount St. Mary's University *T*
Salisbury University *T*
Towson University *T*

Massachusetts
Assumption College *T*
Bridgewater State College *T*
Elms College *T*
Framingham State College *M*
Salem State College *B, M*
Tufts University *T*
University of Massachusetts
  Dartmouth *T*

Michigan
Albion College *B, T*
Alma College *T*
Calvin College *B*
Central Michigan University *B*
Eastern Michigan University *B*
Grand Valley State University *T*
Hope College *B, T*
Michigan State University *B*
Northern Michigan University *B, T*
University of Michigan
  Flint *B, T*
Western Michigan University *B, T*

Minnesota
Augsburg College *T*
Bemidji State University *T*
Bethel University *B*
College of St. Benedict *T*
Concordia College: Moorhead *B, T*
Gustavus Adolphus College *T*
Minnesota State University
  Mankato *B, M, T*
  Moorhead *B*
St. Catherine University *T*
Saint Cloud State University *B, T*
St. John's University *T*
St. Mary's University of Minnesota *B*
University of Minnesota
  Duluth *B, T*
  Morris *T*
University of St. Thomas *B*
Winona State University *B, T*

Mississippi
Blue Mountain College *B*
Millsaps College *T*
Mississippi College *B*
Mississippi State University *T*

Missouri
Lindenwood University *B*
Missouri Southern State
  University *B, T*
Missouri State University *B*
Missouri Western State University *B*
Northwest Missouri State
  University *B, T*
Truman State University *M, T*
University of Central Missouri *B, M, T*
University of Missouri
  Columbia *B*
  Kansas City *B*
Washington University in St.
  Louis *B, M, T*
William Jewell College *B, T*

Montana
Montana State University
  Billings *B, T*
University of Montana *T*

Nebraska
Chadron State College *B*
Concordia University *B, T*
Creighton University *T*
Dana College *B*
Nebraska Wesleyan University *T*
University of Nebraska
  Kearney *B, T*
  Lincoln *B*

New Hampshire
Keene State College *B, M, T*
Rivier College *B, M, T*
Saint Anselm College *T*
University of New Hampshire *T*

New Jersey
Caldwell College *T*
College of St. Elizabeth *T*
County College of Morris *A*
Georgian Court University *T*
Rowan University *T*
Saint Peter's College *T*
William Paterson University of New
  Jersey *T*

New Mexico
Western New Mexico University *B*

New York
Adelphi University *M, T*
Alfred University *B, T*
City University of New York
  Brooklyn College *B, M, T*
  City College *B, M*
  College of Staten Island *B, T*
  Hunter College *B, M, T*
  Lehman College *M*
  Queens College *M, T*
College of Mount St. Vincent *T*
College of Saint Rose *B, T*
D'Youville College *M, T*
Dowling College *B, M*
Dutchess Community College *A*
Elmira College *B, T*
Fordham University *M, T*
Hobart and William Smith Colleges *T*
Hofstra University *B, M*
Houghton College *B, T*
Iona College *B, M, T*
Ithaca College *B, M, T*
Le Moyne College *T*

Long Island University
  Brooklyn Campus *B, T*
  C. W. Post Campus *B, M, T*
Manhattan College *B, T*
Marist College *B*
Molloy College *B*
New York University *M*
Niagara University *B, M, T*
Pace University *B, M, T*
Roberts Wesleyan College *B*
Saint Bonaventure University *M*
St. John Fisher College *B, M, T*
St. John's University *B, M, T*
St. Joseph's College: Suffolk
  Campus *B*
St. Lawrence University *T*
St. Thomas Aquinas College *B, T*
State University of New York
  Albany *M, T*
  Buffalo *M, T*
  College at Brockport *B, M, T*
  College at Buffalo *B*
  College at Cortland *B*
  College at Fredonia *B, T*
  College at Geneseo *B, M, T*
  College at Old Westbury *B, M, T*
  College at Oneonta *B, T*
  College at Plattsburgh *B*
  College at Potsdam *B, M*
  New Paltz *B, T*
  Oswego *B, M*
Ulster County Community College *A*
University of Rochester *M*
Vassar College *T*
Wells College *T*

North Carolina
Appalachian State University *B, T*
Campbell University *B, T*
Davidson College *T*
East Carolina University *B*
Elon University *T*
Gardner-Webb University *B*
Greensboro College *B, T*
Meredith College *T*
North Carolina Central University *B, T*
North Carolina State University *B, T*
Queens University of Charlotte *M*
Salem College *T*
University of North Carolina
  Charlotte *T*
  Greensboro *B*
  Wilmington *B*
Wake Forest University *T*
Western Carolina University *B, T*
Winston-Salem State University *B*

North Dakota
Dickinson State University *B, T*
Minot State University *B*
North Dakota State University *B, T*

Ohio
Ashland University *B, T*
Baldwin-Wallace College *T*
Bowling Green State University *M*
Case Western Reserve University *T*
Cedarville University *B*
Hiram College *T*
Kent State University *T*
Malone University *B*
Miami University
  Oxford Campus *B*
Mount Union College *T*
Mount Vernon Nazarene
  University *B, T*
Ohio Northern University *B, T*
Ohio University *B, T*
Ohio Wesleyan University *B*
Otterbein College *B*
University of Akron *B, M*
University of Dayton *B*
University of Findlay *B, M, T*
University of Toledo *B, M, T*

Youngstown State University *B, M*

Oklahoma

Northeastern State University *B*
Northwestern Oklahoma State
   University *B, T*
Oklahoma Baptist University *B, T*
Oklahoma City University *B*
Oral Roberts University *B, T*
Southeastern Oklahoma State
   University *B, T*
Southern Nazarene University *B*
University of Central Oklahoma *B*
University of Tulsa *T*

Oregon

Eastern Oregon University *B, T*
Linfield College *T*
Oregon State University *M*
Portland State University *T*
Western Oregon University *B, T*

Pennsylvania

Albright College *T*
Cabrini College *T*
DeSales University *T*
Dickinson College *T*
Duquesne University *B, M, T*
Gettysburg College *T*
Grove City College *B, T*
Holy Family University *B*
Juniata College *B, T*
King's College *T*
La Salle University *B, T*
Lebanon Valley College *T*
Lycoming College *T*
Mansfield University of
   Pennsylvania *B, T*
Marywood University *B*
Messiah College *B, T*
Moravian College *T*
Rosemont College *T*
St. Francis University *B, T*
St. Vincent College *T*
Seton Hill University *B, T*
Susquehanna University *T*
Villanova University *T*
Washington & Jefferson College *T*
Westminster College *T*
Widener University *T*
Wilson College *T*

Puerto Rico

American University of Puerto
   Rico *B, T*
Bayamon Central University *B*
Inter American University of Puerto
   Rico
   Arecibo Campus *B*
   Fajardo Campus *B, T*
   Metropolitan Campus *B*
   San German Campus *B*
Pontifical Catholic University of
   Puerto Rico *B, T*
Turabo University *B*
University of Puerto Rico
   Arecibo *B, M*
   Cayey University College *B*

Rhode Island

Rhode Island College *B, M*
Salve Regina University *B*

South Carolina

Bob Jones University *M*
Charleston Southern University *B*
Furman University *T*
Wofford College *T*

South Dakota

Augustana College *B, T*
University of South Dakota *B, M, T*

Tennessee

Belmont University *B, M, T*
Bryan College *T*
Christian Brothers University *T*
King College *T*
Lee University *B*
Lipscomb University *B, T*
Maryville College *B, T*
Southern Adventist University *B*
Union University *B, T*

Texas

Abilene Christian University *B, T*
Baylor University *T*
East Texas Baptist University *B*
Hardin-Simmons University *B, T*
Houston Baptist University *T*
Howard Payne University *B, T*
Lamar University *T*
Laredo Community College *A*
Lubbock Christian University *B*
McMurry University *B, T*
St. Edward's University *B, T*
St. Mary's University *T*
Sam Houston State University *M, T*
Texas A&M International
   University *B, T*
Texas A&M University
   Commerce *T*
   Kingsville *T*
Texas Christian University *B*
Texas State University: San Marcos *T*
Texas Wesleyan University *B, T*
University of Dallas *T*
University of Houston *T*
University of Mary Hardin-Baylor *T*
University of Texas
   Arlington *T*
   San Antonio *T*
University of the Incarnate Word *T*
West Texas A&M University *T*

Utah

Brigham Young University *B*
Southern Utah University *B, T*
Utah Valley University *B*
Weber State University *B*

Vermont

Bennington College *M*
Castleton State College *B, T*
St. Michael's College *T*

Virginia

Bridgewater College *T*
Eastern Mennonite University *T*
Emory & Henry College *B*
Hollins University *T*
Longwood University *B, T*
Old Dominion University *B, T*
University of Virginia's College at
   Wise *T*

Washington

Eastern Washington University *B*
Washington State University *B, M, T*
Western Washington University *B*
Whitworth University *B, T*

West Virginia

Bethany College *B*
Shepherd University *T*

Wisconsin

Carroll University *B, T*
Carthage College *T*
Concordia University Wisconsin *B*
Edgewood College *B*
Lawrence University *T*
Marian University *B, T*
Marquette University *M*
Mount Mary College *B, T*
St. Norbert College *T*
University of Wisconsin
   Green Bay *T*
   Parkside *T*
   Platteville *B, T*
   River Falls *T*
   Whitewater *B*
Viterbo University *B, T*

Special education

Alabama

Alabama Agricultural and Mechanical
   University *B, M*
Alabama State University *B, M*
Athens State University *B*
Auburn University *B, M, D, T*
Birmingham-Southern College *B*
Jacksonville State University *B, M, T*
University of Alabama *B, M, D*
University of Alabama
   Birmingham *B, M*
University of North Alabama *M*
University of South Alabama *B, M, T*
University of West Alabama *B, M, T*

Alaska

University of Alaska
   Anchorage *M*
   Fairbanks *M, T*

Arizona

Arizona State University *B, M*
Central Arizona College *A*
Grand Canyon University *B, M*
Northcentral University *M, D*
Northern Arizona University *B, M, T*
Prescott College *B, M, T*
University of Arizona *B, M, D*
University of Phoenix *M*

Arkansas

Arkansas State University *B, M, T*
Harding University *B, M, T*
Henderson State University *M*
University of Arkansas *M*
University of Arkansas
   Little Rock *M*
   Pine Bluff *B*
University of Central Arkansas *M*
University of the Ozarks *B*

California

Azusa Pacific University *M, D*
California Baptist University *M, T*
California Lutheran University *B, M*
California State University
   Chico *M, T*
   Dominguez Hills *M*
   East Bay *M*
   Fresno *M*
   Fullerton *M, T*
   Long Beach *M, T*
   Los Angeles *M, D*
   Northridge *M*
   Sacramento *M*
   San Bernardino *M*
   San Marcos *T*
Cerritos College *A*
Chapman University *M, D, T*
Cuesta College *A*
Diablo Valley College *A*
Dominican University of California *M*
El Camino College: Compton
   Center *A*
Fresno Pacific University *M, T*
Holy Names University *M*
La Sierra University *M*
Loyola Marymount University *M*
Mills College *M, T*
Mount St. Mary's College *M*
National University *M, T*

Notre Dame de Namur
   University *M, T*
Sacramento City College *A*
St. Mary's College of California *M*
San Diego State University *M*
San Francisco State University *M, D, T*
San Jose State University *M*
Santa Clara University *M*
University of California
   Berkeley *D, T*
   Los Angeles *D*
University of La Verne *M, T*
University of San Diego *M, T*
University of San Francisco *M*
University of the Pacific *D, T*

Colorado

Adams State College *B, M, T*
Metropolitan State College of
   Denver *T*
Regis University *B, T*
University of Colorado
   Colorado Springs *M*
   Denver *M*
University of Denver *M, D*
University of Northern
   Colorado *B, M, D, T*
Western State College of
   Colorado *B, T*

Connecticut

Fairfield University *M, T*
Gateway Community College *A*
Saint Joseph College *B, M, T*
Southern Connecticut State
   University *M, T*
Three Rivers Community College *A*
University of Connecticut *B, M, D, T*
University of Hartford *M*
Western Connecticut State
   University *M*

Delaware

Delaware State University *B*
University of Delaware *B, M, T*
Wilmington University *M*

District of Columbia

American University *M*
Catholic University of America *M*
George Washington University *M*
Howard University *M*
Trinity Washington University *M*
University of the District of
   Columbia *M*

Florida

Barry University *B, M*
Broward College *A, B*
Chipola College *B*
Clearwater Christian College *B*
Flagler College *B, T*
Florida Atlantic University *B, M, D*
Florida Gulf Coast University *B, M*
Florida International
   University *B, M, D*
Florida State University *M, D*
Gulf Coast Community College *A*
Miami Dade College *A, B*
Nova Southeastern University *B*
Pensacola Junior College *A*
Saint Leo University *M*
St. Petersburg College *B*
Saint Thomas University *M*
Southeastern University *B*
Trinity Baptist College *B*
University of Central Florida *B, M*
University of Florida *B, M*
University of North Florida *B, M*
University of South Florida *B, M*
University of West Florida *B, M, T*
Warner University *B*

Georgia

Albany State University *B, M*
Armstrong Atlantic State
 University *B, M, T*
Augusta State University *B, M*
Brenau University *B*
Clark Atlanta University *M*
College of Coastal Georgia *A, B*
Georgia College and State
 University *B, M, T*
Georgia Southern University *B*
Georgia Southwestern State
 University *B*
Georgia State University *D, T*
Kennesaw State University *M*
Middle Georgia College *A*
North Georgia College & State
 University *B, M*
Piedmont College *B, M, T*
University of Georgia *B, M, D, T*
University of West Georgia *B, M, T*
Valdosta State University *B, M*

Hawaii

Chaminade University of Honolulu *M*
University of Hawaii
 Manoa *M, T*

Idaho

Boise State University *B, T*
Brigham Young University-Idaho *A*
Idaho State University *B, M, D*
University of Idaho *B, M, T*

Illinois

Aurora University *B, M*
Benedictine University *B, M, T*
Black Hawk College *A*
DePaul University *B, M, T*
Dominican University *M*
Eastern Illinois University *B, M, T*
Elmhurst College *B*
Eureka College *B*
Governors State University *M, T*
Greenville College *B, T*
Hebrew Theological College *B*
Illinois Central College *A*
Illinois State University *B, M, D, T*
John A. Logan College *A*
Joliet Junior College *A*
Kankakee Community College *A*
Kishwaukee College *A*
Lewis University *B, M*
Loyola University Chicago *B, M*
MacMurray College *B, T*
National-Louis University *M*
Northeastern Illinois University *B, M*
Northern Illinois University *B, M, D*
Quincy University *B, T*
Roosevelt University *B, M*
Sauk Valley Community College *A*
South Suburban College of Cook
 County *A*
Southern Illinois University
 Carbondale *B, M*
Southern Illinois University
 Edwardsville *B, M, T*
Trinity Christian College *B, T*
University of Illinois
 Chicago *M, D*
 Urbana-Champaign *B, M, D, T*
University of St. Francis *B, M*
Waubonsee Community College *B*
Western Illinois University *B, M*

Indiana

Ball State University *M, D, T*
Butler University *M*
Goshen College *B, T*
Grace College *B*
Huntington University *B*
Indiana State University *B, M, T*

Indiana University
 Bloomington *B, M, D, T*
 South Bend *B, M*
 Southeast *B*
Indiana University-Purdue University
 Fort Wayne *M*
Indiana University-Purdue University
 Indianapolis *M*
Indiana Wesleyan University *A*
Manchester College *B, T*
Marian University *T*
Oakland City University *B*
St. Mary-of-the-Woods College *B, T*
University of Evansville *B, T*
University of St. Francis *B, M, T*
Vincennes University *A, B*

Iowa

Buena Vista University *B, T*
Central College *T*
Dordt College *B*
Drake University *M*
Grand View University *T*
Iowa State University *M, T*
Iowa Wesleyan College *T*
Loras College *B*
Morningside College *B, M*
Mount Mercy College *M, T*
St. Ambrose University *M, T*
Simpson College *T*
University of Dubuque *T*
University of Iowa *M, D*
University of Northern Iowa *M*
Upper Iowa University *B, T*
Wartburg College *T*

Kansas

Benedictine College *B*
Bethel College *T*
Emporia State University *M, T*
Fort Hays State University *M*
Highland Community College *B*
Kansas State University *M, D*
Kansas Wesleyan University *T*
McPherson College *B, T*
Pittsburg State University *M*
Southwestern College *M*
Tabor College *B*
University of Kansas *M, D*
University of St. Mary *M*
Washburn University *M*
Wichita State University *M*

Kentucky

Asbury College *M, T*
Bellarmine University *B, M, T*
Brescia University *B, T*
Campbellsville University *M*
Eastern Kentucky University *B, M*
Georgetown College *B, M*
Kentucky State University *M*
Midway College *B*
Morehead State University *B, M*
Murray State University *B, M, T*
Spalding University *B, M*
Union College *B, M*
University of Kentucky *B, M, D*
University of Louisville *M*
University of the Cumberlands *B, M, T*
Western Kentucky University *B, M, T*

Louisiana

Dillard University *B*
Grambling State University *B, M*
Louisiana State University and
 Agricultural and Mechanical
 College *M*
Louisiana Tech University *B*
McNeese State University *B, M, T*
Northwestern State University *M*
Our Lady of Holy Cross College *B, T*
Southeastern Louisiana
 University *B, M*

Southern University and Agricultural
 and Mechanical College *B, M, D*
University of Louisiana at Lafayette *B*
University of Louisiana at Monroe *M*
University of New Orleans *M, D*
Xavier University of Louisiana *B, M*

Maine

University of Maine *M*
University of Maine
 Farmington *B, T*
University of Southern Maine *M*

Maryland

Bowie State University *M*
College of Notre Dame of Maryland *B*
Community College of Baltimore
 County *A, T*
Coppin State University *B, M, T*
Goucher College *B*
Hood College *B, T*
Loyola University Maryland *M*
McDaniel College *M*
Mount St. Mary's University *T*
Towson University *B, M, T*
University of Maryland
 College Park *B, M, D*
 Eastern Shore *B, M, T*

Massachusetts

American International
 College *B, M, T*
Assumption College *M*
Atlantic Union College *M*
Bay Path College *M*
Boston University *B, M, D, T*
Bridgewater State College *B, M, T*
Curry College *B*
Eastern Nazarene College *B, M, T*
Elms College *B, M, T*
Fitchburg State College *B, M, T*
Framingham State College *M*
Gordon College *B*
Lesley University *B, M*
Regis College *M*
Salem State College *M*
Simmons College *B, M*
Springfield College *B*
University of Massachusetts
 Boston *M*
Westfield State College *B, M, T*
Wheelock College *B, M*

Michigan

Andrews University *M*
Aquinas College *B*
Calvin College *B, T*
Central Michigan University *M*
Delta College *A*
Eastern Michigan University *B, M*
Gogebic Community College *A*
Grand Valley State University *B, M, T*
Henry Ford Community College *A*
Lansing Community College *A*
Marygrove College *B, M, T*
Michigan State University *B, M, D*
Northern Michigan University *B, T*
Oakland University *M*
Saginaw Valley State University *B, T*
Spring Arbor University *B, M*
University of Detroit Mercy *B, M*
Wayne State University *B, M, D, T*
Western Michigan University *M, D*

Minnesota

Bemidji State University *M*
Bethel University *M, T*
Capella University *M*
Minnesota State University
 Mankato *M*
 Moorhead *B, M*
Minnesota West Community and
 Technical College *A*

Normandale Community College *A*
Ridgewater College *A*
Saint Cloud State University *B, M, T*
St. Mary's University of Minnesota *M*
University of Minnesota
 Duluth *M, T*
 Twin Cities *M*
University of St. Thomas *M*
Walden University *M, D*
Winona State University *B, M, T*

Mississippi

Alcorn State University *B*
Delta State University *M*
Jackson State University *B, M*
Millsaps College *T*
Mississippi College *B*
Mississippi Delta Community
 College *A*
Mississippi State University *B, M, T*
Mississippi Valley State University *M*
Northwest Mississippi Community
 College *A*
Tougaloo College *B, T*
University of Mississippi *B, T*
University of Southern
 Mississippi *B, M*

Missouri

Avila University *B, T*
Central Methodist University *B*
Culver-Stockton College *T*
Evangel University *B, T*
Fontbonne University *B, T*
Lincoln University *B*
Missouri Baptist University *T*
Missouri Southern State
 University *B, T*
Missouri State University *B, M*
Missouri Valley College *B*
Northwest Missouri State University *T*
Southeast Missouri State
 University *B, M, T*
Truman State University *M, T*
University of Central Missouri *B, M, T*
University of Missouri
 Columbia *M, D*
 Kansas City *M*
 St. Louis *B, M*
Webster University *M*
William Woods University *B*

Montana

Montana State University
 Billings *A, B, M, T*
University of Great Falls *B*
University of Montana: Western *T*

Nebraska

College of Saint Mary *B, T*
Dana College *B*
Doane College *B*
Nebraska Wesleyan University *B*
Peru State College *B, T*
University of Nebraska
 Kearney *B, M, T*
 Omaha *B, M*
Wayne State College *B, M, T*
York College *B, T*

Nevada

Nevada State College *B*
University of Nevada
 Las Vegas *B, M, D, T*
 Reno *B, M, D, T*

New Hampshire

Granite State College *T*
Keene State College *M, T*
New England College *B, T*
Rivier College *T*
University of New Hampshire *M*

New Jersey

Caldwell College *T*
Centenary College *M*
The College of New Jersey *B, M, T*
College of St. Elizabeth *B, T*
Georgian Court University *M, T*
Gloucester County College *A*
Kean University *B, M, T*
Monmouth University *B, M*
Montclair State University *M*
New Jersey City University *B, M*
Rider University *M*
Rowan University *B, M*
Rutgers, The State University of New
    Jersey
    New Brunswick/Piscataway
      Campus *T*
Seton Hall University *B, T*
William Paterson University of New
    Jersey *B, M, T*

New Mexico

Eastern New Mexico University *B, M*
New Mexico Highlands
    University *B, M*
University of New Mexico *B, M, D, T*
University of the Southwest *B*
Western New Mexico
    University *B, M, T*

New York

Adelphi University *M, T*
Canisius College *M, T*
Cazenovia College *B*
City University of New York
    Brooklyn College *B, M*
    College of Staten Island *M, T*
    Hunter College *M, T*
    Lehman College *M, T*
    Medgar Evers College *B*
    Queens College *M, T*
College of Mount St. Vincent *T*
College of New Rochelle *B, M, T*
College of Saint Rose *M, T*
D'Youville College *M, T*
Daemen College *B, M, T*
Dominican College of Blauvelt *B*
Dowling College *B, M*
Fordham University *M*
Hobart and William Smith Colleges *T*
Hofstra University *M, T*
Iona College *M*
Keuka College *B, T*
Le Moyne College *M, T*
Long Island University
    Brooklyn Campus *M, T*
    C. W. Post Campus *M, T*
Manhattan College *B, M, T*
Manhattanville College *M, T*
Marist College *B, M*
Marymount Manhattan College *T*
Medaille College *M, T*
Molloy College *B, T*
Mount Saint Mary College *M*
Nazareth College *B, M, T*
New York University *B, M, T*
Niagara University *B, M, T*
Pace University *B, M, T*
Roberts Wesleyan College *B, M*
Saint Bonaventure University *B, M*
St. John Fisher College *B, M, T*
St. John's University *B, M, T*
St. Joseph's College *B, T*
St. Joseph's College: Suffolk
    Campus *B, T*
St. Thomas Aquinas College *B, M, T*
State University of New York
    Albany *M*
    Binghamton *M*
    Buffalo *D*
    College at Brockport *B, M, T*
    College at Buffalo *M*
    College at Cortland *B*
    College at Fredonia *T*

College at Geneseo *B, T*
College at Old Westbury *B, T*
College at Plattsburgh *B, M*
College at Potsdam *M*
New Paltz *M, T*
Oswego *M*
Syracuse University *B, M, D, T*
Touro College *B, M*
University of Rochester *M*
Utica College *B, M*

North Carolina

Appalachian State University *M, T*
East Carolina University *B*
Elizabeth City State University *B, T*
Elon University *B, M, T*
Fayetteville State University *M*
Fayetteville Technical Community
    College *A*
Forsyth Technical Community
    College *A*
Greensboro College *B, M, T*
High Point University *B*
Methodist University *A, B, T*
North Carolina Agricultural and
    Technical State University *B*
North Carolina Central University *M*
North Carolina State University *M, T*
Pfeiffer University *B*
Stanly Community College *A*
University of North Carolina
    Charlotte *B, M, D*
    Greensboro *B, M, D*
    Pembroke *B*
    Wilmington *B*
Western Carolina University *B*
Wilson Community College *A*
Winston-Salem State University *B*

North Dakota

Jamestown College *B*
Minot State University *M*
University of North Dakota *M*

Ohio

Antioch University McGregor *M*
Ashland University *B, M, T*
Bluffton University *B*
Bowling Green State
    University *B, M, T*
Capital University *B, T*
Cedarville University *B*
Central State University *B*
Cincinnati Christian University *B*
Cleveland State University *B, T*
College of Mount St. Joseph *B, T*
Kent State University *B, M, D*
Miami University
    Oxford Campus *B, M*
Mount Union College *B, T*
Mount Vernon Nazarene
    University *B, T*
Muskingum University *B, T*
Ohio Dominican University *B, M, T*
Ohio State University
    Columbus Campus *B, M*
Ohio University *B, M, D, T*
Ohio University
    Zanesville Campus *M*
Otterbein College *B*
Union Institute & University *B, M*
University of Akron *B, M*
University of Cincinnati *M, D*
University of Dayton *B, M, T*
University of Findlay *B, M, T*
University of Rio Grande *B, T*
University of Toledo *M, T*
Urbana University *B*
Ursuline College *B, M, T*
Wilmington College *M*
Wright State University *M*
Xavier University *B, M*
Youngstown State University *B, M*

Oklahoma

East Central University *B, M, T*
Langston University *B*
Northwestern Oklahoma State
    University *B*
Oklahoma Baptist University *B, T*
Oral Roberts University *B, T*
Southeastern Oklahoma State
    University *B*
Southwestern Oklahoma State
    University *B, M, T*
University of Central Oklahoma *B, M*
University of Oklahoma *B, M, D, T*

Oregon

Eastern Oregon University *T*
Portland State University *M, D, T*
Southern Oregon University *T*
University of Oregon *M, D, T*
Western Oregon University *M, T*

Pennsylvania

Albright College *B, M, T*
Alvernia University *B*
Arcadia University *B, M, D, T*
Bloomsburg University of
    Pennsylvania *B, M, T*
Cabrini College *B, T*
California University of
    Pennsylvania *B, M*
Carlow University *B, M*
Cedar Crest College *T*
Chatham University *B, M*
Chestnut Hill College *T*
Cheyney University of
    Pennsylvania *B, M, T*
Clarion University of
    Pennsylvania *B, M, T*
DeSales University *B, M, T*
Duquesne University *B, M, T*
East Stroudsburg University of
    Pennsylvania *B, M, T*
Eastern University *T*
Edinboro University of
    Pennsylvania *A, B, M*
Geneva College *B, M, T*
Gwynedd-Mercy College *B, M, T*
Holy Family University *B, M, T*
Indiana University of
    Pennsylvania *B, M, T*
King's College *B*
Kutztown University of
    Pennsylvania *B, T*
La Salle University *B, T*
Lebanon Valley College *B, T*
Lehigh Carbon Community College *A*
Lehigh University *M, D*
Lincoln University *B*
Lock Haven University of
    Pennsylvania *B*
Lycoming College *T*
Mansfield University of
    Pennsylvania *B, M*
Marywood University *B, M*
Mercyhurst College *B, M, T*
Millersville University of
    Pennsylvania *B, M, T*
Misericordia University *B, T*
Penn State
    Abington *B*
    Altoona *B*
    Beaver *B*
    Berks *B*
    Brandywine *B*
    DuBois *B*
    Erie, The Behrend College *B*
    Fayette, The Eberly Campus *B*
    Greater Allegheny *B*
    Hazleton *B*
    Lehigh Valley *B*
    Mont Alto *B*
    New Kensington *B*
    Schuylkill *B*
    Shenango *B*

University Park *B, M, D*
Wilkes-Barre *B*
Worthington Scranton *B*
York *B*
Rosemont College *T*
St. Francis University *M*
Saint Joseph's University *B, M, T*
St. Vincent College *M*
Seton Hill University *M, T*
Shippensburg University of
    Pennsylvania *M, T*
Slippery Rock University of
    Pennsylvania *B, M, T*
University of Scranton *B*
Waynesburg University *B*
West Chester University of
    Pennsylvania *B, M, T*
Widener University *B, M, T*
Wilkes University *B, M, T*

Puerto Rico

American University of Puerto
    Rico *B, T*
Bayamon Central University *B, M*
Caribbean University *B, T*
Inter American University of Puerto
    Rico
    Arecibo Campus *B*
    Metropolitan Campus *B, M*
    Ponce Campus *B, T*
    San German Campus *B, M*
Pontifical Catholic University of
    Puerto Rico *B*
Turabo University *B, M*
Universidad Metropolitana *B, M*
Universidad del Este *B, M*
University of Puerto Rico
    Cayey University College *B*
    Rio Piedras *M*

Rhode Island

Community College of Rhode
    Island *A*
Providence College *B, M*
Rhode Island College *B, M*
Salve Regina University *B*

South Carolina

Anderson University *B, T*
Bob Jones University *B*
Clemson University *B, M*
Coastal Carolina University *B, T*
College of Charleston *B, M, T*
Columbia College *B, T*
Converse College *B, M, T*
Erskine College *B, T*
Francis Marion University *M*
Furman University *M, T*
Lander University *B, T*
Presbyterian College *B, T*
South Carolina State
    University *B, M, T*
Southern Wesleyan University *B, T*
University of South Carolina *M, D*
University of South Carolina
    Aiken *B*
    Upstate *B, M, T*
Winthrop University *B, M, T*

South Dakota

Augustana College *B, M, T*
Black Hills State University *B*
Dakota Wesleyan University *B, T*
Mount Marty College *B*
Northern State University *B, T*
Sinte Gleska University *A, B*
University of South Dakota *B, M*

Tennessee

Austin Peay State University *B*
Bethel University *B, T*
Carson-Newman College *B, T*
Christian Brothers University *B*

Cumberland University *B*
East Tennessee State
  University *B, M, T*
Fisk University *B*
Freed-Hardeman University *B, M, T*
Lambuth University *B, T*
LeMoyne-Owen College *B*
Lee University *B*
Middle Tennessee State
  University *B, M*
Southern Adventist University *M*
Tennessee State University *B, M, T*
Tennessee Technological
  University *B, M, T*
Trevecca Nazarene University *B, T*
Tusculum College *B, T*
Union University *B, T*
University of Memphis *B*
University of Tennessee
  Chattanooga *B, M, T*
  Knoxville *B, T*
  Martin *R*
Vanderbilt University *B, M, D, T*

Texas

Abilene Christian University *B, M, T*
Angelo State University *M*
Baylor University *B, T*
El Paso Community College *A*
Houston Baptist University *M*
Jarvis Christian College *B, T*
Lamar University *B, M, T*
Laredo Community College *A*
Lubbock Christian University *B*
Midwestern State University *M*
Our Lady of the Lake University of San
  Antonio *B, M*
Prairie View A&M University *M*
Sam Houston State University *M*
Southern Methodist University *T*
Southwestern University *T*
Stephen F. Austin State University *M, T*
Sul Ross State University *M*
Texas A&M International
  University *B, M, T*
Texas A&M University
  Commerce *B, M, D, T*
  Corpus Christi *M, T*
  Kingsville *M*
  Texarkana *M, T*
Texas Christian University *B, M*
Texas Southern University *M*
Texas State University: San
  Marcos *M, T*
Texas Tech University *M, D*
Texas Woman's University *M, D, T*
University of Houston *M, D*
University of Houston
  Clear Lake *T*
  Victoria *M*
University of Mary Hardin-Baylor *B*
University of North Texas *M, D*
University of Texas
  Austin *M, D*
  Brownsville - Texas Southmost
    College *M*
  El Paso *M*
  Pan American *M*
  San Antonio *M, T*
  Tyler *M*
  of the Permian Basin *M*
West Texas A&M University *M, T*

Utah

Brigham Young University *B, M*
Snow College *A*
Southern Utah University *B*
University of Utah *B, M, D*
Utah State University *B, M, D*
Western Governors University *B, M, T*
Westminster College *B, T*

Vermont

Castleton State College *M, T*

College of St. Joseph in Vermont *M*
Green Mountain College *B, T*
Johnson State College *M*
Lyndon State College *B, M*
St. Michael's College *M, T*
University of Vermont *M, T*

Virginia

Averett University *M*
College of William and Mary *M*
George Mason University *M*
Hampton University *B, M*
James Madison University *M, T*
Liberty University *M, T*
Longwood University *B, M, T*
Lynchburg College *M*
Norfolk State University *B*
Old Dominion University *M, D, T*
Radford University *M*
Regent University *M*
University of Virginia *M, D*
University of Virginia's College at
  Wise *T*
Virginia Commonwealth University *M*
Virginia Intermont College *B, T*

Washington

City University of Seattle *B, M, T*
Eastern Washington University *B, M*
Gonzaga University *B, M, T*
Pacific Lutheran University *M*
Saint Martin's University *B, T*
Seattle Pacific University *B*
Seattle University *M*
Shoreline Community College *A*
Spokane Falls Community College *A*
University of Washington *M, D*
Walla Walla University *B, M*
Washington State
  University *B, M, D, T*
Western Washington University *B, M*
Whitworth University *B, M, T*

West Virginia

Bethany College *B*
Glenville State College *B*
Marshall University *M*
Salem International University *T*
University of Charleston *B*
West Liberty University *B*
West Virginia State University *B*
West Virginia University *M, D*
West Virginia Wesleyan College *B, M*

Wisconsin

Alverno College *M*
Cardinal Stritch University *B, M*
Carthage College *B, T*
Concordia University Wisconsin *M*
Edgewood College *B, M*
University of Wisconsin
  Eau Claire *B, M*
  La Crosse *M*
  Madison *B, M, D*
  Milwaukee *M, T*
  Oshkosh *B, M, T*
  Stout *B*
  Superior *M*
  Whitewater *B, M, T*

Wyoming

Laramie County Community
  College *A*
Northwest College *A*
University of Wyoming *B*

Special education administration

Arizona

Northcentral University *M, D*

California

California Baptist University *M*
California Coast University *M*
Mills College *M*

District of Columbia

Gallaudet University *D*

Illinois

University of Illinois
  Urbana-Champaign *M, D, T*

Massachusetts

Cambridge College *T*
Westfield State College *M*

Michigan

Northern Michigan University *M*

Minnesota

Capella University *D*

Missouri

Lincoln University *M*
University of Missouri
  Columbia *M, D*

New York

Hofstra University *T*
Le Moyne College *M*

Pennsylvania

Marywood University *M*

Virginia

College of William and Mary *D*
Virginia Polytechnic Institute and
  State University *D*

Special products marketing

Illinois

Illinois Institute of Art: Schaumburg *B*

Iowa

Northeast Iowa Community
  College *C*

Maryland

Community College of Baltimore
  County *C*

Minnesota

Century Community and Technical
  College *C*
Rochester Community and Technical
  College *C, A*

Missouri

State Fair Community College *A*

New Jersey

Bergen Community College *A*

New York

Fashion Institute of Technology *B*
Rochester Institute of Technology *B*

Oklahoma

Oklahoma State University
  Oklahoma City *C*

Pennsylvania

Saint Joseph's University *B, M*

Texas

Stephen F. Austin State University *B*
University of North Texas *B*

Speech-language pathology assistant

Arizona

Estrella Mountain Community
  College *C, A*

California

Grossmont College *A*
Orange Coast College *A*
Pasadena City College *A*

Illinois

College of DuPage *A*

Massachusetts

Elms College *A, B*

North Carolina

Caldwell Community College and
  Technical Institute *A*
Fayetteville Technical Community
  College *A*

North Dakota

Williston State College *A*

Oregon

Chemeketa Community College *C, A*

Speech pathology

Alabama

Alabama Agricultural and Mechanical
  University *M*
University of Alabama *M*
University of Montevallo *B, M, T*

Arizona

Northern Arizona University *M*
University of Arizona *B, M, D*

Arkansas

Arkansas State University *M*
Harding University *B, T*

California

California State University
  Northridge *B*
Stanford University *D*
University of the Pacific *B, M*

Colorado

University of Northern Colorado *B, M*

District of Columbia

University of the District of
  Columbia *B*

Florida

Nova Southeastern University *M, D*

Georgia

Georgia State University *T*
University of West Georgia *B, M*
Valdosta State University *B, M*

Idaho

Idaho State University *M*

Illinois

Elmhurst College *B, T*
Governors State University *B, M*
Northwestern University *M, D*
Rush University *M*
Saint Xavier University *B, M*

Indiana

Ball State University *M*

Indiana University-Purdue University
Fort Wayne *M*
Purdue University *B, M, D*

Iowa
St. Ambrose University *M*
University of Northern Iowa *B, M*

Kansas
University of Kansas *M, D*
University of Kansas Medical
Center *M, D*

Louisiana
Centenary College of Louisiana *B*
Southeastern Louisiana University *M*
Xavier University of Louisiana *B*

Maryland
Loyola University Maryland *B*
University of Maryland
College Park *M*

Massachusetts
Boston University *M, D*
Elms College *B*
Emerson College *B, M*
Worcester State College *M*

Michigan
Calvin College *B*
Central Michigan University *M*
Eastern Michigan University *B*
Michigan State University *M, D*
Northern Michigan University *B*
Western Michigan University *M*

Minnesota
Minnesota State University
Mankato *M*
Moorhead *M*

Mississippi
Mississippi University for
Women *B, M*

Missouri
Fontbonne University *B, M*
Rockhurst University *B, M*
University of Central Missouri *B, T*

Nebraska
University of Nebraska
Kearney *B, M, T*
Lincoln *B*

Nevada
Nevada State College *B*
University of Nevada
Reno *B, D*

New Jersey
Montclair State University *T*
Seton Hall University *M*
William Paterson University of New
Jersey *B*

New Mexico
University of New Mexico *M*

New York
City University of New York
Brooklyn College *B, M*
Hunter College *B, M*
Queens College *M, T*
College of New Rochelle *M*
Hofstra University *M*
Ithaca College *B, M, T*
Nazareth College *B, M, T*
State University of New York
College at Buffalo *B, M*

College at Fredonia *M*
College at Geneseo *B, M, T*
College at Plattsburgh *M*
Touro College *M*

North Carolina
Appalachian State University *M, T*

North Dakota
University of North Dakota *M*

Ohio
Case Western Reserve
University *M, D*
Miami University
Oxford Campus *B*
Muskingum University *B*
Ohio University *M*
University of Toledo *M*

Oklahoma
Northeastern State University *M*
Oklahoma State University *B, M*
University of Central Oklahoma *B, M*
University of Oklahoma *M, D*
University of Science and Arts of
Oklahoma *B*

Oregon
Portland State University *M*

Pennsylvania
Bloomsburg University of
Pennsylvania *M, T*
Duquesne University *M*
Edinboro University of
Pennsylvania *M*
Geneva College *B*
La Salle University *B, M*
Misericordia University *M*
University of Pittsburgh *D*

Puerto Rico
Caribbean University *B*
Turabo University *B, M*
University of Puerto Rico
Medical Sciences *M*

Rhode Island
University of Rhode Island *M*

South Carolina
Bob Jones University *B*
Columbia College *B, T*
University of South Carolina *M*

Tennessee
University of Tennessee
Knoxville *B, M*

Texas
Abilene Christian University *B, M*
Lamar University *M*
Our Lady of the Lake University of San
Antonio *B*
Stephen F. Austin State University *M, T*
Texas A&M University
Kingsville *B, M*
Texas Christian University *B, M*
Texas Woman's University *M*
University of Houston *M*
University of North Texas *M*

Utah
Brigham Young University *M*
University of Utah *M*

Virginia
James Madison University *B, M, D, T*

Washington
Eastern Washington University *B, M*
University of Washington *M*
Western Washington University *M*

West Virginia
Marshall University *B*
West Virginia University *M*

Wisconsin
Marquette University *M*
University of Wisconsin
Whitewater *B, T*

Speech/rhetorical studies

Alabama
Faulkner University *B*
Troy University *B*
University of Alabama
Huntsville *B*
University of Montevallo *B, T*
University of North Alabama *B*

Alaska
University of Alaska
Fairbanks *B*

Arizona
Northern Arizona University *B, M*

Arkansas
Arkansas State University *B, M*
Arkansas Tech University *B*
Henderson State University *B*
Ouachita Baptist University *B*
Phillips Community College of the
University of Arkansas *A*
University of Arkansas
Monticello *B*
University of Central Arkansas *B*

California
Cabrillo College *A*
California Lutheran University *B*
California Polytechnic State
University: San Luis Obispo *B*
California State University
Chico *B*
East Bay *B, M*
Fresno *B, M*
Fullerton *B, M*
Long Beach *B, M*
Northridge *B, M*
Cerritos College *A*
Chabot College *A*
College of Marin: Kentfield *A*
College of San Mateo *A*
College of the Desert *A*
College of the Sequoias *A*
College of the Siskiyous *C*
Columbia College *A*
Cypress College *A*
El Camino College *A*
El Camino College: Compton
Center *A*
Foothill College *C, A*
Fresno City College *A*
Fullerton College *A*
Golden West College *A*
Grossmont College *A*
Irvine Valley College *A*
Long Beach City College *A*
The Master's College *B*
Mendocino College *A*
Modesto Junior College *C, A*
Ohlone College *C*
Orange Coast College *A*
Palomar College *A*
Pasadena City College *C, A*
Saddleback College *A*

San Diego City College *A*
San Diego Miramar College *A*
San Diego State University *B*
San Francisco State University *B, M*
San Joaquin Delta College *A*
San Jose State University *B*
Santa Barbara City College *A*
Santa Rosa Junior College *C*
Santiago Canyon College *A*
Sierra College *A*
Skyline College *A*
University of California
Berkeley *B, D*
West Los Angeles College *C, A*
West Valley College *A*

Colorado
Colorado Mountain College *A*
Colorado State University *B, M*
Metropolitan State College of
Denver *B*

District of Columbia
Catholic University of America *M, D*

Florida
Bethune-Cookman University *B*
Miami Dade College *A*
State College of Florida,
Manatee-Sarasota *A*
University of South Florida *B, M, D*

Georgia
Albany State University *B*
Atlanta Metropolitan College *A*
Clark Atlanta University *B*
Columbus State University *B*
Darton College *A*
Georgia College and State
University *B*
Georgia Southern University *B*
Oglethorpe University *B*
University of Georgia *B, M, D*
Valdosta State University *B*
Young Harris College *A*

Hawaii
University of Hawaii
Hilo *B*

Illinois
Augustana College *B*
Chicago State University *B*
City Colleges of Chicago
Harold Washington College *A*
DePaul University *M*
Eastern Illinois University *B, M, T*
Greenville College *B*
Illinois Central College *A*
Illinois College *B*
Illinois State University *B, T*
Illinois Valley Community College *A*
Lake Land College *A*
Lewis University *B, T*
Lincoln College *A*
McKendree University *B*
Monmouth College *B*
Northeastern Illinois University *B, M*
Richland Community College *A*
Southern Illinois University
Carbondale *B, M, D*
Southern Illinois University
Edwardsville *B, M*
Southwestern Illinois College *A*
Triton College *A*
University of Illinois
Urbana-Champaign *B, M, D*

Indiana
Ball State University *B, M*
Butler University *B*
Indiana University
South Bend *B*

Wabash College B

Iowa
Coe College B
Dordt College B
Drake University B
Iowa State University B, M, D
Mount Mercy College B, T
St. Ambrose University B, T
University of Dubuque B
University of Iowa B
University of Northern Iowa B
Wartburg College B, T

Kansas
Bethany College B
Butler Community College A
Central Christian College of
  Kansas A, B
Coffeyville Community College A
Donnelly College A
Kansas Wesleyan University B, T
Pratt Community College A
University of Kansas B, M, D
Washburn University B

Kentucky
Asbury College B
Bluegrass Community and Technical
  College A
Eastern Kentucky University B
Northern Kentucky University B
Thomas More College B

Louisiana
Louisiana State University
  Shreveport B
Louisiana State University and
  Agricultural and Mechanical
  College B, M, D
Louisiana Tech University B, M
McNeese State University B
Northwestern State University B
Southern University and Agricultural
  and Mechanical College B
University of Louisiana at Monroe B

Maine
Bates College B
University of Maine B, M

Maryland
Frederick Community College A
Frostburg State University B, T
Morgan State University B

Massachusetts
Emerson College B, M

Michigan
Calvin College B
Cornerstone University B, T
Eastern Michigan University B, M
Ferris State University A, B
Grand Rapids Community College A
Hillsdale College B
Madonna University B
Michigan State University D
Mid Michigan Community College A
Spring Arbor University B
University of Detroit Mercy B
University of Michigan
  Flint T

Minnesota
College of St. Benedict B
Minnesota State University
  Mankato B, M
  Moorhead B
Ridgewater College A
St. Catherine University B
Saint Cloud State University B

St. John's University B
Southwest Minnesota State
  University B
University of Minnesota
  Twin Cities B, M, D
Winona State University B

Mississippi
Hinds Community College A
Jackson State University B
Mississippi Valley State University B

Missouri
Evangel University B
Missouri Western State University B, T
Northwest Missouri State
  University B
St. Charles Community College A
St. Louis Community College
  St. Louis Community College at
    Florissant Valley A
Southeast Missouri State University B
Three Rivers Community College A
University of Central Missouri B, M
William Jewell College B

Montana
Miles Community College A
University of Montana B, M

Nebraska
Chadron State College B
Concordia University B
Nebraska Wesleyan University B
Northeast Community College A
Union College B
University of Nebraska
  Kearney B, T
  Omaha C, B

New Jersey
The College of New Jersey B
Rider University B
Rutgers, The State University of New
  Jersey
  Camden Regional Campus T

New Mexico
Eastern New Mexico University B
New Mexico State University B, M
University of New Mexico B, M, D

New York
City University of New York
  Brooklyn College B, M
  Lehman College B
  York College B
Ithaca College B
Long Island University
  Brooklyn Campus B
New York University B, M, T
St. John's University B
St. Joseph's College B
State University of New York
  Albany B, M
  College at Oneonta B
  College at Plattsburgh B
  College at Potsdam B
Syracuse University B, M
Touro College B
Yeshiva University B

North Carolina
Fayetteville State University B
Methodist University A, B
North Carolina Agricultural and
  Technical State University B
University of North Carolina
  Greensboro B, M

North Dakota
Minot State University B

North Dakota State University M

Ohio
Bowling Green State University B, M
Defiance College B, T
Kent State University B, M, D
Miami University
  Oxford Campus B
Ohio University B, M
Youngstown State University B

Oklahoma
Carl Albert State College A
Connors State College A
East Central University B
Northeastern State University B
Northwestern Oklahoma State
  University B
Oklahoma Baptist University B, T
Oklahoma City University B
Redlands Community College A
Southern Nazarene University B
Tulsa Community College A

Oregon
Chemeketa Community College A
Linn-Benton Community College A
Oregon State University B
Portland State University B, M
Southern Oregon University B, T
Western Oregon University B
Willamette University B

Pennsylvania
Bloomsburg University of
  Pennsylvania B
Carnegie Mellon University M, D
Clarion University of Pennsylvania B
Community College of Philadelphia A
Duquesne University B, D
Kutztown University of
  Pennsylvania B, T
La Salle University B
Lock Haven University of
  Pennsylvania B
Mansfield University of
  Pennsylvania B
Shippensburg University of
  Pennsylvania B
Temple University B
University of Pittsburgh C, B, M, D
University of Pittsburgh
  Bradford B
West Chester University of
  Pennsylvania B, M

South Carolina
Bob Jones University B, M
Clemson University B

South Dakota
Augustana College T
Black Hills State University B
Northern State University B
South Dakota State University B
University of Sioux Falls B
University of South Dakota B, M, D

Tennessee
Belmont University B
Carson-Newman College B
East Tennessee State University B, T
Lipscomb University B
Tennessee Temple University B
Union University B, T
University of Tennessee
  Chattanooga C

Texas
Amarillo College A
Austin Community College A
Blinn College A

Brazosport College A
Clarendon College A
Coastal Bend College A
Del Mar College A
El Paso Community College A
Galveston College A
Grayson County College A
Hardin-Simmons University B
Howard Payne University B
Lamar State College at Orange A
Lamar University B, M
Lon Morris College A
Midland College A
Navarro College A
North Lake College C
Northwest Vista College A
St. Philip's College A
Sam Houston State University B
Stephen F. Austin State
  University B, M
Sul Ross State University B
Texas A&M University B, M, D
Texas A&M University
  Commerce B, M
Texas Southern University B
Texas State University: San
  Marcos B, M, T
Texas Tech University B, M
Texas Woman's University D
Trinity University B
Trinity Valley Community College A
Tyler Junior College A
University of Houston B, M
University of Houston
  Downtown B
  Victoria B, T
University of North Texas B, M
University of Texas
  Arlington B, D
  Austin M, D
  El Paso D
  San Antonio B
  Tyler B
Weatherford College A
West Texas A&M University B

Utah
Brigham Young University B
Southern Utah University C
Utah State University B, M

Virginia
George Mason University B
Hampton University B
Old Dominion University B
University of Richmond B

Washington
Everett Community College A
Gonzaga University B
University of Washington B, M, D

West Virginia
Marshall University B, M

Wisconsin
Beloit College B
Marquette University B
University of Wisconsin
  River Falls B, M
  Superior B, M
  Whitewater B

Speech teacher
education

Arizona
Northern Arizona University B
University of Arizona B

Arkansas
Arkansas Tech University B

Harding University *B, T*
Ouachita Baptist University *B, T*

California

California State University
   East Bay *B, M, T*
Pepperdine University *B*
San Diego Mesa College *A*
San Francisco State University *T*

Colorado

Adams State College *B, T*
Colorado State University *B, T*
Metropolitan State College of
   Denver *T*

Georgia

Darton College *A*

Idaho

Boise State University *B, T*

Illinois

Augustana College *B, T*
Bradley University *B*
Lewis University *T*
North Park University *T*
University of Illinois
   Urbana-Champaign *M*

Indiana

Indiana University
   Bloomington *B, T*
Indiana University-Purdue University
   Fort Wayne *B, T*
Indiana University-Purdue University
   Indianapolis *B, T*
University of Indianapolis *B, T*
Vincennes University *A*

Iowa

Buena Vista University *B, T*
Central College *T*
Dordt College *B*
Graceland University *T*
Grand View University *T*
Loras College *T*
Northwestern College *T*
Simpson College *T*
University of Iowa *T*
University of Northern Iowa *B*
Upper Iowa University *T*
Wartburg College *T*

Kansas

Bethel College *T*
Coffeyville Community College *A*
McPherson College *B, T*
Southwestern College *B, T*

Louisiana

McNeese State University *B, T*
Northwestern State University *B*
Southeastern Louisiana University *B*
University of Louisiana at Lafayette *B*
University of Louisiana at Monroe *B*

Massachusetts

Emerson College *B, M*

Michigan

Central Michigan University *B*
Lansing Community College *A*

Minnesota

Augsburg College *T*
Concordia College: Moorhead *B, T*
Minnesota State University
   Mankato *B, M*
   Moorhead *B*
Saint Cloud State University *B, T*

Southwest Minnesota State
   University *B, T*
University of Minnesota
   Morris *T*
Winona State University *B, T*

Mississippi

Mississippi Delta Community
   College *A*
Mississippi State University *T*

Missouri

Culver-Stockton College *B, T*
Missouri Southern State
   University *B, T*
Missouri State University *B*
Southeast Missouri State
   University *B, T*
Southwest Baptist University *T*
University of Central Missouri *B, M, T*
William Jewell College *B, T*
William Woods University *T*

Montana

Montana State University
   Billings *T*

Nebraska

Concordia University *B, T*
Creighton University *T*
Nebraska Wesleyan University *T*
Peru State College *B, T*
University of Nebraska
   Kearney *B, M, T*
Wayne State College *B, T*
York College *B, T*

New Jersey

Kean University *B, T*

New York

Elmira College *B, T*
Marymount Manhattan College *T*
Nazareth College *B, M, T*
State University of New York
   College at Fredonia *M, T*
   New Paltz *M, T*

North Carolina

North Carolina Agricultural and
   Technical State University *B, T*

North Dakota

Dickinson State University *B, T*

Ohio

Bowling Green State University *B, M*
Capital University *T*
Defiance College *B, T*
Hiram College *T*
Kent State University *T*
University of Findlay *B, M, T*
University of Rio Grande *B, T*
Youngstown State University *B, M*

Oklahoma

East Central University *B, T*
Eastern Oklahoma State College *A*
Northeastern State University *B*
Oklahoma Baptist University *B, T*
Oklahoma Christian University *B, T*
Oklahoma City University *B*
Southern Nazarene University *B*
Southwestern Oklahoma State
   University *T*

Oregon

Portland State University *T*
Southern Oregon University *T*

Pennsylvania

St. Francis University *B, T*

South Dakota

Augustana College *B, T*
Black Hills State University *B*
Northern State University *B, T*
University of Sioux Falls *T*
University of South Dakota *B, M, T*

Tennessee

Tennessee Technological University *T*
Tennessee Temple University *B*
Trevecca Nazarene University *B, T*

Texas

Austin College *M*
East Texas Baptist University *B*
Hardin-Simmons University *B, T*
Howard Payne University *B, T*
Lamar University *T*
Laredo Community College *A*
Lubbock Christian University *B*
Sam Houston State University *M, T*
Texas A&M University
   Commerce *B*
   Kingsville *T*
University of Mary Hardin-Baylor *B, T*
University of Texas
   Arlington *T*
West Texas A&M University *T*

Utah

Southern Utah University *B, T*

Vermont

Johnson State College *M*

Virginia

University of Virginia's College at
   Wise *T*

Washington

Western Washington University *B*
Whitworth University *B, T*

West Virginia

Concord University *B, T*
Fairmont State University *B*

Wisconsin

University of Wisconsin
   Green Bay *T*
   Platteville *B, T*
   River Falls *T*
   Whitewater *B, T*

Sports and fitness administration

Alabama

Faulkner University *B*
Huntingdon College *B*
Shelton State Community College *C*
Troy University *B, M*
United States Sports Academy *B, M, D*

Arizona

Grand Canyon University *B*
University of Phoenix *A*

Arkansas

Arkansas State University *B, M*
Ecclesia College *B*
Harding University *B*
Henderson State University *M*
John Brown University *B*

California

California State University
   Chico *C*
   East Bay *C*
Fresno Pacific University *B*
Mendocino College *A*
National University *C*
Orange Coast College *C, A*
Pepperdine University *B*
St. Mary's College of California *B*
Solano Community College *A*
Southwestern College *C*
University of San Francisco *M*
University of the Pacific *B*

Colorado

Johnson & Wales University:
   Denver *B*
Mesa State College *B*

Connecticut

Eastern Connecticut State
   University *B*
Gateway Community College *C, A*
Mitchell College *B*
Sacred Heart University *B*
University of New Haven *B, M*

Delaware

Delaware State University *B, M*
University of Delaware *B*

District of Columbia

American University *C, B, M*

Florida

Barry University *B, M*
Clearwater Christian College *B*
Flagler College *B*
Florida Southern College *B*
Florida State University *B, M, D*
Gulf Coast Community College *A*
Johnson & Wales University: North
   Miami *B*
Lake-Sumter Community College *A*
Northwood University
   Florida *B*
Nova Southeastern University *B*
Saint Leo University *B*
Saint Thomas University *B, M*
Southeastern University *B*
State College of Florida,
   Manatee-Sarasota *A*
Stetson University *B*
University of Central Florida *M*
University of Miami *B, M*
University of North Florida *B*
University of Tampa *B*
Warner University *A, B*

Georgia

Clayton State University *B*
Darton College *A*
Emmanuel College *B*
Georgia Southern University *C, B, M*
Georgia State University *M, D*
Kennesaw State University *B*
Reinhardt College *B*
Shorter College *B*
University of Georgia *B*

Idaho

College of Idaho *B*
Northwest Nazarene University *B*
University of Idaho *B*

Illinois

Elmhurst College *B*
Greenville College *B*
Illinois Valley Community College *A*
Judson University *B*
Lewis University *B*

Lincoln College *B*
Loyola University Chicago *B*
MacMurray College *B*
Millikin University *B*
North Central College *B*
Northwestern University *M*
Olivet Nazarene University *B*
Principia College *B*
Quincy University *B*
South Suburban College of Cook
  County *C, A*
University of Illinois
  Urbana-Champaign *B, M, D*
Western Illinois University *M*

Indiana

Grace College *B*
Huntington University *B*
Indiana Institute of Technology *B*
Indiana State University *M*
Indiana Wesleyan University *B*
Marian University *B*
Saint Joseph's College *B*
Taylor University *B*
Trine University *B*
University of Evansville *B*
University of Indianapolis *B*
Valparaiso University *B, M*
Vincennes University *A*

Iowa

Briar Cliff University *B*
Buena Vista University *B*
Clarke College *B*
Des Moines Area Community
  College *A*
Dordt College *B*
Graceland University *B*
Grand View University *C, B*
Iowa Wesleyan College *B*
Loras College *M*
Luther College *B*
North Iowa Area Community
  College *A*
St. Ambrose University *B*
Simpson College *B*
University of Iowa *B, M, D*
Wartburg College *B*

Kansas

Baker University *B*
Barton County Community College *A*
Bethany College *B*
Central Christian College of
  Kansas *A, B*
MidAmerica Nazarene University *B*
Southwestern College *B*
Tabor College *B*
University of St. Mary *B*
Washburn University *B*
Wichita State University *B, M*

Kentucky

Asbury College *B*
Kentucky Wesleyan College *B*
Midway College *B*
Northern Kentucky University *B*
Thomas More College *B*
Union College *B*
University of Louisville *B, M*
University of the Cumberlands *B*
Western Kentucky University *B*

Louisiana

Grambling State University *M*
Louisiana State University and
  Agricultural and Mechanical
  College *B*
Southeastern Louisiana University *B*

Maine

Husson University *B*
Saint Joseph's College of Maine *B*

Thomas College *B*
University of New England *B*

Maryland

Cecil College *C*
Coppin State University *B*
Frostburg State University *B*
Howard Community College *C, A*
Mount St. Mary's University *B*
Towson University *B*
Washington Adventist University *B*

Massachusetts

American International College *B*
Anna Maria College *B*
Becker College *B*
Bridgewater State College *B*
Dean College *A*
Eastern Nazarene College *B*
Elms College *B*
Endicott College *B*
Fitchburg State College *B*
Holyoke Community College *C, A*
Lasell College *B, M*
Mount Ida College *B*
Nichols College *B*
North Shore Community College *C*
Northern Essex Community
  College *A*
Roxbury Community College *C*
Salem State College *B*
Springfield College *B, M*
Springfield Technical Community
  College *A*
University of Massachusetts
  Amherst *B, M, D*
Western New England College *B, M*

Michigan

Aquinas College *B*
Central Michigan University *B, M*
Cornerstone University *B*
Davenport University *B*
Eastern Michigan University *M*
Madonna University *B*
Northern Michigan University *B*
Northwood University: Michigan *B*
Siena Heights University *B*
University of Michigan *B*
Wayne State University *M*
Western Michigan University *M*

Minnesota

Century Community and Technical
  College *C*
Crown College *B*
Minnesota School of Business *C, A*
Minnesota State University
  Mankato *B, M, T*
North Central University *B*
Rochester Community and Technical
  College *A*
Saint Cloud State University *M*
St. Mary's University of Minnesota *B*
University of Minnesota
  Crookston *B*
Winona State University *B*

Mississippi

Belhaven University *B*
Jackson State University *M*
Mississippi College *B, M*
University of Southern
  Mississippi *B, M*

Missouri

Culver-Stockton College *B*
Fontbonne University *B*
Lindenwood University *B, M*
Maryville University of Saint Louis *B*
Missouri Baptist University *B*
Southeast Missouri State University *B*
Southwest Baptist University *B*

William Woods University *B*

Montana

Montana State University
  Billings *B, M*
  Bozeman *B*
Rocky Mountain College *B*

Nebraska

Bellevue University *B*
Concordia University *B*
Dana College *B*
Nebraska Wesleyan University *B*
Union College *B*
University of Nebraska
  Kearney *B*
Wayne State College *B, M*

Nevada

University of Nevada
  Las Vegas *M*

New Hampshire

Colby-Sawyer College *B*
Daniel Webster College *B*
NHTI-Concord's Community
  College *A*
New England College *B*
Southern New Hampshire
  University *B, M*

New Jersey

Fairleigh Dickinson University
  Metropolitan Campus *B*
Rowan University *B*
Seton Hall University *B*
Union County College *A*

New Mexico

New Mexico Highlands
  University *B, M*

New York

Adelphi University *B, M*
Canisius College *M*
Cazenovia College *B*
Finger Lakes Community College *A*
Genesee Community College *A*
Ithaca College *B, M*
Medaille College *B*
Saint Bonaventure University *B*
St. John Fisher College *B*
St. John's University *C, B, M*
State University of New York
  College at Brockport *B*
  College at Cortland *B, M*
  College at Fredonia *B*
  College of Agriculture and
    Technology at Morrisville *A, B*
  College of Technology at Alfred *A*
Syracuse University *B*
Tompkins Cortland Community
  College *A*

North Carolina

Barton College *B*
Campbell University *B*
Catawba College *B*
Chowan University *B*
East Carolina University *B*
Elon University *B*
Greensboro College *C, B*
Guilford College *B*
High Point University *B*
Johnson & Wales University:
  Charlotte *B*
Johnson C. Smith University *B*
Lenoir-Rhyne University *B*
Livingstone College *B*
Methodist University *B*
North Carolina State University *B*
Pfeiffer University *B*

St. Augustine's College *B*
Western Carolina University *B, M*
Wingate University *B*
Winston-Salem State University *B*

North Dakota

Jamestown College *B*
Mayville State University *B*
Minot State University *B*
North Dakota State University *B*
University of Mary *B*

Ohio

Ashland University *B*
Baldwin-Wallace College *B*
Bluffton University *B*
Bowling Green State University *B, M*
Cedarville University *B*
Cincinnati State Technical and
  Community College *C*
Cleveland State University *M*
College of Mount St Joseph *B*
Columbus State Community
  College *C, A*
Defiance College *B*
Heidelberg University *B*
Hocking College *A*
Malone University *B*
Miami University
  Oxford Campus *B, M*
Mount Union College *B*
Mount Vernon Nazarene
  University *A, B*
Ohio Northern University *B*
Ohio State University
  Columbus Campus *B*
Ohio University *M*
Otterbein College *B*
Shawnee State University *B*
Tiffin University *B, M*
University of Akron *C, B*
University of Dayton *B*
University of Findlay *B*
University of Rio Grande *B*
Urbana University *B*
Wilmington College *B*
Xavier University *B, M*
Youngstown State University *B*

Oklahoma

Bacone College *B*
Oklahoma Baptist University *B*
Rogers State University *B*

Oregon

Concordia University *B*
Corban College *B*
Lane Community College *C, A*
Southern Oregon University *B*
Warner Pacific College *B*

Pennsylvania

Alvernia University *B*
Bucks County Community College *A*
Butler County Community College *A*
California University of
  Pennsylvania *B, M*
DeSales University *B*
Drexel University *B, M*
Edinboro University of
  Pennsylvania *B*
Gannon University *B*
Gettysburg College *B*
Holy Family University *B*
Keystone College *A, B*
Lehigh Carbon Community College *A*
Lock Haven University of
  Pennsylvania *B*
Messiah College *B*
Millersville University of
  Pennsylvania *M*
Misericordia University *B*
Neumann University *B, M*

Northampton Community College *A*
Robert Morris University *B, M*
Seton Hill University *B*
Slippery Rock University of
   Pennsylvania *B, M*
University of Pittsburgh
   Bradford *B*
University of the Sciences in
   Philadelphia *B*
Waynesburg University *B*
Wilson College *B*
York College of Pennsylvania *B*

Puerto Rico
Inter American University of Puerto
   Rico
   Bayamon Campus *B*
Universidad Metropolitana *M*

Rhode Island
Johnson & Wales University:
   Providence *B*

South Carolina
Claflin University *B*
Coastal Carolina University *B*
Coker College *B*
Erskine College *B*
Limestone College *B*
Newberry College *B*
North Greenville University *B*
Southern Wesleyan University *B*
University of South Carolina *B*
Winthrop University *B*

South Dakota
Augustana College *B*
Black Hills State University *B*
Dakota Wesleyan University *B*
Northern State University *B*

Tennessee
Belmont University *M*
Cumberland University *B*
East Tennessee State University *B*
Lambuth University *B*
Martin Methodist College *B*
Southern Adventist University *B*
Tennessee Wesleyan College *B*
Trevecca Nazarene University *B*
Tusculum College *B*
Union University *B*
University of Memphis *B*
University of Tennessee
   Knoxville *B, M*

Texas
Abilene Christian University *B*
Hardin-Simmons University *M*
Howard Payne University *B*
LeTourneau University *B*
Lubbock Christian University *B*
Midwestern State University *B*
Rice University *B*
Schreiner University *B*
Texas Lutheran University *B*
Texas State University: San Marcos *B*
University of Houston *B*
University of Mary Hardin-Baylor *B*
University of Texas
   Austin *B*
University of the Incarnate Word *B, M*
Wayland Baptist University *B*

Utah
Salt Lake Community College *A*

Vermont
Castleton State College *B*
College of St. Joseph in Vermont *B*
Johnson State College *B*
Lyndon State College *B*

Norwich University *B*
Southern Vermont College *B*

Virginia
Averett University *B*
Eastern Mennonite University *B*
Emory & Henry College *B*
Ferrum College *B*
Hampton University *B*
Liberty University *B*
Lynchburg College *B*
Old Dominion University *B, M*
Virginia Commonwealth University *M*
Virginia Intermont College *B*
Virginia State University *M*

Washington
Bellingham Technical College *C*
Clark College *A*
Gonzaga University *B, M*
Lake Washington Technical College *C*
Spokane Falls Community College *A*
Washington State University *B, M*

West Virginia
Alderson-Broaddus College *B*
American Public University
   System *B, M*
Bethany College *B*
Concord University *B*
Davis and Elkins College *B*
University of Charleston *B*
West Virginia University *B*

Wisconsin
Cardinal Stritch University *B*
Marian University *B*
University of Wisconsin
   Parkside *B*
Viterbo University *B*

Sports communication

Connecticut
Albertus Magnus College *B*

Illinois
Bradley University *B*

Indiana
Valparaiso University *M*

Massachusetts
Lasell College *B*

New York
Ithaca College *B*
Marist College *B*

Statistics

Alabama
Auburn University *M, T*
University of South Alabama *B*

Alaska
University of Alaska
   Fairbanks *B, M*

Arizona
Arizona State University *M, D*
Northern Arizona University *M*

Arkansas
University of Arkansas *M*

California
California Polytechnic State
   University: San Luis Obispo *B*

California State University
   Chico *B*
   East Bay *B, M*
   Fullerton *B*
   Long Beach *B*
   Northridge *B*
San Diego State University *B, M*
San Francisco State University *B*
Stanford University *M, D*
University of California
   Berkeley *B, M, D*
   Davis *B, M, D*
   Irvine *M, D*
   Los Angeles *B, M, D*
   Riverside *B, M, D*
   San Diego *M*
   Santa Barbara *B, M, D*
University of Southern California *M*

Colorado
Colorado School of Mines *B*
Colorado State University *B, M, D*

Connecticut
University of Connecticut *B, M, D*
Yale University *B, M, D*

Delaware
University of Delaware *B, M, D*

District of Columbia
American University *B, M*
George Washington
   University *B, M, D*

Florida
Daytona State College *A*
Florida International University *B, M*
Florida State University *B, M, D*
University of Central Florida *B, M*
University of Florida *M*
University of Miami *M*
University of North Florida *B*

Georgia
Georgia Institute of Technology *M*
Kennesaw State University *M*
University of Georgia *B, M, D*

Idaho
Idaho State University *B*
University of Idaho *M*

Illinois
DePaul University *M*
Loyola University Chicago *B, M*
Northern Illinois University *M*
Northwestern University *B, M, D*
University of Chicago *B, M, D*
University of Illinois
   Chicago *B*
   Urbana-Champaign *B, M, D*

Indiana
Ball State University *M*
Grace College *B*
Indiana University-Purdue University
   Fort Wayne *B*
Indiana University-Purdue University
   Indianapolis *M*
Purdue University *B, M, D*
Purdue University
   North Central *A*
Saint Mary's College *B*

Iowa
Iowa State University *B, M, D*
Luther College *B*
University of Iowa *B, M, D*

Kansas
Kansas State University *B, M, D*

Kentucky
Bluegrass Community and Technical
   College *B*
Eastern Kentucky University *B*
University of Kentucky *M, D*

Louisiana
Louisiana State University and
   Agricultural and Mechanical
   College *M*
Tulane University *M*
Xavier University of Louisiana *B*

Maine
University of Southern Maine *M*

Maryland
Johns Hopkins University *B*
University of Maryland
   Baltimore County *B, M, D*
   College Park *M, D*

Massachusetts
Harvard College *B, M, D*
Mount Holyoke College *B*
Worcester Polytechnic Institute *M*

Michigan
Central Michigan University *B*
Eastern Michigan University *B, M*
Ferris State University *B*
Grand Valley State University *B*
Michigan State University *B, M, D*
Oakland University *B, M*
University of Michigan *B, M, D*
Wayne State University *M*
Western Michigan University *B, M, D*

Minnesota
Minnesota State University
   Mankato *M*
Saint Cloud State University *B, M*
University of Minnesota
   Duluth *B*
   Morris *B*
   Twin Cities *B, M, D*
University of St. Thomas *B*
Winona State University *B*

Mississippi
Mississippi State University *M*

Missouri
Northwest Missouri State
   University *B*
University of Missouri
   Columbia *B, M, D*
   Kansas City *B, M, D*
   Missouri University of Science and
      Technology *D*
Washington University in St.
   Louis *B, M*

Montana
Montana State University
   Bozeman *M, D*

Nebraska
University of Nebraska
   Lincoln *M, D*

New Jersey
Montclair State University *M*
New Jersey Institute of Technology *M*
Rutgers, The State University of New
   Jersey
   New Brunswick/Piscataway
      Campus *B, M, D*
Stevens Institute of Technology *M*

New Mexico
New Mexico State University *M*
University of New Mexico *B, M, D*

New York
Barnard College *B*
City University of New York
  Baruch College *B, M*
  Hunter College *B, M*
Columbia University *B*
Columbia University
  School of General Studies *B*
Cornell University *M, D*
Rochester Institute of
  Technology *B, M*
St. John Fisher College *B*
State University of New York
  College at Oneonta *B*
Syracuse University *M*
University of Rochester *B, M, D*

North Carolina
Appalachian State University *B*
North Carolina State
  University *B, M, D*
Queens University of Charlotte *B*
University of North Carolina
  Wilmington *B*

North Dakota
North Dakota State University *B, M, D*

Ohio
Bowling Green State University *B, M*
Case Western Reserve
  University *B, M, D*
Miami University
  Oxford Campus *B, M*
Ohio Northern University *B*
Ohio State University
  Columbus Campus *M, D*
Ohio Wesleyan University *B*
University of Akron *B, M*
Wright State University *B, M*

Oklahoma
Oklahoma State University *B, M, D*
University of Central Oklahoma *B*

Oregon
Oregon State University *M, D*
Portland State University *M*

Pennsylvania
Carnegie Mellon University *B, M, D*
La Salle University *B*
Lehigh University *B, M*
Penn State
  Abington *B*
  Altoona *B*
  Beaver *B*
  Berks *B*
  Brandywine *B*
  DuBois *B*
  Erie, The Behrend College *B*
  Fayette, The Eberly Campus *B*
  Greater Allegheny *B*
  Hazleton *B*
  Lehigh Valley *B*
  Mont Alto *B*
  New Kensington *B*
  Schuylkill *B*
  Shenango *B*
  University Park *B, M, D*
  Wilkes-Barre *B*
  Worthington Scranton *B*
  York *B*
Slippery Rock University of
  Pennsylvania *B*
Temple University *M, D*
University of Pennsylvania *B, M, D*
University of Pittsburgh *B, M, D*

West Chester University of
  Pennsylvania *M*

Rhode Island
Brown University *B*
Bryant University *B*
University of Rhode Island *M*

South Carolina
University of South Carolina *B, M, D*

South Dakota
South Dakota State University *M*

Tennessee
University of Tennessee
  Knoxville *B, M*

Texas
Baylor University *B, M, D*
North Lake College *A*
Rice University *B, M, D*
Sam Houston State University *M*
Southern Methodist
  University *B, M, D*
Stephen F. Austin State University *M*
Texas A&M University *M, D*
Texas Tech University *M*
University of Houston
  Clear Lake *B*
University of Texas
  Austin *M*
  Dallas *B, M, D*
  El Paso *M*
  San Antonio *B, M*

Utah
Brigham Young University *B, M*
Snow College *A*
University of Utah *M*
Utah State University *B, M*

Vermont
Castleton State College *B*
University of Vermont *B, M*

Virginia
George Mason University *M, D*
University of Virginia *M, D*
Virginia Polytechnic Institute and
  State University *B, M, D*

Washington
University of Washington *M, D*
Washington State University *M*

West Virginia
West Virginia University *M*

Wisconsin
Marquette University *B*
University of Wisconsin
  Madison *B, M, D*

Wyoming
Eastern Wyoming College *A*
University of Wyoming *B, M, D*

Structural biology

California
Stanford University *D*

New York
State University of New York
  Buffalo *M, D*
  Stony Brook *D*

Structural engineering

California
California State Polytechnic
  University: Pomona *M*
University of California
  San Diego *B, M, D*
University of Southern
  California *B, M*

Florida
University of Central Florida *B*

Illinois
Illinois Institute of Technology *M*
University of Illinois
  Urbana-Champaign *B, M, D*

Massachusetts
Bristol Community College *A*

Michigan
Western Michigan University *B*

Missouri
Washington University in St.
  Louis *M, D*

New Jersey
Stevens Institute of Technology *M*

New York
Polytechnic Institute of New York
  University *M*
State University of New York
  Buffalo *B*

Pennsylvania
Lehigh University *B, M, D*
Penn State
  Harrisburg *B*

Wisconsin
Marquette University *M, D*
Milwaukee School of Engineering *M*

Substance abuse counseling

Alabama
Gadsden State Community College *A*
Wallace State Community College at
  Hanceville *A*

Arizona
Pima Community College *C, A*
Rio Salado College *C, A*
Tohono O'odham Community
  College *C*

Arkansas
Arkansas State University *M*
University of Arkansas
  Pine Bluff *M*
University of Central Arkansas *C, B*

California
Allan Hancock College *C*
Bethany University *C, B*
Butte College *C, A*
California Institute of Integral
  Studies *M, D*
California State University
  East Bay *B*
Charles Drew University of Medicine
  and Science *C, A*
City College of San Francisco *C*
College of San Mateo *C, A*
College of the Redwoods *C*
College of the Siskiyous *C, A*

Cypress College *C*
Diablo Valley College *C*
East Los Angeles College *C*
Fresno City College *C, A*
Glendale Community College *C*
Hartnell College *C, A*
Imperial Valley College *C, A*
Lake Tahoe Community College *A*
Loma Linda University *M*
Los Angeles Pierce College *C, A*
Loyola Marymount University *M*
Mendocino College *C, A*
Merced College *C, A*
Modesto Junior College *C*
Mount San Jacinto College *C, A*
National Polytechnic College of
  Science *A*
Oxnard College *C, A*
Palo Verde College *C*
Saddleback College *C*
San Diego City College *C, A*
San Jose City College *C, A*
Santa Barbara City College *C, A*
Yuba Community College
  District *C, A*

Connecticut
Gateway Community College *C, A*
Housatonic Community College *A*
Manchester Community College *A*
Middlesex Community College *A*
Naugatuck Valley Community
  College *A*
Tunxis Community College *A*

Delaware
Delaware Technical and Community
  College
  Stanton/Wilmington *C, A*
  Terry *C, A*

Florida
Florida Keys Community College *C*
Florida State College at Jacksonville *A*
St. Petersburg College *C, A*

Illinois
City Colleges of Chicago
  Harold Washington College *C, A*
  Kennedy-King College *C*
College of DuPage *C, A*
College of Lake County *C, A*
Dominican University *B*
Elgin Community College *C*
Governors State University *M*
Moraine Valley Community
  College *C, A*
National-Louis University *C, B, M*
Oakton Community College *C*
Prairie State College *A*
Triton College *C, A*
Waubonsee Community College *C*

Indiana
Indiana University-Purdue University
  Fort Wayne *B*
Indiana Wesleyan University *A, B*
Vincennes University *C*

Iowa
Iowa Western Community College *A*
Southeastern Community College
  North Campus *A*
University of Iowa *M*

Kansas
Colby Community College *A*
Dodge City Community College *A*
Kansas City Kansas Community
  College *C, A*
Neosho County Community
  College *C*
Pittsburg State University *B*

Washburn University *A, B*

Louisiana

Northwestern State University *B*
Southern University
  New Orleans *A, B*
University of Louisiana at Monroe *M*

Maine

University of Southern Maine *M*

Maryland

Anne Arundel Community
  College *C, A*
Community College of Baltimore
  County *C, A*
Coppin State University *M*
Towson University *B*
Washington Adventist University *C*
Wor-Wic Community College *C, A*

Massachusetts

Holyoke Community College *C*
Massasoit Community College *C*
Middlesex Community College *C*
North Shore Community College *C, A*
Northern Essex Community
  College *C, A*
Springfield College *M*
University of Massachusetts
  Boston *C*

Michigan

Lake Superior State University *A*
Madonna University *C*
University of Detroit Mercy *B, M*
Washtenaw Community College *A*
Wayne County Community College *C*

Minnesota

Century Community and Technical
  College *C, A*
Fond du Lac Tribal and Community
  College *C*
Mesabi Range Community and
  Technical College *C, A*
Metropolitan State University *B*
Minneapolis Community and
  Technical College *C, A*
North Central University *B*
Ridgewater College *A*
Rochester Community and Technical
  College *C*
Saint Cloud State University *B, M*
University of Minnesota
  Twin Cities *C*
Walden University *M*

Missouri

Missouri Technical School *B*
Missouri Valley College *B*

Montana

Dawson Community College *A*
Flathead Valley Community College *A*
Fort Belknap College *A*
Fort Peck Community College *A*
Little Big Horn College *A*
Stone Child College *A*
University of Great Falls *A, B*

Nebraska

Bellevue University *B, M*
Little Priest Tribal College *A*

Nevada

Truckee Meadows Community
  College *C, A*

New Hampshire

Keene State College *A, B*

NHTI-Concord's Community
  College *A*

New Jersey

Burlington County College *C*
Georgian Court University *C*
Mercer County Community College *C*

New Mexico

Northern New Mexico College *A*
Santa Fe Community College *C*

New York

Broome Community College *A*
City University of New York
  Kingsborough Community
  College *C*
Corning Community College *A*
Dutchess Community College *C*
Erie Community College
  City Campus *A*
Finger Lakes Community College *A*
Genesee Community College *A*
Hudson Valley Community College *A*
Mercy College *M*
Metropolitan College of New York *C*
Mohawk Valley Community College *A*
Niagara County Community
  College *C*
Pace University *M*
St. Joseph's College: Suffolk
  Campus *C*
Suffolk County Community College *A*
Sullivan County Community
  College *A*
Tompkins Cortland Community
  College *A*
Ulster County Community College *A*
Westchester Community College *C, A*

North Carolina

Central Piedmont Community
  College *C, A*
East Carolina University *M*
Guilford Technical Community
  College *C, A*
Roanoke-Chowan Community
  College *A*
Sandhills Community College *A*
South Piedmont Community
  College *C*
Southwestern Community
  College *C, A*
Wayne Community College *A*

North Dakota

Minot State University *B*
University of Mary *B, M*

Ohio

Columbus State Community
  College *C, A*
Kent State University *C*
North Central State College *C*
Southern State Community College *A*
Tiffin University *C, B*
University of Akron *C, A*

Oklahoma

Oklahoma State University
  Oklahoma City *A*

Oregon

Central Oregon Community
  College *C*
Chemeketa Community College *C, A*
Portland Community College *C, A*
Rogue Community College *C*
Southwestern Oregon Community
  College *A*

Pennsylvania

Alvernia University *B*
Community College of Allegheny
  County *C*
Community College of Philadelphia *C*
Drexel University *B*
Misericordia University *C*
Montgomery County Community
  College *C*
St. Vincent College *C*
Seton Hill University *C*
Slippery Rock University of
  Pennsylvania *M*
University of Scranton *C*

Rhode Island

Community College of Rhode
  Island *A*
Rhode Island College *B*

South Dakota

Kilian Community College *C, A*
Oglala Lakota College *A*
Sisseton Wahpeton College *A*
University of South Dakota *B, M, D*

Tennessee

Southwest Tennessee Community
  College *C*

Texas

Alvin Community College *C*
Amarillo College *C, A*
Angelina College *C, A*
Austin Community College *C, A*
Central Texas College *C, A*
Del Mar College *A*
Eastfield College *C, A*
El Paso Community College *A*
Grayson County College *C, A*
Houston Community College
  System *C*
Howard College *C, A*
Lamar State College at Port
  Arthur *C, A*
Lee College *C, A*
Lone Star College System *C, A*
McLennan Community College *C, A*
Midland College *A*
Odessa College *A*
St. Mary's University *M*
San Antonio College *C, A*
San Jacinto College *C*
Texarkana College *C, A*
Texas State Technical College
  West Texas *A*
Tyler Junior College *A*
University of Texas
  Pan American *B*

Vermont

College of St. Joseph in Vermont *B, M*

Virginia

J. Sargeant Reynolds Community
  College *C*
Northern Virginia Community
  College *C, A*

Washington

Bellevue College *C*
Clark College *C, A*
Lower Columbia College *C, A*
Olympic College *C*
Peninsula College *C, A*
Pierce College *C*
Spokane Falls Community
  College *C, A*
Wenatchee Valley College *C, A*
Yakima Valley Community
  College *C, A*

West Virginia

Mountain State College *A*

Wisconsin

Chippewa Valley Technical College *A*
Fox Valley Technical College *A*
Gateway Technical College *C*
Marquette University *M*
Moraine Park Technical College *A*

Wyoming

Casper College *C, A*

Surgical technology

Alabama

Bevill State Community College *C*
Calhoun Community College *C*
Gadsden State Community College *C*
Lurleen B. Wallace Community
  College *C*
Southern Union State Community
  College *C*

Arizona

GateWay Community College *C, A*
Lamson College *C*
Mohave Community College *C, A*

Arkansas

North Arkansas College *C, A*
Southeast Arkansas College *C, A*
University of Arkansas
  Fort Smith *C, A*

California

Concorde Career College: North
  Hollywood *C*
Concorde Career College: San
  Bernardino *C*
Concorde Career College: San
  Diego *C*
Kaplan College: Salida *A*
Saddleback College *C, A*
San Joaquin Valley College *A*
Silicon Valley College
  Western Career College: San Jose *A*
Skyline College *C, A*
Southwestern College *C, A*
Western Career College: Citrus
  Heights *C, A*

Colorado

Anthem College *A*

Connecticut

Manchester Community College *A*

Florida

Brevard Community College *C*
Central Florida Community College *C*
Daytona State College *C*
Florida State College at Jacksonville *C*
Gulf Coast Community College *C*
Indian River State College *C*
Palm Beach Community College *C*
Santa Fe College *C*
Southwest Florida College *A*

Georgia

Albany Technical College *C*
Athens Technical College *C*
Augusta Technical College *C*
Brown Mackie College: Atlanta *C, A*
Central Georgia Technical College *C*
Chattahoochee Technical College *C*
Columbus Technical College *C, A*
DeKalb Technical College *C*
Macon State College *A*
Middle Georgia College *A*
Middle Georgia Technical College *C*

Savannah Technical College *C, A*
Southeastern Technical College *C*
Southwest Georgia Technical
 College *C, A*
Waycross College *A*

Idaho

Eastern Idaho Technical College *A*

Illinois

City Colleges of Chicago
 Malcolm X College *A*
College of DuPage *C, A*
College of Lake County *C*
Elgin Community College *C*
Illinois Central College *C, A*
John A. Logan College *C*
John Wood Community College *C*
Kaskaskia College *C*
Parkland College *C, A*
Prairie State College *C*
Rend Lake College *C*
Richland Community College *C, A*
Robert Morris University: Chicago *A*
Southeastern Illinois College *C*
Trinity College of Nursing and Health
 Sciences *C, A*
Triton College *C*
Waubonsee Community College *C*

Indiana

Harrison College
 Fort Wayne *A*
 Indianapolis East *A*
Ivy Tech Community College
 Central Indiana *A*
 Columbus *A*
 East Central *A*
 Kokomo *A*
 Lafayette *A*
 Northwest *A*
 Southwest *A*
 Wabash Valley *A*
National College: Indianapolis *A*
University of St. Francis *A*
Vincennes University *C, A*

Iowa

Iowa Lakes Community College *C*
Kirkwood Community College *C, A*
Marshalltown Community College *C*
Mercy College of Health Sciences *C, A*
Western Iowa Tech Community
 College *C, A*

Kansas

Hutchinson Community College *C*
Johnson County Community
 College *A*
Seward County Community College *C*
Washburn University *A*

Kentucky

Bluegrass Community and Technical
 College *C, A*
Madisonville Community College *C*
Maysville Community and Technical
 College *C*
Owensboro Community and
 Technical College *C*
St. Catharine College *A*
Somerset Community College *C*
Spencerian College *A*
West Kentucky Community and
 Technical College *C*

Louisiana

Bossier Parish Community College *C*
Delgado Community College *C*
Our Lady of the Lake College *A*
Southern University
 Shreveport *A*

Maine

Southern Maine Community
 College *A*

Maryland

Baltimore City Community College *C*
Carroll Community College *C, A*
Chesapeake College *C*
Community College of Baltimore
 County *C*
Frederick Community College *C, A*
Howard Community College *C, A*
Montgomery College *A*

Massachusetts

Bunker Hill Community College *C*
Massachusetts Bay Community
 College *C*
North Shore Community College *C*
Quincy College *C*
Quinsigamond Community College *C*
Springfield Technical Community
 College *A*

Michigan

Baker College
 of Cadillac *A*
 of Clinton Township *A*
 of Flint *A*
 of Jackson *A*
 of Muskegon *A*
 of Port Huron *A*
Baker College of Allen Park *A*
Delta College *C, A*
Grand Rapids Community College *A*
Henry Ford Community College *A*
Kalamazoo Valley Community
 College *C*
Kirtland Community College *C, A*
Lansing Community College *A*
Macomb Community College *C, A*
Northern Michigan University *A, B*
Oakland Community College *C, A*
Washtenaw Community College *C*
Wayne County Community
 College *C, A*

Minnesota

Anoka Technical College *C*
High-Tech Institute *A*
Lake Superior College *C, A*
Minnesota West Community and
 Technical College *C*
Northland Community & Technical
 College *A*
Rasmussen College
 St. Cloud *A*
Rasmussen College: Brooklyn Park *A*
Rasmussen College: Lake
 Elmo/Woodbury *A*
Rochester Community and Technical
 College *A*
St. Cloud Technical College *C, A*
St. Mary's University of Minnesota *C*

Mississippi

Hinds Community College *C, A*
Virginia College Gulf Coast *A*

Missouri

High-Tech Institute *A*
Metropolitan Community College:
 Penn Valley *C*
Ozarks Technical Community
 College *C*
Southeast Missouri Hospital College of
 Nursing and Health Sciences *C*
Three Rivers Community College *C*

Montana

Flathead Valley Community College *A*

Montana State University
 Billings *A*
 College of Technology: Great
 Falls *A*
University of Montana *A*

Nebraska

Nebraska Methodist College of
 Nursing and Allied Health *C*
Northeast Community College *A*
Southeast Community College *C, A*

Nevada

High-Tech Institute *A*

New Jersey

Bergen Community College *C*
Ocean County College *C*

New Mexico

Central New Mexico Community
 College *C*

New York

City University of New York
 Kingsborough Community
 College *A*
Mohawk Valley Community College *C*
Nassau Community College *A*
Niagara County Community
 College *A*
Onondaga Community College *C*
Trocaire College *A*

North Carolina

Blue Ridge Community College *C, A*
Cabarrus College of Health
 Sciences *C, A*
Carolinas College of Health
 Sciences *C*
Catawba Valley Community College *C*
Coastal Carolina Community
 College *C*
College of the Albemarle *C*
Durham Technical Community
 College *C*
Edgecombe Community College *C*
Fayetteville Technical Community
 College *A*
Guilford Technical Community
 College *C, A*
Isothermal Community College *C*
Lenoir Community College *C*
Miller-Motte Technical College *C, A*
Miller-Motte Technical College:
 Cary *A*
Robeson Community College *A*
Rockingham Community College *C*
Sandhills Community College *C, A*
South College *C*
South Piedmont Community
 College *C*
Wake Technical Community
 College *C*
Wayne Community College *C*
Wilson Community College *C, A*

North Dakota

Bismarck State College *A*
Rasmussen College: Fargo *A*

Ohio

Central Ohio Technical College *C, A*
Cincinnati State Technical and
 Community College *A*
Columbus State Community
 College *C, A*
Cuyahoga Community College
 Metropolitan Campus *A*
Mount Carmel College of Nursing *C*
National College: Cincinnati *A*

Owens Community College
 Toledo *A*
University of Akron *C, A*
University of Akron: Wayne College *A*
University of Cincinnati
 Clermont College *A*

Oklahoma

Northern Oklahoma College *A*
Platt College
 Tulsa *C*

Oregon

Mt. Hood Community College *A*

Pennsylvania

Community College of Allegheny
 County *C, A*
Harrisburg Area Community
 College *C, A*
Lackawanna College *A*
Lock Haven University of
 Pennsylvania *A*
Luzerne County Community
 College *A*
McCann School of Business and
 Technology: Dickson City *A*
Montgomery County Community
 College *C, A*
Mount Aloysius College *C, A*
Northampton Community College *A*
Pennsylvania College of
 Technology *A, B*
University of Pittsburgh
 Johnstown *A*

Puerto Rico

Ponce Paramedical College *C*

Rhode Island

New England Institute of
 Technology *A*

South Carolina

Aiken Technical College *C*
Central Carolina Technical College *A*
Florence-Darlington Technical
 College *C*
Greenville Technical College *C*
Horry-Georgetown Technical
 College *C*
Midlands Technical College *C*
Miller-Motte Technical College *A*
Spartanburg Community College *C*
Tri-County Technical College *C*
York Technical College *C*

South Dakota

Presentation College *A*
Southeast Technical Institute *C*
Western Dakota Technical Institute *C*

Tennessee

Nashville State Community College *C*
National College
 Knoxville *A*
National College: Memphis *A*
Northeast State Community College *C*

Texas

Amarillo College *C, A*
Austin Community College *C, A*
Del Mar College *C, A*
El Centro College *C*
El Paso Community College *A*
Galveston College *C*
Houston Community College
 System *C*
Kilgore College *C, A*
Lamar State College at Port
 Arthur *C, A*
Odessa College *A*

St. Philip's College *C*
San Jacinto College *C, A*
South Plains College *C*
Tarrant County College *C*
Temple College *C*
Texas State Technical College
    Harlingen *C, A*
Trinity Valley Community College *C*
Tyler Junior College *C, A*
Wharton County Junior College *C*

Utah

Dixie State College of Utah *C*
Salt Lake Community College *C*

Virginia

Lord Fairfax Community College *C*
Piedmont Virginia Community
    College *C*
Virginia Western Community
    College *C*

Washington

Bellingham Technical College *C, A*
Centralia College *C*
Clover Park Technical College *A*
Renton Technical College *C, A*
Spokane Community College *A*
Yakima Valley Community
    College *C, A*

West Virginia

Blue Ridge Community and Technical
    College *A*
West Virginia Northern Community
    College *C, A*
West Virginia University at
    Parkersburg *C*

Wisconsin

Chippewa Valley Technical College *A*
Gateway Technical College *A*
Lakeshore Technical College *C*
Mid-State Technical College *C*
Milwaukee Area Technical College *A*
Nicolet Area Technical College *A*
Northcentral Technical College *A*
Northeast Wisconsin Technical
    College *C*
Waukesha County Technical
    College *A*
Western Technical College *C*

Wyoming

Laramie County Community
    College *A*

Surveying engineering

Florida

Florida Atlantic University *B*

Indiana

Purdue University *B*
Vincennes University *A*

Iowa

Des Moines Area Community
    College *A*

Maine

University of Maine *B, M, D*

Michigan

Baker College
    of Flint *A*
Michigan Technological University *B*

Nevada

Great Basin College *B*

New York

Paul Smith's College *A*

North Carolina

Southwestern Community College *A*

Pennsylvania

Penn State
    Wilkes-Barre *B*

Rhode Island

Community College of Rhode
    Island *A*

Texas

Texas A&M University
    Corpus Christi *M*

Washington

Bates Technical College *A*

Surveying technology

Alabama

Troy University *B*

Alaska

University of Alaska
    Anchorage *A, B*

Arkansas

University of Arkansas
    Monticello *A, B*
University of Arkansas Community
    College at Morrilton *C, A*

California

California State University
    Fresno *B*
Chabot College *A*
City College of San Francisco *C*
Coastline Community College *C*
College of the Canyons *C, A*
Cuyamaca College *A*
Diablo Valley College *C*
Palomar College *C, A*
Santiago Canyon College *C*
Shasta College *C*

Colorado

Metropolitan State College of
    Denver *B*
Westwood College: Denver North *A*

Delaware

Delaware Technical and Community
    College
    Owens *A*
    Stanton/Wilmington *A*

Florida

Palm Beach Community College *A*
University of Florida *B*

Georgia

Albany Technical College *C*
Middle Georgia College *A*
Southern Polytechnic State
    University *C, B*

Idaho

Idaho State University *B*

Illinois

Morrison Institute of Technology *A*
Parkland College *A*
Rend Lake College *A*
Triton College *A*
Waubonsee Community College *C*

Indiana

Purdue University *B*
Vincennes University *A*

Iowa

Kirkwood Community College *A*

Louisiana

Nicholls State University *B*

Maryland

College of Southern Maryland *C*
Community College of Baltimore
    County *C*

Massachusetts

Wentworth Institute of Technology *C*

Michigan

Ferris State University *A, B*
Macomb Community College *C, A*
Montcalm Community College *A*
Mott Community College *A*

Minnesota

Dunwoody College of
    Technology *C, A*
Saint Cloud State University *B*
St. Paul College *C, A*

Missouri

Metropolitan Community College:
    Longview *A*

Montana

Flathead Valley Community College *A*

Nevada

College of Southern Nevada *A*

New Hampshire

University of New Hampshire *A*
White Mountains Community
    College *A*

New Jersey

Essex County College *A*
Gloucester County College *A*
Middlesex County College *A*
Ocean County College *A*
Thomas Edison State College *A, B*

New Mexico

Central New Mexico Community
    College *C, A*
New Mexico State University *B*
San Juan College *C, A*

New York

Mohawk Valley Community
    College *C, A*
Monroe Community College *C*
Orange County Community College *C*
Paul Smith's College *A*
State University of New York
    College of Environmental Science
        and Forestry *A*
    College of Technology at
        Alfred *A, B*
Sullivan County Community
    College *A*

North Carolina

Asheville-Buncombe Technical
    Community College *A*
Central Carolina Community
    College *A*
Central Piedmont Community
    College *C, A*
Fayetteville Technical Community
    College *A*

Guilford Technical Community
    College *A*
Sandhills Community College *A*
Tri-County Community College *A*
Wake Technical Community
    College *A*

Ohio

Cincinnati State Technical and
    Community College *C, A*
Columbus State Community
    College *C, A*
James A. Rhodes State College *C*
Ohio State University
    Columbus Campus *B*
Owens Community College
    Toledo *C, A*
Stark State College of Technology *A*
Terra State Community College *C, A*
University of Akron *C, A, B*

Oregon

Chemeketa Community College *C*
Oregon Institute of Technology *B*

Pennsylvania

Penn State
    Wilkes-Barre *A*
Pennsylvania College of
    Technology *A*

Puerto Rico

Universidad Politecnica de Puerto
    Rico *B*

South Carolina

Trident Technical College *C*

South Dakota

Southeast Technical Institute *A*

Tennessee

East Tennessee State University *B*

Texas

Austin Community College *C, A*
Texas A&M University
    Corpus Christi *B*
Tyler Junior College *C, A*

Utah

Salt Lake Community College *A*

Virginia

J. Sargeant Reynolds Community
    College *C*
Virginia Western Community
    College *C*

Washington

Bates Technical College *C, A*
Bellingham Technical College *A*
Centralia College *A*
Clark College *C, A*
Peninsula College *A*
Renton Technical College *C, A*

West Virginia

Glenville State College *A*

Wisconsin

Nicolet Area Technical College *A*

Wyoming

Sheridan College *A*
University of Wyoming *C*

Sustainable/organic agriculture

Iowa
Iowa State University *M, D*

Kentucky
University of Kentucky *B*

Maine
University of Maine *B*

New York
State University of New York
College of Technology at Alfred *A*

North Carolina
Central Carolina Community
College *C, A*

Vermont
Sterling College *B*
University of Vermont *B*

Swedish

Washington
University of Washington *B*

System administration

Alabama
Remington College
Mobile *A*

Alaska
University of Alaska
Southeast *C*

Arizona
Chandler-Gilbert Community College
Pecos *A*
Cochise College *C*
Coconino County Community
College *C, A*
Collins College *A, B*
Eastern Arizona College *A*
GateWay Community College *C, A*
Paradise Valley Community College *C*
Tohono O'odham Community
College *A*
University of Phoenix *A*

Arkansas
East Arkansas Community College *C*

California
Allan Hancock College *C*
DeVry University
Sherman Oaks *A*
Foothill College *C*
Hartnell College *C, A*
Heald College
Hayward *A*
Roseville *A*
Kaplan College: Panorama City *A*
Long Beach City College *C*
MTI College *C, A*
National University *B, M*
Ohlone College *A*
Platt College
Ontario *A*
Sierra College *C, A*
Silicon Valley College
Western Career College:
Emeryville *A*

Colorado
American Sentinel University *B*
Colorado Technical University *B*

Jones International University *B*
Westwood College of Technology
Westwood College: Denver
South *A, B*

Florida
Central Florida Community College *A*
Florida National College *A*
St. Petersburg College *C, A, B*

Georgia
DeVry University
Alpharetta *A*

Illinois
DeVry University
Tinley Park *A*
Harper College *C*
Heartland Community College *C*
Kaskaskia College *C, A*
Lincoln Land Community College *C*
Moraine Valley Community College *C*
Morton College *C*
Richland Community College *C*
Sauk Valley Community College *C*
Triton College *C*
Waubonsee Community College *C*

Indiana
Harrison College
Indianapolis Northwest *A*
Terre Haute *A*
Indiana University-Purdue University
Indianapolis *A, B*
Ivy Tech Community College
Bloomington *C*
Central Indiana *C*
Columbus *C*
East Central *C*
Kokomo *C*
Lafayette *C*
North Central *C*
Northeast *C*
Northwest *C*
Richmond *C*
South Central *C*

Iowa
Dordt College *B*
North Iowa Area Community
College *A*
Northwest Iowa Community
College *A*

Kansas
Central Christian College of Kansas *A*

Kentucky
Draughons Junior College *C, A*
Sullivan College of Technology and
Design *A*

Maryland
Frederick Community College *A*
Kaplan College: Hagerstown *A, B*
TESST College of Technology
Beltsville *C*

Massachusetts
Bunker Hill Community College *C, A*
Springfield Technical Community
College *C, A*

Michigan
Cleary University *A*
Michigan Technological University *B*
Mott Community College *C*
Oakland Community College *C*
Wayne County Community College *A*

Minnesota
Academy College *C, A*

Century Community and Technical
College *C*
Crown College *A, B*
Dunwoody College of Technology *B*
Globe University *C, A, B*
Herzing University *A*
Minnesota School of Business *C, A*

Missouri
Crowder College *A*
Vatterott College *A*

Montana
Montana State University
College of Technology: Great
Falls *C*
University of Great Falls *B*

Nevada
College of Southern Nevada *C*

New Hampshire
Daniel Webster College *C*

New Jersey
Bergen Community College *A*

New York
Globe Institute of Technology *C, A, B*
Rochester Institute of
Technology *B, M*
St. Francis College *B*
State University of New York
College of Agriculture and
Technology at Morrisville *B*
Ulster County Community
College *C, A*

North Carolina
Brunswick Community College *C*
College of the Albemarle *C*

North Dakota
Williston State College *A*

Ohio
Vatterott College: Cleveland *A*

Oregon
Linn-Benton Community College *A*

Pennsylvania
Community College of Philadelphia *A*
Lincoln Technical Institute: Northeast
Philadelphia *A*
Peirce College *C, A*

South Carolina
York Technical College *C*

South Dakota
Dakota State University *C*

Texas
Blinn College *A*
Houston Community College
System *C, A*
San Antonio College *C*
Temple College *C, A*
Victoria College *C, A*

Utah
Salt Lake Community College *C*
Western Governors University *B*

Vermont
Champlain College *B*

Virginia
ECPI College of Technology: Virginia
Beach *C, A*
ECPI Technical College: Roanoke *A*

Washington
Green River Community College *A*
Olympic College *C*
South Seattle Community
College *C, A*

Wisconsin
Nicolet Area Technical College *C*

Wyoming
Laramie County Community
College *C*

Systematic biology

California
University of California
Los Angeles *B*

Systems engineering

Arizona
University of Arizona *B, M, D*

Arkansas
University of Arkansas
Little Rock *B*

California
California State University
Fullerton *M*
Northridge *M*
Loyola Marymount University *M*
National University *B*
Northwestern Polytechnic
University *B, M, D*
University of California
San Diego *B, M, D*
University of Southern
California *B, M, D*

Colorado
United States Air Force Academy *B*

District of Columbia
Howard University *B, M*

Florida
Florida Institute of Technology *M*
University of Florida *B, M*

Georgia
Southern Polytechnic State
University *B, M*

Idaho
University of Idaho *M*

Illinois
University of Illinois
Urbana-Champaign *M, D*

Indiana
Rose-Hulman Institute of
Technology *M*

Iowa
Iowa State University *M*

Louisiana
Louisiana Tech University *M*

Maine
Maine Maritime Academy *B*

University of Maine *B*

Maryland
United States Naval Academy *B*
University of Maryland
 Baltimore County *M*
 College Park *M*

Massachusetts
Massachusetts Institute of
 Technology *M, D*
Worcester Polytechnic Institute *B, M*

Michigan
Lawrence Technological University *M*
Oakland University *M, D*
University of Michigan *M*

Minnesota
University of St. Thomas *M*
Walden University *M*

Missouri
University of Missouri
 Missouri University of Science and
 Technology *M*
Washington University in St.
 Louis *B, M, D*

Nebraska
University of Nebraska
 Lincoln *M*

New Hampshire
University of New Hampshire *B, D*

New Jersey
New Jersey Institute of Technology *M*
Stevens Institute of Technology *M, D*

New York
Cornell University *M*
Polytechnic Institute of New York
 University *M*
Rensselaer Polytechnic Institute *M*
Rochester Institute of
 Technology *B, M*
United States Merchant Marine
 Academy *B*
United States Military Academy *B*

North Carolina
University of North Carolina
 Charlotte *B*

Ohio
Case Western Reserve
 University *B, M, D*
Eastern Gateway Community
 College *A*
Edison State Community College *A*
Ohio State University
 Columbus Campus *B, M, D*
Wright State University *B*

Oregon
Portland State University *M*

Pennsylvania
Lehigh University *B, M, D*
Penn State
 University Park *M*
University of Pennsylvania *B, M, D*

Rhode Island
Johnson & Wales University:
 Providence *B*
Providence College *B*

South Carolina
Clemson University *M, D*

Tennessee
University of Tennessee
 Chattanooga *D*

Texas
St. Mary's University *M*
Southern Methodist University *M*
Texas A&M University
 Galveston *B*
University of Houston *M, D*
University of Texas
 Arlington *M*
 El Paso *M*

Virginia
George Mason University *B, M, D*
Liberty University *B*
Old Dominion University *M*
University of Virginia *B, M, D*
Virginia Polytechnic Institute and
 State University *M*

West Virginia
West Virginia University Institute of
 Technology *M*

Wisconsin
Marquette University *M, D*
University of Wisconsin
 Madison *M*

Wyoming
University of Wyoming *B*

Systems science/theory

California
Stanford University *B*

Florida
University of Central Florida *M, D*

Idaho
Idaho State University *M*

Illinois
Northwestern University *D*

Indiana
Indiana University
 Bloomington *B, D*
St. Mary-of-the-Woods College *M*

Massachusetts
Worcester Polytechnic Institute *M*

Mississippi
Mississippi State University *D*

Missouri
Saint Louis University *D*
Washington University in St.
 Louis *B, M, D*

New York
State University of New York
 Binghamton *M, D*
United States Military Academy *B*

Ohio
Kent State University *M*
Wright State University *B*

Oregon
Portland State University *D*

Pennsylvania
Carnegie Mellon University *B*
La Salle University *B*

West Chester University of
 Pennsylvania *M*

Tennessee
University of Tennessee
 Knoxville *M*

Virginia
James Madison University *B*

West Virginia
Marshall University *B*

Talmudic studies

California
Yeshiva Ohr Elchonon Chabad/West
 Coast Talmudical Seminary *B*

Illinois
Telshe Yeshiva-Chicago *B, M*

New Jersey
Beth Medrash Govoha *B, M*

New York
Beis Medrash Heichal Dovid *B, M*
Central Yeshiva Tomchei
 Tmimim-Lubavitch *B, M*
Kehilath Yakov Rabbinical
 Seminary *B*
Machzikei Hadath Rabbinical
 College *B*
Mesivta Torah Vodaath Seminary *B, D*
Mirrer Yeshiva Central
 Institute *B, M, D*
Ohr Somayach Tanenbaum Education
 Center *B*
Rabbinical Academy Mesivta Rabbi
 Chaim Berlin *B, M*
Rabbinical College Beth Shraga *B*
Rabbinical College Bobover Yeshiva
 B'nei Zion *B, D*
Rabbinical College Ch'san Sofer of
 New York *B, M*
Rabbinical College of Long Island *B*
Rabbinical College of Ohr Shimon
 Yisroel *B*
Rabbinical Seminary of
 America *B, M, D*
Shor Yoshuv Rabbinical College *B, M*
Talmudical Institute of Upstate New
 York *B, D*
Talmudical Seminary Oholei Torah *B*
Torah Temimah Talmudical
 Seminary *B*
U.T.A. Mesivta-Kiryas Jocl *B*
United Talmudical Seminary *B, M*
Yeshiva D'Monsey Rabbinical
 College *B*
Yeshiva Derech Chaim *B, D*
Yeshiva Gedolah Imrei Yosef
 D'Spinka *B*
Yeshiva Gedolah Zichron Moshe *B, D*
Yeshiva Karlin Stolin *B*
Yeshiva Shaar Hatorah *B, M*
Yeshiva Shaarei Torah of Rockland *B*
Yeshiva and Kolel Bais Medrash
 Elyon *B, D*
Yeshiva and Kollel Harbotzas
 Torah *B, D*
Yeshiva of Nitra *B, M*
Yeshiva of the Telshe Alumni *B*
Yeshivas Novominsk *B*
Yeshivat Mikdash Melech *B, M*
Yeshivath Viznitz *B, D*

Ohio
Rabbinical College of Telshe *B, M, D*

Pennsylvania
Talmudical Yeshiva of Philadelphia *B*

Taxation

Alabama
Troy University *M*
University of Alabama *M*

Arizona
Arizona State University *M*

Arkansas
Northwest Arkansas Community
 College *C*

California
California State University
 East Bay *M*
 Fullerton *M*
 Northridge *M*
 San Bernardino *M*
De Anza College *C, A*
Golden Gate University *M*
Los Angeles Pierce College *C*
National University *M*
San Diego State University *M*
San Jose State University *M*
Santa Rosa Junior College *C*
University of San Diego *M*
University of Southern California *M*
Yuba Community College District *A*

Colorado
Colorado Technical University *C*
University of Colorado
 Boulder *M*
University of Denver *M*

Connecticut
Fairfield University *M*
Manchester Community College *C*
University of New Haven *M*

District of Columbia
American University *M*

Florida
Florida Atlantic University *M*
Florida International University *M*
Florida State University *M*
Nova Southeastern University *M*
University of Central Florida *M*
University of Miami *M*

Georgia
Georgia State University *M*

Illinois
DePaul University *M*
Northern Illinois University *M*
Saint Xavier University *M*
University of Illinois
 Urbana-Champaign *M*

Louisiana
University of New Orleans *M*

Maryland
University of Baltimore *M*

Massachusetts
American International College *M*
Bentley University *M*
Boston University *M*
Northeastern University *M*
Suffolk University *M*

Michigan
Grand Valley State University *M*
Walsh College of Accountancy and
 Business Administration *M*
Washtenaw Community College *C*
Wayne State University *M*

Minnesota
University of Minnesota
Twin Cities *M*

Mississippi
Mississippi State University *M*
University of Mississippi *M*

Missouri
Fontbonne University *M*

New Jersey
Fairleigh Dickinson University
College at Florham *M*
Metropolitan Campus *M*
Rutgers, The State University of New
Jersey
New Brunswick/Piscataway
Campus *M*
Newark Regional Campus *M*
Seton Hall University *M*

New York
City University of New York
Baruch College *M*
Hofstra University *M*
Long Island University
Brooklyn Campus *M*
C. W. Post Campus *M*
Pace University *M*
St. John's University *M*
State University of New York
Albany *M*
College at Old Westbury *M*

North Carolina
Cape Fear Community College *C*
North Carolina State University *C*

Ohio
Capital University *M*
Ohio University
Southern Campus at Ironton *C*
Stark State College of Technology *A*
University of Akron *M*
University of Cincinnati
Clermont College *C*
University of Toledo *M*

Oklahoma
University of Tulsa *M*

Pennsylvania
Philadelphia University *M*
Villanova University *M*
Widener University *M*

Puerto Rico
Turabo University *M*
University of the Sacred Heart *M*

Rhode Island
Bryant University *M*

South Carolina
York Technical College *C*

Texas
Baylor University *M*
Texas A&M University *M*
University of Houston *M*
University of North Texas *M*
University of Texas
Arlington *M*
San Antonio *M*

Virginia
ECPI College of Technology: Virginia
Beach *C, A*
ECPI Technical College: Roanoke *A*
George Mason University *M*

Virginia Commonwealth University *M*

Taxidermy

New York
Finger Lakes Community College *C*

North Carolina
Montgomery Community College *C*

Teacher assistance

Alaska
University of Alaska
Fairbanks *C, A*

Arizona
Cochise College *C*
Estrella Mountain Community
College *A*
Mesa Community College *A*
University of Phoenix *A*

Arkansas
Northwest Arkansas Community
College *C*

California
American River College *A*
Antelope Valley College *A*
Barstow Community College *A*
Cerritos College *A*
Chabot College *A*
City College of San Francisco *A*
College of Alameda *A*
Contra Costa College *A*
El Camino College: Compton
Center *A*
Hartnell College *C, A*
Long Beach City College *A*
Los Angeles Mission College *A*
Los Angeles Southwest College *A*
Mount St. Mary's College *A*
West Hills College: Lemoore *C*

Colorado
Community College of Denver *A*
Front Range Community College *C*
Otero Junior College *A*
Red Rocks Community College *C, A*

Connecticut
Goodwin College *A*
Manchester Community College *A*
Sacred Heart University *A*

Florida
South Florida Community College *A*

Georgia
South Georgia College *C*

Illinois
City Colleges of Chicago
Harold Washington College *A*
Malcolm X College *A*
Danville Area Community College *A*
Elgin Community College *C*
Harper College *C, A*
Heartland Community College *A*
Highland Community College *C*
Illinois Eastern Community Colleges
Lincoln Trail College *A*
John A. Logan College *A*
Joliet Junior College *A*
Kankakee Community College *C, A*
Kaskaskia College *C, A*
Lewis and Clark Community
College *A*
Lincoln Land Community College *A*

Moraine Valley Community
College *C, A*
Sauk Valley Community College *A*
South Suburban College of Cook
County *A*
Triton College *C*
Waubonsee Community College *C, A*

Indiana
St. Mary-of-the-Woods College *A*
Valparaiso University *A*
Vincennes University *A*

Iowa
Dordt College *A*
Ellsworth Community College *A*
Western Iowa Tech Community
College *C*

Kansas
Butler Community College *A*
Cloud County Community College *A*
Seward County Community College *A*

Kentucky
Bluegrass Community and Technical
College *C, A*
Elizabethtown Community and
Technical College *A*
Hopkinsville Community College *C, A*
Somerset Community College *A*

Maine
Central Maine Community
College *C, A*
Kennebec Valley Community
College *A*

Massachusetts
Bristol Community College *C*
Massasoit Community College *A*
North Shore Community College *A*

Michigan
Baker College
of Cadillac *A*
of Flint *A*
of Port Huron *A*
Bay de Noc Community College *C*
Gogebic Community College *A*
Grand Rapids Community College *A*
Henry Ford Community College *C*
Kirtland Community College *A*
Mid Michigan Community College *A*
Montcalm Community College *A*
Mott Community College *C, A*
Southwestern Michigan College *A*

Minnesota
Central Lakes College *A*
Century Community and Technical
College *C, A*
Lake Superior College *C*
Mesabi Range Community and
Technical College *A*
Minnesota State Community and
Technical College *A*
Ridgewater College *A*
Rochester Community and Technical
College *C, A*
St. Cloud Technical College *A*

Missouri
East Central College *A*
St. Charles Community College *A*
St. Louis Community College
St. Louis Community College at
Florissant Valley *A*
State Fair Community College *A*

Montana
University of Montana: Western *A*

New Jersey
Brookdale Community College *A*
Middlesex County College *A*
Ocean County College *C*

New Mexico
Clovis Community College *A*
Eastern New Mexico University:
Roswell Campus *A*
New Mexico State University
Alamogordo *A*
Carlsbad *A*

New York
City University of New York
Bronx Community College *C, A*
Kingsborough Community
College *A*
Medgar Evers College *A*
Columbia-Greene Community
College *C*
Dutchess Community College *A*
Erie Community College
City Campus *C*
Finger Lakes Community College *C*
Genesee Community College *C, A*
Herkimer County Community
College *A*
Jefferson Community College *C*
Maria College *A*
Mercy College *C*
Monroe Community College *C*
Nassau Community College *C*
Westchester Community College *C*

North Carolina
Carteret Community College *C, A*
Durham Technical Community
College *A*
Edgecombe Community College *A*
Halifax Community College *A*
Lenoir Community College *A*
Mitchell Community College *A*
Nash Community College *A*
Roanoke-Chowan Community
College *A*
Sandhills Community College *A*
Vance-Granville Community
College *A*

North Dakota
Bismarck State College *A*
Dakota College at Bottineau *A*

Ohio
Hocking College *A*
North Central State College *A*
Southern State Community College *A*
Tiffin University *A*

Oregon
Blue Mountain Community College *A*
Klamath Community College *C, A*
Linn-Benton Community College *A*
Portland Community College *C, A*
Southwestern Oregon Community
College *A*
Umpqua Community College *C*

Pennsylvania
Bucks County Community College *A*
Community College of Allegheny
County *A*
Community College of Beaver
County *A*
Lehigh Carbon Community College *A*
Luzerne County Community
College *A*
McCann School of Business and
Technology: Dickson City *A*
Montgomery County Community
College *A*

Northampton Community
College *C, A*
Pennsylvania Highlands Community
College *A*

Puerto Rico

Turabo University *C*
Universidad Metropolitana *C*
Universidad del Este *C*

South Carolina

Forrest Junior College *A*
Williamsburg Technical College *A*

South Dakota

Black Hills State University *A*
Oglala Lakota College *A*
Sinte Gleska University *A*
University of Sioux Falls *A*

Tennessee

Johnson Bible College *A*
Trevecca Nazarene University *A*

Texas

El Centro College *A*
Midland College *A*
North Lake College *A*
Odessa College *A*
Richland College *A*
St. Philip's College *A*
San Antonio College *A*
Temple College *A*
Texas State Technical College
Harlingen *A*

Virginia

Eastern Mennonite University *A*
J. Sargeant Reynolds Community
College *A*
John Tyler Community College *A*
Lord Fairfax Community College *C*
Tidewater Community College *A*

Washington

Bellingham Technical College *C*
Big Bend Community College *A*
Centralia College *A*
Clover Park Technical College *A*
Grays Harbor College *A*
Green River Community College *C, A*
Highline Community College *A*
Lower Columbia College *A*
Pierce College *A*
Renton Technical College *C, A*
Shoreline Community College *A*
Spokane Falls Community College *A*
Whatcom Community College *A*
Yakima Valley Community College *C*

West Virginia

Fairmont State University *A*
New River Community and Technical
College *A*
West Virginia University at
Parkersburg *C, A*

Wisconsin

Alverno College *A*
Gateway Technical College *A*
Waukesha County Technical
College *A*
Western Technical College *A*

Wyoming

Casper College *C, A*
Central Wyoming College *A*
Sheridan College *A*

Teacher education, multiple levels

Alabama

Alabama State University *M*
Auburn University *D, T*
Faulkner University *B, M, T*
Samford University *B*
Troy University *B, M, T*
University of North Alabama *B, M*

Arizona

Central Arizona College *A*
Northcentral University *M, D*
Prescott College *B, M, T*
University of Phoenix *M*

Arkansas

Arkansas State University
Beebe *A*
East Arkansas Community College *A*
Harding University *B, M, T*
North Arkansas College *A*
Southern Arkansas University *M*
Southern Arkansas University Tech *A*
University of Arkansas
Monticello *M*
University of Central Arkansas *M*

California

Alliant International University *T*
Azusa Pacific University *B, T*
Fresno City College *A*
Glendale Community College *A*
Hope International University *M*
National University *B, T*
Occidental College *M*
Pepperdine University *T*
Simpson University *T*
University of California
Irvine *M*
University of San Francisco *M*
University of the Pacific *B, T*
Vanguard University of Southern
California *T*
Whittier College *T*

Colorado

Adams State College *B, M, T*
Colorado College *M*
University of Colorado
Colorado Springs *M*

Connecticut

Quinnipiac University *B, M*
Western Connecticut State
University *M*

Delaware

Delaware Technical and Community
College
Owens *A*
Stanton/Wilmington *A*
Terry *A*

District of Columbia

George Washington University *M*
Howard University *M*

Florida

Saint Thomas University *M*
Southeastern University *M, T*
University of Miami *M*
University of Tampa *M*

Georgia

Atlanta Metropolitan College *A*
Darton College *A*
East Georgia College *A*
Georgia Highlands College *A*
Georgia Southern University *M*

Gordon College *A*
LaGrange College *M*
Macon State College *A*

Hawaii

Chaminade University of
Honolulu *M, T*
University of Hawaii
Manoa *M, T*

Idaho

Boise State University *T*

Illinois

Chicago State University *B*
Concordia University Chicago *B, M, T*
Dominican University *M*
Eureka College *B*
Lincoln College *A*
North Park University *B, M, T*
Quincy University *B, T*
Southern Illinois University
Carbondale *M, T*
University of Illinois
Urbana-Champaign *B, M, D, T*
Waubonsee Community College *A*

Indiana

Earlham College *M*
Indiana University
Bloomington *B, T*
Manchester College *B, T*
Marian University *M, T*
Purdue University *B, M, D*
Purdue University
Calumet *B*
University of Indianapolis *T*
University of Notre Dame *M*

Iowa

Buena Vista University *T*
Ellsworth Community College *A*
Loras College *B*
Waldorf College *B*

Kansas

Bethany College *T*
Bethel College *T*
Central Christian College of Kansas *A*
Coffeyville Community College *A*
Friends University *T*
Tabor College *B*

Kentucky

Asbury College *M, T*
Eastern Kentucky University *M*
Midway College *B*
Thomas More College *M*
University of Louisville *A*

Louisiana

Centenary College of Louisiana *B, T*
University of Louisiana at Monroe *M*
Xavier University of Louisiana *B, T*

Maine

University of Maine
Fort Kent *B*
University of New England *M*
University of Southern Maine *T*

Maryland

Baltimore City Community College *A*
Coppin State University *M*
Frederick Community College *A*
Goucher College *M*
Hood College *T*
McDaniel College *M*
Washington Bible College *B, T*

Massachusetts

Brandeis University *M*

Bridgewater State College *M*
Eastern Nazarene College *M*
Framingham State College *M*
Lesley University *M*
Merrimack College *T*
Smith College *M*
University of Massachusetts
Dartmouth *M*

Michigan

Adrian College *B*
Baker College
of Auburn Hills *B*
of Clinton Township *B*
of Flint *B*
of Jackson *B*
of Muskegon *B*
of Owosso *B*
Grand Rapids Community College *A*
Hillsdale College *B*
Kirtland Community College *A*
Lake Superior State University *B, M, T*
Western Michigan University *M*

Minnesota

Capella University *M, D*
Century Community and Technical
College *A*
College of St. Scholastica *B, M*
Martin Luther College *B*
Minneapolis Community and
Technical College *A*
Minnesota State University
Mankato *M*
Ridgewater College *A*
Saint Cloud State University *B*
St. Mary's University of Minnesota *M*
University of St. Thomas *B, M*
Walden University *M*
Winona State University *B, M, T*

Mississippi

Alcorn State University *M*
Delta State University *M*
Jackson State University *M*
Millsaps College *T*
Mississippi Gulf Coast Community
College *A*
Pearl River Community College *A*

Missouri

Harris-Stowe State University *B, T*
Maryville University of Saint
Louis *M, T*
Missouri Baptist University *M, T*
Missouri Southern State
University *B, T*
Missouri State University *M*
Saint Louis University *B, M, D*
University of Central Missouri *T*
Washington University in St. Louis *T*
William Jewell College *T*
William Woods University *T*

Montana

Rocky Mountain College *B, T*
University of Montana: Western *B, T*

Nebraska

Concordia University *B, T*
University of Nebraska
Lincoln *B*
York College *B, T*

Nevada

Sierra Nevada College *M*

New Hampshire

Franklin Pierce University *M*
Plymouth State University *M, T*
White Mountains Community
College *A*

New Jersey
Caldwell College *T*
College of St. Elizabeth *T*
Cumberland County College *A*
Fairleigh Dickinson University
  College at Florham *M*
  Metropolitan Campus *M*
Felician College *B*
Gloucester County College *A*
Raritan Valley Community College *A*
Richard Stockton College of New
  Jersey *B, M*
Rider University *M*
Saint Peter's College *M*

New Mexico
New Mexico Institute of Mining and
  Technology *T*
Western New Mexico University *M*

New York
College of Saint Rose *M, T*
Columbia-Greene Community
  College *A*
D'Youville College *M, T*
Dowling College *B, M*
Elmira College *B, M, T*
Hofstra University *B, M*
Ithaca College *B, M, T*
Jewish Theological Seminary of
  America *M, D*
Marist College *M*
Mount Saint Mary College *B, T*
Pace University *M, T*
Saint Bonaventure University *M*
St. Thomas Aquinas College *B, M, T*
Schenectady County Community
  College *A*
State University of New York
  Buffalo *M*
  College at Oneonta *B*
  College at Plattsburgh *B*
  New Paltz *M*

North Carolina
Brevard College *B*
Gardner-Webb University *B*
Halifax Community College *A*
Peace College *B*
University of North Carolina
  Asheville *T*
  Charlotte *M*

North Dakota
North Dakota State University *M*
Sitting Bull College *A*

Ohio
Bowling Green State University *B*
Central State University *B*
Defiance College *B*
John Carroll University *M, T*
Marietta College *B*
Mount Union College *T*
Ohio Wesleyan University *B*
Otterbein College *B*
Owens Community College
  Toledo *A*
Shawnee State University *B*
Union Institute & University *B*
University of Dayton *B, M, T*
University of Findlay *B, M, T*
University of Rio Grande *B, T*
Washington State Community
  College *A*
Wilmington College *B*
Wright State University *M*
Youngstown State University *B, M*

Oklahoma
Family of Faith College *B*
Hillsdale Free Will Baptist College *B*
Oklahoma City Community College *A*
Oral Roberts University *M*
Rose State College *A*
Southwestern Oklahoma State
  University *M*

Oregon
Concordia University *B, M, T*
Corban College *B*
George Fox University *M, T*
Lewis & Clark College *M*
Linfield College *T*
Multnomah University *M*
Northwest Christian
  University *B, M, T*
University of Oregon *M, T*
Warner Pacific College *T*
Western Oregon University *B, M, T*

Pennsylvania
Arcadia University *B, M, T*
Baptist Bible College of
  Pennsylvania *B, M*
Cedar Crest College *M, T*
Chestnut Hill College *B, T*
Duquesne University *B, M, T*
Edinboro University of
  Pennsylvania *M*
Gettysburg College *T*
Juniata College *B, T*
Keystone College *B, T*
La Salle University *B, T*
Mansfield University of
  Pennsylvania *B, T*
Moravian College *T*
Penn State
  Harrisburg *M*
St. Francis University *B, M, T*
Westminster College *B, T*

Puerto Rico
Universidad Metropolitana *B, D*
University of Puerto Rico
  Bayamon University College *B*

Rhode Island
Rhode Island College *B*

South Carolina
Charleston Southern University *B*
Columbia International
  University *B, M*
Furman University *T*
University of South Carolina *M*
Winthrop University *T*

South Dakota
Northern State University *B, M, T*
University of Sioux Falls *B*

Tennessee
Cumberland University *B, M*
Freed-Hardeman University *B, T*
LeMoyne-Owen College *T*
Southern Adventist University *M*
Tennessee Wesleyan College *B, T*
Trevecca Nazarene University *M, T*
University of Memphis *B*
University of Tennessee
  Knoxville *M*
  Martin *M*

Texas
Arlington Baptist College *B, T*
Blinn College *A*
Dallas Christian College *B, T*
Howard Payne University *B, T*
LeTourneau University *B, T*
Lubbock Christian University *B*
St. Edward's University *B, T*
St. Mary's University *T*
Tarleton State University *M, T*

Texas A&M University
  Commerce *B*
Texas Christian University *B, M*
Texas Lutheran University *B, T*
Texas Wesleyan University *B, T*
University of Mary Hardin-Baylor *T*
University of Texas
  of the Permian Basin *M*
Wayland Baptist University *B, T*
West Texas A&M University *T*

Utah
Brigham Young University *M*
Utah State University *B*

Vermont
College of St. Joseph in Vermont *B, M*
Goddard College *M*
Johnson State College *B, M*

Virginia
Averett University *B, T*
Bluefield College *B, T*
Longwood University *B, T*
Virginia Union University *B*

Washington
Antioch University Seattle *M, T*
Evergreen State College *M, T*
Saint Martin's University *T*
Seattle University *M*
University of Puget Sound *M*
University of Washington *M*
Washington State
  University *B, M, D, T*
Whitworth University *B, M, T*

West Virginia
Bethany College *B*
Ohio Valley University *B*
Salem International University *B, T*

Wisconsin
Beloit College *T*
Carroll University *T*
Concordia University Wisconsin *B*
Northland College *B, T*
University of Wisconsin
  Green Bay *T*
  Superior *B, M, T*

Wyoming
Western Wyoming Community
  College *A*

Technical and business writing

Alabama
Auburn University *M*

Arizona
Northern Arizona University *C*
Pima Community College *C*

Arkansas
University of Arkansas
  Fort Smith *B*
  Little Rock *B, M*

California
De Anza College *C, A*
Orange Coast College *A*
San Francisco State University *C, B*

Colorado
Pikes Peak Community College *A*
University of Colorado
  Denver *M*

Connecticut
Three Rivers Community College *C*
University of Hartford *B*

Florida
University of Central Florida *D*

Georgia
Athens Technical College *C*

Idaho
Boise State University *M*

Illinois
Black Hawk College *A*
Chicago State University *B*
College of Lake County *C, A*

Indiana
Indiana University-Purdue University
  Fort Wayne *B*
St. Mary of the Woods College *B*
Valparaiso University *B*

Iowa
Iowa State University *B*

Kansas
Central Christian College of Kansas *A*
Pittsburg State University *B, M*

Kentucky
Murray State University *C*

Maryland
Montgomery College *C*
Towson University *M*

Massachusetts
Fitchburg State College *B*
Northeastern University *M*
Salem State College *B*
University of Massachusetts
  Boston *C*
  Dartmouth *M*
Worcester Polytechnic Institute *B*

Michigan
Eastern Michigan University *B*
Ferris State University *B*
Grand Valley State University *B*
Madonna University *B*
Michigan State University *B, M*
Michigan Technological University *C*
Washtenaw Community College *A*

Minnesota
Inver Hills Community College *C*
Metropolitan State University *B, M*
Minnesota State University
  Mankato *B, M*

Missouri
Missouri Southern State University *B*
Missouri State University *B*
St. Louis Community College
  St. Louis Community College at
    Florissant Valley *B*
  St. Louis Community College at
    Meramec *C*
University of Missouri
  Missouri University of Science and
    Technology *B, M*
Webster University *C*

Montana
Montana Tech of the University of
  Montana *B, M*
University of Montana *M*

New Jersey

New Jersey Institute of
Technology *B, M*

New Mexico

New Mexico Institute of Mining and
Technology *B*

New York

D'Youville College *B*
New York Institute of Technology *C*
State University of New York
College of Agriculture and
Technology at Morrisville *A*
Farmingdale *B*

North Carolina

East Carolina University *D*
Gardner-Webb University *B*
North Carolina State University *M*

North Dakota

North Dakota State University *D*

Ohio

Bowling Green State University *B, M*
Cedarville University *B*
Cincinnati State Technical and
Community College *C, A*
Edison State Community College *C, A*
Miami University
Oxford Campus *M*
Ohio Northern University *B*
Terra State Community College *A*
University of Findlay *C*
Youngstown State University *B*

Oklahoma

East Central University *B*
Oklahoma City University *M*

Oregon

Linn-Benton Community College *A*
Portland Community College *C*
Portland State University *M*

Pennsylvania

Carlow University *B*
Carnegie Mellon University *B, M*
Chatham University *M*
Drexel University *B, M*
Elizabethtown College *B*
Kutztown University of
Pennsylvania *B*
La Salle University *B*
Penn State
Berks *B*
Lehigh Valley *B*
Slippery Rock University of
Pennsylvania *B, M*
York College of Pennsylvania *B*

Rhode Island

University of Rhode Island *B*

South Carolina

Coker College *B*
Winthrop University *B*

Tennessee

Chattanooga State Community
College *A*
Maryville College *B*
Tennessee Technological University *B*

Texas

Austin Community College *C, A*
Lee College *A*
Lubbock Christian University *B*
Texas State University: San
Marcos *M, T*

Texas Tech University *B, M, D*
University of Houston
Downtown *B, M*
University of North Texas *M*
University of Texas
El Paso *M*
San Antonio *B*

Utah

Weber State University *B*

Vermont

Champlain College *B*

Virginia

James Madison University *B, M*
Northern Virginia Community
College *C*
Thomas Nelson Community
College *C*

Washington

Everett Community College *A*
University of Washington *B*
Washington State University *C*

West Virginia

West Virginia State University *B*
West Virginia University *M*

Wisconsin

Gateway Technical College *A*
Mount Mary College *B, M, T*
University of Wisconsin
Stout *B*

Technology/industrial arts education

Alaska

University of Alaska
Southeast *M*

Arizona

Eastern Arizona College *A*
Northern Arizona University *B, M, T*
Prescott College *B, T*

Arkansas

Arkansas State University *A*

California

Azusa Pacific University *M*
California Baptist University *M, T*
California State University
Los Angeles *B, M*
Cypress College *A*
Pepperdine University *M*
San Francisco State University *T*

Colorado

Colorado State University *B, T*

Connecticut

Central Connecticut State
University *B, M, T*
University of Hartford *M*

Delaware

Wilmington University *M*

Florida

Miami Dade College *A*
St. Petersburg College *B*

Georgia

Valdosta State University *M*

Hawaii

University of Hawaii
Honolulu Community College *A*

Idaho

University of Idaho *B, M, T*

Illinois

Chicago State University *B*
Illinois State University *B*
Loyola University Chicago *M*

Indiana

Ball State University *B, M, T*
Indiana State University *M*
Purdue University *B, M, D*
Vincennes University *A*

Iowa

Iowa State University *B, M, D, T*
University of Northern Iowa *B*

Kansas

Fort Hays State University *B*
McPherson College *B, T*
Pittsburg State University *B, M, T*

Kentucky

Berea College *B, T*
Eastern Kentucky University *B, M*
Murray State University *M, T*

Louisiana

Northwestern State University *M*
University of Louisiana at Lafayette *B*

Maine

University of Southern Maine *B, T*

Maryland

Loyola University Maryland *M*
University of Maryland
Eastern Shore *B, M*

Massachusetts

Endicott College *M*
Fitchburg State College *B, M, T*
Westfield State College *B, M, T*

Michigan

Central Michigan University *B, M*
Delta College *A*
Eastern Michigan University *B, T*
Grand Rapids Community College *A*
Michigan Technological University *T*
Northern Michigan University *B, T*
Western Michigan University *B, T*

Minnesota

Bemidji State University *M, T*
Minnesota State University
Mankato *B, M, T*
Saint Cloud State University *B*
University of Minnesota
Crookston *B*
Twin Cities *B, M, D, T*

Mississippi

Jackson State University *M*
Mississippi State University *T*
University of Southern Mississippi *B*

Missouri

College of the Ozarks *B, T*
Lindenwood University *B*
Missouri Southern State
University *B, M, T*
Missouri State University *B*
Southeast Missouri State
University *B, T*
University of Central Missouri *B, M, T*

Montana

Montana State University
Bozeman *B*
University of Montana: Western *B, T*

Nebraska

Chadron State College *B, M*
Concordia University *B, T*
University of Nebraska
Kearney *B*
Lincoln *B*
Wayne State College *B, T*

Nevada

University of Nevada
Reno *B, T*

New Hampshire

Keene State College *B, M, T*

New Jersey

The College of New Jersey *B, M, T*
Montclair State University *B, M, T*

New Mexico

Central New Mexico Community
College *A*
University of New Mexico *B*
Western New Mexico University *B*

New York

City University of New York
New York City College of
Technology *B*
College of Saint Rose *M, T*
Hofstra University *T*
New York Institute of
Technology *B, T*
Pace University *M, T*
State University of New York
College at Buffalo *B, M, T*
Oswego *B, M, T*

North Carolina

Appalachian State University *B, M, T*
Elizabeth City State University *B*
North Carolina Agricultural and
Technical State University *B, M, T*
North Carolina State
University *B, M, D, T*

North Dakota

University of North Dakota *M*

Ohio

Bowling Green State University *B, M*
Kent State University *B*
Ohio Northern University *B, T*
Ohio State University
Columbus Campus *B*
Youngstown State University *M*

Oklahoma

East Central University *B*
Langston University *B*
Northwestern Oklahoma State
University *B, T*
Southwestern Oklahoma State
University *B, M, T*
University of Central Oklahoma *B*

Oregon

Oregon State University *B, M*

Pennsylvania

Arcadia University *M*

Puerto Rico

National College of Business and
Technology: Bayamon *B*

Rhode Island

Rhode Island College *B, M*

South Carolina

Clemson University *B, M*
South Carolina State University *B, T*

South Dakota

Black Hills State University *B*

Tennessee

Middle Tennessee State University *B*
Trevecca Nazarene University *M, T*
University of Tennessee
  Knoxville *M, D, T*
Vanderbilt University *M*

Texas

El Paso Community College *A*
Prairie View A&M University *M*
Sam Houston State University *M, T*
Sul Ross State University *M*
Texas A&M University
  Commerce *M, T*
  Kingsville *M*
University of Texas
  Tyler *M*
Wayland Baptist University *B, T*

Utah

Brigham Young University *B*
Southern Utah University *B, T*
Utah State University *B, D*

Virginia

Old Dominion University *B, M, D, T*

Washington

Western Washington University *B*

West Virginia

Fairmont State University *B*

Wisconsin

University of Wisconsin
  Platteville *B, T*
  Stout *B, M, T*
Viterbo University *B, T*

Wyoming

Casper College *A*
University of Wyoming *B*

Telecommunications technology

Alabama

Gadsden State Community
  College *C, A*

California

City College of San Francisco *C*
National University *M*
Southwestern College *C, A*

Colorado

University of Denver *M*

Florida

Palm Beach Community College *C*

Georgia

Southern Polytechnic State
  University *B*

Idaho

Idaho State University *B*

Illinois

Waubonsee Community College *C*

Indiana

Ivy Tech Community College
  Central Indiana *C, A*
  North Central *C, A*
  Northeast *C, A*
  Northwest *C, A*
  South Central *C, A*
  Southwest *C, A*

Iowa

Western Iowa Tech Community
  College *C, A*

Maryland

Capitol College *A, B*
Howard Community College *C*

Massachusetts

Massasoit Community College *A*
North Shore Community College *A*
Quinsigamond Community
  College *A*
Springfield Technical Community
  College *A*

Michigan

Ferris State University *B*

Minnesota

Lake Superior College *A*
Minnesota State Community and
  Technical College *C, A*

Nebraska

University of Nebraska
  Lincoln *M*

New York

Canisius College *M*
Cayuga County Community College *A*
City University of New York
  New York City College of
    Technology *A, B*
Erie Community College
  South Campus *A*
Pace University *C*
Rochester Institute of
  Technology *B, M*
St. John's University *C, A, B*
Schenectady County Community
  College *A*

Ohio

Marion Technical College *C, A*

Puerto Rico

Turabo University *M*

Rhode Island

Community College of Rhode
  Island *C, A*

South Carolina

York Technical College *C*

Texas

Collin County Community College
  District *C, A*
Lone Star College System *C*
San Antonio College *A*
Texas A&M University *B*
Texas State Technical College
  Harlingen *C, A*
Texas State Technical College:
  Marshall *C, A*

Utah

Salt Lake Community College *C, A*

Virginia

ECPI College of Technology: Virginia
  Beach *C, A*
ECPI Technical College: Roanoke *A*

Washington

Clark College *C, A*

Wisconsin

Herzing University *A, B*
Waukesha County Technical
  College *A*

Textile science

Alabama

Auburn University *M*

California

Fashion Institute of Design and
  Merchandising
  Los Angeles *A*
  San Diego *A*
  San Francisco *A*

Georgia

University of Georgia *D*

Michigan

Michigan State University *B, M*

Pennsylvania

Philadelphia University *C, B, M*

Washington

Bates Technical College *C*

Textile sciences/ engineering

Alabama

Auburn University *B, M, D*

Georgia

Georgia Institute of
  Technology *B, M, D*

Massachusetts

University of Massachusetts
  Dartmouth *B, M*

North Carolina

North Carolina State
  University *B, M, D*

Pennsylvania

Philadelphia University *B, M, D*

Washington

Bates Technical College *A*

Theater arts management

Alabama

Calhoun Community College *A*
Faulkner University *B*

California

California Baptist University *B*
College of the Siskiyous *C, A*
Ohlone College *C*
University of Southern California *B*

Colorado

Colorado Mountain College *C*

District of Columbia

Howard University *B*

Florida

Florida State University *M*
Nova Southeastern University *B*
University of Miami *B*

Georgia

Berry College *B*

Illinois

DePaul University *M*
Lewis University *B*

Indiana

University of Evansville *B*

Iowa

St. Ambrose University *B*
Waldorf College *B*

Kansas

Benedictine College *B*
Central Christian College of Kansas *A*
Pittsburg State University *B*

Maine

University of Maine
  Farmington *B*
University of Southern Maine *B*

Massachusetts

Bay State College *A, B*
Eastern Nazarene College *B*
Emerson College *B*

Michigan

Aquinas College *B*
Eastern Michigan University *M*
Michigan State University *B, M*

Missouri

Crowder College *A*
Lindenwood University *B, M*

Nebraska

Metropolitan Community
  College *C, A*

New Jersey

Bergen Community College *A*
Seton Hall University *B*

New Mexico

College of Santa Fe *B*

New York

Ithaca College *B*
State University of New York
  College at Buffalo *B*

North Carolina

Guilford College *B*

Ohio

Ohio University *B*
University of Akron *M*

Oklahoma

Oklahoma City University *B*

Oregon

University of Portland *B*
Western Oregon University *B*

Pennsylvania

Carnegie Mellon University *M*
Drexel University *B*

Gettysburg College *B*
Juniata College *B*
Seton Hill University *B*
Slippery Rock University of
Pennsylvania *B*

South Carolina
Converse College *B*

Texas
Texas Tech University *M*

Utah
College of Eastern Utah *T*

Virginia
Regent University *B*

Washington
Pacific Lutheran University *B*

West Virginia
West Virginia Wesleyan College *B*

Wisconsin
University of Wisconsin
Whitewater *B*

Theater design and technology

Alabama
Faulkner University *B*

Alaska
University of Alaska
Fairbanks *B*

Arizona
University of Arizona *B*

California
Allan Hancock College *C*
California Institute of the Arts *C, B, M*
California State University
East Bay *B*
Long Beach *B, M*
San Bernardino *B*
College of the Sequoias *A*
Cypress College *C, A*
Diablo Valley College *C, A*
Fashion Institute of Design and
Merchandising
Los Angeles *A*
San Francisco *A*
Foothill College *C, A*
Fresno City College *C, A*
Gavilan College *A*
Glendale Community College *A*
Grossmont College *C, A*
Irvine Valley College *A*
Long Beach City College *A*
Los Angeles Pierce College *C, A*
MiraCosta College *C, A*
Ohlone College *C, A*
Palomar College *C*
Pepperdine University *B*
San Francisco State University *M*
Santa Barbara City College *A*
Santa Rosa Junior College *C*
University of Southern
California *B, M*
Vanguard University of Southern
California *B*

Colorado
Community College of Denver *C*
Red Rocks Community College *C, A*

Connecticut
University of Connecticut *B*

Delaware
University of Delaware *B*

District of Columbia
Howard University *B*

Florida
Florida Southern College *B*
Florida State College at Jacksonville *A*
Florida State University *B*
University of Miami *B*
Valencia Community College *A*

Georgia
Savannah College of Art and
Design *B, M*

Illinois
Columbia College Chicago *B*
DePaul University *B, M*
Illinois Wesleyan University *B*
Lincoln College *A*
Millikin University *B*

Indiana
Huntington University *B*
Indiana University
Bloomington *A*
Vincennes University *A*

Iowa
Coe College *B*
Cornell College *B*
Drake University *B*
University of Iowa *M*
University of Northern Iowa *B*

Kansas
Central Christian College of Kansas *A*
University of Kansas *B, M*

Louisiana
Centenary College of Louisiana *B*

Maryland
Carroll Community College *A*
Harford Community College *A*
Montgomery College *A*
University of Maryland
College Park *M*

Massachusetts
Boston University *B, M*
Brandeis University *M*
Emerson College *B*
Fitchburg State College *B*
Salem State College *B*

Michigan
Central Michigan University *B*
Michigan Technological University *B*
Oakland University *B*
University of Michigan *B*
University of Michigan
Flint *B*

Minnesota
Minnesota State University
Mankato *B*
University of Minnesota
Duluth *B*

Missouri
College of the Ozarks *B*
Lindenwood University *B*
Northwest Missouri State
University *B*
University of Missouri
Kansas City *M*

Montana
Rocky Mountain College *B*

New Hampshire
Keene State College *B*

New Jersey
Essex County College *A*
Kean University *B*
Raritan Valley Community College *A*

New Mexico
College of Santa Fe *B*
University of New Mexico *B*

New York
City University of New York
New York City College of
Technology *C, B*
Cornell University *B*
Fordham University *B*
Genesee Community College *A*
Ithaca College *B*
Sarah Lawrence College *M*
State University of New York
Binghamton *B*
College at Fredonia *B*
Purchase *B, M*
Suffolk County Community College *A*
Wagner College *B*

North Carolina
Elon University *B*
Greensboro College *C, B*
High Point University *B*
Lees-McRae College *B*
University of North Carolina School of
the Arts *C, B, M*

North Dakota
Dickinson State University *B*

Ohio
Ohio University *M*
Otterbein College *B*
University of Cincinnati *B, M*
University of Findlay *B*
University of Rio Grande *A*
Wright State University *B*
Youngstown State University *B*

Oklahoma
Oklahoma City Community College *A*
Oklahoma City University *B, M*
Oral Roberts University *B*

Oregon
Chemeketa Community College *A*

Pennsylvania
Penn State
Abington *B*
Altoona *B*
Beaver *B*
Berks *B*
Brandywine *B*
DuBois *B*
Erie, The Behrend College *B*
Fayette, The Eberly Campus *B*
Greater Allegheny *B*
Hazleton *B*
Lehigh Valley *B*
Mont Alto *B*
New Kensington *B*
Schuylkill *B*
Shenango *B*
University Park *B*
Wilkes-Barre *B*
Worthington Scranton *B*
York *B*
Seton Hill University *B*

Slippery Rock University of
Pennsylvania *B*
Temple University *M*
University of the Arts *B*

Rhode Island
Community College of Rhode
Island *A*

South Carolina
Coker College *B*
Wofford College *B*

Tennessee
Freed-Hardeman University *B*

Texas
Baylor University *B*
Lon Morris College *A*
Texas Christian University *B*
Texas Tech University *B, M*
Trinity University *B*

Utah
Salt Lake Community College *A*

Vermont
Bennington College *B, M*
Johnson State College *A, B*
Marlboro College *B*

Virginia
Shenandoah University *B*

Washington
Cornish College of the Arts *B*
North Seattle Community College *C*
Shoreline Community College *A*

West Virginia
Davis and Elkins College *B*

Wisconsin
Carthage College *B*
University of Wisconsin
Madison *B, M*

Wyoming
Casper College *A*
Central Wyoming College *A*
Western Wyoming Community
College *C, A*

Theater history/ criticism

California
California State University
San Bernardino *B*
College of the Desert *A*
Whittier College *B*

Delaware
University of Delaware *B*

District of Columbia
George Washington University *B*
Howard University *B*

Florida
State College of Florida,
Manatee-Sarasota *A*

Georgia
Clark Atlanta University *B*
Georgia State University *B*
Oglethorpe University *B*

Illinois
DePaul University *B*

Northwestern University *B*
University of Illinois
 Urbana-Champaign *B*

Iowa

Buena Vista University *B, T*

Louisiana

Tulane University *B, M*

Maine

Bowdoin College *B*

Maryland

University of Maryland
 College Park *M, D*

Massachusetts

Bard College at Simon's Rock *B*
Boston University *B*
Emerson College *M*
Salem State College *B*
Suffolk University *B*
Tufts University *B, M, D*

Michigan

Michigan State University *M*
University of Michigan
 Flint *B*
Western Michigan University *B*

Minnesota

Augsburg College *B*

Missouri

Washington University in St.
 Louis *B, M*

New Hampshire

Keene State College *B*

New York

Bard College *B*
Columbia University *B*
Sarah Lawrence College *M*
State University of New York
 Purchase *B*

Ohio

Ohio University *M*

Pennsylvania

Arcadia University *B*
Washington & Jefferson College *B*

Vermont

Bennington College *B, M*
Marlboro College *B*

Virginia

Averett University *B*
Virginia Wesleyan College *B*

Washington

Whitworth University *B, T*

West Virginia

West Virginia University *B*

Wisconsin

University of Wisconsin
 Madison *M, D*
 Whitewater *B, T*

Theological studies

Alabama

Amridge University *M, D*
Faulkner University *B, M*
Huntsville Bible College *B*

Oakwood University *B, M*
Samford University *M*
Spring Hill College *C, B, M*

Arizona

American Indian College of the
 Assemblies of God *B*
Southwestern College *C, A, B*

Arkansas

Ecclesia College *B*
Harding University *B, M, D*
John Brown University *B*
Ouachita Baptist University *B*
Williams Baptist College *A, B*

California

Azusa Pacific University *B, D*
Bethany University *B*
Bethesda Christian University *B*
Biola University *B, M, D*
California Christian College *B*
California Lutheran University *B*
Concordia University *B, M*
Hope International
 University *C, A, B, M*
La Sierra University *M*
Loyola Marymount University *B, M*
The Master's College *B, D*
Pacific Union College *B*
Pepperdine University *M*
Shasta Bible College and Graduate
 School *B*
Simpson University *B, M*
University of San Francisco *B, M*
Vanguard University of Southern
 California *B, M*
William Jessup University *B*
World Mission University *M*

Colorado

Colorado Christian University *B*

Connecticut

Yale University *M*

District of Columbia

Catholic University of America *M, D*
Georgetown University *D*

Florida

Ave Maria University *B, M, D*
Baptist College of Florida *A, B*
Barry University *C, B, M*
Florida Christian College *B*
Hobe Sound Bible College *B*
Northwest Florida State College *A*
Palm Beach Atlantic University *B*
Saint Leo University *M*
Saint Thomas University *M, D*
Universidad FLET *C, A, B, M*
Warner University *C, A, B*

Georgia

Atlanta Christian College *B*
Brewton-Parker College *B*
Emory University *M, D*
Mercer University *M, D*
Shorter College *B*

Hawaii

Chaminade University of Honolulu *M*

Idaho

Boise Bible College *A, B*
New Saint Andrews College *M*

Illinois

Benedictine University *B*
Concordia University Chicago *B*
Dominican University *B*
Elmhurst College *B*

Lincoln Christian University *B, M*
Loyola University Chicago *C, B, M, D*
Moody Bible Institute *B, M*
North Park University *B, M, D*
Olivet Nazarene University *B, M*
Quincy University *M*
Saint Xavier University *B*
Trinity Christian College *B*
Trinity International University *B, M*
University of St. Francis *B*
Wheaton College *M, D*

Indiana

Anderson University *B, M*
Bethel College *B, M*
Hanover College *B*
Holy Cross College *B*
Huntington University *M*
Indiana Wesleyan University *B*
Manchester College *A*
Marian University *A, B*
Oakland City University *D*
St. Mary of the Woods College *A, B, M*
University of Evansville *B*
University of Notre Dame *B, M, D*
University of St. Francis *B, M*
Valparaiso University *B, M*

Iowa

Briar Cliff University *A, B*
Dordt College *B*
Emmaus Bible College *B*
Faith Baptist Bible College and
 Theological Seminary *B, M*
Loras College *M*
St. Ambrose University *M*
University of Dubuque *M, D*

Kansas

Barclay College *B*
Central Christian College of
 Kansas *A, B*
Hesston College *A*
Newman University *B, M*
Tabor College *B*
University of St. Mary *B*

Kentucky

Bellarmine University *B, M*
Brescia University *B*
Campbellsville University *M*
Kentucky Christian University *M*
Kentucky Mountain Bible College *B*

Louisiana

Xavier University of Louisiana *B, M*

Maine

Saint Joseph's College of Maine *B*

Maryland

Mount St. Mary's University *B, M*
Washington Adventist University *B*
Washington Bible College *B, M*

Massachusetts

Anna Maria College *B*
Assumption College *B*
Atlantic Union College *B*
Boston College *D*
Eastern Nazarene College *B, M*
Elms College *M*
Harvard College *M*
Hellenic College/Holy Cross *B, M*

Michigan

Andrews University *B, M, D*
Grace Bible College *B*
Madonna University *B, M*
Rochester College *B*
Sacred Heart Major Seminary *C, A, M*
Spring Arbor University *B*

Minnesota

Bethel University *M*
College of St. Benedict *B*
Concordia University: St. Paul *B*
Crossroads College *B*
Crown College *B, M*
Martin Luther College *C, B*
North Central University *B*
Northwestern College *M*
St. Catherine University *B, M*
St. John's University *B, M*
St. Mary's University of
 Minnesota *C, B, M*

Mississippi

Wesley College *B*

Missouri

Baptist Bible College *B*
Calvary Bible College and Theological
 Seminary *A, B, M*
Central Bible College *B*
Central Christian College of the
 Bible *B*
Global University *C, A, B*
Midwest University *M, D*
Missouri Baptist University *C, B*
Ozark Christian College *C, A, B*
St. Louis Christian College *A, B*
Saint Louis University *B, M, D*
Southwest Baptist University *C, B*

Nebraska

College of Saint Mary *B, T*
Concordia University *B*
Grace University *B*
Nebraska Christian College *A, B*
Union College *B*

New Hampshire

Saint Anselm College *B*

New Jersey

Assumption College for Sisters *C*
Caldwell College *B, M*
College of St. Elizabeth *B, M*
Drew University *M, D*
Georgian Court University *C, M*
Seton Hall University *B, M*

New York

Holy Trinity Orthodox Seminary *C, B*
Jewish Theological Seminary of
 America *D*
Nyack College *B, M*
Saint Bonaventure University *B*
St. John's University *B, M*

North Carolina

Apex School of Theology *B*
Campbell University *M*
Duke University *M, D*
John Wesley College *C, A, B*
Livingstone College *B*
Mid-Atlantic Christian University *B*
Shaw University *M*
Shepherds Theological Seminary *B, M*
Southeastern Baptist Theological
 Seminary *A*
Southeastern Baptist Theological
 Seminary: Theological
 Professions *D*
Wake Forest University *M*

North Dakota

Trinity Bible College *B*
University of Mary *B*

Ohio

Allegheny Wesleyan College *B*
Ashland University *M, D*
Cedarville University *B*

Cincinnati Christian University *M*
Franciscan University of
　Steubenville *A, B, M*
God's Bible School and College *B*
Lourdes College *M*
Malóne University *B, M*
Mount Vernon Nazarene University *M*
Notre Dame College *A, B*
Ohio Christian University *A, B*
Ohio Dominican University *A, B, M*
Pontifical College Josephinum *M*
University of Dayton *M, D*
University of Findlay *B*
Walsh University *B, M*
Xavier University *A, B, M*

Oklahoma
Family of Faith College *C, B*
Hillsdale Free Will Baptist College *B*
Mid-America Christian University *B*
Oklahoma Baptist University *C, A, B*
Oklahoma Christian University *B*
Oklahoma Wesleyan University *B*
Oral Roberts University *B, M, D*
St. Gregory's University *B*
Southern Nazarene University *B*
Southwestern Christian
　University *B, M*

Oregon
Concordia University *B*
Corban College *B*
Eugene Bible College *B*
George Fox University *M*
Mount Angel Seminary *C, B*
Multnomah University *B, M*
Northwest Christian University *B*
University of Portland *B, M*
Warner Pacific College *M*

Pennsylvania
Alvernia University *B*
Baptist Bible College of
　Pennsylvania *M*
Bryn Athyn College of the New
　Church *A, B*
Carlow University *B*
DeSales University *B*
Duquesne University *B, M, D*
Eastern University *B, M*
Gannon University *B*
Immaculata University *B*
King's College *B*
Philadelphia Biblical University *B*
St. Charles Borromeo Seminary -
　Overbrook *M*
St. Vincent College *B*
Valley Forge Christian College *B, M*
Villanova University *M*
Waynesburg University *B*

Puerto Rico
Bayamon Central University *M*
Pontifical Catholic University of
　Puerto Rico *M*
Universidad Adventista de las
　Antillas *B*

Rhode Island
Providence College *B, M*

South Carolina
Bob Jones University *B, D*
Columbia International
　University *M, D*
Erskine College *M, D*
Morris College *B*
Southern Wesleyan University *M*

South Dakota
University of Sioux Falls *B*

Tennessee
American Baptist College *C, A, B*
Carson-Newman College *A, B*
Free Will Baptist Bible College *B*
Freed-Hardeman University *B, M*
Lee University *B, M*
Lipscomb University *M*
Southern Adventist University *B, M*
Tennessee Temple University *B*
Trevecca Nazarene University *M*
Union University *B*
University of the South *M, D*
Vanderbilt University *D*
Visible School - Music and Worship
　Arts College *B*

Texas
Austin Graduate School of
　Theology *B, M*
Baptist Missionary Association
　Theological Seminary *A, B, M*
Baptist University of the
　Americas *A, B*
Baylor University *M, D*
Brazosport College *A*
Dallas Christian College *B*
Hardin-Simmons University *B, M, D*
Houston Baptist University *M*
Howard Payne University *C, A, B*
Lubbock Christian University *B*
St. Edward's University *B*
St. Mary's University *B, M*
Southern Methodist University *M, D*
Southwestern Adventist University *B*
Southwestern Assemblies of God
　University *M*
Southwestern Baptist Theological
　Seminary *D*
Southwestern Baptist Theological
　Seminary: Theological
　Professions *M, D*
University of Dallas *B, M*
University of Mary Hardin-Baylor *B*
University of St. Thomas *B, M*

Vermont
St. Michael's College *M*

Virginia
Bluefield College *B*
Eastern Mennonite University *C, B, M*
Hampton University *B*
Liberty University *M, D*
Regent University *M, D*
Roanoke College *B*
Virginia Union University *M, D*

Washington
Faith Evangelical Seminary *B, M, D*
Northwest University *B, M*
Seattle University *M*
Trinity Lutheran College *A, B*
Walla Walla University *B*
Whitworth University *B, M*

West Virginia
Wheeling Jesuit University *B*

Wisconsin
Concordia University Wisconsin *B*
Maranatha Baptist Bible College *M*
Marquette University *M*
St. Norbert College *M*
Silver Lake College *B*
Wisconsin Lutheran College *B*

Theoretical/
mathematical physics

Arizona
Northern Arizona University *B*

Arkansas
University of Arkansas *M*

California
Chapman University *A*
San Diego State University *B*

Indiana
Indiana University
　Bloomington *D*

Michigan
Spring Arbor University *B*

New York
State University of New York
　Buffalo *B*

Texas
Rice University *M, D*
Southwestern Adventist
　University *B, T*

Vermont
Marlboro College *B*

Virginia
Sweet Briar College *B*

Wisconsin
University of Wisconsin
　Madison *M, D*

Tibetan studies

California
California Institute of Integral
　Studies *M, D*

Tool and die technology

Alabama
Bevill State Community College *C, A*
Calhoun Community College *C, A*
Shelton State Community
　College *C, A*

Illinois
Black Hawk College *C*
College of DuPage *C*
College of Lake County *C*
Elgin Community College *C*
John A. Logan College *C, A*

Indiana
Ivy Tech Community College
　Bloomington *C, A*
　Central Indiana *C, A*
　Columbus *C, A*
　East Central *C, A*
　Kokomo *C, A*
　Lafayette *C, A*
　North Central *C, A*
　Northeast *C, A*
　Northwest *C, A*
　Richmond *C, A*
　South Central *C, A*
　Southwest *C, A*
　Wabash Valley *C, A*
Vincennes University *A*

Iowa
Des Moines Area Community
　College *C, A*
Hawkeye Community College *A*
Marshalltown Community College *C*
North Iowa Area Community
　College *A*
Northwest Iowa Community
　College *C, A*

Southeastern Community College
　North Campus *C, A*

Michigan
Ferris State University *A*
Montcalm Community College *C*
Oakland Community College *C, A*
Southwestern Michigan College *C, A*
Wayne County Community College *A*

Minnesota
Hennepin Technical College *C, A*
Lake Superior College *C*
Minnesota State College - Southeast
　Technical *C*
Ridgewater College *C, A*
St. Paul College *C*

North Carolina
Asheville-Buncombe Technical
　Community College *C*

Ohio
North Central State College *C, A*
Northwest State Community
　College *C, A*
Owens Community College
　Toledo *C, A*
Zane State College *A*

Pennsylvania
Lehigh Carbon Community College *C*
Pennsylvania College of
　Technology *A*
Thaddeus Stevens College of
　Technology *A*

South Carolina
York Technical College *A*

South Dakota
Lake Area Technical Institute *A*

Texas
Texas State Technical College
　Harlingen *A*

Wisconsin
Chippewa Valley Technical College *A*
Lakeshore Technical College *C*
Milwaukee Area Technical College *C*
Northcentral Technical College *C*
Waukesha County Technical
　College *C*
Western Technical College *C, A*
Wisconsin Indianhead Technical
　College *C*

Tourism promotion

Arizona
Phoenix College *C, A*

California
Alliant International University *B*
Butte College *C, A*
City College of San Francisco *A*
Coastline Community College *C*
Cypress College *C, A*
Foothill College *C, A*
Fullerton College *C, A*
Grossmont College *C, A*
Long Beach City College *C, A*
Los Angeles City College *C, A*
Los Medanos College *C, A*
Palomar College *C, A*
Pasadena City College *C, A*
Saddleback College *C*
San Diego City College *C, A*
Southwestern College *C, A*

Colorado
Community College of Aurora C
Metropolitan State College of Denver B

District of Columbia
George Washington University B, M

Florida
Florida National College A
Lynn University B
Miami Dade College C, A

Georgia
Gwinnett Technical College C

Illinois
College of DuPage C, A
Lincoln College A
MacCormac College C, A

Indiana
International Business College C, A

Kansas
Cloud County Community College A

Kentucky
Sullivan University C, A, B

Maine
Andover College C, A
Beal College A
University of Maine
Machias B

Maryland
Allegany College of Maryland C
Chesapeake College A

Massachusetts
Bay State College A
Northern Essex Community
College A

Michigan
Grand Valley State University B
Lansing Community College A

Minnesota
Central Lakes College C

Mississippi
Hinds Community College A

Missouri
University of Central Missouri B

New Hampshire
NHTI-Concord's Community
College C, A

New York
Adirondack Community College A
Bryant & Stratton Business Institute
Bryant & Stratton College:
Syracuse A
City University of New York
Kingsborough Community
College A
LaGuardia Community College A
Dutchess Community College A
Finger Lakes Community College A
Genesee Community College C
Jefferson Community College C, A
Mildred Elley C
Monroe Community College A
Paul Smith's College B
Rochester Institute of
Technology B, M

Schenectady County Community
College C, A
State University of New York
College of Agriculture and
Technology at Morrisville A
College of Technology at Delhi A
Wood Tobe-Coburn School C

North Carolina
Blue Ridge Community College A

Ohio
Bowling Green State University B
Columbus State Community
College C, A
RETS College C
Youngstown State University A, B

Oklahoma
Oklahoma City Community College A

Pennsylvania
Butler County Community College A
Consolidated School of Business
York A
Mansfield University of
Pennsylvania A, B
Reading Area Community College A

Puerto Rico
University of Puerto Rico
Carolina Regional College B
University of the Sacred Heart B

Rhode Island
Community College of Rhode
Island C
Johnson & Wales University:
Providence B

Tennessee
University of Tennessee
Knoxville M

Texas
Amarillo College A
Central Texas College C, A
El Paso Community College C, A
Texas A&M University B

Vermont
Champlain College B

West Virginia
Concord University B
Mountain State College A
West Liberty University B

Wisconsin
Fox Valley Technical College A
Lac Courte Oreilles Ojibwa
Community College C

Wyoming
Northwest College A

Tourism/travel management

Alabama
Columbia Southern University B, M

Arizona
Arizona State University B
Northern Arizona University C
Phoenix College C, A
Pima Community College C, A

California
Berkeley City College C

California State University
Fullerton B
Canada College C, A
Chabot College A
City College of San Francisco A
Coastline Community College C
College of the Redwoods C
Empire College C
Grossmont College C, A
Long Beach City College C, A
Los Angeles City College C, A
MiraCosta College C, A
Mount St. Mary's College A
Saddleback College C, A
San Diego Mesa College C, A
San Joaquin Delta College C
Santiago Canyon College C, A
Southwestern College C, A

Colorado
Metropolitan State College of
Denver B

Connecticut
Lincoln College of New England:
Briarwood A
Mitchell College B
Three Rivers Community College C, A
University of New Haven C

Florida
Broward College A
Edison State College A
Florida National College A
Florida State College at
Jacksonville C, A
Johnson & Wales University: North
Miami B
Miami Dade College C, A
Rasmussen College: Pasco County A
Saint Thomas University B
Schiller International University A, B
University of Central Florida B

Georgia
Gwinnett Technical College C, A

Hawaii
Hawaii Pacific University B
Heald College
Honolulu A
University of Hawaii
Manoa B, M
Maui Community College A

Illinois
City Colleges of Chicago
Harold Washington College C, A
Danville Area Community College C
Lincoln College A, B
MacCormac College C, A
Moraine Valley Community
College C, A
Northwestern College A

Indiana
Indiana University-Purdue University
Indianapolis B
Purdue University B, M, D
University of Indianapolis A, B

Iowa
AIB College of Business A
Kaplan University
Cedar Falls A
Davenport C, A

Maine
Andover College C, A
University of Maine
Machias B

Maryland
Allegany College of Maryland C

Massachusetts
Becker College B
Bunker Hill Community College C, A
Lasell College B
Marian Court College C, A
Massasoit Community College C, A
Middlesex Community College C
Northern Essex Community
College C, A
Quincy College A
Salem State College B

Michigan
Baker College
of Clinton Township A
of Flint A
Central Michigan University M
Grand Valley State University B
Lansing Community College A
Wayne County Community College C

Minnesota
Central Lakes College A
Dakota County Technical College C, A
Minneapolis Business College A
Normandale Community College C
Saint Cloud State University B

Mississippi
University of Southern Mississippi B

Missouri
Patricia Stevens College A

Montana
University of Montana: Western A, B

Nebraska
Kaplan University
Lincoln C
University of Nebraska
Kearney B

New Hampshire
NHTI-Concord's Community
College C, A
Southern New Hampshire
University B

New Jersey
Cumberland County College C, A
Essex County College A
Mercer County Community College C

New York
Bryant & Stratton Business Institute
Bryant & Stratton College:
Syracuse A
City University of New York
Kingsborough Community
College A
New York City College of
Technology B
Dutchess Community College A
Finger Lakes Community College A
Genesee Community College A
Globe Institute of Technology C, A, B
Herkimer County Community
College A
Mohawk Valley Community College C
Monroe Community College A
New York Institute of Technology B
New York University M
Niagara University B
Paul Smith's College A, B
Rochester Institute of
Technology A, B, M
Rockland Community College A

State University of New York
  College at Plattsburgh *B*
  College of Agriculture and
      Technology at Morrisville *A*
  College of Technology at Delhi *A, B*
  Maritime College *B, M*

North Carolina

Central Piedmont Community
  College *C, A*
King's College *A*
Methodist University *B*

North Dakota

Jamestown College *B*

Ohio

Bowling Green State University *B*
Bradford School *C*
Columbus State Community
  College *C, A*
RETS College *C*
University of Akron *C, A*
University of Northwestern Ohio *C, A*
Youngstown State University *A, B*

Oklahoma

Northeastern State University *B*
Oklahoma City Community College *A*
Tulsa Community College *C, A*

Oregon

Blue Mountain Community College *C*
Chemeketa Community College *C, A*
Mt. Hood Community College *C, A*

Pennsylvania

Bucks County Community
  College *C, A*
Erie Business Center *A*
Erie Business Center South *A*
Harrisburg Area Community
  College *C, A*
Mansfield University of
  Pennsylvania *A, B*
Newport Business Institute: Lower
  Burrell *A*
Westmoreland County Community
  College *A*

Puerto Rico

Inter American University of Puerto
  Rico
  Fajardo Campus *A*
National College of Business and
  Technology: Arecibo *A*
National College of Business and
  Technology: Bayamon *A*
National College of Business and
  Technology: Rio Grande *A*
Pontifical Catholic University of
  Puerto Rico *A, B*
Turabo University *C*

Rhode Island

Johnson & Wales University:
  Providence *B*

South Carolina

Trident Technical College *A*

South Dakota

Black Hills State University *A, B, M*

Tennessee

National College: Madison *A*
University of Tennessee
  Knoxville *B*

Texas

Amarillo College *C*

Austin Community College *C*
Central Texas College *C*
El Paso Community College *C, A*
Houston Community College
  System *C, A*
Richland College *A*
St. Philip's College *C, A*
Tarrant County College *C, A*
Texas A&M University *B*
Texas A&M University
  Galveston *B*
University of Texas
  San Antonio *B*

Vermont

Champlain College *B*
Johnson State College *B*

Virginia

Northern Virginia Community
  College *C, A*
Virginia Highlands Community
  College *C*

Washington

Highline Community College *C, A*
Spokane Falls Community
  College *C, A*

West Virginia

Concord University *B*
Mountain State College *A*
New River Community and Technical
  College *A*
West Liberty University *B*

Wisconsin

Milwaukee Area Technical
  College *C, A*
Northeast Wisconsin Technical
  College *A*

Tourism/travel services

California

Orange Coast College *C, A*

Colorado

United States Air Force Academy *B*

Connecticut

Central Connecticut State
  University *B*

Georgia

Athens Technical College *C, A*

Maryland

Community College of Baltimore
  County *C*

Michigan

Western Michigan University *B*

Minnesota

Dakota County Technical College *C, A*

Missouri

Patricia Stevens College *A*
University of Missouri
  Columbia *B, M*

New York

Dutchess Community College *A*
Rochester Institute of
  Technology *B, M*
Schenectady County Community
  College *A*
State University of New York
  College of Agriculture at Cobleskill *A*

College of Agriculture and
    Technology at Morrisville *A*

Pennsylvania

Central Pennsylvania College *A*
Montgomery County Community
  College *A*
Newport Business Institute: Lower
  Burrell *A*
Westmoreland County Community
  College *C*

Puerto Rico

Inter American University of Puerto
  Rico
  Metropolitan Campus *C, A*

Vermont

Champlain College *B*

Washington

Grays Harbor College *C*

Toxicology

California

University of California
  Berkeley *B, M, D*

Colorado

Colorado State University *M, D*
University of Colorado
  Denver *D*

District of Columbia

George Washington University *M, D*

Georgia

University of Georgia *M, D*

Indiana

Indiana University-Purdue University
  Indianapolis *M, D*

Iowa

Iowa State University *M, D*

Kansas

University of Kansas Medical
  Center *M, D*

Kentucky

University of Kentucky *M, D*

Louisiana

University of Louisiana at Monroe *B*

Maryland

University of Maryland
  Baltimore *M, D*
  Baltimore County *M, D*
  Eastern Shore *M, D*

Massachusetts

Northeastern University *B*

Michigan

Eastern Michigan University *B*
University of Michigan *M, D*

Minnesota

Minnesota State University
  Mankato *B, T*
University of Minnesota
  Duluth *M*
  Twin Cities *M, D*

Mississippi

Mississippi State University *D*

Nebraska

University of Nebraska
  Lincoln *M, D*

New Hampshire

Dartmouth College *D*

New Jersey

Felician College *B*
Rutgers, The State University of New
  Jersey
  New Brunswick/Piscataway
    Campus *M, D*
Saint Peter's College *B*

New York

St. John's University *B, M*
State University of New York
  Albany *M, D*
University of Rochester *M, D*

North Carolina

North Carolina State University *M, D*
University of North Carolina
  Chapel Hill *M, D*

Oregon

Oregon State University *M, D*

Pennsylvania

Penn State
  Abington *B*
  Altoona *B*
  Beaver *B*
  Berks *B*
  Brandywine *B*
  DuBois *B*
  Erie, The Behrend College *B*
  Fayette, The Eberly Campus *B*
  Greater Allegheny *B*
  Hazleton *B*
  Lehigh Valley *B*
  Mont Alto *B*
  New Kensington *B*
  Schuylkill *B*
  Shenango *B*
  University Park *B*
  Wilkes-Barre *B*
  Worthington Scranton *B*
  York *B*

South Carolina

Clemson University *M, D*

Tennessee

University of Tennessee
  Knoxville *M*

Texas

Prairie View A&M University *M*
Texas A&M University *M, D*
Texas Southern University *M, D*
Texas Tech University *M, D*
University of Texas
  Health Science Center at
    Houston *M, D*

Utah

Utah State University *M, D*

Trade/industrial education

Alabama

Athens State University *B*

Arizona

Glendale Community College *A*
Northern Arizona University *B, M*

Arkansas

University of Arkansas *B, M, D*
University of Arkansas
   Pine Bluff *B, T*

California

California State University
   Los Angeles *B*
   San Bernardino *B, M*
Fullerton College *A*
Humboldt State University *B, T*
San Diego State University *B*
Vanguard University of Southern
   California *T*

Colorado

Colorado School of Trades *A*
Colorado State University *B, T*

Delaware

Delaware State University *B*

Florida

Florida Agricultural and Mechanical
   University *B, M*
State College of Florida,
   Manatee-Sarasota *A*
University of Central Florida *B, M*
University of South Florida *B, M*
University of West Florida *B*

Georgia

Valdosta State University *B*

Idaho

University of Idaho *B, T*

Illinois

Chicago State University *M, D*
Southern Illinois University
   Carbondale *B, M, D*

Indiana

Indiana State University *B, M, T*
Purdue University *A*

Iowa

Iowa State University *B, T*

Kansas

Fort Hays State University *B, T*

Kentucky

Eastern Kentucky University *B, M*
Murray State University *A, T*
Northern Kentucky University *B*
University of Kentucky *M, D*
University of Louisville *B, M*
Western Kentucky University *B, T*

Massachusetts

Fitchburg State College *B, M, T*

Michigan

Lansing Community College *A*
Western Michigan University *B*

Minnesota

Saint Cloud State University *T*

Mississippi

Hinds Community College *A*
Mississippi Gulf Coast Community
   College *A*

Missouri

Lindenwood University *B*

Nebraska

Chadron State College *B*

University of Nebraska
   Kearney *B*
   Lincoln *B*

Nevada

Great Basin College *B*
University of Nevada
   Reno *B, T*

New Hampshire

Keene State College *M, T*

New York

College of Saint Rose *B, M*
New York Institute of
   Technology *A, B, T*
State University of New York
   College at Buffalo *B, M, T*
   Oswego *B, M, T*

North Carolina

North Carolina Agricultural and
   Technical State University *B, T*
Southwestern Community College *A*

Ohio

Bowling Green State University *B*
Kent State University *B, M*
Ohio State University
   Columbus Campus *B, M*
University of Toledo *B, M*

Oklahoma

East Central University *B*

Pennsylvania

Indiana University of
   Pennsylvania *B, T*
Temple University *B, M*

Puerto Rico

Turabo University *B*

South Carolina

Clemson University *D*

Tennessee

University of Tennessee
   Knoxville *T*

Texas

Sam Houston State University *M, T*
Texas A&M University *M, D*
Texas A&M University
   Commerce *M, T*
   Corpus Christi *M, T*
Texas State University: San
   Marcos *M, T*
University of Houston *B, M*
Wayland Baptist University *B, T*

Utah

Southern Utah University *B, T*

Virginia

Norfolk State University *B*
Virginia Polytechnic Institute and
   State University *M, D*
Virginia State University *B, M*

Washington

Western Washington University *M*

West Virginia

Fairmont State University *B*
Marshall University *M*

Wisconsin

University of Wisconsin
   Stout *M*

Wyoming

University of Wyoming *B*

Traditional Chinese medicine/herbology

Pennsylvania

Keystone Technical Institute *C, A*

Washington

Bastyr University *B, M, D*

Traffic/customs/ transportation clerk

Michigan

Bay de Noc Community College *C*

Transportation

Alaska

University of Alaska
   Anchorage *B, M*

California

El Camino College: Compton
   Center *C*
Fresno City College *C, A*

Colorado

Trinidad State Junior College *C, A*

Delaware

Wilmington University *M*

Florida

Florida State College at Jacksonville *C*

Illinois

Richland Community College *C*

Kansas

Kansas State University *C*

Maryland

Cecil College *C, A*
Morgan State University *M*

Michigan

Baker College
   of Muskegon *C*
Henry Ford Community College *A*

Minnesota

Minnesota School of Business: St.
   Cloud *A*

Mississippi

East Mississippi Community
   College *C*

Nevada

University of Nevada
   Las Vegas *M*

New York

Nassau Community College *A*
Niagara University *B*
United States Merchant Marine
   Academy *B*

North Dakota

Lake Region State College *A*

Ohio

Columbus State Community
   College *A*
Ohio Technical College *C, A*

South Carolina

Trident Technical College *C, A*

Texas

Brookhaven College *A*
Central Texas College *C*
Texas A&M University
   Galveston *B*
Texas Southern University *M*

Virginia

Central Virginia Community
   College *C*
J. Sargeant Reynolds Community
   College *C*

Washington

Bates Technical College *C*
Green River Community College *C, A*
Highline Community College *A*
Spokane Falls Community College *A*

Wisconsin

Milwaukee Area Technical College *A*
Northeast Wisconsin Technical
   College *A*
University of Wisconsin
   Superior *B*

Transportation/highway engineering

Arkansas

University of Arkansas *M*

California

California Polytechnic State
   University: San Luis Obispo *M*
University of Southern California *M*

Illinois

Illinois Institute of Technology *M*
University of Illinois
   Urbana-Champaign *B, M, D*

Massachusetts

Massachusetts Institute of
   Technology *M, D*

Missouri

Washington University in St.
   Louis *M, D*

New Jersey

New Jersey Institute of
   Technology *M, D*

New York

Polytechnic Institute of New York
   University *M, D*
Rensselaer Polytechnic Institute *M, D*

Pennsylvania

Villanova University *M*

Wisconsin

Marquette University *M, D*

Transportation management

Arizona

Coconino County Community
   College *C*

California

University of California
   Davis *M, D*

Colorado
University of Denver *M*

Delaware
Wilmington University *M*

Florida
Florida Institute of Technology *M*
University of North Florida *B*

Illinois
Kankakee Community College *C*
Northwestern University *M*

Iowa
Iowa State University *M*

Maryland
Anne Arundel Community College *C*
Cecil College *C, A*
Hagerstown Community College *C, A*

Massachusetts
Bridgewater State College *B*
Massachusetts Maritime Academy *B*

Michigan
College for Creative Studies *B*

Minnesota
Academy College *C*

North Carolina
North Carolina Agricultural and
    Technical State University *B*

North Dakota
Bismarck State College *A*
North Dakota State University *M, D*

Ohio
North Central State College *C*
Ohio State University
    Columbus Campus *B, M, D*
Ohio Technical College *C*

Pennsylvania
University of Pennsylvania *B*

Puerto Rico
Pontifical Catholic University of
    Puerto Rico *B*

South Carolina
South Carolina State University *M*
Trident Technical College *C, A*

Tennessee
Southwest Tennessee Community
    College *C*

Texas
Texas A&M University
    Galveston *B*
Texas Southern University *M*

West Virginia
American Public University
    System *B, M*

Truck/bus/commercial vehicle operation

Alabama
Bevill State Community College *C*
Shelton State Community College *C*

Arizona
Glendale Community College *C*

Pima Community College *C*

Arkansas
North Arkansas College *C*
Ouachita Technical College *C*
Pulaski Technical College *C*

Delaware
Delaware Technical and Community
    College
    Owens *C*

Florida
Central Florida Community College *C*
Indian River State College *C*

Georgia
Albany Technical College *C*
Athens Technical College *C*
Bainbridge College *C*
Middle Georgia Technical College *C*
North Georgia Technical College *C*
Savannah Technical College *C*
Southeastern Technical College *C*

Idaho
Eastern Idaho Technical College *C*

Illinois
Black Hawk College *C*
Danville Area Community College *C*
Elgin Community College *C*
Illinois Valley Community College *C*
John Wood Community College *C*
Kaskaskia College *C*
Lincoln Land Community College *C*
Sauk Valley Community College *C*
Spoon River College *C*

Iowa
Hawkeye Community College *C*
Indian Hills Community College *C*
Muscatine Community College *C*
Scott Community College *C*

Kentucky
Big Sandy Community and Technical
    College *C*

Maryland
College of Southern Maryland *C*
Hagerstown Community College *C*

Michigan
Baker College
    of Cadillac *C, A*
    of Flint *C, A*

Minnesota
Alexandria Technical College *C*
Dakota County Technical College *C*
Lake Superior College *C*
Minnesota State College - Southeast
    Technical *C*

Mississippi
Copiah-Lincoln Community College *C*
Mississippi Gulf Coast Community
    College *C*

Missouri
Crowder College *C*

Montana
Blackfeet Community College *C*

Nebraska
Central Community College *C*
Northeast Community College *C*
Southeast Community College *C*

New Mexico
Central New Mexico Community
    College *C*

North Carolina
Beaufort County Community
    College *C*
Cape Fear Community College *C*
Catawba Valley Community College *C*
Davidson County Community
    College *C*

Oregon
Rogue Community College *C*

Pennsylvania
Pittsburgh Institute of Aeronautics *C*

South Carolina
Greenville Technical College *C*

South Dakota
Southeast Technical Institute *C*

Texas
Houston Community College
    System *C*
San Jacinto College *C*
Weatherford College *C*

Utah
Salt Lake Community College *C*

Virginia
Dabney S. Lancaster Community
    College *C*
Southside Virginia Community
    College *C*
Southwest Virginia Community
    College *C*
Tidewater Community College *C, A*
Wytheville Community College *C*

Washington
Bates Technical College *C*
Bellingham Technical College *C*
Big Bend Community College *C*
Grays Harbor College *C*
South Seattle Community
    College *C, A*

Wisconsin
Chippewa Valley Technical College *C*
Fox Valley Technical College *C*
Waukesha County Technical
    College *C*

Turf management

Arizona
Northland Pioneer College *C, A*

California
Butte College *C*
College of the Desert *C, A*
Los Angeles Pierce College *C*
MiraCosta College *C, A*
Monterey Peninsula College *C*
Mount San Antonio College *C*
Mount San Jacinto College *C, A*
San Joaquin Delta College *C*
Shasta College *C*
Southwestern College *C, A*

Delaware
Delaware Technical and Community
    College
    Owens *C, A*
    Stanton/Wilmington *C*
    Terry *C*

Florida
Daytona State College *A*
Edison State College *C*
Florida Southern College *B*
Indian River State College *A*
Lake City Community College *C*

Georgia
Abraham Baldwin Agricultural
    College *A, B*
North Georgia Technical College *C, A*
University of Georgia *B*

Illinois
College of DuPage *C*
College of Lake County *A*
Danville Area Community College *A*
Harper College *C, A*
Joliet Junior College *C, A*
Kishwaukee College *C*
McHenry County College *C*
Southwestern Illinois College *A*

Iowa
Iowa Central Community College *A*
Kirkwood Community College *A*
Western Iowa Tech Community
    College *C, A*

Kansas
Colby Community College *C*

Kentucky
Eastern Kentucky University *B*

Maine
University of Maine *B*

Maryland
Harford Community College *A*

Massachusetts
University of Massachusetts
    Amherst *A*

Michigan
Michigan State University *C*
Northwestern Michigan College *A*

Minnesota
Anoka Technical College *C, A*
Rochester Community and Technical
    College *C, A*
University of Minnesota
    Crookston *B*

Mississippi
Mississippi Gulf Coast Community
    College *C, A*

Missouri
Linn State Technical College *A*
Metropolitan Community College:
    Longview *A*
Ozarks Technical Community
    College *C, A*

Nebraska
Nebraska College of Technical
    Agriculture *A*

New Mexico
New Mexico State University *B*

New York
State University of New York
    College of Agriculture and
        Technology at Cobleskill *B*
    College of Technology at Delhi *A*

North Carolina

Blue Ridge Community College *C*
Brunswick Community College *C, A*
Catawba Valley Community College *A*
Central Piedmont Community
College *C, A*
Guilford Technical Community
College *A*
North Carolina State University *A*
Sandhills Community College *A*
Wayne Community College *A*

North Dakota

Dakota College at Bottineau *A*
North Dakota State University *B*

Ohio

Cincinnati State Technical and
Community College *C, A*
Ohio State University
Agricultural Technical Institute *A*
Columbus Campus *B*

Oklahoma

Oklahoma State University
Oklahoma City *A*

Oregon

Southwestern Oregon Community
College *C, A*

Pennsylvania

Community College of Allegheny
County *C, A*
Delaware Valley College *B*
Penn State
Abington *B*
Altoona *B*
Beaver *B*
Berks *B*
Brandywine *B*
DuBois *B*
Erie, The Behrend College *B*
Fayette, The Eberly Campus *B*
Greater Allegheny *B*
Hazleton *B*
Lehigh Valley *B*
Mont Alto *B*
New Kensington *B*
Schuylkill *B*
Shenango *B*
University Park *C, B*
Wilkes-Barre *B*
Worthington Scranton *B*
York *B*
Westmoreland County Community
College *A*
Williamson Free School of Mechanical
Trades *A*

Rhode Island

University of Rhode Island *B*

South Carolina

Horry-Georgetown Technical
College *C, A*
Trident Technical College *C*

South Dakota

Southeast Technical Institute *A*

Tennessee

Chattanooga State Community
College *C*

Texas

Houston Community College
System *C, A*
Palo Alto College *C, A*
Texas A&M University *B*
Texas State Technical College
Waco *C, A*

Virginia

J. Sargeant Reynolds Community
College *A*
Northern Virginia Community
College *C*

Washington

Spokane Community College *A*

Wyoming

Sheridan College *A*

Turkish

Michigan

University of Michigan *B*

Texas

University of Texas
Austin *B*

Utah

University of Utah *B, M, D*

Washington

University of Washington *B*

Ukrainian

Washington

University of Washington *B*

Underwater diving

California

National Polytechnic College of
Science *C, A*
Santa Barbara City College *C, A*

Florida

Florida Keys Community College *A*

Upholstery

Alabama

Gadsden State Community College *C*
Jefferson Davis Community College *C*

Arkansas

Arkansas State University
Beebe *C*

Colorado

Pueblo Community College *C*

North Carolina

Catawba Valley Community College *C*

Washington

Clover Park Technical College *C*

Urban, community, and regional planning

Alabama

Alabama Agricultural and Mechanical
University *B, M*
Auburn University *M*

Arizona

Arizona State University *B, M*
University of Arizona *B, M*

California

California Polytechnic State
University: San Luis Obispo *B, M*
California State Polytechnic
University: Pomona *B, M*

California State University
Chico *B*
San Bernardino *C*
East Los Angeles College *A*
Modesto Junior College *A*
San Diego State University *M*
San Jose State University *M*
University of California
Berkeley *M, D*
Davis *B, M*
Irvine *M, D*
Los Angeles *M, D*
San Diego *B*
University of Southern
California *M, D*

Colorado

University of Colorado
Denver *M*

District of Columbia

University of the District of
Columbia *A, B, M*

Florida

Florida Atlantic University *C, B, M*
Florida State University *M, D*
University of Florida *M*
University of Miami *M*

Georgia

Georgia Institute of Technology *M*
Savannah College of Art and
Design *M*
Southern Polytechnic State
University *C*
University of Georgia *M*

Hawaii

University of Hawaii
Manoa *M, D*

Illinois

University of Illinois
Chicago *M, D*
Urbana-Champaign *B, M, D*

Indiana

Ball State University *B, M*
Indiana University-Purdue University
Indianapolis *M*

Iowa

Iowa State University *B, M*
University of Iowa *M*

Kansas

Kansas State University *M*
University of Kansas *M*

Kentucky

University of Louisville *M*

Louisiana

University of New Orleans *M*

Maine

University of Southern Maine *M*

Maryland

Frostburg State University *B*
University of Maryland
College Park *D*

Massachusetts

Bridgewater State College *B*
Harvard College *M*
Massachusetts Institute of
Technology *B, M, D*
Tufts University *M*

University of Massachusetts

Amherst *M, D*
Westfield State College *B*

Michigan

Eastern Michigan University *B, M*
Grand Valley State University *B*
Michigan State University *B, M*
University of Michigan *M, D*
Wayne State University *M*
Western Michigan University *B*

Minnesota

Minnesota State University
Mankato *B, M*

Mississippi

Jackson State University *M, D*

Missouri

Missouri State University *B, M*
Saint Louis University *M*
University of Missouri
Kansas City *B*
Washington University in St. Louis *M*

Montana

University of Montana *B, M*

Nebraska

University of Nebraska
Lincoln *M*

Nevada

University of Nevada
Las Vegas *B*

New Hampshire

Plymouth State University *B*
University of New Hampshire *B*

New Jersey

New Jersey Institute of Technology *M*
Rutgers, The State University of New
Jersey
New Brunswick/Piscataway
Campus *B, M, D*

New Mexico

New Mexico State University *B*
University of New Mexico *M*

New York

City University of New York
Baruch College *B*
City College *M*
Cornell University *B, M, D*
New York Institute of Technology *M*
New York University *B, M*
Pratt Institute *M*
State University of New York
Albany *M*
Buffalo *M*
College at Buffalo *B*

North Carolina

Appalachian State University *B*
Cape Fear Community College *A*
East Carolina University *B*
University of North Carolina
Chapel Hill *M, D*
Charlotte *M*

Ohio

Kent State University *M*
Miami University
Oxford Campus *B*
Ohio State University
Columbus Campus *M, D*
Stark State College of Technology *A*
University of Akron *C, B, M*

University of Cincinnati *B, M*
University of Cincinnati
   Clermont College *A*

Oklahoma
University of Oklahoma *M*

Oregon
Portland State University *B, M, D*
University of Oregon *M*

Pennsylvania
Bryn Mawr College *B*
Carnegie Mellon University *M*
Haverford College *B*
Indiana University of Pennsylvania *B*
Mansfield University of
   Pennsylvania *B*
Temple University *B, M*
University of Pennsylvania *M, D*

Puerto Rico
University of Puerto Rico
   Rio Piedras *M*

Rhode Island
University of Rhode Island *M*

South Carolina
Clemson University *M*

Tennessee
University of Memphis *M*
University of Tennessee
   Knoxville *M*

Texas
Prairie View A&M University *M*
Rice University *M*
Texas A&M University *M, D*
Texas Southern University *M, D*
Texas State University: San Marcos *B*
University of Texas
   Arlington *M*
   Austin *M, D*

Utah
Utah State University *M*

Virginia
University of Virginia *B, M*
Virginia Polytechnic Institute and
   State University *M*

Washington
Eastern Washington University *B, M*
University of Washington *B, M, D*

Wisconsin
University of Wisconsin
   Madison *M, D*
   Milwaukee *M*

Wyoming
University of Wyoming *M*

Urban education

California
Holy Names University *M*

Florida
Florida International University *M*

Georgia
Georgia State University *M*

Illinois
Columbia College Chicago *M*
Concordia University Chicago *M*

Illinois
University of Illinois
   Chicago *D*
   Urbana-Champaign *M, D*

Louisiana
Southern University
   New Orleans *M*

Maryland
Morgan State University *M, D*

Massachusetts
Harvard College *M, D*

Minnesota
Capella University *M, D*

Nebraska
University of Nebraska
   Omaha *T*

New Jersey
Kean University *D*
Saint Peter's College *M*

New York
Le Moyne College *M*
Mercy College *M*

Oklahoma
Langston University *M*

Pennsylvania
Alvernia University *M*
Eastern University *M*
Temple University *M, D*

Tennessee
University of Memphis *T*
University of Tennessee
   Chattanooga *M*

Virginia
Norfolk State University *M*

Wisconsin
University of Wisconsin
   Milwaukee *D*

Urban forestry

California
University of California
   Davis *B*

Illinois
University of Illinois
   Urbana-Champaign *B, M, D*

Louisiana
Southern University and Agricultural
   and Mechanical College *B, M, D*

Minnesota
University of Minnesota
   Crookston *B*

New York
Paul Smith's College *A*
State University of New York
   College of Technology at Alfred *A*

Pennsylvania
Keystone College *A*

Texas
Texas A&M University *B*

Wisconsin
Mid-State Technical College *A*

Urban studies

Arizona
Arizona State University *B*

California
California State University
   Dominguez Hills *B*
   Northridge *B*
   San Bernardino *M*
College of Alameda *C, A*
Loyola Marymount University *B*
San Diego State University *B*
San Francisco Art Institute *B, M*
San Francisco State University *B*
Stanford University *B*
University of California
   Berkeley *B*
   Irvine *B*
   San Diego *B*
Whittier College *B*

Connecticut
Connecticut College *B*
Trinity College *B*
University of Connecticut *B*

Delaware
Delaware State University *B*
University of Delaware *M, D*

District of Columbia
University of the District of
   Columbia *A, B*

Florida
New College of Florida *B*

Georgia
Georgia State University *B, M*
Morehouse College *B*
Savannah State University *M*

Illinois
DePaul University *B*
Elmhurst College *B*
Loyola University Chicago *M*
Northwestern University *B*
University of Illinois
   Chicago *B, D*

Indiana
Ball State University *B*
Butler University *B*
Indiana University-Purdue University
   Fort Wayne *C*
Indiana Wesleyan University *B*

Kansas
MidAmerica Nazarene University *B*

Kentucky
University of Louisville *D*

Louisiana
Dillard University *B*
Tulane University *B*
University of New Orleans *B, M, D*

Maryland
Towson University *B*
University of Maryland
   College Park *M*

Massachusetts
Boston University *B*
Bridgewater State College *B*

Hampshire College *B*
Tufts University *M*
Worcester State College *B*

Michigan
Spring Arbor University *B*
Wayne State University *B*

Minnesota
Augsburg College *B*
Crown College *B*
Hamline University *B*
Minnesota State University
   Mankato *B, M*
North Central University *B*
Northwestern College *B*
Ridgewater College *A*
Saint Cloud State University *B*
University of Minnesota
   Duluth *B*
   Twin Cities *B*
Winona State University *B*

Mississippi
Jackson State University *B*

Missouri
Calvary Bible College and Theological
   Seminary *B*
Harris-Stowe State University *B*
Saint Louis University *B, M*
University of Missouri
   Kansas City *B*
Washington University in St. Louis *B*

Nebraska
University of Nebraska
   Omaha *C, B, M*

Nevada
University of Nevada
   Reno *M*

New Jersey
Rutgers, The State University of New
   Jersey
   Camden Regional Campus *B*
   New Brunswick/Piscataway
     Campus *B, M*
Saint Peter's College *A, B*

New York
Barnard College *B*
Canisius College *B*
City University of New York
   Hunter College *B, M*
   Queens College *B, M, T*
Columbia University *B*
Columbia University
   School of General Studies *B*
Daemen College *C*
Eugene Lang College The New School
   for Liberal Arts *B*
Fordham University *B*
Hobart and William Smith Colleges *B*
Long Island University
   Brooklyn Campus *M*
Metropolitan College of New
   York *A, B*
New York University *B*
Polytechnic Institute of New York
   University *B*
Rochester Institute of Technology *B*
State University of New York
   Albany *B*
Vassar College *B*

Ohio
Cleveland State University *B, M, D*
College of Wooster *B*
Ohio State University
   Columbus Campus *B*

Ohio University *B*
Ohio Wesleyan University *B*
University of Akron *M, D*
University of Cincinnati *B*
University of Cincinnati
   Clermont College *A*
   Raymond Walters College *A*
University of Toledo *B*
Wittenberg University *B*
Wright State University *B*

Oklahoma

Langston University *B*
University of Central Oklahoma *B, M*

Oregon

Portland State University *B, M, D*
Warner Pacific College *B*

Pennsylvania

Bryn Mawr College *D*
Haverford College *B*
Temple University *B, M*
University of Pennsylvania *B*
University of Pittsburgh *B*

Rhode Island

Brown University *B*
Community College of Rhode
   Island *A*

South Carolina

College of Charleston *B*
Furman University *B*

Tennessee

Lipscomb University *B*
Rhodes College *B*
Tennessee State University *B*
Vanderbilt University *B*

Texas

St. Philip's College *A*
Texas A&M International University *B*
Trinity University *B*
University of Houston *B*
University of Texas
   Arlington *M*
   Austin *B*

Utah

University of Utah *B, M*

Virginia

Norfolk State University *M*
Old Dominion University *M, D*
Virginia Commonwealth
   University *B, M*
Virginia Polytechnic Institute and
   State University *M, D*

Washington

University of Washington Tacoma *B*

Wisconsin

University of Wisconsin
   Green Bay *B*
   Milwaukee *B, M, D*
   Oshkosh *B*

Vehicle emissions inspection/maintenance

California

College of the Desert *C*
Southwestern College *C*

Vehicle parts/ accessories marketing

Florida

Northwood University
   Florida *B*

Iowa

Iowa Lakes Community College *C*

Michigan

Northwood University: Michigan *B*

Nebraska

Central Community College *C, A*
Southeast Community College *A*

Pennsylvania

Pennsylvania College of
   Technology *A*

Washington

Bates Technical College *C*
Spokane Community College *C, A*

Vendor/product certification

Arizona

Chandler-Gilbert Community College
   Pecos *C, A*
Estrella Mountain Community
   College *C, A*
Glendale Community College *C*
Paradise Valley Community College *C*

Arkansas

University of Arkansas
   Cossatot Community College of the
     C

California

City College of San Francisco *C*
College of Marin: Kentfield *C*
College of the Siskiyous *C*
Folsom Lake College *C*
Foothill College *C*
Heald College
   Roseville *C*
   Stockton *C, A*
Kaplan College: Vista *C*
Long Beach City College *C*
San Jose City College *C*
Santa Rosa Junior College *C*
Shasta College *C*
Southwestern College *C*

Colorado

Colorado Technical University *C*

Florida

Herzing University *C*

Hawaii

Heald College
   Honolulu *C, A*

Illinois

Morton College *C*
Richland Community College *C*

Indiana

Ivy Tech Community College
   Bloomington *C*
   Central Indiana *C*
   Columbus *C*
   East Central *C*
   Kokomo *C*
   Lafayette *C*
   North Central *C*

   Northeast *C*
   Northwest *C*
   Richmond *C*
   South Central *C*

Kansas

Neosho County Community
   College *C*

Kentucky

Ashland Community and Technical
   College *A*
Sullivan College of Technology and
   Design *A*

Maryland

Hagerstown Community College *C*

Massachusetts

Bristol Community College *C*

Michigan

Baker College
   of Port Huron *C, A*
Lansing Community College *A*

Minnesota

Pine Technical College *C*
St. Paul College *C*

Montana

Dawson Community College *A*

New Jersey

Cumberland County College *A*
Raritan Valley Community College *C*

New York

Globe Institute of Technology *C, A, B*

North Carolina

Beaufort County Community
   College *C, A*
Pitt Community College *C, A*

North Dakota

Lake Region State College *C, A*
Williston State College *C, A*

Ohio

James A. Rhodes State College *C*
Marion Technical College *C, A*
University of Cincinnati
   Clermont College *C, A*

Pennsylvania

Keystone College *A*
Peirce College *C, A*

South Dakota

Kilian Community College *A*

Texas

Blinn College *C*

Washington

Bellevue College *C*
Big Bend Community College *C*
Clover Park Technical College *C*
Peninsula College *A*

Veterinary medicine (D.V.M.)

Alabama

Auburn University: College of
   Veterinary Medicine *P*
Tuskegee University: School of
   Veterinary Medicine *P*

California

University of California Davis: School
   of Veterinary Medicine *P*

Colorado

Colorado State University: College of
   Veterinary Medicine and
   Biomedical Sciences *P*

Florida

University of Florida: College of
   Veterinary Medicine *P*

Georgia

University of Georgia: College of
   Veterinary Medicine *P*

Illinois

University of Illinois at
   Urbana-Champaign: College of
   Veterinary Medicine *P*

Indiana

Purdue University: School of
   Veterinary Medicine *P*

Iowa

Iowa State University: College of
   Veterinary Medicine *P*

Kansas

Kansas State University: College of
   Veterinary Medicine *P*

Louisiana

Louisiana State University and
   Agricultural and Mechanical
   College: School of Veterinary
   Medicine *P*

Massachusetts

Tufts University: School of Veterinary
   Medicine *P*

Michigan

Michigan State University: School of
   Veterinary Medicine *P*

Minnesota

University of Minnesota Twin Cities:
   College of Veterinary Medicine *P*

Mississippi

Mississippi State University: College of
   Veterinary Medicine *P*

Missouri

University of Missouri Columbia:
   School of Veterinary Medicine *P*

New York

Cornell University: College of
   Veterinary Medicine *P*

North Carolina

North Carolina State University:
   College of Veterinary Medicine *P*

Ohio

Ohio State University Columbus
   Campus: College of Veterinary
   Medicine *P*

Oklahoma

Oklahoma State University: College of
   Veterinary Medicine *P*

Oregon

Oregon State University: College of
   Veterinary Medicine *P*

Pennsylvania

University of Pennsylvania: School of
Veterinary Medicine *P*

Tennessee

University of Tennessee Knoxville:
College of Veterinary Medicine *P*

Texas

Texas A&M University: College of
Veterinary Medicine *P*

Virginia

Virginia Polytechnic Institute:
Virginia-Maryland Regional
College of Veterinary Medicine *P*

Washington

Washington State University: School of
Veterinary Medicine *P*

Wisconsin

University of Wisconsin Madison:
School of Veterinary Medicine *P*

Veterinary technology

Alabama

Jefferson State Community College *A*

Alaska

University of Alaska
Fairbanks *C*

Arizona

Pima Community College *A*

Arkansas

Arkansas State University
Beebe *A*

California

Foothill College *C, A*
Hartnell College *A*
Los Angeles Pierce College *A*
San Joaquin Valley College *A*
Silicon Valley College
Western Career College: San Jose *A*
Western Career College
San Leandro *A*
Western Career College: Citrus
Heights *A*
Western Career College:
Sacramento *A*
Western Career College: Stockton *A*
Yuba Community College District *A*

Colorado

Bel-Rea Institute of Animal
Technology *A*
Colorado Mountain College *A*
Community College of Denver *A*
Front Range Community College *A*
Otero Junior College *A*

Connecticut

Northwestern Connecticut
Community College *A*

Delaware

Delaware Technical and Community
College
Owens *A*

Florida

Daytona State College *A*
Hillsborough Community College *A*
Miami Dade College *A*
St. Petersburg College *C, A, B*

State College of Florida,
Manatee-Sarasota *A*

Georgia

Athens Technical College *A*
Fort Valley State University *A, B*
Gwinnett Technical College *C, A*

Illinois

Fox College *A*
Joliet Junior College *A*
Kaskaskia College *A*
Parkland College *A*
Rockford Career College *A*

Indiana

Harrison College
Indianapolis Northwest *A*
Purdue University *A, B*

Iowa

Des Moines Area Community
College *A*
Kirkwood Community College *A*
Muscatine Community College *A*
Western Iowa Tech Community
College *C*

Kansas

Colby Community College *A*
Johnson County Community
College *A*

Kentucky

Morehead State University *A*
Murray State University *B*

Louisiana

Northwestern State University *A*

Maine

University of Maine
Augusta *A*

Maryland

Community College of Baltimore
County *A*

Massachusetts

Becker College *A, B*
Berkshire Community College *C*
Holyoke Community College *A*
Mount Ida College *A, B*
North Shore Community College *A*

Michigan

Baker College
of Cadillac *A*
of Flint *A*
of Muskegon *A*
of Port Huron *A*
Bay de Noc Community College *C*
Macomb Community College *A*
Michigan State University *C, B*
Oakland Community College *A*
Wayne County Community College *A*

Minnesota

Argosy University: Twin Cities *A*
Globe University *A*
Minnesota School of Business:
Blaine *C, A*
Minnesota School of Business: St.
Cloud *A*
Ridgewater College *A*
Rochester Community and Technical
College *C, A*

Mississippi

Hinds Community College *A*

Mississippi Gulf Coast Community
College *A*

Missouri

Hickey College *A*
Jefferson College *C, A*
Metropolitan Community College:
Maple Woods *A*

Nebraska

Nebraska College of Technical
Agriculture *A*
Northeast Community College *A*
University of Nebraska
Lincoln *B*

New Jersey

Bergen Community College *A*
Camden County College *A*
Thomas Edison State College *A, B*

New Mexico

Central New Mexico Community
College *A*
Navajo Technical College *A*
San Juan College *C, A*

New York

City University of New York
LaGuardia Community College *A*
Medaille College *A, B*
State University of New York
College of Technology at Alfred *A*
College of Technology at
Canton *A, B*
College of Technology at Delhi *A*
Suffolk County Community College *A*
Ulster County Community College *A*

North Carolina

Central Carolina Community
College *A*
Gaston College *A*

North Dakota

North Dakota State University *B*

Ohio

Bradford School *A*
Columbus State Community
College *A*
Stautzenberger College:
Brecksville *C, A*
University of Cincinnati
Raymond Walters College *A*

Oklahoma

Oklahoma State University
Oklahoma City *A*
Redlands Community College *A*

Oregon

Linn-Benton Community College *C*
Portland Community College *A*

Pennsylvania

Harcum College *A*
Johnson College *A*
Lehigh Carbon Community College *A*
Manor College *A*
Northampton Community College *A*
Vet Tech Institute *A*
Wilson College *A, B*

Puerto Rico

University of Puerto Rico
Medical Sciences *B*

South Carolina

Greenville Technical College *C*
Tri-County Technical College *A*

South Dakota

National American University
Rapid City *A*

Tennessee

Chattanooga State Community
College *A*
Columbia State Community College *A*
Lincoln Memorial University *A, B*
University of Tennessee
Knoxville *D*

Texas

Cedar Valley College *C, A*
Houston Community College
System *C*
Lone Star College System *C, A*
Midland College *A*
Sul Ross State University *A*
Weatherford College *C, A*

Utah

Snow College *A*
Utah Career College *A*

Vermont

Vermont Technical College *A*

Virginia

Blue Ridge Community College *C, A*
Northern Virginia Community
College *A*

Washington

Bellingham Technical College *C, A*
Centralia College *C*
Pierce College *A*
Yakima Valley Community
College *C, A*

West Virginia

Fairmont State University *A*

Wisconsin

Northcentral Technical College *C*

Wyoming

Eastern Wyoming College *A*

Violin/viola/guitar/ stringed instruments

California

Bethesda Christian University *B, M*
Orange Coast College *C*
San Francisco Conservatory of
Music *B, M*
University of Southern
California *B, M, D*

Florida

Florida State University *B, M, D*
Stetson University *B*

Illinois

Illinois Wesleyan University *B*
Northwestern University *B, M, D*
Roosevelt University *B, M*

Indiana

Butler University *B, M*

Iowa

Cornell College *B*
Dordt College *B*
University of Iowa *B*

Kansas

University of Kansas *B, M, D*

Louisiana
Xavier University of Louisiana *B*

Maine
University of Southern Maine *B, M*

Massachusetts
Eastern Nazarene College *B*
New England Conservatory of
Music *B, M, D*

Michigan
Hope College *B*
University of Michigan *M*

Minnesota
Northwestern College *B*
Saint Cloud State University *B*

Missouri
University of Missouri
Kansas City *B*

Nebraska
University of Nebraska
Omaha *B*

New York
Bard College *B*
Five Towns College *A, B, M*
Houghton College *B, M*
Juilliard School *B, M, D*
Mannes College The New School for
Music *B, M*

North Carolina
East Carolina University *B*
Gardner-Webb University *B*

Ohio
Oberlin College *B, M*
University of Akron *B, M*
Youngstown State University *B, M*

Oklahoma
Oklahoma City University *B*
University of Central Oklahoma *B*

Oregon
Willamette University *B*

Pennsylvania
Carnegie Mellon University *B, M*

Puerto Rico
Conservatory of Music of Puerto
Rico *B*

South Carolina
Converse College *B, M*

Tennessee
Vanderbilt University *B*

Texas
Hardin-Simmons University *B, M*
Howard Payne University *B*
Texas Christian University *B, M*

Utah
Brigham Young University *B*

Vermont
Bennington College *B*

Washington
Cornish College of the Arts *B*
University of Washington *B, M, D*

Virology

Illinois
University of Chicago *D*

Massachusetts
Harvard College *D*

Ohio
Case Western Reserve University *D*
Ohio State University
Columbus Campus *M, D*

Texas
University of Texas
Health Science Center at
Houston *M, D*

Vision science

Alabama
University of Alabama
Birmingham *M, D*

California
University of California
Berkeley *M, D*

Florida
Nova Southeastern University *M*

Missouri
University of Missouri
St. Louis *M, D*

Texas
University of the Incarnate Word *B*

Visual/performing arts

Alabama
Birmingham-Southern College *B*
Faulkner State Community College *A*

Arizona
Arizona State University *B*
Central Arizona College *A*
Cochise College *A*
Northern Arizona University *B*
Pima Community College *A*
Prescott College *B, M*
Scottsdale Community College *A*
University of Arizona *B*

Arkansas
University of the Ozarks *B*

California
Antelope Valley College *C, A*
Cabrillo College *A*
California Lutheran University *B*
California State University
Bakersfield *B*
San Marcos *B*
California State University: Channel
Islands *B*
College of Alameda *A*
College of the Siskiyous *C, A*
Cypress College *C, A*
Feather River College *A*
Fresno City College *C, A*
Fullerton College *A*
Glendale Community College *A*
Irvine Valley College *A*
Los Angeles City College *C*
Merced College *A*
Modesto Junior College *C, A*
Moorpark College *A*
Platt College
Los Angeles *C, A*

Ontario *C, A, B*
San Diego *C, A, B*
Pomona College *B*
Porterville College *A*
Rio Hondo College *A*
Sacramento City College *A*
St. Mary's College of California *B*
San Diego City College *A*
San Joaquin Delta College *A*
San Jose State University *B*
Santa Ana College *C, A*
Skyline College *A*
Sonoma State University *A*
University of California
Riverside *M*
San Diego *M*
Santa Barbara *B, M*
University of San Francisco *B*
University of Southern California *B*

Colorado
Colorado Mountain College *A*
Naropa University *B*
Regis University *B*
University of Colorado
Colorado Springs *B*

Connecticut
Albertus Magnus College *B*
Eastern Connecticut State
University *B*
Fairfield University *B*
Trinity College *B*
Tunxis Community College *C, A*
University of Hartford *B*

Delaware
Delaware State University *B*
University of Delaware *M*

District of Columbia
American University *B*
Catholic University of America *M, D*
Corcoran College of Art and
Design *A, B*
Gallaudet University *B*
George Washington University *B, M*
Howard University *B*

Florida
Daytona State College *A*
Flagler College *B*
Florida State College at Jacksonville *A*
Miami International University of Art
and Design *B, M*
Palm Beach Atlantic University *B*
Palm Beach Community College *A*
Saint Johns River Community
College *A*
State College of Florida,
Manatee-Sarasota *A*
Tallahassee Community College *A*
University of Tampa *B*

Georgia
Abraham Baldwin Agricultural
College *A*
Andrew College *A*
LaGrange College *B*
Savannah State University *B*
Valdosta State University *B*
Young Harris College *A*

Illinois
City Colleges of Chicago
Kennedy-King College *A*
Columbia College Chicago *B*
Illinois Institute of Art: Schaumburg *B*
Illinois Valley Community College *A*
Kankakee Community College *A*
Kishwaukee College *A*
Lake Forest College *B*
Lincoln College *A*

Northwestern University *B, M*
Richland Community College *A*
School of the Art Institute of
Chicago *B*
University of Chicago *B, M*
University of St. Francis *B*

Indiana
Holy Cross College *B*
Indiana University
Bloomington *B, M*
Purdue University *B, M, D*
Taylor University *B*

Iowa
Graceland University *B*
Iowa State University *B, M*
Loras College *B*
Marshalltown Community College *A*
Waldorf College *B*

Kansas
Central Christian College of
Kansas *A, B*
Coffeyville Community College *A*
Cowley County Community
College *A*
Garden City Community College *A*
Hutchinson Community College *A*
MidAmerica Nazarene University *B, T*
Pratt Community College *A*
Seward County Community College *A*
Washburn University *B*
Wichita State University *B*

Kentucky
Bluegrass Community and Technical
College *A*
Western Kentucky University *B*

Louisiana
Centenary College of Louisiana *B*
Delta College of Arts &
Technology *C, A*
Loyola University New Orleans *B*
University of Louisiana at Lafayette *B*

Maine
University of Maine
Machias *B*
University of Southern Maine *B*

Maryland
Community College of Baltimore
County *A*
Frostburg State University *C, B*
Garrett College *A*
Harford Community College *A*
Montgomery College *A*
Mount St. Mary's University *B, T*
University of Maryland
Baltimore County *B, M*

Massachusetts
Art Institute of Boston at Lesley
University *B*
Assumption College *B*
Bard College at Simon's Rock *B*
Berkshire Community College *A*
Boston University *B, M*
Cape Cod Community College *A*
Clark University *B*
Emerson College *B, M*
Hampshire College *B*
Harvard College *B*
Massachusetts College of Liberal
Arts *B*
Massasoit Community College *C*
Middlesex Community College *A*
New England Institute of Art *A*
Northeastern University *M*
Pine Manor College *B*

Roxbury Community College *A*
Stonehill College *B*
Suffolk University *B*
Tufts University *M*
University of Massachusetts
  Dartmouth *B, M*
  Lowell *B*
Wheelock College *B*
Worcester State College *B*

Michigan
Albion College *B, T*
Alma College *B*
Andrews University *B*
Calvin College *B*
Lansing Community College *A*
Michigan Technological University *B*
Mid Michigan Community College *A*
University of Michigan *B*

Minnesota
Academy College *C, A*
Hamline University *B*
Minnesota School of Business:
  Brooklyn Center *C, A*
Minnesota State University
  Mankato *B*
Minnesota West Community and
  Technical College *A*
Northland Community & Technical
  College *A*
Winona State University *B*

Mississippi
Blue Mountain College *B*
Delta State University *B*
Jackson State University *B*
Mississippi State University *B*
Mississippi University for Women *B*
University of Mississippi *B, M*
University of Southern Mississippi *B*

Missouri
Drury University *B, T*
Lindenwood University *B*
Missouri State University *B*
St. Louis Community College
  St. Louis Community College at
    Florissant Valley *A*
Southeast Missouri State University *B*
Stephens College *B*
Washington University in St.
  Louis *B, M*

Montana
University of Montana *B, M*
University of Montana: Western *B*

Nebraska
Concordia University *B*
University of Nebraska
  Kearney *B, M, T*

Nevada
Art Institute
  of Las Vegas *B*
Sierra Nevada College *B*

New Hampshire
Lebanon College *A*

New Jersey
Bergen Community College *A*
Bloomfield College *C, B*
The College of New Jersey *B*
County College of Morris *A*
Fairleigh Dickinson University
  College at Florham *B*
  Metropolitan Campus *B*
Mercer County Community College *A*
Ramapo College of New Jersey *B*

Richard Stockton College of New
  Jersey *B*
Seton Hall University *B, T*
William Paterson University of New
  Jersey *M*

New Mexico
New Mexico State University *B, M*
Northern New Mexico College *A*

New York
Bard College *B, M*
Barnard College *B*
Briarcliffe College *B*
City University of New York
  Brooklyn College *M*
  City College *B, M*
  Kingsborough Community
    College *A*
  Queensborough Community
    College *A*
Columbia University *B*
Columbia University
  School of General Studies *B*
Cornell University *M*
Dowling College *B*
Eugene Lang College The New School
  for Liberal Arts *B*
Ithaca College *B, M*
Long Island University
  Brooklyn Campus *B, M*
Medaille College *B*
Molloy College *B*
New York University *C*
Pace University *M*
Saint Bonaventure University *B*
Siena College *B*
State University of New York
  College at Brockport *B, M*
  College at Buffalo *B*
  College at Old Westbury *B*
  College at Plattsburgh *B*
  New Paltz *B*
Ulster County Community College *A*
Union College *B*
Wells College *B*
Westchester Community College *A*

North Carolina
Bennett College for Women *B*
Carteret Community College *A*
Fayetteville State University *B*
Johnson C. Smith University *B*
Lees-McRae College *B*
Methodist University *B*
North Carolina Agricultural and
  Technical State University *B*
St. Andrews Presbyterian College *B*
St. Augustine's College *B*

Ohio
Antioch University McGregor *M*
Baldwin-Wallace College *T*
International College of
  Broadcasting *C, A*
Mount Union College *T*
Notre Dame College *B, T*
Ohio University *D*
Otterbein College *B*
Shawnee State University *B*
Wittenberg University *B*
Youngstown State University *B, M*

Oklahoma
Murray State College *A*
Oklahoma City University *B, M*
Rogers State University *B*
St. Gregory's University *B*
Southern Nazarene University *B*
University of Oklahoma *B*

Oregon
Central Oregon Community
  College *A*
Oregon State University *B*
Pacific University *B*
Treasure Valley Community College *A*
Western Oregon University *B*

Pennsylvania
Arcadia University *B*
Bucknell University *B*
Bucks County Community College *A*
Cedar Crest College *B*
East Stroudsburg University of
  Pennsylvania *B*
Gannon University *B*
Gettysburg College *B*
Harrisburg Area Community
  College *A*
Lycoming College *B*
Oakbridge Academy of Arts *A*
Penn State
  Abington *B*
  Altoona *B*
  Beaver *B*
  Berks *B*
  Brandywine *B*
  DuBois *B*
  Erie, The Behrend College *B*
  Fayette, The Eberly Campus *B*
  Greater Allegheny *B*
  Hazleton *B*
  Lehigh Valley *B*
  Mont Alto *B*
  New Kensington *B*
  Schuylkill *B*
  Shenango *B*
  University Park *B*
  Wilkes-Barre *B*
  Worthington Scranton *B*
  York *B*
Saint Joseph's University *B*
Thiel College *B*
University of Pennsylvania *B*
University of Pittsburgh
  Bradford *B*

Puerto Rico
Escuela de Artes Plasticas de Puerto
  Rico *B*
Inter American University of Puerto
  Rico
  San German Campus *B, M*
University of Puerto Rico
  Aguadilla *A*
  Rio Piedras *B*
University of the Sacred Heart *B*

Rhode Island
Brown University *B*
Providence College *B*

South Carolina
College of Charleston *M*

South Dakota
South Dakota State University *B*

Tennessee
Carson-Newman College *B*
King College *B*
Lambuth University *B*
Lincoln Memorial University *B, T*
Milligan College *B*
Nossi College of Art *A*
Tusculum College *B*
University of Tennessee
  Martin *B*
University of the South *B*

Texas
Art Institute
  of Houston *C, A*
Coastal Bend College *A*
College of the Mainland *A*
Hill College *A*
Howard College *A*
Lon Morris College *A*
Rice University *B, M*
South Texas College *A*
Texas A&M University
  Commerce *B*
  Corpus Christi *B*
Texas Lutheran University *B*
Texas Tech University *D*
Texas Wesleyan University *B, T*
Trinity Valley Community College *A*
Tyler Junior College *A*
University of Houston
  Downtown *B*
University of Texas
  Austin *B*
  Dallas *B*

Utah
Provo College *A*
Snow College *A*
University of Utah *B*
Weber State University *B*

Vermont
Bennington College *B*
Castleton State College *B*
Johnson State College *B*
Lyndon State College *B*
Marlboro College *B*

Virginia
Ferrum College *B*
George Mason University *B, M*
Longwood University *B, T*
Mary Baldwin College *M*
Norfolk State University *M*
Old Dominion University *M*
Piedmont Virginia Community
  College *A*
Regent University *M*
Shenandoah University *B*
University of Mary Washington *B*
Virginia State University *B*

Washington
Art Institute of Seattle *A, B*
Centralia College *A*
Cornish College of the Arts *B*
Everett Community College *A*
Evergreen State College *B*
Green River Community College *C, A*
Highline Community College *A*
North Seattle Community
  College *C, A*
Olympic College *A*
Seattle Pacific University *B, T*
Seattle University *B*
Western Washington University *B*
Whitworth University *B, T*

West Virginia
Bethany College *B*
West Virginia University *B, M*

Wisconsin
Edgewood College *B*
University of Wisconsin
  Green Bay *B*
  Milwaukee *M*
  Stevens Point *B*
  Superior *B, M, T*
Viterbo University *B*

Wyoming

Western Wyoming Community
College *A*

Vocational
rehabilitation
counseling

Alabama

Alabama State University *M*
University of Alabama *M*

Arkansas

Arkansas State University *M*
University of Arkansas *M, D*
University of Arkansas
Little Rock *M*

California

California State University
Fresno *B, M*
San Bernardino *M*
San Diego State University *M*

Colorado

University of Northern Colorado *B, M*

Florida

Florida State University *M*
University of South Florida *M*

Georgia

Fort Valley State University *M*
Georgia State University *M*
University of Georgia *M*

Illinois

Illinois Institute of Technology *M*
Southern Illinois University
Carbondale *M*
University of Illinois
Urbana-Champaign *B, M, D*

Kansas

Emporia State University *B, M*

Kentucky

University of Kentucky *M*

Louisiana

Louisiana State University Health
Sciences Center *B, M*
Southern University and Agricultural
and Mechanical College *B, M*

Massachusetts

Boston University *M, D*
Springfield College *M*

Michigan

Michigan State University *M, D*
Wayne State University *M*

Minnesota

Saint Cloud State University *M*

Mississippi

Jackson State University *M*

Missouri

Maryville University of Saint
Louis *B, M*

Montana

Montana State University
Billings *B, M*

New Jersey

Seton Hall University *M*

Union County College *A*
University of Medicine and Dentistry
of New Jersey
School of Health Related
Professions *M*

New York

Hofstra University *M*
State University of New York
Buffalo *M*
Syracuse University *M*

North Carolina

East Carolina University *B, M, D*
University of North Carolina
Chapel Hill *M*
Winston-Salem State University *B, M*

North Dakota

University of North Dakota *D*

Ohio

Bowling Green State University *B, M*
University of Cincinnati *M*
University of Cincinnati
Raymond Walters College *A*
Wilberforce University *M*
Wright State University *B*

Oklahoma

East Central University *B*

Oregon

Western Oregon University *M*

Pennsylvania

Edinboro University of
Pennsylvania *M*

Puerto Rico

University of Puerto Rico
Rio Piedras *M*

Rhode Island

Salve Regina University *M*

Tennessee

University of Tennessee
Knoxville *M*

Texas

Stephen F Austin State University *M*
Texas Tech University Health Sciences
Center *D*
University of North Texas *B, M*
University of Texas
Pan American *B, M*
Southwestern Medical Center at
Dallas *M*

Virginia

Virginia Commonwealth University *M*

Washington

Spokane Falls Community College *A*
Western Washington University *M*

West Virginia

West Virginia University *M*

Wisconsin

University of Wisconsin
Madison *B, M, D*
Stout *B, M*

Vocational/technical
education

Alabama

Auburn University *B, M, D*

Tuskegee University *B*

Arizona

Northern Arizona University *B*
Prescott College *B*

Connecticut

University of Connecticut *D, T*

Delaware

Wilmington University *M*

Florida

Palm Beach Community College *A*

Georgia

University of Georgia *B, M, D, T*

Hawaii

University of Hawaii
Honolulu Community College *A*

Idaho

University of Idaho *B, M, T*

Illinois

City Colleges of Chicago
Kennedy-King College *A*
Eastern Illinois University *B, T*
University of Illinois
Urbana-Champaign *M, D*

Indiana

Ball State University *M*
Oakland City University *B*

Kansas

Pittsburg State University *B, M*

Kentucky

Eastern Kentucky University *A*
Western Kentucky University *A*

Maine

University of Southern Maine *B, T*

Michigan

Cornerstone University *B, T*
Ferris State University *B, M*
Wayne State University *B, M, T*

Minnesota

Bemidji State University *B*
Minnesota State University
Mankato *B, M, T*
Ridgewater College *A*
Saint Cloud State University *B*

Mississippi

Millsaps College *T*
Mississippi State University *B, M, T*

Missouri

Mineral Area College *A*
State Fair Community College *A*
University of Missouri
Columbia *B, M, D*

Nebraska

Chadron State College *M*
Peru State College *B, T*

New Jersey

College of St. Elizabeth *M*

New Mexico

University of New Mexico *M, D, T*
Western New Mexico University *B*

New York

College of Saint Rose *M*
New York Institute of
Technology *A, B, T*
State University of New York
College at Buffalo *B, M, T*
Oswego *B*

North Carolina

East Carolina University *M*

North Dakota

Lake Region State College *A*
University of North Dakota *M*

Ohio

Bowling Green State
University *B, M, T*
Ohio State University
Columbus Campus *M, D*
University of Akron *B, M*

Oklahoma

Oklahoma State University *B*

Oregon

Oregon State University *M*

Pennsylvania

Temple University *M*

Puerto Rico

Inter American University of Puerto
Rico
San German Campus *B*

Rhode Island

Rhode Island College *B, M*

South Carolina

Aiken Technical College *A*
Florence-Darlington Technical
College *A*
Horry-Georgetown Technical
College *A*
Spartanburg Community College *A*
Trident Technical College *A*

South Dakota

South Dakota State University *B*

Tennessee

Middle Tennessee State University *M*

Texas

Texas A&M University
Commerce *T*

Utah

Utah State University *B, M*

Washington

Bellingham Technical College *A*
Renton Technical College *A*
Walla Walla University *B*

Wisconsin

University of Wisconsin
Platteville *B, T*
Stout *B*

Voice/opera

Alabama

Birmingham-Southern College *B*
Samford University *B*
Talladega College *B*
University of Mobile *B*

Arizona
Northern Arizona University *B, M*

Arkansas
Ouachita Baptist University *B*

California
Bethesda Christian University *B, M*
California Baptist University *B*
California State University
   Chico *C*
   Long Beach *B*
   Sacramento *B, M*
Chapman University *B*
College of the Siskiyous *C, A*
Fresno City College *A*
The Master's College *B*
Notre Dame de Namur
   University *B, M*
Ohlone College *C*
Point Loma Nazarene University *B*
San Francisco Conservatory of
   Music *B, M*
Solano Community College *C*
University of Southern
   California *B, M, D*
University of the Pacific *B*

Colorado
Adams State College *B*

Delaware
University of Delaware *B*

District of Columbia
Catholic University of
   America *B, M, D*
Howard University *B*

Florida
Florida State University *B, M, D*
Jacksonville University *B*
Palm Beach Atlantic University *B*
Southeastern University *B*
Stetson University *B*
University of Miami *B, M, D*

Georgia
Shorter College *B*

Idaho
Northwest Nazarene University *B*
University of Idaho *B*

Illinois
Augustana College *B*
Columbia College Chicago *B*
Illinois Wesleyan University *B*
Lincoln College *A*
Millikin University *B*
Moody Bible Institute *B*
North Park University *M*
Northwestern University *B, M, D*
Olivet Nazarene University *B*
Roosevelt University *B, M*
Saint Xavier University *B*
Trinity International University *B*
University of Illinois
   Urbana-Champaign *B, M, D*

Indiana
Anderson University *B*
Butler University *B, M*
Grace College *B*
Huntington University *B*
Indiana University
   Bloomington *B*
Indiana University-Purdue University
   Fort Wayne *B, T*
Indiana Wesleyan University *T*
Valparaiso University *B*

Iowa
Cornell College *B*
Dordt College *B*
University of Iowa *B*
Waldorf College *B*

Kansas
Allen County Community College *A*
Central Christian College of Kansas *A*
MidAmerica Nazarene University *B, T*
Seward County Community College *A*
University of Kansas *B, M, D*
Wichita State University *B*

Kentucky
Berea College *B*
Campbellsville University *B*

Louisiana
Centenary College of Louisiana *B, T*
Louisiana College *B*
Xavier University of Louisiana *B*

Maine
University of Southern Maine *B, M*

Maryland
Johns Hopkins University: Peabody
   Conservatory of Music *B, M, D*
Washington Bible College *B, T*

Massachusetts
Berklee College of Music *B*
Boston Conservatory *B, M*
Boston University *B, M, D*
Eastern Nazarene College *B*
New England Conservatory of
   Music *B, M, D*

Michigan
Calvin College *B, T*
Eastern Michigan University *M*
Grand Rapids Community College *A*
Hope College *B*
Northwestern Michigan College *A*
Oakland Community College *A*
Oakland University *B, M*

Minnesota
Northwestern College *B*
Saint Cloud State University *B*

Mississippi
Mississippi College *B*

Missouri
Calvary Bible College and Theological
   Seminary *B*
Drury University *B*
University of Missouri
   Kansas City *B*
Washington University in St.
   Louis *B, M*

Nebraska
Concordia University *B, T*
Grace University *B*
University of Nebraska
   Omaha *B*
York College *B*

New Jersey
Rider University *B*

New York
Bard College *B, M*
Columbia University
   School of General Studies *B*
Eastman School of Music of the
   University of Rochester *B, M, D*
Five Towns College *A, B, M*

Houghton College *B, M*
Mannes College The New School for
   Music *B, M*
Roberts Wesleyan College *B*
State University of New York
   College at Fredonia *B*
University of Rochester *M*

North Carolina
Campbell University *B*
East Carolina University *B*
Gardner-Webb University *B*

Ohio
Baldwin-Wallace College *B*
Bowling Green State University *B*
Capital University *B*
Cleveland Institute of Music *B, M, D*
Oberlin College *B, M*
Ohio State University
   Columbus Campus *B*
Ohio University *B*
University of Akron *B, M*
University of Cincinnati *B, M, D*
Youngstown State University *B, M*

Oklahoma
East Central University *B, T*
Northwestern Oklahoma State
   University *B*
Oklahoma Baptist University *B*
Oklahoma Christian University *B*
Oklahoma City University *B, M*
Oral Roberts University *B*
Southwestern Oklahoma State
   University *B*
University of Central Oklahoma *B*
University of Tulsa *B*

Oregon
Corban College *B*
Willamette University *B*

Pennsylvania
Carnegie Mellon University *B, M*
Curtis Institute of Music *M*
Gettysburg College *B*
Mansfield University of
   Pennsylvania *B*
Penn State
   University Park *M*
Temple University *B, M, D*
Westminster College *B*

Puerto Rico
Conservatory of Music of Puerto
   Rico *B*

South Carolina
Charleston Southern University *B*
Coker College *B*
Columbia College *B*
Converse College *B, M*
North Greenville University *B*
University of South Carolina *M*

Tennessee
Belmont University *B, M*
Lambuth University *B*
Lipscomb University *B*
University of Tennessee
   Knoxville *B*
Vanderbilt University *B*

Texas
Abilene Christian University *B*
Angelina College *A*
Dallas Baptist University *B*
East Texas Baptist University *B*
Hardin-Simmons University *B, M*
Howard Payne University *B*
Lamar University *B, M*

Lon Morris College *A*
Navarro College *A*
Southern Methodist University *B, M*
Southwestern Assemblies of God
   University *B*
Texas A&M University
   Commerce *B, M*
Texas Christian University *B, M*
Trinity University *B*
University of Texas
   El Paso *B*

Utah
Brigham Young University *B*
Weber State University *B*

Vermont
Bennington College *B*
Johnson State College *B*

Virginia
Bluefield College *B*
Virginia Union University *B*

Washington
Cornish College of the Arts *B*
University of Washington *B, M, D*
Whitworth University *B*

Wisconsin
University of Wisconsin
   Madison *B, M*
   Parkside *T*

Waldorf/Steiner
teacher education

Arizona
Prescott College *B*

Kentucky
Bellarmine University *M*

Warehousing/inventory
management

Illinois
Black Hawk College *C*

Iowa
Iowa Lakes Community College *C*

Washington
Bates Technical College *C*
Clover Park Technical College *C*

Wisconsin
Lakeshore Technical College *A*

Watch/jewelrymaking

Minnesota
Minneapolis Community and
   Technical College *C, A*
St. Paul College *C*

Montana
Flathead Valley Community
   College *C, A*

Oklahoma
Oklahoma State University
   Institute of Technology:
   Okmulgee *A*

Pennsylvania
Commonwealth Technical Institute *C*

Texas

Austin Community College *C, A*
Paris Junior College *A*

Washington

North Seattle Community
College *C, A*

Wisconsin

Milwaukee Area Technical College *C*

Water quality/ treatment/recycling technology

Alabama

Gadsden State Community College *C*
Northwest-Shoals Community
College *C*

Arizona

Arizona Western College *C, A*
GateWay Community College *C, A*
Rio Salado College *C, A*

Arkansas

Southern Arkansas University Tech *C*

California

Citrus College *C*
College of the Canyons *A*
Hartnell College *C, A*
Imperial Valley College *A*
San Diego Mesa College *C, A*
Santa Barbara City College *C*
Shasta College *C*
Solano Community College *C, A*
Ventura College *C, A*
Yuba Community College
District *C, A*

Colorado

Red Rocks Community College *C*

Connecticut

Gateway Community College *C*
Three Rivers Community College *C, A*

Delaware

Delaware Technical and Community
College
Owens *A*

Florida

Hillsborough Community College *C*

Kentucky

Eastern Kentucky University *B*
Murray State University *A, B*

Maryland

Cecil College *C*
Community College of Baltimore
County *A*

Massachusetts

Bristol Community College *A*
Cape Cod Community College *C*
Springfield Technical Community
College *C*

Michigan

Bay de Noc Community College *C, A*
Grand Rapids Community College *A*

Minnesota

St. Cloud Technical College *C, A*

Nevada

College of Southern Nevada *C, A*

New Hampshire

White Mountains Community
College *C*

Ohio

Wright State University *A*

Oregon

Clackamas Community College *C, A*
Linn-Benton Community College *C, A*

Texas

Angelina College *C*

Utah

Utah Valley University *C*

Wisconsin

Milwaukee Area Technical College *A*

Wyoming

Casper College *C, A*

Water resource engineering

Arizona

Prescott College *M*
University of Arizona *B, M, D*

Idaho

University of Idaho *B, M, D*

Illinois

University of Illinois
Urbana-Champaign *B, M, D*

Minnesota

University of Minnesota
Crookston *B*

Nevada

University of Nevada
Reno *B, M, D*

New Jersey

Stevens Institute of Technology *M*

New Mexico

University of New Mexico *M*

Ohio

Central State University *B*

Pennsylvania

Villanova University *M*

Wisconsin

Marquette University *M, D*
University of Wisconsin
Madison *M, D*

Water, wetlands, and marine management

Arizona

Prescott College *M*

California

California State University
Monterey Bay *M*
Santa Rosa Junior College *C*

Colorado

Colorado State University *B, M, D*

Florida

Florida Gulf Coast University *B*
University of Miami *M*

Michigan

Delta College *C, A*

Montana

Helena College of Technology of the
University of Montana *A*

New Hampshire

University of New Hampshire *M*

New York

State University of New York
Stony Brook *B*

North Carolina

Lenoir Community College *C, A*

Oregon

Lane Community College *A*

Pennsylvania

Gettysburg College *B*
Keystone College *A, B*

Rhode Island

University of Rhode Island *B*

Texas

Texas State University: San Marcos *B*

Vermont

Sterling College *B*

Washington

Grays Harbor College *C*
Green River Community College *A*
Spokane Community College *A*

Wisconsin

University of Wisconsin
Madison *M*
Stevens Point *B*

Wyoming

Western Wyoming Community
College *A*

Web/multimedia management

Alabama

Gadsden State Community College *C*
Shelton State Community College *C*

Arizona

Art Institute
of Phoenix *B*
Cochise College *C*
Eastern Arizona College *C*
Paradise Valley Community College *C*
University of Advancing
Technology *A, B*
University of Phoenix *B*

Arkansas

Mid-South Community College *C*
Northwest Arkansas Community
College *A*

California

Allan Hancock College *C*
Art Institute
of California: Orange County *A, B*
of California: San Diego *B*
City College of San Francisco *C*

College of the Siskiyous *C*
Fashion Institute of Design and
Merchandising
San Francisco *A*
Foothill College *C*
Grossmont College *C, A*
Los Angeles Pierce College *C*
Orange Coast College *C*
Santa Rosa Junior College *C*
Shasta College *C*
Sierra College *C, A*
Skyline College *C, A*
Southwestern College *C, A*
Westwood College: Anaheim *B*

Colorado

Colorado Technical University *C*
Morgan Community College *C, A*
Red Rocks Community College *C, A*
Westwood College of Technology
Westwood College: Denver South *B*
Westwood College: Denver North *B*

Connecticut

Northwestern Connecticut
Community College *C*

Florida

Saint Johns River Community
College *C*
St. Petersburg College *C, A*
Santa Fe College *A*
Valencia Community College *C, A*

Georgia

Art Institute
of Atlanta *A, B*

Idaho

Lewis-Clark State College *A, B*

Illinois

Illinois Institute of Art:
Schaumburg *C, A, B*
Lewis and Clark Community
College *A*
Moraine Valley Community College *A*
Oakton Community College *C*
Rasmussen College: Rockford *A*
Rend Lake College *C*
University of St. Francis *B*
Westwood College: DuPage *B*

Indiana

Indiana University-Purdue University
Indianapolis *B*
Indiana Wesleyan University *B*
Ivy Tech Community College
Bloomington *C*
Central Indiana *C*
Columbus *C*
East Central *C*
Kokomo *C*
Lafayette *C*
North Central *C*
Northeast *C*
Northwest *C*
Richmond *C*
South Central *C*
Vincennes University *A*

Iowa

Iowa Central Community College *C, A*
Southwestern Community College *A*

Kentucky

Big Sandy Community and Technical
College *C, A*
Draughons Junior College *C, A*
Elizabethtown Community and
Technical College *C*

Louisiana

Louisiana College *B*

Maryland

Howard Community College *C*
Kaplan College: Hagerstown *A, B*
Montgomery College *C*

Massachusetts

Cape Cod Community College *A*
Holyoke Community College *C*
Massachusetts Bay Community
College *C*
Mount Wachusett Community
College *C*
Quinsigamond Community College *C*

Michigan

Delta College *C, A*
Gogebic Community College *C*
Grand Rapids Community College *A*
Kirtland Community College *C, A*
Northern Michigan University *B*
Northwestern Michigan College *C*
Oakland Community College *C*
Wayne County Community
College *C, A*

Minnesota

Art Institutes International
Minnesota *A, B*
Globe University *C, A*
Ridgewater College *C, A*
South Central College *C*

Mississippi

Antonelli College
Jackson *A*

Missouri

Missouri Southern State University *A*
Ranken Technical College *A*

Montana

Montana Tech of the University of
Montana *A*

Nevada

College of Southern Nevada *A*
Western Nevada College *A*

New Hampshire

Daniel Webster College *C*
Manchester Community College *C*
Nashua Community College *C, A*

New York

Bryant & Stratton Business Institute
Bryant & Stratton College:
Rochester *A*
Columbia-Greene Community
College *C*
Erie Community College
North Campus *C*
Genesee Community College *C, A*
Globe Institute of Technology *C, A, B*
Herkimer County Community
College *A*
Mohawk Valley Community
College *C, A*
Onondaga Community College *C*
Pace University *C*
Rochester Institute of
Technology *B, M*
Sage College of Albany *B*
State University of New York
College of Agriculture and
Technology at Morrisville *B*
College of Technology at Alfred *B*
Farmingdale *C*
Suffolk County Community College *A*

Tompkins Cortland Community
College *A*
Westchester Community College *C*

North Carolina

Carteret Community College *C, A*
Central Piedmont Community
College *C, A*
College of the Albemarle *C*
Durham Technical Community
College *C*
Sandhills Community College *C, A*

North Dakota

Dakota College at Bottineau *A*

Ohio

Davis College *A*
James A. Rhodes State College *C*
Marion Technical College *A*
Shawnee State University *C*
Stark State College of Technology *A*
University of Cincinnati
Raymond Walters College *C, A*
Youngstown State University *C*

Oklahoma

Rose State College *A*

Oregon

Chemeketa Community College *C*
Clackamas Community College *A*
Mt. Hood Community College *C, A*
Southwestern Oregon Community
College *C, A*

Pennsylvania

Community College of Philadelphia *B*
Consolidated School of Business
Lancaster *A*
York *A*
Duquesne University *B*
Kaplan Career Institute: Harrisburg *A*
Kaplan Career Institute: Pittsburgh *A*
Montgomery County Community
College *A*

Puerto Rico

Inter American University of Puerto
Rico
Bayamon Campus *C*

Rhode Island

Community College of Rhode
Island *C, A*
Johnson & Wales University:
Providence *B*

South Carolina

York Technical College *C*

South Dakota

National American University
Rapid City *B*

Tennessee

Northeast State Community
College *A*

Texas

Mountain View College *C*
North Lake College *C*
St. Philip's College *C, A*
San Jacinto College *C*
South Texas College *A*
Temple College *C, A*
Victoria College *C, A*

Vermont

Champlain College *B*

Virginia

ECPI College of Technology: Virginia
Beach *C, A*
ECPI Technical College: Roanoke *A*
Lord Fairfax Community College *C, A*
University of Management and
Technology *A, B, M*

Washington

Bates Technical College *C, A*
Cascadia Community College *C*
Clark College *C, A*
Everett Community College *A*
Olympic College *C*
Peninsula College *C*
South Seattle Community
College *C, A*
Yakima Valley Community College *C*

West Virginia

American Public University
System *C, A*
Mountain State University *A*

Wisconsin

Gateway Technical College *A*
Nicolet Area Technical College *A*
Northcentral Technical College *C*
Rasmussen College: Green Bay *A*

Wyoming

Sheridan College *A*
Western Wyoming Community
College *C*

Web page/multimedia design

Alabama

Gadsden State Community College *C*

Alaska

University of Alaska
Southeast *C*

Arizona

Anthem College *A*
Art Institute
of Phoenix *B*
Art Institute of Tucson *B*
Collins College *B*
DeVry University
Phoenix *A, B*
Estrella Mountain Community
College *C*
GateWay Community College *C*
Glendale Community College *C, A*
Pima Community College *C*
University of Advancing
Technology *A, B*
University of Phoenix *C, A, B*

Arkansas

East Arkansas Community
College *C, A*
Harding University *B*
Rich Mountain Community College *C*
Southern Arkansas University
Tech *C, A*

California

Academy of Art University *A, B*
Art Institute
of California: Los Angeles *A, B*
of California: Orange County *A, B*
of California: San Diego *A, B*
Art Institute of California:
Hollywood *A, B*
Art Institute of California: San
Francisco *A, B*

Art Institute of California:
Sunnyvale *A, B*
Bakersfield College *C*
California State University
East Bay *M*
City College of San Francisco *C*
College of Marin: Kentfield *A*
College of San Mateo *C, A*
College of the Siskiyous *C*
Folsom Lake College *C*
Foothill College *C*
Hartnell College *C, A*
Imperial Valley College *C, A*
Los Angeles Harbor College *C*
Los Angeles Pierce College *C*
Monterey Peninsula College *A*
Mt. Sierra College *B*
Ohlone College *C*
Orange Coast College *C*
Oxnard College *C, A*
Platt College
Ontario *C, B*
San Diego Mesa College *C, A*
San Jose City College *C*
Santa Clara University *B*
Santiago Canyon College *A*
Sierra College *C*
Southwestern College *C, A*
Taft College *C*
University of California
Santa Cruz *B*
University of San Francisco *M*
Westwood College of Technology
Westwood College: Inland
Empire *B*
Westwood College: Los Angeles *B*
Westwood College: Anaheim *B*

Colorado

American Sentinel University *B*
Arapahoe Community College *C, A*
Art Institute
of Colorado *C, A, B*
Colorado Mountain College *C*
Colorado Technical University *C*
DeVry University
Westminster *A, B*
Pueblo Community College *C, A*
Red Rocks Community College *C*
Westwood College of Technology
Westwood College: Denver South *B*
Westwood College: Denver North *B*

Connecticut

Asnuntuck Community College *C*
Gateway Community College *C*
Naugatuck Valley Community
College *A*

Delaware

Wilmington University *B*

Florida

Art Institute of Fort Lauderdale *A, B*
College of Business and Technology:
Flagler *C, A*
DeVry University
Miramar *A, B*
Orlando *A, B*
Florida National College *A*
Full Sail University *A, B, M, T*
Gulf Coast Community College *C, A*
Indian River State College *A*
International Academy of Design and
Technology: Tampa *A, B*
Miami Dade College *C, A*
Miami International University of Art
and Design *B*
Pasco-Hernando Community
College *C*
Rasmussen College: Fort Myers *A*
Rasmussen College: Ocala *A, B*

Rasmussen College: Pasco
County *A, B*
St. Petersburg College *C, A*
Santa Fe College *A*
Southwest Florida College *A*

Georgia
Abraham Baldwin Agricultural
College *A*
Albany Technical College *C*
Art Institute
of Atlanta *C, A, B*
Central Georgia Technical
College *C, A*
DeVry University
Alpharetta *A, B*
Decatur *A*
Gwinnett Technical College *C, A*
Southeastern Technical College *A*
Southwest Georgia Technical
College *C*
West Georgia Technical College *C, A*

Hawaii
Heald College
Honolulu *C, A*

Idaho
Eastern Idaho Technical College *A*
Idaho State University *C, A*

Illinois
Black Hawk College *C*
Columbia College Chicago *B*
DePaul University *B, M*
DeVry University
Addison *A, B*
Chicago *A, B*
Tinley Park *A, B*
DeVry University: Online *A, B*
Elgin Community College *C*
Harper College *C, A*
Harry S. Truman College *C*
Heartland Community College *C*
Highland Community College *C*
Illinois Eastern Community Colleges
Frontier Community College *C*
Illinois Institute of Technology *B, M*
International Academy of Design and
Technology: Schaumburg *A, B*
Judson University *C*
Lake Land College *C*
Lewis and Clark Community
College *A*
Lincoln Land Community College *C*
Moraine Valley Community College *C*
Morton College *C*
North Central College *M*
Oakton Community College *C*
Rasmussen College: Aurora *A*
Spoon River College *C, A*
Triton College *C*
Waubonsee Community College *C, A*

Indiana
DeVry University: Indianapolis *A, B*
Indiana Institute of Technology *A*
Indiana University-Purdue University
Indianapolis *C, A, B*
Indiana Wesleyan University *B*
St. Mary-of-the-Woods College *B*
Valparaiso University *C*
Vincennes University *C*

Iowa
Hawkeye Community College *A*
Iowa Central Community College *C, A*
Iowa Wesleyan College *B*
Kaplan University
Davenport *C*
Southeastern Community College
North Campus *A*

Western Iowa Tech Community
College *A*

Kansas
Baker University *B*
Central Christian College of Kansas *A*
Cloud County Community
College *C, A*
Kansas City Kansas Community
College *C*
Southwestern College *B*

Kentucky
Sullivan College of Technology and
Design *A*
Thomas More College *A*

Louisiana
Bossier Parish Community College *A*

Maine
New England School of
Communications *B*

Maryland
Cecil College *C, A*
Hagerstown Community College *C, A*
Howard Community College *C*
Montgomery College *C*
University of Maryland
University College *C*

Massachusetts
Bristol Community College *C*
Bunker Hill Community College *C, A*
Cape Cod Community College *A*
Fitchburg State College *C*
Massachusetts Bay Community
College *C*
Massasoit Community College *C*
Middlesex Community College *C*
Mount Wachusett Community
College *C, A*
New England Institute of Art *C, B*
North Shore Community College *C*
Quinsigamond Community College *C*
Springfield Technical Community
College *A*
Worcester Polytechnic Institute *B*

Michigan
Baker College
of Jackson *C*
of Muskegon *A*
of Port Huron *C, A*
Baker College of Allen Park *C*
Delta College *A*
Grace Bible College *B*
Grand Rapids Community
College *C, A*
Henry Ford Community College *C*
Jackson Community College *C, A*
Macomb Community College *C, A*
Mott Community College *C*
Schoolcraft College *C, A*
Washtenaw Community College *C, A*
Wayne County Community College *A*

Minnesota
Academy College *C, A*
Alexandria Technical College *C, A*
Art Institutes International
Minnesota *A, B*
Capella University *B*
DeVry University
Edina *A, B*
Globe University *C, A, B*
Hennepin Technical College *C, A*
Hibbing Community College *A*
Minneapolis Community and
Technical College *C*
Minnesota School of Business *C, A*

Minnesota State College - Southeast
Technical *C, A*
Minnesota State Community and
Technical College *C, A*
Rasmussen College
Eagan *A*
Eden Prairie *A*
St. Cloud *A*
Rasmussen College: Brooklyn Park *A*
Rasmussen College: Lake
Elmo/Woodbury *A*
Ridgewater College *C, A*
Rochester Community and Technical
College *A*
St. Paul College *C*

Mississippi
Antonelli College
Jackson *A*

Missouri
DeVry University
Kansas City *A, B*
Fontbonne University *C*
Northwest Missouri State
University *B*
Ozarks Technical Community
College *A*
Sanford-Brown College
St. Peters *A*
State Fair Community College *A*
Webster University *C*

Montana
Flathead Valley Community College *A*

Nebraska
Bellevue University *B*

Nevada
College of Southern Nevada *C*

New Hampshire
Chester College of New England *B*
Nashua Community College *C*

New Jersey
Berkeley College- Garret Mountain
Campus *A*
Gloucester County College *C, A*
Ocean County College *C*
Raritan Valley Community College *C*
Salem Community College *C*

New Mexico
New Mexico State University
Alamogordo *C, A*

New York
Cayuga County Community College *A*
City University of New York
Brooklyn College *B*
College of Westchester *A*
Erie Community College
South Campus *C*
Globe Institute of Technology *C, A, B*
Iona College *B*
Parsons The New School for Design *C*
Polytechnic Institute of New York
University *B, M, D*
Rochester Institute of
Technology *B, M*
State University of New York
College of Agriculture and
Technology at Morrisville *B*

North Carolina
Art Institute
of Charlotte *C, A, B*
Carteret Community College *A*
College of the Albemarle *C*

Durham Technical Community
College *C*
Fayetteville Technical Community
College *C, A*
Methodist University *B*
Southeastern Community
College *C, A*
University of North Carolina
Asheville *B*
Vance-Granville Community
College *A*
Wayne Community College *B*

North Dakota
Bismarck State College *A*
Dakota College at Bottineau *C*
North Dakota State College of
Science *A*
Rasmussen College: Fargo *A*
Williston State College *C, A*

Ohio
Central Ohio Technical College *A*
Cincinnati State Technical and
Community College *C*
College of Mount St. Joseph *C*
DeVry University
Columbus *A*
ETI Technical College of Niles *A*
Edison State Community College *C, A*
Franklin University *B*
James A. Rhodes State College *C, A*
Marion Technical College *A*
Mount Union College *B*
Ohio Business College: Sandusky *A*
Shawnee State University *C*
Stark State College of Technology *A*
University of Akron *C*
University of Cincinnati
Raymond Walters College *C, A*
University of Rio Grande *A*
Youngstown State University *C*

Oklahoma
Cameron University *A, B*
DeVry University: Oklahoma City
Center *A, B*
Northern Oklahoma College *A*
Oklahoma City Community College *A*
Rose State College *C, A*
Vatterott College
Tulsa *A*

Oregon
Art Institute of Portland *A, B*
Clackamas Community College *C, A*
DeVry University: Portland *A, B*
Eastern Oregon University *C, B*
Portland Community College *C, A*

Pennsylvania
Art Institute
of Philadelphia *A, B*
of Pittsburgh *A, B*
Bucks County Community College *C*
Butler County Community College *A*
Central Pennsylvania College *A*
Consolidated School of Business
Lancaster *A*
York *A*
DeVry University
Fort Washington *A*
Drexel University *B, M*
Duquesne University *B, M*
Harrisburg Area Community
College *C, A*
Kaplan Career Institute: Harrisburg *A*
Keystone Technical Institute *C*
La Salle University *B*
Lehigh Carbon Community
College *C, A*
Luzerne County Community
College *C, A*

Montgomery County Community College *A*
Newport Business Institute: Lower Burrell *A*
Northampton Community College *C, A*
Pennsylvania College of Technology *A, B*
Pennsylvania Highlands Community College *A*
Westmoreland County Community College *C, A*

Puerto Rico

Inter American University of Puerto Rico
  Aguadilla Campus *C*
Turabo University *A*

Rhode Island

Johnson & Wales University: Providence *B*
New England Institute of Technology *A*

South Carolina

York Technical College *C*

South Dakota

Dakota State University *C*
Dakota Wesleyan University *B*
National American University
  Rapid City *B*

Tennessee

Chattanooga State Community College *C, A*
Draughons Junior College: Nashville *A*
Pellissippi State Community College *C, A*
Roane State Community College *C, A*
Southwest Tennessee Community College *C, A*
Tennessee Technological University *B*
Trevecca Nazarene University *B*
Union University *B*
University of Tennessee Chattanooga *C*
Walters State Community College *C, A*

Texas

Blinn College *C*
Collin County Community College District *C, A*
DeVry University
  Irving *A*
DeVry University: Houston *A*
Eastfield College *C*
Mountain View College *C, A*
North Lake College *C, A*
Panola College *C*
San Antonio College *C*
South Texas College *C, A*
Tarrant County College *C*
Texas State Technical College
  West Texas *A*
Tyler Junior College *A*
Victoria College *C, A*

Utah

DeVry University: Sandy *A*
Dixie State College of Utah *C*
Eagle Gate College: Layton *A*
Eagle Gate College: Murray *C*
Utah Valley University *A, B*

Vermont

Champlain College *B*

Virginia

DeVry University
  Arlington *A, B*
ECPI College of Technology: Virginia Beach *C, A*
ECPI Technical College: Roanoke *A*
Liberty University *B*
Marymount University *C*
Mountain Empire Community College *C*
Southwest Virginia Community College *C*
University of Management and Technology *A, B, M*

Washington

Art Institute of Seattle *C, A, B*
Bates Technical College *C, A*
Bellevue College *C, A*
Cascadia Community College *C*
Clark College *C*
Clover Park Technical College *C, A*
DeVry University
  Federal Way *A, B*
Northwest Indian College *C*
Olympic College *C*
Peninsula College *C, A*
Shoreline Community College *C, A*
South Seattle Community College *C, A*
Spokane Falls Community College *A*
Yakima Valley Community College *C, A*

West Virginia

Huntington Junior College *A*

Wisconsin

Blackhawk Technical College *A*
Mid-State Technical College *A*
Nicolet Area Technical College *A*
Northcentral Technical College *C, A*
Southwest Wisconsin Technical College *A*
University of Wisconsin
  Parkside
  Stevens Point *B*
  Whitewater *B*
Wisconsin Indianhead Technical College *A*

Wyoming

Casper College *C, A*
Eastern Wyoming College *C*
Laramie County Community College *C, A*
Western Wyoming Community College *C*

Welding technology

Alabama

Bevill State Community College *C*
Gadsden State Community College *C*
Jefferson Davis Community College *C*
Lawson State Community College *C*
Northeast Alabama Community College *C*
Northwest-Shoals Community College *C*
Shelton State Community College *C*

Alaska

University of Alaska
  Anchorage *C, A*

Arizona

Arizona Western College *C, A*
Cochise College *C, A*
Eastern Arizona College *C*
Northland Pioneer College *C, A*
Pima Community College *A*

Arkansas

Arkansas Northeastern College *C*
Arkansas State University
  Beebe *C, A*
  Mountain Home *C, A*
Arkansas Tech University *C*
North Arkansas College *C*
Ouachita Technical College *C*
Pulaski Technical College *C*
Southeast Arkansas College *C*
Southern Arkansas University Tech *C*
University of Arkansas
  Community College at Hope *C*
  Cossatot Community College of the *C*
  Fort Smith *C*
  Monticello *C*
University of Arkansas Community College at Morrilton *C*

California

Antelope Valley College *C, A*
Barstow Community College *C, A*
Butte College *A*
Chabot College *A*
City College of San Francisco *C*
College of the Canyons *C, A*
College of the Siskiyous *C, A*
Imperial Valley College *C, A*
Long Beach City College *C, A*
Los Angeles Pierce College *C*
Merced College *C, A*
Orange Coast College *C*
Palo Verde College *C*
Santa Ana College *C, A*
Shasta College *C, A*
Solano Community College *C, A*
Ventura College *C, A*
Victor Valley College *C, A*

Colorado

Community College of Denver *C, A*
Front Range Community College *C, A*
Morgan Community College *C*
Pikes Peak Community College *C, A*
Pueblo Community College *C, A*
Red Rocks Community College *C, A*
Trinidad State Junior College *C, A*

Connecticut

Asnuntuck Community College *C, A*

Florida

Central Florida Community College *C*
Daytona State College *C*
Palm Beach Community College *C*

Georgia

Albany Technical College *C*
Athens Technical College *C*
Central Georgia Technical College *C*
Columbus Technical College *C*
Dalton State College *C*
Middle Georgia Technical College *C*
North Georgia Technical College *C*
Savannah Technical College *A*
Southeastern Technical College *C*
Southwest Georgia Technical College *C*
West Georgia Technical College *C*

Idaho

Brigham Young University-Idaho *A*
Eastern Idaho Technical College *C, A*
Idaho State University *C, A*
Lewis-Clark State College *C, A, B*

Illinois

Black Hawk College *C*
College of DuPage *C*
College of Lake County *C*
Danville Area Community College *C*
Elgin Community College *C*
Harper College *C*
Heartland Community College *C, A*
Highland Community College *C*
Illinois Eastern Community Colleges
  Lincoln Trail College *C*
John A. Logan College *C, A*
Kankakee Community College *C, A*
Kaskaskia College *C*
Lincoln Land Community College *C*
Moraine Valley Community College *C*
Rend Lake College *C*
Rock Valley College *C*
Sauk Valley Community College *C*
Southwestern Illinois College *C, A*
Spoon River College *C*
Triton College *C, A*
Waubonsee Community College *C, A*

Indiana

Oakland City University *A*
Vincennes University *C*

Iowa

Des Moines Area Community College *C*
Hawkeye Community College *C*
Indian Hills Community College *C*
Iowa Central Community College *C*
Iowa Lakes Community College *C*
North Iowa Area Community College *C*
Northeast Iowa Community College *C*
Northwest Iowa Community College *C*
Scott Community College *C, A*
Southeastern Community College
  North Campus *C*
Western Iowa Tech Community College *C*

Kansas

Coffeyville Community College *C*
Cowley County Community College *C, A*
Hutchinson Community College *C, A*
Kansas City Kansas Community College *C*
Manhattan Area Technical College *C, A*
Neosho County Community College *C*

Kentucky

Bluegrass Community and Technical College *C, A*
Elizabethtown Community and Technical College *C, A*
Hopkinsville Community College *C*
Madisonville Community College *C*
Owensboro Community and Technical College *C, A*
Somerset Community College *C, A*
West Kentucky Community and Technical College *C*

Louisiana

Delgado Community College *C*

Maine

Eastern Maine Community College *C, A*
Southern Maine Community College *C, A*

Michigan

Bay de Noc Community College *C*
Delta College *C, A*
Ferris State University *A*
Grand Rapids Community College *C, A*
Kirtland Community College *C, A*

Montcalm Community College *C*
Oakland Community College *C, A*
St. Clair County Community
College *C, A*
Schoolcraft College *C*
Southwestern Michigan College *C, A*
Wayne County Community
College *C, A*
West Shore Community College *A*

Minnesota

Alexandria Technical College *C*
Central Lakes College *C, A*
Dakota County Technical College *C*
Dunwoody College of Technology *C*
Hennepin Technical College *C, A*
Lake Superior College *A*
Minneapolis Community and
Technical College *C*
Minnesota State College - Southeast
Technical *C*
Northland Community & Technical
College *C, A*
Ridgewater College *C, A*
St. Cloud Technical College *C*
St. Paul College *C*

Mississippi

Southwest Mississippi Community
College *C*

Missouri

East Central College *C, A*
Jefferson College *C, A*
Mineral Area College *C, A*
Ozarks Technical Community
College *C, A*
State Fair Community College *C*
Vatterott College *C, A*

Montana

Flathead Valley Community College *C*
Helena College of Technology of the
University of Montana *C, A*
Montana State University
College of Technology: Great
Falls *C*

Nebraska

Central Community College *C, A*
Mid-Plains Community College
Area *C, A*
Northeast Community College *C*
Southeast Community College *C, A*
Western Nebraska Community
College *C, A*

Nevada

College of Southern Nevada *C, A*
Great Basin College *C, A*
Western Nevada College *C, A*

New Hampshire

Manchester Community College *C, A*

New Mexico

Central New Mexico Community
College *C*
Eastern New Mexico University:
Roswell Campus *C, A*
New Mexico State University
Carlsbad *C, A*
Northern New Mexico College *C, A*
San Juan College *C, A*

New York

Excelsior College *A*
Mohawk Valley Community
College *C, A*
State University of New York
College of Technology at
Alfred *C, A*

North Carolina

Asheville-Buncombe Technical
Community College *C*
Beaufort County Community
College *C, A*
Bladen Community College *C, A*
Brunswick Community College *C*
Cape Fear Community College *C, A*
Catawba Valley Community College *C*
Central Piedmont Community
College *C, A*
Coastal Carolina Community
College *C*
Davidson County Community
College *C*
Fayetteville Technical Community
College *C*
Forsyth Technical Community
College *C*
Guilford Technical Community
College *C*
Halifax Community College *A*
Haywood Community College *C*
Isothermal Community College *C, A*
James Sprunt Community College *C*
Lenoir Community College *C, A*
Pitt Community College *C, A*
Robeson Community College *C*
Rowan-Cabarrus Community
College *C, A*
Southwestern Community College *C*
Surry Community College *C*
Tri-County Community College *C*
Vance-Granville Community
College *C*
Wilkes Community College *C*
Wilson Community College *C*

North Dakota

Bismarck State College *C, A*
North Dakota State College of
Science *C, A*
Turtle Mountain Community
College *C*

Ohio

Columbus State Community
College *C, A*
Eastern Gateway Community
College *C*
Edison State Community College *A*
North Central State College *C*
Owens Community College
Toledo *C*
Terra State Community College *C, A*

Oklahoma

Tulsa Welding School *C, A*

Oregon

Clackamas Community College *C, A*
Clatsop Community College *C*
Lane Community College *C, A*
Mt. Hood Community College *C*
Portland Community College *C, A*
Rogue Community College *C, A*
Southwestern Oregon Community
College *C, A*
Treasure Valley Community
College *C, A*
Umpqua Community College *C*

Pennsylvania

Community College of Allegheny
County *C, A*
Community College of Beaver
County *A*
Harrisburg Area Community
College *C*
Northampton Community College *C*
Pennsylvania College of
Technology *C, A*

Thaddeus Stevens College of
Technology *A*
Triangle Tech
DuBois *A*
Pittsburgh *A*
Triangle Tech: Sunbury *A*
Westmoreland County Community
College *C, A*

South Carolina

Aiken Technical College *C*
Greenville Technical College *C*
Horry-Georgetown Technical
College *C*
Midlands Technical College *C*
Spartanburg Community College *C*
Williamsburg Technical College *C*
York Technical College *C, A*

South Dakota

Lake Area Technical Institute *A*

Texas

Alvin Community College *C*
Angelina College *C, A*
Austin Community College *C, A*
Del Mar College *C, A*
Frank Phillips College *C*
Houston Community College
System *C*
Kilgore College *C*
Lamar Institute of Technology *C, A*
Lone Star College System *C, A*
Midland College *C, A*
Mountain View College *C, A*
Odessa College *C, A*
Panola College *C*
Paris Junior College *C, A*
Ranger College *C, A*
St. Philip's College *C, A*
San Jacinto College *C, A*
Tarrant County College *C, A*
Texarkana College *C*
Texas State Technical College
Harlingen *C*
West Texas *C*
Victoria College *C*
Western Technical College *C*
Western Texas College *C, A*

Utah

College of Eastern Utah *C, A*
Salt Lake Community College *C, A*
Snow College *C*
Utah Valley University *C, A*

Virginia

Eastern Shore Community College *C*
J. Sargeant Reynolds Community
College *C*
Mountain Empire Community
College *C*
New River Community College *C*
Southwest Virginia Community
College *C*
Tidewater Community College *C, A*

Washington

Bates Technical College *C, A*
Bellingham Technical College *C, A*
Big Bend Community College *C, A*
Centralia College *C, A*
Clark College *C, A*
Clover Park Technical College *C*
Grays Harbor College *C, A*
Lower Columbia College *C, A*
Olympic College *C, A*
Peninsula College *C, A*
South Puget Sound Community
College *C, A*
South Seattle Community
College *C, A*

West Virginia

New River Community and Technical
College *C*
West Virginia University at
Parkersburg *C, A*

Wisconsin

Blackhawk Technical College *C*
Chippewa Valley Technical College *C*
Gateway Technical College *C*
Lakeshore Technical College *C*
Mid-State Technical College *C*
Milwaukee Area Technical
College *C, A*
Nicolet Area Technical College *C*
Northcentral Technical College *A*
Southwest Wisconsin Technical
College *C*
Waukesha County Technical
College *C*
Western Technical College *C*
Wisconsin Indianhead Technical
College *C*

Wyoming

Casper College *C, A*
Central Wyoming College *C, A*
Eastern Wyoming College *A*
Sheridan College *C, A*
Western Wyoming Community
College *C, A*

Well drilling

Mississippi

Southwest Mississippi Community
College *A*

Western European
studies

California

Claremont McKenna College *B*

District of Columbia

Georgetown University *M*

Illinois

Illinois Wesleyan University *B*

Indiana

Indiana University
Bloomington *M*

Maryland

St. John's College *B, M*

Massachusetts

Amherst College *B*
Bard College at Simon's Rock *B*
Tufts University *B, M*

Nebraska

University of Nebraska
Lincoln *B*

New York

New York University *M, D*

Ohio

College of Wooster *B*
Denison University *B*
Ohio State University
Columbus Campus *B*

Oregon

Pacific University *B*

Tennessee

Vanderbilt University *B*

Vermont
Marlboro College *B*

Wildlife and wilderness management

Alabama
Auburn University *B*

Alaska
University of Alaska
Fairbanks *B, M*

Arizona
Northern Arizona University *B*
Prescott College *B, M*
University of Arizona *M, D*

Arkansas
Arkansas State University *B*
University of Arkansas
Monticello *B*

California
California State University
Chico *C*
Cerritos College *A*
Feather River College *C, A*
Humboldt State University *B*
Modesto Junior College *C, A*
Napa Valley College *C, A*
San Joaquin Delta College *A*

Colorado
Colorado State University *B, M, D*
Front Range Community College *C, A*

Delaware
Delaware State University *B*
University of Delaware *B*

District of Columbia
University of the District of
Columbia *A*

Florida
University of Florida *M, D*

Georgia
Abraham Baldwin Agricultural
College *A*
University of Georgia *B*

Idaho
North Idaho College *A*
University of Idaho *B, M, D*

Illinois
Lake Land College *A*
Shawnee Community College *A*
Southeastern Illinois College *A*
University of Illinois
Urbana-Champaign *B, M, D*

Indiana
Purdue University *B, M, D*

Iowa
Ellsworth Community College *A*
Iowa State University *M, D*

Kansas
Colby Community College *A*
Garden City Community College *A*
Pratt Community College *A*
Seward County Community College *A*

Kentucky
Bluegrass Community and Technical
College *A*

Eastern Kentucky University *B*
Murray State University *B*

Louisiana
Louisiana State University and
Agricultural and Mechanical
College *M*
McNeese State University *B*

Maine
Unity College *B*
University of Maine *B, M, D*

Maryland
Frostburg State University *B, M*
Garrett College *C, A*

Michigan
Bay de Noc Community College *C*
Grand Rapids Community College *A*
Lake Superior State University *B*
Michigan State University *B, M, D*
Michigan Technological University *B*

Minnesota
University of Minnesota
Crookston *B*
Twin Cities *B, M, D*
Vermilion Community College *C, A*

Mississippi
Mississippi State University *B, M*

Missouri
College of the Ozarks *B*
Missouri State University *B*
Northwest Missouri State
University *B*
University of Missouri
Columbia *B, M, D*

Montana
Miles Community College *A*
Montana State University
Bozeman *M, D*
University of Montana *B, M, D*
University of Montana: Western *B*

Nevada
University of Nevada
Reno *B*

New Hampshire
University of New Hampshire *B, M*

New Mexico
Eastern New Mexico University *B*
New Mexico State University *B, M*
Western New Mexico University *B*

New York
Paul Smith's College *B*
State University of New York
College of Agriculture and
Technology at Cobleskill *B*
College of Environmental Science
and Forestry *B, M, D*

North Carolina
Haywood Community College *A*

North Dakota
Dakota College at Bottineau *A*
Sitting Bull College *A*

Ohio
Hocking College *C, A*
Ohio State University
Columbus Campus *B*
University of Rio Grande *B*

Oklahoma
Eastern Oklahoma State College *A*
Western Oklahoma State College *A*

Oregon
Oregon State University *B, M, D*
Treasure Valley Community
College *C, A*

Pennsylvania
Delaware Valley College *B*
Juniata College *B*
Keystone College *A*
Penn State
DuBois *A*

Puerto Rico
University of Puerto Rico
Humacao *B*

Rhode Island
University of Rhode Island *B*

South Dakota
Dakota Wesleyan University *B*
South Dakota State University *B, M, D*

Tennessee
Lincoln Memorial University *B*
Tennessee Technological University *B*
University of Tennessee
Knoxville *B, M, D*

Texas
Stephen F. Austin State University *B*
Sul Ross State University *B, M*
Tarleton State University *B*
Texas A&M University *B, M, D*
Texas A&M University
Commerce *B*
Kingsville *B, M, D*
Texas Tech University *B, M, D*

Utah
Brigham Young University *B, M, D*
Snow College *A*
Utah State University *B, M, D*

Vermont
Sterling College *B*

Washington
Centralia College *A*
Grays Harbor College *A*
Spokane Community College *A*
University of Washington *B*
Washington State University *B*

West Virginia
Mountain State University *A*
Potomac State College of West
Virginia University *A*
West Virginia University *B, M*

Wisconsin
University of Wisconsin
Madison *B, M*
Stevens Point *B*

Wyoming
Casper College *A*
Eastern Wyoming College *A*
Laramie County Community
College *A*
Northwest College *A*
Western Wyoming Community
College *A*

Wildlife biology

Arizona
Eastern Arizona College *A*
Northern Arizona University *B*
Prescott College *B, M*

Colorado
Colorado State University *B*

Kansas
Baker University *B*
Barton County Community College *A*
Kansas State University *B*

Maine
Unity College *B*

Michigan
University of Michigan
Flint *B*

Montana
University of Montana: Western *B*

New York
State University of New York
College of Environmental Science
and Forestry *B*

North Dakota
Dakota College at Bottineau *A*
University of North Dakota *B*

Ohio
Ohio University *B*

Oklahoma
Northeastern State University *B*

Pennsylvania
Keystone College *A*

Texas
Texas State University: San Marcos *B*
West Texas A&M University *B*

Utah
Brigham Young University *B*

Vermont
Sterling College *B*
University of Vermont *B*

Wyoming
University of Wyoming *B*
Western Wyoming Community
College *A*

Women's studies

Alabama
University of Alabama *M*

Arizona
Arizona State University *B*
Northern Arizona University *B*
Prescott College *B, M*
University of Arizona *B, M*

California
California Institute of Integral
Studies *M, D*
California State University
Chico *B*
Fresno *B*
Fullerton *B*
Long Beach *B*
San Marcos *B*

Claremont McKenna College *B*
Cosumnes River College *A*
Dominican University of California *B*
El Camino College: Compton
    Center *A*
Folsom Lake College *A*
Foothill College *A*
Fresno City College *A*
Humboldt State University *B*
Irvine Valley College *A*
Loyola Marymount University *B*
Mills College *B*
Monterey Peninsula College *A*
Pitzer College *B*
Pomona College *B*
Sacramento City College *A*
Saddleback College *A*
St. Mary's College of California *B*
San Diego State University *B, M*
San Francisco State University *B, M*
Santa Ana College *A*
Santa Clara University *B*
Scripps College *B*
Sonoma State University *B*
Southwestern College *A*
Stanford University *B*
University of California
    Berkeley *B*
    Davis *B*
    Irvine *B*
    Los Angeles *B, M, D*
    Riverside *B*
    San Diego *B*
    Santa Barbara *B*
    Santa Cruz *B*
University of Redlands *B*
University of Southern California *B*
West Valley College *A*

Colorado
Colorado College *B*
Fort Lewis College *B*
Regis University *B*
University of Colorado
    Boulder *B*
    Colorado Springs *B*
University of Denver *B*

Connecticut
Connecticut College *B*
Manchester Community College *A*
Saint Joseph College *B*
Southern Connecticut State
    University *M*
Trinity College *B*
University of Connecticut *B*
University of Hartford *B*
Yale University *B*

Delaware
University of Delaware *B*

District of Columbia
American University *C, B*
George Washington University *M*
Georgetown University *B*

Florida
Eckerd College *B*
Florida Atlantic University *M*
Florida International University *B*
Gulf Coast Community College *A*
State College of Florida,
    Manatee-Sarasota *A*
University of Miami *B*
University of South Florida *B, M*

Georgia
Agnes Scott College *B*
Emory University *B, D*
Georgia State University *B, M*
Mercer University *B*
Spelman College *B*

University of Georgia *B*

Illinois
Augustana College *B*
DePaul University *B, M*
Illinois Wesleyan University *B*
Knox College *B*
Loyola University Chicago *B, M*
Northeastern Illinois University *B*
Northwestern University *B*
Roosevelt University *B, M*
Triton College *A*
University of Illinois
    Urbana-Champaign *B*
Western Illinois University *B*

Indiana
Ball State University *B*
DePauw University *B*
Earlham College *B*
Indiana University
    Bloomington *B*
    South Bend *B*
Indiana University-Purdue University
    Fort Wayne *A, B*
Manchester College *B*
Purdue University *B*

Iowa
Cornell College *B*
Iowa State University *B*
Luther College *B*
University of Iowa *B, D*
University of Northern Iowa *M*

Kansas
Kansas State University *B*
University of Kansas *B*
Wichita State University *B*

Kentucky
Berea College *B*
University of Louisville *B*

Louisiana
Louisiana State University and
    Agricultural and Mechanical
    College *B*
Tulane University *B*
University of New Orleans *B*

Maine
Bates College *B*
Bowdoin College *B*
Colby College *B*
University of Maine *B*
University of Maine
    Farmington *B*
University of Southern Maine *B*

Maryland
Goucher College *B*
Prince George's Community
    College *A*
Towson University *B, M*
University of Maryland
    College Park *B, M, D*

Massachusetts
Amherst College *B*
Bard College at Simon's Rock *B*
Brandeis University *B, M*
Clark University *B, D*
Hampshire College *B*
Harvard College *B*
Simmons College *B*
Smith College *B*
Suffolk University *B, M*
Tufts University *B, M*
University of Massachusetts
    Amherst *B*

Boston *B*
    Dartmouth *B*
Wellesley College *B*
Wheaton College *B*

Michigan
Central Michigan University *B*
Eastern Michigan University *B, M*
Hope College *B*
Michigan State University *B*
Oakland University *B*
University of Michigan *B, D*
Western Michigan University *B*

Minnesota
Augsburg College *B*
Carleton College *B*
College of St. Benedict *B*
College of St. Scholastica *C*
Gustavus Adolphus College *B*
Hamline University *B*
Macalester College *B*
Metropolitan State University *B*
Minnesota State University
    Mankato *B, M*
St. Catherine University *B*
Saint Cloud State University *B*
St. John's University *B*
St. Olaf College *B*
University of Minnesota
    Duluth *B*
    Morris *B*
    Twin Cities *B*
University of St. Thomas *B*

Missouri
Saint Louis University *B*
University of Missouri
    Columbia *B*
Washington University in St. Louis *B*

Montana
University of Montana *B*
University of Montana: Western *B*

Nebraska
University of Nebraska
    Lincoln *B*
    Omaha *B*

Nevada
University of Nevada
    Las Vegas *B*
    Reno *B*

New Hampshire
Dartmouth College *B*
University of New Hampshire *B*

New Jersey
Bergen Community College *A*
The College of New Jersey *B*
College of St. Elizabeth *B*
Drew University *B, M, D*
Montclair State University *B*
Rutgers, The State University of New
    Jersey
    New Brunswick/Piscataway
        Campus *B, M*
    Newark Regional Campus *B*
William Paterson University of New
    Jersey *B*

New Mexico
New Mexico State University *B*
University of New Mexico *B*

New York
Barnard College *B*
City University of New York
    Brooklyn College *B*
    College of Staten Island *B*

Hunter College *B*
    Queens College *B*
Colgate University *B*
College of New Rochelle *B*
College of Saint Rose *B*
Columbia University *B*
Columbia University
    School of General Studies *B*
Cornell University *B*
Fordham University *B*
Hamilton College *B*
Hobart and William Smith Colleges *B*
Hofstra University *B*
Pace University *B*
Saint Bonaventure University *B*
Sarah Lawrence College *M*
Skidmore College *B*
State University of New York
    Albany *B, M*
    Buffalo *B*
    College at Brockport *B*
    College at Plattsburgh *B*
    College at Potsdam *B*
    New Paltz *B*
    Oswego *B*
    Purchase *B*
    Stony Brook *B*
Suffolk County Community College *A*
University of Rochester *B*
Vassar College *B*
Wells College *B*

North Carolina
Appalachian State University *B*
Duke University *B*
East Carolina University *B*
Guilford College *B*
North Carolina State University *B*
Southeastern Baptist Theological
    Seminary *M*
University of North Carolina
    Asheville *B*
    Chapel Hill *B*
    Greensboro *B, M*

North Dakota
North Dakota State University *B*

Ohio
Bowling Green State University *B*
Case Western Reserve University *B*
Cleveland State University *B*
College of Wooster *B*
Denison University *B*
Kenyon College *B*
Miami University
    Oxford Campus *B*
Oberlin College *B*
Ohio State University
    Columbus Campus *B, M, D*
Ohio University *B*
Ohio Wesleyan University *B*
Owens Community College
    Toledo *A*
University of Toledo *B*
Wright State University *B*

Oklahoma
University of Oklahoma *B*

Oregon
Pacific University *B*
Portland State University *B*
University of Oregon *B*
Willamette University *B*

Pennsylvania
Albright College *B*
Allegheny College *B*
Bucknell University *B*
Chatham University *B*
Community College of Philadelphia *A*
Dickinson College *B*

Edinboro University of
  Pennsylvania *B*
Gettysburg College *B*
Lehigh University *B*
Penn State
  Abington *B*
  Altoona *B*
  Beaver *B*
  Berks *B*
  Brandywine *B*
  DuBois *B*
  Erie, The Behrend College *B*
  Fayette, The Eberly Campus *B*
  Greater Allegheny *B*
  Hazleton *B*
  Lehigh Valley *B*
  Mont Alto *B*
  New Kensington *B*
  Schuylkill *B*
  Shenango *B*
  University Park *B*
  Wilkes-Barre *B*
  Worthington Scranton *B*
  York *B*
Rosemont College *B*
Swarthmore College *B*
Temple University *B*
University of Pennsylvania *A, B*
West Chester University of
  Pennsylvania *B*
Widener University *B*

Puerto Rico

Inter American University of Puerto
  Rico
  Metropolitan Campus *M*

Rhode Island

Brown University *B*
Providence College *B*
Rhode Island College *B*
University of Rhode Island *B*

South Carolina

University of South Carolina *B*

Tennessee

University of Memphis *M*
University of Tennessee
  Knoxville *B*
Vanderbilt University *B*

Texas

El Paso Community College *A*
Rice University *B*
Southwestern University *B*
Texas Woman's University *M*
University of Texas
  Austin *B, M*
  Dallas *B*
  San Antonio *B*

Utah

University of Utah *B*

Vermont

Bennington College *B*
Goddard College *B, M*
Middlebury College *B*
University of Vermont *B*

Virginia

College of William and Mary *B*
Hollins University *B*
Old Dominion University *B*
Randolph-Macon College *B*
University of Richmond *B*
Virginia Commonwealth University *B*
Virginia Wesleyan College *B*

Washington

Eastern Washington University *B*

Gonzaga University *B*
Pacific Lutheran University *B*
Seattle University *B*
University of Washington *B, M, D*
Washington State University *B*

Wisconsin

Beloit College *B*
Marquette University *B*
Ripon College *B*
University of Wisconsin
  Eau Claire *B*
  Green Bay *B*
  Madison *B, M*
  Marinette *A*
  Milwaukee *B*
  Whitewater *B*

Wyoming

Casper College *A*
University of Wyoming *B*

Wood science/pulp/ paper technology

Idaho

University of Idaho *B, M*

Maine

University of Maine *C, B*

Massachusetts

University of Massachusetts
  Amherst *B*

Michigan

Bay de Noc Community College *A*

Mississippi

Copiah-Lincoln Community College *A*
Mississippi State University *M*

New York

State University of New York
  College of Agriculture and
    Technology at Morrisville *A*
  College of Environmental Science
    and Forestry *B*

North Carolina

Halifax Community College *C, A*
Haywood Community College *A*
North Carolina State
  University *B, M, D*

Ohio

Miami University
  Oxford Campus *B, M*

South Carolina

York Technical College *C*

West Virginia

Potomac State College of West
  Virginia University *A*
West Virginia University *B*

Wisconsin

University of Wisconsin
  Stevens Point *B*

Woodworking

Alabama

Gadsden State Community College *C*
Wallace State Community College at
  Hanceville *C, A*

Arkansas

Phillips Community College of the
  University of Arkansas *C*

California

Bakersfield College *A*
College of the Redwoods *C*
El Camino College: Compton
  Center *C, A*
Laney College *C, A*
Palomar College *C, A*
San Joaquin Delta College *C, A*
Sierra College *C, A*

Colorado

Red Rocks Community College *A*

Georgia

Gwinnett Technical College *A*

Illinois

Illinois Eastern Community Colleges
  Olney Central College *A*

Kansas

Allen County Community College *A*
Pittsburg State University *A, B*

Maine

Northern Maine Community
  College *A*

Michigan

Bay de Noc Community College *C*

Minnesota

Dakota County Technical College *C*
Hennepin Technical College *C, A*

Mississippi

East Central Community College *C*
Northwest Mississippi Community
  College *C*

New Mexico

Northern New Mexico College *C, A*
Santa Fe Community College *C*

New York

Rochester Institute of
  Technology *A, B, M*
State University of New York
  College of Agriculture and
    Technology at Morrisville *A*

North Carolina

Haywood Community College *C, A*
Mayland Community College *C*
Tri-County Community College *C*

Ohio

University of Rio Grande *C, A*

Oregon

Oregon College of Art & Craft *C, B*

Pennsylvania

Bucks County Community College *A*
Thaddeus Stevens College of
  Technology *A*

Vermont

Burlington College *C, A*

Washington

Peninsula College *C*

Wisconsin

Fox Valley Technical College *C*

Northeast Wisconsin Technical
  College *C*
Western Technical College *C*

Word processing

Alabama

Gadsden State Community College *C*

Arizona

GateWay Community College *C*
Paradise Valley Community
  College *C, A*

California

College of the Siskiyous *C*
Foothill College *C*
Kaplan College: Panorama City *C*
Long Beach City College *C, A*
Monterey Peninsula College *C, A*
Ohlone College *C*

Colorado

Trinidad State Junior College *C, A*

Connecticut

Gateway Community College *C, A*

Georgia

Darton College *C*
Southeastern Technical College *C*

Illinois

Elgin Community College *C*
Lincoln Land Community College *C*
Sauk Valley Community College *C*
Southeastern Illinois College *C*
Waubonsee Community College *C*

Maryland

Frederick Community College *C*
Kaplan College: Hagerstown *C*

Massachusetts

Bunker Hill Community College *C, A*

Michigan

Kirtland Community College *C, A*

Minnesota

North Hennepin Community
  College *C*
Ridgewater College *C*

New Mexico

Navajo Technical College *C*

New York

Globe Institute of Technology *C*
Olean Business Institute *A*
State University of New York
  College of Agriculture and
    Technology at Morrisville *C*
Utica School of Commerce *C, A*

North Carolina

Beaufort County Community
  College *C*
Carteret Community College *C, A*
College of the Albemarle *C*
Durham Technical Community
  College *C*
Rockingham Community College *C*

Ohio

Columbus State Community
  College *C*
James A. Rhodes State College *C*
Marion Technical College *C, A*
Stark State College of Technology *A*

University of Cincinnati
Raymond Walters College *C*

Oregon
Portland Community College *C*

Pennsylvania
Consolidated School of Business
Lancaster *A*
York *A*
Newport Business Institute: Lower
Burrell *A*
Northampton Community College *C*

Rhode Island
Community College of Rhode
Island *C*

South Carolina
Williamsburg Technical College *C*
York Technical College *C*

Texas
North Lake College *C*
Palo Alto College *C*

Virginia
ECPI College of Technology: Virginia
Beach *C, A*
ECPI Technical College: Roanoke *A*
Mountain Empire Community
College *A*

Washington
Lower Columbia College *C*
Spokane Falls Community College *C*
Yakima Valley Community College *C*

West Virginia
West Virginia Business College: Nutter
Fort *C, A*
West Virginia Business College:
Wheeling *C, A*

Wisconsin
Nicolet Area Technical College *C*

Wyoming
Western Wyoming Community
College *C*

Work/family studies

Arizona
Estrella Mountain Community
College *C*

Georgia
Dalton State College *A, B*

Illinois
Triton College *C*

Maryland
Washington Bible College *B*

Michigan
Cornerstone University *B*
Michigan State University *M*

Mississippi
Belhaven University *C*

Ohio
Ursuline College *B*
Youngstown State University *B*

West Virginia
American Public University System *C*

Yoga teacher/therapy

Arizona
Scottsdale Community College *C*

California
California Institute of Integral
Studies *C*

Massachusetts
Mount Wachusett Community
College *A*

Youth ministry

Alabama
Faulkner University *B, M*

Arkansas
Ecclesia College *B*
Harding University *B*
John Brown University *B*
Ouachita Baptist University *B*
Williams Baptist College *B*

California
Azusa Pacific University *M*
Bethany University *B*
California Lutheran University *B*
Hope International University *B*
Point Loma Nazarene University *B*
Simpson University *B*
Vanguard University of Southern
California *B*
William Jessup University *C, B*

Colorado
Colorado Christian University *B*

Florida
Florida Southern College *B*
Southeastern University *B*
Trinity College of Florida *B*

Georgia
Toccoa Falls College *B*

Idaho
Boise Bible College *B*
Northwest Nazarene University *B*

Illinois
Greenville College *B*
Judson University *B*
Lincoln Christian University *B, M*
North Park University *B, M*
Trinity International University *B*

Indiana
Goshen College *B*
Grace College *B*
Huntington University *B*

Iowa
Dordt College *B*
Emmaus Bible College *B*
St. Ambrose University *C*

Kansas
Barclay College *B*
Benedictine College *B*
Bethel College *C*
Central Christian College of
Kansas *A, B*
Friends University *B*
MidAmerica Nazarene University *B*
Tabor College *B*

Kentucky
Asbury College *B*

Maryland
Washington Bible College *B, M*

Massachusetts
Eastern Nazarene College *B*
Gordon College *B*

Michigan
Andrews University *B, M*
Cornerstone University *B*
Grace Bible College *B*
Kuyper College *C, B*
Spring Arbor University *B*

Minnesota
Augsburg College *B*
Bethel University *B*
Crossroads College *B*
Crown College *B*
North Central University *B*
Northwestern College *B*
Oak Hills Christian College *B*
St. Mary's University of Minnesota *B*

Mississippi
Wesley College *B*

Missouri
Calvary Bible College and Theological
Seminary *B*
Central Bible College *A, B*
Lindenwood University *B*

Nebraska
Concordia University *B*

New Jersey
College of St. Elizabeth *C*
Seton Hall University *M*

New Mexico
University of the Southwest *B*

North Carolina
Gardner-Webb University *B*
Mid-Atlantic Christian University *B*
Montreat College *B*
Pfeiffer University *B*
Piedmont Baptist College *B*

Ohio
Bluffton University *B*
Cedarville University *B*
God's Bible School and College *B*
Malone University *B*
Mount Vernon Nazarene University *B*
Ohio Christian University *B*
Ohio Northern University *B*

Oklahoma
Oklahoma Christian University *B*
Oklahoma City University *B*
Southwestern Christian University *B*

Oregon
Corban College *B*
Eugene Bible College *B*
Multnomah University *B*
Northwest Christian University *B*
Warner Pacific College *A*

Pennsylvania
Baptist Bible College of
Pennsylvania *B*
Eastern University *B*
Geneva College *B*

South Carolina
Charleston Southern University *B*
Columbia International University *B*
North Greenville University *B*

Tennessee
King College *B*
Lee University *B, M*
Lipscomb University *B*
Union University *B*

Texas
Abilene Christian University *B*
Arlington Baptist College *B*
East Texas Baptist University *B*
Hardin-Simmons University *B*
Howard Payne University *B, M*
Lubbock Christian University *B*
Southwestern Assemblies of God
University *B*
Texas Lutheran University *B*

Virginia
Bluefield College *B*
Liberty University *B, M*

Washington
Northwest University *B*
Trinity Lutheran College *B*

Wisconsin
Cardinal Stritch University *B*
Concordia University Wisconsin *B*
Maranatha Baptist Bible College *B*

Youth services

California
San Francisco State University *C*

Connecticut
Goodwin College *C, A*

Massachusetts
Brandeis University *M*
Wheelock College *B*

New York
City University of New York
New York City College of
Technology *C*
Dutchess Community College *C*

Oregon
Mt. Hood Community College *C*

South Carolina
Trident Technical College *C*

Washington
Olympic College *C*

Zoology

Alabama
Auburn University *B, M, D*

Alaska
University of Alaska
Fairbanks *D*

Arizona
Northern Arizona University *B*
Prescott College *B*

California
California State Polytechnic
University: Pomona *B*
Cerritos College *A*
Citrus College *A*
El Camino College *A*
Fullerton College *A*
Humboldt State University *B*
Palomar College *A*
San Diego State University *M*

San Francisco State University *B*
San Joaquin Delta College *A*
University of California
   Davis *B, M, D*
   Santa Barbara *B*

Colorado
Colorado State University *B, M, D*

Connecticut
University of Connecticut *M, D*

District of Columbia
George Washington University *M, D*

Florida
Daytona State College *A*
Palm Beach Community College *A*
Pensacola Junior College *A*
University of Florida *B, M*

Hawaii
University of Hawaii
   Manoa *B, M, D*

Idaho
Brigham Young University-Idaho *B*
Idaho State University *B*
North Idaho College *A*
University of Idaho *B, M, D*

Illinois
Olivet Nazarene University *B*
Southern Illinois University
   Carbondale *B, M, D*

Indiana
Indiana University
   Bloomington *M, D*
Purdue University *B*

Iowa
Iowa State University *M, D*

Kentucky
Kentucky Wesleyan College *B*

Maine
University of Maine *B, M, D*

Michigan
Andrews University *B*
Michigan State University *B, M, D*
Northern Michigan University *B*

Minnesota
Minnesota State University
   Mankato *B, T*
University of Minnesota
   Twin Cities *M, D*

Montana
University of Montana *B, M, D*

New Hampshire
University of New Hampshire *B, M, D*

New Jersey
Rutgers, The State University of New
   Jersey
   Newark Regional Campus *B*

New Mexico
Western New Mexico University *B*

New York
Cornell University *M, D*
State University of New York
   Oswego *B*

North Carolina
Davidson County Community
   College *A*
Duke University *D*
Mars Hill College *B*
Methodist University *A, B*
North Carolina State
   University *B, M, D*

North Dakota
Dakota College at Bottineau *A*
North Dakota State University *B, M, D*

Ohio
Kent State University *B, D*
Malone University *B*
Miami University
   Oxford Campus *B, M, D, T*
Ohio State University
   Columbus Campus *B*
Ohio University *B, M, D*
Ohio Wesleyan University *B*
University of Akron *B*

Oklahoma
Carl Albert State College *A*
Langston University *B*
Northern Oklahoma College *A*
Oklahoma State University *B, M, D*
University of Oklahoma *B, M, D*

Oregon
Chemeketa Community College *A*
Oregon State University *B, M, D*

Pennsylvania
Delaware Valley College *B*
Juniata College *B*

Rhode Island
University of Rhode Island *B, M, D*

South Carolina
Clemson University *B, M, D*

Tennessee
Union University *B*

Texas
Tarleton State University *B, T*
Texas A&M University *B, M, D*
Texas A&M University
   Galveston *B*
Texas State University: San Marcos *B*
Texas Tech University *B, M, D*
Texas Woman's University *B*

Utah
Snow College *A*
Utah State University *B, M*
Weber State University *B*

Vermont
Bennington College *B*
University of Vermont *B*

Washington
University of Washington *B, M, D*
Washington State University *B, M, D*
Western Washington University *B*

Wisconsin
University of Wisconsin
   Madison *B, M, D*

Wyoming
University of Wyoming *B, M, D*

Special academic programs

Combined bachelor's/graduate programs

Combined bachelor's/graduate program in accounting

Alabama

Alabama State University
Jacksonville State University
University of Mobile
University of Montevallo

Arkansas

Arkansas State University
  Mountain Home
University of Arkansas
  Cossatot Community College of the
    Monticello
University of Central Arkansas

California

California State University
  Fresno
  Los Angeles
Mount St. Mary's College
Pacific States University
Southern California Institute of
  Technology
University of San Diego
University of Southern California
Vanguard University of Southern
  California

Colorado

University of Colorado
  Boulder
University of Denver

Connecticut

Asnuntuck Community College
Quinnipiac University
Sacred Heart University

District of Columbia

Catholic University of America

Florida

Barry University
Florida Atlantic University
Florida Memorial University
Warner University
Webber International University

Georgia

Albany State University
Clark Atlanta University
Gwinnett College
Reinhardt College
University of Georgia
Waycross College
Wesleyan College

Hawaii

University of Hawaii
  Hilo

Idaho

College of Idaho

Illinois

Benedictine University
Bradley University
Dominican University
Hebrew Theological College
Illinois State University
Loyola University Chicago
University of Illinois
  Urbana-Champaign

Indiana

Purdue University
Purdue University
  Calumet

Iowa

Iowa Wesleyan College
Kaplan University
  Mason City
University of Dubuque
University of Northern Iowa

Kansas

Fort Hays State University
Pittsburg State University

Kentucky

Murray State University
Transylvania University

Louisiana

Herzing University
Louisiana State University
  Shreveport

Maine

Husson University
Thomas College
University of Maine
  Presque Isle
University of Southern Maine

Maryland

Bowie State University
University of Baltimore

Massachusetts

American International College
Atlantic Union College
Babson College
Bentley University
Suffolk University
Western New England College

Michigan

Baker College
  of Clinton Township
  of Flint
  of Muskegon
  of Port Huron
Baker College of Allen Park
Cleary University
Eastern Michigan University
Grace Bible College
Grand Valley State University
Kuyper College
Rochester College

Minnesota

Minnesota School of Business: St.
  Cloud
Minnesota School of Business:
  Shakopee
Minnesota State University
  Mankato
Rochester Community and Technical
  College

Mississippi

Millsaps College
Mississippi State University
University of Mississippi
University of Southern Mississippi

Missouri

Drury University
Missouri State University
Saint Louis University
Stephens College
University of Missouri
  Columbia
Washington University in St. Louis
Webster University

Montana

Rocky Mountain College
Salish Kootenai College

Nebraska

Creighton University
Grace University
Nebraska Christian College
University of Nebraska
  Omaha
Western Nebraska Community
  College

Nevada

Morrison University

New Hampshire

New England College
University of New Hampshire

New Jersey

Caldwell College
Fairleigh Dickinson University
  College at Florham
  Metropolitan Campus
William Paterson University of New
  Jersey

New Mexico

Eastern New Mexico University:
  Roswell Campus
San Juan College
University of the Southwest

New York

Canisius College
City University of New York
  Baruch College
College of Saint Rose
Daemen College
Fordham University
Globe Institute of Technology
Hofstra University
Ithaca College
Le Moyne College

Long Island University
  Brooklyn Campus
  C. W. Post Campus
Mercy College
Molloy College
Mount Saint Mary College
Nazareth College
Pace University
Rochester Institute of Technology
Saint Bonaventure University
St. Francis College
St. John's University
St. Joseph's College: Suffolk Campus
Siena College
State University of New York
  Binghamton
  Buffalo
  College at Old Westbury
  College at Oneonta
  Oswego
Wagner College
Yeshiva University

North Carolina

East Carolina University
Gardner-Webb University
Guilford College
Meredith College
North Carolina State University
Wake Forest University

North Dakota

Bismarck State College
Dakota College at Bottineau
Lake Region State College
University of Mary

Ohio

Baldwin-Wallace College
Case Western Reserve University
Hiram College
Hocking College
James A. Rhodes State College
Kent State University
Mount Vernon Nazarene University
University of Akron
University of Dayton
University of Rio Grande
Urbana University
Xavier University

Oklahoma

Oklahoma State University
Southeastern Oklahoma State
  University
University of Oklahoma

Oregon

Oregon Institute of Technology

Pennsylvania

Chatham University
Elizabethtown College
Lock Haven University of
  Pennsylvania
Mount Aloysius College
Philadelphia University
University of Pennsylvania
University of Pittsburgh
  Greensburg
University of Scranton
Widener University

York College of Pennsylvania

Puerto Rico
Caribbean University
Universidad Metropolitana

Rhode Island
University of Rhode Island

South Carolina
Bob Jones University
College of Charleston
University of South Carolina
  Lancaster

South Dakota
University of South Dakota

Tennessee
Freed-Hardeman University
Lipscomb University
University of Tennessee
  Knoxville

Texas
Abilene Christian University
Angelo State University
Baylor University
Houston Baptist University
Prairie View A&M University
Southwestern Adventist University
Stephen F. Austin State University
Texas A&M University
Texas A&M University
  Commerce
  Kingsville
  Texarkana
Texas State University: San Marcos
Texas Tech University
Trinity University
University of Houston
University of Houston
  Clear Lake
University of North Texas
University of Texas
  Arlington
  El Paso
  Pan American
University of the Incarnate Word
West Texas A&M University

Utah
Southern Utah University
Western Governors University

Vermont
Lyndon State College

Virginia
Randolph-Macon College
Virginia Commonwealth University
Virginia Polytechnic Institute and
  State University

Washington
Olympic College
University of Washington Bothell

West Virginia
Davis and Elkins College
Potomac State College of West
  Virginia University
Wheeling Jesuit University

Wisconsin
Chippewa Valley Technical College
Herzing University
Lakeshore Technical College
Marquette University
Silver Lake College

University of Wisconsin
  Madison
  Whitewater

Combined bachelor's/ graduate program in architecture

California
California College of the Arts
California Polytechnic State
  University: San Luis Obispo

Connecticut
Yale University

District of Columbia
Catholic University of America

Florida
Florida Agricultural and Mechanical
  University
Florida Atlantic University
University of Miami

Georgia
Agnes Scott College
Georgia Institute of Technology
Morehouse College

Hawaii
University of Hawaii
  Hilo

Idaho
University of Idaho

Illinois
Illinois Institute of Technology
Judson University
Knox College
Monmouth College

Indiana
Ball State University
Purdue University
  Calumet

Iowa
Central College
Coe College
Cornell College

Kansas
University of Kansas

Louisiana
Tulane University

Maine
University of Maine
  Augusta

Massachusetts
Northeastern University
Tufts University

Michigan
Adrian College
Andrews University
University of Detroit Mercy

Mississippi
Mississippi State University

Missouri
Drury University
University of Missouri
  St. Louis

Washington University in St. Louis
Webster University

Montana
Montana State University
  Bozeman

Nebraska
College of Saint Mary
Nebraska Wesleyan University

New Jersey
New Jersey Institute of Technology

New York
City University of New York
  City College
Colgate University
Cooper Union for the Advancement of
  Science and Art
Hobart and William Smith Colleges
New York Institute of Technology
Rensselaer Polytechnic Institute

North Carolina
North Carolina State University

North Dakota
North Dakota State University

Ohio
College of Wooster
Kent State University

Pennsylvania
University of Pennsylvania

Puerto Rico
Universidad del Este

Rhode Island
Roger Williams University

Tennessee
University of Tennessee
  Knoxville

Texas
Del Mar College
Prairie View A&M University
Texas Tech University

Vermont
Norwich University

Virginia
Virginia Polytechnic Institute and
  State University

Washington
University of Washington
Washington State University

Combined bachelor's/ graduate program in business administration

Alabama
Birmingham-Southern College
Jacksonville State University
Troy University
University of Alabama
University of Mobile

Alaska
University of Alaska
  Anchorage

Arkansas
Southern Arkansas University
University of Arkansas
University of Arkansas
  Monticello
University of Central Arkansas

California
Alliant International University
American Jewish University
California College of the Arts
California State University
  Fresno
  Los Angeles
Chapman University
Claremont McKenna College
Dominican University of California
Harvey Mudd College
Hope International University
John F. Kennedy University
Mills College
Pacific States University
Pitzer College
Scripps College
Sonoma State University
Southern California Institute of
  Technology
University of California
  Irvine
University of the West
Vanguard University of Southern
  California

Colorado
CollegeAmerica
  Fort Collins
Colorado Heights University
Colorado State University
  Pueblo
Jones International University
Mesa State College
Regis University
University of Colorado
  Denver
University of Denver
Western State College of Colorado

Connecticut
Asnuntuck Community College
Quinnipiac University
Sacred Heart University
University of Bridgeport

Delaware
Goldey-Beacom College

District of Columbia
Georgetown University

Florida
Barry University
Embry-Riddle Aeronautical University
Florida Agricultural and Mechanical
  University
Florida International University
Florida Memorial University
Northwood University
  Florida
Nova Southeastern University
Rollins College
Stetson University
University of Miami
University of South Florida
University of Tampa
Warner University
Webber International University

Georgia
Gwinnett College
Mercer University
Reinhardt College
University of Georgia

Wesleyan College

Hawaii

Hawaii Pacific University

Idaho

College of Idaho
Northwest Nazarene University

Illinois

Benedictine University
Concordia University Chicago
Dominican University
Illinois Institute of Technology
Lewis University
Loyola University Chicago
National-Louis University
North Central College
North Park University
Robert Morris University, Chicago
University of Illinois
  Urbana-Champaign
University of St. Francis

Indiana

Indiana University
  Bloomington
Purdue University
Purdue University
  Calumet
Taylor University
University of Indianapolis
University of St. Francis

Iowa

Drake University
Kaplan University
  Mason City
University of Dubuque
University of Northern Iowa
Upper Iowa University

Kansas

Benedictine College
Fort Hays State University
Pittsburg State University
Tabor College

Kentucky

Bellarmine University
Kentucky State University
Murray State University
University of Kentucky
University of Louisville

Louisiana

Centenary College of Louisiana
Louisiana State University
  Shreveport
Louisiana Tech University
Tulane University
Xavier University of Louisiana

Maine

Husson University
Thomas College
Unity College
University of Maine
University of Southern Maine

Maryland

Bowie State University
Capitol College
Frostburg State University
Mount St. Mary's University
Towson University
University of Baltimore

Massachusetts

American International College
Anna Maria College
Assumption College

Babson College
Bentley University
Clark University
Endicott College
Franklin W. Olin College of
  Engineering
Gordon College
Massachusetts Maritime Academy
Nichols College
Simmons College
Suffolk University
University of Massachusetts
  Boston
  Lowell
Western New England College
Wheaton College
Worcester Polytechnic Institute

Michigan

Baker College
  of Auburn Hills
  of Cadillac
  of Clinton Township
  of Flint
  of Jackson
  of Muskegon
  of Owosso
  of Port Huron
Baker College of Allen Park
Cleary University
Northwood University: Michigan
University of Detroit Mercy
University of Michigan
  Flint
Walsh College of Accountancy and
  Business Administration
Wayne State University

Minnesota

Crown College
Minnesota School of Business
Minnesota School of Business: St.
  Cloud
Minnesota State University
  Mankato
Southwest Minnesota State University

Mississippi

Millsaps College
Mississippi State University
University of Mississippi
University of Southern Mississippi

Missouri

Avila University
Drury University
Maryville University of Saint Louis
Missouri Baptist University
Missouri Southern State University
Missouri State University
Missouri Valley College
Rockhurst University
Stephens College
University of Missouri
  Kansas City
  Missouri University of Science and
    Technology
Washington University in St. Louis
Webster University

Montana

Salish Kootenai College

Nebraska

Creighton University
Kaplan University: Omaha

Nevada

Morrison University

New Hampshire

Daniel Webster College

Franklin Pierce University
New England College
Rivier College
Southern New Hampshire University

New Jersey

Caldwell College
College of St. Elizabeth
Fairleigh Dickinson University
  College at Florham
  Metropolitan Campus
Georgian Court University
Monmouth University
New Jersey Institute of Technology
Richard Stockton College of New
  Jersey
Rutgers, The State University of New
  Jersey
  New Brunswick/Piscataway
    Campus
  Newark Regional Campus
Saint Peter's College
Seton Hall University

New Mexico

Eastern New Mexico University:
  Roswell Campus
New Mexico Highlands University
San Juan College
University of New Mexico
University of the Southwest

New York

Adelphi University
Albany College of Pharmacy and
  Health Sciences
Alfred University
Bard College
Canisius College
Cazenovia College
Clarkson University
College of Saint Rose
Dowling College
Elmira College
Fordham University
Hartwick College
Hilbert College
Hobart and William Smith Colleges
Hofstra University
Houghton College
Iona College
Ithaca College
Laboratory Institute of Merchandising
Long Island University
  C. W. Post Campus
Marist College
Medaille College
Molloy College
Mount Saint Mary College
New York Institute of Technology
Niagara University
Pace University
Paul Smith's College
Rensselaer Polytechnic Institute
Rochester Institute of Technology
Russell Sage College
Saint Bonaventure University
St. John's University
St. Joseph's College: Suffolk Campus
St. Lawrence University
St. Thomas Aquinas College
Siena College
Skidmore College
State University of New York
  Albany
  Binghamton
  Buffalo
  College at Cortland
  College at Fredonia
  College at Geneseo
  College at Oneonta
  College at Plattsburgh
  College at Potsdam
  Empire State College

  Oswego
  Stony Brook
Touro College
Union College
University of Rochester
Wells College

North Carolina

Campbell University
Elon University
Fayetteville State University
Gardner-Webb University
North Carolina State University
Pfeiffer University
University of North Carolina
  Greensboro

North Dakota

Lake Region State College
University of Mary
University of North Dakota

Ohio

Baldwin-Wallace College
Case Western Reserve University
Edison State Community College
Franciscan University of Steubenville
Franklin University
Heidelberg University
Hocking College
John Carroll University
Kent State University
Mount Vernon Nazarene University
Otterbein College
University of Dayton
University of Toledo
Urbana University

Oklahoma

Cameron University
Mid-America Christian University
Oklahoma Christian University
Oral Roberts University
Southeastern Oklahoma State
  University
Southern Nazarene University
University of Tulsa

Oregon

Portland State University
Southern Oregon University
Willamette University

Pennsylvania

California University of Pennsylvania
Carnegie Mellon University
Chatham University
DeSales University
Drexel University
Duquesne University
Elizabethtown College
Gannon University
La Salle University
Lehigh University
Lycoming College
Marywood University
Mercyhurst College
Millersville University of Pennsylvania
Moravian College
Penn State
  Erie, The Behrend College
  University Park
Philadelphia University
St. Francis University
St. Vincent College
University of Pennsylvania
University of Pittsburgh
  Greensburg
University of Scranton
University of the Sciences in
  Philadelphia
Waynesburg University
Widener University

Wilkes University
York College of Pennsylvania

Puerto Rico

Columbia College
Columbia Centro Universitario:
Yauco
Pontifical Catholic University of
Puerto Rico
Universidad Metropolitana
Universidad del Este
University of Puerto Rico
Rio Piedras

Rhode Island

Providence College
Salve Regina University

South Carolina

Bob Jones University
Claflin University
Coastal Carolina University
University of South Carolina
Sumter

South Dakota

University of South Dakota

Tennessee

Bethel University
Cumberland University
Fisk University
Freed-Hardeman University
King College
Tennessee State University
University of Tennessee
Knoxville
Vanderbilt University

Texas

Baylor University
Dallas Baptist University
Midwestern State University
Prairie View A&M University
Rice University
St. Mary's University
Sam Houston State University
Southwestern Adventist University
Texas A&M University
Commerce
Texas Tech University
Texas Wesleyan University
University of Dallas
University of Mary Hardin-Baylor
University of St. Thomas
University of Texas
Arlington
Dallas
El Paso
University of the Incarnate Word

Utah

Brigham Young University
Southern Utah University
Western Governors University

Vermont

Castleton State College
Norwich University
St. Michael's College
Southern Vermont College

Virginia

Hampton University
Longwood University
Marymount University
Old Dominion University
Randolph-Macon College
Regent University
Shenandoah University
University of Management and
Technology

Virginia Commonwealth University
Virginia Polytechnic Institute and
State University

Washington

University of Washington Bothell
Washington State University
Whitman College

West Virginia

Davis and Elkins College
University of Charleston
West Virginia Wesleyan College
Wheeling Jesuit University

Wisconsin

Herzing University
Lakeland College
Marquette University
Milwaukee School of Engineering
University of Wisconsin
River Falls
Whitewater
Viterbo University

Combined bachelor's/ graduate program in chemistry

Alabama

Jacksonville State University

Arkansas

University of Arkansas
Monticello
University of Central Arkansas

California

California State University
Fresno
Los Angeles
Stanford University
Vanguard University of Southern
California

Colorado

Colorado School of Mines
Colorado State University
Pueblo

Connecticut

Sacred Heart University
Saint Joseph College
Wesleyan University

District of Columbia

American University

Florida

Florida International University
University of Tampa

Georgia

Clark Atlanta University
Emory University
University of Georgia
Wesleyan College

Hawaii

University of Hawaii
Hilo

Idaho

Idaho State University

Illinois

Bradley University
DePaul University
Illinois Institute of Technology
Northwestern University

University of Illinois
Urbana-Champaign

Indiana

Purdue University
Purdue University
Calumet

Iowa

Iowa Wesleyan College
University of Northern Iowa

Kansas

Pittsburg State University

Kentucky

Murray State University

Louisiana

Louisiana State University
Shreveport

Maine

University of Maine

Maryland

University of Maryland
Baltimore County

Massachusetts

Clark University
Massachusetts College of Pharmacy
and Health Sciences
Tufts University
University of Massachusetts
Dartmouth
Worcester Polytechnic Institute

Michigan

University of Detroit Mercy
University of Michigan

Minnesota

Minnesota State University
Mankato

Mississippi

University of Mississippi

Missouri

Drury University
Missouri State University
University of Missouri
Missouri University of Science and
Technology

Montana

Montana Tech of the University of
Montana

New Jersey

Fairleigh Dickinson University
Metropolitan Campus
Rutgers, The State University of New
Jersey
Camden Regional Campus
Stevens Institute of Technology

New Mexico

Eastern New Mexico University
New Mexico Highlands University

New York

City University of New York
Hunter College
Rensselaer Polytechnic Institute
Rochester Institute of Technology
St. John's University
State University of New York
Binghamton

College at Fredonia
Stony Brook
University of Rochester
Vassar College

North Carolina

Guilford College
Western Carolina University

North Dakota

Dakota College at Bottineau
University of North Dakota

Ohio

Case Western Reserve University
Mount Vernon Nazarene University
University of Rio Grande
Urbana University
Youngstown State University

Oklahoma

Southeastern Oklahoma State
University

Oregon

Southern Oregon University

Pennsylvania

Bryn Mawr College
Bucknell University
Duquesne University
Lock Haven University of
Pennsylvania
Temple University
University of Pennsylvania
University of Pittsburgh
Greensburg
University of Scranton

Rhode Island

University of Rhode Island

South Carolina

Bob Jones University
University of South Carolina
Lancaster

South Dakota

University of South Dakota

Tennessee

Tennessee State University
University of Tennessee
Knoxville

Texas

Prairie View A&M University
Texas A&M University
Commerce
University of Texas
Arlington

Utah

University of Utah

Virginia

George Mason University
Virginia Commonwealth University
Virginia Polytechnic Institute and
State University

Washington

Olympic College

West Virginia

Davis and Elkins College
Potomac State College of West
Virginia University

Wisconsin
University of Wisconsin
    Parkside

Combined bachelor's/ graduate program in dentistry

California
University of the Pacific

Colorado
Western State College of Colorado

Connecticut
University of Connecticut

District of Columbia
Howard University

Florida
Nova Southeastern University
Saint Leo University
University of North Florida

Georgia
Medical College of Georgia
Mercer University

Idaho
Idaho State University

Illinois
Southern Illinois University
    Edwardsville

Indiana
Purdue University
Purdue University
    Calumet

Iowa
Buena Vista University
Iowa Wesleyan College
University of Iowa

Kansas
McPherson College
Pittsburg State University

Kentucky
Murray State University
Union College
University of Louisville

Maryland
Coppin State University
Salisbury University
University of Maryland
    College Park

Massachusetts
Boston University
Tufts University

Michigan
University of Detroit Mercy

Minnesota
College of St. Benedict
St. John's University
University of Minnesota
    Twin Cities

Mississippi
Mississippi College

Missouri
University of Central Missouri

Nebraska
Chadron State College
Creighton University
University of Nebraska
    Lincoln

Nevada
University of Nevada
    Las Vegas

New Jersey
Caldwell College
Fairleigh Dickinson University
    College at Florham
    Metropolitan Campus
Montclair State University
New Jersey Institute of Technology
Ramapo College of New Jersey
Richard Stockton College of New
    Jersey
Rutgers, The State University of New
    Jersey
    Camden Regional Campus
    New Brunswick/Piscataway
        Campus
    Newark Regional Campus
Saint Peter's College
Stevens Institute of Technology
William Paterson University of New
    Jersey

New York
Adelphi University
Alfred University
Barnard College
Canisius College
Le Moyne College
Manhattanville College
New York University
Saint Bonaventure University
Siena College
State University of New York
    Albany
    Binghamton
    Buffalo
    College at Fredonia
    College at Geneseo
    Stony Brook
Utica College
Wagner College

Ohio
Case Western Reserve University
College of Wooster
Ohio State University
    Columbus Campus

Oregon
Eastern Oregon University
Portland State University

Pennsylvania
Cabrini College
East Stroudsburg University of
    Pennsylvania
Elizabethtown College
Indiana University of Pennsylvania
Juniata College
Lehigh University
Moravian College
Muhlenberg College
Penn State
    Erie, The Behrend College
Rosemont College
St. Francis University
Shippensburg University of
    Pennsylvania
Susquehanna University
Temple University
Thiel College
University of Pennsylvania
University of Pittsburgh

University of Pittsburgh
    Bradford
    Greensburg
Villanova University
Widener University
Wilkes University

Puerto Rico
Universidad Adventista de las Antillas
University of Puerto Rico
    Medical Sciences

South Carolina
Furman University
Morris College

Tennessee
Fisk University
Union University
University of Tennessee
    Knoxville
University of Tennessee Health
    Science Center

Texas
McMurry University
Texas A&M University
    Baylor College of Dentistry
Texas Lutheran University
Texas State University: San Marcos
University of Texas
    Arlington
    Health Science Center at Houston

Virginia
Old Dominion University
Virginia Commonwealth University

West Virginia
Davis and Elkins College
Potomac State College of West
    Virginia University

Wisconsin
Chippewa Valley Technical College
Marquette University
University of Wisconsin
    Green Bay

Combined bachelor's/ graduate program in education

Alabama
Alabama State University
Jacksonville State University
University of Montevallo

Alaska
University of Alaska
    Anchorage
    Southeast

Arizona
College of the Humanities and
    Sciences

Arkansas
Arkansas State University
    Mountain Home
Ozarka College
Southern Arkansas University
University of Arkansas
    Cossatot Community College of the
    Monticello
University of Central Arkansas

California
Academy of Art University
American Jewish University

Antioch Southern California
    Antioch University Los Angeles
Bethany University
Bethesda Christian University
California State University
    Fresno
    Los Angeles
Chapman University
Hope International University
John F. Kennedy University
Mills College
Mount St. Mary's College
Occidental College
Pacific Union College
Pitzer College
Pomona College
Simpson University
Stanford University
University of California
    Santa Cruz
University of San Francisco
Vanguard University of Southern
    California

Colorado
Jones International University
Trinidad State Junior College
University of Denver

Connecticut
Asnuntuck Community College
Quinnipiac University
Sacred Heart University
Saint Joseph College
University of Bridgeport
University of Connecticut

District of Columbia
American University
Catholic University of America
Corcoran College of Art and Design
Gallaudet University

Florida
Florida Memorial University
Florida State University
Nova Southeastern University
Pasco-Hernando Community College
Warner University

Georgia
Albany State University
Atlanta Metropolitan College
Emory University
LaGrange College
Piedmont College
Reinhardt College
University of Georgia
Wesleyan College

Hawaii
Hawaii Pacific University
University of Hawaii
    Hilo

Idaho
College of Idaho
Northwest Nazarene University

Illinois
Benedictine University
Dominican University
Hebrew Theological College
Judson University
Kendall College
Loyola University Chicago
National-Louis University
University of Chicago

Indiana
Oakland City University
Purdue University

Purdue University
  Calumet
Taylor University
University of St. Francis
Valparaiso University

Iowa

Emmaus Bible College
Graceland University
Iowa Wesleyan College
St. Ambrose University
Upper Iowa University
Waldorf College

Kansas

Fort Hays State University
Pittsburg State University

Kentucky

Bellarmine University
Gateway Community and Technical
  College
Murray State University

Maine

University of Maine
University of Southern Maine

Maryland

Bowie State University
College of Notre Dame of Maryland
Maryland Institute College of Art
Towson University
University of Maryland
  Baltimore County

Massachusetts

American International College
Anna Maria College
Art Institute of Boston at Lesley
  University
Assumption College
Boston College
Bridgewater State College
Clark University
Lesley University
Merrimack College
School of the Museum of Fine Arts
Simmons College
Tufts University
University of Massachusetts
  Dartmouth
  Lowell
Wheelock College

Michigan

Baker College
  of Cadillac
  of Flint
  of Port Huron
Bay Mills Community College
Grace Bible College
Great Lakes Christian College
Kalamazoo College
Kendall College of Art and Design of
  Ferris State University
Kuyper College
Lake Superior State University
Northern Michigan University
Rochester College

Minnesota

Bemidji State University
Crown College
Minnesota State University
  Mankato
Rochester Community and Technical
  College
University of Minnesota
  Twin Cities

Mississippi

Mississippi State University
University of Mississippi

Missouri

Avila University
Columbia College
Drury University
Lindenwood University
Maryville University of Saint Louis
Missouri Baptist University
Missouri Southern State University
Missouri Valley College
Ozark Christian College
State Fair Community College
Truman State University
Washington University in St. Louis
Webster University
Wentworth Military Junior College

Montana

Montana State University
  College of Technology: Great Falls
Salish Kootenai College

Nebraska

Creighton University
Grace University
Nebraska Christian College
Western Nebraska Community
  College

Nevada

Sierra Nevada College

New Hampshire

New England College
Rivier College
University of New Hampshire at
  Manchester

New Jersey

Caldwell College
Centenary College
The College of New Jersey
Fairleigh Dickinson University
  College at Florham
  Metropolitan Campus
Kean University
Richard Stockton College of New
  Jersey
Rutgers, The State University of New
  Jersey
  New Brunswick/Piscataway
  Campus
William Paterson University of New
  Jersey

New Mexico

Dona Ana Community College of New
  Mexico State University
Eastern New Mexico University:
  Roswell Campus
New Mexico Highlands University
New Mexico State University
  Alamogordo
Northern New Mexico College
San Juan College
University of the Southwest

New York

Adelphi University
City University of New York
  Hunter College
Colgate University
College of Mount St. Vincent
College of New Rochelle
College of Saint Rose
Five Towns College
Fordham University
Hilbert College
Hobart and William Smith Colleges

Iona College
Le Moyne College
Long Island University
  Brooklyn Campus
  C. W. Post Campus
Manhattan College
Manhattanville College
Marist College
Mercy College
Nazareth College
Pace University
Russell Sage College
Saint Bonaventure University
St. John's University
Sarah Lawrence College
State University of New York
  Albany
  Binghamton
  College at Fredonia
  College at Old Westbury
  College at Plattsburgh
  College at Potsdam
  Stony Brook
Syracuse University
Union College
University of Rochester
Wells College

North Carolina

Elon University
Fayetteville Technical Community
  College
Gardner-Webb University
Guilford College
Pfeiffer University

North Dakota

Bismarck State College
Dakota College at Bottineau
University of Mary

Ohio

Antioch University McGregor
Edison State Community College
Heidelberg University
James A. Rhodes State College
Kenyon College
Mount Vernon Nazarene University
Ohio Christian University
Otterbein College
University of Rio Grande
Urbana University

Oklahoma

Cameron University
Mid-America Christian University
Southeastern Oklahoma State
  University
Southern Nazarene University

Oregon

Corban College
Lewis & Clark College
Mt. Hood Community College
Pacific University
Portland State University
Southern Oregon University
Southwestern Oregon Community
  College
Willamette University

Pennsylvania

Albright College
Allegheny College
Arcadia University
Baptist Bible College of Pennsylvania
California University of Pennsylvania
Cedar Crest College
Chatham University
Chestnut Hill College
Drexel University
Duquesne University
Immaculata University

Lehigh University
Lock Haven University of
  Pennsylvania
Luzerne County Community College
Marywood University
Mount Aloysius College
Philadelphia Biblical University
St. Francis University
Saint Joseph's University
University of Pennsylvania
University of Pittsburgh
  Greensburg
University of Scranton
Widener University
Wilkes University

Puerto Rico

Caribbean University
Universidad Metropolitana
Universidad del Este
University of the Sacred Heart

Rhode Island

University of Rhode Island

South Carolina

Bob Jones University
Coastal Carolina University
College of Charleston
Columbia International University
University of South Carolina
University of South Carolina
  Lancaster
  Sumter

South Dakota

University of South Dakota

Tennessee

Cumberland University
Jackson State Community College
Johnson Bible College
Memphis College of Art
Rhodes College
Tennessee State University
University of Tennessee
  Knoxville

Texas

Concordia University Texas
Grayson County College
Hill College
Mountain View College
Prairie View A&M University
Texas A&M University
  Commerce
  Galveston
Texas Christian University
Trinity University

Utah

Southern Utah University
Western Governors University

Vermont

Bennington College
Lyndon State College

Virginia

Emory & Henry College
Hampton University
Longwood University
Old Dominion University
Randolph College
Regent University
University of Mary Washington
University of Virginia
Virginia Commonwealth University
Virginia Polytechnic Institute and
  State University

Washington

Olympic College
Trinity Lutheran College
University of Washington Bothell
Walla Walla University
Washington State University
Whitman College

West Virginia

Davis and Elkins College
Potomac State College of West
 Virginia University
West Virginia University
West Virginia Wesleyan College

Wisconsin

Lakeland College
Marian University
Silver Lake College
University of Wisconsin
 Marinette
 Parkside
 River Falls
 Superior
 Whitewater
Viterbo University

Combined bachelor's/ graduate program in engineering

Alabama

Birmingham-Southern College
Huntingdon College
Stillman College
Tuskegee University
University of Alabama
 Huntsville

Alaska

University of Alaska
 Anchorage
 Fairbanks

Arkansas

Hendrix College
Lyon College

California

Biola University
California Polytechnic State
 University: San Luis Obispo
California State University
 Fresno
 Los Angeles
Claremont McKenna College
Harvey Mudd College
Loyola Marymount University
Mills College
Occidental College
St. Mary's College of California
Santa Clara University
Scripps College
Southern California Institute of
 Technology
Stanford University
University of California
 Santa Cruz
University of San Francisco
University of Southern California
Whittier College

Colorado

Colorado College
Colorado School of Mines
Colorado State University
Regis University
University of Colorado
 Boulder
 Denver
University of Denver
Western State College of Colorado

Connecticut

Fairfield University
Trinity College
University of Bridgeport
Yale University

Delaware

Delaware State University

District of Columbia

Catholic University of America
Howard University

Florida

Bethune-Cookman University
Eckerd College
Embry-Riddle Aeronautical University
Florida Atlantic University
Florida International University
Florida Memorial University
Palm Beach Atlantic University
University of Miami
Valencia Community College

Georgia

Berry College
Georgia Institute of Technology
LaGrange College
Mercer University
Morehouse College
North Georgia College & State
 University
Paine College
University of Georgia
Wesleyan College

Hawaii

Hawaii Pacific University
University of Hawaii
 Hilo

Idaho

College of Idaho
University of Idaho

Illinois

Augustana College
DePaul University
Illinois College
Illinois Institute of Technology
Illinois Wesleyan University
Knox College
MacMurray College
Monmouth College
North Park University
Northwestern University
Southern Illinois University
 Edwardsville
University of Illinois
 Urbana-Champaign
Wheaton College

Indiana

Anderson University
DePauw University
Earlham College
Goshen College
Purdue University
Purdue University
 Calumet
Saint Mary's College
Taylor University
Trine University
Wabash College

Iowa

Buena Vista University
Central College
Cornell College
Iowa State University
Iowa Wesleyan College
Luther College

Simpson College
University of Iowa
University of Northern Iowa

Kansas

Benedictine College
Bethany College
Kansas State University
Pittsburg State University

Kentucky

Berea College
Brescia University
Murray State University
Transylvania University
University of Kentucky
University of Louisville
West Kentucky Community and
 Technical College

Louisiana

Dillard University
Xavier University of Louisiana

Maine

Bates College
Bowdoin College
Colby College
Saint Joseph's College of Maine
University of Maine

Maryland

Capitol College
Goucher College
Hood College
Johns Hopkins University
University of Maryland
 Baltimore County
Washington College

Massachusetts

Clark University
Gordon College
Massachusetts Institute of Technology
Massachusetts Maritime Academy
Mount Holyoke College
Northeastern University
Tufts University
University of Massachusetts
 Boston
 Dartmouth
 Lowell
Wheaton College
Williams College
Worcester Polytechnic Institute

Michigan

Adrian College
Albion College
Alma College
Grand Valley State University
Kalamazoo College
Kettering University
Michigan State University
Spring Arbor University
University of Detroit Mercy
University of Michigan
Western Michigan University

Minnesota

Augsburg College
Bethany Lutheran College
Bethel University
Central Lakes College
College of St. Benedict
Hamline University
Minnesota State University
 Mankato
Northwestern College
Rochester Community and Technical
 College
St. John's University

St. Olaf College
University of Minnesota
 Morris

Mississippi

Belhaven University
Millsaps College
Mississippi College
Mississippi State University
University of Mississippi

Missouri

Central Methodist University
College of the Ozarks
Drury University
Fontbonne University
Maryville University of Saint Louis
Rockhurst University
University of Central Missouri
University of Missouri
 Missouri University of Science and
  Technology
Washington University in St. Louis
Westminster College

Montana

Montana Tech of the University of
 Montana
Salish Kootenai College
University of Great Falls

Nebraska

College of Saint Mary
Creighton University
Doane College
Nebraska Wesleyan University

New Hampshire

Dartmouth College
New England College

New Jersey

Drew University
Fairleigh Dickinson University
 Metropolitan Campus
Monmouth University
New Jersey Institute of Technology
Richard Stockton College of New
 Jersey
Rutgers, The State University of New
 Jersey
 Newark Regional Campus
Saint Peter's College
Stevens Institute of Technology
William Paterson University of New
 Jersey

New Mexico

Northern New Mexico College

New York

Adelphi University
Bard College
Barnard College
City University of New York
 City College
Clarkson University
Colgate University
Columbia University
Columbia University
 School of General Studies
Cooper Union for the Advancement of
 Science and Art
Fordham University
Hamilton College
Hartwick College
Hobart and William Smith Colleges
Ithaca College
Le Moyne College
Manhattan College
New York Institute of Technology
Pace University

Polytechnic Institute of New York
University
Rensselaer Polytechnic Institute
Roberts Wesleyan College
Rochester Institute of Technology
St. John's University
St. Lawrence University
St. Thomas Aquinas College
Sarah Lawrence College
Siena College
Skidmore College
State University of New York
Albany
Binghamton
Buffalo
College at Geneseo
College at Oneonta
College at Plattsburgh
College at Potsdam
Stony Brook
Union College
University of Rochester
Vassar College
Wells College
Yeshiva University

North Carolina

Duke University
Elon University
North Carolina State University

North Dakota

Dickinson State University
Jamestown College
University of North Dakota

Ohio

Baldwin-Wallace College
Capital University
Case Western Reserve University
Cleveland State University
College of Wooster
Edison State Community College
Heidelberg University
Hiram College
James A. Rhodes State College
John Carroll University
Kenyon College
University of Cincinnati
University of Dayton
Wittenberg University

Oklahoma

Oklahoma Baptist University
Oklahoma Christian University
University of Oklahoma

Oregon

Eastern Oregon University
Lewis & Clark College
Oregon Institute of Technology
Pacific University
Portland State University
Reed College
Southern Oregon University
Willamette University

Pennsylvania

Allegheny College
Arcadia University
Bryn Mawr College
Bucknell University
Carnegie Mellon University
Chatham University
Dickinson College
Drexel University
Duquesne University
Edinboro University of Pennsylvania
Franklin & Marshall College
Gettysburg College
Haverford College
Indiana University of Pennsylvania
Juniata College
Kutztown University of Pennsylvania
La Roche College
Lehigh University
Lock Haven University of
Pennsylvania
Lycoming College
Millersville University of Pennsylvania
Moravian College
Muhlenberg College
Penn State
University Park
Rosemont College
St. Francis University
St. Vincent College
Slippery Rock University of
Pennsylvania
Thiel College
University of Pennsylvania
University of Pittsburgh
Greensburg
Ursinus College
Villanova University
Washington & Jefferson College
Waynesburg University
Widener University
Wilkes University

Puerto Rico

Caribbean University
Universidad Adventista de las Antillas
Universidad del Este
University of Puerto Rico
Cayey University College

Rhode Island

Providence College
University of Rhode Island

South Carolina

Bob Jones University
Charleston Southern University
Clemson University
Converse College
Furman University
Lander University
Presbyterian College
University of South Carolina
University of South Carolina
Beaufort
Lancaster
Wofford College

Tennessee

Bethel University
King College
Lambuth University
Rhodes College
Tennessee State University
University of Tennessee
Knoxville
University of Tennessee Health
Science Center

Texas

Angelo State University
Baylor University
Del Mar College
Jarvis Christian College
Our Lady of the Lake University of San
Antonio
Prairie View A&M University
Rice University
St. Mary's University
Southern Methodist University
Southwestern University
Texas A&M University
Commerce
Texas Lutheran University
Texas State University: San Marcos
Texas Tech University
University of Houston
University of Texas
Arlington
Dallas

Utah

University of Utah
Westminster College

Vermont

Norwich University
University of Vermont

Virginia

College of William and Mary
George Mason University
Hampden-Sydney College
Hollins University
Longwood University
Lynchburg College
Norfolk State University
Old Dominion University
Randolph College
Randolph-Macon College
Roanoke College
Sweet Briar College
University of Management and
Technology
University of Virginia
Virginia Commonwealth University
Virginia Polytechnic Institute and
State University

Washington

Olympic College
Pacific Lutheran University
Saint Martin's University
Whitman College

West Virginia

Bethany College
Potomac State College of West
Virginia University
West Virginia University Institute of
Technology
West Virginia Wesleyan College

Wisconsin

Beloit College
Carthage College
Lawrence University
Marquette University
Milwaukee School of Engineering
Ripon College
University of Wisconsin
Marinette
Platteville
River Falls
Superior

Combined bachelor's/ graduate program in environmental studies

Alabama

Birmingham-Southern College

Arkansas

University of Central Arkansas

California

California State University
Fresno
Los Angeles
Stanford University

Colorado

Western State College of Colorado

Connecticut

University of New Haven
Wesleyan University
Yale University

District of Columbia

American University

Florida

Florida International University

Georgia

Georgia Institute of Technology
University of Georgia

Hawaii

University of Hawaii
Hilo

Illinois

Augustana College
Illinois Institute of Technology
Knox College
Loyola University Chicago

Indiana

Purdue University
Taylor University
University of St. Francis

Iowa

Cornell College
Iowa Wesleyan College
University of Northern Iowa

Kansas

McPherson College
Pittsburg State University

Kentucky

Murray State University

Louisiana

Southern University and Agricultural
and Mechanical College

Maine

University of Maine

Maryland

University of Maryland
Baltimore County

Massachusetts

Anna Maria College
Art Institute of Boston at Lesley
University
Clark University
Lesley University
Tufts University

Michigan

Albion College

Minnesota

Bemidji State University
Central Lakes College
Minnesota State University
Mankato

Missouri

Drury University

Montana

Salish Kootenai College

Nebraska

Creighton University
Doane College

New Jersey

Fairleigh Dickinson University
Metropolitan Campus
Richard Stockton College of New
Jersey

William Paterson University of New
Jersey

New Mexico

Northern New Mexico College

New York

Adelphi University
Bard College
New York Institute of Technology
Pace University
Rochester Institute of Technology
Siena College
State University of New York
College at Cortland
New Paltz

North Carolina

Guilford College
High Point University
Wake Forest University

North Dakota

Dakota College at Bottineau

Ohio

Cleveland State University
College of Wooster
Hocking College
Kenyon College
Miami University
Oxford Campus
Ohio State University
Columbus Campus
University of Rio Grande
Wittenberg University
Xavier University

Oklahoma

Southeastern Oklahoma State
University

Oregon

Eastern Oregon University
Pacific University
Portland State University
Reed College
Southern Oregon University

Pennsylvania

Albright College
Arcadia University
Duquesne University
Franklin & Marshall College
Gettysburg College
Lebanon Valley College
Lycoming College
Muhlenberg College
St. Francis University
Susquehanna University
University of Pennsylvania
University of Pittsburgh
Greensburg

Puerto Rico

University of Puerto Rico
Medical Sciences

South Carolina

College of Charleston
Furman University
Presbyterian College

Tennessee

University of Tennessee
Knoxville

Texas

Texas A&M University
Commerce

Utah

University of Utah

Vermont

Lyndon State College

Virginia

College of William and Mary
Virginia Commonwealth University
Virginia Polytechnic Institute and
State University

Washington

Olympic College
University of Washington Bothell
Whitman College

West Virginia

Davis and Elkins College
Potomac State College of West
Virginia University

Wisconsin

Milwaukee School of Engineering
University of Wisconsin
Green Bay
Parkside

Combined bachelor's/ graduate program in fine arts

Alaska

University of Alaska
Anchorage

California

Academy of Art University
Art Institute of California: San
Francisco
Brooks Institute
California College of the Arts
California State University
Los Angeles
John F. Kennedy University
University of California
Santa Cruz

Colorado

Western State College of Colorado

Florida

Full Sail University

Georgia

University of Georgia

Idaho

University of Idaho

Indiana

University of St. Francis

Maine

Maine College of Art
University of Maine
University of Southern Maine

Maryland

Towson University
University of Baltimore

Massachusetts

Art Institute of Boston at Lesley
University
Lesley University
School of the Museum of Fine Arts
Simmons College
Suffolk University
Tufts University

Wheaton College

Michigan

Northern Michigan University

Minnesota

Bemidji State University
Minneapolis College of Art and Design
Minnesota State University
Mankato

Mississippi

Mississippi State University
University of Mississippi

Missouri

Drury University
Webster University

New Jersey

Fairleigh Dickinson University
College at Florham
Metropolitan Campus

New York

Pace University
Rensselaer Polytechnic Institute
Rochester Institute of Technology

North Carolina

North Carolina State University

Ohio

Kent State University

Oregon

Pacific University
Portland State University

Pennsylvania

California University of Pennsylvania
Chatham University
Marywood University
Wilkes University

Rhode Island

Rhode Island College

South Carolina

Bob Jones University

South Dakota

University of South Dakota

Tennessee

Memphis College of Art
University of Tennessee
Knoxville

Texas

Sam Houston State University
Texas A&M University
Commerce
University of Texas
Dallas

Utah

Southern Utah University

Virginia

Hollins University
Mary Baldwin College
Regent University
Virginia Commonwealth University
Virginia Polytechnic Institute and
State University

West Virginia

Davis and Elkins College

Combined bachelor's/ graduate program in forestry

Arkansas

University of Arkansas
Monticello

Colorado

Western State College of Colorado

Connecticut

Yale University

Florida

Rollins College

Georgia

University of Georgia

Illinois

Augustana College
Illinois Wesleyan University
Knox College

Indiana

Purdue University

Iowa

Cornell College
Iowa Wesleyan College

Kansas

Pittsburg State University

Maine

University of Maine

Massachusetts

Assumption College

Michigan

Albion College

Mississippi

Mississippi State University

Montana

Salish Kootenai College

Nebraska

Doane College

New Jersey

Drew University

New York

Alfred University
Bard College
Paul Smith's College
State University of New York
College at Cortland

North Carolina

Guilford College
High Point University
North Carolina State University

North Dakota

Dakota College at Bottineau

Ohio

College of Wooster
Hocking College
Miami University
Oxford Campus
Ohio State University
Columbus Campus
Xavier University

Oregon
Eastern Oregon University
Portland State University
Reed College
Willamette University

Pennsylvania
Albright College
Allegheny College
Franklin & Marshall College
Gettysburg College
Lebanon Valley College
Lycoming College
Moravian College
Muhlenberg College
St. Francis University
Susquehanna University
Thiel College

South Carolina
Furman University
Presbyterian College

Tennessee
University of Tennessee
  Knoxville

Virginia
College of William and Mary
James Madison University
Randolph-Macon College
Virginia Polytechnic Institute and
  State University

Washington
Whitman College

West Virginia
Davis and Elkins College
Marshall University
Potomac State College of West
  Virginia University

Wisconsin
Beloit College
Lawrence University
Ripon College
University of Wisconsin
  Superior

Combined bachelor's/ graduate program in law

Arkansas
University of Arkansas

California
Claremont McKenna College
Humphreys College
John F. Kennedy University
Occidental College
University of La Verne
University of San Francisco
Whittier College

Colorado
Colorado College
Western State College of Colorado

Connecticut
Quinnipiac University

Florida
Florida Agricultural and Mechanical
  University
Nova Southeastern University
Saint Thomas University
Stetson University
University of Miami

Georgia
University of Georgia

Idaho
College of Idaho
University of Idaho

Illinois
Illinois Institute of Technology
Knox College
Lake Forest College
Roosevelt University
Shimer College

Indiana
Valparaiso University
Wabash College

Iowa
Drake University
Iowa Wesleyan College
Kaplan University
  Mason City

Kansas
McPherson College
Pittsburg State University

Kentucky
Union College

Louisiana
Southern University and Agricultural
  and Mechanical College

Maine
Bowdoin College
University of Southern Maine

Maryland
Salisbury University
University of Baltimore
University of Maryland
  College Park

Massachusetts
Assumption College
Newbury College
Suffolk University
University of Massachusetts
  Dartmouth
Western New England College

Michigan
Grand Valley State University
Siena Heights University
University of Detroit Mercy

Minnesota
Hamline University

Mississippi
Mississippi College
Mississippi State University

Missouri
Central Methodist University
College of the Ozarks
University of Central Missouri
Washington University in St. Louis

Nebraska
Creighton University
University of Nebraska
  Lincoln

New Hampshire
New England College

New Jersey
Rutgers, The State University of New
  Jersey
    New Brunswick/Piscataway
      Campus
    Newark Regional Campus
Saint Peter's College
Seton Hall University
Stevens Institute of Technology

New York
Adelphi University
Albany College of Pharmacy and
  Health Sciences
Barnard College
College of Saint Rose
Columbia University
Eugene Lang College The New School
  for Liberal Arts
Fordham University
Hamilton College
Hartwick College
Hofstra University
Long Island University
  C. W. Post Campus
New York Institute of Technology
Pace University
Rensselaer Polytechnic Institute
Russell Sage College
Saint Bonaventure University
St. John's University
St. Thomas Aquinas College
Siena College
State University of New York
  Albany
    College of Environmental Science
      and Forestry
Union College

North Carolina
Campbell University

North Dakota
Dakota College at Bottineau

Ohio
College of Wooster
Ohio Northern University
University of Toledo

Oklahoma
Oklahoma City University
University of Tulsa

Oregon
Portland State University
Willamette University

Pennsylvania
Carlow University
Dickinson College
Drexel University
Duquesne University
East Stroudsburg University of
  Pennsylvania
Edinboro University of Pennsylvania
Gannon University
Juniata College
Mercyhurst College
St. Francis University
St. Vincent College
Seton Hill University
Thomas Jefferson University: College
  of Health Professions
University of Pennsylvania
University of Pittsburgh
University of Pittsburgh
  Greensburg
Washington & Jefferson College
Waynesburg University
Widener University

Puerto Rico
Pontifical Catholic University of
  Puerto Rico

Rhode Island
Roger Williams University

Tennessee
Lambuth University
University of Tennessee
  Knoxville
Vanderbilt University

Texas
Texas Tech University

Utah
Brigham Young University

Vermont
Southern Vermont College
University of Vermont

Virginia
Old Dominion University
Regent University
Washington and Lee University

Washington
Whitman College

West Virginia
Bethany College
Davis and Elkins College

Wisconsin
Marquette University
University of Wisconsin
  Green Bay

Combined bachelor's/ graduate program in mathematics

Alabama
Alabama State University
Jacksonville State University
University of Alabama
  Birmingham
University of Montevallo

Arkansas
University of Arkansas
  Monticello
University of Central Arkansas

California
California Polytechnic State
  University: San Luis Obispo
California State University
  Fresno
  Los Angeles
Harvey Mudd College
Mills College
Pitzer College
Stanford University
University of Southern California
Vanguard University of Southern
  California

Colorado
Colorado School of Mines
University of Colorado
  Boulder

Connecticut
Wesleyan University
Yale University

District of Columbia
American University

Florida
Florida Atlantic University
Florida International University

Georgia
Clark Atlanta University
Emory University
Reinhardt College
University of Georgia
Wesleyan College

Hawaii
University of Hawaii
Hilo

Illinois
DePaul University
Loyola University Chicago

Indiana
Purdue University
Purdue University
Calumet

Iowa
Iowa Wesleyan College

Kansas
Fort Hays State University
Pittsburg State University

Kentucky
Murray State University

Maine
University of Maine

Maryland
Bowie State University
Hood College
Johns Hopkins University
University of Maryland
Baltimore County

Massachusetts
Tufts University
Worcester Polytechnic Institute

Michigan
Central Michigan University
Northern Michigan University
University of Michigan
Wayne State University

Minnesota
Bemidji State University
Crown College
Minnesota State University
Mankato

Mississippi
University of Mississippi

Missouri
Drury University
Missouri State University
University of Missouri
Missouri University of Science and
Technology

Montana
Salish Kootenai College

Nebraska
Creighton University
Nebraska Christian College

New Jersey
Monmouth University
New Jersey Institute of Technology
Rowan University
Rutgers, The State University of New
Jersey
Camden Regional Campus
Stevens Institute of Technology
William Paterson University of New
Jersey

New Mexico
Eastern New Mexico University
Northern New Mexico College
University of the Southwest

New York
City University of New York
City College
Hunter College
Rensselaer Polytechnic Institute
Roberts Wesleyan College
Rochester Institute of Technology
St. John's University
St. Joseph's College: Suffolk Campus
State University of New York
Buffalo
College at Fredonia
College at Potsdam
Stony Brook
University of Rochester

North Carolina
Guilford College
Western Carolina University

North Dakota
Dakota College at Bottineau

Ohio
Case Western Reserve University
Mount Vernon Nazarene University
University of Akron
University of Rio Grande
Urbana University

Oklahoma
Southeastern Oklahoma State
University
University of Oklahoma

Oregon
Southern Oregon University

Pennsylvania
Bryn Mawr College
Bucknell University
Duquesne University
Lock Haven University of
Pennsylvania
Mount Aloysius College
University of Pennsylvania
University of Pittsburgh
University of Pittsburgh
Greensburg
Villanova University
Wilkes University

Puerto Rico
Caribbean University

Rhode Island
University of Rhode Island

South Carolina
Bob Jones University
College of Charleston
University of South Carolina
Lancaster

Tennessee
King College
Tennessee State University
University of Tennessee
Knoxville

Texas
Prairie View A&M University
Texas A&M University
Commerce

Utah
University of Utah

Vermont
Lyndon State College
University of Vermont

Virginia
Virginia Polytechnic Institute and
State University

Washington
Olympic College

West Virginia
Davis and Elkins College
Potomac State College of West
Virginia University

Wisconsin
University of Wisconsin
Parkside

Combined bachelor's/ graduate program in medicine

Alaska
University of Alaska
Anchorage

California
California Institute of Technology
Charles Drew University of Medicine
and Science
University of California
San Diego
University of Southern California

Colorado
Western State College of Colorado

Connecticut
University of Connecticut

District of Columbia
Howard University

Florida
University of Central Florida
University of Miami
University of South Florida

Georgia
Medical College of Georgia

Illinois
Bradley University
Illinois Institute of Technology
Knox College
Lincoln College
Northwestern University
Rush University
Southern Illinois University
Carbondale
University of Chicago

Indiana
Purdue University
Calumet

Iowa
Iowa Wesleyan College

Kansas
McPherson College
Pittsburg State University

Kentucky
Murray State University
Union College

Louisiana
Louisiana State University
Shreveport

Maryland
University of Maryland
College Park

Massachusetts
Boston College
Boston University
Massachusetts College of Pharmacy
and Health Sciences
Tufts University

Michigan
Northern Michigan University
Wayne State University

Mississippi
Mississippi College
Mississippi State University

Missouri
University of Central Missouri
University of Missouri
Kansas City

Nebraska
Chadron State College
Creighton University
University of Nebraska
Lincoln
Medical Center

New Jersey
The College of New Jersey
Drew University
Fairleigh Dickinson University
College at Florham
Metropolitan Campus
Kean University
Monmouth University
Montclair State University
New Jersey Institute of Technology
Richard Stockton College of New
Jersey
Rutgers, The State University of New
Jersey
Camden Regional Campus
New Brunswick/Piscataway
Campus
Newark Regional Campus
Saint Peter's College
Stevens Institute of Technology

New Mexico
University of New Mexico

New York
Albany College of Pharmacy and
Health Sciences
Canisius College
City University of New York
Brooklyn College

City College
York College
Colgate University
Hobart and William Smith Colleges
Rensselaer Polytechnic Institute
Russell Sage College
Saint Bonaventure University
Siena College
State University of New York
Binghamton
College of Environmental Science
and Forestry
Upstate Medical University
Union College
University of Rochester
Utica College

North Carolina
High Point University

North Dakota
Dakota College at Bottineau

Ohio
College of Wooster
Kent State University
Ohio State University
Columbus Campus
University of Akron
University of Dayton

Oregon
Portland State University

Pennsylvania
Delaware Valley College
Drexel University
Gannon University
Indiana University of Pennsylvania
Juniata College
Lehigh University
Moravian College
Muhlenberg College
Penn State
Erie, The Behrend College
University Park
Rosemont College
St. Francis University
Temple University
Thomas Jefferson University: College
of Health Professions
University of Pittsburgh
University of Pittsburgh
Greensburg
Ursinus College
Villanova University
Washington & Jefferson College
Widener University
Wilkes University

Puerto Rico
Universidad Adventista de las Antillas
University of Puerto Rico
Medical Sciences

Rhode Island
Brown University

South Carolina
Furman University
Morris College

Tennessee
East Tennessee State University
Fisk University
Lambuth University
Union University
University of Tennessee
Knoxville
University of Tennessee Health
Science Center

Texas
McMurry University
Rice University
Texas State University: San Marcos
Texas Tech University Health Sciences
Center
University of Texas
Arlington
Health Science Center at Houston

Virginia
Old Dominion University
Virginia Commonwealth University

Washington
Washington State University

West Virginia
Davis and Elkins College
Potomac State College of West
Virginia University

Wisconsin
University of Wisconsin
Green Bay

Combined bachelor's/ graduate program in nursing

Alabama
Birmingham-Southern College
Jacksonville State University
Stillman College
Talladega College
Troy University

Alaska
University of Alaska
Anchorage

Arizona
Grand Canyon University

Arkansas
Arkansas State University
Mountain Home
University of Arkansas
Monticello
University of Central Arkansas

California
California State University
Fresno
Los Angeles
Loma Linda University
Mount St. Mary's College
St. Mary's College of California
Samuel Merritt University
University of San Diego
Vanguard University of Southern
California

Connecticut
Quinnipiac University
Sacred Heart University
Saint Joseph College

District of Columbia
Catholic University of America

Florida
Barry University
Florida Atlantic University
Florida Gulf Coast University
Florida Memorial University
Florida Southern College
Jacksonville University
Northwest Florida State College

State College of Florida,
Manatee-Sarasota
University of Central Florida
University of Tampa
Valencia Community College

Georgia
Agnes Scott College
Berry College
Emory University
Medical College of Georgia
Reinhardt College
South University: Savannah
Southeastern Technical College

Hawaii
Hawaii Pacific University
University of Hawaii
Hilo

Idaho
College of Idaho

Illinois
Blessing-Rieman College of Nursing
DePaul University
Dominican University
Harper College
Hebrew Theological College
Knox College
Monmouth College
National-Louis University
Rush University
St. Francis Medical Center College of
Nursing
Saint Xavier University
Trinity College of Nursing and Health
Sciences
Wheaton College

Indiana
Purdue University
Purdue University
Calumet
North Central
University of St. Francis
University of Southern Indiana
Valparaiso University

Iowa
Allen College
Cornell College
Dordt College
Emmaus Bible College
Graceland University
Iowa Wesleyan College
St. Luke's College
University of Iowa

Kansas
Fort Hays State University
Pittsburg State University

Kentucky
Beckfield College
Bellarmine University
Gateway Community and Technical
College
Kentucky Mountain Bible College
Murray State University

Louisiana
Loyola University New Orleans
Our Lady of the Lake College
Southern University and Agricultural
and Mechanical College

Maine
Husson University
Saint Joseph's College of Maine
University of Maine
University of Southern Maine

Maryland
Bowie State University
Salisbury University
Towson University
University of Baltimore
Washington College

Massachusetts
Atlantic Union College
Boston College
Northeastern University
Regis College
Simmons College
University of Massachusetts
Boston
Dartmouth

Michigan
Albion College
Kuyper College
Madonna University
Northern Michigan University

Minnesota
Crown College
Minnesota State University
Mankato
North Central University
Rochester Community and Technical
College
St. Paul College

Mississippi
Blue Mountain College
Millsaps College
Mississippi State University
University of Mississippi

Missouri
Culver-Stockton College
Goldfarb School of Nursing at
Barnes-Jewish College
Missouri State University
Ozark Christian College
St. Luke's College
University of Central Missouri
University of Missouri
Missouri University of Science and
Technology
Webster University
Wentworth Military Junior College

Montana
Montana State University
College of Technology: Great Falls
Salish Kootenai College
University of Great Falls

Nebraska
Chadron State College
Clarkson College
Creighton University
Grace University
Nebraska Methodist College of
Nursing and Allied Health
Western Nebraska Community
College

New Hampshire
Rivier College

New Jersey
College of St. Elizabeth
Fairleigh Dickinson University
Metropolitan Campus
Felician College
Ocean County College
Ramapo College of New Jersey
Richard Stockton College of New
Jersey
Saint Peter's College
Thomas Edison State College

University of Medicine and Dentistry
  of New Jersey
  School of Nursing
William Paterson University of New
  Jersey

New Mexico

Dona Ana Community College of New
  Mexico State University
Eastern New Mexico University:
  Roswell Campus
New Mexico State University
  Alamogordo
Northern New Mexico College
San Juan College

New York

Adelphi University
Cochran School of Nursing
D'Youville College
Daemen College
Excelsior College
Hobart and William Smith Colleges
Long Island University
  Brooklyn Campus
Maria College
Mercy College
Molloy College
New York University
Pace University
Russell Sage College
St. Elizabeth College of Nursing
State University of New York
  College at Geneseo
  Institute of Technology at
    Utica/Rome
  Stony Brook
  Upstate Medical University
University of Rochester

North Carolina

Gardner-Webb University
University of North Carolina
  Greensboro

North Dakota

Bismarck State College
Dakota College at Bottineau
Lake Region State College

Ohio

Bowling Green State University
Bryant & Stratton College
  Parma
College of Wooster
Franciscan University of Steubenville
Hocking College
James A. Rhodes State College
Kent State University
MedCentral College of Nursing
Mercy College of Northwest Ohio
Mount Vernon Nazarene University
Ohio Christian University
Otterbein College
University of Akron
University of Findlay
University of Rio Grande
Ursuline College
Wittenberg University

Oklahoma

Cameron University
Northeastern Oklahoma Agricultural
  and Mechanical College
Southeastern Oklahoma State
  University
Southern Nazarene University

Oregon

Eastern Oregon University
Oregon Institute of Technology
Portland State University
Southern Oregon University

Southwestern Oregon Community
  College
Western Oregon University

Pennsylvania

Allegheny College
Arcadia University
Cedar Crest College
Clarion University of Pennsylvania
Drexel University
Gannon University
Gettysburg College
Juniata College
Kutztown University of Pennsylvania
Lock Haven University of
  Pennsylvania
Luzerne County Community College
Mount Aloysius College
Neumann University
Rosemont College
St. Francis University
Susquehanna University
Thomas Jefferson University: College
  of Health Professions
University of Pennsylvania
University of Pittsburgh
University of Scranton
Widener University
Wilkes University

Puerto Rico

Caribbean University
Universidad del Este
University of Puerto Rico
  Medical Sciences

Rhode Island

University of Rhode Island

South Carolina

Bob Jones University
Furman University
University of South Carolina
  Lancaster

Tennessee

Bryan College
Fisk University
King College
Lambuth University
Maryville College
Southern Adventist University
Tennessee State University
University of Tennessee
  Knoxville
Vanderbilt University

Texas

Baylor University
Grayson County College
Jarvis Christian College
Mountain View College
Prairie View A&M University
Texas A&M University
  Commerce
Texas Tech University Health Sciences
  Center
Texas Woman's University
University of Texas
  Health Science Center at Houston
  Health Science Center at San
    Antonio
University of the Incarnate Word

Utah

Western Governors University

Vermont

Lyndon State College
Norwich University
University of Vermont

Virginia

Bridgewater College
Mary Baldwin College
Old Dominion University
Randolph College

Washington

Gonzaga University
Olympic College
University of Washington Bothell

West Virginia

Davis and Elkins College
Glenville State College
Mountain State University
Potomac State College of West
  Virginia University
West Virginia University at
  Parkersburg
Wheeling Jesuit University

Wisconsin

Beloit College
Herzing University
Lakeshore Technical College
Marian University
Marquette University
Silver Lake College
University of Wisconsin
  Marinette
  Parkside
Viterbo University

Combined bachelor's/graduate program in occupational therapy

Alabama

Alabama State University
University of South Alabama

Alaska

University of Alaska
  Anchorage

Arkansas

University of Central Arkansas

California

Dominican University of California
Loma Linda University

Connecticut

Quinnipiac University
Sacred Heart University

District of Columbia

Howard University

Florida

Florida Agricultural and Mechanical
  University
Hodges University
Nova Southeastern University
Saint Leo University

Georgia

Brenau University
Medical College of Georgia

Idaho

College of Idaho

Illinois

Augustana College
Dominican University
Hebrew Theological College
Illinois College
Knox College
McKendree University

Monmouth College
Rush University

Indiana

University of Southern Indiana

Iowa

St. Ambrose University

Kansas

University of Kansas Medical Center

Maine

Husson University
University of New England
University of Southern Maine

Maryland

Mount St. Mary's University
Towson University

Massachusetts

American International College
Bay Path College
Boston University
Springfield College
Tufts University
Worcester State College

Michigan

Alma College
Baker College
  of Flint
Baker College of Allen Park
Calvin College
Eastern Michigan University
Grand Valley State University

Minnesota

College of St. Scholastica
St. Catherine University

Mississippi

Mississippi State University

Missouri

Avila University
Culver-Stockton College
Drury University
Fontbonne University
Maryville University of Saint Louis
Saint Louis University
State Fair Community College
Stephens College
University of Missouri
  Columbia
Washington University in St. Louis

Nebraska

Chadron State College
College of Saint Mary
Creighton University

Nevada

Nevada State College
University of Nevada
  Las Vegas

New Hampshire

University of New Hampshire

New Jersey

Caldwell College
Kean University
Richard Stockton College of New
  Jersey
Saint Peter's College
Seton Hall University

New York
City University of New York
   York College
D'Youville College
Dominican College of Blauvelt
Hartwick College
Ithaca College
Keuka College
Long Island University
   Brooklyn Campus
New York Institute of Technology
Pace University
Russell Sage College
Siena College
State University of New York
   Buffalo
   Stony Brook
Touro College
Utica College

North Carolina
Lenoir-Rhyne University

North Dakota
University of Mary

Ohio
Hocking College
Mount Vernon Nazarene University
University of Findlay
Wittenberg University
Xavier University

Oregon
Pacific University
Portland State University

Pennsylvania
Allegheny College
Alvernia University
Bloomsburg University of
   Pennsylvania
Chatham University
Duquesne University
Elizabethtown College
Gannon University
La Roche College
La Salle University
Misericordia University
Moravian College
Mount Aloysius College
Muhlenberg College
St. Francis University
St. Vincent College
Shippensburg University of
   Pennsylvania
Susquehanna University
Temple University
Thiel College
Thomas Jefferson University: College
   of Health Professions
University of Pittsburgh
   Greensburg
University of Scranton
University of the Sciences in
   Philadelphia
Villanova University

Puerto Rico
University of Puerto Rico
   Medical Sciences

Tennessee
Belmont University
Tennessee State University
University of Tennessee
   Knoxville
University of Tennessee Health
   Science Center

Texas
Texas Tech University Health Sciences
   Center
University of Texas
   Health Science Center at San
      Antonio

Vermont
Castleton State College
Lyndon State College
Southern Vermont College

Virginia
Shenandoah University
Virginia Commonwealth University

West Virginia
Potomac State College of West
   Virginia University
West Virginia University

Wisconsin
Carroll University
Carthage College
Concordia University Wisconsin
Lawrence University
Mount Mary College
University of Wisconsin
   Green Bay

Combined bachelor's/ graduate program in optometry

Colorado
Western State College of Colorado

Florida
Nova Southeastern University

Illinois
Illinois Institute of Technology
Knox College

Indiana
Indiana University
   Bloomington
Purdue University
   Calumet

Iowa
Iowa Wesleyan College

Kansas
McPherson College
Pittsburg State University

Kentucky
Murray State University

Maine
Saint Joseph's College of Maine
University of Maine

Maryland
Salisbury University

Massachusetts
Assumption College
Massachusetts College of Pharmacy
   and Health Sciences
Wheaton College

Mississippi
Mississippi State University

Missouri
Maryville University of Saint Louis
University of Central Missouri

New Jersey
Caldwell College
The College of New Jersey
Fairleigh Dickinson University
   Metropolitan Campus
Felician College
Ramapo College of New Jersey

New York
Adelphi University
Canisius College
City University of New York
   City College
Ithaca College
Le Moyne College
Mount Saint Mary College
Pace University
St. John's University
Siena College
State University of New York
   Albany
   Binghamton
   College at Fredonia
   College at Geneseo
   College at Oneonta
   College at Plattsburgh
   College at Potsdam
   New Paltz
   Oswego
Utica College
Wagner College

Ohio
Ohio State University
   Columbus Campus

Oklahoma
Northeastern State University

Oregon
Pacific University
Portland State University
Southern Oregon University

Pennsylvania
Arcadia University
Gannon University
Gettysburg College
Indiana University of Pennsylvania
Juniata College
Lehigh University
Lycoming College
Millersville University of Pennsylvania
Muhlenberg College
St. Francis University
Shippensburg University of
   Pennsylvania
University of Pittsburgh
   Bradford
   Greensburg
   Johnstown
Villanova University
Washington & Jefferson College
Wilkes University

Puerto Rico
Universidad Adventista de las Antillas

Rhode Island
Providence College

Tennessee
Union University

Virginia
Old Dominion University

Wisconsin
University of Wisconsin
   Green Bay

Combined bachelor's/ graduate program in osteopathic medicine

California
Pitzer College

Florida
Jacksonville University
Nova Southeastern University
Saint Leo University

Illinois
Illinois Institute of Technology

Indiana
University of St. Francis

Kansas
McPherson College

Kentucky
Pikeville College

Maine
University of Maine

Massachusetts
Assumption College
Massachusetts College of Pharmacy
   and Health Sciences

Missouri
Avila University
Central Methodist University
Missouri Western State University
William Jewell College

Nevada
University of Nevada
   Las Vegas

New Jersey
Caldwell College
Ramapo College of New Jersey
Richard Stockton College of New
   Jersey

New York
Marist College
New York Institute of Technology
Pace University
Saint Bonaventure University
State University of New York
   College at Geneseo
   College at Old Westbury
   New Paltz
Touro College
Utica College

Ohio
Heidelberg University
Kent State University
Ohio University

Oregon
Portland State University

Pennsylvania
Allegheny College
Duquesne University
Edinboro University of Pennsylvania
Gannon University
Indiana University of Pennsylvania
Juniata College
Mercyhurst College
Penn State
   Erie, The Behrend College
St. Francis University
St. Vincent College

Seton Hill University
Shippensburg University of
Pennsylvania
Slippery Rock University of
Pennsylvania
Thiel College
University of Pittsburgh
Bradford
Greensburg
Widener University
Wilkes University

Texas

University of Texas
Dallas

Combined bachelor's/ graduate program in pharmacy

Arizona

University of Arizona

Arkansas

Harding University

California

University of California
San Diego
University of Southern California
University of the Pacific

Connecticut

University of Connecticut

Florida

Florida Agricultural and Mechanical
University
Hodges University
Nova Southeastern University
Saint Leo University

Georgia

Mercer University

Hawaii

Hawaii Pacific University
University of Hawaii
Hilo

Idaho

College of Idaho
Idaho State University

Illinois

Hebrew Theological College
Illinois Institute of Technology
Lewis University
Millikin University

Indiana

Butler University
Purdue University
Purdue University
Calumet
University of St. Francis

Iowa

Drake University
Iowa Wesleyan College
University of Iowa

Kansas

McPherson College
Pittsburg State University
University of Kansas

Kentucky

Murray State University

Louisiana

University of Louisiana at Monroe

Maine

Husson University
Saint Joseph's College of Maine

Maryland

Coppin State University
Salisbury University
University of Baltimore
Washington College

Massachusetts

Assumption College
Eastern Nazarene College
Massachusetts College of Pharmacy
and Health Sciences
Northeastern University
Simmons College
Worcester State College

Michigan

University of Michigan
Wayne State University

Minnesota

University of Minnesota
Twin Cities

Mississippi

Mississippi State University
University of Mississippi

Missouri

University of Central Missouri

Montana

University of Montana

Nebraska

Chadron State College
Creighton University
University of Nebraska
Lincoln

Nevada

Nevada State College

New Hampshire

New England College
University of New Hampshire at
Manchester

New Jersey

Fairleigh Dickinson University
Metropolitan Campus
New Jersey Institute of Technology
Rutgers, The State University of New
Jersey
Camden Regional Campus
Saint Peter's College
William Paterson University of New
Jersey

New York

Albany College of Pharmacy and
Health Sciences
Canisius College
Long Island University
Brooklyn Campus
Roberts Wesleyan College
Saint Bonaventure University
St. John's University
St. Thomas Aquinas College
State University of New York
Buffalo
Touro College

North Carolina

Campbell University

Elizabeth City State University
University of North Carolina
Chapel Hill
Wingate University

North Dakota

Dakota College at Bottineau
North Dakota State University

Ohio

Ohio Northern University
Ohio State University
Columbus Campus
University of Findlay
University of Toledo
Ursuline College

Oklahoma

Southwestern Oklahoma State
University

Oregon

Pacific University
Portland State University

Pennsylvania

East Stroudsburg University of
Pennsylvania
Edinboro University of Pennsylvania
Gannon University
Indiana University of Pennsylvania
Juniata College
Keystone College
Mercyhurst College
Penn State
Erie, The Behrend College
St. Francis University
St. Vincent College
Seton Hill University
Shippensburg University of
Pennsylvania
Slippery Rock University of
Pennsylvania
Temple University
Thiel College
Thomas Jefferson University: College
of Health Professions
University of Pittsburgh
University of Pittsburgh
Bradford
Greensburg
Johnstown
Titusville
Wilkes University

Puerto Rico

University of Puerto Rico
Medical Sciences

Rhode Island

University of Rhode Island

South Carolina

Clemson University
Furman University
Presbyterian College
University of South Carolina
Lancaster

South Dakota

South Dakota State University

Tennessee

Belmont University
Bethel University
East Tennessee State University
Fisk University
King College
Lambuth University
Lipscomb University
Milligan College
Union University

University of Tennessee
Knoxville
University of Tennessee Health
Science Center

Texas

Texas Tech University Health Sciences
Center
University of Houston
University of Texas
Austin
El Paso

Vermont

St. Michael's College

Virginia

Old Dominion University
Shenandoah University
Virginia Commonwealth University

Washington

University of Washington
Washington State University

West Virginia

Davis and Elkins College
Potomac State College of West
Virginia University
University of Charleston
West Virginia University

Wisconsin

Carroll University
University of Wisconsin
Green Bay
Madison

Combined bachelor's/ graduate program in physical therapy

Alabama

Alabama State University
University of South Alabama

Arkansas

University of Central Arkansas

California

California State University
Fresno
Loma Linda University
Mount St. Mary's College

Colorado

Western State College of Colorado

Connecticut

Quinnipiac University
Sacred Heart University
University of Connecticut
University of Hartford

Florida

Hodges University
Nova Southeastern University
Saint Leo University
University of Miami

Georgia

Armstrong Atlantic State University
Medical College of Georgia
Mercer University

Idaho

College of Idaho

Illinois

Bradley University

Monmouth College

Indiana
Purdue University
Calumet

Iowa
Iowa Wesleyan College
St. Ambrose University

Kansas
McPherson College
Pittsburg State University

Kentucky
Bellarmine University

Maine
Husson University
University of New England

Maryland
Coppin State University
Mount St. Mary's University
University of Maryland
College Park

Massachusetts
American International College
Assumption College
Atlantic Union College
Boston University
Massachusetts College of Pharmacy
and Health Sciences
Northeastern University
Simmons College
Springfield College
University of Massachusetts
Lowell

Michigan
Andrews University
Grand Valley State University

Minnesota
Dunwoody College of Technology
St. Catherine University

Mississippi
Mississippi State University

Missouri
Avila University
Central Methodist University
Maryville University of Saint Louis
Saint Louis University
State Fair Community College
Stephens College
University of Central Missouri
University of Missouri
Columbia
Washington University in St. Louis

Nebraska
Chadron State College
Creighton University
University of Nebraska
Medical Center

New Hampshire
Franklin Pierce University
New England College

New Jersey
Caldwell College
Fairleigh Dickinson University
Metropolitan Campus
Kean University
Ramapo College of New Jersey
Richard Stockton College of New
Jersey

Saint Peter's College
Seton Hall University
University of Medicine and Dentistry
of New Jersey
School of Health Related
Professions
William Paterson University of New
Jersey

New York
Adelphi University
D'Youville College
Daemen College
Dominican College of Blauvelt
Hartwick College
Iona College
Ithaca College
Le Moyne College
Long Island University
Brooklyn Campus
Manhattanville College
Mount Saint Mary College
Nazareth College
New York Institute of Technology
Pace University
Russell Sage College
Sage College of Albany
Saint Bonaventure University
St. Thomas Aquinas College
Siena College
State University of New York
College at Brockport
College at Geneseo
College at Oneonta
College of Environmental Science
and Forestry
Oswego
Upstate Medical University
Touro College
Utica College

North Dakota
Dakota College at Bottineau
University of Mary
University of North Dakota

Ohio
Bowling Green State University
Hocking College
Mount Vernon Nazarene University
Ohio University
University of Findlay
Walsh University

Oregon
Pacific University
Portland State University

Pennsylvania
Allegheny College
Arcadia University
Bloomsburg University of
Pennsylvania
Cabrini College
Chatham University
Drexel University
Duquesne University
Elizabethtown College
Gannon University
Gettysburg College
Indiana University of Pennsylvania
Juniata College
Keystone College
La Roche College
Lebanon Valley College
Misericordia University
Moravian College
Mount Aloysius College
Muhlenberg College
Penn State
Abington
Brandywine
St. Francis University

St. Vincent College
Slippery Rock University of
Pennsylvania
Temple University
Thiel College
University of Pittsburgh
University of Pittsburgh
Greensburg
University of Scranton
University of the Sciences in
Philadelphia
Villanova University
Waynesburg University
Widener University
Wilkes University

Puerto Rico
Universidad Adventista de las Antillas
University of Puerto Rico
Medical Sciences

Rhode Island
University of Rhode Island

South Carolina
Bob Jones University
Furman University

Tennessee
Belmont University
King College
Lambuth University
Tennessee State University
University of Tennessee
Chattanooga
Knoxville
University of Tennessee Health
Science Center

Texas
Texas A&M University
Commerce
Texas Tech University Health Sciences
Center
University of Texas
El Paso
Health Science Center at San
Antonio

Vermont
Castleton State College
Lyndon State College

Virginia
Bridgewater College
Shenandoah University
Virginia Commonwealth University

Washington
Olympic College
University of Puget Sound

West Virginia
Davis and Elkins College
Potomac State College of West
Virginia University
West Virginia University
Wheeling Jesuit University

Wisconsin
Carroll University
Concordia University Wisconsin
Marquette University
University of Wisconsin
Green Bay

Combined bachelor's/ graduate program in podiatry

District of Columbia
Howard University

Florida
Barry University

Maryland
Salisbury University

Massachusetts
Assumption College
Massachusetts College of Liberal Arts
Massachusetts College of Pharmacy
and Health Sciences

New Jersey
Caldwell College
Fairleigh Dickinson University
Metropolitan Campus
Felician College
Kean University
Richard Stockton College of New
Jersey

New York
Canisius College
Le Moyne College
Mount Saint Mary College
Pace University
St. Francis College
St. John's University
St. Joseph's College: Suffolk Campus
St. Thomas Aquinas College
Siena College
Utica College

Oregon
Portland State University

Pennsylvania
Cabrini College
Chestnut Hill College
East Stroudsburg University of
Pennsylvania
Gannon University
Indiana University of Pennsylvania
Juniata College
Lycoming College
Millersville University of Pennsylvania
St. Francis University
St. Vincent College
Shippensburg University of
Pennsylvania
Temple University
Washington & Jefferson College
Widener University

Tennessee
Union University

Wisconsin
Viterbo University

Combined bachelor's/ graduate program in psychology

Alabama
Jacksonville State University
University of Montevallo

Alaska
University of Alaska
Anchorage

Arkansas
University of Arkansas
  Monticello
University of Central Arkansas

California
California Polytechnic State
  University: San Luis Obispo
California State University
  Fresno
  Los Angeles
Claremont McKenna College
Hope International University
John F. Kennedy University
Mills College
Mount St. Mary's College
Pitzer College
Simpson University
Stanford University
University of the West
Vanguard University of Southern
  California

Colorado
University of Colorado
  Boulder

Connecticut
Asnuntuck Community College
Wesleyan University
Yale University

District of Columbia
American University
Catholic University of America

Florida
Nova Southeastern University
Warner University

Georgia
Reinhardt College
University of Georgia
Wesleyan College

Hawaii
University of Hawaii
  Hilo

Illinois
Benedictine University
DePaul University
Hebrew Theological College
Illinois Institute of Technology
Kendall College
Lewis University
Loyola University Chicago
National-Louis University
Roosevelt University

Indiana
Purdue University
University of St. Francis
Valparaiso University

Iowa
Iowa State University
Iowa Wesleyan College
Waldorf College

Kansas
Fort Hays State University
Pittsburg State University

Kentucky
Mid-Continent University
Murray State University
Union College

Louisiana
Centenary College of Louisiana

Our Lady of the Lake College

Maine
Husson University
University of Maine

Maryland
Bowie State University
Johns Hopkins University
University of Baltimore
University of Maryland
  Baltimore County

Massachusetts
American International College
Anna Maria College
Art Institute of Boston at Lesley
  University
Lesley University
Suffolk University
Tufts University
University of Massachusetts
  Dartmouth

Michigan
Central Michigan University
Northern Michigan University
Rochester College
University of Michigan
Wayne State University

Minnesota
Bemidji State University
Capella University
Crown College
Minnesota State University
  Mankato
Oak Hills Christian College

Mississippi
Mississippi State University
University of Mississippi

Missouri
Avila University
Drury University
Stephens College
University of Missouri
  Missouri University of Science and
    Technology

Montana
Salish Kootenai College
University of Great Falls

Nebraska
Grace University
Nebraska Christian College

New Hampshire
Rivier College

New Jersey
Caldwell College
College of St. Elizabeth
Fairleigh Dickinson University
  College at Florham
  Metropolitan Campus
William Paterson University of New
  Jersey

New Mexico
New Mexico Highlands University
San Juan College
University of the Southwest

New York
City University of New York
  City College
  John Jay College of Criminal Justice
College of New Rochelle

Iona College
Marist College
Pace University
Rochester Institute of Technology
Russell Sage College
St. John's University
St. Thomas Aquinas College
State University of New York
  Albany
  College at Plattsburgh
  Oswego
Touro College

North Carolina
Guilford College

North Dakota
Bismarck State College
Dakota College at Bottineau
University of Mary

Ohio
Case Western Reserve University
Heidelberg University
Hocking College
Marietta College
Mount Vernon Nazarene University
Ohio Christian University
Walsh University

Oklahoma
Mid-America Christian University
Southeastern Oklahoma State
  University
Southern Nazarene University

Oregon
Oregon Institute of Technology
Southern Oregon University

Pennsylvania
Baptist Bible College of Pennsylvania
Bryn Mawr College
California University of Pennsylvania
Chatham University
Chestnut Hill College
Drexel University
Duquesne University
Lock Haven University of
  Pennsylvania
Marywood University
Mount Aloysius College
Rosemont College
Saint Joseph's University
Shippensburg University of
  Pennsylvania
University of Pittsburgh
  Greensburg
University of the Sciences in
  Philadelphia
Widener University

Puerto Rico
Universidad del Este

Rhode Island
Salve Regina University
University of Rhode Island

South Carolina
University of South Carolina
  Lancaster

South Dakota
University of South Dakota

Tennessee
Tennessee State University
University of Tennessee
  Knoxville

Texas
Prairie View A&M University
Texas A&M University
  Commerce
University of Dallas

Utah
University of Utah

Vermont
Lyndon State College

Virginia
George Mason University
Regent University
Virginia Commonwealth University
Virginia Polytechnic Institute and
  State University

Washington
Olympic College
Trinity Lutheran College
Walla Walla University

West Virginia
Davis and Elkins College
Potomac State College of West
  Virginia University

Wisconsin
University of Wisconsin
  Marinette
  Parkside
  Whitewater

Combined bachelor's/ graduate program in social work

Alabama
Alabama State University
Jacksonville State University
University of Montevallo

Arkansas
University of Arkansas
  Monticello

California
California State University
  Fresno
  Los Angeles
Mount St. Mary's College

Colorado
University of Denver

Connecticut
Asnuntuck Community College
Sacred Heart University

Florida
Barry University
Warner University

Georgia
Waycross College

Hawaii
Hawaii Pacific University

Idaho
Northwest Nazarene University

Illinois
Loyola University Chicago
Roosevelt University
University of Chicago

Kansas

Pittsburg State University

Kentucky

Brescia University
Murray State University

Louisiana

Southern University
  New Orleans

Maine

University of Maine
University of Southern Maine

Maryland

Bowie State University
Salisbury University
University of Maryland
  Baltimore County
Washington Adventist University

Massachusetts

Art Institute of Boston at Lesley
  University
Boston College
Lesley University
Regis College
Simmons College
Springfield College
Wheelock College

Michigan

Andrews University
Kuyper College
Northern Michigan University

Minnesota

Minnesota State University
  Mankato
Rochester Community and Technical
  College

Mississippi

Mississippi State University
University of Mississippi

Missouri

Fontbonne University
Maryville University of Saint Louis
Washington University in St. Louis
Webster University

Montana

Salish Kootenai College

Nebraska

Chadron State College
Nebraska Christian College
Western Nebraska Community
  College

New Hampshire

University of New Hampshire

New Jersey

Fairleigh Dickinson University
  Metropolitan Campus
Monmouth University
William Paterson University of New
  Jersey

New Mexico

Eastern New Mexico University:
  Roswell Campus
New Mexico Highlands University
Northern New Mexico College
San Juan College

New York

Adelphi University
Bard College
Concordia College
Fordham University
Molloy College
Mount Saint Mary College
Nazareth College
St. Thomas Aquinas College
Siena College
State University of New York
  Albany
  Buffalo
Touro College
Yeshiva University

North Carolina

North Carolina State University

North Dakota

Bismarck State College
Dakota College at Bottineau
Dickinson State University

Ohio

Baldwin-Wallace College
College of Wooster
Hocking College
James A. Rhodes State College
Mount Vernon Nazarene University
Ohio Christian University
University of Rio Grande

Oregon

Portland State University
Southern Oregon University

Pennsylvania

Bryn Mawr College
California University of Pennsylvania
Cedar Crest College
Kutztown University of Pennsylvania
Lock Haven University of
  Pennsylvania
Marywood University
Millersville University of Pennsylvania
Shippensburg University of
  Pennsylvania
University of Pittsburgh
  Greensburg
Widener University

Puerto Rico

Caribbean University
Universidad del Este

Rhode Island

Rhode Island College

South Dakota

University of South Dakota

Tennessee

Jackson State Community College
Tennessee State University
University of Tennessee
  Knoxville

Texas

Jarvis Christian College
Texas A&M University
  Commerce
University of Texas
  Health Science Center at Houston

Virginia

Virginia Commonwealth University

Washington

Clark College
Olympic College

Trinity Lutheran College
Walla Walla University

West Virginia

Davis and Elkins College
Potomac State College of West
  Virginia University

Wisconsin

University of Wisconsin
  Marinette
  River Falls
  Superior

Combined bachelor's/ graduate program in veterinary medicine

Colorado

Western State College of Colorado

Georgia

University of Georgia

Indiana

Purdue University

Iowa

Iowa Wesleyan College

Kansas

McPherson College
Pittsburg State University

Maryland

Salisbury University
University of Maryland
  College Park

Massachusetts

Massachusetts College of Pharmacy
  and Health Sciences
Tufts University
Worcester Polytechnic Institute

Mississippi

Mississippi College
Mississippi State University

Missouri

University of Central Missouri

New Jersey

Fairleigh Dickinson University
  Metropolitan Campus
William Paterson University of New
  Jersey

New Mexico

San Juan College

North Carolina

North Carolina State University

North Dakota

Dakota College at Bottineau

Ohio

College of Wooster
Kent State University
University of Findlay

Pennsylvania

Delaware Valley College
Gannon University
St. Francis University
University of Pittsburgh
  Greensburg
Widener University

Puerto Rico

Pontifical Catholic University of
  Puerto Rico
University of Puerto Rico
  Cayey University College

Tennessee

Lambuth University
Union University
University of Tennessee
  Knoxville

Texas

Mountain View College

Vermont

University of Vermont

Virginia

Bridgewater College
Old Dominion University

Washington

Washington State University

West Virginia

Davis and Elkins College
Potomac State College of West
  Virginia University

Wisconsin

University of Wisconsin
  Madison
Viterbo University

Double major

Alabama
Alabama Agricultural and Mechanical University
Alabama State University
Amridge University
Athens State University
Auburn University
Auburn University at Montgomery
Birmingham-Southern College
Faulkner State Community College
Faulkner University
George C. Wallace State Community College
  Selma
Huntingdon College
Jacksonville State University
Judson College
Lawson State Community College
Miles College
Oakwood University
Samford University
Shelton State Community College
Southeastern Bible College
Spring Hill College
Stillman College
Talladega College
Troy University
Tuskegee University
University of Alabama
University of Alabama
  Birmingham
  Huntsville
University of Mobile
University of Montevallo
University of North Alabama
University of South Alabama
University of West Alabama
Wallace State Community College at Hanceville

Alaska
Alaska Pacific University
Ilisagvik College
Prince William Sound Community College
University of Alaska
  Anchorage
  Fairbanks
  Southeast

Arizona
American Indian College of the Assemblies of God
Arizona Automotive Institute
Arizona State University
Art Center Design College
Dine College
Eastern Arizona College
Embry-Riddle Aeronautical University: Prescott Campus
GateWay Community College
Grand Canyon University
Northern Arizona University
Pima Community College
Prescott College
Rio Salado College
University of Advancing Technology
University of Arizona
Western International University

Arkansas
Arkansas Baptist College
Arkansas Northeastern College
Arkansas State University
Arkansas State University
  Beebe
Arkansas Tech University
Ecclesia College
Harding University

Hendrix College
John Brown University
Lyon College
National Park Community College
Northwest Arkansas Community College
Ouachita Baptist University
Pulaski Technical College
Southern Arkansas University
Southern Arkansas University Tech
University of Arkansas
University of Arkansas
  Community College at Hope
  Cossatot Community College of the Fort Smith
  Little Rock
  Monticello
  Pine Bluff
University of Central Arkansas
University of the Ozarks
Williams Baptist College

California
Allan Hancock College
American Jewish University
Antelope Valley College
Antioch Southern California
  Antioch University Los Angeles
  Antioch University Santa Barbara
Azusa Pacific University
Bakersfield College
Barstow Community College
Bethany University
Biola University
Brooks Institute
Butte College
California Baptist University
California College of the Arts
California Institute of Technology
California Lutheran University
California Maritime Academy
California Polytechnic State University: San Luis Obispo
California State Polytechnic University: Pomona
California State University
  Bakersfield
  Chico
  Dominguez Hills
  East Bay
  Fresno
  Fullerton
  Long Beach
  Los Angeles
  Monterey Bay
  Northridge
  Sacramento
  San Bernardino
  San Marcos
  Stanislaus
California State University: Channel Islands
Canada College
Cerro Coso Community College
Chabot College
Chapman University
Charles Drew University of Medicine and Science
Citrus College
Claremont McKenna College
Cogswell Polytechnical College
Coleman University
College of San Mateo
College of the Desert
College of the Redwoods
Columbia College
Concordia University
Cosumnes River College
Crafton Hills College
Cuesta College
Cuyamaca College
Dominican University of California
East Los Angeles College
El Camino College

Empire College
Evergreen Valley College
Feather River College
Fresno City College
Fresno Pacific University
Fullerton College
Golden West College
Grossmont College
Harvey Mudd College
Holy Names University
Hope International University
Humboldt State University
Humphreys College
Imperial Valley College
Irvine Valley College
La Sierra University
Laguna College of Art and Design
Lake Tahoe Community College
Lincoln University
Loma Linda University
Los Angeles Harbor College
Los Angeles Southwest College
Loyola Marymount University
The Master's College
Mendocino College
Menlo College
Mills College
MiraCosta College
Modesto Junior College
Monterey Peninsula College
Mount St. Mary's College
Mount San Jacinto College
Napa Valley College
National University
NewSchool of Architecture & Design
Notre Dame de Namur University
Occidental College
Ohlone College
Pacific States University
Pacific Union College
Patten University
Pepperdine University
Pitzer College
Point Loma Nazarene University
Pomona College
Porterville College
Reedley College
Riverside Community College
Sacramento City College
Saddleback College
St. Mary's College of California
San Bernardino Valley College
San Diego Christian College
San Diego City College
San Diego Mesa College
San Diego State University
San Francisco Art Institute
San Francisco State University
San Jose State University
Santa Ana College
Santa Barbara City College
Santa Clara University
Santa Rosa Junior College
Santiago Canyon College
Scripps College
Shasta College
Sierra College
Simpson University
Skyline College
Solano Community College
Sonoma State University
Southern California Institute of Technology
Southwestern College
Stanford University
Taft College
University of California
  Berkeley
  Davis
  Irvine
  Los Angeles
  Riverside
  San Diego

  Santa Barbara
  Santa Cruz
University of California: Merced
University of La Verne
University of Redlands
University of San Diego
University of San Francisco
University of Southern California
University of the Pacific
Vanguard University of Southern California
Victor Valley College
West Valley College
Westmont College
Whittier College
William Jessup University
Woodbury University

Colorado
Adams State College
Aims Community College
Arapahoe Community College
Colorado Christian University
Colorado College
Colorado Heights University
Colorado School of Mines
Colorado State University
Colorado State University
  Pueblo
Colorado Technical University
Community College of Denver
Fort Lewis College
Front Range Community College
Mesa State College
Metropolitan State College of Denver
Morgan Community College
Naropa University
Nazarene Bible College
Northeastern Junior College
Pikes Peak Community College
Pueblo Community College
Regis University
Rocky Mountain College of Art & Design
Trinidad State Junior College
United States Air Force Academy
University of Colorado
  Boulder
  Colorado Springs
  Denver
University of Denver
University of Northern Colorado
Western State College of Colorado

Connecticut
Albertus Magnus College
Asnuntuck Community College
Capital Community College
Central Connecticut State University
Connecticut College
Eastern Connecticut State University
Fairfield University
Goodwin College
Housatonic Community College
Lincoln College of New England: Briarwood
Manchester Community College
Naugatuck Valley Community College
Northwestern Connecticut Community College
Norwalk Community College
Post University
Quinebaug Valley Community College
Quinnipiac University
Sacred Heart University
Saint Joseph College
Southern Connecticut State University
Three Rivers Community College
Trinity College
Tunxis Community College
United States Coast Guard Academy
University of Bridgeport
University of Connecticut
University of Hartford

University of New Haven
Wesleyan University
Yale University

Delaware

Delaware State University
Delaware Technical and Community
  College
  Owens
  Stanton/Wilmington
  Terry
Goldey-Beacom College
University of Delaware
Wesley College
Wilmington University

District of Columbia

American University
Catholic University of America
Gallaudet University
George Washington University
Georgetown University
Howard University
Trinity Washington University
University of the District of Columbia

Florida

Angley College
Ave Maria University
Baptist College of Florida
Barry University
Beacon College
Bethune-Cookman University
Brevard Community College
Brown Mackie College: Miami
Carlos Albizu University
Clearwater Christian College
Eckerd College
Edison State College
Edward Waters College
Embry-Riddle Aeronautical University
Flagler College
Florida Agricultural and Mechanical
  University
Florida Atlantic University
Florida College
Florida Gulf Coast University
Florida Institute of Technology
Florida International University
Florida Keys Community College
Florida Memorial University
Florida Southern College
Florida State College at Jacksonville
Florida State University
Hillsborough Community College
Hobe Sound Bible College
Hodges University
Jacksonville University
Jones College
Lynn University
New College of Florida
Northwood University
  Florida
Nova Southeastern University
Palm Beach Atlantic University
Palm Beach Community College
Pasco-Hernando Community College
Pensacola Junior College
Polk State College
Rasmussen College: Ocala
Rasmussen College: Pasco County
Rollins College
Saint Leo University
Saint Thomas University
Schiller International University
South Florida Community College
Southeastern University
Southwest Florida College
Stetson University
Tallahassee Community College
Trinity College of Florida
University of Central Florida
University of Florida
University of Miami

University of North Florida
University of South Florida
University of Tampa
University of West Florida
Valencia Community College
Warner University
Webber International University

Georgia

Abraham Baldwin Agricultural College
Agnes Scott College
Albany State University
American InterContinental University
Andrew College
Armstrong Atlantic State University
Atlanta Christian College
Augusta State University
Bainbridge College
Berry College
Beulah Heights University
Brenau University
Brewton-Parker College
Clark Atlanta University
Clayton State University
Columbus State University
Covenant College
Dalton State College
Darton College
East Georgia College
Emory University
Fort Valley State University
Georgia College and State University
Georgia Highlands College
Georgia Institute of Technology
Georgia Military College
Georgia Perimeter College
Georgia Southern University
Georgia Southwestern State
  University
Georgia State University
Gwinnett College
Kennesaw State University
LaGrange College
Life University
Mercer University
Middle Georgia College
Morehouse College
North Georgia College & State
  University
Oglethorpe University
Oxford College of Emory University
Piedmont College
Reinhardt College
Savannah College of Art and Design
Savannah State University
Shorter College
Southern Polytechnic State University
Spelman College
Toccoa Falls College
Truett-McConnell College
University of Georgia
University of West Georgia
Valdosta State University
Wesleyan College

Hawaii

Chaminade University of Honolulu
Hawaii Pacific University
University of Hawaii
  Hawaii Community College
  Hilo
  Kapiolani Community College
  Manoa
  Maui Community College
  West Oahu
  Windward Community College

Idaho

Boise Bible College
Boise State University
Brigham Young University-Idaho
College of Idaho
Idaho State University
Northwest Nazarene University

University of Idaho

Illinois

Augustana College
Aurora University
Benedictine University
Black Hawk College: East Campus
Blackburn College
Bradley University
Chicago State University
City Colleges of Chicago
  Harold Washington College
College of DuPage
Concordia University Chicago
Danville Area Community College
DePaul University
Dominican University
East-West University
Eastern Illinois University
Elgin Community College
Elmhurst College
Eureka College
Governors State University
Greenville College
Heartland Community College
Illinois College
Illinois Eastern Community Colleges
  Frontier Community College
  Lincoln Trail College
  Olney Central College
  Wabash Valley College
Illinois Institute of Technology
Illinois State University
Illinois Wesleyan University
John A. Logan College
Judson University
Kaskaskia College
Kishwaukee College
Knox College
Lake Forest College
Lewis University
Lewis and Clark Community College
Lincoln Christian University
Lincoln Land Community College
Loyola University Chicago
MacMurray College
McKendree University
Midstate College
Millikin University
Monmouth College
Moody Bible Institute
Moraine Valley Community College
Morrison Institute of Technology
Morton College
National-Louis University
North Central College
North Park University
Northeastern Illinois University
Northern Illinois University
Northwestern College
Northwestern University
Olivet Nazarene University
Parkland College
Principia College
Quincy University
Richland Community College
Rockford College
Roosevelt University
St. Augustine College
Saint Xavier University
School of the Art Institute of Chicago
Shimer College
South Suburban College of Cook
  County
Southeastern Illinois College
Southern Illinois University
  Carbondale
Southern Illinois University
  Edwardsville
Southwestern Illinois College
Trinity Christian College
Trinity International University
University of Chicago

University of Illinois
  Chicago
  Springfield
  Urbana-Champaign
University of St. Francis
Western Illinois University
Wheaton College

Indiana

Ancilla College
Anderson University
Ball State University
Bethel College
Brown Mackie College: South Bend
Butler University
Calumet College of St. Joseph
DePauw University
Earlham College
Franklin College
Goshen College
Grace College
Hanover College
Huntington University
Indiana Institute of Technology
Indiana State University
Indiana University
  Bloomington
  East
  Kokomo
  Northwest
  South Bend
  Southeast
Indiana University-Purdue University
  Fort Wayne
Indiana University-Purdue University
  Indianapolis
Indiana Wesleyan University
Manchester College
Marian University
Oakland City University
Purdue University
Purdue University
  Calumet
Rose-Hulman Institute of Technology
Saint Joseph's College
Saint Mary's College
St. Mary-of-the-Woods College
Taylor University
Trine University
University of Evansville
University of Indianapolis
University of Notre Dame
University of St. Francis
University of Southern Indiana
Valparaiso University
Wabash College

Iowa

AIB College of Business
Briar Cliff University
Buena Vista University
Central College
Clarke College
Clinton Community College
Coe College
Cornell College
Divine Word College
Dordt College
Drake University
Ellsworth Community College
Emmaus Bible College
Graceland University
Grand View University
Grinnell College
Iowa State University
Iowa Wesleyan College
Kaplan University
  Davenport
Loras College
Luther College
Maharishi University of Management
Morningside College
Mount Mercy College
Muscatine Community College

Northeast Iowa Community College
Northwestern College
St. Ambrose University
Scott Community College
Simpson College
Southwestern Community College
University of Dubuque
University of Iowa
University of Northern Iowa
Upper Iowa University
Waldorf College
Wartburg College
Western Iowa Tech Community
College
William Penn University

Kansas

Allen County Community College
Baker University
Barclay College
Benedictine College
Bethany College
Bethel College
Central Christian College of Kansas
Coffeyville Community College
Cowley County Community College
Dodge City Community College
Emporia State University
Fort Hays State University
Friends University
Highland Community College
Hutchinson Community College
Johnson County Community College
Kansas State University
Kansas Wesleyan University
McPherson College
MidAmerica Nazarene University
Newman University
Ottawa University
Pittsburg State University
Seward County Community College
Southwestern College
Sterling College
Tabor College
University of Kansas
University of St. Mary
Washburn University
Wichita State University

Kentucky

Alice Lloyd College
Asbury College
Bellarmine University
Berea College
Bluegrass Community and Technical
College
Brescia University
Campbellsville University
Centre College
Clear Creek Baptist Bible College
Daymar College
Owensboro
Draughons Junior College
Eastern Kentucky University
Georgetown College
Henderson Community College
Kentucky Christian University
Kentucky State University
Kentucky Wesleyan College
Madisonville Community College
Maysville Community and Technical
College
Mid-Continent University
Midway College
Morehead State University
Murray State University
National College
Danville
Florence
Lexington
Pikeville
Richmond
Northern Kentucky University

Owensboro Community and
Technical College
Pikeville College
Spalding University
Spencerian College: Lexington
Sullivan College of Technology and
Design
Sullivan University
Thomas More College
Transylvania University
Union College
University of Kentucky
University of Louisville
University of the Cumberlands
Western Kentucky University

Louisiana

Baton Rouge Community College
Bossier Parish Community College
Centenary College of Louisiana
Delgado Community College
Dillard University
Grambling State University
Louisiana College
Louisiana State University
Shreveport
Louisiana State University Health
Sciences Center
Louisiana State University and
Agricultural and Mechanical
College
Louisiana Tech University
Loyola University New Orleans
McNeese State University
Northwestern State University
Nunez Community College
South Louisiana Community College
Southeastern Louisiana University
Southern University
New Orleans
Southern University and Agricultural
and Mechanical College
Southwest University
Tulane University
University of Louisiana at Lafayette
University of Louisiana at Monroe
University of New Orleans
Xavier University of Louisiana

Maine

Andover College
Bates College
Beal College
Bowdoin College
Colby College
Husson University
Maine College of Art
Maine Maritime Academy
New England School of
Communications
Northern Maine Community College
Saint Joseph's College of Maine
Southern Maine Community College
Thomas College
Unity College
University of Maine
University of Maine
Augusta
Farmington
Fort Kent
Machias
Presque Isle
University of New England
University of Southern Maine
Washington County Community
College

Maryland

Allegany College of Maryland
Anne Arundel Community College
Baltimore City Community College
Baltimore International College
Bowie State University
Capitol College

Cecil College
College of Notre Dame of Maryland
Coppin State University
Frostburg State University
Garrett College
Goucher College
Hagerstown Community College
Harford Community College
Hood College
Johns Hopkins University
Johns Hopkins University: Peabody
Conservatory of Music
Kaplan College: Hagerstown
Loyola University Maryland
Maryland Institute College of Art
McDaniel College
Montgomery College
Morgan State University
Mount St. Mary's University
Prince George's Community College
St. Mary's College of Maryland
Salisbury University
Stevenson University
Towson University
United States Naval Academy
University of Maryland
Baltimore
Baltimore County
College Park
Eastern Shore
University College
Washington Adventist University
Washington Bible College
Washington College
Wor-Wic Community College

Massachusetts

American International College
Amherst College
Anna Maria College
Art Institute of Boston at Lesley
University
Assumption College
Atlantic Union College
Bay Path College
Benjamin Franklin Institute of
Technology
Bentley University
Berklee College of Music
Berkshire Community College
Boston College
Boston Conservatory
Boston University
Brandeis University
Bridgewater State College
Bunker Hill Community College
Cambridge College
Clark University
College of the Holy Cross
Curry College
Eastern Nazarene College
Elms College
Emerson College
Emmanuel College
Fisher College
Fitchburg State College
Framingham State College
Gordon College
Greenfield Community College
Harvard College
Holyoke Community College
Lasell College
Lesley University
Marian Court College
Massachusetts College of Art and
Design
Massachusetts College of Liberal Arts
Massachusetts College of Pharmacy
and Health Sciences
Massachusetts Institute of Technology
Massachusetts Maritime Academy
Merrimack College
Montserrat College of Art
Mount Holyoke College

Mount Ida College
Mount Wachusett Community College
Newbury College
Nichols College
North Shore Community College
Northeastern University
Northern Essex Community College
Pine Manor College
Quinsigamond Community College
Regis College
Roxbury Community College
Salem State College
School of the Museum of Fine Arts
Simmons College
Smith College
Springfield College
Stonehill College
Suffolk University
Tufts University
University of Massachusetts
Amherst
Boston
Dartmouth
Lowell
Wellesley College
Western New England College
Westfield State College
Wheaton College
Wheelock College
Williams College
Worcester Polytechnic Institute
Worcester State College

Michigan

Adrian College
Albion College
Alma College
Alpena Community College
Andrews University
Aquinas College
Baker College
of Auburn Hills
of Cadillac
of Clinton Township
of Flint
of Jackson
of Muskegon
of Owosso
of Port Huron
Baker College of Allen Park
Bay Mills Community College
Calvin College
Central Michigan University
Cleary University
College for Creative Studies
Cornerstone University
Delta College
Eastern Michigan University
Ferris State University
Finlandia University
Glen Oaks Community College
Gogebic Community College
Grace Bible College
Grand Valley State University
Great Lakes Christian College
Henry Ford Community College
Hillsdale College
Hope College
Kalamazoo College
Kellogg Community College
Kendall College of Art and Design of
Ferris State University
Kettering University
Kuyper College
Lake Michigan College
Lake Superior State University
Lansing Community College
Lawrence Technological University
Madonna University
Marygrove College
Michigan Jewish Institute
Michigan State University
Michigan Technological University
Mid Michigan Community College

Mott Community College
Muskegon Community College
Northern Michigan University
Northwood University: Michigan
Oakland University
Rochester College
Sacred Heart Major Seminary
Saginaw Valley State University
St. Clair County Community College
Schoolcraft College
Siena Heights University
Southwestern Michigan College
Spring Arbor University
University of Detroit Mercy
University of Michigan
University of Michigan
    Dearborn
    Flint
Walsh College of Accountancy and
    Business Administration
Wayne County Community College
Wayne State University
Western Michigan University

Minnesota
Alexandria Technical College
Augsburg College
Bemidji State University
Bethany Lutheran College
Bethel University
Carleton College
College of St. Benedict
College of St. Scholastica
Concordia College: Moorhead
Concordia University: St. Paul
Crossroads College
Crown College
Dakota County Technical College
Dunwoody College of Technology
Gustavus Adolphus College
Hamline University
Inver Hills Community College
Lake Superior College
Leech Lake Tribal College
Macalester College
Martin Luther College
Metropolitan State University
Minnesota State College - Southeast
    Technical
Minnesota State University
    Mankato
    Moorhead
Minnesota West Community and
    Technical College
National American University
    Bloomington
Normandale Community College
North Central University
North Hennepin Community College
Northland Community & Technical
    College
Northwest Technical College
Northwestern College
Oak Hills Christian College
Pine Technical College
Rasmussen College
    Eagan
    Eden Prairie
    Mankato
    St. Cloud
Rasmussen College: Brooklyn Park
Riverland Community College
St. Catherine University
Saint Cloud State University
St. Cloud Technical College
St. John's University
St. Mary's University of Minnesota
St. Olaf College
Southwest Minnesota State University
University of Minnesota
    Crookston
    Duluth
    Morris
    Twin Cities

University of St. Thomas
Winona State University

Mississippi
Alcorn State University
Antonelli College
    Jackson
Belhaven University
Blue Mountain College
Delta State University
Hinds Community College
Jackson State University
Jones County Junior College
Millsaps College
Mississippi College
Mississippi State University
Mississippi University for Women
Mississippi Valley State University
Rust College
Tougaloo College
University of Mississippi
University of Southern Mississippi
Wesley College

Missouri
Avila University
Calvary Bible College and Theological
    Seminary
Central Bible College
Central Methodist University
College of the Ozarks
Columbia College
Culver-Stockton College
Drury University
Evangel University
Fontbonne University
Hannibal-LaGrange College
Jefferson College
Kansas City Art Institute
Lincoln University
Lindenwood University
Maryville University of Saint Louis
Missouri Baptist University
Missouri Southern State University
Missouri State University
Missouri Technical School
Missouri Valley College
Missouri Western State University
North Central Missouri College
Northwest Missouri State University
Ozark Christian College
Park University
Patricia Stevens College
Ranken Technical College
Research College of Nursing
Rockhurst University
St. Charles Community College
Saint Louis University
Southeast Missouri State University
Southwest Baptist University
Stephens College
Truman State University
University of Central Missouri
University of Missouri
    Columbia
    Kansas City
    Missouri University of Science and
        Technology
    St. Louis
Washington University in St. Louis
Webster University
Westminster College
William Jewell College
William Woods University

Montana
Chief Dull Knife College
Dawson Community College
Fort Peck Community College
Montana State University
    Billings
    Bozeman
    College of Technology: Great Falls

Montana Tech of the University of
    Montana
Rocky Mountain College
Salish Kootenai College
Stone Child College
University of Great Falls
University of Montana
University of Montana: Western

Nebraska
Bellevue University
Central Community College
Chadron State College
Clarkson College
College of Saint Mary
Concordia University
Creighton University
Dana College
Doane College
Grace University
Kaplan University: Omaha
Metropolitan Community College
Nebraska Christian College
Nebraska College of Technical
    Agriculture
Nebraska Indian Community College
Nebraska Wesleyan University
Peru State College
Union College
University of Nebraska
    Kearney
    Lincoln
    Omaha
Wayne State College
Western Nebraska Community
    College
York College

Nevada
College of Southern Nevada
Nevada State College
Sierra Nevada College
University of Nevada
    Las Vegas
    Reno
Western Nevada College

New Hampshire
Chester College of New England
Colby-Sawyer College
Daniel Webster College
Dartmouth College
Franklin Pierce University
Granite State College
Keene State College
Lakes Region Community College
Manchester Community College
NHTI-Concord's Community College
Nashua Community College
New England College
Plymouth State University
River Valley Community College
Rivier College
Southern New Hampshire University
University of New Hampshire
University of New Hampshire at
    Manchester
White Mountains Community College

New Jersey
Atlantic Cape Community College
Bloomfield College
Burlington County College
Caldwell College
Centenary College
The College of New Jersey
College of St. Elizabeth
County College of Morris
Cumberland County College
Drew University
Essex County College
Fairleigh Dickinson University
    College at Florham

Felician College
Georgian Court University
Kean University
Mercer County Community College
Middlesex County College
Monmouth University
Montclair State University
New Jersey City University
New Jersey Institute of Technology
Passaic County Community College
Ramapo College of New Jersey
Raritan Valley Community College
Richard Stockton College of New
    Jersey
Rider University
Rowan University
Rutgers, The State University of New
    Jersey
    Camden Regional Campus
    New Brunswick/Piscataway
        Campus
    Newark Regional Campus
Saint Peter's College
Salem Community College
Seton Hall University
Stevens Institute of Technology
Sussex County Community College
University of Medicine and Dentistry
    of New Jersey
    School of Health Related
        Professions
    School of Nursing
Warren County Community College
William Paterson University of New
    Jersey

New Mexico
Art Center Design College
Central New Mexico Community
    College
Clovis Community College
College of Santa Fe
Dona Ana Community College of New
    Mexico State University
Eastern New Mexico University
Institute of American Indian Arts
Navajo Technical College
New Mexico Highlands University
New Mexico Institute of Mining and
    Technology
New Mexico State University
New Mexico State University
    Alamogordo
    Carlsbad
    Grants
Northern New Mexico College
Santa Fe Community College
Southwestern Indian Polytechnic
    Institute
University of New Mexico
University of the Southwest
Western New Mexico University

New York
Adelphi University
Adirondack Community College
Alfred University
Bard College
Barnard College
Bramson ORT College
Bryant & Stratton Business Institute
    Bryant & Stratton College: Albany
    Bryant & Stratton College:
        Rochester
    Bryant & Stratton College:
        Southtowns
Canisius College
Cayuga County Community College
Cazenovia College
City University of New York
    Baruch College
    Borough of Manhattan Community
        College
    Bronx Community College

Brooklyn College
City College
College of Staten Island
Hunter College
Lehman College
Queens College
York College
Clarkson University
Colgate University
College of Mount St. Vincent
College of New Rochelle
College of Saint Rose
College of Westchester
Columbia University
Columbia University
  School of General Studies
Concordia College
Cornell University
Corning Community College
D'Youville College
Daemen College
Dowling College
Eastman School of Music of the
  University of Rochester
Elmira College
Erie Community College
  City Campus
  North Campus
  South Campus
Eugene Lang College The New School
  for Liberal Arts
Finger Lakes Community College
Fordham University
Fulton-Montgomery Community
  College
Genesee Community College
Hamilton College
Hartwick College
Hobart and William Smith Colleges
Hofstra University
Houghton College
Hudson Valley Community College
Institute of Design and Construction
Iona College
Ithaca College
Jefferson Community College
Jewish Theological Seminary of
  America
Keuka College
Le Moyne College
Long Island University
  Brooklyn Campus
  C. W. Post Campus
Manhattan College
Manhattanville College
Mannes College The New School for
  Music
Marist College
Marymount Manhattan College
Medaille College
Mercy College
Mildred Elley
Mohawk Valley Community College
Molloy College
Mount Saint Mary College
Nazareth College
New York Institute of Technology
New York University
Niagara County Community College
Niagara University
North Country Community College
Nyack College
Onondaga Community College
Pace University
Parsons The New School for Design
Paul Smith's College
Polytechnic Institute of New York
  University
Rensselaer Polytechnic Institute
Roberts Wesleyan College
Rochester Institute of Technology
Rockland Community College
Russell Sage College
Sage College of Albany

Saint Bonaventure University
St. Francis College
St. John Fisher College
St. John's University
St. Lawrence University
St. Thomas Aquinas College
Sarah Lawrence College
Siena College
Skidmore College
State University of New York
  Albany
  Binghamton
  Buffalo
  College at Brockport
  College at Buffalo
  College at Cortland
  College at Fredonia
  College at Geneseo
  College at Old Westbury
  College at Oneonta
  College at Plattsburgh
  College at Potsdam
  College of Agriculture and
    Technology at Morrisville
  College of Technology at Delhi
  Empire State College
  Farmingdale
  Institute of Technology at
    Utica/Rome
  Maritime College
  New Paltz
  Oswego
  Purchase
  Stony Brook
Syracuse University
Ulster County Community College
Union College
United States Military Academy
University of Rochester
Utica College
Vassar College
Vaughn College of Aeronautics and
  Technology
Villa Maria College of Buffalo
Wagner College
Webb Institute
Wells College
Westchester Community College
Yeshiva Shaar Hatorah
Yeshiva University

North Carolina
Alamance Community College
Appalachian State University
Asheville-Buncombe Technical
  Community College
Barton College
Belmont Abbey College
Bennett College for Women
Bladen Community College
Blue Ridge Community College
Brevard College
Brunswick Community College
Campbell University
Carteret Community College
Catawba College
Catawba Valley Community College
Central Piedmont Community College
Chowan University
Cleveland Community College
College of the Albemarle
Davidson College
Duke University
East Carolina University
Edgecombe Community College
Elizabeth City State University
Elon University
Fayetteville State University
Fayetteville Technical Community
  College
Forsyth Technical Community College
Gardner-Webb University
Gaston College
Greensboro College

Guilford College
Guilford Technical Community
  College
High Point University
James Sprunt Community College
John Wesley College
Johnson C. Smith University
Johnston Community College
Lees-McRae College
Lenoir-Rhyne University
Livingstone College
Mars Hill College
Martin Community College
Mayland Community College
McDowell Technical Community
  College
Meredith College
Methodist University
Mid-Atlantic Christian University
Miller-Motte Technical College
Montgomery Community College
Montreat College
Mount Olive College
North Carolina Agricultural and
  Technical State University
North Carolina Central University
North Carolina State University
North Carolina Wesleyan College
Peace College
Pfeiffer University
Piedmont Baptist College
Piedmont Community College
Pitt Community College
Queens University of Charlotte
Randolph Community College
Richmond Community College
Robeson Community College
St. Andrews Presbyterian College
St. Augustine's College
Salem College
Sandhills Community College
Shaw University
South College
Southeastern Community College
Southwestern Community College
Surry Community College
Tri-County Community College
University of North Carolina
  Asheville
  Chapel Hill
  Charlotte
  Greensboro
  Pembroke
  Wilmington
Vance-Granville Community College
Wake Forest University
Wake Technical Community College
Warren Wilson College
Wayne Community College
Western Carolina University
Wilkes Community College
Wilson Community College
Wingate University
Winston-Salem State University

North Dakota
Dakota College at Bottineau
Dickinson State University
Jamestown College
Mayville State University
Minot State University
North Dakota State University
Rasmussen College: Bismarck
Rasmussen College: Fargo
Trinity Bible College
University of Mary
University of North Dakota
Williston State College

Ohio
Allegheny Wesleyan College
Antioch University McGregor
Art Academy of Cincinnati
Ashland University

Baldwin-Wallace College
Belmont Technical College
Bluffton University
Bowling Green State University
Bryant & Stratton College
  Eastlake
Bryant & Stratton College: Cleveland
Capital University
Case Western Reserve University
Cedarville University
Central Ohio Technical College
Central State University
Cincinnati Christian University
Cincinnati State Technical and
  Community College
Clark State Community College
Cleveland Institute of Art
Cleveland Institute of Music
Cleveland State University
College of Mount St. Joseph
College of Wooster
Columbus College of Art and Design
Columbus State Community College
Defiance College
Denison University
Eastern Gateway Community College
Edison State Community College
Franciscan University of Steubenville
Franklin University
Gallipolis Career College
God's Bible School and College
Heidelberg University
Hiram College
Hocking College
James A. Rhodes State College
John Carroll University
Kaplan College: Dayton
Kent State University
Kent State University
  Ashtabula
  East Liverpool
  Salem
  Stark
  Trumbull
  Tuscarawas
Kent State University: Geauga
Kenyon College
Kettering College of Medical Arts
Lourdes College
Malone University
Marietta College
Marion Technical College
Mercy College of Northwest Ohio
Miami University
  Hamilton Campus
  Oxford Campus
Mount Union College
Mount Vernon Nazarene University
Muskingum University
Notre Dame College
Oberlin College
Ohio Business College: Sandusky
Ohio Christian University
Ohio Dominican University
Ohio Northern University
Ohio State University
  Agricultural Technical Institute
  Columbus Campus
  Lima Campus
  Mansfield Campus
  Marion Campus
  Newark Campus
Ohio University
Ohio University
  Southern Campus at Ironton
  Zanesville Campus
Ohio Valley College of Technology
Ohio Wesleyan University
Otterbein College
Owens Community College
  Toledo
Pontifical College Josephinum
Rosedale Bible College
Shawnee State University

Stark State College of Technology
Terra State Community College
Tiffin University
University of Akron
University of Cincinnati
University of Cincinnati
  Clermont College
  Raymond Walters College
University of Dayton
University of Findlay
University of Northwestern Ohio
University of Rio Grande
University of Toledo
Urbana University
Ursuline College
Walsh University
Washington State Community College
Wilmington College
Wittenberg University
Wright State University
Wright State University: Lake Campus
Xavier University
Youngstown State University

Oklahoma
Bacone College
Cameron University
East Central University
Hillsdale Free Will Baptist College
Langston University
Mid-America Christian University
Northeastern Oklahoma Agricultural
  and Mechanical College
Northeastern State University
Northwestern Oklahoma State
  University
Oklahoma Baptist University
Oklahoma Christian University
Oklahoma City Community College
Oklahoma City University
Oklahoma Panhandle State University
Oklahoma State University
Oklahoma State University
  Institute of Technology: Okmulgee
  Oklahoma City
Oklahoma Wesleyan University
Oral Roberts University
Redlands Community College
Rose State College
St. Gregory's University
Southeastern Oklahoma State
  University
Southern Nazarene University
Southwestern Christian University
Southwestern Oklahoma State
  University
University of Central Oklahoma
University of Oklahoma
University of Science and Arts of
  Oklahoma
University of Tulsa

Oregon
Blue Mountain Community College
Central Oregon Community College
Chemeketa Community College
Clackamas Community College
Clatsop Community College
Concordia University
Corban College
Eastern Oregon University
Eugene Bible College
George Fox University
Lane Community College
Lewis & Clark College
Linfield College
Marylhurst University
Mount Angel Seminary
Mt. Hood Community College
Multnomah University
Northwest Christian University
Oregon Institute of Technology
Oregon State University
Pacific University

Portland Community College
Portland State University
Reed College
Rogue Community College
Southern Oregon University
Southwestern Oregon Community
  College
Umpqua Community College
University of Oregon
University of Portland
Warner Pacific College
Western Oregon University
Willamette University

Pennsylvania
Albright College
Allegheny College
Alvernia University
Arcadia University
Baptist Bible College of Pennsylvania
Bloomsburg University of
  Pennsylvania
Bryn Mawr College
Bucknell University
Cabrini College
California University of Pennsylvania
Cambria-Rowe Business College:
  Indiana
Carlow University
Carnegie Mellon University
Cedar Crest College
Central Pennsylvania College
Chatham University
Chestnut Hill College
Cheyney University of Pennsylvania
Clarion University of Pennsylvania
Community College of Beaver County
Curtis Institute of Music
DeSales University
Delaware Valley College
Dickinson College
Douglas Education Center
Drexel University
Duquesne University
East Stroudsburg University of
  Pennsylvania
Eastern University
Edinboro University of Pennsylvania
Elizabethtown College
Franklin & Marshall College
Gannon University
Geneva College
Gettysburg College
Grove City College
Gwynedd-Mercy College
Harcum College
Harrisburg Area Community College
Haverford College
Holy Family University
Immaculata University
Indiana University of Pennsylvania
Juniata College
Kaplan Career Institute: Pittsburgh
Keystone College
King's College
Kutztown University of Pennsylvania
La Roche College
La Salle University
Lackawanna College
Lafayette College
Lancaster Bible College
Laurel Business Institute
Lebanon Valley College
Lehigh University
Lock Haven University of
  Pennsylvania
Lycoming College
Manor College
Mansfield University of Pennsylvania
Marywood University
Mercyhurst College
Messiah College
Millersville University of Pennsylvania
Misericordia University

Moore College of Art and Design
Moravian College
Muhlenberg College
Neumann University
PJA School
Penn State
  Abington
  Altoona
  Beaver
  Brandywine
  DuBois
  Erie, The Behrend College
  Fayette, The Eberly Campus
  Greater Allegheny
  Harrisburg
  Hazleton
  Mont Alto
  New Kensington
  Schuylkill
  Shenango
  University Park
  Wilkes-Barre
  Worthington Scranton
  York
Pennsylvania Institute of Technology
Philadelphia Biblical University
Philadelphia University
Point Park University
Robert Morris University
Rosemont College
St. Francis University
Saint Joseph's University
St. Vincent College
Seton Hill University
Shippensburg University of
  Pennsylvania
Slippery Rock University of
  Pennsylvania
South Hills School of Business &
  Technology
Susquehanna University
Swarthmore College
Temple University
Thiel College
University of Pennsylvania
University of Pittsburgh
University of Pittsburgh
  Bradford
  Greensburg
  Johnstown
University of Scranton
University of the Arts
University of the Sciences in
  Philadelphia
Ursinus College
Villanova University
Washington & Jefferson College
Waynesburg University
West Chester University of
  Pennsylvania
Westminster College
Westmoreland County Community
  College
Widener University
Wilkes University
Wilson College
York College of Pennsylvania

Puerto Rico
Bayamon Central University
Inter American University of Puerto
  Rico
  Fajardo Campus
  San German Campus
Pontifical Catholic University of
  Puerto Rico
Universidad Adventista de las Antillas
University College of San Juan
University of Puerto Rico
  Bayamon University College
  Rio Piedras
University of the Sacred Heart

Rhode Island
Brown University
Bryant University
Community College of Rhode Island
New England Institute of Technology
Providence College
Rhode Island College
Rhode Island School of Design
Roger Williams University
Salve Regina University
University of Rhode Island

South Carolina
Aiken Technical College
Anderson University
Benedict College
Charleston Southern University
The Citadel
Claflin University
Clemson University
Coastal Carolina University
Coker College
College of Charleston
Columbia College
Columbia International University
Converse College
Erskine College
Florence-Darlington Technical College
Forrest Junior College
Francis Marion University
Furman University
Horry-Georgetown Technical College
Lander University
Limestone College
Morris College
Newberry College
North Greenville University
Orangeburg-Calhoun Technical
  College
Presbyterian College
South Carolina State University
Southern Wesleyan University
Spartanburg Community College
Technical College of the Lowcountry
Trident Technical College
University of South Carolina
University of South Carolina
  Aiken
  Upstate
Williamsburg Technical College
Winthrop University
Wofford College

South Dakota
Augustana College
Black Hills State University
Dakota State University
Dakota Wesleyan University
Kilian Community College
Mount Marty College
National American University
  Rapid City
Northern State University
Oglala Lakota College
Presentation College
Sinte Gleska University
Sisseton Wahpeton College
South Dakota State University
Southeast Technical Institute
University of Sioux Falls
University of South Dakota

Tennessee
American Baptist College
Aquinas College
Austin Peay State University
Belmont University
Bethel University
Bryan College
Carson-Newman College
Chattanooga State Community
  College
Christian Brothers University

Cleveland State Community College
Crichton College
Cumberland University
East Tennessee State University
Fisk University
Free Will Baptist Bible College
Freed-Hardeman University
Jackson State Community College
Johnson Bible College
King College
Lambuth University
LeMoyne-Owen College
Lee University
Lincoln Memorial University
Lipscomb University
Maryville College
Memphis College of Art
Middle Tennessee State University
Milligan College
Motlow State Community College
Nashville State Community College
National College of Business & Technology
  National College: Bristol
Northeast State Community College
Pellissippi State Community College
Rhodes College
Roane State Community College
South College
Southern Adventist University
Southwest Tennessee Community College
Tennessee State University
Tennessee Technological University
Tennessee Temple University
Tennessee Wesleyan College
Trevecca Nazarene University
Tusculum College
Union University
University of Memphis
University of Tennessee
  Chattanooga
  Knoxville
  Martin
University of Tennessee Health Science Center
University of the South
Vanderbilt University
Volunteer State Community College

Texas

Abilene Christian University
Angelo State University
Arlington Baptist College
Austin College
Baylor University
College of the Mainland
Concordia University Texas
Culinary Institute Alain & Marie LeNotre
Dallas Baptist University
Dallas Christian College
Del Mar College
East Texas Baptist University
El Centro College
El Paso Community College
Hardin-Simmons University
Houston Baptist University
Howard Payne University
Huston-Tillotson University
Jarvis Christian College
Lamar State College at Port Arthur
Lamar University
LeTourneau University
Lone Star College System
Lubbock Christian University
McMurry University
Midwestern State University
Mountain View College
North Lake College
Northwood University: Texas
Our Lady of the Lake University of San Antonio
Prairie View A&M University

Rice University
St. Edward's University
St. Mary's University
St. Philip's College
Sam Houston State University
San Antonio College
San Jacinto College
Schreiner University
South Texas College
Southern Methodist University
Southwestern Adventist University
Southwestern Assemblies of God University
Southwestern University
Stephen F. Austin State University
Tarleton State University
Tarrant County College
Texas A&M International University
Texas A&M University
Texas A&M University
  Commerce
  Corpus Christi
  Galveston
  Kingsville
Texas Christian University
Texas College
Texas Lutheran University
Texas Southern University
Texas State Technical College Waco
Texas State University: San Marcos
Texas Tech University
Texas Wesleyan University
Texas Woman's University
Trinity University
University of Dallas
University of Houston
University of Houston
  Clear Lake
  Victoria
University of Mary Hardin-Baylor
University of North Texas
University of St. Thomas
University of Texas
  Arlington
  Austin
  Brownsville - Texas Southmost College
  Dallas
  El Paso
  Pan American
  San Antonio
  Tyler
  of the Permian Basin
University of the Incarnate Word
Wade College
Wayland Baptist University
West Texas A&M University
Wiley College

Utah

Brigham Young University
College of Eastern Utah
Dixie State College of Utah
Southern Utah University
University of Utah
Utah State University
Utah Valley University
Weber State University
Westminster College

Vermont

Bennington College
Burlington College
Castleton State College
Champlain College
College of St. Joseph in Vermont
Green Mountain College
Johnson State College
Lyndon State College
Marlboro College
Middlebury College
Norwich University
St. Michael's College

Southern Vermont College
Sterling College
University of Vermont
Vermont Technical College

Virginia

Averett University
Blue Ridge Community College
Bluefield College
Bridgewater College
Bryant & Stratton College Richmond
Bryant & Stratton College: Virginia Beach
Christendom College
Christopher Newport University
College of William and Mary
Dabney S. Lancaster Community College
Danville Community College
ECPI College of Technology: Virginia Beach
Eastern Mennonite University
Emory & Henry College
Ferrum College
George Mason University
Germanna Community College
Hampden-Sydney College
Hampton University
Hollins University
J. Sargeant Reynolds Community College
James Madison University
Jefferson College of Health Sciences
Liberty University
Longwood University
Lord Fairfax Community College
Lynchburg College
Mary Baldwin College
Marymount University
Mountain Empire Community College
National College
  Bluefield
  Charlottesville
  Danville
  Harrisonburg
  Lynchburg
  Martinsville
  Roanoke Valley
Norfolk State University
Northern Virginia Community College
Old Dominion University
Patrick Henry Community College
Radford University
Randolph College
Randolph-Macon College
Rappahannock Community College
Regent University
Roanoke College
St. Paul's College
Shenandoah University
Southern Virginia University
Southwest Virginia Community College
Sweet Briar College
Tidewater Community College
University of Mary Washington
University of Richmond
University of Virginia
University of Virginia's College at Wise
Virginia Commonwealth University
Virginia Highlands Community College
Virginia Intermont College
Virginia Military Institute
Virginia Polytechnic Institute and State University
Virginia State University
Virginia Wesleyan College
Washington and Lee University

Washington

Bastyr University

Centralia College
City University of Seattle
Eastern Washington University
Evergreen State College
Gonzaga University
Grays Harbor College
Highline Community College
Northwest College of Art
Northwest University
Pacific Lutheran University
Peninsula College
Pierce College
Saint Martin's University
Seattle Pacific University
Seattle University
University of Puget Sound
University of Washington
University of Washington Bothell
University of Washington Tacoma
Walla Walla University
Washington State University
Wenatchee Valley College
Western Washington University
Whitman College
Whitworth University

West Virginia

Alderson-Broaddus College
Bethany College
Bluefield State College
Concord University
Davis and Elkins College
Eastern West Virginia Community and Technical College
Fairmont State University
Glenville State College
Huntington Junior College
Marshall University
Mountain State College
Mountain State University
Ohio Valley University
Potomac State College of West Virginia University
Salem International University
Shepherd University
University of Charleston
West Liberty University
West Virginia Northern Community College
West Virginia State Community and Technical College
West Virginia State University
West Virginia University
West Virginia University Institute of Technology
West Virginia Wesleyan College
Wheeling Jesuit University

Wisconsin

Alverno College
Beloit College
Cardinal Stritch University
Carroll University
Carthage College
Chippewa Valley Technical College
College of Menominee Nation
Concordia University Wisconsin
Edgewood College
Fox Valley Technical College
Lac Courte Oreilles Ojibwa Community College
Lakeland College
Lakeshore Technical College
Lawrence University
Maranatha Baptist Bible College
Marian University
Marquette University
Mid-State Technical College
Milwaukee Area Technical College
Milwaukee School of Engineering
Moraine Park Technical College
Mount Mary College
Nicolet Area Technical College
Northcentral Technical College

Northeast Wisconsin Technical
    College
Northland College
Ripon College
St. Norbert College
Silver Lake College
Southwest Wisconsin Technical
    College
University of Wisconsin
    Eau Claire
    Green Bay
    La Crosse
    Madison
    Milwaukee
    Oshkosh
    Parkside
    Platteville
    River Falls
    Stevens Point
    Stout
    Superior
    Whitewater
Viterbo University
Waukesha County Technical College
Western Technical College
Wisconsin Indianhead Technical
    College
Wisconsin Lutheran College

Wyoming

Central Wyoming College
Laramie County Community College
Northwest College
Sheridan College
University of Wyoming
WyoTech: Laramie

Alabama

Troy University
University of Alabama

Alaska

Prince William Sound Community
  College
University of Alaska
  Fairbanks

Arizona

GateWay Community College
Penn Foster College
Prescott College
University of Arizona

Arkansas

Pulaski Technical College
Rich Mountain Community College
University of Arkansas
  Fort Smith

California

Bethany University
Bethesda Christian University
California Coast University
California State Polytechnic
  University: Pomona
California State University
  Bakersfield
  Chico
  Dominguez Hills
Hope International University
King's College and Seminary, The
  The King's College and Seminary
Life Pacific College
Pacific Union College
San Diego State University
Sonoma State University
University of San Francisco

Colorado

Adams State College
Colorado State University
Colorado State University
  Pueblo
Community College of Denver
Metropolitan State College of Denver
Pikes Peak Community College
University of Northern Colorado

Connecticut

Charter Oak State College
Eastern Connecticut State University
Southern Connecticut State University

Florida

Flagler College
Florida Southern College
Florida State College at Jacksonville
Hobe Sound Bible College
Northwood University
  Florida
Pasco-Hernando Community College
South Florida Community College
University of Florida

Georgia

Abraham Baldwin Agricultural College
Atlanta Metropolitan College
Brewton-Parker College
Dalton State College
Georgia College and State University
Georgia Military College
North Georgia College & State
  University
Reinhardt College
University of Georgia

University of West Georgia
Valdosta State University

Hawaii

University of Hawaii
  Kapiolani Community College

Idaho

Stevens-Henager College: Boise

Illinois

Eastern Illinois University
Governors State University
Greenville College
McKendree University
Moody Bible Institute
Rock Valley College
Saint Xavier University
Western Illinois University

Indiana

Ball State University
Indiana Institute of Technology
Indiana University
  Bloomington
  East
  Kokomo
  Northwest
  South Bend
  Southeast
Indiana University-Purdue University
  Indianapolis
Oakland City University
St. Mary-of-the-Woods College
University of Evansville
Vincennes University

Iowa

Allen College
Buena Vista University
Hawkeye Community College
Iowa Central Community College
Iowa State University
Kirkwood Community College
Northeast Iowa Community College
University of Iowa
University of Northern Iowa
Upper Iowa University

Kansas

Fort Hays State University
Friends University
Kansas City Kansas Community
  College
Pittsburg State University
Seward County Community College

Kentucky

Murray State University
Somerset Community College
Western Kentucky University

Maine

Eastern Maine Community College

Maryland

Coppin State University
Howard Community College
Salisbury University
University of Maryland
  College Park
  University College
Washington Adventist University

Massachusetts

Atlantic Union College
Bard College at Simon's Rock
Bunker Hill Community College

Michigan

Baker College
  of Cadillac

  of Clinton Township
  of Flint
  of Jackson
  of Muskegon
  of Owosso
  of Port Huron
Eastern Michigan University
Ferris State University
Northwood University: Michigan
Schoolcraft College
Siena Heights University
University of Michigan

Minnesota

Bemidji State University
College of St. Scholastica
Metropolitan State University
Minnesota State University
  Mankato
  Moorhead
Northland Community & Technical
  College
Southwest Minnesota State University
University of Minnesota
  Twin Cities
Winona State University

Mississippi

Mississippi State University

Missouri

Global University
Lindenwood University
Missouri Valley College
Stephens College
University of Missouri
  Columbia

Montana

Montana State University
  Billings
Montana Tech of the University of
  Montana

Nebraska

Clarkson College

New Hampshire

Manchester Community College
New England College
Plymouth State University
University of New Hampshire at
  Manchester

New Jersey

Caldwell College
County College of Morris
Fairleigh Dickinson University
  College at Florham
Mercer County Community College
Ramapo College of New Jersey
Raritan Valley Community College
Thomas Edison State College

New Mexico

San Juan College

New York

City University of New York
  Bronx Community College
Excelsior College
Fulton-Montgomery Community
  College
Hofstra University
Manhattanville College
Skidmore College
State University of New York
  Empire State College
  Oswego

North Carolina

Forsyth Technical Community College

Lenoir-Rhyne University
Mount Olive College
North Carolina State University
University of North Carolina
  Pembroke

North Dakota

Minot State University
University of Mary
University of North Dakota

Ohio

Capital University
Eastern Gateway Community College
Kent State University
Marion Technical College
Ohio University
Tiffin University
Union Institute & University
University of Akron
University of Findlay
University of Toledo
Walsh University

Oklahoma

Mid-America Christian University
Oklahoma City University
Oral Roberts University
Southern Nazarene University
University of Oklahoma

Oregon

Corban College
Eastern Oregon University
Linfield College
Mt. Hood Community College
Oregon Institute of Technology
Oregon State University

Pennsylvania

Bucks County Community College
California University of Pennsylvania
Community College of Allegheny
  County
Duquesne University
Elizabethtown College
Indiana University of Pennsylvania
Lehigh Carbon Community College
Lehigh University
Luzerne County Community College
Penn State
  Abington
  New Kensington
  University Park
St. Vincent College
University of Pittsburgh
University of Pittsburgh
  Bradford
Wilkes University

Puerto Rico

Inter American University of Puerto
  Rico
  Guayama Campus
Universidad Pentecostal Mizpa
University of Puerto Rico
  Rio Piedras
University of the Sacred Heart

Rhode Island

Roger Williams University

South Carolina

Benedict College
University of South Carolina

South Dakota

Augustana College
Northern State University
Presentation College
University of South Dakota

Tennessee

East Tennessee State University
Lee University
Tennessee Temple University
University of Memphis
University of Tennessee
  Knoxville

Texas

Arlington Baptist College
El Centro College
Huston-Tillotson University
Lamar State College at Port Arthur
Northwood University: Texas
Prairie View A&M University
Southwestern Adventist University
Southwestern Assemblies of God
  University
Texas A&M University
  Commerce
Texas Tech University
University of North Texas
Wayland Baptist University

Utah

Brigham Young University
Weber State University

Vermont

Burlington College
Community College of Vermont
Goddard College
Johnson State College
Norwich University

Virginia

ECPI College of Technology: Virginia
  Beach
George Mason University
Liberty University
Mary Baldwin College
University of Richmond
Virginia University of Lynchburg
Virginia Western Community College

Washington

City University of Seattle
Renton Technical College
Seattle Pacific University
Skagit Valley College
Washington State University

West Virginia

Davis and Elkins College
Eastern West Virginia Community and
  Technical College
West Liberty University
West Virginia State University
West Virginia University
West Virginia University Institute of
  Technology
West Virginia University at
  Parkersburg

Wisconsin

Chippewa Valley Technical College
University of Wisconsin
  Baraboo/Sauk County
  Eau Claire
  Green Bay
  Milwaukee
  Platteville
  River Falls
  Stout
  Superior
  Whitewater

Wyoming

Central Wyoming College
University of Wyoming
Western Wyoming Community
  College

Semester at sea

Alabama
Birmingham-Southern College

Alaska
Alaska Pacific University
University of Alaska
Anchorage
Fairbanks

Arizona
Arizona State University
University of Arizona

California
California Lutheran University
California Polytechnic State
University, San Luis Obispo
California State University
Monterey Bay
Chapman University
Loyola Marymount University
Point Loma Nazarene University
Sonoma State University
University of California
Irvine
San Diego
University of San Diego
Victor Valley College
Westmont College
Whittier College

Colorado
Colorado Christian University
Colorado College
Colorado State University
University of Colorado
Boulder
University of Denver
University of Northern Colorado
Western State College of Colorado

Connecticut
Manchester Community College
Quinnipiac University
Trinity College
University of Bridgeport
University of Connecticut
Wesleyan University

Delaware
Delaware State University

Florida
Eckerd College
Florida Keys Community College
Jacksonville University
New College of Florida
Rollins College
University of Florida
University of Tampa

Georgia
Agnes Scott College
Georgia College and State University
Morehouse College

Hawaii
Chaminade University of Honolulu
University of Hawaii
Manoa

Illinois
Greenville College
Lake Forest College
Monmouth College
Saint Xavier University

University of Illinois
Urbana-Champaign

Indiana
Franklin College
Indiana State University
Indiana University
Bloomington
Taylor University
University of Evansville
Wabash College

Iowa
Cornell College
Drake University
University of Iowa

Kentucky
Bellarmine University
Murray State University

Maine
Bates College
Bowdoin College
Colby College
College of the Atlantic
Maine Maritime Academy
Saint Joseph's College of Maine
Unity College
University of Maine
University of Maine
Farmington
University of Southern Maine

Maryland
McDaniel College
University of Maryland
Baltimore County
College Park

Massachusetts
Assumption College
Babson College
Bentley University
Boston University
College of the Holy Cross
Curry College
Eastern Nazarene College
Emmanuel College
Franklin W. Olin College of
Engineering
Massachusetts College of Liberal Arts
Massachusetts Institute of Technology
Massachusetts Maritime Academy
Mount Holyoke College
Mount Ida College
Nichols College
Northeastern University
Pine Manor College
Simmons College
Smith College
Tufts University
University of Massachusetts
Dartmouth
Wellesley College
Westfield State College

Michigan
Albion College
Central Michigan University
Michigan Technological University
University of Michigan

Minnesota
Bethel University
Concordia College: Moorhead
Minnesota State University
Mankato
University of Minnesota
Morris
University of St. Thomas

Mississippi
Millsaps College

Missouri
Culver-Stockton College
Fontbonne University
Maryville University of Saint Louis
Rockhurst University
Stephens College
Truman State University
University of Missouri
St. Louis
William Jewell College

Nebraska
Dana College
Nebraska Wesleyan University

New Hampshire
Colby-Sawyer College
Daniel Webster College
Dartmouth College
New England College
Saint Anselm College
Southern New Hampshire University
University of New Hampshire
University of New Hampshire at
Manchester

New Jersey
The College of New Jersey
Kean University
Richard Stockton College of New
Jersey

New Mexico
University of New Mexico

New York
Alfred University
Clarkson University
Colgate University
Cornell University
Hartwick College
Hobart and William Smith Colleges
Le Moyne College
Marist College
State University of New York
College at Brockport
Maritime College
United States Merchant Marine
Academy
University of Rochester

North Carolina
Duke University
University of North Carolina
Asheville

North Dakota
University of Mary
University of North Dakota

Ohio
Baldwin-Wallace College
Denison University
Kenyon College
Miami University
Oxford Campus
Ohio State University
Columbus Campus
University of Dayton
University of Findlay

Oklahoma
Oklahoma State University
University of Oklahoma

Oregon
Concordia University
Eastern Oregon University

Linfield College
Northwest Christian University
University of Oregon

Pennsylvania
Albright College
Carlow University
Chatham University
DeSales University
Drexel University
Duquesne University
Gettysburg College
Immaculata University
Lafayette College
Marywood University
Mercyhurst College
Penn State
Beaver
Erie, The Behrend College
University Park
Philadelphia University
St. Francis University
Seton Hill University
Shippensburg University of
Pennsylvania
Susquehanna University
Thiel College
University of Pittsburgh
Bradford
University of Scranton
Ursinus College
Westminster College

Puerto Rico
University of Puerto Rico
Rio Piedras
University of the Sacred Heart

Rhode Island
Providence College
Roger Williams University
Salve Regina University
University of Rhode Island

South Carolina
College of Charleston
Presbyterian College

Texas
Texas A&M University
Galveston
Texas Tech University
Trinity University

Utah
Weber State University
Westminster College

Vermont
Middlebury College
St. Michael's College

Virginia
Hampden-Sydney College
Mary Baldwin College
University of Mary Washington
University of Virginia
Washington and Lee University

Washington
Evergreen State College
Gonzaga University
University of Washington Tacoma
Washington State University

West Virginia
West Virginia University
Wheeling Jesuit University

Wisconsin
Alverno College
Lawrence University

Wyoming
University of Wyoming

Student-designed major

Alabama

Birmingham-Southern College
Huntingdon College
Judson College
Lawson State Community College
Snead State Community College
Spring Hill College
United States Sports Academy
University of Alabama
University of Alabama
  Birmingham
University of North Alabama
University of South Alabama

Alaska

Alaska Pacific University
University of Alaska
  Anchorage
  Fairbanks
  Southeast

Arizona

College of the Humanities and
  Sciences
Mesa Community College
Mohave Community College
Pima Community College
Prescott College
University of Advancing Technology

Arkansas

Hendrix College
John Brown University
Lyon College
National Park Community College
North Arkansas College
Rich Mountain Community College
University of Arkansas
University of Arkansas
  Cossatot Community College of the
    Fort Smith
  Little Rock

California

Academy of Art University
American Jewish University
Antioch Southern California
  Antioch University Los Angeles
  Antioch University Santa Barbara
Biola University
California College of the Arts
California Institute of Technology
California Institute of the Arts
California Lutheran University
California State University
  Bakersfield
  Chico
  Dominguez Hills
  East Bay
  Fresno
  Long Beach
  Los Angeles
  Monterey Bay
  Northridge
  Sacramento
  San Marcos
  Stanislaus
Chabot College
Chapman University
Claremont McKenna College
Cogswell Polytechnical College
College of the Sequoias
College of the Siskiyous
Concordia University
Cuesta College
Dominican University of California
Fresno Pacific University

Grossmont College
Harvey Mudd College
Holy Names University
Humboldt State University
La Sierra University
Las Positas College
Los Angeles Pierce College
Loyola Marymount University
Mendocino College
Menlo College
Mills College
MiraCosta College
Mount St. Mary's College
Notre Dame de Namur University
Occidental College
Orange Coast College
Pepperdine University
Pitzer College
Pomona College
Saddleback College
St. Mary's College of California
San Diego Christian College
San Diego City College
San Diego Mesa College
San Francisco State University
San Jose State University
Santa Clara University
Scripps College
Simpson University
Sonoma State University
Stanford University
University of California
  Berkeley
  Davis
  Los Angeles
  San Diego
  Santa Barbara
  Santa Cruz
University of La Verne
University of Redlands
University of Southern California
University of the Pacific
West Los Angeles College
Westmont College
Whittier College
Woodbury University

Colorado

Adams State College
Colorado Christian University
Colorado College
Colorado Northwestern Community
  College
Fort Lewis College
Lamar Community College
Metropolitan State College of Denver
Morgan Community College
Naropa University
Northeastern Junior College
Regis University
United States Air Force Academy
University of Colorado
  Boulder
  Colorado Springs
  Denver
University of Denver
University of Northern Colorado

Connecticut

Albertus Magnus College
Central Connecticut State University
Charter Oak State College
Connecticut College
Eastern Connecticut State University
Fairfield University
Manchester Community College
Middlesex Community College
Mitchell College
Post University
Quinnipiac University
Sacred Heart University
Saint Joseph College
Southern Connecticut State University
Trinity College

University of Bridgeport
University of Connecticut
University of Hartford
Wesleyan University
Western Connecticut State University
Yale University

Delaware

University of Delaware

District of Columbia

American University
Gallaudet University
George Washington University
Georgetown University
Howard University
Trinity Washington University

Florida

Clearwater Christian College
Eckerd College
Embry-Riddle Aeronautical University
Florida Atlantic University
Florida Christian College
Florida Gulf Coast University
Florida National College
Florida Southern College
Jacksonville University
Jones College
New College of Florida
Northwest Florida State College
Palm Beach Atlantic University
Rollins College
Stetson University
University of Florida
University of Miami
University of North Florida
Valencia Community College

Georgia

Agnes Scott College
Berry College
Brenau University
Clayton State University
Covenant College
Georgia College and State University
Georgia Institute of Technology
Georgia Southern University
Georgia State University
LaGrange College
Mercer University
Oglethorpe University
Piedmont College
Shorter College
Spelman College
University of Georgia
Wesleyan College

Hawaii

Chaminade University of Honolulu
Hawaii Pacific University
University of Hawaii
  Hilo
  Honolulu Community College
  Manoa
  Windward Community College

Idaho

Boise State University
Brigham Young University-Idaho
College of Idaho
Idaho State University
Northwest Nazarene University
University of Idaho

Illinois

Augustana College
Aurora University
Blackburn College
Bradley University
Carl Sandburg College
Chicago State University

City Colleges of Chicago
  Olive-Harvey College
College of DuPage
College of Lake County
Columbia College Chicago
DePaul University
Eureka College
Governors State University
Greenville College
Highland Community College
Illinois College
Illinois Eastern Community Colleges
  Frontier Community College
  Lincoln Trail College
  Olney Central College
  Wabash Valley College
Illinois State University
Illinois Wesleyan University
John Wood Community College
Judson University
Kaskaskia College
Knox College
Lake Forest College
Lewis University
Lewis and Clark Community College
MacMurray College
McKendree University
Millikin University
Monmouth College
Moody Bible Institute
North Central College
North Park University
Northeastern Illinois University
Northern Illinois University
Northwestern University
Olivet Nazarene University
Parkland College
Principia College
Quincy University
Rock Valley College
Saint Xavier University
School of the Art Institute of Chicago
Southeastern Illinois College
Southern Illinois University
  Carbondale
Southern Illinois University
  Edwardsville
Trinity International University
University of Chicago
University of Illinois
  Chicago
  Urbana-Champaign
University of St. Francis
Western Illinois University
Wheaton College

Indiana

Anderson University
Ball State University
Bethel College
Butler University
Calumet College of St. Joseph
DePauw University
Earlham College
Goshen College
Hanover College
Indiana Institute of Technology
Indiana University
  Bloomington
  Northwest
  Southeast
Indiana University-Purdue University
  Fort Wayne
Indiana University-Purdue University
  Indianapolis
Indiana Wesleyan University
Manchester College
Saint Joseph's College
Saint Mary's College
St. Mary-of-the-Woods College
Taylor University
University of Evansville
University of Indianapolis
University of Notre Dame

Valparaiso University
Vincennes University

Iowa

Briar Cliff University
Buena Vista University
Central College
Clarke College
Coe College
Cornell College
Dordt College
Drake University
Graceland University
Grand View University
Grinnell College
Iowa State University
Iowa Wesleyan College
Iowa Western Community College
Kaplan University
   Mason City
Kirkwood Community College
Loras College
Luther College
Morningside College
Northeast Iowa Community College
Northwestern College
St. Ambrose University
Simpson College
Southeastern Community College
   North Campus
University of Iowa
University of Northern Iowa
Upper Iowa University
Waldorf College
Wartburg College

Kansas

Allen County Community College
Baker University
Benedictine College
Bethany College
Central Christian College of Kansas
Coffeyville Community College
Emporia State University
Fort Hays State University
Friends University
Garden City Community College
Highland Community College
Kansas Wesleyan University
McPherson College
MidAmerica Nazarene University
Newman University
Ottawa University
Pittsburg State University
Southwestern College
Sterling College
Tabor College
University of St. Mary
Washburn University

Kentucky

Alice Lloyd College
Bellarmine University
Berea College
Brescia University
Centre College
Eastern Kentucky University
Georgetown College
Kentucky State University
Kentucky Wesleyan College
Lindsey Wilson College
Morehead State University
Northern Kentucky University
Pikeville College
St. Catharine College
Thomas More College
Transylvania University
Union College
University of Louisville
University of the Cumberlands
Western Kentucky University

Louisiana

Centenary College of Louisiana
Delgado Community College
Louisiana College
Louisiana State University
   Shreveport
Louisiana State University and
   Agricultural and Mechanical
   College
Loyola University New Orleans
Nunez Community College
Tulane University
University of Louisiana at Lafayette
University of New Orleans

Maine

Bates College
Bowdoin College
Colby College
College of the Atlantic
Eastern Maine Community College
Husson University
Maine Maritime Academy
New England School of
   Communications
Saint Joseph's College of Maine
Unity College
University of Maine
   Augusta
   Farmington
   Fort Kent
   Machias
   Presque Isle
University of New England
University of Southern Maine

Maryland

Anne Arundel Community College
Chesapeake College
College of Notre Dame of Maryland
Goucher College
Griggs University
Hood College
Johns Hopkins University
Maryland Institute College of Art
McDaniel College
Montgomery College
Mount St. Mary's University
St. Mary's College of Maryland
Salisbury University
Stevenson University
Towson University
University of Baltimore
University of Maryland
   Baltimore County
   College Park
Washington Adventist University
Washington College

Massachusetts

Amherst College
Anna Maria College
Art Institute of Boston at Lesley
   University
Assumption College
Babson College
Bard College at Simon's Rock
Bay Path College
Bentley University
Berklee College of Music
Berkshire Community College
Boston College
Boston University
Brandeis University
Bristol Community College
Clark University
College of the Holy Cross
Curry College
Dean College
Emerson College
Emmanuel College
Endicott College
Fitchburg State College

Franklin W. Olin College of
   Engineering
Gordon College
Hampshire College
Harvard College
Holyoke Community College
Lasell College
Lesley University
Massachusetts College of Art and
   Design
Massachusetts College of Liberal Arts
Merrimack College
Montserrat College of Art
Mount Holyoke College
North Shore Community College
Northeastern University
Pine Manor College
Regis College
School of the Museum of Fine Arts
Simmons College
Smith College
Stonehill College
Tufts University
University of Massachusetts
   Amherst
   Boston
   Dartmouth
Wellesley College
Western New England College
Westfield State College
Wheaton College
Williams College
Worcester Polytechnic Institute

Michigan

Adrian College
Albion College
Alma College
Andrews University
Aquinas College
Calvin College
Central Michigan University
Delta College
Eastern Michigan University
Ferris State University
Finlandia University
Gogebic Community College
Grand Valley State University
Hope College
Kalamazoo College
Lake Superior State University
Madonna University
Marygrove College
Michigan State University
Northern Michigan University
Oakland University
Saginaw Valley State University
Siena Heights University
Spring Arbor University
University of Michigan
University of Michigan
   Dearborn
   Flint
Western Michigan University

Minnesota

Alexandria Technical College
Augsburg College
Bethany Lutheran College
Bethel University
Carleton College
College of St. Benedict
College of St. Scholastica
Concordia University: St. Paul
Crossroads College
Gustavus Adolphus College
Hamline University
Hennepin Technical College
Inver Hills Community College
Macalester College
Metropolitan State University
Minnesota State University
   Mankato
   Moorhead

Minnesota West Community and
   Technical College
North Central University
North Hennepin Community College
Northwest Technical College
Northwestern College
Ridgewater College
St. Catherine University
Saint Cloud State University
St. John's University
St. Mary's University of Minnesota
St. Olaf College
Southwest Minnesota State University
University of Minnesota
   Crookston
   Morris
   Twin Cities
University of St. Thomas
Walden University
Winona State University

Mississippi

Belhaven University
Millsaps College
Mississippi State University
Tougaloo College

Missouri

Calvary Bible College and Theological
   Seminary
Central Methodist University
College of the Ozarks
Columbia College
Culver-Stockton College
Drury University
Fontbonne University
Hannibal-LaGrange College
Harris-Stowe State University
Lindenwood University
Maryville University of Saint Louis
Missouri Baptist University
Missouri State University
Missouri State University: West Plains
Missouri Valley College
Park University
Saint Louis University
Southeast Missouri State University
Southwest Baptist University
Stephens College
Truman State University
University of Central Missouri
University of Missouri
   Columbia
   Kansas City
   Missouri University of Science and
      Technology
   St. Louis
Washington University in St. Louis
Webster University
Westminster College
William Jewell College
William Woods University

Montana

Montana State University
   Bozeman
Rocky Mountain College

Nebraska

Chadron State College
College of Saint Mary
Dana College
Doane College
Grace University
Union College
University of Nebraska
   Lincoln
   Omaha
Wayne State College
Western Nebraska Community
   College
York College

Nevada

College of Southern Nevada
Nevada State College
University of Nevada
  Las Vegas

New Hampshire

Chester College of New England
Colby-Sawyer College
Dartmouth College
Franklin Pierce University
Granite State College
Keene State College
Manchester Community College
Nashua Community College
New England College
Plymouth State University
Southern New Hampshire University
University of New Hampshire
University of New Hampshire at
  Manchester
White Mountains Community College

New Jersey

Bloomfield College
Caldwell College
Centenary College
The College of New Jersey
College of St. Elizabeth
Drew University
Fairleigh Dickinson University
  Metropolitan Campus
Felician College
Monmouth University
Passaic County Community College
Princeton University
Ramapo College of New Jersey
Rutgers, The State University of New
  Jersey
  Camden Regional Campus
  New Brunswick/Piscataway
    Campus
  Newark Regional Campus
Saint Peter's College
Thomas Edison State College
University of Medicine and Dentistry
  of New Jersey
  School of Health Related
    Professions

New Mexico

College of Santa Fe
Eastern New Mexico University
New Mexico Institute of Mining and
  Technology
New Mexico State University
New Mexico State University
  Carlsbad
  Grants
University of New Mexico

New York

Alfred University
Bard College
Barnard College
Broome Community College
Cazenovia College
City University of New York
  Baruch College
  Borough of Manhattan Community
    College
  Bronx Community College
  Brooklyn College
  City College
  Hostos Community College
  Hunter College
  John Jay College of Criminal Justice
  Kingsborough Community College
  LaGuardia Community College
  Lehman College
  Medgar Evers College
  New York City College of
    Technology

Queens College
Queensborough Community
  College
York College
Clarkson University
Clinton Community College
Colgate University
College of Saint Rose
Columbia University
Columbia University
  School of General Studies
Columbia-Greene Community College
Concordia College
Cooper Union for the Advancement of
  Science and Art
Cornell University
Daemen College
Davis College
Dowling College
Eastman School of Music of the
  University of Rochester
Elmira College
Erie Community College
  City Campus
  North Campus
  South Campus
Eugene Lang College The New School
  for Liberal Arts
Fordham University
Fulton-Montgomery Community
  College
Hamilton College
Hartwick College
Hobart and William Smith Colleges
Hofstra University
Hudson Valley Community College
Ithaca College
Jefferson Community College
Jewish Theological Seminary of
  America
Keuka College
Long Island University
  Brooklyn Campus
  C. W. Post Campus
Manhattan College
Manhattanville College
Medaille College
Mohawk Valley Community College
Molloy College
Mount Saint Mary College
New York University
North Country Community College
Parsons The New School for Design
Rensselaer Polytechnic Institute
Rochester Institute of Technology
Rockland Community College
Russell Sage College
Sage College of Albany
Saint Bonaventure University
St. Francis College
St. John Fisher College
St. Lawrence University
Sarah Lawrence College
Skidmore College
State University of New York
  Albany
  Binghamton
  Buffalo
  College at Brockport
  College at Cortland
  College at Fredonia
  College at Plattsburgh
  College at Potsdam
  College of Agriculture and
    Technology at Morrisville
  College of Technology at Alfred
  College of Technology at Canton
  Empire State College
  New Paltz
  Purchase
  Stony Brook
Syracuse University
Touro College
Ulster County Community College

Union College
University of Rochester
Vassar College
Wells College
Westchester Community College
Yeshiva University

North Carolina

Appalachian State University
Bennett College for Women
Brevard College
Catawba College
Catawba Valley Community College
Davidson College
Duke University
East Carolina University
Elon University
Fayetteville Technical Community
  College
Forsyth Technical Community College
Greensboro College
Guilford College
High Point University
John Wesley College
Lees-McRae College
Lenoir-Rhyne University
Mars Hill College
Meredith College
Methodist University
Montreat College
North Carolina State University
Queens University of Charlotte
Richmond Community College
Rockingham Community College
St. Andrews Presbyterian College
Salem College
Shaw University
University of North Carolina
  Asheville
  Chapel Hill
Warren Wilson College
Western Carolina University

North Dakota

Dickinson State University
Jamestown College
Mayville State University
Minot State University
North Dakota State College of Science
North Dakota State University
University of North Dakota
Williston State College

Ohio

Antioch University McGregor
Art Academy of Cincinnati
Ashland University
Baldwin-Wallace College
Belmont Technical College
Bluffton University
Bowling Green State University
Bowling Green State University:
  Firelands College
Capital University
Case Western Reserve University
Cedarville University
Cincinnati State Technical and
  Community College
Clark State Community College
Cleveland State University
College of Wooster
Columbus State Community College
Defiance College
Denison University
Edison State Community College
Hiram College
Hocking College
James A. Rhodes State College
John Carroll University
Kent State University
Kent State University
  Ashtabula
  East Liverpool
  Stark

  Trumbull
  Tuscarawas
Kent State University: Geauga
Kenyon College
Lourdes College
Malone University
Marietta College
Marion Technical College
Miami University
  Hamilton Campus
  Oxford Campus
Mount Union College
Muskingum University
North Central State College
Northwest State Community College
Notre Dame College
Oberlin College
Ohio Christian University
Ohio State University
  Agricultural Technical Institute
  Columbus Campus
  Lima Campus
  Mansfield Campus
  Marion Campus
  Newark Campus
Ohio University
Ohio University
  Southern Campus at Ironton
  Zanesville Campus
Ohio Wesleyan University
Otterbein College
Owens Community College
  Toledo
Shawnee State University
Southern State Community College
Stark State College of Technology
Terra State Community College
University of Akron
University of Akron: Wayne College
University of Cincinnati
  Clermont College
  Raymond Walters College
University of Dayton
University of Findlay
University of Rio Grande
University of Toledo
Urbana University
Washington State Community College
Wilmington College
Wittenberg University
Wright State University
Wright State University: Lake Campus
Youngstown State University
Zane State College

Oklahoma

Bacone College
Northeastern State University
Oklahoma Baptist University
Oklahoma City Community College
Oklahoma City University
Oklahoma State University
Oklahoma Wesleyan University
Oral Roberts University
St. Gregory's University
Southern Nazarene University
Southwestern Oklahoma State
  University
University of Oklahoma
University of Science and Arts of
  Oklahoma
University of Tulsa

Oregon

Central Oregon Community College
Clatsop Community College
Corban College
Eastern Oregon University
George Fox University
Lewis & Clark College
Linfield College
Linn-Benton Community College
Marylhurst University
Northwest Christian University

Oregon State University
Pacific Northwest College of Art
Southern Oregon University
Umpqua Community College
University of Oregon
Warner Pacific College
Western Oregon University
Willamette University

Pennsylvania

Albright College
Allegheny College
Alvernia University
Arcadia University
Bryn Athyn College of the New
  Church
Bryn Mawr College
Bucknell University
Bucks County Community College
Cabrini College
California University of Pennsylvania
Carlow University
Carnegie Mellon University
Cedar Crest College
Chatham University
Chestnut Hill College
Dickinson College
Duquesne University
East Stroudsburg University of
  Pennsylvania
Eastern University
Edinboro University of Pennsylvania
Franklin & Marshall College
Geneva College
Gettysburg College
Harrisburg Area Community College
Haverford College
Indiana University of Pennsylvania
Juniata College
King's College
Kutztown University of Pennsylvania
La Roche College
Lafayette College
Lebanon Valley College
Lock Haven University of
  Pennsylvania
Lycoming College
Mansfield University of Pennsylvania
Marywood University
Mercyhurst College
Messiah College
Misericordia University
Montgomery County Community
  College
Moravian College
Mount Aloysius College
Muhlenberg College
Neumann University
Northampton Community College
Penn State
  Abington
  Altoona
  DuBois
  Fayette, The Eberly Campus
  Greater Allegheny
  Harrisburg
  Hazleton
  Schuylkill
  Shenango
  University Park
  Wilkes-Barre
  York
Pennsylvania College of Technology
Point Park University
Reading Area Community College
Rosemont College
St. Francis University
Saint Joseph's University
Seton Hill University
Slippery Rock University of
  Pennsylvania
Susquehanna University
Swarthmore College
Temple University

University of Pennsylvania
University of Pittsburgh
University of Pittsburgh
  Greensburg
  Johnstown
Ursinus College
Washington & Jefferson College
West Chester University of
  Pennsylvania
Westminster College
Westmoreland County Community
  College
Widener University
Wilkes University
Wilson College
York College of Pennsylvania

Puerto Rico

University of Puerto Rico
  Rio Piedras

Rhode Island

Brown University
New England Institute of Technology
Providence College
Rhode Island College
Roger Williams University

South Carolina

Coastal Carolina University
Coker College
Columbia College
Converse College
Furman University
Lander University
Limestone College
Newberry College
North Greenville University
South Carolina State University
Southern Wesleyan University
Tri-County Technical College
University of South Carolina
University of South Carolina
  Aiken
  Beaufort
  Salkehatchie Regional Campus
  Sumter
  Union
  Upstate
Williamsburg Technical College
Wofford College

South Dakota

Dakota Wesleyan University
Mount Marty College
Northern State University
University of Sioux Falls
University of South Dakota

Tennessee

Belmont University
Bethel University
Carson-Newman College
Chattanooga State Community
  College
Crichton College
East Tennessee State University
Fisk University
Freed-Hardeman University
King College
Lambuth University
LeMoyne-Owen College
Maryville College
Nashville State Community College
Rhodes College
Southwest Tennessee Community
  College
Tennessee Wesleyan College
Tusculum College
University of Memphis
University of Tennessee
  Knoxville
  Martin

University of the South
Vanderbilt University

Texas

Abilene Christian University
Austin College
Baylor University
Cedar Valley College
Clarendon College
East Texas Baptist University
Jarvis Christian College
Lubbock Christian University
McMurry University
Northwood University: Texas
Rice University
Schreiner University
Southern Methodist University
Southwestern Adventist University
Southwestern University
Stephen F. Austin State University
Texas A&M University
  Texarkana
Texas Tech University
Trinity University
University of Dallas
University of Houston
  Clear Lake
University of Mary Hardin-Baylor
University of St. Thomas
University of Texas
  Arlington
  Austin
  Dallas
  Tyler
University of the Incarnate Word

Utah

Dixie State College of Utah
University of Utah
Utah State University
Utah Valley University
Weber State University
Westminster College

Vermont

Bennington College
Burlington College
Castleton State College
Community College of Vermont
Goddard College
Green Mountain College
Lyndon State College
Marlboro College
Middlebury College
Norwich University
St. Michael's College
Southern Vermont College
Sterling College
University of Vermont

Virginia

Averett University
Christopher Newport University
College of William and Mary
Emory & Henry College
Ferrum College
George Mason University
Hollins University
Liberty University
Mary Baldwin College
Marymount University
Mountain Empire Community College
Northern Virginia Community College
Old Dominion University
Radford University
Randolph College
Sweet Briar College
University of Mary Washington
University of Richmond
University of Virginia
University of Virginia's College at
  Wise
Virginia Commonwealth University

Virginia Wesleyan College
Washington and Lee University

Washington

Antioch University Seattle
Centralia College
City University of Seattle
Eastern Washington University
Evergreen State College
Highline Community College
Lower Columbia College
Northwest Indian College
Northwest University
Olympic College
Pacific Lutheran University
Pierce College
Renton Technical College
Seattle Pacific University
Seattle University
Spokane Community College
Trinity Lutheran College
University of Puget Sound
University of Washington
University of Washington Bothell
University of Washington Tacoma
Washington State University
Wenatchee Valley College
Western Washington University
Whatcom Community College
Whitman College
Whitworth University

West Virginia

Bethany College
Concord University
Davis and Elkins College
Eastern West Virginia Community and
  Technical College
Glenville State College
Mountain State University
Ohio Valley University
Salem International University
West Liberty University
West Virginia University
West Virginia University Institute of
  Technology
West Virginia Wesleyan College
Wheeling Jesuit University

Wisconsin

Alverno College
Beloit College
Blackhawk Technical College
Cardinal Stritch University
Carroll University
Carthage College
Chippewa Valley Technical College
Concordia University Wisconsin
Edgewood College
Fox Valley Technical College
Lakeshore Technical College
Lawrence University
Marian University
Marquette University
Moraine Park Technical College
Mount Mary College
Nicolet Area Technical College
Northcentral Technical College
Northland College
Ripon College
St. Norbert College
Silver Lake College
Southwest Wisconsin Technical
  College
University of Wisconsin
  Eau Claire
  Green Bay
  Madison
  Milwaukee
  Oshkosh
  Platteville
  Stevens Point
  Superior
  Whitewater

Viterbo University
Waukesha County Technical College
Western Technical College
Wisconsin Lutheran College

Wyoming
Central Wyoming College
University of Wyoming

Alabama

Alabama Agricultural and Mechanical University
Alabama State University
Athens State University
Auburn University
Auburn University at Montgomery
Birmingham-Southern College
Faulkner University
Huntingdon College
Jacksonville State University
Judson College
Miles College
Oakwood University
Samford University
Spring Hill College
Stillman College
Talladega College
Troy University
Tuskegee University
University of Alabama
University of Alabama
    Birmingham
    Huntsville
University of Mobile
University of Montevallo
University of North Alabama
University of South Alabama
University of West Alabama

Alaska

Alaska Pacific University
University of Alaska
    Anchorage
    Fairbanks
    Southeast

Arizona

American Indian College of the Assemblies of God
Arizona State University
Arizona Western College
Chandler-Gilbert Community College
    Pecos
Grand Canyon University
Mesa Community College
Northern Arizona University
Paradise Valley Community College
Pima Community College
Prescott College
Scottsdale Community College
Southwestern College
University of Arizona
University of Phoenix

Arkansas

Arkansas State University
Arkansas State University: Newport
Arkansas Tech University
Harding University
Henderson State University
Hendrix College
John Brown University
Lyon College
Northwest Arkansas Community College
Ouachita Baptist University
Philander Smith College
Southern Arkansas University
University of Arkansas
University of Arkansas
    Fort Smith
    Little Rock
    Monticello
    Pine Bluff
University of Central Arkansas
University of the Ozarks

California

Academy of Art University
Antelope Valley College
Antioch Southern California
    Antioch University Los Angeles
    Antioch University Santa Barbara
Azusa Pacific University
Bethany University
Bethesda Christian University
Biola University
California Baptist University
California Lutheran University
California Polytechnic State University: San Luis Obispo
California State Polytechnic University: Pomona
California State University
    Bakersfield
    Chico
    Dominguez Hills
    East Bay
    Fresno
    Fullerton
    Long Beach
    Los Angeles
    Monterey Bay
    Northridge
    Sacramento
    San Bernardino
    San Marcos
    Stanislaus
California State University: Channel Islands
Chapman University
College of the Redwoods
Concordia University
Dominican University of California
Fresno Pacific University
Holy Names University
Hope International University
Humboldt State University
John F. Kennedy University
La Sierra University
Loyola Marymount University
The Master's College
Mills College
MiraCosta College
Mount St. Mary's College
Mount San Antonio College
National Hispanic University
National University
Notre Dame de Namur University
Otis College of Art and Design
Pacific Oaks College
Pacific Union College
Patten University
Pepperdine University
Point Loma Nazarene University
St. Mary's College of California
San Diego Christian College
San Diego City College
San Diego Mesa College
San Diego State University
San Francisco State University
San Jose State University
Santa Clara University
Shasta Bible College and Graduate School
Simpson University
Sonoma State University
University of California
    Berkeley
    Davis
    Irvine
    Riverside
    San Diego
    Santa Barbara
    Santa Cruz
University of La Verne
University of Redlands
University of San Diego
University of San Francisco
University of the Pacific

Vanguard University of Southern California
West Valley College
Westmont College
Whittier College
William Jessup University

Colorado

Adams State College
Colorado Christian University
Colorado State University
Colorado State University Pueblo
Fort Lewis College
Front Range Community College
Mesa State College
Metropolitan State College of Denver
Morgan Community College
Northeastern Junior College
Red Rocks Community College
Regis University
Rocky Mountain College of Art & Design
University of Colorado
    Boulder
    Colorado Springs
    Denver
University of Denver
University of Northern Colorado
Western State College of Colorado

Connecticut

Albertus Magnus College
Central Connecticut State University
Connecticut College
Eastern Connecticut State University
Fairfield University
Mitchell College
Quinnipiac University
Sacred Heart University
Saint Joseph College
Southern Connecticut State University
Trinity College
University of Bridgeport
University of Connecticut
University of Hartford
University of New Haven
Western Connecticut State University
Yale University

Delaware

Delaware State University
University of Delaware
Wesley College
Wilmington University

District of Columbia

American University
Catholic University of America
Corcoran College of Art and Design
Gallaudet University
Howard University
Trinity Washington University
University of the District of Columbia

Florida

Baptist College of Florida
Barry University
Bethune-Cookman University
Brevard Community College
Broward College
Carlos Albizu University
Central Florida Community College
Chipola College
Clearwater Christian College
Daytona State College
Edward Waters College
Flagler College
Florida Agricultural and Mechanical University
Florida Atlantic University
Florida Christian College
Florida College

Florida Gulf Coast University
Florida Institute of Technology
Florida International University
Florida Keys Community College
Florida Memorial University
Florida Southern College
Florida State College at Jacksonville
Florida State University
Gulf Coast Community College
Hillsborough Community College
Hobe Sound Bible College
Indian River State College
Jacksonville University
Lake City Community College
Lake-Sumter Community College
Lynn University
Miami Dade College
North Florida Community College
Nova Southeastern University
Palm Beach Atlantic University
Pasco-Hernando Community College
Rollins College
Saint Leo University
St. Petersburg College
Saint Thomas University
Santa Fe College
Seminole Community College
South Florida Community College
Southeastern University
Southwest Florida College
State College of Florida, Manatee-Sarasota
Stetson University
University of Central Florida
University of Florida
University of Miami
University of North Florida
University of South Florida
University of Tampa
University of West Florida
Warner University

Georgia

Agnes Scott College
Albany State University
Armstrong Atlantic State University
Atlanta Christian College
Augusta State University
Berry College
Brenau University
Brewton-Parker College
Clark Atlanta University
Clayton State University
College of Coastal Georgia
Columbus State University
Covenant College
Dalton State College
Emmanuel College
Emory University
Fort Valley State University
Gainesville State College
Georgia College and State University
Georgia Southern University
Georgia Southwestern State University
Georgia State University
Kennesaw State University
LaGrange College
Macon State College
Mercer University
North Georgia College & State University
Paine College
Piedmont College
Reinhardt College
Savannah College of Art and Design
Shorter College
South Georgia College
Spelman College
Toccoa Falls College
Truett-McConnell College
University of Georgia
University of West Georgia
Valdosta State University

Wesleyan College

Hawaii
Chaminade University of Honolulu
Hawaii Pacific University
University of Hawaii
  Hilo
  Kapiolani Community College
  Manoa
  West Oahu

Idaho
Boise State University
Brigham Young University-Idaho
College of Idaho
Idaho State University
Lewis-Clark State College
Northwest Nazarene University
University of Idaho

Illinois
Augustana College
Aurora University
Benedictine University
Blackburn College
Bradley University
Carl Sandburg College
Chicago State University
Columbia College Chicago
Concordia University Chicago
DePaul University
Dominican University
Eastern Illinois University
Elmhurst College
Eureka College
Governors State University
Greenville College
Illinois College
Illinois Eastern Community Colleges
  Frontier Community College
Illinois Institute of Technology
Illinois State University
Illinois Wesleyan University
Judson University
Kankakee Community College
Kendall College
Knox College
Lake Forest College
Lewis University
Loyola University Chicago
MacMurray College
McKendree University
Millikin University
Monmouth College
National-Louis University
North Central College
North Park University
Northeastern Illinois University
Northern Illinois University
Northwestern University
Oakton Community College
Olivet Nazarene University
Principia College
Quincy University
Rend Lake College
Richland Community College
Rockford College
Roosevelt University
Saint Xavier University
School of the Art Institute of Chicago
Southern Illinois University
  Carbondale
Southern Illinois University
  Edwardsville
Trinity Christian College
Trinity International University
Triton College
University of Chicago
University of Illinois
  Chicago
  Springfield
  Urbana-Champaign
University of St. Francis
VanderCook College of Music

Western Illinois University
Wheaton College

Indiana
Anderson University
Ball State University
Bethel College
Butler University
Calumet College of St. Joseph
DePauw University
Franklin College
Goshen College
Grace College
Hanover College
Holy Cross College
Huntington University
Indiana State University
Indiana University
  Bloomington
  East
  Kokomo
  Northwest
  South Bend
  Southeast
Indiana University-Purdue University
  Fort Wayne
Indiana University-Purdue University
  Indianapolis
Indiana Wesleyan University
Ivy Tech Community College
  Bloomington
  Central Indiana
  Columbus
  East Central
  Kokomo
  Lafayette
  North Central
  Northeast
  Northwest
  Richmond
  South Central
  Southeast
  Southwest
  Wabash Valley
Manchester College
Marian University
Oakland City University
Purdue University
Purdue University
  Calumet
  North Central
Saint Joseph's College
Saint Mary's College
St. Mary-of-the-Woods College
Taylor University
Trine University
University of Evansville
University of Indianapolis
University of Notre Dame
University of St. Francis
University of Southern Indiana
Valparaiso University
Wabash College

Iowa
Briar Cliff University
Buena Vista University
Central College
Clarke College
Coe College
Cornell College
Dordt College
Drake University
Emmaus Bible College
Faith Baptist Bible College and
  Theological Seminary
Graceland University
Grand View University
Grinnell College
Iowa State University
Iowa Wesleyan College
Kaplan University
  Davenport
  Mason City

Loras College
Luther College
Maharishi University of Management
Morningside College
Mount Mercy College
Northwestern College
St. Ambrose University
Simpson College
University of Dubuque
University of Iowa
University of Northern Iowa
Upper Iowa University
Waldorf College
Wartburg College
William Penn University

Kansas
Baker University
Barclay College
Benedictine College
Bethany College
Bethel College
Central Christian College of Kansas
Cloud County Community College
Cowley County Community College
Emporia State University
Fort Hays State University
Fort Scott Community College
Friends University
Kansas State University
Kansas Wesleyan University
McPherson College
MidAmerica Nazarene University
Newman University
Ottawa University
Pittsburg State University
Southwestern College
Sterling College
Tabor College
University of Kansas
University of St. Mary
Washburn University
Wichita State University

Kentucky
Alice Lloyd College
Asbury College
Bellarmine University
Berea College
Brescia University
Campbellsville University
Centre College
Eastern Kentucky University
Elizabethtown Community and
  Technical College
Georgetown College
Kentucky Christian University
Kentucky Mountain Bible College
Kentucky State University
Kentucky Wesleyan College
Lindsey Wilson College
Mid-Continent University
Midway College
Morehead State University
Murray State University
Northern Kentucky University
Pikeville College
St. Catharine College
Spalding University
Thomas More College
Transylvania University
Union College
University of Kentucky
University of Louisville
University of the Cumberlands
Western Kentucky University

Louisiana
Baton Rouge Community College
Bossier Parish Community College
Centenary College of Louisiana
Dillard University
Grambling State University
Louisiana College

Louisiana State University
  Shreveport
Louisiana State University and
  Agricultural and Mechanical
  College
Louisiana Tech University
Loyola University New Orleans
McNeese State University
Nicholls State University
Northwestern State University
Our Lady of Holy Cross College
Southeastern Louisiana University
Southern University
  New Orleans
Southern University and Agricultural
  and Mechanical College
Tulane University
University of Louisiana at Lafayette
University of Louisiana at Monroe
University of New Orleans

Maine
Bates College
Bowdoin College
Colby College
College of the Atlantic
Husson University
Maine College of Art
Maine Maritime Academy
Saint Joseph's College of Maine
Thomas College
Unity College
University of Maine
University of Maine
  Farmington
  Fort Kent
  Machias
  Presque Isle
University of New England
University of Southern Maine

Maryland
Anne Arundel Community College
Baltimore City Community College
Bowie State University
Cecil College
College of Notre Dame of Maryland
Community College of Baltimore
  County
Coppin State University
Frederick Community College
Frostburg State University
Goucher College
Hood College
Howard Community College
Johns Hopkins University: Peabody
  Conservatory of Music
Loyola University Maryland
Maryland Institute College of Art
McDaniel College
Montgomery College
Morgan State University
Mount St. Mary's University
Prince George's Community College
St. Mary's College of Maryland
Salisbury University
Stevenson University
Towson University
University of Maryland
  Baltimore County
  College Park
  Eastern Shore
  University College
Washington Adventist University
Washington Bible College
Washington College

Massachusetts
American International College
Amherst College
Anna Maria College
Art Institute of Boston at Lesley
  University
Assumption College

Atlantic Union College
Bay Path College
Becker College
Berklee College of Music
Boston College
Boston Conservatory
Boston University
Bridgewater State College
Clark University
College of the Holy Cross
Curry College
Eastern Nazarene College
Elms College
Emerson College
Emmanuel College
Endicott College
Fitchburg State College
Framingham State College
Gordon College
Hampshire College
Harvard College
Holyoke Community College
Lasell College
Lesley University
Massachusetts College of Liberal Arts
Massachusetts Institute of Technology
Merrimack College
Montserrat College of Art
Mount Holyoke College
Mount Ida College
Nichols College
Northeastern University
Pine Manor College
Regis College
Salem State College
School of the Museum of Fine Arts
Simmons College
Smith College
Springfield College
Stonehill College
Tufts University
University of Massachusetts
  Amherst
  Boston
  Dartmouth
  Lowell
Wellesley College
Western New England College
Westfield State College
Wheaton College
Wheelock College
Worcester Polytechnic Institute
Worcester State College

Michigan
Adrian College
Albion College
Alma College
Andrews University
Aquinas College
Baker College
  of Auburn Hills
  of Clinton Township
  of Muskegon
Baker College of Allen Park
Calvin College
Central Michigan University
College for Creative Studies
Cornerstone University
Eastern Michigan University
Ferris State University
Finlandia University
Grand Valley State University
Hillsdale College
Hope College
Kendall College of Art and Design of
  Ferris State University
Kuyper College
Lake Superior State University
Lansing Community College
Madonna University
Marygrove College
Michigan State University
Michigan Technological University

Northern Michigan University
Oakland University
Rochester College
Saginaw Valley State University
Siena Heights University
Spring Arbor University
University of Detroit Mercy
University of Michigan
University of Michigan
  Dearborn
  Flint
Wayne State University
Western Michigan University

Minnesota
Augsburg College
Bemidji State University
Bethany Lutheran College
Bethel University
Carleton College
College of St. Benedict
College of St. Scholastica
Concordia College: Moorhead
Concordia University: St. Paul
Crown College
Gustavus Adolphus College
Hamline University
Leech Lake Tribal College
Martin Luther College
Metropolitan State University
Minnesota State University
  Mankato
  Moorhead
Normandale Community College
North Central University
Northwestern College
St. Catherine University
Saint Cloud State University
St. John's University
St. Mary's University of Minnesota
St. Olaf College
Southwest Minnesota State University
University of Minnesota
  Crookston
  Duluth
  Morris
  Twin Cities
University of St. Thomas
Walden University
Winona State University

Mississippi
Alcorn State University
Belhaven University
Blue Mountain College
Delta State University
Jackson State University
Millsaps College
Mississippi College
Mississippi State University
Mississippi University for Women
Mississippi Valley State University
Rust College
Tougaloo College
University of Mississippi
University of Southern Mississippi

Missouri
Avila University
Calvary Bible College and Theological
  Seminary
Central Methodist University
College of the Ozarks
Columbia College
Culver-Stockton College
Drury University
Evangel University
Fontbonne University
Hannibal-LaGrange College
Harris-Stowe State University
Lincoln University
Lindenwood University
Maryville University of Saint Louis
Missouri Baptist University

Missouri Southern State University
Missouri State University
Missouri Valley College
Missouri Western State University
Northwest Missouri State University
Park University
Rockhurst University
St. Charles Community College
St. Louis Community College
  St. Louis Community College at
    Florissant Valley
Saint Louis University
Southeast Missouri State University
Southwest Baptist University
Stephens College
Truman State University
University of Central Missouri
University of Missouri
  Columbia
  Kansas City
  Missouri University of Science and
    Technology
  St. Louis
Washington University in St. Louis
Webster University
Westminster College
William Jewell College
William Woods University

Montana
Fort Peck Community College
Montana State University
  Billings
  Bozeman
Montana Tech of the University of
  Montana
Rocky Mountain College
University of Great Falls
University of Montana
University of Montana: Western

Nebraska
Chadron State College
College of Saint Mary
Concordia University
Creighton University
Dana College
Doane College
Grace University
Nebraska Christian College
Nebraska Wesleyan University
Peru State College
Union College
University of Nebraska
  Kearney
  Lincoln
  Omaha
Wayne State College
York College

Nevada
Great Basin College
Nevada State College
Sierra Nevada College
University of Nevada
  Las Vegas
  Reno

New Hampshire
Colby-Sawyer College
Dartmouth College
Franklin Pierce University
Granite State College
Keene State College
New England College
Plymouth State University
Rivier College
Saint Anselm College
Southern New Hampshire University
University of New Hampshire
University of New Hampshire at
  Manchester

New Jersey
Bloomfield College
Caldwell College
Centenary College
The College of New Jersey
College of St. Elizabeth
County College of Morris
Drew University
Essex County College
Fairleigh Dickinson University
  College at Florham
  Metropolitan Campus
Felician College
Georgian Court University
Hudson County Community College
Kean University
Monmouth University
Montclair State University
New Jersey City University
Princeton University
Ramapo College of New Jersey
Richard Stockton College of New
  Jersey
Rider University
Rowan University
Rutgers, The State University of New
  Jersey
  Camden Regional Campus
  New Brunswick/Piscataway
    Campus
  Newark Regional Campus
Saint Peter's College
Salem Community College
Seton Hall University
Sussex County Community College
William Paterson University of New
  Jersey

New Mexico
Clovis Community College
Eastern New Mexico University
Navajo Technical College
New Mexico Highlands University
New Mexico Institute of Mining and
  Technology
New Mexico State University
Northern New Mexico College
San Juan College
Santa Fe Community College
University of New Mexico
University of the Southwest
Western New Mexico University

New York
Adelphi University
Alfred University
Barnard College
Boricua College
Canisius College
Cazenovia College
City University of New York
  Brooklyn College
  City College
  College of Staten Island
  Hunter College
  Lehman College
  Medgar Evers College
  New York City College of
    Technology
  Queens College
  York College
Colgate University
College of Mount St. Vincent
College of New Rochelle
College of Saint Rose
Columbia University
Columbia University
  School of General Studies
Concordia College
Cornell University
D'Youville College
Daemen College
Dominican College of Blauvelt
Dowling College

Eastman School of Music of the University of Rochester
Elmira College
Erie Community College
   City Campus
   North Campus
   South Campus
Five Towns College
Fordham University
Hartwick College
Hobart and William Smith Colleges
Hofstra University
Houghton College
Iona College
Ithaca College
Keuka College
Le Moyne College
Long Island University
   Brooklyn Campus
   C. W. Post Campus
Manhattan College
Manhattanville College
Marist College
Marymount Manhattan College
Medaille College
Mercy College
Metropolitan College of New York
Molloy College
Mount Saint Mary College
Nazareth College
New York Institute of Technology
New York University
Niagara University
Nyack College
Ohr Somayach Tanenbaum Education Center
Pace University
Pratt Institute
Roberts Wesleyan College
Rochester Institute of Technology
Russell Sage College
Saint Bonaventure University
St. Francis College
St. John Fisher College
St. John's University
St. Joseph's College
St. Joseph's College: Suffolk Campus
St. Lawrence University
St. Thomas Aquinas College
Sarah Lawrence College
Schenectady County Community College
Siena College
Skidmore College
State University of New York
   Binghamton
   Buffalo
   College at Brockport
   College at Buffalo
   College at Cortland
   College at Fredonia
   College at Geneseo
   College at Old Westbury
   College at Oneonta
   College at Plattsburgh
   College at Potsdam
   College of Environmental Science and Forestry
   Empire State College
   New Paltz
   Oswego
   Stony Brook
Syracuse University
Touro College
Union College
University of Rochester
Utica College
Vassar College
Wagner College
Wells College
Yeshiva University

North Carolina

Appalachian State University

Barton College
Belmont Abbey College
Bennett College for Women
Blue Ridge Community College
Brevard College
Campbell University
Carteret Community College
Catawba College
Catawba Valley Community College
Chowan University
Davidson College
Duke University
East Carolina University
Elizabeth City State University
Elon University
Fayetteville State University
Gardner-Webb University
Greensboro College
Guilford College
Guilford Technical Community College
High Point University
Johnson C. Smith University
Lees-McRae College
Lenoir-Rhyne University
Livingstone College
Mars Hill College
Martin Community College
Meredith College
Methodist University
Montreat College
Mount Olive College
North Carolina Agricultural and Technical State University
North Carolina Central University
North Carolina State University
North Carolina Wesleyan College
Peace College
Pfeiffer University
Piedmont Baptist College
Queens University of Charlotte
Richmond Community College
Rowan-Cabarrus Community College
St. Andrews Presbyterian College
St. Augustine's College
Salem College
Sandhills Community College
Shaw University
University of North Carolina
   Asheville
   Chapel Hill
   Charlotte
   Greensboro
   Pembroke
   Wilmington
Wake Forest University
Warren Wilson College
Wayne Community College
Western Carolina University
Wingate University
Winston-Salem State University

North Dakota

Dickinson State University
Jamestown College
Mayville State University
Minot State University
North Dakota State University
Trinity Bible College
University of Mary
University of North Dakota

Ohio

Antioch University McGregor
Ashland University
Baldwin-Wallace College
Bluffton University
Bowling Green State University
Bowling Green State University: Firelands College
Capital University
Case Western Reserve University
Cedarville University
Central State University

Cincinnati Christian University
Cleveland State University
College of Mount St. Joseph
College of Wooster
Columbus State Community College
Defiance College
Denison University
Franciscan University of Steubenville
Heidelberg University
Hiram College
John Carroll University
Kent State University
Kent State University
   Salem
Kent State University: Geauga
Lourdes College
Malone University
Marietta College
Miami University
   Hamilton Campus
   Oxford Campus
Mount Union College
Mount Vernon Nazarene University
Muskingum University
Notre Dame College
Oberlin College
Ohio Dominican University
Ohio Northern University
Ohio State University
   Columbus Campus
   Lima Campus
   Mansfield Campus
   Marion Campus
   Newark Campus
Ohio University
Ohio University
   Southern Campus at Ironton
   Zanesville Campus
Ohio Wesleyan University
Otterbein College
Shawnee State University
Tiffin University
Union Institute & University
University of Akron
University of Cincinnati
University of Cincinnati
   Raymond Walters College
University of Dayton
University of Findlay
University of Rio Grande
University of Toledo
Urbana University
Ursuline College
Walsh University
Wilmington College
Wittenberg University
Wright State University
Xavier University
Youngstown State University

Oklahoma

Bacone College
Cameron University
East Central University
Langston University
Mid-America Christian University
Northeastern State University
Northwestern Oklahoma State University
Oklahoma Baptist University
Oklahoma Christian University
Oklahoma City University
Oklahoma Panhandle State University
Oklahoma State University
Oklahoma Wesleyan University
Oral Roberts University
St. Gregory's University
Southeastern Oklahoma State University
Southern Nazarene University
Southwestern Oklahoma State University
University of Central Oklahoma
University of Oklahoma

University of Science and Arts of Oklahoma
University of Tulsa

Oregon

Chemeketa Community College
Clatsop Community College
Concordia University
Corban College
Eastern Oregon University
George Fox University
Linfield College
Marylhurst University
Multnomah University
Northwest Christian University
Oregon State University
Pacific University
Portland State University
Southern Oregon University
University of Oregon
University of Portland
Warner Pacific College
Western Oregon University
Willamette University

Pennsylvania

Albright College
Alvernia University
Arcadia University
Baptist Bible College of Pennsylvania
Bloomsburg University of Pennsylvania
Bryn Athyn College of the New Church
Bryn Mawr College
Bucknell University
Cabrini College
California University of Pennsylvania
Carlow University
Carnegie Mellon University
Cedar Crest College
Chatham University
Chestnut Hill College
Cheyney University of Pennsylvania
Clarion University of Pennsylvania
DeSales University
Delaware Valley College
Dickinson College
Drexel University
Duquesne University
East Stroudsburg University of Pennsylvania
Eastern University
Edinboro University of Pennsylvania
Elizabethtown College
Franklin & Marshall College
Gannon University
Geneva College
Gettysburg College
Grove City College
Gwynedd-Mercy College
Haverford College
Holy Family University
Immaculata University
Indiana University of Pennsylvania
Juniata College
Keystone College
King's College
Kutztown University of Pennsylvania
La Roche College
La Salle University
Lancaster Bible College
Lebanon Valley College
Lincoln University
Lock Haven University of Pennsylvania
Lycoming College
Mansfield University of Pennsylvania
Marywood University
Mercyhurst College
Messiah College
Millersville University of Pennsylvania
Misericordia University

Montgomery County Community
College
Moore College of Art and Design
Moravian College
Mount Aloysius College
Muhlenberg College
Neumann University
Northampton Community College
Penn State
Abington
Altoona
Berks
Brandywine
Erie, The Behrend College
Harrisburg
Lehigh Valley
University Park
Philadelphia Biblical University
Point Park University
Robert Morris University
Rosemont College
St. Francis University
Saint Joseph's University
St. Vincent College
Seton Hill University
Shippensburg University of
Pennsylvania
Slippery Rock University of
Pennsylvania
Susquehanna University
Swarthmore College
Temple University
Thiel College
University of Pennsylvania
University of Pittsburgh
University of Pittsburgh
Bradford
Johnstown
University of Scranton
University of the Arts
University of the Sciences in
Philadelphia
Ursinus College
Valley Forge Christian College
Villanova University
Washington & Jefferson College
Waynesburg University
West Chester University of
Pennsylvania
Westminster College
Widener University
Wilkes University
Wilson College
York College of Pennsylvania

Puerto Rico

Bayamon Central University
Caribbean University
Conservatory of Music of Puerto Rico
Escuela de Artes Plasticas de Puerto
Rico
Inter American University of Puerto
Rico
Aguadilla Campus
Arecibo Campus
Fajardo Campus
Guayama Campus
Ponce Campus
San German Campus
Pontifical Catholic University of
Puerto Rico
Universidad Adventista de las Antillas
Universidad Metropolitana
Universidad del Este
University of Puerto Rico
Aguadilla
Cayey University College
Humacao
Rio Piedras
Utuado
University of the Sacred Heart

Rhode Island

Brown University

Providence College
Rhode Island College
Rhode Island School of Design
Roger Williams University
Salve Regina University
University of Rhode Island

South Carolina

Allen University
Anderson University
Benedict College
Bob Jones University
Charleston Southern University
The Citadel
Claflin University
Clemson University
Coastal Carolina University
Coker College
College of Charleston
Columbia College
Columbia International University
Converse College
Erskine College
Francis Marion University
Furman University
Greenville Technical College
Lander University
Limestone College
Morris College
Newberry College
North Greenville University
Presbyterian College
South Carolina State University
Southern Wesleyan University
University of South Carolina
University of South Carolina
Aiken
Beaufort
Sumter
Upstate
Winthrop University
Wofford College

South Dakota

Augustana College
Black Hills State University
Dakota State University
Dakota Wesleyan University
Mount Marty College
Northern State University
Oglala Lakota College
South Dakota State University
University of Sioux Falls
University of South Dakota

Tennessee

Aquinas College
Austin Peay State University
Belmont University
Bethel University
Bryan College
Carson-Newman College
Christian Brothers University
Crichton College
Cumberland University
Dyersburg State Community College
East Tennessee State University
Fisk University
Free Will Baptist Bible College
Freed-Hardeman University
Johnson Bible College
King University
Lambuth University
Lane College
LeMoyne-Owen College
Lee University
Lincoln Memorial University
Lipscomb University
Maryville College
Middle Tennessee State University
Milligan College
Roane State Community College
South College
Southern Adventist University

Tennessee State University
Tennessee Technological University
Tennessee Temple University
Tennessee Wesleyan College
Trevecca Nazarene University
Tusculum College
Union University
University of Memphis
University of Tennessee
Chattanooga
Knoxville
Martin
Vanderbilt University

Texas

Abilene Christian University
Angelo State University
Arlington Baptist College
Austin College
Austin Community College
Baylor University
Blinn College
College of the Mainland
Collin County Community College
District
Concordia University Texas
Dallas Baptist University
Dallas Christian College
Del Mar College
East Texas Baptist University
El Centro College
El Paso Community College
Hardin-Simmons University
Houston Baptist University
Howard Payne University
Huston-Tillotson University
Jarvis Christian College
Lamar State College at Orange
Lamar University
Laredo Community College
LeTourneau University
Lone Star College System
Lubbock Christian University
McLennan Community College
McMurry University
Midwestern State University
Mountain View College
North Lake College
Northwest Vista College
Our Lady of the Lake University of San
Antonio
Prairie View A&M University
Rice University
Richland College
St. Edward's University
St. Mary's University
St. Philip's College
Sam Houston State University
San Antonio College
San Jacinto College
Schreiner University
Southern Methodist University
Southwestern Adventist University
Southwestern Assemblies of God
University
Southwestern University
Stephen F. Austin State University
Sul Ross State University
Tarleton State University
Texas A&M International University
Texas A&M University
Texas A&M University
Commerce
Corpus Christi
Galveston
Kingsville
Texarkana
Texas Christian University
Texas College
Texas Lutheran University
Texas Southern University
Texas State Technical College
Harlingen
Texas State University: San Marcos

Texas Tech University
Texas Wesleyan University
Texas Woman's University
Trinity University
University of Dallas
University of Houston
University of Houston
Clear Lake
Downtown
Victoria
University of Mary Hardin-Baylor
University of North Texas
University of St. Thomas
University of Texas
Arlington
Austin
Brownsville - Texas Southmost
College
Dallas
El Paso
Pan American
San Antonio
Tyler
of the Permian Basin
University of the Incarnate Word
Wayland Baptist University
Weatherford College
West Texas A&M University
Wharton County Junior College
Wiley College

Utah

Brigham Young University
Dixie State College of Utah
Southern Utah University
University of Utah
Utah State University
Utah Valley University
Weber State University
Western Governors University
Westminster College

Vermont

Bennington College
Castleton State College
Champlain College
College of St. Joseph in Vermont
Goddard College
Green Mountain College
Johnson State College
Lyndon State College
Middlebury College
Norwich University
St. Michael's College
University of Vermont

Virginia

Averett University
Blue Ridge Community College
Bluefield College
Bridgewater College
College of William and Mary
Eastern Mennonite University
Emory & Henry College
Ferrum College
George Mason University
Hampton University
Hollins University
James Madison University
Liberty University
Longwood University
Lynchburg College
Mary Baldwin College
Marymount University
New River Community College
Norfolk State University
Old Dominion University
Patrick Henry Community College
Radford University
Randolph College
Randolph-Macon College
Regent University
Roanoke College
St. Paul's College

Shenandoah University
Sweet Briar College
University of Mary Washington
University of Richmond
University of Virginia
University of Virginia's College at
   Wise
Virginia Commonwealth University
Virginia Intermont College
Virginia Military Institute
Virginia Polytechnic Institute and
   State University
Virginia State University
Virginia Union University
Virginia Wesleyan College
Washington and Lee University

Washington

Antioch University Seattle
Bates Technical College
City University of Seattle
Eastern Washington University
Evergreen State College
Gonzaga University
Grays Harbor College
Lower Columbia College
Northwest University
Pacific Lutheran University
Saint Martin's University
Seattle Pacific University
University of Puget Sound
University of Washington
University of Washington Bothell
University of Washington Tacoma
Walla Walla University
Washington State University
Western Washington University
Whitworth University

West Virginia

Alderson-Broaddus College
Appalachian Bible College
Bethany College
Bluefield State College
Concord University
Davis and Elkins College
Fairmont State University
Glenville State College
Marshall University
Ohio Valley University
Salem International University
Shepherd University
Southern West Virginia Community
   and Technical College
West Liberty University
West Virginia State University
West Virginia University
West Virginia University at
   Parkersburg
West Virginia Wesleyan College
Wheeling Jesuit University

Wisconsin

Alverno College
Beloit College
Cardinal Stritch University
Carroll University
Carthage College
Concordia University Wisconsin
Edgewood College
Lakeland College
Lawrence University
Maranatha Baptist Bible College
Marian University
Marquette University
Mount Mary College
Northland College
Ripon College
St. Norbert College
Silver Lake College
University of Wisconsin
   Eau Claire
   Green Bay
   La Crosse

Madison
Milwaukee
Oshkosh
Parkside
Platteville
Richland
River Falls
Stevens Point
Stout
Superior
Whitewater
Viterbo University
Wisconsin Lutheran College

Wyoming

Central Wyoming College
Northwest College

United Nations semester

Arkansas

University of Arkansas

California

Mount St. Mary's College
Occidental College
Point Loma Nazarene University
Scripps College
Sonoma State University
University of Redlands
University of the Pacific

Connecticut

Sacred Heart University
Trinity College
University of Bridgeport

Florida

Eckerd College
Florida Southern College

Georgia

Agnes Scott College

Illinois

Illinois Wesleyan University
Lincoln Land Community College
Millikin University
North Central College
Rockford College

Indiana

Franklin College
Indiana University
  Bloomington
Valparaiso University
Wabash College

Iowa

Morningside College

Kansas

Fort Hays State University

Maryland

McDaniel College

Minnesota

University of Minnesota
  Morris

Mississippi

Millsaps College

Nebraska

Dana College
Nebraska Wesleyan University

New Hampshire

Southern New Hampshire University
University of New Hampshire

New Jersey

College of St. Elizabeth
Drew University

New York

Alfred University
City University of New York
  College of Staten Island
College of New Rochelle
Fordham University
Hobart and William Smith Colleges

Long Island University
  Brooklyn Campus
  C. W. Post Campus
Marist College
State University of New York
  New Paltz
Utica College
Wagner College

North Carolina

Meredith College

Ohio

College of Wooster
Muskingum University
Ohio Wesleyan University

Pennsylvania

Gettysburg College
Lycoming College
Seton Hill University
Susquehanna University
Thiel College
University of Scranton
Ursinus College

South Carolina

Furman University
Winthrop University

Texas

Hardin-Simmons University
Trinity University

Utah

Weber State University

Virginia

Randolph-Macon College

West Virginia

Bethany College
Wheeling Jesuit University

Wisconsin

Carroll University
University of Wisconsin
  Milwaukee

Urban semester

California
Azusa Pacific University
Biola University
California Lutheran University
Laguna College of Art and Design
Marymount College
Pitzer College
San Francisco Art Institute
Scripps College
Sonoma State University
University of California
　Los Angeles
University of Redlands
Westmont College

Colorado
Colorado Christian University
Colorado College

Connecticut
Trinity College
University of Bridgeport
University of Connecticut
Wesleyan University

District of Columbia
Corcoran College of Art and Design

Florida
Florida Southern College
Ringling College of Art and Design

Georgia
Savannah College of Art and Design
Spelman College

Idaho
Brigham Young University-Idaho

Illinois
Greenville College
Illinois Wesleyan University
Judson University
Knox College
Lake Forest College
Millikin University
Monmouth College
North Central College
School of the Art Institute of Chicago
Trinity Christian College
Trinity International University
Wheaton College

Indiana
Anderson University
Bethel College
Earlham College
Goshen College
Manchester College
Purdue University
Taylor University
Valparaiso University
Wabash College

Iowa
Briar Cliff University
Central College
Coe College
Cornell College
Dordt College
Grinnell College
Loras College
Simpson College
University of Dubuque
University of Iowa
Wartburg College

Kansas
Bethany College
Bethel College
Central Christian College of Kansas
McPherson College
Southwestern College
Sterling College

Kentucky
Asbury College
Western Kentucky University

Maine
Bates College

Maryland
Maryland Institute College of Art
McDaniel College
University of Maryland
　Eastern Shore

Massachusetts
Art Institute of Boston at Lesley
　University
Curry College
Eastern Nazarene College
Gordon College
Lesley University
Montserrat College of Art
School of the Museum of Fine Arts
Stonehill College
Worcester Polytechnic Institute

Michigan
Albion College
Alma College
Aquinas College
Calvin College
College for Creative Studies
Cornerstone University
Hope College
Kalamazoo College
Kendall College of Art and Design of
　Ferris State University

Minnesota
Augsburg College
Bethel University
Carleton College
Concordia College: Moorhead
Crown College
Hamline University
Macalester College
Minneapolis College of Art and Design
St. Catherine University
St. Mary's University of Minnesota
St. Olaf College
University of Minnesota
　Morris
University of St. Thomas

Mississippi
Millsaps College
Tougaloo College

Missouri
Kansas City Art Institute
Missouri Baptist University
Rockhurst University
University of Missouri
　Columbia
Westminster College
William Woods University

Nebraska
Dana College
Grace University
Nebraska Wesleyan University

New Hampshire
Saint Anselm College

New Jersey
Berkeley College- Garret Mountain
　Campus
Drew University

New Mexico
College of Santa Fe

New York
Alfred University
Bard College
Berkeley College
City University of New York
　College of Staten Island
Colgate University
Cornell University
Eugene Lang College The New School
　for Liberal Arts
Hamilton College
Hartwick College
King's College
Niagara University
Onondaga Community College
State University of New York
　College at Brockport
　College at Buffalo
　College at Oneonta
　New Paltz
　Stony Brook
University of Rochester
Vassar College
Wagner College

North Carolina
Duke University
Meredith College

Ohio
Art Academy of Cincinnati
Cleveland Institute of Art
College of Wooster
Columbus College of Art and Design
Denison University
Kent State University
Kent State University
　Ashtabula
　East Liverpool
　Salem
　Stark
　Trumbull
　Tuscarawas
Kent State University: Geauga
Kenyon College
Oberlin College
Ohio Wesleyan University
Ursuline College
Wittenberg University
Xavier University
Youngstown State University

Oklahoma
Oklahoma City University
Southern Nazarene University

Oregon
Lewis & Clark College
Pacific Northwest College of Art
Willamette University

Pennsylvania
Albright College
California University of Pennsylvania
Franklin & Marshall College
Indiana University of Pennsylvania
Juniata College
Lafayette College
Lebanon Valley College
Lehigh University
Lycoming College
Mercyhurst College
Messiah College
Seton Hill University

Susquehanna University

South Dakota
Augustana College

Tennessee
Memphis College of Art

Texas
Hardin-Simmons University
Southwestern University
Texas Christian University
Trinity University

Utah
Weber State University

Virginia
Washington and Lee University

Washington
Trinity Lutheran College
Whitman College

West Virginia
West Virginia Wesleyan College

Wisconsin
Beloit College
Lawrence University
Ripon College
Viterbo University

Alabama
Alabama Agricultural and Mechanical
   University
Auburn University
Birmingham-Southern College
Huntingdon College
Judson College
Spring Hill College
University of Alabama

Alaska
University of Alaska
   Anchorage

Arizona
Arizona State University

Arkansas
Arkansas State University
Hendrix College
John Brown University
Lyon College

California
Azusa Pacific University
Biola University
California Baptist University
California Lutheran University
California State University
   Long Beach
Chapman University
Claremont McKenna College
Fresno Pacific University
Loyola Marymount University
The Master's College
Mills College
Mount St. Mary's College
Pepperdine University
Point Loma Nazarene University
Pomona College
San Diego Christian College
San Francisco State University
Santa Clara University
Scripps College
Simpson University
Sonoma State University
Stanford University
University of California
   Davis
   Irvine
   Los Angeles
   Riverside
   San Diego
   Santa Barbara
   Santa Cruz
University of California: Merced
University of Redlands
University of San Diego
University of San Francisco
University of Southern California
University of the Pacific
Vanguard University of Southern
   California
Westmont College
Whittier College
William Jessup University

Colorado
Colorado Christian University
Colorado College
Metropolitan State College of Denver
University of Denver

Connecticut
Connecticut College
Fairfield University
Quinnipiac University
Sacred Heart University
Trinity College
University of Bridgeport
University of Connecticut
University of Hartford
Wesleyan University

Delaware
University of Delaware

District of Columbia
American University
Catholic University of America
Georgetown University
Trinity Washington University

Florida
Eckerd College
Florida Gulf Coast University
Florida Southern College
Jacksonville University
Lynn University
New College of Florida
Palm Beach Atlantic University
Rollins College
Stetson University
University of Florida
University of Miami
University of North Florida
University of South Florida
University of Tampa
Warner University

Georgia
Agnes Scott College
Clark Atlanta University
Covenant College
Emory University
Georgia College and State University
Georgia Southern University
LaGrange College
Savannah College of Art and Design
Spelman College
University of Georgia

Idaho
College of Idaho

Illinois
Blackburn College
Bradley University
Dominican University
Elmhurst College
Eureka College
Greenville College
Illinois College
Illinois State University
Illinois Wesleyan University
Judson University
Knox College
Lake Forest College
Loyola University Chicago
Millikin University
Monmouth College
North Central College
North Park University
Olivet Nazarene University
Quincy University
Rockford College
Trinity Christian College
Trinity International University
University of Chicago
University of Illinois
   Urbana-Champaign
University of St. Francis
Wheaton College

Indiana
Ball State University
Bethel College
Butler University
Franklin College
Goshen College
Hanover College
Huntington University
Indiana University
   Bloomington
   Northwest
Indiana University-Purdue University
   Fort Wayne
Saint Joseph's College
Saint Mary's College
Taylor University
University of Evansville
University of Notre Dame
Valparaiso University
Wabash College

Iowa
Buena Vista University
Central College
Coe College
Cornell College
Dordt College
Drake University
Grand View University
Grinnell College
Iowa State University
Iowa Wesleyan College
Loras College
Luther College
Morningside College
Northwestern College
Simpson College
University of Iowa
University of Northern Iowa
Wartburg College

Kansas
Bethany College
Bethel College
Central Christian College of Kansas
MidAmerica Nazarene University
Southwestern College
Sterling College
Tabor College
University of Kansas
Wichita State University

Kentucky
Alice Lloyd College
Asbury College
Bellarmine University
Campbellsville University
Centre College
Kentucky Wesleyan College
Morehead State University
Pikeville College
Transylvania University
Western Kentucky University

Louisiana
Centenary College of Louisiana
Louisiana State University
   Shreveport
Loyola University New Orleans
Tulane University
University of Louisiana at Lafayette
University of New Orleans

Maine
Bates College
Bowdoin College
Colby College
Saint Joseph's College of Maine
Thomas College
Unity College
University of Southern Maine

Maryland
Goucher College
Hood College
Johns Hopkins University
McDaniel College
Mount St. Mary's University
St. Mary's College of Maryland
Salisbury University
Stevenson University
Washington Adventist University
Washington College

Massachusetts
American International College
Anna Maria College
Assumption College
Bay Path College
Boston College
Boston University
Bridgewater State College
Clark University
College of the Holy Cross
Eastern Nazarene College
Elms College
Emerson College
Emmanuel College
Endicott College
Framingham State College
Gordon College
Lesley University
Massachusetts College of Liberal Arts
Massachusetts Institute of Technology
Merrimack College
Mount Holyoke College
Nichols College
Northeastern University
Pine Manor College
Regis College
Simmons College
Smith College
Stonehill College
Suffolk University
Tufts University
University of Massachusetts
   Amherst
   Dartmouth
Wellesley College
Western New England College
Westfield State College
Wheaton College
Worcester Polytechnic Institute
Worcester State College

Michigan
Adrian College
Albion College
Alma College
Calvin College
Central Michigan University
Cornerstone University
Eastern Michigan University
Grand Valley State University
Hillsdale College
Hope College
Northern Michigan University
Spring Arbor University
University of Detroit Mercy
University of Michigan
University of Michigan
   Dearborn
Western Michigan University

Minnesota
Bethel University
College of St. Scholastica
Concordia College: Moorhead
Gustavus Adolphus College
Hamline University
Macalester College
Northwestern College
St. Catherine University
St. Mary's University of Minnesota
St. Olaf College
University of Minnesota
   Morris
University of St. Thomas

Mississippi
Millsaps College
Tougaloo College

Missouri

Avila University
Culver-Stockton College
Drury University
Evangel University
Maryville University of Saint Louis
Missouri Baptist University
Northwest Missouri State University
Park University
Rockhurst University
Southwest Baptist University
Truman State University
University of Missouri
 Columbia
Washington University in St. Louis
Westminster College
William Jewell College
William Woods University

Nebraska

Creighton University
Nebraska Wesleyan University

New Hampshire

Colby-Sawyer College
Daniel Webster College
Dartmouth College
Franklin Pierce University
New England College
Saint Anselm College
Southern New Hampshire University
University of New Hampshire
University of New Hampshire at
 Manchester

New Jersey

Caldwell College
The College of New Jersey
Drew University
Fairleigh Dickinson University
 College at Florham
 Metropolitan Campus
Kean University
Monmouth University
Montclair State University
New Jersey City University
Richard Stockton College of New
 Jersey
Rutgers, The State University of New
 Jersey
 New Brunswick/Piscataway
 Campus
 Newark Regional Campus
Saint Peter's College
Seton Hall University
William Paterson University of New
 Jersey

New Mexico

University of New Mexico

New York

Adelphi University
Alfred University
Bard College
Cazenovia College
City University of New York
 Brooklyn College
 College of Staten Island
Clarkson University
Colgate University
College of New Rochelle
Cornell University
Daemen College
Hamilton College
Hartwick College
Hilbert College
Hobart and William Smith Colleges
Hofstra University
Houghton College
Ithaca College
Jamestown Community College
Le Moyne College

Long Island University
 C. W. Post Campus
Manhattan College
Marist College
Nazareth College
New York University
Niagara University
Nyack College
Roberts Wesleyan College
Saint Bonaventure University
St. Francis College
St. John Fisher College
St. Lawrence University
St. Thomas Aquinas College
Siena College
Skidmore College
State University of New York
 Albany
 Binghamton
 Buffalo
 College at Brockport
 College at Buffalo
 College at Cortland
 College at Fredonia
 College at Geneseo
 College at Old Westbury
 College at Oneonta
 Oswego
 Stony Brook
United States Military Academy
University of Rochester
Utica College
Vassar College
Wagner College
Wells College

North Carolina

Barton College
Bennett College for Women
Campbell University
Davidson College
Duke University
East Carolina University
Elon University
Guilford College
Lenoir-Rhyne University
Meredith College
Methodist University
Montreat College
Pfeiffer University
Queens University of Charlotte
Salem College
University of North Carolina
 Asheville
 Chapel Hill
 Charlotte
 Greensboro
 Pembroke
Wake Forest University
Warren Wilson College
Winston-Salem State University

Ohio

Baldwin-Wallace College
Bluffton University
Bowling Green State University
Capital University
Case Western Reserve University
Cedarville University
College of Wooster
Denison University
Heidelberg University
Hiram College
John Carroll University
Kent State University
Kent State University
 Ashtabula
 East Liverpool
 Salem
 Stark
 Trumbull
 Tuscarawas
Kent State University: Geauga
Kenyon College

Malone University
Marietta College
Miami University
 Oxford Campus
Mount Vernon Nazarene University
Muskingum University
Oberlin College
Ohio Dominican University
Ohio Northern University
Ohio State University
 Columbus Campus
Ohio Wesleyan University
Otterbein College
Shawnee State University
Tiffin University
University of Cincinnati
University of Dayton
University of Findlay
Walsh University
Wilmington College
Wittenberg University
Xavier University
Youngstown State University

Oklahoma

Oklahoma City University
Oklahoma State University
Oklahoma Wesleyan University
Oral Roberts University
Rogers State University
Southern Nazarene University
University of Oklahoma
University of Tulsa

Oregon

Corban College
George Fox University
Lewis & Clark College
Linfield College
Pacific University
Portland State University
University of Portland
Warner Pacific College
Willamette University

Pennsylvania

Albright College
Allegheny College
Alvernia University
Arcadia University
Bucknell University
Cabrini College
California University of Pennsylvania
Carnegie Mellon University
Cedar Crest College
Chatham University
Dickinson College
Duquesne University
Eastern University
Elizabethtown College
Franklin & Marshall College
Gannon University
Geneva College
Gettysburg College
Grove City College
Immaculata University
Indiana University of Pennsylvania
Juniata College
King's College
La Roche College
Lafayette College
Lebanon Valley College
Lehigh University
Lycoming College
Mansfield University of Pennsylvania
Mercyhurst College
Messiah College
Moravian College
Muhlenberg College
Penn State
 University Park
Rosemont College
St. Francis University
Saint Joseph's University

Seton Hill University
Shippensburg University of
 Pennsylvania
Susquehanna University
Thiel College
University of Pennsylvania
University of Scranton
Ursinus College
Villanova University
Washington & Jefferson College
Waynesburg University
West Chester University of
 Pennsylvania
Westminster College
Wilson College

Puerto Rico

Inter American University of Puerto
 Rico
 Fajardo Campus
Universidad Metropolitana
University of Puerto Rico
 Arecibo
 Rio Piedras

Rhode Island

Providence College
Roger Williams University
Salve Regina University

South Carolina

Anderson University
Clemson University
Columbia College
Francis Marion University
Furman University
Presbyterian College
South Carolina State University
Southern Wesleyan University
University of South Carolina
 Upstate
Wofford College

South Dakota

Augustana College
Dakota Wesleyan University
Northern State University
University of Sioux Falls

Tennessee

Belmont University
Bryan College
Carson-Newman College
Lambuth University
Lee University
Maryville College
Milligan College
Rhodes College
Tennessee Temple University
Union University
University of the South
Vanderbilt University

Texas

Austin College
Dallas Baptist University
East Texas Baptist University
Hardin-Simmons University
Jarvis Christian College
Midland College
St. Mary's University
Southern Methodist University
Southwestern University
Texas Christian University
Texas Lutheran University
Texas State University: San Marcos
Trinity University
University of Houston
University of Texas
 Austin
 Dallas
West Texas A&M University

Utah

Brigham Young University
University of Utah
Weber State University

Vermont

Middlebury College
St. Michael's College
University of Vermont

Virginia

Averett University
Bridgewater College
College of William and Mary
Eastern Mennonite University
Hampden-Sydney College
James Madison University
Randolph College
Randolph-Macon College
Regent University
Roanoke College
Sweet Briar College
University of Mary Washington
University of Richmond
Virginia Polytechnic Institute and
   State University
Washington and Lee University

Washington

Gonzaga University
Northwest University
Saint Martin's University
Seattle Pacific University
University of Washington
Whitman College
Whitworth University

West Virginia

Bethany College
Davis and Elkins College
Fairmont State University
Glenville State College
Marshall University
Ohio Valley University
Salem International University
Shepherd University
West Liberty University
West Virginia University
West Virginia Wesleyan College
Wheeling Jesuit University

Wisconsin

Alverno College
Beloit College
Carroll University
Carthage College
Lawrence University
Marquette University
Ripon College
St. Norbert College
University of Wisconsin
   Milwaukee
Viterbo University

Wyoming

University of Wyoming

Alphabetical index of majors